THE
ENCYCLOPEDIA
OF
MINOR LEAGUE
BASEBALL

THE
ENCYCLOPEDIA
OF
MINOR LEAGUE
BASEBALL

Second Edition

THE OFFICIAL RECORD
OF MINOR LEAGUE BASEBALL

Lloyd Johnson
Miles Wolff
Editors

Steve McDonald
Associate Editor

BASEBALL AMERICA, INC
DURHAM, NORTH CAROLINA

SECOND EDITION

ASSOCIATE EDITOR:
  Steve McDonald

EDITORIAL AND RESEARCH:

		PRODUCTION:
Davis Barker	Cliff Kachline	Jeff Brunk
John Benesch	David Kemp	Valerie Holbert
Bob Davids	Bob McConnell	Casey Mansfield-Thomas
Ed Hasse	Ray Nemec	
James Holl	John Pardon	
Bob Hoie	Joe Simenic	
Howe Sportsdata International	Bill Weiss	
Jerry Jackson		

EDITORS:

W. Lloyd Johnson is a professional baseball historian, writer and consultant. He is a former president of the Society for American Baseball Research. He is a graduate of Oklahoma State University and has a Masters degree in history from the University of Tulsa. He is the author of *Baseball's Dream Team* and the editor of the *Minor League Register*, *Baseball: A Pictorial Tribute* and *Unions to Royals: Kansas City Baseball History*. He has also served as the Executive Director of SABR, the Senior Research Associate for the National Baseball Hall of Fame at Cooperstown, NY., and the first director of the Negro Leagues Baseball Museum.

Miles Wolff is president of *Baseball America*. He is president of the Northern League and president of the Burlington, N.C. Indians baseball club. He is a graduate of the Johns Hopkins University and has a Masters degree in history from the University of Virginia. He is the author of *Lunch at the Five and Ten*, a history of the Greensboro sit-ins, and *Season of the Owl*, a novel set around minor league baseball. He is the former owner of the Durham Bulls, Carolina League and other minor league baseball and hockey teams.

Cover photo uniforms courtesy of Ebbetts Field Flannels, Seattle, WA.

Copyright © 1997 by Miles Wolff, Lloyd Johnson

Baseball America, Inc.
P.O. Box 2089
600 South Duke Street
Durham, NC 27701

Library of Congress Cataloging in Publication Data

Main entry under title:

The Encyclopedia of Minor League Baseball
Bibliography: p.
1. Baseball—United States—Statistics.
I. Johnson, Lloyd   II. Wolff, Miles
ISBN 0-9637189-7-5

Printed in the United States Of America

TABLE OF CONTENTS

I

INTRODUCTION

FOREWARD

ACKNOWLEDGEMENTS

READER'S GUIDE TO ABBREVIATIONS

LEAGUE CLASSIFICATIONS

FOREWARD

For those who love minor league baseball and its history, the study of the minors is always challenging. It is also a delight. The basic challenge has been to find the information. The resources are few and to find an old Baseball Guide or a Blue Book to add to a collection can best be compared to the early joy of discovering a Mickey Mantle in a bubble gum pack. There are old record books and programs, and there is a network of minor league buffs to call when most sources for information have dried up. But there has never been one source.

The delights in minor league history are many. The names together make poetry. Turkey Tyson, Muscle Shoals, Bunny Brief and Jigger Statz roll off the tongue and evoke images of an America that seems far away. It is a unique profession, where men named Ox and Baby Doll, Big Boy and Dirty Al become heroes.

To study minor league baseball is to study the geography of this country, of small towns and mid-sized towns, of towns that have died, and cities that have grown large. It is searching maps to find places unheard of, and to see leagues spring up and wither as people dream of a professional team for their town, and then realize that dreams sometime die.

It a is study of U.S. history, and in the agate type one finds that floods, polio outbreaks, wars and train wrecks have all affected the course of this special game. It is to see how America has changed, from a player killed by a kick of a mule to one who was killed by a drug overdose. The blips in U.S. history become the bumps in minor league history.

Because of these challenges and delights, many who have loved minor league history have also thought of a minor league encyclopedia. The challenge of minor league history would not need to be so great if the information were in one place. Others might find the same delight if the information were available. But the idea of a minor league encyclopedia has also been a daunting proposal. There have been books on specific minor leagues or teams, but never has there been one source or place to go.

But the idea grew, and we made the decision to go ahead. The resources of Baseball America and S.A.B.R were available to the editors, two organizations that have helped focus interest in minor league baseball over the last decade. The main task was to put limits on the material that would be included in the volume. The decision was reached to cover those years and teams of the National Association of Professional Baseball Leagues, the parent organization of minor league baseball since 1902. The nineteenth century minor leagues and outlaw leagues would have to be included at a later date.

Limits were put on the project by the information itself. There was conflicting information, lack of information and incorrect information in minor league material. We have corrected some of the incorrect facts and made judgements on disputed information that some may disagree with. In some early leagues, we were unable to even find such basic information as final standings. We have included what we could find.

It would be impossible to make the book an encyclopedia of players. With a ninety year total of nearly a quarter of a million minor league players, a listing of players would only be a telephone directory. Our focus was to be on the leagues and the cities. We wanted a source where a city or league baseball history could be quickly researched.

In the year and a half since we began this project, there have been times when we questioned our sanity in undertaking the effort. As numbers ran together, eye sight strained, and deadlines became impossible to reach, it seemed a project that was never to end. But we wanted a minor league encyclopedia and kept pushing to complete it.

Here is the first edition. We have visions of future editions, of adding more information, correcting existing information, and expanding our years. We know minor league historians and fans will help to correct errors and find information for the future. For now, the *Encyclopedia of Minor League Baseball* is a source for minor league history in one volume. We hope it proves useful. We also hope there is challenge and delight in the exploration of minor league baseball.

May, 1993

FOREWARD TO THE SECOND EDITION

In his foreward to the *1996 Texas League Record Book*, Tom Keyser writes, "The nature of a statistical and record book is that it is a living, changing document. Through editing, correction and research changes are made . . ., new research turns up additional information or compilation errors made years ago are discovered and recalculated." We have found this to be true with the *Encyclopedia of Minor League Baseball*. It is a living, changing and growing document.

This is our second edition and we know there is much more. Fortunately, we have a huge research staff made up of our readers who will send new material, changes and corrections. The very nature of a project such as this is that it leads to further research. For now, this edition is ready for the reader, and our desires are the same as they were with the first edition. We wish you enjoyment, and hope that this volume will continue the challenge and delight in the exploration of minor league baseball.

May, 1997

ACKNOWLEDGEMENTS – 2ND EDITION

*F*our years have passed since the first edition of the *Encyclopedia of Minor League Baseball* was published. Interest in both the game and the history of minor league professional baseball has reached a 50-year high. This encyclopedia was helped tremendously by the interest as evidenced by letters from readers of the first volume and assistance from many sources.

Joe Overfield, John Benesch, and David Thomas sent page-by-page compilations of suggestions to make the EMLB better. Davis Barker sent an encyclopedia of East Texas baseball in the same format, but in much more depth. Ed Hasse of Detroit wrote that he had balanced standings for all of the leagues. We have added the suggestions and the managerial research of Jerry Jackson.

For the second edition, Bob Hoie, Bob McConnell, and Bob Tiemann threw their weighty knowledge into numerous readings of the manuscript. Many members of the SABR (Society for American Baseball Research) Minor League Committee have gone beyond the limits of research comradeship to produce something special.

Giants among the contributors in the ever-growing field of minor league research include Bob Davids, who founded SABR and compiled playing records of African-Americans in 19th century organized ball, Ray Nemec, who is the nonpareil statistics compiler of minor leagues without published figures, and Bill Weiss, the West Coast statistician who knows more about minor league players than anyone in the world. John Pardon and David Kemp, former chairs of the SABR minor league committee, regularly make contributions that cannot be found in regular research channels.

The additional roster of those who provided standings, managers, first names, nicknames, no-hit scores, and other information read as a "Who's Who in Baseball Research"—Carlos Bauer, Brent Cobb, Denny Cryder, Jack Daugherty, Bill Deane, Alan Denman, Jr., Bob Epler, Russell Field, Steve Garlick, Scott Hanzelka, Ted Hauser, Dennis Hernandez, James Holl, Reed Howard, Chuck Howell, Cliff Kachline, Tom Kayser, James Kiernan, Troy Kirk, Robert Mitchell, Joe Murphy, Terrence O'Brien, Mark Okkonen, Joe Overfield, David Pietrusca, Tim Rask, James Riley, Patrick Rock, Arthur Schott, Corey Seamon, Jamie Selko, Ron Selter, Tom Shrimplin, David Skinner, John E. Spalding, Dick Thompson, and Bill Wakefield. Other giants in the field who gone before are L. D. Addington, Leonard Gettelson, and Vern Luse.

Very special thanks go to Dean Coughenour who lent his in addition to his microfilm copies of the *Sporting News* and *Sporting Life* as well as access to his Guide collection. His Guides have first names hand-written first names in the statistics portions.

The final thank you must go to the readers who purchased the first edition and refused to relegate it to the bookshelf. From readers' responses we know that the book was used over and over. Hundreds of letters were sent with information, corrections, and new research. A few who sent in valuable information and material are Richard Adler, Ted Battles, Max G. Bernhardt, Merritt Clifton, Cecil Darby, John Fox, Bob Gaunt, Charlie Harville, Jim Henley, Marc Alan Jones, Mike Keough, Tony Kissel, Willard W. Lewis, Willie Runquist, Dean Sullivan, Jim Wintermute, Lynn Womack, and David Zink. We had hoped to list all those who wrote in with this information, but it is not possible. Simply put, we thank those who have taken the time to send in their information and hope they will continue to send us more information and suggestions.

The end of season all-star teams from each league can be a better indicator of the top players in the league rather than the league leaders. One fact was learned, a player seldom reaches the Big Leagues without being a headliner at some point in his career. It was not easy to find all-star teams prior to 1967, when they re-appeared in the Guides after a 25-year hiatus. The search took us to league archives, record books, Reach Guides, and to Bill Weiss. He suggested a little-known booklet, National Association Highlights, in which all-star teams and post-season attendance figures were published. A complete set—1948-1968—was found at the National Association office in St. Petersburg. We owe immense thanks to Tom Kilty and Chuck Merrill who spent days copying this information for us.

Bob Hoie and John Pardon provided a break-through in the search for attendances by sending a copy of the appropriate sections from Study of Monopoly Power subcommittee hearings in House of Representatives, 82nd Congress, first session. The 1952 hearings studied attendance figures from the Pacific Coast and International Leagues and American and Southern Associations. Other attendances for this book came from post-season reports in the Sporting News, various league and club histories, and readers with a special interest in one club or league.

In Durham, NC, we need to acknowledge many people, particularly Associate Editor Steve McDonald who spent months pouring over the material, checking and rechecking the endless names and numbers. Dave Chase, John Royster, and Hoffman Wolff all gave valuable time. The production staff headed by Jeff Brunk with Valerie Holbert and Casey Mansfield Thomas enabled this book to make it to the printer.

No matter how many attendance figures, managerial changes, or all-star teams are published here, there are many more pieces to the informational jigsaw puzzle called baseball history. All National Agreement leagues are included in this volume, but most non-signatory associations are absent. When standings, managers, and league leaders are adequately researched those leagues will likely join the database of professional baseball history.

As we stated in the acknowledgments to the first edition we repeat. The editors accept all responsibility for errors. Should you have a correction or an addition to make, please contact the Minor League Encyclopedia, Baseball America, P.O. Box 2089, Durham, North Carolina, 27702. We hope that you will enjoy reading and using this book.

Lloyd Johnson and Miles Wolff
May 1997

ACKNOWLEDGEMENTS – 1ST EDITION

*T*he *Baseball Minor League Encyclopedia* is a result of the efforts of many people who worked together to meet the particular challenges of its publication. The two previously existing principal sources of early information on minor league baseball—the *Reach Guides* and the *Spalding Baseball Guides*—are invaluable, but have several shortcomings. They lack data on many class D leagues, have multiple typographical errors, and include league standings that are unbalanced—the number of games won does not equal the number of games lost, signalling incorrect data.

The Society for American Baseball Research (SABR) began setting the record straight in 1971. That was the year SABR was founded in Cooperstown, New York, by L. Robert Davids. Since that time, SABR members have researched and published a great deal of information on baseball, much of it on the minor leagues. Thousands of hours have been spent combing through microfilmed newspapers to collect unreported or incorrectly reported box scores, line scores and standings. We are appreciative of the efforts of the current SABR Minor League Committee chair, Dave Kemp.

The work of baseball research pioneers made this encyclopedia possible. Among those who have devoted a lifetime to baseball research are Bob Davids, Bob Hoie, Jerry Jackson, Cliff Kachline, Bob McConnell, Ray Nemec, John Pardon, Joe Simenic, Bill Weiss and the late Vern Luse.

Special thanks go to Hoie, McConnell, Nemec, Pardon and Weiss for supplying accurate information on won-lost totals, which are so necessary in balancing league totals, and to John Benesch who supplied data on league leaders, as did Hoie, McConnell, Nemec and Weiss.

The following people were of tremendous assistance: Tom Heitz and the staff at the National Baseball Library of the National Baseball Hall of Fame and Museum; Steve Gietschier, archivist at *The Sporting News*; the staffs of the Kansas State Historical Association and the Missouri State Historical Society.

Bob Hoie and Bill Deane, the Senior Research Associate at the National Baseball Library of the National Baseball Hall of Fame and Museum, extended themselves far beyond expectations. Hoie worked solo, while Deane coordinated a staff that included Gary Van Allen and Matt Reese.

Baseball executives Paul Marshall, general manager of the Burlington club in the Midwest League; Charlie Eshbach, president of the Eastern League; Walt Winkleman, president of the Stockton club in the California League; and Bob Sparks, director of information for the National Association of Professional Baseball Leagues, provided insight and encouragement. League presidents generously provided record books and histories of their leagues. Arnold Springer contributed an unpublished manuscript that served as the basis for "This Date in Minor League History."

Tony Kissell and Eric DeMunn filled in New York State League information. Robert Van Atta made his history of the West Pennsylvania League of 1907 available. Art Schott sent the 1942 Evangeline League standings. Paul Leslie found standings on the 1920 Louisiana State League. Jerry Clark supplied data on the Western League. Jamie Selko, from his listening post in Germany, added Far West League data.

Since 1942, *The Sporting News Official Baseball Guide* has been the principal source of statistical information. No minor league historian can operate without these Guides, and we thank *The Sporting News* for the use of this material.

Luck sometimes plays a role in a momentous discovery. This time, baseball research has been facilitated by the United States government's newspaper microfilming project. We made use of the completed project for the states of Kansas, Missouri and Nebraska, but it is not yet finished in several other states—notably Texas. A special thanks is due to Debbie Cottrell, University of Texas Ph.D candidate, who took time to find the standings for five previously missing leagues.

Dean Coughenour, of AG Press in Manhattan, Kansas, generously provided access to his collection of minor league material. Patrick Rock lent his collection of guides and his expertise. In Kansas City, young Tom Lynch came home from school and worked diligently fact-checking and balancing league standings.

In the Durham, NC area we have had tremendous help from those associated with *Baseball America* and from area baseball historians. Special thanks go to a group of fact checkers who helped in this detailed effort. Bill Grubbs, Bruce Winkworth, Kevin Seymour and Dave Chase have spent many days pouring over statistics. The production department of *Baseball America* did outstanding work in laying out the book and thanks go to Joy Tempkins, Susan Merrell and Shannon Cain for their efforts. Randy Edwards provided countless hours of production work updating the pages. Thanks to all of the staff of *Baseball America* for their patience and advice on this project. Hoffman Wolff spent many hours updating team nicknames, and particular appreciation to young Alexander Merrill for waiting for this project to be completed before coming into the world.

The first edition of *The Encyclopedia of Minor League Baseball* has been a vast undertaking, but is by no means as complete as we envision it. Our goal is to list the managers and team nicknames dating back to 1877. Missing data, such as attendance figures, home runs and strikeouts in the early years of the minor leagues are being sought. Likewise, we will be looking for data on the leagues that are included here, but are without their standings. Missing batting and pitching statistics from disbanded leagues will also be added in future editions.

The editors accept all responsibility for errors. Should you have a correction or an addition to make, please contact the Minor League Encyclopedia, Baseball America, P.O. Box 2089, Durham, North Carolina, 27702.

We hope the encyclopedia will help you make your own discoveries in the story of minor league baseball.

Lloyd Johnson

Miles Wolff
May 1993

READERS' GUIDE TO ABBREVIATIONS

ABBREVIATIONS

2B	–	Double(s)
3B	–	Triple(s)
aka	–	Also Known As
Attend	–	Attendance
BA	–	Batting Average
BB	–	Base On Balls
CS	–	Caught Stealing
DH	–	Designated Hitter
EBH	–	Extra Base Hits
ERA	–	Earned Run Average
GB	–	Games Behind
HB	–	Hit Batsmen
HBP	–	Hit by Pitch
HR	–	Home Run(s)
IBB	–	Intentional Base on Balls
IP	–	Innings Pitched
L	–	Games Lost
MVP	–	Most Valuable Player
PCT	–	Won-Lost Percentage
RBI	–	Run(s) Batted In
Sac	–	Sacrifice Hits
SacF	–	Sacrifice Flies
SB	–	Stolen Base(s)
ShO	–	Shutout(s)
ShO Streak	–	Shutout Innings Pitched
SO	–	Strikeout(s)
Streak	–	Number of Games batting safely
TB	–	Total Bases
Util	–	Utility Player
W	–	Games Won
WP	–	Wild Pitches

SYMBOLS

* (one asterisk) Won first half of split season

** (two asterisks) Won second half of split season

*** (three asterisks) Won both halves of split season

/ (slash) Indicates a change in franchise location or a change in a player's team affiliation. For example Seattle/Tacoma means that the Seattle franchise moved to Tacoma during the season. The same notation by a player's name would mean he changed teams that season.

- (dash) Indicates a dual city franchise, Fargo-Moorhead, for example.

(pound sign) This and other symbols are used when the data requires an explanatory note. Notes are printed immediately below the standings.

TRANSLATIONS

Mexican League nicknames, page 579.

LEAGUE CLASSIFICATIONS

*A*bout 1890, teams that were members of the National Agreement were given classifications. It was a loose system, and these classifications, A to F, while in some cases reflecting the level of play often were assigned in response to the amount of dues paid. The Connecticut League, one of the leading leagues of the 1890s, was given a Class F designation. This well organized league felt it did not need all the protection of the National Agreement and paid dues at the lowest level.

With the formation of the National Association of Professional Baseball Leagues in 1902, the current system of classifications was started. Over the years, there have been changes, and the following is a brief history of each classification:

MAJOR
The Major Leagues. This is the top classification of professional baseball.

O The **OPEN** classification. It was established in 1952 exclusively for the Pacific Coast League. It is one notch above the AAA classification and was established in order to help the Pacific Coast League build itself into a major league. When the National League moved into Los Angeles and San Francisco in 1958, the major league hopes of the Pacific Coast League died and it returned to Class AAA.

AAA This is currently the highest classification. It was established effective in 1946 with the three Class AA leagues of 1945, the American Association, International League, and Pacific Coast League, moving up. The Mexican League moved up to Class AAA in 1967.

AA This classification was established in 1912 with the American Association, Eastern League (forerunner of the present International League), and Pacific Coast League moving up from Class A. In 1946, the A1 classification was changed to AA and the Southern Association and Texas League became Class AA. The Mexican League joined organized baseball in 1955 as a Class AA league. In the classification restructuring of 1963, all Class A and AA leagues were grouped in Class AA. This resulted in the Eastern League and the South Atlantic League moving up to join the Texas League as Class AA.

A1 This classification was established in 1936 and was in existence through the 1945 season. It was one notch above Class A and one below Class AA. The Southern Association and the Texas League moved up to this classification from class A when it was established. They are the only leagues to have had this classification.

A Under the original structure, Class A was the highest classification from 1902 through 1911. The Eastern

League and the Western League were Class [...] period. The American Association joined o[...] 1903 as a Class A league and the Pacific Coa[...] in 1904 as Class A. They remained in this cla[...] 1911. The Southern Association moved up t[...] The Pacific National League was Class A for [...] In the classification restructuring of 1963, all [...] leagues were moved to Class A.

B This was the second highest classification [...] through 1907. Class B leagues in 1902 we[...] England League, New York State League, Pacifi[...] League, Southern Association and Three I Leagu[...] leagues in the B classification at sometime durin[...] 1907 were the Central League, Connecticut Leagu[...] Northwestern League, Pacific National League an[...] League. In the classification restructuring of 196[...] leagues were moved to Class A.

C This was the third ranked classification from [...] through 1907. Class C leagues in 1902 were [...] Connecticut League and the Northern League. In th[...] tion restructuring of 1963, all Class C leagues were [...] Class A.

D This was the lowest classification from 1902 th[...] 1962, except for 1943 when there was a Class E[...] operation. In the classification restructuring of 1963, [...] D leagues were moved to Class A.

E This classification was established at the National [...] Association meeting in December, 1937. Class E [...] were restricted to players with no experience in Class D[...] higher. The classification was created in order to compe[...] the successful Semi-Pro National Baseball Congress. Th[...] Ports League, in 1943, was the only league to operate in t[...] classification. The four team league operated at Duluth, [...] Minnesota and Superior, Wisconsin. The Twin Ports Leag[...] disbanded on July 13, 1943.

R This is the **ROOKIE** classification. This classificatio[...] was established in 1963. It is the lowest classification [...] the present time. Rookie leagues are primarily for first year [...] players.

IND
This designation stands for **INDEPENDENT** leagues which were not members of the National Association. At various times known as outlaw leagues, these leagues were not accepted by the NA but operated under most of the same guidelines that governed NA sanctioned leagues.

II

THE TEAMS AND LEAGUES – 1883-1997

PROFESSIONAL TEAMS BY LEAGUE

PROFESSIONAL TEAMS BY CITY

PROFESSIONAL TEAMS BY STATE AND COUNTRY

PROFESSIONAL LEAGUES BY YEAR

PROFESSIONAL TEAMS BY LEAGUE 1883-1997

ALABAMA-FLORIDA LEAGUE
CLASS D 1936-1939, 1951-1962
ALABAMA STATE LEAGUE
CLASS D 1940-1941, 1946-1950

Abbeville	AL	1936
Andalusia	AL	1936-1941, 1947-1950, 1953, 1962
Andalusia-Opp	AL	1954
Brewton	AL	1940-1941, 1946-1950
Columbus	GA	1958
Crestview	FL	1954-1956
Donalsonville	GA	1955-1956
Dothan	AL	1936-1941, 1946-1956, 1958-1962
Enterprise	AL	1936, 1947-1952
Eufaula	AL	1952-1953
Evergreen	AL	1937-1938
Ft. Walton Beach	FL	1953-1962
Geneva	AL	1946-1950
Graceville	FL	1952-1958
Greenville	AL	1939-1941, 1946-1950
Headland	AL	1950-1952
Montgomery	AL	1957-1962
Ozark	AL	1936-1937, 1946-1952, 1962
Panama City	FL	1936-1939, 1951-1961
Pensacola	FL	1957-1962
Selma	AL	1957-1962
Tallahassee	FL	1951
Tallassee	AL	1939-1941
Troy	AL	1936-1941, 1946-1949
Tuskegee	AL	1941
Union Springs	AL	1936-1938

ALABAMA-TENNESSEE LEAGUE
CLASS D 1921

Albany-Decatur	AL	1921
Columbia	TN	1921
Russellville	AL	1921
Tri-Cities	AL	1921
(Sheffield-Tuscumbia-Muscle Shoals)		

AMERICAN ASSOCIATION
MAJOR 1883-1891

Baltimore	MD	1883-1891
Boston	MA	1891
Brooklyn	NY	1884-1890
Cincinnati	OH	1883-1889, 1891
Cleveland	OH	1887-1888
Columbus	OH	1883-1884, 1889-1891
Indianapolis	IN	1884
Kansas City	MO	1888-1889
Louisville	KY	1883-1891
Milwaukee	WI	1891
New York	NY	1883-1887
Philadelphia	PA	1883-1891
Pittsburgh	PA	1883-1886
Richmond	VA	1884
Rochester	NY	1890
St. Louis	MO	1883-1891
Syracuse	NY	1890
Toledo	OH	1884, 1890
Washington	DC	1884, 1891

AMERICAN ASSOCIATION
IND 1902; CLASS A 1903-1911; CLASS AA 1912-1945;
CLASS AAA 1946-1962; CLASS AAA 1969-

Buffalo	NY	1985-1997
Charleston	WV	1952-1960
Cleveland	OH	1914-1915
Columbus	OH	1902-1954
Dallas	TX	1959
Dallas-Ft. Worth	TX	1960-1962
Denver	CO	1955-1962, 1969-1992
Evansville	IN	1970-1984
Ft. Worth	TX	1959
Houston	TX	1959-1961
Indianapolis	IN	1902-1962, 1969-
Iowa (Des Moines)	IA	1969-
Kansas City	MO	1902-1954
Louisville	KY	1902-1962, 1982-
Milwaukee	WI	1902-1952
Minneapolis	MN	1902-1960
Nashville	TN	1985-

New Orleans	LA	1977, 1993-
Oklahoma City	OK	1962, 1969-
Omaha	NE	1955-1959, 1961-1962, 1969-
St. Paul	MN	1902-1960
Springfield	IL	1978-1981
Toledo	OH	1902-1913, 1916-1955
Tulsa	OK	1969-1976
Wichita	KS	1956-1958, 1970-1984

AMERICAN LEAGUE
IND 1900
(successor of Western League 1885-1899)

Buffalo	NY	1900
Chicago	IL	1900
Cleveland	OH	1900
Detroit	MI	1900
Indianapolis	IN	1900
Kansas City	MO	1900
Milwaukee	WI	1900
Minneapolis	MN	1900

AMERICAN LEAGUE
MAJOR 1901-

Baltimore	MD	1901-1902, 1954-
Boston	MA	1901-
California (aka Anaheim) (aka Los Angeles)	CA	1961-
Chicago	IL	1901-
Cleveland	OH	1901-
Detroit	MI	1901-
Kansas City	MO	1955-1967, 1969-
Milwaukee	WI	1901, 1970-
Minnesota (Minneapolis)	MN	1961-
New York	NY	1903-
Oakland	CA	1968-
Philadelphia	PA	1901-1954
St. Louis	MO	1902-1953
Seattle	WA	1969, 1977-
Texas (Dallas-Ft. Worth)	TX	1972-
Toronto	ONT	1977-
Washington	DC	1901-1971

APPALACHIAN LEAGUE
CLASS D 1911-1914, 1921-1925, 1937-1955, 1957-1962
ROOKIE 1963-

Asheville	NC	1911-1912
Bluefield	WV	1946-1955, 1957-
Bristol	VA	1911-1913, 1921-1925, 1940-1955, 1969-
Burlington	NC	1986-
Cleveland	TN	1911-1913, 1921-1922
Covington	VA	1966-1976
Danville	VA	1993-
Elizabethton	TN	1937-1942, 1945-1951, 1974-
Erwin	TN	1940, 1943-1944
Greeneville	TN	1921-1925, 1938-1942
Harlan	KY	1961-1963, 1965
Harriman	TN	1914
Huntington (aka River City)	WV	1990-1995
Johnson City	TN	1911-1913, 1921-1924, 1937-1955, 1957-1961, 1964-
Kingsport	TN	1921-1925, 1938-1952, 1957, 1960-1963, 1969-1982, 1984-
Knoxville	TN	1911-1914, 1921-1924
Lynchburg	VA	1959
Marion	VA	1955, 1965-1976
Martinsville	VA	1988-
Middlesboro	KY	1913-1914, 1961-1963
Morristown	TN	1911-1914, 1923-1925, 1959-1961
New River	VA	1946-1950
Newport	TN	1937-1942
Paintsville	KY	1978-1984
Pennington Gap	VA	1937-1940
Pikeville	KY	1982-1984
Princeton	WV	1988-
Pulaski	VA	1946-1950, 1952-1955, 1957-1958, 1969-1977, 1982-1992, 1997-
Rome	GA	1913
Salem	VA	1955, 1957-1967
Welch	WV	1946-1955
Wytheville	VA	1953-1955, 1957-1965, 1967, 1969, 1971-1973, 1985-1989

PROFESSIONAL TEAMS BY LEAGUE 1883-1997

ARIZONA LEAGUE
ROOKIE 1988-
(games played at Chandler, Mesa, Peoria, Phoenix, Scottsdale and Tempe, AZ)

Angels	AZ	1989-
Athletics	AZ	1988-
Brewers	AZ	1988-1995
Cardinals	AZ	1989-1994
Diamondbacks	AZ	1996-
Giants	AZ	1991-1994
Mariners	AZ	1989-
Padres	AZ	1988-
Red Sox/Mariners	AZ	1988
Rockies/Cubs	AZ	1992
Rockies	AZ	1993-

ARIZONA STATE LEAGUE
CLASS D 1928-1930
ARIZONA-TEXAS LEAGUE
CLASS D 1931-1932, 1937-1939;
CLASS C 1940-1941, 1947-1950, 1952-1954
(merged with Sunset League to form Southwest International League 1951-1952)
ARIZONA-MEXICO LEAGUE
CLASS C 1955-1958

Albuquerque	NM	1932, 1937-1941
Bisbee	AZ	1928-1932, 1937-1941
Bisbee-Douglas	AZ	1947-1950, 1952-1955
Cananea	MEX	1954-1957
Chihuahua	MEX	1952, 1958
Ciudad Juarez	MEX	1947-1950, 1952-1954, 1958
Douglas	AZ	1956-1958
El Paso	TX	1930-1932, 1937-1941, 1947-1950, 1952-1954
Globe	AZ	1929-1931
Globe-Miami	AZ	1947-1950, 1955
Las Vegas	NV	1957
Mesa	AZ	1929, 1947
Mexicali	MEX	1953-1958
Miami	AZ	1928-1930
Nogales	MEX	1931, 1954-1956, 1958
Phoenix	AZ	1928-1932, 1947-1950, 1952-1957
Tijuana	MEX	1956
Tucson	AZ	1928-1932, 1937-1941, 1947-1950, 1952-1958
Yuma	AZ	1955-1956

ARKANSAS STATE LEAGUE
CLASS D 1908-1909

Alexandria	LA	1909
Argenta	AR	1908-1909
Brinkley	AR	1908
Ft. Smith	AR	1909
Helena	AR	1908-1909
Hot Springs	AR	1908-1909
Jonesboro	AR	1909
Monroe	LA	1909
Newport	AR	1908
Newport-Batesville	AR	1909
Pine Bluff	AR	1908
Poplar Bluff	AR	1908
Texarkana	TX	1909

ARKANSAS STATE LEAGUE
CLASS D 1934-1935
ARKANSAS-MISSOURI LEAGUE
CLASS D 1936-1940

Bentonville	AR	1934-1936
Carthage	MO	1938-1940
Cassville	MO	1935-1936
Fayetteville	AR	1934-1940
Huntsville	AR	1935
Monett	MO	1936-1939
Neosho	MO	1937-1940
Rogers	AR	1934-1938
Siloam Springs	AR	1934-1938, 1940

ARKANSAS-TEXAS LEAGUE
CLASS D 1906

Camden	AR	1906
Hot Springs	AR	1906
Pine Bluff	AR	1906
Texarkana	TX	1906

ATLANTIC ASSOCIATION
1889-1890

Baltimore	MD	1890
Easton	PA	1889
Harrisburg	PA	1890
Hartford	CT	1889-1890
Jersey City	NJ	1889-1890
Lebanon	PA	1890
Lowell	MA	1889
New Haven	CT	1889-1890
Newark	NJ	1889-1890
Norwalk	CT	1889
Washington	DC	1890
Wilkes-Barre	PA	1889
Wilmington	DE	1890
Worcester	MA	1889-1890

ATLANTIC ASSOCIATION
CLASS D 1908

Attleboro	MA	1908
Lewiston	ME	1908
Newport	RI	1908
Pawtucket	RI	1908
Portland	ME	1908
Taunton	MA	1908
Woonsocket	RI	1908

ATLANTIC LEAGUE
1896-1900
(successor of the Pennsylvania State League 1892-1895)

Allentown	PA	1898-1900
Elmira	NY	1900
Harrisburg	PA	1900
Hartford	CT	1896-1898
Jersey City	NJ	1900
Lancaster	PA	1896-1899
New Haven	CT	1896
New York	NY	1896
Newark	NJ	1896-1900
Norfolk	VA	1897-1898
Paterson	NJ	1896-1899
Philadelphia	PA	1896-1897, 1900
Reading	PA	1897-1900
Richmond	VA	1897-1899
Scranton	PA	1899-1900
Wilkes-Barre	PA	1899-1900
Wilmington	DE	1896

ATLANTIC LEAGUE
CLASS D 1914
(successor of the New York-New Jersey League 1913)

Asbury Park	NJ	1914
Bloomfield-Long Branch	NJ	1914
Danbury	CT	1914
Long Branch	NJ	1914
Middletown	NY	1914
Newark	NJ	1914
Newburgh	NY	1914
Paterson	NJ	1914
Perth Amboy	NJ	1914
Poughkeepsie	NY	1914

ATLANTIC COAST LEAGUE
IND 1995

Gaston (Gastonia)	NC	1995
Spartanburg	SC	1995
Florence	SC	1995
Greenwood	SC	1995

BI-STATE LEAGUE (IL-WI)
CLASS D 1915
(successor of the Wisconsin-Illinois League 1907-1914)

Aurora	IL	1915
Elgin	IL	1915
Freeport	IL	1915
Ottawa	IL	1915
Racine	WI	1915
Streator	IL	1915

PROFESSIONAL TEAMS BY LEAGUE 1883-1997

BI-STATE LEAGUE (NC-VA)
CLASS D 1934-1942

Bassett	VA	1935-1940
Burlington	NC	1942
Danville	VA	1934-1938
Danville-Schoolfield	VA	1939-1942
Fieldale	VA	1934-1936
Leaksville-Draper-Spray	NC	1934-1942
Martinsville	VA	1934-1941
Mayodan	NC	1934-1941
Mt. Airy	NC	1934-1941
Reidsville	NC	1935-1940
Rocky Mount	NC	1942
Sanford	NC	1941-1942
South Boston	VA	1937, 1939-1940
South Boston-Halifax	VA	1938
Wilson	NC	1942

BIG SOUTH LEAGUE
IND 1996-

Clarksville	TN	1996
Columbia	TN	1996
Greenville	MS	1996-
LaGrange	GA	1997-
Meridian	MS	1996-
Pine Bluff	AR	1996
Tennessee (Winchester)	TN	1996
Tupelo	MS	1997-

BIG STATE LEAGUE
CLASS B 1947-1957

Abilene	TX	1956-1957
Austin	TX	1947-1955
Beaumont	TX	1956-1957
Bryan	TX	1953-1954
Corpus Christi	TX	1954-1957
Del Rio	TX	1954
Gainesville	TX	1947-1951
Galveston	TX	1954-1955
Greenville	TX	1947-1950, 1953
Harlingen	TX	1954-1955
Longview	TX	1952-1953
Lubbock	TX	1956
Paris	TX	1947-1948, 1952-1953
Port Arthur	TX	1955-1957
Sherman-Denison	TX	1947-1951
Temple	TX	1949-1954, 1957
Texarkana	TX	1947-1953
Texas City	TX	1955-1956
Tyler	TX	1951-1955
Victoria	TX	1956-1957
Waco	TX	1947-1956
Wichita Falls	TX	1947-1953, 1956-1957

BLUE GRASS LEAGUE
CLASS D 1908-1912, 1922-1924

Cynthiana	KY	1922-1924
Frankfort	KY	1908-1912
Lawrenceburg	KY	1908
Lexington	KY	1908-1912, 1922-1923
Maysville	KY	1910-1912, 1922-1923
Mt. Sterling	KY	1912, 1922-1923
Nicholasville	KY	1912
Paris	KY	1909-1912, 1922-1924
Richmond	KY	1908-1912
Shelbyville	KY	1908-1910
Winchester	KY	1908-1912, 1922-1924

BLUE RIDGE LEAGUE (PA-MD-WV)
CLASS D 1915-1918, 1920-1930

Chambersburg	PA	1915-1917, 1920-1930
Cumberland	MD	1917-1918
Frederick	MD	1915-1917, 1920-1930
Gettysburg	PA	1915-1917
Hagerstown	MD	1915-1918, 1920-1930
Hanover	MD	1915-1917, 1920-1929
Martinsburg	WV	1915-1918, 1920-1929
Piedmont-Westernport	WV-MD	1918
Waynesboro	PA	1920-1930

BLUE RIDGE LEAGUE (NC-VA)
CLASS D 1946-1950

Abingdon	VA	1948
Bassett	VA	1950
Elkin	NC	1949-1950
Galax	VA	1946-1950
Leaksville-Spray-Draper	NC	1948
Lenoir	NC	1946-1947
Mt. Airy	NC	1946-1950
North Wilkesboro	NC	1948-1950
Radford	VA	1946-1950
Salem	VA	1946
Wytheville	VA	1948-1950

BORDER LEAGUE
CLASS D 1912-1913
(aka Eastern Michigan League)

Mt. Clemens	MI	1912-1913
Port Huron	MI	1912-1913
Pontiac	MI	1912-1913
Windsor	ONT	1912-1913
Wyandotte	MI	1912-1913
Ypsilanti	MI	1913

BORDER LEAGUE
CLASS C 1946-1951

Auburn	NY	1946-1951
Cornwall	ONT	1951
Geneva	NY	1947-1951
Granby	QUE	1946
Kingston	ONT	1946-1951
Ogdensburg	NY	1946-1951
Ottawa	ONT	1947-1950
Sherbrooke	QUE	1946
Watertown	NY	1946-1951

BUCKEYE LEAGUE
CLASS D 1915

Akron	OH	1915
Canton	OH	1915
Findlay	OH	1915
Lima	OH	1915
Marion	OH	1915
Newark	OH	1915

CALIFORNIA LEAGUE
1887-1889, 1891, 1893, 1899-1901; IND 1902, 1907-1909

Alameda	CA	1907-1908
Fresno	CA	1908-1909
Los Angeles	CA	1893, 1901-1902
Oakland	CA	1887-1889, 1891, 1893, 1899-1902, 1907-1909
Sacramento	CA	1887, 1889, 1891, 1893, 1899-1902, 1907-1909
San Francisco	CA	1889, 1891, 1893, 1899-1902, 1907-1909
San Francisco Haverly	CA	1887-1888
San Francisco Pioneers	CA	1887-1888
San Jose	CA	1891, 1899, 1907-1909
Santa Cruz	CA	1899, 1908-1909
Stockton	CA	1888-1889, 1893, 1900, 1907-1909
Watsonville	CA	1899

CALIFORNIA LEAGUE
CLASS C 1941-1942, 1946-1962; CLASS A 1963-

Anaheim	CA	1941
Bakersfield	CA	1941-1942, 1946-1975, 1978-1979, 1982-
Channel Cities	CA	1954-1955
Fresno	CA	1941-1942, 1946-1988
High Desert (Adelanto)	CA	1991-
Lake Elsinore	CA	1994-
Lancaster	CA	1996-
Las Vegas	NV	1958
Lodi	CA	1966-1984
Merced	CA	1941
Modesto	CA	1946-1964, 1966-
Palm Springs	CA	1986-1993
Rancho Cucamonga	CA	1993-
Reno	NV	1955-1964, 1966-1992
Riverside	CA	1941, 1988-1990
Rohnert Park	CA	1980-1985
Salinas	CA	1954-1958, 1963-1965, 1973-1980, 1982-1987, 1989-1992

San Bernardino	CA	1941, 1987-
San Jose	CA	1942, 1947-1958, 1962-1976, 1979-
Santa Barbara	CA	1941-1942, 1946-1953, 1962-1967
Santa Clara	CA	1979
Stockton	CA	1941, 1946-1972, 1978-
Ventura	CA	1947-1953, 1986
Visalia (aka Central Valley)	CA	1946-1962, 1968-1975, 1977-

CALIFORNIA STATE LEAGUE
CLASS D 1910; CLASS D 1913-1915, 1929

Alameda	CA	1915
Bakersfield	CA	1929
Berkeley	CA	1915
Coronado	CA	1929
Fresno	CA	1910, 1913-1914
Merced	CA	1910
Modesto	CA	1914-1915
Oakland	CA	1910, 1915
Orange County	CA	1929
Pomona	CA	1929
Sacramento	CA	1910
San Bernardino	CA	1929
San Diego	CA	1929
San Francisco	CA	1910, 1915
San Jose	CA	1910, 1913-1915
Stockton	CA	1910, 1913-1915
Vallejo	CA	1913
Watsonville	CA	1913

CANADIAN LEAGUE
1899-1900; CLASS D 1905, 1911; CLASS C 1912-1913; CLASS B 1914-1915
(known as International League 1900)
(aka Western Ontario Baseball Association 1905)

Berlin (Kitchener)	ONT	1911-1913
Brantford	ONT	1905, 1911-1915
Chatham	ONT	1899-1900
Erie	PA	1914
Guelph	ONT	1899, 1911-1913, 1915
Grand Rapids	MI	1900
Hamilton	ONT	1899-1900, 1911-1915
Ingersoll	ONT	1905
London	ONT	1899-1900, 1911-1915
Ottawa	ONT	1912-1915
Peterborough	ONT	1912-1914
Port Huron	MI	1900
Saginaw	MI	1900
St. Thomas	ONT	1899, 1905, 1911-1915
Simcoe	ONT	1905
Stratford	ONT	1899
Toronto	ONT	1914
Woodstock	ONT	1899, 1905

CANADIAN-AMERICAN LEAGUE
CLASS C 1936-1942, 1946-1951

Amsterdam	NY	1938-1942, 1946-1951
Auburn	NY	1938, 1940
Brockville	ONT	1936-1937
Cornwall	ONT	1938-1939
Gloversville	NY	1937
Gloversville-Johnstown	NY	1938-1942, 1946-1951
Kingston	NY	1951
Ogdensburg	NY	1936-1939
Oneonta	NY	1940-1942, 1946-1951
Oswego	NY	1936-1940
Ottawa	ONT	1936-1939
Ottawa-Ogdensburg	ONT-NY	1940
Perth	ONT	1936
Perth-Cornwall	ONT	1937
Pittsfield	MA	1941-1942, 1946-1951
Quebec	QUE	1941-1942, 1946-1950
Rome	NY	1937-1942, 1946-1951
Schenectady	NY	1946-1950
Smiths Falls	ONT	1937
Trois Rivieres	QUE	1941-1942, 1946-1950
Utica	NY	1939-1942
Watertown	NY	1936

CAPE BRETON COLLIERY LEAGUE
CLASS D 1937-1938; CLASS C 1939

Dominion	NS	1937-1938
Glace Bay	NS	1937-1939
New Waterford	NS	1937-1939
Sydney	NS	1937-1939
Sydney Mines	NS	1937-1939

CAROLINA ASSOCIATION
CLASS D 1908-1912
(predecessor of the North Carolina State League 1913-1917)

Anderson	SC	1908-1912
Charlotte	NC	1908-1912
Greensboro	NC	1908-1912
Greenville	SC	1908-1912
Spartanburg	SC	1908-1912
Winston-Salem	NC	1908-1912

CAROLINA LEAGUE
CLASS C 1945-1948; CLASS B 1949-1962; CLASS A 1963-

Alexandria	VA	1978-1983
Asheville	NC	1967
Burlington	NC	1945-1951, 1958-1972
Burlington-Graham	NC	1952-1955
Danville	VA	1945-1958
Durham	NC	1945-1967, 1980-
Fayetteville	NC	1950-1956
Frederick	MD	1989-
Greensboro	NC	1945-1968
Hagerstown	MD	1981-1988
High Point-Thomasville	NC	1954-1958, 1968-1969
Kinston	NC	1956-1957, 1962-1974, 1978-
Leaksville-Draper-Spray	NC	1945-1947
Lynchburg	VA	1966-
Martinsville	VA	1945-1949
Peninsula (Hampton) (aka Virginia)	VA	1963-1971, 1974, 1976-1987, 1989-1992 1988
Portsmouth	VA	1963-1968
Prince William	VA	1984-
Raleigh	NC	1945-1953, 1958-1967
Raleigh-Durham	NC	1968-1971
Red Springs	NC	1969
Reidsville	NC	1948-1955
Rocky Mount	NC	1962-1975, 1980
Salem	VA	1968-
Wilmington	DE	1993-
Wilson	NC	1956-1968, 1973
Winston-Salem	NC	1945-

CENTRAL ASSOCIATION
CLASS D 1908-1917; CLASS C 1947-1949
(successor of the Iowa State League 1904-1907)

Burlington	IA	1908-1916, 1947-1949
Cedar Rapids	IA	1913-1917, 1949
Charles City	IA	1917
Clear Lake	IA	1917
Clinton	IA	1914-1917, 1947-1949
Dubuque	IA	1917
Ft. Dodge	IA	1916-1917
Galesburg	IL	1910-1912, 1914
Hannibal	MO	1909-1912, 1947-1948
Jacksonville	IL	1908-1909
Keokuk	IA	1908-1915, 1947-1949
Kewanee	IL	1908-1913, 1948-1949
La Crosse	WI	1917
Marshalltown	IA	1914-1917
Mason City	IA	1915-1917
Moline	IL	1947-1948
Monmouth	IL	1910-1913
Muscatine	IA	1911-1916
Oskaloosa	IA	1908
Ottumwa	IA	1908-1914, 1916
Quincy	IL	1908-1910
Rock Island	IL	1914
Rockford	IL	1947-1949
Waterloo	IA	1908-1909, 1913-1917

CENTRAL LEAGUE
1888

Allentown	PA	1888
Binghamton	NY	1888
Easton	PA	1888
Hazleton	PA	1888
Jersey City	NJ	1888
Newark	NJ	1888
Scranton	PA	1888
Wilkes-Barre	PA	1888

PROFESSIONAL TEAMS BY LEAGUE 1883-1997

CENTRAL LEAGUE
1900
(successor of the Western Association 1894-1897, 1899)

Bloomington	IN	1900
Danville	IL	1900
Decatur	IL	1900
Jacksonville	IL	1900
Peoria	IL	1900
Springfield	IL	1900
Terre Haute	IN	1900

CENTRAL LEAGUE
CLASS B 1903-1917, 1920-1922, 1926, 1928-1930, 1932, 1934; CLASS A 1948-1951
(mid-season predecessor of the Michigan State League 1926)

Akron	OH	1912, 1928-1929, 1932
Anderson	IN	1903
Canton	OH	1905-1907, 1912, 1928-1930, 1932
Charleston	WV	1949-1951
Dayton	OH	1903-1917, 1928-1930, 1932, 1948-1951
Erie	PA	1912, 1915, 1928-1930, 1932
Evansville	IN	1903-1911, 1913-1917
Flint	MI	1948-1951
Fort Wayne	IN	1903-1905, 1908-1915, 1917, 1928-1930, 1932, 1934, 1948
Grand Rapids	MI	1903-1917, 1920-1922, 1926, 1948-1951
Ionia	MI	1921-1922
Jackson	MI	1921
Kalamazoo	MI	1920-1922, 1926
Lansing	MI	1921-1922
Lima	OH	1934
Ludington	MI	1920-1922, 1926
Marion	OH	1903-1904
Muskegon	MI	1916-1917, 1920-1922, 1926, 1934, 1948-1951
Newark	OH	1911
Peoria	IL	1904, 1917, 1934
Richmond	IN	1917, 1930
Saginaw	MI	1948-1951
South Bend	IN	1903-1912, 1916-1917, 1932
Springfield	OH	1905-1907, 1912-1914, 1916-1917, 1928-1930
Terre Haute	IN	1903-1916
Wheeling	WV	1903-1912, 1915-1916
Youngstown	OH	1912, 1915, 1932
Zanesville	OH	1908-1912

CENTRAL CALIFORNIA LEAGUE
CLASS D 1910-1911

Alameda	CA	1910-1911
Berkeley	CA	1910-1911
Hayward	CA	1910-1911
Healdsburg	CA	1910
Napa	CA	1910
Oakland	CA	1910-1911
Oakland-Elmhurst	CA	1910-1911
Oakland-Fruitvale	CA	1910-1911
Petaluma	CA	1910
Richmond	CA	1910-1911
St. Helena	CA	1910
San Leandro	CA	1910-1911
San Rafael	CA	1910
Santa Rosa	CA	1910
Vallejo	CA	1910-1911

CENTRAL INTERNATIONAL LEAGUE
CLASS C 1912
(predecessor of the Northern League 1913-1917)

Duluth	MN	1912
Grand Forks	ND	1912
Superior	WI	1912
Winnipeg	MB	1912

CENTRAL INTERSTATE LEAGUE
1888-1889

Bloomington	IN	1888
Burlington	IA	1889
Crawfordsville	IN	1888
Danville	IL	1888
Davenport	IA	1888-1889
Decatur	IL	1888
Dubuque	IA	1888
Evansville	IN	1889
Lafayette	IN	1888
Peoria	IL	1888-1889

Quincy	IL	1889
Rockford	IL	1888
Springfield	IL	1889
Terre Haute	IN	1888

CENTRAL KANSAS LEAGUE
CLASS D 1908-1912
(predecessor of the Kansas State League 1913-1914)

Abilene	KS	1909-1910
Beloit	KS	1909-1910
Chapman	KS	1910
Clay Center	KS	1909-1911
Concordia	KS	1910-1911
Ellsworth	KS	1908-1910
Great Bend	KS	1912
Junction City	KS	1909-1912
Little River	KS	1908
Lyons	KS	1912
Manhattan	KS	1909-1912
McPherson	KS	1908
Minneapolis	KS	1908-1909, 1912
Newton	KS	1908, 1912
Salina	KS	1908-1910, 1912

CENTRAL MEXICAN LEAGUE
CLASS C 1956-1957

Aguascalientes	MEX	1956-1957
Chihuahua	MEX	1956-1957
Ciudad Juarez	MEX	1956-1957
Durango	MEX	1956-1957
Fresnillo	MEX	1956-1957
Laguna	MEX	1957
Saltillo	MEX	1956-1957

CENTRAL PENNSYLVANIA LEAGUE
1887

Ashland	PA	1887
Danville	PA	1887
Hazleton	PA	1887
Mahanoy City	PA	1887
Minersville	PA	1887
Mt. Carmel	PA	1887
Shamokin	PA	1887
Sunbury	PA	1887

CENTRAL TEXAS LEAGUE
CLASS D 1914-1917
(aka Central Texas Trolley League 1914-1915)

Corsicana	TX	1914-1915, 1917
Ennis	TX	1914-1917
Hillsboro	TX	1914
Italy	TX	1914
Kaufman	TX	1915
Marlin	TX	1916-1917
Mexia	TX	1915-1917
Temple	TX	1916-1917
Terrell	TX	1915-1916
Waxahachie	TX	1914-1916
West	TX	1914

COASTAL PLAIN LEAGUE
CLASS D 1937-1941, 1946-1952

Ayden	NC	1937-1938
Edenton	NC	1952
Fayetteville	NC	1946
Goldsboro	NC	1937-1941, 1946-1952
Greenville	NC	1937-1940, 1946-1951
Kinston	NC	1937-1941, 1946-1952
New Bern	NC	1937-1941, 1946-1952
Roanoke Rapids	NC	1947-1952
Rocky Mount	NC	1941, 1946-1952
Snow Hill	NC	1937-1940
Tarboro	NC	1937-1941, 1946-1952
Williamston	NC	1937-1941
Wilson	NC	1939-1941, 1946-1952

COCOA ROOKIE LEAGUE
ROOKIE 1964
(games played at Cocoa, FL)

Colts	FL	1964
Mets	FL	1964
Twins	FL	1964
Tigers	FL	1964

PROFESSIONAL TEAMS BY LEAGUE 1883-1997

COLONIAL LEAGUE
CLASS C 1914; IND 1915

Brockton	MA	1914-1915
Fall River	MA	1914-1915
Hartford	CT	1915
New Bedford	MA	1914-1915
New Haven	CT	1915
Pawtucket	RI	1914-1915
Springfield	MA	1915
Taunton	MA	1914-1915
Woonsocket	RI	1914

COLONIAL LEAGUE
CLASS B 1947-1950

Bridgeport	CT	1947-1950
Bristol	CT	1949-1950
Kingston	NY	1948-1950
New Brunswick	NJ	1948
New London	CT	1947
Port Chester	NY	1947-1948
Poughkeepsie	NY	1947-1950
Stamford	CT	1947-1949
Torrington	CT	1950
Waterbury	CT	1947-1950

CONNECTICUT ASSOCIATION
CLASS D 1910
(aka Eastern Connecticut League)

Meriden	CT	1910
Middletown	CT	1910
New London	CT	1910
Norwich	CT	1910
Willimantic	CT	1910

CONNECTICUT STATE LEAGUE
1899-1901; CLASS D 1902-1904; CLASS B 1905-1912
(aka Connecticut League)
(predecessor of the Eastern Association 1913-1914)

Bridgeport	CT	1899-1912
Bristol	CT	1899-1901
Derby	CT	1899-1901
Hartford	CT	1902-1912
Holyoke	MA	1903-1912
Meriden	CT	1899-1905, 1908
New Britain	CT	1908-1912
New Haven	CT	1899-1912
New London	CT	1899-1907
Northampton	MA	1909-1911
Norwich	CT	1899-1907
Springfield	MA	1902-1912
Worcester	MA	1904
Waterbury	CT	1899-1902, 1906-1912

COPPER COUNTRY SOO LEAGUE
CLASS D 1905
(merged with Northern League to form Northern-Copper Country League 1906-1907)

Calumet	MI	1905
Sault Ste. Marie	MI	1905
Hancock	MI	1905
Lake Linden	MI	1905

COTTON STATES LEAGUE
CLASS D 1902-1908, 1910-1913, 1922-1932;
CLASS C 1936-1941, 1947-1955

Alexandria	LA	1925-1930
Baton Rouge	LA	1902-1906, 1929-1932
Brookhaven	MS	1924-1925
Clarksdale	MS	1913, 1922-1923, 1936-1941, 1947-1951
Cleveland	MS	1936
Columbus	MS	1907-1908, 1912-1913
De Quincy	LA	1932
El Dorado	AR	1929-1932, 1936-1941, 1947-1955
Greenville	MS	1902-1905, 1922-1923, 1936-1941, 1947-1955
Greenwood	MS	1910-1912, 1922-1923, 1936-1940, 1947-1952
Gulfport	MS	1906-1907, 1926-1928
Gulfport-Biloxi	MS	1908
Hattiesburg	MS	1905, 1910-1912, 1923-1929
Helena	AR	1936-1941, 1947-1949
Hot Springs	AR	1938-1941, 1947-1955
Jackson	MS	1905-1908, 1910-1913, 1922-1932, 1936, 1953
Lake Charles	LA	1929-1930

Laurel	MS	1923-1929
Marshall	TX	1941
Meridian	MS	1905-1908, 1910-1913, 1922-1929, 1952-1955
Mobile	AL	1905-1907
Monroe	LA	1903-1904, 1908, 1924-1932, 1937-1941, 1950-1955
Natchez	MS	1902-1905, 1948-1953
New Orleans	LA	1912
Opelousas	LA	1932
Pensacola	FL	1913
Pine Bluff	AR	1903-1905, 1930-1932, 1936-1940, 1948-1955
Port Arthur	TX	1932
Selma	AL	1913
Texarkana	TX	1941
Vicksburg	MS	1902-1908, 1910-1912, 1922-1931, 1937, 1941, 1955
Yazoo City	MS	1910-1912

DAKOTA LEAGUE
CLASS D 1921-1922
(successor of the South Dakota League 1920)
(predecessor of the South Dakota League 1923)

Aberdeen	SD	1921-1922
Bismarck	ND	1922
Fargo	ND	1922
Huron	SD	1921
Jamestown	ND	1922
Madison	SD	1921
Mitchell	SD	1921-1922
Redfield	SD	1921
Sioux Falls	SD	1921-1922
Valley City	ND	1922
Wahpeton-Breckenridge	ND-MN	1921-1922
Watertown	SD	1921-1922

DELTA LEAGUE
CLASS D 1904

Brookhaven	MS	1904
Canton	MS	1904
Clarksdale	MS	1904
Hattiesburg	MS	1904
Jackson	MS	1904
Yazoo City	MS	1904

DIXIE LEAGUE (AL-GA)
CLASS D 1916-1917

Bainbridge	GA	1916-1917
Dothan	AL	1916-1917
Eufaula	AL	1916-1917
Moultrie	GA	1916-1917
Quitman	GA	1916-1917
Tifton	GA	1917
Valdosta	GA	1916

DIXIE LEAGUE (AR-LA-MS-TX)
CLASS C 1933
(split into East and West Dixie Leagues)

Baton Rouge	LA	1933
El Dorado	AR	1933
Henderson	TX	1933
Jackson	MS	1933
Longview	TX	1933
Pine Bluff	AR	1933
Shreveport	LA	1933
Tyler	TX	1933
Waco	TX	1933

EAST DIXIE LEAGUE
CLASS C 1934-1935
(successor of the Dixie League 1933)

Baton Rouge	LA	1934
Clarksdale	MS	1934-1935
Cleveland	MS	1935
Columbus	MS	1935
El Dorado	AR	1934-1935
Greenville	MS	1934-1935
Greenwood	MS	1934-1935
Helena	AR	1935
Jackson	MS	1934-1935
Pine Bluff	AR	1934-1935
Shreveport	LA	1934

PROFESSIONAL TEAMS BY LEAGUE 1883-1997

EAST TEXAS LEAGUE
CLASS D 1916, 1923-1926, 1931;
CLASS C 1936-1940, 1946, 1949-1950

Bryan	TX	1949-1950
Crockett	TX	1916
Gladewater	TX	1936, 1949-1950
Greenville	TX	1923-1926, 1946
Henderson	TX	1931, 1936-1940, 1946, 1949-1950
Jacksonville	TX	1936-1940, 1946
Kilgore	TX	1931, 1936-1940, 1949-1950
Longview	TX	1923-1926, 1931, 1936-1940, 1949-1950
Lufkin	TX	1916, 1946
Marshall	TX	1923-1926, 1936-1940, 1949-1950
Mt. Pleasant	TX	1923-1925
Nacogdoches	TX	1916
Palestine	TX	1916, 1936-1940
Paris	TX	1923-1926, 1931, 1946, 1949-1950
Rusk	TX	1916
Sherman	TX	1946
Sulphur Springs	TX	1923-1925
Texarkana	TX	1924-1926, 1937-1940, 1946
Tyler	TX	1924-1926, 1931, 1936-1940, 1946, 1949-1950

EASTERN LEAGUE
1883-1886
(known as Interstate Association 1883)

Allentown	PA	1884
Atlantic City	NJ	1885
Baltimore	MD	1884
Bridgeport	CT	1885-1886
Brooklyn	NY	1883-1884
Camden	NJ	1883
Harrisburg	PA	1883-1884
Hartford	CT	1886
Jersey City	NJ	1885-1886
Pottsville	PA	1883
Providence	RI	1886
Reading	PA	1883-1884
Richmond	VA	1884-1885
Lancaster	PA	1884-1885
Long Island (Maspeth)	NY	1886
Meriden	CT	1886
Newark	NJ	1884-1886
Norfolk	VA	1885
Trenton	NJ	1883-1885
Washington	DC	1885
Waterbury	CT	1885-1886
Wilmington	DE	1883-1885
York	PA	1884

EASTERN LEAGUE
1892-1911
(see International League)

EASTERN LEAGUE
CLASS B 1916-1918; CLASS A 1919-1932

Albany	NY	1920-1932
Allentown	PA	1929-1932
Bridgeport	CT	1916-1932
Fitchburg	MA	1922
Hartford	CT	1916-1932
Lawrence	MA	1916-1917
Lowell	MA	1916
Lynn	MA	1916
New Haven	CT	1916-1932
New London	CT	1916-1918
Norfolk	VA	1931-1932
Pittsfield	MA	1919-1930
Portland	ME	1916-1917
Providence	RI	1918-1919, 1926-1930
Richmond	VA	1931-1932
Springfield	MA	1916-1932
Waterbury	CT	1918-1922
Worcester	MA	1916-1926

EASTERN LEAGUE
CLASS A 1938-1962; CLASS AA 1963-
(successor of the New York-Pennsylvania League 1923-1937)

Akron	OH	1997-
Albany	NY	1938-1959
Albany-Colonie	NY	1983-1994
Allentown	PA	1954-1960
Binghamton	NY	1938-1963, 1967-1968, 1992-
Bristol	CT	1973-1982
Bowie	MD	1993-
Buffalo	NY	1979-1984
Canton-Akron	OH	1989-1996
Charleston	WV	1962-1964
Elmira	NY	1938-1955, 1961-1972
Glens Falls	NY	1980-1988
Hagerstown	MD	1989-1992
Harrisburg	PA	1987-
Hartford	CT	1938-1952
Hazleton	PA	1938
Holyoke	MA	1977-1982
Jersey City	NJ	1977-1978
Johnstown	PA	1955-1956, 1961
Lancaster	PA	1958-1961
London	ONT	1989-1993
Lynn	MA	1980-1983
Manchester	NH	1969-1971
Nashua	NH	1983-1986
New Britain (aka Hardware City)	CT	1984-
New Haven	CT	1994-
Norwich	CT	1995-
Pawtucket	RI	1966-1967, 1970-1972
Pittsfield	MA	1965-1976, 1985-1988
Portland	ME	1994-
Quebec	QUE	1971-1977
Reading	PA	1952-1961, 1963-1965, 1967-
Schenectady	NY	1951-1957
Scranton	PA	1939-1953
Sherbrooke	QUE	1972-1973
Springfield	MA	1939-1943, 1957-1965
Syracuse	NY	1956-1957
Thetford Mines	QUE	1974-1975
Trenton	NJ	1938, 1994-
Trois Rivieres	QUE	1971-1977
Utica	NY	1943-1950
Vermont (Burlington)	VT	1984-1988
Waterbury	CT	1966-1971, 1973-1986
West Haven	CT	1972-1982
Wilkes-Barre	PA	1938-1951, 1953-1955
Williamsport	PA	1938-1942, 1944-1956, 1958-1962, 1964-1967, 1976, 1987-1991
York	PA	1958-1959, 1962-1969

EASTERN ASSOCIATION
CLASS B 1913-1914
(successor of the Connecticut State League 1899-1912)

Bridgeport	CT	1913-1914
Hartford	CT	1913-1914
Holyoke	MA	1913
Meriden	CT	1913
New Britain	CT	1914
New Haven	CT	1913-1914
New London	CT	1913-1914
Pittsfield	MA	1913-1914
Springfield	MA	1913-1914
Waterbury	CT	1913-1914

EASTERN CANADA LEAGUE
CLASS B 1922-1923

Cap de la Madeleine	QUE	1922
Montreal	QUE	1922-1923
Ottawa	ONT	1922-1923
Quebec	QUE	1923
Trois Rivers	QUE	1922-1923
Valleyfield	QUE	1922

EASTERN CAROLINA LEAGUE
CLASS D 1908-1910, 1928-1929

Fayetteville	NC	1909-1910, 1928-1929
Goldsboro	NC	1908-1910, 1928-1929
Greenville	NC	1928-1929
Kinston	NC	1908, 1928-1929
New Bern	NC	1908
Raleigh	NC	1908-1910
Rocky Mount	NC	1909-1910, 1928-1929
Wilmington	NC	1908-1910, 1928-1929
Wilson	NC	1908-1910

PROFESSIONAL TEAMS BY LEAGUE 1883-1997

EASTERN ILLINOIS LEAGUE
CLASS D 1907-1908

Centralia	IL	1907
Charleston	IL	1907-1908
Danville	IL	1908
Linton	IN	1908
Mattoon	IL	1907-1908
Pana	IL	1907-1908
Paris	IL	1907-1908
Shelbyville	IL	1907-1908
Staunton	IL	1908
Taylorville	IL	1907-1908
Vincennes	IN	1908

EASTERN KANSAS LEAGUE
CLASS D 1910

Blue Rapids	KS	1910
Hiawatha	KS	1910
Holton	KS	1910
Horton	KS	1910
Marysville	KS	1910
Sabetha	KS	1910
Seneca	KS	1910

EASTERN SHORE LEAGUE
CLASS D 1922-1928, 1937-1941, 1946-1949

Cambridge	MD	1922-1928, 1937-1941, 1946-1949
Centreville	MD	1937-1941, 1946
Crisfield	MD	1922-1928, 1937
Dover	DE	1923-1926, 1937-1941, 1946-1948
Easton	MD	1924-1928, 1937-1941, 1946-1949
Federalsburg	MD	1937-1941, 1946-1949
Laurel	DE	1922-1923
Milford	DE	1923, 1938-1941, 1946-1948
Northampton	VA	1927-1928
Parksley	VA	1922-1928
Pocomoke City	MD	1922-1923, 1937-1940
Rehoboth Beach	DE	1947-1949
Salisbury	MD	1922-1928, 1937-1941, 1946-1949
Seaford	DE	1946-1949

EMPIRE STATE LEAGUE (GA)
CLASS D 1913
(predecessor of the Georgia State League 1914)

Americus	GA	1913
Brunswick	GA	1913
Cordele	GA	1913
Thomasville	GA	1913
Valdosta	GA	1913
Waycross	GA	1913

EVANGELINE LEAGUE
CLASS D 1934-1942, 1946-1948; CLASS C 1949-1957

Abbeville	LA	1935-1939, 1946-1950, 1952
Alexandria	LA	1934-1942, 1946-1957
Baton Rouge	LA	1946-1957
Crowley	LA	1951-1957
Hammond	LA	1946-1951
Houma	LA	1940, 1946-1952
Jeanerette	LA	1934-1939
Lafayette	LA	1934-1942, 1948-1957
Lake Charles	LA	1934-1942, 1954-1957
Monroe	LA	1956
Natchez	MS	1940-1942, 1946-1947
New Iberia	LA	1934-1942, 1946-1956
Opelousas	LA	1934-1941
Port Arthur	TX	1940-1942, 1954
Rayne	LA	1934-1941
Texas City	TX	1954
Thibodaux	LA	1946-1954, 1956-1957

FAR WEST LEAGUE
CLASS D 1948-1951

Eugene	OR	1950-1951
Klamath Falls	OR	1948-1951
Marysville	CA	1948-1950
Medford	OR	1948-1951
Oroville	CA	1948
Pittsburg	CA	1948-1951
Redding	CA	1948-1951
Reno	NV	1950-1951
Roseville	CA	1948
Santa Rosa	CA	1948-1949
Vallejo	CA	1949
Willows	CA	1948-1950

FEDERAL LEAGUE
IND 1913; MAJOR 1914-1915

Baltimore	MD	1914-1915
Brooklyn	NY	1914-1915
Buffalo	NY	1914-1915
Chicago	IL	1913-1915
Cleveland	OH	1913
Covington	KY	1913
Indianapolis	IN	1913-1914
Kansas City	MO	1913-1915
Newark	NJ	1915
Pittsburgh	PA	1913-1915
St. Louis	MO	1913-1915

FLAG LEAGUE (FLORIDA-ALABAMA-GEORGIA)
CLASS D 1915
(successor of the Georgia State League 1914)
(started 1915 season as the Georgia State League; changed its name June 15.)

Americus	GA	1915
Brunswick	GA	1915
Dothan	AL	1915
Gainesville	FL	1915
Thomasville	GA	1915
Valdosta	GA	1915
Waycross	GA	1915

FLORIDA EAST COAST LEAGUE
CLASS D 1940-1942

Cocoa	FL	1941-1942
DeLand	FL	1942
Ft. Lauderdale	FL	1940-1942
Ft. Pierce	FL	1940-1942
Hollywood	FL	1940
Miami	FL	1940-1942
Miami Beach	FL	1940-1942
Orlando	FL	1942
West Palm Beach	FL	1940-1942

FLORIDA EAST COAST LEAGUE
ROOKIE 1972
(games played at Cocoa and Melbourne, FL)

Reds	FL	1972
Twins	FL	1972
Astros	FL	1972
Expos	FL	1972

FLORIDA INTERNATIONAL LEAGUE
CLASS C 1946-1948; CLASS B 1949-1954

Ft. Lauderdale	FL	1947-1953
Havana	Cuba	1946-1953
Key West	FL	1952
Lakeland	FL	1946-1952
Miami	FL	1946-1954
Miami Beach	FL	1946-1952, 1954
St. Petersburg	FL	1947-1954
Tallahassee	FL	1954
Tampa	FL	1946-1954
West Palm Beach	FL	1946-1954

FLORIDA ROOKIE LEAGUE
ROOKIE 1965
(successor of the Sarasota Rookie League 1964)
(predecessor of the Gulf Coast League 1966-)
(games played at Bradenton and Sarasota, FL)

Astros	FL	1965
Braves	FL	1965
Twins	FL	1965
White Sox	FL	1965
Cardinals	FL	1965
Yankees	FL	1965

FLORIDA STATE LEAGUE
CLASS D 1919-1920, 1925-1928, 1936-1941, 1946-1962; CLASS C 1921-1924; CLASS A 1963-

Bartow	FL	1920
Bartow-Winter Haven	FL	1919
Baseball City	FL	1988-1992
Bradenton (formerly Bradentown)	FL	1919-1920, 1923-1924, 1926
Brevard County	FL	1994-
Clearwater	FL	1924, 1985-
Cocoa	FL	1951-1958, 1965-1972, 1977
Daytona Beach	FL	1920-1924, 1928, 1936-1941, 1946-1973,

22

PROFESSIONAL TEAMS BY LEAGUE 1883-1997

		1977-1987, 1993-
DeLand	FL	1936-1941, 1946-1954, 1970
Deerfield Beach	FL	1966
Dunedin	FL	1978-1979, 1987-
Ft. Lauderdale	FL	1928, 1962-1993
Ft. Myers	FL	1926, 1978-1987, 1992-
Gainesville	FL	1936-1941, 1946-1952, 1955-1958
Jacksonville	FL	1921-1922
Jacksonville Beach	FL	1952-1954
Key West	FL	1969, 1971-1975
Kissimmee (aka Osceola)	FL	1985-
Lakeland	FL	1919-1926, 1953-1955, 1960, 1962-1964, 1967-
Leesburg	FL	1937-1941, 1946-1953, 1956-1957, 1960-1961, 1965-1968
Miami	FL	1927-1928, 1962-1991
Ocala	FL	1940-1941
Orlando	FL	1919-1924, 1926-1928, 1937-1941, 1946-1961, 1963-1972
Palatka	FL	1936-1939, 1946-1953, 1956-1962
Port Charlotte	FL	1987-
Pompano Beach	FL	1969-1973, 1976-1978
St. Augustine	FL	1936-1941, 1946-1950, 1952
St. Lucie	FL	1988-
St. Petersburg	FL	1920-1928, 1955-
Sanford	FL	1919-1920, 1925-1928, 1936-1941, 1946-1953, 1955, 1959-1960
Sarasota	FL	1926-1927, 1961-1965, 1989-
Tampa	FL	1919-1927, 1957-1988, 1994-
Vero Beach	FL	1980-
West Palm Beach	FL	1928, 1955-1956, 1965-
Winter Haven	FL	1966-1967, 1969-1992

FRONTIER LEAGUE
IND 1993-

Canton	OH	1997-
Chillicothe	OH	1993-
Erie	PA	1994
Evansville	IN	1995-
Johnstown	PA	1995-
Kalamazoo	MI	1996-
Kentucky (Paintsville)	KY	1993-1994
Lancaster	OH	1993-1994
Newark	OH	1994-1995
Ohio Valley (Parkersburg)	WV	1993-
Portsmouth	OH	1993-1995
Richmond	IN	1995-
Springfield	IL	1996-
Tri-State (Ashland)	KY	1993
West Virginia (Wayne)	WV	1993
Zanesville	OH	1993-1996

GEORGIA STATE LEAGUE
CLASS D 1906, 1914
(successor of the Empire State League 1913)
(predecessor of the FLAG League 1915)

Albany	GA	1906
Americus	GA	1906, 1914
Brunswick	GA	1906, 1914
Columbus	GA	1906
Cordele	GA	1906, 1914
Thomasville	GA	1914
Valdosta	GA	1906, 1914
Waycross	GA	1906, 1914

GEORGIA STATE LEAGUE
CLASS D 1948-1956

Baxley	GA	1948
Baxley-Hazlehurst	GA	1949-1950
Douglas	GA	1948-1956
Dublin	GA	1949-1956
Eastman	GA	1948-1953
Fitzgerald	GA	1948-1952
Hazlehurst-Baxley	GA	1951-1956
Jesup	GA	1950-1953
Sandersville	GA	1953-1956
Sparta	GA	1948-1949
Statesboro	GA	1952-1955
Thomson	GA	1956
Tifton	GA	1949-1950
Vidalia	GA	1952-1956
Vidalia-Lyons	GA	1948-1950

GEORGIA-ALABAMA LEAGUE
CLASS D 1913-1917, 1928-1930, 1946-1951
GEORGIA STATE LEAGUE
CLASS D 1920-1921

Alexander City	AL	1947-1951
Anniston	AL	1913-1917, 1928-1930
Carrollton	GA	1920-1921, 1928-1930, 1946-1950
Cedartown	GA	1920-1921, 1928-1930
Gadsden	AL	1913-1914, 1928-1929
Griffin	GA	1915-1917, 1920-1921, 1947-1951
Huntsville	AL	1930
La Grange	GA	1913-1917, 1920-1921, 1946-1951
Lindale	GA	1920-1921, 1928-1930
Newnan	GA	1913-1916, 1946-1950
Opelika	AL	1913-1914, 1946-1951
Rome	GA	1914-1917, 1920-1921, 1950-1951
Selma	AL	1914
Talladega	AL	1913-1917, 1928-1930
Tallassee	AL	1946-1949
Tri-Cities	AL	1917
Valley	AL-GA	1946-1951
(Valley-Lanett-West Point)		

GEORGIA-FLORIDA LEAGUE
CLASS D 1935-1942, 1946-1958, 1962; CLASS A 1963

Albany	GA	1935-1942, 1946-1958
Americus	GA	1935-1942, 1946-1951
Brunswick	GA	1951-1958, 1962-1963
Cordele	GA	1936-1942, 1946-1953, 1955
Cordele-Americus	GA	1954
Dothan	AL	1942
Dublin	GA	1958, 1962
Fitzgerald	GA	1953-1954, 1956-1957
Moultrie	GA	1935-1942, 1946-1952, 1956-1957, 1962-1963
Panama City	FL	1935
Tallahassee	FL	1935-1942, 1946-1950
Thomasville	GA	1935-1941, 1946-1950, 1952-1958, 1962-1963
Tifton	GA	1951-1956
Valdosta	GA	1939-1942, 1946-1958
Waycross	GA	1939-1942, 1946-1958, 1963

GOLDEN STATE LEAGUE
IND 1995

Brawley (Antelope Valley)	CA	1995
Rosamond (Imperial Valley)	CA	1995
Southern Nomadic (Yuma)	AZ	1995
Yuma	AZ	1995

GREAT CENTRAL LEAGUE
IND 1994

Champaign-Urbana	IL	1994
Lafayette	IN	1994
Mason City	IA	1994
Minneapolis	MN	1994

GULF COAST LEAGUE
CLASS D 1907-1908, 1926; CLASS C 1950; CLASS B 1951-1953

Alexandria	LA	1907-1908
Beaumont	TX	1908
Beeville	TX	1926
Brownsville	TX	1951-1953
Corpus Christi	TX	1926, 1951-1953
Crowley	LA	1908, 1950
Edinburg	TX	1926
Galveston	TX	1950-1953
Harlingen	TX	1951-1953
Jacksonville	TX	1950
Kingsville	TX	1926
Lafayette	LA	1907
Lake Charles	LA	1907-1908, 1950-1953
Laredo	TX	1926, 1951-1953
Leesville	LA	1950
Lufkin	TX	1950
McAllen	TX	1926
Mission	TX	1926
Monroe	LA	1907
Morgan City	LA	1908
Opelousas	LA	1907
Orange	TX	1907-1908
Port Arthur	TX	1950-1953
Texas City	TX	1951-1953
Victoria	TX	1926

PROFESSIONAL TEAMS BY LEAGUE 1883-1997

GULF COAST LEAGUE
ROOKIE 1966-
(successor of the Florida Rookie League 1965)

(games played at Baseball City, Bradenton, Dunedin, Ft. Myers, Kissimmee, Lakeland, Lee County, Melbourne, Plant City, Port Charlotte, Port St. Lucie, St. Petersburg, Sarasota, Tampa, West Palm Beach and Winter Haven, FL)

Astros	FL	1977-
Athletics	FL	1968
Blue Jays	FL	1981-1985, 1991-1995
Braves	FL	1966-1967, 1976-
Cardinals	FL	1966-1976
Cubs	FL	1972-1982, 1993-
Devil Rays	FL	1996-
Dodgers	FL	1983-1992
Expos	FL	1969-1970, 1974, 1977, 1986-
Indians	FL	1967-1975, 1988-1990
Marlins	FL	1992-
Mets	FL	1983, 1988-
Orioles	FL	1991-
Padres	FL	1981-1982
Phillies	FL	1984
Pirates	FL	1968-
Rangers	FL	1973-
Red Sox	FL	1989-
Reds	FL	1968-1973, 1984-1990
Royals	FL	1967, 1971-
Tigers	FL	1968, 1995-
Twins	FL	1966-1971, 1989-
White Sox	FL	1966-1977, 1980-
Yankees	FL	1966, 1980-1982, 1984-

GULF STATES LEAGUE
CLASS A 1976
(predecessor of the Lone Star League 1977)

Baton Rouge	LA	1976
Beeville	TX	1976
Corpus Christi	TX	1976
Rio Grande Valley	TX	1976
Seguin	TX	1976
Victoria	TX	1976

HEARTLAND LEAGUE
IND 1996-

Anderson	IN	1996-
Clarksville	TN	1997-
Columbia	TN	1997-
DuBois County	IN	1996-
Altoona	PA	1997-
Lafayette	IN	1996-
Tennessee (Winchester)	TN	1997-
Will County	IL	1996-

HUDSON RIVER LEAGUE
CLASS D 1903; CLASS C 1904-1907

Catskill	NY	1903
Glens Falls-Saratoga Springs	NY	1906
Hudson	NY	1903-1907
Kingston	NY	1903-1907
Newburgh	NY	1903-1907
Ossining	NY	1903
Paterson	NJ	1904-1907
Peekskill	NY	1903, 1905
Pittsfield	MA	1905
Poughkeepsie	NY	1903-1907
Saugerties	NY	1903-1905
Yonkers	NY	1905, 1907

ILLINOIS STATE LEAGUE
CLASS D 1947-1948
(predecessor of the Mississippi-Ohio Valley League 1949-1955)

Belleville	IL	1947-1948
Centralia	IL	1947-1948
Marion	IL	1947-1948
Mattoon	IL	1947-1948
Mt. Vernon	IL	1947-1948
West Frankfort	IL	1947-1948

ILLINOIS-INDIANA LEAGUE
(see Two-I League)

ILLINOIS-IOWA-INDIANA LEAGUE
(see Three-I League)

ILLINOIS-MISSOURI LEAGUE
CLASS D 1908-1914

Beardstown	IL	1909-1910
Canton	IL	1908-1913
Champaign	IL	1912-1914
Champaign-Urbana	IL	1911
Clinton	IL	1910-1912
Galesburg	IL	1908-1909
Hannibal	MO	1908
Havana	IL	1908
Jacksonville	IL	1910
Kankakee	IL	1912-1914
La Salle	IL	1914
Lincoln	IL	1910-1914
Macomb	IL	1908-1910
Monmouth	IL	1908-1909
Ottawa	IL	1914
Pekin	IL	1909-1913
Streator	IL	1912-1914
Taylorville	IL	1911

INDIANA STATE LEAGUE
(see Northern State of Indiana League)

INDIANA-MICHIGAN LEAGUE
CLASS D 1910

Berrien Springs	MI	1910
Dowagiac	MI	1910
Elkhart	IN	1910
Gary	IN	1910
Ligonier	IN	1910
Niles	MI	1910

INDIANA-OHIO LEAGUE
(see Ohio-Indiana League)

INLAND EMPIRE LEAGUE
CLASS D 1908
(predecessor of the Western Tri-State League 1912-1914)

Baker City	OR	1908
La Grande	OR	1908
Pendleton	OR	1908
Walla Walla	WA	1908

INTER-AMERICAN LEAGUE
CLASS AAA 1979

Caracas	VEN	1979
Maracaibo	VEN	1979
Miami	FL	1979
Panama	PAN	1979
San Juan	PR	1979
Santo Domingo	DR	1979

INTER-MOUNTAIN LEAGUE
1901

Ogden	UT	1901
Salt Lake City	UT	1901
Lagoon	UT	1901
Park City	UT	1901

INTER-MOUNTAIN LEAGUE
CLASS D 1909

Boise	ID	1909
Bozeman	MT	1909
Butte	MT	1909
Helena	MT	1909
Livingston	MT	1909
Salt Lake City	UT	1909

INTERNATIONAL ASSOCIATION
(see International League)

INTERNATIONAL LEAGUE 1900
(see Canadian League)

INTERNATIONAL LEAGUE
CLASS D 1908

Guelph	ONT	1908
Hamilton	ONT	1908
London	ONT	1908
Niagara Falls	NY	1908
St. Thomas	ONT	1908

PROFESSIONAL TEAMS BY LEAGUE 1883-1997

INTERNATIONAL LEAGUE
1885-1901; CLASS A 1902-1911; CLASS AA 1912-1945; CLASS AAA 1946-
(known as New York State League 1885)
(known as International Association 1886-1890)
(known as Eastern Association 1891)
(known as Eastern League 1892-1911)
(known as the New International League 1918-1919)

Akron	OH	1920
Albany	NY	1885, 1888, 1891-1893, 1896, 1933-1936
Allentown	PA	1894
Atlanta	GA	1962-1965
Baltimore	MD	1903-1914, 1916-1953
Binghamton	NY	1885-1887, 1892-1894, 1918-1919
Brockton	MA	1901
Buffalo	NY	1886-1899, 1901-1970
Charleston	WV	1961, 1971-1983
Charlotte	NC	1993-
Columbus	OH	1955-1970, 1977-
Detroit	MI	1889-1890
Elmira	NY	1885, 1892
Erie	PA	1893-1894
Grand Rapids	MI	1890
Hamilton	ONT	1886-1890, 1918
Harrisburg	PA	1915
Hartford	CT	1899-1901
Havana	Cuba	1954-1960
Indianapolis	IN	1963
Jacksonville	FL	1962-1968
Jersey City	NJ	1887, 1902-1915, 1918-1933, 1937-1950, 1960-1961
Lebanon	PA	1891
Little Rock	AR	1963
London	ONT	1888-1890
Louisville	KY	1968-1972
Maine (Old Orchard Beach)	ME	1984-1988
Memphis	TN	1974-1976
Miami	FL	1956-1960
Montreal	QUE	1890, 1897-1917, 1928-1960
New Haven	CT	1891-1892
Newark	NJ	1887, 1902-1919, 1921-1949
Norfolk (aka Tidewater)	VA	1969-
Oswego	NY	1885-1887
Ottawa	ONT	1898, 1951-1954, 1993-
Pawtucket	RI	1973-
Peninsula (Hampton)	VA	1972-1973
Philadelphia	PA	1892
Providence	RI	1891-1917
Reading	PA	1919-1931
Richmond	VA	1915-1917, 1954-1964, 1966-
Rochester	NY	1885-1889, 1891-1892, 1895-
Saginaw-Bay City	MI	1890
San Juan	PR	1961
Scranton	PA	1887, 1894-1897
Scranton-Wilkes-Barre	PA	1989-
Springfield	MA	1893-1900, 1950-1953
Syracuse	NY	1885-1889, 1891-1892, 1894-1901, 1918, 1920-1927, 1934-1955, 1961-
Toledo	OH	1889, 1965-
Toronto	ONT	1886-1890, 1895-1967
Troy	NY	1888, 1891-1894
Utica	NY	1885-1887
Wilkes-Barre	PA	1887, 1893-1898
Winnipeg	MB	1970-1971
Worcester	MA	1899-1903

INTERNATIONAL NORTHWEST LEAGUE
(see Pacific Coast International League)

INTERSTATE ASSOCIATION
CLASS C 1906

Anderson	IN	1906
Bay City	MI	1906
Flint	MI	1906
Fort Wayne	IN	1906
Lima	OH	1906
Marion	IN	1906
Muncie	IN	1906
Saginaw	MI	1906

INTERSTATE LEAGUE
1896-1901
(aka Western Association 1901)

Columbus	OH	1899-1901
Dayton	OH	1897-1901
Fort Wayne	IN	1896-1901
Grand Rapids	MI	1898-1899, 1901

Indianapolis	IN	1901
Jackson	MI	1896
Louisville	KY	1901
Mansfield	OH	1897-1900
Marion	IN	1900-1901
New Castle	OH	1896-1900
Saginaw	MI	1896
Springfield	OH	1897-1899
Toledo	OH	1896-1901
Washington	MI	1896
Wheeling	WV	1896-1897, 1899-1901
Youngstown	OH	1896-1900

INTERSTATE LEAGUE
CLASS D 1905-1908, 1914-1916

Bradford	PA	1905-1908, 1914-1916
Coudersport	PA	1905
DuBois	PA	1905-1907
Erie	PA	1905-1908, 1916
Franklin	PA	1907-1908
Hornell	NY	1906, 1914-1915
Jamestown	NY	1905, 1914-1915
Johnsonburg	PA	1916
Kane	PA	1905-1907
Oil City	PA	1907-1908
Oil City-Jamestown	PA-NY	1906
Olean	NY	1905-1908, 1914-1916
Patton	PA	1906
Punxsutawney	PA	1906-1907
Ridgway	PA	1916
St. Marys	PA	1916
Warren	PA	1908, 1914-1916
Wellsville	NY	1914-1916

INTERSTATE LEAGUE
CLASS B 1913

Akron	OH	1913
Canton	OH	1913
Columbus	OH	1913
Erie	PA	1913
Steubenville	OH	1913
Wheeling	WV	1913
Youngstown	OH	1913
Zanesville	OH	1913

INTERSTATE LEAGUE
CLASS D 1932

Lancaster	PA	1932
Norristown	PA	1932
Pottstown	PA	1932
St. Clair	PA	1932
Slatington	PA	1932
Stroudsburg	PA	1932
Tamaqua	PA	1932
Washington	NJ	1932

INTERSTATE LEAGUE
CLASS C 1939; CLASS B 1940-1952

Allentown	PA	1939-1952
Bridgeport	CT	1941
Hagerstown	MD	1941-1952
Harrisburg	PA	1940-1942, 1946-1952
Hazleton	PA	1939-1940
Lancaster	PA	1940-1952
Reading	PA	1940-1941
Salisbury	MD	1951-1952
Sunbury	PA	1939-1940, 1946-1952
Trenton	NJ	1939-1950
Wilmington	DE	1940-1952
York	PA	1940, 1943-1952

IOWA STATE LEAGUE
CLASS D 1904-1907
(formal name was Iowa League of Professional Baseball Clubs)
(predecessor of the Central Association)

Boone	IA	1904-1906
Burlington	IA	1904-1907
Clinton	IA	1906
Ft. Dodge	IA	1904-1906
Jacksonville	IL	1907
Keokuk	IA	1904-1906
Marshalltown	IA	1904-1907
Oskaloosa	IA	1904-1907

Ottumwa	IA	1904-1907
Quincy	IL	1907
Waterloo	IA	1904-1907

IOWA-SOUTH DAKOTA LEAGUE
CLASS D 1902-1903

Council Bluffs	IA	1903
Flandreau	SD	1902
Le Mars	IA	1902-1903
Rock Rapids	IA	1902
Sheldon	IA	1902
Sheldon-Primghar	IA	1903
Sioux City	IA	1902-1903
Sioux Falls	SD	1902-1903

IRON & OIL ASSOCIATION
1884

East Liberty	OH	1884
Franklin	PA	1884
Johnstown	PA	1884
New Brighton	PA	1884
New Castle	PA	1884
Oil City	PA	1884
Youngstown	OH	1884

KANSAS STATE LEAGUE
CLASS D 1905-1906, 1909-1911, 1913-1914
(see also Central Kansas League)

Arkansas City	KS	1909-1910
Arkansas City-Winfield	KS	1909
Bartlesville	OK	1906
Chanute	KS	1906
Cherryvale	KS	1906
Clay Center	KS	1913
Coffeyville	KS	1906
El Dorado	KS	1911
Ellsworth	KS	1905
Emporia	KS	1914
Ft. Scott	KS	1906
Great Bend	KS	1905, 1909-1911, 1913-1914
Hoisington	KS	1905
Hutchinson	KS	1905, 1909-1911, 1914
Independence	KS	1906
Iola	KS	1906
Junction City	KS	1913
Kingman	KS	1905
Larned	KS	1909-1911
Lincoln Center	KS	1905
Lyons	KS	1909-1911, 1913
Manhattan	KS	1913
McPherson	KS	1909-1911
Minneapolis	KS	1905
Newton	KS	1909-1911
Parsons	KS	1906
Pittsburg	KS	1906
Salina	KS	1913-1914
Strong City-Cottonwood Falls	KS	1909
Wellington	KS	1909-1911
Winfield	KS	1909

KANSAS-OKLAHOMA-MISSOURI LEAGUE
(KOM LEAGUE)
CLASS D 1946-1952

Bartlesville	OK	1946-1952
Blackwell	OK	1952
Carthage	MO	1946-1951
Chanute	KS	1946-1950
Independence	KS	1947-1950, 1952
Iola	KS	1946-1952
Miami	OK	1946-1952
Pittsburg	KS	1946-1952
Ponca City	OK	1947-1952

KENTUCKY-ILLINOIS-TENNESSEE LEAGUE
(KITTY LEAGUE)
CLASS D 1903-1906, 1910-1914, 1916, 1922-1924, 1935-1942, 1946-1955

Bowling Green	KY	1939-1942
Cairo	IL	1903-1906, 1911-1914, 1922-1924, 1946-1950
Central City	KY	1954
Clarksville	TN	1903-1904, 1910-1914, 1916, 1946-1949
Danville	IL	1906
Dawson Springs	KY	1916
Dyersburg	TN	1924

Evansville	IN	1912
Fulton	KY	1911, 1922-1924, 1936-1942, 1946-1955
Harrisburg	IL	1910-1911, 1913
Henderson	KY	1903-1905, 1911-1914, 1916
Hopkinsville	KY	1903-1905, 1910-1914, 1916, 1922-1923, 1935-1942, 1946-1954
Jackson	TN	1903, 1911, 1923-1924, 1935-1942, 1950-1954
Jacksonville	IL	1906
Lexington	TN	1935-1938
Madisonville	KY	1916, 1922, 1946-1955
Mattoon-Charleston	IL	1906
Mayfield	KY	1922-1924, 1936-1941, 1946-1955
McLeansboro	IL	1910-1911
Milan	TN	1923
Owensboro	KY	1903, 1913-1914, 1916, 1936-1942, 1946-1955
Paducah	KY	1903-1906, 1910-1914, 1922-1923, 1935-1941, 1951-1955
Paris	TN	1922-1924
Portageville	MO	1935-1936
Princeton	KY	1905
Springfield	TN	1923
Trenton	TN	1922-1923
Union City	TN	1935-1942, 1946-1955
Vincennes	IN	1903-1906, 1910-1911, 1913

KEYSTONE ASSOCIATION
1884

Chambersburg	PA	1884
Chester	PA	1884
Lancaster	PA	1884
Littlestown	PA	1884
York	PA	1884

LONE STAR LEAGUE
CLASS D 1927-1929; CLASS C 1947-1948

Bryan	TX	1947-1948
Corsicana	TX	1927-1928
Gladewater	TX	1948
Henderson	TX	1947-1948
Jacksonville	TX	1947
Kilgore	TX	1947-1948
Longview	TX	1927, 1947-1948
Lufkin	TX	1947-1948
Marshall	TX	1927, 1947-1948
Mexia	TX	1927-1928
Palestine	TX	1927-1929
Paris	TX	1927-1929
Sherman	TX	1929
Texarkana	TX	1927-1929
Tyler	TX	1927-1929, 1947-1948

LONE STAR LEAGUE
CLASS A 1977
(successor of the Gulf States League 1976)

Beeville	TX	1977
Corpus Christi	TX	1977
Harlingen	TX	1977
McAllen	TX	1977
Texas City	TX	1977
Victoria	TX	1977

LONGHORN LEAGUE
CLASS D 1947-1950; CLASS C 1951-1955
(predecessor of the Southwestern League 1956-1957)

Artesia	NM	1951-1955
Ballinger	TX	1947-1950
Big Spring	TX	1947-1955
Carlsbad	NM	1953-1955
Del Rio	TX	1948
Hobbs	NM	1955
Lamesa	TX	1953
Midland	TX	1947-1955
Odessa	TX	1947-1955
Roswell	NM	1949-1955
San Angelo	TX	1948-1955
Sweetwater	TX	1947-1952, 1954
Vernon	TX	1947-1952
Wichita Falls	TX	1954
Winters-Ballinger	TX	1953

LOUISIANA STATE LEAGUE
CLASS D 1920

Abbeville	LA	1920
Alexandria	LA	1920

Lafayette	LA	1920
New Iberia	LA	1920
Oakdale	LA	1920
Rayne	LA	1920

MAINE STATE LEAGUE
CLASS D 1907

Bangor	ME	1907
Biddeford	ME	1907
Pine Tree	ME	1907
Portland	ME	1907

MEXICAN LEAGUE
IND 1937-54; CLASS AA 1955-1966; CLASS AAA 1967-
(The Mexican League has competed since 1925, yet has been recognized by the National Association only since 1955.)

Aguascalientes	MEX	1975-
Anahuac	MEX	1939, 1953
Campeche	MEX	1980-
Chihuahua	MEX	1940, 1973-1982
Ciudad Juarez	MEX	1973-1984
Coahuila	MEX	1974-1979
Coatzacoalcos	MEX	1979-1983
Cordoba	MEX	1937-1939, 1972-1979, 1984-1986, 1991-1992
Durango	MEX	1976-1979
Jalisco (Guadalajara)	MEX	1949-1952, 1964-1975, 1988, 1991-1995
Leon	MEX	1979-1980, 1983-1991
Mexico City Agrario	MEX	1937-1938
Mexico City Agricultura	MEX	1937
Mexico City Azul	MEX	1954
Mexico City Comintra	MEX	1937-1939
Mexico City Diablos Rojos	MEX	1940-
Mexico City Necaxa	MEX	1937
Mexico City Petroleros	MEX	1937
Mexico City Tigres	MEX	1955-
Mexico City Transito	MEX	1937
Minatitlan	MEX	1992-
Monclova	MEX	1980, 1982-
Monterrey	MEX	1939-
Monterrey Industriales	MEX	1989-1994
Nogales	MEX	1937-1938
Nuevo Laredo (aka Dos Laredos with Laredo, TX)	MEX	1940, 1944-1946, 1949-1959, 1976-
Oaxaca	MEX	1996-
Poza Rica	MEX	1958-1983, 1996-
Puebla	MEX	1942-1948, 1960-1969, 1972-1980, 1985-1987, 1993-1995
Quintana Roo (Cancun)	MEX	1996-
Reynosa	MEX	1963-1976, 1980-1982, 1995-
Rio Blanco	MEX	1937-1938
Sabinas	MEX	1971-1973
Saltillo	MEX	1970-
San Luis Potosi	MEX	1946-1951, 1986-1991
Santa Rosa	MEX	1937-1939
Tabasco (Villahermosa)	MEX	1975, 1977-
Tampico	MEX	1937-1948, 1971-1979, 1983-1985
Toluca	MEX	1980, 1984
Torreon	MEX	1940-1943, 1946, 1949-1953
Union Laguna (Torreon)	MEX	1970-1981, 1985-
Veracruz	MEX	1937-1939, 1941, 1949-1957, 1959-1974, 1979-1986, 1992-1995
Veracruz Azules	MEX	1940-1951
Yucatan (Merida)	MEX	1954-1958, 1970-1974, 1979-

MEXICAN CENTER LEAGUE
CLASS D 1960; CLASS C 1961-1962; CLASS A 1963-1978

Acambaro	MEX	1975-1976
Aguascalientes	MEX	1960-1963, 1965-1967, 1969-1974
Arandas	MEX	1977
Celaya	MEX	1960-1961, 1975
Cerro Azul	MEX	1978
Ciudad Madero	MEX	1968-1970
Ciudad Mante	MEX	1969-1971, 1973-1974, 1977
Ciudad Victoria	MEX	1971, 1973-1974, 1976-1978
Ciudad Valles	MEX	1974, 1978
Cortazar	MEX	1975
Diaz Ordaz	MEX	1978
Durango	MEX	1965-1967, 1972-1974
Ebano	MEX	1971-1974, 1977
Fresnillo	MEX	1962, 1964-1968, 1976-1978
Guadalajara	MEX	1977-1978
Guanajuato	MEX	1960-1967, 1975-1976, 1978
Jalisco	MEX	1977

La Barca	MEX	1978
Lagos de Moreno	MEX	1975-1977
Leon	MEX	1960-1971, 1975
Matamoros	MEX	1978
Miguel Aleman	MEX	1978
Monterrey Industriales	MEX	1970-1972
Morella	MEX	1966
Naranjos	MEX	1972-1973
Nuevo Laredo	MEX	1968
Parras	MEX	1974
Salamanca	MEX	1960-1962, 1964-1965, 1975
Saltillo	MEX	1964, 1968-1969
San Luis Potosi	MEX	1960-1966, 1969-1971
San Pedro	MEX	1974
Silao	MEX	1978
Tampico	MEX	1967-1970
Tamuin	MEX	1973
Teocaltiche	MEX	1977-1978
Torreon	MEX	1968
Uriangato	MEX	1975
Zacatecas	MEX	1965-1973, 1976-1978

MEXICAN NORTHERN LEAGUE
CLASS A 1968-1969

Ensenada	MEX	1968-1969
Mazatlan	MEX	1968
Mexicali	MEX	1968-1969
Nogales	MEX	1968-1969
Puerto Penasco	MEX	1969
San Luis Rio Colorado	MEX	1968-1969

MEXICAN NATIONAL LEAGUE
CLASS B 1946
(The league was sponsored by Organized Baseball, in opposition to the Independent Mexican League of the Pascual brothers.)

Chihuahua	MEX	1946
El Paso	TX	1946
Juarez	MEX	1946
Mexico City	MEX	1946
Saltillo	MEX	1946
Torreon	MEX	1946

MEXICAN PACIFIC LEAGUE
CLASS A 1976

Ciudad Obregon	MEX	1976
Guamuchil	MEX	1976
Guasave	MEX	1976
Guaymas	MEX	1976
Hermosillo	MEX	1976
Los Mochis	MEX	1976
Mazatlan	MEX	1976
Navojoa	MEX	1976

MEXICAN ROOKIE LEAGUE
ROOKIE 1968

Agua Prieta	MEX	1968
Caborca	MEX	1968
Campeche	MEX	1968
Cananea	MEX	1968
Empalme	MEX	1968

MEXICAN SOUTHEAST LEAGUE
CLASS A 1964-1970

Campeche	MEX	1964-1970
Ciudad del Carmen	MEX	1967-1970
Las Choapas	MEX	1967-1969
Minatitlan	MEX	1968-1969
Orizaba	MEX	1966-1967
Puerto Mexico	MEX	1964-1970
Tabasco	MEX	1964-1970
Yucatan	MEX	1964-1969

MICHIGAN STATE LEAGUE
1889-1890, 1895; CLASS D 1902, 1910-1914; CLASS B 1926; CLASS C 1940-1941
(known as the West Michigan League 1910)
(formed by mid season merger of the Michigan-Ontario and Central Leagues 1926)
(sometimes known as the Michigan League)

Battle Creek	MI	1895, 1902
Bay City	MI	1926
Belding	MI	1914
Boyne City	MI	1911-1914

Cadillac	MI	1910-1914
Charlotte	MI	1926
Flint	MI	1889-1890, 1902, 1926, 1940-1941
Grand Rapids	MI	1889-1890, 1902, 1926, 1940-1941
Greenville	MI	1889
Holland	MI	1910-1911
Jackson	MI	1889, 1895, 1902
Kalamazoo	MI	1889, 1895, 1926
Lansing	MI	1889-1890, 1895, 1902, 1940-1941
Ludington	MI	1912-1914, 1926
Manistee	MI	1890, 1911-1914
Muskegon	MI	1890, 1902, 1910-1914, 1926,1940-1941
Oswosso	MI	1895
Port Huron	MI	1890, 1895, 1926
Saginaw	MI	1889, 1902, 1926, 1940-1941
St. Joseph	MI	1940-1941
Traverse City	MI	1910-1914

MICHIGAN-ONTARIO LEAGUE
CLASS B 1919-1926
(merged with Central League to form the Michigan State League 1926)

Battle Creek	MI	1919-1920
Bay City	MI	1919-1926
Brantford	ONT	1919-1922
Flint	MI	1919-1926
Grand Rapids	MI	1923-1924
Hamilton	ONT	1919-1925
Kalamazoo	MI	1923-1924
Kitchener	ONT	1919-1922, 1925
London	ONT	1919-1925
Muskegon	MI	1923-1924
Port Huron	MI	1921, 1926
Port Huron-Sarnia	MI-ONT	1922
Saginaw	MI	1919-1926

MID-AMERICA LEAGUE
IND 1995

Lafayette	IN	1995
Anderson	IN	1995
Merrillville	IN	1995
East Chicago	IN	1995

MIDDLE ATLANTIC LEAGUE
CLASS C 1925-1942, 1946-1951

Akron	OH	1935-1941
Altoona	PA	1931
Beaver Falls	PA	1931
Beckley	WV	1931-1935
Butler	PA	1946-1951
Canton	OH	1936-1942
Charleroi	PA	1927-1931
Charleston	WV	1931-1942
Clarksburg	WV	1925-1932
Cumberland	MD	1925-1932
Dayton	OH	1933-1942
Erie	PA	1938-1939, 1941-1942, 1946-1951
Fairmont	WV	1925-1931
Hagerstown	MD	1931
Huntington	WV	1931-1936
Jeannette	PA	1926-1931
Johnstown	PA	1925-1938, 1946-1950
Lockport	NY	1951
New Castle	PA	1948-1951
Niagara Falls	NY	1946-1947, 1950-1951
Oil City	PA	1946-1951
Parkersburg	WV	1931
Portsmouth	OH	1935-1940
Scottdale	PA	1925-1931
Springfield	OH	1933-1934, 1937-1939, 1941-1942
Uniontown	PA	1926, 1947-1949
Vandergrift	PA	1947-1950
Wheeling	WV	1925-1931, 1933-1934
Youngstown	OH	1931, 1939-1941, 1946-1951
Zanesville	OH	1933-1937, 1941-1942

MIDDLE TEXAS LEAGUE
CLASS D 1914-1915

Austin	TX	1915
Bartlett	TX	1914-1915
Belton	TX	1914-1915
Brenham	TX	1914-1915
Georgetown	TX	1914
Lampasas	TX	1914

Schulenburg	TX	1915
Taylor	TX	1915
Temple	TX	1914-1915

MIDWEST LEAGUE
CLASS D 1956-1962; CLASS A 1963-
(successor of the Mississippi-Ohio Valley League 1949-1955)

Appleton	WI	1962-
(aka Fox Cities/Wisconsin)		
Beloit	WI	1982-
Burlington	IA	1962-
Cedar Rapids	IA	1962-
Clinton	IA	1956-
Danville	IL	1970-1976, 1982
Decatur	IL	1956-1974
Dubuque	IA	1956-1968, 1974-1976
Fort Wayne	IN	1993-
Kane County (Geneva)	IL	1991-
Kenosha	WI	1985-1992
Keokuk	IA	1958-1962
Kokomo	IN	1956-1961
Lafayette	IN	1956-1957
Lansing	MI	1996-
Madison	WI	1982-1994
Mattoon	IL	1956-1957
Michigan (Battle Creek)	MI	1995-
Michigan City	IN	1956-1959
Paris	IL	1956-1959
Peoria	IL	1983-
Quad City/Cities	IA-IL	1960-
(Davenport-Bettendorf-Moline-Rock Island)		
Quincy	IL	1960-1973
Rockford	IL	1988-
South Bend	IN	1988-
Springfield	IL	1982-1995
Waterloo	IA	1958-1993
Wausau	WI	1975-1990
West Michigan (Grand Rapids)	MI	1994-
Wisconsin Rapids	WI	1963-1983

MINNESOTA-WISCONSIN LEAGUE
CLASS D 1909-1910, 1912; CLASS C 1911
(successor of the Northern League 1908)

Duluth	MN	1909-1911
Eau Claire	WI	1909-1912
La Crosse	WI	1909-1912
Red Wing	MN	1910-1911
Rochester	MN	1910-1912
Superior	WI	1909-1911
Wausau	WI	1909-1911
Winona	MN	1909-1912

MISSISSIPPI STATE LEAGUE
CLASS D 1921
(all four teams moved into the Cotton States League 1922)

Clarksdale	MS	1921
Greenwood	MS	1921
Jackson	MS	1921
Meridian	MS	1921

MISSISSIPPI VALLEY LEAGUE
CLASS D 1922-1932; CLASS B 1933

Burlington	IA	1924-1932
Cedar Rapids	IA	1922-1932
Davenport	IA	1929-1933
Dubuque	IA	1922-1932
Keokuk	IA	1929-1933
Marshalltown	IA	1922-1928
Moline	IL	1924-1932
Ottumwa	IA	1922-1928
Peoria	IL	1933
Quincy	IL	1933
Rock Island	IL	1922-1933
Springfield	IL	1933
Waterloo	IA	1922-1932

MISSISSIPPI-OHIO VALLEY LEAGUE
CLASS D 1949-1955
(successor of the Illinois State League 1947-1948)
(predecessor of the Midwest League 1956-)

Belleville	IL	1949
Canton	IL	1952
Centralia	IL	1949-1952

PROFESSIONAL TEAMS BY LEAGUE 1883-1997

Clinton	IA	1954-1955
Danville	IL	1951-1954
Decatur	IL	1952-1955
Dubuque	IA	1954-1955
Hannibal	MO	1952-1955
Kokomo	IN	1955
Lafayette	IN	1955
Mattoon	IL	1949-1955
Mt. Vernon	IL	1949-1954
Paducah	KY	1949-1950
Paris	IL	1950-1955
Springfield	IL	1950
Vincennes	IN	1950-1952
West Frankfort	IL	1949-1950

MISSOURI STATE LEAGUE
CLASS D 1911

Brookfield	MO	1911
Jefferson City	MO	1911
Kirksville	MO	1911
Macon	MO	1911
Sedalia	MO	1911

MISSOURI VALLEY LEAGUE
CLASS D 1902-1903; CLASS C 1904-1905
(predecessor of the Western Association 1905-1911)

Chanute	KS	1902
Coffeyville	KS	1902
Ft. Scott	KS	1902-1905
Ft. Smith	AR	1905
Iola	KS	1902-1904
Jefferson City	MO	1902
Joplin	MO	1902-1904
Leavenworth	KS	1903-1904
Muskogee	OK	1905
Nevada	MO	1902-1903
Parsons	KS	1905
Pittsburg	KS	1903-1905
Sedalia	MO	1902-1904
South McAlester	OK	1905
Springfield	MO	1902-1904
Topeka	KS	1904
Tulsa	OK	1905
Vinita	OK	1905
Webb City	MO	1903, 1905

MISSOURI-IOWA-NEBRASKA-KANSAS LEAGUE
(MINK LEAGUE)
CLASS D 1910-1913

Auburn	NE	1910-1913
Beatrice-Fairbury	NE	1912
Clarinda	IA	1910-1911
Falls City	NE	1910-1913
Hiawatha	KS	1912
Humboldt	NE	1911-1913
Maryville	MO	1910-1911
Nebraska City	NE	1910-1913
Shenandoah	IA	1910-1911

MONTANA STATE LEAGUE
1900

Great Falls	MT	1900
Helena	MT	1900
Anaconda	MT	1900
Butte	MT	1900

MOUNTAIN STATES LEAGUE
CLASS D 1911-1912

Ashland-Catlettsburg	KY	1911-1912
Charleston	WV	1911-1912
Huntington	WV	1911-1912
Ironton	OH	1911-1912
Middleport-Pomeroy	OH	1911-1912
Montgomery	WV	1911-1912
Point Pleasant-Gallipolis	WV-OH	1911
Williamson	WV	1912

MOUNTAIN STATE LEAGUE
CLASS D 1937-1941, CLASS C 1942

Ashland	KY	1939-1942
Beckley	WV	1937-1938
Bluefield	WV	1937-1942
Huntington	WV	1937-1942

Logan	WV	1937-1942
Welch	WV	1937-1942
Williamson	WV	1937-1942

MOUNTAIN STATES LEAGUE
CLASS D 1948-1953, CLASS C 1954

Big Stone Gap	VA	1949-1953
Harlan	KY	1948-1954
Hazard	KY	1948-1952
Jenkins	KY	1948-1951
Kingsport	TN	1953-1954
Knoxville	TN	1953
Lexington	KY	1954
Maryville-Alcoa	TN	1953-1954
Middlesboro	KY	1949
Morristown	TN	1948-1954
Newport	TN	1948-1950
Norton	VA	1951-1953
Oak Ridge	TN	1948, 1954
Pennington Gap	VA	1948-1951

NATIONAL LEAGUE
MAJOR 1883-

Atlanta	GA	1966-
Baltimore	MD	1892-1899
Boston	MA	1883-1952
Brooklyn	NY	1890-1957
Buffalo	NY	1883-1885
Chicago	IL	1883-
Cincinnati	OH	1890-
Cleveland	OH	1883-1884, 1889-1899
Colorado (Denver)	CO	1993-
Detroit	MI	1883-1888
Florida (Miami)	FL	1993-
Houston	TX	1962-
Indianapolis	IN	1887-1889
Kansas City	MO	1886
Los Angeles	CA	1958-
Louisville	KY	1892-1899
Milwaukee	WI	1953-1965
Montreal	QUE	1969-
New York	NY	1883-1957, 1962-
Philadelphia	PA	1883-
Pittsburgh	PA	1887-
Providence	RI	1883-1885
St. Louis	MO	1885-1886, 1892-
San Diego	CA	1969-
San Francisco	CA	1958-
Washington	DC	1886-1889, 1892-1899

NATIONAL COLORED LEAGUE
1887

Baltimore	MD	1887
Boston	MA	1887
Louisville	KY	1887
New York	NY	1887
Philadelphia	PA	1887
Pittsburgh	PA	1887

NEBRASKA STATE LEAGUE
CLASS D 1910-1915, 1922-1923, 1928-1938, 1956-1959
(predecessor of the Western League 1939-1941)

Beatrice	NE	1913-1915, 1922-1923, 1928, 1932-1938
Columbus	NE	1910-1915
Fairbury	NE	1915, 1922-1923, 1928-1930, 1936-1937
Fremont	NE	1910-1913
Grand Island	NE	1910-1915, 1922-1923, 1928-1934, 1938, 1956-1959
Hastings	NE	1910-1915, 1922-1923, 1956-1959
Holdrege	NE	1956-1959
Kearney	NE	1910-1915, 1956-1959
Lexington	NE	1956-1958
Lincoln	NE	1922-1923, 1928-1936, 1938
McCook	NE	1928-1932, 1956-1959
Mitchell	SD	1936-1937
Norfolk	NE	1914-1915, 1922-1923, 1928-1938
North Platte	NE	1928-1932, 1956-1959
Norton	KS	1929-1930
Red Cloud	NE	1910
Seward	NE	1910-1913
Sioux City	IA	1938
Sioux Falls	SD	1933-1938
Superior	NE	1910-1914, 1956-1958
York	NE	1911-1915, 1928-1931

PROFESSIONAL TEAMS BY LEAGUE 1883-1997

NEW BRUNSWICK-MAINE LEAGUE
CLASS D 1913

Bangor	ME	1913
Calais-St. Stephen	ME-NB	1913
Fredericton	NB	1913
St. John	NB	1913

NEW ENGLAND ASSOCIATION
1895

Fitchburg	MA	1895
Haverhill	MA	1895
Lawrence	MA	1895
Lowell	MA	1895
Nashua	NH	1895
Salem	MA	1895

NEW ENGLAND LEAGUE
1886-1888, 1891-1899, 1901; CLASS B 1902-1915,
1919, 1926-1930, 1933, 1946-1949
(predecessor of the Northeastern League 1934)

Attleboro	MA	1928, 1933
Augusta	ME	1895-1896, 1901
Bangor	ME	1894-1896, 1901
Boston	MA	1886-1887, 1893
Brockton	MA	1886, 1892-1899, 1901, 1903, 1907-1913, 1928-1929, 1933, 1946-1949
Cambridge	MA	1899
Concord	NH	1902-1905
Dover	NH	1893, 1902
Fall River	MA	1893-1899, 1902-1913, 1946-1949
Fitchburg	MA	1914-1915, 1919, 1929
Gloucester	MA	1929
Haverhill	MA	1886-1887, 1894, 1901-1912, 1914, 1919, 1926-1929
Lawrence	MA	1886-1887, 1892, 1899, 1902-1915, 1919, 1926-1927, 1933, 1946-1947
Lewiston	ME	1891-1896, 1901, 1914-1915, 1919, 1926-1930
Lewiston-Auburn	ME	1919
Lowell	MA	1887-1888, 1891-1893, 1901-1915, 1919, 1926, 1933, 1947
Lynn	MA	1886-1888, 1891, 1901, 1905-1915, 1926-1930, 1946-1949
Manchester	NH	1887-1888, 1891-1893, 1899, 1901-1906, 1914-1915, 1926-1930, 1946-1949
Nashua	NH	1901-1905, 1926-1927, 1929-1930, 1933, 1946-1949
New Bedford	MA	1895-1898, 1903-1913, 1929, 1933
Newburyport	MA	1886
Newport	RI	1897-1899
Pawtucket	RI	1892, 1894-1899, 1946-1949
Portland	ME	1886-1888, 1891-1896, 1899, 1901, 1913-1915, 1919, 1926-1930, 1946-1949
Portsmouth	NH	1888
Providence	RI	1946-1949
Quincy	MA	1933
Salem	MA	1887-1888, 1891-1892, 1926-1928, 1930
Springfield	MA	1948-1949
Taunton	MA	1897-1899, 1905, 1933
Watertown	MA	1934
Wayland	MA	1934
Woonsocket	RI	1891-1892, 1933
Worcester	MA	1888, 1891, 1894, 1898, 1906-1915, 1933

NEW PACIFIC LEAGUE
(see Pacific Northwest League)

NEW YORK STATE LEAGUE 1885
(see Eastern League)

NEW YORK STATE LEAGUE
1889

Auburn	NY	1889
Elmira	NY	1889
Canandaigua	NY	1889
Oneida	NY	1889
Seneca Falls	NY	1889
Utica	NY	1889

NEW YORK STATE LEAGUE
1899-1901; CLASS B 1902-1917

Albany	NY	1899-1916
Amsterdam-Johnstown- Gloversville	NY	1902-1907
Auburn	NY	1899
Binghamton	NY	1899-1917
Cortland	NY	1899-1901
Elmira	NY	1900, 1908-1917
Harrisburg	PA	1916-1917
Ilion	NY	1901-1904
Johnstown-Gloversville	NY	1908
Oswego	NY	1899-1900
Reading	PA	1916-1917
Rome	NY	1899-1901
Schenectady	NY	1899-1904
Scranton	PA	1904-1917
Syracuse	NY	1902-1917
Troy	NY	1899-1916
Utica	NY	1899-1917
Waverly	NY	1901
Wilkes-Barre	PA	1905-1917

NEW YORK-NEW JERSEY LEAGUE
CLASS D 1913
(predecessor of Atlantic League 1914)

Danbury	CT	1913
Kingston	NY	1913
Long Branch	NJ	1913
Middletown	NY	1913
Newburgh	NY	1913
Poughkeepsie	NY	1913

NEW YORK-PENNSYLVANIA LEAGUE
1891

Bradford	PA	1891
Erie	PA	1891
Elmira	NY	1891
Jamestown	NY	1891
Meadville	NY	1891
Olean	NY	1891

NEW YORK-PENNSYLVANIA LEAGUE
CLASS B 1923-1932; CLASS A 1933-1937
(predecessor of the Eastern League 1938-)

Albany	NY	1937
Allentown	PA	1935-1936
Binghamton	NY	1923-1937
Elmira	NY	1923-1937
Harrisburg	PA	1924-1935
Hazleton	PA	1929-1932, 1934-1937
Oneonta	NY	1924
Scranton	PA	1923-1937
Shamokin	PA	1925-1927
Syracuse	NY	1928-1929
Trenton	NJ	1936-1937
Utica	NY	1924
Wilkes-Barre	PA	1923-1937
Williamsport	PA	1923-1937
York	PA	1923-1933, 1936

NEW YORK-PENNSYLVANIA LEAGUE
CLASS D 1939-1962; CLASS A 1963-
(known as PONY League 1939-1956)

Auburn	NY	1958-1980, 1982-
Batavia	NY	1939-1953, 1957-1959, 1961-
Binghamton	NY	1964-1966
Bradford	PA	1939-1942, 1944-1957
Corning	NY	1951-1960, 1968-1969
Elmira	NY	1957-1960, 1973-1995
Erie	PA	1944-1945, 1954-1963, 1967, 1981-1993, 1995-
Geneva	NY	1958-1973, 1977-1993
Glens Falls	NY	1993
Hamilton	ONT	1939-1942, 1946-1956, 1988-1992
Hornell	NY	1942-1957
Hudson Valley (Fishkill)	NY	1994-
Jamestown	NY	1939-1957, 1961-1973, 1977-
Little Falls	NY	1977-1988
Lockport	NY	1942-1950
London	ONT	1940-1941
Lowell	MA	1996-
New Jersey (Augusta)	NJ	1994-
Newark	NY	1968-1979, 1983-1987
Niagara Falls	NY	1939-1940, 1970-1979, 1982-1985, 1989-1993
Olean	NY	1939-1959, 1961-1962
Oneonta	NY	1966-
Pittsfield	MA	1989-
St. Catharines	ONT	1986-
Vermont (Burlington)	VT	1994-
Utica	NY	1977-
Watertown	NY	1983-

PROFESSIONAL TEAMS BY LEAGUE 1883-1997

Welland	ONT	1989-1994
Wellsville	NY	1942-1961, 1963-1965
Williamsport	PA	1968-1972, 1994-

NORTH ATLANTIC LEAGUE
CLASS D 1946-1950

Bangor	PA	1949-1950
Berwick	PA	1950
Bloomingdale	NJ	1946-1948
Carbondale	PA	1946-1950
Hazleton	PA	1949-1950
Kingston	NY	1947
Lansdale	PA	1948
Lebanon	PA	1949-1950
Mahanoy City	PA	1946-1950
Nazareth	PA	1946-1950
Newburgh	NY	1946
Nyack	NY	1946-1948
Peekskill	NY	1946-1949
Stroudsburg	PA	1946-1950
Walden	NY	1946

NORTH ATLANTIC LEAGUE
IND 1995-1996

Altoona	PA	1996
Catskill (Mountaindale)	NY	1996
Massachusetts (Lynn)	MA	1996
Nashua	NH	1995-1996
Newark	NY	1995-1996
Niagara Falls	NY	1995
Welland	ONT	1995-1996

NORTH CAROLINA LEAGUE
CLASS C 1902

Charlotte	NC	1902
Durham	NC	1902
Greensboro	NC	1902
New Bern	NC	1902
Raleigh	NC	1902
Wilmington	NC	1902

NORTH CAROLINA STATE LEAGUE
CLASS D 1913-1917, 1937-1942, 1945-1952
(successor of the Carolina Baseball Association 1908-1912)
(sometimes known as the North Carolina League)
(combined with Western Carolina to form TAR HEEL League 1953)

Albemarle	NC	1948
Asheville	NC	1913-1917
Charlotte	NC	1913-1917
Concord	NC	1939-1942, 1945-1951
Cooleemee	NC	1937-1941
Durham	NC	1913-1917
Elkin	NC	1951-1952
Gastonia	NC	1938
Greensboro	NC	1913-1917
Hickory	NC	1942, 1945-1950
High Point-Thomasville	NC	1948-1952
Kannapolis	NC	1939-1941
Landis	NC	1937-1942, 1945-1947, 1949-1951
Lexington	NC	1937-1942, 1945-1952
Mooresville	NC	1937-1942, 1945-1952
Newton-Conover	NC	1937-1938
Raleigh	NC	1913-1917
Salisbury	NC	1937-1942, 1945-1952
Shelby	NC	1937-1938
Statesville	NC	1942, 1945-1952
Thomasville	NC	1937-1942, 1945-1947
Winston-Salem	NC	1913-1917

NORTH CENTRAL LEAGUE
IND 1994-1995

Brainerd	MN	1994-1995
Chaska Valley	MN	1995
Huron	ND	1994
Marshall	MN	1994
Minneapolis	MN	1994
Minnesota (Hibbing)	MN	1995

Regina	SK	1994
Saskatoon	SK	1994
Will County	IL	1995

NORTH DAKOTA LEAGUE
CLASS D 1923

Bismarck	ND	1923
Carrington	ND	1923
Jamestown	ND	1923
Minot	ND	1923
New Rockford	ND	1923
Valley City	ND	1923

NORTH TEXAS LEAGUE
CLASS D 1905, 1907

Clarksville	TX	1905
Corsicana	TX	1907
Greenville	TX	1905, 1907
Hope	AR	1905
Paris	TX	1905, 1907
Terrell	TX	1907
Texarkana	TX	1905

NORTHEAST LEAGUE
IND 1995-

Adirondack (Glens Falls)	NY	1995-
Albany	NY	1995-
Allentown	PA	1997-
Bangor	ME	1996-
Elmira	NY	1996-
Lynn	MA	1997-
Mohawk Valley (Little Falls)	NY	1995
Newburgh	NY	1995-
Rhode Island (West Warwick)	RI	1996
Sullivan (Mountaindale)	NY	1995, 1997-
Waterbury	CT	1997-
Yonkers	NY	1995

NORTHEAST ARKANSAS LEAGUE
CLASS D 1909-1911, 1936-1941

Batesville	AR	1936, 1938, 1940-1941
Blytheville	AR	1910-1911, 1937-1938
Caruthersville	MO	1910, 1936-1940
Helena	AR	1911
Jonesboro	AR	1909-1911, 1936-1941
Marianna	AR	1909
Newport	AR	1909, 1936-1941
Osceola	AR	1936-1937
Paragould	AR	1909-1911, 1936-1941
West Plains	MO	1936

NORTHEASTERN LEAGUE
CLASS B 1934
(successor of the New England League 1933)

Cambridge	MA	1934
Hartford	CT	1934
Lowell	MA	1934
Manchester	NH	1934
New Bedford	MA	1934
Springfield	MA	1934
Waltham	MA	1934
Watertown	MA	1934
Wayland	MA	1934
Worcester	MA	1934

NORTHERN ASSOCIATION
CLASS D 1910

Clinton	IA	1910
Decatur	IL	1910
Elgin	IL	1910
Freeport	IL	1910
Jacksonville	IL	1910
Joliet	IL	1910
Kankakee	IL	1910
Muscatine	IA	1910
Sterling	IL	1910

PROFESSIONAL TEAMS BY LEAGUE 1883-1997

NORTHERN LEAGUE
IND 1902; CLASS D 1903-1905, 1908, 1917, 1933-1940; CLASS C 1913-1916, 1941-1942, 1946-1962; CLASS A 1963-1971; IND 1993-
(merged with Copper Country Soo League to form Northern-Copper Country League 1906-1907)
(predecessor of the Minnesota-Wisconsin League 1909-1912)
(successor of the Central International League 1912)

Aberdeen	SD	1946-1971
Bismarck-Mandan	ND	1962-1964, 1966
Brainerd	MN	1933, 1935
Brainerd-Little Falls	MN	1934
Brandon	MB	1908, 1933-1934
Cavalier	ND	1902
Crookston	MN	1902-1905, 1933-1941
Devils Lake	ND	1902
Duluth	MN	1903-1905, 1908, 1913-1916, 1934-1942, 1946-1955
Duluth-Superior	MN-WI	1956-1970, 1993-
East Grand Forks	MN	1933, 1935
Eau Claire	WI	1933-1942, 1946-1962
Fargo	ND	1902-1905, 1908
Fargo-Moorhead	ND-MN	1914-1917, 1933-1942, 1946-1960, 1996-
Ft. William-Pt. Arthur	ONT	1914-1916
Grand Forks	ND	1902-1905, 1913-1915, 1934-1935, 1938-1942, 1946-1964
Huron	SD	1965-1970
Jamestown	ND	1936-1937
La Crosse	WI	1913
Madison	WI	1996-
Mankato	MN	1967-1968
Minneapolis	MN	1913
Minot	ND	1917, 1958-1960, 1962
Rochester	MN	1993
St. Boniface	MB	1915
St. Cloud	MN	1946-1971
St. Cloud-Brainerd	MN	1905
St. Paul	MN	1913, 1993-
Sioux City	IA	1993-
Sioux Falls	SD	1942, 1946-1953, 1966-1971, 1993-
Superior	WI	1903-1905, 1913-1916, 1933-1942, 1946-1955
Thunder Bay (formerly Ft. William-Pt. Arthur)	ONT	1993-
Virginia	MN	1913-1916
Warren	MN	1917
Watertown	SD	1970-1971
Wausau	WI	1936-1942, 1956-1957
Winnipeg	MB	1902-1905, 1908, 1913-1917, 1933-1942, 1954-1964, 1969, 1994-
Winona	MN	1913-1914

NORTHERN-COPPER COUNTRY LEAGUE
CLASS C 1906; CLASS D 1907
(aka Northern Copper League)
(formed by merger of the Northern and Copper Country Soo Leagues)

Calumet	MI	1906-1907
Duluth	MN	1906-1907
Fargo	ND	1906
Grand Forks	ND	1906
Hancock	MI	1906
Houghton	MI	1906-1907
Lake Linden	MI	1906
Winnipeg	MB	1906-1907

NORTHERN STATE OF INDIANA LEAGUE
CLASS D 1909-1911
(informally known as the Indiana State League)

Anderson	IN	1911
Bluffton	IN	1909-1911
Huntington	IN	1909-1911
Kokomo	IN	1909
Lafayette	IN	1909-1911
Logansport	IN	1910
Marion	IN	1909-1911
Wabash	IN	1909-1911

NORTHWEST LEAGUE
CLASS B 1955-1962; CLASS A 1963-
(successor of the Western International League 1946-1954)

Bellingham	WA	1973-1996
Bend (aka Central Oregon)	OR	1970-1971, 1978-1994
Boise	ID	1975-1976, 1978, 1987-
Coos Bay-North Bend	OR	1970-1972
Eugene	OR	1955-1968, 1974-
Everett	WA	1984-
Grays Harbor (Aberdeen)	WA	1976-1980
Lewiston	ID	1955-1974
Medford (aka Rogue Valley) (aka Southern Oregon)	OR	1967-1968, 1971, 1979- / 1970 / 1988-
New Westminster	BC	1974
Portland	OR	1973-1977, 1995-
Salem	OR	1955-1965, 1977-1989, 1997-
Seattle	WA	1972-1976
Spokane	WA	1955-1956, 1972, 1983-
Tri-Cities (Kennewick-Pasco-Richland)	WA	1955-1974, 1983-1986
Victoria	BC	1978-1980
Walla Walla	WA	1969-1983
Wenatchee	WA	1955-1965
Yakima	WA	1955-1966, 1990-

NORTHWESTERN LEAGUE
1883-1884, 1886-1887

Bay City	MI	1883-1884
Des Moines	IA	1887
Duluth	MN	1886-1887
Eau Claire	WI	1886-1887
Evansville	IN	1884
Fort Wayne	IN	1883-1884
Grand Rapids	MI	1883-1884
La Crosse	WI	1887
Milwaukee	WI	1884, 1886-1887
Minneapolis	MN	1884, 1886-1887
Muskegon	MI	1884
Oshkosh	WI	1886-1887
Peoria	IL	1883-1884
Quincy	IL	1883-1884
Saginaw	MI	1883-1884
St. Paul	MN	1884, 1886-1887
Springfield	IL	1883
Stillwater	MN	1884
Terre Haute	IN	1884
Toledo	OH	1883
Winona	MN	1884

NORTHWESTERN LEAGUE
CLASS B 1905-1917

Aberdeen	WA	1907, 1915
Ballard	WA	1914
Bellingham	WA	1905
Butte	MT	1906-1908, 1916-1917
Everett	WA	1905
Grays Harbor	WA	1906, 1908-1909
Great Falls	MT	1916-1917
Portland	OR	1909, 1911-1914
Seattle	WA	1907-1917
Spokane	WA	1905-1917
Tacoma	WA	1906-1917
Vancouver	BC	1905, 1907-1917
Victoria	BC	1905, 1911-1915

OHIO STATE ASSOCIATION
1884

Chillicothe	OH	1884
Dayton	OH	1884
Ironton	OH	1884
Portsmouth	OH	1884
Springfield	OH	1884

OHIO STATE LEAGUE
(see Tri-State League)

OHIO STATE LEAGUE
CLASS D 1908-1916, 1936-1941, 1944-1947

Canton	OH	1936
Charleston	WV	1913-1916
Chillicothe	OH	1910-1916
Dayton	OH	1946-1947
Findlay	OH	1937-1941
Fostoria	OH	1936-1941
Frankfort	KY	1915-1916
Fremont	OH	1936-1941
Hamilton	OH	1911, 1913
Huntington	WV	1913-1916
Ironton	OH	1912-1915
Lancaster	OH	1908-1911
Lexington	KY	1913-1916

Lima	OH	1908-1912, 1939-1941, 1944-1947
Mansfield	OH	1908-1909, 1912, 1936-1937, 1939-1941
Marion	OH	1908-1912, 1937, 1944-1947
Maysville	KY	1913-1916
Middletown	OH	1944-1946
Muncie	IN	1947
New Philadelphia	OH	1936
Newark	OH	1908-1912, 1936, 1944-1947
Newport	KY	1914
Paris	KY	1914
Piqua	OH	1910-1911
Portsmouth	OH	1908-1916
Richmond	IN	1946-147
Sandusky	OH	1936-1937
Springfield	OH	1908, 1911, 1944-1947
Tiffin	OH	1936-1941
Zanesville	OH	1944-1947

OHIO-INDIANA LEAGUE
CLASS D 1908, 1948-1951
(aka Indiana-Ohio League)

Huntington	IN	1908
Lima	OH	1948-1951
Marion	OH	1948-1951
Muncie	IN	1908, 1948-1950
Newark	OH	1948-1951
Portsmouth	OH	1948-1950
Richmond	IN	1908, 1948-1951
Springfield	OH	1948-1951
Van Wert	OH	1908
Zanesville	OH	1948-1950

OHIO-MICHIGAN LEAGUE
1893

Akron	OH	1893
Bay City	MI	1893
Canton	OH	1893
East Liverpool	OH	1893
Mansfield	OH	1893
Saginaw	MI	1893
Sandusky	OH	1893

OHIO-PENNSYLVANIA LEAGUE
CLASS C 1905-1911; CLASS D 1912

Akron	OH	1905-1911
Alliance-Sebring	OH	1912
Barberton	OH	1905
Braddock	PA	1905
Bridgeport	OH	1912
Bucyrus	OH	1905
Butler	PA	1905, 1908
Canton	OH	1905, 1908-1911
Connellsville	PA	1912
East Liverpool	OH	1908-1912
Fairmont	WV	1912
Girard	OH	1908
Homestead	PA	1905
Kent	OH	1905
Lancaster	OH	1905-1907
Lima	OH	1905
Mansfield	OH	1906-1907, 1910-1911
Marion	OH	1906-1907
Massillon	OH	1905
McKeesport	PA	1905, 1908-1910, 1912
Mt. Vernon	OH	1905
New Castle	PA	1906-1912
New Martinsville	WV	1912
Newark	OH	1905-1907
Niles	OH	1905
Pittsburgh	PA	1912
Salem	OH	1912
Sharon	PA	1905-1908, 1911-1912
Steubenville	OH	1905, 1909, 1911
Steubenville-Follansbee	OH-WV	1912
Washington	PA	1905
Wooster	OH	1905
Youngstown	OH	1905-1911
Zanesville	OH	1905-1906

OKLAHOMA STATE LEAGUE
CLASS D 1912, 1922-1924

Anadarko	OK	1912
Ardmore	OK	1924
Blackwell	OK	1924

Bristow	OK	1923-1924
Chickasha	OK	1922
Clinton	OK	1922-1923
Cushing	OK	1923-1924
Drumright	OK	1923
Duncan	OK	1922-1924
El Reno	OK	1922-1923
Enid	OK	1924
Guthrie	OK	1912, 1922-1924
Holdenville	OK	1912
McAlester	OK	1912, 1924
Muskogee	OK	1912
Oklahoma City	OK	1912
Okmulgee	OK	1912
Pawhuska	OK	1924
Ponca City	OK	1923-1924
Shawnee	OK	1923-1924
Tulsa	OK	1912
Wewoka-Holdenville	OK	1924
Wilson	OK	1922

OKLAHOMA-ARKANSAS-KANSAS LEAGUE (OAK)
CLASS D 1907
(predecessor of the Oklahoma-Kansas League 1908)

Bartlesville	OK	1907
Coffeyville	KS	1907
Ft. Smith	AR	1907
Independence	KS	1907
McAlester	OK	1907
Muskogee	OK	1907
Parsons	KS	1907
Tulsa	OK	1907

OKLAHOMA-KANSAS LEAGUE
CLASS D 1908
(successor of the Oklahoma-Arkansas-Kansas League 1907)

Bartlesville	OK	1908
Independence	KS	1908
Iola	KS	1908
McAlester	OK	1908
Muskogee	OK	1908
Tulsa	OK	1908

ONTARIO LEAGUE
CLASS C 1930

Brantford	ONT	1930
Guelph	ONT	1930
Hamilton	ONT	1930
London	ONT	1930
St. Catharines	ONT	1930
St. Thomas	ONT	1930

OREGON STATE LEAGUE
CLASS D 1904

Albany	OR	1904
Eugene	OR	1904
Roseburg	OR	1904
Salem	OR	1904
Vancouver	WA	1904

PACIFIC COAST LEAGUE
IND 1903; CLASS A 1904-1911; CLASS AA 1912-1945; CLASS AAA 1946-1951; OPEN CLASSIFICATION 1952-1957; CLASS AAA 1958-

Albuquerque	NM	1972-
Calgary	ALB	1985-
Colorado Springs	CO	1988-
Dallas	TX	1964
Dallas-Ft. Worth	TX	1963
Denver	CO	1963-1968
Edmonton	ALB	1981-
Eugene	OR	1969-1973
Fresno	CA	1906
Hollywood	CA	1926-1935, 1938-1957
Hawaii (Honolulu)	HI	1961-1987
Indianapolis	IN	1964-1968
Las Vegas	NV	1983-
Little Rock	AR	1964-1965
Los Angeles	CA	1903-1957
Mission (San Francisco)	CA	1914, 1926-1937
Oakland	CA	1903-1955
Ogden	UT	1979-1980
Oklahoma City	OK	1963-1968
Phoenix	AZ	1958-1959, 1966-
Portland	OR	1903-1972, 1978-1993

Sacramento	CA	1903, 1909-1914, 1918-1960, 1974-1976
Salt Lake City	UT	1915-1925, 1958-1965, 1970-1984, 1994-
San Diego	CA	1936-1968
San Francisco	CA	1903-1957
San Jose	CA	1977-1978
Seattle	WA	1903-1906, 1919-1968
Spokane	WA	1958-1971, 1973-1982
Tacoma	WA	1904-1905, 1960-
Tucson	AZ	1969-
Tulsa	OK	1966-1968
Vancouver	BC	1956-1962, 1965-1969, 1978-
Venice	CA	1913-1915
Vernon	CA	1909-1912, 1915-1925

PACIFIC COAST INTERNATIONAL LEAGUE
CLASS B 1918-1921
(aka Pacific International League)
(known as the Northwest International League 1919)
(predecessor of the Western International League 1922)

Aberdeen	WA	1918
Portland	OR	1918
Seattle	WA	1918-1920
Spokane	WA	1918, 1920
Tacoma	WA	1918-1921
Vancouver	BC	1918-1921
Vancouver	WA	1918
Victoria	BC	1919-1921
Yakima	WA	1920-1921

PACIFIC NATIONAL LEAGUE
CLASS A 1903; CLASS B 1904
(successor of the Pacific Northwest League 1902)

Boise	ID	1904
Butte	MT	1903-1904
Helena	MT	1903
Los Angeles	CA	1903
Portland	OR	1903
Salt Lake City	UT	1903-1904
San Francisco	CA	1903
Seattle	WA	1903
Spokane	WA	1903-1904
Tacoma	WA	1903

PACIFIC NORTHWEST LEAGUE
CLASS B 1892, 1896, 1901; CLASS B 1902
(aka New Pacific League 1896)
(predecessor of the Pacific National League 1903-1905)

Butte	MT	1902
Helena	MT	1902
Portland	OR	1892, 1896, 1901-1902
Seattle	WA	1892, 1896, 1901-1902
Spokane	WA	1892, 1901-1902
Tacoma	WA	1892, 1896, 1901-1902
Victoria	BC	1896

PALMETTO LEAGUE
CLASS D 1931

Anderson	SC	1931
Augusta	GA	1931
Florence	SC	1931
Greenville	SC	1931
Spartanburg	SC	1931

PANHANDLE-PECOS VALLEY LEAGUE
CLASS D 1923
(successor of the West Texas League 1920-1922)

Amarillo	TX	1923
Clovis	NM	1923
Lubbock	TX	1923
Roswell	NM	1923

PENNSYLVANIA STATE ASSOCIATION
CLASS D 1934-1942

Beaver Falls	PA	1937-1941
Butler	PA	1935-1942
Charleroi	PA	1934-1936
Greensburg	PA	1934-1939
Jeannette	PA	1934-1937
Johnstown	PA	1939-1940
McKeesport	PA	1934-1940
Monessen	PA	1934-1938
Oil City	PA	1940-1942
Warren	PA	1940-1941
Washington	PA	1934-1935, 1939-1942

PENNSYLVANIA STATE LEAGUE
1892-1895
(predecessor of the Atlantic League 1896-1900)

Allentown	PA	1892-1895
Altoona	PA	1892-1894
Ashland	PA	1894
Danville	PA	1892-1893
Easton	PA	1893-1894
Harrisburg	PA	1893-1895
Hazleton	PA	1894-1895
Johnstown	PA	1892-1893
Lancaster	PA	1894-1895
Lebanon	PA	1892
Philadelphia	PA	1894
Pottsville	PA	1894-1895
Reading	PA	1892-1895
Scranton	PA	1892-1894
Shenandoah	PA	1894-1895
Wilkes-Barre	PA	1892
York	PA	1893

PENNSYLVANIA-OHIO-MARYLAND LEAGUE (POM)
CLASS D 1906-1907

Braddock	PA	1906-1907
Butler	PA	1906
Charleroi	PA	1906-1907
Cumberland	MD	1906
East Liverpool	OH	1906-1907
McKeesport	PA	1907
Piedmont	WV	1906
Steubenville	OH	1906-1907
Uniontown	PA	1906-1907
Washington	PA	1906-1907
Waynesburg	PA	1906
Zanesville	OH	1907

PENNSYLVANIA-WEST VIRGINIA LEAGUE
CLASS D 1908-1909

Charleroi	PA	1908-1909
Clarksburg	WV	1908-1909
Connellsville	PA	1908-1909
Fairmont	WV	1908-1909
Grafton	WV	1908-1909
Parkersburg	WV	1909
Scottdale	PA	1908
Uniontown	PA	1908-1909

PIEDMONT LEAGUE
CLASS D 1920; CLASS C 1921-1931; CLASS B 1932-1955

Asheville	NC	1931-1932, 1934-1942
Charlotte	NC	1931-1935, 1937-1942
Colonial Heights-Petersburg	VA	1954
Columbia	SC	1934
Danville	VA	1920-1925
Durham	NC	1920-1933, 1936-1943
Greensboro	NC	1920-1926, 1928-1934, 1941-1942
Hagerstown	MD	1953-1955
Henderson	NC	1929-1931
High Point	NC	1920-1932
Lancaster	PA	1954-1955
Lynchburg	VA	1943-1955
Newport News	VA	1944-1955
Norfolk	VA	1934-1955
Portsmouth	VA	1935-1955
Raleigh	NC	1920-1932
Richmond	VA	1933-1953
Roanoke	VA	1943-1953
Rocky Mount	NC	1927, 1936-1940
Salisbury-Spencer	NC	1925-1929
Sunbury	PA	1955
Wilmington	NC	1932-1935
Winston	NC	1920
Winston-Salem	NC	1921-1933, 1937-1942
York	PA	1953-1955

PIONEER LEAGUE
CLASS C 1939-1942, 1946-1962, CLASS A 1963; ROOKIE 1964-

Billings	MT	1948-1963, 1969-
Boise	ID	1939-1942, 1946-1963
Butte	MT	1978-1985, 1987-
Caldwell (aka Treasure Valley)	ID	1964-1971
Calgary	ALB	1977-1984
Great Falls	MT	1948-1963, 1969-
Helena	MT	1978-

PROFESSIONAL TEAMS BY LEAGUE 1883-1997

Idaho Falls	ID	1940-1942, 1946-
Lethbridge	ALB	1975-1983, 1992-
Lewiston	ID	1939
Medicine Hat	ALB	1977-
Missoula	MT	1956-1960
Ogden	UT	1939-1942, 1946-1955, 1966-1974, 1994-
Pocatello (aka Gate City)	ID	1939-1942, 1946-1965, 1984-1985, 1987-1991, 1993
Salt Lake City	UT	1939-1942, 1946-1957, 1967-1969, 1985-1992
Twin Falls (aka Magic Valley)	ID	1939-1942, 1946-1958, 1961-1966, 1968-71

PLAYER'S LEAGUE
MAJOR 1890

Boston	MA	1890
Brooklyn	NY	1890
Buffalo	NY	1890
Chicago	IL	1890
Cleveland	OH	1890
New York	NY	1890
Philadelphia	PA	1890
Pittsburgh	PA	1890

PONY LEAGUE (PENNSYLVANIA-ONTARIO-NEW YORK)
CLASS D 1939-1956
(see New York-Pennsyvania League 1939-)

POTOMAC LEAGUE
CLASS D 1916

Cumberland	MD	1916
Frostburg	MD	1916
Lonaconing	MD	1916
Piedmont	WV	1916

PRAIRIE LEAGUE
IND 1995-

Aberdeen	SD	1995-
Brainerd	MN	1996
Brandon	MB	1995-
Dakota (Bismarck)	ND	1995-1996
Grand Forks	ND	1996-
Green Bay	WI	1996
Minneapolis	MN	1995
Minot	ND	1995-
Moose Jaw	SK	1995-
Regina	SK	1995-
Saskatoon	SK	1995-
Southern Minny (Austin)	MN	1996-

PROVINCIAL LEAGUE
IND 1948-1949; CLASS C 1950-1955
(The Quebec Provincial League existed in different names from 1922-1924, 1935-1955, 1958-1970, sometimes in Organized Baseball and sometimes out.)

Burlington	VT	1955
Drummondville	QUE	1948-1954
Farnham	QUE	1948-1951
Granby	QUE	1948-1953
Quebec	QUE	1951-1955
St. Hyacinthe	QUE	1948-1953
St. Jean-Sur-Richelieu	QUE	1948-1955
Sherbrooke	QUE	1948-1951, 1953-1955
Thetford Mines	QUE	1953-1955
Trois Rivieres	QUE	1951-1955

QUEBEC PROVINCIAL LEAGUE
CLASS B 1940

Drummondville	QUE	1940
Granby	QUE	1940
Quebec	QUE	1940
St. Hyacinthe	QUE	1940
Sherbrooke	QUE	1940
Trois Rivieres	QUE	1940

QUEBEC-ONTARIO-VERMONT LEAGUE
CLASS B 1924
(aka Quebec-Ontario League)

Montpelier	VT	1924
Montreal	QUE	1924
Ottawa-Hull	ONT-QUE	1924
Outremont	QUE	1924
Quebec	QUE	1924
Rutland	VT	1924

RIO GRANDE ASSOCIATION
CLASS D 1915

Albuquerque	NM	1915
Douglas	AZ	1915
El Paso	TX	1915
Las Cruces	NM	1915
Phoenix	AZ	1915
Tucson	AZ	1915

RIO GRANDE VALLEY LEAGUE
CLASS D 1931, 1949; CLASS C 1950

Brownsville	TX	1949-1950
Corpus Christi	TX	1931, 1949-1950
Del Rio	TX	1949-1950
Donna	TX	1949-1950
Harlingen	TX	1931, 1950
La Feria	TX	1931
Laredo	TX	1949-1950
McAllen	TX	1931, 1949-1950
Robstown	TX	1949-1950
San Benito	TX	1931

ROCKY MOUNTAIN LEAGUE
CLASS D 1912

Canon City	CO	1912
Cheyenne	WY	1912
Colorado Springs	CO	1912
Dawson	NM	1912
La Junta	CO	1912
Pueblo	CO	1912
Raton	NM	1912
Trinidad	CO	1912

SAN JOAQUIN VALLEY LEAGUE
CLASS D 1910-1911

Bakersfield	CA	1910
Coalinga	CA	1910-1911
Hanford	CA	1911
Lemoore	CA	1911
Porterville	CA	1911
Tulare	CA	1910-1911
Visalia	CA	1910-1911

SARASOTA ROOKIE LEAGUE
ROOKIE 1964
(games played at Sarasota, FL)

Braves	FL	1964
Cardinals	FL	1964
White Sox	FL	1964
Yankees	FL	1964

SOONER STATE LEAGUE
CLASS D 1947-1957

Ada	OK	1947-1954
Ardmore	OK	1947-1957
Chickasha	OK	1948-1952
Duncan	OK	1947-1950
Gainesville	TX	1953-1955
Greenville	TX	1957
Lawton	OK	1947-1957
McAlester	OK	1947-1956
Muskogee	OK	1955-1957
Paris	TX	1955-1957
Pauls Valley	OK	1948-1954
Ponca City	OK	1955-1957
Seminole	OK	1947-1951, 1954-1957
Shawnee	OK	1950-1957
Sherman	TX	1952
Sherman-Denison	TX	1953

SOPHOMORE LEAGUE
CLASS D 1958-1961
(successor of the Southwestern League 1956-1957)

Albuquerque	NM	1960-1961
Alpine	TX	1959-1961
Artesia	NM	1958-1961
Carlsbad	NM	1958-1961
El Paso	TX	1961
Hobbs	NM	1958-1961
Midland	TX	1958-1959
Odessa	TX	1959-1960
Plainview	TX	1958-1959
Roswell	NM	1959
San Angelo	TX	1958-1959

PROFESSIONAL TEAMS BY LEAGUE 1883-1997

SOUTH ATLANTIC LEAGUE (SALLY LEAGUE)
CLASS C 1904-1917, 1919-1920; CLASS B 1921-1930, 1936-1942;
CLASS A 1946-1962; CLASS AA 1963
(known as the South Atlantic Association 1926-1930)
(predecessor of the Southern League 1964-)

Albany	GA	1911-1916
Asheville	NC	1924-1930, 1959-1963
Augusta	GA	1904-1911, 1914-1917, 1919-1930, 1936-1942, 1946-1963
Charleston	SC	1904-1909, 1911, 1913-1917, 1919-1923, 1940-1942, 1946-1953, 1959-1961
Charlotte	NC	1919-1930, 1954-1963
Chattanooga	TN	1909, 1943, 1963
Columbia	SC	1904-1912, 1914-1917, 1919-1923, 1925-1930, 1936-1942, 1946-1957, 1960-1961
Columbus	GA	1909-1917, 1936-1942, 1946-1957, 1959
Gastonia	NC	1923, 1959
Greenville	SC	1919-1930, 1938-1942, 1946-1950, 1961-1962
Jacksonville	FL	1904-1917, 1936-1942, 1946-1961
Knoxville	TN	1909, 1925-1929, 1956-1963
Lynchburg	VA	1962-1963
Macon	GA	1904-1917, 1923-1930, 1936-1942, 1946-1960, 1962-1963
Montgomery	AL	1916, 1951-1956
Nashville	TN	1963
Portsmouth-Norfolk	VA	1961-1962
Savannah	GA	1904-1915, 1936-1942, 1946-1960, 1962
Spartanburg	SC	1919-1929, 1938-1940

SOUTH ATLANTIC LEAGUE (SALLY LEAGUE)
CLASS A 1980-
(successor of the Western Carolinas League 1960-1979)

Albany	GA	1992-1995
Anderson	SC	1980-1984
Asheville	NC	1980-
Augusta	GA	1988-
Charleston	SC	1980-
Charleston	WV	1987-
Columbia (aka Capital City)	SC	1983-
Columbus	GA	1991-
Delmarva (Salisbury)	MD	1996-
Fayetteville (Cape Fear)	NC	1987-
Florence	SC	1981-1986
Gastonia	NC	1980-1992
Greensboro	NC	1980-
Greenwood	SC	1981-1983
Hagerstown	MD	1993-
Hickory	NC	1993-
Macon	GA	1980-1987, 1991-
Myrtle Beach	SC	1987-1992
Piedmont (Kannapolis)	NC	1995-
Savannah	GA	1984-
Shelby	NC	1980-1982
Spartanburg	SC	1980-1994
Sumter	SC	1985-1991

SOUTH CAROLINA LEAGUE
CLASS D 1907-1908

Anderson	SC	1907
Chester	SC	1908
Darlington	SC	1907
Florence	SC	1907
Greenville	SC	1907
Orangeburg	SC	1907-1908
Rock Hill	SC	1908
Spartanburg	SC	1907
Sumter	SC	1907-1908

SOUTH CENTRAL LEAGUE
CLASS D 1906, 1912

Texarkana	TX	1912
Cleburne	TX	1912
Ft. Smith	AR	1906
Guthrie	OK	1906
Longview	TX	1912
Marshall	TX	1912
Muskogee	OK	1906
Paris	TX	1912
Shawnee	OK	1906
South McAlester	OK	1906
Tulsa	OK	1906
Tyler	TX	1912

SOUTH DAKOTA LEAGUE
CLASS D 1920, 1923
(predecessor of the Dakota League 1921-1922)
(successor of the Dakota League 1921-1922)

Aberdeen	SD	1920, 1923
Huron	SD	1920
Madison	SD	1920
Miller	SD	1920
Mitchell	SD	1920, 1923
Redfield	SD	1920
Sioux Falls	SD	1920, 1923
Watertown	SD	1923
Wessington Springs	SD	1920

SOUTH TEXAS LEAGUE
CLASS C 1903-1906

Austin	TX	1906
Beaumont	TX	1903-1906
Brenham	TX	1905
Galveston	TX	1903-1906
Houston	TX	1903-1906
Lake Charles	LA	1906
San Antonio	TX	1903-1906

SOUTHEASTERN LEAGUE
CLASS D 1910-1912; CLASS B 1926-1930, 1932, 1937-1942, 1946-1950

Albany	GA	1926-1928
Anniston	AL	1911-1912, 1938-1942, 1946-1950
Asheville	NC	1910
Bessemer	AL	1912
Columbus	GA	1926-1930, 1932
Decatur	AL	1911
Gadsden	AL	1910-1912, 1938-1941, 1946-1950
Huntsville	AL	1911-1912
Jackson	MS	1932, 1937-1942, 1946-1950
Jacksonville	FL	1926-1930
Johnson City	TN	1910
Knoxville	TN	1910
Macon	GA	1932
Meridian	MS	1937-1942, 1946-1950
Mobile	AL	1932, 1937-1942
Montgomery	AL	1926-1930, 1932, 1937-1942, 1946-1950
Morristown	TN	1910
Pensacola	FL	1927-1930, 1934-1942, 1946-1950
Rome	GA	1910-1912
St. Augustine	FL	1926-1927
Savannah	GA	1926-1928
Selma	AL	1911-1912, 1927-1930, 1932, 1937-1941, 1946-1950
Talladega	AL	1912
Tampa	FL	1928-1930
Vicksburg	MS	1946-1950
Waycross	GA	1927

SOUTHERN ASSOCIATION
1885-1886, 1892-1896; 1901; CLASS A 1902-1935;
CLASS A1 1936-1945; CLASS AA 1946-1961
(frequently called Southern League prior to 1920)

Atlanta	GA	1885-1886, 1892-1896, 1902-1961
Augusta	GA	1885-1886, 1893-1894
Birmingham	AL	1885-1888, 1892-1893, 1896, 1901-1961
Charleston	SC	1886-1888, 1893-1894
Chattanooga	TN	1885-1886, 1892-1893, 1895, 1901-1902, 1910-1961
Columbus	GA	1885, 1896
Evansville	IN	1895
Knoxville	TN	1932-1944
Little Rock	AR	1895, 1901-1910, 1915-1958, 1960-1961
Macon	GA	1885-1886, 1892-1894
Memphis	TN	1885-1888, 1892-1895, 1901-1960
Mobile	AL	1887, 1892-1896, 1908-1931, 1944-1961
Montgomery	AL	1892-1893, 1895-1896, 1903-1914, 1943, 1956
Nashville	TN	1885-1887, 1893-1895, 1901-1961
New Orleans	LA	1887-1888, 1892-1896, 1901-1959
Pensacola	FL	1893
Savannah	GA	1886-1887, 1893-1894
Shreveport	LA	1901-1907, 1959-1961
Selma	AL	1901

PROFESSIONAL TEAMS BY LEAGUE 1883-1997

SOUTHERN LEAGUE
CLASS AA 1964-
(successor of the South Atlantic League 1946-1963)

Asheville	NC	1964-1966, 1968-1975
Birmingham	AL	1964-1965, 1967-1975, 1981-
Carolina (Zebulon)	NC	1991-
Charlotte	NC	1964-1972, 1976-1992
Chattanooga	TN	1964-1965, 1976-
Columbus	GA	1964-1966, 1969-1990
Evansville	IN	1966-1968
Greenville	SC	1984-
Huntsville	AL	1985-
Jacksonville	FL	1970-
Knoxville	TN	1964-1967, 1972-
Lynchburg	VA	1964-1965
Macon	GA	1961, 1964, 1966-1967
Memphis	TN	1978-
Mobile	AL	1966, 1970. 1997-
Montgomery	AL	1965-1980
Nashville	TN	1978-1984, 1993-1994
Orlando	FL	1973-
Port City (Wilmington)	NC	1995-1996
Savannah	GA	1968-1983

SOUTHERN CALIFORNIA LEAGUE
CLASS D 1913

Long Beach	CA	1913
Pasadena	CA	1913
San Bernardino	CA	1913
San Diego	CA	1913
Santa Barbara	CA	1913

SOUTHERN CALIFORNIA TROLLEY LEAGUE
CLASS D 1910

Long Beach	CA	1910
Los Angeles-Maiers	CA	1910
Los Angeles-McCormicks	CA	1910
Pasadena	CA	1910
Redondo Beach	CA	1910
Santa Ana	CA	1910

SOUTHERN ILLINOIS LEAGUE
CLASS D 1910

Eldorado	IL	1910
Harrisburg	IL	1910
Herrin	IL	1910
McLeansboro	IL	1910
Mt. Vernon	IL	1910

SOUTHERN MICHIGAN ASSOCIATION
CLASS D 1910, 1912-1913; CLASS C 1911, 1914-1915
SOUTHERN MICHIGAN LEAGUE
CLASS D 1906-1909
(aka South Michigan League)

Adrian	MI	1909-1914
Battle Creek	MI	1906-1915
Bay City	MI	1907-1915
Flint	MI	1907-1915
Jackson	MI	1906-1915
Kalamazoo	MI	1906-1914
Lansing	MI	1907-1914
Mt. Clemens	MI	1906-1907, 1914
Saginaw	MI	1906, 1908-1915
South Bend	IN	1914-1915
Tecumseh	MI	1906-1908
Toledo	OH	1914

SOUTHWEST INTERNATIONAL LEAGUE
CLASS C 1951-1952
(The Arizona-Texas and Sunset Leagues merged to form the Southwest International. The Arizona-Texas League reformed in 1952 and continued play through 1954.)

Bisbee-Douglas	AZ	1951
Ciudad Juarez	MEX	1951
El Centro	CA	1951-1952
El Paso	TX	1951
Las Vegas	NV	1951
Mexicali	MEX	1951-1952
Phoenix	AZ	1951
Porterville	CA	1952
Riverside-Ensenada	CA-MEX	1952
Riverside-Porterville	CA	1952
Tijuana	MEX	1951-1952
Tucson	AZ	1951
Yuma	AZ	1951-1952

SOUTHWEST IOWA LEAGUE
CLASS D 1903

Atlantic	IA	1903
Clarinda	IA	1903
Creston	IA	1903
Osceola	IA	1903
Red Oak	IA	1903
Shenandoah	IA	1903

SOUTHWEST TEXAS LEAGUE
CLASS D 1910-1911

Bay City	TX	1910-1911
Beeville	TX	1910-1911
Brownsville	TX	1910-1911
Corpus Christi	TX	1910-1911
Laredo	TX	1910-1911
Victoria	TX	1910-1911

SOUTHWEST WASHINGTON LEAGUE
CLASS D 1903-1906

Aberdeen	WA	1903-1906
Centralia	WA	1903-1904
Hoquiam	WA	1903-1906
Montesano	WA	1905
Olympia	WA	1903-1906

SOUTHWESTERN LEAGUE
CLASS D 1904, 1921, 1924-1926; CLASS C 1922-1923
(aka Oklahoma State League 1904)

Arkansas City	KS	1924-1926
Bartlesville	OK	1921-1923
Blackwell	OK	1924-1926
Chickasha	OK	1904
Coffeyville	KS	1921-1924
Cushing	OK	1921, 1925
Emporia	KS	1924
Enid	OK	1904, 1924-1926
Eureka	KS	1924-1926
Guthrie	OK	1904
Hutchinson	KS	1922-1923
Independence	KS	1921-1924
Miami	OK	1921
Muskogee	OK	1921-1923
Newton	KS	1924
Oklahoma City	OK	1904
Ottawa	KS	1924
Parsons	KS	1921
Pittsburg	KS	1921
Ponca City	OK	1926
Salina	KS	1922-1926
Sapulpa	OK	1921-1923
Shawnee	OK	1904, 1925
Topeka	KS	1922-1923, 1925-1926

SOUTHWESTERN LEAGUE
CLASS B 1956-1957
(successor of the Longhorn League 1947-1955)
(predecessor of the Sophomore League 1958-1961)

Ballinger	TX	1956-1957
Carlsbad	NM	1956-1957
Clovis	NM	1956-1957
El Paso	TX	1956-1957
Hobbs	NM	1956-1957
Lamesa	TX	1957
Midland	TX	1956-1957
Pampa	TX	1956-1957
Plainview	TX	1956-1957
Roswell	NM	1956
San Angelo	TX	1956-1957

SUNSET LEAGUE
CLASS C 1947-1950
(merged with Arizona-Texas League to form Southwest International League 1951-1952)

Anaheim	CA	1947-1948
El Centro	CA	1947-1950
Las Vegas	NV	1947-1950
Mexicali	MEX	1948-1950
Ontario	CA	1947
Porterville	CA	1949-1950

Reno	NV	1947-1949
Riverside	CA	1947-1950
Salinas	CA	1949
San Bernardino	CA	1948-1950
Tijuana	MEX	1949-1950
Yuma	AZ	1950

TAR HEEL LEAGUE
CLASS D 1939-1940, 1953-1954
(formed in 1953 from combined North Carolina State and Western Carolina Leagues)

Forest City	NC	1953-1954
Gastonia	NC	1939-1940
Hickory	NC	1939-1940, 1953-1954
High Point-Thomasville	NC	1953
Lenoir	NC	1939-1940
Lexington	NC	1953
Lincolnton	NC	1953
Marion	NC	1953-1954
Mooresville	NC	1953
Newton-Conover	NC	1939-1940
Salisbury	NC	1953
Shelby	NC	1939-1940, 1953-1954
Statesville	NC	1939-1940, 1953

TEXAS ASSOCIATION
CLASS D 1923-1926

Austin	TX	1923-1926
Corsicana	TX	1923-1926
Marlin	TX	1923-1924
Mexia	TX	1923-1926
Palestine	TX	1925-1926
Sherman	TX	1923
Temple	TX	1924-1926
Terrell	TX	1925-1926
Waco	TX	1923-1924

TEXAS LEAGUE
1888-1890; CLASS D 1902-1903, 1906; CLASS C 1904-1905, 1907-1910; CLASS B 1911-1920; CLASS A 1921-1935; CLASS A1 1936-1942; CLASS AA 1946-

(The Texas League split into the Texas and South Texas Leagues, 1903-1906. The Texas League was sometimes known as the North Texas League to distinguish it from the South Texas League. There was an official North Texas League in 1905 and 1907.)

Albuquerque	NM	1962-1971
Alexandria	LA	1972-1975
Amarillo	TX	1959-1963, 1965-1974, 1976-1982
Ardmore	OK	1904, 1961
Arkansas (Little Rock)	AR	1966-
Austin	TX	1888-1890, 1905, 1907-1908, 1911-1914, 1956-1967
Beaumont	TX	1912-1917, 1919-1955, 1983-1986
Cleburne	TX	1906
Corpus Christi	TX	1958-1959
Corsicana	TX	1902-1905
Dallas	TX	1888-1890, 1902-1942, 1946-1958
Dallas-Ft. Worth	TX	1965-1971
Denison	TX	1896
El Paso	TX	1962-1970, 1972-
Ft. Worth	TX	1888-1890, 1902-1942, 1946-1958, 1964
Galveston	TX	1888-1890, 1907-1917, 1919-1924, 1931-1937
Greenville	TX	1906
Houston	TX	1888-1890, 1907-1958
Jackson	MS	1975-
Lafayette	LA	1975-1976
Longview	TX	1932
Memphis	TN	1968-1973
Midland	TX	1972-
New Orleans	LA	1888
Oklahoma City	OK	1909-1911, 1933-1957
Paris	TX	1902-1904
Rio Grande Valley (Harlingen)	TX	1960-1961
San Antonio	TX	1888, 1907-1942, 1946-1964, 1967-
Sherman-Denison	TX	1902
Shreveport	LA	1908-1910, 1915-1932, 1938-1942, 1946-1957, 1968-
Temple	TX	1905-1907
Texarkana	TX	1902
Tulsa	OK	1933-1942, 1946-1965, 1977-
Tyler	TX	1932
Victoria	TX	1958-1961, 1974
Waco	TX	1889-1890, 1902-1903, 1905-1919, 1925-1930
Wichita	KS	1987-
Wichita Falls	TX	1920-1932

TEXAS VALLEY LEAGUE
CLASS D 1927-1928, 1938

Brownsville	TX	1928, 1938
Corpus Christi	TX	1927-1928, 1938
Edinburg	TX	1927
Harlingen	TX	1938
Laredo	TX	1927
McAllen	TX	1928, 1938
Mission	TX	1927-1928
Refugio	TX	1938
Taft	TX	1938

TEXAS-LOUISIANA LEAGUE
IND 1994-

Abilene	TX	1995-
Alexandria	LA	1994-
Amarillo	TX	1994-
Beaumont	TX	1994
Corpus Christi	TX	1994-1995
Laredo	TX	1995
Lubbock	TX	1995-
Mobile	AL	1994-1995
Pueblo	CO	1995
Rio Grande Valley (Harlingen)	TX	1994-
San Antonio	TX	1994
Tyler	TX	1994-

TEXAS-OKLAHOMA LEAGUE
CLASS D 1911-1914, 1921-1922

Altus	OK	1911
Ardmore	OK	1911-1914, 1921-1922
Bonham	TX	1911-1914, 1921-1922
Cleburne	TX	1911, 1921-1922
Corsicana	TX	1922
Denison	TX	1912-1914
Durant	OK	1911-1914
Gainesville	TX	1911
Graham	TX	1921
Greenville	TX	1912, 1922
Hugo	OK	1913-1914
Lawton	OK	1911
McKinney	TX	1912
Mexia	TX	1922
Mineral Wells	TX	1921
Paris	TX	1913-1914, 1921-1922
Sherman	TX	1912-1914, 1921-1922
Texarkana	TX	1913-1914
Wichita Falls	TX	1911-1913

TEXAS-SOUTHERN LEAGUE
1895-1896

Austin	TX	1895-1896
Dallas	TX	1895-1896
Denison	TX	1896
Ft. Worth	TX	1895-1896
Galveston	TX	1895-1896
Houston	TX	1895-1896
San Antonio	TX	1895-1896
Sherman	TX	1895-1896
Shreveport	LA	1895

THREE-I LEAGUE (ILLINOIS-IOWA-INDIANA)
1901; CLASS B 1902-1917, 1919-1932, 1935, 1937-1942, 1946-1961
(aka 3 Eye League)

Alton	IL	1917
Appleton (aka Fox Cities)	WI	1958-1961
Bloomington	IN	1901-1910, 1912-1917, 1919-1931, 1935, 1937-1939
Burlington	IA	1952-1961
Cedar Rapids	IA	1901-1909, 1920-1921, 1938-1942, 1950-1961
Clinton	IA	1907-1908, 1937-1941
Danville	IL	1910-1914, 1922-1932, 1946-1950
Davenport	IA	1901-1906, 1909-1916, 1946-1952, 1957-1958
Decatur	IL	1901-1909, 1911-1915, 1922-1932, 1935, 1937-1942, 1946-1950
Des Moines	IA	1959-1961
Dubuque	IA	1903-1915
Evansville	IN	1901-1902, 1919-1931, 1938-1942, 1946-1957
Fort Wayne	IN	1935
Freeport	IL	1915
Green Bay	WI	1958-1960
Hannibal	MO	1916-1917
Joliet	IL	1903
Keokuk	IA	1952-1957

Lincoln	NE	1959-1961
Madison	WI	1940-1942
Moline	IL	1914-1917, 1919-1923, 1937-1941
Peoria	IL	1905-1917, 1919-1932, 1935, 1937, 1953-1957
Quincy	IL	1911-1917, 1925-1932, 1946-1956
Rochester	MN	1958
Rock Island	IL	1901-1911, 1916-1917, 1920-1921
Rockford	IL	1901-1904, 1915-1917, 1919-1923
Sioux City	IA	1959-1960
Springfield	IL	1903-1914, 1925-1932, 1935, 1938-1942, 1946-1949
Terre Haute	IN	1901-1902, 1919-1932, 1935, 1937, 1946-1956
Topeka	KS	1959-1961
Waterloo	IA	1910-1911, 1938-1942, 1946-1956
Winona	MN	1958

TOBACCO STATE LEAGUE
CLASS D 1946-1950

Angier-Fuquay Springs	NC	1946
Clinton	NC	1946-1950
Dunn-Erwin	NC	1946-1949
Fayetteville	NC	1949
Lumberton	NC	1947-1950
Red Springs	NC	1947-1950
Rockingham	NC	1950
Sanford	NC	1946-1950
Smithfield	NC	1946
Smithfield-Selma	NC	1947-1950
Warsaw	NC	1947-1948
Whiteville	NC	1950
Wilmington	NC	1946-1950

TRI-STATE LEAGUE (OH)
1887-1890
(aka Ohio State League 1887)

Akron	OH	1887, 1890
Canton	OH	1887-1890
Columbus	OH	1887-1888
Dayton	OH	1889-1890
Hamilton	OH	1889
Jackson	MI	1888
Kalamazoo	MI	1887-1888
Lima	OH	1888
Mansfield	OH	1887-1890
McKeesport	PA	1890
Sandusky	OH	1887-1888
Springfield	OH	1889-1890
Steubenville	OH	1887
Toledo	OH	1888
Wheeling	WV	1887-1890
Youngstown	OH	1890
Zanesville	OH	1887-1888

TRI-STATE LEAGUE (AR-MS-TN)
CLASS D 1925-1926

Blytheville	AR	1925-1926
Corinth	MS	1925-1926
Dyersburg	TN	1925
Jackson	TN	1925-1926
Jonesboro	AR	1925-1926
Sheffield-Tuscumbia	AL	1926
Tupelo	MS	1925-1926

TRI-STATE LEAGUE (NC-SC-TN)
CLASS B 1946-1955

Anderson	SC	1946-1954
Asheville	NC	1946-1955
Charlotte	NC	1946-1953
Fayetteville	NC	1947-1948
Florence	SC	1948-1950
Gastonia	NC	1952-1953
Greenville	SC	1951-1952, 1954-1955
Greenwood	SC	1951
Knoxville	TN	1946-1952, 1954-1955
Reidsville	NC	1947
Rock Hill	SC	1947-1955
Shelby	NC	1946
Spartanburg	SC	1946-1955
Sumter	SC	1949-1950

TRI-STATE LEAGUE (NE-IA-SD)
CLASS D 1924

Beatrice	NE	1924
Grand Island	NE	1924
Hastings	NE	1924
Norfolk	NE	1924
Sioux City	IA	1924
Sioux Falls	SD	1924

TRI-STATE LEAGUE (PA-DE-NJ)
IND 1904-1906; CLASS B 1907-1914

Allentown	PA	1912-1914
Altoona	PA	1904-1912
Atlantic City	NJ	1912-1913
Camden	NJ	1904
Chester	PA	1912
Harrisburg	PA	1904-1914
Johnstown	PA	1905-1912
Lancaster	PA	1905-1912, 1914
Lebanon	PA	1904
Reading	PA	1907-1912, 1914
Shamokin	PA	1905
Trenton	NJ	1907-1914
Williamsport	PA	1904-1910
Wilmington	DE	1904-1905, 1907-1908, 1911-1914
York	PA	1904-1907, 1909-1914

TWIN PORTS LEAGUE
CLASS E 1943

Duluth-Heralds	MN	1943
Duluth-Dukes	MN	1943
Duluth-Marion Iron	MN	1943
Superior	WI	1943

TWIN STATES LEAGUE
CLASS D 1911

Bellows Falls	VT	1911
Brattleboro	VT	1911
Keene	NH	1911
Springfield-Charlestown	VT-NH	1911

TWO-I LEAGUE (ILLINOIS-INDIANA LEAGUE)
1892

Aurora	IL	1892
Evansville	IN	1892
Jacksonville	IL	1892
Joliet	IL	1892
Peoria	IL	1892
Quincy	IL	1892
Rock Island-Moline	IL	1892
Rockford	IL	1892
Terre Haute	IN	1892

UNION ASSOCIATION
MAJOR 1884

Altoona	PA	1884
Baltimore	MD	1884
Boston	MA	1884
Chicago	IL	1884
Cincinnati	OH	1884
Kansas City	MO	1884
Milwaukee	WI	1884
Philadelphia	PA	1884
Pittsburgh	PA	1884
St. Louis	MO	1884
St. Paul	MN	1884
Washington	DC	1884
Wilmington	DE	1884

UNION ASSOCIATION
CLASS D 1911-1914

Boise	ID	1911, 1914
Butte	MT	1911-1914
Great Falls	MT	1911-1913
Helena	MT	1911-1914
Missoula	MT	1911-1913
Murray	UT	1914
Ogden	UT	1912-1914
Salt Lake City	UT	1911-1914

UNITED STATES LEAGUE
IND 1912

Chicago	IL	1912
Cincinnati	OH	1912
Cleveland	OH	1912
Pittsburgh	PA	1912
Richmond	VA	1912
Reading	PA	1912
New York	NY	1912
Washington	DC	1912

PROFESSIONAL TEAMS BY LEAGUE 1883-1997

UTAH-IDAHO LEAGUE
CLASS C 1926-1928

Boise	ID	1928
Idaho Falls	ID	1926-1928
Logan	UT	1926-1927
Ogden	UT	1926-1928
Pocatello	ID	1926-1928
Salt Lake City	UT	1926-1928
Twin Falls	ID	1926-1928

VIRGINIA LEAGUE
1894-1896, 1900; CLASS C 1906-1919, 1941-1942;
CLASS B 1920-1928; CLASS D 1939-1940; 1948-1951
(19th century predecessor of Virginia-North Carolina League 1901-1902)

Blackstone	VA	1948
Colonial Heights-Petersburg	VA	1951
Danville	VA	1906-1912
Edenton	NC	1951
Elizabeth City	NC	1950-1951
Emporia	VA	1948-1951
Franklin	VA	1948-1951
Harrisonburg	VA	1939-1941
Hampton	VA	1896
Hopewell	VA	1916, 1949-1950
Kinston	NC	1925-1927
Lawrenceville	VA	1948-1949
Lynchburg	VA	1894-1896, 1906-1912, 1917, 1939-1942
Newport News	VA	1900, 1912-1922, 1941-1942
Newport News-Hampton	VA	1894
Norfolk	VA	1894-1896, 1900, 1906-1928
Petersburg	VA	1894-1896, 1900, 1910-1921, 1923-1924, 1926-1928, 1941-1942, 1948-1950
Portsmouth	VA	1895-1896, 1900, 1906-1910, 1912-1917, 1919-1928
Pulaski	VA	1942
Richmond	VA	1894-1896, 1900, 1906-1914, 1918-1928
Roanoke	VA	1894-1896, 1906-1914
Rocky Mount	NC	1915-1917, 1920-1925
Salem-Roanoke	VA	1939-1942
Staunton	VA	1894, 1939-1942
Suffolk	VA	1915, 1919-1921, 1948-1951
Tarboro	NC	1921
Wilson	NC	1920-1927

VIRGINIA MOUNTAIN LEAGUE
CLASS D 1914

Charlottesville	VA	1914
Clifton Forge	VA	1914
Covington	VA	1914
Harrisonburg	VA	1914
Staunton	VA	1914

VIRGINIA VALLEY LEAGUE
CLASS D 1910

Ashland-Catlettsburg	KY	1910
Charleston	WV	1910
Huntington	WV	1910
Montgomery	WV	1910
Parkersburg	WV	1910
Point Pleasant-Gallipolis	WV-OH	1910

VIRGINIA-NORTH CAROLINA LEAGUE
1901; CLASS D 1905

Charlotte	NC	1901, 1905
Danville	VA	1905
Greensboro	NC	1905
Newport News	VA	1901
Norfolk	VA	1901
Portsmouth	VA	1901
Raleigh	NC	1901
Richmond	VA	1901
Salisbury-Spencer	NC	1905
Tarboro	NC	1901
Wilmington	NC	1901
Winston-Salem	NC	1905

WASHINGTON STATE LEAGUE
CLASS D 1910-1912

Aberdeen	WA	1910, 1912
Centralia	WA	1911-1912
Chehalis	WA	1910-1912
Hoquiam	WA	1910, 1912
Montesano	WA	1910
Raymond	WA	1910-1911

South Bend	WA	1911
Tacoma	WA	1910

WEST DIXIE LEAGUE
CLASS C 1934-1935
(successor of the Dixie League 1933)

Gladewater	TX	1935
Henderson	TX	1934-1935
Jacksonville	TX	1934-1935
Longview	TX	1934-1935
Lufkin	TX	1934
Palestine	TX	1934-1935
Paris	TX	1934
Shreveport	LA	1935
Tyler	TX	1934-1935

WEST MICHIGAN LEAGUE
(SEE MICHIGAN STATE LEAGUE)

WEST TEXAS LEAGUE
CLASS D 1920-1922, 1928-1929
(predecessor of the Panhandle-Pecos Valley League 1923)

Abilene	TX	1920-1922, 1928-1929
Amarillo	TX	1922
Ballinger	TX	1921, 1929
Big Spring	TX	1928-1929
Clovis	NM	1922
Cisco	TX	1920-1921
Coleman	TX	1928-1929
Eastland	TX	1920
Gorman	TX	1920
Hamlin	TX	1928
Lubbock	TX	1922, 1928
Midland	TX	1928-1929
Mineral Wells	TX	1920-1921
Ranger	TX	1920-1922
San Angelo	TX	1921-1922, 1928-1929
Stamford	TX	1922
Sweetwater	TX	1920-1922

WEST TEXAS-NEW MEXICO LEAGUE
CLASS D 1937-1942; CLASS C 1946-1954; CLASS B 1955

Abilene	TX	1939, 1946-1955
Albuquerque	NM	1942, 1946-1955
Amarillo	TX	1939-1942, 1946-1955
Big Spring	TX	1938-1942
Borger	TX	1939, 1942, 1946-1954
Clovis	NM	1938-1942, 1946-1955
El Paso	TX	1955
Hobbs	NM	1937-1938
Lamesa	TX	1939-1942, 1946-1952
Lubbock	TX	1938-1942, 1946-1955
Midland	TX	1937-1940
Monahans	TX	1937
Odessa	TX	1937, 1940
Pampa	TX	1939-1942, 1946-1955
Plainview	TX	1953-1955
Roswell	NM	1937
Wichita Falls	TX	1941-1942
Wink	TX	1937-1938

WEST VIRGINIA LEAGUE
CLASS D 1910

Clarksburg	WV	1910
Fairmont	WV	1910
Grafton	WV	1910
Mannington	WV	1910

WESTERN ASSOCIATION 1888-1891, 1893
(see Western League)

WESTERN ASSOCIATION 1901
(see Interstate League)

WESTERN ASSOCIATION
1894-1897, 1899
(predecessor of the Central League 1900)

Bloomington	IN	1899
Burlington	IA	1895-1897
Cedar Rapids	IA	1896-1897, 1899
Denver	CO	1895
Des Moines	IA	1894-1897
Dubuque	IA	1895-1897, 1899
Jacksonville	IL	1894-1895

Lincoln	NE	1894-1895
Omaha	NE	1894-1895
Ottumwa	IA	1899
Peoria	IL	1894-1897
Quincy	IL	1894-1897, 1899
Rock Island	IL	1899
Rock Island-Moline	IL	1894
Rockford	IL	1895-1897, 1899
St. Joseph	MO	1894-1897
Springfield	IL	1895

WESTERN ASSOCIATION
1901

Columbus	OH	1901
Dayton	OH	1901
Grand Rapids	MI	1901
Fort Wayne	IN	1901
Indianapolis	IN	1901
Louisville	KY	1901
Marion	IN	1901
Toledo	OH	1901
Wheeling	WV	1901

WESTERN ASSOCIATION
CLASS C 1905-1910, 1922-1932, 1934-1942, 1946-1954;
CLASS D 1911, 1914-1917, 1920-1921
(successor of the Missouri Valley League 1902-1904)

Ardmore	OK	1917, 1923-1926
Bartlesville	OK	1909-1910, 1924, 1931-1932, 1934-1938
Blackwell	OK	1954
Carthage	MO	1941
Chickasha	OK	1920-1921
Coffeyville	KS	1911
Denison	TX	1915-1917
Drumright	OK	1920-1921
El Reno	OK	1909-1910
Enid	OK	1908-1910, 1920-1923, 1950-1951
Ft. Smith	AR	1911, 1914-1917, 1920-1932, 1938-1942, 1946-1949, 1951-1952
Ft. Smith-Van Buren	AR	1953
Guthrie	OK	1905, 1909-1910, 1914
Henryetta	OK	1914, 1920-1923
Hutchinson	KS	1906-1908, 1924, 1932, 1934-1942, 1946-1954
Independence	KS	1911, 1925, 1928-1932
Iola	KS	1954
Joplin	MO	1905-1911, 1922-1924, 1926-1932, 1934-1942, 1946-1954
Joplin-Webb City	MO	1914
Leavenworth	KS	1905-1907, 1946-1949
Maud	OK	1929
McAlester	OK	1914-1917, 1922-1923, 1926
Muskogee	OK	1909-1911, 1914-1917, 1924-1929, 1932, 1934-1942, 1946-1954
Oklahoma City	OK	1905-1908, 1914-1917
Okmulgee	OK	1920-1927
Paris	TX	1915-1917
Pawhuska	OK	1920-1922
Pittsburg	KS	1909
Ponca City	OK	1934-1938, 1954
St. Joseph	MO	1906, 1927, 1939-1941, 1946-1951, 1953-1954
Salina	KS	1938-1941, 1946-1952
Sapulpa	OK	1909-1911
Sedalia	MO	1905
Shawnee	OK	1929-1930
Sherman	TX	1915-1917
Springfield	MO	1905-1909, 1911, 1920-1932, 1934-1942, 1948, 1950
Topeka	KS	1905-1908, 1924, 1927-1928, 1932, 1939, 1942, 1946-1954
Tulsa	OK	1910-1911, 1914-1917
Webb City	MO	1906-1908
Wichita	KS	1906-1909

WESTERN LEAGUE
1885-1899
(known as Western Association 1888-1891, 1893)
(predecessor of the American League 1900)

Buffalo	NY	1899
Chicago	IL	1888
Cleveland	OH	1885
Columbus	OH	1892, 1896-1899
Davenport	IA	1888
Denver	CO	1886-1891
Des Moines	IA	1888-1890
Detroit	MI	1894-1899
Duluth	MN	1891

Emporia	KS	1887
Fort Wayne	IN	1892
Grand Rapids	MI	1894-1897, 1899
Hastings	NE	1887
Indianapolis	IN	1885, 1892, 1894-1899
Kansas City	MO	1885, 1887-1899
Keokuk	IA	1885
Lawrence	KS	1893
Leadville	CO	1886
Leavenworth	KS	1886-1887
Lincoln	NE	1886-1887, 1890-1891
Milwaukee	WI	1885, 1888-1892, 1894-1899
Minneapolis	MN	1888-1892, 1894-1899
Omaha	NE	1885, 1887-1892, 1898
St. Joseph	MO	1886-1887, 1889, 1893, 1898
St. Louis	MO	1888
St. Paul	MN	1888-1892, 1895-1899
Sioux City	IA	1888-1891, 1894
Terre Haute	IN	1895
Toledo	OH	1885, 1892, 1894-1895
Topeka	KS	1886-1887, 1893
Wichita	KS	1887

WESTERN LEAGUE
1888

Denver	CO	1888
Hutchinson	KS	1888
Leavenworth	KS	1888
Lincoln	NE	1888
Newton	KS	1888

WESTERN LEAGUE
1900-1901; CLASS A 1902-1937, 1947-1958

Albuquerque	NM	1956-1958
Amarillo	TX	1927-1928, 1956-1958
Bartlesville	OK	1933
Cedar Rapids	IA	1934-1937
Colorado Springs	CO	1901-1905, 1916, 1950-1958
Council Bluffs	IA	1935
Davenport	IA	1934-1937
Denver	CO	1900-1917, 1922-1932, 1947-1954
Des Moines	IA	1900-1937, 1947-1958
Hutchinson	KS	1917-1918, 1933
Joplin	MO	1917-1921, 1933
Kansas City	MO	1901-1903
Keokuk	IA	1935
Lincoln	NE	1906-1917, 1924-1927, 1947-1958
Milwaukee	WI	1902-1903
Minneapolis	MN	1901
Muskogee	OK	1933
Oklahoma City	OK	1918-1932
Omaha	NE	1900-1936, 1947-1954
Peoria	IL	1902-1903
Pueblo	CO	1900, 1905-1909, 1911, 1928-1932, 1947-1958
Rock Island	IL	1934-1937
St. Paul	MN	1901
St. Joseph	MO	1900-1905, 1910-1926, 1930-1935
Sioux City	IA	1900, 1904-1923, 1934-1937, 1947-1958
Springfield	MO	1933
Topeka	KS	1909-1916, 1918, 1929-1931, 1933-1934, 1956-1958
Tulsa	OK	1919-1929, 1932
Waterloo	IA	1936-1937
Wichita	KS	1909-1933, 1950-1955

WESTERN LEAGUE
CLASS D 1939-1941
(successor of the Nebraska State League 1928-1938)

Cheyenne	WY	1941
Denver	CO	1941
Lincoln	NE	1939-1940
Mitchell	SD	1939-1940
Norfolk	NE	1939-1941
Pueblo	CO	1941
Sioux City	IA	1939-1941
Sioux Falls	SD	1939-1941
Worthington	MN	1939-1940

WESTERN LEAGUE
IND 1995-

Bend	OR	1995-
Chico	CA	1997-
Grays Harbor	WA	1995-
Long Beach	CA	1995-1996
Mission Viejo	CA	1997-

PROFESSIONAL TEAMS BY LEAGUE 1883-1997

Palm Springs	CA	1995-1996
Reno	NV	1996-
Salinas	CA	1995-
Sonoma County	CA	1995-
Surrey	BC	1995
Tri-City	WA	1995-

WESTERN CANADA LEAGUE
CLASS D 1907, 1909-1914; CLASS C 1919; CLASS B 1920-1921

Bassano	ALB	1912
Brandon	MB	1909-1911
Calgary	ALB	1907, 1909-1914, 1920-1921
Edmonton	ALB	1907, 1909-1914, 1920-1921
Lethbridge	ALB	1907, 1909-1910
Medicine Hat	ALB	1907, 1909-1910, 1913-1914
Moose Jaw	SK	1909-1911, 1913-1914, 1919-1921
Red Deer	ALB	1912
Regina	SK	1909-1910, 1913-1914, 1919-1921
Saskatoon	SK	1910-1911, 1913-1914, 1919-1921
Winnipeg	MB	1909-1911, 1919-1921

WESTERN CAROLINA(S) LEAGUE
CLASS D 1948-1952, 1960-1962; CLASS A 1963-1979
(predecessor of the South Atlantic League 1980-)
(known as the Western Carolinas League 1963-1979)
(combined with North Carolina State League in 1953 to form Tar Heel League)

Anderson	SC	1970-1975
Asheville	NC	1976-1979
Belmont	NC	1961
Charleston	SC	1973-1978
Charlotte	NC	1972
Forest City	NC	1948
Gastonia	NC	1950, 1960, 1963-1970, 1972-1974, 1977-1979
Granite Falls	NC	1951
Greensboro	NC	1979
Greenville	SC	1963-1972
Greenwood	SC	1968-1979
Hendersonville	NC	1948-1949
Hickory	NC	1952, 1960
Lenoir	NC	1948-1951
Lexington	NC	1960-1961, 1963-1967
Lincolnton	NC	1948-1952
Marion	NC	1948-1952
Monroe	NC	1969, 1971
Morganton	NC	1948-1952
Newton-Conover	NC	1948-1951, 1960-1962
Orangeburg	SC	1973-1974
Rock Hill	SC	1963-1968
Rutherford County (Spindale)	NC	1949-1952, 1960
Salisbury	NC	1960-1966, 1968
Shelby	NC	1948-1952, 1960-1965, 1969, 1977-1979
Spartanburg	SC	1963-1979
Statesville	NC	1960-1964, 1966-1967, 1969
Sumter	SC	1970-1971
Thomasville	NC	1965-1966

WESTERN INTERNATIONAL LEAGUE
CLASS B 1922, 1937-1942, 1946-1951; CLASS A 1952-1954
(successor of the Pacific Coast International League 1918-1921)
(predecessor of the Northwest League 1955-)

Bellingham	WA	1938-1939
Bremerton	WA	1946-1949
Calgary	ALB	1922, 1953-1954
Edmonton	ALB	1922, 1953-1954
Lewiston	ID	1937, 1952-1954
Salem	OR	1940-1942, 1946-1954
Spokane	WA	1937-1942, 1946-1954
Tacoma	WA	1922, 1937-1942, 1946-1951

Tri-City	WA	1950-1954
(Kennewick-Richland-Pasco)		
Vancouver	BC	1922, 1937-1942, 1946-1954
Victoria	BC	1946-1954
Wenatchee	WA	1937-1941, 1946-1954
Yakima	WA	1937-1941, 1946-1954

WESTERN PENNSYLVANIA LEAGUE
CLASS D 1907

Beaver Falls	PA	1907
Butler	PA	1907
Clarksburg	WV	1907
Connellsville	PA	1907
Cumberland	MD	1907
Fairmont	WV	1907
Greensburg	PA	1907
Kittanning	PA	1907
Latrobe	PA	1907
Piedmont	WV	1907
Scottdale	PA	1907
Somerset	PA	1907

WESTERN TRI-STATE LEAGUE
CLASS D 1912-1914
(successor of the Inland Empire League 1902, 1908)

Baker City	OR	1913-1914
Boise	ID	1912-1913
La Grande	OR	1912-1913
North Yakima	WA	1913-1914
Pendleton	OR	1912-1914
Walla Walla	WA	1912-1914

WISCONSIN STATE LEAGUE
CLASS D 1905-1907, 1940-1942, 1946-1953
(aka Wisconsin Association 1905-1906)

Appleton	WI	1940-1942, 1946-1953
Beloit	WI	1905
Eau Claire	WI	1907
Eau Claire-Chippewa Falls	WI	1906
Fond du Lac	WI	1907, 1940-1942, 1946-1953
Freeport	IL	1905-1907
Green Bay	WI	1905-1907, 1940-1942, 1946-1953
Janesville	WI	1941-1942, 1946-1953
La Crosse	WI	1905-1907, 1940-1942
Madison	WI	1907
Oshkosh	WI	1905-1907, 1941-1942, 1946-1953
Sheboygan	WI	1940-1942, 1946-1953
Wausau	WI	1905-1907, 1946-1953
Wisconsin Rapids	WI	1940-1942, 1946-1953

WISCONSIN-ILLINOIS LEAGUE
CLASS D 1908-1909; CLASS C 1910-1914
(successor of the Wisconsin State League 1907)
(predecessor of the Bi-State League 1915)

Appleton	WI	1909-1914
Aurora	IL	1910-1912
Fond du Lac	WI	1908-1911, 1913
Freeport	IL	1908-1909
Green Bay	WI	1908-1914
La Crosse	WI	1908
Madison	WI	1908-1914
Marinette-Menominee	WI-MI	1914
Milwaukee	WI	1913
Oshkosh	WI	1908-1914
Racine	WI	1909-1914
Rockford	IL	1908-1914
Wausau	WI	1908, 1912-1914

A

City	State	League	Years
Abbeville	AL	Alabama-Florida	1936
Abbeville	LA	Louisiana State	1920
		Evangeline	1935-1939, 1946-1950, 1952
Aberdeen	SD	South Dakota	1920, 1923
		Dakota	1921-1922
		Northern	1946-1971
		Prairie	1995-
Aberdeen	WA	Southwest Washington	1903-1905
see also Grays Harbor		Northwestern	1907, 1915
		Washington State	1910, 1912
		Pacific Coast International	1918
Abilene	KS	Central Kansas	1909-1910
Abilene	TX	West Texas	1920-1922, 1928-1929
		West Texas-New Mexico	1939, 1946-1955
		Big State	1956-1957
		Texas-Louisiana	1995-
Abingdon	VA	Blue Ridge	1948
Acambaro	MEX	Mexican Center	1975-1976
Ada	OK	Sooner State	1947-1954
Adelanto	CA	California	1991-
(aka High Desert)			
Adirondack	NY		
see Glens Falls			
Adrian	MI	Michigan State	1895
		Southern Michigan	1909
		Southern Michigan Assn.	1910-1914
Agua Prieta	MEX	Mexican Rookie	1968
Aguascalientes	MEX	Central Mexican	1956-1957
		Mexican Center	1960-1963, 1965-1967, 1969-1974
		Mexican	1975-
Akron	OH	Ohio State	1887
see also Canton-Akron		Tri-State	1890
		Ohio-Michigan	1893
		Ohio-Pennsylvania	1905-1911
		Central	1912, 1928-1929, 1932
		Interstate	1913
		Buckeye	1915
		International	1920
		Middle Atlantic	1935-1941
		Eastern	1997-
Alabama City	AL		
see Tri-Cities			
Alameda	CA	California	1907-1908
		Central California	1910-1911
		California State	1915
Albany	GA	Georgia State	1906
		South Atlantic	1911-1916, 1992-1995
		Southeastern	1926-1928
		Georgia-Florida	1935-1942, 1946-1958
Albany	NY	New York State	1885, 1899-1916
(aka Albany-Colonie)		International	1888, 1933-1936
		Eastern	1891-1893, 1896, 1920-1932, 1938-1959, 1983-1994
		New York-Pennsylvania	1937
		Northeast	1995-
Albany	OR	Oregon State	1904
Albany-Decatur	AL	Alabama-Tennessee	1921
Albemarle	NC	North Carolina State	1948
Albuquerque	NM	Rio Grande Association	1915
		Arizona-Texas	1932, 1937-1941
		West Texas-New Mexico	1942, 1946-1955
		Western	1956-1958
		Sophomore	1960-1961
		Texas	1962-1971
		Pacific Coast	1972-
Alcoa	TN		
see Maryville-Alcoa			
Alexander City	AL	Georgia-Alabama	1947-1951
Alexandria	LA	Gulf Coast	1907-1908
		Arkansas State	1909
		Louisiana State	1920
		Cotton States	1925-1930
		Evangeline	1934-1942, 1946-1957
		Texas	1972-1975
		Texas-Louisiana	1994-
Alexandria	VA	Carolina	1978-1983
Allentown	PA	Eastern	1884, 1894, 1929-1932, 1954-1960
		Central	1888
		Pennsylvania State	1892-1895
		Atlantic	1898-1900
		Tri-State	1912-1914
		New York-Pennsylvania	1935-1936

City	State	League	Years
		Interstate	1939-1952
		Northeast	1997-
Alliance-Sebring	OH	Ohio-Pennsylvania	1912
Alpine	TX	Sophomore	1959-1961
Alton	IL	Three-I	1917
Altoona	PA	Union Association	1884
		Pennsylvania State	1892-1894
		Tri-State	1904-1912
		Middle Atlantic	1931
		North Atlantic	1996-
Altus	OK	Texas-Oklahoma	1911
Amarillo	TX	West Texas	1922
		Panhandle-Pecos Valley	1923
		Western	1927-1928, 1956-1958
		West Texas-New Mexico	1939-1942, 1946-1955
		Texas	1959-1963, 1965-1974, 1976-1982
		Texas-Louisiana	1994-
Americus	GA	Georgia State	1906, 1914
		Empire State	1913
		FLAG	1915
		Georgia-Florida	1935-1942, 1946-1951
see also Cordele-Americus			
Amsterdam	NY	Canadian-American	1938-1942, 1946-1951
Amsterdam-Johnstown-Gloversville	NY	New York State	1902-1907
see also Gloversville; Gloversville-Johnstown			
Anaconda	MT	Montana State	1900
Anadarko	OK	Oklahoma State	1912
Anaheim	CA	California	1941
		Sunset	1947-1948
		American	1966-
Anahuac	MEX	Mexican	1939, 1953
Andalusia	AL	Alabama-Florida	1936-1939, 1953, 1962
		Alabama State	1940-1941, 1947-1950
Andalusia-Opp	AL	Alabama-Florida	1954
Anderson	IN	Central	1903
		Interstate Association	1906
		Northern State of Indiana	1911
		Mid-America	1995
		Heartland	1996-
Anderson	SC	South Carolina	1907
		Carolina Association	1908-1912
		Palmetto	1931
		Tri-State	1946-1954
		Western Carolinas	1970-1975
		South Atlantic	1980-1984
Angier-Fuquay Springs	NC	Tobacco State	1946
Anniston	AL	Southeastern	1911-1912, 1938-1942, 1946-1950
		Georgia-Alabama	1913-1917, 1928-1930
Antelope Valley	CA		
see Brawley			
Appleton	WI	Wisconsin-Illinois	1909-1914
		Wisconsin State	1940-1942, 1946-1953
		Three-I	1958-1961
(aka Fox Cities/Wisconsin)		Midwest	1962-
Arandas	MEX	Mexican Center	1977
Ardmore	OK	Texas	1904, 1961
		Texas-Oklahoma	1911-1914, 1921-1922
		Western Association	1917, 1923-1926
		Oklahoma State	1924
		Sooner State	1947-1957
Argenta	AR	Arkansas State	1908-1909
Arkansas	AR		
see Little Rock			
Arkansas City	KS	Kansas State	1909-1910
		Southwestern	1924-1926
Arkansas City-Winfield	KS	Kansas State	1909
Artesia	NM	Longhorn	1951-1955
		Sophomore	1958-1961
Asbury Park	NJ	Atlantic	1914
Asheville	NC	Southeastern	1910
		Appalachian	1911-1912
		North Carolina State	1913-1917
		South Atlantic	1924-1930, 1959-1963, 1980-
		Piedmont	1931-1932, 1934-1942
		Tri-State	1946-1955
		Southern	1964-1966, 1968-1975
		Carolina	1967
		Western Carolinas	1976-1979
Ashland	KY	Mountain State	1939-1942
(aka Tri-State)		Frontier	1993
Ashland-Catlettsburg	KY	Virginia Valley	1910
		Mountain States	1911-1912
Ashland	PA	Central Pennsylvania	1887

City	State	League	Years
		Pennsylvania State	1894
Atlanta	GA	Southern	1885-1886, 1892-1896
		Southern Association	1902-1961
		International	1962-1965
		National	1966-
Atlantic	IA	Southwest Iowa	1903
Atlantic City	NJ	Eastern	1885
		Tri-State	1912-1913
Attalla see Tri-Cities	AL		
Attleboro	MA	Atlantic Association	1908
		New England	1928, 1933
Auburn see Lewiston-Auburn	ME		
Auburn	NE	MINK	1910-1913
Auburn	NY	New York State	1889, 1899
		Canadian-American	1938, 1940
		Border	1946-1951
		New York-Pennsylvania	1958-1980, 1982-
Augusta	GA	Southern	1885-1886, 1893
		South Atlantic	1904-1911, 1914-1917, 1919-1930, 1936-1942, 1946-1963, 1988-
		Palmetto	1931
Augusta	ME	New England	1895-1896, 1901
Augusta (aka New Jersey)	NJ	New York-Pennsylvania	1994-
Aurora	IL	Two-I	1892
		Wisconsin-Illinois	1910-1912
		Bi-State	1915
Austin (aka Southern Minny)	MN	Prairie	1996-
Austin	TX	Texas	1888-1890, 1905, 1907-1908, 1911-1914, 1956-1967
		Texas-Southern	1895-1896
		South Texas	1906
		Middle Texas	1915
		Texas Association	1923-1926
		Big State	1947-1955
Ayden	NC	Coastal Plain	1937-1938

B

City	State	League	Years
Bainbridge	GA	Dixie	1916-1917
Baker City	OR	Inland Empire	1908
		Western Tri-State	1913-1914
Bakersfield	CA	San Joaquin Valley	1910
		California State	1929
		California	1941-1942, 1946-1975, 1978-1979, 1982-
Ballard	WA	Northwestern	1914
Ballinger see also Winters-Ballinger	TX	West Texas	1921, 1929
		Longhorn	1947-1950
		Southwestern	1956-1957
Baltimore	MD	American Association	1883-1891
		Union Association	1884
		Eastern	1884, 1903-1911
		National Colored	1887
		Atlantic Association	1890
		National	1892-1899
		American	1901-1902, 1954-
		International	1912-1914, 1916-1953
		Federal	1914-1915
Bangor	ME	New England	1894-1896, 1901
		Maine State	1907
		New Brunswick-Maine	1913
		Northeast	1996-
Bangor	PA	North Atlantic	1949-1950
Barberton	OH	Ohio-Pennsylvania	1905
Bartow	FL	Florida State	1920
Bartow-Winter Haven	FL	Florida State	1919
Bartlesville	OK	Kansas State	1906
		Oklahoma-Arkansas-Kansas	1907
		Oklahoma-Kansas	1908
		Western Association	1909-1910, 1924, 1931-1932, 1934-1938
		Southwestern	1921-1923
		Western	1933
		Kansas-Oklahoma-Missouri	1946-1952
Bartlett	TX	Middle Texas	1914-1915
Baseball City	FL	Florida State	1988-1992
Bassano	ALB	Western Canada	1912
Bassett	VA	Bi-State	1935-1940
		Blue Ridge	1950

City	State	League	Years
Batavia	NY	PONY	1939-1953
		New York-Pennsylvania	1957-1959, 1961-
Batesville see also Newport-Batesville	AR	Northeast Arkansas	1936, 1938, 1940-1941
Baton Rouge	LA	Cotton States	1902-1906, 1929-1932
		Dixie	1933
		East Dixie	1934
		Evangeline	1946-1957
		Gulf States	1976
Battle Creek	MI	Michigan State	1895, 1902
		Southern Michigan	1906-1909
		Southern Michigan Assn.	1910-1915
		Michigan-Ontario	1919-1920
(aka Michigan)		Midwest	1995-
Baxley	GA	Georgia State	1948
Baxley-Hazlehurst see also Hazlehurst-Baxley	GA	Georgia State	1949-1950
Bay City see also Saginaw-Bay City	MI	Northwestern	1883-1884
		Ohio-Michigan	1893
		Interstate Association	1906
		Southern Michigan	1907-1909
		Southern Michigan Assn.	1910-1915
		Michigan-Ontario	1919-1926
		Michigan State	1926
Bay City	TX	Southwest Texas	1910-1911
Beardstown	IL	Illinois-Missouri	1909-1910
Beatrice	NE	Nebraska State	1913-1915, 1922-1923, 1928, 1932-1937
		Tri-State	1924
		Western (Class D)	1939
Beatrice-Fairbury see also Fairbury	NE	MINK	1912
Beaumont	TX	South Texas	1903-1906
		Gulf Coast	1908
		Texas	1912-1917, 1919-1955, 1983-1986
		Big State	1956-1957
		Texas-Louisiana	1994
Beaver Falls	PA	Western Pennsylvania	1907
		Middle Atlantic	1931
		Pennsylvania State Assn.	1937-1941
Beckley	WV	Middle Atlantic	1931-1935
		Mountain State	1937-1938
Beeville	TX	Southwest Texas	1910-1911
		Gulf Coast	1926
		Gulf States	1976
		Lone Star	1977
Belding	MI	Michigan State	1914
Belleville	IL	Illinois State	1947-1948
		Mississippi-Ohio Valley	1949
Bellingham	WA	Northwestern	1905
		Western International	1938-1939
		Northwest	1973-1996
Bellows Falls	VT	Twin States	1911
Belmont	NC	Western Carolina	1961
Beloit	KS	Central Kansas	1909-1910
Beloit	WI	Wisconsin State	1905
		Midwest	1982-
Belton	TX	Middle Texas	1914-1915
Bend (aka Central Oregon)	OR	Northwest	1970-1971, 1978-1994
		Western	1995-
Bentonville	AR	Arkansas State	1934-1935
		Arkansas-Missouri	1936
Berkeley	CA	Central California	1910-1911
		California State	1915
Berkshire see Pittsfield			
Berlin see also Kitchener (formerly Berlin)	ONT	Canadian	1911-1913
Berrien Springs	MI	Indiana-Michigan	1910
Berwick	PA	North Atlantic	1950
Bessemer	AL	Southeastern	1912
Bettendorf see Quad City	IA		
Biddeford	ME	Maine State	1907
Big Spring	TX	West Texas	1928-1929
		West Texas-New Mexico	1938-1942
		Longhorn	1947-1955
Big Stone Gap	VA	Mountain States	1949-1953
Billings	MT	Pioneer	1948-1963, 1969-
Biloxi see Gulfport-Biloxi	MS		
Binghamton	NY	New York State	1885, 1899-1917
		International	1886-1887, 1918-1919
		Central	1888

PROFESSIONAL TEAMS BY CITY

City	State	League	Years
		Eastern	1892-1894, 1938-1963, 1967-1968, 1992-
		New York-Pennsylvania	1923-1937, 1964-1966
Birmingham	AL	Southern	1885, 1887-1888, 1892-1893, 1896
		Southern Association	1901-1961
		Southern	1964-1965, 1967-1975, 1981-
Bisbee	AZ	Arizona State	1928-1930
		Arizona-Texas	1931-1932, 1937-1941
Bisbee-Douglas	AZ	Arizona-Texas	1947-1950, 1952-1954
see also Douglas		Southwest International	1951
		Arizona-Mexico	1955
Bismarck	ND	Dakota	1922
		North Dakota	1923
(aka Dakota)		Prairie	1995-1996
Bismarck-Mandan	ND	Northern	1962-1964, 1966
Blackstone	VA	Virginia	1948
Blackwell	OK	Oklahoma State	1924
		Southwestern	1924-1926
		Kansas-Oklahoma-Missouri	1952
		Western Association	1954
Bloomfield-Long Branch	NJ	Atlantic	1914
see also Long Branch			
Bloomingdale	NJ	North Atlantic	1946-1948
Bloomington	IN	Central Interstate	1888
		Western Association	1899
		Central	1900
		Three-I	1901-1910, 1912-1917, 1919-1931, 1935, 1937-1939
Blue Rapids	KS	Eastern Kansas	1910
Bluefield	WV	Mountain State	1937-1942
		Appalachian	1946-1955, 1957-
Bluffton	IN	Northern State of Indiana	1909-1911
Blytheville	AR	Northeast Arkansas	1910-1911, 1937-1938
		Tri-State	1925-1926
Boise	ID	Pacific National	1904
		Inter-Mountain	1909
		Union Association	1911, 1914
		Western Tri-State	1912-1913
		Utah-Idaho	1928
		Pioneer	1939-1942, 1946-1963
		Northwest	1975-1976, 1978, 1987-
Bonham	TX	Texas-Oklahoma	1911-1914, 1921-1922
Boone	IA	Iowa State	1904-1906
Borger	TX	West Texas-New Mexico	1939, 1942, 1946-1954
Boston	MA	National	1883-1952
		Union Association	1884
		New England	1886-1887, 1893
		National Colored	1887
		Player's	1890
		American Association	1891
		American	1901-
Bowie	MD	Eastern	1993-
Bowling Green	KY	Kitty	1939-1942
Boyne City	MI	Michigan State	1911-1914
Bozeman	MT	Inter-Mountain	1909
Braddock	PA	Ohio-Pennsylvania	1905
		Penn-Ohio-Maryland	1906-1907
Bradenton	FL	Florida State	1919-1920, 1923-1924, 1926
(formerly Bradentown)			
Bradford	PA	New York-Pennsylvania	1891, 1957
		Interstate	1905-1908, 1914-1916
		PONY	1939-1942, 1944-1956
Brainerd	MN	Northern	1933, 1935
see also St. Cloud-Brainerd		North Central	1994-1995
		Prairie	1996
Brainerd-Little Falls	MN	Northern	1934
Brandon	MB	Northern	1908, 1933-1934
		Western Canada	1909-1911
		Prairie	1995-
Brantford	ONT	Canadian	1905, 1911-1915
		Michigan-Ontario	1919-1922
		Ontario	1930
Brattleboro	VT	Twin States	1911
Brawley	CA	Golden State	1995
(aka Antelope Valley)			
Breckenridge	MN		
see Wahpeton-Breckenridge			
Bremerton	WA	Western International	1946-1949
Brenham	TX	South Texas	1905
		Middle Texas	1914-1915
Brevard County	FL		
see Melbourne			
Brewton	AL	Alabama State	1940-1941, 1946-1950
Bridgeport	CT	Eastern	1885-1886, 1916-1932
		Connecticut State	1899-1912
		Eastern Association	1913-1914
		Interstate	1941
		Colonial	1947-1950
Bridgeport	OH	Ohio-Pennsylvania	1912
Brinkley	AR	Arkansas State	1908
Bristol	CT	Connecticut State	1899-1901
		Colonial	1949-1950
		Eastern	1973-1982
Bristol	VA	Appalachian	1911-1913, 1921-1925, 1940-1955, 1969-
Bristow	OK	Oklahoma State	1923-1924
Brockton	MA	New England	1886, 1892-1899, 1901, 1903, 1907-1913, 1928-1929, 1933
		Eastern	1901
		Colonial	1914-1915
Brockville	ONT	Canadian-American	1936-1937
Brookfield	MO	Missouri State	1911
Brookhaven	MS	Delta	1904
		Cotton States	1924-1925
Brooklyn	NY	Interstate Association	1883
		Eastern	1884
		American Association	1884-1890
		Player's	1890
		National	1890-1957
		Federal	1914-1915
Brownsville	TX	Southwest Texas	1910-1911
		Texas Valley	1938
		Rio Grande Valley	1949-1950
		Gulf Coast	1951-1953
Brunswick	GA	Empire State	1913
		Georgia State	1906, 1914
		FLAG	1915
		Georgia-Florida	1951-1958, 1962-1963
Bryan	TX	Lone Star	1947-1948
		East Texas	1949-1950
		Big State	1953-1954
Bucyrus	OH	Ohio-Pennsylvania	1905
Buffalo	NY	National	1883-1885
		International	1886-1890, 1912-1970
		Player's	1890
		Eastern	1891-1898, 1901-1911, 1979-1984
		Western	1899
		American	1900
		Federal	1914-1915
		American Association	1985-
Burlington	IA	Central Interstate	1889
		Western Association	1895-1897
		Iowa State	1904-1907
		Central Association	1908-1916, 1947-1949
		Mississippi Valley	1924-1932
		Three-I	1952-1961
		Midwest	1962-
Burlington	NC	Bi-State	1942
		Carolina	1945-1951, 1958-1972
(aka Alamance)		Appalachian	1986-
Burlington-Graham	NC	Carolina	1952-1955
Burlington	VT	Provincial	1955
		Eastern	1984-1988
(aka Vermont)		New York-Pennsylvania	1994-
Butler	PA	Ohio-Pennsylvania	1905, 1908
		Penn-Ohio-Maryland	1906
		Western Pennsylvania	1907
		Pennsylvania State Assn.	1935-1942
		Middle Atlantic	1946-1951
Butte	MT	Montana State	1900
		Pacific Northwest	1902
		Pacific National	1903-1904
		Northwestern	1906-1908, 1916-1917
		Inter-Mountain	1909
		Union Association	1911-1914
		Pioneer	1978-1985, 1987-

C

City	State	League	Years
Caborca	MEX	Mexican Rookie	1968
Cadillac	MI	West Michigan	1910
		Michigan State	1911-1914
Cairo	IL	Kitty	1903-1906, 1911-1914, 1922-1924, 1946-1950
Calais-St. Stephen	ME-NB	New Brunswick-Maine	1913
Caldwell	ID	Pioneer	1964-1971
(aka Treasure Valley)			
Calgary	ALB	Western Canada	1907, 1909-1914, 1920-1921

		Western International	1922, 1953-1954
		Pioneer	1977-1984
		Pacific Coast	1985-
California	CA		
see also Anaheim			
Calumet	MI	Copper Country Soo	1905
		Northern-Copper Country	1906-1907
Cambridge	MD	Eastern Shore	1922-1928, 1937-1941, 1946-1949
Cambridge	MA	New England	1899
		Northeastern	1934
Camden	AR	Arkansas-Texas	1906
Camden	NJ	Interstate Association	1883
		Tri-State	1904
Campeche	MEX	Mexican Southeast	1964-1970
		Mexican	1980-
Canandaigua	NY	New York State	1889
Cananea	MEX	Arizona-Texas	1954
		Arizona-Mexico	1955-1957
		Mexican Rookie	1968
Canon City	CO	Rocky Mountain	1912
Canton	IL	Illinois-Missouri	1908-1913
		Mississippi-Ohio Valley	1952
Canton	MS	Delta	1904
Canton	OH	Ohio State	1887
		Tri-State	1888-1890
		Ohio-Michigan	1893
		Central	1905-1907, 1912, 1928-1930, 1932
		Ohio-Pennsylvania	1905, 1908-1911
		Interstate	1913
		Buckeye	1915
		Ohio State	1936
		Middle Atlantic	1936-1942
		Frontier	1997-
Canton-Akron	OH	Eastern	1989-1996
see also Akron			
Cap de la Madeleine	QUE	Eastern Canada	1922
Capital City	SC		
see Columbia			
Caracas	VEN	Inter-American	1979
Carbondale	PA	Pennsylvania State	1895
		North Atlantic	1946-1950
Carlsbad	NM	Longhorn	1953-1955
		Southwestern	1956-1957
		Sophomore	1958-1961
Carmen	MEX	Mexican Southeast	1967-1970
Carolina	NC		
see Zebulon			
Carrington	ND	North Dakota	1923
Carrollton	GA	Georgia State	1920-1921
		Georgia-Alabama	1928-1930, 1946-1950
Carthage	MO	Arkansas-Missouri	1938-1940
		Western Association	1941
		Kansas-Oklahoma-Missouri	1946-1951
Caruthersville	MO	Northeast Arkansas	1910, 1936-1940
Cassville	MO	Arkansas State	1935
		Arkansas-Missouri	1936
Catlettsburg	KY		
see Ashland-Catlettsburg			
Catskill	NY	Hudson River	1903
see also Mountaindale			
Cavalier	ND	Northern	1902
Cedar Rapids	IA	Western Association	1896-1897, 1899
		Three-I	1901-1909, 1920-1921, 1938-1942, 1950-1961
		Central Association	1913-1917, 1949
		Mississippi Valley	1922-1932
		Western	1934-1937
		Midwest	1962-
Cedartown	GA	Georgia State	1920-1921
		Georgia-Alabama	1928-1930
Celaya	MEX	Mexican Center	1960-1961, 1975
Central City	KY	Kitty	1954
Centralia	IL	Eastern Illinois	1907
		Illinois State	1947-1948
		Mississippi-Ohio Valley	1949-1952
Centralia	WA	Southwest Washington	1903-1904
		Washington State	1911-1912
Central Oregon	OR		
see Bend			
Centreville	MD	Eastern Shore	1937-1941, 1946
Cerro Azul	MEX	Mexican Center	1978
Chambersburg	PA	Keystone Association	1884
		Blue Ridge	1915-1917, 1920-1930
Champaign	IL	Illinois-Missouri	1912-1914

Champaign-Urbana	IL	Illinois-Missouri	1911
		Great Central	1994
Channel Cities	CA		
see also Santa Barbara; Ventura			
Chanute	KS	Missouri Valley	1902
		Kansas State	1906
		Kansas-Oklahoma-Missouri	1946-1950
Chapman	KS	Central Kansas	1910
Charleroi	PA	Penn-Ohio-Maryland	1906-1907
		Pennsylvania-West Virginia	1908-1909
		Middle Atlantic	1927-1931
		Pennsylvania State Assn.	1934-1936
Charles City	IA	Central Association	1917
Charleston	IL	Eastern Illinois	1907-1908
see also Mattoon-Charleston			
Charleston	SC	Southern	1886-1888, 1893-1894
		South Atlantic	1904-1909, 1911, 1913-1917, 1919-1923, 1940-1942, 1946-1953, 1959-1961, 1980-
		Western Carolinas	1973-1978
Charleston	WV	Virginia Valley	1910
		Mountain States	1911-1912
		Ohio State	1913-1916
		Middle Atlantic	1931-1942
		Central	1949-1951
		American Association	1952-1960
		International	1961, 1971-1983
		Eastern	1962-1964
		South Atlantic	1987-
Charlestown	NH		
see Springfield-Charlestown			
Charlotte	FL		
see Port Charlotte			
Charlotte	MI	Michigan State	1926
Charlotte	NC	Virginia-North Carolina	1901, 1905
		North Carolina	1902
		Carolina Association	1908-1912
		North Carolina State	1913-1917
		South Atlantic	1919-1930, 1954-1963
		Piedmont	1931-1935, 1937-1942
		Tri-State	1946-1953
		Southern	1964-1972, 1976-1992
		Western Carolinas	1972
		International	1993-
Charlottesville	VA	Virginia Mountain	1914
Chaska Valley	MN	North Central	1995
Chatham	ONT	Canadian	1899-1900
Chattanooga	TN	Southern	1885-1886, 1892-1893, 1895
		Southern Association	1901-1902, 1910-1961
		South Atlantic	1909, 1943, 1963
		Southern	1964-1965, 1976-
Chehalis	WA	Washington State	1910-1912
Cherryvale	KS	Kansas State	1906
Chester	PA	Keystone Association	1884
		Tri-State	1912
Chester	SC	South Carolina	1908
Cheyenne	WY	Rocky Mountain	1912
		Western (Class D)	1941
Chicago	IL	National	1883-
		Union Association	1884
		Western Association	1888
		Player's	1890
		American	1900-
		United States	1912
		Federal	1913-1915
Chickasha	OK	Southwestern	1904
		Western Association	1920-1921
		Oklahoma State	1922
		Sooner State	1948-1952
Chico	CA	Golden State	1995
		Western	1997-
Chihuahua	MEX	Mexican	1940, 1973-1982
		Mexican National	1946
		Arizona-Texas	1952
		Central Mexican	1956-1957
		Arizona-Mexico	1958
Chillicothe	OH	Ohio State Association	1884
		Ohio State	1910-1916
		Frontier	1993-
Chippewa Falls	WI		
see Eau Claire-Chippewa Falls			
Cincinnati	OH	American Association	1883-1889, 1891
		Union Association	1884
		National	1890-
		United States	1912

City	State	League	Years
Cisco	TX	West Texas	1920-1921
Ciudad Juarez	MEX	Mexican National	1946
		Arizona-Texas	1947-1950, 1952-1954
		Southwest International	1951
		Central Mexican	1956-1957
		Arizona-Mexico	1958
		Mexican	1973-1984
Ciudad Madero	MEX	Mexican Center	1968-1970
Ciudad Mante	MEX	Mexican Center	1969-1971, 1973-1974, 1977
Ciudad Obregon	MEX	Mexican Pacific	1976
Ciudad Victoria	MEX	Mexican Center	1971, 1973-1974, 1976-1978
Ciudad Valles	MEX	Mexican Center	1974, 1978
Clarinda	IA	Southwest Iowa	1903
		MINK	1910-1911
Clarksburg	WV	Western Pennsylvania	1907
		Pennsylvania-West Virginia	1908-1909
		West Virginia	1910
		Middle Atlantic	1925-1932
Clarksdale	MS	Delta	1904
		Cotton States	1913, 1922-1923, 1936-1941, 1947-1951
		Mississippi State	1921
		East Dixie	1934-1935
Clarksville	TN	Kitty	1903-1904, 1910-1914, 1916, 1946-1949
		Big South	1996
		Heartland	1997-
Clarksville	TX	North Texas	1905
Clay Center	KS	Central Kansas	1909-1911
		Kansas State	1913
Clear Lake	IA	Central Association	1917
Clearwater	FL	Florida State	1924, 1985-
Cleburne	TX	Texas	1906
		Texas-Oklahoma	1911, 1921-1922
		South Central	1912
Cleveland	MS	East Dixie	1935
		Cotton States	1936
Cleveland	OH	National	1883-1884, 1889-1899
		Western	1885
		American Association	1887-1888, 1914-1915
		Player's	1890
		American	1900-
		United States	1912
		Federal	1913
Cleveland	TN	Appalachian	1911-1913, 1921-1922
Clifton Forge	VA	Virginia Mountain	1914
Clinton	IA	Iowa State	1906
		Central Association	1914-1917, 1947-1949
		Three-I	1907-1908, 1937-1941
		Northern Association	1910
		Mississippi-Ohio Valley	1954-1955
		Midwest	1956-
Clinton	IL	Illinois-Missouri	1910-1912
Clinton	NC	Tobacco State	1946-1950
Clinton	OK	Oklahoma State	1922-1923
Clovis	NM	West Texas	1922
		Panhandle-Pecos Valley	1923
		West Texas-New Mexico	1938-1942, 1946-1955
		Southwestern	1956-1957
Coahuila	MEX	Mexican	1974-1979
Coalinga	CA	San Joaquin Valley	1910-1911
Coatzacoalcos	MEX	Mexican	1979-1983
Cocoa	FL	Florida East Coast	1941-1942
		Florida State	1951-1958, 1965-1972, 1977
Coffeyville	KS	Missouri Valley	1902
		Kansas State	1906
		Oklahoma-Arkansas-Kansas	1907
		Western Association	1911
		Southwestern	1921-1924
Coleman	TX	West Texas	1928-1929
Colonial Heights-Petersburg see also Petersburg	VA	Virginia	1951
		Piedmont	1954
Colonie see Albany-Colonie	NY		
Colorado see Denver	CO		
Colorado Springs	CO	Western	1901-1905, 1916, 1950-1958
		Rocky Mountain	1912
		Pacific Coast	1988-
Columbia	TN	Tennessee-Alabama	1921
		Big South	1996
		Heartland	1997-
Columbia	SC	South Atlantic	1904-1912, 1914-1917, 1919-1923, 1925-1930, 1936-1942, 1946-1957, 1960-1961, 1983-
(aka Capital City)		Piedmont	1934
Columbus	GA	Southern	1885, 1896
		Georgia State	1906
		South Atlantic	1909-1917, 1936-1942, 1946-1957, 1959, 1991-
		Southeastern	1926-1930, 1932
		Alabama-Florida	1958
		Southern	1964-1966, 1969-1990
Columbus	MS	Cotton States	1907-1908, 1912-1913
		East Dixie	1935
Columbus	NE	Nebraska State	1910-1915
Columbus	OH	American Association	1883-1884, 1889-1891, 1902-1954
		Tri-State	1887-1888
		Western	1892, 1896-1899
		Interstate	1899-1900, 1913
		Western Association	1901
		International	1955-1970, 1977-
Concord	NC	North Carolina State	1939-1942, 1945-1951
Concord	NH	New England	1902-1905
Concordia	KS	Central Kansas	1910-1911
Connellsville	PA	Western Pennsylvania	1907
		Pennsylvania-West Virginia	1908-1909
		Ohio-Pennsylvania	1912
Conover see Newton-Conover	NC		
Cooleemee	NC	North Carolina State	1937-1941
Coos Bay-North Bend	OR	Northwest	1970-1972
Cordele	GA	Georgia State	1906, 1914
		Empire State	1913
		Georgia-Florida	1936-1942, 1946-1953, 1955
Cordele-Americus see also Americus	GA	Georgia-Florida	1954
Cordoba	MEX	Mexican	1937-1939, 1972-1979, 1984-1986, 1991-1992
Corinth	MS	Tri-State	1925-1926
Corning	NY	PONY	1951-1956
		New York-Pennsylvania	1957-1960, 1968-1969
Cornwall see also Perth-Cornwall	ONT	Canadian-American	1938-1939
		Border	1951
Coronado	CA	California State	1929
Corpus Christi	TX	Southwest Texas	1910-1911
		Gulf Coast	1926, 1951-1953
		Texas Valley	1927, 1938
		Rio Grande Valley	1931, 1949-1950
		Big State	1954-1957
		Texas	1958-1959
		Gulf States	1976
		Lone Star	1977
		Texas-Louisiana	1994-1995
Corsicana	TX	Texas	1902-1905
		North Texas	1907
		Central Texas	1914-1915, 1917
		Texas-Oklahoma	1922
		Texas Association	1923-1926
		Lone Star	1927-1928
Cortazar	MEX	Mexican Center	1975
Cortland	NY	New York State	1899-1901
Cottonwood Falls see Strong City-Cottonwood Falls	KS		
Coudersport	PA	Interstate	1905
Council Bluffs	IA	Iowa-South Dakota	1903
		Western	1935
Covington	KY	Federal	1913
Covington	VA	Virginia Mountain	1914
		Appalachian	1966-1976
Crawfordsville	IN	Central Interstate	1888
Creston	IA	Southwest Iowa	1903
Crestview	FL	Alabama-Florida	1954-1956
Crisfield	MD	Eastern Shore	1922-1928, 1937
Crockett	TX	East Texas	1916
Crookston	MN	Northern	1902-1905, 1933-1941
Crowley	LA	Gulf Coast	1908, 1950
		Evangeline	1951-1957
Cumberland	MD	Penn-Ohio-Maryland	1906
		Western Pennsylvania	1907
		Potomac	1916
		Blue Ridge	1917-1918
		Middle Atlantic	1925-1932
Cushing	OK	Southwestern	1921, 1925
		Oklahoma State	1923-1924
Cynthiana	KY	Blue Grass	1922-1924

D

City	State	League	Years
Dakota	ND		
see Bismarck			
Dallas	TX	Texas	1888-1890, 1902-1942, 1946-1958
		Texas-Southern	1895-1896
		American Association	1959
		Pacific Coast	1964
Dallas-Ft. Worth	TX	American Association	1960-1962
(aka Texas)		Pacific Coast	1963
see also Ft. Worth		Texas	1965-1971
		American	1972-
Danbury	CT	New York-New Jersey	1913
		Atlantic	1914
Danville	IL	Central Interstate	1888
		Central	1900
		Kitty	1906
		Eastern Illinois	1908
		Three-I	1910-1914, 1922-1932, 1946-1950
		Mississippi-Ohio Valley	1951-1954
		Midwest	1970-1976, 1982
Danville	PA	Central Pennsylvania	1887
		Pennsylvania State	1892-1893
Danville	VA	Virginia-North Carolina	1905
		Virginia	1906-1912
		Piedmont	1920-1925
		Bi-State	1934-1938
		Carolina	1945-1958
		Appalachian	1993-
Danville-Schoolfield	VA	Bi-State	1939-1942
Darlington	SC	South Carolina	1907
Davenport	IA	Central Interstate	1888-1889
see also Quad City		Western Association	1888
		Three-I	1901-1906, 1909-1916, 1946-1952, 1957-1958
		Mississippi Valley	1929-1933
		Western	1934-1937
		Midwest	1960
Dawson	NM	Rocky Mountain	1912
Dawson Springs	KY	Kitty	1916
Dayton	OH	Ohio State Association	1884
		Tri-State	1889-1890
		Interstate	1897-1900
		Western Association	1901
		Central	1903-1917, 1928-1930, 1932, 1948-1951
		Middle Atlantic	1933-1942
		Ohio State	1946-1947
Daytona Beach	FL	Florida State	1920-1924, 1928, 1936-1941, 1946-1973, 1977-1987, 1993-
(aka Daytona)			
DeLand	FL	Florida State	1936-1941, 1946-1954, 1970
		Florida East Coast	1942
Decatur	AL	Southeastern	1911
see also Albany-Decatur			
Decatur	IL	Central Interstate	1888
		Central	1900
		Three-I	1901-1909, 1911-1915, 1922-1932, 1935, 1937-1942, 1946-1950
		Northern Association	1910
		Mississippi-Ohio Valley	1952-1955
		Midwest	1956-1974
Deerfield Beach	FL	Florida State	1966
Del Rio	TX	Longhorn	1948
		Rio Grande Valley	1949-1950
		Big State	1954
Delmarva	MD		
see Salisbury			
Denison	TX	Texas-Southern	1896
see also Sherman-Denison		Texas-Oklahoma	1912-1914
		Western Association	1915-1917
Denver	CO	Western	1886-1891, 1900-1917, 1922-1932, 1947-1954
		Western Association	1895
		Western (Class D)	1941
		American Association	1955-1962, 1969-1992
		Pacific Coast	1963-1968
(aka Colorado)		National	1993-
De Quincy	LA	Cotton States	1932
Derby	CT	Connecticut State	1899-1901
Des Moines	IA	Northwestern	1887
		Western Association	1888-1890, 1894-1897
		Western	1900-1937, 1947-1958
(aka Iowa)		Three-I	1959-1961
		American Association	1969-
Detroit	MI	National	1883-1888
		International	1889-1890
		Western	1894-1899
		American	1900-
Devils Lake	ND	Northern	1902
Diaz Ordaz	MEX	Mexican Center	1978
Dominion	NS	Cape Breton Colliery	1937-1938
Donalsonville	GA	Alabama-Florida	1955-1956
Donna	TX	Rio Grande Valley	1949-1950
Dos Laredos	MEX		
see Nuevo Laredo			
Dothan	AL	FLAG	1915
		Dixie	1916-1917
		Alabama-Florida	1936-1939, 1951-1956, 1958-1962
		Alabama State	1940-1941, 1946-1950
		Georgia-Florida	1942
Douglas	AZ	Rio Grande Association	1915
see also Bisbee-Douglas		Arizona-Mexico	1956-1958
Douglas	GA	Georgia State	1948-1956
Dover	DE	Eastern Shore	1923-1926, 1937-1941, 1946-1948
Dover	NH	New England	1893, 1902
Dowagiac	MI	Indiana-Michigan	1910
Draper	NC		
see Leaksville-Draper-Spray			
Drummondville	QUE	Quebec Provincial	1940
		Provincial	1948-1954
Drumright	OK	Western Association	1920-1921
		Oklahoma State	1923
DuBois	PA	Interstate	1905-1907
DuBois County	IN		
see Huntingburg			
Dublin	GA	Georgia State	1949-1956
		Georgia-Florida	1958, 1962
Dubuque	IA	Central Interstate	1888
		Western Association	1895-1897, 1899
		Three-I	1903-1915
		Central Association	1917
		Mississippi Valley	1922-1932
		Mississippi-Ohio Valley	1954-1955
		Midwest	1956-1968, 1974-1976
Duluth	MN	Northwestern	1886-1887
		Western Association	1891
		Northern	1903-1905, 1908, 1913-1916, 1934-1942, 1946-1955
		Northern-Copper Country	1906-1907
		Minnesota-Wisconsin	1909-1911
		Central International	1912
Duluth-Superior	MN-WI	Northern	1956-1970, 1993-
see also Superior			
Duluth-Heralds	MN	Twin Ports	1943
Duluth-Dukes	MN	Twin Ports	1943
Duluth-Marine Iron	MN	Twin Ports	1943
Duncan	OK	Oklahoma State	1922-1924
		Sooner State	1947-1950
Dunedin	FL	Florida State	1978-1979, 1987-
Dunn-Erwin	NC	Tobacco State	1946-1949
Durango	MEX	Central Mexican	1956-1957
		Mexican Center	1965-1967, 1972-1974
		Mexican	1976-1979
Durant	OK	Texas-Oklahoma	1911-1914
Durham	NC	North Carolina	1902
see also Raleigh-Durham		North Carolina State	1913-1917
		Piedmont	1920-1933, 1936-1943
		Carolina	1945-1967, 1980-
Dyersburg	TN	Kitty	1924
		Tri-State	1925

E

City	State	League	Years
East Chicago	IN	Mid-America	1995
East Grand Forks	MN	Northern	1933, 1935
East Liberty	OH	Iron & Oil Association	1884
East Liverpool	OH	Ohio-Michigan	1893
		Penn-Ohio-Maryland	1906-1907
		Ohio-Pennsylvania	1908-1912
Eastland	TX	West Texas	1920
Eastman	GA	Georgia State	1948-1953
Easton	MD	Eastern Shore	1924-1928, 1937-1941, 1946-1949
Easton	PA	Central	1888

City	State	League	Years
		Atlantic Association	1889
		Pennsylvania State	1893-1894
Eau Claire	WI	Northwestern	1886-1887
		Wisconsin State	1907
		Minnesota-Wisconsin	1909-1912
		Northern	1933-1942, 1946-1962
Eau Claire-Chippewa Falls	WI	Wisconsin State	1906
Ebano	MEX	Mexican Center	1971-1974, 1977
Eden	NC		
see Leaksville-Draper-Spray			
Edenton	NC	Virginia	1951
		Coastal Plain	1952
Edinburg	TX	Gulf Coast	1926
		Texas Valley	1927
Edmonton	ALB	Western Canada	1907, 1909-1914, 1920-1921
		Western International	1922, 1953-1954
		Pacific Coast	1981-
El Centro	CA	Sunset	1947-1950
		Southwest International	1951-1952
El Dorado	AR	Cotton States	1929-1932, 1936-1941, 1947-1955
		Dixie	1933
		East Dixie	1934-1935
El Dorado	KS	Kansas State	1911
El Paso	TX	Rio Grande Association	1915
		Arizona State	1930
		Arizona-Texas	1931-1932, 1937-1941, 1947-1950, 1952-1954
		Mexican National	1946
		Southwest International	1951
		West Texas-New Mexico	1955
		Southwestern	1956-1957
		Sophomore	1961
		Texas	1962-1970, 1972-
El Reno	OK	Western Association	1909-1910
		Oklahoma State	1922-1923
Eldorado	IL	Southern Illinois	1910
Elgin	IL	Northern Association	1910
		Bi-State	1915
Elizabeth City	NC	Virginia	1950-1951
Elizabethton	TN	Appalachian	1937-1942, 1945-1951, 1974-
Elkin	NC	Blue Ridge	1949-1950
		North Carolina State	1951-1952
Elkhart	IN	Indiana-Michigan	1910
Ellsworth	KS	Kansas State	1905
		Central Kansas	1908-1910
Elmhurst	CA		
see Oakland-Elmhurst			
Elmira	NY	New York State	1885, 1889, 1900, 1908-1917
		New York-Pennsylvania	1891, 1923-1937, 1957-1960, 1973-1995
		Eastern	1892, 1938-1955, 1961-1972
		Atlantic	1900
		Northeast	1996-
Empalme	MEX	Mexican Rookie	1968
Emporia	KS	Western	1887
		Kansas State	1914
		Southwestern	1924
Emporia	VA	Virginia	1948-1951
Enid	OK	Southwestern	1904, 1924-1926
		Western Association	1908-1910, 1920-1923, 1950-1951
		Oklahoma State	1924
Ennis	TX	Central Texas	1914-1917
Ensenada	MEX	Mexican Northern	1968-1969
see also Riverside-Ensenada			
Enterprise	AL	Alabama-Florida	1936, 1951-1952
		Alabama State	1947-1950
Erie	PA	New York-Pennsylvania	1891, 1957-1963, 1967, 1981-1993, 1995-
		Eastern	1893-1894
		Interstate	1905-1908, 1913, 1916
		Ohio-Pennsylvania	1908-1911
		Central	1912, 1915, 1928-1930, 1932
		Canadian	1914
		Middle Atlantic	1938-1939, 1941-1942, 1946-1951
		PONY	1944-1945, 1954-1956
		Frontier	1994
Erwin	NC		
see Dunn-Erwin			
Erwin	TN	Appalachian	1940, 1943-1944
Eufaula	AL	Dixie	1916-1917
		Alabama-Florida	1952-1953
Eugene	OR	Oregon State	1904
		Far West	1950-1951
		Northwest	1955-1968, 1974-
		Pacific Coast	1969-1973
Eureka	KS	Southwestern	1924-1926
Evansville	IN	Northwestern	1884
		Central Interstate	1889
		Two-I	1892
		Southern	1895, 1966-1968
		Three-I	1901-1902, 1919-1931, 1938-1942, 1946-1957
		Central	1903-1911, 1913-1917
		Kitty	1912
		American Association	1970-1984
		Frontier	1995-
Everett	WA	Northwestern	1905
		Northwest	1984-
Evergreen	AL	Alabama-Florida	1937-1938

F

City	State	League	Years
Fairbury	NE	Nebraska State	1915, 1922-1923, 1928-1930, 1936-1937
see also Beatrice-Fairbury			
Fairmont	WV	Western Pennsylvania	1907
		Pennsylvania-West Virginia	1908-1909
		West Virginia	1910
		Ohio-Pennsylvania	1912
		Middle Atlantic	1925-1931
Fall River	MA	New England	1893-1898, 1902-1913, 1946-1949
		Colonial	1914-1915
Falls City	NE	MINK	1910-1913
Fargo	ND	Northern	1902-1905, 1908
		Northern-Copper Country	1906
		Dakota	1922
Fargo-Moorhead	ND-MN	Northern	1914-1917, 1933-1942, 1946-1960, 1996-
Farnham	QUE	Provincial	1948-1951
Fayetteville	AR	Arkansas State	1934-1935
		Arkansas-Missouri	1936-1940
Fayetteville	NC	Eastern Carolina	1909-1910, 1928-1929
		Coastal Plain	1946
		Tri-State	1947-1948
		Tobacco State	1949
		Carolina	1950-1956
(aka Cape Fear)		South Atlantic	1987-
Federalsburg	MD	Eastern Shore	1937-1941, 1946-1949
Fieldale	VA	Bi-State	1934-1936
Findlay	OH	Buckeye	1915
		Ohio State	1937-1941
Fishkill	NY	New York-Pennsylvania	1994-
(aka Hudson Valley)			
Fitchburg	MA	New England Association	1895
		New England	1899, 1914-1915, 1919, 1929
		Eastern	1922
Fitzgerald	GA	Georgia State	1948-1952
		Georgia-Florida	1953-1954, 1956-1957
Flandreau	SD	Iowa-South Dakota	1902
Flint	MI	Michigan State	1889-1890, 1902, 1926, 1940-1941
		Interstate Association	1906
		Southern Michigan	1907-1909
		Southern Michigan Assn.	1910-1915
		Michigan-Ontario	1919-1926
		Central	1948-1951
Florence	SC	South Carolina	1907
		Palmetto	1931
		Tri-State	1948-1950
		South Atlantic	1981-1986
		Atlantic Coast	1995
Florida	FL		
see Miami			
Follansbee	WV		
see Steubenville-Follansbee			
Fond du Lac	WI	Wisconsin State	1907, 1940-1942, 1946-1953
		Wisconsin-Illinois	1908-1911, 1913
Forest City	NC	Western Carolina	1948
		Tar Heel	1953-1954
Ft. Dodge	IA	Iowa State	1904-1906
		Central Association	1916-1917
Ft. Lauderdale	FL	Florida State	1928, 1962-1993
		Florida East Coast	1940-1942
		Florida International	1947-1953
Ft. Myers	FL	Florida State	1926, 1978-1987, 1992-

City	State	League	Years
Ft. Pierce	FL	Florida East Coast	1940-1942
Ft. Scott	KS	Missouri Valley	1902-1905
		Kansas State	1906
Ft. Smith	AR	Missouri Valley	1905
		South Central	1906
		Oklahoma-Arkansas-Kansas	1907
		Arkansas State	1909
		Western Association	1911, 1914-1917, 1920-1932, 1938-1942, 1946-1949, 1951-1952
Ft. Smith-Van Buren	AR	Western Association	1953
Ft. Walton Beach	FL	Alabama-Florida	1953-1962
Fort Wayne	IN	Northwestern	1883-1884
		Western	1892
		Interstate	1896-1900
		Western Association	1901
		Central	1903-1905, 1908-1915, 1917, 1928-1930, 1932, 1934, 1948
		Interstate Association	1906
		Three-I	1935
		Midwest	1993-
Ft. William-Pt. Arthur	ONT	Northern	1914-1916
see also Thunder Bay (formerly Ft. William-Pt. Arthur)			
Ft. Worth	TX	Texas	1888-1890, 1902-1942, 1946-1958, 1964
see also Dallas-Ft. Worth			
		Texas-Southern	1895-1896
		American Association	1959
		Pacific Coast	1963
Fostoria	OH	Ohio State	1936-1941
Fox Cities	WI		
see Appleton			
Frankfort	KY	Blue Grass	1908-1912
		Ohio State	1915-1916
Franklin	PA	Iron & Oil Association	1884
		Interstate	1907-1908
Franklin	VA	Virginia	1948-1951
Frederick	MD	Blue Ridge	1915-1917, 1920-1930
		Carolina	1989-
Fredericton	NB	New Brunswick-Maine	1913
Freeport	IL	Wisconsin State	1905-1907
		Wisconsin-Illinois	1908-1909
		Northern Association	1910
		Bi-State	1915
		Three-I	1915
Fremont	NE	Nebraska State	1910-1913
Fremont	OH	Ohio State	1936-1941
Fresnillo	MEX	Central Mexican	1956-1957
		Mexican Center	1962, 1964-1968, 1976-1978
Fresno	CA	Pacific Coast	1906
		California	1908-1909, 1941-1942, 1946-1988
		California State	1910, 1913-1914
Frostburg	MD	Potomac	1916
Fruitvale	CA		
see Oakland-Fruitvale			
Fulton	KY	Kitty	1911, 1922-1924, 1936-1942, 1946-1955
Fuquay Springs	NC		
see Angier-Fuquay Springs			

G

City	State	League	Years
Gadsden	AL	Southeastern	1910-1912, 1938-1941, 1946-1950
		Georgia-Alabama	1913-1914, 1928-1929
see also Tri-Cities			
Gainesville	FL	FLAG	1915
		Florida State	1936-1941, 1946-1952, 1955-1958
Gainesville	TX	Texas-Oklahoma	1911
		Big State	1947-1951
		Sooner State	1953-1955
Galax	VA	Blue Ridge	1946-1950
Galesburg	IL	Illinois-Missouri	1908-1909
		Central Association	1910-1912, 1914
Gallipolis	OH		
see Point Pleasant-Gallipolis			
Galveston	TX	Texas	1888-1890, 1907-1917, 1919-1924, 1931-1937
		Texas-Southern	1895-1896
		South Texas	1903-1906
		Gulf Coast	1950-1953
		Big State	1954-1955
Gary	IN	Indiana-Michigan	1910

City	State	League	Years
Gastonia	NC	South Atlantic	1923, 1959, 1980-1992
		North Carolina State	1938
		Tar Heel	1939-1940
		Western Carolina(s)	1950, 1960, 1963-1970, 1972-1974, 1977-1979
		Tri-State	1952-1953
		Atlantic Coast	1995
Gate City	ID		
see Pocatello			
Geneva	AL	Alabama State	1946-1950
Geneva	IL	Midwest	1991-
(aka Kane County)			
Geneva	NY	Border	1947-1951
		New York-Pennsylvania	1958-1973, 1977-1993
Georgetown	TX	Middle Texas	1914
Gettysburg	PA	Blue Ridge	1915-1917
Girard	OH	Ohio-Pennsylvania	1908
Glace Bay	NS	Cape Breton Colliery	1937-1939
Gladewater	TX	West Dixie	1935
		East Texas	1936, 1949-1950
		Lone Star	1948
Glens Falls	NY	Eastern	1980-1988
		New York-Pennsylvania	1993
(aka Adirondack)		Northeast	1995-
Glens Falls-Saratoga Springs	NY	Hudson River	1906
Globe	AZ	Arizona State	1929-1930
see also Miami-Globe		Arizona-Texas	1931
Gloucester	MA	New England	1929
Gloversville	NY	Canadian-American	1937
Gloversville-Johnstown	NY	New York State	1908
		Canadian-American	1938-1942, 1946-1951
see also Amsterdam-Johnstown-Gloversville			
Goldsboro	NC	Eastern Carolina	1908-1910, 1928-1929
		Coastal Plain	1937-1941, 1946-1952
Gomez Palacio	MEX		
see Union Laguna			
Gorman	TX	West Texas	1920
Graceville	FL	Alabama-Florida	1952-1958
Grafton	WV	Pennsylvania-West Virginia	1908-1909
		West Virginia	1910
Graham	NC		
see Burlington-Graham			
Graham	TX	Texas-Oklahoma	1921
Granby	QUE	Quebec Provincial	1940
		Border	1946
		Provincial	1948-1953
Grand Forks	ND	Northern	1902-1905, 1913-1915, 1934-1935, 1938-1942, 1946-1964
		Northern-Copper Country	1906
		Central International	1912
		Prairie	1996-
Grand Island	NE	Nebraska State	1910-1915, 1922-1923, 1928-1934, 1938, 1956-1959
		Tri-State	1924
Grand Rapids	MI	Northwestern	1883-1884
		Michigan State	1889-1890, 1902, 1926, 1940-1941
		International	1890
		Western	1894-1897, 1899
		Interstate	1898-1899
		Canadian	1900
		Western Association	1901
		Central	1903-1917, 1920-1922, 1926, 1934, 1948-1951
		Michigan-Ontario	1923-1924
(aka West Michigan)		Midwest	1994-
Granite Falls	NC	Western Carolina	1951
Grays Harbor	WA	Northwestern	1906, 1908-1909
see also Aberdeen; Hoquiam		Northwest	1976-1980
		Western	1995-
Great Bend	KS	Kansas State	1905, 1909-1911, 1913-1914
		Central Kansas	1912
Great Falls	MT	Montana State	1900
		Union Association	1911-1913
		Northwestern	1916-1917
		Pioneer	1948-1963, 1969-
Green Bay	WI	Wisconsin State	1905-1907, 1940-1942, 1946-1953
		Wisconsin-Illinois	1908-1914
		Three-I	1958-1960
		Prairie	1996-
Greeneville	TN	Appalachian	1921-1925, 1938-1942
Greensboro	NC	North Carolina	1902
		Virginia-North Carolina	1905

City	State	League	Years
		Carolina Association	1908-1912
		North Carolina State	1913-1917
		Piedmont	1920-1926, 1928-1934, 1941-1942
		Carolina	1945-1968
		Western Carolinas	1979
		South Atlantic	1980-
Greensburg	PA	Western Pennsylvania	1907
		Pennsylvania State Assn.	1934-1939
Greenville	AL	Alabama-Florida	1939
		Alabama State	1940-1941, 1946-1950
Greenville	MI	Michigan State	1889
Greenville	MS	Cotton States	1902-1905, 1922-1923, 1936-1941, 1947-1955
		East Dixie	1934-1935
		Big South	1996-
Greenville	NC	Eastern Carolina	1928-1929
		Coastal Plain	1937-1940, 1946-1951
Greenville	SC	South Carolina	1907
		Carolina Association	1908-1912
		South Atlantic	1919-1930, 1938-1942, 1946-1950, 1961-1962
		Palmetto	1931
		Tri-State	1951-1952, 1954-1955
		Western Carolinas	1963-1972
		Southern	1984-
Greenville	TX	North Texas	1905, 1907
		Texas	1906
		Texas-Oklahoma	1912, 1922
		East Texas	1923-1926, 1946
		Big State	1947-1950, 1953
		Sooner State	1957
Greenwood	MS	Cotton States	1910-1912, 1922-1923, 1936-1940, 1947-1952
		Mississippi State	1921
		East Dixie	1934-1935
Greenwood	SC	Tri-State	1951
		Western Carolinas	1968-1979
		South Atlantic	1981-1983
		Atlantic Coast	1995
Griffin	GA	Georgia-Alabama	1915-1917, 1947-1951
		Georgia State	1920-1921
Guadalajara	MEX	Mexican Center	1977-1978
Guamuchil	MEX	Mexican Pacific	1976
Guanajuato	MEX	Mexican Center	1960-1967, 1975-1976, 1978
Guasave	MEX	Mexican Pacific	1976
Guaymas	MEX	Mexican Pacific	1976
Guelph	ONT	Canadian	1899, 1911-1913, 1915
		International (Class D)	1908
		Ontario	1930
Gulfport	MS	Cotton States	1906-1907, 1926-1928
Gulfport-Biloxi	MS	Cotton States	1908
Guthrie	OK	Southwestern	1904
		Western Association	1905, 1909-1910, 1914
		South Central	1906
		Oklahoma State	1912, 1922-1924

H

City	State	League	Years
Hagerstown	MD	Blue Ridge	1915-1918, 1920-1930
		Middle Atlantic	1931
		Interstate	1941-1952
		Piedmont	1953-1955
		Carolina	1981-1988
		Eastern	1989-1992
		South Atlantic	1993-
Halifax	VA		
see South Boston-Halifax			
Hamilton	OH	Tri-State	1889
		Ohio State	1911, 1913
Hamilton	ONT	International	1886-1890, 1918
		Canadian	1899-1900, 1911-1915
		International (Class D)	1908
		Michigan-Ontario	1919-1925
		Ontario	1930
		PONY	1939-1942, 1946-1956
		New York-Pennsylvania	1988-1992
Hamlin	TX	West Texas	1928
Hammond	LA	Evangeline	1946-1951
Hampton	VA	Virginia	1896
see also Newport News-Hampton; Peninsula			
Hancock	MI	Copper Country Soo	1905
		Northern-Copper Country	1906
Hanford	CA	San Joaquin Valley	1911
Hannibal	MO	Illinois-Missouri	1908
		Central Association	1909-1912, 1947-1948

City	State	League	Years
		Three-I	1916-1917
		Mississippi-Ohio Valley	1952-1955
Hanover	MD	Blue Ridge	1915-1917, 1920-1929
Hardware City	CT		
see New Britain			
Harlan	KY	Mountain States	1948-1954
		Appalachian	1961-1963, 1965
Harlingen	TX	Rio Grande Valley	1931, 1950
		Texas Valley	1938
		Gulf Coast	1951-1953
		Big State	1954-1955
		Texas	1960-1961
		Gulf States	1976
		Lone Star	1977
(aka Rio Grande Valley)		Texas-Louisiana	1994-
Harriman	TN	Appalachian	1914
Harrisburg	IL	Southern Illinois	1910
		Kitty	1910-1911, 1913
Harrisburg	PA	Interstate Association	1883
		Eastern	1884, 1987-
		Atlantic Association	1890
		Pennsylvania State	1893-1895
		Atlantic	1900
		Tri-State	1904-1914
		International	1915
		New York State	1916-1917
		New York-Pennsylvania	1924-1935
		Interstate	1940-1942, 1946-1952
Harrisonburg	VA	Virginia Mountain	1914
		Virginia	1939-1941
Hartford	CT	Eastern	1886
		Atlantic Association	1889-1890
		Atlantic	1896-1898
		Eastern	1899-1901, 1916-1932, 1938-1952
		Connecticut State	1902-1912
		Eastern Association	1913-1914
		Colonial	1915
		Northeastern	1934
Hastings	NE	Western	1887
		Nebraska State	1910-1915, 1922-1923, 1956-1959
		Tri-State	1924
Hattiesburg	MS	Delta	1904
		Cotton States	1905, 1910-1912, 1923-1929
Havana	Cuba	Florida International	1946-1953
		International	1954-1960
Havana	IL	Illinois-Missouri	1908
Haverhill	MA	New England	1886-1887, 1894, 1901-1912, 1914, 1919, 1926-1929
		New England Association	1895
Hawaii	HI		
see Honolulu			
Hayward	CA	Central California	1910-1911
Hazard	KY	Mountain States	1948-1952
Hazlehurst-Baxley	GA	Georgia State	1951-1956
see also Baxley-Hazlehurst			
Hazleton	PA	Central Pennsylvania	1887
		Central	1888
		Pennsylvania State	1894-1895
		New York-Pennsylvania	1929-1932, 1934-1937
		Eastern	1938
		Interstate	1939-1940
		North Atlantic	1949-1950
Headland	AL	Alabama State	1950
		Alabama-Florida	1951-1952
Healdsburg	CA	Central California	1910
Helena	AR	Arkansas State	1908-1909
		Northeast Arkansas	1911
		East Dixie	1935
		Cotton States	1936-1941, 1947-1949
Helena	MT	Montana State	1900
		Pacific Northwest	1902
		Pacific National	1903
		Inter-Mountain	1909
		Union Association	1911-1914
		Pioneer	1978-
Henderson	KY	Kitty	1903-1905, 1911-1914, 1916
Henderson	NC	Piedmont	1929-1931
Henderson	TX	East Texas	1931, 1936-1940, 1946, 1949-1950
		Dixie	1933
		West Dixie	1934-1935
		Lone Star	1947-1948
Hendersonville	NC	Western Carolina	1948-1949
Henryetta	OK	Western Association	1914, 1920-1923

City	State	League	Years
Hermosillo	MEX	Mexican Pacific	1976
Herrin	IL	Southern Illinois	1910
Hiawatha	KS	Eastern Kansas	1910
		MINK	1912
Hibbing (aka Minnesota)	MN	North Central	1995
Hickory	NC	Tar Heel	1939-1940, 1953-1954
		North Carolina State	1942, 1945-1950
		Western Carolina	1952, 1960
		South Atlantic	1993-
High Desert see Adelanto	CA		
High Point	NC	Piedmont	1920-1932
High Point-Thomasville see also Thomasville	NC	North Carolina State	1948-1952
		Tar Heel	1953
		Carolina	1954-1958, 1968-1969
Hillsboro	TX	Central Texas	1914
Hobbs	NM	West Texas-New Mexico	1937-1938
		Longhorn	1955
		Southwestern	1956-1957
		Sophomore	1958-1961
Hoisington	KS	Kansas State	1905
Holdenville	OK	Oklahoma State	1912
Holdrege	NE	Nebraska State	1956-1959
Holland	MI	West Michigan	1910
		Michigan State	1911
Hollywood	CA	Pacific Coast	1926-1935, 1938-1957
Hollywood	FL	Florida East Coast	1940
Holton	KS	Eastern Kansas	1910
Holyoke	MA	Connecticut State	1903-1912
		Eastern Association	1913
		Eastern	1977-1982
Homestead	PA	Ohio-Pennsylvania	1905
Honolulu (aka Hawaii)	HI	Pacific Coast	1961-1987
Hope	AR	North Texas	1905
Hopewell	VA	Virginia	1900, 1916, 1949-1950
Hopkinsville	KY	Kitty	1903-1905, 1910-1914, 1916, 1922-1923, 1935-1942, 1946-1954
Hoquiam see also Grays Harbor; Aberdeen	WA	Southwest Washington	1903-1905
		Washington State	1910, 1912
Hornell	NY	Interstate	1906, 1914-1915
		PONY	1942-1956
		New York-Pennsylvania	1957
Horton	KS	Eastern Kansas	1910
Hot Springs	AR	Arkansas-Texas	1906
		Arkansas State	1908-1909
		Cotton States	1938-1941, 1947-1955
Houghton	MI	Northern-Copper Country	1906-1907
Houma	LA	Evangeline	1940, 1946-1952
Houston	TX	Texas	1888-1890, 1907-1958
		Texas-Southern	1895-1896
		South Texas	1903-1906
		American Association	1959-1961
		National	1962-
Hudson	NY	Hudson River	1903-1907
Hudson Valley see Fishkill	NY		
Hugo	OK	Texas-Oklahoma	1913-1914
Hull see Ottawa-Hull	QUE		
Humboldt	NE	MINK	1911-1913
Huntingburg (aka DuBois County)	IN	Heartland	1996-
Huntington	IN	Ohio-Indiana	1908
		Northern State of Indiana	1909-1911
Huntington	WV	Virginia Valley	1910
		Mountain States	1911-1912, 1937-1942
		Ohio State	1913-1916
		Middle Atlantic	1931-1936
(aka River City)		Appalachian	1990-1995
Huntsville	AL	Southeastern	1911-1912
		Georgia-Alabama	1930
		Southern	1985-
Huntsville	AR	Arkansas State	1935
Huron	SD	South Dakota	1920
		Dakota	1921
		Northern	1965-1970
		North Central	1994
Hutchinson	KS	Western	1888, 1917-1918, 1933
		Kansas State	1905, 1909-1911, 1914
		Western Association	1906-1908, 1924, 1932, 1934-1942, 1946-1954
		Southwestern	1922-1923

I

City	State	League	Years
Idaho Falls	ID	Utah-Idaho	1926-1928
		Pioneer	1940-1942, 1946-
Ilion	NY	New York State	1901-1904
Imperial Valley see Rosamond	CA		
Independence	KS	Kansas State	1906
		Oklahoma-Arkansas-Kansas	1907
		Oklahoma-Kansas	1908
		Western Association	1911, 1925, 1928-1932
		Southwestern	1921-1924
		Kansas-Oklahoma-Missouri	1947-1950, 1952
Indianapolis	IN	American Association	1884, 1902-1962, 1969-
		Western	1885, 1892, 1894-1899
		National	1887-1889
		American	1900
		Western Association	1901
		Federal	1913-1914
		International	1963
		Pacific Coast	1964-1968
Ingersoll	ONT	Canadian	1905
Iola	KS	Missouri Valley	1902-1904
		Kansas State	1906
		Oklahoma-Kansas	1908
		Kansas-Oklahoma-Missouri	1946-1952
		Western Association	1954
Ionia	MI	Central	1921-1922
Iowa see Des Moines	IA		
Ironton	OH	Ohio State Association	1884
		Mountain States	1911-1912
		Ohio State	1912-1915
Italy	TX	Central Texas	1914

J

City	State	League	Years
Jackson	MI	Tri-State	1888
		Michigan State	1889, 1895, 1902
		Interstate	1896
		Southern Michigan	1906-1909
		Southern Michigan Assn.	1910-1915
		Central	1921
Jackson	MS	Cotton States	1905-1908, 1910-1913, 1922-1932, 1936, 1953
		Delta	1904
		Mississippi State	1921
		Dixie	1933
		East Dixie	1934-1935
		Southeastern	1932, 1937-1942, 1946-1950
		Texas	1975-
Jackson	TN	Kitty	1903, 1911, 1923-1924, 1935-1942, 1950-1954
		Tri-State	1925-1926
Jacksonville	FL	South Atlantic	1904-1917, 1936-1942, 1946-1961
		Florida State	1921-1922
		Southeastern	1926-1930
		International	1962-1968
		Southern	1970-
Jacksonville	IL	Two-I	1892
		Western Association	1894-1895
		Central	1900
		Kitty	1906
		Iowa State	1907
		Central Association	1908-1909
		Northern Association	1910
		Illinois-Missouri	1910
Jacksonville	TX	East Texas	1916, 1936-1940, 1946
		West Dixie	1934-1935
		Lone Star	1947
		Gulf Coast	1950
Jacksonville Beach	FL	Florida State	1952-1954
Jalisco	MEX	Mexican	1949-1952, 1964-1975, 1988, 1991-1995
		Mexican Center	1977
Jamestown	ND	Dakota	1922
		North Dakota	1923
		Northern	1936-1937
Jamestown see also Oil City-Jamestown	NY	New York-Pennsylvania	1891, 1957, 1961-1973, 1977-
		Interstate	1905, 1914-1915
		PONY	1939-1956
Janesville	WI	Wisconsin State	1941-1942, 1946-1953
Jeanerette	LA	Evangeline	1934-1939

Jeannette	PA	Middle Atlantic	1926-1931
		Pennsylvania State Assn.	1934-1937
Jefferson City	MO	Missouri Valley	1902
		Missouri State	1911
Jenkins	KY	Mountain States	1948-1951
Jersey City	NJ	Eastern	1885-1886, 1902-1911, 1977-1978
		International	1887, 1912-1915, 1918-1933, 1937-1950, 1960-1961
		Central	1888
		Atlantic Association	1889-1890
		Atlantic	1900
Jesup	GA	Georgia State	1950-1953
Johnson City	TN	Southeastern	1910
		Appalachian	1911-1913, 1921-1924, 1937-1955, 1957-1961, 1964-
Johnsonburg	PA	Interstate	1916
Johnstown	NY		
see Amsterdam-Johnstown-Gloversville; Gloversville-Johnstown			
Johnstown	PA	Iron & Oil Association	1884
		Pennsylvania State	1892-1893
		Tri-State	1905-1912
		Middle Atlantic	1925-1938, 1946-1950
		Pennsylvania State Assn.	1939-1940
		Eastern	1955-1956, 1961
		Frontier	1995-
Joliet	IL	Two-I	1892
		Three-I	1903
		Northern Association	1910
Jonesboro	AR	Arkansas State	1909
		Northeast Arkansas	1909-1911, 1936-1941
		Tri-State	1925-1926
Joplin	MO	Missouri Valley	1902-1904
		Western Association	1905-1911, 1922-1924, 1926-1932, 1934-1942, 1946-1954
		Western	1917-1921, 1933
Joplin-Webb City	MO	Western Association	1914
see also Webb City			
Juarez	MEX		
see Ciudad Juarez			
Junction City	KS	Central Kansas	1909-1912
		Kansas State	1913

K

City	State	League	Years
Kalamazoo	MI	Ohio State	1887
		Tri-State	1888
		Michigan State	1889, 1895, 1926
		Southern Michigan	1906-1909
		Southern Michigan Assn.	1910-1914
		Central	1920-1922, 1926
		Michigan-Ontario	1923-1924
		Frontier	1996-
Kane	PA	Interstate	1905-1907
Kane County	IL		
see Geneva			
Kankakee	IL	Northern Association	1910
		Illinois-Missouri	1912-1914
Kannapolis	NC	North Carolina State	1939-1941
(aka Piedmont)		South Atlantic	1995-
Kansas City	MO	Union Association	1884
		Western	1885, 1887, 1892, 1894-1899, 1901-1903
		National	1886
		Western Association	1888-1891, 1893
		American Association	1888-1889, 1902-1954
		American	1900, 1955-1967, 1969-
		Federal	1913-1915
Kaufman	TX	Central Texas	1915
Kearney	NE	Nebraska State	1910-1915, 1956-1959
Keene	NH	Twin States	1911
Kennewick	WA		
see Tri-City			
Kenosha	WI	Midwest	1985-1992
Kent	OH	Ohio-Pennsylvania	1905
Kentucky	KY		
see Pikeville			
Keokuk	IA	Western	1885, 1935
		Iowa State	1904-1907
		Central Association	1908-1915, 1947-1949
		Mississippi Valley	1929-1933
		Three-I	1952-1957
		Midwest	1958-1962

Kewanee	IL	Central Association	1908-1913, 1948-1949
Key West	FL	Florida International	1952
		Florida State	1969, 1971-1975
Kilgore	TX	East Texas	1931, 1936-1940, 1949-1950
		Lone Star	1947-1948
Kingman	KS	Kansas State	1905
Kingsport	TN	Appalachian	1921-1925, 1938-1952, 1957, 1960-1963, 1969-1982, 1984-
		Mountain States	1953-1954
Kingston	NY	Hudson River	1903-1907
		New York-New Jersey	1913
		North Atlantic	1947
		Colonial	1948-1950
		Canadian-American	1951
Kingston	ONT	Border	1946-1951
Kinston	NC	Eastern Carolina	1908, 1928-1929
		Virginia	1925-1927
		Coastal Plain	1937-1941, 1946-1952
		Carolina	1956-1957, 1962-1974, 1978-
Kirksville	MO	Missouri State	1911
Kissimmee (aka Osceola)	FL	Florida State	1985-
Kitchener see also Berlin	ONT	Michigan-Ontario	1919-1922, 1925
Kittanning	PA	Western Pennsylvania	1907
Klamath Falls	OR	Far West	1948-1951
Knoxville	TN	South Atlantic	1909, 1925-1929, 1956-1963
		Southeastern	1910
		Appalachian	1911-1914, 1921-1924
		Southern Association	1932-1944
		Tri-State	1946-1952, 1954-1955
		Mountain States	1953
		Southern	1964-1967, 1972-
Kokomo	IN	Northern State of Indiana	1909
		Mississippi-Ohio Valley	1955
		Midwest	1956-1961

L

City	State	League	Years
La Barca	MEX	Mexican Center	1978
La Crosse	WI	Northwestern	1887
		Wisconsin State	1905-1907
		Wisconsin-Illinois	1908
		Minnesota-Wisconsin	1909-1912
		Northern	1913
		Central Association	1917
		Wisconsin State	1940-1942
La Feria	TX	Rio Grande Valley	1931
La Grande	OR	Inland Empire	1908
		Western Tri-State	1912-1913
La Grange	GA	Georgia-Alabama	1913-1917, 1946-1951
		Georgia State	1920-1921
		Big South	1997-
La Junta	CO	Rocky Mountain	1912
La Salle	IL	Illinois-Missouri	1914
Lafayette	IN	Central Interstate	1888
		Northern State of Indiana	1909-1911
		Mississippi-Ohio Valley	1955
		Midwest	1956-1957
		Great Central	1994
		Mid-America	1995
		Heartland	1996-
Lafayette	LA	Gulf Coast	1907
		Louisiana State	1920
		Evangeline	1934-1942, 1948-1957
		Texas	1975-1976
Lagoon	UT	Inter-Mountain	1901
Lagos de Moreno	MEX	Mexican Center	1975-1977
Laguna	MEX	Central Mexican	1957
Lake Charles	LA	South Texas	1906
		Gulf Coast	1907-1908, 1950-1953
		Cotton States	1929-1930
		Evangeline	1934-1942, 1954-1957
Lake Elsinore	CA	California	1994-
Lake Linden	MI	Copper Country Soo	1905
		Northern-Copper Country	1906
Lakeland	FL	Florida State	1919-1926, 1953-1955, 1960, 1962-1964, 1967-
		Florida International	1946-1952
Lamesa	TX	West Texas-New Mexico	1939-1942, 1946-1952
		Longhorn	1953
		Southwestern	1957
Lampasas	TX	Middle Texas	1914

City	State	League	Years
Lancaster	CA	California	1996-
Lancaster	OH	Ohio-Pennsylvania	1905-1907
		Ohio State	1908-1911
		Frontier	1993-1994
Lancaster	PA	Keystone Association	1884
		Eastern	1884-1885, 1958-1961
		Pennsylvania State	1894-1895
		Atlantic	1896-1899
		Tri-State	1905-1912, 1914
		Interstate	1932, 1940-1952
		Piedmont	1954-1955
Landis	NC	North Carolina State	1937-1942, 1945-1947, 1949-1951
Lanett *see Valley*	AL		
Lansdale	PA	North Atlantic	1948
Lansing	MI	Michigan State	1889-1890, 1895, 1902, 1940-1941
		Southern Michigan	1907-1909
		Southern Michigan Assn.	1910-1914
		Central	1921-1922
		Midwest	1996-
Laredo	TX	Southwest Texas	1910-1911
		Gulf Coast	1926, 1951-1953
		Texas Valley	1927
		Rio Grande Valley	1949-1950
		Texas-Louisiana	1995
see also Nuevo Laredo		Mexican	1986-1994
Larned	KS	Kansas State	1909-1911
Las Choapas	MEX	Mexican Southeast	1967-1969
Las Cruces	NM	Rio Grande Association	1915
Las Vegas	NV	Sunset	1947-1950
		Southwest International	1951
		Arizona-Mexico	1957
		California	1958
		Pacific Coast	1983-
Latrobe	PA	Western Pennsylvania	1907
Laurel	DE	Eastern Shore	1922-1923
Laurel	MS	Cotton States	1923-1929
Lawrence	KS	Western Association	1893
Lawrence	MA	New England	1886-1887, 1892, 1899, 1902-1915, 1919, 1926-1927, 1933, 1946-1947
		New England Association	1895
		Eastern	1916-1917
Lawrenceburg	KY	Blue Grass	1908
Lawrenceville	VA	Virginia	1948-1949
Lawton	OK	Texas-Oklahoma	1911
		Sooner State	1947-1957
Le Mars	IA	Iowa-South Dakota	1902-1903
Leadville	CO	Western	1886
Leaksville-Draper-Spray (now Eden, NC)	NC	Bi-State	1934-1942
		Carolina	1945-1947
		Blue Ridge	1948
Leavenworth	KS	Western	1886-1888
		Missouri Valley	1903-1904
		Western Association	1905-1907, 1946-1949
Lebanon	PA	Atlantic Association	1890
		Eastern	1891
		Pennsylvania State	1892
		Tri-State	1904
		North Atlantic	1949-1950
Leesburg	FL	Florida State	1937-1941, 1946-1953, 1956-1957, 1960-1961, 1965-1968
Leesville	LA	Gulf Coast	1950
Lemoore	CA	San Joaquin Valley	1911
Lenoir	NC	Tar Heel	1939-1940
		Blue Ridge	1946-1947
		Western Carolina	1948-1951
Leon	MEX	Mexican Center	1960-1971, 1975
		Mexican	1979-1980, 1983-1991
Lethbridge	ALB	Western Canada	1907, 1909-1910
		Pioneer	1975-1983, 1992-
Lexington	KY	Blue Grass	1908-1912, 1922-1923
		Ohio State	1913-1916
		Mountain States	1954
Lexington	NC	North Carolina State	1937-1942, 1945-1952
		Tar Heel	1953
		Western Carolina(s)	1960-1961, 1963-1967
Lexington	NE	Nebraska State	1956-1958
Lexington	TN	Kitty	1935-1938
Lewiston	ID	Western International	1937, 1952-1954
		Pioneer	1939
		Northwest	1955-1974
Lewiston	ME	New England	1891-1896, 1901, 1914-1915, 1919, 1926-1930
		Atlantic Association	1908
Lewiston-Auburn	ME	New England	1919
Ligonier	IN	Indiana-Michigan	1910
Lima	OH	Tri-State	1888
		Ohio-Pennsylvania	1905
		Interstate Association	1906
		Ohio State	1908-1912, 1939-1941, 1944-1947
		Buckeye	1915
		Central	1934
		Ohio-Indiana	1948-1951
Lincoln	IL	Illinois-Missouri	1910-1914
Lincoln	NE	Western	1886-1888, 1906-1917, 1924-1927, 1947-1958
		Western Association	1890-1891, 1894-1895
		Nebraska State	1922-1923, 1928-1936, 1938
		Western (Class D)	1939-1940
		Three-I	1959-1961
Lincoln Center	KS	Kansas State	1905
Lincolnton	NC	Western Carolina	1948-1952
		Tar Heel	1953
Lindale	GA	Georgia State	1920-1921
		Georgia-Alabama	1928-1930
Linton	IN	Eastern Illinois	1908
Little Falls *see Brainerd-Little Falls*	MN		
Little Falls (aka Mohawk Valley)	NY	New York-Pennsylvania	1977-1988
		Northeast	1995
Little River	KS	Central Kansas	1908
Little Rock	AR	Southern	1895
		Southern Association	1901-1910, 1915-1958, 1960-1961
		International	1963
		Pacific Coast	1964-1965
(aka Arkansas)		Texas	1966-
Littlestown	PA	Keystone Association	1884
Livingston	MT	Inter-Mountain	1909
Lockport	NY	PONY	1942-1950
		Middle Atlantic	1951
Lodi	CA	California	1966-1984
Logan	UT	Utah-Idaho	1926-1927
Logan	WV	Mountain State	1937-1942
Logansport	IN	Northern State of Indiana	1910-1911
Lonaconing	MD	Potomac	1916
London	ONT	International	1888-1890
		Canadian	1899-1900, 1911-1915
		International (Class D)	1908
		Michigan-Ontario	1919-1925
		Ontario	1930
		PONY	1940-1941
		Eastern	1989-1993
Long Beach	CA	Southern California Trolley	1910
		Southern California	1913
		Western	1995-
Long Branch	NJ	New York-New Jersey	1913
		Atlantic	1914
see also Bloomfield-Long Branch			
Long Island *see Maspeth*	NY		
Longview	TX	South Central	1912
		East Texas	1923-1926, 1931, 1936-1940, 1949-1950
		Lone Star	1927, 1947-1948
		Texas	1932
		Dixie	1933
		West Dixie	1934-1935
		Big State	1952-1953
Los Angeles	CA	California	1893, 1901-1902
		Pacific National	1903
		Pacific Coast	1903-1957
		American	1961-1965
		National	1958-
Los Angeles-Maiers	CA	Southern California Trolley	1910
Los Angeles-McCormicks	CA	Southern California Trolley	1910
Los Mochis	MEX	Mexican Pacific	1976
Louisville	KY	American Association	1883-1891, 1902-1962, 1982-
		National Colored	1887
		National	1892-1899
		Western Association	1901
		International	1968-1972
Lowell	MA	New England	1887-1888, 1891-1893, 1901-1915, 1919, 1926, 1933, 1947
		Atlantic Association	1889
		New England Association	1895
		Eastern	1916
		Northeastern	1934

PROFESSIONAL TEAMS BY CITY

City	State	League	Years
		New York-Pennsylvania	1996-
Lubbock	TX	West Texas	1922, 1928
		Panhandle-Pecos Valley	1923
		West Texas-New Mexico	1938-1942, 1946-1955
		Big State	1956
		Texas-Louisiana	1995-
Ludington	MI	Michigan State	1912-1914, 1926
		Central	1920-1922, 1926
Lufkin	TX	East Texas	1916, 1946
		West Dixie	1934
		Lone Star	1947-1948
		Gulf Coast	1950
Lumberton	NC	Tobacco State	1947-1950
Lynchburg	VA	Virginia	1894-1896, 1906-1912, 1917, 1939-1942
		Piedmont	1943-1955
		Appalachian	1959
		South Atlantic	1962-1963
		Southern	1964-1965
		Carolina	1966-
Lynn	MA	New England	1886-1888, 1891, 1901, 1905-1915, 1926-1930, 1946-1949
		Eastern	1916, 1980-1983
		North Atlantic	1996
(aka Massachusetts)		Northeast	1997-
Lyons GA see Vidalia-Lyons			
Lyons	KS	Kansas State	1909-1911, 1913
		Central Kansas	1912

M

City	State	League	Years
Macomb	IL	Illinois-Missouri	1908-1910
Macon	GA	Southern	1885-1886, 1892-1894
		South Atlantic	1904-1917, 1923-1930, 1936-1942, 1946-1960, 1962-1963, 1980-1987, 1991-
		Southeastern	1932
		Southern Association	1961
		Southern	1964, 1966-1967
Macon	MO	Missouri State	1911
Madison	SD	South Dakota	1920
		Dakota	1921
Madison	WI	Wisconsin State	1907
		Wisconsin-Illinois	1908-1914
		Three-I	1940-1942
		Midwest	1982-1994
		Northern	1996-
Madisonville	KY	Kitty	1916, 1922, 1946-1955
Magic Valley ID see Twin Falls			
Mahanoy City	PA	Central Pennsylvania	1887
		North Atlantic	1946-1950
Maine ME see Old Orchard Beach			
Manchester	NH	New England	1887-1888, 1891-1893, 1899, 1901-1906, 1914-1915, 1926-1930, 1946-1949
		Northeastern	1934
		Eastern	1969-1971
Mandan ND see Bismarck-Mandan			
Manhattan	KS	Central Kansas	1909-1912
		Kansas State	1913
Manistee	MI	Michigan State	1890, 1911-1914
Mankato	MN	Northern	1967-1968
Mannington	WV	West Virginia	1910
Mansfield	OH	Ohio State	1887, 1908-1909, 1912, 1936-1937, 1939-1941
		Tri-State	1888-1890
		Ohio-Michigan	1893
		Interstate	1897-1900
		Ohio-Pennsylvania	1906-1907, 1910-1911
Maracaibo	VEN	Inter-American	1979
Marianna	AR	Northeast Arkansas	1909
Marinette-Menominee	WI-MI	Wisconsin-Illinois	1914
Marion	IL	Illinois State	1947-1948
Marion	IN	Interstate Association	1906
		Northern State of Indiana	1909-1911
Marion	NC	Western Carolina	1948-1952
		Tar Heel	1953-1954
Marion	OH	Interstate	1900
		Western Association	1901
		Central	1903-1904
		Ohio-Pennsylvania	1906-1907
		Ohio State	1908-1912, 1937, 1944-1947
		Buckeye	1915
		Ohio-Indiana	1948-1951
Marion	VA	Appalachian	1955, 1965-1976
Marlin	TX	Central Texas	1916-1917
		Texas Association	1923-1924
Marshall	MN	North Central	1994
Marshall	TX	South Central	1912
		East Texas	1923-1926, 1936-1940, 1949-1950
		Lone Star	1927, 1947-1948
		Cotton States	1941
Marshalltown	IA	Iowa State	1904-1907
		Central Association	1914-1917
		Mississippi Valley	1922-1928
Martinsburg	WV	Blue Ridge	1915-1918, 1920-1929
Martinsville	VA	Bi-State	1934-1941
		Carolina	1945-1949
		Appalachian	1988-
Maryville	MO	MINK	1910-1911
Maryville-Alcoa	TN	Mountain States	1953-1954
Marysville	CA	Far West	1948-1950
Marysville	KS	Eastern Kansas	1910
Mason City	IA	Central Association	1915-1917
		Great Central	1994
Maspeth NY (aka Long Island)		Eastern	1886
Massachusetts MA see Lynn			
Massillon	OH	Ohio-Pennsylvania	1905
Matamoros	MEX	Mexican Center	1978
Mattoon		Eastern Illinois	1907-1908
		Illinois State	1947-1948
		Mississippi-Ohio Valley	1949-1955
		Midwest	1956-1957
Mattoon-Charleston IL see also Charleston		Kitty	1906
Maud	OK	Western Association	1929
Mayfield	KY	Kitty	1922-1924, 1936-1941, 1946-1955
Mayodan	NC	Bi-State	1934-1941
Maysville	KY	Blue Grass	1910-1912, 1922-1923
		Ohio State	1913-1916
Mazatlan	MEX	Mexican Pacific	1976
McAlester	OK	Oklahoma-Arkansas-Kansas	1907
		Oklahoma-Kansas	1908
		Oklahoma State	1912, 1924
		Western Association	1914-1917, 1922-1923, 1926
		Sooner State	1947-1956
McAllen	TX	Gulf Coast	1926
		Texas Valley	1938
		Rio Grande Valley	1931, 1949-1950
		Lone Star	1977
McCook	NE	Nebraska State	1928-1932, 1956-1959
McKeesport	PA	Tri-State	1890
		Ohio-Pennsylvania	1905, 1908-1910, 1912
		Penn-Ohio-Maryland	1907
		Pennsylvania State Assn.	1934-1940
McKinney	TX	Texas-Oklahoma	1912
McLeansboro	IL	Southern Illinois	1910
		Kitty	1910-1911
McPherson	KS	Central Kansas	1908
		Kansas State	1909-1911
Meadville	PA	New York-Pennsylvania	1891
Medford	OR	Far West	1948-1951
		Northwest	1967-1971, 1979-
(aka Rogue Valley/Southern Oregon)			
Medicine Hat	ALB	Western Canada	1907, 1909-1910, 1913-1914
		Pioneer	1977-
Melbourne FL (aka Brevard County)		Florida State	1994-
Memphis	TN	Southern	1885-1888, 1892-1895
		Southern Association	1901-1960
		Texas	1968-1973
		International	1974-1976
		Southern	1978-
Menominee MI see Marinette-Menominee			
Merced	CA	California State	1910
		California	1941
Meriden	CT	Eastern	1886
		Connecticut State	1899-1905, 1908
		Connecticut Association	1910
		Eastern Association	1913
Meridian	MS	Cotton States	1905-1908, 1910-1913,

City	State	League	Years
		Mississippi State	1922-1929, 1952-1955
		Southeastern	1921
		Big South	1937-1942, 1946-1950
Merrillville	IN	Mid-America	1996-
Mesa	AZ	Arizona State	1995
		Arizona-Texas	1929
Mexia	TX	Central Texas	1947
		Texas-Oklahoma	1915-1917
		Texas Association	1922
		Lone Star	1923-1926
Mexicali	MEX	Sunset	1927-1928
		Southwest International	1948-1950
		Arizona-Texas	1951-1952
		Arizona-Mexico	1953-1954
		Mexican Northern	1955-1958
			1968-1969
Mexico City	MEX	Mexican National	1946
Mexico City Agrario	MEX	Mexican	1937-1938
Mexico City Agricultura	MEX	Mexican	1937
Mexico City Azul	MEX	Mexican	1954
Mexico City Comintra	MEX	Mexican	1937-1939
Mexico City Diablos Rojos	MEX	Mexican	1940-
Mexico City Necaxa	MEX	Mexican	1937
Mexico City Petroleros	MEX	Mexican	1937
Mexico City Tigres	MEX	Mexican	1955-
Mexico City Transito	MEX	Mexican	1937
Miami	AZ	Arizona State	1928-1930
Miami	FL	Florida State	1927-1928, 1962-1991
		Florida East Coast	1940-1942
		Florida International	1946-1954
		International	1956-1960
		Inter-American	1979
(aka Florida)		National	1993-
Miami	OK	Southwestern	1921
		Kansas-Oklahoma-Missouri	1946-1952
Miami Beach	FL	Florida East Coast	1940-1942
		Florida International	1946-1952, 1954
Miami-Globe	AZ	Arizona-Texas	1947-1950
see also Globe		Arizona-Mexico	1955
Michigan	MI		
see Battle Creek			
Michigan City	IN	Midwest	1956-1959
Middleport-Pomeroy	OH	Mountain States	1911-1912
Middlesboro	KY	Appalachian	1913-1914, 1961-1963
		Mountain States	1949
Middletown	CT	Connecticut Association	1910
Middletown	NY	New York-New Jersey	1913
		Atlantic	1914
Middletown	OH	Ohio State	1944-1946
Midland	TX	West Texas	1928-1929
		West Texas-New Mexico	1937-1940
		Longhorn	1947-1955
		Southwestern	1956-1957
		Sophomore	1958-1959
		Texas	1972-
Miguel Aleman	MEX	Mexican Center	1978
Milan	TN	Kitty	1923
Milford	DE	Eastern Shore	1923, 1938-1941, 1946-1948
Miller	SD	South Dakota	1920
Milwaukee	WI	Union Association	1884
		Northwestern	1884, 1886-1887
		Western	1885, 1892, 1894-1899, 1902-1903
		Western Association	1888-1891
		American Association	1891, 1902-1952
		American	1900-1901, 1970-
		Wisconsin-Illinois	1913
		National	1953-1965
Minatitlan	MEX	Mexican Southeast	1968-1969
		Mexican	1992-
Mineral Wells	TX	West Texas	1920-1921
		Texas-Oklahoma	1921
Minersville	PA	Central Pennsylvania	1887
Minneapolis	KS	Kansas State	1905
		Central Kansas	1908-1909, 1912
Minneapolis	MN	Northwestern	1884, 1886-1887
		Western Association	1888-1891
		Western	1892, 1894-1899, 1901
		American	1900, 1961-
		American Association	1902-1960
		Northern	1913
		Great Central	1994
		North Central	1994
(aka Minnesota)		Prairie	1995
Minnesota	MN		
see Hibbing; Minneapolis			
Minot	ND	Northern	1917, 1958-1960, 1962
		North Dakota	1923
		Prairie	1995-
Mission (San Francisco)	CA	Pacific Coast	1914, 1926-1937
Mission	TX	Gulf Coast	1926
		Texas Valley	1927
Missoula	MT	Union Association	1911-1913
		Pioneer	1956-1960
Mitchell	SD	South Dakota	1920, 1923
		Dakota	1921-1922
		Nebraska State	1936-1937
		Western (Class D)	1939-1940
Mobile	AL	Southern	1887, 1892-1896, 1966, 1970, 1997-
		Cotton States	1905-1907
		Southern Association	1908-1931, 1944-1961
		Southeastern	1932, 1937-1942
		Texas-Louisiana	1994-1995
Modesto	CA	California State	1914-1915
		California	1946-1964, 1966-
Mohawk Valley	NY		
see Little Falls			
Moline	IL	Three-I	1914-1917, 1919-1923, 1937-1941
		Mississippi Valley	1924-1932
		Central Association	1947-1948
see also Quad City; Rock Island-Moline			
Monahans	TX	West Texas-New Mexico	1937
Monclova	MEX	Mexican	1980, 1982-
Monessen	PA	Pennsylvania State Assn.	1934-1938
Monett	MO	Arkansas-Missouri	1936-1939
Monmouth	IL	Illinois-Missouri	1908-1909
		Central Association	1910-1913
Monroe	LA	Cotton States	1903-1904, 1908, 1924-1932, 1937-1941, 1950-1955
		Arkansas State	1909
		Gulf Coast	1907
		Evangeline	1956
Monroe	NC	Western Carolina	1969, 1971
Monterrey	MEX	Mexican	1939-
		Mexican Center	1970-1972
Monterrey Industriales	MEX	Mexican	1989-1994
Montesano	WA	Southwest Washington	1905
		Washington State	1910
Montgomery	AL	Southern	1892-1893, 1895-1896
		Southern Association	1903-1914, 1943, 1956
		South Atlantic	1916, 1951-1956
		Southeastern	1926-1930, 1932, 1937-1942, 1946-1950
		Alabama-Florida	1957-1962
		Southern	1965-1980
Montgomery	WV	Virginia Valley	1910
		Mountain States	1911-1912
Montpelier	VT	Quebec-Ontario-Vermont	1924
Montreal	QUE	Eastern	1890, 1897-1911
		International	1912-1917, 1928-1960
		Eastern Canada	1922-1923
		Quebec-Ontario-Vermont	1924
		National	1969-
Mooresville	NC	North Carolina State	1937-1942, 1945-1952
		Tar Heel	1953
Moorhead	MN		
see Fargo-Moorhead			
Moose Jaw	SK	Western Canada	1909-1911, 1913-1914, 1919-1921
		Prairie	1995-
Morella	MEX	Mexican Center	1966
Morgan City	LA	Gulf Coast	1908
Morganton	NC	Western Carolina	1948-1952
Morristown	TN	Southeastern	1910
		Appalachian	1911-1914, 1923-1925, 1959-1961
		Mountain States	1948-1954
Moultrie	GA	Dixie	1916-1917
		Georgia-Florida	1935-1942, 1946-1952, 1956-1957, 1962-1963
Mountaindale	NY	Northeast	1995, 1997-
(aka Sullivan; Catskill)		North Atlantic	1996
Mt. Airy	NC	Bi-State	1934-1941
		Blue Ridge	1946-1950
Mt. Carmel	PA	Central Pennsylvania	1887
Mt. Clemens	MI	Southern Michigan	1906-1907
		Border	1912-1913
		Southern Michigan Assn.	1914
Mt. Pleasant	TX	East Texas	1923-1925

City	State	League	Years
Mt. Sterling	KY	Blue Grass	1912, 1922-1923
Mt. Vernon	IL	Southern Illinois	1910
		Illinois State	1947-1948
		Mississippi-Ohio Valley	1949-1954
Mt. Vernon	OH	Ohio-Pennsylvania	1905
Muncie	IN	Interstate Association	1906
		Ohio-Indiana	1908, 1948-1950
		Ohio State	1947
Murray	UT	Union Association	1914
Muscatine	IA	Northern Association	1910
		Central Association	1911-1916
Muscle Shoals see Tri-Cities	AL		
Muskegon	MI	Northwestern	1884
		Michigan State	1890, 1902, 1911-1914, 1926, 1940-1941
		West Michigan	1910
		Central	1916-1917, 1920-1922, 1926, 1934, 1948-1951
		Michigan-Ontario	1923-1924
Muskogee	OK	Missouri Valley	1905
		South Central	1906
		Oklahoma-Arkansas-Kansas	1907
		Oklahoma-Kansas	1908
		Western Association	1909-1911, 1914-1917, 1924-1929, 1932, 1934-1942, 1946-1954
		Oklahoma State	1912
		Southwestern	1921-1923
		Western	1933
		Sooner State	1955-1957
Myrtle Beach	SC	South Atlantic	1987-1992

N

City	State	League	Years
Nacogdoches	TX	East Texas	1916
Napa	CA	Central California	1910
Naranjos	MEX	Mexican Center	1972-1973
Narrows-Pearisburg (aka New River)	VA	Appalachian	1946-1950
Nashua	NH	New England Association	1895
		New England	1901-1905, 1926-1927, 1929-1930, 1933, 1946-1949
		Eastern	1983-1986
		North Atlantic	1995-
Nashville	TN	Southern	1885-1887, 1893-1895
		Southern Association	1901-1961
		South Atlantic	1963
		Southern	1978-1984, 1993-1994
		American Association	1985-
Natchez	MS	Cotton States	1902-1905, 1948-1953
		Evangeline	1940-1942, 1946-1947
Navojoa	MEX	Mexican Pacific	1976
Nazareth	PA	North Atlantic	1946-1950
Nebraska City	NE	MINK	1910-1913
Neosho	MO	Arkansas-Missouri	1937-1940
Nevada	MO	Missouri Valley	1902-1903
New Bedford	MA	New England	1895-1898, 1903-1913, 1929, 1933
		Colonial	1914-1915
		Northeastern	1934
New Bern	NC	North Carolina	1902
		Eastern Carolina	1908
		Coastal Plain	1937-1941, 1946-1952
New Brighton	PA	Iron & Oil Association	1884
New Britain	CT	Connecticut State	1908-1912
		Eastern Association	1914
(aka Hardware City)		Eastern	1984-
New Brunswick	NJ	Colonial	1948
New Castle	PA	Iron & Oil Association	1884
		Interstate	1896-1900
		Ohio-Pennsylvania	1906-1912
		Middle Atlantic	1948-1951
New Haven	CT	Atlantic Association	1889-1890
		Eastern	1891-1892, 1916-1932, 1994-
		Atlantic	1896
		Connecticut State	1899-1912
		Eastern Association	1913-1914
		Colonial	1915
New Iberia	LA	Louisiana State	1920
		Evangeline	1934-1942, 1946-1956
New Jersey see Augusta	NJ		
New London	CT	Connecticut State	1899-1907
		Connecticut Association	1910

City	State	League	Years
		Eastern Association	1913-1914
		Eastern	1916-1918
		Colonial	1947
New Martinsville	WV	Ohio-Pennsylvania	1912
New Orleans	LA	Southern	1887-1888, 1892-1896
		Texas	1888
		Southern Association	1901-1959
		Cotton States	1912
		American Association	1977, 1993-
New Philadelphia	OH	Ohio State	1936
New River see Narrows-Pearisburg	VA		
New Rockford	ND	North Dakota	1923
New Waterford	NS	Cape Breton Colliery	1937-1939
New Westminster	BC	Northwest	1974
New York	NY	American Association	1883-1887
		National	1883-1957, 1962-
		National Colored	1887
		Player's	1890
		Atlantic	1896
		American	1903-
		United States	1912
Newark	NJ	Eastern	1884-1886, 1902-1911
		International	1887, 1912-1919, 1921-1949
		Central	1888
		Atlantic Association	1889-1890
		Atlantic	1896-1900, 1914
		Federal	1915
Newark	NY	New York-Pennsylvania	1968-1979, 1983-1987
		North Atlantic	1995-
Newark	OH	Ohio-Pennsylvania	1905-1907
		Ohio State	1908-1912, 1936, 1944-1947
		Central	1911
		Buckeye	1915
		Ohio-Indiana	1948-1951
		Frontier	1994-1995
Newburgh	NY	Hudson River	1903-1907
		New York-New Jersey	1913
		Atlantic	1914
		North Atlantic	1946
		Northeast	1995-
Newburyport	MA	New England	1886
Newnan	GA	Georgia-Alabama	1913-1916, 1946-1950
Newport	AR	Arkansas State	1908
		Northeast Arkansas	1909, 1936-1941
Newport	KY	Ohio State	1914
Newport	RI	New England	1897-1899
		Atlantic Association	1908
Newport	TN	Appalachian	1937-1942
		Mountain States	1948-1950
Newport-Batesville see also Batesville	AR	Arkansas State	1909
Newport News	VA	Virginia	1900, 1912-1922, 1941-1942
		Virginia-North Carolina	1901
		Piedmont	1944-1955
Newport News-Hampton (aka Peninsula; Virginia) see also Hampton	VA	Virginia	1894
		Carolina	1963-1971, 1974, 1976-1992
		International	1972-1973
Newton	KS	Western	1888
		Central Kansas	1908, 1912
		Kansas State	1909-1911
		Southwestern	1924
Newton-Conover	NC	North Carolina State	1937-1938
		Tar Heel	1939-1940
		Western Carolina	1948-1951, 1960-1962
Niagara Falls	NY	International (Class D)	1908
		PONY	1939-1940
		Middle Atlantic	1946-1947, 1950-1951
		New York-Pennsylvania	1970-1979, 1982-1985, 1989-1993
		North Atlantic	1995
Nicholasville	KY	Blue Grass	1912
Niles	MI	Indiana-Michigan	1910
Niles	OH	Ohio-Pennsylvania	1905
Nogales	MEX	Arizona-Texas	1931, 1954
		Mexican	1937-1938
		Arizona-Mexico	1955-1956, 1958
		Mexican Northern	1968-1969
Norfolk	NE	Nebraska State	1914-1915, 1922-1923, 1928-1938
		Tri-State	1924
		Western (Class D)	1939-1941
Norfolk (aka Tidewater) see also Portsmouth-Norfolk	VA	Eastern	1885, 1931-1932
		Virginia	1894-1896, 1900, 1906-1928
		Atlantic	1897-1898
		Virginia-North Carolina	1901

City	State	League	Years
		Piedmont	1934-1955
		International	1969-
Norristown	PA	Interstate	1932
North Platte	NE	Nebraska State	1928-1932, 1956-1959
North Wilkesboro	NC	Blue Ridge	1948-1950
North Yakima	WA	Western Tri-State	1913-1914
Northampton	MA	Connecticut State	1909-1911
Northampton	VA	Eastern Shore	1927-1928
Norton	KS	Nebraska State	1929-1930
Norton	VA	Mountain States	1951-1953
Norwalk	CT	Atlantic Association	1889
Norwich	CT	Connecticut State	1899-1907
		Connecticut Association	1910
		Eastern	1995-
Nuevo Laredo	MEX	Mexican	1940, 1944-1946, 1949-1959, 1976-
(aka Dos Laredos)		Mexican Center	1968
Nyack	NY	North Atlantic	1946-1948

O

City	State	League	Years
Oak Ridge	TN	Mountain States	1948, 1954
Oakdale	LA	Louisiana State	1920
Oakland	CA	California	1887-1889, 1891, 1893, 1899-1902, 1907-1909
		Pacific Coast	1903-1955
		Central California	1910-1911
		California State	1910, 1915
		American	1968-
Oakland-Elmhurst	CA	Central California	1910-1911
Oakland-Fruitvale	CA	Central California	1910-1911
Oaxaca	MEX	Mexican	1996-
Ocala	FL	Florida State	1940-1941
Odessa	TX	West Texas-New Mexico	1937, 1940
		Longhorn	1947-1955
		Sophomore	1959-1960
Ogden	UT	Inter-Mountain	1901
		Union Association	1912-1914
		Utah-Idaho	1926-1928
		Pioneer	1939-1942, 1946-1955, 1966-1974, 1994-
		Pacific Coast	1979-1980
Ogdensburg	NY	Canadian-American	1936-1939
see also Ottawa-Ogdensburg		Border	1946-1951
Ohio Valley	WV		
see Parkersburg			
Oil City	PA	Iron & Oil Association	1884
		Interstate	1907-1908
		Pennsylvania State Assn.	1940-1942
		Middle Atlantic	1946-1951
Oil City-Jamestown	PA-NY	Interstate	1906
see also Jamestown			
Oklahoma City	OK	Southwestern	1904
		Western Association	1905-1908, 1914-1917
		Texas	1909-1911, 1933-1957
		Oklahoma State	1912
		Western	1918-1932
		American Association	1962, 1969-
		Pacific Coast	1963-1968
Okmulgee	OK	Oklahoma State	1912
		Western Association	1920-1927
Old Orchard Beach	ME	International	1984-1988
(aka Maine)			
Olean	NY	New York-Pennsylvania	1891, 1957-1959, 1961-1962
		Interstate	1905-1908, 1914-1916
		PONY	1939-1956
Olympia	WA	Southwest Washington	1903-1905
Omaha	NE	Western	1885, 1887-1892, 1898, 1900-1936, 1947-1954
		Western Association	1894-1895
		American Association	1955-1959, 1961-1962, 1969-
Oneida	NY	New York State	1889
Oneonta	NY	New York-Pennsylvania	1924, 1966-
		Canadian-American	1940-1942, 1946-1951
Ontario	CA	Sunset	1947
Opelika	AL	Georgia-Alabama	1913-1914, 1946-1951
Opelousas	LA	Gulf Coast	1907
		Cotton States	1932
		Evangeline	1934-1941
Opp	AL		
see Andalusia-Opp			
Orange	TX	Gulf Coast	1907-1908
Orange County	CA	California State	1929
Orangeburg	SC	South Carolina	1907-1908
		Western Carolinas	1973-1974

City	State	League	Years
Orizaba	MEX	Mexican Southeast	1966-1967
Orlando	FL	Florida State	1919-1924, 1926-1928, 1937-1941, 1946-1961, 1963-1972
		Florida East Coast	1942
		Southern	1973-
Oroville	CA	Far West	1948
Osceola	AR	Northeast Arkansas	1936-1937
Osceola	FL		
see Kissimmee			
Osceola	IA	Southwest Iowa	1903
Oshkosh	WI	Northwestern	1886-1887
		Wisconsin State	1905-1907, 1941-1942, 1946-1953
		Wisconsin-Illinois	1908-1914
Oskaloosa	IA	Iowa State	1904-1907
		Central Association	1908
Ossining	NY	Hudson River	1903
Oswego	NY	New York State	1885, 1899-1900
		International	1886-1887
		Canadian-American	1936-1940
Ottawa	IL	Illinois-Missouri	1914
		Bi-State	1915
Ottawa	KS	Southwestern	1924
Ottawa	ONT	Eastern	1898
		Canadian	1912-1915
		Eastern Canada	1922-1923
		Canadian-American	1936-1939
		Border	1947-1950
		International	1951-1954, 1993-
Ottawa-Hull	ONT-QUE	Quebec-Ontario-Vermont	1924
Ottawa-Ogdensburg	ONT-NY	Canadian-American	1940
Ottumwa	IA	Western Association	1899
		Iowa State	1904-1907
		Central Association	1908-1914, 1916
		Mississippi Valley	1922-1928
Outremont	QUE	Quebec-Ontario-Vermont	1924
Owensboro	KY	Kitty	1903, 1913-1914, 1916, 1936-1942, 1946-1955
Owosso	MI	Michigan State	1895
Ozark	AL	Alabama-Florida	1936-1937, 1951-1952, 1962
		Alabama State	1946-1950

P

City	State	League	Years
Paducah	KY	Kitty	1903-1906, 1910-1914, 1922-1923, 1935-1941, 1951-1955
		Mississippi-Ohio Valley	1949-1950
Paintsville	KY	Appalachian	1978-1984
see also Pikeville			
Palatka	FL	Florida State	1936-1939, 1946-1953, 1956-1962
Palestine	TX	East Texas	1916, 1936-1940
		Texas Association	1925-1926
		Lone Star	1927-1929
		West Dixie	1934-1935
Palm Springs	CA	California	1986-1993
		Western	1995-
Palmdale	CA	Golden State	1995
Pampa	TX	West Texas-New Mexico	1939-1942, 1946-1955
		Southwestern	1956-1957
Pana	IL	Eastern Illinois	1907-1908
Panama	PAN	Inter-American	1979
Panama City	FL	Georgia-Florida	1935
		Alabama-Florida	1936-1939, 1951-1961
Paragould	AR	Northeast Arkansas	1909-1911, 1936-1941
Paris	IL	Eastern Illinois	1907-1908
		Mississippi-Ohio Valley	1950-1955
		Midwest	1956-1959
Paris	KY	Blue Grass	1909-1912, 1922-1924
		Ohio State	1914
Paris	TN	Kitty	1922-1924
Paris	TX	Texas-Southern	1896
		Texas	1902-1904
		North Texas	1905, 1907
		South Central	1912
		Texas-Oklahoma	1913-1914, 1921-1922
		Western Association	1915-1917
		East Texas	1923-1926, 1931, 1946, 1949-1950
		Lone Star	1927-1929
		West Dixie	1934
		Sooner State	1955-1957
		Big State	1947-1948, 1952-1953

City	State	League	Years
Park City	UT	Inter-Mountain	1901
Parkersburg	WV	Pennsylvania-West Virginia	1909
		Virginia Valley	1910
		Middle Atlantic	1931
(aka Ohio Valley)		Frontier	1993-
Parksley	VA	Eastern Shore	1922-1928
Parras	MEX	Mexican Center	1974
Parsons	KS	Missouri Valley	1905
		Kansas State	1906
		Oklahoma-Arkansas-Kansas	1907
		Southwestern	1921
Pasadena	CA	Southern California Trolley	1910
		Southern California	1913
Pasco	WA		
see Tri-City			
Paterson	NJ	Atlantic	1896-1899, 1914
		Hudson River	1904-1907
Patton	PA	Interstate	1906
Pauls Valley	OK	Sooner State	1948-1954
Pawhuska	OK	Oklahoma State	1924
		Western Association	1920-1922
Pawtucket	RI	New England	1892, 1894-1899, 1946-1949
		Atlantic Association	1908
		Colonial	1914-1915
		Eastern	1966-1967, 1970-1972
		International	1973-
Pearisburg	VA		
see Narrows-Pearisburg			
Peekskill	NY	Hudson River	1903, 1905
		North Atlantic	1946-1949
Pekin	IL	Illinois-Missouri	1909-1913
Pendleton	OR	Inland Empire	1908
		Western Tri-State	1912-1914
Peninsula	VA		
see Newport News-Hampton; see also Hampton; Newport News			
Pennington Gap	VA	Appalachian	1937-1940
		Mountain States	1948-1951
Pensacola	FL	Southern	1893
		Cotton States	1913
		Southeastern	1927-1930, 1934-1942, 1946-1950
		Alabama-Florida	1957-1962
Peoria	IL	Northwestern	1883-1884
		Central Interstate	1888-1889
		Two-I	1892
		Western Association	1894-1897
		Central	1900, 1904, 1917, 1934
		Western	1902-1903
		Three-I	1905-1917, 1919-1932, 1935, 1937, 1953-1957
		Mississippi Valley	1933
		Midwest	1983-
Perth	ONT	Canadian-American	1936
Perth-Cornwall	ONT	Canadian-American	1937
see also Cornwall			
Perth Amboy	NJ	Atlantic	1914
Petaluma	CA	Central California	1910
Peterborough	ONT	Canadian	1912-1914
Petersburg	VA	Virginia	1894-1896, 1900, 1910-1921, 1923-1924, 1926-1928, 1941-1942, 1948-1950
see also Colonial Heights-Petersburg			
Philadelphia	PA	American Association	1883-1891
		National	1883-
		Union Association	1884
		National Colored	1887
		Player's	1890
		Eastern	1892
		Pennsylvania State	1894
		Atlantic	1896-1897, 1900
		American	1901-1954
Phoenix	AZ	Rio Grande Association	1915
		Arizona State	1928-1930
		Arizona-Texas	1931-1932, 1947-1950, 1952-1954
		Southwest International	1951
		Arizona-Mexico	1955-1957
		Pacific Coast	1958-1959, 1966-
Piedmont	NC		
see Kannapolis			
Piedmont	WV	Penn-Ohio-Maryland	1906
		Western Pennsylvania	1907
		Potomac	1916
Piedmont-Westernport	WV-MD	Blue Ridge	1918
Pikeville	KY	Appalachian	1982-1984
(aka Kentucky)		Frontier	1993-1994
Pine Bluff	AR	Cotton States	1903-1905, 1930-1932, 1936-1940, 1948-1955
		Arkansas-Texas	1906
		Arkansas State	1908
		Dixie	1933
		East Dixie	1934-1935
		Big South	1996-
Pine Tree	ME	Maine State	1907
Piqua	OH	Ohio State	1911
Pittsburg	CA	Far West	1948-1951
Pittsburg	KS	Missouri Valley	1903-1905
		Kansas State	1906
		Western Association	1909
		Southwestern	1921
		Kansas-Oklahoma-Missouri	1946-1952
Pittsburgh	PA	American Association	1883-1886
		Union Association	1884
		National Colored	1887
		National	1887-
		Player's	1890
		Ohio-Pennsylvania	1912
		United States	1912
		Federal	1913-1915
Pittsfield	MA	Hudson River	1905
		Eastern Association	1913-1914
		Eastern	1919-1930, 1965-1976, 1985-1988
		Canadian-American	1941-1942, 1946-1951
		New York-Pennsylvania	1989-
Plainview	TX	West Texas-New Mexico	1953-1955
		Southwestern	1956-1957
		Sophomore	1958-1959
Pocatello	ID	Utah-Idaho	1926-1928
(aka Gate City)		Pioneer	1939-1942, 1946-1965, 1984-1985, 1987-1991, 1993
Pocomoke City	MD	Eastern Shore	1922-1923, 1937-1940
Point Pleasant-Gallipolis	WV-OH	Virginia Valley	1910
		Mountain States	1911
Pomeroy	OH		
see Middleport-Pomeroy			
Pomona	CA	California State	1929
Pompano Beach	FL	Florida State	1969-1973, 1976-1978
Ponca City	OK	Oklahoma State	1923-1924
		Southwestern	1926
		Western Association	1934-1938, 1954
		Kansas-Oklahoma-Missouri	1947-1952
		Sooner State	1955-1957
Pontiac	MI	Border	1912-1913
Poplar Bluff	AR	Arkansas State	1908
Pt. Arthur	ONT		
see Ft. William-Pt. Arthur			
Port Arthur	TX	Gulf Coast	1950-1953
		Cotton States	1932
		Evangeline	1940-1942, 1954
		Big State	1955-1957
Port Charlotte	FL	Florida State	1987-
Port Chester	NY	Colonial	1947-1948
Port City	NC		
see Wilmington			
Port Huron	MI	Michigan State	1890, 1895, 1926
		Canadian	1900
		Border	1912-1913
		Michigan-Ontario	1921, 1926
Port Huron-Sarnia	MI-ONT	Michigan-Ontario	1922
Portageville	MO	Kitty	1935-1936
Porterville	CA	San Joaquin Valley	1911
		Sunset	1949-1950
		Southwest International	1952
see also Riverside-Porterville			
Portland	ME	New England	1886-1888, 1891-1896, 1899, 1901, 1913-1915, 1919, 1926-1930, 1946-1949
		Maine State	1907
		Atlantic Association	1908
		Eastern	1916-1917, 1994-
Portland	OR	Pacific Northwest	1892, 1901-1902
		New Pacific	1896
		Pacific National	1903
		Pacific Coast	1903-1972, 1978-1993
		Northwestern	1909, 1911-1914
		Pacific Coast International	1918
		Northwest	1973-1977, 1995-
Portsmouth	NH	New England	1888
Portsmouth	OH	Ohio State Association	1884
		Ohio State	1908-1916
		Middle Atlantic	1935-1940
		Ohio-Indiana	1948-1950
		Frontier	1993-1995
Portsmouth	VA	Virginia	1895-1896, 1900, 1906-

City	State	League	Years
			1910, 1912-1917, 1919-1928
		Virginia-North Carolina	1901
		Piedmont	1935-1955
		Carolina	1963-1968
Portsmouth-Norfolk see also Norfolk	VA	South Atlantic	1961-1962
Pottsville	PA	Interstate Association	1883
		Pennsylvania State	1894-1895
Pottstown	PA	Interstate	1932
Poughkeepsie	NY	Hudson River	1903-1907
		New York-New Jersey	1913
		Atlantic	1914
		Colonial	1947-1950
Poza Rica	MEX	Mexican	1958-1983, 1996-
Primghar see Sheldon-Primghar	IA		
Prince William see Woodbridge	VA		
Princeton	KY	Kitty	1905
Princeton	WV	Appalachian	1988-
Providence	RI	National	1883-1885
		Eastern	1886, 1891-1911, 1918-1919, 1926-1930
		International	1912-1917
		New England	1946-1949
Puebla	MEX	Mexican	1942-1948, 1960-1969, 1972-1980, 1985-1987, 1993-1995
Pueblo	CO	Western	1900, 1905-1909, 1911, 1928-1932, 1947-1958
		Rocky Mountain	1912
		Western (Class D)	1941
		Texas-Louisiana	1995
Puerto Mexico	MEX	Mexican Southeast	1964-1970
Puerto Penasco	MEX	Mexican Northern	1969
Puerto Rico see San Juan	PR		
Pulaski	VA	Virginia	1942
		Appalachian	1946-1950, 1952-1955, 1957-1958, 1969-1977, 1982-1992, 1997-
Punxsutawney	PA	Interstate	1906-1907

Q

City	State	League	Years
Quad City/Cities (Davenport-Bettendorf- IA, Moline-Rock Island)-IL see also Davenport; Moline; Rock Island		Midwest	1961-
Quebec	QUE	Eastern Canada	1923
		Quebec-Ontario-Vermont	1924
		Quebec Provincial	1940
		Canadian-American	1941-1942, 1946-1950
		Provincial	1951-1955
		Eastern	1971-1977
Quincy	IL	Northwestern	1883-1884
		Central Interstate	1889
		Two-I	1892
		Western Association	1894-1897, 1899
		Iowa State	1907
		Central Association	1908-1910
		Three-I	1911-1917, 1925-1932, 1946-1956
		Mississippi Valley	1933
		Midwest	1960-1973
Quincy	MA	New England	1933
Quintana Roo	MEX	Mexican	1996-
Quitman	GA	Dixie	1916-1917

R

City	State	League	Years
Racine	WI	Wisconsin-Illinois	1909-1914
		Bi-State	1915
Radford	VA	Blue Ridge	1946-1950
Raleigh	NC	Virginia-North Carolina	1901
		North Carolina	1902
		Eastern Carolina	1908-1910
		North Carolina State	1913-1917
		Piedmont	1920-1932
		Carolina	1945-1953, 1958-1967
Raleigh-Durham see also Durham	NC	Carolina	1968-1971
Rancho Cucamonga	CA	California	1993-
Ranger	TX	West Texas	1920-1922
Raton	NM	Rocky Mountain	1912
Raymond	WA	Washington State	1910-1911
Rayne	LA	Louisiana State	1920
		Evangeline	1934-1941
Reading	PA	Interstate Association	1883
		Eastern	1884,1952-1961, 1963-1965, 1967-
		Pennsylvania State	1892-1895
		Atlantic	1897-1900
		Tri-State	1907-1912, 1914
		United States	1912
		New York State	1916-1917
		International	1919-1931
		New York-Pennsylvania	1933-1935
		Interstate	1940-1941
Red Cloud	NE	Nebraska State	1910
Red Deer	ALB	Western Canada	1912
Red Oak	IA	Southwest Iowa	1903
Red Springs	NC	Tobacco State	1947-1950
		Carolina	1969
Red Wing	MN	Minnesota-Wisconsin	1910-1911
Redding	CA	Far West	1948-1951
Redfield	SD	South Dakota	1920
		Dakota	1921
Redondo Beach	CA	Southern California Trolley	1910
Refugio	TX	Texas Valley	1938
Regina	SK	Western Canada	1909-1910, 1913-1914, 1919-1921
		North Central	1994
		Prairie	1995-
Rehoboth Beach	DE	Eastern Shore	1947-1949
Reidsville	NC	Bi-State	1935-1940
		Tri-State	1947
		Carolina	1948-1955
Reno	NV	Sunset	1947-1949
		Far West	1950-1951
		California	1955-1964, 1966-1992
		Western	1996-
Reynosa	MEX	Mexican	1963-1976, 1980-1982, 1995-
Rhode Island see West Warwick	RI		
Richland see Tri-City	WA		
Richmond	CA	Central California	1910-1911
Richmond	IN	Ohio-Indiana	1908, 1948-1951
		Central	1917, 1930
		Ohio State	1946-1947
		Frontier	1995-
Richmond	KY	Blue Grass	1908-1912
Richmond	VA	American Association	1884
		Eastern	1884-1885, 1931-1932
		Virginia	1894-1896, 1900, 1906-1914, 1918-1928
		Atlantic	1897-1899
		Virginia-North Carolina	1901
		United States	1912
		Internatonal	1915-1917, 1954-1964, 1966-
		Piedmont	1933-1953
Ridgway	PA	Interstate	1916
Rio Blanco	MEX	Mexican	1937-1938
Rio Grande Valley see Harlingen	TX		
River City see Huntington	WV		
Riverside	CA	California	1941, 1988-1990
		Sunset	1947-1950
Riverside-Ensenada see also Ensenada	CA-MEX	Southwest International	1952
Riverside-Porterville see also Porterville	CA	Southwest International	1952
Roanoke see also Salem-Roanoke	VA	Virginia	1894-1896, 1906-1914
		Piedmont	1943-1953
Roanoke Rapids	NC	Coastal Plain	1947-1952
Robstown	TX	Rio Grande Valley	1949-1950
Rochester	MN	Minnesota-Wisconsin	1910-1912
		Three-I	1958
		Northern	1993
Rochester	NY	New York State	1885
		International	1886-1889, 1912-
		American Association	1890
		Eastern	1891-1892, 1895-1911
Rock Hill	SC	South Carolina	1908
		Tri-State	1947-1955
		Western Carolinas	1963-1968
Rock Island see also Quad City	IL	Western Association	1899
		Three-I	1901-1911, 1916-1917, 1920-1921

City	State	League	Years
		Central Association	1914
		Mississippi Valley	1922-1933
		Western	1934-1937
Rock Island-Moline see also Moline; Quad City	IL	Two-I Western Association	1892 1894
Rock Rapids	IA	Iowa-South Dakota	1902
Rockford	IL	Central Interstate	1888
		Two-I	1892
		Western Association	1895-1897, 1899
		Three-I	1901-1904, 1915-1917, 1919-1923
		Wisconsin-Illinois	1908-1914
		Central Association	1947-1949
		Midwest	1988-
Rockingham	NC	Tobacco State	1950
Rocky Mount	NC	Eastern Carolina	1909-1910, 1928-1929
		Virginia	1915-1917, 1920-1925
		Piedmont	1927, 1936-1940
		Coastal Plain	1941, 1946-1952
		Bi-State	1942
		Carolina	1962-1975, 1980
Rogers	AR	Arkansas State	1934-1935
		Arkansas-Missouri	1936-1938
Rogue Valley see Medford	OR		
Rohnert Park (aka Sonoma County) (aka Redwood)	CA	Western California	1995- 1980-1985
Rome	GA	Southeastern	1910-1912
		Appalachian	1913
		Georgia-Alabama	1914-1917, 1950-1951
		Georgia State	1920-1921
Rome	NY	New York State	1899-1901
		Canadian-American	1937-1942, 1946-1951
Romeoville (aka Will County)	IL	North Central Heartland	1995 1996-
Rosamond (aka Imperial Valley)	CA	Golden State	1995
Roseburg	OR	Oregon State	1904
Roseville	CA	Far West	1948
Roswell	NM	Panhandle-Pecos Valley	1923
		West Texas-New Mexico	1937
		Longhorn	1949-1955
		Southwestern	1956
		Sophomore	1959
Rusk	TX	East Texas	1916
Russellville	AL	Alabama-Tennessee	1921
Rutherford County see Spindale	NC		
Rutland	VT	Quebec-Ontario-Vermont	1924

S

City	State	League	Years
Sabetha	KS	Eastern Kansas	1910
Sabinas	MEX	Mexican	1971-1973
Sacramento	CA	California	1887, 1889, 1891, 1893, 1899-1902, 1907-1909
		Pacific Coast	1903, 1909-1914, 1918-1960, 1974-1976
		California State	1910
Saginaw	MI	Northwestern	1883-1884
		Michigan State	1889, 1902, 1926, 1940-1941
		Ohio-Michigan	1893
		Interstate	1896
		Canadian	1900
		Interstate Association	1906
		Southern Michigan	1906, 1908-1909
		Southern Michigan Assn.	1910-1915
		Michigan-Ontario	1919-1926
		Central	1948-1951
Saginaw-Bay City see also Bay City	MI	Eastern	1890
St. Augustine	FL	Southeastern	1926-1927
		Florida State	1936-1941, 1946-1950, 1952
St. Boniface	MB	Northern	1915
St. Catharines	ONT	Ontario	1930
		New York-Pennsylvania	1986-
St. Clair	PA	Interstate	1932
St. Cloud	MN	Northern	1946-1971
St. Cloud-Brainerd see also Brainerd	MN	Northern	1905
St. Helena	CA	Central California	1910
St. Hyacinthe	QUE	Quebec Provincial	1940
		Provincial	1948-1953
St. Jean-Sur-Richelieu	QUE	Provincial	1948-1955
St. John	NB	New Brunswick-Maine	1913
St. Joseph	MI	Michigan State	1940-1941
St. Joseph	MO	Western	1886-1887, 1898, 1900-1905, 1910-1926, 1930-1935
		Western Association	1889, 1893-1897, 1906, 1927, 1939-1941, 1946-1951, 1953-1954
St. Louis	MO	American Association	1883-1891
		Union Association	1884
		National	1885-1886, 1892-
		Western Association	1888
		American	1902-1953
		Federal	1913-1915
St. Lucie	FL	Florida State	1988-
St. Marys	PA	Interstate	1916
St. Paul	MN	Union Association	1884
		Northwestern	1884, 1886-1887
		Western Association	1888-1891
		Western	1892, 1895-1899, 1901
		American Association	1902-1960
		Northern	1913, 1993-
St. Petersburg	FL	Florida State	1920-1928, 1955-
		Florida International	1947-1954
St. Stephen see Calais-St. Stephen	NB		
St. Thomas	ONT	Canadian	1899, 1905, 1911-1915
		International (Class D)	1908
		Ontario	1930
Salamanca	MEX	Mexican Center	1960-1962, 1964-1965, 1975
Salem	MA	New England	1887-1888, 1891-1892, 1926-1928, 1930
		New England Association	1895
Salem	OH	Ohio-Pennsylvania	1912
Salem	OR	Oregon State	1904
		Western International	1940-1942, 1946-1954
		Northwest	1955-1965, 1977-1989, 1997-
Salem	VA	Blue Ridge	1946
		Appalachian	1955, 1957-1967
		Carolina	1968-
Salem-Roanoke see also Roanoke	VA	Virginia	1939-1942
Salina	KS	Central Kansas	1908-1910, 1912
		Kansas State	1913-1914
		Southwestern	1922-1926
		Western Association	1938-1941, 1946-1952
Salinas	CA	Sunset	1949
		California	1954-1958, 1963-1965, 1973-1980, 1982-1987, 1989-1992
		Western	1995-
Salisbury (aka Delmarva)	MD	Eastern Shore	1922-1928, 1937-1941, 1946-1949
		Interstate	1951-1952
		South Atlantic	1996-
Salisbury	NC	North Carolina State	1937-1942, 1945-1952
		Tar Heel	1953
		Western Carolina(s)	1960-1966, 1968
Salisbury-Spencer	NC	Virginia-North Carolina	1905
		Piedmont	1925-1929
Salt Lake City	UT	Inter-Mountain	1901, 1909
		Pacific National	1903-1904
		Union Association	1911-1914
		Pacific Coast	1915-1925, 1958-1965, 1970-1984, 1994-
		Utah-Idaho	1926-1928
		Pioneer	1939-1942, 1946-1957, 1967-1969, 1985-1992
Saltillo	MEX	Mexican National	1946
		Central Mexican	1956-1957
		Mexican Center	1964, 1968-1969
		Mexican	1970-
San Angelo	TX	West Texas	1921-1922, 1928-1929
		Longhorn	1948-1955
		Southwestern	1956-1957
		Sophomore	1958-1959
San Antonio	TX	Texas	1888, 1907-1942, 1946-1964, 1967-
		Texas-Southern	1895-1896
		South Texas	1903-1906
		Texas-Louisiana	1994
San Benito	TX	Rio Grande Valley	1931
San Bernardino	CA	Southern California	1913
		California State	1929
		California	1941, 1987-
		Sunset	1948-1950
San Diego	CA	Southern California	1913

PROFESSIONAL TEAMS BY CITY

City	State	League	Years
		California State	1929
		Pacific Coast	1936-1968
		National	1969-
San Francisco see also Mission	CA	California	1889, 1891, 1893, 1899-1902, 1907-1909
		Pacific National	1903
		Pacific Coast	1903-1957
		California State	1910, 1915
		National	1958-
San Francisco Haverly	CA	California	1887-1888
San Francisco Pioneers	CA	California	1887-1888
San Jose	CA	California	1891, 1899, 1907-1909, 1942, 1947-1958, 1962-1976, 1979-
		California State	1910, 1913-1915
		Pacific Coast	1977-1978
San Juan (aka Puerto Rico)	PR	International	1961
		Inter-American	1979
San Leandro	CA	Central California	1910-1911
San Luis Potosi	MEX	Mexican	1946-1951, 1986-1991
		Mexican Center	1960-1966, 1969-1971
San Luis Rio Colorado	MEX	Mexican Northern	1968-1969
San Pedro	MEX	Mexican Center	1974
San Rafael	CA	Central California	1910
Sandersville	GA	Georgia State	1953-1956
Sandusky	OH	Ohio State	1887, 1936-1937
		Tri-State	1888
		Ohio-Michigan	1893
Sanford	FL	Florida State	1919-1920, 1925-1928, 1936-1941, 1946-1953, 1955, 1959-1960
Sanford	NC	Bi-State	1941-1942
		Tobacco State	1946-1950
Santa Ana	CA	Southern California Trolley	1910
Santa Barbara	CA	Southern California	1913
		California	1941-1942, 1946-1953, 1962-1967
Santa Barbara-Ventura (aka Channel Cities)	CA	California	1954-1955
Santa Clara	CA	California	1979
Santa Cruz	CA	California	1899, 1908-1909
Santo Domingo	DR	Inter-American	1979
Santa Rosa	CA	Central California	1910
		Far West	1948-1949
Santa Rosa	MEX	Mexican	1937-1939
Sapulpa	OK	Western Association	1909-1911
		Southwestern	1921-1923
Sarasota	FL	Florida State	1926-1927, 1961-1965, 1989-
Saratoga Springs see Glens Falls-Saratoga Springs	NY		
Sarnia see Port Huron-Sarnia	ONT		
Saskatoon	SK	Western Canada	1910-1911, 1913-1914, 1919-1921
		North Central	1994
		Prairie	1995-
Saugerties	NY	Hudson River	1903-1905
Sault Ste. Marie	MI	Copper Country Soo	1905
Savannah	GA	Southern	1886-1887, 1893-1894, 1968-1983
		South Atlantic	1904-1915, 1936-1942, 1946-1960, 1962, 1984-
		Southeastern	1926-1928
Schenectady	NY	New York State	1899-1904
		Canadian-American	1946-1950
		Eastern	1951-1957
Schoolfield see Danville-Schoolfield	VA		
Schulenburg	TX	Middle Texas	1915
Scottdale	PA	Western Pennsylvania	1907
		Pennsylvania-West Virginia	1908
		Middle Atlantic	1925-1931
Scranton	PA	International	1887
		Central	1888
		Pennsylvania State	1892-1894
		Eastern	1894-1897, 1939-1953
		Atlantic	1899-1900
		New York State	1904-1917
		New York-Pennsylvania	1923-1937
Scranton-Wilkes-Barre see also Wilkes-Barre	PA	International	1989-
Seaford	DE	Eastern Shore	1946-1949
Seattle	WA	Pacific Northwest	1892, 1901-1902
		New Pacific	1896
		Pacific National	1903
		Pacific Coast	1903-1906, 1919-1968
		Northwestern	1907-1917
		Pacific Coast International	1918-1920
		American	1969, 1977-
		Northwest	1972-1976
Sebring see Alliance-Sebring	OH		
Sedalia	MO	Missouri Valley	1902-1904
		Western Association	1905
		Missouri State	1911
Seguin	TX	Gulf States	1976
Selma	AL	Southern Association	1901
		Southeastern	1911-1912, 1927-1930, 1932, 1937-1941, 1946-1950
		Cotton States	1913
		Georgia-Alabama	1914
		Alabama-Florida	1957-1962
Selma see Smithfield-Selma	NC		
Seminole	OK	Sooner State	1947-1951, 1954-1957
Seneca	KS	Eastern Kansas	1910
Seneca Falls	NY	New York State	1889
Seward	NE	Nebraska State	1910-1913
Shamokin	PA	Central Pennsylvania	1887
		Tri-State	1905
		New York-Pennsylvania	1925-1927
Sharon	PA	Ohio-Pennsylvania	1905-1908, 1911-1912
Shawnee	OK	Southwestern	1904, 1925
		South Central	1906
		Oklahoma State	1923-1924
		Western Association	1929-1930
		Sooner State	1950-1957
Sheboygan	WI	Wisconsin State	1940-1942, 1946-1953
Sheffield-Tuscumbia see also Tri-Cities	AL	Tri-State	1926
Shelby	NC	North Carolina State	1937-1938
		Tar Heel	1939-1940, 1953-1954
		Tri-State	1946
		Western Carolina(s)	1948-1952, 1960-1965, 1969, 1977-1979
		South Atlantic	1980-1982
Shelbyville	IL	Eastern Illinois	1907-1908
Shelbyville	KY	Blue Grass	1908-1910
Sheldon	IA	Iowa-South Dakota	1902
Sheldon-Primghar	IA	Iowa-South Dakota	1903
Shenandoah	IA	Southwest Iowa	1903
		MINK	1910-1911
Shenandoah	PA	Pennsylvania State	1894-1895
Sherbrooke	QUE	Quebec Provincial	1940
		Border	1946
		Provincial	1948-1951, 1953-1955
		Eastern	1972-1973
Sherman	TX	Texas-Southern	1895-1896
		Texas-Oklahoma	1912-1914, 1921-1922
		Western Association	1915-1917
		Texas Association	1923
		Lone Star	1929
		East Texas	1946
		Sooner State	1952
Sherman-Denison see also Denison	TX	Texas	1902
		Big State	1947-1951
		Sooner State	1953
Shreveport	LA	Texas-Southern	1895
		Southern Association	1901-1907, 1959-1961
		Texas	1908-1910, 1915-1932, 1938-1942, 1946-1957, 1968-
		Dixie	1933
		East Dixie	1934
		West Dixie	1935
Silao	MEX	Mexican Center	1978
Siloam Springs	AR	Arkansas State	1934-1935
		Arkansas-Missouri	1936-1938, 1940
Simcoe	ONT	Canadian	1905
Sioux City	IA	Western Association	1888-1891
		Western	1894, 1900, 1904-1923, 1934-1937, 1947-1958
		Iowa-South Dakota	1902-1903
		Tri-State	1924
		Nebraska State	1938
		Western (Class D)	1939-1941
		Three-I	1959-1960
		Northern	1993-
Sioux Falls	SD	Iowa-South Dakota	1902-1903
		South Dakota	1920, 1923
		Dakota	1921-1922
		Tri-State	1924
		Nebraska State	1933-1938

City	State	League	Years
		Western (Class D)	1939-1941
		Northern	1942, 1946-1953, 1966-1971, 1993-
Slatington	PA	Interstate	1932
Smiths Falls	ONT	Canadian-American	1937
Smithfield	NC	Tobacco State	1946
Smithfield-Selma	NC	Tobacco State	1947-1950
Snow Hill	NC	Coastal Plain	1937-1940
Somerset	PA	Western Pennsylvania	1907
Sonoma County see Rohnert Park	CA		
South Bend	IN	Central	1903-1912, 1916-1917, 1932
		Southern Michigan Assn.	1914-1915
		Midwest	1988-
South Bend	WA	Washington State	1911
South Boston (aka South Boston-Halifax)	VA	Bi-State	1937-1940
South McAlester	OK	Missouri Valley	1905
		South Central	1906
Southern Minny see Austin	MN		
Southern Nomadic see Yuma	AZ	Golden State	1995
Southern Oregon see Medford	OR		
Sparta	GA	Georgia State	1948-1949
Spartanburg	SC	South Carolina	1907
		Carolina Association	1908-1912
		South Atlantic	1919-1929, 1938-1940, 1980-1994
		Palmetto	1931
		Tri-State	1946-1955
		Western Carolinas	1963-1979
		Atlantic Coast	1995
Spencer see Salisbury-Spencer	NC		
Spindale (aka Rutherford County)	NC	Western Carolina	1949-1952, 1960
Spokane	WA	Pacific Northwest	1892, 1901-1902
		Pacific National	1903-1904
		Northwestern	1905-1917
		Pacific Coast International	1918, 1920
		Western International	1937-1942, 1946-1954
		Pacific Coast	1958-1971, 1973-1982
		Northwest	1955-1956, 1972, 1983-
Spray see Leaksville-Draper-Spray	NC		
Springfield	IL	Northwestern	1883
		Central Interstate	1889
		Western Association	1895
		Central	1900, 1934
		Three-I	1903-1914, 1925-1932, 1935, 1938-1942, 1946-1949
		Mississippi Valley	1933
		Mississippi-Ohio Valley	1950
		American Association	1978-1981
		Midwest	1982-1995
		Frontier	1996-
Springfield	MA	Eastern	1893-1900, 1916-1932, 1939-1943, 1957-1965
		Connecticut State	1902-1912
		Eastern Association	1913-1914
		Colonial	1915
		Northeastern	1934
		New England	1948-1949
		International	1950-1953
Springfield	MO	Missouri Valley	1902-1904
		Western Association	1905-1909, 1911, 1920-1932, 1934-1942, 1948, 1950
		Western	1933
Springfield	OH	Ohio State Association	1884
		Tri-State	1889-1890
		Interstate	1897-1899
		Central	1905-1907, 1912-1914, 1916-1917, 1928-1930
		Ohio State	1908, 1911, 1944-1947
		Middle Atlantic	1933-1934, 1937-1939, 1941-1942
		Ohio-Indiana	1948-1951
Springfield	TN	Kitty	1923
Springfield-Charlestown	VT-NH	Twin States	1911
Stamford	CT	Colonial	1947-1949
Stamford	TX	West Texas	1922
Statesboro	GA	Georgia State	1952-1955
Statesville	NC	Tar Heel	1939-1940, 1953
		North Carolina State	1942, 1945-1952
		Western Carolina(s)	1960-1964, 1966-1967, 1969
Staunton	IL	Eastern Illinois	1908
Staunton	VA	Virginia	1894, 1939-1942
		Virginia Mountain	1914
Sterling	IL	Northern Association	1910
Steubenville	OH	Ohio State	1887
		Ohio-Pennsylvania	1905, 1909, 1911
		Penn-Ohio-Maryland	1906-1907
		Interstate	1913
Steubenville-Follansbee	OH-WV	Ohio-Pennsylvania	1912
Stillwater	MN	Northwestern	1884
Stockton	CA	California	1888-1889, 1893, 1900, 1907-1909, 1941, 1946-1972, 1978-
		California State	1910, 1913-1915
Stratford	ONT	Canadian	1899
Streator	IL	Illinois-Missouri	1912-1914
		Bi-State	1915
Strong City-Cottonwood Falls	KS	Kansas State	1909
Stroudsburg	PA	Interstate	1932
		North Atlantic	1946-1950
Suffolk	VA	Virginia	1915, 1919-1921, 1948-1951
Sullivan see Mountaindale	NY		
Sulphur Springs	TX	East Texas	1923-1925
Sumter	SC	South Carolina	1907-1908
		Tri-State	1949-1950
		Western Carolinas	1970-1971
		South Atlantic	1985-1991
Sunbury	PA	Central Pennsylvania	1887
		Interstate	1939-1940, 1946-1952
		Piedmont	1955
Superior	NE	Nebraska State	1910-1914, 1956-1958
Superior see also Duluth-Superior	WI	Northern	1903-1905, 1913-1916, 1933-1942, 1946-1955
		Minnesota-Wisconsin	1909-1911
		Central International	1912
		Twin Ports	1943
Surrey	BC	Western	1995
Sweetwater	TX	West Texas	1920-1922
		Longhorn	1947-1952, 1954
Sydney	NS	Cape Breton Colliery	1937-1939
Sydney Mines	NS	Cape Breton Colliery	1937-1939
Syracuse	NY	New York State	1885, 1902-1917
		International	1886-1889, 1918, 1920-1927, 1934-1955, 1961-
		American Association	1890
		Eastern	1891-1892, 1894-1901, 1956-1957
		New York-Pennsylvania	1928-1929

T

City	State	League	Years
Tabasco see also Villahermosa	MEX	Mexican Southeast	1964-1970
Tacoma	WA	Pacific Northwest	1892, 1901-1902
		New Pacific	1896
		Pacific National	1903
		Pacific Coast	1904-1905, 1960-
		Northwestern	1906-1917
		Washington State	1910
		Pacific Coast International	1918-1921
		Western International	1922, 1937-1942, 1946-1951
Taft	TX	Texas Valley	1938
Talladega	AL	Southeastern	1912
		Georgia-Alabama	1913-1917, 1928-1930
Tallahassee	FL	Georgia-Florida	1935-1942, 1946-1950
		Alabama-Florida	1951
		Florida International	1954
Tallassee	AL	Alabama-Florida	1939
		Alabama State	1940-1941
		Georgia-Alabama	1946-1949
Tamaqua	PA	Interstate	1932
Tampa	FL	Florida State	1919-1927, 1957-1988, 1994-
		Southeastern	1928-1930
		Florida International	1946-1954
Tampico	MEX	Mexican	1937-1948, 1971-1979, 1983-1985
		Mexican Center	1967-1970
Tamuin	MEX	Mexican Center	1973
Tarboro	NC	Virginia-North Carolina	1901
		Virginia	1921
		Coastal Plain	1937-1941, 1946-1952
Taunton	MA	New England	1897-1899, 1905, 1933

City	State	League	Years
		Atlantic Association	1908
		Colonial	1914-1915
Taylor	TX	Middle Texas	1915
Taylorville	IL	Eastern Illinois	1907-1908
		Illinois-Missouri	1911
Tecumseh	MI	Southern Michigan	1906-1908
Temple	TX	Texas	1905-1907
		Middle Texas	1914-1915
		Central Texas	1916-1917
		Texas Association	1924-1926
		Big State	1949-1954, 1957
Tennessee see Winchester	TN		
Teocaltiche	MEX	Mexican Center	1977-1978
Terre Haute	IN	Northwestern	1884
		Central Interstate	1888
		Two-I	1892
		Western	1895
		Central	1900, 1903-1916
		Three-I	1901-1902, 1919-1932, 1935, 1937, 1946-1956
Terrell	TX	North Texas	1907
		Central Texas	1915-1916
		Texas Association	1925-1926
Texarkana	TX	Texas	1902
		North Texas	1905
		Arkansas-Texas	1906
		Arkansas State	1909
		South Central	1912
		Texas-Oklahoma	1913-1914
		East Texas	1924-1926, 1937-1940, 1946
		Lone Star	1927-1929
		Cotton States	1941
		Big State	1947-1953
Texas see Dallas-Ft. Worth	TX		
Texas City	TX	Gulf Coast	1951-1953
		Evangeline	1954
		Big State	1955-1956
		Lone Star	1977
Thetford Mines	QUE	Provincial	1953-1955
		Eastern	1974-1975
Thibodaux	LA	Evangeline	1946-1954, 1956-1957
Thomasville	GA	Empire State	1913
		Georgia State	1914
		FLAG	1915
		Georgia-Florida	1935-1941, 1946-1950, 1952-1958, 1962-1963
Thomasville see also High Point-Thomasville	NC	North Carolina State	1937-1942, 1945-1947
		Western Carolinas	1965-1966
Thomson	GA	Georgia State	1956
Thunder Bay see also Ft. William-Pt. Arthur	ONT	Northern	1993-
Tidewater see Norfolk	VA		
Tiffin	OH	Ohio State	1936-1941
Tifton	GA	Dixie	1917
		Georgia State	1949-1950
		Georgia-Florida	1951-1956
Tijuana	MEX	Sunset	1949-1950
		Southwest International	1951-1952
		Arizona-Mexico	1956
Toledo	OH	Northwestern	1883
		American Association	1884, 1890, 1902-1913, 1916-1955
		Western	1885, 1892, 1894-1895
		Tri-State	1888
		International	1889, 1965-
		Interstate	1896-1900
		Western Association	1901
		Southern Michigan Assn.	1914
Toluca	MEX	Mexican	1980, 1984
Topeka	KS	Western	1886-1887, 1893, 1909-1916, 1918, 1929-1931, 1933-1934, 1956-1958
		Missouri Valley	1904
		Western Association	1905-1908, 1924, 1927-1928, 1932, 1939, 1942, 1946-1954
		Southwestern	1922-1923, 1925-1926
		Three-I	1959-1961
Toronto	ONT	International	1886-1890, 1912-1967
		Eastern	1895-1911
		Canadian	1914
		American	1977-
Torreon	MEX	Mexican	1940-1943, 1946, 1949-1953

City	State	League	Years
see also Union Laguna		Mexican National	1946
		Mexican Center	1968
Torrington	CT	Colonial	1950
Traverse City	MI	West Michigan	1910
		Michigan State	1911-1914
Treasure Valley see Caldwell	ID		
Trenton	NJ	Interstate Association	1883
		Eastern	1884-1885, 1938, 1994-
		Tri-State	1907-1914
		New York-Pennsylvania	1936-1937
		Interstate	1939-1950
Trenton	TN	Kitty	1922-1923
Tri-Cities (Sheffield-Tuscumbia-Muscle Shoals) see also Sheffield; Sheffield-Tuscumbia	AL	Alabama-Tennessee	1921
Tri-Cities (Gadsden-Alabama City-Attalla) see also Gadsden	AL	Georgia-Alabama	1917
Tri-City/Cities (Kennewick-Pasco-Richland)	WA	Western International	1950-1954
		Northwest	1955-1974, 1983-1986
		Western	1995-
Trinidad	CO	Rocky Mountain	1912
Tri-State see Ashland	KY		
Trois Rivieres	QUE	Eastern Canada	1922-1923
		Quebec Provincial	1940
		Canadian-American	1941-1942, 1946-1950
		Provincial	1951-1955
		Eastern	1971-1977
Troy	AL	Alabama-Florida	1936-1939
		Alabama State	1940-1941, 1946-1949
Troy	NY	Eastern	1888, 1891-1894
		New York State	1899-1916
Tucson	AZ	Rio Grande Association	1915
		Arizona State	1928-1930
		Arizona-Texas	1931-1932, 1937-1941, 1947-1950, 1952-1954
		Southwest International	1951
		Arizona-Mexico	1955-1958
		Pacific Coast	1969-
Tulare	CA	San Joaquin Valley	1910-1911
Tulsa	OK	Missouri Valley	1905
		South Central	1906
		Oklahoma-Arkansas-Kansas	1907
		Oklahoma-Kansas	1908
		Western Association	1910-1911, 1914-1917
		Oklahoma State	1912
		Western	1919-1929, 1932
		Texas	1933-1942, 1946-1965, 1977-
		Pacific Coast	1966-1968
		American Association	1969-1976
Tupelo	MS	Tri-State	1925-1926
Tuscumbia see Sheffield-Tuscumbia; Tri-Cities	AL		
Tuskegee	AL	Alabama State	1941
Twin Falls (aka Magic Valley)	ID	Utah-Idaho	1926-1928
		Pioneer	1939-1942, 1946-1958, 1961-1966, 1968-1971
Tyler	TX	South Central	1912
		East Texas	1924-1926, 1931, 1936-1940, 1946, 1949-1950
		Lone Star	1927-1929, 1947-1948
		Texas	1932
		Dixie	1933
		West Dixie	1934-1935
		Big State	1951-1955
		Texas-Louisiana	1994-

U

City	State	League	Years
Union City	TN	Kitty	1935-1942, 1946-1955
Union Laguna (Gomez Palacio-Torreon) see also Torreon	MEX	Mexican	1970-1981, 1985-
Union Springs	AL	Alabama-Florida	1936-1938
Uniontown	PA	Penn-Ohio-Maryland	1906-1907
		Pennsylvania-West Virginia	1908-1909
		Middle Atlantic	1926, 1947-1949
Urbana see Champaign-Urbana	IL		
Uriangato	MEX	Mexican Center	1975
Utica	NY	New York State	1885, 1889, 1899-1917
		International	1886-1887
		Canadian-American	1939-1942

City	State	League	Years
		New York-Pennsylvania	1924, 1977-
		Eastern	1943-1950

V

City	State	League	Years
Valdosta	GA	Georgia State	1906, 1914
		Empire State	1913
		FLAG	1915
		Dixie	1916
		Georgia-Florida	1939-1942, 1946-1958
Vallejo	CA	Central California	1910-1911
		California State	1913
		Far West	1949
Valley (Valley-Lanett-West Point)	AL	Georgia-Alabama	1946-1951
Valley City	ND	Dakota	1922
		North Dakota	1923
Valleyfield	QUE	Eastern Canada	1922
Van Buren see Ft. Smith-Van Buren	AR		
Van Wert	OH	Ohio-Indiana	1908
Vancouver	BC	Northwestern	1905, 1907-1917
		Pacific Coast International	1918-1921
		Western International	1922, 1937-1942, 1946-1954
		Pacific Coast	1956-1962, 1965-1969, 1978-
Vancouver	WA	Oregon State	1904
		Pacific Coast International	1918
Vandergrift	PA	Middle Atlantic	1947-1950
Venice	CA	Pacific Coast	1913-1915
Ventura see also Santa Barbara-Ventura	CA	California	1947-1953, 1986
Veracruz	MEX	Mexican	1937-1939, 1941, 1949-1957, 1959-1974, 1979-1986, 1992-1995
Veracruz Azules	MEX	Mexican	1940-1951
Vermont see Burlington	VT		
Vernon	CA	Pacific Coast	1909-1912, 1915-1925
Vernon	TX	Longhorn	1947-1952
Vero Beach	FL	Florida State	1980-
Vicksburg	MS	Cotton States	1902-1908, 1910-1912, 1922-1931, 1937, 1941, 1955
		Southeastern	1946-1950
Victoria	BC	New Pacific	1896
		Northwestern	1905, 1911-1915
		Pacific Coast International	1919-1921
		Western International	1946-1954
		Northwest	1978-1980
Victoria	TX	Southwest Texas	1910-1911
		Gulf Coast	1926
		Big State	1956-1957
		Texas	1958-1961, 1974
		Gulf States	1976
		Lone Star	1977
Vidalia	GA	Georgia State	1952-1956
Vidalia-Lyons	GA	Georgia State	1948-1950
Villahermosa (aka Tabasco)	MEX	Mexican	1975, 1977-
Vincennes	IN	Kitty	1903-1906, 1910-1911, 1913
		Eastern Illinois	1908
		Mississippi-Ohio Valley	1950-1952
Vinita	OK	Missouri Valley	1905
		Kansas State	1906
Virginia	MN	Northern	1913-1916
Virginia see Newport News-Hampton	VA		
Visalia (aka Central Valley)	CA	San Joaquin Valley	1910-1911
		California	1946-1962, 1968-1975, 1977-

W

City	State	League	Years
Wabash	IN	Northern State of Indiana	1909-1911
Waco	TX	Texas	1889-1890, 1902-1903, 1905-1919, 1925-1930
		Texas Association	1923-1924
		Dixie	1933
		Big State	1947-1956
Wahpeton-Breckenridge	ND-MN	Dakota	1921-1922
Walla Walla	WA	Inland Empire	1908
		Western Tri-State	1912-1914
		Northwest	1969-1983
Walden	NY	North Atlantic	1946
Waltham	MA	Northeastern	1934
Warren	MN	Northern	1917

City	State	League	Years
Warren	PA	Interstate	1908, 1914-1916
		Pennsylvania State Assn.	1940-1941
Warsaw	NC	Tobacco State	1947-1948
Washington	DC	Union Association	1884
		American Association	1884, 1891
		Eastern	1885
		National	1886-1889, 1892-1899
		Atlantic Association	1890
		American	1901-1971
		United States	1912
Washington	NJ	Interstate	1932
Washington	PA	Interstate	1896
		Ohio-Pennsylvania	1905
		Penn-Ohio-Maryland	1906-1907
		Pennsylvania State Assn.	1934-1935, 1939-1942
Waterbury	CT	Eastern	1885-1886, 1918-1922, 1966-1971, 1973-1986
		Connecticut State	1899-1902, 1906-1912
		Eastern Association	1913-1914
		Colonial	1947-1950
		Northeast	1997-
Waterloo	IA	Iowa State	1904-1907
		Central Association	1908-1909, 1913-1917
		Three-I	1910-1911, 1938-1942, 1946-1956
		Mississippi Valley	1922-1932
		Western	1936-1937
		Midwest	1958-1993
Watertown	MA	Northeastern	1934
Watertown	NY	Canadian-American	1936
		Border	1946-1951
		New York-Pennsylvania	1983-
Watertown	SD	Dakota	1921-1922
		South Dakota	1923
		Northern	1970-1971
Watsonville	CA	California	1899
		California State	1913
Wausau	WI	Wisconsin State	1905-1907, 1946-1953
		Wisconsin-Illinois	1908, 1912-1914
		Minnesota-Wisconsin	1909-1911
		Northern	1936-1942, 1956-1957
		Midwest	1975-1990
Waverly	NY	New York State	1901
Waxahachie	TX	Central Texas	1914-1916
Waycross	GA	Georgia State	1906, 1914
		Empire State	1913
		FLAG	1915
		Southeastern	1927
		Georgia-Florida	1939-1942, 1946-1958, 1963
Wayland	MA	Northeastern	1934
Wayne (aka West Virginia)	WV	Frontier	1993
Waynesboro	PA	Blue Ridge	1920-1930
Waynesburg	PA	Penn-Ohio-Maryland	1906
Webb City see also Joplin-Webb City	MO	Missouri Valley	1903, 1905
		Western Association	1906-1909
Welch	WV	Mountain State	1937-1942
		Appalachian	1946-1955
Welland	ONT	New York-Pennsylvania	1989-1994
		North Atlantic	1995-
Wellington	KS	Kansas State	1909-1911
Wellsville	NY	Interstate	1914-1916
		PONY	1942-1956
		New York-Pennsylvania	1957-1961, 1963-1965
Wenatchee	WA	Western International	1937-1941, 1946-1954
		Northwest	1955-1965
Wessington Springs	SD	South Dakota	1920
West	TX	Central Texas	1914
West Frankfort	IL	Illinois State	1947-1948
		Mississippi-Ohio Valley	1949-1950
West Haven	CT	Eastern	1972-1982
West Michigan see Grand Rapids	MI		
West Palm Beach	FL	Florida State	1928, 1955-1956, 1965-
		Florida East Coast	1940-1942
		Florida International	1946-1954
West Plains	MO	Northeast Arkansas	1936
West Point see Valley	GA		
West Virginia see Wayne	WV		
West Warwick (aka Rhode Island)	RI	Northeast	1996
Westernport see Piedmont-Westernport	MD		
Wewoka	OK	Oklahoma State	1924

City	State	League	Years
Wheeling	WV	Ohio State	1887
		Tri-State	1888-1890
		Interstate	1896-1897, 1899-1900, 1913
		Western Association	1901
		Central	1903-1912, 1915-1916
		Middle Atlantic	1925-1931, 1933-1934
Whiteville	NC	Tobacco State	1950
Wichita	KS	Western	1887, 1909-1933, 1950-1955
		Western Association	1905-1908
		American Association	1956-1958, 1970-1984
		Texas	1987-
Wichita Falls	TX	Texas-Oklahoma	1911-1913
		Texas	1920-1932
		West Texas-New Mexico	1941-1942
		Big State	1947-1953, 1956-1957
		Longhorn	1954
Wilkes-Barre see also Scranton-Wilkes-Barre	PA	International	1887
		Central	1888
		Atlantic Association	1889
		Pennsylvania State	1892
		Eastern	1893-1898, 1938-1951, 1953-1955
		Atlantic	1899-1900
		New York State	1905-1917
		New York-Pennsylvania	1923-1937
Will County see Romeoville	IL		
Williamson	WV	Mountain States	1912, 1937-1942
Williamsport	PA	Tri-State	1904-1910
		New York-Pennsylvania	1923-1937, 1968-1972, 1994-
		Eastern	1938-1942, 1944-1956, 1958-1962, 1964-1967, 1976, 1987-1991
Williamston	NC	Coastal Plain	1937-1941
Willimantic	CT	Connecticut Association	1910
Willows	CA	Far West	1948-1950
Wilmington	DE	Interstate Association	1883
		Union Association	1884
		Eastern	1884-1885
		Atlantic Association	1890
		Atlantic	1896
		Tri-State	1904-1905, 1907-1908, 1911-1914
		Interstate	1940-1952
		Carolina	1993-
Wilmington	NC	Virginia-North Carolina	1901
		North Carolina	1902
		Eastern Carolina	1908-1910, 1928-1929
		Piedmont	1932-1935
		Tobacco State	1946-1950
(aka Port City)		Southern	1995-1996
Wilson	NC	Eastern Carolina	1908-1910
		Virginia	1920-1927
		Coastal Plain	1939-1941, 1946-1952
		Bi-State	1942
		Carolina	1956-1968, 1973
Wilson	OK	Oklahoma State	1922
Winchester	KY	Blue Grass	1908-1912, 1922-1924
Winchester (aka Tennessee)	TN	Big South	1996
		Heartland	1997-
Windsor	ONT	Border	1912-1913
Winfield see Arkansas City-Winfield	KS		
Wink	TX	West Texas-New Mexico	1937-1938
Winnipeg	MB	Northern	1902-1905, 1908, 1913-1917, 1933-1942, 1954-1964, 1969, 1994-
		Northern-Copper Country	1906-1907
		Western Canada	1909-1911, 1919-1921
		Central International	1912
		International	1970-1971
Winona	MN	Northwestern	1884
		Minnesota-Wisconsin	1909-1912
		Northern	1913-1914
		Three-I	1958
Winston-Salem	NC	Virginia-North Carolina	1905
		Carolina Association	1908-1912
		North Carolina State	1913-1917
		Piedmont	1920-1933, 1937-1942
(aka Winston)		Carolina	1945-
Winter Haven see also Bartow-Winter Haven	FL	Florida State	1966-1967, 1969-1992
Winters-Ballinger see also Ballinger	TX	Longhorn	1953
Wisconsin see Appleton	WI		
Wisconsin Rapids	WI	Wisconsin State	1940-1942, 1946-1953
		Midwest	1963-1983
Woodbridge (aka Prince William)	VA	Carolina	1984-
Woodstock	ONT	Canadian	1899, 1905
Woonsocket	RI	New England	1891-1892, 1933
		Atlantic Association	1908
		Colonial	1914
Wooster	OH	Ohio-Pennsylvania	1905
Worcester	MA	New England	1888, 1891, 1894, 1898, 1906-1915, 1933
		Atlantic Association	1889-1890
		Eastern	1899-1903, 1916-1926
		Connecticut State	1904
		Northeastern	1934
Worthington	MN	Western (Class D)	1939-1940
Wyandotte	MI	Border	1912-1913
Wytheville	VA	Blue Ridge	1948-1950
		Appalachian	1953-1955, 1957-1965, 1967, 1969, 1971-1973, 1985-1989

Y

City	State	League	Years
Yakima	WA	Pacific Coast International	1920-1921
		Western International	1937-1941, 1946-1954
		Northwest	1955-1966, 1990-
Yazoo City	MS	Delta	1904
		Cotton States	1910-1912
Yonkers	NY	Hudson River	1905, 1907
		Northeast	1995
York	NE	Nebraska State	1911-1915, 1928-1931
York	PA	Eastern	1884, 1958-1959, 1962-1969
		Keystone Association	1884
		Pennsylvania State	1893
		Tri-State	1904-1907, 1909-1914
		New York-Pennsylvania	1923-1933, 1936
		Interstate	1940, 1943-1952
		Piedmont	1953-1955
Youngstown	OH	Iron & Oil Association	1884
		Tri-State	1890
		Interstate	1896-1900, 1913
		Ohio-Pennsylvania	1905-1911
		Central	1912, 1915, 1932
		Middle Atlantic	1931, 1939-1941, 1946-1951
Ypsilanti	MI	Border	1913
Yucatan	MEX	Mexican	1954-1958, 1970-1974, 1979-
		Mexican Southeast	1964-1969
Yuma	AZ	Sunset	1950
		Southwest International	1951-1952
		Arizona-Mexico	1955-1956
		Golden State	1995

Z

City	State	League	Years
Zacatecas	MEX	Mexican Center	1965-1973, 1976-1978
Zanesville	OH	Ohio State	1887
		Tri-State	1888
		Ohio-Pennsylvania	1905-1906
		Penn-Ohio-Maryland	1907
		Central	1908-1912
		Interstate	1913
		Middle Atlantic	1933-1937, 1941-1942
		Ohio State	1944-1947
		Ohio-Indiana	1948-1950
		Frontier	1993-1996
Zebulon (aka Carolina)	NC	Southern	1991-

PROFESSIONAL TEAMS BY STATE

ALABAMA

City	League	Years
Abbeville	Alabama-Florida	1936
Alabama City see Tri-Cities		
Albany-Decatur	Alabama-Tennessee	1921
Alexander City	Georgia-Alabama	1947-1951
Andalusia	Alabama-Florida	1936-1939, 1953, 1962
	Alabama State	1940-1941, 1947-1950
Andalusia-Opp	Alabama-Florida	1954
Anniston	Southeastern	1911-1912, 1938-1942, 1946-1950
	Georgia-Alabama	1913-1917, 1928-1930
Attalla see Tri-Cities		
Bessemer	Southeastern	1912
Birmingham	Southern	1885, 1887-1888, 1892-1893, 1896
	Southern Association	1901-1961
	Southern	1964-1965, 1967-1975, 1981-
Brewton	Alabama State	1940-1941, 1946-1950
Decatur	Southeastern	1911
see also Albany-Decatur		
Dothan	FLAG	1915
	Dixie	1916-1917
	Alabama-Florida	1936-1939, 1951-1956, 1958-1962
	Alabama State	1940-1941, 1946-1950
	Georgia-Florida	1942
Enterprise	Alabama-Florida	1936, 1951-1952
	Alabama State	1947-1950
Eufaula	Dixie	1916-1917
	Alabama-Florida	1952-1953
Evergreen	Alabama-Florida	1937-1938
Gadsden	Southeastern	1910-1912, 1938-1941, 1946-1950
	Georgia-Alabama	1913-1914, 1928-1929
see also Tri-Cities		
Geneva	Alabama State	1946-1950
Greenville	Alabama-Florida	1939
	Alabama State	1940-1941, 1946-1950
Headland	Alabama State	1950
	Alabama-Florida	1951-1952
Huntsville	Southeastern	1911-1912
	Georgia-Alabama	1930
	Southern	1985-
Lanett see Valley		
Mobile	Southern	1887, 1892-1896, 1966, 1970, 1997-
	Cotton States	1905-1907
	Southern Association	1908-1931, 1944-1961
	Southeastern	1932, 1937-1942
	Texas-Louisiana	1994-1995
Montgomery	Southern	1892-1893, 1895-1896
	Southern Association	1903-1914, 1943, 1956
	South Atlantic	1916, 1951-1956
	Southeastern	1926-1930, 1932, 1937-1942, 1946-1950
	Alabama-Florida	1957-1962
	Southern	1965-1980
Opelika	Georgia-Alabama	1913-1914, 1946-1951
Opp see Andalusia-Opp		
Ozark	Alabama-Florida	1936-1937, 1951-1952, 1962
	Alabama State	1946-1950
Russellville	Alabama-Tennessee	1921
Selma	Southern Association	1901
	Southeastern	1911-1912, 1927-1930, 1932, 1937-1941, 1946-1950
	Cotton States	1913
	Georgia-Alabama	1914
	Alabama-Florida	1957-1962
Sheffield-Tuscumbia	Tri-State	1926
see also Tri-Cities		
Talladega	Southeastern	1912
	Georgia-Alabama	1913-1917, 1928-1930
Tallassee	Alabama-Florida	1939
	Alabama State	1940-1941
	Georgia-Alabama	1946-1949
Tri-Cities (Sheffield-Tuscumbia-Muscle Shoals) see also Sheffield; Sheffield-Tuscumbia	Alabama-Tennessee	1921
Tri-Cities (Gadsden-Alabama City-Attalla)	Georgia-Alabama	1917
Troy	Alabama-Florida	1936-1939
	Alabama State	1940-1941, 1946-1949
Tuskegee	Alabama State	1941
Union Springs	Alabama-Florida	1936-1938
Valley (Valley-Lanett-West Point)	Georgia-Alabama	1946-1951

ARIZONA

City	League	Years
Bisbee	Arizona State	1928-1930
	Arizona-Texas	1931-1932, 1937-1941
Bisbee-Douglas	Arizona-Texas	1947-1950, 1952-1954
	Southwest International	1951
	Arizona-Mexico	1955
Douglas	Rio Grande Association	1915
	Arizona-Mexico	1956-1958
see also Bisbee-Douglas		
Globe	Arizona State	1929-1930
	Arizona-Texas	1931
see also Miami-Globe		
Mesa	Arizona State	1929
	Arizona-Texas	1947
Miami	Arizona State	1928-1930
Miami-Globe	Arizona-Texas	1947-1950
	Arizona-Mexico	1955
see also Globe		
Phoenix	Rio Grande Association	1915
	Arizona State	1928-1930
	Arizona-Texas	1931-1932, 1947-1950, 1952-1954
	Southwest International	1951
	Arizona-Mexico	1955-1957
	Pacific Coast	1958-1959, 1966-
Southern Nomadic see Yuma		
Tucson	Rio Grande Association	1915
	Arizona State	1928-1930
	Arizona-Texas	1931-1932, 1937-1941, 1947-1950, 1952-1954
	Southwest International	1951
	Arizona-Mexico	1955-1958
	Pacific Coast	1969-
Yuma	Sunset	1950
	Southwest International	1951-1952
	Arizona-Mexico	1955-1956
	Golden State	1995

ARKANSAS

City	League	Years
Argenta	Arkansas State	1908-1909
Arkansas see Little Rock		
Batesville	Northeast Arkansas	1936, 1938, 1940-1941
see also Newport-Batesville		
Bentonville	Arkansas State	1934-1935
	Arkansas-Missouri	1936
Blytheville	Northeast Arkansas	1910-1911, 1937-1938
	Tri-State	1925-1926
Brinkley	Arkansas State	1908
Camden	Arkansas-Texas	1906
El Dorado	Cotton States	1929-1932, 1936-1941, 1947-1955
	Dixie	1933
	East Dixie	1934-1935
Fayetteville	Arkansas State	1934-1935
	Arkansas-Missouri	1936-1940
Ft. Smith	Missouri Valley	1905
	South Central	1906
	Oklahoma-Arkansas-Kansas	1907
	Arkansas State	1909
	Western Association	1911, 1914-1917, 1920-1932, 1938-1942, 1946-1949, 1951-1952
Ft. Smith-Van Buren	Western Association	1953
Helena	Arkansas State	1908-1909
	Northeast Arkansas	1911
	East Dixie	1935
	Cotton States	1936-1941, 1947-1949
Hope	North Texas	1905
Hot Springs	Arkansas-Texas	1906
	Arkansas State	1908-1909
	Cotton States	1938-1941, 1947-1955
Huntsville	Arkansas State	1935
Jonesboro	Arkansas State	1909
	Northeast Arkansas	1909-1911, 1936-1941
	Tri-State	1925-1926
Little Rock	Southern	1895
	Southern Association	1901-1910, 1915-1958, 1960-1961
	International	1963
	Pacific Coast	1964-1965
(aka Arkansas)	Texas	1966-
Marianna	Northeast Arkansas	1909
Newport	Arkansas State	1908
	Northeast Arkansas	1909, 1936-1941
Newport-Batesville	Arkansas State	1909

67

see also Batesville

City	League	Years
Osceola	Northeast Arkansas	1936-1937
Paragould	Northeast Arkansas	1909-1911, 1936-1941
Pine Bluff	Cotton States	1903-1905, 1930-1932, 1936-1940, 1948-1955
	Arkansas-Texas	1906
	Arkansas State	1908
	Dixie	1933
	East Dixie	1934-1935
	Big South	1996-
Poplar Bluff	Arkansas State	1908
Rogers	Arkansas State	1934-1935
	Arkansas-Missouri	1936-1938
Siloam Springs	Arkansas State	1934-1935
	Arkansas-Missouri	1936-1938, 1940
Van Buren see Ft. Smith-Van Buren		

CALIFORNIA

City	League	Years
Adelanto (aka High Desert)	California	1991-
Alameda	California	1907-1908
	Central California	1910-1911
	California State	1915
Anaheim	California	1941
	Sunset	1947-1948
	American	1966-
Antelope Valley see Brawley		
Bakersfield	San Joaquin Valley	1910
	California State	1929
	California	1941-1942, 1946-1975, 1978-1979, 1982-
Berkeley	Central California	1910-1911
	California State	1915
Brawley (aka Antelope Valley)	Golden State	1995
Channel Cities see Santa Barbara-Ventura; see also Santa Barbara; Ventura		
Chico	Golden State	1995
	Western	1997-
Coalinga	San Joaquin Valley	1910-1911
Coronado	California State	1929
El Centro	Sunset	1947-1950
	Southwest International	1951-1952
Elmhurst see Oakland-Elmhurst		
Fresno	Pacific Coast	1906
	California	1908-1909, 1941-1942, 1946-1988
	California State	1910, 1913-1914
Fruitvale see Oakland-Fruitvale		
Hanford	San Joaquin Valley	1911
Hayward	Central California	1910-1911
Healdsburg	Central California	1910
High Desert see Adelanto		
Hollywood	Pacific Coast	1926-1935, 1938-1957
Imperial Valley see Rosamond		
Lake Elsinore	California	1994-
Lancaster	California	1996-
Lemoore	San Joaquin Valley	1911
Lodi	California	1966-1984
Long Beach	Southern California Trolley	1910
	Southern California	1913
	Western	1995-
Los Angeles	California	1893, 1901-1902
	Pacific National	1903
	Pacific Coast	1903-1957
	National	1958-
	American	1961-1965
Los Angeles-Maiers	Southern California Trolley	1910
Los Angeles-McCormicks	Southern California Trolley	1910
Marysville	Far West	1948-1950
Merced	California State	1910
	California	1941
Mission (San Francisco)	Pacific Coast	1914, 1926-1937
Mission Viejo	Western	1997-
Modesto	California State	1914-1915
	California	1946-1964, 1966-
Napa	Central California	1910
Oakland	California	1887-1889, 1891, 1893, 1899-1902, 1907-1909
	Pacific Coast	1903-1955

City	League	Years
	Central California	1910-1911
	California State	1910, 1915
	American	1968-
Oakland-Elmhurst	Central California	1910-1911
Oakland-Fruitvale	Central California	1910-1911
Ontario	Sunset	1947
Orange County	California State	1929
Oroville	Far West	1948
Palm Springs	California	1986-1993
	Western	1995-
Palmdale	Golden State	1995
Pasadena	Southern California Trolley	1910
	Southern California	1913
Petaluma	Central California	1910
Pittsburg	Far West	1948-1951
Pomona	California State	1929
Porterville	San Joaquin Valley	1911
	Sunset	1949-1950
	Southwest International	1952
see also Riverside-Porterville		
Rancho Cucamonga	California	1993-
Redding	Far West	1948-1951
Redondo Beach	Southern California Trolley	1910
Richmond	Central California	1910-1911
Riverside	California	1941, 1988-1990
	Sunset	1947-1950
Riverside-Ensenada see also Ensenada	Southwest International	1952
Riverside-Porterville see also Porterville	Southwest International	1952
Rohnert Park (aka Redwood) (aka Sonoma County)	Western	1995-
	California	1980-1985
Rosamond (aka Imperial Valley)	Golden State	1995
Roseville	Far West	1948
Sacramento	California	1887, 1889, 1891, 1893, 1899-1902, 1907-1909
	Pacific Coast	1903, 1909-1914, 1918-1960, 1974-1976
	California State	1910
St. Helena	Central California	1910
Salinas	Sunset	1949
	California	1954-1958, 1963-1965, 1973-1980, 1982-1987, 1989-1992
	Western	1995-
San Bernardino	Southern California	1913
	California State	1929
	California	1941, 1987-
	Sunset	1948-1950
San Diego	Southern California	1913
	California State	1929
	Pacific Coast	1936-1968
	National	1969-
San Francisco	California	1889, 1891, 1893, 1899-1902, 1907-1909
	Pacific National	1903
	Pacific Coast	1903-1957
	California State	1910, 1915
	National	1958-
see also Mission		
San Francisco Haverly	California	1887-1888
San Francisco Pioneers	California	1887-1888
San Jose	California	1891, 1899, 1907-1909, 1942, 1947-1958, 1962-1976, 1979-
	California State	1910, 1913-1915
	Pacific Coast	1977-1978
San Leandro	Central California	1910-1911
San Rafael	Central California	1910
Santa Ana	Southern California Trolley	1910
Santa Barbara	Southern California	1913
	California	1941-1942, 1946-1953, 1962-1967
Santa Barbara-Ventura (aka Channel Cities)	California	1954-1955
Santa Clara	California	1979
Santa Cruz	California	1899, 1908-1909
Santa Rosa	Central California	1910
	Far West	1948-1949
Stockton	California	1888-1889, 1893, 1900, 1907-1909, 1941, 1946-1972, 1978-
	California State	1910, 1913-1915
Tulare	San Joaquin Valley	1910-1911
Vallejo	Central California	1910-1911
	California State	1913
	Far West	1949
Venice	Pacific Coast	1913-1915
Ventura	California	1947-1953, 1986
see also Santa Barbara-Ventura		

City	League	Years
Vernon	Pacific Coast	1909-1912, 1915-1925
Visalia	San Joaquin Valley	1910-1911
(aka Central Valley)	California	1946-1962, 1968-1975, 1977-
Watsonville	California	1899
	California State	1913
Willows	Far West	1948-1950

COLORADO

City	League	Years
Canon City	Rocky Mountain	1912
Colorado see Denver		
Colorado Springs	Western	1901-1905, 1916, 1950-1958
	Rocky Mountain	1912
	Pacific Coast	1988-
Denver	Western	1886-1891, 1900-1917, 1922-1932, 1947-1954
	Western Association	1895
	Western (Class D)	1941
	American Association	1955-1962, 1969-1992
	Pacific Coast	1963-1968
(aka Colorado)	National	1993-
La Junta	Rocky Mountain	1912
Leadville	Western	1886
Pueblo	Western	1900, 1905-1909, 1911, 1928-1932, 1947-1958
	Rocky Mountain	1912
	Western (Class D)	1941
	Texas-Louisiana	1995
Trinidad	Rocky Mountain	1912

CONNECTICUT

City	League	Years
Bridgeport	Eastern	1885-1886, 1916-1932
	Connecticut State	1899-1912
	Eastern Association	1913-1914
	Interstate	1941
	Colonial	1947-1950
Bristol	Connecticut State	1899-1901
	Colonial	1949-1950
	Eastern	1973-1982
Danbury	New York-New Jersey	1913
	Atlantic	1914
Derby	Connecticut State	1899-1901
Hartford	Eastern	1886
	Atlantic Association	1889-1890
	Atlantic	1896-1898
	Eastern	1899-1901, 1916-1932, 1938-1952
	Connecticut State	1902-1912
	Eastern Association	1913-1914
	Colonial	1915
	Northeastern	1934
Meriden	Eastern	1886
	Connecticut State	1899-1905, 1908
	Connecticut Association	1910
	Eastern Association	1913
Middletown	Connecticut Association	1910
New Britain	Connecticut State	1908-1912
	Eastern Association	1914
(aka Hardware City)	Eastern	1984-
New Haven	Atlantic Association	1889-1890
	Eastern	1891-1892, 1916-1932, 1994-
	Atlantic	1896
	Connecticut State	1899-1912
	Eastern Association	1913-1914
	Colonial	1915
New London	Connecticut State	1899-1907
	Connecticut Association	1910
	Eastern Association	1913-1914
	Eastern	1916-1918
	Colonial	1947
Norwalk	Atlantic Association	1889
Norwich	Connecticut State	1899-1907
	Connecticut Association	1910
	Eastern	1995-
Stamford	Colonial	1947-1949
Torrington	Colonial	1950
Waterbury	Eastern	1885-1886, 1918-1922, 1966-1971, 1973-1986
	Connecticut State	1899-1902, 1906-1912
	Eastern Association	1913-1914
	Colonial	1947-1950

City	League	Years
	Northeast	1997-
West Haven	Eastern	1972-1982
Willimantic	Connecticut Association	1910

DELAWARE

City	League	Years
Dover	Eastern Shore	1923-1926, 1937-1941, 1946-1948
Laurel	Eastern Shore	1922-1923
Milford	Eastern Shore	1923, 1938-1941, 1946-1948
Rehoboth Beach	Eastern Shore	1947-1949
Seaford	Eastern Shore	1946-1949
Wilmington	Interstate Association	1883
	Eastern	1884-1885
	Atlantic Association	1890
	Atlantic	1896
	Tri-State	1904-1905, 1907-1908, 1911-1914
	Interstate	1940-1952
	Carolina	1993-

DISTRICT OF COLUMBIA

City	League	Years
Washington	Union Association	1884
	American Association	1884, 1891
	Eastern	1885
	National	1886-1889, 1892-1899
	Atlantic Association	1890
	American	1901-1971
	United States	1912

FLORIDA

City	League	Years
Bartow	Florida State	1920
Bartow-Winter Haven	Florida State	1919
Baseball City	Florida State	1988-1992
Bradenton (formerly Bradentown)	Florida State	1919-1920, 1923-1924, 1926
Brevard County see Melbourne		
Charlotte see Port Charlotte		
Clearwater	Florida State	1924, 1985-
Cocoa	Florida East Coast	1941-1942
	Florida State	1951-1958, 1965-1972, 1977
Crestview	Alabama-Florida	1954-1956
Daytona Beach	Florida State	1920-1924, 1928, 1936-1941, 1946-1973, 1977-1987, 1993-
De Land	Florida State	1936-1941, 1946-1954, 1970
	Florida East Coast	1942
Deerfield Beach	Florida State	1966
Dunedin	Florida State	1978-1979, 1987-
Florida see Miami		
Ft. Lauderdale	Florida State	1928, 1962-1993
	Florida East Coast	1940-1942
	Florida International	1947-1953
Ft. Myers	Florida State	1926, 1978-1987, 1992-
Ft. Pierce	Florida East Coast	1940-1942
Ft. Walton Beach	Alabama-Florida	1953-1962
Gainesville	FLAG	1915
	Florida State	1936-1941, 1946-1952, 1955-1958
Graceville	Alabama-Florida	1952-1958
Hollywood	Florida East Coast	1940
Jacksonville	South Atlantic	1904-1917, 1936-1942, 1946-1961
	Florida State	1921-1922
	Southeastern	1926-1930
	International	1962-1968
	Southern	1970-
Jacksonville Beach	Florida State	1952-1954
Key West	Florida International	1952
	Florida State	1969, 1971-1975
Kissimmee (aka Osceola)	Florida State	1985-
Lakeland	Florida State	1919-1926, 1953-1955, 1960, 1962-1964, 1967-
	Florida International	1946-1952
Leesburg	Florida State	1937-1941, 1946-1953, 1956-1957, 1960-1961, 1965-1968
Melbourne (aka Brevard County)	Florida State	1994-
Miami	Florida State	1927-1928, 1962-1991

City	League	Years
	Florida East Coast	1940-1942
	Florida International	1946-1954
	International	1956-1960
	Inter-American	1979
(aka Florida)	National	1993-
Miami Beach	Florida East Coast	1940-1942
	Florida International	1946-1952, 1954
Ocala	Florida State	1940-1941
Orlando	Florida State	1919-1924, 1926-1928, 1937-1941, 1946-1961, 1963-1972
	Florida East Coast	1942
	Southern	1973-
Osceola see Kissimmee		
Palatka	Florida State	1936-1939, 1946-1953, 1956-1962
Panama City	Georgia-Florida	1935
	Alabama-Florida	1936-1939, 1951-1961
Pensacola	Southern	1893
	Cotton States	1913
	Southeastern	1927-1930, 1934-1942, 1946-1950
	Alabama-Florida	1957-1962
Pompano Beach	Florida State	1969-1973, 1976-1978
Port Charlotte	Florida State	1987-
St. Augustine	Southeastern	1926-1927
	Florida State	1936-1941, 1946-1950, 1952
St. Lucie	Florida State	1988-
St. Petersburg	Florida State	1920-1928, 1955-
	Florida International	1947-1954
Sanford	Florida State	1919-1920, 1925-1928, 1936-1941, 1946-1953, 1955, 1959-1960
Sarasota	Florida State	1926-1927, 1961-1965, 1989-
Tallahassee	Georgia-Florida	1935-1942, 1946-1950
	Alabama-Florida	1951
	Florida International	1954
Tampa	Florida State	1919-1927, 1957-1988, 1994-
	Southeastern	1928-1930
	Florida International	1946-1954
Vero Beach	Florida State	1980-
West Palm Beach	Florida State	1928, 1955-1956, 1965-
	Florida East Coast	1940-1942
	Florida International	1946-1954
Winter Haven	Florida State	1966-1967, 1969-1992
see also Bartow-Winter Haven		

GEORGIA

City	League	Years
Albany	Georgia State	1906
	South Atlantic	1911-1916, 1992-1995
	Southeastern	1926-1928
	Georgia-Florida	1935-1942, 1946-1958
Americus	Georgia State	1906, 1914
	Empire State	1913
	FLAG	1915
	Georgia-Florida	1935-1942, 1946-1951
see also Cordele-Americus		
Atlanta	Southern	1885-1886, 1892-1896
	Southern Association	1902-1961
	International	1962-1965
	National	1966-
Augusta	Southern	1885-1886, 1893
	South Atlantic	1904-1911, 1914-1917, 1919-1930, 1936-1942, 1946-1963, 1988-
	Palmetto	1931
Bainbridge	Dixie	1916-1917
Baxley	Georgia State	1948
Baxley-Hazlehurst	Georgia State	1949-1950
see also Hazlehurst-Baxley		
Brunswick	Empire State	1913
	Georgia State	1906, 1914
	FLAG	1915
	Georgia-Florida	1951-1958, 1962-1963
Carrollton	Georgia State	1920-1921
	Georgia-Alabama	1928-1930, 1946-1950
Cedartown	Georgia State	1920-1921
	Georgia-Alabama	1928-1930
Columbus	Southern	1885, 1896
	Georgia State	1906
	South Atlantic	1909-1917, 1936-1942, 1946-1957, 1959, 1991-
	Southeastern	1926-1930, 1932
	Alabama-Florida	1958
	Southern	1964-1966, 1969-1990
Cordele	Georgia State	1906, 1914
	Empire State	1913
	Georgia-Florida	1936-1942, 1946-1953, 1955
Cordele-Americus	Georgia-Florida	1954

see also Americus

City	League	Years
Donalsonville	Alabama-Florida	1955-1956
Douglas	Georgia State	1948-1956
Dublin	Georgia State	1949-1956
	Georgia-Florida	1958, 1962
Eastman	Georgia State	1948-1953
Fitzgerald	Georgia State	1948-1952
	Georgia-Florida	1953-1954, 1956-1957
Griffin	Georgia-Alabama	1915-1917, 1947-1951
	Georgia State	1920-1921
Hazlehurst-Baxley	Georgia State	1951-1956
see also Baxley-Hazlehurst		
Jesup	Georgia State	1950-1953
La Grange	Georgia-Alabama	1913-1917, 1946-1951
	Georgia State	1920-1921
	Big South	1997-
Lindale	Georgia State	1920-1921
	Georgia-Alabama	1928-1930
Lyons see Vidalia-Lyons		
Macon	Southern	1885-1886, 1892-1894
	South Atlantic	1904-1917, 1923-1930, 1936-1942, 1946-1960, 1962-1963, 1980-1987, 1991-
	Southeastern	1932
	Southern Association	1961
	Southern	1964, 1966-1967
Moultrie	Dixie	1916-1917
	Georgia-Florida	1935-1942, 1946-1952, 1956-1957, 1962-1963
Newnan	Georgia-Alabama	1913-1916, 1946-1950
Quitman	Dixie	1916-1917
Rome	Southeastern	1910-1912
	Appalachian	1913
	Georgia-Alabama	1914-1917, 1950-1951
	Georgia State	1920-1921
Sandersville	Georgia State	1953-1956
Savannah	Southern	1886-1887, 1893-1894, 1968-1983
	South Atlantic	1904-1915, 1936-1942, 1946-1960, 1962, 1984-
	Southeastern	1926-1928
Sparta	Georgia State	1948-1949
Statesboro	Georgia State	1952-1955
Thomasville	Empire State	1913
	Georgia State	1914
	FLAG	1915
	Georgia-Florida	1935-1941, 1946-1950, 1952-1958, 1962-1963
Thomson	Georgia State	1956
Tifton	Dixie	1917
	Georgia State	1949-1950
	Georgia-Florida	1951-1956
Valdosta	Georgia State	1906, 1914
	Empire State	1913
	FLAG	1915
	Dixie	1916
	Georgia-Florida	1939-1942, 1946-1958
Vidalia	Georgia State	1952-1956
Vidalia-Lyons	Georgia State	1948-1950
Waycross	Georgia State	1906, 1914
	Empire State	1913
	FLAG	1915
	Southeastern	1927
	Georgia-Florida	1939-1942, 1946-1958, 1963
West Point see Valley, AL		

HAWAII

City	League	Years
Honolulu (aka Hawaii)	Pacific Coast	1961-1987

IDAHO

City	League	Years
Boise	Pacific National	1904
	Inter-Mountain	1909
	Union Association	1911, 1914
	Western Tri-State	1912-1913
	Utah-Idaho	1928
	Pioneer	1939-1942, 1946-1963
	Northwest	1975-1976, 1978, 1987-
Caldwell (aka Treasure Valley)	Pioneer	1964-1971
Gate City see Pocatello		
Idaho Falls	Utah-Idaho	1926-1928

City	League	Years
	Pioneer	1940-1942, 1946-
Lewiston	Western International	1937, 1952-1954
	Pioneer	1939
	Northwest	1955-1974
Magic Valley see Twin Falls		
Pocatello (aka Gate City)	Utah-Idaho	1926-1928
	Pioneer	1939-1942, 1946-1965, 1984-1985, 1987-1991, 1993
Treasure Valley see Caldwell		
Twin Falls (aka Magic Valley)	Utah-Idaho	1926-1928
	Pioneer	1939-1942, 1946-1958, 1961-1966, 1968-1971

ILLINOIS

City	League	Years
Alton	Three-I	1917
Aurora	Two-I	1892
	Wisconsin-Illinois	1910-1912
	Bi-State	1915
Beardstown	Illinois-Missouri	1909-1910
Belleville	Illinois State	1947-1948
	Mississippi-Ohio Valley	1949
Cairo	Kitty	1903-1906, 1911-1914, 1922-1924, 1946-1950
Canton	Illinois-Missouri	1908-1913
	Mississippi-Ohio Valley	1952
Centralia	Eastern Illinois	1907
	Illinois State	1947-1948
	Mississippi-Ohio Valley	1949-1952
Champaign	Illinois-Missouri	1912-1914
Champaign-Urbana	Illinois-Missouri	1911
	Great Central	1994
Charleston see also Mattoon-Charleston	Eastern Illinois	1907-1908
Chicago	National	1883-
	Union Association	1884
	Western Association	1888
	Player's	1890
	American	1900-
	United States	1912
	Federal	1913-1915
Clinton	Illinois-Missouri	1910-1912
Danville	Central Interstate	1888
	Central	1900
	Kitty	1906
	Eastern Illinois	1908
	Three-I	1910-1914, 1922-1932, 1946-1950
	Mississippi-Ohio Valley	1951-1954
	Midwest	1970-1976, 1982
Decatur	Central Interstate	1888
	Central	1900
	Three-I	1901-1909, 1911-1915, 1922-1932, 1935, 1937-1942, 1946-1950
	Northern Association	1910
	Mississippi-Ohio Valley	1952-1955
	Midwest	1956-1974
Eldorado	Southern Illinois	1910
Elgin	Northern Association	1910
	Bi-State	1915
Freeport	Wisconsin State	1905-1907
	Wisconsin-Illinois	1908-1909
	Northern Association	1910
	Bi-State	1915
	Three-I	1915
Galesburg	Illinois-Missouri	1908-1909
	Central Association	1910-1912, 1914
Geneva (aka Kane County)	Midwest	1991-
Harrisburg	Southern Illinois	1910
	Kitty	1910-1911, 1913
Havana	Illinois-Missouri	1908
Herrin	Southern Illinois	1910
Jacksonville	Two-I	1892
	Western Association	1894-1895
	Central	1900
	Kitty	1906
	Iowa State	1907
	Central Association	1908-1909
	Northern Association	1910
	Illinois-Missouri	1910
Joliet	Two-I	1892
	Three-I	1903
	Northern Association	1910
Kane County see Geneva		

City	League	Years
Kankakee	Northern Association	1910
	Illinois-Missouri	1912-1914
Kewanee	Central Association	1908-1913, 1948-1949
La Salle	Illinois-Missouri	1914
Lincoln	Illinois-Missouri	1910-1914
Macomb	Illinois-Missouri	1908-1910
Marion	Illinois State	1947-1948
Mattoon	Eastern Illinois	1907-1908
	Illinois State	1947-1948
	Mississippi-Ohio Valley	1949-1955
	Midwest	1956-1957
Mattoon-Charleston see also Charleston	Kitty	1906
McLeansboro	Southern Illinois	1910
	Kitty	1910-1911
Moline	Three-I	1914-1917, 1919-1923, 1937-1941
	Mississippi Valley	1924-1932
	Central Association	1947-1948
see also Quad City, Iowa; Rock Island-Moline		
Monmouth	Illinois-Missouri	1908-1909
	Central Association	1910-1913
Mt. Vernon	Southern Illinois	1910
	Illinois State	1947-1948
	Mississippi-Ohio Valley	1949-1954
Ottawa	Illinois-Missouri	1914
	Bi-State	1915
Pana	Eastern Illinois	1907-1908
Paris	Eastern Illinois	1907-1908
	Mississippi-Ohio Valley	1950-1955
	Midwest	1956-1959
Pekin	Illinois-Missouri	1909-1913
Peoria	Northwestern	1883-1884
	Central Interstate	1888-1889
	Two-I	1892
	Western Association	1894-1897
	Central	1900, 1904, 1917, 1934
	Western	1902-1903
	Three-I	1905-1917, 1919-1932, 1935, 1937, 1953-1957
	Mississippi Valley	1933
	Midwest	1983-
Quincy	Northwestern	1883-1884
	Central Interstate	1889
	Two-I	1892
	Western Association	1894-1897, 1899
	Iowa State	1907
	Central Association	1908-1910
	Three-I	1911-1917, 1925-1932, 1946-1956
	Mississippi Valley	1933
	Midwest	1960-1973
Rock Island see also Quad City, Iowa	Western Association	1899
	Three-I	1901-1911, 1916-1917, 1920-1921
	Central Association	1914
	Mississippi Valley	1922-1933
	Western	1934-1937
Rock Island-Moline see also Moline; Quad City, Iowa	Two-I	1892
	Western Association	1894
Rockford	Central Interstate	1888
	Two-I	1892
	Western Association	1895-1897, 1899
	Three-I	1901-1904, 1915-1917, 1919-1923
	Wisconsin-Illinois	1908-1914
	Central Association	1947-1949
	Midwest	1988-
Romeoville (aka Will County)	North Central	1995
	Heartland	1996-
Shelbyville	Eastern Illinois	1907-1908
Springfield	Northwestern	1883
	Central Interstate	1889
	Western Association	1895
	Central	1900, 1934
	Three-I	1903-1914, 1925-1932, 1935, 1938-1942, 1946-1949
	Mississippi Valley	1933
	Mississippi-Ohio Valley	1950
	American Association	1978-1981
	Midwest	1982-1995
	Frontier	1996-
Staunton	Eastern Illinois	1908
Sterling	Northern Association	1910
Streator	Illinois-Missouri	1912-1914
	Bi-State	1915
Taylorville	Eastern Illinois	1907-1908
	Illinois-Missouri	1911

Urbana		
see Champaign-Urbana		
West Frankfort	Illinois State	1947-1948
	Mississippi-Ohio Valley	1949-1950
Will County		
see Romeoville		

INDIANA

City	League	Years
Anderson	Central	1903
	Interstate Association	1906
	Northern State of Indiana	1911
	Mid-America	1995
	Heartland	1996-
Bloomington	Central Interstate	1888
	Western Association	1899
	Central	1900
	Three-I	1901-1910, 1912-1917, 1919-1931, 1935, 1937-1939
Bluffton	Northern State of Indiana	1909-1911
Crawfordsville	Central Interstate	1888
Dubois County		
see Huntingburg		
East Chicago	Mid-American	1995
Elkhart	Indiana-Michigan	1910
Evansville	Northwestern	1884
	Central Interstate	1889
	Two-I	1892
	Southern	1895, 1966-1968
	Three-I	1901-1902, 1919-1931, 1938-1942, 1946-1957
	Central	1903-1911, 1913-1917
	Kitty	1912
	American Association	1970-1984
	Frontier	1995-
Fort Wayne	Northwestern	1883-1884
	Western	1892
	Interstate	1896-1900
	Western Association	1901
	Central	1903-1905, 1908-1915, 1917, 1928-1930, 1932, 1934, 1948
	Interstate Association	1906
	Three-I	1935
	Midwest	1993-
Gary	Indiana-Michigan	1910
Huntingburg (aka Dubois County)	Heartland	1996-
Huntington	Ohio-Indiana	1908
	Northern State of Indiana	1909-1911
Indianapolis	American Association	1884, 1902-1962, 1969-
	Western	1885, 1892, 1894-1899
	American	1900
	Western Association	1901
	Federal	1913-1914
	International	1963
	Pacific Coast	1964-1968
Kokomo	Northern State of Indiana	1909
	Mississippi-Ohio Valley	1955
	Midwest	1956-1961
Lafayette	Central Interstate	1888
	Northern State of Indiana	1909-1911
	Mississippi-Ohio Valley	1955
	Midwest	1956-1957
	Great Central	1994
	Mid-America	1995
	Heartland	1996-
Ligonier	Indiana-Michigan	1910
Linton	Eastern Illinois	1908
Logansport	Northern State of Indiana	1910-1911
Marion	Interstate Association	1906
	Northern State of Indiana	1909-1911
Merrillville	Mid-America	1995
Michigan City	Midwest	1956-1959
Muncie	Interstate Association	1906
	Ohio-Indiana	1908, 1948-1950
	Ohio State	1947
Richmond	Ohio-Indiana	1908, 1948-1951
	Central	1917, 1930
	Ohio State	1946-1947
	Frontier	1995-
South Bend	Central	1903-1912, 1916-1917, 1932
	Southern Michigan Assn.	1914-1915
	Midwest	1988-
Terre Haute	Northwestern	1884
	Central Interstate	1888
	Two-I	1892

	Western	1895
	Central	1900, 1903-1916
	Three-I	1901-1902, 1919-1932, 1935, 1937, 1946-1956
Vincennes	Kitty	1903-1906, 1910-1911, 1913
	Eastern Illinois	1908
	Mississippi-Ohio Valley	1950-1952
Wabash	Northern State of Indiana	1909-1911

IOWA

City	League	Years
Atlantic	Southwest Iowa	1903
Bettendorf		
see Quad City		
Boone	Iowa State	1904-1906
Burlington	Central Interstate	1889
	Western Association	1895-1897
	Iowa State	1904-1907
	Central Association	1908-1916, 1947-1949
	Mississippi Valley	1924-1932
	Three-I	1952-1961
	Midwest	1962-
Cedar Rapids	Western Association	1896-1897, 1899
	Three-I	1901-1909, 1920-1921, 1938-1942, 1950-1961
	Central Association	1913-1917, 1949
	Mississippi Valley	1922-1932
	Western	1934-1937
	Midwest	1962-
Charles City	Central Association	1917
Clarinda	Southwest Iowa	1903
	MINK	1910-1911
Clear Lake	Central Association	1917
Clinton	Iowa State	1906
	Central Association	1914-1917, 1947-1949
	Three-I	1907-1908, 1937-1941
	Northern Association	1910
	Mississippi-Ohio Valley	1954-1955
	Midwest	1956-
Council Bluffs	Iowa-South Dakota	1903
	Western	1935
Creston	Southwest Iowa	1903
Davenport	Central Interstate	1888-1889
	Western Association	1888
	Three-I	1901-1906, 1909-1916, 1946-1952, 1957-1958
	Mississippi Valley	1929-1933
	Western	1934-1937
	Midwest	1960
see also Quad City		
Des Moines	Northwestern	1887
	Western Association	1888-1890, 1894-1897
	Western	1900-1937, 1947-1958
	Three-I	1959-1961
(aka Iowa)	American Association	1969-
Dubuque	Central Interstate	1888
	Western Association	1895-1897, 1899
	Three-I	1903-1915
	Central Association	1917
	Mississippi Valley	1922-1932
	Mississippi-Ohio Valley	1954-1955
	Midwest	1956-1968, 1974-1976
Ft. Dodge	Iowa State	1904-1906
	Central Association	1916-1917
Iowa		
see Des Moines		
Keokuk	Western	1885, 1935
	Iowa State	1904-1907
	Central Association	1908-1915, 1947-1949
	Mississippi Valley	1929-1933
	Three-I	1952-1961
	Midwest	1958-1962
Le Mars	Iowa-South Dakota	1902-1903
Marshalltown	Iowa State	1904-1907
	Central Association	1914-1917
	Mississippi Valley	1922-1928
Mason City	Central Association	1915-1917
	Great Central	1994
Muscatine	Northern Association	1910
	Central Association	1911-1916
Osceola	Southwest Iowa	1903
Oskaloosa	Iowa State	1904-1907
	Central Association	1908
Ottumwa	Western Association	1899
	Iowa State	1904-1907
	Central Association	1908-1914, 1916

City	League	Years
	Mississippi Valley	1922-1928
Primghar see Sheldon-Primghar		
Quad City/Cities (Davenport-Bettendorf- Moline-Rock Island) see also Davenport; Moline; Rock Island	Midwest	1961-
Red Oak	Southwest Iowa	1903
Rock Rapids	Iowa-South Dakota	1902
Sheldon	Iowa-South Dakota	1902
Sheldon-Primghar	Iowa-South Dakota	1903
Shenandoah	Southwest Iowa	1903
	MINK	1910-1911
Sioux City	Western Association	1888-1891
	Western	1894, 1900, 1904-1923, 1934-1937, 1947-1958
	Iowa-South Dakota	1902-1903
	Tri-State	1924
	Nebraska State	1938
	Western (Class D)	1939-1941
	Three-I	1959-1960
	Northern	1993-
Waterloo	Iowa State	1904-1907
	Central Association	1908-1909, 1913-1917
	Three-I	1910-1911, 1938-1942, 1946-1956
	Mississippi Valley	1922-1932
	Western	1936-1937
	Midwest	1958-1993

KANSAS

City	League	Years
Abilene	Central Kansas	1909-1910
Arkansas City	Kansas State	1909-1910
	Southwestern	1924-1926
Arkansas City-Winfield	Kansas State	1909
Beloit	Central Kansas	1909-1910
Blue Rapids	Eastern Kansas	1910
Chanute	Missouri Valley	1902
	Kansas State	1906
	Kansas-Oklahoma-Missouri	1946-1950
Chapman	Central Kansas	1910
Cherryvale	Kansas State	1906
Clay Center	Central Kansas	1909-1911
	Kansas State	1913
Coffeyville	Missouri Valley	1902
	Kansas State	1906
	Oklahoma-Arkansas-Kansas	1907
	Western Association	1911
	Southwestern	1921-1924
Concordia	Central Kansas	1910-1911
Cottonwood Falls see Strong City-Cottonwood Falls		
El Dorado	Kansas State	1911
Ellsworth	Kansas State	1905
	Central Kansas	1908-1910
Emporia	Western	1887
	Kansas State	1914
	Southwestern	1924
Eureka	Southwestern	1924-1926
Ft. Scott	Missouri Valley	1902-1905
	Kansas State	1906
Great Bend	Kansas State	1905, 1909-1911, 1913-1914
	Central Kansas	1912
Hiawatha	Eastern Kansas	1910
	MINK	1912
Hoisington	Kansas State	1905
Holton	Eastern Kansas	1910
Horton	Eastern Kansas	1910
Hutchinson	Western	1888, 1917-1918, 1933
	Kansas State	1905, 1909-1911, 1914
	Western Association	1906-1908, 1924, 1932, 1934-1942, 1946-1954
	Southwestern	1922-1923
Independence	Kansas State	1906
	Oklahoma-Arkansas-Kansas	1907
	Oklahoma-Kansas	1908
	Western Association	1911, 1925, 1928-1932
	Southwestern	1921-1924
	Kansas-Oklahoma-Missouri	1947-1950, 1952
Iola	Missouri Valley	1902-1904
	Kansas State	1906
	Oklahoma-Kansas	1908
	Kansas-Oklahoma-Missouri	1946-1952
	Western Association	1954
Junction City	Central Kansas	1909-1912
	Kansas State	1913
Kingman	Kansas State	1905

City	League	Years
Larned	Kansas State	1909-1911
Lawrence	Western Association	1893
Leavenworth	Western	1886-1888
	Missouri Valley	1903-1904
	Western Association	1905-1907, 1946-1949
Lincoln Center	Kansas State	1905
Little River	Central Kansas	1908
Lyons	Kansas State	1909-1911, 1913
	Central Kansas	1912
Manhattan	Central Kansas	1909-1912
	Kansas State	1913
Marysville	Eastern Kansas	1910
McPherson	Central Kansas	1908
	Kansas State	1909-1911
Minneapolis	Kansas State	1905
	Central Kansas	1908-1909, 1912
Newton	Western	1888
	Central Kansas	1908, 1912
	Kansas State	1909-1911
	Southwestern	1924
Norton	Nebraska State	1929-1930
Ottawa	Southwestern	1924
Parsons	Missouri Valley	1905
	Kansas State	1906
	Oklahoma-Arkansas-Kansas	1907
	Southwestern	1921
Pittsburg	Missouri Valley	1903-1905
	Kansas State	1906
	Western Association	1909
	Southwestern	1921
	Kansas-Oklahoma-Missouri	1946-1952
Sabetha	Eastern Kansas	1910
Salina	Central Kansas	1908-1910, 1912
	Kansas State	1913-1914
	Southwestern	1922-1926
	Western Association	1938-1941, 1946-1952
Seneca	Eastern Kansas	1910
Strong City-Cottonwood Falls	Kansas State	1909
Topeka	Western	1886-1887, 1893, 1909-1916, 1918, 1929-1931, 1933-1934, 1956-1958
	Missouri Valley	1904
	Western Association	1905-1908, 1924, 1927-1928, 1932, 1939, 1942, 1946-1954
	Southwestern	1922-1923, 1925-1926
	Three-I	1959-1961
Wellington	Kansas State	1909-1911
Wichita	Western	1887, 1909-1933, 1950-1955
	Western Association	1905-1908
	American Association	1956-1958, 1970-1984
	Texas	1987-
Winfield see Arkansas City-Winfield		

KENTUCKY

City	League	Years
Ashland (aka Tri-State)	Mountain State	1939-1942
	Frontier	1993
Ashland-Catlettsburg	Virginia Valley	1910
	Mountain States	1911-1912
Bowling Green	Kitty	1939-1942
Catlettsburg see Ashland-Catlettsburg		
Central City	Kitty	1954
Covington	Federal	1913
Cynthiana	Blue Grass	1922-1924
Dawson Springs	Kitty	1916
Frankfort	Blue Grass	1908-1912
	Ohio State	1915-1916
Fulton	Kitty	1911, 1922-1924, 1936-1942, 1946-1955
Harlan	Mountain States	1948-1954
	Appalachian	1961-1963, 1965
Hazard	Mountain States	1948-1952
Henderson	Kitty	1903-1905, 1911-1914, 1916
Hopkinsville	Kitty	1903-1905, 1910-1914, 1916, 1922-1923, 1935-1942, 1946-1954
Jenkins	Mountain States	1948-1951
Kentucky see Pikeville		
Lawrenceburg	Blue Grass	1908
Lexington	Blue Grass	1908-1912, 1922-1923
	Ohio State	1913-1916
	Mountain States	1954
Louisville	American Association	1883-1891, 1902-1962, 1982-
	National Colored	1887
	National	1892-1899

City	League	Years
	Western Association	1901
	International	1968-1972
Madisonville	Kitty	1916, 1922, 1946-1955
Mayfield	Kitty	1922-1924, 1936-1941, 1946-1955
Maysville	Blue Grass	1910-1912, 1922-1923
	Ohio State	1913-1916
Middlesboro	Appalachian	1913-1914, 1961-1963
	Mountain States	1949
Mt. Sterling	Blue Grass	1912, 1922-1923
Newport	Ohio State	1914
Nicholasville	Blue Grass	1912
Owensboro	Kitty	1903, 1913-1914, 1916, 1936-1942, 1946-1955
Paducah	Kitty	1903-1906, 1910-1914, 1922-1923, 1935-1941, 1951-1955
	Mississippi-Ohio Valley	1949-1950
Paintsville see also Pikeville	Appalachian	1978-1984
Paris	Blue Grass	1909-1912, 1922-1924
	Ohio State	1914
Pikeville (aka Kentucky)	Appalachian	1982-1984
	Frontier	1993-1994
Princeton	Kitty	1905
Richmond	Blue Grass	1908-1912
Shelbyville	Blue Grass	1908-1910
Winchester	Blue Grass	1908-1912, 1922-1924

LOUISIANA

City	League	Years
Abbeville	Louisiana State	1920
	Evangeline	1935-1939, 1946-1950, 1952
Alexandria	Gulf Coast	1907-1908
	Arkansas State	1909
	Louisiana State	1920
	Cotton States	1925-1930
	Evangeline	1934-1942, 1946-1957
	Texas	1972-1975
	Texas-Louisiana	1994-
Baton Rouge	Cotton States	1902-1906, 1929-1932
	Dixie	1933
	East Dixie	1934
	Evangeline	1946-1957
	Gulf States	1976
Crowley	Gulf Coast	1908, 1950
	Evangeline	1951-1957
DeQuincy	Cotton States	1932
Hammond	Evangeline	1946-1951
Houma	Evangeline	1940, 1946-1952
Jeanerette	Evangeline	1934-1939
Lafayette	Gulf Coast	1907
	Louisiana State	1920
	Evangeline	1934-1942, 1948-1957
	Texas	1975-1976
Lake Charles	South Texas	1906
	Gulf Coast	1907-1908, 1950-1953
	Cotton States	1929-1930
	Evangeline	1934-1942, 1954-1957
Leesville	Gulf Coast	1950
Monroe	Cotton States	1903-1904, 1908, 1924-1932, 1937-1941, 1950-1955
	Arkansas State	1909
	Gulf Coast	1907
	Evangeline	1956
Morgan City	Gulf Coast	1908
New Iberia	Louisiana State	1920
	Evangeline	1934-1942, 1946-1956
New Orleans	Southern	1887-1888, 1892-1896
	Texas	1888
	Southern Association	1901-1959
	Cotton States	1912
	American Association	1977, 1993-
Oakdale	Louisiana State	1920
Opelousas	Gulf Coast	1907
	Cotton States	1932
	Evangeline	1934-1941
Rayne	Louisiana State	1920
	Evangeline	1934-1941
Shreveport	Texas-Southern	1895
	Southern Association	1901-1907, 1959-1961
	Texas	1908-1910, 1915-1932, 1938-1942, 1946-1957, 1968-
	Dixie	1933
	East Dixie	1934
	West Dixie	1935
Thibodaux	Evangeline	1946-1954, 1956-1957

MAINE

City	League	Years
Auburn see Lewiston-Auburn		
Augusta	New England	1895-1896, 1901
Bangor	New England	1894-1896, 1901
	Maine State	1907
	New Brunswick-Maine	1913
	Northeast	1996-
Biddeford	Maine State	1907
Calais-St. Stephen (NB)	New Brunswick-Maine	1913
Lewiston	New England	1891-1896, 1901, 1914-1915, 1919, 1926-1930
	Atlantic Association	1908
Lewiston-Auburn	New England	1919
Maine see Old Orchard Beach		
Old Orchard Beach (aka Maine)	International	1984-1988
Pine Tree	Maine State	1907
Portland	New England	1886-1888, 1891-1896, 1899, 1901, 1913-1915, 1919, 1926-1930, 1946-1949
	Maine State	1907
	Atlantic Association	1908
	Eastern	1916-1917, 1994-

MARYLAND

City	League	Years
Baltimore	American Association	1883-1891
	Union Association	1884
	Eastern	1884, 1903-1911
	National Colored	1887
	Atlantic Association	1890
	National	1892-1899
	American	1901-1902, 1954-
	International	1912-1914, 1916-1953
	Federal	1914-1915
Bowie	Eastern	1993-
Cambridge	Eastern Shore	1922-1928, 1937-1941, 1946-1949
Centreville	Eastern Shore	1937-1941, 1946
Crisfield	Eastern Shore	1922-1928, 1937
Cumberland	Penn-Ohio-Maryland	1906
	Western Pennsylvania	1907
	Potomac	1916
	Blue Ridge	1917-1918
	Middle Atlantic	1925-1932
Delmarva see Salisbury		
Easton	Eastern Shore	1924-1928, 1937-1941, 1946-1949
Federalsburg	Eastern Shore	1937-1941, 1946-1949
Frederick	Blue Ridge	1915-1917, 1920-1930
	Carolina	1989-
Frostburg	Potomac	1916
Hagerstown	Blue Ridge	1915-1918, 1920-1930
	Middle Atlantic	1931
	Interstate	1941-1952
	Piedmont	1953-1955
	Carolina	1981-1988
	Eastern	1989-1992
	South Atlantic	1993-
Hanover	Blue Ridge	1915-1917, 1920-1929
Lonaconing	Potomac	1916
Pocomoke City	Eastern Shore	1922-1923, 1937-1940
Salisbury	Eastern Shore	1922-1928, 1937-1941, 1946-1949
	Interstate	1951-1952
(aka Delmarva)	South Atlantic	1996-
Westernport see Piedmont (WV)-Westernport		

MASSACHUSETTS

City	League	Years
Attleboro	Atlantic Association	1908
	New England	1928, 1933
Boston	National	1883-1952
	Union Association	1884
	New England	1886-1887, 1893
	National Colored	1887
	Player's	1890
	American Association	1891
	American	1901-
Brockton	New England	1886, 1892-1899, 1901, 1903, 1907-1913, 1928-1929, 1933
	Eastern	1901
	Colonial	1914-1915

PROFESSIONAL TEAMS BY STATE

City	League	Years
Cambridge	New England	1899
	Northeastern	1934
Fall River	New England	1893-1898, 1902-1913, 1946-1949
	Colonial	1914-1915
Fitchburg	New England Association	1895
	New England	1899, 1914-1915, 1919, 1929
	Eastern	1922
Gloucester	New England	1929
Haverhill	New England	1886-1887, 1894, 1901-1912, 1914, 1919, 1926-1929
	New England Association	1895
Holyoke	Connecticut State	1903-1912
	Eastern Association	1913
	Eastern	1977-1982
Lawrence	New England	1886-1887, 1892, 1899, 1902-1915, 1919, 1926-1927, 1933, 1946-1947
	New England Association	1895
	Eastern	1916-1917
Lowell	New England	1887-1888, 1891-1893, 1901-1915, 1919, 1926, 1933, 1947
	Atlantic Association	1889
	New England Association	1895
	Eastern	1916
	Northeastern	1934
	New York-Pennsylvania	1996-
Lynn (aka Massachusetts)	New England	1886-1888, 1891, 1901, 1905-1915, 1926-1930, 1946-1949
	Eastern	1916, 1980-1983
	North Atlantic	1996-
	Northeast	1997-
New Bedford	New England	1895-1898, 1903-1913, 1929, 1933
	Colonial	1914-1915
	Northeastern	1934
Newburyport	New England	1886
Northampton	Connecticut State	1909-1911
Pittsfield	Hudson River	1905
	Eastern Association	1913-1914
	Eastern	1919-1930, 1965-1976, 1985-1988
	Canadian-American	1941-1942, 1946-1951
	New York-Pennsylvania	1989-
Quincy	New England	1933
Salem	New England	1887-1888, 1891-1892, 1926-1928, 1930
	New England Association	1895
Springfield	Eastern	1893-1900, 1916-1932, 1939-1943, 1957-1965
	Connecticut State	1902-1912
	Eastern Association	1913-1914
	Colonial	1915
	Northeastern	1934
	New England	1948-1949
	International	1950-1953
Taunton	New England	1897-1899, 1905, 1933
	Atlantic Association	1908
	Colonial	1914-1915
Waltham	Northeastern	1934
Watertown	Northeastern	1934
Wayland	Northeastern	1934
Worcester	New England	1888, 1891, 1894, 1898, 1906-1915, 1933
	Atlantic Association	1889-1890
	Eastern	1899-1903, 1916-1926
	Connecticut State	1904
	Northeastern	1934

MICHIGAN

City	League	Years
Adrian	Michigan State	1895
	Southern Michigan	1909
	Southern Michigan Assn.	1910-1914
Battle Creek	Michigan State	1895, 1902
	Southern Michigan	1906-1909
	Southern Michigan Assn.	1910-1915
	Michigan-Ontario	1919-1920
(aka Michigan)	Midwest	1995-
Bay City	Northwestern	1883-1884
	Ohio-Michigan	1893
	Interstate Association	1906
	Southern Michigan	1907-1909
	Southern Michigan Assn.	1910-1915
	Michigan-Ontario	1919-1926
	Michigan State	1926
see also Saginaw-Bay City		
Belding	Michigan State	1914
Berrien Springs	Indiana-Michigan	1910
Boyne City	Michigan State	1911-1914
Cadillac	West Michigan	1910
	Michigan State	1911-1914
Calumet	Copper Country Soo	1905
	Northern-Copper Country	1906-1907
Charlotte	Michigan State	1926
Detroit	National	1883-1888
	International	1889-1890
	Western	1894-1899
	American	1900-
Dowagiac	Indiana-Michigan	1910
Flint	Michigan State	1889-1890, 1902, 1926, 1940-1941
	Interstate Association	1906
	Southern Michigan	1907-1909
	Southern Michigan Assn.	1910-1915
	Michigan-Ontario	1919-1926
	Central	1948-1951
Grand Rapids	Northwestern	1883-1884
	Michigan State	1889-1890, 1902, 1926, 1940-1941
	International	1890
	Western	1894-1897, 1899
	Interstate	1898-1899
	Canadian	1900
	Western Association	1901
	Central	1903-1917, 1920-1922, 1926, 1934, 1948-1951
	Michigan-Ontario	1923-1924
(aka West Michigan)	Midwest	1994-
Greenville	Michigan State	1889
Hancock	Copper Country Soo	1905
	Northern-Copper Country	1906
Holland	West Michigan	1910
	Michigan State	1911
Houghton	Northern-Copper Country	1906-1907
Ionia	Central	1921-1922
Jackson	Tri-State	1888
	Michigan State	1889, 1895, 1902
	Interstate	1896
	Southern Michigan	1906-1909
	Southern Michigan Assn.	1910-1915
	Central	1921
Kalamazoo	Ohio State	1887
	Tri-State	1888
	Michigan State	1889, 1895, 1926
	Southern Michigan	1906-1909
	Southern Michigan Assn.	1910-1914
	Central	1920-1922, 1926
	Michigan-Ontario	1923-1924
	Frontier	1996-
Lake Linden	Copper Country Soo	1905
	Northern-Copper Country	1906
Lansing	Michigan State	1889-1890, 1895, 1902, 1940-1941
	Southern Michigan	1907-1909
	Southern Michigan Assn.	1910-1914
	Central	1921-1922
	Midwest	1996-
Ludington	Michigan State	1912-1914, 1926
	Central	1920-1922, 1926
Manistee	Michigan State	1890, 1911-1914
Menominee see Marinette (WI)-Menominee		
Michigan see Battle Creek		
Mt. Clemens	Southern Michigan	1906-1907
	Border	1912-1913
	Southern Michigan Assn.	1914
Muskegon	Northwestern	1884
	Michigan State	1890, 1902, 1911-1914, 1926, 1940-1941
	West Michigan	1910
	Central	1916-1917, 1920-1922, 1926, 1934, 1948-1951
	Michigan-Ontario	1923-1924
Niles	Indiana-Michigan	1910
Owosso	Michigan State	1895
Pontiac	Border	1912-1913
Port Huron	Michigan State	1890, 1895, 1926
	Canadian	1900
	Border	1912-1913
	Michigan-Ontario	1921, 1926
Port Huron-Sarnia (ONT)	Michigan-Ontario	1922
Saginaw	Northwestern	1883-1884
	Michigan State	1889, 1902, 1926, 1940-1941
	Ohio-Michigan	1893
	Interstate	1896
	Canadian	1900
	Interstate Association	1906
	Southern Michigan	1906, 1908-1909
	Southern Michigan Assn.	1910-1915
	Michigan-Ontario	1919-1926
	Central	1948-1951

City	League	Years
Saginaw-Bay City see also Bay City	Eastern	1890
St. Joseph	Michigan State	1940-1941
Sault Ste. Marie	Copper Country Soo	1905
Tecumseh	Southern Michigan	1906-1908
Traverse City	West Michigan	1910
	Michigan State	1911-1914
West Michigan see Grand Rapids		
Wyandotte	Border	1912-1913
Ypsilanti	Border	1913

MINNESOTA

City	League	Years
Austin (aka Southern Minny)	Prairie	1996-
Brainerd	Northern	1933-1935
	North Central	1994-1995
	Prairie	1996
see also St. Cloud-Brainerd		
Brainerd-Little Falls	Northern	1934
Breckenridge see Wahpeton-Breckenridge		
Chaska Valley	North Central	1995
Crookston	Northern	1902-1905, 1933-1941
Duluth	Northwestern	1886-1887
	Western Association	1891
	Northern	1903-1905, 1908, 1913-1916, 1934-1942, 1946-1955
	Northern-Copper Country	1906-1907
	Minnesota-Wisconsin	1909-1911
	Central International	1912
Duluth-Superior see also Superior (WI)	Northern	1956-1970, 1993-
Duluth-Heralds	Twin Ports	1943
Duluth-Dukes	Twin Ports	1943
Duluth-Marine Iron	Twin Ports	1943
East Grand Forks	Northern	1933, 1935
Hibbing (aka Minnesota)	North Central	1995
Little Falls see Brainerd-Little Falls		
Mankato	Northern	1967-1968
Marshall	North Central	1994
Minneapolis	Northwestern	1884, 1886-1887
	Western Association	1888-1891
	Western	1892, 1894-1899, 1901
	American	1900, 1961-
	American Association	1902-1960
	Northern	1913
	Great Central	1994
	North Central	1994
(aka Minnesota)	Prairie	1995
Minnesota see Hibbing; Minneapolis		
Moorhead see Fargo (ND)-Moorhead		
Red Wing	Minnesota-Wisconsin	1910-1911
Rochester	Minnesota-Wisconsin	1910-1912
	Three-I	1958
	Northern	1993
St. Cloud	Northern	1946-1971
St. Cloud-Brainerd	Northern	1905
St. Paul	Union Association	1884
	Northwestern	1884, 1886-1887
	Western Association	1888-1891
	Western	1892, 1895-1899, 1901
	American Association	1902-1960
	Northern	1913, 1993-
Southern Minny see Austin		
Stillwater	Northwestern	1884
Virginia	Northern	1913-1916
Warren	Northern	1917
Winona	Northwestern	1884
	Minnesota-Wisconsin	1909-1912
	Northern	1913-1914
	Three-I	1958
Worthington	Western (Class D)	1939-1940

MISSISSIPPI

City	League	Years
Biloxi see Gulfport-Biloxi		
Brookhaven	Delta	1904
Canton	Delta	1904
Clarksdale	Delta	1904
	Cotton States	1913, 1922-1923, 1936-1941, 1947-1951
	Mississippi State	1921
	East Dixie	1934-1935
Cleveland	East Dixie	1935
	Cotton States	1936
Columbus	Cotton States	1907-1908, 1912-1913
	East Dixie	1935
Corinth	Tri-State	1925-1926
Greenville	Cotton States	1902-1905, 1922-1923, 1936-1941, 1947-1955
	East Dixie	1934-1935
	Big South	1996-
Greenwood	Cotton States	1910-1912, 1922-1923, 1936-1940, 1947-1952
	Mississippi State	1921
	East Dixie	1934-1935
Gulfport	Cotton States	1906-1907, 1926-1928
Gulfport-Biloxi	Cotton States	1908
Hattiesburg	Delta	1904
	Cotton States	1905, 1910-1912, 1923-1929
Jackson	Cotton States	1905-1908, 1910-1913, 1922-1932, 1936, 1953
	Delta	1904
	Mississippi State	1921
	Dixie	1933
	East Dixie	1934-1935
	Southeastern	1932, 1937-1942, 1946-1950
	Texas	1975-
Laurel	Cotton States	1923-1929
Meridian	Cotton States	1905-1908, 1910-1913, 1922-1929, 1952-1955
	Mississippi State	1921
	Southeastern	1937-1942, 1946-1950
	Big South	1996-
Natchez	Cotton States	1902-1905, 1948-1953
	Evangeline	1940-1942, 1946-1947
Tupelo	Tri-State	1925-1926
Vicksburg	Cotton States	1902-1908, 1910-1912, 1922-1931, 1937, 1941, 1955
	Southeastern	1946-1950
Yazoo City	Delta	1904
	Cotton States	1910-1912

MISSOURI

City	League	Years
Brookfield	Missouri State	1911
Carthage	Arkansas-Missouri	1938-1940
	Western Association	1941
	Kansas-Oklahoma-Missouri	1946-1951
Caruthersville	Northeast Arkansas	1910, 1936-1940
Cassville	Arkansas State	1935
	Arkansas-Missouri	1936
Hannibal	Illinois-Missouri	1908
	Central Association	1909-1912, 1947-1948
	Three-I	1916-1917
	Mississippi-Ohio Valley	1952-1955
Jefferson City	Missouri Valley	1902
	Missouri State	1911
Joplin	Missouri Valley	1902-1904
	Western Association	1905-1911, 1922-1924, 1926-1932, 1934-1942, 1946-1954
	Western	1917-1921, 1933
Joplin-Webb City see also Webb City	Western Association	1914
Kansas City	Union Association	1884
	Western	1885, 1887, 1892, 1894-1899, 1901-1903
	National	1886
	Western Association	1888-1891, 1893
	American Association	1888-1889, 1902-1954
	American	1900, 1955-1967, 1969-
	Federal	1913-1915
Kirksville	Missouri State	1911
Macon	Missouri State	1911
Maryville	MINK	1910-1911
Monett	Arkansas-Missouri	1936-1939
Neosho	Arkansas-Missouri	1937-1940
Nevada	Missouri Valley	1902-1903
Portageville	Kitty	1935-1936
St. Joseph	Western	1886-1887, 1898, 1900-1905, 1910-1926, 1930-1935
	Western Association	1889, 1893-1897, 1906, 1927, 1939-1941, 1946-1951, 1953-1954
St. Louis	American Association	1883-1891

	Union Association	1884
	National	1885-1886, 1892-
	Western Association	1888
	American	1902-1953
	Federal	1913-1915
Sedalia	Missouri Valley	1902-1904
	Western Association	1905
	Missouri State	1911
Springfield	Missouri Valley	1902-1904
	Western Association	1905-1909, 1911, 1920-1932, 1934-1942, 1948, 1950
	Western	1933
Webb City	Missouri Valley	1903, 1905
	Western Association	1906-1909
see also Joplin-Webb City		
West Plains	Northeast Arkansas	1936

MONTANA

City	League	Years
Anaconda	Montana State	1900
Billings	Pioneer	1948-1963, 1969-
Bozeman	Inter-Mountain	1909
Butte	Montana State	1900
	Pacific Northwest	1902
	Pacific National	1903-1904
	Northwestern	1906-1908, 1916-1917
	Inter-Mountain	1909
	Union Association	1911-1914
	Pioneer	1978-1985, 1987-
Great Falls	Montana State	1900
	Union Association	1911-1913
	Northwestern	1916-1917
	Pioneer	1948-1963, 1969-
Helena	Montana State	1900
	Pacific Northwest	1902
	Pacific National	1903
	Inter-Mountain	1909
	Union Association	1911-1914
	Pioneer	1978-
Livingston	Inter-Mountain	1909
Missoula	Union Association	1911-1913
	Pioneer	1956-1960

NEBRASKA

City	League	Years
Auburn	MINK	1910-1913
Beatrice	Nebraska State	1913-1915, 1922-1923, 1928, 1932-1937
	Tri-State	1924
	Western (Class D)	1939
Beatrice-Fairbury	MINK	1912
see also Fairbury		
Columbus	Nebraska State	1910-1915
Fairbury	Nebraska State	1915, 1922-1923, 1928-1930, 1936-1937
see also Beatrice-Fairbury		
Falls City	MINK	1910-1913
Fremont	Nebraska State	1910-1913
Grand Island	Nebraska State	1910-1915, 1922-1923, 1928-1934, 1938, 1956-1959
	Tri-State	1924
Hastings	Western	1887
	Nebraska State	1910-1915, 1922-1923, 1956-1959
	Tri-State	1924
Holdrege	Nebraska State	1956-1959
Humboldt	MINK	1911-1913
Kearney	Nebraska State	1910-1915, 1956-1959
Lexington	Nebraska State	1956-1959
Lincoln	Western	1886-1888, 1906-1917, 1924-1927, 1947-1958
	Western Association	1890-1891, 1894-1895
	Nebraska State	1922-1923, 1928-1936, 1938
	Western (Class D)	1939-1940
	Three-I	1959-1961
McCook	Nebraska State	1928-1932, 1956-1959
Nebraska City	MINK	1910-1913
Norfolk	Nebraska State	1914-1915, 1922-1923, 1928-1938
	Tri-State	1924
	Western (Class D)	1939-1941
North Platte	Nebraska State	1928-1932, 1956-1959
Omaha	Western	1885, 1887-1892, 1898, 1900-1936, 1947-1954
	Western Association	1894-1895
	American Association	1955-1959, 1961-1962, 1969-
Red Cloud	Nebraska State	1910
Seward	Nebraska State	1910-1913
Superior	Nebraska State	1910-1914, 1956-1958
York	Nebraska State	1911-1915, 1928-1931

NEVADA

City	League	Years
Las Vegas	Sunset	1947-1950
	Southwest International	1951
	Arizona-Mexico	1957
	California	1958
	Pacific Coast	1983-
Reno	Sunset	1947-1949
	Far West	1950-1951
	California	1955-1964, 1966-1992
	Western	1996-

NEW HAMPSHIRE

City	League	Years
Charlestown		
see Springfield (VT)-Charlestown		
Concord	New England	1902-1905
Dover	New England	1893, 1902
Keene	Twin States	1911
Manchester	New England	1887-1888, 1891-1893, 1899, 1901-1906, 1914-1915, 1926-1930, 1946-1949
	Northeastern	1934
	Eastern	1969-1971
Nashua	New England Association	1895
	New England	1901-1905, 1926-1927, 1929-1930, 1933, 1946-1949
	Eastern	1983-1986
	North Atlantic	1995-
Portsmouth	New England	1888

NEW JERSEY

City	League	Years
Asbury Park	Atlantic	1914
Atlantic City	Eastern	1885
	Tri-State	1912-1913
Augusta (aka New Jersey)	New York-Pennsylvania	1994-
Bloomfield-Long Branch	Atlantic	1914
see also Long Branch		
Bloomingdale	North Atlantic	1946-1948
Camden	Interstate Association	1883
	Tri-State	1904
Jersey City	Eastern	1885-1886, 1902-1911, 1977-1978
	International	1887, 1912-1915, 1918-1933, 1937-1950, 1960-1961
	Central	1888
	Atlantic Association	1889-1890
	Atlantic	1900
Long Branch	New York-New Jersey	1913
	Atlantic	1914
see also Bloomfield-Long Branch		
New Brunswick	Colonial	1948
New Jersey		
see Augusta		
Newark	Eastern	1884-1886, 1902-1911
	International	1887, 1912-1919, 1921-1949
	Central	1888
	Atlantic Association	1889-1890
	Atlantic	1896-1900, 1914
	Federal	1915
Paterson	Atlantic	1896-1899, 1914
	Hudson River	1904-1907
Perth Amboy	Atlantic	1914
Trenton	Interstate Association	1883
	Eastern	1884-1885, 1938, 1994-
	Tri-State	1907-1914
	New York-Pennsylvania	1936-1937
	Interstate	1939-1950
Washington	Interstate	1932

NEW MEXICO

City	League	Years
Albuquerque	Rio Grande Association	1915
	Arizona-Texas	1932, 1937-1941
	West Texas-New Mexico	1942, 1946-1955
	Western	1956-1958
	Sophomore	1960-1961
	Texas	1962-1971
	Pacific Coast	1972-
Artesia	Longhorn	1951-1955
	Sophomore	1958-1961
Carlsbad	Longhorn	1953-1955
	Southwestern	1956-1957
	Sophomore	1958-1961

Clovis	West Texas	1922
	Panhandle-Pecos Valley	1923
	West Texas-New Mexico	1938-1942, 1946-1955
	Southwestern	1956-1957
Dawson	Rocky Mountain	1912
Hobbs	West Texas-New Mexico	1937-1938
	Longhorn	1955
	Southwestern	1956-1957
	Sophomore	1958-1961
Las Cruces	Rio Grande Association	1915
Raton	Rocky Mountain	1912
Roswell	Panhandle-Pecos Valley	1923
	West Texas-New Mexico	1937
	Longhorn	1949-1955
	Southwestern	1956
	Sophomore	1959

NEW YORK

City	League	Years
Adirondack see Glens Falls		
Albany	New York State	1885, 1899-1916
	International	1888, 1933-1936
	Eastern	1891-1893, 1896, 1920-1932, 1938-1959, 1983-1994
	New York-Pennsylvania	1937
	Northeast	1995-
(aka Albany-Colonie)		
Amsterdam	Canadian-American	1938-1942, 1946-1951
Amsterdam-Johnstown-Gloversville	New York State	1902-1907
see also Gloversville; Gloversville-Johnstown		
Auburn	New York State	1889, 1889
	Canadian-American	1938, 1940
	Border	1946-1951
	New York-Pennsylvania	1958-1980, 1982-
Batavia	PONY	1939-1953
	New York-Pennsylvania	1957-1959, 1961-
Binghamton	New York State	1885, 1899-1917
	International	1886-1887, 1918-1919
	Central	1888
	Eastern	1892-1894, 1938-1963, 1967-1968, 1992-
	New York-Pennsylvania	1923-1937, 1964-1966
Brooklyn	Interstate Association	1883
	Eastern	1884
	American Association	1884-1890
	Player's	1890
	National	1890-1957
	Federal	1914-1915
Buffalo	National	1883-1885
	International	1886-1890, 1912-1970
	Player's	1890
	Eastern	1891-1898, 1901-1911, 1979-1984
	Western	1899
	American	1900
	Federal	1914-1915
	American Association	1985-
Canandaigua	New York State	1889
Catskill	Hudson River	1903
see also Mountaindale		
Colonie see Albany-Colonie		
Corning	PONY	1951-1956
	New York-Pennsylvania	1957-1960, 1968-1969
Cortland	New York State	1899-1901
Elmira	New York State	1885, 1889, 1900, 1908-1917
	New York-Pennsylvania	1891, 1923-1937, 1957-1960, 1973-1995
	Eastern	1892, 1938-1955, 1961-1972
	Atlantic	1900
	Northeast	1996-
Fishkill	New York-Pennsylvania	1994-
(aka Hudson Valley)		
Geneva	Border	1947-1951
	New York-Pennsylvania	1958-1973, 1977-1993
Glens Falls	Eastern	1980-1988
	New York-Pennsylvania	1993
(aka Adirondack)	Northeast	1995-
Glens Falls-Saratoga Springs	Hudson River	1906
Gloversville	Canadian-American	1937
Gloversville-Johnstown	New York State	1908
	Canadian-American	1938-1942, 1946-1951
see also Amsterdam-Johnstown-Gloversville		
Hornell	Interstate	1906, 1914-1915
	PONY	1942-1956
	New York-Pennsylvania	1957

Hudson	Hudson River	1903-1907
Hudson Valley see Fishkill		
Ilion	New York State	1901-1904
Jamestown	New York-Pennsylvania	1891, 1957, 1961-1973, 1977-
	Interstate	1905, 1914-1915
	PONY	1939-1956
see also Oil City (PA)-Jamestown		
Johnstown		
see Amsterdam-Johnstown-Gloversville; Gloversville-Johnstown		
Kingston	Hudson River	1903-1907
	New York-New Jersey	1913
	North Atlantic	1947
	Colonial	1948-1950
	Canadian-American	1951
Little Falls	New York-Pennsylvania	1977-1988
(aka Mohawk Valley)	Northeast	1995
Lockport	PONY	1942-1950
	Middle Atlantic	1951
Long Island see Maspeth		
Maspeth	Eastern	1886
(aka Long Island)		
Middletown	New York-New Jersey	1913
	Atlantic	1914
Mohawk Valley see Little Falls		
Mountaindale	Northeast	1995, 1997-
(aka Sullivan)	North Atlantic	1996
New York	American Association	1883-1887
	National	1883-1957, 1962-
	National Colored	1887
	Player's	1890
	Atlantic	1896
	American	1903-
	United States	1912
Newark	New York-Pennsylvania	1968-1979, 1983-1987
	North Atlantic	1995-
Newburgh	Hudson River	1903-1907
	New York-New Jersey	1913
	Atlantic	1914
	North Atlantic	1946
	Northeast	1995-
Niagara Falls	International (Class D)	1908
	PONY	1939-1940
	Middle Atlantic	1946-1947, 1950-1951
	New York-Pennsylvania	1970-1979, 1982-1985, 1989-1993
	North Atlantic	1995
Nyack	North Atlantic	1946-1948
Ogdensburg	Canadian-American	1936-1939
	Border	1946-1951
see also Ottawa-Ogdensburg		
Olean	New York-Pennsylvania	1891, 1957-1959, 1961-1962
	Interstate	1905-1908, 1914-1916
	PONY	1939-1956
Oneida	New York State	1889
Oneonta	New York-Pennsylvania	1924, 1966-
	Canadian-American	1940-1942, 1946-1951
Ossining	Hudson River	1903
Oswego	New York State	1885, 1899-1900
	International	1886-1887
	Canadian-American	1936-1940
Peekskill	Hudson River	1903, 1905
	North Atlantic	1946-1949
Port Chester	Colonial	1947-1948
Poughkeepsie	Hudson River	1903-1907
	New York-New Jersey	1913
	Atlantic	1914
	Colonial	1947-1950
Rochester	New York State	1885
	International	1886-1889, 1912-
	American Association	1890
	Eastern	1891-1892, 1895-1911
Rome	New York State	1899-1901
	Canadian-American	1937-1942, 1946-1951
Saratoga Springs see Glens Falls-Saratoga Springs		
Saugerties	Hudson River	1903-1905
Schenectady	New York State	1899-1904
	Canadian-American	1946-1950
	Eastern	1951-1957
Seneca Falls	New York State	1889
Sullivan see Mountaindale		
Syracuse	New York State	1885, 1902-1917
	International	1886-1889, 1918, 1920-1927, 1934-1955, 1961-

PROFESSIONAL TEAMS BY STATE

	American Association	1890
	Eastern	1891-1892, 1894-1901, 1956-1957
	New York-Pennsylvania	1928-1929
Troy	Eastern	1888, 1891-1894
	New York State	1899-1916
Utica	New York State	1885, 1889, 1899-1917
	International	1886-1887
	Canadian-American	1939-1942
	New York-Pennsylvania	1924, 1977-
	Eastern	1943-1950
Walden	North Atlantic	1946
Watertown	Canadian-American	1936
	Border	1946-1951
	New York-Pennsylvania	1983-
Waverly	New York State	1901
Wellsville	Interstate	1914-1916
	PONY	1942-1956
	New York-Pennsylvania	1957-1961, 1963-1965
Yonkers	Hudson River	1905, 1907
	Northeast	1995

NORTH CAROLINA

City	League	Years
Alamance see Burlington		
Albemarle	North Carolina State	1948
Angier-Fuquay Springs	Tobacco State	1946
Asheville	Southeastern	1910
	Appalachian	1911-1912
	North Carolina State	1913-1917
	South Atlantic	1924-1930, 1959-1963, 1980-
	Piedmont	1931-1932, 1934-1942
	Tri-State	1946-1955
	Southern	1964-1966, 1968-1975
	Carolina	1967
	Western Carolinas	1976-1979
Ayden	Coastal Plain	1937-1938
Belmont	Western Carolina	1961
Burlington	Bi-State	1942
	Carolina	1945-1951, 1958-1972
(aka Alamance)	Appalachian	1986-
Burlington-Graham	Carolina	1952-1955
Cape Fear see Fayetteville		
Carolina see Zebulon		
Charlotte	Virginia-North Carolina	1901, 1905
	North Carolina	1902
	Carolina Association	1908-1912
	North Carolina State	1913-1917
	South Atlantic	1919-1930, 1954-1963
	Piedmont	1931-1935, 1937-1942
	Tri-State	1946-1953
	Southern	1964-1972, 1976-1992
	Western Carolinas	1972
	International	1993
Clinton	Tobacco State	1946-1950
Concord	North Carolina State	1939-1942, 1945-1951
Conover see Newton-Conover		
Cooleemee	North Carolina State	1937-1941
Draper see Leaksville-Draper-Spray		
Dunn-Erwin	Tobacco State	1946-1949
Durham	North Carolina	1902
	North Carolina State	1913-1917
	Piedmont	1920-1933, 1936-1943
	Carolina	1945-1967, 1980-
see also Raleigh-Durham		
Eden see Leaksville-Draper-Spray		
Edenton	Virginia	1951
	Coastal Plain	1952
Elizabeth City	Virginia	1950-1951
Elkin	Blue Ridge	1949-1950
	North Carolina State	1951-1952
Erwin see Dunn-Erwin		
Fayetteville	Eastern Carolina	1909-1910, 1928-1929
	Coastal Plain	1946
	Tri-State	1947-1948
	Tobacco State	1949
	Carolina	1950-1956
(aka Cape Fear)	South Atlantic	1987-
Forest City	Western Carolina	1948
	Tar Heel	1953-1954

City	League	Years
Fuquay Springs see Angier-Fuquay Springs		
Gastonia	South Atlantic	1923, 1959, 1980-1992
	North Carolina State	1938
	Tar Heel	1939-1940
	Western Carolina(s)	1950, 1960, 1963-1970, 1972-1974, 1977-1979
	Tri-State	1952-1953
	Atlantic Coast	1995
Goldsboro	Eastern Carolina	1908-1910, 1928-1929
	Coastal Plain	1937-1941, 1946-1952
Graham see Burlington-Graham		
Granite Falls	Western Carolina	1951
Greensboro	North Carolina	1902
	Virginia-North Carolina	1905
	Carolina Association	1908-1912
	North Carolina State	1913-1917
	Piedmont	1920-1926, 1928-1934, 1941-1942
	Carolina	1945-1968
	Western Carolinas	1979
	South Atlantic	1980-
Greenville	Eastern Carolina	1928-1929
	Coastal Plain	1937-1940, 1946-1951
Henderson	Piedmont	1929-1931
Hendersonville	Western Carolina	1948-1949
Hickory	Tar Heel	1939-1940, 1953-1954
	North Carolina State	1942, 1945-1950
	Western Carolina	1952, 1960
	South Atlantic	1993-
High Point	Piedmont	1920-1932
High Point-Thomasville	North Carolina State	1948-1952
	Tar Heel	1953
	Carolina	1954-1958, 1968-1969
see also Thomasville		
Kannapolis	North Carolina State	1939-1941
(aka Piedmont)	South Atlantic	1995-
Kinston	Eastern Carolina	1908, 1928-1929
	Virginia	1925-1927
	Coastal Plain	1937-1941, 1946-1952
	Carolina	1956-1957, 1962-1974, 1978-
Landis	North Carolina State	1937-1942, 1945-1947, 1949-1951
Leaksville-Draper-Spray	Bi-State	1934-1942
(now Eden, NC)	Carolina	1945-1947
	Blue Ridge	1948
Lenoir	Tar Heel	1939-1940
	Blue Ridge	1946-1947
	Western Carolina	1948-1951
Lexington	North Carolina State	1937-1942, 1945-1952
	Tar Heel	1953
	Western Carolina(s)	1960-1961, 1963-1967
Lincolnton	Western Carolina	1948-1952
	Tar Heel	1953
Lumberton	Tobacco State	1947-1950
Marion	Western Carolina	1948-1952
	Tar Heel	1953-1954
Mayodan	Bi-State	1934-1941
Monroe	Western Carolinas	1969, 1971
Mooresville	North Carolina State	1937-1942, 1945-1952
	Tar Heel	1953
Morganton	Western Carolina	1948-1952
Mt. Airy	Bi-State	1934-1941
	Blue Ridge	1946-1950
New Bern	North Carolina	1902
	Eastern Carolina	1908
	Coastal Plain	1937-1941, 1946-1952
Newton-Conover	North Carolina State	1937-1938
	Tar Heel	1939-1940
	Western Carolina	1948-1951, 1960-1962
North Wilkesboro	Blue Ridge	1948-1950
Piedmont see Kannapolis		
Port City see Wilmington		
Raleigh	Virginia-North Carolina	1901
	North Carolina	1902
	Eastern Carolina	1908-1910
	North Carolina State	1913-1917
	Piedmont	1920-1932
	Carolina	1945-1953, 1958-1967
Raleigh-Durham	Carolina	1968-1971
see also Durham		
Red Springs	Tobacco State	1947-1950
	Carolina	1969
Reidsville	Bi-State	1935-1940
	Tri-State	1947
	Carolina	1948-1955

PROFESSIONAL TEAMS BY STATE

City	League	Years
Roanoke Rapids	Coastal Plain	1947-1952
Rockingham	Tobacco State	1950
Rocky Mount	Eastern Carolina	1909-1910, 1928-1929
	Virginia	1915-1917, 1920-1925
	Piedmont	1927, 1936-1940
	Coastal Plain	1941, 1946-1952
	Bi-State	1942
	Carolina	1962-1975, 1980
Rutherford County see Forest City see Spindale		
Salisbury	North Carolina State	1937-1942, 1945-1952
	Tar Heel	1953
	Western Carolina(s)	1960-1966, 1968
Salisbury-Spencer	Virginia-North Carolina	1905
	Piedmont	1925-1929
Sanford	Bi-State	1941-1942
	Tobacco State	1946-1950
Selma see Smithfield-Selma		
Shelby	North Carolina State	1937-1938
	Tar Heel	1939-1940, 1953-1954
	Tri-State	1946
	Western Carolina(s)	1948-1952, 1960-1965, 1969, 1977-1979
	South Atlantic	1980-1982
Smithfield	Tobacco State	1946
Smithfield-Selma	Tobacco State	1947-1950
Snow Hill	Coastal Plain	1937-1940
Spencer see Salisbury-Spencer		
Spindale (aka Rutherford County)	Western Carolina	1949-1952, 1960
Spray see Leaksville-Spray-Draper		
Statesville	Tar Heel	1939-1940, 1953
	North Carolina State	1942, 1945-1952
	Western Carolina(s)	1960-1964, 1966-1967, 1969
Tarboro	Virginia-North Carolina	1901
	Virginia	1921
	Coastal Plain	1937-1941, 1946-1952
Thomasville	North Carolina State	1937-1942, 1945-1947
	Western Carolinas	1965-1966
see also High Point-Thomasville		
Warsaw	Tobacco State	1947-1948
Whiteville	Tobacco State	1950
Williamston	Coastal Plain	1937-1941
Wilmington	Virginia-North Carolina	1901
	North Carolina	1902
	Eastern Carolina	1908-1910, 1928-1929
	Piedmont	1932-1935
	Tobacco State	1946-1950
(aka Port City)	Southern	1995-1996
Wilson	Eastern Carolina	1908-1910
	Virginia	1920-1927
	Coastal Plain	1939-1941, 1946-1952
	Bi-State	1942
	Carolina	1956-1968, 1973
Winston-Salem	Virginia-North Carolina	1905
	Carolina Association	1908-1912
	North Carolina State	1913-1917
	Piedmont	1920-1933, 1937-1942
(aka Winston)	Carolina	1945-
Zebulon (aka Carolina)	Southern	1991-

NORTH DAKOTA

City	League	Years
Bismarck	Dakota	1922
	North Dakota	1923
(aka Dakota)	Prairie	1995-1996
Bismarck-Mandan	Northern	1962-1964, 1966
Carrington	North Dakota	1923
Cavalier	Northern	1902
Dakota see Bismarck		
Devils Lake	Northern	1902
Fargo	Northern	1902-1905, 1908
	Northern-Copper Country	1906
	Dakota	1922
Fargo-Moorhead	Northern	1914-1917, 1933-1942, 1946-1960, 1996-
Grand Forks	Northern	1902-1905, 1913-1915, 1934-1935, 1938-1942, 1946-1964
	Northern-Copper Country	1906
	Central International	1912
	Prairie	1996-
Jamestown	Dakota	1922
	North Dakota	1923
	Northern	1936-1937
Mandan see Bismarck-Mandan		
Minot	Northern	1917, 1958-1960, 1962
	North Dakota	1923
	Prairie	1995-
New Rockford	North Dakota	1923
Valley City	Dakota	1922
	North Dakota	1923
Wahpeton-Breckenridge	Dakota	1921-1922

OHIO

City	League	Years
Akron see also Canton-Akron	Ohio State	1887
	Tri-State	1890
	Ohio-Michigan	1893
	Ohio-Pennsylvania	1905-1911
	Central	1912, 1928-1929, 1932
	Interstate	1913
	Buckeye	1915
	International	1920
	Middle Atlantic	1935-1941
	Eastern	1997-
Alliance-Sebring	Ohio-Pennsylvania	1912
Barberton	Ohio-Pennsylvania	1905
Bridgeport	Ohio-Pennsylvania	1912
Bucyrus	Ohio-Pennsylvania	1905
Canton	Ohio State	1887
	Tri-State	1888-1890
	Ohio-Michigan	1893
	Central	1905-1907, 1912, 1928-1930, 1932
	Ohio-Pennsylvania	1905, 1908-1911
	Interstate	1913
	Buckeye	1915
	Ohio State	1936
	Middle Atlantic	1936-1942
	Frontier	1997-
Canton-Akron see also Akron	Eastern	1989-1996
Chillicothe	Ohio State Association	1884
	Ohio State	1910-1916
	Frontier	1993-
Cincinnati	American Association	1883-1889, 1891
	Union Association	1884
	National	1890-
	United States	1912
Cleveland	National	1883-1884, 1889-1899
	Western	1885
	American Association	1887-1888, 1914-1915
	Player's	1890
	American	1900-
	United States	1912
	Federal	1913
Columbus	American Association	1883-1884, 1889-1891, 1902-1954
	Tri-State	1887-1888
	Western	1892, 1896-1899
	Interstate	1899-1900, 1913
	Western Association	1901
	International	1955-1970, 1977-
Dayton	Ohio State Association	1884
	Tri-State	1889-1890
	Interstate	1897-1900
	Western Association	1901
	Central	1903-1917, 1928-1930, 1932, 1948-1951
	Middle Atlantic	1933-1942
	Ohio State	1946-1947
East Liberty	Iron & Oil Association	1884
East Liverpool	Ohio-Michigan	1893
	Penn-Ohio-Maryland	1906-1907
	Ohio-Pennsylvania	1908-1912
Findlay	Buckeye	1915
	Ohio State	1937-1941
Fostoria	Ohio State	1936-1941
Fremont	Ohio State	1936-1941
Gallipolis see Point Pleasant (WV)-Gallipolis		
Girard	Ohio-Pennsylvania	1908
Hamilton	Tri-State	1889
	Ohio State	1911, 1913
Ironton	Ohio State Association	1884
	Mountain States	1911-1912
	Ohio State	1912-1915
Kent	Ohio-Pennsylvania	1905
Lancaster	Ohio-Pennsylvania	1905-1907
	Ohio State	1908-1911
	Frontier	1993-1994
Lima	Tri-State	1888

	Ohio-Pennsylvania	1905
	Interstate Association	1906
	Ohio State	1908-1912, 1939-1941, 1944-1947
	Buckeye	1915
	Central	1934
	Ohio-Indiana	1948-1951
Mansfield	Ohio State	1887, 1908-1909, 1912, 1936-1937, 1939-1941
	Tri-State	1888-1890
	Ohio-Michigan	1893
	Interstate	1897-1900
	Ohio-Pennsylvania	1906-1907, 1910-1911
Marion	Interstate	1900
	Western Association	1901
	Central	1903-1904
	Ohio-Pennsylvania	1906-1907
	Ohio State	1908-1912, 1937, 1944-1947
	Buckeye	1915
	Ohio-Indiana	1948-1951
Massillon	Ohio-Pennsylvania	1905
Middleport-Pomeroy	Mountain States	1911-1912
Middletown	Ohio State	1944-1946
Mt. Vernon	Ohio-Pennsylvania	1905
New Philadelphia	Ohio State	1936
Newark	Ohio-Pennsylvania	1905-1907
	Ohio State	1908-1912, 1936, 1944-1947
	Central	1911
	Buckeye	1915
	Ohio-Indiana	1948-1951
	Frontier	1994-1995
Niles	Ohio-Pennsylvania	1905
Piqua	Ohio State	1911
Pomeroy see Middleport-Pomeroy		
Portsmouth	Ohio State Association	1884
	Ohio State	1908-1916
	Middle Atlantic	1935-1940
	Ohio-Indiana	1948-1950
	Frontier	1993-1995
Salem	Ohio-Pennsylvania	1912
Sandusky	Ohio State	1887, 1936-1937
	Tri-State	1888
	Ohio-Michigan	1893
Sebring see Alliance-Sebring		
Springfield	Ohio State Association	1884
	Tri-State	1889-1890
	Interstate	1897-1899
	Central	1905-1907, 1912-1914, 1916-1917, 1928-1930
	Ohio State	1908, 1911, 1944-1947
	Middle Atlantic	1933-1934, 1937-1939, 1941-1942
	Ohio-Indiana	1948-1951
Steubenville	Ohio State	1887
	Ohio-Pennsylvania	1905, 1909, 1911
	Penn-Ohio-Maryland	1906-1907
	Interstate	1913
Steubenville-Follansbee	Ohio-Pennsylvania	1912
Tiffin	Ohio State	1936-1941
Toledo	Northwestern	1883
	American Association	1884, 1890, 1902-1913, 1916-1955
	Western	1885, 1892, 1894-1895
	Tri-State	1888
	International	1889, 1965-
	Interstate	1896-1900
	Western Association	1901
	Southern Michigan Assn.	1914
Van Wert	Ohio-Indiana	1908
Wooster	Ohio-Pennsylvania	1905
Youngstown	Iron & Oil Association	1884
	Tri-State	1890
	Interstate	1896-1900, 1913
	Ohio-Pennsylvania	1905-1911
	Central	1912, 1915, 1932
	Middle Atlantic	1931, 1939-1941, 1946-1951
Zanesville	Ohio State	1887
	Tri-State	1888
	Ohio-Pennsylvania	1905-1906
	Penn-Ohio-Maryland	1907
	Central	1908-1912
	Interstate	1913
	Middle Atlantic	1933-1937, 1941-1942
	Ohio State	1944-1947
	Ohio-Indiana	1948-1950
	Frontier	1993-1996

OKLAHOMA

City	League	Years
Ada	Sooner State	1947-1954
Altus	Texas-Oklahoma	1911
Anadarko	Oklahoma State	1912
Ardmore	Texas	1904, 1961
	Texas-Oklahoma	1911-1914, 1921-1922
	Western Association	1917, 1923-1926
	Oklahoma State	1924
	Sooner State	1947-1957
Bartlesville	Kansas State	1906
	Oklahoma-Arkansas-Kansas	1907
	Oklahoma-Kansas	1908
	Western Association	1909-1910, 1924, 1931-1932, 1934-1938
	Southwestern	1921-1923
	Western	1933
	Kansas-Oklahoma-Missouri	1946-1952
Blackwell	Oklahoma State	1924
	Southwestern	1924-1926
	Kansas-Oklahoma-Missouri	1952
	Western Association	1954
Bristow	Oklahoma State	1923-1924
Chickasha	Southwestern	1904
	Western Association	1920-1921
	Oklahoma State	1922
	Sooner State	1948-1952
Clinton	Oklahoma State	1922-1923
Cushing	Southwestern	1921, 1925
	Oklahoma State	1923-1924
Drumright	Western Association	1920-1921
	Oklahoma State	1923
Duncan	Oklahoma State	1922-1924
	Sooner State	1947-1950
Durant	Texas-Oklahoma	1911-1914
El Reno	Western Association	1909-1910
	Oklahoma State	1922-1923
Enid	Southwestern	1904, 1924-1926
	Western Association	1908-1910, 1920-1923, 1950-1951
	Oklahoma State	1924
Guthrie	Southwestern	1904
	Western Association	1905, 1909-1910, 1914
	South Central	1906
	Oklahoma State	1912, 1922-1924
Henryetta	Western Association	1914, 1920-1923
Holdenville	Oklahoma State	1912
Hugo	Texas-Oklahoma	1913-1914
Lawton	Texas-Oklahoma	1911
	Sooner State	1947-1957
Maud	Western Association	1929
McAlester	Oklahoma-Arkansas-Kansas	1907
	Oklahoma-Kansas	1908
	Oklahoma State	1912, 1924
	Western Association	1914-1917, 1922-1923, 1926
	Sooner State	1947-1956
Miami	Southwestern	1921
	Kansas-Oklahoma-Missouri	1946-1952
Muskogee	Missouri Valley	1905
	South Central	1906
	Oklahoma-Arkansas-Kansas	1907
	Oklahoma-Kansas	1908
	Western Association	1909-1911, 1914-1917, 1924-1929, 1932, 1934-1942, 1946-1954
	Oklahoma State	1912
	Southwestern	1921-1923
	Western	1933
	Sooner State	1955-1957
Oklahoma City	Southwestern	1904
	Western Association	1905-1908, 1914-1917
	Texas	1909-1911, 1933-1957
	Oklahoma State	1912
	Western	1918-1932
	American Association	1962, 1969-
	Pacific Coast	1963-1968
Okmulgee	Oklahoma State	1912
	Western Association	1920-1927
Pauls Valley	Sooner State	1948-1954
Pawhuska	Oklahoma State	1924
	Western Association	1920-1922
Ponca City	Oklahoma State	1923-1924
	Southwestern	1926
	Western Association	1934-1938, 1954
	Kansas-Oklahoma-Missouri	1947-1952
	Sooner State	1955-1957
Sapulpa	Western Association	1909-1911
	Southwestern	1921-1923

Seminole	Sooner State	1947-1951, 1954-1957
Shawnee	Southwestern	1904, 1925
	South Central	1906
	Oklahoma State	1923-1924
	Western Association	1929-1930
	Sooner State	1950-1957
South McAlester	Missouri Valley	1905
	South Central	1906
Tulsa	Missouri Valley	1905
	South Central	1906
	Oklahoma-Arkansas-Kansas	1907
	Oklahoma-Kansas	1908
	Western Association	1910-1911, 1914-1917
	Oklahoma State	1912
	Western	1919-1929, 1932
	Texas	1933-1942, 1946-1965, 1977-
	Pacific Coast	1966-1968
	American Association	1969-1976
Vinita	Missouri Valley	1905
	Kansas State	1906
Wewoka	Oklahoma State	1924
Wilson	Oklahoma State	1922

OREGON

City	League	Years
Albany	Oregon State	1904
Baker City	Inland Empire	1908
	Western Tri-State	1913-1914
Bend	Northwest	1970-1971, 1978-1994
(aka Central Oregon)	Western	1995-
Coos Bay-North Bend	Northwest	1970-1972
Eugene	Oregon State	1904
	Far West	1950-1951
	Northwest	1955-1968, 1974-
	Pacific Coast	1969-1973
Klamath Falls	Far West	1948-1951
La Grande	Inland Empire	1908
	Western Tri-State	1912-1913
Medford	Far West	1948-1951
	Northwest	1967-1971, 1979-
(aka Rogue Valley/Southern Oregon)		
Pendleton	Inland Empire	1908
	Western Tri-State	1912-1914
Portland	Pacific Northwest	1892, 1901-1902
	New Pacific	1896
	Pacific National	1903
	Pacific Coast	1903-1972, 1978-1993
	Northwestern	1909, 1911-1914
	Pacific Coast International	1918
	Northwest	1973-1977, 1995-
Rogue Valley see Medford		
Roseburg	Oregon State	1904
Salem	Oregon State	1904
	Western International	1940-1942, 1946-1954
(aka Salem-Keizer)	Northwest	1955-1965, 1977-1989, 1997-
Southern Oregon see Medford		

PENNSYLVANIA

City	League	Years
Allentown	Eastern	1884, 1894, 1929-1932, 1954-1960
	Central	1888
	Pennsylvania State	1892-1895
	Atlantic	1898-1900
	Tri-State	1912-1914
	New York-Pennsylvania	1935-1936
	Interstate	1939-1952
	Northeast	1997-
Altoona	Union Association	1884
	Pennsylvania State	1892-1894
	Tri-State	1904-1912
	Middle Atlantic	1931
	North Atlantic	1996-
Ashland	Central Pennsylvania	1887
	Pennsylvania State	1894
Bangor	North Atlantic	1949-1950
Beaver Falls	Western Pennsylvania	1907
	Middle Atlantic	1931
	Pennsylvania State Assn.	1937-1941
Berwick	North Atlantic	1950
Braddock	Ohio-Pennsylvania	1905
	Penn-Ohio-Maryland	1906-1907
Bradford	New York-Pennsylvania	1891, 1957

	Interstate	1905-1908, 1914-1916
	PONY	1939-1942, 1944-1956
Butler	Ohio-Pennsylvania	1905, 1908
	Penn-Ohio-Maryland	1906
	Western Pennsylvania	1907
	Pennsylvania State Assn.	1935-1942
	Middle Atlantic	1946-1951
Carbondale	Pennsylvania State	1895
	North Atlantic	1946-1950
Chambersburg	Keystone Association	1884
	Blue Ridge	1915-1917, 1920-1930
Charleroi	Penn-Ohio-Maryland	1906-1907
	Pennsylvania-West Virginia	1908-1909
	Middle Atlantic	1927-1931
	Pennsylvania State Assn.	1934-1936
Chester	Keystone Association	1884
	Tri-State	1912
Connellsville	Western Pennsylvania	1907
	Pennsylvania-West Virginia	1908-1909
	Ohio-Pennsylvania	1912
Coudersport	Interstate	1905
Danville	Central Pennsylvania	1887
	Pennsylvania State	1892-1893
DuBois	Interstate	1905-1907
Easton	Central	1888
	Atlantic Association	1889
	Pennsylvania State	1893-1894
Erie	New York-Pennsylvania	1891, 1957-1963, 1967, 1981-1993, 1995-
	Eastern	1893-1894
	Interstate	1905-1908, 1913, 1916
	Ohio-Pennsylvania	1908-1911
	Central	1912, 1915, 1928-1930, 1932
	Canadian	1914
	Middle Atlantic	1938-1939, 1941-1942, 1946-1951
	PONY	1944-1945, 1954-1956
	Frontier	1994
Franklin	Iron & Oil Association	1884
	Interstate	1907-1908
Gettysburg	Blue Ridge	1915-1917
Greensburg	Western Pennsylvania	1907
	Pennsylvania State Assn.	1934-1939
Harrisburg	Interstate Association	1883
	Eastern	1884, 1987-
	Atlantic Association	1890
	Pennsylvania State	1893-1895
	Atlantic	1900
	Tri-State	1904-1914
	International	1915
	New York State	1916-1917
	New York-Pennsylvania	1924-1935
	Interstate	1940-1942, 1946-1952
Hazleton	Central Pennsylvania	1887
	Central	1888
	Pennsylvania State	1894-1895
	New York-Pennsylvania	1929-1932, 1934-1937
	Eastern	1938
	Interstate	1939-1940
	North Atlantic	1949-1950
Homestead	Ohio-Pennsylvania	1905
Jeannette	Middle Atlantic	1926-1931
	Pennsylvania State Assn.	1934-1937
Johnsonburg	Interstate	1916
Johnstown	Iron & Oil Association	1884
	Pennsylvania State	1892-1893
	Tri-State	1905-1912
	Middle Atlantic	1925-1938, 1946-1950
	Pennsylvania State Assn.	1939-1940
	Eastern	1955-1956, 1961
	Frontier	1995-
Kane	Interstate	1905-1907
Kittanning	Western Pennsylvania	1907
Lancaster	Keystone Association	1884
	Eastern	1884-1885, 1958-1961
	Pennsylvania State	1894-1895
	Atlantic	1896-1899
	Tri-State	1905-1912, 1914
	Interstate	1932, 1940-1952
	Piedmont	1954-1955
Lansdale	North Atlantic	1948
Latrobe	Western Pennsylvania	1907
Lebanon	Atlantic Association	1890
	Eastern	1891
	Pennsylvania State	1892
	Tri-State	1904
	North Atlantic	1949-1950
Littlestown	Keystone Association	1884

Mahanoy City	Central Pennsylvania	1887
	North Atlantic	1946-1950
McKeesport	Tri-State	1890
	Ohio-Pennsylvania	1905, 1908-1910, 1912
	Penn-Ohio-Maryland	1907
	Pennsylvania State Assn.	1934-1940
Meadville	New York-Pennsylvania	1891
Minersville	Central Pennsylvania	1887
Monessen	Pennsylvania State Assn.	1934-1938
Mt. Carmel	Central Pennsylvania	1887
Nazareth	North Atlantic	1946-1950
New Brighton	Iron & Oil Association	1884
New Castle	Iron & Oil Association	1884
	Interstate	1896-1900
	Ohio-Pennsylvania	1906-1912
	Middle Atlantic	1948-1951
Norristown	Interstate	1932
Oil City	Iron & Oil Association	1884
	Interstate	1907-1908
	Pennsylvania State Assn.	1940-1942
	Middle Atlantic	1946-1951
Oil City-Jamestown	Interstate	1906
see also Jamestown (NY)		
Patton	Interstate	1906
Philadelphia	American Association	1883-1891
	National	1883-
	Union Association	1884
	National Colored	1887
	Player's	1890
	Eastern	1892
	Pennsylvania State	1894
	Atlantic	1896-1897, 1900
	American	1901-1954
Pittsburgh	American Association	1883-1886
	Union Association	1884
	National Colored	1887
	National	1887-
	Player's	1890
	Ohio-Pennsylvania	1912
	United States	1912
	Federal	1913-1915
Pottsville	Interstate Association	1883
	Pennsylvania State	1894-1895
Pottstown	Interstate	1932
Punxsutawney	Interstate	1906-1907
Reading	Interstate Association	1883
	Eastern	1884, 1952-1961, 1963-1965, 1967-
	Pennsylvania State	1892-1895
	Atlantic	1897-1900
	Tri-State	1907-1912, 1914
	United States	1912
	New York State	1916-1917
	International	1919-1931
	Interstate	1940-1941
	New York-Pennsylvania	1933-1935
Ridgway	Interstate	1916
St. Clair	Interstate	1932
St. Marys	Interstate	1916
Scottdale	Western Pennsylvania	1907
	Pennsylvania-West Virginia	1908
	Middle Atlantic	1925-1931
Scranton	International	1887
	Central	1888
	Pennsylvania State	1892-1894
	Eastern	1894-1897, 1939-1953
	Atlantic	1899-1900
	New York State	1904-1917
	New York-Pennsylvania	1923-1937
Scranton-Wilkes-Barre	International	1989-
see also Wilkes-Barre		
Shamokin	Central Pennsylvania	1887
	Tri-State	1905
	New York-Pennsylvania	1925-1927
Sharon	Ohio-Pennsylvania	1905-1908, 1911-1912
Shenandoah	Pennsylvania State	1894-1895
Slatington	Interstate	1932
Somerset	Western Pennsylvania	1907
Stroudsburg	Interstate	1932
	North Atlantic	1946-1950
Sunbury	Central Pennsylvania	1887
	Interstate	1939-1940, 1946-1952
	Piedmont	1955
Tamaqua	Interstate	1932
Uniontown	Penn-Ohio-Maryland	1906-1907
	Pennsylvania-West Virginia	1908-1909
	Middle Atlantic	1926, 1947-1949

Vandergrift	Middle Atlantic	1947-1950
Warren	Interstate	1908, 1914-1916
	Pennsylvania State Assn.	1940-1941
Washington	Interstate	1896
	Ohio-Pennsylvania	1905
	Penn-Ohio-Maryland	1906-1907
	Pennsylvania State Assn.	1934-1935, 1939-1942
Waynesboro	Blue Ridge	1920-1930
Waynesburg	Penn-Ohio-Maryland	1906
Wilkes-Barre	International	1887
	Central	1888
	Atlantic Association	1889
	Pennsylvania State	1892
	Eastern	1893-1898, 1938-1951, 1953-1955
	Atlantic	1899-1900
	New York State	1905-1917
	New York-Pennsylvania	1923-1937
see also Scranton-Wilkes-Barre		
Williamsport	Tri-State	1904-1910
	New York-Pennsylvania	1923-1937, 1968-1972, 1994-
	Eastern	1938-1942, 1944-1956, 1958-1962, 1964-1967, 1976, 1987-1991
York	Eastern	1884, 1958-1959, 1962-1969
	Keystone Association	1884
	Pennsylvania State	1893
	Tri-State	1904-1907, 1909-1914
	New York-Pennsylvania	1923-1933, 1936
	Interstate	1940, 1943-1952
	Piedmont	1953-1955

RHODE ISLAND

City	League	Years
Newport	New England	1897-1899
	Atlantic Association	1908
Pawtucket	New England	1892, 1894-1899, 1946-1949
	Atlantic Association	1908
	Colonial	1914-1915
	Eastern	1966-1967, 1970-1972
	International	1973-
Providence	National	1883-1885
	Eastern	1886, 1891-1911, 1918-1919, 1926-1930
	International	1912-1917
	New England	1946-1949
West Warwick (aka Rhode Island)	Northeast	1996
Woonsocket	New England	1891-1892, 1933
	Atlantic Association	1908
	Colonial	1914

SOUTH CAROLINA

City	League	Years
Anderson	South Carolina	1907
	Carolina Association	1908-1912
	Palmetto	1931
	Tri-State	1946-1954
	Western Carolinas	1970-1975
	South Atlantic	1980-1984
Capital City see Columbia		
Charleston	Southern	1886-1888, 1893-1894
	South Atlantic	1904-1909, 1911, 1913-1917, 1919-1923, 1940-1942, 1946-1953, 1959-1961, 1980-
	Western Carolinas	1973-1978
Chester	South Carolina	1908
Columbia	South Atlantic	1904-1912, 1914-1917, 1919-1923, 1925-1930, 1936-1942, 1946-1957, 1960-1961, 1983-
(aka Capital City)	Piedmont	1934
Darlington	South Carolina	1907
Florence	South Carolina	1907
	Palmetto	1931
	Tri-State	1948-1950
	South Atlantic	1981-1986
	Atlantic Coast	1995
Greenville	South Carolina	1907
	Carolina Association	1908-1912
	South Atlantic	1919-1930, 1938-1942, 1946-1950, 1961-1962
	Palmetto	1931
	Tri-State	1951-1952, 1954-1955
	Western Carolinas	1963-1972
	Southern	1984-
Greenwood	Tri-State	1951
	Western Carolinas	1968-1979

PROFESSIONAL TEAMS BY STATE

City	League	Years
	South Atlantic	1981-1983
	Atlantic Coast	1995
Myrtle Beach	South Atlantic	1987-1992
Orangeburg	South Carolina	1907-1908
	Western Carolinas	1973-1974
Rock Hill	South Carolina	1908
	Tri-State	1947-1955
	Western Carolinas	1963-1968
Spartanburg	South Carolina	1907
	Carolina Association	1908-1912
	South Atlantic	1919-1929, 1938-1940, 1980-1994
	Palmetto	1931
	Tri-State	1946-1955
	Western Carolinas	1963-1979
	Atlantic Coast	1995
Sumter	South Carolina	1907-1908
	Tri-State	1949-1950
	Western Carolinas	1970-1971
	South Atlantic	1985-1991

SOUTH DAKOTA

City	League	Years
Aberdeen	South Dakota	1920, 1923
	Dakota	1921-1922
	Northern	1946-1971
	Prairie	1995-
Flandreau	Iowa-South Dakota	1902
Huron	South Dakota	1920
	Dakota	1921
	Northern	1965-1970
	North Central	1994
Madison	South Dakota	1920
	Dakota	1921
Miller	South Dakota	1920
Mitchell	South Dakota	1920, 1923
	Dakota	1921-1922
	Nebraska State	1936-1937
	Western (Class D)	1939-1940
Redfield	South Dakota	1920
	Dakota	1921
Sioux Falls	Iowa-South Dakota	1902-1903
	South Dakota	1920, 1923
	Dakota	1921-1922
	Tri-State	1924
	Nebraska State	1933-1938
	Western (Class D)	1939-1941
	Northern	1942, 1946-1953, 1966-1971, 1993-
Watertown	Dakota	1921-1922
	South Dakota	1923
	Northern	1970-1971
Wessington Springs	South Dakota	1920

TENNESSEE

City	League	Years
Alcoa see Maryville-Alcoa		
Chattanooga	Southern	1885-1886, 1892-1893, 1895
	Southern Association	1901-1902, 1910-1961
	South Atlantic	1909, 1943, 1963
	Southern	1964-1965, 1976-
Clarksville	Kitty	1903-1904, 1910-1914, 1916, 1946-1949
	Big South	1996
	Heartland	1997-
Cleveland	Appalachian	1911-1913, 1921-1922
Columbia	Tennessee-Alabama	1921
	Big South	1996
	Heartland	1997-
Dyersburg	Kitty	1924
	Tri-State	1925
Elizabethton	Appalachian	1937-1942, 1945-1951, 1974-
Erwin	Appalachian	1940, 1943-1944
Greeneville	Appalachian	1921-1925, 1938-1942
Harriman	Appalachian	1914
Jackson	Kitty	1903, 1911, 1923-1924, 1935-1942, 1950-1954
	Tri-State	1925-1926
Johnson City	Southeastern	1910
	Appalachian	1911-1913, 1921-1924, 1937-1955, 1957-1961, 1964-
Kingsport	Appalachian	1921-1925, 1938-1952, 1957, 1960-1963, 1969-1982, 1984-
	Mountain States	1953-1954
Knoxville	South Atlantic	1909, 1925-1929, 1956-1963
	Southeastern	1910
	Appalachian	1911-1914, 1921-1924

City	League	Years
	Southern Association	1932-1944
	Tri-State	1946-1952, 1954-1955
	Mountain States	1953
	Southern	1964-1967, 1972-
Lexington	Kitty	1935-1938
Maryville-Alcoa	Mountain States	1953-1954
Memphis	Southern	1885-1888, 1892-1895
	Southern Association	1901-1960
	Texas	1968-1973
	International	1974-1976
	Southern	1978-
Milan	Kitty	1923
Morristown	Southeastern	1910
	Appalachian	1911-1914, 1923-1925, 1959-1961
	Mountain States	1948-1954
Nashville	Southern	1885-1887, 1893-1895
	Southern Association	1901-1961
	South Atlantic	1963
	Southern	1978-1984, 1993-1994
	American Association	1985-
Newport	Appalachian	1937-1942
	Mountain States	1948-1950
Oak Ridge	Mountain States	1948, 1954
Paris	Kitty	1922-1924
Springfield	Kitty	1923
Trenton	Kitty	1922-1923
Union City	Kitty	1935-1942, 1946-1955
Winchester (aka Tennessee)	Big South	1996-
	Heartland	1997-

TEXAS

City	League	Years
Abilene	West Texas	1920-1922, 1928-1929
	West Texas-New Mexico	1939, 1946-1955
	Big State	1956-1957
	Texas-Louisiana	1995-
Alpine	Sophomore	1959-1961
Amarillo	West Texas	1922
	Panhandle-Pecos Valley	1923
	Western	1927-1928, 1956-1958
	West Texas-New Mexico	1939-1942, 1946-1955
	Texas	1959-1963, 1965-1974, 1976-1982
	Texas-Louisiana	1994-
Austin	Texas	1888-1890, 1905, 1907-1908, 1911-1914, 1956-1967
	Texas-Southern	1895-1896
	South Texas	1906
	Middle Texas	1915
	Texas Association	1923-1926
	Big State	1947-1955
Ballinger	West Texas	1921, 1929
	Longhorn	1947-1950
	Southwestern	1956-1957
Bartlett	Middle Texas	1914-1915
Bay City	Southwest Texas	1910-1911
Beaumont	South Texas	1903-1906
	Gulf Coast	1908
	Texas	1912-1917, 1919-1955, 1983-1986
	Big State	1956-1957
	Texas-Louisiana	1994
Beeville	Southwest Texas	1910-1911
	Gulf Coast	1926
	Gulf States	1976
	Lone Star	1977
Belton	Middle Texas	1914-1915
Big Spring	West Texas	1928-1929
	West Texas-New Mexico	1938-1942
	Longhorn	1947-1955
Bonham	Texas-Oklahoma	1911-1914, 1921-1922
Borger	West Texas-New Mexico	1939, 1942, 1946-1954
Brenham	South Texas	1905
	Middle Texas	1914-1915
Brownsville	Southwest Texas	1910-1911
	Texas Valley	1938
	Rio Grande Valley	1949-1950
	Gulf Coast	1951-1953
Bryan	Lone Star	1947-1948
	East Texas	1949-1950
	Big State	1953-1954
Cisco	West Texas	1920-1921
Clarksville	North Texas	1905
Cleburne	Texas	1906
	Texas-Oklahoma	1911, 1921-1922
	South Central	1912
Coleman	West Texas	1928-1929
Corpus Christi	Southwest Texas	1910-1911

PROFESSIONAL TEAMS BY STATE

City	League	Years
	Gulf Coast	1926, 1951-1953
	Texas Valley	1927, 1938
	Rio Grande Valley	1931, 1949-1950
	Big State	1954-1957
	Texas	1958-1959
	Gulf States	1976
	Lone Star	1977
	Texas-Louisiana	1994-1995
Corsicana	Texas	1902-1905
	North Texas	1907
	Central Texas	1914-1915, 1917
	Texas-Oklahoma	1922
	Texas Association	1923-1926
	Lone Star	1927-1928
Crockett	East Texas	1916
Dallas	Texas	1888-1890, 1902-1942, 1946-1958
	Texas-Southern	1895-1896
	American Association	1959
	Pacific Coast	1964
Dallas-Ft. Worth (aka Texas) see also Ft. Worth	American Association	1960-1962
	Pacific Coast	1963
	Texas	1965-1971
	American	1972-
Del Rio	Longhorn	1948
	Rio Grande Valley	1949-1950
	Big State	1954
Denison	Texas-Southern	1896
	Texas-Oklahoma	1912-1914
	Western Association	1915-1917
see also Sherman-Denison		
Donna	Rio Grande Valley	1949-1950
Eastland	West Texas	1920
Edinburg	Gulf Coast	1926
	Texas Valley	1927
El Paso	Rio Grande Association	1915
	Arizona State	1930
	Arizona-Texas	1931-1932, 1937-1941, 1947-1950, 1952-1954
	Mexican National	1946
	Southwest International	1951
	West Texas-New Mexico	1955
	Southwestern	1956-1957
	Sophomore	1961
	Texas	1962-1970, 1972-
Ennis	Central Texas	1914-1917
Ft. Worth	Texas	1888-1890, 1902-1942, 1946-1958, 1964
	Texas-Southern	1895-1896
	American Association	1959
	Pacific Coast	1963
see also Dallas-Ft. Worth		
Gainesville	Texas-Oklahoma	1911
	Big State	1947-1951
	Sooner State	1953-1955
Galveston	Texas	1888-1890, 1907-1917, 1919-1924, 1931-1937
	Texas-Southern	1895-1896
	South Texas	1903-1906
	Gulf Coast	1950-1953
	Big State	1954-1955
Georgetown	Middle Texas	1914
Gladewater	West Dixie	1935
	East Texas	1936, 1949-1950
	Lone Star	1948
Gorman	West Texas	1920
Graham	Texas-Oklahoma	1921
Greenville	North Texas	1905, 1907
	Texas	1906
	Texas-Oklahoma	1912, 1922
	East Texas	1923-1926, 1946
	Big State	1947-1950, 1953
	Sooner State	1957
Hamlin	West Texas	1928
Harlingen	Rio Grande Valley	1931, 1950
	Texas Valley	1938
	Gulf Coast	1951-1953
	Big State	1954-1955
	Texas	1960-1961
	Gulf States	1976
	Lone Star	1977
(aka Rio Grande Valley)	Texas-Louisiana	1994-
Henderson	East Texas	1931, 1936-1940, 1946, 1949-1950
	Dixie	1933
	West Dixie	1934-1935
	Lone Star	1947-1948
Hillsboro	Central Texas	1914
Houston	Texas	1888-1890, 1907-1958
	Texas-Southern	1895-1896
	South Texas	1903-1906
	American Association	1959-1961
	National	1962-
Italy	Central Texas	1914
Jacksonville	East Texas	1916, 1936-1940, 1946
	West Dixie	1934-1935
	Lone Star	1947
	Gulf Coast	1950
Kaufman	Central Texas	1915
Kilgore	East Texas	1931, 1936-1940, 1949-1950
	Lone Star	1947-1948
La Feria	Rio Grande Valley	1931
Lamesa	West Texas-New Mexico	1939-1942, 1946-1952
	Longhorn	1953
	Southwestern	1957
Lampasas	Middle Texas	1914
Laredo see also Nuevo Lardo, Mex.	Southwest Texas	1910-1911
	Gulf Coast	1926, 1951-1953
	Texas Valley	1927
	Rio Grande Valley	1949-1950
	Texas-Louisiana	1995
	Mexican	1986-1994
Longview	South Central	1912
	East Texas	1923-1926, 1931, 1936-1940, 1949-1950
	Lone Star	1927, 1947-1948
	Texas	1932
	Dixie	1933
	West Dixie	1934-1935
	Big State	1952-1953
Lubbock	West Texas	1922, 1928
	Panhandle-Pecos Valley	1923
	West Texas-New Mexico	1938-1942, 1946-1955
	Big State	1956
	Texas-Louisiana	1995-
Lufkin	East Texas	1916, 1946
	West Dixie	1934
	Lone Star	1947-1948
	Gulf Coast	1950
Marlin	Central Texas	1916-1917
	Texas Association	1923-1924
Marshall	South Central	1912
	East Texas	1923-1926, 1936-1940, 1949-1950
	Lone Star	1927, 1947-1948
	Cotton States	1941
McAllen	Gulf Coast	1926
	Texas Valley	1938
	Rio Grande Valley	1931, 1949-1950
	Lone Star	1977
McKinney	Texas-Oklahoma	1912
Mexia	Central Texas	1915-1917*
	Texas-Oklahoma	1922
	Texas Association	1923-1926
	Lone Star	1927-1928
Midland	West Texas	1928-1929
	West Texas-New Mexico	1937-1940
	Longhorn	1947-1955
	Southwestern	1956-1957
	Sophomore	1958-1959
	Texas	1972-
Mineral Wells	West Texas	1920-1921
	Texas-Oklahoma	1921
Mission	Gulf Coast	1926
	Texas Valley	1927
Monahans	West Texas-New Mexico	1937
Mt. Pleasant	East Texas	1923-1925
Nacogdoches	East Texas	1916
Odessa	West Texas-New Mexico	1937, 1940
	Longhorn	1947-1955
	Sophomore	1959-1960
Orange	Gulf Coast	1907-1908
Palestine	East Texas	1916, 1936-1940
	Texas Association	1925-1926
	Lone Star	1927-1929
	West Dixie	1934-1935
Pampa	West Texas-New Mexico	1939-1942, 1946-1955
	Southwestern	1956-1957
Paris	Texas-Southern	1896
	Texas	1902-1904
	North Texas	1905, 1907
	South Central	1912
	Texas-Oklahoma	1913-1914, 1921-1922
	Western Association	1915-1917
	East Texas	1923-1926, 1931, 1946, 1949-1950
	Lone Star	1927-1929
	Sooner State	1955-1957

PROFESSIONAL TEAMS BY STATE

City	League	Years
	West Dixie	1934
	Big State	1947-1948, 1952-1953
Plainview	West Texas-New Mexico	1953-1955
	Southwestern	1956-1957
	Sophomore	1958-1959
Port Arthur	Gulf Coast	1950-1953
	Cotton States	1932
	Evangeline	1940-1942, 1954
	Big State	1955-1957
Ranger	West Texas	1920-1922
Refugio	Texas Valley	1938
Rio Grande Valley see Harlingen		
Robstown	Rio Grande Valley	1949-1950
Rusk	East Texas	1916
San Angelo	West Texas	1921-1922, 1928-1929
	Longhorn	1948-1955
	Southwestern	1956-1957
	Sophomore	1958-1959
San Antonio	Texas	1888, 1907-1942, 1946-1964, 1967-
	Texas-Southern	1895-1896
	South Texas	1903-1906
	Texas-Louisiana	1994
San Benito	Rio Grande Valley	1931
Schulenburg	Middle Texas	1915
Seguin	Gulf States	1976
Sherman	Texas-Southern	1895-1896
	Texas-Oklahoma	1912-1914, 1921-1922
	Western Association	1915-1917
	Texas Association	1923
	Lone Star	1929
	East Texas	1946
	Sooner State	1952
Sherman-Denison	Texas	1902
	Big State	1947-1951
	Sooner State	1953
see also Denison		
Stamford	West Texas	1922
Sulphur Springs	East Texas	1923-1925
Sweetwater	West Texas	1920-1922
	Longhorn	1947-1952, 1954
Taft	Texas Valley	1938
Taylor	Middle Texas	1915
Temple	Texas	1905-1907
	Middle Texas	1914-1915
	Central Texas	1916-1917
	Texas Association	1924-1926
	Big State	1949-1954, 1957
Terrell	North Texas	1907
	Central Texas	1915-1916
	Texas Association	1925-1926
Texarkana	Texas	1902
	North Texas	1905
	Arkansas-Texas	1906
	Arkansas State	1909
	South Central	1912
	Texas-Oklahoma	1913-1914
	East Texas	1924-1926, 1937-1940, 1946
	Lone Star	1927-1929
	Cotton States	1941
	Big State	1947-1953
Texas see Dallas-Ft. Worth		
Texas City	Gulf Coast	1951-1953
	Evangeline	1954
	Big State	1955-1956
	Lone Star	1977
Tyler	South Central	1912
	East Texas	1924-1926, 1931, 1936-1940, 1946, 1949-1950
	Lone Star	1927-1929, 1947-1948
	Texas	1932
	Dixie	1933
	West Dixie	1934-1935
	Big State	1951-1955
	Texas-Louisiana	1994-
Vernon	Longhorn	1947-1952
Victoria	Southwest Texas	1910-1911
	Gulf Coast	1926
	Big State	1956-1957
	Texas	1958-1961, 1974
	Gulf States	1976
	Lone Star	1977
Waco	Texas	1889-1890, 1902-1903, 1905-1919, 1925-1930
	Texas Association	1923-1924
	Dixie	1933
	Big State	1947-1956
Waxahachie	Central Texas	1914-1916
West	Central Texas	1914
Wichita Falls	Texas-Oklahoma	1911-1913
	Texas	1920-1932
	West Texas-New Mexico	1941-1942
	Big State	1947-1953, 1956-1957
	Longhorn	1954
Wink	West Texas-New Mexico	1937-1938
Winters-Ballinger see also Ballinger	Longhorn	1953

UTAH

City	League	Years
Lagoon	Inter-Mountain	1901
Logan	Utah-Idaho	1926-1927
Murray	Union Association	1914
Ogden	Inter-Mountain	1901
	Union Association	1912-1914
	Utah-Idaho	1926-1928
	Pioneer	1939-1942, 1946-1955, 1966-1974, 1994-
	Pacific Coast	1979-1980
Park City	Inter-Mountain	1901
Salt Lake City	Inter-Mountain	1901, 1909
	Pacific National	1903-1904
	Union Association	1911-1914
	Pacific Coast	1915-1925, 1958-1965, 1970-1984, 1994-
	Utah-Idaho	1926-1928
	Pioneer	1939-1942, 1946-1957, 1967-1969, 1985-1992

VERMONT

City	League	Years
Bellows Falls	Twin States	1911
Brattleboro	Twin States	1911
Burlington	Provincial	1955
	Eastern	1984-1988
(aka Vermont)	New York-Pennsylvania	1994-
Montpelier	Quebec-Ontario-Vermont	1924
Rutland	Quebec-Ontario-Vermont	1924
Springfield-Charlestown	Twin States	1911

VIRGINIA

City	League	Years
Abingdon	Blue Ridge	1948
Alexandria	Carolina	1978-1983
Bassett	Bi-State	1935-1940
	Blue Ridge	1950
Big Stone Gap	Mountain States	1949-1953
Blackstone	Virginia	1948
Bristol	Appalachian	1911-1913, 1921-1925, 1940-1955, 1969-
Charlottesville	Virginia Mountain	1914
Clifton Forge	Virginia Mountain	1914
Colonial Heights-Petersburg see also Petersburg	Virginia	1951
	Piedmont	1954
Covington	Virginia Mountain	1914
	Appalachian	1966-1976
Danville	Virginia-North Carolina	1905
	Virginia	1906-1912
	Piedmont	1920-1925
	Bi-State	1934-1938
	Carolina	1945-1958
	Appalachian	1993-
Danville-Schoolfield	Bi-State	1939-1942
Emporia	Virginia	1948-1951
Fieldale	Bi-State	1934-1936
Franklin	Virginia	1948-1951
Galax	Blue Ridge	1946-1950
Halifax see South Boston-Halifax		
Hampton see also Newport News-Hampton; Peninsula	Virginia	1896
Harrisonburg	Virginia Mountain	1914
	Virginia	1939-1941
Hopewell	Virginia	1900, 1916, 1949-1950
Lawrenceville	Virginia	1948-1949
Lynchburg	Virginia	1894-1896, 1906-1912, 1917, 1939-1942
	Piedmont	1943-1955
	Appalachian	1959
	South Atlantic	1962-1963
	Southern	1964-1965
	Carolina	1966-
Marion	Appalachian	1955, 1965-1976

PROFESSIONAL TEAMS BY STATE

Martinsville	Bi-State	1934-1941
	Carolina	1945-1949
	Appalachian	1988-
Narrows-Pearisburg (aka New River)	Appalachian	1946-1950
Newport News	Virginia	1900, 1912-1922, 1941-1942
	Virginia-North Carolina	1901
	Piedmont	1944-1955
Newport News-Hampton (aka Peninsula; Virginia)	Virginia	1894
	Carolina	1963-1971, 1974, 1976-1992
	International	1972-1973
see also Hampton		
Norfolk	Eastern	1885, 1931-1932
	Virginia	1894-1896, 1900, 1906-1928
	Atlantic	1897-1898
	Virginia-North Carolina	1901
	Piedmont	1934-1955
(aka Tidewater)	International	1969-
see also Portsmouth-Norfolk		
Northampton	Eastern Shore	1927-1928
Norton	Mountain States	1951-1953
Parksley	Eastern Shore	1922-1928
Pearisburg		
see Narrows-Pearisburg		
Peninsula		
see Newport News-Hampton; see also Hampton; Newport News		
Pennington Gap	Appalachian	1937-1940
	Mountain States	1948-1951
Petersburg	Virginia	1894-1896, 1900, 1910-1921, 1923-1924, 1926-1928, 1941-1942, 1948-1950
see also Colonial Heights-Petersburg		
Portsmouth	Virginia	1895-1896, 1900, 1906-1910, 1912-1917, 1919-1928
	Virginia-North Carolina	1901
	Piedmont	1935-1955
	Carolina	1963-1968
Portsmouth-Norfolk	South Atlantic	1961-1962
see also Norfolk		
Prince William		
see Woodbridge		
Pulaski	Virginia	1942
	Appalachian	1946-1950, 1952-1955, 1957-1958, 1969-1977, 1982-1992, 1997-
Radford	Blue Ridge	1946-1950
Richmond	American Association	1884
	Eastern	1884-1885, 1931-1932
	Virginia	1894-1896, 1900, 1906-1914, 1918-1928
	Atlantic	1897-1899
	Virginia-North Carolina	1901
	United States	1912
	Internatonal	1915-1917, 1954-1964, 1966-
	Piedmont	1933-1953
Roanoke	Virginia	1894-1896, 1906-1914
	Piedmont	1943-1953
see also Salem-Roanoke		
Salem	Blue Ridge	1946
	Appalachian	1955, 1957-1967
	Carolina	1968-
Salem-Roanoke	Virginia	1939-1942
Schoolfield		
see Danville-Schoolfield		
South Boston	Bi-State	1937-1940
(aka South Boston-Halifax)		
Staunton	Virginia	1894, 1939-1942
	Virginia Mountain	1914
Suffolk	Virginia	1915, 1919-1921, 1948-1951
Tidewater		
see Norfolk		
Virginia		
see Newport News-Hampton		
Woodbridge	Carolina	1984-
(aka Prince William)		
Wytheville	Blue Ridge	1948-1950
	Appalachian	1953-1955, 1957-1965, 1967, 1969, 1971-1973, 1985-1989

WASHINGTON

City	League	Years
Aberdeen	Southwest Washington	1903-1905
see also Grays Harbor	Northwestern	1907, 1915
	Washington State	1910, 1912
	Pacific Coast International	1918
Ballard	Northwestern	1914
Bellingham	Northwestern	1905
	Western International	1938-1939
	Northwest	1973-1996

Bremerton	Western International	1946-1949
Centralia	Southwest Washington	1903-1904
	Washington State	1911-1912
Chehalis	Washington State	1910-1912
Everett	Northwestern	1905
	Northwest	1984-
Grays Harbor (Aberdeen-Hoquiam)	Northwestern	1906, 1908-1909
	Northwest	1976-1980
	Western	1995-
see also Aberdeen; Hoquiam		
Hoquiam	Southwest Washington	1903-1905
	Washington State	1910, 1912
see also Grays Harbor		
Kennewick		
see Tri-City		
Montesano	Southwest Washington	1905
	Washington State	1910
North Yakima	Western Tri-State	1913-1914
Olympia	Southwest Washington	1903-1905
Pasco		
see Tri-City		
Raymond	Washington State	1910-1911
Richland		
see Tri-City		
Seattle	Pacific Northwest	1892, 1901-1902
	New Pacific	1896
	Pacific National	1903
	Pacific Coast	1903-1906, 1919-1968
	Northwestern	1907-1917
	Pacific Coast International	1918-1920
	American	1969, 1977-
	Northwest	1972-1976
South Bend	Washington State	1911
Spokane	Pacific Northwest	1892, 1901-1902
	Pacific National	1903-1904
	Northwestern	1905-1917
	Pacific Coast International	1918, 1920
	Western International	1937-1942, 1946-1954
	Pacific Coast	1958-1971, 1973-1982
	Northwest	1955-1956, 1972, 1983-
Tacoma	Pacific Northwest	1892, 1901-1902
	New Pacific	1896
	Pacific National	1903
	Pacific Coast	1904-1905, 1960-
	Northwestern	1906-1917
	Washington State	1910
	Pacific Coast International	1918-1921
	Western International	1922, 1937-1942, 1946-1951
Tri-City/Cities	Western International	1950-1954
(Kennewick-Pasco-	Northwest	1955-1974, 1983-1986
Richland)	Western	1995-
Vancouver	Oregon State	1904
	Pacific Coast International	1918
Walla Walla	Inland Empire	1908
	Western Tri-State	1912-1914
	Northwest	1969-1983
Wenatchee	Western International	1937-1941, 1946-1954
	Northwest	1955-1965
Yakima	Pacific Coast International	1920-1921
	Western International	1937-1941, 1946-1954
	Northwest	1955-1966, 1990-

WEST VIRGINIA

City	League	Years
Beckley	Middle Atlantic	1931-1935
	Mountain State	1937-1938
Bluefield	Mountain State	1937-1942
	Appalachian	1946-1955, 1957-
Charleston	Virginia Valley	1910
	Mountain States	1911-1912
	Ohio State	1913-1916
	Middle Atlantic	1931-1942
	Central	1949-1951
	American Association	1952-1960
	International	1961, 1971-1983
	Eastern	1962-1964
	South Atlantic	1987-
Clarksburg	Western Pennsylvania	1907
	Pennsylvania-West Virginia	1908-1909
	West Virginia	1910
	Middle Atlantic	1925-1932
Fairmont	Western Pennsylvania	1907
	Pennsylvania-West Virginia	1908-1909
	West Virginia	1910
	Ohio-Pennsylvania	1912
	Middle Atlantic	1925-1931

PROFESSIONAL TEAMS BY STATE/COUNTRY

Follansbee
see Steubenville (OH)-Follansbee

City	League	Years
Grafton	Pennsylvania-West Virginia	1908-1909
	West Virginia	1910
Huntington	Virginia Valley	1910
	Mountain States	1911-1912, 1937-1942
	Ohio State	1913-1916
	Middle Atlantic	1931-1936
(aka River City)	Appalachian	1990-1995
Logan	Mountain State	1937-1942
Mannington	West Virginia	1910
Martinsburg	Blue Ridge	1915-1918, 1920-1929
Montgomery	Virginia Valley	1910
	Mountain States	1911-1912
New Martinsville	Ohio-Pennsylvania	1912

Ohio Valley
see Parkersburg

City	League	Years
Parkersburg	Pennsylvania-West Virginia	1909
	Virginia Valley	1910
	Middle Atlantic	1931
(aka Ohio Valley)	Frontier	1993-
Piedmont	Penn-Ohio-Maryland	1906
	Western Pennsylvania	1907
	Potomac	1916
Piedmont-Westernport	Blue Ridge	1918
Point Pleasant-Gallipolis	Virginia Valley	1910
	Mountain States	1911
Princeton	Appalachian	1988-

River City
see Huntington

City	League	Years
Wayne	Frontier	1993
(aka West Virginia)		
Welch	Mountain State	1937-1942
	Appalachian	1946-1955
Wheeling	Ohio State	1887
	Tri-State	1888-1890
	Interstate	1896-1897, 1899-1900, 1913
	Western Association	1901
	Central	1903-1912, 1915-1916
	Middle Atlantic	1925-1931, 1933-1934
Williamson	Mountain States	1912, 1937-1942

WISCONSIN

City	League	Years
Appleton	Wisconsin-Illinois	1909-1914
(aka Fox Cities/Wisconsin)	Wisconsin State	1940-1942, 1946-1953
	Three-I	1958-1961
	Midwest	1962-
Beloit	Wisconsin Association	1905
	Midwest	1982-

Chippewa Falls
see Eau Claire-Chippewa Falls

City	League	Years
Eau Claire	Northwestern	1886-1887
	Wisconsin State	1907
	Minnesota-Wisconsin	1909-1912
	Northern	1933-1942, 1946-1962
Eau Claire-Chippewa Falls	Wisconsin State	1906
Fond du Lac	Wisconsin State	1907, 1940-1942, 1946-1953
	Wisconsin-Illinois	1908-1911, 1913

Fox Cities
see Appleton

City	League	Years
Green Bay	Wisconsin State	1905-1907, 1940-1942, 1946-1953
	Wisconsin-Illinois	1908-1914
	Three-I	1958-1960
	Prairie	1996
	Heartland	1997-
Janesville	Wisconsin State	1941-1942, 1946-1953
Kenosha	Midwest	1985-1992
La Crosse	Northwestern	1887
	Wisconsin State	1905-1907
	Wisconsin-Illinois	1908
	Minnesota-Wisconsin	1909-1912
	Northern	1913
	Central Association	1917
	Wisconsin State	1940-1942
Madison	Wisconsin State	1907
	Wisconsin-Illinois	1908-1914
	Three-I	1940-1942
	Midwest	1982-1994
	Northern	1996-
Marinette-Menominee	Wisconsin-Illinois	1914
Milwaukee	Union Association	1884
	Northwestern	1884, 1886-1887

City	League	Years
	Western	1885, 1892, 1894-1899, 1902-1903
	Western Association	1888-1891
	American Association	1891, 1902-1952
	American	1900-1901, 1970-
	Wisconsin-Illinois	1913
	National	1953-1965
Oshkosh	Northwestern	1886-1887
	Wisconsin State	1905-1907, 1941-1942, 1946-1953
	Wisconsin-Illinois	1908-1914
Racine	Wisconsin-Illinois	1909-1914
	Bi-State	1915
Sheboygan	Wisconsin State	1940-1942, 1946-1953
Superior	Northern	1903-1905, 1913-1916, 1933-1942, 1946-1955
	Minnesota-Wisconsin	1909-1911
	Central International	1912
	Twin Ports	1943
see also Duluth-Superior		
Wausau	Wisconsin State	1905-1907, 1946-1953
	Wisconsin-Illinois	1908, 1912-1914
	Minnesota-Wisconsin	1909-1911
	Northern	1936-1942, 1956-1957
	Midwest	1975-1990

Wisconsin
see Appleton

City	League	Years
Wisconsin Rapids	Wisconsin State	1940-1942, 1946-1953
	Midwest	1963-1983

WYOMING

City	League	Years
Cheyenne	Rocky Mountain	1912
	Western (Class D)	1941

CANADA: ALBERTA

City	League	Years
Bassano	Western Canada	1912
Calgary	Western Canada	1907, 1909-1914, 1920-1921
	Western International	1922, 1953-1954
	Pioneer	1977-1984
	Pacific Coast	1985-
Edmonton	Western Canada	1907, 1909-1914, 1920-1921
	Western International	1922, 1953-1954
	Pacific Coast	1981-
Lethbridge	Western Canada	1907, 1909-1910
	Pioneer	1975-1983, 1992-
Medicine Hat	Western Canada	1907, 1909-1910, 1913-1914
	Pioneer	1977-
Red Deer	Western Canada	1912

CANADA: BRITISH COLUMBIA

City	League	Years
New Westminster	Northwest	1974
Surrey	Western	1995
Vancouver	Northwestern	1905, 1907-1917
	Pacific Coast International	1918-1921
	Western International	1922, 1937-1942, 1946-1954
	Pacific Coast	1956-1962, 1965-1969, 1978-
Victoria	New Pacific	1896
	Northwestern	1905, 1911-1915
	Pacific Coast International	1919-1921
	Western International	1946-1954
	Northwest	1978-1980

CANADA: MANITOBA

City	League	Years
Brandon	Northern	1908, 1933-1934
	Western Canada	1909-1911
	Prairie	1995-
St. Boniface	Northern	1915
Winnipeg	Northern	1902-1905, 1908, 1913-1917, 1933-1942, 1954-1964, 1969, 1994-
	Northern-Copper Country	1906-1907
	Western Canada	1909-1911, 1919-1921
	Central International	1912
	International	1970-1971

CANADA: NEW BRUNSWICK

City	League	Years
Fredericton	New Brunswick-Maine	1913
St. John	New Brunswick-Maine	1913

St. Stephen
see Calais (ME)-St. Stephen

CANADA: NOVA SCOTIA

City	League	Years
Dominion	Cape Breton Colliery	1937-1938
Glace Bay	Cape Breton Colliery	1937-1939
New Waterford	Cape Breton Colliery	1937-1939
Sydney	Cape Breton Colliery	1937-1939
Sydney Mines	Cape Breton Colliery	1937-1939

CANADA: ONTARIO

City	League	Years
Berlin	Canadian	1911-1913
see also Kitchener (formerly Berlin)		
Brantford	Canadian	1905, 1911-1915
	Michigan-Ontario	1919-1922
	Ontario	1930
Brockville	Canadian-American	1936-1937
Chatham	Canadian	1899-1900
Cornwall	Canadian-American	1938-1939
	Border	1951
see also Perth-Cornwall		
Ft. William-Pt. Arthur	Northern	1914-1916
see also Thunder Bay		
Guelph	Canadian	1899, 1911-1913, 1915
	International (Class D)	1908
	Ontario	1930
Hamilton	International	1886-1890, 1918
	Canadian	1899-1900, 1911-1915
	International (Class D)	1908
	Michigan-Ontario	1919-1925
	Ontario	1930
	PONY	1939-1942, 1946-1956
	New York-Pennsylvania	1988-1992
Ingersoll	Canadian	1905
Kingston	Border	1946-1951
Kitchener	Michigan-Ontario	1919-1922, 1925
see also Berlin		
London	International	1888-1890
	Canadian	1899-1900, 1911-1915
	International (Class D)	1908
	Michigan-Ontario	1919-1925
	Ontario	1930
	PONY	1940-1941
	Eastern	1989-1993
Ottawa	Eastern	1898
	Canadian	1912-1915
	Eastern Canada	1922-1923
	Canadian-American	1936-1939
	Border	1947-1950
	International	1951-1954, 1993-
Ottawa-Hull	Quebec-Ontario-Vermont	1924
Ottawa-Ogdensburg	Canadian-American	1940
Perth	Canadian-American	1936
Perth-Cornwall	Canadian-American	1937
see also Cornwall		
Peterborough	Canadian	1912-1914
Pt. Arthur		
see Ft. William-Pt. Arthur		
St. Catharines	Ontario	1930
	New York-Pennsylvania	1986-
St. Thomas	Canadian	1899, 1905, 1911-1915
	International (Class D)	1908
	Ontario	1930
Sarnia		
see Port Huron-Sarnia		
Simcoe	Canadian	1905
Smiths Falls	Canadian-American	1937
Stratford	Canadian	1899
Thunder Bay	Northern	1993-
see also Ft. William-Pt. Arthur		
Toronto	International	1886-1890, 1912-1967
	Eastern	1895-1911
	Canadian	1914
	American	1977-
Welland	New York-Pennsylvania	1989-1994
	North Atlantic	1995-
Windsor	Border	1912-1913
Woodstock	Canadian	1899, 1905

CANADA: QUEBEC

City	League	Years
Cap de la Madeleine	Eastern Canada	1922

Drummondville	Quebec Provincial	1940
	Provincial	1948-1954
Farnham	Provincial	1948-1951
Granby	Quebec Provincial	1940
	Border	1946
	Provincial	1948-1953
Hull		
see Ottawa (ONT)-Hull		
Montreal	Eastern	1890, 1897-1911
	International	1912-1917, 1928-1960
	Eastern Canada	1922-1923
	Quebec-Ontario-Vermont	1924
	National	1969-
Outremont	Quebec-Ontario-Vermont	1924
Quebec	Eastern Canada	1923
	Quebec-Ontario-Vermont	1924
	Quebec Provincial	1940
	Canadian-American	1941-1942, 1946-1950
	Provincial	1951-1955
	Eastern	1971-1977
St. Hyacinthe	Quebec Provincial	1940
	Provincial	1948-1953
St. Jean-Sur-Richelieu	Provincial	1948-1955
Sherbrooke	Quebec Provincial	1940
	Border	1946
	Provincial	1948-1951, 1953-1955
	Eastern	1972-1973
Thetford Mines	Provincial	1953-1955
	Eastern	1974-1975
Trois Rivieres	Eastern Canada	1922-1923
	Quebec Provincial	1940
	Canadian-American	1941-1942, 1946-1950
	Provincial	1951-1955
	Eastern	1971-1977
Valleyfield	Eastern Canada	1922

CANADA: SASKATCHEWAN

City	League	Years
Moose Jaw	Western Canada	1909-1911, 1913-1914, 1919-1921
	Prairie	1995-
Regina	Western Canada	1909-1910, 1913-1914, 1919-1921
	North Central	1994
	Prairie	1995-
Saskatoon	Western Canada	1910-1911, 1913-1914, 1919-1921
	North Central	1994
	Prairie	1995-

CUBA

City	League	Years
Havana	Florida International	1946-1953
	International	1954-1960

DOMINICAN REPUBLIC

City	League	Years
Santo Domingo	Inter-American	1979

MEXICO

City	League	Years
Acambaro	Mexican Center	1975-1976
Agua Prieta	Mexican Rookie	1968
Aguascalientes	Central Mexican	1956-1957
	Mexican Center	1960-1963, 1965-1967, 1969-1974
	Mexican	1975-
Anahuac	Mexican	1939, 1953
Arandas	Mexican Center	1977
Caborca	Mexican Rookie	1968
Campeche	Mexican Southeast	1964-1970
	Mexican	1980-
Cananea	Arizona-Texas	1954
	Arizona-Mexico	1955-1957
	Mexican Rookie	1968
Carmen	Mexican Southeast	1967-1970
Celaya	Mexican Center	1960-1961, 1975
Cerro Azul	Mexican Center	1978
Chihuahua	Mexican	1940, 1973-1982
	Mexican National	1946
	Arizona-Texas	1952
	Central Mexican	1956-1957
	Arizona-Mexico	1958
Ciudad Juarez	Mexican National	1946
	Arizona-Texas	1947-1950, 1952-1954
	Southwest International	1951
	Central Mexican	1956-1957

	Arizona-Mexico	1958
	Mexican	1973-1984
Ciudad Madero	Mexican Center	1968-1970
Ciudad Mante	Mexican Center	1969-1971, 1973-1974, 1977
Ciudad Obregon	Mexican Pacific	1976
Ciudad Victoria	Mexican Center	1971, 1973-1974, 1976-1978
Ciudad Valles	Mexican Center	1974, 1978
Coahuila	Mexican	1974-1979
Coatzacoalcos	Mexican	1979-1983
Cordoba	Mexican	1937-1939, 1972-1979, 1984-1986, 1991-1992
Cortazar	Mexican Center	1975
Diaz Ordaz	Mexican Center	1978
Dos Laredos see Nuevo Laredo		
Durango	Central Mexican	1956-1957
	Mexican Center	1965-1967, 1972-1974
	Mexican	1976-1979
Ebano	Mexican Center	1971-1974, 1977
Empalme	Mexican Rookie	1968
Ensenada	Mexican Northern	1968-1969
see also Riverside (CA)-Ensenada		
Fresnillo	Central Mexican	1956-1957
	Mexican Center	1962, 1964-1968, 1976-1978
Gomez Palacio see Union Laguna		
Guadalajara	Mexican Center	1977-1978
Guamuchil	Mexican Pacific	1976
Guanajuato	Mexican Center	1960-1967, 1975-1976, 1978
Guasave	Mexican Pacific	1976
Guaymas	Mexican Pacific	1976
Hermosillo	Mexican Pacific	1976
Jalisco	Mexican	1949-1952, 1964-1975, 1988, 1991-1995
(Guadalajara)	Mexican Center	1977
Juarez see Ciudad Juarez		
La Barca	Mexican Center	1978
Lagos de Moreno	Mexican Center	1975-1977
Laguna	Central Mexican	1957
Las Choapas	Mexican Southeast	1967-1969
Leon	Mexican Center	1960-1971, 1975
	Mexican	1979-1980, 1983-1991
Los Mochis	Mexican Pacific	1976
Matamoros	Mexican Center	1978
Mazatlan	Mexican Pacific	1976
Mexicali	Sunset	1948-1950
	Southwest International	1951-1952
	Arizona-Texas	1953-1954
	Arizona-Mexico	1955-1958
	Mexican Northern	1968-1969
Mexico City	Mexican National	1946
Mexico City Agrario	Mexican	1937-1938
Mexico City Agricultura	Mexican	1937
Mexico City Azul	Mexican	1954
Mexico City Comintra	Mexican	1937-1939
Mexico City Diablos Rojos	Mexican	1940-
Mexico City Necaxa	Mexican	1937
Mexico City Petroleros	Mexican	1937
Mexico City Tigres	Mexican	1955-
Mexico City Transito	Mexican	1937
Miguel Aleman	Mexican Center	1978
Minatitlan	Mexican Southeast	1968-1969
	Mexican	1992-
Monclova	Mexican	1980, 1982-
Monterrey	Mexican	1939-
	Mexican Center	1970-1972
Monterrey Industriales	Mexican	1989-1994
Morella	Mexican Center	1966
Naranjos	Mexican Center	1972-1973
Navojoa	Mexican Pacific	1976
Nogales	Arizona-Texas	1931, 1954

	Mexican	1937-1938
	Arizona-Mexico	1955-1956, 1958
	Mexican Northern	1968-1969
Nuevo Laredo	Mexican	1940, 1944-1946, 1949-1959, 1976-
(aka Dos Laredos)	Mexican Center	1968
Oaxaca	Mexican	1996-
Orizaba	Mexican Southeast	1966-1967
Parras	Mexican Center	1974
Poza Rica	Mexican	1958-1983, 1996-
Puebla	Mexican	1942-1948, 1960-1969, 1972-1980, 1985-1987, 1993-1995
Puerto Mexico	Mexican Southeast	1964-1970
Puerto Penasco	Mexican Northern	1969
Quintana Roo (Cancun)	Mexican	1996-
Reynosa	Mexican	1963-1976, 1980-1982, 1995-
Rio Blanco	Mexican	1937-1938
Sabinas	Mexican	1971-1973
Salamanca	Mexican Center	1960-1962, 1964-1965, 1975
Saltillo	Mexican National	1946
	Central Mexican	1956-1957
	Mexican Center	1964, 1968-1969
	Mexican	1970-
San Luis Potosi	Mexican	1946-1951, 1986-1991
	Mexican Center	1960-1966, 1969-1971
San Luis Rio Colorado	Mexican Northern	1968-1969
San Pedro	Mexican Center	1974
Santa Rosa	Mexican	1937-1939
Silao	Mexican Center	1978
Tabasco	Mexican Southeast	1964-1970
see also Villahermosa		
Tampico	Mexican	1937-1939, 1971-1979, 1983-1985
	Mexican Center	1967-1970
Tamuin	Mexican Center	1973
Teocaltiche	Mexican Center	1977-1978
Tijuana	Sunset	1949-1950
	Southwest International	1951-1952
	Arizona-Mexico	1956
Toluca	Mexican	1980, 1984
Torreon	Mexican	1940-1943, 1946, 1949-1953
	Mexican National	1946
	Mexican Center	1968
Union Laguna	Mexican	1970-1981, 1985-
(Gomez Palacio-Torreon) see also Torreon		
Uriangato	Mexican Center	1975
Veracruz	Mexican	1937-1939, 1941, 1949-1957, 1959-1974, 1979-1986, 1992-1995
Veracruz Azules	Mexican	1940-1951
Villahermosa	Mexican	1975, 1977-
(aka Tabasco)		
Yucatan	Mexican	1954-1958, 1970-1974, 1979-
(Merida)	Mexican Southeast	1964-1969
Zacatecas	Mexican Center	1965-1973, 1976-1978

PANAMA

City	League	Years
Panama	Inter-American	1979

PUERTO RICO

City	League	Years
San Juan	International	1961
(aka Puerto Rico)	Inter-American	1979

VENEZUELA

City	League	Years
Caracas	Inter-American	1979
Maracaibo	Inter-American	1979

PROFESSIONAL LEAGUES BY YEAR

1883

League	Start-End
American Association	1883-1891
National League	1883-
Interstate Association	1883
Northwestern League	1883-1884

1884

League	Start-End
American Association	1883-1891
National League	1883-
Union Association	1884
Eastern League	1884-1886
Iron & Oil Association	1884
Keystone Association	1884
Northwestern League	1883-1884
Ohio State Association	1884

1885

League	Start-End
American Association	1883-1891
National League	1883-
Eastern League	1884-1886
New York State League	1885
Southern League	1885-1888
Western League	1885-1887

1886

League	Start-End
American Association	1883-1891
National League	1883-
Eastern League	1884-1886
International League (Assn.)	1886-1890
New England League	1886-1888
Northwestern League	1886-1887
Southern League	1885-1888
Western League	1885-1887

1887

League	Start-End
American Association	1883-1891
National League	1883-
California League	1887-1889
Central Pennsylvania League	1887
International League (Assn.)	1886-1890
National Colored League	1887
New England League	1886-1888
Northwestern League	1886-1887
Ohio State League	1887
Southern League	1885-1888
Western League	1885-1887

1888

League	Start-End
American Association	1883-1891
National League	1883-
California League	1887-1889
Central League	1888
Central Interstate League	1888-1889
International Association	1886-1890
New England League	1886-1888
Southern League	1885-1888
Texas League	1888-1890
Tri-State League	1888-1890
Western Association	1888-1891
Western League	1888

1889

League	Start-End
American Association	1883-1891
National League	1883-
Atlantic Association	1889-1890
California League	1887-1889
Central Interstate League	1888-1889
International Association	1886-1890
Michigan State League	1889-1890
New York State League	1889
Texas League	1888-1890
Tri-State League	1888-1890

Western Association	1888-1891

1890

League	Start-End
American Association	1883-1891
National League	1883-
Player's League	1890
Atlantic Association	1889-1890
International Association	1886-1890
Michigan State League	1889-1890
Texas League	1888-1890
Tri-State League	1888-1890
Western Association	1888-1891

1891

League	Start-End
American Association	1883-1891
National League	1883-
California League	1891
Eastern Association	1891
New England League	1891-1899
New York-Pennsylvania League	1891
Western Association	1888-1891

1892

League	Start-End
National League	1883-
Eastern League	1892-1911
Illinois-Indiana League	1892
New England League	1891-1899
Pacific Northwest League	1892
Pennsylvania State League	1892-1895
Southern League	1892-1896
Western League	1892

1893

League	Start-End
National League	1883-
California League	1893
Eastern League	1892-1911
New England League	1891-1899
Ohio-Michigan League	1893
Pennsylvania State League	1892-1895
Southern League	1892-1896
Western Association	1893

1894

League	Start-End
National League	1883-
Eastern League	1892-1911
New England League	1891-1899
Pennsylvania State League	1892-1895
Southern League	1892-1896
Virginia League	1894-1896
Western Association	1894-1897
Western League	1894-1899

1895

League	Start-End
National League	1883-
Eastern League	1892-1911
Michigan State League	1895
New England Association	1895
New England League	1891-1899
Pennsylvania State League	1892-1895
Southern League	1892-1896
Texas-Southern League	1895-1896
Virginia League	1894-1896
Western Association	1894-1897
Western League	1894-1899

1896

League	Start-End
National League	1883-
Atlantic League	1896-1900
Eastern League	1892-1911
Interstate League	1896-1900
New England League	1891-1899
New Pacific League	1896

Southern League	1892-1896
Texas-Southern League	1895-1896
Virginia League	1894-1896
Western Association	1894-1897
Western League	1894-1899

1897

League	Start-End
National League	1883-
Atlantic League	1896-1900
Eastern League	1892-1911
Interstate League	1896-1900
New England League	1891-1899
Western Association	1894-1897
Western League	1894-1899

1898

League	Start-End
National League	1883-
Atlantic League	1896-1900
Eastern League	1892-1911
Interstate League	1896-1900
New England League	1891-1899
Western League	1894-1899

1899

League	Start-End
National League	1883-
Atlantic League	1896-1900
California League	1899-1902
Canadian League	1899
Connecticut State League	1899-1912
Eastern League	1892-1911
Interstate League	1896-1900
New England League	1891-1899
New York State League	1899-1917
Western Association	1899
Western League	1894-1899

1900

League	Start-End
National League	1883-
American League	1900
Atlantic League	1896-1900
California League	1899-1902
Central League	1900
Connecticut State League	1899-1912
Eastern League	1892-1911
International League	1900
Interstate League	1896-1900
Montana State League	1900
New York State League	1899-1917
Virginia League	1900
Western League	1900-1937

1901

League	Start-End
American League	1901-
National League	1883-
California League	1899-1902
Connecticut League	1899-1912
Eastern League	1892-1911
New England League	1901-1915
New York State League	1899-1917
Pacific Northwest League	1901-1902
Southern Association	1901-1961
Three-I League	1901-1917
Inter-Mountain League	1901
Virginia-North Carolina League	1901
Western Association	1901
Western League	1900-1937

1902

Class	League	Start-End
Maj	American League	1901-
Maj	National League	1883-
A	Eastern League	1892-1911
A	Western League	1900-1937
B	New England League	1901-1915

PROFESSIONAL LEAGUES BY YEAR

Class	League	Start-End
B	New York State League	1899-1917
B	Pacific Northwest League	1901-1902
B	Southern Association	1901-1961
B	Three-I League	1901-1917
C	North Carolina League	1902
D	Connecticut League	1899-1912
D	Cotton States League	1902-1908
D	Iowa-South Dakota League	1902-1903
D	Michigan State League	1902
D	Missouri Valley League	1902-1905
D	Texas League	1902-1942
Ind	American Association	1902-1962
Ind	California League	1899-1902
Ind	Northern League	1902-1905

1903

Class	League	Start-End
Maj	American League	1901-
Maj	National League	1883-
A	American Association	1902-1962
A	Eastern League	1892-1911
A	Pacific National League	1903-1904
A	Western League	1900-1937
B	Central League	1903-1917
B	New England League	1901-1915
B	New York State League	1899-1917
B	Southern Association	1901-1961
B	Three-I League	1901-1917
C	South Texas League	1903-1906
D	Connecticut League	1899-1912
D	Cotton States League	1902-1908
D	Hudson River League	1903-1907
D	Iowa-South Dakota League	1902-1903
D	Kitty League	1903-1906
D	Missouri Valley League	1902-1905
D	Northern League	1902-1905
D	Southwest Iowa League	1903
D	Southwest Washington League	1903-1905
D	Texas League	1902-1942
Ind	Pacific Coast League	1903-

1904

Class	League	Start-End
Maj	American League	1901-
Maj	National League	1883-
A	American Association	1902-1962
A	Eastern League	1892-1911
A	Pacific Coast League	1903-
A	Western League	1900-1937
B	Central League	1903-1917
B	New England League	1901-1915
B	New York State League	1899-1917
B	Pacific National League	1903-1904
B	Southern Association	1901-1961
B	Three-I League	1901-1917
C	Hudson River League	1903-1907
C	Missouri Valley League	1902-1905
C	South Atlantic League	1904-1917
C	South Texas League	1903-1906
C	Texas League	1902-1942
D	Connecticut League	1899-1912
D	Cotton States League	1902-1908
D	Delta League	1904
D	Iowa State League	1904-1907
D	Kitty League	1903-1906
D	Northern League	1902-1905
D	Oregon State League	1904
D	Southwest Washington League	1903-1905
D	Southwestern League	1904
Ind	Tri-State League	1904-1914

1905

Class	League	Start-End
Maj	American League	1901-
Maj	National League	1883-
A	American Association	1902-1962
A	Eastern League	1892-1911
A	Pacific Coast League	1903-
A	Southern Association	1901-1961
A	Western League	1900-1937
B	Central League	1903-1917
B	Connecticut League	1899-1912
B	New England League	1901-1915
B	New York State League	1899-1917
B	Northwestern League	1905-1917
B	Three-I League	1901-1917
C	Hudson River League	1903-1907
C	Missouri Valley League	1902-1905
C	Ohio-Pennsylvania League	1905-1912
C	South Atlantic League	1904-1917
C	South Texas League	1903-1906
C	Texas League	1902-1942
C	Western Association	1905-1911
D	Canadian League	1905
D	Copper Country Soo League	1905
D	Cotton States League	1902-1908
D	Interstate League	1905-1908
D	Iowa State League	1904-1907
D	Kansas State League	1905-1906
D	Kitty League	1903-1906
D	North Texas League	1905
D	Northern League	1902-1905
D	Southwest Washington League	1903-1905
D	Virginia-North Carolina League	1905
D	Wisconsin State League	1905-1907
Ind	Tri-State League	1904-1914

1906

Class	League	Start-End
Maj	American League	1901-
Maj	National League	1883-
A	American Association	1902-1962
A	Eastern League	1892-1911
A	Pacific Coast League	1903-
A	Southern Association	1901-1961
A	Western League	1900-1937
B	Central League	1903-1917
B	Connecticut League	1899-1912
B	New England League	1901-1915
B	New York State League	1899-1917
B	Northwestern League	1905-1917
B	Three-I League	1901-1917
C	Hudson River League	1903-1907
C	Interstate Association	1906
C	Northern-Copper Country League	1906-1907
C	Ohio-Pennsylvania League	1905-1912
C	South Atlantic League	1904-1917
C	South Texas League	1903-1906
C	Virginia League	1906-1928
C	Western Association	1905-1911
D	Arkansas-Texas League	1906
D	Cotton States League	1902-1908
D	Georgia State League	1906
D	Interstate League	1905-1908
D	Iowa State League	1904-1907
D	Kansas State League	1905-1906
D	Kitty League	1903-1906
D	POM League	1906-1907
D	South Central League	1906
D	Southern Michigan League	1906-1909
D	Texas League	1902-1942
D	Wisconsin State League	1905-1907
Ind	Tri-State League	1904-1914

1907

Class	League	Start-End
Maj	American League	1901-
Maj	National League	1883-
A	American Association	1902-1962
A	Eastern League	1892-1911
A	Pacific Coast League	1903-
A	Southern Association	1901-1961
A	Western League	1900-1937
B	Central League	1903-1917
B	Connecticut League	1899-1912
B	New England League	1901-1915
B	New York State League	1899-1917
B	Northwestern League	1905-1917
B	Three-I League	1901-1917
B	Tri-State League	1904-1914
C	Hudson River League	1903-1907
C	Ohio-Pennsylvania League	1905-1912
C	South Atlantic League	1904-1917
C	Texas League	1902-1942
C	Virginia League	1906-1928
C	Western Association	1905-1911
D	Cotton States League	1902-1908
D	Eastern Illinois League	1907-1908
D	Gulf Coast League	1907-1908
D	Interstate League	1905-1908
D	Iowa State League	1904-1907
D	Maine State League	1907
D	Northern-Copper Country League	1906-1907
D	North Texas League	1907
D	Oklahoma-Arkansas-Kansas League	1907
D	POM League	1906-1907
D	South Carolina State League	1907-1908
D	Southern Michigan League	1906-1909
D	Western Canada League	1907
D	Western Pennsylvania League	1907
D	Wisconsin State League	1905-1907
Ind	California League	1907-1909

1908

Class	League	Start-End
Maj	American League	1901-
Maj	National League	1883-
A	American Association	1902-1962
A	Eastern League	1892-1911
A	Pacific Coast League	1903-
A	Southern Association	1901-1961
A	Western League	1900-1937
B	Central League	1903-1917
B	Connecticut League	1899-1912
B	New England League	1901-1915
B	New York State League	1899-1917
B	Northwestern League	1905-1917
B	Three-I League	1901-1917
B	Tri-State League	1904-1914
C	Ohio-Pennsylvania League	1905-1912
C	South Atlantic League	1904-1917
C	Texas League	1902-1942
C	Virginia League	1906-1928
C	Western Association	1905-1911
D	Arkansas State League	1908-1909
D	Atlantic Association	1908
D	Blue Grass League	1908-1912
D	Carolina Association	1908-1912
D	Central Association	1908-1917
D	Central Kansas League	1908-1912
D	Cotton States League	1902-1908
D	Eastern Carolina League	1908-1910
D	Eastern Illinois League	1907-1908
D	Gulf Coast League	1907-1908
D	Illinois-Missouri League	1908-1914
D	Indiana-Ohio League	1908
D	Inland Empire League	1908
D	International League	1908
D	Interstate League	1905-1908
D	Northern League	1908
D	Ohio State League	1908-1916
D	Oklahoma-Kansas League	1908
D	Pennsylvania-West Virginia League	1908-1909
D	South Carolina League	1907-1908
D	Southern Michigan League	1906-1909
D	Wisconsin-Illinois League	1908-1914
Ind	California League	1907-1909

1909

Class	League	Start-End
Maj	American League	1901-
Maj	National League	1883-
A	American Association	1902-1962
A	Eastern League	1892-1911

PROFESSIONAL LEAGUES BY YEAR

Class	League	Start-End
A	Pacific Coast League	1903-
A	Southern Association	1901-1961
A	Western League	1900-1937
B	Central League	1903-1917
B	Connecticut League	1899-1912
B	New England League	1901-1915
B	New York State League	1899-1917
B	Northwestern League	1905-1917
B	Three-I League	1901-1917
B	Tri-State League	1904-1914
C	Minnesota-Wisconsin League	1909-1912
C	Ohio-Pennsylvania League	1905-1912
C	South Atlantic League	1904-1917
C	Texas League	1902-1942
C	Virginia League	1906-1928
C	Western Association	1905-1911
D	Arkansas State League	1908-1909
D	Blue Grass League	1908-1912
D	Carolina Association	1908-1912
D	Central Association	1908-1917
D	Central Kansas League	1908-1912
D	Eastern Carolina League	1908-1910
D	Illinois-Missouri League	1908-1914
D	Inter-Mountain League	1909
D	Kansas State League	1909-1911
D	Northeast Arkansas League	1909-1911
D	Northern State of Indiana League	1909-1911
D	Ohio State League	1908-1916
D	Pennsylvania-West Virginia League	1908-1909
D	Southern Michigan League	1906-1909
D	Western Canada League	1909-1914
D	Wisconsin-Illinois League	1908-1914
Ind	California League	1907-1909

1910

Class	League	Start-End
Maj	American League	1901-
Maj	National League	1883-
A	American Association	1902-1962
A	Eastern League	1892-1911
A	Pacific Coast League	1903-
A	Southern Association	1901-1961
A	Western League	1900-1937
B	Central League	1903-1917
B	Connecticut League	1899-1912
B	New England League	1901-1915
B	New York State League	1899-1917
B	Northwestern League	1905-1917
B	Three-I League	1901-1917
B	Tri-State League	1904-1914
C	Minnesota-Wisconsin League	1909-1912
C	Ohio-Pennsylvania League	1905-1912
C	South Atlantic League	1904-1917
C	Texas League	1902-1942
C	Virginia League	1906-1928
C	Western Association	1905-1911
C	Wisconsin-Illinois League	1908-1914
D	Blue Grass League	1908-1912
D	California State League	1910
D	Carolina Association	1908-1912
D	Central Association	1908-1917
D	Central California League	1910-1911
D	Central Kansas League	1908-1912
D	Connecticut Association	1910
D	Cotton States League	1910-1913
D	Eastern Carolina League	1908-1910
D	Eastern Kansas League	1910
D	Illinois-Missouri League	1908-1914
D	Indiana-Michigan League	1910
D	Kansas State League	1909-1911
D	Kitty League	1910-1914
D	MINK League	1910-1913
D	Nebraska State League	1910-1915
D	Northeast Arkansas League	1909-1911
D	Northern Association	1910
D	Northern State of Indiana League	1909-1911
D	Ohio State League	1908-1916
D	San Joaquin Valley League	1910-1911
D	Southeastern League	1910-1912
D	Southern California Trolley League	1910
D	Southern Illinois League	1910
D	Southern Michigan League	1910-1915
D	Southwest Texas League	1910-1911
D	Virginia Valley League	1910
D	Washington State League	1910-1912
D	West Michigan League	1910
D	West Virginia League	1910
D	Western Canada League	1909-1914

1911

Class	League	Start-End
Maj	American League	1901-
Maj	National League	1883-
A	American Association	1902-1962
A	Eastern League	1892-1911
A	Pacific Coast League	1903-
A	Southern Association	1901-1961
A	Western League	1900-1937
B	Central League	1903-1917
B	Connecticut League	1899-1912
B	New England League	1901-1915
B	New York State League	1899-1917
B	Northwestern League	1905-1917
B	Texas League	1902-1942
B	Three-I League	1901-1917
B	Tri-State League	1904-1914
C	Minnesota-Wisconsin League	1909-1912
C	Ohio-Pennsylvania League	1905-1912
C	South Atlantic League	1904-1917
C	Southern Michigan League	1910-1915
C	Virginia League	1906-1928
C	Wisconsin-Illinois League	1908-1914
D	Appalachian League	1911-1914
D	Blue Grass League	1908-1912
D	Canadian League	1911-1915
D	Carolina Association	1908-1912
D	Central Association	1908-1917
D	Central California League	1910-1911
D	Central Kansas League	1908-1912
D	Cotton States League	1910-1913
D	Illinois-Missouri League	1908-1914
D	Kansas State League	1909-1911
D	Kitty League	1910-1914
D	Michigan State League	1911-1914
D	Missouri State League	1911
D	MINK League	1910-1913
D	Mountain States League	1911-1912
D	Nebraska State League	1910-1915
D	Northeast Arkansas League	1909-1911
D	Northern State of Indiana League	1909-1911
D	Ohio State League	1908-1916
D	San Joaquin Valley League	1910-1911
D	Southeastern League	1910-1912
D	Southwest Texas League	1910-1911
D	Texas-Oklahoma League	1911-1914
D	Twin States League	1911
D	Union Association	1911-1914
D	Washington State League	1910-1912
D	Western Association	1905-1911
D	Western Canada League	1909-1914

1912

Class	League	Start-End
Maj	American League	1901-
Maj	National League	1883-
AA	American Association	1902-1962
AA	International League	1912-
AA	Pacific Coast League	1903-
A	Southern Association	1901-1961
A	Western League	1900-1937
B	Central League	1903-1917
B	Connecticut League	1899-1912
B	New England League	1901-1915
B	New York State League	1899-1917
B	Northwestern League	1905-1917
B	Texas League	1902-1942
B	Three-I League	1901-1917
B	Tri-State League	1904-1914
C	Canadian League	1911-1915
C	Central International League	1912
C	South Atlantic League	1904-1917
C	Virginia League	1906-1928
C	Wisconsin-Illinois League	1908-1914
D	Appalachian League	1911-1914
D	Blue Grass League	1908-1912
D	Border League	1912-1913
D	Carolina Association	1908-1912
D	Central Association	1908-1917
D	Central Kansas League	1908-1912
D	Cotton States League	1910-1913
D	Illinois-Missouri League	1908-1914
D	Kitty League	1910-1914
D	Michigan State League	1911-1914
D	MINK League	1910-1913
D	Minnesota-Wisconsin League	1909-1912
D	Mountain States League	1911-1912
D	Nebraska State League	1910-1915
D	Ohio State League	1908-1916
D	Ohio-Pennsylvania League	1905-1912
D	Oklahoma State League	1912
D	Rocky Mountain League	1912
D	South Central League	1912
D	Southeastern League	1910-1912
D	Southern Michigan League	1910-1915
D	Texas-Oklahoma League	1911-1914
D	Union Association	1911-1914
D	Washington State League	1910-1912
D	Western Canada League	1909-1914
D	Western Tri-State League	1912-1914
Ind	United States League	1912

1913

Class	League	Start-End
Maj	American League	1901-
Maj	National League	1883-
AA	American Association	1902-1962
AA	International League	1912-
AA	Pacific Coast League	1903-
A	Southern Association	1901-1961
A	Western League	1900-1937
B	Central League	1903-1917
B	Eastern Association	1913-1914
B	Interstate League	1913
B	New England League	1901-1915
B	New York State League	1899-1917
B	Northwestern League	1905-1917
B	Texas League	1902-1942
B	Three-I League	1901-1917
B	Tri-State League	1904-1914
C	Canadian League	1911-1915
C	Northern League	1913-1917
C	South Atlantic League	1904-1917
C	Virginia League	1906-1928
C	Wisconsin-Illinois League	1908-1914
D	Appalachian League	1911-1914
D	Border League	1912-1913
D	California State League	1913-1915
D	Central Association	1908-1917
D	Cotton States League	1910-1913
D	Empire State League	1913
D	Georgia-Alabama League	1913-1917
D	Illinois-Missouri League	1908-1914
D	Kansas State League	1913-1914
D	Kitty League	1910-1914
D	Michigan State League	1911-1914
D	MINK League	1910-1913
D	Nebraska State League	1910-1915
D	New Brunswick-Maine League	1913
D	New York-New Jersey League	1913
D	North Carolina League	1913-1917
D	Ohio State League	1908-1916
D	Southern California League	1913
D	Southern Michigan Association	1910-1915
D	Texas-Oklahoma League	1911-1914

PROFESSIONAL LEAGUES BY YEAR

Class	League	Start-End
D	Union Association	1911-1914
D	Western Canada League	1909-1914
D	Western Tri-State League	1912-1914
Ind	Federal League	1913-1915

1914

Class	League	Start-End
Maj	American League	1901-
Maj	Federal League	1913-1915
Maj	National League	1883-
AA	American Association	1902-1962
AA	International League	1912-
AA	Pacific Coast League	1903-
A	Southern Association	1901-1961
A	Western League	1900-1937
B	Canadian League	1911-1915
B	Central League	1903-1917
B	Eastern Association	1913-1914
B	New England League	1901-1915
B	New York State League	1899-1917
B	Northwestern League	1905-1917
B	Texas League	1902-1942
B	Three-I League	1901-1917
B	Tri-State League	1904-1914
C	Colonial League	1914-1915
C	Northern League	1913-1917
C	South Atlantic League	1904-1917
C	Southern Michigan Association	1910-1915
C	Virginia League	1906-1928
C	Wisconsin-Illinois League	1908-1914
D	Appalachian League	1911-1914
D	Atlantic League	1914
D	California State League	1913-1915
D	Central Association	1908-1917
D	Central Texas League	1914-1917
D	Georgia State League	1914
D	Georgia-Alabama League	1913-1917
D	Illinois-Missouri League	1908-1914
D	Interstate League	1914-1916
D	Kansas State League	1913-1914
D	Kitty League	1910-1914
D	Michigan State League	1911-1914
D	Middle Texas League	1914-1915
D	Nebraska State League	1910-1915
D	North Carolina State League	1913-1917
D	Ohio State League	1908-1916
D	Texas-Oklahoma League	1911-1914
D	Union Association	1911-1914
D	Virginia Mountain League	1914
D	Western Association	1914-1917
D	Western Canada League	1909-1914
D	Western Tri-State League	1912-1914

1915

Class	League	Start-End
Maj	American League	1901-
Maj	Federal League	1913-1915
Maj	National League	1883-
AA	American Association	1902-1962
AA	International League	1912-
AA	Pacific Coast League	1903-
A	Southern Association	1901-1961
A	Western League	1900-1937
B	Canadian League	1911-1915
B	Central League	1903-1917
B	New England League	1901-1915
B	New York State League	1899-1917
B	Northwestern League	1905-1917
B	Texas League	1902-1942
B	Three-I League	1901-1917
C	Northern League	1913-1917
C	South Atlantic League	1904-1917
C	Southern Michigan Association	1910-1915
C	Virginia League	1906-1928
D	Bi-State League	1915
D	Blue Ridge League	1915-1918
D	Buckeye League	1915
D	California State League	1913-1915

Class	League	Start-End
D	Central Association	1908-1917
D	Central Texas League	1914-1917
D	FLAG League	1915
D	Georgia-Alabama League	1913-1917
D	Interstate League	1914-1916
D	Middle Texas League	1914-1915
D	Nebraska State League	1910-1915
D	North Carolina State League	1913-1917
D	Ohio State League	1908-1916
D	Rio Grande Association	1915
D	Western Association	1914-1917
Ind	Colonial League	1914-1915

1916

Class	League	Start-End
Maj	American League	1901-
Maj	National League	1883-
AA	American Association	1902-1962
AA	International League	1912-
AA	Pacific Coast League	1903-
A	Southern Association	1901-1961
A	Western League	1900-1937
B	Central League	1903-1917
B	Eastern League	1916-1932
B	New York State League	1899-1917
B	Northwestern League	1905-1917
B	Texas League	1902-1942
B	Three-I League	1901-1917
C	Northern League	1913-1917
C	South Atlantic League	1904-1917
C	Virginia League	1906-1928
D	Blue Ridge League	1915-1918
D	Central Association	1908-1917
D	Central Texas League	1914-1917
D	Dixie League	1916-1917
D	East Texas League	1916
D	Georgia-Alabama League	1913-1917
D	Interstate League	1914-1916
D	Kitty League	1916
D	North Carolina State League	1913-1917
D	Ohio State League	1908-1916
D	Potomac League	1916
D	Western Association	1914-1917

1917

Class	League	Start-End
Maj	American League	1901-
Maj	National League	1883-
AA	American Association	1902-1962
AA	International League	1912-
AA	Pacific Coast League	1903-
A	Southern Association	1901-1961
A	Western League	1900-1937
B	Central League	1903-1917
B	Eastern League	1916-1932
B	New York State League	1899-1917
B	Northwestern League	1905-1917
B	Texas League	1902-1942
B	Three-I League	1901-1917
C	South Atlantic League	1904-1917
C	Virginia League	1906-1928
D	Blue Ridge League	1915-1918
D	Central Association	1908-1917
D	Central Texas League	1914-1917
D	Dixie League	1916-1917
D	Georgia-Alabama League	1913-1917
D	North Carolina State League	1913-1917
D	Northern League	1913-1917
D	Western Association	1914-1917

1918

Class	League	Start-End
Maj	American League	1901-
Maj	National League	1883-
AA	American Association	1902-1962
AA	International League	1912-
AA	Pacific Coast League	1903-
A	Southern Association	1901-1961

Class	League	Start-End
A	Western League	1900-1937
B	Eastern League	1916-1932
B	Pacific Coast International League	1918
B	Texas League	1902-1942
C	Virginia League	1906-1928
D	Blue Ridge League	1915-1918

1919

Class	League	Start-End
Maj	American League	1901-
Maj	National League	1883-
AA	American Association	1902-1962
AA	International League	1912-
AA	Pacific Coast League	1903-
A	Eastern League	1916-1932
A	Southern Association	1901-1961
A	Western League	1900-1937
B	Northwest International League	1919
B	Michigan-Ontario League	1919-1926
B	New England League	1919
B	Texas League	1902-1942
B	Three-I League	1919-1932
C	South Atlantic League	1919-1930
C	Virginia League	1906-1928
C	Western Canada League	1919-1921
D	Florida State League	1919-1928

1920

Class	League	Start-End
Maj	American League	1901-
Maj	National League	1883-
AA	American Association	1902-1962
AA	International League	1912-
AA	Pacific Coast League	1903-
A	Eastern League	1916-1932
A	Southern Association	1901-1961
A	Western League	1900-1937
B	Central League	1920-1922
B	Michigan-Ontario League	1919-1926
B	Pacific Coast International League	1920-1921
B	Texas League	1902-1942
B	Three-I League	1919-1932
B	Virginia League	1906-1928
B	Western Canada League	1919-1921
C	South Atlantic League	1919-1930
D	Blue Ridge League	1920-1930
D	Florida State League	1919-1928
D	Georgia State League	1920-1921
D	Louisiana State League	1920
D	Piedmont League	1920-1955
D	South Dakota League	1920
D	West Texas League	1920-1922
D	Western Association	1920-1932

1921

Class	League	Start-End
Maj	American League	1901-
Maj	National League	1883-
AA	American Association	1902-1962
AA	International League	1912-
AA	Pacific Coast League	1903-
A	Eastern League	1916-1932
A	Southern Association	1901-1961
A	Texas League	1902-1942
A	Western League	1900-1937
B	Central League	1920-1922
B	Michigan-Ontario League	1919-1926
B	Pacific Coast International League	1920-1921
B	South Atlantic League	1919-1930
B	Three-I League	1919-1932
B	Virginia League	1906-1928
B	Western Canada League	1919-1921
C	Florida State League	1919-1928
C	Piedmont League	1920-1955
D	Alabama-Tennessee League	1921
D	Appalachian League	1921-1925
D	Blue Ridge League	1920-1930
D	Dakota League	1921-1922

PROFESSIONAL LEAGUES BY YEAR

D	Georgia State League	1920-1921
D	Mississippi State League	1921
D	Southwestern League	1921-1926
D	Texas-Oklahoma League	1921-1922
D	West Texas League	1920-1922
D	Western Association	1920-1932

1922

Class	League	Start-End
Maj	American League	1901-
Maj	National League	1883-
AA	American Association	1902-1962
AA	International League	1912-
AA	Pacific Coast League	1903-
A	Eastern League	1916-1932
A	Southern Association	1901-1961
A	Texas League	1902-1942
A	Western League	1900-1937
B	Central League	1920-1922
B	Eastern Canada League	1922-1923
B	Michigan-Ontario League	1919-1926
B	South Atlantic League	1919-1930
B	Three-I League	1919-1932
B	Virginia League	1906-1928
B	Western International League	1922
C	Florida State League	1919-1928
C	Piedmont League	1920-1955
C	Southwestern League	1921-1926
C	Western Association	1920-1932
D	Appalachian League	1921-1925
D	Blue Grass League	1922-1924
D	Blue Ridge League	1920-1930
D	Cotton States League	1922-1932
D	Dakota League	1921-1922
D	Eastern Shore League	1922-1928
D	Kitty League	1922-1924
D	Mississippi Valley League	1922-1933
D	Nebraska State League	1922-1923
D	Oklahoma State League	1922-1924
D	Texas-Oklahoma League	1921-1922
D	West Texas League	1920-1922

1923

Class	League	Start-End
Maj	American League	1901-
Maj	National League	1883-
AA	American Association	1902-1962
AA	International League	1912-
AA	Pacific Coast League	1903-
A	Eastern League	1916-1932
A	Southern Association	1901-1961
A	Texas League	1902-1942
A	Western League	1900-1937
B	Eastern Canada League	1922-1923
B	Michigan-Ontario League	1919-1926
B	New York-Pennsylvania League	1923-1937
B	South Atlantic League	1919-1930
B	Three-I League	1919-1932
B	Virginia League	1906-1928
C	Florida State League	1919-1928
C	Piedmont League	1920-1955
C	Southwestern League	1921-1926
C	Western Association	1920-1932
D	Appalachian League	1921-1925
D	Blue Grass League	1922-1924
D	Blue Ridge League	1920-1930
D	Cotton States League	1922-1932
D	East Texas League	1923-1926
D	Eastern Shore League	1922-1928
D	Kitty League	1922-1924
D	Mississippi Valley League	1922-1933
D	Nebraska State League	1922-1923
D	North Dakota League	1923
D	Oklahoma State League	1922-1924
D	Panhandle-Pecos Valley League	1923
D	South Dakota League	1923
D	Texas Association	1923-1926

1924

Class	League	Start-End
Maj	American League	1901-
Maj	National League	1883-
AA	American Association	1902-1962
AA	International League	1912-
AA	Pacific Coast League	1903-
A	Eastern League	1916-1932
A	Southern Association	1901-1961
A	Texas League	1902-1942
A	Western League	1900-1937
B	Michigan-Ontario League	1919-1926
B	New York-Pennsylvania League	1923-1937
B	Quebec-Ontario-Vermont League	1924
B	South Atlantic League	1919-1930
B	Three-I League	1919-1932
B	Virginia League	1906-1928
C	Florida State League	1919-1928
C	Piedmont League	1920-1955
C	Western Association	1920-1932
D	Appalachian League	1921-1925
D	Blue Grass League	1922-1924
D	Blue Ridge League	1920-1930
D	Cotton States League	1922-1932
D	East Texas League	1923-1926
D	Eastern Shore League	1922-1928
D	Kitty League	1922-1924
D	Mississippi Valley League	1922-1933
D	Oklahoma State League	1922-1924
D	Southwestern League	1921-1926
D	Texas Association	1923-1926
D	Tri-State League	1924

1925

Class	League	Start-End
Maj	American League	1901-
Maj	National League	1883-
AA	American Association	1902-1962
AA	International League	1912-
AA	Pacific Coast League	1903-
A	Eastern League	1916-1932
A	Southern Association	1901-1961
A	Texas League	1902-1942
A	Western League	1900-1937
B	Michigan-Ontario League	1919-1926
B	New York-Pennsylvania League	1923-1937
B	South Atlantic League	1919-1930
B	Three-I League	1919-1932
B	Virginia League	1906-1928
C	Middle Atlantic League	1925-1942
C	Piedmont League	1920-1955
C	Western Association	1920-1932
D	Appalachian League	1921-1925
D	Blue Ridge League	1920-1930
D	Cotton States League	1922-1932
D	East Texas League	1923-1926
D	Eastern Shore League	1922-1928
D	Florida State League	1919-1928
D	Mississippi Valley League	1922-1933
D	Southwestern League	1921-1926
D	Texas Association	1923-1926
D	Tri-State League	1925-1926

1926

Class	League	Start-End
Maj	American League	1901-
Maj	National League	1883-
AA	American Association	1902-1962
AA	International League	1912-
AA	Pacific Coast League	1903-
A	Eastern League	1916-1932
A	Southern Association	1901-1961
A	Texas League	1902-1942
A	Western League	1900-1937
B	Michigan State League	1926
B	Michigan-Ontario League	1919-1926
B	New England League	1926-1930
B	New York-Pennsylvania League	1923-1937

B	South Atlantic Association	1919-1930
B	Southeastern League	1926-1930
B	Three-I League	1919-1932
B	Virginia League	1906-1928
C	Central League	1926
C	Middle Atlantic League	1925-1942
C	Piedmont League	1920-1955
C	Utah-Idaho League	1926-1928
C	Western Association	1920-1932
D	Blue Ridge League	1920-1930
D	Cotton States League	1922-1932
D	East Texas League	1923-1926
D	Eastern Shore League	1922-1928
D	Florida State League	1919-1928
D	Gulf Coast League	1926
D	Mississippi Valley League	1922-1933
D	Southwestern League	1921-1926
D	Texas Association	1923-1926
D	Tri-State League	1925-1926

1927

Class	League	Start-End
Maj	American League	1901-
Maj	National League	1883-
AA	American Association	1902-1962
AA	International League	1912-
AA	Pacific Coast League	1903-
A	Eastern League	1916-1932
A	Southern Association	1901-1961
A	Texas League	1902-1942
A	Western League	1900-1937
B	New England League	1926-1930
B	New York-Pennsylvania League	1923-1937
B	South Atlantic Association	1919-1930
B	Southeastern League	1926-1930
B	Three-I League	1919-1932
B	Virginia League	1906-1928
C	Middle Atlantic League	1925-1942
C	Piedmont League	1920-1955
C	Utah-Idaho League	1926-1928
C	Western Association	1920-1932
D	Blue Ridge League	1920-1930
D	Cotton States League	1922-1932
D	Eastern Shore League	1922-1928
D	Florida State League	1919-1928
D	Lone Star League	1927-1929
D	Mississippi Valley League	1922-1933
D	Texas Valley League	1927

1928

Class	League	Start-End
Maj	American League	1901-
Maj	National League	1883-
AA	American Association	1902-1962
AA	International League	1912-
AA	Pacific Coast League	1903-
A	Eastern League	1916-1932
A	Southern Association	1901-1961
A	Texas League	1902-1942
A	Western League	1900-1937
B	Central League	1928-1930
B	New England League	1926-1930
B	New York-Pennsylvania League	1923-1937
B	South Atlantic Association	1919-1930
B	Southeastern League	1926-1930
B	Three-I League	1919-1932
B	Virginia League	1906-1928
C	Middle Atlantic League	1925-1942
C	Piedmont League	1920-1955
C	Utah-Idaho League	1926-1928
C	Western Association	1920-1932
D	Arizona State League	1928-1930
D	Blue Ridge League	1920-1930
D	Cotton States League	1922-1932
D	Eastern Carolina League	1928-1929
D	Eastern Shore League	1922-1928
D	Florida State League	1919-1928
D	Georgia-Alabama League	1928-1930

PROFESSIONAL LEAGUES BY YEAR

D	Lone Star League	1927-1929
D	Mississippi Valley League	1922-1933
D	Nebraska State League	1928-1938
D	West Texas League	1928-1929

1929

Class	League	Start-End
Maj	American League	1901-
Maj	National League	1883-
AA	American Association	1902-1962
AA	International League	1912-
AA	Pacific Coast League	1903-
A	Eastern League	1916-1932
A	Southern Association	1901-1961
A	Texas League	1902-1942
A	Western League	1900-1937
B	Central League	1928-1930
B	New England League	1926-1930
B	New York-Pennsylvania League	1923-1937
B	South Atlantic Association	1919-1930
B	Southeastern League	1926-1930
B	Three-I League	1919-1932
C	Middle Atlantic League	1925-1942
C	Piedmont League	1920-1955
C	Western Association	1920-1932
D	Arizona State League	1928-1930
D	Blue Ridge League	1920-1930
D	California State League	1929
D	Cotton States League	1922-1932
D	Eastern Carolina League	1928-1929
D	Georgia-Alabama League	1928-1930
D	Lone Star League	1927-1929
D	Mississippi Valley League	1922-1933
D	Nebraska State League	1928-1938
D	West Texas League	1928-1929

1930

Class	League	Start-End
Maj	American League	1901-
Maj	National League	1883-
AA	American Association	1902-1962
AA	International League	1912-
AA	Pacific Coast League	1903-
A	Eastern League	1916-1932
A	Southern Association	1901-1961
A	Texas League	1902-1942
A	Western League	1900-1937
B	Central League	1928-1930
B	New England League	1926-1930
B	New York-Pennsylvania League	1923-1937
B	South Atlantic Association	1919-1930
B	Southeastern League	1926-1930
B	Three-I League	1919-1932
C	Middle Atlantic League	1925-1942
C	Ontario League	1930
C	Piedmont League	1920-1955
C	Western Association	1920-1932
D	Arizona State League	1928-1930
D	Blue Ridge League	1920-1930
D	Cotton States League	1922-1932
D	Georgia-Alabama League	1928-1930
D	Mississippi Valley League	1922-1933
D	Nebraska State League	1928-1938

1931

Class	League	Start-End
Maj	American League	1901-
Maj	National League	1883-
AA	American Association	1902-1962
AA	International League	1912-
AA	Pacific Coast League	1903-
A	Eastern League	1916-1932
A	Southern Association	1901-1961
A	Texas League	1902-1942
A	Western League	1900-1937
B	New York-Pennsylvania League	1923-1937
B	Three-I League	1919-1932
C	Middle Atlantic League	1925-1942

C	Piedmont League	1920-1955
C	Western Association	1920-1932
D	Arizona-Texas League	1931-1932
D	Cotton States League	1922-1932
D	East Texas League	1931
D	Mississippi Valley League	1922-1933
D	Nebraska State League	1928-1938
D	Palmetto League	1931
D	Rio Grande Valley League	1931

1932

Class	League	Start-End
Maj	American League	1901-
Maj	National League	1883-
AA	American Association	1902-1962
AA	International League	1912-
AA	Pacific Coast League	1903-
A	Eastern League	1916-1932
A	Southern Association	1901-1961
A	Texas League	1902-1942
A	Western League	1900-1937
B	Central League	1932
B	New York-Pennsylvania League	1923-1937
B	Piedmont League	1920-1955
B	Southeastern League	1932
B	Three-I League	1919-1932
C	Middle Atlantic League	1925-1942
C	Western Association	1920-1932
D	Arizona-Texas League	1931-1932
D	Cotton States League	1922-1932
D	Interstate League	1932
D	Mississippi Valley League	1922-1933
D	Nebraska State League	1928-1938

1933

Class	League	Start-End
Maj	American League	1901-
Maj	National League	1883-
AA	American Association	1902-1962
AA	International League	1912-
AA	Pacific Coast League	1903-
A	New York-Pennsylvania League	1923-1937
A	Southern Association	1901-1961
A	Texas League	1902-1942
A	Western League	1900-1937
B	Mississippi Valley League	1922-1933
B	New England League	1933
B	Piedmont League	1920-1955
C	Dixie League	1933
C	Middle Atlantic League	1925-1942
D	Nebraska State League	1928-1938
D	Northern League	1933-1942

1934

Class	League	Start-End
Maj	American League	1901-
Maj	National League	1883-
AA	American Association	1902-1962
AA	International League	1912-
AA	Pacific Coast League	1903-
A	New York-Pennsylvania League	1923-1937
A	Southern Association	1901-1961
A	Texas League	1902-1942
A	Western League	1900-1937
B	Central League	1934
B	Northeastern League	1934
B	Piedmont League	1920-1955
C	East Dixie League	1934-1935
C	Middle Atlantic League	1925-1942
C	West Dixie League	1934-1935
C	Western Association	1934-1942
D	Arkansas State League	1934-1935
D	Bi-State League	1934-1942
D	Evangeline League	1934-1942
D	Nebraska State League	1928-1938
D	Northern League	1933-1942
D	Pennsylvania State Association	1934-1942

1935

Class	League	Start-End
Maj	American League	1901-
Maj	National League	1883-
AA	American Association	1902-1962
AA	International League	1912-
AA	Pacific Coast League	1903-
A	New York-Pennsylvania League	1923-1937
A	Southern Association	1901-1961
A	Texas League	1902-1942
A	Western League	1900-1937
B	Piedmont League	1920-1955
B	Three-I League	1935
C	East Dixie League	1934-1935
C	Middle Atlantic League	1925-1942
C	West Dixie League	1934-1935
C	Western Association	1934-1942
D	Arkansas State League	1934-1935
D	Bi-State League	1934-1942
D	Evangeline League	1934-1942
D	Georgia-Florida League	1935-1942
D	Kitty League	1935-1942
D	Nebraska State League	1928-1938
D	Northern League	1933-1942
D	Pennsylvania State Association	1934-1942

1936

Class	League	Start-End
Maj	American League	1901-
Maj	National League	1883-
AA	American Association	1902-1962
AA	International League	1912-
AA	Pacific Coast League	1903-
A1	Southern Association	1901-1961
A1	Texas League	1902-1942
A	New York-Pennsylvania League	1923-1937
A	Western League	1900-1937
B	Piedmont League	1920-1955
B	South Atlantic League	1936-1942
C	Canadian-American League	1936-1942
C	Cotton States League	1936-1941
C	East Texas League	1936-1940
C	Middle Atlantic League	1925-1942
C	Western Association	1934-1942
D	Alabama-Florida League	1936-1939
D	Arkansas-Missouri League	1936-1940
D	Bi-State League	1934-1942
D	Evangeline League	1934-1942
D	Florida State League	1936-1941
D	Georgia-Florida League	1935-1942
D	Kitty League	1935-1942
D	Nebraska State League	1928-1938
D	Northeast Arkansas League	1936-1941
D	Northern League	1933-1942
D	Ohio State League	1936-1941
D	Pennsylvania State Association	1934-1942

1937

Class	League	Start-End
Maj	American League	1901-
Maj	National League	1883-
AA	American Association	1902-1962
AA	International League	1912-
AA	Pacific Coast League	1903-
A1	Southern Association	1901-1961
A1	Texas League	1902-1942
A	New York-Pennsylvania League	1923-1937
A	Western League	1900-1937
B	Piedmont League	1920-1955
B	South Atlantic League	1936-1942
B	Southeastern League	1937-1942
B	Three-I League	1937-1942
B	Western International League	1937-1942
C	Canadian-American League	1936-1942
C	Cotton States League	1936-1941
C	East Texas League	1936-1940
C	Middle Atlantic League	1925-1942
C	Western Association	1934-1942

PROFESSIONAL LEAGUES BY YEAR

Class	League	Start-End
D	Alabama-Florida League	1936-1939
D	Appalachian League	1937-1955
D	Arizona-Texas League	1937-1941
D	Arkansas-Missouri League	1936-1940
D	Bi-State League	1934-1942
D	Cape Breton Colliery League	1937-1939
D	Coastal Plain League	1937-1941
D	Eastern Shore League	1937-1941
D	Evangeline League	1934-1942
D	Florida State League	1936-1941
D	Georgia-Florida League	1935-1942
D	Kitty League	1935-1942
D	Mountain State League	1937-1942
D	Nebraska State League	1928-1938
D	North Carolina State League	1937-1942
D	Northeast Arkansas League	1936-1941
D	Northern League	1933-1942
D	Ohio State League	1936-1941
D	Pennsylvania State Association	1934-1942
D	West Texas-New Mexico League	1937-1942
Ind	Mexican League	1937-

1938

Class	League	Start-End
Maj	American League	1901-
Maj	National League	1883-
AA	American Association	1902-1962
AA	International League	1912-
AA	Pacific Coast League	1903-
A1	Southern Association	1901-1961
A1	Texas League	1902-1942
A	Eastern League	1938-
B	Piedmont League	1920-1955
B	South Atlantic League	1936-1942
B	Southeastern League	1937-1942
B	Three-I League	1937-1942
B	Western International League	1937-1942
C	Canadian-American League	1936-1942
C	Cotton States League	1936-1941
C	East Texas League	1934-1940
C	Middle Atlantic League	1925-1942
C	Western Association	1934-1942
D	Alabama-Florida League	1936-1939
D	Appalachian League	1937-1955
D	Arizona-Texas League	1937-1941
D	Arkansas-Missouri League	1936-1940
D	Bi-State League	1934-1942
D	Cape Breton Colliery League	1937-1939
D	Coastal Plain League	1937-1941
D	Eastern Shore League	1937-1941
D	Evangeline League	1934-1942
D	Florida State League	1936-1941
D	Georgia-Florida League	1935-1942
D	Kitty League	1935-1942
D	Mountain State League	1937-1942
D	Nebraska State League	1928-1938
D	North Carolina State League	1937-1942
D	Northeast Arkansas League	1936-1941
D	Northern League	1933-1942
D	Ohio State League	1936-1941
D	Pennsylvania State Association	1934-1942
D	Texas Valley League	1938
D	West Texas-New Mexico League	1937-1942
Ind	Mexican League	1937-

1939

Class	League	Start-End
Maj	American League	1901-
Maj	National League	1883-
AA	American Association	1902-1962
AA	International League	1912-
AA	Pacific Coast League	1903-
A1	Southern Association	1901-1961
A1	Texas League	1902-1942
A	Eastern League	1938-
B	Piedmont League	1920-1955
B	South Atlantic League	1936-1942
B	Southeastern League	1937-1942

Class	League	Start-End
B	Three-I League	1937-1942
B	Western International League	1937-1942
C	Canadian-American League	1936-1942
C	Cape Breton Colliery League	1937-1939
C	Cotton States League	1936-1941
C	East Texas League	1934-1940
C	Interstate League	1939-1952
C	Middle Atlantic League	1925-1942
C	Pioneer League	1939-1942
C	Western Association	1934-1942
D	Alabama-Florida League	1936-1939
D	Appalachian League	1937-1955
D	Arizona-Texas League	1937-1941
D	Arkansas-Missouri League	1936-1940
D	Bi-State League	1934-1942
D	Coastal Plain League	1937-1941
D	Eastern Shore League	1937-1941
D	Evangeline League	1934-1942
D	Florida State League	1936-1941
D	Georgia-Florida League	1935-1942
D	Kitty League	1935-1942
D	Mountain State League	1937-1942
D	North Carolina State League	1937-1942
D	Northeast Arkansas League	1936-1941
D	Northern League	1933-1942
D	Ohio State League	1936-1941
D	Pennsylvania State Association	1934-1942
D	PONY League	1939-1956
D	Tar Heel League	1939-1940
D	Virginia League	1939-1942
D	West Texas-New Mexico League	1937-1942
D	Western League	1939-1941
Ind	Mexican League	1937-

1940

Class	League	Start-End
Maj	American League	1901-
Maj	National League	1883-
AA	American Association	1902-1962
AA	International League	1912-
AA	Pacific Coast League	1903-
A1	Southern Association	1901-1961
A1	Texas League	1902-1942
A	Eastern League	1938-
B	Interstate League	1939-1952
B	Piedmont League	1920-1955
B	Quebec Provincial League	1940
B	South Atlantic League	1936-1942
B	Southeastern League	1937-1942
B	Three-I League	1937-1942
B	Western International League	1937-1942
C	Arizona-Texas League	1937-1941
C	Canadian-American League	1936-1942
C	Cotton States League	1936-1941
C	East Texas League	1934-1940
C	Michigan State League	1940-1941
C	Middle Atlantic League	1925-1942
C	Pioneer League	1939-1942
C	Western Association	1934-1942
D	Alabama State League	1940-1941
D	Appalachian League	1937-1955
D	Arkansas-Missouri League	1936-1940
D	Bi-State League	1934-1942
D	Coastal Plain League	1937-1941
D	Eastern Shore League	1937-1941
D	Evangeline League	1934-1942
D	Florida East Coast League	1940-1942
D	Florida State League	1936-1941
D	Georgia-Florida League	1935-1942
D	Kitty League	1935-1942
D	Mountain State League	1937-1942
D	North Carolina State League	1937-1942
D	Northeast Arkansas League	1936-1941
D	Northern League	1933-1942
D	Ohio State League	1936-1941
D	Pennsylvania State Association	1934-1942
D	PONY League	1939-1956
D	Tar Heel League	1939-1940

Class	League	Start-End
D	Virginia League	1939-1942
D	West Texas-New Mexico League	1937-1942
D	Western League	1939-1941
D	Wisconsin State League	1940-1942
Ind	Mexican League	1937-

1941

Class	League	Start-End
Maj	American League	1901-
Maj	National League	1883-
AA	American Association	1902-1962
AA	International League	1912-
AA	Pacific Coast League	1903-
A1	Southern Association	1901-1961
A1	Texas League	1902-1942
A	Eastern League	1938-
B	Interstate League	1939-1952
B	Piedmont League	1920-1955
B	South Atlantic League	1936-1942
B	Southeastern League	1937-1942
B	Three-I League	1937-1942
B	Western International League	1937-1942
C	Arizona-Texas League	1937-1941
C	California League	1941-1942
C	Canadian-American League	1936-1942
C	Cotton States League	1936-1941
C	Michigan State League	1940-1941
C	Middle Atlantic League	1925-1942
C	Northern League	1933-1942
C	Pioneer League	1939-1942
C	Virginia League	1939-1942
C	Western Association	1934-1942
D	Alabama State League	1940-1941
D	Appalachian League	1937-1955
D	Bi-State League	1934-1942
D	Coastal Plain League	1937-1941
D	Eastern Shore League	1937-1941
D	Evangeline League	1934-1942
D	Florida East Coast League	1940-1942
D	Florida State League	1936-1941
D	Georgia-Florida League	1935-1942
D	Kitty League	1935-1942
D	Mountain State League	1937-1942
D	North Carolina State League	1937-1942
D	Northeast Arkansas League	1936-1941
D	Ohio State League	1936-1941
D	Pennsylvania State Association	1934-1942
D	PONY League	1939-1956
D	West Texas-New Mexico League	1937-1942
D	Western League	1939-1941
D	Wisconsin State League	1940-1942
Ind	Mexican League	1937-

1942

Class	League	Start-End
Maj	American League	1901-
Maj	National League	1883-
AA	American Association	1902-1962
AA	International League	1912-
AA	Pacific Coast League	1903-
A1	Southern Association	1901-1961
A1	Texas League	1902-1942
A	Eastern League	1938-
B	Interstate League	1939-1952
B	Piedmont League	1920-1955
B	South Atlantic League	1936-1942
B	Southeastern League	1937-1942
B	Three-I League	1937-1942
B	Western International League	1937-1942
C	California League	1941-1942
C	Canadian-American League	1936-1942
C	Middle Atlantic League	1925-1942
C	Mountain State League	1937-1942
C	Northern League	1933-1942
C	Pioneer League	1939-1942
C	Virginia League	1939-1942
C	Western Association	1934-1942
D	Appalachian League	1937-1955

D	Bi-State League	1934-1942
D	Evangeline League	1934-1942
D	Florida East Coast League	1940-1942
D	Georgia-Florida League	1935-1942
D	Kitty League	1935-1942
D	North Carolina State League	1937-1942
D	Pennsylvania State Association	1934-1942
D	PONY League	1939-1956
D	West Texas-New Mexico League	1937-1942
D	Wisconsin State League	1940-1942
Ind	Mexican League	1937-

1943

Class	League	Start-End
Maj	American League	1901-
Maj	National League	1883-
AA	American Association	1902-1962
AA	International League	1912-
AA	Pacific Coast League	1903-
A1	Southern Association	1901-1961
A	Eastern League	1938-
B	Interstate League	1939-1952
B	Piedmont League	1920-1955
D	Appalachian League	1937-1955
D	PONY League	1939-1956
E	Twin Ports League	1943
Ind	Mexican League	1937-

1944

Class	League	Start-End
Maj	American League	1901-
Maj	National League	1883-
AA	American Association	1902-1962
AA	International League	1912-
AA	Pacific Coast League	1903-
A1	Southern Association	1901-1961
A	Eastern League	1938-
B	Interstate League	1939-1952
B	Piedmont League	1920-1955
D	Appalachian League	1937-1955
D	Ohio State League	1944-1947
D	PONY League	1939-1956
Ind	Mexican League	1937-

1945

Class	League	Start-End
Maj	American League	1901-
Maj	National League	1883-
AA	American Association	1902-1962
AA	International League	1912-
AA	Pacific Coast League	1903-
A1	Southern Association	1901-1961
A	Eastern League	1938-
B	Interstate League	1939-1952
B	Piedmont League	1920-1955
C	Carolina League	1945-
D	Appalachian League	1937-1955
D	North Carolina State League	1945-1952
D	Ohio State League	1944-1947
D	PONY League	1939-1956
Ind	Mexican League	1937-

1946

Class	League	Start-End
Maj	American League	1901-
Maj	National League	1883-
AAA	American Association	1902-1962
AAA	International League	1912-
AAA	Pacific Coast League	1903-
AA	Southern Association	1901-1961
AA	Texas League	1946-
A	Eastern League	1938-
A	South Atlantic League	1946-1963
B	Interstate League	1939-1952
B	Mexican National League	1946
B	New England League	1946-1949
B	Piedmont League	1920-1955
B	Southeastern League	1946-1950

B	Three-I League	1946-1961
B	Tri-State League	1946-1955
B	Western International League	1946-1954
C	Border League	1946-1951
C	California League	1946-
C	Canadian-American League	1946-1951
C	Carolina League	1945-
C	East Texas League	1946
C	Florida International League	1946-1954
C	Middle Atlantic League	1946-1951
C	Northern League	1946-1971
C	Pioneer League	1946-
C	West Texas-New Mexico League	1946-1955
C	Western Association	1946-1954
D	Alabama State League	1946-1950
D	Appalachian League	1937-1955
D	Blue Ridge League	1946-1950
D	Coastal Plain League	1946-1952
D	Eastern Shore League	1946-1949
D	Evangeline League	1946-1957
D	Florida State League	1946-
D	Georgia-Alabama League	1946-1951
D	Georgia-Florida League	1946-1958
D	Kansas-Oklahoma-Missouri League	1946-1952
D	Kitty League	1946-1955
D	North Atlantic League	1946-1950
D	North Carolina State League	1945-1952
D	Ohio State League	1944-1947
D	PONY League	1939-1956
D	Tobacco State League	1946-1950
D	Wisconsin State League	1946-1953
Ind	Mexican League	1937-

1947

Class	League	Start-End
Maj	American League	1901-
Maj	National League	1883-
AAA	American Association	1902-1962
AAA	International League	1912-
AAA	Pacific Coast League	1903-
AA	Southern Association	1901-1961
AA	Texas League	1946-
A	Eastern League	1938-
A	South Atlantic League	1946-1963
A	Western League	1947-1958
B	Big State League	1947-1957
B	Colonial League	1947-1950
B	Interstate League	1939-1952
B	New England League	1946-1949
B	Piedmont League	1920-1955
B	Southeastern League	1946-1950
B	Three-I League	1946-1961
B	Tri-State League	1946-1955
B	Western International League	1946-1954
C	Arizona-Texas League	1947-1950
C	Border League	1946-1951
C	California League	1946-
C	Canadian-American League	1946-1951
C	Carolina League	1945-
C	Central Association	1947-1949
C	Cotton States League	1947-1955
C	Florida International League	1946-1954
C	Lone Star League	1947-1948
C	Middle Atlantic League	1946-1951
C	Northern League	1946-1971
C	Pioneer League	1946-
C	Sunset League	1947-1950
C	West Texas-New Mexico League	1946-1955
C	Western Association	1946-1954
D	Alabama State League	1946-1950
D	Appalachian League	1937-1955
D	Blue Ridge League	1946-1950
D	Coastal Plain League	1946-1952
D	Eastern Shore League	1946-1949
D	Evangeline League	1946-1957
D	Florida State League	1946-
D	Georgia-Alabama League	1946-1951
D	Georgia-Florida League	1946-1958

D	Illinois State League	1947-1948
D	Kansas-Oklahoma-Missouri League	1946-1952
D	Kitty League	1946-1955
D	Longhorn League	1947-1955
D	North Atlantic League	1946-1950
D	North Carolina State League	1945-1952
D	Ohio State League	1944-1947
D	PONY League	1939-1956
D	Sooner State League	1947-1957
D	Tobacco State League	1946-1950
D	Wisconsin State League	1946-1953
Ind	Mexican League	1937-

1948

Class	League	Start-End
Maj	American League	1901-
Maj	National League	1883-
AAA	American Association	1902-1962
AAA	International League	1912-
AAA	Pacific Coast League	1903-
AA	Southern Association	1901-1961
AA	Texas League	1946-
A	Central League	1948-1951
A	Eastern League	1938-
A	South Atlantic League	1946-1963
A	Western League	1947-1958
B	Big State League	1947-1957
B	Colonial League	1947-1950
B	Interstate League	1939-1952
B	New England League	1946-1949
B	Piedmont League	1920-1955
B	Southeastern League	1946-1950
B	Three-I League	1946-1961
B	Tri-State League	1946-1955
B	Western International League	1946-1954
C	Arizona-Texas League	1947-1950
C	Border League	1946-1951
C	California League	1946-
C	Canadian-American League	1946-1951
C	Carolina League	1945-
C	Central Association	1947-1949
C	Cotton States League	1947-1955
C	Florida International League	1946-1954
C	Lone Star League	1947-1948
C	Middle Atlantic League	1946-1951
C	Northern League	1946-1971
C	Pioneer League	1946-
C	Sunset League	1947-1950
C	West Texas-New Mexico League	1946-1955
C	Western Association	1946-1954
D	Alabama State League	1946-1950
D	Appalachian League	1937-1955
D	Blue Ridge League	1946-1950
D	Coastal Plain League	1946-1952
D	Eastern Shore League	1946-1949
D	Evangeline League	1946-1957
D	Far West League	1948-1951
D	Florida State League	1946-
D	Georgia State League	1948-1956
D	Georgia-Alabama League	1946-1951
D	Georgia-Florida League	1946-1958
D	Illinois State League	1947-1948
D	Kansas-Oklahoma-Missouri League	1946-1952
D	Kitty League	1946-1955
D	Longhorn League	1947-1955
D	Mountain States League	1948-1954
D	North Atlantic League	1946-1950
D	North Carolina State League	1945-1952
D	Ohio-Indiana League	1948-1951
D	PONY League	1939-1956
D	Sooner State League	1947-1957
D	Tobacco State League	1946-1950
D	Virginia League	1948-1951
D	Western Carolina League	1948-1952
D	Wisconsin State League	1946-1953
Ind	Mexican League	1937-
Ind	Provincial League	1948-1955

PROFESSIONAL LEAGUES BY YEAR

1949

Class	League	Start-End
Maj	American League	1901-
Maj	National League	1883-
AAA	American Association	1902-1962
AAA	International League	1912-
AAA	Pacific Coast League	1903-
AA	Southern Association	1901-1961
AA	Texas League	1946-
A	Central League	1948-1951
A	Eastern League	1938-
A	South Atlantic League	1946-1963
A	Western League	1947-1958
B	Big State League	1947-1957
B	Carolina League	1945-
B	Colonial League	1947-1950
B	Florida International League	1946-1954
B	Interstate League	1939-1952
B	New England League	1946-1949
B	Piedmont League	1920-1955
B	Southeastern League	1946-1950
B	Three-I League	1946-1961
B	Tri-State League	1946-1955
B	Western International League	1946-1954
C	Arizona-Texas League	1947-1950
C	Border League	1946-1951
C	California League	1946-
C	Canadian-American League	1946-1951
C	Central Association	1947-1949
C	Cotton States League	1947-1955
C	East Texas League	1949-1950
C	Evangeline League	1946-1957
C	Middle Atlantic League	1946-1951
C	Northern League	1946-1971
C	Pioneer League	1946-
C	Sunset League	1947-1950
C	West Texas-New Mexico League	1946-1955
C	Western Association	1946-1954
D	Alabama State League	1946-1950
D	Appalachian League	1937-1955
D	Blue Ridge League	1946-1950
D	Coastal Plain League	1946-1952
D	Eastern Shore League	1946-1949
D	Far West League	1948-1951
D	Florida State League	1946-
D	Georgia State League	1948-1956
D	Georgia-Alabama League	1946-1951
D	Georgia-Florida League	1946-1958
D	Kansas-Oklahoma-Missouri League	1946-1952
D	Kitty League	1946-1955
D	Longhorn League	1947-1955
D	Mississippi-Ohio Valley League	1949-1955
D	Mountain States League	1948-1954
D	North Atlantic League	1946-1950
D	North Carolina State League	1945-1952
D	Ohio-Indiana League	1948-1951
D	PONY League	1939-1956
D	Rio Grande Valley League	1949-1950
D	Sooner State League	1947-1957
D	Tobacco State League	1946-1950
D	Virginia League	1948-1951
D	Western Carolina League	1948-1952
D	Wisconsin State League	1946-1953
Ind	Mexican League	1937-
Ind	Provincial League	1948-1955

1950

Class	League	Start-End
Maj	American League	1901-
Maj	National League	1883-
AAA	American Association	1902-1962
AAA	International League	1912-
AAA	Pacific Coast League	1903-
AA	Southern Association	1901-1961
AA	Texas League	1946-
A	Central League	1948-1951
A	Eastern League	1938-
A	South Atlantic League	1946-1963
A	Western League	1947-1958
B	Big State League	1947-1957
B	Carolina League	1945-
B	Colonial League	1947-1950
B	Florida International League	1946-1954
B	Interstate League	1939-1952
B	Piedmont League	1920-1955
B	Southeastern League	1946-1950
B	Three-I League	1946-1961
B	Tri-State League	1946-1955
B	Western International League	1946-1954
C	Arizona-Texas League	1947-1950
C	Border League	1946-1951
C	California League	1946-
C	Canadian-American League	1946-1951
C	Cotton States League	1947-1955
C	East Texas League	1949-1950
C	Evangeline League	1946-1957
C	Gulf Coast League	1950-1953
C	Middle Atlantic League	1946-1951
C	Northern League	1946-1971
C	Pioneer League	1946-
C	Provincial League	1948-1955
C	Rio Grande Valley League	1949-1950
C	Sunset League	1947-1950
C	West Texas-New Mexico League	1946-1955
C	Western Association	1946-1954
D	Alabama State League	1946-1950
D	Appalachian League	1937-1955
D	Blue Ridge League	1946-1950
D	Coastal Plain League	1946-1952
D	Far West League	1948-1951
D	Florida State League	1946-
D	Georgia State League	1948-1956
D	Georgia-Alabama League	1946-1951
D	Georgia-Florida League	1946-1958
D	Kansas-Oklahoma-Missouri League	1946-1952
D	Kitty League	1946-1955
D	Longhorn League	1947-1955
D	Mississippi-Ohio Valley League	1949-1955
D	Mountain States League	1948-1954
D	North Atlantic League	1946-1950
D	North Carolina State League	1945-1952
D	Ohio-Indiana League	1948-1951
D	PONY League	1939-1956
D	Sooner State League	1947-1957
D	Tobacco State League	1946-1950
D	Virginia League	1948-1951
D	Western Carolina League	1948-1952
D	Wisconsin State League	1946-1953
Ind	Mexican League	1937-

1951

Class	League	Start-End
Maj	American League	1901-
Maj	National League	1883-
AAA	American Association	1902-1962
AAA	International League	1912-
AAA	Pacific Coast League	1903-
AA	Southern Association	1901-1961
AA	Texas League	1946-
A	Central League	1948-1951
A	Eastern League	1938-
A	South Atlantic League	1946-1963
A	Western League	1947-1958
B	Big State League	1947-1957
B	Carolina League	1945-
B	Florida International League	1946-1954
B	Gulf Coast League	1950-1953
B	Interstate League	1939-1952
B	Piedmont League	1920-1955
B	Three-I League	1946-1961
B	Tri-State League	1946-1955
B	Western International League	1946-1954
C	Border League	1946-1951
C	California League	1946-
C	Canadian-American League	1946-1951
C	Cotton States League	1947-1955
C	Evangeline League	1946-1957
C	Longhorn League	1947-1955
C	Middle Atlantic League	1946-1951
C	Northern League	1946-1971
C	Pioneer League	1946-
C	Provincial League	1948-1955
C	Southwest International League	1951-1952
C	West Texas-New Mexico League	1946-1955
C	Western Association	1946-1954
D	Alabama-Florida League	1951-1962
D	Appalachian League	1937-1955
D	Coastal Plain League	1946-1952
D	Far West League	1948-1951
D	Florida State League	1946-
D	Georgia State League	1948-1956
D	Georgia-Alabama League	1946-1951
D	Georgia-Florida League	1946-1958
D	Kansas-Oklahoma-Missouri League	1946-1952
D	Kitty League	1946-1955
D	Mississippi-Ohio Valley League	1949-1955
D	Mountain States League	1948-1954
D	North Carolina State League	1945-1952
D	Ohio-Indiana League	1948-1951
D	PONY League	1939-1956
D	Sooner State League	1947-1957
D	Virginia League	1948-1951
D	Western Carolina League	1948-1952
D	Wisconsin State League	1946-1953
Ind	Mexican League	1937-

1952

Class	League	Start-End
Maj	American League	1901-
Maj	National League	1883-
Open	Pacific Coast League	1903-
AAA	American Association	1902-1962
AAA	International League	1912-
AA	Southern Association	1901-1961
AA	Texas League	1946-
A	Eastern League	1938-
A	South Atlantic League	1946-1963
A	Western League	1947-1958
A	Western International League	1946-1954
B	Big State League	1947-1957
B	Carolina League	1945-
B	Florida International League	1946-1954
B	Gulf Coast League	1950-1953
B	Interstate League	1939-1952
B	Piedmont League	1920-1955
B	Three-I League	1946-1961
B	Tri-State League	1946-1955
C	Arizona-Texas League	1952-1954
C	California League	1946-
C	Cotton States League	1947-1955
C	Evangeline League	1946-1957
C	Longhorn League	1947-1955
C	Northern League	1946-1971
C	Pioneer League	1946-
C	Provincial League	1948-1955
C	Southwest International League	1951-1952
C	West Texas-New Mexico League	1946-1955
C	Western Association	1946-1954
D	Alabama-Florida League	1951-1962
D	Appalachian League	1937-1955
D	Coastal Plain League	1946-1952
D	Florida State League	1946-
D	Georgia State League	1948-1956
D	Georgia-Florida League	1946-1958
D	Kansas-Oklahoma-Missouri League	1946-1952
D	Kitty League	1946-1955
D	Mississippi-Ohio Valley League	1949-1955
D	Mountain States League	1948-1954
D	North Carolina State League	1945-1952
D	PONY League	1939-1956
D	Sooner State League	1947-1957
D	Western Carolina League	1948-1952
D	Wisconsin State League	1946-1953
Ind	Mexican League	1937-

PROFESSIONAL LEAGUES BY YEAR

1953

Class	League	Start-End
Maj	American League	1901-
Maj	National League	1883-
Open	Pacific Coast League	1903-
AAA	American Association	1902-1962
AAA	International League	1912-
AA	Southern Association	1901-1961
AA	Texas League	1946-
A	Eastern League	1938-
A	South Atlantic League	1946-1963
A	Western League	1947-1958
A	Western International League	1946-1954
B	Big State League	1947-1957
B	Carolina League	1945-
B	Florida International League	1946-1954
B	Gulf Coast League	1950-1953
B	Piedmont League	1920-1955
B	Three-I League	1946-1961
B	Tri-State League	1946-1955
C	Arizona-Texas League	1952-1954
C	California League	1946-
C	Cotton States League	1947-1955
C	Evangeline League	1946-1957
C	Longhorn League	1947-1955
C	Northern League	1946-1971
C	Pioneer League	1946-
C	Provincial League	1948-1955
C	West Texas-New Mexico League	1946-1955
C	Western Association	1946-1954
D	Alabama-Florida League	1951-1962
D	Appalachian League	1937-1955
D	Florida State League	1946-
D	Georgia State League	1948-1956
D	Georgia-Florida League	1946-1958
D	Kitty League	1946-1955
D	Mississippi-Ohio Valley League	1949-1955
D	Mountain States League	1948-1954
D	PONY League	1939-1956
D	Sooner State League	1947-1957
D	Tar Heel League	1953-1954
D	Wisconsin State League	1946-1953
Ind	Mexican League	1937-

1954

Class	League	Start-End
Maj	American League	1901-
Maj	National League	1883-
Open	Pacific Coast League	1903-
AAA	American Association	1902-1962
AAA	International League	1912-
AA	Southern Association	1901-1961
AA	Texas League	1946-
A	Eastern League	1938-
A	South Atlantic League	1946-1963
A	Western League	1947-1958
A	Western International League	1946-1954
B	Big State League	1947-1957
B	Carolina League	1945-
B	Florida International League	1946-1954
B	Piedmont League	1920-1955
B	Three-I League	1946-1961
B	Tri-State League	1946-1955
C	Arizona-Texas League	1952-1954
C	California League	1946-
C	Cotton States League	1947-1955
C	Evangeline League	1946-1957
C	Longhorn League	1947-1955
C	Mountain States League	1948-1954
C	Northern League	1946-1971
C	Pioneer League	1946-
C	Provincial League	1948-1955
C	West Texas-New Mexico League	1946-1955
C	Western Association	1946-1954
D	Alabama-Florida League	1951-1962
D	Appalachian League	1937-1955
D	Florida State League	1946-
D	Georgia State League	1948-1956

1955

Class	League	Start-End
Maj	American League	1901-
Maj	National League	1883-
Open	Pacific Coast League	1903-
AAA	American Association	1902-1962
AAA	International League	1912-
AA	Mexican League	1937-
AA	Southern Association	1901-1961
AA	Texas League	1946-
A	Eastern League	1938-
A	South Atlantic League	1946-1963
A	Western League	1947-1958
B	Big State League	1947-1957
B	Carolina League	1945-
B	Northwest League	1955-
B	Piedmont League	1920-1955
B	Three-I League	1946-1961
B	Tri-State League	1946-1955
B	West Texas-New Mexico League	1946-1955
C	Arizona-Mexico League	1955-1958
C	California League	1946-
C	Cotton States League	1947-1955
C	Evangeline League	1946-1957
C	Longhorn League	1947-1955
C	Northern League	1946-1971
C	Pioneer League	1946-
C	Provincial League	1948-1955
D	Alabama-Florida League	1951-1962
D	Appalachian League	1937-1955
D	Florida State League	1946-
D	Georgia State League	1948-1956
D	Georgia-Florida League	1946-1958
D	Kitty League	1946-1955
D	Mississippi-Ohio Valley League	1949-1955
D	PONY League	1939-1956
D	Sooner State League	1947-1957

1956

Class	League	Start-End
Maj	American League	1901-
Maj	National League	1883-
Open	Pacific Coast League	1903-
AAA	American Association	1902-1962
AAA	International League	1912-
AA	Mexican League	1937-
AA	Southern Association	1901-1961
AA	Texas League	1946-
A	Eastern League	1938-
A	South Atlantic League	1946-1963
A	Western League	1947-1958
B	Big State League	1947-1957
B	Carolina League	1945-
B	Northwest League	1955-
B	Southwestern League	1956-1957
B	Three-I League	1946-1961
C	Arizona-Mexico League	1955-1958
C	California League	1946-
C	Central Mexican League	1956-1957
C	Evangeline League	1946-1957
C	Northern League	1946-1971
C	Pioneer League	1946-
D	Alabama-Florida League	1951-1962
D	Florida State League	1946-
D	Georgia State League	1948-1956
D	Georgia-Florida League	1946-1958
D	Midwest League	1956-
D	Nebraska State League	1956-1959
D	PONY League	1939-1956
D	Sooner State League	1947-1957

1957

Class	League	Start-End
Maj	American League	1901-
Maj	National League	1883-
Open	Pacific Coast League	1903-
AAA	American Association	1902-1962
AAA	International League	1912-
AA	Mexican League	1937-
AA	Southern Association	1901-1961
AA	Texas League	1946-
A	Eastern League	1938-
A	South Atlantic League	1946-1963
A	Western League	1947-1958
B	Big State League	1947-1957
B	Carolina League	1945-
B	Northwest League	1955-
B	Southwestern League	1956-1957
B	Three-I League	1946-1961
C	Arizona-Mexico League	1955-1958
C	California League	1946-
C	Central Mexican League	1956-1957
C	Evangeline League	1946-1957
C	Northern League	1946-1971
C	Pioneer League	1946-
D	Alabama-Florida League	1951-1962
D	Appalachian League	1957-
D	Florida State League	1946-
D	Georgia-Florida League	1946-1958
D	Midwest League	1956-
D	Nebraska State League	1956-1959
D	New York-Pennsylvania League	1957-
D	Sooner State League	1947-1957

1958

Class	League	Start-End
Maj	American League	1901-
Maj	National League	1883-
AAA	American Association	1902-1962
AAA	International League	1912-
AAA	Pacific Coast League	1903-
AA	Mexican League	1937-
AA	Southern Association	1901-1961
AA	Texas League	1946-
A	Eastern League	1938-
A	South Atlantic League	1946-1963
A	Western League	1947-1958
B	Carolina League	1945-
B	Northwest League	1955-
B	Three-I League	1946-1961
C	Arizona-Mexico League	1955-1958
C	California League	1946-
C	Northern League	1946-1971
C	Pioneer League	1946-
D	Alabama-Florida League	1951-1962
D	Appalachian League	1957-
D	Florida State League	1946-
D	Georgia-Florida League	1946-1958
D	Midwest League	1956-
D	Nebraska State League	1956-1959
D	New York-Pennsylvania League	1957-
D	Sophomore League	1958-1961

1959

Class	League	Start-End
Maj	American League	1901-
Maj	National League	1883-
AAA	American Association	1902-1962
AAA	International League	1912-
AAA	Pacific Coast League	1903-
AA	Mexican League	1937-
AA	Southern Association	1901-1961
AA	Texas League	1946-
A	Eastern League	1938-
A	South Atlantic League	1946-1963
B	Carolina League	1945-
B	Northwest League	1955-
B	Three-I League	1946-1961
C	California League	1946-

C	Northern League	1946-1971
C	Pioneer League	1946-
D	Alabama-Florida League	1951-1962
D	Appalachian League	1957-
D	Florida State League	1946-
D	Midwest League	1956-
D	Nebraska State League	1956-1959
D	New York-Pennsylvania League	1957-
D	Sophomore League	1958-1961

1960

Class	League	Start-End
Maj	American League	1901-
Maj	National League	1883-
AAA	American Association	1902-1962
AAA	International League	1912-
AAA	Pacific Coast League	1903-
AA	Mexican League	1937-
AA	Southern Association	1901-1961
AA	Texas League	1946-
A	Eastern League	1938-
A	South Atlantic League	1946-1963
B	Carolina League	1945-
B	Northwest League	1955-
B	Three-I League	1946-1961
C	California League	1946-
C	Northern League	1946-1971
C	Pioneer League	1946-
D	Alabama-Florida League	1951-1962
D	Appalachian League	1957-
D	Florida State League	1946-
D	Mexican Center League	1960-1978
D	Midwest League	1956-
D	New York-Pennsylvania League	1957-
D	Sophomore League	1958-1961
D	Western Carolina League	1960-1979

1961

Class	League	Start-End
Maj	American League	1901-
Maj	National League	1883-
AAA	American Association	1902-1962
AAA	International League	1912-
AAA	Pacific Coast League	1903-
AA	Mexican League	1937-
AA	Southern Association	1901-1961
AA	Texas League	1946-
A	Eastern League	1938-
A	South Atlantic League	1946-1963
B	Carolina League	1945-
B	Northwest League	1955-
B	Three-I League	1946-1961
C	California League	1946-
C	Mexican Center League	1960-1978
C	Northern League	1946-1971
C	Pioneer League	1946-
D	Alabama-Florida League	1951-1962
D	Appalachian League	1957-
D	Florida State League	1946-
D	Midwest League	1956-
D	New York-Pennsylvania League	1957-
D	Sophomore League	1958-1961
D	Western Carolina League	1960-1979

1962

Class	League	Start-End
Maj	American League	1901-
Maj	National League	1883-
AAA	American Association	1902-1962
AAA	International League	1912-
AAA	Pacific Coast League	1903-
AA	Mexican League	1937-
AA	Texas League	1946-
A	Eastern League	1938-
A	South Atlantic League	1946-1963
B	Carolina League	1945-
B	Northwest League	1955-
C	California League	1946-

C	Mexican Center League	1960-1978
C	Northern League	1946-1971
C	Pioneer League	1946-
D	Alabama-Florida League	1951-1962
D	Appalachian League	1957-
D	Florida State League	1946-
D	Georgia-Florida League	1962-1963
D	Midwest League	1956-
D	New York-Pennsylvania League	1957-
D	Western Carolina League	1960-1979

1963

Class	League	Start-End
Maj	American League	1901-
Maj	National League	1883-
AAA	International League	1912-
AAA	Pacific Coast League	1903-
AA	Eastern League	1938-
AA	Mexican League	1937-
AA	South Atlantic League	1946-1963
AA	Texas League	1946-
A	California League	1946-
A	Carolina League	1945-
A	Florida State League	1946-
A	Georgia-Florida League	1962-1963
A	Mexican Center League	1960-1978
A	Midwest League	1956-
A	New York-Pennsylvania League	1957-
A	Northern League	1946-1971
A	Northwest League	1955-
A	Pioneer League	1946-
A	Western Carolinas League	1960-1979
R	Appalachian League	1957-

1964

Class	League	Start-End
Maj	American League	1901-
Maj	National League	1883-
AAA	International League	1912-
AAA	Pacific Coast League	1903-
AA	Eastern League	1938-
AA	Mexican League	1937-
AA	Southern League	1964-
AA	Texas League	1946-
A	California League	1946-
A	Carolina League	1945-
A	Florida State League	1946-
A	Mexican Center League	1960-1978
A	Mexican Southeast League	1964-1970
A	Midwest League	1956-
A	New York-Pennsylvania League	1957-
A	Northern League	1946-1971
A	Northwest League	1955-
A	Western Carolinas League	1960-1979
R	Appalachian League	1957-
R	Cocoa Rookie League	1964
R	Pioneer League	1946-
R	Sarasota Rookie League	1964

1965

Class	League	Start-End
Maj	American League	1901-
Maj	National League	1883-
AAA	International League	1912-
AAA	Pacific Coast League	1903-
AA	Eastern League	1938-
AA	Mexican League	1937-
AA	Southern League	1964-
AA	Texas League	1946-
A	California League	1946-
A	Carolina League	1945-
A	Florida State League	1946-
A	Mexican Center League	1960-1978
A	Mexican Southeast League	1964-1970
A	Midwest League	1956-
A	New York-Pennsylvania League	1957-
A	Northern League	1946-1971
A	Northwest League	1955-

A	Western Carolinas League	1960-1979
R	Appalachian League	1957-
R	Florida Rookie League	1965
R	Pioneer League	1946-

1966

Class	League	Start-End
Maj	American League	1901-
Maj	National League	1883-
AAA	International League	1912-
AAA	Pacific Coast League	1903-
AA	Eastern League	1938-
AA	Mexican League	1937-
AA	Southern League	1964-
AA	Texas League	1946-
A	California League	1946-
A	Carolina League	1945-
A	Florida State League	1946-
A	Mexican Center League	1960-1978
A	Mexican Southeast League	1964-1970
A	Midwest League	1956-
A	New York-Pennsylvania League	1957-
A	Northern League	1946-1971
A	Northwest League	1955-
A	Western Carolinas League	1960-1979
R	Appalachian League	1957-
R	Gulf Coast League	1966-
R	Pioneer League	1946-

1967

Class	League	Start-End
Maj	American League	1901-
Maj	National League	1883-
AAA	International League	1912-
AAA	Mexican League	1937-
AAA	Pacific Coast League	1903-
AA	Eastern League	1938-
AA	Southern League	1964-
AA	Texas League	1946-
A	California League	1946-
A	Carolina League	1945-
A	Florida State League	1946-
A	Mexican Center League	1960-1978
A	Mexican Southeast League	1964-1970
A	Midwest League	1956-
A	New York-Pennsylvania League	1957-
A	Northern League	1946-1971
A	Northwest League	1955-
A	Western Carolinas League	1960-1979
R	Appalachian League	1957-
R	Gulf Coast League	1966-
R	Pioneer League	1946-

1968

Class	League	Start-End
Maj	American League	1901-
Maj	National League	1883-
AAA	International League	1912-
AAA	Mexican League	1937-
AAA	Pacific Coast League	1903-
AA	Eastern League	1938-
AA	Southern League	1964-
AA	Texas League	1946-
A	California League	1946-
A	Carolina League	1945-
A	Florida State League	1946-
A	Mexican Center League	1960-1978
A	Mexican Northern League	1968-1969
A	Mexican Southeast League	1964-1970
A	Midwest League	1956-
A	New York-Pennsylvania League	1957-
A	Northern League	1946-1971
A	Northwest League	1955-
A	Western Carolinas League	1960-1979
R	Appalachian League	1957-
R	Gulf Coast League	1966-
R	Mexican Rookie League	1968
R	Pioneer League	1946-

PROFESSIONAL LEAGUES BY YEAR

1969

Class	League	Start-End
Maj	American League	1901-
Maj	National League	1883-
AAA	American Association	1969-
AAA	International League	1912-
AAA	Mexican League	1937-
AAA	Pacific Coast League	1903-
AA	Eastern League	1938-
AA	Southern League	1964-
AA	Texas League	1946-
A	California League	1946-
A	Carolina League	1945-
A	Florida State League	1946-
A	Mexican Center League	1960-1978
A	Mexican Northern League	1968-1969
A	Mexican Southeast League	1964-1970
A	Midwest League	1956-
A	New York-Pennsylvania League	1957-
A	Northern League	1946-1971
A	Northwest League	1955-
A	Western Carolinas League	1960-1979
R	Appalachian League	1957-
R	Gulf Coast League	1966-
R	Pioneer League	1946-

1970

Class	League	Start-End
Maj	American League	1901-
Maj	National League	1883-
AAA	American Association	1969-
AAA	International League	1912-
AAA	Mexican League	1937-
AAA	Pacific Coast League	1903-
AA	Eastern League	1938-
AA	Southern League	1964-
AA	Texas League	1946-
A	California League	1946-
A	Carolina League	1945-
A	Florida State League	1946-
A	Mexican Center League	1960-1978
A	Mexican Southeast League	1964-1970
A	Midwest League	1956-
A	New York-Pennsylvania League	1957-
A	Northern League	1946-1971
A	Northwest League	1955-
A	Western Carolinas League	1960-1979
R	Appalachian League	1957-
R	Gulf Coast League	1966-
R	Pioneer League	1946-

1971

Class	League	Start-End
Maj	American League	1901-
Maj	National League	1883-
AAA	American Association	1969-
AAA	International League	1912-
AAA	Mexican League	1937-
AAA	Pacific Coast League	1903-
AA	Eastern League	1938-
AA	Southern League	1964-
AA	Texas League	1946-
A	California League	1946-
A	Carolina League	1945-
A	Florida State League	1946-
A	Mexican Center League	1960-1978
A	Midwest League	1956-
A	New York-Pennsylvania League	1957-
A	Northern League	1946-1971
A	Northwest League	1955-
A	Western Carolinas League	1960-1979
R	Appalachian League	1957-
R	Gulf Coast League	1966-
R	Pioneer League	1946-

1972

Class	League	Start-End
Maj	American League	1901-

1972 (continued)

Class	League	Start-End
Maj	National League	1883-
AAA	American Association	1969-
AAA	International League	1912-
AAA	Mexican League	1937-
AAA	Pacific Coast League	1903-
AA	Eastern League	1938-
AA	Southern League	1964-
AA	Texas League	1946-
A	California League	1946-
A	Carolina League	1945-
A	Florida State League	1946-
A	Mexican Center League	1960-1978
A	Midwest League	1956-
A	New York-Pennsylvania League	1957-
A	Northwest League	1955-
A	Western Carolinas League	1960-1979
R	Appalachian League	1957-
R	Florida East Coast League	1972
R	Gulf Coast League	1966-
R	Pioneer League	1946-

1973-1975

Class	League	Start-End
Maj	American League	1901-
Maj	National League	1883-
AAA	American Association	1969-
AAA	International League	1912-
AAA	Mexican League	1937-
AAA	Pacific Coast League	1903-
AA	Eastern League	1938-
AA	Southern League	1964-
AA	Texas League	1946-
A	California League	1946-
A	Carolina League	1945-
A	Florida State League	1946-
A	Mexican Center League	1960-1978
A	Midwest League	1956-
A	New York-Pennsylvania League	1957-
A	Northwest League	1955-
A	Western Carolinas League	1960-1979
R	Appalachian League	1957-
R	Gulf Coast League	1966-
R	Pioneer League	1946-

1976

Class	League	Start-End
Maj	American League	1901-
Maj	National League	1883-
AAA	American Association	1969-
AAA	International League	1912-
AAA	Mexican League	1937-
AAA	Pacific Coast League	1903-
AA	Eastern League	1938-
AA	Southern League	1964-
AA	Texas League	1946-
A	California League	1946-
A	Carolina League	1945-
A	Florida State League	1946-
A	Gulf States League	1976
A	Mexican Center League	1960-1978
A	Mexican Pacific League	1976
A	Midwest League	1956-
A	New York-Pennsylvania League	1957-
A	Northwest League	1955-
A	Western Carolinas League	1960-1979
R	Appalachian League	1957-
R	Gulf Coast League	1966-
R	Pioneer League	1946-

1977

Class	League	Start-End
Maj	American League	1901-
Maj	National League	1883-
AAA	American Association	1969-
AAA	International League	1912-
AAA	Mexican League	1937-
AAA	Pacific Coast League	1903-
AA	Eastern League	1938-
AA	Southern League	1964-
AA	Texas League	1946-
A	California League	1946-
A	Carolina League	1945-
A	Florida State League	1946-
A	Lone Star League	1977
A	Mexican Center League	1960-1978
A	Midwest League	1956-
A	New York-Pennsylvania League	1957-
A	Northwest League	1955-
A	Western Carolinas League	1960-1979
R	Appalachian League	1957-
R	Gulf Coast League	1966-
R	Pioneer League	1946-

1978

Class	League	Start-End
Maj	American League	1901-
Maj	National League	1883-
AAA	American Association	1969-
AAA	International League	1912-
AAA	Mexican League	1937-
AAA	Pacific Coast League	1903-
AA	Eastern League	1938-
AA	Southern League	1964-
AA	Texas League	1946-
A	California League	1946-
A	Carolina League	1945-
A	Florida State League	1946-
A	Mexican Center League	1960-1978
A	Midwest League	1956-
A	New York-Pennsylvania League	1957-
A	Northwest League	1955-
A	Western Carolinas League	1960-1979
R	Appalachian League	1957-
R	Gulf Coast League	1966-
R	Pioneer League	1946-

1979

Class	League	Start-End
Maj	American League	1901-
Maj	National League	1883-
AAA	American Association	1969-
AAA	Inter-American League	1979
AAA	International League	1912-
AAA	Mexican League	1937-
AAA	Pacific Coast League	1903-
AA	Eastern League	1938-
AA	Southern League	1964-
AA	Texas League	1946-
A	California League	1946-
A	Carolina League	1945-
A	Florida State League	1946-
A	Midwest League	1956-
A	New York-Pennsylvania League	1957-
A	Northwest League	1955-
A	Western Carolinas League	1960-1979
R	Appalachian League	1957-
R	Gulf Coast League	1966-
R	Pioneer League	1946-

1980-1987

Class	League	Start-End
Maj	American League	1901-
Maj	National League	1883-
AAA	American Association	1969-
AAA	International League	1912-
AAA	Mexican League	1937-
AAA	Pacific Coast League	1903-
AA	Eastern League	1938-
AA	Southern League	1964-
AA	Texas League	1946-
A	California League	1946-
A	Carolina League	1945-
A	Florida State League	1946-
A	Midwest League	1956-
A	New York-Pennsylvania League	1957-
A	Northwest League	1955-

PROFESSIONAL LEAGUES BY YEAR

Class	League	Start-End
A	South Atlantic League	1980-
R	Appalachian League	1957-
R	Gulf Coast League	1966-
R	Pioneer League	1946-

1988-1992

Class	League	Start-End
Maj	American League	1901-
Maj	National League	1883-
AAA	American Association	1969-
AAA	International League	1912-
AAA	Mexican League	1937-
AAA	Pacific Coast League	1903-
AA	Eastern League	1938-
AA	Southern League	1964-
AA	Texas League	1946-
A	California League	1946-
A	Carolina League	1945-
A	Florida State League	1946-
A	Midwest League	1956-
A	New York-Pennsylvania League	1957-
A	Northwest League	1955-
A	South Atlantic League	1980-
R	Appalachian League	1957-
R	Arizona League	1988-
R	Gulf Coast League	1966-
R	Pioneer League	1946-

1993

Class	League	Start-End
Maj	American League	1901-
Maj	National League	1883-
AAA	American Association	1969-
AAA	International League	1912-
AAA	Mexican League	1937-
AAA	Pacific Coast League	1903-
AA	Eastern League	1938-
AA	Southern League	1964-
AA	Texas League	1946-
A	California League	1946-
A	Carolina League	1945-
A	Florida State League	1946-
A	Midwest League	1956-
A	New York-Pennsylvania League	1957-
A	Northwest League	1955-
A	South Atlantic League	1980-
R	Appalachian League	1957-
R	Arizona League	1988-
R	Gulf Coast League	1966-

Class	League	Start-End
R	Pioneer League	1946-
Ind	Frontier League	1993-
Ind	Northern League	1993-

1994

Class	League	Start-End
Maj	American League	1901-
Maj	National League	1883-
AAA	American Association	1969-
AAA	International League	1912-
AAA	Mexican League	1937-
AAA	Pacific Coast League	1903-
AA	Eastern League	1938-
AA	Southern League	1964-
AA	Texas League	1946-
A	California League	1946-
A	Carolina League	1945-
A	Florida State League	1946-
A	Midwest League	1956-
A	New York-Pennsylvania League	1957-
A	Northwest League	1955-
A	South Atlantic League	1980-
R	Appalachian League	1957-
R	Arizona League	1988-
R	Gulf Coast League	1966-
R	Pioneer League	1946-
Ind	Frontier League	1993-
Ind	Great Central League	1994
Ind	North Central League	1994-1995
Ind	Northern League	1993-
Ind	Texas-Louisiana League	1994-

1995

Class	League	Start-End
Maj	American League	1901-
Maj	National League	1883-
AAA	American Association	1969-
AAA	International League	1912-
AAA	Mexican League	1937-
AAA	Pacific Coast League	1903-
AA	Eastern League	1938-
AA	Southern League	1964-
AA	Texas League	1946-
A	California League	1946-
A	Carolina League	1945-
A	Florida State League	1946-
A	Midwest League	1956-
A	New York-Pennsylvania League	1957-
A	Northwest League	1955-

Class	League	Start-End
A	South Atlantic League	1980-
R	Appalachian League	1957-
R	Arizona League	1988-
R	Gulf Coast League	1966-
R	Pioneer League	1946-
Ind	Atlantic Coast League	1995
Ind	Frontier League	1993-
Ind	Golden State League	1995
Ind	Mid-America League	1995
Ind	North Atlantic League	1995-
Ind	North Central League	1994-1995
Ind	Northeast League	1995-
Ind	Northern League	1993-
Ind	Prairie League	1995-
Ind	Texas-Louisiana League	1994-
Ind	Western League	1995-

1996-1997

Class	League	Start-End
Maj	American League	1901-
Maj	National League	1883-
AAA	American Association	1969-
AAA	International League	1912-
AAA	Mexican League	1937-
AAA	Pacific Coast League	1903-
AA	Eastern League	1938-
AA	Southern League	1964-
AA	Texas League	1946-
A	California League	1946-
A	Carolina League	1945-
A	Florida State League	1946-
A	Midwest League	1956-
A	New York-Pennsylvania League	1957-
A	Northwest League	1955-
A	South Atlantic League	1980-
R	Appalachian League	1957-
R	Arizona League	1988-
R	Gulf Coast League	1966-
R	Pioneer League	1946-
Ind	Big South League	1996-
Ind	Frontier League	1993-
Ind	Heartland League	1996-
Ind	North Atlantic League	1995-1996
Ind	Northeast League	1995-
Ind	Northern League	1993-
Ind	Prairie League	1995-
Ind	Texas-Louisiana League	1994-
Ind	Western League	1995-

III
THE YEARS

The Beginnings: 1883-1901

The Early Years: 1902-1913

The First Decline: 1914-1919

The Roaring Twenties: 1920-1929

The Depression and Beyond: 1930-1941

The War Years: 1942-1945

The Golden Age: 1946-1951

The Decline: 1952-1962

The Subsistence Years: 1963-1977

The Revival: 1978-1991

The Boom: 1992-1996

THE BEGINNINGS: 1883-1901

*M*inor league baseball, like the major league version of the national pastime, did not start on a specific date or in a single year. It evolved. After the Civil War the United States and Canada became more urbanized and industrialized. Fast-growing cities began to need leisure activity and entertainment for the masses. Baseball became that outlet. Town teams grew, and as competition increased, players started being recruited and paid for their services, which consisted primarily of defeating the neighboring town nine.

By the 1870s professional baseball appeared in most large North American cities. At first, there was no such designation as major or minor league, but larger cities with the finances to recruit better players began meeting each other and loose leagues formed. Schedules were not standardized, league umpires were nonexistent and administrative controls were loose. Often a league would dictate that each club must play only a four-game series with each team in the association. The Chicago White Stockings and Philadelphia Athletics left the country for a tour in England in the middle of the 1874 season.

Scheduling and uniform rules were cause for concern, but the most important problem was protecting player contracts. Often in middle of a season players would jump to other leagues, or teams would fold, leaving players and fans high and dry. In March 1883, the three most successful leagues, the National League, the American Association and the Northwestern League, signed the tripartite agreement in which they agreed to honor contracts, establish territories and create an arbitration committee for disputes. Minimum salaries were established and guaranteed by a bond filed by the league with the newly created National Agreement organization. Because the National League and American Association had higher salary limits than the Northwestern League, a working definition of major and minor league was established. The Interstate League joined the next year and the first structure for Organized Baseball was in existence. (For the purposes of this volume, the National Agreement teams are considered the first minor league teams, and their standings are listed. Those leagues not signing the National Agreement are listed at the end of this section.)

Attendance, player salaries and team profits blossomed in the 1880s, and by 1890 there were 17 National Agreement leagues. In 1887 the National Colored League, fearing that its contracts were not protected, joined the National Agreement. The league folded (as many other leagues would do in this era,) but its membership helped point out the importance of being a member of the National Agreement. Leagues and clubs paid dues and bonds for the protections and guarantees that the National Agreement offered. Players were more interested in playing for a team in an NA league because the salaries were guaranteed by the bond that each club posted. Some leagues, such as the California or Connecticut State League, had reputations for stability and quality play, and thus did not need the guarantees to attract top players. Such well-off leagues chose to pay the minimum dues to the NA.

Minor league baseball did not show the same growth in the 1890s. A pattern that would hold for the next hundred years developed. The depression of 1892-93 and the Spanish-American War proved that baseball could not be isolated from outside forces. Internal forces also had important negative effects, as bad operators and fly-by-night leagues showed baseball could not flourish without solid business practices.

In 1900 the National Agreement started unraveling. The American League (formerly the Western League) announced that it was withdrawing. It would no longer allow its players to be drafted by a higher league, and it would not respect territorial rights or the reserve clause. In short, the American League was going to make its own rules and become a major league.

The National League could not sit by and refuse to take action against a serious competitor. In September 1901, the National League announced it would not abide by the National Agreement. With the American League pirating players and appropriating cities, the National League felt compelled to do the same. Minor league operators knew they were in trouble and on Sept. 5, 1901, seven minor league presidents met in Chicago to discuss protection for their leagues and franchises. The group formed the National Association of Professional Baseball Leagues, the modern organization that still governs minor league baseball.

1883-1901

1883

American Association
President: H.D. McKnight

Standings	W	L	Pct.	GB	Manager
Philadelphia Athletics........	66	32	.673	—	Lew Simmons
St. Louis Browns	65	33	.663	1	Ted Sullivan/Charlie Comiskey
Cincinnati Red Stockings ...	61	37	.622	5	Pop Snyder
New York Metropolitans	54	42	.563	11	Jim Mutrie
Louisville Eclipse	52	45	.536	13½	Bill Reccius/Sam "Leech" Maskrey/
					Joe Gerhardt
Columbus Senators............	32	65	.330	33½	Horace Phillips
Pittsburgh Alleghenies........	31	67	.316	35	Al Pratt/Ormond Butler/Joe Battin
Baltimore Orioles	28	68	.292	37	Billy Barnie

BA: Ed Swartwood, Pittsburgh, .356
Runs: Harry Stovey, Philadelphia, 110
Hits: Harry Stovey, Philadelphia, 148
HRs: Harry Stovey, Philadelphia, 14

Wins: Will White, Cincinnati, 43
SOs: Tim Keefe, New York, 361
ERA: Will White, Cincinnati, 2.09
Pct: Tony Mullane, St. Louis, .700, 35-15

National League
President: Abraham G. Mills

Standings	W	L	Pct.	GB	Attend.	Manager
Boston Beaneaters	63	35	.643	—	138,284	Jack Burdock/John Morrill
Chicago White Stockings ...	59	39	.602	4	126,376	Cap Anson
Providence Grays...............	58	40	.592	5	61,341	Harry Wright
Cleveland Blues	55	42	.567	7½	88,000	Frank Bancroft
Buffalo Bisons	52	45	.536	10½		Jim O'Rourke
New York Gothams	46	50	.479	16		John Clapp
Detroit Wolverines	40	58	.408	23		Jack Chapman
Philadelphia Quakers	17	81	.173	46	55,992	Bob Ferguson/Blondie Purcell

BA: Dan Brouthers, Buffalo, .374
Runs: Joe Hornung, Boston, 107
Hits: Dan Brouthers, Buffalo, 159
HRs: Buck Ewing, New York, 10

Wins: Old Hoss Radbourn, Providence, 49
SOs: Jim Whitney, Boston, 345
ERA: Jim McCormick, Cleveland, 1.84
Pct: Jim McCormick, Cleveland, .675, 27-13

Interstate Association

Standings	W	L	Pct.	GB	Manager
Brooklyn Grays..................	44	28	.611	—	George Taylor
Harrisburg..........................	43	33	.566	3	Henry Meyers
Reading Actives.................	33	35	.485	9	Sam Fields/Henry Boyle/Frank Fox
Trenton...............................	34	38	.472	10	Albert Douress/Joseph Simmons
Wilmington Quicksteps	27	48	.360	18½	Charles Waitt/John McHugh/
					Fergy Malone
Pottsville Anthracites..........	28	46	.378	17	T.B. Fielders/Hugh Galbraith/
					John Sullivan
Camden Merritts#...............	27	8	.771	NA	James Farrington/Wes Fisler

#Camden disbanded after the July 20 game.

BA: Henry Boyle, Reading, .356
Runs: Frank Fennely, Camden/Brooklyn, 91
Hits: Frank Fennely, Camden/Brooklyn, 102
HRs: Frank Fennely, Camden/Brooklyn, 6

Wins: Sam Kimber, Camden/Brooklyn, 28
SOs: John Harkins, Trenton, 213
Pct: Bob Emslie, Camden, .824

Northwestern League
President: Elias Matter

Standings	W	L	Pct.	GB	Manager
Toledo Blue Stockings........	56	28	.667	—	William Voltz/Charles Morton
Saginaw Greys...................	54	30	.643	2	Art Whitney
Peoria Reds........................	49	35	.583	7	Charles Flynn/Charles Levis/A.C. Harding
Grand Rapids	48	36	.571	8	Charles Eden/Henry Jones
Springfield	37	47	.440	19	C.J. Frichtel/John Peters/John Crawford
Bay City	35	49	.417	21	Dave Foutz/W.B. Montgomery/
					Chester Morgan
Fort Wayne Hoosiers..........	34	50	.405	22	James Remsen/Milton Scott
Quincy	23	61	.274	33	Charles Overrecker/Edward Hengel/
					Richard J. Pearce

BA: Charles Eden, Grand Rapids, .359
Runs: Henry M. Jones, Grand Rapids, 87

Hits: Charles Eden, Grand Rapids, 130

1884

American Association
President: H.D. McKnight

Standings	W	L	Pct.	GB	Manager
New York Mets	75	32	.701	—	Jim Mutrie
Columbus Senators	69	39	.639	6½	Gus Schmelz
Louisville Eclipse	68	40	.630	7½	Joe Gerhardt/Mike Walsh
St. Louis Browns	67	40	.626	8	Jimmy Williams
Cincinnati Reds..................	68	41	.624	8	Will White/Pop Snyder
Baltimore Orioles	63	43	.594	11½	Billy Barnie
Philadelphia Athletics.........	61	46	.570	14	Charlie Mason/Bill Sharsig
Toledo Blue Stockings........	46	58	.442	27½	Charlie Morton
Brooklyn Atlantics..............	40	64	.385	33½	George Taylor
Pittsburgh Alleghenies........	30	78	.278	45½	Joe Battin/George Creamer/
					Denny McKnight/Bob Ferguson/
					Horace Phillips
Indianapolis Hoosiers	29	78	.271	46	Jim Gifford/Bill Watkins
Richmond Virginians#.........	12	30	.286	NA	Felix Moses
Washington Nationals#.......	12	51	.190	NA	Holly Hollingshead

#Washington disbanded August 2 and was replaced by Richmond August 5.

BA: Harry Stovey, Philadelphia, .404
Runs: Harry Stovey, Philadelphia, 126
Hits: Harry Stovey, Philadelphia, 179

HRs: Harry Stovey, Philadelphia, 11
Long John Reilly, Cincinnati, 11
Wins: Guy Hecker, Louisville, 52
SOs: Guy Hecker, Louisville, 385
Pct: Jack Lynch, New York, .725, 37-14

National League
President: Abraham G. Mills

Standings	W	L	Pct.	GB	Attend.	Manager
Providence Grays...............	84	28	.750	—	71,000	Frank Bancroft
Boston Beaneaters	73	38	.658	10½	146,777	John Morrill
Buffalo Bison....................	64	47	.577	19½		Jim O'Rourke
Chicago White Stockings ...	62	50	.554	22	88,218	Cap Anson
New York Giants	62	50	.554	22		James Price/Monte Ward
Philadelphia Quakers	39	73	.348	45	100,475	Harry Wright
Cleveland Spiders	35	77	.313	49		Charlie Hackett
Detroit Wolverines	28	84	.250	56		Jack Chapman

BA: King Kelly, Chicago, .354
Runs: King Kelly, Chicago, 120
Hits: Jim O'Rourke, Buffalo, 162
HRs: Ned Williamson, Chicago, 27
Wins: Old Hoss Radbourn, Providence, 60

SOs: Old Hoss Radbourn, Providence, 441
ERA: Old Hoss Radbourn, Providence, 1.38
Pct: Old Hoss Radbourn, Providence, .833, 60-12

Union Association
President: Henry Lucas

Standings	W	L	Pct.	GB	Manager
St. Louis Maroons...............	94	19	.832	—	Henry Lucas
Cincinnati Outlaw Reds......	69	36	.657	21	Dan O'Leary/Sam Crane
Baltimore Unions................	58	47	.552	32	Charlie Levis/Bill Henderson
Boston Reds.......................	58	51	.532	34	Tim Murnane/Tom Furniss/Jake Morse
Washington Nationals.........	47	65	.420	46½	Mike Scanlon
Milwaukee Cream Citys&....	8	4	.667	NA	Tom Loftus
Chicago Browns/					
Pittsburgh Stogies+&.......	41	50	.451	NA	Ed Hengle/Joe Battin/Joe Ellick
Philadelphia Keystones@ ...	21	46	.313	NA	Fergy Malone/Tom Pratt
St. Paul Saints$	2	6	.250	NA	A.M. Thompson
Altoona Unions#................	6	19	.240	NA	Ed Curtis
Kansas City Cowboys#.......	16	63	.203	NA	Ted Sullivan
Wilmington Quicksteps@$ ..	2	16	.111	NA	Joseph Simmons

#Altoona disbanded May 31 and was replaced by Kansas City June 7.
@Philadelphia disbanded August 7 and was replaced by Wilmington August 18.
+Chicago moved to Pittsburgh August 20.
$Wilmington disbanded September 15 and was replaced by St. Paul September 27.
&Pittsburgh disbanded September 19 and was replaced by Milwaukee September 27.

BA: Fred Dunlap, St. Louis, .412
Runs: Fred Dunlap, St. Louis, 160
Hits: Fred Dunlap, St. Louis, 185
HRs: Fred Dunlap, St. Louis, 13
Wins: Bill Sweeney, Baltimore, 40

SOs: One Arm Daily, Chicago/Pittsburgh/
Washington, 483
ERA: Jim McCormick, Cincinnati, 1.54
Pct: Jim McCormick, Cincinnati, .875, 21-3

Eastern League
President: William C. Seddon

Standings	W	L	Pct.	GB	Manager
Trenton Trentonians	46	39	.541	—	Patrick Powers
Lancaster Ironsides$	30	31	.492	4	Robert Clark
Newark Domestics..............	40	43	.482	5	Dave Pierson
Allentown Dukes	31	44	.413	10	H.J. Dehlman/K.H. Debelle
Harrisburg Olympics/					
York White Roses+	26	46	.361	13½	R.M. Sturgeon/John Murphy
Wilmington Quicksteps% ..	50	12	.806	NA	Joseph Simmons
Reading Actives&	28	27	.509	NA	Frank Helfer
Richmond Virginias&	28	30	.483	NA	Ted Sullivan/Abner Powell
Baltimore Monumentals@	3	10	.231	NA	Harry Spence
Brooklyn Greys#..................	0	2	.000	NA	Endler

#Brooklyn disbanded in early May.
@Baltimore disbanded May 20.
+Harrisburg (16-25) disbanded July 4 and was replaced by York July 18.
$Lancaster entered the league July 22.
&Reading and Richmond disbanded August 4.
%Wilmington disbanded August 12 to join the Union Association.

BA: John W. Coogan, Newark, .375
Runs: Thomas P. Burns, Wilmington, 107
Hits: John W. Coogan, Newark, 128
HRs: Thomas P. Burns, Wilmington, 11

Wins: Con Murphy, Trenton/Newark, 21
SOs: Ed Dugan, Richmond, 260
Pct: Dan Casey, Wilmington, .833

Iron & Oil Association
President: Horace G. Miller

Standings	W	L	Pct.	GB	Manager
Franklin......................					Baker
New Brighton/Johnstown#					William Boyle/W.C. Blagg
Oil City@					N.L. Baker/Baisley
Youngstown....................					T.T. Dorsey/T.F. Brownlee
New Castle Nashannocks					Levi Dunham/Ellis
East Liberty Stars....................					William Deems

#New Brighton disbanded August 1 and was replaced by Johnstown.
@Oil City disbanded August 4, causing the league to disband August 8.

Keystone Association
President: Thomas Hargraves

Standings	W	L	Pct.	GB	Manager
Lancaster Red Stockings# ..	15	4	.789	—	Diffenderfer
York White Roses...............	10	10	.500	5½	Frank Burnham
Chester Blue Stockings#.......	8	10	.444	6½	
Chambersburg	8	10	.444	6½	
Littlestown Brown Stockings	6	8	.429	6½	

#Chester disbanded June 2 and Lancaster disbanded June 7, ending the league.

Northwestern League
Presidents: Jonathan J. Just/W.D. Whitmore

Standings	W	L	Pct.	GB	Manager
Grand Rapids+	48	15	.762	—	Horace Phillips
Saginaw	47	21	.691	3½	William Dyer
Quincy	45	23	.662	5½	George Brackett
Peoria Reds	40	25	.615	9	James Whitfield/Charles Flynn
Milwaukee Brewers	42	30	.583	10½	James McKee/Tom Loftus
Minneapolis Millers............	30	42	.417	22½	Benjamin Tuthill
Muskegon@	23	40	.365	25	A.J. Bradford/Edward Cushman/John Rainey
Fort Wayne Hoosiers	22	43	.338	27	John McDonough/Harry Smith
St. Paul Apostles	24	48	.333	28½	Robert Hunter/A.M. Thompson
Stillwater	21	46	.313	29	Joseph May/Joseph Miller/Fred Gunkle/John Peters
Terre Haute	15	50	.231	34	Al Buckenberger/George Hammerstein
Evansville@	4	1	.800	NA	Stephen Hagan
Bay City#......................	39	16	.709	NA	Bill Watkins

#Bay City disbanded July 22.
@Evansville joined the league on July 30.
+Grand Rapids and Muskegon disbanded August 2, forcing a second season.

Second Season

Standings	W	L	Pct.	GB	Manager
Milwaukee Brewers	11	4	.733	—	Tom Loftus
Minneapolis Millers#..........	7	4	.636	2	Benjamin Tuthill
St. Paul Apostles	7	7	.500	3½	A.M. Thompson
Winona Clippers	1	11	.083	8½	

#Minneapolis disbanded September 3, ending the season.

BA: Jonathan Morrison, Bay City, .328
Runs: Bob Hogan, Milwaukee, 83
Hits: Bill Reid, Minneapolis, 95

HRs: Con Doyle, Quincy, 4
Charles Eden, Grand Rapids, 4
Wins: John Clarkson, Saginaw, 34
SOs: John Clarkson, Saginaw, 388
Pct: Ed Cushman, Milwaukee, .957, 22-1

Ohio State Association
President: Colonel A.E. Butt

Standings	W	L	Pct.	GB	Manager
Dayton Gem Citys	55	21	.724	—	Ben Shade
Springfield	53	23	.705	1	H.H. Laney/H.C. Fisher
Portsmouth Riversides	12	19	.387	NA	Daniel Spry
Hamilton 26	42	.382	19		William Kane
Ironton	21	45	.318	NA	John Murphy/P.A. McCarthy
Chillicothe Logans#...........	13	38	.255	NA	

#Chillicothe disbanded in August.

1885

American Association
President: H.D. McKnight

Standings	W	L	Pct.	GB	Manager
St. Louis Browns	79	33	.705	—	Charlie Comiskey
Cincinnati Reds.................	63	49	.563	16	O.P. Caylor
Pittsburgh Alleghenies........	56	55	.505	22½	Horace Phillips
Philadelphia Athletics........	55	57	.491	24	Lon Knight/Charlie Mason/Bill Sharsig
Brooklyn Grays	53	59	.473	26	Joe Doyle/Charlie Hackett/Charlie Byrne
Louisville Colonels	53	59	.473	26	Jim Hart
New York Mets	44	64	.407	33	Jim Gifford
Baltimore Orioles	41	68	.376	36½	Billy Barnie

BA: Pete Browning, Louisville, .362
Runs: Harry Stovey, Philadelphia, 130
Hits: Pete Browning, Louisville, 174
HRs: Harry Stovey, Philadelphia, 13

Wins: Bob Caruthers, St. Louis, 40
SOs: Ed Morris, Pittsburgh, 298
ERA: Bob Caruthers, St. Louis, 2.07
Pct: Bob Caruthers, St. Louis, .755, 40-13

National League
President: Nicholas E. Young

Standings	W	L	Pct.	GB	Attend.	Manager
Chicago White Stockings ...	87	25	.777	—	119,318	Cap Anson
New York Giants	85	27	.759	2		Jim Mutrie
Philadelphia Quakers.........	56	54	.509	30	150,698	Harry Wright
Providence Grays.............	53	57	.482	33		Frank Bancroft
Boston Beaneaters	46	66	.411	41	110,290	John Morrill
Detroit Wolverines	41	67	.380	44	43,000	Charlie Morton/Bill Watkins
Buffalo Bison.....................	38	74	.339	49		Pud Galvin/Jack Chapman
St. Louis Maroons..............	36	72	.333	49		Henry Lucas

BA: Roger Connor, New York, .371
Runs: King Kelly, Chicago, 124
Hits: Roger Connor, New York, 169
HRs: Abner Dalrymple, Chicago, 11

Wins: John Clarkson, Chicago, 53
SOs: John Clarkson, Chicago, 318
ERA: Tim Keefe, New York, 1.58
Pct: Mickey Welch, New York, .800, 44-11

Eastern League
President: W.C. Seddon

Standings	W	L	Pct.	GB	Manager
Washington Nationals...	70	25	.736	—	Mike Scanlon
Richmond Virginians...	67	26	.720	2	Joseph Simmons
Trenton Trentonians...	43	49	.467	25½	Patrick Powers
Newark Domestics............	42	49	.462	26	John Farrow/Charles Hackett
Waterbury%....................	8	9	.471	NA	Danny Jones
Norfolk&......................	32	44	.421	NA	Andrew Swan/James Powell
Lancaster Lancasters+ ...	28	39	.417	NA	John Murphy/Denny Mack
Bridgeport Giants$	12	17	.413	NA	Dan Shannon
Jersey City Skeeters@	9	27	.250	NA	Thomas Cummings
Wilmington Blue Hens/					
Atlantic City#	5	31	.139	NA	Joseph Fralinger/James Farrington

#Wilmington (5-28) moved to Atlantic City June 19, then disbanded June 24.
@Jersey City disbanded June 23.
+Lancaster disbanded August 4.
$Bridgeport entered the league August 14.
&Norfolk disbanded August 29.
%Waterbury entered the league September 4.

BA: Richard Johnston, Richmond, .329
Runs: Bill Greenwood, Richmond/Newark, 108
Hits: James Knowles, Washington, 120
HRs: Richard Johnston, Richmond, 16

Wins: Harry Pyle, Richmond/Newark, 37
SOs: Mike Tiernan, Trenton, 268
ERA: Hank O'Day, Washington, 0.74
Pct: Bob Barr, Washington, .833, 20-4

New York State League
President: W.S. Arnold

Standings	W	L	Pct.	GB	Manager
Syracuse Stars....................	52	37	.584	—	Henry Ormsbee/John Humphries
Utica Pentups	49	41	.544	3½	Dave Dischler/Dick Dwyer
Rochester Flour Cities ...	45	42	.517	6	James Jackson
Binghamton Bingoes ...	41	46	.471	10	Leonard Baldwin
Oswego Sweegs ...	35	51	.407	15½	M.A. Gorman/Salladin/Michael Gill
Albany Senators@	24	20	.545	NA	W.S. Arnold
Elmira Colonels#................	0	9	.000	NA	Wightman/Michael Kennedy

#Elmira entered the league July 6 and disbanded July 16.
@Albany disbanded July 28.

BA: Michael Kennedy, Elmira, .387   **Hits:** Sandy Griffin, Utica, 91
Runs: Charles Osterhout, Toronto, 74

Southern League
President: Henry W. Grady

Standings	W	L	Pct.	GB	Manager
Atlanta Atlantas	66	32	.673	—	Gus Schmelz
Augusta Browns	68	36	.654	1	P. Kelly/J.H. O'Brien
Nashville Americans	62	39	.614	5½	William Bryan/Nat Kellogg
Macon	55	47	.539	13	Clarence Walsh/Ed Pendleton/
					William Bryan
Memphis Browns	38	54	.413	25	Michael Bell/Ted Sullivan
Columbus Stars@	49	47	.510	NA	Charles Hager/Powell DeFrance/
					James Donnelly
Chattanooga Lookouts+	33	61	.351	NA	Frank Monroe/Frank Harris/
					Adolph Deublebliss/William Voltz/
					Charles Levis
Birmingham#	18	76	.191	NA	W. Harrison/Charles Barber

#Birmingham disbanded September 3.
@Columbus disbanded September 7.
+Chattanooga disbanded September 9.

BA: Leonard Sowders, Nashville, .309   **HRs:** John Cahill, Atlanta, 6
Runs: Joe Mack, Macon, 91   Walton Goldsby, Atlanta, 6
Hits: Leonard Sowders, Nashville, 130   Charles Levis, Chattanooga/Macon, 6
Wins: John Hofford, Augusta, 38
SOs: John Hofford, Augusta, 389
Pct: Tom Sullivan, Atlanta, .778, 21-6

Western League
President: Ted Sullivan

Standings	W	L	Pct.	GB	Manager
Indianapolis Hoosiers$	27	4	.871	—	Bill Watkins
Milwaukee Brewers	22	13	.629	7	Tom Loftus
Kansas City Cowboys	17	13	.567	9½	Ted Sullivan
Omaha Omahogs/					
Keokuk Hawkeyes@	7	27	.206	21½	George Hay/Bill Harrington
Cleveland Forest Citys#	13	16	.448	NA	T.L. Lawrence/Joe Battin/Doc Kennedy
Toledo Avengers+	8	21	.276	NA	Dan O'Leary

#Cleveland disbanded June 6.
@Omaha (4-22) moved to Keokuk June 6.
+Toledo disbanded June 7.
$Indianapolis disbanded June 15, causing the league to disband the same day.

BA: William O'Brien, Kansas City, .362   **Wins:** Lawrence McKeon, Indianapolis, 11
Runs: Emmett Seery, Kansas City, 43   Lady Baldwin, Milwaukee, 11
Hits: William O'Brien, Kansas City, 51   **SOs:** Bill Stemmyer, Toledo, 104
HRs: James Keenan, Indianapolis, 3   **Pct:** Lawrence McKeon, Indianapolis, .846, 11-2
Games: William "Peek-a-Boo" Veach, Kansas City, 18

1886

American Association
President: Wheeler C. Wyckoff

Standings	W	L	Pct.	GB	Manager
St. Louis Browns	93	46	.669	—	Charlie Comiskey
Pittsburgh Alleghenies	80	57	.584	12	Horace Phillips
Brooklyn Grays	76	61	.555	16	Charlie Byrne
Louisville Colonels	66	70	.485	25½	Jim Hart
Cincinnati Reds	65	73	.471	27½	O.P. Caylor
Philadelphia Athletics	63	72	.467	28	Lew Simmons/Bill Sharsig
New York Mets	53	82	.393	38	Jim Gifford/Bob Ferguson
Baltimore Orioles	48	83	.366	41	Billy Barnie

BA: Guy Hecker, Louisville, .342   **Wins:** Dave Foutz, St. Louis, 41
Runs: Arlie Latham, St. Louis, 152   Ed Morris, Pittsburgh, 41
Hits: Dave Orr, New York, 193   **SOs:** Matt Kilroy, Baltimore, 513
HRs: Harry Stovey, Philadelphia, 7   **ERA:** Dave Foutz, St. Louis, 2.11
     Bid McPhee, Cincinnati, 7   **Pct:** Dave Foutz, St. Louis, .719, 41-16
     Dave Orr, New York, 7

National League
President: Nicholas E. Young

Standings	W	L	Pct.	GB	Attend.	Manager
Chicago White Stockings	90	34	.726	—	142,438	Cap Anson
Detroit Wolverines	87	36	.707	2½		Bill Watkins
New York Giants	75	44	.630	12½		Jim Mutrie
Philadelphia Quakers	71	43	.623	14	175,623	Harry Wright
Boston Beaneaters	56	61	.479	30½	133,682	John Morrill
St. Louis Maroons	43	79	.352	46		Gus Schmelz
Kansas City Cowboys	30	91	.248	58½		Dave Rowe
Washington Statesmen	28	92	.233	60		Mike Scanlon/John Gaffney

BA: King Kelly, Chicago, .388   **Wins:** Tim Keefe, New York, 42
Runs: King Kelly, Chicago, 155   Lady Baldwin, Detroit, 42
Hits: Hardy Richardson, Detroit, 189   **SOs:** John Clarkson, Chicago, 340
RBIs: Cap Anson, Chicago, 147   **ERA:** Charlie Ferguson, Philadelphia, 1.98
HRs: Dan Brouthers, Detroit, 11   **Pct:** Jocko Flynn, Chicago, .800, 24-6
     Hardy Richardson, Detroit, 11

Eastern League
President: George M. Ballard

Standings	W	L	Pct.	GB	Manager
Newark Little Giants	68	26	.723	—	Charles Hackett
Waterbury	55	36	.600	11½	Joseph Simmons/Joseph Battin
Jersey City Jerseys	49	39	.557	16	Patrick Powers
Hartford Dark Blues	40	48	.455	25	John Remsen/William Krieg/
					Charles Daniels
Bridgeport Giants	33	57	.367	33	James Donnelly
Providence Grays@	7	14	.333	NA	John Doyle
Meriden+	12	34	.261	NA	Walter Burnham/John Remsen
Long Island (Maspeth) A's#.	1	11	.083	NA	Thomas Cummings

#Long Island disbanded May 22.
@Providence disbanded June 2.
+Meriden disbanded July 13.

BA: Thomas P. Burns, Newark, .352   **SOs:** John F. "Phenomenal" Smith,
Runs: Mike Tiernan, Jersey City, 85   Newark, 317
Hits: Mike Tiernan, Jersey City, 123   **Pct:** George Knowlton, Newark, .769, 20-6
HRs: Thomas P. Burns, Newark, 10   **Games:** Mike Hughes, Waterbury, 54
Wins: Mike Hughes, Waterbury, 33

International League
President: George G. Campbell

Standings	W	L	Pct.	GB	Manager
Utica Pentups	62	34	.645	—	Emory Hengle
Rochester Maroons	56	39	.589	5½	Frank Bancroft/Alonzo Knight
Toronto Canucks	53	41	.563	8	John Humphries
Hamilton Clippers	52	43	.547	9½	Charles Collings/Thomas Crooks
Buffalo Bisons	50	45	.526	11½	John Chapman
Syracuse Stars	46	47	.491	14½	Henry Ormsbee/Frank Olin/James Gifford
Binghamton Crickets	37	58	.389	24½	C.F. McCormack/David Sullivan
Oswego Starchboxes	23	72	.272	38½	Milton West/Henry Ormsbee

BA: Jon Morrison, Toronto, .346   **Wins:** Billy Serad, Utica, 30
Runs: Jon Morrison, Toronto, 108   **SOs:** Billy Serad, Utica, 260
Hits: Jon Morrison, Toronto, 141   **ERA:** Billy Serad, Utica, 0.96
HRs: John Fields, Buffalo/Utica, 8   **Pct:** John Davis, Toronto, .696, 16-7
     Joe Visner, Rochester, 8   **Games:** Mike F. Walsh, Buffalo, 51

New England League
Secretary: J.C. Morse

Standings	W	L	Pct.	GB	Manager
Portland	66	36	.647	—	Harrison Spence
Haverhill	59	38	.608	4½	Frank Selee/A.G. "Fred" Doe/John Irwin
Newburyport Clamdiggers/					
Lynn#	53	52	.505	14½	Dan Shannon/Edward Flanagan/
					A.G. "Fred" Doe
Brockton	45	56	.455	20½	Bill McGunnigle/James Cudworth
Lawrence	42	55	.433	21½	Frank Cox
Boston Blues	35	63	.357	29	Walter Burnham

#Newburyport (35-34) moved to Lynn August 14.

BA: Tom McCarthy, Brockton, .330   **SBs:** Mike Slattery, Haverhill, 63
Runs: Warren "Bobby" Wheelock, Portland, 93   **Wins:** Tom Lovett, Newburyport/Lynn, 32
Hits: Sam LaRoque, Newburyport/Lynn, 134   **SOs:** Tom Lovett, Newburyport/Lynn, 300
HRs: Guerdon Whiteley, Newburyport/Lynn, 11   **ERA:** Tom Lovett, Newburyport/Lynn, 1.27
     Theodore Scheffler, Portland, 11   **Pct:** Tom Lovett, Newburyport/Lynn, .780, 32-9
     George Wilson, Newburyport/Lynn, 11

Northwestern League
President: Ted Sullivan

Standings	W	L	Pct.	GB	Manager
Duluth Jayhawks	46	33	.582	—	William Lucas
Eau Claire	43	36	.544	3	Abe Devine
Oshkosh	39	39	.500	6½	William Harrington/William Roche
St. Paul Freezers	37	43	.463	9½	John Barnes
Minneapolis Millers	36	42	.462	9½	Edward Whitcomb
Milwaukee Brewers	35	43	.447	10½	Ted Sullivan

BA: Charles Ingram, Oshkosh, .313   **Hits:** J. Doran, Eau Claire, 95
Runs: Bill Reid, Duluth, 85   Llewellyn Legg, Duluth, 95

Southern League
President: Henry W. Grady

Standings	W	L	Pct.	GB	Manager
Atlanta Atlantas	64	28	.696	—	William "Blondie" Purcell
Savannah	59	33	.641	5	Charles Morton/Pete Hotaling

	W	L	Pct.	GB	Manager
Nashville Americans	46	43	.517	16½	Walton Goldsby
Memphis Grays	43	46	.483	19½	Jonathan Sneed
Charleston Seagulls	44	49	.473	20½	Charles Cushman/James Powell
Macon	32	59	.352	31½	John Peltz
Augusta Browns#	21	31	.404	NA	John O'Brien
Chattanooga Lookouts@	20	40	.333	NA	H. Levis

#Augusta disbanded July 5.
@Chattanooga disbanded July 9.

BA: John Cline, Atlanta, .353
Runs: Blondie Purcell, Atlanta, 97
Hits: John Cline, Atlanta, 129
HRs: Blondie Purcell, Atlanta, 9
Denny Lyons, Atlanta, 9

Wins: Hank O'Day, Savannah, 26
SOs: Ed Knouff, Memphis, 342
ERA: Gus Weyhing, Charleston, 0.78
Pct: Frank Wells, Atlanta, .789, 15-4

Western League
Presidents: Edward Murphy/William M. McClintock

Standings	W	L	Pct.	GB	Manager
Denver Mountain Lions	54	26	.675	—	W.W. Wallace
St. Joseph Reds	50	30	.625	4	William "Nin" Alexander
Leadville Blues	39	41	.488	15	D.W. Morgan
Topeka Capitals	35	45	.438	19	W.J. Sheard/Henry Strong & Hiram Dillon
Leavenworth Soldiers	31	49	.388	23	Michael Hurley/Charles Hall
Lincoln Tree Planters	31	49	.388	23	Harry Durfee/Partington

BA: William O'Brien, Denver, .352
Runs: Charles Hall, Leavenworth, 96
Hits: Jake Beckley, Leavenworth, 113

HRs: Perry Werden, Lincoln, 11
2B: James "Bug" Holliday, St. Joseph, 28
3B: John "Bud" Fowler, Topeka, 12

1887

American Association
President: Wheeler C. Wyckoff

Standings	W	L	Pct.	GB	Manager
St. Louis Browns	95	40	.704	—	Charlie Comiskey
Cincinnati Reds	81	54	.600	14	Gus Schmelz
Baltimore Orioles	77	58	.570	18	Billy Barnie
Louisville Colonels	76	60	.559	19½	John Kelly
Philadelphia Athletics	64	69	.481	30	Frank Bancroft/Bill Sharsig
Brooklyn Grays	60	74	.448	34½	Charlie Byrne
New York Mets	44	89	.331	50	Bob Ferguson/Dave Orr/O.P. Caylor
Cleveland Blues	39	92	.298	54	Jimmy Williams

BA: Tip O'Neill, St. Louis, .435
Runs: Tip O'Neill, St. Louis, 167
Hits: Tip O'Neill, St. Louis, 225
HRs: Tip O'Neill, St. Louis, 14

Wins: Matt Kilroy, Baltimore, 46
SOs: Toad Ramsey, Louisville, 355
ERA: Elmer Smith, Cincinnati, 2.94
Pct: Bob Caruthers, St. Louis, .763, 29-9

National League
President: Nicholas E. Young

Standings	W	L	Pct.	GB	Attend.	Manager
Detroit Wolverines	79	45	.637	—	95,000	Bill Watkins
Philadelphia Quakers	75	48	.610	3½	253,671	Harry Wright
Chicago White Stockings	71	50	.587	6½	217,079	Cap Anson
New York Giants	68	55	.553	10½		Jim Mutrie
Boston Beaneaters	61	60	.504	16½	261,000	John Morrill
Pittsburgh Alleghenies	55	69	.444	24		Horace Phillips
Washington Statesmen	46	76	.377	32		John Gaffney
Indianapolis Hoosiers	37	89	.294	43		Walter Burnham/Fred Thomas/Horace Fogel

BA: Sam Thompson, Detroit, .372
Runs: Dan Brouthers, Detroit, 153
Hits: Sam Thompson, Detroit, 203
RBIs: Sam Thompson, Detroit, 166
HRs: Billy O'Brien, Washington, 19

Wins: John Clarkson, Chicago, 38
SOs: John Clarkson, Chicago, 237
ERA: Dan Casey, Philadelphia, 2.86
Pct: Charlie Getzien, Detroit, .690, 29-13

California League
President: John J. Mone

Standings	W	L	Pct.	GB	Manager
San Francisco Pioneers	24	21	.533	—	Mike Finn
San Francisco Haverly	23	22	.511	1	Henry Harris
Sacramento Altas	19	19	.500	1½	Tom Gleeson
Oakland G & Ms	21	25	.457	3½	Tom Robinson

BA: Nick Smith, SF Pioneers, .307
Runs: George Taylor, SF Pioneers, 51
Hits: Bob Blackiston, Oakland, 57
Wins: Jimmy Mullee, Sacramento, 18

SOs: Billy Incell, SF Haverly, 203
ERA: George Van Haltren, Oakland, 1.00
Pct: Eddie Lorrigan, SF Pioneers, .882, 15-2

Central Pennsylvania League

Standings	W	L	Pct.	GB	Manager
Shamokin Maroons	33	20	.622	—	Krouse
Hazleton	31	20	.607	1	Frank Stahr
Ashland	27	20	.574	3	
Mt. Carmel	21	21	.500	6½	
Sunbury	21	23	.477	7½	H.B. Young
Danville	15	26	.365	12	A.G. McCoy
Mahanoy City	16	28	.363	12½	James Quirk
Minersville	0	6	.000	NA	Charles Steel

International League
President: Frank T. Gilbert

Standings	W	L	Pct.	GB	Manager
Toronto Canucks	65	36	.643	—	Charles Cushman
Buffalo Bisons	63	40	.611	3	John Chapman
Syracuse Stars	61	40	.604	4	James Gifford/Joseph Simmons
Newark Little Giants	59	39	.602	4½	Charles Hackett/Lawrence Murphy
Hamilton Hams	57	42	.575	7	George Stroud/Chub Collins/Peter Wood
Jersey City Skeeters	48	49	.494	15	Patrick Powers
Rochester Maroons	49	52	.485	16	John Humphries
Utica Pent Ups/Wilkes-Barre Coal Barons@	26	75	.257	39	David Dischler/Bill Hoover/Fergy Malone/Denny Mack
Binghamton Crickets+	27	46	.369	NA	Henry Ormsbee/Alonzo Knight
Scranton Indians#	19	55	.256	NA	Denny Mack/Chris Neisel/Fergy Malone
Oswego Starchboxes#	3	23	.115	NA	Wes Curry/Mike Gill

#Oswego disbanded May 31. Scranton then joined the league, with the provision that they start with a clean slate.
@Utica (12-39) moved to Wilkes-Barre after the game of July 15.
+Binghamton disbanded August 20.

BA: Edward "Cannonball" Crane, Toronto, .428
Runs: Michael Slattery, Toronto, 134
Hits: William "Rasty" Wright, Hamilton, 198
HRs: Frank Grant, Buffalo, 11
SBs: Michael Slattery, Toronto, 112

Wins: Edward "Cannonball" Crane, Toronto, 33
George Stovey, Newark, 33
ERA: Con Murphy, Syracuse, 2.19
Pct: Michael Walsh, Buffalo, .750, 27-9
Games: John Fanning, Buffalo, 50

National Colored League
President: Walter S. Brown

Standings	W	L	Pct.	GB	Manager
Philadelphia Pythians#	4	1	.800	—	Herman Close
New York Gorhams#	2	2	.500	1½	Benjamin Butler
Pittsburgh Keystones	3	4	.429	2	Walter S. Brown
Louisville Falls City	1	2	.333	2	William Franklin/C.W. Hines
Baltimore Lord Baltimores	2	4	.333	2½	Joseph Callis/Hugh Cumming
Boston Resolutes	1	0	1.000	NA	Marshall Thompson

#Philadelphia and New York disbanded May 18.
Cincinnati and Washington were admitted May 6, after the season started, but played no games. The league disbanded May 23.

BA: Wood, Philadelphia, .500
Hits: Stannard, Pittsburgh, 17

Wins: John Nelson, New York, 2
Stewart, Baltimore, 2

New England League
Secretary: J.C. Morse

Standings	W	L	Pct.	GB	Manager
Lowell Browns	71	33	.683	—	Bill McGunnigle
Portland	68	36	.654	3	Harry Spence
Boston Blues/Haverhill Blues+	47	36	.566	13½	Walter Burnham
Manchester Farmers	55	46	.545	14½	Frank Leonard
Lawrence/Salem$	45	50	.473	21½	P.E. Pettee/W. Putnam
Lynn Lions	40	64	.384	31	George Brackett/Henry Murphy
Haverhill@	15	41	.268	NA	Arthur Williams/A.G. "Fred" Doe
Salem Fairies#	10	45	.181	NA	Wallace Fessendon/Ed Flanagan

#Salem disbanded July 9.
@Haverhill disbanded July 11.
+Boston (35-18) moved to Haverhill July 11.
$Lawrence (29-34) moved to Salem July 26.

BA: Hugh Duffy, Salem/Lowell, .470
Runs: Wyman Andrus, Portland, 165
Hits: Wyman Andrus, Portland, 233
HRs: Ed Kennedy, Lowell, 15
SBs: Gil Hatfield, Portland, 141

Wins: Henry Burns, Lowell, 32
SOs: Henry Burns, Lowell, 137
ERA: James Devlin, Lynn, 1.84
Pct: Henry Burns, Lowell, .780, 32-9

Northwestern League
President: James A. Hart

Standings	W	L	Pct.	GB	Manager
Oshkosh	76	41	.649	—	Frank Selee
Milwaukee Cream Citys	78	43	.644	—	James Hart
St. Paul Saints	75	45	.610	2½	John Barnes
Des Moines Hawkeyes	73	47	.608	4½	William Bryan/Charles Morton
Minneapolis Millers	54	65	.453	23	Robert Foster
La Crosse	45	78	.365	34	William Harrington/Frank Hatch
Duluth Freezers	42	76	.356	34½	William Lucas/Joseph Quinn/J.W. Anderson
Eau Claire	38	85	.309	41	Abe Devine/Joseph Quest

BA: Elmer Foster, Minneapolis, .415
Runs: Clarence Murphy, St. Paul, 142
Hits: Elmer Foster, Minneapolis, 213
HRs: Elmer Foster, Minneapolis, 17
3B: Dummy Hoy, Oshkosh, 18
Walter Wilmot, St. Paul, 18

SBs: W.J. Van Dyke, Des Moines, 108
Wins: Bill Sowders, St. Paul, 34
SOs: Bill Sowders, St. Paul, 266
ERA: Tom Lovett, Oshkosh, 1.48
Pct: Tom Lovett, Oshkosh, .909, 20-2

Ohio State League
Secretary: L.A. Moore

Standings	W	L	Pct.	GB	Manager
Kalamazoo Kazoos	73	34	.682	—	Al Buckenberger
Zanesville Kickapoos	58	46	.558	13½	Patrick Welsh/Peter McShannick
Wheeling	53	48	.525	17	John Crogan/William English/ Tom Nicholson/Henry Myers
Sandusky Suds	53	49	.520	17½	James Curry
Columbus Buckeyes	50	55	.476	22	W.A. Calhoun/J.W. Morrison/ James Gifford/Milton West
Mansfield	46	56	.451	24½	Thomas McDermott/Robert Allen/ Frank O'Brien
Canton@	22	14	.611	NA	H.H. Kerr/William Zecher
Akron Acorns+	32	60	.348	NA	A.B. Showers/Charles Morton/ Thomas McDermott/William Irwin
Steubenville Stubs#	9	34	.209	NA	Tom Nicholson/A.S. Woods/Joseph Woods

#Steubenville disbanded June 29.
@Canton entered the league August 4.
+Akron disbanded September 3.

BA: Ed Hutchinson, Columbus, .395
Runs: Ed Stapleton, Kalamazoo, 121
Hits: John Crogan, Wheeling, 184
HRs: Ed Stapleton, Kalamazoo, 12

Wins: A.G. Watson, Kalamazoo, 29
SOs: Bill Irwin, Akron/Kalamazoo, 283
Pct: A.G. Watson, Kalamazoo, .763, 29-9

Southern League
President: John Morrow

Standings	W	L	Pct.	GB	Manager
New Orleans Pelicans	78	37	.678	—	Thomas Brennan
Charleston Sea Gulls	65	38	.631	7	James Powell
Memphis Browns	64	51	.557	14	Jonathan Sneed/Davy Force/John Peltz
Nashville Blues$	33	31	.516	NA	George Bradley/Jim Clinton
Savannah@	9	26	.257	NA	Charles Morton/John Peltz
Birmingham Ironmakers+	19	63	.232	NA	Joe Diestel/Tim Manning/Jim Clinton
Mobile Swamp Angels#	5	21	.192	NA	Jack Kelly

#Mobile disbanded May 17.
@Savannah disbanded May 31.
+Birmingham entered the league June 1.
$Nashville disbanded August 2.
The league disbanded August 21.

BA: Walter Andrews, Memphis, .422
Runs: Walter Andrews, Memphis, 143
Hits: Walter Andrews, Memphis, 218
HRs: Walter Andrews, Memphis, 28
SBs: Ed Cartwright, New Orleans, 109

Wins: Frederick Smith, Charleston, 33
SOs: Frederick Smith, Charleston, 221
Pct: John Ewing, New Orleans, .769, 20-6
IP: Frederick Smith, Charleston, 448

Western League
President: J.H. Threw

Standings	W	L	Pct.	GB	Manager
Topeka Golden Giants	90	25	.783	—	Walton Goldsby
Lincoln Tree Planters	71	36	.664	15	David Rowe
Kansas City Cowboys	58	54	.518	30½	Joe Ellick/Bradley Patterson
Denver Mountaineers	55	55	.500	32½	Robert McClintock
Omaha Omahogs	41	66	.383	45	Frank Bandle/J.J. Philbin
Hastings	36	65	.356	47	Fred Corey/Ulysses Rohrer/Ed Hengle/ Fergy Malone/Charles Reynolds
Leavenworth Soldiers#	27	27	.500	NA	John Brandon
Emporia$	6	12	.333	NA	B.F. Sullivan
St. Joseph Reds+	21	48	.304	NA	William "Nin" Alexander
Wichita Braves@	7	24	.226	NA	George Mold/John Griffin

#Leavenworth disbanded July 8.
@Wichita entered the league July 26, then disbanded September 5.
+St. Joseph disbanded July 28.
$Emporia entered the league August 13, then disbanded September 9.

BA: James F. Macullar, Topeka, .464
Runs: Daniel Stearns, Topeka, 189
Hits: Daniel Stearns, Topeka, 265
HRs: Jake Beckley, Leavenworth/Lincoln, 16
James "Bug" Holliday, Topeka, 16
Wins: Tom Sullivan, Topeka, 36

SOs: Parke Swartzel, Leavenworth/ Lincoln, 205
ERA: John McCarty, Emporia/Kansas City, 2.51
Pct: Bill Hart, Lincoln, .824, 28-6
IP: Phil Ehret, St. Joseph/Denver, 405

1888

American Association
President: Wheeler C. Wyckoff

Standings	W	L	Pct.	GB	Manager
St. Louis Browns	92	43	.681	—	Charlie Comiskey
Brooklyn Bridegrooms	88	52	.629	6½	Bill McGunnigle
Philadelphia Athletics	81	52	.609	10	Bill Sharsig
Cincinnati Reds	80	54	.597	11½	Gus Schmelz
Baltimore Orioles	57	80	.416	36	Billy Barnie
Cleveland Blues	50	82	.379	40½	Jimmy Williams/Tom Loftus
Louisville Colonels	48	87	.356	44	John Kerins/Mordecai Davidson
Kansas City Cowboys	43	89	.326	47½	Dave Rowe/Sam Barkley/Bill Watkins

BA: Tip O'Neill, St. Louis, .335
Runs: George Pinckney, Brooklyn, 134
Hits: Tip O'Neill, St. Louis, 177
RBIs: Long John Reilly, Cincinnati, 103
HRs: Long John Reilly, Cincinnati, 13

Wins: Silver King, St. Louis, 45
SOs: Ed Seward, Philadelphia, 272
ERA: Silver King, St. Louis, 1.64
Pct: Nat Hudson, St. Louis, .714, 25-10

National League
President: Nicholas E. Young

Standings	W	L	Pct.	GB	Attend.	Manager
New York Giants	84	47	.641	—	305,455	Jim Mutrie
Chicago White Stockings	77	58	.570	9	229,863	Cap Anson
Philadelphia Quakers	69	61	.531	14½	151,804	Harry Wright
Boston Beaneaters	70	64	.522	15½	265,015	John Morrill
Detroit Wolverines	68	63	.519	16		Bill Watkins/Bob Leadley
Pittsburgh Alleghenys	66	68	.493	19½	113,000	Horace Phillips
Indianapolis Hoosiers	50	85	.370	36		Harry Spence
Washington Senators	48	86	.358	37½		Walter Hewett/Ted Sullivan

BA: Cap Anson, Chicago, .344
Runs: Dan Brouthers, Detroit, 118
Hits: Jimmy Ryan, Chicago, 182
RBIs: Cap Anson, Chicago, 84
HRs: Jimmy Ryan, Chicago, 16

Wins: Tim Keefe, New York, 35
SOs: Tim Keefe, New York, 333
ERA: Tim Keefe, New York, 1.74
Pct: Tim Keefe, New York, .745, 35-12

California League
President: John J. Mone

Standings	W	L	Pct.	GB	Manager
Stockton	41	24	.631	—	J.P. Carroll
San Francisco Haverly	36	29	.554	5	Henry Harris
San Francisco Pioneers	30	37	.448	12	Mike Finn
Oakland G & Ms	25	42	.373	17	Tom Robinson

BA: Pete Sweeney, Stockton, .272
Runs: Henry Moore, Stockton, 58
Hits: Pete Sweeney, Stockton, 76

Wins: Billy Incell, SF Haverly, 19
ERA: Norman Baker, Stockton, 0.44
Pct: Eddie Lorrigan, Stockton, .611, 11-7

Central League
President: John W. Collins

Standings	W	L	Pct.	GB	Manager
Newark Trunkmakers	83	23	.783	—	Christopher Meisel
Jersey City Skeeters	84	25	.771	½	Patrick Powers
Wilkes-Barre Barons	59	48	.551	24½	James Donnelly/John Irwin
Scranton Miners	55	51	.519	28	Samuel Crane
Allentown Peanuts	51	51	.500	30	Fergy Malone/Charles Reuter
Easton	38	67	.362	44½	L.F. Abbott/J.B. Henry/H.W. Putnam
Binghamton Crickets#	15	49	.234	NA	Leonard Baldwin/John Lavin
Hazleton Pugilists@	7	32	.184	NA	Charles Gessner

#Binghamton disbanded August 3.
@Hazleton entered the league August 9.

BA: John Crogan, Newark, .335
Runs: John Crogan, Newark, 116
Hits: John Crogan, Newark, 158
HRs: Jim Knowles, Jersey City, 4

SBs: John McKee, Wilkes-Barre, 112
Wins: William Daley, Jersey City, 42
Pct: Harry Pyle, Jersey City, .818, 18-4

Central Interstate League
President: William H. Allen

Standings	W	L	Pct.	GB	Manager
Davenport	40	18	.690	—	William Lucas
Peoria Reds	38	22	.633	3	Charles Flynn
Crawfordsville/ Terre Haute Hoosiers+	32	26	.552	8	Albert Miller
Bloomington Reds	26	28	.538	12	Edward Wochner/Cheney/Joseph Farrell
Dubuque&	21	18	.538	NA	C.R. McQuade
Danville Browns$	15	25	.375	NA	L.O. Platt
Rockford@	11	23	.324	NA	William Allen
Decatur/Lafayette#&	7	30	.189	NA	Michael Hurley/William McMillen

#Decatur (6-23) moved to Lafayette June 13.
@Rockford disbanded June 26.
+Crawfordsville (21-21) moved to Terre Haute July 2.
$Danville disbanded July 5.
&Lafayette and Dubuque disbanded July 9.
The league disbanded in late July.

BA: W.A. Schwartz, Peoria, .389
Runs: Owen Williams, Davenport, 65
Hits: W.A. Schwartz, Peoria, 82

HRs: A.W. Snyder, Crawfordsville/
Terre Haute, 6

International Association
President: E. Strachen Cox

Standings	W	L	Pct.	GB	Manager
Syracuse Stars	81	30	.730	—	Charles Hackett
Toronto Canucks	75	35	.682	5½	Charles Cushman
Hamilton Mountaineers	66	44	.600	14½	Harry Fisher
Rochester Jingoes	62	45	.579	17	Henry Leonard
London Tecumsehs	53	53	.500	25½	Philip Powers
Buffalo Bisons	48	62	.436	32½	John Chapman
Troy Trojans	29	79	.268	50½	Ted Sullivan/L.E. Burkett/
					Mortimer Hackett/Perry Werden
Albany Governors	19	86	.181	59	Thomas York

BA: Patsy Donovan, London, .359
Runs: William "Rasty" Wright, Syracuse, 143
Hits: Ollie Beard, Syracuse, 174
HRs: Mike Lehane, Buffalo, 13

SBs: Eddie Burke, Toronto, 107
Wins: Con Murphy, Syracuse, 34
SOs: Al Atkinson, Toronto, 307
ERA: Con Murphy, Syracuse, 1.27

New England League
President: Edward Chesney

Standings	W	L	Pct.	GB	Manager
Lowell Chippies	51	36	.573	—	James Cudworth
Worcester Grays	48	40	.545	3½	Walter Burnham
Manchester Maroons	47	50	.485	9	Jim Clinton/Herbert Clough
Lynn Lions@	37	26	.587	NA	George Brackett
Salem Witches+	36	34	.514	NA	Wallace Fessendon
Portsmouth Lillies#	12	20	.375	NA	Frank Leonard
Portland#	2	18	.200	NA	Henry Myers/David Mahoney

#Portland disbanded June 9 and was replaced by Portsmouth July 20.
@Lynn disbanded July 25.
+Salem disbanded August 3.

BA: Ted Scheffler, Manchester, .375
Runs: Ted Scheffler, Manchester, 107
Hits: Edward Kennedy, Lowell, 121
HRs: Mark Polhemus, Lowell, 14
Wins: Alexander Ferson, Lynn/Manchester, 25

SOs: Henry Burns, Lowell, 224
ERA: Alexander Ferson, Lynn/Manchester, 1.10
Pct: Alexander Ferson, Lynn/Manchester,
.781, 25-7

Southern League
President: J.T. Wilson

Standings	W	L	Pct.	GB	Manager
Birmingham Maroons	32	19	.627	—	Walton Goldsby
Memphis Grays#	26	24	.520	5½	Davey Force
New Orleans Pelicans	25	32	.438	10	Abner Powell
Charleston Seagulls	20	28	.416	10½	James Powell

#Memphis disbanded June 30.
The league disbanded July 4.

BA: John Cline, Memphis, .339
Runs: John Cline, Memphis, 55
Hits: John Cline, Memphis, 74
HRs: Perry Werden, New Orleans, 5

Wins: Tom Sullivan, Birmingham, 13
SOs: Charles "Kid" Nichols, Memphis, 84
Pct: John Ewing, Memphis, .750, 12-4

Texas League
Presidents: Fred W. Turner/Robert Adair

Standings	W	L	Pct.	GB	Manager
Dallas Hams	55	29	.655	—	Charles Levis/Doug Crothers
Austin Senators/					
San Antonio Missionaries+	43	33	.566	8	John McCloskey
Galveston Giants%	39	46	.459	16½	Charles Dooley/Edward Tray
Houston Red Stockings&	35	45	.438	18	Traut/Lew Whistler
New Orleans Pelicans$	18	9	.667	NA	Abner Powell
Ft. Worth Panthers@	21	27	.438	NA	Burney/Firie
San Antonio Cowboys#	6	28	.176	NA	John Cavanaugh/Hofford

#San Antonio disbanded May 24.
@Ft. Worth disbanded July 4.
+Austin (29-22) moved to San Antonio July 4.
$New Orleans entered the league from the disbanded Southern League in mid-July.
&Houston disbanded August 7.
%Galveston disbanded August 27.

BA: Art Sunday, Ft. Worth/Dallas, .332
Runs: Farmer Weaver, Austin/San Antonio, 66
Hits: Farmer Weaver, Austin/San Antonio, 90
HRs: Lew Whistler, San Antonio/
Houston/Galveston, 7

Wins: Doug Crothers, Dallas, 24
SOs: Frank Hoffman, Austin/San Antonio, 231
ERA: Frank Hoffman, Austin/San Antonio, 0.70
Pct: Doug Crothers, Dallas, .706, 24-10

Tri-State League
President: W.H. McDermith

Standings	W	L	Pct.	GB	Manager
Lima Lushers	74	35	.679	—	William Harrington
Wheeling Nail Cities	71	43	.623	5½	Al Buckenberger
Columbus Senators	64	50	.561	12½	James Curry/Frank Arnold
Canton	50	64	.439	26½	William Zecher
Toledo Maumees	46	68	.403	30½	Harry Smith/Frank Mountain/Robert Woods
Mansfield	43	74	.368	35	Frank O'Brien/James Green/Ed Darrow
Jackson Jaxons	30	83	.264	46	George Burbridge/James Curry/
					Jay Moore/James Tray
Kalamazoo Kazoos#	62	37	.626	NA	Norris O'Neil
Zanesville Kickapoos#	63	39	.618	NA	Harry Baumgardner/Al Swift
Sandusky Fish Eaters#	44	54	.449	NA	James Hever/W.E. Rutter

#Kalamazoo, Zanesville, and Sandusky disbanded prior to the end of the season.

BA: Wayne Kirby, Lima, .369
Runs: Sam Nichol, Wheeling, 112

Hits: Buck West, Columbus/Wheeling, 150
Sam Nichol, Wheeling, 150
HRs: George Rooks, Lima, 13
SBs: William Fuller, Lima, 103

Western Association
President: Samuel Morton

Standings	W	L	Pct.	GB	Manager
Kansas City Blues	76	42	.644	—	Jim Manning
Des Moines Prohibitionists	73	40	.646	½	Charles Morton
St. Paul Apostles	61	38	.616	5½	A.M. Thompson
Omaha Omahogs	55	48	.534	13½	Frank Selee
Milwaukee Brewers	53	54	.495	17½	James Hart
Chicago Maroons	41	71	.366	32	Emory Hengle
St. Louis Whites#	10	18	.357	NA	Tom Loftus
Sioux City Corn Huskers#..	21	38	.356	NA	William Bryan/James Powell
Minneapolis Millers@	28	52	.350	NA	Al Gooding/David Rowe
Davenport Onion Weeders@	4	21	.160	NA	William Lucas

#St. Louis disbanded June 20 and was replaced by Sioux City, which began play July 4 and later disbanded.
@Minneapolis played its last game August 18, selling its franchise to Davenport, which also had a team in the Central Interstate League. Davenport played its first game August 25.

BA: Ralph Johnson, Kansas City, .342
Runs: Jim Manning, Kansas City, 123
Hits: James "Bug" Holliday, Des Moines, 147
George Shaffer, Des Moines, 147
HRs: John Carroll, St. Paul, 16
SBs: Jim Manning, Kansas City, 101

Wins: Tom Lovett, Omaha, 30
SOs: Tom Lovett, Omaha, 273
ERA: Charles "Kid" Nichols, Kansas City, 1.14
Pct: Charles "Kid" Nichols, Kansas City,
.889, 16-2

Western League
President: William Bryan

Standings	W	L	Pct.	GB	Manager
Denver Mountaineers	18	6	.750	—	William McClintock
Leavenworth Soldiers	7	7	.500	6	L.M. Cretors
Hutchinson	9	10	.474	6½	William Bryan/Edward Dugan
Newton#	3	5	.375	NA	Dick Juvenal
Lincoln Tree Planters#	2	11	.154	NA	James Keith

#Lincoln disbanded June 6 and Newton entered the league June 11.
The league disbanded June 21.

BA: McAndries, .371
Runs: Charles Faatz, 33

Hits: Charles Faatz, 35

1889

American Association
President: Wheeler C. Wyckoff

Standings	W	L	Pct.	GB	Manager
Brooklyn Bridegrooms	93	44	.679	—	Bill McGunnigle
St. Louis Browns	90	45	.667	2	Charlie Comiskey
Philadelphia Athletics	75	58	.564	16	Bill Sharsig
Cincinnati Reds	76	63	.547	18	Gus Schmelz
Baltimore Orioles	70	65	.519	22	Billy Barnie
Columbus Senators	60	78	.435	33½	Al Buckenberger
Kansas City Cowboys	55	82	.401	38	Bill Watkins
Louisville Colonels	27	111	.196	66½	Dude Esterbrook/Chicken Wolf/
					Dan Shannon/Jack Chapman

BA: Tommy Tucker, Baltimore, .372
Runs: Mike Griffin, Baltimore, 152
    Harry Stovey, Philadelphia, 152
Hits: Tommy Tucker, Baltimore, 196
RBIs: Harry Stovey, Philadelphia, 119

HRs: Harry Stovey, Philadelphia, 19
    James "Bug" Holliday, Cincinnati, 19
Wins: Bob Caruthers, Brooklyn, 40
SOs: Mark Baldwin, Columbus, 368
ERA: Jack Stivetts, St. Louis, 2.25
Pct: Bob Caruthers, Brooklyn, .784, 40-11

National League
President: Nicholas E. Young

Standings	W	L	Pct.	GB	Attend.	Manager
New York Giants	83	43	.659	—	201,989	Jim Mutrie
Boston Beaneaters	83	45	.648	1	283,257	Jim Hart
Chicago White Stockings	67	65	.508	19	149,175	Cap Anson
Philadelphia Quakers	63	64	.496	20½	281,869	Harry Wright
Pittsburgh Alleghenies	61	71	.462	25	117,338	Horace Phillips/Fred Dunlap/ Ned Hanlon
Cleveland Spiders	61	72	.459	25½	144,425	Tom Loftus
Indianapolis Hoosiers	59	75	.440	28	105,850	Frank Bancroft/Jack Glasscock
Washington Senators	41	83	.331	41	68,652	John Morrill/Arthur Irwin

BA: Dan Brouthers, Boston, .373
Runs: Mike Tiernan, New York, 147
Hits: Jack Glasscock, Indianapolis, 205
RBIs: Roger Connor, New York, 130
HRs: Sam Thompson, Philadelphia, 20

Wins: John Clarkson, Boston, 49
SOs: John Clarkson, Boston, 284
ERA: John Clarkson, Boston, 2.73
Pct: John Clarkson, Boston, .721, 49-19

Atlantic Association
President: James M. Braden

Standings	W	L	Pct.	GB	Manager
Worcester	58	35	.624	—	Walter Burnham
Newark Little Giants	54	40	.574	4½	Samuel Trott
Hartford	52	44	.542	7½	John Henry
New Haven	40	52	.435	17½	Harrison Spence/Jack Burdock
Lowell	35	59	.373	23½	John Cosgrove/Nathaniel Kellogg/ D.A. Sullivan
Wilkes-Barre Coal Barons$	32	20	.605	NA	John Irwin/M.H. Bergunder
Jersey City Skeeters+	33	23	.589	NA	Patrick Powers
Easton@	10	26	.378	NA	Henry Putnam
Norwalk#	2	17	.105	NA	James Donnelly/George Moolic

#Norwalk disbanded.
@Easton disbanded June 22.
+Jersey City disbanded July 25.
$Wilkes-Barre disbanded August 1.

BA: Robert Hamilton, Lowell, .341
Runs: Ted Scheffler, Worcester, 87
Hits: Robert Hamilton, Lowell, 117
HRs: Dan Lally, New Haven, 7

Wins: Jesse Burkett, Worcester, 30
    Henry Deems, Newark, 30
SOs: Jesse Burkett, Worcester, 240
Pct: Bill Daley, Jersey City, .750, 18-6

California League
President: John J. Mone

Standings	W	L	Pct.	GB	Manager
Oakland Colonels	56	38	.595	—	Tom Robinson
San Francisco	55	39	.585	1	Henry Harris/Mike Finn
Stockton	42	50	.457	13	Ben Young/Henry Harris
Sacramento Altas	33	59	.358	22	Charley Gagus/Steve Lang/ Charles Schreiver

BA: Lou Hardie, Oakland, .365
Runs: Danny Long, Oakland, 116
Hits: Lou Hardie, Oakland, 152
HRs: Lou Hardie, Oakland, 10
SBs: Danny Long, Oakland, 118

Wins: Roscoe Coughlin, Oakland, 32
SOs: George Harper, Stockton, 212
ERA: Bill Wehrle, Oakland, 1.35
Pct: Bill Wehrle, Oakland, .750, 15-5

Central Interstate League
President: Joseph C. Pritchard

Standings	W	L	Pct.	GB	Manager
Quincy Ravens	66	50	.569	—	George Brackett
Springfield Senators	65	53	.551	2	Harry Smith
Burlington Babies	55	62	.470	11½	William Lucas
Peoria Canaries	55	64	.462	12½	Charles Flynn/Charles Levis
Evansville Hoosiers	51	69	.425	17	Walton Goldsby/Jacob Aydelotte/ Douglas Crothers
Davenport#	57	45	.559	NA	Charles Holacher/Robert Allen

#Davenport disbanded September 11.

BA: Allen McCauley, .317
Runs: Phil Routcliffe, 122

Hits: Floyd Lauman, 132
HRs: Lew Whistler, Evansville, 22

International Association
President: Riley V. Miller

Standings	W	L	Pct.	GB	Manager
Detroit Wolverines	72	39	.649	—	Bob Leadley
Syracuse Stars	63	44	.589	7	Jack Chapman
Rochester Jingoes	60	49	.550	11	Henry Leonard/Patrick Powers
Toledo Black Pirates	54	51	.514	15	Charles Morton
Toronto Canucks	56	55	.505	16	Charles Cushman
London Tecumsehs	51	55	.481	18½	Philip Powers/Thomas "Dude" Esterbrook/ Wallace Fessenden
Buffalo Bisons	41	65	.404	28½	Jim White/Jack Rowe/Will White
Hamilton Hams	35	74	.321	36	Swartwood/Abner Powell

BA: Perry Werden, Toledo, .394
Runs: Warren "Bobby" Wheelock, Detroit, 130
Hits: Perry Werden, Toledo, 167
HRs: Bill Hoover, Toronto, 10

Wins: Bob Barr, Rochester, 29
SOs: Ed Cushman, Toledo, 194
    Tom Vickery, Toronto, 194
ERA: Cannonball Titcomb, Toronto, 1.27
Pct: Edgar Smith, Detroit, .692, 18-8

Michigan State League

Standings	W	L	Pct.	GB	Manager
Jackson Jaxons	60	37	.619	—	James Tray
Saginaw	59	40	.586	2	Louis Williams/J.A. Murphy
Grand Rapids	53	44	.546	7	John Roushkolb/Harry Smith/ Edward Easan
Lansing	42	56	.429	18½	W.H. Mumby
Greenville	42	58	.400	19½	John Foster
Kalamazoo Kazoos#	32	42	.432	NA	J.A. Lombard/Timothy Manning
Flint Flyers#	6	17	.261	NA	J.A. Lombard

#Flint replaced Kalamazoo in mid-season.

BA: Joe Katz, Greenville, .364
Runs: Fred Popkay, Jackson, 109

Hits: Joe Katz, Greenville, 154

New York State League

Standings	W	L	Pct.	GB	Manager
Auburn	32	19	.627	—	Frank Leonard
Elmira	30	21	.588	2	Harry Taylor
Canandaigua	27	24	.529	5	E.P. Gardner
Utica Pentups	22	28	.440	9½	George Geer
Seneca Falls Maroons@	18	28	.391	11½	John Toole
Oneida#	8	17	.320	NA	

#Oneida was expelled July 12.
@Seneca Falls disbanded August 19.

BA: Harry Taylor, Elmira, .377
Runs: T.L. Keay, Auburn, 70

Hits: Dan Phalen, Auburn, 92

Texas League
President: Louis Newburg

Standings	W	L	Pct.	GB	Manager
Houston Mud Cats@	54	44	.551	—	John McCloskey
Dallas Tigers+	49	42	.538	1½	Doug Crothers
Austin Senators	50	46	.521	3	John Masuer/Big Mike O'Connor/ Ed Reeder
Galveston Sand Crabs	50	48	.510	4	Charles Levis/John Wentz
Ft. Worth Panthers	45	51	.469	8	J. Horsfield/Patrick Welch
Waco Babies#	33	50	.398	NA	John Pettiford/Ezekial Ellsworth/ Robert Rose

#Waco disbanded August 4.
@Houston disbanded August 9.
+Dallas disbanded August 11, causing the league to disband August 12.

BA: Bill Works, Galveston, .372
Hits: Bill Works, Galveston, 136
HRs: Bill Joyce, Houston, 18
SBs: Herman Bader, Dallas, 146

Wins: Pop Weikart, Houston, 27
SOs: Edgar McNabb, Waco, 261
ERA: Edgar McNabb, Waco, 1.53
Pct: Pop Weikart, Houston, .711, 27-11

Tri-State League
President: W.H. McDermith

Standings	W	L	Pct.	GB	Manager
Canton Nadjys	67	37	.644	—	William Harrington
Mansfield	59	50	.541	10½	Christopher Meisel/Robert Carey/ John Rense
Springfield	55	48	.534	11½	Walter Jennison/Lewis Hill/Harry Fisher
Dayton Reds	48	54	.471	18	Frank Jones/Timothy Donovan/ Frank O'Brien
Wheeling Nailers	41	67	.380	28	Benjamin Sullivan/Samuel Nichol/Howell/ John Dunn/John Wright/John Crogan
Hamilton#	41	57	.418	NA	D.C. Blondy/Edward Hengle

#Hamilton was expelled for non-payment of dues August 28.

BA: John Ryn, Canton, .358
Runs: Charles Miller, Canton, 129

Hits: John Ryn, Canton, 150

Western Association
President: J.S. McCormick

Standings	W	L	Pct.	GB	Manager
Omaha Omahogs	83	38	.686	—	Frank Selee
St. Paul Apostles	74	46	.617	8½	A.M. Thompson/John Barnes

	W	L	Pct.	GB	Manager
Minneapolis Millers	66	56	.541	17½	Samuel Morton/Emory Hengle
Sioux City Corn Huskers	59	61	.492	23½	James Powell
Milwaukee Creams	56	63	.471	26	Ezra Sutton
St. Joseph Clay Eaters	42	65	.393	34	Charles Lord/A.H. Truckenmiller/ James McGarr
Denver Grizzlies	42	68	.382	35½	David Rowe
Des Moines Prohibitionists	41	76	.350	40	James Macullar

BA: John Cline, Sioux City, .364
Runs: John Cline, Sioux City, 172
Hits: Abner Dalrymple, Denver, 173
HRs: Charles T. Reilly, St. Paul, 27

Wins: Charles "Kid" Nichols, Omaha, 39
SOs: Charles "Kid" Nichols, Omaha, 368
Pct: Charles "Kid" Nichols, Omaha, .830, 39-8

1890

American Association
President: Zach Phelps

Standings	W	L	Pct.	GB	Attend.	Manager
Louisville Colonels	88	44	.667	—	206,208	Jack Chapman
Columbus Senators	79	55	.590	10		Al Buckenberger/Gus Schmelz
St. Louis Browns	78	58	.574	12	140,000	Tommy McCarthy/ Chief Roseman/ Charles "Count" Campau
Toledo Maumees	68	64	.515	20	70,000	Charlie Morton
Rochester Hop Bitters	63	63	.500	22		Pat Powers
Syracuse Stars	55	72	.433	30½		George Frazer
Philadelphia Athletics	54	78	.409	34	134,000	Bill Sharsig
Brooklyn Gladiators/ Baltimore Orioles#	41	92	.308	47½	71,500	Jim Kennedy/Billy Barnie

#Brooklyn (26-73) was replaced by Baltimore August 26.

BA: Chicken Wolf, Louisville, .363
Runs: Jim McTamany, Columbus, 140
Hits: Chicken Wolf, Louisville, 197
HRs: Charles "Count" Campau, St. Louis, 10

Wins: Sadie McMahon, Brooklyn/ Baltimore/Philadelphia, 36
SOs: Sadie McMahon, Brooklyn/ Baltimore/Philadelphia, 291
ERA: Scott Stratton, Louisville, 2.36
Pct: Scott Stratton, Louisville, .708, 34-14

National League
President: Nicholas E. Young

Standings	W	L	Pct.	GB	Attend.	Manager
Brooklyn Bridegrooms	86	43	.667	—	121,412	Bill McGunnigle
Chicago White Stockings	84	53	.613	6	102,536	Cap Anson
Philadelphia Phillies	78	54	.591	9½	148,366	Harry Wright
Cincinnati Reds	77	55	.583	10½	131,980	Tom Loftus
Boston Beaneaters	76	57	.571	12	147,539	Frank Selee
New York Giants	63	68	.481	24	60,667	Jim Mutrie
Cleveland Spiders	44	88	.333	43½	47,478	Gus Schmelz/Bob Leadley
Pittsburgh Innocents	23	113	.169	66½	16,064	Guy Hecker

BA: Jack Glasscock, New York, .336
Runs: Hub Collins, Brooklyn, 148
Hits: Jack Glasscock, New York, 172
Sam Thompson, Philadelphia, 172
RBIs: Thomas P. Burns, Brooklyn, 128

HRs: Walt Wilmot, Chicago, 14
Wins: Bill Hutchison, Chicago, 42
SOs: Amos Rusie, New York, 345
ERA: Billy Rhines, Cincinnati, 1.95
Pct: Tom Lovett, Brooklyn, .732, 30-11

Player's League
President: Colonel Edward A. McAlpin

Standings	W	L	Pct.	GB	Attend.	Manager
Boston Reds	81	48	.628	—	197,346	King Kelly
Brooklyn Wonders	76	56	.576	6½	79,272	Monte Ward
New York Giants	74	57	.565	8	148,197	Buck Ewing
Chicago Pirates	75	62	.547	10	148,876	Charlie Comiskey
Philadelphia Quakers	68	63	.519	14	170,399	Ben Hilt/Jim Fogarty/ Charlie Buffinton
Pittsburgh Burghers	60	68	.469	20½	117,123	Ned Hanlon
Cleveland Infants	55	75	.423	26½	58,430	Jay Faatz/Henry Larkin/ Patsy Tebeau
Buffalo Bisons	36	96	.273	46½	61,244	Jack Rowe

BA: Pete Browning, Cleveland, .387
Runs: Hugh Duffy, Chicago, 161
Hits: Monte Ward, Brooklyn, 207
RBIs: Hardy Richardson, Boston, 143
HRs: Roger Connor, New York, 13

Wins: Silver King, Chicago, 32
Mark Baldwin, Chicago, 32
SOs: Mark Baldwin, Chicago, 211
ERA: Silver King, Chicago, 2.69
Pct: Old Hoss Radbourn, Boston, .692, 27-12
Bill Daley, Boston, .692, 18-8

Atlantic Association
President: James M. Braden

Standings	W	L	Pct.	GB	Manager
New Haven	82	36	.695	—	Walter Burnham
Worcester/Lebanon@	60	51	.541	18½	James Cudworth
Newark Little Giants	60	61	.496	23½	Samuel Trott

	W	L	Pct.	GB	Manager
Jersey City/Harrisburg Ponies#	58	72	.446	30	Steve Brady/Jack Burdock
Baltimore Orioles%	77	24	.762	NA	Billy Barnie
Washington Senators+	38	47	.447	NA	Ted Sullivan
Wilmington Peach Growers&	29	66	.305	NA	
Hartford$	22	60	.268	NA	Ezra Sutton

#Jersey City (27-46) disbanded July 22. Harrisburg, from the disbanded Interstate League, applied for the vacant franchise and joined the league July 24.
@Worcester (37-31) moved to Lebanon July 28.
+Washington disbanded August 2.
$Hartford disbanded August 25.
&Wilmington disbanded August 27.
%Baltimore left the league to join the American Association August 27.

BA: Joe Sommer, Baltimore, .347
Runs: Joseph "Reddy" Mack, Baltimore, 120
T. Long, Baltimore, 120
Hits: Dan Lally, New Haven, 159
HRs: Dan Lally, New Haven, 12

Wins: Les German, Baltimore, 35
SOs: John Doran, New Haven, 241
ERA: John Doran, New Haven, 1.12
Pct: Mike O'Rourke, Baltimore, .923, 12-1

International Association
President: Charles D. White

Standings	W	L	Pct.	GB	Manager
Detroit Wolverines	31	19	.620	—	Bob Leadley
Saginaw-Bay City Hyphens	32	20	.615	—	Malcolm McArthur
Toronto Canucks	30	20	.600	1	Charles Collins
Hamilton Mountaineers/ Montreal Canadians@	24	26	.480	7	Jimmy Dean
Buffalo Bisons/ Grand Rapids Shamrocks#..	14	29	.326	13½	Louis Bacon
London Tecumsehs+	15	32	.319	14½	Wallace Fessenden

#Buffalo (8-16) moved to Grand Rapids June 11.
@Hamilton (21-18) moved to Montreal June 23.
+London disbanded July 8, causing the league to fold July 10.

BA: Bill Andrus, Buffalo, .339
Runs: Ed Cartwright, 45
Hits: Don Casey, 68

HRs: Dan Quinn, Buffalo/Montreal/ Detroit, 3
E. Doyle, 3

Michigan State League
President: Orlando F. Barnes

Standings	W	L	Pct.	GB	Manager
Grand Rapids	17	8	.680	—	
Manistee	16	8	.667	½	
Flint Flyers	13	10	.565	3	
Port Huron	11	14	.440	6	
Muskegon	10	14	.417	6½	John Roushkolb
Lansing	4	17	.190	11	

The league disbanded June 13.

Texas League
President: Joseph Seinsheimer

Standings	W	L	Pct.	GB	Manager
Galveston Sand Crabs	31	13	.705	—	Bill Works
Dallas Tigers	22	18	.550	7	Will Holland
Waco Babies	24	20	.545	7	Charles Levis
Houston Mud Cats	23	23	.500	9	John McCloskey
Ft. Worth Panthers	17	28	.378	14½	John Fogerty
Austin Senators#	13	18	.317	NA	Ed Reeder

#Austin disbanded June 2. When Ft. Worth disbanded shortly thereafter, the league disbanded June 10.

BA: Bill Works, Galveston, .358
Runs: Jake Stenzel, Galveston, 58
Hits: Bill Works, Galveston, 63
HRs: Bill Works, Galveston, 5
Jake Stenzel, Galveston, 5

Wins: Ossie France, Houston, 13
Jack Huston, Galveston, 13
SOs: Pat Luby, Galveston, 116
ERA: Ossie France, Houston, 0.99
Pct: Jack Huston, Galveston, .813, 13-3

Tri-State League
President: W.H. McDermith

Standings	W	L	Pct.	GB	Manager
Mansfield	49	25	.662	—	George Greer
Youngstown Giants	39	32	.549	8½	Harry Morton/Michael Cody
Wheeling Nailers	41	34	.547	8½	Robert Glenalvin/Bill George
Akron Akrons	33	37	.471	14	Charles Pike
McKeesport	34	42	.447	16	Alexander Voss/Frank Torreyson
Canton	27	47	.365	22	William Heingaitonk/James Peoples/ Cicero Hiner/Jack Grogran
Dayton Reds#	17	19	.472	NA	Timothy Donovan
Springfield@	16	20	.444	NA	Harry Fisher

#Dayton disbanded July 8.
@ Springfield disbanded July 10.

BA: Fred Osborne, Wheeling, .397   **Hits:** Fred Betts, Springfield/Wheeling, 113
Runs: Frank Goodryder, Mansfield, 81   **HRs:** Frank Motz, Akron, 14

Western Association
Presidents: J.S. McCormick/L.C. Krauthoff

Standings	W	L	Pct.	GB	Manager
Kansas City Blues	78	39	.667	—	James Manning
Minneapolis Millers	80	43	.650	1	Tim Hurst
Milwaukee Brewers	76	47	.618	5	Charles Cushman
Denver Grizzlies	57	64	.471	23	Dave Rowe
Sioux City Cornhuskers	55	64	.462	24	James Powell
Omaha Omahas	51	69	.425	28½	Frank Selee
Des Moines Prohibitionists/					
Lincoln#	48	73	.397	32	James Macullar
St. Paul Apostles	37	84	.306	43	A.M. Thompson

#Des Moines (31-52) moved to Lincoln August 1.

BA: Bill Hoover, Kansas City, .336   **Wins:** John Thornton, Milwaukee, 29
Runs: Elmer "Nick" Smith, Denver, 128   **SOs:** Martin Duke, Minneapolis, 308
Hits: Dan Minnehan, Minneapolis, 178   **ERA:** Martin Duke, Minneapolis, 0.81
HRs: John Carroll, St. Paul, 21   **Pct:** Nat Hudson, Minneapolis, .765, 13-4

1891

American Association
Presidents: Louis Kramer/Ed Renau/Zach Phelps

Standings	W	L	Pct.	GB	Attend.	Manager
Boston Reds	93	42	.689	—	188,000	Arthur Irwin
St. Louis Browns	86	52	.623	8½	245,000	Charlie Comiskey
Baltimore Orioles	72	63	.533	21	165,000	Billy Barnie/George Van Haltren
Philadelphia Athletics	73	66	.525	22	186,000	Bill Sharsig/George Wood/
						Billy Barnie
Cincinnati/						
Milwaukee Brewers#	64	72	.471	29½	119,000	King Kelly/Charlie Cushman
Columbus Senators	61	76	.445	33	115,000	Gus Schmelz
Louisville Colonels	55	84	.396	40	155,000	Jack Chapman
Washington Senators	43	92	.319	50	123,000	Sam Trott/Pop Snyder/
						Dan Shannon/Sandy Griffin

#Cincinnati (43-57) was replaced by Milwaukee August 18.

BA: Dan Brouthers, Boston, .350   **Wins:** Sadie McMahon, Baltimore, 34
Runs: Tom Brown, Boston, 177   George Haddock, Boston, 34
Hits: Tom Brown, Boston, 189   **SOs:** Jack Stivetts, St. Louis, 259
RBIs: Duke Farrell, Boston, 110   **ERA:** Edward "Cannonball" Crane,
HRs: Duke Farrell, Boston, 12   Cincinnati/Milwaukee, 2.45
   Pct: Charlie Buffinton, Boston, .757, 28-9

National League
President: Nicholas E. Young

Standings	W	L	Pct.	GB	Attend.	Manager
Boston Beaneaters	87	51	.630	—	184,472	Frank Selee
Chicago White Stockings	82	53	.607	3½	201,188	Cap Anson
New York Giants	71	61	.538	13	210,568	Jim Mutrie
Philadelphia Phillies	68	69	.496	18½	217,282	Harry Wright
Cleveland Spiders	65	74	.468	22½	132,000	Bob Leadley/Patsy Tebeau
Brooklyn Grooms	61	76	.445	25½	181,477	Monte Ward
Cincinnati Reds	56	81	.409	30½	97,500	Tom Loftus
Pittsburgh Pirates	55	80	.407	30½	128,000	Ned Hanlon/Bill McGunnigle

BA: Billy Hamilton, Philadelphia, .340   **Wins:** Bill Hutchinson, Chicago, 43
Runs: Billy Hamilton, Philadelphia, 141   **SOs:** Amos Rusie, New York, 337
Hits: Billy Hamilton, Philadelphia, 179   **ERA:** John Ewing, New York, 2.27
RBIs: Cap Anson, Chicago, 120   **Pct:** John Ewing, New York, .724, 21-8
HRs: Mike Tiernan, New York, 17

California League
President: John J. Mone

Standings	W	L	Pct.	GB	Manager
San Jose Dukes	90	57	.612	—	Mike Finn
San Francisco Friscos	84	62	.575	5½	Henry Harris
Sacramento Senators	75	73	.506	15½	John J. McCloskey/Tom McGuirk
Oakland Colonels	45	102	.306	45	Tom Robinson

BA: Ed Cartwright, San Francisco, .285   **Wins:** George Harper, San Jose, 47
Runs: James Sharp, San Francisco, 144   **SOs:** George Harper, San Jose, 313
Hits: James Sharp, San Francisco, 180   **ERA:** George Harper, San Jose, 0.96
HRs: Ed Cartwright, San Francisco, 7   **Pct:** J.D. "Nick" Lookabaugh, San Jose,
   Bill Everett, San Jose, 7   .632, 43-25
   Rube Levy, San Francisco, 7   **IPs:** George Harper, San Jose, 704

Eastern Association
President: Charles D. White

Standings	W	L	Pct.	GB	Manager
Buffalo Bisons***	89	35	.718	—	Patrick Powers
Albany Senators	72	49	.595	15½	Joe Gearhart

Lebanon Cedars	48	73	.397	39½	James Randall
Troy Trojans	51	77	.398	40	David Mahoney
Syracuse Stars+	56	42	.571	NA	George Frazier
New Haven Nutmegs@	48	39	.552	NA	Walter Burnham
Rochester Hop Bitters+	36	60	.375	NA	Tom Power/Kerstein
Providence Clamdiggers#	29	54	.349	NA	Bill McGunnigle

#Providence disbanded August 13.
@New Haven disbanded August 14.
+Syracuse and Rochester disbanded August 25.

BA: Buck West, Syracuse, .339   **SBs:** Herman Bader, Albany, 106
Runs: Ted Scheffler, Buffalo, 156   **Wins:** Lester German, Buffalo, 35
Hits: Harry Lyons, Buffalo, 166   **SOs:** Tony Fricken, Albany, 197
HRs: Dan Lally, New Haven, 5   **Pct:** Lester German, Buffalo, .761, 35-11
   Pete Sweeney, Rochester, 5

New England League
President: E.B. Fuller

Standings	W	L	Pct.	GB	Manager
Worcester	47	25	.653	—	Charles Greenleaf
Portland	46	25	.648	½	Frank Leonard
Manchester Amskoegs	42	30	.583	5	Louis Bacon
Lowell Lowells	37	29	.561	7	King Kerville
Salem	27	34	.443	14½	Niehaus/Hopkins/Jack Burdock
Woonsocket#	11	23	.324	NA	Tom Rowe
Lynn@	18	45	.286	NA	Harry Putnam/M.H. Nichols/Charles Cook
Lewiston#	11	28	.282	NA	Jeremiah Scannell

#Woonsocket and Lewiston joined the league June 12.
@Lynn disbanded July 20.

BA: Joe Kelley, Lowell, .323   **Wins:** Charles Willis, Portland, 21
Runs: James Connor, Manchester, 80   **SOs:** Feen, Worcester, 137
Hits: John O'Brien, Portland, 91   **Pct:** Charles Willis, Portland, .724, 21-8
HRs: John Newell, Portland, 7

New York-Pennsylvania League
President: James A. Lindsey

Standings	W	L	Pct.	GB	Manager
Erie*	62	36	.633	—	Frank Torreyson
Elmira Gladiators	47	49	.488	14	J.C. Velder/Jim White
Jamestown**	43	55	.439	19	Roberts
Olean	42	55	.433	19½	Edward Troy
Bradford@	47	30	.610	NA	Charles Levis
Meadville#	32	48	.400	NA	Striffler

#Meadville disbanded August 18.
@Bradford disbanded August 19.

Western Association
President: L.C. Krauthoff

Standings	W	L	Pct.	GB	Manager
Sioux City Cornhuskers	66	57	.537	—	Al Buckenberger
Kansas City Blues	66	59	.528	1	Jim Manning
Omaha Lambs	51	59	.464	8½	Dan Shannon/Bob Leadley
Denver Mountaineers	53	63	.457	9½	George Tebeau/L. Van Horn/Sim Cantrell
Milwaukee Brewers@	59	37	.615	NA	Charles Cushman
Minneapolis Millers+	52	47	.525	NA	William Harrington
Lincoln Rustlers+	46	49	.484	NA	Dave Rowe
St. Paul Apostles/					
Duluth Whalebacks#	39	61	.390	NA	William Watkins/Jay Anderson

#St. Paul (17-34) moved to Duluth June 8; Duluth disbanded August 20.
@Milwaukee disbanded August 16.
+Minneapolis and Lincoln disbanded August 20.

BA: William "Rasty" Wright, Duluth/   **HRs:** Dell Darling, Minneapolis, 18
   Omaha, .353   **Wins:** Billy Hart, Sioux City, 25
Runs: Jim Manning, Kansas City, 138   **SOs:** Tom Vickery, Milwaukee, 153
Hits: Dan Stearns, Kansas City, 156   **Pct:** George Davies, Milwaukee, .767, 23-7

1892

National League
President: Nicholas E. Young

Standings	W	L	Pct.	GB	Attend.	Manager
Boston Beaneaters*	102	48	.680	—	146,421	Frank Selee
Cleveland Spiders**	93	56	.624	8½	139,928	Patsy Tebeau
Brooklyn Grooms	95	59	.617	9	183,727	Monte Ward
Philadelphia Phillies	87	66	.569	16½	193,731	Harry Wright
Cincinnati Reds	82	68	.547	20	196,473	Charlie Comiskey
Pittsburgh Pirates	80	73	.523	23½	177,205	Thomas E. Burns/
						Al Buckenberger
Chicago Colts	70	76	.479	30	109,067	Cap Anson

	W	L	Pct.	GB	Attend.	Manager
New York Giants	71	80	.470	31½	130,566	Pat Powers
Louisville Colonels	63	89	.414	40	131,159	Jack Chapman/Fred Pfeffer
Washington Senators	58	93	.384	44½	128,279	Billy Barnie/Arthur Irwin/ Danny Richardson
St. Louis Browns	56	94	.373	46	192,442	Chris Von Der Ahe
Baltimore Orioles	46	101	.313	54½	93,589	George Van Haltren/ John Waltz/Ned Hanlon

Playoff: Boston 5 games, Cleveland 0, one tie.

BA: Dan Brouthers, Brooklyn, .335
Runs: Cupid Childs, Cleveland, 136
Hits: Dan Brouthers, Brooklyn, 197
RBIs: Dan Brouthers, Brooklyn, 124
HRs: James "Bug" Holliday, Cincinnati, 13

Wins: Bill Hutchison, Chicago, 37
SOs: Bill Hutchison, Chicago, 316
ERA: Cy Young, Cleveland, 1.93
Pct: Cy Young, Cleveland, .766, 36-11

Eastern League
Presidents: Charles D. White/Patrick T. Powers

Standings	W	L	Pct.	GB	Manager
Rochester Hop Bitters	68	57	.544	—	Sam Wise
Binghamton Bingoes**	60	52	.536	1½	Mike Lehane
Troy Trojans	62	57	.521	3	Joe McGlone
Albany Senators	60	58	.509	4½	Jim Fields
Providence Clamdiggers*	57	59	.491	6½	Walter Burnham
Buffalo Bisons	53	60	.469	9	Dan Stearns/Dan Shannon
Elmira Gladiators@	33	27	.556	NA	Bobby Wheelock
Syracuse Stars@	24	36	.400	NA	Jay Faatz
New Haven Nutmegs#	20	17	.541	NA	Dan Shannon
Philadelphia Reserves#	12	26	.316	NA	Harry Lyons

#Philadelphia and New Haven disbanded June 16.
@Elmira and Syracuse disbanded July 22.

Playoff: Binghamton 4 games, Providence 2.

BA: Willie Keeler, Binghamton, .373
Runs: Ted Scheffler, Troy, 115
Hits: Joseph Knight, Syracuse/ Binghamton, 172
HRs: Bill Hoover, Rochester/Providence, 5

Wins: Henry Fournier, Buffalo/New Haven/ Syracuse, 30
SOs: Dailey, Albany/Binghamton/ Philadelphia, 196
ERA: Dad Clarkson, Troy, 0.88
Pct: Jouett Meekin, Rochester, .719, 23-9

Illinois-Indiana League
President: W.W. Kent

Standings	W	L	Pct.	GB	Manager
Joliet Stone Citys*	55	27	.671	—	William Murray
Rockford Hustlers	46	38	.549	10	Hugh Nicol
Rock Island-Moline Twins**	37	42	.468	16½	Henry Sage
Jacksonville	30	57	.345	27½	Jack Pettiford/Guy Hecker
Evansville+	30	20	.600	NA	Jack Wentz
Peoria Canaries/ Aurora Hoodoos#	26	27	.491	NA	Mike Trost/Charles Flynn
Terre Haute Hottentots$	25	27	.481	NA	George Brackett
Quincy Ravens@	12	23	.343	NA	Tom Baldwin/Godar/Jerry Harrington

#Peoria (17-8) moved to Aurora May 31; Aurora disbanded July 5.
@Quincy disbanded June 24.
+Evansville disbanded July 8.
$Terre Haute disbanded July 10.

BA: Fred Underwood, Rockford, .282
Runs: Ed Wiswell, Rockford, 77
Hits: Ernest Moriarty, Evansville/ Jacksonville, 93
HRs: Charles Thorpe, Rockford, 9

Wins: Charles "Bumpus" Jones, Joliet, 24
SOs: George Nicol, Rockford, 230
Pct: Charles "Bumpus" Jones, Joliet, .889, 24-3

New England League
President: Tim H. Murnane

Standings	W	L	Pct.	GB	Manager
Woonsocket	63	31	.670	—	Thomas O'Brien
Portland	56	38	.596	7	Michael Garrity
Lewiston	53	45	.541	12	Keay/Bradley
Brockton	46	45	.505	15½	Bill McGunnigle
Salem	47	57	.452	21	Louis Bacon
Lowell@	30	30	.500	NA	R.M. Lincoln
Manchester/Lawrence#	26	45	.366	NA	James Cudworth
Pawtucket@	17	47	.266	NA	W.H. Rowe

#Manchester moved to Lawrence July 2, and later disbanded.
@Lowell and Pawtucket disbanded July 2.

BA: Jim Rogers, Portland, .323
Runs: Thomas O'Brien, Woonsocket, 106

Hits: Hi Ladd, Woonsocket, 140
HRs: Abel Lizotte, Lewiston, 10

Pacific Northwest League
President: W.B. Bushnell

Standings	W	L	Pct.	GB	Manager
Tacoma Daisies	41	32	.562	—	Bill Works
Portland Webfeet*	41	34	.547	1	John Barnes
Seattle**	38	37	.507	4	Abner Powell/Gilbert Hatfield
Spokane Bunchgrassers	29	46	.387	13	Ollie Beard

BA: Jake Stenzel, Portland, .339
Runs: Bill Goodenough, Tacoma, 77
Hits: Bill Works, Tacoma, 101
HRs: Ed Cartwright, Tacoma, 7

Wins: August McGinnis, Seattle, 19
SOs: August McGinnis, Seattle, 169
Pct: John Leiper, Portland, .700, 14-6

Pennsylvania State League
President: J. Monroe Kreiter

Standings	W	L	Pct.	GB	Manager
Wilkes-Barre Coal Barons	24	9	.727	—	James Randall
Allentown Colts	24	12	.667	1½	John Hanlon
Altoona	23	15	.606	3½	Alexander Donahue
Johnstown Johnnies	21	15	.583	4½	Thayer Torreyson
Danville	9	22	.290	14	
Scranton Miners	5	26	.161	18	
Reading Actives#	8	11	.445	NA	
Lebanon Pretzel Eaters#	4	8	.333	NA	Bill Sharsig

#Lebanon and Reading disbanded.

BA: John Coleman, Lebanon, .362
Runs: George Shaffer, Altoona, 60
Jack Drauby, Wilkes-Barre, 60

Hits: George Shaffer, Altoona, 99

Southern League
Presidents: Hart/Charles B. Genslinger

Standings	W	L	Pct.	GB	Manager
Birmingham Grays**	73	50	.593	—	Sam Mills/Jim Manning
Mobile Blackbirds	66	57	.537	7	J.F. "King" Kelly/Harry Powers
New Orleans Pelicans	66	57	.537	7	Abner Powell
Montgomery Lambs	66	58	.532	7½	Charles Levis
Chattanooga Chatts*	63	57	.525	8½	Ted Sullivan
Atlanta Firecrackers	58	65	.472	15	Sam "Leech" Maskrey
Macon Central City	51	69	.425	20½	Foley/Frank Graves/G.E. Burbridge
Memphis Giants	46	76	.377	26½	Taylor Hutton/P.H. Winston/Frank Graves

Playoff: Birmingham was awarded the championship on the basis of best overall won-lost percentage.

BA: Dick Phelan, Memphis, .342
Runs: C.J. Conley, Montgomery, 86
Hits: Al Weddige, Macon, 130

SBs: Charles "Count" Campau, New Orleans, 39

Western League
President: James A. Williams

Standings	W	L	Pct.	GB	Manager
Columbus Reds+***	46	20	.697	—	Gus Schmelz
Kansas City Cowboys	33	33	.500	13	Jim Manning
Omaha Omahogs	31	31	.500	13	Stout/Dave Rowe
Toledo Black Pirates	28	29	.491	13½	Ed MacGregor
Minneapolis Minnies+	21	25	.457	15	Charles Morton
Indianapolis Hoosiers	15	39	.278	25	Bill Harrington/Bill Sharsig
Milwaukee Brewers@	32	21	.604	NA	Billy Barnie
St. Paul Saints/Fort Wayne#	20	31	.392	NA	A.M. Thompson/Bill Alvord

#St. Paul moved to Fort Wayne May 25; Fort Wayne disbanded July 7.
@Milwaukee disbanded July 7.
+Columbus and Minneapolis disbanded July 15.
The league disbanded July 15.

BA: Charles Newman, Minneapolis, .347
Runs: Jim Manning, Kansas City, 76
Hits: Jim Manning, Kansas City, 83
HRs: Ed Breckinridge, Columbus, 18

Wins: George Stephens, Columbus, 18
SOs: Jim Hughes, Kansas City, 111
Pct: Fred Clausen, Columbus, .773, 17-5

1893

National League
President: Nicholas E. Young

Standings	W	L	Pct.	GB	Attend.	Manager
Boston Beaneaters	86	43	.667	—	193,300	Frank Selee
Pittsburgh Pirates	81	48	.628	5	184,000	Al Buckenberger
Cleveland Spiders	73	55	.570	12½	130,000	Patsy Tebeau
Philadelphia Phillies	72	57	.558	14	293,019	Harry Wright
New York Giants	68	64	.515	19½	290,000	Monte Ward
Brooklyn Grooms	65	63	.508	20½	235,000	Dave Foutz
Cincinnati Reds	65	63	.508	20½	194,250	Charlie Comiskey
Baltimore Orioles	60	70	.462	26½	143,000	Ned Hanlon
Chicago Colts	56	71	.441	29	223,500	Cap Anson
St. Louis Browns	57	75	.432	30½	195,000	Bill Watkins
Louisville Colonels	50	75	.400	34	53,683	Billy Barnie
Washington Senators	40	89	.310	46	90,000	Jim O'Rourke

BA: Billy Hamilton, Philadelphia, .380
Runs: Herman Long, Boston, 149
Hits: Sam Thompson, Philadelphia, 222
RBIs: Ed Delahanty, Philadelphia, 146
HRs: Ed Delahanty, Philadelphia, 19

Wins: Frank Killen, Pittsburgh, 34
SOs: Amos Rusie, New York, 208
ERA: Ted Breitenstein, St. Louis, 3.18
Pct: Hank Gastright, Boston/Pittsburgh, .750, 15-5

California League
President: Robert Wieland

Standings	W	L	Pct.	GB	Manager
Oakland Colonels**	60	39	.606	—	Tom Robinson/Joe Cantillon
Los Angeles Angels*	51	44	.537	7	Robert Glenalvin
San Francisco Friscos	50	49	.505	10	Henry Harris
Stockton River Pirates#	21	44	.323	NA	Michael Finn/John Moore
Sacramento Senators@	8	14	.364	NA	John Moore

#Stockton played the first half only.
@Sacramento played the second half only.

BA: William "Rasty" Wright, Los Angeles, .350
Runs: Charles Irwin, Oakland, 124
Hits: Howard Earl, Oakland, 140
William "Rasty" Wright, Los Angeles, 140

HRs: Fred Carroll, San Francisco, 8
Wins: Clark Griffith, Oakland, 30
Jack Horner, Oakland, 30
SOs: Clark Griffith, Oakland, 151
Pct: George Nicol, Los Angeles, .652, 15-8

Eastern League
President: Patrick T. Powers

Standings	W	L	Pct.	GB	Manager
Erie Blackbirds	63	41	.606	—	Charles Morton
Springfield Ponies	64	44	.593	1	Thomas E. Burns
Troy Trojans	67	50	.573	2½	J.D. Maloney
Buffalo Bisons	61	50	.550	5½	Jack Chapman
Albany Senators	54	62	.466	15	L.T. Fassett
Providence Clamdiggers	47	67	.412	21	Walter Burnham
Binghamton Bingoes	41	61	.402	21	A.S. Patton
Wilkes-Barre Coal Barons	41	63	.394	22	Dan Shannon

BA: Joseph Knight, Binghamton, .389
Runs: Bill Eagan, Albany, 137

Hits: Joseph Knight, Binghamton, 170
HRs: Frank Bonner, Wilkes-Barre, 16

New England League
President: Tim H. Murnane

Standings	W	L	Pct.	GB	Manager
Fall River Indians	60	30	.667	—	Michael McDermott
Lewiston	56	37	.602	5½	John Leighton
Portland	44	43	.506	14½	Michael Garrity
Dover	40	43	.482	16½	Frank Leonard
Brockton Shoemakers	30	51	.370	25½	A.G. "Fred" Doe
Lowell/Manchester/ Boston Reds#	29	55	.345	28	Bill McGunnigle/Thomas O'Brien

#Lowell (14-20) moved to Manchester June 26; Manchester (3-13) moved to Boston July 16.

BA: Willard Mains, Portland, .377
Runs: Tim Sheehan, Lewiston, 118
Hits: Abel Lizotte, Lewiston, 147
HRs: Abel Lizotte, Lewiston, 25

Wins: Lincoln, Fall River, 24
SOs: George "Win" Mercer, Dover, 136
Pct: Lincoln, Fall River, .774, 24-7

Ohio-Michigan League
President: Captain W.H. Taylor

Standings	W	L	Pct.	GB	Manager
Akron Summits	20	10	.667	—	Charles Hazen
Mansfield Electricians	20	18	.526	4	Carl McVey
Sandusky Sandies	16	17	.485	5½	Walter Miller
Bay City Riders#	19	9	.526	NA	Willard Davis
Canton Deubers@	13	14	.481	NA	Bill Delaney
Saginaw Alerts#	5	15	.250	NA	Frank Thyne/Fred Popkay
East Liverpool East End All Stars+	1	2	.333	NA	Jack Darragh

#Bay City and Saginaw disbanded June 11.
@Canton disbanded June 22.
+East Liverpool joined the league June 26.
The league disbanded July 4.

BA: Charles Hazen, Akron, .460
Runs: Charles Hazen, Akron, 50
Hits: Pete Munderscheid, Sandusky, 58
HRs: Ed McFarland, Akron, 12

Wins: Tim Nevins, Mansfield, 7
Bob Walsh, Akron, 7
SOs: Bill Phillips, Akron, 47
Pct: Charles Wilhelm, Canton, .833, 5-1

Pennsylvania State League
President: Henry B. Diddlebock

Standings	W	L	Pct.	GB	Manager
Easton**	70	36	.660	—	Charles Faatz
Johnstown Terrors*	62	39	.614	5½	Thayer Torreyson
Altoona Mud Turtles	57	41	.582	9	Alexander Donahue
Allentown Colts	57	46	.563	11½	John Hanlon
Harrisburg Hustlers	49	52	.485	18½	Felix Marks
York White Roses	51	55	.481	19	William Stevens/Bill Sharsig
Scranton Miners	45	57	.441	23	Martin Swift
Danville/Reading Actives#	16	81	.165	49½	A.G. McCoy/Elias Maier/ William Abbott Whitman

#Danville (5-47) moved to Reading July 7.

Playoff: Johnstown 3 games, Easton 2; Easton refused to continue the series.

BA: Fred Betts, Easton, .402
Runs: Herman Pitz, Scranton, 127
Hits: Fred Betts, Easton, 160
HRs: George Carey, Altoona, 10
Asa Stewart, Easton, 10

Wins: John Lyston, Altoona/Harrisburg, 24
SOs: John Fee, Scranton/Allentown, 134
Pct: Henry Miller, Harrisburg, .762, 16-5
John Slagle, Easton, .762, 16-5

Southern League
Presidents: Hart/James B. Nicklin

Standings	W	L	Pct.	GB	Manager
Charleston Seagulls*	51	33	.607	—	J.J. Carney
Macon Central City**	54	38	.587	1	Dan Shannon
Atlanta Windjammers	55	39	.585	1	William Murray
Memphis Giants	53	38	.582	1½	Frank Graves
Savannah Electrics	53	38	.582	1½	Jim Manning
Augusta Electricians	51	39	.567	3	George Stallings
Chattanooga Warriors	49	45	.521	7	Gus Schmelz
New Orleans Pelicans	40	51	.440	14½	Abner Powell
Mobile Blackbirds	38	53	.418	16½	Jack Kelly
Montgomery Colts	38	57	.400	18½	John McCloskey
Birmingham/Pensacola#	34	58	.370	21	Billy Earl
Nashville Tigers	33	60	.355	22½	Ted Sullivan/Henry "Hunky" Hines

#Birmingham (25-39) moved to Pensacola July 28.

BA: Ed Cartwright, Memphis, .373
Runs: Ed Cartwright, Memphis, 110

Hits: Ed Cartwright, Memphis, 144
HRs: Fred "Bones" Ely, Atlanta, 19

Western Association
Presidents: L.C. Krauthoff/Robert G. Scott

Standings	W	L	Pct.	GB	Manager
Kansas City Cowboys	12	8	.600	—	William Lucas
St. Joseph Saints	11	8	.579	½	Harry Gatewood
Topeka Populists	8	12	.400	4	Dick Cooley
Lawrence Farmers	7	12	.368	4½	John Rodemaker/John Hayden

The league disbanded June 20.

Playoff: Kansas City 4 games, St. Joseph 2.

BA: William Holmes, St. Joseph, .481
Runs: Cornelius Holohan, St. Joseph, 28
Hits: Harry Howe, St. Joseph, 37
HRs: Costello, Lawrence, 4

Wins: Bert Cunningham, Kansas City, 7
SOs: Bert Cunningham, Kansas City, 35
Gus Mackey, Lawrence, 35
Pct: Harry Howe, St. Joseph, 1.000, 3-0

1894

National League
President: Nicholas E. Young

Standings	W	L	Pct.	GB	Attend.	Manager
Baltimore Orioles	89	39	.695	—	328,000	Ned Hanlon
New York Giants	88	44	.667	3	387,000	Monte Ward
Boston Beaneaters	83	49	.629	8	152,800	Frank Selee
Philadelphia Phillies	71	57	.555	18	352,773	Arthur Irwin
Brooklyn Grooms	70	61	.534	20½	214,000	Dave Foutz
Cleveland Spiders	68	61	.527	21½	82,000	Patsy Tebeau
Pittsburgh Pirates	65	65	.500	25	159,000	Al Buckenberger/Connie Mack
Chicago Colts	57	75	.432	34	239,000	Cap Anson
St. Louis Browns	56	76	.424	35	155,000	George Miller
Cincinnati Reds	55	75	.423	35	158,000	Charlie Comiskey
Washington Senators	45	87	.341	46	125,000	Gus Schmelz
Louisville Colonels	36	94	.277	54	75,000	Billy Barnie

BA: Hugh Duffy, Boston, .438
Runs: Billy Hamilton, Philadelphia, 196
Hits: Hugh Duffy, Boston, 236
RBIs: Hugh Duffy, Boston, 145
HRs: Hugh Duffy, Boston, 18

Wins: Jouett Meekin, New York, 36
SOs: Amos Rusie, New York, 195
ERA: Amos Rusie, New York, 2.78
Pct: Jouett Meekin, New York, .783, 36-10

Eastern League
President: Patrick T. Powers

Standings	W	L	Pct.	GB	Manager
Providence Clamdiggers	78	34	.696	—	William Murray
Erie Blackbirds	57	49	.538	18	Charles Morton
Syracuse Stars	63	56	.529	18½	Jay Faatz
Springfield Ponies	57	54	.514	20½	Thomas E. Burns
Buffalo Bisons	64	61	.512	20½	John Chapman
Wilkes-Barre Coal Barons	54	56	.495	23	Dan Shannon

Troy/Scranton
Washer Women# .... 51 63 .447 28   Thomas Cahill
Binghamton Bingoes/
Allentown Buffalos@ ...... 26 78 .250 53   Herman Doescher/King Kelly

#Troy (43-32) disbanded July 26 and was replaced by Scranton August 2.
@Binghamton (18-62) moved to Allentown August 16.

BA: Joe Knight, Wilkes-Barre/Providence, .371   **Hits:** Jimmy Collins, Buffalo, 198
Runs: Ted Scheffler, Troy/Springfield, 138   **HRs:** Jack Drauby, Buffalo, 21

New England League
President: Tim H. Murnane

Standings	W	L	Pct.	GB	Manager
Fall River Indians	62	35	.639	—	Michael McDermott
Haverhill	53	41	.564	7½	John Irwin
Portland	51	43	.543	9½	Mike Garrity
Bangor Millionaires...........	48	48	.500	13½	Louis Bacon/John Sharrott
Lewiston	46	50	.479	15½	John Leighton/Sam LaRoque
Pawtucket Maroons	46	52	.469	16½	Frank Leonard/R.E. Perrin
Worcester#	27	32	.458	NA	John Murphy/Michael Slattery
Brockton Shoemakers@	30	62	.326	NA	William Allen/Charles Wilson

#Worcester disbanded July 13.
@Brockton disbanded August 25.

BA: Buck Freeman, Haverhill, .386   **HRs:** Buck Freeman, Haverhill, 34
Runs: Tom Bannon, Pawtucket, 137   **SOs:** Stafford, Lewiston, 127
Hits: Buck Freeman, Haverhill, 167   **Pct:** Stevens, Fall River, .727, 16-6

Pennsylvania State League
Presidents: E.K. Meyers/A.L. Johnson/John H. Hanlon

Standings	W	L	Pct.	GB	Manager
Pottsville Colts**	62	44	.585	—	John F. "Phenomenal" Smith
Harrisburg Senators*	56	45	.554	3½	Jack Huston
Reading Actives.................	61	50	.550	3½	William Whitman
Allentown Kelly's Killers/					
Easton/Ashland$	53	46	.535	5½	Mike "King" Kelly/Jack Milligan
Hazleton Barons	53	53	.500	9	Bill Sharsig
Scranton Indianas/					
Shenandoah+	55	55	.500	9	W. Brennan
Altoona/Lancaster Chicks@	51	54	.486	10½	A.T. Bentley/Alexander Donahue
Easton/Philadelphia Colts#.	40	74	.351	26	Billy Parks/Charles Levis

#Easton (8-36) moved to Philadelphia July 4.
@Altoona (17-31) moved to Lancaster July 7.
+Scranton (45-28) was replaced by Shenandoah August 2.
$Allentown (53-29) was replaced by Easton August 16; Easton (0-8) moved to Ashland September 1.

Playoff: Pottsville defeated Harrisburg in a disputed title game.

BA: John Walters, Allentown, .383   **Hits:** William Massey, Scranton/Philadelphia, 176
Runs: Tom Golden, Pottsville, 145   **HRs:** Henry Cote, Altoona/Lancaster, 21

Southern League
President: James B. Nicklin

Standings	W	L	Pct.	GB	Manager
Mobile Bluebirds/Atlanta@	43	23	.652	—	Jake Wells/William Murray
Memphis Giants..................	42	23	.646	½	Frank Graves
New Orleans Pelicans	33	38	.465	12½	Henry Powers
Nashville Tigers.................	30	37	.448	13½	George Stallings
Charleston Seagulls#	33	22	.600	NA	Ollie Beard
Savannah Modocs#	30	26	.536	NA	John McCloskey
Atlanta Atlantas#	21	37	.362	NA	Ted Sullivan
Macon Hornets#	15	41	.268	NA	William Hoggins/John Hill

#Charleston, Savannah, Atlanta, and Macon disbanded June 27.
@Mobile (38-20) moved to Atlanta June 27.

BA: Ollie Beard, Charleston/Atlanta, .424   **Wins:** Jack Wadsworth, Memphis, 16
Runs: Ollie Beard, Charleston/Atlanta, 83   Bill Kling, Mobile/Atlanta, 16
   Gus Klopf, Charleston, 83   **SOs:** Jack Wadsworth, Memphis, 110
Hits: Ollie Beard, Charleston/Atlanta, 118   **Pct:** Bill Kling, Mobile/Atlanta, .800, 16-4
HRs: Charles "Count" Campau,
   New Orleans, 11

Virginia League
Presidents: Ted Sullivan/Camden Sommers

Standings	W	L	Pct.	GB	Manager
Petersburg Champs	72	44	.621	—	Dennis Perkinson
Norfolk Oystermen	66	45	.595	3½	Camden Sommers
Richmond Colts	67	48	.583	4½	Timothy West
Staunton Hayseeds/					
Newport News-Hampton#..	50	64	.439	21	Pat Ziegler/William Donovan
Roanoke Braves	45	71	.388	27	Jake Byrd
Lynchburg Hill Climbers....	43	71	.377	28	Varney Anderson

#Staunton (36-53) moved to Newport News-Hampton August 11.

Hits: Sanford, Petersburg, 121

Western Association
Presidents: David E. Rowe/W.W. Kent

Standings	W	L	Pct.	GB	Manager
Rock Island-Moline Islanders..	72	50	.590	—	Henry Sage
Peoria Distillers	68	55	.553	4½	George Brackett
Lincoln Treeplanters...........	67	56	.545	5½	Buck Ebright
Jacksonville Jacks..............	67	57	.540	6	J.C. "Con" Strothers
Omaha Omahogs	66	59	.528	7½	Pa Rourke
St. Joseph Saints	57	66	.463	15½	Bill Kneisley/Hugh Nicol
Des Moines Prohibitionists.	55	73	.430	20	Hugh Nicol/Bill Traffley
Quincy Ravens...................	42	78	.350	29	Burt Merrifield

BA: Joe Katz, Rock Island/Moline, .404   **Hits:** George McVey, Omaha, 215
Runs: John Seery, Omaha, 196   **HRs:** Joe Strauss, Jacksonville, 33

Western League
President: Byron Bancroft Johnson

Standings	W	L	Pct.	GB	Manager
Sioux City Cornhuskers......	74	52	.587	—	William Watkins
Toledo White Stockings......	67	54	.554	4½	Jack Carney
Kansas City Blues..............	68	59	.535	6½	Jim Manning
Minneapolis Millers...........	61	68	.473	14½	John Barnes
Grand Rapids Rippers.........	64	62	.508	10	William "Rasty" Wright
Detroit Wolverines	56	68	.455	17	Robert Glenalvin
Indianapolis Hoosiers	53	66	.445	17½	William Sharsig
Milwaukee Brewers............	51	65	.440	18	Charles Cushman

BA: Henry "Hunky" Hines, Minneapolis, .427   **SBs:** George Hogriever, Sioux City, 93
Runs: William "Rasty" Wright,   **Wins:** Pete Daniels, Kansas City, 36
   Grand Rapids, 217   **SOs:** Frank Foreman, Toledo, 190
Hits: Henry Hines, Minneapolis, 250   **Pct:** Pete Daniels, Kansas City, .735, 36-13
HRs: Perry Werden, Minneapolis, 43

1895

National League
President: Nicholas E. Young

Standings	W	L	Pct.	GB	Attend.	Manager
Baltimore Orioles	87	43	.669	—	293,000	Ned Hanlon
Cleveland Spiders	84	46	.646	3	143,000	Patsy Tebeau
Philadelphia Phillies	78	53	.595	9½	474,971	Arthur Irwin
Chicago Colts	72	58	.554	15	382,300	Cap Anson
Brooklyn Grooms	71	60	.542	16½	230,000	Dave Foutz
Boston Beaneaters	71	60	.542	16½	242,000	Frank Selee
Pittsburgh Pirates...............	71	61	.538	17	188,000	Connie Mack
Cincinnati Reds..................	66	64	.508	21	281,000	Buck Ewing
New York Giants................	66	65	.504	21½	240,000	George Davis/Jack Doyle/
						Harvey Watkins
Washington Senators	43	85	.336	43	153,000	Gus Schmelz
St. Louis Browns	39	92	.298	48½	170,000	Al Buckenberger/Joe Quinn/
						Lew Phelan/Chris Von Der Ahe
Louisville Colonels............	35	96	.267	52½	92,000	John McCloskey

BA: Jesse Burkett, Cleveland, .423   **Wins:** Cy Young, Cleveland, 35
Runs: Billy Hamilton, Philadelphia, 166   **SOs:** Amos Rusie, New York, 201
Hits: Jesse Burkett, Cleveland, 235   **ERA:** Al Maul, Washington, 2.45
RBIs: Sam Thompson, Philadelphia, 165   **Pct:** Bill Hoffer, Baltimore, .811, 30-7
HRs: Sam Thompson, Philadelphia, 18

Eastern League
President: Patrick T. Powers

Standings	W	L	Pct.	GB	Manager
Springfield Maroons	79	36	.687	—	Thomas E. Burns
Providence Grays................	74	44	.627	6½	William Murray
Wilkes-Barre Coal Barons..	61	49	.555	15½	Dan Shannon
Syracuse Stars...................	62	53	.539	17	Sandy Griffin
Buffalo Bisons	63	61	.508	20½	Charles Morton
Scranton Coal Heavers	44	72	.379	35½	Billy Barnie
Toronto Canucks................	43	76	.361	38	Charles Maddock/John Chapman
Rochester Browns	47	82	.364	39	John Chapman/Timothy Shinnick/
					Pete Sweeney/John Berger

Playoff: Springfield 4 games, Providence 2.

BA: Frank "Piggy" Ward, Scranton, .372   **Wins:** Nixey Callahan, Springfield, 30
Runs: John Shearon, Buffalo, 131   **SOs:** George Harper, Rochester, 233
Hits: James Daly, Rochester, 191   **Pct:** Nixey Callahan, Springfield, .769, 30-9
HRs: Judson Smith, Toronto, 14

Michigan State League
President: Walter H. Mumby

Standings	W	L	Pct.	GB	Manager
Adrian Reformers	57	30	.655	—	R.G. Taylor
Lansing Senators	56	36	.609	3½	R.N. Parshall
Kalamazoo Celery Eaters ...	50	41	.549	9	O.G. Hungerford

Battle Creek Adventists/

	W	L	Pct.	GB	Manager
Jackson Jaxons	36	53	.404	22	Mittenthal
Owosso Colts#	34	47	.420	NA	Craves
Port Huron Marines#	27	51	.346	NA	Charles Schaub/Boocher

#Owosso and Port Huron disbanded September 3.

BA: Jack Daly, Lansing, .397
Runs: Jack Daly, Lansing, 124
Hits: Jack Daly, Lansing, 143
HRs: Jack Daly, Lansing, 25
Wins: George Wilson, Adrian, 29
Pct: George Wilson, Adrian, .879, 29-4

New England Association
President: J.C. Morse

Standings	W	L	Pct.	GB	Manager
Lawrence	31	19	.620	—	John Irwin
Nashua	27	21	.563	3	E.C. Norton
Lowell	24	24	.500	6	Michael Mahoney/William Meade
Salem/Haverhill@	20	28	.417	10	Frank Leonard
Fitchburg	12	25	.324	NA	Lawrence Thyne
Haverhill#	12	26	.316	NA	W.T. Dwyer/William Laverty

#Fitchburg and Haverhill disbanded June 20.
@Salem moved to Haverhill June 20.
The league disbanded July 8.

BA: Ed Flanagan, Lowell, .470
Runs: John Gilbert, Nashua, 88
Hits: Mike Birmingham, Nashua, 97
HRs: Dan Roche, Nashua, 18

New England League
President: Tim H. Murnane

Standings	W	L	Pct.	GB	Manager
Fall River Indians	67	39	.632	—	Michael McDermott
New Bedford Whalers	60	45	.571	6½	A.G. "Fred" Doe
Bangor Millionaires	55	49	.529	11	John Sharrott/William Long
Pawtucket Maroons	52	53	.495	14½	Louis Bacon/Harry Davis
Lewiston	47	54	.465	17½	Michael Slattery/Michael Gerrity
Brockton Shoemakers	48	56	.463	18	R.E. Perrin
Portland	47	60	.439	20½	Michael Gerrity/Frank Leonard/Merrill
Augusta Kennebecs	44	64	.407	24	Walter Burnham

BA: Harry Davis, Pawtucket, .391
Runs: Hobart Whiting, Pawtucket, 139
Hits: Harry Davis, Pawtucket, 189
HRs: Harry Davis, Pawtucket, 16
Wins: Fred Klobedanz, Fall River, 28
Pct: Tom Braham, Bangor, .800, 16-4

Pennsylvania State League
President: J.J. Hanlon

Standings	W	L	Pct.	GB	Manager
Hazleton Quay-kers**	61	44	.581	—	Bill Sharsig
Carbondale Anthracites	55	48	.533	5	M. Swift
Lancaster Chicks	49	54	.476	11	A.T. Bentley
Pottsville Colts/Allentown/ Reading&	44	64	.407	18½	John F. "Phenomenal" Smith
Allentown Goobers$*	29	28	.509	NA	Jack Milligan
Reading Actives+	37	27	.578	NA	William Whitman
Harrisburg Senators@	19	16	.543	NA	Frank Seiss
Shenandoah Huns#	1	14	.067	NA	William Brennan

#Shenandoah disbanded May 20.
@Harrisburg disbanded June 14.
+Reading disbanded July 20.
$Allentown disbanded July 24.
&Pottsville (35-33) moved to Allentown July 27; Allentown (5-7) moved to Reading August 10.

BA: John Milligan, Allentown/Reading, .457
Runs: Gus Moran, Hazleton, 139
Hits: Bill Massey, Carbondale, 174

Southern League
President: James B. Nicklin

Standings	W	L	Pct.	GB	Manager
Atlanta Crackers	70	37	.654	—	James Knowles
Nashville Seraphs	69	38	.645	1	George Stallings
Evansville Blackbirds	66	38	.635	2½	Ollie Beard
New Orleans Pelicans	46	55	.455	21	Abner Powell
Chattanooga Warriors/ Mobile Bluebirds@	37	63	.455	29½	Lew Whistler
Montgomery Grays	40	70	.364	31½	Jack Hayes
Memphis Giants#	32	37	.464	NA	Charles Levis
Little Rock Travellers#	25	47	.347	NA	Frank Thyne

#Memphis and Little Rock disbanded in July.
@Chattanooga moved to Mobile July 19.

BA: Lew Whistler, Chattanooga/Mobile, .404
Runs: Claude McFarland, Evansville, 149
Hits: Ollie Beard, Evansville, 140
HRs: Hercules Burnett, Evansville, 25
Wins: James Callahan, Atlanta, 23
SOs: Fred Clausen, Montgomery, 139
Pct: James Callahan, Atlanta, .812, 23-5

Texas-Southern League
Presidents: J.C. McNealus/C.P. Gregory

Standings	W	L	Pct.	GB	Manager
Dallas Steers*	82	33	.713	—	Ted Sullivan
Ft. Worth Panthers**	77	39	.664	5½	T.P. Richards/George Reilley/Fernandez
Galveston Sandcrabs	72	47	.605	12	Bill Works/Jack Huston
Sherman Orphans	53	64	.453	30	Llewellyn Legg/Ryan/Mike O'Connor/ Douglass
Shreveport Grays#	58	38	.604	NA	Pete Weckbecker/Keefe/Kennedy
Austin Beavers#	32	63	.337	NA	Joseph Schachern/Brennan/McBride
Houston Magnolias#	26	65	.286	NA	W.F. Hepworth/McCormick/Pickering
San Antonio Missionaries#	21	72	.226	NA	W.J. Clare/Garson/Land

#Austin, Houston, San Antonio, and Shreveport disbanded August 6.

Playoff: Ft. Worth led Dallas 7 games to 6 in a 15-game playoff when a dispute arose that ended the series. Ft. Worth was declared champion several months later.

BA: Al McBride, Austin, .444
Runs: Ernest Hodge, Dallas, 167
Hits: Jack Killacky, Dallas, 197
HRs: Charles Meyers, Shreveport/ Galveston, 15
SBs: Will Blakey, Galveston, 103
Wins: Al McFarlan, Ft. Worth, 34
Pct: Frank Woodruff, Dallas, 1.000, 11-0

Virginia League
President: Judge Samuel B. Witt, Jr.

Standings	W	L	Pct.	GB	Manager
Richmond Blue Birds	78	45	.634	—	Jake Wells
Lynchburg Hill Climbers	67	52	.563	9	William A. Smith
Norfolk Clams/Crows	56	61	.479	19	Camden Sommers/William Hoggins/ Edward Tate
Portsmouth Truckers	57	68	.456	22	Captain Brady/Charles Bland/George Reed
Petersburg Farmers	55	69	.444	23½	Robert Pender
Roanoke Magicians	52	70	.431	25½	James Breen/Richard Padden

BA: Edward Tate, Portsmouth/Norfolk, .412
Runs: Harry O'Hagan, Norfolk, 125
Hits: Edward Tate, Portsmouth/Norfolk, 194
HRs: Bob Berryhill, Lynchburg, 19
Charles McIntyre, Lynchburg, 19
Wins: Con Flynn, Richmond, 25
SOs: Con Flynn, Richmond, 203
Pct: Albert Orth, Lynchburg, .774, 24-7

Western Association
President: W.W. Kent

Standings	W	L	Pct.	GB	Manager
Lincoln Treeplanters	80	48	.625	—	Buck Ebright
Peoria Distillers	74	55	.574	6½	Charles Flynn
Des Moines Prohibitionists	71	55	.563	8	Bill Trafley
Rockford Forest City	66	60	.524	13	Hugh Nicol
Quincy Browns	63	63	.500	16	George Brackett
Omaha Omahogs/Denver/ Dubuque@	55	68	.447	22½	David Rowe/Joe Cantillon/Tom Morrissey
Jacksonville/Springfield/ Burlington Colts#	46	72	.390	29	Bob Caruthers/J.C. Aydelotte/Paul Hines
St. Joseph Saints	45	79	.363	33	Harry Gatewood

#Jacksonville moved to Springfield, then to Burlington.
@Omaha moved to Denver, then to Dubuque.

BA: Bill Krieg, Rockford, .452
Runs: Charles Flynn, Peoria, 145
Hits: Bill Krieg, Rockford, 237
HRs: Sam Mertes, Quincy, 13
Wins: Beam, Peoria, 36
Pct: Beam, Peoria, .692, 36-16

Western League
President: Byron Bancroft Johnson

Standings	W	L	Pct.	GB	Manager
Indianapolis Hoosiers	78	43	.645	—	William Watkins
St. Paul Apostles	74	50	.597	5½	Charles Comiskey
Kansas City Blues	73	52	.584	7	Jim Manning
Minneapolis Millers	64	59	.520	15	John Barnes/Ed Murphy
Detroit Tigers	59	66	.472	21	J.C. "Con" Strothers/George Vanderbeck
Milwaukee Brewers	57	67	.460	22½	Larry Twitchell
Toledo Swamp Angels/ Terre Haute Hottentots#	52	72	.419	27½	Dennis Long/W. Schneider
Grand Rapids Gold Bugs	38	86	.306	41½	George Ellis

#Toledo (23-28) moved to Terre Haute.

BA: Perry Werden, Minneapolis, .428
Runs: Dan Lally, Minneapolis, 205
Hits: Perry Werden, Minneapolis, 241
William George, Grand Rapids/ St. Paul, 241
HRs: Perry Werden, Minneapolis, 45
Wins: Chauncey Fisher, Indianapolis, 36
ERA: Tony Mullane, St. Paul, 2.30
Pct: Chauncey Fisher, Indianapolis, .818, 36-8

1896

National League
President: Nicholas E. Young

Standings	W	L	Pct.	GB	Attend.	Manager
Baltimore Orioles	90	39	.698	—	249,448	Ned Hanlon
Cleveland Spiders	80	48	.625	9½	152,000	Patsy Tebeau
Cincinnati Reds	77	50	.606	12	373,000	Buck Ewing
Boston Beaneaters	74	57	.565	17	240,000	Frank Selee
Chicago Colts	71	57	.555	18½	317,500	Cap Anson
Pittsburgh Pirates	66	63	.512	24	197,000	Connie Mack
New York Giants	64	67	.489	27	274,000	Arthur Irwin/Bill Joyce
Philadelphia Phillies	62	68	.477	28½	357,025	Billy Nash
Brooklyn Bridegrooms	58	73	.443	33	201,000	Dave Foutz
Washington Senators	58	73	.443	33	223,000	Gus Schmelz
St. Louis Browns	40	90	.308	50½	184,000	Harry Diddlebock/ Arlie Latham/ Chris Von Der Ahe/ Roger Connor/Tommy Dowd
Louisville Colonels	38	93	.290	53	133,000	John McCloskey/Bill McGunnigle

BA: Jesse Burkett, Cleveland, .410
Runs: Jesse Burkett, Cleveland, 160
Hits: Jesse Burkett, Cleveland, 240
RBIs: Ed Delahanty, Philadelphia, 126
HRs: Bill Joyce, Washington/New York, 14

Wins: Charles "Kid" Nichols, Boston, 30
SOs: Cy Young, Cleveland, 137
ERA: Billy Rhines, Cincinnati, 2.45
Pct: Bill Hoffer, Baltimore, .781, 25-7

Atlantic League
President: Samuel B. Crane

Standings	W	L	Pct.	GB	Manager
Newark Colts	82	61	.573	—	Thomas P. Burns
Hartford Bluebirds	73	54	.566	1	Billy Barnie
Paterson Silk Weavers	74	60	.552	3½	Edward Barrow
New York Metropolitans/ Philadelphia Athletics@	57	69	.452	13	John Irwin/Bill Sharsig
Wilmington Peaches	58	79	.423	20	Dennis Long
New Haven Texas Steers/ Lancaster Maroons#	47	68	.409	21	Theodore Sullivan/Frank Ring

#New Haven (21-38) moved to Lancaster July 3.
@New York (30-32) was expelled July 13 and replaced by Philadelphia.

Playoff: Paterson 5 games, Hartford 2.

BA: John Newell, Wilmington, .391
Runs: William "Rasty" Wright, Newark, 163
Hits: William "Rasty" Wright, Newark, 189
HRs: John Rothfuss, Newark, 13

Wins: Tom Vickery, Hartford, 34
SOs: Jeremiah Nops, Wilmington, 199
Pct: Tom Vickery, Hartford, .642, 34-19

Eastern League
President: Patrick T. Powers

Standings	W	L	Pct.	GB	Manager
Providence Grays	71	47	.602	—	William Murray
Buffalo Bisons	70	53	.569	3½	Jack Rowe
Rochester Browns	68	58	.540	7	Dan Shannon
Toronto Maple Leafs/ Albany Senators#	59	57	.509	11	Al Buckenberger
Syracuse Stars	59	62	.488	13½	Charles Reilly/George Kuntsch
Springfield Ponies	54	64	.458	17	Thomas E. Burns
Wilkes-Barre Coal Barons	49	66	.426	20½	Jack Chapman/Howard Earl
Scranton Miners	44	67	.396	23½	Michael McDermott/Sandy Griffin

#Toronto played in Albany (7-11) July 9 through July 31.

Playoff: Providence 4 games, Buffalo 2.

BA: Abel Lizotte, Wilkes-Barre, .390
Runs: Chick Stahl, Buffalo, 130

Hits: Abel Lizotte, Wilkes-Barre, 195
HRs: Jack Drauby, Providence, 18

Interstate League
President: Charles B. Powers

Standings	W	L	Pct.	GB	Manager
Toledo Swamp Angels**	86	36	.705	—	Charles Strobel/Frank Torreyson
Fort Wayne Farmers*	70	36	.660	8	George Tebeau
Wheeling Nailers	57	60	.487	26½	Isaac Hughes/John Darrah
Youngstown Puddlers	54	57	.486	26½	Art Anderson/Charles Hazen
New Castle Quakers	53	59	.473	28	Jay Faatz
Jackson Wolverines	53	66	.445	31½	Alex McDonald/Leigh Lynch
Washington Little Senators	43	70	.381	38½	Byron McKeown
Saginaw Lumbermen	40	73	.354	41½	George Black

Playoff: Toledo 4 games, Fort Wayne 0.

BA: Ervin Beck, Toledo, .371
Runs: Jake Ganzel, New Castle, 82

Hits: Ervin Beck, Toledo, 171

New England League
President: Tim H. Murnane

Standings	W	L	Pct.	GB	Manager
Fall River Indians	68	39	.636	—	Charles Marston
Bangor Millionaires	63	39	.618	2½	William Long/Michael McDermott
Brockton Shoemakers	63	43	.594	4½	Walter Burnham
New Bedford Browns	57	48	.543	14	A.G. "Fred" Doe
Pawtucket Maroons	55	54	.505	14	John A. Smith
Augusta Kennebecs	35	68	.340	31	Walter Harrington/Daniel Clare
Portland@	32	58	.356	NA	Frank Leonard
Lewiston#	29	53	.354	NA	Michael Garrity/Edward Flanagan/Henry Slater

#Lewiston disbanded August 14.
@Portland disbanded August 23.

BA: Napoleon Lajoie, Fall River, .429
Runs: Irving Waldron, Pawtucket, 137
Hits: Irving Waldron, Pawtucket, 182

HRs: Ed Breckinridge, Brockton, 25
George Yeager, Pawtucket, 25
Wins: Fred Klobedanz, Fall River, 25
SOs: James Kerwan, Brockton, 168
Pct: Fred Klobedanz, Fall River, .806, 25-6

New Pacific League
President: M.J. Roach

Standings	W	L	Pct.	GB	Manager
Portland Gladiators	19	9	.679	—	Robert Glenalvin
Tacoma Robbers/Colts	16	17	.485	5½	Charles Strobel
Victoria Chappies	13	16	.448	6½	August Klopf
Seattle Yannigans/ Rainmakers	13	19	.406	8	Charles "Count" Campau

The league disbanded June 15.

BA: Robert Glenalvin, Portland, .448
Runs: Charles "Count" Campau, Seattle, 55
Hits: John Morrissey, Tacoma, 57
F.A. Whaling, Victoria, 57

HRs: Charles "Count" Campau, Seattle, 13
Wins: Isaac Butler, Seattle, 9
SOs: George Derby, Victoria, 64
Pct: George Borchers, Portland, .875, 7-1

Southern League
President: Henry Powers

Standings	W	L	Pct.	GB	Manager
New Orleans Pelicans	68	31	.686	—	Abner Powell
Montgomery Grays	60	36	.625	6½	Richard Gorman
Mobile Blackbirds	39	56	.410	27	Charles Cushman/William Whitrock/ Paul Hines
Columbus Babies	34	63	.350	33	J.C. "Con" Strothers/Frank Flournoy/ Charles Cushman
Atlanta Crackers#	36	36	.500	NA	James Knowles
Birmingham Bluebirds@	26	41	.388	NA	William Rourke/William Fuller

#Atlanta disbanded August 11.
@Birmingham disbanded August 14.

BA: Ed Deady, Montgomery, .371
Jim Knowles, Atlanta, .371
Runs: Abner Powell, New Orleans, 97
Hits: Ed Deady, Montgomery, 154

HRs: Newton Fisher, Mobile, 10
Wins: Lucien "Lee" Smith, New Orleans, 22
SOs: Tully Sparks, Birmingham/Mobile, 160
Pct: Winford Kellum, Montgomery, .808, 21-5

Texas-Southern League
President: John L. Ward

Standings	W	L	Pct.	GB	Manager
Houston Magnolias*	81	49	.623	—	Carson/Charles Shaffer
Galveston Sand Crabs**	69	61	.623	12	Bill Works/Jack Huston/Pete Weckbecker
Austin Senators	60	70	.462	21	Henri Blackburn/Burns/Pop Weikart
San Antonio Missionaries	57	71	.445	23	Brophy/Lawrence/Mike O'Connor
Ft. Worth Panthers@	71	29	.710	NA	Carmen/McAllister
Sherman Students/ Paris Midlands#@	44	49	.473	NA	Ryan/Russ Steinhoff
Denison Tigers@	41	51	.446	NA	Peacock/Mike O'Connor
Dallas Navigators@	25	68	.269	NA	Earle/Pritchard/Henri Blackburn

#Sherman disbanded June 10; a Paris semi-pro team replaced them the next day.
@Denison, Ft. Worth, Dallas, and Paris disbanded August 2.

Playoff: Houston defeated Galveston in a seven-game series that had been designed to last 30 contests.

BA: Mike O'Connor, Sherman/
Denison/San Antonio, .395
Runs: James Slagle, Houston, 171
Hits: James Slagle, Houston, 216

HRs: Mike O'Connor, Sherman/Denison/
San Antonio, 18
Wins: John Roach, Houston, 29
Pct: Dale Gear, Ft. Worth, .828, 24-5

Virginia League
President: James McLaughlin

Standings	W	L	Pct.	GB	Manager
Richmond Bluebirds**	71	55	.563	—	Jacob Wells
Norfolk Clams***	70	60	.538	3	Claude McFarland
Portsmouth Browns	65	64	.504	7½	Charles "Lefty" Marr/William "Pete" Hall

Petersburg Farmers/Hampton# 39 90 .302 33½ James Breen/George Kelly
Lynchburg Hill Climbers+* 68 37 .648 NA William A. Smith
Roanoke Magicians@ .... 49 56 .467 NA Charles Boyer/Edward Tate

#Petersburg (32-60) moved to Hampton August 13.
@Roanoke disbanded August 20.
+Lynchburg disbanded August 22.

BA: Edward Tate, Roanoke, .384
Runs: Claude McFarland, Norfolk, 123
Hits: Claude McFarland, Norfolk, 194

HRs: Zeke Wrigley, Roanoke, 16
Joe Dolan, Lynchburg, 16
Reuben Stephenson, Norfolk/
Portsmouth/Petersburg, 16
Wins: Jesse Tannehill, Richmond, 27
SOs: Cy Malarkey, Richmond, 208
Pct: W.T. McFarland, Lynchburg, .741, 20-7

Western Association
President: Thomas J. Hickey

Standings	W	L	Pct.	GB	Manager
Des Moines Prohibitionists*	56	22	.718	—	Bill Traffley
Dubuque+**	47	34	.580	10½	Sam LaRoque
Peoria Distillers+	43	35	.551	13	Daniel Dugdale
Rockford Forest City+	44	37	.543	13½	Hugh Nicol
Cedar Rapids Bunnies	29	49	.372	27	Buck Ebright
Burlington Colts	28	51	.354	28½	Paul Hines
Quincy Blue Birds#	31	37	.456	NA	George Brackett
St. Joseph Saints@	31	44	.413	NA	Frank Haller

#Quincy disbanded July 16.
@St. Joseph disbanded July 18.
+Dubuque, Peoria, and Rockford disbanded July 25.
The league disbanded August 1.

BA: Bill Krieg, Rockford, .350
Runs: Tom Letcher, Des Moines, 88
Hits: Bill Krieg, Rockford, 123
HRs: Bill Krieg, Rockford, 15

Wins: Beam, Peoria, 36
ERA: Dolan, Dubuque, 1.31
Pct: Beam, Peoria, .692, 36-16

Western League
President: Byron Bancroft Johnson

Standings	W	L	Pct.	GB	Manager
Minneapolis Millers	89	47	.654	—	Walter Wilmot
Indianapolis Hoosiers	78	54	.591	9	William Watkins
Detroit Tigers	80	58	.580	10	J.C. "Con" Strothers/George Stallings
St. Paul Apostles	73	63	.537	16	Jack Glasscock/Charles Comiskey
Kansas City Blues	69	66	.511	19½	Jim Manning
Milwaukee Brewers	62	78	.443	29	Larry Twitchell/Robert Glenalvin
Columbus Buckeyes	52	88	.371	39	W. Schneider/Tom Loftus
Grand Rapids Gold Bugs	45	94	.324	45½	G.E. Ellis/John Carney

Playoff: Minneapolis 4 games, Indianapolis 2.

BA: Jack Glasscock, St. Paul, .431
Runs: Jack Glasscock, St. Paul, 172
Hits: Jack Glasscock, St. Paul, 263

HRs: Perry Werden, Minneapolis, 18
William Schriver, Minneapolis, 18
Wins: Bill Hutchinson, Minneapolis, 38
SOs: Roger Denzer, St. Paul, 200
Pct: Bill Hutchinson, Minneapolis, .731, 38-14

1897

National League
President: Nicholas E. Young

Standings	W	L	Pct.	GB	Attend.	Manager
Boston Beaneaters	93	39	.705	—	334,800	Frank Selee
Baltimore Orioles	90	40	.692	2	273,046	Ned Hanlon
New York Giants	83	48	.634	9½	390,340	Bill Joyce
Cincinnati Reds	76	56	.576	17	336,800	Buck Ewing
Cleveland Spiders	69	62	.527	23½	115,250	Patsy Tebeau
Brooklyn Bridegrooms	61	71	.462	32	220,831	Billy Barnie
Washington Senators	61	71	.462	32	151,028	Gus Schmelz/Tom Brown
Pittsburgh Pirates	60	71	.458	32½	165,950	Patsy Donovan
Chicago Colts	59	73	.447	34	327,160	Cap Anson
Philadelphia Phillies	55	77	.417	38	290,027	George Stallings
Louisville Colonels	52	78	.400	40	145,210	Jim Rogers/Fred Clarke
St. Louis Browns	29	102	.221	63½	136,400	Tommy Dowd/Hugh Nicol/ Bill Hallman/Chris Von Der Ahe

BA: Willie Keeler, Baltimore, .432
Runs: Billy Hamilton, Boston, 152
Hits: Willie Keeler, Baltimore, 243
RBIs: George Davis, New York, 134
HRs: Hugh Duffy, Boston, 11

Wins: Charles "Kid" Nichols, Boston, 30
SOs: Cy Seymour, New York, 157
ERA: Amos Rusie, New York, 2.54
Pct: Fred Klobedanz, Boston, .788, 26-7

Atlantic League
President: Edward Barrow

Standings	W	L	Pct.	GB	Manager
Lancaster Maroons	90	45	.667	—	Frank Rinn
Newark Colts	89	52	.631	4	George Ellis

Hartford Bluebirds	78	55	.586	11	Thomas P. Burns
Richmond Bluebirds	71	59	.546	16½	Jake Wells
Norfolk Jewels	66	72	.478	25½	William A. Smith
Paterson Silk Weavers	68	79	.463	28	Charles McKee
Philadelphia Athletics	49	89	.355	42½	Bill Sharsig
Reading Coal Heavers	40	100	.286	52½	Daniel Long

BA: William "Rasty" Wright, Newark, .372
Runs: Harry O'Hagan, Newark, 150
Hits: Harry O'Hagan, Newark, 202
HRs: Ralph Seybold, Lancaster, 14

Wins: William Carrick, Newark, 31
SOs: Sam Leever, Richmond, 179
Pct: Joe Yeager, Lancaster, .757, 28-9

Eastern League
President: Patrick T. Powers

Standings	W	L	Pct.	GB	Manager
Syracuse Stars	83	50	.624	—	Al Buckenberger
Toronto Maple Leafs	75	49	.605	3½	Arthur Irwin
Buffalo Bisons	74	57	.565	8	Jack Rowe
Springfield Ponies	68	55	.553	10	Thomas E. Burns
Providence Grays	68	60	.521	12½	William Murray
Scranton Miners	53	60	.469	20	Sandy Griffin
Rochester Blackbirds/ Montreal Royals#	45	76	.372	32	Dan Shannon/George Weidman/ Charles Dooley
Wilkes-Barre Coal Barons	30	85	.233	44	Abner Powell/Dan Shannon

#Rochester (24-42) moved to Montreal July 16.

Playoff: With the series between Syracuse and Toronto tied at 3 games apiece, a dispute arose where the final game would be played. League officials cancelled the Steinert Cup Series and awarded the league title to Toronto.

BA: Dan Brouthers, Springfield, .415
Runs: Edward "Danny" Green, Springfield, 134
Hits: Dan Brouthers, Springfield, 208

HRs: John "Buck" Freeman, Toronto, 20
Wins: John Malarkey, Syracuse, 27
SOs: Vic Willis, Syracuse, 171
Pct: Elisha Norton, Toronto, .762, 16-5

Interstate League
President: Charles B. Powers

Standings	W	L	Pct.	GB	Manager
Toledo Mud Hens	83	43	.659	—	Charles Strobel
Dayton Old Soldiers	74	51	.592	8½	Frank Torreyson/Bill Armour
New Castle Quakers	72	54	.571	11	Paul Russell
Fort Wayne Indians	63	59	.516	18	Fred Cooke
Mansfield Haymakers	63	61	.508	19	J.C. "Con" Strothers/Bert Howard
Youngstown Puddlers	59	66	.472	23½	John Scheible/Edward Zinram
Springfield Governors	46	79	.368	36½	Harry Rinehart/Lew Whistler
Wheeling Nailers#	38	85	.309	43½	William Harrington/Frank Torreyson

#Wheeling went on strike due to unpaid salaries. The franchise was awarded to Frank Torreyson, manager of Dayton, who sold the best players.

Playoff: Toledo 4 games, Dayton 2.

BA: Bill Myers, Toledo, .411
Runs: Bill Hartman, Toledo, 152
Hits: Robert Gilks, Toledo, 208

HRs: George "Dummy" Kihm, Fort Wayne, 17
Joe Reiman, Dayton, 17
Joe Werrick, Mansfield, 17
Wins: Harry "Kid" Keenan, Toledo, 20
ERA: Chase Alloway, Fort Wayne, 1.00
Pct: John Blue, Toledo, .857, 18-3

New England League
President: Tim H. Murnane

Standings	W	L	Pct.	GB	Manager
Brockton Shoemakers	70	37	.654	—	Walter Burnham
Newport Colts	70	37	.654	—	Michael Finn
Pawtucket Phenoms	54	51	.514	15	John A. Smith
Fall River Indians	47	59	.443	22½	Michael McDermott/Charles Marston
Taunton Herrings	40	68	.370	30½	John Irwin
New Bedford Whalers	38	67	.362	31	Con Murphy/Michael McDermott

BA: Jimmy Sheckard, Brockton, .370
Runs: Jimmy Sheckard, Brockton, 122
Hits: Jimmy Sheckard, Brockton, 166
HRs: Tom News, Pawtucket, 17

Wins: Marvin "Blue" Hawley, Newport, 24
SOs: Frank Todd, Pawtucket, 99
Pct: Charles Pittinger, Brockton, .778, 14-4

Western Association
President: Thomas J. Hickey

Standings	W	L	Pct.	GB	Manager
Cedar Rapids Bunnies	84	41	.672	—	Belden Hill
St. Joseph Saints	80	45	.640	4	Palmer
Rockford Forest City	70	55	.560	14	Varney Anderson
Des Moines Prohibitionists	67	57	.540	16½	Pete Lohman
Peoria Blackbirds	56	68	.452	27½	Daniel Dugdale/Buck Ebright
Quincy Little Giants	56	69	.448	28	Bill Traffley
Dubuque	47	79	.373	37½	Joe Cantillon
Burlington Colts	39	85	.315	44½	Bob Berryhill

BA: Irving Waldron, St. Joseph, .353
Runs: Rony Viox, St. Joseph, 130
Hits: Bill Klusman, St. Joseph, 175
HRs: Jimmy Williams, St. Joseph, 31

Wins: L.W. Mahaffey, Cedar Rapids, 30
ERA: M. Carish, St. Joseph, 1.19
Pct: L.W. Mahaffey, Cedar Rapids, .750, 30-10

Western League
President: Byron Bancroft Johnson

Standings	W	L	Pct.	GB	Attend.	Manager
Indianapolis Hoosiers	98	37	.726	—	140,000	Bill Watkins
Columbus Senators	89	47	.654	9½	110,000	George Tebeau
Milwaukee Creams	85	50	.630	13	160,000	Connie Mack
St. Paul Saints	86	51	.628	13	120,000	Charles Comiskey
Detroit Tigers	70	66	.515	28½	110,000	Robert Allen/Frank Graves
Minneapolis Millers	43	95	.312	56½	90,000	Walt Wilmer/George Miller
Kansas City Blues	40	99	.288	60	100,000	Jim Manning
Grand Rapids Gold Bugs	34	100	.254	63½	75,000	Bob Leadley

BA: Al McBride, St. Paul, .387
Runs: Al McBride, St. Paul, 166
Hits: William George, St. Paul, 207
HRs: William Gray, Indianapolis, 19

Wins: Francis Foreman, Indianapolis, 30
SOs: Tommy Thomas, Detroit, 147
Pct: Francis Foreman, Indianapolis, .769, 30-9

1898

National League
President: Nicholas E. Young

Standings	W	L	Pct.	GB	Attend.	Manager
Boston Beaneaters	102	47	.685	—	229,275	Frank Selee
Baltimore Orioles	96	53	.644	6	123,416	Ned Hanlon
Cincinnati Reds	92	60	.605	11½	336,378	Buck Ewing
Chicago Orphans	85	65	.567	17½	424,352	Thomas E. Burns
Cleveland Spiders	81	68	.544	21	70,496	Patsy Tebeau
Philadelphia Phillies	78	71	.523	24	265,414	George Stallings/Bill Shettsline
New York Giants	77	73	.513	25½	206,700	Bill Joyce/Cap Anson
Pittsburgh Pirates	72	76	.486	29½	150,900	Bill Watkins
Louisville Colonels	70	81	.464	33	128,980	Fred Clarke
Brooklyn Bridegrooms	54	91	.372	46	122,514	Billy Barnie/Mike Griffin/Charlie Ebbets
Washington Senators	51	101	.336	52½	103,250	Tom Brown/Jack Doyle/Deacon McGuire/Arthur Irwin
St. Louis Perfectos	39	111	.260	63½	151,700	Tim Hurst

BA: Willie Keeler, Baltimore, .379
Runs: John McGraw, Baltimore, 143
Hits: Jesse Burkett, Cleveland, 215
RBIs: Napoleon Lajoie, Philadelphia, 127
HRs: Jimmy Collins, Boston, 15

Wins: Charles "Kid" Nichols, Boston, 29
SOs: Cy Seymour, New York, 244
ERA: Clark Griffith, Chicago, 1.88
Pct: Al Maul, Baltimore, .769, 20-6

Atlantic League
President: Edward Barrow

Standings	W	L	Pct.	GB	Manager
Richmond Bluebirds	77	44	.636	—	Jacob Wells
Lancaster Maroons	82	50	.621	½	Frank Rinn/Pierce Chiles/Carl McVey
Reading Coal Heavers	72	56	.559	8½	Daniel Long
Paterson Silk Weavers	65	70	.481	19	Sam LaRoque
Allentown Peanuts	55	67	.451	22½	Bill Sharsig
Newark Colts	58	71	.450	23	Thomas P. Burns
Hartford Cooperatives	57	76	.427	26	Bill Traffley/Mike Roach
Norfolk Jewels	47	79	.373	32½	W.A. Jewell

BA: Pat Meany, Newark, .330
Runs: John Buttermore, Lancaster, 118
Hits: Pierce Chiles, Lancaster, 184

HRs: Ralph "Socks" Seybold, Richmond, 17
SBs: Frank "Piggy" Ward, Lancaster, 59

Eastern League
President: Patrick T. Powers

Standings	W	L	Pct.	GB	Manager
Montreal Royals	68	48	.586	—	Charley Dooley
Wilkes-Barre Coal Barons	62	48	.564	3	Dan Shannon
Toronto Maple Leafs	64	55	.538	5½	Arthur Irwin
Buffalo Bisons	62	60	.508	9	Jack Rowe
Providence Clamdiggers	58	60	.492	11	William Murray
Syracuse Stars	52	63	.452	15½	George Kuntzsch
Springfield Ponies	48	63	.432	17½	
Rochester Patriots/Ottawa Wanderers#	53	70	.431	18½	Bill Clymer/Sandy Griffin

#Rochester (23-38) moved to Ottawa July 7.

BA: Buck Freeman, Toronto, .347
Runs: Doc Casey, Toronto, 123

Hits: Reddy Grey, Toronto, 174
HRs: Buck Freeman, Toronto, 23

Interstate League
President: Charles B. Powers

Standings	W	L	Pct.	GB	Manager
Dayton Old Soldiers	85	66	.564	—	Bill Armour
Toledo Mud Hens	86	68	.558	½	Charles Strobel

Springfield Governors	81	66	.551	2	Lew Whistler
New Castle Quakers	81	69	.540	3½	Pop Lytle
Grand Rapids Cabinet Makers	75	79	.487	11½	Frank Torreyson
Mansfield Haymakers	71	75	.486	11½	Bert Howard
Fort Wayne Indians	71	84	.458	16	Ed O'Meara/George Geer
Youngstown Puddlers	53	96	.356	31	George Geer/Paul Russell

BA: Bill Hartman, Toledo, .340
Runs: Bill Hartman, Toledo, 167
Hits: Bill Hartman, Toledo, 214
HRs: Joe Reiman, Dayton, 14

Wins: John Ewing, Toledo, 25
Ferguson, Toledo, 25
SOs: Eimer Smith, New Castle, 184
Pct: Nick Altrock, .850, 17-3

New England League
President: Tim H. Murnane

Standings	W	L	Pct.	GB	Manager
Brockton Shoemakers	32	16	.667	—	Walter Burnham
Pawtucket Tigers	26	23	.530	6½	H.B. Whiting
Fall River Indians	28	25	.528	6½	John A. Smith
Newport Colts	26	28	.481	9	Finn Kelley
New Bedford Whalers/Worcester#	20	22	.476	9	A.G. "Fred" Doe/Charles Rice
Taunton Herrings	15	33	.312	17	Frank Leonard

#New Bedford (18-20) moved to Worcester June 14.

BA: Tom News, Pawtucket, .401
Runs: Mike Kelley, Newport, 56
Hits: Tom News, Pawtucket, 85
HRs: Tom News, Pawtucket, 8

Wins: Frank Todd, Pawtucket, 13
SOs: Jack Cronin, Fall River, 67
Pct: Grant Thatcher, Brockton, .833, 10-2

Western League
President: Byron Bancroft Johnson

Standings	W	L	Pct.	GB	Attend.	Manager
Kansas City Blues	88	51	.633	—	180,000	Jim Manning
Indianapolis Hoosiers	84	50	.627	1½	120,000	Bill Watkins/Bob Allen
Milwaukee Brewers	82	57	.590	6	160,000	Connie Mack
St. Paul Apostles	81	58	.583	7	90,000	Charles Comiskey
Columbus Senators	73	60	.549	12	60,000	Tom Loftus/George Tebeau
Detroit Tigers	50	87	.365	37	85,000	Frank Graves/Ollie Beard/Tony Mullane/George Stallings
Minneapolis Millers	48	92	.343	40½	40,000	Gus Schmelz/Walter Wilmot
St. Joseph Saints/Omaha Omahogs#	42	93	.311	44	50,000	Pa Rourke/Tom Tucker/Chauncey Fisher

#St. Joseph (23-38) moved to Omaha July 7.

BA: Jimmy Slagle, Kansas City, .378
Runs: Jimmy Slagle, Kansas City, 137
Hits: Jimmy Slagle, Kansas City, 206
HRs: Frank Shugart, St. Paul, 12

SBs: Charles "Count" Campau, Kansas City, 60
Wins: Roger Denzer, St. Paul, 33
Pct: Bill Phillips, Indianapolis, .784, 29-8
CGs: Bill Phillips, Indianapolis, 39

1899

National League
President: Nicholas E. Young

Standings	W	L	Pct.	GB	Attend.	Manager
Brooklyn Superbas	101	47	.682	—	269,641	Ned Hanlon
Boston Beaneaters	95	57	.625	8	200,384	Frank Selee
Philadelphia Phillies	94	58	.618	9	388,903	Bill Shettsline
Baltimore Orioles	86	62	.581	15	121,935	John McGraw
St. Louis Perfectos	84	67	.556	18½	373,909	Patsy Tebeau
Cincinnati Reds	83	67	.553	19	259,536	Buck Ewing
Pittsburgh Pirates	76	73	.510	25½	251,834	Bill Watkins/Patsy Donovan
Chicago Cubs	75	73	.507	26	352,130	Thomas E. Burns
Louisville Colonels	75	77	.493	28	109,319	Fred Clarke
New York Giants	60	90	.400	42	121,384	John Day/Fred Hoey
Washington Senators	54	98	.355	49	86,392	Arthur Irwin
Cleveland Spiders	20	134	.130	84	6,088	Lave Cross/Joe Quinn

BA: Ed Delahanty, Philadelphia, .408
Runs: John McGraw, Baltimore, 140
Willie Keeler, Brooklyn, 140
Hits: Ed Delahanty, Philadelphia, 234
RBIs: Ed Delahanty, Philadelphia, 137
HRs: Buck Freeman, Washington, 25

Wins: Jim Hughes, Brooklyn, 28
Joe McGinnity, Baltimore, 28
SOs: Noodles Hahn, Cincinnati, 145
ERA: Al Orth, Philadelphia, 2.49
Pct: Jim Hughes, Brooklyn, .824, 28-6

Atlantic League
President: Edward Barrow

Standings	W	L	Pct.	GB	Manager
Richmond Bluebirds	63	25	.716	—	Jacob Wells
Wilkes-Barre Coal Barons	49	37	.570	13	Dan Shannon/William Goeckel
Lancaster Maroons	51	42	.548	14½	Carl McVey
Reading Coal Heavers	46	40	.535	16	Frank Rinn
Allentown Peanuts	37	47	.440	24	Bill Sharsig
Newark Colts	42	54	.437	25	Jim Fields/John Chapman/Abner Powell
Scranton Miners@	25	38	.397	NA	Marty Swift
Paterson Giants#	21	51	.292	NA	William "Rasty" Wright/Jack Thornton/Edward Barrow/Abner Powell

#Paterson disbanded July 4.
@Scranton disbanded July 9.

BA: Jack Thornton, Paterson/Newark, .379
Runs: John Buttermore, Lancaster, 83
Hits: Frank "Piggy" Ward, Lancaster, 136
HRs: Ralph "Socks" Seybold, Richmond, 11
2B: Frank "Piggy" Ward, Lancaster, 29

3B: Joe Delahanty, Allentown, 30
Wins: Harry Wilhelm, Lancaster, 21
SOs: Case Patton, Wilkes-Barre, 101
Pct: Virgil Garvin, Reading, .824, 14-3

California League
President: James T. Moran

Standings	W	L	Pct.	GB	Manager
Sacramento Brewers	48	30	.615	—	Edward Kripp
San Francisco Friscos	45	41	.524	7	Henry Harris
Oakland Dudes	44	48	.478	11	Cal Ewing
Santa Cruz Beachcombers	35	49	.417	16	Fred Swanton
Watsonville Hayseeds	25	25	.500	NA	Ed Struve
San Jose Prune Pickers	23	27	.460	NA	W.F. McGraw

BA: Irwin Harvey, Sacramento, .350
Runs: Heine Krug, San Francisco, 67
　Jim Sullivan, San Francisco, 67
Hits: Henry Krug, San Francisco, 122

HRs: Truck Eagan, Sacramento, 7
　Hen Stultz, Sacramento, 7
Wins: Charley Doyle, Sacramento, 28
Pct: Charley Doyle, Sacramento, .718, 28-11

Canadian League
Secretary: Cal Davis

Standings	W	L	Pct.	GB	Manager
London Cockneys***	64	28	.696	—	George "Pete" Lohman
Hamilton Blackbirds	49	43	.533	15	Charles Collins
Guelph Maple Leafs	42	48	.467	21	George Black
Stratford/Woodstock#	34	53	.391	27½	
Chatham Reds@	19	23	.452	NA	Leslie Snyder
St. Thomas Saints@	11	24	.314	NA	Joseph Knight

#Stratford (5-20) moved to Woodstock June 8.
@Chatham and St. Thomas disbanded July 4.

BA: Bill Congalton, Hamilton, .391
Runs: Kid Mohler, London, 73
Hits: J. William Reed, London, 99
HRs: four players tied with 5

Wins: Thomas Cooper, London, 23
SOs: Thomas Cooper, London, 103
Pct: Thomas Cooper, London, .885, 23-3

Connecticut State League
President: Tim H. Murnane

Standings	W	L	Pct.	GB	Manager
New Haven Blues	55	38	.591	—	W.R. Reilly
Waterbury Rough Riders	53	43	.552	3½	Roger Connor
Derby Lushers	51	43	.542	4½	Billy Lush/Larry Battam
Bristol Bellmakers	48	45	.516	7	John Gunshannon
Meriden Silverites	46	48	.489	9½	
New London Whalers	45	52	.464	12	
Bridgeport Orators	43	55	.438	14½	Jim O'Rourke
Norwich Witches	41	58	.414	17	Jack Rose

BA: Roger Connor, Waterbury, .392
Runs: Roger Connor, Waterbury, 79
Hits: Fred Parent, New Haven, 138

HRs: Frank Woodruff, New London/
　Bridgeport, 11
Wins: Charles McDonald, New Haven, 26
Pct: Charles McDonald, New Haven,
　.703, 26-11

Eastern League
President: Patrick T. Powers

Standings	W	L	Pct.	GB	Manager
Rochester Bronchos	72	43	.628	—	Al Buckenberger
Montreal Royals	61	50	.550	9	Charley Dooley
Worcester Farmers	58	51	.532	11	Frank Leonard
Toronto Maple Leafs	55	55	.500	14½	Wally Taylor
Springfield Ponies	52	56	.481	16½	Tom Brown
Hartford Indians	50	56	.472	17½	Billy Barnie
Providence Clamdiggers	54	62	.466	18½	William Murray
Syracuse Stars	39	68	.364	29	Lew Whistler/Sandy Griffin

BA: Charlie Frisbee, Worcester, .362
Runs: Jim Bannon, Toronto, 112

Hits: John Walters, Providence, 160
HRs: Tom Campbell, Springfield, 11

Interstate League
President: Charles B. Powers

Standings	W	L	Pct.	GB	Manager
New Castle Quakers	87	53	.621	—	Pat Wright
Mansfield Haymakers	86	54	.614	1	Dan Lowney
Fort Wayne Indians	82	58	.586	5	Jack Glasscock
Toledo Mud Hens	82	58	.586	5	Charles Strobel
Youngstown Little Giants	60	79	.432	26½	Harry Truby/Jim McAleer
Wheeling Stogies	58	81	.417	28½	Pop Lytle/Tom Nicholson
Dayton Veterans	55	85	.393	32	Bill Armour
Grand Rapids/Columbus/ Springfield#	49	91	.350	38	Frank Torreyson

#Grand Rapids moved to Columbus July 20, then to Springfield July 30.

BA: Billy Taylor, Youngstown/
　Grand Rapids/Wheeling, .331
Runs: Bill Hartman, Toledo, 117
Hits: Ervin Beck, Toledo, 185

HRs: Ervin Beck, Toledo, 25
Wins: R. Miller, Mansfield, 28
Pct: Theodore Guese, Fort Wayne, .714, 25-10

New England League
President: Tim H. Murnane

Standings	W	L	Pct.	GB	Manager
Portland Phenoms*	61	39	.610	—	John A. Smith
Manchester Manchesters	55	41	.573	4	John Irwin
Newport Colts**	52	46	.531	8	Mike Finn
Taunton Herrings	34	67	.337	27½	Bobby Moore/George Grant
Brockton Shoemakers+	35	27	.625	NA	Walter Burnham
Pawtucket Colts+	37	40	.481	NA	Hobe Whiting
Fitchburg/Lawrence#	3	14	.176	NA	Ed Norton
Cambridge@	4	16	.200	NA	George Spalding

#Fitchburg (3-7) moved to Lawrence May 24, then disbanded June 1.
@Cambridge disbanded June 1.
+Brockton and Pawtucket disbanded after the first half, August 8.
Manchester attempted to win the second half title on the last day of the season by playing six games with Portland. Manchester won all six, but the results were thrown out by the league directors.

BA: John A. Smith, Portland, .382
Runs: Mike Hickey, Manchester, 110
Hits: Mike Hickey, Manchester, 143
　George Noblitt, Portland, 143

HRs: George Noblitt, Portland, 12
　Ed Breckinridge, Brockton, 12
Wins: Tom Flanagan, Portland, 20
SOs: Sam Curran, Manchester, 104
　Tom Gallagher, Newport, 104
Pct: Jim Gannon, Newport, .739, 17-6

New York State League
President: John H. Farrell

Standings	W	L	Pct.	GB	Manager
Rome Romans	76	32	.705	—	Tom O'Brien
Utica Pentups	70	43	.620	8½	Howard Earl
Cortland Wagonmakers	56	46	.550	17	Henry Ramsey
Binghamton Bingoes	56	55	.505	21½	Louis Bacon
Oswego Oswegos	57	57	.500	22	George Sayers
Albany Senators	54	62	.466	26	Charles Faatz/J.H. Haas/John Rafter
Auburn Prisoners/ Troy Washerwomen#	43	69	.384	35	Timothy Shinnick
Schenectady Electricians	29	77	.274	46	Billy Bottenus

#Auburn (27-43) moved to Troy August 1.

BA: Eddie Hill, Binghamton, .378
Runs: Bill Fox, Rome, 113
Hits: Eddie Hill, Binghamton, 158

Wins: John Rudderham, Rome, 26
Pct: Edward Wheeler, Rome, .765, 13-4

Western Association
President: Thomas J. Hickey

Standings	W	L	Pct.	GB	Manager
Rock Island Islanders	28	8	.778	—	Harry Sage
Rockford Rough Riders	20	16	.556	8	Henry "Hunky" Hines
Cedar Rapids Bunnies	22	14	.611	6	Belden Hill
Bloomington Blues	14	23	.378	14½	William Krieg/Frank Blanford
Ottumwa Giants	13	24	.351	15½	Patrick Flaherty
Quincy/Dubuque#	11	23	.324	16	Ed Deady

#Quincy (3-10) moved to Dubuque May 19; Dubuque disbanded June 13.
The league disbanded June 16.

BA: Charles Buelow, Rockford, .331
Runs: Bob Rothermel, Rock Island, 40
Hits: Charles Buelow, Rockford, 48
　Harry Bay, Rock Island, 48

Wins: Elmer Stricklett, Rock Island, 14
Pct: Elmer Stricklett, Rock Island, .933, 14-1
CGs: Elmer Stricklett, Rock Island, 13
　Jack Hart, Rock Island, 13

Western League
President: Byron Bancroft Johnson

Standings	W	L	Pct.	GB	Manager
Indianapolis Hoosiers	75	47	.615	—	Bob Allen
Minneapolis Millers	76	50	.613	1	Perry Werden
Detroit Tigers	64	60	.516	12	George Stallings
Columbus Senators/ Grand Rapids Furnituremakers#	63	62	.504	13½	Tom Loftus/George Tebeau
St. Paul Saints	57	69	.452	20	Charles Comiskey
Milwaukee Brewers	55	68	.447	20½	Connie Mack
Kansas City Blues	53	70	.431	22½	Jim Manning
Buffalo Bisons	53	70	.431	22½	Billy Nash/Jim Garry/Jim Franklin/ Dan Shannon

#Columbus (36-35) moved to Grand Rapids July 17.

BA: Sam Dungan, Detroit, .347
Runs: Alfonso Davis, Minneapolis, 126
Hits: Alfonso Davis, Minneapolis, 176
HRs: Bob Stafford, Milwaukee, 8

Wins: Rube Waddell, Columbus/
Grand Rapids, 26
Jack Cronin, Detroit, 26
SOs: Rube Waddell, Columbus/
Grand Rapids, 200
Pct: Jock Menefee, Minneapolis, .781, 25-7

1900

National League
President: Nicholas E. Young

Standings	W	L	Pct.	GB	Attend.	Manager
Brooklyn Superbas	82	54	.603	—	183,000	Ned Hanlon
Pittsburgh Pirates	79	60	.568	4½	264,000	Fred Clarke
Philadelphia Phillies	75	63	.543	8	301,913	Bill Shettsline
Boston Beaneaters	66	72	.478	17	202,000	Frank Selee
Chicago Cubs	65	75	.464	19	248,577	Tom Loftus
St. Louis Cardinals	65	75	.464	19	270,000	Patsy Tebeau/Louie Heilbroner
Cincinnati Reds	62	77	.446	21½	170,000	Bob Allen
New York Giants	60	78	.435	23	190,000	Buck Ewing/George Davis

BA: Honus Wagner, Pittsburgh, .381
Runs: Roy Thomas, Philadelphia, 134
Hits: Willie Keeler, Brooklyn, 208
RBIs: Elmer Flick, Philadelphia, 110
HRs: Herman Long, Boston, 12

Wins: Joe McGinnity, Brooklyn, 29
SOs: Rube Waddell, Pittsburgh, 130
ERA: Rube Waddell, Pittsburgh, 2.37
Pct: Jesse Tannehill, Pittsburgh, .769, 20-6

American League
President: Byron Bancroft Johnson

Standings	W	L	Pct.	GB	Attend.	Manager
Chicago White Stockings	82	53	.607	—	175,000	Charles Comiskey
Milwaukee Brewers	79	58	.577	4	149,000	Connie Mack
Indianapolis Hoosiers	71	64	.526	11	106,000	Bill Watkins
Detroit Tigers	71	67	.514	12½	146,000	George Stallings
Kansas City Blues	69	70	.496	15	118,000	Jim Manning
Cleveland Lake Shores	63	73	.463	19½	84,000	Jimmy McAleer
Buffalo Bisons	61	78	.439	23	78,000	Dan Shannon/Jim Franklin/Joe Franklin/George Carey
Minneapolis Millers	53	86	.381	31	71,000	Walter Wilmot

BA: Sam Dungan, Kansas City, .337
Runs: Ollie Pickering, Cleveland, 117
Hits: Ollie Pickering, Cleveland, 194

HRs: Perry Werden, Minneapolis, 9
Ralph "Socks" Seybold, Indianapolis, 9
2B: Perry Werden, Minneapolis, 39
Wins: Wyatt Lee, Kansas City, 23
Pct: Roy Patterson, Chicago, .739, 17-6

Atlantic League
President: Horace S. Fogel

Standings	W	L	Pct.	GB	Manager
Scranton Miners	26	7	.788	—	Walter Burnham
Wilkes-Barre Coal Barons	24	13	.649	4	Bill Clymer
Reading Coal Heavers	16	16	.500	9½	Ben Fleishman
Allentown Peanuts	14	20	.412	12½	Bill Sharsig
Philadelphia Athletics/Harrisburg#	10	17	.370	13	Dick Cooley
Elmira	11	19	.367	13½	George Sayers
Newark Colts@	8	12	.400	NA	John Irwin
Jersey City@	7	12	.368	NA	Sam Mills

#Philadelphia moved to Harrisburg.
@Newark and Jersey City disbanded June 2.
The league disbanded June 12.

BA: Joe Delahanty, Allentown, .469
Runs: Fred Ketcham, Wilkes-Barre, 49
Hits: Joe Delahanty, Allentown, 67
Fred Ketcham, Wilkes-Barre, 67

Wins: Dan Kerwin, Scranton, 8
Frank Owen, Wilkes-Barre, 8
SOs: Frank Owen, Wilkes-Barre, 41
Pct: Bill Milligan, Scranton, 1.000, 7-0

California League
President: James T. Moran

Standings	W	L	Pct.	GB	Manager
Sacramento Brewers	50	35	.588	—	J. Butler/Arthur Beebe
San Francisco Friscos	47	43	.522	5½	Henry Harris
Stockton Wasps	39	48	.448	12	George Harper
Oakland Dudes	41	51	.446	12½	Cal Ewing

BA: Henry Krug, San Francisco, .304
Runs: Brick Devereaux, Sacramento, 71
Hits: Henry Krug, San Francisco, 105

HRs: Truck Eagan, Sacramento, 11
Wins: Ham Iburg, San Francisco, 25
Pct: Jim Hughes, Sacramento, .719, 23-9

Central League
President: F.H. Schmidt

Standings	W	L	Pct.	GB	Manager
Bloomington Blues*	64	34	.654	—	George Reed
Danville Champions**	57	44	.564	8½	Charles Leverenz
Decatur Commodores	46	51	.474	17½	Pop Weikart
Terre Haute Hottentots	46	61	.440	21½	Jap Poor
Peoria Distillers@	29	25	.537	NA	Alfred Lawson/William Krieg
Springfield/Jacksonville Reds#	15	43	.259	NA	W.D. Highfield

#Springfield (4-14) moved to Jacksonville May 21; Jacksonville disbanded July 8.
@Peoria disbanded July 8.

BA: Red Wright, .329
Runs: Fred Abbott, Danville, 91

Hits: Charles Elsey, Bloomington, 130
Red Wright, 130
HRs: Frank Huelsman, Peoria/Danville, 5

Connecticut State League
President: Sturgis Whitlock

Standings	W	L	Pct.	GB	Manager
Norwich Witches	64	33	.660	—	A.G. "Fred" Doe
New Haven Blues	58	39	.598	6	W.R. Reilley
Bridgeport Orators	57	41	.582	7½	Jim O'Rourke
Bristol Bellmakers	48	47	.505	15	John Gunshannon
Meriden Silverites	47	48	.495	16	A. Penny
Waterbury Rough Riders	43	53	.448	20½	Roger Connor
Derby Angels	36	60	.375	27½	Jeremiah Denny
New London Whalers	32	64	.333	31½	George Bindloss

BA: Hi Ladd, Derby, .371
Runs: Danny Murphy, Norwich, 112

Hits: Danny Murphy, Norwich, 138
HRs: Danny Murphy, Norwich, 14

Eastern League
President: Patrick T. Powers

Standings	W	L	Pct.	GB	Manager
Providence Clamdiggers	84	52	.618	—	William Murray
Rochester Bronchos	77	56	.579	5½	Al Buckenberger
Hartford Indians	68	55	.556	9½	Billy Barnie/Billy Shindle
Worcester Farmers	62	63	.496	16½	Frank Leonard
Springfield Ponies	61	63	.492	17	Thomas E. Burns
Toronto Maple Leafs	63	67	.485	18	Edward Barrow
Montreal Royals	53	71	.427	25	Charles Dooley
Syracuse Stars	43	84	.339	36½	Arthur Irwin

BA: Kitty Bransfield, Worcester, .371
Runs: Kitty Bransfield, Worcester, 115

Hits: Kitty Bransfield, Worcester, 186
HRs: Kitty Bransfield, Worcester, 17

International League
President: Bo Needham

Standings	W	L	Pct.	GB	Manager
London Tecumsehs	26	14	.650	—	George Stroud
Hamilton Hams	28	16	.609	—	Charles Collins
Saginaw#	25	23	.521	5	Fred Eddy
Grand Rapids Boers#	18	17	.514	5½	E.W. Dickerson
Chatham Reds	18	26	.409	10	George Black
Port Huron Tunnelites#	12	29	.292	14½	Patsy Flaherty

#Grand Rapids disbanded July 3, causing Port Huron and Saginaw to disband.
The league disbanded July 5.

BA: Frank Hemphill, London, .405
Runs: Frank Hemphill, London, 55
Hits: Frank Norcum, 99

HRs: Charles Jones, London, 5
Frank Hemphill, London, 5

Interstate League
President: Charles B. Powers

Standings	W	L	Pct.	GB	Manager
Dayton Veterans	90	43	.677	—	Bill Armour
Fort Wayne Indians	85	53	.616	7½	Jack Glasscock/Joe Hubbard
Toledo Mud Hens	81	58	.583	12	Charles Strobel
Wheeling Stogies	76	58	.568	14½	E.B. Lytle/Pete Healey
Mansfield Haymakers	67	68	.496	24	D.J. Lowney
Columbus Senators	58	78	.427	33½	James "Bob" Quinn
Youngstown/Marion Glass Blowers#	44	92	.324	47½	Mike Finn/Pat Wright
New Castle Quakers	44	95	.317	49	Pat Wright/John Wadsworth

#Youngstown (28-67) moved to Marion August 5.

Playoff: Fort Wayne 4 games, Dayton 3.

BA: Ervin Beck, Toledo, .360
Runs: Otto Krueger, Fort Wayne, 131
Hits: Ervin Beck, Toledo, 207
HRs: Ed Bradley, Columbus/Anderson, 18

Wins: Cy Swaim, Fort Wayne, 24
Pct: Charles "Bumpus" Jones, Fort Wayne, .786, 11-3

Montana State League
President: William Henry Lucas

Standings	W	L	Pct.	GB	Manager
Great Falls Indians**	39	32	.549	—	Kinsella/John McCloskey
Helena Senators*	38	33	.535	1	Carl Wood/Paddy Ryan/Jack Flannery
Anaconda Serpents	34	36	.485	4½	Jack Grim
Butte Smoke Eaters	30	40	.428	8½	James Powell

BA: Charles McIntrye, Anaconda/Helena, .441
Runs: Dave Zearfoss, Great Falls, 88
Hits: Dave Zearfoss, Great Falls, 106
HRs: Bert Schils, Anaconda, 19
Wins: Bill Salisbury, Helena, 19
Pct: C.E. Wright, Great Falls, .696, 16-7

New York State League
President: John H. Farrell

Standings	W	L	Pct.	GB	Manager
Utica Pentups	74	43	.633	—	Howard Earl
Cortland Wagonmakers	70	43	.621	2	J.D. Roche
Rome Romans	70	44	.617	2½	J. O'Brien
Schenectady Electricians	55	61	.474	18½	Lew Whistler
Albany Senators	54	62	.466	19½	William A. Smith
Binghamton Crickets	43	54	.443	21	Louis Bacon
Troy Washerwomen	48	66	.421	24½	Henry Ramsey
Oswego Grays/					
Elmira Pioneers#	31	72	.300	36	Timothy Shinnick/W. Preston/Abner Powell

#Oswego (20-45) moved to Elmira July 30.

BA: John Dobbs, Utica, .366
Runs: John Dobbs, Utica, 113
Hits: John Dobbs, Utica, 171
HRs: Lew Whistler, Schenectady, 9
Wins: Willard Mains, Rome, 27
Pct: Willard Mains, Rome, .844, 27-5

Virginia League
President: E.H. Cunningham

Standings	W	L	Pct.	GB	Manager
Norfolk Mary Janes***	43	15	.741	—	John A. Smith
Portsmouth Pirates	29	29	.500	14	Pete Weckbecker/Win Clark
Hopewell	29	29	.500	14	Ed Ashenback
Newport News Shipbuilders	23	39	.371	22	W.H. Richardson
Richmond Colts@	21	15	.583	NA	Charles W. Boyer
Petersburg#	8	26	.235	NA	Fred Foster

#Petersburg disbanded June 11.
@Richmond disbanded June 13.

RBIs: Jim Murray, Portsmouth, 98
HRs: Jim Murray, Portsmouth, 11
Pct: Christy Mathewson, Norfolk, .909, 20-2

Western League
President: Thomas J. Hickey

Standings	W	L	Pct.	GB	Manager
Denver Grizzlies	61	44	.581	—	George Tebeau
Des Moines Hawkeyes	59	45	.567	1½	Belden Hill
Sioux City Cornhuskers	49	48	.505	8	Jack Glasscock
Omaha Omahogs	51	53	.490	9½	Pa Rourke
St. Joseph Saints	51	58	.468	12	Byron McKibben
Pueblo Indians	41	64	.390	20	Billy Hulen

BA: Matty McVicker, Omaha, .389
Runs: Sam Strang, St. Joseph, 103
Hits: Joe Schrall, St. Joseph, 149
Wins: Henry Maupin, St. Joseph, 23
Elwood Eyler, Denver, 23
SOs: Tom Hughes, Omaha, 219
Pct: Frank Parvin, Sioux City, .692, 18-8

1901

American League
President: Byron Bancroft Johnson

Standings	W	L	Pct.	GB	Attend.	Manager
Chicago White Stockings	83	53	.610	—	354,350	Clark Griffith
Boston Americans	79	57	.581	4	289,448	Jimmy Collins
Detroit Tigers	74	61	.548	8½	259,430	George Stallings
Philadelphia Athletics	74	62	.544	9	206,329	Connie Mack
Baltimore Orioles	68	65	.511	13½	141,952	John McGraw
Washington Senators	61	73	.455	21	161,661	Jimmy Manning
Cleveland Bluebirds	55	82	.401	28½	131,380	Jimmy McAleer
Milwaukee Brewers	48	89	.350	35½	139,034	Hugh Duffy

BA: Napoleon Lajoie, Philadelphia, .422
Runs: Napoleon Lajoie, Philadelphia, 145
Hits: Napoleon Lajoie, Philadelphia, 229
RBIs: Napoleon Lajoie, Philadelphia, 125
HRs: Napoleon Lajoie, Philadelphia, 13
Wins: Cy Young, Boston, 33
SOs: Cy Young, Boston, 158
ERA: Cy Young, Boston, 1.62
Pct: Clark Griffith, Chicago, .774, 24-7

National League
President: Nicholas E. Young

Standings	W	L	Pct.	GB	Attend.	Manager
Pittsburgh Pirates	90	49	.647	—	251,955	Fred Clarke
Philadelphia Phillies	83	57	.593	7½	234,937	Bill Shettsline
Brooklyn Superbas	79	57	.581	9½	198,200	Ned Hanlon
St. Louis Cardinals	76	64	.543	14½	379,988	Patsy Donovan
Boston Beaneaters	69	69	.500	20½	146,502	Frank Selee
Chicago Cubs	53	86	.381	37	205,071	Tom Loftus
New York Giants	52	85	.380	37	297,650	George Davis
Cincinnati Reds	52	87	.374	38	205,728	Bid McPhee

BA: Jesse Burkett, St. Louis, .382
Runs: Jesse Burkett, St. Louis, 139
Hits: Jesse Burkett, St. Louis, 228
RBIs: Honus Wagner, Pittsburgh, 126
HRs: Sam Crawford, Cincinnati, 16
Wins: Wild Bill Donovan, Brooklyn, 25
SOs: Noodles Hahn, Cincinnati, 239
ERA: Jesse Tannehill, Pittsburgh, 2.18
Pct: Jack Chesbro, Pittsburgh, .677, 21-10

California League
President: James T. Moran

Standings	W	L	Pct.	GB	Manager
San Francisco Wasps	95	66	.573	—	Henry Harris
Los Angeles Angels	81	67	.547	7½	James Morley
Sacramento Senators	66	78	.458	20½	Arthur Beebe
Oakland Commuters	63	94	.401	30	Cal Ewing

BA: Ernest Courtney, Sacramento, .309
Runs: Lou Nordyke, San Francisco, 103
Hits: Henry Krug, San Francisco, 181
HRs: Henry Krug, San Francisco, 15
Wins: Ham Iburg, San Francisco, 37
SOs: Oscar Jones, Los Angeles, 180
ERA: Frank McPartlin, Los Angeles, 0.90
Pct: Charley Doyle, Sacramento, .625, 20-12

Connecticut League
President: Tim H. Murnane

Standings	W	L	Pct.	GB	Manager
Bristol Woodchoppers	63	41	.606	—	Frank Reisling
Bridgeport Orators	61	43	.587	2	Jim O'Rourke
Norwich Witches	62	46	.574	3	Jack Tighe
Meriden Silverites	56	48	.538	7	W.R. Reilly
New Haven Blues	56	54	.509	10	James Canavan
Waterbury Hustlers	47	60	.439	17½	Roger Connor
New London Whalers	45	63	.417	20	P.L. Shea
Derby Angels	37	72	.330	28½	Jerry Denny

BA: Dougherty, Bridgeport, .375
Runs: Danny Murphy, Norwich, 104
Hits: Hi Ladd, Derby, 171
HRs: Danny Murphy, Norwich, 12
Frank Woodruff, Norwich/
New London, 12

Eastern League
President: Patrick T. Powers

Standings	W	L	Pct.	GB	Manager
Rochester Bronchos	89	49	.645	—	Al Buckenberger
Toronto Maple Leafs	74	52	.587	9	Edward Barrow
Providence Clamdiggers	73	58	.557	12½	William Murray
Worcester Quakers	62	64	.492	21	Mal Kittridge
Montreal Royals	64	66	.492	21	Charles Dooley
Buffalo Bisons	40	73	.354	36½	George Carey/Thomas E. Burns/
					Walter Burnham/Jim Franklin/Joe Franklin
Syracuse Stars/					
Brockton B's#	45	87	.341	41	Frank Leonard
Hartford Wooden Nutmegs@	58	56	.509	NA	Billy Shindle

#Syracuse (28-39) moved to Brockton July 25.
@Hartford disbanded September 10.

BA: Homer Smoot, Worcester, .356
Runs: Billy Lush, Rochester, 137
Hits: George Barclay, Rochester, 194
HRs: Reddy Grey, Buffalo/Rochester, 12

New England League
President: Tim H. Murnane

Standings	W	L	Pct.	GB	Manager
Portland	55	37	.598	—	Thomas P. Burns
Manchester	48	39	.552	4½	John A. Smith
Lowell Tigers	47	47	.500	9	Fred Lake
Haverhill Hustlers	45	48	.484	10½	F.H. Burrill
Lewiston	42	50	.457	13	A.G. "Fred" Doe
Nashua	39	49	.443	14	
Bangor/Brockton B's#	24	16	.600	NA	Walter Burnham
Augusta/Lynn Live Oaks@	11	25	.306	NA	Jack Leighton

#Bangor (22-14) moved to Brockton June 30, then disbanded July 6.
@Augusta (10-23) moved to Lynn June 30, then disbanded July 6.

BA: John A. Smith, Manchester, .363
Runs: John Wiley, Portland, 94
Hits: Jim Barry, Portland, 141
HRs: Nick Wise, Lewiston/Haverhill, 12

New York State League
President: John H. Farrell

Standings	W	L	Pct.	GB	Manager
Albany Senators	72	43	.626	—	Thomas O'Brien
Utica Pent-ups	68	44	.607	2½	Wally Taylor
Binghamton Bingoes	69	45	.605	2½	Charles "Count" Campau
Rome Romans	62	47	.569	7	George Wheeler
Schenectady Electricians	65	50	.565	7	Howard Earl
Troy Trojans	46	62	.426	22½	Louis Bacon
Cortland/Waverly					
Wagonmakers#	36	68	.346	30½	William A. Smith
Ilion Typewriters	23	82	.219	44	Timothy Shinnick

#Cortland (22-34) moved to Waverly July 11.

BA: Hugh Ahern, Troy, .380
Runs: Chick Cargo, Albany, 110
Hits: Jim Jones, Albany, 154

Wins: George Merritt, Utica, 23
Pct: George Merritt, Utica, .742, 23-8

Pacific Northwest League
President: William Henry Lucas

Standings	W	L	Pct.	GB	Manager
Portland Webfoots	73	35	.675	—	Jack Grim
Tacoma Tigers	57	51	.530	16	John McCloskey
Seattle Clamdiggers	45	63	.417	28	Daniel Dugdale
Spokane Blue Stockings	41	67	.379	32	Tom Turner/Joe Marshall/Maloney

BA: Charles McIntyre, Tacoma, .341
Runs: Joe McCarthy, Tacoma, 98
Hits: Charles McIntyre, Tacoma, 149
HRs: Joe Marshall, Spokane, 15

SBs: Joe Tinker, Portland, 37
  Joe McCarthy, Tacoma, 37
Wins: Clyde Engel, Portland, 28
  Bill Salisbury, Portland, 28
SOs: Jimmy St. Vrain, Tacoma, 299
Pct: Clyde Engel, Portland, .718, 28-11

Southern Association
Presidents: R.W. Kent/John B. Nicklin/W.J. Boles

Standings	W	L	Pct.	GB	Manager
Nashville Vols	78	45	.634	—	Newt Fisher
Little Rock Travelers	76	45	.628	1	Michael Finn
Memphis Egyptians	75	48	.610	3	Charley Frank
New Orleans Pelicans	68	56	.548	10½	Abner Powell
Shreveport Giants	55	66	.455	22	George Reed
Birmingham Barons	45	70	.391	29	Sam Mills/Charley Moss
Chattanooga Lookouts	47	73	.392	29½	Lew Whistler
Selma Christians	37	78	.322	37	E.T. Peters

BA: Frank Huelsman, Shreveport, .392
Runs: Ed Abbaticchio, Nashville, 127
Hits: Frank Huelsman, Shreveport, 191

HRs: Jim Ballantyne, Nashville, 11
Wins: Guy Sample, Shreveport/Nashville, 25
Pct: Harry Allemang, Little Rock, .833, 20-4

Three-I League
President: Michael Sexton

Standings	W	L	Pct.	GB	Manager
Terre Haute Hottentots	72	39	.649	—	William Krieg
Bloomington Blues	68	44	.607	4½	William Connors
Cedar Rapids Rabbits	67	45	.598	5½	Belden Hill
Rockford Red Sox	57	55	.509	15½	Hugh Nicol
Davenport River Rats	51	61	.455	21½	William Smith
Evansville River Rats	47	65	.420	25½	Lou Camp/R.B. Hubbard/
					J.C. "Con" Strothers/Phil Reccius/
					Sam Kennedy
Rock Island Islanders	45	66	.405	27	Henry Tate/Harry Sage/Dom Mullaney
Decatur Commodores	40	72	.357	32½	Tom Kieranan/Frank Badger

BA: Davey Jones, Rockford, .384
Runs: George Nill, Davenport, 125
Hits: Frank Roth, Evansville, 141
HRs: Frank Roth, Evansville, 27

Wins: Eugene McGreevy, Bloomington, 28
SOs: Claude Elliott, Rockford, 297
Pct: Mordecai "Three Finger" Brown,
  Terre Haute, .758, 25-8

Inter-Mountain League
President: William Henry Lucas

Standings	W	L	Pct.	GB	Manager
Ogden	31	10	.756	—	
Salt Lake City	26	15	.634	5	
Lagoon	23	19	.548	8½	
Park City	3	39	.071	28½	

Virginia-North Carolina League
President: E.H. Cunningham

Standings	W	L	Pct.	GB	Manager
Raleigh Senators**	59	46	.562	—	George "King" Kelley
Wilmington Giants*	58	46	.558	½	H.B. Peschau
Newport News Shipbuilders/					
Charlotte Hornets#	50	55	.476	9	Ed Ashenback
Portsmouth Browns/					
Tarboro Tartars@	42	58	.420	24½	Win Clark
Norfolk Skippers+	31	27	.534	NA	Ed Gilligan/William Spratt
Richmond Bluebirds+	27	35	.435	NA	Barley Kain

#Newport News (32-26) moved to Charlotte June 21.
@Portsmouth (22-31) moved to Tarboro June 21.
+Norfolk and Richmond disbanded in early July. The league continued as the North
Carolina League until disbanding August 17.

BA: John Mullen, Norfolk, .342
Runs: James Smith, Norfolk, 61
Hits: John Mullen, Norfolk, 93
HRs: Joe Staley, Raleigh, 10

Wins: J.H. Dannehower, Norfolk, 17
SOs: J.H. Dannehower, Norfolk, 156
Pct: J.H. Dannehower, Norfolk, .708, 17-7

Western Association
President: William F. Myer

Standings	W	L	Pct.	GB	Manager
Louisville Colonels/					
Grand Rapids@	84	54	.609	—	Walter Wilmot
Dayton Old Soldiers	84	55	.604	½	William Armour
Toledo Mud Hens	78	61	.564	6½	Charles Strobel
Grand Rapids Woodworkers/					
Wheeling Stogies#	70	64	.522	12	George Ellis/Bill White
Fort Wayne Railroaders	74	68	.521	12	George Miller
Indianapolis Hoosiers	57	79	.419	26	Bill Watkins
Columbus Senators	55	86	.390	30½	Frank Metz/Jimmy Gardner/Ed Zinram
Marion	53	88	.376	32½	Pat Wright

#Grand Rapids (22-13) moved to Wheeling June 3.
@Louisville (38-23) moved to Grand Rapids July 2.

BA: Tuck Turner, Toledo, .348
Runs: Natty Nattress, Fort Wayne, 124

Hits: Pat Meaney, Mansfield, 181
HRs: Tuck Turner, Toledo, 14

Western League
President: Thomas J. Hickey

Standings	W	L	Pct.	GB	Manager
Kansas City Blues	79	44	.642	—	George Tebeau
St. Paul Saints	69	54	.561	10	Jimmy Ryan
St. Joseph Saints	69	58	.543	12	Byron McKibben
Denver Grizzlies	60	59	.504	17	Buck Weaver/Tom Brown/Bill Everitt
Omaha Omahogs	61	62	.496	18	Pa Rourke
Minneapolis Millers	56	62	.475	20½	Jack Glasscock/Beall
Des Moines Hawkeyes	48	75	.390	31	Mike Kelly
Colorado Springs					
Millionaires	45	73	.381	31½	Billy Hulen

BA: Frank Hemphill, Colorado Springs, .332
Runs: Bill Hartman, Kansas City, 101
Hits: Dakin Miller, Kansas City, 153
HRs: Dave Brain, St. Paul, 13

Wins: Henry Maupin, St. Joseph, 31
SOs: Fred Glade, Des Moines, 196
Pct: Bob Ewing, Kansas City, .808, 21-5

No-Hitters 1883-1901

1883

Date	Pitcher	Team	League	Opponent	Score
7-25	Old Hoss Radbourn	Providence	National	Cleveland	8-0
9-13	One Arm Daily	Cleveland	National	Philadelphia	1-0
9-26	Sam Kimber	Brooklyn	Interstate	Reading	13-0 (7)

1884

Date	Pitcher	Team	League	Opponent	Score
5-24	Al Atkisson	Philadelphia	American Assoc.	Pittsburgh	10-1
5-29	Ed Morris	Columbus	American Assoc.	Pittsburgh	5-0
6-5	Frank Mountain	Columbus	American Assoc.	Washington	12-0
6-25	Ed Dugan	Richmond	Eastern	Newark	9-1 (8)
6-26	William Fox	Trenton	Eastern	Harrisburg	2-1
6-27	Larry Corcoran	Chicago	National	Providence	6-0
7-31	Elmer Foster	St. Paul	Northwestern	Milwaukee	2-1 (10)
8-4	Pud Galvin	Buffalo	National	Detroit	18-0
8-26	Dick Burns	Cincinnati	Union Assoc.	Kansas City	3-1
9-28	Ed Cushman	Milwaukee	Union Assoc.	Washington	5-0
10-4	Sam Kimber	Brooklyn	American Assoc.	Toledo	0-0 (10)

1885

Date	Pitcher	Team	League	Opponent	Score
5-29	Charlie Parsons	Birmingham	Southern	Augusta	3-0
5-30	Thomas Ramsey	Chattanooga	Southern	Nashville	4-1
6-29	John Hofford	Augusta	Southern	Memphis	3-0
7-27	John Clarkson	Chicago	National	Providence	4-0
8-22	Bob Barr	Washington	Eastern	Richmond	3-0
8-28	John Pendergrass	Rochester	New York State	Utica	4-0
8-29	Charlie Ferguson	Philadelphia	National	Providence	1-0
9-3	Phenomenal Smith	Newark	Eastern	Baltimore	(P)

1886

Date	Pitcher	Team	League	Opponent	Score
4-25	Billy Hart	Leavenworth	Western	St. Louis	0-3
5-1	Al Atkisson	Philadelphia	American Assoc.	New York	3-2
6-8	Doyle	Haverhill	New England	Boston	
7-16	Tuckerman	Brockton	New England	Boston	4-2
7-24	Adonis Terry	Brooklyn	American Assoc.	St. Louis	1-0
8-5	Ed Knouff	Memphis	Southern	Macon	3-0
8-6	Matt Kilroy	Baltimore	American Assoc.	Pittsburgh	6-0
8-12	Mike Hughes	Waterbury	Eastern	Bridgeport	4-1
8-16	Frank Wells	Atlanta	Southern	Charleston	6-0
8-17	Frank Gruber	Lynn	New England	Boston	3-0
8-17	J.H. Green	Oswego	International	Hamilton	5-1
8-18	John Shafer	Atlanta	Southern	Savannah	2-0 (6)
8-26	Murphy	Eau Claire	Northwestern	Minneapolis	

1887

Date	Pitcher	Team	League	Opponent	Score
8-21	George Borchers	Oakland	California	SF Haverly	7-0

1888

Date	Pitcher	Team	League	Opponent	Score
5-27	Adonis Terry	Brooklyn	American Assoc.	Louisville	4-0
6-6	Henry Porter	Kansas City	American Assoc.	Baltimore	4-0
7-6	George Hayes	Rochester	International Assoc.	London	6-0
7-14	Eddie Lorrigan	Stockton	California	SF Pioneers	8-0
7-26	Ed Seward	Philadelphia	American Assoc.	Cincinnati	12-2
7-31	Gus Weyhing	Philadelphia	American Assoc.	Kansas City	4-0
8-30	Landmann	Jersey City	Central	Allentown	
10-10	George Borchers	Stockton	California	Oakland	1-1

1889

Date	Pitcher	Team	League	Opponent	Score
6-18	Ed Cushman	Toledo	International Assoc.	Rochester	8-0
6-27	Burchard	Mansfield	Tri-State	Dayton	5-0
7-14	Philip Knell	St. Joseph	Western Assoc.	Sioux City	11-0
7-29	Willie McGill	Evansville	Central Interstate	Davenport	3-0
9-29	Martin Duke	Minneapolis	Western Assoc.	St. Paul	5-1

1890

Date	Pitcher	Team	League	Opponent	Score
6-21	Silver King	Chicago	Player's	Brooklyn	0-1 (8)
7-25	Cy Young	Canton	Tri-State	McKeesport	
9-15	Cannonball Titcomb	Rochester	American Assoc.	Syracuse	7-0
	Frank Killen	Minneapolis	Western Assoc.		

1891

Date	Pitcher	Team	League	Opponent	Score
4-27	Tom Vickery	Milwaukee	Western Assoc.	Denver	1-0
6-22	Tom Lovett	Brooklyn	National	New York	4-0
7-31	Amos Rusie	New York	National	Brooklyn	6-0
8-22	Billy Hart	Sioux City	Western Assoc.	Omaha	2-1
10-4	Ted Breitenstein	St. Louis	American Assoc.	Louisville	8-0
	William Bond	Omaha	Western Assoc.	Sioux City	

1892

Date	Pitcher	Team	League	Opponent	Score
5-30	Michael Kilroy	Providence	Eastern	Philadelphia	6-0
7-8	Darby	Omaha	Western	Columbus	3-1
8-6	Jack Stivetts	Boston	National	Brooklyn	11-0
8-22	Ben Sanders	Louisville	National	Baltimore	6-2
10-15	Bumpus Jones	Cincinnati	National	Pittsburgh	7-1

1893

Date	Pitcher	Team	League	Opponent	Score
8-16	Bill Hawke	Baltimore	National	Washington	5-0

1894

Date	Pitcher	Team	League	Opponent	Score
7-12	Patrick Fox	Pottsville	Pennsylvania State	Harrisburg	7-0
7-25	John See	Hazelton	Pennsylvania State	Pottsville	1-0

1897

Date	Pitcher	Team	League	Opponent	Score
9-18	Cy Young	Cleveland	National	Cincinnati	6-0

1898

Date	Pitcher	Team	League	Opponent	Score
4-22	Ted Breitenstein	Cincinnati	National	Pittsburgh	11-0
4-22	Jim Hughes	Baltimore	National	Boston	8-0
6-5	Bumpus Jones	Columbus	Western	Kansas City	0-2
7-8	Red Donahue	Philadelphia	National	Boston	5-0
7-27	H.G. McNeely	Minneapolis	Western	Columbus	6-0
8-20	William Phyle	St. Paul	Western	Milwaukee	11-0
8-21	Walter Thornton	Chicago	National	Brooklyn	2-0

1899

Date	Pitcher	Team	League	Opponent	Score
5-8	George Gray	Buffalo	Western	Indianapolis	1-0
5-25	Deacon Phillippe	Louisville	National	New York	7-0
5-25	Red Brown	Ottumwa	Western Assoc.	Rockford	4-0
6-3	Red Brown	Ottumwa	Western Assoc.	Dubuque	5-1
6-9	Newton	Indianapolis	Western	Milwaukee	5-0
7-29	George Harper	Watsonville	California	Oakland	6-0
	Watkins	Dayton	Interstate		
	R. Smith	Mansfield	Interstate		

1900

Date	Pitcher	Team	League	Opponent	Score
4-19	Morris "Doc" Amole	Buffalo	American	Detroit	8-0
6-8	Earl Moore	Dayton	Interstate	Mansfield	1-0
6-16	Win Kellum	Indianapolis	American	Chicago	6-0
6-18	Hank Morrison	Portsmouth	Virginia	Norfolk	
6-21	Christy Mathewson	Norfolk	Virginia	Newport News	1-0
7-12	Noodles Hahn	Cincinnati	National	Philadelphia	4-0
7-28	Pete Dowling	Milwaukee	American	Cleveland	5-0
8-31	John McDonald	Sioux City	Western	Denver	5-0

1901

Date	Pitcher	Team	League	Opponent	Score
5-3	John McCloskey	Little Rock	Southern Assoc.	Memphis	7-0
5-9	Earl Moore	Cleveland	American	Chicago	2-4 (10)
7-15	Christy Mathewson	New York	National	St. Louis	5-0
9-1	Clarence Wright	Dayton	Western Assoc.	Columbus	9-0
9-4	Clarence Wright	Dayton	Western Assoc.	Grand Rapids	2-0 (C)

Number in parentheses indicates innings if other than nine; "P" indicates perfect game; "C" indicates no-hitters in consecutive starts.

THIS DATE IN MINOR LEAGUE HISTORY — 1883-1901

April 21, 1883, William (Yank) Robinson of Saginaw, Northwestern League, hit two doubles and a triple in the sixth inning of a game against Dayton in which Saginaw scored 20 runs. Robinson scored three times in the frame.

May 1883, The first black player in the minor leagues, Moses Fleetwood Walker, began his season with Toledo of the Northwestern League.

May 16, 1883, In a game played under artificial light, George Pensinger's Paint Shop defeated Clay Henninger's nine in Chambersburg, Pennsylvania. The score of the contest is not known, but the light was supplied by a portable dynamo which rested on a flat car.

June 2, 1883, The first game under electric lights was played in Fort Wayne, Indiana. Fort Wayne beat Quincy, Illinois 19-11 in a seven inning Northwestern League game.

January 5, 1884, The International League was formed at the Bingham House in Philadelphia and christened the Eastern League. Franchises were allotted to Domestic of Newark, Allentown, Monumental of Baltimore, Harrisburg, Quicksteps of Wilmington, Actives of Reading, and Virginia of Richmond. Henry N. Diddlebock of Philadelphia was elected president. In 1885 the league was known as the New York State League and in 1886 the International League. Through the years it was also known as the International Association, the Eastern Association, the Eastern League and the New International League.

May 16, 1884, The Georgia State League was organized.

September 19, 1884, Dayton and Ironton played an Ohio State Association game in 47 minutes at Dayton, Ohio.

February 12, 1885, The Western League was organized in Indianapolis, with Indianapolis, Kansas City, Cleveland, Milwaukee, Toledo and Omaha the original clubs.

April 21, 1885, The first one-hitter in the Southern League was thrown by Atlanta's Tom Sullivan at Macon. Centerfielder Keinzmann singled for Macon's only hit.

May 3, 1885, The uniforms for Syracuse, New York State League, were not ready for their opening game with Rochester. The Stars played while attired in nine different suits.

May 27, 1885, A game between Allentown and Lancaster was postponed on account of only one attendee being in the stands. A large parade kept people away.

May 29, 1885, Charlie Parsons of Birmingham tossed the first no-hitter in the Southern League, against Augusta at Birmingham.

June 3, 1886, One of the first verified no-hit games in the minor leagues was pitched by Billy Crowell of Altoona in the Pennsylvania State League. In the same game, Wilkes-Barre pitcher Staltz allowed only one safety.

June 18, 1886, Pitcher Mark Baldwin of Duluth struck out twelve successive batters in a Northwestern League game against St. Paul. A total of 30 strikeouts were recorded in the nine-inning game. Baldwin, later with Cap Anson's Chicago team, fanned 18 for Duluth and Fitzsimmons struck out 12 for St. Paul.

July 4, 1886, A game between Leadville and St. Joseph of the Western League was delayed for 30 minutes by a snow storm in the Colorado city.

April 29, 1887, The first Ladies Day in the history of minor league baseball was held in New Orleans, the idea being conceived by Abner Powell, early-day manager in the Southern League. Powell is also credited with inventing the rain check.

May 4, 1887, Binghamton defeated Utica 26-8 in the International League, with pitcher Bones Ely going 6-for-6 at the plate.

May 17, 1887, Mobile of the Southern League disbanded, Memphis having scored 119 runs in four games against the Alabama club. In a 38-8 win, Memphis tallied 16 runs in the fourth inning. Memphis also won a 31-5 debacle.

May 30, 1887, Ledell Titcomb lost two games in one day in two different cities for Jersey City in the International League. In the morning he was beaten by Mickey Hughes of Newark 3-2 at Jersey City, and in the afternoon he lost 11-1 to George Stovey at Newark.

June 15, 1887, Lowell, New England League, was routed Haverhill by the score of 41-7 in a seven-inning game.

June 25, 1887, James "Bug" Holliday of Topeka collected six hits in seven trips in a Western League contest. Holliday hit .422 in 98 games, winning a trip to the major leagues.

July 4, 1887, Hamilton leftfielder Joseph W. Knight became the first International League player to hit three home runs in a game. Hamilton won the game, at Buffalo, 15-4.

January 18, 1888, The Texas League was formally organized in Houston, Texas. The original six clubs were Austin, Dallas, Ft. Worth, Galveston, Houston and San Antonio.

July 28, 1888, In Austin, Texas League, a wild bull charged the outfielders of the Austin team during the game. The contest was ended at that point.

May 9, 1889, Outfielder William Murphy of Hartford, Atlantic Association, hit three home runs in a game against New Haven.

June 9, 1889, Johnny Crooks, an infielder with Omaha, Western Association, became the first player in Organized Ball to hit four home runs in one game, achieving the feat against St. Paul. Crooks also had a single to bat in 13 runs in the contest, won by Omaha 19-15.

June 27, 1889, Fitzgerald hit two home runs in one inning for Wilkes-Barre in the Atlantic Association.

July 4, 1889, Austin swept both games from Houston in the Texas League's first twinbill.

September 2, 1889, James Thomas McGuire, catcher for Toronto, International Association, hit three home runs and a single off Hamilton pitcher Gibbs, leading the Canucks to a 22-5 win.

April 30, 1890, Cy Young broke into Organized Ball with Canton of the Tri-State League, hurling the first game of a doubleheader against Wheeling and recording his first victory by a 4-2 score. Cy gave but three hits, striking out eight and walking one.

May 24, 1890, Ledell Titcomb, Toronto, International Association, shut out Buffalo 5-0 on three hits in the morning and then won 1-0 in the afternoon, scattering nine safeties.

June 10, 1890, The first Texas League expired.

July 25, 1890, Cy Young pitched a no-hitter for Canton of the Tri-State League against McKeesport. He fanned 18. This game, the last Young pitched in the minors, gained him a job with Cleveland in the National League.

May 16, 1891, Tacoma and Seattle played a 22-inning game in the Pacific Northwest League, with Tacoma winning 6-5. Neil Donahue hurled the full 22 innings. This was the second longest game played at the time. Harvard and Manchester had played a 24-inning scoreless tie on May 11, 1877.

June 9, 1891, Manager Bill McGunnigle, Providence, Eastern Association, fined pitcher Sullivan $5 for not running out a missed third strike, took him out of the game, fined him $10 for his back talk, then suspended him indefinitely.

June 27, 1891, Outfielder Joe Hornung of Buffalo, Eastern Association, was fined $20 by umpire Herm Doescher for telling the arbiter he should wear glasses when making close decisions.

October 6, 1891, The Providence ball park was sold for $300 to Warner Brown of New York City.

November 23, 1891, The California League season, which began March 22, finally came to an end. George Harper won 47 games and Nick Lookabaugh 43 for San Jose. The two hurlers accounted for all of their club's 90 victories. San Jose played 147 games.

May 21, 1892, Ollie Pickering, Houston, Texas League, made seven consecutive singles in one game against Ft. Worth.

May 31, 1892, Danny Cronin, Pawtucket, New England League, hit four homers in one game, the only ones he would hit during the season.

June 6, 1892, Willie Keeler made his pro debut as a lefthanded shortstop for Binghamton in the Eastern League. He made one hit and one error.

June 19, 1892, Charles "Bumpus" Jones won his first 15 decisions for Joliet, Illinois-Indiana League, then racked up nine more after Terre Haute halted him on this date. He had 10 shutouts, including three in a row. He had 24 wins and five defeats for Joliet, and won three and lost four for Atlanta after the Two-I League collapsed. Purchased by Cincinnati, Jones made one appearance with the Reds on the last day of the season, and he startled the baseball world by pitching a no-hitter against Pittsburgh, winning over Mark Baldwin.

July 22, 1892, Galveston, Texas League, defeated Houston 9-8 in a five-inning regulation game under the lights. The next Texas League night game would come in 1930.

January 1893, The first interleague post season series in the minor leagues was played. In 19 games played during the month, the 1892 champions of the California and Pacific Northwest Leagues met. San Jose, the California champ, defeated Portland.

July 21, 1893, Joseph Knight, Binghamton, Eastern League, made six hits in one game, including a double and three triples.

July 25, 1893, Billy Bottenus, Springfield, Eastern League, hit three home runs in two innings (two in the fourth and one in the fifth) in game with Binghamton. But, he didn't get to bat again because he became involved in a rhubarb with the umpire and was banished from the field.

July 30, 1893, At Macon, Georgia, Twitchell threw a ball 405 feet and two inches.

September 12, 1893, Springfield and Albany played an Eastern League game at Holyoke to avoid conflict with bicycle races in Springfield. Springfield won the contest 11-9.

November 9, 1893, San Francisco and Oakland played a California League game in 47 minutes at San Francisco.

July 30, 1894, Buck Freeman of Haverhill, New England League, hit four home runs and a double in five at bats. The next afternoon, Freeman belted two more round-trippers. Freeman totaled 34 homers and led the league in batting at .386.

August 31, 1894, Brothers Matt Kilroy of Syracuse and Mike Kilroy of Allentown faced each other in the Eastern League, and the first named won 6-4.

February 10, 1895, John Peter "Honus" Wagner, a 20-year-old coal miner and barber's apprentice from Carnegie, Pennsylvania, signed a contract with Steubenville, Interstate League, to play baseball for $35 a month. Wagner hit .402 in 44 games. He was later purchased by Edward Barrow, owner of the Paterson, New Jersey club of the Atlantic League. Wagner would play with four clubs in 1895.

April 27, 1895, Fall River opened the New England League season by trimming Lewiston 29-1.

May 1, 1895, The new Western League season opened. At Milwaukee, Minneapolis defeated the home team before over 5,000 fans by a score of 4-3. St. Paul, managed by Charles "The Old Roman" Comiskey, won 4-3 in Kansas City. Veteran pitcher Tony Mullane played first base for St. Paul.

May 12, 1895, Billy Bottenus of Buffalo, Eastern League, smashed four home runs and a double in six at bats against Wilkes-Barre. The Bisons won 18-13 in seven innings.

May 28, 1895, Hercules Burnett of Evansville, Southern League, ripped four round-trippers at home.

May 29, 1895, Billy Bottenus, Buffalo, Eastern League, batted in 12 runs in a game with Wilkes-Barre.

June 24, 1895, Umpire John Gaffney forfeited an Eastern League game at Rochester to Springfield because both balls had been "used up" and there were no more. Second baseman Jerry O'Brien hit one out of the park in the seventh inning. The other was played with until it split apart.

July 23, 1895, Perry Werden of Minneapolis, Western League, clouted four home runs and a single in five times at bat.

August 1, 1895, Harry Hulen, Minneapolis, Western League, scored six runs in a game against Grand Rapids without having an official at bat. In addition, Hulen stole five bases. He was given six bases on balls.

November 29, 1895, Charles "Pacer" Smith, 38, a former amateur and professional baseball player who served with numerous teams from 1876 to 1893, was executed by hanging at Decatur, Illinois, for the murder of his sister-in-law and daughter on September 28, 1895.

May 11, 1896, Napoleon Lajoie drew parental wrath when he quit his job as a hack driver in Woonsocket, Rhode Island, to play baseball for Fall River of the New England League for $70 a month. Lajoie played his first game in center field. A few months later, The Phillies paid $1,500 for outfielder Phil Geier with Lajoie coming as a "throw-in" to seal the bargain.

July 4, 1896, Edward Barrow, owner of the Paterson club in the Atlantic League, introduced night baseball in the East, as Paterson played Wilmington under some improvised lights in the Delaware city.

July 5, 1896, In the Western League, St. Paul massacred Minneapolis 41-8, the winners scoring in every inning. Jack Glasscock, St. Paul first baseman and a former major league player, had eight hits in nine at bats, including two doubles and a home run, and scored seven runs. The Apostles belted eight homers in the game.

September 8, 1896, Howard Earl, acting manager of Wilkes-Barre, Eastern League, threw a wrapped-up uniform in the face of president Rogert. Earl didn't boss the Barons the next day. He also drew a $100 fine.

September 26, 1896, Providence, Eastern League, defeated Buffalo 11-4 to win the Steinert Cup Series, four games to two.

October 1, 1896, Minneapolis, Western League, defeated Indianapolis 13-11 to win the Detroit Free Press Cup Series, four games to two.

October 3, 1896, Paterson, Atlantic League, defeated Hartford 4-3 to win the Soby Cup Series, five games to two.

April, 1897, Connie Mack assumed management of Milwaukee in the Western League. Mack played in 27 games, seeing action at first base and behind the plate. He batted .254 in his last year in Organized Ball as a player.

July, 1897, Fire destroyed the Rochester, Eastern League, ball park. The Jingos finished their home schedule in Montreal with an agreement to return to Rochester in 1898. When the season was over, Montreal refused to give up its new team. Rochester was forced to buy the Scranton franchise in order to stay in the league.

August 6, 1897, The first three minor league players to hit home runs in succession in the same inning were Harry Steinfeldt (later the third baseman in the immortal Chicago Cubs infield of Tinker, Evers and Chance), Davis and Macauley of Detroit. They performed the feat against Kansas City pitcher Abbey in a Western League game.

May 10, 1898, The Texas closed up for the season.

May 22, 1898, Atlanta of the Southern League disbanded, immediately causing the league to fold.

June 18, 1898, Springfield, Eastern League, players struck for salary and forfeited their first game to Rochester. The team played its second contest when Charles Shean, an Eastern League director, guaranteed salaries for a day.

June 26, 1898, In a 21-inning game at Peoria, the home club scored five runs in the final frame to defeat St. Joseph 8-4 in a Western Association game. Both clubs went scoreless for 16 innings, between the fifth and 21st. Joe McGinnity pitched for Peoria.

July 5, 1898, Edward Barrow signed Lizzie Stroud, a lady pitcher, to go around the circuit with his Paterson team of the Atlantic League. Miss Stroud, renamed Lizzie Arlington by Barrow, was an accomplished pupil of Jack Stivetts, famous hurler for the Baltimore Orioles. She played with Reading.

September 4, 1899, On the last day of the season in the New England League, Manchester and Portland played six games, starting at 9 a.m. Two games were played before lunch and four more came in the afternoon. All were nine inning games except the sixth, which terminated after two innings when Portland walked off the field in protest of an umpire's decision. Manchester, which won the first five games, was given the sixth by forfeit. Newport, the league leader, scheduled a tripleheader with Taunton and won all three games. League officials then stepped in and threw out seven of the final day games involving Newport and Manchester and allowed just one victory for each club. Newport won the league championship.

October 11, 1899, The Western League changed its name to the American League, occupied the vacant Cleveland territory by purchasing the ball park there, and then decided to move Charles Comiskey's St. Paul club to Chicago.

December 4, 1899, The nine-month California League season ended with Sacramento the pennant winner with a record of 48-30. The league had many franchises changes during the year and only four clubs completed the season.

April 19, 1900, Morris "Doc" Amole pitched a no-hit game for Buffalo in the American League on opening day against Detroit, recording the first shutout in the loop's history. Buffalo won 8-0.

April 21, 1900, Chicago began its American League existence by losing its home opener to Milwaukee, managed by Connie Mack, 5-4 in ten innings The game drew a crowd of 5,000.

May 5, 1900, Pitcher Youngie Johnson, in a Western League game at Pueblo, Colorado, made an unassisted triple play against St. Joseph, the first in minor league history.

May 29, 1900, Judson Smith of Buffalo, American League, committed seven errors at shortstop in a game which Cleveland won 5-0. Smith had one putout and five assists in addition to his seven bobbles.

June 21, 1900, Christy Mathewson, playing under the name of Mathews, pitched a no-hit game for Norfolk of the Virginia League against Newport News, winning 1-0. Norfolk scored its lone run in the ninth inning when Matty's manager, John A. Smith, batted the tally across the plate.

October 14, 1900, The American League decided to occupy the vacant territory of Washington and Baltimore, also placing clubs in Boston and Philadelphia several weeks later.

January 30, 1901, The Three-I League was formally organized at a meeting in Peoria, Illinois, with the following cities being awarded franchises: Cedar Rapids, Davenport, Rock Island, Rockford, Peoria, Decatur, Bloomington and Terre Haute. Evansville replaced Peoria before the league season opened on May 2. Michael Sexton was elected president. The first season consisted of a 110-game schedule.

May, 1901, Early in the 1901 season, Abner Powell fired every member of his tail-end New Orleans club of the Southern Association, then recruited an entirely new team on the same day.

May 5, 1901, Mordecai "Three Finger" Brown pitched his first pro game for Terre Haute against Rockford in the Three-I League, winning 12-2. Brown would go 25-8 in his first pro season.

September 5, 1901, The National Association of Professional Baseball Leagues was formed at a meeting at the Leland Hotel in Chicago. Representatives from seven leagues were in attendance. Patrick T. Powers was elected president; he would reign from 1901 to 1909.

Non-Signatory 19th Century Leagues

1877
International Association
League Alliance

1878
International Association
New England Association
Pacific League

1879
National Association
Northwestern League
Pacific/California League

1880
National Association
Pacific/California League

1881
Eastern Association
League Alliance
California League

1882
American Alliance
Eastern Association
League Alliance
Northwestern League
Western League

1883
American Alliance
Eastern Association
* Interstate Association
Mass. State Association

1884
Connecticut State League
Mass. State Association

1885
Colorado State League
Connecticut State League
East. New England League
Interstate League
New England League
Northwestern League
Ontario League
So. New England League
Virginia League

1886
California League
Canadian League
Hudson River League
New Hamp. State League
Penn. State Association
Virginia League

1887
Eastern League
Kansas State League
Montana State League
Northeastern League
 aka Vermont State League
Northern Michigan League
Penn. State Association
Southwestern League

1888
Central New York League
Central Penn. League
Connecticut State League
Eastern Int. League
Hudson River League
Indiana State League
New Eng. Interstate League
Ohio State League

1889
Colorado State League

Eastern Interstate League
Illinois-Iowa League
Middle States League
New England League
Ohio State League
Southern League
Western Penn. League

1890
California League
Colorado State League
Eastern Interstate League
 aka Penn. State League
Illinois-Iowa League
Indiana State League
New Brunswick League
New England League
New York-Penn. League
New York State League
Pacific Northwest League
Rhode Island League
Upper Peninsula League
* Western Association
Western Interstate League
Western New York League

1891
Central New Jersey League
Colorado State League
Connecticut State League
Illinois-Iowa League
Michigan League
Northwestern League
Pacific Interstate League
Pacific Northwestern
Penn. State League
Southwestern League
Tri-State League
Upper Peninsula League
Wisconsin State League

1892
California League
Central New Jersey
Florida State League
Montana State League
Nebraska State League
Ohio State League
South Atlantic League
Texas League
Wisconsin-Michigan

1893
Michigan State League
Mississippi State League

1894
Interstate League
Michigan State League
Mississippi State League
New York State League
Tri-State League

1895
Colorado State League
Eastern Interstate League
Eastern Iowa League
Iron and Oil League
Kansas State League
New York State League
Northern Michigan League
Ohio State League
South Atlantic League
Southern Illinois League
Southwest Interstate
Upper Peninsula League
Western Interstate League

1896
Blue Grass League

Canadian League
Central Connecticut
Central Penn. League
Colorado State League
Illinois League
Indiana State League
International League
Kansas State League
Kentucky-Indiana League
Maine State League
Michigan State League
Missouri State League
New York State League
Ohio-West Virginia League
Penn. State League
Pennyrile League
Schuykill Valley League
Southern Illinois League
Wisconsin State League

1897
Arizona League
Arkansas League
Canadian League
Central League
Central Penn. League
Connecticut State League
Indiana State League
Kansas State League
Kootenay & Washington League
Lehigh Valley League
Maine State League
Michigan State League
New Jersey State League
New York State League
Ohio State League
Ohio-West Virginia League
Red River Valley League
Southeastern League
Southeastern League
Virginia League
Texas-Southern League
Washington State League

1898
California League
Canadian League
Central Penn. League
Colorado State League
Connecticut State League
International League
Iron and Oil League
Kansas State League
Maine State League
Montana State League
Naugatuck Valley League
New York State League
Ohio State League
Pacific Coast League
Pacific Northwest League
Pacific States League
Southern League
Southwestern League
Texas Association
Western Association

1899
Colorado State League
Indiana State League
Montana State League
Southern League
Southwestern League
Texas Association
* Western Association

1900
Indiana State League
New England League
No. Carolina Association
* Virginia League

* listed with National Agreement Leagues

THE EARLY YEARS: 1902 - 1913

*T*he September 5, 1901 meeting in Chicago that formed the National Association had been called by Mike Sexton, president of the Three I League and Thomas J. Hickey, president of the Western League. At that meeting Patrick T. Powers was elected president and a new agreement between the major leagues and the new minor league association was written. The new document established league classifications, roster and salary limits and a system for drafting players. It recognized reserve lists and created a Board of Arbitration that was given power to suspend players, clubs or officials for violations.

By the beginning of the 1902 season, the National Association had 15 leagues. With a peace agreement ratified between the American and National Leagues in 1903, the National Association agreement formalized relations between the major and minor leagues, and the minor leagues began a period of stability. The National Association continued to grow over the decade as leagues that had operated outside its jurisdiction joined, and new leagues began. In 1903, 21 leagues started the season. In 1904 the number was 27, and by 1905 the member leagues numbered 34. The high mark, until the late 1940s, was reached in 1910 when 52 leagues started the season. Minor league baseball was growing and prospering, and the National Association survived.

The draft was one of the early problems. The major leagues favored an unlimited draft, the ability to purchase any player on a minor league roster for a fixed price. By 1905, the rules allowed only one player to be drafted from a club per year. A graduated system of payments, where the lowest levels had the lowest draft prices, evolved into a system where the draft had the positive effect of allowing players to advance to whatever levels their abilities would take them.

The clubs at the higher levels were not satisfied with the prices received, and the Eastern League nearly withdrew from the National Association, feeling that the forced sale of top players at the draft price was well below true market value. Almost annually there were revisions to the draft rules, prices and limits on optional player assignments.

During this era, there were no true farm teams because of limits on the number of players that a major league club could have on option In 1911 the number was eight. These extra players were farmed out, and informal arrangements between major and minor league clubs enabled major league clubs to obtain many of the promising young players. Major league clubs, as always, found ways around the rules, and secret major league ownership of minor league clubs was one method.

In 1909 Patrick Powers resigned as president of the National Association after the American Association and the Eastern League attempted to withdraw from the N.A. He was replaced by Michael Sexton, who had been president of the Three I League. Sexton was to remain as president until 1931. The future looked bright for minor league baseball. It was difficult to forsee that the rest of the 20th century would be a roller coaster ride of highs and lows. Baseball in the cities across North America survived, but it would be affected by wars, depressions, inventions, changes in public taste and most important, the varying attitudes of major league baseball.

1902

American League
President: Byron Bancroft Johnson

Standings	W	L	Pct.	GB	Attend.	Manager
Philadelphia Athletics.........	83	53	.610	—	420,078	Connie Mack
St. Louis Browns	78	58	.574	5	272,283	Jimmy McAleer
Boston Somersets	77	60	.562	6½	348,567	Jimmy Collins
Chicago White Stockings ...	74	60	.552	8	337,898	Clark Griffith
Cleveland Broncos..............	69	67	.507	14	275,395	Bill Armour
Washington Senators	61	75	.449	22	188,158	Tom Loftus
Detroit Tigers.....................	52	83	.385	30½	189,469	Frank Dwyer
Baltimore Orioles	50	88	.362	34	174,606	John McGraw/Wilbert Robinson

BA: Ed Delahanty, Washington, .376
Runs: Dave Fultz, Philadelphia, 109
Topsy Hartsel, Philadelphia, 109
Hits: Piano Legs Hickman, Boston/
Cleveland, 195
RBIs: Buck Freeman, Boston, 121

HRs: Socks Seybold, Philadelphia, 16
Wins: Cy Young, Boston, 32
SOs: Rube Waddell, Philadelphia, 210
ERA: Ed Siever, Detroit, 1.91
Pct: Bill Bernhard, Philadelphia/
Cleveland, .783, 18-5

National League
Presidents: Nicholas E. Young/Harry C. Pulliam

Standings	W	L	Pct.	GB	Attend.	Manager
Pittsburgh Pirates.............	103	36	.741	—	243,826	Fred Clarke
Brooklyn Superbas	75	63	.543	27½	199,868	Ned Hanlon
Boston Beaneaters	73	64	.533	29	116,960	Al Buckenberger
Cincinnati Reds.................	70	70	.500	33½	217,300	Bid McPhee/Frank Bancroft/ Joe Kelley
Chicago Cubs....................	68	69	.496	34	263,700	Frank Selee
St. Louis Cardinals	56	78	.418	44½	226,417	Patsy Donovan
Philadelphia Phillies	56	81	.409	46	112,066	Bill Shettsline
New York Giants	48	88	.353	53½	302,875	Horace Fogel/Heinie Smith/ John McGraw

BA: Ginger Beaumont, Pittsburgh, .357
Runs: Honus Wagner, Pittsburgh, 105
Hits: Ginger Beaumont, Pittsburgh, 194
RBIs: Honus Wagner, Pittsburgh, 91
HRs: Tommy Leach, Pittsburgh, 6

Wins: Jack Chesbro, Pittsburgh, 28
SOs: Vic Willis, Boston, 225
ERA: Jack Taylor, Chicago, 1.33
Pct: Jack Chesbro, Pittsburgh, .824, 28-6
IP: Vic Willis, Boston, 410

A Eastern League
President: Patrick T. Powers

Standings	W	L	Pct.	GB	Manager
Toronto Maple Leafs	85	42	.669	—	Edward Barrow
Buffalo Bisons	88	45	.662	—	George Stallings
Jersey City Skeeters...........	72	65	.526	18	Thomas Reilly/Lew Carr
Worcester Hustlers	68	65	.511	20	Frank Leonard
Providence Grays..............	67	67	.500	21½	William Murray
Rochester Bronchos............	57	74	.435	30	Edward McKeon/Harold O'Hagen
Montreal Royals	58	78	.426	31½	Charles Dooley
Newark Sailors	39	98	.285	51	Walter Burnham

Attendance: Buffalo, 258,769.

BA: Bill "Jocko" Halligan, Jersey City, .351
Runs: Dave Brain, Buffalo, 127
Hits: Bill "Jocko" Halligan, Jersey City, 182

HRs: Clarence "Pop" Foster, Providence/ Montreal, 14
Wins: Frank Corrigan, Providence, 28
Pct: Louis Bruce, Toronto, .900, 18-2

A Western League
President: Michael H. Sexton

Standings	W	L	Pct.	GB	Manager
Kansas City Blue Stockings	82	54	.603	—	Charles "Kid" Nichols
Omaha Indians	84	56	.600	—	William Rourke
Milwaukee Creams............	80	54	.597	1	Hugh Duffy
Denver Grizzlies	81	57	.587	2	Parke Wilson
St. Joseph Saints	71	68	.511	12½	Byron McKibben
Colorado Springs Millionaires.	63	75	.456	20	Bill Everitt
Des Moines Midgets	54	83	.394	28½	Joe Quinn
Peoria Distillers	35	103	.254	48	William Hart

BA: Emil Frisk, Denver, .373
Runs: John O'Brien, Milwaukee, 125
Hits: George Stone, Peoria/Omaha, 198
HRs: Emil Frisk, Denver, 14

Wins: Charles "Kid" Nichols, Kansas City, 27
SOs: Jake Weimer, Kansas City, 209
Pct: Charles "Kid" Nichols, Kansas City, .794, 27-7

B New England League
President: Tim H. Murnane

Standings	W	L	Pct.	GB	Manager
Manchester........................	75	37	.670	—	John A. Smith
Haverhill Hustlers..............	62	49	.559	12½	C.A. Driscoll/Billy Hamilton
Lawrence Colts	60	51	.541	14½	William Parsons
Concord Marines	58	53	.523	16½	John Carney
Dover	55	56	.495	19½	A.G. "Fred" Doe
Lowell Tigers.....................	52	59	.468	22½	Frederick Lake
Nashua	46	66	.411	29	Henry Burns
Fall River Indians	37	74	.333	37½	Thomas McDermott

BA: John A. Smith, Manchester, .369
Runs: Jim Murray, Manchester, 91
Hits: Wid Conroy, Lawrence, 155

HRs: Jim Murray, Manchester, 12
Wins: Frank Morrissey, Manchester, 27
Pct: Frank Morrissey, Manchester, .884, 27-5

B New York State League
President: John H. Farrell

Standings	W	L	Pct.	GB	Manager
Albany Senators.................	73	42	.635	—	Thomas O'Brien
Binghamton Bingoes	71	41	.634	½	Charles "Count" Campau
Ilion Typewriters	59	47	.557	9½	Howard Earl
Syracuse Stars...................	61	55	.526	12½	Sandy Griffin
Schenectady Electricians	56	55	.505	15	Lew Whistler
Utica Pent-Ups..................	49	63	.438	22½	Walter Taylor
Troy Trojans	40	63	.388	27	Louis Bacon
Amsterdam-Johnstown- Gloversville Jags..............	29	72	.287	37	Thomas Dowd

BA: Curt Bernard, Albany, .323
Runs: Robert "Chick" Cargo, Albany, 94
Arthur Ross, Syracuse, 94
Hits: Curt Bernard, Albany, 148

HRs: John Evers, Troy, 10
Wins: Ernie Crabill, Binghamton, 22
Pct: Ernie Crabill, Binghamton, .759, 22-7

B Pacific Northwest League
President: William H. Lucas

Standings	W	L	Pct.	GB	Manager
Butte Miners	73	47	.608	—	John McCloskey
Seattle Clamdiggers	70	50	.583	3	Daniel Dugdale
Helena Senators	65	54	.546	7½	John Flannery
Portland Webfoots	58	62	.483	15	Sam Vigneux
Tacoma Tigers	48	72	.400	25	Jay Andrews
Spokane Smoke Eaters	46	75	.380	27½	John J. Grim

BA: Frank "Piggy" Ward, Butte, .332
Runs: Bill Kane, Butte, 102
Hits: Frank "Piggy" Ward, Butte, 157

HRs: Joe Marshall, Butte, 6
SBs: Frank "Piggy" Ward, Butte, 51

B Southern Association
Presidents: J.B. Nicklin/William M. Kavanagh

Standings	W	L	Pct.	GB	Manager
Nashville Volunteers	80	40	.667	—	Newton Fisher
New Orleans Pelicans	75	47	.615	6	Abner Powell
Little Rock Travelers	77	49	.611	6	Michael Finn
Atlanta Firemen	59	59	.500	20	Edward Pabst/Ed Peters
Memphis Egyptians	52	67	.437	27½	Charles Frank
Chattanooga Lookouts........	50	67	.427	28½	William Kreig/Jack Dolan/ J.C. "Con" Strothers
Shreveport Giants	48	71	.403	31½	Justin Bennett/George Reed/ Edward Ashenbach
Birmingham Barons............	39	80	.328	40½	Frank Haller/Erwin Wilhelm

Standings include 12 Memphis wins which were reversed due to an ineligible player violation.

BA: Hugh Hill, Nashville, .416
Runs: Julius Wiseman, Nashville, 110
Hits: Frank Huelsman, Shreveport, 155
HRs: Frank Weikart, Shreveport, 11

Wins: Larry Stewart, New Orleans/ Shreveport, 23
Pct: Bill Dammann, Memphis, .782, 18-5

B Three-I League
President: Michael H. Sexton

Standings	W	L	Pct.	GB	Manager
Rockford Red Sox	74	52	.587	—	Hugh Nicol
Terre Haute Hottentots	70	53	.569	2½	Lou Walters/James Hackett
Cedar Rapids Rabbits	64	55	.538	6½	Belden Hill
Rock Island Islanders	58	61	.487	12½	Frank Donnelly
Davenport River Rats	59	63	.484	13	James Hayes
Evansville River Rats	57	67	.460	16	Sam Kennedy/Harley Parker
Decatur Commodores	55	69	.444	18	Fred Pfeiffer
Bloomington Blues	54	71	.432	19½	William Connors

BA: Louis Lippert, Rockford, .340
Runs: Louis Lippert, Rockford, 109
Hits: Louis Lippert, Rockford, 172
HRs: Charles Buelow, Rockford, 16

Wins: Amos Scott, Terre Haute, 23
SOs: John McCord, Davenport, 239
ERA: Charles McFarland, Cedar Rapids, 3.07

*Won first-half   **Won second-half   ***Won both halves

C North Carolina League
President: Perrin Busbee

Standings	W	L	Pct.	GB	Manager
Charlotte Hornets*#	44	12	.786	—	Edward Ashenbach
New Bern Truckers	34	25	.576	11½	C. Stevens & F. Market
Raleigh Red Birds	35	27	.565	12	R.C. Rivers
Greensboro Farmers**	33	30	.524	14½	King Kelly
Durham Bulls	23	39	.371	24	Otis Stockdale
Wilmington Sailors@	10	46	.179	34	Edgar Baer/Harry Mace

#Charlotte disbanded July 9.
@Wilmington disbanded July 10.
The league disbanded July 15.

BA: Buck Weaver, Charlotte, .325

D Connecticut League
Presidents: James O'Rourke/Sturgis Whitlock

Standings	W	L	Pct.	GB	Manager
New Haven Blues	70	39	.642	—	James Canavan
Springfield Ponies	65	45	.591	5½	Roger Connor
New London Whalers	57	54	.514	14	John Shea
Hartford Senators	57	55	.509	14½	Frank Reisling
Bridgeport Orators	53	59	.473	18½	James O'Rourke
Norwich Reds	51	58	.469	19	Harry Davenport
Meriden Silverites	51	58	.469	19	Cornelius Miller/Thomas Tucker
Waterbury Rough Riders	37	73	.336	33½	George Harrington

BA: Danny Hoffman, Springfield, .336
Runs: George Turner, Norwich, 110
Hits: H.E. Slater, Waterbury, 147
HRs: Bob Drew, Meriden, 7
Pct: Ed Walsh, Meriden, .750, 15-5
ShO: Nelson Long, New London, 7

D Cotton States League
President: R.W. Tilford

Standings	W	L	Pct.	GB	Manager
Natchez Indians	55	51	.519	—	George Blackburn
Baton Rouge Cajuns	53	54	.495	2½	Robert Pender
Vicksburg Hill Climbers	52	53	.495	2½	Jesse Reynolds
Greenville Cotton Pickers	53	55	.491	3	Bell Hebron

BA: Howard Murphy, Baton Rouge, .400

D Iowa-South Dakota League
President: W.E. Lockhart

Standings	W	L	Pct.	GB	Manager
Sioux Falls Canaries*	65	24	.730	—	Ed Craig
Flandreau Indians**	51	19	.729	4½	
Sioux City Cornhuskers	56	40	.583	12½	Ed Kirby
Le Mars Blackbirds	43	48	.473	23	Bob Black
Rock Rapids Browns	32	59	.352	34	
Sheldon	14	71	.165	49	

Flandreau started late, on June 20, and was awarded a record of 9-9, which made its overall first-half record 31-22. Flandreau won the second half but could not hold its team for the playoffs.

BA: Dorman, Flandreau, .314
Runs: John "Moose" Baxter, Sioux City, 63
Wins: Harry Swalm, Sioux Falls, 23
Pct: Jack Corbett, Sioux Falls, .882, 15-2

D Michigan State League
President: G.E. Morrison

Standings	W	L	Pct.	GB	Manager
Battle Creek Cero Frutos	53	31	.631	—	W.E. Woods
Saginaw White Sox/Jackson#..	50	39	.562	5½	George "Doggie" Miller
Flint	47	41	.534	8	Arlie Latham/Ed Zinram
Muskegon Reds	40	47	.460	14½	Arthur DeBaker
Lansing Senators+	35	62	.361	24½	H.A. Bowie/Walter Niles
Grand Rapids Colts@	29	34	.460	NA	Emerson Dickerson

#Saginaw (35-28) moved to Jackson July 20.
@Grand Rapids disbanded July 20.
+Lansing disbanded August 20, causing the league to disband.

D Missouri Valley League
President: Dr. D.M. Shiveley

Standings	W	L	Pct.	GB	Manager
Nevada Lunatics	86	38	.694	—	James Driscoll
Springfield Reds	83	40	.678	2½	Frank Hurlburt

Ft. Scott Giants	80	44	.645	6	Fred Hornaday
Sedalia Gold Bugs	72	48	.600	12	Joseph Roe/Fultz
Joplin Miners	56	66	.459	29	Claude Marcum/Wickhizer
Coffeyville Indians/ Chanute Oilers#	41	81	.336	44	Fred Porter/Larry Powers/J. G. Galbreath/ Jack Jamison
Jefferson City Convicts	40	85	.320	46½	A.B. Carey/E.J. Miller
Iola Gasbags	34	90	.274	52	Jenkins

#Coffeyville (9-30) moved to Chanute June 23.

D Texas League
President: John L. Ward

Standings	W	L	Pct.	GB	Manager
Corsicana Oil Cities	87	23	.791	—	Mike O'Connor
Dallas Griffins	60	53	.531	28½	Lee Dawkins
Ft. Worth Panthers	48	62	.436	39	Ted Sullivan
Paris Eisenfelder's Homeseekers	42	65	.393	43½	Wade Moore/Wilson Mathews/ Emmett Rodgers
Waco Tigers#	27	36	.429	NA	Emmitt Rodgers
Sherman-Denison Students/ Texarkana Casketmakers@..	21	46	.313	NA	Cy Mulkey/Frederick Cavender/F.M. Ball

#Waco disbanded July 8, at the end of the first half.
@Sherman-Denison (1-10) moved to Texarkana May 6; Texarkana disbanded July 8.
The season was shortened to August 31.

(second half statistics:)
BA: Allen Nickell, Dallas, .397
Runs: Jim "Curley" Maloney, Corsicana, 44
Hits: Jim "Curley" Maloney, Corsicana, 61
HRs: Jim "Curley" Maloney, Corsicana, 4
Ben Shelton, Corsicana, 4

Ind American Association
President: Thomas J. Hickey

Standings	W	L	Pct.	GB	Manager
Indianapolis Indians	96	45	.681	—	Bill Watkins
Louisville Colonels	92	45	.671	2	William Clymer
St. Paul Apostles	72	66	.521	22½	Mike Kelley
Kansas City Cowboys	69	67	.507	24½	Dale Gear
Columbus Senators	66	74	.471	29½	John J. Grim/Frank Leonard
Milwaukee Brewers	65	75	.464	30½	William Clingman/Joe Cantillon
Minneapolis Millers	54	86	.385	41½	Walter Wilmot
Toledo Mud Hens	42	85	.330	53½	Charles Strobel

BA: John Ganzel, Louisville, .366
Runs: George Hogriever, Indianapolis, 124
Hits: John Ganzel, Louisville, 194
HRs: Harry Lumley, St. Paul, 8
SBs: Bill Fox, Indianapolis, 49
Wins: Ed Dunkle, Louisville, 30
Pct: Ed Dunkle, Louisville, .750, 30-10

Ind California League
President: James T. Moran

Standings	W	L	Pct.	GB	Manager
Oakland Clamdiggers	108	74	.593	—	Pete Lohman
Los Angeles	91	83	.523	13	James Morley
San Francisco	88	98	.473	22	Henry Harris
Sacramento Gilt Edges	68	100	.405	33	Mike Fisher

BA: Walter McCredie, Oakland, .319
Wins: Oscar Jones, Los Angeles, 36
Pct: Henry Schmidt, Oakland, .636, 35-20

Ind Northern League

Standings	W	L	Pct.	GB	Manager
Winnipeg Maroons	37	20	.649	—	Ned Egan
Crookston Crooks	31	25	.554	5½	
Fargo	30	26	.536	6½	Oscar Bandelin
Grand Forks	28	26	.519	7½	J. Callihan
Devils Lake#	19	31	.380	14½	Charles Henley
Cavalier#	15	32	.319	17	O. Luxdale

#Cavalier and Devils Lake disbanded July 21.

BA: Oscar Bandelin, Fargo, .421
Runs: Fred Quigley, Crookston, 54
Hits: Jim Novacek, Crookston, 68
Wins: Phil Dellers, Winnipeg, 13
SOs: Sessions, Devils Lake, 106
Pct: Phil Dellers, Winnipeg, .722, 13-5

1902 No-Hitters

Date	Pitcher	Team	League	Opponent	Score
6-2	Bill Cristall	Oakland	California	Sacramento	4-0
6-8	Fred Burchell	Evansville	Three-I	Bloomington	1-0 (10)
7-4	Gus Hamilton	Dallas	Texas	Ft. Worth	3-0
7-19	Norwood Gibson	Kansas City	Western	Omaha	2-3
8-25	Jake Weimer/				
	Norwood Gibson	Kansas City	Western	St. Joseph	3-0 (10)
9-20	Jim Callahan	Chicago	American	Detroit	3-0

Jesse Stovall	Seattle	Pacific Northwest
Weldon Henley	Atlanta	Southern Association
Doc Adkins	Milwaukee	Western
Charles McFarland	Cedar Rapids	Three-I
Warren McLaughlin	New London	Connecticut
Buck Hooker	Concord	New England

Number in parentheses indicates innings if other than nine.

THIS DATE IN MINOR LEAGUE HISTORY

January 27, 1902, George Stallings was awarded the Buffalo franchise in the Eastern League.

June 8, 1902, Fred Burchell, Evansville, Three-I League, shut out Bloomington without a hit or run in ten innings and brought in the only run in the game with a triple in the tenth frame. McGreevey, the Bloomington hurler, held Evansville to five safeties, two by Burchell.

June 15, 1902, Justin "Nig" Clarke, Corsicana, Texas League, catcher, hit eight home runs in twelve times at bat against Texarkana in a Sunday game played at Ennis, Texas (Sunday ball was banned at Corsicana). Clarke drove in 16 runs. Corsicana won the affair 51-3, making 53 hits, 21 home runs, 45 runs batted in and 25 extra base wallops. Corsicana's Bill Alexander and Ike Pendleton also had eight hits and George Malarkey and manager Mike O'Connor scored seven runs each.

July 5, 1902, Charles Harrington was fatally injured when struck in the stomach by a batted ball in a Texas League game at Dallas.

July 20, 1902, James Wiggs, Helena, Pacific Northwest League, yielded a run to Seattle in the sixth frame, after having hurled 44 consecutive scoreless innings, including four straight nine-inning shutouts.

July 26, 1902, Buffalo walloped Providence 33-6 in an Eastern League game.

August 18, 1902, Harry O'Hagan, Rochester first baseman, executed an unassisted triple play in the Eastern League at Jersey City. This was the first authenticated unassisted triple play in Organized Ball.

August 23, 1902, Irwin Wilhelm, Birmingham, Southern Association, hurled both games of a doubleheader against Nashville, allowing one hit in each game. Both contests were nine innings, and the scores were 5-0 and 5-1.

September 17, 1902, Miller Huggins, St. Paul, American Association, handled 19 chances at second base, 11 putouts and 8 assists, without an error against Louisville.

December 7, 1902, The four-team independent California League campaign, which began in March, ended with Oakland the pennant winner. The champs had a record of 108-74.

Financial Report of the 1900 Cortland Wagonmakers of the New York State League

Disbursements		Receipts	
Salaries of players	$5,407.36	National fair	$1482.04
League guarantee	100.00	Cash donations	600.45
Uniforms	72.27	Fence signs	223.25
Rent park	50.00	Score cards	60.00
Bases	4.40	Season and benefit tickets	144.67
Dues to President of league	100.00	A.O.H. games	37.40
Dues to National League	40.00	Gross earnings on road	3553.24
Stamps and license	16.00	Sale of Eason and McFall	600.00
Cleaning uniforms	2.80	From league treasurer	92.50
Balls and bats	36.91	Loan	300.00
Labor at park	50.50	Gross earnings at home	4567.84
Police at park	29.00		
Advertising	75.64		
Local hotels	43.89		
Telegrams and telephones	40.44		
Bus hire	116.75		
Hotels on road	904.45		
Transportation	1,284.00		
Paid to visiting clubs	2,371.40		
Road umpires	332.00		
Paid loan	300.00		
Miscellaneous expenses	243.95		
Total Disbursements	**$11,621.76**	**Total Revenues**	**$11,661.39**

1903

American League
President: Byron Bancroft Johnson

Standings	W	L	Pct.	GB	Attend.	Manager
Boston Pilgrims	91	47	.659	—	379,338	Jimmy Collins
Philadelphia Athletics........	75	60	.556	14½	422,473	Connie Mack
Cleveland Naps..................	77	63	.550	15	311,280	Bill Armour
New York Highlanders	72	62	.537	17	211,808	Clark Griffith
Detroit Tigers....................	65	71	.478	25	224,523	Edward Barrow
St. Louis Browns	65	74	.468	26½	380,405	Jimmy McAleer
Chicago White Stockings ...	60	77	.438	30½	286,183	Nixey Callahan
Washington Senators	43	94	.314	47½	128,878	Tom Loftus

BA: Napoleon Lajoie, Cleveland, .355
Runs: Patsy Dougherty, Boston, 108
Hits: Patsy Dougherty, Boston, 195
RBIs: Buck Freeman, Boston, 104
HRs: Buck Freeman, Boston, 13

Wins: Cy Young, Boston, 28
SOs: Rube Waddell, Philadelphia, 302
ERA: Earl Moore, Cleveland, 1.77
Pct: Cy Young, Boston, .757, 28-9

National League
President: Harry C. Pulliam

Standings	W	L	Pct.	GB	Attend.	Manager
Pittsburgh Pirates	91	49	.650	—	326,855	Fred Clarke
New York Giants	84	55	.604	6½	579,530	John McGraw
Chicago Cubs.....................	82	56	.594	8	386,205	Frank Selee
Cincinnati Reds..................	74	65	.532	16½	351,680	Joe Kelley
Brooklyn Superbas	70	66	.515	19	224,670	Ned Hanlon
Boston Beaneaters	58	80	.420	32	143,155	Al Buckenberger
Philadelphia Phillies	49	86	.363	39½	151,729	Chief Zimmer
St. Louis Cardinals	43	94	.314	46½	226,538	Patsy Donovan

BA: Honus Wagner, Pittsburgh, .355
Runs: Ginger Beaumont, Pittsburgh, 137
Hits: Ginger Beaumont, Pittsburgh, 209
RBIs: Sam Mertes, New York, 104
HRs: Jimmy Sheckard, Brooklyn, 9

Wins: Joe McGinnity, New York, 31
SOs: Christy Mathewson, New York, 267
ERA: Sam Leever, Pittsburgh, 2.06
Pct: Sam Leever, Pittsburgh, .781, 25-7
IP: Joe McGinnity, New York, 434

A American Association
President: Thomas J. Hickey

Standings	W	L	Pct.	GB	Attend.	Manager
St. Paul Apostles...............	88	46	.657	—	135,000	Mike Kelley
Louisville Colonels............	87	54	.617	4½	131,000	William Clymer
Milwaukee Brewers............	77	60	.562	12½	105,000	Joe Cantillon
Indianapolis Indians...........	78	61	.561	12½	88,000	Bill Watkins
Kansas City Cowboys.........	69	66	.511	19½	100,000	Dale Gear
Columbus Senators	56	84	.400	35	154,876	Frank Leonard/Robert Quinn/ James Bannon
Minneapolis Millers...........	50	91	.355	41½	91,000	Walter Wilmot/George Yeager
Toledo Mud Hens	48	91	.345	42½	96,124	Frank Reisling

BA: Jiggs Donahue, Milwaukee, .344
Runs: Spike Shannon, St. Paul, 132
Hits: Phil Geier, St. Paul, 191
HRs: Mike Grady, Kansas City, 16

Wins: Tom Walker, Louisville, 26
SOs: Claude Elliott, Milwaukee, 226
Pct: Tom Walker, Louisville, .788, 26-7

A Eastern League
President: Patrick T. Powers

Standings	W	L	Pct.	GB	Manager
Jersey City Skeeters...........	92	33	.736	—	William Murray
Toronto Maple Leafs	82	45	.646	11	James Gardner/Arthur Irwin
Buffalo Bisons	79	43	.648	11½	George Stallings
Baltimore Orioles	71	54	.568	21	Wilbert Robinson/Hugh Jennings
Newark Sailors	74	63	.540	24	Walter Burnham
Providence Grays...............	45	86	.344	50	Richard Cogan
Worcester Riddlers/ Montreal Royals#...........	37	93	.285	57½	George Wrigley/Bill Clancy/ Gene DeMontreville
Rochester Bronchos............	34	97	.260	61	Arthur Irwin/Abbie Johnson/ George Smith

#Worcester (25-39) moved to Montreal July 21.
Attendance: Buffalo, 305,119.

BA: Harry McCormick, Jersey City, .362
Runs: Joseph Bean, Jersey City, 112
Hits: Harry McCormick, Jersey City, 172
HRs: Ed Atherton, Buffalo, 9

Wins: George Pfanmiller, Jersey City, 28
SOs: Herb Briggs, Toronto, 205
Pct: Jake Thielman, Jersey City, .821, 23-5

A Pacific National League
President: William H. Lucas

Standings	W	L	Pct.	GB	Manager
Butte Miners	85	62	.578	—	William Kane/Walter Wilmot
Spokane Indians.................	82	68	.547	4½	W.V. Garrett/C.H. Williams
Seattle Chinooks	78	71	.523	8	Daniel Dugdale
Portland Green Gages/ Salt Lake City Elders#.....	56	91	.381	29	John J. Grim/John McCloskey
Los Angeles+....................	65	42	.607	NA	Charles Reilly
San Francisco Pirates+........	56	52	.519	NA	John McCloskey
Tacoma Tigers@.................	46	60	.434	NA	Byron McKibben
Helena Senators@	40	62	.392	NA	John Flannery/M. Carish

#Portland (21-42) moved to Salt Lake City July 2.
@Tacoma and Helena disbanded August 16.
+Los Angeles and San Francisco disbanded August 21.

BA: Frank Huelsman, Spokane, .392
Runs: Charles Donahue, Portland/ Salt Lake City, 114
Hits: Charles Donahue, Portland/ Salt Lake City, 192

HRs: Joe Marshall, San Francisco, 25
Wins: Pete Dowling, Butte, 30
SOs: Pete Dowling, Butte, 249
Pct: Ernest Nichols, Spokane, .833, 20-4

A Western League
President: Michael H. Sexton

Standings	W	L	Pct.	GB	Manager
Milwaukee Creams	83	43	.659	—	Hugh Duffy
Colorado Springs Millionaires.	76	52	.594	8	Bill Everitt
Kansas City Blue Stockings..	65	61	.516	18	Charles "Kid" Nichols
St. Joseph Saints...............	62	59	.512	20½	George Rohe
Denver Grizzlies	61	70	.466	24½	Thomas Delahanty/Robert Lowe
Peoria Distillers	57	69	.452	26	William Wilson
Des Moines Undertakers	55	76	.420	30½	Joe Quinn
Omaha Indians...................	49	78	.386	34½	Pa Rourke

The season was shortened to September 17 due to widespread poor weather.

BA: Bill Congalton, Colorado Springs, .363
Runs: Tom V. Fleming, Colorado Springs, 107
Tom O'Neill, Milwaukee, 107
Hits: Bill Congalton, Colorado Springs, 184

HRs: Mike Jacobs, Kansas City, 8
Wins: Ed Kenna, Milwaukee, 28
SOs: H.B. Cushman, Des Moines, 195
Pct: Ed Kenna, Milwaukee, .757, 28-9

B Central League
President: George W. Bement

Standings	W	L	Pct.	GB	Manager
Fort Wayne Railroaders......	89	49	.645	—	Bade Myers
South Bend Greens	88	50	.638	1	Angus Grant
Marion Oilworkers	71	65	.522	17	John H. Grim
Wheeling Stogies	69	68	.504	19½	Barley Kain/Ted Price
Evansville River Rats	64	68	.485	22	Tom News/C. McKinley/Ed Ashenbach
Dayton Veterans	61	76	.445	27½	W.S. Lauder
Terre Haute Hottentots	58	80	.420	31	Lou Walters/Peter Somers/Bill James/ Ed Beecher
Anderson/Grand Rapids Orphans#........................	48	92	.343	42	M. Lindsey

#Anderson (15-12) moved to Grand Rapids May 30.

BA: J.P. Bonner, Evansville, .329
Runs: Ed Coffee, South Bend, 105
Hits: J.P. Bonner, Evansville, 172

B New England League
President: Tim H. Murnane

Standings	W	L	Pct.	GB	Manager
Lowell Tigers....................	72	41	.637	—	Frederick Lake
Nashua	68	46	.596	4½	Edward Ashenbach/Charles Collins
Manchester.......................	66	45	.595	5	John A. Smith
Concord Marines	63	47	.573	7½	John Carney/Frank Eustace
Fall River Indians	57	56	.504	15	Thomas McDermott
Lawrence Colts	48	62	.436	22½	William Parsons/Stephen Flanagan
Brockton/New Bedford Whalers#.......................	46	63	.422	24	A.G. "Fred" Doe
Haverhill Hustlers..............	26	86	.232	45½	Billy Hamilton/Charles O'Reilly/ Otto Deininger

#Brockton (18-23) moved to New Bedford June 27.

BA: Fred Iott, Fall River, .317
Runs: Clark Rapp, Manchester, 86

Hits: Edward Swander, Manchester, 140
HRs: Lou Knau, Manchester, 7

B New York State League
President: John H. Farrell

Standings	W	L	Pct.	GB	Manager
Schenectady Frog Alleys	80	52	.606	—	Benjamin Ellis
Syracuse Stars....................	80	54	.597	1	Sandy Griffin

*Won first-half   **Won second-half   ***Won both halves

137

Standings	W	L	Pct.	GB	Manager
Troy Trojans	72	47	.605	1½	Louis Bacon
Albany Senators	63	60	.512	12½	Michael Doherty
Utica Pentups	61	63	.492	15	James Say/Elmer Horton
Binghamton Bingoes	52	72	.419	24	John Quinn/Fred Popkay/ Charles "Count" Campau
Ilion Typewriters	52	73	.416	24½	Howard Earl
Amsterdam-Johnstown- Gloversville Hyphens	43	82	.350	33½	William Hazleton/Frank Shannon/ Clarence Williams

BA: Charles Loudenslager, Syracuse, .326
Runs: Archie Marshall, Troy, 90
Hits: Charles Loudenslager, Syracuse, 167
HRs: Archie Marshall, Troy, 8
Wins: Jack Fifield, Syracuse, 26
SOs: Leon Ames, Ilion, 214
Pct: Del Mason, Schenectady, .774, 24-7

B Southern Association
President: William B. Kavanaugh

Standings	W	L	Pct.	GB	Manager
Memphis Egyptians	73	52	.584	—	Charles Frank
Little Rock Travelers	70	51	.579	1	Michael Finn
Shreveport Giants	67	58	.536	6	Robert Gilks
Atlanta Crackers	59	59	.500	10½	Abner Powell
Nashville Volunteers	60	62	.492	11½	Newton Fisher
Birmingham Barons	57	64	.471	14	Thomas O'Brien
Montgomery Black Sox	53	67	.442	17½	Lew Whistler
New Orleans Pelicans	48	74	.393	23½	Charles "Count" Campau/ George "Zeke" Wrigley/Joe Rickert

Playoff: Little Rock 3 games, Memphis 2.

BA: Jim Delahanty, Little Rock, .382
Runs: Frank Norcum, Shreveport, 105
Hits: Ervin Beck, Shreveport, 164
HRs: Lew Whistler, Montgomery, 18
Wins: Bill Fisher, Nashville, 24
Pct: Bill Fisher, Nashville, .686, 24-11

B Three-I League
President: Michael H. Sexton

Standings	W	L	Pct.	GB	Manager
Bloomington Bloomers	72	47	.605	—	William Connors
Decatur Commodores	67	51	.568	4½	Monte McFarland
Davenport River Rats	65	53	.551	6½	James Hayes
Rock Island Islanders	64	54	.542	7½	Frank Donnelly
Cedar Rapids Rabbits	60	60	.500	12½	Belden Hill
Rockford Red Sox	58	60	.492	13½	Hugh Nicol
Dubuque Shamrocks	49	72	.405	24	Clarence "Pants" Rowland/Charles Buelow
Joliet Standards/ Springfield Foot Trackers#	42	80	.344	31½	Albert Tebeau/Frank Belt

#Joliet (14-19) moved to Springfield June 12.

BA: Dutch Hines, Davenport, .339
Runs: Frank Donnelly, Rock Island, 97
Hits: Charles McFarland, Decatur, 151
Wins: Charles Case, Rock Island, 22
SOs: Charles Case, Rock Island, 187
ERA: Albert Jacobson, Decatur, 2.18

C South Texas League
Presidents: James Nolan/Max Stubenraugh

Standings	W	L	Pct.	GB	Manager
San Antonio Bronchos*	70	54	.565	—	Wade Moore
Galveston Sandcrabs**	67	58	.536	3½	E.M. Riley
Houston Buffalos	57	64	.471	11½	Gerald Hayes
Beaumont Oil Gushers	53	71	.427	17	Denny Lyons

Playoff: San Antonio 7 games, Galveston 2.

BA: Ed Pleiss, Galveston, .360
Runs: Ed Pleiss, Galveston, 105
Hits: Ed Pleiss, Galveston, 168
Wins: Orth Thomas, San Antonio, 22
Pct: Baldo Luitich, Galveston, .708, 17-7

D Connecticut League
President: Sturgis Whitlock

Standings	W	L	Pct.	GB	Manager
Holyoke Paperweights	66	37	.641	—	Orville Woodruff/Daniel O'Neill
Meriden Silverites	62	42	.595	4½	Sam Kennedy
Bridgeport Orators	59	47	.557	8½	James O'Rourke
Norwich Reds	57	48	.543	10	Dennis Morrissey
New London Whalers	57	52	.523	12	John Shea/Charles Humphrey
New Haven Blues	52	57	.477	17	James Canavan
Springfield Ponies	41	64	.370	26	Roger Connor
Hartford Senators	30	77	.280	38	Thomas Reilly

Twelve Holyoke games (8-4) were deducted after the season due to ineligible player violations.

BA: Claude Rossman, Holyoke, .385
Runs: Emil Batch, Holyoke, 98
Hits: Claude Rossman, Holyoke, 158
HRs: Jack Tighe, Norwich, 5
SBs: Tom Bannon, New London, 73

D Cotton States League
President: George Wheatley

Standings	W	L	Pct.	GB	Manager
Baton Rouge Red Sticks	74	42	.638	—	Robert Pender
Vicksburg Hill Billies	70	46	.603	4	Billy Earle
Natchez Indians	59	59	.500	16	Albert Haupt
Pine Bluff Lumbermen	54	60	.474	19	George Blackburn/Frank Christian
Greenville Grays	53	64	.453	21½	William A. Smith
Monroe Hill Cities	36	75	.324	35½	Henry Hunt/J.C. "Con" Strothers/ Jim McDermott

BA: William A. Smith, Greenville, .308
Hits: Ed Zinram, Natchez, 144
Wins: Howard Camnitz, Vicksburg, 26
SOs: Howard Camnitz, Vicksburg, 294
Pct: Howard Camnitz, Vicksburg, .788, 26-7

D Hudson River League
Presidents: Henry D. Ramsey/C.S. Harvey

Standings	W	L	Pct.	GB	Manager
Kingston Colonials	63	30	.677	—	Henry Ramsey
Hudson Marines	63	33	.656	1½	Gus Schnack
Peekskill@	48	39	.552	12	F. Valentine
Saugerties	48	47	.505	16	Charles Brady
Poughkeepsie Colts	39	51	.433	22½	William McCabe
Newburgh Taylor-mades	37	54	.407	25	Charles Fisher
Ossining/Catskill#	22	69	.242	40	J.M. Evans

#Ossining (7-37) moved to Catskill August 2.
@Peekskill entered the league August 10 on equal footing with Poughkeepsie, 21-24. Peekskill's actual record was 27 wins and 15 losses.

D Iowa-South Dakota League
President: J.U. Sammis

Standings	W	L	Pct.	GB	Manager
Le Mars Blackbirds	48	34	.585	—	Bob Black
Council Bluffs Bluffers/ Sheldon-Primghar Hyphens#	44	35	.557	2½	Buck Keith
Sioux City Sioux	44	41	.518	5½	Frank Lohr
Sioux Falls Canaries	40	42	.488	8	Ed Craig

#Council Bluffs withdrew on June 20 with a record of 1-22. The official record was expunged with the transfer to Sheldon-Primghar, which was awarded a record of 14-11 on June 25.

BA: Tony Fremmer, Sheldon-Primghar, .325
Runs: Frank Lohr, Sioux City, 62
Hits: Jim Metcalf, Le Mars, 100
Wins: Helmsdorfer, Sheldon-Primghar, 19
Pct: Ralph Hutchinson, Le Mars, .909, 10-1

D Kitty League
President: W.I. Thompson

Standings	W	L	Pct.	GB	Manager
Cairo Egyptians	67	41	.620	—	G.P. Eichenbarger
Clarksville Villagers	60	43	.583	4½	
Jackson Railroaders	53	52	.505	12½	
Henderson Blue Birds	48	60	.444	19	
Paducah Chiefs	47	59	.443	19	Meredeth
Hopkinsville Browns	45	63	.417	22	
Owensboro Distillers#	8	3	.727	NA	
Vincennes Alices@	11	18	.379	NA	

#Owensboro disbanded June 1.
@Vincennes was dropped from the league June 22.

D Missouri Valley League
President: Dr. D.M. Shiveley

Standings	W	L	Pct.	GB	Manager
Sedalia Gold Bugs	86	47	.647	—	W.J. Ferguson/R.N. Harrison
Springfield Midgets	82	48	.631	2½	Frank Hurlburt
Iola Gaslighters	79	52	.603	6	A.H. Harris
Joplin Miners	69	62	.527	16	Dave Joseph
Ft. Scott Giants	71	64	.526	16	Fred Hornaday
Pittsburg Coal Diggers	39	95	.291	47½	Claude East
Nevada Lunatics/ Webb City Goldbugs#	21	43	.328	NA	A.B. Cockerell
Leavenworth White Sox@	15	50	.231	NA	Clyde Hughes

#Nevada (21-39) moved to Webb City July 13, then disbanded July 16.
@Leavenworth disbanded July 16.

D Northern League
President: D.J. Laxdal

Standings	W	L	Pct.	GB	Manager
Winnipeg Maroons	65	28	.699	—	Ned Egan
Grand Forks Forkers	57	36	.613	8	Scott Kairnes
Crookston Crooks	55	41	.573	11½	William Lycan/William Bray
Duluth Cardinals	41	51	.446	23½	Leonard Van Praugh

Fargo .... 36 61 .371 31 Thomas Reynolds/George Pirie/
                                                                    Spencer Abbott

Superior Longshoremen ..... 26 63 .292 37 Tim Keefe/John Lagger/Henry Rusch

BA: Jess Hoffmeister, Crookston, .327   **Wins:** Dave Martin, Crookston, 24
Runs: Hank Scharnweber, Grand Forks, 71   **SOs:** Isaac Slette, Grand Forks, 221
Hits: Hank Scharnweber, Grand Forks, 112   **Pct:** Ted Corbett, Winnipeg, .800, 20-5

D Southwest Iowa League
President: E.H. Whiteside

Standings	W	L	Pct.	GB	Manager
Atlantic**	34	26	.567	—	
Clarinda	31	30	.508	3½	
Red Oak Blue Indians........	22	33	.400	9½	
Shenandoah#*...................	22	14	.611	NA	
Creston Cyclones@	24	19	.558	NA	
Osceola	18	29	.383	NA	

Osceola and Creston joined for the second half June 29.
#Shenandoah disbanded July 18.
@Creston disbanded August 29.

D Southwest Washington League
President: John P. Fink

Standings	W	L	Pct.	GB	Manager
Aberdeen Pippins................	11	7	.611	—	Will Campbell
Hoquiam Perfect Gentlemen..	11	7	.611	—	A.C. Girard
Centralia Midgets	7	11	.389	4	Paul Ruff
Olympia Senators	7	11	.389	4	Jessie Mill

The league played six times a week, but only the weekend games counted.

Playoff: Hoquiam refused to play off the tie; the championship was awarded to Aberdeen.

BA: Ira Harmon, Centralia, .341   **Wins:** Sammy "Indian" Morris, Hoquiam, 12
Runs: Culton, Centralia, 16   **SOs:** Sammy "Indian" Morris, Hoquiam, 106
Hits: Culton, Centralia, 25   **Pct:** Sammy "Indian" Morris, Hoquiam,
HRs: Ira Harmon, Centralia, 2   .706, 12-5

D Texas League
President: Newton D. Lassiter

Standings	W	L	Pct.	GB	Manager
Dallas Giants**..................	61	47	.565	—	Charles Moran
Corsicana Oil Cities........	54	53	.505	6½	Mike O'Connor
Paris Parasites*/Waco Steers#.	51	56	.477	9½	Ted Sullivan
Ft. Worth Panthers.............	49	59	.454	12	Con Lucid/Fred Schatzke/George Disch

#Paris (32-20) moved to Waco at the start of the second half, June 26.

Playoff: Dallas 7 games, Waco 3.

(second half averages:)
BA: Art Pennell, Waco, .347   **Hits:** Harry "Pep" Clark, Dallas, 82
Runs: Harry "Pep" Clark, Dallas, 43

Ind Pacific Coast League
President: Eugene F. Bert

Standings	W	L	Pct.	GB	Manager
Los Angeles Angels..........	133	78	.630	—	Frank "Cap" Dillon
Sacramento Senators........	105	105	.500	27½	Charley Graham
Seattle Siwashes	98	100	.495	28½	Parke Wilson
San Francisco Seals	107	110	.493	29	Charlie Irwin
Portland Browns	95	108	.468	34	Sam Vigneaux/Bones Ely
Oakland Oaks	89	126	.414	46	Pete Lohman

BA: Frank "Cap" Dillon, Los Angeles, .363   **Wins:** Doc Newton, Los Angeles, 34
Runs: William "Dummy" Hoy,   Jay Hughes, Seattle, 34
   Los Angeles, 157   **SOs:** Joe Corbett, Los Angeles, 196
Hits: Frank "Cap" Dillon, Los Angeles, 273   **ERA:** Jake Thielman, Portland, 2.12
HRs: Truck Eagan, Sacramento, 13   **Pct:** Doc Newton, Los Angeles, .739, 34-12
                                   CGs: Oscar Graham, Oakland, 53
                                   IP: Oscar Graham, Oakland, 505

1903 Interleague Post Season Play

World Series
Boston (American) 5 games, Pittsburgh (National) 3

New England Championship
Holyoke (Connecticut State) 4 games, Lowell (New England) 2

1903 No-Hitters

Date	Pitcher	Team	League	Opponent	Score
5-17	Arthur Ragan	Dallas	Texas	Ft. Worth	1-0
7-4	Fred Falkenberg	Worcester	Eastern	Providence	7-0
7-11	Clyde Bateman	Corsicana	Texas	Ft. Worth	2-0
7-31	Bussey	Binghamton	New York State	Syracuse	
8-7	Eugene Burns	Houston	South Texas	San Antonio	2-0
8-7	Haslem	Syracuse	New York State	Troy	
8-11	H. Conover	Dallas	Texas	Ft. Worth	8-0
9-6	Eddie Taylor	San Antonio	South Texas	Galveston	3-0 (PO)
9-15	Arthur Goodwin	Schenectady	New York State	Binghamton	1-0
9-18	Chick Fraser	Philadelphia	National	Chicago	10-0
11-8	Doc Newton	Los Angeles	Pacific Coast	Oakland	2-0

Number in parentheses indicates innings if other than nine; "PO" indicates playoff game.

THIS DATE IN MINOR LEAGUE HISTORY

February 12, 1903, At Ft. Scott, Kansas, Charles Parmenter was convicted of the murder of umpire Frank Brunner.

April 23, 1903, At Los Angeles, Butte of the Pacific National League made two triple plays in one game. The first went from Reilley to Hillingsworth to Messerly; the second, Reilley to Messerly. Gavvy Cravath, later a star for the Minneapolis Millers and Philadelphia Phillies, lined into one of the triple erasures.

May 5, 1903, The Hudson River League was admitted to the National Association as a Class D circuit. The loop opened May 21 and closed September 19.

May 14, 1903, At Corsicana in the Texas League, Paris, managed by the famous Ted Sullivan, defeated the home club 13-7, hitting nine home runs. Four circuit drives were made by Clyde Bateman, teammate Wolfe added three, and Harry Coyle and Walsh had one each.

June 5, 1903, In the Cotton States League, Monroe and Baton Rouge played to an 18-inning 0-0 tie.

June 28, 1903, At Iola, Kansas, shortstop George Pennington of Ft. Scott made an unassisted triple play against the home club in a Missouri Valley League game.

August 10, 1903, At Kingston, New York, the Kingston and Hudson teams of the Hudson River League played a 20-inning game that ended in a 2-2 tie.

August 21, 1903, San Francisco and Los Angeles dropped out of the Pacific National League, which decided to finish the season with four clubs. Tacoma and Helena had dropped out five days earlier.

August 29, 1903, Manager George Yeager of Minneapolis, American Association, was arrested at Toledo for assault upon a stone-throwing 10-year-old boy.

September 7, 1903, Peekskill won three Hudson River League games in one day, a

morning victory from Poughkeepsie and twin victories over Catskill in the afternoon.

September 20, 1903, Hudson and Poughkeepsie played a "quadrupleheader". In the morning twin-bill, Hudson won 2-1 and 6-4, and in the afternoon, 3-1 and 4-2. Bingham and Sewall each lost two games for Poughkeepsie, while Donahue and Berger won in the morning and ace Erwin Donnelly pitched both winners in the afternoon for Hudson.

October 1, 1903, Thomas J. Hickey resigned the presidency of the American Association, which he founded, to enter into private business in St. Paul, Minnesota.

October 25, 1903, Seattle, Pacific Coast League, won its 19th successive game (includes one tie).

October 26, 1903, Dolly Gray, pitching for Los Angeles, Pacific Coast League, stopped Seattle 7-5, after the latter club had won 19 straight decisions.

October 26, 1903, Third baseman William Phyle, Memphis, Southern Association, was expelled by the National Board for refusing to appear and substantiate his charge that Southern League games had been "thrown".

November 10, 1903, Veteran William "Billy" Hamilton signed to manage Haverhill in the New England League.

November 29, 1903, The six-club Pacific Coast League, which began on March 9, ended with the Los Angeles Angels the pennant winners by a margin of 27-1/2 games with a record of 133-78.

December 19, 1903, Dane Calhoun, a minor league player of note from Philadelphia, was found murdered near Indian Springs, Indiana.

December 24, 1903, Henry D. Ramsey of Kingston, Hudson River League, took his ball team to Cuba for a winter season.

1904

American League
President: Byron Bancroft Johnson

Standings	W	L	Pct.	GB	Attend.	Manager
Boston Pilgrims	95	59	.617	—	623,295	Jimmy Collins
New York Highlanders	92	59	.609	1½	438,919	Clark Griffith
Chicago White Sox	89	65	.578	6	557,123	Nixey Callahan/Fielder Jones
Cleveland Naps	86	65	.570	7½	264,749	Bill Armour
Philadelphia Athletics	81	70	.536	12½	512,294	Connie Mack
St. Louis Browns	65	87	.428	29	318,108	Jimmy McAleer
Detroit Tigers	62	90	.408	32	177,796	Edward Barrow/Bobby Lowe
Washington Senators	38	113	.252	55½	131,744	Mal Kittridge/Patsy Donovan

BA: Napoleon Lajoie, Cleveland, .381
Runs: Patsy Dougherty, Boston/New York, 113
Hits: Napoleon Lajoie, Cleveland, 211
RBIs: Napoleon Lajoie, Cleveland, 102
HRs: Harry Davis, Philadelphia, 10

Wins: Jack Chesbro, New York, 41
SOs: Rube Waddell, Philadelphia, 349
ERA: Addie Joss, Cleveland, 1.59
Pct: Jack Chesbro, New York, .774, 41-12
CG: Jack Chesbro, New York, 48
IP: Jack Chesbro, New York, 455

National League
President: Harry C. Pulliam

Standings	W	L	Pct.	GB	Attend.	Manager
New York Giants	106	47	.693	—	609,826	John McGraw
Chicago Cubs	93	60	.608	13	439,100	Frank Selee
Cincinnati Reds	88	65	.575	18	391,915	Joe Kelley
Pittsburgh Pirates	87	66	.569	19	340,615	Fred Clarke
St. Louis Cardinals	75	79	.487	31½	386,750	Charles "Kid" Nichols
Brooklyn Superbas	56	97	.366	50	214,600	Ned Hanlon
Boston Beaneaters	55	98	.359	51	140,694	Al Buckenberger
Philadelphia Phillies	52	100	.342	53½	140,771	Hugh Duffy

BA: Honus Wagner, Pittsburgh, .349
Runs: George Browne, New York, 99
Hits: Ginger Beaumont, Pittsburgh, 185
RBIs: Bill Dahlen, New York, 80
HRs: Harry Lumley, Brooklyn, 9

Wins: Joe McGinnity, New York, 35
SOs: Christy Mathewson, New York, 212
ERA: Joe McGinnity, New York, 1.61
Pct: Joe McGinnity, New York, .814, 35-8
IP: Joe McGinnity, New York, 408

A American Association
President: J. Edward Grillo

Standings	W	L	Pct.	GB	Manager
St. Paul Apostles	95	52	.646	—	Mike Kelley
Columbus Senators	88	61	.591	8	William Clymer
Milwaukee Brewers	89	63	.586	8½	Joe Cantillon
Minneapolis Millers	78	67	.538	16	Bill Watkins
Louisville Colonels	77	70	.524	18	George Tebeau
Indianapolis Indians	69	85	.448	29½	Bill Phillips
Kansas City Blues	60	91	.387	37	Dale Gear/Arthur Irwin
Toledo Mud Hens	42	109	.272	55	Herman Long/John Burns/William Clingman

BA: George Stone, Milwaukee, .406
Runs: Germany Schaefer, Milwaukee, 159
Hits: George Stone, Milwaukee, 254
HRs: Jim Jackson, St. Paul, 13

Wins: Charles Chech, St. Paul, 27
SOs: Clifton Curtis, Milwaukee, 210
Pct: Charles Chech, St. Paul, .771, 27-8

A Eastern League
President: Patrick T. Powers

Standings	W	L	Pct.	GB	Manager
Buffalo Bisons	88	46	.657	—	George Stallings
Baltimore Orioles	78	52	.600	8	Hugh Jennings
Jersey City Skeeters	76	57	.571	11½	William Murray
Newark Sailors	77	59	.566	12	Walter Burnham
Montreal Royals	67	62	.519	18½	Charles Atherton/Edward Barrow
Toronto Maple Leafs	67	71	.486	23	Arthur Irwin/Richard Harley
Providence Grays	52	81	.391	35½	Thomas Daly
Rochester Bronchos	28	105	.211	59½	George Smith

Attendance: Buffalo, 234,935.

BA: Joe Yeager, Montreal, .332
Runs: Myron Grimshaw, Buffalo, 98
Hits: Myron Grimshaw, Buffalo, 177
HRs: Frank LaPorte, Buffalo, 9

Wins: Mal Eason, Jersey City, 26
SOs: Cy Falkenberg, Toronto, 175
Pct: Stan Yerkes, Buffalo, .769, 10-3

A Pacific Coast League
President: Eugene F. Bert

Standings	W	L	Pct.	GB	Manager
Tacoma Tigers***	130	94	.580	—	Mike Fisher
Los Angeles Angels	119	97	.551	7	James Morely
Seattle Siwashes	114	106	.518	14	Parke Wilson
Oakland Oaks	116	109	.516	14½	Pete Lohman
San Francisco Seals	101	117	.463	26	Henry Harris
Portland Browns	79	136	.368	46½	Fred Ely/Daniel Dugdale/Ike Butler

Playoff: Tacoma 4 games, Los Angeles 1, one tie.

BA: Emil Frisk, Seattle, .337
Runs: Emil Frisk, Seattle, 179
Hits: Emil Frisk, Seattle, 272

HRs: Truck Eagan, Tacoma, 25
Wins: Doc Newton, Los Angeles, 39
Pct: Doc Newton, Los Angeles, .696, 39-17

A Western League
President: Michael H. Sexton

Standings	W	L	Pct.	GB	Manager
Omaha Rangers	90	60	.600	—	Pa Rourke
Colorado Springs Millionaires	85	58	.594	1½	Jimmy Ryan
Denver Grizzlies	87	61	.588	2	William Hallman
Des Moines Prohibitionists	79	69	.534	10	Bill Hoffer
St. Joseph Saints	53	93	.363	35	E.D. Webster
Sioux City Soos	45	98	.315	41½	Jay Andrews/Jay Parker/Tom Fleming

Attendance: Des Moines, 74,000.

BA: Bill Congalton, Colorado Springs, .327
Runs: George Nill, Colorado Springs, 117
Hits: Del Howard, Omaha, 184
HRs: Del Howard, Omaha, 9

Wins: Mordecai "Three Finger" Brown, Omaha, 27
SOs: Jack Pfiester, Omaha, 178
Pct: Mordecai "Three Finger" Brown, Omaha, .643, 27-15

B Central League
President: George W. Bement

Standings	W	L	Pct.	GB	Manager
Fort Wayne Railroaders	88	51	.633	—	Bade Myers
Terre Haute Hottentots	76	63	.547	12	Frank Warrender
South Bend Greens	75	65	.536	13½	Angus Grant
Wheeling Stogies	72	65	.526	15	Ted Price
Dayton Veterans	67	70	.489	20	John Spaatz/Charles Jewell/Hub Knoll
Marion Oilworkers/Peoria Distillers#	61	75	.449	25½	John H. Grim/Mike Lawrence
Grand Rapids Orphans	58	81	.417	30	John Flannery/John Morrissey
Evansville River Rats	56	83	.403	32	Frank Schoeller/Robert Berryhill/Frank Cross

#Marion (12-15) moved to Peoria (27-33) June 1, then returned to Marion July 31.

BA: Charles Cogswell, South Bend, .355
Hits: Henry Melchior, Grand Rapids/Evansville, 174

B New England League
President: Tim H. Murnane

Standings	W	L	Pct.	GB	Manager
Haverhill Hustlers	82	41	.667	—	Billy Hamilton
New Bedford Whalers	64	58	.525	17½	A.G. "Fred" Doe
Fall River Indians	65	60	.520	18	Thomas McDermott
Manchester	61	60	.504	20	John A. Smith
Concord Marines	62	62	.500	20½	Nathan Pulsifer
Nashua	62	62	.500	20½	John Carney/Sid Rollins
Lowell Tigers	59	62	.488	22	Frederick Lake
Lawrence Colts	36	86	.295	45½	Stephen Flanagan

BA: Billy Hamilton, Haverhill, .412
Runs: Billy Hamilton, Haverhill, 113
Hits: Billy Hamilton, Haverhill, 168
HRs: Izzy Van Zant, Nashua, 7

B New York State League
President: John H. Farrell

Standings	W	L	Pct.	GB	Manager
Syracuse Stars	91	44	.674	—	Sandy Griffin
Albany Senators	81	52	.609	9	Michael Doherty
Ilion Typewriters	75	56	.573	14	James Sharrott
Amsterdam-Johnstown-Gloversville Hyphens	65	61	.516	21½	Howard Earl
Troy Trojans	61	73	.455	29½	Louis Bacon
Utica Pent-Ups	59	73	.447	30½	Elmer Horton/John Lawler
Schenectady Electricians/Scranton Miners#	47	75	.385	35½	Benjamin Ellis/Lou O'Neal/Bill Bannon
Binghamton Bingoes	40	85	.320	46	Charles "Count" Campau

#Schenectady (20-39) moved to Scranton July 17.

BA: Elmer Smith, Ilion, .326
Runs: Pat Crisham, Syracuse, 89

Hits: Frank Schulte, Syracuse, 159
J.T. Fox, Utica, 159
Wins: Jack Fifield, Syracuse, 26
Pct: Jack Fifield, Syracuse, .788, 26-7

*Won first-half   **Won second-half   ***Won both halves

B Pacific National League
President: William H. Lucas

Standings	W	L	Pct.	GB	Manager
Boise Fruit Pickers	82	49	.626	—	John McCloskey
Spokane Indians	73	57	.562	8½	Charles Reilly
Butte Miners	54	75	.419	27	Walter Wilmot
Salt Lake City Elders	51	79	.392	30½	Frank "Dad" Gimlin/Frederick Clarke

BA: Bill Carney, Spokane, .366
Runs: Ike Rockenfield, Spokane, 113
Hits: Bill Weaver, Boise, 188
HRs: Ralph Frary, Spokane, 13
Wins: Dan McFarlan, Boise, 30
SOs: Bill Hogg, Spokane, 259
Pct: Moses Vasbinder, Butte, .727, 8-3

B Southern Association
President: William M. Kavanagh

Standings	W	L	Pct.	GB	Manager
Memphis Egyptians	81	54	.600	—	Lew Whistler
Atlanta Crackers	78	57	.578	3	Abner Powell
New Orleans Pelicans	79	58	.577	3	Charles Frank
Birmingham Barons	73	64	.533	9	Thomas O'Brien/Harry Vaughn
Nashville Volunteers	72	67	.518	11	Newton Fisher
Little Rock Travelers	61	74	.452	20	Michael Finn
Shreveport Pirates	55	81	.404	26½	Robert Gilks
Montgomery Senators	44	88	.333	35½	William Stickney/Thomas O'Brien

BA: John Gilbert, Little Rock, .327
Runs: Jim Duffy, Birmingham, 100
Hits: Justin "Pug" Bennett, Nashville, 166
HRs: Frank Weikart, Shreveport/New Orleans, 7
Wins: Charles Smith, Atlanta, 31
Pct: Pat Reagan, Birmingham, .800, 8-2

B Three-I League
President: Michael H. Sexton

Standings	W	L	Pct.	GB	Manager
Springfield Hustlers	72	48	.600	—	Frank Donnelly
Cedar Rapids Rabbits	70	52	.574	4	Belden Hill
Dubuque Shamrocks	69	54	.561	4½	Charles Buelow
Bloomington Bloomers	60	61	.496	12½	William Connors
Decatur Commodores	59	62	.488	13½	Monte McFarland
Rock Island Islanders	57	65	.467	16	Ross Thornton/Kahley Miller/Hugh Nicol
Davenport River Rats	52	69	.430	20½	James Hayes
Rockford Red Sox	48	76	.387	26	Hugh Nicol/Jack Meek

BA: William Connors, Bloomington, .329
Runs: Louis Lippert, Springfield, 92
Hits: Jack Meek, Rockford, 167
Wins: Louis Fiene, Cedar Rapids, 23
SOs: Charles Jaeger, Rockford, 218
ERA: Louis Fiene, Cedar Rapids, 2.45

C Hudson River League
President: C.S. Harvey

Standings	W	L	Pct.	GB	Manager
Poughkeepsie Colts	70	47	.598	—	William McCabe
Paterson Intruders#	70	49	.588	1	Richard Cogan
Hudson Marines	68	52	.567	3½	Gus Schnack
Kingston Colonials	58	58	.500	11½	Henry Ramsey
Saugerties	50	68	.424	20½	John O'Halloran
Newburgh Taylor-mades	39	81	.325	32½	Charles Fisher/John Green/Fred Taylor

#Paterson played home games at Paterson and Clifton, New Jersey.

BA: Dan Brouthers, Poughkeepsie, .373
Hits: Dan Brouthers, Poughkeepsie, 158

C Missouri Valley League
President: Dr. D.M. Shiveley

Standings	W	L	Pct.	GB	Manager
Iola Gasbags	83	41	.669	—	D.C. "Dad" Risley
Springfield Midgets	77	46	.626	5½	F. Smith/John Perrine
Joplin Miners	77	49	.611	7	John Fillman
Sedalia Gold Bugs	71	53	.573	12	E.E. Codding
Pittsburg Coal Diggers	57	64	.471	24½	O.H. Baldwin/John Kane
Leavenworth Orioles	48	74	.393	34	Eli Cates/Elmer Smith
Topeka Saints	45	78	.366	37½	Gus Alberts/C. Cole/John Shrant/Spencer Abbott
Ft. Scott Giants	36	89	.288	47½	Jack Bene/Louis Armstrong

BA: Jacob Bauer, Sedalia, .346
Hits: Jacob Bauer, Sedalia, 178
Wins: Amos Morgan, Iola, 32
SOs: John Root, Iola, 224
Pct: Ed Craig, Springfield, .826, 19-4

C South Atlantic League
President: Charles W. Boyer

Standings	W	L	Pct.	GB	Manager
Macon Highlanders	67	45	.598	—	William A. Smith
Savannah Pathfinders	63	48	.568	3½	Sam LaRoque/Dominick Mullaney
Charleston Sea Gulls	59	50	.541	6½	Edward Ashenbach
Jacksonville Jays	58	57	.504	11½	George Kelly/Jack Robinson/Robert Black
Columbia Skyscrapers	47	62	.431	18½	John J. Grim/William Engle
Augusta Tourists	41	73	.360	27	J.C. "Con" Strothers/Harlan Wingard

BA: Andy Oyler, Savannah, .301
Runs: Ed McKernan, Charleston, 82
Hits: Sidney Smith, Charleston, 137
HRs: Chris Miller, Columbia/Augusta/Savannah, 5
Wins: Brindle Bayne, Macon, 30
SOs: Brindle Bayne, Macon, 288
Pct: Conrad Welch, Savannah, .706, 24-10

C South Texas League
Presidents: Max Stubenraugh/Bliss P. Gorman

Standings	W	L	Pct.	GB	Manager
Galveston Sandcrabs**	82	43	.656	—	Marcene Johnson
Beaumont Millionaires	66	56	.541	14½	F.W. Greer
Houston Wanderers*	66	59	.528	16	Claude Reilly
San Antonio Bronchos	32	88	.267	47½	Wade Moore

The league started the season at Class D, then became a C league in June.

Playoff: Galveston 4 games, Houston 3.

BA: Bob Edmundson, Houston, .340
Runs: Ed Cermack, Galveston, 104
Hits: Les Smith, Beaumont/San Antonio/Houston, 171
HRs: Dick Latham, Galveston, 18
Wins: Clayton Robb, Beaumont/Houston, 26
Baldo Luitich, Galveston/Beaumont, 26
SOs: Bill Sorrells, Houston, 243
Pct: John Reuther, Galveston, .774, 24-7

C Texas League
Presidents: William A. Abey/J. Doak Roberts

Standings	W	L	Pct.	GB	Manager
Ft. Worth Panthers	71	30	.703	—	Fred Willis
Dallas Giants	58	45	.563	14	Charles Moran
Corsicana Oil Cities	48	53	.475	23	James "Curley" Maloney/Walter Salm
Paris Parasites/Ardmore Territorians#	26	75	.257	45	Mike O'Connor/Pete Walsh/Billy Hughes

#Paris (23-65) moved to Ardmore August 5.

Playoff: Corsicana 11 games, Ft. Worth 8.

BA: Trapper Longley, Corsicana, .372
Runs: Lon Ury, Dallas, 71
Hits: Trapper Longley, Corsicana, 106
Fred Willis, Ft. Worth, 106
Wins: Charles Jackson, Ft. Worth, 26
SOs: Jack Jarvis, Ft. Worth, 185
Pct: Walt "Harold" Chrisman, Ft. Worth, .778, 21-6

D Connecticut League
President: James O'Rourke

Standings	W	L	Pct.	GB	Manager
Bridgeport Orators	71	45	.612	—	James O'Rourke
Springfield Ponies	69	46	.600	1½	Daniel O'Neill
New Haven Blues	69	47	.595	2	James Canavan
Holyoke Paperweights	58	55	.513	11½	Frank Fitzpatrick/P. Prindiville/W. Winkler
New London Whalers	56	60	.483	15	Charles Humphrey
Hartford Senators	53	61	.465	17	William Kennedy
Worcester/Norwich Reds#	53	62	.461	17½	Mal Kittridge/Robert Tracey/Jack Tighe/Fred Crolius
Meriden Silverites	31	84	.270	39½	Sam Kennedy

#Worcester (26-11) moved to Norwich June 21.

BA: Clarence "Pop" Foster, Bridgeport, .376
Runs: Royal Clark, Bridgeport, 101
Hits: Clarence "Pop" Foster, Bridgeport, 158
HRs: Emil Batch, Holyoke, 7
SOs: Bill Foxen, Hartford, 180

D Cotton States League
President: George Wheatley

Standings	W	L	Pct.	GB	Manager
Pine Bluff Lumbermen	73	43	.629	—	Bert Blue/George Reed
Vicksburg Hill Billies	68	48	.586	5	Billy Earle
Monroe Hill Cities	62	56	.525	12	George Leidy
Greenville Cotton Pickers	51	61	.455	20	Robert Rothermel
Baton Rouge Red Sticks	49	63	.438	22	Robert Pender
Natchez Indians	42	74	.362	31	George Blackburn/William Breitenstein

BA: Howard Murphy, Pine Bluff, .343
Runs: Ollie Gfroerer, Pine Bluff, 102
Hits: Howard Murphy, Pine Bluff, 156
SBs: Forrest Plass, Vicksburg, 72
Wins: Robert Lee Vernuelle, Pine Bluff, 24
Gordon Hickman, Monroe, 24
SOs: Ross Helm, Monroe, 221
Pct: Walt Deaver, Pine Bluff, .762, 16-5

D Delta League
Presidents: S.L. Dodds/V.M. Scanlan

Standings	W	L	Pct.	GB	Manager
Clarksdale	67	31	.684	—	William "Dave" Gaston
Yazoo City Zoos	62	34	.646	4	Wilson
Canton#	43	45	.489	19	Freeman
Jackson Senators	47	53	.470	21	Jackson
Hattiesburg#	36	49	.424	24½	Conrad Best
Brookhaven	27	70	.278	39½	

#Canton and Hattiesburg were added to the league May 16, one week after the season opened.

1904

All-Star Team: 1B-Harry Salliard, Jackson; **2B**-Leo Huber, Jackson; **3B**-Dan Davies, Hattiesburg; **SS**-J.A. Tilford, Clarksdale; **OF**-John Sens, Hattiesburg; William "Dave" Gaston, Clarksdale; Ernest Schultz, Canton; **C**-John Burns, Clarksdale; Freeman, Canton; **P**-Harry Kane (Cohen), Clarksdale; Baxter Sparks, Yazoo City; Conrad Best, Hattiesburg; F.R. Burnam, Canton; Jack Ryan, Jackson.

BA: Harry Vitter, Canton, .330
Runs: H. Foster, Jackson, 83
Hits: William "Dave" Gaston, Clarksdale, 91
Wins: Baxter Sparks, Yazoo City, 25

SOs: Harry Kane (Cohen), Clarksdale, 131
Pct: Harry Kane (Cohen), Clarksdale, .857, 18-3

D Iowa State League
President: Frank S. Norton

Standings	W	L	Pct.	GB	Attend.	Manager
Ottumwa Standpatters	70	36	.660	—	17,630	A.L. "Snapper" Kennedy
Waterloo Microbes	64	43	.598	6½	18,695	James Myers
Marshalltown Grays	60	49	.550	11½	23,117	Robert Warner
Keokuk Indians	58	50	.537	13	15,741	Tom Hackett
Ft. Dodge Gypsum Eaters	57	52	.523	14½	13,582	Frank Boyle
Boone Coal Miners	50	61	.450	22½	16,581	Thomas Reynolds/ Walter Holcomb
Oskaloosa Quakers	38	69	.355	32½	16,620	William Tilley/ Tom "Red" Donohue
Burlington River Rats	36	73	.330	35½	21,352	F.L. Sullivan/George Stovall/ Bob Black

BA: A.L. "Snapper" Kennedy, Ottumwa, .325
Runs: Joe Beaver, Ottumwa, 76; Al Spencer, Ottumwa, 76
Hits: A.L. "Snapper" Kennedy, Ottumwa, 142
Wins: Louis Schaub, Ottumwa, 23
SOs: Louis Schaub, Ottumwa, 298
Pct: Louis Schaub, Ottumwa, .767, 23-7

D Kitty League
President: W.I. Thompson

Standings	W	L	Pct.	GB	Manager
Paducah Indians	73	48	.603	—	Meredeth/John Ray
Cairo Champions	72	49	.595	1	P. Scullin
Clarksville Grays	64	58	.517	9½	
Henderson Blue Birds	54	68	.443	19½	Clyde McNutt
Hopkinsville Browns	52	68	.433	20½	Cummings/Jack Ferrell
Vincennes Reds	50	73	.407	24	Willie Popp/Luke Duffy/Eichler

D Northern League
President: D.J. Laxdal

Standings	W	L	Pct.	GB	Manager
Duluth White Sox	54	20	.730	—	Leonard Van Praagh
Winnipeg Maroons	40	36	.526	15	Ned Egan/R.J. Smith/William Wilson
Grand Forks Forkers	36	37	.493	17½	Scott Kairnes/E.G. Cooper
Crookston Crooks	33	36	.478	18½	Bill McNeil/William Lycan
Superior Longshoremen#	29	44	.397	24½	Don Cameron/William Bray
Fargo	29	48	.377	26½	Perry Werden/Lee DeMontreville

#Superior disbanded August 8.
The season was shortened to August 13.

BA: Earl Howard, Winnipeg, .363
Runs: Newton Randall, Duluth, 61
Hits: Newton Randall, Duluth, 91
Wins: Henry Gehring, Duluth, 13; Frank Green, Winnipeg, 13; John Bartos, Winnipeg, 13
SOs: John Bartos, Winnipeg, 114; Roy Morton, Grand Forks, 114
Pct: Henry Gehring, Duluth, .867, 13-2

D Oregon State League

Standings	W	L	Pct.	GB	Manager
Salem Raglans	27	13	.675	—	Jack Fay
Eugene Blues@	22	19	.537	5½	Dushane
Vancouver Soldiers/ Albany Rollers#	17	24	.415	10½	E.P. Preble
Roseburg Shamrocks@	15	25	.375	12	Turkey Morrow

#Vancouver (3-8) moved to Albany May 18.
@Eugene and Roseburg disbanded July 6, causing the league to disband the same day. The league was not admitted to the National Association until it vacated Vancouver, Washington, which was within the territorial limit of Portland, Oregon of the Pacific Coast League.

D Southwest Washington League
Presidents: John P. Fink/Colonel Fox

Standings	W	L	Pct.	GB	Manager
Hoquiam Perfect Gentlemen	14	4	.778	—	Ralph Philbrick
Aberdeen Pippins	10	8	.556	4	Robert Brown
Centralia Midgets	6	12	.333	8	Bloomfield
Olympia Senators	6	12	.333	8	Jessie Mill

The league played six times a week, but only the weekend games counted.

D Southwestern League
Presidents: Will Kimmel/D.F. Smith

Standings	W	L	Pct.	GB	Manager
Guthrie Blues**	56	44	.560	—	Ernest Jones/Billy Hughes/Frank Overbay/ Thomas Neal
Enid Evangelists*	46	37	.554	1½	Walter Frantz/Howard Price
Oklahoma City Mets**	45	49	.479	8	Emmett Rodgers/Andy Warner/Gene Barnes
Shawnee/Chickasha Indians/ Shawnee Browns#	25	42	.373	NA	W.M. Hazlett/L.A. Lackey/Van Ness/ Charles Palmer

#Shawnee (1-2) moved to Chickasha (13-20) June 30, then moved back to Shawnee August 3; the franchise disbanded September 5.

Ind Tri-State League
President: Charles F. Carpenter

Standings	W	L	Pct.	GB	Manager
York Penn Parks	64	40	.615	—	George Heckert
Williamsport Millionaires	61	46	.570	4½	Curt Weigand
Harrisburg Senators	58	51	.532	8½	Peter Agnew
Altoona Mountaineers	50	48	.516	11	Charles Carpenter
Lebanon	48	61	.440	18½	Charles Kelchner
Wilmington Peaches	41	61	.402	22	Jess Frysinger
Camden#	4	19	.176	NA	Black

#Camden disbanded early in the season.

Wins: Stoney McGlynn, York, 30
Pct: Stoney McGlynn, York, .732, 30-11

1904 Interleague Post Season Play

Junior World Series
Buffalo (Eastern) 2 games, St. Paul (American Association) 1

1904 No-Hitters

Date	Pitcher	Team	League	Opponent	Score
5-5	Cy Young	Boston	American	Philadelphia	3-0 (P)
5-8	George Feye	Monroe	Cotton States	Greenville	3-0
5-13	Danny Friend	New Bedford	New England	Fall River	4-0
6-11	Bob Wicker	Chicago	National	New York	1-0 (10)
6-21	Henry Gehring	Duluth	Northern	Superior	1-0
6-29	Ralph Bell	A-J-G	New York State	Syracuse	1-0
6-30	Jim Scott	Binghamton	New York State	Schenectady	6-0 (7)
7-8	Glenn Liebhardt	Rock Island	Three-I	Bloomington	2-0
7-9	Harry Brown	New Orleans	Southern Assoc.	Shreveport	5-0
7-13	Frank Barber	San Francisco	Pacific Coast	Oakland	1-0
7-15	H.A. Souders	Fargo	Northern	Grand Forks	1-0 (10)
7-17	Frank Lange	Dayton	Central	Peoria	3-0
8-5	Bart Farrell	Grand Rapids	Central	Wheeling	6-0
8-17	Jesse Tannehill	Boston	American	Chicago	6-0
8-21	L.R. Childs	Charleston	South Atlantic	Jacksonville	2-0
8-27	Baxter Sparks	Yazoo City	Delta	Clarksdale	1-0
9-3	Jimmy Dygert	Poughkeepsie	Hudson River	Newburgh	
9-11	Jim Wiggs	New Orleans	Southern Assoc.	Little Rock	7-0
9-27	Jerry Nops	Providence	Eastern	Toronto	5-0
	Jack Pfiester	Omaha	Western	St. Joseph	

Number in parentheses indicates innings if other than nine; "P" indicates perfect game.

THIS DATE IN MINOR LEAGUE HISTORY

January 2, 1904, Toledo, American Association, signed veteran Herman Long as player-manager.

January 10, 1904, Clinton H. Bradley, a former Eastern League player, committed suicide at Utica, New York, owing to business reverses.

March 27, 1904, Hal Chase made his Organized Ball debut with the Los Angeles Angels of the Pacific Coast League and went 0-for-3 against the Oakland Oaks.

April 17, 1904, Thirty people were injured by the collapse of the bleachers at the Paterson, Hudson River League, New Jersey ball park.

April 26, 1904, Tyrus Raymond Cobb, 17-year-old rookie for Augusta in the South Atlantic League, made his Organized Ball debut against Columbia with a double and a home run, but he drew his release the following day. Cobb then signed with Anniston of the independent Southeastern League, on April 29th at a salary of $50 per month.

May 5, 1904, President George Tebeau of Louisville was suspended for ten days by American Association prexy J. Edward Grillo for throwing umpire George Bausewine's clothing into the street and locking him out of his dressing room.

June 1, 1904, Future Hall of Fame umpire William J. Klem of New York signed to umpire in the American Association.

June 4, 1904, Toledo, American Association, hit into two triple plays in one game at Kansas City. The Blues' Loewe and Ryan turned the first triple killing while Loewe and Sullivan did the second.

June 24, 1904, Veteran player-manager Herman Long resigned from the Toledo, American Association, club.

July 1, 1904, Tom Mylett of Syracuse, New York State League, accepted 20 chances at shortstop in a game.

July 6, 1904, Wilbert Robinson, veteran catcher with Baltimore, Eastern League, retired from active play.

July 8, 1904, Baltimore, Eastern League, beat Jersey City 10-9; each Jersey City player scored one of the nine runs.

July 9, 1904, Frank Herbert, Dayton, Central League, died from injuries received while running the bases.

July 11, 1904, In the Cotton States League, Greenville and Vicksburg played to a 20-inning 2-2 tie.

July 16, 1904, In Little Rock, pitcher Duke Carter of Montgomery, Southern Association, while walking in his sleep, fell from a window on the third floor of the Capitol Hotel and was badly injured.

July 19, 1904, Shortstop Downey, Nashville, Southern Association, was arrested and fined at Memphis for throwing a bat at spectators.

July 28, 1904, Captain "Buck" Thiel of Des Moines, Western League, was arrested and pleaded guilty to assaulting a local reporter. He was then traded to Omaha.

July 30, 1904, Pitcher Jake Volz of Manchester, New England League, pitched a doubleheader and won both games from Nashua, 3-0 and 3-1, allowing only a total of five hits in the two contests.

August 5, 1904, Atlanta, Southern Association, made 24 hits and 19 runs off pitcher Hughey of Shreveport.

August 13, 1904, Edward Barrow, formerly of Detroit, assumed management of the Montreal club in the Eastern League.

August 27, 1904, Baxter Sparks, who won 21 straight games this season for Yazoo City of the Delta League, tossed a no-hit game against Clarksdale.

September 4, 1904, Pitcher "Babe" Brown of New Orleans, Southern Association, died of spinal meningitis in New Orleans.

September 5, 1904, Omaha scored 12 runs in one inning against Sioux City in the Western League.

September 21, 1904, Omaha, Western League, won its 14th successive game, defeating St. Joseph.

September 24, 1904, Atlanta and Shreveport of the Southern League played a nine-inning game in a record time of 44 minutes at Atlanta.

November 5, 1904, At Los Angeles, during the Los Angeles-Tacoma Pacific Coast League game, Frank Chance collided with shortstop Truck Eagan of Tacoma, breaking the latter's arm.

November 15, 1904, Pitcher Orvie Overall of Tacoma, Pacific Coast League, struck out 15 in a game with Oakland.

November 27, 1904, The Pacific Coast League season closed with Tacoma the pennant winner for the combined two seasons. The league played a 225-game schedule.

November 28, 1904, Pitcher Steve Ashe of New Haven, Connecticut State League, committed suicide at Grace Hospital in New Haven while temporarily insane.

December 8, 1904, Edward Barrow of Montreal, Eastern League, purchased a one-third interest in the Indianapolis team of the American Association.

An Umpire's Union

At the National League meetings in New York, Tim Hurst was quoted as saying, "In view of this union spirit which fills the air, we umpires ought to organize for mutual benefit and protection. We could do a lot if we were only banded together. If a player got fresh we could pass the word along the line and that player would never get anything but strikes called. Suppose McGraw, for example, called me a bullet-headed loafer, an A.P.A., and a burlesque on humanity. Say – I'll kick you in the face if you say that he'd only be telling the truth! Well, I'd send word to the union. Next town Bob Emslie's umpiring, he would call two strikes on McGraw on balls over the catcher's head, and then, when Muggsy drove one through center field, it would be foul. So on, he'd get it in every city until he agreed to apologize, pay a fine of $250 and sign the union scale."

"What's the Union Scale?" asked sportswriters.

"Five dollars to call the umpire a lobster, $10 to call him a fat-head, $25 to call him a stiff, and $50 to kick him in the shins . . .."

Sporting Life 1904

1905

American League

President: Byron Bancroft Johnson

Standings	W	L	Pct.	GB	Attend.	Manager
Philadelphia Athletics	92	56	.622	—	554,576	Connie Mack
Chicago White Sox	92	60	.605	2	687,419	Fielder Jones
Detroit Tigers	79	74	.516	15½	193,384	Bill Armour
Boston Pilgrims	78	74	.513	16	468,828	Jimmy Collins
Cleveland Naps	76	78	.494	19	316,306	Napoleon Lajoie/Bill Bradley
New York Highlanders	71	78	.477	21½	309,100	Clark Griffith
Washington Senators	64	87	.424	29½	252,027	Jake Stahl
St. Louis Browns	54	99	.353	40½	339,112	Jimmy McAleer

BA: Elmer Flick, Cleveland, .306
Runs: Harry Davis, Philadelphia, 92
Hits: George Stone, St. Louis, 187
RBIs: Harry Davis, Philadelphia, 83
HRs: Harry Davis, Philadelphia, 8
Wins: Rube Waddell, Philadelphia, 26
SOs: Rube Waddell, Philadelphia, 287
ERA: Rube Waddell, Philadelphia, 1.48
Pct: Andy Coakley, Philadelphia, .741, 20-7

National League

President: Harry C. Pulliam

Standings	W	L	Pct.	GB	Attend.	Manager
New York Giants	105	48	.686	—	552,700	John McGraw
Pittsburgh Pirates	96	57	.627	9	369,124	Fred Clarke
Chicago Cubs	92	61	.601	13	509,900	Frank Selee/Frank Chance
Philadelphia Phillies	83	69	.546	21½	317,932	Hugh Duffy
Cincinnati Reds	79	74	.516	26	313,927	Joe Kelley
St. Louis Cardinals	58	96	.377	47½	292,800	Charles "Kid" Nichols/Jimmy Burke/Matt Robison
Boston Beaneaters	51	103	.331	54½	150,003	Fred Tenney
Brooklyn Superbas	48	104	.316	56½	227,924	Ned Hanlon

BA: Cy Seymour, Cincinnati, .377
Runs: Mike Donlin, New York, 124
Hits: Cy Seymour, Cincinnati, 219
RBIs: Cy Seymour, Cincinnati, 121
HRs: Fred Odwell, Cincinnati, 9
Wins: Christy Mathewson, New York, 31
SOs: Christy Mathewson, New York, 206
ERA: Christy Mathewson, New York, 1.27
Pct: Christy Mathewson, New York, .795, 31-8

A American Association

President: Joseph D. O'Brien

Standings	W	L	Pct.	GB	Manager
Columbus Senators	100	52	.658	—	William Clymer
Milwaukee Brewers	91	59	.607	8	Joe Cantillon
Minneapolis Millers	88	62	.587	11	Bill Watkins
Louisville Colonels	76	75	.503	23½	Charles Dexter
St. Paul Apostles	73	77	.487	26	Mike Kelley
Indianapolis Indians	69	83	.454	31	Edward Barrow
Toledo Mud Hens	60	91	.397	39½	Michael Finn/Edward Grillo
Kansas City Blues	44	102	.301	53	Arthur Irwin

BA: Charlie Hemphill, St. Paul, .364
Runs: Davy Jones, Minneapolis, 126
Hits: Charlie Hemphill, St. Paul, 204
HRs: Wyatt Lee, Toledo, 13
Wins: Gus Dorner, Columbus, 29
SOs: Charles Berger, Columbus, 200
Pct: Gus Dorner, Columbus, .784, 29-8

A Eastern League

President: Patrick T. Powers

Standings	W	L	Pct.	GB	Manager
Providence Clamdiggers	83	47	.638	—	Jack Dunn
Baltimore Orioles	82	47	.636	½	Hugh Jennings
Jersey City Skeeters	81	49	.623	2	William Murray
Newark Sailors	69	62	.527	14½	Walter Burnham
Buffalo Bisons	63	74	.460	23½	George Stallings
Montreal Royals	56	80	.412	30	James Bannon
Rochester Bronchos	51	86	.372	35½	Al Buckenberger
Toronto Maple Leafs	48	88	.350	38	Richard Harley/Edward Barrow

Attendance: Buffalo, 200,537.

BA: Frank Laporte, Buffalo, .331
Runs: Herm McFarland, Providence, 91
Hits: Jack Dunn, Providence, 157
HRs: Jim Murray, Buffalo/Toronto, 9
Wins: John Cronin, Providence, 29
SOs: Walt Clarkson, Jersey City, 195
Pct: Vic Lindaman, Jersey City, .774, 24-7

A Pacific Coast League

President: Eugene F. Bert

Standings	W	L	Pct.	GB	Manager
Los Angeles Angels**	120	94	.561	—	Frank "Cap" Dillon
San Francisco Seals	125	100	.556	½	Parke Wilson
Tacoma Tigers*	106	107	.498	13½	Mike Fisher
Oakland Oaks	103	119	.464	21	Pete Lohman/George Van Haltren
Portland Giants	94	110	.461	21	Walter McCredie
Seattle Siwashes	93	111	.456	22	Russ Hall

Playoff: Los Angeles 5 games, Tacoma 1, one tie.

BA: Kitty Brashear, Los Angeles, .303
Runs: George Van Haltren, Oakland, 125
Hits: Lou Nordyke, Tacoma, 227
HRs: Truck Eagan, Tacoma, 21
Wins: Jimmy Whalen, San Francisco, 30
SOs: Charles "Sea Lion" Hall, Seattle, 275
Pct: Walter Nagle, Los Angeles, 1.000, 11-0

A Southern Association

President: William B. Kavanaugh

Standings	W	L	Pct.	GB	Manager
New Orleans Pelicans	84	45	.651	—	Charles Frank
Montgomery Senators	73	54	.575	10	Thomas O'Brien/Ike Durrett
Atlanta Crackers	71	60	.539	14	Otto Jordan
Shreveport Pirates	69	60	.535	15	Robert Gilks
Birmingham Barons	70	61	.534	15	Harry Vaughn
Memphis Egyptians	69	62	.527	16	Lew Whistler
Nashville Volunteers	47	88	.348	40	Newton Fisher/Michael Finn
Little Rock Travelers	37	90	.307	46	Dale Gear

Due to a quarantine, after August 7 New Orleans played its home games in Meridian, Mississippi, and Shreveport in Chattanooga, Tennessee. New Orleans and Shreveport retained their franchise rights.

BA: Carleton Molesworth, Montgomery, .312
Runs: Frank Norcum, Nashville, 86
Hits: Frank Norcum, Nashville, 157
HRs: Frank Weikart, Shreveport, 7
Wins: Ginger Clark, Birmingham, 22
Pct: Jimmy Dygert, New Orleans, .818, 18-4

A Western League

President: Norris O'Neil

Standings	W	L	Pct.	GB	Manager
Des Moines Underwriters	95	54	.638	—	Herman Long
Denver Grizzlies	92	58	.613	3½	Bill Everitt
Omaha Rourkes	87	62	.584	8	Pa Rourke
Sioux City Packers	80	68	.541	14½	John Carney
Colorado Springs Millionaires/Pueblo Indians#	52	92	.361	40½	Ed McKean/Jack Tanner/William Shriver
St. Joseph Saints	37	109	.253	56½	William Douglas/Charles Dexter/Ralph Gibson/Ed Zinram

#Colorado Springs (22-48) moved to Pueblo July 15.

BA: Claude Rossman, Des Moines, .357
Runs: George Hogriever, Des Moines, 122
Hits: Claude Rossman, Des Moines, 229
HRs: Bill Shipke, Omaha, 10
Wins: Lefty Leifield, Des Moines, 26
Pct: Lefty Leifield, Des Moines, .743, 26-9
CGs: Ralph Cadwaller, Sioux City, 37
IPs: Peter Manske, Des Moines, 357

B Central League

President: Frank R. Carson

Standings	W	L	Pct.	GB	Manager
Wheeling Stogies	81	56	.591	—	William Schriver
Grand Rapids Orphans	77	59	.566	3½	John Ganzel
South Bend Greens	77	63	.550	5½	Angus Grant
Dayton Veterans	72	64	.529	8½	Hub Knoll
Evansville River Rats	71	69	.507	11½	Jimmy Ryan
Springfield Babes	67	68	.496	13	Jack Hendricks
Fort Wayne Railroaders/Canton Red Stockings#	56	78	.418	23½	Bade Myers/George Williams
Terre Haute Hottentots	49	89	.355	32½	Frank Warrender/Bert Dennis

#Fort Wayne (31-41) moved to Canton July 10.

BA: John Connors, South Bend, .338
Runs: John Connors, South Bend, 96
Hits: John Connors, South Bend, 184
HRs: Jimmy Ryan, Evansville, 10
Wins: Walter Miller, Grand Rapids, 24
Pct: Elmer Moffitt, South Bend, .677, 21-10
Walter Miller, Wheeling, .677, 21-10

B Connecticut League

President: Sturgis Whitlock

Standings	W	L	Pct.	GB	Manager
Holyoke Paperweights	79	35	.693	—	Jesse Freysinger
Springfield Ponies	74	44	.627	7	Daniel O'Neill
Bridgeport Orators	64	50	.561	15	James O'Rourke
Hartford Senators	58	56	.509	21	William Kennedy
Meriden Silverites	49	64	.434	29½	Sam Kennedy
New London Whalers	49	68	.419	31½	Charles Humphrey

*Won first-half   **Won second-half   ***Won both halves

	W	L	Pct.	GB	Manager
New Haven Blues	46	70	.397	34	James Canavan/Jack Tighe
Norwich Reds	42	74	.362	38	George Allen/James Canavan

BA: Fred Crolius, New London, .348
Runs: Bill Yale, Bridgeport, 96
Hits: Fred Crolius, New London, 160

HRs: Walt Hartley, Holyoke, 9
Wins: Carson Hodge, Holyoke, 24
Pct: Carson Hodge, Holyoke, .727, 24-9

B New England League
President: Tim H. Murnane

Standings	W	L	Pct.	GB	Manager
Concord Marines	69	39	.639	—	Frank Eustace
Fall River Indians	66	40	.623	2	Thomas McDermott
Lynn Shoemakers	60	48	.556	9	Frederick Lake/Frank Leonard
New Bedford Whalers	60	50	.545	10	A.G. "Fred" Doe
Haverhill Hustlers	53	51	.510	14	Connie Murphy
Manchester/Lawrence Colts#..	52	54	.491	16	Win Clark
Nashua	41	66	.383	27½	Stephen Flanagan
Lowell/Taunton Tigers@....	28	81	.257	41½	William Connor/George Grant

#Manchester (33-28) moved to Lawrence July 20.
@Lowell (24-45) moved to Taunton August 3.

BA: Harry Armbruster, Manchester/ Lawrence, .339
Runs: Harry Armbruster, Manchester/ Lawrence, 99

Hits: Harry Armbruster, Manchester/ Lawrence, 134
Wins: Joe Harris, Fall River, 25
Pct: Joe Harris, Fall River, .735, 25-9

B New York State League
President: John H. Farrell

Standings	W	L	Pct.	GB	Manager
Amsterdam-Johnstown- Gloversville Jags..............	71	51	.582	—	Howard Earl
Syracuse Stars....................	70	51	.579	½	Sandy Griffin
Wilkes-Barre Barons	70	52	.574	1	John Sharrott
Albany Senators..................	69	60	.535	5½	James Conners/Mike Doherty
Utica Pent-Ups...................	60	60	.500	10	John Lawler
Scranton Miners..................	56	67	.455	15½	James Garry/Edward Ashenbach
Binghamton Bingoes	48	75	.390	23½	Charles "Count" Campau/Robert Drury
Troy Trojans	51	79	.392	24	James Bacon/Harry Mason/Collins

BA: John Seigle, Wilkes-Barre, .344
Runs: Art DeGroff, Troy, 85
Hits: John Seigle, Wilkes-Barre, 159

Wins: George Bell, A-J-G, 25
Pct: George Bell, A-J-G, .676, 25-12

B Northwestern League
President: William H. Lucas

Standings	W	L	Pct.	GB	Manager
Everett Smokestackers***..	60	37	.619	—	Billy Hulen
Bellingham Yankees	49	48	.505	11	Kirby Drennen/Frederick Clarke
Vancouver Horse Doctors*	45	52	.464	15	John McCloskey
Victoria Legislators/ Spokane Indians#.............	41	58	.414	20	G.G. Howlett/Ed Hutchinson/ Charles McIntyre

#Victoria (14-38) moved to Spokane July 11.
The season was shortened to September 10.

Playoffs: None; the first half finished in a tie, and it was decided that if Everett won the second half, the pennant would be awarded to Everett.

BA: Harry Heitmuller, Everett, .304
Runs: Billy Hulen, Everett, 85
Hits: Ed Hutchinson, Victoria/Spokane, 107
HRs: Joe Marshall, Vancouver, 7

Wins: Collie Druhot, Bellingham, 18
Hick Belt, Everett, 18
SOs: Ira Harmon, Vancouver, 194
Pct: John McInnis, Everett, .800, 12-3

B Three-I League
President: Edward Holland

Standings	W	L	Pct.	GB	Manager
Dubuque Shamrocks...........	70	53	.569	—	Charles Buelow/Henry Hines
Rock Island Islanders.........	68	55	.553	2	J.B. McConnell
Springfield Senators	64	58	.525	5½	Frank Donnelly
Decatur Commodores	63	58	.521	6	Monte McFarland
Cedar Rapids Rabbits	63	61	.508	7½	Belden Hill
Bloomington Bloomers......	60	65	.480	11	William Connors
Davenport Riversides	56	67	.455	14	James Hayes
Peoria Distillers	48	75	.390	22	Hugh Nicol/Henry Simon

BA: Ross Thornton, Decatur, .307
Runs: Lou Lippert, Springfield, 85
Hits: Ross Thornton, Decatur, 143

Wins: Al Lundin, Rock Island, 22
SOs: Frank Oberlin, Springfield, 110
Pct: Harry Swalm, Dubuque, .690, 20-9

C Hudson River League
President: C.S. Harvey

Standings	W	L	Pct.	GB	Manager
Hudson Marines..................	68	50	.576	—	Gus Schnack/Dave Patterson
Paterson Invaders	62	51	.549	1	Richard Cogan
Poughkeepsie Colts	59	52	.532	5½	William McCabe

	W	L	Pct.	GB	Manager
Newburgh Taylor-mades	60	54	.526	6	Fred Taylor/Henry Ramsey
Kingston Colonials	57	57	.500	9	M.M. Allen/Matt Kelley
Yonkers#..........................	10	8	.556	NA	Henry Ramsey
Peekskill#.........................	5	13	.278	NA	Walter Dobbins
Saugerties/Pittsfield Hillies@..	13	49	.210	NA	D.J. Schulman/Daniel Cassiday

#Peekskill and Yonkers disbanded June 1.
@Saugerties (8-34) moved to Pittsfield July 4, then disbanded July 25.

BA: Joseph McCarthy, Poughkeepsie, .340
Hits: Mike O'Malley, Hudson, 144

C Missouri Valley League
President: Richard Robertson, Jr.

Standings	W	L	Pct.	GB	Manager
Pittsburg Miners	75	26	.743	—	H.O. Baldwin
Parsons Preachers	61	40	.604	14	John Hamilton
Muskogee Reds#.................	52	46	.531	21½	G.A. Sabin/Mel Cooley/Dillard/ Alex Sandheimer
Ft. Scott Hay Diggers	49	52	.485	26	Harry Chapman
Webb City Gold Bugs........	47	54	.465	28	Elmer Meredith
Tulsa Oilers........................	44	58	.431	31½	Charlie Schafft
Vinita Cherokees	41	63	.394	35½	Ed Finney
South McAlester/ Ft. Smith Giants@	33	63	.344	39½	Joe B. Roe

#Muskogee disbanded September 1, causing the season to be shortened to September 5.
@South McAlester moved to Ft. Smith.
Attendance: Tulsa, 25,500.

Wins: J.W. "Cy" Stinson, Pittsburg, 22
Pct: William Burns, Pittsburg, .875, 21-3

CGs: J.W. "Cy" Stinson, Pittsburg, 30
IP: J.W. "Cy" Stinson, Pittsburg, 279

C Ohio-Pennsylvania League
President: Charles H. Morton

Standings	W	L	Pct.	GB	Manager
Youngstown Ohio Works ...	88	35	.615	—	Martin Hogan
Akron Buckeyes	66	42	.611	14½	Frank Metz/Walter East
Zanesville Moguls	51	36	.586	NA	Fred Drumm
Niles Crowites	52	37	.584	NA	Charles Crowe
Braddock Infants................	23	22	.511	NA	Don McKim
Washington Patriots...........	3	3	.500	NA	Dan Kline
Lancaster Lanks	36	37	.493	NA	Fred Killen
Homestead Steel Workers ..	29	32	.475	NA	Howard Fisher
Newark Idlewilds	37	46	.446	NA	Jack Doyle
Sharon Steels	29	39	.426	NA	Frank Killen
McKeesport Colts	20	27	.426	NA	Ed Crawford/Frank Metz
Mt. Vernon Clippers	16	24	.400	NA	Bill Goodrich
Massillon Farmers	26	41	.388	NA	Walter Lipps
Canton Protectives	19	40	.322	NA	
Lima Lees	2	6	.333	NA	Eddie Bailey
Bucyrus Bucks	5	12	.294	NA	
Butler Bucks	1	7	.125	NA	Ward Buckminister
Steubenville Factory Men....	1	7	.125	NA	Jack Kelley
Wooster Trailers	0	2	.000	NA	Jess Bowers
Barberton Magic Cities........	0	3	.000	NA	Bill Feignley
Kent Kings	0	6	.000	NA	Henry Metz

The league was admitted to the National Association July 21.

C South Atlantic League
President: Charles W. Boyer

Standings	W	L	Pct.	GB	Manager
Macon Brigands.................	75	45	.625	—	William A. Smith
Savannah Pathfinders	71	56	.559	7½	W. Schaeffer
Jacksonville Jays...............	68	59	.535	10½	Robert Pender
Augusta Tourists................	57	71	.445	22	Andy Roth/George Leidy
Charleston Sea Gulls	53	70	.431	23½	Edward Ashenbach/Leon DeMontreville/ Peter Tibald
Columbia Gamecocks.........	52	75	.409	26½	Bill Earle/Charlie Dexter

BA: Ty Cobb, Augusta, .326
Runs: Paul Sentell, Macon, 71
Hits: Paul Sentell, Macon, 137

Wins: Rob Spade, Macon, 25
SOs: Harry Kane (Cohen), Savannah, 228
Pct: Vess Loucks, Macon, .842, 16-3

C South Texas League
President: Bliss P. Gorham

Standings	W	L	Pct.	GB	Manager
Houston Buffalos***	83	42	.664	—	Claude Reilly
San Antonio Bronchos........	68	61	.527	17	Wade Moore
Galveston Sandcrabs	57	69	.452	26½	Marcene Johnson
Beaumont Millionaires/ Brenham Orphans#.........	45	81	.357	38½	J.W. Greer

#Beaumont (40-68) moved to Brenham (1-6) August 21, then became an orphan team, playing in Austin and San Antonio.

BA: Earl Gardner, San Antonio, .306
Runs: Newt Hunter, Houston, 79
Bob Edmundson, Houston, 79

Hits: Newt Hunter, Houston, 139
Bob Edmundson, Houston, 139
Wins: Ed Karger, Houston, 24
SOs: Ivy Tevis, Galveston, 201
Pct: Ed Karger, Houston, .750, 24-8

C Texas League
President: J. Doak Roberts

Standings	W	L	Pct.	GB	Manager
Ft. Worth Panthers	72	59	.550	—	B. Hubbard/Fred Wills
Temple Boll Weevils	71	59	.546	½	Ben Shelton
Waco Tigers	65	65	.500	6½	Don Curtis/Mike O'Connor
Dallas Giants	65	65	.500	6½	James "Curley" Maloney
Austin Senators@	17	22	.436	NA	Mike O'Connor
Corsicana Oilers#	10	30	.250	NA	Con Lucid/Jim Mahaffey

#Corsicana surrendered its franchise June 1 and was dropped June 6.
@Austin was dropped by the league June 6.

BA: Scott Ragsdale, Waco, .292
Runs: Red Andreas, Dallas, 87
Hits: Ben Shelton, Temple, 148

HRs: Ben Shelton, Temple, 5
Sam Stovall, Waco, 5
Wins: Walt "Harold" Chrisman, Ft. Worth, 23
Pct: Rick Adams, Temple, .813, 13-3

C Western Association
President: Dr. D.M. Shiveley

Standings	W	L	Pct.	GB	Manager
Wichita Jobbers	79	56	.585	—	William Kimmel
Oklahoma City Mets	77	58	.570	2	Gene Barnes/D.C. "Dad" Risley
Leavenworth Orioles	75	59	.560	3½	Louis Armstrong
Sedalia Goldbugs	70	64	.522	8½	Dutch Henry/Richard Rohn
Guthrie Senators	66	70	.485	13½	John Hamilton/Ben Bennett
Joplin Miners	65	73	.471	15½	John Fillman/John Baerwald
Topeka White Sox	54	80	.403	24½	Spencer Abbott/Frank Quigley/ George Blackburn
Springfield Highlanders	54	80	.403	24½	Frank Hurlburt/Zoellers

The league started the season at Class D, then became a C league June 2.

BA: Ed Hurlburt, Oklahoma City, .349
Hits: J.W. Seabaugh, Springfield, 166
HRs: Henry Gehring, Wichita, 9
Wins: Henry Gehring, Wichita, 32

Pct: Henry Gehring, Wichita, .865, 32-5
ShOs: Henry Gehring, Wichita, 10
CGs: Robert Groom, Springfield, 41

D Canadian League

Standings	W	L	Pct.	GB	Manager
Woodstock Maroons	48	32	.600	—	Will Roche
Ingersoll	45	38	.542	4½	Weldon
St. Thomas Saints	39	39	.500	8	Ponsford
Brantford Indians	31	38	.449	11½	"Knotty" Lee
Simcoe#	10	27	.270	NA	Barwell

#Simcoe disbanded around July 15.

D Copper Country Soo League
President: Dr. G.W. Orr

Standings	W	L	Pct.	GB	Manager
Calumet Aristocrats	61	36	.629	—	Charles Fichtel
Lake Linden Lakers	57	36	.613	2	Percy Glass
Hancock Infants	38	58	.396	22½	John Condon/Charles Rogers
Sault Ste. Marie Soos#	29	55	.345	25½	Bill Earle

#Sault Ste. Marie disbanded August 22.
An attempted merger with the Northern League on June 1 was unsuccessful. Both leagues went back to their regular schedules.

Playoff: Lake Linden 4 games, Calumet 0.

D Cotton States League
President: George Wheatley

Standings	W	L	Pct.	GB	Manager
Greenville Cotton Pickers	50	25	.667	—	George Reed
Meridian White Ribbons	49	35	.583	5½	Thomas Stouch
Pine Bluff Lumbermen@	42	31	.575	7	Guy Sample
Jackson Blind Tigers	46	37	.554	8	Thomas Reynolds/Asa Stewart
Baton Rouge Cajuns	44	38	.537	9½	Wilson Matthews
Vicksburg Hill Billies	32	43	.427	18	Frank Belt/Joseph Keenan
Hattiesburg Tar Heels@	21	46	.313	25	Cooney Best/Perry Werden
Natchez Indians/ Mobile Sea Gulls#	24	53	.312	27	George "King" Kelley/George Reed

#Natchez (18-27) moved to Mobile June 26.
@Hattiesburg surrendered its franchise to the league July 8, but the league kept the team playing through July 17. At a league meeting held July 16, it was decided to drop the Hattiesburg and Pine Bluff teams to even out the league.
The league disbanded July 31, with National Association permission, due to the yellow fever epidemic.

BA: Lyndon Welday, Greenville, .349
Runs: Lyndon Welday, Greenville, 62
Hits: Lyndon Welday, Greenville, 99

Wins: Slim Sallee, Meridian, 10
Pct: Slim Sallee, Meridian, .714, 10-4

D Interstate League
Presidents: Frank Baumeister/George F. Rindernecht

Standings	W	L	Pct.	GB	Manager
Coudersport Giants	59	38	.608	—	Harry Knight/John Lawley
Erie Fishermen	58	39	.598	1	Daniel Koster/Bob McLaughlin/Jack Burke
Olean Refiners	54	50	.519	8½	Al Lawson/Paul Wrath
Bradford Drillers	46	54	.460	14½	William Leary/Frederick Paige
Kane Mountaineers	40	56	.417	18½	C.R. Eichelberger
Jamestown Hill Climbers/ DuBois Miners#	40	60	.400	20½	J. Lawrence Alexander/Paul Wrath/ Menzo Sibley

#Jamestown (18-23) moved to DuBois July 12.

BA: Duke Servatius, Kane, .352
Runs: Julius Streib, Coudersport, 63

D Iowa State League
President: Frank S. Norton

Standings	W	L	Pct.	GB	Attend.	Manager
Ottumwa Snappers	74	45	.621	—	22,261	A.L. "Snapper" Kennedy
Ft. Dodge Gypsumites	73	49	.599	2½	19,270	Frank Boyle
Boone Greyhounds	65	54	.546	9	19,588	Frank Haller
Oskaloosa Quakers	65	56	.537	10	23,256	Howard Cassibone
Keokuk Indians	59	62	.488	16	18,931	Ned Egan
Marshalltown Grays	55	66	.454	20		Bobby Warner
Waterloo Microbes	56	69	.448	21	19,754	Harry Meek/Deacon Lohr
Burlington Flint Hills	37	83	.368	37½	26,635	Rusty Owens/ Thomas Reynolds/ Charles Frisbie

BA: Jack Meek, Waterloo/Boone, .320
Runs: John Bassey, Boone, 83
Red Fisher, Boone, 83
Hits: Jack Meek, Waterloo/Boone, 152

Wins: Harry Cornes, Boone, 25
SOs: Melvin Blexuld, Keokuk, 207
Pct: Fred Steel, Oskaloosa, .857, 18-3

D Kansas State League
President: George T. Tremble

Standings	W	L	Pct.	GB	Manager
Ellsworth	34	15	.694	—	
Great Bend Millers#	19	9	.679	4½	Carl Moore
Minneapolis Minnies	24	22	.522	8½	Roy Gafford
Hutchinson Salt Miners	22	24	.478	10½	Cook/Fred Abbott
Lincoln Center#	11	19	.375	13½	Simpson
Kingman/Hoisington@	13	34	.276	20	

#Lincoln Center and Great Bend joined the league July 6.
@Kingman disbanded July 22. Hoisington took Kingman's place in the league July 24.

Wins: Cy Mason, Hutchinson, 10
Jones, Ellsworth, 10
Relihan, Ellsworth, 10

Pct: Jones, Ellsworth, .909, 10-1
ShO: Jones, Ellsworth, 5
CGs: Cy Mason, Hutchinson, 15

D Kitty League
Presidents: W.I. Thompson/Charles C. Gosnell

Standings	W	L	Pct.	GB	Manager
Paducah Indians	68	35	.660	—	Harry Lloyd
Vincennes Alices	65	41	.613	4½	Eddie Kolb
Cairo Giants	46	57	.447	22	Dan McCarthy
Princeton Infants	46	61	.430	24	Meredeth/John Ray
Henderson Hens#	29	47	.382	NA	Jake Zimbro/Harry Kubitz
Hopkinsville Hoppers#	31	44	.413	NA	

#Henderson and Hopkinsville withdrew July 18.
The season was shortened to August 17, with National Association permission, due to the yellow fever epidemic.

Playoff: Vincennes 7 games, Paducah 6.

D Northern League
President: W.W. Kent

Standings	W	L	Pct.	GB	Manager
Duluth White Sox	64	34	.653	—	Leonard Van Praugh/Arthur O'Dea
Grand Forks Forkers	55	41	.573	8	M. Stansfield
Fargo	51	45	.531	12	Charles Traeger/W.J. Price
Winnipeg Maroons	46	50	.479	17	William Wilson/Harry Clayton
St. Cloud-Brainerd/ Superior Longshoremen#	40	61	.396	25½	M.J. Reilly/J.B. Pattison
Crookston Crooks	38	63	.376	27½	Bill McNeil/N. Davies

#St. Cloud-Brainerd (13-20) moved to Superior June 25.

BA: Lou Harris, Superior, .332
Runs: Sam Meniece, Duluth, 96
Hits: Arthur O'Dea, Duluth, 133

Wins: Peter Hansen, Fargo, 24
Pct: Frank Miller, Duluth, .800, 12-3

D North Texas League
President: Capt. J.B. King

Standings	W	L	Pct.	GB	Manager
Paris Parasites/Hope#*** ...	48	32	.600	—	E.W. Dunaway/A.L. "Dad" Ritter
Greenville Midlands	41	40	.506	7½	William Owen/Richard Bendel/Cy Mulkey
Clarksville@**	34	42	.447	12	Roy Taylor
Texarkana+	36	46	.439	13	Robert Shelton

#Paris (5-2 in the second half) moved to Hope July 20.
@Clarksville disbanded July 31.
+Texarkana disbanded August 2, causing the league to disband August 6.

D Southwest Washington League
President: Will Campbell

Standings	W	L	Pct.	GB	Manager
Montesano Farmers	24	10	.706	—	
Olympia Senators	20	16	.556	5	
Aberdeen Pippins	17	17	.500	7	Robert P. Brown
Hoquiam Loggers	9	27	.250	16	

The league played six times a week, but only the weekend games counted.

D Virginia-North Carolina League
President: L.J. Brandt

Standings	W	L	Pct.	GB	Manager
Danville Tobacconists	48	27	.640	—	Ed Ransick
Charlotte Hornets...............	40	42	.488	11½	E.L. Keesler
Salisbury-Spencer/ Winston-Salem Twins# ...	34	42	.447	14½	J.C. "Con" Strothers/Earle Holt
Greensboro Farmers	36	47	.434	16	John J. Grim

#Salisbury-Spencer (24-28) moved to Winston-Salem July 17.
The league disbanded August 19.

D Wisconsin State League
President: John T. Powers

Standings	W	L	Pct.	GB	Manager
La Crosse Pinks	68	41	.624	—	Pink Hawley
Oshkosh Indians	60	47	.561	7	Morey Crall/John Lavie
Freeport Pretzels	54	56	.491	14½	Nick Malvern/William Moriarty

	W	L	Pct.	GB	
Beloit Collegians	50	59	.459	18	George Wilbur/George Bubsir
Wausau Lumberjacks	47	61	.435	20½	Jack Corbett/John Mott/Nick Malvern
Green Bay Colts.................	47	62	.431	21	W. Kennelly/William McGinnis/ Marty McQuade/Ernest Van Erman/ Warren Beckwith

BA: Frank Duchein, Oshkosh, .303
Runs: F.E. Graves, Oshkosh, 71
Hits: Frank Duchein, Oshkosh, 125

HRs: George Perring, Beloit, 2
Tom Sullivan, Freeport, 2
Frank Schneiberg, Freeport, 2
Wins: Fred Beebe, Oshkosh, 27
SOs: Fred Beebe, Oshkosh, 291
Pct: Fred Beebe, Oshkosh, .794, 27-7

Ind Tri-State League
President: Charles F. Carpenter

Standings	W	L	Pct.	GB	Manager
Williamsport Millionaires...	78	46	.629	—	Curt Weigand
Johnstown Johnnies	78	47	.624	½	Jack Menefee
York White Roses..............	78	49	.614	1½	George Heckert
Harrisburg Senators	76	51	.595	3½	Peter Agnew
Shamokin	56	69	.448	22½	
Altoona Mountaineers	52	73	.416	26½	Arthur Irwin
Lancaster Red Roses...........	51	76	.402	28½	Thomas Feeley
Wilmington Peaches	33	91	.266	45	

Wins: Stoney McGlynn, York, 36
SOs: Stoney McGlynn, York, 206
Pct: Stoney McGlynn, York, .783, 36-10

1905 Interleague Post Season Play

World Series
New York (National) 4 games, Philadelphia (American) 1

New England Championship Series (round-robin)
Holyoke (Connecticut) 4-1
Fall River (New England) 2-2
Springfield (Connecticut) 2-2
Concord (New England) 1-4

Iowa State Series
Burlington (Iowa State) 4 games, Cedar Rapids (Three-I) 3
Des Moines (Western) 3 games, Burlington (Iowa State) 1

1905 No-Hitters

Date	Pitcher	Team	League	Opponent	Score
4-5	Charles "Sea Lion" Hall	Seattle	Pacific Coast	Oakland	8-0
5-4	Charles Porter	Dallas	Texas	Ft. Worth	5-2
5-23	Brindle Bayne	Binghamton	New York State	A-J-G	1-0
5-28	Harry Dunham	Pine Bluff	Cotton States	Vicksburg	4-0
5-30	Walter Boles	Ft. Worth	Texas	Austin	9-0
6-5	Harold Chrisman	Ft. Worth	Texas	Temple	0-0
6-13	Christy Mathewson	New York	National	Chicago	1-0
6-19	Fred Blanchard	Kingston	Hudson River	Paterson	8-0
6-19	J.H. Dannehower	Meridian	Cotton States	Pine Bluff	1-0
6-22	Cy Alberts	Dayton	Central	Fort Wayne	1-0
6-22	Hickory Clark	San Antonio	South Texas	Beaumont	0-0 (11)
7-4	Moxie Manuel	Baton Rouge	Cotton States	Vicksburg	0-4
7-5	Harold Chrisman	Ft. Worth	Texas	Temple	0-0
7-14	Harry Cornes	Boone	Iowa State	Ft. Dodge	9-0
7-16	Jimmy Whalen	San Francisco	Pacific Coast	Seattle	2-0 (7)
7-16	Happy Westcott	Sedalia	Western Assoc.	Topeka	5-0 (5)
7-22	Weldon Henley	Philadelphia	American	St. Louis	6-0
7-23	Roy McFarland	Beaumont	South Texas	San Antonio	4-1
7-25	Scott Holmes	Augusta	South Atlantic	Savannah	1-0
8-2	Ducky Holmes	Great Bend	Kansas State	Hoisington	4-0
8-6	Arthur Owens	Dubuque	Three-I	Decatur	2-0
8-11	Bill Clark	Jacksonville	South Atlantic	Macon	0-0 (10)
8-11	Rudy Schwenk	Ft. Worth	Texas	Dallas	13-0
8-15	Harry Kane	Savannah	South Atlantic	Jacksonville	0-1 (13)
8-19	John Cronin	Providence	Eastern	Montreal	2-0
9-6	Frank Smith	Chicago	American	Detroit	15-0
9-27	Bill Dinneen	Boston	American	Chicago	2-0
11-18	Robert Keefe	Tacoma	Pacific Coast	Oakland	3-0

Number in parentheses indicates innings if other than nine.

THIS DATE IN MINOR LEAGUE HISTORY

February 2, 1905, Manager Hugh Jennings of Baltimore was admitted to the Maryland Bar.

April 13, 1905, Pitcher Jimmy Whalen, San Francisco, Pacific Coast League, completed a feat of hurling 46 consecutive scoreless innings. Whalen began the season with four straight nine-inning shutouts.

April 15, 1905, Manager George Cole, Waterloo, Iowa State League, died in a Waterloo hospital from the effects of an appendicitis operation.

April 24, 1905, Hugh Jennings suffered a broken arm when hit by a pitch in an exhibition game between Baltimore and Cumberland.

April 30, 1905, In the Memphis-Shreveport Southern Association game, Harold Smith of Shreveport, scored a home run after striking out; the catcher missed the ball, which went into the grandstand.

April 30, 1905, Pitcher Arthur Goodwin of Brooklyn and Memphis was sued for breach of promise by Mayme Del Mont, an actress.

May 4, 1905, Shortstop Robert Cargo, York, Tri-State League, made a home run and four triples in five times at bat against four Lancaster pitchers.

May 10, 1905, John Lower, Waco, Texas League, pitched 14 no-hit frames in a 15-inning scoreless tie with Dallas.

May 17, 1905, First baseman Marty Murphy, San Francisco, was expelled from the Pacific Coast League by president Eugene Bert for a brutal assault upon umpire Fred Perrine.

June 8, 1905, Manager Hugh Jennings, Baltimore, Eastern League, in a collision at second base, suffered a broken arm again where it had just healed.

June 10, 1905, At Indianapolis, umpire Gifford forfeited the game to Indianapolis because the Milwaukee, American Association, battery of John Hickey and Wolf plotted to hit the umpire with the ball.

June 11, 1905, At Newark, after the Toronto-Newark Eastern League game, umpire John H. Conway was escorted to the railroad station by the police and hurried out of town to escape an angry mob.

June 12, 1905, When no umpires appeared for a Hudson River League game between Poughkeepsie and Paterson, the Reverend C.S. Rahm, pastor of the Evangelical Lutheran Church of Poughkeepsie, stepped from the stands and offered his services. They were accepted and he gave satisfactory service.

June 14, 1905, Kansas City executed two triple plays in an American Association game.

June 21, 1905, Second baseman Larry Schafley of Portland, Pacific Coast League, turned an unassisted triple play against Seattle.

June 24, 1905, At Las Vegas, New Mexico, Michael Flood, a minor league player, was shot and killed in a saloon during a quarrel with Robert McSherry.

June 27, 1905, Herman McFarland, Providence, Eastern League, reached base for the 16th successive time, nine times on hits and seven on walks.

July 3, 1905, Pitcher Alexander Hardy of the Troy, New York State League club was shot by Charles Thero of Danbury, Connecticut for alleged attention to Thero's wife.

July 4, 1905, Moxie Manuel pitched both games for Baton Rouge against Vicksburg in the Cotton States League and won the first contest, but lost the second on errors despite giving up no hits.

July 4, 1905, Harry Ables, Dallas, Texas League, set a league mark by yielding only five hits to Ft. Worth in a doubleheader, winning both nine-inning games, 6-0 and 8-0. He allowed only one safety in the nightcap.

July 5, 1905, In the Lynn-Nashua game in the New England League, pitcher M.J. Phelan of Nashua gave 14 bases on balls and allowed 17 stolen bases.

July 8, 1905, Charlie Shields of Seattle defeated Portland 4-1, striking out 19, an all-time Pacific Coast League record.

July 8, 1905, Pitcher Bugs Raymond of Jackson, Cotton States League, pitched a doubleheader against Meridian, scoring two shutouts, yielding only one hit in the second game.

July 9, 1905, At Topeka, pitcher William Howie of Topeka, Western Association, blanked Sedalia in a doubleheader, allowing only one hit in the opener and five in the second.

July 11, 1905, At Kansas City, the wife of second baseman Frank Bonner of Kansas City, American Association, committed suicide.

July 15, 1905, President Eugene F. Bert of the Pacific Coast League shot himself in San Francisco with alleged suicidal intent, but he subsequently recovered.

July 17, 1905, Shortstop Mike Donovan, Wilkes-Barre, New York State League, accepted 17 chances in a game against Troy without an error.

July 19, 1905, Grand Rapids, Central League, lost a doubleheader to Dayton after having won 17 straight games at home.

July 29, 1905, Third baseman Griffin, Little Rock, Southern Association, was seriously injured and five other teammates were hurt in a train wreck at Ozark, Arkansas.

July 30, 1905, At Los Angeles, Pacific Coast League, Oakland and Los Angeles played a doubleheader in record time, the first game in 47 minutes 30 seconds, the second in 51 minutes.

July 31, 1905, The Cotton States League ended its season owing to the yellow fever epidemic.

August 7, 1905, The home games of New Orleans and Shreveport of the Southern Association were transferred respectively to Meridian, Mississippi and Chattanooga, Tennessee on account of yellow fever.

August 8, 1905, Kansas City, American Association, won its first game in 16 tries by beating Columbus.

August 9, 1905, Word reached Ty Cobb, Augusta, South Atlantic League, outfielder, that his father had been accidentally killed by a shotgun blast by his wife, who mistook him for a prowler at the Cobb home in Royston, Georgia. Professor William Herschel Cobb was a scholar, state senator, editor and philosopher. Ty was 18 years of age at this time. A few days later he was sold to Detroit.

August 10, 1905, Newark, Eastern League, advertised a doubleheader at home with Providence, but the Clamdiggers didn't appear.

August 13, 1905, Wiley Piatt, Toledo, defeated Kansas City, American Association, to win his third game in as many days.

August 15, 1905, Harry Kane, Savannah, South Atlantic League, held Jacksonville without a hit for 13 innings, but lost 1-0 on errors.

August 17, 1905, The Kitty League closed because of the yellow fever epidemic.

August 17, 1905, At Toledo, umpire Kane was pelted with eggs, mud and cushions during the Toledo-Indianapolis game and was afterward escorted to his hotel by a police guard.

August 29, 1905, Captain Dan Brouthers of Poughkeepsie, Hudson River League, retired after 25 years of service in the major and minor leagues.

August 31, 1905, At Kansas City, eight Louisville players were injured in a collision between their coach and a trolley car.

September 3, 1905, Two pitchers in the Western Association. Jack Forrester, Topeka, and Paul Companion, Joplin, turned in one-hit games. Neither of the hurlers posted a shutout due to errors afield.

September 19, 1905, The American Association season ended with Columbus the pennant winner. The Columbus squad closed the season by shutting out Louisville four consecutive games in the last three days.

September 22, 1905, Nine Louisville, American Association, players injured in a trolley wreck at Kansas City sued the Metropolitan Traction Company of that city for damages totalling $39,500.

September 23, 1905, In Cincinnati, pitcher Gus Bonno broke his ankle jumping from a second-story window of a young woman's home to avoid being shot by a jealous rival suitor.

October 2, 1905, In Des Moines, catcher Charles Dexter of Louisville, American Association, in a quarrel slashed first baseman Bateman of Milwaukee with a knife. Dexter was arrested but released when Bateman refused to prosecute.

November 8, 1905, A record low attendance for a Pacific Coast League game, one, was recorded at the Portland at Oakland game.

November 22, 1905, Portland scored twice in the third inning on an error by pitcher William Loyzer of Los Angeles after the hurler had pitched 46 consecutive scoreless innings in Pacific Coast League play. Included in the streak was a 14-inning shutout against Tacoma.

December 3, 1905, The Pacific Coast League season ended with Los Angeles winning the championship.

December 26, 1905, Mike Kelley purchased the Minneapolis club from W.H. Watkins at a price said to be $25,000.

December 31, 1905, Frank Bonner, second baseman for Kansas City, died in that city of blood poisoning at age 41. Bonner's wife had committed suicide the previous July.

1906

American League
President: Byron Bancroft Johnson

Standings	W	L	Pct.	GB	Attend.	Manager
Chicago White Sox	93	58	.616	—	585,202	Fielder Jones
New York Highlanders	90	61	.596	3	434,700	Clark Griffith
Cleveland Naps	89	64	.582	5	325,733	Napoleon Lajoie
Philadelphia Athletics	78	67	.538	12	489,129	Connie Mack
St. Louis Browns	76	73	.510	16	389,157	Jimmy McAleer
Detroit Tigers	71	78	.477	21	174,043	Bill Armour
Washington Senators	55	95	.367	37½	129,903	Jake Stahl
Boston Pilgrims	49	105	.318	45½	410,209	Jimmy Collins/Chick Stahl

BA: George Stone, St. Louis, .358
Runs: Elmer Flick, Cleveland, 98
Hits: Napoleon Lajoie, Cleveland, 214
RBIs: Harry Davis, Philadelphia, 96
HRs: Harry Davis, Philadelphia, 12

Wins: Al Orth, New York, 27
SOs: Rube Waddell, Philadelphia, 196
ERA: Doc White, Chicago, 1.52
Pct: Eddie Plank, Philadelphia, .760, 19-6

National League
President: Harry C. Pulliam

Standings	W	L	Pct.	GB	Attend.	Manager
Chicago Cubs	116	36	.763	—	654,300	Frank Chance
New York Giants	96	56	.632	20	402,850	John McGraw
Pittsburgh Pirates	93	60	.608	23½	394,877	Fred Clarke
Philadelphia Phillies	71	82	.464	45½	294,680	Hugh Duffy
Brooklyn Superbas	66	86	.434	50	277,400	Patsy Donovan
Cincinnati Reds	64	87	.424	51½	330,056	Ned Hanlon
St. Louis Cardinals	52	98	.347	63	283,770	John McCloskey
Boston Beaneaters	49	102	.325	66½	143,280	Fred Tenney

BA: Honus Wagner, Pittsburgh, .339
Runs: Frank Chance, Chicago, 103
    Honus Wagner, Pittsburgh, 103
Hits: Harry Steinfeldt, Chicago, 176
RBIs: Harry Steinfeldt, Chicago, 83
    Jim Nealon, Pittsburgh, 83

HRs: Tim Jordan, Brooklyn, 12
Wins: Joe McGinnity, New York, 27
SOs: Fred Beebe, Chicago/St. Louis, 171
ERA: Mordecai "Three Finger" Brown, Chicago, 1.04
Pct: Ed Reulbach, Chicago, .826, 19-4

A American Association
President: Joseph D. O'Brien

Standings	W	L	Pct.	GB	Manager
Columbus Senators	91	57	.615	—	William Clymer
Milwaukee Brewers	85	67	.559	8	Joe Cantillon
Minneapolis Millers	79	66	.545	10½	Mike Kelley
Toledo Mud Hens	79	69	.534	12	Edward Grillo
Louisville Colonels	71	79	.473	21	Suter Sullivan/Roy Brashear
Kansas City Blues	69	79	.466	22	James Burke
St. Paul Apostles	66	80	.452	24	Richard Padden
Indianapolis Indians	53	96	.356	38½	Bill Watkins/Charles Carr

BA: Billy Hallman, Louisville, .342
Runs: Ed Green, Milwaukee, 119
Hits: Alfonzo Davis, Minneapolis, 204
HRs: Ed Green, Milwaukee, 8

Wins: Charles Berger, Columbus, 28
SOs: Charles Berger, Columbus, 264
Pct: Pat Flaherty, Columbus, .719, 23-9

A Eastern League
President: Harry L. Taylor

Standings	W	L	Pct.	GB	Manager
Buffalo Bisons	85	55	.607	—	George Stallings
Jersey City Skeeters	80	57	.584	3½	William Murray
Baltimore Orioles	76	61	.555	7½	Hugh Jennings
Rochester Bronchos	77	62	.554	7½	Al Buckenberger
Newark Sailors	66	71	.482	17½	Walter Burnham
Providence Grays	65	75	.464	20	Jack Dunn
Montreal Canucks	57	83	.407	28	James Bannon/Mal Kittridge
Toronto Maple Leafs	46	88	.343	36	Edward Barrow

Attendance: Buffalo, 253,554.

BA: Jack Thoney, Toronto, .294
Runs: Natty Nattress, Buffalo, 95
Hits: Jack Thoney, Toronto, 173
HRs: Jim Murray, Buffalo, 7

Wins: Del Mason, Baltimore, 26
SOs: Fred Burchell, Baltimore, 183
Pct: Del Mason, Baltimore, .743, 26-9

A Pacific Coast League
President: Eugene F. Bert

Standings	W	L	Pct.	GB	Manager
Portland Beavers	115	60	.657	—	Walter McCredie
Seattle Siwashes	99	83	.544	19½	Russ Hall
Los Angeles Angels	95	87	.522	23½	Frank "Cap" Dillon
San Francisco Seals	91	84	.520	24	Parke Wilson
Oakland Oaks	77	110	.412	44	George Van Haltren
Fresno Raisin Eaters	64	117	.354	54	Mike Fisher

BA: Mike Mitchell, Portland, .351
Runs: Hank Spencer, San Francisco, 133
Hits: Art Krueger, Oakland, 211
HRs: Mike Mitchell, Portland, 6

Wins: Rube Vickers, Seattle, 39
SOs: Rube Vickers, Seattle, 409
Pct: Bill Essick, Portland, .760, 19-6
IP: Rube Vickers, Seattle, 517

A Southern Association
President: William B. Kavanaugh

Standings	W	L	Pct.	GB	Manager
Birmingham Barons	86	46	.652	—	Harry Vaughn
Memphis Egyptians	79	55	.590	8	Charles Babb
Atlanta Crackers	80	56	.588	8	William A. Smith
New Orleans Pelicans	75	61	.551	13	Charles Frank
Shreveport Pirates	70	66	.515	18	Robert Gilks
Montgomery Senators	64	65	.495	20½	Ike Durrett/Dominick Mullaney
Nashville Volunteers	45	92	.328	43½	Michael Finn
Little Rock Travelers	40	98	.292	49	Charles Zimmer

BA: Sid Smith, Atlanta, .326
Runs: Fred Houtz, Montgomery, 86
Hits: Phil Douglass, Little Rock, 160
    Charley Babb, Memphis, 160

HRs: Charley Babb, Memphis, 5
Wins: Glenn Liebhardt, Memphis, 35
Pct: Tom Hughes, Atlanta, .833, 25-5
CGs: Glenn Liebhardt, Memphis, 45

A Western League
President: Norris L. O'Neil

Standings	W	L	Pct.	GB	Manager
Des Moines Champions	97	50	.660	—	Jack Doyle
Lincoln Ducklings	75	74	.503	23	James "Ducky" Holmes
Omaha Rourkes	73	74	.497	24	Pa Rourke
Sioux City Packers	69	81	.460	29½	John Carney
Denver Grizzlies	68	81	.456	30	Bill Everitt
Pueblo Indians	63	85	.426	34½	Frank Selee

BA: Bill McGilvray, Pueblo, .373
Runs: James Cook, Pueblo, 149
Hits: Henry Melchior, Pueblo, 220

HRs: George Noblitt, Sioux City, 11
Wins: Roscoe Miller, Des Moines, 28
Pct: Mark Hall, Sioux City, .900, 9-1

B Central League
President: Frank R. Carson

Standings	W	L	Pct.	GB	Manager
Grand Rapids Wolverines	99	52	.656	—	John Ganzel
Springfield Babes	91	60	.603	8	Jack Hendricks
Canton Chinamen	85	63	.574	12½	Bade Myers
Dayton Veterans	78	71	.523	20	John Thornton/James Barrett/Hub Knoll/ McKinley/Ed McKean
Wheeling Stogies	75	77	.493	24½	William Shriver
Evansville River Rats	65	82	.442	32	Jimmy Ryan/John Walker/Harry Stahlhefer
South Bend Greens	62	88	.413	36½	Angus Grant
Terre Haute Hottentots	44	106	.293	54½	Jack Boyle/Frank Warrander

BA: John Ganzel, Grand Rapids, .323
Runs: Ed Anderson, South Bend, 100
Hits: Ed Anderson, South Bend, 169
HRs: John Ganzel, Grand Rapids, 13

Wins: Ralph Willis, Canton, 27
SOs: Tony Freeman, Evansville, 214
Pct: Roy Hale, Dayton, .857, 12-2

B Connecticut League
President: James O'Rourke

Standings	W	L	Pct.	GB	Manager
Norwich Reds	72	53	.576	—	George Allen/Jack Tighe
Springfield Ponies	70	56	.556	2½	Daniel O'Neill
New Haven Blues	68	57	.544	4	William Slack
Hartford Senators	62	57	.521	7	Bert Daly/J.H. Clarkson
Waterbury Authors	60	63	.488	11	Harold Durant
Holyoke Paperweights	58	65	.472	13	Tom Fleming/Thomas Dowd/M. Prindiville
Bridgeport Orators	54	72	.429	18½	James O'Rourke
New London Whalers	53	74	.417	20	Jimmy Humphrey/Sam Kennedy

BA: Frank Burke, New Haven, .349
Runs: Frank Fitzpatrick, Springfield/ New Haven, 88
Hits: Hi Ladd, Bridgeport, 157

HRs: Percy Rising, New London, 5
Wins: Phil Corcoran, New Haven, 26
Pct: Phil Corcoran, New Haven, .667, 26-13
ShO: Otto Hess, Springfield, 9

B New England League
President: Tim H. Murnane

Standings	W	L	Pct.	GB	Manager
Worcester Busters	74	42	.638	—	Jesse Burkett
Lynn Shoemakers	66	49	.574	7½	Frank Leonard

*Won first-half   **Won second-half   ***Won both halves

	W	L	Pct.	GB	Manager
Lawrence Colts	65	52	.556	9½	John A. Smith/Albert Weddige/ James Rolley
New Bedford Whalers	63	54	.538	11½	James Canavan
Manchester Textiles	57	56	.504	15½	Stephen Flanagan
Fall River Indians	55	59	.482	18	Thomas McDermott
Haverhill Hustlers	53	63	.457	21	J.H. Sayer
Lowell Tigers	28	86	.246	45	Frederick Lake

BA: Jesse Burkett, Worcester, .344
Runs: Tommy Madden, Haverhill, 80
Hits: Elmer Zacher, Worcester, 143
Wins: Henry Labelle, Lynn, 23
Pct: Samuel Frock, Worcester, .741, 20-7

B New York State League
President: John H. Farrell

Standings	W	L	Pct.	GB	Manager
Scranton Miners	82	48	.631	—	Edward Ashenbach
Albany Senators	73	63	.537	12	Michael Doherty
Syracuse Stars	70	65	.519	14½	Sandy Griffin
Troy Trojans	67	64	.511	15½	John O'Brien
Amsterdam-Johnstown-Gloversville Jags	66	68	.493	17½	Howard Earl
Utica Pent-Ups	61	72	.459	22	John Lawler
Binghamton Bingoes	58	72	.446	23½	Robert Drury
Wilkes-Barre Barons	52	76	.406	29	John Sharrott/Mike Donovan

BA: Archie "Moonlight" Graham, Scranton, .336
Runs: Frank Hafford, A-J-G, 86
Hits: Art DeGroff, Troy, 160
Wins: Robert Chappelle, Albany, 27
Pct: Robert Chappelle, Albany, .794, 27-7

B Northwestern League
President: William H. Lucas

Standings	W	L	Pct.	GB	Manager
Tacoma Tigers	54	36	.600	—	Mike Lynch
Butte Miners	43	42	.506	8½	Charles McIntrye
Grays Harbor Lumbermen#	41	47	.466	12	Robert Brown
Spokane Indians	37	50	.425	15½	Bill Hurley

#represented Aberdeen-Hoquiam, Washington.

BA: Mike Lynch, Tacoma, .355
Runs: Mike Lynch, Tacoma, 76
Hits: Mike Lynch, Tacoma, 130
HRs: Mike Lynch, Tacoma, 7
Wins: Ike Butler, Tacoma, 20
SOs: Irv Higginbotham, Tacoma, 153
Pct: Oscar Bandelin, Butte, .733, 11-4

B Three-I League
President: Edward Holland

Standings	W	L	Pct.	GB	Manager
Cedar Rapids Rabbits	79	43	.648	—	Belden Hill
Peoria Distillers	74	48	.607	5	Charles Buelow
Dubuque Dubs	64	55	.538	13½	Monte McFarland
Springfield Senators	64	56	.533	14	Frank Donnelly
Rock Island Islanders	58	66	.468	22	Jack McConnell
Decatur Commodores	48	67	.418	27½	Harry Lewee
Bloomington Bloomers	51	74	.408	29½	William Connors
Davenport Knickerbockers	45	74	.378	32½	A.L. "Snapper" Kennedy/Peter Burg

BA: Steve Reagan, Dubuque, .340
Runs: William Davidson, Dubuque, 79
Hits: Steve Reagan, Dubuque, 156
Wins: Harry Swalm, Dubuque, 23
SOs: Harry Swalm, Dubuque, 247
ERA: Harry Swalm, Dubuque, 1.81

C Hudson River League
President: C.S. Harvey

Standings	W	L	Pct.	GB	Manager
Paterson Invaders	64	47	.577	—	Richard Cogan
Poughkeepsie Colts	60	45	.571	3	William McCabe
Kingston Colonials	56	51	.523	6	John Cuneo
Hudson Marines	54	56	.491	9½	Gus Schnack
Newburgh Hill Climbers	43	59	.422	16½	Dan Brouthers/Fred Ochs/Taylor/ John McGratty
Glens Falls-Saratoga Springs	43	62	.410	18	Henry Ramsey

The season was shortened to September 9.

BA: John Connors, Kingston, .343
Hits: John Connors, Kingston, 124

C Interstate Association
President: Emerson W. Dickerson

Standings	W	L	Pct.	GB	Manager
Fort Wayne	35	24	.593	—	Jack Hardy/Louis Heilbronner
Marion	35	24	.593	—	Clarence Jessup
Flint Vehics	35	25	.583	½	Joseph Ganzel
Anderson	30	31	.492	6	Sid Hubbard/Joseph O'Neill
Lima	26	34	.433	9½	Harry Truby
Saginaw@	18	30	.375	NA	A.B. Kimber/Bootie Wolf
Bay City#	6	9	.400	NA	J.C. "Con" Strothers
Muncie Fruit Jars#	4	12	.250	NA	Frederick Paige

#Muncie and Bay City were expelled May 18.
@Saginaw withdrew June 21.
The league disbanded July 8.

C Northern-Copper Country League
President: W.J. Price

Standings	W	L	Pct.	GB	Manager
Calumet Aristocrats	61	37	.622	—	Jack Morrison
Houghton Giants	56	35	.615	1½	J.T. Haley
Winnipeg Maroons	57	38	.600	2½	S. Anderson/Bill Hanrahan
Duluth White Sox	52	44	.542	8	A.W. Kuehnow
Lake Linden Sandy Cities	40	56	.417	20	Percy Glass
Fargo	35	59	.372	24	Matt Camitsch
Hancock Infants#	29	34	.460	NA	Paul Wreath
Grand Forks Forkers#	13	40	.245	NA	F.J. Dudley/Bill Hanrahan

#Hancock and Grand Forks disbanded July 29.
The league, which became a C league on May 25, was formed as a merger between the Northern and Copper Country Soo Leagues.

BA: Jesse Becker, Lake Linden, .326
Runs: Louis Piper, Winnipeg, 75
Hits: Sam Meniece, Winnipeg, 118
Wins: Paul Grimes, Calumet, 18
Harry Bond, Winnipeg, 18
Barry, Houghton, 18
Ed Beecher, Houghton, 18
Pct: Eddie Brennan, Winnipeg, .727, 8-3

C Ohio-Pennsylvania League
President: Charles H. Morton

Standings	W	L	Pct.	GB	Manager
Youngstown Ohio Works	84	53	.613	—	Martin Hogan
Akron Rubbernecks	83	55	.601	1½	Walter East
Lancaster Lanks	73	66	.525	12	Willie Gray/Curt Elston
New Castle Outlaws	73	67	.521	12½	Percy Stetler/Ralph Lindaman
Zanesville/Marion Moguls#..	71	69	.507	14½	Ferdinand Drumm
Newark Cotton Tops	65	74	.468	20	Gene Bates/Bill Bottenus/Peter Sommers/ W. Snodgrass
Mansfield Giants	59	77	.434	24½	Carl McVey
Sharon Steels	46	93	.331	39	Frank Yoho/Charles Crow/Dick Glassburner

#Zanesville (58-55) moved to Marion August 28.

BA: William Thomas, Youngstown, .303
Runs: Fred Abbott, Lancaster, 83
Hits: William Thomas, Youngstown, 158
Wins: Fred Ehman, Akron, 29
Pct: Fred Ehman, Akron, .707, 29-12

C South Atlantic League
President: Charles W. Boyer

Standings	W	L	Pct.	GB	Manager
Savannah Indians	72	41	.637	—	Bill Hallman/Wilson Matthews
Augusta Tourists	70	45	.609	3	Edward Ransick
Macon Brigands	58	53	.523	13	Perry Lipe
Columbia Gamecocks	52	59	.468	19	Ed Granville
Charleston Sea Gulls	48	61	.440	22	Robert Pender
Jacksonville Jax	36	77	.319	36	Arlie Latham/Joe Hennager

BA: Ed Sabrie, Savannah, .290
Runs: F.J. King, Savannah, 56
Hits: Ed Sabrie, Savannah, 117
Wins: Nap Rucker, Augusta, 27
Pct: Walt Deaver, Savannah, .818, 18-4

C South Texas League
President: Dr. William R. Robbie

Standings	W	L	Pct.	GB	Manager
Houston Buffalos*	78	43	.645	—	Con Harlow
Austin Senators**	76	47	.618	3	Warren Gill
Beaumont Oilers	72	50	.590	6½	Gerald Hayes/Sam LaRoque
Galveston Sand Crabs	58	68	.460	22½	Wade Moore
San Antonio Bronchos	57	69	.452	23½	William Alexander/George Page
Lake Charles Creoles	30	94	.242	49½	Edward Switzer/Dick Latham/ Dennis Lyons

Playoff: Austin 4 games, Houston 4; Austin was awarded the championship because Houston refused to stop using non-league players. An eighth game was played after Austin had been awarded the title by forfeit.

BA: Sam LaRoque, Beaumont, .313
Runs: Joe Mowry, Houston, 84
Hits: Joe Mowry, Houston, 156
HRs: Pat Newnam, Houston, 5
Wins: Prince Gaskill, Houston, 19
Pct: Peaches Nelson, Houston, .818, 18-4

C Virginia League
President: Jacob Wells

Standings	W	L	Pct.	GB	Manager
Lynchburg Shoemakers	72	36	.667	—	John J. Grim
Norfolk Tars	62	44	.585	9	Win Clark
Richmond Colts	57	54	.514	16½	Charles Shaffer
Danville Red Sox	50	58	.463	22	John Benny/Frank Doyle
Portsmouth Truckers	44	63	.411	27½	Ernest Landgraf/Barley Kain
Roanoke Tigers	42	72	.368	33	C.R. Williams/George "King" Kelley/ J.R. "Con" Strothers/W.D. "Red" McMahon

BA: Win Clark, Norfolk, .303
Runs: Fred Dingle, Norfolk, 71
    A.N. Bowen, Lynchburg, 71
Hits: Win Clark, Norfolk, 117

HRs: Willie Fetzer, Danville, 5
Wins: Walter Moser, Lynchburg, 24
SOs: Otto Willis, Roanoke, 212
Pct: Walter Moser, Lynchburg, .750, 24-8

C Western Association
President: Dr. D.M. Shiveley

Standings	W	L	Pct.	GB	Manager
Topeka White Sox	82	56	.594	—	Dick Cooley
Joplin Miners	75	62	.547	6½	John Baerwald/Louis Armstrong
Wichita Jabbers	75	65	.536	8	William Kimmel/Jack Holland
Springfield Midgets	72	67	.518	10½	G. Bennett/J.W. Seabaugh/John Shinn
Oklahoma City Mets	70	69	.504	12½	J.H. Chinn
Leavenworth Old Soldiers	68	72	.486	15	Louis Armstrong/George Pennington/ Bill Zink/Nick Kahl
Webb City Goldbugs	57	79	.419	24	Tom Hayden/Richard Rohn
St. Joseph Packers/ Hutchinson Salt Packers#	55	84	.396	27½	Frank Hurlburt/Spencer Abbott/Frank Genins

#St. Joseph (16-24) moved to Hutchinson June 12.

BA: Dick Cooley, Topeka, .305
Runs: Dick Bayless, Joplin, 104
Hits: Dakin Miller, Wichita, 173

HRs: Jerry Downs, Topeka, 9
Wins: Blaine Durbin, Joplin, 32
Pct: Blaine Durbin, Joplin, .800, 32-8

D Arkansas-Texas League
President: A.J. Kaiser

Standings	W	L	Pct.	GB	Manager
Pine Bluff Barristers**	34	25	.576	—	Sandy Reeves/Leroy Taylor/Lee Dawkins/ James Drake
Camden Ouachitas	29	28	.509	4	Arthur Riggs/Cleve Turner
Texarkana Shine-Oners#	28	31	.475	6	Cap Shelton
Hot Springs Vapors*	25	32	.439	8	Wade Moore/Jack Love

#Texarkana (28-30) disbanded August 25.
The league disbanded August 26.

Playoff: Pine Bluff 4 games, Hot Springs 1.

D Cotton States League
President: D. Stacey Compton

Standings	W	L	Pct.	GB	Manager
Mobile Sea Gulls	74	44	.627	—	George Reed/Joe Wright/Charles Miller
Meridian Ribboners	65	54	.546	9½	Guy Sample
Jackson Senators	58	60	.492	16	Asa Stewart
Gulfport Crabs	58	61	.487	16½	Erie Miller/John Bolin/Link Stickney
Baton Rouge Cajuns	57	63	.475	18	Bernie McCay
Vicksburg Hill Billies	44	74	.373	30	Billy Earle/Cy Hooker

BA: Guy Woodruff, Baton Rouge, .314
Runs: J.D. Jefferies, Jackson, 73
Hits: Curt Gardner, Meridian, 137

Wins: Robert Lee Vernuelle, Mobile, 26
SOs: McCain Robinson, Jackson, 197
Pct: Bill Phillips, Mobile, .917, 11-1

D Georgia State League
President: J.W. Thomas

Standings	W	L	Pct.	GB	Manager
Waycross Machinists	37	12	.755	—	Carl Beusse
Columbus River Snipes/ Brunswick#	29	17	.630	6½	Dudley Lewis/Bill Hessler
Cordele	24	24	.500	12½	Trammel Scott
Valdosta Stars@	22	25	.468	14	A.L. Starr/Harry Piepho/Peck Walters/ E. Bagwell
Albany	17	32	.347	20	E.D. Alexander/Walter Snodgrass
Americus Pallbearers+	13	32	.289	22	Harry Powell/Coniff/James Whalen

#Columbus (24-16) moved to Brunswick June 25.
@Valdosta disbanded July 4.
+Americus disbanded July 7.
The league disbanded July 9.

Playoff: Waycross 3 games, Brunswick 1.

D Interstate League
President: George F. Rindernecht

Standings	W	L	Pct.	GB	Manager
Erie Sailors	65	41	.613	—	Tom O'Hara
Punxsutawney Policemen	53	45	.541	8	C. Brown
Bradford Drillers	61	53	.535	8	Thomas News
DuBois Miners	52	52	.500	12	James Breen/Edward "Bunny" Larkin
Kane Mountaineers	58	58	.500	12	James Collopy
Hornell Pigmies/Patton#	53	56	.486	13½	John Quinn
Olean Refiners	50	62	.446	18	John Ziegler/John Dailey
Oil City-Jamestown Oseejays	44	69	.389	24½	Alfred Lawson/C.L. Rexford

#Hornell (35-31) moved to Patton August 6.
Attendance: Erie, 106,000.

D Iowa State League
President: L.S. Peckham

Standings	W	L	Pct.	GB	Manager
Burlington Pathfinders	83	39	.680	—	Ned Egan
Oskaloosa Quakers	75	49	.605	9	Hamilton Patterson
Ft. Dodge Gypsumites	68	49	.581	12½	Frank Boyle
Marshalltown Brownies	65	55	.542	17	Rollo Brown
Keokuk Indians	53	67	.442	24	Pat McAndrews
Boone/Clinton Miners#	46	70	.397	34	William Wooley/Pat Ryan/Harold Johnson
Waterloo Microbes	48	76	.387	36	Charlie Frisbee/F.G. Anklam
Ottumwa Champs	44	77	.364	38½	Niles/W. Everett

#Boone (25-33) moved to Clinton July 14.

BA: William Davidson, Ft. Dodge, .344
Runs: Cy Neighbors, Burlington, 96
Hits: Cy Neighbors, Burlington, 161

Wins: Frank Shaw, Oskaloosa, 29
SOs: Joe Bills, Keokuk, 209
Pct: Frank Dick, Marshalltown, .857, 18-3

D Kansas State League
President: Edward Bero, Jr.

Standings	W	L	Pct.	GB	Manager
Independence Coyotes**	69	48	.590	—	Charles McLinn/Crutcher/John Hendley
Iola Grays/ Cherryvale Boosters@	62	50	.554	4½	William Burns
Parsons Preachers	60	50	.545	5½	C. Pinkerton/P.P. Duffy & B.L. Taft
Coffeyville Bricks	58	50	.537	6½	Ed Mahley/Harry Barndollar/Haisman/ Finney
Bartlesville Indians	51	64	.443	17	Gus Alberts
Chanute Browns	31	82	.274	36	A. Allen
Ft. Scott Giants+*	35	18	.660	NA	M. McDonald
Pittsburg Champs/Vinita#+	30	25	.545	NA	H. Bartley/William Burns

#Pittsburg (16-15) moved to Vinita June 6.
@Iola (23-18) moved to Cherryvale June 15.
+Vinita and Ft. Scott disbanded July 5.
Games played before July 10 were discarded and the season was restarted.

(second half statistics:)
BA: Bert Haas, Independence, .341
Runs: Ed Foster, Coffeyville, 44
Hits: Wilder Gray, Coffeyville, 97

Wins: Chick Brandom, Independence, 16
SOs: Chick Brandom, Independence, 121
Pct: Harry Womack, Coffeyville, 1.000, 10-0

D Kitty League
President: Charles C. Gosnell

Standings	W	L	Pct.	GB	Manager
Vincennes Alices	76	49	.608	—	Eddie Kolb
Jacksonville Jacks	67	58	.536	9	Frank Belt
Cairo Giants	68	61	.527	10	Dan McCarthy
Danville Old Soldiers	58	69	.457	19	Jake Wortham/Ed Bauer
Paducah Indians	57	69	.452	19½	Harry Lloyd
Mattoon-Charleston Canaries	54	74	.422	23½	Bob Berryhill/Jack McCarthy

BA: Bill Dithridge, Cairo, .329
Runs: Andy Lotshaw, Jacksonville, 70
Hits: Frank Long, Cairo, 162
HRs: Andy Lotshaw, Jacksonville, 11

Wins: Hub Perdue, Vincennes, 25
SOs: Hub Perdue, Vincennes, 260
Pct: Hub Perdue, Vincennes, .758, 25-8

D POM League
President: Richard R. Guy

Standings	W	L	Pct.	GB	Manager
Uniontown Coal Barons	56	42	.571	—	James Groninger
Washington	57	44	.564	½	Bill Seamon
Braddock Infants	55	43	.561	1	Don McKim
East Liverpool	53	45	.541	3	Percy Stetler
Cumberland Rooters	50	48	.510	6	
Waynesburg	48	50	.490	8	Phillips
Steubenville Stubs	48	51	.485	8½	John W. Smith
Butler/Piedmont/Charleroi#	26	70	.271	29	Thomas Lindsay

#Butler (16-16) moved to Piedmont July 14; Piedmont (1-20) moved to Charleroi August 6.

D South Central League
Presidents: J.M. McAllister/Orville Frantz/P.D. Harper

Standings	W	L	Pct.	GB	Manager
South McAlester Miners***	59	32	.648	—	Smith
Muskogee Indians	50	38	.568	7½	Nixey Callahan/Muggsy Monroe
Ft. Smith Razorbacks	47	39	.547	9½	Fernandez/Walter Ahern
Tulsa Oilers	45	42	.517	12	F.H. "Cap" Smith/William Rupp
Shawnee Blues#	29	42	.408	NA	J.B. Roe/J.B. McAlester
Guthrie Senators#	18	55	.247	NA	Dad Bennett/James Geer/J.W. Faulkner

#Guthrie and Shawnee disbanded July 21.
The league disbanded in August.
Attendance: Tulsa, 19,750.

D Southern Michigan League
President: Joseph S. Jackson

Standings	W	L	Pct.	GB	Manager
Mt. Clemens Bathers	69	34	.670	—	D. Trembly
Kalamazoo White Sox	63	41	.612	6½	Clarence Pickell/Maurice Myers

	W	L	Pct.	GB	Manager
Tecumseh	57	47	.548	12½	Brewer
Jackson Convicts	52	52	.500	17½	Maurice Myers/Rube Deneau
Battle Creek Crickets#	39	56	.411	26	Bob Black/Maurice Myers
Saginaw#	34	60	.362	30½	Clarence Jessup

#Saginaw began play July 18. It was awarded a record of 15-20 when added. The Battle Creek record of 4-38 was expunged on July 21 and the reorganized team was awarded a record of 15-20 on July 22. The official standings were unequal due to the adjusted won-lost records.

BA: Bill Roth, Mt. Clemens, .302
Hits: Bill Roth, Mt. Clemens, 115

D Texas League
President: J. Doak Roberts

Standings	W	L	Pct.	GB	Manager
Ft. Worth Panthers*	78	48	.619	—	Frederick Cavender
Dallas Giants	79	49	.617	—	Curley Maloney
Cleburne Railroaders**	77	49	.611	1	Ben Shelton
Waco Navigators	32	96	.250	47	Lee Dawkins/Walt Hickey/William Doyle
Greenville Hunters#	30	31	.492	NA	Don Curtis
Temple Boll Weevils#	20	43	.317	NA	Con Lucid/Wade Moore

#Greenville disbanded June 30, then Temple was dropped to even the league.

Playoff: Cleburne was awarded the pennant when Ft. Worth completed the season but could not field a competitive team for the playoff.

BA: George Whiteman, Cleburne, .281
Runs: Walt Boles, Ft. Worth, 77
Hits: George Whiteman, Cleburne, 131

Wins: Alex Dupree, Ft. Worth, 25
Rick Adams, Cleburne, 25
SOs: Rick Adams, Cleburne, 138
Pct: Alex Dupree, Ft. Worth, .781, 25-7

D Wisconsin State League
President: John T. Powers

Standings	W	L	Pct.	GB	Manager
La Crosse Pinks	76	42	.644	—	Pink Hawley
Freeport Pretzels	73	43	.629	2	William Moriarity
Oshkosh Indians	56	63	.471	20½	Chip Hanford
Green Bay Colts	55	63	.466	21	George Bubsir/Phil Stremmel
Wausau Lumberjacks	48	70	.407	28	Nick Malvern/Belanger
Eau Claire-Chippewa Falls Orphans	44	71	.383	30½	Andy Porter/Tebeau/Rasmussen/Nick Malvern

BA: Tom Tennant, Green Bay, .312
Runs: George Moriarity, Freeport, 79
Hits: Tom Tennant, Green Bay, 141
George Moriarity, Freeport, 141

HRs: William Gleason, Oshkosh, 2
Fred Goldsmith, Eau Claire, 2
Frank Baker, Eau Claire, 2
Wins: Jim Scott, Freeport, 27
SOs: Jack Warhop, Freeport, 231
Pct: Jim Scott, Freeport, .771, 27-8

Ind Tri-State League
President: Charles F. Carpenter

Standings	W	L	Pct.	GB	Manager
York White Roses	75	52	.591	—	George Heckert
Williamsport Millionaires	72	55	.567	3	James Sebring
Lancaster Red Roses	70	57	.551	5	Fred Crolius
Altoona Mountaineers	64	62	.508	10½	Arthur Irwin
Harrisburg Senators	52	74	.413	22½	William Hamilton
Johnstown Johnnies	47	80	.370	28	Ed Holly

BA: Hartley, Lancaster, .307
Runs: Tom O'Hara, Lancaster, 90
Hits: Mike O'Neill, York, 157
HRs: Bob Unglaub, Williamsport, 14

3B: Jim Delahanty, Williamsport, 17
Wins: Stoney McGlynn, York, 36
SOs: Stoney McGlynn, York, 206
Pct: Stoney McGlynn, York, .783, 36-10

1906 Interleague Post Season Play

World Series
Chicago (American) 4 games, Chicago (National) 2

Junior World Series
Buffalo (Eastern) 3 games, Columbus (American Association) 2, one tie
The series ended abruptly due to a dispute over the site of the seventh game and distribution of the gate receipts.

New England Championship Series
Elimination Round (round robin)

Lynn (New England)	5-1
Springfield (Connecticut)	3-3
Norwich (Connecticut)	2-4
Worcester (New England)	2-4

Final Round: Lynn (New England) 3 games, Springfield (Connecticut) 2

Dixie Championship
Richmond (Virginia) 3 games, Savannah (South Atlantic) 2

1906 No-Hitters

Date	Pitcher	Team	League	Opponent	Score
4-28	Ivy Tevis	Galveston	South Texas	Houston	0-1
5-1	Johnny Lush	Philadelphia	National	Brooklyn	6-0
5-12	Charles "Sea Lion" Hall	Seattle	Pacific Coast	Oakland	2-0
5-23	Rick Adams	Cleburne	Texas	Temple	6-0
5-28	Alex Dupree	Ft. Worth	Texas	Greenville	5-1
6-26	Eddie Rodebaugh	Dallas	Texas	Cleburne	3-1
6-26	Alex Dupree	Ft. Worth	Texas	Waco	1-0
6-30	Hickory Dickson	Cleburne	Texas	Temple	3-1
7-9	Irvin Wilhelm	Birmingham	Southern Assoc.	Montgomery	7-0 (P)
7-20	Mal Eason	Brooklyn	National	St. Louis	2-0
8-1	Harry McIntyre	Brooklyn	National	Pittsburgh	0-1 (11)
8-5	Red Jarvis	Ft. Worth	Texas	Waco	4-0
8-10	Harry Swan	Kansas City	American Asso.	Columbus	5-0
8-22	Ed Moriarity	Newark	Eastern	Montreal	1-0
8-27	John Cronin	Providence	Eastern	Newark	0-1 (10)
8-28	Bernie McCoy	Baton Rouge	Cotton States	Vicksburg	3-0
9-1	Tom Fisher	Shreveport	Southern Assoc.	Montgomery	4-0 (P)
9-2	Eli Cates	Oakland	Pacific Coast	Fresno	7-0
9-4	Robert Bandy	Pine Bluff	Arkansas-Texas	Hot Springs	3-0
9-12	Fred Burchell	Baltimore	Eastern	Toronto	2-0 (7)
10-13	Fred Brown	San Francisco	Pacific Coast	Oakland	3-0
	Eddie Cicotte	Des Moines	Western	Omaha	
	Adolph Vollendorf	Pueblo	Western	Des Moines	
	Edward Eyler	Lincoln	Western	Des Moines	
	Tony Freeman	Evansville	Central		
	Boyd Chambers	Springfield	Central		

Number in parentheses indicates innings if other than nine; "P" indicates perfect game.

THIS DATE IN MINOR LEAGUE HISTORY

April 18, 1906, The city of San Francisco was virtually destroyed by earthquake and fire, forcing the Pacific Coast League to suspend operations. Catcher Pat Donahue of the Oakland club suffered two broken legs when he jumped from a hotel window during the quake.

May 4, 1906, Pitcher William Thomas of Buffalo, Eastern League, disappeared from the steamboat, Richard Peck, en route from Providence to New York. He was never heard from again, and was supposed to have drowned during the night.

May 21, 1906, Manager George Stallings, Buffalo, Eastern League, was sued for divorce in Atlanta by his wife on statutory grounds.

May 27, 1906, Five persons were killed and 25 injured by a bolt of lightning which struck a crowd watching a game near Mobile, Alabama.

June 3, 1906, The Amsterdam-Johnstown-Gloversville team, New York State League, shut out Troy for third straight time.

August 4, 1906, The Hornell franchise in the Interstate League was sold for $250 and later moved to Patton.

August 11, 1906, Thomas Burke, Lynn, New England League, died from the effects of being hit in the head by a pitched ball two days earlier by Joseph Yeager of Fall River.

August 23, 1906, President Cornelius Danaher of the New Haven, Connecticut League, club sold pitcher C.C. Hodge to Holyoke for 25 cents.

August 25, 1906, Umpire Langdon deserted his post and fled the park during the Fall River-Worcester game in the New England League because of the threatening crowd.

September 1, 1906, La Crosse played Freeport on the last day of the season with the Wisconsin State League pennant in the balance. 5,000 fans saw a 0-0 game after nine innings. La Crosse pushed across five runs in the tenth to win.

October 2, 1906, Manager George Stallings of Buffalo sold his stock in that club and retired from the game to take up mining in British Columbia.

December 4, 1906, The Norwich franchise of the Connecticut State League was sold at a sheriff's sale for $25.

1907

American League
President: Byron Bancroft Johnson

Standings	W	L	Pct.	GB	Attend.	Manager
Detroit Tigers	92	58	.613	—	297,079	Hugh Jennings
Philadelphia Athletics	88	57	.607	1½	625,581	Connie Mack
Chicago White Sox	87	64	.576	5½	666,307	Fielder Jones
Cleveland Naps	85	67	.559	8	382,046	Napoleon Lajoie
New York Highlanders	70	78	.473	21	350,020	Clark Griffith
St. Louis Browns	69	83	.454	24	419,025	Jimmy McAleer
Boston Red Sox	59	90	.396	32½	436,777	Cy Young/George Huff/ Bob Unglaub/Deacon McGuire
Washington Senators	49	102	.325	43½	221,929	Joe Cantillon

BA: Ty Cobb, Detroit, .350
Runs: Sam Crawford, Detroit, 102
Hits: Ty Cobb, Detroit, 212
RBIs: Ty Cobb, Detroit, 116
HRs: Harry Davis, Philadelphia, 8

Wins: Addie Joss, Cleveland, 27
Doc White, Chicago, 27
SOs: Rube Waddell, Philadelphia, 232
ERA: Ed Walsh, Chicago, 1.60
Pct: Wild Bill Donovan, Detroit, .862, 25-4

National League
President: Harry C. Pulliam

Standings	W	L	Pct.	GB	Attend.	Manager
Chicago Cubs	107	45	.704	—	422,550	Frank Chance
Pittsburgh Pirates	91	63	.591	17	319,506	Fred Clarke
Philadelphia Phillies	83	64	.565	21½	341,216	Billy Murray
New York Giants	82	71	.536	25½	538,350	John McGraw
Brooklyn Superbas	65	83	.439	40	312,500	Patsy Donovan
Cincinnati Reds	66	87	.431	41½	317,500	Ned Hanlon
Boston Doves	58	90	.392	47	203,221	Fred Tenney
St. Louis Cardinals	52	101	.340	55½	185,377	John McCloskey

BA: Honus Wagner, Pittsburgh, .350
Runs: Spike Shannon, New York, 104
Hits: Ginger Beaumont, Pittsburgh, 187
RBIs: Sherry Magee, Philadelphia, 85
HRs: Dave Brain, Boston, 10

Wins: Christy Mathewson, New York, 24
SOs: Christy Mathewson, New York, 178
ERA: Jack Pfiester, Chicago, 1.15
Pct: Ed Reulbach, Chicago, .810, 17-4

A American Association
President: Joseph D. O'Brien

Standings	W	L	Pct.	GB	Manager
Columbus Senators	90	64	.584	—	William Clymer
Toledo Mud Hens	88	65	.575	1½	Bill Armour
Minneapolis Millers	79	73	.520	10	Mike Cantillon
Kansas City Blues	78	76	.510	12	James Burke
Louisville Colonels	77	77	.500	13	Thomas Chivington
Indianapolis Indians	73	80	.477	16½	Charles Carr
Milwaukee Brewers	71	83	.461	19	Jack Doyle
St. Paul Apostles	58	96	.377	32	Edward Ashenbach

BA: Jake Beckley, Kansas City, .365
Runs: Ed Green, Milwaukee, 107
Hits: William Friel, Columbus, 189
HRs: Buck Freeman, Minneapolis, 18

Wins: George Upp, Columbus, 27
SOs: Ambrose Puttman, Louisville, 174
Pct: George Upp, Columbus, .730, 27-10

A Eastern League
President: Patrick Powers

Standings	W	L	Pct.	GB	Manager
Toronto Maple Leafs	83	51	.619	—	Joseph Kelley
Buffalo Bisons	73	59	.553	9	Lew McAllister
Providence Grays	72	63	.533	11½	Hugh Duffy
Newark Sailors	67	66	.504	15½	Walter Burnham
Jersey City Skeeters	67	66	.504	15½	Joseph Bean
Baltimore Orioles	68	69	.495	16½	Jack Dunn
Rochester Bronchos	59	76	.437	24½	Al Buckenberger
Montreal Royals	46	85	.351	35½	Mal Kittridge/James Morgan

Attendance: Buffalo, 212,986.

BA: Jack Thoney, Toronto, .329
Runs: Jack Thoney, Toronto, 93
Hits: Wally Clement, Jersey City, 160
HRs: Bill Abstein, Providence, 7
Natty Nattress, Buffalo, 7

Wins: Joe Lake, Jersey City, 25
SOs: Joe Lake, Jersey City, 187
Pct: George McQuillan, Providence, .731, 19-7

A Pacific Coast League
President: J. Cal Ewing

Standings	W	L	Pct.	GB	Manager
Los Angeles Angels	115	74	.608	—	Frank "Cap" Dillon
San Francisco Seals	104	99	.515	17	Daniel Long
Oakland Oaks	97	101	.489	21½	George Van Haltren
Portland Beavers	72	114	.388	41½	Walter McCredie

BA: Truck Eagan, Oakland, .335
Runs: Walter "Rosy" Carlisle, Los Angeles, 113
Hits: Truck Eagan, Oakland, 237
HRs: Walter "Rosy" Carlisle, Los Angeles, 14

Wins: Dolly Gray, Los Angeles, 32
SOs: Eli Cates, Oakland, 226
Pct: Dolly Gray, Los Angeles, .696, 32-14

A Southern Association
President: William B. Kavanaugh

Standings	W	L	Pct.	GB	Manager
Atlanta Crackers	78	54	.591	—	William A. Smith
Memphis Egyptians	74	57	.565	3½	Charles Babb
New Orleans Pelicans	68	66	.507	11	Charles Frank
Little Rock Travelers	66	66	.500	12	Michael Finn
Birmingham Barons	64	71	.474	15½	Harry Vaughn
Shreveport Pirates	62	70	.470	16	Thomas Fisher
Montgomery Senators	62	71	.466	16½	John Malarkey
Nashville Finnites	59	78	.431	21½	Johnny Dobbs

BA: Jack Meek, Birmingham, .340
Runs: Carleton Molesworth, Birmingham, 89
Hits: Jake Atz, New Orleans, 158
HRs: Dode Paskert, Atlanta, 6

Wins: Irvin "Little Eva" Wilhelm, Birmingham, 23
Pct: Charles Shields, Memphis, .727, 8-3

A Western League
President: Norris L. O'Neill

Standings	W	L	Pct.	GB	Manager
Omaha Rourkes	84	63	.571	—	Pa Rourke
Lincoln Treeplanters	79	63	.556	2½	James "Ducky" Holmes
Des Moines Champs	76	63	.547	4	Mike Kelley
Denver Grizzlies	67	75	.472	14½	Eddie Wheeler
Pueblo Indians	65	73	.471	14½	Frank Selee/Lewis Drill
Sioux City Packers	56	90	.384	27½	Billy Hart

BA: Billy Hart, Sioux City, .323
Runs: Bill McGilvray, Pueblo, 94
Hits: Bill McGilvray, Pueblo, 174
HRs: John Thomas, Lincoln, 9

SBs: Jim Austin, Omaha, 63
Wins: Charles "Babe" Adams, Denver, 23
Pct: Charles "Babe" Adams, Denver, .657, 23-12

B Central League
President: Frank R. Carson

Standings	W	L	Pct.	GB	Manager
Springfield Babes	86	49	.637	—	Jack Hendricks
Wheeling Stogies	77	57	.575	8½	Ted Price
Canton Chinamen	69	64	.519	16	Bade Myers
Evansville River Rats	69	69	.500	18½	Charles "Punch" Knoll
Dayton Veterans	66	71	.482	21	Ed McKean/E. Richardson/Mal Kittridge
Terre Haute Hottentots	65	72	.474	22	Jack McConnell/Cameron
Grand Rapids Wolverines	60	77	.438	27	George "Cuppy" Groeschow/Elmer Bliss
South Bend Greens	53	86	.381	35	Angus Grant

BA: Champ Osteen, Springfield, .338
Runs: Joe Collins, Springfield, 96
Hits: Champ Osteen, Springfield, 170

Wins: Rube Marquard, Canton, 23
Pct: Matt Muldowney, Springfield, .783, 18-5

B Connecticut League
President: W.J. Tracey

Standings	W	L	Pct.	GB	Manager
Holyoke Papermakers	83	42	.664	—	Thomas Dowd
Waterbury Authors	77	47	.621	5½	Harold Durant
Springfield Ponies	72	49	.595	9	Daniel O'Neill
Norwich Reds	71	51	.582	10½	August Soffel
Hartford Senators	66	55	.545	15	James Clarkin
Bridgeport Orators	48	75	.390	34	James O'Rourke
New Haven Blues	44	80	.355	38½	Cornelius Danaher
New London Whalers	31	93	.250	51½	Sam Kennedy/Charles "Al" Page

BA: Hi Ladd, Bridgeport, .341
Runs: Mike McAndrews, Waterbury, 100
Hits: Hi Ladd, Bridgeport, 168

HRs: Lou Lapine, Holyoke, 8
Wins: Ira Plank, New Haven, 26
Pct: Ed Farley, Waterbury, .774, 24-7

B New England League
President: Tim H. Murnane

Standings	W	L	Pct.	GB	Manager
Worcester Busters	76	36	.679	—	Jesse Burkett
Lynn Shoemakers	61	49	.555	14	Frank Leonard
Brockton Tigers	59	51	.536	16	Stephen Flanagan
Haverhill Hustlers	55	55	.500	20	Billy Hamilton
Fall River Indians	56	56	.500	20	John O'Brien

*Won first-half   **Won second-half   ***Won both halves

	W	L	Pct.	GB	Manager
Lowell Tigers	48	60	.444	26	Alexander Winn
New Bedford Whalers	48	62	.436	27	John Coveny
Lawrence Colts	40	74	.351	37	James Rolley

BA: Billy Hamilton, Haverhill, .333
Runs: Tommy Madden, Haverhill, 76
Hits: Dave Pickett, Lowell, 116
    Fred Reynolds, Worcester, 116

HRs: Simeon Murch, Brockton, 4
    Harry Billet, Lawrence/Haverhill, 4
Wins: Elmer Steele, Lynn, 24
Pct: Harry Wormwood, Worcester, .769, 10-3

B New York State League
President: John H. Farrell

Standings	W	L	Pct.	GB	Manager
Albany Senators	79	50	.612	—	Michael Doherty
Scranton Miners	81	54	.600	1	Henry Ramsey
Utica Pent-Ups	78	54	.591	2½	Charles Dooley
Troy Trojans	75	56	.573	5	John O'Brien
Wilkes-Barre Coal Barons	69	66	.511	13	Abel Lizotte
Syracuse Stars	61	75	.449	21½	Sandy Griffin
Binghamton Bingoes	51	83	.381	30½	Robert Drury
Amsterdam-Johnstown-Gloversville Jags	39	95	.291	42½	Howard Earl

BA: Wallace Hollingsworth, Wilkes-Barre, .327
Runs: Fred Eley, Wilkes-Barre, 76
Hits: Art DeGroff, Troy, 151
Wins: Vic Schlitzer, Utica, 27
SOs: Vic Schlitzer, Utica, 207
Pct: Vic Schlitzer, Utica, .711, 27-11

B Northwestern League
President: William H. Lucas

Standings	W	L	Pct.	GB	Manager
Aberdeen Black Cats	85	51	.625	—	Robert Brown
Tacoma Tigers	90	59	.604	1½	George Shreeder
Seattle Siwashes	83	65	.561	8	Daniel Dugdale
Butte Miners	70	73	.490	18½	Russ Hall
Spokane Indians	68	76	.472	21	E.E. Quinn
Vancouver Horse Doctors	34	106	.243	53	Parke Wilson/Butch McIntyre/James Evans/J.C. "Con" Strothers/William Hurley

BA: Ed Householder, Aberdeen, .347
Runs: Royal "Hunky" Shaw, Tacoma, 105
Hits: Royal "Hunky" Shaw, Tacoma, 174
HRs: John Clynes, Tacoma/Vancouver, 10
Wins: Ike Butler, Tacoma, 32
SOs: Irv Higginbotham, Aberdeen, 295
Pct: Bill "Dode" Brinker, Aberdeen, .714, 15-6

B Three-I League
President: Edward Holland

Standings	W	L	Pct.	GB	Manager
Rock Island Islanders	86	46	.652	—	Jack Tighe
Decatur Commodores	80	47	.630	3½	George Reed
Springfield Senators	81	50	.618	4½	Hank Scharnweber
Peoria Distillers	77	52	.597	7½	Frank Donnelly
Cedar Rapids Rabbits	72	61	.541	14½	Belden Hill
Clinton Infants	53	78	.405	27½	Monte McFarland/Harry Stauffer
Bloomington Bloomers	51	79	.392	29	Fred Donovan
Dubuque Dubs	22	109	.169	63½	Claude Stark/George Jennings/Frank Genins/John Ray

BA: Harry Swacina, Peoria, .292
Runs: Walter Thiery, Peoria, 84
Hits: Harry Swacina, Peoria, 147
Wins: Roy Beecher, Springfield, 28
SOs: Charles Bomar, Decatur, 190
Pct: Happy Campbell, Springfield, .769, 10-3

B Tri-State League
President: Charles F. Carpenter

Standings	W	L	Pct.	GB	Manager
Williamsport Millionaires	86	38	.694	—	Harry Wolverton
Harrisburg Senators	79	47	.627	8	George Heckert
Lancaster Red Roses	73	53	.579	14	Clarence "Pop" Foster
Trenton Tigers	70	54	.565	16	John Carney
Altoona Mountaineers	61	61	.500	24	Arthur Irwin/John Farrell
Johnstown Johnnies	46	77	.374	39½	Charles Atherton/Thomas Daly/Fred Raymer
Wilmington Peaches	43	79	.352	42	William Connolly/Charles Atherton/Michael Grady
York White Roses/Reading Pretzels#	38	87	.304	48½	Curt Weigand

#York (18-57) moved to Reading July 24.

BA: Joe Delahanty, Williamsport, .355
Runs: Joe Hennessey, Williamsport, 91
Hits: Mike O'Neill, Harrisburg, 143
HRs: Kip Selbach, Harrisburg, 7
Wins: Rube Vickers, Williamsport, 25
Pct: Slim Sallee, Williamsport, .815, 22-5

C Hudson River League
President: C.S. Harvey

Standings	W	L	Pct.	GB	Manager
Poughkeepsie Colts	17	10	.630	—	William McCabe
Newburgh Hillies	15	11	.577	1½	Jim Connor
Yonkers	12	12	.500	3½	Jack Lawler
Hudson Marines	12	12	.500	3½	Gus Schnack
Paterson Intruders@	4	9	.308	NA	Dick Cogan
Kingston Colonial Colts#	4	10	.286	NA	Ryan

#Kingston disbanded June 1.
@Paterson disbanded June 2.
The league disbanded June 18.

C Ohio-Pennsylvania League
President: Charles H. Morton

Standings	W	L	Pct.	GB	Manager
Youngstown Champs	86	52	.623	—	Samuel Wright
Newark Newks	86	53	.619	½	Bob Berryhill
Akron Champs	83	53	.610	2	Walter East
Lancaster Lanks	72	62	.537	12	James Breen/Curt Elston
New Castle Nocks	64	74	.464	22	William Smith
Mansfield Pioneers	55	84	.396	31½	Carl McVey
Sharon Giants	55	84	.396	31½	R.A. "Jimmy" Kling/Van Patterson
Marion Moguls	48	87	.356	36½	Ferdinand Drumm/Bob Quinn/Thomas Mylett

BA: Curt Elston, Lancaster, .318
Runs: Charles Starr, Youngstown, 75
Hits: Del Drake, Marion, 164
Wins: B. Thomas, Youngstown, 28
Pct: Ed Asher, Newark, .714, 25-10

C South Atlantic League
President: Charles W. Boyer

Standings	W	L	Pct.	GB	Manager
Charleston Sea Gulls	75	46	.620	—	Wilson Matthews/Richard Crozier
Jacksonville Jays	68	51	.571	6	Dominick Mullaney
Macon Brigands	68	54	.557	7½	Perry Lipe
Augusta Tourists	59	61	.492	15½	Edward Ransick/Richard Crozier
Savannah Indians	56	63	.471	18	Robert Stafford
Columbia Gamecocks	36	87	.293	40	Jay Kanzler/Bill Hallman/Edward Ransick

BA: Tom Raftery, Charleston, .301
Runs: Tom Raftery, Charleston, 69
Hits: Tom Raftery, Charleston, 128
Wins: Bugs Raymond, Charleston, 35
SOs: Bugs Raymond, Charleston, 335
Pct: Bugs Raymond, Charleston, .761, 35-11

C Texas League
President: Dr. William R. Robbie

Standings	W	L	Pct.	GB	Manager
Austin Senators	88	52	.629	—	Brooks Gordon
Dallas Giants	84	55	.604	3½	Curley Maloney
San Antonio Bronchoes	82	58	.586	6	Sam LaRoque/Pat Newnam
Houston Buffalos	79	60	.568	8½	Wade Moore
Ft. Worth Panthers	61	78	.439	26½	Walter Salm/Walt Boles
Galveston Sand Crabs	59	81	.421	29	Frank Weikart
Waco Navigators	53	87	.379	35	Frederick Cavender
Temple Boll Weevils	52	87	.374	35½	Ben Shelton

BA: Tris Speaker, Houston, .314
Runs: Bill Louden, Dallas, 89
Hits: Earl Gardner, Austin, 160
Wins: Ivy Tevis, Houston, 24
SOs: Bill Bailey, Austin, 234
Pct: Parson McGill, Austin, .789, 15-4

C Virginia League
President: Jacob Wells

Standings	W	L	Pct.	GB	Manager
Norfolk Tars	67	48	.583	—	Robert Pender
Danville Red Sox	67	58	.536	5	James McKevitt
Lynchburg Shoemakers	65	62	.512	8	John J. Grim
Richmond Colts	62	62	.500	9½	Charles Schaffer/John Wells/Ralph Reeve
Roanoke Tigers	62	62	.500	9½	Win Clark/Walter Brodie
Portsmouth Truckers	46	77	.374	25	Charles Moss/Win Clark

BA: Jacob Henn, Danville, .284
Runs: Guy Titman, Richmond, 67
Hits: Jacob Henn, Danville, 131
HRs: Jacob Henn, Danville, 8
Wins: Bill Otey, Norfolk, 22
SOs: Bill Otey, Norfolk, 197
Pct: Hal Bertrand, Norfolk, .818, 9-2

C Western Association
President: Dr. D.M. Shiveley

Standings	W	L	Pct.	GB	Manager
Wichita Jobbers	98	35	.737	—	Jack Holland
Oklahoma City Mets	86	54	.614	15½	C.A. McFarland
Hutchinson White Sox	77	59	.566	22½	Jay Andrews
Topeka White Sox	75	65	.536	30½	Dick Cooley
Joplin Miners	71	64	.526	31½	Ted Price/Lou Armstrong
Webb City Goldbugs	65	70	.481	37½	Richard Rohn/George Dalrymple
Springfield Midgets	46	92	.333	54½	F.R. Pierce
Leavenworth Convicts	29	108	.212	71	John Ray/Ernest Quigley/A. Schaumeyer

BA: Beals Becker, Wichita, .310
Runs: Jack Pendry, Oklahoma City, 91
Hits: Gus Hetling, Wichita, 149
Wins: Harley Young, Wichita, 29
Pct: Harley Young, Wichita, .879, 29-4
ShO: Jack Halla, Topeka, 16

D Cotton States League
President: A.C. Crowder

Standings	W	L	Pct.	GB	Manager
Mobile Sea Gulls	82	52	.612	—	Bernie McCay
Vicksburg Hill Billies.........	77	57	.575	5	George Blackburn
Jackson Senators.................	71	62	.534	10½	Harry Salliard/Roy Montgomery
Gulfport Crabs	68	67	.504	14½	Robert Gilks
Meridian White Ribbons	64	70	.478	18	Guy Sample
Columbus Discoverers........	42	96	.304	42	Jack Law

BA: Roy Montgomery, Jackson, .340
Runs: Woody Thornton, Mobile, 76
Hits: Woody Thornton, Mobile, 150
Wins: William Bruner, Mobile, 25
SOs: Jackson Ryan, Gulfport, 220
Pct: Rufus Nolley, Mobile, .767, 23-7

D Eastern Illinois League
Presidents: Charles Welvert/L.A.G. Schoaff

Standings	W	L	Pct.	GB	Manager
Mattoon Giants	74	44	.627	—	Charles O'Day
Charleston Broom Corn Cutters..................	71	49	.592	4	Nig Langdon
Taylorville Tailors	60	58	.508	14	Phil Ketter/W.J. Ryan
Centralia White Stockings/ Paris Colts#..................	51	67	.432	23	Kelly/Bob Shaw
Pana Coal Miners................	51	70	.421	24½	Joe Adams
Shelbyville Queen Citys	50	69	.420	24½	Joe Young

#Centralia (6-27) moved to Paris June 20.

BA: Phil Ketter, Taylorville, .284
Runs: John Bartley, Charleston, 51
Hits: Phil Ketter, Taylorville, 111
HRs: Andy Lotshaw, Charleston, 10
Wins: Grover Lowdermilk, Mattoon, 33
SOs: Grover Lowdermilk, Mattoon, 458
ERA: Grover Lowdermilk, Mattoon, 0.93

D Gulf Coast League
President: Paul O. Moss

Standings	W	L	Pct.	GB	Manager
Lake Charles Creoles**......	74	46	.617	—	Dan Collins
Alexandria White Sox*	64	50	.564	7	Jack Auslit
Monroe Municipals............	63	55	.534	10	Jim Lighton
Orange Hoos-Hoos	50	65	.435	21½	Tim Cook/Roland Vitter/Mac McDonald
Lafayette Browns...............	48	64	.429	22	Roland Vitter/B. Hubbard
Opelousas Indians..............	48	67	.417	23½	D. Edmonds

Playoff: Lake Charles 4 games, Alexandria 1.

BA: William "Silver" Braun, Alexandria, .348
Runs: Burleigh Emery, Lake Charles, 80
Hits: William "Silver" Braun, Alexandria, 125
Wins: H.B. Weeks, Alexandria, 20
Pct: A.H. Richardson, Orange, .900, 9-1

D Interstate League
President: Frank Baumeister

Standings	W	L	Pct.	GB	Manager
Erie Sailors**	64	51	.557	—	Thomas Reynolds
Bradford Drillers................	63	54	.538	2	Eddie Foster
Franklin Millionaires	51	52	.495	7	L.L. Jacklin/George Rindernecht
Oil City Oilers*	54	57	.486	8	James Collopy
DuBois Miners&................	36	26	.581	NA	Edward "Bunny" Larkin
Kane Mountaineers#...........	17	26	.395	NA	Charles Kelchner
Olean Refiners@	12	35	.255	NA	J.M. Flynn
Punxsutawney Policemen+.	33	26	.559	NA	Milt Montgomery

#Kane disbanded July 16.
@Olean disbanded July 18.
+Punxsutawney disbanded August 3.
&DuBois disbanded August 5.
The league played a third season, August 7 through September 8, won by Bradford.

Playoffs: Oil City was declared the first half champion because DuBois disbanded. Oil City 4 games, Bradford 3.

BA: Jake Weimer, DuBois/Oil City, .338
Runs: Ben Jewell, Oil City, 66
Hits: Earl Sykes, Oil City, 108
Wins: Dwight Hazleton, Bradford, 16
Pct: W.E. Parsons, Oil City, .750, 15-5

D Iowa State League
President: L.S. Peckham

Standings	W	L	Pct.	GB	Attend.	Manager
Waterloo Cubs	79	45	.637	—	27,992	Frank Boyle
Burlington Pathfinders........	77	51	.602	4	43,420	Ned Egan
Oskaloosa Quakers.............	70	55	.560	9½	22,585	Hamilton Patterson
Jacksonville Lunatics..........	63	61	.508	16	29,448	Frank Belt
Marshalltown Snappers	62	61	.504	16½	14,992	A.L. "Snapper" Kennedy
Quincy Gems.....................	61	66	.480	19½	37,000	Harry Hofer
Ottumwa Packers................	51	74	.408	28½	24,974	Jack Corbett
Keokuk Indians..................	39	89	.305	42	20,760	Cy Black/Charles Yeager

BA: John House, Burlington, .308
Runs: John House, Burlington, 91
Hits: John House, Burlington, 158
Wins: Frank Green, Burlington, 28
Pct: Fred Steel, Oskaloosa, .817, 9-2

D Maine State League
President: Fred K. Owen

Standings	W	L	Pct.	GB	Manager
Bangor White Sox	47	31	.603	—	Jack "Biddo" Iott
Biddeford..........................	30	27	.526	6½	
Portland Blue Sox	39	41	.488	9	
Pine Tree...........................	27	32	.458	10½	

D Northern-Copper Country League
President: Percy Glass

Standings	W	L	Pct.	GB	Manager
Winnipeg Maroons	70	27	.722	—	Edward Herr
Duluth White Sox	49	53	.480	23½	A.W. Kuehnow
Houghton Giants................	47	55	.464	25½	John "Kid" Taylor
Calumet Aristocrats	34	65	.343	37	Dick Egan

The season was shortened to September 2.

BA: Rollie Zeider, Winnipeg, .314
Runs: Rollie Zeider, Winnipeg, 75
Hits: Gene Cox, Winnipeg, 117
SBs: Rollie Zeider, Winnipeg, 59
Wins: Alvin Cummings, Duluth, 20
Pct: R. Terry, Winnipeg, .842, 16-3

D North Texas League
President: W.E. Craddock

Standings	W	L	Pct.	GB	Manager
Corsicana Oilers/Desperados..	38	21	.644	—	Dee Poindexter
Paris Athletics...................	36	23	.610	2	Robert Shelton/Everett Sheffield
Greenville Hunters#...........	24	35	.407	14	Horace Kelton/William Owen
Terrell Red Stockings	19	38	.333	18	Luke Rash/Cy Mulkey/Rube Walters/ T.R. Bell

#Greenville disbanded June 28, causing the league to disband June 30.

BA: Harry Welch, Greenville, .309
Runs: Bill Yohe, Greenville, 42
Hits: Elmer Coyle, Corsicana, 78
HRs: J. Heigelfort, Terrell, 4
Wins: W. Jenkins, Corsicana, 16
SOs: Joe Buench, Greenville, 130
ERA: W. Jenkins, Corsicana, 2.09
Pct: W. Jenkins, Corsicana, .800, 16-4

D Oklahoma-Arkansas-Kansas League
President: Fred McDaniel

Standings	W	L	Pct.	GB	Manager
Bartlesville Boosters***.....	83	51	.619	—	Jack Love/Harry Truby
Coffeyville Glassblowers ..	71	57	.555	9	Stuart
Independence Champs........	68	63	.519	13½	Billy Rupp
Muskogee Redskins............	63	70	.474	19½	Lon Ury
Ft. Smith Soldiers@............	40	46	.465	NA	C. Pinkerton
McAlester Miners#.............	11	17	.393	NA	Deacon White
Tulsa Oilers@	37	60	.381	NA	Jake Beckley
Parsons Preachers#............	10	19	.345	NA	Gus Alberts

#Parsons and McAlester withdrew June 2.
@Ft. Smith and Tulsa disbanded August 6.
The season was shortened to September 15.
Attendance: Tulsa, 24,000.

BA: Ernie Wilson, Independence, .292
Runs: Fred Hutchinson, Bartlesville, 84
Hits: Dave White, Bartlesville, 135
Wins: Howard McClintock, Bartlesville, 32
Pct: Howard McClintock, Bartlesville, .842, 32-6

D POM League
President: Richard R. Guy

Standings	W	L	Pct.	GB	Manager
Steubenville Stubs	69	33	.676	—	Percy Stetler
Uniontown Coal Barons	64	43	.598	7½	Alex Pearson
Zanesville.........................	63	43	.594	8	Martin Hogan
East Liverpool...................	62	45	.579	9½	C.C. Bippus
Washington........................	45	57	.441	24	William Seaman
Charleroi	45	63	.417	27	Tom Sloan
McKeesport Tubers	38	68	.358	33	Jock Menefee
Braddock Infants................	37	71	.343	35	Don McKim/Tom Cosgrove

BA: C.S. "Pop" Schriver, Zanesville, .335
Runs: R. Hess Morgan, McKeesport, 70
Hits: R. Hess Morgan, McKeesport, 118
SBs: Harry E. Ball, East Liverpool, 54

D South Carolina League
President: M.L. Smith

Standings	W	L	Pct.	GB	Manager
Sumter Gamecocks	44	23	.657	—	Guy Gunter
Orangeburg Cottonpickers..	42	25	.627	2	J.P. Doyle
Spartanburg Spartans	36	34	.514	9½	J.W. McMakin
Darlington/Florence Fiddlers@..	23	45	.338	21½	Heisman/Russell/Schmitz
Greenville Edistoes#..........	25	28	.472	NA	Thomas Stouch
Anderson Electricians#.......	21	36	.368	NA	Bagwell

#Anderson and Greenville withdrew July 27.
@Darlington (18-38) moved to Florence July 27.

BA: J.C. Watson, Spartanburg, .327
Hits: Ralph McLaurin, Sumter, 88
Wins: L.G. Lanford, Orangeburg, 18
Pct: L.G. Lanford, Orangeburg, .783, 18-5

D Southern Michigan League
President: Joseph S. Jackson

Standings	W	L	Pct.	GB	Manager
Tecumseh............................	69	42	.622	—	Bo Slear
Kalamazoo White Sox	62	47	.569	6	Maurice Myers
Battle Creek Crickets..........	63	49	.563	6½	James Henderson
Mt. Clemens Bathers	51	51	.500	13½	Joe Ganzel/Thomas
Bay City..............................	46	57	.447	19	M.E. Taylor
Lansing Senators................	46	57	.447	19	John Morrisey
Flint Vehics.......................	42	64	.396	24½	Fred Mason
Jackson Convicts#	18	30	.375	NA	Bruce Hayes

#Jackson withdrew July 15.

BA: John Landry, Mt. Clemens, .297
Runs: John Landry, Mt. Clemens, 60
Hits: John Landry, Mt. Clemens, 120
HRs: John Cocash, Flint, 6
Fred Merkle, Tecumseh, 6

Wins: Harvey Teal, Tecumseh, 21
Tom Railing, Tecumseh, 21
SOs: Irwin Gough, Mt. Clemens, 253
Pct: Harry Steiger, Battle Creek, .810, 17-4

D Western Canada League
President: Bruce L. Robinson

Standings	W	L	Pct.	GB	Manager
Medicine Hat Hatters........	58	32	.644	—	John Benny
Edmonton Grays................	50	35	.588	5½	
Lethbridge Miners	37	45	.451	17	Art O'Dea
Calgary Bronchos	26	59	.306	29½	

Attendance: Edmonton, 30,000; Calgary, 30,000.

BA: Art O'Dea, Lethbridge, .339
Runs: William Hamilton, Medicine Hat, 72
Hits: Art O'Dea, Lethbridge, 95

Wins: Ralph Works, Medicine Hat, 26
SOs: Ralph Works, Medicine Hat, 217
Pct: Ralph Works, Medicine Hat, .703, 26-11

D Western Pennsylvania League
Presidents: Alex J. Lawson/Charles B. Powers

Standings	W	L	Pct.	GB	Manager
Fairmont Champions***	68	36	.654	—	Joseph "Reddy" Mack
Butler White Sox	58	44	.569	9	Alfred Lawson/Jake Jacobsen/
					Eddie Linneborn/William Harkins
Scottdale Giants.................	48	49	.495	16½	Billy Earle/S.B. "Duff" Buttermore
Clarksburg Bees.................	50	54	.481	18	Tom Hulings/Tom Essler/Bull Smith
Greensburg Red Sox	42	50	.457	20	Anderson/Bill Powell/Lefty Wallace
Connellsville Cokers...........	44	59	.427	23½	Bill Malarkey/Denny O'Hara/Jack Dolan
Beaver Falls Beavers@.......	41	36	.532	NA	Charles Jewell
Latrobe/Cumberland Rooters/					
Piedmont/Somerset#........	18	46	.281	NA	Whaley/W.A. Morrow/Tom Dillon/
					Don Curtis/Bill Malarkey
Kittanning Infants@	2	5	.286	NA	Bill Malarkey

#The Latrobe (7-10) franchise was forfeited to the league May 28; the league then awarded it to Cumberland. Cumberland (5-20) moved to Piedmont (4-6) June 27, then to Somerset (0-5) July 11. It disbanded later that month.
@Beaver Falls and Kittanning withdrew August 11; Kittanning entered the league August 1.

D Wisconsin State League
President: Charles F. Moll

Standings	W	L	Pct.	GB	Manager
Freeport Pretzels	79	41	.658	—	Tom Schoonhover
Wausau Lumberjacks	76	43	.639	2½	Charles Ferguson
La Crosse Badgers	67	50	.528	10½	E.P. "Pink" Hawley
Eau Claire Tigers	62	56	.525	16	Robert Lynch
Oshkosh Indians	58	65	.472	21½	George Bubsir
Madison Senators	52	66	.441	26	Howard Cassibone
Green Bay Orphans	48	73	.397	31½	John Corrigan
Fond du Lac Webfoots	34	82	.293	43	Tom Fletcher

BA: Joe Whitmore, Madison, .293
Runs: Bob Lynch, Eau Claire, 63
Hits: John Cahill, La Crosse, 124
Wins: Jack Warhop, Freeport, 30

SOs: Jack Warhop, Freeport, 339
Pct: Frank Miller, Wausau, .875, 14-2
ShO: Jack Warhop, Freeport, 13

Ind California League
President: Frank Herman

Standings	W	L	Pct.	GB	Manager
Stockton Millers	43	13	.768	—	Cy Moreing
Sacramento Cordovas.........	38	18	.679	5	Bill Curtin
San Jose Prune Pickers	32	24	.571	11	Emil Mayer
Alameda Grays	15	23	.395	19	Lou Schroeder
Oakland Commuters............	9	28	.243	24½	Walt McMemony
San Francisco......................	3	34	.081	30½	James McGowan

BA: Jimmy McHale, Stockton, .318
Wins: Fred Brown, Sacramento, 24

Pct: Fred Brown, Sacramento, .800, 24-6

1907 Interleague Post Season Play

World Series
Chicago (National) 4 games, Detroit (American) 0

Junior World Series
Toronto (Eastern) 4 games, Columbus (American Association) 1

Midwest Championship
Freeport (Wisconsin) 2 games, Waterloo (Iowa State) 2
The series was called due to poor attendance.

1907 No-Hitters

Date	Pitcher	Team	League	Opponent	Score
4-11	Bugs Raymond	Jackson	Cotton States	Columbus	4-0
4-23	Fred Brown	Sacramento	California	Stockton	1-0 (P, 10)
5-2	Willie Humes	Bloomington	Three-I	Springfield	12-1
5-8	Jeff Pfeffer	Boston	National	Cincinnati	6-0
5-15	Bob Harmon	Waterloo	Iowa State	Ottumwa	9-0
5-20	C.H. Clark	Wichita	Western Assoc.	Leavenworth	3-0
5-23	Frank Lange	Wausau	Wisconsin State	Eau Claire	
5-27	Bill Otey	Norfolk	Virginia	Lynchburg	1-0 (5)
5-28	Jack Warhop	Freeport	Wisconsin State	Fond du Lac	
5-31	William Luby	Springfield	Connecticut	New Haven	2-0
6-3	Lou Schettler	Youngstown	Ohio-Penn.	New Castle	12-0
6-4	George McQuillan	Providence	Eastern	Rochester	2-0
6-4	Rube Zeller	Atlanta	Southern Assoc.	Little Rock	0-1
6-4	C.A. Licht	Greenville	North Texas	Paris	4-0
6-12	Charles Shuman	Portsmouth	Virginia	Richmond	5-1
6-15	Maury Kent	Marshalltown	Iowa State	Keokuk	1-2
6-16	Harry Keener	South Bend	Central	Dayton	4-0
6-16	Robert Groom	Portland	Pacific Coast	Los Angeles	1-0
6-25	Eli Cates	Oakland	Pacific Coast	Portland	2-1
6-26	Pat Ragan	Omaha	Western	Lincoln	4-1
6-30	Frank Christian	Clarksburg	Western Penn.	Connellsville	3-0
7-4	Bugs Raymond	Charleston	South Atlantic	Jacksonville	4-0
7-4	Dusty Rhodes	Trenton	Tri-State	Wilmington	1-0 (7)
7-4	Frank Arellanes	San Jose	California	Alameda	11-0
7-13	Doc Moskiman	Stockton	California	Sacramento	2-0
7-18	Jonathan Wizotsky	DuBois	Interstate	Franklin	0-1
7-19	Charles Hallman	Portsmouth	Virginia	Danville	0-2
7-19	Ed Farley	Waterbury	Connecticut	Bridgeport	3-0
7-20	Ike Butler	Tacoma	Northwestern	Seattle	5-1
7-26	Bill Bailey	Mansfield	Ohio-Penn.	New Castle	1-0 (8)
7-27	Michaels	Beaver Falls	Western Penn.	Butler	1-0
7-29	Tom Keady	Haverhill	New England	Fall River	1-0
8-1	Jack Halla	Topeka	Western Assoc.	Oklahoma City	4-0
8-10	Kich White	Lancaster	Ohio-Penn.	Akron	4-1
8-11	Buck Friel	Wheeling	Central	Canton	1-0
8-11	Buck Harris	San Antonio	Texas	Dallas	6-0
8-17	W.L. Hoffer	Oklahoma City	Western Assoc.	Hutchinson	8-0
8-26	Lefty George	Joplin	Western Assoc.	Wichita	3-0
8-29	Bill Robertson	Wheeling	Central	Evansville	2-0
8-30	Bill Baker	Clinton	Three-I	Rock Island	2-1
9-10	Charlie Alberts	Zanesville	POM	Steubenville	1-0 (7)
9-11	George Watt	Zanesville	POM	Charleroi	1-0
9-12	Frank Reisling	Lancaster	Tri-State	Harrisburg	0-0 (7)
9-12	John McCloskey	Baltimore	Eastern	Rochester	7-1
9-16	Frank Ray	Mobile	Cotton States	Meridian	11-0
9-20	Nick Maddox	Pittsburgh	National	Brooklyn	2-1
10-6	Ben Henderson	Stockton	California	Oakland	8-1

Number in parentheses indicates innings if other than nine; "P" indicates perfect game.

THIS DATE IN MINOR LEAGUE HISTORY

January 10, 1907, Bob Langsdorf, a well-known minor league player, committed suicide in Louisville by drinking carbolic acid, because of unrequited love for movie actress Elsie Cressy.

January 10, 1907, Jack Dunn, formerly with Providence, was appointed manager of Baltimore, Eastern League.

January 17, 1907, Jesse Burkett was elected president-treasurer-manager of Worcester in the New England League.

March 12, 1907, Outfielder Pat Hynes, Milwaukee, American Association, was shot and killed in a barroom brawl in St. Louis.

April 23, 1907, Fred Brown of the Sacramento Cordovas, California State League, an independent circuit, pitched a perfect ten inning game against Stockton.

April 29, 1907, Worcester made 13 fielding errors against New Bedford in a New England League game.

May 1, 1907, Brockton, New England League, pounded out 11 doubles, plus two homers and three singles, to score 13 runs against pitcher Ed Connelly of Haverhill.

May 4, 1907, Henry "Butch" Kern, Dallas catcher, had 11 assists, a Texas League record.

May 29, 1907, In the Western Association, Oklahoma City defeated Hutchinson 2-1 in 23 innings. R.A. Bandy hurled all the way for the winners.

June 1, 1907, Frank Selee, famous National League manager, resigned the management of the Denver club of the Western League.

June 3, 1907, At Cumberland, Maryland, bees caused a panic during game between Clarksburg and Cumberland of the Western Pennsylvania League. A large swarm of bees settled upon the diamond and bleachers, driving both spectators and players to the opposite side of the field. Umpire Johnson halted the game for 15 minutes until the unwelcome visitors departed, and the game resumed.

June 8, 1907, Harrisburg, Tri-State League, lost to Williamsport after 18 consecutive victories.

June 12, 1907, Shreveport, Southern Association, made 24 infield assists in a 7-1 victory over Birmingham. Only three fly balls were hit to the outfield.

June 14, 1907, In the Three-I League, Rock Island beat Springfield 6-5 in 19 innings, a record for that circuit.

June 15, 1907, Moxie Manuel of New Orleans, Southern Association, pitched and won a doubleheader from Birmingham, each game by a score of 1-0, yielding two hits in the opener and six in the second.

June 16, 1907, Second baseman Heinie Zimmerman, Wilkes-Barre, New York State League, made six hits in six at bats against Syracuse.

June 22, 1907, In the Ohio-Pennsylvania League, Lancaster beat Akron 1-0 in 18 innings.

June 25, 1907, Troy beat Scranton 6-5 in 19 innings, a record for the New York State League.

June 26, 1907, In the Iowa State League at Jacksonville, Illinois, Jacksonville defeated Burlington 3-2 in 21 innings.

June 28, 1907, Tim Flood, captain and second baseman of Toronto, Eastern League, was sentenced to 15 days in the Toronto city jail for assaulting umpire Conway on the preceding day.

June 30, 1907, Burlington, Iowa State League, won a 4-0, 18-inning game at Quincy, although pitcher Bennett of Quincy gave up only four hits, losing on two errors.

July 4, 1907, After Corkman, Newark, Eastern League, received a base on balls, Merritt, first baseman for Jersey City, lifted him up bodily and carried him six feet when the umpire wasn't looking. Merritt then called for a decision that the base runner was nipped off first. Umpire Cusack called Corkman out, and the decision stood.

July 6, 1907, After winning 16 straight games, Williamsport, Tri-State League, lost to Wilmington in ten innings.

July 10, 1907, Shreveport, Southern Association, lost its fourth straight game to Little Rock, making only one run and being held scoreless over the last 34 innings.

July 19, 1907, Charles Hallman of Portsmouth, Virginia League, lost a no-hitter to Danville, 2-0. Winning pitcher Jimmy Lavender gave up only one safety in the game.

July 23, 1907, Austin, Texas League, set an Organized Ball record - still unbroken - by stealing 23 bases in a 44-0 win over San Antonio.

July 25, 1907, Peoria, Three-I League, defeated Clinton 3-0 in 22 innings.

July 27, 1907, Catcher Foley White of Temple made 11 assists in a Texas League game.

August 10, 1907, Bugs Raymond, Charleston, South Atlantic League, held Macon to one hit in a game called after 11 innings with no score.

August 16, 1907, Pitcher Beeker of Shreveport, Southern Association, pitched a doubleheader and shut out New Orleans in both games, yielding only one hit in the second contest. Each tilt went nine innings.

August 18, 1907, Outfielder Walter Carlisle, Los Angeles, Pacific Coast League, smashed three home runs in the second game against Oakland.

August 29, 1907, Ft. Worth, Texas League, scored five runs against Temple on only one hit and a walk. There were five errors and a passed ball before John Blakeney got Ft. Worth out by fanning the third of the three batters he struck out that inning.

September 1, 1907, The game at Columbus, American Association, against Toledo drew a crowd of 20,531.

September 5, 1907, Rock Island, Three-I League, won its fourth successive game by a 2-0 score to post its sixth straight shutout victory, holding opposing clubs scoreless at their home park for 68 consecutive innings.

September 8, 1907, Sheldon Lejeune of Springfield, Central League, threw a baseball 142 yards by actual measurement.

September 8, 1907, The Decatur-Peoria game in the Three-I League drew a paid crowd of 5,303 at Peoria.

September 9, 1907, Charles Bomar, Decatur, Three-I League, had 20 victories and two ties in his last 22 decisions.

September 11, 1907, Irving Wilhelm, Birmingham, Southern Association, defeated Little Rock 8-0 for his fourth successive shutout. Wilhelm hurled a total of 11 shutouts on the season.

September 12, 1907, Springfield, Central League, outslugged Wheeling 12-11, making 25 hits to the losers' 24.

September 14, 1907, Irvin "Little Eva" Wilhelm, Birmingham, celebrated the close of the Southern League season by pitching a doubleheader against Shreveport, scoring two shutouts.

September 17, 1907, Jack Thoney, Toronto, Eastern League, circled the bases in 13-3/5 seconds, a new record.

September 21, 1907, Pitcher Jack Halla of Topeka closed the Western Association season with 16 shutouts, the all-time minor league record.

October 1, 1907, Fred Pope, a former left fielder with South Bend of the Central League, lost both legs when run over by a freight train in Dillonville, Ohio.

November 3, 1907, The Pacific Coast League season ended with Los Angeles the pennant winner.

November 9, 1907, A fire believed to have been started by tramps destroyed the Montreal, International League, stands and bleachers. The loss was placed at $8,000, of which $2,000 was covered by insurance.

November 19, 1907, Arthur Wilson, star catcher for Bloomington of the Three-I League, was kicked in the stomach by a mule near his home in Macon County, Illinois, receiving severe but not fatal injuries.

1908

American League
President: Byron Bancroft Johnson

Standings	W	L	Pct.	GB	Attend.	Manager
Detroit Tigers	90	63	.588	—	436,199	Hugh Jennings
Cleveland Naps	90	64	.584	½	422,262	Napoleon Lajoie
Chicago White Sox	88	64	.579	1½	636,096	Fielder Jones
St. Louis Browns	83	69	.546	6½	618,947	Jimmy McAleer
Boston Red Sox	75	79	.487	15½	473,048	Deacon McGuire/Frederick Lake
Philadelphia Athletics	68	85	.444	22	455,062	Connie Mack
Washington Senators	67	85	.441	22½	264,252	Joe Cantillon
New York Highlanders	51	103	.331	39½	305,500	Clark Griffith/Kid Elberfeld

BA: Ty Cobb, Detroit, .324
Runs: Matty McIntyre, Detroit, 105
Hits: Ty Cobb, Detroit, 188
RBIs: Ty Cobb, Detroit, 108
HRs: Sam Crawford, Detroit, 7

Wins: Ed Walsh, Chicago, 40
SOs: Ed Walsh, Chicago, 269
ERA: Addie Joss, Cleveland, 1.16
Pct: Ed Walsh, Chicago, .727, 40-15
IP: Ed Walsh, Chicago, 464

National League
President: Harry C. Pulliam

Standings	W	L	Pct.	GB	Attend.	Manager
Chicago Cubs	99	55	.643	—	665,325	Frank Chance
New York Giants	98	56	.636	1	910,000	John McGraw
Pittsburgh Pirates	98	56	.636	1	382,444	Fred Clarke
Philadelphia Phillies	83	71	.539	16	420,660	Billy Murray
Cincinnati Reds	73	81	.474	26	399,200	John Ganzel
Boston Doves	63	91	.409	36	253,750	Joe Kelley
Brooklyn Superbas	53	101	.344	46	275,600	Patsy Donovan
St. Louis Cardinals	49	105	.318	50	205,129	John McCloskey

Playoff: Chicago beat New York 4-2 in a one game playoff for the National League pennant.

BA: Honus Wagner, Pittsburgh, .354
Runs: Fred Tenney, New York, 101
Hits: Honus Wagner, Pittsburgh, 201
RBIs: Honus Wagner, Pittsburgh, 109
HRs: Tim Jordan, Brooklyn, 12

Wins: Christy Mathewson, New York, 37
SOs: Christy Mathewson, New York, 259
ERA: Christy Mathewson, New York, 1.43
Pct: Ed Reulbach, Chicago, .774, 24-7

A American Association
President: Joseph D. O'Brien

Standings	W	L	Pct.	GB	Attend.	Manager
Indianapolis Indians	92	61	.601	—	263,783	Charles Carr
Louisville Colonels	88	65	.575	4	182,254	James Burke
Columbus Senators	86	68	.558	6½	193,536	Bill Clymer
Toledo Mud Hens	81	72	.530	11	162,009	Bill Armour
Minneapolis Millers	77	77	.500	15½	125,203	Mike Cantillon
Milwaukee Brewers	71	83	.461	21½	131,168	Barry McCormick
Kansas City Blues	70	83	.456	22	160,685	Monte Cross
St. Paul Apostles	48	104	.316	43½	90,510	Tim Flood/Mike Kelley

BA: John Hayden, Indianapolis, .316
Runs: Donie Bush, Indianapolis, 99
Hits: John Hayden, Indianapolis, 186

HRs: Berton James, Columbus, 10
Buck Freeman, Minneapolis, 10
Wins: Rube Marquard, Indianapolis, 28
SOs: Rube Marquard, Indianapolis, 250
Pct: Brown Rogers, Columbus, .792, 19-5

A Eastern League
President: Patrick T. Powers

Standings	W	L	Pct.	GB	Manager
Baltimore Orioles	83	57	.593	—	Jack Dunn
Providence Grays	79	57	.581	2	Hugh Duffy
Newark Indians	79	58	.577	2½	George Stallings
Buffalo Bisons	75	65	.536	8	George Smith
Montreal Royals	64	75	.461	18½	James Casey
Toronto Maple Leafs	59	79	.428	23	Mike Kelley/Larry Schafley
Jersey City Skeeters	58	79	.423	23½	Joseph Bean/Eugene McCann
Rochester Bronchos	55	82	.401	26½	Al Buckenberger/John Ganzel

Attendance: Buffalo, 186,750.

BA: Jim Jones, Montreal, .309
Runs: Josh DeVore, Newark, 91
Hits: Jim Jones, Montreal, 160
HRs: William Phyle, Toronto, 16

Wins: Merle Adkins, Baltimore, 29
SOs: Tom Hughes, Newark, 161
Pct: Jim Mueller, Newark, .720, 18-7

A Pacific Coast League
President: J. Cal Ewing

Standings	W	L	Pct.	GB	Manager
Los Angeles Angels	110	78	.585	—	Frank "Cap" Dillon
Portland Beavers	95	90	.514	13½	Walter McCredie
San Francisco Seals	100	104	.490	18	Daniel Long
Oakland Oaks	83	116	.417	32½	George Van Haltren

BA: Babe Danzig, Portland, .298
Runs: Kid Mohler, San Francisco, 118
Hits: Henry Heitmuller, Oakland, 225
HRs: Henry Heitmuller, Oakland, 12

SBs: Rollie Zeider, San Francisco, 93
Wins: Bob Groom, Portland, 29
Pct: Frank Browning, San Francisco, .818, 9-2

A Southern Association
President: William M. Kavanaugh

Standings	W	L	Pct.	GB	Manager
Nashville Volunteers	75	56	.573	—	Bill Bernhardt
New Orleans Pelicans	76	57	.571	—	Charley Frank
Memphis Egyptians	73	62	.540	4	Charles Babb
Montgomery Senators	68	65	.511	8	James Ryan/Ed Gremlinger
Mobile Sea Gulls	67	67	.500	9½	Thomas Fisher
Atlanta Crackers	63	72	.467	14	William A. Smith
Little Rock Travelers	62	76	.449	16½	Michael Finn
Birmingham Barons	53	82	.393	24	Harry Vaughn/Carleton Molesworth

BA: Tris Speaker, Little Rock, .350
Runs: Tris Speaker, Little Rock, 81
Hits: Tris Speaker, Little Rock, 165

HRs: Harry Lord, New Orleans, 6
Jake Daubert, Nashville, 6
Wins: Ralph Savidge, Memphis, 20
Pct: Ted Breitenstein, New Orleans, .739, 17-6

A Western League
President: Norris L. O'Neill

Standings	W	L	Pct.	GB	Manager
Sioux City Soos	88	57	.607	—	James "Ducky" Holmes
Omaha Rourkes	86	59	.593	2	Pa Rourke
Lincoln Greenbackers	74	73	.503	15	Guy Green/Billy Fox
Denver Grizzlies	71	75	.486	17½	Charles Irwin/Charles Jones
Pueblo Indians	63	78	.447	23	Hamilton Patterson/Frank Selee
Des Moines Boosters	54	94	.365	35½	Charles Dexter

BA: Harry Welch, Omaha, .362
Runs: Tom Campbell, Sioux City, 113
Hits: Harry Welch, Omaha, 180

HRs: John Thomas, Lincoln, 7
Ira Belden, Denver, 7
Hamilton Patterson, Pueblo, 7
SBs: Jim Austin, Omaha, 97
Wins: Al Furchner, Sioux City, 30
Pct: Pat Reagan, Omaha, .806, 29-7

B Central League
President: Dr. Frank R. Carson

Standings	W	L	Pct.	GB	Manager
Evansville River Rats	84	56	.600	—	Charles "Punch" Knoll
South Bend Greens	80	60	.571	4	Angus Grant
Dayton Veterans	77	63	.550	7	Bade Myers
Fort Wayne Billikens	75	65	.536	9	Jack Hendricks
Grand Rapids Wolverines	68	71	.489	15½	Robert Lowe
Zanesville Infants	67	73	.479	17	Martin Hogan/Montgomery
Terre Haute Hottentots	63	75	.457	20	Louis Drill
Wheeling Stogies	44	95	.317	39½	Ted Price/Tom Fleming

BA: Charles French, Evansville, .339
Runs: Bert Noblett, Grand Rapids, 92
Hits: Charles French, Evansville, 170
HRs: Charles "Punch" Knoll, Evansville, 12

SBs: Midge Craven, South Bend, 87
Wins: Charles Wacker, Evansville, 27
SOs: John Rowan, Dayton, 232
Pct: Charles Wacker, Evansville, .771, 27-8

B Connecticut League
President: W.J. Tracey

Standings	W	L	Pct.	GB	Manager
Springfield Ponies	84	41	.672	—	Daniel O'Neill
Hartford Senators	84	42	.667	½	Thomas Dowd/Thomas Connery
New Haven Blues	63	63	.500	21½	Albert Daly/Billy Lush/George Bone
New Britain Perfectos	61	64	.488	23	Charles Humphrey/William Hanna
Holyoke Papermakers	60	66	.476	24½	Jack Tighe/Fred Winkler
Bridgeport Orators	55	71	.437	29½	James O'Rourke
Meriden	54	72	.429	30½	Charles Cheney
Waterbury Authors	42	84	.333	42½	Harold Durant

BA: Jim McCabe, New Britain, .320
Runs: George Simmons, New Haven, 78
Hits: George Simmons, New Haven, 155

HRs: George Simmons, New Haven, 10
Wins: John Waller, Bridgeport, 23
Pct: Ray Fisher, Hartford, .923, 12-1

B New England League
President: Tim H. Murnane

Standings	W	L	Pct.	GB	Manager
Worcester Busters	80	44	.645	—	Jesse Burkett
Lawrence Colts	75	49	.605	5	Mal Eason

*Won first-half **Won second-half ***Won both halves

Haverhill Hustlers	71	52	.577	8½	Billy Hamilton
Brockton Tigers	66	56	.541	13	Stephen Flanagan
Lynn Shoemakers	54	70	.435	26	Frank Leonard
Fall River Indians	53	70	.431	26½	John H. O'Brien
Lowell Tigers	49	75	.395	31	Arthur Daly/Alexander Winn
New Bedford Whalers	46	78	.371	34	James Canavan/Thomas Corcoran

BA: Tommy Catterson, Brockton, .327
Runs: John Flynn, Lawrence, 92
Hits: Tommy Catterson, Brockton, 140
HRs: Garry Wilson, Lawrence, 5; Simeon Murch, Lawrence, 5
SBs: John Flynn, Lawrence, 76
Wins: Marty O'Toole, Brockton, 31
Pct: Buck Friel, Haverhill, .857, 12-2

B New York State League
President: John H. Farrell

Standings	W	L	Pct.	GB	Manager
Scranton Miners	84	51	.622	—	Mal Kittridge
Binghamton Bingoes	80	61	.567	7	James Bannon
Troy Trojans	78	61	.561	9	John J. O'Brien
Syracuse Stars	76	64	.543	10½	Sandy Griffin
Utica Pent-Ups	74	64	.536	11½	Charles Dooley
Albany Senators	67	73	.479	19½	Michael Doherty
Wilkes-Barre Barons	60	77	.438	25	Abel Lizotte/Robert Drury
Gloversville-Johnstown Jags/ Elmira Colonels#	36	104	.257	50½	Louis Bacon/Henry Ramsey

#Gloversville-Johnstown (11-54) moved to Elmira July 22.

BA: Gene Goode, Troy, .305
Runs: Jim Tamsett, Albany, 88
Hits: Gene Goode, Troy, 153
SBs: Art Marcan, Troy, 65

B Northwestern League
President: William H. Lucas

Standings	W	L	Pct.	GB	Manager
Vancouver Beavers	85	62	.578	—	Richard Dickson
Tacoma Tigers	74	66	.529	7½	George Shreeder
Grays Harbor Grays	73	69	.514	9½	Robert Brown
Spokane Indians	72	75	.490	13	E.E. Quinn
Butte Miners	63	73	.463	16½	Russ Hall
Seattle Siwashes	65	87	.428	22½	Daniel Dugdale

BA: Jim Flanagan, Vancouver, .352
Runs: Ham Hyatt, Vancouver, 102
Hits: Ham Hyatt, Vancouver, 185
HRs: Ham Hyatt, Vancouver, 15
Wins: George Engel, Vancouver, 22; Ed Erickson, Vancouver, 22; Fred Harkness, Butte, 22
SOs: Gus Thompson, Grays Harbor, 263
Pct: George Engel, Vancouver, .733, 22-8

B Three-I League
President: Thomas J. Loftus

Standings	W	L	Pct.	GB	Manager
Springfield Senators	82	54	.603	—	John McCarthy
Decatur Commodores	77	59	.572	5	George Reed
Cedar Rapids Rabbits	69	63	.523	11	Belden Hill/Ted Price
Peoria Distillers	66	67	.496	14½	Frank Donnelly
Dubuque Dubs	67	69	.493	16	Clarence "Pants" Rowland
Bloomington Bloomers	64	73	.467	18½	William Connors
Rock Island Islanders	59	76	.437	22½	Louis Cook/Jack Tighe
Clinton Infants	55	78	.414	25½	Charles Buelow

BA: Tom Tennant, Decatur, .310
Runs: Richard Crozier, Decatur, 82
Hits: Tom Tennant, Decatur, 164
HRs: Charles Buelow, Clinton, 9
Wins: William Fleet, Clinton, 23; Pete Higgins, Bloomington, 23
Pct: Forrest More, Springfield, .741, 20-7

B Tri-State League
President: Charles F. Carpenter

Standings	W	L	Pct.	GB	Manager
Williamsport Millionaires	82	45	.646	—	Harry Wolverton
Harrisburg Senators	80	47	.630	2	George Heckert
Lancaster Red Roses	72	55	.567	10	Clarence "Pop" Foster
Reading Pretzels	67	60	.528	15	Thomas Owen/Curt Weigand
Johnstown Johnnies	64	63	.504	18	Edward Ashenbach
Trenton Tigers	54	73	.425	28	John Carney
Altoona Mountaineers	49	78	.386	33	John Farrell
Wilmington Peaches	40	87	.315	42	Michael Grady/William Waller/John O'Rourke

BA: Harry Wolverton, Williamsport, .349
Runs: Dave Shean, Williamsport, 97
Hits: Frank Huelsman, Harrisburg, 153
HRs: Charles Johnson, Johnstown, 9
SBs: Dick Egan, Harrisburg, 93
Wins: Jack Warhop, Williamsport, 29
Pct: Harry Krause, Harrisburg, .810, 17-4

C Ohio-Pennsylvania League
President: Charles H. Morton

Standings	W	L	Pct.	GB	Manager
Akron Champs	81	36	.692	—	J. Breckinridge
East Liverpool Potters	70	42	.625	8½	Bill Phillips
Canton Watchmakers	65	54	.546	17	Edward Murphy/Thomas Lindsay
Sharon Giants	62	56	.525	19½	Van Patterson
Youngstown Champs	58	60	.492	23½	Samuel Wright
New Castle Nocks	47	70	.402	34	Peter Porter/R. "Kid" Hagan
McKeesport Tubers	44	72	.379	36½	Bernie McCay
Girard/Butler/Erie Sailors#	42	79	.347	41	Daniel Koster/Walter East/Richard Nallin

#Girard (0-9) moved to Butler May 19; Butler (5-17) moved to Erie June 15. The season was shortened to September 7.

BA: Wilbur Good, Akron, .370
Runs: Teddy Hinton, Youngstown, 82
Hits: Jack McAleese, Youngstown, 150
HRs: Harry Bailey, Canton, 8
Wins: Fred Ehman, Akron, 25
Pct: Bill Phillips, East Liverpool, .818, 18-4

C South Atlantic League
President: Charles W. Boyer

Standings	W	L	Pct.	GB	Manager
Jacksonville Jays	77	34	.694	—	Dominick Mullaney
Savannah Indians	64	45	.587	12	Walter Morris
Augusta Tourists	51	59	.464	25½	Charles Dexter/Henry Busch
Columbia Gamecocks	46	58	.442	27½	Win Clark
Macon Peaches	48	68	.412	31½	John Malarkey/Wilbur Murdoch
Charleston Sea Gulls	44	66	.400	32½	Pat Meaney

BA: Wilbur Murdoch, Macon, .302
Runs: Bill McMahon, Columbia/Augusta, 55; George Bigbee, Columbia, 55
Hits: Wilbur Murdoch, Macon, 140
Wins: Phil Sitton, Augusta, 19; Ed Welcher, Columbia, 19
Pct: Carl Sitton, Jacksonville, .773, 17-5

C Texas League
President: Dr. William R. Robbie

Standings	W	L	Pct.	GB	Manager
San Antonio Bronchoes	95	48	.664	—	George Leidy/Pat Newnam
Dallas Giants	90	55	.620	6	Curley Maloney
Houston Buffaloes	77	67	.535	18½	Doak Roberts/Blake/Al McFarland/Ben Shelton
Waco Navigators	71	72	.497	24	Frederick Cavender/Bill Yohe
Ft. Worth Panthers	68	74	.479	26½	Dan Curtis/Henry Deiters
Shreveport Pirates	66	78	.458	29½	Dale Gear
Galveston Sand Crabs	59	86	.407	37	Frank Weikart
Austin Senators	49	95	.340	46½	Brooks Gordon/Wilson Mathews/Rick Adams

BA: Bob Edmundson, Galveston, .391
Runs: E.C. Collins, San Antonio, 113
Hits: Curley Maloney, Dallas, 169
HRs: Pat Newnam, San Antonio, 18
Wins: Rube Peters, Dallas, 24
Pct: Hank Griffin, Ft. Worth, .719, 23-9

C Virginia League
President: Jacob Wells

Standings	W	L	Pct.	GB	Manager
Richmond Colts	87	41	.680	—	Perry Lipe
Danville Red Sox	74	52	.587	12	Robert Stafford
Roanoke Tigers	63	67	.485	25	Charles Shaffer/Elmore Hines
Portsmouth Truckers	57	71	.445	30	Steve Griffin/Andy Lawrence
Lynchburg Shoemakers	52	76	.406	35	Al Orth/John J. Grim/Robert Westlake
Norfolk Tars	52	78	.400	36	Robert Pender

BA: Jacob Henn, Danville, .290
Runs: Perry Lipe, Richmond, 65
Hits: Bill Hessler, Roanoke, 133
RBIs: Jacob Henn, Danville, 72
HRs: Jacob Henn, Danville, 8
Wins: Martin Walsh, Danville, 30
SOs: Dutch Revell, Richmond, 199
Pct: John Quinn, Richmond, 1.000, 14-0

C Western Association
President: Dr. D.M. Shiveley

Standings	W	L	Pct.	GB	Manager
Topeka Jayhawkers	89	50	.640	—	Dick Cooley
Wichita Jobbers	87	53	.621	2½	Jack Holland
Oklahoma City Mets	81	58	.583	8	Jack McConnell
Joplin Miners	71	65	.522	16½	John Fillman
Hutchinson Salt Packers	69	70	.496	20	Jay Andrews/Frank Barber
Webb City Webbfeet	66	69	.489	21	Larry Milton
Springfield Midgets	48	85	.361	38	D.C. "Dad" Risley/Tony Vanderhill
Enid Railroaders	38	99	.277	50	William Kimmel/Specs Hurlbert/Red Wright/Walter Frantz

BA: Gus Hetling, Wichita, .318
Runs: Red Davis, Topeka, 85
Hits: Gus Hetling, Wichita, 163
HRs: Milt Porkorney, Webb City, 16
Wins: Jim Scott, Wichita, 30; Joe Hagerman, Topeka, 30
Pct: John Bolin, Wichita, .846, 11-2

D Arkansas State League
President: T.J. Craighead

Standings	W	L	Pct.	GB	Manager
Hot Springs	78	38	.672	—	Arthur Riggs/W. Forbes
Newport Pearl Diggers	65	44	.596	9½	Robert Shelton
Helena	67	48	.583	10½	Rudolph Kling
Pine Bluff Pine Knotts	51	61	.455	24	Walter Deaver/Al Sullivan
Argenta	49	68	.419	28½	James Kerwin/Roy Geyer/Charles Reece/Arthur Riggs
Poplar Bluff/Brinkley#	28	79	.262	45½	Al Sullivan/Lee Dawkins

#Poplar Bluff (16-58) was replaced by Brinkley June 8.

All-Star Team: 1B-Elmer Coyle, Hot Springs; **2B-**C.V. Ware, Hot Springs; **3B-**Lee Dawkins, Poplar Bluff/Brinkley; **SS-**G.W. Smitheal, Hot Springs; **OF-**Herbert Benham, Helena; Rupert Blakely, Hot Springs; Otto Besse, Hot Springs; **C-**Berry, Pine Bluff; **P-**W. "Lucky" Wright, Hot Springs; Shaw, Newport; A.K. Walters, Pine Bluff; William Luhrsen, Argenta.

BA: Elmer Coyle, Hot Springs, .376
SBs: Herbert Benham, Helena, 65
Runs: Elmer Coyle, Hot Springs, 134
Wins: W. "Lucky" Wright, Hot Springs, 27
Hits: Elmer Coyle, Hot Springs, 178
Pct: Hippo Vaughn, Hot Springs, .900, 9-1

D Atlantic Association
President: Hugh McBreen

Standings	W	L	Pct.	GB	Manager
Portland Blue Sox	8	3	.727	—	F. Driscoll
Lewiston	8	4	.667	½	George Beede/Mike McDonough
Pawtucket Colts+	6	3	.667	1	William Connors
Newport Ponies	5	5	.500	2½	Ben Anthony/George Reed
Taunton/Attleboro Angels#	1	12	.077	8	Maury McDermott/Wilson/McEleney
Woonsocket Trotters@	0	1	.000	NA	John Leighton/Buster Burrill

#Taunton moved to Attleboro.
@Woonsocket disbanded May 4.
+Pawtucket disbanded May 19.
The circuit started May 2 and disbanded May 21.

BA: Billy Lush, Taunton/Attleboro, .418
Hits: F. Burns, Taunton/Attleboro, 16
Runs: Bob Black, Pawtucket, 13
    P. Sullivan, Lewiston, 16
    P. Sullivan, Lewiston, 13
HRs: P. Sullivan, Lewiston, 4
Wins: Sanford, Pawtucket/Attleboro, 4
SOs: Sanford, Pawtucket/Attleboro, 40

D Blue Grass League
President: George L. Hammond

Standings	W	L	Pct.	GB	Manager
Frankfort Statesmen	47	23	.671	—	N.G. Kennedy
Lexington Colts	37	31	.544	9	Anderson
Richmond Pioneers	36	34	.514	11	W. Parrish
Lawrenceburg	33	35	.485	13	Guy Woodruff
Shelbyville Grays	32	37	.464	14½	Anton Kuhn
Winchester Hustlers	22	47	.319	24½	

BA: P. Long, Shelbyville, .336
Hits: P. Long, Shelbyville, 82
Runs: P. Long, Shelbyville, 60

D Carolina Association
President: Joseph H. Wearn

Standings	W	L	Pct.	GB	Manager
Greensboro Champs	51	38	.573	—	James McKevitt
Greenville Spinners	48	36	.571	½	Thomas Stouch
Spartanburg Spartans	49	39	.557	1½	Carleton Buesse
Winston-Salem Twins	41	48	.461	10	Robert Carter
Charlotte Hornets	40	47	.460	10	Jess Reynolds
Anderson Electricians	32	53	.376	17	Elmer Hines

BA: Joe Jackson, Greenville, .346
RBIs: Joe Jackson, Greenville, 72
Runs: Barre, Greenville, 62
Wins: Walt Hammersley, Greensboro, 22
Hits: Joe Jackson, Greenville, 120
Pct: Phifer Fullenwider, Charlotte, .765, 13-4

D Central Association
President: M.E. Justice

Standings	W	L	Pct.	GB	Manager
Waterloo Lulus	88	37	.704	—	Frank Boyle
Burlington Pathfinders	83	41	.669	4½	Ned Egan
Quincy Gems	73	55	.570	16½	Harry Hofer
Keokuk Indians	57	68	.456	31	Frank Belt
Jacksonville Lunatics	56	69	.448	32	Harry Berte
Oskaloosa Quakers	51	75	.398	37½	A.L. "Snapper" Kennedy/Taylor Kensel
Kewanee Boilermakers	48	79	.378	41	Harry Busse/Andy Steveson/ William Connors
Ottumwa Packers	48	80	.375	41½	Billy Earle/Chuck Fleming

BA: John House, Burlington, .306
Wins: Harry Gaspar, Waterloo, 32
Runs: Al Linderbeck, Quincy, 75
SOs: Harry Gaspar, Waterloo, 217
Hits: Charles Rose, Burlington, 146
Pct: Harry Gaspar, Waterloo, .889, 32-4
HRs: Al Linderbeck, Quincy, 10

D Central Kansas League

Standings	W	L	Pct.	GB	Manager
Minneapolis Minnies	31	19	.620	—	Ben Young
Newton Browns	25	22	.532	4½	Karl Becker
Ellsworth Blues	25	22	.532	4½	F.S. Foster
Salina Trade Winners	24	23	.511	5½	Frank Everhart
McPherson Merry Macks	20	27	.426	9½	Davis
Little River	18	30	.375	12	G.W. Hamilton/I.C. Meyer

D Cotton States League
President: A.C. Crowder

Standings	W	L	Pct.	GB	Manager
Jackson Senators	68	42	.618	—	Roy Montgomery
Vicksburg Hill Climbers	66	49	.574	4½	George Blackburn

	63	52	.548	7½	Robert Gilks
Gulfport-Biloxi Sand Crabs	63	52	.548	7½	Robert Gilks
Columbus Discoverers	58	56	.509	12	John Toft/Asa Stewart/William May/Louis Hall
Meridian White Ribbons	46	68	.404	24	Fred Schmidt/John Hankey/Charles Fuller
Monroe Municipals	41	75	.353	30	Jack Auslet/Dan Collins/W. Dobard

BA: George Manush, Columbus, .296
Wins: Al Demaree, Columbus, 23
Runs: George Manush, Columbus, 74
Pct: Guy Sample, Vicksburg, .760, 19-6
Hits: George Manush, Columbus, 136

D Eastern Carolina League
President: J.W. Washington

Standings	W	L	Pct.	GB	Manager
Wilson Tobacconists*	36	18	.667	—	Earl Holt
Wilmington Sailors**	35	21	.625	2	Dick Smith
Goldsboro Giants	29	28	.509	8½	H.E. Kling
Raleigh Red Birds	23	36	.390	15½	George "King" Kelly/Frank Thompson/ Wallace Warren
New Bern#	5	16	.238	NA	
Kinston#	6	12	.333	NA	

#New Bern and Kinston withdrew July 15.

Playoff: Abandoned August 27 due to inclement weather with Wilmington leading Wilson 2 games to 1.

BA: Earl Holt, Wilson, .286
Wins: Harvey Bussey, Wilmington, 14
Runs: Walker Moore, Wilson, 28
SOs: Fred Anderson, Wilson, 120
Hits: Walker Moore, Wilson, 57
Pct: Hatton Ogle, Wilson, .846, 11-2
HRs: L. Fox, Kinston/Raleigh, 3

D Eastern Illinois League
President: L.A.G. Shoaff

Standings	W	L	Pct.	GB	Manager
Danville Speakers*/Staunton@	65	27	.707	—	W.C. Dithridge
Taylorville Tailors	56	39	.589	10½	Ryan
Shelbyville Queen Citys&	52	43	.547	14½	Joe Adams
Vincennes Alices	47	48	.495	19½	Harry Lloyd
Paris Parisians	43	48	.473	21½	Erickstone/Eckson/Dan Jenkins/Roberts
Pana Coal Miners/Linton#	25	70	.263	41½	Sunday Hawker/Nig Landon/Butts
Mattoon Giants+	32	45	.416	NA	Russell/George Kizer
Charleston Evangelists+	37	37	.500	NA	Madden

#Pana (18-44) moved to Linton July 17, for the second half.
@Danville (42-18) moved to Staunton July 17, for the second half.
+Charleston and Mattoon disbanded July 30.
&Shelbyville disbanded August 20, causing the league to disband.

BA: Arthur Ahring, Charleston, .355
Wins: Ralph Grimes, Danville/Staunton, 19
Runs: Chuck Fleming, Danville/Staunton, 57
SOs: Joe Jenkins, Paris/Pana/Staunton, 139
Hits: Charles Stanley, Paris, 93
Pct: Chester Carmichael, Vincennes, .800, 16-4
HRs: Andrew Biltz, Shelbyville, 6

D Gulf Coast League
President: Paul O. Moss

Standings	W	L	Pct.	GB	Manager
Lake Charles Creoles	18	9	.667	—	L.A. McCoy
Orange Hoo-Hoos	15	14	.517	4	W. Rucker
Alexandria White Sox	14	15	.483	5	B. Carbo/A. Hoffman
Beaumont Cubs#	11	13	.458	5½	M.L. Gibbs/Bob Smith
Morgan City Oyster Shuckers@	13	16	.448	6	H.G. Stearn/Bill Hitchcroft
Crowley Rice Birds@	13	17	.433	6½	W.E. Trotter/Alexander

#Beaumont disbanded May 28.
@Crowley and Morgan City disbanded June 2, causing the league to disband.

D Illinois-Missouri League
President: A.E. Blain

Standings	W	L	Pct.	GB	Manager
Hannibal Cannibals	68	49	.581	—	Bert Hough
Macomb Potters	66	53	.555	3	Jap Wagner
Havana Perfectos	58	61	.487	11	Mike Sampson/Fred Kommers
Canton Chinks	56	61	.479	12	Rodney Turner/Chuck Murphy
Monmouth Browns	55	62	.470	13	Robert Hyde/Charles Karnell
Galesburg Hornets	50	67	.427	18	Clyde Horne/Andy Mueller/John Grogan/ Jerry Smith

BA: Fred Kommers, Havana, .349
Wins: Henry Rossback, Galesburg, 21
Runs: Fred Kommers, Havana, 75
SOs: Charles Fanning, Canton, 200
Hits: Fred Kommers, Havana, 153
Pct: Curley Curtis, Macomb, .714, 15-6
HRs: Fred Kommers, Havana, 11

D Indiana-Ohio League
President: Frank Gamble

Standings	W	L	Pct.	GB	Manager
Huntington Miamis	14	10	.583	—	Jack Smith
Van Wert Buckeyes	15	14	.517	1½	Louis Hunt
Richmond Quakers	13	15	.464	3	Clarence Jessup
Muncie Fruit Jars	10	14	.417	4	J.F. "Dick" Baird/Wills

The league started May 9 and folded June 8. National Association status was granted June 3.

BA: Gray, Van Wert, .363
Runs: Gray, Van Wert, 19
Hits: Gray, Van Wert, 33
HRs: Paddy Bauman, Richmond, 5
Wins: Howard, Van Wert, 7

SOs: Brown, Richmond, 53
ERA: Bill Prough, Huntington, 1.08
Pct: Romaine, Huntington, .714, 5-2
Aresmith, Richmond, .714, 5-2

D Inland Empire League
President: W.L. Thompson

Standings	W	L	Pct.	GB	Manager
La Grande Babes	19	12	.631	—	O'Brien
Baker City Nuggets	15	15	.500	3½	Cryderman/Tatum
Walla Walla Walla Wallas	14	17	.452	5	Rogers
Pendleton Pets	14	18	.438	5½	Lorimer/Hosier

The league disbanded July 12 due to extreme heat.

D International League
President: George Long

Standings	W	L	Pct.	GB	Manager
Hamilton Hams	22	18	.550	—	Frederick Paige/Wilson
Guelph Maple Leafs/ St. Thomas Saints#	22	20	.524	1	John Murray
London Cockneys	20	21	.488	2½	Paul Wreath
Niagara Falls	19	24	.442	4½	William Murray

#Guelph (11-11) moved to St. Thomas June 12.
The league disbanded July 31.

BA: Charlie Bird, London, .309
Runs: Gus Joy, Niagara Falls, 29
Hits: Charlie Bird, London, 51
HRs: 8 tied with 1 each

Wins: Frank Sterling, Guelph/St. Thomas, 10
SOs: N. Gianelli, London/Niagara Falls, 91
Pct: Bill Payne, London, .692, 9-4

D Interstate League
President: C.L. Rexford

Standings	W	L	Pct.	GB	Manager
Olean Candidates	15	2	.882	—	Percy Stetler
Bradford Drillers	13	7	.650	3½	George Rinderknecht
Warren Blues	8	8	.500	6½	Thomas McNeal
Franklin Millionaires	6	12	.333	9½	William H. Smith
Oil City Cubs	6	13	.316	10	C.L. Rexford
Erie Fishermen#	4	12	.250	10½	Frank Baumeister

#Erie home games were played in Corry, Pennsylvania.
The league disbanded June 5.

BA: Jake Weimer, Olean, .461
Runs: Price, Olean, 27
Hits: Jake Weimer, Olean, 30

HRs: Jake Weimer, Olean, 3
Wins: Tom Fleming, Olean, 6
Pct: Tom Fleming, Olean, 1.000, 6-0

D Northern League
President: John M. Lamb

Standings	W	L	Pct.	GB	Manager
Brandon Angels	50	31	.617	—	Arthur O'Dea
Winnipeg Maroons	47	33	.588	2½	Edward Herr
Duluth White Sox	45	45	.500	9½	W.E. Morrow/Alfred Kuehnow
Fargo Browns	23	56	.291	26	Bill McNeil/Fields

The season was shortened to August 13.

Playoff: Abandoned August 22 with Brandon and Winnipeg tied at five games each.

BA: W. Crum, Winnipeg, .343
Runs: George Metzger, Winnipeg, 49
Hits: Jack Ness, Duluth, 95

Wins: Robert Nelson, Brandon, 17
Pct: Robert Nelson, Brandon, .773, 17-5

D Ohio State League
President: Robert Quinn

Standings	W	L	Pct.	GB	Manager
Lancaster Red Roses	92	57	.617	—	Kurt Ellston/George Fox
Lima Cigarmakers	80	67	.544	11	Nicholas Kahl/James Jackson
Marion Diggers	78	71	.523	14	Charles O'Day
Mansfield Pioneers	76	73	.510	16	Carl McVey/Tim Flood
Newark Newks	74	75	.497	18	Bob Berryhill/Harry Eells
Springfield Reapers/ Portsmouth Cobblers#	46	103	.309	46	Ed Ransick/R. Quinn

#Springfield (17-30) moved to Portsmouth June 16.

BA: Hugh Tate, Marion, .320
Runs: Charles Brown, Lancaster, 103
Hits: Hugh Tate, Marion, 169
HRs: Frank Foutz, Lima, 12
SBs: Alex Reilley, Lima, 80

Wins: "Kich" White, Lancaster, 28
SOs: Walter Justus, Lancaster, 293
Pct: "Kich" White, Lancaster, .700, 28-12
Charles Pickett, Lima, .700, 21-9

D Oklahoma-Kansas League
President: Dr. D.M. Shiveley

Standings	W	L	Pct.	GB	Manager
Bartlesville Boosters*	71	50	.587	—	Harry Truby
Tulsa Oilers**	69	55	.556	3½	Deacon White/Stu McBirney
Independence Jewelers	66	58	.532	6½	Art Quiesser
Muskogee Redskins	58	66	.467	14½	Lon Ury/Jay Andrews
Iola Champs@	32	34	.485	NA	Tom Hayden
McAlester Miners#	17	47	.266	NA	Cy Mason

Attendance: Tulsa, 23,250.

#McAlester disbanded July 5.
@Iola disbanded July 8.

Playoff: Bartlesville 2 games, Muskogee 0, for the first half title.
Finals: Tulsa 3 games, Bartlesville 0.

D Pennsylvania-West Virginia League
President: James D. Groninger

Standings	W	L	Pct.	GB	Manager
Uniontown Coal Barons	68	41	.624	—	Frank Sisley
Clarksburg Drummers	71	48	.597	2	Lucas Hogue/Ferdinand Drumm
Charleroi Cherios	56	53	.514	12	Arch Osborne
Connellsville Cokers	54	56	.491	14½	H.E. Irwin/W. Marietta/Milt Montgomery
Fairmont Badies	55	64	.462	18	Thomas Haymond/Reddy Mack/ Walter Snodgrass
Scottdale Millers/ Grafton Wanderers#	36	78	.316	34½	S.B. "Duff" Buttermore

#Scottdale (24-46) moved to Grafton July 31.

Playoff: Clarksburg 3 games, Uniontown 1.

BA: Joe Phillips, Uniontown, .307
Runs: Fred Dawson, Clarksburg, 80

Hits: E.A. Jacobson, Scottdale/Grafton, 119

D South Carolina League
President: Mendel L. Smith

Standings	W	L	Pct.	GB	Manager
Sumter Gamecocks	41	27	.603	—	Frank Dingle
Chester	40	30	.571	2	H.P. Caldwell
Rock Hill Catawbas	28	40	.412	13	Guy Gunter
Orangeburg Cotton Pickers	27	39	.409	13	

BA: L.B. Simmons, Orangeburg, .354
Runs: L.C. Drake, Chester, 38
Hits: Fred Prim, Orangeburg/Chester, 69

Wins: Bill Temple, Chester, 15
Pct: Elmer Long, Sumter, .750, 9-3

D Southern Michigan League
President: Joseph S. Jackson

Standings	W	L	Pct.	GB	Manager
Saginaw Wa-was	72	52	.581	—	Bruce Hayes/E. Dillon/Blair
Kalamazoo White Sox	70	56	.556	3	Maurice Meyers
Jackson Convicts	68	57	.544	4½	Bo Slear
Tecumseh	64	62	.508	9	Smith
Battle Creek Crickets	62	63	.496	10½	
Lansing Senators	60	65	.480	12½	John Morrissey
Flint Vehicles	57	68	.448	15½	Rube Deneau/Charles Cassell
Bay City	48	78	.381	25	M. Taylor/Clyde McNutt

BA: Len Cote, Kalamazoo, .327
Runs: Bob Parker, Jackson, 79
Hits: Raymond Evans, Jackson, 141
John Morrissey, Lansing, 141

HRs: Jim Bowser, Flint, 11
Wins: Belmont Method, Kalamazoo, 24
SOs: George Pearce, Lansing, 298
Pct: Ed Taylor, Kalamazoo, .800, 12-3

D Wisconsin-Illinois League
President: Charles F. Moll

Standings	W	L	Pct.	GB	Manager
Wausau Lumberjacks	71	48	.597	—	Charles Ferguson
Madison Senators	66	54	.550	5½	Howard Cassibone/John Moran
La Crosse Pinks	66	57	.537	7	E.P."Pink" Hawley
Green Bay Tigers	65	58	.528	8	John Corrigan/Jack Pickett
Fond du Lac Cubs	58	65	.472	15	Robert Lynch/Frank Newhouse
Freeport Pretzels	57	64	.471	15	Tom Schoonover/F. Rodemyer
Oshkosh Indians	55	66	.455	17	George Bubsir/Charles "Kid" Nichols
Rockford Reds	48	74	.393	24½	Frank Shugart/James Hutten/Henry Hines

BA: Ward Miller, Wausau, .383
Runs: Ward Miller, Wausau, 91

Hits: Ward Miller, Wausau, 156

Ind California League
President: Frank Herman

Standings	W	L	Pct.	GB	Manager
Stockton Millers	62	17	.785	—	Cy Moreing
San Jose Prune Pickers	58	17	.773	2	Emil Mayer/A. Jarman
Sacramento Senators	55	20	.733	5	Bill Curtin
Fresno Tigers	47	31	.603	15½	Spider Baum
Santa Cruz Sand Crabs	60	46	.566	15½	H.R. Bradford/W. Keating

1908

Alameda Encinals .... 24 50 .324 35½ Lou Schroeder/Fred Lange
San Francisco .... 9 67 .118 51½ Phil Knell
Oakland Commuters .... 4 71 .053 56 Walt McMemony

BA: Joe Nealon, Sacramento, .372   **Pct:** Harry Wolter, San Jose, .926, 25-2
Wins: Ben Henderson, Stockton, 35

1908 Interleague Post Season Play

World Series
Chicago (National) 4 games, Detroit (American) 1

1908 No-Hitters

Date	Pitcher	Team	League	Opponent	Score
3-29	Doc Moskiman	Stockton	California	Oakland	7-0
4-28	Jesse Stovall	Louisville	American Assoc.	Minneapolis	2-0
4-30	George Bitteroff	Decatur	Three-I	Springfield	2-1 (12)
5-1	Rube Kroh	Johnstown	Tri-State	Wilmington	1-0 (10)
5-3	Wilson	Rock Island	Three-I	Dubuque	5-0
5-9	Cliff Curtis	Milwaukee	American Assoc.	Indianapolis	6-0
5-9	Clarence Wright	Spokane	Northwestern	Vancouver	5-0
5-10	Jim Buchanan	Little Rock	Southern Assoc.	Memphis	1-0
5-11	Cy Alberts	South Bend	Central	Wheeling	4-0
5-14	Chick Brandom	Kansas City	American Assoc.	Indianapolis	5-0
5-21	Joe Wood	Kansas City	American Assoc.	Milwaukee	1-0
5-31	Edward Eis	Burlington	Central Assoc.	Ottumwa	11-0
5-31	Brazelle	Monroe	Cotton States	Vicksburg	3-0
5-31	"Kich" White	Lancaster	Ohio State	Newark	4-0
6-1	Homer Mock	Lancaster	Ohio State	Newark	6-0
6-4	H.B. Rush	Seattle	Northwestern	Spokane	4-0
6-6	Moore	Lynn	New England	Haverhill	2-0
6-9	Edward Collins	Gloversville-Johnstown	New York State	Albany	5-0
6-10	John Jones	Lincoln	Western	Sioux City	2-0
6-11	Pep Hornsby	Ft. Worth	Texas	Waco	1-0
6-13	Cyrus Clyde	Sharon	Ohio-Penn.	East Liverpool	1-0
6-14	Slim Nelson	Alameda	California	Oakland	1-0
6-21	Dell Paddock	Vancouver	Northwestern	Spokane	4-0
6-21	Fred Cook	San Antonio	Texas	Waco	0-2 (11)
6-27	A.J. Patrick	Jacksonville	Central Assoc.	Ottumwa	4-1
6-28	Ed Barry	Providence	Eastern	Jersey City	4-0
6-30	Cy Young	Boston	American	New York	8-0
6-30	Sandy Bannister	Rochester	Eastern	Buffalo	0-1 (7)
7-3	E.F. Mayberry	Wilson	Eastern Carolina	Raleigh	
7-4	Hooks Wiltse	New York	National	Philadelphia	1-0 (10)
7-5	Joe Hagerman	Grand Rapids	Central	South Bend	5-0
7-6	J.F. Crouch	Rock Hill	South Carolina	Orangeburg	
7-6	Fred Mitchell	Toronto	Eastern	Montreal	2-0
7-16	Walter Sullivan	Austin	Texas	Waco	7-0
7-17	George Watt	Zanesville	Central	Terre Haute	1-0 (7)
7-19	Walter Justus	Lancaster	Ohio State	Mansfield	6-0
7-21	Charles Evans	Hartford	Connecticut	Bridgeport	5-0 (P)
7-23	Gus Thompson	Grays Harbor	Northwestern	Seattle	3-0
7-29	John McFarland	Helena	Arkansas	Pine Bluff	9-0
7-30	McGreary	Winston-Salem	Carolina Association	Anderson	
7-30	Ivy Tevis	Austin	Texas	Waco	1-0
8-1	James Ward	New Britain	Connecticut	Holyoke	6-0
8-1	Carl Sitton	Jacksonville	South Atlantic	Macon	3-0
8-2	Walter Justus	Lancaster	Ohio State	Portsmouth	6-0
8-3	Phil Sitton	Augusta	South Atlantic	Columbia	1-0
8-5	Schultz	Gulfport-Biloxi	Cotton States	Jackson	3-0 (8)
8-6	Frederick Stoehr	Anderson	Carolina Assoc.	Charlotte	0-1 (13)
8-8	Gene Packard	Independence	Oklahoma-Kansas	Bartlesville	4-0 (P)
8-8	Ira Plank	Meriden	Connecticut	New Haven	2-0
8-9	Harry Killilay	Tulsa	Oklahoma-Kansas	Muskogee	7-1
8-12	Harry Coveleski	Lancaster	Tri-State	Reading	2-0 (8)
8-13	Buck Friel	Haverhill	New England	Fall River	2-0
8-14	Grover Lowdermilk	Decatur	Three-I	Peoria	6-2
8-16	Hi West	Toledo	American Assoc.	Milwaukee	7-0
8-18	George Upp	Columbus	American Assoc.	Kansas City	3-0
8-21	Fred Burnham	Webb City	Western Assoc.	Hutchinson	5-0
8-22	Dick Slater	Galveston	Texas	Austin	1-0
8-26	Frank Barber	Hutchinson	Western Assoc.	Springfield	5-0
8-27	Cliff Bayless	Dallas	Texas	Shreveport	1-0
8-27	Dusty Rhodes	Omaha	Western	Sioux City	6-0
8-28	John Quinn	Richmond	Virginia	Norfolk	3-0
9-1	James Lucas	Marion	Ohio State	Newark	2-0
9-3	Rube Marquard	Indianapolis	American Assoc.	Columbus	7-0
9-5	Nap Rucker	Brooklyn	National	Boston	6-0
9-8	Walter Justus	Lancaster	Ohio State	Lima	5-0
9-10	John Duggan	Nashville	Southern Assoc.	Little Rock	1-0
9-13	Dell Paddock	Vancouver	Northwestern	Tacoma	3-1
9-13	Walter Justus	Lancaster	Ohio State	Marion	3-0
9-18	Dusty Rhoades	Cleveland	American	Boston	2-1
9-20	Frank Smith	Chicago	American	Philadelphia	1-0
10-2	Addie Joss	Cleveland	American	Chicago	1-0 (P)
11-1	Johnny Hopkins	Santa Cruz	California	San Francisco	11-0

Number in parentheses indicates innings if other than nine; "P" indicates perfect game.

THIS DATE IN MINOR LEAGUE HISTORY

January 21, 1908, Don Gallagos, a Mexican pitcher with Ft. Worth of the Texas League, died in Ft. Worth from the effects of a gunshot wound inflicted by Palmer Maddox during a fight.

April 20, 1908, The Cuban baseball season closed with Alamendares of Havana as the champion team.

May 26, 1908, The season opening game at Butte, Northwestern League, against Spokane was prevented by a six-inch snowfall.

June 3, 1908, The outlaw Union League collapsed and disbanded.

June 15, 1908, Fort Wayne, Central League, which started the season with six straight victories, ended a 15-game losing streak by winning on a forfeit when pitcher Eugene Moore of South Bend brutally assaulted umpire Tug Arundel.

June 16, 1908, Joe Jackson, Greenville outfielder, smashed three home runs in a Carolina Association game against Winston-Salem.

June 24, 1908, William F. Traffley, former Baltimore manager and pilot of the Des Moines club in 1896 which won 25 consecutive games, died of tuberculosis in Denver.

July 4, 1908, Attendance at the doubleheader at Richmond between the Virginia League teams of Danville and Richmond was placed at 24,000.

July 6, 1908, The Western League game at Omaha was postponed because of cold weather.

July 19, 1908, John Bender was suspended indefinitely by Columbia, South Atlantic

League, for the stabbing of manager Win Clark on board a steamer bound from Jacksonville to Charleston. Bender, an outfielder, was reinstated in 1909.

July 28, 1908, Pitcher John Picus Quinn joined Richmond in the Virginia League and during the balance of the season won 14 games without a loss. Quinn, who later hurled in the majors for many years, also hurled two extra-inning tie games, 0-0 in 13 frames and 1-1 in 10 rounds.

July 29, 1908, Pitcher John McFarland, Helena, Arkansas State League, lost credit for a perfect game when the 27th Pine Bluff batter refused to face him, causing the game to be forfeited, 9-0.

August 1, 1908, Columbia's John Bender, brother of the Athletics' Chief Bender, was held at Augusta, Georgia, under $1,000 bond for the July stabbing of his manager, Win Clark.

September 9, 1908, Pitcher Louis "Bull" Durham of Indianapolis, American Association, pitched and won his fifth doubleheader of the season. Five of the ten victories were shutouts.

September 13, 1908, Pitcher Walter "Smoke" Justus, Lancaster, Ohio State League, shut out Marion, hurling his fourth no-hit game of the season. It was also the sixth no-hitter for the Lancaster pitching staff on the year.

September 19, 1908, The Scranton vs. Wilkes-Barre game in the New York State League was called off due to smoke from forest fires.

December 23, 1908, William Mack, 43, once a noted minor league player, later a tramp, died of starvation in St. John's Hospital in Pittsburgh.

1909

American League
President: Byron Bancroft Johnson

Standings	W	L	Pct.	GB	Attend.	Manager
Detroit Tigers	98	54	.645	—	490,490	Hugh Jennings
Philadelphia Athletics	95	58	.621	3½	674,915	Connie Mack
Boston Red Sox	88	63	.583	9½	668,965	Frederick Lake
Chicago White Sox	78	74	.513	20	478,400	Billy Sullivan
New York Highlanders	74	77	.490	23½	501,700	George Stallings
Cleveland Naps	71	82	.464	27½	354,627	Napoleon Lajoie/ Deacon McGuire
St. Louis Browns	61	89	.407	36	366,274	Jimmy McAleer
Washington Senators	42	110	.276	56	205,199	Joe Cantillon

BA: Ty Cobb, Detroit, .377
Runs: Ty Cobb, Detroit, 116
Hits: Ty Cobb, Detroit, 216
RBIs: Ty Cobb, Detroit, 107
HRs: Ty Cobb, Detroit, 9

Wins: George Mullin, Detroit, 29
SOs: Frank Smith, Chicago, 177
ERA: Harry Krause, Philadelphia, 1.39
Pct: George Mullin, Detroit, .784, 29-8

National League
Presidents: Harry C. Pulliam/John A. Heydler

Standings	W	L	Pct.	GB	Attend.	Manager
Pittsburgh Pirates	110	42	.724	—	534,950	Fred Clarke
Chicago Cubs	104	49	.680	6½	633,480	Frank Chance
New York Giants	92	61	.601	18½	783,700	John McGraw
Cincinnati Reds	77	76	.503	33½	424,643	Clark Griffith
Philadelphia Phillies	74	79	.484	36½	303,177	Billy Murray
Brooklyn Superbas	55	98	.359	55½	321,300	Harry Lumley
St. Louis Cardinals	54	98	.355	56	299,982	Roger Bresnahan
Boston Rustlers	45	108	.294	65½	195,188	Frank Bowerman/Harry Smith

BA: Honus Wagner, Pittsburgh, .339
Runs: Tommy Leach, Pittsburgh, 126
Hits: Larry Doyle, New York, 172
RBIs: Honus Wagner, Pittsburgh, 100
HRs: Red Murray, New York, 7

Wins: Mordecai "Three Finger" Brown, Chicago, 27
SOs: Orval Overall, Chicago, 205
ERA: Christy Mathewson, New York, 1.14
Pct: Christy Mathewson, New York, .806, 25-6
Howie Camnitz, Pittsburgh, .806, 25-6

A American Association
President: Thomas J. Hickey

Standings	W	L	Pct.	GB	Attend.	Manager
Louisville Colonels	93	75	.554	—	196,682	Thomas Chivington
Milwaukee Brewers	90	77	.539	2½	260,495	John McCloskey
Minneapolis Millers	88	79	.527	4½	217,130	James Collins
Indianapolis Indians	83	85	.494	10	250,317	Charles Carr
St. Paul Apostles	80	83	.491	10½	146,691	Mike Kelley
Toledo Mud Hens	80	86	.482	12	164,051	Fred Abbott/Ralph Seybold
Columbus Senators	80	87	.479	12½	183,478	Bill Clymer/William Friel
Kansas City Blues	71	93	.432	20	151,473	Monte Cross/Jake Beckley/ Danny Shay

BA: Mike O'Neill, Minneapolis, .296
Runs: Newt Randall, Milwaukee, 91
Hits: Arthur Krueger, Columbus, 194
HRs: Berton James, Columbus, 7
Wins: Stony McGlynn, Milwaukee, 27

SOs: Stony McGlynn, Milwaukee, 183
Pct: Ed Karger, St. Paul, .700, 7-3
IP: Stony McGlynn, Milwaukee, 446
ShOs: Stony McGlynn, Milwaukee, 14

A Eastern League
President: Patrick T. Powers

Standings	W	L	Pct.	GB	Manager
Rochester Bronchos	90	61	.596	—	John Ganzel
Newark Indians	86	67	.562	5	Harry Wolverton/Joe McGinnity
Providence Clamdiggers	80	70	.533	9½	Hugh Duffy
Toronto Maple Leafs	79	72	.523	11	Joe Kelley
Buffalo Bisons	72	79	.477	18	George Smith
Montreal Royals	68	83	.450	22	James Casey
Baltimore Orioles	67	86	.438	24	Jack Dunn
Jersey City Skeeters	63	87	.420	26½	Eugene McCann/John Calhoun/John Ryan

Attendance: Buffalo, 188,946.

BA: Myron Grimshaw, Toronto, .309
Runs: Herb Moran, Providence, 92
Hits: Ed Hoffman, Providence, 164
HRs: Les Simmons, Rochester, 8
Wins: Joe McGinnity, Newark, 29

SOs: Joe McGinnity, Newark, 195
Pct: George McConnell, Jersey City/ Rochester, .750, 9-3
IP: Joe McGinnity, Newark, 422

A Pacific Coast League
President: J. Cal Ewing

Standings	W	L	Pct.	GB	Manager
San Francisco Seals	132	80	.622	—	Daniel Long
Portland Beavers	112	87	.563	13½	Walter McCredie
Los Angeles Angels	118	97	.549	15½	Frank "Cap" Dillon
Sacramento Sacts	97	107	.475	31	Charles Graham
Oakland Oaks	88	125	.413	44½	George Van Haltren/William Reidy
Vernon Tigers	80	131	.379	51½	W.L. "Happy" Hogan

BA: Henry Melchior, San Francisco, .298
Runs: Rollie Zeider, San Francisco, 141
Hits: Chick Gandil, Sacramento, 214
HRs: Otis Johnson, Portland, 13

SBs: Rollie Zeider, San Francisco, 93
Wins: Frank Browning, San Francisco, 32
SOs: Jimmy Wiggs, Oakland, 268
Pct: Cack Henley, San Francisco, .756, 31-10

A Southern Association
President: William B. Kavanaugh

Standings	W	L	Pct.	GB	Manager
Atlanta Crackers	87	49	.640	—	William A. Smith
Nashville Volunteers	82	55	.594	5½	Bill Bernhardt
Montgomery Climbers	76	60	.559	11	Ed Gremlinger
New Orleans Pelicans	73	64	.533	14½	Charley Frank
Mobile Sea Gulls	64	77	.454	25½	George Reed
Birmingham Barons	60	79	.429	28½	Carleton Molesworth
Little Rock Travelers	59	80	.424	29½	Michael Finn
Memphis Turtles	51	88	.367	37½	Charles Babb

BA: Bill McGilvray, Birmingham, .291
Runs: Dick Bayless, Atlanta, 85
Hits: Noah Henline, Birmingham, 159

HRs: Frank Huelsman, New Orleans, 5
Wins: Hub Perdue, Nashville, 23
Pct: Oliver Jones, Atlanta, .741, 20-7

A Western League
President: Norris L. O'Neill

Standings	W	L	Pct.	GB	Manager
Des Moines Boosters	93	59	.613	—	Bill Dwyer
Sioux City Soos	94	60	.610	—	James "Ducky" Holmes
Omaha Rourkes	84	68	.553	9	Pa Rourke/Billy Fox
Topeka Jayhawks	76	73	.510	15½	Dick Cooley
Wichita Jobbers	71	82	.464	22½	Jack Holland
Denver Grizzlies	69	82	.457	23½	Charley Jones/Henry Thompson
Lincoln Greenbackers	61	89	.407	31	James Sullivan
Pueblo Indians	58	93	.384	34½	Walter Carlisle

Attendance: Omaha, 136,000.

BA: Harry Welch, Omaha, .373
Runs: Tony Smith, Sioux City, 135
Hits: Harry Welch, Omaha, 196
HRs: Bill Hunter, Sioux City, 13

SBs: Bill Fisher, Omaha, 88
Wins: Fred Lange, Des Moines, 29
SOs: Fred Lange, Des Moines, 328
Pct: Henry Olmstead, Denver, .750, 24-8

B Central League
President: Dr. Frank R. Carson

Standings	W	L	Pct.	GB	Manager
Wheeling Stogies	83	50	.624	—	Bill Phillips
Zanesville Infants	75	58	.564	8	Roy Montgomery
Fort Wayne Billikens	71	66	.518	14	Jack Hendricks
Grand Rapids Wolverines	67	65	.508	15½	Joe Raidy
Terre Haute Hottentots	65	73	.471	20½	George "Cuppy" Groeschow
South Bend Greens	64	72	.470	20½	Angus Grant
Evansville River Rats	58	78	.426	26½	Charles "Punch" Knoll
Dayton Veterans	56	77	.421	27	Bade Myers

BA: Arista DeHaven, Terre Haute, .336
Runs: Curley Blount, Fort Wayne, 92
Hits: Arista DeHaven, Terre Haute, 173
HRs: Charles "Punch" Knoll, Evansville, 11
Hank Butcher, Evansville, 11

Wins: John Fisher, Wheeling, 24
Bill Kenworthy, Zanesville, 24
SOs: Bucky O'Brien, Evansville, 180
Pct: Bill Phillips, Wheeling, .800, 12-3

B Connecticut League
President: James O'Rourke

Standings	W	L	Pct.	GB	Manager
Hartford Senators	74	44	.627	—	Thomas Connery
Holyoke Papermakers	68	53	.562	7½	M.J. "Kid" McCormick
New Britain Perfectos	64	55	.533	10½	William Hanna
Waterbury Invincibles	64	61	.512	13½	Michael Doherty
Springfield Ponies	60	63	.488	16½	John Zeller
New Haven Black Crows	59	65	.476	18	George Bone
Northampton Meadowlarks	54	68	.443	22	Edward Bowler & Gil Edwards
Bridgeport Orators	44	78	.361	32	James O'Rourke

BA: Jim McCabe, New Britain, .366
Runs: William McCormick, Northampton, 95
Hits: Jim McCabe, New Britain, 176
HRs: Cy Perkins, Hartford, 23

Wins: Ray Fisher, Hartford, 24
SOs: Ray Fisher, Hartford, 243
Pct: Ray Fisher, Hartford, .828, 24-5

*Won first-half   **Won second-half   ***Won both halves

B New England League
President: Tim H. Murnane

Standings	W	L	Pct.	GB	Manager
Worcester Busters	77	47	.621	—	Jesse Burkett
Brockton Tigers	75	48	.610	1½	Stephen Flanagan
Lynn Shoemakers	74	49	.602	2½	Billy Hamilton
Fall River Indians	71	53	.573	6	John H. O'Brien
Haverhill Hustlers	62	62	.500	15	Frank Connaughton
New Bedford Whalers	51	72	.416	25½	Thomas Dowd
Lowell Tigers	43	81	.348	34	Tom Fleming/Tom Bannon/Roy Smith
Lawrence Colts	41	82	.333	35½	Mal Eason

BA: Billy Hamilton, Lynn, .332
Runs: Roland Barrows, New Bedford, 88
Olaf Henriksen, Brockton, 88
Hits: Simeon Murch, Brockton, 144
Hugh Bradley, Worcester, 144
HRs: Bob Messenger, Fall River, 8
Wins: Marty O'Toole, Brockton, 26
Pct: Marty O'Toole, Brockton, .684, 26-12

B New York State League
President: John H. Farrell

Standings	W	L	Pct.	GB	Manager
Wilkes-Barre Barons	88	53	.624	—	Mal Kittridge
Utica Pent-Ups	84	56	.600	3½	Charles Dooley
Albany Senators	76	63	.547	11	William Clark
Elmira Pioneers	68	68	.500	17½	Henry Ramsey/Jerry Hurley
Binghamton Bingoes	61	77	.442	25½	William Roach
Troy Trojans	60	76	.441	25½	Edward Murphy
Syracuse Stars	60	78	.435	26½	Sandy Griffin
Scranton Miners	55	81	.404	30½	August Zeimer

BA: Bill Kay, Albany, .351
Runs: Tom Madden, Utica, 103
Hits: Bill Kay, Albany, 185
Del Drake, Wilkes-Barre, 185
SBs: Tom Madden, Utica, 57

B Northwestern League
President: William H. Lucas

Standings	W	L	Pct.	GB	Manager
Seattle Turks	109	58	.653	—	Michael Lynch
Spokane Indians	100	66	.602	8½	Robert Brown
Grays Harbor Grays	78	81	.491	27	Clarence "Pants" Rowland
Portland Colts	79	88	.473	30	Perle Casey
Vancouver Beavers	70	96	.422	38½	Lou Nordyke
Tacoma Tigers	64	111	.366	49	Russ Hall/Jerry Hurley/Issac Butler

BA: Justin "Pug" Bennett, Seattle, .314
Runs: Justin "Pug" Bennett, Seattle, 111
Hits: Justin "Pug" Bennett, Seattle, 201
HRs: Ralph Capron, Seattle, 15
Wins: John Thompson, Seattle, 26
SOs: Jesse Baker, Tacoma/Spokane, 249
Pct: Frank Allen, Seattle, .769, 20-6

B Three-I League
President: Michael H. Sexton

Standings	W	L	Pct.	GB	Manager
Rock Island Islanders	90	48	.652	—	Jack Tighe
Springfield Senators	81	53	.604	7	Richard Smith
Davenport Prodigals	77	59	.566	12	Charles Shaffer
Bloomington Bloomers	70	67	.511	19½	W.R. McNamara/James Novacek
Peoria Distillers	69	67	.507	20	Frank Donnelly
Dubuque Dubs	64	71	.474	24½	Forrest Plass/Charles Buelow
Decatur Commodores	63	73	.464	26	Doc Childs/Fred Moore/John Barkwell
Cedar Rapids Rabbits	31	107	.225	59	Rollo Brown/C. Brown/Chet Spencer

BA: Frank Murphy, Rock Island, .300
Runs: Frank Murphy, Rock Island, 86
Hits: Frank Murphy, Rock Island, 172
HRs: Elmer Johnson, Springfield, 10
Wins: George Hardin, Rock Island, 26
SOs: George Hardin, Rock Island, 235
Pct: Cornelius Walsh, Peoria, .722, 13-5

B Tri-State League
President: Charles F. Carpenter

Standings	W	L	Pct.	GB	Manager
Lancaster Red Roses	75	39	.658	—	Martin Hogan
Reading Dutchmen	71	43	.623	4	Clarence "Pop" Foster
Williamsport Millionaires	61	53	.535	14	William Coughlin
Altoona Mountaineers	59	55	.518	16	Edward Ashenbach
Johnstown Johnnies	57	57	.500	18	Curt Weigand
Harrisburg Senators	49	65	.430	26	George Heckert
Trenton Tigers	43	71	.377	32	Percy Stetler/George Magoon
York White Roses	41	73	.360	34	Frank Reisling/William Poole

BA: Pete Lister, Williamsport, .350
Runs: Morrie Rath, Reading, 98
Hits: Virgil Cannell, Williamsport, 145
Tom O'Hara, Williamsport, 145
HRs: Mert Whitney, Hartford, 10
SBs: Archie Marshall, Lancaster, 71
Wins: Stan Coveleski, Lancaster, 23
Pct: A.P. Dank, Reading, .917, 11-1

C Minnesota-Wisconsin League
President: John A. Elliott

Standings	W	L	Pct.	GB	Manager
Duluth White Sox	65	52	.556	—	Bunny Kuehn
Eau Claire Puffs	62	57	.521	4	Tom Schoonhover
La Crosse Outcasts	60	56	.517	4½	Joe Safford
Winona Pirates	60	56	.517	4½	Joe Killian
Wausau Lumberjacks	54	66	.450	12½	Joe McCarthy
Superior Blues	51	65	.440	13½	

BA: Russ Bailey, Eau Claire, .308
Runs: Mike Malloy, La Crosse, 75
Hits: Russ Bailey, Eau Claire, 143
HRs: A.J. McCrone, Duluth, 6
Wins: Phil Stremmel, Superior, 22
Pct: John Nicholson, Eau Claire, .800, 8-2

C Ohio-Pennsylvania League
President: Samuel L. Wright

Standings	W	L	Pct.	GB	Manager
Akron Champs	81	40	.670	—	J. Breckinridge/William Schwartz
East Liverpool Potters	80	45	.640	3	Arch Osborne
McKeesport Tubers	73	53	.579	10½	William Thomas
New Castle Nocks/Alliance	59	65	.476	23½	James Barton/Ferdinand Drumm
Canton Watchmakers	55	67	.451	26½	Van Patterson
Erie Sailors	48	69	.410	31	Milt Montgomery/Red Davis/W. Broderick
Steubenville Stubs	48	73	.397	33	John Hanlon/Jim Lynch/Frank Blair
Youngstown Indians	46	78	.371	36½	Charles Crowe/William Terry

BA: Burt Shotten, Steubenville, .347
Runs: Gene Elliott, McKeesport, 75
Hits: Burt Shotten, Steubenville, 154
Wins: Howard Camnitz, McKeesport, 27
Pct: Arch Osborne, East Liverpool, .760, 19-6

C South Atlantic League
Presidents: N.J. Etheridge/W.R. Joyner

Standings	W	L	Pct.	GB	Manager
Chattanooga Lookouts*	84	36	.700	—	Johnny Dobbs
Columbus Foxes	73	50	.593	12½	James Fox
Augusta Tourists**	65	48	.575	15½	Louis Castro
Savannah Indians	60	61	.496	24½	Robert Gilks/Ernest Howard
Charleston Sea Gulls/ Knoxville Appalachians#	52	61	.460	28½	G.S. Malarkey/Steve Griffin
Macon Peaches	50	68	.424	33	John Lawler
Jacksonville Jays	47	70	.402	35½	Dominick Mullaney
Columbia Gamecocks	41	78	.345	42½	Ed Granville

#Charleston moved to Knoxville July 5 after completing the first half.

Playoff: Chattanooga 4 games, Augusta 2.

BA: Joe Jackson, Savannah, .358
Runs: Leo Huber, Savannah, 93
Hits: Doc Johnston, Chattanooga, 166
Wins: Roy Radabaugh, Columbus, 25
SOs: L.R. Wagner, Columbia/Augusta, 202
Pct: Prince Gaskill, Chattanooga, .840, 21-4

C Texas League
Presidents: Wilbur Allen/J. Doak Roberts

Standings	W	L	Pct.	GB	Manager
Houston Buffaloes	86	57	.601	—	Charles Barrett/Hunter Hill
Oklahoma City Indians	79	63	.556	6½	George Kelsey/Jay Andrews
San Antonio Bronchoes	76	63	.547	8	George Leidy
Dallas Giants	75	64	.540	9	Curley Maloney
Shreveport Pirates	73	68	.518	12	Dale Gear
Ft. Worth Panthers	73	71	.507	13½	Frederick Cavender
Galveston Sand Crabs	53	89	.373	32½	Tom Carlin/Robert Gilks
Waco Navigators	51	91	.359	34½	Ben Shelton

BA: Red Downey, Oklahoma City, .346
Runs: Bill McCormick, Oklahoma City, 93
Hits: Bill McCormick, Oklahoma City, 169
HRs: Dick Hoffman, Waco/Galveston, 18
Wins: Harry Stewart, Houston, 23
SOs: Fred Winchell, San Antonio, 264
Pct: Louis Drucke, Dallas, .778, 14-4

C Virginia League
President: Jacob Wells

Standings	W	L	Pct.	GB	Manager
Roanoke Tigers	73	49	.598	—	Frank Shaughnessy
Norfolk Tars	72	49	.595	½	Bob Pender/Win Clark
Richmond Colts	63	61	.508	11	Perry Lipe
Danville Red Sox	60	62	.496	13	Robert Stafford
Portsmouth Truckers	49	72	.406	23½	Maurice White/Thomas Guiheen
Lynchburg Shoemakers	50	74	.403	24	Al Orth/Dickinson

BA: Charles Seitz, Norfolk, .328
Runs: Charles Seitz, Norfolk, 73
Hits: Charles Seitz, Norfolk, 154
RBIs: Charles Seitz, Norfolk, 78
HRs: Frank Shaughnessy, Roanoke, 5
Wins: Dutch Revell, Richmond, 29
SOs: Walter Doane, Roanoke, 208
Pct: John Fox, Norfolk, .769, 20-6

C Western Association
President: Dr. D.M. Shiveley

Standings	W	L	Pct.	GB	Manager
Enid Railroaders	82	44	.651	—	J.H. Shaw/Ted Price
Muskogee Navigators	74	51	.592	7½	George Dalrymple
Guthrie Senators	70	55	.560	11½	Howard Price
Bartlesville Boosters	66	59	.528	15½	Frank Barber
Webb City Webfeet/ Sapulpa Oilers@	64	59	.520	16½	Perry Parker/Frank Everhart
Springfield Midgets	56	70	.444	24½	Frank Hurlburt

	W	L	Pct.	GB	
Pittsburg Pirates	52	73	.416	28	Elmer Meredith
Joplin Miners/					
El Reno Packers#	36	89	.288	44	Thomas Hayden/Bailey Vinson/
					Jack McConnell/William Burns

#Joplin (20-43) moved to El Reno July 4.
@Webb City (35-39) moved to Sapulpa July 18.

BA: Claire Patterson, Guthrie, .355
Runs: Frank Loften, Webb City/Sapulpa, 108
Hits: Claire Patterson, Guthrie, 180

HRs: Tex Jones, Enid, 11
Wilder Gray, Springfield, 11
Wins: Floyd Willis, Guthrie, 22
SOs: Clyde Geist, Guthrie, 247
Pct: Floyd Willis, Guthrie, .815, 22-5

D Arkansas State League
Presidents: W.W. Hurst/R.M. Rider

Standings	W	L	Pct.	GB	Manager
Jonesboro	42	27	.609	—	Senter Rainey
Helena Hellions*	39	25	.609	½	C.A. Vandergriff
Texarkana	34	35	.493	8	Robert Shelton
Hot Springs Vaporites	33	37	.471	9½	Arthur Riggs/Elmer Coyle
Monroe/Newport-Batesville					
Pearl Diggers@	25	38	.397	14	W. Dobard
Ft. Smith Soldiers	27	42	.391	15	Hugo Bezdek/A.L. "Dad" Ritter
Argenta Shamrocks#	26	19	.578	NA	A.L. "Dad" Ritter
Alexandria Hoo Hoos#	20	23	.465	NA	John Auslet

#Argenta and Alexandria disbanded June 7.
@Monroe moved to Newport-Batesville July 1.
The league disbanded July 7.

D Blue Grass League
President: George L. Hammond

Standings	W	L	Pct.	GB	Manager
Winchester Hustlers	75	44	.630	—	Newton "Daddy" Horn
Richmond Pioneers	75	45	.625	½	
Paris Bourbonites	61	57	.516	13½	J. Barnett
Frankfort Statesmen	56	60	.482	17½	N.G. Kennedy/Ben Marshall
Lexington Colts	48	69	.410	26	Thomas Sheets/Stults/Downing
Shelbyville	39	79	.321	35½	Anton Kuhn

BA: Hub Dawson, Richmond, .334
Runs: Fred Ochs, Paris, 74
Hits: J.F. Whittaker, Richmond, 142

Wins: Charles Burden, Winchester, 25
Pct: Bill Knox, Richmond, .714, 10-4

D Carolina Association
President: Joseph H. Wearn

Standings	W	L	Pct.	GB	Manager
Greensboro Champs	65	44	.596	—	James McKevitt
Anderson Electricians	63	48	.568	3	Jim "King" Kelly
Greenville Spinners	61	51	.545	5½	Thomas Stouch
Winston-Salem Twins	54	52	.509	9½	Robert Carter
Charlotte Hornets	46	63	.422	19	Danny Collins/Lave Cross
Spartanburg Spartans	40	71	.360	26	Carlton Beusse

BA: Al Humphrey, Charlotte, .296
Runs: Charles Sisson, Greensboro, 81
Hits: Jim "King" Kelly, Anderson, 117
RBIs: Jim "King" Kelly, Anderson, 71

HRs: Harvey Ritter, Spartanburg, 11
Wins: R.C. Walters, Greensboro, 25
SOs: R.C. Walters, Greensboro, 148
Pct: George Schmick, Anderson, .789, 15-4

D Central Association
President: M.E. Justice

Standings	W	L	Pct.	GB	Attend.	Manager
Burlington Pathfinders	83	51	.620	—	36,884	Ned Egan
Hannibal Cannibals	83	53	.610	1	30,130	Bert Hough/Ben Prout
Keokuk Indians	80	57	.584	4½	42,029	Frank Belt
Kewanee Boilermakers	73	61	.544	10	31,228	William Connors
Waterloo Lulus	64	69	.481	18½	33,756	Frank Boyle
Quincy Vets	62	73	.459	21½	45,527	Louis Cook/Harry Hofer
Jacksonville Braves	46	84	.354	35	26,908	Harry Berte
Ottumwa Packers	48	91	.345	37½	35,576	Hugh Shannon/Arthur Owens

BA: Fred Fenney, Ottumwa/Burlington, .300
Runs: George Manush, Burlington, 91
Hits: George Manush, Burlington, 149
HRs: Al Linderbeck, Hannibal, 10
H.W. Gray, Jacksonville, 10

Wins: Collis Spencer, Burlington, 27
SOs: Joe Vyskocil, Hannibal, 209
Pct: Burleigh Grimes, Ottumwa/Kewanee, .742, 23-8

D Central Kansas League
President: Ralph W. Hoffman

Standings	W	L	Pct.	GB	Manager
Ellsworth Worthies	44	23	.657	—	George Seigle
Salina Trade Winners	40	28	.588	4½	Ernest Quigley
Abilene Red Sox	37	30	.552	7	F.D. Parent/Affie Wilson
Minneapolis Minnies	36	32	.529	8½	Harry Short/Roy Gafford
Junction City Soldiers	34	32	.515	9½	Lewis Armstrong/Tom Campbell
Beloit	33	36	.478	12	Buck Ebright

	W	L	Pct.	GB	
Clay Center Cubs	32	37	.464	13	Lee Gramley
Manhattan Maroons	16	54	.229	29½	Earle Bryant/Murphy

BA: Tom Campbell, Junction City, .335
Runs: James Whalen, Junction City, 49
Hits: Claude Jennings, Minneapolis, 72

Wins: Ora Williams, Abilene, 19
SOs: Ora Williams, Abilene, 178
Pct: Ora Williams, Abilene, .826, 19-4

D Eastern Carolina League
President: Dr. Joel Whitaker

Standings	W	L	Pct.	GB	Manager
Wilson Tobacconists	50	39	.562	—	Earl Holt
Wilmington Sailors	50	40	.556	½	Dick Smith
Fayetteville Highlanders	49	41	.544	1½	Charles E. Moss/Charles Clancy
Raleigh Red Birds	49	41	.544	1½	Richard Crozier
Goldsboro Giants	43	46	.486	7	H.E. Kling
Rocky Mount Railroaders	27	61	.307	22½	W.B. Fenner/Walsh

Wilson was awarded the pennant after ineligible player violation rules were enacted.

BA: Bill Schumaker, Fayetteville, .340
Runs: Pete Clemens, Fayetteville, 46
Hits: Charles Armstrong, Wilson, 76

Wins: Harry "Cannonball" Otis, Goldsboro, 19
Pct: Bill Luyster, Fayetteville, .786, 11-3

D Illinois-Missouri League
President: A.E. Blain

Standings	W	L	Pct.	GB	Manager
Monmouth Browns	77	50	.606	—	Jack Corbett
Beardstown Infants	77	52	.597	1	Harry Riggons
Pekin Celestials	73	57	.562	5½	Doug Jefries/Skinny Horton/Spider Diehl/
					W.C. Dithridge
Macomb Potters	63	67	.485	15½	Wolfe
Canton Chinks	51	79	.392	27½	Harry Lloyd
Galesburg Boosters	47	83	.362	31½	

BA: Andy Lotshaw, Beardstown, .329
Runs: Andy Lotshaw, Beardstown, 72
Hits: Andy Lotshaw, Beardstown, 146
HRs: Cy Forsythe, Pekin, 7
Will Johnston, Monmouth, 7
Fred Johnson, Canton, 7

Wins: Homer Hargrove, Monmouth, 27
J.W. Jenkins, Pekin, 27
SOs: Charles Fanning, Canton, 249
Pct: Homer Hargrove, Monmouth, .750, 27-9

D Inter-Mountain League
President: William H. Lucas

Standings	W	L	Pct.	GB	Manager
Helena Senators	43	19	.694	—	John Huston
Salt Lake City Mormons/					
Livingston#	39	23	.629	4	E.S. Farnsworth
Butte Miners+	21	36	.368	19½	John S. Barnes
Boise Irrigators/Bozeman@	16	41	.281	24½	J.C. "Con" Strothers

#Salt Lake City (34-17) moved to Livingston July 10, first home game July 15.
@Boise (13-38) moved to Bozeman July 10, first home game July 15.
+Butte disbanded July 18.
The league disbanded July 25.

D Kansas State League
President: P.H. Hostutler

Standings	W	L	Pct.	GB	Manager
Lyons Lions	61	37	.622	—	Cecil Bankhead
Hutchinson Salt Packers	60	37	.619	½	Bill Zink
McPherson Merry Macks	59	37	.615	1	O.P. Depew/Earl Green
Great Bend Millers	49	48	.505	11½	Rudy Kling/Stillings
Wellington Dukes	44	54	.449	17	Cy Mason & John Meade
Newton Railroaders	42	54	.438	18	Con Harlow/A. Stillwell
Arkansas City-					
Winfield Twins@	41	56	.423	19½	M.E. Parks/Frank Layne/Bennie Owens
Strong City-Cottonwood Falls					
Twin Citys/Larned Cowboys#	32	65	.330	28½	Butch Freese/Buck Weaver

#Strong City-Cottonwood Falls (22-41) moved to Larned July 12.
@Winfield bought part interest in the Arkansas City (30-44) franchise July 22.

BA: Tom Miller, Newton, .342
Runs: Jasper Hainsey, McPherson, 66
Hits: Tom Miller, Newton, 119

HRs: Pete LaFlambois, Arkansas City-
Winfield, 6
Wins: Robert Hassler, Lyons, 25
SOs: Robert Hassler, Lyons, 193
Pct: Pearl Stanley, Hutchinson, .793, 23-6

D Northeast Arkansas League
President: R.M. Rider

Standings	W	L	Pct.	GB	Manager
Jonesboro Zebras	30	23	.566	—	H. Brown
Newport Pearl Diggers	29	25	.537	1½	Arthur Riggs
Marianna Brickeys	24	29	.453	6	McAdams
Paragould Scouts	24	30	.444	6½	Senter Rainey

The league was formed after the Arkansas State League disbanded July 7, beginning play July 26.

BA: H.V. Rogers, Newport, .337
Runs: Abe Jolley, Jonesboro, 44
Hits: Abe Jolley, Jonesboro, 67

Wins: Charles Deardorff, Jonesboro, 12
Pct: Charles Deardorff, Jonesboro, .800, 12-3

BA: Harry Martin, Kalamazoo, .330
Runs: Harry Ball, Adrian, 94
Hits: Harry Ball, Adrian, 141

Wins: Gene Krapp, Flint, 23
Pct: Elmer Criger, Jackson, .759, 22-7
Ed Kusel, Saginaw, .759, 22-7

D Northern State of Indiana League
President: C.A. Klunk

Standings	W	L	Pct.	GB	Manager
Bluffton Babes	65	38	.631	—	Duck Ebers/Herman Weber
Lafayette Wets	66	39	.629	—	
Huntington Johnnies	61	46	.570	6	
Kokomo Wild Cats	50	53	.485	15	
Marion Boosters	38	67	.362	28	Mike Lawrence
Wabash Rockeries	35	72	.327	32	

D Ohio State League
President: Robert Quinn

Standings	W	L	Pct.	GB	Manager
Lima Cigarmakers	79	50	.612	—	Lee Fohl
Marion Diggers	71	59	.546	8½	Charles O'Day/Joseph Lewis
Mansfield Pioneers	63	58	.521	12	Tim Flood
Portsmouth Cobblers	48	76	.387	28½	William Doyle/John McAllister/ Charles O'Day
Lancaster Lanks#	53	53	.500	NA	George Fox
Newark Newks#	46	64	.418	NA	Homer Davidson/Erve Wratten

#Newark and Lancaster disbanded August 23.

BA: Frank "Red" Farrell, Marion, .316
Runs: Charles Fink, Lima, 91
Hits: Charles Staley, Marion, 142
HRs: Ed Williams, Marion, 6

SBs: Alex Reilley, Lima, 76
Wins: Ed Zmich, Marion, 21
Pct: Robert Nelson, Lima, .800, 8-2

D Pennsylvania-West Virginia League
President: James D. Groninger

Standings	W	L	Pct.	GB	Manager
Uniontown Coal Barons**	63	44	.589	—	Frank Sisley
Fairmont Champions*	58	50	.537	5½	Louis Hunt
Grafton	56	54	.509	8½	S.B. "Duff" Buttermore
Connellsville Cokers	53	56	.486	11	Alexander Sweeney
Clarksburg Bees#	22	31	.415	NA	Ferdinand Drumm
Charleroi/ Parkersburg Parkers#	16	33	.327	NA	H. Osborne/Frank McHale

#Charleroi (13-25) moved to Parkersburg June 30, then was dropped July 10 after Clarksburg disbanded.

Playoff: Uniontown 4 games, Fairmont 3.

BA: Waldo Jackley, Fairmont, .326
Runs: Del Gainer, Grafton, 59
Hits: Joe Phillips, Uniontown, 127

Wins: Joe Phillips, Uniontown, 29
Pct: Joe Phillips, Uniontown, .806, 29-7

D Southern Michigan League
President: Joseph S. Jackson

Standings	W	L	Pct.	GB	Manager
Saginaw Wa-was	73	52	.584	—	A.A. Burkhardt
Flint Vehicles	72	52	.581	½	Red Wright
Jackson Convicts	71	52	.577	1	Bo Slear
Kalamazoo Kazoos	64	60	.516	8½	Harry Martin
Bay City	59	66	.478	14	Edward Herr/Fred Buelow
Lansing Senators	55	69	.443	17½	John Morrissey
Adrian Yeggs	52	73	.416	21	Charles Cassell
Battle Creek Crickets	52	74	.413	21½	Rube Deneau

D Western Canada League
President: C.J. Eckstrom

Standings	W	L	Pct.	GB	Attend.	Manager
Medicine Hat Hatters	68	33	.673	—	11,696	William Hamilton
Winnipeg Maroons	66	38	.635	3½	53,132	Frank Lohr/J. Shuster
Calgary Cowboys	56	44	.560	11½	25,379	Charles "Spokane" Crist
Lethbridge Miners	51	46	.526	15	13,192	Jack Corrigan
Moose Jaw Robin Hoods	50	50	.500	17½	19,568	M.O. Taylor
Regina Bonepilers	42	53	.442	23	21,204	Charles Blackburn/ Gardner Katcher
Brandon Angels	37	67	.356	32½	23,428	Charles Traeger
Edmonton Eskimos	28	67	.295	37	18,808	Dennis McGuire

The far western clubs kept no player records and no averages were issued.

D Wisconsin-Illinois League
President: Charles F. Moll

Standings	W	L	Pct.	GB	Manager
Madison Senators	74	45	.627	—	Howard Cassibone
Green Bay Bays	69	54	.561	7	John Pickett
Appleton Papermakers	66	57	.537	10	Charles Ferguson
Racine Malted Milks	65	58	.523	11	William Armstrong
Rockford Reds	61	61	.500	14½	George Bubsir
Fond du Lac Giants	58	64	.475	17½	Fred Barnes
Oshkosh Indians	52	72	.419	24½	E.P. "Pink" Hawley
Freeport Pretzels	45	79	.363	31½	Frank Genins

BA: Fred Luderus, Freeport, .321
Hits: Tom Coates, Oshkosh, 151

Wins: Frank Shaw, Madison, 23
Pct: Jesse Theobald, Freeport, .750, 12-4

Ind California League
President: Frank Herman

Standings	W	L	Pct.	GB	Manager
Oakland Invaders**	94	63	.599	—	Cy Moreing
Stockton Tigers*	85	60	.586	3	Danny Shay
Fresno Raisin Growers	66	89	.426	27	W.W. Kelley
San Francisco Orphans/ Sacramento Senators#	53	91	.368	34½	Charles Irwin/Frank Bacon
Santa Cruz Sand Crabs@	62	36	.633	NA	Fred Swanton
San Jose Prune Pickers@	34	55	.382	NA	T.C. Barnett

#San Francisco (34-63) moved to Sacramento July 19.
@Santa Cruz and San Jose disbanded in mid-season.
Oakland was awarded the pennant when Stockton refused to take part in a playoff.

BA: Monte Pfyl, Stockton, .358
Wins: Oscar Jones, Santa Cruz/Fresno, 40

Pct: Oscar Jones, Santa Cruz/Fresno, .755, 40-13

1909 Interleague Post Season Play

World Series
Pittsburgh (National) 4 games, Detroit (American) 3

Dixie Championship
Chattanooga (South Atlantic) 3 games, Atlanta (Southern Association) 2

New York vs. Pennsylvania
Wilkes-Barre (New York State) 4 games, Lancaster (Tri-State) 1

Carolina Championship
Wilmington (Eastern Carolina) 4 games, Greensboro (Carolina Association) 2

1909 No-Hitters

Date	Pitcher	Team	League	Opponent	Score
4-15	Red Ames	New York	National	Brooklyn	0-3 (10)
4-16	Elmer Koestner	Los Angeles	Pacific Coast	San Francisco	4-0
4-24	Ike Butler	Tacoma	Northwestern	Vancouver	2-0
4-25	Burt Keeley	Vancouver	Northwestern	Tacoma	0-1
5-7	R.C. Walters	Greensboro	Carolina Assoc.	Anderson	5-1
5-10	Fred Toney	Winchester	Blue Grass	Lexington	1-0 (17)
5-10	Bob Harmon	Shreveport	Texas	Galveston	6-0
5-10	Rufus Gilbert	Peoria	Three-I	Dubuque	2-0
5-13	Jim Wiggs	Oakland	Pacific Coast	San Francisco	3-0
5-13	Andrew McCarthy	Anderson	Carolina Assoc.	Greenville	3-2
5-13	Prince Gaskill	Chattanooga	South Atlantic	Jacksonville	5-0
5-16	Henry Yount	Dubuque	Three-I	Decatur	1-2
5-18	Walter Justus	Lancaster	Ohio State	Marion	7-0
5-19	Mellie Wolfgang	Albany	New York State	Syracuse	0-1
5-22	Hippo Vaughn	Macon	South Atlantic	Columbia	5-0
5-27	T. Cummings	Duluth	Minnesota-Wisc.	Wausau	5-0
5-27	Ed Kinsella	Portland	Northwestern	Spokane	3-0
5-28	Pat Paige	Charleston	South Atlantic	Macon	2-0
6-1	Art Fennell	Ottumwa	Central Assoc.	Burlington	1-0
6-3	Harry Hammond	Fort Wayne	Central	Grand Rapids	0-1
6-4	Jack Taylor	Grand Rapids	Central	Fort Wayne	4-0
6-4	Ivan Loos	Danville	Virginia	Roanoke	8-0 (P)
6-5	Edward Asher	Terre Haute	Central	Wheeling	2-0
6-6	Harry Steiger	Springfield	Three-I	Davenport	4-0
6-8	Charles Deardorff	Jonesboro	Arkansas State	Ft. Smith	10-0
6-9	Cook	Helena	Arkansas State	Texarkana	1-0
6-9	J.T. Touchstone	Greenville	Carolina Assoc.	Charlotte	1-0
6-11	Phil Stremmel	Superior	Minnesota-Wisc.	Eau Claire	2-0
6-15	Del Howard	Wilmington	Eastern Carolina	Goldsboro	2-0
6-18	Ray Boyd	Burlington	Central Assoc.	Jacksonville	3-0
6-19	Tony Freeman	Mansfield	Ohio State	Portsmouth	2-0
6-21	J.C. Ashley	Enid	Western Assoc.	Guthrie	4-0
6-26	Willie Mitchell	San Antonio	Texas	Shreveport	4-0
6-29	George Daly	Springfield	Three-I	Rock Island	2-0
6-29	Stine	Lawrence	New England	Lowell	7-0
7-2	Del Howard	Wilmington	Eastern Carolina	Fayetteville	2-1
7-5	Frank Browning	San Francisco	Pacific Coast	Sacramento	3-0
7-5	Joe Hagerman	Grand Rapids	Central	South Bend	1-0
7-5	Ed Erickson	Vancouver	Northwestern	Tacoma	3-0
7-5	L.R. Wagner	Columbia	South Atlantic	Knoxville	1-0
7-7	T.Z. Abercombie	Spartanburg	Carolina Assoc.	Anderson	5-2
7-9	George Zackert	Waterloo	Central Assoc.	Kewanee	4-0
7-12	Edward Lafitte	Providence	Eastern	Jersey City	0-2
7-15	Frank Schneiberg	Paris	Blue Grass	Lexington	4-0
7-19	Al Demaree	Savannah	South Atlantic	Knoxville	4-0
7-21	John Barthold	Reading	Tri-State	Altoona	2-0
7-22	Alexander Carson	Portland	Pacific Coast	Los Angeles	1-0 (10)
7-22	Grover Alexander	Galesburg	Illinois-Missouri	Canton	2-0
7-25	Roberts	Uniontown	Penn.-W. Virginia	Fairmont	5-3 (7)
7-28	Jack Lively	Montgomery	Southern Assoc.	Little Rock	3-0
7-28	Rube Peters	Dallas	Texas	Waco	2-0
7-30	Bill Luyster	Fayetteville	Eastern Carolina	Raleigh	1-0
8-1	Phil Chenault	Portland	Northwestern	Vancouver	4-0
8-2	Len Schroeder	Eau Claire	Minnesota-Wis.	Duluth	
8-3	Harry Otis	Goldsboro	Eastern Carolina	Wilson	2-0
8-7	Edward Collins	Utica	New York State	Albany	1-0
8-10	Charles Jaeger	Cedar Rapids	Three-I	Davenport	3-1
8-10	George Bauswine	Charlotte	Carolina Assoc.	Greenville	3-0
8-12	Bill Prough	Keokuk	Central Assoc.	Waterloo	1-0
8-12	Bill Phillips	Wheeling	Central	South Bend	1-0
8-13	Ed Zmich	Marion	Ohio State	Lancaster	4-0
8-14	Earl Hamilton	Portsmouth	Virginia	Danville	4-0
8-15	Ted Breitenstein	New Orleans	Southern Assoc.	Montgomery	2-0
8-18	Charles Fanning	Canton	Illinois-Missouri	Macomb	0-2
8-19	Hayes	Charlotte	Carolina Assoc.	Winston-Salem	6-0
8-21	Rube Kisinger	Buffalo	Eastern	Rochester	5-0
8-23	Ashton	Green Bay	Wisconsin-Illinois	Racine	6-0
8-29	Robert Holmes	Waco	Texas	Houston	4-1
8-30	Dugger	Paris	Blue Grass	Shelbyville	7-0
8-31	Charlie Case	Nashville	Southern Assoc.	New Orleans	1-0
8-31	L.R. Wagner	Augusta	South Atlantic	Columbia	6-0
9-1	Ginger Clark	Chattanooga	South Atlantic	Knoxville	3-0
9-1	Frank Allen	Mobile	Southern Assoc.	Montgomery	1-0 (7)
9-3	Rufus Nolley	Wheeling	Central	Evansville	1-0
9-4	Buck Friel	Haverhill	New England	Fall River	7-0 (7)
9-6	Bill Schardt	La Crosse	Minnesota-Wisc.	Winona	3-1
9-7	Fred Bramble	Keokuk	Central Assoc.	Jacksonville	1-0 (7)
9-10	Weisenberger	Beardstown	Illinois-Missouri	Monmouth	2-0
9-10	Hagen	Portland	Northwestern	Vancouver	12-0
9-11	Robert Keefe	Montreal	Eastern	Buffalo	3-0
9-19	Marks	Galesburg	Illinois-Missouri	Monmouth	
9-27	Frank Lange	Des Moines	Western	Lincoln	1-0
	Edward Smith	South Bend	Central		

Number in parentheses indicates innings if other than nine; "P" indicates perfect game.

THIS DATE IN MINOR LEAGUE HISTORY

January 2, 1909, Edward Strickland, 26, pitcher with Greenville of the Carolina Association, shot and killed his sweetheart, Ida Williamson, and then himself.

May 28, 1909, At Ft. Worth, Texas League, Overton of Dallas made a "home run" on a strikeout. He swung and missed at the third strike, and the ball hit the plate, bounding up on top of the grandstand and lodging in the gutter while Overton circled the bases.

May 31, 1909, Decatur and Bloomington played a 26-inning game in the Three-I League, the longest contest on record in Organized Ball to date. Otto Burns of Decatur hurled 25 consecutive scoreless innings after yielding a run in the first frame, winning the 2-1 duel with Ed Clarke, who also went the route. Decatur made 11 hits and 3 errors; Bloomington had 13 hits and 2 errors.

July 7, 1909, Grand Rapids and Zanesville played seven innings in the Central League at Grand Rapids after sundown with the assistance of artificial light.

July 8, 1909, Tom Tennant, San Francisco, Pacific Coast League, handled 35 fielding chances at first base in an extra-inning game with Oakland.

July 22, 1909, Grover Alexander, beginning his Organized Ball career with a tail-end club, Galesburg of the Illinois-Missouri League, pitched a no-hitter, winning 2-0.

July 25, 1909, Grover Alexander, Galesburg, Illinois-Missouri League, won an 18 inning 1-0 game, striking out 19 Macomb batters and issuing no bases on balls.

July 27, 1909, James Phelps of Raymill died from a snake bite received during an independent league game at Monroe, Louisiana.

July 27, 1909, Lyons, Kansas State League, defeated McPherson 2-1 in 21 innings. Although umpire Cleary stopped the game in the 18th frame to borrow a chew of tobacco, the contest was played in two hours and 50 minutes.

August 21, 1909, Willie Mitchell of San Antonio fanned 20 Galveston batters in a nine-inning game to set an all-time Texas League record. Southpaw Mitchell, only 20, accomplished the feat in his first pro season, having graduated in June from Memphis A&M College. In his next outing, August 23, Mitchell fanned 12 Galveston batters for total of 32 over two consecutive games.

August 27, 1909, Ironman Joe McGinnity pitched a doubleheader for Newark, Eastern League, against Buffalo and won both games.

September 15, 1909, Charles Pinkney, Dayton, Central League died from a skull fracture as a result of being beaned the previous day.

November 9, 1909, The National Association admitted the independent California League to Organized Ball membership. It would change its name to the California State League.

November 15, 1909, An announcement was made in Baltimore that the Orioles' Eastern League franchise had been sold by Edward Hanlon to Jack Dunn, former manager of the Baltimore team. Wilbert Robinson, former Oriole catcher, was named as one of the club's new directors.

November 26, 1909, Edward Barrow, former manager of Toronto, signed to manage Montreal of the Eastern League, succeeding James Casey.

1910

American League
President: Byron Bancroft Johnson

Standings	W	L	Pct.	GB	Attend.	Manager
Philadelphia Athletics	102	48	.680	—	588,905	Connie Mack
New York Highlanders	88	63	.583	14½	355,857	George Stallings/Hal Chase
Detroit Tigers	86	68	.558	18	391,288	Hugh Jennings
Boston Red Sox	81	72	.529	22½	584,619	Patsy Donovan
Cleveland Naps	71	81	.467	32	293,456	Deacon McGuire
Chicago White Sox	68	85	.444	35½	552,084	Hugh Duffy
Washington Senators	66	85	.437	36½	254,591	Jimmy McAleer
St. Louis Browns	47	107	.305	57	249,889	Jack O'Connor

BA: Ty Cobb, Detroit, .385
Runs: Ty Cobb, Detroit, 106
Hits: Napoleon Lajoie, Cleveland, 227
RBIs: Sam Crawford, Detroit, 120
HRs: Jake Stahl, Boston, 10

Wins: Jack Coombs, Philadelphia, 31
SOs: Walter Johnson, Washington, 313
ERA: Ed Walsh, Chicago, 1.27
Pct: Charles "Chief" Bender, Philadelphia, .821, 23-5

National League
President: Thomas J. Lynch

Standings	W	L	Pct.	GB	Attend.	Manager
Chicago Cubs	104	50	.675	—	526,152	Frank Chance
New York Giants	91	63	.591	13	511,785	John McGraw
Pittsburgh Pirates	86	67	.562	17½	436,586	Fred Clarke
Philadelphia Phillies	78	75	.510	25½	296,597	Red Dooin
Cincinnati Reds	75	79	.487	29	380,622	Clark Griffith
Brooklyn Superbas	64	90	.416	40	279,321	Bill Dahlen
St. Louis Cardinals	63	90	.412	40½	355,668	Roger Bresnahan
Boston Rustlers	53	100	.346	50½	149,027	Frederick Lake

BA: Sherry Magee, Philadelphia, .331
Runs: Sherry Magee, Philadelphia, 110
Hits: Honus Wagner, Pittsburgh, 178
Bobby Byrne, Pittsburgh, 178
RBIs: Sherry Magee, Philadelphia, 123

HRs: Wildfire Schulte, Chicago, 10
Fred Beck, Boston, 10
Wins: Christy Mathewson, New York, 27
SOs: Earl Moore, Philadelphia, 185
ERA: George McQuillan, Philadelphia, 1.60
Pct: King Cole, Chicago, .833, 20-4

A American Association
President: Thomas M. Chivington

Standings	W	L	Pct.	GB	Attend.	Manager
Minneapolis Millers	107	61	.637	—	195,058	Joe Cantillon
Toledo Mud Hens	91	75	.548	15	165,935	James Holmes/ Harry Hinchman
Columbus Senators	88	77	.533	17½	156,333	William Friel
St. Paul Apostles	88	80	.524	19	165,619	Mike Kelley
Kansas City Blues	85	81	.512	21	194,233	Danny Shay
Milwaukee Brewers	76	91	.455	30½	137,687	John McCloskey
Indianapolis Indians	69	96	.418	36½	184,252	Charles Carr
Louisville Colonels	60	103	.368	44½	111,869	Henry Peitz/Del Howard

BA: Gavvy Cravath, Minneapolis, .326
Runs: Dave Altizer, Minneapolis, 111
Hits: Gavvy Cravath, Minneapolis, 200
HRs: Gavvy Cravath, Minneapolis, 14

Wins: Tom Hughes, Minneapolis, 31
SOs: Tom Hughes, Minneapolis, 222
Pct: Tom Hughes, Minneapolis, .721, 31-12

A Eastern League
President: Patrick T. Powers

Standings	W	L	Pct.	GB	Manager
Rochester Bronchos	92	61	.601	—	John Ganzel
Newark Indians	88	66	.571	4½	Joe McGinnity
Baltimore Orioles	83	70	.542	9	Jack Dunn
Toronto Maple Leafs	80	72	.526	11½	Joseph Kelley
Montreal Royals	71	80	.470	20	Edward Barrow
Buffalo Bisons	69	81	.460	21½	William Smith
Jersey City Skeeters	66	88	.432	26½	John Ryan
Providence Grays	61	92	.399	31	James Collins

Attendance: Buffalo, 212,577.

BA: Will Osborn, Rochester, .302
Runs: Dan Moeller, Jersey City/Rochester, 96
Hits: Will Osborn, Rochester, 176
HRs: Al Shaw, Toronto, 11

Wins: Joe McGinnity, Newark, 30
SOs: Lefty Russell, Baltimore, 219
Pct: Buck Donnelly, Baltimore, .733, 11-4

A Pacific Coast League
President: Thomas F. Graham

Standings	W	L	Pct.	GB	Manager
Portland Beavers	114	87	.567	—	Walter McCredie
Oakland Oaks	122	98	.555	1½	Harry Wolverton
San Francisco Seals	114	106	.518	9½	Daniel Long
Vernon Tigers	113	107	.514	10½	W.L. "Happy" Hogan
Los Angeles Angels	101	121	.455	23½	Frank "Cap" Dillon
Sacramento Sacts	83	128	.393	36	Charles Graham

BA: Hunky Shaw, San Francisco, .281
Runs: Walter Carlisle, Vernon, 134
Hits: Tom Tennant, San Francisco, 231
HRs: Ping Bodie, San Francisco, 30

Sac: Clyde "Buzzy" Wares, Oakland, 74
Wins: Cack Henley, San Francisco, 34
SOs: Vean Gregg, Portland, 376
Pct: Everett Lively, Oakland, .674, 31-15

A Southern Association
President: William B. Kavanaugh

Standings	W	L	Pct.	GB	Manager
New Orleans Pelicans	87	53	.621	—	Charley Frank
Birmingham Barons	79	61	.564	8	Carleton Molesworth
Atlanta Crackers	75	63	.543	11	Otto Jordan
Chattanooga Lookouts	66	71	.482	19½	Johnny Dobbs
Nashville Volunteers	64	76	.457	23	Bill Bernhardt
Mobile Sea Gulls	63	75	.457	23	George Reed
Memphis Turtles	62	76	.449	24	Charles Babb
Montgomery Climbers	59	80	.424	27½	Ed Gremlinger

All-Star Team: 1B-William Schwartz, Nashville; **2B**-Otto Jordan, Atlanta; **3B**-Frank Manush, New Orleans; **SS**-Steve Yerkes, Chattanooga; **OF**-Jud Daley, Montgomery; Joe Jackson, New Orleans; Charles Messenger, Birmingham; **C**-Smith, Atlanta; Elliott, Birmingham; **P**-Harry Coveleski, Birmingham; Otto Hess, New Orleans; Frank Allen, Memphis; Thomas Fisher, Atlanta.

BA: Joe Jackson, New Orleans, .354
Runs: Joe Jackson, New Orleans, 82
Hits: Joe Jackson, New Orleans, 165

HRs: George Rohe, New Orleans, 4
Charles Messenger, Birmingham, 4
Jake Weimer, New Orleans, 4
Hank Butcher, New Orleans, 4
Wins: Otto Hess, New Orleans, 25
Pct: Frank Sparks, Chattanooga, .800, 8-2

A Western League
President: Norris O'Neill

Standings	W	L	Pct.	GB	Manager
Sioux City Packers	108	60	.643	—	Jay Towne
Denver Grizzlies	102	65	.611	6½	Jack Hendricks
Lincoln Railsplitters	95	71	.572	12	James Sullivan
Wichita Jobbers	89	78	.533	18½	Frank Isbell
Omaha Rourkes	84	82	.506	23	Pa Rourke
St. Joseph Drummers	76	91	.455	31½	Jack Holland
Des Moines Boosters	72	96	.429	36	Bill Dwyer
Topeka Jayhawks	42	125	.251	65½	Dick Cooley

BA: Art Fenlon, Sioux City, .365
Runs: Red Andreas, Sioux City, 137
Hits: Cy Neighbors, Sioux City, 206
HRs: John Thomas, Lincoln, 22

SBs: Cozy Dolan, Denver, 80
Wins: Charles Durham, Wichita, 24
SOs: James Freeman, Sioux City, 246
Pct: Marty O'Toole, Sioux City, .792, 19-5

B Central League
President: Dr. Frank R. Carson

Standings	W	L	Pct.	GB	Manager
South Bend Bronchos	88	50	.638	—	Edward Wheeler/Midge Craven
Fort Wayne Billikens	79	58	.577	8½	James Burke
Dayton Veterans	74	63	.540	13½	Charles "Punch" Knoll
Evansville River Rats	70	67	.511	17½	Angus Grant
Terre Haute Stags	63	74	.470	24½	George "Cuppy" Groeschow
Zanesville Potters	61	76	.445	26½	Roy Montgomery
Grand Rapids Raiders	60	77	.438	27½	Joe Raidy
Wheeling Stogies	52	82	.388	34	Bill Phillips

BA: Larry LeJeune, Evansville, .328
Runs: Larry LeJeune, Evansville, 81
Hits: Del Young, Fort Wayne, 166
HRs: Larry LeJeune, Evansville, 18

Wins: Buck Sterzer, Evansville, 28
SOs: Walter Justus, Dayton, 177
Pct: Dick Robertson, Fort Wayne, .800, 20-5

B Connecticut League
President: W.J. Tracy

Standings	W	L	Pct.	GB	Manager
Waterbury Finnegans	70	52	.574	—	Michael Finn
Bridgeport Orators	67	52	.563	1½	Eugene McCann
New Britain Perfectos	69	55	.556	2	William Hanna
New Haven Prairie Hens	67	55	.549	3	Bill Carrick
Hartford Senators	64	58	.525	6	Tom Connery
Springfield Ponies	58	68	.460	14	John Zeller
Northampton Meadowlarks	50	73	.407	20½	Bill Luby
Holyoke Papermakers	46	78	.371	25	Clarence "Pop" Foster

BA: Clarence "Pop" Foster, Holyoke, .342
Runs: Bill Rodgers, Waterbury, 79
Hits: Hi Ladd, Bridgeport, 158
HRs: Clarence "Pop" Foster, Holyoke, 15

Wins: John Waller, Bridgeport, 21
   Alex "Sandy" Bannister, Waterbury, 21
SOs: Bucky O'Brien, Hartford, 264
Pct: M. Parker, New Britain, .621, 18-11

B New England League
President: Tim H. Murnane

Standings	W	L	Pct.	GB	Manager
New Bedford Whalers	77	46	.634	—	Thomas Dowd
Lynn Shoemakers	68	52	.567	7½	Billy Hamilton
Worcester Busters	67	54	.554	9	Jesse Burkett
Lowell Tigers	65	56	.535	11	Fred Tenney
Fall River Indians	61	60	.504	15	John H. O'Brien
Lawrence Colts	53	70	.431	24	James Bannon
Haverhill Hustlers	47	73	.392	28½	Tom Fleming
Brockton Shoemakers	45	72	.385	29	Stephen Flanagan

BA: Jimmy Wallace, Lynn, .312
Runs: Billy Page, Worcester, 102
Hits: Billy Page, Worcester, 139
   Percy Rising, New Bedford, 139

HRs: William McCormick, New Bedford, 7
Wins: Pembroke Finlayson, Lawrence, 21
Pct: Ben Van Dyke, Worcester, .833, 20-4

B New York State League
President: John H. Farrell

Standings	W	L	Pct.	GB	Manager
Wilkes-Barre Barons	85	53	.616	—	Bill Clymer
Syracuse Stars	78	57	.577	5½	Edward Ashenbach
Elmira Colonials	76	57	.571	7½	Michael O'Neill
Scranton Miners	72	66	.529	13	Monte Cross
Albany Senators	70	65	.519	13½	William Clark
Utica Utes	69	69	.500	16	Charles Dooley
Troy Trojans	48	85	.361	34½	James Kennedy
Binghamton Bingoes	44	90	.328	39	John Warner/J.H. Mooney/Harry Lumley

BA: Bill Kay, Albany, .363
Runs: Bill Zimmerman, Utica, 98
Hits: Jay Kirke, Sr., Scranton, 182
SBs: Bill Zimmerman, Utica, 105

Wins: George Chalmers, Scranton, 25
Pct: George Chalmers, Scranton, .806, 25-6
ShOs: Grover Alexander, Syracuse, 12

B Northwestern League
President: William H. Lucas

Standings	W	L	Pct.	GB	Manager
Spokane Indians	96	65	.596	—	Daniel Dugdale
Vancouver Beavers	89	71	.556	6½	Robert Brown
Tacoma Tigers	73	84	.465	21	Cliff Blankenship
Seattle Giants	61	99	.381	34½	Mike Lynch

BA: Lou Nordyke, Spokane, .290
Runs: Charles Swain, Vancouver, 88
Hits: Lou Nordyke, Spokane, 163
HRs: Charles Swain, Vancouver, 11

Wins: Jesse Baker, Spokane, 28
SOs: Jesse Baker, Spokane, 227
Pct: Jesse Baker, Spokane, .737, 28-10

B Three-I League
President: Albert R. Tearney

Standings	W	L	Pct.	GB	Manager
Springfield Senators	88	48	.647	—	Richard Smith
Rock Island Islanders	81	56	.591	7½	Jack Tighe
Peoria Distillers	75	64	.540	14½	Daniel Rowan
Waterloo Boosters	72	67	.518	17½	Frank Boyle
Bloomington Bloomers	60	76	.441	28	Joseph Keenan
Dubuque Dubs	60	79	.432	29½	Charles Buelow
Davenport Prodigals	59	80	.424	30½	Charles Shaffer
Danville Speakers	57	82	.410	32½	John McCarthy

BA: Paul Meloan, Springfield, .376
Runs: Charles Moore, Peoria, 82
Hits: George Manush, Rock Island, 159

Wins: Grover Lowdermilk, Springfield, 25
SOs: Teller Cavet, Rock Island, 248
Pct: Harry Steiger, Springfield, .923, 12-1

B Tri-State League
President: Charles F. Carpenter

Standings	W	L	Pct.	GB	Manager
Altoona Rams	72	38	.655	—	Henry Ramsey
Lancaster Red Roses	63	47	.573	9	Martin Hogan
Williamsport Millionaires	60	50	.545	12	William Coughlin
Trenton Tigers	58	52	.527	14	George Heckert
Johnstown Johnnies	55	57	.491	18	Bert Conn
Harrisburg Senators	52	59	.468	20½	Albert Selbach
Reading Pretzels	45	65	.409	27	Harry Barton
York White Roses	37	74	.333	35½	Louis Simmel/Jacob Weitzel/Curt Weigand

BA: Virgil Cannell, Williamsport, .355
Runs: Bob Coulson, Altoona, 81
Hits: Virgil Cannell, Williamsport, 129
   Jack Ness, Williamsport, 129

HRs: Scotty Ingerton, Altoona, 10
Wins: Elmer Steele, Altoona, 25
Pct: Elmer Steele, Altoona, .781, 25-7

C Minnesota-Wisconsin League
President: John H. Elliott

Standings	W	L	Pct.	GB	Manager
Eau Claire Commissioners	79	44	.642	—	Tom Schoonhover
Winona Pirates	69	54	.561	10	Joe Killian
Wausau Lumberjacks	69	55	.557	10½	Carl Bond
Superior Red Sox	64	57	.529	14	Arthur O'Dea/John "Kid" Taylor
La Crosse Outcasts	56	68	.451	23½	Joe Safford
Red Wing Manufacturers	51	67	.432	25½	Mike Walsh
Duluth White Sox	50	70	.417	27½	William "Darby" O'Brien
Rochester Roosters	46	69	.400	29	Jack Corrigan/Frank O'Leary

BA: Dave Callahan, Eau Claire, .365
Runs: Dave Callahan, Eau Claire, 92
Hits: Dave Callahan, Eau Claire, 168

HRs: Walter Altermott, Duluth, 12
Wins: Nicholas Lakoff, Winona, 23
Pct: Cy Dahlgren, Superior, .759, 22-7

C Ohio-Pennsylvania League
Presidents: Samuel L. Wright/George L. Moreland

Standings	W	L	Pct.	GB	Manager
Akron Champs	73	53	.579	—	William Schwartz/Lee Fohl
Canton Deubers	72	54	.571	1	Van Patterson/Ferdinand Drumm
East Liverpool Potters	63	61	.508	9	Guy Sample/Henry Lattimore
McKeesport Tubers	64	62	.508	9	Duke Servatius/Edward Connors
Mansfield Reformers	60	66	.476	13	George Fox
New Castle Nocks	57	67	.460	15	Frank Blair/James Barton
Youngstown Steelmen	55	67	.451	16	Frank Eustace
Erie Sailors	55	69	.444	17	Matthew Broderick

BA: Frank Warrender, East Liverpool, .341
Runs: Charles Conway, Youngstown, 82
Hits: Fred Corbin, Akron, 150
HRs: Duke Servatius, McKeesport, 16

Wins: Irvin "Kaiser" Wilhelm, Canton, 23
SOs: Irvin "Kaiser" Wilhelm, Canton, 284
Pct: Irvin "Kaiser" Wilhelm, Canton, .767, 23-7

C South Atlantic League
President: W.R. Joyner

Standings	W	L	Pct.	GB	Manager
Columbus Foxes	70	49	.588	—	James Fox
Macon Peaches	68	50	.576	1½	Perry Lipe
Jacksonville Jays	60	58	.508	9½	Dominick Mullaney/Joe Burke/ Kohley Miller
Savannah Indians	61	59	.508	9½	George Magoon
Augusta Tourists	51	68	.429	19	Frank Norcum
Columbia Gamecocks	46	72	.390	23½	William Breitenstein/Frederick Cavender

BA: Juan Viola, Augusta, .305
Runs: Jesse Becker, Columbus, 63
Hits: Jack Lee, Macon, 128

Wins: Sam Weems, Macon, 25
Pct: Rufus Nolley, Shreveport, .864, 19-3

C Texas League
President: Wilbur P. Allen

Standings	W	L	Pct.	GB	Manager
Dallas Giants	82	58	.586	—	Curley Maloney
Houston Buffaloes	82	58	.586	—	Hunter Hill
Ft. Worth Panthers	76	62	.551	5	Walter Morris
San Antonio Bronchoes	74	62	.544	6	George Leidy
Shreveport Pirates	75	66	.532	7½	Dale Gear
Galveston Sand Crabs	64	75	.460	17½	Frank Donnelly
Oklahoma City Mets	63	74	.460	17½	Jay Andrews/Red Downey
Waco Navigators	38	99	.277	42½	Brooks Gordon

BA: Hank Gowdy, Dallas, .312
Runs: Otto McIver, San Antonio, 87
Hits: Hub Northen, Houston, 160

HRs: Hank Gowdy, Dallas, 11
   Harry Storch, Dallas, 11
   George Stinson, San Antonio, 11
Wins: Sanford Burk, Ft. Worth, 25
SOs: Harry Ables, San Antonio, 325
Pct: John Eubanks, Houston, .714, 10-4

C Virginia League
President: Jacob Wells

Standings	W	L	Pct.	GB	Manager
Danville Red Sox	69	45	.605	—	Steve Griffin
Roanoke Tigers	68	52	.567	4	Frank Shaughnessy
Norfolk Tars	58	56	.513	11	Win Clark
Lynchburg Shoemakers	57	60	.487	13½	Walter Smith
Richmond Colts	49	67	.422	21	John Lawler
Portsmouth Truckers/ Petersburg Goobers#	47	68	.409	22½	Robert Stafford/John J. Grim

#Portsmouth (23-31) moved to Petersburg July 5.

BA: Joe Holland, Roanoke, .291
Runs: Sam Powell, Roanoke, 69
Hits: Joe Holland, Roanoke, 133
RBIs: Joe Holland, Roanoke, 73

HRs: Sam Powell, Roanoke, 3
   Joe Holland, Roanoke, 3
   Clarence "Red" Munson, Norfolk, 3
Wins: Harvey Bussey, Danville, 23
SOs: Dutch Revelle, Richmond, 198
Pct: Walter Doane, Roanoke, .923, 12-1

C Western Association
Presidents: Dr. D.M. Shiveley/J.H. Shaw

Standings	W	L	Pct.	GB	Manager
Joplin Miners	90	34	.726	—	Elmer Meredith
Enid Railroaders	64	53	.547	22½	R.E. "Snapper" Kennedy
Sapulpa Oilers	65	61	.516	26	Larry Millton
Guthrie Senators	47	73	.392	41	Howard Price
El Reno Packers@	65	43	.602	NA	Arthur Riggs
Bartlesville Boosters@	51	51	.500	NA	Frank Barbour/Jake Beckley
Muskogee Navigators#	36	63	.364	NA	Peck Harrington & Ed Nichols
Tulsa Oilers#	28	68	.292	NA	Gus Weyhing/Con Harlow

Attendance: Tulsa, 31,200.

#Muskogee and Tulsa disbanded July 22.
@El Reno and Bartlesville disbanded July 31.
The season ended August 16.

BA: R.E. "Snapper" Kennedy, Enid, .326
Runs: Harry Ellis, Joplin, 104
Hits: H.E. Goodrich, Sapulpa, 139
HRs: H.E. Goodrich, Sapulpa, 11
Wins: Mark Hall, Joplin, 21
   Ralph Bell, Joplin, 21
SOs: Mark Hall, Joplin, 241
Pct: Howard Gregory, Joplin, .857, 18-3

C Wisconsin-Illinois League
President: Charles F. Moll

Standings	W	L	Pct.	GB	Manager
Appleton Papermakers	74	45	.622	—	Edward Lewee
Rockford Reds	72	50	.590	3½	George Bubsir
Fond du Lac Giants	66	55	.546	9	Thomas O'Hara
Madison Senators	62	59	.511	13	Howard Cassibone
Green Bay Bays	59	61	.492	15½	John Pickett
Racine Malted Milks	59	62	.489	16	William Armstrong
Oshkosh Indians	50	72	.410	25½	Edward Burwell
Aurora Islanders	43	81	.347	33½	A.L. "Snapper" Kennedy/Edward Jacobson

BA: Jim McAuley, Appleton, .344
Hits: Jim McAuley, Appleton, 153
Wins: Mike Murphy, Appleton, 32
Pct: Mike Murphy, Appleton, .842, 32-6

D Blue Grass League
President: Dr. W.C. Ussery

Standings	W	L	Pct.	GB	Manager
Paris Bourbonites	80	47	.630	—	Edward McKernan
Lexington Colts	69	56	.552	10	Hogan Yancy
Winchester Hustlers	63	59	.516	14½	Newton "Daddy" Horn
Richmond Pioneers	63	60	.512	15	W.J. Maloney
Frankfort Statesmen	60	61	.496	17	Wallace Warren/Danny Harrell
Shelbyville/					
Maysville Rivermen#	37	89	.294	42½	Anton Kuhn/McDaniels

#Shelbyville (34-65) moved to Maysville August 24.

All-Star Team: 1B-J.G. Barrett, Paris; 2B-Edward McKernan, Paris; 3B-Goosetree, Winchester; SS-Jim Viox, Lexington; OF-J.T. Whittaker, Richmond; Kaiser, Paris; Hogan Yancy, Lexington; C-Leo Angemeier, Frankfort; George Keifel, Lexington; P-Fred Toney, Winchester; Milton McCormick, Paris; Cornell, Frankfort; Mark Allison, Richmond; John Kline, Lexington.

BA: Leo Angemeier, Frankfort, .321
Runs: B.F. Goodman, Paris, 74
Hits: Leo Angemeier, Frankfort, 147
   Wesley Callahan, Winchester, 147
Wins: Fred Toney, Winchester, 23
Pct: Milton McCormick, Paris, .850, 17-3

D California State League
President: Frank Herman

Standings	W	L	Pct.	GB	Manager
Stockton Millers	33	19	.635	—	Jimmy McCall
Fresno Tigers+	32	21	.604	1½	Bill McDonough
Oakland Invaders/					
Merced Fig Growers@	25	25	.500	7	Cy Mooreing
San Jose Prune Pickers	22	30	.423	11	Willis Browne
Sacramento Baby Senators#	16	23	.410	NA	Charles Doyle
San Francisco Baby Seals#	14	24	.368	NA	Tom Sheehan

#Sacramento and San Francisco disbanded May 31.
@Oakland (24-19) moved to Merced June 7.
+Fresno disbanded June 24, and the league ceased operations the same day.
The league was at Class B until June 6, when it became a Class D league.

BA: Bill McDonough, Fresno, .349
Wins: Oscar Jones, Fresno, 16
Pct: Gene Kratzberg, Stockton, .733, 11-4

D Carolina Association
President: Joseph H. Wearn

Standings	W	L	Pct.	GB	Manager
Greenville Spinners	63	40	.612	—	Thomas Stouch
Charlotte Hornets	56	50	.528	8½	Lave Cross
Anderson Electricians	56	54	.509	10½	Jim "King" Kelly
Winston-Salem Twins	51	57	.472	14½	James McKivett
Spartanburg Spartans	50	57	.467	15	Andy Roth/Bob Wood
Greensboro Champs	46	64	.418	20½	Carlton Beusse/Pug Hicks

BA: Jim "King" Kelly, Anderson, .325
Runs: Fred Wehrell, Anderson, 62
Hits: Jim "King" Kelly, Anderson, 132
RBIs: Jim "King" Kelly, Anderson, 66
HRs: Carlisle Smith, Anderson, 4
Wins: Jim Redfern, Spartanburg, 21
   O.W. Brazille, Charlotte, 21
SOs: George Bauswine, Charlotte, 192
Pct: Bert Gardin, Spartanburg, .750, 15-5

D Central Association
President: M.E. Justice

Standings	W	L	Pct.	GB	Attend.	Manager
Quincy Vets	88	50	.638	—	37,213	Bade Myers
Ottumwa Packers	80	57	.584	7½	37,000	Ned Egan
Hannibal Cannibals	77	60	.562	10½	28,547	Bill Prout/Bill Forney
Galesburg Pavers	69	67	.507	18	35,031	Bert Hough
Keokuk Indians	67	70	.493	20½	28,160	Frank Belt
Monmouth Browns	62	72	.459	24	25,000	Lew Drill
Burlington Pathfinders	56	81	.409	31½	25,043	Phil Geier
Kewanee Boilermakers	49	91	.350	40	26,307	Bill Connors/Ted Price

BA: Dan Kerwin, Hannibal, .331
Runs: Don Senno, Ottumwa, 84
Hits: Thomas Owens, Quincy, 148
HRs: Thomas Owens, Quincy, 9
   Bill Donahue, Quincy, 9
Wins: Charles Fanning, Galesburg, 30
SOs: Charles Fanning, Galesburg, 320
Pct: Charles Fanning, Galesburg, .714, 30-12

D Central California League
Presidents: D.C. Anderson/E.H. Raymond/E.T. Shortall

Standings	W	L	Pct.	GB	Manager
Richmond Merchants**	18	10	.643	—	
Healdsburg Grapevines/					
San Leandro#	17	11	.607	1	Pop Wieland
St. Helena/Fruitvale/					
Alameda Alerts@*	19	13	.594	1	Nathan Coombs
Santa Rosa Prune Pickers/					
Alameda Bracketts/					
Oakland Basches/Berkeley+	14	15	.483	4½	William H. Bailey/T. Walton
Petaluma Incubators/					
Elmhurst%	8	18	.308	9	Dennis Healey/W.D. Thomas
San Rafael/Hayward/					
Fruitvale&	7	17	.292	9	George Englefield/William Hull/C. Heyer
Vallejo$	4	2	.667	NA	Charles McCauley
Napa$	3	4	.429	NA	Earl H. Raymond

#Healdsburg moved to San Leandro April 24.
@St. Helena moved to Fruitvale April 24, then to Alameda July 10.
+Santa Rosa moved to Alameda May 5, then to Oakland July 10, then to Berkeley July 31.
$Vallejo and Napa disbanded May 29.
%Petaluma moved to Elmhurst June 5.
&San Rafael moved to Hayward June 12, then to Fruitvale July 10. The franchise disbanded October 9.
The league played a full schedule, but only the weekend games counted.

Playoff: Alameda Alerts 2 games, Richmond 0.

D Central Kansas League
President: J.H. Kreamer

Standings	W	L	Pct.	GB	Manager
Ellsworth Blues	53	28	.654	—	Dick Ford
Clay Center Cubs	48	33	.593	5	Lee Gramley
Abilene Reds	44	33	.571	7	Affie Wilson
Salina Trade Winners	44	34	.564	7½	Elmer Meredith
Concordia Travelers	43	38	.531	10	Harry Short
Manhattan Maroons	35	43	.449	16½	Jim Gardiner
Junction City Soldiers	34	48	.415	19½	Cecil Bankhead
Beloit/Chapman#	18	62	.225	34½	Ben Dimond

#Beloit (11-39) moved to Chapman July 20.

BA: A.B. Conley, Abilene, .348
Runs: Walter Wentz, Clay Center, 53
Hits: Muggsy Monroe, Abilene, 110
Wins: Paul Stokesberry, Clay Center, 19
Pct: Otis Peebles, Ellsworth, .769, 10-3

D Connecticut Association
President: Daniel Dunn

Standings	W	L	Pct.	GB	Manager
New London Whalers*	32	25	.561	—	Charles Humphrey
Middletown Jewels**	26	24	.520	2½	Tom Bannon/Walter Bellis
Norwich Bonbons/					
Meriden Doublins#	19	25	.413	6½	Dennis Hayes/John Stone/Patsy Flanagan
Willimantic Colts	19	28	.404	8	Daniel Dunn

#Norwich (19-21) disbanded July 10; the team's remnants moved to Meriden July 15, first home game July 19; the team disbanded July 24.
The season officially ended August 4.

BA: O'Donnell, Willimantic, .323
Runs: Dunlap, Middletown, 38
   J. Sullivan, Willimantic, 38
Hits: Jim Nealon, New London, 83
HRs: Dunlap, Middletown, 4
SBs: Harris, Middletown, 44
Wins: H. Ferris, Middletown, 17
   Fred Rieger, New London, 17
Pct: Kid Smith, Norwich/Willimantic, .682, 15-7

D Cotton States League
President: A.C. Crowder

Standings	W	L	Pct.	GB	Manager
Greenwood Chauffeurs......	71	36	.664	—	Woody Thornton
Jackson Tigers	71	37	.658	½	William Nance
Hattiesburg Timberjacks.....	50	60	.455	22½	Link Stickney
Yazoo City ZuZus	44	62	.415	26½	Walter Hickey
Vicksburg Hill Billies.........	46	65	.414	27	Bruce Hayes/Otto Mills
Meridian White Ribbons	45	67	.402	28½	Bernie McCay

BA: Charles Bates, Jackson, .340
Runs: Bert Graham, Jackson, 91
Hits: Bert Graham, Jackson, 122
Wins: Robert Lee Vernuelle, Greenwood, 24
Pct: Bill Sorrells, Jackson, .742, 23-8

D Eastern Carolina League
President: Dr. Joel D. Whitaker

Standings	W	L	Pct.	GB	Manager
Fayetteville Highlanders*...	47	37	.560	—	Charles Clancy
Wilson Tobacconists..........	44	39	.530	2½	Charles McGeehan
Wilmington Sailors............	42	43	.494	5½	Bert Kite/L.T. Mills
Rocky Mount Railroaders**..	43	45	.489	6	M.J. Phelan/James Connors
Goldsboro Giants.............	39	44	.470	7½	William "King" Kelley
Raleigh Red Birds.............	38	45	.458	8½	Richard Crozier

Playoff: Fayetteville 4 games, Rocky Mount 1, one tie.

All-Star Team: 1B-L.T. Mills, Wilmington; **2B**-B.A. Castenmeyer, Rocky Mount; **3B**-Jim Gillespie, Rocky Mount; **SS**-W. Dubbs, Wilmington; **OF**-T.L. Sharpe, Goldsboro; Pete Clemens, Raleigh; V. Tyderman, Wilmington; **C**-Bert Kite, Wilmington; J.A. Westlake, Wilson; **Util**-Walter Keating, Raleigh; **P**-Harvey Brooks, Wilmington; Del Howard, Wilmington; Bunn Hearn, Wilson; Erskine Mayer, Fayetteville; Bill Luyster, Fayetteville.

BA: Curly Brown, Goldsboro, .294
Runs: J.T. Mullins, Fayetteville, 40
Hits: Pete Clemens, Raleigh, 74
Wins: Bunn Hearn, Wilson, 16
Pct: Erskine Mayer, Fayetteville, .882, 15-2

D Eastern Kansas League
Presidents: Bert E. Black/Irwin R. Curry

Standings	W	L	Pct.	GB	Manager
Sabetha....................	53	28	.653	—	R.J. "Nick" Kahl
Seneca	46	39	.541	9	
Hiawatha Boosters	44	44	.500	12½	Pepper Williford
Marysville@	38	39	.494	13	William Davidson
Horton@	35	38	.479	14	Papa Church
Holton/Blue Rapids#	26	54	.325	26½	Ted McGrew

#Holton (15-31) moved to Blue Rapids August 25.
@Marysville and Horton disbanded September 1.

BA: R.J. "Nick" Kahl, Sabetha, .322
Hits: Bill Barackman, Sabetha, 74

D Illinois-Missouri League
President: A.E. Blaine

Standings	W	L	Pct.	GB	Manager
Pekin Celestials............	66	47	.584	—	William Hickey/Bill Lethridge
Clinton Champs.............	58	57	.504	9	Monte McFarland/C. Suttles/Charles Cline
Canton Chinks	55	62	.470	13	Elmer Smith/M. McDonald
Lincoln Abes................	43	71	.377	23½	James Novacek/Bill Salliard
Macomb Potters@	50	43	.538	NA	Stewart
Beardstown/Jacksonville Jacks#	44	36	.550	NA	Jack Corbett/Clarence "Pants" Rowland

#Beardstown (38-26) moved to Jacksonville July 21; Jacksonville disbanded August 17.
@Macomb disbanded August 17.

BA: Cy Forsythe, Pekin, .380
Runs: Will Lindberg, Clinton, 61
Hits: Will Lindberg, Clinton, 138
HRs: Al Dean, Pekin/Clinton, 5
Wins: John Jenkins, Pekin, 27
SOs: John Jenkins, Pekin, 242
Pct: John Jenkins, Pekin, .771, 27-8

D Indiana-Michigan League
President: Robert Proctor

Standings	W	L	Pct.	GB	Manager
Berrien Springs Grays	15	4	.789	—	G.O. "Fatty" McComber
Elkhart Blue Sox..............	10	8	.556	4½	Charles Karnell
Niles Blues...................	8	10	.444	6½	Fred "Bunny" Marshall
Dowagiac.....................	7	11	.389	7½	John Shottz
Gary Sand Fleas#.............	2	5	.286	NA	C.R. Woods/F.E. copeland
Ligonier@....................	2	6	.250	NA	Bert Inks

#Gary disbanded June 19.
@Ligonier disbanded June 30.
The league, which played Sunday games only, disbanded August 21.

D Kansas State League
President: P.H. Hostutler

Standings	W	L	Pct.	GB	Manager
Hutchinson Salt Packers	70	39	.642	—	Bill Zink
McPherson Merry Macks ...	58	49	.542	11	D. Conklin/F.J. Synek
Lyons Lions	57	53	.518	13½	Cecil Bankhead/Joe Riggert/Buck Ebright/John Jones
Newton Railroaders............	56	54	.509	14½	Mel Backus
Great Bend Millers.............	54	55	.495	16	Charles Lyons
Wellington Dukes..............	48	56	.461	19½	C. Pinkerton/Spencer Abbott/Harry Vitter/Lewis Armstrong
Larned Wheat Kings...........	46	56	.451	20½	Buck Weaver/Harry McLean
Arkansas City Grays...........	40	67	.374	29	L. Evans/Dennis McGuire/Doc Baker

BA: Joe Riggert, Lyons, .362
Runs: Charles Weisner, Lyons, 132
Hits: Bill Zink, Hutchinson, 141
HRs: Joe Riggert, Lyons, 13
Wins: E.J. Smith, Hutchinson, 18
Walt Sizemore, Lyons, 18
SOs: Rolla Maple, Great Bend, 205
Pct: E.J. Smith, Hutchinson, .750, 18-6

D Kitty League
President: Charles C. Gosnell

Standings	W	L	Pct.	GB	Manager
Vincennes Alices*..........	64	54	.542	—	John Nairn
Clarksville Volunteers......	55	60	.478	7½	M.O. Bridges/William McAndrews
Paducah Indians..............	55	64	.462	9½	Louis Angemeier/Eddie Gilligan
Hopkinsville Hoppers........	50	68	.424	14	Dave Anderson/John Ray
McLeansboro Billikens#**.	40	18	.690	NA	Ollie Gfroerer
Harrisburg Miners#..........	29	29	.500	NA	

#McLeansboro and Harrisburg were added for the second half July 24.

Playoffs: Cancelled; Vincennes and McLeansboro were declared co-champions.

BA: John Nairn, Vincennes, .285
Runs: Arista DeHaven, Vincennes, 54
Hits: Stewart Brown, Hopkinsville, 99
Jantzen, Vincennes, 99
HRs: Brown "Rebel" Keen, Clarksville, 4
Clarence "Big Boy" Kraft, McLeansboro, 4
Wins: Lyman Johnson, Vincennes, 20
SOs: Lyman Johnson, Vincennes, 182
Pct: Clarence "Big Boy" Kraft, McLeansboro, .867, 13-2

D MINK League
President: T.A. Wilson

Standings	W	L	Pct.	GB	Manager
Falls City Colts	57	40	.588	—	Bill Annis
Clarinda Antelopes	56	42	.571	1½	Rudy Kling
Shenandoah Pin Rollers......	47	52	.475	11	E.C. Fishbaugh
Auburn Athletics...............	46	51	.474	11	
Maryville Comets	45	54	.455	13	Joe Wentz
Nebraska City Forresters	43	55	.439	14½	Bonwell

BA: Joe Wentz, Maryville, .304
Runs: Frank Hutchinson, Clarinda, 69
Hits: Ed Bright, Auburn, 111
Wins: Verne Hirsch, Auburn, 25
Pct: Lawrence Casey, Clarinda, .750, 12-4

D Nebraska State League
President: Henry A. Sievers

Standings	W	L	Pct.	GB	Attend.	Manager
Fremont Pathfinders	63	43	.594	—	16,966	L.D. "Dad" Bennett
Columbus Discoverers.......	59	48	.551	4½	14,110	Joe Dolan
Kearney Kapitalists.............	60	51	.541	5½	14,946	C.R. Murphy
Grand Island Collegians	60	52	.536	6	20,129	Buck Beltzer
Superior Brickmakers..........	56	54	.509	9	13,150	Dennis Bockewitz
Seward Statesmen	50	62	.446	16	10,251	John Fink
Red Cloud	47	62	.431	17½	10,126	B.F. Grant
Hastings Brickmakers...........	42	65	.398	21½	14,318	George Harms

BA: Fred Jarrott, Red Cloud, .326
Runs: Leo Cook, Hastings, 88
Hits: Fred Jarrott, Red Cloud, 126
HRs: Fresco Thompson, Fremont, 10
SBs: Archie Turpin, Fremont, 75
Wins: Winifred Noyes, Kearney, 24
SOs: Winifred Noyes, Kearney, 323
Pct: Frank Green, Kearney, .900, 9-1

D Northeast Arkansas League
Presidents: J.E. Doherty/J.R. Bertig

Standings	W	L	Pct.	GB	Manager
Caruthersville*.................	68	48	.586	—	A.L. "Dad" Ritter
Paragould Scouts**...........	65	46	.586	½	Howard Schaaf
Jonesboro Zebras..............	53	55	.491	11	Senter Rainey
Blytheville	38	75	.336	28½	J.K. Malone/Scoops Carey

Playoff: Caruthersville 2 games, Paragould 2; the series was called when the deciding game was broken up by a riot.

BA: Clyde Curtis, Jonesboro, .330
Runs: B.B. Bevill, Paragould, 68
Hits: Clyde Curtis, Jonesboro, 118

D Northern Association
President: C.A. Burton

Standings	W	L	Pct.	GB	Manager
Elgin Kittens+*................	37	20	.649	—	Mal Kittridge
Muscatine Pearl Finders**.	37	21	.638	½	Lou Walters
Kankakee Kays+...............	34	24	.586	3½	Danny Collins
Jacksonville Jacks.............	32	31	.508	8	Clarence "Pants" Rowland
Decatur Commodores	30	32	.484	9½	Del Williams/Charles O'Day

Joliet Jolly-ites/
Sterling Infants# .... 24 34 .414 13½ Hunky Hines
Freeport Pretzels@ .... 22 25 .468 NA   Forest Plass
Clinton Teddies@ .... 10 39 .204 NA   Ted Sullivan/John Marmen

#Joliet (21-18) moved to Sterling June 21.
@Freeport and Clinton disbanded June 28.
+Elgin and Kankakee disbanded July 11.
The league disbanded July 19.

BA: Phil Nadeau, Joliet/Sterling, .333   **Wins:** Pop Eyler, Muscatine, 11
Runs: Fritz Maisel, Elgin, 49   Metigne, Kankakee, 11
Hits: Harmony Van Dine, Jacksonville, 80   Archie Hickman, Joliet/Sterling, 11
HRs: John Hopkins, Elgin, 7   **Pct:** Metigne, Kankakee, .786, 11-3

D Northern State of Indiana League
President: C.A. Klunk

Standings	W	L	Pct.	GB	Manager
Wabash Rockeries	46	25	.648	—	Eddie Pferferle
Bluffton Babes....................	42	28	.600	3½	Daddy Orr
Lafayette Farmers...............	39	30	.565	6	Carl Cominger
Marion Boosters	32	37	.464	13	Mike Lawrence
Huntington Johnnies...........	23	41	.359	19½	Johnnie Strands
Logansport Whitecaps	24	45	.348	21	Nathanial Fleming/Fred Payne

Games played prior to July 1 were not counted. Bluffton and Marion joined the league July 2.

D Ohio State League
President: Robert W. Reid

Standings	W	L	Pct.	GB	Manager
Portsmouth Cobblers	86	52	.623	—	Pete Childs
Lima Cigarmakers	82	56	.594	4	Alfred Newnham
Marion Diggers..................	80	58	.580	6	Joseph Lewis
Newark Newks	58	80	.420	28	Bob Berryhill/Charles Riehl/Charles O'Day
Lancaster Lanks	55	82	.401	30½	Al McClintock/Guy Sample/Heinie Pietz
Chillicothe Infants	52	85	.380	33½	W. Cochran/Frank Grubb/Louis Kibler/ Zeke Wrigley

BA: F. O'Day, Portsmouth, .324   **HRs:** Frank Nesser, Lima, 6
Runs: Henry "Dick" Breen, Portsmouth, 88   **Wins:** Theodore Goulait, Marion, 24
Hits: Henry "Dick" Breen, Portsmouth, 151   **Pct:** Harry Lloyd, Lima, .769, 10-3

D San Joaquin Valley League
President: J. Newton Young

Standings	W	L	Pct.	GB	Manager
Bakersfield Drillers.............	21	10	.667	—	Brick Devereaux
Visalia Pirates	13	17	.433	7½	Newt Young
Tulare Merchants#.............	13	15	.464	NA	Smith
Coalinga Savages@	9	14	.391	NA	Eddie Householder

#Tulare disbanded August 8.
@Coalinga disbanded August 15.
The league officially disbanded September 12.

Wins: Willard Meikle, Bakersfield, 11
Pct: Willard Meikle, Bakersfield, .733, 11-4

D Southeastern League
President: J.H. O'Neill

Standings	W	L	Pct.	GB	Manager
Knoxville Appalachians	50	30	.625	—	Frank Moffett
Morristown Jobbers	46	37	.554	5½	E. Fisher/E. Sherrill
Johnson City Soldiers	45	39	.536	7	Nat Taylor/Ed Garner
Asheville Moonshiners	44	41	.519	8½	William "Dave" Gaston
Rome Romans	43	41	.512	9	Joe Patton/C. Milford/Walter Justus
Gadsden Steel Makers	21	61	.256	30	Paul Stevenson/J. Foreman/Baldorf

D Southern California Trolley League
President: James McCormick

Standings	W	L	Pct.	GB	Manager
Redondo Beach Sand Dabs...	9	2	.818	—	
Santa Ana Walnut Growers ..	8	3	.727	1	Ed Crolic
Long Beach Clothiers	4	5	.444	4	S.J. Abrams
Los Angeles McCormicks	2	7	.222	6	
Los Angeles Maiers#...........	1	3	.250	NA	
Pasadena Silk Sox#..............	0	4	.000	NA	Joe Judge/Frank Abbott

#Los Angeles Maiers and Pasadena disbanded May 3.
The league disbanded June 13.

D Southern Illinois League
President: C.C. Wright

Standings	W	L	Pct.	GB	Manager
McLeansboro Merchants	20	5	.800	—	Ollie Gfroerer
Eldorado...........................	14	12	.538	6½	
Herrin................................	8	11	.421	9	Pa Bradshaw

Mt. Vernon Merchants#........ | 8 | 11 | .421 | 9 | Ira Hastings
Harrisburg Merchants .... 6 | 17 | .261 | 13 |

#Mt. Vernon disbanded June 30.
The league folded July 11. Harrisburg and McLeansboro joined the Kitty League July 24.

D Southern Michigan League
President: Joseph S. Jackson

Standings	W	L	Pct.	GB	Manager
Kalamazoo Kazoos	87	52	.626	—	Charles Wagner
Lansing Senators...............	87	52	.626	—	John Morrissey
Adrian Yeggs	83	56	.597	4	Carl Vandergrift
Battle Creek Crickets..........	72	64	.529	13½	Billy Earle
Flint Vehics	69	71	.493	18½	Edward Herr
Bay City	59	81	.421	28½	Elbert Nugent/Leon Foy
Jackson Convicts	51	85	.375	34½	Bo Slear
Saginaw Wa-was	46	93	.331	41	William Smith/Frank Wessell

Playoff: Kalamazoo 4 games, Lansing 2.

BA: Jim Bowser, Flint, .342   **Wins:** B. Valliere, Kalamazoo, 23
Runs: Harry Ball, Adrian, 117   Homer Warner, Lansing, 23
Hits: Vic Saier, Lansing, 175   **SOs:** Verne Hughey, Kalamazoo, 193
HRs: Jim Bowser, Flint, 14   **Pct:** B. Valliere, Kalamazoo, .793, 23-6

D Southwest Texas League
President: B.S. Dickinson

Standings	W	L	Pct.	GB	Manager
Victoria Rose Buds*...........	72	45	.615	—	Jack Burke
Brownsville Brownies**......	68	47	.591	3	S.H. Bell/Leo Hellman/Kerr Price
Bay City Rice Eaters..........	59	56	.513	12	E. Haralson/John Blakeney/Louis Hamilton
Laredo Bermudas..............	54	61	.470	17	George Page/Tomlin
Beeville Orange Growers ...	52	64	.448	19½	Trapper Longley/J.C. Woessner
Corpus Christi Pelicans	42	74	.362	29½	Patrick Murphy/Billy Page

Playoffs: Brownsville 3 games, Victoria 2.

BA: Jack Burke, Victoria, .294   **Wins:** Larry Gilbert, Victoria, 18
Runs: L.A. Hamilton, Bay City, 75   **SOs:** Roy Morton, Brownsville, 173
Hits: Jack Burke, Victoria, 125   **Pct:** Roy Morton, Brownsville, .850, 17-3
SBs: J.P. Sheffield, Victoria, 94

D Virginia Valley League
Presidents: John A. Spinney/John C. Bond

Standings	W	L	Pct.	GB	Manager
Huntington	61	42	.592	—	Cy Young
Charleston Senators	62	53	.539	6	John Benny
Point Pleasant-Gallipolis	57	51	.527	6½	Joseph "Reddy" Mack
Ashland-Catlettsburg Twins ..	52	55	.486	11	Zeke Wilson
Parkersburg Parkers	49	64	.433	17	Louis Haidt/Frank Locke/Boyd Chambers
Montgomery Miners	47	63	.427	17½	Jimmy O'Connor

BA: Benny Kauff, Parkersburg, .336
SBs: Benny Kauff, Parkersburg, 36

D Washington State League
President: Walter R. McFarlane

Standings	W	L	Pct.	GB	Manager
Raymond Cougars	36	19	.655	—	Fred Dunbar
Chehalis Gophers...............	35	19	.618	½	Fielder Jones
Aberdeen Black Cats	24	29	.453	11	
Montesano Farmers	22	31	.415	13	
Hoquiam Loggers#	12	18	.400	NA	
Tacoma Cubs@	8	21	.276	NA	

#Hoquiam disbanded July 15.
@Tacoma disbanded July 18.

BA: Fielder Jones, Chehalis, .358   **Wins:** James Jachs, Raymond, 15
Runs: White McBride, Chehalis, 48   **SOs:** James Jachs, Raymond, 164
Hits: Frank Jansa, Chehalis, 70   **Pct:** Clarence Krause, Chehalis, .833, 5-1

D West Michigan League
President: Thomas Jones

Standings	W	L	Pct.	GB	Manager
Cadillac Chiefs	53	42	.558	—	Calvin Wenger
Traverse City Resorters	50	45	.526	3	Henry Collett/Pat Thacker
Muskegon Speed Boys	48	48	.500	5½	Arthur DeBaker
Holland Wooden Shoes	40	56	.417	13½	Charles Doyle/Emerson Dickerson/ Clyde McNutt

BA: Martin Kubiak, Cadillac, .378   **Wins:** Harry Gerloski, Cadillac, 18
Runs: Frank Wittowski, Cadillac, 85   **SOs:** LaRue Kirby, Traverse City, 150
Hits: Frank Wittowski, Cadillac, 114   **Pct:** Harry Gerloski, Cadillac, .720, 18-7
HRs: Martin Kubiak, Cadillac, 5

D West Virginia League
President: Thomas S. Haymond

Standings	W	L	Pct.	GB	Manager
Fairmont Champions	37	18	.673	—	Lewis Hunt
Mannington......................	33	21	.611	3½	George Pritchard
Grafton..............................	20	30	.400	14½	Dan Raily
Clarksburg Bees................	14	35	.286	20	Bull Smith

The league disbanded July 5 after Grafton disbanded.

D Western Canada League
President: C.J. Eckstorm

Standings	W	L	Pct.	GB	Manager
Calgary Bronchos*	68	29	.701	—	William Carney
Edmonton Eskimos**.........	61	32	.656	5	Deacon White
Moose Jaw Robin Hoods....	49	44	.527	17	M.O. Taylor
Winnipeg Maroons	53	50	.515	18	Frank Lohr/W. Rowland
Medicine Hat Mad Hatters/					
Saskatoon Berry Pickers#	45	47	.489	20½	William Hamilton
Lethbridge Miners	40	53	.430	26	Chester Cox
Brandon Angels	41	59	.410	28½	Charles Traeger
Regina Bone Pilers	26	69	.274	41	Roxey Walters/Thomas Letcher

#Medicine Hat (30-30) moved to Saskatoon July 23.

Playoffs: None. Calgary originally finished first in the second half; however, late decisions on protested games gave Edmonton the second half title. Calgary and Edmonton were declared co-champions.

BA: Hap Morse, Edmonton, .340
Runs: Theodore Smith, Calgary, 81
Hits: Jack Clynes, Calgary, 125
HRs: Theodore Smith, Calgary, 10

Wins: Dell Manning, Calgary, 26
SOs: Phil Lezie, Lethbridge, 191
Pct: Phil Dellers, Edmonton, .786, 22-6

1910 Interleague Post Season Play

World Series
Philadelphia (American) 4 games, Chicago (National) 1

Kansas vs. Nebraska
Sabetha (Eastern Kansas) 2 games, Falls City (MINK) 2

Northern Championship
Wausau (Minnesota-Wisconsin) 4 games, Appleton (Wisconsin-Illinois) 0

1910 No-Hitters

Date	Pitcher	Team	League	Opponent	Score
4-20	Addie Joss	Cleveland	American	Chicago	1-0
5-1	Bill Sorrells	Jackson	Cotton States	Vicksburg	10-1
5-2	Hank Chelette	Oklahoma City	Texas	Waco	7-0
5-5	Jeff Pfeffer	Fort Wayne	Central	Zanesville	0-1
5-12	Chief Bender	Philadelphia	American	Cleveland	4-0
5-12	Sam Beer	Fairmont	West Virginia	Clarksburg	10-0
5-13	Boothby	Elgin	Northern Assoc.	Freeport	7-2
5-19	John Jenkins	Pekin	Illinois-Missouri		8-0
5-20	Ed "Chief" Williams	Newton	Kansas State	Great Bend	2-0 (P)
5-27	H. Schantze	Akron	Ohio-Penn.	Mansfield	4-0
5-30	Wilson	Elgin	Northern Assoc.	Freeport	3-0
5-30	Tex Pruiett	New Bedford	New England	Fall River	1-0
6-4	John Sterling	Kalamazoo	Southern Michigan	Bay City	2-0
6-4	Harvey Brooks	Wilmington	Eastern Carolina	Raleigh	1-0
6-7	Linn Listen	Guthrie	Western Assoc.	El Reno	7-0
6-8	Harry Wormwood	Fall River	New England	Worcester	1-0 (11)
6-8	Ross Pennybaker	Lima	Ohio State	Newark	6-0
6-15	Fred Olmstead	Denver	Western	St. Joseph	10-0
6-18	Rube Robinson	Toledo	American Assoc.	Kansas City	8-0
6-20	George Kaiserling	Great Bend	Kansas State	McPherson	1-0 (10)
6-22	Schultz	Galesburg	Central Assoc.	Monmouth	2-1
6-22	Harvey Brooks	Wilmington	Eastern Carolina	Goldsboro	2-0
6-22	Lou Shakespeare	Muskogee	Western Assoc.	Guthrie	4-2
6-24	Dode Brindle	Adrian	Southern Michigan	Jackson	15-0
6-27	John Taff	Brownsville	Southwest Texas	Corpus Christi	1-0
6-28	Charles Gibson	Superior	Nebraska State	Fremont	3-0
6-28	Harry Miller	Clinton	Illinois-Missouri	Pekin	2-1
6-30	L.E. "Lefty" Webb	Goldsboro	Eastern Carolina	Wilmington	6-0
7-1	Joe Connolly	Zanesville	Central	Wheeling	4-0
7-4	John McCloskey	Wilkes-Barre	New York State	Scranton	4-2
7-4	Ed Zmich	Marion	Ohio State	Newark	5-2
7-4	Bill Luyster	Fayetteville	Eastern Carolina	Wilmington	5-0
7-6	Jim Wiggs	Montreal	Eastern	Rochester	3-0
7-8	Rube Robinson	El Reno	Western Assoc.	Guthrie	12-0
7-9	Bull Wagner	Winona	Minnesota-Wisc.	Wausau	2-0
7-12	Ivar Swanson	Hartford	Connecticut	Bridgeport	4-0
7-12	C.W. Brown	New Britain	Connecticut	Springfield	4-0
7-14	Joe Corbett	South Bend	Central	Zanesville	0-0 (11)
7-15	John Taff	Brownsville	Southwest Texas	Beeville	5-0
7-22	Eaton	Hattiesburg	Cotton States	Jackson	2-1
7-24	Gene Dale	Dallas	Texas	Houston	6-1
7-26	Maury Kent	Ottumwa	Central Assoc.	Kewanee	2-0
7-27	Louis Leroy	St. Paul	American Assoc.	Indianapolis	4-2
7-27	Eberly	Racine	Wisconsin-Illinois	Oshkosh	2-0
7-30	Harry Coveleski	Birmingham	Southern Assoc.	Chattanooga	7-3
8-2	Winifred Noyes	Kearney	Nebraska State	Red Cloud	6-0
8-5	James Ward	Hartford	Connecticut	New Haven	6-0
8-8	Penny Farthing	Lincoln	Western	Topeka	1-0 (P)
8-9	George Hinrickson	Galveston	Texas	Ft. Worth	2-0
8-9	Chet Carmichael	Buffalo	Eastern	Jersey City	1-0 (P)
8-12	Rankin Johnson	Dallas	Texas	Galveston	2-0
8-14	George Baumgardner	Huntington	Virginia Valley	Ashland-Catlettsburg	3-0
8-17	Clarence Mitchell	Des Moines	Western	Topeka	3-0
8-18	Urban (Red) Faber	Dubuque	Three-I	Davenport	3-0 (P)
8-19	Walter Doane	Roanoke	Virginia	Petersburg	5-0
8-19	H.C. Watson	Larned	Kansas State	Great Bend	3-0 (7)
8-20	Frank Miller	San Francisco	Pacific Coast	Vernon	3-1
8-20	Patrick Kelly	Lima	Ohio State	Marion	4-1
8-21	John Waller	Bridgeport	Connecticut	Hartford	1-0
8-21	Elmer Moffitt	Grand Rapids	Central	Zanesville	6-0
8-21	Bill Lattimore	Ft. Worth	Texas	Oklahoma City	1-0
8-25	C.M. Wagner	Lancaster	Ohio State	Marion	0-2
8-27	Fred Wehrell	Anderson	Carolina Assoc.	Greensboro	3-0
8-29	Jack Killilay	Spokane	Northwestern	Vancouver	1-0
8-29	Bill McCorry	Lynn	New England	Brockton	6-2
8-29	Buck Stanley	Montgomery	Virginia Valley	Parkersburg	3-0
8-30	Tom Hughes	New York	American	Cleveland	0-5 (10)
8-30	Ray Schardt	Milwaukee	American Assoc.	Indianapolis	3-0
8-30	William Riley	Green Bay	Wisconsin-Illinois	Aurora	4-0
9-2	Vean Gregg	Portland	Pacific Coast	Los Angeles	2-0
9-3	Louis Tretter	Quincy	Central Assoc.	Keokuk	3-0
9-5	George McConnell	Rochester	Eastern	Toronto	5-0
9-6	Frank Nicholson	Eau Claire	Minnesota-Wisc.	Winona	9-0
9-6	Lyman Johnson	Vincennes	Kitty	Clarksville	1-0
9-7	F.B. Archer	Davenport	Three-I	Danville	2-0
9-8	Ellis	Superior	Nebraska State	Hastings	2-0
9-11	Edward Asher	Dayton	Central	Zanesville	7-0
9-12	Dick Rudolph	Toronto	Eastern	Montreal	0-1 (10)
9-13	Frank Schneiberg	Paris	Blue Grass	Richmond	1-0
9-15	George Beck	McLeansboro	Kitty	Vincennes	1-0
9-18	Fay	Hopkinsville	Kitty	Paducah	1-0
9-18	Joe Willis	Springfield	Three-I	Bloomington	2-0
9-21	Johnny Baker	St. Joseph	Western	Topeka	11-0
10-17	Frank Arellanes	Sacramento	Pacific Coast	Vernon	0-2

Number in parentheses indicates innings if other than nine; "P" indicates perfect game.

THIS DATE IN MINOR LEAGUE HISTORY

March 15, 1910, Members of the Los Angeles and Vernon clubs were put to flight by a huge cloud of bees during a Pacific Coast League game.

April 23, 1910, Kansas City, American Association, released veteran first baseman Jake Beckley.

May 5, 1910, Only one hit was made in a Central Association game between Fort Wayne and Zanesville, the latter club winning 1-0. Joe Connolly of Zanesville gave one hit to decision Jeff Pfeffer, who hurled no-hit ball, only to lose on two errors in the first frame.

May 8, 1910, Rock Island, Three-I League, after having played two successive 12-inning tie games at Davenport, defeated Waterloo 2-1 in 17 frames.

May 8, 1910, Wilson of Canton, Ohio-Pennsylvania League, defeated East Liverpool 3-2 in a ten inning game, recording 19 strikeouts.

May 10, 1910, Casey Stengel made his debut as a professional with Kankakee of the Northern Association, appearing in the curtain-raiser. Stengel, then 19 and playing center field and batting cleanup, had one hit, a single, and stole a base as his club was nosed out 3-2 by Jacksonville. Casey remained with Kankakee until the league folded in July. He batted .267. Because the club owed him $67 in back salary (Stengel's pay was $150 a month), Stengel confiscated the team's uniforms. After Kankakee collapsed, Casey moved on to Maysville in the Blue Grass League. He batted only .223 the rest of that season, but bloomed with Aurora in the Wisconsin-Illinois League in 1911. His loop leading batting mark of .352 attracted Dodgers scout Larry Sutton, and Stengel was drafted for a mere $300.

May 27, 1910, After pitching and winning the first game of a Central League doubleheader from Wheeling, pitcher Joe Connolly of Zanesville played in the outfield in the second game and won it with a home run.

June 20, 1910, After 13 successive victories, Danville, Virginia League was stopped on a one-hitter by Harry Lloyd of Lynchburg.

June 21, 1910, Manager Pete Childs, relieving the Portsmouth pitcher with the bases full and none out, made one pitch, which was hit into a triple play, in an Ohio State League game at Marion, Ohio.

June 29, 1910, At Lancaster in the Ohio-Pennsylvania League, umpire Raphun created a sensation by pulling a revolver on a spectator. The umpire and a bystander were discussing a play that had occurred on the previous day when another person mixed himself up in the argument. He slapped the umpire, at which point the latter pulled a revolver and threatened to shoot. Policemen were called and Raphun was arrested, but later released until a hearing could be held. He went back to the grounds and umpired the game without further incident.

July 3, 1910, In the West Virginia League, Mannington and Clarksburg played to a 24-inning 1-1 tie, called on account of darkness. Cassel pitched for Clarksburg and Nicholson for Mannington.

July 5, 1910, After allowing Waco to score a run in the first frame, Harry Ables of San Antonio, Texas League, held the opposition scoreless for 22 more in a game called after 23 innings tied at one. Arthur Loudell went the route for Waco against Ables, giving up a run to San Antonio in the sixth frame. Ables yielded 16 hits, gave three walks and fanned 17, while Loudell was touched for 15 safeties, walked two and struck out 11.

July 10, 1910, Marty O'Toole, Sioux City, Western League, struck out 18 but lost 7-6 to Lincoln.

July 10, 1910, First baseman John Connors, South Bend, Central League, had no putouts, assists or errors in a nine inning game with Terre Haute.

July 11, 1910, The Kankakee club of the Northern Association, of which Casey Stengel was a member, folded, as did the league a short time later.

July 13, 1910, South Bend, Central League, defeated Zanesville 1-0 in 21 innings.

July 14, 1910, Joe Corbett, South Bend, Central League, pitched a no-hitter in game called with the score tied at zero after eleven innings to permit Zanesville to catch a train.

July 14, 1910, Jeff Holmquist of Mansfield, Ohio-Pennsylvania League, after working the last six innings of the first game of a doubleheader, pitched the entire distance of the second contest, defeating Canton 3-2 in 18 innings.

July 16, 1910, Muscatine, Northern Association, defeated Sterling 2-1 in 20 innings. The circuit collapsed three days later.

July 17, 1910, Henry Benz of Green Bay, Wisconsin-Illinois League, shut out Racine twice, 2-0 and 2-0, allowing two hits in the first game and four in the second.

July 20, 1910, Grover Alexander, Syracuse, New York State League, pitched and won a doubleheader from Wilkes-Barre.

July 21, 1910, First baseman Mullen, Shelbyville, Blue Grass League, made 21 putouts and one assist in a nine-inning game with Winchester. Shelbyville outfielders had no fielding chances.

July 21, 1910, After winning 19 successive Western Association games, Joplin lost to Tulsa 5-4.

August 3, 1910, Parkersburg, Virginia Valley League, made 28 hits to defeat Point Pleasant-Gallipolis 21-7.

August 8, 1910, Harry Ables, San Antonio, Texas League, fanned the first ten Dallas batters to face him and a total of 15 in the game.

August 9, 1910, Chet Carmichael of Buffalo, Eastern League, pitched a perfect game against Jersey City, winning 1-0. Forty-two years passed before the league saw its next perfect game.

August 11, 1910, Birmingham, Southern Association, won its fourth straight shutout.

August 18, 1910, Urban (Red) Faber pitched a perfect game for Dubuque, Three-I League, retiring 27 Davenport batters in a row to record a 3-0 victory. The umpire was ex-American Association star Robert Caruthers, and Ray Chapman, who was killed when hit by a pitched ball in 1920 with Cleveland, played third base for the losers.

August 20, 1910, A crowd of 18,552 attended an Eastern League doubleheader at Rochester with Newark.

August 21, 1910, John Waller, Bridgeport, Connecticut League, pitched a doubleheader, defeating Hartford 4-2, and 1-0, facing only 28 men in the nightcap while notching a no-hitter.

August 24, 1910, New Orleans, Southern Association, blanked Memphis for the third time in as many days.

September 1, 1910, Dubuque, Three-I League, defeated Rock Island 4-2 in 19 innings. Bill Cault, pitching for the losers, fanned 23 batters.

September 2, 1910, Sylveanus "Vean" Gregg, Portland, Pacific Coast League, struck out eight Los Angeles batters in a row.

September 5, 1910, Lowell, New England League, won a tripleheader from Lawrence. The morning game was played at Lawrence, and the other two came in the afternoon at Lowell.

September 5, 1910, Houston, Texas League, played three games with Galveston, winning two and losing one.

September 10, 1910, Fayetteville and Rocky Mount played the final game of the season tied for the championship of the Eastern Carolina League. In the last of the ninth, with Rocky Mount at bat with two on and none out, trailing 2-1, a triple play was recorded to end the game and the season.

September 12, 1910, Dick Rudolph, Toronto, Eastern League, pitched 10 innings of no-hit ball against Montreal, but lost 1-0 in twelve frames. Rudolph, who later starred with the Boston Braves, gave up singles in the eleventh and twelfth rounds.

September 15, 1910, Dick Rudolph, Toronto, lost his second consecutive well-pitched game, permitting Montreal but one hit but losing 2-1. In the two contests, Montreal batted .046, but won both games.

September 18, 1910, At the end of the New York State League season, records showed that Bill Zimmerman, Utica rightfielder, had 105 stolen bases in 135 games.

September 19, 1910, The fastest game on record, Mobile at Atlanta in the Southern Association, was played in 32 minutes. Mobile won 2-1. At Nashville, New Orleans and the home club rushed through their game in 42 minutes.

September 25, 1910, Lansing, Southern Michigan League, won a tripleheader from Flint on the final day of the season. Lansing capped a double bill the previous day for five victories in two days.

November 5, 1910, Vean Gregg, Portland, Pacific Coast League, struck out five Vernon batters for a final season total of 376. Gregg recorded 14 shutouts and a won-lost mark of 32-18.

1911

American League
President: Byron Bancroft Johnson

Standings	W	L	Pct.	GB	Attend.	Manager
Philadelphia Athletics	101	50	.669	—	605,749	Connie Mack
Detroit Tigers	89	65	.578	13½	484,988	Hugh Jennings
Cleveland Naps	80	73	.523	22	406,296	Deacon McGuire/ George Stovall
Chicago White Sox	77	74	.510	24	583,208	Hugh Duffy
Boston Red Sox	78	75	.510	24	503,961	Patsy Donovan
New York Highlanders	76	76	.500	25½	302,444	Hal Chase
Washington Senators	64	90	.416	38½	244,884	Jimmy McAleer
St. Louis Browns	45	107	.296	56½	207,984	Bobby Wallace

BA: Ty Cobb, Detroit, .420
Runs: Ty Cobb, Detroit, 147
Hits: Ty Cobb, Detroit, 248
RBIs: Ty Cobb, Detroit, 144
HRs: Frank Baker, Philadelphia, 11

Wins: Jack Coombs, Philadelphia, 28
SOs: Ed Walsh, Chicago, 255
ERA: Vean Gregg, Cleveland, 1.81
Pct: Charles "Chief" Bender, Philadelphia, .773, 17-5

National League
President: Thomas J. Lynch

Standings	W	L	Pct.	GB	Attend.	Manager
New York Giants	99	54	.647	—	675,000	John McGraw
Chicago Cubs	92	62	.597	7½	576,000	Frank Chance
Pittsburgh Pirates	85	69	.552	14½	432,000	Fred Clarke
Philadelphia Phillies	79	73	.520	19½	416,000	Red Dooin
St. Louis Cardinals	75	74	.503	22	447,768	Roger Bresnahan
Cincinnati Reds	70	83	.458	29	300,000	Clark Griffith
Brooklyn Dodgers	64	86	.427	33½	269,000	Bill Dahlen
Boston Braves	44	107	.291	54	116,000	Fred Tenney

BA: Honus Wagner, Pittsburgh, .334
Runs: Jimmy Sheckard, Chicago, 121
Hits: Doc Miller, Boston, 192
RBIs: Wildfire Schulte, Chicago, 121
HRs: Wildfire Schulte, Chicago, 21

Wins: Grover Alexander, Philadelphia, 28
SOs: Rube Marquard, New York, 237
ERA: Christy Mathewson, New York, 1.99
Pct: Rube Marquard, New York, .774, 24-7

A American Association
President: Thomas M. Chivington

Standings	W	L	Pct.	GB	Attend.	Manager
Minneapolis Millers	99	66	.600	—	208,588	Joe Cantillon
Kansas City Blues	94	70	.573	4½	257,703	Danny Shay
Columbus Senators	87	78	.527	12	159,932	William Friel
St. Paul Apostles	79	85	.482	19½	153,240	Mike Kelley
Milwaukee Brewers	79	87	.476	20½	170,234	James Barrett
Toledo Mud Hens	78	86	.476	20½	120,658	Harry Hinchman
Indianapolis Indians	78	88	.470	21½	218,357	James Burke
Louisville Colonels	67	101	.398	33½	134,765	Del Howard

BA: Gavvy Cravath, Minneapolis, .363
Runs: Hamilton Hyatt, Kansas City, 159
Hits: Gavvy Cravath, Minneapolis, 221
HRs: Gavvy Cravath, Minneapolis, 29

Wins: Roy Patterson, Minneapolis, 24
SOs: Marty O'Toole, St. Paul, 199
Pct: Rube Peters, Minneapolis, .786, 11-3

A Eastern League
President: Patrick T. Powers

Standings	W	L	Pct.	GB	Manager
Rochester Bronchos	98	54	.645	—	John Ganzel
Baltimore Orioles	95	58	.621	3½	Jack Dunn
Toronto Maple Leafs	94	59	.614	4½	Joe Kelley
Buffalo Bisons	74	75	.497	22½	George Stallings
Montreal Royals	72	80	.474	26	Ed McCafferty
Jersey City Skeeters	63	88	.417	34½	John Ryan
Newark Indians	57	95	.375	41	Joe McGinnity
Providence Grays	54	98	.356	44	James Collins/Jake Atz

Attendance: Buffalo, 233,160.

BA: Hank Perry, Providence, .343
Runs: Herb Moran, Rochester, 109
Hits: Ward Miller, Montreal, 191
HRs: Tim Jordan, Toronto, 20

Wins: Harry Vickers, Baltimore, 32
SOs: Jimmy Dygert, Baltimore, 218
Pct: George McConnell, Rochester, .789, 30-8

A Pacific Coast League
President: Thomas F. Graham

Standings	W	L	Pct.	GB	Manager
Portland Beavers	113	79	.589	—	Walter McCredie
Vernon Tigers	118	88	.573	2	W.L. "Happy" Hogan
Oakland Oaks	111	99	.528	11	Harry Wolverton
Sacramento Sacts	95	109	.466	24	Patsy O'Rourke
San Francisco Seals	95	112	.459	25½	Daniel Long
Los Angeles Angels	82	127	.392	39½	Frank "Cap" Dillon

BA: Buddy Ryan, Portland, .333
Runs: Walter Carlisle, Vernon, 181
Hits: Buddy Ryan, Portland, 247
HRs: Buddy Ryan, Portland, 23

Wins: Bill Steen, Portland, 30
SOs: Harry Sutor, San Francisco, 339
Pct: Bill Steen, Portland, .667, 30-15
Harry Ables, Oakland, .667, 22-11

A Southern Association
President: William B. Kavanaugh

Standings	W	L	Pct.	GB	Manager
New Orleans Pelicans	78	54	.591	—	Charley Frank
Montgomery Billikens	77	58	.570	2½	Johnny Dobbs
Birmingham Barons	76	62	.551	5	Carleton Molesworth
Nashville Volunteers	69	64	.519	9½	William Schwartz
Chattanooga Lookouts	67	71	.485	14	William A. Smith
Memphis Turtles	62	71	.466	16½	Bill Bernhardt
Mobile Sea Gulls	57	76	.428	21½	James Holmes/George Rohe/Harry Swacina
Atlanta Crackers	54	84	.391	27	Otto Jordan

BA: Del Pratt, Montgomery, .316
Runs: Pete Daley, Montgomery, 96
Del Pratt, Montgomery, 96
Hits: Del Pratt, Montgomery, 167

HRs: Roy Moran, Atlanta/Chattanooga, 11
Wins: Otto Hess, New Orleans, 23
Pct: Joe Bills, Montgomery, .800, 8-2

A Western League
President: Norris O'Neill

Standings	W	L	Pct.	GB	Manager
Denver Grizzlies	111	54	.673	—	Jack Hendricks
St. Joseph Drummers	93	72	.564	18	Jack Holland/Charles Shaffer
Wichita Jobbers/ Pueblo Indians#	92	75	.551	20	Frank Isbell
Omaha Rourkes	85	80	.515	26	Pa Rourke
Sioux City Packers	85	80	.515	26	Jay "Babe" Towne
Lincoln Railsplitters	84	81	.509	27	James Sullivan/Robert Unglaub
Topeka Kaws	60	104	.365	50½	Dick Cooley/Frank Richert
Des Moines Boosters	49	113	.302	60½	George Dwyer

#Wichita (15-9) moved to Pueblo May 22.

BA: Art Thomason, Omaha/Topeka, .342
Runs: Joe Berger, Wichita/Pueblo, 128
Hits: Art Thomason, Omaha/Topeka, 218
James Kane, Omaha, 218
RBIs: Dutch Zwilling, St. Joseph, 92

HRs: John Thomas, Lincoln, 12
Wins: Henry Chellette, St. Joseph, 27
SOs: Bucky O'Brien, Denver, 261
Pct: Bucky O'Brien, Denver, .788, 26-7

B Central League
President: Dr. Frank R. Carson

Standings	W	L	Pct.	GB	Manager
Dayton Veterans	86	51	.628	—	Charles "Punch" Knoll
Fort Wayne Brakies	83	54	.606	3	James "Doc" Casey
Zanesville Potters	74	58	.561	9½	Joe Raidy
South Bend Benders/ Grand Rapids Grads@	73	61	.545	11½	Edward Smith
Evansville Strikers/ South Bend Bux+	62	72	.463	22½	Angus Grant/Harry Arndt
Wheeling Stogies	56	73	.434	26	Roy Montgomery
Grand Rapids Furniture Makers/ Newark Skeeters#	59	78	.431	27	Harley Parker/John Pendry
Terre Haute Miners	45	91	.331	40½	Edward Wheeler/Angus Grant

#Grand Rapids (25-36) moved to Newark, Ohio June 27.
@South Bend (42-36) moved to Grand Rapids July 13.
+Evansville (54-54) moved to South Bend August 11.

BA: Joe Connolly, Zanesville/Terre Haute, .355
Runs: Ed Justice, Fort Wayne, 96
Marion Kilpatrick, Dayton, 96
Hits: Ray Spencer, Dayton, 176

HRs: Al "Bull" Durham, Wheeling, 11
Charles "Punch" Knoll, Dayton, 11
H. Hadley, Evansville/South Bend, 11
Emil Grefe, Evansville/South Bend, 11
Wins: Harry "Jack" Compton, Dayton, 22
George Harden, Fort Wayne, 22
SOs: George Harden, Fort Wayne, 172
Pct: Fred Albert, Fort Wayne, .800, 16-4

B Connecticut League
President: James O'Rourke

Standings	W	L	Pct.	GB	Manager
Springfield Ponies	71	45	.614	—	John Zeller
Bridgeport Orators	71	47	.602	1	Eugene McCann/Tracy
Hartford Senators	68	52	.568	5	Tom Connery

*Won first-half   **Won second-half   ***Won both halves

New Haven Murlins............ 56 61 .480 15½ Clarence "Pop" Foster
New Britain Perfectos......... 53 66 .444 19½ Daniel O'Neill
Waterbury Champs .... 45 75 .375 28   Carl Pace
Northampton Meadowlarks#... 21 24 .467 NA   Bill Luby
Holyoke Papermakers#....... 16 31 .340 NA   Wade Moore

#Northampton and Holyoke disbanded June 26.

BA: Clarence "Pop" Foster, New Haven, .325
Runs: Wilford Genest, Springfield, 95
Hits: Hi Ladd, Bridgeport, 143
HRs: Clarence "Pop" Foster, New Haven, 7
    Fred Eley, Bridgeport, 7
Wins: Eddie Dent, New Haven, 21
SOs: Jacob Reisigl, New Haven, 199
Pct: Curtis Walker, Holyoke/Bridgeport, .750, 15-5

B New England League
President: Tim H. Murnane

Standings	W	L	Pct.	GB	Manager
Lowell Tigers....................	77	46	.626	—	John Gray
Worcester Busters..............	73	47	.603	2½	Jesse Burkett
Lawrence Barristers...........	65	55	.542	10½	Louis Piper
Fall River Brinies.............	59	57	.509	14½	John H. O'Brien
Lynn Leonardites..............	60	60	.500	15½	Frank Leonard
Brockton Shoemakers........	59	60	.496	16	Stephen Flanagan
New Bedford Whalers	45	75	.375	30½	James Sullivan
Haverhill Hustlers..............	38	76	.333	34½	Tom Bannon

BA: Roland Barrows, Lowell, .370
Runs: Ollie Moulton, Lowell, 116
Hits: Roland Barrows, Lowell, 163
HRs: George Walsh, Fall River, 12
Wins: Meldon Wolfgang, Lowell, 27
Pct: Meldon Wolfgang, Lowell, .844, 27-5

B New York State League
President: John H. Farrell

Standings	W	L	Pct.	GB	Manager
Wilkes-Barre Barons	82	61	.573	—	Bill Clymer
Elmira Colonels	74	62	.544	4½	Henry Ramsey
Troy Trojans	74	66	.529	6½	Charles Dooley
Albany Senators	70	70	.500	10½	William Clark
Utica Utes	67	74	.475	14	Charles Carr
Syracuse Stars...................	65	74	.467	15	Edward Ashenbach/John Deal
Scranton Miners	63	74	.460	16	Monte Cross
Binghamton Bingos	63	77	.450	17½	Harry Lumley

BA: Larry Schlafly, Troy, .344
Runs: Mike O'Neill, Utica, 99
Hits: Chick Hartley, Albany, 173
Wins: Prince Gaskill, Scranton, 20
    J.J. McCloskey, Wilkes-Barre, 20
    James Swift, Elmira, 20
Pct: Joe Kutz, Utica/Wilkes-Barre, .625, 10-6

B Northwestern League
Presidents: Robert H. Lindsay/Daniel E. Dugdale

Standings	W	L	Pct.	GB	Manager
Vancouver Beavers...........	103	61	.628	—	Kitty Brashear
Spokane Indians................	96	71	.574	8½	Joseph Cohn
Seattle Giants....................	90	77	.533	14½	Jack Tighe/Frank Raymond
Portland Pippins................	84	77	.521	17½	Nick Williams
Tacoma Tigers	81	84	.490	22½	Mike Lynch
Victoria Bees	41	125	.247	63	T.S. McPherson

BA: Art Bues, Seattle, .352
Runs: Phil Cooney, Spokane, 130
Hits: Art Bues, Seattle, 219
HRs: Art Bues, Seattle, 27
Wins: Ralph Willis, Spokane, 23
Pct: George Engel, Vancouver, .786, 22-6

B Texas League
President: Wilbur P. Allen

Standings	W	L	Pct.	GB	Manager
Austin Senators..................	84	62	.575	—	Dale Gear
Ft. Worth Panthers.............	80	67	.548	4½	Walter Morris
San Antonio Bronchos........	77	68	.531	6½	George Leidy
Dallas Giants.....................	77	69	.528	7	Curley Maloney
Waco Navigators...............	75	71	.514	9	Ellis Hardy
Houston Buffaloes	71	75	.486	13	Hunter Hill/Sled Allen
Oklahoma City Indians.......	72	77	.483	13½	Lee Garvin
Galveston Sand Crabs........	50	97	.340	34½	Frank Donnelly/W.J. Donahue/
					Otto Krueger

BA: Bill Yohe, Oklahoma City, .324
Runs: Otto Krueger, Galveston, 102
Hits: Bill Yohe, Oklahoma City, 181
HRs: Frank Metz, San Antonio, 22
Wins: Rube Robinson, Ft. Worth, 28
SOs: Harley Young, Oklahoma City, 245
Pct: Rube Robinson, Ft. Worth, .800, 28-7

B Three-I League
President: Albert R. Tearney

Standings	W	L	Pct.	GB	Manager
Peoria Distillers	76	59	.563	—	David Drohan/Charles Stis
Springfield Senators/					
Decatur Nomads#...........	69	60	.535	4	Richard Smith
Quincy Infants	71	63	.530	4½	Bade Myers
Danville Speakers.............	69	62	.526	5	John McCarthy
Davenport Prodigals..........	69	69	.500	8½	Daniel O'Leary

Dubuque Hustlers .... 67 70 .489 10 Clarence "Pants" Rowland
Waterloo Boosters .... 59 76 .437 17 Frank Boyle
Rock Island Islanders......... 58 79 .424 19 William Carney/John Gondling

#Springfield (12-4) moved to Decatur May 31.

BA: Elmer Johnson, Springfield/Decatur, .320
Runs: Russell Fountain, Peoria, 83
Hits: Alfred Bromwich, Davenport, 153
Wins: Joseph Willis, Springfield/Decatur, 24
    Collis Spencer, Springfield/Decatur, 24
SOs: Joseph Willis, Springfield/Decatur, 208
Pct: Joe Hovlik, Peoria, .696, 16-7

B Tri-State League
President: Charles F. Carpenter

Standings	W	L	Pct.	GB	Manager
Reading Pretzels	74	35	.679	—	Harry Barton
Trenton Tigers	65	46	.586	10	George Heckert
Johnstown Johnnies	57	49	.538	15½	Bert Conn
Lancaster Red Roses...........	54	54	.500	19½	Martin Hogan
Altoona Rams	51	56	.477	22	Henry Ramsey
York White Roses	50	58	.463	23½	Curt Weigand
Harrisburg Ponies	47	61	.435	26½	Albert Selbach
Wilmington Chicks	34	73	.318	39	Peter Cassidy/Tom Bannon

Playoff: Trenton 4 games, Reading 3.

BA: John Davis, Trenton, .363
Runs: Al Jube, Reading, 88
Hits: George Cockill, Reading, 144
HRs: George Cockill, Reading, 12
Wins: Jack Northrop, Reading, 27
Pct: Jack Northrop, Reading, .871, 27-4

C Minnesota-Wisconsin League
President: Frank Force

Standings	W	L	Pct.	GB	Manager
Superior Red Sox...............	72	36	.667	—	John "Kid" Taylor
Winona Pirates..................	71	45	.612	5	Joe Killian
Duluth White Sox	60	49	.550	12½	William "Darby" O'Brien
Eau Claire Commissioners ...	53	57	.482	20	Tom Schoonhover
La Crosse Outcasts	47	68	.409	28½	Charles "Bumpus" Jones/Carl Bond
Rochester Bears	40	71	.360	33½	Ted Corbett
Wausau Lumberjacks#	21	22	.488	NA	Carl Bond/Buddy Dolan
Red Wing Manufacturers#..	13	29	.310	NA	Fred Cook

#Red Wing and Wausau disbanded June 26.

C Ohio-Pennsylvania League
President: George L. Moreland

Standings	W	L	Pct.	GB	Manager
Akron Champs	90	42	.682	—	Jack McCallister/Lee Fohl
Youngstown Steelmen........	82	50	.621	8	Bill Phillips
Erie Sailors	77	54	.588	12½	William Gilbert
Canton Deubers	75	59	.560	16	Ferdinand Drumm
Mansfield Brownies............	55	82	.401	37½	Edward Hahn
New Castle Nocks/					
Sharon Travelers#............	35	101	.257	57	Joseph Sugden/Steve Griffin/
					William Thomas/Peter Porter
East Liverpool Potters@.....	63	49	.563	NA	Alexander Sweeney
Steubenville Stubs@...........	40	80	.333	NA	John Castle

#New Castle (25-85) moved to Sharon August 12.
@East Liverpool and Steubenville disbanded August 20.

BA: Joe Wilson, East Liverpool, .365
Runs: Ezra Midkiff, Akron, 96
Hits: Ray Miller, Akron, 162
HRs: Hugh Tate, Youngstown, 23
Wins: Elmer Brown, Akron, 22
    Ralph McConnaughey, Erie, 22
SOs: Earl Moseley, Youngstown, 242
Pct: Elmer Brown, Akron, .815, 22-5

C South Atlantic League
Presidents: W.R. Joyner/Nick P. Corish

Standings	W	L	Pct.	GB	Manager
Columbia Commies**	87	49	.639	—	Frederick Cavender/William Clark
Columbus Foxes*	86	50	.632	1	James Fox
Albany Babies	82	53	.609	4½	Harry Mathews/Bernie McCay
Macon Peaches	72	62	.537	14	Perry Lipe
Jacksonville Tarpons	56	79	.415	30½	Kohler Miller/C. Spencer
Savannah Indians	56	81	.409	31½	George Magoon/P. Mullaney
Augusta Tourists/					
SAL Orphans#.................	52	74	.413	NA	James LaFitte
Charleston Sea Gulls#	41	84	.328	NA	Edward Rinsick/Edward Sabrie/
					James Durham/Charles Laskey

#Augusta withdrew July 26, but the league operated the club as SAL Orphans. When storms destroyed the Charleston ball park, both clubs disbanded August 30.

Playoff: Columbus 4 games, Columbia 2.

BA: Scottie Alcock, Albany, .333
Runs: Bernie McCay, Albany, 97
Hits: Scottie Alcock, Albany, 178
Wins: Phil Douglas, Macon, 28
Pct: Roy Radabaugh, Columbus, .818, 27-6

C Southern Michigan League
President: James P. Bowen

Standings	W	L	Pct.	GB	Manager
Kalamazoo Celery Eaters ...	88	51	.633	—	Charles Wagner
Lansing Senators.................	79	55	.590	6½	John Morrissey
Flint Vehicles......................	77	59	.566	9½	Dan Collins
Bay City Billikens...............	73	64	.533	14	Maurice Meyers/Bo Slear
Saginaw Krazy Kats	72	67	.518	16	Mal Kittridge
Adrian Yeggs......................	65	76	.461	24	William Smith
Battle Creek Crickets..........	57	80	.416	30	Jack Burke
Jackson Convicts	39	98	.285	48	Charles Fox

BA: John Connors, Jackson, .377
Runs: J.W. "Sis" Hopkins, Saginaw, 120
Hits: J.J. Kutina, Saginaw, 193
HRs: Clarence "Big Boy" Kraft, Flint, 19
SBs: Dan Jenkins, Adrian, 76

Wins: Albert Jacobson, Kalamazoo, 26
  Edward Warner, Lansing, 26
SOs: Edward Warner, Lansing, 231
Pct: Albert Jacobson, Kalamazoo, .743, 26-9

C Virginia League
President: C.R. Williams

Standings	W	L	Pct.	GB	Manager
Petersburg Hustlers.............	68	51	.572	—	Henry Busch
Norfolk Tars	67	54	.554	2	Charles Babb
Roanoke Tigers...................	63	56	.529	5	Frank Shaughnessy
Richmond Colts	55	63	.466	12½	J.W. Sullivan/Bradley
Lynchburg Shoemakers........	56	65	.463	13	Otis Stockdale
Danville Bugs	50	70	.417	18½	Joseph Laughlin/G. Schrader

BA: Bruno Block, Norfolk, .330
Runs: Frank Shaughnessy, Roanoke, 93
Hits: Frank Shaughnessy, Roanoke, 160
RBI: Mike Kelliher, Petersburg, 84
HRs: Ralph Mattis, Richmond, 9

Wins: Earl Hamilton, Petersburg, 21
  Andy Bruckmiller, Petersburg, 21
  Joe Finneran, Norfolk, 21
  Edward Poole, Norfolk, 21
SOs: Edward Poole, Norfolk, 207
Pct: J.G. Vance, Petersburg, 1.000, 11-0

C Wisconsin-Illinois League
President: Charles F. Moll

Standings	W	L	Pct.	GB	Manager
Rockford Wolverines..........	74	46	.617	—	George Bubsir/Frank Richards
Madison Senators	66	57	.537	9½	Smiley Smith
Green Bay Bays	61	56	.521	11½	John Pickett
Appleton Papermakers........	63	58	.521	11½	George Hogriever
Oshkosh Indians	61	64	.488	15½	Frank Cassiboine/Noel Warren
Racine Malted Milks	58	64	.475	17	Larry Hoffman
Aurora Blues......................	55	67	.451	20	Albert Tebeau
Fond du Lac Mudhens	47	73	.392	27	Bobby Lynch

BA: Casey Stengel, Aurora, .352
Runs: Clyde Curtis, Rockford, 92
Hits: Casey Stengel, Aurora, 148

Wins: Bruce Noel, Oshkosh, 28
Pct: Cy Slapnicka, Rockford, .788, 26-7

D Appalachian League
President: W.W. Miller

Standings	W	L	Pct.	GB	Manager
Johnson City Soldiers	61	38	.616	—	Ed Gardner
Knoxville Appalachians	58	38	.604	1½	Frank Moffett
Asheville Moonshiners.......	53	45	.546	7½	Apey Mills/Lou Hobbs
Morristown Jobbers	46	50	.479	13½	J.F. McFarlin
Cleveland Counts	39	56	.411	20	Count Zimeski
Bristol Boosters	33	63	.344	26½	Clarence "Red" Munson

BA: Buck Thrasher, Cleveland, .351
Runs: E.N. "Pop" Shaw, Johnson City, 71
Hits: E.N. "Pop" Shaw, Johnson City, 126
HRs: B.B. Woodward, Asheville, 11

Wins: Nick Cullop, Knoxville/Bristol, 18
SOs: Frank Davis, Knoxville, 181
Pct: S.E. Silvers, Knoxville, .722, 13-5

D Blue Grass League
Presidents: Dr. W.C. Ussery/William Neal

Standings	W	L	Pct.	GB	Manager
Paris Bourbonites**.............	71	44	.617	—	Ed McKernan
Lexington Colts	65	50	.565	6	Thomas Sheets/Hogan Yancy
Winchester Hustlers*..........	59	59	.500	13½	Frank Coleman
Maysville Rivermen	55	63	.466	17½	James Carmony
Frankfort Statesmen	48	65	.425	22	Ed Coleman
Richmond Pioneers.............	47	64	.423	22	Connie Lewis/Sylvester Olsen

Playoff: Paris 4 games, Winchester 0.

BA: Walter Mayer, Paris, .352
Runs: E.E. Coleman, Winchester, 95
Hits: Walter Mayer, Paris, 160
HRs: Charles Ellis, Lexington, 13

Wins: Charles Burden, Winchester, 23
SOs: Frank Romine, Maysville, 253
Pct: John Scheneberg, Paris, 1.000, 12-0

D Canadian League
President: Donald Ferguson

Standings	W	L	Pct.	GB	Manager
Berlin Green Sox	70	40	.637	—	George Deneau
London Cockneys	59	51	.536	11	Louis Bierbauer/Joe Keenan
Hamilton Kolts	58	52	.527	12	George Lee
Brantford Red Sox	53	58	.477	17½	Ambrose Kane
Guelph Maple Leafs	45	62	.421	23½	Abbie Johnson/William Lane/Hugh Shannon
St. Thomas Saints	43	65	.398	26	Edwin Elliott

BA: Louis Bierbauer, London, .367
Runs: Ray Cameron, Berlin, 89

Hits: Malcolm Barry, Brantford, 141
HRs: Ambrose Kane, Brantford, 7

D Carolina Association
President: Joseph H. Wearn

Standings	W	L	Pct.	GB	Manager
Winston-Salem Twins	72	37	.661	—	Charles Clancy
Greensboro Patriots	66	43	.581	6	Frank Doyle
Charlotte Hornets...............	52	58	.473	20½	Lave Cross
Anderson Electricians.........	48	59	.449	23	Jim "King" Kelly
Spartanburg Spartans	44	63	.411	27	Bill Laval
Greenville Spinners	42	64	.396	28½	Thomas Stouch

BA: F.P. Wofford, Charlotte, .392
Runs: Walt Rickard, Greensboro, 105
Hits: Bill Schumaker, Winston-Salem, 145
RBIs: Bill Schumaker, Winston-Salem, 91

HRs: Richard Smith, Greenville, 17
Wins: Joshua Swindell, Winston-Salem, 29
Pct: Joshua Swindell, Winston-Salem, .784, 29-8

D Central Association
President: M.E. Justice

Standings	W	L	Pct.	GB	Manager
Ottumwa Speedboys	87	41	.680	—	Ned Egan
Burlington Cow Boys	81	44	.648	4½	Richard Rohn
Galesburg Pavers	66	63	.512	21½	Bert Hough
Keokuk Indians	64	64	.500	23	Frank Belt
Kewanee Boilermakers........	59	67	.468	27	Jay Andrews
Monmouth Browns	59	69	.461	28	Claude Starke
Muscatine Camels...............	48	80	.375	39	Harry C. Blake
Hannibal Cannibals.............	45	81	.357	41	Jake Beckley

BA: Pearl Holycross, Muscatine, .361
Runs: George Watson, Burlington, 108
Hits: Taylor Kensel, Ottumwa, 163
HRs: Don Senno, Ottumwa, 14

SBs: A.J. Ahring, Muscatine, 79
Wins: Ray Boyd, Ottumwa, 30
Pct: Ray Boyd, Ottumwa, .811, 30-7

D Central California League
Presidents: Anderson/Hon. E.P. Shortall

Standings	W	L	Pct.	GB	Manager
San Leandro Cherry Pickers .	10	3	.769	—	
Alameda Alerts...................	8	5	.615	2	
Vallejo Pastimes	8	5	.615	2	
Richmond Merchants	8	6	.571	2½	
Berkeley Clarions+.............	5	6	.455	4	
Elmhurst Carroll Tildens/					
Oakland Emery Arms@	4	7	.364	5	
Hayward Cubs	4	9	.308	6	
Fruitvale Travelers/					
Alameda Monday Models#	4	10	.286	6½	

#Fruitvale (1-7) moved to Alameda May 28.
@Elmhurst moved to Oakland June 4, then disbanded June 18.
+Berkeley disbanded June 23.
The league disbanded July 9.

D Central Kansas League
Presidents: C.A. Case/Roy C. Gafford

Standings	W	L	Pct.	GB	Manager
Concordia Travelers***	44	27	.620	—	Harry Short/Roy Gafford
Junction City Soldiers.........	40	31	.563	4	Cecil Bankhead
Clay Center Cubs..............	33	38	.465	11	Lee Gramley
Manhattan Maroons.............	25	46	.352	19	Dee Poindexter

The league disbanded July 23.

Playoff: Concordia 4 games, Junction City 3.

BA: Gilbert Britton, Clay Center, .347
Runs: Claude Jennings, Clay Center, 53
Hits: Gilbert Britton, Clay Center, 90

SBs: Claude Jennings, Clay Center, 30
Wins: G.H. Jepson, Junction City, 21
Pct: G.H. Jepson, Junction City, .724, 21-8

D Cotton States League
President: Frank A. Scott

Standings	W	L	Pct.	GB	Manager
Vicksburg Hill Billies	73	42	.635	—	Otto Mills
Hattiesburg Woodpeckers...	65	51	.560	8½	B.D. Moore/Carlos Smith
Yazoo City Zoos	60	54	.526	12½	Dominick Mullaney
Jackson Drummers	58	60	.492	16½	Frank Norcum
Greenwood Scouts	46	68	.404	26½	Woodie Thornton
Meridian White Ribbons	46	73	.387	29	Forrest Plass

BA: Carlos Smith, Vicksburg/Hattiesburg, .401
Runs: Otto Mills, Vicksburg, 87
  Guy Tutweiler, Hattiesburg, 87
Hits: Otto Mills, Vicksburg, 155

HRs: Guy Tutweiler, Hattiesburg, 11
Wins: Jim Bagby, Hattiesburg, 22
SOs: Joe Martina, Yazoo City, 205
Pct: Ralph Comstock, Vicksburg, .840, 21-4

1911

D Illinois-Missouri League
President: R.E. Rollins

Standings	W	L	Pct.	GB	Manager
Clinton Champs	74	55	.574	—	Jack Carter
Pekin Celestials	72	55	.567	1	Jack Herbert
Champaign-Urbana Velvets	66	60	.524	6½	John Thiner/Fred Donovan
Canton Chinks	60	62	.492	10½	Blackie Wilson
Lincoln Abes	59	64	.480	12	Conley/Bill Salliard/James Brady/
					Charles Vaught/Jack Corbett
Taylorville Christians	47	82	.364	27	Fred Donovan/Joe Adams

BA: Andy Lotshaw, Canton, .355
Runs: Will Lindberg, Clinton, 94
Hits: Andy Lotshaw, Canton, 160
HRs: Andy Lotshaw, Canton, 29
Wins: Joab McManus, Canton, 32
SOs: Joab McManus, Canton, 243
Pct: Fred Marks, Clinton, .727, 24-9

D Kansas State League
Presidents: C.A. Case/Roy C. Gafford

Standings	W	L	Pct.	GB	Manager
Great Bend Millers	39	20	.661	—	Affie Wilson/William Luhrsen
Newton Railroaders	39	21	.650	½	
Lyons Lions	37	27	.578	4½	Spencer Abbott
McPherson Merry Macks	31	28	.525	8	Joseph Harris
Hutchinson Salt Packers	29	29	.500	9½	Bill Zink
Larned Wheat Kings	23	32	.418	14	Harry Berte
El Dorado Crushers	15	33	.313	18½	Bill Annis/Walter Sizemore
Wellington Dukes#	15	38	.283	21	Peter Ketter/C.E. Powell/Ned Price

#Wellington played 10 home games (2-8) in Wichita June 11-23.
The league disbanded July 11 due to crop failures and drought.

D Kitty League
President: Charles C. Gosnell

Standings	W	L	Pct.	GB	Manager
Hopkinsville Hoppers*	78	46	.629	—	John Nairn
Fulton Colonels**	67	58	.536	11½	Senter Rainey
McLeansboro Miners/					
Henderson Hens#	65	58	.528	12½	Miles Bradshaw/Stelle
Vincennes Hoosiers	62	59	.512	14½	Charlie Gosnell
Paducah Polecats	58	64	.475	19	Ollie Pickering
Cairo Egyptians	58	67	.464	20½	Morris Michaels
Harrisburg Merchants/					
Jackson@	53	68	.438	23½	Reiser/Ira Hastings
Clarksville Billies	51	71	.422	26	Johnny Siegle/Gene Curtis

#McLeansboro (19-15) moved to Henderson June 20 because Sunday baseball was not permitted in McLeansboro.
@Harrisburg moved to Jackson August 13.

Playoffs: Fulton and Hopkinsville were declared co-champions when the playoffs were cancelled due to poor field conditions in Fulton and inclement weather.

BA: Ernie Gust, Harrisburg/Jackson, .354
Runs: Harry Heckert, Fulton, 86
Hits: Ernie Gust, Harrisburg/Jackson, 148
HRs: Ernie Calbert, Harrisburg/Jackson, 10

D Michigan State League
President: Emerson W. Dickerson

Standings	W	L	Pct.	GB	Manager
Manistee Colts	74	45	.622	—	Ed Somerlott/Earl Zook/Connie Lewis
Muskegon Reds	73	45	.619	½	Arthur DeBaker
Cadillac Chiefs	73	45	.619	½	Calvin Wenger
Traverse City Resorters	62	56	.525	11½	William Hawker/Henry Collett
Holland Wooden Shoes	48	71	.403	26	Clyde McNutt/Ted Penfold/
					McDonough/W. Schaefer
Boyne City Boosters	24	92	.207	48½	Peter Partlow/Jack Ryan/Lou Criger

BA: Earl Comstock, Muskegon, .354
Runs: Bunny Brief, Traverse City, 97
Hits: Bunny Brief, Traverse City, 169
HRs: Bunny Brief, Traverse City, 10
SBs: Otto Pfeifer, Traverse City, 85
Wins: Ray Williams, Manistee, 25
SOs: Ray Williams, Manistee, 169
Pct: Ray Williams, Manistee, .833, 25-5

D Missouri State League
Presidents: W.G. Lynch/James Lay

Standings	W	L	Pct.	GB	Manager
Sedalia/Brookfield Cubs@	11	8	.579	—	R.T. Easley
Macon Athletics	10	8	.556	½	Brooks Gordon
Jefferson City Senators+	11	9	.550	½	Jack "Chief" Meyers
Kirksville Osteopaths	9	12	.429	3	Senter Rainey
Brookfield Hustlers#	0	4	.000	NA	Ginger Lyons

#Brookfield disbanded May 19.
@Sedalia (7-3) moved to Brookfield May 24.
+Jefferson City disbanded June 2, causing the league to disband June 4.

HRs: David Kraft, Kirksville, 3

D MINK League
Presidents: T.A. Wilson/Frederick Carey

Standings	W	L	Pct.	GB	Manager
Maryville Comets/					
Humboldt Infants#	59	41	.590	—	Harry Sievers/A.F. Bridges
Falls City Colts	57	43	.570	2	
Auburn Athletics	52	48	.520	7	L. Higgins
Shenandoah Pin Rollers	49	51	.490	10	Fred Wells
Clarinda Antelopes	43	57	.430	16	Frank Hutchinson
Nebraska City Foresters	40	60	.400	19	Dan Nee/C. Pinkerton/T.A. Wilson

#Maryville (21-24) moved to Humboldt July 10.

BA: Joe Stricker, Clarinda, .349
Runs: Les Mann, Nebraska City, 78
Hits: Joe Stricker, Clarinda, 128
Wins: Walter Hirsch, Auburn, 22
Pct: Jay Errett, Maryville/Humboldt, .800, 8-2

D Mountain States League
President: Lon H. Barringer

Standings	W	L	Pct.	GB	Manager
Montgomery Miners	67	53	.558	—	Ralph Fleming/Henry Runser
Huntington Blue Sox*	63	50	.558	½	Albert Knoessell
Ashland-Catlettsburg Twins	63	55	.534	3	James Kitler
Point Pleasant-Gallipolis/					
Middleport-Pomeroy#**	59	60	.496	7½	Joseph "Reddy" Mack
Charleston Senators	57	58	.496	7½	George Bigbee
Ironton Nailers	44	77	.364	23½	John Benny

#Point Pleasant-Gallipolis (16-32) moved to Middleport-Pomeroy July 1, first home game July 8. The season ended September 12 when an investigation ordered by the National Association disclosed two cases of improper conduct in late season games to prevent Middleport-Pomeroy from winning the second half title. These games were deducted at the fall meeting.

BA: H. Hollis, Charleston, .362
Runs: Grover Erb, Ashland-Catlettsburg, 99
Hits: Earl Steward, Ashland-Catlettsburg, 147
HRs: Grover Erb, Ashland-Catlettsburg, 17
Wins: George Baumgardner, Huntington, 24
Howard Cochran, Montgomery, 24
SOs: George Baumgardner, Huntington, 292
Pct: George Baumgardner, Huntington, .727, 24-9

D Nebraska State League
President: Henry A. Sievers

Standings	W	L	Pct.	GB	Manager
Superior Brickmakers	70	40	.636	—	Dennis Bockewitz
Fremont Pathfinders	69	43	.616	2	L.D. "Dad" Bennett
Hastings Third Citys	54	58	.482	17	Rudy Kling
Seward Statesmen	53	57	.482	17	John Fink
Grand Island Collegians	52	60	.464	19	Armstrong
Columbus Discoverers	52	60	.464	19	Joe Dolan
Kearney Buffaloes	48	64	.429	23	C.R. Murphy
York Prohibitionists	48	64	.429	23	George Harms/Lefty Davis

BA: Norm Coyle, Superior, .354
Runs: C.G. Allen, Superior, 95
Hits: Norm Coyle, Superior, 153
HRs: George Harms, York, 21
Wins: Emery Orth, Hastings, 23
SOs: Harry Smith, Fremont, 235
Pct: George Stevens, Superior, .750, 18-6

D Northeast Arkansas League
President: J.R. Bertig

Standings	W	L	Pct.	GB	Manager
Helena	37	29	.561	—	Charley Reese/Con Harlow
Blytheville	31	30	.508	3½	Senter Rainey/Polly Perrott
Paragould Scouts	28	32	.467	6	
Jonesboro Zebras	28	33	.459	6½	D.D. Lewis/Nig Miller

The league disbanded July 5.

D Northern State of Indiana League
President: C.A. Klunk

Standings	W	L	Pct.	GB	Manager
Marion Boosters	46	24	.657	—	Mike Lawrence
Huntington Indians	40	30	.571	6	
Bluffton Babes#	31	31	.500	11	Jake Schock/Lew Scott
Wabash Rockeries	30	35	.462	13½	
Lafayette Farmers	28	37	.431	15½	
Logansport/					
Anderson Whitecaps#	22	40	.355	20	

#Logansport moved to Anderson July 2, then disbanded July 28, forcing Bluffton to withdraw. The league folded July 29.

D Ohio State League
President: Robert W. Read

Standings	W	L	Pct.	GB	Manager
Springfield Reapers	84	55	.604	—	Charles O'Day
Marion Diggers	80	59	.576	4	Joseph Lewis
Portsmouth Cobblers	78	61	.561	6	Pete Childs
Chillicothe Infants	78	62	.557	6½	George "Zeke" Wrigley
Newark Newks/Piqua Picks#	72	65	.526	11	Alfred Newnham
Lima Cigarmakers	62	77	.446	22	Frank Nesser
Lancaster Lanks	53	84	.387	30	Charles Riehl/Gus Epler
Hamilton Mechanics	48	92	.343	36½	James Barton

#Newark (29-33) moved to Piqua June 22.

BA: B.W. Blue, Newark/Piqua, .347
Runs: W. Colligan, Marion, 119
Hits: B.W. Blue, Newark/Piqua, 176
HRs: J. Kelly, Marion, 12

Wins: Roy Ashenfelder, Hamilton/
Springfield, 24
Pct: H. McCall, Marion, .800, 8-2

D San Joaquin Valley League
President: J. Newton Young

Standings	W	L	Pct.	GB	Manager
Tulare Merchants#	9	4	.692	—	Heath
Coalinga Tigers	8	6	.571	1½	
Lemoore Cubs	7	6	.538	2	Frank Blakeley
Hanford Braves	6	7	.462	3	Sidney Jehl
Visalia Colts	5	8	.385	4	Lou Maire
Porterville Orange Pickers#	4	8	.333	4½	

#Tulare and Porterville disbanded July 11.
The league disbanded July 18.

D Southeastern League
President: J.H. O'Neill

Standings	W	L	Pct.	GB	Manager
Anniston Models	68	39	.636	—	Walter Ford/Thomas Fisher
Gadsden Steelmakers	62	42	.596	4½	L.C. "King" Bailey
Selma Centralites	53	51	.510	13½	Bill May/Howard/Frank Anderson/ Ralph Savidge
Rome Hillies	47	57	.452	19½	Carleton Beusse/Don Burt
Huntsville Westerns	46	56	.451	19½	V. Campbell/W.H. Watkins/Newt Horn/ Bill Evans/Arthur Riggs
Decatur Twins	37	68	.352	30	Don Burt/Gordon Hickman/Con Harlow

BA: Tommy Long, Gadsden, .364
Runs: Tommy Long, Gadsden, 97
Hits: Tommy Long, Gadsden, 149
HRs: Tommy Long, Gadsden, 18

Wins: Clarence Smith, Anniston, 24
SOs: Clarence Smith, Anniston, 248
Pct: Sam Nelson, Anniston, .750, 12-4

D Southwest Texas League
President: B.S. Dickinson

Standings	W	L	Pct.	GB	Manager
Bay City Rice Eaters*	67	51	.568	—	Louis Hamilton/E. Haralson
Brownsville Brownies	64	52	.552	2	O.H. Boston
Beeville Orange Growers**	63	54	.538	3½	Ted Schultz/Billy Disch
Laredo Bermudas	55	63	.466	12	John Blakeney/W. "Lucky" Wright
Victoria Rosebuds@	54	59	.478	NA	Hart McCormick/J. Linebaugh/Jack Burke
Corpus Christi Pelicans#	46	70	.397	NA	Henry Hunt

#Corpus Christi surrendered its franchise to the league July 17. The club was dropped from the league August 13.
@Victoria withdrew August 11.

Playoff: Beeville was awarded the pennant when Bay City refused to play.

BA: Howard Wakefield, Victoria, .338
Runs: Dave Harper, Corpus Christi, 66
Hits: Lou Vetter, Beeville, 121
HRs: Harry Sweet, Bay City, 9

Wins: Ezequiel Ramos, Laredo, 20
SOs: Samuel Napier, Brownsville, 213
Pct: Raymond Stubbs, Beeville, .750, 15-5

D Texas-Oklahoma League
President: F.P. St. Clair

Standings	W	L	Pct.	GB	Manager
Wichita Falls Irish Lads*	65	38	.631	—	Fred Morris, Sr./Dick Naylor
Durant Educators	65	46	.586	4	W. Washington/Joe Connors/ Benny Brownlow
Cleburne Railroaders**	61	50	.550	8	Will Reed/Jiggs Donahue/A.L. "Dad" Ritter
Bonham Boosters	54	60	.474	16½	Jimmy Humphries
Ardmore Blues	49	58	.458	12	Emmett Rogers/Hillis/George McAvoy
Altus Chiefs+	31	44	.413	NA	Muggsy Monroe/Dad Campbell/ George Partain
Gainesville Blue Ribbons#.	19	30	.388	NA	John Stone/George Morris
Lawton Medicine Men@	17	31	.354	NA	Cap Metcalf/C. Pinkerton

#Gainesville disbanded June 14.
@Lawton disbanded June 16.
+Altus disbanded July 18.
The season was shortened to August 23.

Playoff: Abandoned with Wichita Falls leading Cleburne 2 games to 1, when Wichita Falls refused to continue due to an ineligible player and non-payment of gate receipts for a game in Cleburne. Cleburne was declared champion.

D Twin States League
President: Major F.M. Keys

Standings	W	L	Pct.	GB	Manager
Brattleboro Islanders	22	14	.611	—	E.L. Breckinridge
Keene Champs	20	16	.556	2	Tom Leonard
Bellows Falls Sulphites	15	20	.428	6½	Hank Shea
Springfield-Charlestown Hyphens	14	21	.388	7½	Warren Potter/Larry Grow

BA: Timothy Horan, Brattleboro, .300

D Union Association
President: William H. Lucas

Standings	W	L	Pct.	GB	Manager
Great Falls	90	46	.662	—	George Reed
Salt Lake City Skyscrapers	85	58	.594	8½	Cliff Blankenship
Butte Miners	77	60	.562	13½	John McCloskey
Boise Irrigators	64	78	.451	29	Hugh Kellackey
Helena Senators	60	78	.435	31	Charles Irby
Missoula	42	98	.300	50	William Joyce/Charles McCafferty

BA: Frank Huelsman, Great Falls, .411
Runs: Howard Murphy, Great Falls, 146
Hits: Howard Murphy, Great Falls, 220
RBIs: Frank Huelsman, Great Falls, 125

HRs: Frank Huelsman, Great Falls, 17
Wins: Roswell Hildebrand, Great Falls, 30
SOs: Amos Morgan, Salt Lake City, 267
Pct: Leo Dressen, Salt Lake City, .813, 13-3

D Washington State League
President: O.J. Albers

Standings	W	L	Pct.	GB	Manager
Centralia Pets	38	17	.691	—	W.R. Patton/Guy Muck
Chehalis Proteges	36	20	.648	2½	B.E. "Dusty" Miller/Lenny Taylor
Raymond Venetians	25	29	.463	12½	C.D. Wineholt
South Bend River Rats	11	44	.200	27	

BA: Reed, South Bend, .333
Runs: Tate Berry, Chehalis, 49
C.D. Wineholt, Raymond/Chehalis, 49
Hits: I.H. Guynn, Centralia, 72
HRs: C.D. Wineholt, Raymond/Chehalis, 8

Wins: Raymond Callahan, Centralia/Chehalis, 13
Ray Baker, Raymond, 13
SOs: Raymond Callahan, Centralia/Chehalis, 131
Pct: Berger, Centralia, .778, 7-2

D Western Association
Presidents: Tom C. Hayden/Herbert Slater

Standings	W	L	Pct.	GB	Manager
Ft. Smith Scouts*	29	14	.674	—	Arthur Riggs
Muskogee Redskins**	23	21	.523	6½	Lon Ury
Sapulpa Oilers	23	21	.523	6½	George McAvoy/Harry Bradbury
Tulsa Railroaders	20	25	.444	10	Bert Shaner
Independence Packers@	15	22	.405	NA	Ned Price/Wilson
Coffeyville White Sox@	15	24	.385	NA	Harry Bradbury
Joplin Miners#	3	2	.600	NA	Tony Anderson
Springfield Jobbers#	2	3	.400	NA	Lawrence Milton

Attendance: Tulsa, 6,800.

#Joplin and Springfield disbanded May 10.
@Coffeyville and Independence disbanded June 14. On June 19 Ft. Smith and Tulsa withdrew, and the league disbanded.

D Western Canada League
President: C.J. Eckstrom

Standings	W	L	Pct.	GB	Manager
Moose Jaw Robin Hoods	83	28	.748	—	William Hurley
Calgary Bronchos	64	36	.640	13½	Matt Stanley
Edmonton Eskimos	52	51	.505	27	Deacon White
Winnipeg Maroons#	51	52	.495	28	Ralph Bell
Saskatoon Berrypickers	37	71	.343	44½	Frank Miley
Brandon Angels#	25	74	.253	52	Charles Traeger

#Winnipeg and Brandon disbanded August 21.

BA: Jake Fournier, Moose Jaw, .377
Runs: Jake Fournier, Moose Jaw, 106
Hits: Jake Fournier, Moose Jaw, 149
HRs: Joseph Collins, Moose Jaw, 10

Wins: Al Naverson, Moose Jaw, 25
SOs: Dell Manning, Calgary, 179
Pct: Al Naverson, Moose Jaw, .758, 25-8

1911 Interleague Post Season Play

World Series
Philadelphia (American) 4 games, New York (National) 2

Carolina vs. Virginia
Winston-Salem (Carolina Association) 4 games, Norfolk (Virginia) 2

1911 No-Hitters

Date	Pitcher	Team	League	Opponent	Score
4-21	Charlie Jackson	St. Joseph	Western	Sioux City	7-0
4-23	George Boehler	Springfield	Ohio State	Lima	7-1
4-25	James Ward	Brockton	New England	Haverhill	1-0
4-25	Harry Sutor	San Francisco	Pacific Coast	Oakland	1-0
4-29	Roswell Hildebrand	Great Falls	Union Association	Helena	2-1
5-5	L.V. Hamilton	Petersburg	Virginia	Lynchburg	2-1
5-7	Dave Skeets	Seattle	Northwestern	Victoria	12-1
5-14	Fred Lamline	Portland	Northwestern	Vancouver	8-1
5-18	L.G. Daniels	Aurora	Wisconsin-Illinois	Green Bay	2-0
5-19	Deacon Morrissey	Greensboro	Carolina Assoc.	Winston-Salem	4-1
5-20	Peltz	Kewanee	Central Assoc.	Muscatine	6-0
5-21	R.R. Brown	Winchester	Blue Grass	Richmond	10-0
5-23	Jim Parks	Richmond	Blue Grass	Maysville	13-0
5-23	Erskine Mayer	Albany	South Atlantic	Augusta	2-0
5-27	Mike Kramer	Duluth	Minnesota-Wisc.	Rochester	3-2
5-27	Will Wehrman	Bay City	Southwest Texas	Laredo	6-0
5-31	Clarence McGrew	Junction City	Central Kansas	Manhattan	6-0
6-1	D.E. Byrd	Helena	Union Association	Boise	2-1
6-3	Carl Renfer	Saginaw	Southern Michigan	Adrian	10-2
6-3	Paul Stowers	Waterloo	Three-I	Davenport	3-2
6-5	Arthur Johnson	Madison	Wisconsin-Illinois	Fond du Lac	4-0 (P)
6-6	Gene Woodburn	Duluth	Minnesota-Wisc.	Winona	5-0
6-7	F. Reiger	Fall River	New England	Haverhill	3-2
6-8	Rudy Niehaus	Charleston	Mountain States	Huntington	1-0 (11)
6-8	George Baumgardner	Huntington	Mountain States	Charleston	0-1 (10)
6-9	Phifer Fullenwider	Independence	Western Assoc.	Tulsa	1-0
6-13	Harry Ables	Oakland	Pacific Coast	Los Angeles	2-0
6-14	Jack Northrop	Reading	Tri-State	Lancaster	3-0 (P)
6-20	Charles Gibson	Superior	Nebraska State	Grand Island	2-1
6-21	Ralph Comstock	Vicksburg	Cotton States	Hattiesburg	9-0
6-25	Addison Brennan	Buffalo	Eastern	Jersey City	1-0
6-27	Fred Applegate	Clarksville	Kitty	Fulton	9-0
6-28	T.J. Hill	Anniston	Southeastern	Selma	4-0
6-29	Harry Camnitz	Youngstown	Ohio-Penn.	Steubenville	9-0
7-1	Ralph Comstock	Vicksburg	Cotton States	Meridian	2-0
7-4	Bucky O'Brien	Denver	Western	Lincoln	5-1
7-5	F.R. Newmeyer	Bay City	Southwest Texas	Brownsville	3-2
7-5	Ferdinand Henkle	Portland	Pacific Coast	Sacramento	1-0
7-10	C.L. Bemis	Newark	Central	Terre Haute	2-0
7-13	Ahlstrom	Ashland-Catlettsburg	Mountain States	Montgomery	2-0
7-13	L.R. Wagner	Columbia	South Atlantic	Jacksonville	2-0
7-16	Charlie Grover	Ironton	Mountain States	Ashland-Catlettsburg	8-0
7-16	Clarence Fitzwater	Youngstown	Ohio-Penn.	Steubenville	8-0
7-18	Dickinson	Edmonton	Western Canada	Saskatoon	3-0
7-18	Louis Leroy	Bay City	Southern Michigan	Jackson	1-0
7-24	Harry Syfert	Winnipeg	Western Canada	Brandon	3-1
7-29	Smoky Joe Wood	Boston	American	St. Louis	5-0
7-30	Matheus Theisen	Lancaster	Ohio State	Hamilton	2-0
8-3	Jim Hauser	Paris	Blue Grass	Lexington	9-0
8-4	Padden	Aurora	Wisconsin-Illinois	Green Bay	3-0
8-10	Bill Foxen	Birmingham	Southern Assoc.	Chattanooga	1-0
8-10	Ben Pattison	Terre Haute	Central	Grand Rapids	0-1
8-12	Harold Chrisman	Racine	Wisconsin-Illinois	Green Bay	3-0
8-14	O.W. Brazell	Wilmington	Tri-State	Johnstown	2-1
8-15	Charles Deardorff	Cleburne	Texas-Oklahoma	Bonham	14-1 (7)
8-23	Fred Blum	Fall River	New England	Lawrence	2-0
8-23	Cy Dahlgren	Superior	Minnesota-Wisc.	Rochester	1-0 (P)
8-25	Brown	Hannibal	Central Assoc.	Monmouth	3-0
8-26	Addison Brennan	Buffalo	Eastern	Jersey City	0-1 (10)
8-27	Ed Walsh	Chicago	American	Boston	5-0
8-28	Ernie Calbert	Jackson	Kitty	Hopkinsville	0-1
8-28	Ed Coleman	Fulton	Kitty	Paducah	1-0
8-28	M. Parker	New Britain	Connecticut	Waterbury	1-0
8-29	Clarence Dunbar	Superior	Minnesota-Wisc.	Winona	6-0
8-30	Joe Houser	Sharon	Ohio-Penn.	Mansfield	8-0
8-31	Phifer Fullenwider	Columbia	South Atlantic	Savannah	4-0
9-5	Roy Irvin	Superior	Nebraska State	Grand Island	4-0
9-5	Sundelar	Hastings	Nebraska State	Fremont	12-0
9-12	Joseph Willis	Decatur	Three-I	Peoria	4-1
9-12	Jeff Clark	Sioux City	Western	Des Moines	1-0
9-17	Heinie Steiger	Sioux City	Western	Denver	4-0
9-22	Jess Nichol	Paducah	Kitty	Jackson	8-0

Number in parentheses indicates innings if other than nine; "P" indicates perfect game.

THIS DATE IN MINOR LEAGUE HISTORY

March 12, 1911, Simon Burdette Nicholls, noted player and shortstop with the Baltimore, Eastern League club, died of typhoid fever at age 29.

April 20, 1911, Pitcher Clyde Emsley, Wichita, Western League, died at age 22 of spinal meningitis.

April 21, 1911, Pitcher George "Lefty" Craig, Indianapolis, American Association, died of a bullet wound received in a struggle with a burglar at a mineral springs resort, the club's training camp, near Indianapolis.

April 26, 1911, Joe McCarthy, playing third base for Toledo, American Association, committed four errors in a game with Minneapolis.

May 5, 1911, Third baseman Lil Sager of Evansville was spiked in the hand in the first inning, missing his first Central League game since 1904. Sager had not missed an inning since July 20, 1904, playing in 895 straight games for Evansville and South Bend. It was the longest consecutive game streak in Organized Ball at the time.

May 20, 1911, The Lynn-Fall River New England League game was called in the seventh inning after a fly ball, which was ruled a home run, disappeared in a fog bank.

May 20, 1911, No games were played in the Eastern League because of the funeral of King Edward VII.

June 15, 1911, Arthur Brown, 26-year-old first baseman with Albany of the New York State League, died in an Albany hospital from four bullet wounds received at the hands of John V. McStea, a New Orleans actor who claimed to have found his wife in an apartment with Brown. Brown had also played for Detroit, American League, Montreal, Eastern League, and Trenton, Tri-State League.

July 5, 1911, In Huntsville, Alabama, Horace Bealey, former catcher with Columbus of the South Atlantic League, and later with Yazoo City, Cotton States League, was shot and killed by Lucy Anderson in the red-light district. The couple had engaged in a jealous quarrel.

July 11, 1911, At Springfield, the Connecticut League game with Bridgeport was called by the umpire after the 12th inning, tied 3-3, "because of intense heat."

August 9, 1911, J. Michael Smalling, first baseman for Lancaster, Tri-State League, drowned while canoeing in the Conestoga River at Lancaster, Pennsylvania. He was 22.

August 26, 1911, Thomas Lessord of Columbus, scheduled to pitch for Cincinnati in 1912, died of quinsy.

September 11, 1911, At Richmond, Kentucky, Richmond and Frankfort of the Blue Grass League played a game in 57 minutes in which a total of 39 hits were made.

September 23, 1911, Louis Angemeier, 25, noted minor league player, this season with Huntsville of the Southeastern League, died of swamp fever in Louisville, Kentucky.

September 25, 1911, John C. Bender, an Indian pitcher and brother of Charles "Chief" Bender, died unexpectedly of heart failure during a game in Edmonton. Bender formerly played in the Northern and South Atlantic Leagues. With Columbus in 1908, Bender stabbed manager Win Clark and was suspended until the 1910 season. Bender began this season with Charleston and finished with Edmonton of the Western Canada League. Bender, married, conducted a cafe in Charleston, South Carolina, where he was buried.

November 23, 1911, Edward Cermak, 29, former player and Cotton States League umpire, died from the effects of an injury to his throat caused by a foul tip.

December 1, 1911, A. McCoy Pitts, age 22, a player with Johnson City of the Appalachian League, died of an accidental gunshot wound.

December 11, 1911, The Eastern League changed its name to the International League. Edward G. Barrow was elected president for five years.

1912

American League
President: Byron Bancroft Johnson

Standings	W	L	Pct.	GB	Attend.	Manager
Boston Red Sox	105	47	.691	—	597,096	Jake Stahl
Washington Senators	91	61	.599	14	350,663	Clark Griffith
Philadelphia Athletics	90	62	.592	15	517,653	Connie Mack
Chicago White Sox	78	76	.506	28	602,241	Nixey Callahan
Cleveland Naps	75	78	.490	30½	336,844	Harry Davis/Joe Birmingham
Detroit Tigers	69	84	.451	36½	402,870	Hugh Jennings
St. Louis Browns	53	101	.344	53	214,070	Bobby Wallace/George Stovall
New York Highlanders	50	102	.329	55	242,194	Harry Wolverton

BA: Ty Cobb, Detroit, .410
Runs: Eddie Collins, Philadelphia, 137
Hits: Ty Cobb, Detroit, 227
RBIs: Frank Baker, Philadelphia, 133
HRs: Frank Baker, Philadelphia, 10
Tris Speaker, Boston, 10

Wins: Smoky Joe Wood, Boston, 34
SOs: Walter Johnson, Washington, 303
ERA: Walter Johnson, Washington, 1.39
Pct: Smoky Joe Wood, Boston, .872, 34-5
IP: Ed Walsh, Chicago, 393

National League
President: Thomas J. Lynch

Standings	W	L	Pct.	GB	Attend.	Manager
New York Giants	103	48	.682	—	638,000	John McGraw
Pittsburgh Pirates	93	58	.616	10	384,000	Fred Clarke
Chicago Cubs	91	59	.607	11½	514,000	Frank Chance
Cincinnati Reds	75	78	.490	29	344,000	Hank O'Day
Philadelphia Phillies	73	79	.480	30½	250,000	Red Dooin
St. Louis Cardinals	63	90	.412	41	241,759	Roger Bresnahan
Brooklyn Dodgers	58	95	.379	46	243,000	Bill Dahlen
Boston Braves	52	101	.340	52	121,000	Johnny Kling

BA: Heinie Zimmerman, Chicago, .372
Runs: Bob Bescher, Cincinnati, 120
Hits: Heinie Zimmerman, Chicago, 207
RBIs: Heinie Zimmerman, Chicago, 103
HRs: Heinie Zimmerman, Chicago, 14

Wins: Larry Cheney, Chicago, 26
Rube Marquard, New York, 26
SOs: Grover Alexander, Philadelphia, 195
ERA: Jeff Tesreau, New York, 1.96
Pct: Claude Hendrix, Pittsburgh, .727, 24-9

AA American Association
President: Thomas M. Chivington

Standings	W	L	Pct.	GB	Attend.	Manager
Minneapolis Millers	105	60	.636	—	198,005	Joe Cantillon
Toledo Mud Hens	98	66	.598	6½	158,338	Topsy Hartsel
Columbus Senators	98	68	.590	7½	188,348	William Friel
Kansas City Blues	85	82	.509	21	185,950	Charles Carr
Milwaukee Brewers	78	85	.479	26	126,940	Hugh Duffy/Harry Clark
St. Paul Apostles	77	90	.461	29	106,149	Mike Kelley
Louisville Colonels	66	101	.395	40	109,434	Jack Tighe/John Hayden
Indianapolis Indians	56	111	.335	50	162,557	James Burke/Charlie O'Leary/Charles O'Day

BA: Arthur Butler, St. Paul, .329
Runs: Otis Clymer, Minneapolis, 127
Hits: Otis Clymer, Minneapolis, 200
HRs: Berton James, Kansas City, 10

Wins: Fred Olmstead, Minneapolis, 28
SOs: William Powell, Kansas City, 174
Pct: Hal Krausse, Toledo, .765, 13-4

AA International League
President: Edward G. Barrow

Standings	W	L	Pct.	GB	Manager
Toronto Maple Leafs	91	62	.595	—	Joe Kelley
Rochester Hustlers	86	67	.562	5	John Ganzel
Newark Indians	80	72	.526	10½	Joe McGinnity
Baltimore Orioles	74	75	.497	15	Jack Dunn
Buffalo Bisons	71	78	.477	18	George Stallings
Montreal Royals	71	81	.467	19½	Billy Lush/Joe Yeager/Kitty Bransfield
Jersey City Skeeters	70	84	.455	21½	Larry Schlafly
Providence Grays	63	87	.420	26½	Frederick Lake/Wild Bill Donovan

Attendance: Buffalo, 241,080.

BA: Eddie Murphy, Baltimore, .361
Runs: Frank Truesdale, Buffalo, 120
Hits: Harry Swacina, Newark, 193
HRs: Tim Jordan, Toronto, 19

Wins: Dick Rudolph, Toronto, 25
SOs: Bill Bailey, Providence, 169
Pct: Dick Rudolph, Toronto, .714, 25-10

AA Pacific Coast League
President: Allan T. Baum

Standings	W	L	Pct.	GB	Manager
Oakland Oaks	120	83	.591	—	Bud Sharpe
Vernon Tigers	118	83	.587	1	W.L. "Happy" Hogan
Los Angeles Angels	110	93	.542	10	Frank "Cap" Dillon
Portland Beavers	85	100	.459	26	Walter McCredie
San Francisco Seals	89	115	.436	31½	Daniel Long
Sacramento Sacts	73	121	.376	42½	Patsy O'Rourke/Deacon Van Buren

*Won first-half **Won second-half ***Won both halves

BA: Henry Heitmuller, Los Angeles, .335
Runs: Walter Carlisle, Vernon, 177
Hits: Henry Bayless, Vernon, 228
HRs: Bert Coy, Oakland, 19

Wins: Harry Ables, Oakland, 25
Charles Chech, Los Angeles, 25
SOs: Harry Ables, Oakland, 303
Pct: Jack Killilay, Oakland, .789, 15-4

A Southern Association
President: William B. Kavanaugh

Standings	W	L	Pct.	GB	Manager
Birmingham Barons	85	51	.625	—	Carleton Molesworth
Mobile Sea Gulls	79	58	.576	6½	Michael Finn
New Orleans Pelicans	71	64	.526	13½	Charley Frank
Memphis Chickasaws	68	71	.490	18½	Bill Bernhardt
Nashville Volunteers	67	70	.489	18½	William Schwartz
Montgomery Rebels	64	75	.460	22½	Johnny Dobbs
Chattanooga Lookouts	59	75	.440	25	William A. Smith
Atlanta Crackers	54	83	.394	31½	Charles Hemphill/Charles "Whitey" Alperman

BA: Harry Welchonce, Atlanta, .325
Runs: King Bailey, Atlanta, 89
Hits: Harry Welchonce, Atlanta, 157
HRs: Del Young, Nashville, 7

SBs: Jimmy Johnston, Birmingham, 81
Wins: Al Demaree, Mobile, 24
Pct: Al Demaree, Mobile, .706, 24-10

A Western League
President: Norris L. O'Neill

Standings	W	L	Pct.	GB	Manager
Denver Grizzlies	99	63	.611	—	Jack Hendricks
St. Joseph Drummers	94	72	.566	7	Jay Andrews
Omaha Rourkes	92	71	.564	7½	Pa Rourke
Des Moines Boosters	82	80	.506	17	Frank Isbell
Lincoln Railsplitters	83	81	.506	17	Bill Dwyer
Sioux City Packers	74	85	.465	23½	George "Red" Andreas/James "Ducky" Holmes
Wichita Jobbers	75	89	.457	25	George Hughes
Topeka Jayhawks	51	109	.319	47	Dale Gear

BA: Babe Borton, St. Joseph, .364
Runs: Ray Powell, St. Joseph, 139
Hits: Hy Myers, Sioux City, 224
HRs: John Beall, Denver, 18

Wins: Mark Hall, Omaha, 25
Elmer Brown, Sioux City, 25
SOs: Joe Hagerman, Lincoln, 315
Pct: Harry Hicks, Omaha, .783, 18-5

B Central League
President: Louis Heilbroner

Standings	W	L	Pct.	GB	Manager
Fort Wayne Railroaders	77	52	.597	—	Frank Shaughnessy
Youngstown Steelmen	74	54	.578	2½	Bill Phillips
Erie Sailors	75	55	.577	2½	William Gilbert
Springfield Reapers	72	54	.571	3½	Charles O'Day/John Pendry
Dayton Veterans	73	56	.565	4	Charles "Punch" Knoll
Wheeling Stogies	66	61	.519	10	J.E. Anderson
Canton Statesmen	64	66	.492	13½	Ed Gremlinger
Akron Rubbermen	59	68	.464	17	Lee Fohl
Grand Rapids Black Sox	58	68	.460	17½	Edward Smith/Bert Annis
Terre Haute Terre-iers	59	70	.457	18	Angus Grant/John Nee
Zanesville Potters	52	78	.400	25½	Willus Kelley/John Pendry/Martin Hogan
South Bend Benders	41	88	.318	36	Harry Arndt

BA: Larry LeJeune, Grand Rapids, .361
Runs: Frank Gilhooey, Erie, 104
Hits: Larry LeJeune, Grand Rapids, 168
HRs: Larry LeJeune, Grand Rapids, 25
Wins: Buck Sterzer, Erie, 24

SOs: Earl Moseley, Youngstown, 235
Pct: Fred Sherry, Youngstown, .769, 10-3
Lou Shettler, Erie, .769, 10-3
Ted Goulait, Springfield, .769, 10-3

B Connecticut League
President: James O'Rourke

Standings	W	L	Pct.	GB	Manager
New Haven Murlins	76	41	.650	—	Jerry O'Connell
Hartford Senators	67	51	.568	9½	Thomas Connery
Bridgeport Orators	61	55	.526	14½	Eugene McCann
Holyoke Papermakers	57	58	.496	18	Daniel O'Neil
Springfield Ponies	50	70	.417	27½	John Zeller
New Britain/Waterbury Spuds#	39	75	.342	35½	John Hoey

#New Britain (12-22) moved to Waterbury June 15.

BA: Hugh High, Hartford, .327
Runs: Hugh High, Hartford, 80
Hits: Hugh High, Hartford, 145
HRs: Clarence "Pop" Foster, New Haven, 9
Wins: Jacob Reisigl, New Haven, 21

SOs: Frank Green, Holyoke, 212
Pct: Clarence "Pop" Foster, New Haven, .750, 15-5
Cliff Averett, Hartford, .750, 12-4

B New England League
President: Tim H. Murnane

Standings	W	L	Pct.	GB	Manager
Lawrence Barristers	76	47	.618	—	Louis Piper
Lowell Grays	75	50	.600	2	James Gray
Worcester Busters	67	56	.545	9	Jesse Burkett/John O'Donnell
Lynn Leonardites	63	62	.504	14	Terry McGovern/Frank Leonard
Brockton Shoemakers	62	62	.500	14½	Jed McLane
New Bedford Whalers	57	67	.460	19½	Frank Connaughton/Jim Sullivan
Haverhill Hustlers	48	76	.387	28½	Lave Cross
Fall River Brinies	46	74	.383	28½	John H. O'Brien

BA: Art DeGroff, Lowell, .348
Runs: Pete Clemens, Haverhill/Lowell, 104
Hits: Art DeGroff, Lowell, 170
HRs: Art DeGroff, Lowell, 13
Wins: Ray Keating, Lawrence, 26
Pct: Jeff Pfeffer, Lowell, .733, 11-4

B New York State League
President: John H. Farrell

Standings	W	L	Pct.	GB	Manager
Utica Utes	82	57	.590	—	Michael O'Neill
Wilkes-Barre Barons	81	57	.587	½	Bill Clymer
Elmira Colonels	75	58	.564	4	John Calhoun
Troy Trojans	70	62	.530	8½	Henry Ramsey
Scranton Miners	62	69	.473	16	John Freeman
Albany Senators	62	72	.463	17½	James Tamsett
Syracuse Stars	54	82	.397	26½	Edward McCafferty/Fred Burchell
Binghamton Bingoes	50	79	.388	27	Harry Lumley/Hollis Gitchell/Gus Zelmer

BA: Harry Lumley, Binghamton/Troy, .326
Runs: George Anderson, Wilkes-Barre, 107
Hits: Charles Loudenslager, Syracuse, 166
SOs: George Pearce, Scranton, 238

B Northwestern League
President: Fielder Jones

Standings	W	L	Pct.	GB	Manager
Seattle Giants	99	66	.600	—	Jack Barry/Frank Raymond
Spokane Indians	95	72	.568	5	Harry Ostdick
Vancouver Champions	94	73	.563	6	Kitty Brashear
Portland Colts	74	88	.457	23½	Nick Williams
Victoria Bees	72	93	.436	27	Lou Nordyke
Tacoma Tigers	62	104	.373	37½	Mike Lynch

BA: Jack Meek, Victoria, .344
Runs: Ralph Myers, Spokane, 121
Hits: Ralph Myers, Spokane, 207
HRs: Les Mann, Seattle, 23
SBs: Ralph Myers, Spokane, 116
Wins: Bill James, Seattle, 26
SOs: Bill James, Seattle, 201
Pct: Bill James, Seattle, .765, 26-8

B Texas League
President: Wilbur P. Allen

Standings	W	L	Pct.	GB	Manager
Houston Buffalos	87	52	.626	—	John Fillman
San Antonio Bronchos	84	57	.596	4	George Leidy/Frank Metz
Waco Navigators	82	63	.566	8	Ellis Hardy
Dallas Giants	73	67	.522	14½	Frederick Cavender
Austin Senators	66	79	.455	24	Red Downey
Galveston Pirates/Sand Crabs	59	79	.428	27½	Curley Maloney
Ft. Worth Panthers	59	81	.421	28½	Walter Morris
Beaumont Oilers	55	87	.387	33½	Edward Wheeler

BA: Frank Metz, San Antonio, .323
Runs: Jewel Ens, Dallas, 96
Hits: Frank Metz, San Antonio, 171
HRs: Frank Metz, San Antonio, 21
Wins: Poll Perritt, Ft. Worth, 24
Rube Foster, Houston, 24
SOs: Gene Moore, Galveston, 213
Pct: Rube Foster, Houston, .774, 24-7

B Three-I League
President: Albert R. Tearney

Standings	W	L	Pct.	GB	Manager
Springfield Senators	90	44	.672	—	Richard Smith
Davenport Prodigals	75	60	.556	15½	Daniel O'Leary
Decatur Commodores	69	67	.507	22	Charles Fraser
Quincy Old Soldiers	67	70	.489	24½	Bade Myers
Dubuque Dubs	65	73	.471	27	Clarence "Pants" Rowland
Danville Speakers	63	71	.470	27	John Massing
Bloomington Bloomers	58	78	.427	33	Harry Bay/James Cuthbert
Peoria Distillers	56	80	.415	35	Charles Stis

BA: Dan Kerwin, Quincy, .350
Runs: Frank Lofton, Springfield, 91
Hits: Dan Kerwin, Quincy, 185
Wins: Bunn Hearn, Springfield, 27
SOs: Ferdie Shupp, Decatur, 265
ERA: John Middleton, Davenport, 1.24

B Tri-State League
President: Charles F. Carpenter

Standings	W	L	Pct.	GB	Manager
Harrisburg Senators	75	37	.670	—	George Cockhill
Allentown	65	47	.580	10	William Coughlin
Trenton Tigers	61	51	.545	14	George Heckert
Lancaster Lanks/					
Atlantic City@	59	52	.532	15½	John Castle
Wilmington Chicks	58	54	.518	17	James Jackson
Altoona Rams/					
Reading Pretzels#	52	59	.468	22½	Charles Babb
York White Roses	45	65	.409	29	John Manning
Johnstown Johnnies/Chester+	31	81	.277	44	Bert Conn/Curt Wiegand

#Altoona (12-22) moved to Reading June 13.
@Lancaster (15-19) moved to Atlantic City June 18.
+Johnstown (25-60) moved to Chester August 2.

BA: Charlie Johnson, Trenton, .403
Runs: Fred Clay, Trenton, 114
Hits: Charlie Johnson, Trenton, 161
HRs: Mert Whitney, Trenton, 15
Wins: J.L. Stanley, Atlantic City, 23
Pct: John Fox, Harrisburg, .909, 10-1

C Canadian League
President: J.P. Fitzgerald

Standings	W	L	Pct.	GB	Manager
Ottawa Senators	63	35	.643	—	Louis Cook
Brantford Red Sox	54	44	.551	9	Ambrose Kane
Hamilton Kolts	51	46	.526	11½	George "Knotty" Lee
London Tecumsehs	48	49	.495	14½	Frank Bowerman/Albert Barrett
St. Thomas Saints	46	50	.479	16	Carl Stewart
Berlin Busy Bees	42	50	.457	18	George Deneau
Guelph Maple Leafs	39	51	.433	20	George Needham/Fred Applegate
Peterborough Whitecaps	40	58	.408	23	Curtis Templin/David Rowan

BA: Jack Fryer, Guelph, .372
Runs: Frank Burke, Ottawa, 79
Hits: Harry Corns, Hamilton, 113
Wins: Matt Hynes, London, 19
SOs: Harry Donovan, Brantford, 138
Pct: Joab McManus, Ottawa, .875, 14-2

C Central International League
President: H.A. Blume

Standings	W	L	Pct.	GB	Manager
Duluth White Sox	58	41	.586	—	William "Darby" O'Brien
Superior Red Sox	51	54	.486	10	Joe Sommer
Grand Forks Flicker Tails	50	55	.476	11	Harmony Van Dine
Winnipeg Maroons	50	59	.459	13	Otto Krueger

C South Atlantic League
President: Nick P. Corish

Standings	W	L	Pct.	GB	Manager
Jacksonville Tarpons*	70	41	.631	—	Percy Wilder
Savannah Indians	66	50	.569	6½	Perry Lipe
Columbus Foxes**	61	51	.545	9½	James Fox
Albany Babies	52	62	.456	19½	Bernie McCay/William Duggleby
Macon Peaches	51	62	.451	20	George Kalkhoff
Columbia Comers	41	75	.353	31½	Langdon Clark/Ted McGrew/Herman Badel

Playoff: Jacksonville 4 games, Columbus 1.

BA: Roy Massey, Savannah, .324
Runs: Bernie McCay, Albany, 97
Hits: Roy Massey, Savannah, 146
HRs: Walton Cruise, Macon, 8
Wins: Albert Schulz, Savannah, 25
SOs: Albert Schulz, Savannah, 318
Pct: Henry "Bugs" Weidell, Columbus, .750, 15-5

C Virginia League
President: Jacob O. Boatwright

Standings	W	L	Pct.	GB	Manager
Roanoke Tigers	81	55	.596	—	William "Buck" Pressley
Petersburg Goobers	79	54	.594	½	Henry Busch
Richmond Colts	77	55	.579	2	Steve Griffin
Portsmouth Pirates	65	63	.508	12	Lou Castro
Norfolk Tars	67	65	.508	12	Charles Shaffer
Newport News Shipbuilders	46	84	.354	32	John J. Grim/Buck Hooker
Danville Red Sox#	16	32	.333	NA	William "Dave" Gaston
Lynchburg Shoemakers#	11	34	.244	NA	Otis Stockdale/James Kelley

#Danville and Lynchburg disbanded June 15.

BA: Steve Griffin, Richmond, .356
Runs: Steve Griffin, Richmond, 97
Hits: Steve Griffin, Richmond, 167
RBIs: Steve Griffin, Richmond, 97
HRs: Frank Burke, Richmond, 12
Wins: Erskine Mayer, Portsmouth, 26
Pct: Erskine Mayer, Portsmouth, .743, 26-9

C Wisconsin-Illinois League
President: Frank S. Edmison

Standings	W	L	Pct.	GB	Manager
Oshkosh Indians	87	45	.659	—	Joseph Killian
Racine Belles	78	51	.605	7½	Billy Fox
Appleton Papermakers	67	60	.528	17½	George Hogriever
Wausau Lumberjacks	66	67	.496	21½	Mickey Malloy
Green Bay Bays	61	68	.473	24½	James Garry
Rockford Wolverines	63	71	.470	25	Frank Richardson
Aurora Blues	54	80	.403	34	Guy Dickey/Thomas Asmussen
Madison Senators	51	85	.375	38	Smiley Smith

BA: Harry Sylvester, Appleton, .355
Runs: George Brautigan, Appleton, 104
Hits: Harry Sylvester, Appleton, 177
HRs: Earl Smith, Green Bay, 12

Wins: Charles Watson, Oshkosh, 22
SOs: Lynn Brenton, Wausau, 224
Pct: Al Kench, Racine, .750, 21-7

D Appalachian League
President: Jacob Smith

Standings	W	L	Pct.	GB	Manager
Bristol Boosters	57	43	.570	—	Clarence "Red" Munson
Knoxville Reds	56	46	.549	2	Frank Moffett
Johnson City Soldiers	54	48	.529	4	James Duffy
Cleveland Counts	51	51	.500	7	Count Zimeski
Asheville Moonshiners	47	58	.448	12½	Rudy Kling/Burt Kite
Morristown Jobbers	41	60	.409	16½	Apey Mills

BA: E.N. "Pop" Shaw, Johnson City, .401
Runs: Buck Thrasher, Cleveland, 68
Hits: Buck Thrasher, Cleveland, 126
HRs: E.J. Pope, Morristown, 9

Wins: F.E. Wilson, Knoxville, 21
SOs: Claude Williams, Morristown, 224
Pct: Frank Davis, Knoxville, .813, 13-3

D Blue Grass League
President: William Neal

Standings	W	L	Pct.	GB	Manager
Frankfort Lawmakers	85	42	.670	—	Ollie Gfroerer
Maysville Rivermen	82	47	.634	4	James Carmony/Harry Kunkel
Richmond Pioneers	66	64	.508	20½	William Fisher
Lexington Colts	60	65	.480	24	Hogan Yancy/Ted McGrew
Paris Bourbonites	60	69	.465	26	Joe Lewis/Danning Harrell
Winchester Hustlers/Nicholasville/					
Mt. Sterling Orphans#	31	97	.242	54½	Harry Kunkel/McBrayer/Bob Spade

#Winchester moved to Nicholasville June 8, then to Mt. Sterling June 26.

BA: Danning Harrell, Paris, .401
Runs: Ovid Nicholson, Frankfort, 128
Hits: Norman Munn, Richmond, 188
HRs: Norman Munn, Richmond, 22

SBs: Ovid Nicholson, Frankfort, 111
Wins: Jim Hauser, Paris, 23
SOs: Harry Camnitz, Lexington, 204
Pct: Bert Grover, Maysville, .720, 18-7

D Border League
President: Richard Jackson

Standings	W	L	Pct.	GB	Manager
Wyandotte	19	5	.792	—	H.R. Browne
Pontiac Indians	14	9	.609	4½	Henry McIntoch
Mt. Clemens Bathers	11	15	.423	9	W. Trombley
Windsor	9	14	.391	9½	J. Wilkie
Port Huron Independents	7	17	.292	12	Bill Brown

BA: Frank Loranger, Wyandotte, .376
Runs: Orville Woodruff, Wyandotte, 21

Hits: Frank Loranger, Wyandotte, 37

D Carolina Association
President: Joseph H. Wearn

Standings	W	L	Pct.	GB	Manager
Anderson Electricians	66	44	.600	—	George Ramsey
Winston-Salem Twins	63	47	.573	3	Charles Clancy
Charlotte Hornets	61	46	.570	3½	Jim Osteen
Spartanburg Red Sox	54	55	.495	11½	Bill Laval
Greensboro Patriots	51	59	.464	15	Frank Doyle
Greenville Spinners	34	78	.304	33	Tom Stouch/Glenn Colby

BA: Ralph Stuart, Greensboro, .326
Runs: Bill Schumaker, Winston-Salem, 73
Hits: Bill Schumaker, Winston-Salem, 125
HRs: Bill Schumaker, Winston-Salem, 16

RBIs: Bill Schumaker, Winston-Salem, 106
Wins: Pete Boyle, Winston-Salem, 16
SOs: Paul Fittery, Anderson, 191
Pct: Pete Boyle, Winston-Salem, .762, 16-5

D Central Association
President: M.E. Justice

Standings	W	L	Pct.	GB	Attend.	Manager
Ottumwa Speedboys	79	50	.612	—	23,000	Ned Egan
Kewanee Boilermakers	74	51	.592	3	19,000	George Pennington/Art Queisser
Burlington Pathfinders	73	53	.579	4½	25,000	Richard Rohn
Monmouth Browns	71	55	.563	6½	18,000	Bert Hough/Jack Corbett/R.L. Noven
Hannibal Cannibals	67	61	.523	11½		Eddie Herr/Ed Painter
Galesburg Pavers	61	67	.477	17½	18,000	Ducky Eberts
Keokuk Indians	49	76	.392	28	17,000	Art Queisser/Bill Proutt
Muscatine Wallopers	33	94	.260	45	22,000	Ed Coleman/Bill Krieg/Joe Wall/Bill Clayton

BA: George Manush, Ottumwa, .375
Runs: Harry Ellis, Burlington, 100
Hits: Harry Shanley, Muscatine, 176
HRs: John Sullivan, Ottumwa, 21

Wins: Bert Dunn, Ottumwa, 26
SOs: Joe Sloan, Keokuk, 197
Pct: Tom Drohan, Kewanee, .800, 24-6

D Central Kansas League
President: Roy C. Gafford

Standings	W	L	Pct.	GB	Manager
Great Bend Millers	54	36	.600	—	Affie Wilson
Manhattan Elks	52	38	.578	2	Fred Moore/Nick Kohl
Newton Railroaders/					
Minneapolis Minnies#	50	40	.555	4	A. Stillwell
Junction City Soldiers	47	43	.522	7	Cecil Bankhead
Lyons Lions	36	54	.400	18	Fred Wilson
Salina Insurgents	31	59	.344	23	Bert Lamb

#Newton (16-11) moved to Minneapolis July 12.

BA: Muggsy Monroe, Newton/Minneapolis, .352
Runs: Burnham Smith, Manhattan, 88
Hits: Muggsy Monroe, Newton/Minneapolis, 118

Wins: Fred Haag, Manhattan, 18
   Elmer Brown, Great Bend, 18
Pct: Fred Haag, Manhattan, .750, 18-6

D Cotton States League
President: Lewis

Standings	W	L	Pct.	GB	Manager
Vicksburg Hill Billies$*	66	42	.611	—	Otto Mills
Meridian Metropolitans+	52	46	.531	9	Bob Kennedy/Harry Steinfeldt/Orth Collins
Jackson Senators	57	55	.509	11	Roy Montgomery
Hattiesburg Timberjacks/					
Columbus Joy Riders@	56	59	.487	13½	Carlos Smith
Greenwood Scouts**	51	64	.443	18½	Orth Collins/M.G. Dudley
New Orleans Little Pels/					
Yazoo City Zoos#	41	57	.418	20	Gene DeMontreville

#New Orleans (14-9) moved to Yazoo City May 9, then disbanded August 3.
@Hattiesburg (19-24) moved to Columbus June 5.
+Meridian disbanded August 3.
$Vicksburg disbanded August 13.

Playoff: Greenwood was declared champion as first half champion Vicksburg had disbanded.

BA: Carlos Smith, Hattiesburg/Columbus, .348
Runs: W.J. Blanchfield, Hattiesburg/Columbus, 116
Hits: W.J. Blanchfield, Hattiesburg/Columbus, 140
   Will Kuhn, Vicksburg/Columbus, 140

Wins: Walt Kinney, Vicksburg, 22
   Larry Cheney, New Orleans/Yazoo City/Jackson, 22
Pct: Walter Hirsch, Meridian, 1.000, 12-0

D Illinois-Missouri League
President: Charles Cline

Standings	W	L	Pct.	GB	Manager
Lincoln Abes	70	47	.598	—	Louis Ehrgott
Pekin Celestials	61	55	.526	8½	Hebert
Canton Highlanders	57	56	.504	11	
Clinton Champs/					
Kankakee Kanks#	56	56	.500	11½	Claude Suttles/Fred "Blackie" Wilson
Champaign Velvets	53	64	.453	17	Chuck Fleming
Streator Speedboys	46	65	.414	21	Jack Leuter

#Clinton (2-5) moved to Kankakee May 16.

BA: Roy Wolfe, Lincoln, .374
Runs: Roy Wolfe, Lincoln, 89
Hits: Roy Wolfe, Lincoln, 164
HRs: Andy Lotshaw, Canton, 11

Wins: Clarence Vaught, Lincoln, 22
SOs: Fred Witte, Champaign, 211
Pct: N. Utrecht, Champaign, .786, 11-3

D Kitty League
President: Frank Bassett

Standings	W	L	Pct.	GB	Manager
Clarksville Rebels	68	29	.701	—	Senter Rainey
Henderson Hens	52	48	.520	17½	Offa Neal/Ward Snyder
Evansville Yankees	47	52	.475	22	Charles Barton
Paducah Chiefs	45	55	.450	24½	John Nairn/Dave Anderson
Hopkinsville Hoppers	54	54	.449	24½	Dudley Lewis/Nig Langdon/Tom Atkins
Cairo Egyptians	41	59	.410	28½	Carl Page/Bill Everett/Tim Flood

BA: L. Bohannon, Paducah, .326
Runs: A.G. Weber, Hopkinsville, 72
Hits: Henry Hughes, Cairo, 110

Wins: Ira Nicks, Clarksville, 22
SOs: Charles Humphrey, Clarksville, 157
Pct: Jim Coleman, Clarksville, .760, 19-6

D Michigan State League
President: Emerson W. Dickerson

Standings	W	L	Pct.	GB	Manager
Manistee Champs	83	35	.703	—	Connie Lewis
Traverse City Resorters	79	40	.664	4½	James Hamilton
Ludington Mariners	60	59	.504	23½	Frank Warrender/Claude Stark
Boyne City Boosters	50	69	.420	33½	Bo Slear
Muskegon Speeders	48	70	.407	35	Arthur DeBaker
Cadillac Chiefs	35	82	.299	47½	Calvin Wenger/Thomas Railing

BA: Alfred Platte, Cadillac, .367
Runs: Carl Jones, Manistee, 80
Hits: Bunny Brief, Traverse City, 152
HRs: Bunny Brief, Traverse City, 13

SBs: Alfred Platte, Cadillac, 42
Wins: Omer Benn, Manistee, 22
SOs: Alva Bowman, Muskegon, 213
Pct: LaRue Kirby, Traverse City, .857, 18-3

D MINK League
President: Warren Cummings

Standings	W	L	Pct.	GB	Manager
Nebraska City Forresters	61	38	.616	—	James "Ducky" Holmes
Falls City Colts	61	41	.598	1½	Tony Vanderhill
Auburn A's	59	41	.590	2½	
Humboldt Infants...............	44	57	.435	18	Jay Plank
Beatrice-Fairbury Milkskimmers..................	42	59	.415	20	George Shriver
Hiawatha Athletics	35	66	.346	27	

BA: Milt Drumm, Nebraska City, .341
Runs: Milt Drumm, Nebraska City, 65
    Ledger Free, Auburn, 65
Hits: Steve Brewer, Auburn, 121
HRs: Bill Stillwell, Auburn, 6

Wins: Vern Willey, Auburn, 22
SOs: George Zonderman, Auburn, 195
Pct: Patrick Conway, Nebraska City, .714, 15-6

D Minnesota-Wisconsin League
President: John A. Elliott

Standings	W	L	Pct.	GB	Manager
Winona Pirates..................	29	14	.674	—	Fred Curtis
Eau Claire Commissioners .	25	17	.595	3½	Russell Bailey
La Crosse Outcasts	15	26	.366	13	Carl Bond
Rochester Bugs	14	26	.350	13½	Art Lizzett

The league disbanded July 1.

D Mountain States League
President: S.J. Wright

Standings	W	L	Pct.	GB	Manager
Ironton Forgers	35	12	.745	—	"Peg" Moore
Ashland-Catlettsburg Twins+..	26	19	.578	8	James Kitler
Huntington Blue Sox+........	27	20	.574	8	Albert Knoessell
Williamson........................	11	30	.268	21	Henry Runser
Charleston Senators@	18	22	.450	NA	Charles Stockton
Middleport-Pomeroy/ Montgomery Miners#......	10	24	.294	NA	Joseph "Reddy" Mack

#Middleport-Pomeroy (7-21) moved to Mongomery June 16; Montgomery disbanded June 29.
@Charleston disbanded July 1.
+Ashland-Catlettsburg and Huntington disbanded July 8, ending the season.

D Nebraska State League
President: A.C. Felt

Standings	W	L	Pct.	GB	Manager
Hastings Third Citys#.........	67	44	.604	—	Bert Shaner
Fremont Pathfinders	66	45	.595	1	L.D. "Dad" Bennett
Kearney Kapitalists............	63	49	.563	4½	Harry Berte
Columbus Discoverers	56	54	.509	10½	Jack Palmer/Affie Wilson
Seward Statesmen	53	59	.473	14½	Bill Zink
Grand Island Collegians	52	59	.468	15	James Cockman
York Prohibitionists...........	45	66	.405	22	Al "Lefty" Davis
Superior Brickmakers.........	43	69	.384	24½	Dennis Bockewitz

#A Kearney win over Hastings was reversed at the 1913 spring meeting, giving Hastings the championship.

BA: L.D. "Dad" Bennett, Fremont, .360
Runs: Charles Block, York, 116
Hits: Bill Zink, Seward, 139

Wins: Joe Lotz, Kearney, 26
Pct: Bert Shaner, Hastings, .773, 17-5

D Ohio State League
President: Robert W. Read

Standings	W	L	Pct.	GB	Manager
Portsmouth Cobblers***	81	52	.609	—	Pete Childs
Mansfield Brownies............	72	67	.518	12	Barry McCormick/Walter East
Newark Skeeters	70	68	.507	13½	Jack Grim/Sandy Murray/ Barry McCormick
Marion Diggers/ Ironton Orphans#.............	65	72	.474	18	William Johnston/Fred Odwell/ "Peg" Moore
Lima Cigarmakers	64	73	.467	19	George "Zeke" Wrigley
Chillicothe Infants	57	77	.425	24½	Ray Ryan/Jesse Tannehill/Alfred Newnham

#Marion moved to Ironton July 15.

BA: Waldo Jackley, Marion/Ironton, .357
Runs: John Shovelin, Newark, 80
Hits: Frank Nesser, Lima, 170
HRs: Waldo Jackley, Marion/Ironton, 11

Wins: George Boehler, Newark, 27
Pct: Charles Burden, Marion/Ironton, .769, 20-6

D Ohio-Pennsylvania League
President: G.Y. Travis

Standings	W	L	Pct.	GB	Manager
Salem Quakers/ Fairmont Fairies@*..........	64	44	.593	—	Hugh Shannon/Buchanon
Steubenville- Follansbee Stubs**..........	62	50	.554	4	Gene Curtis
East Liverpool Potters/Pittsburgh/ New Martinsville%..........	49	57	.462	14	Tony Crane/Charles Donnelly
Sharon/Bridgeport Giants&	47	59	.443	16	Charles Eichenberger/Paige/Ralph Rainson
McKeesport Tubers$	39	22	.639	NA	Hack Adler/McGrath/Monte Pfeiffer
Alliance-Sebring Twins+....	26	33	.441	NA	Larry Maley
Connellsville Cokers#........	12	21	.364	NA	W.C. Wilson/Mack
New Castle Nocks#	9	22	.290	NA	Charles Smith/Jack Murray

#Connellsville and New Castle disbanded June 18.
@Salem moved to Fairmont July 9.
+Alliance-Sebring disbanded July 15 due to a player strike.
$McKeesport disbanded July 17.
&Sharon moved to Bridgeport August 10.
%East Liverpool moved to Pittsburgh (2-0) August 14, then to New Martinsville August 18. The league rescinded its membership in the National Association August 13 when it placed a franchise in Pittsburgh.

Playoff: Fairmont was declared champion when Steubenville-Follansbee was unable to field a team for the playoffs.

BA: Baby Foster, Connellsville/Alliance/ Steubenville, .377
Runs: William Carroll, Salem/Fairmont, 68
Hits: Harry Edwards, Salem/Fairmont, 127
HRs: William Carroll, Salem/Fairmont, 6
    Clarence Marshall, Steubenville, 6

SBs: Jim McKelvey, Steubenville/ Bridgeport, 40
Wins: Ed Sisley, Steubenville, 20
SOs: Ed Sisley, Steubenville, 217
Pct: Ed Bauer, McKeesport, .789, 15-4

D Oklahoma State League
President: Leo Meyer

Standings	W	L	Pct.	GB	Manager
Okmulgee Glassblowers	38	10	.792	—	Frank Garner
Tulsa Terriers....................	33	15	.688	5	Howard Price
Anadarko Indians...............	24	23	.511	13½	Roy Ellison/Thomas Reed/Ted Price
Holdenville Hitters	21	23	.477	15	Al Vorhees/James Bouldin/John Hendley
McAlester Miners...............	21	25	.457	16	Jerry Kane
Muskogee Indians..............	19	24	.442	16½	Victor Kelly/Dick Speer
Oklahoma City Senators.....	15	33	.313	23	Bill Reukauff/Joe "Leo" Langley
Guthrie	15	33	.313	23	Chick Leutke

The league disbanded June 29.
Attendance: Tulsa, 19,200.

SOs: Ben Tincup, Muskogee, 163

D Rocky Mountain League
President: Ira Bidwell

Standings	W	L	Pct.	GB	Manager
Pueblo/Trinidad/ Cheyenne Indians@	22	7	.759	—	John Galena/Ira Bidwell
Canon City Swastikas/Raton# .	20	14	.588	4½	Farrell
Colorado Springs Millionaires/ Dawson Stags+	10	20	.333	12½	Brammell
La Junta Railroaders	11	22	.333	13	Bill Annis/Waller/Tubby Graves

#Canon City moved to Raton June 4.
@Pueblo moved to Trinidad June 8, then to Cheyenne June 28.
+Colorado Springs moved to Dawson June 15.
The league disbanded July 5.

D South Central League
Presidents: Dr. D.M. Shiveley/Luther Ellison/W.H. "Bill" Lattimore

Standings	W	L	Pct.	GB	Manager
Longview Cannibals	63	51	.553	—	Tully Spear/Jim Gardiner
Marshall Athletics..............	56	58	.491	7	Harry Kane
Texarkana Twins**	51	65	.440	13	Pat Woods/McLendon/Rudy Kling/ Dee Poindexter
Paris Boosters	46	63	.422	14½	Rick Adams & W.W. Hawker/Jack Jutze
Cleburne Railroaders@*	51	28	.646	NA	A.L. "Dad" Ritter
Tyler Elbertas#	40	42	.488	NA	Dee Poindexter

#Tyler disbanded July 17.
@Cleburne disbanded July 17.

Playoff: Texarkana was declared champion as first half winner Cleburne had disbanded.

BA: Ray Nagle, Marshall, .368
Runs: Ray Nagle, Marshall, 42
Hits: Ray Nagle, Marshall, 76
Wins: C.N. Harbin, Cleburne, 15

SOs: Bill Daniels, Cleburne/Paris, 123
Pct: Henry "Lindy" Hiett, Cleburne, .875, 7-1

D Southeastern League
President: H.W. Roberts

Standings (first half)	W	L	Pct.	GB	Manager
Gadsden Steel Makers	43	33	.566	—	John Siegle
Selma Centralites*.............	42	35	.545	1½	Lindsay Stickney
Anniston Models+	41	35	.539	2	Tom Fisher
Rome Romans....................	37	36	.507	4½	Harry Matthews

Huntsville Mountaineers/
    Talladega Highlanders#... 33 44 .429 10½ Arthur Riggs
Bessemer Pipemakers@ ..... 29 42 .408 NA Gordon Hickman

#Huntsville (24-29) moved to Talladega July 9.
@Bessemer disbanded July 14.
+Anniston disbanded July 19.
Second half games started July 22. The league disbanded August 2 with the following official second half standings: Gadsden (7-4), Talladega (5-5), Selma (5-6), and Rome (5-7).

BA: Earl Hanna, Selma, .345   **Hits:** Earl Hanna, Selma, 115
Runs: Earl Hanna, Selma, 62   **HRs:** John Cochran, Bessemer/Anniston, 12

D Southern Michigan League
President: Judge James P. Bowen

Standings	W	L	Pct.	GB	Manager
Adrian Lions	78	47	.624	—	Dan Jenkins
Jackson Convicts	71	55	.563	7½	Maurice Myers
Flint Vehicles....................	69	56	.552	9	Jack Burke/Danny Collins
Lansing Senators...............	63	62	.504	15	John Morrissey
Kalamazoo Celery Eaters ...	60	63	.488	17	Charles Wagner
Battle Creek Crickets.........	59	68	.465	20	Ed McKernan
Bay City Billikens#	19	43	.306	NA	James Slevins
Saginaw Trailers#..............	19	44	.302	NA	Walter Hartwell

#Bay City and Saginaw were disbanded by league directors July 13.
The league was lowered from Class C to Class D for reserve purposes August 25.

BA: Jack Onslow, Lansing, .385   **Wins:** Robert Troy, Adrian, 23
Runs: Fred Ochs, Flint, 89   **SOs:** Robert Troy, Adrian, 268
Hits: John Connors, Jackson, 156 **Pct:** Walter Scott, Adrian, .826, 19-4
HRs: Al "Bull" Durham, Bay City/Lansing, 25

D Texas-Oklahoma League
Presidents: Tom D. Newcomb/C.O. Johnson

Standings	W	L	Pct.	GB	Manager
Ardmore Giants**	62	32	.660	—	George McAvoy
Sherman Cubs....................	56	37	.602	5½	Jimmy Humphries
Bonham Tigers	53	35	.602	6	Roy Leslie
Wichita Falls Drillers*.......	52	38	.578	8	Fred "Cap" Morris
Denison Katydids	44	49	.473	17½	Horace Covington/Hart McCormick
Durant Choctaws/Hustlers..	26	64	.289	34	Hettie Green/Mitchell/Charles Deardorff/ Bill Harper
Greenville Highlanders#.....	14	25	.359	NA	Richard Atkins/Bill Harper
McKinney#	6	33	.154	NA	Alfred Scott/Art Pennell/Blair Kerr

#McKinney and Greenville disbanded June 7.

Playoffs: Wichita Falls was leading Ardmore 2 games to 1 when Ardmore disbanded August 1. The title was awarded to Wichita Falls.

(second half statistics)
BA: William Verna Brown, Wichita Falls, .324   **Hits:** William Verna Brown, Wichita Falls, 46
Runs: George McAvoy, Ardmore, 31

D Union Association
Presidents: William H. Lucas/Van Patte

Standings	W	L	Pct.	GB	Manager
Missoula............................	83	51	.620	—	Cliff Blankenship
Salt Lake City Skyscrapers.	77	61	.558	8	A.C. Weaver
Great Falls........................	72	61	.541	10½	George Reed
Ogden Canners	71	68	.511	14½	John McCloskey
Butte Miners	53	82	.393	30½	Charles McCafferty/Jesse Stovall
Helena Senators	50	83	.376	32½	Charles Irby

BA: Howard Murphy, Great Falls, .390   **HRs:** A.E. Spencer, Helena, 14
Runs: Jacob Bauer, Salt Lake City, 143 **3B:** Mike Killilay, Helena, 25
Hits: Howard Murphy, Great Falls, 240 **Wins:** Joe Bush, Missoula, 29
RBIs: Frank Huelsman, Great Falls, 114 **Pct:** Joe Bush, Missoula, .707, 29-12

D Washington State League

Standings	W	L	Pct.	GB	Manager
Chehalis Farmers	25	16	.610	—	James Burns
Centralia Railroaders	19	17	.528	3½	W.R. Patton/George Dysart
Aberdeen Black Cats#........	16	21	.432	7	Tom Kelly
Hoquiam Cougars	17	23	.425	7½	Eddie Ford/Joe Wilkins

#Aberdeen disbanded July 10.
The league disbanded July 14.

D Western Canada League
Presidents: Fred Johnson/John Dewar

Standings	W	L	Pct.	GB	Manager
Calgary Bronchos**	59	34	.634	—	John Streib
Bassano Boosters	45	46	.495	13	Chester Cox
Red Deer Eskimos*	48	52	.480	14½	Jerry Hurley
Edmonton Gray Birds.........	40	60	.400	22½	Mackin

Playoff: Calgary 4 games, Red Deer 2.

BA: Chester Cox, Bassano, .348   **HRs:** Jim Flanagan, Calgary, 5
Runs: Bill Daniels, Red Deer, 99   **Wins:** Al Standridge, Calgary, 21
Hits: Bill Daniels, Red Deer, 118   Ferdy Manning, Red Deer, 21
    Harry Raymond, Bassano, 118   **SOs:** Ferdy Manning, Red Deer, 144
    Roy Dudley, Edmonton, 118   **Pct:** W.F. Barenkamp, Calgary, .800, 12-3

D Western Tri-State League
President: W.N. Sweet

Standings	W	L	Pct.	GB	Manager
Walla Walla Bears..............	61	37	.622	—	Gus Badz
Boise Irrigators	56	46	.548	7	Hugh Kellacky/Frank "Dad" Gimlin
Pendleton Buckaroos	53	51	.510	11	Jess Garrett
La Grande Pippins	31	67	.316	30	James Bradley

BA: George Pembroke, Pendleton, .328 **Pct:** Elmer "Brick" Leonard, Walla Walla,
Hits: Phil Nadeau, Pendleton, 124   .765, 13-4
Wins: Carl Mays, Boise, 22

Ind United States League
President: William A. Whitman

Standings	W	L	Pct.	GB	Manager
Pittsburgh Filipinos............	27	17	.614	—	Deacon Phillippe
Richmond Rebels................	21	14	.600	1½	Alfred Newnham
Chicago Green Sox.............	17	15	.531	4	Bert Keeley
Cincinnati Pippins..............	14	13	.519	4½	James Barton
Reading$............................	12	12	.500	NA	Leo Groom
Washington Senators@	6	8	.429	NA	George Brown/Kid Carsay
Cleveland Forest City+........	8	13	.381	NA	Jack O'Connor
New York Knickerbockers#....	2	15	.118	NA	William Jordan

#New York withdrew May 26.
@Washington withdrew May 27.
+Cleveland withdrew June 2.
$Reading withdrew June 6.
The league disbanded June 24.

BA: Robert Adler, Washington, .543   **Wins:** Bill Taylor, Richmond, 9
Runs: Herman Walters, Chicago, 42   G. Rapp, Pittsburgh, 9
Hits: James Brown, Pittsburgh, 54   **SOs:** Bill Taylor, Richmond, 85
HRs: Herman McFarland, Richmond, 8 **Pct:** Bill Taylor, Richmond, .750, 9-3
    G. Rapp, Pittsburgh, .750, 9-3

1912 Interleague Post Season Play

World Series
Boston (American) 4 games, New York (National) 3, one tie

Western Championship
Denver (Western) 4 games, Minneapolis (American Association) 1

Virginia Series
Bristol (Appalachian) 5 games, Roanoke (Virginia) 2

Class D Series
Clarksville (Kitty) 4 games, Frankfort (Blue Grass) 2

1912 No-Hitters

Date	Pitcher	Team	League	Opponent	Score
4-30	Powell Burnett	Okmulgee	Oklahoma State	Muskogee	5-0
4-30	Wingo Anderson	Bonham	Texas-Oklahoma	McKinney	9-0
5-4	Clark	Dubuque	Three-I	Peoria	5-2
5-10	Paul Trammell	Longview	South Central	Cleburne	2-3
5-18	Harry Kane	Marshall	South Central	Longview	4-0
5-21	Tom Toner	Spokane	Northwestern	Portland	9-0
5-25	Paul Trammell	Longview	South Central	Texarkana	6-0
5-25	Ray Keating	Lawrence	New England	Worcester	1-0
5-29	Harry Wormwood	Fall River	New England	Worcester	2-2 (12)
5-31	Grover Brandt	Houston	Texas	Ft. Worth	2-1 (12)
6-8	Fred Johnson	Davenport	Three-I	Bloomington	4-0
6-11	Cy Watson	Houston	Texas	Ft. Worth	5-0
6-14	F.L. Delotel	Ashland-Catlettsburg	Mountain States	Williamson	12-0
6-22	Bill Upham	Brockton	New England	New Bedford	4-0
6-24	Charles Pickett	Bloomington	Three-I	Davenport	4-0
6-24	Joe Willis	Auburn	MINK	Hiawatha	6-0
6-25	Hatton Ogle	Waco	Texas	Galveston	11-0
6-30	William Malarkey	Oakland	Pacific Coast	San Francisco	0-0 (10)
7-4	George Mullin	Detroit	American	St. Louis	7-0
7-5	Moore	Ironton	Mountain States	Williamson	6-0
7-6	John Frill	Jersey City	International	Providence	4-0 (P, 7)
7-18	Wyatt Lee	Newark	International	Providence	4-0
7-19	R.M. Paine	Columbus	Cotton States	Greenwood	1-1 (10)
7-23	Wheezer Dell	Butte	Union Assoc.	Ogden	1-0
7-23	Buck Taylor	Spartanburg	Carolina Assoc.	Winston-Salem	10-3
8-2	Bill Lelivelt	Minneapolis	American Assoc.	Toledo	4-0
8-3	Joe Neely	Clarksville	Kitty	Henderson	7-0
8-5	Fred Merchant	Johnson City	Appalachian	Bristol	5-1
8-13	Claude Williams	Bridgeport	Ohio-Penn.	Steubenville	2-0 (P)
8-14	Thomas Caesar	Mt. Clemens	Border	Wyandotte	12-0
8-15	Charles Pickett	Bloomington	Three-I	Peoria	4-0
8-15	Bill Essick	Grand Rapids	Central	Canton	4-1
8-16	Lou North	Mt. Clemens	Border	Wyandotte	5-0
8-18	Tom Toner	San Francisco	Pacific Coast	Portland	2-0
8-18	Liese	Oshkosh	Wisconsin-Illinois	Madison	3-2
8-20	Ed Hovlik	Milwaukee	American Assoc.	Louisville	2-0
8-20	Careau	Spokane	Northwestern	Tacoma	2-0
8-22	Finis Wilson	Bristol	Appalachian	Johnson City	5-0
8-29	Tom Drohan	Kewanee	Central Assoc.	Hannibal	4-0
8-30	Earl Hamilton	St. Louis	American	Detroit	5-1
9-6	Jeff Tesreau	New York	National	Philadelphia	3-0
9-6	R.M. Paine	Columbus	Cotton States	Greenwood	1-0 (10)
9-6	Meldon Wolfgang	Lowell	New England	Lynn	1-0 (10)
9-14	Moore	Springfield	Connecticut	Holyoke	1-0 (10)
9-16	Gene Cochreham	Topeka	Western	Omaha	1-0
	Chief Johnson	St. Joseph	Western	Sioux City	

Number in parentheses indicates innings if other than nine; "P" indicates perfect game.

THIS DATE IN MINOR LEAGUE HISTORY

April 11, 1912, Kansas City and Columbus, American Association, played an entire game with one ball. A total of 15 runs and 28 hits were made.

April 25, 1912, John V. McStea, a theatrical manager, was acquitted in Albany, New York of the killing of Arthur Brown of the Albany club. McStea shot Brown on June 15, 1911, after he found his wife in Brown's room in a boarding house.

May 9, 1912, Third baseman Roy Akin of Waco, Texas League, executed an unassisted triple play on a squeeze bunt in the first inning against Houston. The previous season, with Los Angeles of the Pacific Coast League, Akin lined into an unassisted triple killing.

May 12, 1912, Andrew Briswalter, 22, pitcher with Los Angeles, Pacific Coast League, died of consumption in Monrovia, California.

June 11, 1912, At Yazoo City, Mississippi, one catcher was behind the plate for both teams for 16 innings in a Cotton States League doubleheader between Columbus and Yazoo City. In the second frame of the first game the Columbus catcher was injured, and when no replacement was available, Yazoo City backstop Taylor volunteered to catch for both clubs, which was agreed to by all in authority. Yazoo City won both games.

June 12, 1912, Pitcher Edward Lafitte, Richmond, Blue Grass League, retired the first twelve Paris batters to face him with twelve pitches and made six assists that resulted in the first twelve putouts. He made ten of his team's 20 assists in the game.

June 24, 1912, The outlaw United States League, which adopted a schedule running from May 1 to September 28 with clubs in Chicago, New York, Reading, Washington, Pittsburgh, Cincinnati, Richmond and Cleveland, folded with heavy financial losses.

June 28, 1912, Frank Davis, Knoxville, Appalachian League, tied a minor league record when he struck out 20 Bristol batters.

July 1, 1912, Roger Harris smashed two home runs in the seventh inning, each with the bases full, as Richmond, Blue Grass League, scored ten times in the round and pummelled Mt. Sterling 19-6.

July 6, 1912, John Frill, Jersey City, International League, pitched a perfect game against Providence which was called after seven innings to allow the umpire to catch a train.

July 10, 1912, John Foreman, shortstop for Kankakee, Illinois-Missouri League, made an unassisted triple play against Champaign.

July 17, 1912, Fleet outfielders often make catches while running at top speed, but William T. Madden, an engineer on a train, caught a ball while traveling 45 miles an hour. Madden leaned out of his cab while passing a field at Gistig's Park, near Louisville, Kentucky, thrust out his hand and made a neat catch of a foul ball.

July 23, 1912, Joe McGinnity, Newark, International League, pitched two games against Rochester and won both.

July 23, 1912, A fan appreciation day was held in Jersey City to permit the city to see if they could support baseball. Most of the cash customers came from Newark.

August 6, 1912, In the Appalachian League, Bristol and Johnson City played a 15-inning 1-1 tie. Nick Cullop of Bristol did not yield a hit for 14 frames and Hall did not yield a safety for ten innings for Johnson City. Each hurler struck out 16.

August 15, 1912, In Steubenville, Ohio, William Craig, pitcher for Steubenville, Ohio-Pennsylvania League, died from injuries received while throwing a curve ball. The swing of his body broke one of his legs and caused an internal rupture.

August 15, 1912, Pitcher Brown of Hiawatha, MINK League, struck out 25 in a game with Auburn which was called after 16 innings with the score tied 0-0.

August 31, 1912, Joab McManus had won 14 consecutive games for Ottawa of the Canadian League, all during the month of August.

September 7, 1912, Binghamton, New York State League, defeated Albany 4-1 in 42 minutes.

September 14, 1912, First baseman William Rapp of Portland, Pacific Coast League, made an unassisted triple play against Oakland.

September 14, 1912, Connecticut League President James O'Rourke, 60, showed that he still possessed his old skill when he caught the full nine innings for the champion New Haven club in the first game of a doubleheader on the windup of the season at New Haven.

September 22, 1912, Association Park, the home of the Kansas City club in the American Association, was destroyed by fire.

October 8, 1912, Outfielder Henry Heitmuller, Los Angeles, Pacific Coast League, died in that city of typhoid fever at the age of 32.

November 13, 1912, Joe McGinnity was named manager of Tacoma in the Northwestern League.

1913

American League
President: Byron Bancroft Johnson

Standings	W	L	Pct.	GB	Attend.	Manager
Philadelphia Athletics	96	57	.627	—	571,896	Connie Mack
Washington Senators	90	64	.584	6½	325,831	Clark Griffith
Cleveland Naps	86	66	.566	9½	541,000	Joe Birmingham
Boston Red Sox	79	71	.527	15½	437,194	Jake Stahl/Bill Carrigan
Chicago White Sox	78	74	.513	17½	644,501	Nixey Callahan
Detroit Tigers	66	87	.431	30	398,502	Hugh Jennings
New York Yankees	57	94	.377	38	357,551	Frank Chance
St. Louis Browns	57	96	.373	39	250,330	George Stovall/Jimmy Austin/ Branch Rickey

BA: Ty Cobb, Detroit, .390
Runs: Eddie Collins, Philadelphia, 125
Hits: Joe Jackson, Cleveland, 197
RBIs: Frank Baker, Philadelphia, 126
HRs: Frank Baker, Philadelphia, 12

Wins: Walter Johnson, Washington, 36
SOs: Walter Johnson, Washington, 243
ERA: Walter Johnson, Washington, 1.09
Pct: Walter Johnson, Washington, .837, 36-7

National League
President: Thomas J. Lynch

Standings	W	L	Pct.	GB	Attend.	Manager
New York Giants	101	51	.664	—	630,000	John McGraw
Philadelphia Phillies	88	63	.583	12½	470,000	Red Dooin
Chicago Cubs	88	65	.575	13½	419,000	Johnny Evers
Pittsburgh Pirates	78	71	.523	21½	296,000	Fred Clarke
Boston Braves	69	82	.457	31½	208,000	George Stallings
Brooklyn Superbas	65	84	.436	34½	347,000	Bill Dahlen
Cincinnati Reds	64	89	.418	37½	258,000	Joe Tinker
St. Louis Cardinals	51	99	.340	49	203,531	Miller Huggins

BA: Jake Daubert, Brooklyn, .350
Runs: Tommy Leach, Chicago, 99
Hits: Gavvy Cravath, Philadelphia, 179
RBIs: Gavvy Cravath, Philadelphia, 128
HRs: Gavvy Cravath, Philadelphia, 19

Wins: Tom Seaton, Philadelphia, 27
SOs: Tom Seaton, Philadelphia, 168
ERA: Christy Mathewson, New York, 2.06
Pct: Bert Humphries, Chicago, .800, 16-4

AA American Association
President: Thomas M. Chivington

Standings	W	L	Pct.	GB	Attend.	Manager
Milwaukee Brewers	100	67	.599	—	213,349	Harry Clark
Minneapolis Millers	97	70	.581	3	175,046	Joe Cantillon
Louisville Colonels	95	72	.569	5	194,703	John Hayden
Columbus Senators	93	74	.557	7	180,462	William Hinchman
St. Paul Saints	77	90	.461	23	123,568	William Friel
Toledo Mud Hens	69	98	.413	31	104,342	Topsy Hartsel/Herman Bronkie
Kansas City Blues	69	98	.413	31	182,296	Charles Carr/Tom Downey
Indianapolis Indians	68	99	.407	32	116,554	Mike Kelley

BA: Duke Reilley, Indianapolis, .337
Runs: Dave Altizer, Minneapolis, 141
Hits: Will Osborne, Louisville, 214
HRs: Joe Riggert, St. Paul, 12

Wins: Cy Slapnicka, Milwaukee, 25
SOs: Grover Lowdermilk, Louisville, 197
Pct: Hugh Quillan, Columbus, .750, 12-4

AA International League
President: Edward G. Barrow

Standings	W	L	Pct.	GB	Manager
Newark Indians	95	57	.625	—	Harry Smith
Rochester Hustlers	92	62	.597	4	John Ganzel
Baltimore Orioles	77	73	.513	17	Jack Dunn
Buffalo Bisons	78	75	.510	17½	Bill Clymer
Montreal Royals	74	77	.490	20½	Kitty Bransfield
Providence Grays	69	80	.463	24½	Wild Bill Donovan
Toronto Maple Leafs	70	83	.458	25½	Joe Kelley
Jersey City Skeeters	53	101	.344	43	Larry Schlafly/William Purtell

Attendance: Buffalo, 220,799.

BA: George Simmons, Rochester, .339
Runs: Fritz Maisel, Baltimore, 119
Hits: George Simmons, Rochester, 185
HRs: Del Paddock, Rochester, 8

Wins: Braggo Roth, Baltimore, 22
   Wyatt Lee, Newark, 22
SOs: George Davis, Jersey City, 199
Pct: Raleigh Aitchison, Newark, .808, 21-5

AA Pacific Coast League
President: Allan T. Baum

Standings	W	L	Pct.	GB	Manager
Portland Beavers	109	86	.571	—	Walter McCredie
Sacramento Sacts	103	94	.523	7	Harry Wolverton
Venice Tigers	107	102	.512	9	W.L. "Happy" Hogan
San Francisco Seals	104	103	.502	11	Daniel Long
Los Angeles Angels	100	108	.484	15½	Frank "Cap" Dillon
Oakland Oaks	90	120	.429	26½	Honus Mitze/Art Devlin

BA: Harry Bayless, Venice, .324
Runs: Harl Maggert, Los Angeles, 128
Hits: Bill Rodgers, Portland, 239
HRs: Bert Coy, Oakland, 18

SBs: Jimmy Johnston, San Francisco, 124
Wins: Charles Fanning, San Francisco, 28
SOs: Bill James, Portland, 215
Pct: John Williams, Sacramento, .708, 17-7

A Southern Association
President: William B. Kavanaugh

Standings	W	L	Pct.	GB	Manager
Atlanta Crackers	81	56	.591	—	William A. Smith
Mobile Sea Gulls	81	57	.587	½	Michael Finn
Birmingham Barons	74	64	.536	7½	Carleton Molesworth
Chattanooga Lookouts	70	64	.523	9½	Norman "Kid" Elberfeld
Montgomery Rebels	68	69	.496	13	Johnny Dobbs
Memphis Chickasaws	64	74	.463	17½	Bill Bernhardt
Nashville Volunteers	62	76	.444	19½	William Schwartz
New Orleans Pelicans	45	85	.346	32½	Charley Frank

BA: Harry Welchonce, Atlanta, .338
Runs: Tommy Long, Atlanta, 112
Hits: Harry Welchonce, Atlanta, 194
HRs: Dave Robertson, Mobile, 11

Wins: Harry Covelski, Chattanooga, 28
SOs: Elmer Brown, Montgomery, 156
Pct: Bill Prough, Birmingham, .793, 23-6

A Western League
President: Norris L. O'Neill

Standings	W	L	Pct.	GB	Manager
Denver Bears	104	62	.627	—	Jack Hendricks
Des Moines Boosters	93	72	.564	10½	Frank Isbell
St. Joseph Drummers	89	78	.533	15½	Jack Holland
Lincoln Greenbackers	87	80	.521	17½	Charles Mullen
Omaha Rourkes	79	86	.478	24½	Charles Arbogast/Pa Rourke
Sioux City Packers	73	92	.442	30½	James "Ducky" Holmes/Josh Clarke
Topeka Jayhawks	73	92	.442	30½	Dale Gear
Wichita Jobbers	65	101	.389	39	George Hughes/Charlie Babb/Nick Maddox

Attendance: Denver, 150,000.

BA: Roxy Middleton, Wichita, .370
Runs: Les Channell, Denver, 137
Hits: Bill Congalton, Omaha, 227
HRs: Les Channell, Denver, 26

Wins: George Boehler, St. Joseph, 27
SOs: Red Faber, Des Moines, 265
ERA: Harry Hicks, Omaha, 2.27

B Central League
President: Louis Heilbroner

Standings	W	L	Pct.	GB	Manager
Grand Rapids Bill-eds	92	48	.657	—	Edward Smith
Fort Wayne Champs	77	63	.550	15	James Burke
Springfield Reapers	67	71	.486	24	Joe Stanley
Dayton Veterans	62	77	.446	29½	John Nee
Terre Haute Terre-iers	60	79	.432	31½	Edward Anderson
Evansville River Rats	60	80	.429	32	Charles "Punch" Knoll

BA: Larry LeJeune, Grand Rapids, .346
Runs: George Brautigan, Springfield, 99
Hits: E.N. Shaw, Dayton, 175
HRs: Bill Keene, Springfield, 15

Wins: Jeff Pfeffer, Grand Rapids, 25
SOs: Jeff Pfeffer, Grand Rapids, 232
Pct: Sherry Smith, Grand Rapids, .818, 9-2
   W. Riley, Grand Rapids, .818, 9-2

B Eastern Association
President: James H. O'Rourke

Standings	W	L	Pct.	GB	Manager
Hartford Senators	83	48	.634	—	Simon McDonald
New Haven White Wings	79	52	.603	4	Jerry O'Connell
Waterbury Contenders	70	61	.534	13	Sam Kennedy
Bridgeport Crossmen	69	63	.523	14½	Eugene McCann/John Freeman/Monte Cross
New London Planters	65	66	.496	18	John Burns/Eugene McCann
Springfield Ponies	60	70	.462	22½	Frank Corriden/Jack O'Hara
Pittsfield Electrics	62	73	.459	23	John Zeller
Holyoke Papermakers/ Meriden Hopes#	40	95	.296	45	James Garry

#Holyoke (24-52) moved to Meriden July 11.

BA: Benny Kauff, Hartford, .345
Runs: Bill Morley, Hartford, 103
Hits: Benny Kauff, Hartford, 176
HRs: Tom Stankard, Holyoke/Meriden/ Springfield, 8

Wins: W. Booth Hopper, New Haven, 31
SOs: W.I. Smith, Pittsfield, 175
ERA: W. Booth Hopper, New Haven, 2.03

*Won first-half   **Won second-half   ***Won both halves

B Interstate League
President: Charles A. Dawson

Standings	W	L	Pct.	GB	Manager
Erie Sailors	57	21	.781	—	Larry Quinlan
Akron Giants	47	32	.595	10½	John Siegle
Youngstown Steelmen	43	33	.566	13	Curley Blount
Columbus Cubs	37	38	.493	18½	Lee Fohl
Steubenville Stubs	31	42	.425	22½	Roy Montgomery
Wheeling Stogies	32	47	.405	25½	Ray Ryan
Canton Senators	29	44	.397	25½	Bade Myers
Zanesville Flood Sufferers#	27	46	.370	27½	Marty Hogan

#Zanesville disbanded July 13.
The league disbanded July 21.

BA: Tom Sheehan, Youngstown, .355
Runs: John Dawson, Erie, 67
Hits: Tom Sheehan, Youngstown, 106
HRs: Art Watson, Steubenville, 6

Wins: Lou Schettler, Erie, 14
SOs: Clark Sterzer, Erie, 121
Pct: Lou Schettler, Erie, .824, 14-3

B New England League
President: Tim H. Murnane

Standings	W	L	Pct.	GB	Manager
Lowell Grays	81	45	.643	—	James Gray
Portland Duffs	71	49	.592	7	Hugh Duffy
Worcester Busters	71	54	.568	9½	Jesse Burkett
Lawrence Barristers	67	53	.558	11	Louis Piper
Lynn Shoemakers	61	60	.504	17½	Patsy Flaherty
New Bedford Whalers	47	75	.385	32	Frank Connaughton/John H. O'Brien
Fall River Adopted Sons	45	76	.372	33½	Dan Clohecy
Brockton Shoemakers	44	75	.370	33½	Nick Rufiange

BA: George Wilson, Lynn, .365
Runs: Pete Clemens, Lowell, 104
Hits: Jim Magee, Lowell, 174

HRs: Art DeGroff, Lowell, 10
      Alban Carlstrom, Lawrence, 10
Wins: Jack Bushelman, Worcester, 26
Pct: Joe Finneran, Lowell, .875, 14-2

B New York State League
President: John H. Farrell

Standings	W	L	Pct.	GB	Manager
Binghamton Bingoes	84	53	.613	—	John Calhoun
Wilkes-Barre Barons	84	56	.600	1½	Joe McCarthy
Troy Trojans	76	61	.556	8	Henry Ramsey
Utica Utes	74	65	.532	11	Michael O'Neill
Albany Senators	72	67	.518	13	James Tamsett/Ed McDonough
Syracuse Stars	61	78	.439	24	Fred Burchell/Fred Payne
Elmira Colonels	56	85	.397	30	Louis Ritter/Bill Conroy
Scranton Miners	49	91	.350	36½	Richard Smith/Bob Peterson/John Kelly

BA: Cad Coles, Elmira, .356
Runs: George Anderson, Wilkes-Barre, 92
Hits: John Leary, Utica, 181

SOs: Walter Nagle, Elmira, 170
Pct: Bill Upham, Binghamton, .778, 14-4

B Northwestern League
President: Fielder Jones

Standings	W	L	Pct.	GB	Manager
Vancouver Bees	99	66	.600	—	Robert Brown
Portland Colts	86	73	.541	10	R.L. "Nick" Williams
Seattle Giants	89	78	.533	11	Frank Raymond
Victoria Bees	81	90	.474	21	Mike Lynch/Bert Delmas
Tacoma Tigers	75	96	.439	27	Joe McGinnity
Spokane Indians	70	97	.419	30	Harry Ostdick/Watt Powell/Mike Lynch

BA: Jack Meek, Victoria, .358
Runs: Charles Swain, Victoria, 112
Hits: Ed Kippert, Vancouver, 202
HRs: Charles Swain, Victoria, 34

Wins: Erv Kentlehner, Victoria, 23
SOs: Erv Kentlehner, Victoria, 253
Pct: Wayne Barham, Victoria, .700, 7-3

B Texas League
President: Wilbur P. Allen

Standings	W	L	Pct.	GB	Manager
Houston Buffaloes	93	57	.620	—	Johnny Fillman
Dallas Giants	92	61	.601	2½	Dred Cavender
Waco Navigators	81	71	.533	13	Thomas Carson/Ellis Hardy
San Antonio Bronchos	74	78	.487	20	George Stinson
Austin Senators	70	82	.461	24	George Leidy/Otto McIvor
Ft. Worth Panthers	70	83	.458	24½	Walter Morris/William Nance
Galveston Pirates	67	85	.441	27	Curley Maloney/Heinie Maag
Beaumont Oilers	60	90	.400	33	Edward Wheeler/Ralph Glaze/ George Leidy

BA: Van Duke Duncan, Dallas, .307
Runs: Van Duke Duncan, Dallas, 91
Hits: Van Duke Duncan, Dallas, 169
HRs: Fred Wohleben, Waco, 12

Wins: Chuck Rose, Houston, 24
SOs: C.H. Harben, Galveston, 204
      Dave Davenport, San Antonio, 204
Pct: Dodie Criss, Houston, .800, 16-4

B Three-I League
President: Albert R. Tearney

Standings	W	L	Pct.	GB	Manager
Quincy Gems	79	60	.568	—	Thomas Hackett/Nicholas Kahl
Dubuque Dubs	74	62	.544	3½	Clarence "Pants" Rowland
Davenport Blue Sox	68	66	.507	8½	Daniel O'Leary
Danville Speakers	69	68	.504	9	Connie Walsh
Decatur Commodores	67	68	.496	10	George Reed
Springfield Watchmakers	66	70	.485	11½	Frank Donnelly
Bloomington Bloomers	64	71	.474	13	Harry Syfert
Peoria Distillers	57	79	.419	20½	Barry McCormick/John Fountain

BA: Jim Flanagan, Decatur, .352
Runs: Jim Flanagan, Decatur, 94
Hits: Jim Flanagan, Decatur, 180
HRs: Frank Lofton, Springfield, 12

Wins: Jim Bluejacket, Bloomington, 23
SOs: Jim Bluejacket, Bloomington, 198
Pct: Louis Tretter, Quincy, .710, 22-9

B Tri-State League
President: Charles F. Carpenter

Standings	W	L	Pct.	GB	Manager
Wilmington Chicks	66	45	.595	—	James Jackson
Allentown	59	52	.532	7	William Coughlin
Harrisburg Senators	59	52	.532	7	George Cockill
York White Roses	59	52	.532	7	George Heckert
Trenton Tigers	50	61	.450	16	Bert Conn
Atlantic City	42	73	.365	26	John Castle

BA: Marty Kavanaugh, York, .357
Runs: Jim Murray, Allentown, 92
Hits: Marty Kavanagh, York, 153

HRs: Harry Fritz, Wilmington, 7
Wins: Alan Russell, Wilmington, 22
Pct: Robert Scott, Allentown, .792, 19-5

C Canadian League
President: J.P. Fitzgerald

Standings	W	L	Pct.	GB	Manager
Ottawa Senators	66	39	.629	—	Frank Shaughnessy
London Tecumsehs	64	39	.621	1	George Deneau
St. Thomas Saints	56	48	.538	9½	George Orth
Peterborough Petes	55	48	.534	10	John Barthold
Guelph Maple Leafs	54	49	.524	11	Louis Cook
Hamilton Hams	52	52	.500	13½	George "Knotty" Lee
Berlin Busy Bees	38	66	.365	27½	Joe Keenan
Brantford Red Sox	30	74	.288	35½	Ambrose Kane/William Wagner

BA: Bill Wright, Guelph, .396
Runs: Merlin Kopp, St. Thomas, 104
Hits: Bill Wright, Guelph, 152
HRs: Bill Wright, Guelph, 10

Wins: Bob Heck, London, 24
SOs: Carl Renfer, Ottawa, 185
Pct: Bob Heck, London, .800, 24-6

C Northern League
President: George A. Barton

Standings	W	L	Pct.	GB	Manager
Winona Pirates	83	38	.686	—	W.D. "Lefty" Davis
Superior Red Sox	72	42	.632	7½	Fred Curtis
Winnipeg Maroons	69	53	.566	14½	Tim Flood/Frank Kurke/Charles Jones
Duluth White Sox	65	54	.546	17	William "Darby" O'Brien
Minneapolis Millers	65	59	.524	19½	Bob Unglaub
Grand Forks Flickertails	54	67	.446	29	Sam Foster/William Carney/F. Lohr
St. Paul/La Crosse Colts#	40	78	.339	41½	Charles Jones/Frank Kurke
Virginia Ore Diggers	30	87	.256	51	Bill Shannon/Bobby Roth/Edward Stewart

#St. Paul (28-54) moved to La Crosse July 23.

BA: Elmer Miller, Duluth, .347
Runs: Jim Collins, Winona, 102
Hits: Jim Collins, Winona, 170
HRs: Elmer Smith, Duluth, 13

Wins: Ralph Bell, Winona, 28
SOs: Ralph Bell, Winona, 271
Pct: George Zabel, Winnipeg, .909, 10-1

C South Atlantic League
President: Nick P. Corish

Standings	W	L	Pct.	GB	Manager
Savannah Colts***	78	38	.672	—	Perry Lipe/Joseph Herold
Columbus Foxes	60	55	.522	17½	James Fox
Jacksonville Tarpons	60	58	.509	19	Percy Wilder
Macon Peaches	55	60	.478	22½	Joseph Herold
Charleston Sea Gulls	48	68	.414	30	George Needham/Charles Kipp/ James Hamilton
Albany Babies	46	68	.404	31	Phil Wells

BA: Al Handiboe, Savannah, .314
Runs: Hal Matthews, Macon, 69
Hits: Al Handiboe, Savannah, 146

Wins: Dick Robertson, Savannah, 28
SOs: Dick Robertson, Savannah, 235
Pct: Dick Robertson, Savannah, .778, 28-8

C Virginia League
President: Jacob O. Boatwright

Standings	W	L	Pct.	GB	Manager
Petersburg Goobers	89	46	.659	—	Henry Busch
Roanoke Tigers	82	57	.590	9	William "Buck" Pressley
Richmond Colts	74	60	.552	14½	Steve Griffin
Portsmouth Pirates	57	77	.425	31½	Lee Garvin

Newport News Shipbuilders .. 53 83 .390 36½ Paul Davis/Harry Matthews
Norfolk Tars .... 51 83 .381 37½ Charles Shaffer/George Kirscher/Ray Ryan

BA: Ralph Mattis, Roanoke, .300
Runs: Tinsley Ginn, Roanoke, 94
Hits: Ralph Mattis, Roanoke, 157

HRs: Tom Tennant, Portsmouth, 7
　Jim Barnett, Petersburg, 7
　Ducky Eberts, Richmond, 7
Wins: Yancey Ayres, Richmond, 29
SOs: Yancey Ayres, Richmond, 390
Pct: Yancey Ayres, Richmond, .784, 29-8

C Wisconsin-Illinois League
President: Frank R. Weeks

Standings	W	L	Pct.	GB	Manager
Oshkosh Indians	75	46	.620	—	Joe Killian
Racine Belles	72	51	.585	4	William Fox
Green Bay Bays	69	57	.548	8½	Robert Lynch
Rockford Wolverines...........	63	57	.525	11½	Clarence Marshall
Milwaukee Creams/					
Fond du Lac Molls#........	63	60	.512	13	Harry Clark/Ernest Landgraf/Marty Hogan
Madison Senators	64	61	.512	13	Harry Bay
Wausau Lumberjacks	45	80	.360	32	Mike Malloy/Ernest Landgraf
Appleton Papermakers........	43	82	.344	34	Bill Cristall

#Milwaukee (28-20) moved to Fond du Lac June 28.

BA: Al Swalm, Madison, .327
Runs: Fred Thomas, Green Bay, 81
Hits: Fritz Mollwitz, Green Bay, 154
HRs: Al "Bull" Durham, Oshkosh, 26

Wins: James Jachs, Milwaukee/
　Fond du Lac, 23
SOs: Arthur Johnson, Madison, 207
Pct: C.R. Clark, Racine, .750, 21-7

D Appalachian League
President: Jacob Smith

Standings	W	L	Pct.	GB	Manager
Johnson City Soldiers*	66	38	.635	—	P.L. "Legs" Martin
Knoxville Reds**	64	39	.622	1½	Frank Moffett
Cleveland Counts/					
Morristown Jobbers#.......	55	46	.545	9½	Robert Riggs
Bristol Boosters	45	55	.450	19	Clarence "Red" Munson
Rome Romans.....................	45	56	.446	19½	Jack Reidy
Middlesboro Colonels.........	30	71	.398	34½	Warren Sanders

#Cleveland (10-12) moved to Morristown June 9.

Playoff: Knoxville was leading Johnson City 2 games to 1 when they forfeited rather than play in Johnson City, due to alleged physical threats by Johnson City fans.

BA: Ephie Holmes, Cleveland/
　Morristown, .412
Runs: John Cochran, Rome, 87
Hits: John Cochran, Rome, 151
HRs: John Cochran, Rome, 20

Wins: Elmer Lawrence, Knoxville, 24
SOs: Cliff Markle, Cleveland/
　Morristown, 214
Pct: Elmer Lawrence, Knoxville, .774, 24-7

D Border League
President: A.L. Ulbrich

Standings	W	L	Pct.	GB	Manager
Ypsilanti.............................	24	10	.706	—	W.C. Pearce
Wyandotte..........................	24	13	.649	1½	H.R. Browne
Port Huron Independents	15	19	.441	9	Bill Brown
Pontiac Indians	13	18	.418	9½	Henry McIntoch
Windsor	10	24	.294	14	J. Wilkie
Mt. Clemens Bathers#	7	9	.437	NA	W. Trombley

#Mt. Clemens disbanded July 12.

BA: Jack Shafer, Ypsilanti, .395
Runs: Carl Stimpson, Ypsilanti, 30
Hits: Orville Woodruff, Wyandotte, 49

HRs: Ralph Bell, Ypsilanti, 2
　Jack Shafer, Ypsilanti, 2
　Frank Loranger, Wyandotte, 2
　Otto Gallant, Ypsilanti, 2
Wins: Ferdy Manning, Wyandotte, 10
SOs: George Mueller, Port Huron, 149
Pct: Ralph Bell, Ypsilanti, 1.000, 6-0

D California State League
President: Allan T. Baum

Standings	W	L	Pct.	GB	Manager
Stockton Producers	79	44	.642	—	Jack Thomas
Fresno Packers...................	73	50	.593	6	George Wheeler
Vallejo Marines/					
Watsonville Pippins#.......	52	71	.423	27	Bill Devereaux
San Jose Bears	42	81	.341	37	Walter Nagle

#Vallejo (24-33) moved to Watsonville July 6.

BA: Hap Smith, San Jose, .323
Runs: Tom Pierce, Fresno, 87
Hits: Joe Wilhoit, Stockton, 158
HRs: Rino Williams, Vallejo/Watsonville, 7

Wins: Nelson Jones, Stockton, 24
SOs: Ashley Pope, Stockton, 235
Pct: Nelson Jones, Stockton, .750, 24-8

D Central Association
President: M.E. Justice

Standings	W	L	Pct.	GB	Attend.	Manager
Ottumwa Packers................	72	54	.571	—		Ned Egan
Muscatine Wallopers	68	54	.557	2	30,000	Frank Boyle
Monmouth Browns	64	62	.508	8		Bert Hough
Keokuk Indians..................	62	63	.496	9½		George Manush
Burlington Pathfinders.......	63	66	.488	10½		Richard Rohn
Cedar Rapids Rabbits	59	65	.476	12	45,000	Belden Hill
Kewanee Boilermakers.......	59	65	.476	12		George Pennington/
						Frank Richardson
Waterloo Jays	53	71	.427	18	44,000	Jay Andrews

BA: Dave Milligan, Cedar Rapids, .320
Runs: Harry Ellis, Burlington, 100
Hits: Harry Ellis, Burlington, 156
Wins: George Zackert, Muscatine, 22

SOs: George Zackert, Muscatine, 230
　William Jacobs, Burlington, 230
Pct: George Zackert, Muscatine, .759, 22-7

D Cotton States League
President: S.J. Redus

Standings	W	L	Pct.	GB	Manager
Jackson Lawmakers............	71	24	.748	—	Otto Mills
Pensacola Snappers............	67	29	.698	4½	James Hamilton
Selma Centralites................	49	46	.516	22	Arthur Riggs/Jack Spratt
Columbus Joy Riders..........	40	57	.412	32	Bob Kennedy
Clarksdale Swamp Angels..	40	58	.408	32½	Edward Kerr/Carlos Smith
Meridian Metropolitans	22	75	.227	50	Carlos Smith/Walter Hirsh

The season was shortened to August 15.

BA: Carlos Smith, Meridian/Clarksdale, .361
Runs: Charles Miller, Pensacola, 74
Hits: Dutch Bernsen, Clarksdale, 117

Wins: Omer Benn, Pensacola, 26
SOs: Edward Poole, Columbus, 163
Pct: Omer Benn, Pensacola, .867, 26-4

D Empire State League
Presidents: C.C. Vaughn/Oscar Grover

Standings	W	L	Pct.	GB	Manager
Valdosta Millionaires*	58	40	.592	—	Whitey Morse/Otto Jordan
Thomasville Hornets**	56	40	.583	1	Martin Dudley/George Durley
Cordele Babies	49	50	.495	9½	Eddie Reagan
Americus Muckalees	45	54	.455	13½	Harry Webber/Hal Griffin/William Kuhlman
Waycross Blowhards	43	52	.453	13½	Charles Wahoo/Jack Hawkins/William Clark
Brunswick Pilots................	42	57	.424	16½	Bert Kite/Charles Moran/Whitey Morse

Playoff: Thomasville 4 games, Valdosta 2.

BA: C.M. Chancey, Americus, .383
Runs: Van Landingham, Valdosta, 72
Hits: C.M. Chancey, Americus, 142

Wins: V. Roth, Thomasville, 18
Pct: Red Dacey, Americus, .750, 9-3

D Georgia-Alabama League
President: W.J. Boykin

Standings	W	L	Pct.	GB	Manager
Gadsden Steel Makers	51	38	.573	—	George "Elmer" Randall
Newnan Cowetas	46	44	.511	5½	E.S. Bagwell/Ed Shulze
Opelika Opelicans	46	45	.505	6	Ed Ery
Anniston Moulders	45	45	.500	6½	Chick Hannon
La Grange Terrapins	42	48	.467	9½	William "Ducky" Holmes
Talladega Indians...............	40	50	.444	11½	Charles Reese

BA: George Randall, Gadsden, .410
Runs: Larry Pezold, Gadsden, 76
Hits: Midge Craven, Newnan, 121

Wins: Ed Ery, Opelika, 19
Pct: Ed Ery, Opelika, .792, 19-5

D Illinois-Missouri League
President: Charles A. Cline

Standings	W	L	Pct.	GB	Manager
Lincoln Abes***	57	26	.686	—	Lou Ehrgott
Champaign Velvets**.........	53	32	.623	5	Fred "Blackie" Wilson
Kankakee Kanks	35	51	.407	23½	Red Kelly
Streator Boosters................	30	57	.345	29	Bob Coyle/Dick Kahl
Pekin Celestials#................	23	26	.469	NA	Jack Herbert
Canton Chinks#	20	26	.435	NA	Ted Raines

#Pekin and Canton disbanded July 10.

Playoff: Lincoln won the first half, then Lincoln and Champaign tied for the second half title. The championship was awarded to Lincoln when Champaign refused to play off the second half tie.

BA: Charles Moore, Lincoln, .440
Runs: Dick Higgins, Lincoln, 65
Hits: A.J. Holtzhouser, Kankakee, 118
HRs: Roy Phillips, Streator, 13

Wins: Clarence Vaught, Lincoln, 21
SOs: Clarence Vaught, Lincoln, 166
Pct: Ernest Hook, Lincoln, .889, 16-2

D Kansas State League
President: Roy C. Gafford

Standings	W	L	Pct.	GB	Manager
Great Bend Millers	53	36	.596	—	Affie Wilson
Clay Center Cubs	51	37	.580	1½	Max Addington
Lyons Lions	50	39	.562	3	William Nelson
Salina Insurgents	26	63	.292	27	Lon Ury/Mike Welday
Manhattan Elks#	27	24	.529	NA	Fred Moore
Junction City Soldiers#	21	29	.420	NA	Norm Price/Cecil Bankhead

#Junction City disbanded July 9, causing the league to drop Manhattan July 10.

BA: John Singleton, Clay Center, .335
Runs: John Singleton, Clay Center, 78
Hits: John Singleton, Clay Center, 133
Wins: J.L. O'Byrne, Lyons, 17
Pct: C.H. Riley, Great Bend, 1.000, 9-0

D Kitty League
President: Dr. Frank H. Bassett

Standings	W	L	Pct.	GB	Manager
Paducah Chiefs	80	47	.630	—	Arthur Brouthers
Clarksville Boosters	78	47	.624	1	Senter Rainey/William McAndrews
Hopkinsville Hoppers	73	53	.579	6½	George Kalkhoff
Henderson Hens	70	55	.560	9	Dave Anderson/Ward Snyder
Owensboro Distillers	69	56	.552	10	William Long/Senter Rainey
Cairo Egyptians	57	68	.456	22	John Nairn/Kessling
Harrisburg Coal Miners	42	85	.331	38	Lewis Brooks/Stelle
Vincennes Alices	34	92	.269	45½	Ollie Pickering/Bob Anderson/ William McAndrews/John Nairn

BA: H.E. Heckert, Clarksville, .345
Runs: Lee Hart, Clarksville, 103
Hits: J. Grady Burgess, Paducah, 172
HRs: P. Vogt, Hopkinsville, 13
Wins: Leslie Johnson, Hopkinsville, 23
SOs: Charles Humphrey, Clarksville, 240
Pct: Clifford Snyder, Henderson, .917, 11-1

D Michigan State League
President: Emerson W. Dickerson

Standings	W	L	Pct.	GB	Manager
Manistee Champs	73	47	.608	—	Connie Lewis
Traverse City Resorters	62	57	.521	10½	Jack Pendry/James Hamilton/Carl Wenger
Muskegon Speeders	61	59	.508	12	Peg Bemis/Sandy Murray
Boyne City Boosters	57	63	.475	16	Grover Gillen
Cadillac Chiefs	53	66	.445	19½	Homer Warner
Ludington Mariners	53	67	.442	20	Bob Grogan/Harry Arndt

BA: Sid Miller, Muskegon, .359
Runs: Pete Allison, Cadillac, 84
Bill Varley, Boyne City, 84
Carl Dunckel, Muskegon, 84
Hits: Pete Allison, Cadillac, 157
HRs: Grover Prough, Manistee, 14
Wins: Hugh "Babe" Roberts, Boyne City, 18
John Walter Radloff, Manistee, 18
SOs: John Walter Radloff, Manistee, 235
Pct: Henry Negake, Muskegon, .750, 9-3

D MINK League
President: Warren Cummings

Standings	W	L	Pct.	GB	Manager
Auburn Athletics	24	8	.750	—	Jack Kraninger
Nebraska City Forresters	15	17	.469	9	Jack Forrester
Falls City Colts#	13	19	.406	11	Ira Bidwell
Humboldt Infants#	12	20	.375	12	Warren Cummings

#Falls City and Humboldt withdrew June 17, causing the league to disband.

D Nebraska State League
President: A.C. Felt

Standings	W	L	Pct.	GB	Manager
Kearney Kapitalists	67	45	.598	—	Harry Berte
Hastings Third Citys	64	48	.571	3	Bert Shaner
York Prohibitionists	57	55	.509	10	Frank Gardner
Fremont Pathfinders	56	56	.500	11	H. Welch
Superior Brickmakers	54	58	.482	13	Dennis Bockewitz
Columbus Discoverers	54	58	.482	13	John Gondling/Red Smythe/Jack Kraninger
Seward Statesmen/ Beatrice Milkskimmers#..	52	60	.464	15	Bill Zink
Grand Island Collegians	44	68	.393	23	O.J. Firestine/Jack Forrester

#Seward (27-37) moved to Beatrice July 21.

BA: Homer Gray, Kearney, .411
Hits: Jim McCabe, Hastings, 155
Wins: R.N. Maples, Kearney, 17
L.R. Plympton, Kearney, 17
Berney Everdon, York, 17
Pct: Bert Reed, Columbus, .737, 14-5

D New Brunswick-Maine League
President: W.L. Hooper

Standings	W	L	Pct.	GB	Manager
Fredericton Pets	41	24	.631	—	Bob Ganley/William Duggan
St. John Marathons	41	29	.586	2½	Frank Leonard
Calais-St. Stephen	31	30	.508	8	Ernest Doyle
Bangor Maroons	18	48	.273	23½	George Magoon/Frank Connaughton/Lamorey

The league disbanded August 23.

BA: Matthews, Bangor, .378
Runs: W.J. O'Brien, St. John, 60
Hits: Louis Tetrault, Calais-St. Stephen, 86
SOs: William Lee, Calais-St. Stephen, 118
Pct: Joe Tarbell, St. John, .688, 11-5

D New York-New Jersey League
President: Rosslyn M. Cox

Standings	W	L	Pct.	GB	Manager
Long Branch Cubans	65	29	.691	—	Ricardo Henriquez
Poughkeepsie Honey Bugs	48	49	.495	18½	Eugene Ressique
Kingston Colonials	45	46	.494	18½	Walter Bennett
Middletown Middies	42	51	.452	22½	Jack Lawlor
Danbury Hatters	43	55	.439	24	Ernest Landgraf
Newburgh Dutchmen	41	54	.432	24½	Archie Marshall

BA: Frank Ely, Middletown, .385
Runs: Eugene Ressique, Poughkeepsie, 101
Hits: Juan Viola, Long Branch, 131
HRs: Frank Ely, Middletown, 7
Edward Harrison, Newburgh, 7
Wins: Dolf Luque, Long Branch, 22
Pct: Dolf Luque, Long Branch, .815, 22-5

D North Carolina League
President: Joseph H. Wearn

Standings	W	L	Pct.	GB	Manager
Winston-Salem Twins	66	49	.574	—	Charles Clancy
Durham Bulls	65	49	.570	½	James Kelly
Raleigh Capitals	60	53	.531	5	Earle Mack
Asheville Mountaineers	58	55	.513	7	Thomas Stouch/Lonnie Noojin
Charlotte Hornets	47	67	.412	18½	Burleigh Emery
Greensboro Patriots	46	69	.400	20	Frank Doyle

BA: James Kelly, Durham, .321
Runs: Warren Butts, Raleigh/Durham, 90
Hits: Bill Schumaker, Winston-Salem, 130
HRs: Bill Schumaker, Winston-Salem, 18
Wins: J.R. Lee, Winston-Salem, 25
SOs: J.R. Lee, Winston-Salem, 199
Pct: Jerry Belanger, Raleigh, .750, 12-4

D Ohio State League
President: Robert W. Read

Standings	W	L	Pct.	GB	Manager
Chillicothe Babes	83	49	.629	—	Alfred Newnham
Charleston Senators	84	50	.627	—	Henry "Buzz" Wetzel
Portsmouth Cobblers	83	55	.601	3	Pete Childs
Huntington Blue Sox	68	68	.500	17	Samuel Wright/S. Redman
Lexington Colts	68	70	.483	18	Jack Reynolds/W. McKernan/ Hubbard Dawson
Ironton Nailers	63	75	.456	23	Al McClintock/Archie Osborne
Hamilton Maroons	55	79	.441	29	George "Zeke" Wrigley
Maysville	38	96	.284	46	Frank Moore

BA: Carl Gray, Charleston, .366
Runs: John Baggan, Portsmouth, 105
Hits: Frank Nesser, Chillicothe, 178
HRs: Carl Gray, Charleston, 33
Wins: Eddie Donalds, Portsmouth, 30
Pct: Eddie Donalds, Portsmouth, .789, 30-8

D Southern California League
President: Jay Davidson

Standings	W	L	Pct.	GB	Manager
San Diego Bears*	56	33	.629	—	Spencer Abbott/Dick Cooley
San Bernardino Kittens	48	38	.558	6½	Ed Householder/Kitty Brashear
Long Beach Beachcombers	43	46	.483	13	Louis "Bull" Durham/Harry G. Connor/ Jesse Stovall
Pasadena Millionaires/ Santa Barbara Barbareans#**	27	57	.321	26½	John Schuster/Louis "Bull" Durham/ Spencer Abbott

#Pasadena (15-38) moved to Santa Barbara June 13, first home game June 24. The league disbanded July 23.

D Southern Michigan Association
President: James Frank

Standings	W	L	Pct.	GB	Manager
Battle Creek Crickets	77	46	.626	—	Ed McKernan
Adrian Champs	68	55	.553	9	Dan Jenkins
Jackson Convicts	66	60	.524	12½	Maurice Myers
Saginaw Ducks	60	65	.480	18	Howard "Ducky" Holmes
Flint Vehicles	57	64	.471	19	Danny Collins
Kalamazoo Kazoos	59	67	.468	19½	Charles Wagner
Lansing Senators	54	68	.439	22½	John Morrissey
Bay City Beavers	54	70	.435	23½	Hugh Shannon

BA: Fred Bramble, Kalamazoo, .349
Runs: Dan Jenkins, Adrian, 88
Hits: T.H. McNellis, Lansing, 146
HRs: Cecil Coombs, Adrian, 10
Wins: Richard Niehaus, Battle Creek, 24
SOs: Rudolph Schwenk, Saginaw, 283
Pct: Richard Niehaus, Battle Creek, .727, 24-9

D Texas-Oklahoma League
President: C.O. Johnson

Standings	W	L	Pct.	GB	Manager
Denison Blue Sox	82	39	.678	—	Babe Peebles
Paris Boosters	80	45	.640	4	Jack Jutze
Texarkana Tigers	73	53	.579	11½	A.L. "Dad" Ritter/Dee Poindexter

	W	L	Pct.	GB	Manager
Sherman Lions	68	58	.540	16½	Jimmy Humphries
Bonham Blues	56	68	.452	27½	Roy Leslie
Wichita Falls Drillers/					
Hugo Hugoites#	54	70	.435	29½	Fred Morris, Sr.
Ardmore Giants	43	80	.350	40	Art Naylor/Whitney Hewitt/Lew Pelkey/ Brooks Gordon
Durant Choctaws	41	84	.328	43	Dick Speer

#Wichita Falls (33-46) moved to Hugo July 7.

BA: Ray Nagle, Paris, .310
Runs: Fred Nicholson, Wichita Falls/Hugo, 90
Hits: Fred Nicholson, Wichita Falls/Hugo, 147
SBs: Ray Wakefield, Denison, 80
Wins: Joe Pate, Texarkana, 23

SOs: Ben Tincup, Sherman, 233
Pct: James Haislip, Denison, .769, 20-6
Grady Higginbotham, Denison, .769, 20-6

D Union Association
President: E.C. Mulroney

Standings	W	L	Pct.	GB	Manager
Great Falls Electrics	78	42	.650	—	Harry Hester
Salt Lake City Skyscrapers	75	47	.615	4	John McCloskey
Butte Miners	54	64	.458	23	Arthur Merkle
Missoula	54	68	.443	25	Cliff Blankenship/Nig Perrine
Helena Senators	52	67	.437	25½	Danny Shay
Ogden Canners	49	74	.398	30½	G.C. "Kitty" Knight/Frank "Dad" Gimlin

BA: Frank Huelsman, Salt Lake City, .423
Runs: Frank Huelsman, Salt Lake City, 123
Hits: Frank Huelsman, Salt Lake City, 200
RBIs: Frank Huelsman, Salt Lake City, 126
HRs: Frank Huelsman, Salt Lake City, 22

Wins: Amos Morgan, Salt Lake City, 26
SOs: Leo Bohen, Missoula, 228
Pct: Amos Morgan, Salt Lake City, .722, 26-10

D Western Canada League
President: Frank M. Gray

Standings	W	L	Pct.	GB	Manager
Moose Jaw Robin Hoods**	68	35	.660	—	James Brown/Fred Weed
Saskatoon Quakers*	63	37	.630	3½	Jerry Hurley
Medicine Hat Hatters	59	46	.562	10	Bert Dunn
Calgary Bronchos	51	56	.477	19	John Streib
Edmonton Gray Birds	39	57	.406	25½	Ray Whisman
Regina Red Sox	29	78	.271	41	Billy Hulen

Playoff: Moose Jaw 4 games, Saskatoon 2. On September 8, a replay of the last playoff game was ordered by the league president, but Moose Jaw had already disbanded for the season. Both teams were declared co-champions.

BA: Roy Mills, Saskatoon, .362
Runs: Fred Weed, Moose Jaw, 90
Hits: Fred Weed, Moose Jaw, 146
HRs: Brad Hollis, Calgary, 13

Wins: Walt Frink, Calgary, 21
SOs: Robert Steele, Moose Jaw, 190
Pct: James Concannon, Moose Jaw, .813, 13-3

D Western Tri-State League
President: W.N. Sweet

Standings	W	L	Pct.	GB	Manager
Boise Irrigators**	72	45	.615	—	Frank "Dad" Gimlin/F.R. Clark
Walla Walla Bears*	71	48	.597	2	Gus Bade
North Yakima Braves	57	61	.483	15½	George Engel
Pendleton Buckarooes	54	60	.474	16½	Terry McKune
Baker City Golddiggers@	15	40	.273	NA	Con Harlow/Charles Harold
La Grande Spuds#	16	31	.340	NA	Carl King

#La Grande (16-29) disbanded June 22.
@Baker City disbanded June 23.

Playoffs: None; Boise and Walla Walla were unable to agree on financial terms. Boise was declared champion on the basis of regular season play.

BA: Henry Martini, Walla Walla, .29648
F.R. Clark, Boise, .29647
Runs: Henry Martini, Walla Walla, 93
Hits: M.E. Reams, Boise, 136

HRs: Henry Martini, Walla Walla, 16
Wins: Blane Gordon, North Yakima, 22
Pct: Elmer Leonard, Walla Walla, .792, 19-5

Ind Federal League
Presidents: John T. Powers/James Gilmore

Standings	W	L	Pct.	GB	Manager
Indianapolis Hoosiers	75	45	.625	—	Bill Phillips
Cleveland Green Sox	64	54	.546	10	Cy Young
St. Louis Terriers	59	60	.496	15½	Jack O'Connor
Chicago Chifeds	57	62	.479	17½	Burton Keeley
Covington Blue Sox/					
Kansas City Packers#	53	65	.449	21	Sam Leever/Hugo Swartling
Pittsburgh Stogies	49	71	.408	26	Deacon Philippe

#Covington (21-20) moved to Kansas City June 26.

BA: Bid Dolan, Indianapolis, .346
Runs: Cliff Barringer, Covington/ Kansas City, 86
Hits: John Kading, Chicago, 154
HRs: John Kading, Chicago, 9

Wins: Pete Henning, Covington/ Kansas City, 18
Thomas McGuire, Chicago, 18
SOs: Thomas McGuire, Chicago, 170
Pct: Ray King, St. Louis, .786, 11-3
CGs: Thomas McGuire, Chicago, 27

1913 Interleague Post Season Play

World Series
Philadelphia (American) 4 games, New York (National) 1

Minor League Championship Series
Milwaukee (American Association) 4 games, Denver (Western) 2

Class B Championship Series
Lowell (New England) 4 games, Hartford (Eastern Association) 2

Michigan State Championship
Manistee (Michigan State) 4 games, Battle Creek (Southern Michigan Association) 1

1913 No-Hitters

Date	Pitcher	Team	League	Opponent	Score
4-22	Smith	Meridian	Cotton States	Clarksdale	3-0
4-26	Wells	Grand Forks	Northern	St. Paul	3-0
4-26	Axtel Hayes	Portland	Northwestern	Vancouver	6-0
4-27	Harry Smith	Lincoln	Western	Wichita	7-0
4-27	W. Booth Hopper	New Haven	Eastern Assoc.	Pittsfield	1-0
4-28	Carl Ray	Winston-Salem	N. Carolina State	Durham	5-0
5-13	Jesse Baker	St. Thomas	Canadian	Berlin	10-1
5-14	W. Booth Hopper	New Haven	Eastern Assoc.	Pittsfield	3-0
5-16	Russell Northrop	Moose Jaw	Western Canada	Medicine Hat	4-0
5-16	Moe	Winona	Northern	Minneapolis	2-0
5-17	W.E. Baker	St. Thomas	Canadian	Peterborough	4-0
5-18	Jack Ryan	Los Angeles	Pacific Coast	Portland	6-0
5-20	Robert Steele	Moose Jaw	Western Canada	Calgary	2-0
5-23	Carter Wilson	Grand Forks	Northern	Virginia	6-0
6-2	Lore	Selma	Cotton States	Jackson	2-0
6-3	Hod Leverett	Minneapolis	Northern	Duluth	7-0
6-7	W.H. Smith	Great Bend	Kansas State	Manhattan	3-0
6-8	Earl Moseley	Youngstown	Interstate	Wheeling	1-0
6-12	Dan Duffy	Great Falls	Union Assoc.	Helena	2-0
6-22	Ralph Comstock	Minneapolis	Northern	Superior	6-0
6-23	Hippo Vaughn	Kansas City	American Assoc.	Toledo	2-0
6-23	Roger Salmon	Hartford	Eastern Assoc.	New London	5-0
6-29	John Loomis	Adrian	Southern Michigan	Bay City	3-0
7-2	Jeff Davis	Columbus	American Assoc.	Indianapolis	4-0
7-3	Kip Dowd	Utica	New York State	Syracuse	5-0
7-4	Karl Adams	Savannah	South Atlantic	Charleston	8-0
7-5	Jimmy Lavender	Huntington	Ohio State	Hamilton	2-0
7-5	Blount	Long Beach	Southern California	San Diego	4-0
7-6	Miller	Long Beach	Southern California	San Diego	2-0 (7)
7-6	Ed Appleton	Sherman	Texas-Oklahoma	Denison	4-0
7-11	Dan Duffy	Great Falls	Union Assoc.	Helena	2-0
7-13	Jim Baskette	Toledo	American Assoc.	Minneapolis	0-1
7-13	Louis Tretter	Quincy	Three-I	Danville	4-0 (7)
7-15	Leonard Cole	Columbus	American Assoc.	Milwaukee	3-1
7-17	W.E. Hollenbeck	Waterloo	Central Assoc.	Keokuk	4-0
7-22	Bentley	Monmouth	Central Assoc.	Ottumwa	3-0
7-23	Dana Fillingim	Cordele	Empire State	Waycross	4-0
7-23	Percy Wilder	Cordele	Empire State	Waycross	5-0 (7)
7-25	Jack Cameron	Danbury	N. Y.-New Jersey	Poughkeepsie	10-0
7-27	Harold Hinkeley	Fremont	Nebraska State	Beatrice	12-0
7-29	Harry Chapman	Danville	Three-I	Bloomington	5-0
7-30	Richard Walls	Muskegon	Michigan State	Cadillac	5-0
7-31	Phil Sitton	Troy	New York State	Wilkes-Barre	4-0
8-6	W.T. Smith	Pittsfield	Eastern Assoc.	Waterbury	3-0
8-6	Harry Watson	Asheville	N. Carolina State	Winston-Salem	3-0
8-6	Paul Fittery	Evansville	Central	Terre Haute	5-0
8-6	Kirley	Guelph	Canadian	St. Thomas	5-2
8-12	Fred House	Kewanee	Central Assoc.	Muscatine	6-0
8-13	Harry Hedgepethe	Petersburg	Virginia	Richmond	10-0
8-14	Albert Mamaux	Huntington	Ohio State	Maysville	(P)
8-16	Ducky Swan	Beaumont	Texas	Waco	8-0
8-16	Cecil Battson	Anniston	Georgia-Alabama	La Grange	8-0
8-17	Cy Dahlgren	Superior	Northern	Grand Forks	9-0
8-20	Caporel	Racine	Wisconsin-Illinois	Rockford	2-0
8-21	Cliff Markle	Morristown	Appalachian	Knoxville	3-0
8-31	Kull	Danbury	N. Y.-New Jersey	Poughkeepsie	2-0
9-7	Tom Rogers	Henderson	Kitty	Owensboro	2-0
9-7	C.H. Harben	Galveston	Texas	San Antonio	4-0

Number in parentheses indicates innings if other than nine; "P" indicates perfect game.

THIS DATE IN MINOR LEAGUE HISTORY

May 6, 1913, In the Western League, Omaha scored seven runs in one inning without a hit against St. Joseph. Eight bases on balls, two errors, a sacrifice fly and a wild pitch accounted for the runs. Omaha failed to score any other tallies and lost 13-7.

May 9, 1913, After 18 consecutive defeats, Newport News of the Virginia League won its first game of the season, defeating Norfolk 2-1.

May 10, 1913, Waterbury, Eastern Association, scored seven runs in the 12th frame and Hartford tallied three times. Waterbury won the extra-inning affair 14-10.

May 17, 1913, In the Central League, pitcher Hexon of Springfield hit six Grand Rapids batters, but won his game 1-0.

May 18, 1913, Chillicothe defeated Hamilton 24-21 in an Ohio State League game. The winners collected 26 hits, the losers 20.

May 24, 1913, In the MINK League, Auburn outfielder Kraninger hit 17 fouls in succession, then was retired on a foul tip.

May 24, 1913, New Orleans made 19 assists in a six-inning Southern League game with Chattanooga.

May 25, 1913, Pitcher Rogge, Des Moines, Western League, was scored on by Wichita after having hurled 31 consecutive shutout innings.

May 29, 1913, Dallas, Texas League, stole 12 bases in a 10-4 win over Austin.

May 31, 1913, Virginia, Northern League, scored 14 runs in the fifth inning and downed Winona 22-14.

May 31, 1913, In the Eastern Association, outfielder Benny Kauff of Hartford made two doubles and two triples and stole home in pacing his team to an 8-3 win over New London.

June 8, 1913, Lansing, Southern Michigan Association, made 11 hits but lost to Battle Creek 6-0. In the second inning, Lansing had a triple, a double and a single, but failed to score as two runners were thrown out at the plate.

June 9, 1913, Virginia, Northern League, scored 11 runs in the first inning and made 25 hits in the game to crush St. Paul 23-2.

June 9, 1913, Jackson, Southern Michigan Association, ended Battle Creek's 15 game inning streak with a 3-2 decision.

June 12, 1913, Grand Rapids, Central League, defeated Evansville 2-0 in the second game of a twinbill, extending its run of scoreless innings over Evansville to 32. Outfielder Larry LeJeune stole three sacks in each contest, including second, third and home in succession in game two.

June 19, 1913, Champaign, Three-I League, defeated Kankakee 6-5 in 20 innings.

June 26, 1913, The outlaw Federal League moved its Covington, Kentucky franchise to Kansas City.

June 28, 1913, Ex-major league southpaw Rube Waddell of Virginia, Northern League, defeated Duluth 2-1 in a 12-inning game. Waddell fanned 12 and gave nine hits, while his pitching opponent, Dusty Rhoades, yielded only five safeties and fanned 17.

July 2, 1913, Bill Pressley, Roanoke, Virginia League, had no putouts and just one assist at first base in a game against Norfolk.

July 8, 1913, In the Ohio State League, the four scheduled games all resulted in 4-3 scores, the four Ohio teams winning and the four West Virginia teams losing.

July 9, 1913, Rudolph Schwenk of Saginaw, Southern Michigan Association, pitched his fourth complete game in as many days. In 36 total innings, he struck out 33 men and allowed 21 hits, allowing his opponents just seven runs.

July 13, 1913, Topeka, Western League, scored 12 runs in the second inning and seven in the third, making 21 hits in a 4-1/2 inning game to wallop Des Moines 20-3.

July 13, 1913, In the New York-New Jersey League, third baseman Culcahy of Danbury stole second, third and home on three successive pitches against Poughkeepsie.

July 13, 1913, Jim Baskette of Toledo, American Association, pitched a no-hitter against Minneapolis, but lost 1-0 on a walk, sacrifice, stolen base and sacrifice fly.

July 14, 1913, Four Buffalo, International League, hurlers walked 15 Rochester batters, and in the ninth inning, three pitchers threw 20 consecutive balls without a strike.

July 15, 1913, Frank Schwab of Kingston, New York-New Jersey League, struck out 17 batters in seven innings of relief pitching against Danbury. Kingston won 9-4.

July 17, 1913, Lovin of Adrian, Southern Michigan Association, fanned 19 and McDonald, his pitching opponent, whiffed 16.

July 24, 1913, Holmquist of Traverse City, Michigan State League, pitched two full games against Ludington and won both by shutouts, 6-0 and 1-0.

July 26, 1913, Pitcher Shaw of York, Tri-State League, struck out 10 Allentown batters in a row and a total of 14 in the game.

July 26, 1913, Pitcher Gardin of Roanoke, Virginia League, shut out Newport News in a doubleheader, winning both nine-inning games, 8-0 and 5-0.

July 27, 1913, Buffalo and Providence played an International League league game in Detroit. The contest was transferred from Buffalo. Frank Navin, Tigers president, was also owner of the Buffalo club.

August 6, 1913, Four no-hit games were recorded in the minor leagues, one each in the Eastern Association, North Carolina State, Central and Canadian Leagues.

August 8, 1913, Minneapolis, American Association, defeated Indianapolis 11-1 in a contest that was a replay of the April 25th game which was played four times to determine a winner. The tilt was called on April 25 after six innings, tied 1-1. On June 15th, the teams tied 6-6 in nine frames. On the third attempt, August 7, the clubs played to a 13-inning, 2-2 tie. The game finally was decided on this date, as Minneapolis took an easy victory.

August 9, 1913, Pitcher Goshen, Chillicothe, Ohio State League, was stopped by Huntington 3-2, after having won six games in 15 days.

August 12, 1913, Jersey City and Toronto played a 20-inning scoreless tie in the International League. Bunn Hearn, who once pitched in the majors, went the distance for Toronto. A year earlier, Hearn had hit three homers in one game, including two in one inning, for Springfield in the Three-I League.

August 12, 1913, In the Central Association, William Whittaker of Keokuk shut out Waterloo twice in a doubleheader, each time by a 1-0 score. The second game went 12 innings. In 21 innings total, Whittaker allowed only five hits.

August 12, 1913, William Powers, New London, Eastern Association, shut out New Haven in a doubleheader, 1-0 and 4-0, yielding only eight hits in 18 innings.

August 13, 1913, Harry Hedgepethe, Petersburg, Virginia League, allowed only one hit in an 18 inning doubleheader against Richmond, winning 1-0 and 10-0. He pitched 14 consecutive no-hit innings and walked only three in the two games. He allowed one scratch hit in the fourth inning of the opener, none in game two. In the first game, pitcher Yancey Ayres of Richmond was the loser after having won 13 straight games.

August 22, 1913, In the New England League, Lowell scored 11 runs in one inning and made 24 hits in the game to clobber Brockton 25-0. In the same circuit, Portland staged a 13-run inning to wallop Lawrence 19-4.

August 23, 1913, In the Canadian League, Peterborough defeated Berlin 30-5 in a seven-inning game. The Petes scored eight runs in the third and sixth, ten in the fifth, and two in the first and fourth.

August 26, 1913, First baseman Kuhagen, Boyne City, Michigan State League, made five of the team's six hits as his club lost 4-2 to Muskegon. The winners garnered only three safeties.

August 28, 1913, Ogden defeated Missoula in an 11-inning Union Association game by a 20-19 score. Ogden had 27 hits and Missoula 21, while outfielder Morehead collected six hits in seven trips to the plate.

September 3, 1913, Outfielder Charles Swain, Victoria, Northwestern League, hit his 32nd home run of the season against Spokane.

September 3, 1913, In the Central League, catcher Hargrove drove in all of his team's runs to feature Fort Wayne's 9-7 victory over Terre Haute. Hargrove sent in all nine tallies on a homer, triple and double off pitchers Loudermilk and Young.

September 9, 1913, Catcher Waldo Jackley of Ironton, Ohio State League, hit four homers, plus a single, and batted in 12 runs in a game at Hamilton.

September 11, 1913, Pitcher Dan Duffy left Great Falls for Pittsburgh to join the Pirates, after earning his 14th consecutive victory, a Union Association record, that afternoon.

October 16, 1913, The consecutive scoreless inning streak by Portland, Pacific Coast League, pitchers ended at 82 when Los Angeles scored in the fourth inning. This was an all-time Organized Ball record.

October 26, 1913, The Pacific Coast League season closed. Five of the six clubs won 100 or more games and the last-place Oakland team posted 90 victories.

THE FIRST DECLINE: 1914-1919

*T*he relative peace of the minor leagues was brought to a halt in 1914 by the war between the Federal League and the Major Leagues. The Federal League raided both the major and minor leagues and encouraged players to jump their contracts. The minor league cities of Baltimore, Newark, N.J. Kansas City, Indianapolis, and Buffalo were invaded by the Federals. It was devastating to some of these franchises. On Opening Day in Baltimore in 1914, the Federal League game drew 30,000 fans, while only 1,500 showed up for the International League.

The Federal League lasted only through the 1915 season, but the minor leagues were experiencing other difficulties. The country was changing. Silent movies were now the rage and the automobile was becoming universal. Attending a ballgame was not the only thing to do. In Europe, a war was on. President Woodrow Wilson vowed to keep the U.S. out of the conflict, but it was difficult.

Forty-four leagues had started the 1914 season. By 1915 the number was down to 32, and in 1916 it was 26. The United States was being drawn into the war both economically and emotionally, and on April 4, 1917, Congress ratified Wilson's declaration of war. That year 21 leagues began play but only 11 would finish the season. There were wartime travel restrictions and manpower cutbacks. Fans no longer were interested in baseball games. In 1918, at the height of the war, nine minor leagues started play but only the International League completed its schedule.

The war ended in November, 1918, and fifteen leagues started play in 1919. Baseball was poised for a postwar boom. The wartime attrition of leagues left the National Association dominated by the higher minors for the first time. During the winter of 1918-1919, the minors adopted a resolution demanding that the majors relinquish the right of the draft and end the practice of optioning players. The majors rejected these demands and the National Association withdrew from the National Agreement with the majors. The National Commission suspended the major league draft. With no players on option, the majors needed to buy more players from the minors. Some players they had previously sold, they now had to buy back at higher prices. Without the draft, minor league clubs could virtually name their own prices. It was the beginning of a new era for minor league baseball.

1914

American League
President: Byron Bancroft Johnson

Standings	W	L	Pct.	GB	Attend.	Manager
Philadelphia Athletics	99	53	.651	—	346,641	Connie Mack
Boston Red Sox	91	62	.595	8½	481,359	Bill Carrigan
Washington Senators	81	73	.526	19	243,888	Clark Griffith
Detroit Tigers	80	73	.523	19½	416,225	Hugh Jennings
St. Louis Browns	71	82	.464	28½	244,714	Branch Rickey
Chicago White Sox	70	84	.455	30	469,290	Nixey Callahan
New York Yankees	70	84	.455	30	359,477	Frank Chance/ Roger Peckinpaugh
Cleveland Naps	51	102	.333	48½	185,997	Joe Birmingham

BA: Ty Cobb, Detroit, .368
Runs: Eddie Collins, Philadelphia, 122
Hits: Tris Speaker, Boston, 193
RBIs: Sam Crawford, Detroit, 104
HRs: Frank Baker, Philadelphia, 9

Wins: Walter Johnson, Washington, 28
SOs: Walter Johnson, Washington, 225
ERA: Dutch Leonard, Boston, 1.01
Pct: Charles "Chief" Bender, Philadelphia, .850, 17-3

National League
President: John K. Tener

Standings	W	L	Pct.	GB	Attend.	Manager
Boston Braves	94	59	.614	—	382,913	George Stallings
New York Giants	84	70	.545	10½	364,313	John McGraw
St. Louis Cardinals	81	72	.529	13	256,099	Miller Huggins
Chicago Cubs	78	76	.506	16½	202,516	Hank O'Day
Brooklyn Robins	75	79	.487	19½	122,671	Wilbert Robinson
Philadelphia Phillies	74	80	.481	20½	138,474	Red Dooin
Pittsburgh Pirates	69	85	.448	25½	139,620	Fred Clarke
Cincinnati Reds	60	94	.390	34½	100,791	Buck Herzog

BA: Jake Daubert, Brooklyn, .329
Runs: George Burns, New York, 100
Hits: Sherry Magee, Philadelphia, 171
RBIs: Sherry Magee, Philadelphia, 103
HRs: Gavvy Cravath, Philadelphia, 19

Wins: Dick Rudolph, Boston, 27
Grover Alexander, Philadelphia, 27
SOs: Grover Alexander, Philadelphia, 214
ERA: Bill Doak, St. Louis, 1.72
Pct: Bill James, Boston, .788, 26-7

Federal League
President: James Gilmore

Standings	W	L	Pct.	GB	Manager
Indianapolis Hoosierfeds	88	65	.575	—	Bill Phillips
Chicago ChiFeds	87	67	.565	1½	Joe Tinker
Baltimore Terrapins	84	70	.545	4½	Otto Knabe
Buffalo BufFeds	80	71	.530	7	Larry Schlafly
Brooklyn Tip-Tops	77	77	.500	11½	Bill Bradley
Kansas City Packers	67	84	.444	20	George Stovall
Pittsburgh Stogies	64	86	.427	22½	Doc Gessler/Rebel Oakes
St. Louis Terriers	62	89	.411	25	Mordecai Brown/Fielder Jones

BA: Benny Kauff, Indianapolis, .370
Runs: Benny Kauff, Indianapolis, 120
Hits: Benny Kauff, Indianapolis, 211
RBIs: Frank LaPorte, Indianapolis, 107
HRs: Duke Kenworthy, Kansas City, 15
Dutch Zwilling, Chicago, 15

Wins: Claude Hendrix, Chicago, 29
SOs: Cy Falkenberg, Indianapolis, 236
ERA: Adam Johnson, Chicago, 1.58
Pct: Russell Ford, Buffalo, .769, 20-6

AA American Association
President: Thomas M. Chivington

Standings	W	L	Pct.	GB	Attend.	Manager
Milwaukee Brewers	98	68	.590	—	177,875	Harry Clark
Louisville Colonels	95	73	.565	4	190,438	John Hayden
Indianapolis Indians	88	77	.533	9½	98,189	Jack Hendricks
Columbus Senators	86	77	.528	10½	156,861	William Hinchman
Cleveland Bearcats	82	81	.503	14½	99,732	Herman Bronkie
Kansas City Blues	84	84	.500	15	99,438	Bill Armour
Minneapolis Millers	75	93	.446	24	104,975	Joe Cantillon
St. Paul Apostles	56	111	.331	42½	75,621	William Friel

BA: Bill Hinchman, Columbus, .366
Runs: Bill Hinchman, Columbus, 139
Hits: Bill Hinchman, Columbus, 227
HRs: Oscar "Hap" Felsh, Milwaukee, 19

Wins: Melvin Gallia, Kansas City, 26
Jack Northrup, Louisville, 26
SOs: Grover Lowdermilk, Louisville, 254
ERA: W.A. "Lefty" James, Cleveland, 2.35

AA International League
President: Edward G. Barrow

Standings	W	L	Pct.	GB	Manager
Providence Grays	95	59	.617	—	Wild Bill Donovan
Buffalo Bisons	89	61	.593	4	Bill Clymer
Rochester Hustlers	91	63	.591	4	John Ganzel
Toronto Maple Leafs	74	70	.514	16	Joe Kelley
Newark Indians	73	77	.487	20	Harry Smith
Baltimore Orioles	72	77	.483	20½	Jack Dunn
Montreal Royals	60	89	.403	32½	Kitty Bransfield/Dan Howley
Jersey City Skeeters	48	106	.312	47	Rudy Hulswitt

Attendance: Buffalo, 117,188.

BA: Dave Shean, Providence, .334
Runs: Al Platte, Providence, 128
Hits: Al Platte, Providence, 190
HRs: Wally Pipp, Rochester, 15

Wins: Carl Mays, Providence, 24
SOs: Tom Hughes, Rochester, 182
Pct: Carl Mays, Providence, .750, 24-8

AA Pacific Coast League
President: Allan T. Baum

Standings	W	L	Pct.	GB	Manager
Portland Beavers	113	84	.573	—	Walter McCredie
Los Angeles Angels	116	94	.552	3½	Frank "Cap" Dillon
San Francisco Seals	115	96	.545	5	Daniel Long
Venice Tigers	113	98	.535	7	W.L. "Happy" Hogan
Sacramento/Mission Wolves#	90	121	.426	30	Harry Wolverton
Oakland Oaks	79	133	.372	41½	Art Devlin/Carl Mitze/Tyler Christian

#Sacramento (69-89) moved to San Francisco and became the Mission club September 6.

BA: Harry Wolter, Los Angeles, .328
Runs: Harl Maggert, Los Angeles, 127
Hits: Harry Wolter, Los Angeles, 263
HRs: Ty Lober, Portland, 9

Wins: Irv Higginbotham, Portland, 31
SOs: Ed Klepfer, Venice, 212
ERA: John Ryan, Los Angeles, 1.84

A Southern Association
President: William B. Kavanaugh

Standings	W	L	Pct.	GB	Manager
Birmingham Barons	88	63	.583	—	Carleton Molesworth
Mobile Sea Gulls	86	67	.562	3	Bris Lord
New Orleans Pelicans	80	65	.552	5	Johnny Dobbs
Atlanta Crackers	78	66	.542	6½	William A. Smith
Nashville Volunteers	77	72	.517	10	William Schwartz
Chattanooga Lookouts	73	78	.487	15	Harry "Moose" McCormick
Memphis Chickasaws	61	87	.412	25½	Michael Finn
Montgomery Billikens	54	99	.353	35	Robert Gilks

BA: Harry "Moose" McCormick, Chattanooga, .332
Runs: Lil Marcan, Birmingham, 103
Hits: Baby Doll Jacobson, Chattanooga, 188

HRs: Baby Doll Jacobson, Chattanooga, 15
Wins: Curley Brown, Birmingham, 21
SOs: Roy Walker, New Orleans, 200
Pct: Curley Brown, Birmingham, .750, 21-7

A Western League
President: Norris L. O'Neill

Standings	W	L	Pct.	GB	Manager
Sioux City Indians	105	60	.636	—	Josh Clarke
Denver Bears	96	72	.571	10½	Jack Coffey
St. Joseph Drummers	89	75	.543	15½	Jack Holland
Des Moines Boosters	82	81	.503	22	Frank Isbell
Lincoln Tigers	81	87	.482	25½	Charles Mullen/David Lloyd
Omaha Rourkes	77	87	.470	27½	Pa Rourke
Topeka Jayhawks	68	97	.412	37	Dale Gear/Dick Cooley
Wichita Wolves	63	102	.382	42	Nick Maddox/George Graham

BA: Larry LeJeune, Sioux City, .361
Runs: Larry LeJeune, Sioux City, 124
Hits: Jim Kane, Sioux City, 221
HRs: Bill Fisher, Denver, 21

Wins: Buck Sterzer, Denver, 28
SOs: Buck Sterzer, Denver, 206
ERA: Jim Scoggins, Lincoln, 2.58

B Canadian League
President: J.P. Fitzgerald

Standings	W	L	Pct.	GB	Manager
Ottawa Senators	76	45	.628	—	Frank Shaughnessy
London Tecumsehs	71	43	.623	1½	Frank Reisling
Erie Yankees	64	57	.529	12	Charles Smith/Frank Gygli
Toronto Beavers	55	55	.500	15½	Joe Keenan/George "Knotty" Lee
St. Thomas Saints	48	60	.444	21½	George Orth/Midge Craven
Peterborough Petes	49	62	.441	22	John Barthold/Curley Blount
Hamilton Hams	47	66	.416	25	Robert Yates/John White
Brantford Red Sox	46	68	.404	26½	William Wagner/George Deneau

BA: J. Trout, Toronto, .349
Runs: John Dawson, Erie, 90
Hits: Owen Harris, Erie, 138
HRs: George Deneau, Brantford, 7

Wins: Urban Shocker, Ottawa, 20
Lou Shettler, Peterborough, 20
SOs: Lou Shettler, Peterborough, 174
Pct: Joab McManus, Ottawa, .875, 14-2

*Won first-half   **Won second-half   ***Won both halves

B Central League
President: Louis Heilbroner

Standings	W	L	Pct.	GB	Manager
Dayton Veterans	85	49	.634	—	John Nee
Evansville River Rats	73	54	.575	8½	Charles "Punch" Knoll
Fort Wayne Railroaders	64	70	.478	21	Harry Martin
Terre Haute Terre-iers	61	71	.462	23	Larry Quinlan
Grand Rapids Champs	58	72	.446	25	George Hughes/James Jones
Springfield Reapers#	42	67	.385	NA	Joe Stanley

#Springfield disbanded August 8.

BA: John Sheehan, Terre Haute, .337
Runs: Arista DeHaven, Dayton, 96
Hits: John Sheehan, Terre Haute, 179
HRs: Howard Baker, Evansville, 15

Wins: Jake Fromholtz, Evansville, 23
SOs: Paul Fittery, Evansville, 249
Pct: Paul Fittery, Evansville, .759, 22-7

B Eastern Association
President: James H. O'Rourke

Standings	W	L	Pct.	GB	Manager
New London Planters	81	35	.698	—	Eugene McCann
Waterbury Frolickers..........	69	51	.575	14	Lee Fohl
Bridgeport Bolts	67	56	.545	17½	Jacob Boultes
Hartford Senators	62	56	.525	20	Simon McDonald/Daniel O'Neill
Springfield Ponies	63	61	.508	22	Billy Hamilton/Simon McDonald
Pittsfield Electrics	60	63	.488	24½	John Zeller
New Haven White Wings	54	64	.458	28	Jerry O'Connell
New Britain Sinks	27	97	.218	58	George Brown/James Garry

BA: Elmer Smith, Waterbury, .332
Runs: Martin Becker, New London, 90
Hits: Ed Barney, Hartford, 140
HRs: Francis Shields, Waterbury, 7

Wins: William Jensen, New Haven, 21
SOs: Robert Troy, Pittsfield, 212
ERA: W. Powers, New Haven, 2.03

B New England League
President: Tim H. Murnane

Standings	W	L	Pct.	GB	Manager
Lawrence Barristers...........	84	39	.683	—	Louis Piper
Worcester Busters	73	44	.624	8	Jesse Burkett
Portland Duffs....................	70	48	.593	11½	Hugh Duffy
Lynn Fighters	60	62	.492	23½	Patsy Flaherty/Ralph Reeve
Lewiston Cupids	57	66	.463	27	John "Red" McMahon/Joe Judge/Terry McGovern
Lowell Grays	57	66	.463	27	James Gray
Haverhill Hustlers	47	72	.395	35	Christy Wilson/Dan Clohecy/Dan Noonan/Eddie Cuddy
Fitchburg Burghers/Manchester Textiles#.......	36	87	.293	48	Frederick Lake

#Fitchburg (24-52) moved to Manchester July 30.

BA: Chick Shorten, Worcester, .345
Runs: Joe Burns, Portland, 99
Hits: Chick Shorten, Worcester, 157

HRs: Bob Conley, Lawrence, 9
Wins: Ben Van Dyke, Worcester, 22
Pct: Alex Pearson, Lawrence, .818, 18-4

B New York State League
President: John H. Farrell

Standings	W	L	Pct.	GB	Manager
Elmira Pioneers..................	90	48	.652	—	Bill Conroy
Wilkes-Barre Barons	79	55	.590	9	Joe McCarthy
Utica Utes	77	55	.584	10	Michael O'Neill
Binghamton Bingoes	78	56	.582	10	John Calhoun
Albany Senators................	61	73	.453	27	Edward McDonough
Troy Trojans	59	74	.444	28½	Henry Ramsey/James Tamsett
Syracuse Stars	48	79	.378	36½	Fred Payne
Scranton Miners................	42	94	.309	47	John Kelly/William Coughlin

BA: Richard Kauffman, Elmira, .329
Runs: Emil "Irish" Meusel, Elmira, 86
Hits: Emil "Irish" Meusel, Elmira, 156

HRs: Otey Johnson, Elmira, 13
SOs: Lou North, Syracuse, 181

B Northwestern League
Presidents: Fielder Jones/E.H. Hughes

Standings	W	L	Pct.	GB	Manager
Vancouver Beavers	96	56	.632	—	Hank Scharnweber
Seattle Giants...................	95	61	.609	3	Frank Raymond
Spokane Indians................	84	68	.553	12	Mike Lynch
Victoria Bees	64	87	.424	31½	Bert Delmas
Tacoma Tigers	64	93	.408	34½	Joe McGinnity/Russ Hall
Portland Colts/Ballard Pippins#.	58	96	.377	39	R.L. "Nick" Williams

#Portland (36-60) moved to Ballard July 20.

BA: Emil Frisk, Vancouver/Spokane, .322
Runs: Willis Butler, Spokane, 95
Hits: Emil Frisk, Vancouver/Spokane, 178
HRs: Charles Swain, Seattle, 12

Wins: Wheezer Dell, Seattle, 21
SOs: Stan Covaleski, Spokane, 214
Pct: Oscar Harstad, Vancouver, .867, 13-2

B Texas League
President: William R. Davidson

Standings	W	L	Pct.	GB	Manager
Houston Buffaloes	102	50	.670	—	Pat Newnam
Waco Navigators	102	50	.670	—	Ellis Hardy
Beaumont Oilers................	89	54	.622	8½	George Leidy
Galveston Pirates	86	63	.577	14½	Paul Sentell
Ft. Worth Panthers.............	71	77	.480	29	William Nance/Jake Atz
Dallas Giants....................	67	83	.447	34	Otto Jordan/Hunter Hill
San Antonio Bronchos........	46	103	.309	54½	Clyde Goodwin/Dred Cavender
Austin Senators.................	31	114	.214	67½	Walter Frantz/Charles Moran

BA: Bob Clemens, Waco, .327
Runs: Bob Clemens, Waco, 115
Hits: Bob Clemens, Waco, 196
HRs: Ed Edmondson, Beaumont, 10

Sac: Ona Dodd, Beaumont, 75
Wins: Eddie Donalds, Waco, 30
SOs: Gene Moore, Galveston, 240
Pct: Eddie Donalds, Waco, .882, 30-4

B Three-I League
President: Albert R. Tearney

Standings	W	L	Pct.	GB	Manager
Davenport Blue Sox	83	52	.615	—	Daniel O'Leary
Peoria Distillers	81	56	.591	3	Clarence "Pants" Rowland
Springfield Watchmakers ...	72	60	.545	9½	Howard Wakefield
Decatur Commodores	72	64	.529	11½	George Reed
Dubuque Dubs	64	69	.481	18	Forrest Plass
Quincy Gems	61	71	.462	20½	Nicholas Kahl
Bloomington Bloomers.......	56	77	.421	26	Harry Syfert/Peter Lister
Danville Speakers/Moline Plowboys#...........	46	86	.348	35½	Connie Walsh/William Neal

#Danville (26-53) moved to Moline July 14.

BA: Howard Wakefield, Springfield, .347
Runs: Dick Breen, Springfield, 114
Hits: Howard Wakefield, Springfield, 172
HRs: Howard Wakefield, Springfield, 10

Wins: James Middleton, Davenport, 26
SOs: Fred Lamline, Dubuque, 190
ERA: James Middleton, Davenport, 1.24

B Tri-State League
President: George M. Graham

Standings	W	L	Pct.	GB	Manager
Harrisburg Senators	78	32	.709	—	George Cockill
Allentown	75	35	.682	3	John Castle
Reading Pretzels	59	51	.536	19	Harry Hoffman
Wilmington Chicks.............	47	62	.431	30½	James Jackson
Trenton Tigers	44	66	.400	34	Zeke Wrigley/Clarence "Pop" Foster
York White Roses/Lancaster Red Roses#......	26	83	.218	51½	George Heckert/Ed Hooper

#York (16-37) moved to Lancaster July 8.

BA: Clarence "Pop" Foster, Trenton, .388
Runs: Jim Murray, Allentown, 95
Hits: Jim Murray, Allentown, 155

HRs: Charles Miller, Harrisburg, 7
Wins: Joe Chabek, Harrisburg, 28
Pct: Joe Chabek, Harrisburg, .903, 28-3

C Colonial League
President: Charles B. Coppen

Standings	W	L	Pct.	GB	Manager
Fall River Spindles	62	37	.625	—	John Kiernan
New Bedford Whalers	60	40	.600	2½	John J. O'Brien
Woonsocket Speeders	49	48	.505	12	Roy Dickinson/T.M. Walsh
Taunton	44	54	.449	17½	Ambrose Kane/Tom Gilroy
Pawtucket Tigers	45	56	.446	18	Jeff Pfeffer/Nixey Callahan/William Fortin
Brockton Shoemakers........	36	61	.371	25	Willie Reardon/Bert Weeden

BA: Joe Gaudette, Woonsocket, .321
Runs: Aime Proulx, Taunton, 92
Hits: Joe Gaudette, Woonsocket, 117
HRs: John Gilmore, Pawtucket, 9

Wins: John Tillman, New Bedford, 21
SOs: Merdic McLeod, Fall River, 193
Pct: Joe Gulden, Fall River, .786, 11-3

C Northern League
President: John Burmeister

Standings	W	L	Pct.	GB	Manager
Duluth White Sox	82	43	.656	—	Bill Clymer
Winnipeg Maroons	81	45	.613	1½	Fred Curtis
Grand Forks Flickertails	65	60	.520	17	Edward Wheeler
Winona Pirates	61	62	.496	20	W.D. "Lefty" Davis
Virginia Ore Diggers	55	68	.447	26	John "Kid" Taylor/John Sundheim/Frank McGee
Fargo-Moorhead Graingrowers..	55	71	.437	27½	Bob Unglaub
Superior Red Sox	52	69	.430	28	John Landry/John "Kid" Taylor
Ft. William-Pt. Arthur Canucks .	46	79	.358	36	Abel Lizotte

BA: H.H. Bond, Duluth, .346
Runs: Joe Wilkes, Winnipeg, 108
Hits: Al Swalm, Winnipeg, 156
HRs: Julius DeRose, Ft. William-Pt. Arthur, 16

Wins: George Cunningham, Duluth, 23
SOs: George Cunningham, Duluth, 296
Pct: E.B. Ezell, Duluth, .842, 16-3

C South Atlantic League
President: Nick P. Corish

Standings	W	L	Pct.	GB	Manager
Charleston Sea Gulls	78	46	.629	—	James Hamilton
Savannah Colts*	72	50	.590	5	Perry Lipe
Albany Babies**	64	57	.529	12½	Phil Wells/Frank Manush
Columbia Comers	60	66	.476	19	Doug Harbison
Jacksonville Tarpons	58	64	.475	19	Percy Wilder/Ed Crowder
Columbus Foxes	55	67	.451	22	James Fox
Macon Peaches	52	68	.433	24	George Stinson
Augusta Tourists	52	73	.416	26½	Arthur Brouthers

Playoff: Savannah 4 games, Albany 2.

BA: George Stinson, Macon, .322
Runs: Tim Bowden, Macon, 79
    Al Handiboe, Savannah, 79
Hits: Sam Mayer, Savannah, 162
Wins: Clarence Burmeister, Jacksonville, 24
SOs: Phil Redding, Columbus, 184
Pct: Robert Spaid, Charleston, .786, 11-3

C Southern Michigan Association
President: James Frank

Standings	W	L	Pct.	GB	Manager
Bay City Beavers*	96	50	.658	—	Dan Jenkins
Saginaw Ducks**	90	55	.621	5½	Howard "Ducky" Holmes
Battle Creek Crickets	92	57	.617	5½	Danny Collins
South Bend Benders	85	60	.586	10½	Edward Smith/Ben Kohler
Flint Vehics	75	70	.517	20½	Jack Burke
Jackson Chiefs	71	72	.497	23½	Maurice Myers/Don Brown
Lansing Senators/					
Mt. Clemens Bathers#	63	80	.441	31½	John Morrissey
Toledo Mud Hens	53	93	.363	43	Topsy Hartsel
Adrian Fencevilles	53	94	.361	43½	Bill Cristall/C. Henderson
Kalamazoo Kazoos	49	97	.336	47	Charles Wagner

#Lansing (33-35) moved to Mt. Clemens July 10.

Playoff: Saginaw 4 games, Bay City 1.

BA: Joe Harris, Bay City, .386
Runs: Dan Jenkins, Bay City, 140
Hits: Joe Harris, Bay City, 197
HRs: Edward Hoffman, Flint, 12
Wins: Walter Scott, Saginaw, 26
SOs: Russell Robbins, Saginaw, 338
Pct: John Jenkins, Bay City, .852, 23-4

C Virginia League
President: Jacob O. Boatwright

Standings	W	L	Pct.	GB	Manager
Norfolk Tars***	93	48	.660	—	William "Buck" Pressley
Richmond Colts	78	56	.582	11½	Ray Ryan
Newport News Shipbuilders	70	69	.504	22	Matthew Broderick/Harry Mathews/
					Jack Spratt
Roanoke Tigers	65	72	.474	26	Otto Mills/W. Welcher
Petersburg Goobers	63	74	.460	28	Henry Busch
Portsmouth Truckers	46	96	.324	47½	Jesse Tannehill/Joe Holland/H. McIlveen

BA: Frank Thrasher, Norfolk, .325
Runs: Art Smith, Norfolk, 96
Hits: Cecil Gray, Richmond, 169
HRs: Pryor McElveen, Portsmouth, 8
Wins: Cliff Markle, Norfolk, 31
SOs: Cliff Markle, Norfolk, 265
Pct: Sam Rice, Petersburg, .818, 9-2

C Wisconsin-Illinois League
President: Frank R. Weeks

Standings	W	L	Pct.	GB	Manager
Oshkosh Indians	75	43	.636	—	Joe Killian
Green Bay Bays	73	51	.589	5	Bobby Lynch
Appleton Papermakers	64	55	.538	11½	George Brautigan
Racine Malted Milks	64	58	.525	13	Frank Reynolds
Marinette-Menominee Twins	61	59	.508	15	John Wickenhoefer/Jack Sheehan
Madison Senators	57	62	.479	18½	Harry Bay
Rockford Wolves	48	71	.403	27½	Orville Wolf/Pat Dunlin
Wausau Lumberjacks	39	82	.322	37½	George Bubsir

BA: H.B. Harrison, Madison, .310
Runs: Al "Bull" Durham, Oshkosh, 87
Hits: Tom McCabe, Racine, 142
HRs: Al "Bull" Durham, Oshkosh, 25
Wins: Joe Lotz, Oshkosh, 24
SOs: Joe Lotz, Oshkosh, 267
Pct: H. Smith, Appleton, .850, 17-3

D Appalachian League
President: E.F. Fisher

Standings	W	L	Pct.	GB	Manager
Middlesboro Colonels#	15	13	.536	—	Lovell Draper
Morristown Jobbers#	15	13	.536	—	Harry Kunkle
Harriman Boosters	14	13	.519	½	Pit Pasini
Knoxville Reds	11	16	.407	3½	Frank Moffett/Ambrose Gaines

#Morristown and Middlesboro disbanded June 17, causing the league to fold the same day.

D Atlantic League
President: Rosslyn M. Cox

Standings	W	L	Pct.	GB	Manager
Poughkeepsie Honey Bugs	65	31	.677	—	Bill McCabe
Newark/Long Branch Cubans@	59	32	.648	3½	Ricardo Henriquez
Middletown Middies	47	45	.511	16	Jack Lawler
Danbury Hatters	49	48	.505	16½	Tom Guiheen
Perth Amboy Pacers	44	49	.473	19½	Bob Ganley/Henry Ramsey
Newburgh Hillclimbers	40	48	.455	21	Andrew Marshall/
					William "Todd" Waterman
Paterson Silk Citys	32	54	.372	28	Richard Cogan
Bloomfield-Long Branch Cubans/					
Asbury Park Sea Urchins#..	30	59	.337	31½	Sam Jaeger

#Bloomfield-Long Branch (15-22) moved to Asbury Park July 2.
@Newark (26-11) moved to Long Branch July 22.

BA: Angel Aragon, Newark/Long Branch, .443
Runs: Joe McCarthy, Poughkeepsie, 83
Hits: William Duggan, Poughkeepsie, 120
HRs: Jim Elcock, Newburgh, 7
Wins: Jim Clinton, Poughkeepsie, 15
SOs: Andy Coakley, Asbury Park, 138
Pct: Jim Clinton, Poughkeepsie, .938, 15-1

D California State League
President: Allan T. Baum

Standings	W	L	Pct.	GB	Manager
Fresno Tigers	20	15	.571	—	George Wheeler
San Jose Bears	20	16	.556	½	Mike Steffani
Stockton Millers	17	19	.472	3½	George Harper
Modesto Reds	14	21	.400	6	Jimmy Byrnes

The league disbanded June 1.

BA: Tony Boeckel, Stockton, .364
Runs: Tony Boeckel, Stockton, 25
Hits: Tony Boeckel, Stockton, 51
HRs: Tom Pierce, Fresno, 2
Wins: Horace Miller, Fresno, 9
SOs: Walt Waldschmidt, Fresno, 75
Pct: Harry Stewart, San Jose, 1.000, 8-0

D Central Association
President: M.E. Justice

Standings	W	L	Pct.	GB	Manager
Waterloo Jays	78	51	.605	—	Jay Andrews
Burlington Pathfinders	75	53	.586	2½	Tom Hayden/Heinie Manush
Muscatine Buttonmakers	72	53	.576	4	Frank Boyle
Clinton Pilots	67	61	.523	10½	Bert Hough
Cedar Rapids Bunnies	64	60	.516	11½	Belden Hill
Keokuk Indians	52	76	.406	25½	Spencer Abbott/Harry Sweet
Marshalltown Ansons	52	76	.406	25½	Frank Richardson
Ottumwa Packers/					
Rock Island Islanders/					
Galesburg Pavers#	49	79	.373	28½	Ned Egan

#Ottumwa (23-47) moved to Rock Island July 17. However, the National Association would not let the Central Association invade the territory of the Three-I League, so Rock Island (6-1) moved to Galesburg July 24.
Attendance: Cedar Rapids, 67,314.

BA: Paddy Siglin, Waterloo, .322
Runs: Walt Meinert, Burlington, 94
Hits: John Singleton, Burlington, 158
Wins: Fred Miller, Burlington, 23
SOs: George Zackert, Muscatine, 305
Pct: W. Halper, Cedar Rapids, .722, 13-5

D Central Texas League
President: A.M. Frazier

Standings	W	L	Pct.	GB	Manager
Waxahachie Buffaloes*	35	23	.603	—	Luther Burleson/Dee Poindexter
West**	29	26	.527	4½	Eli Walker
Ennis Tigers	31	28	.525	4½	Ed Wicker
Italy	29	29	.500	6	T.A. Craig
Corsicana Athletics	26	32	.448	9	Gus Kennedy
Hillsboro	21	33	.389	12	L.C. Eastland

The second half was shortened to July 25.

Playoff: Waxahachie 3 games, West 2.

D Georgia State League
President: I.J. Kalmon

Standings	W	L	Pct.	GB	Manager
Cordele Ramblers	57	44	.564	—	Ed Reagan
Americus Muckalees**	57	47	.548	1½	William "Dave" Gaston
Thomasville Hornets*	53	50	.515	5	Martin Dudley
Brunswick Pilots	53	51	.510	5½	Whitey Morse/Bert Kite/Earl Bitting/
					Otto Jordan
Waycross Grasshoppers/					
Moguls	53	53	.500	6½	Langdon "Wild Bill" Clark/Jack Coveney
Valdosta Millionaires	41	69	.410	20½	Joe Herold/Frank Moffett

Playoff: Americus 4 games, Thomasville 0.

BA: Will Bankston, Cordele, .359
Runs: Walt Brouthers, Cordele, 87
Hits: Will Bankston, Cordele, 144
HRs: Will Bankston, Cordele, 31

D Georgia-Alabama League
President: W.J. Boykin

Standings	W	L	Pct.	GB	Manager
Selma River Rats	60	35	.632	—	W. Guiterrez/Arthur Riggs
Newnan Cowetas	56	37	.602	3	Warren Sanders

La Grange Terrapins........... 55 43 .561 6½ James Lafitte
Opelika Pelicans................. 52 45 .536 9 Kirk Newell/F.C. Steele
Rome Romans.................... 46 50 .479 14½ Jack Reidy
Anniston Moulders .... 41 54 .432 19 Bob Ragsdale/Louis Procter
Talladega Indians............... 37 55 .402 21 Carl Pace/Lovell Draper/Howard Baker/
                                                   H. Garrett
Gadsden Steel Makers#...... 32 60 .348 26½ Bruce Hayes/Louis Jordan/L. Mills

#Gadsden became a road club August 3.

BA: Lloyd Howell, Newnan, .332   **Hits:** Jack Reidy, Rome, 117
Runs: Jack Reidy, Rome, 76

D Illinois-Missouri League
President: Charles A. Cline

Standings	W	L	Pct.	GB	Manager
Champaign Velvets***	62	27	.696	—	Fred "Blackie" Wilson
Ottawa Indians	47	38	.553	13	Chuck Fleming
Streator Boosters	40	48	.454	21½	John Ray/Heinie Seebach
La Salle Blue Sox	26	60	.302	34½	Tony Hinley/John Fitzpatrick
Lincoln Abes#	32	15	.681	NA	Louis Ehrgott
Kankakee Kanks#	14	33	.301	NA	Harry Randall/Gene Connelly/ Teddy Raines/William Hinley

#Lincoln and Kankakee withdrew July 3.

BA: Andy Lotshaw, Champaign, .320   **Wins:** Grover Baichley, Champaign, 15
Runs: Chuck Fleming, Ottawa, 68   **SOs:** Grover Baichley, Champaign, 174
Hits: Andy Lotshaw, Champaign, 108   **Pct:** Grover Baichley, Champaign, .938, 15-1
HRs: Andy Lotshaw, Champaign, 10

D Interstate League
Presidents: Milton A. Jordan/W. Duke Jr.

Standings	W	L	Pct.	GB	Manager
Jamestown Giants*	59	40	.596	—	Joseph Lohr
Bradford Drillers**	59	42	.584	1	Art Goodwin/Duke Servatius
Warren Bingoes	57	45	.559	3½	William Webb
Olean Refiners	43	53	.448	14½	Harry Giles/Joe Reynolds
Wellsville Rainmakers	41	60	.406	19	William Clarke/Elmer Bliss
Hornell Green Sox	39	58	.402	19	O'Keefe/Albert Barrett/Joe Prozeller

Playoff: Jamestown 4 games, Bradford 3.

D Kansas State League
President: Roy C. Gafford

Standings	W	L	Pct.	GB	Manager
Emporia Bidwells	54	32	.628	—	Ira Bidwell
Salina Coyotes	47	41	.534	8	Dick Robin
Hutchinson Packers	40	49	.449	15½	Jesse Clifton
Great Bend Millers	35	54	.393	20½	Affie Wilson

BA: Pete LaFlambois, Emporia, .342   **Wins:** Otis Lambeth, Emporia, 14
Runs: Paul Turgeon, Emporia, 61   Ralph Shimeal, Emporia, 14
Hits: Rick Freeman, Hutchinson, 98   **SOs:** Powell Burnett, Salina, 166
          Pct: Otis Lambeth, Emporia, .737, 14-5

D Kitty League
President: Dr. Frank H. Bassett

Standings	W	L	Pct.	GB	Manager
Cairo Egyptians	77	46	.626	—	John Herbert
Owensboro Distillers	66	55	.545	10	William Long/Ollie Pickering
Henderson Hens	64	58	.525	12½	Ward Snyder
Paducah Indians	59	65	.476	18½	Dow Vandyne/Arthur Brouthers
Clarksville Boosters#	22	39	.361	NA	James Coleman
Hopkinsville Hoppers#	20	45	.308	NA	George Kalkhoff

#Clarksville and Hopkinsville disbanded July 10.

BA: James Allen, Henderson, .307   **Wins:** John Grogan, Cairo, 22
Runs: Ed Wise, Cairo, 70   **SOs:** John Grogan, Cairo, 143
Hits: Charles Gosnell, Paducah, 135   **Pct:** Win Frewen, Cairo, .792, 19-5

D Michigan State League
President: Emerson W. Dickerson

Standings	W	L	Pct.	GB	Manager
Muskegon Speeders	73	46	.613	—	Sandy Murray
Ludington Mariners	69	50	.580	4	Bob Grogan/Jim Sager
Cadillac Chiefs	67	51	.568	5½	Jay Parker
Manistee/Belding Champs@	57	64	.471	17	Louis Haidt
Boyne City Boosters#	48	51	.485	NA	Grover Gillen
Traverse City Resorters#	22	74	.229	NA	Leo Speer/Carl Wenger/Harry Kunkel

#Traverse City and Boyne City, which had become a road club July 8, both withdrew September 1.
@Manistee (56-51) was expelled and the franchise moved to Belding September 9.

BA: Gilbert Patterson, Traverse City/   **HRs:** Carl Tennant, Ludington, 7
  Manistee/Belding, .314   **Wins:** Neal Leifers, Muskegon, 25
Runs: Raleigh Baum, Cadillac, 86   **SOs:** Neal Leifers, Muskegon, 194
Hits: Raleigh Baum, Cadillac, 138   **Pct:** Neal Leifers, Muskegon, .758, 25-8

D Middle Texas League
President: W.F. Blum, Jr.

Standings	W	L	Pct.	GB	Manager
Temple Tigers*	54	27	.667	—	Charlie Nichols
Georgetown Collegians	50	30	.625	3½	James Callahan/E. Gober
Brenham Brewers	50	34	.595	5½	Ike Pendleton
Belton Braves**	37	47	.440	18½	Leslie Mitchell/L. Hubbard/Hart/ Jack Forrester/Cal Calahan
Lampasas Resorters	35	51	.407	21½	Jesse Estill/Luke Roberts
Bartlett	22	59	.272	32	Robert Roundtree/Brooks Gordon

The season was shortened to August 8.

Playoff: Belton 5 games, Temple 1.

BA: Fred Wende, Georgetown, .380   **HRs:** Ellis Boggess, Temple, 16
Runs: Ellis Boggess, Temple, 58   **Wins:** J. Reems, Brenham, 14
Hits: Fred Wende, Georgetown, 116   **Pct:** Frank Wolfram, Georgetown, .833, 10-2

D Nebraska State League
President: Clarence J. Miles

Standings	W	L	Pct.	GB	Manager
Grand Island Islanders	66	46	.589	—	Harry Claire
Beatrice Milkskimmers	65	47	.580	1	Frank Coe
Hastings Reds	64	48	.571	2	Leo Bennett
York Prohibitionists	60	52	.536	6	Jim Pierce
Superior Brickmakers	54	58	.482	12	James Feeney/F.H. Bigby
Norfolk Drummers	52	60	.464	14	Warren Cummings/Jay "Babe" Towne
Columbus Pawnees	49	63	.437	17	Jake Kraninger
Kearney Kapitalists	38	74	.339	28	Harry Berte

BA: Jacob Gettman, Hastings, .336   **Wins:** John McDonnell, Beatrice, 21
Runs: Clint Neff, Beatrice, 80   **SOs:** Dazzy Vance, Hastings, 194
Hits: Charles Payne, Grand Island, 134   **Pct:** Dazzy Vance, Hastings, .810, 17-4
HRs: Clint Neff, Beatrice, 19

D North Carolina State League
President: Arthur Lyon

Standings	W	L	Pct.	GB	Manager
Winston-Salem Twins	70	47	.598	—	Charles Clancy
Charlotte Hornets	72	49	.593	—	Burleigh Emery
Durham Bulls	70	50	.583	1½	James "King" Kelly
Raleigh Capitals	52	68	.433	19½	Earle Mack
Greensboro Patriots	47	67	.412	21½	Red Owens/Pete Baylis
Asheville Mountaineers	43	73	.371	26½	Louis Cook/Jack Corbett

BA: Harry Weiser, Charlotte, .333   **Wins:** Carl Ray, Winston-Salem, 28
Runs: Harry Weiser, Charlotte, 102   **SOs:** Carl Ray, Winston-Salem, 317
Hits: Harry Weiser, Charlotte, 148   **Pct:** Robert Ledbetter, Charlotte, .684, 26-12
HRs: Jimmy Hickman, Winston-Salem, 20

D Ohio State League
President: Robert W. Read

Standings	W	L	Pct.	GB	Manager
Portsmouth Cobblers	86	53	.723	—	Pete Childs
Charleston Senators**	79	62	.560	8	Henry "Buzz" Wetzel/Charles "Biddy" Beers
Chillicothe Babes*	73	64	.533	12	Alfred Newnham
Lexington Colts	66	68	.493	17½	Howard Guyn
Ironton Nailers#	35	33	.514	NA	Richard Smith
Huntington Blue Sox+	39	47	.453	NA	John Seigle/James Calbert
Maysville+	30	51	.370	NA	Ollie Chapman/Roy Montgomery
Newport/Paris@	19	49	.279	NA	Charles Applegate/Clarence "Red" Munson

#Ironton disbanded July 5.
@Newport (16-27), which entered the league May 26, moved to Paris June 16; Paris disbanded July 5.
+Huntington and Maysville disbanded July 22.

Playoffs: None; Charleston was awarded the title when Chillicothe was unable to field a competitive team.

BA: E. Crouch, Lexington/Portsmouth, .327   **Wins:** Abel Applegate, Charleston, 22
Runs: John Baggan, Portsmouth, 116   Paul Carter, Portsmouth, 22
Hits: John Baggan, Portsmouth, 182   **Pct:** T. Thompson, Maysville/Charleston/
HRs: Ernie Calbert, Huntington/Charleston, 17   Chillicothe, .684, 13-6

D Texas-Oklahoma League
President: C.O. Johnson

Standings	W	L	Pct.	GB	Manager
Paris Snappers**	77	39	.664	—	Johnny Fillman
Texarkana Tigers*	79	41	.658	—	A.L. "Dad" Ritter
Denison Champions	68	49	.581	9½	Babe Peebles
Durant Gladiators	46	73	.387	32½	Fred Morris, Sr./Bert Humphries
Bonham Sliders@	47	58	.448	NA	Senter Rainey/Charlie Nichols
Sherman Lions@	30	75	.286	NA	Stanley "Dolly" Gray/Charlie Moran/ Harry Webber
Ardmore Indians#	26	25	.510	NA	Brooks Gordon
Hugo Scouts#	19	32	.373	NA	Lon Ury

#Hugo and Ardmore disbanded June 11.
@Bonham and Sherman disbanded July 30.

1914

Playoff: Texarkana 3 games, Paris 1.

BA: Bill Stellbauer, Texarkana, .351
Runs: Ray Nagle, Paris, 80
Hits: Bill Stellbauer, Texarkana, 151
HRs: C.H. O'Neill, Texarkana, 7

Wins: Dickie Kerr, Paris, 22
SOs: Neeley, Bonham/Denison, 198
Pct: Tex Covington, Hugo/Denison, .800, 16-4

Attendance: Tulsa, 48,000.
Playoff: Oklahoma City 4 games, Muskogee 2.

BA: Glenn Dameron, Oklahoma City, .357
Runs: Lee Morris, Tulsa, 105
Hits: H. Thompson, Muskogee, 155

HRs: Ed Palmer, Muskogee, 21
Wins: Nelson Jones, Tulsa, 29
Pct: Nelson Jones, Tulsa, .784, 29-8

D Union Association
President: Edward F. Murphy

Standings	W	L	Pct.	GB	Manager
Ogden Canners**	54	32	.628	—	Frank "Dad" Gimlin
Salt Lake City Skyscrapers*	52	34	.605	2	Harry Hester
Butte Miners@	44	40	.524	9	James "Ducky" Holmes
Helena Senators	27	53	.338	24	Jesse Garrett/William Quigley
Boise Irrigators#	32	39	.451	NA	Ervin Jensen
Murray Infants#	31	42	.425	NA	Cliff Blankenship

#Boise and Murray disbanded July 20.
@The league disbanded August 5 after Butte disbanded, but Ogden and Salt Lake City played 16 games with each other to complete their seasons. Ogden won 10 and Salt Lake City won 6.

Playoff: Ogden 4 games, Salt Lake City 2.

BA: Frank Huelsman, Salt Lake City, .424
Runs: Swede Risberg, Ogden, 84
Hits: Fred Carmen, Ogden/Boise, 130
HRs: Frank Huelsman, Salt Lake City, 23

Wins: Amos Morgan, Salt Lake City, 16
G.C. Knight, Ogden, 16
SOs: Tom Tomer, Boise/Salt Lake City, 124
Pct: Amos Morgan, Salt Lake City, .762, 16-5

D Virginia Mountain League
President: B.F. Donovan

Standings	W	L	Pct.	GB	Manager
Covington Papermakers*	37	26	.587	—	Moore/Carter
Charlottesville Tuckahoes**	31	30	.508	5	W. Steinhause
Clifton Forge Railroaders	28	34	.452	8½	Clarence Irwin/Harry Bailey/ Edward Eschback/Buck Hooker
Staunton/ Harrisonburg Lunatics#	26	32	.448	8½	Dave Crockett/Pat Krebs

#Staunton (15-22) moved to Harrisonburg July 1.
The league disbanded July 25 due to poor attendance and rumors of fixed games.

D Western Association
Presidents: A.J. Baker/W.P. Hill

Standings	W	L	Pct.	GB	Manager
Tulsa Oilers	74	49	.602	—	Howard Price
Oklahoma City Boosters*	75	52	.591	1	W.C. Holliday/Heinie Maag
Ft. Smith Twins	73	52	.584	2	R.J. Mack
Muskogee Mets**	74	54	.578	2½	George McAvoy
McAlester Miners	47	79	.373	28½	Jerry Kane/Leo Miller/John Henley
Joplin-Webb City Miners/ Guthrie Senators/ Henryetta Boosters#	35	92	.278	41	Claude Marcum

#Joplin-Webb City (22-46) moved to Guthrie July 10; Guthrie (2-10) moved to Henryetta July 22.

D Western Canada League
President: James E. Fleming

Standings	W	L	Pct.	GB	Manager
Saskatoon Quakers	71	52	.577	—	Jerry Hurley
Moose Jaw Robin Hoods	63	52	.548	4	Fred Weed
Regina Red Sox	67	57	.540	4½	Charles Stis
Medicine Hat Hatters	61	53	.535	5½	Bert Dunn
Edmonton Eskimoes	53	57	.482	11½	Deacon White
Calgary Bronchos	37	81	.313	31½	Bill Devereaux/Jules Streib

BA: Harry Morse, Regina, .344
Runs: Bill Daniels, Medicine Hat, 91
Hits: Les Wilson, Saskatoon, 157
HRs: Ken Williams, Edmonton, 12

Wins: Jess Buckles, Medicine Hat, 25
SOs: Jess Buckles, Medicine Hat, 196
Pct: Sam Beer, Saskatoon, .767, 23-7

D Western Tri-State League
President: Roy W. Ritner

Standings	W	L	Pct.	GB	Manager
Pendleton Buckaroos	59	37	.615	—	Al Lodell
Walla Walla Bears	53	43	.552	6	Gus Bade
Baker City Miners	44	52	.456	15	Carl King
North Yakima Braves	36	60	.395	23	Eddie Ford

BA: George Pembrooke, Pendleton, .349
Runs: George Naughton, Pendleton, 86
Hits: Edson Johnson, Walla Walla, 123
HRs: Earl Sheely, Walla Walla, 11

Wins: Henry Peterson, North Yakima, 17
SOs: Clyde Schroeder, Pendleton, 206
Pct: Arch Osborne, Pendleton, .714, 15-6

1914 Interleague Post Season Play

World Series
Boston (National) 4 games, Philadelphia (American) 0

Minor League Championship Series
Milwaukee (American Association) 4 games, Birmingham (Southern Association) 2

Minor League Championship Series
Indianapolis (American Association) 4 games, Denver (Western) 2

Class B Championship Series
Lawrence (New England) 4 games, New London (Eastern Association) 2

Michigan State Championship
Saginaw (Southern Michigan Association) 4 games, Muskegon (Michigan State) 1

Virginia-North Carolina Series
Winston-Salem (North Carolina State) 4 games, Norfolk (Virginia) 2

1914 No-Hitters

Date	Pitcher	Team	League	Opponent	Score
4-13	Frank Johnson	Jacksonville	South Atlantic	Albany	6-0
4-26	Hattan Ogle	Waco	Texas	Austin	6-0
4-30	Festus Higgins	Binghamton	New York State	Utica	1-0
5-10	Harry Grover	Omaha	Western	Sioux City	7-0
5-14	Jim Scott	Chicago	American	Washington	0-1 (10)
5-14	Carl Ray	Winston-Salem	N. Carolina State	Charlotte	2-0
5-22	Schull	Middletown	Atlantic	Newburgh	10-0
5-23	John McIlvaine	Chillicothe	Ohio State	Charleston	4-1
5-27	Grover Brandt	Beaumont	Texas	Galveston	7-0
5-31	Joe Benz	Chicago	American	Cleveland	6-1
5-31	Henry Benz	Green Bay	Wisconsin-Illinois	Appleton	4-1
6-1	Walter Scott	Saginaw	S. Michigan	South Bend	1-0
6-1	Reidland	Belton	Middle Texas	Brenham	2-0
6-2	Clunn	Reading	Tri-State	Trenton	7-0
6-5	Frank McDermott	Beatrice	Nebraska State	York	8-0
6-7	R.T. "Red" Adams	Denison	Texas-Oklahoma	Durant	8-1
6-10	D.L. Gage	Calgary	Western Canada	Regina	4-3
6-11	John Fitzpatrick	Owensboro	Kitty	Paducah	5-0
6-14	Hooks Beltz	Emporia	Kansas State	Great Bend	3-0 (5)
6-16	Guy Morton	Waterbury	Eastern Assoc.	New Haven	2-0
6-16	Reynolds	Manistee	Michigan State	Muskegon	1-0
6-20	Dode Criss	Houston	Texas	Dallas	3-1
6-22	Fritz Redford	Bonham	Texas-Oklahoma	Sherman	7-0
6-25	Stanley Dugan	Fargo-Moorhead	Northern	Winnipeg	8-0
6-26	Abner Gould	Muscatine	Central Assoc.	Cedar Rapids	7-0
7-3	Haley	Fall River	Colonial	Taunton	1-0
7-9	Hopkins	Bartlett	Middle Texas	Georgetown	2-0
7-9	George Cunningham	Duluth	Northern	Ft. William-Pt. Arthur	3-0
7-11	Alvah Cochran	Charleston	South Atlantic	Jacksonville	5-0
7-17	Within	Duluth	Northern	Virginia	9-0
7-18	Howie Camnitz	Columbus	South Atlantic	Charleston	1-0
7-19	Roy Hitt	Venice	Pacific Coast	San Francisco	2-0
7-21	Joe Doyle	Elmira	New York State	Syracuse	6-0
7-23	George Crabble	San Antonio	Texas	Dallas	2-1
7-23	Shafer	Olean	Interstate	Wellsville	3-0
7-24	Bob Geary	Americus	Georgia State	Valdosta	8-0
7-25	Dickie Kerr	Paris	Texas-Oklahoma	Denison	12-0
8-3	C.M. Spencer	Cedar Rapids	Central Assoc.	Keokuk	10-0
8-6	C.J. Yon	Raleigh	N. Carolina State	Asheville	4-0
8-13	Abner Gould	Muscatine	Central Assoc.	Clinton	3-0
8-14	Clay Blancke	Duluth	Northern	Ft. William-Pt. Arthur	3-0
8-14	Berlyn Horne	Wellsville	Interstate	Jamestown	5-0
8-15	Elmer Meyers	Raleigh	N. Carolina State	Winston-Salem	0-1
8-21	Dwight Stone	Augusta	South Atlantic	Charleston	0-1
8-21	Bravener	Mt. Clemens	S. Michigan	Battle Creek	1-0 (11)
8-21	Russell Robbins	Saginaw	S. Michigan	Jackson	6-0
8-22	Russell Robbins	Saginaw	S. Michigan	Jackson	3-0 (C)
9-5	Mike Cantwell	Oshkosh	Wisconsin-Illinois	Racine	4-0
9-9	George Davis	Boston	National	Philadelphia	7-0
9-19	Ed Lafitte	Brooklyn	Federal	Kansas City	6-2
9-20	Johnny Lush	Portland	Pacific Coast	Venice	0-1
10-16	Rube Evans	Portland	Pacific Coast	Oakland	3-0
10-25	Skeeter Fanning	San Francisco	Pacific Coast	Portland	7-0

Number in parentheses indicates innings if other than nine; "C" indicates no-hitters in consecutive starts.

THIS DATE IN MINOR LEAGUE HISTORY

January 15, 1914, Buffalo, International League, signed Joseph V. McCarthy, future New York Yankees manager, as an utility infielder for 1914.

February 14, 1914, Jack Dunn, manager and owner of the Baltimore Orioles of the International League, signed George Herman "Babe" Ruth from St. Mary's Industrial School in Baltimore to a baseball contract.

February 16, 1914, Gardner C. Louie, a noted minor league pitcher, last with Butte, Union Association, died in Delmar, Delaware, from an infection supposed to have been caused from being hit by a pitched ball the previous summer.

April 22, 1914, Babe Ruth, 19, fresh out of a Baltimore orphanage, hurled the Orioles to a 6-0 win over Buffalo in his Organized Ball debut. The Bambino allowed only six hits and contributed two singles to the Orioles' attack. Joe McCarthy, later the Babe's manager with the Yankees, went 0-for-4 and made the game's final out. Paul Krichell, later a Yankees scout, reached Ruth for a double. A crowd of only 200 at Baltimore saw Ruth begin his career.

April 29, 1914, Dallas, Texas League, released 18-year-old rookie Rogers Hornsby following a tryout. Hornsby later caught on with Hugo, Texas-Oklahoma League, and moved on to Denison of the same league on July 2.

April 30, 1914, In the opener of the New York State League season, F. Higgins of Binghamton pitched a no-hitter to defeat Utica 1-0. Utica pitcher Oberlin gave up only one single.

May 25, 1914, Kankakee and Streator played a 21-inning, 2-2 tie in the Illinois-Missouri League. Hay hurled for Kankakee and Brownfield for Streator.

May 27, 1914, Oakland, Pacific Coast League, defeated Venice 4-2 in a 20-inning game.

June 5, 1914, John Cantley, a pitcher with Opelika of the Georgia-Alabama League, pitched and batted his club to a 19-1 victory over Talladega. He hit three grand slams and a single while batting in 15 runs.

June 8, 1914, McCabe, pitching for Burlington, Central Association, struck out 17 in a game with Muscatine.

June 9, 1914, Minneapolis, American Association, defeated Louisville 3-2 in a 20-inning game. Joe Lake went the route for Minneapolis against Fred Toney and Grover Lowdermilk.

June 9, 1914, Outfielder Fremer of Virginia, Northern League, hit two home runs and two doubles in four at bats off Winona pitcher Torasson.

June 11, 1914, Pitcher William Couchman, Montreal, International League, threw the ball over the fence after being removed from the hill by manager Kitty Bransfield, allowing all three Toronto runners on base to score.

June 12, 1914, Pitcher Harper of Greensboro, North Carolina State League, struck out 17 in a game with Winston-Salem.

June 14, 1914, Pitcher Higley of Huntington, Ohio State League, fanned nine batters in 3-2/3 innings in a game with Marysville.

June 15, 1914, Waterloo, Central Association, scored 13 runs in one inning against Cedar Rapids.

June 17, 1914, Pitcher Grover Lowdermilk of Louisville, American Association, struck out 16 in a game with Kansas City.

June 27, 1914, Houston stole seven bases in one inning in a Texas League game.

July 3, 1914, In the Kansas State League, Hutchinson defeated Great Bend 4-3 in 23 innings.

July 12, 1914, After having lost 30 consecutive games, Austin, Texas League, beat Ft. Worth 9-3.

July 25, 1914, Pitcher Dickie Kerr of Paris, Texas-Oklahoma League, fanned 17 in a game with Denison.

July 27, 1914, Infielder Ward of Cedar Rapids, Central Association, stole home twice in a game with Marshalltown.

August 4, 1914, Pitcher Davidson of Baltimore, International League, walked 20 men and lost 7-4 to Buffalo. Carlstrem, Bisons' first baseman, was up four times with the bases full and fanned each time, stranding 12 base runners.

August 10, 1914, Waco, Texas League, won its 12th straight game, defeating Austin.

August 11, 1914, After having won 14 successive decisions, pitcher Ware of Houston lost to Beaumont in the Texas League.

August 15, 1914, In a Western Canada League doubleheader, Medicine Hat beat Calgary 19-5 and 9-0. Jess Buckles pitched both games for the winners, allowing 14 hits in the opener and only one in the second; plus, he had three hits in four tries in each game. Outfielder Martin of Medicine Hat made four hits in the opener, including two doubles and two homers, plus two homers in game two.

August 20, 1914, Fielder Jones, ex-manager of the Hitless Wonders White Sox, resigned as president of the Northwestern League to assume the management of the St. Louis Federal League team.

August 22, 1914, Pitcher Russell Robbins of Saginaw pitched his second no-hitter in as many days against Jackson, winning 3-0 and fanning 14. The no-hitter was the third in the Southern Michigan Association in a two-day span.

August 24, 1914, Pitcher Ritter of Scranton, New York State League, struck out 18 in a 14-inning game with Troy.

September 1, 1914, Trenton, Tri-State League, cracked 24 hits to wallop Wilmington 22-4.

September 3, 1914, Pitcher Abner Gould of Muscatine, Central Association, struck out 17 in a ten-inning 2-1 victory over Clinton.

September 5, 1914, Babe Ruth hit a home run with two aboard at Toronto, his first and only homer in the minor leagues. The victim was Ellis Johnson, a pitcher who belonged to the White Sox. Ruth pitched a one-hitter to blank Toronto 4-0.

September 7, 1914, Third baseman Cully of Jamestown, Interstate League, in a Labor Day doubleheader, made three singles, a double, two triples and a home run in eight at bats.

September 9, 1914, Outfielder Jimmy Hickman smashed three consecutive home runs in a game for Winston-Salem in the North Carolina State League.

September 26, 1914, Providence, International League, defeated Baltimore in a 23-19 slugfest. The contest produced 55 hits, 29 by Providence.

December 17, 1914, Salt Lake City was admitted to the Pacific Coast League to replace Sacramento.

1915

American League
President: Byron Bancroft Johnson

Standings	W	L	Pct.	GB	Attend.	Manager
Boston Red Sox	101	50	.669	—	539,885	Bill Carrigan
Detroit Tigers	100	54	.649	2½	476,105	Hugh Jennings
Chicago White Sox	93	61	.604	9½	539,461	Clarence "Pants" Rowland
Washington Senators	85	68	.556	17	167,332	Clark Griffith
New York Yankees	69	83	.454	32½	256,035	Wild Bill Donovan
St. Louis Browns	63	91	.409	39½	150,358	Branch Rickey
Cleveland Indians	57	95	.375	44½	159,285	Joe Birmingham/Lee Fohl
Philadelphia Athletics	43	109	.283	58½	146,223	Connie Mack

BA: Ty Cobb, Detroit, .369
Runs: Ty Cobb, Detroit, 144
Hits: Ty Cobb, Detroit, 208
RBIs: Bobby Veach, Detroit, 112
      Sam Crawford, Detroit, 112
HRs: Braggo Roth, Chicago/Cleveland, 7

SBs: Ty Cobb, Detroit, 96
Wins: Walter Johnson, Washington, 28
SOs: Walter Johnson, Washington, 203
ERA: Smoky Joe Wood, Boston, 1.49
Pct: Smoky Joe Wood, Boston, .750, 15-5

National League
President: John K. Tener

Standings	W	L	Pct.	GB	Attend.	Manager
Philadelphia Phillies	90	62	.592	—	449,898	Pat Moran
Boston Braves	83	69	.546	7	376,283	George Stallings
Brooklyn Robins	80	72	.526	10	297,766	Wilbert Robinson
Chicago Cubs	73	80	.477	17½	217,058	Roger Bresnahan
Pittsburgh Pirates	73	81	.474	18	225,743	Fred Clarke
St. Louis Cardinals	72	81	.471	18½	252,666	Miller Huggins
Cincinnati Reds	71	83	.461	20	218,878	Buck Herzog
New York Giants	69	83	.454	21	391,850	John McGraw

BA: Larry Doyle, New York, .320
Runs: Gavvy Cravath, Philadelphia, 89
Hits: Larry Doyle, New York, 189
RBIs: Gavvy Cravath, Philadelphia, 115
HRs: Gavvy Cravath, Philadelphia, 24

Wins: Grover Alexander, Philadelphia, 31
SOs: Grover Alexander, Philadelphia, 241
ERA: Grover Alexander, Philadelphia, 1.22
Pct: Grover Alexander, Philadelphia, .756, 31-10

Federal League
President: James Gilmore

Standings	W	L	Pct.	GB	Manager
Chicago Whales	86	66	.566	—	Joe Tinker
St. Louis Terriers	87	67	.565	—	Fielder Jones
Pittsburgh Stogies	86	67	.562	½	Rebel Oakes
Kansas City Packers	81	72	.529	5½	George Stovall
Newark Peppers	80	72	.526	6	Bill Phillips/Bill McKechnie
Buffalo Blues	74	78	.487	12	Larry Schlafly/Walter Blair/Harry Lord
Brooklyn Tip-Tops	70	82	.461	16	Lee Magee/John Ganzel
Baltimore Terrapins	47	107	.305	40	Otto Knabe

BA: Benny Kauff, Brooklyn, .342
Runs: Babe Borton, St. Louis, 97
Hits: Jack Tobin, St. Louis, 184
RBIs: Dutch Zwilling, Chicago, 94
HRs: Hal Chase, Buffalo, 17

Wins: George McConnell, Chicago, 25
SOs: Dave Davenport, St. Louis, 229
ERA: Earl Moseley, Newark, 1.91
Pct: George McConnell, Chicago, .714, 25-10

AA American Association
President: Thomas M. Chivington

Standings	W	L	Pct.	GB	Attend.	Manager
Minneapolis Millers	92	62	.597	—	149,931	Joe Cantillon
St. Paul Saints	90	63	.588	1½	137,295	Mike Kelley
Indianapolis Indians	81	70	.536	9½	96,893	Jack Hendricks
Louisville Colonels	78	72	.520	12	111,785	John Hayden/Ezra Midkiff
Kansas City Blues	71	79	.473	19	56,219	Bill Armour/Danny Shay
Milwaukee Brewers	67	81	.453	22	80,937	Harry Clark
Cleveland Spiders	67	82	.450	22½	86,977	Jack Knight
Columbus Senators	54	91	.372	33½	74,246	Rudy Hulswitt

BA: Jack Lelivelt, Kansas City, .346
Runs: Dave Altizer, Minneapolis, 118
Hits: Jack Lelivelt, Kansas City, 199
HRs: Bash Compton, Kansas City, 9
      Joe Riggert, St. Paul, 9

Wins: Mutt Williams, Minneapolis, 29
SOs: Robert Steele, St. Paul, 183
ERA: Chink Yingling, Minneapolis, 2.17
IP: Mutt Williams, Minneapolis, 441

AA International League
President: Edward G. Barrow

Standings	W	L	Pct.	GB	Manager
Buffalo Bisons	86	50	.632	—	Patsy Donovan
Providence Grays	85	53	.616	2	David Shean
Toronto Maple Leafs	72	67	.518	15½	Bill Clymer
Rochester Hustlers	69	69	.500	18	John Ganzel/Robert Williams
Montreal Royals	67	70	.489	19½	Dan Howley
Newark Indians/ Harrisburg Senators#	61	76	.445	25½	Harry Smith
Richmond Climbers	59	81	.422	29	Jack Dunn
Jersey City Skeeters	52	85	.380	34½	George "Hooks" Wiltse/Joe Yeager

#Newark (26-26) moved to Harrisburg July 2.
Attendance: Buffalo, 185,326.

BA: Morrie Rath, Toronto, .332
Runs: George Whiteman, Montreal, 106
Hits: Chick Shorten, Providence, 175
HRs: George Whiteman, Montreal, 14

Wins: Fred Beebe, Buffalo, 27
SOs: Allen Russell, Richmond, 239
Pct: Fred Beebe, Buffalo, .794, 27-7

AA Pacific Coast League
President: Allan T. Baum

Standings	W	L	Pct.	GB	Manager
San Francisco Seals	118	89	.570	—	Harry Wolverton
Salt Lake City Bees	108	89	.548	5	Cliff Blankenship
Los Angeles Angels	110	98	.529	8½	Frank "Cap" Dillon
Venice/Vernon Tigers#	102	104	.495	15½	W.L. "Happy" Hogan/Dick Bayless/ Doc White
Oakland Oaks	93	113	.451	24½	Tyler Christian/Rowdy Elliott
Portland Beavers	78	116	.402	33½	Walter McCredie

#Venice (43-50) moved to Vernon July 11.

BA: Harry Wolter, Los Angeles, .359
Runs: Harl Maggert, Los Angeles, 147
Hits: Jimmy Johnston, Oakland, 274
HRs: Biff Schaller, San Francisco, 20

Wins: Lefty Williams, Salt Lake City, 33
SOs: Lefty Williams, Salt Lake City, 294
ERA: Slim Love, Los Angeles, 1.95

A Southern Association
President: William B. Kavanaugh

Standings	W	L	Pct.	GB	Attend.	Manager
New Orleans Pelicans	91	63	.591	—	134,405	Johnny Dobbs
Birmingham Barons	86	67	.562	4½	135,856	Carleton Molesworth
Memphis Chickasaws	81	73	.526	10	170,678	Bris Lord
Nashville Volunteers	75	78	.490	15½	103,399	William Schwartz
Atlanta Crackers	74	79	.483	16½	99,480	William A. Smith
Chattanooga Lookouts	73	80	.476	17½	52,781	Harry McCormick/ Norman "Kid" Elberfeld
Mobile Sea Gulls	68	86	.441	23	52,056	Charles Schmidt
Little Rock Travelers	65	87	.427	25	89,129	Bob Allen/Charles Starr

BA: Elmer Miller, Mobile, .326
Runs: Tim Hendryx, New Orleans, 109
Hits: Yale Sloan, Birmingham, 185
HRs: Fred Thomas, New Orleans, 11

Wins: George Cunningham, Chattanooga, 24
SOs: George Cunningham, Chattanooga, 167
Pct: George Cunningham, Chattanooga, .667, 24-12

A Western League
President: Norris L. O'Neill

Standings	W	L	Pct.	GB	Manager
Des Moines Boosters	87	53	.621	—	Frank Isbell
Denver Bears	82	55	.599	3½	Jack Coffey/Larry Spahr
Topeka Jayhawks	75	63	.543	11	Jimmy Jackson
Omaha Rourkes	71	69	.507	16	Marty Krug
Lincoln Tigers	70	69	.504	16½	Matty McIntyre
Sioux City Packers	66	68	.493	18	Josh Clarke/Harry Gaspar
Wichita Wolves	57	80	.416	28½	Clyde "Buzzy" Wares/Hamilton Patterson
St. Joseph Drummers	43	94	.314	42½	Jack Holland

BA: Larry LeJeune, Sioux City, .355
Runs: Tex Jones, Des Moines, 103
Hits: Vern Spencer, Denver, 185
HRs: Harry "Moose" McCormick, Denver, 16

Wins: George Mogridge, Des Moines, 24
      Tom Blodgett, Omaha, 24
SOs: Dazzy Vance, St. Joseph, 199
ERA: George Mogridge, Des Moines, 1.94
Pct: Paul Musser, Des Moines, .909, 20-2

B Canadian League
President: J.P. Fitzgerald

Standings	W	L	Pct.	GB	Manager
Ottawa Senators	72	39	.649	—	Frank Shaughnessy
Guelph Maple Leafs	59	51	.537	12½	George "Knotty" Lee
Hamilton Hams/Tigers	55	48	.534	13	Bill Cristall/Gus Ziemer
Brantford Red Sox	52	55	.485	18	George Deneau/John Warner
London Tecumsehs	50	58	.463	20½	Frank Reisling/Walter Hartwell
St. Thomas Saints	38	75	.337	35	Carlton Stewart/Louis Bierbauer, Jr.

BA: Ralph Burrill, Brantford, .344
Runs: Jim Murphy, Guelph, 66
Hits: D.J. Bullock, Ottawa, 130

Wins: Urban Shocker, Ottawa, 15
SOs: Urban Shocker, Ottawa, 186
Pct: Tom Caesar, London, .727, 8-3

B Central League
President: Louis Heilbroner

Standings	W	L	Pct.	GB	Manager
Evansville River Rats	72	50	.590	—	Charles "Punch" Knoll
Grand Rapids Black Sox	68	54	.557	4	William Essick
Youngstown Steelmen	66	56	.546	6	Curley Blount
Terre Haute Highlanders	66	58	.532	7	R.W. Gilbert
Erie Sailors	64	58	.525	8	Larry Quinlan
Fort Wayne Cubs	62	60	.509	10	Bade Myers
Wheeling Stogies	50	76	.397	24	C.S. "Pop" Shriver/Arch Riley
Dayton Veterans	43	79	.352	29	Harry Compton

BA: Tom Miller, Erie, .336
Runs: Jim Smyth, Fort Wayne, 84
Hits: Frank Edington, Grand Rapids, 142
HRs: Fred Bratchie, Fort Wayne, 10

Wins: Earl Ainsworth, Fort Wayne, 24
Lou Schettler, Youngstown, 24
SOs: Art Nehf, Terre Haute, 218
ERA: Art Nehf, Terre Haute, 1.38

B New England League
President: Tim H. Murnane

Standings	W	L	Pct.	GB	Manager
Portland Duffs	77	42	.647	—	Hugh Duffy
Lawrence Barristers	62	54	.531	13½	Alex Pearson
Lynn Pirates	62	57	.521	15	Louis Piper
Worcester Busters	58	56	.509	16½	Jesse Burkett
Lowell Grays	54	55	.495	18	Roland Barrows/Charles Kelchner
Lewiston Cupids	50	59	.459	22	Arthur Irwin
Manchester Textiles	48	67	.417	27	John Kiernan
Fitchburg Burghers	48	69	.410	28	Hugh McCune

BA: Roland Barrows, Lowell, .332
Runs: Pete Clemens, Portland, 88
Hits: Taylor Farrell, Portland, 135

HRs: Roland Barrows, Lowell, 11
Wins: Forrest More, Portland, 18
Pct: George Martin, Portland, 1.000, 10-0

B New York State League
President: John H. Farrell

Standings	W	L	Pct.	GB	Manager
Binghamton Bingoes	79	44	.642	—	John Calhoun
Utica Utes	73	46	.614	4	Edward McDonough
Elmira Colonels	72	53	.576	8	Bill Conroy
Scranton Miners	68	55	.553	11	William Coughlin
Syracuse Stars	60	60	.500	17½	Mike O'Neill
Wilkes-Barre Barons	54	60	.474	20½	Peter Noonan
Troy Trojans	44	76	.359	33½	Lewis Wachter
Albany Senators	33	89	.279	45½	Joseph O'Rourke

BA: Bill Kay, Binghamton, .378
Runs: Bill Kay, Binghamton, 98
Hits: Bill Kay, Binghamton, 169

Wins: Frank Dessau, Elmira, 21
SOs: Jess Buckles, Troy, 158
Pct: Monte Priest, Syracuse, .929, 13-1

B Northwestern League
President: R.L. Blewett

Standings	W	L	Pct.	GB	Manager
Seattle Giants	88	68	.564	—	Frank Raymond
Tacoma Tigers	86	72	.544	3	Russ Hall/Joe McGinnity
Spokane Indians	81	74	.523	6½	Robert Wicker
Vancouver Champions	74	79	.484	12½	Hank Scharnweber
Victoria Bees#	41	61	.402	NA	Martin Nye
Aberdeen Black Cats#	46	62	.389	NA	Charles Stis/Justin "Pug" Bennett

#Victoria and Aberdeen withdrew, with league permission, August 1.

Playoff: Seattle 3 games, Tacoma 2; abandoned when the sixth game broke up in a dispute.

BA: Ed Kippert, Seattle/Aberdeen/Tacoma, .332
Runs: Jack Smith, Aberdeen/Seattle, 99
Hits: Ted Kaylor, Spokane/Victoria, 197

HRs: Bill Brinker, Vancouver, 11
Wins: Richard Kaufman, Tacoma, 25
SOs: Walter Mails, Seattle, 250
Pct: Chuck Rose, Seattle, .667, 20-10

B Texas League
President: William R. Davidson

Standings	W	L	Pct.	GB	Manager
Waco Navigators	87	60	.592	—	Ellis Hardy
San Antonio Bronchos	81	67	.548	6½	George Leidy
Ft. Worth Panthers	81	72	.530	9	William Nance/Jake Atz
Dallas Giants	73	75	.493	14½	Joe Dunn
Houston Buffaloes	68	74	.479	16½	Pat Newnam
Shreveport Gassers	62	85	.422	25	Lee Garvin/Syd Smith
Beaumont Oilers	61	84	.421	25	Ducky Swan
Galveston Pirates#	67	63	.515	NA	Paul Sentell

#Galveston withdrew, with league permission, when a hurricane destroyed its ball park August 14.

BA: Bert James, Waco, .313
Runs: Gene Madden, Galveston, 95
Hits: Archie Tanner, Waco, 163

HRs: Fred Wohleben, Waco, 8
Bert James, Waco, 8
Otto McIver, Ft. Worth, 8
Harry Storch, Dallas, 8
Wins: Emmett Munsell, San Antonio, 25
SOs: Cliff Markle, Waco, 228
Pct: Earl Duffy, Shreveport, .846, 11-2

B Three-I League
President: Albert R. Tearney

Standings	W	L	Pct.	GB	Manager
Moline Plowboys**	75	51	.595	—	George Hughes
Davenport Blue Sox*	76	52	.594	—	Daniel O'Leary
Rockford Wakes	72	58	.554	5	Howard Wakefield
Quincy Gems	65	56	.537	7½	John Castle
Peoria Distillers	68	63	.519	9½	Harry Hoffman
Dubuque Dubs/ Freeport Comeons#	48	76	.387	26	Larry Mullen/Howard Derringer/ A. "Doc" Cummings
Bloomington Bloomers	48	76	.387	26	Pete Lister
Decatur Commodores@	37	57	.394	NA	Elmer Duggan

#Dubuque (2-5) moved to Freeport July 14.
@Decatur disbanded August 10.

Playoff: Moline 4 games, Davenport 2.

BA: Roy Sherer, Quincy, .321
Runs: Ernest Baxter, Rockford, 84
Hits: Howard Wakefield, Rockford, 151
Roy Sherer, Quincy, 151
HRs: Otto Jacobs, Rockford, 7

Wins: Louis Tretter, Quincy, 19
Abner Gould, Davenport, 19
Hod Eller, Moline, 19
SOs: Abner Gould, Davenport, 218
ERA: Frank Romine, Peoria, 1.13

C Northern League
President: John Burmeister

Standings	W	L	Pct.	GB	Manager
Fargo-Moorhead Graingrowers	74	49	.602	—	Bob Unglaub
St. Boniface Saints/Bonnies	61	55	.526	9½	Charles Moll
Ft. William-Pt. Arthur Canucks	61	58	.513	11	Denny Sullivan
Duluth White Sox	60	62	.492	13½	William "Darby" O'Brien
Winnipeg Maroons	58	61	.487	14	Roy Patterson/Fred Curtis
Virginia Ore Diggers	53	69	.434	20½	John Sundheim
Superior Red Sox#	20	26	.435	NA	Fred Curtis
Grand Forks Flickertails#	21	28	.429	NA	William Fox

#Grand Forks and Superior withdrew July 5.

BA: Kenzie Kirkham, Duluth, .344
Runs: Del Wertz, Ft. William-Pt. Arthur, 95
Hits: Hack Miller, St. Boniface, 150
HRs: Keith Dancy, Ft. William-Pt. Arthur, 16

Wins: Ralph Bell, Fargo-Moorhead, 22
SOs: Charles Boardman, St. Boniface, 240
Pct: Roy Patterson, Fargo-Moorhead, .808, 21-5

C South Atlantic League
President: Nick P. Corish

Standings	W	L	Pct.	GB	Manager
Columbus Foxes**	52	36	.591	—	James Fox
Charleston Sea Gulls	51	36	.587	½	Edward Reagan/Ed Sobrie/George Stinson
Macon Peaches*	48	39	.552	3½	George Stinson/Eddie Foster
Columbia Comers	44	42	.512	7	Connie Lewis/Doug Harbison
Augusta Tourists	41	45	.477	10	Martin Dudley/George Baumgardner
Albany Babies	41	45	.477	10	Frank Manush
Jacksonville Tarpons	35	51	.407	16	William "Dave" Gaston/Willard Manes
Savannah Colts	34	52	.395	17	Perry Lipe/Al Handiboe

Playoff: Columbus 4 games, Macon 1.

BA: C.M. Chancey, Macon, .359
Runs: Hardin Herndon, Columbus, 63
Hits: C.M. Chancey, Macon, 126

Wins: Phil Redding, Columbus, 19
SOs: Dana Fillingim, Charleston, 129
Pct: Phil Redding, Columbus, .760, 19-6

C Southern Michigan Association
President: James Frank

Standings	W	L	Pct.	GB	Manager
South Bend Factors	44	24	.667	—	Ed Smith
Battle Creek Crickets	34	33	.507	9½	Charles Wagner
Jackson Vets	31	33	.484	11	Danny Collins
Bay City Beavers	31	35	.470	12	Dan Jenkins
Saginaw Ducks	31	38	.449	13½	Howard "Ducky" Holmes
Flint Vehicles	31	39	.443	14	Ed Wheeler

The league disbanded July 7.

BA: Charles Donnelly, Bay City, .387
Runs: Joe Helmer, South Bend, 48
Hits: Charles Donnelly, Bay City, 87
HRs: Ed Hoffman, Flint, 7

Wins: Charles Vallandingham, South Bend, 13
SOs: Ben Higley, Saginaw, 127
Pct: Charles Vallandingham, South Bend, .813, 13-3

C Virginia League
President: Jacob O. Boatwright

Standings	W	L	Pct.	GB	Manager
Rocky Mount Carolinians*.	74	48	.607	—	Ray Ryan
Portsmouth Truckers**	68	58	.540	8	Win Clark
Norfolk Tars	66	56	.541	8	M.D. "Red" McMahon
Newport News Shipbuilders	63	62	.504	12½	Carl Carnes/Brooke Crist
Suffolk Tigers	59	62	.488	14½	Harry Welcher/George "King" Kelly
Petersburg Goobers	40	84	.323	35	Henry Busch

Playoff: Rocky Mount 4 games, Portsmouth 1.

BA: Buck Thrasher, Norfolk, .348
Runs: Charles Bittle, Rocky Mount, 117
Hits: Buck Thrasher, Norfolk, 150
HRs: Carl Gray, Rocky Mount, 15

Wins: Roy Gardinier, Newport News, 20
SOs: Roy Gardinier, Newport News, 216
Pct: Al Leake, Rocky Mount, .737, 14-5

D Bi-State League
President: B.M. Parsons

Standings	W	L	Pct.	GB	Manager
Streator Boosters	30	18	.625	—	Jack Herbert
Racine Belles	30	20	.600	1	Frank Reynolds/James Sheffield
Elgin Watch Makers#	27	26	.509	5½	Dennis Blake
Aurora Foxes#	25	27	.481	7	Clarence Marshall
Freeport Pretzels	23	29	.442	9	Doc Cummings
Ottawa Indians	20	35	.364	13½	Lou Erghott

#Elgin and Aurora disbanded July 5.
The league disbanded July 7.

BA: Al "Bull" Durham, Racine, .356
Runs: James Sheffield, Racine, 40
Hits: Clay Schoonover, Racine, 67

HRs: Eddie Wise, Streator, 5
Art Mueller, Elgin, 5
Clay Schoonover, Racine, 5

D Blue Ridge League
President: Charles W. Boyer

Standings	W	L	Pct.	GB	Manager
Frederick Hustlers	53	23	.697	—	Jack Morrison
Martinsburg Champs	44	30	.595	8	W.J. "Country" Morris
Hanover Hornets	42	35	.545	11½	William Starr
Hagerstown Blues	34	42	.477	19	John Laughlin/Gene Hanks
Gettysburg Patriots	28	48	.368	25	Ira Plank
Chambersburg Maroons	28	51	.354	26½	Gus Doner/George Stroh/Bill Clay

All-Star Team: 1B-Myers, Frederick; **2B**-Rabbit Agnew, Frederick; **3B**-Cy Rigler, Gettysburg; **SS**-Connolly, Frederick; **OF**-George Rawlings, Martinsburg; Posnall, Hanover; W.H. Lamar, Frederick; Mackert, Hanover; **C**-George Stroh, Chambersburg; Johnson, Martinsburg; **Util**-Olson, Frederick; **P**-Bill King, Frederick; Harry Llewellyn, Frederick; Ed Stricker, Chambersburg.

BA: Jack Morrison, Frederick, .341
Runs: J.K. Snyder, Chambersburg, 50
Hits: Jack Morrison, Frederick, 104
HRs: Clyde Barnhart, Frederick, 6

Wins: Bill King, Frederick, 17
SOs: Ed Stricker, Chambersburg, 170
Pct: Willie Sherdel, Hanover, .833, 15-3

D Buckeye League
President: Alfred W. Lawson

Standings	W	L	Pct.	GB	Manager
Lima Cigarmakers	25	18	.581	—	Sandy Murray
Findlay Oilers	22	19	.537	2	Ollie Chapman
Akron Rubbermen	22	21	.512	3	Al Newnham
Newark Skeeters	14	24	.368	8½	Paul Wreath
Marion#	10	5	.667	NA	Henry "Buzz" Wetzel
Canton#	5	11	.313	NA	Bill Prout

#Marion and Canton disbanded June 11.
The league disbanded July 5.

BA: Bill Munday, Canton/Akron, .355
Runs: Newt Jaekel, Akron, 35
Hits: Sandy Murray, Lima, 52
HRs: Costello, Findlay, 4
Egan, Findlay, 4

Wins: Red Hart, Findlay, 15
SOs: Reynolds, Lima, 110
Pct: Red Hart, Findlay, .882, 15-2

D California State League
President: Louis W. Schroeder, Jr.

Standings	W	L	Pct.	GB	Manager
Modesto Reds	6	1	.857	—	Jack Lesher
San Jose Bears	4	1	.800	1	Mike Steffani
Oakland Commuters	2	3	.400	3	Walt McMemony
Alameda	2	3	.400	3	Billy Hammond
Stockton Millers	2	4	.333	3½	Buck Franks
Berkeley/San Francisco#	1	5	.167	4½	C.W. Brainard/Joe Solari

#Berkeley (0-2) moved to San Francisco April 28.
The league disbanded May 30 due to heavy rains.

D Central Association
President: M.E. Justice

Standings	W	L	Pct.	GB	Manager
Burlington Pathfinders	81	38	.681	—	Richard Rohn
Muscatine Muskies	63	57	.525	18½	Ned Egan/Jess Runser
Keokuk Indians	51	52	.495	22	Frank Boyle
Mason City Claydiggers	58	63	.479	24	Harry Bay
Cedar Rapids Rabbits	54	62	.466	25½	James Hamilton/Jack Herbert
Marshalltown Ansons	46	67	.407	32	Frank Richardson/Bob Lynch
Waterloo Jays	52	74	.413	32½	Jay Andrews/Eddie Brennan
Clinton Pilots#	13	69	.159	NA	George Manush

#Clinton disbanded in mid-season.
Wins thrown out: Clinton 40, Keokuk 18, Marshalltown 5, Waterloo 1.

BA: Bill Collins, Cedar Rapids, .337
Runs: Walt Meinert, Burlington, 97
Hits: Walt Meinert, Burlington, 137
Harmon Hagmon, Burlington, 137

HRs: Cliff Lee, Muscatine, 9
Lyle Sours, Muscatine, 9
Wins: Grover Baichley, Burlington, 23
Dick Blunk, Burlington, 23
SOs: Grover Baichley, Burlington, 310
Pct: Grover Baichley, Burlington, .697, 23-10

D Central Texas League
Presidents: Earl Brown/Hulen P. Robertson

Standings	W	L	Pct.	GB	Manager
Ennis Tigers*	35	26	.574	—	Ed Wicker
Corsicana A's	32	29	.525	3	Roy Morton
Terrell Cubs	32	30	.516	3½	Hank Griffin
Kaufman Kings	30	32	.484	5½	Dee Poindexter
Mexia Gassers**	28	33	.459	7	Roy Akin
Waxahachie Athletics	27	34	.443	8	Anson Cole

The league folded July 24.

D FLAG League
President: Richard Jemison

Standings	W	L	Pct.	GB	Manager
Dothan	45	26	.634	—	Jack Reidy
Waycross Moguls	41	30	.577	4	Hammond Reynolds
Valdosta Millionaires**	35	33	.515	8½	Otto Jordan
Brunswick Pilots*	36	37	.493	10	Wade Reynolds
Americus Muckalees/ Gainesville Sharks#	29	42	.408	16	John Wagnon/Oscar Baker
Thomasville Hornets	25	43	.368	18½	Red Murch

#Americus (11-18) surrendered its franchise to the league May 18; it was moved to Gainesville May 31. The league started the season as the Georgia State League but changed its name to FLAG League June 15.
The league disbanded July 17.

Playoff: Valdosta 2 games, Brunswick 1; the series was ended by a player strike.

BA: Guy Dunning, Americus/Gainesville, .316
Runs: John Reidy, Dothan, 69
Hits: Guy Dunning, Americus/Gainesville, 100

HRs: Ben Paschal, Dothan, 7
Jesse Hammond Reynolds, Waycross, 7
Wins: G.H. Hall, Dothan, 14
SOs: Edward Poole, Dothan, 119
Pct: G.H. Hall, Dothan, .737, 14-5

D Georgia-Alabama League
President: C.L. Bruner

Standings	W	L	Pct.	GB	Manager
Newnan Cowetas	39	20	.661	—	Harry Matthews
Talladega Tigers	39	22	.639	1	Tige Garrett
Griffin Lightfoots	32	28	.533	7½	W.P. Martin/Ed Reagan
Rome Romans	27	31	.466	11½	Art Burleson
Anniston Moulders	22	38	.367	17½	P.C. "Jack" Steele
La Grange Terrapins	18	38	.327	19½	James Lafitte

The league disbanded July 14.

BA: Don Flynn, Newnan, .358
Runs: John Cochran, Rome, 47
Hits: Don Flynn, Newnan, 76
HRs: Don Flynn, Newnan, 15

Wins: John Nabors, Talladega/Newnan, 12
SOs: Charles Glazner, Anniston, 101
Pct: Harry Watson, Griffin, 1.000, 7-0

D Interstate League
President: James A. Lindsey

Standings	W	L	Pct.	GB	Manager
Wellsville Rainmakers**	54	32	.628	—	Joe Lohr
Olean White Sox*	52	30	.634	2	Gus Dundon
Bradford Drillers	42	42	.500	11	Duke Servatius/R. Topham
Hornell Maple Leafs	38	51	.427	14½	Joe Prozeller/Lenny Burrell
Warren Bingoes	33	50	.398	16½	R.W. Archer/George Bell
Jamestown Rabbits#	28	42	.400	18	William Webb

#Jamestown disbanded August 14.

Playoff: None; Olean refused to engage in a playoff, claiming that Jamestown's second half games should have been thrown out for failing to complete the schedule and Olean should have won both halves. The claim was denied and the title was awarded to Wellsville.

BA: Bill Colligan, Olean, .322
Runs: Bill Colligan, Olean, 62
Joe Apple, Wellsville, 62
Hits: John Steinfeldt, Wellsville, 101
HRs: F. Moran, Warren, 3
Wins: Everett Keener, Wellsville, 14
L. Webb, Jamestown/Hornell, 14
SOs: L. Webb, Jamestown/Hornell, 152
Pct: Everett Keener, Wellsville, .778, 14-4

D Middle Texas League

President: Hulen P. Robertson

Standings	W	L	Pct.	GB	Manager
Belton Braves***	40	19	.678	—	Charles "Hickory" Lawson
Temple Governors	32	27	.542	8	Luther Burleson/Frank Rogers
Bartlett	29	26	.527	9	Ike Pendleton
Austin Reps/Taylor Producers/ Brenham Kaisers#	21	36	.368	18	Billy Disch/Jack Sniper
Schulenburg Giants@	23	18	.561	NA	J. Robbins
Brenham Huskies@	12	31	.279	NA	Art Wickes/John Tuller

#Austin (2-5) moved to Taylor May 1, when floods forced the team to relocate; Taylor (15-23) moved to Brenham June 8.
@Brenham and Schulenburg disbanded June 7.
The league disbanded June 19.

BA: Russ Breaux, Taylor, .358
Runs: Williamson, Belton, 49
Hits: Williamson, Belton, 79
HRs: Tom Osborne, Temple, 11
Wins: Lester Gaines, Belton, 13
SOs: Ray Francis, Temple, 106
Pct: Dennis, Belton, 1.000, 11-0

D Nebraska State League

President: Clarence J. Miles

Standings	W	L	Pct.	GB	Manager
Beatrice Milkskimmers	35	18	.660	—	John Fillman
Hastings Reds	30	27	.526	7	Leonard Bennett
York Prohibitionists	25	31	.446	11½	John Pierce
Fairbury Shaners	22	31	.415	13	Bert Shaner
Norfolk Drummers@	24	13	.649	NA	Jay "Babe" Towne
Grand Island Champions@	16	16	.500	NA	Harry Claire
Kearney Buffaloes#	4	10	.286	NA	Grover Matney
Columbus Pawnees#	3	13	.188	NA	Frank Justus

#Columbus and Kearney disbanded June 4.
@Grand Island and Norfolk disbanded June 28.
The league ceased operations July 18.

D North Carolina State League

President: Arthur Lyon

Standings	W	L	Pct.	GB	Manager
Asheville Tourists***	74	46	.617	—	Jack Corbett
Durham Bulls	69	52	.570	5½	James Kelly
Raleigh Capitals	63	57	.525	11	Earle Mack
Charlotte Hornets	56	66	.459	19	Burleigh Emery/Martin Dudley
Winston-Salem Twins	53	69	.434	22	Charles Clancy
Greensboro Patriots	46	71	.393	26½	William "Red" Rowe/Fred Messer

BA: Turner Barber, Winston-Salem, .324
Runs: Jimmy Hickman, Asheville, 95
Hits: Jimmy Hickman, Asheville, 127
Dallas Bradshaw, Asheville, 127
HRs: Jimmy Hickman, Asheville, 14
Wins: Elmer Myers, Raleigh, 29
SOs: Elmer Myers, Raleigh, 268
Pct: Elmer Myers, Raleigh, .744, 29-10

D Ohio State League

President: Joseph T. Carr

Standings	W	L	Pct.	GB	Manager
Portsmouth Cobblers*	71	42	.628	—	Chester Spencer
Lexington Colts	63	48	.568	7	Howard Guyn
Chillicothe Babes/Huntington/ Maysville Angels#**	58	55	.513	13	Josh Devore
Charleston Senators	58	63	.479	17	Charles "Biddy" Beers
Frankfort Old Taylors	45	65	.409	24½	Pat Bohannon/Jack Hayden
Ironton Nailers	47	69	.405	25½	Dick Smith

#Chillicothe (27-34) moved to Huntington July 13; Huntington (2-4) moved to Maysville July 19.

Playoff: Portsmouth 4 games, Maysville 1.

BA: Ralph Sharman, Portsmouth, .374
Runs: Pickles Dilhofer, Portsmouth, 83
Hits: Ralph Sharman, Portsmouth, 147
HRs: Ernie Calbert, Ironton, 13
Wins: Hubert Test, Portsmouth, 21
Pct: Howard McGraynor, Chillicothe/ Huntington/Maysville, .800, 12-3

D Rio Grande Association

Presidents: John McCloskey/E.P. Hughes

Standings	W	L	Pct.	GB	Manager
Phoenix Senators	38	21	.644	—	Herbert Hester
El Paso Mackmen	36	22	.621	1½	John McCloskey
Albuquerque Dukes	32	25	.561	5	George Reed
Tucson Old Pueblos	19	40	.322	19	Kitty Brashear/Spots MacMurdo
Douglas Miners#	5	13	.278	NA	William Quigley
Las Cruces Farmers#	5	14	.263	NA	William Hurley

#Douglas and Las Cruces disbanded May 24.
The league disbanded July 6.

BA: George Duddy, El Paso, .404
Runs: John Stadille, Tucson, 61
Hits: George Duddy, El Paso, 97
HRs: Frank Huelsman, Albuquerque, 10
Wins: Herb Hall, Phoenix, 14
Grover Knight, El Paso, 14
SOs: Herb Hall, Phoenix, 99
Sam Beer, Las Cruces/El Paso, 99
Pct: Grover Knight, El Paso, .875, 14-2

D Western Association

President: William P. Hill

Standings	W	L	Pct.	GB	Manager
Denison Railroaders	76	53	.589	—	Babe Peebles
Oklahoma City Senators	76	62	.551	4½	Heinie Maag
Sherman Hitters	70	65	.519	9	A.L. "Dad" Ritter
Muskogee Mets	68	66	.507	10½	Frank Coe/Dave Tacke
Paris Red Snappers	66	66	.500	11½	Earl "Red" Snapp/William Nance/ Johnny Fillman
Tulsa Producers	63	71	.470	15½	George Kelsey/Norman Price
Ft. Smith Twins	61	75	.449	18½	Charles Mosley/Ted Schultz
McAlester Miners	57	79	.419	22½	Rudy Kling/Phil Ketter/Jimmy Humphries

Attendance: Tulsa, 40,200.

Playoff: Oklahoma City 4 games, Muskogee 3.

BA: John Robinson, Muskogee, .323
Runs: Clyde McCarty, Ft. Smith, 104
Hits: John Robinson, Muskogee, 160
HRs: Otto Beese, McAlester, 34
Wins: Roy Clements, Tulsa, 21
Dick Robertson, Ft. Smith, 21
SOs: L.G. Daniels, Paris, 222
ERA: Ray Fagan, Oklahoma City, 1.06
Pct: Ray Fagan, Oklahoma City, 1.000, 13-0

Ind Colonial League

President: Charles B. Coppen

Standings	W	L	Pct.	GB	Manager
Hartford Senators	55	42	.567	—	Jim Delehanty
Brockton Pilgrims	57	44	.564	—	Bert Weeden
New Bedford Whalers	56	45	.554	1	John J. O'Brien
New Haven MaxFeds	52	50	.510	5½	Bert Maxwell
Springfield Tips	47	50	.485	8	Henry Ramsey
Pawtucket Rovers	37	57	.394	16½	Jim Connor
Fall River Spindles#	22	24	.478	NA	Frank Connaughton/William Phoenix
Taunton Herrings#	14	28	.333	NA	Thomas Gilroy

#Fall River and Taunton disbanded July 10.

BA: Jim Delehanty, Hartford, .379
Runs: Jiggs, New Bedford, 65
Hits: Hugh Miller, Taunton/Springfield, 116
HRs: Frank Kiley, Taunton/Brockton, 4
Wins: John Tillman, New Bedford, 22
SOs: John Tillman, New Bedford, 176
Pct: John Tillman, New Bedford, .786, 22-6

1915 Interleague Post Season Play

World Series
Boston (American) 4 games, Philadelphia (National) 1

Virginia-North Carolina Series
Asheville (North Carolina) 4 games, Rocky Mount (Virginia) 2

1915 No-Hitters

Date	Pitcher	Team	League	Opponent	Score
4-15	Rube Marquard	New York	National	Brooklyn	2-0
4-16	Neil	Austin	Middle Texas	Bartlett	0-1
4-19	Dode Criss	Houston	Texas	San Antonio	3-0
4-24	Frank Allen	Pittsburgh	Federal	St. Louis	2-0
5-1	Zieser	Lowell	New England	Worcester	4-0
5-7	Tim McCabe	Decatur	Three-I	Moline	4-0
5-9	Spec Harkness	Aberdeen	Northwestern	Seattle	4-0
5-15	Claude Hendrix	Chicago	Federal	Pittsburgh	10-0
5-19	Harry Harper	Minneapolis	American Assoc.	St. Paul	4-0
5-20	C.H. Frye	Durham	N. Carolina State	Asheville	3-0
5-26	George Ross	Muscatine	Central Assoc.	Cedar Rapids	5-0
5-30	Dazzy Vance	St. Joseph	Western	Wichita	2-1
5-31	Doug Smith	Springfield	Colonial	Hartford	6-0
6-1	John Cantley	Waycross	FLAG	Valdosta	0-1
6-1	Eddie Donalds	Waco	Texas	Shreveport	11-0
6-2	Frank May	Macon	South Atlantic	Albany	2-0
6-5	Sline	Manchester	New England	Fitchburg	2-0
6-7	Charles Veasey	Beaumont	Texas	Shreveport	6-0
6-14	Jake Smith	Brenham	Middle Texas	Temple	3-0
6-15	John Nabors	Newnan	Georgia-Alabama	Talladega	1-0 (13)
6-17	Pep Hornsby	Ft. Smith	Western Assoc.	Paris	3-0
6-18	McLeod	Fall River	Colonial	Springfield	3-0
6-19	Dumont	Fargo-Moorhead	Northern	Ft. William-Pt. Arthur	1-0
6-19	Paige	Corsicana	Central Texas	Ennis	4-0
6-20	Ben Harris	Saginaw	Southern Michigan	Flint	3-2
6-21	Ted Bowen	Mexia	Central Texas	Ennis	2-1 (11)
6-25	Dan Tipple	Indianapolis	American Assoc.	Cleveland	6-0
6-30	Bill Terry	Newnan	Georgia-Alabama	Anniston	2-0
7-2	Marty O'Toole	Columbus	American Assoc.	Cleveland	1-0
7-5	Hart	Newark	Buckeye	Findlay	5-0
7-7	Buck Weaver	New Orleans	Southern Assoc.	Nashville	1-0
7-12	Win Noyes	Spokane	Northwestern	Vancouver	11-1
7-14	Joe Oeschger	Providence	International	Toronto	1-0
7-15	Billings	Kaufman	Central Texas	Ennis	4-0
7-19	Preacher Perryman	Atlanta	Southern Assoc.	Nashville	2-1
7-24	Art Nehf	Terre Haute	Central	Erie	1-0
7-25	William Piercey	Vernon	Pacific Coast	Oakland	3-0
7-27	Tom Dougherty	Hamilton	Canadian	London	2-1
8-3	Ed Stricker	Chambersburg	Blue Ridge	Gettysburg	1-0
8-7	Oscar Tuero	Lewiston	New England	Lowell	5-0
8-12	Carl Ray	Greensboro	N. Carolina State	Raleigh	9-0
8-15	Larry Henderson	Charleston	Ohio State	Ironton	5-0
8-16	Alex Main	Kansas City	Federal	Buffalo	5-0
8-18	Fred Beebe	Buffalo	International	Montreal	7-0
8-19	George Cunningham	Chattanooga	Southern Assoc.	Birmingham	1-1
8-20	Carl Thompson	Atlanta	Southern Assoc.	Little Rock	5-0
8-21	Bob Ingersoll	Omaha	Western	Topeka	7-0
8-25	J. Meyers	Wilkes-Barre	New York State	Albany	5-0
8-28	Bert Humphries	Norfolk	Virginia	Petersburg	3-0
8-31	Jimmy Lavender	Chicago	National	New York	2-0
9-7	Dave Davenport	St. Louis	Federal	Chicago	3-0

Number in parentheses indicates innings if other than nine.

THIS DATE IN MINOR LEAGUE HISTORY

January 19, 1915, Bud O'Laughlin, 24, a member of the Owensboro, Kitty League, club, was shot dead on a Booneville, Indiana, street by Clyde Barnhill, with whose wife O'Laughlin was walking.

April 24, 1915, Pitcher Gary Fortune, Asheville, North Carolina State League, struck out 21 and allowed only eight hits in a 12-inning game, yet lost 5-4 to Winston-Salem.

June 9, 1915, Pitcher Palmer, Freeport, Bi-State League, clouted two homers, one with the bases full, to help win his own game, 9-8 over Streator.

June 14, 1915, First baseman O. Kelleher, Worcester, New England League, had no fielding chances in a nine-inning game with Fitchburg. Fitchburg won the contest 5-4, the club's 17th successive victory.

June 27, 1915, In the Central Association, Burlington and Keokuk played a 22-inning 0-0 tie. Pitchers Miller of Burlington and Watkins of Keokuk both went the distance.

June 29, 1915, Pitcher Roy Clements, Tulsa, Western Association, shut out Denison in a doubleheader to run his consecutive scoreless innings streak to 32-2/3.

June 30, 1915, Bill Terry, later player-manager of the New York Giants, pitched a no-hitter for Newnan, Georgia-Alabama League, defeating Anniston 2-0.

July 1, 1915, Tacoma, Northwestern League, made 29 hits to win the first game of a doubleheader from Victoria 26-8, then made 17 more in the second game for a 9-4 triumph.

July 3, 1915, Tacoma, Northwestern League, defeated Victoria 21-18, despite being outhit 26-24. In the four-game set, Tacoma tallied 72 runs and made 92 hits. Shortstop J. Butler collected 16 hits in 20 at bats, including eight extra-base blows, and scored 15 runs.

July 5, 1915, In the North Carolina State League, Durham and Raleigh played 35 innings in one day. In the opener of a doubleheader, Raleigh won 3-2 in 14 innings, and the second game was called after 21 innings tied 2-2.

July 5, 1915, Pitcher Harper, Minneapolis, American Association, walked 20 St. Paul batters in a nine-inning game, helping the Saints post a 13-5 victory.

July 9, 1915, Pitcher Roth, Augusta, South Atlantic League, made the only two hits credited to his club off Causey of Savannah, and drove in both of his team's runs.

July 11, 1915, Fred Mellinger, Cedar Rapids, Central Association, pitched 24 innings, winning a doubleheader from Marshalltown, 4-0 and 3-2. He allowed four hits in the opener and 11 safeties in the 15-inning nightcap.

July 19, 1915, After 13 consecutive victories, St. Paul, American Association, lost to Columbus.

July 22, 1915, First baseman John Mers of Oakland, Pacific Coast League, was stopped by Art Fromme, Los Angeles, after having hit safely in 49 consecutive games. The streak began May 31.

July 24, 1915, Daniel Howley, catching for Montreal, International League, hit two grand slams in a 15-6 win over Toronto.

July 26, 1915, Seattle, Northwestern League, lost 5-2 to Victoria after having won 18 consecutive games. The streak elevated Seattle from last place to first.

August 4, 1915, Pitcher Davis of Columbus, American Association, fanned seven St. Paul batters in a row.

August 12, 1915, Pitcher Carl Ray of Greensboro, North Carolina State League, pitched a no-hit game against Raleigh, his third no-hitter in as many seasons.

August 14, 1915, The ball parks at Galveston and Houston, Texas League, were destroyed by a Gulf of Mexico hurricane. Galveston discontinued play for the final two weeks of the season.

August 14, 1915, Norfolk and Suffolk, Virginia League, played a 2-2 tie called after 23 innings because of darkness, Cochran pitching against Poole.

August 14, 1915, Greensboro, North Carolina State League, shut out Raleigh for the third time in as many days. No Raleigh player reached third base in the three games and only seven got to second. Raleigh had no hits in the first game, four in the second and three in the third.

August 15, 1915, Larry Henderson of Charleston, Ohio State League, shut out Ironton in a doubleheader, 5-0 and 2-0, pitching a no-hitter in the first game. He yielded five hits in the second tilt.

August 26, 1915, After 13 consecutive victories, Minneapolis, American Association, lost to Louisville.

August 29, 1915, Pitcher Slattery of Marshalltown, Central Association, struck out 19 in a game with Muscatine.

September 4, 1915, Norfolk and Suffolk, Virginia League, who played a 23-inning tie on August 14, battled to a 3-3 deadlock in a game called after 22 frames.

September 8, 1915, First baseman Bunny Brief of Salt Lake City, Pacific Coast League, had no fielding chances in a nine inning game with Vernon.

September 12, 1915, Dave Danforth, Louisville, whiffed 18 Kansas City batters to set a new American Association record. In his next game, September 15, Danforth struck out 16 St. Paul Saints for a total 34 in two consecutive games, 49 in three consecutive tilts and a total of 59 over a four-game stretch. He whiffed 130 in a 101-inning span.

September 25, 1915, Chattanooga, Southern Association, pitchers yielded a run in a game with Mobile after holding the opposition scoreless for 54 consecutive innings. Chattanooga scored seven consecutive shutouts, three seven-inning games and one five-inning forfeit included.

October 10, 1915, A crowd estimated by police at more than 100,000 watched a semipro championship game between the Cleveland White Autos and Omaha, Nebraska, Panhandlers in Brookside Stadium, a natural bowl on the West Side in Cleveland, Ohio.

1916

American League
President: Byron Bancroft Johnson

Standings	W	L	Pct.	GB	Attend.	Manager
Boston Red Sox	91	63	.591	—	496,397	Bill Carrigan
Chicago White Sox	89	65	.578	2	679,923	Clarence "Pants" Rowland
Detroit Tigers	87	67	.565	4	616,772	Hugh Jennings
New York Yankees	80	74	.519	11	469,211	Wild Bill Donovan
St. Louis Browns	79	75	.513	12	335,740	Fielder Jones
Cleveland Indians	77	77	.500	14	492,106	Lee Fohl
Washington Senators	76	77	.497	14½	177,265	Clark Griffith
Philadelphia Athletics	36	117	.235	54½	184,471	Connie Mack

BA: Tris Speaker, Cleveland, .386
Runs: Ty Cobb, Detroit, 113
Hits: Tris Speaker, Cleveland, 211
RBIs: Del Pratt, St. Louis, 103
HRs: Wally Pipp, New York, 12

Wins: Walter Johnson, Washington, 25
SOs: Walter Johnson, Washington, 228
ERA: Babe Ruth, Boston, 1.75
Pct: Eddie Cicotte, Chicago, .682, 15-7

National League
President: John K. Tener

Standings	W	L	Pct.	GB	Attend.	Manager
Brooklyn Robins	94	60	.610	—	447,747	Wilbert Robinson
Philadelphia Phillies	91	62	.595	2½	515,365	Pat Moran
Boston Braves	89	63	.586	4	313,495	George Stallings
New York Giants	86	66	.566	7	552,056	John McGraw
Chicago Cubs	67	86	.438	26½	453,685	Joe Tinker
Pittsburgh Pirates	65	89	.422	29	289,132	Nixey Callahan
Cincinnati Reds	60	93	.392	33½	255,846	Buck Herzog/Ivy Wingo/ Christy Mathewson
St. Louis Cardinals	60	93	.392	33½	224,308	Miller Huggins

BA: Hal Chase, Cincinnati, .339
Runs: George Burns, New York, 105
Hits: Hal Chase, Cincinnati, 184
RBIs: Heinie Zimmerman, Chicago/ New York, 83
HRs: Cy Williams, Chicago, 12
    Dave Robertson, New York, 12
Wins: Grover Alexander, Philadelphia, 33
SOs: Grover Alexander, Philadelphia, 167
ERA: Grover Alexander, Philadelphia, 1.55
Pct: Tom Hughes, Boston, .842, 16-3

AA American Association
President: Thomas M. Chivington

Standings	W	L	Pct.	GB	Attend.	Manager
Louisville Colonels	101	66	.605	—	140,622	Bill Clymer
Indianapolis Indians	95	71	.572	5½	123,463	Jack Hendricks
Minneapolis Millers	88	76	.537	11½	131,627	Joe Cantillon
St. Paul Saints	86	79	.521	14	126,372	Mike Kelley
Kansas City Blues	86	81	.515	15	124,869	Danny Shay
Toledo Iron Men	78	86	.476	21½	124,363	Roger Bresnahan
Columbus Senators	71	90	.441	27	133,339	Rudy Hulswitt/Bob Quinn/ William Johns
Milwaukee Brewers	54	110	.329	45½	122,143	Harry Clark/Jack Martin

BA: Beals Becker, Kansas City, .343
Runs: Dave Altizer, Minneapolis, 108
Hits: John Leary, Indianapolis, 195
HRs: Beals Becker, Kansas City, 15

SBs: Jim Thorpe, Milwaukee, 48
Wins: Chink Yingling, Minneapolis, 24
SOs: Cy Falkenberg, Indianapolis, 178
ERA: Paul Carter, Indianapolis, 1.65

AA International League
President: Edward G. Barrow

Standings	W	L	Pct.	GB	Manager
Buffalo Bisons	82	58	.586	—	Patsy Donovan
Providence Grays	76	62	.551	5	David Shean
Montreal Royals	75	64	.539	7½	Dan Howley
Baltimore Orioles	74	66	.529	8	Jack Dunn
Toronto Maple Leafs	73	66	.525	8½	Joe Birmingham/Lena Blackburn
Richmond Climbers	64	75	.460	17½	William A. Smith
Rochester Hustlers	60	78	.435	21	Thomas Leach
Newark Indians	52	87	.374	29½	Fred Tenney

Attendance: Buffalo, 274,172.

BA: Jim Smyth, Montreal, .3440
    Walter Holke, Rochester, .3438
Runs: Herb Moran, Montreal, 115
Hits: Will Bankston, Richmond, 166

HRs: George Twombly, Baltimore, 12
Wins: Leon Cadore, Montreal, 25
SOs: Jack McTigue, Toronto, 187
ERA: Urban Shocker, Toronto, 1.31

AA Pacific Coast League
President: Allan T. Baum

Standings	W	L	Pct.	GB	Manager
Los Angeles Angels	119	79	.601	—	Frank Chance
Vernon Tigers	115	91	.558	8	Hamilton Patterson
Salt Lake City Bees	99	96	.507	18½	Cliff Blankenship
San Francisco Seals	104	102	.504	19	Harry Wolverton
Portland Beavers	93	98	.487	22½	Walter McCredie
Oakland Oaks	72	136	.346	52	Rowdy Elliott/Del Howard

BA: Duke Kenworthy, Oakland, .314
Runs: Bunny Brief, Salt Lake City, 149
Hits: Larry Quinlan, Salt Lake City, 241
HRs: Bunny Brief, Salt Lake City, 33

Wins: Allen Sothoron, Portland, 30
SOs: Paul Fittery, Salt Lake City, 203
ERA: Art Fromme, Vernon, 1.92

A Southern Association
President: Robert H. Baugh

Standings	W	L	Pct.	GB	Attend.	Manager
Nashville Volunteers	84	54	.609	—	111,418	Roy Ellam
New Orleans Pelicans	73	61	.544	9	111,387	Johnny Dobbs
Birmingham Barons	69	62	.526	11½	100,751	Carleton Molesworth
Little Rock Travelers	70	65	.518	12½	90,497	Charles Starr
Atlanta Crackers	70	67	.511	13½	136,741	Charley Frank
Memphis Chickasaws	68	70	.493	16	170,493	Dolly Stark/George Moriarity
Chattanooga Lookouts	65	74	.467	19½	53,479	Norman "Kid" Elberfeld/ Frank "Pop" Kitchens
Mobile Sea Gulls	45	91	.331	38	38,930	Charles Schmidt/Matt McIntyre

BA: Baby Doll Jacobson, Little Rock, .346
Runs: Milo Allison, New Orleans, 87
Hits: Baby Doll Jacobson, Little Rock, 176
HRs: Joe Harris, Chattanooga, 9

Wins: Dickie Kerr, Memphis, 24
    Scott Perry, Atlanta, 24
    Tom Rogers, Nashville, 24
SOs: Roy Walker, New Orleans, 173
Pct: Hank Robinson, Little Rock, .917, 11-1

A Western League
President: Norris L. O'Neill

Standings	W	L	Pct.	GB	Manager
Omaha Rourkes	92	57	.617	—	Marty Krug
Lincoln Tigers	87	63	.580	5½	James "Ducky" Holmes
Sioux City Indians	79	71	.527	13½	Harry Gaspar
Denver Bears	78	75	.510	16	Rebel Oakes
Des Moines Boosters	75	75	.500	17½	Frank Isbell
Topeka Savages	70	84	.455	24½	Bill Lattimore/Clyde Engel
St. Joseph Drummers	67	86	.440	27	Denny Sullivan
Wichita Wolves/Colorado Springs Millionaires#	57	94	.377	36	Jimmy Jackson

#Wichita (55-84) moved to Colorado Springs September 10.

BA: Hank Butcher, Denver, .377
Runs: Walter Carlisle, Lincoln, 121
Hits: Kenzie Kirkham, St. Joseph, 205
    Rebel Oakes, Denver, 205

HRs: Ben Dyer, Denver, 16
Wins: Carl East, Lincoln, 24
SOs: Paul Musser, Des Moines, 249
ERA: Otto Merz, Omaha, 2.45

B Central League
President: Emerson W. Dickerson

Standings	W	L	Pct.	GB	Manager
Grand Rapids Black Sox#	77	55	.583	—	William Essick
Dayton Veterans*	73	57	.562	3	John Nee
Springfield Reapers**	74	58	.561	3	Joe Dunn
Wheeling Stogies	65	64	.504	10½	Harry Smith
Evansville Evas	63	66	.488	12½	Charles "Punch" Knoll
Terre Haute Highlanders	62	71	.466	15½	Rufus Gilbert
South Bend Benders	56	77	.421	21½	Ben Koehler/Lee Tannehill
Muskegon Reds	55	77	.417	22	Bade Myers

#Grand Rapids played some of its home games in Battle Creek, Michigan.

Playoff: Dayton 4 games, Springfield 2.

BA: Ray Spencer, Dayton, .343
Runs: Ray Spencer, Dayton, 84
Hits: Ray Spencer, Dayton, 170
HRs: Earl Sykes, Dayton, 18

Wins: Nick Lakaff, Dayton, 25
SOs: Theodore Turner, Evansville, 203
ERA: O.A. McArthur, Grand Rapids, 1.56

B Eastern League
President: Tim H. Murnane

Standings	W	L	Pct.	GB	Manager
New London Planters	86	34	.717	—	Eugene McCann
Portland Duffs	81	37	.687	4	Hugh Duffy
Springfield Ponies	70	53	.569	17½	John Flynn
Lynn Pipers	66	57	.537	21½	Louis Piper
Worcester Boosters	61	60	.504	25½	Billy Hamilton

*Won first-half   **Won second-half   ***Won both halves

New Haven Murlins............ 56 65 .463 30½ Danny Murphy
Bridgeport Hustlers............ 44 78 .361 43 Neal Ball/Mike Healy
Hartford Senators................ 38 79 .325 46½ Charles Wagner/James Clarkin/
George Spires/Jesse Burkett/
Simon McDonald
Lawrence Barristers#...... 51 57 .472 NA Jesse Burkett/Ned O'Donnell/
Larry Mahoney/Jack O'Hara
Lowell Grays# .... 36 69 .343 NA Harry Lord/Joe Kilhullen/Jesse Burkett

#Lawrence and Lowell disbanded September 4.

BA: Patrick Maloney, Worcester, .332
Runs: Patrick Maloney, Worcester, 93
Hits: Patrick Maloney, Worcester, 151

Wins: Bunn Hearn, New London, 22
Oscar Tuero, Lynn, 22
SOs: Richard Durning, Portland, 187
Pct: Pat Martin, New London, .778, 21-6

B New York State League
President: John H. Farrell

Standings	W	L	Pct.	GB	Manager
Syracuse Stars.....................	81	52	.609	—	Mike O'Neill
Scranton Miners...................	67	52	.563	7	William Coughlin
Binghamton Bingoes	69	61	.530	10½	John Calhoun
Wilkes-Barre Barons	62	63	.496	15	Joe McCarthy
Utica Utes	63	68	.481	17	Ambrose McConnell
Albany Senators/					
Reading Pretzels@...........	58	70	.453	20½	George Wiltse
Elmira Colonels	59	75	.440	22½	Bill Conroy
Troy Trojans/					
Harrisburg Islanders#	56	74	.431	23½	Louis Wachter/George Cockill/Walter Blair

#Troy (8-27) moved to Harrisburg June 20.
@ Albany (51-57) moved to Reading August 21.

BA: Bill Kay, Binghamton, .360
Runs: Bill Kay, Binghamton, 85
Hits: Bill Kay, Binghamton, 166

Wins: Howard Ehmke, Syracuse, 31
SOs: Howard Ehmke, Syracuse, 195
Pct: Howard Ehmke, Syracuse, .816, 31-7

B Northwestern League
President: R.L. Blewett

Standings	W	L	Pct.	GB	Manager
Spokane Indians.................	79	48	.622	—	R.L. "Nick" Williams
Butte Miners	68	59	.535	11	Joe McGinnity
Tacoma Tigers	63	61	.508	14½	Russ Hall
Great Falls.........................	60	61	.496	16	Dick Hurley/Herb Hester
Seattle Giants.....................	60	72	.455	21½	Frank Raymond
Vancouver Beavers.............	50	79	.388	30	Robert Brown

BA: Ed Kippert, Butte, .358
Runs: Roy Grover, Butte, 119
Hits: Rod Murphy, Vancouver, 182
RBIs: Dave Hillyard, Butte, 101

HRs: Dave Hillyard, Butte, 17
Wins: Harvey Sutherland, Tacoma, 23
SOs: Rudolph Kallio, Great Falls, 190
Pct: Harvey Sutherland, Tacoma, .767, 23-7

B Texas League
President: Walter Morris

Standings	W	L	Pct.	GB	Manager
Waco Navigators	85	58	.594	—	Ellis Hardy
Shreveport Gassers	84	60	.583	1½	Syd Smith
Galveston Pirates	72	66	.522	10½	Paul Sentell
Houston Buffaloes	73	72	.503	13	Pat Newnam
Ft. Worth Panthers............	71	74	.490	15	Jake Atz/Otto McIvor
Beaumont Oilers	65	79	.451	20½	Michael Finn/Jim Delahanty/Clay Perry
San Antonio Bronchos	65	79	.451	20½	George Leidy/Monroe Stark/Harry Stewart
Dallas Giants......................	58	85	.406	27	Harry Welchonce/Bennie Brownlow

BA: Charles Bittle, Waco, .335
Runs: Charles Bittle, Waco, 90
John Baggan, San Antonio, 90
Hits: Charles Bittle, Waco, 185

HRs: Al Nixon, Beaumont, 9
Wins: Cliff Hill, Waco, 23
SOs: Cliff Hill, Waco, 251
ERA: Walt Dickson, Houston, 1.06

B Three-I League
President: Albert R. Tearney

Standings	W	L	Pct.	GB	Manager
Peoria Distillers	84	50	.627	—	William Jackson
Hannibal Mules..................	79	57	.581	6	Theodore Waring
Bloomington Bloomers.......	76	56	.576	7	Howard Darringer
Rockford Wakes	67	66	.504	16½	Howard Wakefield
Moline Plowboys	59	76	.437	25½	George Hughes
Rock Island Islanders.........	57	76	.429	26½	Pete Lister/Harry Bay
Quincy Gems	57	77	.425	27	John Castle
Davenport Blue Sox...........	56	77	.421	27½	Daniel O'Leary

BA: Howard Wakefield, Rockford, .352
Runs: Ralph Craig, Peoria, 101
Hits: Howard Wakefield, Rockford, 179
HRs: Fred Beck, Peoria, 10
Rhino Williams, Rockford, 10

Wins: Bert Graham, Moline, 23
Hal Carlson, Rockford, 23
SOs: Dave Black, Peoria, 159
ERA: Art Smith, Hannibal, 1.50

C Northern League
President: John Burmeister

Standings	W	L	Pct.	GB	Manager
Winnipeg Maroons*	72	46	.610	—	John Sheehan
Fargo-Moorhead Graingrowers**	68	47	.591	2½	Bob Unglaub
Duluth White Sox..............	55	61	.474	16	William "Darby" O'Brien
Superior Red Sox...............	45	65	.409	23	George Brautigan
Virginia Ore Diggers#........	28	32	.467	NA	A.D. "Lefty" Davis
Ft. William-Pt. Arthur					
Canadians#......................	22	39	.361	NA	Frank Reynolds

#Virginia and Ft. William-Pt. Arthur withdrew July 10.

Playoff: Abandoned with Fargo-Moorhead and Winnipeg tied at two games each.

BA: Hack Miller, Winnipeg, .335
Runs: Warren Adams, Winnipeg, 82
Hits: Hack Miller, Winnipeg, 150
HRs: Hack Miller, Winnipeg, 10

Wins: Harry Donovan, Winnipeg, 21
SOs: Charlie Boardman, Fargo-Moorhead, 222
Pct: Harry Donovan, Winnipeg, .778, 21-6

C South Atlantic League
President: Nick P. Corish

Standings	W	L	Pct.	GB	Manager
Columbia Gamecocks**.....	72	50	.590	—	Doug Harbison
Charleston Sea Gulls	68	55	.553	4½	James Hamilton
Augusta Tourists*	69	56	.552	4½	Carl Eubanks
Columbus Foxes	62	62	.500	11	Hardin Herndon
Jacksonville Tarpons	57	65	.467	15	James Manes/Paul Cobb
Macon Tigers	55	67	.451	17	George Stinson
Montgomery Rebels#	42	47	.472	NA	Tiomon Bowden
Albany Babies#..................	30	53	.361	NA	Perry Lipe

#Montgomery and Albany disbanded July 23.

Playoff: Augusta 4 games, Columbia 0.

BA: Harry Purcell, Jacksonville, .316
Runs: Hardin Herndon, Columbus, 94
Hits: W.D. Brazier, Augusta, 150

Wins: Reid Zellars, Macon, 22
SOs: Reid Zellars, Macon, 237
Pct: Jesse James, Columbia, .750, 15-5

C Virginia League
President: Burrus Corprew

Standings	W	L	Pct.	GB	Manager
Newport News Shipbuilders**	79	39	.669	—	Brooke Crist/Fred Payne
Portsmouth Foxes*	76	42	.644	3	James Fox
Rocky Mount Tar Heels	61	60	.504	19½	Ray Ryan
Petersburg Goobers............	54	68	.443	27	George Kelly/William Helfrich
Norfolk Tars	38	77	.330	39½	M.D. "Nelly" McMahon/William "Buck" Pressley
Hopewell Powder Puffs#....	30	52	.366	NA	Win Clark/R. Barrett

#Hopewell disbanded July 22 and Roanoke Rapids, North Carolina was added August 14 as a replacement. The league directors would not allow the move and Roanoke Rapids was dropped August 16 after playing one game, which it won.

Playoff: Newport News 4 games, Portsmouth 1.

BA: Manuel Cueto, Portsmouth, .321
Runs: Al Moore, Portsmouth, 71
Hits: Manuel Cueto, Portsmouth, 126
HRs: Rasty Walters, Newport News, 15

Wins: William Wood, Portsmouth, 22
SOs: Clarence Teague, Rocky Mount, 205
Pct: Molly Craft, Norfolk, .800, 8-2

D Blue Ridge League
Presidents: Charles W. Boyer/J. Vincent Jamison, Jr.

Standings	W	L	Pct.	GB	Manager
Chambersburg Maroons	53	40	.570	—	Ed Hooper
Martinsburg Blue Sox........	56	44	.560	½	W.J. "Country" Morris
Hagerstown Terriers	49	46	.516	5	Bert Weeden
Hanover Raiders................	46	48	.489	7½	Bill Starr
Frederick Hustlers..............	46	51	.454	9	Jack Morrison
Gettysburg Ponies.............	35	56	.385	17	Ira Plank

BA: Ed Hooper, Chambersburg, .332
Runs: Charles Dysert, Hagerstown, 71
Hits: Ed Hooper, Chambersburg, 113
HRs: Clyde Barnhart, Frederick, 9
Jack Morrison, Frederick, 9

Wins: Marv Goodwin, Martinsburg, 19
SOs: Earl Howard, Hagerstown, 188
Pct: Chalkey McCleary, Hagerstown, .692, 18-8

D Central Association
President: M.E. Justice

Standings	W	L	Pct.	GB	Manager
Marshalltown Ansons	77	50	.606	—	Frank Boyle
Clinton Pilots	73	51	.589	2½	Jim Drohan/Larry Brown
Cedar Rapids Rabbits	62	64	.492	14½	Jack Herbert/Billy Collins
Burlington Pathfinders/					
Ottumwa Packers@...........	62	64	.492	14½	Richard Rohn/George Boelzle
Waterloo Shamrocks	58	67	.464	18	Eddie Brennan

Mason City Claydiggers ..... 50 76 .397 26½ Harry Bay
Ft. Dodge Dodgers .... 41 86 .323 36 Paul Turgeon/Jay "Babe" Towne
Muscatine Muskies# .... 45 44 .506 NA Ned Egan

#Muscatine forfeited 34 wins.
@Burlington (41-29) moved to Ottumwa July 20.

BA: Herbert Ellison, Muscatine, .361
Runs: Charles Reinhart, Muscatine, 104
Hits: Herbert Ellison, Muscatine, 178

HRs: Al "Bull" Durham, Muscatine/
Marshalltown, 18
Wins: Dick Blunk, Ottumwa, 24
SOs: H.W. Flanagan, Muscatine, 266
ERA: Ken Penner, Marshalltown, 1.41

D Central Texas League
Presidents: Earl C. Brown/J.C. Castellaw

Standings	W	L	Pct.	GB	Manager
Temple Governors	36	25	.590	—	Paul Trammell
Ennis Tigers	35	26	.574	1	Ed Wicker
Mexia Gassers	32	29	.525	4	Roy Akin/Grady White
Terrell Terrors	29	32	.475	7	Hank Griffin/William Nance
Waxahachie Athletics	26	35	.426	10	Dee Poindexter
Marlin Marlins	25	36	.410	11	Bob Tarleton/Bob Countryman/
					Fielder Murray

BA: Roy Leslie, Ennis, .359
Runs: Babe Green, Ennis, 65
Hits: A. Edens, Ennis, 68
HRs: A. Edens, Ennis, 10
W.C. Comstock, Marlin, 10

Wins: Lester Gaines, Ennis, 15
SOs: Bill Francis, Temple, 126
ERA: Ted Bowen, Mexia, 1.26
Pct: Lester Gaines, Ennis, .750, 15-5
Ossee Ball, Temple, .750, 9-3

D Dixie League
President: T.A. Ward

Standings	W	L	Pct.	GB	Manager
Dothan	38	22	.633	—	Jack Reidy
Eufaula	34	24	.586	3	
Bainbridge	31	29	.517	7	Fred Glass
Moultrie Packers	28	29	.491	8½	H.J. Wienges/Bob Schuyler
Valdosta Millionaires	25	34	.424	12½	
Quitman	20	38	.345	17	

BA: Fred Chambers, Dothan, .348
Runs: John Reidy, Dothan, 56
Hits: W.E. Barrow, Bainbridge, 83
HRs: Fred Chambers, Dothan, 9

Wins: Earl Moseley, Dothan, 13
SOs: R.J. Williamson, Quitman, 109
Pct: George Dickerson, Dothan, 1.000, 11-0

D East Texas League
President: Lawrence Jordan

Standings	W	L	Pct.	GB	Manager
Palestine Athletics	14	9	.609	—	Dick Brewer
Lufkin Lumbermen	14	9	.609	—	Lee Lemon
Nacogdoches Cogs	10	9	.526	2	Tom Cherry
Crockett@	9	13	.409	4½	Bob Countryman
Rusk Governors	7	11	.389	4½	Jack Ashton
Jacksonville Tomato Pickers#..	3	6	.333	NA	Art Wickes

#Jacksonville joined the league June 29 and disbanded July 13.
@Crockett disbanded July 15.
The league disbanded July 19.

(limited box scores available)
BA: Lee Lemon, Lufkin, .407
Runs: J.T. Ellis, Nacogdoches, 10
Hits: J.T. Ellis, Nacogdoches, 13
Haywood McDaniel, Palestine, 13

HRs: Hank Utzman, Lufkin, 3
Wins: George Crevenstine, Lufkin, 6
Pct: George Crevenstine, Lufkin, 1.000, 6-0

D Georgia-Alabama League
President: Dick Jemison

Standings	W	L	Pct.	GB	Manager
Rome Romans	43	22	.662	—	Frank Manush
Newnan Cowetas	41	26	.612	3	Harry Mathews
La Grange Grangers	39	29	.574	5½	Grady Bowen
Talladega Tigers	26	38	.406	16½	Tige Garrett
Anniston Moulders	23	39	.371	18½	Wade Reynolds
Griffin Lightfoots	23	41	.359	19½	Kid Reagan/Phil Wells

BA: Don Flynn, Newnan, .365
Runs: Don Flynn, Newnan, 52
Hits: H.L. Shaw, Rome, 89

Wins: Joseph Wiley, Rome, 15
Robert Watkins, Newnan, 15
Pct: Rufus Nolly, La Grange, .857, 12-2

D Interstate League
President: James A. Lindsey

Standings	W	L	Pct.	GB	Manager
Ridgway***	56	24	.700	—	Izzy Hoffman
St. Marys Saints	49	30	.620	6½	Curly Blount

Bradford Drillers .... 45 38 .542 12½ Larry Schlafly
Wellsville Rainmakers .... 27 48 .360 26½ Joe Lohr
Johnsonburg Johnnies .... 27 49 .355 27 Thomas "Davy" Jones
Warren Bingoes@ .... 24 19 .558 NA Frank Shaughnessy
Erie Sailors+ .... 26 37 .413 NA Bill Bradley
Olean White Sox# .... 16 25 .390 NA Gus Dundon

#Olean disbanded July 12.
@Warren disbanded August 4; none of its second half games (6-9) were counted.
+Erie disbanded August 9.
Games thrown out: Wins: Warren 6, Wellsville 3, Bradford 2, Erie 2, St. Marys 1,
Johnsonburg 1; Losses: Warren 9, Wellsville 4, St. Marys 1.

BA: Jacob Jennis, Bradford, .357
Runs: Sam McConnell, Ridgway, 64
Hits: Jim McCabe, Ridgway, 95

HRs: John Gilmore, Warren/St. Marys/
Wellsville, 4
Frank Gleich, Erie, 4
Wins: John Verbout, St. Marys, 18
SOs: A. Braithwood, Bradford, 133
Pct: Bill Chapelle, Wellsville/Ridgway,
.800, 12-3

D Kitty League
President: Dr. Frank H. Bassett

Standings	W	L	Pct.	GB	Manager
Clarksville Volunteers*	50	24	.676	—	Lemarr Boykin
Henderson Hens	44	30	.595	6	Connie Walsh
Owensboro Distillers**	43	31	.581	7	Sandy Murray/Henry "Buzz" Wetzel
Dawson Springs	33	41	.446	17	Art Goodwin/Louis Eith/Senter Rainey/
					William Schwartz
Madisonville Miners#	31	41	.431	18	Artie Cummings/Leo Angemeier
Hopkinsville Hoppers	22	56	.282	30	William Schwartz

#Madisonville disbanded August 2.
The league disbanded August 4.

D North Carolina State League
President: William G. Bramham

Standings	W	L	Pct.	GB	Manager
Charlotte Hornets**	68	44	.607	—	Martin Dudley
Winston-Salem Twins	63	48	.568	4½	Charles Clancy
Durham Bulls	62	51	.549	6½	Richard Hoffman/Frank Manush
Asheville Tourists*	58	54	.518	10	Jack Corbett
Greensboro Patriots	45	67	.402	23	James Kelly/Bill Laval
Raleigh Capitals	39	71	.355	28	Henry Busch/Duke Duncan/
					George "King" Kelly

Playoff: Charlotte 4 games, Asheville 0.

BA: Jimmy Hickman, Asheville, .350
Runs: Warren Butts, Durham, 90
Hits: Harvey Hiller, Winston-Salem, 145
HRs: Ben Paschal, Charlotte, 15
Wins: Phil Redding, Charlotte, 23

SOs: Herman Schwartje, Winston-Salem, 183
ERA: Phil Redding, Charlotte, 1.34
Pct: Charles Glazner, Winston-Salem,
.750, 21-7

D Ohio State League
President: Joseph T. Carr

Standings	W	L	Pct.	GB	Manager
Portsmouth Truckers*	47	19	.712	—	Chester Spencer
Maysville Burley Cubs	26	36	.419	19	Jimmy Jones
Charleston Senators/					
Chillicothe Babes@**	29	35	.453	NA	Watt Powell
Frankfort Old Taylors#	24	35	.407	NA	James "Ducky" Holmes
Huntington Blue Sox#	22	38	.367	NA	John DeArmond/Ezra Midkiff
Lexington Colts+	39	24	.619	NA	Howard Guyn

#Huntington and Frankfort disbanded July 6.
@Charleston (24-34) moved to Chillicothe July 13.
+Lexington disbanded July 16.
The league disbanded July 19.

BA: Stewart Dilts, Portsmouth, .420
Runs: Stewart Dilts, Portsmouth, 57
Hits: Stewart Dilts, Portsmouth, 95
HRs: Rube Lindholm, Frankfort, 6

Wins: Burge, Lexington, 12
John Ferguson, Portsmouth, 12
SOs: Paul Carpenter, Charleston/
Chillicothe, 95
Pct: John Ferguson, Portsmouth, .923, 12-1

D Potomac League
President: Fuller Barnard, Jr.

Standings	W	L	Pct.	GB	Manager
Frostburg Demons*	33	25	.569	—	Pat Brophy
Piedmont Drybugs	26	30	.464	6	Owen "Cy" Harris/Dutch Kane
Cumberland Colts**	23	35	.397	10	Tom Russler
Lonaconing Giants#	26	18	.691	NA	James McGuire/Roy Keener

#Lonaconing disbanded July 23.
The league disbanded August 16.

BA: Joe Phillips, Cumberland, .367
Runs: Roy Keener, Lonaconing/
Cumberland, 51
Hits: Roy Keener, Lonaconing/
Cumberland, 82

HRs: Paul Cobb, Lonaconing/Cumberland, 6
Wins: Ben Schaufele, Piedmont, 14
SOs: John Baylor, Frostburg, 114
Pct: Bill Stair, Frostburg, .889, 8-1

BA: Ross Youngs, Sherman, .362
Runs: Ross Youngs, Sherman, 103
Hits: Ross Youngs, Sherman, 195

HRs: Pete Adams, Ft. Smith, 22
Henry Moore, Tulsa, 22
J.W. Harper, Tulsa/Muskogee, 22
Wins: Walt Kinney, Denison, 22
SOs: Rollie Naylor, McAlester, 228
ERA: Rolla Mapel, McAlester, 2.03

D Western Association
Presidents: William P. Hill/J.W. Bell

Standings	W	L	Pct.	GB	Manager
Denison Railroaders*	86	49	.637	—	Babe Peebles
Tulsa Producers**	80	58	.580	7½	Norman Price
McAlester Miners	79	58	.577	8	Jimmy Humphries
Oklahoma City Senators	64	73	.467	23	Earl "Red" Snapp/Rudy Baerwald
Muskogee Mets	63	77	.450	25½	Heinie Maag
Ft. Smith Twins	61	76	.445	26	Herschel Thompson/Hugh McMurray
Sherman Lions	61	76	.445	26	Walter Frantz/Jack Love
Paris Survivors	56	83	.403	32	Johnny Fillman/Dick Speer

Attendance: Tulsa, 62,100.

Playoff: Denison 4 games, Tulsa 2.

1916 Interleague Post Season Play

World Series
Boston (American) 4 games, Brooklyn (National) 1

Minor League Championship Series
Louisville (American Association) 4 games, Omaha (Western) 1

1916 No-Hitters

Date	Pitcher	Team	League	Opponent	Score
5-11	Harry Stewart	San Antonio	Texas	Waco	2-0
5-19	C.F. Jeter	Quitman	Dixie	Bainbridge	9-0
5-30	J. Howard	Greensboro	N. Carolina State	Raleigh	3-0
6-1	Frank Johnson	Superior	Northern	Virginia	2-0
6-4	Berlyn Horne	Wellsville	Interstate	Johnsonburg	2-0
6-4	Bill Prough	Oakland	Pacific Coast	San Francisco	1-0 (10)
6-5	Wallace Norris	Charleston	South Atlantic	Macon	3-0
6-5	Joiner	Columbia	South Atlantic	Albany	6-0
6-9	John Woods	Portsmouth	Virginia	Norfolk	2-0
6-16	Tom Hughes	Boston	National	Pittsburgh	2-0
6-16	Rube Foster	Boston	American	New York	2-0
6-20	Charles Harding	San Antonio	Texas	Shreveport	2-0
6-23	Skeeter Fanning	San Francisco	Pacific Coast	Vernon	1-0
6-26	Cy Lambert	Topeka	Western	St. Joseph	4-0
6-28	Wick Winslow	Hagerstown	Blue Ridge	Chambersburg	4-0
7-11	Charlie Boardman	Fargo-Moorhead	Northern	Duluth	0-0
7-11	Tom Rogers	Nashville	Southern Assoc.	Chattanooga	2-0 (P)
7-11	Ben Davenport	Mexia	Central Texas	Terrell	8-0 (7)
7-20	O.A. McArthur	Grand Rapids	Central	South Bend	2-0
7-22	Urban Shocker	Toronto	International	Rochester	1-0 (11)
8-3	Fred Winchell	Evansville	Central	Springfield	1-0
8-7	Socks Seibold	Wheeling	Central	Muskegon	4-0
8-18	C.E. Barmeister	Jacksonville	South Atlantic	Columbia	2-0
8-25	Earl Howard	Hagerstown	Blue Ridge	Gettysburg	4-0
8-26	Joe Bush	Philadelphia	American	Cleveland	5-0
8-26	Jimmy Flowers	Tulsa	Western Assoc.	Muskogee	2-0
8-30	Dutch Leonard	Boston	American	St. Louis	4-0
9-2	Vic Aldridge	Indianapolis	American Assoc.	Columbus	3-0
9-2	Carl Ray	Newport News	Virginia	Norfolk	3-0
9-4	Reid Zellars	Macon	South Atlantic	Columbus	1-0

Number in parentheses indicates innings if other than nine; "P" indicates perfect game.

THIS DATE IN MINOR LEAGUE HISTORY

March 6, 1916, Cleveland, American Association, was transferred back to Toledo with Roger Bresnahan as manager.

May 4, 1916, Shortstop DeFate hit three successive home runs in one game for Virginia in the Northern League.

May 28, 1916, Negro Jimmy Claxton pitched briefly for Oakland in both games of a doubleheader against Los Angeles, then managed by Frank Chance.

June 3, 1916, Oakland released Negro pitcher Jimmy Claxton.

June 4, 1916, H.C. "Bill" Prough, Oakland, Pacific Coast League, pitched no-hit ball against San Francisco for the first ten innings, allowed one hit in the eleventh, then threw three more hitless frames as the Oaks defeated San Francisco 1-0 in an 18-inning game. Prough was later relieved by Besser. Barnes pitched the entire game for the losers.

June 19, 1916, Johnny Dodge, 26, former National League infielder, died after being struck by a pitch in the face while playing for Mobile in the Southern League.

June 19, 1916, Centerfielder Hack Miller of Winnipeg, Northern League, who had a tryout with the Brooklyn Dodgers in 1915, broke the world record for fungo hitting by batting the ball 438-1/2 feet, bettering Ed Walsh's record mark of 419-1/2 feet.

June 23, 1916, Eufaula, Dixie League, defeated Bainbridge 21-11.

June 30, 1916, Richmond, International League, crushed Baltimore 22-3.

July 5, 1916, Los Angeles, Pacific Coast League, scored 12 runs on nine singles, a double and a home run in the first inning against Salt Lake City.

July 10, 1916, Hannibal, Three-I League, defeated Rock Island 8-3 in 22 innings, Smith pitching against Ware.

July 11, 1916, Tom Rogers of Nashville, Southern Association, pitched a perfect game to defeat Chattanooga 2-0. Nashville made only one hit off Lookouts pitcher Allen. Three weeks previously, Rogers had thrown the pitch that struck and killed Mobile's Johnny Dodge.

July 20, 1916, Vancouver, Northwestern League, amassed 31 hits and scored 27 runs in a game with Butte. Outfielders Calvo and Brinker each had six hits in six at bats. Calvo's bag included three doubles and a homer. The next day, Vancouver made 21 more safeties to trim Butte 13-8.

August 7, 1916, Newport News, Virginia League, scored 10 runs in one inning and beat Norfolk 15-1.

August 8, 1916, Harry "Cotton" Knaupp, playing second base for New Orleans, Southern Association, made an unassisted triple play against Chattanooga.

August 13, 1916, Waco defeated Galveston 4-1 in a 20-inning Texas League game.

August 15, 1916, Portland, Eastern League, swamped Bridgeport 20-1.

August 16, 1916, Seattle, Northwestern League, made 25 hits to chalk up a 24-8 victory over Butte.

August 17, 1916, Jimmy Hickman, an outfielder sent by Brooklyn to Asheville, North Carolina State League, made a home run, a double and six singles in nine times at bat and stole four bases in a doubleheader.

August 20, 1916, Butte, Northwestern League, had 24 hits in a 27-12 victory over Seattle.

August 22, 1916, Rocky Mount collected 28 hits in a Virginia League game to whip Norfolk 15-2.

August 26, 1916, Little Rock, Southern Association, made 22 hits to swamp Chattanooga 17-0.

August 29, 1916, Reading, New York State League, walloped Utica 25-3 in a seven-inning game, scoring 11 runs in one frame.

September 4, 1916, Columbus, South Atlantic League, bagged 26 hits in a 14-11 win over Macon in the second game of a doubleheader, after having been held without a safety by Reid Zellars in the opener.

1917

American League
President: Byron Bancroft Johnson

Standings	W	L	Pct.	GB	Attend.	Manager
Chicago White Sox	100	54	.649	—	684,521	Clarence "Pants" Rowland
Boston Red Sox	90	62	.592	9	387,856	Jack Barry
Cleveland Indians	88	66	.571	12	477,298	Lee Fohl
Detroit Tigers	78	75	.510	21½	457,289	Hugh Jennings
Washington Senators	74	79	.484	25½	89,682	Clark Griffith
New York Yankees	71	82	.464	28½	330,294	Wild Bill Donovan
St. Louis Browns	57	97	.370	43	210,486	Fielder Jones
Philadelphia Athletics	55	98	.359	44½	221,432	Connie Mack

BA: Ty Cobb, Detroit, .383
Runs: Donie Bush, Detroit, 112
Hits: Ty Cobb, Detroit, 225
RBIs: Bobby Veach, Detroit, 103
HRs: Wally Pipp, New York, 9
Wins: Eddie Cicotte, Chicago, 28
SOs: Walter Johnson, Washington, 188
ERA: Eddie Cicotte, Chicago, 1.53
Pct: Reb Russell, Chicago, .750, 15-5

National League
President: John K. Tener

Standings	W	L	Pct.	GB	Attend.	Manager
New York Giants	98	56	.636	—	500,264	John McGraw
Philadelphia Phillies	87	65	.572	10	354,428	Pat Moran
St. Louis Cardinals	82	70	.539	15	288,491	Miller Huggins
Cincinnati Reds	78	76	.506	20	269,056	Christy Mathewson
Chicago Cubs	74	80	.481	24	360,218	Fred Mitchell
Boston Braves	72	81	.471	25½	174,253	George Stallings
Brooklyn Robins	70	81	.464	26½	221,619	Wilbert Robinson
Pittsburgh Pirates	51	103	.331	47	192,807	Nixey Callahan/Honus Wagner/ Hugo Bezdek

BA: Edd Roush, Cincinnati, .341
Runs: George Burns, New York, 103
Hits: Heinie Groh, Cincinnati, 182
RBIs: Heinie Zimmerman, New York, 102
HRs: Dave Robertson, New York, 12
Gavvy Cravath, Philadelphia, 12
Wins: Grover Alexander, Philadelphia, 30
SOs: Grover Alexander, Philadelphia, 201
ERA: Grover Alexander, Philadelphia, 1.86
Pct: Ferdie Schupp, New York, .750, 21-7
IP: Grover Alexander, Philadelphia, 388

AA American Association
President: Thomas J. Hickey

Standings	W	L	Pct.	GB	Attend.	Manager
Indianapolis Indians	90	63	.588	—	96,099	Jack Hendricks
Louisville Colonels	88	66	.571	2½	111,242	Bill Clymer
St. Paul Saints	88	66	.571	2½	99,254	Mike Kelley
Columbus Senators	84	69	.549	8	104,947	Joe Tinker
Milwaukee Brewers	71	81	.467	18½	84,035	Danny Shay/William Friel/ Paddy Livingston
Minneapolis Millers	68	86	.442	22½	88,138	Joe Cantillon
Kansas City Blues	66	86	.434	23½	85,106	John Ganzel
Toledo Iron Men	57	95	.375	32½	93,921	Roger Bresnahan

BA: Beals Becker, Kansas City, .323
Runs: Lee Dressen, St. Paul, 118
Hits: Beals Becker, Kansas City, 178
HRs: Beals Becker, Kansas City, 15
Wins: Frank Davis, Louisville, 25
Grover Lowdermilk, Columbus, 25
SOs: Grover Lowdermilk, Columbus, 250
ERA: Grover Lowdermilk, Columbus, 1.70

AA International League
President: Edward G. Barrow

Standings	W	L	Pct.	GB	Manager
Toronto Maple Leafs	93	61	.604	—	Napoleon Lajoie
Providence Grays	90	61	.596	1½	Jack Egan
Baltimore Orioles	88	61	.591	2½	Jack Dunn
Newark Bears	86	68	.558	7	Thomas Needham
Rochester Hustlers	72	82	.468	21	Mike Doolan
Buffalo Bisons	67	84	.444	24½	Patsy Donovan
Montreal Royals	56	94	.373	35	Dan Howley
Richmond Virginians	53	94	.361	36½	William A. Smith/Otto Knabe

Attendance: Buffalo, 116,000.

BA: Napoleon Lajoie, Toronto, .380
Runs: Baldomero Acosta, Baltimore, 119
Hits: Napoleon Lajoie, Toronto, 221
HRs: Harry Damrau, Montreal, 16
2B: Napoleon Lajoie, Toronto, 39
Wins: Harry Thompson, Toronto, 25
SOs: Vean Gregg, Providence, 249
ERA: Vean Gregg, Providence, 1.72

AA Pacific Coast League
President: Allan T. Baum

Standings	W	L	Pct.	GB	Manager
San Francisco Seals	119	93	.561	—	Harry Wolverton/Jerry Downs
Los Angeles Angels	116	94	.552	2	Frank Chance/Red Killefer
Salt Lake City Bees	102	97	.490	10½	Bill Bernard
Portland Beavers	98	102	.490	15	Walter McCredie
Oakland Oaks	103	108	.488	15½	Del Howard
Vernon Tigers	84	128	.396	35	George Stovall

BA: Morrie Rath, Salt Lake City, .341
Runs: John Tobin, Salt Lake City, 149
Hits: John Tobin, Salt Lake City, 265
HRs: Ken Williams, Portland, 24
Wins: Eric Erickson, San Francisco, 31
SOs: Eric Erickson, San Francisco, 307
ERA: Eric Erickson, San Francisco, 1.93

A Southern Association
President: Robert H. Baugh

Standings	W	L	Pct.	GB	Attend.	Manager
Atlanta Crackers	98	56	.637	—	154,596	Charley Frank
New Orleans Pelicans	89	61	.593	7	120,064	Johnny Dobbs
Birmingham Barons	87	66	.569	10½	115,090	Carleton Molesworth
Memphis Chickasaws	81	73	.527	17	152,752	Mike Donlin/Cy Barger
Nashville Volunteers	77	73	.513	19	79,018	Roy Ellam
Chattanooga Lookouts	76	74	.507	20	74,275	Norman "Kid" Elberfeld
Little Rock Travelers	64	86	.427	32	66,274	Charles Starr/Clyde "Buzzy" Wares
Mobile Sea Gulls	34	117	.226	62½	27,121	Matty McIntyre/ Frank "Pop" Kitchens

BA: Ham Hyatt, Chattanooga, .334
Runs: William "Tex" Covington, Little Rock, 90
Hits: Roy Moran, Atlanta, 177
HRs: Fred Bratchie, Mobile, 14
Wins: Carmen Hill, Birmingham, 26
SOs: Roy Walker, New Orleans, 231
ERA: Roy Walker, New Orleans, 1.64

A Western League
Presidents: F.C. Zehrung/Emerson W. Dickerson

Standings	W	L	Pct.	GB	Manager
Des Moines Boosters*	84	62	.575	—	Jack Coffey
Lincoln Links	83	64	.565	1½	James "Ducky" Holmes
Sioux City Indians/ St. Joseph Drummers@	80	66	.548	4	Ed Holly
Joplin Miners	79	68	.537	5½	Jack Dalton/Yank Davis/John Savage
Omaha Rourkes	73	75	.493	12	Marty Krug/Pa Rourke
St. Joseph Drummers/ Hutchinson Wheatshockers#**	66	80	.452	18	Jack Holland/Wid Conroy/ Charles "Babe" Adams
Denver Bears	62	86	.419	23	Rebel Oakes/Roy Hartzell
Wichita Witches	61	87	.412	24	Frank Isbell/Bobby Wallace/Joe Berger

#St. Joseph (34-56) moved to Hutchinson July 24 for the second half.
@Sioux City moved to St. Joseph August 5.

Playoff: Hutchinson 3 games, Joplin 0, for the second half title.
Finals: Des Moines 4 games, Hutchinson 2.

BA: Hank Butcher, Denver, .321
Runs: Frank Gilmore, St. Joseph, 116
Hits: Hank Butcher, Denver, 183
HRs: Hank Butcher, Denver, 13
Wins: Otto Merz, Omaha, 26
SOs: Paul Musser, Des Moines, 337
Pct: Howard Gregory, Lincoln, .742, 23-8

B Central League
Presidents: Emerson W. Dickerson/Harry W. Stahlhefer

Standings	W	L	Pct.	GB	Manager
Grand Rapids Black Sox	80	44	.645	—	William Essick
Springfield Reapers	74	50	.597	6	Jack Dunn
South Bend Benders/ Peoria Distillers#	66	55	.545	12½	Harry Smith/William Jackson
Muskegon Muskies	65	57	.533	14	James Hamilton
Evansville Evas	56	61	.479	20½	Charles "Punch" Knoll
Richmond Quakers	46	70	.397	30	Bade Myers/Joe Evers/Larry Gilbert
Dayton Veterans	44	68	.393	30	John Nee
Fort Wayne Chiefs	47	73	.392	31	Carl Vandergrift

#South Bend (26-35) moved to Peoria July 8.

Playoff: Grand Rapids 4 games, Peoria 3.

*Won first-half   **Won second-half   ***Won both halves

BA: Frank Walker, Springfield, .370
Runs: Frank Walker, Springfield, 94
Hits: Frank Walker, Springfield, 161
HRs: Frank Walker, Springfield, 10

Wins: Paul Carpenter, Grand Rapids, 23
SOs: Paul Wachtel, Muskegon, 176
Pct: Guy Hoffman, Peoria, .786, 11-3

B Eastern League
President: Daniel O'Neill

Standings	W	L	Pct.	GB	Manager
New Haven Murlins	66	35	.653	—	Danny Murphy
Lawrence Barristers	64	45	.587	6	John Flynn
New London Planters	53	52	.505	15	Eugene McCann
Bridgeport Americans	50	52	.490	16½	Paul Krichell
Worcester Busters	51	55	.481	17½	John McMahon
Portland Paramounts	51	58	.468	19	Mike Garrity
Springfield Green Sox	48	57	.457	20	William Carey/John O'Hara
Hartford Senators	37	66	.359	30	Louis Piper

BA: Rip Conway, Worcester, .309
Runs: Patrick Maloney, Worcester, 81
Hits: Hank Schreiber, Lawrence, 133
HRs: John Flynn, Lawrence, 9

Wins: Rollie Naylor, New Haven, 18
SOs: Robert Spaid, Portland, 168
Pct: James Weaver, New Haven, .824, 14-3

B New York State League
President: John H. Farrell

Standings	W	L	Pct.	GB	Manager
Wilkes-Barre Barons***	81	37	.686	—	John Calhoun
Binghamton Bingoes	71	44	.617	8½	Chick Hartman
Syracuse Stars	64	51	.557	15½	Mike O'Neill
Elmira Colonels	62	54	.534	18	James Jackson
Reading Pretzels	51	70	.421	31½	George "Hooks" Wiltse
Scranton Miners	38	84	.311	45	William Coughlin/Jack Connors
Utica Utes#	27	24	.529	NA	Ambrose McConnell
Harrisburg Islanders#	11	41	.212	NA	George Cockill

#Harrisburg and Utica disbanded after games of July 4.

BA: Harry Weiser, Wilkes-Barre, .375
Runs: Wheat Orcutt, Wilkes-Barre, 83
Hits: Hoke Warner, Wilkes-Barre, 144

Wins: John Verbout, Wilkes-Barre, 26
SOs: Oscar Tuero, Wilkes-Barre, 156
Pct: John Verbout, Wilkes-Barre, .788, 26-7

B Northwestern League
President: R.L. Blewett

Standings	W	L	Pct.	GB	Manager
Great Falls Electrics	42	29	.592	—	Herb Hester
Seattle Giants	46	34	.575	½	Bill Leard/Rube Gardner
Tacoma Tigers	38	35	.521	5	Frank Raymond
Spokane Indians	36	41	.468	9	R.L. "Nick" Williams
Butte Miners	31	38	.449	10	Joe McGinnity/Cliff McCarl
Vancouver Beavers	33	49	.402	14½	Robert Brown

The season was shortened to July 15 with National Association approval, but the league did not disband.

BA: Harry Harper, Tacoma, .382
Runs: C. Jackson, Spokane, 74
Hits: Harry Harper, Tacoma, 113
HRs: Dave Hillyard, Butte, 12

Wins: Herman Pillette, Tacoma, 13
James Clark, Great Falls, 13
SOs: Harry Gardner, Great Falls/Tacoma, 108
Pct: Pat Eastley, Seattle, .750, 9-3

B Texas League
President: Walter Morris

Standings	W	L	Pct.	GB	Manager
Dallas Giants	96	64	.600	—	Hamilton Patterson
Ft. Worth Panthers	90	71	.559	6½	Jake Atz
Waco Navigators	84	73	.535	10½	Ellis Hardy
Houston Buffaloes	77	87	.470	21	Pat Newnam
San Antonio Bronchos	75	89	.457	23	Charley O'Leary/Clay Perry
Shreveport Gassers	73	89	.451	24	Syd Smith
Beaumont Oilers#	19	23	.452	NA	Clay Perry
Galveston Pirates#	11	29	.275	NA	Paul Sentell

#Beaumont and Galveston disbanded May 18.

BA: Ralph Sharman, Ft. Worth, .341
Runs: John Baggan, San Antonio, 102
Hits: Ralph Sharman, Ft. Worth, 203
HRs: Roy Leslie, San Antonio, 18

Wins: John "Snipe" Conley, Dallas, 27
SOs: John "Snipe" Conley, Dallas, 171
ERA: Paul Jones, Shreveport, 1.83

B Three-I League
President: Albert R. Tearney

Standings	W	L	Pct.	GB	Manager
Peoria Distillers	43	23	.652	—	William Jackson
Rockford Rox	39	21	.650	1	Frank Reynolds
Hannibal Mules	39	27	.591	4	John Castle
Rock Island Islanders	36	26	.581	5	Jack Tighe
Quincy Gems	27	38	.415	15½	Ted Waring

	W	L	Pct.	GB	Manager
Moline Plowboys	27	38	.415	15½	Ned Pettigrew/Bob Tarleton
Bloomington Bloomers	25	37	.403	16	Howard Darringer
Alton Blues	18	44	.290	23	Harry Bay/Elmer Duggan

The season was shortened to July 8 with National Association approval, but the league did not disband.

BA: Bert Graham, Quincy, .386
Runs: Del Bemis, Rockford, 55
Hits: Del Bemis, Rockford, 87
HRs: Norman Glockson, Rockford, 8

Wins: Pat Griffin, Rockford, 15
SOs: Ollie Reeb, Rock Island, 75
ERA: Ollie Reeb, Rock Island, 1.25

C South Atlantic League
President: Nick P. Corish

Standings	W	L	Pct.	GB	Manager
Charleston Sea Gulls*	47	20	.701	—	Robert Crowell
Columbia Comers**	40	28	.588	7½	John Corbett
Jacksonville Roses	33	35	.485	14½	Lee Tannehill
Augusta Tourists	27	41	.397	20½	Carl Eubanks
Columbus Foxes#	8	19	.296	NA	Hardin Herndon
Macon Tigers#	7	19	.269	NA	George Stinson

#Columbus and Macon withdrew May 19.
The season was shortened to July 4 with National Association approval.

Playoff: Columbia 3 games, Charleston 0, for the second half title.
Finals: Columbia 4 games, Charleston 2.

BA: Howard Camp, Charleston, .357
Runs: Guy Dunning, Columbia, 63
Hits: Howard Camp, Charleston, 105

Wins: John Meador, Charleston, 13
SOs: Berlyn Horne, Jacksonville, 93
Pct: John Meador, Charleston, .867, 13-2

C Virginia League
President: William B. Bradley

Standings	W	L	Pct.	GB	Manager
Newport News Shipbuilders	10	5	.667	—	Fred Payne
Portsmouth Truckers	9	7	.563	1½	James Foxx
Lynchburg Shoemakers	7	7	.500	2½	Joe Stanley
Norfolk Tars	7	9	.438	3½	Art Devlin
Petersburg Goobers	6	8	.429	3½	Hamilton Reynolds
Rocky Mount Tar Heels	6	9	.400	4	Ray Ryan

The league disbanded May 15.

BA: Harry Hartsell, Norfolk, .378
Runs: Dick Moore, Portsmouth, 15
Hits: R.H. Holmes, Norfolk, 21
HRs: Brook Crist, Newport News, 3

Wins: F. Jarman, Rocky Mount, 4
Louis Magalis, Norfolk, 4
Carl Ray, Newport News, 4
SOs: Carl Ray, Newport News, 57
Pct: Carl Ray, Newport News, 1.000, 4-0

D Blue Ridge League
President: J. Vincent Jamison, Jr.

Standings	W	L	Pct.	GB	Manager
Hagerstown Terriers	61	36	.629	—	Jack Hurley/Charles Dysert
Martinsburg Blue Sox	59	40	.596	3	W.J. "Country" Morris
Gettysburg Ponies	48	46	.511	11½	Joe Ward/John Mumsford
Hanover Raiders	44	52	.458	16½	Rabbit Agnew/Monte Cross/Earle Mack/Buck Elliott
Frederick Hustlers	44	55	.444	18	Tom Crooks
Chambersburg Maroons/ Cumberland Colts#	36	63	.364	26	Eddie Hooper/Brook Crist

#Chambersburg (16-25) moved to Cumberland June 30.

BA: Jack Hurley, Hagerstown, .385
Runs: Lee Percy, Martinsburg, 84
Charles Dysert, Hagerstown, 84
Hits: Jack Hurley, Hagerstown, 125

HRs: John Bates, Martinsburg, 15
Wins: Earl Howard, Hagerstown, 25
SOs: Earl Howard, Hagerstown, 163
Pct: Earl Howard, Hagerstown, .714, 25-10

D Central Association
President: John F. Ford

Standings	W	L	Pct.	GB	Manager
Marshalltown Ansons	64	34	.653	—	Frank Boyle
Mason City Claydiggers	54	38	.587	7	Dan O'Leary
Waterloo Loons	50	42	.543	11	Ned Egan
Cedar Rapids/ Clear Lake Rabbits+	39	52	.429	21½	W. Collins/Jay Andrews/Harry Shanley
Dubuque Dubs/ Charles City Tractorites#	40	54	.426	22	George Hughes
Ft. Dodge Dodgers	37	57	.394	25	Charles Stis
Clinton Pilots@	40	33	.548	NA	Larry Brown
La Crosse Infants@	29	43	.403	NA	Mike Malloy/Jay Andrews

#Dubuque (23-40) moved to Charles City July 4.
@La Crosse and Clinton disbanded July 17.
+Cedar Rapids (38-48) moved to Clear Lake July 27.
The season was shortened to August 7 with National Association permission.

BA: Bing Miller, Clinton, .337
Runs: Joe Wilkes, Clinton/Charles City, 69
Hits: Bing Miller, Clinton, 106
HRs: John Mokan, Ft. Dodge, 9

Wins: Red Torkelson, Marshalltown, 20
ERA: Frank Ulch, La Crosse/
    Cedar Rapids, 1.25

D Central Texas League
President: Earl C. Smith

Standings	W	L	Pct.	GB	Manager
Mexia Gassers	8	6	.571	—	Roy Akin
Ennis Tigers	8	7	.533	½	Ed Wicker
Marlin Marlins	7	8	.467	1½	H. Sinclair/Roy Wakefield
Temple Governors/					
Corsicana Athletics#	6	8	.429	2	Charles Roberts

#Temple (4-4) moved to Corsicana June 1.
The league opened May 21 and closed June 6.

Wins: A.V. Freeman, Ennis, 3
    Carl Hill, Mexia, 3
    F.D. Poteet, Mexia, 3

Pct: Carl Hill, Mexia, .750, 3-1
IP: A.V. Freeman, Ennis, 57

D Dixie League
President: T.A. Ward

Standings	W	L	Pct.	GB	Manager
Moultrie Packers	36	20	.643	—	Bobby Schuyler
Eufaula	31	23	.574	4	John Robinson
Bainbridge	32	25	.561	4½	William Foxworthy/Ed Foster
Dothan	25	30	.455	10½	Jack Reidy/Frank Manush
Quitman	25	32	.439	11½	Jack Donaldson
Tifton Tifters	18	37	.327	17½	E.H. "Doc" Newton

The league disbanded July 4.

BA: Lance Richbourg, Dothan, .345
Runs: L.C. Brinson, Eufaula, 46

Hits: Lance Richbourg, Dothan, 78

D Georgia-Alabama League
Presidents: Dick Jemison/Dred Johnson

Standings	W	L	Pct.	GB	Manager
Anniston Moulders	13	5	.722	—	Bill Pierre
Griffin Griffs	10	7	.588	2½	Matty Matthews
Tri-Cities Triplets#	10	8	.556	3	Martin Dudley
Rome-Lindale Romans	9	9	.500	4	Dannie Overton
Talladega Tigers	6	12	.333	7	Ed Goosetree
La Grange Grangers	5	12	.294	7½	Isom "Heisman" Jones

#represented Gadsden-Alabama City-Attalla, Alabama.
The league disbanded May 23.

BA: W.W. Waldron, Griffin, .388
Runs: W.W. Waldron, Griffin, 21
Hits: W.W. Waldron, Griffin, 26
HRs: four tied with 2

Wins: E.A. Verrett, Talladega, 4
SOs: Conrad Fields, La Grange, 39
Pct: Bennett, Tri-Cities, 1.000, 3-0

D North Carolina State League
President: William G. Bramham

Standings	W	L	Pct.	GB	Attend.	Manager
Durham Bulls	24	12	.667	—	8,019	Frank Manush
Charlotte Hornets	20	16	.556	4	9,850	Earle Mack
Greensboro Patriots	20	17	.541	4½	13,050	Billy Laval
Winston-Salem Twins	17	20	.459	7½	10,633	Charles Clancy
Asheville Tourists#	12	16	.429	NA	6,900	Ernest "Doc" Ferris
Raleigh Capitals#	8	20	.286	NA	8,200	Lee Gooch

#Raleigh and Asheville disbanded May 18.
The league ceased operations May 30.

BA: Harry Chancey, Winston-Salem, .366
Runs: Warren Butts, Durham, 36
Hits: Warren Butts, Durham, 48
    Harry Chancey, Winston-Salem, 48

HRs: Ray Grimes, Durham, 6
Wins: N.L. Elliott, Durham, 10
SOs: G.M. McWorter, Greensboro, 54
Pct: N.L. Elliott, Durham, .909, 10-1

D Northern League
President: George A. Barton

Standings	W	L	Pct.	GB	Manager
Fargo-Moorhead Graingrowers	36	16	.692	—	Denny Sullivan
Winnipeg Maroons	24	26	.480	11	Charles Burden
Minot Why Nots	19	23	.452	12	George Brautigan
Warren Wanderers	16	30	.348	17	Frank Withrow

The league disbanded July 4.

D Western Association
President: J.W. Bell

Standings	W	L	Pct.	GB	Manager
McAlester Miners	95	57	.625	—	Jimmy Humphries
Muskogee Reds	89	69	.563	9	Henry "Buzz" Wetzel/Ernie Calbert
Sherman Browns	80	72	.526	15	Leo Hellman
Denison Railroaders	79	75	.513	17	Babe Peebles
Ft. Smith Twins	77	82	.484	21½	Hyder "Scotty" Barr
Oklahoma City Boosters	72	80	.474	23	Jimmy Murray
Tulsa Producers	68	84	.447	27	Lige Wooley/Ray Cahill/
					Harley "Cy III" Young
Paris Athletics/					
Ardmore Foundlings#	57	98	.368	39½	Dick Speer/Richard Crittenden

#Paris (16-12) moved to Ardmore May 10.
Attendance: Tulsa, 45,600.

BA: Emmet Mulvey, McAlester, .320
Runs: Ernie Calbert, Muskogee, 101
Hits: Ernie Calbert, Muskogee, 177
RBIs: Ernie Calbert, Muskogee, 109
HRs: Ernie Calbert, Muskogee, 43

Wins: Charlie Robertson, Sherman, 26
    John Watson, Ft. Smith, 26
SOs: Walt Kinney, Denison, 260
Pct: Charlie Robertson, Sherman, .813, 26-6

1917 Interleague Post Season Play

World Series
Chicago (American) 4 games, New York (National) 2

Junior World Series
Indianapolis (American Association) 4 games, Toronto (International) 1

1917 No-Hitters

Date	Pitcher	Team	League	Opponent	Score
4-14	Eddie Cicotte	Chicago	American	St. Louis	11-0
4-15	Chief Johnson	Vernon	Pacific Coast	Portland	6-0
4-19	Jimmy Zinn	Waco	Texas	Ft. Worth	4-0
4-24	George Mogridge	New York	American	Boston	2-1
4-25	Joseph Thornton	Durham	N. Carolina State	Winston-Salem	4-0
5-2	Fred Toney	Cincinnati	National	Chicago	1-0 (10)
5-2	Hippo Vaughn	Chicago	National	Cincinnati	0-1 (10)
5-5	Ernie Koob	St. Louis	American	Chicago	1-0
5-6	Bob Groom	St. Louis	American	Chicago	3-0
5-8	Harvey Sutherland	Tacoma	Northwestern	Great Falls	3-0
5-12	Harvey Couchman	Galveston	Texas	Ft. Worth	1-0
5-13	Paul Strand	Seattle	Northwestern	Spokane	1-0 (P)
5-13	Kernagher	Evansville	Central	South Bend	1-0
5-19	Ray Boyd	Bloomington	Three-I	Peoria	2-0
5-26	Frank Graham	St. Joseph	Western	Wichita	4-0
6-15	Ralph Comstock	Birmingham	Southern Assoc.	Nashville	1-0
6-18	Ben Tincup	Little Rock	Southern Assoc.	Birmingham	3-0 (P)
6-23	Ernie Shore	Boston	American	Washington	3-0 (P)
6-24	John "Snipe" Conley	Dallas	Texas	Ft. Worth	4-0
6-24	Pat Eastley	Seattle	Northwestern	Great Falls	6-0
7-3	John Fitzpatrick	Mason City	Central Assoc.	La Crosse	4-0
7-4	Brown	Harrisburg	New York State	Reading	5-0
7-8	Tink Turner	Ft. Dodge	Central Assoc.	Charles City	0-1
7-22	John Nabors	Denver	Western	Sioux City	1-0
7-27	Roy Johnson	McAlester	Western Assoc.	Ft. Smith	3-0
7-30	Carmen Hill	Birmingham	Southern Assoc.	Little Rock	12-0
8-11	Hugh McQuillan	Worcester	Eastern	New Haven	1-0
8-20	Pat Martin	New London	Eastern	Springfield	2-0
8-24	Jesse Winters	Denison	Western Assoc.	Ardmore	7-0
8-26	Paul Wachtel	Muskegon	Central	Richmond	2-0
	Roy Johnson	McAlester	Western Assoc.		

Number in parentheses indicates innings if other than nine; "P" indicates perfect game.

THIS DATE IN MINOR LEAGUE HISTORY

April 16, 1917, At Los Angeles, five people were shot, wounding two of them seriously, scores of lives were endangered, and several hundred women and children were trampled in the panic when two men, armed with revolvers, fought a running battle in the grandstand at the Vernon, Pacific Coast League, ball park during a game between two semi-pro teams, one a Negro club.

April 22, 1917, Outfielder Ernie Calbert of Muskogee, Western Association, smashed three homers plus a single in a game with Tulsa.

April 23, 1917, Columbia, South Atlantic League, outslugged Charleston 21-11.

May 3, 1917, Dan Shay, manager of Milwaukee, American Association, shot and fatally wounded Clarence Euell, a black waiter, in an Indianapolis hotel during an argument over a sugar bowl. Shay, pleading self-defense, was tried and acquitted on November 22.

May 4, 1917, Beaumont, Texas League, scored 12 runs in the first inning and beat Shreveport 18-1.

May 12, 1917, Veteran Joe McGinnity of Butte, Northwestern League, pitched a doubleheader against Vancouver and won both games.

May 16, 1917, South Bend, Central League, scored 12 runs in the seventh inning to defeat Dayton 13-1.

June 1, 1917, In the New York State League, 19 runs were scored in the first inning of the Binghamton-Utica game. Utica tallied 10 times in top of the frame and Binghamton came back with nine. The contest was called at the beginning of the fourth inning because of darkness.

June 3, 1917, Ken Williams of Portland, Pacific Coast League, hit three homers in a 14-inning game with Vernon. Williams' third four-bagger, in the final inning, gave his team a 4-3 victory.

June 7, 1917, Tacoma, Northwestern League, made 31 hits and crushed Butte 31-12. Tacoma catcher Stower bagged seven hits in eight at bats.

June 9, 1917, Pitcher Joe McGinnity sold his interest in the Butte, Northwestern League club.

June 18, 1917, Ben Tincup, an Indian, pitched a 3-0 perfect game for Little Rock against Birmingham in the Southern Association. The catcher for Tincup was Raymond Lincoln Kennedy, later to become a business executive for the Pittsburgh Pirates. Billy Southworth, later a major league manager, played in the game for the Barons.

June 21, 1917, With the bases full, Ray McKee of San Francisco, Pacific Coast League, stole third and got away with it. The umpire called a balk on Salt Lake City's pitcher, Tom Hughes.

June 24, 1917, The consecutive game playing streak of the Louisville, American Association, infield was terminated at 232 consecutive tilts when third baseman John Corridon was absent from the Colonels lineup. The four players, Corridon, first baseman Jay Kirke, second baseman Joe McCarthy, and shortstop Wilbur "Roxy" Roach, had played as a unit for 167 games in 1916 and 65 this season.

July 3, 1917, Frank Chance resigned as manager of the Los Angeles, Pacific Coast League club.

July 6, 1917, Phil Cooney, playing second base for Omaha, made an unassisted triple play in a Western League game against Denver.

July 8, 1917, John "Snipe" Conley, Dallas, Texas League, won his 19th successive game, defeating Waco 5-4 in ten innings. His 17th win was a no-hitter.

July 8, 1917, Kansas City set a new American Association record by winning its 15th straight game in the first game of a doubleheader with St. Paul. The Saints won the second game to end the streak.

July 8, 1917, Minneapolis, American Association, scored in every inning and defeated Milwaukee 15-2.

July 11, 1917, John "Snipe" Conley, Dallas, Texas League, lost 8-3 to Waco, ending his winning streak at 19 straight games.

August 6, 1917, Chattanooga, Southern Association, suffered its fourth successive shutout.

August 6, 1917, Babe Adams, ex-Pittsburgh hurler, pitched a 17-inning game for Hutchinson in the Western League, defeating Des Moines 2-1. Adams gave up six hits and struck out 12.

August 7, 1917, Outfielder Thrasher, Atlanta, Southern Association, went 4-for-4 in each game of a doubleheader with Nashville.

August 11, 1917, Hugh McQuillan, Worcester, Eastern League, hurled a 1-0 no-hitter against New Haven. His run-scoring triple won the contest.

August 12, 1917, Lincoln, Western League, defeated Joplin 2-1 in 21 innings.

August 16, 1917, After playing 57 consecutive errorless innings, Lincoln, Western League, committed a miscue in a game with Hutchinson.

August 20, 1917, McAlester, Western Association, shut out Ardmore 2-0 in a nine-inning game that required only 36 minutes to play.

August 23, 1917, Los Angeles, Pacific Coast League, made 28 assists in a nine-inning game versus Salt Lake City.

August 24, 1917, Eleven members of the Dayton, Central League, club were injured when a fast freight train of the Big Four Railroad crashed into a passenger train at Mansfield, Illinois. The team was en route from Peoria to Fort Wayne. One player, rightfielder Ray Spencer, later died from the effects of his injuries.

August 25, 1917, Jim "Rube" Parnham, a strapping righthander sent by Connie Mack to Jack Dunn's Baltimore club for seasoning, pitched both games of a doubleheader, a total of 24 innings, and won each game by a 3-2 score. The first contest went 15 frames. The Pennsylvania youngster gave up six blows in the opener and seven in the second.

August 28, 1917, Scranton, New York State League, ended its 22-game losing streak by defeating Reading 11-5.

August 28, 1917, Louisville, American Association, made nine errors in losing to Milwaukee 9-6.

September 1, 1917, Elmira, New York State League, scored in every inning but one to wallop Scranton 20-2.

September 2, 1917, In an International League thriller, Newark defeated Providence 1-0 in 18 innings. Vean Gregg fanned 20 men, but lost his own game by making a wild throw on an attempted sacrifice. During the first 13 innings, Newark pitcher John Enzmann allowed but two safeties and hurled eleven consecutive hitless frames.

September 3, 1917, Manager and leftfielder Ernie Calbert of Muskogee, Western Association, smashed two home runs on the final day of the season to give him a total of 43 for the year, two shy of Perry Werden's single season record of 45.

September 3, 1917, Mobile, Southern Association, broke its 20-game losing streak by beating Atlanta in ten innings in the first game of a doubleheader.

September 3, 1917, Wilkes-Barre, New York State League, defeated Scranton three times, 6-1 in the morning and twice in the afternoon, 16-5 and 7-1. The last tilt was an exhibition game.

September 4, 1917, Ray Bressler of Atlanta, Southern Association, won his 24th game of the season, needing only 72 pitches.

September 10, 1917, Toronto, International League, defeated Montreal 19-16 in a 12-inning game. A total of eight home runs were hit, each team getting three in the first frame. Frigid weather hindered the pitchers.

September 13, 1917, In the Southern Association, Mobile and Atlanta, which in 1910 set the record for the shortest nine-inning game in Organized Ball, put on another fast game when they went the distance in 52 minutes.

September 16, 1917, The International League season closed with Toronto, managed by Napoleon Lajoie, the pennant winner by eight percentage points over Providence. The immortal Lajoie, now 42, played in 151 games and hit .380, leading the league in batting. It was the first time in his 22 seasons of pro baseball that Lajoie played on a pennant-winning club.

September 19, 1917, Kansas City, American Association, stranded 19 baserunners in a game with Louisville.

December 12, 1917, Edward Barrow resigned as president of the International League when club owners voted to cut his salary from $7,500 to $2,500.

1918

American League
President: Byron Bancroft Johnson

Standings	W	L	Pct.	GB	Attend.	Manager
Boston Red Sox	75	51	.595	—	249,513	Edward Barrow
Cleveland Indians	73	54	.575	2½	295,515	Lee Fohl
Washington Senators	72	56	.563	4	182,122	Clark Griffith
New York Yankees	60	63	.488	13½	282,047	Miller Huggins
St. Louis Browns	58	64	.475	15	122,076	Fielder Jones/Jimmy Austin/ Jimmy Burke
Chicago White Sox	57	67	.460	17	195,081	Clarence "Pants" Rowland
Detroit Tigers	55	71	.437	20	203,719	Hugh Jennings
Philadelphia Athletics	52	76	.406	24	177,926	Connie Mack

BA: Ty Cobb, Detroit, .382
Runs: Ray Chapman, Cleveland, 84
Hits: George Burns, Philadelphia, 178
RBIs: Bobby Veach, Detroit, 78

HRs: Tilly Walker, Philadelphia, 11
    Babe Ruth, Boston, 11
Wins: Walter Johnson, Washington, 23
SOs: Walter Johnson, Washington, 162
ERA: Walter Johnson, Washington, 1.27
Pct: Sad Sam Jones, Boston, .762, 16-5

National League
President: John K. Tener

Standings	W	L	Pct.	GB	Attend.	Manager
Chicago Cubs	84	45	.651	—	337,256	Fred Mitchell
New York Giants	71	53	.573	10½	256,618	John McGraw
Cincinnati Reds	68	60	.531	15½	163,009	Christy Mathewson/Heinie Groh
Pittsburgh Pirates	65	60	.520	17	213,610	Hugo Bezdek
Brooklyn Robins	57	69	.452	25½	83,831	Wilbert Robinson
Philadelphia Phillies	55	68	.447	26	122,266	Pat Moran
Boston Braves	53	71	.427	28½	84,938	George Stallings
St. Louis Cardinals	51	78	.395	33	110,599	Jack Hendricks

BA: Zack Wheat, Brooklyn, .335
Runs: Heinie Groh, Cincinnati, 88
Hits: Charlie Hollocher, Chicago, 161
RBIs: Sherry Magee, Cincinnati, 76
HRs: Gavvy Cravath, Philadelphia, 8

Wins: Hippo Vaughn, Chicago, 22
SOs: Hippo Vaughn, Chicago, 148
ERA: Hippo Vaughn, Chicago, 1.74
Pct: Claude Hendrix, Chicago, .731, 19-7

AA American Association
President: Thomas J. Hickey

Standings	W	L	Pct.	GB	Manager
Kansas City Blues	43	30	.589	—	John Ganzel
Columbus Senators	41	32	.562	2	Joe Tinker
Indianapolis Indians	41	34	.547	3	Napoleon Lajoie
Louisville Colonels	41	36	.532	4	Bill Clymer
Milwaukee Brewers	38	34	.528	4½	Jack Egan
St. Paul Saints	39	38	.506	6	Mike Kelley
Minneapolis Millers	34	42	.447	10½	Joe Cantillon
Toledo Iron Men	23	54	.299	22	Roger Bresnahan

The league suspended operations July 21.

BA: Doc Johnston, Milwaukee, .374
Runs: Bob Bescher, Louisville, 48
    Joe Riggert, St. Paul, 48
Hits: Joe Riggert, St. Paul, 101
HRs: Joe Riggert, St. Paul, 6

Wins: Dickie Kerr, Milwaukee, 17
SOs: Dickie Kerr, Milwaukee, 99
ERA: George Merritt, St. Paul, 1.50
    Gene Dale, Indianapolis, 1.50

AA International League
President: John H. Farrell

Standings	W	L	Pct.	GB	Manager
Toronto Maple Leafs	88	39	.693	—	Dan Howley
Binghamton Bingoes	85	38	.691	1	Chick Hartman
Baltimore Orioles	74	53	.583	14	Jack Dunn
Newark Bears	64	63	.504	24	Tom McCarthy
Rochester Hustlers	60	61	.496	25	Arthur Irwin
Buffalo Bisons	53	68	.438	32	George Wilson
Syracuse Stars/ Hamilton Tigers#	38	76	.333	43½	Patsy Donovan
Jersey City Skeeters	30	94	.242	56½	Harry Lord/Dave Driscoll

#Syracuse (28-56) moved to Hamilton August 6.

BA: Polly McLarry, Binghamton, .385
Runs: Emmet Mulvey, Baltimore, 81
Hits: Otis Lawrey, Baltimore, 149
    Emmet Mulvey, Baltimore, 149

HRs: Fred Lear, Toronto, 5
Wins: Ralph Worrell, Baltimore, 25
SOs: Godfrey Brogan, Rochester, 157
ERA: Harry Heitman, Rochester, 1.32

AA Pacific Coast League
President: Allan T. Baum

Standings	W	L	Pct.	GB	Manager
Vernon Tigers	58	44	.569	—	Bill Essick
Los Angeles Angels	57	47	.548	2	Red Killefer
San Francisco Seals	51	51	.500	7	Charles Graham/Jerry Downs
Sacramento Senators	48	48	.500	7	Bill Rodgers
Salt Lake City Bees	48	49	.495	7½	Walter McCreedie
Oakland Oaks	40	63	.388	18½	Del Howard

The league suspended operations July 14.

Playoff: Los Angeles 5 games, Vernon 2.

BA: Art Griggs, Sacramento, .378
Runs: Charles Pick, San Francisco, 65
Hits: Hack Miller, Oakland, 131
HRs: Art Griggs, Sacramento, 12
    Earl Sheely, Salt Lake City, 12

Wins: Doc Crandall, Los Angeles, 16
    Walt Leverenz, Salt Lake City, 16
SOs: John Picus Quinn, Vernon, 99
ERA: John Picus Quinn, Vernon, 1.48

A Southern Association
President: Robert H. Baugh

Standings	W	L	Pct.	GB	Attend.	Manager
New Orleans Pelicans	49	21	.700	—	50,484	Johnny Dobbs
Little Rock Travelers	41	28	.594	7½	35,867	Norman "Kid" Elberfeld
Mobile Bears	35	32	.522	12½	29,838	Patsy Flaherty
Birmingham Barons	33	31	.516	13	39,202	Carleton Molesworth
Chattanooga Lookouts	35	34	.507	13½	27,284	Michael Finn
Memphis Chickasaws	32	38	.457	17	33,831	Cy Barger
Nashville Volunteers	30	40	.429	19	24,119	Roy Ellam
Atlanta Crackers	18	49	.269	29½	39,112	Charley Frank

The league suspended operations June 28.

BA: Ira Flagstead, Chattanooga, .381
Runs: Johnny Bates, Mobile, 50
    Tommy Leach, Chattanooga, 50
Hits: Billy Southworth, Birmingham, 81
HRs: Fred Bratchie, Memphis, 7

Wins: Hub Perdue, New Orleans, 12
SOs: Bill Bailey, New Orleans, 55
Pct: Claude Robertson, New Orleans, .909, 10-1

A Western League
President: Emerson W. Dickerson

Standings	W	L	Pct.	GB	Manager
Wichita Jobbers	41	24	.631	—	Joe Berger
Topeka Kaw-nees/ Hutchinson Salt Packers@	37	31	.544	5½	Johnny Nee
Des Moines Boosters	36	31	.537	6	Jack Coffey
Joplin Miners	34	31	.523	7	Rudy Hulswitt
Omaha Rourkes	33	32	.508	8	William Jackson
Hutchinson Salt Packers/ Oklahoma City Indians#	33	37	.471	10½	Otto Jacobs/Jack Holland
St. Joseph Saints	30	38	.441	12½	Bert Daniels
Sioux City Indians	22	42	.344	18½	James "Ducky" Holmes

#Hutchinson (14-19) moved to Oklahoma City June 2.
@Topeka (19-13) moved to Hutchinson June 2.
The league suspended operations July 7.

BA: Clarence Pitts, Hutchinson/ Oklahoma City, .380
Runs: Al Bashang, Omaha, 49
Hits: George Watson, St. Joseph, 74
    Harry McClellan, Hutchinson/ Oklahoma City, 74

HRs: Bob Murphy, Des Moines, 8
Wins: Ed Hovlik, Wichita, 13
    Jesse Haines, Topeka/Hutchinson, 13
SOs: Ed Hovlik, Wichita, 128
ERA: Jesse Haines, Topeka/Hutchinson, 1.59

B Eastern League
President: Daniel O'Neill

Standings	W	L	Pct.	GB	Manager
New London Planters	46	12	.793	—	John Flynn
Bridgeport Americans	44	12	.786	1	Paul Krichell
Providence Grays	34	22	.607	11	Edwin Eayrs
New Haven Murlins	31	24	.564	13½	Danny Murphy
Hartford Senators	29	26	.527	15½	Jim Clarkin
Springfield Ponies	21	35	.375	24	Fred Parent
Waterbury Nattatucks	14	43	.246	31½	Harry Hinchman
Worcester Boosters	7	52	.119	39½	John McMahon

The league suspended operations July 22.

*Won first-half   **Won second-half   ***Won both halves

1918

BA: Edwin Eayrs, Providence, .354
Runs: Pete Brausen, Providence, 45
Hits: Frank O'Rourke, New London, 68
HRs: Ray Grimes, Hartford, 3

Wins: James Ferguson, Bridgeport, 19
SOs: James Ferguson, Bridgeport, 102
Pct: Gary Fortune, New London, .867, 13-2

B Pacific Coast International League
President: R.L. Blewitt

Standings	W	L	Pct.	GB	Manager
Seattle Giants	40	28	.588	—	Bill Leard
Portland Buckaroos	37	28	.569	1½	Bill Fisher
Aberdeen Black Cats	32	35	.478	7½	Dick Egan
Vancouver Beavers@	26	41	.388	13½	Robert Brown
Tacoma Tigers#	13	9	.591	NA	Bill Speas
Spokane Indians#	9	16	.360	NA	R.L. "Nick" Williams

#Tacoma and Spokane disbanded May 26.
@Vancouver, British Columbia (26-28) moved to Vancouver, Washington June 25.
The league suspended operations July 7.

BA: Cliff Lee, Portland, .359
Runs: Bob Smale, Seattle, 62
Hits: Bevo LeBourveau, Seattle, 91
HRs: Bill Fisher, Portland, 4

Wins: Cyrus Young, Seattle, 13
SOs: Frank Rapp, Portland, 80
Pct: Cyrus Young, Seattle, .867, 13-2

B Texas League
President: Walter Morris

Standings	W	L	Pct.	GB	Manager
Dallas Giants	52	37	.584	—	Hamilton Patterson
Ft. Worth Panthers	47	39	.547	3½	Jake Atz
Waco Navigators	45	40	.529	5	Ellis Hardy
San Antonio Bronchos	43	45	.489	8½	Clay Perry
Houston Buffaloes	38	46	.452	11½	Pat Newnam
Shreveport Gassers	35	53	.398	16½	Mike O'Neill

The league suspended operations July 7.

BA: Olen Nokes, Dallas, .333
Runs: Jewel Ens, Dallas, 67
Hits: Jewel Ens, Dallas, 102
HRs: John Mokan, Waco, 9

Wins: Harry Lee, Ft. Worth, 9
SOs: Joe Martina, Houston, 115
ERA: Ed Matteson, Dallas, 2.09

C Virginia League
President: W.B. Bradley

Standings	W	L	Pct.	GB	Manager
Richmond Colts	29	21	.580	—	George Stinson
Newport News Shipbuilders	28	21	.571	½	Roy Whitcraft
Petersburg Goobers	27	22	.551	1½	Burleigh Emery
Norfolk Tars	13	33	.239	14	Art Devlin

The league suspended operations in late June.

BA: Curt Daughton, Newport News, .328
Runs: Curt Daughton, Newport News, 38
Hits: Curt Daughton, Newport News, 62
HRs: Curt Daughton, Newport News, 3

Wins: Edwin Tomlin, Newport News, 10
SOs: George Jackson, Richmond, 83
Pct: Joe Trivett, Newport News, .800, 4-1

D Blue Ridge League
President: J. Vincent Jamison, Jr.

Standings	W	L	Pct.	GB	Manager
Cumberland Colts	11	7	.611	—	Eddie Hooper
Piedmont-Westernport Drybugs	10	7	.588	½	Arthur "Shorty" Smith
Hagerstown Terriers	7	10	.412	3½	Ernest "Doc" Ferris
Martinsburg Mountaineers	6	10	.375	4	W.J. "Country" Morris

The league disbanded June 16.

BA: Joe Brophy, Cumberland, .343
Runs: H.L. Hickey, Hagerstown, 15
Hits: Joe Brophy, Cumberland, 23
HRs: Eddie Hooper, Cumberland, 3

Wins: Vic Keen, Hagerstown, 4
Hugh Markwood, Martinsburg, 4
Ben Schaufele, Piedmont-Westernport, 4
SOs: Vic Keen, Hagerstown, 33
Pct: Ben Schaufele, Piedmont-Westernport, 1.000, 4-0

1918 Interleague Post Season Play

World Series
Boston (American) 4 games, Chicago (National) 2

1918 No-Hitters

Date	Pitcher	Team	League	Opponent	Score
5-16	Paul Wachtel	Ft. Worth	Texas	Dallas	2-0
6-3	Dutch Leonard	Boston	American	Detroit	5-0
6-4	Harry Gere	Springfield	Eastern	Hartford	8-0
6-10	Wally Waldbauer	Wichita	Western	Omaha	4-0
6-23	Charles "Sea Lion" Hall	St. Paul	American Assoc.	Columbus	2-0

THIS DATE IN MINOR LEAGUE HISTORY

1918, Ten minor leagues began the season, but only the International League completed its schedule due to the World War.

April 7, 1918, Otis "Doc" Crandall of Los Angeles, Pacific Coast League, pitched a one-hit game to defeat Salt Lake City 14-0. The lone safety, a single between short-stop and third base, came with two out in the ninth and one ball and two strikes on the batter, Salt Lake City third baseman Karl Crandall, Doc's brother. The contest was played on a Sunday morning at the Vernon park.

May 8, 1918, Ft. Worth, Texas League, and Shreveport played 20 innings to a 1-1 tie. Each club garnered nine hits. Polson hurled the distance for Shreveport.

May 21, 1918, Jack Enright, pitching for Shreveport in the Texas League, walked seven, hit a batter, made a wild pitch and allowed San Antonio 12 runs in the first inning. The Bronchos won 24-4.

May 22, 1918, Miss Gladys Palmer of the University of Wisconsin set a record for women by throwing a baseball 215 feet 11 inches.

May 27, 1918, Nashville, Southern Association, collected 27 hits to crush Chattanooga 20-0.

June 1, 1918, Oakland, Pacific Coast League, scored 12 runs in one inning and walloped Salt Lake City 25-3.

June 1, 1918, Joplin, Western League, defeated St. Joseph 3-1 in a 20-inning game.

June 1, 1918, The Southern Association became the first victim of the World War. At a special meeting, the directors decided to suspend operations on June 28. Travel difficulty was the chief reason cited for the action.

June 8, 1918, St. Paul, American Association, stole eight bases in a 12-9 victory over Columbus.

June 11, 1918, Aberdeen, Pacific Coast International League, trounced Vancouver 20-8.

June 15, 1918, Louisville, American Association, defeated Minneapolis 11-9, scoring all 11 runs in the second inning.

June 20, 1918, Vernon, Pacific Coast League, defeated Sacramento 19-2.

June 29, 1918, Pitcher Harry Heitman, Rochester, International League, hurled his second doubleheader within five days and won all four games. On June 25, Heitman beat Jersey City 3-2 and 14-10. Jersey City scored six runs in the ninth inning of the second game. The Newark club was the victim on this date, 5-3 and 4-1.

July 1, 1918, Dallas, Texas League, scored 10 runs in one inning to trim Shreveport 18-4.

July 7, 1918, Sacramento, Pacific Coast League, downed Salt Lake City 23-5.

July 7, 1918, The Texas League season closed due to many players joining the Armed Forces.

July 14, 1918, The Pacific Coast League suspended play for the balance of the season.

July 22, 1918, The Eastern League closed its season.

August 25, 1918, Buffalo of the International League, the only minor league still in operation, made 24 hits to defeat Hamilton 19-2.

August 27, 1918, Jersey City, International League, pounded out 27 hits, scoring eight runs in the fifth and nine in the seventh to trounce Hamilton 22-8, continuing the Tigers' woes.

September 2, 1918, The International League ended its season on orders from the Secretary of War, Newton Baker. The loop was the only minor league circuit to play out the season.

1919

American League
President: Byron Bancroft Johnson

Standings	W	L	Pct.	GB	Attend.	Manager
Chicago White Sox	88	52	.629	—	627,186	Kid Gleason
Cleveland Indians	84	55	.604	3½	538,135	Lee Fohl/Tris Speaker
New York Yankees	80	59	.576	7½	619,164	Miller Huggins
Detroit Tigers	80	60	.571	8	643,805	Hugh Jennings
St. Louis Browns	67	72	.482	20½	349,350	Jimmy Burke
Boston Red Sox	66	71	.482	20½	417,291	Edward Barrow
Washington Senators	56	84	.400	32	234,096	Clark Griffith
Philadelphia Athletics	36	104	.257	52	225,209	Connie Mack

BA: Ty Cobb, Detroit, .384
Runs: Babe Ruth, Boston, 103
Hits: Bobby Veach, Detroit, 191
Ty Cobb, Detroit, 191
RBIs: Babe Ruth, Boston, 114
HRs: Babe Ruth, Boston, 29

Wins: Eddie Cicotte, Chicago, 29
SOs: Walter Johnson, Washington, 147
ERA: Walter Johnson, Washington, 1.49
Pct: Eddie Cicotte, Chicago, .806, 29-7
CG: Eddie Cicotte, Chicago, 30

National League
President: John A. Heydler

Standings	W	L	Pct.	GB	Attend.	Manager
Cincinnati Reds	96	44	.686	—	532,501	Pat Moran
New York Giants	87	53	.621	9	708,857	John McGraw
Chicago Cubs	75	65	.536	21	424,430	Fred Mitchell
Pittsburgh Pirates	71	68	.511	24½	276,810	Hugo Bezdek
Brooklyn Robins	69	71	.493	27	360,721	Wilbert Robinson
Boston Braves	57	82	.410	38½	167,401	George Stallings
St. Louis Cardinals	54	83	.394	40½	167,059	Branch Rickey
Philadelphia Phillies	47	90	.343	47½	240,424	Jack Coombs/Gavvy Cravath

BA: Edd Roush, Cincinnati, .321
Runs: George Burns, New York, 86
Hits: Ivy Olson, Brooklyn, 164
RBIs: Hy Myers, Brooklyn, 73
HRs: Gavvy Cravath, Philadelphia, 12

Wins: Jesse Barnes, New York, 25
SOs: Hippo Vaughn, Chicago, 141
ERA: Grover Alexander, Philadelphia, 1.72
Pct: Dutch Ruether, Cincinnati, .760, 19-6

AA American Association
President: Thomas J. Hickey

Standings	W	L	Pct.	GB	Attend.	Manager
St. Paul Saints	94	60	.610	—	139,915	Mike Kelley
Kansas City Blues	86	65	.570	6½	143,217	John Ganzel
Louisville Colonels	86	67	.562	7½	132,759	Patsy Flaherty/Joe McCarthy
Indianapolis Indians	85	68	.556	8½	159,902	Jack Hendricks
Minneapolis Millers	72	82	.468	22	108,459	Joe Cantillon
Columbus Senators	70	84	.455	24	87,123	Grover Hartley
Toledo Mud Hens	59	91	.393	33	89,712	Rollie Zeider/Roger Bresnahan
Milwaukee Brewers	58	93	.384	34½	103,337	Clarence "Pants" Rowland

BA: Tim Hendryx, Louisville, .368
Runs: Ward Miller, Kansas City, 116
Hits: Wilbur Good, Kansas City, 204
HRs: Elmer Miller, St. Paul, 15

Wins: Teller Cavet, Indianapolis, 28
SOs: Frank Davis, Louisville, 165
ERA: Roy Wilkinson, Columbus, 2.09

AA International League
President: David Fultz

Standings	W	L	Pct.	GB	Manager
Baltimore Orioles	100	49	.671	—	Jack Dunn
Toronto Maple Leafs	92	57	.617	8	George Gibson
Buffalo Bisons	81	67	.548	18½	George Wiltse
Binghamton Bingoes	75	71	.514	23½	Frank Schulte/Chick Hartman
Newark Bears	71	80	.470	30	Patsy Donovan
Rochester Hustlers	67	83	.447	33½	Arthur Irwin
Jersey City Skeeters	56	93	.376	44	Wild Bill Donovan
Reading Coal Barons	51	93	.354	46½	Red Dooin/Charles Kelchner

BA: Otis Lawrey, Baltimore, .364
Runs: Fritz Maisel, Baltimore, 135
Hits: Mervyn Jacobson, Baltimore, 203
HRs: George Kelly, Rochester, 15

SBs: Edward Miller, Newark, 87
Wins: Rube Parnham, Baltimore, 28
SOs: Rube Parnham, Baltimore, 187
ERA: Roy Jordan, Baltimore, 1.43

AA Pacific Coast League
President: Allan T. Baum

Standings	W	L	Pct.	GB	Attend.	Manager
Vernon Tigers	111	70	.613	—	244,949	Bill Essick
Los Angeles Angels	108	72	.600	2½	230,647	Red Killefer
Salt Lake City Bees	88	83	.515	18	133,086	Edward Herr
Sacramento Senators	85	83	.506	19½	111,571	Bill Rodgers
Oakland Oaks	86	96	.473	25½	289,680	Del Howard
San Francisco Seals	84	94	.473	25½	350,960	Charles Graham
Portland Beavers	78	96	.448	29½	141,179	Walter McCredie
Seattle Rainiers	62	108	.365	43½	185,005	Bill Clymer/Charles Mullen

BA: Bill Rumler, Salt Lake City, .362
Runs: Harl Maggert, Salt Lake City, 127
Hits: Sam Crawford, Los Angeles, 239
HRs: Earl Sheely, Salt Lake City, 28

Wins: Doc Crandall, Los Angeles, 28
SOs: Bill Piercy, Sacramento, 163
ERA: Curly Brown, Los Angeles, 2.03

A Eastern League
President: Daniel O'Neill

Standings	W	L	Pct.	GB	Manager
Pittsfield Hillies	64	44	.593	—	Joe Birmingham
Worcester Boosters	61	44	.581	1½	John McMahon
Providence Grays	61	45	.575	2	Edwin Eayrs
Bridgeport Americans	59	47	.557	4	Ray Grimes
Springfield Ponies	54	52	.509	9	Ed Holly/Jack O'Hara
Waterbury Nattatucks	46	59	.438	16½	John Flynn/Jud Daily
New Haven Weissmen	47	62	.431	17½	John Meyers/Danny Murphy
Hartford Senators	34	73	.318	29½	Danny Murphy/Oscar Grimes

BA: Edwin Eayrs, Providence, .322
Runs: Everett Nutter, New Haven, 78
Hits: Ray Grimes, Hartford/Bridgeport, 127
Everett Nutter, New Haven, 127

HRs: Joe Hauser, Providence, 6
Wins: Gary Fortune, Pittsfield, 24
SOs: Gary Fortune, Pittsfield, 182
Pct: Dinty Gearin, Providence, .846, 11-2

A Southern Association
President: John D. Martin

Standings	W	L	Pct.	GB	Attend.	Manager
Atlanta Crackers	85	53	.616	—	195,033	Charley Frank
Little Rock Travelers	74	56	.569	7	99,437	Norman "Kid" Elberfeld
New Orleans Pelicans	74	61	.548	9½	108,358	Johnny Dobbs
Mobile Bears	67	69	.493	17	70,502	Bob Coleman
Memphis Chickasaws	66	73	.475	19½	114,274	Cy Barger
Chattanooga Lookouts	65	73	.471	20	76,848	Sam Strang Nicklin
Birmingham Barons	59	77	.434	25	93,661	Carleton Molesworth
Nashville Volunteers	55	83	.399	30	79,014	Roy Ellam

BA: Larry Gilbert, New Orleans, .349
Runs: Lloyd Christenbury, Memphis, 90
Hits: Lloyd Christenbury, Memphis, 174
HRs: Tex McDonald, Nashville, 8

Wins: Rube Robinson, Little Rock, 23
SOs: Rube Marshall, Chattanooga, 124
ERA: Hub Perdue, Nashville, 1.56

A Western League
President: Albert R. Tearney

Standings	W	L	Pct.	GB	Manager
St. Joseph Saints	78	57	.578	—	Alvin Dolan
Tulsa Oilers	77	63	.550	3½	Spencer Abbott
Wichita Jobbers	75	65	.536	5½	Joe Berger
Des Moines Boosters	71	67	.514	8½	Jack Coffey
Oklahoma City Indians	69	69	.500	10½	Jack Holland
Sioux City Indians	68	72	.486	12½	Charley Schmidt
Joplin Miners	57	78	.422	21	Rudy Hulswitt
Omaha Rourkes	56	80	.412	22½	William Jackson

Playoff: Tulsa 3 games, St. Joseph 1; series was cancelled due to inclement weather and lack of support.

BA: Joe Wilhoit, Wichita, .422
Runs: Joe Wilhoit, Wichita, 126
Hits: Joe Wilhoit, Wichita, 222
HRs: Ev "Yam" Yaryan, Wichita, 12

Wins: Louis North, St. Joseph, 23
SOs: Paul Musser, Des Moines/Wichita, 212
Pct: Guy Hoffman, St. Joseph, .737, 14-5

B Northwest International League
President: J.M. Osmond

Standings	W	L	Pct.	GB	Manager
Vancouver Beavers	20	14	.588	—	Bill Speas
Seattle Drydockers	16	12	.571	1	Joe Devine
Victoria Tyees	14	12	.538	2	Duncan Hamilton
Tacoma Tigers#	5	17	.227	9	Dick Egan

#Tacoma disbanded June 5, causing the league to disband June 8.

B Michigan-Ontario League
President: Joseph S. Jackson

Standings	W	L	Pct.	GB	Manager
Saginaw Aces	77	32	.706	—	Henry "Buzz" Wetzel
Hamilton Tigers	75	36	.676	3	Frank Shaughnessy

*Won first-half   **Won second-half   ***Won both halves

1919

	W	L	Pct.	GB	Manager
Battle Creek Custers	67	45	.598	11½	Danny Jenkins
Brantford Red Sox	61	46	.570	15	Knotty Lee
Bay City Wolves	43	69	.384	35½	Bill Cristall/Cal Wenger
Kitchener Beavers	41	68	.376	36	Jack Beatty
London Tecumsehs	41	70	.369	37	Joe Keenan/Starr Mason/Kenneth Hagel/ C.E. "Dad" Stewart
Flint Halligans	35	74	.321	42	Jim Pierce

BA: Ted Kaylor, Battle Creek, .376
Runs: William Pike, Saginaw, 95
Hits: Ted Kaylor, Battle Creek, 146
HRs: Andy Lotshaw, Flint/Brantford, 13

Wins: John Glasier, Hamilton, 25
SOs: John Glasier, Hamilton, 213
ERA: Len Okrie, London, 1.00

B New England League
President: John H. Donnelly

Standings	W	L	Pct.	GB	Manager
Lowell Grays/Lewiston-Auburn Twins@	38	25	.603	—	Mike Hayden
Portland Blue Sox	38	27	.585	1	Charles "Heinie" Wagner
Fitchburg Foxes	31	36	.463	9	John Quinn/Bill Phoenix/Bill Burger/ Bill Page
Haverhill Climbers	27	40	.403	13	Jesse Burkett
Lewiston Red Sox#	21	23	.477	NA	Fred Parent
Lawrence Barristers#	20	24	.455	NA	Bill Page

#Lewiston and Lawrence disbanded July 12.
@Lowell (24-18) moved to Lewiston-Auburn July 14.
The league disbanded August 2.

BA: Dick Loftus, Fitchburg, .350
Runs: Joe Duffee, Lawrence/Portland/Haverhill, 56
Hits: Bill Bailey, Portland, 81
HRs: Bossie, Lowell/Lewiston-Auburn, 5

SBs: Bill Page, Lawrence/Fitchburg, 21
Wins: Bob Clark, Lowell/Lawrence, 14
SOs: Cyril Morgan, Portland, 97
Pct: Tom Gallagher, Portland, .818, 9-2

B Texas League
President: Walter Morris

Standings	W	L	Pct.	GB	Manager
Ft. Worth Panthers**	94	60	.610	—	Jake Atz
Houston Buffaloes	89	71	.556	8	Al Bridwell
Shreveport Gassers*	81	64	.559	8½	Billy Smith
Beaumont Oilers	79	71	.527	13	John McCloskey/Joe Mathes
Dallas Marines	74	75	.497	17½	Hamilton Patterson
San Antonio Bronchos	66	87	.431	27½	Michael Finn
Galveston Pirates	63	89	.414	30	Bob Tarleton
Waco Navigators	59	88	.401	31½	Archie Tanner

Playoff: Shreveport 4 games, Ft. Worth 2.

BA: Al Nixon, Beaumont, .362
Runs: Al Nixon, Beaumont, 99
Hits: Al Nixon, Beaumont, 215
HRs: Roy Leslie, Houston, 16; Jewel Ens, Dallas, 16

Wins: Joe Martina, Beaumont, 28
SOs: Bill Bailey, Beaumont, 277
ERA: Bryan Harris, Houston, 1.56; John Verbout, Shreveport, 1.56

B Three-I League
President: Albert R. Tearney

Standings	W	L	Pct.	GB	Manager
Bloomington Bloomers	80	41	.661	—	Joseph Dunn
Peoria Tractors	68	54	.557	12½	James Hamilton
Evansville Evas	63	58	.521	17	John Nee
Rockford Rox	63	60	.512	18	John Castle
Terre Haute Browns	50	70	.417	29½	Mordecai Brown
Moline Plowboys	40	81	.331	40	George Hughes

BA: J.A. Thompson, Bloomington, .346
Runs: John Nee, Evansville, 93
Hits: Bevo LeBourveau, Peoria, 163
HRs: Fred Felsch, Rockford, 8

Wins: Frank Romine, Bloomington, 25
SOs: Cliff Murchison, Peoria, 218
ERA: Theodore Turner, Bloomington, 1.92

C South Atlantic League
President: W.H. Walsh

Standings	W	L	Pct.	GB	Manager
Columbia Comers	55	39	.585	—	Tom Clarke
Charlotte Hornets	55	41	.573	1	Ernest Burke
Greenville Spinners	52	45	.536	4½	Billy Laval
Charleston Gulls	49	48	.505	7½	Jimmy Manes
Augusta Dollies	45	52	.464	11½	Fred DeWitt/Bill Pierre/Dolly Stark
Spartanburg Spartans	33	64	.340	23½	H.A. "Dandy" Overton/Warren Wilson/ E.K. Perryman/Doug Harbison

BA: Walter Johnson, Columbia, .362
Runs: Ernest Burke, Charlotte, 73
Hits: Walter Johnson, Columbia, 150
HRs: Red Wingo, Greenville, 11

Wins: Rube Eldridge, Charlotte, 20
SOs: J.D. Thompson, Greenville, 128
Pct: Jesse Doyle, Greenville, .750, 18-6

C Virginia League
President: W.B. Bradley

Standings	W	L	Pct.	GB	Manager
Petersburg Goobers*	62	47	.569	—	Ambrose McConnell
Richmond Colts**	60	50	.545	2½	Frank Dobson/Charles "Chief" Bender
Portsmouth Truckers	57	51	.528	4½	Eddie Hooper
Norfolk Tars	58	53	.523	5	William Schwartz
Suffolk Nuts	49	58	.458	12	Rube Oldring
Newport News Shipbuilders	42	69	.378	21	Roy Whitcraft

Playoffs: None, due to disagreement between teams over sites and distribution of gate receipts.

BA: George McConnell, Petersburg, .338
Runs: Harold Leathers, Norfolk, 71
Hits: Jim Poole, Richmond, 127
HRs: Jack Ballinger, Norfolk, 5
Wins: Charles "Chief" Bender, Richmond, 29

SOs: Charles "Chief" Bender, Richmond, 295
ERA: Orion Mitchell, Norfolk, 1.01
Pct: Charles "Chief" Bender, Richmond, .935, 29-2

C Western Canada League
Presidents: Charles F. Moll/Frank H. Miley

Standings	W	L	Pct.	GB	Manager
Saskatoon Quakers**	69	34	.670	—	George Brautigan
Winnipeg Maroons*	54	47	.535	14	John Sheehan
Regina Senators	43	60	.417	26	Bill Speas
Moose Jaw Robin Hoods	38	63	.376	30	Dick Hurley

Playoff: Saskatoon 5 games, Winnipeg 3.

BA: Arthur Henning, Winnipeg, .315
Runs: Bernie Neis, Saskatoon, 86
Hits: Arthur Henning, Winnipeg, 132

Wins: Spencer Heath, Winnipeg, 18
Pct: Ed Williams, Saskatoon, .800, 8-2

D Florida State League
President: Walter W. Rose

Standings	W	L	Pct.	GB	Manager
Sanford Celeryfeds*	46	30	.605	—	Bert Chapman
Orlando Caps**	46	30	.605	—	Bert Humphries/Bob Schuyler
Lakeland Highlanders	40	39	.506	7½	Bill Pierre/Hugh Wicker
Bradentown Growers	34	43	.442	12½	Jim Moore
Bartow-Winter Haven Polkers	35	45	.438	13	L'Hommedieu
Tampa Smokers	32	46	.410	15	Bryant Bowden/Hoke Dellinger

Playoff: Sanford 5 games, Orlando 3; Sanford won the series but two wins were thrown out on October 11 due to ineligible player violations. The series was declared a tie with both teams declared co-champions.

BA: George Foss, Tampa, .365
Runs: Stuffy Stewart, Sanford, 63
Hits: George Foss, Tampa, 92

1919 Interleague Post Season Play

World Series
Cincinnati (National) 5 games, Chicago (American) 3

Junior World Series
Vernon (Pacific Coast) 5 games, St. Paul (American Association) 4
The American Association refused to continue the series due to perceived ill-treatment at the hands of the Vernon club.

Dixie Championship
Columbia (South Atlantic) 4 games, Atlanta (Southern Association) 1

1919 No-Hitters

Date	Pitcher	Team	League	Opponent	Score
5-2	Sam Crews	Birmingham	Southern Assoc.	Mobile	14-0
5-11	Hod Eller	Cincinnati	National	St. Louis	6-0
5-12	Eddie Rommel	Newark	International	Toronto	1-0
5-14	Ray Jordan	Buffalo	International	Jersey City	3-0
5-20	Winn Taylor	Waterbury	Eastern	New Haven	1-0
5-27	Cliff Murchison	Peoria	Three-I	Moline	6-0
6-13	Frank Colley	Worcester	Eastern	Providence	3-0
6-15	Frank Sparks	Tulsa	Western	Joplin	6-0
6-15	William Pierson	Suffolk	Virginia	Portsmouth	3-2
6-15	Harvey Sutherland	Portland	Pacific Coast	San Francisco	11-0
7-19	Jim Roberts	Atlanta	Southern Assoc.	Chattanooga	2-0 (7)
7-19	Gus Bono	Shreveport	Texas	San Antonio	2-1
8-1	John Glasier	Hamilton	Michigan-Ontario	Brantford	4-0
8-8	Rosy Ryan	Buffalo	International	Reading	7-0 (7)
8-19	Fred Falkenberg	Oakland	Pacific Coast	Seattle	6-0
8-20	William Morrisette	Hamilton	Michigan-Ontario	Bay City	4-0
8-22	Frank Winchell	Evansville	Three-I	Moline	2-0
8-31	Howard Gregory	Wichita	Western	Joplin	5-1
9-10	Ray Caldwell	Cleveland	American	New York	3-0

Number in parentheses indicates innings if other than nine.

THIS DATE IN MINOR LEAGUE HISTORY

April 18, 1919, Babe Ruth, Boston, American League, walloped four home runs against Baltimore, International League, in six times at bat. This was the only time in Ruth's career that he slugged four homers in a single game.

May 12, 1919, Newark's Eddie Rommel, later a star pitcher for the Philadelphia Athletics, pitched a 1-0 no-hitter against Toronto. In his next outing, he lost to Buffalo 1-0, allowing one hit, which did not figure in the scoring.

May 12, 1919, Oakland, Pacific Coast League, scored 13 runs in the eighth inning to defeat Vernon 17-9.

May 17, 1919, Peoria, Three-I League, made 27 hits to clobber Evansville 19-1. Cliff Murchison held the losers to one safety.

May 17, 1919, Pitcher Fisher of Flint, Michigan-Ontario League, fanned 16 in a game against London.

June 8, 1919, The International Northwest League, also known as the Pacific Coast International League, disbanded.

June 10, 1919, Seattle, Pacific Coast League, scored 11 runs in one inning and routed Sacramento 18-3.

June 13, 1919, The longest game in Southern Association history, a 23-inning 2-2 struggle between Atlanta and Chattanooga, was played. Each club used only nine players. Rube Marshall, Chattanooga pitcher, gave no walks and only two hits, both bunts, in the last nine frames. Roberts worked the game for Atlanta. Jimmy Dykes, later a major league player and manager, played second base for Atlanta. Leading off, he went 2-for-10 and handled 22 chances afield without an error. Each club had 16 hits.

June 23, 1919, Reading, International League, scored 12 runs in one inning and made 24 hits to decision Buffalo 15-6.

June 24, 1919, Rochester first baseman George Kelly, nephew of famed major leaguer Bill Lange, cracked four homers, plus a double, driving in nine runs to feature Rochester's 19-0 International League victory over Reading. The Hustlers registered 25 hits.

June 29, 1919, Atlanta, Southern Association, scored in every inning to submerge Birmingham 24-4. The Georgians notched a total of 27 hits.

July 6, 1919, Pittsfield, Eastern League, scored in every inning and made 24 hits in the contest as they topped Waterbury 17-4.

July 7, 1919, Terre Haute, Three-I League, outhit Peoria 17-8, but lost the game 7-5.

July 10, 1919, Jack Bentley made five extra-base hits, two doubles, a triple and two home runs, in one game for Baltimore, International League.

July 12, 1919, Chattanooga, Southern Association, defeated Nashville 6-5 in a 20-inning game, Lohman pitching against Lankerman. Lohman yielded only two hits.

July 17, 1919, Salt Lake City, Pacific Coast League, edged Los Angeles 18-17. The game produced 40 hits, 21 by Los Angeles. First baseman Jack Fournier hit three homers for the Angels.

July 20, 1919, Chattanooga, Southern Association, scored 10 runs in the first inning, made 24 hits in the game, and drubbed Birmingham 21-4.

July 22, 1919, Joe McCarthy, Louisville second baseman, was named manager of the third-place Colonels.

July 27, 1919, St. Joseph, Western League, downed Des Moines 20-5, as each St. Joseph player had at least two hits. The winners amassed 22 safeties.

July 29, 1919, Outfielder Stroud, Peoria, Three-I League, belted three doubles and a homer, plus a sacrifice fly, in five trips against Rockford.

August 2, 1919, After having succeeded through the Great War when most other leagues collapsed, the New England League succumbed to low attendance and shaky management.

August 3, 1919, Beaumont tallied 11 runs in the first inning and crushed Waco 21-2. Shortstop Rapp made four hits, stole four bases and scored six runs. Beaumont made 24 hits for total of 34 safeties and 39 runs in two successive games.

August 10, 1919, Dallas, Texas League, scored 11 runs in one frame in a 17-5 defeat of Houston.

August 12, 1919, Chattanooga, Southern Association, scored nine runs in one frame, made 23 hits in the game, and beat Mobile 18-0.

August 13, 1919, Pinch hitter Ben Tincup, a pitcher, and manager-second baseman Joe McCarthy hit home runs on two successive pitches for Louisville, American Association, against St. Paul.

August 16, 1919, First baseman Ed Miller of Newark, International League, stole a base in the first game of a doubleheader, giving him 19 in eleven games, including two in eight successive tilts beginning on August 9. In his last game of the season, Miller pilfered five sacks to total 87 for the year.

August 20, 1919, Outfielder Joe Wilhoit of Wichita, Western League, was held hitless by Elam Van Gilder and reliever Williams of Tulsa, after having hit safely in 69 consecutive games, the all-time record for Organized Ball. In the 69 contests, Wilhoit had 151 hits in 299 at bats for an average of .505.

August 30, 1919, Charlotte, South Atlantic League, played a 5-5, 20-inning tie with Columbia.

August 31, 1919, Worcester, Eastern League, defeated New Haven 4-3 in 21 innings. The game saw no scoring from the fifth frame through the 20th.

September 10, 1919, Joplin, Western League, made 22 hits, scored in every inning but one, and downed St. Joseph 22-4.

September 13, 1919, Vernon, Pacific Coast League, scored in all eight innings of an 18-7 romp over Portland.

September 30, 1919, Columbus and Toledo, American Association, played a game in 53 minutes.

October 7, 1919, Smokey Joe Williams, Negro pitcher, pitched for the Lincoln Giants against John McGraw's New York Giants in an exhibition game. Williams hurled a no-hitter and fanned 20, but he lost 1-0 on miscues by his infielders.

October 17, 1919, Vernon, Pacific Coast League, won the Junior World Series by defeating St. Paul of the American Association five games to four. All nine tilts were played in California.

THE ROARING TWENTIES: 1920 - 1929

*F*or some, the 1920s are considered the best era of minor league baseball. Baseball emerged from World War I booming and throughout the decade nearly 30 leagues would start each season. Three or four might fold, but others would soon replace them.

At the higher levels of minor league baseball there were tremendous success stories. In the Pacific Coast League, the Los Angeles franchise built a new twenty thousand seat stadium. The club and park were valued at two million dollars. The Oakland club was sold for $500,000 in 1928. Three years later the Newark, N.J., club was purchased for a reported $600,000. It would be more than half a century before franchise prices reached that level again. Minor league teams were developing their own players, and selling them to the majors at impressive prices. Lefty Grove was sold for $100,000, and it was not uncommon for good minor league players to go for more than $50,000.

The election in November, 1920, of Judge Kenesaw Mountain Landis as commissioner of baseball brought stability to the game. Landis quickly brought the majors and minors together to sign a new National Agreement. The draft was reinstituted. The International League agreed to a modified draft. By the end of 1924, the International League had accepted the draft, but prices for players remained high until the end of the decade.

Changes were happening in the minors that would profoundly affect the future. The most important was the beginning of the farm system. In 1921 the National Agreement allowed minor league teams to be owned by major league clubs. The St. Louis Cardinals, under the direction of Branch Rickey, acquired an interest in Houston, Fort Smith, Ark., and a half interest in Syracuse. Rickey's approach was original: He was the first to assemble teams at different levels and push talent through his system. In 1926 the Cards, who had never finished higher than third, won the World Series with much of the talent coming from the farm system. Players the Cardinals could not use themselves were sold to other major league teams at market value. From 1922-1942 the Cardinals made more than $2 million dollars in player sales to other major league franchises.

At first, major league clubs operated as they always had, signing players out of amateur ball, optioning them for seasoning and buying top prospects from minor league clubs. By 1929 this was changing. Judge Landis was speaking out against major league ownership of minor league teams, but at the Winter Meetings that year, Jacob Rupert of the New York Yankees declared that no ballclub could afford the prices being paid for minor league players. He was going to be forced into owning minor league clubs, and so was every other major league owner.

The farm system had been created largely out of necessity by Rickey; the Cardinals did not have the financial resources to compete with other clubs for top prospects. It was now recognized as the most efficient method of acquiring talent. The farm system would force the minors to undergo further change.

1920

American League
President: Byron Bancroft Johnson

Standings	W	L	Pct.	GB	Attend.	Manager
Cleveland Indians	98	56	.636	—	912,832	Tris Speaker
Chicago White Sox	96	58	.623	2	833,492	Kid Gleason
New York Yankees	95	59	.617	3	1,289,422	Miller Huggins
St. Louis Browns	76	77	.497	21½	419,311	Jimmy Burke
Boston Red Sox	72	81	.471	25½	402,445	Edward Barrow
Washington Senators	68	84	.447	29	359,260	Clark Griffith
Detroit Tigers	61	93	.396	37	579,650	Hugh Jennings
Philadelphia Athletics	48	106	.312	50	287,888	Connie Mack

BA: George Sisler, St. Louis, .407
Runs: Babe Ruth, New York, 158
Hits: George Sisler, St. Louis, 257
RBIs: Babe Ruth, New York, 137
HRs: Babe Ruth, New York, 54
Wins: Jim Bagby, Cleveland, 31
SOs: Stan Coveleski, Cleveland, 133
ERA: Bob Shawkey, New York, 2.45
Pct: Jim Bagby, Cleveland, .721, 31-12

National League
President: John A. Heydler

Standings	W	L	Pct.	GB	Attend.	Manager
Brooklyn Robins	93	61	.604	—	808,722	Wilbert Robinson
New York Giants	86	68	.558	7	929,609	John McGraw
Cincinnati Reds	82	71	.536	10½	568,107	Pat Moran
Pittsburgh Pirates	79	75	.513	14	429,037	George Gibson
Chicago Cubs	75	79	.487	18	480,783	Fred Mitchell
St. Louis Cardinals	75	79	.487	18	326,836	Branch Rickey
Boston Braves	62	90	.408	30	162,483	George Stallings
Philadelphia Phillies	62	91	.405	30½	330,998	Gavvy Cravath

BA: Rogers Hornsby, St. Louis, .370
Runs: George Burns, New York, 115
Hits: Rogers Hornsby, St. Louis, 218
RBIs: George Kelly, New York, 94
Rogers Hornsby, St. Louis, 94
HRs: Cy Williams, Philadelphia, 15
Wins: Grover Alexander, Philadelphia, 27
SOs: Grover Alexander, Philadelphia, 173
ERA: Grover Alexander, Philadelphia, 1.91
Pct: Burleigh Grimes, Brooklyn, .676, 23-11

AA American Association
President: Thomas J. Hickey

Standings	W	L	Pct.	GB	Attend.	Manager
St. Paul Saints	115	49	.701	—	229,285	Mike Kelley
Louisville Colonels	88	79	.527	28½	123,704	Joe McCarthy
Toledo Mud Hens	87	79	.524	29	241,718	Roger Bresnahan
Minneapolis Millers	85	79	.518	30	223,671	Joe Cantillon
Indianapolis Indians	83	83	.500	33	143,869	Jack Hendricks
Milwaukee Brewers	78	88	.470	38	201,333	Jack Egan
Columbus Senators	66	99	.400	49½	106,566	Bill Clymer
Kansas City Blues	60	106	.361	56	119,179	Alex McCarthy/Otto Knabe

BA: Joseph Rapp, St. Paul, .335
Runs: Lee Dressen, St. Paul, 131
Hits: Wilbur Good, Kansas City, 229
RBIs: Bunny Brief, Kansas City, 120
HRs: Bunny Brief, Kansas City, 23
Wins: Charles "Sea Lion" Hall, St. Paul, 27
SOs: Dave Danforth, Columbus, 188
ERA: Charles "Sea Lion" Hall, St. Paul, 2.06

AA International League
President: David L. Fultz

Standings	W	L	Pct.	GB	Manager
Baltimore Orioles	110	43	.719	—	Jack Dunn
Toronto Maple Leafs	108	46	.701	2½	Hugh Duffy
Buffalo Bisons	96	57	.627	14	George Wiltse
Akron Buckeyes	88	63	.583	21	Rich Hoblitzell
Reading Marines	65	85	.433	43½	Jack Hummel
Jersey City Skeeters	62	91	.407	48	Wild Bill Donovan
Rochester Hustlers	45	106	.298	64	George Stallings
Syracuse Stars	33	116	.221	75	Tony Cummings/Ambrose McConnell/John Engman/Tom Madden

Attendance: Buffalo, 184,011; Toronto, 207,570.

BA: Merwyn Jacobson, Baltimore, .404
Runs: Merwyn Jacobson, Baltimore, 161
Hits: Merwyn Jacobson, Baltimore, 235
RBIs: Jack Bentley, Baltimore, 161
HRs: Frank Brower, Reading, 22
Mike Konnick, Reading, 22
Wins: Red Shea, Toronto, 27
SOs: Jack Ogden, Baltimore, 137
ERA: Jack Bentley, Baltimore, 2.11

AA Pacific Coast League
President: William H. McCarthy

Standings	W	L	Pct.	GB	Attend.	Manager
Vernon Tigers	110	88	.556	—	265,681	Bill Essick
Seattle Rainiers	102	91	.528	5½	284,950	Clyde Wares
Los Angeles Angels	102	95	.517	7½	279,879	Red Killefer
San Francisco Seals	103	96	.517	7½	371,931	Charles Graham
Salt Lake City Bees	95	92	.508	9½	159,351	Ernie Johnson
Oakland Oaks	95	103	.480	14	280,024	Del Howard
Sacramento Senators	89	109	.449	21	137,013	Bill Rodgers
Portland Beavers	81	103	.440	21	138,157	Walter McCreedie

BA: Earl Sheely, Salt Lake City, .371
Runs: Dennis Wilie, Oakland, 135
Hits: Hack Miller, Oakland, 280
HRs: Earl Sheely, Salt Lake City, 33
Wins: Buzz Arlett, Oakland, 29
SOs: Willis Mitchell, Vernon, 161
ERA: Jim Scott, San Francisco, 2.29

A Eastern League
President: Daniel O'Neill

Standings	W	L	Pct.	GB	Manager
New Haven Weissmen	79	61	.564	—	Charles "Chief" Bender
Springfield Hampdens	74	63	.540	3½	John Flynn
Worcester Boosters	72	66	.522	6	John McMahon
Hartford Senators	70	68	.507	8	
Bridgeport Americans	70	70	.500	9	Ed Walsh
Pittsfield Hillies	69	69	.500	9	Joe Birmingham
Albany Senators	61	78	.439	17½	Bill McCorry
Waterbury Brasscos	60	80	.429	19	Jud Daly

BA: Ray Grimes, Bridgeport, .364
Runs: Everett Nutter, New Haven, 108
Hits: Everett Nutter, New Haven, 179
HRs: Fred Wilder, Springfield, 13
Wins: Charles "Chief" Bender, New Haven, 25
SOs: Charles "Chief" Bender, New Haven, 252
ERA: Frank Woodward, New Haven, 1.08
Games: Charles "Chief" Bender, New Haven, 47

A Southern Association
President: John D. Martin

Standings	W	L	Pct.	GB	Attend.	Manager
Little Rock Travelers	88	59	.599	—	165,127	Norman "Kid" Elberfeld
New Orleans Pelicans	86	62	.581	2½	181,486	Johnny Dobbs
Atlanta Crackers	85	62	.578	3	221,638	Dick Kauffman
Birmingham Barons	85	69	.552	6½	172,475	Carleton Molesworth
Memphis Chickasaws	72	77	.484	17	213,936	John McCloskey
Mobile Bears	68	86	.441	23½	83,661	Bob Coleman
Nashville Vols	65	89	.422	26½	102,529	Roy Ellam
Chattanooga Lookouts	53	98	.351	39	74,515	Sam Strang Nicklin

BA: Harry Harper, Little Rock, .346
Runs: Dixie Carroll, Memphis, 106
Hits: Harry Harper, Little Rock, 196
HRs: Bing Miller, Little Rock, 19
Wins: Roy Walker, New Orleans, 26
John Morrison, Birmingham, 26
Rube Robinson, Little Rock, 26
Tom Sheehan, Atlanta, 26
SOs: Roy Walker, New Orleans, 237
Pct: Moses Yellowhorse, Little Rock, .750, 21-7

A Western League
President: Albert R. Tearney

Standings	W	L	Pct.	GB	Manager
Tulsa Oilers	92	61	.601	—	Spencer Abbott
Wichita Jobbers	92	62	.597	½	Joe Berger
Oklahoma City Indians	82	68	.547	8½	James Humphries/Dan Moell/Dick Breen
Omaha Rourkes	76	77	.497	16	Jack Lelivelt
St. Joseph Saints	74	80	.481	18½	John Kelleher
Joplin Miners	73	81	.474	19½	James Hamilton
Sioux City Packers	63	88	.417	28	George Andreas/Frank Metz
Des Moines Boosters	58	93	.384	33	Jack Coffey

Attendance: Tulsa, 110,000.

BA: Yam Yaryan, Wichita, .357
Runs: Yam Yaryan, Wichita, 124
Hits: Yam Yaryan, Wichita, 206
HRs: Yam Yaryan, Wichita, 41
Wins: Emilio Palmero, Omaha, 28
SOs: George Boehler, Joplin, 258
Pct: C.A. Ramsey, Oklahoma City, .821, 23-5

B Central League
President: Emerson W. Dickerson

Standings	W	L	Pct.	GB	Manager
Grand Rapids Joshers	76	50	.603	—	Josh Devore
Kalamazoo Celery Pickers	64	60	.516	11	Rube Vickers
Ludington Mariners	62	62	.500	13	Charles "Punch" Knoll
Muskegon Muskies	47	77	.379	28	Doc White

*Won first-half   **Won second-half   ***Won both halves

BA: Lance Richbourg, Grand Rapids, .416
Runs: Harry Carey, Grand Rapids, 91
Hits: Dave Claire, Ludington, 137
HRs: Vincent Tydeman, Ludington, 11

Wins: William Shoup, Ludington, 20
SOs: John Bogart, Ludington, 199
Pct: Frank Rose, Grand Rapids, .704, 19-8

B Michigan-Ontario League
President: George H. Maines

Standings	W	L	Pct.	GB	Manager
London Tecumsehs	86	32	.729	—	Frank "Buzz" Wetzel
Hamilton Tigers	71	46	.607	14½	Frank Shaughnessy
Brantford Red Sox	65	48	.575	18½	Knotty Lee
Kitchener Beavers	53	63	.457	32	John Beatty
Flint Halligans	53	63	.457	32	Jim Pierce/Ted Anderson
Bay City Wolves	51	69	.425	36	Cal Wenger
Battle Creek Custers	46	74	.383	41	Gene Krapp/John Heving/Hump Pierce
Saginaw Aces	43	73	.371	42	Ray McKee

BA: Frank "Buzz" Wetzel, Flint, .387
Runs: E.H. Kennedy, London, 100
Hits: Frank "Buzz" Wetzel, Flint, 164
RBIs: Frank "Buzz" Wetzel, Flint, 72
HRs: Frank "Buzz" Wetzel, Flint, 12

Wins: George Carmen, London, 26
SOs: William Morrisette, Hamilton, 181
ERA: Joe Reddy, Hamilton, 1.24
  Thomas Estelle, Brantford, 1.24
Pct: George Carmen, London, .929, 26-2

B Pacific Coast International League
President: Louis H. Burnett

Standings	W	L	Pct.	GB	Manager
Victoria Islanders	69	46	.600	—	Bill Leard
Yakima Indians	65	48	.575	3	Frank Raymond
Vancouver Beavers	65	50	.565	4	Bob Brown
Tacoma Tigers	66	53	.555	5	Bob Vaughn
Spokane Indians	56	58	.491	12½	Cliff Blankenship
Seattle Giants	24	90	.211	44½	Dave Hillyard/Bill Kenworthy/ William Hoffman

BA: Paul Strand, Yakima, .339
Runs: Charles Gorman, Yakima, 101
Hits: James Harrigan, Yakima, 156
  Tiny Graham, Tacoma, 156

HRs: Lee Dempsey, Victoria, 19
Wins: Bert Cole, Tacoma, 24
SOs: Harry Morton, Victoria, 198
Pct: Bert Cole, Tacoma, .774, 24-7

B Texas League
President: Walter Morris

Standings	W	L	Pct.	GB	Manager
Ft. Worth Panthers***	108	40	.730	—	Jake Atz
Wichita Falls Spudders	85	63	.574	23	Walt Salm
Shreveport Gassers	81	66	.551	26½	Billy Smith
Beaumont Exporters	81	70	.537	28½	Joe Mathes
San Antonio Bears	79	71	.527	30	John Nee
Dallas Submarines	63	85	.426	45	Ham Patterson
Houston Buffaloes	50	101	.331	59½	Jewel Ens
Galveston Pirates	49	100	.329	59½	Bob Tarleton/Hunter Hill

BA: Godfrey Josephson, Wichita Falls, .345
Runs: Godfrey Josephson, Wichita Falls, 104
Hits: Ed Brown, San Antonio, 200
RBIs: Dan Clark, Wichita Falls, 99
HRs: Dave Callahan, Galveston, 12

Wins: Joe Pate, Ft. Worth, 26
  Paul Wachtel, Ft. Worth, 26
SOs: Paul Bailey, Beaumont, 216
ERA: Joe Pate, Ft. Worth, 1.71

B Three-I League
President: Albert R. Tearney

Standings	W	L	Pct.	GB	Manager
Bloomington Bloomers	82	57	.590	—	Joseph Dunn
Evansville Evas	80	56	.588	½	Lewis Groh
Rockford Rox	70	70	.500	12½	Jim Schollenberger/Harry Brandt
Moline Plowboys	69	70	.497	13	Earle Mack
Cedar Rapids Rabbits	68	69	.497	13	Frank Boyle
Peoria Tractors	67	71	.486	14½	William Jackson
Terre Haute Browns	58	77	.430	22	Mordecai Brown/Charles Oberta/ Howard Darringer
Rock Island Islanders	57	81	.413	24½	Jack Tighe/Norman Glockson

BA: Bob Fothergill, Bloomington, .332
Runs: Gus Kellerman, Bloomington, 111
Hits: Bob Fothergill, Bloomington, 180
RBIs: Bob Fothergill, Bloomington, 116

HRs: Norman Glockson, Rock Island, 11
  Earl Sykes, Bloomington, 11
Wins: Jack Tesar, Cedar Rapids, 25
SOs: Alex Pearson, Moline, 209
ERA: Allen Conkwright, Bloomington, 1.72

B Virginia League
President: William B. Bradley

Standings	W	L	Pct.	GB	Manager
Richmond Colts*	76	38	.667	—	Lee Gooch
Portsmouth Truckers**	73	45	.619	5	Jim Barton/Jim Viox
Petersburg Goobers	68	50	.576	10	Tom Clarke
Norfolk Mary Janes	54	59	.478	21½	Bill Schwartz/Heinie Wagner
Rocky Mount Tar Heels	53	66	.445	25½	Al Bridwell/Phifer Fullenwider
Newport News Shipbuilders	51	68	.429	27½	Joe Wall/Jim Brannigan/Bill Schwartz/ Harry Lake

Standings	W	L	Pct.	GB	Manager
Suffolk Nuts	47	69	.405	30	Gabby Street
Wilson Bugs	44	71	.383	32½	John Castle

Playoff: Portsmouth 4 games, Richmond 3.

BA: Rasty Walters, Wilson, .435
Runs: Irving Smith, Richmond, 90
Hits: Henry Roth, Wilson, 154
HRs: Lee Gooch, Richmond, 8
  Pie Traynor, Portsmouth, 8
  Luke Stewart, Richmond, 8

Wins: Paul Bennett, Petersburg, 25
SOs: W.M. McGloughlin, Portsmouth, 155
ERA: Lee Stone, Richmond, 1.47
Pct: Mike Kircher, Richmond, .895, 17-2

B Western Canada League
President: Frank H. Miley

Standings	W	L	Pct.	GB	Manager
Calgary Bronchos**	73	37	.664	—	Joe Devine
Regina Senators*	72	41	.637	2½	Bill Speas
Moose Jaw Robin Hoods	56	57	.496	18½	Nick Williams
Winnipeg Maroons	53	57	.482	20	Jack Sheehan
Saskatoon Quakers	44	72	.379	32	Joe Kerman/Sammy Beer
Edmonton Esquimos	39	73	.348	35	Pete Standridge

Playoff: Calgary 4 games, Regina 3.

BA: Nelson Hawks, Calgary, .359
Runs: Harvey Christensen, Calgary, 104
Hits: Nelson Hawks, Calgary, 161
RBIs: Ernest Vache, Regina, 80

Wins: Charles Sweeney, Calgary, 19
SOs: Charles Sweeney, Calgary, 159
ERA: Evan Evans, Regina, 1.42

C South Atlantic League
President: W.H. Walsh

Standings	W	L	Pct.	GB	Manager
Columbia Comers	76	44	.633	—	Zinn Beck
Greenville Spinners	72	55	.567	7½	Bill Lava/Patsy O'Rourke
Spartanburg Pioneers	56	65	.463	20½	Doug Harbison
Charlotte Hornets	58	68	.460	21	Herb Murphy
Augusta Georgians	55	68	.447	22½	Dolly Stark
Charleston Palmettos	54	71	.432	24½	Frank Matthews/Ezra Midkiff

BA: Clarence Marshall, Charlotte, .320
Runs: Alva Nalley, Columbia, 92
Hits: Norm McMillan, Greenville, 148
RBIs: Everett Bankston, Greenville, 86
HRs: Norm McMillan, Greenville, 14

Wins: Jesse Doyle, Greenville, 25
SOs: Lawrence Cheney, Columbia, 183
ERA: A.E. Townsend, Charleston, 2.15
Pct: Lawrence Cheney, Columbia, .793, 23-6

D Blue Ridge League
President: J. Vincent Jamison, Jr.

Standings	W	L	Pct.	GB	Manager
Hagerstown Champs	56	40	.583	—	Mike Mowrey
Frederick Hustlers	53	40	.569	1½	George "Buck" Ramsey
Waynesboro Red Birds	53	42	.558	2½	Country Morris
Martinsburg Mountaineers	49	48	.505	7½	Bill Louden
Chambersburg Maroons	38	56	.405	17	Eddie Hooper
Hanover Raiders	37	60	.381	19½	Karl Kolesett/Bert Weeden

BA: Bill Satterlee, Chambersburg, .355
Runs: John Blair, Waynesboro, 61
Hits: Bill Satterlee, Chambersburg, 122
HRs: Harold Yordy, Waynesboro, 12

Wins: Charles Dye, Hagerstown, 18
SOs: Alan Clarke, Waynesboro, 150
Pct: Charles Dye, Hagerstown, .720, 18-7

D Florida State League
President: Walter W. Rose

Standings	W	L	Pct.	GB	Manager
Tampa Smokers***	79	28	.746	—	Thomas Leach
Bradentown Growers	57	44	.564	19	Frank Larisey/K. Cashion
Daytona Beach Islanders	58	45	.563	19	Rudy Hulswitt
Bartow Polkers	54	52	.509	24½	Tom Phelan
Orlando Stars	45	58	.437	32	Joe Black/Jim Donnelly
Lakeland Highlanders	41	60	.406	35	Jim Manes
Sanford Celeryfeds	40	63	.388	37	John Burns
St. Petersburg Saints	39	63	.382	37½	Art Burleson

BA: Eugene Elliott, Bradentown, .325
Runs: Bob Lamotte, Tampa, 81
Hits: Arthur Quinn, Bradentown, 129
RBIs: Arthur Quinn, Bradentown, 65

HRs: Elliott Bigelow, St. Petersburg, 10
Wins: F.W. Larisey, Bradentown, 21
SOs: Russell Drake, Bradentown, 240
ERA: Bert Humphries, Tampa, 0.76

D Georgia State League
President: J.P. Nichols, Jr.

Standings	W	L	Pct.	GB	Manager
Carrollton	53	39	.576	—	Charles Bell
Rome	50	40	.555	2	Tim Bowden
Lindale Pepperels	47	43	.522	5	Hardin Herndon
Cedartown Cedars	44	48	.478	9	D. Jones
Griffin	42	52	.447	12	Tighe Garrett
La Grange	39	53	.424	14	Red Smith/J. Culpepper

BA: Ike Boone, Cedartown, .403
Runs: Ike Boone, Cedartown, 63
Hits: Ike Boone, Cedartown, 117

HRs: Ike Boone, Cedartown, 10
Wins: Earl Johnson, Carrollton, 20

D Louisiana State League
President: Jay Davidson

Standings	W	L	Pct.	GB	Manager
Oakdale Lumberjacks#*	37	24	.607	—	Lew Bremerhoff
Lafayette Hubs	36	31	.537	4	Charles French/Buck Danville
Abbeville Sluggers**	33	35	.485	7½	F. DeMay/Lefty Herbert/Schaffer
Alexandria Tigers	23	47	.329	19½	John Carbo/G. Harris/Henry Chelette
Rayne Rice Birds@	30	33	.476	NA	Kitty Knight
New Iberia Sugar Boys@	36	25	.590	NA	Dan Gandolfi

#Oakdale lost seven wins due to ineligible players.
@Rayne and New Iberia disbanded July 6.
The league disbanded July 15.

D Piedmont League
President: William G. Bramham

Standings	W	L	Pct.	GB	Manager
Greensboro Patriots*	69	51	.575	—	Charles Carroll
Raleigh Nats**	67	53	.558	2	Joe Ward
High Point Furniture Makers	57	57	.500	9	Dick Miller/Bill Pierce
Winston Twins	56	65	.463	13½	Bill Shumaker/Eddie Brennan/Jim Kelly
Danville Tobacconists	54	65	.454	14½	J. Moore/Rebel Williams
Durham Bulls	53	65	.449	15	Frank Manush

Playoff: Greensboro 4 games, Raleigh 3.

BA: Hobart Whitman, Winston, .342
Runs: John Koval, Winston, 92
Hits: Sparky Adams, Danville, 157
HRs: Doc Smith, Greensboro, 16

Wins: George Nelson, Durham, 19
Roy Sadler, Greensboro, 19
William Hughes, Raleigh, 19
SOs: Frank Allen, Raleigh, 205
ERA: Jess Eldridge, High Point, 1.35

D South Dakota League
President: M.E. Cantillon

Standings	W	L	Pct.	GB	Manager
Mitchell Kernels	61	36	.629	—	Hank Scharnweber
Sioux Falls Soos	58	40	.592	3½	Fred Carisch
Huron Packers	56	40	.583	4½	Bill Shipke
Wessington Springs Saints	49	48	.505	12	Mattie McGrath
Redfield Reds/Red Sox	46	49	.484	14	Ollie Pickering/Harry Halstead
Madison Greys	42	50	.457	16½	Ralph Works/Dave Altizer
Aberdeen Boosters	42	54	.438	18½	Dave Altizer/Ed Karger
Miller Climbers/Jugglers	28	65	.301	31	George "Red" Fisher/Frank Gurney

BA: George "Red" Fisher, Miller, .378
Hits: G.M. Hollicker, Mitchell, 121
Wins: George Stueland, Sioux Falls, 22

SOs: George Stueland, Sioux Falls, 212
Pct: J. "Lefty" Wilkus, Mitchell, .778, 14-4

D West Texas League
President: Walter Morris

Standings	W	L	Pct.	GB	Manager
Abilene Eagles*	70	50	.583	—	Robert "Bugs" Young/Ed Kiznar
Ranger Nitros**	66	60	.524	7	Jim "Bad News" Galloway
Mineral Wells Resorters	60	60	.500	10	Charles Stis/Bill Burns
Cisco Scouts	55	61	.474	13	Jack York/Tom Carson
Gorman Buddies/ Sweetwater Swatters#	51	58	.467	13½	Bert Hise
Eastland Judges	54	67	.446	16½	

#Gorman (36-44) moved to Sweetwater August 7, first home game August 15.

Playoff: Abilene 4 games, Ranger 3.

BA: Jim "Bad News" Galloway, Ranger, .341
Runs: Charles Gressett, Gorman/ Sweetwater, 77
Hits: Joe Bratcher, Cisco/Eastland, 126

HRs: Jim "Bad News" Galloway, Ranger, 9
Wins: Henry Meade, Mineral Wells, 20
SOs: John Kolzelnick, Cisco, 200
ERA: Carl Hill, Abilene, .778, 14-4

D Western Association
President: J.C. Letcher

Standings	W	L	Pct.	GB	Manager
Okmulgee Drillers*	83	46	.643	—	Art Hemsley/Eddie Brennan
Ft. Smith Twins	80	58	.580	7½	Charles Schmidt
Enid Harvesters**	71	53	.573	9½	Ted Waring
Henryetta Hens	75	56	.573	9	Emmett Rodgers
Drumright Drummers	66	62	.516	16½	Dick Crittenden
Springfield Merchants/Orioles	58	76	.433	27½	Doc Seabough/Steve O'Rourke
Chickasha Chicks	52	72	.419	28½	Ned Pettigrew/Drap Hayes
Pawhuska Huskers	33	95	.258	50½	Norm Price/Don Moseley

Playoff: Okmulgee 3 games, Enid 3; Enid won the seventh game but the president invalidated the victory.

BA: Clyde McCarthy, Okmulgee, .372
Runs: Bill "Red" Lowrance, Enid, 100
Hits: Clyde McCarthy, Okmulgee, 164
RBIs: Dave Williams, Okmulgee, 94

HRs: Willis Windle, Okmulgee, 18
Wins: George Gray, Henryetta, 26
SOs: George Gray, Henryetta, 195
ERA: A.G. McGuire, Enid, 1.60

1920 Interleague Post Season Play

World Series
Cleveland (American) 5 games, Brooklyn (National) 2

Junior World Series
Baltimore (International) 5 games, St. Paul (American Association) 1

Dixie Series
Ft. Worth (Texas) 4 games, Little Rock (Southern Association) 2, one tie
Total Attendance: 36,836

1920 No-Hitters

Date	Pitcher	Team	League	Opponent	Score
4-15	Joe Thorn	Atlanta	Southern Assoc.	Chattanooga	5-0
5-3	Leo Mangum	Albany	Eastern	Pittsfield	5-0
5-11	Ernie Koob	Louisville	American Assoc.	Kansas City	1-0
5-13	Emilio Palmero	Omaha	Western	Joplin	1-0
5-20	Charles Gassaway	Rayne	Louisiana State	New Iberia	1-0
5-26	Cy Blankston	Abbeville	Louisiana State	Oakdale	4-0
5-28	Pete Schneider	Daytona Beach	Florida State	St. Petersburg	3-0
6-14	Frazier	Orlando	Florida State	Lakeland	5-0
6-18	Orrin Hays	Flint	Michigan-Ontario	Bay City	1-0
7-1	Walter Johnson	Washington	American	Boston	1-0
7-5	George Little	Houston	Texas	Galveston	1-0
7-24	Tom Long	Louisville	American Assoc.	Toledo	12-0
7-26	Dennis Burns	Rockford	Three-I	Terre Haute	2-0
8-19	Charles "Chief" Bender	New Haven	Eastern	Bridgeport	3-0 (P)
8-21	Jess Doyle	Greenville	South Atlantic	Spartanburg	3-0
8-22	Jimmy Zinn	Wichita Falls	Texas	Houston	5-0
8-26	Charles "Sea Lion" Hall	St. Paul	American Assoc.	Columbus	6-0
9-1	Jim Park	Drumright	Western Assoc.	Pawhuska	3-0
9-4	Allen Conkwright	Bloomington	Three-I	Rockford	5-0
9-5	Gene Dale	Dallas	Texas	Wichita Falls	1-0 (10)
9-6	Jake Knowlton	Augusta	South Atlantic	Charleston	2-0
9-9	Clarence Darrough	Wichita Falls	Texas	Ft. Worth	2-0

Number in parentheses indicates innings if other than nine; "P" indicates perfect game.

THIS DATE IN MINOR LEAGUE HISTORY

February 13, 1920, The first stable black league, the Negro National League, was organized in Kansas City, Missouri, by Andrew "Rube" Foster. Representatives from seven clubs met at the Paseo YMCA to draw up a constitution and by-laws for the National Association of Professional Colored Baseball Teams.

August 3, 1920, Harold "Hal" Chase was barred from all Pacific Coast League games because of alleged attempts by the former major league first baseman to seduce Pacific Coast League players into throwing games. Following this, Chase was also expelled from the California Mission League for the same reasons.

August 27, 1920, Because of a mistake in the schedule that was not discovered until it was too late to correct it, Toronto, International League, played a doubleheader at Hanlan's Island with two different clubs, winning over Jersey City 9-4, but losing 6-4 to Syracuse.

October 15, 1920, Charges of "wholesale bribery of players" were made by Deputy District Attorney W.C. Doran to unnamed gamblers as the Los Angeles Grand Jury commenced its inquiry into gambling incidents that involved, but were not limited to,

Vernon and Salt Lake City during the 1919 Pacific Coast League season.

November, 1920, Vernon first baseman W.B. Bouton and outfielders W.G. Rumler and Karl V. Maggart were suspended by the Pacific Coast League for gambling and other questionable activities (conspiring to throw games) during the 1919 season. Previously, San Francisco had released pitchers Tom Seaton and Casey Smith "for the good of the game." All five players were barred from Organized Ball the following January. Rumler and Maggart had formerly played in the American League.

November, 1920, Gene Dale, a former Cardinal and Cincinnati pitcher, was expelled from Organized Ball for allegedly conspiring to throw games while with Salt Lake City of the Pacific Coast League.

December 1, 1920, Southern Association President John D. Martin refused to permit Little Rock to employ pitchers Tom Seaton and Casey Smith, two players expelled by the Pacific Coast League for alleged collusion with gamblers.

1921

American League
President: Byron Bancroft Johnson

Standings	W	L	Pct.	GB	Attend.	Manager
New York Yankees	98	55	.641	—	1,230,696	Miller Huggins
Cleveland Indians	94	60	.610	4½	748,705	Tris Speaker
St. Louis Browns	81	73	.526	17½	355,978	Lee Fohl
Washington Senators	80	73	.523	18	456,069	George McBride
Boston Red Sox	75	79	.487	23½	279,273	Hugh Duffy
Detroit Tigers	71	82	.464	27	661,527	Ty Cobb
Chicago White Sox	62	92	.403	36½	543,650	Kid Gleason
Philadelphia Athletics	53	100	.346	45	344,430	Connie Mack

BA: Harry Heilmann, Detroit, .394
Runs: Babe Ruth, New York, 177
Hits: Harry Heilmann, Detroit, 237
RBIs: Babe Ruth, New York, 171
HRs: Babe Ruth, New York, 59

Wins: Carl Mays, New York, 27
Urban Shocker, St. Louis, 27
SOs: Walter Johnson, Washington, 143
ERA: Red Faber, Chicago, 2.48
Pct: Carl Mays, New York, .750, 27-9

National League
President: John A. Heydler

Standings	W	L	Pct.	GB	Attend.	Manager
New York Giants	94	59	.614	—	973,477	John McGraw
Pittsburgh Pirates	90	63	.588	4	701,567	George Gibson
St. Louis Cardinals	87	66	.569	7	384,773	Branch Rickey
Boston Braves	79	74	.516	15	318,627	Fred Mitchell
Brooklyn Robins	77	75	.507	16½	613,245	Wilbert Robinson
Cincinnati Reds	70	83	.458	24	311,227	Pat Moran
Chicago Cubs	64	89	.418	30	410,107	Johnny Evers/Bill Killefer
Philadelphia Phillies	51	103	.331	43½	273,961	Wild Bill Donovan/ Irvin "Kaiser" Wilhelm

BA: Rogers Hornsby, St. Louis, .397
Runs: Rogers Hornsby, St. Louis, 131
Hits: Rogers Hornsby, St. Louis, 235
RBIs: Rogers Hornsby, St. Louis, 126
HRs: George Kelly, New York, 23

Wins: Burleigh Grimes, Brooklyn, 22
Wilbur Cooper, Pittsburgh, 22
SOs: Burleigh Grimes, Brooklyn, 136
ERA: Bill Doak, St. Louis, 2.59
Pct: Bill Doak, St. Louis, .714, 15-6

AA American Association
President: Thomas J. Hickey

Standings	W	L	Pct.	GB	Attend.	Manager
Louisville Colonels	98	70	.583	—	170,614	Joe McCarthy
Minneapolis Millers	92	73	.558	4½	273,159	Joe Cantillon
Kansas City Blues	84	80	.512	12	279,043	Otto Knabe
Indianapolis Indians	83	85	.494	15	139,488	Jack Hendricks
Milwaukee Brewers	81	86	.485	16½	176,485	Jack Egan
St. Paul Saints	80	87	.479	17½	179,527	Mike Kelley
Toledo Mud Hens	80	88	.476	18	198,148	Bill Clymer/Fred Luderus
Columbus Senators	67	96	.411	33½	105,853	Clarence "Pants" Rowland

BA: Jay Kirke Sr., Louisville, .386
Runs: Bunny Brief, Kansas City, 166
Hits: Jay Kirke Sr., Louisville, 282
RBIs: Bunny Brief, Kansas City, 191
HRs: Bunny Brief, Kansas City, 42
TBs: Jay Kirke Sr., Louisville, 422

Wins: Adlai Bono, Kansas City, 25
Dave Danforth, Columbus, 25
SOs: Dave Danforth, Columbus, 204
ERA: Dave Danforth, Columbus, 2.66
CGs: Dave Danforth, Columbus, 35

AA International League
President: John Conway Toole

Standings	W	L	Pct.	GB	Attend.	Manager
Baltimore Orioles	119	47	.717	—	308,970	Jack Dunn
Rochester Colts	100	68	.595	20	217,845	George Stallings
Buffalo Bisons	99	69	.589	21	167,399	George Wiltse
Toronto Maple Leafs	89	77	.536	30	147,639	Larry Doyle/Lena Blackburne
Newark Bears	72	92	.433	46	103,060	Jim Walsh
Syracuse Stars	71	96	.425	48½	115,985	Tom Madden/Frank Shaughnessy
Jersey City Skeeters	59	106	.358	59½	71,631	Patsy Donovan
Reading Aces	56	110	.337	63	84,695	Rich Hoblitzell

BA: Jack Bentley, Baltimore, .412
Runs: Maurice Archdeacon, Rochester, 166
Hits: Jack Bentley, Baltimore, 246
RBIs: Fred Merkle, Rochester, 152

HRs: Jack Bentley, Baltimore, 24
Wins: Jack Ogden, Baltimore, 31
SOs: Lefty Grove, Baltimore, 254
ERA: Joe Reddy, Baltimore, 1.98

AA Pacific Coast League
President: William H. McCarthy

Standings	W	L	Pct.	GB	Attend.	Manager
Los Angeles Angels	108	80	.574	—	288,044	Red Killefer
Sacramento Senators	105	80	.568	1½	125,123	Bill Rodgers
San Francisco Seals	106	82	.564	2	399,420	Charles Graham
Seattle Rainiers	103	82	.557	3½	235,096	Clyde Wares/Bill Kenworthy
Oakland Oaks	101	85	.543	6	300,214	Del Howard
Vernon Tigers	96	90	.516	11	250,389	Bill Essick
Salt Lake City Bees	73	110	.399	32½	102,261	Gavvy Cravath
Portland Beavers	51	134	.276	55½	85,243	Walter McCreedie

BA: Hack Miller, Oakland, .347
Runs: Paddy Siglin, Salt Lake City, 156
Hits: Paddy Siglin, Salt Lake City, 270
HRs: Paddy Siglin, Salt Lake City, 22

Wins: Wheezer Dell, Vernon, 28
SOs: Paul Fittery, Sacramento, 164
ERA: Vic Aldridge, Los Angeles, 2.16

A Eastern League
President: Daniel O'Neill

Standings	W	L	Pct.	GB	Manager
Pittsfield Hillies	92	59	.609	—	Walker Hammond
Worcester Boosters	88	65	.575	5	John McMahon
Bridgeport Americans	85	66	.563	7	Eugene McCann
New Haven Indians	81	72	.529	12	Charles "Chief" Bender
Hartford Senators	73	78	.483	19	Arthur Irwin/Jack Dowd/Chet Thomas
Springfield Hampdens	70	82	.461	22½	John Flynn
Waterbury Brasscos	64	85	.430	27	Joe Cosgrove/Billy Gilbert
Albany Senators	52	98	.347	39½	Joe Birmingham/Paddy O'Connor

BA: Walter Hammond, Pittsfield, .351
Runs: Robert Murray, Worcester, 129
Hits: Henry Long, Waterbury, 211
HRs: John Flynn, Springfield, 15

Wins: Colonel Snover, Pittsfield, 25
SOs: Frank Woodward, New Haven, 171
ERA: Herman Bornheoft, Bridgeport, 1.73
Pct: Al Pierotti, Pittsfield, .767, 23-7

A Southern Association
President: John D. Martin

Standings	W	L	Pct.	GB	Attend.	Manager
Memphis Chickasaws	104	49	.679	—	253,338	Spencer Abbott
New Orleans Pelicans	97	57	.630	7½	167,076	Johnny Dobbs
Birmingham Barons	90	63	.558	14	160,734	Carleton Molesworth
Little Rock Travelers	74	77	.490	29	110,760	Norman "Kid" Elberfeld
Atlanta Crackers	73	78	.483	30	184,740	Charley Frank
Nashville Volunteers	62	90	.409	41½	97,057	Hub Purdue
Mobile Bears	58	94	.382	45½	62,356	Herman Bronkie
Chattanooga Lookouts	52	102	.338	52½	69,938	Sam Strang Nicklin/ Ed McDonald

BA: Ike Boone, New Orleans, .389
Runs: Andy High, Memphis, 136
Hits: Bert Griffith, New Orleans, 224
RBIs: Polly McLarry, Memphis, 135
HRs: Dutch Bernsen, Birmingham, 22

3B: Ike Boone, New Orleans, 27
Wins: Oscar Tuero, Memphis, 27
SOs: Claude Jonnard, Little Rock, 234
ERA: Tom Phillips, New Orleans, 2.63
CGs: Claude Jonnard, Little Rock, 37

A Texas League
President: J. Doak Roberts

Standings	W	L	Pct.	GB	Manager
Ft. Worth Panthers***	107	51	.677	—	Jake Atz
Houston Buffaloes	92	67	.579	15½	George Whiteman
Wichita Falls Spudders	86	74	.541	22	Walt Salm
Dallas Submarines	81	78	.508	26½	Ham Patterson
Shreveport Gassers	74	84	.468	33	Billy Smith
Galveston Pirates	68	87	.439	37½	Roy Ellam
Beaumont Exporters	64	93	.408	40½	Pat Newnam
San Antonio Bears	60	98	.380	47	John Nee

BA: Clarence "Big Boy" Kraft, Ft. Worth, .352
Runs: Clarence "Big Boy" Kraft, Ft. Worth, 132
Hits: Clarence "Big Boy" Kraft, Ft. Worth, 212

RBIs: Henry Eibel, Shreveport, 145
HRs: Henry Eibel, Shreveport, 35
Wins: Joe Pate, Ft. Worth, 30
SOs: John Hollingsworth, Wichita Falls, 218
ERA: John Hollingsworth, Wichita Falls, 2.13

A Western League
President: Albert R. Tearney

Standings	W	L	Pct.	GB	Manager
Wichita Witches	106	61	.615	—	Joe Berger
Omaha Buffaloes	95	73	.565	11½	Jack Lelivelt/Barney Burch
Oklahoma City Indians	93	75	.554	13½	Dick Breen
Sioux City Packers	81	83	.494	23½	Frank Metz/George Andreas
St. Joseph Saints	79	88	.473	27	Yip Owens
Joplin Miners	76	91	.455	30	James Hamilton
Des Moines Boosters	71	92	.436	33	Jack Coffey
Tulsa Oilers	65	103	.387	41½	Jimmy Burke/Bill Clymer

Attendance: Tulsa, 104,975.

BA: Jack Lelivelt, Omaha, .416
Runs: Royce Washburn, Wichita, 170
Hits: Jack Lelivelt, Omaha, 274
HRs: Fred Beck, Wichita, 35

2B: Jack Lelivelt, Omaha, 70
Wins: Roy Allen, Oklahoma City, 25
SOs: Jack Tesar, Sioux City, 163
Pct: Nelson Pott, Des Moines, .737, 14-5

*Won first-half   **Won second-half   ***Won both halves

B Central League
President: Emerson W. Dickerson

Standings	W	L	Pct.	GB	Manager
Ludington Mariners	87	42	.675	—	James Sharpe
Kalamazoo Celery Pickers..	69	58	.543	17	George Tomer
Lansing Senators	65	63	.508	21½	Fred Hunter
Muskegon Muskies..............	63	67	.485	24½	Dannie Claire
Grand Rapids Joshers	59	71	.454	28½	Josh Devore/Louis Wolfe
Jackson/Ionia Mayors#......	44	86	.338	43½	Dan Jenkins/Bill Hartwell

#Jackson (27-45) moved to Ionia July 20, first home game July 30.

BA: Harry Purcell, Jackson/Ionia, .380
Runs: Joe Napier, Ludington, 112
Hits: Harry Purcell, Jackson/Ionia, 176
RBIs: Grover Prough, Kalamazoo, 97
HRs: Joseph Hamel, Ludington, 21
Wins: William Shoup, Ludington, 25
SOs: Lawrence Reno, Lansing, 133
ERA: William Shoup, Ludington, 2.71
Pct: Clarence Brown, Ludington, .759, 22-7

B Michigan-Ontario League
President: George H. Maines

Standings	W	L	Pct.	GB	Manager
London Tecumsehs**........	72	46	.610	—	Frank "Buzz" Wetzel
Brantford Red Sox	64	52	.552	7	George Orme
Bay City Wolves*.............	65	53	.551	7	Punch Knoll
Hamilton Tigers.................	64	55	.538	8½	Patsy O'Rourke
Port Huron Saints...............	58	63	.479	15½	Jim Pierce/Steve Harter & Bill Kelly
Saginaw Aces	57	62	.479	15½	Ray McKee
Kitchener Beavers	45	68	.398	24½	Otto Jordan
Flint Vehicles...................	48	74	.393	26	Ted Anderson/Dolly Gray

Playoff: London 4 games, Bay City 2.

BA: Frank Nesser, Saginaw, .385
Runs: Frank Nesser, Saginaw, 90
Hits: Frank Nesser, Saginaw, 173
HRs: Frank Emmer, Flint, 15
Wins: Cy Boothby, Bay City, 21
SOs: Claude Gillenwater, Saginaw, 157
ERA: Pete Behan, Hamilton, 1.18

B Pacific Coast International League
President: Louis H. Burnett

Standings	W	L	Pct.	GB	Manager
Yakima Indians***............	79	36	.687	—	Frank Raymond
Tacoma Tigers	63	53	.543	16½	Charles Mullen
Victoria Bees.............	45	71	.388	34½	Cliff Blankenship/Elmer Hansen
Vancouver Beavers...........	45	72	.385	35	Bill Purtell

BA: George Lafayette, Yakima, .428
Runs: George Lafayette, Yakima, 132
Hits: George Lafayette, Yakima, 179
HRs: Ed Handley, Victoria, 15
Wins: Guy Cooper, Yakima, 22
SOs: Guy Cooper, Yakima, 162
Pct: Henry Robcke, Tacoma, .762, 16-5

B South Atlantic League
President: W.H. Walsh

Standings	W	L	Pct.	GB	Manager
Columbia Comers	95	53	.642	—	Zinn Beck
Charleston Pals	83	64	.562	11½	Ezra Midkiff/Larry Cheney
Augusta Georgians	78	68	.534	16	Emil Huhn
Greenville Spinners	71	76	.483	23½	Lew Wendell/Doc Pressly
Spartanburg Pioneers	61	86	.415	33½	Al Bridwell/Mike Kelly
Charlotte Hornets	52	93	.359	41	Ed Hooper/Red Day/Ezra Midkiff

BA: Goose Goslin, Columbia, .390
Runs: Goose Goslin, Columbia, 124
Hits: Goose Goslin, Columbia, 214
RBIs: Goose Goslin, Columbia, 131
HRs: August Felix, Charleston, 19
Wins: Lee Johnson, Columbia, 24
SOs: Willard Davis, Augusta, 174
ERA: Roy Jordan, Columbia, 2.10
Pct: Roy Jordan, Columbia, .918, 21-2

B Three-I League
President: Albert R. Tearney

Standings	W	L	Pct.	GB	Manager
Moline Plowboys	78	55	.587	—	Earle Mack
Rockford Rox	72	64	.529	7½	Harry Brandt
Terre Haute Tots.................	70	65	.519	9	Bob Coleman
Peoria Tractors...................	70	69	.504	11	William Jackson
Evansville Evas.................	67	69	.493	12½	Al Bashang
Bloomington Bloomers........	65	69	.485	13½	Joseph Dunn
Cedar Rapids Rabbits	62	72	.463	16½	Frank Boyle
Rock Island Islanders..........	57	78	.422	22	George McQuillan

BA: John Anderson, Rockford, .339
Runs: J.F. Hall, Rockford, 99
Hits: John Anderson, Rockford, 170
RBIs: John Anderson, Rockford, 109
HRs: Howard Jones, Moline, 17
Wins: Fred Heimach, Moline, 24
SOs: James Sullivan, Moline, 185
ERA: Fred Heimach, Moline, 2.38

B Virginia League
President: William B. Bradley

Standings	W	L	Pct.	GB	Manager
Wilson Bugs	74	52	.587	—	Tom Clarke
Portsmouth Truckers*.........	78	56	.582	—	Jim Viox
Rocky Mount Tar Heels	77	57	.575	1	Phifer Fullenwider
Richmond Colts	74	58	.561	3	Ray Ryan
Norfolk Tars**	74	64	.536	6	Jack Warhop
Suffolk Wildcats	59	78	.431	20½	Gabby Street
Newport News Shipbuilders ...	52	81	.391	25½	Harry Lake
Petersburg Goobers/					
Tarboro Tarbabies#............	46	88	.343	32	Bill Martin/Ambrose McConnell

#Petersburg moved to Tarboro August 2, first home game August 4.
Commissioner K.M. Landis intervened because of salary limitation violations; he threw out Rocky Mount and Wilson as first half winners and gave the title to Portsmouth.

Playoff: Portsmouth 4 games, Norfolk 1.

BA: Jim Viox, Portsmouth, .370
Runs: Ben Spencer, Rocky Mount, 153
Hits: Ben Spencer, Rocky Mount, 194
HRs: Joe Kelly, Norfolk, 17
Wins: William McGloughlin, Portsmouth, 25
SOs: Al Benton, Portsmouth, 196
Pct: Leroy Finnegan, Richmond, .857, 18-3

B Western Canada League
President: Robert Pearson

Standings	W	L	Pct.	GB	Manager
Calgary Bronchos*	70	39	.642	—	Joe Devine
Winnipeg Maroons**	72	42	.632	½	George Brautigan
Saskatoon Quakers	57	59	.491	16½	John Hummel
Edmonton Eskimos.............	51	60	.459	20	Gus Gleichman
Regina Senators#...............	37	43	.463	NA	Bill Speas
Moose Jaw Millers#...........	21	65	.244	NA	Nick Williams/Elmer Leifer

#Regina and Moose Jaw disbanded August 10.

Playoff: Calgary 5 games, Winnipeg 2, one tie.

BA: Frank Jude, Saskatoon, .355
Runs: Phil Apperson, Edmonton, 111
Hits: Babe Herman, Edmonton, 135
HRs: Heinie Manush, Edmonton, 9

C Florida State League
President: Walter W. Rose

Standings	W	L	Pct.	GB	Manager
Orlando Tigers...................	73	42	.635	—	Joe Tinker
Tampa Smokers	64	50	.561	8½	Thomas Leach
Lakeland Highlanders.........	59	57	.509	14½	Harry Swacina/Perry Wilder/Bill Zimmerman/ Milton Reed
Daytona Beach Islanders	55	60	.478	18	Jack Martin
St. Petersburg Saints	50	65	.435	23	Cy Barger
Jacksonville Scouts	45	72	.385	29	Dominick Mullaney

BA: Walt Ammons, Tampa, .345
Runs: Ernie Burke, Orlando, 101
Hits: Ed Morris, St. Petersburg, 152
HRs: Walter Shannon, Daytona Beach, 9
Wins: Frank Henry, Orlando, 25
SOs: Frank Henry, Orlando, 200
Pct: C.D. Wilder, Daytona Beach, .813, 13-3

C Piedmont League
President: William G. Bramham

Standings	W	L	Pct.	GB	Manager
Raleigh Red Birds..............	68	52	.567	—	Joe Ward
High Point Furniture Makers**	65	55	.542	3	Bill Pierre
Greensboro Patriots*	64	58	.525	5	Charles Carroll
Winston-Salem Twins	62	58	.517	6	Charles Clancy
Durham Bulls....................	57	64	.471	11½	Frank Manush
Danville Tobacconists	46	75	.380	22½	Herb Murphy

Playoff: Greensboro 4 games, High Point 1.

BA: Lloyd Smith, Greensboro, .404
Runs: Hoke Floyd, Raleigh, 102
Hits: Lloyd Smith, Greensboro, 195
HRs: Jim Holt, High Point, 26
Wins: William Hughes, Raleigh, 26
SOs: Gilbert Price, Durham, 158
Pct: Thomas Day, High Point, .875, 14-2

D Alabama-Tennessee League
President: G.R. Cowie

Standings	W	L	Pct.	GB	Manager
Albany-Decatur Twins*	50	39	.663	—	
Tri-Cities Triplets#	44	46	.489	6½	
Columbia Mules	42	46	.477	7½	Red Smith
Russellville Miners**	41	46	.471	8	

#represented Sheffield-Tuscumbia-Muscle Shoals, Alabama.

Playoff: Albany-Decatur 5 games, Russellville 1.

D Appalachian League
President: W.T. Ellison

Standings	W	L	Pct.	GB	Manager
Johnson City Soldiers**	63	44	.589	—	Dave Taylor
Kingsport Indians	58	48	.547	4½	Harold Irelan
Greeneville Burley Cubs*	58	48	.547	4½	Nick Leonard
Bristol State Liners	57	52	.523	7	Nick Bell/Cliff Raley
Knoxville Pioneers	50	58	.463	13½	Roy Clunk
Cleveland Manufacturers	36	72	.333	27½	Bob Hunter

Playoff: Johnson City won the second half by a President's ruling.
Finals: Johnson City 5 games, Greeneville 1.

BA: Joe Price, Johnson City, .363
Runs: Oscar Rodriguez, Greeneville, 77
Hits: John Inman, Kingsport, 122
HRs: Joe Price, Johnson City, 18
Wins: L.G. Ellis, Kingsport, 18
SOs: F.E. Hodge, Greeneville/Cleveland, 124
Pct: L.G. Ellis, Kingsport, .900, 18-2

D Blue Ridge League
President: J. Vincent Jamison, Jr.

Standings	W	L	Pct.	GB	Manager
Frederick Hustlers	58	38	.604	—	George "Buck" Ramsey
Hanover Raiders	52	40	.565	4	Bert Weeden
Waynesboro Villagers	52	45	.536	6½	Bill Morris
Martinsburg Mountaineers	44	49	.473	12½	Joe Ward
Chambersburg Marooners	46	52	.469	13	Harry Hinchman
Hagerstown Champs	30	58	.341	24	Mike Mowery

BA: Bill Goff, Hanover, .384
Runs: Frank Lloyd, Martinsburg/Waynesboro, 92
Hits: Walter Kimmick, Waynesboro, 146
HRs: Walter Kimmick, Waynesboro, 20
Wins: Alan Clarke, Waynesboro, 25
SOs: Alan Clarke, Waynesboro, 258
Pct: William King, Frederick, .793, 23-6

D Dakota League
President: M.E. Cantillon

Standings	W	L	Pct.	GB	Manager
Mitchell Kernels	65	33	.663	—	Hank Scharnweber
Sioux Falls Canaries	61	35	.649	3	Fred Carish
Wahpeton-Breckenridge Twins	55	43	.561	10	Roy Patterson
Redfield	47	46	.505	15½	Harry Halstead
Madison	45	50	.474	18½	Dave Altizer
Watertown Cubs	44	53	.454	20½	Matty McGrath
Aberdeen Grays	35	62	.361	29½	Ed Karger
Huron	34	64	.347	31	Jay Andrews

BA: Albert Nolt, Mitchell, .395
Runs: Albert Nolt, Mitchell, 121
Hits: Albert Nolt, Mitchell, 154
HRs: Albert Wenz, Madison, 9
Wins: George Stueland, Sioux Falls, 22
SOs: George Stueland, Sioux Falls, 169
Pct: Earl Keiser, Mitchell, .909, 20-2

D Georgia State League
President: H.P. Meikleham

Standings	W	L	Pct.	GB	Manager
Lindale Pepperells*	69	29	.704	—	Hardin Herndon
Griffin	53	48	.525	17½	Harry Matthews
La Grange**	52	49	.515	18½	Fred Hager
Cedartown Cedars	52	49	.515	18½	Bill Schwartz
Rome	50	49	.505	19½	Jim Fox
Carrollton	24	76	.240	46	Cy Hawkins/Jule Warren

Playoff: La Grange 4 games, Lindale 1.

BA: Ollie Tucker, Cedartown, .434
Runs: Ollie Tucker, Cedartown, 76
Hits: Ollie Tucker, Cedartown, 146
HRs: Ollie Tucker, Cedartown, 22

D Mississippi State League
President: John G. Dailey

Standings	W	L	Pct.	GB	Manager
Clarksdale Cubs**	65	44	.596	—	Baxter Sparks
Greenwood Indians*	59	49	.546	5½	Charles Hall
Meridian Mets	45	60	.429	18	C. Reflogal/Ollie Mills
Jackson Red Sox	45	61	.425	18½	Rebel Oakes

Playoff: Greenwood 5 games, Clarksdale 0.

BA: John Kane, Greenwood/Meridian, .355
Runs: Ben Allen, Meridian, 121
Hits: Ben Allen, Meridian, 124
Wins: Harold Goldsmith, Clarksdale, 16
SOs: Frank Albernese, Jackson, 128
Pct: Hugh Boyd, Greenwood, .688, 11-5

D Southwestern League
President: Ensley Barbour

Standings	W	L	Pct.	GB	Manager
Independence Producers***	103	38	.730	—	Ted Waring
Muskogee Mets	93	56	.624	19	Bobby Wallace
Pittsburg Pirates	87	63	.580	25½	Frank Matthews
Coffeyville Refiners	71	72	.497	38	John Clarke
Sapulpa Sappers	68	76	.472	41½	Gerald Jones/Larry Quigley
Bartlesville Braves	64	80	.444	45½	John McCloskey/Al Lindsay

	W	L	Pct.	GB	Manager
Miami Indians	59	84	.413	50	Bobby Byrne
Parsons Parsons/ Cushing Oilers#	34	110	.236	70½	G.C. Knight/Lefty Wilson

#Parsons (26-57) moved to Cushing, first home game July 27.

BA: Bill Bagwell, Pittsburg, .357
Runs: Bill "Red" Lowrance, Independence, 125
Hits: Chuck Corgan, Muskogee, 193
HRs: Glenn Wright, Independence, 22
3B: Bill Bagwell, Pittsburg, 27
SBs: Bill "Red" Lowrance, Independence, 98
Wins: Happy Campbell, Independence, 28
SOs: Jake Beedle, Pittsburg, 263
Pct: Happy Campbell, Independence, .778, 28-8

D Texas-Oklahoma League
President: A.M. Keisker

Standings	W	L	Pct.	GB	Manager
Paris Snappers*	89	38	.701	—	Earl "Red" Snapp
Ardmore Peps**	87	40	.685	2	Coon Barnes/Walter Thompson/ Joe Chelette/Fletcher "Sled" Allen
Bonham Favorites	57	71	.445	32½	Pittman/Moss
Cleburne Generals	51	75	.398	37½	Robertson/Pete Dillon/William Hopper
Graham Hijackers/ Mineral Wells Resorters#	49	79	.383	40½	Roy Brashear
Sherman Lions	48	78	.381	40½	Babe Peebles/Curley Maloney

#Graham (5-24) moved to Mineral Wells May 27, first home game May 30.

Playoff: Ardmore 4 games, Paris 4; Ardmore refused to play at Paris. Paris was named champion.

D West Texas League
President: Richard Hodges

Standings	W	L	Pct.	GB	Manager
Sweetwater Swatters*	72	56	.563	—	Clarence "Pop Boy" Smith/Earl Fleharty
Abilene Eagles**	69	56	.552	1½	Hub Northen
San Angelo Bronchos	70	58	.547	2	Luke Robinson
Mineral Wells Resorters/ Ballinger Bearcats#	57	72	.442	15½	Roy Brashear/Clarence "Pop Boy" Smith
Ranger Nitros+	37	43	.463	NA	Sled Allen
Cisco Scouts@	27	47	.365	NA	Josh Billings

#Mineral Wells moved to Ballinger May 19.
@Cisco disbanded July 6.
+Ranger disbanded July 9.

Playoff: Sweetwater defeated San Angelo in a one game playoff for the first half title.
Finals: Abilene 4 games, Sweetwater 3.

D Western Association
President: George LaMotte

Standings	W	L	Pct.	GB	Manager
Springfield Midgets	85	60	.586	—	Charles Stis/Wilson White
Ft. Smith Twins**	83	61	.576	1½	Charles Schmidt
Henryetta Hens	77	66	.538	7	Dick Crittenden/Steve O'Rourke
Pawhuska Huskers	76	71	.517	10	Rudy Hulswitt
Enid Harvesters	77	74	.510	11	Barney Cleveland
Chickasha Chicks*	74	74	.500	12½	Drap Hayes
Okmulgee Drillers	71	76	.483	15	Harry Womack/Ed Klepfer/Red Herriott/ John Wuffli
Drumright Oilers	44	105	.295	43	Dick Speer

Playoff: Chickasha 4 games, Ft. Smith 3.

BA: Oscar Felber, Pawhuska, .341
Runs: C.E. Johnson, Chickasha, 129
Hits: Green, Chickasha, 191
HRs: Frank Reiger, Enid, 20
Wins: Grady Adkins, Henryetta, 26
SOs: Gorham Leverett, Ft. Smith, 199
Pct: Lewis Jones, Springfield, .759, 22-7

1921 Interleague Post Season Play

World Series
New York (National) 5 games, New York (American) 3

Junior World Series
Louisville (American Association) 5 games, Baltimore (International) 3
Total Attendance: 44,985

Dixie Series
Ft. Worth (Texas) 4 games, Memphis (Southern Association) 2
Total Attendance: 43,683

Class B Championship
London (Michigan-Ontario) 5 games, Ludington (Central) 3

Class D Series
Springfield (Western Association) 2 games, Independence (Southwestern) 1

Border Series
Ardmore (Texas-Oklahoma) 2 games, Chickasha (Western Association) 0

1921 No-Hitters

Date	Pitcher	Team	League	Opponent	Score
4-22	Harry Biemiller	Jersey City	International	Buffalo	1-0
4-24	Leo Rossi	Pawhuska	Western Assoc.	Springfield	4-0
5-12	Happy Campbell	Independence	Southwestern	Miami	4-0
5-26	Ray Werre	Brantford	Michigan-Ontario	Saginaw	5-0
5-28	Johnny Suggs	Atlanta	Southern Assoc.	Memphis	4-0
6-1	Bert Humphries	Lakeland	Florida State	Jacksonville	2-0
6-18	Robert Clark	Columbus	American Assoc.	Indianapolis	3-0
6-20	Al Williamson	La Grange	Georgia State	Cedartown	5-0
6-25	George Swartz	Dallas	Texas	Houston	1-0
7-5	Myles Thomas	Hartford	Eastern	Springfield	3-0
7-20	Phil Morrison	Birmingham	Southern Assoc.	Mobile	14-0 (7)
7-23	Al Pierotti	Pittsfield	Eastern	Albany	2-0
7-24	Tom Phillips	New Orleans	Southern Assoc.	Mobile	1-0
7-31	J.J. Woodhead	Rocky Mount	Virginia	Norfolk	3-0
8-4	Glenn Harris	Ft. Smith	Western Assoc.	Okmulgee	4-0
8-14	Paul Carter	Ardmore	Texas-Oklahoma	Bonham	5-0
8-22	Oscar Roettger	Muskogee	Southwestern	Cushing	4-1
8-22	Wilcy Moore	Paris	Texas-Oklahoma	Bonham	1-0
8-23	A.F. Miller	Enid	Western Assoc.	Henryetta	5-1
8-27	Clarence Brown	Ludington	Central	Grand Rapids	3-0 (P)
8-27	Hub Pruett	Tulsa	Western	St. Joseph	6-0
9-1	Frank Woodward	New Haven	Eastern	Waterbury	10-0

Number in parentheses indicates innings if other than nine; "P" indicates perfect game.

THIS DATE IN MINOR LEAGUE HISTORY

March 12, 1921, The Worcester club in the Eastern League signed Charles Leo "Gabby" Hartnett, a tall, young semipro catcher from Millville, Massachusetts. Hartnett's father was the motorman on the electric trolley between Worcester and Woonsocket, and Hartnett was signed by Worcester as a favor to Gabby's father.

April 23, 1921, First baseman Clarence "Big Boy" Kraft of Ft. Worth, Texas League, went 5-for-5, including a double and three homers, to help his team defeat Wichita Falls 14-11.

April 24, 1921, Tommy McMillan, Memphis, Southern Association, had a 6-for-6 day against Birmingham, plus one putout and nine assists at shortstop.

May 9, 1921, Centerfielder Ted LeMenye of Peoria, Three-I League, made five assists in one game, throwing out four Rockford base runners at the plate and one at third base.

May 14, 1921, Outfielder Ross Wallers of Portsmouth made seven hits, five singles and two doubles, in seven times at bat in a 12-inning Virginia League game against Wilson.

May 27, 1921, Wichita outfielder Jim Blakesley had five doubles in a 23-7 Western League win over Omaha. Blakesley also had a single for a 6-for-6 day. His teammate Carlton East belted three homers and a double.

May 28, 1921, Syracuse, International League, beat Reading 13-12, as outfielder Frank "Wildfire" Schulte, outfielder Arthur Smith and third baseman Jewel Ens hit home runs on three successive pitches in the seventh inning off Reading's Dean Barnhardt.

June 3, 1921, Lou Gehrig made his pro debut with Hartford of the Eastern League under the name of Lou Lewis. He had been sent by the Giants after a tryout at the Polo Grounds. Gehrig went 0-for-3 versus Pittsfield in his first pro game. His first hit, a triple against Waterbury, came the following day. He played in 12 games and hit .261 before returning to Columbia University.

June 6, 1921, Paris, Texas-Oklahoma League, scored 16 runs in the sixth inning and defeated Bonham 16-0. No other runs were scored in the game. All scoring came off Blankenship, who allowed 12 hits, four of which were doubles.

June 15, 1921, Led by light-hitting catcher Walter Tragesser's 6-for-6 day, Buffalo defeated Baltimore 19-8 in the second game of an International League doubleheader, ending the Orioles' string of consecutive victories at 27. Buffalo had 24 hits. The fabulous Orioles tied the Organized Ball record for consecutive wins set by Corsicana, Texas League, in 1902.

June 15, 1921, Catcher Pete Lapan went 6-for-6 in Galveston's 15-2 win over Wichita Falls in the Texas League.

June 27, 1921, Jack Bentley, Baltimore, International League, hit three consecutive homers against Rochester, for a total of eight in the last week.

July 4, 1921, Shortstop Henry Sands of Salt Lake City, Pacific Coast League, made an unassisted triple play against Sacramento. Sands also hit two homers as Salt Lake City, scoring 11 runs in the eighth inning, won 16-14. Salt Lake City had 24 hits, Sacramento 21.

July 4, 1921, Charleston, South Atlantic League, lost to Augusta in the morning game after 14 successive victories.

July 7, 1921, First baseman Leslie went 6-for-6 as New Orleans, Southern Association, defeated Chattanooga 17-1.

July 10, 1921, From July 7, 1919 to this date, Garrett "Gary" Fortune won 24 straight games in the Eastern League. Fortune spent a portion of this time in the major leagues.

July 13, 1921, Outfielder Jim Thorpe, the famed Indian athlete, smashed three home runs as Toledo whipped Milwaukee 17-4. Also in the American Association, Bunny Brief of Kansas City hit three homers against Columbus.

July 16, 1921, Manager Arthur Irwin of Hartford, Eastern League, fell or jumped from the steamer cabin during a voyage from New York to Boston.

July 22, 1921, Jersey City, International League, beat Baltimore pitcher Jack Ogden 3-2, after the righthander had won 18 successive decisions.

July 24, 1921, After having hit safely in 32 consecutive games, third baseman Harry Long of Waterbury, Eastern League, was stopped by Hartford pitcher Sloan.

July 30, 1921, Pitcher Ray Bird of Johnson City, Appalachian League, was scored on by Bristol after having hurled 46 consecutive scoreless innings. In 130 frames, Bird allowed but six earned runs.

July 31, 1921, Pitcher Harry Gardner of Oakland, Pacific Coast League, had 11 assists in a 7-2 win over Seattle.

August 7, 1921, In the Texas League, a new attendance record was set at Dallas when 10,073 spectators turned out to witness the Ft. Worth tilt.

August 13, 1921, Rochester, International League, outslugged Reading 16-15. First baseman Fred Merkle had five hits in six at bats for the winners.

August 14, 1921, First baseman Bunny Brief of Kansas City, American Association, was stopped by Minneapolis pitcher Grover Lowdermilk after having hit safely in 31 consecutive games.

August 15, 1921, In the Blue Ridge League, the Hanover pitching staff completed a string of 42 consecutive scoreless innings by blanking Hagerstown, Martinsburg (twice) and Waynesboro.

August 24, 1921, With two out in the ninth inning, Neal Ball of New Haven, Eastern League, singled to prevent Waterbury hurler Kahn from notching a no-hit game.

August 31, 1921, Second baseman Bob Fisher of Minneapolis, American Association, was stopped by Louisville pitcher Ben Tincup after having batted safely in 36 consecutive games.

September 2, 1921, Maurice Archdeacon of Rochester, International League, circled the bases in 13.4 seconds during a pre-game exhibition at Rochester to set a new record. The old mark of 13.8 seconds was set by Hans Lobert in 1910.

September 3, 1921, Edward Wurm of Jersey City, International League, in a doubleheader against Syracuse, received seven consecutive bases on balls. He was a pitcher playing in the outfield.

September 5, 1921, Portland and Los Angeles of the Pacific Coast League completed a 13-game series which began August 29. The Angels took 10 of the 13 contests.

September 14, 1921, In the first game of a doubleheader, Bates, Baker and Snower of Pittsfield, Eastern League, all hit grand slams off pitcher Lindstrom of Worcester.

September 24, 1921, Worcester, Eastern League, pushed across 12 runs in the fourth inning as they crushed Albany 26-2. Worcester had 27 hits, six by catcher Gabby Hartnett in six at bats.

September 25, 1921, The International League season closed with Baltimore winning the pennant with 119 victories, a record for the circuit and one of the highest winning marks in Organized Ball. The Orioles finished 20 games ahead of runner-up Rochester, which posted 100 victories. Jack Ogden of the Orioles hurled his 31st victory, tying the modern league record held by Rube Vickers.

October 9, 1921, The fourth Junior World Series game was forfeited to Baltimore when 3,500 fans at Louisville, angered by a close decision, swarmed the field and pelted the umps and policemen with seat cushions. The Orioles were leading 12-4 when the game was called.

October 17, 1921, Louisville captured the Junior World Series, five games to three, by winning 11-5 over Baltimore. Louisville batted .329 in the eight-game series. The victory for manager Joe McCarthy and the Colonels was one of baseball's greatest upsets.

1922

American League
President: Byron Bancroft Johnson

Standings	W	L	Pct.	GB	Attend.	Manager
New York Yankees	94	60	.610	—	1,026,134	Miller Huggins
St. Louis Browns	93	61	.604	1	712,918	Lee Fohl
Detroit Tigers	79	75	.513	15	861,206	Ty Cobb
Cleveland Indians	78	76	.506	16	528,145	Tris Speaker
Chicago White Sox	77	77	.500	17	602,860	Kid Gleason
Washington Senators	69	85	.448	25	458,552	Clyde Milan
Philadelphia Athletics	65	89	.422	29	425,356	Connie Mack
Boston Red Sox	61	93	.396	33	259,184	Hugh Duffy

BA: George Sisler, St. Louis, .420
Runs: George Sisler, St. Louis, 134
Hits: George Sisler, St. Louis, 246
RBIs: Ken Williams, St. Louis, 155
HRs: Ken Williams, St. Louis, 39

Wins: Eddie Rommel, Philadelphia, 27
SOs: Urban Shocker, St. Louis, 149
ERA: Red Faber, Chicago, 2.80
Pct: Bullet Joe Bush, New York, .788, 26-7

National League
President: John A. Heydler

Standings	W	L	Pct.	GB	Attend.	Manager
New York Giants	93	61	.604	—	945,809	John McGraw
Cincinnati Reds	86	68	.558	7	493,754	Pat Moran
Pittsburgh Pirates	85	69	.552	8	523,675	George Gibson/Bill McKechnie
St. Louis Cardinals	85	69	.552	8	536,998	Branch Rickey
Chicago Cubs	80	74	.519	13	542,283	Bill Killefer
Brooklyn Robins	76	78	.494	17	498,865	Wilbert Robinson
Philadelphia Phillies	57	96	.373	35½	232,471	Irvin "Kaiser" Wilhelm
Boston Braves	53	100	.346	39½	167,965	Fred Mitchell

BA: Rogers Hornsby, St. Louis, .401
Runs: Rogers Hornsby, St. Louis, 141
Hits: Rogers Hornsby, St. Louis, 250
RBIs: Rogers Hornsby, St. Louis, 152
HRs: Rogers Hornsby, St. Louis, 42

Wins: Eppa Rixey, Cincinnati, 25
SOs: Dazzy Vance, Brooklyn, 134
ERA: Rosy Ryan, New York, 3.01
Pct: Pete Donohue, Cincinnati, .667, 18-9

AA American Association
President: Thomas J. Hickey

Standings	W	L	Pct.	GB	Attend.	Manager
St. Paul Saints	107	60	.641	—	213,029	Mike Kelley
Minneapolis Millers	92	75	.551	15	225,523	Joe Cantillon
Kansas City Blues	92	76	.548	15½	306,919	Otto Knabe/Wilbur Good
Indianapolis Indians	87	80	.521	20	166,001	Jack Hendricks
Milwaukee Brewers	85	83	.506	22½	214,892	Harry Clark
Louisville Colonels	77	91	.458	30½	139,229	Joe McCarthy
Toledo Mud Hens	65	101	.392	41½	155,631	Fred Luderus/Roger Bresnahan/ George "Possum" Whitted
Columbus Senators	63	102	.382	43	108,154	Clarence "Pants" Rowland

BA: Beals Becker, Kansas City, .367
Runs: Wilbur Good, Kansas City, 149
Hits: Wilbur Good, Kansas City, 249
RBIs: Bunny Brief, Kansas City, 151

HRs: Bunny Brief, Kansas City, 40
Wins: Tom Sheehan, St. Paul, 26
SOs: Joseph Giard, Toledo, 141
ERA: Tom Sheehan, St. Paul, 3.01

AA International League
President: John Conway Toole

Standings	W	L	Pct.	GB	Attend.	Manager
Baltimore Orioles	115	52	.689	—	230,118	Jack Dunn
Rochester Tribe	105	62	.629	10	204,021	George Stallings
Buffalo Bisons	95	72	.569	20	136,997	George Wiltse
Jersey City Colts	83	82	.503	31	118,133	Arthur Egan
Toronto Maple Leafs	76	88	.463	37½	119,608	Eddie Onslow
Reading Aces	71	93	.433	42½	133,793	Charles "Chief" Bender
Syracuse Stars	64	102	.386	50½	97,587	Frank Shaughnessy
Newark Bears	54	112	.325	60½	66,817	Bill Clymer

BA: Frank Gilhooley, Reading, .362
Runs: Maurice Archdeacon, Rochester, 151
Hits: Frank Gilhooley, Reading, 230
RBIs: Fred Merkle, Rochester, 130
HRs: Red Wingo, Toronto, 34

Wins: Jack Ogden, Baltimore, 24
SOs: Lefty Grove, Baltimore, 205
ERA: Jack Bentley, Baltimore, 1.73

AA Pacific Coast League
President: William H. McCarthy

Standings	W	L	Pct.	GB	Attend.	Manager
San Francisco Seals	127	72	.638	—	446,021	John Miller
Vernon Tigers	123	76	.618	4	276,498	Bill Essick
Los Angeles Angels	111	88	.558	16	289,637	Red Killefer
Salt Lake City Bees	95	106	.473	33	106,055	Duffy Lewis
Seattle Indians	90	107	.457	36	166,817	Walter McCreedie/John Adams
Oakland Oaks	88	112	.446	39½	210,597	Del Howard
Portland Beavers	87	112	.437	40	205,929	Bill Kenworthy/Tom Turner/ Al Demaree/Jim Middleton
Sacramento Senators	76	124	.380	51½	160,004	Charley Pick

BA: Paul Strand, Salt Lake City, .384
Runs: Bill Lane, Seattle, 166
Hits: Paul Strand, Salt Lake City, 289
RBIs: Bert Ellison, San Francisco, 141

HRs: Paul Strand, Salt Lake City, 28
Wins: Jackie May, Vernon, 35
SOs: Jackie May, Vernon, 238
ERA: Jackie May, Vernon, 1.84

A Eastern League
President: Daniel O'Neill

Standings	W	L	Pct.	GB	Manager
New Haven Indians	100	51	.622	—	Wild Bill Donovan
Waterbury Brasscos	84	66	.560	15½	Billy Gilbert
Bridgeport Americans	78	73	.516	22	Eugene McCann
Pittsfield Hillies	77	74	.510	23	Gus Gardella
Springfield Ponies	77	76	.503	24	John Hummel
Hartford Senators	73	76	.490	26	Jack Coffey
Albany Senators	69	84	.451	32	Paddy O'Connor
Fitchburg/Worcester Boosters#	47	105	.399	53½	Jack Mack/Jack Flynn

#Fitchburg (29-59) moved to Worcester July 30, first home game August 3.

All-Star Team: **1B**-Jose Rodriguez, Bridgeport; **2B**-Henry Demoe, Hartford; **3B**-Henry Long, Waterbury; **SS**-Ramon Gonzales, Springfield; **OF**-Leo "Brick" Kane, Hartford; Joe Cosgrove, Waterbury; Simon Rosenthal, Hartford; **C**-Charles Hargreaves, Pittsfield; Walter Simpson, Springfield; **Util**-John Donahue, Waterbury; **P**-John Cooney, New Haven; Frank Woodward, New Haven; Ralph Head, Hartford; Herman Bornhoeft, Bridgeport; A.P. Etten, Albany; Cy Morgan, Waterbury; William Anderson, Waterbury.

BA: Elmer Bowman, New Haven, .365
Runs: Walter Shay, New Haven, 105
Adelbert Capes, Pittsfield, 105
Hits: Elmer Bowman, New Haven, 209

HRs: Walter Simpson, Springfield, 21
Wins: Frank Woodward, New Haven, 23
SOs: Frank Woodward, New Haven, 186
ERA: Robert Vines, Bridgeport, 1.65

A Southern Association
President: John D. Martin

Standings	W	L	Pct.	GB	Attend.	Manager
Mobile Bears	97	55	.638	—	125,976	Bert Niehoff
Memphis Chickasaws	94	58	.618	3	239,459	Spencer Abbott
New Orleans Pelicans	89	64	.582	8½	148,825	Johnny Dobbs
Little Rock Travelers	86	67	.562	11½	101,198	Norman "Kid" Elberfeld
Birmingham Barons	74	80	.481	24	146,678	Carleton Molesworth/ Smutter Matthews/Joseph Dunn
Chattanooga Lookouts	59	93	.388	38	61,024	Sam Strang Nicklin
Nashville Volunteers	56	96	.368	41	87,893	Larry Doyle
Atlanta Crackers	55	97	.362	42	138,827	Roy Ellam/Bill Rariden/ Bill Bersen

BA: Dutch Schliebner, Little Rock, .354
Runs: Eddie Bogart, Mobile, 119
Hits: Dutch Schliebner, Little Rock, 194
HRs: Emil Huhn, Mobile, 12
Joe Connolly, Little Rock, 12
John Schulte, Mobile, 12

Wins: Rube Robinson, Little Rock, 26
SOs: Wallace Warmoth, Nashville/ Little Rock, 170
ERA: Roy Walker, New Orleans, 1.57

A Texas League
President: J. Doak Roberts

Standings	W	L	Pct.	GB	Attend.	Manager
Ft. Worth Panthers***	109	46	.703	—	143,382	Jake Atz
Wichita Falls Spudders	94	61	.606	15	94,643	Walt Salm
Dallas Steers	82	74	.525	27½	148,162	Walter Morris
Galveston Sand Crabs	79	76	.510	30	54,898	Dave Griffith/Pat Newnam
San Antonio Bears	76	79	.490	33	41,874	Hub Northen
Beaumont Exporters	65	88	.425	43	48,753	Joe Mathes
Houston Buffaloes	57	95	.375	50½	52,711	George Whiteman/Roy Thomas
Shreveport Gassers	56	99	.361	53	72,233	Billy Smith/Johnny Vann

BA: Homer Summa, Wichita Falls, .362
Runs: Homer Summa, Wichita Falls, 131
Hits: Homer Summa, Wichita Falls, 225
RBIs: Clarence "Big Boy" Kraft, Ft. Worth, 131

HRs: Clarence "Big Boy" Kraft, Ft. Worth, 32
Wins: Paul Wachtel, Ft. Worth, 26
SOs: Rip Wheeler, Wichita Falls, 132
ERA: Gus Johns, Ft. Worth, 2.34

A Western League
President: Albert R. Tearney

Standings	W	L	Pct.	GB	Manager
Tulsa Oilers	103	64	.617	—	Jack Lelivelt
St. Joseph Saints	98	70	.584	5½	Wally Smith
Wichita Witches	94	73	.568	9	Joe Berger/Howard Gregory
Omaha Buffaloes	91	77	.549	12½	Barney Burch
Sioux City Packers	86	79	.518	16	Walter Mattick

Oklahoma City Indians .... 73 94 .435 30   Gus Fisher/Jack Egan
Denver Bears .... 63 105 .374 40½   Joseph Dunn/C.H. Adkins/Bill Rodgers
Des Moines Boosters .... 61 107 .363 42½   Dick Breen/Jack Graney

Attendance: Tulsa, 135,000.

BA: Carlton East, Wichita, .391
Runs: Herschel Bennett, Tulsa, 177
Hits: Carlton East, Wichita, 270
HRs: Yank Davis, Tulsa, 35
2B: Lyman Lamb, Tulsa, 68

Wins: George Boehler, Tulsa, 38
SOs: George Boehler, Tulsa, 333
Pct: Dan Tipple, Omaha, .793, 23-6
IP: George Boehler, Tulsa, 441

B Central League
President: Emerson W. Dickerson

Standings	W	L	Pct.	GB	Manager
Ludington Mariners**	77	53	.592	—	Ambrose McConnell/Andy Woehre
Grand Rapids Billbobs*	73	55	.570	3	Bob Wells
Muskegon Daniels/Muskies	67	62	.519	9½	Dannie Claire/Carrington Sweeney
Kalamazoo Celery Pickers	61	67	.477	15	Grover Prough
Lansing Senators	60	67	.472	15½	Fred Hunter
Ionia Mayors	47	81	.367	29	Carrington Sweeney/William Wilcox

Playoff: Grand Rapids 5 games, Ludington 3.

BA: Leo Payne, Grand Rapids, .370
Runs: Howard Pennington, Grand Rapids, 109
Hits: Harry Schwab, Ludington, 190
HRs: Charles Miller, Lansing, 12

Wins: Oscar Johnson, Ludington, 25
SOs: Wilcy Moore, Grand Rapids, 158
ERA: Wilcy Moore, Grand Rapids, 1.92

B Eastern Canada League
President: Joseph H. Page

Standings	W	L	Pct.	GB	Manager
Trois Rivieres Trios	69	53	.566	—	Bill Innes/Eugene Grenier
Ottawa Senators	68	57	.544	2½	Dick Dawson
Valleyfield/ Cap de la Madeleine Madcaps#	56	69	.448	14½	Ubaldi Rose
Montreal Royals	55	69	.443	15	Larry Carmel/Bill Innes

#Valleyfield (34-41) moved to Cap de la Madeleine July 29.

BA: Norman Sauvage, Valleyfield/ Cap de la Madeleine, .331
Runs: Joseph Delisle, Montreal, 90
Hits: Norman Sauvage, Valleyfield/ Cap de la Madeleine, 164

HRs: Frank Delisle, Montreal/Trois Rivieres, 16
Wins: Alan Grenier, Trois Rivieres, 18
    Fred Frankhouse, Ottawa, 18
Pct: Louis Kimball, Trois Rivieres, .706, 12-5

B Michigan-Ontario League
President: Thomas J. Halligan

Standings	W	L	Pct.	GB	Manager
Hamilton Tigers**	84	49	.632	—	Ernie Calbert
London Tecumsehs	83	50	.624	1	Frank "Buzz" Wetzel
Saginaw Aces*	74	58	.561	9½	Bobby Byrnes
Bay City Wolves	69	62	.527	14	Punch Knoll
Port Huron-Sarnia Saints	67	65	.508	16½	Bill Kelly
Brantford Brants	54	77	.412	29	Mickey LaLonge
Flint Vehics	53	81	.396	31½	George Orme
Kitchener Terriers	46	88	.343	38½	Ray Dunn/Hump Pierce

Playoff: Hamilton 5 games, Saginaw 3.

BA: Jack Shafer, London, .410
Runs: Clifford Hegedorn, Bay City, 105
Hits: Ernie Calbert, Hamilton, 174
    John Roseberry, Saginaw, 174
RBIs: Ernie Calbert, Hamilton, 110

HRs: Ernie Calbert, Hamilton, 28
Wins: Herman Schwartje, Saginaw, 23
SOs: John Saladna, Brantford, 164
ERA: Richard Glazier, Port Huron-Sarnia, 1.31

B South Atlantic League
President: W.H. Walsh

Standings	W	L	Pct.	GB	Manager
Charleston Pals	80	48	.625	—	James Hamilton
Charlotte Hornets	73	59	.553	9	Dick Hoblitzell
Columbia Comers	72	59	.550	9½	Zinn Beck
Spartanburg Spartans	63	68	.481	18½	Mike Kelly
Augusta Tygers	54	76	.415	27	Neal Ball/Forest Cady
Greenville Spinners	50	82	.379	32	Cliff Blankenship

BA: Ernest Padgett, Charlotte, .333
Runs: Ben Paschal, Charlotte, 131
Hits: Ben Paschal, Charlotte, 174
RBIs: Ben Paschal, Charlotte, 114
HRs: Ben Paschal, Charlotte, 18

Wins: Charles Brown, Charlotte, 21
SOs: George Pipgras, Charleston, 175
ERA: Godfrey Brogan, Charleston, 2.90
Pct: Charles Brown, Charlotte, .724, 21-8

B Three-I League
President: Albert R. Tearney

Standings	W	L	Pct.	GB	Attend.	Manager
Terre Haute Tots	85	51	.625	—	80,056	Bob Coleman
Decatur Commodores	78	58	.574	7	64,024	Daniel O'Leary

Peoria Tractors	76	60	.559	9		William Jackson
Evansville Evas	74	64	.536	12	64,442	John Nee
Rockford Rox	74	65	.532	12½	39,500	Harry Brandt
Bloomington Bloomers	63	75	.457	23		Earl Sykes
Danville Veterans	50	87	.365	25½	43,925	Charles O'Day
Moline Plowboys	49	89	.355	37		Earle Mack

BA: Alfred Platte, Peoria, .360
Runs: John Command, Rockford, 113
Hits: Guy Dunning, Terre Haute, 194
HRs: Frank McCue, Moline, 20

Sac: Peter Hughes, Evansville, 75
Wins: Adolph Holtzhauser, Decatur, 24
SOs: James "Jumbo" Elliott, Terre Haute, 214
ERA: Adolph Holtzhauser, Decatur, 2.18

B Virginia League
President: W.S. Moye

Standings	W	L	Pct.	GB	Manager
Wilson Bugs	68	52	.567	—	Bunn Hearn
Newport News Shipbuilders	63	56	.529	4½	Roy Whitcraft
Norfolk Tars	58	57	.504	7½	Win Clark
Rocky Mount Tar Heels	58	61	.496	8½	Frank Walker
Portsmouth Truckers	57	61	.483	10	Jim Viox
Richmond Colts	49	68	.419	17½	Ray Ryan/Rube Oldring

BA: Rasty Walters, Wilson, .374
Runs: Emil Yoter, Portsmouth, 98
Hits: Rasty Walters, Wilson, 173
RBIs: Harry Swacina, Rocky Mount, 88
HRs: Emil Yoter, Portsmouth, 13

Wins: Bill Manning, Portsmouth, 20
SOs: Alex Peterson, Norfolk, 154
ERA: Bunn Hearn, Wilson, 2.12
Pct: Chester Lucas, Newport News, .704, 19-8

B Western International League
Presidents: Louis H. Burnett/Deacon White

Standings	W	L	Pct.	GB	Manager
Calgary Bronchos	24	16	.600	—	Bill Rodgers
Edmonton Eskimos	23	16	.590	½	Gus Gleichman
Vancouver Beavers	22	23	.489	4½	Bob Brown
Tacoma Tigers	16	30	.343	11	Tealey Raymond

Playoff: Calgary 4 games, Edmonton 1. Playoff took place after the league disbanded June 18.

BA: Adolph Schinkel, Calgary, .354
Runs: John Kerr, Calgary, 43
Hits: Adolph Schinkel, Calgary, 58
HRs: Bob Snyder, Tacoma, 6

Wins: Al Miller, Edmonton, 7
    Ira Colwell, Calgary, 7
SOs: Al Miller, Edmonton, 48
Pct: Al Miller, Edmonton, .778, 7-2

C Florida State League
President: Walter W. Rose

Standings	W	L	Pct.	GB	Manager
St. Petersburg Saints***	67	43	.609	—	George Block
Orlando Bulldogs	59	50	.541	7½	Ernie Burke
Daytona Beach Islanders	53	58	.477	14½	Jack Martin
Tampa Smokers	54	60	.474	15	Thomas Leach
Lakeland Highlanders	52	61	.460	16½	Doug Harbison
Jacksonville Indians	50	63	.442	18½	George Stovall

BA: Elliott Bigelow, St. Petersburg, .343
Runs: Frank McGee, Daytona Beach, 94
Hits: Elliott Bigelow, St. Petersburg, 150
HRs: John Roser, St. Petersburg, 10
    Ernie Burke, Orlando, 10

Wins: George Cusack, Daytona Beach, 21
SOs: Cesar Alvarez, Tampa, 151
Pct: Charles Ollinger, St. Petersburg, .680, 17-8

C Piedmont League
President: William G. Bramham

Standings	W	L	Pct.	GB	Manager
High Point Furniture Makers*	70	55	.560	—	Hardin Herndon
Durham Bulls**	69	58	.543	2	Lee Gooch
Winston-Salem Twins	66	59	.528	4	Charles Clancy
Greensboro Patriots	60	63	.488	9	Charles Carroll
Raleigh Capitals	60	66	.476	10½	Duke Duncan
Danville Tobacconists	50	74	.403	19½	Tom Abbott

Playoff: Durham 4 games, High Point 3, one tie.

BA: Al Smith, High Point, .366
Runs: Hardin Herndon, High Point, 87
Hits: Hoke Floyd, Raleigh, 169

HRs: Floyd Trexler, Danville, 11
    Edward Regan, Danville, 11
Wins: Jess Eldridge, High Point, 26
SOs: D. Fair Crews, Greensboro, 128
Pct: Jess Eldridge, High Point, .743, 26-9

C Southwestern League
President: Ensley Barbour

Standings	W	L	Pct.	GB	Manager
Muskogee Mets**	84	53	.613	—	Roy Corgan
Coffeyville Refiners	83	56	.597	2	Joe Clarke/H. Ennis
Sapulpa Sappers*	81	58	.583	4	Barney Cleveland
Independence Producers	79	58	.576	5	Ted Waring/Walt Fromm
Bartlesville Grays	63	72	.467	20	Ned Pettigrew
Topeka Kaws	62	74	.456	21½	Dick Cooley

	W	L	Pct.	GB	Manager
Hutchinson Wheat Shockers	47	85	.356	34½	Emmett Rodgers/Red Harriott
Salina Millers	45	88	.338	37	John McCloskey/Charles Olson

Playoff: Sapulpa 4 games, Muskogee 2.

BA: Bill Bagwell, Salina/Independence, .402
Runs: Ike Khadot, Coffeyville, 111
Hits: Bill Bagwell, Salina/Independence, 217
HRs: Dutch Wetzel, Muskogee, 23

Wins: Andy Rush, Muskogee, 23
Oscar Middleton, Coffeyville, 23
SOs: Arnold Luchien, Topeka, 196
ERA: Andy Rush, Muskogee, 1.88

C Western Association
President: E.A. Daniels

Standings	W	L	Pct.	GB	Manager
Enid Harvesters**	104	27	.794	—	Tom Downey
Joplin Miners*	93	42	.689	13	Charles "Gabby" Street
Henryetta Hens	74	56	.569	29½	Drap Hayes
Springfield Midgets	68	69	.496	39	Wilson White
Okmulgee Drillers	56	79	.415	50	John Wuffli/Troy Agnew
Ft. Smith Twins	54	79	.406	51	William "Ducky" Holmes/Roy Thomas
McAlester Miners	49	82	.374	55	Cecil Briggs/Harry Coveleski
Pawhuska Osages#	29	93	.238	NA	Clyde Wren/John Wuffli/Otis Stucker

#Pawhuska disbanded August 16; all games after that date were forfeited to scheduled opponents.

Playoff: Joplin 4 games, Enid 2.

BA: Leo Cotter, Springfield, .396
Runs: Glen McNally, Joplin, 129
Hits: Glen McNally, Joplin, 201
HRs: Frank Reiger, Enid, 31

3B: Glenn McNally, Joplin, 24
Wins: Don Songer, Enid, 31
SOs: Don Songer, Enid, 176
Pct: Byrd Hodges, Joplin, .897, 26-3

D Appalachian League
President: Jacob Smith

Standings	W	L	Pct.	GB	Manager
Bristol State Liners	68	54	.557	—	Patsy O'Rourke
Kingsport Indians	65	58	.528	3½	Harold Irelan
Cleveland Manufacturers	61	59	.508	6	Charles Leonard
Johnson City Soldiers	60	61	.496	7½	Bill Schumaker
Knoxville Pioneers	59	61	.492	8	Frank Moffett
Greeneville Burley Cubs	50	70	.417	17	Art Riggs/Sam Alexander

BA: Herman Lane, Bristol, .354
Runs: Herman Lane, Bristol, 83
Hits: Herman Lane, Bristol, 161
HRs: Harry Lane, Cleveland, 14

Wins: Thomas Rich, Cleveland, 18
SOs: F.E. Hodge, Cleveland, 149
ERA: Thomas Rich, Cleveland, .692, 18-8

D Blue Grass League
President: Thomas M. Russell

Standings	W	L	Pct.	GB	Manager
Paris Bourbons	36	28	.563	—	B. Goodman/Harold Willis
Maysville Cardinals*	33	28	.541	1½	Norbert Bosken
Cynthiana Merchants**	34	30	.531	2	Sprouts McIlvain
Mt. Sterling Essex	30	31	.492	4½	Hod Eller
Winchester Dodgers	28	36	.438	8	Howard Camitz/Rip Van Winkle
Lexington Reds	28	36	.438	8	Pat Devereaux

Playoff: Maysville 3 games, Cynthiana 1.

BA: M.J. Hogan, Winchester, .356
Runs: Ray Class, Maysville, 58
Hits: Charles Rorer, Cynthiana, 83
HRs: Ray Class, Maysville, 14

Wins: Ray Miner, Paris/Maysville, 15
SOs: Claude Monhollen, Lexington/Cynthiana, 237
Pct: James Park, Lexington, .727, 8-3

D Blue Ridge League
President: J. Vincent Jamison, Jr.

Standings	W	L	Pct.	GB	Manager
Martinsburg Blue Sox	58	41	.586	—	Earle Mack
Waynesboro Villagers	56	42	.571	1½	Bill Morris
Frederick Hustlers	54	44	.551	3½	George "Buck" Ramsey
Hanover Raiders	47	49	.490	9½	Joe Miller
Chambersburg Maroons	46	49	.484	10	Mike Mowrey
Hagerstown Terriers	30	66	.313	26½	Mike Corcoran/Tony Walsh

BA: George Rawlings, Martinsburg, .371
Runs: George Rawlings, Martinsburg, 82
Hits: George Rawlings, Martinsburg, 146
HRs: Hack Wilson, Martinsburg, 30

Wins: R.S. Roberts, Martinsburg, 15
SOs: William King, Frederick, 139
Pct: Virgil Clarke, Waynesboro, .750, 9-3
Walter Seeman, Martinsburg, .750, 9-3

D Cotton States League
President: Syd L. Dodds

Standings	W	L	Pct.	GB	Manager
Greenwood Indians**	73	40	.646	—	Charles Bell
Meridian Mets*	72	40	.643	½	Frank Kohlbecker
Greenville Bucks	60	56	.517	14½	Frank "Bud" Stapleton
Vicksburg Hill Billies	56	60	.483	18½	Les Crichlow/"Red" Torkelson

	W	L	Pct.	GB	Manager
Clarksdale Cubs	49	70	.412	27	Tom Toland/Harry Collenberger
Jackson Red Sox	35	79	.307	38½	F. "Red" McDermott/Jack Steele

Playoff: Greenwood 4 games, Meridian 0.

BA: Frank Kohlbecker, Meridian, .324
Runs: Bill Propst, Greenville, 75
William Waldron, Greenwood, 75
Hits: William Waldron, Greenwood, 141

HRs: William Waldron, Greenwood, 4
Wins: Hugh Boyd, Greenwood, 24
SOs: D.D. Hunter, Meridian, 163
Pct: Winfred Ballou, Vicksburg, .818, 9-2

D Dakota League
President: M.E. Cantillon

Standings	W	L	Pct.	GB	Manager
Mitchell Kernels	60	37	.619	—	Hank Scharnweber
Aberdeen Grays	56	42	.571	4½	Bill Shipke/E. Harkin
Fargo Athletics	56	42	.571	4½	Ed Whiting
Sioux Falls Soos	55	42	.567	5	Fred Carish
Jamestown Jimkotans	46	51	.474	14	Wilbur Smith
Watertown Cubs	42	54	.443	17½	John Mokate
Wahpeton-Breckenridge Twins	42	55	.439	18	Ray Patterson
Valley City Hi-Liners/ Bismarck#	30	64	.319	28½	Charles Boardman/Ernie Menone/J. Sampson/ Louis Bachant

#Valley City (25-46) moved to Bismarck August 3.

BA: Stan Lewan (Lewandowski), Watertown, .394
Runs: Lyman Nason, Wahpeton-Breckenridge, 92
Hits: Al Simmons, Aberdeen, 144

HRs: Lyman Nason, Wahpeton-Breckenridge, 17
Wins: Cecil Duff, Mitchell, 15
Ed Lane, Wahpeton-Breckenridge, 15
SOs: Roy Birkenstock, Jamestown, 160
Pct: Al Zweifel, Mitchell, .824, 14-3

D Eastern Shore League
President: Walter B. Miller

Standings	W	L	Pct.	GB	Manager
Parksley Spuds	42	25	.627	—	Thomas "Poke" Whalen
Cambridge Canners	37	32	.536	6	Herb Armstrong
Crisfield Crabbers	36	32	.529	6½	Jack Ryan
Laurel Blue Hens	34	34	.500	8½	Sam Frocke
Pocomoke City Salamanders	29	41	.414	14½	Jack Ryan/Ducky Davis/Sam Frocke
Salisbury Indians	27	41	.397	15½	Harry Hoffman/George Eichnor

BA: Joseph Tagg, Crisfield, .329
Runs: Jake Flowers, Cambridge, 50
Hits: Herbert Fisher, Parksley, 83
HRs: Jake Flowers, Cambridge, 14

Wins: Bill Klingehoffer, Parksley, 15
SOs: Bill Klingehoffer, Parksley, 158
Pct: Bill Klingehoffer, Parksley, .750, 15-5

D Kitty League
President: Dr. Frank H. Bassett

Standings	W	L	Pct.	GB	Manager
Madisonville Miners**	73	39	.652	—	Neil Deighan
Hopkinsville Hoppers	62	51	.549	11½	Bill Catton/Art Nilson
Mayfield Pantmakers*	60	50	.545	12	Rudy Hulswitt
Paris Travelers	58	52	.527	14	Tuffy Fowlkes
Cairo Egyptians	56	56	.500	17	George Hughes/Jim Moore/Jack Herbert
Trenton Reds	56	56	.500	17	H. Reese/Andy Jarrell/G. Watson
Fulton Railroaders	41	68	.376	30½	Ralph Works/Senter Rainey
Paducah Indians	39	73	.348	34	Ollie Pickering/Lee Fairchild/Fred DeWitt/ Hoke Dillinger

Playoff: First place Madisonville was disqualified from the second half title for using an ineligible player. Second place Cairo was disqualified for salary limit violations. The second half title was awarded to Paris.
Finals: Mayfield 4 games, Paris 2.

BA: Mahlon Higby, Hopkinsville, .383
Runs: Mahlon Higby, Hopkinsville, 99
Hits: Mahlon Higby, Hopkinsville, 156
HRs: Mahlon Higby, Hopkinsville, 16

Wins: R. Donovan, Madisonville, 15
SOs: Ervin Braime, Hopkinsville, 135
Pct: Kay Beach, Cairo, 1.000, 7-0

D Mississippi Valley League
President: Michael H. Sexton

Standings	W	L	Pct.	GB	Manager
Cedar Rapids Bunnies***	92	37	.713	—	Bill Speas
Marshalltown Ansons	73	55	.570	18½	Frank Boyle
Rock Island Islanders	66	63	.512	26	Jimmy Conzelman
Waterloo Hawks	59	68	.465	32	Pat Ragan
Ottumwa Cardinals	49	76	.392	41	Jim Drohan/Carl Bond
Dubuque Climbers	44	84	.344	47½	Larry Mullen/Harry Henge

BA: Fred Leach, Waterloo, .383
Runs: Bill Speas, Cedar Rapids, 128
Hits: Bill Speas, Cedar Rapids, 182
HRs: Fred Leach, Waterloo, 13

Wins: Frank Johnson, Cedar Rapids, 24
SOs: Charles Schwiete, Marshalltown, 180
ERA: Frank Johnson, Cedar Rapids, .828, 24-5

D Nebraska State League
President: Clarence J. Miles

Standings	W	L	Pct.	GB	Manager
Norfolk Elk Horns**	70	48	.593	—	Ernie Adams/Runt Marr
Lincoln Links	70	49	.588	½	O.A. Beltzer
Fairbury Jeffersons*	69	49	.585	1	George Segrist
Beatrice Blues	53	63	.457	16	R. Kirchner/William "Ducky" Holmes
Hastings Cubs	52	67	.437	18½	A. Smith
Grand Island Champions	40	78	.339	30	Ed Willett

Playoff: Fairbury 4 games, Norfolk 3.

BA: Cliff Marr, Norfolk, .364
Runs: Cliff Marr, Norfolk, 116
Hits: Cliff Marr, Norfolk, 167
HRs: Claude Mitchell, Norfolk, 21

Wins: Bill Bailey, Lincoln, 23
SOs: Fred Wigington, Hastings, 260
Pct: L.W. Jenney, Fairbury, .773, 17-5

D Oklahoma State League
Presidents: C.E. Plott/E.A. Daniels

Standings	W	L	Pct.	GB	Manager
Duncan Oilers	65	44	.596	—	John Fant
Clinton Bulldogs**	64	46	.582	1½	Jim Lawrence
Chickasha Chicks*	55	55	.500	10½	Jim Fitzgerald/Larry McLean
El Reno Railroaders	53	56	.486	12	Virgil Moss
Guthrie	48	59	.449	16	Mike Balenti
Wilson Drillers	40	65	.381	23	Jim Payne/Jew Hellman

Playoff: Chickasha 4 games, Clinton 0.

D Texas-Oklahoma League
President: J. Doak Roberts

Standings	W	L	Pct.	GB	Manager
Paris Snappers**	72	36	.667	—	Earl "Red" Snapp
Greenville Togs*	66	40	.623	5	Bennie Brownlow
Corsicana Gumbo Busters	56	46	.549	13	Charles Miller/Harvey Grubb
Ardmore Producers	49	60	.450	23½	Curley Maloney/Elia Boggus
Sherman Red Sox	48	60	.444	24	Grady Higginbotham
Mexia Gushers	47	60	.439	24½	Roy Akin
Bonham Bingers@	39	53	.424	NA	Les Tullos
Cleburne Generals/Scouts#	36	58	.386	NA	Lindy Hiett

#Cleburne disbanded July 22.
@Bonham was dropped July 22 when Cleburne disbanded, even with the franchise on solid financial ground.
The season was shortened to August 6 with National Association permission due to a railroad strike. The league did not disband.

Playoff: Paris 4 games, Greenville 1.

BA: Charles "Chink" Taylor, Paris, .369
Runs: Joe Bratcher, Paris, 100
Hits: Joe Bratcher, Paris, 138
HRs: Edward Seely, Greenville, 21

Wins: Sam Gray, Paris, 23
SOs: Sam Gray, Paris, 219
Pct: Edwin Bryan, Greenville, .864, 19-3

D West Texas League
President: Gordon W. Northen

Standings	W	L	Pct.	GB	Manager
Amarillo Gassers*	88	51	.633	—	Jack Meanor
Clovis Buzzers**	79	56	.585	7	Frank "Buzz" Wetzel
Lubbock Hubbers	79	59	.572	8½	Sled Allen
San Angelo Bronchos	63	74	.460	24	Walt Alexander/Luke Robinson
Sweetwater Swatters	62	73	.459	24	Clarence "Pop Boy" Smith
Abilene Eagles	61	74	.450	25	C. Anderson
Ranger Nitros	58	80	.420	29½	Bob Allen/Joe Clayton
Stamford Colonels	56	79	.415	30	Tom Price/Poston Baker

Playoff: Amarillo 5 games, Clovis 1, one tie.

1922 Interleague Post Season Play

World Series
New York (National) 4 games, New York (American) 0

Junior World Series
Baltimore (International) 5 games, St. Paul (American Association) 2
Total Attendance: 48,791

Class C Series
Joplin (Western Association) 4 games, Sapulpa (Southwestern) 3

Junior World Series Tune-Up
New Haven (Eastern) 2 games, Baltimore (International) 1

Dixie Series
Mobile (Southern Association) 4 games, Ft. Worth (Texas) 2, one tie
Total Attendance: 46,742

Class A Series
Tulsa (Western) 4 games, Mobile (Southern Association) 1, one tie

Class B Southern Championship
Charleston (South Atlantic) 4 games, Wilson (Virginia) 2, one tie.

Five-State Championship
Martinsburg (Blue Ridge) 4 games, Parksley (Eastern Shore) 0

1922 No-Hitters

Date	Pitcher	Team	League	Opponent	Score
4-23	F.R. Rose	Jackson	Cotton States	Clarksdale	2-0
4-25	Cockrell	Springfield	Western Assoc.	Ft. Smith	4-0
4-26	Thomas Green	Winston-Salem	Piedmont	Greensboro	(P)
4-30	Charlie Robertson	Chicago	American	Detroit	2-0 (P)
5-7	Jesse Barnes	New York	National	Philadelphia	6-0
5-9	Willis Morgan	Beaumont	Texas	Shreveport	4-0
5-9	Glenn Harle	Ft. Smith	Western Assoc.	Enid	3-0
5-17	Bert Humphries	Lakeland	Florida State	Tampa	3-1
5-21	Randolph Young	Bloomington	Three-I	Decatur	1-0
5-23	Harry O'Neil	Augusta	South Atlantic	Greenville	1-0
5-27	Duke Gross	Tacoma	Western Int'l.	Calgary	3-0
6-6	Frank Thornton	Chickasha	Oklahoma State	Clinton	4-0
6-18	Howard Etten	Albany	Eastern	Fitchburg	5-0
7-10	Thomas Rich	Cleveland	Appalachian	Bristol	3-0
7-11	Ed Stauffer	Bridgeport	Eastern	New Haven	4-0
7-24	Mose Poolaw	Joplin	Western Assoc.	Henryetta	5-0
8-17	Robert Harrison	Mt. Sterling	Blue Grass	Lexington	4-0
8-23	Kay Beach	Cairo	Kitty	Madisonville	4-0
8-26	Roy Birkenstock	Jamestown	Dakota	Sioux Falls	2-0
9-21	Dan Tipple	Omaha	Western	Des Moines	3-0
9-21	Wheezer Dell	Vernon	Pacific Coast	Oakland	7-0

Number in parentheses indicates innings if other than nine; "P" indicates perfect game.

THIS DATE IN MINOR LEAGUE HISTORY

April 26, 1922, Thomas Green of Winston-Salem used his underhand delivery to retire 27 consecutive Greensboro batters in a 5-0 perfect game victory in the Piedmont League.

May 30, 1922, The umpires failed to appear for a scheduled twinbill between Sapulpa and Topeka in the Southwestern League. The games were played with substitute arbiters; one was none other than Ensley Barbour, the president of the league.

June 10, 1922, Pitcher Gary Fortune of Springfield lost to Fitchburg after a run of 24 consecutive victories in the Eastern League over a three-season period. Fortune won 16 straight in 1919, six in 1920 and his first two in 1922.

June 15, 1922, Salt Lake City, Pacific Coast League, had 26 hits to trounce Los Angeles 17-6. Third sacker Cot Deal went 6-for-6.

August 6, 1922, Shortstop Charles Pechous, Columbus, American Association, made an unassisted triple play against Minneapolis. Columbus won the game 15-5, ending its 13-game losing streak.

August 9, 1922, Pitcher Nick Cullop of Louisville, American Association, pitched and won three straight games, August 6, 8, and 9; the team did not play on August 7.

August 31, 1922, Paducah, Kitty League, lost its 25th consecutive game by bowing 18-4 to Cairo.

August 31, 1922, First baseman Otto Pahlman of Danville, Three-I League, ran his hitting streak to 40 straight games.

September 10, 1922, Beals Becker, Kansas City, American Association, made eight hits in eight consecutive at bats in a doubleheader against Minneapolis.

October 30, 1922, Jack Bentley, star pitcher-first baseman of the Baltimore Orioles, was sold to the New York Giants.

1923

American League
President: Byron Bancroft Johnson

Standings	W	L	Pct.	GB	Attend.	Manager
New York Yankees	98	54	.645	—	1,007,066	Miller Huggins
Detroit Tigers	83	71	.539	16	911,377	Ty Cobb
Cleveland Indians	82	71	.536	16½	558,856	Tris Speaker
Washington Senators	75	78	.490	23½	357,406	Donie Bush
St. Louis Browns	74	78	.487	24	430,296	Lee Fohl/Jimmy Austin
Philadelphia Athletics	69	83	.454	29	534,122	Connie Mack
Chicago White Sox	69	85	.448	30	573,778	Kid Gleason
Boston Red Sox	61	91	.401	37	229,688	Frank Chance

BA: Harry Heilmann, Detroit, .403
Runs: Babe Ruth, New York, 151
Hits: Charley Jamieson, Cleveland, 222
RBIs: Babe Ruth, New York, 130
Tris Speaker, Cleveland, 130

HRs: Babe Ruth, New York, 41
Wins: George Uhle, Cleveland, 26
SOs: Walter Johnson, Washington, 130
ERA: Stan Coveleski, Cleveland, 2.76
Pct: Herb Pennock, New York, .760, 19-6

National League
President: John A. Heydler

Standings	W	L	Pct.	GB	Attend.	Manager
New York Giants	95	58	.621	—	820,780	John McGraw
Cincinnati Reds	91	63	.591	4½	575,063	Pat Moran
Pittsburgh Pirates	87	67	.565	8½	611,082	Bill McKechnie
Chicago Cubs	83	71	.539	12½	703,705	Bill Killefer
St. Louis Cardinals	79	74	.516	16	338,551	Branch Rickey
Brooklyn Robins	76	78	.494	19½	564,666	Wilbert Robinson
Boston Braves	54	100	.351	41½	227,802	Fred Mitchell
Philadelphia Phillies	50	104	.325	45½	228,168	Art Fletcher

BA: Rogers Hornsby, St. Louis, .384
Runs: Ross Youngs, New York, 121
Hits: Frank Frisch, New York, 223
RBIs: Emil "Irish" Meusel, New York, 125
HRs: Cy Williams, Philadelphia, 41

Wins: Dolf Luque, Cincinnati, 27
SOs: Dazzy Vance, Brooklyn, 197
ERA: Dolf Luque, Cincinnati, 1.93
Pct: Dolf Luque, Cincinnati, .771, 27-8

AA American Association
President: Thomas J. Hickey

Standings	W	L	Pct.	GB	Attend.	Manager
Kansas City Blues	112	54	.675	—	425,064	Wilbur Good
St. Paul Saints	111	57	.661	2	219,979	Mike Kelley
Louisville Colonels	91	77	.542	22	167,737	Joe McCarthy
Columbus Senators	79	89	.470	34	142,149	Carleton Molesworth
Milwaukee Brewers	75	91	.452	37	144,865	Harry Clark
Minneapolis Millers	74	92	.446	38	165,643	Joe Cantillon/Clyde Milan
Indianapolis Indians	72	94	.434	40	103,807	Jack Hendricks
Toledo Mud Hens	54	114	.321	59	98,694	George "Possum" Whitted/Bill Terry

BA: William Lamar, Toledo, .391
Runs: Bunny Brief, Kansas City, 161
Hits: Earle Combs, Louisville, 241
RBIs: Bunny Brief, Kansas City, 164

HRs: Carlton East, Minneapolis, 31
Wins: Tom Sheehan, St. Paul, 31
SOs: Cliff Markle, St. Paul, 184
ERA: Tom Sheehan, St. Paul, 2.90

AA International League
President: John Conway Toole

Standings	W	L	Pct.	GB	Attend.	Manager
Baltimore Orioles	111	53	.677	—	253,584	Jack Dunn
Rochester Tribe	101	65	.608	11	217,977	George Stallings
Reading Keystones	85	79	.518	26	157,892	Spencer Abbott
Toronto Maple Leafs	81	79	.506	28	114,908	Dan Howley
Buffalo Bisons	83	81	.506	28	112,410	George Wiltse
Syracuse Stars	73	92	.442	38½	95,236	Frank Shaughnessy
Newark Bears	60	101	.373	49½	105,996	Mickey Devine/Fred Brainerd
Jersey City Skeeters	61	105	.367	51	67,147	Arthur "Ben" Egan

BA: Clarence Pitt, Rochester/Baltimore, .357
Runs: Maurice Archdeacon, Rochester, 162
Hits: Maurice Archdeacon, Rochester, 228
RBIs: Fred Merkle, Rochester, 166

HRs: Max Bishop, Baltimore, 22
Bill Webb, Buffalo, 22
Wins: Rube Parnham, Baltimore, 33
SOs: Lefty Grove, Baltimore, 330
ERA: Joe Lucey, Jersey City, 2.73

AA Pacific Coast League
President: William H. McCarthy

Standings	W	L	Pct.	GB	Manager
San Francisco Seals	124	77	.617	—	John Miller/Herbert Ellison
Sacramento Senators	112	87	.563	11	Charley Pick
Portland Beavers	107	89	.546	14½	Jimmy Middleton
Seattle Indians	99	97	.505	22½	Harry Wolverton/Red Killefer
Salt Lake City Bees	94	105	.472	29	Duffy Lewis
Los Angeles Angels	93	109	.460	31½	Marty Krug
Oakland Oaks	91	111	.450	33½	Ivan Howard
Vernon Tigers	77	122	.387	46	Bill Essick

Total Attendance: 1,849,000.

BA: Paul Strand, Salt Lake City, .394
Runs: Paul Strand, Salt Lake City, 180
Hits: Paul Strand, Salt Lake City, 325
RBIs: Paul Strand, Salt Lake City, 187
HRs: Paul Strand, Salt Lake City, 43

TBs: Paul Strand, Salt Lake City, 546
Wins: Ray Kremer, Oakland, 25
SOs: Walter Mails, Oakland, 206
ERA: Vean Gregg, Seattle, 2.75
CGs: Ray Kremer, Oakland, 35

A Eastern League
President: Daniel O'Neill

Standings	W	L	Pct.	GB	Manager
Hartford Senators	98	55	.640	—	Paddy O'Connor
New Haven Profs	90	63	.588	8	Wild Bill Donovan
Worcester Panthers	79	74	.516	19	Jesse Burkett
Springfield Ponies	76	77	.497	22	Patsy Donovan
Bridgeport Americans	71	81	.467	26½	Eugene McCann
Albany Senators	68	84	.447	29½	William Rodgers
Pittsfield Hillies	66	87	.440	32	Art Wilson
Waterbury Brasscos	63	90	.412	35	Herman Bronkie

BA: Wade Lefler, Worcester, .369
Runs: Walt Simpson, Springfield, 131
Hits: Elmer Bowman, New Haven, 211
HRs: Walt Simpson, Springfield, 44

Wins: Steve Stryker, Worcester, 26
SOs: Sam Hyman, New Haven, 171
ERA: Hugh Canavan, Hartford, 2.75

A Southern Association
President: John D. Martin

Standings	W	L	Pct.	GB	Attend.	Manager
New Orleans Pelicans	89	57	.610	—	218,295	Larry Gilbert
Mobile Bears	88	66	.571	5	123,619	Bert Niehoff
Memphis Chickasaws	76	70	.521	13	176,607	Johnny Dobbs
Atlanta Crackers	78	73	.516	13½	239,911	Otto Miller
Birmingham Barons	75	74	.503	15½	199,079	Joseph Dunn/Stuffy Stewart
Nashville Volunteers	75	77	.493	17	160,302	James Hamilton
Chattanooga Lookouts	63	88	.417	28½	71,627	Les Nunamaker
Little Rock Travelers	53	92	.365	35½	68,509	Norman "Kid" Elberfeld

BA: Emil Huhn, Mobile, .345
Runs: Denny Williams, Mobile, 129
Hits: Denny Williams, Mobile, 212
RBIs: Dutch Bernsen, Nashville, 113

HRs: Danny Clark, Birmingham/Atlanta, 19
Wins: Tommy Long, Mobile, 27
SOs: Joe Martina, New Orleans, 149
ERA: Dan McGrew, Memphis, 2.29

A Texas League
President: J. Doak Roberts

Standings	W	L	Pct.	GB	Attend.	Manager
Ft. Worth Panthers	96	56	.632	—	164,448	Jake Atz
San Antonio Bears	81	68	.556	13½	78,783	Bob Coleman
Dallas Steers	78	70	.527	16	194,282	Walter Morris
Wichita Falls Spudders	79	72	.523	16½	84,219	Walt Salm
Houston Buffaloes	74	75	.497	20½	95,747	Hunter Hill
Beaumont Exporters	71	77	.480	23	49,304	Frank Edington/Frank "Pop" Kitchens
Galveston Crabs	68	80	.459	26	49,300	Pat Newnam
Shreveport Gassers	50	99	.336	44½	80,566	Ira Thomas

BA: Ike Boone, San Antonio, .402
Runs: Ike Boone, San Antonio, 134
Hits: Ike Boone, San Antonio, 241
RBIs: Ike Boone, San Antonio, 135

HRs: Clarence "Big Boy" Kraft, Ft. Worth, 32
Wins: Lil Stoner, Ft. Worth, 27
SOs: Slim Love, Dallas, 172
ERA: Lil Stoner, Ft. Worth, 2.70

A Western League
President: Albert R. Tearney

Standings	W	L	Pct.	GB	Attend.	Manager
Oklahoma City Indians	102	64	.614	—	98,913	Fred Luderus
Tulsa Oilers	101	67	.601	2	142,228	Jack Lelivelt
Wichita Izzies	100	68	.595	3	97,760	Howard Gregory
Omaha Buffaloes	92	74	.554	10	88,526	Ed Konetchy
Des Moines Boosters	87	79	.527	15	79,996	Johnny "Red" Corriden
St. Joseph Saints	65	101	.392	37	44,788	Wally Smith
Sioux City Packers	59	105	.358	42	35,982	Frank Metz/Eddie Palmer/Wray Query
Denver Bears	59	107	.355	43	76,735	Billy Gilbert

*Won first-half   **Won second-half   ***Won both halves

BA: Joe Horan, Des Moines, .411
Runs: Jim Blakesley, Wichita, 151
Hits: Joe Horan, Des Moines, 256
HRs: Jim McDowell, Wichita, 37

2B: Lyman Lamb, Tulsa, 71
Wins: Karl Black, Tulsa, 29
SOs: Ed Hovlik, Wichita, 161
Pct: Ernest Maun, Wichita, .703, 26-11

B Eastern Canada League
President: Joseph H. Page

Standings	W	L	Pct.	GB	Manager
Montreal Royals**	66	52	.559	—	Harry Hoffman
Ottawa Canadiens#*	62	52	.544	2	Jim O'Rourke
Trois Rivieres Trios/Montreal@	52	62	.456	12	Pat Grenier/Thomas Reilly
Quebec Bulldogs	47	62	.431	14½	Bill Innes

#The Ottawa club played its home games in Montreal before erecting its own park.
@Trois Rivieres moved to Montreal for the second half.

Playoff: Montreal Royals 8 games, Ottawa 7.

BA: John Jones, Montreal, .370
Runs: Jim Grant, Montreal, 76
Hits: Bill Hunnefield, Montreal, 116
HRs: Frank Delisle, Trois Rivieres/ Ottawa, 24

Wins: Bartlett "Tex" McMillan, Montreal, 14
SOs: Bartlett "Tex" McMillan, Montreal, 128
Pct: George Crowe, Ottawa, .733, 11-4

B Michigan-Ontario League
President: Thomas J. Halligan

Standings	W	L	Pct.	GB	Manager
Bay City Wolves	80	51	.611	—	Punch Knoll
Saginaw Aces	78	54	.591	2½	Frank "Buzz" Wetzel
Muskegon Anglers	73	57	.562	6½	George "Red" Fisher
Flint Vehics	70	63	.526	11	Dan O'Leary
Kalamazoo Celery Pickers	69	64	.518	12	Marty Becker
London Tecumsehs	55	73	.430	23½	Leo Mackey/Jack Beatty
Grand Rapids Billbobs	55	76	.420	25	Bob Wells
Hamilton Tigers	45	87	.341	35½	Jim Carlin

BA: Frank Luce, Flint, .382
Runs: Al Bashang, Saginaw, 106
Hits: Art Jahn, Flint, 172
        Ernest "Tex" Jeanes, Saginaw, 172
RBIs: Ernest "Tex" Jeanes, Saginaw, 108

HRs: Art Jahn, Flint, 18
Wins: Seraphin Good, Bay City, 20
SOs: Seraphin Good, Bay City, 168
ERA: Ovila Lahaie, Bay City, 1.85

B New York-Pennsylvania League
President: John H. Farrell

Standings	W	L	Pct.	GB	Manager
Williamsport Billies	82	42	.661	—	Harry Hinchman
York White Roses	73	51	.589	9	Frank Dessau
Scranton Miners	68	54	.557	13	Joe Ward
Binghamton Triplets	67	55	.549	14	John Hummel
Wilkes-Barre Barons	47	74	.388	33½	Tom Downey
Elmira Red Jackets	30	91	.248	50½	John Riley

BA: Earl Babbington, Elmira/York, .383
Runs: Stan Benton, Williamsport, 133
Hits: Stan Benton, Williamsport, 171
HRs: Bill Batch, York, 19

Wins: Gene Costello, York, 22
SOs: Dudley Foulk, Williamsport, 167
Pct: Gene Costello, York, .759, 22-7

B South Atlantic League
President: W.H. Walsh

Standings	W	L	Pct.	GB	Manager
Charlotte Hornets*	89	56	.614	—	Dick Hoblitzell
Greenville Spinners	77	65	.538	10½	Zinn Beck
Augusta Tigers	73	62	.533	11	Patsy O'Rourke
Spartanburg Spartans	74	66	.528	12½	Mike Kelly
Charleston Pals/ Macon Peaches#**	64	76	.457	22½	Jack Coffey
Columbia/Gastonia Combers@	44	96	.314	42½	Scotty Alcock

#Charleston (7-28) moved to Macon May 28.
@Columbia (8-15 in second half) moved to Gastonia July 26.

Playoff: Charlotte 4 games, Macon 1.

BA: Zinn Beck, Greenville, .370
Runs: Ben Paschal, Charlotte, 147
Hits: George Rhinehardt, Greenville, 212
RBIs: Ben Paschal, Charlotte, 122
HRs: Ben Paschal, Charlotte, 26

Wins: Lee Bolt, Charlotte, 20
SOs: Lee Bolt, Charlotte, 133
ERA: Rufus Clarke, Augusta, 2.90
Pct: Rush Yeargin, Greenville, .667, 18-9

B Three-I League
President: Albert R. Tearney

Standings	W	L	Pct.	GB	Manager
Decatur Commodores	81	54	.600	—	Charles Miller
Rockford Rox	76	63	.547	7	Harry Rigsby
Terre Haute Tots	71	60	.541	8	Ernie Robertson
Bloomington Bloomers	72	64	.529	9½	William Jackson
Evansville Evas	72	65	.525	10	John Nee

Peoria Tractors	71	65	.522	10½	H.F. Breen
Danville Veterans	55	81	.404	26½	Rudy Hulswitt
Moline Plowboys	45	91	.331	36½	Robert Coltrin/Jim Shollenberger

BA: Guy Dunning, Terre Haute, .371
Runs: Ed Barnes, Peoria, 100
Hits: Guy Dunning, Terre Haute, 198

HRs: Ernie Calbert, Decatur, 18
        Harry Rice, Danville, 18
Wins: John Kotzelnick, Decatur, 20
SOs: James "Jumbo" Elliott, Terre Haute, 154
Pct: Oliver Adkins, Rockford, .773, 17-5

B Virginia League
President: W.S. Moye

Standings	W	L	Pct.	GB	Manager
Wilson Tobacconists	70	52	.774	—	Rube Oldring
Richmond Colts	71	53	.773	—	Dave Robertson
Rocky Mount Tar Heels	63	59	.516	7	Frank Walker
Norfolk Tars	62	60	.508	8	Win Clark
Portsmouth Truckers	58	62	.483	11	Ed Goosetree
Petersburg Trunkmakers	43	81	.347	28	George Block/Baldy Alterman

BA: Hack Wilson, Portsmouth, .388
Runs: Frank Walker, Rocky Mount, 126
Hits: Frank Walker, Rocky Mount, 177
RBIs: Hack Wilson, Portsmouth, 101

HRs: Hack Wilson, Portsmouth, 19
Wins: Alex Peterson, Norfolk, 19
SOs: Alex Peterson, Norfolk, 129
Pct: Bill Manning, Richmond, .727, 16-6

C Florida State League
President: Al E. Lang

Standings	W	L	Pct.	GB	Manager
Orlando Bulldogs***	78	38	.672	—	Ernie Burke
Bradentown Growers	63	55	.534	16	Roy Thomas
Lakeland Highlanders	60	55	.522	17½	Tom Leach
St. Petersburg Saints	56	61	.479	22½	Hugh Bradley
Daytona Beach Islanders	50	66	.431	28	Leon "Red" Ames/Bob Munn
Tampa Smokers	40	72	.357	36	Doc Nance/Kylie Myers

BA: Al Green, Orlando, .382
Runs: Gale Staley, Orlando, 92
Hits: Al Green, Orlando, 170
HRs: Al Green, Orlando, 14

Wins: Jesse Woolf, Orlando, 20
SOs: John Luther, Lakeland, 127
Pct: Bert Humphries, Orlando, .737, 14-5

C Piedmont League
President: William G. Bramham

Standings	W	L	Pct.	GB	Manager
Danville Tobacconists**	73	50	.593	—	Herb Murphy
Greensboro Patriots*	66	57	.537	7	Charles Carroll
High Point Pointers	65	58	.528	8	Hardin Herndon
Winston-Salem Twins	59	63	.484	13½	Bill Leard/Mike Fahey
Raleigh Capitals	57	66	.463	16	Duke Duncan
Durham Bulls	48	74	.393	24½	Bill Pierre

Playoff: Danville 4 games, Greensboro 0.

BA: Carr Smith, Raleigh, .418
Runs: Carr Smith, Raleigh, 107
        Dutch Dorman, Danville, 107
Hits: John Kane, High Point, 189
RBIs: Carr Smith, Raleigh, 137

HRs: Carr Smith, Raleigh, 24
Wins: Jess Eldridge, High Point, 27
SOs: Braxton Gibson, Danville, 120
Pct: Grier Friday, Raleigh, .800, 8-2

C Southwestern League
President: Ensley Barbour

Standings	W	L	Pct.	GB	Manager
Hutchinson Wheat Shockers**	84	50	.627	—	Marty Purtell
Sapulpa Yanks	76	55	.580	6½	Barney Cleveland
Coffeyville Refiners*	73	61	.541	11	Frank Matthews
Bartlesville Bearcats	68	66	.507	16	Ted Waring
Topeka Kaws	67	66	.504	16½	Gus Suhr
Salina Millers	60	72	.455	23	Benny Meyer
Muskogee Mets	57	79	.419	28	Ray Brownlee
Independence Producers	49	85	.366	35	Drummond Brown

Playoff: Coffeyville 4 games, Hutchinson 0.

BA: Moses Solomon, Hutchinson, .421
Runs: Moses Solomon, Hutchinson, 143
Hits: Moses Solomon, Hutchinson, 222
HRs: Moses Solomon, Hutchinson, 49

Wins: Homer Owens, Sapulpa, 23
        Ray Pierce, Topeka, 23
SOs: D. Walker, Salina, 200
Pct: Alvin Bauer, Hutchinson, .733, 11-4

C Western Association
President: E.A. Daniels

Standings	W	L	Pct.	GB	Manager
Joplin Miners	83	60	.580	—	Gabby Street
Ardmore Snappers**	82	60	.577	½	Earl "Red" Snapp
Okmulgee Drillers*	81	63	.563	2½	Troy Agnew
Enid Harvesters	80	65	.552	4	Tom Downey
Springfield Midgets	70	74	.486	13½	Runt Marr
Ft. Smith Twins	53	92	.366	31	Fred Hunter/Mickey Doolan

Henryetta Hens@ .... 43 48 .473 NA   Drap Hayes/Louis Jones
McAlester Diggers# .... 27 57 .321 NA   Les Tullos

#McAlester disbanded July 19.
@Henryetta disbanded July 21.

Playoff: Ardmore 4 games, Okmulgee 0.

BA: John Jones, Joplin, .398
Runs: Frank Reiger, Enid, 123
Hits: John Jones, Joplin, 214
HRs: Osborne McDaniel, Enid, 36

Wins: Jimmy Walkup, Okmulgee, 25
SOs: Jack Killeen, Enid, 231
Pct: Jack Williams, Enid, .800, 12-3

D Appalachian League
President: George C. Davis

Standings	W	L	Pct.	GB	Manager
Knoxville Pioneers	66	38	.635	—	Frank Moffett
Bristol State Liners	55	50	.524	11½	George Ramsey
Kingsport Indians	52	55	.486	15½	Tom Conway
Greeneville Burley Cubs	51	56	.477	16½	Pat Carroll
Johnson City Soldiers	47	57	.452	19	Jack Ryan
Morristown Roosters	45	60	.429	21½	Jim Barton

BA: Walt Mittwede, Morristown, .344
Runs: Aubrey Hood, Greeneville, 84
Hits: T.V. McGuire, Bristol, 139
HRs: Joe Price, Johnson City, 15

Wins: R.E. Leach, Knoxville, 17
    A.C. Stoner, Knoxville, 17
SOs: Lee Ormand, Kingsport, 140
Pct: R.E. Leach, Knoxville, .810, 17-4

D Blue Grass League
President: Thomas M. Russell

Standings	W	L	Pct.	GB	Manager
Cynthiana Cobblers	54	43	.557	—	Bill Schumaker
Winchester Dodgers	53	44	.546	1	Pat Devereaux
Maysville Cardinals	48	45	.516	4	Norbert Bosken
Paris Bourbons	45	47	.480	6½	Nick Winger
Lexington Reos	44	49	.473	8	Doug Harbison
Mt. Sterling Essex	38	54	.413	13½	Hod Eller

D Blue Ridge League
President: J. Vincent Jamison, Jr.

Standings	W	L	Pct.	GB	Manager
Martinsburg Blue Sox	67	30	.691	—	Earle Mack
Waynesboro Villagers	52	45	.536	15	Bill Morris
Hanover Raiders	49	50	.495	19	George Wilson/Frank Caporal
Frederick Hustlers	41	53	.436	24½	Norm McNeill
Chambersburg Maroons	41	55	.427	25½	Mike Mowrey/Wayne Dowell
Hagerstown Terriers	41	58	.414	27	Tony Walsh/Larry Steinbeck

BA: George Rawlings, Martinsburg, .376
Runs: George Rawlings, Martinsburg, 104
Hits: George Rawlings, Martinsburg, 145
HRs: George Rawlings, Martinsburg, 25

Wins: Horace Ozmer, Martinsburg, 20
SOs: Horace Ozmer, Martinsburg, 142
Pct: Horace Ozmer, Martinsburg, .800, 20-5

D Cotton States League
President: Frank A. Scott

Standings	W	L	Pct.	GB	Manager
Greenville Swamp Angels ..	46	35	.563	—	Harold Irelan
Laurel Lumberjacks	43	35	.544	1½	Charles Hodge/Bill Statham
Greenwood Indians	43	35	.544	1½	Tom Toland
Clarksdale Cubs	41	38	.519	4	Baxter Sparks
Jackson Senators	37	40	.489	7	Charles Bell
Vicksburg Hill Billies	37	43	.481	8½	Cy Slapnicka/Ollie Mills
Meridian Metropolitans	36	43	.456	9	John Jones/Bill Bongeno
Hattiesburg Hubmen	31	45	.408	12½	"Red" Torkelson/Fred Smith

The league disbanded July 24.

BA: Arthur Bourg, Laurel, .370
Runs: Leonard Glassbrenner, Clarksdale, 56
Hits: Chap Marable, Greenville, 93

Wins: Bill Statham, Laurel, 17
Pct: Bill Statham, Laurel, .773, 17-5

D East Texas League
President: Ike Hockwald

Standings	W	L	Pct.	GB	Manager
Paris Grays***	76	43	.639	—	Paul Trammell
Greenville Staplers	70	48	.593	5½	Bennie Brownlow
Marshall Indians	63	55	.534	12½	Hick Munsell/Jackie Reid/Johnny Jones/ Larry Parker
Mt. Pleasant Cats	53	66	.445	23	Frank Youree/Roy Storey
Sulphur Springs Lions	53	67	.442	23½	Roy Eichord
Longview Cannibals	41	77	.348	34½	Jack Lockhart/Grady White/Hick Munsell

Attendance: Mt. Pleasant, 13,029.

BA: Fred Craig, Greenville, .328
Runs: Chalmers Williams, Paris, 105
Hits: Fred Craig, Greenville, 156
HRs: Lillard Belcher, Marshall/Paris, 31

Wins: Jackie Reid, Marshall, 20
SOs: Jack Robertson, Greenville, 193
Pct: Jack Robertson, Greenville, .731, 19-7

D Eastern Shore League
President: M.B. Thawley

Standings	W	L	Pct.	GB	Manager
Dover Senators	51	24	.680	—	Jiggs Donohue
Cambridge Canners	47	26	.644	3	Herb Armstrong
Laurel Blue Hens	42	30	.583	7½	J.P. "Poke" Whalen
Salisbury Indians	34	39	.446	16	Burt Shipley
Parksley Spuds	31	45	.408	20½	Thomas "Poke" Whalen
Crisfield Crabbers	26	47	.356	24	
Pocomoke City Salamanders@	27	37	.422	NA	James Sharpe
Milford Sandpipers#	9	19	.321	NA	Bob Clark/John McCloskey

#Milford withdrew July 14 rather than forfeit all of its wins because of an ineligible player.
@Pocomoke City disbanded August 21.

BA: Harvey McDonald, Dover, .388
Runs: Harvey McDonald, Dover, 60
Hits: Harvey McDonald, Dover, 95
HRs: Charles Tolson, Salisbury, 27

Wins: Oscar Shertzer, Cambridge, 13
SOs: Ted Firth, Parksley, 133
Pct: Charles Humphreys, Dover, .800, 12-3

D Kitty League
President: Dr. Frank H. Bassett

Standings	W	L	Pct.	GB	Manager
Mayfield Pantmakers**	59	43	.578	—	Oren Mitchell
Fulton Railroaders	61	45	.575	—	Charles Holloway
Dyersburg Forked Deers*...	51	47	.520	6	Dutch Quellmalz
Paducah Indians	55	53	.509	7	Dolly Stark
Hopkinsville Hoppers	52	51	.505	7½	Ben Smith
Cairo Egyptians	48	57	.457	12½	Jack Herbert/Elmer "Doc" Bennett
Paris Parisians	46	55	.455	12½	Tuffy Fowlkes/Dehaney
Milan/Trenton Twins@	22	21	.512	NA	
Springfield Blanket Makers#...	14	36	.280	NA	Frank Stapleton

#Springfield disbanded July 9.
@Milan replaced Springfield July 19 for the second half, and later moved to Trenton.

Playoff: Dyersburg defeated Mayfield.

D Mississippi Valley League
President: Michael H. Sexton

Standings	W	L	Pct.	GB	Manager
Dubuque Climbers	78	50	.609	—	Joe McGinnity
Ottumwa Cardinals	73	53	.579	4	Walt Mattick
Cedar Rapids Bunnies	69	56	.552	7½	Bill Speas
Waterloo Hawks	58	69	.457	19½	Bert Weeden
Rock Island Islanders..........	53	73	.421	24	Tommy Thompson
Marshalltown Ansons	48	78	.381	29	Frank Boyle

BA: Bill Speas, Cedar Rapids, .363
Runs: John Armstrong, Dubuque, 93
Hits: Bill Speas, Cedar Rapids, 182
HRs: Andrew McEwan, Waterloo, 8

Wins: John Dill, Ottumwa, 22
SOs: George Brown, Waterloo, 175
Pct: Emil Levson, Cedar Rapids, .826, 19-4

D Nebraska State League
Presidents: Clarence J. Miles/Richard R. Grotte

Standings	W	L	Pct.	GB	Manager
Lincoln Links	71	64	.526	—	O.A. Beltzer
Norfolk Elk Horns	68	66	.507	2½	Ed Reichle
Grand Island Champions ...	68	66	.507	2½	Leo McDonnell/Boser
Hastings Cubs	65	66	.498	4	Leo Bennett
Beatrice Blues	64	68	.485	5½	Ed Willett/Matty McGrath
Fairbury Jeffersons	63	69	.477	6½	George Segrist

BA: Fred Conkey, Lincoln, .390
Runs: Fresco Thompson, Grand Island, 91
Hits: Fred Conkey, Lincoln, 169
HRs: Jim Hudgens, Fairbury, 13

Wins: Art Stokes, Lincoln, 23
SOs: Art Stokes, Lincoln, 207
Pct: Edward Shupe, Grand Island, .720, 18-7

D North Dakota League
President: Logan Powell

Standings	W	L	Pct.	GB	Manager
Minot Magicians***	48	21	.696	—	Herb Hester
Jamestown Jimkotas	32	35	.478	15	Ed Whiting/Henry Wingfield
New Rockford-Carrington Twins/ Valley City Hi-Liners#	30	38	.441	17½	Earl Pickering
Bismarck Capitals	26	42	.382	21½	Tom Shanley/Mo McKnight

#New Rockford-Carrington moved to Valley City July 17.

BA: Harry Wingfield, Jamestown, .402
Runs: George Coleman, Minot, 72

Hits: Fred Gunther, Minot, 88
    Albert Chenoweth, Jamestown, 88
HRs: Albert Wenz, Jamestown, 6
    Henry Oliver, Minot, 6

D Oklahoma State League
President: E.A. Daniels

Standings	W	L	Pct.	GB	Manager
Cushing Refiners	65	53	.551	—	Ned Pettigrew
Bristow Producers**	65	54	.546	½	Jim Payne/Ralph Heatley

1923

	W	L	Pct.	GB	Manager
Duncan Oilers*	64	55	.538	1½	Larry McLean
Clinton Bulldogs	63	55	.534	2	Huber Dennis
El Reno Railroaders	58	59	.496	6½	Harry Burge
Shawnee Indians	57	62	.479	8½	Clyde Wren
Guthrie	54	65	.454	11½	Bill Williams
Drumright Boosters/ Ponca City Poncans#	43	72	.374	20½	F. McGaha/J. Wiggins/J. Jones

#Drumright (11-21) moved to Ponca City June 7.

Playoff: Bristow 4 games, Duncan 0.

D Panhandle-Pecos Valley League
President: S.D. Hunter

Standings	W	L	Pct.	GB	Manager
Amarillo Gassers	62	42	.596	—	Snappy Anheier/Skinny Moore
Lubbock Hubbers*	57	47	.548	5	Sled Allen
Clovis Cubs**	48	56	.461	14	Clarence "Pop Boy" Smith/Frank Fuller
Roswell Giants	41	63	.394	21	Charles O'Day

The league disbanded August 15.

Playoff: Lubbock 5 games, Amarillo 4.

BA: Ben Bedford, Roswell, .354
Runs: Robert Clary, Clovis, 83
Hits: Ben Bedford, Roswell, 134
Wins: Dick Morgan, Lubbock, 17
Mike File, Clovis, 17
SOs: Harry Swenson, Lubbock, 162
Pct: Dick Morgan, Lubbock, .654, 17-9

D South Dakota League
President: M.E. Cantillon

Standings	W	L	Pct.	GB	Manager
Sioux Falls Soos*	35	22	.614	—	Jack Beatty
Aberdeen Grays**	35	23	.603	½	Nig Nolte
Mitchell Kernels	28	27	.509	6	Hank Scharnweber
Watertown Cubs	15	41	.268	19½	Wilbur Smith

The league disbanded July 17.

D Texas Association
President: W.R. Davidson

Standings	W	L	Pct.	GB	Manager
Mexia Gushers	80	60	.571	—	Hub Northen
Austin Rangers**	72	66	.522	7	Rankin Johnson
Sherman Twins*	72	67	.518	7½	A.B. Sands/Otto McIvor
Corsicana Oilers	68	70	.493	11	Harvey Grubb
Marlin Bathers	65	73	.471	14	Walt Alexander
Waco Indians	59	80	.424	20½	Ray Falk/H. House/Bill Reynolds/ Warwick Comstock

Playoff: Austin 3 games, Sherman 3. The series was declared a draw when the two clubs could not agree upon a site for the deciding game.

BA: Tom Pyle, Sherman, .359
Runs: Tom Pyle, Sherman, 94
Hits: Tom Pyle, Sherman, 199
HRs: Don Flynn, Waco/Austin, 22
Wins: Clarence Tiner, Mexia, 23
SOs: Murray Richburg, Sherman, 197
Pct: Harvey Muns, Sherman, .690, 20-9

1923 Interleague Post Season Play

World Series
New York (American) 4 games, New York (National) 2

Junior World Series
Kansas City (American Association) 5 games, Baltimore (International) 4
Total Attendance: 84,705

Junior World Series Tune-Up
Hartford (Eastern) 2 games, Baltimore (International) 0

Dixie Series
Ft. Worth (Texas) 4 games, New Orleans (Southern Association) 2, one tie
Total Attendance: 55,436

Class B Southern Championship
Charlotte (South Atlantic) 4 games, Wilson (Virginia) 2

Five-State Championship
Dover (Eastern Shore) 4 games, Martinsburg (Blue Ridge) 2

1923 No-Hitters

Date	Pitcher	Team	League	Opponent	Score
4-14	Jim Scott	San Francisco	Pacific Coast	Oakland	5-0
5-2	Randolph Young	Bloomington	Three-I	Rockford	16-0 (P)
5-10	Oscar Anderson	Paris	East Texas	Longview	3-0
5-20	George Munger	Bristow	Oklahoma State	Duncan	1-0
5-23	Rufus Clarke	Augusta	South Atlantic	Columbia	9-0
5-25	George Dennison	Minot	North Dakota	Bismarck	2-1
6-8	John Gross	Mt. Sterling	Blue Grass	Paris	2-0
6-15	Russell Haines	London	Michigan-Ontario	Flint	2-1 (11)
6-24	George Edmundson	Albany	Eastern	Springfield	5-0
6-30	George Phillips	Paris	East Texas	Marshall	1-5 (10)
7-16	Stanton	Fairbury	Nebraska State	Hastings	6-3
7-23	Ray Pierce	Topeka	Southwestern	Independence	4-0
8-4	Horace Browne	Kalamazoo	Michigan-Ontario	Grand Rapids	1-0
8-6	Mark Webb	Rocky Mount	Virginia	Norfolk	6-0
9-4	Sam Jones	New York	American	Philadelphia	2-0
9-7	Howard Ehmke	Boston	American	Philadelphia	4-0

Number in parentheses indicates innings if other than nine; "P" indicates perfect game.

THIS DATE IN MINOR LEAGUE HISTORY

April 19, 1923, Lefty Grove of Baltimore, International League, fanned 17 to beat Syracuse 8-1 in his first start of the season. Lefty would record 330 strikeouts in 303 innings this season, setting the all-time loop record.

April 29, 1923, Lefty Grove, Baltimore, fanned 13 batters for a total of 59 in his first four engagements of the season. His totals were 17-15-14-13.

May 11, 1923, Outfielder Pete Schneider, a former big league pitcher, hit five home runs, including two grand slams, plus a double, for Vernon, Pacific Coast League. The Tigers defeated Salt Lake City 35-11. Schneider hit two round-trippers in the sixth inning and one in the seventh. He batted eight times, scored six runs and batted in 14 tallies. Vernon piled up 33 hits in the game, including nine homers.

May 16, 1923, Joe McGinnity, 52, pitched a three-hit game for Dubuque against Marshalltown in the Mississippi Valley League.

May 28, 1923, Lester Bell, later a third base star with the St. Louis Cardinals, clouted five consecutive doubles in Houston's 22-4 win over Dallas in the Texas League.

June 15, 1923, Joe McGinnity of Dubuque, Mississippi Valley League, shut out Rock Island on three hits, issuing just one base on balls.

July 2, 1923, Outfielder Ed Bratcher of Ardmore, Western Association, hit three homers, three doubles, and three singles in nine at bats in a doubleheader.

July 8, 1923, Nick Cullop of Omaha, Western League, hit three triples and a single in a game at Denver.

August 2, 1923, Lou Gehrig was returned to Hartford of the Eastern League by the New York Yankees.

August 9, 1923, Pitcher John Gillespie of Bridgeport, Eastern League, hit four home runs plus a double in one game against Springfield. His fourth homer was the game winner in the tenth inning.

August 18, 1923, Harrison Field, home of the Newark International League club, was destroyed by fire. The loss was estimated at $100,000.

September 2, 1923, After playing 238 games without being shut out, Kansas City was whitewashed 5-0 by Milwaukee slabster Nelson Potts. The streak tied the American Association record of 238 games set by Minneapolis from September 1920 to June 1922.

September 2, 1923, Second baseman Roy Ostergard hit three home runs in a game for Galveston, Texas League.

September 5, 1923, Muskogee of the Southwestern League lost its 38th consecutive game under manager Ray Brownlee, the longest losing streak in the history of Organized Ball.

September 23, 1923, Rube Parnham of Baltimore, International League, pitched a doubleheader against Jersey City and won both games. The victories extended his run of consecutive wins to 20, boosting his final record to 33-7.

October 6, 1923, Shortstop Jimmy Cooney of Milwaukee, American Association, who later played for the St. Louis Cardinals, Chicago Cubs and Philadelphia Phillies, made 12 consecutive hits during a two-day batting spree.

October 14, 1923, The Pacific Coast League's 202-game season concluded.

October 14, 1923, Paul Strand set an all-time Organized Ball record when the outfielder finished with 325 hits for Salt Lake City, Pacific Coast League.

1924

American League
President: Byron Bancroft Johnson

Standings	W	L	Pct.	GB	Attend.	Manager
Washington Senators	92	62	.597	—	584,310	Bucky Harris
New York Yankees	89	63	.586	2	1,053,533	Miller Huggins
Detroit Tigers	86	68	.558	6	1,015,136	Ty Cobb
St. Louis Browns	74	78	.487	17	533,349	George Sisler
Philadelphia Athletics	71	81	.467	20	531,992	Connie Mack
Cleveland Indians	67	86	.438	24½	481,905	Tris Speaker
Boston Red Sox	67	87	.435	25	448,556	Lee Fohl
Chicago White Sox	66	87	.431	25½	606,658	Johnny Evers/Ed Walsh/ Eddie Collins

BA: Babe Ruth, New York, .378
Runs: Babe Ruth, New York, 143
Hits: Sam Rice, Washington, 216
RBIs: Goose Goslin, Washington, 129
HRs: Babe Ruth, New York, 46

Wins: Walter Johnson, Washington, 23
SOs: Walter Johnson, Washington, 158
ERA: Walter Johnson, Washington, 2.72
Pct: Walter Johnson, Washington, .767, 23-7

National League
President: John A. Heydler

Standings	W	L	Pct.	GB	Attend.	Manager
New York Giants	93	60	.608	—	844,068	John McGraw
Brooklyn Robins	92	62	.597	1½	818,883	Wilbert Robinson
Pittsburgh Pirates	90	63	.588	3	736,883	Bill McKechnie
Cincinnati Reds	83	70	.542	10	473,707	Jack Hendricks
Chicago Cubs	81	72	.529	12	716,922	Bill Killefer
St. Louis Cardinals	65	89	.422	28½	272,885	Branch Rickey
Philadelphia Phillies	55	96	.364	37	299,818	Art Fletcher
Boston Braves	53	100	.346	40	177,478	Dave Bancroft

BA: Rogers Hornsby, St. Louis, .424
Runs: Rogers Hornsby, St. Louis, 121
    Frank Frisch, New York, 121
Hits: Rogers Hornsby, St. Louis, 227
RBIs: George Kelly, New York, 136

HRs: Jake Fournier, Brooklyn, 27
Wins: Dazzy Vance, Brooklyn, 28
SOs: Dazzy Vance, Brooklyn, 262
ERA: Dazzy Vance, Brooklyn, 2.16
Pct: Emil Yde, Pittsburgh, .842, 16-3

AA American Association
President: Thomas J. Hickey

Standings	W	L	Pct.	GB	Attend.	Manager
St. Paul Saints	96	70	.578	—	242,268	Nick Allen
Indianapolis Indians	92	74	.554	4	214,623	Donie Bush
Louisville Colonels	91	76	.545	5½	188,587	Joe McCarthy
Milwaukee Brewers	83	83	.500	13	144,495	Harry Clark
Toledo Mud Hens	82	83	.497	13½	205,658	James Burke
Minneapolis Millers	77	89	.464	19	181,094	Mike Kelley
Columbus Senators	75	93	.446	22	131,957	Carleton Molesworth
Kansas City Blues	68	96	.415	27	254,826	Wilbur Good/John "Doc" Lavan

BA: Les Bell, Milwaukee, .365
Runs: Les Bell, Milwaukee, 145
    Walter Christensen, St. Paul, 145
Hits: Les Bell, Milwaukee, 230
RBIs: Chuck Dressen, St. Paul, 151

HRs: Elmer Smith, Louisville, 28
Wins: Jesse Petty, Indianapolis, 29
SOs: Rube Walberg, Milwaukee, 175
ERA: Jesse Petty, Indianapolis, 2.83

AA International League
President: John Conway Toole

Standings	W	L	Pct.	GB	Attend.	Manager
Baltimore Orioles	117	48	.709	—	229,382	Jack Dunn
Toronto Maple Leafs	98	67	.594	19	102,153	Dan Howley
Buffalo Bisons	84	83	.503	34	126,300	George Wiltse/Bill Webb
Rochester Tribe	83	84	.497	35	160,064	George Stallings
Newark Bears	80	83	.491	36	160,730	Fred Brainerd
Syracuse Stars	79	83	.488	36½	99,378	Frank Shaughnessy
Reading Keystones	63	98	.391	52	124,009	Spencer Abbott
Jersey City Colts	53	111	.323	63½	74,810	Patsy Donovan

All-Star Team: 1B-Fred Merkle, Rochester; **2B**-Dick Porter, Baltimore; **3B**-George Makin, Syracuse; **SS**-Joe Boley, Baltimore; **OF**-Bill Zitman, Newark; Jocko Conlan, Rochester; Joe Kelly, Toronto; **C**-Mickey Devine, Newark; Joe Cobb, Baltimore; **Util**-Ray Whitman, Newark; Frank O'Rourke, Toronto; **P**-Lefty Grove, Baltimore; Walter Beall, Rochester; Jack Ogden, Baltimore; Wally Stewart, Toronto.

BA: Richard Porter, Baltimore, .364
Runs: Bill Zitman, Newark, 137
Hits: Jocko Conlan, Rochester, 214
RBIs: William Kelly, Buffalo, 155

HRs: William Kelly, Buffalo, 28
Wins: Lefty Grove, Baltimore, 26
SOs: Walter Beall, Rochester, 227
ERA: Walter Beall, Rochester, 2.76

AA Pacific Coast League
President: Harry A. Williams

Standings	W	L	Pct.	GB	Manager
Seattle Indians	109	91	.545	—	Red Killefer
Los Angeles Angels	107	92	.538	1½	Marty Krug
San Francisco Seals	108	93	.537	1½	Herbert Ellison
Oakland Oaks	103	99	.510	7	Ivan Howard
Salt Lake City Bees	101	100	.502	8½	Duffy Lewis
Vernon Tigers	97	104	.483	12½	Bill Essick
Portland Beavers	88	110	.444	20	Bill Kenworthy/Frank Brazil
Sacramento Senators	88	112	.440	21	Charley Pick/Buddy Ryan

Total Attendance: 2,235,510.

BA: Duffy Lewis, Salt Lake City, .392
Runs: Howard Lindemore, Salt Lake City, 183
Hits: Herbert Ellison, San Francisco, 307
RBIs: Herbert Ellison, San Francisco, 188
HRs: Jim Poole, Portland, 38

TBs: Herbert Ellison, San Francisco, 496
Wins: Willis Mitchell, San Francisco, 28
SOs: George Boehler, Oakland, 216
ERA: Doc Crandall, Los Angeles, 2.71

A Eastern League
President: Daniel O'Neill

Standings	W	L	Pct.	GB	Manager
Waterbury Brasscos	89	63	.586	—	Kitty Bransfield
Springfield Ponies	87	66	.569	2½	Eugene McCann
Hartford Senators	85	67	.559	4	Paddy O'Connor
New Haven Profs	75	78	.490	14½	Clyde Milan
Pittsfield Hillies	70	81	.464	18½	Billy Gilbert/Frank Stapleton/Andy Coakley
Worcester Coal Heavers	70	82	.461	19	Jesse Burkett
Albany Empires	67	83	.447	21	William Rodgers/Bill McCorry
Bridgeport Bears	65	88	.425	24½	John O'Hara/Joe Smith/Dick Hoblitzel

BA: Wade Lefler, Worcester, .370
Runs: Robert Emmerich, Worcester, 137
Hits: Wade Lefler, Worcester, 210
HRs: John Roser, Worcester, 38

Wins: Gary Fortune, Springfield, 23
SOs: Kent Greenfield, New Haven, 138
ERA: Earl Johnson, Hartford, 2.27

A Southern Association
President: John D. Martin

Standings	W	L	Pct.	GB	Attend.	Manager
Memphis Chickasaws	104	49	.680	—	224,224	Johnny Dobbs
Atlanta Crackers	99	54	.647	5	244,278	Bert Niehoff
New Orleans Pelicans	93	60	.608	11	178,529	Larry Gilbert
Nashville Volunteers	78	75	.510	26	107,403	James Hamilton
Mobile Bears	68	84	.447	35½	76,168	Emil Huhn
Chattanooga Lookouts	63	89	.414	40½	71,031	Les Nunamaker
Birmingham Barons	54	98	.356	49½	125,540	Stuffy Stewart
Little Rock Travelers	51	101	.336	52½	52,434	Norman "Kid" Elberfeld

BA: Carlisle Smith, Atlanta, .385
Runs: Ben Paschal, Atlanta, 136
Hits: Roy Carlyle, Memphis, 233
RBIs: Roy Carlyle, Memphis, 122

HRs: John Anderson, Chattanooga, 26
Wins: Benny Karr, Little Rock, 23
SOs: Benny Karr, Little Rock, 127
ERA: Teller Cavet, New Orleans, 2.65

A Texas League
President: J. Doak Roberts

Standings	W	L	Pct.	GB	Attend.	Manager
Ft. Worth Panthers***	109	41	.727	—	166,313	Jake Atz
Houston Buffaloes	80	73	.523	30½	111,959	Hunter Hill/Marvin Goodwin
Beaumont Exporters	77	73	.513	32	64,770	Dutch Bernsen
Wichita Falls Spudders	77	74	.510	32½	76,236	Archie Tanner
San Antonio Bears	75	75	.500	34	88,280	Bob Coleman
Dallas Steers	75	79	.487	36	182,346	Walter Morris/Roy Mitchell
Galveston Sand Crabs	61	93	.396	50	48,483	Paddy Baumann/ George "Tex" Wisterzil
Shreveport Gassers	54	100	.351	57	82,095	Ira Thomas

BA: Art Weis, Wichita Falls, .377
Runs: Clarence "Big Boy" Kraft, Ft. Worth, 150
Hits: Matt Donohue, Dallas, 209
RBIs: Clarence "Big Boy" Kraft, Ft. Worth, 196

HRs: Clarence "Big Boy" Kraft, Ft. Worth, 55
Wins: Joe Pate, Ft. Worth, 30
SOs: Slim Love, Dallas, 208
ERA: Jack Knight, Houston, 2.34

A Western League
President: Albert R. Tearney

Standings	W	L	Pct.	GB	Manager
Omaha Buffaloes	103	61	.628	—	Art Griggs
Denver Bears	100	67	.599	4½	Joe Berger
Tulsa Oilers	98	69	.587	6½	Jack Lelivelt
St. Joseph Saints	86	79	.521	17½	Joe Mathes
Oklahoma City Indians	82	86	.488	23	Fred Luderus
Wichita Izzies	79	88	.473	25½	Howard Gregory
Des Moines Boosters	59	106	.358	44½	John "Red" Corriden
Lincoln Links	57	108	.345	46½	Howard Wakefield/Art Rasmussen/ Josh Clarke

Attendance: Denver, 150,000; Tulsa, 135,000.

*Won first-half   **Won second-half   ***Won both halves

BA: Charles Miller, St. Joseph, .385
Runs: Royce Washburn, Tulsa, 184
Hits: Lyman Lamb, Tulsa, 261
HRs: Royce Washburn, Tulsa, 48
2B: Lyman Lamb, Tulsa, 100

TBs: Royce Washburn, Tulsa, 458
Wins: Herb Hall, Denver, 26
SOs: Bill Bailey, Omaha, 191
Pct: George Blaeholder, Tulsa, .750, 18-6

B Michigan-Ontario League
President: Thomas J. Halligan

Standings	W	L	Pct.	GB	Manager
Bay City Wolves**	86	50	.632	—	Punch Knoll
Flint Vehics*	78	52	.600	5	Dan O'Leary
Hamilton Clippers	76	60	.559	10	Frank "Buzz" Wetzel
Saginaw Aces	72	64	.529	14	Al Bashang
London Tecumsehs	62	70	.470	22	Jack Beatty
Grand Rapids Homoners	60	74	.448	25	Josh Devore
Muskegon Anglers	58	79	.423	28½	George "Red" Fisher/Jack Ryan
Kalamazoo Kazoos	45	88	.338	39½	Marty Becker/Fred Hunter

Playoff: Bay City 4 games, Flint 3.

BA: Leo Payne, Grand Rapids, .397
Runs: Frank McGee, Hamilton, 111
Hits: George Tomer, Bay City, 174
RBIs: Frank Gleich, Hamilton, 95

HRs: Frank Luce, Flint, 23
Wins: Joseph Kiefer, Bay City, 19
SOs: Ovila Lahaie, Bay City, 148
ERA: Berlyn Horne, Saginaw, 1.77

B New York-Pennsylvania League
President: John H. Farrell

Standings	W	L	Pct.	GB	Manager
Williamsport Grays	87	46	.654	—	Harry Hinchman
York White Roses	80	48	.625	4½	Frank Desseau
Scranton Miners	72	61	.541	15	Jack Egan
Harrisburg Senators	70	60	.538	15½	Steve Yerkes/Mickey LaLonge/ Glenn Killinger
Binghamton Triplets	62	65	.488	22	John Hummel/Mick Konnick/Bud Weiser
Elmira Colonels	57	76	.428	30	Armando Marsans/Leo Hanley
Wilkes-Barre Barons	51	82	.383	36	Tom Downey/Dutch Bannon/Joe Wall
Utica Utes/Oneonta Indians#	43	84	.339	41	Ambrose McConnell/Ben Egan/Roy Thomas

#Utica (25-62) moved to Oneonta August 7, first home game August 11.
Total Attendance: 477,616.

BA: Dewey Steffens, York, .376
Runs: Bill Hunnefield, Williamsport, 123
Hits: Dewey Steffens, York, 191
HRs: Roy Leavitt, Williamsport, 18

Wins: Thomas George, York, 25
SOs: Thomas George, York, 167
Pct: Thomas George, York, .758, 25-8

B Quebec-Ontario-Vermont League
President: Joseph H. Page

Standings	W	L	Pct.	GB	Manager
Quebec Bulldogs***	66	40	.623	—	Mike Corcoran
Montreal Royals	54	55	.495	13½	Patsy O'Rourke/White Zilenger
Outremont Canadiens	49	58	.458	17½	Pete Farrand
Ottawa-Hull Senators	46	55	.455	17½	Jean Dubuc
Rutland Sheiks#	34	20	.630	NA	A.W. "Punch" Daly
Montpelier Goldfish@	16	37	.302	NA	Mike McCorry

#Rutland disbanded July 15.
@Montpelier was dropped July 15, changing the league to the Quebec-Ontario League.

BA: Buck Fraser, Rutland/Quebec, .417
Runs: John Henzes, Quebec, 101
Hits: Buck Fraser, Rutland/Quebec, 140
  John Sherlock, Quebec, 140

HRs: Buck Fraser, Rutland/Quebec, 15
Wins: Charles Parkes, Ottawa-Hull, 14
SOs: Charles Parkes, Ottawa-Hull, 107
ERA: Al Grabowski, Montpelier, 1.94

B South Atlantic League
Presidents: W.H. Walsh/William G. Bramham

Standings	W	L	Pct.	GB	Manager
Augusta Tygers	74	47	.612	—	Johnny Nee
Charlotte Hornets	73	48	.604	1	Ray Kennedy
Spartanburg Spartans	62	59	.512	12	Mike Kelly
Greenville Spinners	59	61	.492	14½	Zinn Beck
Asheville Tourists	58	63	.479	16	Bob Higgins
Macon Peaches	37	85	.303	37½	Henry Eibel/Joe Brennan/Ernie Burke

BA: George Rhinehardt, Greenville, .404
Runs: George Rhinehardt, Greenville, 110
Hits: George Rhinehardt, Greenville, 200
RBIs: Charles Tolson, Charlotte, 111
HRs: Clarence McCrone, Asheville, 28

Wins: Charles Fulton, Augusta, 24
SOs: Sam Gibson, Asheville, 140
ERA: Charles Fulton, Augusta, 3.07
Pct: Charles Fulton, Augusta, .750, 24-8

B Three-I League
Presidents: Albert R. Tearney/L.J. Wiley

Standings	W	L	Pct.	GB	Manager
Terre Haute Tots	75	62	.547	—	Roy Whitcraft
Evansville Little Evas	75	64	.540	1	Joseph Dunn
Bloomington Bloomers	71	64	.526	3	Patrick Harkins
Peoria Tractors	71	66	.518	4	Richard Breen

| Danville Veterans | 59 | 75 | .440 | 14½ | Edward Wright/Forrest Cady/Lance Utt |
| Decatur Commodores | 58 | 78 | .426 | 16½ | Harold Ireland/Guy Rigsby/Ernest Calbert/ Jack Coffey |

BA: Paddy Reagan, Evansville, .329
Runs: Paddy Reagan, Evansville, 104
Hits: Paddy Reagan, Evansville, 188
RBIs: Alfred Platte, Peoria, 98

HRs: Paddy Reagan, Evansville, 18
Wins: Phil Collins, Bloomington, 19
SOs: Walter Miller, Terre Haute, 147
ERA: Emil Levsen, Terre Haute, 2.03

B Virginia League
President: W.S. Moye

Standings	W	L	Pct.	GB	Manager
Richmond Colts	76	59	.563	—	Jack Onslow
Portsmouth Truckers	75	60	.555	1	Ed Goosetree
Rocky Mount Bronchos	74	62	.544	2½	Frank Walker
Norfolk Tars	69	66	.511	7	Win Clark
Wilson Bugs	66	70	.485	10½	Moose Marshall/Les Nunamaker
Petersburg Goobers	46	89	.340	30	Ed Konetchy

BA: Frank Walker, Rocky Mount, .370
Runs: Frank Walker, Rocky Mount, 117
Hits: Ben Malonee, Richmond, 201
RBIs: Ed Konetchy, Petersburg, 98

HRs: Ed Konetchy, Petersburg, 33
Wins: Cecil Duff, Rocky Mount, 23
SOs: Frank Dodson, Richmond, 153
ERA: Kenneth Ash, Rocky Mount, 2.39

C Florida State League
President: Al E. Lang

Standings	W	L	Pct.	GB	Manager
Lakeland Highlanders	69	31	.690	—	Thomas Leach
St. Petersburg Saints	64	41	.609	7½	Jack Martin
Orlando Bulldogs	50	51	.495	19½	Ernie Burke
Bradentown Growers	47	55	.461	23	Gene Elliott
Tampa Smokers	39	63	.382	31	George Carey
Daytona Beach Islanders/ Clearwater Pelicans#	37	65	.363	33	Bill Holloway/Tom McMillan

#Daytona Beach (26-55) moved to Clearwater July 15.
The league disbanded August 8.

BA: Elliott Bigelow, St. Petersburg, .388
Runs: Elliott Bigelow, St. Petersburg, 85
Hits: Elliott Bigelow, St. Petersburg, 154
HRs: Walt Hunter, Orlando, 19

Wins: W.E. Wilson, St. Petersburg, 26
SOs: Roy Sullivan, Bradentown, 86
Pct: John Luther, Lakeland, .800, 16-4

C Piedmont League
President: William G. Bramham

Standings	W	L	Pct.	GB	Manager
Durham Bulls	74	46	.617	—	Bill Pierre
High Point Pointers	71	52	.577	4½	Hardin Herndon
Greensboro Patriots	61	59	.508	13	Charles Carroll
Winston-Salem Twins	59	62	.488	15½	Bill Jackson
Danville Tobacconists	53	67	.442	21	Herb Murphy
Raleigh Capitals	45	77	.369	30	Duke Duncan

BA: Hobe Brummitt, Durham, .356
Runs: Loren Thrasher, High Point, 93
Hits: Loren Thrasher, High Point, 160
RBIs: Arnold Townsend, High Point, 102
HRs: Arnold Townsend, High Point, 27
  Dave Harris, Greensboro, 27
Wins: Bill Hackney, Durham, 19
SOs: John Wertz, Winston-Salem, 129
ERA: Orion Masters, Durham, 1.90

C Western Association
President: J.W. Seabaugh

Standings	W	L	Pct.	GB	Manager
Okmulgee Drillers***	110	48	.696	—	Troy Agnew
Ft. Smith Twins	97	63	.606	14	Runt Marr
Muskogee Athletics	97	65	.599	15	Gabby Street
Hutchinson Wheat Shockers	81	80	.503	30½	Mark Purtell
Bartlesville/Ardmore Bearcats#	75	82	.478	34½	Frank Matthews/Ted Waring
Joplin/Bartlesville Boosters@	69	87	.442	40	Tom Toland/Al Williams
Topeka Senators	59	98	.376	50½	Barney Cleveland/Bob Browne
Springfield Midgets	47	112	.296	63½	Charles Schmidt/Alvin Maline/Pete Adams

#Bartlesville (19-23) moved to Ardmore June 8, first home game June 18.
@Joplin (25-24) moved to Bartlesville June 16.

BA: Wilbur Davis, Okmulgee, .400
Runs: Cecil "Stormy" Davis, Okmulgee, 187
Hits: Wilbur Davis, Okmulgee, 260
RBIs: Wilbur Davis, Okmulgee, 190
HRs: Wilbur Davis, Okmulgee, 51
  Cecil "Stormy" Davis, Okmulgee, 51
TBs: Wilbur Davis, Okmulgee, 485
Wins: Clyde Day, Muskogee, 28
SOs: Flint Rhem, Ft. Smith, 282
ERA: Jimmy Walkup, Okmulgee, 2.59

D Appalachian League
President: George C. Davis

Standings	W	L	Pct.	GB	Manager
Knoxville Pioneers*	67	43	.609	—	Frank Moffett
Morristown Roosters	55	52	.514	10½	Roy Clunk

	W	L	Pct.	GB	
Greeneville Burley Cubs	54	52	.509	11	Harvey Russell
Bristol State Liners**	53	57	.482	14	Chuck McDaniels/Jim O'Rourke
Johnson City Soldiers	51	57	.472	15	Sam Hall
Kingsport Indians	44	63	.411	21½	Otto Miller

Playoff: Knoxville 4 games, Bristol 3, one tie.

BA: Art Ruble, Knoxville, .350
Runs: Art Ruble, Knoxville, 78
Hits: Art Ruble, Knoxville, 148
HRs: Elbert Slayback, Morristown, 13

Wins: Fred Reunning, Bristol, 17
SOs: Frank Watt, Greeneville, 146
ERA: Hoyt Williams, Morristown, 1.64

D Blue Grass League
President: Thomas M. Russell

Standings	W	L	Pct.	GB	Manager
Paris Bourbons...................	51	43	.543	—	Bob Corkhill/Pat Devereaux/Fritz Mueller
Cynthiana Cobblers	50	43	.538	½	Bill Schumaker/John Koval
Lexington Studebakers	43	50	.462	7½	Jesse Young/Jim Viox
Winchester Dodgers	43	51	.457	8	George Bell

BA: Don Hurst, Paris, .382
Runs: Pete Monahan, Paris, 81
Hits: Pete Monahan, Paris, 133
HRs: Don Hurst, Paris, 20

Wins: Sam Reid, Lexington, 20
SOs: Sam Reid, Lexington, 170
Pct: Weldon, Winchester, .824, 14-3

D Blue Ridge League
President: J. Vincent Jamison, Jr.

Standings	W	L	Pct.	GB	Manager
Martinsburg Blue Sox..........	59	38	.608	—	Bill Curtis
Hagerstown Hubs	60	39	.606	—	"Bugs" Snyder
Chambersburg Maroons........	47	52	.475	13	Red McDermott/George "Buck" Ramsey
Hanover Raiders.................	44	52	.458	14½	Frank Caporal/Walter Halas
Frederick Hustlers..............	44	56	.440	16½	Herb Armstrong
Waynesboro Villagers	39	56	.411	19	Joe Ward/Joe Conti

BA: George Rawlings, Martinsburg, .379
Runs: George Thomas, Chambersburg, 89
Hits: George Rawlings, Martinsburg, 152
HRs: George Rawlings, Martinsburg, 21

Wins: Leroy Byham, Chambersburg, 16
SOs: Jackson Mathews, Waynesboro, 115
Pct: Clarence Griffin, Waynesboro, .750, 9-3

D Cotton States League
President: Frank A. Scott

Standings	W	L	Pct.	GB	Manager
Hattiesburg Hubmen***.....	64	33	.660	—	Herschel Bobo
Monroe Drillers	59	39	.602	5½	Bill Akey/L.A. Ripperton
Jackson Red Sox	46	52	.469	18½	Nemo Cannon/Buck Stapleton
Brookhaven Truckers	43	50	.462	19	Sam Vick
Laurel Lumberjacks............	43	57	.430	22½	Baxter Sparks/Pat Boyd/Ed McDonald
Vicksburg Hill Billies.........	38	62	.380	27½	Red Torkelson/Ollie Mills/Jim Johnston/Grady Adkins

BA: Clyde Freeman, Jackson, .366
Runs: Herschel Bobo, Hattiesburg, 91
Hits: Hoot Gibson, Hattiesburg, 141
HRs: Sammy Vick, Brookhaven, 16

Wins: Buddy Williamson, Hattiesburg, 21
SOs: Albert Youngblood, Brookhaven, 131
Pct: Buddy Williamson, Hattiesburg, .808, 21-5

D East Texas League
President: T. Lamar Denman

Standings	W	L	Pct.	GB	Manager
Tyler Trojans***	83	37	.692	—	Frank "Pop" Kitchens
Greenville Hunters.............	71	50	.587	12½	Bennie Brownlow
Texarkana Twins	63	56	.529	19½	Hub Northen
Longview Cannibals	56	63	.471	26½	Les Tullos/Jack Johnston
Mt. Pleasant Cats	56	63	.471	26½	Paul Trammell/Edgar "Dutch" Behrens
Sulphur Springs Saints........	56	66	.459	28	Johnny Meanor/Abe Bowman
Marshall Indians	48	69	.410	33½	Robert "Bugs" Young/Johnnie Baggan
Paris North Stars................	43	72	.374	37½	Bill Byers/Rollie Zeider

Attendance: Tyler, 63,000; Mt. Pleasant, 17,003.

BA: Tom Osborne, Mt. Pleasant, .432
Runs: George "Hickory" Jackson, Tyler, 103
Hits: Tom Osborne, Mt. Pleasant, 171
HRs: Pete Daniels, Marshall, 35

Wins: Verne "Red" Roberts, Greenville, 23
SOs: Lloyd Brown, Paris, 224
Pct: Carl Yowell, Tyler, .813, 13-3

D Eastern Shore League
President: J. Harry Rew

Standings	W	L	Pct.	GB	Manager
Parksley Spuds...................	46	34	.575	—	Thomas "Poke" Whalen
Cambridge Canners	45	35	.563	1	James Sharpe
Salisbury Indians	44	36	.550	2	Alva Burris
Crisfield Crabbers..............	41	39	.515	5	Joe Riley
Dover Senators	41	39	.515	5	Jiggs Donohue
Easton Farmers	23	57	.281	23	Frank Baker

BA: Ralph Mattis, Parksley, .322
Runs: Fred Fitzberger, Salisbury, 58
Hits: Art Sullivan, Dover, 97
HRs: Roy Zanzalari, Crisfield, 24

Wins: Clinton Brown, Parksley, 17
SOs: Bunn Hearn, Salisbury, 175
Pct: Thomas Glass, Cambridge, .700, 14-6

D Kitty League
President: Dr. Frank H. Bassett

Standings	W	L	Pct.	GB	Manager
Dyersburg Deers*	60	48	.556	—	George Block/John Woodson
Paris Parisians**.................	59	50	.541	1½	Dutch Quellmalz
Fulton Railroaders	62	54	.534	2	Dan Grenier
Cairo Egyptians	55	56	.495	6½	John Dowell/Brown
Jackson Blue Jays	51	61	.455	11	Ward McDowell/George Block
Mayfield Pantmakers#........	41	59	.410	NA	Ben Koehler/Norm Thelan

#Mayfield disbanded August 26.

Playoff: Dyersburg 4 games, Paris 0.

BA: Paul Kirby, Paris, .342
Runs: Louis Neibert, Dyersburg, 62
Hits: Paul Kirby, Paris, 137

Wins: Carl Dunagan, Dyersburg, 19
Pct: Carl Dunagan, Dyersburg, .905, 19-2

D Mississippi Valley League
President: Michael H. Sexton

Standings	W	L	Pct.	GB	Manager
Waterloo Hawks	84	40	.678	—	Cletus Dixon
Dubuque Dubs	70	51	.579	12½	John Armstrong
Rock Island Islanders.........	64	57	.529	18½	Preston Gray
Ottumwa Cardinals	58	61	.487	23½	Walt Mattick
Moline Plowboys...............	59	65	.478	25	Jim Shollenberger
Burlington Bees	54	67	.446	28½	Henry Wingfield
Cedar Rapids Bunnies	54	67	.446	28½	Bill Speas
Marshalltown Ansons	43	78	.355	39½	Jack Lacy/Frank Boyle

BA: Fred Schult, Waterloo, .368
Runs: Harold Anderson, Ottumwa, 126
Hits: Fred Schult, Waterloo, 167
HRs: Stan Keyes, Rock Island, 20

Wins: Orville McCracken, Waterloo, 23
SOs: Richard Didier, Ottumwa, 145
Pct: Claude Willoughby, Waterloo, .750, 21-7

D Oklahoma State League
President: E.A. Daniels

Standings	W	L	Pct.	GB	Manager
Ardmore Bearcats/ Pawhuska Huskies#.......	52	21	.712	—	Drap Hayes
Bristow Producers..............	48	21	.696	2	Ralph Heatley
Cushing Refiners**	49	27	.645	4½	Ned Pettigrew
Shawnee Indians	40	37	.519	14	Larry McLean
Duncan Oilers+	33	37	.471	17½	John Fant
Ponca City Poncans	32	44	.421	21½	Huber Dennis
Blackwell Gassers..............	20	53	.274	32	J. Rustenhaven/Hal Grun
Guthrie/McAlester/Wewoka@	18	48	.272	30½	M. Robertson/Ted Lipps

#Ardmore (30-13) moved to Pawhuska June 8.
@Guthrie (8-18) moved to McAlester May 24; McAlester (3-13) moved to Wewoka June 8, first home game June 12.
+Duncan (0-2 in second half) disbanded July 6.
The league disbanded July 8.

D Southwestern League
President: J.W. Harris

Standings	W	L	Pct.	GB	Manager
Newton Railroaders*/ Blackwell/Ottawa Gassers#..	79	50	.612	—	John McCloskey
Salina Millers....................	72	56	.563	6½	Floyd Dorland
Arkansas City Osages**.....	70	61	.534	10	Rube Geyer/Ed Yuna
Enid Harvesters.................	65	67	.492	15½	Bert Ellison/George Dye
Eureka Oilers	51	75	.405	26½	Ross Crawford/Dutch Sherman
Emporia Traders	40	89	.310	39	Tom Oran/Hunky Shaw/Pat Mason/Ole Olsen
Independence Producers@ .	45	21	.682	NA	Pat Mason
Coffeyville Refiners@........	29	32	.475	NA	Pat O'Byrne

#A windstorm in Newton wrecked the grandstand, causing the team to move to Blackwell July 26; Blackwell (7-4) moved to Ottawa August 5; Ottawa (13-12) moved back to Newton August 28.
@Independence and Coffeyville disbanded July 5.

Playoff: Newton was awarded the first half championship when co-leader Independence disbanded. Arkansas City 4 games, Newton 3.

BA: Fuzzy Hufft, Arkansas City, .367
Runs: Bill Rogell, Salina, 104
Hits: Brodie Thompson, Newton, 170
HRs: Fuzzy Hufft, Arkansas City, 28

Wins: Joe Kling, Newton, 25
SOs: Joe Kling, Newton, 254
Pct: Bill Doak, Independence, .833, 10-2

D Texas Association
President: A.B. Johnson

Standings	W	L	Pct.	GB	Manager
Corsicana Oilers***	83	42	.664	—	Johnny Vann
Marlin Bathers	73	55	.570	11½	Walt Alexander
Waco Indians	65	64	.504	20	Otto McIvor/Tom Carson
Mexia Gushers	60	68	.469	24½	R.A. Fowlkes

Austin Rangers .... 54 72 .429 29½ Cecil Griggs/Fats Fleharty/Otto McIvor
Temple Surgeons .... 48 82 .369 37½ Rankin Johnson

BA: Joe Munson (Carlson), Marlin, .346   **Wins:** Charles Gressett, Marlin, 22
Runs: Bill Etheredge, Corsicana, 106   **SOs:** G.M. Nugent, Temple, 176
Hits: Bill Etheredge, Corsicana, 159   **Pct:** William Hollis, Corsicana, .789, 15-4
HRs: Stephen Barrett, Corsicana, 27

D Tri-State League
President: Richard R. Grotto

Standings	W	L	Pct.	GB	Manager
Beatrice Blues	35	30	.538	—	Ed Reichle
Sioux Falls Canaries	35	30	.538	—	Frank Boyle
Norfolk Elk Horns	31	30	.508	2	Nig Lane
Grand Island Islanders	32	32	.500	2½	Jake Kraninger
Hastings Cubs	29	34	.460	5	Harry Cheek
Sioux City Cardinals	29	35	.453	5½	Joe McDermott

The league disbanded July 17.

BA: Graeme Snow, Sioux Falls, .339   **Wins:** Edward Shupe, Grand Island, 15
Runs: Everette Purdy, Beatrice, 39   **Pct:** Dunnagan, Beatrice, .800, 8-2
Hits: Everette Purdy, Beatrice, 65

1924 Interleague Post Season Play

World Series
Washington (American) 4 games, New York (National) 3

Junior World Series
St. Paul (American Association) 5 games, Baltimore (International) 4, one tie
Total Attendance: 52,240

Junior World Series Tune-up
Waterbury (Eastern) 3 games, Baltimore (International) 0

Class AA Series
St. Paul (American Association) 1 game, Seattle (Pacific Coast) 0
Called on account of poor weather.

Dixie Series
Ft. Worth (Texas) 4 games, Memphis (Southern Association) 3, one tie
Total Attendance: 71,826

Waterbury (Eastern) 1 game, Richmond (Virginia) 1

Lone Star Series
Tyler (East Texas) 4 games, Corsicana (Texas Association) 0, one tie

Five-State Championship
Parksley (Eastern Shore) 4 games, Martinsburg (Blue Ridge) 2

1924 No-Hitters

Date	Pitcher	Team	League	Opponent	Score
5-31	Art Stokes	Des Moines	Western	Denver	4-0
6-14	Ruest	Emporia	Southwestern	Independence	4-1
6-15	Floyd Worley	Eureka	Southwestern	Independence	1-0
7-10	Paul Wachtel	Ft. Worth	Texas	Shreveport	6-0
7-17	Jesse Haines	St. Louis	National	Boston	5-0
7-24	Russ Pence	Tulsa	Western	Omaha	22-0
7-29	Clarence Satterfield	Toronto	International	Jersey City	1-0 (7)
8-2	Carl Hill	Mexia	Texas Association	Corsicana	3-0
8-27	William Moore	Rochester	International	Syracuse	4-0
9-1	Frank Karpp	Rochester	International	Syracuse	8-0 (7)
9-1	Roy Allen	Oklahoma City	Western	Wichita	6-0
	Jim Marquis	St. Joseph	Western	Omaha	
	Walter Halas	Hanover	Blue Ridge		

Number in parentheses indicates innings if other than nine.

THIS DATE IN MINOR LEAGUE HISTORY

April 19, 1924, Lefty Grove of Baltimore, International League, struck out 17 Syracuse batters.

April 21, 1924, Rochester, International League, scored a 30-2 win over Newark.

April 21, 1924, First baseman Niehaus of Chattanooga, Southern Association, successfully accepted all of 24 chances, 21 putouts and three assists, in a game with Little Rock.

April 21, 1924, Francis Shay, Charlotte, South Atlantic League, hit four doubles in a nine-inning game.

May 10, 1924, John Neun of St. Paul, American Association, stole second, third and home in succession during the first inning against Louisville.

May 14, 1924, Clarence "Big Boy" Kraft, Ft. Worth, Texas League, bagged his eighth homer in a span of nine games.

May 16, 1924, Eleven home runs were hit in the Salt Lake City-Vernon Pacific Coast League game.

May 24, 1924, San Francisco, Pacific Coast League, piled up 37 hits to submerge Salt Lake City 30-14. The losers made 17 blows for a total of 54 for the game.

May 24, 1924, Seven homers were hit as Minneapolis beat Milwaukee 8-6. Earl Smith of the Millers drove out circuit clouts in three consecutive innings.

May 25, 1924, Bert Ellison, San Francisco, Pacific Coast League, had 25 hits in 37 at bats in a seven-game series with Salt Lake City. Ellison hit eight homers in one three-game span. He belted 10 four-baggers in the seven-game set from May 20-25.

May 30, 1924, Pittsfield, Eastern League, defeated Albany 9-8 in 21 innings. Pittsfield had 26 hits, the losers 21.

June 1, 1924, Wes Griffin of Vernon, Pacific Coast League, had 18 chances at second base in a game with Portland.

June 6, 1924, Seattle, Pacific Coast League, defeated Vernon 4-3 in 19 innings.

July 4, 1924, Third baseman Chuck Dressen of St. Paul, American Association, was stopped by Minneapolis pitching after having made 11 successive hits and reaching base 14 consecutive times.

July 12, 1924, Flint, Michigan-Ontario League, defeated Saginaw 3-2 in 20 innings.

August 15, 1924, Louisville, American Association, defeated St. Paul 25-0.

September 14, 1924, Clarence "Big Boy" Kraft of Ft. Worth, Texas League, hit his 55th home run of the season off Beaumont's Oran O'Neal. Kraft finished the season with 203 hits, 150 runs scored, 196 runs batted in, 414 total bases, and a .349 average. He had 36 doubles, five triples and 55 homers. Kraft hit two home runs in one game nine times.

September 14, 1924, In the Texas League, Joe Pate won 30 games for Ft. Worth for the second time, having also won 30 in 1921. Pate is one of two minor leaguers to have achieved that lofty win total twice in the last 70 years. Rube Vickers did it in 1906 with Seattle, and again in 1911 with Baltimore.

September 14, 1924, Denver beat Wichita 16-15 in a 15-inning Western League game.

September 15, 1924, Two unrelated players named Davis finished outstanding seasons for Okmulgee, Western Association. First baseman Wilbur Davis led the league in batting with a .400 mark, belted 51 homers and drove in 190 runs. Outfielder Cecil "Stormy" Davis also clubbed 51 round-trippers, hit .364, drove in 162 runs and scored 187 markers. Cecil never reached the majors, and Wilbur's only fling in the big leagues came previously in 1915 as a pitcher when he was 1-2 for the Philadelphia Athletics.

September 20, 1924, Portland, Pacific Coast League, made two or more hits in each of nine innings against Salt Lake City. Emmett McCann collected seven safeties for the Beavers.

September 24, 1924, Cliff Markle of St. Paul, American Association, fanned 15 Toledo batters.

September 28, 1924, The International League season ended with Baltimore the champion for the sixth straight year. The Orioles had a record of 117-48 and finished 19 games ahead of second-place Toronto.

October 3, 1924, St. Paul, American Association, defeated Baltimore, International League, in the ninth and deciding game to win the Junior World Series, 5 games to 4, after having lost four of the first six games.

1925

American League
President: Byron Bancroft Johnson

Standings	W	L	Pct.	GB	Attend.	Manager
Washington Senators	96	55	.636	—	817,199	Bucky Harris
Philadelphia Athletics	88	64	.579	8½	869,703	Connie Mack
St. Louis Browns	82	71	.536	15	462,898	George Sisler
Detroit Tigers	81	73	.526	16½	820,766	Ty Cobb
Chicago White Sox	79	75	.513	18½	832,231	Eddie Collins
Cleveland Indians	70	84	.455	27½	419,005	Tris Speaker
New York Yankees	69	85	.448	28½	697,267	Miller Huggins
Boston Red Sox	47	105	.309	49½	267,782	Lee Fohl

BA: Harry Heilmann, Detroit, .393
Runs: Johnny Mostil, Chicago, 135
Hits: Al Simmons, Philadelphia, 253
RBIs: Bob Meusel, New York, 138
HRs: Bob Meusel, New York, 33

Wins: Eddie Rommel, Philadelphia, 21
    Ted Lyons, Chicago, 21
SOs: Lefty Grove, Philadelphia, 116
ERA: Stan Coveleski, Washington, 2.84
Pct: Stan Coveleski, Washington, .800, 20-5

National League
President: John A. Heydler

Standings	W	L	Pct.	GB	Attend.	Manager
Pittsburgh Pirates	95	58	.621	—	804,354	Bill McKechnie
New York Giants	86	66	.566	8½	778,993	John McGraw
Cincinnati Reds	80	73	.523	15	464,920	Jack Hendricks
St. Louis Cardinals	77	76	.503	18	404,959	Branch Rickey/Rogers Hornsby
Boston Braves	70	83	.458	25	313,528	Dave Bancroft
Brooklyn Robins	68	85	.444	27	659,435	Wilbert Robinson
Philadelphia Phillies	68	85	.444	27	304,905	Art Fletcher
Chicago Cubs	68	86	.442	27½	622,610	Bill Killefer/Rabbit Maranville/ George Gibson

BA: Rogers Hornsby, St. Louis, .403
Runs: Kiki Cuyler, Pittsburgh, 144
Hits: Jim Bottomley, St. Louis, 227
RBIs: Rogers Hornsby, St. Louis, 143
HRs: Rogers Hornsby, St. Louis, 39

Wins: Dazzy Vance, Brooklyn, 22
SOs: Dazzy Vance, Brooklyn, 221
ERA: Dolf Luque, Cincinnati, 2.63
Pct: Willie Sherdel, St. Louis, .714, 15-6

AA American Association
President: Thomas J. Hickey

Standings	W	L	Pct.	GB	Attend.	Manager
Louisville Colonels	106	61	.635	—	233,051	Joe McCarthy
Indianapolis Indians	92	74	.554	13½	169,817	Donie Bush
St. Paul Saints	91	75	.548	14½	195,236	Nick Allen
Minneapolis Millers	86	80	.518	19½	233,065	Mike Kelley
Kansas City Blues	80	87	.474	26	262,051	John "Doc" Lavan
Toledo Mud Hens	77	90	.461	29	149,299	James Burke
Milwaukee Brewers	74	94	.440	32½	158,746	Harry Clark
Columbus Senators	61	106	.365	45	121,393	Carleton Molesworth

BA: Joe Guyon, Louisville, .363
Runs: Joe Guyon, Louisville, 152
Hits: Joe Guyon, Louisville, 228
RBIs: Bunny Brief, Milwaukee, 175

HRs: Bunny Brief, Milwaukee, 37
Wins: Bill Burwell, Indianapolis, 24
SOs: Robert McGraw, Minneapolis, 141
ERA: Bill Burwell, Indianapolis, 2.73

AA International League
President: John Conway Toole

Standings	W	L	Pct.	GB	Attend.	Manager
Baltimore Orioles	105	61	.633	—	221,438	Jack Dunn
Toronto Maple Leafs	99	63	.611	4	115,592	Dan Howley
Rochester Tribe	83	77	.519	19	158,420	George Stallings
Buffalo Bisons	78	84	.481	25	127,612	Bill Webb
Reading Keystones	78	90	.464	28	164,641	Spencer Abbott
Syracuse Stars	74	87	.460	28½	110,892	Frank Shaughnessy/Harry Myers
Jersey City Skeeters	74	92	.446	31	147,992	Patsy Donovan
Newark Bears/ Providence Grays#	63	100	.387	40½	124,727	Eddie Onslow/Frank Shaughnessy

#Newark (8-20) moved to Providence May 16, first home game May 23.

BA: Jim Walsh, Buffalo, .356
Runs: Fritz Maisel, Baltimore, 141
Hits: Vern Spencer, Buffalo, 227
RBIs: William Kelly, Buffalo, 125
HRs: Joe Kelly, Toronto, 29

Wins: Al Thomas, Baltimore, 32
SOs: Al Thomas, Baltimore, 268
ERA: Walter Stewart, Toronto, 2.51

AA Pacific Coast League
President: Harry A. Williams

Standings	W	L	Pct.	GB	Manager
San Francisco Seals	128	71	.643	—	Herbert Ellison
Salt Lake City Bees	116	84	.580	12½	Oscar Vitt
Seattle Indians	103	91	.531	22½	Red Killefer
Los Angeles Angels	105	93	.530	22½	Marty Krug
Portland Beavers	92	104	.470	34½	Duffy Lewis/Truck Hannah
Oakland Oaks	88	112	.442	40½	Ivan Howard
Sacramento Senators	82	119	.408	47	Buddy Ryan
Vernon Tigers	80	120	.400	48½	Bill Essick/Rube Ellis

Total Attendance: 1,828,000.

All-Star Team: 1B-Babe Herman, Seattle; **2B**-Pete Kilduff, San Francisco; **3B**-Eddie Mulligan, San Francisco; **SS**-Hal Rhyne, San Francisco; **OF**-Paul Waner, San Francisco; Arnold "Jigger" Statz, Los Angeles; Lefty O'Doul, Salt Lake City; **C**-E.P. Baldwin, Seattle; Archie Yello, San Francisco; **Util**-Charles Lucas, Seattle; **P**-Clyde Barfoot, Vernon; Charley Root, Los Angeles; William Piercy, Salt Lake City; Doug McWeeney, San Francisco; William Hughes, Sacramento.

BA: Paul Waner, San Francisco, .401
Runs: Tony Lazzeri, Salt Lake City, 202
Hits: Lefty O'Doul, Salt Lake City, 309
RBIs: Tony Lazzeri, Salt Lake City, 222
HRs: Tony Lazzeri, Salt Lake City, 60

2B: Paul Waner, San Francisco, 75
TBs: Tony Lazzeri, Salt Lake City, 512
Wins: Clyde Barfoot, Vernon, 26
SOs: George Boehler, Oakland, 278
ERA: Doug McWeeney, San Francisco, 2.70

A Eastern League
President: Daniel O'Neill

Standings	W	L	Pct.	GB	Manager
Waterbury Brasscos	88	66	.571	—	Kitty Bransfield
Hartford Senators	86	67	.562	1½	Paddy O'Connor
Worcester Panthers	80	72	.526	7	Ed Eayrs/Casey Stengel
New Haven Profs	81	73	.526	7	Neal Ball
Springfield Ponies	76	76	.500	11	Eugene McCann
Bridgeport Bears	76	78	.494	12	Irvin "Kaiser" Wilhelm
Albany Senators	71	82	.464	16½	Bill McCorry
Pittsfield Hillies	54	98	.355	33	Frank Stapleton

BA: Ed Eayrs, Worcester, .357
Runs: Herbert Thomas, Worcester, 121
Hits: Ramon Herrera, Springfield, 200
HRs: Adolph Schinkel, Albany/Hartford, 12

Wins: Earl Johnson, Hartford, 23
SOs: Bunn Hearn, Bridgeport, 160
ERA: Andy Rush, Waterbury, 2.80

A Southern Association
President: John D. Martin

Standings	W	L	Pct.	GB	Attend.	Manager
Atlanta Crackers	87	67	.565	—	284,611	Bert Niehoff
New Orleans Pelicans	85	68	.556	1½	223,577	Larry Gilbert
Nashville Volunteers	81	72	.529	5½	178,663	James Hamilton
Memphis Chickasaws	80	73	.523	6½	203,322	Clyde Milan
Mobile Bears	73	78	.483	12½	96,981	Norman "Kid" Elberfeld
Chattanooga Lookouts	71	82	.464	15½	102,233	Sam Strang Nicklin
Birmingham Barons	67	85	.441	19	182,560	Johnny Dobbs
Little Rock Travelers	67	86	.438	19½	79,653	Lena Blackburne

BA: Wilbur Good, Atlanta, .379
Runs: Frankie Zoeller, Atlanta, 131
Hits: Wilbur Good, Atlanta, 236
RBIs: Charles Tolson, Nashville, 143

HRs: Nick Cullop, Atlanta, 30
Wins: Joe Martina, New Orleans, 23
SOs: George Pipgras, Atlanta/Nashville, 141
ERA: Rube Robinson, Little Rock, 2.73

A Texas League
President: J. Doak Roberts

Standings	W	L	Pct.	GB	Attend.	Manager
Ft. Worth Panthers***	103	48	.682	—	169,534	Jake Atz
Houston Buffaloes	87	66	.569	17	127,671	Marvin Goodwin/Pete Compton
Dallas Steers	85	66	.563	18	203,271	Larry Gardner/ James "Snipe" Conley
San Antonio Bears	81	64	.559	19	94,158	Bob Coleman
Wichita Falls Spudders	81	68	.544	21	94,620	Archie Tanner
Waco Cubs	62	86	.419	39½	77,214	Del Pratt
Shreveport Sports	59	94	.386	45	105,642	Fred Luderus/Sid Smith
Beaumont Exporters	42	108	.280	60½	51,506	Dutch Bernsen/Andy Woehr

Playoff: Ft. Worth 3 games, Dallas 0, for the second half championship.

BA: Danny Clark, San Antonio, .399
Runs: Billy Mullen, Ft. Worth, 147
Hits: Danny Clark, San Antonio, 225
RBIs: Ed Konetchy, Ft. Worth, 166

HRs: Ed Konetchy, Ft. Worth, 41
Wins: Paul Wachtel, Ft. Worth, 23
SOs: Gus Johns, Ft. Worth, 211
ERA: Russ Pence, Dallas, 2.88

A Western League
President: Albert R. Tearney

Standings	W	L	Pct.	GB	Manager
Des Moines Demons	98	70	.583	—	Joe Mathes
Denver Bears	97	71	.577	1	Joe Berger
Oklahoma City Indians	88	76	.537	8	Ned Pettigrew/Fred Luderus

*Won first-half   **Won second-half   ***Won both halves

239

	W	L	Pct.	GB	
Wichita Izzies	80	84	.488	16	Howard Gregory
St. Joseph Saints	77	87	.470	19	Jack Lelivelt
Omaha Buffaloes	74	89	.454	21½	Art Griggs
Tulsa Oilers	75	91	.452	22	Lyman Lamb/Marty Berghammer
Lincoln Links	70	91	.435	24½	Josh Clarke/Frank Haley

Attendance: Denver, 150,000; Tulsa, 130,000.

All-Star Team: 1B-Charles Stuvengen, Des Moines; **2B**-John Monroe, Oklahoma City; **3B**-Joe Tate, Oklahoma City; **SS**-George Corrigan, Wichita; **OF**-Leo Payne, Wichita; Elton Langford, Des Moines; F.A. Griffin, Wichita; **C**-F.J. Wilder, Oklahoma City; Homer Haworth, Des Moines; **Util**-Luke Stuart, Tulsa; **P**-Carl Hubbell, Oklahoma City; Herm Holzhouser, Des Moines; Ken Penner, Wichita; Claude Thomas, Des Moines; Carl Christian, Lincoln; Harold Haid, St. Joseph.

BA: Frank Osborn, Omaha, .372
Runs: Elton Langford, Des Moines, 160
Hits: Frank Osborn, Omaha, 245
HRs: Leo Payne, Wichita, 33

3B: Walter Shaner, Lincoln, 30
Wins: Byrd Hodges, Denver, 26
SOs: Stew Bolen, Tulsa, 184
Pct: Joe Brown, Oklahoma City, .824, 14-3

B Michigan-Ontario League
President: Thomas J. Halligan

Standings	W	L	Pct.	GB	Manager
London Indians**	83	52	.615	—	Mike Baker
Hamilton Clippers*	82	57	.590	3	Frank "Buzz" Wetzel
Saginaw Aces	76	66	.535	10½	Les Nunamaker
Bay City Wolves	74	67	.525	12	Dick Breen
Flint Vehics	68	73	.482	18	Jack Hruska
Kitchener Colts	35	103	.254	49½	Knotty Lee/George Orme

Playoff: Hamilton 4 games, London 3.

BA: Joe Klein, London, .363
Runs: Guy Froman, Hamilton, 107
Hits: Walter Sandquist, London, 178
RBIs: Guy Froman, Hamilton, 112

HRs: Guy Froman, Hamilton, 18
Wins: Will Coogan, London, 24
SOs: W. Marty, Bay City, 137
ERA: Will Coogan, London, 2.48

B New York-Pennsylvania League
President: John H. Farrell

Standings	W	L	Pct.	GB	Manager
York White Roses	77	55	.583	—	Frank Desseau
Williamsport Grays	77	55	.583	—	Harry Hinchman
Binghamton Triplets	65	63	.508	10	John Haddock/Mick Konnick
Elmira Colonels	66	65	.504	10½	Ed Barney
Scranton Miners	64	69	.481	13½	Jack Egan
Harrisburg Senators	61	69	.469	15	Rankin Johnson
Wilkes-Barre Barons	60	71	.458	16½	James Sharpe/George Maisel
Shamokin Shammies	54	77	.412	22½	Amos Strunk/Clyde Mearke

Total Attendance: 629,180.

Playoff: York 3 games, Williamsport 1.

BA: Joe Munson (Carlson), Harrisburg, .400
Runs: Joe Munson (Carlson), Harrisburg, 132
Hits: Joe Munson (Carlson), Harrisburg, 188
RBIs: Joe Munson (Carlson), Harrisburg, 129

HRs: Joe Munson (Carlson), Harrisburg, 33
Wins: Thomas George, York, 27
SOs: Henry Hoffman, Williamsport, 153
ERA: Thomas George, York, 2.27

B South Atlantic League
President: William G. Bramham

Standings	W	L	Pct.	GB	Manager
Spartanburg Spartans	80	49	.621	—	Mike Kelly
Charlotte Hornets	79	50	.613	1	Ray Kennedy
Macon Peaches	69	58	.543	10	Ernie Burke
Augusta Tygers	69	59	.539	10½	Troy Agnew/Emil Huhn/Odie Strain
Asheville Tourists	66	63	.512	14	Bob Higgins/Larry Gardner
Grennville Spinners	60	68	.469	19½	Zinn Beck/Pat Crawford
Columbia Comers	47	82	.364	33	Olin Perrin
Knoxville Smokies	44	85	.341	36	Ed McDonald/Bill Holden/W. Barbare

BA: Everett Bankston, Columbia, .388
Runs: Mike Kelly, Spartanburg, 134
Hits: Art Ruble, Charlotte, 192
RBIs: R.J. Ducote, Charlotte, 124
HRs: Pete Daniels, Greenville, 29

Wins: Jack Killeen, Spartanburg, 27
SOs: Jim Lyle, Augusta, 131
ERA: Harry Smythe, Augusta, 2.83
Pct: Clarence Blethen, Macon, .762, 16-5

B Three-I League
President: L.J. Wylie

Standings	W	L	Pct.	GB	Manager
Peoria Tractors	89	48	.605	—	William Rodgers
Terre Haute Tots	81	54	.600	7	Roy Whitcraft
Evansville Pocketeers	72	63	.533	16	Joseph Dunn
Danville Veterans	69	66	.516	19	Charles Knoll
Decatur Commodores	62	73	.459	26	Daniel O'Leary
Bloomington Bloomers	56	74	.431	29½	Patrick Harkins
Springfield Senators	56	79	.415	32	William Jackson
Quincy Red Birds	54	82	.397	34½	Frederick Hunter

BA: John Jenkins, Danville, .360
Runs: Frank McGee, Peoria, 134
Hits: John Jenkins, Danville, 192
HRs: Frank McGee, Peoria, 20
Joe Bratcher, Peoria, 20

Wins: James "Jumbo" Elliott, Terre Haute, 25
SOs: Ron Chesterfield, Danville, 138
ERA: James "Jumbo" Elliott, Terre Haute, 3.03

B Virginia League
President: William G. Bramham

Standings	W	L	Pct.	GB	Manager
Richmond Colts	78	54	.591	—	Percy Dawson
Portsmouth Truckers	73	59	.553	5	Lester Bangs
Norfolk Tars	72	60	.545	6	Dave Robertson
Wilson Bugs	68	64	.515	10	H.E. "Winnie" Winston
Rocky Mount Broncos	53	79	.402	25	Jim Viox/Bill Pike
Kinston Eagles	52	80	.394	26	John Nee

BA: Hal Weafer, Richmond, .391
Runs: Guy Lacy, Richmond, 120
Hits: Art Hauger, Kinston, 183
RBIs: Dave Robertson, Norfolk, 118
HRs: Otis Carter, Richmond, 38

Wins: Ben Shields, Richmond, 21
SOs: Ben Shields, Richmond, 187
ERA: Cy Fried, Norfolk, 2.87
Pct: Alex Peterson, Norfolk, 1.000, 11-0

C Middle Atlantic League
President: Ray H. Archibald

Standings	W	L	Pct.	GB	Manager
Johnstown Johnnies***	64	31	.674	—	Norm McNeill
Cumberland Colts	56	40	.583	8½	Tom Ray/Hank McEnroe/Jim McGuire
Clarksburg Cyrians/Ghosts.	48	45	.516	15	Blake Lytle/Harry "Pop" Shriver
Fairmont Maroons	47	53	.470	19½	Cy Perry/Ira Erret
Wheeling Stogies#	39	62	.386	28	Art Rooney/Frank Eastley
Scottdale Scotties#	18	41	.305	NA	Joe Brahaney

#Scottdale was added to the league July 12.

BA: Mike Martineck, Johnstown, .372
Runs: Art Rooney, Wheeling, 109
Hits: Art Rooney, Wheeling, 143
HRs: Mike Martineck, Johnstown, 18

SBs: Art Rooney, Wheeling, 58
Wins: John Schmutte, Johnstown, 19
SOs: Charles Harkins, Clarksburg, 123
Pct: Paul Secrist, Cumberland, .909, 10-1

C Piedmont League
President: William G. Bramham

Standings	W	L	Pct.	GB	Manager
Winston-Salem Twins**	77	49	.611	—	Charles Carroll
Durham Bulls*	68	58	.540	9	Art Bourg
Greensboro Patriots	61	63	.492	15	Lee Gooch/Hardin Herndon/Dick Smith
High Point Pointers/ Danville Leafs#	58	67	.464	18½	Lloyd Smith/Hardin Herndon
Raleigh Capitals	57	69	.452	20	
Salisbury Colonials	54	69	.439	21½	Pat O'Rourke/Red Stewart/Rowdy Elliott

#High Point (18-32) moved to Danville June 18, first home game June 19.

Playoff: Durham 4 games, Winston-Salem 3.

BA: Harry Smith, Durham, .385
Runs: Arthur Bourg, Durham, 108
Hits: Harry Smith, Durham, 192
HRs: Otis Cashion, Salisbury, 25

Wins: Roy Sullivan, Winston-Salem, 21
SOs: Roy Sullivan, Winston-Salem, 127
ERA: Bernie Thompson, Winston-Salem, 2.39

C Western Association
President: J.W. Seabaugh

Standings	W	L	Pct.	GB	Manager
Ft. Smith Twins	94	56	.627	—	Carl Metz
Ardmore Boomers*	86	64	.573	8	George Whiteman
Okmulgee Drillers	80	71	.530	14½	Roy Corgan/Earl "Red" Snapp
Muskogee Athletics**	79	72	.523	15½	Gabby Street
Springfield Midgets	67	82	.450	26½	Mark Purtell
Independence Producers	44	105	.295	49½	Mick Reidy/Pat O'Byrne

Playoff: Ardmore 4 games, Muskogee 1.

BA: Jim Hudgens, Ft. Smith, .389
Runs: Leo Najo, Okmulgee, 195
Hits: Jim Hudgens, Ft. Smith, 230
RBIs: Jim Hudgens, Ft. Smith, 168
HRs: Leo Najo, Okmulgee, 34

2B: Jim Hudgens, Ft. Smith, 63
Wins: Edgar Clough, Ft. Smith, 28
SOs: J.E. Carroll, Muskogee, 239
ERA: Lloyd Brown, Ardmore, 2.45

D Appalachian League
Presidents: George C. Davis/E.B. Fisher

Standings	W	L	Pct.	GB	Manager
Greeneville Burley Cubs	28	16	.636	—	Harvey Russell
Morristown Roosters	22	22	.500	6	Hack Henderson
Kingsport Indians	20	22	.476	7	Frank Moffett
Bristol State Liners	16	26	.381	11	Buck Ramsey

The league disbanded July 15.

D Blue Ridge League
President: J. Vincent Jamison, Jr.

Standings	W	L	Pct.	GB	Manager
Hagerstown Hubs	65	35	.650	—	Ray Werre
Frederick Hustlers..............	56	40	.583	7	George "Buck" Ramsey
Martinsburg Blue Sox.........	50	47	.515	13½	Pat Ragan/Frank Burke
Waynesboro Red Birds	47	49	.490	16	John Breckenridge
Chambersburg Maroons	39	59	.398	25	Ed Goosetree/Pat O'Rourke/John Reistenberg
Hanover Raiders	33	60	.355	28½	Roy Clunk/Howard Brown

BA: Walt Hammen, Waynesboro, .375
Runs: George Scheminant, Hagerstown, 93
Hits: Walt Hammen, Waynesboro, 141
HRs: George Thomas, Hagerstown, 19

Wins: Joseph Zubris, Hagerstown, 20
Henry Sherry, Frederick, 20
SOs: Joseph Zubris, Hagerstown, 163
Pct: Alfred Kendricks, Hagerstown, .818, 18-4

D Cotton States League
President: Frank A. Scott

Standings	W	L	Pct.	GB	Manager
Meridian Mets**	71	53	.573	—	Dutch Quellmalz/Pat Patterson
Hattiesburg Hubbers	70	53	.569	½	Herschel Bobo
Jackson Senators*	68	54	.557	2	Bill Pierre/Fred Heck
Vicksburg Hill Billies.........	60	62	.492	10	Runt Marr
Laurel Lumberjacks............	58	64	.475	12	Jake Propst/Jim Moore/Pat Devereaux/Sam Vick
Monroe Drillers	56	65	.463	13½	Bill Wise/Paul Trammell
Brookhaven Truckers	56	69	.448	15½	Tom Toland/Tex Covington
Alexandria Reds	51	70	.421	18½	Pat Flaherty/Phil Wells

Playoff: Jackson 3 games, Meridian 0; called due to lack of police protection in Meridian. The title was awarded to Jackson.

BA: Hoot Gibson, Hattiesburg, .351
Runs: J. Poland, Hattiesburg, 90
Hits: Hoot Gibson, Hattiesburg, 164
HRs: Herschel Bobo, Hattiesburg, 17

3B: Mel Simons, Meridian, 21
Wins: James Patterson, Meridian, 19
SOs: Stanley Anderson, Meridian, 168
Pct: Roger Williams, Jackson, .733, 11-4

D East Texas League
President: H.E. Crosby

Standings	W	L	Pct.	GB	Manager
Paris Bearcats***	76	46	.623	—	Les Tullos
Tyler Trojans	69	55	.556	8	Frank "Pop" Kitchens
Greenville Hunters	63	61	.508	14	Walt Alexander/Lee Ballanfant
Longview Cannibals/Mt. Pleasant#	63	61	.508	14	Jack Johnston/Willie "Tex" Crosby
Texarkana Twins	58	64	.475	18	Mike Prendergast
Marshall Indians	51	69	.425	24	Johnnie Baggan/Cecil Coombs
Mt. Pleasant Cats#	22	22	.500	NA	Bob Countryman
Sulphur Springs Spartans#..	11	35	.239	NA	Abe Bowman

#Sulphur Springs disbanded June 7. Mt. Pleasant and Longview were consolidated June 7, playing games in both cities as the Longview-Mt. Pleasant Longcats until July 12, when the club settled permanently in Longview. The records on June 7 were Longview 18-27 and Mt. Pleasant 22-22.

Playoff: Paris 2 games, Texarkana 1, one tie, for the first half championship.

BA: Tom Pyle, Greenville, .388
Runs: Jack Holloway, Tyler, 115
Hits: Joe Granade, Texarkana/Tyler, 182
HRs: Jack Holloway, Tyler, 41

Wins: Gus Burleson, Paris, 19
Kearby Lybrand, Tyler, 19
SOs: Kearby Lybrand, Tyler, 154
Pct: Gus Burleson, Paris, .760, 19-6

D Eastern Shore League
President: M.B. Thawley

Standings	W	L	Pct.	GB	Manager
Cambridge Canners	51	38	.573	—	Ted Smith
Parksley Spuds...................	48	42	.533	3½	Thomas "Poke" Whalen
Salisbury Indians	46	44	.511	5½	Homer Smoot
Dover Dobbins	46	44	.511	5½	Jiggs Donohue
Crisfield Crabbers.............	42	48	.467	9½	Marty Breslin/Herb Armstong
Easton Farmers	36	53	.404	15	Frank Baker/Charles Gault/Buck Herzog

BA: Victor St. Martin, Parksley, .363
Runs: Victor St. Martin, Parksley, 78
Hits: Phillip Voyles, Salisbury, 119

HRs: Victor St. Martin, Parksley, 25
Charles Fitzberger, Salisbury, 25
Wins: Ted Firth, Parksley, 21
SOs: Ted Firth, Parksley, 131
Pct: John Trippe, Cambridge, .722, 13-5

D Florida State League
President: Al E. Lang

Standings	W	L	Pct.	GB	Manager
Tampa Smokers**	71	50	.587	—	Charles Allen
Lakeland Highlanders*.......	70	52	.574	1½	Bill Brazier
St. Petersburg Saints	66	54	.550	4½	George Block
Sanford Celeryfeds	36	87	.293	36	Nick Carter/Jim Moore

Playoff: Tampa 4 games, St. Petersburg 3.

D Mississippi Valley League
President: Belden Hill

Standings	W	L	Pct.	GB	Attend.	Manager
Cedar Rapids Bunnies	74	51	.592	—	43,429	William Speas
Moline Plowboys	73	52	.584	1	39,738	Jim Shollenberger
Rock Island Islanders.........	65	60	.520	9	43,157	Preston Gray
Ottumwa Cardinals	61	64	.488	13	30,572	Walter Mattick
Dubuque Ironmen	60	65	.480	14	46,175	Joe McGinnity/John Armstrong
Waterloo Hawks	59	66	.472	15	54,702	Cletus Dixon
Marshalltown Ansons	55	70	.440	19	30,442	Frank Boyle
Burlington Bees	53	72	.424	22	42,179	Dick Speer/Whitey Mann/Ed Reichle

BA: Al Groski, Ottumwa, .360
Runs: John Armstrong, Dubuque, 104
Hits: Ed Farber, Rock Island, 174
HRs: Chester Guppy, Moline, 17

Wins: George Valentine, Cedar Rapids, 26
SOs: Archie Kelsey, Waterloo, 174
Pct: George Valentine, Cedar Rapids, .765, 26-8

D Southwestern League
President: Dale D. Gear

Standings	W	L	Pct.	GB	Manager
Salina Millers*	73	55	.570	—	Jimmy Payton
Topeka Senators**	69	59	.539	4	Bill Meyer/Butch Wetzel
Arkansas City Osages	65	63	.508	8	Ed Yuna
Cushing Refiners	64	65	.496	9½	Frank Thompson
Blackwell Gassers..............	61	66	.480	11½	Ralph Heatley
Enid Boosters/Shawnee Braves#.............	52	76	.406	21	Ben Dimond/George Dye

#Enid (20-27) moved to Shawnee June 17, first home game June 23.

Playoff: Topeka 4 games, Salina 1.

BA: Lloyd Branch, Cushing, .383
Runs: Roy Hutson, Topeka, 132
Hits: Ed Yuna, Arkansas City, 205

HRs: Ed Yuna, Arkansas City, 28
Wins: Joe Bloomer, Salina, 22
Pct: Joe Bloomer, Salina, .710, 22-9

D Texas Association
Presidents: J.G. McIntosh/Charles L. Clover

Standings	W	L	Pct.	GB	Manager
Corsicana Oilers***	85	48	.639	—	Johnny Vann
Mexia Gushers...................	76	57	.571	9	Frank "Matty" Matthews
Temple Surgeons	74	59	.556	11	Roy Mitchell
Austin Senators	63	70	.474	22	Bennie Brownlow
Marlin Bathers/Palestine Pals#	58	75	.436	27	Fred Pipkin/Tommie McMillan
Terrell Terrors...................	43	90	.323	42	Otto McIvor/Ed Fulton/Pete Adams

#Marlin (7-15) moved to Palestine May 13.

BA: Clyde Glass, Mexia, .367
Runs: Cotton Tucker, Temple, 129
Hits: Smead Jolley, Corsicana, 180
Clyde Glass, Mexia, 180

HRs: Stan Keyes (Kewaya), Terrell, 28
Wins: Joe Cantrell, Corsicana, 22
SOs: Dick Whitworth, Austin, 152
Pct: Bob Arnold, Mexia, .706, 12-5

D Tri-State League
President: John D. Martin

Standings	W	L	Pct.	GB	Manager
Tupelo Wolves*	67	39	.632	—	Red Reese
Jonesboro Buffaloes**	63	43	.594	4	Buck Stapleton
Dyersburg Deers	59	46	.562	7½	P.H. White
Corinth Corinthians	57	49	.538	10	M.R. Striplin
Jackson Giants	40	63	.388	25½	Luke Pratt
Blytheville Tigers	31	77	.287	37	J.G. "Stormy" Kromer

Playoff: Jonesboro 4 games, Tupelo 2.

BA: John Kloza, Blytheville, .373
Runs: T.P. Bynaum, Tupelo, 102
Hits: T.P. Bynaum, Tupelo, 144
HRs: C.T. Swafford, Jonesboro, 14
Bill Akers, Jonesboro, 14

Wins: Elmer Hymel, Tupelo, 16
William Stewart, Corinth, 16
John Bates, Corinth, 16
SOs: John Bates, Corinth, 129
Pct: Henry Baumgartner, Jonesboro, .909, 10-1

1925 Interleague Post Season Play

World Series
Pittsburgh (National) 4 games, Washington (American) 3

Junior World Series
Baltimore (International) 5, Louisville (American Association) 3

Junior World Series Tune-up
Waterbury (Eastern) 3 games, Baltimore (International) 0

Dixie Series
Ft. Worth (Texas) 4 games, Atlanta (Southern Association) 2
Total Attendance: 73,930

Southern Championship
Spartanburg (South Atlantic) 4 games, Richmond (Virginia) 1

Five-State Championship
Hagerstown (Blue Ridge) 4 games, Cambridge (Eastern Shore) 3

San Francisco-Louisville Series
San Francisco (Pacific Coast) 5 games, Louisville (American Association) 4

1925 No-Hitters

Date	Pitcher	Team	League	Opponent	Score
4-15	Lefty Webb	Hamilton	Michigan-Ontario	Flint	7-0
5-28	George Boehler	Oakland	Pacific Coast	Sacramento	0-2 (10)
6-7	James Marquis	St. Joseph	Western	Omaha	4-0
6-20	Ray Pipkin	Temple	Texas Association	Terrell	5-0
6-22	Joe Cantrell	Corsicana	Texas Association	Palestine	14-0
6-24	Oscar Tuero	Waco	Texas	Shreveport	4-0
7-9	James Keenan	Kansas City	American Assoc.	Indianapolis	1-2 (10)
7-21	Harold Johnson	Ottumwa	Mississippi Valley	Moline	5-0
7-23	Albert Phillips	Salisbury	Piedmont	Winston-Salem	4-0
7-27	Herman Schwartz	Bloomington	Three-I	Springfield	4-0 (P)
7-30	Henry Hoffman	Williamsport	New York-Penn.		
8-2	Johnnie Biggers	Palestine	Texas Association	Terrell	5-0 (7)
8-17	Bartlett McMillan	Rocky Mount	Virginia	Portsmouth	4-0
8-21	H.M. Purcell	Spartanburg	South Atlantic	Columbia	7-0 (7)
8-22	Al Grabowski	Syracuse	International	Providence	1-0
8-22	Elmer Tutwiler	Laurel	Cotton States	Alexandria	5-0
9-3	Joe Poetz	Portsmouth	Virginia	Richmond	4-1
9-7	Paul Secrist	Cumberland	Middle Atlantic	Scottdale	8-0
9-7	J. Ryan	Hamilton	Michigan-Ontario	Saginaw	4-0
9-13	Dazzy Vance	Brooklyn	National	Philadelphia	10-1

Number in parentheses indicates innings if other than nine; "P" indicates perfect game.

THIS DATE IN MINOR LEAGUE HISTORY

April 16, 1925, Outfielder C.A. Davis of Ft. Worth, Texas League, hit three homers, including two in one inning, in a game with Dallas.

April 19, 1925, Outfielder Simon Rosenthal, San Antonio, Texas League, hit three homers versus Beaumont.

May 4, 1925, Outfielder John Rieder, Waco, Texas League, belted three homers against Beaumont.

May 8, 1925, In the Mississippi Valley League, Waterloo and Rock Island played a 17-inning 0-0 tie.

May 11, 1925, Joe McGinnity, 54, won for Dubuque against Ottumwa in the Mississippi Valley League. He would compile a 6-6 record on the mound this season.

May 14, 1925, Houston, Texas League, piled up 21 hits to trounce Shreveport 23-1. Pitcher Stanton walked 10 Houston batters in one inning.

May 16, 1925, The Newark franchise in the International League moved to Providence.

May 18, 1925, Ping Bodie, Wichita Falls, Texas League, walloped a trio of four-baggers in a tilt with Beaumont.

May 19, 1925, J.W. "Ziggy" Sears, later a major league umpire, drove in 11 runs with three homers and a double for Ft. Worth, Texas League, as the Panthers overwhelmed San Antonio 19-8.

May 20, 1925, Ft. Worth again beat San Antonio by a lop-sided margin, 29-9, with Ziggy Sears getting six hits in eight at bats. The Panthers made 31 hits.

May 20, 1925, The Worcester club of the Eastern League was sold to Casey Stengel.

May 21, 1925, The Ft. Worth Panthers handed San Antonio another unmerciful trimming. The fans, angered by the ejection of the San Antonio shortstop, swarmed onto the field in the fifth inning. Police were needed to escort the umpires to their hotel. League President J. Doak Roberts, in the stands, ordered the game forfeited to Ft. Worth, then told the teams to continue play, with players serving as umpires. The final score was 24-12 in favor of the Panthers, who collected 72 runs off Bears hurlers in last three games.

May 28, 1925, George Boehler, Oakland, Pacific Coast League, held Sacramento hitless for 9-2/3 innings but lost 2-0 on two hits and an error in the tenth.

May 29, 1925, Ft. Worth, Texas League, scored 34 runs in a game with San Antonio.

June 4, 1925, Catcher Charles Morgan, Macon, South Atlantic League, made his 12th successive hit.

June 7, 1925, Bruno Haas, St. Paul, American Association, went 6-for-6 in a game at Milwaukee.

June 7, 1925, Third baseman Monger hit two homers in one inning for Quincy, Three-I League.

June 28, 1925, George Earnshaw, pitching for Baltimore, International League, won two games over Providence.

June 30, 1925, Joe McCarthy's Louisville Colonels, American Association, completed the month's play with 29 victories in 31 games.

July 8, 1925, Joe McGinnity resigned as manager of the Dubuque club in the Mississippi Valley League.

July 9, 1925, First baseman J.C. "Bad News" Galloway, Waco, Texas League, walloped three consecutive homers in a game against Beaumont.

July 9, 1925, Danville second baseman Milsap belted three homers in a Piedmont League game.

July 9, 1925, Outfielder Howard Camp of Reading, International League, entered the stands at Rochester, accompanied by pitcher Leo Mangum, carrying a bat to get at a fan who had been "roasting" the players. Police had to rescue the two athletes from the stands.

July 15, 1925, Outfielder Earl Waltz of Waynesboro, Blue Ridge League, drove out four home runs and a single in a 16-5 win over Martinsburg. Waltz had seven homers a span of three games.

July 30, 1925, Outfielder P. Johnson, Columbus, American Association, had 10 putouts and one assist in a nine-inning game.

August 6, 1925, Charles Miller, Dallas, Texas League, hit three homers in a game.

August 19, 1925, Lefty O'Doul of Salt Lake City scored six runs in a game with Portland. John Peters also tallied six times for the Bees.

August 23, 1925, First baseman Tim Jourdan hit four doubles in one game for Minneapolis, American Association.

September 9, 1925, Eddie Moen, Richmond, Virginia League, hit three consecutive homers, plus a double, against Kinston.

September 12, 1925, Charles Miller, Dallas, Texas League, belted three consecutive homers in a game for the second time their year when he connected in a game against Shreveport.

September 15, 1925, Tony Lazzeri, Salt Lake City, Pacific Coast League, who had hit eight home runs in a span of five games, was walked all four times he came to the plate.

September 19, 1925, A total of 26 walks were issued in the St. Joseph-Lincoln game in the Western League.

September 20, 1925, The International League season closed with Baltimore the pennant winner for the seventh successive year. The Orioles aggregation, managed by Jack Dunn, was considered by many as one of the greatest clubs in minor league history.

October 11, 1925, Baltimore, International League, captured the Junior World Series 5 games to 3, defeating Louisville, American Association, 5-2 in the eighth game, behind Big George Earnshaw.

October 18, 1925, The Pacific Coast League season ended with San Francisco the champions with 128 wins and 71 defeats. The Seals finished 12-1/2 games ahead of second-place Salt Lake City.

1926

American League
President: Byron Bancroft Johnson

Standings	W	L	Pct.	GB	Attend.	Manager
New York Yankees	91	63	.591	—	1,027,675	Miller Huggins
Cleveland Indians	88	66	.571	3	627,426	Tris Speaker
Philadelphia Athletics	83	67	.553	6	714,508	Connie Mack
Washington Senators	81	69	.540	8	551,580	Bucky Harris
Chicago White Sox	81	72	.529	9½	710,339	Eddie Collins
Detroit Tigers	79	75	.513	12	711,914	Ty Cobb
St. Louis Browns	62	92	.403	29	283,986	George Sisler
Boston Red Sox	46	107	.301	44½	285,155	Lee Fohl

BA: Heinie Manush, Detroit, .378
Runs: Babe Ruth, New York, 139
Hits: Sam Rice, Washington, 216
    George Burns, Cleveland, 216
RBIs: Babe Ruth, New York, 145

HRs: Babe Ruth, New York, 47
Wins: George Uhle, Cleveland, 27
SOs: Lefty Grove, Philadelphia, 194
ERA: Lefty Grove, Philadelphia, 2.51
Pct: George Uhle, Cleveland, .711, 27-11

National League
President: John A. Heydler

Standings	W	L	Pct.	GB	Attend.	Manager
St. Louis Cardinals	89	65	.578	—	668,428	Rogers Hornsby
Cincinnati Reds	87	67	.565	2	672,987	Jack Hendricks
Pittsburgh Pirates	84	69	.549	4½	798,542	Bill McKechnie
Chicago Cubs	82	72	.532	7	885,063	Joe McCarthy
New York Giants	74	77	.490	13½	700,362	John McGraw
Brooklyn Robins	71	82	.464	17½	650,819	Wilbert Robinson
Boston Braves	66	86	.434	22	303,598	Dave Bancroft
Philadelphia Phillies	58	93	.384	29½	240,600	Art Fletcher

BA: Bubbles Hargrave, Cincinnati, .353
Runs: Kiki Cuyler, Pittsburgh, 113
Hits: Eddie Brown, Boston, 201
RBIs: Jim Bottomley, St. Louis, 120
HRs: Hack Wilson, Chicago, 21

Wins: Spec Meadows, Pittsburgh, 20
    Pete Donohue, Cincinnati, 20
    Ray Kremer, Pittsburgh, 20
    Flint Rhem, St. Louis, 20
SOs: Dazzy Vance, Brooklyn, 140
ERA: Ray Kremer, Pittsburgh, 2.61
Pct: Ray Kremer, Pittsburgh, .769, 20-6

AA American Association
President: Thomas J. Hickey

Standings	W	L	Pct.	GB	Attend.	Manager
Louisville Colonels	105	62	.629	—	220,606	Bill Meyer
Indianapolis Indians	94	71	.570	10	153,454	Donie Bush
Milwaukee Brewers	93	71	.567	10½	327,891	Jack Lelivelt
Toledo Mud Hens	87	77	.530	16½	230,610	Casey Stengel
Kansas City Blues	87	78	.527	17	232,981	Spencer Abbott
St. Paul Saints	82	81	.503	21	166,197	Nick Allen
Minneapolis Millers	72	94	.434	32½	177,626	Mike Kelley
Columbus Senators	39	125	.238	64½	93,205	Hank Gowdy/George McQuillan

BA: Bevo LeBourveau, Toledo, .377
Runs: Lance Richbourg, Milwaukee, 151
Hits: Lance Richbourg, Milwaukee, 247
RBIs: Pat Duncan, Minneapolis, 123

HRs: Bunny Brief, Milwaukee, 26
Wins: Tom Sheehan, Kansas City, 26
SOs: George Pipgras, St. Paul, 156
ERA: Ernest Maun, Toledo, 2.71

AA International League
President: John Conway Toole

Standings	W	L	Pct.	GB	Attend.	Manager
Toronto Maple Leafs	109	57	.657	—	221,846	Dan Howley
Baltimore Orioles	101	65	.608	8	153,360	Jack Dunn
Newark Bears	99	66	.600	9½	274,099	Fred Burchell
Buffalo Bisons	92	72	.561	16	241,013	Bill Clymer
Rochester Tribe	81	83	.494	27	134,779	George Stallings
Jersey City Skeeters	72	92	.439	36	103,806	Patsy Donovan
Syracuse Stars	70	91	.435	36½	123,214	Burt Shotten
Reading Keystones	31	129	.194	75	32,329	Frank Shaughnessy/Byrd Lynn/George Wiltse

BA: Jimmy Walsh, Buffalo, .388
Runs: Fresco Thompson, Buffalo, 150
Hits: Fresco Thompson, Buffalo, 217
RBIs: William Kelly, Buffalo, 151

HRs: William Kelly, Buffalo, 44
Wins: Jack Ogden, Baltimore, 24
SOs: Roy Chesterfield, Newark, 141
ERA: Al Mamaux, Newark, 2.22

AA Pacific Coast League
President: Harry A. Williams

Standings	W	L	Pct.	GB	Manager
Los Angeles Angels	121	81	.599	—	Marty Krug
Oakland Oaks	111	92	.547	9½	Ivan Howard
Mission Bells	106	94	.530	14	Walter McCreedie/Walter Schmidt/Bill Leard
Portland Beavers	100	101	.498	20½	Ernie Johnson
Sacramento Senators	99	102	.493	21½	Buddy Ryan

*Won first-half **Won second-half ***Won both halves

Hollywood Stars	94	107	.468	26½	Oscar Vitt
Seattle Indians	89	111	.445	31	Red Killefer
San Francisco Seals	84	116	.420	36	Herbert Ellison/Nick Williams

Total Attendance: 1,879,000.

All-Star Team: **1B**-Jimmy McDowell, Mission; **2B**-John Monroe, Sacramento; **3B**-Tommy "Doc" Prothro, Portland; **SS**-Johnny Mitchell, Los Angeles; **OF**-Art Jahn, Los Angeles; Arnold "Jigger" Statz, Los Angeles; Buzz Arlett, Oakland; **C**-Art Koehler, Sacramento; Truck Hannah, Los Angeles; **Util**-Brick Eldred, Seattle; Jimmy Caveney, Oakland; **P**-Wayne Wright, Los Angeles; Doc Crandall, Los Angeles; Elmer Jacobs, Los Angeles; James "Jumbo" Elliott, Seattle; Bert Cole, Mission; **Manager**-Red Killefer, Seattle.

BA: Buzz Arlett, Oakland, .382
Runs: Evar Swanson, Mission, 157
Hits: Arnold "Jigger" Statz, Los Angeles, 291
RBIs: Buzz Arlett, Oakland, 140
HRs: Elmer Smith, Portland, 46

Wins: Bert Cole, Mission, 29
SOs: James "Jumbo" Elliott, Seattle, 203
ERA: Elmer Jacobs, Los Angeles, 2.20
CGs: James "Jumbo" Elliott, Seattle, 37

A Eastern League
Presidents: Daniel O'Neill/Herman J. Weisman

Standings	W	L	Pct.	GB	Manager
Providence Rubes	97	55	.638	—	Rube Marquard
New Haven Profs	91	60	.603	5½	Jack Flynn
Bridgeport Bears	91	63	.591	7	Frank Stapleton
Springfield Ponies	78	71	.523	17½	Eugene McCann
Albany Senators	77	75	.507	20	Bill McCorry
Hartford Senators	65	88	.425	32½	S. McDonald
Waterbury Brasscos	58	93	.384	38½	Kitty Bransfield
Pittsfield Hillies	50	102	.329	47	Neal Ball/Harold Elliott

BA: Elmer Bowman, New Haven, .377
Runs: Herbert Thomas, Providence, 125
Hits: William Albert, Springfield, 209
HRs: Harold Yordy, Bridgeport, 18

Wins: Foster Edwards, Providence, 25
SOs: Orin O'Neal, Springfield, 127
ERA: Fay Thomas, New Haven, 2.29

A Southern Association
President: John D. Martin

Standings	W	L	Pct.	GB	Attend.	Manager
New Orleans Pelicans	101	53	.656	—	236,681	Larry Gilbert
Memphis Chickasaws	95	57	.625	5	196,365	Clyde Milan
Birmingham Barons	87	61	.588	11	233,559	Johnny Dobbs
Nashville Volunteers	83	68	.550	16½	134,803	James Hamilton
Atlanta Crackers	75	76	.497	24½	183,699	Bert Niehoff
Chattanooga Lookouts	55	94	.369	43½	76,632	Norman "Kid" Elberfeld
Mobile Bears	56	96	.368	44	78,749	Duffy Lewis/Milt Stock
Little Rock Travelers	51	98	.342	47½	49,545	Joe Cantillon

BA: Tom Taylor, Memphis, .383
Runs: Harvey Hendrick, New Orleans, 137
Hits: Harvey Hendrick, New Orleans, 231
RBIs: Tom Taylor, Memphis, 135

HRs: Yam Yaryan, Birmingham, 20
Wins: Lute Roy, New Orleans, 24
SOs: Guy Morton, Memphis, 110
ERA: Clarence Griffin, Memphis, 3.28

A Texas League
President: J. Doak Roberts

Standings	W	L	Pct.	GB	Attend.	Manager
Dallas Steers	89	66	.574	—	286,806	James "Snipe" Conley
San Antonio Bears	86	70	.551	3½	148,533	Honus Mitze
Ft. Worth Panthers	83	73	.532	6½	204,386	Jake Atz
Shreveport Sports	77	79	.494	12½	143,794	Bob Tarleton/Art Phelan
Beaumont Exporters	76	80	.487	13½	97,961	Jim "Bad News" Galloway
Houston Buffaloes	75	80	.484	14	99,238	Joe Mathes
Wichita Falls Spudders	72	84	.462	17½	99,105	Fred Brainard/Carl Williams
Waco Cubs	65	91	.417	24½	80,082	Del Pratt

BA: Tom Jenkins, Wichita Falls, .374
Runs: Pete Turgeon, Wichita Falls, 133
Hits: Tom Connolly, Beaumont, 211
RBIs: Charles "Hack" Miller, Dallas, 118
HRs: Charles "Hack" Miller, Dallas, 30

Wins: Jimmy Walkup, Ft. Worth, 22
    Tiny Owens, San Antonio, 22
SOs: Slim Love, Dallas, 216
ERA: Jimmy Walkup, Ft. Worth, 2.43

A Western League
President: Dale D. Gear

Standings	W	L	Pct.	GB	Manager
Des Moines Demons	99	64	.607	—	Shano Collins
Oklahoma City Indians	100	66	.602	½	Fred Luderus
St. Joseph Saints	89	75	.543	10½	Joe Kelly/Dick Breen
Tulsa Oilers	86	78	.524	13½	Marty Berghammer
Denver Bears	88	80	.524	13½	Joe Berger
Omaha Buffaloes	77	89	.464	23½	Barney Burch
Lincoln Links	64	101	.388	36	Dutch Zwilling
Wichita Izzies	58	108	.349	42½	Howard Gregory/Pat Haley

Attendance: Denver, 100,000; Tulsa, 130,000.

All-Star Team: 1B-Guy Sturdy, Tulsa; **2B**-Walter Nufer, St. Joseph; **3B**-Pee Wee Lewis, Tulsa; **SS**-Eddie Hock, Oklahoma City; **OF**-Jim Blakesley, Omaha; Ray O'Brien, Denver; F.A. Griffin, Des Moines; **C**-Peter Groft, Oklahoma City; **F.** Meyers, Omaha; **Util**-Ray Falk, Denver; **P**-George Blaeholder, Tulsa; Herbert Hall, Denver; Pat Malone, Denver; George Peery, St. Joseph; Leo Moon, Des Moines; Joe Brown, Oklahoma City.

BA: Jim Blakesley, Omaha, .384
Runs: Guy Sturdy, Tulsa, 163
Hits: Fred "Snake" Henry, Omaha, 247
HRs: Guy Sturdy, Tulsa, 49

TBs: Guy Sturdy, Tulsa, 452
Wins: Herbert Hall, Denver, 29
SOs: Pat Malone, Denver, 190
Pct: Frank Tubbs, Oklahoma City, .818, 9-2

B Michigan State League
President: Thomas J. Halligan

Standings	W	L	Pct.	GB	Manager
Bay City Wolves	64	30	.681	—	Robert Prysock
Port Huron Saints	56	38	.596	8	Johnny Carlin
Saginaw Aces	55	41	.573	10	Les Nunamaker
Grand Rapids Black Sox	51	43	.543	13	Pat Devereaux
Ludington Tars	45	51	.469	20	Ovid Nicholson
Muskegon Reds	39	56	.411	25½	Curtis "Buck" Wheat
Kalamazoo Celery Pickers	39	59	.398	27	Charles Schmidt/Fred Hutton
Flint Vehics/Charlotte Giants#	32	63	.337	32½	Ray Dunn

#Flint (18-26) moved to Charlotte July 22, first home game July 25.
The league was created June 15 through the mid-season merger of the Central and Michigan-Ontario leagues.

BA: Dan Beal, Ludington, .375
Runs: Al Bashang, Bay City, 107
Hits: Dan Beal, Ludington, 134
HRs: Harry Green, Kalamazoo, 11

Wins: Saraphin Good, Bay City, 19
SOs: Sid Dyer, Saginaw, 148
Pct: Saraphin Good, Bay City, .826, 19-4

B Michigan-Ontario League
President: Thomas J. Halligan

Standings	W	L	Pct.	GB	Manager
Port Huron Saints	20	10	.667	—	Johnny Carlin
Saginaw Aces	19	11	.633	1	Les Nunamaker
Bay City Wolves	10	18	.357	9	Robert Prysock
Flint Vehics	9	19	.321	10	Ray Dunn

Last game played June 13. The league merged with the Central League to form the Michigan State League, which began play June 15.

BA: Edward Zupancic, Saginaw, .349
Runs: Stanley Casper, Saginaw, 29
Hits: Edward Zupancic, Saginaw, 38
HRs: Karl Weber, Bay City, 5

Wins: Frank Matuzek, Saginaw, 8
Frank Tubbs, Port Huron, 8
SOs: Frank Matuzek, Saginaw, 44
Pct: Frank Tubbs, Port Huron, .889, 8-1

B New England League
President: Claude B. Davidson

Standings	W	L	Pct.	GB	Manager
Manchester Blue Sox	57	35	.620	—	Jean Dubuc
Lynn Papooses	53	42	.558	5½	King Bader
Lewiston Twins	50	43	.538	7½	Joe Murphy
Haverhill Hillies	49	46	.516	9½	John Kiernan
Lawrence Merry Macks	46	49	.484	12½	George Tyler
Lowell Highwaymen/ Salem Witches#	44	47	.484	12½	Thomas "Poke" Whalen
Portland Eskimos	38	56	.404	20	George Faulkner
Nashua Millionaires	37	56	.398	20½	Fred Lake/Walter Keating/Sandy McGregor/ John Mitchell

#Lowell (6-8) moved to Salem June 3.

BA: Jay O'Connor, Haverhill, .394
Runs: Willard Millsap, Lynn, 87
Hits: Harry Lavallie, Manchester, 138
RBIs: Shanty Hogan, Lynn, 89

HRs: Shanty Hogan, Lynn, 19
Wins: Donald McPhee, Haverhill, 16
SOs: John Prudhomme, Lawrence, 122
ERA: Lore Bader, Lynn, 2.64

B New York-Pennsylvania League
President: John H. Farrell

Standings	W	L	Pct.	GB	Manager
Scranton Miners	84	50	.627	—	Jack Egan
York White Roses	79	57	.581	6	Frank Desseau
Williamsport Grays	69	65	.515	15	Harry Hinchman
Elmira Colonels	68	67	.504	16½	Joseph Dunn
Binghamton Triplets	67	67	.500	17	Mike Konnick
Shamokin Indians	61	68	.473	20½	W.G. "Allen" Killinger
Wilkes-Barre Barons	56	73	.434	25½	George Maisel/Earl Potteiger
Harrisburg Senators	47	84	.359	35½	Rankin Johnson/Joe Lightner

Total Attendance: 561,712.

BA: Red Shilling, York, .366
Runs: Don Donaldson, Scranton, 106
Hits: Joe Faber, York, 172
RBIs: Francis Farrell, Scranton, 93

HRs: John Roseberry, Shamokin, 10
Wins: Eddie Williams, Elmira, 22
SOs: Henry Hoffman, Williamsport, 129
ERA: Ed Matteson, Scranton/York, 1.80

B South Atlantic Association
President: William G. Bramham

Standings	W	L	Pct.	GB	Manager
Greenville Spinners	98	50	.662	—	Frank Walker
Asheville Tourists	80	66	.547	17	Larry Gardner
Augusta Tygers	80	67	.544	17½	Gabby Street
Charlotte Hornets	77	72	.517	21½	Ray Kennedy
Spartanburg Spartans	74	74	.500	24	Mike Kelly
Macon Peaches	71	74	.489	25½	Ernie Burke
Knoxville Smokies	68	79	.463	29½	Frank Moffet
Columbia Comers	40	106	.274	57	Herbert Brenner

BA: Bill Rhiel, Greenville, .386
Runs: Russell Scarritt, Greenville, 150
Hits: Russell Scarritt, Greenville, 243
RBIs: Roy Moore, Greenville, 134
HRs: Roy Moore, Greenville, 35

Wins: Wilcy Moore, Greenville, 30
SOs: Lee Ormand, Greenville, 160
ERA: Mark Rainey, Asheville/Augusta, 2.84
Pct: Wilcy Moore, Greenville, .882, 30-4

B Southeastern League
President: Cliff Green

Standings	W	L	Pct.	GB	Manager
Columbus Foxes*	72	49	.595	—	Hardin Herndon
Montgomery Lions**	70	49	.588	1	Joe Brennan/Nig Leonard
Jacksonville Tars	64	60	.516	9½	Bob Fisher/Red Smith
Albany Nuts	53	64	.453	17	George Stinson/Sumter Clark
St. Augustine Saints	55	70	.440	19	Fred Graff/Bob Folmar
Savannah Indians	49	71	.408	22½	Bill Robertson/Bill Holland/H. Magness

Playoff: Columbus 4 games, Montgomery 1.

BA: John Kloza, Montgomery, .380
Runs: Burney Acton, Montgomery, 103
Hits: Henry Parrish, Columbus, 174
HRs: Henry Parrish, Columbus, 28

Wins: Lawton McWhirter, Montgomery, 19
SOs: Paul Doss, Columbus, 110
Pct: Ed Wepfer, Montgomery, .818, 9-2

B Three-I League
President: L.J. Wylie

Standings	W	L	Pct.	GB	Manager
Springfield Senators	77	59	.566	—	Alex McCarthy
Peoria Tractors	75	62	.547	2½	William Rodgers
Terre Haute Tots	73	61	.545	3	Roy Whitcraft
Danville Veterans	72	65	.526	5½	Charles Knoll
Evansville Hubs	72	66	.522	6	Oscar Stanage
Decatur Commodores	69	67	.507	8	Harold Irelan
Quincy Red Birds	62	75	.453	15½	Henry Wingfield/Henry Wetzel
Bloomington Bloomers	43	88	.328	31½	R.H. Goodbread

BA: Harry Layne, Peoria, .360
Runs: Al Maderas, Springfield, 119
Hits: Frank Murphy, Danville, 193
HRs: Al Maderas, Springfield, 30

Wins: Hal Smith, Peoria, 19
Elmer Ambrose, Decatur, 19
Carl Boone, Terre Haute, 19
William Clark, Terre Haute, 19
Clarence Hoots, Springfield, 19
SOs: William Clark, Terre Haute, 134
ERA: Arnold Stone, Evansville, 2.44

B Virginia League
President: William G. Bramham

Standings	W	L	Pct.	GB	Manager
Richmond Colts	85	68	.556	—	Troy Agnew/Guy Lacy/Rube Oldring
Wilson Bugs	85	69	.552	½	Bunn Hearn
Norfolk Tars	79	73	.520	5½	Dave Robertson
Portsmouth Truckers	74	78	.487	10½	Lester Bangs
Kinston Eagles	69	83	.454	15½	John Nee
Petersburg Broncos	66	87	.431	19	Charles Connolly/Tom Abbott

BA: Davy Robertson, Norfolk, .382
Runs: Richard Attreau, Norfolk, 154
Hits: Richard Attreau, Norfolk, 225
RBIs: Davy Robertson, Norfolk, 127

HRs: Pete Stack, Richmond, 44
Wins: Alex Peterson, Norfolk, 22
SOs: Herman Kemner, Richmond, 152
ERA: Bunn Hearn, Wilson, 2.68

C Central League
President: Emerson W. Dickerson

Standings	W	L	Pct.	GB	Manager
Kalamazoo Celery Pickers	16	8	.667	—	Charles Schmidt
Ludington Tars	12	12	.500	4	Ovid Nicholson
Muskegon Reds	12	13	.480	4½	Curtis "Buck" Wheat
Grand Rapids Black Sox	10	17	.370	7½	Jess Runser/Pat Devereaux

Last game played June 13. The league merged with the Michigan-Ontario League to form the Michigan State League, which began play June 15.

BA: Stanley Sykes, Muskegon, .391
Runs: Harry Harding, Kalamazoo, 25
Hits: Harry Harding, Kalamazoo, 34
HRs: Eddie Radtke, Kalamazoo, 4

Wins: Frank Negake, Ludington, 5
John Oravetz, Muskegon, 5
SOs: Victor Ferretti, Ludington, 30
Pct: Harvey Freeman, Kalamazoo, 1.000, 4-0
Fred Hutton, Kalamazoo, 1.000, 4-0

C Middle Atlantic League
President: Elmer M. Daily

Standings	W	L	Pct.	GB	Manager
Fairmont Diamonds**	68	44	.607	—	Joe Phillips
Johnstown Johnnies*	63	43	.594	2	Norm McNeill
Cumberland Colts	62	48	.564	5	Pat Ragan
Clarksburg Generals	56	51	.523	9½	Pop Shriver/Bill Pike
Scottdale Scotties	51	61	.455	17	Mike Mowrey
Uniontown Cokers	47	61	.435	19	Jim McGuire/Lee King/John Bail
Jeannette Jays	45	64	.413	21½	Jack Snyder/Warwick Comstock
Wheeling Stogies	44	64	.407	22	John Hummell

Playoff: Johnstown 4 games, Fairmont 2.

BA: Dennis Sothern, Cumberland, .374
Runs: Edward Sobb, Clarksburg, 113
Hits: Dewey Stover, Clarksburg, 152
HRs: Jack Smith, Uniontown, 28
Wins: Arthur Cousins, Fairmont, 21
SOs: John Hopkins, Scottdale, 193
Pct: Arthur Cousins, Fairmont, .750, 21-7

C Piedmont League
President: William G. Bramham

Standings	W	L	Pct.	GB	Manager
Greensboro Patriots*	86	60	.589	—	Lee Gooch
Danville Leafs/					
High Point Pointers#	85	61	.582	1	Bob Higgins
Durham Bulls**	73	71	.507	12	Art Bourg/Lew McCarty
Salisbury Colonials	69	75	.479	16	Moose Marshall
Winston-Salem Twins	64	81	.441	21½	Cy Chisolm/Red Irby/Walt Christensen/
					Art Bourg
Raleigh Capitals	57	86	.399	27½	Runt Marr/Bennie Allen/Charles Carroll/
					Cy Chisolm

#Danville (11-10) moved to High Point May 12, first home game May 14.

Playoff: Greensboro 4 games, Durham 1.

BA: Danny Boone, Danville/High Point, .399
Runs: Danny Boone, Danville/High Point, 112
Hits: Danny Boone, Danville/High Point, 214
RBIs: Danny Boone, Danville/High Point, 117
HRs: David Barbee, Greensboro, 29
Wins: Raymond Phelps, Danville/High Point, 27
SOs: Raymond Phelps, Danville/ High Point, 151
ERA: William Taylor, Winston-Salem, 2.21

C Utah-Idaho League
President: Fred M. Nye

Standings	W	L	Pct.	GB	Manager
Idaho Falls Spuds***	75	39	.658	—	Bill Leard/Danny Collins
Twin Falls Bruins	63	50	.558	11½	Carl Zamlock
Pocatello Bannocks	58	53	.523	15½	Al Bonner/Bert McIvor/Doug Taitt
Logan Collegians	48	65	.425	26½	Harry Wolter/Nick Williams/
					Nate Shandling
Salt Lake City Bees	52	70	.426	27	Bud Orr/Bert Whaling/Chet Chadbourne
Ogden Gunners	46	65	.414	27½	Ray Bates/Dad Gimlin/Guy Cooper

BA: Charles King, Logan, .402
Runs: Roy Johnson, Idaho Falls, 133
Hits: Eddie Rose, Idaho Falls, 177
HRs: Larman Cox, Ogden, 20
Wins: Robert Hurst, Idaho Falls, 22
SOs: Bruce Cunningham, Pocatello, 140
ERA: John Morrison, Idaho Falls, 2.83

C Western Association
President: J.W. Seabaugh

Standings	W	L	Pct.	GB	Manager
Springfield Midgets**	92	66	.582	—	Mark Purtell
Ft. Smith Twins	92	68	.575	1	Everett Booe
Ardmore Boomers/					
Joplin Ozarks@*	77	81	.487	15	George Whiteman
Okmulgee Drillers	73	85	.462	19	Chick Mattick
Muskogee Athletics#	51	45	.531	NA	Walt Kreuger/Connie Fields/
					George Armstrong
McAlester Miners#	28	68	.292	NA	Clyde Wren/Connie Fields/Frank Thompson/
					Mose Poolaw

#Muskogee and McAlester withdrew July 20.
@Ardmore (8-12 in the second half) moved to Joplin July 14, first home game July 22.

Playoff: Springfield 3 games, Joplin 2.

BA: L.A. Benson, Ft. Smith, .391
Runs: Carey Selph, Ft. Smith, 169
Hits: L.A. Benson, Ft. Smith, 231
HRs: John Reider, Springfield, 36
Wins: Norman Sitts, Springfield, 24
SOs: Allyn Stout, Ft. Smith, 155
ERA: Bill Clowers, Ardmore/Joplin, 2.98

D Blue Ridge League
President: J. Vincent Jamison, Jr.

Standings	W	L	Pct.	GB	Manager
Hagerstown Hubs*	64	31	.674	—	Ray Werre
Frederick Hustlers**	54	41	.568	10	Barney Cleveland
Martinsburg Blue Sox	47	46	.505	16	Dave Black
Hanover Raiders	46	51	.474	19	George "Buck" Ramsey
Chambersburg Maroons	38	55	.409	25	Dick Julian/Rankin Johnson
Waynesboro Villagers	34	59	.366	29	Ed Greene/William Suhre/Bill Morris

Playoff: Hagerstown 3 games, Frederick 1.

BA: Mickey Kelliher, Martinsburg, .370
Runs: Charles Fullis, Frederick, 80
Hits: John M. Smith, Frederick, 126
HRs: George Rawlings, Martinsburg, 19
Wins: Harry Fishbaugh, Hagerstown, 17
SOs: Raymond Kepner, Chambersburg, 140
Pct: Philip Dolan, Hagerstown, .833, 15-3

D Cotton States League
President: Frank A. Scott

Standings	W	L	Pct.	GB	Manager
Hattiesburg Pinetoppers*	77	46	.626	—	Herschel Bobo
Meridian Mets	67	57	.540	10½	"Spoke" Berry
Jackson Senators	65	64	.504	15	Frank Heck/Ray Gillwater/Walt Barbare
Alexandria Reds	64	65	.496	16	Bill Pierre
Laurel Lumberjacks	59	61	.492	16½	Sam Vick/Bill Statham
Gulfport Tarpons	57	67	.460	20½	Henry Knaupp/Jack Ryan
Vicksburg Hill Billies**	58	71	.450	22	Bob Clarke/Bunny Fabrique
Monroe Drillers	56	72	.438	23½	Charles Carroll/Eddie Palmer

Playoffs: None; second half irregularities were not ruled upon until it was too late to play. No formal champion was named.

BA: George Biggerstaff, Laurel, .357
Runs: Sammy Mack, Hattiesburg, 98
  Hoot Gibson, Hattiesburg, 98
Hits: Mel Simons, Meridian, 161
HRs: George Ferrell, Monroe, 20
Wins: Ed Greer, Meridian, 24
SOs: Lester Rouprich, Gulfport/Jackson, 146
Pct: Merle Settlemire, Meridian, .875, 14-2

D East Texas League
President: T.H. Fisher

Standings	W	L	Pct.	GB	Manager
Longview Cannibals***	83	39	.680	—	Bennie Brownlow
Texarkana Twins	66	54	.550	16	George "Tex" Wisterzil
Greenville Hunters	62	57	.521	19½	George Jackson
Tyler Trojans	57	64	.471	25½	Frank "Pop" Kitchens
Marshall Snappers/Indians	55	67	.451	28	Earl "Red" Snapp/Buster Wisrock &
					Mike Massey/Dutch Bernsen
Paris Bearcats	39	81	.325	43	Les Tullos/Faustin Gallegos/
					Earl "Red" Snapp

Attendance: Tyler, 40,720.

BA: John "Moose" Clabaugh, Tyler, .376
Runs: John "Moose" Clabaugh, Tyler, 106
Hits: Joe Granade, Texarkana, 180
HRs: John "Moose" Clabaugh, Tyler, 62
Wins: Elmer Bowman, Longview, 20
SOs: Noel Haynes, Paris, 120
Pct: Elmer Bowman, Longview, .833, 20-4

D Eastern Shore League
President: J. Harry Rew

Standings	W	L	Pct.	GB	Manager
Crisfield Crabbers	63	21	.750	—	Dan Pasquella
Salisbury Indians	57	29	.670	7	Jack White
Dover Senators	40	46	.465	24	Jiggs Donohue
Parksley Spuds	40	46	.465	24	Win Clark
Cambridge Canners	32	54	.372	32	Thomas "Poke" Whalen
Easton Farmers	24	60	.286	39	Buck Herzog

34 Easton wins were reversed August 16, 19 Parksley wins were reversed August 22, 23 Dover wins and 22 Cambridge wins were reversed September 2 — all due to salary limit violations.

BA: Tony Rensa, Crisfield, .388
Runs: Bill Hohman, Easton, 69
Hits: Floyd McDougall, Parksley, 113
  Aikens, Cambridge, 113
HRs: Pete Stack, Parksley, 22
Wins: Ted Firth, Parksley, 21
SOs: Ted Firth, Parksley, 143
Pct: A.L. Carlton, Easton, .765, 13-4

D Florida State League
President: J.B. Asher

Standings	W	L	Pct.	GB	Manager
Sanford Celeryfeds***	67	36	.650	—	Lee Crowe
Lakeland Highlanders	67	47	.588	5½	Roy Ellam
Ft. Myers Palms	66	51	.564	8	Buck Conroy/John Johnson/Mike Doyle/
					Pat Doran
Tampa Smokers	63	57	.525	12½	Charles Allen/Tom Leach
Orlando Colts	59	57	.509	14½	Phil Wells/Jim Black
St. Petersburg Saints	55	57	.491	16½	George Block
Bradenton Growers	44	76	.367	31½	Frank Larisey/Dixie Parker
Sarasota Gulls	38	78	.328	35½	Ivan Olson/Hatty Manush

BA: Otto Dumas, Sanford, .361
Runs: Ralph Dunbar, Sanford, 95
Hits: O.O. Brown, St. Petersburg, 152
HRs: Otto Dumas, Sanford, 4
  Philip Grandio, Ft. Myers, 4
  Dick Luckey, St. Petersburg, 4
  R. Tinker, Orlando, 4
Wins: Ben Cantwell, Sanford, 24
SOs: Walter Brown, Sarasota, 181
Pct: Ben Cantwell, Sanford, .828, 24-5

D Gulf Coast League
President: Pat Newnam

Standings	W	L	Pct.	GB	Manager
Beeville Bees/					
Laredo Oilers#**	59	41	.590	—	Emmett Rodgers/E. Newberry
Victoria Rosebuds/					
Edinburg Bobcats+*	51	48	.515	7½	Bart Cahill/Cam Hill
Kingsville Jerseys/					
Mission Grapefruiters@	46	52	.469	12	Tom Deering/Fred Paschal/Ed Harburger
Corpus Christi Seahawks	43	58	.426	16½	Chick Brandon

#Beeville (4-9) moved to Laredo May 29.
@Kingsville (14-26) moved to Mission July 9, first home game July 16.
+Victoria (17-19 in the second half) moved to Edinburg August 24.

Playoff: Edinburg 4 games, Laredo 3, one tie.

D Mississippi Valley League
President: Belden Hill

Standings	W	L	Pct.	GB	Manager
Ottumwa Packers	75	45	.625	—	Pat Harkins
Moline Plowboys	71	50	.587	4½	Jim Shollenberger
Waterloo Hawks	67	52	.563	7½	Cletus Dixon
Burlington Bees	68	53	.562	7½	Ed Reichle
Rock Island Islanders	65	55	.542	10	Preston Gray
Dubuque Speasmen	56	63	.471	18½	Bill Speas
Marshalltown Ansons	41	79	.342	34	E.F. Lane/Casey Coffin/Dike Brannigan/ Dan O'Leary
Cedar Rapids Bunnies	38	84	.311	38	Fred Beck/Jack Lacy/Jim "Dutch" While

BA: Bob Worthington, Waterloo, .389
Runs: Les Smith, Ottumwa, 99
Hits: Bob Worthington, Waterloo, 185
HRs: Les Smith, Ottumwa, 20
Wins: Alvin Bauer, Ottumwa, 25
SOs: Robert Shanklin, Rock Island, 188
Pct: Alvin Bauer, Ottumwa, .862, 25-4

D Southwestern League
President: Dale D. Gear

Standings	W	L	Pct.	GB	Manager
Salina Millers**	76	41	.650	—	Jimmy Payton
Enid Boosters*	70	49	.588	7	George Dye
Topeka Senators	57	59	.491	18½	Dina Wright/Butch Wetzel
Arkansas City Osages	54	62	.466	21½	Russ McMullan/Zuidal Zunigha
Ponca City Poncans/					
Eureka Oilers#	49	69	.415	27½	Bob Browne/Tiny Simmons
Blackwell Gassers	45	71	.388	30½	J.G. "Stormy" Kromer/Mike Balenti

#Ponca City (11-33) moved to Eureka June 22.

Playoff: Salina 3 games, Enid 1.

BA: Bill Diester, Salina, .444
Runs: Bill Diester, Salina, 110
Hits: Bill Diester, Salina, 190
HRs: Dick Wykoff, Salina, 28
Wins: Dick Wykoff, Salina, 25
SOs: Holman Bass, Blackwell, 143
Pct: W.A. Peters, Enid, .813, 13-3

D Texas Association
President: Mark H. Dewitt

Standings	W	L	Pct.	GB	Manager
Austin Senators*	73	49	.598	—	Walt Alexander
Palestine Pals**	72	53	.576	2½	Jack Stansbury/Bob Countryman
Mexia Gushers	63	62	.504	11½	Frank "Matty" Matthews
Terrell Terrors	56	68	.452	18	Edgar "Dutch" Behrens
Temple Surgeons	56	69	.448	18½	Roy Mitchell
Corsicana Oilers	53	72	.424	21½	Johnny Vann

Playoff: Palestine 3 games, Austin 0.

BA: Clyde Glass, Mexia, .361
Runs: James Long, Mexia, 99
Hits: James Long, Mexia, 164
HRs: Norman Peterson, Austin, 29
Wins: Dick Whitworth, Austin, 24
SOs: Dick Whitworth, Austin, 176
    Leslie Cox, Palestine, 176
Pct: Carl Littlejohn, Austin, .824, 14-3

D Tri-State League
President: John D. Martin

Standings	W	L	Pct.	GB	Manager
Jonesboro Buffaloes	35	23	.603	—	Buck Stapleton
Corinth Corinthians	35	23	.603	—	Roy Clunk
Sheffield-Tuscumbia Twins	27	29	.482	7	P.H. White
Jackson Jays	27	30	.474	7½	H.T. Reece
Blytheville Tigers	26	31	.456	8½	Ralph Minatree
Tupelo Wolves	22	36	.379	13	O.V. Pressley

Playoff: The first half ended in a tie when Corinth wanted to use outside players for the playoff but Jonesboro refused. The league then disbanded July 6 at the end of the first half.

BA: M.E. Rittenhouse, Sheffield-Tuscumbia, .435
Runs: Basil Milazzo, Sheffield-Tuscumbia, 49
Hits: Sam Byrd, Jonesboro, 73
HRs: Duncan Doty, Jonesboro, 9
Wins: John Bates, Corinth, 11
    William Stewart, Corinth, 11
SOs: John Bates, Corinth, 71
Pct: John Bates, Corinth, .846, 11-2

1926 Interleague Post Season Play

World Series
St. Louis (National) 4 games, New York (American) 3

Junior World Series
Toronto (International) 5 games, Louisville (American Association) 0

Dixie Series
Dallas (Texas) 4 games, New Orleans (Southern Association) 2, one tie
Total Attendance: 63,625

Northern Championship
Springfield (Three-I) 4 games, Bay City (Michigan State) 0

Mid-Western Championship
Springfield (Three-I) 3 games, Des Moines (Western) 1
Series called on account of cold weather.

Eastern Championship
Scranton (New York-Pennsylvania) 4 games, Manchester (New England) 0

Eastern Championship
Scranton (New York-Pennsylvania) 2 games, Providence (Eastern) 1

Southern Championship
Greenville (South Atlantic Association) 4 games, Richmond (Virginia) 1

Lone Star Series
Longview (East Texas) 4 games, Palestine (Texas Association) 2, one tie

Five-State Championship
Hagerstown (Blue Ridge) 4 games, Crisfield (Eastern Shore) 2

1926 No-Hitters

Date	Pitcher	Team	League	Opponent	Score
5-17	Raymond Starr	Danville	Three-I	Bloomington	2-0 (P)
5-31	Frank Tubbs	Port Huron	Michigan-Ontario	Flint	4-0
6-12	Meade	Kinston	Virginia	Petersburg	14-0 (7)
6-16	Holman Bass	Blackwell	Southwestern	Topeka	2-0
6-20	Gene Walker	Palestine	Texas Association	Austin	2-0
6-20	Walter Leverenz	Buffalo	International	Reading	7-0
6-21	Marty Kinnear	Harrisburg	New York-Penn.	Shamokin	2-0
7-2	Jim Crawford	Parksley	Eastern Shore	Easton	
7-3	Maurice Higgins	Charlotte	South Atlantic	Augusta	1-0
7-10	Rufe Wafer	Greenville	East Texas	Tyler	6-0 (7)
7-10	Lefty Maxwell	Corpus Christi	Gulf Coast	Mission	4-1
7-18	Lennon	Salisbury	Eastern Shore	Crisfield	
8-3	Chuck Warden	Waynesboro	Blue Ridge	Hagerstown	
8-11	Fred Adamson	Moline	Mississippi Valley	Ottumwa	7-1
8-13	Roy Spruell	Hattiesburg	Cotton States	Monroe	12-0
8-15	Jack Knott	Corsicana	Texas Association	Terrell	1-0
8-16	Ted Pritchard	Elmira	New York-Penn.	Scranton	2-0
8-17	Peter Jablonski	Waterbury	Eastern	Bridgeport	3-0
8-21	Ted Lyons	Chicago	American	Boston	6-0
8-21	Denny Gearin	Milwaukee	American Assoc.	Columbus	10-0
8-26	Bob Fitzke	Scranton	New York-Penn.	Shamokin	(7)
8-27	Bill Everham	Crisfield	Eastern Shore	Salisbury	

Number in parentheses indicates innings if other than nine; "P" indicates perfect game.

THIS DATE IN MINOR LEAGUE HISTORY

April 23, 1926, Toronto, International League, defeated Newark 17-13 in a game which produced 19 doubles, 12 by Toronto.

May 1, 1926, Satchel Paige, 19, made his debut for Chattanooga in the Negro Southern Association, beating Birmingham 5-4.

May 3, 1926, Bangs, Brandon and Poetz hit successive homers in the third inning for Portsmouth of the Virginia League.

May 5, 1926, John Reider smashed two circuit drives for Springfield, Western Association, for a total of five in two games.

May 6, 1926, John Reider, Springfield, Western Association, continued his home run hitting streak by rapping three in one game for the second time in three days and a total of eight round-trippers in a span of three games.

May 7, 1926, Manager Casey Stengel, Toledo, American Association, used 21 players in a nine-inning game.

May 7, 1926, Greenville, South Atlantic Association, hit eight homers in a 17-1 victory over Columbia.

May 8, 1926, Buffalo posted its 12th successive victory in the International League, defeating Jersey City.

May 9, 1926, Toledo pilfered 10 bases in an American Association tilt.

May 17, 1926, Outfielder Howard "Ben" Mallonee of Richmond, Virginia League, smashed a double and four home runs in six at bats against Portsmouth.

June 2, 1926, Seattle, Pacific Coast League, made five hits in the fifth inning of a game with Oakland, but scored only one run.

June 5, 1926, Jersey City and Reading played 19 innings to a 3-3 tie in the International League. Reading was blanked after scoring three runs in the fifth frame. Erwin Brame hurled the full game for Jersey City.

June 10, 1926, Baltimore turned in double plays in six consecutive innings in an International League tilt with Syracuse, executing a twin killing in each frame from the third through the eighth.

June 15, 1926, Dan Clark, Syracuse, International League, collected his eleventh consecutive hit, the streak consisting of nine singles and two home runs.

June 15, 1926, Hilton Brandon hit two home runs and scored three times in the fifth inning for Portsmouth in a Virginia League game.

June 16, 1926, Milwaukee won its 21st successive game, the all-time record for the American Association.

June 24, 1926, Newark, International League, lost to Baltimore after having won 13 straight games.

June 29, 1926, Louisville, American Association, scored in all nine innings to defeat Columbus 24-3.

July 4, 1926, Max Flack, Syracuse, International League, made six hits in six trips in a game with Buffalo.

July 6, 1926, The Tri-State League season came to an end. M.E. Rittenhouse, playing for Sheffield-Tuscumbia, hit .435 in 50 games.

July 9, 1926, Dan Clark, Syracuse, International League, hit two homers, giving him four in his last two games.

July 10, 1926, Greenville, South Atlantic Association, scored 10 runs in the fourth inning and repeated the feat in the fifth.

July 14, 1926, Shortstop Al Maderas of Springfield, Three-I League, slammed four successive homers in a game at Quincy.

July 14, 1926, After having lost 14 straight games, Reading, International League, defeated Syracuse.

July 15, 1926, Portland, Pacific Coast League, scored 10 runs in the ninth inning to beat Mission 12-6.

July 21, 1926, In one of the wildest games in minor league history, Springfield defeated Peoria 33-23 in a Three-I League battle. Springfield had 22 hits, received 14 bases on balls and overcame a 10-run deficit. Catcher Thomas of the winners hit a home run and a bases-loaded triple in one frame, and teammate Chatham received five consecutive walks. Peoria had 27 safeties and led 10-0 going into the bottom of the third. Peoria rightfielder Harry Layne whacked three successive homers and also had two doubles in seven trips. Thirteen pitchers saw action, ten homers were hit, and eight errors were committed.

July 21, 1926, San Francisco, Pacific Coast League, scored eight runs in the ninth to beat Mission 9-8.

July 22, 1926, Kruska cracked four doubles in one game for Columbus, American Association.

August 6, 1926, First baseman Gus Suhr, San Francisco, Pacific Coast League, hit three homers in one game against Portland.

August 14, 1926, Reading, International League, defeated Syracuse, ending a 15-game losing skid.

August 17, 1926, Robert Lamotte had 11 assists at shortstop for Milwaukee, American Association.

August 22, 1926, John "Moose" Clabaugh hit his 61st home run of the season for Tyler in the East Texas League.

August 25, 1926, Elmer Smith, Portland, Pacific Coast League, hit his ninth home run in the last five games. He had walloped three on the 19th and three on the 21st of August.

August 26, 1926, Pitcher "Cowboy" Ed Tomlin, Newark, International League, was fined $500 and suspended for the remainder of the season for attacking manager Fred Burchell, who had removed him from a game at Newark.

August 29, 1926, Columbus set an American Association record with 12 errors in a nine-inning game.

September 3, 1926, William Kelly, Buffalo, International League, swatted his 41st home run of the season.

September 14, 1926, Reading suffered its 23rd straight defeat, bowing to Jersey City.

September 15, 1926, The Southwestern League season ended with Dick Wykoff of Salina leading the circuit in both home runs (28) and wins (25).

October 3, 1926, Toronto, International League, defeated Louisville, American Association, in the Junior World Series, sweeping the set five games to none, winning by scores of 2-0, 3-2, 2-1, 4-3 and 7-0.

1927

American League
Presidents: Byron Bancroft Johnson/Ernest S. Barnard

Standings	W	L	Pct.	GB	Attend.	Manager
New York Yankees	110	44	.714	—	1,164,015	Miller Huggins
Philadelphia Athletics	92	63	.591	19	605,529	Connie Mack
Washington Senators	85	69	.552	25	528,976	Bucky Harris
Detroit Tigers	82	71	.536	27½	773,716	George Moriarty
Chicago White Sox	70	83	.458	39½	614,423	Ray Schalk
Cleveland Indians	66	87	.431	43½	373,138	Jack McCallister
St. Louis Browns	59	94	.386	50½	247,879	Dan Howley
Boston Red Sox	51	103	.331	59	305,275	Bill Carrigan

BA: Harry Heilmann, Detroit, .398
Runs: Babe Ruth, New York, 158
Hits: Earl Combs, New York, 231
RBIs: Lou Gehrig, New York, 175
HRs: Babe Ruth, New York, 60

Wins: Waite Hoyt, New York, 22
Ted Lyons, Chicago, 22
SOs: Lefty Grove, Philadelphia, 174
ERA: Waite Hoyt, New York, 2.63
Pct: Waite Hoyt, New York, .759, 22-7

National League
President: John A. Heydler

Standings	W	L	Pct.	GB	Attend.	Manager
Pittsburgh Pirates	94	60	.610	—	869,720	Donie Bush
St. Louis Cardinals	92	61	.601	1½	749,340	Bob O'Farrell
New York Giants	92	62	.597	2	858,190	John McGraw/Rogers Hornsby
Chicago Cubs	85	68	.556	8½	1,159,168	Joe McCarthy
Cincinnati Reds	75	78	.490	18½	442,164	Jack Hendricks
Brooklyn Robins	65	88	.425	28½	637,230	Wilbert Robinson
Boston Braves	60	94	.390	34	288,685	Dave Bancroft
Philadelphia Phillies	51	103	.331	43	305,420	Stuffy McInnis

BA: Paul Waner, Pittsburgh, .380
Runs: Rogers Hornsby, New York, 133
Lloyd Waner, Pittsburgh, 133
Hits: Paul Waner, Pittsburgh, 237
RBIs: Paul Waner, Pittsburgh, 131

HRs: Hack Wilson, Chicago, 30
Cy Williams, Philadelphia, 30
Wins: Charlie Root, Chicago, 26
SOs: Dazzy Vance, Brooklyn, 184
ERA: Ray Kremer, Pittsburgh, 2.47
Pct: Larry Benton, Boston/New York, .708, 17-7

AA American Association
President: Thomas J. Hickey

Standings	W	L	Pct.	GB	Attend.	Manager
Toledo Mud Hens	101	67	.601	—	316,328	Casey Stengel
Kansas City Blues	99	69	.589	2	314,285	Dutch Zwilling
Milwaukee Brewers	99	69	.589	2	365,473	Jack Lelivelt
St. Paul Saints	90	78	.536	11	163,423	Nick Allen
Minneapolis Millers	88	80	.524	13	185,363	Mike Kelley
Indianapolis Indians	70	98	.417	31	101,984	Bruno Betzel
Louisville Colonels	65	103	.387	36	115,429	Bill Meyer
Columbus Senators	60	108	.357	41	121,678	Ivy Wingo

All-Star Team: 1B-Joe Hauser, Kansas City; **2B**-Fred Maguire, Toledo; **3B**-Gene Robertson, St. Paul; **SS**-Frank Emmer, Indianapolis; **OF**-Bobby Veach, Toledo; Bevo LeBourveau, Toledo; Elias "Liz" Funk, St. Paul; **C**-Alex Gaston, St. Paul; Eddie Kenna, Minneapolis; **Util**-Harry Riconda, Milwaukee; Russell Scarritt, St. Paul; **P**-Tom Sheehan, Kansas City; Jimmy Zinn, Kansas City; Paul Zahniser, St. Paul; Oswald Orwoll, Milwaukee; Claude Jonnard, Milwaukee; Pat Malone, Minneapolis.

BA: Reb Russell, Indianapolis, .385
Runs: Frank Emmer, Minneapolis, 154
Hits: Harry Riconda, Milwaukee, 255
RBIs: Bobby Veach, Toledo, 145

HRs: Frank Emmer, Minneapolis, 32
Wins: Tom Sheehan, Kansas City, 26
SOs: Pat Malone, Minneapolis, 214
ERA: Jimmy Zinn, Kansas City, 3.08

AA International League
President: John Conway Toole

Standings	W	L	Pct.	GB	Attend.	Manager
Buffalo Bisons	112	56	.667	—	247,449	Bill Clymer
Syracuse Stars	102	66	.607	10	174,059	Burt Shotton
Newark Bears	90	77	.539	21½	224,950	John Egan
Toronto Maple Leafs	89	78	.533	22½	124,098	Lee Fohl/Bill O'Hara
Baltimore Orioles	85	82	.509	26½	103,177	Jack Dunn
Rochester Red Wings	81	86	.485	30½	129,364	George Stallings/George Mogridge
Jersey City Skeeters	66	100	.398	45	80,021	Spencer Abbott
Reading Keystones	43	123	.259	68	82,642	Fred Merkle/Fritz Maisel/Harry Hinchman

BA: Dick Porter, Baltimore, .376
Runs: Del Bissonette, Buffalo, 168
Hits: Del Bissonette, Buffalo, 229
RBIs: Del Bissonette, Buffalo, 167

HRs: Del Bissonette, Buffalo, 31
Wins: Al Mamaux, Newark, 25
SOs: Bill Hallahan, Syracuse, 195
ERA: Al Mamaux, Newark, 2.61

AA Pacific Coast League
President: Harry A. Williams

Standings	W	L	Pct.	GB	Manager
Oakland Oaks	120	75	.615	—	Ivan Howard
San Francisco Seals	106	90	.541	14½	Nick Williams
Seattle Indians	98	92	.516	19½	Red Killefer
Sacramento Senators	100	95	.513	20	Buddy Ryan
Portland Beavers	95	95	.500	22½	Ernie Johnson
Hollywood Stars	92	104	.469	28½	Oscar Vitt
Mission Bells	86	110	.439	34½	Bill Leard/Harry Hooper
Los Angeles Angels	80	116	.408	40½	Marty Krug

Total Attendance: 1,919,000.

MVP-Lefty O'Doul, San Francisco.

BA: Smead Jolley, San Francisco, .397
Runs: Lefty O'Doul, San Francisco, 164
Hits: Lefty O'Doul, San Francisco, 278
RBIs: Smead Jolley, San Francisco, 163

HRs: Elmer Smith, Portland, 40
Wins: George Boehler, Oakland, 22
SOs: George Boehler, Oakland, 160
ERA: John Miljus, Seattle, 2.36

A Eastern League
President: Herman J. Weisman

Standings	W	L	Pct.	GB	Manager
Albany Senators	88	65	.576	—	Bill McCorry
Springfield Ponies	86	68	.558	2½	Joe Benes
Pittsfield Hillies	84	67	.556	3	Bill Whitman
Bridgeport Bears	84	70	.545	4½	Frank Stapleton
New Haven Profs	74	80	.481	14½	Neal Ball
Hartford Senators	72	81	.471	16	Kitty Bransfield
Waterbury Brasscos	63	90	.412	25	Harry Hinchman/Bob Gill
Providence Grays	61	91	.401	26½	Patsy Donovan

Playoff: Springfield 3 games, Albany 0.

BA: George Davis, Hartford, .349
Runs: Dennis Sothern, Pittsfield, 117
Hits: James Keesey, Hartford, 204
RBIs: James Keesey, Hartford, 115

HRs: Harold Yordy, Albany, 22
Wins: Earl Johnson, Albany, 23
SOs: John Hopkins, Albany, 161
ERA: Andy Rush, Bridgeport, 1.57

A Southern Association
President: John D. Martin

Standings	W	L	Pct.	GB	Attend.	Manager
New Orleans Pelicans	96	57	.627	—	266,905	Larry Gilbert
Birmingham Barons	91	63	.591	5½	299,150	Johnny Dobbs
Memphis Chickasaws	89	64	.582	7	146,387	Clyde Milan
Nashville Volunteers	84	69	.549	12	175,875	James Hamilton
Atlanta Crackers	70	81	.484	25	159,308	Bert Niehoff
Mobile Bears	67	87	.435	29½	75,489	Milt Stock
Chattanooga Lookouts	59	94	.386	37	82,284	Jim Johnston
Little Rock Travelers	56	97	.366	40	42,943	Joe Cantillon

BA: John Davis, New Orleans, .376
Runs: Elliott Bigelow, Birmingham, 137
Hits: Denny Williams, Mobile, 223
RBIs: Elliott Bigelow, Birmingham, 143
HRs: Elliott Bigelow, Birmingham, 19

Wins: Joe Martina, New Orleans, 23
SOs: Joe Martina, New Orleans, 103
Oscar Fuhr, Nashville, 103
ERA: Eddie Wells, Birmingham, 2.13
Pct: Eddie Wells, Birmingham, .929, 13-1

A Texas League
President: J. Doak Roberts

Standings	W	L	Pct.	GB	Attend.	Manager
Wichita Falls Spudders	102	54	.654	—	131,385	Carl Williams
Waco Cubs	88	68	.564	14	92,755	Del Pratt
Houston Buffaloes	85	70	.548	16½	141,857	Joe Mathes
Ft. Worth Panthers	77	79	.494	25	127,427	Jake Atz
Dallas Steers	74	80	.481	27	180,129	James "Snipe" Conley/Ewell "Turkey" Gross
Shreveport Sports	73	82	.471	28½	105,172	Art Phelan
San Antonio Bears	65	90	.419	36½	88,403	Honus Mitze/Bob Couchman & Ray Flaskamper
Beaumont Exporters	56	97	.366	44½	57,936	Jim "Bad News" Galloway/Claude "Ug" Robertson

BA: Del Pratt, Waco, .386
Runs: Tom Jenkins, Wichita Falls, 147
Hits: Max West, Waco, 228
RBIs: Del Pratt, Waco, 140
HRs: Del Pratt, Waco, 32

2B: Spencer Harris, Shreveport, 60
Wins: George Payne, Wichita Falls, 23
SOs: William Shores, Waco, 125
ERA: Ken Penner, Houston, 2.52

*Won first-half **Won second-half ***Won both halves

A Western League
President: Dale D. Gear

Standings	W	L	Pct.	GB	Manager
Tulsa Oilers	101	53	.656	—	Marty Berghammer
Wichita Larks	91	63	.591	10	Otis "Doc" Crandall
Des Moines Demons	82	72	.532	19	John "Shano" Collins
Denver Bears	77	75	.507	23	Joe Berger
Oklahoma City Indians	68	86	.442	33	Fred Luderus
Amarillo Texans	66	87	.431	34½	Joe Kelly
Omaha Buffaloes	66	88	.429	35	Kal Segrist/Barney Burch/Petey Brausen
Lincoln Links	63	90	.412	37½	John Lavan

Attendance: Tulsa, 140,000.

All-Star Team: 1B-Guy Sturdy, Tulsa; **2B**-Otis Brannon, Tulsa; **3B**-George Gottleber, Lincoln; **SS**-Lou Brower, Oklahoma City; **OF**-Fred Bennett, Tulsa; Adam Comorosky, Wichita; Elton Langford, Des Moines; **C**-Joe Sprinz, Des Moines; Pete Groft, Oklahoma City; **Util**-Al Vancamp, Des Moines; **P**-George Blaeholder, Tulsa; Dixie Walker, Denver; Ed "Bear Tracks" Greer, Denver; Lester Berry, Wichita; Clarence Griffin, Lincoln; Fred Ortman, Des Moines; John Smithson, Tulsa.

BA: Elton Langford, Des Moines, .409
Runs: Joe Rabbitt, Omaha, 172
Hits: Joe Rabbitt, Omaha, 251
HRs: Joe Munson (Carlson), Tulsa, 32

Wins: George Blaeholder, Tulsa, 26
SOs: Dixie Walker, Denver, 193
Pct: Karl Black, Tulsa, .857, 12-2

B New England League
President: Claude B. Davidson

Standings	W	L	Pct.	GB	Manager
Lynn Papooses*	59	30	.663	—	Thomas "Poke" Whalen
Portland Eskimos**	54	40	.574	7½	Duffy Lewis
Nashua Millionaires	47	43	.522	12½	Bill Stewart
Lewiston Twins	46	45	.505	14	Joe Murphy
Manchester Blue Sox	46	47	.495	15	Hank Lavallee
Salem Witches	42	50	.457	18½	Tom DeNoville
Lawrence Merry Macks	36	53	.404	23	Fred Parent
Haverhill Hillies	35	57	.380	25½	John Kiernan

Playoff: Lynn 4 games, Portland 0.

BA: Len Dugan, Manchester, .364
Runs: Ed Bogart, Portland, 81
Hits: Bob Unglaub, Salem, 125
RBIs: Bill Scholtz, Nashua, 73
HRs: Tony Cuccinello, Lawrence, 8

Wins: William Dunlap, Lynn, 15
Vic Fraser, Portland, 15
Frank Shuman, Lynn, 15
Charles Wolfe, Manchester, 15
SOs: Harry Slate, Nashua, 119
ERA: William Dunlap, Lynn, 1.23

B New York-Pennsylvania League
President: John H. Farrell

Standings	W	L	Pct.	GB	Manager
Harrisburg Senators	87	51	.630	—	Win Clark
Wilkes-Barre Barons	80	56	.588	6	Earl Potteiger
York White Roses	79	58	.577	7½	Frank Desseau/Johnny Tillman
Elmira Colonels	67	73	.479	21	Joseph Dunn
Scranton Miners	61	72	.459	23½	Gus Getz
Shamokin Indians	62	78	.443	26	Irvin Trout
Binghamton Triplets	57	81	.413	30	Mike McNally
Williamsport Grays	56	80	.412	30	George Burns

Attendance: Wilkes-Barre, 150,000; Total, 562,409.

BA: Mike Martineck, Harrisburg, .366
Runs: Glenn Killinger, Harrisburg, 107
Edward Burke, Harrisburg, 107
Hits: Mike Martineck, Harrisburg, 186
RBIs: Jim Conley, Elmira, 105
HRs: Glenn Killinger, Harrisburg, 11

Wins: Louis Polli, Harrisburg, 18
Seymour Bailey, Harrisburg, 18
Eddie Williams, Elmira, 18
SOs: Louis Polli, Harrisburg, 109
ERA: Roy Richards, York, 1.68

B South Atlantic Association
President: William G. Bramham

Standings	W	L	Pct.	GB	Manager
Greenville Spinners	92	56	.622	—	Frank Walker
Spartanburg Spartans	81	67	.547	11	Mike Kelly
Knoxville Smokies	79	68	.537	12½	Bob Coleman
Asheville Tourists	76	73	.510	16½	Larry Gardner
Macon Peaches	76	73	.510	16½	Wilbur Good
Charlotte Hornets	72	78	.480	21	Ray Kennedy
Columbia Comers	65	81	.445	26	Gabby Street
Augusta Tygers	52	97	.349	40½	Bob Taggert

BA: Bob Barrett, Knoxville, .360
Runs: Charles Fullis, Macon, 123
Hits: Ted Kearns, Charlotte, 191
RBIs: Ernest Shirley, Greenville, 128
HRs: Bob Barrett, Knoxville, 39

Wins: William Bayne, Greenville, 26
SOs: John Walker, Spartanburg, 139
ERA: William Bayne, Greenville, 2.87
Pct: Clarence Hodge, Spartanburg, .762, 16-5

B Southeastern League
President: Cliff Green

Standings	W	L	Pct.	GB	Manager
Jacksonville Tars	90	63	.588	—	Tom McMillan
Montgomery Lions	86	67	.562	4	Nig Leonard/Bill Pierre
Columbus Foxes	80	71	.530	9	Hardin Herndon
Pensacola Pilots	79	73	.520	10½	Bill Holden
Savannah Indians	72	79	.477	17	Joe Brennan/Harry Snyder
Albany Nuts	69	81	.460	19½	Sumter Clark
St. Augustine/ Waycross Saints#	66	85	.437	23	Bob Folmar/Roy Elam
Selma Selmians	65	88	.425	25	Fred Graff/Dutch Hoffman

#St. Augustine (42-53) moved to Waycross July 25, first home game August 15.
Total Attendance: 900,000+.

BA: John Kloza, Albany, .404
Runs: Henry Parrish, Columbus, 114
Hits: Mel Simons, Montgomery, 198
HRs: Henry Parrish, Columbus, 34

Wins: Ben Cantwell, Jacksonville, 25
SOs: Bill Clowers, Pensacola, 172
Pct: Ben Cantwell, Jacksonville, .833, 25-4

B Three-I League
President: L.J. Wylie

Standings	W	L	Pct.	GB	Manager
Danville Veterans	86	50	.632	—	Everett Booe
Peoria Tractors	87	51	.630	—	William Rodgers
Springfield Senators	72	66	.522	15	Alex McCarthy
Terre Haute Tots	70	66	.515	16	Robert Wells
Decatur Commodores	62	70	.470	22	Harold Ireland
Quincy Red Birds	63	75	.457	24	Charles Schmidt/Mack Allison/ Charles Knoll
Bloomington Bloomers	55	83	.403	32	Clarence Brooks/William Campbell
Evansville Hubs	50	84	.373	35	Roy Whitcraft

Attendance: Danville, 71,915; Springfield, 71,858; Total, 430,825.

All-Star Team: 1B-Joseph Walker, Danville; **2B**-Henry Demon, Peoria; **3B**-Tom Smith, Peoria; **SS**-Karl Urban, Danville; **OF**-William Mizeur, Peoria; Paul Easterling, Bloomington; Ted Menze, Springfield; **C**-Ray Thompson, Springfield; **Util**-Ed Yuna, Decatur; **P**-Ralph Judd, Danville; Sylvester Heitzman, Danville; Guilford Paulsen, Danville; George Grant, Terre Haute; Orville McCracken, Danville.

BA: Tom Smith, Peoria, .370
Runs: William Mizeur, Peoria, 125
Hits: William Mizeur, Peoria, 186
RBIs: William Mizeur, Peoria, 128

HRs: William Mizeur, Peoria, 23
Ted Menze, Springfield, 23
Wins: Ralph Judd, Peoria, 21
SOs: Ralph Judd, Peoria, 121
ERA: Ralph Judd, Peoria, 2.01

B Virginia League
President: William G. Bramham

Standings	W	L	Pct.	GB	Manager
Portsmouth Truckers	76	52	.594	—	Zinn Beck
Petersburg Bronchos	72	61	.541	6½	Olin Pratt
Richmond Colts	65	65	.500	12	Ed Mooers/Lew McCarty
Wilson Bugs	65	67	.492	13	Bunn Hearn
Norfolk Tars	58	72	.446	19	Dave Robertson
Kinston Eagles	56	75	.427	21½	Mike Konnick/Art Hauger

BA: Earl Clark, Richmond, .386
Runs: Jack Bandrimer, Portsmouth, 123
Hits: Jack Bandrimer, Portsmouth, 179
RBIs: George Thrasher, Petersburg, 114

HRs: George Thomas, Portsmouth, 24
Pete Stack, Richmond, 24
Wins: Frank Riel, Wilson, 20
SOs: Kenneth Ash, Petersburg, 109
ERA: Kenneth Ash, Petersburg, 2.78

C Middle Atlantic League
President: Elmer M. Daily

Standings	W	L	Pct.	GB	Manager
Cumberland Colts*	66	47	.584	—	Gus Thompson
Fairmont Black Diamonds	64	50	.561	2½	Joe Phillips
Clarksburg Generals	63	55	.534	5½	Earl Neale
Wheeling Stogies	59	55	.518	7½	Bobby Prysock
Scottdale Scotties	57	54	.514	8	Moose Marshall
Johnstown Johnnies**	57	55	.509	8½	Charles Babe Adams/ Charles "Chief" Bender
Jeannette Jays	48	65	.425	18	Jim Ferguson/Lee Strait/Elmer Knetzer
Charleroi Babes	42	75	.359	26	John McIlvain/Cowboy Comstock

Playoff: Cumberland 4 games, Johnstown 2.

BA: Karl Weber, Wheeling, .340
Runs: Edward Sobb, Clarksburg, 74
Hits: Karl Weber, Wheeling, 155
HRs: Edward Conley, Cumberland, 16

Wins: William Helmick, Fairmont, 18
SOs: Carl Fisher, Johnstown, 133
ERA: Claude Gillenwater, Wheeling, 1.66

C Piedmont League
President: William G. Bramham

Standings	W	L	Pct.	GB	Manager
Rocky Mount Buccaneers	84	60	.583	—	Lee Gooch
Salisbury-Spencer Colonials**	83	62	.572	1½	George Whiteman

Winston-Salem Twins .... 79 64 .552 4½ Charles McMillan
Raleigh Capitals* .... 77 70 .524 7½ Al Watt
High Point Pointers .... 62 82 .431 22 Frank "Pop" Kitchens/J. Smith/
                                                                    Danny Boone
Durham Bulls .... 48 95 .336 35½ Lew McCarty/Barney Cleveland/
                                                                    George "Possum" Whitted

Playoff: Salisbury-Spencer 3 games, Raleigh 2.

All-Star Team: 1B-John "Moose" Clabaugh, High Point; **2B**-Jack Teague, Rocky Mount; **3B**-Claude Butler, Raleigh; **SS**-Bill Akers, Durham; **OF**-Leroy Jones, Salisbury-Spencer; Faber O'Hara, Durham; **C**-Tom Ray, High Point; **P**-Harry Smythe, Winston-Salem; Roy Sullivan, Winston-Salem; Bob Huffman, Salisbury-Spencer.

BA: John "Moose" Clabaugh, High Point, .363
Runs: Otis Cashion, Rocky Mount, 113
Hits: John "Moose" Clabaugh, High Point, 187
RBIs: Dick Wade, Winston-Salem, 111
HRs: Dick Wade, Winston-Salem, 24

Wins: James Richardson, Salisbury-Spencer, 23
          Harry Moger, Raleigh, 23
SOs: James Richardson, Salisbury-Spencer, 161
ERA: Roy Sullivan, Winston-Salem, 2.04

C Utah-Idaho League
President: Fred M. Nye

Standings	W	L	Pct.	GB	Manager
Ogden Gunners	58	45	.563	—	Art Murphy/Del Baker
Salt Lake City Bees	59	50	.541	2	Harry O'Neill
Idaho Falls Spuds*	52	47	.525	4	Dan O'Leary
Logan Collegians	49	51	.490	7½	Harry Wolter
Pocatello Bannocks**	48	50	.490	7½	Ivan Olsen
Twin Falls Bruins	40	63	.388	18	Curly Gardiner/Bill Leard

Playoff: Idaho Falls 4 games, Pocatello 3.

All-Star Team: 1B-Dolph Camilli, Logan; **2B**-Ernie Hutton, Idaho Falls; **3B**-Jimmie Cronin, Idaho Falls; **SS**-Dan Jessee, Salt Lake City; **OF**-Wally Berger, Pocatello; John Schinski, Logan; Ira Caffey, Salt Lake City; **C**-Carroll Thompson, Idaho Falls; Del Baker, Ogden; **P**-George Hollerson, Salt Lake City; Harry O'Neill, Salt Lake City; Merton Nelson, Idaho Falls; Charley Newbill, Idaho Falls; Wallace Canfield, Twin Falls.

BA: Wally Berger, Pocatello, .38504
          John Schinski, Logan, .38482
Runs: John Schinski, Logan, 93
          R. Dennis Gearron, Logan, 93
Hits: Ira Caffey, Salt Lake City, 152

HRs: Wally Berger, Pocatello, 24
Wins: George Hollerson, Salt Lake City, 18
SOs: Dave Salazar, Pocatello, 129
ERA: George Hollerson, Salt Lake City, 2.52

C Western Association
President: Dale D. Gear

Standings	W	L	Pct.	GB	Manager
Ft. Smith Twins	81	51	.614	—	Runt Marr
Topeka Jayhawks	74	58	.560	7	Joe Schultz
St. Joseph Saints/					
Joplin Miners#	73	60	.549	8½	Marty Purtell
Springfield Midgets	63	69	.477	18	Chuck Funk
Okmulgee Drillers	57	75	.432	24	Troy Agnew
Muskogee Chiefs	48	83	.366	32½	Roy Corgan/Otto Williams

#St. Joseph (38-32) moved to Joplin July 7, causing the league classification to drop from "B" to "C".

MVP-John King, St. Joseph/Joplin.

BA: David Miner, Okmulgee, .410
Runs: William Brengle, St. Joseph/Joplin, 113
Hits: Fred Honea, Muskogee, 180
RBIs: John King, St. Joseph/Joplin, 114

HRs: John King, St. Joseph/Joplin, 26
Wins: Charles Johnson, 23
SOs: Laurence Irvine, Topeka, 120
ERA: James Moore, Ft. Smith, 2.07

D Blue Ridge League
President: J. Vincent Jamison, Jr.

Standings	W	L	Pct.	GB	Manager
Chambersburg Maroons* ...	65	34	.657	—	Mickey Kelliher
Martinsburg Blue Sox**	57	43	.570	8½	Frank Burke
Frederick Hustlers	53	47	.530	12½	Henry Sherry
Hanover Raiders	50	49	.505	15	George Hammen/Mike Konnick
Waynesboro Villagers	41	57	.418	23½	Jack Perrin/John Ebert
Hagerstown Hubs	32	68	.320	33½	Tommy Thomas/Al Kreuz

Playoff: Chambersburg 2 games, Martinsburg 0.

BA: Walt Hammen, Hanover, .369
Runs: Charles Hamel, Chambersburg, 87
Hits: Frank Roscoe, Hanover, 139

HRs: Frank Roscoe, Hanover, 13
          Joe Roetz, Hanover, 13
Wins: Lester Shatzer, Chambersburg, 16
SOs: Robert McIntire, Martinsburg, 117
Pct: Lester Shatzer, Chambersburg, .889, 16-2

D Cotton States League
President: Frank A. Scott

Standings	W	L	Pct.	GB	Manager
Jackson Senators**	76	47	.618	—	Walt Barbare
Monroe Drillers*	74	48	.607	1½	Eddie Palmer
Hattiesburg Pinetoppers	68	52	.567	6½	Herschel Bobo

Alexandria Reds .... | 59 | 60 | .496 | 15 | Bill Pierre/Sam Barnes
Gulfport Tarpons .... | 57 | 64 | .471 | 18 | Joe Evans
Vicksburg Hill Billies .... | 54 | 70 | .435 | 22½ | Bunny Gabrique/John Wooley
Meridian Mets .... | 48 | 66 | .421 | 23½ | Herrick "Spoke" Emery/Cotton Klindworth
Laurel Lumberjacks ** .... | 41 | 70 | .369 | 29 | Frank Mathews/Buck Stapleton

Standings	W	L	Pct.	GB	Manager
Alexandria Reds	59	60	.496	15	Bill Pierre/Sam Barnes
Gulfport Tarpons	57	64	.471	18	Joe Evans
Vicksburg Hill Billies	54	70	.435	22½	Bunny Gabrique/John Wooley
Meridian Mets	48	66	.421	23½	Herrick "Spoke" Emery/Cotton Klindworth
Laurel Lumberjacks**	41	70	.369	29	Frank Mathews/Buck Stapleton

Playoff: Jackson 4 games, Monroe 1.

BA: Hoot Gibson, Hattiesburg, .358
Runs: Fred Polvogt, Alexandria, 94
Hits: Joe Granade, Monroe, 180
HRs: Hoot Gibson, Hattiesburg, 12

Wins: Ed Greer, Jackson, 23
SOs: Wayne LaMaster, Jackson, 139
Pct: Philip Hensick, Monroe, .759, 22-7

D Eastern Shore League
President: J. Harry Rew

Standings	W	L	Pct.	GB	Manager
Parksley Spuds***	60	28	.681	—	Lester Bangs
Salisbury Indians	48	38	.552	11	Thomas "Poke" Whalen
Crisfield Crabbers	44	43	.506	15½	Dan Pasquella
Cambridge Canners	41	47	.466	19	Bill Johnson
Easton Farmers	36	48	.462	22	Ted Cather/Jiggs Donohue
Northampton Red Sox	30	55	.353	28½	Jack Sauer

BA: Bill Bickham, Parksley, .361
Runs: Mike McAllister, Parksley, 71
Hits: Bill Bickham, Parksley, 119
HRs: Paul Richards, Crisfield, 24

Wins: Cecil Rose, Crisfield, 17
SOs: Stephen Toner, Salisbury, 132
Pct: Clinton Brown, Parksley, .800, 16-4

D Florida State League
President: J.B. Asher

Standings	W	L	Pct.	GB	Manager
Orlando Colts*	72	52	.581	—	Phil Wells
Sanford Celeryfeds	68	53	.562	2½	Lee Crowe
Sarasota Tarpons	62	62	.500	10	Harry Manush/Ernie Burke
Tampa Smokers	57	65	.467	14	Tom Leach
Miami Hustlers**	57	69	.452	16	Bill Holloway/Cotton Knaupp
St. Petersburg Saints	52	67	.427	17½	Ben Shaw/Bill Frazier/Gene Hodges

Playoff: Orlando 4 games, Miami 3.

BA: Faustin Casaras, Miami, .318
Runs: Cecil Frisbie, Sanford, 78
          Faustin Casaras, Miami, 78
Hits: Clarence Beasley, Sanford, 145

HRs: Faustin Casaras, Miami, 15
Wins: E.E. Brower, Miami, 28
SOs: Frank Austin, St. Petersburg, 125
Pct: Herman Myers, Sanford, .765, 13-4

D Lone Star League
President: Pat Newnam

Standings	W	L	Pct.	GB	Manager
Palestine Pals	69	51	.575	—	Lyman "Rip" Ripperton
Texarkana Twins	67	53	.558	2	Charlie Miller
Mexia Gushers**	68	55	.553	2½	Les Hayes/Jim Kendrick/Abe Bowman
Tyler Trojans*	63	55	.534	5	George Jackson
Paris Snappers	54	67	.446	15½	Earl "Red" Snapp
Corsicana Oilers	48	72	.400	21	Les Nunamaker/Bennie Brownlow
Marshall Indians#	12	17	.414	NA	Abe Bowman
Longview Cannibals#	9	20	.310	NA	Bennie Brownlow

#Longview withdrew May 21, and the league then voted Marshall out to even the number of teams. Both teams disbanded May 22.

Playoff: Tyler 4 games, Mexia 2.

BA: Carl Reynolds, Palestine, .376
Runs: Buster Wisrock, Marshall/Tyler, 87
Hits: Carl Reynolds, Palestine, 180
HRs: Tom Pyle, Tyler, 26

Wins: Gene McClung, Corsicana/Mexia, 21
SOs: E.H. McBride, Longview/Corsicana, 139
Pct: Altus "Nick" Carter, Mexia, .810, 17-4

D Mississippi Valley League
President: Michael H. Sexton

Standings	W	L	Pct.	GB	Manager
Dubuque Dubs	66	41	.617	1½	Bill Speas
Waterloo Hawks	75	47	.615	—	Cletus Dixon
Burlington Bees	71	52	.577	4½	Ed Reichle
Marshalltown Ansons	65	54	.546	8½	Bill Shollenberger
Moline Plowboys	63	55	.534	10	Fred Mollwitz
Cedar Rapids Bunnies	50	70	.417	24	Pete Hughes/Herrick "Spoke" Emery
Rock Island Islanders	40	75	.348	31½	Joe Kernan
Ottumwa Packers	41	77	.347	32	Pat Harkins

BA: Jim Stroner, Rock Island, .380
Runs: James Worth, Dubuque, 127
Hits: James Worth, Dubuque, 171
HRs: Len Koenecke, Moline, 20

Wins: Duncan Grant, Waterloo, 22
SOs: Harold McKain, Waterloo, 147
          Duncan Grant, Waterloo, 147
Pct: Elbert Fisch, Dubuque, .800, 20-5

D Texas Valley League

Standings	W	L	Pct.	GB	Manager
Mission Grapefruiters	62	55	.523	—	Ed Marburger
Corpus Christi Seahawks** ..	63	56	.529	—	Jimmy Payton

Edinburg Bobcats .... 57 58 .496   4   Cam Hill
Laredo Oilers* .... 53 66 .445 10   George "Tex" Wisterzil

Playoff: Corpus Christi 3 games, Laredo 0.

BA: Garland Orr, Mission, .372   **Wins:** Herbert Pyle, Mission, 15
Runs: Leslie Mallon, Mission, 94   Glenn Brown, Corpus Christi, 15
Hits: Leslie Mallon, Mission, 162   **SOs:** Fay Haddock, Laredo, 113
HRs: Jack Holloway, Mission, 17   **Pct:** R.S. Hill, Laredo, .750, 12-4

1927 Interleague Post Season Play

World Series
New York (American) 4 games, Pittsburgh (National) 0

Junior World Series
Toledo (American Association) 5 games, Buffalo (International) 1

Dixie Series
Wichita Falls (Texas) 4 games, New Orleans (Southern Association) 0
Total Attendance: 32,687

Dixie Series
Waco (Texas-2nd place) 3 games, Tulsa (Western) 2, one tie
Total Attendance: 10,000

Eastern Championship
Buffalo (International) 2 games, Albany (Eastern) 1

Class B Championship
Harrisburg (New York-Pennsylvania) 2 games, Portsmouth (Virginia) 1

Southern Championship
Greenville (South Atlantic Association) 4 games, Portsmouth (Virginia) 1

Southern Championship
Jacksonville (Southeastern) 4 games, Greenville (South Atlantic Association) 3

Five-State Championship
Parksley (Eastern Shore) 4 games, Chambersburg (Blue Ridge) 2

1927 No-Hitters

Date	Pitcher	Team	League	Opponent	Score
4-23	Alex Orr	Tyler	Lone Star	Palestine	
5-13	Lefty Holman	Corpus Christi	Texas Valley	Mission	5-0
5-21	Frank Tubbs	Oklahoma City	Western	Lincoln	9-0
5-24	Fred DeLoach	Savannah	Southeastern	Selma	8-0
6-21	John Trippe	Cambridge	Eastern Shore	Easton	(7)
6-24	Walter Tauscher	Columbia	South Atlantic	Knoxville	7-0
6-25	William Helmick	Fairmont	Middle Atlantic	Scottdale	3-0 (7)
6-28	Charley Newbill	Idaho Falls	Utah-Idaho	Twin Falls	4-0
7-4	Rex Adkins	Hattiesburg	Cotton States	Gulfport	
7-30	Dick Woodward	Haverhill	New England	Lynn	7-2
7-31	Syl Johnson	Syracuse	International	Buffalo	2-0
8-3	Steve Ellis	Oklahoma City	Western	Omaha	7-1
8-12	Maurice Clark	Texarkana	Lone Star	Mexia	7-0
8-22	Earl Hanson	Harrisburg	New York-Penn.	Binghamton	4-0 (7)
8-23	John Prudhomme	Toronto	International	Reading	14-0
8-27	K.E. McNeill	Augusta	South Atlantic	Asheville	1-0 (7)
8-29	Bill Fitzpatrick	Spartanburg	South Atlantic	Charlotte	9-1
9-8	Bill Lucas	Binghamton	New York-Penn.	Shamokin	1-0

Number in parentheses indicates innings if other than nine; "P" indicates perfect game.

THIS DATE IN MINOR LEAGUE HISTORY

March 5, 1927, Fred Merkle, former Giants first baseman, was appointed manager of Reading, International League.

April 25, 1927, George Magerkurth, American Association umpire, was fined $25 plus costs and sentenced to 30 days in jail in Indianapolis on charges of assault and battery on Guy Griffin, Milwaukee first baseman. The jail sentence was suspended. Magerkurth was arrested the previous night following a fight in Griffin's hotel room, which was the aftermath of an argument during the day's game. Griffin was hospitalized with a broken shoulder and was sidelined for about one month.

May 3, 1927, Outfielder Frank Wilson hit four doubles in a game for Milwaukee, American Association.

May 5, 1927, Shortstop Edward Hock of Houston, Texas League, made an unassisted triple play at Dallas.

May 10, 1927, Shortstop Leo Durocher of St. Paul, American Association, had only one chance in a 14-inning game, a putout in the seventh frame.

May 18, 1927, Syracuse led the International League for the first time since the circuit was reorganized.

May 28, 1927, Pitcher Ned Potter, in a relief role for Birmingham, Southern Association, managed to strike out the side despite walking five, hitting one batter and uncorking a wild pitch.

May 30, 1927, Reading, managed by Fred Merkle, ended a 32-game losing streak by defeating Baltimore in International League action.

June 10, 1927, George Stallings resigned as manager of Rochester, International League.

June 11, 1927, Fred Werber of Augusta, South Atlantic Association, stole seven bases in a nine-inning game, setting an all-time Organized Ball record.

July 17, 1927, Buffalo lost two games to Newark after having won 14 games in succession.

July 18, 1927, Outfielder Clay Hopper of Danville, Three-I League, hit four home runs in one game against Quincy.

July 18, 1927, Del Bissonette drove in eight runs in one game for Buffalo, International League.

July 23, 1927, Thomas Daly of Jersey City, International League, hit two grand slams against Baltimore, in the fifth and ninth innings.

August 10, 1927, The St. Louis Stars played to the largest crowd ever to witness a regular Negro National League baseball game. Approximately 14,000 fans jammed the stands, including noted Black Baseball historian Tweed Webb. First baseman Willie Bobo knocked a home run over the car shed to beat Rube Foster's Chicago Giants 1-0.

August 10, 1927, At the age of 42, Jack Warhop, once a New York Yankee mound ace, twirled a doubleheader victory for Bridgeport over Albany in the Eastern League. In the nightcap, Warhop won 1-0 in ten innings.

August 11, 1927, Chuck Klein made his Organized Ball debut with Evansville of the Three-I League. He played in 14 games with a batting average of .327 before spraining an ankle.

August 15, 1927, Shortstop Jess Runser of Evansville, Three-I League, made an unassisted triple play when he caught a liner, stepped on second, then tagged the runner going from first to second.

August 20, 1927, Minneapolis, American Association, hit six home runs, catcher Kenna getting two in one frame.

August 20, 1927, Ray Rohwer of Sacramento, Pacific Coast League, sacrificed four times against Hollywood; he also had one walk and was hit by a pitch, for no official at bats in six trips.

August 28, 1927, An American Association game at Kansas City drew 28,973 fans.

September 2, 1927, Second baseman Lew Malone of Buffalo, International League, accepted 16 chances in a nine inning game.

September 4, 1927, Elmer Smith of Portland, Pacific Coast League, walloped his 40th home run of the season.

September 7, 1927, Paul Block, a newspaper and magazine publisher, purchased the Newark International League club for a sum said to be $360,000.

October 12, 1927, San Francisco's Lefty O'Doul was named the MVP of the Pacific Coast League for 1927. He was voted a cash prize of $1,000 by the directors of the league.

October 26, 1927, Former Washington pitcher Walter Johnson was signed to a two-year contract to manage Newark of the International League.

November 25, 1927, The Jersey City franchise in the International League was moved to Montreal.

1928

American League
President: Ernest S. Barnard

Standings	W	L	Pct.	GB	Attend.	Manager
New York Yankees	101	53	.656	—	1,072,132	Miller Huggins
Philadelphia Athletics	98	55	.641	2½	689,756	Connie Mack
St. Louis Browns	82	72	.532	19	339,497	Dan Howley
Washington Senators	75	79	.487	26	378,501	Bucky Harris
Chicago White Sox	72	82	.468	29	494,152	Ray Schalk/Lena Blackburne
Detroit Tigers	68	86	.442	33	474,323	George Moriarty
Cleveland Indians	62	92	.403	39	375,907	Roger Peckinpaugh
Boston Red Sox	57	96	.373	43½	396,920	Bill Carrigan

BA: Goose Goslin, Washington, .379
Runs: Babe Ruth, New York, 163
Hits: Heinie Manush, St. Louis, 241
RBIs: Lou Gehrig, New York, 142
 Babe Ruth, New York, 142
HRs: Babe Ruth, New York, 54

Wins: Lefty Grove, Philadelphia, 24
 George Pipgras, New York, 24
SOs: Lefty Grove, Philadelphia, 183
ERA: Garland Braxton, Washington, 2.51
Pct: General Alvin Crowder, St. Louis, .808, 21-5

National League
President: John A. Heydler

Standings	W	L	Pct.	GB	Attend.	Manager
St. Louis Cardinals	95	59	.617	—	761,574	Bill McKechnie
New York Giants	93	61	.604	2	916,191	John McGraw
Chicago Cubs	91	63	.591	4	1,143,740	Joe McCarthy
Pittsburgh Pirates	85	67	.559	9	495,070	Donie Bush
Cincinnati Reds	78	74	.513	16	490,490	Jack Hendricks
Brooklyn Robins	77	76	.503	17½	664,863	Wilbert Robinson
Boston Braves	50	103	.327	44½	227,001	Jack Slattery/Rogers Hornsby
Philadelphia Phillies	43	109	.283	51	182,168	Burt Shotton

BA: Rogers Hornsby, Boston, .387
Runs: Paul Waner, Pittsburgh, 142
Hits: Fred Lindstrom, New York, 231
RBIs: Jim Bottomley, St. Louis, 136
HRs: Hack Wilson, Chicago, 31
 Jim Bottomley, St. Louis, 31

Wins: Larry Benton, New York, 25
 Burleigh Grimes, Pittsburgh, 25
SOs: Dazzy Vance, Brooklyn, 200
ERA: Dazzy Vance, Brooklyn, 2.09
Pct: Larry Benton, New York, .735, 25-9

AA American Association
President: Thomas J. Hickey

Standings	W	L	Pct.	GB	Attend.	Manager
Indianapolis Indians	99	68	.593	—	162,992	Bruno Betzel
Minneapolis Millers	97	71	.577	2½	252,875	Mike Kelley
Milwaukee Brewers	90	78	.536	9½	307,374	Jack Lelivelt
Kansas City Blues	88	80	.524	11½	249,113	Dutch Zwilling
St. Paul Saints	88	80	.524	11½	175,638	Nick Allen
Toledo Mud Hens	79	88	.473	20	182,814	Casey Stengel
Columbus Senators	68	100	.405	31½	120,609	Nemo Leibold
Louisville Colonels	62	106	.369	37½	95,594	Bill Meyer

All-Star Team: 1B-Joe Kuhel, Kansas City; **2B**-Eddie Sicking, Louisville; **3B**-Fred Haney, Indianapolis; **SS**-Rabbit Warstler, Indianapolis; **OF**-Adam Comorosky, Indianapolis; Denver Grigsby, Kansas City; Ernie Orsatti, Minneapolis; **C**-Rick Ferrell, Columbus; **P**-Fred Heimach, St. Paul; Emil Yde, Indianapolis; Jimmy Zinn, Kansas City; Steve Swetonic, Indianapolis; Huck Betts, St. Paul; Ben Tincup, Louisville.

BA: Bobby Veach, Toledo, .382
Runs: Spencer Harris, Minneapolis, 133
Hits: Eddie Sicking, Louisville, 242
RBIs: Dudley Branom, Louisville, 128

HRs: Spencer Harris, Minneapolis, 32
Wins: James Wingard, Milwaukee, 24
SOs: Claude Jonnard, Milwaukee, 150
ERA: Fred Heimach, St. Paul, 2.76

AA International League
President: John Conway Toole

Standings	W	L	Pct.	GB	Attend.	Manager
Rochester Red Wings	90	74	.549	—	235,566	Billy Southworth
Buffalo Bisons	92	76	.548	—	247,979	Bill Clymer
Toronto Maple Leafs	86	80	.518	5	202,864	Bill O'Hara
Reading Keys	84	83	.503	7½	176,668	Harry Hinchman
Baltimore Orioles	82	82	.500	8	137,514	Jack Dunn
Montreal Royals	84	84	.500	8	214,057	George Stallings/Ed Holly
Newark Bears	81	84	.491	9½	262,656	Walter Johnson
Jersey City Skeeters	66	102	.393	26	68,868	Frank Gilhooley

All-Star Team: 1B-Dale Alexander, Toronto; **2B**-Herb Thomas, Buffalo; **3B**-Joe Brown, Rochester; **SS**-Charlie Gelbert, Rochester; **OF**-Billy Southworth, Rochester; Dick Porter, Baltimore; Hobart Whitman, Reading; **C**-Louis Leggett, Reading; Lee Head, Jersey City; **P**-Harry Seibold, Reading; Warren Collins, Toronto; Jack Ogden, Buffalo.

BA: Dale Alexander, Toronto, .380
Runs: Charlie Gelbert, Rochester, 145
Hits: Dale Alexander, Toronto, 236
RBIs: Dale Alexander, Toronto, 144

HRs: Dale Alexander, Toronto, 31
Wins: Harry Seibold, Reading, 22
SOs: Guy Cantrell, Baltimore, 165
ERA: Maurice Bream, Jersey City, 2.32

AA Pacific Coast League
President: Harry A. Williams

Standings	W	L	Pct.	GB	Attend.	Manager
San Francisco Seals*	120	71	.628	—	414,854	Nick Williams
Sacramento Senators**	112	79	.586	8	275,839	Buddy Ryan
Hollywood Stars	112	79	.586	8	363,319	Oscar Vitt
Mission Reds	99	92	.518	21	250,276	Red Killefer
Oakland Oaks	91	100	.476	29	230,088	Ivan Howard
Los Angeles Angels	87	104	.455	33	286,855	Marty Krug
Portland Beavers	79	112	.414	41	130,479	Ernie Johnson/Bill Rogers
Seattle Indians	64	127	.335	56	96,660	Jimmy Middleton

Playoff: Sacramento 2 games, San Francisco 0, for the second half title.
Finals: San Francisco 4 games, Sacramento 2.

All-Star Team: 1B-Earl Sheely, Sacramento; **2B**-Johnny Kerr, Hollywood; **3B**-Jim McLaughlin, Sacramento; **SS**-Lynn Lary, Oakland; Dudley Lee, Hollywood; **OF**-Roy Johnson, San Francisco; Earl Averill, San Francisco; Smead Jolley, San Francisco; **C**-John Bassler, Hollywood; **Util**-Sloppy Thurston, San Francisco; **P**-Dutch Ruether, San Francisco.

BA: Smead Jolley, San Francisco, .404
Runs: Earl Averill, San Francisco, 178
Hits: Smead Jolley, San Francisco, 309
RBIs: Smead Jolley, San Francisco, 188
HRs: Smead Jolley, San Francisco, 45

TBs: Smead Jolley, San Francisco, 516
Wins: Dutch Ruether, San Francisco, 29
SOs: Elmer Jacobs, San Francisco, 159
ERA: Elmer Jacobs, San Francisco, 2.56

A Eastern League
President: Herman J. Weisman

Standings	W	L	Pct.	GB	Manager
New Haven Profs	92	61	.601	—	Eugene McCann
Pittsfield Hillies	87	65	.572	4½	Shano Collins
Albany Senators	81	70	.537	10	Bill McCorry
Providence Grays	79	71	.527	11½	King Bader
Hartford Senators	78	72	.520	12½	Paddy O'Connor
Springfield Ponies	78	73	.516	13	Joe Benes
Bridgeport Bears	77	76	.503	15	Bill Whitman/Bob Emmerich
Waterbury Brasscos	34	118	.224	57½	Dick Rudolph/William Stewart

All-Star Team: 1B-Francis Farrell, Albany; **2B**-Walter Gautreau, Providence; **3B**-Eugene Sheridan, Pittsfield; **SS**-Coburn Jones, Bridgeport; **OF**-Jim Blakesley, New Haven; Sam Byrd, Albany; George Loepp, Pittsfield; **C**-Robert Munn, Albany; C.A. Niebergall, Springfield; **P**-Joseph Zubris, New Haven; Herman Kemner, New Haven; Earl Johnson, Albany; Joe Cascarella, Pittsfield; Hal Jeffcoat, Albany; James Bishop, Bridgeport; **MVP**-Earl Johnson, Albany.

BA: Jim Blakesley, New Haven, .382
Runs: Sam Byrd, Albany, 120
Hits: Jim Blakesley, New Haven, 217
RBIs: John Wight, Springfield, 114

HRs: John Roser, Hartford, 27
Wins: Earl Johnson, Albany, 21
SOs: Herman Kemner, New Haven, 142
ERA: Herman Kemner, New Haven, 2.52

A Southern Association
President: John D. Martin

Standings	W	L	Pct.	GB	Attend.	Manager
Birmingham Barons*	99	54	.647	—	261,824	Johnny Dobbs
Memphis Chickasaws**	97	55	.638	1½	187,753	Tommy "Doc" Prothro
New Orleans Pelicans	73	74	.497	23	176,018	Larry Gilbert
Mobile Bears	74	76	.493	23½	85,892	Milt Stock/Rudy Hulswitt
Little Rock Travelers	72	82	.468	27½	61,474	Bill Rogers/Jack Steele
Chattanooga Lookouts	67	85	.441	31½	102,324	Jim Johnston/Joe Mathes
Atlanta Crackers	66	87	.431	33	172,710	Bert Niehoff/Wilbur Good
Nashville Volunteers	59	94	.386	40	96,396	James Hamilton/Clarence "Pants" Rowland

Playoff: Birmingham 4 games, Memphis 0.

All-Star Team: 1B-Jim Poole, Atlanta; **2B**-Stuffy Stewart, Birmingham; **3B**-Tommy "Doc" Prothro, Memphis; **SS**-Ray Gardner, New Orleans; **OF**-Nick Cullop, Atlanta; Johnny Frederick, Memphis; Elliott Bigelow, Birmingham; **C**-Yam Yaryan, Birmingham; Bill Dickey, Little Rock; **Util**-Billy Rhiel, Atlanta; **P**-Eddie Wells, Birmingham; Harry Kelly, Memphis; Clarence Griffin, Memphis; Whitey Glazner, Mobile; Luther Roy, Birmingham; Dave Danforth, New Orleans.

BA: Elliott Bigelow, Birmingham, .395
Runs: Stuffy Stewart, Birmingham, 138
Hits: Johnny Frederick, Memphis, 221
RBIs: Mule Shirley, Birmingham, 133

HRs: Dick Wade, Nashville, 24
Wins: Eddie Wells, Birmingham, 25
SOs: Eddie Wells, Birmingham, 129
ERA: Harry Kelly, Memphis, 2.38

A Texas League
President: J. Doak Roberts

Standings	W	L	Pct.	GB	Attend.	Manager
Houston Buffaloes*	104	54	.658	—	186,469	Frank Snyder
Wichita Falls Spudders**	104	56	.650	1	103,228	Carl Williams/Jim "Bad News" Galloway

	W	L	Pct.	GB		
Ft. Worth Panthers	83	73	.532	20	119,446	Jake Atz
Shreveport Sports	79	81	.494	26	81,920	Art Phelan
San Antonio Bears	76	83	.478	28½	106,517	Frank Gibson
Waco Cubs	71	87	.449	33	60,978	Del Pratt
Dallas Steers	66	93	.415	38½	135,069	Herbert Ellison/Bob Tarleton/Hap Morse
Beaumont Exporters	50	106	.321	53	41,551	Claude "Ug" Robertson

Playoff: Houston 3 games, Wichita Falls 1.

BA: George Blackerby, Waco, .368
Runs: Tom Jenkins, Wichita Falls, 121
Hits: Bob Worthington, Houston, 211
RBIs: Tom Jenkins, Wichita Falls, 122
HRs: Tom Jenkins, Wichita Falls, 27
Wins: Jim Lindsay, Houston, 25
SOs: Bill Hallahan, Houston, 244
ERA: Bill Hallahan, Houston, 2.25

A Western League
President: Dale D. Gear

Standings	W	L	Pct.	GB	Manager
Oklahoma City Indians*	95	67	.586	—	Howard Gregory
Tulsa Oilers**	96	69	.582	½	Marty Berghammer
Wichita Larks	94	70	.573	2	Otis "Doc" Crandall/Art Griggs
Pueblo Steel Workers	85	78	.521	10½	Spencer Abbott
Denver Bears	81	84	.491	15½	Jack Knight
Omaha Crickets	71	86	.452	21½	Fred Luderus/Barney Burch
Amarillo Texans	60	93	.392	30½	Sled Allen/Tom Connelly/L.A. Ripperton
Des Moines Demons	63	98	.391	31½	Lute Boone/Archie Yelle/Lee Fohl

Attendance: Tulsa, 145,000.

Playoff: Tulsa 4 games, Oklahoma City 1, one game was ruled no contest.

All-Star Team: 1B-Fred "Snake" Henry, Omaha; **2B**-Jack Saltzgaver, Oklahoma City; **3B**-Oscar Grimes, Tulsa; **SS**-George Knothe, Pueblo; **OF**-Joe Munson (Carlson), Tulsa; Leon Riley, Pueblo; Estel Crabtree, Oklahoma City; **C**-Arndt Jorgens, Oklahoma City; Irving "Jack" Burns, Omaha; **Util**-Joe Mayes, Tulsa; **P**-Chad Kimsey, Tulsa; William Hargrove, Pueblo; Barney Bornholdt, Oklahoma City; Lou Fette, Pueblo; George Darrow, Oklahoma City; Max Thomas, Omaha.

BA: Joe Munson (Carlson), Tulsa, .385
Runs: Joe Munson (Carlson), Tulsa, 171
Jim Stroner, Wichita, 171
Hits: Jim Stroner, Wichita, 255
HRs: Jim Stroner, Wichita, 42
Wins: Barney Bornholdt, Oklahoma City, 24
SOs: Barney Bornholdt, Oklahoma City, 154
Pct.: Chad Kimsey, Tulsa, .767, 23-7

B Central League
President: L.J. Wylie

Standings	W	L	Pct.	GB	Manager
Erie Sailors**	76	59	.563	—	Frank "Buzz" Wetzel
Dayton Aviators	76	59	.563	—	Everett Booe
Fort Wayne Chiefs*	72	62	.537	3½	Punch Knoll
Akron Tyrites	67	65	.508	7½	John McCloskey
Springfield Buckeyes	67	66	.504	8	Joe Dunn
Canton Terriers	43	90	.323	32	Joe Agler/Dan O'Leary

Playoff: Fort Wayne 4 games, Erie 2.

All-Star Team: 1B-Lee Walsh, Fort Wayne; **2B**-Myers, Fort Wayne; **3B**-Lee Cunningham, Dayton; **SS**-Hap Briscoe, Erie; **OF**-Chuck Klein, Fort Wayne; Clarence Beasley, Erie; Frank Brozovitch, Erie/Canton; **P**-Bert Grimm, Akron; Marv Gudat, Dayton.

BA: James Jordan, Dayton, .362
Runs: James Jordan, Dayton, 130
Hits: James Jordan, Dayton, 212
HRs: James Jordan, Dayton, 27
Wins: Alex McColl, Akron, 19
Bert Grimm, Akron, 19
SOs: Edgar Clough, Dayton, 130
ERA: Alex McColl, Akron, 2.73

B New England League
President: Claude B. Davidson

Standings	W	L	Pct.	GB	Manager
Lynn Papooses**	56	44	.560	—	Thomas "Poke" Whalen
Manchester Blue Sox	51	43	.543	2	Henry LaVallie
Lewiston Twins	51	46	.526	3½	Jesse Burkett
Brockton Shoemakers	51	48	.515	4½	Lew Courtney
Salem Witches	51	50	.505	5½	Stuffy McInnis
Attleboro Burros*	47	49	.490	7	Patsy Donovan
Haverhill Hillies	46	48	.489	7	John Kiernan/Jack Ryan
Portland Mariners	39	64	.379	18½	Duffy Lewis

Playoff: Lynn 4 games, Attleboro 3.

BA: Bob Gill, Attleboro/Portland/Lewiston, .344
Runs: Roy Hutson, Attleboro, 85
Hits: Billy Jurges, Manchester, 127
RBIs: August Snyder, Manchester, 75
HRs: Henry Bosse, Brockton, 12
Wins: William Diehl, Lewiston, 21
John Pomorski, Attleboro, 21
SOs: Leon Chagnon, Lynn, 124
ERA: William Diehl, Lewiston, 1.19

B New York-Pennsylvania League
President: John H. Farrell

Standings	W	L	Pct.	GB	Manager
Harrisburg Senators	82	54	.603	—	Glenn Killinger
Binghamton Triplets	83	57	.593	1	Mike McNally
Wilkes-Barre Barons	71	65	.522	11	Mike Konnick
Williamsport Grays	69	71	.493	15	George Burns
York White Roses	65	72	.474	17½	Win Clark
Syracuse Stars	64	74	.464	19	Mike O'Neill
Scranton Miners	58	77	.430	23½	Gus Getz
Elmira Colonels	58	80	.420	25	Jack Sheehan

Total Attendance: 503,909.

BA: Dave Robertson, York, .360
Runs: Hubert Mason, Scranton, 95
Hits: John Burke, Harrisburg, 163
RBIs: Glenn Killinger, Harrisburg, 82
HRs: Ray Flood, Harrisburg, 11
Bernard Hungling, Syracuse, 11
Wins: Clinton Brown, Harrisburg, 23
SOs: Herm Holzhouser, Binghamton, 153
ERA: John Milligan, Syracuse, 2.10

B South Atlantic Association
President: William G. Bramham

Standings	W	L	Pct.	GB	Manager
Asheville Tourists	97	49	.664	—	Ray Kennedy
Macon Peaches	80	68	.541	18	Wilbur Good
Augusta Tygers	75	69	.521	21	Joe Berger/Odie Strain
Spartanburg Spartans	73	72	.503	23½	Mike Kelly
Knoxville Smokies	73	75	.493	25	Gabby Street
Columbia Comers	67	78	.462	29½	Joe Kelly
Charlotte Hornets	60	86	.411	37	Heinie Groh/Abe Hood
Greenville Spinners	60	88	.405	38	Frank Walker

All-Star Team: 1B-Bob "Stuffy" McCrone, Macon; **2B**-Mack Hillis, Columbia; **3B**-Tom Osborne, Knoxville; **SS**-Ben Chapman, Asheville; **OF**-Oscar Felber, Knoxville; Allen Cooke, Asheville; Stan Keyes, Asheville; **C**-Roy Luebbe, Asheville; Al Lopez, Macon; **Util**-J.W. Watson, Asheville; **P**-William Harris, Asheville; Harry Smythe, Asheville; Norman Rauch, Macon; Leroy Mahaffey, Columbia, **Manager**-Ray Kennedy, Asheville.

BA: Oscar Felber, Knoxville, .366
Runs: Jarrett Hamilton, Knoxville, 118
Hits: Holt "Cat" Milner, Augusta, 193
RBIs: Cecil "Stormy" Davis, Augusta, 125
HRs: Clarence Walker, Greenville, 33
Wins: Norman Rauch, Macon, 26
SOs: Norman Rauch, Macon, 147
Leroy Mahaffey, Columbia, 147
ERA: Joseph Heving, Asheville, 2.46
Pct.: William Harris, Asheville, .735, 25-9

B Southeastern League
President: Cliff Green

Standings	W	L	Pct.	GB	Manager
Pensacola Flyers*	92	54	.630	—	Jim Johnston
Montgomery Lions**	91	57	.615	2	Bill Pierre
Tampa Krewes	72	76	.486	21	Roy Ellam
Jacksonville Tars	71	78	.477	22½	Art Bourg/Hardin Herndon
Columbus Foxes	61	84	.421	30½	Hardin Herndon/Bill White
Selma Cloverleafs	59	83	.415	31	Polly McLarry/Zinn Beck
Albany Nuts#	62	60	.508	NA	Joe Schepner/Tom McMillan
Savannah Indians#	49	65	.430	NA	Ray Schmandt

#Albany and Savannah withdrew August 12.

Playoff: Montgomery 4 games, Pensacola 2.

All-Star Team: 1B-Ray Schmandt, Savannah; **2B**-Wally Dashiell, Pensacola; **3B**-Otto Lind, Pensacola; **SS**-Joe Longnecker, Pensacola; **OF**-John "Moose" Clabaugh, Jacksonville; Tom Pyle, Pensacola; Pete Susko, Montgomery; **C**-Joe Palm, Montgomery; **P**-G. Johnston, Albany; Bill Clowers, Pensacola.

BA: John "Moose" Clabaugh, Jacksonville, .366
Runs: Tom Pyle, Pensacola, 110
Hits: Tom Pyle, Pensacola, 197
RBIs: Parker Perry, Albany/Selma, 118
HRs: Sam Stuart, Columbus, 17
Wins: Floyd Van Pelt, Montgomery, 26
SOs: Floyd Van Pelt, Montgomery, 183
ERA: Ralph Stewart, Montgomery, 2.24

B Three-I League
President: L.J. Wylie

Standings	W	L	Pct.	GB	Manager
Decatur Commodores**	81	49	.623	—	Frank Desseau
Terre Haute Tots*	75	59	.560	8	Pat Haley
Danville Veterans	69	57	.548	10	Joseph Schultz
Peoria Tractors	69	66	.511	14½	Ernest Krueger
Evansville Hubs	62	68	.477	19	Bob Coleman
Bloomington Bloomers	61	69	.469	20	William Campbell
Springfield Senators	60	74	.448	23	Carlisle Smith/Roy Whitcraft
Quincy Indians	50	85	.370	33½	Joseph Riggert/Harold Irelan

Attendance: Springfield, 61,171; Total, 360,836.

Playoff: Decatur 4 games, Terre Haute 1, one tie.

All-Star Team: 1B-James "Rip" Collins, Danville; **2B**-Tony Cuccinello, Danville; **3B**-Urban Pickering, Decatur; **SS**-John Burnett, Terre Haute; **OF**-Art Veltman, Springfield; Wade, Evansville; Floyd Patterson, Decatur; **C**-Claude "Bob" Linton, Decatur; Otto Krueger, Peoria; **P**-Harold McKain, Decatur; Wes Ferrell, Terre Haute; Al Grabowski, Danville; Leo Skidmore, Peoria; Whitlow Wyatt, Evansville.

BA: James "Rip" Collins, Danville, .388
Runs: Vern Blenkiron, Springfield, 117
Hits: Floyd Patterson, Decatur, 181
RBIs: James "Rip" Collins, Danville, 101
HRs: James "Rip" Collins, Danville, 19
　　Marucis Duffy, Peoria, 19

Wins: Wes Ferrell, Terre Haute, 20
　　Chester Howard, Decatur, 20
SOs: Whitlow Wyatt, Evansville, 138
ERA: Leo Skidmore, Peoria, 1.59

B Virginia League
President: William G. Bramham

Standings	W	L	Pct.	GB	Manager
Norfolk Tars	26	13	.667	—	Zinn Beck
Portsmouth Truckers	25	14	.641	1	J.F. "Stump" Edington
Petersburg Bronchos	15	27	.357	12½	Earl Hanson
Richmond Colts	15	27	.357	12½	Olin Perritt/Charles "Chief" Bender

The league disbanded June 3.

BA: Arthur Crump, Norfolk, .381
Runs: Carr Smith, Norfolk, 41
Hits: Hank Collenberger, Norfolk, 74
HRs: William Hohman, Richmond, 7

Wins: Joseph Heving, Portsmouth, 8
　　Jim Turner, Norfolk, 8
SOs: Pat Townsend, Norfolk, 51
ERA: Joseph Heving, Portsmouth, 1.82

C Middle Atlantic League
President: Elmer M. Daily

Standings	W	L	Pct.	GB	Manager
Cumberland Colts	75	49	.605	—	Johnny Byrne
Fairmont Black Diamonds**	70	51	.578	3½	Joe Phillips
Wheeling Stogies	68	52	.567	5	Bobby Prysock
Jeannette Jays	65	54	.546	7½	Lee Strait
Charleroi Babes	62	60	.508	12	Bill Phillips
Johnstown Johnnies	55	59	.482	15	Claude Roth/Mike Thompson/ Charles "Chief" Bender
Clarksburg Generals	42	76	.356	30	Moose Marshall/Web Cashion/Earl Neale
Scottdale Scotties	40	76	.345	31	Mike Flaherty

Playoff: Fairmont 4 games, Wheeling 2.

All-Star Team: 1B-Johnny Byrne, Cumberland; 2B-Lafe Byard, Johnstown; 3B-Ed Zupancic, Wheeling; SS-John Cortazzo, Johnstown; OF-Lewis, Wheeling; Eddie Conley, Cumberland; C-Mike Thompson, Johnstown; P-W.C. "Bill" Thomas, Wheeling; Gowell Claset, Wheeling.

BA: Bill Pritchard, Clarksburg/Wheeling, .370
Runs: Eddie Conley, Cumberland, 99
Hits: Dewey Stover, Clarksburg, 165
RBIs: Bob Holland, Fairmont, 96

HRs: Bob Holland, Fairmont, 20
Wins: Joseph Drugmond, Charleroi, 23
SOs: Joseph Drugmond, Charleroi, 149
ERA: Charles Herrell, Cumberland, 2.23

C Piedmont League
President: William G. Bramham

Standings	W	L	Pct.	GB	Manager
Winston-Salem Twins	82	51	.617	—	Bunn Hearn
High Point Pointers	83	52	.615	—	Danny Boone
Greensboro Patriots	76	56	.576	5½	Charlie Carroll
Salisbury-Spencer Colonials	61	74	.452	22	George Whiteman
Raleigh Capitals	56	74	.431	24½	Jim Viox/H. Dawson/Frank Edington
Durham Bulls	40	91	.305	41	George "Possum" Whitted

Playoff: Winston-Salem 4 games, High Point 3.

BA: Danny Boone, High Point, .419
Runs: Jim Stewart, High Point, 126
Hits: Danny Boone, High Point, 196
RBIs: Danny Boone, High Point, 131

HRs: Danny Boone, High Point, 38
Wins: Al Smith, Winston-Salem, 20
SOs: Max Wilson, Greensboro, 101
ERA: Jack Fogelman, Winston-Salem, 2.68

C Utah-Idaho League
President: Fred M. Nye

Standings	W	L	Pct.	GB	Manager
Salt Lake City Bees**	68	49	.581	—	Bob Coltrin
Boise Senators*	60	55	.522	7	Harry O'Neill
Pocatello Bannocks	57	58	.496	10	Jack Roche
Ogden Gunners	57	59	.491	10½	Del Baker
Twin Falls Bruins#	29	29	.500	NA	Bill Leard
Idaho Falls Spuds#	17	38	.309	NA	Pete Maloney

#Twin Falls and Idaho Falls disbanded July 5 at the end of the first half.

Playoff: Salt Lake City 4 games, Boise 1.

All-Star Team: 1B-Dolph Camilli, Salt Lake City; 2B-Arthur Parker, Pocatello; 3B-Johnny Vergez, Ogden; SS-James "Cat" Tierney, Pocatello; OF-Foy Frazier, Ogden; Forrest Jensen, Pocatello; Ed Coleman, Boise/Twin Falls; C-Harvey Hand, Salt Lake City; P-Val Glynn, Salt Lake City; Richard Young, Ogden.

BA: Ed Coleman, Boise/Twin Falls, .385
Runs: Arthur Parker, Pocatello, 122
Hits: Ed Coleman, Boise/Twin Falls, 167
HRs: Ed Coleman, Boise/Twin Falls, 26

Wins: Val Glynn, Salt Lake City, 16
　　Curt Davis, Salt Lake City, 16
　　George Hollerson, Boise, 16
SOs: Lefty Gomez, Salt Lake City, 172
ERA: George Hollerson, Boise, 3.34

C Western Association
President: Dale D. Gear

Standings	W	L	Pct.	GB	Manager
Ft. Smith Twins	74	63	.540	—	Runt Marr
Topeka Jayhawks	70	61	.534	1	Eddie Dyer
Joplin Miners*	70	65	.519	3	Mark Purtell
Independence Producers**	66	67	.496	6	Jimmy Payton
Springfield Midgets	61	66	.480	8	Bob Wells
Muskogee Chiefs	58	77	.430	15	Otto Williams

Playoff: Joplin 4 games, Independence 2.

All-Star Team: 1B-Ted Willis, Joplin; 2B-Dewey Bondurant, Independence; 3B-Paul Richards, Muskogee; SS-Ed Delker, Topeka; OF-Joe Robbins, Joplin; Bill Diester, Independence/Joplin; Ted Gullic, Independence; C-Jack Crouch, Joplin; P-Lefty House, Joplin; Lefty Connelly, Joplin; Sonny Ellis, Muskogee; Dick Gifford, Ft. Smith.

BA: Jack Crouch, Joplin, .358
Runs: Paul Richards, Muskogee, 119
Hits: Bill Diester, Independence/Joplin, 188
RBIs: Paul Richards, Muskogee, 109
HRs: Paul Richards, Muskogee, 36

Wins: Dick Gifford, Ft. Smith, 19
　　Floyd Rose, Topeka, 19
SOs: Steve Ellis, Independence, 155
ERA: Dick Gifford, Ft. Smith, 2.75

D Arizona State League
President: Paul Davis

Standings	W	L	Pct.	GB	Manager
Phoenix Senators	39	29	.574	—	Bert Whaling
Bisbee Bees	37	31	.544	2	Roy Johnson
Miami Miners	30	38	.441	9	Pete Compton
Tucson Waddies	30	38	.441	9	Cowboy "Rube" Foster

BA: John Alloway, Phoenix, .381
Runs: Lefty Colvard, Miami, 58
Hits: Eddie Miller, Bisbee, 104

HRs: Larmon Cox, Phoenix, 14
Wins: Tom Vaughn, Bisbee, 14

D Blue Ridge League
President: J. Vincent Jamison, Jr.

Standings	W	L	Pct.	GB	Manager
Hanover Raiders*	59	38	.608	—	Jess Altenberg/Walt Hammen/George Burns
Chambersburg Maroons**	57	37	.606	½	Mickey Keliher
Frederick Hustlers	47	49	.490	11½	Joe Neptune/Henry Sherry
Martinsburg Blue Sox	43	52	.453	15	Jess Runser/Jiggs Donohue
Hagerstown Hubs	43	52	.453	15	Bill Purtell/Lester Bangs/Joel Shelton
Waynesboro Red Birds	37	58	.389	21	Ed Miller/Harold Funk

Playoff: Hanover 4 games, Chambersburg 1.

BA: Walt Hammen, Hanover, .355
Runs: Raymond Zorman, Hanover, 76
Hits: Edward Millek, Martinsburg, 125
HRs: George Thomas, Hagerstown, 13

Wins: Sheriff Blake, Chambersburg, 17
SOs: Luke Hamlin, Hanover, 123
Pct: Sheriff Blake, Chambersburg, .773, 17-5

D Cotton States League
President: Frank A. Scott

Standings	W	L	Pct.	GB	Manager
Jackson Senators	77	45	.631	—	James "Snipe" Conley/Buck Stapleton
Meridian Mets	71	52	.577	6½	Howard Camp
Hattiesburg Pinetoppers*	66	52	.559	9	Herschel Bobo
Vicksburg Hill Billies**	67	56	.545	10½	Bob Taggert/Wray Query
Monroe Drillers	64	56	.533	12	Eddie Palmer
Gulfport Tarpons	50	65	.435	23½	Howard Knaupp
Laurel Cardinals	44	78	.361	33	John Ganzel/Bob Schang
Alexandria Reds	42	77	.353	33½	Sam Barnes/Frank Karpp

Playoff: Vicksburg 4 games, Hattiesburg 3.

BA: Mike Powers, Gulfport/Jackson, .383
Runs: Joe Granade, Monroe, 96
Hits: Mike Powers, Gulfport/Jackson, 174
　　Joe Granade, Monroe, 174

HRs: Horace Long, Jackson, 21
Wins: Ed Greer, Jackson, 20
SOs: Edward Durham, Jackson, 114
Pct: H.C. Perkins, Meridian, .800, 16-4

D Eastern Carolina League
President: William G. Bramham

Standings	W	L	Pct.	GB	Manager
Wilmington Pirates	68	46	.596	—	Hal Weafer
Goldsboro Manufacturers	66	48	.579	2	Jim Teague
Rocky Mount Buccaneers	55	56	.495	11½	Charles McMilan
Kinston Eagles	55	59	.482	13	Paul Bennett/Marty Walters
Fayetteville Highlanders	53	60	.469	14½	Lee Gooch/Pooly Hubert
Greenville Tobacconists	43	71	.377	25	Taylor Jolliff/Tom Abbott

Playoff: Goldsboro 4 games, Wilmington 2.

BA: Frank Roscoe, Wilmington, .387
Runs: Charles Hamel, Goldsboro, 101
Hits: Frank Roscoe, Wilmington, 154
RBIs: Frank Roscoe, Wilmington, 101
HRs: Frank Roscoe, Wilmington, 36
Wins: Ralph Carver, Goldsboro, 17

SOs: Bobo Newsom, Greenville/ Wilmington, 114
ERA: Eddie Alsobrook, Fayetteville/ Rocky Mount, 2.70
Pct: Ralph Carver, Goldsboro, .944, 17-1

D Eastern Shore League
President: J. Harry Rew

Standings	W	L	Pct.	GB	Manager
Northampton Red Sox	22	9	.710	—	Lester Bangs
Salisbury Indians	22	10	.688	½	Thomas "Poke" Whalen
Crisfield Crabbers	14	17	.452	8	Billy Lush
Cambridge Canners	13	19	.406	9½	Jiggs Donohue
Easton Farmers	13	20	.394	10	Dan Pasquella
Parksley Spuds	12	21	.364	11	John Pasquella

The league disbanded July 10.

D Florida State League
President: J.B. Asher

Standings	W	L	Pct.	GB	Manager
Ft. Lauderdale Tarpons/					
St. Petersburg Saints#	38	23	.623	—	Tom Leach
Orlando Colts	37	23	.617	½	Phil Wells
West Palm Beach Sheriffs	31	32	.492	8	Ernie Burke
Miami Hustlers	29	35	.453	10½	Lee Crowe
Daytona Beach Islanders	26	36	.419	12½	T. Simmons
Sanford Celeryfeds	25	37	.403	13½	Pop Wallace

#Ft. Lauderdale (13-12) moved to St. Petersburg May 24.
The league disbanded July 4, at the end of the first half.

D Georgia-Alabama League
President: C.I. Scarborough

Standings	W	L	Pct.	GB	Manager
Cedartown Sea Cows	55	34	.618	—	W.F. Kleton/Sherrod Smith
Carrollton Frogs*	54	34	.614	½	Paul Fittery
Anniston Nobles	47	42	.528	8	Ben Bruner/Bud Ammons
Talladega Indians**	45	43	.511	9½	Earl Hawkins/Lewis Walker
Gadsden Eagles	37	49	.430	16½	Doc Newton/Joe Schepner
Lindale Dragons	26	62	.295	28½	Earl Donaldson

Playoff: Talladega 2 games, Anniston 1, for the second half title.
Finals: Carrollton 4 games, Talladega 2.

BA: Clark Taliaferro, Carrollton, .392
Runs: Joyner White, Carrollton, 92
Hits: Murray Howell, Carrollton, 152
HRs: Joyner White, Carrollton, 27
Wins: Paul Fittery, Carrollton, 21
SOs: Adel White, Carrollton, 141
ERA: Paul Fittery, Carrollton, 1.60
Pct: Paul Fittery, Carrollton, .913, 21-2

D Lone Star League
President: Pat Newnam

Standings	W	L	Pct.	GB	Manager
Texarkana Twins**	75	47	.615	—	Charlie Miller
Palestine Pals*	72	51	.585	3½	Walt Alexander
Tyler Trojans	67	53	.558	7	George "Hickory" Jackson
Mexia Gushers	55	66	.455	19½	Roy Leslie
Corsicana Oilers	55	68	.447	20½	Ray Faltz
Paris Colts/Rustlers	42	81	.341	33½	Abe Bowman/Ewell "Turkey" Gross

Playoff: Palestine 4 games, Texarkana 1.

All-Star Team: 1B-Walt Alexander, Palestine; **2B**-Bobby Goff, Palestine; **3B**-James Adair, Paris; **SS**-Roy Smalley, Palestine; **OF**-Charlie Dorman, Tyler, Pete McLanahan, Palestine; **C**-Dooley Ferguson, Texarkana, Chandler, Paris; **P**-George Wood, Palestine.

BA: Charlie Dorman, Tyler, .408
Runs: Charlie Dorman, Tyler, 122
Hits: Charlie Dorman, Tyler, 188
HRs: Charlie Dorman, Tyler, 39
Wins: Ed Hopkins, Texarkana, 19
SOs: Ed Hopkins, Texarkana, 134
Pct: Philip Gallivan, Texarkana, .750, 15-5

D Mississippi Valley League
President: Belden Hill

Standings	W	L	Pct.	GB	Manager
Waterloo Hawks	81	41	.664	—	Cletus Dixon
Moline Plowboys	69	54	.561	12½	Richard Manchester
Rock Island Islanders	67	59	.532	16	Lester "Pat" Patterson
Dubuque Dubs	63	60	.512	18½	Bill Speas/John Armstrong
Burlington Bees	59	61	.492	21	Ed Reichle
Marshalltown Ansons	58	65	.472	22½	Jim Shollenberger/George Topmer/Ken Diamond
Ottumwa Packers	48	72	.400	32	Preston Gray/Bill Speas
Cedar Rapids Bunnies	45	78	.366	36½	Herrick "Spoke" Emery/Bob Hasbrook

BA: Len Koenecke, Moline, .389
Runs: Walter Genin, Rock Island, 115
Hits: Len Koenecke, Moline, 182
HRs: Len Koenecke, Moline, 22
Wins: Duncan Grant, Waterloo, 21
Ray Wolf, Moline, 21
SOs: Bob Weiland, Moline, 209
Pct: Duncan Grant, Waterloo, .808, 21-5

D Nebraska State League
President: James E. Beltzer

Standings	W	L	Pct.	GB	Manager
McCook Generals	71	49	.592	—	Elmer "Doc" Bennett
Lincoln Links	66	54	.550	5	Bob Browne
Beatrice Blues	64	56	.533	7	Hal Brokaw
North Platte Buffaloes	64	57	.529	7½	Joe Pizer
York Dukes	58	62	.483	13	Art Rasmussen
Norfolk Elkhorns	55	66	.455	16½	J. "Lefty" Wilkus
Grand Island Champs	52	68	.433	19	Clarence Clair/Alf Pierpoint/Fred Thomson/Clay Schoonover
Fairbury Jeffersons	51	69	.425	20	Lee Fairchild

BA: John Stoneham, McCook, .396
Runs: Herb Pember, McCook, 116
Hits: Herb Pember, McCook, 172
HRs: Walt Cookson, North Platte, 19
Wins: Ernest Krenk, Lincoln, 20
Harlan Pyle, McCook, 20
SOs: Joe Wilman, York, 164
ERA: Ernest Krenk, Lincoln, 2.57

D West Texas League
Presidents: J. McAllister Stevenson/E.E. Lowrie

Standings	W	L	Pct.	GB	Manager
San Angelo Red Snappers**	69	47	.595	—	Earl "Red" Snapp
Coleman Bobcats	67	49	.578	2	Bob Couchman
Abilene Aces*	61	54	.530	7½	Les Tullos
Midland Colts	52	64	.448	17	Jimmy Maloney/James "Snipe" Conley
Lubbock Hubbers	48	63	.432	18½	Bennie Brownlow/Ray "Red" Hill
Hamlin Pied Pipers/					
Big Spring Springers#	46	66	.411	21	Army Magness/Poston Baker/J.L. Thornton

#Hamlin (4-6 in the second half, 28-40 overall) moved to Big Spring July 3.

Playoff: San Angelo 3 games, Abilene 2.

BA: Bob Sanguinette, Midland, .394
Runs: Garland Orr, Abilene, 121
Hits: Garland Orr, Abilene, 171
HRs: Bob Sanguinette, Midland, 35
Wins: Jubilo Clements, San Angelo, 20
SOs: J.H. Hokey Garcia, San Angelo, 178
Pct: Clarence Williams, San Angelo, .737, 14-5

1928 Interleague Post Season Play

World Series
New York (American) 4 games, St. Louis (National) 0

Junior World Series
Indianapolis (American Association) 5 games, Rochester (International) 1, one tie
Total Attendance: 28,000 est.

Dixie Series
Houston (Texas) 4 games, Birmingham (Southern Association) 2
Total Attendance: 67,087

Southern Championship
Montgomery (Southeastern) 4 games, Asheville (South Atlantic Association) 2

Texas Class D Championship Series
Palestine (Lone Star) 4 games, San Angelo (West Texas) 0

Tri-State Series
Fairmont (Middle Atlantic) 4 games, Hanover (Blue Ridge) 0

1928 No-Hitters

Date	Pitcher	Team	League	Opponent	Score
5-15	Rudy Kneisch	Springfield	Central	Akron	4-0
5-20	Claude Davenport	Mission	Pacific Coast	Los Angeles	4-0 (7)
5-30	George Dresher	Wheeling	Middle Atlantic	Scottdale	4-0
6-15	Wayne Pollan	Mexia	Lone Star	Tyler	6-0
6-25	Fred Barron	Sanford	Florida State	Orlando	3-2 (8)
6-28	Howard Conklin	High Point	Piedmont	Winston-Salem	13-0
7-5	Bo Melinda	Texarkana	Lone Star	Paris	2-0
7-22	Jack Knight	Portland	Pacific Coast	Oakland	5-0
7-27	Nelson Greene	Des Moines	Western	Amarillo	3-0 (7)
7-29	Joe Smith	North Platte	Nebraska State	Beatrice	3-0
8-17	Chuck Roberts	Fairmont	Middle Atlantic	Charleroi	(7)
8-22	John Prudhomme	Toronto	International	Jersey City	5-0 (7)
8-25	Glenn Spencer	Columbia	South Atlantic	Charlotte	2-0 (7)
8-31	Lefty Lane	Talladega	Georgia-Alabama	Cedartown	4-0

Number in parentheses indicates innings if other than nine.

THIS DATE IN MINOR LEAGUE HISTORY

April 28, 1928, Denver, Western League, stranded 19 runners in a nine inning game against Tulsa.

June 11, 1928, Tommie Harris of Midland, West Texas League, stroked four home runs in a single game.

August 26, 1928, Louisville, American Association, lost its third straight double-header to Kansas City in as many days.

September 10, 1928, Macon hit 10 doubles in a South Atlantic Association game.

September 16, 1928, Walter Johnson made his final appearance as an active player. The former Washington star, manager of the Newark club in the International League, batted for pitcher Carl Fischer in the ninth inning and grounded out to third baseman Danny Clark. Baltimore won 7-1 behind Stu Bolen. Johnson pinch hit in six games, connecting once for a .167 average.

October 6, 1928, Indianapolis, American Association, beat Rochester, International League, in the Junior World Series, five games to one (with one tie). Steve Swetonic earned three of the Indianapolis victories.

October 22, 1928, John "Jack" Dunn, 54, owner of the Baltimore International League club, died suddenly astride the horse he was riding in Towson, Maryland. His club won seven successive International League pennants beginning in 1915. He sold many star players to the majors, including Babe Ruth, Lefty Grove, Frank Baker, Joe Boley, Max Bishop, Fritz Maisel, Bob Shawkey, Ben Egan, Jack Bentley, John Ogden and George Earnshaw. Dunn started as a pitcher in the minors in 1895 and played infield with Brooklyn, Philadelphia and New York of the National League, Baltimore of the American League, and Toronto of the Eastern League.

Toronto's Maple Leaf Stadium was opened on April 29, 1926 and built at a cost of $750,000. Capacity was about 20,000. This photo is from the mid 1950s.

1929

American League
President: Ernest S. Barnard

Standings	W	L	Pct.	GB	Attend.	Manager
Philadelphia Athletics	104	46	.693	—	839,176	Connie Mack
New York Yankees	88	66	.571	18	960,148	Miller Huggins/Art Fletcher
Cleveland Indians	81	71	.533	24	536,210	Roger Peckinpaugh
St. Louis Browns	79	73	.520	26	280,697	Dan Howley
Washington Senators	71	81	.467	34	355,506	Walter Johnson
Detroit Tigers	70	84	.455	36	869,318	Bucky Harris
Chicago White Sox	59	93	.388	46	426,795	Lena Blackburne
Boston Red Sox	58	96	.377	48	394,620	Bill Carrigan

BA: Lou Fonseca, Cleveland, .369
Runs: Charlie Gehringer, Detroit, 131
Hits: Dale Alexander, Detroit, 215
    Charlie Gehringer, Detroit, 215
RBIs: Al Simmons, Philadelphia, 157

HRs: Babe Ruth, New York, 46
Wins: George Earnshaw, Philadelphia, 24
SOs: Lefty Grove, Philadelphia, 170
ERA: Lefty Grove, Philadelphia, 2.81
Pct: Lefty Grove, Philadelphia, .769, 20-6

National League
President: John A. Heydler

Standings	W	L	Pct.	GB	Attend.	Manager
Chicago Cubs	98	54	.645	—	1,485,166	Joe McCarthy
Pittsburgh Pirates	88	65	.575	10½	491,377	Donie Bush/Jewel Ens
New York Giants	84	67	.556	13½	868,806	John McGraw
St. Louis Cardinals	78	74	.513	20	399,887	Billy Southworth/Gabby Street/Bill McKechnie
Philadelphia Phillies	71	82	.464	27½	281,200	Burt Shotton
Brooklyn Robins	70	83	.458	28½	731,886	Wilbert Robinson
Cincinnati Reds	66	88	.429	33	295,040	Jack Hendricks
Boston Braves	56	98	.364	43	372,351	Judge Emil Fuchs

BA: Lefty O'Doul, Philadelphia, .398
Runs: Rogers Hornsby, Chicago, 156
Hits: Lefty O'Doul, Philadelphia, 254
RBIs: Hack Wilson, Chicago, 159
HRs: Chuck Klein, Philadelphia, 43

Wins: Pat Malone, Chicago, 22
SOs: Pat Malone, Chicago, 166
ERA: Bob Walker, New York, 3.09
Pct: Charley Root, Chicago, .760, 19-6

AA American Association
President: Thomas J. Hickey

Standings	W	L	Pct.	GB	Attend.	Manager
Kansas City Blues	111	56	.665	—	281,376	Dutch Zwilling
St. Paul Saints	102	64	.614	8½	197,099	Eugene "Bubbles" Hargrave
Minneapolis Millers	89	78	.533	22	187,246	Mike Kelley
Indianapolis Indians	78	89	.467	33	105,982	Bruno Betzel
Louisville Colonels	75	90	.455	35	108,756	Allan Sothoron
Columbus Senators	75	91	.452	35½	138,849	Nemo Leibold
Milwaukee Brewers	69	98	.413	42	156,340	Jack Lelivelt/Marty Berghammer
Toledo Mud Hens	67	100	.402	44	106,021	Casey Stengel

All-Star Team: 1B-Dudley Branom, Louisville; **2B**-Tony Cuccinello, Columbus; **3B**-Ben Chapman, St. Paul; **SS**-Billy Rogell, St. Paul; **OF**-Marty Callaghan, Columbus; Dusty Cooke, St. Paul; Ollie Tucker, Kansas City; **C**-Eugene "Bubbles" Hargrave, St. Paul; Joseph Spring, Indianapolis; **Util**-Edgar Pick, Milwaukee; Estel Crabtree, Columbus; **P**-Archie Campbell, St. Paul; Huck Betts, St. Paul; Si Johnson, Columbus; Bill Burwell, Indianapolis; J.C. Benton, Minneapolis; Marion Thomas, Kansas City.

BA: Dusty Cooke, St. Paul, .358
Runs: Ben Chapman, St. Paul, 162
Hits: Tony Cuccinello, Columbus, 227
RBIs: Dusty Cooke, St. Paul, 148
HRs: Dusty Cooke, St. Paul, 33
Wins: Louis Polli, St. Paul, 22
SOs: Jack Brillheart, Minneapolis, 134
ERA: Archie Campbell, St. Paul, 2.79

AA International League
President: Charles H. Knapp

Standings	W	L	Pct.	GB	Attend.	Manager
Rochester Red Wings	103	65	.613	—	298,803	Billy Southworth
Toronto Maple Leafs	92	76	.548	11	163,562	Steve O'Neill
Baltimore Orioles	90	78	.536	13	155,855	Fritz Maisel
Montreal Royals	88	79	.527	14½	230,138	Ed Holly
Buffalo Bisons	83	84	.497	19½	186,876	Bill Clymer
Newark Bears	81	85	.488	21	223,931	Tris Speaker
Reading Keystones	80	86	.482	22	154,453	Harry Hinchman
Jersey City Skeeters	51	115	.307	51	67,627	Frank Gilhooley/Ted Jourdan

All-Star Team: 1B-James "Rip" Collins, Rochester; **2B**-Herb Thomas, Buffalo; **3B**-Joe Brown, Rochester; **SS**-Billy Urbanski, Montreal; **OF**-Danny Taylor, Reading; George Watkins, Rochester; George Fisher, Buffalo; **C**-Albert Bool, Baltimore; **P**-Tex Carleton, Rochester; Guy Cantrell, Toronto; Elon Hogsett, Montreal; Charles Fischer, Newark; **MVP**-George "Specs" Toporcer, Rochester.

BA: Danny Taylor, Reading, .371
Runs: George "Specs" Toporcer, Rochester, 142
Hits: Hobart Whitman, Reading, 230
RBIs: James "Rip" Collins, Rochester, 134

HRs: James "Rip" Collins, Rochester, 38
Wins: Elon Hogsett, Montreal, 22
SOs: Charles Fischer, Newark, 191
ERA: Hub Pruett, Newark, 2.43

AA Pacific Coast League
President: Harry A. Williams

Standings	W	L	Pct.	GB	Attend.	Manager
Mission Reds*	123	78	.612	—	275,996	Red Killefer
San Francisco Seals	114	87	.567	9	365,556	Nick Williams
Hollywood Stars**	113	89	.559	10½	313,243	Oscar Vitt
Oakland Oaks	111	91	.549	12½	231,728	Ivan Howard
Los Angeles Angels	104	98	.510	19½	341,173	Marty Krug/Jack Lelivelt
Portland Beavers	90	112	.446	33½	164,038	Bill Rogers
Sacramento Senators	85	117	.421	38½	164,158	Buddy Ryan
Seattle Indians	67	135	.332	56½	97,776	Ernie Johnson

Playoff: Hollywood 4 games, Mission 3.

All-Star Team: 1B-Jim Keesey, Portland; **2B**-Jimmy Reese, Oakland; **3B**-Johnny Vergez, Oakland; **SS**-Dudley Lee, Hollywood; **OF**-Elias "Liz" Funk, Hollywood; Arnold "Jigger" Statz, Los Angeles; Ike Boone, Mission; **C**-Hank Severeid, Hollywood; **P**-Frank Shellenback, Hollywood; Roy Mahaffey, Portland; Dutch Ruether, Mission.

BA: Ike Boone, Mission, .407
Runs: Gus Shur, San Francisco, 196
Hits: Ike Boone, Mission, 323
RBIs: Ike Boone, Mission, 218
HRs: Ike Boone, Mission, 55

TBs: Ike Boone, Mission, 553
Wins: Frank Shellenback, Hollywood, 26
SOs: Howard Craghead, Oakland, 190
ERA: Lefty Gomez, San Francisco, 3.43

A Eastern League
President: Herman J. Weisman

Standings	W	L	Pct.	GB	Manager
Albany Senators	97	57	.630	—	Bill McCorry
Bridgeport Bears	91	63	.591	6	Hans Lobert
Providence Grays	81	70	.537	16½	King Bader
Pittsfield Hillies	77	75	.507	19	Shano Collins
New Haven Profs	73	80	.477	24½	Gene Martin
Springfield Ponies	71	83	.461	27	George Burns
Allentown Dukes	61	90	.404	34½	Jim Trout
Hartford Senators	60	93	.392	36½	Heinie Groh

All-Star Team: 1B-Frank Farrell, Albany; **2B**-Frank Parenti, Albany; **3B**-Bernard Helgeth, Albany; **SS**-Eddie Marshall, Bridgeport; **OF**-Adolph Schinkle, Bridgeport; John Gill, Albany; Harold Yordy, Albany; **C**-Robert Munn, Albany; Arthur Pond, Providence; **Util**-Walter Kimmick, Bridgeport; **P**-Joe Bloomer, Springfield; Andy Rush, Allentown/Bridgeport; Clay Touchstone, Providence; James Weaver, New Haven; Earl Johnson, Albany.

BA: Walter Kimmick, Bridgeport, .376
Runs: John Gill, Albany, 150
Hits: John Gill, Albany, 232
RBIs: Harold Yordy, Albany, 170

HRs: Bruce Caldwell, New Haven, 41
Wins: Andy Rush, Allentown/Bridgeport, 23
SOs: Clay Touchstone, Providence, 132
ERA: James Weaver, New Haven, 3.28

A Southern Association
President: John D. Martin

Standings	W	L	Pct.	GB	Attend.	Manager
Birmingham Barons	93	60	.608	—	202,571	Johnny Dobbs
Nashville Volunteers	90	63	.588	3	154,113	Clarence "Pants" Rowland
New Orleans Pelicans	89	64	.582	4	194,803	Larry Gilbert
Memphis Chickasaws	88	66	.571	5½	154,249	Tommy "Doc" Prothro
Atlanta Crackers	78	75	.510	15	183,902	Wilbur Good
Little Rock Travelers	63	91	.409	30½	78,688	Jack Steele
Mobile Bears	57	95	.375	35½	74,405	Rudy Hulswitt
Chattanooga Lookouts	55	99	.357	38½	78,010	Jim Johnston

BA: Art Weis, Birmingham, .345
Runs: Tex Jeanes, Memphis, 120
Hits: Tom Oliver, Little Rock, 218
RBIs: Jim Poole, Atlanta/Nashville, 127
HRs: Jim Poole, Atlanta/Nashville, 33

Wins: Clarence Blethen, Atlanta, 22
    Benny Frey, Nashville, 22
    Bob Hasty, Birmingham, 22
SOs: William Hughes, Little Rock, 90
ERA: Benny Frey, Nashville, 3.05

*Won first-half   **Won second-half   ***Won both halves

A Texas League
President: William B. Ruggles

Standings	W	L	Pct.	GB	Attend.	Manager
Wichita Falls Spudders** ...	94	65	.591	—	94,795	Jim "Bad News" Galloway
Shreveport Sports	91	66	.580	2	106,403	Art Phelan
Dallas Steers*	91	69	.569	3½	181,548	Milt Stock
Ft. Worth Panthers............	84	76	.525	10½	107,075	Jake Atz/Frank Snyder
Waco Cubs........................	77	83	.481	17½	72,737	Del Pratt
Houston Buffaloes	73	86	.459	21	110,015	Frank Snyder/Eugene Bailey
Beaumont Exporters	72	87	.453	22	78,432	Claude "Ug" Robertson
San Antonio Indians	56	106	.346	39½	77,086	William Alexander/Pat Newnam

Playoff: Dallas 3 games, Wichita Falls 1.

All-Star Team: 1B-William Kelley, Beaumont; **2B**-Cecil Stewart, Shreveport; **3B**-Ernie Holman, Shreveport; **SS**-Bill Akers, Beaumont; **OF**-Jim Moore, Dallas; Randy Moore, Dallas; George Blackerby, Waco; **C**-Pete Lapan, Wichita Falls; **Util**-Irving Jeffries, Dallas; Fred Bennett, Wichita Falls; **P**-Whitey Glazner, Dallas; George Payne, Wichita Falls; Vic Frasier, Dallas.

BA: Randy Moore, Dallas, .369
Runs: Edward Moore, Ft. Worth, 143
Hits: Randy Moore, Dallas, 245
RBIs: Fred Bennett, Wichita Falls, 145

HRs: George Blackerby, Waco, 33
Wins: George Payne, Wichita Falls, 28
SOs: Andy Messenger, Wichita Falls, 138
ERA: Vic Frasier, Dallas, 2.61

A Western League
President: Dale D. Gear

Standings	W	L	Pct.	GB	Manager
Tulsa Oilers......................	95	66	.590	—	Marty Berghammer/Nick Allen
Oklahoma City Indians.......	88	68	.564	4½	Lefty Leifield
Omaha Crickets	81	75	.519	11½	Barney Burch/Pug Griffin
Wichita Aviators................	77	79	.494	15½	Art Griggs
Denver Bears	73	81	.474	18½	Eddie Palmer
Topeka Jayhawks	75	85	.469	19½	Jimmy Payton
Des Moines Demons	72	86	.456	21½	Lee Fohl/Claude Davenport
Pueblo Steelworkers	69	90	.434	25	James "Cat" Tierney/Spencer Abbott

Attendance: Denver, 50,000; Tulsa, 145,000.

BA: Buster Chatham, Pueblo, .386
Runs: Joe Munson (Carlson), Tulsa, 167
Hits: Lin Storti, Tulsa, 230
HRs: Irving "Jack" Burns, Tulsa, 36

Wins: Glenn Spencer, Wichita, 24
John McGrew, Omaha, 24
SOs: Pat Caraway, Topeka, 159
Pct: Joe O'Dowd, Tulsa, .750, 15-5

B Central League
President: L.J. Wylie

Standings	W	L	Pct.	GB	Manager
Canton Terriers	80	58	.580	—	James Hamilton
Erie Sailors	78	61	.561	2½	Jocko Munch
Dayton Aviators	68	69	.496	11½	Merito Acosta
Fort Wayne Chiefs.............	68	70	.493	12	Everett Booe
Springfield Dunnmen	59	77	.434	20	Joseph Dunn
Akron Tyrites....................	58	76	.433	20	John McCloskey

Total Attendance: 248,013.

All-Star Team: 1B-Ted Donovan, Springfield; **2B**-Les Mallon, Akron; **3B**-Sylvester Simon, Erie; **SS**-Ed Taylor, Canton; **OF**-John Reider, Fort Wayne; Charles Hostetler, Akron; Tripp Sigman, Canton; **C**-Dewey Hill, Erie; **P**-Axel Lindstrom, Canton; Earl Browne, Dayton.

BA: Charles Hostetler, Akron, .360
Runs: Ken Hogan, Erie, 125
Hits: John Reider, Fort Wayne, 185
RBIs: John Reider, Fort Wayne, 134

HRs: Tripp Sigman, Canton, 41
Wins: Axel Lindstrom, Canton, 24
SOs: Carl Schoof, Erie, 120
ERA: Fred Pipgras, Canton, 2.51

B New England League
President: Claude B. Davidson

Standings	W	L	Pct.	GB	Attend.	Manager
Manchester Blue Sox**	82	47	.636	—	50,000	Win Clark
Lynn Papooses*	81	47	.633	½	42,000	Thomas "Poke" Whalen
New Bedford Millmen	62	51	.549	12	36,000	Jack Ryan
Lewiston Twins	61	56	.521	15	40,000	Jesse Burkett
Portland Mariners	61	64	.488	19	48,000	Ted Baldwin/Duffy Lewis
Brockton Shoemakers.........	55	69	.444	24½	27,000	Art Ryan
Lowell Millers/ Nashua Millionaires#......	41	69	.373	31½	20,000	Bill Merritt/Tom DeNoville
Haverhill Hillies/Fitchburg Wanderers/ Gloucester Hillies@.........	39	79	.331	37½	20,000	Jack Driscoll

#Lowell (13-22) moved to Nashua June 19.
@Haverhill (11-10) moved to Fitchburg July 28; Fitchburg (5-20) moved to Gloucester August 25.

Playoff: Manchester 4 games, Lynn 1.

BA: Russ Saunders, Portland, .399
Runs: August Snyder, Portland, 115
Hits: Joe Dwyer, Lynn, 192
RBIs: Russ Saunders, Portland, 145
HRs: Bernie McHugh, Portland/Lynn, 19

Wins: John Miller, Manchester, 23
SOs: William Diehl, Lewiston, 137
ERA: Walter Hayes, Manchester, 2.30
Pct: Leslie Shatzer, Manchester, .846, 11-2

B New York-Pennsylvania League
President: John H. Farrell

Standings	W	L	Pct.	GB	Manager
Binghamton Triplets	83	56	.597	—	Mike McNally
Williamsport Grays............	79	60	.568	4	Glenn Killinger
Harrisburg Senators	75	62	.547	7	Johnny Tillman
York White Roses..............	71	66	.518	11	John Bentley
Elmira Colonels................	66	72	.478	16½	Jake Pitler
Scranton Miners................	64	75	.460	19	Mike O'Neill
Syracuse Stars/ Hazleton Mountaineers#..	63	74	.460	19	Irvin "Kaiser" Wilhelm
Wilkes-Barre Barons	50	86	.367	31½	Mike Konnick/Don Sykes/ Charles "Punch" Knoll

#Syracuse (19-23) moved to Hazleton June 16 when Star Park collapsed, first home game June 23.
Total Attendance: 525,427.

All-Star Team: 1B-Cy Anderson, Williamsport; **2B**-Glenn Killinger, Williamsport; **3B**-Bobby Reece, Binghamton; **SS**-Johnny Shovlin, Binghamton; **OF**-Larry "Babe" Fischer, York; Arthur McHenry, Scranton; Carr Smith, Williamsport; **C**-Mickey O'Brien, Binghamton; Joe Glenn, Syracuse/Hazleton; **P**-Johnny Tillman, Harrisburg; James Lyle, Williamsport; Charles Schessler, Harrisburg; Harry Holsclaw, Syracuse/Hazleton; Thomas "Lefty" George, York.

BA: Cy Anderson, Williamsport, .382
Runs: Larry "Babe" Fischer, York, 115
Hits: Arthur McHenry, Scranton, 184
RBIs: Glenn Killinger, Williamsport, 82

HRs: Ray Flood, Harrisburg, 18
Arthur McHenry, Scranton, 18
Wins: Norman Lehr, Williamsport, 18
Johnny Tillman, Harrisburg, 18
SOs: Beryk Richmond, York, 124
ERA: Jim Brice, Binghamton, 2.59

B South Atlantic Association
President: William G. Bramham

Standings	W	L	Pct.	GB	Manager
Knoxville Smokies**	85	61	.582	—	Joe Schepner
Asheville Tourists*	84	62	.575	1	Mike Kennedy
Charlotte Hornets..............	79	67	.541	6	Dick Hoblitzel
Greenville Spinners	71	73	.486	13	Frank Walker
Macon Peaches	69	79	.466	17	Tom Rogers
Augusta Tygers	68	78	.466	17	Odie Strain
Columbia Comers	68	79	.463	17½	Joe Kelly
Spartanburg Spartans	59	84	.413	24½	Mike Kelly

Playoff: Knoxville 4 games, Asheville 1.

All-Star Team: 1B-Robert Hipps, Asheville; **2B**-Thorpe Hamilton, Knoxville; **3B**-Harry Daughtry, Charlotte; **SS**-Eric McNair, Knoxville; **OF**-Odie Strain, Augusta; C.F. Walker, Greenville; Stan Keyes, Asheville; **C**-Art McCrea, Knoxville; **Util**-Chick Outen, Asheville; **P**-Harry Smythe, Asheville; John Walker, Knoxville; Al Bates, Knoxville; Earl Brown, Charlotte; John Allen, Asheville.

BA: Stan Keyes, Asheville, .377
Runs: Elwood Smith, Knoxville, 119
Hits: Odie Strain, Augusta, 202
RBIs: Murray Howell, Greenville, 135
HRs: Frank Welch, Greenville, 29

Wins: John Walker, Knoxville, 25
SOs: John Allen, Asheville, 173
ERA: Dick Niehaus, Spartanburg, 2.80
Pct: John Walker, Knoxville, .735, 25-9

B Southeastern League
President: Cliff Green

Standings	W	L	Pct.	GB	Manager
Tampa Smokers**	79	56	.585	—	Frank "Pop" Kitchens
Selma Cloverleafs..............	77	60	.562	3	Zinn Beck
Montgomery Lions*	73	64	.533	7	Roy Ellam
Jacksonville Tars	68	68	.500	11½	Tom McMillan/Rube Marquard
Columbus Foxes	58	74	.439	19½	Frank Kohlbecker
Pensacola Flyers	52	85	.380	28	Jim Johnston/Tom Pyle

Total Attendance: 291,751.

Playoff: Montgomery 4 games, Tampa 3.

All-Star Team: 1B-Arthur Bourg, Jacksonville; **2B**-Harry Collenberger, Selma; **3B**-W.J. Meekin, Jacksonville; **SS**-Robert Lennox, Columbus; **OF**-Dick Tangeman, Pensacola; Jack Kloza, Montgomery; Parker Perry, Selma; **C**-Bailey Tipton, Montgomery; **P**-Pat Moulton, Montgomery; Henry Shoaf, Selma; Ray Phelps, Jacksonville.

BA: Dick Tangeman, Pensacola, .373
Runs: Arthur Bourg, Jacksonville, 108
Hits: Tom Pyle, Pensacola, 190
RBIs: Parker Perry, Selma, 107
HRs: Parker Perry, Selma, 12

Wins: Roy Appleton, Tampa, 26
SOs: Ray Phelps, Jacksonville, 136
ERA: Edward Chambers, Montgomery/
Pensacola, 2.16

B Three-I League
President: L.J. Wylie

Standings	W	L	Pct.	GB	Manager
Quincy Indians	82	56	.594	—	Walter Holke
Decatur Commodores	81	57	.587	1	Frank Desseau
Evansville Hubs	79	57	.581	2	Bob Coleman
Terre Haute Tots	72	66	.522	10	Earl Wolgamot
Bloomington Bloomers	70	70	.500	13	Pat Harkins
Peoria Tractors	61	76	.445	20½	Cliff Brady
Springfield Senators	59	77	.434	22	Roy Whitcraft
Danville Veterans	46	91	.336	35½	Joseph Schultz

Attendance: Decatur, 50,876; Total, 322,999.

All-Star Team: 1B-Walter Holke, Quincy; 2B-Cliff Brady, Peoria; 3B-George Detore, Decatur; SS-Walter Krehmeyer, Bloomington; OF-Bill Mizeur, Springfield; Marucis Duffy, Peoria; Nat Hickey, Decatur; C-Sanford Hamby, Springfield; P-Whitlow Wyatt, Evansville; Bob Coleman, Evansville.

BA: Floyd Patterson, Decatur, .348
Runs: George Detore, Decatur, 106
Hits: Clarence Beasley, Terre Haute, 180
RBIs: Lafe Byard, Decatur, 101
HRs: Marucis Duffy, Peoria, 21

Wins: Whitlow Wyatt, Evansville, 22
Elmer Ambrose, Quincy, 22
SOs: Whitlow Wyatt, Evansville, 177
ERA: Bill Martin, Evansville, 2.32

C Middle Atlantic League
President: Elmer M. Daily

Standings	W	L	Pct.	GB	Manager
Charleroi Governors*	67	47	.587	—	Bobby Rice
Wheeling Stogies**	67	47	.587	—	Pat Haley
Cumberland Colts	65	53	.551	4	Johnny Byrne
Fairmont Black Diamonds	58	55	.513	8½	Joe Phillips
Scottdale Scotties	57	58	.496	10½	Eddie Dyer
Clarksburg Generals	53	63	.457	15	Chap Marable
Jeannette Jays	50	66	.431	18	Lee Strait/Leo Hanley
Johnstown Johnnies	44	72	.379	24	Norm McNeil/Marty Fielder

Playoff: Charleroi 4 games, Wheeling 1.

BA: Fred Lucas, Charleroi, .407
Runs: George Durning, Cumberland, 96
Hits: Fred Lucas, Charleroi, 178
RBIs: Fred Lucas, Charleroi, 113

HRs: Fred Lucas, Charleroi, 21
Julius Solters, Fairmont, 21
Wins: Irvin Rase, Cumberland, 22
SOs: Clarence Heise, Scottdale, 154
ERA: Irvin Rase, Cumberland, 2.63

C Piedmont League
President: William G. Bramham

Standings	W	L	Pct.	GB	Manager
Durham Bulls	85	51	.625	—	George "Possum" Whitted
Greensboro Patriots	83	54	.606	2½	Charlie Carroll
Winston-Salem Twins	77	63	.550	10	George Whiteman
High Point Pointers	67	72	.482	19½	Danny Boone
Henderson Bunnies	54	85	.388	32½	Bunn Hearn/Lew Murphy/Lee Gooch/ Guy Winston
Salisbury-Spencer Colonials	48	89	.350	37½	Jess Altenburg

Playoff: Greensboro 4 games, Durham 1.

BA: Danny Boone, High Point, .372
Runs: Danny Boone, High Point, 116
Henry Parrish, Greensboro, 116
Hits: Danny Boone, High Point, 191
RBIs: Tom Wolfe, Durham, 134

HRs: Danny Boone, High Point, 46
Wins: Jim Turner, Greensboro, 25
SOs: Howell Conklin, High Point, 160
ERA: Monte Weaver, Durham, 1.94
Pct: Jim Turner, Greensboro, .735, 25-9

C Western Association
President: Dale D. Gear

Standings	W	L	Pct.	GB	Manager
Ft. Smith Twins**	88	59	.599	—	John Cimpi
Shawnee Robins*	87	61	.588	1½	Ray Powell
Springfield Midgets	71	77	.480	17½	Joe Mathes
Independence Producers	71	78	.477	18	Mark Purtell
Joplin Miners	68	82	.453	21½	George Cochran/Roy Corgan
Muskogee/Maud Chiefs#	61	89	.407	28½	John Smithson

#Muskogee moved to Maud August 22. One game was played, which drew poorly. It was decided to play the remaining home games at Independence or Joplin when those teams were on the road.
Attendance: Joplin, 40,000.

Playoff: Ft. Smith 5 games, Shawnee 2, one tie.

BA: Elmer Gray, Shawnee, .360
Runs: Chet Titus, Shawnee, 129
Hits: Elmer Gray, Shawnee, 219
RBIs: Elmer Gray, Shawnee, 128

HRs: Bill Hooten, Springfield, 25
Wins: Raymond Starr, Shawnee, 24
SOs: Fritz Ostermueller, Shawnee, 195
ERA: John F. Smith, Ft. Smith, 1.73

D Arizona State League
President: Fred Joyce

Standings	W	L	Pct.	GB	Manager
Bisbee Bees**	60	30	.667	—	Roy "Hardrock" Johnson
Miami Miners*	50	40	.556	10	Drap Hayes
Globe Bears	48	42	.533	12	Mickey Shader
Tucson Cowboys	43	47	.478	17	Tom Holley/Cliff McCarl/Pug Cavet
Phoenix Senators	40	49	.449	19½	Ross Lyall/Tom Burke/Ross Gardner/ Chet Thomas
Mesa Jewels#	28	61	.315	31½	Bill Whittaker/Ernie Lloyd/Lee Dempsey

#Mesa (20-38) withdrew July 24. Mesa's opponents were given 3 wins and 1 loss for each scheduled series with the disbanded team.

Playoff: Miami 4 games, Bisbee 3; Miami was awarded the title when the September 17 game was declared no contest and both teams refused to replay the game.

BA: Arthur Parker, Bisbee, .390
Runs: Arthur Parker, Bisbee, 99
Hits: Henry "Prince" Oana, Globe, 127
HRs: Leo Burns, Bisbee, 23

Wins: Glenn Gabler, Bisbee, 20
SOs: John Mitchell, Phoenix, 147
ERA: John Mitchell, Phoenix, 3.18

D Blue Ridge League
President: J. Vincent Jamison, Jr.

Standings	W	L	Pct.	GB	Manager
Martinsburg Blue Sox**	69	47	.595	—	Dan O'Leary
Frederick Warriors	63	53	.543	6	Bob Wells
Hagerstown Hubs*	60	55	.522	8½	Mickey Keliher
Hanover Raiders	58	58	.500	11	Bob Prysock
Chambersburg Young Yanks	53	61	.465	15	Tom Clarke
Waynesboro Red Birds	40	69	.367	25½	Ken Kirkham/Irwin Wimer

Playoff: Hagerstown 4 games, Martinsburg 2.

BA: Roger Cramer, Martinsburg, .404
Runs: Daniel Tapson, Hanover, 94
Hits: Daniel Tapson, Hanover, 155
Joe Vosmik, Frederick, 155

HRs: Patrick Shea, Chambersburg, 17
Wins: Harry Griffith, Martinsburg, 18
SOs: Frank Wertman, Hagerstown, 167
Pct: Alfred Biot, Frederick, .813, 13-3

D California State League
President: Orville McPherson

Standings	W	L	Pct.	GB	Manager
San Diego Aces	34	25	.576	—	Sam Agnew
Bakersfield Bees	32	28	.533	2½	Lew Giusto/Red Porter
San Bernardino Padres	32	29	.525	3	Rube Ellis
Santa Ana Orange Countians/Pomona Arabs/ Coronado Arabs#	22	38	.367	12½	Jesse Orndorf/Chet Thomas

#Santa Ana (4-20) moved to Pomona, which played six games at San Bernardino, May 8; Pomona (2-4) moved to Coronado County May 15, playing their games at the San Diego ball park.
The league disbanded June 17.

BA: Lou Martin, Bakersfield, .389
Runs: Red Porter, Bakersfield, 63
Hits: L.B. Tomlinson, Bakersfield, 83
HRs: Red Porter, Bakersfield, 15

Wins: George Caster, San Bernardino, 12
SOs: George Caster, San Bernardino, 80
Pct: George Caster, San Bernardino, .706, 12-5

D Cotton States League
President: Frank A. Scott

Standings	W	L	Pct.	GB	Manager
Alexandria Reds	74	50	.597	—	Pete Kilduff
Jackson Senators*	70	57	.551	5½	Herschel Bobo
El Dorado Lions**	66	55	.545	6½	George "Hickory" Jackson
Laurel Cardinals	59	63	.484	14	Clay Hopper
Hattiesburg Pinetoppers/ Baton Rouge Essos#	57	61	.483	14	Ed Cousineau/Bill Pierre
Monroe Drillers	55	63	.466	16	Art Ewold/Tillie Metteer/John Kane
Vicksburg Hill Billies	55	68	.447	18½	Wray Query
Meridian Mets/ Lake Charles Newporters@	51	70	.421	21½	Jake Hurt

#Hattiesburg (15-19) moved to Baton Rouge May 30.
@Meridian (23-27) moved to Lake Charles June 17, first home game June 24.

Playoff: El Dorado 4 games, Jackson 3. (Pitcher Jackie Reid won all four games for El Dorado.)

MVP- Clyde "Buck" Crouse, Alexandria.

BA: Joe Granade, Monroe, .368
Runs: Arvel "Bad News" Hale, Monroe, 116
Hits: Joseph Hutcheson, Jackson, 171

HRs: Cecil "Stormy" Davis, Meridian/
 Lake Charles, 28
Wins: Joe Berry, Vicksburg, 21
SOs: Gus Burleson, El Dorado, 143
ERA: Joe Berry, Vicksburg, 2.66

BA: Ed Hendee, Davenport, .362
Runs: Paul Speraw, Dubuque, 112
Hits: Ed Hendee, Davenport, 183
HRs: Ken Storm, Waterloo, 23

Wins: Albert Eckert, Dubuque, 19
 H.H. Miller, Cedar Rapids, 19
 Fred Witte, Davenport, 19
SOs: Lester Neisslie, Moline, 141
Pct: John Niggeling, Waterloo, .789, 15-4

D Eastern Carolina League
President: William G. Bramham

Standings	W	L	Pct.	GB	Manager
Rocky Mount Buccaneers**	69	47	.595	—	Zip King/Charles Moore
Goldsboro Goldbugs	68	50	.576	2	Jim Teague/Herrick "Spoke" Emery
Wilmington Pirates*	67	52	.563	3½	Hal Weafer
Fayetteville Highlanders	55	62	.470	14½	Cy Chisholm/Marty Walters
Greenville Tobacconists	45	68	.398	22½	Lester Bangs/Guy Smith/Dan Pasquella
Kinston Eagles	46	71	.393	23½	Clarence Roper

Playoff: Rocky Mount 4 games, Wilmington 2.

BA: Clarence Roper, Kinston, .368
Runs: Sam Fayonsky, Rocky Mount, 94
Hits: Roland Robins, Wilmington, 154
RBIs: Toni Bayard Young, Fayetteville/
 Wilmington, 89

HRs: Toni Bayard Young, Fayetteville/
 Wilmington, 21
Wins: Edward Heller, Goldsboro, 17
 Eddie Alsobrook, Rocky Mount, 17
SOs: Henry Thormahlen, Wilmington, 135
ERA: Edward Heller, Goldsboro, 2.37

D Georgia-Alabama League
President: C.I. Scarborough

Standings	W	L	Pct.	GB	Manager
Lindale Collegians**	60	39	.606	—	Jack Moulton
Carrollton Champs*	56	44	.560	4½	Paul Fittery
Talladega Indians	49	49	.500	10½	Howard Camp
Gadsden Eagles	49	50	.495	11	Louis Walker
Anniston Nobles	44	56	.440	16½	Bud Ammons/Verdo Elmore
Cedartown Sea Cows	40	60	.400	20½	Frank Thrasher/Sherrod Smith

Playoff: Carrollton 4 games, Lindale 0.

BA: Bernard Lewis, Talladega, .420
Runs: Charles Knowles, Cedartown, 92
Hits: Bernard Lewis, Talladega, 159
HRs: Charles Knowles, Cedartown, 25

Wins: James Soward, Gadsden, 17
SOs: Adel White, Carrollton, 101
Pct: Paul Fittery, Carrollton, .889, 16-2

D Lone Star League
President: T.H. Fisher

Standings	W	L	Pct.	GB	Manager
Tyler Trojans	12	8	.600	—	Roy Leslie
Palestine Pals	12	8	.600	—	Dillard "Dee" Payne
Sherman Snappers	9	9	.500	2	Earl "Red" Snapp
Texarkana Twins#	6	14	.300	6	Ray Corgan

#Texarkana disbanded May 16, and league then disbanded on that date.

BA: Clyde Pratt, Sherman, .442
Runs: Embert Mueller, Tyler, 25
Hits: Clyde Pratt, Sherman, 34

HRs: Ed Kallina, Sherman, 6
 John King, Tyler, 6
Wins: Leon Pettit, Tyler, 5
SOs: Leon Pettit, Tyler, 40
Pct: Leon Pettit, Tyler, 1.000, 5-0

D Mississippi Valley League
President: Belden Hill

Standings	W	L	Pct.	GB	Manager
Dubuque Tigers	75	51	.595	—	Lester "Pat" Patterson
Waterloo Hawks	72	54	.571	3	Cletus Dixon
Davenport Blue Sox	69	57	.548	6	Ed Reichle
Moline Plowboys	63	63	.500	12	Richard Manchester
Burlington Bees	62	64	.492	13	George Young
Keokuk Indians	60	65	.480	14½	Ben Dimond
Cedar Rapids Bunnies	58	67	.464	16½	Bill Speas/Tibb Serre
Rock Island Islanders	44	82	.349	31	Walt Genin/Buck Wheat

All-Star Team: 1B-Cletus Dixon, Waterloo; **2B**-Johnny Armstrong, Davenport; **3B**-Jim Grant, Waterloo; **SS**-George Young, Burlington; **OF**-John Bengel, Burlington; Edward Stock, Dubuque; Elmer Klumpp, Burlington; **C**-Mike Dempsey, Cedar Rapids; **P**-John MacDonald, Burlington; Greg Becker, Waterloo; Harold Applegren, Keokuk; Albert Eckert, Dubuque; Joe Huff, Burlington.

D Nebraska State League
President: James E. Beltzer

Standings	W	L	Pct.	GB	Manager
McCook Generals	74	42	.638	—	Elmer "Doc" Bennett
Fairbury Jeffersons	70	51	.579	6½	Preston Gray
Lincoln Links	68	51	.571	7½	Bob Browne/Les Nunamaker
York Dukes	61	53	.535	12	Art Rassmussen
Norton Jayhawks	54	60	.474	19	Hal Brokaw
Grand Island Islanders	54	62	.466	20	Clay Schoonover/Bob Browne
Norfolk Elkhorns	43	73	.371	31	J. "Lefty" Wilkus
North Platte Buffaloes	42	74	.362	32	Joe Pizer

All-Star Team: 1B-Herman Cholcher, Lincoln; **2B**-Herb Pember, McCook; **3B**-Hugh Graham, Norton; **SS**-Roy Tarr, McCook; **OF**-John Stoneham, McCook; Ed Taylor, Lincoln; Eddie Lass, Fairbury; **C**-Otto Cholcher, Lincoln; Morgan Snyder, York; **Util**-John Gabler, Lincoln; **P**-Andy Bednar, McCook; Jean Jones, Norton; Vito SanFilippo, Fairbury; Dean Beckwith, York; Glen Dacus, Norfolk.

BA: John Stoneham, McCook, .410
Runs: Herb Pember, McCook, 117
Hits: Herb Pember, McCook, 194
HRs: Joe Smith, Norfolk, 15

Wins: Andy Bednar, McCook, 21
 Stanford Primm, Fairbury, 21
SOs: Vito SanFilippo, Fairbury, 201
ERA: Jean Jones, Norton, 2.15

D West Texas League
President: D.L. Snodgrass

Standings	W	L	Pct.	GB	Manager
Midland Colts**	67	52	.563	—	Kal Segrist, Sr./John King
Coleman Bobcats*	62	56	.525	4½	Honus Mitze/Jack Holloway
Ballinger Bearcats	62	56	.525	4½	Bill Dean
San Angelo Sheep Herders	55	61	.474	10½	Walt Alexander
Abilene Aces	55	64	.462	12	Carl Williams
Big Spring Cowboys	54	66	.450	13½	Jim Payne/Ralph Rose/Nick Carter

Playoff: Coleman 3 games, Midland 3; Coleman won the title when Midland failed to appear for the seventh game.

All-Star Team: 1B-Lee Stebbins, Coleman; **2B**-Robert Rawlins, San Angelo; **3B**-Sam Coleman, San Angelo; **SS**-John Norek, Abilene; **OF**-Cameron Best, Coleman; E. McMillan, San Angelo; George Nebel, Abilene; **C**-Art Bradbury, Abilene; Neal Rabe, Big Spring; **P**-Tom Vaughn, Ballinger; Ed McMillan, San Angelo; Gene Moore, Midland.

BA: Ed Kallina, Midland, .433
Runs: Julian Flowers, Midland, 136
Hits: Ed Kallina, Midland, 159
HRs: Ed Kallina, Midland, 44

Wins: Jimmie Parker, Ballinger, 18
SOs: Gene Moore, Midland, 147
ERA: Tom Vaughn, Ballinger, 2.11

1929 Interleague Post Season Play

World Series
Philadelphia (American) 4 games, Chicago (National) 1

Junior World Series
Kansas City (American Association) 5 games, Rochester (International) 4
Total Attendance: 90,000

Eastern Championship
Rochester (International) 2 games, Albany (Eastern) 0

Dixie Series
Birmingham (Southern Association) 4 games, Dallas (Texas) 2
Total Attendance: 59,051

Eastern Series
Manchester (New England) 2 games, Albany (Eastern) 2

Midwest Championship
Canton (Central) 4 games, Quincy (Three-I) 2

Tri-State Series
Charleroi (Middle Atlantic) 4 games, Hagerstown (Blue Ridge) 1

1929 No-Hitters

Date	Pitcher	Team	League	Opponent	Score
5-4	John Trippe	Charlotte	South Atlantic	Greenville	9-0 (7)
5-7	Vance Page	Durham	Piedmont	High Point	2-0
5-8	Carl Hubbell	New York	National	Pittsburgh	11-0
5-9	Walter Wolfe	Quincy	Three-I	Terre Haute	10-0
5-24	Delano Wetherall	Rock Island	Mississippi Valley	Cedar Rapids	5-0
6-10	Bill Ferebee	Selma	Southeastern	Jacksonville	6-0
6-30	Lena Stiles	Tulsa	Western	Des Moines	6-0
7-3	Ray Pierce	Independence	Western Assoc.	Shawnee	9-0
7-19	C.H. Freeman	Baton Rouge	Cotton States	Lake Charles	4-0 (P, 7)
7-28	Andy Bednar	McCook	Nebraska State	Lincoln	2-0
8-1	Lefty Cox	Alexandria	Cotton States	Monroe	3-0
8-11	Pete Newman	Lake Charles	Cotton States	Vicksburg	5-0
8-16	Preston Chalk	Grand Island	Nebraska State	Norfolk	5-0
8-18	Al Grabowski	Danville	Three-I	Terre Haute	1-0 (7)
9-14	Tex Carleton	Rochester	International	Toronto	3-1

Number in parentheses indicates innings if other than nine; "P" indicates perfect game.

THIS DATE IN MINOR LEAGUE HISTORY

April 17, 1929, Joe Rabbit hit three homers for Toronto, International League, at Baltimore.

May 7, 1929, Ben Chapman hit three triples in a game for St. Paul, American Association.

May 12, 1929, William Burwell, Indianapolis, set an American Association record for most chances accepted by a pitcher in a game with 10.

June 11, 1929, Spencer Harris, Minneapolis, American Association, hit four doubles in one game.

July 4, 1929, Ralph "Babe" Pinelli of San Francisco, Pacific Coast League, hit two grand slams in one game. Pinelli collected six hits in six at bats, including three homers, and batted in twelve runs.

July 4, 1929, One of the longest estimated home runs was tagged by minor leaguer Roy Carlyle, who reportedly hit one 618 feet for Oakland of the Pacific Coast League at Emeryville Park in Oakland. Carlyle's blast, off Mission's Ernie Nevers, famed Stanford University All-America football star, sailed over the clubhouse in deepest center field.

July 13, 1929, Tony Cuccinello of Columbus, American Association, had six hits in six at bats.

July 13, 1929, Buffalo set an International League record by making 11 consecutive hits against the Baltimore Orioles.

July 30, 1929, Milwaukee, American Association, executed six double plays in a game with Louisville.

July 30, 1929, Columbus cracked 10 doubles in an American Association game with Minneapolis.

August 12, 1929, Reading outfielder George Quellich completed a streak of 15 con-

secutive hits, apparently the record for most consecutive hits by a player in Organized Ball. The spree started August 9 with a single, double and homer against Toronto, then continued against Montreal. He had five singles and a homer in the first game, two homers and two singles on August 11, and a homer and a single on this day. Finally, he was stopped when pitcher Elam Vangilder got him to loft an outfield fly to Henry Haines.

August 14, 1929, Minneapolis made 27 assists in a nine inning American Association game.

August 24, 1929, Chester Chatham, brother of Charles "Buster" Chatham, made six consecutive assists at third base for Pueblo, Western League, in a game with Wichita.

September 2, 1929, Elmer Yoter went 6-for-6 for Minneapolis, American Association.

September 22, 1929, Joe Kuhel stole four bases for Kansas City, American Association.

October 7, 1929, Smead Jolley had over 300 hits in the Pacific Coast League for the second consecutive season.

October 7, 1929, Mission's Ike Boone completed the Pacific Coast League season with 218 runs batted in. Boone is one of only four players in Organized Ball history to drive in more than 200 runs in a season.

October 13, 1929, Kansas City, American Association, won the Junior World Series, five games to four, defeating Rochester, International League, 6-5 in eleven innings in the deciding game.

October, 1929, Outfielder George Whiteman retired after a minor league career which began in 1905. He played in 3,282 games, the all-time mark for a minor league player. Whiteman played in 100 or more games in 24 different seasons. He had 3,388 hits for an average of .283.

Rochester's Red Wing Stadium opened on May 2, 1929. The stadium, built at a cost of $415,000, had an initial capacity of 15,000. The name was changed to Silver Stadium in 1968. This photo was taken circa 1950.

THE DEPRESSION AND BEYOND: 1930 - 1941

*O*n Oct. 23, 1929, the New York stock market crashed. As the prices of stocks fell, the economy of the United States went into a huge decline. As always, the minors were affected. Twenty-three leagues started the 1930 season, down from the 26 that had started the previous year. Two failed during the season, and only 16 finished the 1931 season. By 1933, 14 leagues opened the season.

The minor leagues might have been hurt far more except for one major factor: the introduction of night baseball. There had been attempts at night baseball earlier, but the lighting systems were inadequate. On May 2, 1930 in Des Moines, the first true night game was played. Many scoffed at the idea, but owner Lee Keyser had installed a high quality system. The results were immediate. Play was not adversely affected and fans came out in large numbers.

Other clubs quickly followed. Sacramento had the first Pacific Coast League night game on May 22, and Buffalo inaugurated International League night baseball on July 3 before a crowd of more than 11,000. Los Angeles' lights were ready on July 22 and drew a crowd of 17,000. Night baseball changed minor league baseball, and saved it from some of the impact of the Depression.

By the end of the 1931 season, minor league leaders realized that drastic revitalization steps were necessary. New blood was needed along with reconstruction of the organization. At the 1931 winter meetings, administrative duties of the National Association were placed in the hands of an Executive Committee for one year. The committee was empowered to change the association where needed. A promotional department and a press bureau were created.

In 1932, Judge William G. Bramham, who had been president of four minor leagues, was elected National Association president to succeed Mike Sexton. The office was moved to Durham, N.C., and sweeping reforms were instituted. The Board of Arbitration was abolished and replaced by an Executive Committee of three. Bramham's reforms were aimed at getting rid of shoestring operators. He insisted on guaranteed deposits to protect player salaries, and he protected territories. Under Bramham's new, forceful leadership, the minors stabilized. Between 1933 and 1940 the minors grew from 14 to 44 leagues and only two failed to finish a season.

Major league farm systems continued to grow during this period, and big league ownership and subsidies helped many teams survive the Depression. Judge Landis continued to rail against major league ownership. He accused Branch Rickey of raping the minors and robbing small towns of their precious heritage of independent baseball. With farm systems no longer against baseball law, Landis fined teams that had an interest in more than one team in a minor league, and granted free agency to players who were in violation of the option rules. Free agency was granted to 74 Cardinal farm hands in 1938, and to 91 Tiger minor leaguers in 1940. But the farm system and major league control of minor league players had become a permanent part of the minor league landscape.

1930

American League
President: Ernest S. Barnard

Standings	W	L	Pct.	GB	Attend.	Manager
Philadelphia Athletics	102	52	.662	—	721,663	Connie Mack
Washington Senators	94	60	.610	8	614,474	Walter Johnson
New York Yankees	86	68	.558	16	1,169,230	Bob Shawkey
Cleveland Indians	81	73	.526	21	528,657	Roger Peckinpaugh
Detroit Tigers	75	79	.487	27	649,450	Bucky Harris
St. Louis Browns	64	90	.416	38	152,088	Bill Killefer
Chicago White Sox	62	92	.403	40	406,123	Donie Bush
Boston Red Sox	52	102	.338	50	444,045	Heinie Wagner

BA: Al Simmons, Philadelphia, .381
Runs: Al Simmons, Philadelphia, 152
Hits: Johnny Hodapp, Cleveland, 225
RBIs: Lou Gehrig, New York, 174
HRs: Babe Ruth, New York, 49

TBs: Lou Gehrig, New York, 419
Wins: Lefty Grove, Philadelphia, 28
SOs: Lefty Grove, Philadelphia, 209
ERA: Lefty Grove, Philadelphia, 2.54
Pct: Lefty Grove, Philadelphia, .848, 28-5

National League
President: John A. Heydler

Standings	W	L	Pct.	GB	Attend.	Manager
St. Louis Cardinals	92	62	.597	—	508,501	Gabby Street
Chicago Cubs	90	64	.584	2	1,463,624	Joe McCarthy/Rogers Hornsby
New York Giants	87	67	.565	5	868,714	John McGraw
Brooklyn Robins	86	68	.558	6	1,097,329	Wilbert Robinson
Pittsburgh Pirates	80	74	.519	12	357,795	Jewel Ens
Boston Braves	70	84	.455	22	464,835	Bill McKechnie
Cincinnati Reds	59	95	.383	33	386,727	Dan Howley
Philadelphia Phillies	52	102	.338	40	299,007	Burt Shotton

BA: Bill Terry, New York, .401
Runs: Chuck Klein, Philadelphia, 158
Hits: Bill Terry, New York, 254
RBIs: Hack Wilson, Chicago, 190
HRs: Hack Wilson, Chicago, 56
2B: Chuck Klein, Philadelphia, 59

TBs: Chuck Klein, Philadelphia, 445
Wins: Ray Kremer, Pittsburgh, 20
Pat Malone, Chicago, 20
SOs: Bill Hallahan, St. Louis, 177
ERA: Dazzy Vance, Brooklyn, 2.61
Pct: Bob Fitzsimmons, New York, .731, 19-7

AA American Association
President: Thomas J. Hickey

Standings	W	L	Pct.	GB	Attend.	Manager
Louisville Colonels	93	60	.607	—	187,430	Allan Sothoron
St. Paul Saints	91	63	.591	2½	180,685	Lefty Leifield
Toledo Mud Hens	88	66	.571	5½	179,433	Casey Stengel
Minneapolis Millers	77	76	.503	16	184,116	Mike Kelley
Kansas City Blues	75	79	.487	18½	113,655	Dutch Zwilling
Columbus Senators	67	86	.438	26	122,946	Nemo Leibold
Milwaukee Brewers	63	91	.409	30½	142,701	Marty Berghammer
Indianapolis Indians	60	93	.393	33	108,016	John Corriden

All-Star Team: 1B-Dudley Branom, Louisville; **2B**-Jack Saltzgaver, St. Paul; **3B**-Meredith Hopkins, St. Paul; **SS**-Jose Olivares, Louisville; **OF**-Bevo LeBourveau, Toledo; Mel Simons, Louisville; Nick Cullop, Minneapolis; **C**-Walter Henline, Toledo; **P**-Phil Weinert, Louisville; Wilcy Moore, St. Paul.

BA: Bevo LeBourveau, Toledo, .380
Runs: Nick Cullop, Minneapolis, 150
Hits: Mel Simons, Louisville, 248
RBIs: Nick Cullop, Minneapolis, 152

HRs: Nick Cullop, Minneapolis, 54
Wins: Wilcy Moore, St. Paul, 22
SOs: Phil Weinert, Louisville, 132
ERA: Hugh McQuillan, Toledo, 3.33

AA International League
President: Charles H. Knapp

Standings	W	L	Pct.	GB	Attend.	Manager
Rochester Red Wings	105	62	.629	—	328,424	Billy Southworth
Baltimore Orioles	97	70	.581	8	171,283	Fritz Maisel
Montreal Royals	96	72	.571	9½	207,757	Ed Holly
Toronto Maple Leafs	87	80	.521	18	121,431	Steve O'Neill
Newark Bears	80	88	.476	25½	242,183	Tris Speaker/Al Mamaux
Buffalo Bisons	74	91	.448	30	149,387	Bill Clymer/Jim Cooney
Reading Keys	68	98	.410	36½	112,900	Harry Hinchman
Jersey City Skeeters	59	105	.360	44½	133,525	Nick Allen/Joe Tinker

All-Star Team: 1B-James "Rip" Collins, Rochester; **2B**-George "Specs" Toporcer, Rochester; **3B**-Jim Stroner, Baltimore; **SS**-Billy Urbanski, Montreal; **OF**-Robert Worthington, Rochester; Pepper Martin, Rochester; Vince Barton, Baltimore; **C**-Frank Grube, Buffalo; **P**-Paul Derringer, Rochester; Stew Bolen, Baltimore.

BA: James "Rip" Collins, Rochester, .376
Runs: Joe Hauser, Baltimore, 173
Hits: James "Rip" Collins, Rochester, 234
RBIs: James "Rip" Collins, Rochester, 180
HRs: Joe Hauser, Baltimore, 63

TBs: Joe Hauser, Baltimore, 443
Wins: Paul Derringer, Rochester, 23
SOs: Paul Derringer, Rochester, 164
ERA: John Berly, Rochester, 2.49

AA Pacific Coast League
President: Harry A. Williams

Standings	W	L	Pct.	GB	Attend.	Manager
Hollywood Stars**	119	81	.595	—	289,131	Oscar Vitt
Los Angeles Angels*	113	84	.574	4½	314,944	Jack Lelivelt
Sacramento Senators	102	96	.515	16	241,130	Buddy Ryan
San Francisco Seals	101	98	.508	17½	220,495	Nick Williams
Oakland Oaks	97	103	.485	22	250,062	Carl Zamloch
Seattle Indians	92	107	.462	26½	103,341	Ernie Johnson
Mission Reds	91	110	.453	28½	139,768	Red Killefer
Portland Beavers	81	117	.409	37	136,029	Larry Woodall

Playoff: Hollywood 4 games, Los Angeles 1.

All-Star Team: 1B-Earl Sheely, San Francisco; **2B**-Frank Sigafoos, Los Angeles; **3B**-Fred Haney, Los Angeles; **SS**-Frank Crosetti, San Francisco; **OF**-John Moore, Los Angeles; Myril Hoag, Sacramento; Wes Schulmerich, Los Angeles; **C**-John Bassler, Hollywood; **P**-Ed Baecht, Los Angeles; Jimmy Zinn, San Francisco; Jim Turner, Hollywood; Frank Shellenback, Hollywood.

BA: Earl Sheely, San Francisco, .403
Runs: Frank Crosetti, San Francisco, 171
Hits: Earl Sheely, San Francisco, 289
RBIs: Earl Sheely, San Francisco, 180
HRs: David Barbee, Seattle/Hollywood, 41

Wins: Ed Baecht, Los Angeles, 26
Jimmy Zinn, San Francisco, 26
SOs: Fay Thomas, Sacramento, 228
ERA: Ed Baecht, Los Angeles, 3.23

A Eastern League
President: William E. Carey

Standings	W	L	Pct.	GB	Attend.	Manager
Allentown Dukes*	95	75	.559	—	80,000	Joe Bush
Bridgeport Bears**	91	74	.552	1½	75,000	Hans Lobert
Springfield Ponies	78	89	.467	15½	35,000	Bill Gleason
Albany Senators	77	91	.458	17	100,000	Bill McCorry
New Haven Profs@	56	43	.566	NA		Gene Martin
Providence Grays@	49	46	.516	NA		Ed Onslow
Hartford Senators#	35	44	.443	NA		Loren Bader
Pittsfield Hillies#	32	51	.386	NA		Otto Frietag/Bob Emmerich

#Hartford and Pittsfield withdrew June 30.
@New Haven and Providence withdrew July 18.

Playoff: Allentown 4 games, Bridgeport 1.

All-Star Team: 1B-Bruce Caldwell, Albany; **2B**-Guy Lacy, Allentown; **3B**-William Dressen, Springfield; **SS**-William Werber, Albany; **OF**-William Jarrett, Allentown; Ray Fitzgerald, Bridgeport; Ralph Boyle, Providence/Albany; **C**-Frank Kohlbecker, Springfield; Art Veltman, Bridgeport; William Karlon, Springfield; **P**-Sam Hyman, Allentown; John Michaels, Bridgeport; Tim McNamara, Albany; Miles Hunter, Bridgeport.

BA: Joe Kelly, New Haven, .373
Runs: Ralph Boyle, Providence/Albany, 130
Hits: William Jarrett, Allentown, 217
RBIs: William Jarrett, Allentown, 135

HRs: Frank Rodgers, New Haven, 23
Wins: Sam Hyman, Allentown, 24
SOs: Frank Loftus, Springfield, 104
ERA: Leslie Signor, Bridgeport, 2.45

A Southern Association
President: John D. Martin

Standings	W	L	Pct.	GB	Attend.	Manager
Memphis Chickasaws	98	55	.641	—	185,149	Tommy "Doc" Prothro
New Orleans Pelicans	91	61	.599	6½	175,239	Larry Gilbert
Birmingham Barons	85	68	.556	13	183,158	Clyde Milan
Atlanta Crackers	84	69	.549	14	163,643	Johnny Dobbs
Little Rock Travelers	81	73	.526	17½	92,122	Jack Steele
Chattanooga Lookouts	67	87	.435	31½	146,181	Bill Rogers
Nashville Volunteers	66	87	.431	32	95,060	Clarence "Pants" Rowland
Mobile Bears	40	112	.263	57½	58,478	James Hamilton

All-Star Team: 1B-Jim Poole, Nashville; **2B**-Jack Sheehan, Atlanta; **3B**-Harry Strohm, Little Rock; **SS**-Luke Appling, Atlanta; **OF**-Art Weis, Birmingham; Tex Jeanes, Memphis; Fred Eichrodt, New Orleans; **C**-Eddie Kenna, Chattanooga; William Campbell, Memphis; **Util**-Tom Taylor, New Orleans; Eddie Rose, Little Rock; **P**-Billy Bayne, Chattanooga; Earl Caldwell, Birmingham; Harry Kelly, Memphis; Whitey Glazner, New Orleans; Leo Moon, Little Rock; Clay Touchstone, Birmingham; William Hughes, Little Rock.

*Won first-half   **Won second-half   ***Won both halves

BA: Joe Hutcheson, Memphis, .380
Runs: Jay Partridge, Nashville, 155
Hits: Johnny Chapman, Mobile, 223
RBIs: Jim Poole, Nashville, 167

HRs: Jim Poole, Nashville, 50
Wins: Billy Bayne, Chattanooga, 21
SOs: Billy Bayne, Chattanooga, 112
ERA: Leo Moon, Little Rock, 2.98

A Texas League
President: J. Alvin Gardner

Standings	W	L	Pct.	GB	Attend.	Manager
Wichita Falls Spudders*	95	58	.621	—	74,994	Carl Williams
Houston Buffaloes	89	65	.578	6½	166,993	Joe Schultz
Shreveport Sports	86	65	.570	8	75,890	Art Phelan
Ft. Worth Panthers**	84	69	.549	11	103,279	Frank Snyder
Waco Cubs	68	81	.457	25	62,568	Del Pratt
Beaumont Exporters	68	84	.447	26½	58,134	Del Baker
San Antonio Indians	60	93	.392	35	59,828	George Burns
Dallas Steers	58	93	.384	36	89,188	Jake Atz

Playoff: Ft. Worth 3 games, Wichita Falls 2.

All-Star Team: 1B-Irving "Jack" Burns, Wichita Falls; **2B**-Les Mallon, Ft. Worth; **3B**-Chester Fowler, Ft. Worth; **SS**-James Levey, Wichita Falls; **OF**-Jack Kloza, Wichita Falls; Homer Peel, Houston; Oscar "Ox" Eckhardt, Beaumont; **C**-Jack Crouch, Wichita Falls; Royce Morrow, Houston; **P**-Lil Stoner, Ft. Worth; Dick Whitworth, Ft. Worth; Bob McCabe, Ft. Worth; Dizzy Dean, Houston; Hal Wiltse, Wichita Falls; Tony Kaufman, Houston.

BA: Oscar "Ox" Eckhardt, Beaumont, .379
Runs: Jack Kloza, Wichita Falls, 144
Hits: Oscar "Ox" Eckhardt, Beaumont, 217
RBIs: Larry Bettencourt, Wichita Falls, 145
HRs: Larry Bettencourt, Wichita Falls, 43

Wins: Bob McCabe, Ft. Worth, 20
Dick Whitworth, Ft. Worth, 20
SOs: Allyn Stout, Houston, 166
ERA: Ralph Judd, Houston, 2.61

A Western League
President: Dale D. Gear

Standings	W	L	Pct.	GB	Manager
Wichita Aviators	89	56	.614	—	Art Griggs
Omaha Packers	76	66	.535	11½	Spencer Abbott
Oklahoma City Indians	79	71	.527	12½	Joe Kelly/Lou Brower/Ned Pettigrew
Des Moines Demons	77	71	.520	13½	Claude Davenport/Shano Collins
Pueblo Braves	75	75	.500	16½	Jimmy Payton
Denver Bears	74	74	.500	16½	Eddie Palmer
Topeka Senators	66	84	.440	25½	Bruno Betzel
St. Joseph Saints	53	92	.366	36	Eugene Bailey/Joe Sugden/Everett Booe

Attendance: Topeka, 35,000.

All-Star Team: 1B-Jim Oglesby, Des Moines; **2B**-J. Faber, Omaha; **3B**-Hetherly, Omaha; **SS**-Lou Brower, Oklahoma City; **OF**-Stan Keyes, Des Moines; Forrest Jensen, Wichita; Gus Dugas, Wichita; **C**-John Fitzpatrick, Oklahoma City; Jack Mealey, Wichita; **Util**-Dewey Bondurant, Omaha; **P**-Walter Brown, Oklahoma City; Charles Wood, Wichita; Dizzy Dean, St. Joseph; Andy Bednar, Wichita; John Jones, Oklahoma City; Bud Tinning, Des Moines.

BA: Forrest Jensen, Wichita, .354
Runs: Carl Frey, Pueblo, 133
Hits: Forrest Jensen, Wichita, 207
RBIs: Stan Keyes, Des Moines, 140
HRs: Stan Keyes, Des Moines, 35
Wins: Charles Wood, Wichita, 22
SOs: Charles Wood, Wichita, 197
ERA: Walter Brown, Oklahoma City, 2.57

B Central League
President: Donald C. Jacobs

Standings	W	L	Pct.	GB	Manager
Springfield Blue Sox***	82	55	.599	—	Joe Dunn
Erie Sailors	76	63	.547	7	Jocko Munch
Fort Wayne Chiefs	72	67	.518	11	Punch Knoll
Canton Terriers	65	73	.471	17½	Heinie Groh
Richmond Roses	63	75	.457	19½	John McCloskey
Dayton Aviators	56	81	.409	26	Nick Cullop

All-Star Team: 1B-Ted Donovan, Springfield; **2B**-Jimmy Vorhoff, Dayton; **3B**-Sylvester Simon, Fort Wayne; **SS**-Bill Ussat, Erie; **OF**-James Bryan, Springfield; Dewey Stover, Erie; Mansfield, Springfield; **C**-Frank Pytlak, Erie; **P**-Robert Kline, Erie; Howard Hardway, Fort Wayne; James Minogue, Springfield; Gus Goeckel, Springfield; Clyde Hatter, Dayton.

BA: Pat Wright, Fort Wayne, .419
Runs: Leroy "Cowboy" Jones, Fort Wayne, 162
Hits: Pat Wright, Fort Wayne, 228
RBIs: Pat Wright, Fort Wayne, 169
HRs: Pat Wright, Fort Wayne, 52

2B: John Reider, Fort Wayne, 52
TBs: Pat Wright, Fort Wayne, 425
Wins: Robert Kline, Erie, 23
SOs: Clyde Hatter, Dayton, 217
ERA: Gus Goeckel, Springfield, 3.14

B New England League
President: Claude B. Davidson

Standings	W	L	Pct.	GB	Manager
Salem Witches	21	9	.700	—	Sam Post
Lynn Papooses	19	12	.613	2½	Thomas "Poke" Whalen
Portland Mariners	13	14	.481	6½	Dick Rudolph
Manchester Blue Sox	9	19	.321	11	Leo Hartline
Lewiston Twins#	12	12	.500	NA	Bill Slattery
Nashua Millionaires#	5	13	.278	NA	Shano Collins

#Lewiston and Nashua disbanded June 16.
The league disbanded June 22.

BA: Bill Scholz, Salem, .433
Runs: Tom Adams, Lynn, 31
Hits: Bill Scholz, Salem, 45
RBIs: John Henry Lehman, Salem, 31

HRs: John Henry Lehman, Salem, 5
Wins: Chili Hardin, Salem, 7
SOs: Bill Diehl, Lewiston, 40
Pct: Mike Balaski, Lynn, 1.000, 4-0

B New York-Pennsylvania League
President: Perry B. Farrell

Standings	W	L	Pct.	GB	Attend.	Manager
Wilkes-Barre Barons	79	59	.572	—		Mike McNally
Elmira Colonels	73	64	.533	5½		Jake Pitler
Williamsport Grays	74	65	.532	5½	51,660	Glenn Killinger
Harrisburg Senators	70	69	.504	9½	61,242	Johnny Tillman
Binghamton Triplets	67	72	.482	12½	53,100	Billy Webb
York White Roses	66	73	.475	13½		John Bentley
Hazleton Mountaineers	63	76	.453	16½		Walter Holke
Scranton Miners	62	76	.449	17		Buck Elliott

All-Star Team: 1B-Mike Martineck, Scranton; **2B**-Glenn Killinger, Williamsport; **3B**-John Hughes, Scranton; **SS**-Hap Briscoe, Wilkes-Barre; **OF**-Horace "Red" McBride, Harrisburg; Arthur McHenry, Binghamton; Matt Donahue, Wilkes-Barre; **C**-Thomas McCarthy, Wilkes-Barre; **P**-John Miller, Wilkes-Barre; Ad Holshauser, Elmira.

BA: Horace "Red" McBride, Harrisburg, .378
Runs: Frank Kern, York, 121
Hits: Donald Brown, York, 214
RBIs: Ken Strong, Hazleton, 130

HRs: Ken Strong, Hazleton, 41
Wins: John Miller, Wilkes-Barre, 22
SOs: John Milligan, Wilkes-Barre, 133
ERA: Chant Parkes, Williamsport, 2.71

B South Atlantic Association
President: William D. Bramham

Standings	W	L	Pct.	GB	Manager
Macon Peaches**	87	52	.612	—	Charles Moore
Greenville Spinners*	85	57	.598	3½	Joe Schepner
Asheville Tourists	79	61	.564	8½	George Speirs
Augusta Wolves	68	70	.493	18½	Sam Agnew/Odie Strain
Charlotte Hornets	61	78	.459	26	Dick Hoblitzell
Columbia Comers	39	101	.279	48½	Marty Fielder/Lem Stebbins

Playoff: Greenville 4 games, Macon 2.

All-Star Team: 1B-Robert Hipps, Asheville; **2B**-Harry Snyder, Macon; **3B**-Lealon Breakfield, Asheville; **SS**-Jay Boggs, Greenville; **OF**-Hal Sullivan, Asheville; Murray Howell, Greenville; George Rhinehardt, Greenville; **C**-Art McCrea, Asheville; Paul Richards, Macon; **P**-Hugh Harmon, Greenville; Frank Pearce, Greenville; June Greene, Macon; Phillip Gallivan, Macon; Jim Mooney, Charlotte; Roland Flinn, Augusta.

BA: Hal Sullivan, Asheville, .374
Runs: Murray Howell, Greenville, 123
Hits: Murray Howell, Greenville, 193
RBIs: Murray Howell, Greenville, 147
HRs: James Hudgens, Greenville, 39

Wins: Hugh Harmon, Greenville, 25
SOs: Jim Mooney, Charlotte, 185
ERA: Phillip Gallivan, Macon, 2.94
Pct: Hugh Harmon, Greenville, .735, 25-9

B Southeastern League
President: Cliff Green

Standings	W	L	Pct.	GB	Manager
Selma Cloverleafs***	94	43	.686	—	Zinn Beck
Tampa Smokers	73	65	.529	21½	Frank "Pop" Kitchens
Jacksonville Tars	69	66	.511	24	Rube Marquard
Montgomery Lions	61	73	.455	31½	Roy Ellam
Columbus Foxes	63	79	.444	34½	Bobby Lennox
Pensacola Flyers	53	87	.379	42½	Tom Pyle

All-Star Team: 1B-Raymond "Rip" Radcliffe, Selma; **2B**-Bill Andrus, Selma; **3B**-Emmett Culbreth, Columbus; **SS**-Joe Longnecker, Selma; **OF**-Woody Abernathy, Montgomery; Buck Finiator, Selma; Brown Braley, Tampa; **C**-Red Johnson, Jacksonville; **P**-Howell Conklin, Tampa; Henry Brewer, Selma.

BA: Raymond "Rip" Radcliffe, Selma, .369
Runs: Ralph Dunbar, Columbus, 104
Hits: Raymond "Rip" Radcliffe, Selma, 199
RBIs: Raymond "Rip" Radcliffe, Selma, 116

HRs: Raymond "Rip" Radcliffe, Selma, 15
Wins: Henry Brewer, Selma, 25
SOs: Thornton Lee, Tampa, 145
ERA: Roy Appleton, Tampa, 2.22

B Three-I League
President: L.J. Wylie

Standings	W	L	Pct.	GB	Manager
Evansville Hubs**	79	55	.590	—	Bob Coleman
Quincy Indians	78	58	.574	2	Ray Schmidt
Decatur Commodores	77	59	.566	3	Frank Desseau
Danville Veterans*	71	61	.538	7	Frank Murphy
Springfield Senators	62	70	.470	16	Dan Clark
Peoria Tractors	57	77	.425	22	L.H. "Pat" Paterson/Deeble Foss
Bloomington Cubs	57	78	.422	22½	Pat Harkins/John Toban
Terre Haute Tots	53	76	.411	23½	Earl Wolgamot

1930

Attendance: Decatur, 70,396.

Playoff: Danville 4 games, Evansville 2.

All-Star Team: 1B-Pete Susko, Springfield; 2B-Joe Morrissey, Evansville; 3B-Lee Cunningham, Danville; SS-Gerald Meyers, Danville; OF-Joe Vosmik, Terre Haute; Hub "Harvey" Walker, Evansville; J.J. Tangeman, Bloomington; C-Ernie Lorbeer, Evansville; Sanford Hamby, Springfield; P-Slim Love, Quincy; Bill Swift, Springfield; Joe Cantrell, Decatur; Al Baker, Decatur; Luke "Hot Potato" Hamlin, Decatur.

BA: Joe Vosmik, Terre Haute, .397
Runs: Hub "Harvey" Walker, Evansville, 136
Hits: Hub "Harvey" Walker, Evansville, 191
RBIs: John "Moose" Clabaugh, Quincy, 154
HRs: John "Moose" Clabaugh, Quincy, 30
Wins: Slim Love, Quincy, 22
SOs: Tommy Bridges, Evansville, 189
ERA: John Niggeling, Evansville, 2.89

C Middle Atlantic League
President: Elmer M. Daily

Standings	W	L	Pct.	GB	Manager
Johnstown Johnnies*	64	53	.547	—	Wilbur Good
Clarksburg Generals**	64	53	.547	—	Earl Neale
Fairmont Black Diamonds	61	55	.526	2½	Del Gainer/Tony Cyran/Jim Walsh
Scottdale Scotties	59	55	.518	3½	Eddie Dyer
Charleroi Governors	58	57	.504	5	Dave Lamb
Cumberland Colts	59	59	.500	5½	Joe Phillips
Wheeling Stogies	50	65	.435	13	Bobby Prysock
Jeannette Jays	49	67	.422	14½	Dan Pasquella

Playoff: Johnstown 4 games, Clarksburg 3.

BA: Joe Medwick, Scottdale, .419
Runs: Sam Thomas, Johnstown, 125
Hits: Frank Doljack, Wheeling, 176
RBIs: Hal Stricklin, Charleroi, 108
HRs: Hal Stricklin, Charleroi, 31
Wins: Richard Proctor, Clarksburg, 24
SOs: Edwin Chapman, Scottdale, 207
ERA: Cecil Slaughter, Fairmont, 3.23

C Ontario League
President: Walter McMullen

Standings	W	L	Pct.	GB	Manager
London Tecumsehs**	37	17	.685	—	Knotty Lee
St. Catharines Brewers*	35	17	.673	1	Pat Doherty
Brantford Red Sox	22	25	.468	11½	Dixie Walker/Herrick "Spoke" Emery
St. Thomas Blue Sox	23	30	.434	13½	Fred Burchell/Joe Untz
Guelph Biltmores	21	29	.420	14	Clare Hoose
Hamilton Tigers#	10	30	.250	NA	Joe Altenburg

#Hamilton disbanded July 3 at the end of the first half.

Playoff: St. Thomas 3 games, London 1. (St. Catharines players went home when the league ceased operations July 23. The two leading teams in the second half participated in the play-off.)

BA: Frank Wojack, London, .371
Runs: Frank Wojack, London, 58
Hits: Frank Wojack, London, 89
HRs: Pat Doherty, St. Catharines, 8
Wins: Reggie Grabowski, London, 14
SOs: Stan Lucas, London, 84
Pct: Stan Lucas, London, .786, 11-3

C Piedmont League
President: William G. Bramham

Standings	W	L	Pct.	GB	Manager
Henderson Gamecocks	78	63	.553	—	Jim Teague
Durham Bulls	71	68	.511	6	George "Possum" Whitted
Greensboro Patriots	70	71	.496	8	Everett Booe/Hobe Brummitt
Winston-Salem Twins	70	71	.496	8	Hal Weafer/Claude Joyner/Charlie Carroll/ Johnny Brock
Raleigh Capitals	68	72	.486	9½	Pat Haley
High Point Pointers	64	76	.457	13½	Danny Boone

Playoff: Durham 4 games, Henderson 3.

BA: Danny Boone, High Point, .385
Runs: Jack Lindley, Durham, 148
Hits: Fred Tauby (Taubansee), Durham, 203
RBIs: Tom Wolfe, Durham, 154
HRs: Tom Wolfe, Durham, 39
Wins: Elmer Bray, Winston-Salem, 22
Richard Durham, High Point, 22
SOs: DeWitt Perry, Durham, 211
ERA: Arthur Yeager, Winston-Salem, 3.47

C Western Association
President: Dale D. Gear

Standings	W	L	Pct.	GB	Manager
Independence Producers**	76	56	.576	—	Mark Purtell
Joplin Miners*	76	59	.563	1½	James "Cat" Tierney
Shawnee Robins	65	71	.478	13	Ray Powell
Ft. Smith Twins	64	72	.471	14	Runt Marr
Springfield Midgets	64	73	.467	14½	Norman "Kid" Elberfeld
Muskogee Chiefs	60	74	.448	17	Herb Smith

Attendance: Joplin, 65,000.

Playoff: Independence 5 games, Joplin 4.

BA: Monk Edwards, Independence, .384
Runs: Joyner White, Ft. Smith, 123
Bill Norman, Shawnee/Muskogee, 123
Hits: Robert Boken, Joplin, 189
RBIs: Robert Boken, Joplin, 124
HRs: Gordon Nell, Joplin/Muskogee, 27
Wins: Lynn Griffith, Joplin, 21
SOs: Lynn Griffith, Joplin, 245
Pct: Ron Vance, Independence, .667, 16-8

D Arizona State League
President: Wilford S. Sullinger

Standings	W	L	Pct.	GB	Manager
Bisbee Bees**	60	45	.571	—	Roy "Hardrock" Johnson
El Paso Texans	58	47	.552	2	Royce "Mule" Washburn
Phoenix Senators	58	47	.552	2	Louis Giusto
Globe Bears*	56	49	.533	4	Mickey Shader
Tucson Cowboys	45	60	.429	15	Pug Cavet/Walter Rehg
Miami Miners	38	67	.362	22	Drap Hayes/Bob Gillespie/George Cochrane

Playoff: Globe 3 games, Phoenix 0, for the first half title.
Finals: Bisbee 3 games, Globe 3; Bisbee won on a forfeit when Globe refused to play in Bisbee September 17.

BA: Tony Antista, Bisbee, .430
Runs: Tony Antista, Bisbee, 127
Hits: Tony Antista, Bisbee, 191
RBIs: Bob Stevenson, Phoenix, 101
HRs: George Steward, Bisbee, 22
Wins: Charlie Biggs, Globe, 20
SOs: Charlie Biggs, Globe, 157
Pct: Al McNeeley, Bisbee, .875, 14-2

D Blue Ridge League
President: J. Vincent Jamison, Jr.

Standings	W	L	Pct.	GB	Manager
Chambersburg Young Yanks***	69	44	.611	—	Leo Mackey
Waynesboro Red Birds*	56	57	.496	13	Bob Rice
Hagerstown Hubs	52	64	.448	18½	Jake Miller/Joe Cambria
Frederick Warriors	50	62	.446	18½	Bob Wells

Playoff: Chambersburg tied with Waynesboro for the first half title; Chambersburg 2 games, Waynesboro 1.

BA: Babe Phelps, Hagerstown, .376
Runs: Ted Norbert, Chambersburg, 99
Hits: Babe Phelps, Hagerstown, 175
HRs: Ted Norbert, Chambersburg, 27
Wins: William Trotter, Waynesboro, 16
SOs: William Perrin, Frederick, 117
Pct: Gene Padberg, Chambersburg, .786, 11-3

D Cotton States League
President: Frank A. Scott

Standings	W	L	Pct.	GB	Manager
El Dorado Lions*	83	51	.619	—	George "Hickory" Jackson
Monroe Drillers	67	61	.523	13	Jim Bagby/Bill Huber
Pine Bluff Judges**	68	63	.519	13½	Wray Query
Baton Rouge Highlanders	68	65	.511	14½	H.E. "Babe" Irwin
Jackson Senators	64	68	.485	18	Herschel Bobo
Vicksburg Hill Billies	48	82	.369	33	John Brock/Rod Murphy/John King
Alexandria Reds#	35	30	.538	NA	Josh Billings
Lake Charles Newporters#	24	37	.393	NA	Al Nixon/Clyde Glass

#Alexandria and Lake Charles disbanded June 17, at the end of the first half.

Playoff: Pine Bluff 4 games, El Dorado 0.

All-Star Team: 1B-Mellon Tatum, Baton Rouge; 2B-Shaw, Monroe; 3B-Ralph Winegarner, El Dorado; SS-Horne, Alexandria/Vicksburg; OF-Virgil Gilliland, Lake Charles/Monroe; C-Dick Luckey, Alexandria/Monroe; P-G.M. "Tex" Nugent, El Dorado; Andy Price, Alexandria/Monroe.

BA: Dick Luckey, Alexandria/Monroe, .358
Runs: Thomas Morris, Jackson, 112
Hits: Buster Wisrock, El Dorado, 181
RBIs: Ralph Winegarner, El Dorado, 128
HRs: Ralph Winegarner, El Dorado, 40
Wins: G.M. "Tex" Nugent, El Dorado, 21
SOs: Jackie Reid, El Dorado, 181
ERA: John Singleton, Vicksburg, 3.11

D Georgia-Alabama League
President: L.H. Carre

Standings	W	L	Pct.	GB	Manager
Lindale Pepperells**	63	38	.624	—	Jack Moulton
Cedartown Braves*	60	41	.594	3	Sherrod Smith
Anniston Nobles	57	44	.564	6	Paul Fittery/Dixie Walker
Huntsville Springers	35	66	.347	28	Bill Pierre/Erskine Thompson/Tubby Walton/ Dixie Carroll/Clarence Hart
Carrollton Champs#	38	46	.452	NA	Carl East/Erskine Thompson
Talladega Indians#	33	51	.393	NA	Walt Barbare/Cliff Verner

#Carrollton and Talladega disbanded August 14.

Playoff: Cedartown 4 games, Lindale 3, one tie.

All-Star Team: 1B-Bill McGhee, Anniston; 2B-Roger Fuqua, Anniston; 3B-W.E. Gentry, Cedartown; SS-Frank Costa, Lindale; OF-Bernard Lewis, Lindale; Jack Shipley,

Cedartown; Gordon Pugh, Lindale; **C**-G.E. Goggans, Anniston; **Util**-William Alexander, Carrollton; **P**-Robert Ledbetter, Anniston; Grady Bassett, Anniston; J.G. Baker, Lindale; K.E. Chitwood, Cedartown; George Granger, Lindale.

BA: Bernard Lewis, Lindale, .422	**Wins:** Paul Fittery, Anniston, 16
Runs: Jack Shipley, Cedartown, 131	**SOs:** Abe White, Lindale, 143
Hits: Bernard Lewis, Lindale, 175	**ERA:** Sherry Smith, Cedartown, 3.34
HRs: George Kelly, Cedartown, 26	**Pct:** Sherry Smith, Cedartown, .875, 14-2

D Mississippi Valley League
President: Belden Hill

Standings	W	L	Pct.	GB	Manager
Cedar Rapids Bunnies	71	55	.564	—	Paul Speraw
Rock Island Islanders	70	56	.556	1	Clarence Roper
Davenport Blue Sox	64	61	.512	6½	Ed Reichle
Moline Plowboys	63	62	.504	7½	Riley Parker
Waterloo Hawks	63	63	.500	8	Cletus Dixon
Burlington Bees	61	65	.484	10	George Young
Keokuk Indians	56	70	.445	15	Sam Schwartz/Lester "Pat" Patterson/ Henry Wingfield/John Schinski
Dubuque Tigers	55	71	.437	16	Richard Manchester/Ed Worber

All-Star Team: 1B-Pickett, Moline; **2B**-Riley Parker, Moline; **3B**-Eddie Hunter, Burlington; **SS**-Mitchell, Waterloo; **OF**-John Grilli, Keokuk; Charles Conners, Burlington; Joe Prerost, Waterloo; **C**-George Treadwell, Moline; Mueller, Cedar Rapids; **Util**-Chris Serre, Dubuque; **P**-Delano Wetherell, Rock Island; Ludsick, Dubuque; Newton, Keokuk; Wilkins, Waterloo; William Prince, Waterloo; Walter Murphy, Rock Island.

BA: Riley Parker, Moline, .376	**Wins:** Delano Wetherell, Rock Island, 21
Runs: Dick Esrey, Moline, 114	**SOs:** Delano Wetherell, Rock Island, 217
Hits: Dick Esrey, Moline, 183	**Pct:** Walter Murphy, Rock Island, .667, 10-5
HRs: Joe Prerost, Waterloo, 15	

D Nebraska State League
President: James E. Beltzer

Standings	W	L	Pct.	GB	Manager
McCook Generals***	85	34	.714	—	Elmer "Doc" Bennett
Fairbury Jeffersons	68	51	.571	17	Preston Gray
Grand Island Islanders	62	58	.517	23½	Kenzie Kirkham
York Dukes	60	59	.504	25	Art Rasmussen

Standings	W	L	Pct.	GB	Manager
North Platte Buffaloes	60	60	.500	25½	Baldy Fowlkes
Norfolk Elkhorns	56	65	.463	30	Hal Brokaw
Lincoln Links	56	66	.459	30½	Les Nunamaker
Norton Jayhawks#	33	87	.275	52½	Earl Harrison/Frank Sidle

#Norton suspended operations August 25; final seven games were forfeited to scheduled opponents.

All-Star Team: 1B-Bert Gregory, North Platte; **2B**-Herbert Hansen, Fairbury; **3B**-Elmer Peters, North Platte; **SS**-Roy Schalk, Fairbury; **OF**-Buster Lucas, McCook; Ed Taylor, Lincoln; Walter Cookson, North Platte; **C**-George Caithamer, Fairbury; **P**-Vito SanFilippo, Fairbury; William Eissler, McCook.

BA: Washington Seelman, North Platte, .373	**Wins:** Vito SanFilippo, Fairbury, 23
Runs: Ed Taylor, Lincoln, 125	**SOs:** Vito SanFilippo, Fairbury, 243
Hits: Washington Seelman, North Platte, 174	**ERA:** Jim Cameron, McCook, 2.25
HRs: Mike Kreevich, McCook, 15	**Pct:** Jim Cameron, McCook, .905, 19-2

1930 Interleague Post Season Play

World Series
Philadelphia (American) 4 games, St. Louis (National) 2

Junior World Series
Rochester (International) 5 games, Louisville (American Association) 3
Total Attendance: 53,347

Dixie Series
Ft. Worth (Texas) 4 games, Memphis (Southern Association) 1
Total Attendance: 36,590

Eastern Championship
Allentown (Eastern) 2 games, Wilkes-Barre (New York-Pennsylvania) 0

Midwest Championship
Springfield (Central) 3 games, Danville (Three-I) 2
Series called off because of low attendance.

Southern Championship
Selma (Southeastern) 4 games, Greenville (South Atlantic Association) 1

1930 No-Hitters

Date	Pitcher	Team	League	Opponent	Score
5-14	Jimmy Zinn	San Francisco	Pacific Coast	Sacramento	8-0
5-22	Cecil Slaughter	Fairmont	Middle Atlantic	Jeannette	3-0 (7)
5-24	Clay Christiansen	Lincoln	Nebraska State	Norfolk	13-1
6-29	Thornton Lee	Tampa	Southeastern	Montgomery	1-0
8-8	Andy Price	Monroe	Cotton States	El Dorado	14-1
8-15	Lon Warneke	Reading	International	Buffalo	1-0 (7)
8-18	Gene Jones	Springfield	Three-I	Decatur	4-1
8-25	Lefty Logan	Fairbury	Nebraska State	York	2-1 (13)
9-2	Bob Mayo	High Point	Piedmont	Winston-Salem	14-0
9-6	Paul Richards/Bob Parham/Bobby Reis/Mattingly/Newsome/Pattison/ Phillip Gallivan	Macon	South Atlantic	Columbia	4-0 (7)

Number in parentheses indicates innings if other than nine.

THIS DATE IN MINOR LEAGUE HISTORY

April 8, 1930, Sacramento beat Mission 21-14 on opening day of the Pacific Coast League season. The Senators had 24 hits, Mission 17.

April 28, 1930, The first official night game in minor league history was played in Independence, Kansas. Muskogee defeated Independence 13-3 in the Western Association tilt.

May 2, 1930, Des Moines of the Western League inaugurated night baseball. The idea was conceived by E. Lee Keyser, president and business manager of the Des Moines club. The night game was the first in Organized Ball history played under permanent light standards. The contest on April 28 at Independence, Kansas, was completed under temporary lights provided by J.L. Wilkinson, owner of the Kansas City Monarchs.

May 13, 1930, Walter Holke of Hazleton, New York-Pennsylvania League, smashed four homers in a home game.

May 18, 1930, Frank Shellenback won the first of 14 consecutive decisions for Hollywood of the Pacific Coast League.

May 24, 1930, Nick Cullop hit three consecutive homers for Minneapolis, American Association, then made it four in a row the next day by hitting one in his first at bat.

June 8, 1930, Ken Strong hit four home runs in one game for Hazleton, Eastern League. Strong's teammate Walter Holke had achieved the same feat less than a month earlier.

June 26, 1930, Veteran Grover Alexander made his debut in a Dallas uniform and was hammered out of the box in the fifth round of the Texas League game.

July 3, 1930, Buffalo and Montreal, International League, inaugurated night baseball in Buffalo.

July 3, 1930, Tommy Bridges of Evansville, Three-I League, struck out 20 in a game with Springfield. Bridges was promoted to Detroit after having struck out 189 in 140 innings.

July 19, 1930, Southpaw Jim Mooney of Charlotte, South Atlantic Association, struck out 23 batters in a nine inning game against Augusta. The contest was the league's first night game. Charlotte won 7-3.

July 21, 1930, Dallas, Texas League, released Grover Cleveland Alexander, ending the great hurler's Organized Ball career. He hurled 24 innings for Dallas and went 1-2, with an earned run average of 8.28.

August 5, 1930, Joe Hauser of Baltimore, International League, hit three homers in a night game at Jersey City.

August 6, 1930, Outfielder Gene Rye of Waco, Texas League, hit three home runs in one inning against Beaumont. Rye, a stocky and bowlegged leftfielder, led off in the eighth frame and hit Jerry Mallet's second serve over the right field fence. The second time up, Rye hit a three-run homer off Walter Newman over the right field fence. Ten runs had scored before the first putout. On his third time up in the frame, Rye hit a grand slam off Newman over the center field fence. The inning featured 18 runs on 12 hits for 28 total bases, six walks, two errors and a wild pitch. Waco won 20-7. It was the first night game ever broadcast in the Texas League. Rye stood only 5-6 and weighed just 170 pounds.

August 22, 1930, St. Paul hit six triples against Toledo, an American Association record.

September 4, 1930, Mickey Heath of Hollywood, Pacific Coast League, made his twelfth successive hit.

September 20, 1930, Dave Danforth of Buffalo, International League, struck out 20 in a game with Rochester to set a new league record.

September 20, 1930, Joe Hauser of Baltimore, International League, walloped his 63rd homer of the season.

1931

American League
Presidents: Ernest S. Barnard/William Harridge

Standings	W	L	Pct.	GB	Attend.	Manager
Philadelphia Athletics	107	45	.704	—	627,464	Connie Mack
New York Yankees	94	59	.614	13½	912,437	Joe McCarthy
Washington Senators	92	62	.597	16	492,657	Walter Johnson
Cleveland Indians	78	76	.506	30	483,027	Roger Peckinpaugh
St. Louis Browns	63	91	.409	45	179,126	Bill Killefer
Boston Red Sox	62	90	.408	45	350,975	Shano Collins
Detroit Tigers	61	93	.396	47	434,056	Bucky Harris
Chicago White Sox	56	97	.366	51½	403,550	Donie Bush

BA: Al Simmons, Philadelphia, .390
Runs: Lou Gehrig, New York, 163
Hits: Lou Gehrig, New York, 211
RBIs: Lou Gehrig, New York, 184
HRs: Lou Gehrig, New York, 46
Babe Ruth, New York, 46

Wins: Lefty Grove, Philadelphia, 31
SOs: Lefty Grove, Philadelphia, 175
ERA: Lefty Grove, Philadelphia, 2.06
Pct: Lefty Grove, Philadelphia, .886, 31-4

National League
President: John A. Heydler

Standings	W	L	Pct.	GB	Attend.	Manager
St. Louis Cardinals	101	53	.656	—	608,535	Gabby Street
New York Giants	87	65	.572	13	812,163	John McGraw
Chicago Cubs	84	70	.545	17	1,086,422	Rogers Hornsby
Brooklyn Robins	79	73	.520	21	753,133	Wilbert Robinson
Pittsburgh Pirates	75	79	.487	26	260,392	Jewel Ens
Philadelphia Phillies	66	88	.429	35	284,849	Burt Shotton
Boston Braves	64	90	.416	37	515,005	Bill McKechnie
Cincinnati Reds	58	96	.377	43	263,316	Dan Howley

BA: Chick Hafey, St. Louis, .349
Runs: Chuck Klein, Philadelphia, 121
Bill Terry, New York, 121
Hits: Lloyd Waner, Pittsburgh, 214
RBIs: Chuck Klein, Philadelphia, 121
HRs: Chuck Klein, Philadelphia, 31

Wins: Bill Hallahan, St. Louis, 19
Heinie Meine, Pittsburgh, 19
James "Jumbo" Elliott, Philadelphia, 19
SOs: Bill Hallahan, St. Louis, 159
ERA: Bob Walker, New York, 2.26
Pct: Paul Derringer, St. Louis, .692, 18-8

AA American Association
President: Thomas J. Hickey

Standings	W	L	Pct.	GB	Attend.	Manager
St. Paul Saints	104	63	.623	—	176,512	Lefty Leifield
Kansas City Blues	90	77	.539	14	117,921	Dutch Zwilling
Indianapolis Indians	86	80	.518	17½	138,415	John Corriden/Emmett McCann
Columbus Red Birds	84	82	.506	19½	174,511	Nemo Leibold
Milwaukee Brewers	83	85	.494	21½	235,345	Marty Berghammer/ Frank O'Rourke
Minneapolis Millers	80	88	.476	24½	132,740	Mike Kelley
Louisville Colonels	74	94	.440	30½	144,247	Allan Sothoron
Toledo Mud Hens	68	100	.405	36½	80,067	Casey Stengel

All-Star Team: 1B-Oscar Roettger, St. Paul; **2B**-Jack Saltzgaver, St. Paul; **3B**-Meredith Hopkins, St. Paul; **SS**-Joe Morrissey, St. Paul; **OF**-Len Koenecke, Indianapolis; Spencer Harris, Minneapolis; Bevo LeBourveau, Toledo/Columbus; **C**-Clyde Manion, Milwaukee; Robert Fenner, St. Paul; **Util**-Harold Anderson, St. Paul; Burgess Whitehead, Columbus; **P**-Dutch Henry, Minneapolis; Huck Betts, St. Paul; Bryan Harris, St. Paul; Louis Polli, Milwaukee; Bill Burwell, Indianapolis; Walter Miller, Indianapolis.

BA: Art Shires, Milwaukee, .385
Runs: Spencer Harris, Minneapolis, 156
Hits: Art Shires, Milwaukee, 240
RBIs: Pat Crawford, Columbus, 154

HRs: Pat Crawford, Columbus, 28
Wins: Dutch Henry, Minneapolis, 23
SOs: Claude Jonnard, Milwaukee, 130
ERA: John Cooney, Toledo, 2.49

AA International League
President: Charles H. Knapp

Standings	W	L	Pct.	GB	Attend.	Manager
Rochester Red Wings	101	67	.601	—	293,091	Billy Southworth
Newark Bears	99	69	.589	2	330,386	Al Mamaux
Baltimore Orioles	94	72	.566	6	214,666	Fritz Maisel
Montreal Royals	85	80	.515	14½	179,586	Eddie Holly
Toronto Maple Leafs	83	84	.497	17½	102,143	Steve O'Neill
Reading Keys	79	88	.473	21½	122,202	Clarence "Pants" Rowland
Jersey City Skeeters	65	102	.389	35½	130,031	George "Specs" Toporcer/ Bob Shawkey
Buffalo Bisons	61	105	.367	39	120,637	James Cooney

All-Star Team: 1B-Baxter Jordan, Newark; **2B**-Andy Cohen, Newark; **3B**-Joe Brown, Jersey City; **SS**-Ed Delker, Rochester; **OF**-Ray Pepper, Rochester; John Gill, Baltimore; Ike Boone, Newark; **C**-Paul Florence, Rochester; Charles Hargreaves, Newark; **P**-Johnny

Allen, Jersey City/Toronto; Walter "Jumbo" Brown, Jersey City; Monte Weaver, Baltimore; Ray Starr, Rochester; **MVP**-Ray Pepper, Rochester.

BA: Ike Boone, Newark, .356
Runs: Ray Pepper, Rochester, 123
Hits: Ray Pepper, Rochester, 233
RBIs: Jim Poole, Reading, 126
HRs: Joe Hauser, Baltimore, 31

Wins: Johnny Allen, Jersey City/Toronto, 21
Monte Weaver, Baltimore, 21
SOs: Don Brennan, Newark, 143
ERA: Ray Starr, Rochester, 2.83

AA Pacific Coast League
President: Harry A. Williams

Standings	W	L	Pct.	GB	Attend.	Manager
San Francisco Seals**	107	80	.572	—	251,759	Nick Williams
Hollywood Stars*	104	83	.556	3	301,843	Oscar Vitt
Portland Beavers	100	87	.535	7	238,340	Spencer Abbott
Los Angeles Angels	98	89	.524	9	256,416	Jack Lelivelt
Sacramento Senators	86	101	.460	21	114,270	Buddy Ryan
Oakland Oaks	86	101	.460	21	175,284	Carl Zamloch
Mission Reds	84	103	.449	23	162,914	George Burns/Joe Devine
Seattle Indians	83	104	.444	24	147,787	Ernie Johnson

Playoff: San Francisco 4 games, Hollywood 0.

All-Star Team: 1B-Jim Keesey, San Francisco; **2B**-John Monroe, Portland/Mission; **3B**-Stan Hack, Sacramento; **SS**-Frank Crosetti, San Francisco; **OF**-Arnold "Jigger" Statz, Los Angeles, Ed Coleman, Portland, David Barbee, Hollywood; **C**-John Bassler, Hollywood, Frank Cox, Seattle; **Util**-Billy Rhiel, Portland; **P**-Frank Shellenback, Hollywood, Sam Gibson, San Francisco, Win Ballou, Los Angeles, Tony Freitas, Sacramento.

BA: Oscar "Ox" Eckhardt, Mission, .369
Runs: Arnold "Jigger" Statz, Los Angeles, 141
John Monroe, Portland/Mission, 141
Frank Crosetti, San Francisco, 141
Homer Summa, Los Angeles, 141
Hits: Ed Coleman, Portland, 275
Oscar "Ox" Eckhardt, Mission, 275

RBIs: Ed Coleman, Portland, 183
HRs: David Barbee, Hollywood, 47
Wins: Sam Gibson, San Francisco, 28
SOs: Sam Gibson, San Francisco, 204
ERA: Sam Gibson, San Francisco, 2.48

A Eastern League
Executive Chairman: Fred J. Voos, Jr.

Standings	W	L	Pct.	GB	Manager
Hartford Senators***	97	40	.708	—	Charley Moore
Bridgeport Bears	81	60	.574	18	Hans Lobert
Springfield Ponies	65	74	.468	33	Frank Stapleton
New Haven Bulldogs	63	73	.463	33½	Ray Ryan/Bill Stewart
Allentown Buffaloes	64	75	.460	34	Joe Bush
Norfolk Tars	62	73	.459	35	Win Clark
Albany Senators	62	76	.449	35½	Bill McCorry
Richmond Byrds	55	78	.414	40	Cy Williams/Bobby Murray

All-Star Team: 1B-Bruce Caldwell, New Haven; **2B**-Robert Murray, Richmond; **3B**-Robert Reis, Hartford; **SS**-Glenn Messner, Allentown; **OF**-Robert Parham, Hartford, Albert Cohen, Hartford, Carr Smith, Norfolk; **C**-Paul Richards, Hartford; **Util**-John Mann, Hartford; **P**-Earl Mattingly, Hartford, Philip Gallivan, Hartford, Van Lingle Mungo, Hartford, Jim Mooney, Bridgeport, Ned Porter, Springfield.

BA: Bruce Caldwell, New Haven, .356
Runs: Robert Parham, Hartford, 105
Hits: Carr Smith, Norfolk, 192
RBIs: Bruce Caldwell, New Haven, 130

HRs: Bruce Caldwell, New Haven, 38
Wins: Arthur Jones, Hartford, 18
SOs: Van Lingle Mungo, Hartford, 151
ERA: Jim Mooney, Bridgeport, 1.69

A Southern Association
President: John D. Martin

Standings	W	L	Pct.	GB	Attend.	Manager
Birmingham Barons	97	55	.638	—	175,877	Clyde Milan
Little Rock Travelers	87	66	.569	10½	113,738	Harry Strohm
Memphis Chickasaws	84	69	.549	13½	137,673	Tommy "Doc" Prothro
Chattanooga Lookouts	79	74	.516	18½	172,286	Bert Niehoff
New Orleans Pelicans	78	75	.510	19½	134,579	Larry Gilbert
Atlanta Crackers	78	76	.506	20	161,859	Johnny Dobbs
Mobile Marines/ Knoxville Smokies#	57	94	.377	39½	79,773	Milt Stock
Nashville Volunteers	51	102	.333	46½	67,338	Joe Klugman

#Mobile (34-61) moved to Knoxville July 22.

All-Star Team: 1B-B.M. Connaster, New Orleans; **2B**-Billy Bancroft, Birmingham; **3B**-John Gooch, Birmingham; **SS**-John Cortazzo, Birmingham; **OF**-Art Weis, Birmingham; Walter French, Little Rock; Elliott Bigelow, Chattanooga; **C**-Henry Erickson, Mobile/Knoxville; Ed Taylor, Birmingham; **P**-Ray Caldwell, Birmingham; Bob Hasty, Birmingham; Jimmy Walkup, Birmingham; Belve Bean, New Orleans; Fred Johnson, New Orleans.

*Won first-half **Won second-half ***Won both halves

BA: John "Moose" Clabaugh, Nashville, .378
Runs: Walter French, Little Rock, 133
Hits: Walter French, Little Rock, 235
RBIs: Elliott Bigelow, Chattanooga, 125

HRs: John "Moose" Clabaugh, Nashville, 23
Wins: Fred Johnson, New Orleans, 21
  Bob Hasty, Birmingham, 21
SOs: Bobo Newsom, Little Rock, 152
ERA: Jimmy Walkup, Birmingham, 2.86

A Texas League
President: J. Alvin Gardner

Standings	W	L	Pct.	GB	Attend.	Manager
Houston Buffaloes***	108	51	.679	—	229,540	Joe Schultz
Beaumont Exporters	94	65	.591	14	84,070	Del Baker
Ft. Worth Panthers	90	70	.563	18½	97,672	Art Phelan
Dallas Steers	83	77	.519	25½	113,285	Hap Morse
Wichita Falls Spudders	76	85	.472	33	33,560	Carl Williams
Shreveport Sports	66	94	.413	42½	57,572	Jake Atz
San Antonio Indians	66	94	.413	42½	55,202	Claude "Ug" Robertson
Galveston Buccaneers	57	104	.354	52	97,163	Del Pratt

Playoff: Houston 3 games, Beaumont 1, one tie, for the first half title.

All-Star Team: 1B-George Stanton, Wichita Falls; **2B**-Carey Selph, Houston; **3B**-Eddie Hock, Houston; **SS**-Ben Taylor, Beaumont; **OF**-Homer Peel, Houston; Joe Medwick, Houston; Raymond "Rip" Radcliff, Shreveport; **C**-Harold Funk, Houston; Bernard Hungling, Wichita Falls; **P**-Dizzy Dean, Houston; Bob McCabe, Ft. Worth; George Payne, Houston; Tex Carleton, Houston; Whitlow Wyatt, Beaumont; **MVP**-Dizzy Dean, Houston.

BA: Raymond "Rip" Radcliff, Shreveport, .361
Runs: Carey Selph, Houston, 116
Hits: Raymond "Rip" Radcliff, Shreveport, 215
RBIs: Joe Medwick, Houston, 126
HRs: Joe Medwick, Houston, 19

Wins: Dizzy Dean, Houston, 26
SOs: Dizzy Dean, Houston, 303
ERA: Dizzy Dean, Houston, 1.53
  Whitlow Wyatt, Beaumont, 1.53

A Western League
President: Dale D. Gear

Standings	W	L	Pct.	GB	Manager
Des Moines Demons**	94	51	.648	—	Bill Rodgers
Wichita Aviators*	92	58	.613	4½	Art Griggs/Howard Gregory
St. Joseph Saints	79	64	.552	14	Frank Haley
Pueblo Braves	76	69	.524	18	Jimmy Payton/Walter Smallwood
Oklahoma City Indians	70	80	.467	26½	Cletus Dixon/Frank Tobin
Denver Bears	64	77	.454	28	John Butler
Topeka Senators	58	86	.397	35½	Howard Gregory/Howard Lindimore
Omaha Packers	49	97	.336	45½	H.C. "Doc" Smith/Pug Griffin

Playoff: Des Moines 4 games, Wichita 2.

All-Star Team: 1B-Jim Oglesby, Des Moines; **2B**-Tony Piet, Wichita; **3B**-John Kroner, Oklahoma City; **SS**-Angus McIsaac, Pueblo; **OF**-Stan Keyes, Des Moines; Ernie Parker, Denver; Mike Kreevich, Des Moines; **C**-Andy Vargas, Denver; Benny Warren, Wichita; **Util**-Lem Young, Wichita; **P**-Bud Tinning, Des Moines; Harold McKain, Pueblo; Rufus Meadows, Topeka; Elmer Knight, Des Moines; Ed "Bear Tracks" Greer, Denver; Arthur Jacobs, Wichita.

BA: Stan Keyes, Des Moines, .369
Runs: Arky Vaughan, Wichita, 145
Hits: Stan Keyes, Des Moines, 203
RBIs: Stan Keyes, Des Moines, 160
HRs: Stan Keyes, Des Moines, 38

Wins: Bud Tinning, Des Moines, 24
SOs: Rufus Meadows, Topeka, 177
ERA: Bud Tinning, Des Moines, 3.14
Pct: Bud Tinning, Des Moines, .923, 24-2

B New York-Pennsylvania League
President: Perry B. Farrell

Standings	W	L	Pct.	GB	Manager
Harrisburg Senators	83	56	.597	—	Joe Cobb/Eddie Onslow
Wilkes-Barre Barons	80	59	.576	3	Mike McNally
Williamsport Grays	76	64	.543	7½	Glenn Killinger
Binghamton Triplets	76	64	.543	7½	Heinie Groh
York White Roses	73	67	.521	10½	Jack Bentley/Frank Uzmann
Scranton Miners	69	70	.496	14	Buck Elliott/Ernie Vick
Hazleton Mountaineers	57	82	.410	26	Hugh Fitzgerald/Jake Pitler
Elmira Colonels	44	96	.314	39½	Jake Pitler/Freddy Coumbe/Joe Sugden

All-Star Team: 1B-Mike Martineck, Williamsport; **2B**-Fred Dorman, York; **3B**-Heinie Groh, Binghamton; **SS**-Walter Novak, Williamsport; **OF**-Joe Dwyer, Wilkes-Barre; Lou Finney, York; Horace "Red" McBride, Harrisburg; **C**-Bill Steinecke, Binghamton; John McCarthy, Harrisburg; **P**-Harry Holsclaw, Wilkes-Barre; Carl Schoof, Scranton; Ivan Rase, Harrisburg; Bert Grimm, Binghamton.

BA: Bill Steinecke, Binghamton, .361
Runs: William Outen, Scranton, 108
Hits: Horace "Red" McBride, Harrisburg, 181
  Joe Dwyer, Wilkes-Barre, 181
RBIs: George McQuinn, Scranton, 101

HRs: John Wright, Wilkes-Barre/Hazleton, 19
Wins: Harry Holsclaw, Wilkes-Barre, 25
SOs: Bob Brown, Binghamton, 176
ERA: Chant Parkes, Williamsport, 2.22

B Three-I League
President: L.J. Wylie

Standings	W	L	Pct.	GB	Manager
Springfield Senators*	72	45	.615	—	Earl Wambsganss
Quincy Indians**	67	49	.578	4½	Walter Holke
Evansville Hubs	67	58	.536	9	Bob Coleman
Decatur Commodores	64	57	.529	10	Frank Desseau
Bloomington Cubs	58	61	.487	15	Joseph Dunn
Terre Haute Tots	55	68	.447	20	Frank Kohlbecker
Peoria Tractors	51	68	.429	22	Charles Fraser
Danville Veterans	44	72	.379	27½	Frank Murphy

Playoff: Quincy 4 games, Springfield 2.

All-Star Team: 1B-John Brewer, Springfield; **2B**-Ollie Bejma, Quincy; **3B**-Lee Cunningham, Danville; **SS**-Ossie Bluege, Peoria; **OF**-George Stumpf, Quincy; Milt Galatzer, Terre Haute; Charles Conners, Decatur; **C**-Howard Maple, Bloomington; Sanford Hamby, Terre Haute; **P**-Charles Reddock, Terre Haute/Decatur; Thadden Campbell, Decatur; Glen Larsen, Springfield; Albert Williamson, Bloomington; Leon Pettit, Quincy.

BA: Milt Galatzer, Terre Haute, .375
Runs: George Stumpf, Quincy, 100
Hits: Charles Conners, Decatur, 169
RBIs: Ollie Bejma, Quincy, 86
HRs: Ollie Bejma, Quincy, 16

Wins: Thadden Campbell, Decatur, 19
SOs: Glen Larsen, Springfield, 168
ERA: Charles Reddock, Terre Haute/
  Decatur, 2.52

C Middle Atlantic League
President: Elmer M. Daily

Standings	W	L	Pct.	GB	Manager
Charleston Senators**	82	44	.651	—	Dick Hoblitzell
Cumberland Colts*	82	46	.641	1	Leo Mackey
Beckley Black Knights	81	49	.623	3	Frank Welch
Scottdale Cardinals	78	55	.586	7½	Clay Hopper
Johnstown Johnnies	73	54	.575	9½	Wilbur Good
Huntington Boosters	68	62	.523	16	Johnny Stuart
Fairmont Black Diamonds	65	60	.520	16½	James Walsh/Tony Cyran
Clarksburg Generals	66	63	.512	17½	Dick Proctor
Hagerstown Hubs/Parkersburg Parkers/					
Youngstown Tubers@	56	65	.463	23½	Joe Cambria
Wheeling Stogies	50	77	.394	32½	Dan Tapson/Pat Haley
Charleroi Governors	30	92	.246	50	Bill Phillips/Benny Arrigiani/Joe Fillingham
Jeannette Jays/Altoona Engineers/					
Beaver Falls Beavers#	32	96	.250	51	William Phillips/Kemp Wicker

#Jeannette (1-11) moved to Altoona May 23, first home game May 28; Altoona moved to Beaver Falls July 18, first home game July 29.

@Hagerstown (27-22) moved to Parkersburg June 28; Parkersburg (9-5) moved to Youngstown July 12.

Playoff: Cumberland 4 games, Charleston 2.

All-Star Team: 1B-Harold Bejin, Wheeling; **2B**-Joe Paiment, Cumberland; **3B**-Milton Gordon, Clarksburg; **SS**-Eli Harris, Beckley; **OF**-J. Rimmer, Huntington; Sam Thomas, Johnstown; Frank Welch, Beckley; **C**-Babe Phelps, Youngstown; Burton Bruckman, Scottdale; **P**-Vito Tamulis, Cumberland; Marvin Duke, Cumberland; Bill Lee, Scottdale; Edward Marleau, Charleston.

BA: Babe Phelps, Youngstown, .408
Runs: Sam Thomas, Johnstown, 122
Hits: Babe Phelps, Youngstown, 178
RBIs: Bill Pritchard, Johnstown, 125

HRs: Frank Welch, Beckley, 38
Wins: Edward Marleau, Charleston, 23
SOs: Bill Lee, Scottdale, 256
ERA: Vito Tamulis, Cumberland, 1.93

C Piedmont League
President: William G. Bramham

Standings	W	L	Pct.	GB	Manager
Charlotte Hornets	100	37	.730	—	Guy Lacy
Raleigh Capitals	86	50	.630	13½	Odie Strain
Greensboro Patriots	81	56	.591	19	Johnny Kane
Asheville Tourists	66	67	.496	32	Ray Kennedy/Bobby Hipps
Durham Bulls	56	72	.438	39½	George "Possum" Whitted
Winston-Salem Twins	55	79	.410	43½	Bunn Hearn/Bob "Stuffy" McCrone
Henderson Gamecocks	51	82	.383	47	Jimmy Teague
High Point Pointers	39	91	.300	57½	Danny Boone/Hobe Brummitt/Tom Young

Playoff: Charlotte 4 games, Raleigh 2.

BA: Frank Packard, Charlotte, .366
Runs: Frank Packard, Charlotte, 145
Hits: Frank Packard, Charlotte, 185
RBIs: Frank Packard, Charlotte, 123
HRs: Frank Packard, Charlotte, 21

Wins: Charles Shaney, Charlotte, 24
SOs: Frank Coleman, Raleigh, 173
ERA: Jim Lyle, Charlotte, 1.92
Pct: Thurman Wical, Charlotte, .842, 16-3

C Western Association
President: Dale D. Gear

Standings	W	L	Pct.	GB	Manager
Springfield Red Wings***	87	57	.604	—	Eddie Dyer
Joplin Miners	80	62	.563	6	Lyman Lamb

Independence Producers ..... 77 69 .527 11   Mark Purtell
Ft. Smith Twins .... 74 76 .493 16   Runt Marr
Muskogee Chiefs .... 64 86 .427 26   Roy Corgan
Bartlesville Bronchos .... 59 91 .393 31   Art Ewoldt

All-Star Team: 1B-W.F. Burt, Ft. Smith; **2B**-Jack Wright, Bartlesville; **3B**-Harold Bohl, Springfield; **SS**-John Keane, Springfield; **OF**-Grover Seitz, Springfield; Sam Scaling, Ft. Smith; Ab Wright, Muskogee; **C**-Mike Ryba, Springfield; F. Cato, Joplin; **P**-Bill Beckman, Springfield; Glen Gabler, Bartlesville; Rudy Jones, Independence; Paul Dean, Springfield.

BA: Ab Wright, Muskogee, .376
Runs: Grover Seitz, Springfield, 143
Hits: Ab Wright, Muskogee, 216
RBIs: David Cheeves, Joplin, 122
HRs: Gordon Nell, Muskogee, 44

Wins: Bill Beckman, Springfield, 24
SOs: William Alexander, Independence, 217
ERA: Marvin Carlson, Joplin, 2.01
Pct: Paul Dean, Springfield, .786, 11-3

D Arizona-Texas League
Presidents: Wilford S. Sullinger/Allan Stewart

Standings	W	L	Pct.	GB	Manager
El Paso Texans**	79	52	.603	—	Royce "Mule" Washburn
Tucson Missions	72	59	.550	7	Bobby Coltrin
Phoenix Senators	65	63	.508	12½	Louis Guisto
Bisbee Bees*	63	68	.481	16	Roy "Hardrock" Johnson
Nogales Internationals	62	67	.481	16	Dick Cox
Globe Bears	49	81	.377	29½	Mickey Shader

Playoff: El Paso 5 games, Bisbee 0.

All-Star Team: 1B-John Keane, Bisbee; **2B**-Dick Gyselman, Tucson; **3B**-Carl Kott, El Paso; **SS**-Claire McDermott, El Paso; **OF**-Tony Antista, El Paso; George Steinback, Bisbee; Cal Lahman, Tucson; **C**-Willard Hershberger, El Paso; Angus McIsaac, Bisbee; **Util**-Charles King, El Paso; **P**-Joe Sullivan, Tucson; Phelps, Phoenix; George Nielsen, El Paso; Sumont, Nogales.

BA: John Keane, Bisbee, .408
Runs: Emil Mailho, Phoenix, 108
Hits: Red Anderson, Tucson/Nogales, 190
HRs: Walter Carson, Globe, 34

Wins: Joe Sullivan, Tucson, 23
SOs: George Nielsen, El Paso, 196
Pct: Joe Sullivan, Tucson, .767, 23-7

D Cotton States League
President: Frank A. Scott

Standings	W	L	Pct.	GB	Manager
Jackson Senators*	79	45	.637	—	Herschel Bobo
Vicksburg Hill Billies**	66	52	.559	10	Joe Schepner
Pine Bluff Judges	62	62	.500	17	Wray Query
Baton Rouge Standards	58	62	.483	19	Joe Martina/Wilbur Davis
Monroe Twins	54	66	.450	23	Eddie Palmer/Frank Meyers/Ted Jourdan
El Dorado Lions	44	76	.367	33	George "Hickory" Jackson

Playoff: Jackson 4 games, Vicksburg 0.

All-Star Team: 1B-Carroll Burrows, Pine Bluff; **2B**-Hugh Ferrell, Jackson; **3B**-Herschel Bobo, Jackson; **SS**-Frank Costa, Vicksburg; **OF**-Herb Welch, Baton Rouge; Redmond Hume, Vicksburg; C.E. Seeley, El Dorado; **C**-Josh Billings, Vicksburg; Wray Query, Pine Bluff; **P**-Jackie Reid, Jackson; Gus Burleson, El Dorado/Monroe; Joe Berry, Pine Bluff; Adel White, Monroe.

BA: Hugh Ferrell, Jackson, .345
Runs: Herschel Bobo, Jackson, 103
Hits: Hugh Ferrell, Jackson, 161
RBIs: Cecil "Stormy" Davis, Pine Bluff, 100

HRs: Horace Long, Jackson, 17
Wins: Gus Burleson, El Dorado/Monroe, 20
SOs: Adel White, Monroe, 163
ERA: Adel White, Monroe, 2.56

D East Texas League
President: Harry Wanderling

Standings	W	L	Pct.	GB	Manager
Henderson Oilers	4	1	.800	—	Hick Munsell/Bennie Bedford
Longview Cannibals	4	3	.571	1	Abe Bowman
Kilgore Gushers	1	3	.250	2½	Ewell "Turkey" Gross
Tyler Trojans	1	3	.250	2½	Frank "Pop" Kitchens

Tyler announced that it would disband May 5; the rest of the league followed suit May 7.

BA: M.B. Hauser, Henderson, .462
   Kenneth Westbrook, Longview, .462
Runs: Gilbert Humphries, Longview, 9
Hits: Lester Seward, Longview, 11

HRs: M.B. Hauser, Henderson, 4
Wins: Jackie Reid, Longview, 2
SOs: R.M. "Rudy" Leopold, Kilgore, 22
Pct: Jackie Reid, Longview, 1.000, 2-0

D Mississippi Valley League
President: Belden Hill

Standings	W	L	Pct.	GB	Attend.	Manager
Keokuk Indians	73	51	.589	—		Bobby Rice
Cedar Rapids Bunnies	74	52	.587	—	63,000	Paul Speraw
Moline Plowboys	68	58	.540	6		Riley Parker
Burlington Bees	64	60	.516	9		Art Mueller
Rock Island Islanders	61	65	.484	13		Clarence Roper
Waterloo Hawks	57	68	.456	16½		Dick Manchester/Babe Thomas
Davenport Blue Sox	53	73	.421	21	80,000	Ed Reichle/Cletus Dixon
Dubuque Tigers	51	74	.408	22½	12,000	Preston Gray/Ed Hendee/ Elmer Peters

BA: Riley Parker, Moline, .374
Runs: Pep Young, Keokuk, 125
Hits: Dick Esrey, Moline, 176
HRs: Malcolm Pickett, Moline, 13

Wins: Guilford Paulsen, Burlington, 19
   John Ziegler, Cedar Rapids, 19
SOs: Al Gizelbach, Burlington, 185
ERA: Guilford Paulsen, Burlington, 2.21

D Nebraska State League
President: Robert C. Russell

Standings	W	L	Pct.	GB	Manager
Grand Island Islanders*	66	41	.617	—	Dick "Sonny" Brookhaus
McCook Generals	59	50	.541	8	Elmer "Doc" Bennett
Lincoln Links	55	51	.519	10½	Les Nunamaker
North Platte Buffaloes**	53	55	.491	13½	Bart Green/Spud Owens
Norfolk Elkhorns	47	58	.448	18	Joe McDermott
York Dukes	42	67	.385	25	Vern "Pop" Gleason/Bob Browne

Playoff: Grand Island 4 games, North Platte 1.

BA: Ignatius Walters, McCook, .400
Runs: Roy Kippert, Grand Island/ McCook, 117
Hits: Ignatius Walters, McCook, 193

HRs: Sebastian Wagner, Norfolk, 22
Wins: Henry Matuzak, McCook, 18
SOs: Harley Hagan, Lincoln, 189
ERA: Robert Pickering, Grand Island, 2.56

D Palmetto League
President: Charles H. Garrison

Standings	W	L	Pct.	GB	Manager
Augusta Wolves***	53	23	.697	—	Holt "Cat" Milner
Florence Pee Deans	44	32	.579	9	Frank Walker/Carl East
Greenville Spinners	37	39	.487	16	Nelson Leach/Sherry Smith
Anderson Electrics/ Spartanburg Spartans#	18	58	.237	35	Joe Guyon/Ken McNeill/Frank Walker

#Anderson (14-40) moved to Spartanburg June 29 for the second half, first home game July 2. The league disbanded July 23.

BA: Bill McGhee, Augusta, .405
Runs: Zach Smith, Augusta, 85
Hits: Bill McGhee, Augusta, 133
RBIs: Bill McGhee, Augusta, 73

HRs: Charles English, Florence, 11
Wins: Jinx Harris, Augusta, 17
SOs: Jinx Harris, Augusta, 119
Pct: James Ryan, Augusta, .846, 11-2

D Rio Grande Valley League
Presidents: George P. Blevins/C.F.C. Ladd

Standings	W	L	Pct.	GB	Manager
McAllen Palms**	55	37	.598	—	Tex Covington
Corpus Christi Seahawks/ La Feria Nighthawks#* ...	49	46	.516	7½	Pat Withers/Ray Pipkin
Harlingen Ladds	43	49	.467	12	Paul Trammel
San Benito Saints	40	55	.421	16½	Bishop Clements/Elgar Waitman

#Corpus Christi (20-23) moved to La Feria June 5, first home game June 10. La Feria played its home games in Harlingen.
The league disbanded July 30.

Playoff: McAllen 3 games, La Feria 0.

BA: John Rizzo, Corpus Christi/La Feria, .385
Runs: Frank Denson, McAllen, 99
Hits: Frank Denson, McAllen, 109
HRs: Harry Bonds, McAllen, 8

SBs: Frank Denson, McAllen, 70
Wins: Adrian Johnston, Harlingen, 14
SOs: Adrian Johnston, Harlingen, 148
Pct: Horace Hardy, McAllen, .786, 11-3

1931 Interleague Post Season Play

World Series
St. Louis (National) 4 games, Philadelphia (American) 3

Junior World Series
Rochester (International) 5 games, St. Paul (American Association) 3

Dixie Series
Birmingham (Southern Association) 4 games, Houston (Texas) 3
Total Attendance: 81,025

1931 No-Hitters

Date	Pitcher	Team	League	Opponent	Score
4-29	Wes Ferrell	Cleveland	American	St. Louis	9-0
5-5	Ivan Young	High Point	Piedmont	Raleigh	4-0
5-17	Darrell Hawley	Dubuque	Mississippi Valley	Moline	7-0
6-5	Euel Moore	San Antonio	Texas	Galveston	3-0
6-6	Bill Dietrich	Harrisburg	New York-Penn.	Wilkes-Barre	1-0
6-6	Willie Ludolph	Oakland	Pacific Coast	Mission	4-0
6-12	Malcolm Moss	Los Angeles	Pacific Coast	Sacramento	5-1
6-19	Rufus Meadows	Newark	International	Montreal	8-0 (7)
6-21	Ralph Erickson	Shreveport	Texas	Houston	2-0
7-9	Walter Newman	El Paso	Arizona-Texas	Globe	13-0
7-21	Bill Winford	McAllen	Rio Grande Valley	Harlingen	14-0
7-25	Bill Storey	Keokuk	Mississippi Valley	Davenport	6-0
8-6	Al Pina	Nogales	Arizona-Texas	Bisbee	2-0 (6)
8-8	Bobby Burke	Washington	American	Boston	5-0
8-12	Ralph Blatz	Dubuque	Mississippi Valley	Moline	7-0
8-19	Edwin Chapman	Greensboro	Piedmont	Henderson	2-0
8-25	George Nielsen	El Paso	Arizona-Texas	Nogales	4-0 (7)
8-25	Andy Rush	Harrisburg	New York-Penn.	Scranton	6-0 (7)
8-29	Lefty Melton	Asheville	Piedmont	High Point	4-0 (5)
8-30	John Paul Jones	Oklahoma City	Western	Omaha	13-0
9-3	Reggie Mapp	Winston-Salem	Piedmont	High Point	6-0 (P, 5)
9-11	Charles Shaney	Charlotte	Piedmont	High Point	7-0 (5)
	Gus Burleson	El Dorado	Cotton States		

Number in parentheses indicates innings if other than nine; "P" indicates perfect game.

THIS DATE IN MINOR LEAGUE HISTORY

April 2, 1931, President Joe Engel of Chattanooga, Southern Association, signed 17-year-old Jackie Mitchell as a pitcher. She appeared in only one exhibition game, against the Yankees, "striking out" Babe Ruth and Lou Gehrig. The Engel stunt drew a crowd of 3,000 to the Chattanooga park. Unfortunately, Mitchell never had a chance to repeat her performance as a professional baseball player. A few days after her debut, Commissioner Landis informed Engel that he had disallowed Mitchell's contract on the grounds that life in baseball was too strenuous for women.

April 26, 1931, In the opening game of the Eastern League season at New Haven, Hartford built up a 13-0 lead and led 22-14 after eight innings. New Haven scored nine runs in the ninth frame to win 23-22, when Van Lingle Mungo walked in the tying and winning runs. Paul Richards was a member of the Hartford club.

May 6, 1931, Gregory Mulleavy made six errors at second base for Toledo, American Association.

May 30, 1931, Walter French of Little Rock, Southern Association, made 21 hits in 29 times at bat over the previous week for an average of .724.

June 10, 1931, Homer Peel of Houston, Texas League, singled into a triple play against Dallas. Ed Hock (who himself had completed an unassisted triple play while playing third base for Houston against Dallas on May 6, 1927) scored from third on Peel's drive to right, but Peel and two other Houston base runners were retired in rundowns on the base paths. The weird play included three putouts and seven assists as six Dallas players took part in the play. Two future major leaguers, third baseman Mike Higgins and catcher Al Todd, helped Dallas execute the triple killing.

June 21, 1931, Columbus and Minneapolis played three games in the American Association, but the Association director later declared the third game void. After the first game of a scheduled doubleheader had been played, Columbus forfeited the second contest after a dispute with the umpire. In order to give the fans the scheduled twinbill, a game was advanced. Later, on league ruling, this third game was thrown out.

June 29, 1931, Outfielder Len Koenecke of Indianapolis, American Association, had six hits in six at bats.

August 16, 1931, Minneapolis, American Association, lost its third twinbill in as many days.

August 18, 1931, Ernie Smith hit four doubles in one game for Minneapolis, American Association.

August 23, 1931, Righthander Bud Tinning of Des Moines, Western League, had his personal winning streak snapped at 16.

August 27, 1931, Newark manager Al Mamaux used 22 players, including eight pitchers, in a 13-12 victory over Buffalo.

August 29, 1931, Johnny Gill had six hits in a game for Baltimore, International League.

September 4, 1931, Hollywood, Pacific Coast League, scored 11 runs in the first inning against Los Angeles on four hits, eight walks and an error.

September 7, 1931, Johnny Gill of Baltimore, International League, had a six-hit game for the second time in a nine-day span.

September 12, 1931, Toledo outfielder Mel Simons bagged 11 putouts, equalling the American Association record.

September 19, 1931, Edgar Pick of Kansas City, American Association, went 6-for-6 in a game.

September 20, 1931, Evar Swanson, fleet outfielder for Columbus, American Association, set the base-circling record at 13.3 seconds in Columbus, Ohio.

October 9, 1931, Rochester, International League, won the Junior World Series, defeating St. Paul, American Association, five games to three.

November 12, 1931, Beer baron and New York Yankees owner Jacob Ruppert purchased the Newark club of the International League.

1932

American League
President: William Harridge

Standings	W	L	Pct.	GB	Attend.	Manager
New York Yankees............	107	47	.695	—	962,320	Joe McCarthy
Philadelphia Athletics.......	94	60	.610	13	405,500	Connie Mack
Washington Senators	93	61	.604	14	371,396	Walter Johnson
Cleveland Indians	87	65	.572	19	468,953	Roger Peckinpaugh
Detroit Tigers.....................	76	75	.503	29½	397,157	Bucky Harris
St. Louis Browns	63	91	.409	44	112,558	Bill Killefer
Chicago White Sox	49	102	.325	56½	233,198	Lew Fonseca
Boston Red Sox	43	111	.279	64	182,150	Shano Collins/Marty McManus

BA: Dale Alexander, Detroit/Boston, .367
Runs: Jimmie Foxx, Philadelphia, 151
Hits: Al Simmons, Philadelphia, 216
RBIs: Jimmie Foxx, Philadelphia, 169
HRs: Jimmie Foxx, Philadelphia, 58

Wins: General Alvin Crowder, Washington, 26
SOs: Red Ruffing, New York, 190
ERA: Lefty Grove, Philadelphia, 2.84
Pct: Johnny Allen, New York, .810, 17-4

National League
President: John A. Heydler

Standings	W	L	Pct.	GB	Attend.	Manager
Chicago Cubs.....................	90	64	.584	—	974,688	Rogers Hornsby/Charlie Grimm
Pittsburgh Pirates...............	86	68	.558	4	287,262	George Gibson
Brooklyn Dodgers..............	81	73	.526	9	681,827	Max Carey
Philadelphia Phillies	78	76	.506	12	268,914	Burt Shotton
Boston Braves....................	77	77	.500	13	507,606	Bill McKechnie
New York Giants................	72	82	.468	18	484,868	John McGraw/Bill Terry
St. Louis Cardinals	72	82	.468	18	279,219	Gabby Street
Cincinnati Reds..................	60	94	.390	30	356,950	Dan Howley

BA: Lefty O'Doul, Philadelphia, .368
Runs: Chuck Klein, Philadelphia, 152
Hits: Chuck Klein, Philadelphia, 226
RBIs: Don Hurst, Philadelphia, 143
HRs: Chuck Klein, Philadelphia, 38
Mel Ott, New York, 38

TBs: Chuck Klein, Philadelphia, 420
Wins: Lon Warneke, Chicago, 22
SOs: Dizzy Dean, St. Louis, 191
ERA: Lon Warneke, Chicago, 2.37
Pct: Lon Warneke, Chicago, .786, 22-6

AA American Association
President: Thomas J. Hickey

Standings	W	L	Pct.	GB	Attend.	Manager
Minneapolis Millers..........	100	68	.595	—	204,567	Donie Bush
Columbus Red Birds (16)...	88	77	.533	10½	309,869	Nemo Leibold/Billy Southworth
Milwaukee Brewers...........	88	78	.530	11	99,274	Frank O'Rourke
Toledo Mud Hens..............	87	80	.521	12½	94,210	Bibb Falk
Indianapolis Indians...........	86	80	.518	13	183,842	Emmett McCann
Kansas City Blues..............	81	86	.485	18½	86,993	Dutch Zwilling
St. Paul Saints	70	97	.419	29½	85,487	Lefty Leifield
Louisville Colonels	67	101	.399	33	96,567	Bruno Betzel

All-Star Team: **1B**-Pat Crawford, Columbus; **2B**-M.T. Connolly, Milwaukee; **3B**-Arvel Hale, Toledo; **SS**-Ernie Smith, Minneapolis; **OF**-Joe Mowry, Minneapolis; Art Ruble, Minneapolis; Evar Swanson, Columbus; **C**-Paul Richards, Minneapolis; **P**-Rosy Ryan, Minneapolis; Roy Parmelee, Columbus; Russ Van Atta, St. Paul; Belve Bean, Toledo.

BA: Art Ruble, Minneapolis, .376
Runs: Joe Mowry, Minneapolis, 175
Hits: Joe Mowry, Minneapolis, 257
RBIs: Babe Ganzel, Minneapolis, 143
HRs: Joe Hauser, Minneapolis, 49

Wins: Russ Van Atta, St. Paul, 22
Rosy Ryan, Minneapolis, 22
SOs: Paul Dean, Columbus, 169
Pct: Roy Parmelee, Columbus, .933, 14-1

AA International League
President: Charles H. Knapp

Standings	W	L	Pct.	GB	Attend.	Manager
Newark Bears (5)..............	109	59	.649	—	342,001	Al Mamaux
Baltimore Orioles	93	74	.557	15½	124,616	Fritz Maisel
Buffalo Bisons	91	75	.548	17	238,010	Ray Schalk
Montreal Royals	90	78	.536	19	196,876	Ed Holly/Walter "Doc" Gautreau
Rochester Red Wings (16)..	88	79	.527	20½	153,739	Billy Southworth/George "Specs" Toporcer
Jersey City Skeeters (10)....	73	94	.437	35½	138,977	Hans Lobert/Charley Moore
Reading Keys/ Albany Senators#	71	97	.423	38	92,401	Clarence "Pants" Rowland
Toronto Maple Leafs (4).....	54	113	.323	54½	49,963	Tom Daly/Lena Blackburne

#Reading (50-66) moved to Albany August 6.

All-Star Team: **1B**-Baxter Jordan, Baltimore; **2B**-Otis Miller, Buffalo; **3B**-Marv Owen, Toronto/Newark; **SS**-Red Rolfe, Newark; **OF**-George Puccinelli, Rochester; John Winsett, Buffalo; Fred Walker, Newark; **C**-William Outen, Jersey City; **P**-Don Brennan, Newark; **MVP**-Marvin Owen, Toronto/Newark.

BA: George Puccinelli, Rochester, .391
Runs: Buzz Arlett, Baltimore, 141
Hits: Johnny Neun, Newark, 212
RBIs: Buzz Arlett, Baltimore, 144

HRs: Buzz Arlett, Baltimore, 54
Wins: Don Brennan, Newark, 26
SOs: Beryl Richmond, Baltimore, 155
ERA: Don Brennan, Newark, 2.79

AA Pacific Coast League
President: Hyland H. Baggerly

Standings	W	L	Pct.	GB	Attend.	Manager
Portland Beavers (6).........	111	78	.587	—	207,384	Spencer Abbott
Hollywood Stars	106	83	.561	5	151,292	Oscar Vitt
Sacramento Senators	101	88	.534	10	68,476	Buddy Ryan/Earl McNeely
San Francisco Seals	96	90	.516	13½	103,627	James Caveney
Los Angeles Angels (11)...	96	93	.508	15	143,829	Jack Lelivelt
Seattle Indians...................	90	95	.486	19	74,012	Ernie Johnson/George Burns
Oakland Oaks	80	107	.428	30	63,865	Carl Zamloch
Mission Reds	71	117	.378	39½	84,202	Joe Devine/Fred Hoffmann

All-Star Team: **1B**-George Burns, Seattle; **2B**-Fred Muller, Seattle; **3B**-Frank Higgins, Portland; **SS**-Ray French, Sacramento; **OF**-Lou Finney, Portland; Arnold "Jigger" Statz, Los Angeles; Oscar "Ox" Eckhardt, Mission; **C**-John Bassler, Hollywood; **P**-Frank Shellenback, Hollywood.

BA: Oscar "Ox" Eckhardt, Mission, .371
Runs: Arnold "Jigger" Statz, Los Angeles, 153
Hits: Lou Finney, Portland, 268
RBIs: George Burns, Seattle, 140
HRs: Fred Muller, Seattle, 38

Wins: Frank Shellenback, Hollywood, 26
SOs: Fay Thomas, Oakland, 196
ERA: Curt Davis, San Francisco, 2.24
CGs: Frank Shellenback, Hollywood, 35

A Eastern League
President: Fred J. Voss, Jr.

Standings	W	L	Pct.	GB	Manager
Springfield Rifles (5)..........	53	26	.671	—	Bill Meyer
Albany Senators	47	32	.595	6	Bill McCorry
Richmond Colts	45	37	.549	9½	Bobby Murray
Allentown Buffaloes...........	37	38	.493	14	Glenn Killinger
New Haven Bulldogs	34	43	.442	18	Gene Martin
Bridgeport Bears (13).........	33	42	.440	18	Frank Stapleton/Harry Layne
Norfolk Tars	31	45	.408	20½	Win Clark/Harry Blake
Hartford Senators (10)........	31	48	.392	22	Charley Moore/Bill Marlotte

The league disbanded July 17.

BA: Ted Norbert, Springfield/Albany, .376
Runs: Sol Mishkin, Springfield, 76
Hits: Gerald Fitzgerald, Hartford/Norfolk, 116
RBIs: Julius "Moose" Solters, Albany, 76
HRs: Wilbur Davis, Norfolk, 18
Yam Yaryan, New Haven, 18

Wins: Ernie Jenkins, Springfield, 11
Alex Ferguson, Richmond, 11
Ed Marleau, Allentown, 11
SOs: Ernie Jenkins, Springfield, 70
Hormidas Aube, Springfield, 70
Pct: Floyd Newkirk, Springfield, .800, 8-2

A Southern Association
President: John D. Martin

Standings	W	L	Pct.	GB	Attend.	Manager
Memphis Chickasaws	101	53	.656	—	136,712	Tommy "Doc" Prothro
Chattanooga Lookouts (8)..	98	51	.658	½	179,601	Bert Niehoff
Little Rock Travelers	77	75	.507	23	72,865	Harry Strohm
Nashville Volunteers	75	78	.490	25½	99,615	Joe Klugman/Chuck Dressen
Birmingham Barons............	68	83	.450	31½	77,746	Clyde Milan
New Orleans Pelicans	66	84	.440	33	112,155	Jake Atz
Atlanta Crackers	62	90	.408	38	78,925	David Barron
Knoxville Smokies	60	93	.392	40½	57,780	Joe Schepner

All-Star Team: **1B**-Harley Boss, Chattanooga; **2B**-Wes Kingdon, Chattanooga; **3B**-Cecil Travis, Chattanooga; **SS**-Bill Rodda, Nashville; **OF**-John "Moose" Clabaugh, Nashville; Peck Hamel, Memphis; Frank Doljack, New Orleans; **C**-Cliff Bolton, Chattanooga; **P**-Walter "Boom-Boom" Beck, Memphis; Alex "Red" McColl, Chattanooga.

BA: John "Moose" Clabaugh, Nashville, .382
Runs: Stan Keyes, Nashville, 147
Hits: Walter French, Little Rock, 211
RBIs: Stan Keyes, Nashville, 147
HRs: Stan Keyes, Nashville, 35

Wins: Walter "Boom-Boom" Beck, Memphis, 27
SOs: Walter "Boom-Boom" Beck, Memphis, 139
ERA: Clyde Barfoot, Chattanooga, 2.76

A Texas League
President: J. Alvin Gardner

Standings	W	L	Pct.	GB	Attend.	Manager
Beaumont Exporters*(4)...	100	51	.662	—	120,082	Del Baker
Dallas Steers**	98	53	.648	2	151,434	Hap Morse
Houston Buffaloes (16)	88	66	.574	13½	112,341	Joe Schultz

*Won first-half   **Won second-half   ***Won both halves
Numbers after nicknames indicate farm system.
Affiliation listed at end of each year.

272

	W	L	Pct.	GB		Manager
Ft. Worth Cats	68	81	.457	31	46,356	Dick McCabe/Art Phelan
Wichita Falls Spudders/						
Longview Cannibals@(7)	69	83	.454	31½	46,211	Hank Severeid
Galveston Buccaneers	67	86	.438	34	59,081	Del Pratt
San Antonio Indians	57	91	.385	41½	31,761	Claude "Ug" Robertson
Shreveport/Tyler Sports#	57	93	.380	42½	45,517	George Sisler/J. Walter Morris/
						Frank "Pop" Kitchens

#Shreveport's park burned May 4. After one game in Longview, Shreveport (9-21) moved to Tyler May 16, first home game May 21.
@Wichita Falls (16-19) moved to Longview May 20, first home game May 25.

Playoff: Beaumont 3 games, Dallas 0.

All-Star Team: 1B-Hank Greenberg, Beaumont; **2B**-Byrne James, Dallas; **3B**-Ernie Holman, Dallas; **SS**-Carleton Molesworth, Galveston; **OF**-Joe Medwick, Houston; Ervin Fox, Beaumont; Homer Peel, Houston; **C**-Frank Reiber, Beaumont; **Util**-Fred Tauby (Taubansee), Beaumont; **P**-George Murray, Dallas; Oscar Fuhr, Dallas; Luke "Hot Potato" Hamlin, Beaumont; **MVP**-Hank Greenberg, Beaumont.

BA: Ervin Fox, Beaumont, .357
Runs: Hank Greenberg, Beaumont, 123
Hits: Homer Peel, Houston, 199
RBIs: Paul Easterling, Beaumont, 134
HRs: Hank Greenberg, Beaumont, 39
Wins: George Murray, Dallas, 24
SOs: Henry Thormahlen, Galveston, 186
ERA: Lynwood "Schoolboy" Rowe, Beaumont, 2.34

A Western League
President: Dale D. Gear

Standings	W	L	Pct.	GB	Manager
Tulsa Oilers*(15)	98	48	.671	—	Art Griggs
Denver Bears (16)	83	64	.565	15½	Earl Smith
Oklahoma City Indians**	83	67	.553	17	Fred Luderus
Des Moines Demons	71	72	.497	25½	Bill Rodgers
St. Joseph Saints	72	75	.490	26½	Frank Haley
Wichita Aviators (11)	63	86	.423	36½	Jimmy Payton
Pueblo Braves	62	90	.408	39	Walter Smallwood/Francis "Pug" Griffin
Omaha Packers	58	88	.397	40	Francis "Pug" Griffin/Eddie Brown

Attendance: Tulsa, 101,450.

Playoff: Oklahoma City 2 games, Tulsa 1, for the second half title.
Finals: Tulsa 4 games, Oklahoma City 0.

All-Star Team: 1B-Jim Oglesby, Des Moines; **2B**-Roy Schalk, Oklahoma City; **3B**-Russell Rollings, Denver; **SS**-George Binder, Denver; **OF**-Stan Schino, Tulsa; Ernie Parker, Denver; John Stoneham, Tulsa; **C**-Horton, Wichita; Tony Rego, Tulsa; **P**-Andy Bednar, Tulsa; Ralph Birkofer, Tulsa; Ed "Bear Tracks" Greer, Denver.

BA: Jim Oglesby, Des Moines, .385
Runs: Bill Allington, Pueblo, 167
Hits: Melvin Nydahl, Denver, 231
RBIs: Stan Schino, Tulsa, 143
HRs: Dick Goldberg, Wichita, 30
Wins: Andy Bednar, Tulsa, 22
SOs: Ralph Birkofer, Tulsa, 186
ERA: Andy Bednar, Tulsa, .846, 22-4

B Central League
President: Frederick Howell

Standings	W	L	Pct.	GB	Manager
Erie Sailors (5)#	85	56	.603	—	Charles "Chief" Bender/Bill McCorry
Fort Wayne Chiefs** (3)	77	60	.562	6	Bill Wambsganss
Dayton Ducks*	77	64	.546	8	Howard "Ducky" Holmes/Roy Grimes
Youngstown Buckeyes	70	69	.504	14	Tony Citrano
South Bend Twins@	29	57	.337	NA	Jess Altenburg/Clarence Roper/Whitey Felber
Akron Tyrites/					
Canton Terriers#	28	60	.318	NA	John McCloskey

#Akron (19-34) moved to Canton June 21; the franchise disbanded July 21.
@South Bend disbanded July 21.

Playoff: Dayton 4 games, Fort Wayne 0.

BA: Babe Phelps, Youngstown, .372
Runs: Pep Young, Evansville, 128
Hits: Babe Phelps, Youngstown, 199
HRs: Babe Phelps, Youngstown, 26
Wins: Marvin Duke, Erie, 23
SOs: Marvin Duke, Erie, 176
ERA: Marvin Duke, Erie, 2.36

B New York-Pennsylvania League
President: Perry B. Farrell

Standings	W	L	Pct.	GB	Manager
Wilkes-Barre Barons	78	61	.561	—	Mike McNally
Harrisburg Senators (9)	74	66	.529	4½	Eddie Onslow
York White Roses	72	66	.522	5½	Russ Wrightstone/Frank Dessau
Scranton Miners	72	68	.514	6½	Bill Clymer/Bob Shawkey
Binghamton Triplets (5)	69	71	.493	9½	Heinie Groh/Bill Meyer
Hazleton Mountaineers (1)	67	72	.482	11	Jake Pitler
Williamsport Grays (3)	63	76	.453	15	Herb Moran/Harry Hinchman/Glenn Killinger
Elmira Red Wings (16)	62	77	.446	16	Jack Bentley/Clay Hopper

All-Star Team: 1B-Harold Grant, Wilkes-Barre; **2B**-Frank Parenti, Wilkes-Barre; **3B**-

Henry Peploski, Harrisburg; **SS**-Walter Novak, Scranton; **OF**-Johnny Mize, Elmira; Babe Fischer, Harrisburg; Jake Plummer, Wilkes-Barre; **C**-Claude Linton, Hazleton; **Util**-Frank Kern, Harrisburg; **P**-Chant Parkes, Williamsport; Clarence Heise, Elmira; **Manager**-Mike McNally, Wilkes-Barre.

BA: Babe Fischer, Harrisburg, .360
Runs: Babe Fischer, Harrisburg, 134
Hits: Babe Fischer, Harrisburg, 191
RBIs: Dutch Prather, Hazleton, 104
HRs: Jake Plummer, Wilkes-Barre, 19
Wins: John Milligan, Wilkes-Barre, 22
SOs: Clarence Heise, Elmira, 187
ERA: Vito Tamulis, Binghamton, 1.92

B Piedmont League
President: William G. Bramham

Standings	W	L	Pct.	GB	Manager
Charlotte Hornets**	80	53	.602	—	Guy Lacy
Greensboro Patriots*(16)	76	59	.563	5	Fred Myers
Winston-Salem Twins/					
High Point Pointers@(13)	68	66	.507	12½	Harry Wilke
Raleigh Capitals	65	71	.478	16½	Odie Strain
Wilmington Pirates (1)	62	77	.446	21	Hal Weafer/Tweet Walsh
Durham Bulls (14)	56	77	.421	24	George "Possum" Whitted
Asheville Tourists#	35	33	.515	NA	Joe Guyon
High Point Pointers#	33	39	.458	NA	Buddy Tanner

#Asheville and High Point disbanded July 7.
@Winston-Salem (18-28) moved to High Point August 20.

Playoff: Greensboro 4 games, Charlotte 3.

All-Star Team: 1B-Bob "Stuffy" McCrone, Wilmington; **2B**-Harry Snyder, Charlotte; **3B**-Emory Culbreth, Charlotte; **SS**-Art Kilpatrick, Raleigh; **OF**-Parker Perry, High Point/Wilmington; Eddie Wilson, Charlotte; Tom Wolfe, Raleigh/Durham; **C**-Bill Lewis, Greensboro; **Util**-Paul O'Malley, Durham; **P**-DeWitt Perry, Raleigh; Fritz Ostermueller, Greensboro; **Manager**-Guy Lacy, Charlotte.

BA: Tom Wolfe, Raleigh/Durham, .381
Runs: Benny Borgmann, Greensboro, 122
Hits: Harry Smith, Raleigh, 198
RBIs: Emory Culbreth, Charlotte, 118
HRs: Parker Perry, High Point/Wilmington, 19
Wins: Jim Lyle, Charlotte, 22
SOs: Ted Kleinhans, Greensboro, 226
ERA: Al Smith, Winston-Salem/High Point, 2.21

B Southeastern League
President: Roy Williams

Standings	W	L	Pct.	GB	Manager
Mobile Red Warriors (16)	19	13	.594	—	Clay Hopper
Columbus Foxes	19	14	.576	½	Jack Sheehan
Selma Cloverleafs	16	16	.500	3	Art Phelan
Macon Peaches	15	18	.455	4½	Sherry Smith
Jackson Senators	15	18	.455	4½	Hank DeBerry
Montgomery Capitals	13	18	.419	5½	Jim Johnston

The league disbanded May 21, last games played May 18.

BA: Robert Schleischer, Selma, .398
Runs: Jack Sheehan, Columbus, 37
Clarence Beasley, Columbus, 37
Hits: Buster Mills, Mobile, 47
RBIs: J.W. McKee, Columbus, 39
HRs: Fred Sington, Columbus, 6
Wins: Albert Fisher, Mobile, 6
SOs: Jackie Reid, Jackson, 47
ERA: Albert Fisher, Mobile, 2.14

B Three-I League
President: L.J. Wylie

Standings	W	L	Pct.	GB	Manager
Terre Haute Tots*	42	27	.609	—	Walter Holke
Peoria Tractors**	40	28	.588	1½	Riley Parker
Quincy Indians@(3)	38	31	.551	4	Sylvester Simon
Springfield Senators#	32	37	.464	10	Frank Dessau
Danville Veterans (16)	29	39	.426	12½	Elmer Yoter/Wattie Holm
Decatur Commodores#(4)	24	43	.358	17	Bob Coleman

#Springfield (3-7 in second half) and Decatur (4-6 in second half) disbanded July 12.
@Quincy withdrew July 15, causing the league to disband.

BA: Ab Wright, Danville, .357
Runs: James Crawford, Terre Haute, 63
Hits: James Crawford, Terre Haute, 99
HRs: Hal Trosky, Quincy, 15
Wins: Rex McDonald, Terre Haute, 12
SOs: Rex McDonald, Terre Haute, 102
Pct: Elmer Ambrose, Springfield, .733, 11-4
Lester Davis, Terre Haute, .733, 11-4

C Middle Atlantic League
President: Elmer M. Daily

Standings	W	L	Pct.	GB	Manager
Charleston Senators**	70	54	.565	—	Danny Boone
Beckley Black Knights*	70	54	.565	—	Frank Welch/Holt "Cat" Milner
Johnstown Johnnies	66	59	.528	4½	Karl Weber
Cumberland Colts (5)	62	60	.508	7	Leo Mackey
Clarksburg Generals	60	66	.476	11	Frank Walker/Herbert "Doc" Smith
Huntington Boosters (4)	45	80	.360	25½	Johnny Stuart

Playoff: Charleston 4 games, Beckley 2.

BA: Fred Sington, Beckley, .368
Runs: Fred Sington, Beckley, 110
    Lou Chiozza, Beckley, 110
Hits: Lou Chiozza, Beckley, 187
RBIs: Fred Sington, Beckley, 110

HRs: Fred Sington, Beckley, 29
Wins: Carl Spencer, Clarksburg, 18
SOs: Wayne LaMaster, Charleston, 177
ERA: Wayne LaMaster, Charleston, 2.27

C Western Association
President: Dale D. Gear

Standings	W	L	Pct.	GB	Manager
Springfield Cardinals*(16) .	79	51	.608	—	Eddie Dyer
Bartlesville Bronchos**	77	53	.592	2	Art Schmidt/Art Ewoldt
Independence Producers/					
Joplin Miners/Hutchinson@ .	58	68	.424	19	Mark Purtell
Ft. Smith Twins/					
Muskogee Chiefs$(7)	48	80	.375	30	Runt Marr/Jerry Mallett
Joplin Miners/					
Topeka Jayhawks#..........	38	38	.500	NA	Grover Wilson
Muskogee Chiefs/					
Hutchinson Wheat Shockers+	37	48	.435	NA	Lyn Boggess

#Joplin (2-1) moved to Topeka May 6, first home game May 10. Topeka disbanded July 18.
@Independence (12-10) moved to Joplin May 23, first home game May 26. Joplin (7-10) moved back to Independence June 10. Independence (4-12) moved to Hutchinson July 20.
+Muskogee (18-16) moved to Hutchinson June 8, then disbanded July 18.
$Ft. Smith (23-29) moved to Muskogee July 1, first home game July 7.
Attendance: Springfield, 60,000.

Playoff: Springfield 5 games, Bartlesville 4.

All-Star Team: 1B-Carl Kentling, Muskogee/Hutchinson; 2B-Ed Williford, Bartlesville; 3B-Charles English, Muskogee/Hutchinson; SS-Johnny Keane, Springfield; OF-John Rizzo, Muskogee/Hutchinson/Bartlesville; Ival Goodman, Bartlesville; Dallas Patton, Hutchinson; C-Bill Delancey, Springfield; Util-Eldon Breese, Bartlesville; P-James Lyons, Springfield; George Jahn, Bartlesville; Manager-Runt Marr, Ft. Smith/Muskogee.

BA: Dallas Patton, Hutchinson, .345
Runs: Eldon Breese, Bartlesville, 119
Hits: John Rizzo, Muskogee/Hutchinson/
    Bartlesville, 172
RBIs: Ival Goodman, Bartlesville, 120

HRs: Ival Goodman, Bartlesville, 22
Wins: Keith Frazier, Bartlesville, 20
SOs: Keith Frazier, Bartlesville, 172
ERA: Art Evans, Independence, 1.98

D Arizona-Texas League
President: P.A. Nathan

Standings	W	L	Pct.	GB	Manager
Albuquerque Dons***	57	42	.576	—	Bobby Coltrin
Bisbee Bees......................	50	49	.505	7	Roy "Hardrock" Johnson
El Paso Texans.................	51	53	.490	8½	Royce "Mule" Washburn
Tucson Lizards	44	53	.454	12	Mickey Shader
Phoenix Senators#	8	13	.381	NA	Dick Cox

#Phoenix disbanded May 9.
The league disbanded July 24.

BA: Dick Gyselman, Albuquerque, .392
Runs: Dick Gyselman, Albuquerque, 104
Hits: Dick Gyselman, Albuquerque, 165
HRs: Vince DiMaggio, Tucson, 25

Wins: Bill Chamberlain, Phoenix/
    Albuquerque, 15
SOs: Guido Simoni, Phoenix/Tucson, 157
ERA: Boyd Biggers, El Paso, 3.78

D Cotton States League
President: Frank A. Scott

Standings	W	L	Pct.	GB	Manager
Baton Rouge Senators*** ..	51	20	.718	—	Josh Billings
Pine Bluff Judges...............	39	29	.574	10½	Wray Query
Vicksburg Hill Billies/					
Jackson Mississippians#..	30	33	.476	17	Don McShane/Joe Schepner
El Dorado Lions...............	33	36	.478	17	George "Hickory" Jackson/Clyde Glass
Monroe Twins (16)............	30	37	.448	19	Frank "Pop" Kitchens
Port Arthur Refiners/De Quincy Railroaders/					
Opelousas Orphans@	17	45	.274	29½	Frank Meyers/Cecil Jones/Milt Delmas

#Vicksburg (13-11) moved to Jackson June 1, first home game June 4.
@Port Arthur (14-28) moved to De Quincy June 19; De Quincy (2-12) moved to Opelousas July 7; the franchise disbanded July 10.
The league disbanded July 13.

BA: Clyde Glass, El Dorado, .416
Runs: Earl Persons, Pine Bluff, 65
Hits: Cal Chapman, Baton Rouge, 93

HRs: Horace Long, El Dorado/
    Baton Rouge, 12
Wins: Otho Nitcholas, Baton Rouge, 12
SOs: Gus Burleson, El Dorado, 87
ERA: Arthur Galeria, Pine Bluff, 2.33

D Interstate League
President: William J. Willenbecher

Standings	W	L	Pct.	GB	Manager
Stroudsburg Poconos	19	7	.731	—	Ed Murphy
Pottstown Legionaries	18	8	.692	1	Earl Potteiger/Whitey Witt
Tamaqua/Slatington Dukes@ ..	10	16	.385	9	Leo Strait
Washington Potomacs	9	17	.346	10	Edward Neff
Lancaster Red Sox+.............	7	16	.304	10½	Bud Shaw/Jimmy Sheckard
Norristown/St. Clair Saints#...	11	10	.524	NA	Steve Yerkes

#Norristown (2-4) moved to St. Clair May 28, then disbanded June 12.
@Tamaqua (8-12) moved to Slatington June 8.
+Lancaster disbanded June 17.
The league disbanded June 20.

BA: Dom D'Alessandro, Norristown/
    St. Clair, .418
    Mickey Haslin, Stroudsburg, .418
Runs: Frank DeManicore, Stroudsburg, 39
Hits: Mickey Haslin, Stroudsburg, 48
RBIs: Paul Piontek, Stroudsburg, 37

HRs: Frank DeManicore, Stroudsburg, 7
    Mickey Haslin, Stroudsburg, 7
    Paul Piontek, Stroudsburg, 7
Wins: Ed Cole, Stroudsburg, 7
    Matt Ramsey, Pottstown, 7
SOs: Jack Crimmins, Tamaqua/Slatington, 47
Pct: Matt Ramsey, Pottstown, .875, 7-1

D Mississippi Valley League
President: Charles A. Logan

Standings	W	L	Pct.	GB	Manager
Davenport Blue Sox**.........	78	47	.624	—	Cletus Dixon
Rock Island Islanders*(7)...	70	56	.556	8½	George Young/Riley Parker
Burlington Bees (3)	69	60	.535	11	Art Mueller/Jack Tesar
Keokuk Indians (16)	67	61	.523	12½	Bobby Rice
Cedar Rapids Bunnies (12).	65	60	.520	13	Paul Speraw
Moline Plowboys (4)	55	66	.455	21	Ernie Lorbeer
Waterloo Hawks (2).............	52	73	.416	26	Elmer "Doc" Bennett
Dubuque Tigers	47	80	.370	32	Clarence Roper/Dave Lamb

Attendance: Davenport, 64,895.

Playoff: Rock Island 4 games, Davenport 2.

All-Star Team: 1B-Malcolm Pickett, Dubuque; 2B-John Kane, Davenport; 3B-Harold Patchett, Moline; SS-Harold Anderson, Burlington; OF-William Mizeur, Cedar Rapids; Thomas Leonard, Rock Island; Brown Braley, Keokuk; C-Sanford Hamby, Burlington; Ken O'Dea, Keokuk; P-Fred Newton, Davenport; Brown, Keokuk; Adolph Wrobel, Rock Island; Edward Linke, Davenport; Norbert Kleinke, Cedar Rapids.

BA: Brown Braley, Keokuk, .374
Runs: Harold Patchett, Moline, 90
Hits: Thomas Leonard, Rock Island, 163
RBIs: William Mizeur, Cedar Rapids, 86

HRs: Lawrence Wilbanks, Moline, 9
Wins: Fred Newton, Davenport, 20
SOs: Edward Linke, Davenport, 228
Pct: Fred Newton, Davenport, .800, 20-5

D Nebraska State League
President: Robert C. Russell

Standings	W	L	Pct.	GB	Manager
Norfolk Elkhorns***	75	35	.682	—	Joe McDermott
Beatrice Blues....................	59	46	.562	13½	Ed Reichle/Dick "Sonny" Brookhaus
Grand Island Islanders	59	52	.532	16½	Dick "Sonny" Brookhaus/Larry Getz
North Platte Buffaloes	49	61	.454	26	Spud Owen
Lincoln Links....................	45	60	.429	27½	Bill Rumler/Bob Sanquist
McCook Generals	37	70	.346	36½	Hooks Bailey/Jack Hruska

Playoff: Beatrice 2 games, Lincoln 1.
Finals: Beatrice 4 games, Norfolk 3.

All-Star Team: 1B-Fred West, Grand Island; 2B-Eugene Strother, Lincoln; James Calhoun, Beatrice; 3B-Henry Fiarito, North Platte; SS-Ray Bertram, Norfolk; OF-Art Moore, North Platte; Walter Gannon, Norfolk; Forrest Ewing, McCook; James Brown, Norfolk; C-Bennie Warren, Lincoln; Util-Spud Owen, North Platte; P-Pat Flanagan, McCook; Mike Pociask, Beatrice; Henry Pippen, Beatrice; Manager-Joe McDermott, Norfolk.

BA: Walter Gannon, Norfolk, .355
Runs: John Cross, Beatrice, 100
Hits: Walter Gannon, Norfolk, 150
HRs: Bill Swinger, Beatrice, 16

Wins: Otto Davis, Norfolk, 24
SOs: Pat Flanagan, McCook, 261
ERA: Luke Bucklin, Norfolk, 1.89

1932 Interleague Post Season Play

World Series
New York (American) 4 games, Chicago (National) 0

Junior World Series
Newark (International) 4 games, Minneapolis (American Association) 2
Total Attendance: 40,067

Dixie Series
Chattanooga (Southern Association) 4 games, Beaumont (Texas) 1
Total Attendance: 34,002

1932 Major League Farm Systems

American League

1 Boston (2): Hazleton, Wilmington.
2 Chicago (1): Waterloo.
3 Cleveland (4): Williamsport, Quincy, Burlington, Fort Wayne.
4 Detroit (5): Toronto, Beaumont, Decatur, Huntington, Moline.
5 New York (5): Newark, Springfield (MA), Cumberland, Binghamton, Erie.
6 Philadelphia (1): Portland.
7 St. Louis (3): Wichita Falls/Longview, Ft. Smith/Muskogee, Rock Island.
8 Washington (1): Chattanooga.

National League

9 Boston (1): Harrisburg.
10 Brooklyn (2): Jersey City, Hartford.
11 Chicago (2): Los Angeles, Wichita.
12 Cincinnati (1): Cedar Rapids.
13 New York (2): Bridgeport, Winston-Salem/High Point.
14 Philadelphia (1): Durham.
15 Pittsburgh (1): Tulsa.
16 St. Louis (11): Columbus, Rochester, Houston, Denver, Elmira, Greensboro, Mobile, Danville, Springfield (MO), Monroe, Keokuk.

1932 No-Hitters

Date	Pitcher	Team	League	Opponent	Score
4-30	Italio Chelin	Albuquerque	Arizona-Texas	Bisbee	4-0 (7)
5-5	Tony Freitas	Sacramento	Pacific Coast	Oakland	2-0
5-18	Bryan Harris	St. Paul	American Assoc.	Kansas City	9-0
5-20	Red Proctor	Clarksburg	Middle Atlantic	Johnstown	8-0
6-19	Rufus Meadows	Newark	International	Montreal	9-0 (7)
6-22	Joe Noonan	Danville	Three-I	Decatur	0-1
6-24	Charley Butler	Durham	Piedmont	Raleigh	3-0
6-29	Al Barker	Danville	Three-I	Peoria	3-0 (7)
7-7	Bill Gilvray	Dayton	Central	Youngstown	3-0 (7)
7-8	Victor Salmon	Lincoln	Nebraska State	Beatrice	(7)
8-2	Joe Martin	Charleston	Middle Atlantic	Cumberland	6-0 (7)
8-11	Bill Brigham	Clarksburg	Middle Atlantic	Huntington	6-0 (7)
8-25	George Granger	Memphis	Southern Assoc.	Nashville	1-0 (P, 7)
8-30	Paul Dean	Columbus	American Assoc.	Kansas City	3-0
9-7	Edward Linke	Davenport	Mississippi Valley	Rock Island	7-0
	Tony Tuma	Grand Island	Nebraska State	North Platte	(7)

Number in parentheses indicates innings if other than nine; "P" indicates perfect game.

THIS DATE IN MINOR LEAGUE HISTORY

April 6, 1932, In one of the highest scoring games in pro baseball history, Albuquerque defeated El Paso 43-15 to open the Arizona-Texas League season. Playing at Tingley Field in Albuquerque, El Paso scored 11 runs in the top of the first inning. The game was played in two hours and 40 minutes, despite the two clubs combining for 46 hits, 58 runs and 12 errors. The contest saw only one home run, but 13 triples and 10 doubles were hit.

April 21, 1932, Paul Dean of Columbus, American Association, Dizzy's brother, shut out the champion St. Paul club on one hit.

April 28, 1932, Joe Mowry of Minneapolis, American Association, completed his streak of reaching base 14 consecutive times. He had 12 hits, not in succession, reached on an error and walked.

May 10, 1932, Pitcher Cy Blanton of Independence, Western Association, set a new record with 13 assists in a game against Bartlesville.

May 12, 1932, The Montreal Royals, International League, won their 13th straight game.

May 13, 1932, Moose Weber smacked three homers in one game for Burlington, Mississippi Valley League.

May 23, 1932, Hans Lobert resigned as manager of Jersey City.

May 26, 1932, The International League race was so close, Newark lost a game and dropped from first place to fourth.

June 1, 1932, Outfielder Russell "Buzz" Arlett of Baltimore, International League, smashed four home runs in four at bats in a game at Reading. Baltimore won 14-13 as Arlett had seven RBIs. His first three homers were hit while batting lefthanded and the last came righthanded.

June 28, 1932, George Sisler resigned as manager of the Tyler club of the Texas League.

July 4, 1932, Buzz Arlett of Baltimore, International League, clouted four successive homers in the first game of a doubleheader against Reading. It was the second time in five weeks he hit four homers in one game. Arlett drove in nine runs as the Orioles won 21-10. He also homered and doubled in game two, won by Baltimore 9-8. Arlett connected for two circuit clouts batting righthanded and the other three came lefthanded, making five consecutive home runs for the doubleheader.

July 6, 1932, Ken Strong hit three homers for Toronto, International League, at Buffalo.

July 13, 1932, Owing to the failure to obtain a loan of $7,500 from the National Association, the five survivors of the Cotton States League voted to suspend activities.

July 17, 1932, Major league support having been withdrawn from Hartford and Bridgeport, the Eastern League decided to abandon its season.

July 18, 1932, The Western Association decided to finish the season with four clubs after Topeka and Hutchinson disbanded.

August 6, 1932, Pat Crawford hit two homers in one inning for Columbus, American Association.

August 12, 1932, George Hubbell, younger brother of the Giants' Carl Hubbell, was traded by manager Runt Marr from Muskogee to Hutchinson, Western Association, in exchange for four new baseballs.

August 20, 1932, Shortstop Dick Gyselman of Mission, Pacific Coast League, made seven hits, four singles, two doubles, and one triple, in seven at bats against Los Angeles.

August 23, 1932, A dozen errors were the melancholy feature of the Moline-Cedar Rapids contest in the Mississippi Valley League.

August 27, 1932, For the second time within five days, Harry Kelly of Memphis, Southern Association, pitched and won a doubleheader. In the first game his teammate Tangeman smacked three triples.

October 1, 1932, Joe DiMaggio played his first game in Organized Ball, for the San Francisco Seals of the Pacific Coast League. Joe played shortstop, replacing Augie Galan, but the following year he was shifted to the outfield. The 17-year old lashed out a triple in his pro debut.

October 7, 1932, Newark won the Junior World Series by defeating Minneapolis 8-7 in the sixth game, in Minneapolis. Paid attendance for the six games was 40,067, with receipts of $57,782.50.

October 18, 1932, Atlanta's Southern Association club surrendered its franchise to bond holders after the loss of $70,000 in operations during 1932.

October 19, 1932, The Northern League was reorganized to begin play in 1933.

October 23, 1932, American Association club owners adopted a monthly salary limit of $6,500 for 1933.

November 21, 1932, At their annual meeting, Pacific Coast League magnates chopped the waiver price on players from $3,000 to $1,250 and decided to open the 1933 season on April 14.

December 7, 1932, The Tulsa and Oklahoma City clubs moved from the Western League to the Texas League.

1933

American League
President: William Harridge

Standings	W	L	Pct.	GB	Attend.	Manager
Washington Senators	99	53	.651	—	437,533	Joe Cronin
New York Yankees	91	59	.607	7	728,014	Joe McCarthy
Philadelphia Athletics	79	72	.523	19½	297,138	Connie Mack
Cleveland Indians	75	76	.497	23½	387,936	Roger Peckinpaugh/Bib Falk/ Walter Johnson
Detroit Tigers	75	79	.487	25	320,972	Bucky Harris/Del Baker
Chicago White Sox	67	83	.447	31	397,789	Lew Fonseca
Boston Red Sox	63	86	.423	34½	268,715	Marty McManus
St. Louis Browns	55	96	.364	43½	88,113	Bill Killefer/Allen Sothoron/ Rogers Hornsby

BA: Jimmie Foxx, Philadelphia, .356
Runs: Lou Gehrig, New York, 138
Hits: Heinie Manush, Washington, 221
RBIs: Jimmie Foxx, Philadelphia, 163
HRs: Jimmie Foxx, Philadelphia, 48

Wins: Lefty Grove, Philadelphia, 24
General Alvin Crowder, Washington, 24
SOs: Lefty Gomez, New York, 163
ERA: Monte Pearson, Cleveland, 2.33
Pct: Lefty Grove, Philadelphia, .750, 24-8

National League
President: John A. Heydler

Standings	W	L	Pct.	GB	Attend.	Manager
New York Giants	91	61	.599	—	604,471	Bill Terry
Pittsburgh Pirates	87	67	.565	5	288,747	George Gibson
Chicago Cubs	86	68	.558	6	594,112	Charlie Grimm
Boston Braves	83	71	.539	9	517,803	Bill McKechnie
St. Louis Cardinals	82	71	.536	9½	256,171	Gabby Street/Frank Frisch
Brooklyn Dodgers	65	88	.425	26½	526,815	Max Carey
Philadelphia Phillies	60	92	.395	31	156,421	Burt Shotton
Cincinnati Reds	58	94	.382	33	218,281	Donie Bush

BA: Chuck Klein, Philadelphia, .368
Runs: Pepper Martin, St. Louis, 122
Hits: Chuck Klein, Philadelphia, 223
RBIs: Chuck Klein, Philadelphia, 120
HRs: Chuck Klein, Philadelphia, 28

Wins: Carl Hubbell, New York, 23
SOs: Dizzy Dean, St. Louis, 199
ERA: Carl Hubbell, New York, 1.66
Pct: Ben Cantwell, Boston, .667, 20-10

AA American Association
President: Thomas J. Hickey

East Standings	W	L	Pct.	GB	Attend.	Manager
Columbus Red Birds (16)	101	51	.664	—	178,190	Ray Blades
Indianapolis Indians	82	72	.532	20	97,835	Wade Killefer
Toledo Mud Hens	70	83	.458	31½	88,890	Steve O'Neill
Louisville Colonels	70	83	.458	31½	66,413	Bruno Betzel

West Standings	W	L	Pct.	GB	Attend.	Manager
Minneapolis Millers	86	67	.562	—	151,803	Dave Bancroft
St. Paul Saints	78	75	.510	8	89,562	Emmett McCann/Phil Todt
Milwaukee Brewers	67	87	.435	19½	51,229	Frank O'Rourke
Kansas City Blues	57	93	.360	27½	53,041	Tris Speaker/Nick Allen

Playoff: Columbus 4 games, Minneapolis 2.

All-Star Team: 1B-Joe Hauser, Minneapolis; **2B**-Frank Sigafoos, Indianapolis; **3B**-George Detore, Toledo; **SS**-Benny Borgmann, Columbus; **OF**-Spencer Harris, Minneapolis; Jack Rothrock, Columbus; Raymond "Rip" Radcliff, St. Paul; **C**-Bill DeLancey, Columbus; Joe Glenn, Minneapolis; **P**-Paul Dean, Columbus; Clarence Heise, Columbus; Bill Lee, Columbus; John Marcum, Louisville.

BA: Frank Sigafoos, Indianapolis, .370
Runs: Joe Hauser, Minneapolis, 153
Hits: Irvine Jeffries, St. Paul, 236
RBIs: Joe Hauser, Minneapolis, 182
HRs: Joe Hauser, Minneapolis, 69

TBs: Joe Hauser, Minneapolis, 439
Wins: Paul Dean, Columbus, 22
SOs: Paul Dean, Columbus, 222
ERA: Paul Dean, Columbus, 3.15

AA International League
President: Charles H. Knapp

North Standings	W	L	Pct.	GB	Attend.	Manager
Rochester Red Wings (16)	88	77	.533	—	152,575	George "Specs" Toporcer
Buffalo Bisons	83	85	.494	6½	245,082	Ray Schalk
Toronto Maple Leafs (4)	82	85	.491	7	109,258	Dan Howley
Montreal Royals (6)	81	84	.491	7	179,396	Doc Gautreau/Oscar Roettger

South Standings	W	L	Pct.	GB	Attend.	Manager
Newark Bears (5)	102	62	.622	—	163,200	Al Mamaux
Baltimore Orioles	84	80	.512	18	104,127	Frank McGowan
Albany Senators	80	84	.488	22	83,433	Bill McCorry
Jersey City Skeeters	61	104	.370	41½	69,915	Bernard "Mike" Kelly

Playoffs: Buffalo 3 games, Baltimore 0; Rochester 3 games, Newark 1.
Finals: Buffalo 4 games, Rochester 2.

All-Star Team: 1B-Johnny Neun, Newark; **2B**-Don Heffner, Baltimore; **3B**-Stan Hack, Albany; **SS**-Red Rolfe, Newark; **OF**-Ike Boone, Toronto; Len Koenecke, Buffalo; Julius "Moose" Solters, Baltimore; **C**-Bennie Tate, Montreal; **P**-James Weaver, Newark; Harry Smythe, Baltimore; **MVP**-Red Rolfe, Newark.

BA: Julius "Moose" Solters, Baltimore, .363
Runs: Buzz Arlett, Baltimore, 135
Hits: Greg Mulleavy, Buffalo, 206
RBIs: Julius "Moose" Solters, Baltimore, 157

HRs: Buzz Arlett, Baltimore, 39
Wins: James Weaver, Newark, 25
SOs: James Weaver, Newark, 175
ERA: Fred Ostermueller, Rochester, 2.44

AA Pacific Coast League
President: Hyland L. Baggerly

Standings	W	L	Pct.	GB	Attend.	Manager
Los Angeles Angels (11)	114	73	.609	—	222,416	Jack Lelivelt
Portland Beavers	105	77	.577	6½	154,705	Spencer Abbott
Hollywood Stars	107	80	.572	7	173,501	Oscar Vitt
Sacramento Senators	96	85	.530	15	92,445	Earl McNeely
Oakland Oaks	93	92	.502	20	108,640	Ray Brubaker
San Francisco Seals	81	106	.433	33	112,004	James Caveney
Mission Reds	79	108	.422	35	82,508	Fred Hoffmann
Seattle Rainiers	65	119	.353	47½	79,064	George Burns

Playoffs: None.

All-Star Team: 1B-George Burns, Seattle; **2B**-John Monroe, Portland; **3B**-Lennie Backer, Sacramento; **SS**-Alan Strange, Hollywood; **OF**-Oscar "Ox" Eckhardt, Mission; Bernard Uhalt, Oakland; Luis Almada, Mission; **C**-Art Veltman, Oakland; **P**-Buck Newsom, Los Angeles; Dick Ward, Los Angeles.

BA: Oscar "Ox" Eckhardt, Mission, .414
Runs: Augie Galan, San Francisco, 164
Hits: Oscar "Ox" Eckhardt, Mission, 315
RBIs: Joe DiMaggio, San Francisco, 169

HRs: Gene Lillard, Los Angeles, 43
Wins: Buck Newsom, Los Angeles, 30
SOs: Buck Newsom, Los Angeles, 212
ERA: William Ludolph, Oakland, 3.09

A New York-Pennsylvania League
President: Perry B. Farrell

Standings	W	L	Pct.	GB	Manager
Binghamton Triplets (5)	79	55	.590	—	Bill Meyer
Reading Red Sox (1)	80	56	.588	—	Nemo Leibold
Wilkes-Barre Barons	71	67	.514	10	Elmer Yoter
Elmira Red Wings (16)	67	69	.493	13	Bobby Rice/Eddie Dyer
Scranton Miners	64	70	.478	15	Bob Shawkey
Williamsport Grays (6)	64	73	.467	16½	Mike McNally
Harrisburg Senators (9)	60	76	.441	20	Eddie Onslow
York White Roses (10)	59	78	.431	21½	Frank Dessau

Total Attendance: 379,186.

Playoffs: None.

All-Star Team: 1B-George McQuinn, Binghamton; **2B**-Arthur Hord, York; **3B**-Henry Peploski, Scranton; **SS**-John "Bunny" Griffiths, Wilkes-Barre; **OF**-Joe Dwyer, Wilkes-Barre; George Stumpf, Reading; Sol Mishkin, Binghamton; **C**-Willard Hershberger, Binghamton; **Util**-Frank Kern, Harrisburg; **P**-Jack LaRocca, Binghamton; James Lyons, Elmira; **Manager**-Bill Meyer, Binghamton.

BA: George McQuinn, Binghamton, .357
Runs: Ray Flood, Reading, 110
Hits: Ray Flood, Reading, 189
RBIs: Horace "Red" McBride, Williamsport, 103

HRs: Bob Gibson, Binghamton, 14
Wins: Earl Johnson, Wilkes-Barre, 20
James Densmore, Binghamton, 20
SOs: Jack LaRocca, Binghamton, 200
ERA: Joe Semler, Wilkes-Barre, 2.32

A Southern Association
President: John D. Martin

Standings	W	L	Pct.	GB	Attend.	Manager
Memphis Chickasaws*	95	58	.621	—	67,624	Tommy "Doc" Prothro
New Orleans Pelicans**	88	65	.575	7	116,604	Larry Gilbert
Nashville Vols	77	69	.521	14½	113,292	Chuck Dressen
Birmingham Barons	76	75	.503	18	71,805	Clyde Milan
Chattanooga Lookouts (8)	74	77	.423	20	78,531	Bert Niehoff
Knoxville Smokies	68	82	.453	25½	70,255	Tommy Taylor
Atlanta Crackers	62	86	.419	30½	79,207	Charles Moore/Wilbert Robinson
Little Rock Travelers	62	90	.408	32½	48,324	Harry Strohm/Guy Sturdy

Playoff: New Orleans 3 games, Memphis 2.

All-Star Team: 1B-Guy Sturdy, Little Rock; **2B**-Cal Chapman, Memphis; **3B**-Chuck Dressen, Nashville; **SS**-Linus Frey, Nashville; **OF**-Walter French, Little Rock/Knoxville; Ab Wright, Little Rock; Lance Richbourg, Nashville; **C**-Raymond Berres, Birmingham; **P**-Fred Johnson, New Orleans; Ted Kleinhans, Atlanta.

*Won first-half   **Won second-half   ***Won both halves
Numbers after nicknames indicate farm system.
Affiliation listed at end of each year.

276

BA: Frank Waddey, Knoxville/
Chattanooga, .361
Runs: Peck Hamel, Memphis, 127
Hits: Walter French, Little Rock/
Knoxville, 215
RBIs: John Gill, Chattanooga, 110
Eddie Rose, New Orleans, 110

HRs: Dutch Prather, Nashville, 23
Wins: Fred Johnson, New Orleans, 21
Clay Touchtone, Birmingham, 21
Harry Kelley, Memphis, 21
SOs: Jackie Reid, Nashville, 135
ERA: Fred Johnson, New Orleans, 3.03

A Texas League
President: J. Alvin Gardner

Standings	W	L	Pct.	GB	Attend.	Manager
Houston Buffaloes (16)	94	57	.623	—	96,675	Carey Selph
Galveston Buccaneers	88	64	.579	6½	77,360	Billy Webb
Dallas Steers	82	70	.539	12½	86,746	Hap Morse/Fred Brainard
San Antonio Missions (7)	79	72	.523	15	78,363	Hank Severeid
Beaumont Exporters (4)	73	79	.480	21½	32,637	Bob Coleman
Tulsa Oilers	65	86	.430	29	57,509	Art Griggs
Ft. Worth Cats	63	88	.417	31	32,791	Walter Holke/Jake Atz
Oklahoma City Indians	62	90	.408	32½	60,341	Fred Luderus/Luther Harvel

Playoffs: San Antonio 3 games, Houston 0; Galveston 3 games, Dallas 2.
Finals: San Antonio 4 games, Galveston 2.

All-Star Team: 1B-Zeke Bonura, Dallas; **2B**-Carey Selph, Houston; **3B**-Buck Fausett, Galveston; **SS**-George Binder, Houston; **OF**-Everett "Pid" Purdy, San Antonio; Tony Governor, Galveston; John Stoneham, Tulsa; **C**-Jimmy O'Dea, Houston; Clarence "Bubber" Jonnard, Dallas; **Util**-Clarence "Cap" Crossley, San Antonio; **P**-Fabian Kowalik, San Antonio; George Darrow, Galveston; Ed "Bear Tracks" Greer, Houston; **MVP**-Zeke Bonura, Dallas; **Pitcher of the Year**-George Darrow, Galveston.

BA: Everett "Pid" Purdy, San Antonio, .358
Runs: Zeke Bonura, Dallas, 141
Hits: Buck Fausett, Galveston, 197
RBIs: Zeke Bonura, Dallas, 111
HRs: Zeke Bonura, Dallas, 24

Wins: George Darrow, Galveston, 22
Ed "Bear Tracks" Greer, Houston, 22
SOs: Elton Walkup, San Antonio, 146
ERA: Mike Cvengros, Houston, 2.43

A Western League
President: Dale D. Gear

Standings	W	L	Pct.	GB	Manager
Des Moines Demons	81	47	.633	—	John Butler
St. Joseph Saints*	77	47	.621	2	Dutch Zwilling
Springfield Cardinals (16)	73	50	.593	5½	Joe Schultz, Sr.
Topeka Senators**(12)	68	55	.553	10½	Art Ewoldt
Omaha Packers	63	61	.508	16	Pug Griffin
Joplin Miners (7)	55	69	.444	24	Runt Marr
Hutchinson Wheatshockers/					
Bartlesville Bronchos@(4)	51	70	.421	26½	Mark Purtell
Wichita Oilers/					
Muskogee Oilers#	26	95	.215	51½	Rube Marquard/Odie Strain/Ed Hawk/
					Red Wilson

#Wichita (6-13) moved to Muskogee June 6, then were evicted from their park and became a road team July 31.
@Hutchinson (25-32) moved to Bartlesville July 7.
Attendance: Springfield, 60,712; Omaha, 59,426.

Playoff: St. Joseph 4 games, Topeka 1.

All-Star Team: 1B-Vic Shiell, Topeka; **2B**-Richard Harrell, St. Joseph; **3B**-Stanley Tutaj, Omaha; **SS**-John Keane, Springfield; **OF**-Dallas Patton, Springfield; Walter Carson, St. Joseph; Leo Ogorek, Des Moines; **C**-Mike Ryba, Springfield; **P**-Herbert May, St. Joseph; Cy Blanton, St. Joseph.

BA: Mike Ryba, Springfield, .380
Runs: John Keane, Springfield, 118
Hits: Walter Carson, St. Joseph, 186
HRs: Vic Shiell, Topeka, 22

Wins: Herbert May, St. Joseph, 24
SOs: Cy Blanton, St. Joseph, 284
Pct: Herbert May, St. Joseph, .800, 24-6

B Mississippi Valley League
President: Charles R. Logan

Standings	W	L	Pct.	GB	Manager
Davenport Blue Sox***	82	32	.719	—	Cletus Dixon
Rock Island Islanders (12)	64	53	.547	19½	Riley Parker
Peoria Tractors	62	53	.539	20½	Paul Speraw/Frank Murphy
Quincy Indians	53	59	.473	28	Joe Klugman
Springfield Senators (16)	43	70	.381	38½	Clay Hopper
Keokuk Indians	40	77	.342	43½	Eddie Sicking/Ray Caldwell

Attendance: Davenport, 73,000; Rock Island, 51,077.

Playoff: Davenport 4 games, Rock Island 1.

All-Star Team: 1B-Malcolm Pickett, Peoria/Quincy; **2B**-Eddie Sicking, Keokuk; **3B**-Tony Robello, Rock Island; **SS**-George Meyer, Davenport; **OF**-Floyd Patterson, Rock Island; Como Cotelle, Davenport; Simon Rosenthal, Quincy; **C**-Jack Redmond, Rock Island; **Util**-Frank Myers, Springfield; **P**-Clarence Struss, Peoria; Al Hollingsworth, Rock Island; **Manager**-Cletus Dixon, Davenport.

BA: Como Cotelle, Davenport, .407
Runs: George Meyer, Davenport, 130
Hits: Simon Rosenthal, Quincy, 166
RBIs: Ed Hall, Davenport, 151

HRs: Ed Hall, Davenport, 28
Wins: Al Piechota, Davenport, 19
SOs: Ray Harrell, Quincy, 193
ERA: Al Hollingsworth, Rock Island, 3.11

B New England League
President: Claude B. Davidson

Standings	W	L	Pct.	GB	Manager
New Bedford Whalers**	58	33	.637	—	Fred Maguire
Worcester Chiefs*	54	33	.621	2	Chief Werre
Lowell Lauriers	49	40	.551	8	Buster Yarnell/Jesse Burkett/Pete Cote
Taunton Blues	43	48	.473	15	Kenneth Black/Bill Duggan
Quincy Shipbuilders/Nashua Millionaires/					
Brockton Shoemakers@(4)	28	47	.373	22	Hal Weafer/Billy Flynn/Paul Wolff
Attleboro/Lawrence Weavers/					
Woonsocket#(13)	27	58	.318	28	Bill Hunnefield/Mark Devlin

#Attleboro (2-6) moved to Lawrence May 26; Lawrence moved to Woonsocket July 18.
@Quincy (12-6) moved to Nashua June 6; Nashua moved to Brockton August 8.

Elimination Playoffs: Lowell 3-1, Worcester 2-2, Taunton 1-3.
Finals: Lowell 1 game, Worcester 1, one tie. Lowell and Worcester were declared co-champions as the final round was abandoned due to prolonged weather delays. New Bedford players refused to take any part in the playoffs.

BA: Edward Baker, New Bedford, .413
Runs: Leon Ballard, Lowell, 99
Hits: George Thomas, Worcester, 141
HRs: Amit Savard, Lowell, 24

Wins: Frank Milliken, Lowell, 20
SOs: Frank Milliken, Lowell, 118
Pct: William Graham, Lowell/Worcester, .800, 16-4

B Piedmont League
President: Dan W. Hill

Standings	W	L	Pct.	GB	Manager
Greensboro Patriots***(16)	90	48	.652	—	Eddie Dyer/Bobby Rice
Charlotte Hornets	80	61	.567	11½	Johnny Dobbs/Guy Lacy
Richmond Colts	73	68	.518	18½	Jack Onslow
Wilmington Pirates	70	68	.507	20	Blackie Carter
Durham Bulls (5)	65	76	.461	26½	Bob Murray/Bill Skiff
Winston-Salem Twins	42	99	.298	49½	Jim Poole/Art Bourg

Playoffs: None.

All-Star Team: 1B-Ed Hendee, Richmond; **2B**-Jim Bucher, Greensboro; **3B**-Frank Packard, Charlotte; **SS**-Jimmy Brown, Greensboro; **OF**-Taft Wright, Charlotte; Ernie Koy, Durham; Charles Wade, Richmond; **C**-Robert Collins, Durham; **P**-Ad Holshauser, Richmond; Junie Barnes, Wilmington.

BA: Jim Bucher, Greensboro, .369
Runs: Emile Barnes, Charlotte, 122
Hits: Jim Bucher, Greensboro, 188
RBIs: Charles Wade, Richmond, 119
HRs: Jim Bucher, Greensboro, 25

Wins: John Chambers, Greensboro, 23
SOs: Dykes Potter, Greensboro, 189
ERA: Al Veach, Charlotte, 2.42
Pct: Al Veach, Charlotte, .750, 12-4

C Dixie League
President: J. Alvin Gardner

Standings	W	L	Pct.	GB	Manager
Baton Rouge Solons*	77	47	.621	—	Josh Billings
Shreveport Sports**(4)	74	49	.602	2½	Gus Whelan
Jackson Senators	70	56	.556	8	Herschel Bobo
Henderson Oilers	64	61	.512	13½	Art Phelan
Tyler Governors	59	65	.476	18	Wray Query
Waco Cubs/Pine Bluff Judges#	56	69	.448	21½	Archie "Buddy" Tanner
El Dorado Lions	49	74	.398	27½	Dusty Boggess/Joe Granade
Longview Cannibals	48	76	.387	29	Abe Bowman/Joe Cantrell/Art Jahn

#Waco (24-38) moved to Pine Bluff June 27. The franchise folded August 22. The six cancelled games were awarded to their opponents.

Playoff: Baton Rouge 4 games, Shreveport 2, one tie.

All-Star Team: 1B-Charles Gilbert, Baton Rouge; **2B**-Carroll Kott, Waco/Pine Bluff; **3B**-Joe Bilgere, Henderson; **SS**-Jimmy Dalrymple, Henderson; **OF**-Mike Bouza, El Dorado; Hub "Buddy" Bates, Shreveport; Mel Mazzera, Baton Rouge; **C**-Adolph Krauss, Baton Rouge; **Util**-George Boutwell, Jackson; **P**-Steve Larkin, Shreveport; Merritt Hubbell, Baton Rouge; **Manager**-Josh Billings, Baton Rouge.

BA: George Brown, Longview, .360
Runs: Charles Gilbert, Baton Rouge, 116
Hits: Jimmy Dalrymple, Henderson, 180
RBIs: Sam Jones, Henderson, 105

HRs: Cecil "Stormy" Davis, Waco/
Pine Bluff, 17
Wins: Steve Larkin, Shreveport, 22
SOs: George Mills, Tyler, 143
ERA: Gene McClung, Baton Rouge, 2.34

C Middle Atlantic League
President: Elmer M. Daily

Standings	W	L	Pct.	GB	Manager
Wheeling Stogies**(5)	78	55	.586	—	Jack Sheehan
Zanesville Grays*(3)	76	59	.563	3	Johnny Walker/Frank "Buzz" Wetzel/
					Harry Layne/Bert Grimm

Dayton Ducks .... 71 63 .530 7½ Howard "Ducky" Holmes
Springfield Chicks (8) .... 67 64 .511 10 Jake Pitler
Charleston Senators .... 67 67 .500 11½ Danny Boone/Watt Powell
Johnstown Johnnies .... 67 67 .500 11½ Karl Weber/Leo Mackey
Beckley Black Knights .... 63 71 .470 15½ Eli Harris
Huntington Boosters (4) ..... 46 89 .341 33 Johnny Stuart/Earl Smith/Bernie Neis/
                                                 Stuart/Rube Benton

Playoff: Zanesville 4 games, Wheeling 1.

All-Star Team: 1B-Buddy Hassett, Wheeling; **2B**-Don Curry, Wheeling; **3B**-Marcel "Mickey" Ballande, Zanesville; **SS**-Billy Hitchcock, Wheeling; **OF**-Al Powell, Dayton; Tony Fiarito, Zanesville; Sam Thomas, Johnstown; **C**-Walter Millies, Dayton; **P**-Al Milnar, Zanesville; William Helmick, Charleston.

BA: Pepper Barry, Johnstown, .361
Runs: Edward Wilson, Springfield, 112
Hits: Pepper Barry, Johnstown, 194
RBIs: Marcel "Mickey" Ballande, Zanesville, 96

HRs: Michael Noonan, Springfield, 26
Wins: Rex McDonald, Springfield, 19
SOs: Al Milnar, Zanesville, 194
ERA: Kemp Wicker, Wheeling, 2.00

D Nebraska State League
President: James E. Beltzer

Standings	W	L	Pct.	GB	Manager
Norfolk Elks*	60	45	.571	—	George McDermott
Beatrice Blues**	60	46	.566	½	Dick "Sonny" Brookhaus
Sioux Falls Canaries	57	49	.538	3½	Rex Stucker
Lincoln Links.....................	34	71	.324	26	Elmer "Doc" Bennett/Joe Hruska

Playoff: Beatrice 5 games, Norfolk 4.

All-Star Team: 1B-Shirley Bosse, Sioux Falls; **2B**-Larry Getz, Beatrice; **3B**-Howard Moore, Beatrice; **SS**-Ray Bertram, Norfolk; **OF**-Hockett Brown, Sioux Falls; Lynn King, Sioux Falls; Don Gutteridge, Lincoln; Walter Gannon, Norfolk; Joe Burris, Norfolk; **C**-Ralph Brandon, Sioux Falls; **Util**-George Proost, Beatrice; **P**-Luke Bucklin, Norfolk; Mike Pociask, Beatrice; **Manager**-Joe McDermott, Norfolk.

BA: Don Gutteridge, Lincoln, .360
Runs: Larry Getz, Beatrice, 100
Hits: Ray Bertram, Norfolk, 152
HRs: Howard Moore, Beatrice, 19

Wins: Wilmer Schroeder, Sioux Falls, 20
SOs: Mike Pociask, Beatrice, 195
ERA: Stan Conaway, Sioux Falls, 2.43

D Northern League
Presidents: Russell L. Voelz/Lute J. Boone

Standings	W	L	Pct.	GB	Manager
Winnipeg Maroons	67	44	.604	—	Bruno Haas
Superior Blues*	60	49	.550	6	Dick Wade
Brainerd Muskies/					
Brandon Grays#**	55	46	.545	7	Ed Reichle
Eau Claire Cardinals	52	45	.536	8	Johnny Mostil
Crookston Pirates................	48	48	.500	11½	Lute Boone
East Grand Forks Colts.......	50	55	.476	14	John Anderson/John Vanusek
Fargo-Moorhead Twins	30	75	.286	34	Alvin Theis/Ralph Williams

#Brainerd (14-21) moved to Brandon June 27.

Playoff: Superior 5 games, Brandon 4.

All-Star Team: 1B-Gene Corbett, Winnipeg; **2B**-Stanley Sperry, Eau Claire; **3B**-Jack Calvey, Brainerd/Brandon; Jerry Kopko, Superior; **SS**-Morris Arnovich, Superior; **OF**-Frank Rendler, Eau Claire; Ray Helixon, East Grand Forks; Julian Johnson, Crookston; **C**-John Rosette, Winnipeg; Chester Bujaci, Brainerd/Brandon; **Util**-Mark Almli, Superior; **P**-Leroy Goldsworth, Winnipeg; Art Braga, Superior; Roman Bertrand, Crookston; Norman Masters, Crookston.

BA: John Anderson, East Grand Forks, .403
Hits: Elmer Greenwald, Winnipeg, 147
  Gene Corbett, Winnipeg, 147
HRs: Gene Corbett, Winnipeg, 18

Wins: Leroy Goldsworth, Winnipeg, 22
SOs: Leroy Goldsworth, Winnipeg, 195
Pct: Leroy Goldsworth, Winnipeg, .786, 22-6

1933 Interleague Post Season Play

World Series
New York (National) 4 games, Washington (American) 1

Junior World Series
Columbus (American Association) 5 games, Buffalo (International) 3
Total Attendance: 46,645

Dixie Series
New Orleans (Southern Association) 4 games, San Antonio (Texas) 2
Total Attendance: 25,529

Midwest Series
St. Joseph (Western) 4 games, Davenport (Mississippi Valley) 2

1933 Major League Farm Systems

American League
1 Boston (1): Reading.
3 Cleveland (1): Zanesville.
4 Detroit (6): Toronto, Beaumont, Hutchinson/Bartlesville, Quincy/Nashua/Brockton, Shreveport, Huntington.
5 New York (4): Newark, Binghamton, Durham, Wheeling.
6 Philadelphia (2): Montreal, Williamsport.
7 St. Louis (2): San Antonio, Joplin.
8 Washington (2): Chattanooga, Springfield (OH).

National League
9 Boston (1): Harrisburg.
10 Brooklyn (1): York.
11 Chicago (1): Los Angeles.
12 Cincinnati (2): Topeka, Rock Island.
13 New York (1): Attleboro/Lawrence/Woonsocket.
16 St. Louis (7): Columbus, Rochester, Houston, Elmira, Springfield (MO), Greensboro, Springfield (IL).

1933 No-Hitters

Date	Pitcher	Team	League	Opponent	Score
5-15	Joe Sullivan/				
	Ray Fritz	Beaumont	Texas	Dallas	6-3
5-22	Floyd Newkirk	St. Paul	American Assoc.	Kansas City	5-0
5-24	Bill Bayne	Memphis	Southern Assoc.	Birmingham	8-0
6-6	Charles Wood	Tulsa	Texas	Houston	9-2 (7)
6-9	Henry Thormahlen	Galveston	Texas	Tulsa	2-0
6-13	Harry Gumbert	Williamsport	New York-Penn.	York	2-0
6-28	Fred Fussell	Albany	International	Jersey City	4-0
7-27	Cy Blanton	St. Joseph	Western	Joplin	9-0
8-8	Roman Bertrand	Crookston	Northern	Fargo-Moorhead	2-0
8-16	Larry Bishop	Lowell	New England	Brockton	6-0 (7)
8-17	Ed Walsh, Jr.	Oakland	Pacific Coast	San Francisco	5-0
8-18	Fred Johnson	New Orleans	Southern Assoc.	Birmingham	6-0 (7)
8-19	Paul Sullivan	Shreveport	Dixie	Jackson	7-0
8-21	Jack LaRocca	Binghamton	New York-Penn.	Reading	8-0
9-3	Lew Krausse	Harrisburg	New York-Penn.	York	3-0

Number in parentheses indicates innings if other than nine.

THIS DATE IN MINOR LEAGUE HISTORY

May 19, 1933, Second baseman Frank Novosel of Richmond, Piedmont League, executed an unassisted triple play against Greensboro.

June 18, 1933, Frank Sigafoos of Indianapolis extended his consecutive game hitting streak to 38 games, breaking the American Association record.

July 14, 1933, Joe DiMaggio of San Francisco hit safely in his 50th straight game, breaking the Pacific Coast League record which had stood since 1914, the year he was born.

July 25, 1933, Joe DiMaggio, 18-year-old San Francisco, Pacific Coast League, outfielder, hit safely in his 61st consecutive game. The streak would end the next day as Oakland's Ed Walsh, Jr. would hold DiMaggio hitless.

August 18, 1933, Julius "Moose" Solters of Baltimore, International League, hit two home runs in one inning against Rochester.

September 4, 1933, In a Labor Day twinbill, Joe Hauser of Minneapolis hit three home runs to raise his total for the season to 65, a new record in Organized Baseball.

September 8, 1933, Cy Blanton of St. Joseph, Western League, fanned 12 Topeka hitters. This was the twelfth time this season he whiffed ten or more in one game. He also had two in postseason games for a total of 14 double-figure strikeout tilts.

November 1933, The Shaughnessy Plan was introduced in the American Association, International and Texas Leagues. Under this system, playoffs were held after the close of the regular schedule to decide the championship and to determine who would play in postseason interleague series.

1934

American League

President: William Harridge

Standings	W	L	Pct.	GB	Attend.	Manager
Detroit Tigers	101	53	.656	—	919,161	Mickey Cochrane
New York Yankees	94	60	.610	7	854,682	Joe McCarthy
Cleveland Indians	85	69	.552	16	391,338	Walter Johnson
Boston Red Sox	76	76	.500	24	610,640	Bucky Harris
Philadelphia Athletics	68	82	.453	31	305,847	Connie Mack
St. Louis Browns	67	85	.441	33	115,305	Rogers Hornsby
Washington Senators	66	86	.434	34	330,074	Joe Cronin
Chicago White Sox	53	99	.349	47	236,559	Lew Fonseca/Jimmy Dykes

BA: Lou Gehrig, New York, .363
Runs: Charlie Gehringer, Detroit, 134
Hits: Charlie Gehringer, Detroit, 214
RBIs: Lou Gehrig, New York, 165
HRs: Lou Gehrig, New York, 49
Wins: Lefty Gomez, New York, 26
SOs: Lefty Gomez, New York, 158
ERA: Lefty Gomez, New York, 2.33
Pct: Lefty Gomez, New York, .839, 26-5

National League

President: John A. Heydler

Standings	W	L	Pct.	GB	Attend.	Manager
St. Louis Cardinals	95	58	.621	—	325,056	Frank Frisch
New York Giants	93	60	.608	2	730,851	Bill Terry
Chicago Cubs	86	65	.570	8	707,525	Charlie Grimm
Boston Braves	78	73	.517	16	303,205	Bill McKechnie
Pittsburgh Pirates	74	76	.493	19½	322,622	George Gibson/Pie Traynor
Brooklyn Dodgers	71	81	.467	23½	434,188	Casey Stengel
Philadelphia Phillies	56	93	.376	37	169,885	Jimmie Wilson
Cincinnati Reds	52	99	.344	42	206,773	Bob O'Farrell/Burt Shotton/ Chuck Dressen

BA: Paul Waner, Pittsburgh, .362
Runs: Paul Waner, Pittsburgh, 122
Hits: Paul Waner, Pittsburgh, 217
RBIs: Mel Ott, New York, 135
HRs: Mel Ott, New York, 35
James "Rip" Collins, St. Louis, 35
Wins: Dizzy Dean, St. Louis, 30
SOs: Dizzy Dean, St. Louis, 195
ERA: Carl Hubbell, New York, 2.30
Pct: Dizzy Dean, St. Louis, .811, 30-7

AA American Association

President: Thomas J. Hickey

East Standings	W	L	Pct.	GB	Attend.	Manager
Columbus Red Birds (16)	85	68	.556	—	142,561	Ray Blades
Louisville Colonels	78	74	.513	6½	88,803	Bruno Betzel/Ken Penner
Indianapolis Indians	77	75	.507	7½	124,372	Wade Killefer
Toledo Mud Hens	68	84	.447	16½	61,886	Steve O'Neill
West Standings	**W**	**L**	**Pct.**	**GB**	**Attend.**	**Manager**
Minneapolis Millers	85	64	.570	—	164,390	Donie Bush
Milwaukee Brewers	82	70	.539	4½	132,514	Allan Sothoron
St. Paul Saints	67	84	.444	19	74,801	Bob Coleman
Kansas City Blues	65	88	.425	22	67,472	Roger Peckinpaugh

Playoff: Columbus 4 games, Minneapolis 3.

All-Star Team: 1B-Harry Davis, Toledo; **2B**-Lin Storti, Milwaukee; **3B**-Fred Bedore, Indianapolis; **SS**-William Myers, Columbus; **OF**-Vern Washington, Indianapolis; Ab Wright, Minneapolis; Luis Almada, Kansas City; **C**-William Hargrave, Minneapolis; **P**-Walter Tauscher, Minneapolis; Garland Braxton, Milwaukee.

BA: Earl Webb, Milwaukee, .368
Runs: Spencer Harris, Minneapolis, 138
Hits: Billy Sullivan, Milwaukee, 222
RBIs: Jack Kloza, Milwaukee, 148
HRs: Buzz Arlett, Minneapolis, 41
Wins: Walter Tauscher, Minneapolis, 21
SOs: Stew Bolen, Indianapolis, 177
ERA: James "Jumbo" Elliott, Columbus, 3.27

AA International League

President: Charles H. Knapp

Standings	W	L	Pct.	GB	Attend.	Manager
Newark Bears (5)	93	60	.608	—	126,070	Bob Shawkey
Rochester Red Wings (16)	88	63	.583	4	162,627	George "Specs" Toporcer
Toronto Maple Leafs (12)	85	67	.559	7½	136,301	Ike Boone
Albany Senators	81	72	.529	12	125,000	Bill McCorry
Buffalo Bisons	76	77	.497	17	245,439	Ray Schalk
Montreal Royals (6)	73	77	.487	18½	158,997	Frank Shaughnessy
Syracuse Chiefs	60	94	.390	33½	91,390	Andy High/Bill Sweeney
Baltimore Orioles	53	99	.349	39½	78,349	Frank McGowan/Joe Judge/ Guy Sturdy

Playoffs: Rochester 4 games, Albany 1; Toronto 4 games, Newark 3.
Finals: Toronto 4 games, Rochester 1.

All-Star Team: 1B-Dale Alexander, Newark; **2B**-Fresco Thompson, Montreal; **3B**-Greg Mulleavy, Buffalo; **SS**-Tom Carey, Rochester; **OF**-Ike Boone, Toronto; Al Powell, Albany; Jess Hill, Newark; **C**-Buddy Lewis, Rochester; **P**-Walter "Jumbo" Brown, Newark; Gene Schott, Toronto; **MVP**-Ike Boone, Toronto.

BA: Ike Boone, Toronto, .372
Runs: Greg Mulleavy, Buffalo, 131
Hits: Jesse Hill, Newark, 205
RBIs: Fred Sington, Albany, 147
HRs: Woody Abernathy, Baltimore, 32
Vince Barton, Newark, 32
Wins: Walter "Jumbo" Brown, Newark, 20
SOs: Cy Blanton, Albany, 165
ERA: Walter "Jumbo" Brown, Newark, 2.56

AA Pacific Coast League

President: Hyland L. Baggerly

Standings	W	L	Pct.	GB	Attend.	Manager
Los Angeles Angels***(11)	137	50	.733	—	129,672	Jack Lelivelt
Mission Reds	101	85	.543	35½	88,021	Gabby Street
Hollywood Stars	97	88	.524	39	128,140	Oscar Vitt
San Francisco Seals	93	95	.495	44½	99,493	James Caveney
Oakland Oaks	90	98	.479	47½	55,610	Ray Brubaker/Art Veltman
Seattle Indians	81	102	.443	54	182,920	George Burns/Dutch Reuther
Sacramento Senators	79	109	.420	58½	59,810	Earl McNeely
Portland Beavers	66	117	.361	69	50,731	Walter McCreedie/ Tom Turner/George Burns

Playoff: Los Angeles 4 games, PCL All-Stars 2.

All-Star Team: 1B-Babe Dahlgren, Mission; **2B**-Al Wright, Mission; **3B**-Jose Coscarart, Seattle; Fred Haney, Hollywood; **SS**-Jim Levey, Hollywood; **OF**-Oscar "Ox" Eckhardt, Mission; Smead Jolley, Hollywood; Art Hunt, Seattle; Luis Almada, Mission; **C**-Johnny Bassler, Hollywood; Lawrence Woodall, San Francisco; **P**-Leroy Herrmann, San Francisco; Joe Sullivan, Hollywood; Herman Pillette, Seattle; Sam Gibson, San Francisco; Clarence Mitchell, Mission; **Manager**-Dutch Reuther, Seattle.

BA: Frank Demaree, Los Angeles, .383
Runs: Frank Demaree, Los Angeles, 190
Hits: Frank Demaree, Los Angeles, 269
RBIs: Frank Demaree, Los Angeles, 173
HRs: Frank Demaree, Los Angeles, 45
Wins: Fay Thomas, Los Angeles, 28
SOs: Fay Thomas, Los Angeles, 204
ERA: Dutch Lieber, Mission, 2.50

A New York-Pennsylvania League

President: Perry B. Farrell

Standings	W	L	Pct.	GB	Manager
Williamsport Grays**(6)	78	60	.565	—	Mike McNally
Binghamton Triplets*(5)	76	62	.551	2	Bill Meyer
Reading Red Sox (1)	72	66	.522	6	Nemo Leibold
Scranton Miners	71	67	.514	7	Jake Pitler
Wilkes-Barre Barons	66	67	.496	9½	Elmer Yoter
Elmira Red Wings (16)	63	75	.457	15	Ira Smith/Joe Mathes
Hazleton Mountaineers (14)	61	75	.449	16	Frank Uzmann
Harrisburg Senators (9)	60	75	.444	16½	Leslie Mann

Total Attendance: 401,211.

Playoff: Williamsport 4 games, Binghamton 2.

All-Star Team: 1B-Neil Caldwell, Elmira; **2B**-Frank Parenti, Wilkes-Barre; **3B**-Elmer Yoter, Wilkes-Barre; **SS**-John "Bunny" Griffiths, Wilkes-Barre; **OF**-Horace "Red" McBride, Williamsport; Ernie Koy, Binghamton; Arthur Graham, Reading; **C**-Bill Baker, Williamsport; **Util**-Sol Mishkin, Binghamton; **P**-Albert Fisher, Elmira; Milburn Shoffner, Scranton; **Manager**-Mike McNally, Williamsport.

BA: John Rizzo, Elmira, .379
Runs: Horace "Red" McBride, Williamsport, 114
Larry Fischer, Scranton, 114
Hits: Horace "Red" McBride, Williamsport, 197
RBIs: Horace "Red" McBride, Williamsport, 129
HRs: Horace "Red" McBride, Williamsport, 26
Wins: Bunn Hearn, Williamsport, 21
SOs: Kemp Wicker, Binghamton, 136
ERA: Bill Thomas, Williamsport, 2.64

A Southern Association

President: John D. Martin

Standings	W	L	Pct.	GB	Attend.	Manager
New Orleans Pelicans**(3)	94	60	.610	—	92,423	Larry Gilbert
Nashville Volunteers*(13)	87	65	.579	6	98,781	Chuck Dressen/Lance Richbourg
Memphis Chickasaws	79	72	.523	13½	85,724	Tommy "Doc" Prothro
Atlanta Crackers	77	74	.510	15½	195,386	Spencer Abbott/Eddie Moore
Chattanooga Lookouts (8)	78	75	.510	15½	94,894	Zinn Beck/Mule Shirley
Knoxville Smokies	73	80	.477	20½	52,239	Pee Wee Wanninger/Lee Head
Birmingham Barons	64	90	.416	30	59,135	Clyde Milan
Little Rock Travelers	59	95	.383	35	81,024	Emmett McCann/John Moore

Playoff: New Orleans 3 games, Nashville 2.

All-Star Team: 1B-Edward Taylor, Atlanta; **2B**-Louis Berger, New Orleans; **3B**-Ernie

*Won first-half **Won second-half ***Won both halves
Numbers after nicknames indicate farm system.
Affiliation listed at end of each year.

Holman, New Orleans; **SS**-Bill Rodda, Nashville; **OF**-Eddie Rose, New Orleans; Walter French, Knoxville; Lance Richbourg, Nashville; **C**-Lee Head, Knoxville; Joe Palmisano, Atlanta; **Util**-Peck Hamel, Memphis; **P**-Harry Kelley, Memphis/Atlanta; Bill Hughes, Birmingham; Byron Speece, Nashville; Al Milnar, New Orleans; Leo Moon, Knoxville; **Manager**-Larry Gilbert, New Orleans.

BA: Phil Weintraub, Nashville, .401
Runs: Cal Chapman, Memphis, 115
Hits: Bill Rodda, Nashville, 190
Louis Berger, New Orleans, 190
Cal Chapman, Memphis, 190

RBIs: Andy Reese, Memphis, 108
HRs: Henry "Prince" Oana, Atlanta, 17
Wins: Harry Kelley, Memphis/Atlanta, 23
SOs: Harry Kelley, Memphis/Atlanta, 143
ERA: Al Milnar, New Orleans, 2.61

A Texas League
President: J. Alvin Gardner

Standings	W	L	Pct.	GB	Attend.	Manager
Galveston Buccaneers	88	64	.579	—	60,842	Billy Webb
San Antonio Missions (7)	89	65	.578	—	125,259	Hank Severeid
Beaumont Exporters (4)	81	69	.540	6	58,150	Dutch Lorbeer
Dallas Steers	80	73	.523	8½	215,094	Fred Brainard
Tulsa Oilers	77	75	.519	11	65,738	Jake Atz
Houston Buffaloes (16)	76	78	.478	13	61,180	Carey Selph
Ft. Worth Cats	59	92	.391	28½	51,304	Del Pratt
Oklahoma City Indians	59	93	.388	29	52,610	Luther Harvel

Playoffs: Galveston 3 games, Dallas 1; San Antonio 3 games, Beaumont 2.
Finals: Galveston 4 games, San Antonio 2.

All-Star Team: 1B-Alex Hooks, Tulsa; **2B**-Charles English, Galveston; **3B**-Donald Ross, Beaumont; **SS**-Lamar Newsome, Tulsa; **OF**-Chester Morgan, Beaumont/San Antonio; Beau Bell, Galveston; Charles Hostetler, Tulsa; **C**-Tommy Heath, San Antonio; **Util**-Joe Vance, Dallas; **P**-Ash Hillin, San Antonio; Clarence "Red" Phillips, Beaumont; **MVP**-Charles English, Galveston; **Pitcher of the Year**-Ash Hillin, San Antonio.

BA: Chester Morgan, Beaumont/
San Antonio, .342
Runs: Charles Hostetler, Tulsa, 124
Hits: Chester Morgan, Beaumont/
San Antonio, 216

RBIs: Larry Bettencourt, San Antonio, 129
HRs: Paul Easterling, Tulsa, 29
Wins: Ash Hillin, San Antonio, 24
SOs: Vern Kennedy, Oklahoma City, 167
ERA: Clarence "Red" Phillips, Beaumont, 2.16

A Western League
President: Dale D. Gear

Standings	W	L	Pct.	GB	Attend.	Manager
Sioux City Cowboys	74	50	.597	—	87,196	Dutch Zwilling
Davenport Blue Sox**	70	53	.569	3½	48,920	Cletus Dixon
Des Moines Demons	68	56	.548	6	30,797	Harold Irelan/Alex Gaston
St. Joseph Saints	65	56	.537	7½	43,772	Wes Griffin/Earle Brucker
Topeka Senators (12)	59	64	.480	14½	28,889	Art Ewoldt/Jimmy Ewold
Rock Island Islanders	58	65	.471	15½	36,619	Riley Parker/Clifford Knox
Omaha Packers	49	73	.402	24	34,675	Frank "Dutch" Wetzel/ Malcolm Pickett
Cedar Rapids Raiders	47	73	.392	25	47,360	Bubbles Hargraves/ William Mizeur

Playoffs: Playoffs involved the three teams tied for first place in the first half and the second half winner. St. Joseph 3 games, Sioux City 1; Davenport 3 games, Des Moines 1.
Finals: St. Joseph 4 games, Davenport 3.

All-Star Team: 1B-Malcolm Pickett, Omaha; **2B**-Hugh Luby, Sioux City; **3B**-Clarence "Cap" Crossley, Davenport; **SS**-Angus McIsaac, St. Joseph; **OF**-Floyd Patterson, Rock Island; Albert McNeely, Omaha; John Dickshot, Rock Island/Cedar Rapids; **C**-Morgan Snyder, Topeka; **P**-Frank Lamanski, Davenport; Max Thomas, Sioux City.

BA: Floyd Patterson, Rock Island, .366
Runs: John Dickshot, Rock Island/
Cedar Rapids, 112
Hits: Howard McFarland, St. Joseph, 164
Charles Bates, St. Joseph, 164
Leo Ogorek, Des Moines, 164

RBIs: Roy Hudson, Des Moines, 94
HRs: Vern Johnson, Sioux City, 24
Wins: Frank Lamanski, Davenport, 24
SOs: Frank Lamanski, Davenport, 216
Pct: Frank Lamanski, Davenport, .774, 24-7

B Central League
President: Emerson W. Dickerson

Standings	W	L	Pct.	GB	Manager
Fort Wayne Chiefs	19	4	.826	—	Bill Burwell
Springfield Red Birds	14	12	.538	6½	Joe Mathes
Grand Rapids Tigers	11	13	.458	8½	Earl Wolgamot
Peoria Tractors	11	13	.458	8½	Frank Murphy
Muskegon Reds@	4	9	.308	NA	Cy Boothby
Lima Buckeyes#	0	8	.000	NA	Jess Orndorf

#Lima disbanded May 26.
@Muskegon disbanded May 30.
The league disbanded June 10.

BA: Paul O'Malley, Grand Rapids, .389
Runs: Ralph Rhein, Fort Wayne, 26
Hits: Ralph Rhein, Fort Wayne, 37
HRs: Ralph Rhein, Fort Wayne, 6

Wins: Allan Baringer, Fort Wayne, 5
SOs: Claude Passeau, Grand Rapids, 50
Pct: Norm Jung, Fort Wayne, 1.000, 4-0

B Northeastern League
President: Roger E. Baker

Standings	W	L	Pct.	GB	Manager
Waltham/Worcester Rosebuds#**	66	43	.555	—	Freddie Knight
Lowell Honeys/Hustlers*	63	46	.529	3	Bill Hunnefield
Manchester Indians	58	49	.542	7	Chief Werre
Hartford Senators	50	53	.485	13	Fred "Snake" Henry/Pepper Rae/ Bill Morrell
New Bedford Whalers	46	60	.434	18½	Jean Dubuc
Springfield Ponies	41	62	.398	22	Bobby Murray
Watertown Townies@	40	28	.588	NA	Bill Barrett
Cambridge Cantabs/ Wayland Birds@+	19	42	.311	NA	Bill Morrell/Mack Hillis/Dick Phelan

#Waltham (6-2) moved to Worcester May 24, first home game June 1.
@Watertown and Cambridge entered the league at the start of the second half.
+Cambridge (1-12) moved to Wayland July 17.

Playoff: Lowell 4 games, Worcester 1.

All-Star Team: 1B-Fred "Snake" Henry, Worcester; **2B**-Fred Maguire, Worcester; **3B**-Bill Hunnefield, Lowell; **SS**-Regis Smith, Lowell; **OF**-Bill Scholz, New Bedford; John Jones, Springfield/Worcester/Watertown; Harold Shaffer, Lowell; **C**-Howard Storie, Manchester; **Util**-William Rea, Hartford; **P**-Gerald Gruenwald, Worcester; Frank Coleman, Hartford; **Manager**-Chief Werre, Manchester.

BA: John Jones, Springfield/Worcester/
Watertown, .365
Runs: Thomas Adams, Worcester/
Springfield, 92
Hits: Fred "Snake" Henry, Worcester, 131

HRs: Amit Savard, Lowell, 17
Wins: Gerald Gruenwald, Worcester, 17
SOs: Frank Coleman, Hartford, 174
Pct: Justin McLaughlin, Manchester,
.706, 12-5

B Piedmont League
President: Dan W. Hill

Standings	W	L	Pct.	GB	Manager
Norfolk Tars**(5)	89	49	.645	—	Bill Skiff
Charlotte Hornets*	87	51	.630	2	Tommy Taylor
Wilmington Pirates (12)	64	74	.464	25	Blackie Carter/Harry McCurdy
Richmond Colts	60	78	.435	29	Ed Hendee/Charles Wade
Columbia Sandlappers/ Asheville Tourists#(1)	55	78	.414	31½	Bill Laval/George "Possum" Whitted
Greensboro Patriots (16)	56	81	.409	32½	Bobby Rice

#Columbia (21-19) moved to Asheville June 7.

Playoff: Norfolk 4 games, Charlotte 2.

All-Star Team: 1B-Buddy Hassett, Norfolk; **2B**-Don Curry, Norfolk; **3B**-William Andrus, Richmond; **SS**-Robert Stevens, Norfolk; **OF**-Emile Barnes, Charlotte; George Ferrell, Columbia/Asheville; Jim Bryan, Norfolk; **C**-Dick Luckey, Charlotte; **Util**-Claude Staylor, Wilmington; **P**-Robert Durham, Charlotte; John "Pretzels" Pezzullo, Richmond; **Manager**-Bill Skiff, Norfolk.

BA: Jim Bryan, Norfolk, .376
Runs: Dan Hall, Norfolk, 126
Hits: Jim Bryan, Norfolk, 200
RBIs: Jim Bryan, Norfolk, 144
HRs: Jim Bryan, Norfolk, 30

Wins: Robert Durham, Charlotte, 21
SOs: Junie Barnes, Wilmington, 232
ERA: Ray White, Norfolk, 2.77
Pct: Thomas "Sugar" Kain, Norfolk,
.846, 11-2

C East Dixie League
President: J. Alvin Gardner

Standings	W	L	Pct.	GB	Manager
Pine Bluff Judges	79	48	.622	—	Lena Styles
Jackson Mississippians*	72	54	.571	6½	Guy Lacy
Greenville Buckshots**	70	58	.547	9½	Bill Eisemann/Frank Brazill
El Dorado Lions	58	71	.450	22	George Harper
Shreveport Sports/ Greenwood Chiefs@(4)	57	70	.449	22	Jerry Mallett/Slim Brewer
Baton Rouge Red Sticks/ Clarksdale Ginners#	47	82	.364	33	Josh Billings

#Baton Rouge (19-29) moved to Clarksdale June 11, first home game June 14.
@Shreveport moved to Greenwood July 13, first home game July 18.

Playoff: Jackson 4 games, Greenville 2.

All-Star Team: 1B-Cecil Bolton, Greenville; **2B**-Benny McCoy, Shreveport/Greenwood; **3B**-Neal Stover, Pine Bluff; **SS**-William Marshall, Baton Rouge/Clarksdale; **OF**-L.F. McDaniels, Jackson; Leslie Horn, Greenville; George Harper, El Dorado; **C**-Harold Sueme, Pine Bluff; **Util**-George Boutwell, Jackson; **P**-Hugo Klaerner, Pine Bluff; Frank Cook, Greenwood; **Manager**-Frank Brazill, Greenville.

BA: Leslie Horn, Greenville, .364
Runs: Joe Valenti, El Dorado, 100
Hits: Leslie Horn, Greenville, 182
RBIs: Hugh Ferrell, Jackson, 95
HRs: Cecil Bolton, Greenville, 19

Wins: Hugo Klaerner, Pine Bluff, 24
SOs: Hugo Klaerner, Pine Bluff, 172
ERA: George Mills, Baton Rouge/
Clarksdale, 1.89

C Middle Atlantic League
President: Elmer M. Daily

Standings	W	L	Pct.	GB	Manager
Zanesville Grays**(3)	72	51	.585	—	Harry Layne/Burt Grimm/Earl Wolgamot
Dayton Ducks*(10)	71	54	.568	2	Howard "Ducky" Holmes
Huntington Red Birds (16)	69	53	.566	2½	Eddie Dyer
Beckley Black Knights (12)	65	57	.533	6½	Milt Stock
Johnstown Johnnies	62	62	.500	10½	Guy Sturdy/Vernon Mackie
Springfield Pirates (15)	57	65	.467	14½	Al DeVormer/Rube Bressler
Charleston Senators (4)	55	67	.451	16½	Charles Neibergall
Wheeling Stogies (5)	39	81	.325	31½	John Sheehan

Playoff: Zanesville 4 games, Dayton 3.

All-Star Team: 1B-John McCarthy, Dayton; **2B**-Eli Harris, Beckley; **3B**-Ed Mayo, Johnstown; **SS**-Eddie Miller, Springfield; **OF**-Nicholas Hickey, Johnstown; Dan Pavlovic, Charleston; Holt "Cat" Milner, Dayton/Zanesville; **C**-Vernon Mackie, Johnstown; **Util**-Tony Fiarito, Zanesville; **P**-Clarence Bergman, Dayton; Wayne LaMaster, Charleston; **Manager**-Earl Wolgamot, Zanesville.

BA: Vernon Mackie, Johnstown, .365
Runs: Sam Thomas, Johnstown, 123
Hits: Arnold Anderson, Huntington, 174
RBIs: Vernon Mackie, Johnstown, 94
HRs: Michael Noonan, Springfield, 17; John McCarthy, Dayton, 17
Wins: Wayne LaMaster, Charleston, 17; Roger Wolff, Dayton, 17
SOs: Wayne LaMaster, Charleston, 168
ERA: Earl Cook, Beckley, 2.48

C West Dixie League
President: J. Alvin Gardner

Standings	W	L	Pct.	GB	Manager
Jacksonville Jax***(13)	83	42	.664	—	Wally Dashiell
Henderson Oilers	67	58	.536	16	Pat Moulton
Longview Cannibals (2)	66	59	.528	17	Ray Flaskamper/Dallas Warren
Tyler Governors	63	62	.504	20	Wray Query
Palestine Pals	53	72	.424	30	Bobby Goff
Paris Pirates/ Lufkin Lumbermen#(16)	43	82	.344	40	Wayne Windle

#Paris (17-45) moved to Lufkin June 27 at the start of the second half.
Attendance: Jacksonville, 24,357.

Playoffs: None.

All-Star Team: 1B-Charles Baron(ovic), Jacksonville; **2B**-Bobby Goff, Palestine; **3B**-Joe Bilgere, Henderson; **SS**-Larry Kinser, Jacksonville; **OF**-Fern Bell, Tyler; John Cummings, Jacksonville; Tom Pyle, Jacksonville; **C**-Orace Powers, Henderson; **Util**-J.R. Phelps, Henderson; **P**-Thomas McPhaul, Henderson; Walter Becker, Jacksonville; **Manager**-Wally Dashiell, Jacksonville.

BA: Fern Bell, Tyler, .373
Runs: Kerby Farrell, Tyler, 105
Hits: Tom Pyle, Jacksonville, 174
RBIs: John Cummings, Jacksonville, 131
HRs: Lou Frierson, Paris/Lufkin, 40
Wins: Linville Watkins, Jacksonville, 19
SOs: Grady Bassett, Tyler, 178
ERA: Jackie Reid, Jacksonville, 1.98

C Western Association
President: Tom Fairweather

Standings	W	L	Pct.	GB	Manager
Springfield Red Wings**(16)	76	58	.567	—	Mike Ryba
Ponca City Angels*(11)	73	61	.545	3	Roy Johnson
Joplin Miners (1)	66	68	.493	10	Wally Schang
Hutchinson Larks	66	68	.493	10	Bob Morrow
Bartlesville Reds (12)	63	69	.477	12	Marty Purtell
Muskogee Tigers	56	76	.424	19	Conrad Fisher

Total Attendance: 251,000.

Playoff: Ponca City defeated Springfield in a one game playoff for the first half title.
Finals: Springfield 4 games, Ponca City 3.

All-Star Team: 1B-Carl Kentling, Bartlesville/Hutchinson; **2B**-Ben Catchings, Muskogee; **3B**-Harold Bohl, Springfield; **SS**-Ike Kahdot, Bartlesville; **OF**-David Cheeves, Springfield/Hutchinson; Sebastian Wagner, Hutchinson; Cliff Ograin, Ponca City; **C**-Frank LaVeque, Bartlesville; Mike Ryba, Springfield; **Util**-Frank Howard, Springfield; Emmett Mueller, Springfield; **P**-Newt Kimball, Ponca City; Joe Berry, Joplin; Bill McGee, Springfield; **Manager**-Marty Purtell, Bartlesville.

BA: David Cheeves, Springfield/Hutchinson, .361
Runs: Sebastian Wagner, Hutchinson, 113
Hits: Steve Mesner, Ponca City, 197
RBIs: Arthur Shoap, Ponca City, 139
HRs: Ed Gray, Muskogee, 16
Wins: Bill McGee, Springfield, 23
SOs: Joe Berry, Joplin, 233
ERA: Mike Ryba, Springfield, 2.96

D Arkansas State League
Presidents: Frank E. Matthews/Charles Morgan

Standings	W	L	Pct.	GB	Manager
Bentonville Officeholders**	40	35	.533	—	Red Wilson/Tom McGill/Ed Hawks
Siloam Springs Buffaloes	37	34	.521	1	Clyde Glass
Rogers Rustlers*	36	35	.507	2	Ed Hawks/Pete Casey
Fayetteville Educators	33	42	.440	7	Fred Hawn/Frank Matthews

Playoff: Rogers defeated Siloam Springs 5-2 in a one game playoff for the first half title. Bentonville was declared second half winner when Fayetteville and Siloam Springs folded August 19.
Finals: Rogers 4 games, Bentonville 3.

All-Star Team: 1B-Parker Rushing, Fayetteville; **2B**-Bill Homan, Rogers; **3B**-Russell Mosier, Siloam Springs; **SS**-David Bush, Rogers; **OF**-John Graves, Siloam Springs; Bill Beams, Bentonville; Rudolph Woodrow, Siloam Springs; **C**-Bill Landthrip, Siloam Springs; **Util**-Clyde Glass, Siloam Springs; **P**-Marvin Brewer, Rogers; J.W. White, Rogers; **Manager**-Pete Casey, Rogers.

BA: John Graves, Siloam Springs, .387
Runs: Bill Beams, Bentonville, 61
Hits: Parker Rushing, Fayetteville, 96
RBIs: Clyde Glass, Siloam Springs, 67
HRs: Bill Beams, Bentonville, 12
Wins: Maurice Wollard, Bentonville, 12
Pct: Everette Hill, Siloam Springs, .889, 8-1

D Bi-State League
President: J. Frank Wilson

Standings	W	L	Pct.	GB	Manager
Danville Leafs**	53	25	.679	—	Herb Brett
Martinsville Manufacturers*	46	29	.613	5½	Jim Sanders
Fieldale Virginians	36	41	.468	16½	D.L. Hodge
Mt. Airy Graniteers	33	43	.434	19	Cecil Harris/G. Thomas
Leaksville-Draper-Spray Triplets	32	45	.416	20½	Oscar Langley/Blackie Carter
Mayodan Senators	29	46	.387	22½	Cecil "Zip" Payne/Charles Eadmon/ Monroe Mitchell

Playoff: Danville 4 games, Martinsville 1.

All-Star Team: 1B-Taylor Sanford, Danville; **2B**-Joe Concannon, Martinsville; **3B**-Sam Narron, Martinsville; **SS**-Cleveland Jarvis, Fieldale; **OF**-Jimmy Sanders, Martinsville; Mike Smith, Danville; Eddie Weston, Mayodan; **C**-Luke Hendrix, Martinsville; Delos Jones, Martinsville; **P**-Cletus Voss, Fieldale; Earl Overman, Danville; Delbert Breece, Mayodan.

BA: Jimmy Sanders, Martinsville, .423
Runs: Woodrow Williams, Leaksville-Spray-Draper, 86
Hits: Cecil "Zip" Payne, Mayodan, 134
HRs: Eddie Weston, Mayodan, 26
Wins: Cletus Voss, Fieldale, 17
SOs: Cletus Voss, Fieldale, 126
Pct: Spencer Bruce, Danville, .813, 13-3

D Evangeline League
President: William T. Daly

Standings	W	L	Pct.	GB	Manager
Lafayette White Sox**	62	45	.579	—	Lee Schulte
Opelousas Indians*	62	50	.554	2½	Pat Flaherty/Clay Guilbeau
Lake Charles Explorers/ Jeanerette Blues#	53	55	.491	9½	Don McShane/Charles Schilling/ Monk Milazzo
Rayne Red Sox	50	52	.490	9½	Dutch Bernson
New Iberia Cardinals	50	58	.463	12½	Hank Dory/Sam Camalo
Alexandria Aces	47	64	.423	17	Art Phelan & Cecil Combs

#Lake Charles (14-13) moved to Jeanerette May 29, after the Lake Charles grandstand was destroyed by fire.

Playoff: Lafayette 4 games, Opelousas 3.

All-Star Team: 1B-Harry Nolan, Rayne; **2B**-Don McShane, Rayne; **3B**-Roy Smith, New Iberia; **SS**-Doug Dean, Opelousas; **OF**-Lee Schulte, Lafayette; Roy Weatherly, Opelousas; Elwood Kelly, Rayne; **C**-Walter Stephenson, Lafayette; **Util**-Basil Milazzo, Jeanerette; **P**-Paul LeBlanc, Lafayette; John Burrows, Opelousas; **Manager**-Art Phelan, Alexandria.

BA: Clinton Jones, Opelousas, .350
Runs: Lee Schulte, Lafayette, 79; Clinton Jones, Opelousas, 79
Hits: Clinton Jones, Opelousas, 151
RBIs: Harry Nolan, Rayne, 101
HRs: Harry Nolan, Rayne, 25
Wins: Roderick Irwin, Rayne, 21
SOs: Bryan Flanagan, Alexandria, 216
Pct: Boyd Biggers, Jeanerette, .750, 12-4

D Nebraska State League
President: J. Roy Carter

Standings	W	L	Pct.	GB	Manager
Lincoln Links***	69	41	.627	—	Cy Lingle/Pug Griffin
Norfolk Elkhorns	60	49	.550	8½	Joe McDermott
Sioux Falls Canaries	50	60	.455	19	Rex Stucker
Beatrice Blues	38	67	.362	28½	Dick "Sonny" Brookhaus

Playoffs: None.

All-Star Team: 1B-George Silvey, Norfolk; **2B**-Darrel Ginzlinger, Lincoln; **3B**-Al Phillips, Lincoln; **SS**-Ray Bertram, Norfolk; **OF**-Buck Ewing, Norfolk; George Rhode, Sioux Falls; George Proost, Beatrice; **C**-Benny Warren, Norfolk; **Util**-Bill Swinger, Beatrice; **P**-Jack Farmer, Norfolk; Tom Seats, Lincoln; **Manager**-Pug Griffin, Lincoln.

BA: Buck Ewing, Norfolk, .360
Runs: Frank Morehouse, Lincoln, 99
Hits: George Silvey, Norfolk, 143
HRs: Bill Swinger, Beatrice, 14
Wins: Jack Farmer, Norfolk, 19
SOs: Tom Seats, Lincoln, 221
ERA: Nelson Potter, Lincoln, 1.71

D Northern League
President: Lute J. Boone

Standings	W	L	Pct.	GB	Manager
Fargo-Moorhead Twins**(3)..	64	53	.547	—	Jack Knight
Eau Claire Bears	63	58	.521	3	Johnny Mostil
Crookston Pirates	62	58	.517	3½	Lute Boone
Brainerd-Little Falls Muskies..	58	58	.500	5½	Charlie Patton
Winnipeg Maroons	57	57	.500	5½	Bruno Haas
Grand Forks Chiefs............	59	60	.496	6	John Anderson
Superior Blues*	56	64	.467	9½	Dick Wade
Duluth Dukes.....................	53	64	.453	11	Harry Strong

Playoff: Fargo-Moorhead 4 games, Superior 2.

All-Star Team: 1B-Charles Larson, Superior; **2B**-Stanley Sperry, Eau Claire; **3B**-John Kopko, Fargo-Moorhead; **SS**-Joe Rezotko, Brainerd-Little Falls; **OF**-Ray Helixon, Grand Forks; Tom Corbett, Brainerd-Little Falls; Morris Arnovich, Superior; **C**-Herb Crompton, Fargo-Moorhead; **Util**-George "Red" Treadwell, Crookston; **P**-Ensio Juntenan, Eau Claire; Norman Masters, Crookston; **Manager**-Jack Knight, Fargo-Moorhead.

BA: Morris Arnovich, Superior, .374
Hits: Morris Arnovich, Superior, 182
HRs: Gus Koch, Fargo-Moorhead, 36
Wins: Norman Masters, Crookston, 21
SOs: Norman Masters, Crookston, 227
Pct: Ralph Mead, Eau Claire, .733, 11-4

D Pennsylvania State Association
President: Elmer M. Daily

Standings	W	L	Pct.	GB	Manager
Greensburg Trojans**(16)..	57	45	.559	—	Clay Hopper
Jeannette Reds (12)............	59	47	.557	—	Ray Ryan
Washington Generals*(5)...	59	47	.557	—	Benny Bengough
McKeesport Tubers (15).....	52	52	.500	6	Leo Mackey
Charleroi Tigers (4)	45	62	.421	14½	Dixie Parker
Monessen Indians (3).........	43	62	.410	15½	Ed Onslow/Bill Ward/Earl Wolgamot/Walt Laskowski

Playoff: Washington 2 games, Jeannette 1 for the first half championship.
Finals: Greensburg 4 games, Washington 2.

All-Star Team: 1B-Edwin Morgan, Greensburg; **2B**-Lynn Myers, Greensburg; **3B**-Merritt McCloy, McKeesport; **SS**-Frank Dudick, Washington; **OF**-Homer Ledbetter, Charleroi; Tommy Henrich, Monessen; Carl Huffman, Monessen; **C**-Grady Bolton, Jeannette; **Util**-Crippen, Jeannette; **P**-Henry Compton, Jeannette; Lee, Charleroi; **Manager**-Clay Hopper, Greensburg.

BA: Carl Huffman, Monessen, .373
Runs: Carl Huffman, Monessen, 93
Hits: Carl Huffman, Monessen, 153
RBIs: Charles Bauder, Monessen, 81
HRs: Tommy Henrich, Monessen, 15
Wins: Henry Compton, Jeannette, 17
SOs: Howard Peckman, McKeeport, 144
ERA: Jack Haley, Washington, 2.44

1934 Interleague Post Season Play

World Series
St. Louis (National) 4 games, Detroit (American) 3

Junior World Series
Columbus (American Association) 5 games, Toronto (International) 4
Total Attendance: 35,211

Dixie Series
New Orleans (Southern Association) 4 games, Galveston (Texas) 2
Total Attendance: 19,448

Little Dixie Series
Jacksonville (West Dixie) 4 games, Jackson (East Dixie) 0

International Border Series
Jacksonville (West Dixie) 5 games, Mexico City Aztecas (Mexican) 4

Mississippi–Louisiana Series
Lafayette (Evangeline) 3 games, Jackson (East Dixie) 1

Northern Championship
Fargo-Moorhead (Northern) 2 games, Lincoln (Nebraska State) 0

1934 Major League Farm Systems

American League
1 Boston (3): Reading, Columbia/Asheville, Joplin.
2 Chicago (1): Longview.
3 Cleveland (4): New Orleans, Zanesville, Fargo-Moorhead, Monessen.
4 Detroit (4): Beaumont, Shreveport/Greenwood, Charleston, Charleroi.
5 New York (5): Newark, Binghamton, Norfolk, Wheeling, Washington.
6 Philadelphia (2): Montreal, Williamsport.
7 St. Louis (1): San Antonio.
8 Washington (1): Chattanooga.

National League
9 Boston (1): Harrisburg.
10 Brooklyn (1): Dayton.
11 Chicago (2): Los Angeles, Ponca City.
12 Cincinnati (6): Toronto, Topeka, Wilmington, Beckley, Bartlesville, Jeannette.
13 New York (2): Nashville, Jacksonville.
14 Philadelphia (1): Hazleton.
15 Pittsburgh (2): Springfield (OH), McKeesport.
16 St. Louis (9): Columbus, Rochester, Elmira, Houston, Greensboro, Huntington, Paris/Lufkin, Springfield (MO), Greensburg.

1934 No-Hitters

Date	Pitcher	Team	League	Opponent	Score
5-10	Newt Kimball	Ponca City	Western Assoc.	Hutchinson	7-0
5-11	Linville Watkins	Jacksonville	West Dixie	Paris	4-0
5-20	Wally Pate	Opelousas	Evangeline	Lafayette	1-0
5-22	Max Beard	El Dorado	East Dixie	Greenville	12-1
7-4	Arthur Jones	Albany	International	Baltimore	2-0
7-10	Earl Miner	Norfolk	Nebraska State	Sioux Falls	(7)
7-24	Cecil Spittler	Norfolk	Piedmont	Richmond	7-0
8-2	Fred Newton	Rock Island	Western	Omaha	5-1
8-4	Cy Blanton	Albany	International	Montreal	0-0 (5)
8-14	Howard LaFlamme	Wheeling	Middle Atlantic	Springfield	15-1
8-15	Bert Grimm	Zanesville	Middle Atlantic	Charleston	2-0 (7)
8-28	Tom Lanning	Asheville	Piedmont	Charlotte	2-0 (5)
8-29	Bob Miller	Binghamton	New York-Penn.	Hazleton	2-0
8-30	Nelson Potter	Lincoln	Nebraska State	Norfolk	6-0
9-17	Hormidas Aube	Binghamton	New York-Penn.	Williamsport	3-1 (PO)
9-18	Bobo Newsom	St. Louis	American	Boston	1-2 (10)
9-21	Paul Dean	St. Louis	National	Brooklyn	3-0
9-25	Herman Dreis	St. Joseph	Western	Davenport	2-0 (PO)

Number in parentheses indicates innings if other than nine; "PO" indicates playoff game.

THIS DATE IN MINOR LEAGUE HISTORY

February 25, 1934, The International League's Jersey City franchise was transferred to Syracuse.

April 18, 1934, The Albany-Toronto International League game wound up in a riot when irate fans threw pop bottles and cushions onto the field in the tenth inning with Toronto leading 13-11. Albany, unable to clear the field for action, forfeited the game by the customary 9-0 score.

May 15, 1934, Buffalo set an International League record when they hit five home runs in one inning, four of them in succession, in a game against Albany. The blows were slammed by Butch Meyers, Gregg Mulleavy, Les Mallon, Jack Smith and Bill Regan.

May 24, 1934, Joe DiMaggio, star outfielder of the San Francisco Seals, injured his knee getting out of an automobile. He would be sidelined for about a month.

May 30, 1934, Lou Frierson of Paris, West Dixie League, hit five homers in his hometown park.

June 2, 1934, In the first baseball game ever played between England and Scotland, the Scots team of university players was triumphant over the English, 24-3.

June 28, 1934, Andy High was deposed as manager of the seventh-place Syracuse Chiefs of the International League. High had suffered an ankle injury earlier in the season, keeping him inactive for three weeks, proving to be a big handicap to the team.

August 17, 1934, Buzz Arlett of Minneapolis, American Association, hit three homers and a double against Toledo.

August 25, 1934, Harry Nolan of Rayne hit six home runs in an Evangeline League doubleheader at Rayne.

September 1, 1934, Albany's Cy Blanton, who fanned 284 batters in the Western League last season, struck out 20 Syracuse batters to equal the International League record set by Dave Danforth of Buffalo in 1930.

1935

American League
President: William Harridge

Standings	W	L	Pct.	GB	Attend.	Manager
Detroit Tigers	93	58	.616	—	1,034,929	Mickey Cochrane
New York Yankees	89	60	.597	3	657,508	Joe McCarthy
Cleveland Indians	82	71	.536	12	397,615	Walter Johnson/Steve O'Neill
Boston Red Sox	78	75	.510	16	558,568	Joe Cronin
Chicago White Sox	74	78	.487	19½	470,281	Jimmy Dykes
Washington Senators	67	86	.438	27	255,011	Bucky Harris
St. Louis Browns	65	87	.428	28½	80,922	Rogers Hornsby
Philadelphia Athletics	58	91	.389	34	233,173	Connie Mack

BA: Buddy Myer, Washington, .349
Runs: Lou Gehrig, New York, 125
Hits: Joe Vosmik, Cleveland, 216
RBIs: Hank Greenberg, Detroit, 170

HRs: Hank Greenberg, Detroit, 36
Jimmie Foxx, Philadelphia, 36
Wins: Wes Ferrell, Boston, 25
SOs: Tommy Bridges, Detroit, 163
ERA: Lefty Grove, Boston, 2.70
Pct: Eldon Auker, Detroit, .720, 18-7

National League
President: Ford Frick

Standings	W	L	Pct.	GB	Attend.	Manager
Chicago Cubs	100	54	.649	—	692,604	Charlie Grimm
St. Louis Cardinals	96	58	.623	4	506,084	Frank Frisch
New York Giants	91	62	.595	8½	748,748	Bill Terry
Pittsburgh Pirates	86	67	.562	13½	352,885	Pie Traynor
Brooklyn Dodgers	70	83	.458	29½	470,517	Casey Stengel
Cincinnati Reds	68	85	.444	31½	448,247	Chuck Dressen
Philadelphia Phillies	64	89	.418	35½	205,470	Jimmie Wilson
Boston Braves	38	115	.248	61½	232,754	Bill McKechnie

BA: Arky Vaughan, Pittsburgh, .385
Runs: Augie Galan, Chicago, 133
Hits: Billy Herman, Chicago, 227
RBIs: Wally Berger, Boston, 130
HRs: Wally Berger, Boston, 34

Wins: Dizzy Dean, St. Louis, 28
SOs: Dizzy Dean, St. Louis, 182
ERA: Cy Blanton, Pittsburgh, 2.58
Pct: Bill Lee, Chicago, .769, 20-6

AA American Association
President: Thomas J. Hickey

Standings	W	L	Pct.	GB	Attend.	Manager
Minneapolis Millers	91	63	.591	—	161,036	Donie Bush
Indianapolis Indians	85	67	.559	5	137,918	Wade Killefer
Kansas City Blues	84	70	.545	7	138,424	Dutch Zwilling
Columbus Red Birds	84	70	.545	7	134,773	Ray Blades
St. Paul Saints	75	78	.490	15½	120,954	Marty McManus
Milwaukee Brewers	75	79	.487	16	117,003	Allan Sothoron
Toledo Mud Hens	64	86	.427	25	53,068	Fred Haney
Louisville Colonels	52	97	.349	36½	40,765	Ken Penner

Playoffs: None.

All-Star Team: 1B-Dale Alexander, Kansas City; **2B**-Jack Warner, St. Paul; **3B**-Fred Haney, Toledo; **SS**-Eddie Marshall, Milwaukee; **OF**-John Gill, Minneapolis; John Cooney, Indianapolis; Ted Gullic, Milwaukee; Mike Kreevich, Kansas City; George Stumpf, Kansas City; **C**-Bruce Ogrodowski, Columbus; Bob Garbark, Toledo; **Util**-Mike Ryba, Columbus; **P**-Monty Stratton, St. Paul; Lee Stine, St. Paul; Garland Braxton, Milwaukee; Walter Tauscher, Minneapolis.

BA: John Cooney, Indianapolis, .371
Runs: John Gill, Minneapolis, 148
Hits: John Cooney, Indianapolis, 224
RBIs: John Gill, Minneapolis, 154

HRs: John Gill, Minneapolis, 43
Wins: Mike Ryba, Columbus, 20
SOs: Jack Tising, Louisville, 230
ERA: Clyde Hatter, Milwaukee, 2.88

AA International League
President: Charles H. Knapp

Standings	W	L	Pct.	GB	Attend.	Manager
Montreal Royals	92	62	.597	—	234,115	Frank Shaughnessy
Syracuse Chiefs	87	67	.565	5	206,179	Nemo Leibold
Buffalo Bisons	86	67	.562	5½	212,544	Ray Schalk
Newark Bears (5)	81	71	.533	10	159,858	Bob Shawkey
Baltimore Orioles	78	74	.513	13	140,097	Guy Sturdy
Toronto Maple Leafs (12)	78	76	.513	14	126,928	Ike Boone
Rochester Red Wings (16)	61	91	.401	30	94,351	Eddie Dyer/Burt Shotton
Albany Senators	49	104	.320	42½	91,099	Albert Mamaux/Johnny Evers

Playoffs: Montreal 4 games, Buffalo 2; Syracuse 4 games, Newark 0.
Finals: Syracuse 4 games, Montreal 3.

MVP-George Puccinelli, Baltimore.

BA: George Puccinelli, Baltimore, .359
Runs: George Puccinelli, Baltimore, 135
Hits: George Puccinelli, Baltimore, 209
RBIs: George Puccinelli, Baltimore, 172

HRs: George Puccinelli, Baltimore, 53
Wins: Pete Appleton, Montreal, 23
SOs: William Harris, Buffalo, 137
ERA: Joe Cascarella, Syracuse, 2.35

AA Pacific Coast League
Presidents: Hyland L. Baggerly/William C. Tuttle

Standings	W	L	Pct.	GB	Attend.	Manager
San Francisco Seals**	103	70	.593	—	151,179	Lefty O'Doul
Los Angeles Angels*(11)	98	76	.563	5½	153,101	Jack Lelivelt
Oakland Oaks (5)	91	83	.523	12½	122,792	Oscar Vitt
Portland Beavers (4)	87	86	.503	16	228,127	George Burns/Buddy Ryan/Bill Cissell
Mission Reds	87	87	.500	16½	90,719	Gabby Street
Seattle Indians (9)	80	93	.462	23	235,279	Dutch Reuther
Sacramento Senators (10)	75	100	.429	29	49,324	Earl McNeely/Kittle Wirts
Hollywood Stars	73	99	.424	29½	136,917	Frank Shellenback

Playoff: San Francisco 4 games, Los Angeles 2.

MVP-Joe DiMaggio, San Francisco.

BA: Oscar "Ox" Eckhardt, Mission, .399
Runs: Joe DiMaggio, San Francisco, 173
Hits: Oscar "Ox" Eckhardt, Mission, 283
RBIs: Joe DiMaggio, San Francisco, 154

HRs: Gene Lillard, Los Angeles, 56
Wins: Walter Beck, Mission, 23
SOs: Walter Beck, Mission, 202
ERA: Mike Meola, Los Angeles, 3.00

A New York-Pennsylvania League
President: Perry B. Farrell

Standings	W	L	Pct.	GB	Manager
Scranton Miners*	81	54	.600	—	Joe Shaute
Wilkes-Barre Barons	79	57	.581	2½	Elmer Yoter
Hazleton Mountaineers (14)	74	56	.569	4½	Andy High
Binghamton Triplets**(5)	75	60	.556	6	Bill Meyer
Williamsport Grays (6)	64	69	.481	16	Mike McNally
Harrisburg Senators (9)	59	77	.434	22½	Art Shires
Elmira Pioneers	58	79	.423	24	Bill Hunnefield/Frank Bedenk/ Emmet McCann/Fred Coumbe
Reading/ Allentown Brooks#(10)	49	87	.360	32½	Zach Taylor

#Reading (2-4 in second half) moved to Allentown July 9, first home game July 14.

Playoff: Binghamton 4 games, Scranton 3.

All-Star Team: 1B-John McCarthy, Allentown; **2B**-Frank Parenti, Wilkes-Barre; **3B**-Henry Peploski, Scranton; **SS**-John "Bunny" Griffiths, Wilkes-Barre; **OF**-John Tyler, Scranton; Art McHenry, Williamsport; Joe Dwyer, Wilkes-Barre; **C**-John Pasek, Elmira; **Util**-John Reder, Williamsport; **P**-Ralph Judd, Hazleton; Charles Willis, Wilkes-Barre; **Manager of the Year**-Mike McNally, Williamsport.

BA: Mike Martineck, Scranton, .369
Runs: Hubert Fitzgerald, Wilkes-Barre, 120
Hits: Henry Peploski, Scranton, 195
RBIs: Pete Susko, Hazleton, 110

HRs: Roberto Estalella, Hazleton, 18
Wins: Charles Willis, Wilkes-Barre, 22
SOs: Charles Ahearn, Binghamton, 112
ERA: Joseph Shaute, Scranton, 2.84

A Southern Association
President: John D. Martin

Standings	W	L	Pct.	GB	Attend.	Manager
Atlanta Crackers	91	60	.605	—	330,795	Eddie Moore
New Orleans Pelicans (3)	86	67	.562	6	92,423	Larry Gilbert
Memphis Chickasaws	84	70	.545	8½	85,724	Fred Hofmann
Nashville Volunteers (13)	82	69	.543	9	98,781	Frank Brazill/Johnny Butler
Chattanooga Lookouts (8)	75	75	.500	15½	100,060	Mule Shirley/Clyde Milan
Little Rock Travelers	75	78	.490	17	81,024	Tommy "Doc" Prothro
Birmingham Barons	59	95	.385	33½	77,481	Clyde Milan/Bill Pierre/ Bill Hughes
Knoxville Smokies	57	95	.375	34½	52,239	Lee Head

Playoffs: Atlanta 3 games, Nashville 0; New Orleans 3 games, Memphis 0.
Finals: Atlanta 3 games, New Orleans 0.

All-Star Team: 1B-Alex Hooks, Atlanta; **2B**-John Mihalic, Chattanooga; **3B**-Joe Martin, Nashville; **SS**-Bill Rodda, Nashville; **OF**-Doug Taitt, Nashville; Peck Hamel, Atlanta; Jim Gleeson, New Orleans; **C**-Martin "Chick" Autry, Nashville; Joe Palmisano, Atlanta; **Util**-Andy Reese, Memphis; **P**-Al Milnar, New Orleans; Harry Kelley, Atlanta; Clay Touchstone, Memphis.

*Won first-half   **Won second-half   ***Won both halves
Numbers after nicknames indicate farm system.
Affiliation listed at end of each year.

283

1935

BA: Doug Taitt, Nashville, .355
Runs: John Mihalic, Chattanooga, 113
Hits: Doug Taitt, Nashville, 194
RBIs: Jim Gleeson, New Orleans, 105
HRs: Doug Taitt, Nashville, 17

Wins: Al Milnar, New Orleans, 24
Tiny Chaplin, Nashville, 24
SOs: Al Milnar, New Orleans, 140
ERA: Harry Kelley, Atlanta, 2.50

A Texas League
President: J. Alvin Gardner

Standings	W	L	Pct.	GB	Attend.	Manager
Oklahoma City Indians	95	66	.590	—	121,289	Bert Niehoff
Beaumont Exporters (4)	90	69	.566	4	74,909	Dutch Lorbeer
Galveston Buccaneers	86	75	.534	9	55,637	Jack Mealey
Tulsa Oilers	82	79	.509	13	74,069	Art Griggs
Houston Buffaloes (16)	77	84	.478	18	66,295	Ira Smith
San Antonio Missions (7)	75	84	.472	19	109,665	Hank Severeid
Dallas Steers (2)	71	88	.447	23	173,433	Byrne James/Alex Gaston
Ft. Worth Cats	64	95	.403	30	42,385	John Heving/Harry "Pid" McCurdy

Playoffs: Beaumont 3 games, Galveston 2; Oklahoma City 3 games, Tulsa 1.
Finals: Oklahoma City 4 games, Beaumont 1.

All-Star Team: 1B-Rudy York, Beaumont; **2B**-Charley English, Galveston; **3B**-Ernie Holman, Oklahoma City; **OF**-Lou Brower, Oklahoma City; Lynn King, Houston; Fred Tauby, Dallas; Art Weis, Ft. Worth; **C**-Claude Linton, Galveston; **P**-Russ Evans, Oklahoma City; Max Butcher, Galveston; Earl Caldwell, San Antonio; **MVP**-Rudy York, Beaumont.

BA: Art Weis, Ft. Worth, .331
Runs: Tony Governor, Galveston, 109
Hits: Al Vincent, Beaumont, 191
RBIs: Rudy York Beaumont, 117
HRs: Rudy York, Beaumont, 32

Wins: Russ Evans, Oklahoma City, 24
Max Butcher, Galveston, 24
SOs: Lee Grissom, Ft. Worth, 166
ERA: Earl Caldwell, San Antonio, 2.25

A Western League
President: Dale D. Gear

Standings	W	L	Pct.	GB	Manager
Davenport Blue Sox	70	46	.603	—	Cletus Dixon
St. Joseph Saints	58	48	.547	7	Earle Brucker
Des Moines Demons	58	55	.513	10½	Otis "Doc" Crandall
Sioux City Cowboys	54	52	.509	11	William "Hack" Wilson
Cedar Rapids Raiders	53	57	.482	14	Clarence "Cap" Crossley
Keokuk Indians	49	66	.426	20½	Jimmy Payton
Omaha Packers/					
Council Bluffs Rails#	55	46	.545	NA	Joe McDermott
Rock Island Islanders@	19	46	.292	NA	Tommy Taylor/Karl Swanson

#Omaha (22-15) moved to Council Bluffs June 25, first home game July 3. Council Bluffs disbanded August 27.
@Rock Island disbanded July 17.

Playoffs: St. Joseph 3 games, Des Moines 0; Sioux City 3 games, Davenport 0.
Finals: St. Joseph 4 games, Sioux City 3.

MVP-Earle Brucker, St. Joseph.

BA: Harold Epps, Cedar Rapids, .346
Runs: Milton Bocek, Cedar Rapids, 93
Hits: James Webb, Cedar Rapids, 151
RBIs: Louis Vezilich, St. Joseph/Council Bluffs, 78

HRs: Hugh Willingham, Sioux City, 20
Wins: Claude Passeau, Des Moines, 20
SOs: Claude Passeau, Des Moines, 239
Pct: Al Piechota, Davenport, .739, 17-6

B Piedmont League
President: Dan W. Hill

Standings	W	L	Pct.	GB	Manager
Asheville Tourists*(16)	75	62	.547	—	Billy Southworth
Wilmington Pirates (12)	69	65	.515	4½	Harry McCurdy/Riley Parker
Richmond Colts**(6)	70	66	.515	4½	Ed Rommel
Norfolk Tars (5)	67	70	.489	8	Bill Skiff
Portsmouth Truckers (11)	67	72	.482	9	Horace "Pip" Koehler
Charlotte Hornets (1)	62	75	.453	13	Frank O'Rourke

Playoff: Richmond 4 games, Asheville 2.

All-Star Team: 1B-Les Scarsella, Wilmington; **2B**-Frank Ware (Worznak), Portsmouth; **3B**-Maurice Sturdy, Asheville; **SS**-Louis Bush, Asheville; **OF**-George Ferrell, Richmond; Fred Petoskey, Wilmington; J.C. Clark, Asheville; **C**-Francis LaVeque, Charlotte; **Util**-Claude Staylor, Norfolk; **P**-Charles Foreman, Richmond; Herbie Moore, Asheville; **Manager**-Bill Skiff, Norfolk.

BA: George Ferrell, Richmond, .377
Runs: Les Scarsella, Wilmington, 120
Hits: Lee Gamble, Wilmington, 191
RBIs: J.C. Clark, Asheville, 129

HRs: Buddy Rosar, Norfolk, 26
Wins: Herbie Moore, Asheville, 21
SOs: Atley Donald, Norfolk, 160
Pct: Herbie Moore, Asheville, .808, 21-5

B Three-I League
President: L.J. Wylie

Standings	W	L	Pct.	GB	Manager
Bloomington Bloomers**(16)	75	44	.630	—	Burleigh Grimes
Springfield Senators*(4)	74	45	.622	1	Bob Coleman

Decatur Commodores	59	56	.513	14	John Butler/Clifford Knox
Terre Haute Tots	57	61	.483	17½	Bill Burwell
Fort Wayne Chiefs	52	71	.423	25	Bruno Betzel
Peoria Tractors (11)	38	78	.328	35½	Jack Sheehan/Bill Rodgers

Playoff: Springfield 4 games, Bloomington 2. Bloomington was declared winner when Springfield refused to replay protested final game that was upheld by the president.

All-Star Team: 1B-Bernard Cobb, Fort Wayne; **2B**-Frank Croucher, Springfield; **3B**-Chet Laabs, Fort Wayne; **SS**-Lindsay Brown, Springfield; **OF**-Herschel Martin, Bloomington; Lou Skoffic, Bloomington; Tom Leonard, Fort Wayne; **C**-Cliff "Bud" Knox, Decatur; **Util**-James Outlaw, Decatur; **P**-Donald French, Springfield; Max Macon, Bloomington; **Manager**-Bob Coleman, Springfield.

BA: Chet Laabs, Fort Wayne, .384
Runs: Herschel Martin, Bloomington, 112
Hits: James Outlaw, Decatur, 157
RBIs: Chet Laabs, Fort Wayne, 96

HRs: Chet Laabs, Fort Wayne, 24
Wins: Max Macon, Bloomington, 19
SOs: John Hutchings, Peoria, 166
Pct: Clyde Smoll, Springfield, .765, 13-4

C East Dixie League
President: J. Alvin Gardner

Standings	W	L	Pct.	GB	Manager
Pine Bluff Judges*	84	54	.609	—	Lena Styles
El Dorado Lions*	80	57	.584	3½	George Harper/Wray Query
Jackson Mississippians**	72	64	.529	11	Herschel Bobo/Guy Lacy
Greenville Buckshots	71	68	.511	13½	Glen Bolton/Tommy Taylor
Helena Seaporters	66	70	.485	17	Rod Whitney
Columbus/Cleveland Bengals#	64	73	.467	19½	Slim Brewer
Clarksdale Ginners	60	79	.432	24½	Harry Strohm
Greenwood Chiefs (16)	52	84	.382	31	Clay Hopper

#Columbus (28-32) moved to Cleveland June 18, first home game June 23.

Playoff: Pine Bluff 4 games, Jackson 0.

All-Star Team: 1B-Glenn Bolton, Greenville; **2B**-Joe Vitter, Pine Bluff; **3B**-Carl Fairly, Pine Bluff; **SS**-Fred Wiesler, Helena; **OF**-Earl Nelson, Greenville; George Harper, El Dorado; Leslie Horn, Greenville; **C**-Harold Sueme, Pine Bluff; **Util**-Jess Haley, Columbus/Cleveland; **P**-Paul Spencer, Pine Bluff; Lester Willis, El Dorado; **Manager**-Lena Styles, Pine Bluff.

BA: Allen Hunt, El Dorado, .363
Runs: Cliff Greer, El Dorado, 117
Hits: Fred Williams, Columbus/Cleveland, 187
RBIs: Milt Stroner, El Dorado, 128

HRs: Earl Nelson, Greenville, 28
Wins: Harold Ginn, El Dorado, 21
SOs: Harold Ginn, El Dorado, 162
ERA: George Boutwell, Jackson, 1.98

C Middle Atlantic League
President: Elmer M. Daily

Standings	W	L	Pct.	GB	Manager
Zanesville Grays (3)	70	54	.565	—	Earl Wolgamot
Dayton Ducks**(10)	69	55	.556	1	Riley Parker/Howard "Ducky" Holmes
Johnstown Johnnies	67	56	.545	2½	Joe O'Rourke/John Picus Quinn/Leo Mackey
Akron Yankees (5)	64	59	.520	5½	Johnny Neun
Huntington Red Birds*(16)	60	58	.508	7	Benny Borgmann
Portsmouth Pirates (15)	54	63	.462	12½	Jake Pitler
Charleston Senators (4)	49	65	.430	16	Russ Young/Val Picinich
Beckley Miners	45	68	.398	19½	Ralph McAdams/Robert Rawlins

Playoff: Huntington 4 games, Dayton 2.

All-Star Team: 1B-Jimmy Wasdell, Zanesville; **2B**-Frank Madura, Portsmouth; **3B**-Mike Noonan, Portsmouth; **SS**-Benny Borgmann, Huntington; **OF**-Milt McIntyre, Zanesville; Tommy Henrich, Zanesville; Sam Thomas, Johnstown; **C**-William Atwood, Johnstown; **Util**-Robert Rawlins, Beckley; **P**-Jess Bream, Johnstown; Mike Martynik, Huntington; **Manager**-Earl Wolgamot, Zanesville.

BA: Jimmy Wasdell, Zanesville, .357
Runs: Jim Gruzdis, Huntington, 111
Hits: Jimmy Wasdell, Zanesville, 182
RBIs: Milt McIntyre, Zanesville, 110

HRs: Milt McIntyre, Zanesville, 24
Wins: Mike Martynik, Huntington, 21
SOs: Mike Martynik, Huntington, 299
ERA: Mike Martynik, Huntington, 2.63

C West Dixie League
President: J. Walter Morris

Standings	W	L	Pct.	GB	Manager
Tyler Trojans*(13)	76	54	.585	—	Wally Dashiell
Palestine Pals**(7)	76	56	.576	1	Bobby Goff
Longview Cannibals (2)	72	60	.545	5	Tex Jeanes
Jacksonville Jax (16)	66	66	.500	11	Jimmy Sanders/Jackie Reid
Henderson Oilers (4)	60	70	.462	16	Ray Flaskamper
Shreveport Sports/					
Gladewater Bears#(1)	44	88	.333	33	Fred Nicholson/Neal Rabe

#Shreveport (8-28) moved to Gladewater June 4.

Playoffs: Postseason play involved the first half winner and the three other teams with the best second half record. Jacksonville 3 games, Palestine 2; Tyler 3 games, Longview 2.
Finals: Jacksonville 3 games, Tyler 0, one tie.

All-Star Team: **1B**-Charles Baron(ovic), Tyler; **2B**-Bobby Goff, Palestine; **3B**-Christman, Henderson; **SS**-Lawrence France, Palestine; **OF**-Allan McElreath, Palestine; Marshall Mauldin, Longview; Tom Pyle, Tyler; **C**-Orace Powers, Palestine; **Util**-Emil DeJonghe, Henderson; **P**-Grady Bassett, Tyler; Jennings Poindexter, Shreveport/Gladewater; **Manager**-Wally Dashiell, Tyler.

BA: Tom Pyle, Tyler, .376
Runs: Charles Baron(ovic), Tyler, 98
Hits: Marshall Mauldin, Longview, 179
RBIs: Tom Pyle, Tyler, 106

HRs: Mervyn Connors, Palestine, 29
Wins: Grady Bassett, Tyler, 23
SOs: Grady Bassett, Tyler, 180
ERA: Hugo Klaerner, Longview, 1.80

C Western Association
President: Tom Fairweather

Standings	W	L	Pct.	GB	Attend.	Manager
Springfield Cardinals*(16)	87	48	.644	—	52,497	George Payne
Ponca City Angels**(11)	76	55	.580	9	30,000	Mike Gazella
Hutchinson Larks (16)	68	61	.527	16	37,218	Bob Morrow
Muskogee Tigers	60	71	.458	25	29,612	Wally Schang
Bartlesville Reds (12)	56	79	.415	31	33,436	Mark Purtell
Joplin Miners (5)	48	81	.372	36	20,000	Runt Marr/Stanley Hino

Playoff: Ponca City 5 games, Springfield 4.

All-Star Team: **1B**-Carl Kentling, Hutchinson; **2B**-Ben Catchings, Muskogee; **3B**-Edward Gray, Muskogee/Bartlesville/Ponca City; **SS**-William "Bill" Matheson, Joplin; **OF**-George Antone, Bartlesville; Longacre, Joplin; Harry Hughes, Bartlesville; **C**-Dee Moore, Ponca City; **P**-Marvin Breuer, Joplin; Lefty Carnett, Ponca City; Morris Young, Bartlesville/Hutchinson.

BA: Ben Catchings, Muskogee, .350
Runs: Harry Hughes, Bartlesville, 135
Hits: Joe Mene, Ponca City, 183
RBIs: J.R. "Doc" Graves, Muskogee, 122
HRs: Tony Masucci, Muskogee, 19
Buster Adams, Springfield, 19

SBs: Lyle Judy, Springfield, 107
Wins: Tom Seats, Springfield, 25
SOs: Tom Seats, Springfield, 279
ERA: Morris Young, Bartlesville/Hutchinson, 2.31

D Arkansas State League
President: Charles Morgan

Standings	W	L	Pct.	GB	Manager
Siloam Springs Travelers**	66	43	.606	—	Ray Powell
Rogers Cardinals*	59	50	.541	7	Fred Cato
Cassville Tigers	54	48	.529	8½	Ed Hawk
Bentonville Officeholders	51	56	.477	14	Wilbur Davis
Fayetteville Bears	45	56	.446	17	Pete Casey/Fred Cato
Huntsville Red Birds	41	63	.394	22½	Jim Nicely/Charles Wilson/Bill Werner

Total Attendance: 60,000.

Playoff: Rogers 4 games, Siloam Springs 3.

All-Star Team: **1B**-Frank Stapleton, Rogers; **2B**-Monte Johnson, Fayetteville; **3B**-Doug White, Fayetteville; **SS**-David Bush, Rogers; **OF**-Howard Roberts, Cassville; Ben Turner, Siloam Springs; Rudolph Woodrow, Siloam Springs; **C**-Walker Cooper, Rogers; **Util**-Leslie Wilson, Fayetteville; **P**-Warren Fralick, Fayetteville; George Gibson, Bentonville; **Manager of the Year**-Ray Powell, Siloam Springs.

BA: Duane Kratzer, Cassville, .397
Runs: Howard Roberts, Cassville, 89
Hits: Wilbur Davis, Bentonville, 146
RBIs: Wilbur Davis, Bentonville, 93
HRs: Howard Roberts, Cassville, 21

Wins: Walter "Jumbo" Brown, Bentonville, 20
George Gibson, Bentonville, 20
SOs: Johnny John, Cassville, 147
ERA: Walter "Jumbo" Brown, Bentonville, 2.97

D Bi-State League
President: Dr. J.E. Taylor

Standings	W	L	Pct.	GB	Manager
Leaksville-Draper-Spray Triplets	71	44	.617	—	Blackie Carter
Danville Leafs*	68	46	.596	2½	Herb Brett
Bassett Furniture Makers**	68	47	.591	3	Ernie "Lefty" Jenkins
Mt. Airy Reds	67	47	.588	3½	Mickey Shader
Mayodan Mills	51	62	.451	19	Phil Lundeen
Fieldale Towlers	50	64	.439	20½	Dixie Parker
Martinsville Manufacturers	42	71	.372	28	Harold Bohl
Reidsville Luckies	39	75	.342	31½	Glenn Biggerstaff/L.J. Perry

Playoff: Danville 4 games, Bassett 3.

All-Star Team: **1B**-Taylor Sanford, Danville; **2B**-Mickey Witek, Bassett; **3B**-Woody Williams, Leaksville-Draper-Spray; **SS**-Len Kahny, Mt. Airy; **OF**-Ray Cote, Mt. Airy; Ralph Hodgin, Fieldale; Cecil "Zip" Payne, Mayodan; **C**-Jack Crosswhite, Bassett; **Util**-Frank Schummell, Danville; **P**-Thornton Honeycutt, Mt. Airy; Ernie "Lefty" Jenkins, Bassett; **Manager**-Mickey Shader, Mt. Airy.

BA: Ralph Hodgin, Fieldale, .387
Runs: Woody Williams, Leaksville-Spray-Draper, 111
Hits: Ralph Hodgin, Fieldale, 187

HRs: Blackie Carter, Leaksville-Spray-Draper, 30
Wins: Fred Pipgras, Danville, 25
SOs: Jeff Jeffcoat, Leaksville-Spray-Draper, 222
Pct: Fred Pipgras, Danville, .806, 25-6

D Evangeline League
President: William T. Daly

Standings	W	L	Pct.	GB	Manager
Jeanerette Blues	86	42	.672	—	Ivy Griffin
Lafayette White Sox	74	53	.583	11½	Leonard Mock
Alexandria Aces	72	57	.558	14½	Art Phelan
Opelousas Indians (3)	69	60	.535	17½	Jay Kirke, Sr./Milt Delmas
Rayne Rice Birds	65	63	.508	21	Don McShane
Abbeville Athletics (13)	54	73	.425	31½	Jimmy Vorhoff
New Iberia Cardinals (16)	48	80	.375	38	Sam Camalo/Bud Teachout
Lake Charles Skippers (12)	44	84	.344	42	Josh Billings

Playoffs: Jeanerette 4 games, Opelousas 0, one tie; Lafayette 4 games, Alexandria 3.
Finals: Jeanerette 4 games, Lafayette 2.

All-Star Team: **1B**-Ivy Griffin, Jeanerette; **2B**-Leonard Mock, Lafayette; **3B**-James Fisher, Jeanerette; **SS**-Douglas Dean, Opelousas; **OF**-Dan Escobar, Lake Charles; Arthur Luce, Jeanerette; Cecil "Dynamite" Dunn, Alexandria; **C**-Sidney Gautreaux, Jeanerette; **Util**-Walter Lamey, Jeanerette; **P**-Bernard Cornitus, Jeanerette; Red Dowie, Lafayette; **Manager**-Ivy Griffin, Jeanerette.

BA: Douglas Dean, Opelousas, .383
Runs: Cecil "Dynamite" Dunn, Alexandria, 113
Hits: Douglas Dean, Opelousas, 189
RBIs: Cecil "Dynamite" Dunn, Alexandria, 122
Sidney Gautreaux, Jeanerette, 122

HRs: Cecil "Dynamite" Dunn, Alexandria, 18
Art Bartelli, Rayne, 18
Wins: Clauson Vines, Jeanerette, 25
SOs: Clauson Vines, Jeanerette, 184
Pct: Red Dowie, Lafayette, .800, 24-6

D Georgia-Florida League
President: Hollis Fort

Standings	W	L	Pct.	GB	Manager
Albany Travelers*	68	52	.567	—	Bobby Rice
Tallahassee Capitols**(13)	67	52	.563	½	Ed "Dutch" Hoffman
Americus Cardinals	59	57	.509	7	Don Sikes/Ed Grayson
Thomasville Orioles	57	61	.483	10	Bob Vines/Harry O'Donnell
Panama City Pilots (8)	53	64	.453	13½	Bill Snyder/Harry Snyder
Moultrie Steers (2)	48	66	.421	17	Bob Murray

Total Attendance: 121,971.

Playoff: Tallahassee 4 games, Albany 3.

All-Star Team: **1B**-Edward Davis, Panama City; **2B**-Rex Bowen, Albany; **3B**-Frank Waites, Tallahassee; **SS**-Sidney Coleman, Panama City; **OF**-Beverley Ferrell, Thomasville; Hooper Triplett, Tallahassee; Glenn Dale Murray, Tallahassee; **C**-George Berry, Americus; **Util**-Sam Narron, Albany; **P**-Walter Ammon, Albany; Kip Saurbrun, Tallahassee; **Manager**-Bobby Rice, Albany.

BA: Sam Narron, Albany, .347
Runs: Frank Waites, Tallahassee, 97
Hits: Herman Cole, Americus, 153
HRs: Frank Puttman, Albany, 18

Wins: Walter Ammon, Albany, 21
SOs: Kendall Chase, Panama City, 220
Pct: Leo Scherer, Tallahassee, .900, 9-1

D Kitty League
President: Dr. Frank H. Bassett

Standings	W	L	Pct.	GB	Manager
Jackson Generals**	50	42	.543	—	Tony Leidl/Joe Wesche/Wilbur Bickham
Union City Greyhounds	49	43	.533	1	Rip Fanning
Hopkinsville Hoppers	46	45	.505	3½	John Suther
Portageville Pirates	44	46	.489	5	Pat Patterson
Lexington Giants*	43	46	.483	5½	John Antonelli
Paducah Red Birds	41	51	.446	9	George Griffin

Playoff: Jackson was disqualified on September 1, as was Union City on September 3, due to violation of the veteran player limit; the second half was awarded to Portageville. Lexington then refused to play Portageville, contending they were not the true second half champion. Subsequent discovery of extensive violations caused the league to name no formal champion.

All-Star Team: **1B**-Glenn Burns, Lexington; **2B**-Sikes, Jackson; **3B**-Willie Morgan, Hopkinsville; **SS**-Clyde Martin, Portageville; **OF**-Joe Grace, Paducah; James Liddell, Jackson; Floyd Perryman, Paducah; **C**-Bill Scheele, Portageville; **Util**-William Hankins, Lexington; **P**-Joe Wesche, Jackson; Al Veach, Paducah; **Manager**-Rip Fanning, Union City.

BA: Floyd Perryman, Paducah, .353
Hits: William Hankins, Lexington, 108
HRs: Glenn Burns, Lexington, 8

Wins: Lester Gray, Lexington, 13
Pct: George Dumler, Union City, .800, 8-2

D Nebraska State League
President: J. Roy Carter

Standings	W	L	Pct.	GB	Manager
Sioux Falls Canaries**	72	40	.643	—	Ralph Brandon
Norfolk Elkhorns*	58	49	.542	11½	Lester "Pat" Patterson
Lincoln Links	50	64	.439	23	Cy Lingle
Beatrice Blues (16)	42	69	.378	29½	Charles Stis/Benny Warren

Attendance: Sioux Falls, 39,300.

Playoff: Norfolk 4 games, Sioux Falls 3.

All-Star Team: 1B-Victor Kosloski, Sioux Falls; **2B**-Howard Dobbins, Lincoln/Beatrice; **3B**-Cobby Moore, Beatrice; **SS**-Darrol Shimer, Norfolk; **OF**-Ash Joerndt, Beatrice, Marvin Pelton, Sioux Falls, Hoskett Brown, Sioux Falls; **C**-Benny Warren, Beatrice; **Util**-Justin Keenoy, Beatrice; **P**-Frank Wagner, Norfolk, Kenneth Cabble, Norfolk; **Manager**-Lester "Pat" Patterson, Norfolk.

BA: Ash Joerndt, Beatrice, .331
Runs: Justin Keenoy, Beatrice, 100
Hits: Ash Joerndt, Beatrice, 153
RBIs: John Grilli, Norfolk, 102
HRs: Bill Swinger, Beatrice, 22
Wins: Claude Bradford, Sioux Falls, 17
SOs: Orie Arntzen, Norfolk, 184
ERA: Tony Johnson, Sioux Falls, 2.14

D Northern League
President: Herman D. White

Standings	W	L	Pct.	GB	Manager
Winnipeg Maroons*	80	38	.678	—	Bruno Haas
Fargo-Moorhead Twins**(3)	72	39	.649	4½	Harold Ireland
Duluth Dukes	59	57	.509	20	Harry Strom
Superior Blues	53	59	.473	24	Dick Wade
Eau Claire Muskies	54	63	.462	25½	Johnny Mostil
Grand Forks Chiefs	46	66	.411	31	John Anderson
Crookston Pirates	45	65	.409	31	Lute Boone
Brainerd Blues	45	67	.402	32	Charlie Patton

Playoff: Winnipeg 5 games, Fargo-Moorhead 1.

BA: Jim Shilling, Fargo-Moorhead, .345
Hits: Jim Shilling, Fargo-Moorhead, 160
RBIs: Gene Corbett, Winnipeg, 126
HRs: Gus Koch, Fargo-Moorhead, 30
Wins: Lloyd Sterling, Winnipeg, 24
SOs: Sylvester Donnelly, Superior, 184
Pct: Lloyd Sterling, Winnipeg, .923, 24-2

D Pennsylvania State Association
President: Elmer M. Daily

Standings	W	L	Pct.	GB	Manager
Monessen Reds**(12)	68	39	.636	—	Milt Stock
Butler Indians (3)	57	46	.553	9	Leo Mackey
Washington Generals*(5)	55	52	.519	13	Benny Bengough
Charleroi Tigers (4)	53	53	.500	14½	Earl Smith
McKeesport Braves (9)	44	62	.415	23½	Wilbur Cooper
Greensburg Red Wings (16)	39	64	.379	27	Arnold Anderson/Heinie Mueller

Playoff: Monessen 4 games, Washington 2.

All-Star Team: 1B-John Cindric, Washington; **2B**-Charles Gillespie, Charleroi; **3B**-Mike McCormick, Butler; **SS**-Skeets McDaniels, Monessen; **OF**-Charles Harig, Washington; Harry Craft, Monessen; Carl Huffman, Butler; **C**-Clyde Chell, Monessen; **Util**-Al Rubeling, Monessen; **P**-George Davis, Butler; Walter Purcey, Monessen; **Manager**-Earl Smith, Charleroi.

BA: Mike McCormick, Butler, .344
Runs: Charles Gillespie, Charleroi, 95
Hits: Harry Craft, Monessen, 137
RBIs: Skeets McDaniels, Monessen, 87
HRs: Harry Craft, Monessen, 14
Wins: Ralph Williams, Monessen, 16
Walter Purcey, Monessen, 16
SOs: Ken Heintzleman, McKeesport, 147
ERA: Harold Gartrell, Butler, 2.60

1935 Interleague Post Season Play

World Series
Detroit (American) 4 games, Chicago (National) 2

Dixie Series
Oklahoma City (Texas) 4 games, Atlanta (Southern Association) 2
Total Attendance: 43,812

Little Dixie Series
Jacksonville (West Dixie) 4 games, Pine Bluff (East Dixie) 1

1935 Major League Farm systems

American League

1 Boston (2): Charlotte, Shreveport/Gladewater.
2 Chicago (3): Dallas, Longview, Moultrie.
3 Cleveland (5): New Orleans, Zanesville, Opelousas, Fargo-Moorhead, Butler.
4 Detroit (6): Portland, Beaumont, Springfield (IL), Charleston, Henderson, Charleroi.
5 New York (7): Newark, Oakland, Binghamton, Norfolk (VA), Akron, Joplin, Washington.
6 Philadelphia (2): Williamsport, Richmond.
7 St. Louis (2): San Antonio, Palestine.
8 Washington (2): Chattanooga, Panama City.

National League

9 Boston (3): Seattle, Harrisburg, McKeesport.
10 Brooklyn (3): Sacramento, Reading/Allentown, Dayton.
11 Chicago (4): Los Angeles, Portsmouth (VA), Peoria, Ponca City.
12 Cincinnati (5): Toronto, Wilmington, Bartlesville, Lake Charles, Monessen.
13 New York (4): Nashville, Tyler, Abbeville, Tallahassee.
14 Philadelphia (1): Hazleton.
15 Pittsburgh (1): Portsmouth (OH).
16 St. Louis (12): Rochester, Houston, Asheville, Bloomington, Greenwood, Huntington, Jacksonville, Springfield (MO), Hutchinson, New Iberia, Beatrice, Greensburg.

1935 No-Hitters

Date	Pitcher	Team	League	Opponent	Score
4-21	Red Dowie	Lafayette	Evangeline	Rayne	3-0
5-18	Clarence Vaughn	Fieldale	Bi-State	Mt. Airy	1-0
5-22	Lefty Albritton	Opelousas	Evangeline	Jeanerette	3-0
5-24	Mike Martynik	Huntington	Middle Atlantic	Akron	12-0
5-31	Bubba Mason	Union City	Kitty	Paducah	1-0
6-17	Elton Hamilton	Wilmington	Piedmont	Charlotte	5-0 (5)
6-21	Gus Burleson	Henderson	West Dixie	Gladewater	8-0
6-23	Al Shealy	Tulsa	Texas	San Antonio	7-0 (7)
6-30	Lester Gray	Lexington	Kitty	Portageville	
7-2	Bill Zuber	Zanesville	Middle Atlantic	Charleston	4-0
7-10	Eddie Cole	Galveston	Texas	Tulsa	1-0 (P)
7-18	Russ Brown	Akron	Middle Atlantic	Beckley	6-0
7-23	Harold Turpin	Des Moines	Western	Keokuk	7-0 (5)
8-8	Ole Olson	Greensburg	Penn. State Assoc.	McKeesport	1-0 (7)
8-21	Hugo Klaerner	Longview	West Dixie	Jacksonville	3-0 (P)
8-31	Vern Kennedy	Chicago	American	Cleveland	5-0
9-7	Louis Polli	Milwaukee	American Assoc.	St. Paul	2-0 (10)

Number in parentheses indicates innings if other than nine; "P" indicates perfect game.

THIS DATE IN MINOR LEAGUE HISTORY

May 12, 1935, Syracuse, International League, broke local attendance records with 12,000 customers at a home game.

June 14, 1935, Dale Alexander of Kansas City, American Association, set a new loop record with four successive home runs in one game. Alexander batted six times. The Blues pounded out 22 hits to crush the Millers 15-2 at Minneapolis.

June 17, 1935, Judge Kenesaw Mountain Landis overruled the Minor League Executive Commission and Judge W.G. Bramham and held that Edwin C. "Alabama" Pitts, a paroled Sing Sing prison inmate, was eligible to play with Albany, International League.

July 25, 1935, Umpire Singbush of the Northern League reversed the general order when he thumbed the league president out of the park. Manager Danny Boone of Crookston, who was also the league president, was coaching for his team against Winnipeg when he became embroiled with Singbush over a decision and was eventually bounced.

August 11, 1935, Outfielder Eddie Rose of New Orleans, Southern Association, playing against Birmingham, hoisted a high fly which struck a soaring pigeon, killing it instantly. The bird fell to the diamond, and Rose was credited with a hit.

September 7, 1935, Catcher Leo Head of Knoxville concluded the season having fanned only once in 122 games and 402 at bats in the Southern Association. In 1933, he whiffed only 3 times in 131 games.

December 12, 1935, The Texas League and the Southern Association were given Class A-1 ratings.

December 12, 1935, George Trautman was elected president of the American Association, replacing Thomas Hickey, who had resigned.

1936

American League
President: William Harridge

Standings	W	L	Pct.	GB	Attend.	Manager
New York Yankees..........	102	51	.667	—	976,913	Joe McCarthy
Detroit Tigers.....................	83	71	.539	19½	875,948	Mickey Cochrane/Del Baker
Chicago White Sox.............	81	70	.536	20	440,810	Jimmy Dykes
Washington Senators..........	82	71	.536	20	379,525	Bucky Harris
Cleveland Indians	80	74	.519	22½	500,391	Steve O'Neill
Boston Red Sox	74	80	.481	28½	626,895	Joe Cronin
St. Louis Browns	57	95	.375	44½	93,267	Rogers Hornsby
Philadelphia Athletics.........	53	100	.346	49	285,173	Connie Mack

BA: Luke Appling, Chicago, .388
Runs: Lou Gehrig, New York, 167
Hits: Earl Averill, Cleveland, 232
RBIs: Hal Trosky, Cleveland, 162
HRs: Lou Gehrig, New York, 49

Wins: Tommy Bridges, Detroit, 23
SOs: Tommy Bridges, Detroit, 175
ERA: Lefty Grove, Boston, 2.81
Pct: Monte Pearson, New York, .731, 19-7

National League
President: Ford Frick

Standings	W	L	Pct.	GB	Attend.	Manager
New York Giants	92	62	.597	—	837,952	Bill Terry
Chicago Cubs.....................	87	67	.565	5	699,370	Charlie Grimm
St. Louis Cardinals	87	67	.565	5	448,078	Frank Frisch
Pittsburgh Pirates	84	70	.545	8	372,524	Pie Traynor
Cincinnati Reds	74	80	.481	18	466,345	Chuck Dressen
Boston Bees	71	83	.461	21	340,585	Bill McKechnie
Brooklyn Dodgers...............	67	87	.435	25	489,618	Casey Stengel
Philadelphia Phillies	54	100	.351	38	249,219	Jimmie Wilson

BA: Paul Waner, Pittsburgh, .373
Runs: Arky Vaughan, Pittsburgh, 122
Hits: Joe Medwick, St. Louis, 223
RBIs: Joe Medwick, St. Louis, 138
HRs: Mel Ott, New York, 33

Wins: Carl Hubbell, New York, 26
SOs: Van Lingle Mungo, Brooklyn, 238
ERA: Carl Hubbell, New York, 2.31
Pct: Carl Hubbell, New York, .813, 26-6

AA American Association
President: George Trautman

Standings	W	L	Pct.	GB	Attend.	Manager
Milwaukee Brewers (3)	90	64	.584	—	275,191	Allan Sothoron
St. Paul Saints (2)	84	68	.553	5	168,734	Gabby Street
Kansas City Blues (5)........	84	69	.549	5½	219,369	Dutch Zwilling
Indianapolis Indians (8)......	79	75	.513	11	142,730	Wade Killefer
Minneapolis Millers (1)......	78	76	.506	12	142,926	Donie Bush
Columbus Red Birds (16)...	76	78	.494	14	121,083	Burt Shotton
Louisville Colonels (15).....	63	91	.409	27	78,732	Burleigh Grimes
Toledo Mud Hens (7)	59	92	.391	29½	67,393	Fred Haney

Playoffs: Indianapolis 4 games, St. Paul 1; Milwaukee 4 games, Kansas City 0.
Finals: Milwaukee 4 games, Indianapolis 1.

MVP: Rudy York, Milwaukee; **Manager of the Year**-Allan Sothoron, Milwaukee.

BA: John Winsett, Columbus, .354
Runs: John Winsett, Columbus, 144
Hits: Mel Simons, Louisville, 220
RBIs: John Winsett, Columbus, 154

HRs: John Winsett, Columbus, 50
Wins: Lou Fette, St. Paul, 25
SOs: Clyde Hatter, Milwaukee, 190
ERA: Bill McGee, Columbus, 2.93

AA International League
Presidents: Charles H. Knapp/Warren Giles

Standings	W	L	Pct.	GB	Attend.	Manager
Buffalo Bisons	94	60	.610	—	280,586	Ray Schalk
Rochester Red Wings (16)..	89	66	.574	5½	160,491	Ray Blades
Newark Bears (5)...............	88	67	.568	6½	178,454	Oscar Vitt
Baltimore Orioles	81	72	.529	12½	158,804	Guy Sturdy
Toronto Maple Leafs	77	76	.503	16½	105,897	Ike Boone
Montreal Royals	71	81	.467	22	162,977	Frank Shaughnessy/Harry Smythe
Syracuse Chiefs (1)............	59	95	.383	35	135,387	Nemo Leibold/Mike Kelly
Albany Senators.................	56	98	.364	38	90,309	Albert Mamaux

Playoffs: Rochester defeated Newark in a one game playoff for second place. Buffalo 4 games, Newark 1; Baltimore 4 games, Rochester 2.
Finals: Buffalo 4 games, Baltimore 2.

MVP-Frank McGowan, Buffalo.

BA: Smead Jolley, Albany, .373
Runs: Woody Abernathy, Baltimore, 132
Hits: Smead Jolley, Albany, 221
RBIs: Buster Mills, Rochester, 134

HRs: Woody Abernathy, Baltimore, 42
Wins: Bob Weiland, Rochester, 23
SOs: Bob Weiland, Rochester, 171
ERA: Steve Sundra, Newark, 2.84

AA Pacific Coast League
President: William C. Tuttle

Standings	W	L	Pct.	GB	Attend.	Manager
Portland Beavers	96	79	.549	—	181,296	Max Bishop/Bill Sweeney
San Diego Padres (1)..........	95	81	.540	1½	178,075	Frank Shellenback
Oakland Oaks (5)................	95	81	.540	1½	141,396	Bill Meyer
Seattle Indians	93	82	.531	3	262,240	Dutch Reuther
Mission Reds (5).................	88	88	.500	8½	113,394	Willie Kamm
Los Angeles Angels (11)....	88	88	.500	8½	128,565	Jack Lelivelt
San Francisco Seals (13).....	83	93	.472	13½	123,321	Lefty O'Doul
Sacramento Solons (16)......	65	111	.369	31½	42,370	Bill Killefer

Playoffs: Oakland 4 games, San Diego 1; Portland 4 games, Seattle 0.
Finals: Portland 4 games, Oakland 1.

MVP-Willie Ludolph, Oakland.

BA: Joe Marty, San Francisco, .359
Runs: Arnold "Jigger" Statz, Los Angeles, 134
Hits: Bobby Doerr, San Diego, 238
RBIs: Art Hunt, Seattle, 135

HRs: Art Hunt, Seattle, 30
Fred Muller, Seattle, 30
Wins: George Caster, Portland, 25
SOs: George Caster, Portland, 234
ERA: Lou Koupal, Seattle, 2.42

A1 Southern Association
President: John D. Martin

Standings	W	L	Pct.	GB	Attend.	Manager
Atlanta Crackers	94	59	.614	—	301,211	Eddie Moore
Nashville Volunteers (13)...	86	65	.570	7	141,369	Lance Richbourg
Birmingham Barons	82	70	.539	11½	198,391	Riggs Stephenson
New Orleans Pelicans (3)...	81	71	.533	12½	135,890	Larry Gilbert
Little Rock Travelers	77	76	.503	17	104,445	Tommy "Doc" Prothro
Knoxville Smokies	63	87	.420	29½	78,275	Jesse Petty/Neil Caldwell
Chattanooga Lookouts (8) ..	64	89	.418	30	144,953	Clyde Milan/John Mihalic/Alex McColl/Joe Engel/Joe Bonowitz
Memphis Chickasaws	60	90	.400	32½	59,726	Fred Hofmann/Billy Southworth

Playoffs: Birmingham 3 games, Nashville 2; New Orleans 3 games, Atlanta 2.
Finals: Birmingham 3 games, New Orleans 0, one tie.

All-Star Team: 1B-Alex Hooks, Atlanta; **2B**-John Mihalic, Chattanooga; **3B**-Bud Connolly, New Orleans; **SS**-Buster Chatham, Atlanta; **OF**-Marshall Mauldin, Knoxville; Joe Dwyer, Nashville; Fred Sington, Chattanooga; **C**-Paul Richards, Atlanta; **P**-Clyde Shoun, Birmingham; Luther Thomas, Atlanta; Byron Speece, Nashville; **MVP**-Leo Nonnekamp, Little Rock.

BA: Fred Sington, Chattanooga, .384
Runs: Joe Dwyer, Nashville, 127
Hits: Joe Dwyer, Nashville, 230
RBIs: Doug Taitt, Nashville, 132
HRs: Doug Taitt, Nashville, 20
Earl Webb, Knoxville, 20

2B: Joe Dwyer, Nashville, 65
3B: Fred Sington, Chattanooga, 22
Wins: Byron Speece, Nashville, 22
SOs: Jennings Poindexter, Little Rock, 144
ERA: Dutch Leonard, Atlanta, 2.28

A1 Texas League
President: J. Alvin Gardner

Standings	W	L	Pct.	GB	Attend.	Manager
Dallas Steers (2)................	93	61	.604	—	199,088	Alex Gaston
Houston Buffaloes (16)	83	69	.547	9	75,057	Ira Smith
Tulsa Oilers.......................	80	74	.519	13	80,778	Marty McManus
Oklahoma City Indians.......	79	75	.513	14	137,195	Bert Niehoff
Ft. Worth Cats	76	78	.494	17	83,339	Harry "Pid" McCurdy/Homer Peel
San Antonio Missions (7)...	73	77	.487	18	97,743	Bob Coleman
Beaumont Exporters (4)......	69	80	.463	21½	72,715	Dutch Lorbeer
Galveston Buccaneers.........	57	96	.373	35½	29,733	Jack Mealey/Jake Atz

Playoffs: Dallas 3 games, Oklahoma City 1; Tulsa 3 games, Houston 1.
Finals: Tulsa 4 games, Dallas 3.

All-Star Team: 1B-John Watwood, Houston; **2B**-Frank Croucher, Beaumont; **3B**-Jim Stroner, Dallas; **SS**-Sig Gryska, San Antonio; **OF**-Paul Easterling, Oklahoma City; Fred Tauby, Dallas; Deb Garms, San Antonio; **C**-George Rensa, Dallas; George "Birdie" Tebbetts, Beaumont; **P**-Curt Fullerton, Dallas; Fred "Firpo" Marberry, Dallas; Ira Smith, Houston; Jackie Reid, Ft. Worth; Howard Mills, San Antonio; Beryl Richmond, Galveston; **MVP**-Les Mallon, Dallas.

BA: Les Mallon, Dallas, .344
Runs: Jim Stroner, Dallas, 115
Hits: Deb Garms, San Antonio, 203
RBIs: Murray Howell, Tulsa, 127

HRs: Jim Stroner, Dallas, 27
Wins: Curt Fullerton, Dallas, 20
SOs: Beryl Richmond, Galveston, 172
ERA: Fred "Firpo" Marberry, Dallas, 2.12

*Won first-half **Won second-half ***Won both halves
Numbers after nicknames indicate farm system.
Affiliation listed at end of each year.

A New York-Pennsylvania League
President: Perry B. Farrell

Standings	W	L	Pct.	GB	Manager
Binghamton Triplets (5)	81	58	.583	—	Bill Skiff
Scranton Miners*(15).........	78	60	.565	2½	Elmer Yoter
Elmira Pioneers**(1)..........	79	61	.564	2½	Rabbit Maranville
Williamsport Grays (6).......	78	62	.557	3½	Mike McNally
Allentown Brooks (10)........	71	68	.511	10	Bruno Betzel
Hazleton Mountaineers (14) ..	66	72	.478	14½	Andy High/Frank Uzmann
Wilkes-Barre Barons	62	75	.453	18	Jake Pitler
York White Roses/					
Trenton Senators#............	40	99	.288	41	Dutch Dorman/Walter Smallwood

#York (24-45) moved to Trenton July 2, at the start of the second half, first home game July 11.
Total Attendance: 417,172.

Playoff: Scranton 4 games, Elmira 0, one tie.

All-Star Team: 1B-Gerald Hannahoe, Elmira; **2B**-Rabbit Maranville, Elmira; **3B**-Al Reiss, Allentown; **SS**-Bill Matheson, Binghamton; **OF**-Jack Grossman, Elmira; Art McHenry, Williamsport; Paul Dunlap, Binghamton; **C**-Bill Steinecke, Williamsport; **Util**-Buddy Rosar, Binghamton; **P**-Hugh Mulcahy, Hazleton; Ed Smith, Williamsport.

BA: Paul Dunlap, Binghamton, .381
Runs: Hubert Fitzgerald, Wilkes-Barre, 120
Hits: Henry Peploski, Williamsport, 211
RBIs: Bill Steinecke, Williamsport, 110

HRs: Morris Arnovich, Hazleton, 19
Horace "Red" McBride, Williamsport, 19
Wins: Hugh Mulcahy, Hazleton, 25
SOs: Atley Donald, Binghamton, 189
ERA: Walter Singer, Allentown, 2.96

A Western League
President: Dr. A.J. McLaughlin

Standings	W	L	Pct.	GB	Manager
Davenport Blue Sox***(10) ..	74	52	.587	—	Cletus Dixon
Cedar Rapids Raiders (16)..	70	58	.547	5	Clarence "Cap" Crossley
Des Moines Demons...........	64	64	.500	11	Spencer Abbott
Omaha Robin Hoods/					
Rock Island Rocks#.........	62	64	.492	12	Hank Severeid/Clarence Mitchell & Keith Clark
Sioux City Cowboys...........	61	64	.488	12½	Marty Berghammer/Dave Bancroft
Waterloo Hawks	50	79	.388	25½	Ralph Michaels/John Berger

#Omaha (23-15 in second half) moved to Rock Island August 18.
Attendance: Cedar Rapids, 44,134; Total, 204,941.

Playoffs: None.

All-Star Team: 1B-Argus "Dutch" Prather, Omaha/Rock Island; **2B**-Hugh Luby, Sioux City; **3B**-Nick Polly, Davenport; **SS**-Skeeter Webb, Cedar Rapids; **OF**-Goldie Howard, Cedar Rapids; James Asbell, Des Moines; Dave Goodman, Omaha/Rock Island; **C**-William Wilson, Des Moines; **Util**-Joe Spadafore, Omaha/Rock Island; **P**-Hal Turpin, Des Moines; Richard Elston, Cedar Rapids; **MVP**-Argus "Dutch" Prather, Omaha/Rock Island; **Manager**-Cletus Dixon, Davenport.

BA: Joe Prerost, Davenport, .341
Runs: Argus "Dutch" Prather, Omaha/ Rock Island, 102
Hits: Hugh Luby, Sioux City, 155
RBIs: Phil Seghi, Sioux City, 104

HRs: Argus "Dutch" Prather, Omaha/ Rock Island, 22
Wins: Hal Turpin, Des Moines, 20
SOs: James Hayes, Cedar Rapids, 172
Pct: Hal Turpin, Des Moines, .667, 20-10

B Piedmont League
President: Dan W. Hill

Standings	W	L	Pct.	GB	Manager
Norfolk Tars (5)................	93	50	.650	—	Johnny Neun
Durham Bulls (12)..............	79	63	.556	13½	John Gooch
Richmond Colts (6)	76	66	.535	16½	George Farrell/Frank Rodgers
Rocky Mount Red Sox (1)..	74	69	.517	19	George "Specs" Toporcer
Portsmouth Cubs (11)........	66	77	.462	27	Horace "Pip" Koehler
Asheville Tourists (16)	40	103	.280	53	Billy Southworth

Playoffs: Norfolk 3 games, Richmond 0; Durham 3 games, Rocky Mount 1.
Finals: Norfolk 3 games, Durham 0.

All-Star Team: 1B-Frank McCormick, Durham; **2B**-Michael Witek, Norfolk; **3B**-Thomas Hafey, Norfolk; **SS**-Louis Blair, Norfolk; **OF**-George Ferrell, Richmond; Ted Petoskey, Durham; Stan Spence, Rocky Mount; **C**-Dick Luckey, Rocky Mount; **Util**-Horace "Pip" Koehler, Portsmouth; **P**-Joe Beggs, Norfolk; Johnny Vander Meer, Durham; **Manager**-Johnny Neun, Norfolk.

BA: Frank McCormick, Durham, .381
Runs: Emile Barnes, Rocky Mount, 126
Hits: Frank McCormick, Durham, 211
RBIs: Frank McCormick, Durham, 138
HRs: Jim Bryan, Norfolk, 38

Wins: Joe Beggs, Norfolk, 22
SOs: Johnny Vander Meer, Durham, 295
ERA: Johnny Vander Meer, Durham, 2.65
Pct: Bill Yocke, Norfolk, .947, 18-1

B South Atlantic League
President: Dr. E.M. Wilder

Standings	W	L	Pct.	GB	Manager
Columbus Red Birds**(16)	97	53	.647	—	Eddie Dyer
Jacksonville Tars*	88	57	.607	6½	Babe Ganzel
Macon Peaches (12)...........	87	64	.576	10½	George "Possum" Whitted/Milt Stock
Savannah Indians................	64	84	.432	32	Bill Gould/Bob LaMotte
Augusta Tigers (4).............	56	94	.373	41	Dixie Parker/Herb Thomas
Columbia Senators.............	55	95	.367	42	John Billings/Otis "Blackie" Carter

Attendance: Savannah, 99,358; Jacksonville, 50,000.

Playoff: Columbus 4 games, Jacksonville 2.

All-Star Team: 1B-William Prout, Macon; **2B**-Jim Gruzdis, Columbus; **3B**-Stanley Tutaj, Columbus; **SS**-Joseph Orengo, Columbus; **OF**-Ralph Dunbar, Jacksonville; Lee Gamble, Macon; Nick Etten, Savannah; **C**-Fran Healey, Columbus; **Util**-Dee Moore, Macon; **P**-Henry Bazner, Jacksonville; Ralph Braun, Jacksonville; **Manager**-Babe Ganzel, Jacksonville.

BA: William Prout, Macon, .342
Runs: Jim Gruzdis, Columbus, 147
Hits: Jim Gruzdis, Columbus, 216
RBIs: Stanley Tutaj, Columbus, 129
HRs: Dee Moore, Macon, 18

Wins: Arthur Evans, Macon, 21
SOs: Ralph Braun, Jacksonville, 172
ERA: Joseph Sims, Columbus, 2.44
Pct: Henry Bazner, Jacksonville, .741, 20-7

C Canadian-American League
President: Walter Gilhooley

Standings	W	L	Pct.	GB	Manager
Perth Blue Cats/Royals.......	50	30	.625	—	Steve Yerkes
Ottawa Senators	53	37	.589	2	Walter Masters
Brockville Pirates (8).........	43	36	.544	6½	Jesse Spring
Ogdensburg Colts	38	45	.458	13½	Knotty Lee
Watertown/Massena Bucks/					
Grays#(9)......................	35	52	.402	18½	J. Pepper Martin
Oswego Netherlands...........	32	51	.386	19½	John Dasher/George Kunes

#Watertown (13-15) moved to Massena June 24. Massena (4-9) returned to Watertown July 12.

Playoffs: Brockville 3 games, Ottawa 1; Perth 3 games, Ogdensburg 2.
Finals: Perth 3 games, Brockville 0.

All-Star Team: 1B-Jim Stevenson, Ottawa; **2B**-Mike Sperrick, Perth; **3B**-Art Petrosky, Watertown/Massena; **SS**-Jim Nolan, Ottawa; **OF**-Joe Gunn, Perth; Ed Tibbetts, Ogdensburg; Frank Perkowski, Brockville; **C**-John Benson, Ogdensburg; **Util**-Walter Masters, Ottawa; **P**-Leo Pukas, Ogdensburg; Ed Carr, Ottawa; **Manager**-Steve Yerkes, Perth.

BA: John Tulacz, Watertown/Massena, .405
Runs: William Caldwell, Ottawa, 80
Hits: Jim Nolan, Ottawa, 111
RBIs: Frank Marinette, Perth, 80

HRs: Jim Stevenson, Ottawa, 15
Wins: Norman Hibbs, Perth, 20
SOs: Joe Krakauskas, Brockville, 216
ERA: John Tulacz, Watertown/Massena, 2.61

C Cotton States League
President: J. Walter Morris

Standings	W	L	Pct.	GB	Manager
Greenwood Chiefs (13)	79	61	.564	—	Frank Brazill
Greenville Bucks	78	62	.557	1	Lena Styles
Pine Bluff Judges (16).......	77	62	.554	1½	LeRoy "Cowboy" Jones
El Dorado Lions (12)..........	75	64	.540	3½	Frank O'Rourke
Helena Seaporters	68	70	.493	10	Rod Whitney
Jackson Senators (4).........	66	71	.482	11½	Guy Lacey
Cleveland A's (6)...............	57	80	.416	20½	Slim Brewer/Hays Copeland
Clarksdale Ginners (3).......	54	84	.391	24	Harry Strohm/Slim Brewer

Attendance: Pine Bluff, 45,265; Total, 250,000.

Playoffs: El Dorado 3 games, Greenwood 1; Greenville 3 games, Pine Bluff 1.
Finals: El Dorado 4 games, Greenville 1.

All-Star Team: 1B-Milt Stroner, El Dorado; **2B**-Robert Kahle, Greenville: **3B**-Herb Rushing, El Dorado; **SS**-Fred Weisler, Helena; **OF**-Allen Hutson, Pine Bluff; Don Hutson, Pine Bluff; Les Horn, Greenwood; **C**-Mickey O'Neil, Jackson; **Util**-F.H. "Doodle" Harper, Helena; **P**-Lloyd Moore, El Dorado; Zach Schuessler, Helena; **Manager**-Frank Brazill, Greenwood.

BA: Curt Sutherlin, Clarksdale, .364
Runs: F.H. "Doodle" Harper, Helena, 120
Hits: Curt Sutherlin, Clarksdale, 190
RBIs: Milt Stroner, El Dorado, 131
HRs: Milt Stroner, El Dorado, 29

Wins: Lloyd Moore, El Dorado, 20
Wimpy Willis, Pine Bluff, 20
SOs: Lloyd Moore, El Dorado, 244
ERA: Tom Ferrick, Greenwood, 2.17

C East Texas League
President: J. Walter Morris

Standings	W	L	Pct.	GB	Manager
Tyler Trojans**(13)...........	94	56	.627	—	Wally Dashiell
Gladewater Bears*.............	93	59	.612	2	Eddie Hock
Longview Cannibals (2)	86	64	.573	8	Tex Jeanes
Jacksonville Jax (16)	80	69	.537	13½	Ray Flaskamper/Horace Simmons
Palestine Pals (7)	74	77	.490	20½	Bobby Goff
Henderson Oilers	70	80	.467	24	Jimmy Dalrymple/Gus Burleson
Marshall Orphans/Tigers	59	90	.396	34½	Harvey Albrecht/Tex Nugent/Bama Jones
Kilgore Braves	45	106	.298	49½	Lee Cunningham/Dutch Seebold/ Jack Fitzpatrick/Robert Rawlins

Playoffs: Tyler 4 games, Jacksonville 2; Gladewater 4 games, Longview 1.
Finals: Gladewater 4 games, Tyler 2.

All-Star Team: 1B-Charles Baron(ovic), Tyler; **2B**-Clyde McDowell, Gladewater; **3B**-Horace Simmons, Jacksonville; **SS**-Larry Kinzer, Tyler; **OF**-Bob Lusk, Gladewater; Al Unser, Jacksonville; Clary Hack, Gladewater; **C**-Frank Krole, Jacksonville; **Util**-Emile De Jonghe, Henderson; **P**-Jim Reninger, Gladewater; Kip Saurbrun, Tyler; **Manager**-Wally Dashiell, Tyler.

BA: Tex Jeanes, Longview, .362
Runs: Charles Baron(ovic), Tyler, 133
Hits: Walter Paschal, Longview, 194
   Larry Kinzer, Tyler, 194
RBIs: Larry Kinzer, Tyler, 121

HRs: Mervyn Connors, Longview, 24
Wins: Kip Saurbrun, Tyler, 23
SOs: Stidham Talley, Palestine, 203
Pct: James Gravin, Jacksonville, .846, 11-2

C Middle Atlantic League
President: Elmer M. Daily

Standings	W	L	Pct.	GB	Manager
Zanesville Greys***(3)	81	48	.628	—	Earl Wolgamot
Charleston Senators (4)	71	58	.550	10	Ignatius Walters
Dayton Ducks	70	59	.543	11	Howard "Ducky" Holmes
Canton Terriers (1)	68	59	.535	12	Floyd Patterson
Akron Yankees (5)	64	63	.504	16	Nick Allen
Huntington Red Birds (16)	60	69	.465	21	Benny Borgmann
Johnstown Johnnies	59	69	.461	21½	Wilbur Good/Dutch Dorman
Portsmouth Pirates (15)	40	88	.313	40½	Eddie Kenna

Playoff: Zanesville 2 games, Dayton 1, for the second half and league championships.

All-Star Team: 1B-Iggy Walters, Charleston; **2B**-James Schilling, Zanesville; **3B**-Joe Greenberg, Johnstown; **SS**-Doody Williams, Dayton; **OF**-Frank Kelleher, Akron; Barney McCosky, Charleston; Jeff Heath, Zanesville; **C**-Sig Broskie, Canton; **Util**-Frank Demanicor, Zanesville; **P**-Stan Corbett, Charleston; Mike Martynik, Huntington; **Manager**-Earl Wolgamot, Zanesville.

BA: Barney McCosky, Charleston, .400
Runs: Oscar Grimes, Zanesville, 150
Hits: Jeff Heath, Zanesville, 208
RBIs: Jeff Heath, Zanesville, 187

HRs: Walter Alston, Huntington, 35
Wins: Tom Reis, Zanesville, 21
SOs: Mike Martynik, Huntington, 226
ERA: John Haley, Canton, 2.63

C Western Association
President: Tom Fairweather

Standings	W	L	Pct.	GB	Attend.	Manager
Ponca City Angels**(11)	87	57	.604	—	26,866	Mike Gazella
Joplin Miners*(5)	83	58	.589	2½	40,000	Benny Bengough
Hutchinson Larks (15)	79	65	.549	8	55,644	Dick Goldberg
Springfield Cardinals (16)	64	78	.451	22	45,501	Joe Brown
Muskogee Tigers (13)	61	80	.433	24½	32,000	David Miner/Carl Kentling
Bartlesville Bucs	53	89	.373	33	31,674	Bob Morrow

Playoff: Ponca City 5 games, Joplin 2.

All-Star Team: 1B-Art Shoap, Bartlesville; **2B**-Proctor Richmond, Hutchinson; **3B**-Bill Homan, Joplin; **SS**-Mike Milosevich, Joplin; **OF**-Albert "Dutch" Mele, Muskogee; Dan Curtis, Hutchinson; Lynn South, Springfield; **C**-Myron "Red" Hayworth, Joplin; **Util**-Kenny Richardson, Ponca City; **P**-Johnny Lindell, Joplin; Myron Myer, Ponca City; **Manager**-Benny Bengough, Joplin.

BA: Lynn South, Springfield, .380
Runs: Proctor Richmond, Hutchinson, 156
Hits: Lynn South, Springfield, 215
RBIs: Proctor Richmond, Hutchinson, 154
HRs: Ted Jennings, Muskogee, 31

Wins: Stroud Fields, Joplin, 20
   Joe Yerosky, Hutchinson, 20
   Cliff Haendiges, Hutchinson, 20
SOs: Louis Tost, Muskogee, 217
ERA: Ralph Hutcheson, Joplin, 3.34

D Alabama-Florida League
President: George M. Grant

Standings	W	L	Pct.	GB	Manager
Troy Trojans***	68	42	.618	—	Ernie Wingard
Enterprise Browns	64	46	.582	4	Shovel Hodge/Vic Walker
Dothan Boll Weevils	61	51	.545	8	Bobby Murry
Ozark Cardinals	55	55	.500	13	Edward Porter
Panama City Papermakers	55	57	.491	14	Bill Gleason/Darwin Cobb/Bill Morrell
Andalusia Reds	54	56	.491	14	Bill Koneman/Yam Yaryan
Union Springs Springers	49	61	.445	19	Harold Bohl
Abbeville Red Sox#	37	75	.330	32	Monroe Mitchell

#Abbeville disbanded August 10, at which time its remaining 34 games, including six previous rainouts, were forfeited to the scheduled opponents.

Playoffs: Dothan 2 games, Panama City 1; Enterprise 2 games, Ozark 0; Enterprise 1 game, Dothan 0; Andalusia 1 game, Enterprise 0.
Finals: Andalusia 4 games, Troy 2, one tie.

All-Star Team: 1B-Hal Tyler, Panama City; **2B**-Fred Spagnoli, Panama City; **3B**-Felix Rios, Ozark; **SS**-John Collins, Andalusia; **OF**-Broughton "Brick" Owens, Troy; Claude Pittman, Andalusia; Joe Gonzales, Ozark; **C**-William Casey, Troy; **Util**-George Kovach, Dothan; **P**-Bob Schremser, Troy; Edward Brockhoeft, Abbeville/Andalusia; **Manager**-Ernie Wingard, Troy.

BA: Broughton "Brick" Owens, Troy, .378
Runs: Broughton "Brick" Owens, Troy, 110
Hits: William Casey, Troy, 151
RBIs: Alvin Tennant, Enterprise, 97
HRs: Joe Gonzales, Ozark, 20

Wins: Joe Bingham, Enterprise, 20
SOs: Joe Bingham, Enterprise, 169
ERA: Edward Brockhoeft, Abbeville/Andalusia, 2.55

D Arkansas-Missouri League
President: Bernal Seamster

Standings	W	L	Pct.	GB	Manager
Siloam Springs Travelers**	74	44	.627	—	Ray Powell
Bentonville Mustangs	69	49	.585	5	Art Hauger
Cassville Blues*	61	59	.508	14	Gary Coker
Monett Red Birds	56	63	.471	18½	Adolph Arlitt/Ken Blackman
Fayetteville Bears	53	67	.442	22	Fred Hawn
Rogers Lions	44	75	.370	30½	Doc Ledbetter/Frank Stapleton

Playoff: Siloam Springs 4 games, Cassville 3, one tie.

All-Star Team: 1B-Lester Rock, Bentonville; **2B**-Al Klier, Cassville; **3B**-Robert Ludwig, Siloam Springs; **SS**-Mel Tonnsen, Bentonville; **OF**-Kermit Lewis, Siloam Springs; Woody Tone, Siloam Springs; Ace Villipigue, Bentonville; **C**-John Dellesaga, Cassville; **Util**-Andy Sinay, Siloam Springs; **P**-Clint Raper, Siloam Springs; Henry Davis, Monett; **Manager**-Ray Powell, Siloam Springs.

BA: Lester Rock, Bentonville, .333
Runs: Kermit Lewis, Siloam Springs, 130
Hits: Kermit Lewis, Siloam Springs, 164
RBIs: Woody Tone, Siloam Springs, 125

HRs: Kermit Lewis, Siloam Springs, 28
Wins: Clint Raper, Siloam Springs, 23
SOs: Robert Olson, Fayetteville, 163
ERA: John Murray, Siloam Springs, 1.35

D Bi-State League
President: Jake Wells

Standings	W	L	Pct.	GB	Manager
Bassett Furniture Makers**	74	43	.632	—	Ernie "Lefty" Jenkins
Danville Leafs	74	45	.622	1	Herb Brett
Leaksville-Draper-Spray Triplets*	65	51	.560	8½	Clyde Sukeforth
Martinsville Manufacturers	59	58	.504	15	Jimmie Sanders
Reidsville Luckies	54	61	.470	19	Jimmy Maus
Mt. Airy Reds	53	63	.457	20½	Mickey Shader/Elbert Conway/Frank Packard
Fieldale Towlers	52	62	.456	20½	Joe Guyon/Richard "Red" Smith
Mayodan Orphans	35	83	.297	39½	Phil Lundeen/Bill Ragsdale

Playoff: Bassett 4 games, Leaksville-Draper-Spray 2.

All-Star Team: 1B-Paul Campbell, Danville; **2B**-Howard Briggs, Reidsville; **3B**-Ken Keltner, Fieldale; **SS**-Frank Thompson, Bassett; **OF**-Ray Cote, Mt. Airy; Woody Traylor, Danville; Mike Chartak, Bassett; **C**-Clyde Sukeforth, Leaksville-Draper-Spray; **Util**-Guy Owens, Danville; **P**-Weaver Nowlin, Leaksville-Draper-Spray; Ernie "Lefty" Jenkins, Bassett; **Manager**-Herb Brett, Danville.

BA: Gene Handley, Mt. Airy, .403
Runs: Ken Keltner, Fieldale, 120
Hits: Ken Keltner, Fieldale, 175
RBIs: Woody Traylor, Danville, 120
HRs: Woody Traylor, Danville, 34

Wins: Ernie "Lefty" Jenkins, Bassett, 25
SOs: Weaver Nowlin, Leaksville-Spray-Draper, 167
Pct: Ernie "Lefty" Jenkins, Bassett, .833, 25-5

D Evangeline League
President: J. Walter Morris

Standings	W	L	Pct.	GB	Manager
Alexandria Aces (4)	96	42	.696	—	Arthur Phelan
Opelousas Indians (3)	89	48	.650	6½	Carlos Moore
Rayne Rice Birds (2)	83	55	.601	13	Harold Funk
Jeanerette Blues (10)	76	63	.547	20½	Emmett Lipscomb
New Iberia Cardinals (16)	68	69	.496	27½	Vernon Taylor
Lafayette White Sox (7)	58	81	.417	38½	Len Mock/Don Motlow
Abbeville Athletics	48	89	.350	47½	Gerald Mallett
Lake Charles Skippers	34	105	.245	62½	Joe Carter/Cotton Tatum/George Jenkins

Playoffs: Alexandria 4 games, Jeanerette 3; Opelousas 4 games, Rayne 3.
Finals: Alexandria 4 games, Opelousas 2.

All-Star Team: 1B-Walter Walsh, Opelousas; **2B**-Emmett Lipscomb, Jeanerette; **3B**-Charles Treadway, Alexandria; **SS**-Boyd Perry, Alexandria; **OF**-Dutch Dunn, Alexandria; Aubrey Hazel, Opelousas; Les Fleming, Alexandria; **C**-Ken Silvestri, Rayne; **Util**-Frank Hackney, Rayne; **P**-Quinn Lee, Alexandria; Glenmore Squires, Jeanerette; **Manager**-Harold Funk, Rayne.

BA: Cecil "Dynamite" Dunn, Alexandria, .378
Runs: Ken Huff, Alexandria, 169
Hits: Cecil "Dynamite" Dunn, Alexandria, 219
RBIs: Cecil "Dynamite" Dunn, Alexandria, 185

HRs: Cecil "Dynamite" Dunn, Alexandria, 47
TBs: Cecil "Dynamite" Dunn, Alexandria, 431
Wins: Rudy Woods, Rayne, 23
SOs: Harold Capdeville, Opelousas, 252
Pct: James Morris, Alexandria, .842, 16-3

D Florida State League
President: G.E. "Eddie" Gilliland

Standings	W	L	Pct.	GB	Manager
Gainesville G-Men	65	55	.542	—	Don McShane
Daytona Beach Islanders (16)	62	54	.534	1	Arnold Anderson
Palatka Azaleas	60	60	.500	5	Jeff Emerson/Teen Gallegos
St. Augustine Saints	58	60	.492	6	Fred Francis
Sanford Lookouts (8)	56	62	.475	8	Clarence McCrone/Bill Rogers
DeLand Reds (12)	53	63	.457	10	Lester "Pat" Patterson

Playoffs: Daytona Beach 3 games, Palatka 2; St. Augustine 3 games, Gainesville 1, two ties.
Finals: St. Augustine 4 games, Daytona Beach 0.

BA: George Andrews, Palatka/ St. Augustine, .350
Runs: Shaw Buck, Gainesville, 98
Hits: George Andrews, Palatka/ St. Augustine, 144
RBIs: George Andrews, Palatka/ St. Augustine, 78

HRs: George Andrews, Palatka/ St. Augustine, 10
Lonnie Smith, Gainesville/Palatka, 10
Wins: Forrest Brewer, St. Augustine, 25
SOs: Frank Gornicki, Daytona Beach, 167
ERA: John Schneider, St. Augustine, 2.25

D Georgia-Florida League
President: Hollis Fort

Standings	W	L	Pct.	GB	Manager
Tallahassee Capitols*(13)	69	50	.580	—	Ed "Dutch" Hoffman
Albany Travelers (16)	60	53	.531	6	Bobby Rice
Americus Cardinals (16)	58	58	.500	9½	Joe Bonowitz/George Berry/Dixie Parker
Cordele Reds**(12)	56	61	.479	12	Ivy Griffin
Thomasville Orioles	51	61	.455	14½	Frank Sidle
Moultrie Packers (2)	51	62	.451	15	Grant Gillis

Playoff: Tallahassee 4 games, Cordele 0.

All-Star Team: 1B-Ed Grayson, Americus; **2B-**Rex Bowen, Albany; **3B-**Frank Waits, Tallahassee; **SS-**Walter Rospond, Tallahassee **OF-**Red Ferrell, Thomasville; Red Marion, Americus; Dan Amaral, Cordele; **C-**Bob Scheffing, Albany **Util-**Dick West, Americus; **P-**Woodrow Davis, Cordele; Lefty McClure, Americus.

BA: Beverley Ferrell, Thomasville, .338
Runs: Walter Rospond, Tallahassee, 106
Hits: James Guinn, Americus, 161
RBIs: Ed Grayston, Americus, 96

HRs: Beverley Ferrell, Thomasville, 14
Wins: James McClure, Americus, 22
SOs: James McClure, Americus, 179
ERA: Woodrow Davis, Cordele, 1.87

D Kitty League
President: Dr. Frank H. Bassett

Standings	W	L	Pct.	GB	Manager
Paducah Indians*(12)	73	45	.619	—	Ben Tincup
Union City Greyhounds**(16)	73	45	.619	—	Heinie Mueller/Fred Hofmann
Lexington Giants	68	52	.567	6	Rip Fanning/John Antonelli
Jackson Generals	62	55	.530	10½	Wilbur Bickham/Herbert "Dutch" Welch
Fulton Eagles	63	56	.529	10½	Norman "Kid" Elberfeld
Portageville/Owensboro Pirates#(13)	52	67	.437	21½	Hugh Wise
Hopkinsville Hoppers	46	72	.390	27	Ralph McKnight/Jesse Petty/Budd Adams
Mayfield Clothiers (10)	37	82	.311	36½	L.L. Sweetland/Bum Robinson/Rip Wheeler

#Portageville (26-35) moved to Owensboro July 17, at the start of the second half.

Playoff: Union City 1 game, Paducah 0. Paducah refused to play the remaining games because of an adverse decision by the league president regarding the eligibility of two Union City players.

All-Star Team: 1B-Gordon Swope, Paducah; **2B-**Wayne Blackburn, Paducah; **3B-**James Hoff, Paducah; **SS-**John Antonelli, Lexington; **OF-**William Shewey, Union City; Budd Adams, Hopkinsville; Averette Thompson, Union City; **C-**Hugh Wise, Portageville/Owensboro; **Util-**Robert Richards, Union City; **P-**Jesse Webb, Jackson; John Swank, Union City; **Manager-**Ben Tincup, Paducah.

BA: Clyde Batts, Fulton, .368
Runs: Wayne Blackburn, Paducah, 124
Hits: Clyde Batts, Fulton, 176
RBIs: Averette Thompson, Union City, 125
HRs: Joe Bestudik, Paducah, 16

Wins: Allen Hayes, Paducah, 18
Gene Thompson, Paducah, 18
Jesse Webb, Jackson, 18
SOs: Jesse Webb, Jackson, 227
Pct: Dick Stewart, Lexington, .762, 16-5

D Nebraska State League
President: J. Roy Carter

Standings	W	L	Pct.	GB	Manager
Sioux Falls Canaries	71	49	.592	—	Ralph Brandon
Mitchell Kernels (16)	68	50	.576	2	Cliff "Bud" Knox
Norfolk Elks (16)	63	57	.525	8	Joe McDermott
Beatrice Blues (10)	56	65	.463	15½	Dick "Sonny" Brookhaus
Lincoln Red Links#(12)	26	38	.406	NA	Everett "Pid" Purdy
Fairbury Jeffs#	19	44	.302	NA	Eddie Brown

#Lincoln and Fairbury disbanded July 16.
Attendance: Sioux Falls, 74,306.

Playoffs: Sioux Falls 3 games, Beatrice 2; Mitchell 3 games, Norfolk 1.

Finals: Mitchell 4 games, Sioux Falls 2.

All-Star Team: 1B-Bert Haas, Beatrice; **2B-**Howard Zeng, Norfolk; **3B-**Dexter Savage, Norfolk; **SS-**Justin Keenoy, Mitchell; **OF-**Cotney Hopp, Norfolk; William James, Norfolk; Marvin Pelton, Mitchell; **C-**Tony Koenig, Sioux Falls; **Util-**Buddy Kahn, Mitchell; **P-**Vern Vogeler, Beatrice; Robert Swan, Sioux Falls; **Manager-**Cliff "Bud" Knox, Mitchell.

BA: Marvin Pelton, Mitchell, .373
Runs: William James, Norfolk, 137
Hits: Bert Haas, Beatrice, 178
RBIs: Dexter Savage, Norfolk, 128

HRs: William James, Norfolk, 29
Wins: Frank Wagner, Sioux Falls, 21
SOs: Robert Swan, Sioux Falls, 267
ERA: Frank Wagner, Sioux Falls, 3.08

D Northeast Arkansas League
President: Joseph R. Bertig

Standings	W	L	Pct.	GB	Manager
Newport Cardinals**(16)	67	30	.691	—	Thorpe Hamilton
Osceola Indians	58	37	.611	8	Royce Williams
Jonesboro Giants	50	46	.521	16½	Dale Barron/Al Williamson/Thad Campbell
West Plains Badgers/ Caruthersville Pilots*#	51	48	.515	17	Harrison Wickel
Batesville White Sox	34	64	.347	33½	Bennie Karr/Paul Fisher/Pat Hogan/ John Cordell/Tex Nugent/ L.S. Davenport/Lonnie Ethridge
Paragould Rebels	31	66	.320	36	Orlin Collier/Grayson McDonald/ Rip Fanning

#West Plains (18-10) moved to Caruthersville June 11.

Playoff: Caruthersville 2 games, Jonesboro 0, for the first half title.
Finals: Caruthersville 3 games, Newport 2.

All-Star Team: 1B-Clair Bates, Jonesboro; **2B-**Roy Herndon, West Plains/Caruthersville; **3B-**George Oldenburg, Newport; **SS-**Harrison Wickel, West Plains/Caruthersville; **OF-**Vernon Beavers, Jonesboro; John McGowan, West Plains/Caruthersville; Charles Valci, Newport; **C-**Paul Rucker, Osceola; **Util-**Willard Vandenberg, Jonesboro; **P-**Ernest Bingham, Osceola; Morris Smith, Newport; **Manager-**Harrison Wickel, West Plains/ Caruthersville.

BA: Charles Valci, Newport, .390
Runs: Paul Rucker, Osceola, 90
Hits: John McGowan, West Plains/ Caruthersville, 131
RBIs: Harvey Hall, Jonesboro/Batesville, 97

HRs: Herbert Naegele, Paragould, 16
Wins: Ernest Bingham, Osceola, 23
SOs: Orlin Collier, Paragould, 177
ERA: Morris Smith, Newport, 2.28

D Northern League
President: Herman D. White

Standings	W	L	Pct.	GB	Manager
Jamestown Jimmies (16)	73	50	.593	—	John Anderson/Ernie Olson/George Foster
Eau Claire Bears (1)	67	52	.563	4	Johnny Mostil
Winnipeg Maroons (15)	65	54	.546	6	Wes Griffin
Wausau Lumberjacks (3)	61	59	.508	10½	Lute Boone
Fargo-Moorhead Twins (3)	59	61	.492	12½	Harold Ireland
Superior Blues	59	63	.484	13½	George "Red" Treadwell
Crookston Pirates (2)	54	68	.443	18½	Ken Penner
Duluth Dukes	42	73	.365	27	Dick Wade

Playoffs: Eau Claire 4 games, Wausau 1; Winnipeg 4 games, Jamestown 3.
Finals: Eau Claire 4 games, Winnipeg 3.

All-Star Team: 1B-Charles Larson, Superior; **2B-**Hank Majeski, Eau Claire; **3B-**Chet Cichosz, Fargo-Moorhead; **SS-**Ernie Olson, Jamestown; **OF-**Henry Meyer, Eau Claire; Hugh Alexander, Fargo-Moorhead; Cal Lahman, Jamestown; **C-**George "Red" Treadwell, Superior; **Util-**Arve Mortrude, Superior; **P-**Clay Smith, Fargo-Moorhead; Ambrose Ebnet, Winnipeg; **Manager-**Wes Griffin, Winnipeg.

BA: Cal Lahman, Jamestown, .391
Runs: Cal Lahman, Jamestown, 154
Hits: Cal Lahman, Jamestown, 182
RBIs: Cal Lahman, Jamestown, 162

HRs: Cal Lahman, Jamestown, 48
Wins: Henry Ruffing, Winnipeg, 18
SOs: Elmer Johnson, Crookston, 247
ERA: Clay Smith, Fargo-Moorhead, 3.13

D Ohio State League
President: Harry Smith

Standings	W	L	Pct.	GB	Manager
Tiffin Mud Hens***(7)	60	35	.635	—	Myles Thomas
Sandusky Sailors	51	47	.520	10½	James "Chappie" Geygan
Fostoria Cardinals (16)	45	50	.474	15	Harry Aldrick/George Silvey
Fremont Reds (12)	42	56	.429	19½	Marty Purtell
New Philadelphia Red Birds#(16)	2	6	.250	NA	George Silvey
Mansfield Tigers#(3)	2	8	.200	NA	Jack Orr

#Mansfield and New Philadelphia disbanded May 26.

Playoffs: None.

All-Star Team: 1B-John Zipay, Fostoria; **2B-**Anthony Rogala, Tiffin; **3B-**Ray Westphall, Tiffin; **SS-**John Korba, Tiffin; **OF-**George Silvey, New Philadelphia/Fostoria; Jack Suydam, Tiffin; John Clements, Tiffin; **C-**Roy House, Tiffin; **Util-**John Adams, Fremont; **P-**Steve Vargo, Fostoria; George Jenkins, Fostoria; **Manager-**Myles Thomas, Tiffin.

BA: John Zipay, Fostoria, .419
Runs: John Clements, Tiffin, 97
    Anthony Rogala, Tiffin, 97
Hits: Jack Suydam, Tiffin, 141
RBIs: John Clements, Tiffin, 112

HRs: John Clements, Tiffin, 37
Wins: Edward Bastian, Tiffin, 18
SOs: Steve Vargo, Fostoria, 156
ERA: Charles Cronin, Tiffin, 3.27

BA: John Dudick, Monessen, .383
Runs: Alfred Derenne, Jeannette, 106
Hits: Alex Clowson, Monessen, 158
RBIs: Charles Marsella, McKeesport, 84

HRs: William Fuchs, Monessen, 24
Wins: Ken Heintzelman, Jeannette, 20
SOs: Ken Heintzelman, Jeannette, 229
ERA: Frank Melton, Greensburg, 2.16

D Pennsylvania State Association
President: Elmer M. Daily

Standings	W	L	Pct.	GB	Manager
Jeannette Little Pirates*(15)....	65	44	.596	—	Wilbur Cooper
Greensburg Red Wings**(16).	64	44	.593	½	Clay Hopper
Butler Yankees (5)..............	58	52	.527	7½	Leo Mackey
Monessen Indians (3)..........	50	59	.459	15	Jack Hruska
Charleroi Tigers (4)	45	62	.421	19	Joe Klinger/John McIlvaine
McKeesport Tubers (1).......	44	65	.404	21	Ray Ryan

Playoff: Jeannette 4 games, Greensburg 3.

All-Star Team: 1B-Gene Colletti, Jeannette; **2B**-Alex Clowson, Monessen; **3B**-Paul Bearint, Butler; **SS**-Harold Reitz, Jeannette; **OF**-Horace Blair, Greensburg; Frank Myers, Greensburg; Fritz Oetting, Charleroi; **C**-Ed Martin, Butler; **Util**-Charles Harig, Butler; **P**-Frank Melton, Greensburg; Ken Heintzelman, Jeannette; **Manager**-Wilbur Cooper, Jeannette.

1936 Interleague Post Season Play

World Series
New York (American) 4 games, New York (National) 2

Junior World Series
Milwaukee (American Association) 4 games, Buffalo (International) 1
Total Attendance: 55,051

Dixie Series
Tulsa (Texas) 4 games, Birmingham (Southern Association) 0
Total Attendance: 16,411

Southeast Championship
St. Augustine (Florida State) 4 games, Tallahassee (Georgia-Florida) 2

1936 Major League Farm Systems

American League

1 Boston (8): Minneapolis, Syracuse, San Diego, Elmira, Rocky Mount, Canton, Eau Claire, McKeesport.
2 Chicago (6): St. Paul, Dallas, Longview, Rayne, Moultrie, Crookston.
3 Cleveland (9): Milwaukee, New Orleans, Clarksdale, Zanesville, Opelousas, Fargo-Moorhead, Wausau, Mansfield, Monessen.
4 Detroit (7): Beaumont, Augusta, Jackson, Charleston, Alexandria, Palatka, Charleroi.
5 New York (9): Kansas City, Newark, Oakland, Mission, Binghamton, Norfolk (VA), Akron, Joplin, Butler.
6 Philadelphia (3): Williamsport, Richmond, Cleveland (MS).
7 St. Louis (5): Toledo, San Antonio, Palestine, Lafayette, Tiffin.
8 Washington (4): Indianapolis, Chattanooga, Brockville, Sanford.

National League

9 Boston (1): Watertown/Massena.
10 Brooklyn (5): Allentown, Davenport, Jeanerette, Mayfield, Beatrice.
11 Chicago (3): Los Angeles, Portsmouth (VA), Ponca City.
12 Cincinnati (8): Durham, Macon, El Dorado, DeLand, Cordele, Paducah, Lincoln, Fremont.
13 New York (7): San Francisco, Nashville, Greenwood, Tyler, Muskogee, Tallahassee, Portageville/Owensboro.
14 Philadelphia (1): Hazleton.
15 Pittsburgh (6): Louisville, Scranton, Portsmouth (OH), Hutchinson, Winnipeg, Jeannette.
16 St. Louis (23): Columbus (OH), Rochester, Sacramento, Houston, Cedar Rapids, Asheville, Columbus (GA), Pine Bluff, Jacksonville (TX), Huntington, Springfield, New Iberia, Daytona Beach, Americus, Albany (GA), Union City, Mitchell, Norfolk (NE), Newport, Jamestown, Fostoria, New Philadelphia, Greensburg.

1936 No-Hitters

Date	Pitcher	Team	League	Opponent	Score
4-22	Paul LeBlanc	Lafayette	Evangeline	Abbeville	5-1 (7)
5-2	Leroy Hermann	Toronto	International	Newark	1-0 (10)
5-3	Henry Johnson	Montreal	International	Syracuse	2-0 (11)
5-9	Doug Johnson	Cleveland	Cotton States	Greenville	14-2
5-25	Bill Burr	Winnipeg	Northern	Eau Claire	8-0
5-26	Charley Cummings	Tyler	East Texas	Palestine	5-0
5-27	Bob Harris	Alexandria	Evangeline	Rayne	2-0 (5)
6-3	Bill Harris	Buffalo	International	Toronto	2-0 (P, 7)
6-24	William Benne	Greenwood	Cotton States	Jackson	9-0

Date	Pitcher	Team	League	Opponent	Score
6-25	Woodrow Davis	Cordele	Georgia-Florida	Thomasville	
7-14	Roger Wolff	Oklahoma City	Texas	Galveston	0-2 (10)
7-16	Sig Jakucki	Oklahoma City	Texas	Galveston	10-0 (7)
7-18	Charles Hawley	Greenville	Cotton States	Clarksdale	8-0
7-30	Bill Harris	Buffalo	International	Newark	4-0
8-6	Gus Burleson	Henderson	East Texas	Kilgore	10-0
9-6	Floyd Wallace	Jacksonville	East Texas	Kilgore	13-0

Number in parentheses indicates innings if other than nine; "P" indicates perfect game.

THIS DATE IN MINOR LEAGUE HISTORY

April 15, 1936, Lance Richbourg scored seven runs for Nashville in a Southern Association game against Knoxville.

April 29, 1936, First baseman Cecil "Dynamite" Dunn of Alexandria, Evangeline League, slammed six hits, including five homers and a single, in a game with Lake Charles. He batted in 12 runs to help the Aces to a 28-5 victory.

May 10, 1936, Raymond Starr of Syracuse, International League, pitched a double-header against Toronto and threw two shutouts of 9-0 and 2-0.

May 12, 1936, Louisville, American Association, ended St. Paul's 16-game winning streak with a 6-5 11-inning victory over the Saints.

May 14, 1936, Indianapolis stole 10 bases against Milwaukee to tie the American Association record. Five of the thefts were made by Robert "Buck" Fausett for another record.

June 6, 1936, Stanley Keyes and Hack Wilson of Des Moines, Western League, staged a two-man slugging exhibition against Sioux City. Each player smacked five hits including one home run. Keyes scored five times and Wilson drove home five runs.

June 11, 1936, Johnny Vander Meer of Durham, Piedmont League, struck out 19 Norfolk Tars and allowed only one hit in a 1-0 victory. Joe Bob Mitchell, the rival hurler, was the only man to nick Vander Meer for a safety. Mitchell allowed but two hits on his own account and fanned 10, losing on a homer by Durham outfielder Harry Hughes.

June 27, 1936, Ted Williams made his Organized Ball debut with San Diego of the Pacific Coast League. He came to bat in the second inning as a pinch hitter for Jack Hill, the San Diego pitcher. He fanned on three pitches by Sacramento's Henry Pippen.

July 11, 1936, Jennings Poindexter of Little Rock, Southern Association, set a league record with 17 strikeouts in a two-hit, 3-0 win over Nashville.

July 23, 1936, Johnny Vander Meer of Durham, Piedmont League, struck out 20 Asheville Tourists. Just nine days previously, he had compiled 17 strikeouts in a game against Portsmouth. Vander Meer would go on to rack up two separate 16-strikeout efforts against Portsmouth later in the season. He would also lead the minors with 295 strikeouts for the season.

July 26, 1936, Newport, Northeast Arkansas League, began an 11-game winning streak which ended August 7; the club then won 12 in a row for a record of 23 wins in 24 games.

August 3, 1936, Hank Majeski of Eau Claire, Northern League, had seven hits in seven times at bat, including three singles, two doubles, a triple and a homer.

August 22, 1936, Max Bishop received six bases on balls for Baltimore in an International League game.

August 24, 1936, Infielder Taylor Sanford hit four home runs in one game for Danville, Bi-State League. On his fifth appearance, his bid for another round-tripper hit the flagpole in center field and bounded back onto the field for a double.

August 27, 1936, Gene Corbett of Hazleton, New York-Pennsylvania League, hit two home runs in one inning to establish a league record. He had performed the same feat in 1935 with Winnipeg of the Northern League.

August 27, 1936, Second baseman George Tkach of Superior, Northern League, died in Winnipeg, Manitoba, from injuries received when he was hit by a pitched ball.

1937

American League
President: William Harridge

Standings	W	L	Pct.	GB	Attend.	Manager
New York Yankees..........	102	52	.662	—	998,148	Joe McCarthy
Detroit Tigers....................	89	65	.578	13	1,072,276	Mickey Cochrane/Del Baker
Chicago White Sox	86	68	.558	16	589,245	Jimmy Dykes
Cleveland Indians	83	71	.539	19	564,849	Steve O'Neill
Boston Red Sox	80	72	.526	21	559,659	Joe Cronin
Washington Senators.........	73	80	.477	28½	397,799	Bucky Harris
Philadelphia Athletics........	54	97	.358	46½	430,738	Connie Mack
St. Louis Browns	46	108	.299	56	123,121	Rogers Hornsby/Jim Bottomley

BA: Charlie Gehringer, Detroit, .371
Runs: Joe DiMaggio, New York, 151
Hits: Beau Bell, St. Louis, 218
RBIs: Hank Greenberg, Detroit, 183
HRs: Joe DiMaggio, New York, 46

Wins: Lefty Gomez, New York, 21
SOs: Lefty Gomez, New York, 194
ERA: Lefty Gomez, New York, 2.33
Pct: Johnny Allen, Cleveland, .938, 15-1

National League
President: Ford Frick

Standings	W	L	Pct.	GB	Attend.	Manager
New York Giants	95	57	.625	—	926,887	Bill Terry
Chicago Cubs	93	61	.604	3	895,020	Charlie Grimm
Pittsburgh Pirates	86	68	.558	10	459,679	Pie Traynor
St. Louis Cardinals	81	73	.526	15	430,811	Frank Frisch
Boston Bees	79	73	.520	16	385,339	Bill McKechnie
Brooklyn Dodgers.............	62	91	.405	33½	482,481	Burleigh Grimes
Philadelphia Phillies...........	61	92	.399	34½	212,790	Jimmie Wilson
Cincinnati Reds.................	56	98	.364	40	411,221	Chuck Dressen/Bobby Wallace

BA: Joe Medwick, St. Louis, .374
Runs: Joe Medwick, St. Louis, 111
Hits: Joe Medwick, St. Louis, 237
RBIs: Joe Medwick, St. Louis, 154

HRs: Joe Medwick, St. Louis, 31
Mel Ott, New York, 31
Wins: Carl Hubbell, New York, 22
SOs: Carl Hubbell, New York, 159
ERA: Jim Turner, Boston, 2.38
Pct: Carl Hubbell, New York, .733, 22-8

AA American Association
President: George Trautman

Standings	W	L	Pct.	GB	Attend.	Manager
Columbus Red Birds (16)...	90	64	.584	—	218,601	Burt Shotton
Toledo Mud Hens (7)	89	65	.578	1	259,267	Fred Haney
Minneapolis Millers (1)	87	67	.565	3	193,896	Donie Bush
Milwaukee Brewers (3)	80	73	.523	9½	221,791	Allan Sothoron
Kansas City Blues (5)........	72	82	.468	18	157,714	Dutch Zwilling
Indianapolis Indians (8)......	67	85	.441	22	111,128	Wade Killefer
St. Paul Saints (2)	67	87	.435	23	144,395	Gabby Street/Phil Todt
Louisville Colonels (15).....	62	91	.405	27½	117,949	Bert Niehoff

Playoffs: Columbus 4 games, Minneapolis 2; Milwaukee 4 games, Toledo 2.
Finals: Columbus 4 games, Milwaukee 2.

BA: Enos Slaughter, Columbus, .382
Runs: Enos Slaughter, Columbus, 147
Hits: Enos Slaughter, Columbus, 245
RBIs: Ralph Kress, Minneapolis, 157

HRs: Roy Pfleger, Minneapolis, 29
Wins: Max Macon, Columbus, 21
SOs: Jack Tising, Louisville, 174
ERA: Bill McGee, Columbus, 2.97

AA International League
President: Frank J. Shaughnessy

Standings	W	L	Pct.	GB	Attend.	Manager
Newark Bears (5).............	109	43	.717	—	267,729	Ossie Vitt
Montreal Royals	82	67	.550	25½	196,889	Rabbit Maranville
Syracuse Chiefs (12)..........	78	74	.513	31	215,745	Mike Kelly
Baltimore Orioles	76	75	.503	32½	179,554	Guy Sturdy/Clyde "Buck" Crouse
Buffalo Bisons	74	79	.484	35½	189,336	Ray Schalk
Rochester Red Wings (16)..	74	80	.481	36	117,207	Ray Blades
Toronto Maple Leafs	63	88	.417	45½	144,157	Dan Howley
Jersey City Giants (13)	50	100	.333	58	207,840	Travis Jackson

Playoffs: Newark 4 games, Syracuse 0; Baltimore 4 games, Montreal 1.
Finals: Newark 4 games, Baltimore 0.

MVP-Clyde "Buck" Crouse, Buffalo/Baltimore.

BA: Charles Keller, Newark, .353
Runs: Charles Keller, Newark, 120
Hits: Charles Keller, Newark, 189
RBIs: Ab Wright, Baltimore, 127
HRs: Ab Wright, Baltimore, 37

Wins: Joe Beggs, Newark, 21
Marvin Duke, Montreal, 21
SOs: Norbert Kleinke, Rochester, 150
ERA: Ben Cantwell, Jersey City, 1.65

AA Pacific Coast League
President: William C. Tuttle

Standings	W	L	Pct.	GB	Attend.	Manager
Sacramento Solons (16)....	102	76	.573	—	143,827	Bill Killefer
San Francisco Seals	98	80	.551	4	217,819	Lefty O'Doul
San Diego Padres...............	97	81	.545	5	216,870	Frank Shellenback
Portland Beavers................	90	86	.511	11	185,824	Bill Sweeney
Los Angeles Angels (11).....	90	88	.506	12	196,793	Truck Hannah
Seattle Indians	81	96	.458	20½	144,866	Spencer Abbott/Johnny Bassler
Oakland Oaks (5)...............	79	98	.446	22½	115,848	Bill Meyer
Mission Reds	73	105	.410	29	124,052	Willie Kamm

Playoffs: San Diego 4 games, Sacramento 0; Portland 4 games, San Francisco 0.
Finals: San Diego 4 games, Portland 0.

MVP-Art Garibaldi, Sacramento.

BA: George Detore, San Diego, .334
Runs: Tony Bongiovanni, Portland, 136
Hits: Tony Bongiovanni, Portland, 236
RBIs: Art Hunt, Seattle, 131

HRs: Art Hunt, Seattle, 39
Wins: Ad Liska, Portland, 24
SOs: Manuel Salvo, San Diego, 196
ERA: Bill Shores, San Francisco, 2.47

A1 Southern Association
President: John D. Martin

Standings	W	L	Pct.	GB	Attend.	Manager
Little Rock Travelers (1)	97	55	.595	—	162,503	Tommy "Doc" Prothro
Memphis Chickasaws	88	64	.579	9	107,549	Billy Southworth
Atlanta Crackers	84	66	.560	12	261,015	Eddie Moore
New Orleans Pelicans (3)...	84	66	.560	12	119,809	Larry Gilbert
Nashville Volunteers	80	73	.523	17½	106,392	Lance Richbourg
Birmingham Barons	75	76	.497	21½	113,364	Riggs Stephenson
Chattanooga Lookouts (8)..	56	95	.371	40½	42,064	Clyde Milan/Bill Rogers/Calvin Griffith
Knoxville Smokies (10)......	42	111	.274	55½	51,879	Neil Caldwell

Playoffs: Atlanta defeated New Orleans in a one game playoff for third place. Atlanta 3 games, Memphis 1; Little Rock 3 games, New Orleans 1.
Finals: Little Rock 4 games, Atlanta 3.

MVP-Coaker Triplett, Memphis.

BA: Coaker Triplett, Memphis, .356
Runs: Leo Nonnenkamp, Little Rock, 145
Hits: Hugh Luby, Atlanta, 208
RBIs: Eddie Rose, New Orleans, 112

HRs: Willie Duke, Nashville, 19
Wins: John Humphries, New Orleans, 20
SOs: Carl Doyle, Memphis, 186
ERA: Hugh Casey, Birmingham, 2.55

A1 Texas League
President: J. Alvin Gardner

Standings	W	L	Pct.	GB	Attend.	Manager
Oklahoma City Indians	101	58	.635	—	139,769	Jim Keesey
Tulsa Oilers........................	89	69	.563	11½	104,898	Bruce Connatser
Ft. Worth Cats..................	85	74	.535	16	129,370	Homer Peel
San Antonio Missions (7)...	85	76	.528	17	141,341	Zach Taylor
Beaumont Exporters (4)......	82	77	.516	19	68,113	Al Vincent
Galveston Buccaneers.........	73	86	.459	28	44,843	Hank Severeid
Houston Buffaloes (16)	67	91	.424	33½	77,801	Ira Smith
Dallas Steers (2).................	55	106	.342	47	85,489	Alex Gaston/Fred "Firpo" Marberry/Ray Brubaker

Playoffs: Oklahoma City 3 games, San Antonio 2; Ft. Worth 3 games, Tulsa 2.
Finals: Ft. Worth 4 games, Oklahoma City 2.

MVP-Ash Hillin, Oklahoma City.

BA: Homer Peel, Ft. Worth, .370
Runs: Barney McCosky, Beaumont, 116
Hits: Barney McCosky, Beaumont, 201
RBIs: Homer Peel, Ft. Worth, 118

HRs: Cecil "Dynamite" Dunn, Beaumont, 33
Wins: Ash Hillin, Oklahoma City, 31
SOs: Ed Cole, Galveston, 205
ERA: Ash Hillin, Oklahoma City, 2.34

A New York-Pennsylvania League
President: John H. Farrell

Standings	W	L	Pct.	GB	Attend.	Manager
Elmira Colonels (10)	84	51	.622	—	93,277	Bruno Betzel
Wilkes-Barre Barons	77	57	.575	6½	86,948	Mike McNally
Hazleton Red Sox (1)	76	61	.555	9	41,976	George "Specs" Toporcer
Binghamton Triplets (5)	67	69	.493	17½	72,714	Bill Skiff
Williamsport Grays (6).......	67	69	.493	17½	50,856	Ollie Marquardt
Scranton Miners (9)..........	63	75	.457	22½	34,000	Bob Coleman
Trenton Senators (8)	54	80	.403	29½	35,422	Bud Shaney/Spencer Abbott
Albany Senators................	54	80	.403	29½	119,166	Bill McCorry

*Won first-half **Won second-half ***Won both halves
Numbers after nicknames indicate farm system.
Affiliation listed at end of each year.

Playoffs: Binghamton defeated Williamsport in a one game playoff for fourth place. Elmira 3 games, Hazleton 1; Wilkes-Barre 3 games, Binghamton 1.
Finals: Elmira 4 games, Wilkes-Barre 1.

All-Star Team: 1B-Charles Hasson, Williamsport; 2B-George Fallon, Elmira; 3B-Stan Rogers, Elmira; SS-Nathan Blair, Binghamton; OF-George Case, Trenton; Como Cotelle, Albany; Bill Sodd, Wilkes-Barre; C-Rae Blaemire, Wilkes-Barre; Util-Otto Denning, Elmira; P-Jim Bagby, Hazleton; Bill Gilvary, Elmira; **Manager**-George "Specs" Toporcer, Hazleton.

BA: Como Cotelle, Albany, .338
Runs: George Fallon, Elmira, 114
Hits: Leslie Horn, Albany, 171
RBIs: Bill Sodd, Wilkes-Barre, 108

HRs: Bill Sodd, Wilkes-Barre, 21
Wins: Jim Bagby, Hazleton, 21
SOs: Joe Krakauskas, Trenton, 184
ERA: Dick Erickson, Scranton, 2.43

A Western League
President: Dr. A.J. McLaughlin

Standings	W	L	Pct.	GB	Manager
Cedar Rapids Raiders***(16)..	78	38	.672	—	Clarence "Cap" Crossley
Waterloo Reds	61	55	.526	17	Lennie Backer
Davenport Blue Sox (10)....	57	59	.491	21	Jack Fitzpatrick
Des Moines Demons (7).....	57	62	.479	22½	Del Bissonette
Sioux City Cowboys (4)	50	63	.442	26½	Dutch Lorbeer/Pete Monahan
Rock Island Islanders#	20	46	.303	NA	Bill Burwell

#Rock Island disbanded July 7, at the end of the first half.

Playoffs: None.

All-Star Team: 1B-Russell DeForrest, Cedar Rapids; 2B-Frank Hall, Davenport; 3B-Lennie Backer, Waterloo; SS-Justin Keenoy, Cedar Rapids; OF-Ray Flood, Davenport; Mike Chartak, Cedar Rapids; Ed Hall, Sioux City; C-Armand Payton, Des Moines; Util-Walter Menke, Des Moines; P-Dwight Van Fleet, Cedar Rapids; Arthur McDougall, Des Moines; **Manager**-Clarence "Cap" Crossley, Cedar Rapids.

BA: Joe Mack, Waterloo, .337
Runs: Mike Chartak, Cedar Rapids, 113
Hits: James Howard, Cedar Rapids, 142
RBIs: Cal Lahman, Cedar Rapids, 101

HRs: Cal Lahman, Cedar Rapids, 22
Wins: Dwight Van Fleet, Cedar Rapids, 22
SOs: Dykes Potter, Cedar Rapids, 138
ERA: Dykes Potter, Cedar Rapids, 2.28

B Piedmont League
President: Dan W. Hill

Standings	W	L	Pct.	GB	Manager
Asheville Tourists (16)	89	50	.640	—	Harold Anderson
Norfolk Tars (5)	83	53	.610	4½	Johnny Neun
Portsmouth Cubs (11).........	75	62	.547	13	Elmer Yoter
Richmond Colts (13)	72	66	.522	16½	Eddie Mooers
Durham Bulls (12)	68	69	.496	20	Red O'Malley
Rocky Mount Red Sox (1)..	67	75	.472	23½	Nemo Leibold
Charlotte Hornets (8)..........	66	75	.468	24	Lee Head/Bill Rodgers/Alex McColl
Winston-Salem Twins (4)...	35	105	.250	54½	General Alvin Crowder/Pepper Rhea/ Phil Lundeen/Walt VanGrofski

Attendance: Asheville, 66,600.

Playoffs: Norfolk 3 games, Richmond 1; Portsmouth 3 games, Asheville 2.
Finals: Norfolk 3 games, Portsmouth 0.

All-Star Team: 1B-Jim Grilk, Asheville; 2B-Mickey Witek, Norfolk; 3B-Harl Maggert, Asheville; SS-Pete Suder, Norfolk; OF-Allen Hunt, Durham; Tommy Holmes, Norfolk; Roberto Estalella, Charlotte; C-Sam Narron, Asheville; Util-Gilberto Torres, Charlotte; P-Paul Gehrman, Durham; Harry Brecheen, Portsmouth; **Manager**-Johnny Neun, Norfolk.

BA: Roberto Estalella, Charlotte, .349
Runs: Jim Gruzdis, Asheville, 125
Hits: Harl Maggert, Asheville, 191
RBIs: Harl Maggert, Asheville, 139
HRs: Roberto Estalella, Charlotte, 33

Wins: Alfred Sherer, Asheville, 23
SOs: Clem Dreisewerd, Richmond, 195
ERA: Hiram Bithorn, Norfolk, 1.47
Pct: Hiram Bithorn, Norfolk, .909, 10-1

B South Atlantic League
President: Dr. E.M. Wilder

Standings	W	L	Pct.	GB	Manager
Columbus Red Birds (16)...	79	59	.572	—	Fred Hofmann
Macon Peaches	77	59	.566	1	Milt Stock
Savannah Indians (15)........	78	60	.566	1	Bill Steinecke/Martin "Chick" Autry
Jacksonville Tars (8)..........	65	73	.471	14	Alex McColl/Bill Steinecke
Augusta Tigers (5)	62	78	.448	18	Jack Mealey/Troy Agnew
Columbia Senators (9)........	52	84	.382	26	Eddie Onslow

Attendance: Savannah, 217,000.

Playoffs: Savannah 3 games, Columbus 1; Macon 3 games, Jacksonville 2.
Finals: Savannah 3 games, Macon 1.

All-Star Team: 1B-Larry Barton, Columbus; 2B-Pee Wee Wanninger, Augusta; 3B-Grey Clarke, Macon; SS-Alton Biggs, Savannah; OF-David Smith, Columbus; Herbert Maxwell, Jacksonville; Jack Bolling, Macon; C-Herbert Bremer, Columbus; Util-Dee Moore, Macon; P-Jake Levy, Savannah; Art Evans, Macon; **Manager**-Fred Hofmann, Columbus.

BA: Jack Bolling, Macon, .343
Runs: Charles Biggs, Savannah, 106
Hits: David Smith, Columbus, 184
RBIs: Herbert Bremer, Columbus, 101
HRs: Nick Etten, Savannah, 21

Wins: Art Evans, Macon, 23
SOs: Lakey Harkrader, Columbia, 133
ERA: Clarence Blethen, Savannah, 2.29
Pct: Art Evans, Macon, .742, 23-8

B Southeastern League
President: Maurice I. Bloch

Standings	W	L	Pct.	GB	Manager
Pensacola Flyers	83	52	.615	—	Frank Kitchens
Selma Cloverleafs (1, 8).....	78	57	.578	5	Babe Ganzel
Mobile Shippers (16)..........	77	59	.566	6½	Marty Purtell
Jackson Senators (5)	61	75	.449	22½	Ike Boone/Jack Mealey
Meridian Scrappers (7).......	58	78	.426	25½	Leonard McNair/Emmett Lipscomb/ Harry Whitehouse
Montgomery Bombers (3) ..	51	87	.370	33½	Ken Penner/Harry Griswold/Bud Connolly

Playoffs: Pensacola 3 games, Jackson 0; Mobile 3 games, Selma 1.
Finals: Mobile 4 games, Pensacola 3.

All-Star Team: 1B-Joe Dotlich, Selma; 2B-Larry Gilbert, Jr., Jackson; 3B-Myer Chozen, Jackson; SS-Don Blanchard, Selma; OF-Paul Carpenter, Pensacola; Fred Stroble, Meridian; Leonard Hill, Mobile; C-Harry Griswold, Montgomery; Util-Del Unser, Mobile; P-Francis Barrett, Mobile; James Mooney, Mobile; **Manager**-Babe Ganzel, Selma.

BA: Norman James, Pensacola, .349
Runs: Hal Willett, Pensacola, 106
Hits: Fred Williams, Jackson/Meridian, 175
RBIs: Norman James, Pensacola, 97

HRs: Fred Stroble, Meridian, 20
Wins: Kinner Graf, Pensacola, 21
SOs: Francis Barrett, Mobile, 189
ERA: Everette Grossman, Selma, 2.08

B Three-I League
President: Tom Fairweather

Standings	W	L	Pct.	GB	Manager
Clinton Owls**(10)	75	36	.676	—	Clyde Sukeforth
Moline Plowboys*(11).......	74	41	.643	3	Mike Gazella
Decatur Commodores (16)..	53	64	.453	25	George Payne
Peoria Reds (12)	45	66	.405	30	Ben Tincup/Wayne Blackburn
Bloomington Bengals#	21	38	.356	NA	Joseph Sims
Terre Haute Tots (7)#	15	38	.283	NA	Walter Holke

#Bloomington and Terre Haute disbanded July 3, at the end of the first half.
Attendance: Clinton, 70,000; Moline, 40,000.

Playoff: Moline 4 games, Clinton 2.

All-Star Team: 1B-Bert Haas, Clinton; 2B-Hank Majeski, Moline; 3B-Stanley Tutaj, Decatur; SS-Jack Grossman, Clinton; OF-Walter Schuerbaum, Decatur; Joe Mene, Moline; Henry Meyer, Moline; C-Jim Steiner, Moline; Util-Leroy Savage, Peoria; P-Sam Nahem, Clinton; Don Jones, Moline; **Manager**-George Payne, Decatur.

BA: Hank Majeski, Moline, .345
Runs: George Cisar, Clinton, 98
Hits: Joe Mene, Moline, 164
HRs: Bert Haas, Clinton, 13

Wins: Kirby Higbe, Moline, 21
SOs: Kirby Higbe, Moline, 257
Pct: Kirby Higbe, Moline, .808, 21-5

B Western International League
President: Roger W. Peck

Standings	W	L	Pct.	GB	Manager
Spokane Hawks	79	58	.577	—	Bernie DeViveiros
Yakima Pippins..................	80	61	.567	1	Raymond Jacobs
Vancouver Maple Leafs......	74	60	.552	3½	John Kerr
Tacoma Tigers**	75	63	.543	4½	Ed Taylor/Sloppy Thurston
Wenatchee Chiefs*	66	72	.478	13½	Glenn Wright
Lewiston Broncs	38	98	.279	40½	Don Rader/Babe Tomlinson/Wes Schulmerich

Total Attendance: 500,000.

Playoff: Tacoma 4 games, Wenatchee 1.

All-Star Team: 1B-Bob Garretson, Yakima; 2B-John Williams, Wenatchee; 3B-Harvey Storey, Tacoma; SS-Joe Abreu, Spokane; OF-Wes Schulmerich, Lewiston; Henry Bonetti, Wenatchee; Dave Goodman, Tacoma; C-Frank Volpi, Spokane; Util-Charles Petersen, Yakima; P-Henry Smith, Vancouver; Oscar Miller, Yakima; **Manager**-Glenn Wright, Wenatchee.

BA: Wes Schulmerich, Lewiston, .367
Runs: Henry Bonetti, Wenatchee, 121
Harvey Storey, Tacoma, 121
Hits: Henry Bonetti, Wenatchee, 206
RBIs: Wes Schulmerich, Lewiston, 117

HRs: Wes Schulmerich, Lewiston, 28
Wins: Oscar Miller, Yakima, 24
SOs: Oscar Miller, Yakima, 234
ERA: Hensil Hulvey, Tacoma, 2.33

C Canadian-American League
President: Rev. Harold J. Martin

Standings	W	L	Pct.	GB	Attend.	Manager
Perth-Cornwall Bisons........	69	37	.651	—	19,194	Steve Yerkes
Oswego Netherlands (3)	67	40	.626	2½	21,076	Riley Parker
Gloversville Glovers...........	68	42	.618	3	24,113	J. Pepper Martin

Ogdensburg Colts .... 55 47 .539 12 27,827 Knotty Lee
Smiths Falls Beavers (5)..... 57 49 .538 12 14,197 Johnny Haddock
Rome Colonels .... 40 59 .404 25½ 18,387 Bill Buckley/Joseph Brown
Brockville Blues (1)........... 30 69 .303 35½ 6,242 John Grilli
Ottawa Braves (9) .... 32 75 .299 37½ 15,949 W. Claire Foster

Playoffs: Gloversville 3 games, Perth-Cornwall 1; Ogdensburg 3 games, Oswego 1.
Finals: Ogdensburg 4 games, Gloversville 3.

All-Star Team: 1B-Frank Marinette, Oswego; **2B**-Al Smith, Smiths Falls; **3B**-Dan Carnevale, Perth-Cornwall; **SS**-James Nolan, Ottawa; **OF**-Maurice Van Robays, Ogdensburg; Arnold Cohen, Oswego; Edward Tibbetts, Ogdensburg; **C**-Guy Shatzer, Gloversville; **Util**-Herbert Cheek, Ogdensburg; **P**-Windy Johnson, Oswego; Albert "Duke" Farrington, Gloversville; **Manager**-Steve Yerkes, Perth-Cornwall.

BA: Maurice Van Robays, Ogdensburg, .368
Runs: Maurice Van Robays, Ogdensburg, 135
Hits: Maurice Van Robays, Ogdensburg, 159
RBIs: Maurice Van Robays, Ogdensburg, 150
HRs: Maurice Van Robays, Ogdensburg, 43
Wins: Joe Dickinson, Perth-Cornwall, 20
SOs: John Tulacz, Gloversville, 216
ERA: Xavier Rescigno, Smiths Falls, 1.56

C Cotton States League
President: J. Walter Morris

Standings	W	L	Pct.	GB	Manager
Pine Bluff Judges (16)	87	51	.630	—	LeRoy "Cowboy" Jones
El Dorado Lions (12)...........	78	62	.557	10	Frank O'Rourke
Greenwood Giants (13)	76	62	.551	11	Frank Brazill
Greenville Bucks	72	66	.522	15	Lena Styles
Helena Seaporters	70	69	.504	17½	Rod Whitney
Clarksdale Red Sox	64	76	.457	24	Red Barnes
Vicksburg Hill Billies (2) ...	55	84	.396	32½	Ray Brubaker/Alfred Libby
Monroe Twins....................	53	85	.384	34	Ed Hock/Walt Butler/Buford Rhea

Playoffs: Pine Bluff 4 games, Greenville 1; El Dorado 4 games, Greenwood 2.
Finals: El Dorado 4 games, Pine Bluff 1.

All-Star Team: 1B-Harold Grant, Pine Bluff; **2B**-Glen Stewart, Greenwood; **3B**-Fred Yazell, Pine Bluff; **SS**-Larry Kinzer, Greenville; **OF**-Charles Bauder, Clarksdale; Marion McElreath, Greenwood; Dan Escobar, El Dorado; **C**-Harry Chozen, El Dorado; **Util**-Foy Harper, Helena; **P**-Henry Zajac, Pine Bluff; Wimpy Willis, Pine Bluff; **Manager**-Frank Brazill, Greenwood.

BA: Harry Chozen, El Dorado, .339
Runs: Jack Murphy, Pine Bluff, 125
Hits: Larry Kinzer, Greenville, 169
    Kermit Lewis, El Dorado, 169
RBIs: Larry Kinzer, Greenville, 123
HRs: Kermit Lewis, El Dorado, 26
Wins: Henry Zajac, Pine Bluff, 24
SOs: Wimpy Willis, Pine Bluff, 200
ERA: Henry Zajac, Pine Bluff, 2.59

C East Texas League
President: J. Walter Morris

Standings	W	L	Pct.	GB	Manager
Tyler Trojans	85	52	.620	—	Wally Dashiell
Jacksonville Jax (16)	85	55	.607	1½	Tony Robello
Marshall Tigers (2)	76	62	.551	9½	Bama Jones/Jimmy Dalrymple
Henderson Oilers (4)	74	62	.544	10½	Gus Burleson/Guy Curtright
Palestine Pals (7)	75	64	.540	11	Archie "Abe" Miller
Longview Cannibals (2)	70	70	.500	16½	Harry Faulkner/Wally Paschal
Texarkana Liners	46	91	.336	39	Bill Windle/Eddie Hock
Kilgore Rangers.................	42	97	.302	44	Tom Estell/Jimmy Kerr

Playoffs: Marshall 4 games, Tyler 1; Jacksonville 4 games, Henderson 3.
Finals: Jacksonville 4 games, Marshall 2.

All-Star Team: 1B-Charles Baron(ovic), Tyler; **2B**-Jesse Newman, Palestine; **3B**-Mervin Connors, Longview; **SS**-Jimmy Dalrymple, Marshall; **OF**-Guy Curtright, Henderson; Norman Peterson, Jacksonville; Lou Brierson, Texarkana; **C**-Neil Andrews, Tyler; **Util**-Emil DeJonghe, Henderson; **P**-Japhet "Red" Lynn, Jacksonville, Rufus Meadows, Tyler; **Manager**-Wally Dashiell, Tyler.

BA: Jesse Newman, Palestine, .363
Runs: Walter Bliss, Palestine, 124
Hits: Norman Peterson, Jacksonville, 207
RBIs: Tony Robello, Jacksonville, 130
HRs: Tony Robello, Jacksonville, 33
Wins: Japhet "Red" Lynn, Jacksonville, 32
SOs: Walter Shaffer, Henderson, 274
ERA: Japhet "Red" Lynn, Jacksonville, 2.65
Pct: Rufus Meadows, Tyler, .806, 25-6

C Middle Atlantic League
President: Elmer M. Daily

Standings	W	L	Pct.	GB	Manager
Canton Terriers (1)	81	46	.591	—	Floyd Patterson
Springfield Indians (3)........	81	47	.587	½	Earl Wolgamot
Portsmouth Red Birds (15).	72	57	.558	10	Benny Borgmann
Akron Yankees (5)...............	64	61	.512	16	Leo Mackey
Dayton Ducks (2)................	61	65	.484	19½	Howard "Ducky" Holmes
Charleston Senators (4)	60	66	.476	20½	Ignatius Walters
Johnstown Johnnies (7)	52	74	.413	28½	Jacques Fournier
Zanesville Grays (9)	33	88	.273	45	George "Possum" Whitted

Playoffs: Akron 3 games, Springfield 1; Canton 3 games, Portsmouth 1.
Finals: Canton 3 games, Akron 2.

All-Star Team: 1B-Walter Walsh, Springfield; **2B**-Dominique Paiement, Dayton; **3B**-Nick Polly, Dayton; **SS**-Frank Scalzi, Springfield; **OF**-Hugh Holiday, Charleston; Hugh Alexander, Springfield; Edward Silber, Johnstown; **C**-George Lacy, Canton; **Util**-Jack Tighe, Charleston; **P**-Lee Sherrill, Portsmouth; Ray Moffett, Akron; **Manager**-Earl Wolgamot, Springfield.

BA: Frank Scalzi, Springfield, .377
Runs: Frank Scalzi, Springfield, 147
Hits: Frank Scalzi, Springfield, 197
RBIs: Marvin Pelton, Portsmouth, 114
HRs: Frank Scalzi, Springfield, 34
Wins: Wayman Kerksieck, Canton, 24
SOs: Lee Sherrill, Portsmouth, 274
ERA: Robert Katz, Canton, 2.73

C Western Association
President: Tom Fairweather

Standings	W	L	Pct.	GB	Attend.	Manager
Muskogee Reds (12)	79	61	.564	—	45,000	Bill Hughes
Hutchinson Larks (15)........	78	64	.549	2	67,000	Dick Goldberg/Dick Klinger/ Hugh McMullen
Joplin Miners (5)	76	66	.535	4	59,745	Benny Bengough
Springfield Cardinals (16) ..	76	67	.531	4½	54,982	Clay Hopper
Ponca City Angels (11).......	71	69	.507	8	21,961	Art Veltman
Bartlesville Blues (5)	45	98	.315	35½	30,509	Wes Kingdon/Dick Goldberg

Playoffs: Joplin 4 games, Muskogee 3; Springfield 3 games, Hutchinson 1.
Finals: Springfield 4 games, Joplin 3.

All-Star Team: 1B-Gene Coletti, Hutchinson; **2B**-Charles Glock, Muskogee; **3B**-Don Lang, Ponca City; **SS**-Frank Mabrey, Springfield; **OF**-Lou Novikoff, Ponca City; Carl Jorgensen, Muskogee; Albert "Dutch" Mele, Muskogee; **C**-John Dellasega, Bartlesville; **Util**-Freddie Vaughn, Hutchinson; **P**-Red Barrett, Muskogee; James McGloin, Muskogee; **Manager**-Benny Bengough, Joplin.

BA: Albert "Dutch" Mele, Muskogee, .354
Runs: Frank Mabrey, Springfield, 139
Hits: Gene Coletti, Hutchinson, 189
RBIs: Freddie Vaughn, Hutchinson, 123
HRs: Albert "Dutch" Mele, Muskogee, 30
SBs: Elmer Miller, Springfield, 87
Wins: Red Barrett, Muskogee, 24
SOs: Cotton Hill, Muskogee, 220
ERA: Al Lien, Joplin, 2.53

D Alabama-Florida League
President: George M. Grant

Standings	W	L	Pct.	GB	Manager
Union Springs Springers**.	77	46	.626	—	Tommy West
Troy Trojans	70	56	.556	8½	Charles Moss
Andalusia Bulldogs*...........	68	56	.548	9½	Yam Yaryan
Panama City Pelicans	70	59	.543	10	Willard Morrell
Dothan Browns..................	55	67	.451	21½	Robert Murray
Ozark Cardinals/					
Evergreen Greenies#..........	31	87	.263	43½	Monroe Mitchell

#Ozark (15-48) moved to Evergreen June 29, at the start of the second half.

Playoff: Andalusia 4 games, Union Springs 2.

All-Star Team: 1B-Charles Cupp, Union Springs; **2B**-Fred Spagnoli, Panama City; **3B**-Bobby Bragan, Panama City; **SS**-Louis Paul Lukas(iuk), Union Springs; **OF**-Andy Skurski, Troy; Broughton Owens, Troy; Stephen Summerhill, Union Springs; **C**-Tommy West, Union Springs; **Util**-George Kovach, Dothan; **P**-Walter Ammon, Union Springs; Edward Wissman, Union Springs; **Manager**-Robert Murray, Dothan.

BA: Tommy West, Union Springs, .358
Runs: Ernie Gene Bryan, Troy, 117
Hits: Tommy West, Union Springs, 160
    Ernie Gene Bryan, Troy, 160
    Stephen Summerhill, Union Springs, 160
RBIs: Andy Skurski, Troy, 107
HRs: Yam Yaryan, Andalusia, 17
Wins: Walter Ammon, Union Springs, 22
SOs: Joe Bingham, Panama City, 202
ERA: Adrian Zabala, Panama City, 2.01

D Appalachian League
President: Ray Ryan

Standings	W	L	Pct.	GB	Manager
Elizabethton Betsy Red Sox (1).	57	45	.559	—	Hobe Brummitt
Johnson City Soldiers	52	51	.505	5½	Bill Dobbs
Pennington Gap Lee Bears .	49	55	.471	9	John Anderson/Reese Harris
Newport Canners	49	56	.467	9½	Tom Henry/Paul Morley/Loy Atchley

Playoff: Pennington Gap 3 games, Elizabethton 2. In the playoff, the 'short season' leader met the leader of the entire season. The 'short season' consisted of games played during the last two months of the regular season.

All-Star Team: 1B-Tom Pearman, Newport; **2B**-Burton Hodge, Elizabethton; **3B**-Reece Harris, Pennington Gap; **SS**-H.B. Dickenson, Johnson City; **OF**-Mark Kegley, Johnson City; Virgil Caton, Newport; Russell Brown (Erastus Grigg), Elizabethton; **C**-Tom Easterbrook, Pennington Gap; **Util**-Abe Brown, Elizabethton; **P**-Paul Layman, Newport; Jack Rader, Pennington Gap; **Manager**-Hobe Brummitt, Elizabethton.

BA: Hobe Brummitt, Elizabethton, .377
Runs: Virgil Caton, Newport, 80
Hits: Harold Lee, Elizabethton, 123
RBIs: Harold Lee, Elizabethton, 79
HRs: Harold Lee, Elizabethton, 5
Wins: Paul Layman, Newport, 22
SOs: Lynn Lunsford, Johnson City, 144
ERA: Earl Walker, Pennington Gap, 2.14

D Arizona-Texas League
President: Dr. R.E. Soners

Standings	W	L	Pct.	GB	Manager
El Paso Texans*	73	49	.598	—	Jimmy Zinn
Tucson Cowboys	57	58	.496	12½	Harry Krause
Albuquerque Cardinals**	56	59	.487	13½	Bill DeLancey
Bisbee Bees	51	71	.418	22	Mickey Shader

Playoff: Albuquerque defeated El Paso in a one game playoff for the second half title.
Finals: Albuquerque 4 games, El Paso 3.

All-Star Team: 1B-Ken Manning, El Paso; **2B**-Vernon Madan, Tucson; **3B**-James Nicholson, El Paso; **SS**-Robert Sturgeon, Albuquerque; **OF**-Sheldon McConnell, Bisbee; Richard Lang, Albuquerque; Frank Sancet, Tucson; **C**-Joe Annunzio, Tucson; **Util**-Marion Coltrin, Bisbee; **P**-Ray Medeghini, Tucson; Laurence Powell, Tucson; **Manager**-Jimmy Zinn, El Paso.

BA: Richard Lang, Albuquerque, .374
Runs: Hubert Singer, Albuquerque, 122
Hits: Ken Manning, El Paso, 179
RBIs: Richard Lang, Albuquerque, 109
HRs: James Nicholson, El Paso, 10
Wins: Milo Candini, El Paso, 21
SOs: Floyd Bevens, El Paso, 179
ERA: Laurence Powell, Tucson, 2.56

D Arkansas-Missouri League
President: Bernal Seamster

Standings#	W	L	Pct.	GB	Manager
Rogers Lions	79	48	.622	—	Ted Mayer
Fayetteville Angels	70	56	.556	8½	Fred Hawn/Ken Blackman
Siloam Springs Travelers	66	61	.520	13	Ray Powell
Neosho Night Hawks	52	71	.423	25	Dennis Burns
Monett Red Birds	45	76	.372	31	Ken Blackman/Joe Davis

#Vinita, the sixth franchise, withdrew May 5 before the season started. The league played with only five clubs.

Playoffs: Fayetteville 3 games, Siloam Springs 0; Rogers 3 games, Neosho 1.
Finals: Rogers 4 games, Fayetteville 1.

All-Star Team: 1B-Paul Fugit, Fayetteville; **2B**-Jerry Priddy, Rogers; **3B**-Robert McCarron, Fayetteville; **SS**-Tony Sams, Rogers; **OF**-Arnold Evans, Neosho; Floyd Hundley, Siloam Springs; Bernard Lutz, Fayetteville; **C**-Albert Harvatin, Siloam Springs; **Util**-Ken Blackman, Fayetteville; **P**-Loy Hanning, Fayetteville; Claude Tarrant, Neosho; **Manager**-Ted Mayer, Rogers.

BA: Arnold Evans, Neosho, .385
Runs: Jerry Priddy, Rogers, 109
Hits: Paul Fugit, Fayetteville, 183
RBIs: Tony Sams, Rogers, 99
HRs: Gene Gibson, Siloam Springs, 20
Wins: Loy Hanning, Fayetteville, 16
Dewey Derry, Rogers, 16
SOs: Edward Smith, Fayetteville, 179
ERA: Loy Hanning, Fayetteville, 1.63

D Bi-State League
President: Win Clark

Standings	W	L	Pct.	GB	Manager
Bassett Furniture Makers	68	45	.602	—	Ray White
Mayodan Senators	69	46	.600	—	Harry Daughtry
Danville Leafs	68	47	.591	1	Herb Brett
Martinsville Manufacturers	63	50	.558	5	Arnold Anderson
Mt. Airy Reds	52	61	.460	16	Walt Novak
Reidsville Luckies	51	65	.440	18½	Charley Moore
South Boston Twins	43	68	.387	24	Jimmy Shelton
Leaksville-Draper-Spray Triplets	41	73	.360	27½	Clarence Blethen/Dave Lawless/Charles Willis

Playoffs: Bassett 3 games, Danville 1; Martinsville 3 games, Mayodan 2, one tie.
Finals: Bassett 4 games, Martinsville 3.

All-Star Team: 1B-Doug Wheeler, Mayodan; **2B**-George Kapura, South Boston; **3B**-Sidney Signaigo, Danville; **SS**-Phil Rizzuto, Bassett; **OF**-Maury Jungman, Mt. Airy; Cecil "Zip" Payne, Mayodan; Edward Stewart, Danville; **C**-Jack Crosswhite, Bassett; **Util**-Frank Reynolds, Mayodan; **P**-Jesse Plummer, Mayodan; Francis Logue, Bassett; **Manager**-Ray White, Bassett.

BA: Doug Wheeler, Mayodan, .359
Runs: Doug Wheeler, Mayodan, 111
Hits: Cecil Payne, Mayodan, 167
RBIs: Doug Wheeler, Mayodan, 71
HRs: Herbert Leary, Reidsville, 29
Wins: Jesse Plummer, Mayodan, 21
SOs: Weaver Nowlin, Reidsville, 168
ERA: Jack Zerblis, Bassett, 2.23

D Cape Breton Colliery League
President: A.D. Campbell

Standings	W	L	Pct.	GB	Manager
Glace Bay Miners	29	19	.604	—	Fred Maguire
Sydney Steel Citians	27	21	.563	2	Hank Hamilton/Guido Panciera
Sydney Mines Ramblers	27	21	.563	2	Bill Buckley
Dominion Hawks	23	25	.478	6	Bill Ziteman/John Turcin
New Waterford Dodgers	14	34	.292	15	Herb Moran/Mickey Morris

Playoff: Sydney 2 games, Sydney Mines 0, for second place.
Finals: Sydney 4 games, Glace Bay 3.

BA: Guido Panciera, Sydney, .394
Runs: Ray Ross, Glace Bay, 44
Hits: Guido Panciera, Sydney, 80
RBIs: Guido Panciera, Sydney, 48
HRs: Chris Pickering, New Waterford, 8
Wins: Roy Moore, Glace Bay, 14
SOs: William Jarvis, Sydney, 114
ERA: Roy Moore, Glace Bay, 1.33

D Coastal Plain League
President: J. Bruce Eure

Standings	W	L	Pct.	GB	Manager
Snow Hill Billies	62	36	.633	—	D.C. "Peahead" Walker
Williamston Martins	55	41	.573	6	Art Hauger
Tarboro Serpents	53	42	.558	7½	Fred "Snake" Henry
New Bern Bears	48	45	.516	11½	Doc Smith
Ayden Aces	47	46	.505	12½	Nick Harrison/Alfred "Monk" Joyner
Goldsboro Goldbugs	47	51	.480	15	Bill Roper
Greenville Greenies	40	58	.408	22	Bo Farley
Kinston Eagles	32	65	.330	29½	Krim Bess/Vern Taylor

Playoffs: Snow Hill 3 games, New Bern 1; Tarboro 3 games, Williamston 0.
Finals: Snow Hill 4 games, Tarboro 1.

All-Star Team: 1B-Harry Soufas, Snow Hill; **2B**-Frank Ware (Worznak), Tarboro; **3B**-Aaron Robinson, Snow Hill; **SS**-Howard Earp, Williamston; **OF**-Alfred "Monk" Joyner, Ayden; Glenn Mullinax, New Bern; Worlise Knowles, New Bern; **C**-Joe Bistroff, Snow Hill; **Util**-Larry Wade, Williamston; **P**-Owen Elliott, Goldsboro; William Flora, Goldsboro; **Manager**-D.C. "Peahead" Walker, Snow Hill.

BA: Alfred "Monk" Joyner, Ayden, .380
Runs: Dwight Wall, Snow Hill, 88
Hits: Alfred "Monk" Joyner, Ayden, 136
RBIs: Alfred "Monk" Joyner, Ayden, 97
HRs: Alfred "Monk" Joyner, Ayden, 24
Joe Bistroff, Snow Hill, 24
Wins: Owen Elliott, Goldsboro, 18
SOs: James Rollins, Williamston, 202
Pct: Emil Zak, Snow Hill, .842, 16-3

D Eastern Shore League
President: J. Thomas Kibler

Standings	W	L	Pct.	GB	Manager
Salisbury Indians#(8)	59	37	.615	—	Jake Flowers
Easton Browns (7)	56	41	.577	3½	George Jacobs
Cambridge Cardinals (16)	53	43	.552	6	Fred Lucas
Centreville Colts (1)	52	43	.547	6½	Ed "Patsy" O'Rourke
Federalsburg Athletics (6)	52	45	.536	7½	George Short
Pocomoke City Red Sox (10)	42	55	.433	17½	Vic Keene
Crisfield Crabbers (13)	40	57	.412	19½	Dan Pasquella/Bob Clark
Dover Orioles	32	65	.330	27½	Jiggs Donahue

#Salisbury had 21 wins reversed June 19 due to violations of the veteran player limit, yet still won the pennant.

Playoffs: Salisbury 2 games, Cambridge 1; Centreville 2 games, Easton 1.
Finals: Salisbury 3 games, Centreville 2.

All-Star Team: 1B-Robert Ivanicki, Cambridge; **2B**-Jerry Lynn, Salisbury; **3B**-Henry Schluter, Pocomoke City; **SS**-Frank Treschock, Salisbury; **OF**-Alex Pitko, Centreville; Bill Luzansky, Salisbury; Harvey Legates, Federalsburg; **C**-Fermin Guerra, Salisbury; **Util**-Edward Feinberg, Centreville; **P**-Joe Kohlman, Salisbury; Ken Raffensberger, Cambridge; **Manager**-Jake Flowers, Salisbury.

BA: Jerry Lynn, Salisbury, .342
Runs: Alex Pitko, Centreville, 103
Hits: Frank Treschock, Salisbury, 131
RBIs: Frank Treschock, Salisbury, 84
HRs: Alex Pitko, Centreville, 20
Wins: Joe Kohlman, Salisbury, 25
SOs: Joe Kohlman, Salisbury, 257
ERA: John Davis, Cambridge, 2.02
Pct: Joe Kohlman, Salisbury, .962, 25-1

D Evangeline League
President: J. Walter Morris

Standings	W	L	Pct.	GB	Attend.	Manager
Lafayette White Sox (7)	73	61	.545	—	100,000	Bob Goff
Rayne Rice Birds (2)	73	61	.545	—	65,000	Harold Funk
Opelousas Indians (3)	73	65	.529	2	100,000	Harry Strohm
Lake Charles Skippers (4)	68	64	.515	4	60,000	Joe Bratcher
Alexandria Aces	69	68	.504	5½	55,000	Art Phelan
Abbeville Athletics	63	72	.467	10½	65,000	Gerald Mallett/Charles Brewster
Jeanerette Blues	62	75	.453	12½	15,000	Carlos Moore
New Iberia Cardinals (16)	61	76	.445	13½	100,000	Don Motlow/Fred Hawn

Playoffs: Lafayette defeated Rayne 8-7 in a one game playoff for first place. Lake Charles 4 games, Lafayette 2; Opelousas 4 games, Rayne 1.
Finals: Opelousas 4 games, Lake Charles 3.

All-Star Team: 1B-Frank Houska, Rayne; **2B**-Bobby Goff, Lafayette; **3B**-Charles Smith, Jeanerette; **SS**-Woodie Head, Jeanerette; **OF**-John Zontini, Alexandria; Patrick Mullins, Lake Charles; Jack Suydan, Alexandria; **C**-Ken Silvestri, Rayne; **Util**-Robert Ludwig, Opelousas; **P**-Hugo Klaerner, Rayne; Jack Kraus, Opelousas; **Manager**-Harry Strohm, Opelousas.

BA: Paul Bruno, Abbeville, .384
Runs: John Zontini, Alexandria, 141
Hits: John Zontini, Alexandria, 189
RBIs: Ken Silvestri, Rayne, 123
HRs: Ken Silvestri, Rayne, 23
Wins: George Munger, New Iberia, 19
SOs: Jack Kraus, Opelousas, 193
ERA: George Gick, Rayne, 2.41

D Florida State League
President: Henry Gray

Standings	W	L	Pct.	GB	Manager
Gainesville G-Men	85	53	.616	—	Don McShane
Sanford Lookouts (8)	79	60	.568	6½	Bill Rogers/Lee Head
DeLand Reds (12)	74	65	.532	11½	Lester "Pat" Patterson
Leesburg Gondoliers	71	67	.514	14	Spec Meadows
Palatka Azaleas (5)	71	69	.507	15	Sam Agnew/Shaw Buck
St. Augustine Saints	69	70	.496	16½	Jerry Fitzgerald
Daytona Beach Islanders (16) .	67	72	.482	18½	Jimmy Sanders
Orlando Gulls	40	100	.286	46	Nelson Leach/Joe Tinker

Playoffs: Gainesville 3 games, Leesburg 2; Sanford 3 games, DeLand 2.
Finals: Gainesville 4 games, Sanford 2.

All-Star Team: 1B-Walt McMullen, Gainesville; **2B**-Shaw Buck, Palatka; **3B**-Charles Aleno, DeLand; **SS**-Ellis Clary, Sanford; **OF**-Ed Martin, Sanford; Jim Sanders, Daytona Beach; Pete Hughes, DeLand; **C**-C.B. Martin, Daytona Beach; **Util**-Bob Pittman, Gainesville; **P**-Elbert Padgett, Gainesville; Andrew Sierra, Gainesville; **Manager**-Bill Rogers, Sanford.

BA: Dick Adair, DeLand, .334
Runs: Ellis Clary, Sanford, 122
Hits: Dick Adair, DeLand, 193
RBIs: Ike Livingston, Gainesville, 93
HRs: Buster Kinard, Palatka, 10
Wins: Elbert Padgett, Gainesville, 26
SOs: Edward Harper, DeLand, 231
ERA: Elbert Padgett, Gainesville, 1.48

D Georgia-Florida League
President: A.D. Walker

Standings	W	L	Pct.	GB	Manager
Thomasville Orioles*	73	49	.598	—	Cy Morgan
Cordele Reds**(10)	73	50	.593	½	Ivy Griffin
Moultrie Packers (1)	61	61	.500	12	Grant Gillis
Albany Travelers	59	66	.472	15½	Bobby Rice
Tallahassee Capitols	51	70	.421	21½	Ed "Dutch" Hoffman
Americus Cardinals (10)	50	71	.413	22½	Dixie Parker/Bill Porter/Guy Lacey

Total Attendance: 187,423.

Playoff: Cordele 4 games, Thomasville 1.

All-Star Team: 1B-Ed Grayston, Americus; **2B**-Charlie Letchas, Thomasville; **3B**-Stan Benjamin, Thomasville; **SS**-Henry Wayton, Albany; **OF**-John Lazor, Moultrie; Bill Morgan, Thomasville; Tom Corbett, Thomasville; **C**-Willie Taylor, Cordele; **Util**-Richard West, Americus; **P**-Ace Adams, Cordele; Frank Sansosti, Thomasville; **Manager**-Bobby Rice, Albany.

BA: Tom Corbett, Thomasville, .350
Runs: Charlie Letchas, Thomasville, 98
Hits: Tom Corbett, Thomasville, 166
RBIs: Tom Corbett, Thomasville, 113
HRs: Tom Corbett, Thomasville, 26
Wins: Ace Adams, Cordele, 26
SOs: Ace Adams, Cordele, 218
ERA: Fred Ogle, Tallahassee, 2.14

D Kitty League
President: Dr. Frank H. Bassett

Standings	W	L	Pct.	GB	Manager
Union City Greyhounds (16) ...	73	46	.613	—	John Antonelli
Hopkinsville Hoppers (3) ...	71	50	.587	3	Red Smith
Fulton Eagles	64	56	.533	9½	Herb Porter
Mayfield Clothiers (7)	63	57	.525	10½	Clarence Mitchell/Walter Holke
Jackson Generals	63	57	.525	10½	Herbert "Dutch" Welch
Lexington Giants	60	61	.496	14	Rip Fanning
Owensboro Oilers (3)	56	65	.463	18	Hugh Wise
Paducah Indians (15)	31	89	.258	42½	Hugh McMullen/Ervin Brame/Lee Keller/Ralph Bishop/George Block/Pete Mondino

Playoffs: Mayfield defeated Jackson in a one game playoff for fourth place. Mayfield 3 games, Union City 0; Fulton 3 games, Hopkinsville 1.
Finals: Mayfield 4 games, Fulton 1.

All-Star Team: 1B-Eddie O'Connell, Mayfield; **2B**-Harry Johnson, Owensboro; **3B**-Jerome Witte, Mayfield; **SS**-John Antonelli, Union City; **OF**-Art Grangard, Hopkinsville; Elmer Hankins (Rush), Lexington; Glenn Grimes, Owensboro; **C**-Joe Just (Juszczak), Hopkinsville; **Util**-Orville Dantic, Owensboro; **P**-George Sauer, Union City; Elmer Wenning, Fulton; **Manager**-Clarence Mitchell, Mayfield.

BA: David Bartosch, Union City, .337
Runs: Vincent "Moon" Mullen, Mayfield, 106
Hits: David Bartosch, Union City, 170
RBIs: David Bartosch, Union City, 103
HRs: William Cooper, Fulton, 13
Wins: Elmer Wenning, Fulton, 20
SOs: Jesse Webb, Jackson, 241
ERA: George Sauer, Union City, 2.37

D Mountain State League
President: Ray Ryan

Standings	W	L	Pct.	GB	Manager
Beckley Bengals***(4)	68	36	.654	—	Eli Harris
Welch Miners	59	43	.578	8	Eddie Krajnik
Williamson Colts	54	46	.540	12	Nat Hickey
Bluefield Blue-Grays	49	46	.516	14½	Ernie Powell
Logan Indians	37	61	.378	28	Bert Grimm
Huntington Boosters#	23	58	.284	NA	Joe Watson/Paul Ryan/Mike Broski

#Huntington withdrew August 1.
The split-season format was abandoned August 24.
Welch withdrew September 3 during playoff series with Williamson.
Williamson withdrew September 6 during the finals.

Playoffs: Beckley, bye; Welch 2 games, Bluefield 0; Williamson 2 games, Logan 0.
Williamson 1 game, Welch 0.
Finals: Beckley 2 games, Williamson 0.

All-Star Team: 1B-Major B. Hutton, Bluefield; **2B**-Andrew Garchar, Logan; **3B**-Alfred Caliteaux, Bluefield; **SS**-Carlos Ratliff, Bluefield; **OF**-Edison Guinther, Logan; Stan Arnzen, Welch; Nat Hickey, Williamson; **C**-Larry Steinbeck, Beckley; **Util**-Earl Martin, Beckley; **P**-Charles Bowles, Beckley; Ben Garner, Bluefield; **Manager**-Eli Harris, Beckley.

BA: Earl Martin, Beckley, .400
Runs: Raleigh Singleton, Beckley, 113
Hits: Stan Arnzen, Welch, 150
RBIs: Earl Martin, Beckley, 96
HRs: Larry Steinbeck, Beckley, 20
Wins: Charles Bowles, Beckley, 16
SOs: Dixie Howell, Logan, 153
ERA: Ed Schumacher, Beckley, 2.70

D Nebraska State League
President: J. Roy Carter

Standings	W	L	Pct.	GB	Manager
Sioux Falls Canaries***	83	36	.697	—	Ralph Brandon
Mitchell Kernels (16)	75	41	.647	6½	Cliff "Bud" Knox
Beatrice Blues (10)	54	61	.470	27	Leon Riley
Norfolk Elks (5)	50	65	.435	31	Elmer "Doc" Bennett
Fairbury Jeffs (7)	48	70	.407	34½	Dick "Sonny" Brookhaus
Grand Island Red Birds (16)	40	77	.342	42	Joe McDermott

Attendance: Sioux Falls, 50,000.

Playoffs: None.

All-Star Team: 1B-Leon Riley, Beatrice; **2B**-John Lucadello, Fairbury; **3B**-Doug White, Mitchell; **SS**-Howard Eaton, Fairbury; **OF**-James Guyman, Mitchell; Harold Schmiel, Sioux Falls; Marvin Rumsey, Mitchell; **C**-Ralph Brandon, Sioux Falls; **Util**-Ted Haas, Beatrice; **P**-Robert Olson, Mitchell; Bobby Swan, Sioux Falls; **Manager**-Cliff "Bud" Knox, Mitchell.

BA: Leon Riley, Beatrice, .372
Runs: Frank Mahacek, Sioux Falls, 129
Hits: James Guyman, Mitchell, 175
RBIs: Harold Schmiel, Sioux Falls, 140
HRs: James Guyman, Mitchell, 22
Wins: Frank Wagner, Sioux Falls, 25
SOs: Murry Dickson, Grand Island, 209
ERA: Bobby Swan, Sioux Falls, 2.35

D North Carolina State League
President: Gene Lawing

Standings	W	L	Pct.	GB	Manager
Mooresville Moors	74	35	.679	—	Jim Poole
Thomasville Chair Makers .	63	48	.568	12	Jimmy Maus
Landis Sens	60	51	.541	15	Marvin Lentz
Shelby Cardinals (16)	55	52	.514	18	George Silvey
Salisbury Bees (9)	57	55	.509	18½	Otis "Blackie" Carter
Lexington Indians	50	59	.459	24	Baxter Moose/Phil Lundeen
Cooleemee Weavers	45	67	.402	30½	O. Coulter/Walt Purcey
Newton-Conover Twins (3)...	36	73	.230	38	Phil Lundeen/Buzz Phillips/Ray Lindsey

Playoffs: Mooresville 3 games, Landis 1; Shelby 3 games, Thomasville 2.
Finals: Mooresville 4 games, Shelby 3.

All-Star Team: 1B-Jim Poole, Mooresville; **2B**-Darr Shealy, Thomasville; **3B**-Earl Connor, Thomasville; **SS**-Mack Myers, Mooresville; **OF**-Charles Whitaker, Landis; Roy Pinkston, Thomasville; William Carrier, Lexington; **C**-Jimmy Maus, Thomasville; **Util**-Frank Crespi, Shelby; **P**-Paige Dennis, Thomasville; Butler Cook, Mooresville; **Manager**-Otis "Blackie" Carter, Salisbury.

BA: William Carrier, Lexington, .388
Runs: Jack Angle, Shelby, 109
Hits: Roy Pinkston, Thomasville, 152
RBIs: Floyd Beal, Shelby, 107
HRs: Floyd Beal, Shelby, 21
Wins: Joe Rucidio, Mooresville, 20
SOs: Wilbur Reeser, Lexington, 177
ERA: Paige Dennis, Thomasville, 1.96

D Northeast Arkansas League
President: Joseph R. Bertig

Standings	W	L	Pct.	GB	Attend.	Manager
Blytheville Giants***(13) ..	62	45	.579	—	13,654	Herschel Bobo
Caruthersville Pilots (16)....	59	47	.557	2½	17,652	Harrison Wickel
Jonesboro Giants	56	53	.514	7	25,760	Miles "Spike" Hunter
Newport Cardinals (16)	53	55	.491	9½		Thorpe Hamilton
Osceola Indians (7)	49	60	.450	14	7,830	Emil Kirchoff
Paragould Rebels	44	63	.411	18	15,312	Royce Williams

Playoffs: None.

All-Star Team: 1B-Clarence Harris, Newport; **2B**-Hal Gruber, Blytheville; **3B**-Whitey Kurowski, Caruthersville; **SS**-Pete Pavich, Blytheville; **OF**-Ben Turner, Caruthersville; V.E. Beavers, Jonesboro; Jack Grantham, Paragould; **C**-Frank Mancuso, Blytheville; **Util**-Elmer Kirchoff, Osceola; **P**-Alfred Kelley, Blytheville; Burley Grimes, Jonesboro; **Manager**-Herschel Bobo, Blytheville.

BA: Albert Tolles, Jonesboro, .368
Runs: Whitey Kurowski, Caruthersville, 125
Hits: Tommy Turner, Caruthersville, 149
RBIs: Harrison Wickel, Caruthersville, 124

HRs: Jack Grantham, Paragould, 22
Wins: Russell May, Newport, 22
SOs: Burley Grimes, Jonesboro, 238
ERA: Miles Hunter, Jonesboro, 1.75

D Northern League
President: Herman D. White

Standings	W	L	Pct.	GB	Manager
Duluth Dukes (16)	81	39	.675	—	Dutch Dorman
Fargo-Moorhead Twins (3)	70	41	.631	6½	Jack Knight
Eau Claire Bears (11)	65	53	.551	15	Johnny Mostil
Crookston Pirates (16)	61	57	.517	19	Erwin Schueren
Jamestown Jimmies	49	65	.430	29	Ed Kraus
Winnipeg Maroons	49	70	.412	31½	Bruno Haas
Superior Blues (7)	48	69	.410	31½	George "Red" Treadwell
Wausau Lumberjacks (3)	46	75	.380	35½	Dickie Kerr

Playoffs: Duluth 4 games, Eau Claire 1; Fargo-Moorhead 4 games, Crookston 3.
Finals: Duluth 4 games, Fargo-Moorhead 2.

All-Star Team: 1B-Hugh Gustafson, Winnipeg; **2B**-Blas Monaco, Fargo-Moorhead; **3B**-Frank Bolla, Winnipeg; **SS**-John Dzuira, Jamestown; **OF**-Clarence Levan(dowski), Eau Claire; Chet Wieczorek, Duluth; Delbert Jones, Fargo-Moorhead; **C**-Marvin Felderman, Duluth; **Util**-Phil Masi, Wausau; **P**-Floyd Stromme, Fargo-Moorhead; Russell Loafman, Fargo-Moorhead; **Manager**-Johnny Mostil, Eau Claire.

BA: Chet Wieczorek, Duluth, .355
Runs: Dutch Dorman, Duluth, 124
Hits: Chet Wieczorek, Duluth, 175
RBIs: Chet Wieczorek, Duluth, 152

HRs: Phil Masi, Wausau, 31
Wins: Russell Loafman, Fargo-Moorhead, 21
SOs: Oscar Gregory, Crookston, 205
ERA: Floyd Stromme, Fargo-Moorhead, 2.10

D Ohio State League
President: Harry Smith

Standings	W	L	Pct.	GB	Manager
Mansfield Red Sox (1)	59	24	.711	—	Dewey Stover
Sandusky Sailors/ Marion Presidents#	61	30	.670	2	James "Chappie" Geygan
Tiffin Mud Hens (7)	43	38	.531	15	Emilio Palmero/Charley Eckert
Findlay Browns (7)	43	47	.478	19½	Grover Hartley
Fremont Reds (12)	36	55	.396	27	Harold Bohl
Fostoria Red Birds (16)	20	68	.227	41½	John Cavanaugh/Red Jenkins/Rex Bowen/ Harry Aldrick

#Sandusky (15-7) moved to Marion June 22.

Playoffs: Mansfield 2 games, Tiffin 0; Findlay 2 games, Marion 1.
Finals: Mansfield 3 games, Findlay 0.

All-Star Team: 1B-William Ebranyl, Tiffin; **2B**-Andy Gilbert, Mansfield; **3B**-Costic Navrocki, Fostoria; **SS**-Steve Vesek, Mansfield; **OF**-Steve Patras, Mansfield; Harry Walker, Tiffin; John Barrett, Mansfield; **C**-John Spartachino, Mansfield; **Util**-Don Lupo, Tiffin; **P**-Gordon Mann, Sandusky/Marion; Lester Heath, Mansfield; **Manager**-Grover Hartley, Findlay.

BA: Dewey Stover, Mansfield, .383
Runs: John Barrett, Mansfield, 97
Hits: John Barrett, Mansfield, 129
RBIs: James "Chappie" Geygan, Sandusky/ Marion, 91
Stanley Platek, Sandusky/Marion, 91

HRs: John Barrett, Mansfield, 13
Steve Patras, Mansfield, 13
Wins: Gordon Mann, Sandusky/Marion, 18
Marion Spence, Sandusky/Marion, 18
SOs: Charles Cronin, Tiffin, 178
ERA: Gordon Mann, Sandusky/Marion, 2.30
Pct: Gordon Mann, Sandusky/Marion, .900, 18-2

D Pennsylvania State Association
President: Elmer M. Daily

Standings	W	L	Pct.	GB	Manager
Butler Yankees*(5)	62	35	.639	—	Lefty Jenkins
Greensburg Green Sox (10)	54	45	.545	9	Wilbur Cooper
Beaver Falls Bees**(9)	48	45	.516	12	Tom Kennedy
Monessen Cardinals (16)	35	64	.354	28	John Lynch/Ollie Vanek
Jeannette Bisons#	13	11	.542	NA	Jake Pitler
McKeesport Tubers#	7	19	.269	NA	Al Falquist/Edward Lee

#Jeannette and McKeesport disbanded June 10.

Playoff: Butler 4 games, Beaver Falls 3.

All-Star Team: 1B-Joe Zagami, Beaver Falls; **2B**-Johnny Russian, Butler; **3B**-Frank Graves, Greensburg; **SS**-Frank Wecheck, Greensburg; **OF**-Hillman Walker, Greensburg; Ed Urban, Beaver Falls; Lynford Rumfield, Greensburg; **C**-L.J. Bartola, Butler; **Util**-William Gaylord, Greensburg; **P**-Darrel Hawley, Greensburg; Ernest Jenkins, Butler; **Manager**-Wilbur Cooper, Greensburg.

BA: Johnny Russian, Butler, .393
Runs: William Denof, Butler, 106
Hits: Johnny Russian, Butler, 134
RBIs: William Johnson, Butler, 91

HRs: Ed Urban, Beaver Falls, 24
Wins: Darrel Hawley, Greensburg, 16
SOs: Darrel Hawley, Greensburg, 161
ERA: Darrel Hawley, Greensburg, 2.72

D West Texas-New Mexico League
President: Milton Price

Standings	W	L	Pct.	GB	Manager
Wink Spudders	68	50	.576	—	D.E. Perry/Joe Tate
Roswell Sunshiners	55	62	.470	12½	Neal Rabe
Monahans Trojans	55	64	.462	13½	Paul Trammel/Charles Bryan
Hobbs Drillers	45	74	.378	23½	Ned Pettigrew/Fat Withers
Odessa Oilers#	28	17	.622	NA	Charles Bryan
Midland Cardinals@(16)	41	25	.621	NA	Wray Query/Joe Davis

#Odessa withdrew June 17.
@Midland withdrew July 9.
Attendance: Wink, 15,877; Total, 48,544.

Playoffs: Wink 3 games, Hobbs 0; Roswell 3 games, Monahans 2.
Finals: Wink 3 games, Roswell 0.

All-Star Team: 1B-Carmin Henderson, Roswell; **2B**-Stuart LeBarron, Monahans; **3B**-Lance Donaldson, Roswell; **SS**-Jack Davis, Roswell; **OF**-Mel Reist, Odessa/Monahans; Cecil Smyly, Roswell; Robert Hood, Wink; **C**-Walter Reinhardt, Roswell; **Util**-Stephen Hoffman, Monahans; **P**-Red Hay, Wink; Marshall Scott, Roswell; **Manager**-Neal Rabe, Roswell.

BA: Robert Hood, Wink, .372
Runs: Robert Hood, Wink, 137
Hits: Mel Reist, Odessa/Monahans, 182
RBIs: Robert Hood, Wink, 145
HRs: Robert Hood, Wink, 30

Wins: Red Hay, Wink, 18
Marshall Scott, Roswell, 18
SOs: Gene Devine, Roswell, 218
ERA: Paul Reeves, Wink, 3.51

Ind Mexican League
President: Higinio Ureta

South Standings	W	L	Pct.	GB	Manager
Veracruz Aguila	20	4	.833	—	Agustin Verde
Cordoba Cafeteros	16	8	.667	4	Lazaro Penagos
Nogales Cerveceros	13	10	.565	6½	Raymundo Martinez
Mexico City Agricultura	12	13	.480	8½	Ernesto Carmona
Mexico City Transito	6	19	.240	14½	Goyito Valdez
Mexico City Petroleros	5	18	.217	14½	Miguel Gonzalez

North Standings	W	L	Pct.	GB	Manager
Mexico City Agrario	21	4	.840	—	Salvador Teuffer/Fernando Barradas/ Adolfo Alvarez
Mexico City Comintra	20	5	.800	1	Manuel Oliveros
Santa Rosa Gallos	14	9	.609	6	Leonardo Olvera
Tampico Alijadores	8	15	.348	12	Manolo Borges/Silviano Roldan/ Porfirio Martinez
Mexico City Necaxa	4	16	.200	14½	Eutiquio Becerril/Jose Luis Gomez
Rio Blanco Cidosa	2	20	.091	17½	Angel Abreu/Armando Corrales

Playoff: Veracruz 3 games, Mexico City Agrario 0.

BA: Alfonso Nieto, MC Agricultura, .476
Hits: Alfonso Nieto, MC Agricultura, 40
Eduardo Fuentes, MC Comintra, 40
RBIs: Roberto Cabal, MC Agrario, 31
HRs: Carlos Galina, MC Petroleros, 6

Wins: Esteban Reyes, MC Comintra, 11
Basilio Rosell, MC Agrario, 11
SOs: Basilio Rosell, MC Agrario, 71
ERA: Alberto Romo Chavez, MC Agrario, 0.78

1937 Interleague Post Season Play

World Series
New York (American) 4 games, New York (National) 1

Junior World Series
Newark (International) 4 games, Columbus (American Association) 3
Total Attendance: 63,340

Dixie Series
Ft. Worth (Texas) 4 games, Little Rock (Southern Association) 1
Total Attendance: 34,622

Southern Championship
Mobile (Southeastern) 4 games, Savannah (South Atlantic) 2

Little Dixie Series
Jacksonville (East Texas) 4 games, Opelousas (Evangeline) 1

Western vs. Three-I Series
Cedar Rapids (Western) 3 games, Moline (Three-I) 1, one tie

Arizona-Texas vs. West Texas-New Mexico Series
Albuquerque (Arizona-Texas) 2 games, Wink (West Texas-New Mexico) 0

Class D Championship of North Carolina and Virginia
Bassett (Bi-State) 1 game, Mooresville (North Carolina State) 1
Series cancelled due to inclement weather.

Class D Mountain Championship
Beckley (Mountain State) 4 games, Pennington Gap (Appalachian) 0

Southeast Championship
Cordele (Georgia-Florida) 4 games, Gainesville (Florida State) 3

1937 Major League Farm Systems

American League

1 Boston (11): Minneapolis, Little Rock, Hazleton, Rocky Mount, Selma, Brockville, Canton, Elizabethton, Centreville, Moultrie, Mansfield.
2 Chicago (7): St. Paul, Dallas, Vicksburg, Marshall, Longview, Dayton, Rayne.
3 Cleveland (11): Milwaukee, New Orleans, Montgomery, Oswego, Springfield (OH), Opelousas, Owensboro, Hopkinsville, Newton-Conover, Wausau, Fargo-Moorhead.
4 Detroit (7): Beaumont, Sioux City, Winston-Salem, Henderson, Charleston, Lake Charles, Beckley.
5 New York (14): Kansas City, Newark, Oakland, Binghamton, Norfolk (VA), Augusta, Jackson, Smiths Falls, Akron, Joplin, Bartlesville, Palatka, Norfolk (NE), Butler.
6 Philadelphia (2): Williamsport, Federalsburg.
7 St. Louis (15): Toledo, San Antonio, Des Moines, Meridian, Terre Haute, Palestine, Johnstown, Easton, Lafayette, Mayfield, Fairbury, Osceola, Superior, Tiffin, Findlay.
8 Washington (8): Indianapolis, Chattanooga, Trenton, Charlotte, Jacksonville (FL), Selma, Salisbury (MD), Sanford.

National League

9 Boston (6): Scranton, Columbia, Ottawa, Zanesville, Salisbury (NC), Beaver Falls.
10 Brooklyn (9): Knoxville, Elmira, Davenport, Clinton, Pocomoke City, Cordele, Americus, Beatrice, Greensburg.
11 Chicago (5): Los Angeles, Portsmouth (VA), Moline, Ponca City, Eau Claire.
12 Cincinnati (7): Syracuse, Durham, Peoria, El Dorado, Muskogee, DeLand, Fremont.
13 New York (5): Jersey City, Richmond, Greenwood, Crisfield, Blytheville.
15 Pittsburgh (5): Louisville, Savannah, Portsmouth (OH), Hutchinson, Paducah.
16 St. Louis (26): Columbus (OH), Rochester, Sacramento, Houston, Cedar Rapids, Asheville, Columbus (GA), Mobile, Decatur, Pine Bluff, Jacksonville (TX), Springfield (MO), Daytona Beach, New Iberia, Cambridge, Union City, Mitchell, Grand Island, Shelby, Newport, Caruthersville, Duluth, Crookston, Fostoria, Monessen, Midland.

1937 No-Hitters

Date	Pitcher	Team	League	Opponent	Score
5-14	Charles Wagener	Palestine	East Texas	Texarkana	1-0
5-16	Danny York	Tarboro	Coastal Plain	Snow Hill	1-0
6-1	Bill Dietrich	Chicago	American	St. Louis	8-0
6-12	Fred "Firpo" Marberry	Dallas	Texas	Galveston	3-0
6-12	Bill Prince	Davenport	Western	Cedar Rapids	2-1
6-12	Manuel Perez	Palestine	East Texas	Kilgore	5-0
6-19	Louis Polli	Montreal	International	Jersey City	6-0
6-29	Bill Faser	Hutchinson	Western Assoc.	Bartlesville	1-0
7-4	Tiny Bonham	Oakland	Pacific Coast	Seattle	2-0 (7)
7-25	Lloyd Moore	Syracuse	International	Jersey City	1-0
7-27	Ken Ash	Buffalo	International	Syracuse	2-0 (7)
7-29	Ed "Bear Tracks" Greer	Ft. Worth	Texas	Houston	0-1
7-30	John Humphries	New Orleans	Southern Assoc.	Chattanooga	1-0
8-2	Clair Bertram	Pensacola	Southeastern	Selma	6-0
8-11	Clair Bertram	Pensacola	Southeastern	Montgomery	6-0
8-11	Dee Moore	Macon	South Atlantic	Columbus	(7)
8-16	Roy Goat Walker	Jacksonville	South Atlantic	Columbus	2-0
8-21	Sulo Mattson	New Iberia	Evangeline	Opelousas	0-1
8-22	Leo Pukas	Ogdensburg	Canadian-American	Ottawa	9-0
8-28	Manuel Perez	Palestine	East Texas	Texarkana	11-0 (7)
8-28	Gordon Bradshaw	St. Augustine	Florida State	Orlando	4-0
9-2	Jim McMullen	DeLand	Florida State	Orlando	0-3
9-2	Joe Kohlman	Salisbury	Eastern Shore	Easton	7-0
9-6	Ed Tantillo	Dover	Eastern Shore	Centreville	11-0 (P)
9-18	Joe Kohlman	Salisbury	Eastern Shore	Centreville	7-0 (PO)
9-18	Al Reis	Wilkes-Barre	New York-Penn.	Binghamton	8-0 (PO)

Number in parentheses indicates innings if other than nine; "P" indicates perfect game; "PO" indicates playoff game.

THIS DATE IN MINOR LEAGUE HISTORY

January 5, 1937, Travis Jackson signed a three-year contract to manage Jersey City of the International League.

April 23, 1937, Jersey City marked its return to the International League by playing to an all-time minor league record breaking crowd of 31,234 paid admissions at Jersey City.

April 29, 1937, The scheduled Texas League game of Tulsa at Galveston was postponed for the second straight night due to heavy fog.

May 2, 1937, Francis Kelleher of Newark, International League, scored six runs, tying the league record.

May 6, 1937, The International League's Baltimore Orioles were forced to use gloves borrowed from members of the Toronto team for their game at Toronto. The Orioles' equipment was stolen the night before while they helped Toronto players celebrate at a pre-opening game banquet.

May 20, 1937, Joe Kohlman, a 22-year old righthander for Salisbury, Eastern Shore League, lost his first decision of the season. He would then complete the regular season with 25 consecutive victories for a 25-1 season mark.

May 27, 1937, Outfielder John Rizzo of Columbus, American Association, was stopped after having hit in 36 successive contests since April 17.

June 1, 1937, Pitcher Joe Vitelli of Albany, New York-Pennsylvania League, pitched and won an 18-inning game over Binghamton, striking out 20 men. He also hit two doubles and a single to lead his team to a 5-4 victory. Albany scored twice in the bottom of the 18th after Binghamton had tallied once in its half of the inning.

June 1, 1937, Winston-Salem, Piedmont League, managed by General Alvin Crowder, won just its second game of the season after having lost 31 of its first 32 contests, including 28 in a row.

June 19, 1937, Salisbury, Eastern Shore League, had its 21 wins reversed by forfeit, changing its record from 21-5 to 0-26. Yet, the club came back to finish in first place and win the playoffs, completing a comeback unparalleled in minor league history.

June 27, 1937, Leftfielder James Taylor and centerfielder Charles Wanny of Bassett were struck by lightning in a Bi-State League game with Mayodan. The bolt, which hit the flagpole in Bassett Park, knocked Taylor unconscious and threw Wanny to the ground. The game was called in the fourth inning when the bolt struck.

June 29, 1937, Bill Faser of Hutchinson, Western Association, pitched a no-hitter, striking out 19 Bartlesville batters. It was his first win in Organized Ball, coming in his eleventh appearance.

June 29, 1937, Jorge Comellas of Salisbury, Eastern Shore League, fanned 21 batters in a nine-inning game.

July 11, 1937, Outfielder Edgar Biedleman of Easton, Eastern Shore League, was knocked unconscious when a drive off the bat of Centreville's Alex Pitko caromed off the fence and struck Biedleman on the head. Pitko circled the bases for a home run.

July 25, 1937, Atley Donald of Newark, International League, was beaten by Henry Johnson of Montreal, for his first loss of the season after 14 consecutive victories.

July 26, 1937, The Baltimore-Toronto International League game at Toronto was postponed due to cold weather.

August 5, 1937, The Newport-Johnson City game in the Appalachian League came to an abrupt halt when the supply of baseballs was exhausted in the last half of the sixth inning.

August 20, 1937, Jorge Comellas of Salisbury, Eastern Shore League, suffered his first loss of the season after having won his first 20 decisions. He would finish the season with a 22-1 mark.

August 23, 1937, Newark clinched the International League pennant.

September 12, 1937, Hank Severeid of Galveston, Texas League, caught both games of a doubleheader on the last day of the season at age 46. He then retired after having caught 2,300 games in 28 seasons in Organized Ball.

September 18, 1937, Salisbury's Joe Kohlman threw his second no-hitter of the season, a 7-0 win over Centreville, giving his club the Eastern Shore League's playoff championship. Kohlman's first no-hitter had come just 16 days earlier against Easton.

October 2, 1937, Paul Richards succeeded Eddie Moore as manager of the Atlanta Crackers of the Southern Association.

November 8, 1937, At their annual meeting, Pacific Coast League officials approved the transfer of the Mission club of San Francisco to Hollywood.

December 24, 1937, John W. Kyler, 23, an outfielder with Bartlesville and Hutchinson of the Western Association during the past season, was fatally injured when he fell down a flight of rear stairs to the basement, suffering a broken neck and fractured skull, during a Christmas Eve party at the home of a friend in St. Louis, Missouri.

1938

American League
President: William Harridge

Standings	W	L	Pct.	GB	Attend.	Manager
New York Yankees.............	99	53	.651	—	970,916	Joe McCarthy
Boston Red Sox	88	61	.591	9½	646,459	Joe Cronin
Cleveland Indians	86	66	.566	13	652,006	Ossie Vitt
Detroit Tigers	84	70	.545	16	799,557	Mickey Cochrane/Del Baker
Washington Senators	75	76	.497	23½	522,694	Bucky Harris
Chicago White Sox	65	83	.439	32	338,278	Jimmy Dykes
St. Louis Browns	55	97	.362	44	130,417	Gabby Street
Philadelphia Athletics........	53	99	.349	46	385,357	Connie Mack

BA: Jimmie Foxx, Boston, .349
Runs: Hank Greenberg, Detroit, 144
Hits: Joe Vosmik, Boston, 201
RBIs: Jimmie Foxx, Boston, 175
HRs: Hank Greenberg, Detroit, 58

Wins: Red Ruffing, New York, 21
SOs: Bob Feller, Cleveland, 240
ERA: Lefty Grove, Boston, 3.08
Pct: Red Ruffing, New York, .750, 21-7

National League
President: Ford Frick

Standings	W	L	Pct.	GB	Attend.	Manager
Chicago Cubs.....................	89	63	.586	—	951,640	Charlie Grimm/Gabby Hartnett
Pittsburgh Pirates...............	86	64	.573	2	641,033	Pie Traynor
New York Giants	83	67	.553	5	799,633	Bill Terry
Cincinnati Reds..................	82	68	.547	6	706,756	Bill McKechnie
Boston Bees	77	75	.507	12	341,149	Casey Stengel
St. Louis Cardinals	71	80	.470	17½	291,418	Frank Frisch/Mike Gonzalez
Brooklyn Dodgers	69	80	.463	18½	663,087	Burleigh Grimes
Philadelphia Phillies	45	105	.300	43	166,111	Jimmie Wilson/Hans Lobert

BA: Ernie Lombardi, Cincinnati, .342
Runs: Mel Ott, New York, 116
Hits: Frank McCormick, Cincinnati, 209
RBIs: Joe Medwick, St. Louis, 122
HRs: Mel Ott, New York, 36

Wins: Bill Lee, Chicago, 22
SOs: Clay Bryant, Chicago, 135
ERA: Bill Lee, Chicago, 2.66
Pct: Bill Lee, Chicago, .710, 22-9

AA American Association
President: George Trautman

Standings	W	L	Pct.	GB	Attend.	Manager
St. Paul Saints (2)	90	61	.596	—	251,308	Babe Ganzel
Kansas City Blues (5).........	84	67	.556	6	257,913	Bill Meyer
Milwaukee Brewers (3)	81	70	.536	9	161,845	Allan Sothoron
Indianapolis Indians (8)......	80	74	.519	11½	154,819	Ray Schalk
Toledo Mud Hens (7)	79	74	.516	12	183,192	Fred Haney
Minneapolis Millers (1)......	78	74	.513	12½	181,681	Donie Bush
Columbus Red Birds (16)...	64	89	.418	27	74,024	Burt Shotton
Louisville Colonels (15)	53	100	.346	38	59,330	Bert Niehoff

Playoffs: Kansas City 4 games, Indianapolis 2; St. Paul 4 games, Milwaukee 3.
Finals: Kansas City 4 games, St. Paul 3.

BA: Ted Williams, Minneapolis, .366
Runs: Ted Williams, Minneapolis, 130
Hits: Joe Gallagher, Kansas City, 200
RBIs: Ted Williams, Minneapolis, 142

HRs: Ted Williams, Minneapolis, 43
Wins: Whitlow Wyatt, Milwaukee, 23
SOs: Whitlow Wyatt, Milwaukee, 208
ERA: Whitlow Wyatt, Milwaukee, 2.37

AA International League
President: Frank J. Shaughnessy

Standings	W	L	Pct.	GB	Attend.	Manager
Newark Bears (5)..............	104	48	.684	—	236,943	Johnny Neun
Syracuse Chiefs (12)...........	87	67	.564	18	183,050	Jim Bottomley/Dick Porter
Rochester Red Wings (16)..	80	74	.519	25	157,939	Ray Blades
Buffalo Bisons	79	74	.516	25½	191,099	Steve O'Neill
Toronto Maple Leafs	72	81	.471	32½	109,417	Dan Howley
Montreal Royals	69	84	.451	35½	166,068	Rabbit Maranville/Alex Hooks
Jersey City Giants (13)	68	85	.444	36½	315,522	Travis Jackson/Hank DeBerry
Baltimore Orioles	52	98	.347	51	105,793	Clyde "Buck" Crouse

Playoffs: Buffalo 4 games, Syracuse 0; Newark 4 games, Rochester 3.
Finals: Newark 4 games, Buffalo 1.

MVP-Ollie Carnegie, Buffalo.

BA: Buddy Rosar, Newark, .387
Runs: Charlie Keller, Newark, 149
Hits: Charlie Keller, Newark, 211
RBIs: Ollie Carnegie, Buffalo, 136

HRs: Ollie Carnegie, Buffalo, 45
Wins: Joseph Sullivan, Toronto, 18
SOs: Atley Donald, Newark, 133
ERA: Red Barrett, Syracuse, 2.34

AA Pacific Coast League
President: William C. Tuttle

Standings	W	L	Pct.	GB	Attend.	Manager
Los Angeles Angels (11)..	105	73	.590	—	188,808	Truck Hannah
Seattle Rainiers	100	75	.571	3½	309,723	Jack Lelivelt
Sacramento Solons (16)......	95	82	.537	9½	108,354	Bill Killefer
San Francisco Seals	93	85	.522	12	202,799	Lefty O'Doul
San Diego Padres	92	85	.520	12½	150,380	Frank Shellenback
Portland Beavers................	79	96	.451	24½	175,781	Bill Sweeney
Hollywood Stars	79	99	.444	26	103,008	Red Killefer
Oakland Oaks	65	113	.365	40	92,244	Dutch Zwilling

Playoffs: Sacramento 4 games, Los Angeles 1; San Francisco 4 games, Seattle 1.
Finals: Sacramento 4 games, San Francisco 1.

MVP-Fred Hutchinson, Seattle.

BA: Smead Jolley, Hollywood/Oakland, .350
Runs: Arnold "Jigger" Statz, Los Angeles, 131
Hits: Glen Russell, Los Angeles, 216
RBIs: Ted Norbert, San Francisco, 163

HRs: Ted Norbert, San Francisco, 30
Wins: Fred Hutchinson, Seattle, 25
SOs: Manuel Salvo, San Diego, 191
ERA: Byron Humphreys, San Diego, 2.33

A1 Southern Association
President: Jack Troy

Standings	W	L	Pct.	GB	Attend.	Manager
Atlanta Crackers	91	62	.595	—	231,363	Paul Richards
Nashville Volunteers (10)..	84	66	.560	5½	128,686	Chuck Dressen
New Orleans Pelicans (3) ...	79	70	.530	10	142,153	Larry Gilbert
Memphis Chickasaws	77	75	.507	13½	77,417	Billy Southworth
Little Rock Travelers (1) ...	75	76	.497	15	111,988	Tommy "Doc" Prothro
Birmingham Barons (11)....	73	79	.480	17½	129,343	Fresco Thompson
Chattanooga Lookouts (8)	66	85	.437	24	121,064	Walter Millies/Rogers Hornsby
Knoxville Smokies (15)......	59	91	.393	30½	70,429	Neil Caldwell

Playoffs: Atlanta 3 games, Memphis 2; Nashville 3 games, New Orleans 2.
Finals: Atlanta 4 games, Nashville 1, one tie.

MVP-Russell "Red" Evans, New Orleans.

BA: John Hill, Atlanta, .338
Runs: Hubert "Buddy" Bates, Memphis, 111
Hits: Paul Campbell, Little Rock, 192
RBIs: Maurice Van Robays, Knoxville, 110
HRs: Tom Hafey, Memphis, 24

Wins: Tom Sunkel, Atlanta, 21
Russell "Red" Evans, New Orleans, 21
William Crouch, Nashville, 21
SOs: Tom Sunkel, Atlanta, 178
ERA: Tom Sunkel, Atlanta, 2.33

A1 Texas League
President: J. Alvin Gardner

Standings	W	L	Pct.	GB	Attend.	Manager
Beaumont Exporters (4)......	99	57	.635	—	102,711	Al Vincent
San Antonio Missions (7)...	93	67	.581	8	136,249	Zach Taylor
Oklahoma City Indians.......	89	70	.569	11½	103,243	Jim Keesey/Jack Fitzpatrick
Tulsa Oilers	86	75	.534	15½	112,889	Bruce Connatser
Houston Buffaloes (16)	74	84	.468	26	98,889	Cliff Watwood
Shreveport Sports	69	90	.434	31½	132,237	Claude Jonnard/Hub Northen
Dallas Steers (2).................	65	94	.409	35½	98,780	Ray Brubaker/Jim Levey
Ft. Worth Cats...................	61	99	.381	40	64,631	Homer Peel/Neil Coombs/ Jackie Reid

Playoffs: Beaumont 3 games, Tulsa 0; San Antonio 3 games, Oklahoma City 0.
Finals: Beaumont 4 games, San Antonio 3, one tie.

MVP-Paul "Dizzy" Trout, Beaumont.

BA: Harlan Pool, Dallas, .330
Runs: Frank Secory, Beaumont, 100
Sig Gryska, San Antonio, 100
Hits: Morris Jones, Tulsa, 189
RBIs: Stanley Schino, Tulsa, 118

HRs: Stanley Schino, Tulsa, 25
Wins: Max Thomas, Tulsa, 23
SOs: Mort Cooper, Houston, 201
ERA: Max Thomas, Tulsa, 1.98

A Eastern League
President: Thomas H. Richardson

Standings	W	L	Pct.	GB	Attend.	Manager
Binghamton Triplets (5)	84	51	.622	—	114,791	Bruno Betzel
Hazleton Red Sox (1)	81	58	.583	5	45,438	George "Specs" Toporcer
Elmira Pioneers (10)...........	71	65	.522	13½	57,367	Clyde Sukeforth
Hartford Laurels (9)............	67	67	.500	16½	60,442	Eddie Onslow
Albany Senators (12)...........	68	70	.493	17½	179,189	Bill McCorry
Williamsport Grays (6).......	65	74	.468	21	95,317	Marty McManus

*Won first-half   **Won second-half   ***Won both halves
Numbers after nicknames indicate farm system.
Affiliation listed at end of year.

299

Trenton Senators (8) .... 62 77 .446 24   46,096   Spencer Abbott
Wilkes-Barre Barons .... 51 87 .370 34½   119,760   Mike McNally

Playoffs: Hazleton 3 games, Hartford 0; Elmira 3 games, Binghamton 2.
Finals: Elmira 4 games, Hazleton 1.

All-Star Team: 1B-Ed Levy, Binghamton; **2B**-Fred Vaughn, Binghamton; **3B**-Pete Suder, Binghamton; **SS**-Len Kahny, Hazleton; **OF**-Charles Bauder, Hazleton; Tommy Holmes, Binghamton; Archie Allen, Binghamton; **C**-Arthur DePhillips, Binghamton; **Util**-Fred Collins, Binghamton; **P**-Lew Krausse, Elmira; John Day, Wilkes-Barre; **Manager**-George "Specs" Toporcer, Hazleton.

BA: Tommy Holmes, Binghamton, .368
Runs: John Barrett, Hazleton, 111
Hits: Tommy Holmes, Binghamton, 200
RBIs: Larry Bettencourt, Trenton/ Wilkes-Barre, 118

HRs: Bill Nicholson, Williamsport, 22
Wins: Marvin Ulrich, Hazleton, 21
SOs: Frank Dasso, Hazleton, 179
ERA: George Barley, Binghamton, 2.24

B Piedmont League
President: Ralph Daughton

Standings	W	L	Pct.	GB	Manager
Norfolk Tars (5)	84	52	.618	—	Ray White
Charlotte Hornets (8)	84	53	.613	½	Calvin Griffith
Rocky Mount Red Sox (1)..	70	64	.522	13	Herb Brett
Portsmouth Cubs (11).........	69	67	.507	15	Dick Luckey
Richmond Colts (13)	66	72	.478	19	Lance Richbourg
Durham Bulls (12).............	64	71	.474	20½	Bill Hughes
Asheville Tourists (16).......	63	75	.457	22	Harold Anderson
Winston-Salem Twins (10).	46	92	.333	39	Walt VanGrofski/Joe Prerost

Total Attendance: 700,000.

Playoffs: Charlotte 3 games, Portsmouth 2; Rocky Mount 3 games, Norfolk 1.
Finals: Charlotte 4 games, Rocky Mount 3.

All-Star Team: 1B-Norman Young, Richmond; **2B**-Jerry Priddy, Norfolk; **3B**-Harry Morris, Durham; **SS**-Phil Rizzuto, Norfolk; **OF**-Roberto Estalella, Charlotte; Art Metheny, Norfolk; Antonio Castano, Asheville; **C**-Jake Early, Charlotte; **Util**-Gil Torres, Charlotte; **P**-Henry Gornicki, Asheville; William Yocke, Norfolk; **Manager**-Ray White, Norfolk.

BA: Roberto Estalella, Charlotte, .378
Runs: Roberto Estalella, Charlotte, 134
Hits: Antonio Castano, Asheville, 180
RBIs: Roberto Estalella, Charlotte, 123
HRs: Roberto Estalella, Charlotte, 38

Wins: Don Hendrickson, Norfolk, 21
    Newton Jacobs, Charlotte, 21
SOs: Manuel Norris, Winston-Salem, 222
ERA: Henry Gornicki, Asheville, 2.57

B South Atlantic League
President: Dr. E.M. Wilder

Standings	W	L	Pct.	GB	Manager
Savannah Indians (15)	81	60	.574	—	Martin "Chick" Autry
Macon Peaches	81	61	.570	½	Milt Stock
Columbia Reds (12)...........	74	66	.529	6½	John Burnett
Augusta Tigers (5).............	74	66	.529	6½	Sam Agnew
Jacksonville Tars	70	69	.504	10	Bob Smith/Roy Walker
Columbus Red Birds (16)...	70	70	.500	10½	George Payne
Spartanburg Spartans (3)	54	82	.397	24½	Eddie Moore/Chick Galloway
Greenville Spinners	53	83	.390	25½	Jiggs Donohue

Attendance: Savannah, 196,136.

Playoffs: Columbia defeated Augusta in a one game playoff for third place. Savannah 4 games, Columbia 3; Macon 4 games, Augusta 2.
Finals: Macon 4 games, Savannah 3.

All-Star Team: 1B-William Prout, Columbus; **2B**-Charles Glock, Columbia; **3B**-Carl Fairly, Macon; **SS**-Claude Corbitt, Augusta; **OF**-Bob Elliott, Savannah; John Rucker, Macon; Walt Schuerbaum, Columbus; **C**-Joe Cusick, Columbus; **Util**-Roy Walker, Jacksonville; **P**-Junior Thompson, Columbia; John "Pretzels" Pezzullo, Savannah; **Manager**-Milt Stock, Macon.

BA: Doug Dean, Savannah/Greenville, .385
Runs: Charles Glock, Columbia, 110
Hits: William Prout, Columbus, 196
RBIs: William Prout, Columbus, 110
HRs: Dan Pavlovic, Augusta/Macon/ Spartanburg/Savannah, 17

Wins: John "Pretzels" Pezzullo, Savannah, 26
SOs: John "Pretzels" Pezzullo, Savannah, 218
ERA: Leo Twardy, Augusta, 1.96
Pct: John "Pretzels" Pezzullo, Savannah, .743, 26-9

B Southeastern League
President: Stuart X. Stephenson

Standings	W	L	Pct.	GB	Manager
Pensacola Fliers (10)	95	53	.642	—	Wally Dashiell
Selma Cloverleafs..............	83	62	.572	10½	Ivy Griffin
Jackson Senators (5)	75	68	.524	17½	Max Rosenfeld
Mobile Shippers (16).........	75	73	.507	20	Marty Purtell
Meridian Scrappers (7).......	69	78	.469	25½	Harry Whitehouse
Gadsden Pilots	69	80	.463	26½	Bill Morrell
Anniston Rams (2).............	62	86	.419	33	Lena Styles/Ray Brubaker

Montgomery Bombers (14)... 60 88 .405 35   Bud Connolly
Playoffs: Mobile 4 games, Pensacola 2; Selma 4 games, Jackson 3.
Finals: Mobile 4 games, Selma 3.

All-Star Team: 1B-Joe Dotlich, Selma; **2B**-Clarence Blair, Jackson; **3B**-Phil Seghi, Pensacola; **SS**-Don Blanchard, Selma; **OF**-David Smith, Mobile; Henry "Prince" Oana, Jackson; Art Luce, Selma; **C**-Aubrey Epps, Jackson; **Util**-Rudy Laskowski, Pensacola; **P**-Marcus Beddington, Jackson; Charlie Gassaway, Pensacola; **Manager**-Marty Purtell, Mobile.

BA: Phil Seghi, Pensacola, .341
Runs: Art Luce, Selma, 119
Hits: Harry Whitehouse, Meridian, 178
RBIs: Henry "Prince" Oana, Jackson, 116

HRs: Henry "Prince" Oana, Jackson, 26
Wins: Marcus Beddington, Jackson, 24
SOs: John Burrows, Selma, 187
ERA: Julian Tubb, Selma, 1.96

B Three-I League
President: Tom Fairweather

Standings	W	L	Pct.	GB	Manager
Evansville Bees (9)	77	47	.621	—	Bob Coleman
Decatur Commodores (16) .	68	58	.540	10	Anthony Kaufman
Moline Plowboys (11)	67	59	.532	11	Michael Gazella
Springfield Browns (7)	63	60	.512	13½	Walter Holke
Waterloo Red Hawks (12)...	59	65	.476	18	Lennie Backer
Cedar Rapids Raiders (16)...	56	63	.471	18½	Clarence "Cap" Crossley
Bloomington Bloomers (3).	56	65	.463	19½	Robert O'Farrell
Clinton Owls (10)	46	75	.380	29½	Oliver Marquardt

Attendance: Evansville, 95,000; Springfield, 62,000.

Playoffs: Decatur 3 games, Springfield 2; Moline 3 games, Evansville 1.
Finals: Decatur 4 games, Moline 1.

All-Star Team: 1B-Leo Marion, Waterloo; **2B**-Einar Sorenson, Waterloo; **3B**-Frank Piet, Springfield; **SS**-Ed Lake, Decatur; **OF**-Lou Novikoff, Moline; Norman Peterson, Decatur; Ralph Hodgin, Evansville; **C**-Salvador Hernandez, Bloomington; **Util**-Albert Unser, Decatur; **P**-Floyd Giebell, Evansville; Emil Bildilli, Springfield; **Manager**-Bob Coleman, Evansville.

BA: Lou Novikoff, Moline, .367
Runs: Ed Lake, Decatur, 117
Hits: Lou Novikoff, Moline, 186
RBIs: Lou Novikoff, Moline, 114
HRs: Frank Piet, Springfield, 25

Wins: Floyd Giebell, Evansville, 18
    Emil Bildilli, Springfield, 18
SOs: Emil Bildilli, Springfield, 185
ERA: Floyd Giebell, Evansville, 1.98

B Western International League
President: F.H. Knickerbocker

Standings	W	L	Pct.	GB	Manager
Yakima Pippins..................	77	55	.583	—	Raymond Jacobs
Bellingham Chinooks	68	65	.511	9½	Ken Penner
Wenatchee Chiefs (5)	66	67	.496	11½	Forrest Wright
Vancouver Maple Leafs......	65	68	.489	12½	John Kerr
Spokane Hawks	62	72	.463	16	Bernie DeViveiros
Tacoma Tigers	62	73	.459	16½	Hack Wilson/Hal Rhyne

Attendance: Spokane, 200,000.

Playoffs: Yakima 3 games, Wenatchee 1; Bellingham 3 games, Vancouver 1.
Finals: Bellingham 4 games, Yakima 3.

All-Star Team: 1B-Frank Milani, Wenatchee; **2B**-Bobby Baer, Wenatchee; **3B**-Alex McDonald, Bellingham; **SS**-William Lyman, Yakima; **OF**-Hal Lee, Wenatchee; Ralph Mountain, Vancouver; David Goodman, Tacoma; **C**-Ted Clawitter, Spokane; **Util**-Charles Petersen, Yakima; **P**-Bill Fleming, Bellingham; Oscar Miller, Yakima; **Manager**-Raymond Jacobs, Yakima.

BA: David Goodman, Tacoma, .337
Runs: William Lyman, Yakima, 97
Hits: David Goodman, Tacoma, 173
RBIs: Wayne McCue, Wenatchee/ Vancouver, 85

HRs: James Tyack, Bellingham, 15
Wins: Bill Fleming, Bellingham, 20
SOs: Floyd Isekite, Tacoma, 248
ERA: Bill Fleming, Bellingham, 1.79

C Canadian-American League
President: Rev. Harold J. Martin

Standings	W	L	Pct.	GB	Attend.	Manager
Amsterdam Rugmakers (16).	79	40	.664	—	25,672	Pepper Martin
Cornwall Bisons	74	47	.612	6	23,687	Steve Yerkes
Ogdensburg Colts	66	52	.559	12½	27,016	Knotty Lee
Gloversville-Johnstown Glovers.....................	63	62	.504	19	29,178	John Roser
Rome Colonels	61	63	.492	20½	51,363	Bill Buckley
Oswego Netherlands (3)	54	69	.439	27	16,522	Riley Parker
Auburn Bouleys	49	68	.419	29	16,178	John Cimpi
Ottawa Braves...................	38	83	.314	42	24,827	George Army

Playoffs: Amsterdam 4 games, Gloversville-Johnstown 0; Cornwall 4 games, Ogdensburg 0.
Finals: Cornwall 2 games, Amsterdam 1, one tie (abandoned September 21 due to extended weather delay).

All-Star Team: 1B-Harold Tyler, Cornwall; **2B**-John Zulberti, Ogdensburg; **3B**-Bill Homan, Auburn; **SS**-John Stonebreaker, Amsterdam; **OF**-Ray Klinkert, Amsterdam; William Powley, Ottawa; Barney Hearn, Cornwall; **C**-Emile Graff, Cornwall; **Util**-John Grilli, Gloversville-Johnstown; **P**-John Tulacz, Cornwall; Albert "Duke" Farrington, Amsterdam; **Manager**-Steve Yerkes, Cornwall.

BA: Bill Homan, Auburn, .389   **HRs:** Tony Gridaitis, Ogdensburg, 34
Runs: Tony Gridaitis, Ogdensburg, 118   **Wins:** John Dickinson, Cornwall, 21
Hits: Alfred Lehman, Auburn/Cornwall, 173   **SOs:** Mike Naymick, Oswego, 230
RBIs: Tony Gridaitis, Ogdensburg, 130   **ERA:** John Tulacz, Cornwall, 2.74

C Cotton States League
Presidents: J. Walter Morris/F.F. Bustany

Standings	W	L	Pct.	GB	Manager
Greenville Bucks	88	50	.638	—	Jimmy Powell
Helena Seaporters (11)	80	57	.584	7½	Riggs Stephenson
Monroe White Sox	78	60	.565	10	Luke Harvel/Doug Taitt
El Dorado Lions (12)	74	61	.548	12½	Frank O'Rourke
Clarksdale Red Sox (1)	66	71	.482	21½	Nemo Leibold
Pine Bluff Judges (16)	60	73	.451	25½	LeRoy "Cowboy" Jones
Greenwood Dodgers (10)	55	83	.399	33	Elmer Yoter
Hot Springs Bathers (11)	45	91	.331	42	Spike Hunter

Playoffs: Monroe 3 games, Helena 1; Greenville 3 games, El Dorado 1.
Finals: Monroe 4 games, Greenville 2.

All-Star Team: 1B-Kerby Farrell, Greenville; **2B**-Frank Hackney, Monroe; **3B**-Elmer Yoter, Greenwood; **SS**-Bob Cummings, Greenville; **OF**-Paul Bruno, Greenville; Buford Rhea, Monroe; Curtis Sutherlin, Helena; **C**-Orace Powers, El Dorado; **Util**-Foy Harper, El Dorado; **P**-Willard Vandenburg, Helena; Chick Galeria, Greenville; **Manager**-Frank O'Rourke, El Dorado.

BA: Orace Powers, El Dorado, .345   **SBs:** Buford Rhea, Monroe, 79
Runs: Rudy Tone, El Dorado, 139   **Wins:** Chuck Hawley, El Dorado, 22
Hits: Kerby Farrell, Greenville, 182   **SOs:** Chuck Hawley, El Dorado, 174
RBIs: Orace Powers, El Dorado, 111   **ERA:** Tom Perry, Monroe, 1.71
HRs: Jay Kirke, Jr., Pine Bluff, 18   **Pct:** Tom Perry, Monroe, .895, 17-2

C East Texas League
President: C.P. Mosley

Standings	W	L	Pct.	GB	Manager
Marshall Tigers	84	55	.604	—	Guy Sturdy/Willard Coker/Abe Miller
Texarkana Liners	80	60	.571	4½	Sam Gray
Henderson Oilers	75	65	.536	9½	Ed Hall
Tyler Trojans	72	66	.522	11½	Doug Taitt/Fred Browning/Red Rollings
Kilgore Rangers	64	74	.464	19½	Jimmy Dalrymple
Longview Cannibals (2)	63	75	.457	20½	Harold Funk
Palestine Pals (7)	60	79	.432	24	Archie "Abe" Miller/Neil Andrews/John Kosey
Jacksonville Jax (16)	58	82	.414	26½	Tony Robello

Playoffs: Tyler 4 games, Marshall 1; Henderson 4 games, Texarkana 3.
Finals: Tyler 4 games, Henderson 3.

All-Star Team: 1B-Tony Robello, Jacksonville; **2B**-Carl McNabb, Tyler; **3B**-Joe Rezotko, Marshall; **SS**-Leslie Floyd, Tyler; **OF**-Gordon Houston, Texarkana; Hal Simpson, Marshall; Ed Hall, Henderson; **C**-Cal Lowman, Marshall; **Util**-Vance Randolph, Kilgore; **P**-Jack Van Orsdol, Marshall; Eugene Davis, Texarkana; **Manager**-Guy Sturdy, Marshall.

BA: Gordon Houston, Texarkana, .384   **HRs:** Tony Robello, Jacksonville, 38
Runs: Gabby Lusk, Texarkana, 152   **Wins:** Jack Van Orsdol, Marshall, 21
Hits: Ed Hall, Henderson, 196   **SOs:** Eugene Davis, Texarkana, 231
RBIs: Tony Robello, Jacksonville, 146   **ERA:** Fred Isert, Kilgore, 2.30

C Middle Atlantic League
President: Elmer M. Daily

Standings	W	L	Pct.	GB	Manager
Portsmouth Red Birds (16)	79	50	.612	—	Benny Borgmann
Canton Terriers (1)	79	51	.608	½	Floyd Patterson
Springfield Indians (3)	71	59	.546	8½	Earl Wolgamot
Akron Yankees (5)	66	62	.516	12½	Horace "Pip" Koehler
Charleston Senators (4)	59	67	.468	18½	Paul O'Malley
Dayton Ducks (10)	58	72	.446	21½	Red Rollings/Howard "Ducky" Holmes/Jim Lindsey
Erie Sailors (9)	52	75	.409	26	Jocko Munch
Johnstown Johnnies (7)	50	78	.391	28½	Bobby Goff

Playoffs: Akron 3 games, Canton 0; Portsmouth 3 games, Springfield 1.
Finals: Portsmouth 4 games, Akron 3.

All-Star Team: 1B-Harry Ashworth, Akron; **2B**-Harry Stoeber, Springfield; **3B**-Whitey Kurowski, Portsmouth; **SS**-Woodrow Williams, Dayton; **OF**-Frank Silvanic, Akron; Charles Workman, Springfield; George Staller, Dayton; **C**-Herbert White, Akron; **Util**-Horace "Pip" Koehler, Akron; **P**-Tex Hughson, Canton; John Andrew Rager, Dayton; **Manager**-Floyd Patterson, Canton.

BA: Whitey Kurowski, Portsmouth, .386   **Wins:** Tex Hughson, Canton, 22
Runs: Whitey Kurowski, Portsmouth, 133   **SOs:** Vearal Puckett, Canton, 188
Hits: Whitey Kurowski, Portsmouth, 209   Jep Jefferson, Johnstown, 188
RBIs: Chet Wieczorek, Portsmouth, 130   **ERA:** James Morris, Charleston, 2.75
HRs: Frank Silvanic, Akron, 35

C Western Association
President: Tom Fairweather

Standings	W	L	Pct.	GB	Attend.	Manager
Ponca City Angels (11)	84	54	.609	—		Goldie Holt
Springfield Cardinals (16)	79	56	.585	3½	62,647	Clay Hopper
Ft. Smith Giants (13)	74	65	.532	10½	83,578	Frank Brazill
Hutchinson Larks (15)	70	67	.511	13½		Hugh McMullen
Muskogee Reds (12)	71	68	.511	13½		Ben Tincup
Joplin Miners (5)	63	74	.460	20½		Ted Meyer
Bartlesville Chiefs	61	78	.439	23½		Cobe Jones/Mickey Duggan
Salina Millers	47	87	.351	35	41,000	Harry Sutter/Jack Calvey

Total Attendance: 350,104.

Playoffs: Ponca City 3 games, Ft. Smith 1; Hutchinson 3 games, Springfield 2.
Finals: Ponca City 4 games, Hutchinson 1.

All-Star Team: 1B-John "Zeke" Clement, Hutchinson; **2B**-Lou Stringer, Ponca City; **3B**-Glen Stewart, Ft. Smith; **SS**-Frank Crespi, Springfield; **OF**-John "Doc" Graves, Salina; Lynn South, Springfield; Harry Schmiel, Springfield; **C**-John Toncoff, Ft. Smith; **Util**-Floyd Perryman, Ft. Smith; **P**-Frank Sokol, Hutchinson; Louis Stefurak, Muskogee; **Manager**-Goldie Holt, Ponca City.

BA: Harry Schmiel, Springfield, .353   **HRs:** Russ Derry, Joplin, 24
Runs: Al White, Bartlesville, 126   **Wins:** Jake Drake, Springfield, 21
     Lou Stringer, Ponca City, 126   **SOs:** Roland Van Slate, Springfield, 220
Hits: Glen Stewart, Ft. Smith, 182   **ERA:** Joe Luber, Ft. Smith, 2.06
RBIs: Clarence Springer, Bartlesville, 121

D Alabama-Florida League
President: George M. Grant

Standings	W	L	Pct.	GB	Manager
Dothan Browns	77	53	.592	—	Ernie Wingard
Troy Trojans	71	59	.546	6	Charley Hilcher
Andalusia Bulldogs	70	60	.538	7	Yam Yaryan
Union Springs Redbirds	70	60	.538	7	Red Lucas
Panama City Pelicans	55	75	.423	22	Rudy Laskowski
Evergreen Greenies	47	83	.362	30	Hardy Rice

Playoffs: Andalusia was awarded third place for playoff pairings by a coin toss. Andalusia 2 games, Dothan 2; Troy 3 games, Union Springs 1. During the semi-final playoff, Dothan refused to flip a coin to decide the location of the deciding game; Andalusia was awarded with advancement to the finals.
Finals: Troy 4 games, Andalusia 2.

All-Star Team: 1B-E.B. Langston, Andalusia; **2B**-Harvey Johnson, Panama City; **3B**-Melvin Serafine, Union Springs; **SS**-Carmen Soltis, Evergreen/Andalusia; **OF**-Robert Jones, Union Springs; Howard Gorman, Union Springs; Steve Summerhill, Union Springs; **C**-George Waldron, Union Springs; **Util**-Oscar Moseley, Andalusia; **P**-Virgil Trucks, Andalusia; Thomas Adams, Troy; **Manager**-Ernie Wingard, Dothan.

BA: Steve Summerhill, Union Springs, .362   **HRs:** Gilbert Leathergood, Troy, 14
Runs: Bill Hodgkins, Troy, 112   **Wins:** Virgil Trucks, Andalusia, 25
Hits: Steve Summerhill, Union Springs, 187   **SOs:** Virgil Trucks, Andalusia, 418
RBIs: Steve Summerhill, Union Springs, 108   **ERA:** Virgil Trucks, Andalusia, 1.25

D Appalachian League
President: John Bernard

Standings	W	L	Pct.	GB	Manager
Elizabethton Red Sox (1)	65	36	.644	—	Hobe Brummitt
Kingsport Cherokees	63	44	.589	5	Jerry Witner
Greeneville Burley Cubs (11)	60	45	.571	7	Sam Alexander
Pennington Gap Lee Bears	46	60	.434	21½	Oliver Goldsmith/Lynn Lunsford
Newport Canners	42	66	.389	26½	Frosty Holt/Reese Harris
Johnson City Soldiers (16)	42	67	.385	27	Joe Sims/Phil Clark

Playoffs: Greeneville 2 games, Elizabethton 0; Kingsport 2 games, Pennington Gap 0.
Finals: Greeneville 3 games, Kingsport 1.

All-Star Team: 1B-Stan Lujack, Kingsport; **2B**-Burton Hodge, Elizabethton; **3B**-Ken Eck, Kingsport; **SS**-Clovis White, Elizabethton; **OF**-Erastus Grigg, Elizabethton; Lew Flick, Elizabethton; Howard Cantrell, Elizabethton/Greeneville; **C**-Tom Esterbrook, Elizabethton; **Util**-Anthony Carr, Pennington Gap; **P**-Clarence Hefflefinger, Kingsport; Lynn Lunsford, Pennington Gap; **Manager**-Jerry Witner, Kingsport.

BA: Erastus Grigg, Elizabethton, .351
Runs: Clovis White, Elizabethton, 67
Hits: Lew Flick, Elizabethton, 128
RBIs: Clovis White, Elizabethton, 68

HRs: Erastus Grigg, Elizabethton, 6
Clovis White, Elizabethton, 6
John Hobson, Johnson City, 6
Wins: Rudy Parsons, Elizabethton, 16
SOs: Rudy Parsons, Elizabethton, 138
Pct: Rudy Parsons, Elizabethton, .842, 16-3

D Arizona-Texas League
President: Dr. R.E. Soners

Standings	W	L	Pct.	GB	Manager
Bisbee Bees**	72	58	.554	—	Charlie Moglia
El Paso Texans*	68	64	.515	5	Jimmy Zinn
Albuquerque Cardinals	67	65	.508	6	Bill DeLancey
Tucson Cowboys	55	75	.423	17	Harry Krause

Attendance: Albuquerque, 60,000.

Playoff: El Paso 4 games, Bisbee 3.

All-Star Team: 1B-Ray Alves, Tucson; 2B-Bill Creager, Bisbee; 3B-William Reyes, Albuquerque; SS-Bobby Sturgeon, Albuquerque; OF-Mike Simon, Tucson; Eddie Goddard, El Paso; Paul Schiffner, Bisbee; C-Roy Partee, Bisbee; Util-John Burleson, Albuquerque/Tucson; P-Jesse Flores, Bisbee; Jack Hawkins, El Paso; Manager-Jimmy Zinn, El Paso.

BA: Mike Simon, Tucson, .367
Runs: Dick Warfield, Bisbee, 120
Ed Morris, Albuquerque, 120
Hits: Mike Simon, Tucson, 195
RBIs: Mike Simon, Tucson, 121

HRs: Bill Creager, Bisbee, 20
Wins: Jesse Flores, Bisbee, 24
Walter Stewart, El Paso, 24
SOs: Walter Stewart, El Paso, 270
ERA: Jesse Flores, Bisbee, 2.37

D Arkansas-Missouri League
President: Bernal Seamster

Standings	W	L	Pct.	GB	Manager
Neosho Yankees (5)	73	42	.635	—	Denny Burns
Carthage Pirates (15)	69	49	.585	5½	Adolph Arlitt
Fayetteville Angels	66	53	.555	9	Cliff "Bud" Knox
Rogers Reds (12)	63	54	.538	11	Lester "Pat" Patterson
Monett Red Birds (16)	44	74	.373	30½	Heinie Mueller
Siloam Springs Travelers	36	79	.331	37	Vincent "Moon" Mullen

Attendance: Carthage, 35,000.

Playoffs: Neosho 3 games, Rogers 0; Carthage 3 games, Fayetteville 2.
Finals: Carthage 4 games, Neosho 1.

All-Star Team: 1B-Cyril Moran, Rogers; 2B-Steve Luby, Neosho; 3B-Ray Lawrence, Carthage; SS-Florian Zielinski, Neosho; OF-Frank DaLuga, Carthage; Earl Naylor, Fayetteville; Ray Kommy, Neosho; C-Dan Radakovich, Neosho; Util-Cliff "Bud" Knox, Fayetteville; P-Bill Gill, Neosho; Leon Skidgel, Carthage; Manager-Denny Burns, Neosho.

BA: Cyril Moran, Rogers, .392
Runs: Steve Luby, Neosho, 127
Hits: Marv Wolverton, Rogers, 160
RBIs: Adolph Arlitt, Carthage, 132
HRs: Cyril Moran, Rogers, 22

SBs: Steve Luby, Neosho, 76
Wins: Bill Gill, Neosho, 20
SOs: Bill Gill, Neosho, 266
ERA: Bill Gill, Neosho, 2.80

D Bi-State League
President: Joseph Garrett

Standings	W	L	Pct.	GB	Manager
Bassett Furniture Makers	76	40	.655	—	Walter Novak
Mayodan Millers	73	46	.613	4½	Harry Lee Daughtry
Reidsville Luckies	71	48	.597	6½	Jim Poole
Danville Leafs	63	55	.534	14	Red Barnes
Martinsville Manufacturers	61	56	.521	15½	Andy Anderson
Mt. Airy Graniteers	49	69	.415	28	Dick Goldberg
South Boston-Halifax Wrappers	43	77	.358	35	Jim Calleran
Leaksville-Spray-Draper Triplets	37	82	.311	40½	Joe Feori

Playoffs: Bassett 3 games, Reidsville 2; Danville 3 games, Mayodan 0.
Finals: Bassett 4 games, Danville 2.

All-Star Team: 1B-Arnold Anderson, Martinsville; 2B-Ben Zentara, Bassett; 3B-Harry Lee Daughtry, Mayodan; SS-Ed Pelligrini, Danville; OF-Ray Scantling, Reidsville; Cecil "Zip" Payne, Mayodan; Eddie Weston, Mayodan; C-Frank Warren, Mt. Airy; Util-John Cortazzo, Leaksville-Spray-Draper; P-Wes Livengood, Bassett; Robert Hampton, Danville; Manager-Walter Novak, Bassett.

BA: Americo Rossomando, Bassett, .390
Runs: Ray Scantling, Reidsville, 130
Hits: Harry Lee Daughtry, Mayodan, 174
RBIs: Ray Scantling, Reidsville, 147
HRs: Ray Scantling, Reidsville, 33
Wins: Wes Livengood, Bassett, 21
SOs: Ramon Voight, Reidsville, 200
ERA: Wes Livengood, Bassett, 3.06

D Cape Breton Colliery League
President: A.D. Campbell

Standings	W	L	Pct.	GB	Manager
Glace Bay Miners	30	21	.588	—	Del Bissonette
Sydney Steel Citians	27	25	.519	3½	Guido Panciera
New Waterford Dodgers	28	26	.518	3½	Nick Morris
Sydney Mines Ramblers	25	27	.480	5½	Fred Loftus
Dominion Hawks#	4	15	.211	NA	Fred Maguire

#Dominion disbanded July 10.

Playoff: New Waterford 2, Sydney 0.
Finals: Glace Bay 4 games, New Waterford 1.

BA: Ralph Bellrose, Glace Bay, .328
Runs: Gerard Kiley, New Waterford, 41
Hits: Gerard Kiley, New Waterford, 63
RBIs: Lester Crabb, Glace Bay, 41
HRs: Lester Crabb, Glace Bay, 6

Wins: Merle Settlemire, Sydney, 13
SOs: Roy Moore, Glace Bay, 107
Pct: Herb Hammerstrom, Sydney Mines, .733, 11-4

D Coastal Plain League
President: J. Bruce Eure

Standings	W	L	Pct.	GB	Manager
New Bern Bears	63	49	.563	—	Doc Smith
Tarboro Serpents	60	47	.561	½	Fred "Snake" Henry
Snow Hill Billies	61	49	.555	1	D.C. "Peahead" Walker
Kinston Eagles	60	50	.545	2	Tommy West
Williamston Martins	56	56	.500	7	Art Hauger
Goldsboro Goldbugs	47	65	.420	16	Bill Roper/Tex "Mule" Shirley
Greenville Greenies	45	68	.398	18½	Alfred "Monk" Joyner/Rube Wilson
Ayden Aces	38	76	.333	26	Frank Sidle/Bill Herring/Jim Tatum/Frank Rogers

Official standings are unequal as Ayden, Goldsboro, Greenville, and Williamston were assigned 41-38 win-loss records on August 3. There were many forfeits due to the constant use of ineligible players. The SABR Minor League Committee opted for accepting the forfeits and standings through July 27 but not the arbitrary assignment of 41-38 records on August 3.

Playoffs: Kinston was awarded third place over Snow Hill for playoff purposes by a coin toss. New Bern 4 games, Kinston 0; Snow Hill 4 games, Tarboro 2.
Finals: New Bern 4 games, Snow Hill 0.

All-Star Team: 1B-Benny Roth, New Bern; 2B-Frank Ware (Worznak), Tarboro; 3B-Bill Harper, New Bern; SS-Howard Earp, Williamston; OF-Clarence Campbell, Tarboro; John Wyrostek, Kinston; Worlise Knowles, New Bern; C-Jesse Overton, Goldsboro; Util-Sid Stringfellow, Kinston; P-Bill Herring, Ayden; Don King, Greenville; Manager-Fred "Snake" Henry, Tarboro.

BA: Phil Morris, Ayden, .377
Runs: Alfred Anderson, New Bern, 101
Hits: John Wyrostek, Kinston, 149
RBIs: Bill Harper, New Bern, 84
HRs: Les Burge, New Bern, 22
Wins: Bernard Mooney, Tarboro, 19
SOs: Cliff Wentz, Kinston, 179
ERA: Ed Hurley, Kinston, .750, 15-5

D Eastern Shore League
President: Harry S. Russell

Standings	W	L	Pct.	GB	Manager
Salisbury Indians (8)	65	47	.580	—	Jake Flowers
Cambridge Cardinals (16)	61	51	.545	4	Joe Davis
Milford Giants (13)	60	52	.536	5	Val Picinich
Dover Orioles	58	54	.518	7	Wes Kingdon/Walter Millies
Federalsburg Athletics (6)	56	56	.500	9	Charley Moss
Easton Cubs (7)	55	56	.495	9½	George Jacobs
Centreville Colts (14)	51	60	.459	13½	Joe O'Rourke
Pocomoke City Red Sox	41	71	.366	24	Joe Boley/Wes Kingdon

Playoffs: Salisbury 2 games, Milford 0; Cambridge 2 games, Dover 0.
Finals: Salisbury 3 games, Cambridge 1.

All-Star Team: 1B-Irv Kolberg, Federalsburg; 2B-Edgar Leip, Salisbury; 3B-Henry Schluter, Pocomoke City; SS-Danny Murtaugh, Cambridge; OF-Charles Quimby, Salisbury; Jim Conlan, Salisbury; George LeGates, Dover; C-Walter Millies, Dover; Util-Alex Monchak, Dover; P-Joseph Davis, Cambridge; John Bassler, Salisbury; Manager-Jake Flowers, Salisbury.

BA: Sid Gordon, Milford, .352
Runs: George Reisinger, Dover, 110
Hits: Sid Gordon, Milford, 145
RBIs: Jim Conlan, Salisbury, 99
HRs: Bill Phillips, Federalsburg, 31
Wins: Joseph Davis, Cambridge, 17
John Bassler, Salisbury, 17
SOs: Bill Yarewick, Milford, 207
ERA: Joseph Davis, Cambridge, 2.02

D Evangeline League
President: Frank F. Boustany

Standings	W	L	Pct.	GB	Manager
Lake Charles Skippers	78	58	.574	—	Joe Bratcher
Abbeville Athletics	76	61	.555	2½	Mike Cvengros
Alexandria Aces	72	60	.545	4	Art Phelan
Rayne Rice Birds (2)	74	62	.544	4	John Fitzpatrick

Standings	W	L	Pct.	GB	Manager
Lafayette White Sox (7)	69	69	.500	10	Frank Oceak
Opelousas Indians	64	67	.489	11½	Harry Strohm
New Iberia Cardinals (16)	57	72	.442	17½	Harrison Wickel
Jeanerette Blues	45	86	.344	30½	Lee Head

Playoffs: Abbeville 4 games, Alexandria 3; Lake Charles 4 games, Rayne 1.
Finals: Lake Charles 4 games, Abbeville 3.

All-Star Team: 1B-Joe Yourkovich, Rayne; **2B**-John Zapor, Alexandria; **3B**-Robert Patrick, Alexandria; **SS**-Dick Korte, Alexandria; **OF**-Chris Flanagan, Abbeville; William Black, Lake Charles; Danny Litwhiler, Alexandria; **C**-James Lawrence, Lake Charles; **Util**-Mason Bugg, Alexandria; **P**-Donald Pulford, Abbeville; Leon Scherer, Lake Charles; **Manager**-Art Phelan, Alexandria.

BA: Chris Flanagan, Abbeville, .352
Runs: Dick Korte, Alexandria, 114
Hits: Chris Flanagan, Abbeville, 178
RBIs: Carl Barnhart, Lafayette, 109
HRs: Robert Hood, Lake Charles, 18
Wins: Nathan Love, Abbeville, 22
SOs: Donald Pulford, Abbeville, 204
ERA: Garth Mann, Rayne, 2.09

D Florida State League
President: Henry Gray

Standings	W	L	Pct.	GB	Manager
Leesburg Gondoliers	87	52	.626	—	Nelson Leach
Gainesville G-Men (3)	86	54	.615	1½	Don McShane
Orlando Senators	73	66	.525	14	Bucky Buscher/Harold Conn/John Ganzel
Daytona Beach Islanders (16)	72	67	.518	15	Jimmy Sanders/Harrison Wickel
St. Augustine Saints	70	70	.500	17½	Lyle Judy
Palatka Azaleas	63	76	.454	24	George Andrews/Herbert Thomas
DeLand Reds (2)	54	86	.385	33½	Harold Chapman
Sanford Lookouts (8)	53	87	.378	34½	Guy Lacy/Bill Rodgers

Playoffs: Gainesville 3 games, Orlando 1; Leesburg 3 games, Daytona Beach 2.
Finals: Gainesville 4 games, Leesburg 2.

All-Star Team: 1B-Walt McMullen, Gainesville; **2B**-Lyle Judy, St. Augustine; **3B**-Bob Pittman, Sanford; **SS**-Lou Rogino, Gainesville; **OF**-Chet Clemens, Leesburg; Clarence Bray, Gainesville; Jack DeVincenzi, Gainesville; **C**-Manny Onis, Leesburg; **Util**-Joe Niedson, Daytona Beach; **P**-Jake Bunch, Leesburg; Forrest Brewer, St. Augustine; **Manager**-Don McShane, Gainesville.

BA: Jack DeVincenzi, Gainesville, .314
Runs: Whitey McMullen, Gainesville, 121
Hits: Jack DeVincenzi, Gainesville, 172
RBIs: Clarence Bray, Gainesville, 101
HRs: Harry Rice, DeLand, 8
Wins: Forrest Brewer, St. Augustine, 25
SOs: Forrest Brewer, St. Augustine, 234
ERA: Jake Bunch, Leesburg, 1.53

D Georgia-Florida League
President: A.D. "Doc" Walker

Standings	W	L	Pct.	GB	Manager
Albany Travelers (16)	84	42	.667	—	Johnny Keane
Thomasville Orioles	69	54	.561	13½	Cy Morgan
Americus Cardinals (8)	65	61	.516	19	Alex "Red" McColl
Tallahassee Capitols (10)	56	69	.448	27½	Tim Murchison
Cordele Reds	51	73	.411	32	Bob Hasty
Moultrie Packers	49	75	.395	34	Dewey Stover

Playoffs: Albany 3 games, Americus 0; Thomasville 3 games, Tallahassee 2.
Finals: Albany 4 games, Thomasville 2.

All-Star Team: 1B-Eddie Murphy, Albany; **2B**-Hillis Layne, Americus; **3B**-A. Stanley Benjamin, Thomasville; **SS**-Lewis Lucas, Albany; **OF**-William Endicott, Albany; Bob Joratz, Albany; D.T. Evans, Cordele; **C**-Harold Michel, Albany; **Util**-Joe Kracher, Thomasville; **P**-Alex "Red" McColl, Americus; Milt Haefner, Tallahassee; **Manager**-Cy Morgan, Thomasville.

BA: William Endicott, Albany, .354
Runs: Pat Riley, Albany, 128
Hits: John Rowe, Americus, 173
RBIs: Eddie Murphy, Albany, 113
HRs: Pat Riley, Albany, 8
Ed Hartness, Americus, 8
Wins: Henry Novak, Albany, 20
SOs: Henry Novak, Albany, 165
ERA: Alex "Red" McColl, Americus, 2.04

D Kitty League
President: J.E. Hannephin

Standings	W	L	Pct.	GB	Manager
Hopkinsville Hoppers (3)	76	53	.589	—	Dick Smith
Jackson Generals	74	54	.578	1½	Herbert "Dutch" Welch
Lexington Giants	66	59	.528	8	Rip Fanning
Mayfield Clothiers (7)	65	60	.520	9	Bennie Tate
Paducah Indians (16)	66	63	.512	10	Pete Mondino
Owensboro Oilers (3)	66	64	.508	10½	Hugh Wise
Fulton Eagles	55	75	.423	21½	George Clonts
Union City Greyhounds (12)	45	85	.346	31½	Hap Bohl

Playoffs: Hopkinsville 3 games, Mayfield 1; Jackson 3 games, Lexington 0.
Finals: Jackson 2 games, Hopkinsville 1. The final round was abandoned September 22 due to extensive weather delays and lack of interest. Jackson was declared playoff winner after Hopkinsville forfeited the final two games.

All-Star Team: 1B-Cy Redifer, Union City; **2B**-Clint Andercek, Lexington; **3B**-Art Grangard, Paducah; **SS**-Willard Padgett, Fulton; **OF**-Lou Perryman, Jackson; Glenn Grimes, Owensboro; Harold Peck, Hopkinsville; **C**-Archie Williams, Jackson; **Util**-Fred Walker, Jackson; **P**-Lester Gray, Jackson; Elmer Haas, Hopkinsville; **Manager**-Dick Smith, Hopkinsville.

BA: Augie Bergamo, Paducah, .355
Runs: Harold Peck, Hopkinsville, 125
Hits: Harold Peck, Hopkinsville, 187
RBIs: Herb Wilson, Owensboro, 95
HRs: Jim Poole, Lexington, 18
Wins: Glen Dacus, Jackson, 22
SOs: Chauncey Scott, Paducah, 282
ERA: Glen Dacus, Jackson, 2.42

D Mountain State League
President: Ray Ryan

Standings	W	L	Pct.	GB	Manager
Logan Indians	72	46	.610	—	Eddie Hock
Beckley Bengals	61	52	.540	8½	Eli Harris
Williamson Colts	58	60	.492	14	Nat Hickey
Welch Miners	56	64	.467	17	Eddie Krajnik/Charles Bowie/Carlos Ratliff
Bluefield Blue-Grays	55	64	.462	17½	Earl Smith
Huntington Bees	50	66	.431	21	Dickie Kerr

Attendance: Logan, 50,000.

Playoffs: Logan 3 games, Williamson 2; Beckley 2 games, Welch 0.
Finals: Beckley 3 games, Logan 2.

All-Star Team: 1B-Robert Hershey, Logan; **2B**-Garfield Ganoe, Bluefield; **3B**-Erwin Paul, Huntington; **SS**-Murray Franklin, Beckley; **OF**-John Mervar, Welch; Earl Martin, Beckley; Walter Sessi, Williamson; **C**-Joe Ereno, Beckley; **Util**-Deedum Krynzel, Bluefield; **P**-Vic Sorrell, Bluefield; Vern Kohler, Logan; **Manager**-Eddie Hock, Logan.

BA: Murray Franklin, Beckley, .439
Runs: Raleigh Singleton, Beckley, 128
Hits: Garfield Ganoe, Bluefield, 170
RBIs: Walter Sessi, Williamson, 126
HRs: Murray Franklin, Beckley, 26
Wins: Earl Brinegar, Welch, 18
John Gorszyca, Beckley, 18
SOs: Vern Kohler, Logan, 216
ERA: Vern Kohler, Logan, 2.24

D Nebraska State League
President: J. Roy Carter

Standings	W	L	Pct.	GB	Manager
Sioux City Cowboys**	70	47	.598	—	Pete Monahan
Norfolk Elkhorns*(5)	67	49	.578	2½	Elmer "Doc" Bennett
Beatrice Blues (10)	62	54	.534	7½	Leon Riley
Lincoln Links (7)	52	64	.448	17½	Pug Griffin
Grand Island Cardinals (16)	49	67	.422	20½	Benny Hassler
Sioux Falls Canaries	49	68	.419	21	Ralph Brandon

Playoff: Norfolk 4 games, Sioux City 2.

All-Star Team: 1B-Pete Monahan, Sioux City; **2B**-Ed Wernett, Norfolk; **3B**-Ted Kakaloris, Lincoln; **SS**-Tony Sams, Norfolk; **OF**-John Kreevich, Norfolk; Leon Riley, Beatrice; John Schinski, Sioux City; **C**-Eddie Gibb, Beatrice; **Util**-Jack White, Grand Island; **P**-Reuben Fisher, Sioux City; Clayton Freis, Beatrice; **Manager**-Elmer "Doc" Bennett, Norfolk.

BA: Leon Riley, Beatrice, .365
Runs: Marion DeJarnett, Lincoln, 124
Ralph Fallon, Sioux City, 124
Hits: Ned Tighe, Norfolk, 161
RBIs: Leon Riley, Beatrice, 122
HRs: Pete Monahan, Sioux City, 19
Wins: Reuben Fisher, Sioux City, 21
SOs: Reuben Fisher, Sioux City, 242
ERA: Cletus Voss, Sioux Falls, 2.33

D North Carolina State League
President: Gene Lawing

Standings	W	L	Pct.	GB	Manager
Thomasville Orioles	75	36	.676	—	Jimmy Maus
Shelby/Gastonia Cardinals#(16)	66	45	.595	9	George Silvey
Lexington Indians (6)	66	46	.589	9½	Phil Lundeen
Mooresville Moors	59	53	.527	16½	John Hicks
Salisbury Bees (9)	51	60	.459	24	Otis "Blackie" Carter
Newton-Conover Twins	46	66	.411	29½	Rube Wilson/Mack Arnette
Cooleemee Weavers (10)	42	69	.378	33	Joe Bird
Landis Sens	41	71	.366	34½	Reese Harris

#Shelby (47-23) moved to Gastonia July 22.

Playoffs: Thomasville 3 games, Lexington 0; Mooresville 3 games, Gastonia 0.
Finals: Mooresville 3 games, Thomasville 3. Final round was abandoned September 18 due to fan violence in Thomasville. Both teams were declared playoff co-winners.

All-Star Team: 1B-George Silvey, Shelby/Gastonia; **2B**-Darr Shealy, Thomasville; **3B**-Bob White, Mooresville; **SS**-Paul Rampey, Salisbury; **OF**-Harry Leonard, Lexington; Gene Nafie, Shelby/Gastonia; Roy Pinkston, Thomasville; **C**-Jimmy Maus, Thomasville; **Util**-William Ayers, Shelby/Gastonia; **P**-Paige Dennis, Thomasville; Wilbur Reeser, Lexington; **Manager**-Otis "Blackie" Carter, Salisbury.

BA: Darr Shealy, Thomasville, .357
Runs: Gene Nafie, Shelby/Gastonia, 120
Hits: Bob White, Mooresville, 156
    James Canty, Thomasville, 156
RBIs: Darr Shealy, Thomasville, 114
HRs: Gene Nafie, Shelby/Gastonia, 27

SBs: George Silvey, Shelby/Gastonia, 80
Wins: Paige Dennis, Thomasville, 28
SOs: Ray Lindsay, Thomasville, 247
ERA: Paige Dennis, Thomasville, 1.33
Pct: Paige Dennis, Thomasville, .933, 28-2

D Northeast Arkansas League
President: Joseph R. Bertig

Standings	W	L	Pct.	GB	Manager
Blytheville Giants (13)	70	35	.667	—	Herschel Bobo
Caruthersville Pilots (16)	62	42	.590	7½	Joseph "Bunny" Simmons/Al Iezzi/
					Wilson Koewing
Newport Cardinals	61	46	.570	10	Thorpe Hamilton/Mike Blazo
Paragould Rebels	52	56	.481	19½	Bobby Schleicher/Paul Rucker
Batesville White Sox (7)	47	62	.431	25	Elmer Kirchoff
Jonesboro Giants	28	79	.262	43	Pete Cooper/Gus Albright/Fred Millican

Playoffs: Blytheville 2 games, Paragould 0; Newport 2 games, Caruthersville 1.
Finals: Blytheville 3 games, Newport 1.

All-Star Team: 1B-James Hamblen, Blytheville; **2B**-Elmer Kirchoff, Batesville; **3B**-George Oldenburg, Newport; **SS**-Herman Dvorak, Blytheville; **OF**-Jimmy Guyman, Newport; George Reichelt, Jonesboro; Allen Zarilla, Batesville; **C**-Angel Aragon, Blytheville; **Util**-Robert O'Brien, Newport; **P**-Johnny Sain, Newport; Tom Gorman, Blytheville; **Manager**-Herschel Bobo, Blytheville.

BA: George Reichelt, Jonesboro, .360
Runs: Allen Zarilla, Batesville, 100
Hits: Cy Block, Paragould, 144
RBIs: Angel Aragon, Blytheville, 80
HRs: George Oldenburg, Newport, 16
    Pete McHaney, Paragould, 16
Wins: Cliff Roberson, Paragould, 17
SOs: Tom Gorman, Blytheville, 166
ERA: Harry Feldman, Blytheville, 2.02
Pct: Harry Feldman, Blytheville, .929, 13-1

D Northern League
President: Herman D. White

Standings	W	L	Pct.	GB	Manager
Superior Blues (10)	78	36	.684	—	George "Red" Treadwell
Duluth Dukes (16)	72	44	.621	7	Dutch Dorman
Crookston Pirates (1)	69	47	.595	10	Bill Burwell
Wausau Lumberjacks	60	55	.522	18½	Bunny Brief
Fargo-Moorhead Twins (3)	60	56	.517	19	Jack Knight
Grand Forks Chiefs	49	66	.426	29½	Johnny Mostil
Winnipeg Maroons	37	76	.327	40½	Bruno Haas
Eau Claire Bears (11)	39	84	.317	43½	Ed Garrity

Playoffs: Duluth 4 games, Wausau 0; Crookston 4 games, Superior 2.
Finals: Duluth 4 games, Crookston 3.

All-Star Team: 1B-Hugh Gustafson, Winnipeg; **2B**-John Nieman, Eau Claire; **3B**-Louis Adrian, Wausau; **SS**-Ray Mack, Fargo-Moorhead; **OF**-William Barnacle, Crookston; Melvin Wasley, Duluth; Lynford Rumfield, Superior; **C**-Bennie Bedrava, Wausau; **Util**-Kenneth Williams, Fargo-Moorhead/Superior; **P**-Will Butland, Crookston; Mike Kash (Kaiserski), Crookston; **Manager**-George "Red" Treadwell, Superior.

BA: Melvin Wasley, Duluth, .357
Runs: Melvin Wasley, Duluth, 110
Hits: Melvin Wasley, Duluth, 168
RBIs: Melvin Wasley, Duluth, 115
HRs: Melvin Wasley, Duluth, 31
Wins: Mike Kash (Kaiserski), Crookston, 20
SOs: Will Butland, Crookston, 203
Pct: Steve Warchol, Duluth, .917, 11-1

D Ohio State League
President: Paul Shank

Standings	W	L	Pct.	GB	Manager
Fostoria Red Birds**(16)	55	41	.573	—	Jack Farmer
Fremont Reds/Green Sox*.	51	43	.543	3	James "Chappie" Geygan
Findlay Browns (7)	44	54	.449	12	Grover Hartley
Tiffin Mud Hens (7)	44	56	.440	13	Tony Rogala

Playoff: Fremont 3 games, Fostoria 0.

All-Star Team: 1B-Frederick Klann, Findlay; **2B**-Garland Sewell, Fremont; **3B**-Harold Freeman, Fremont; **SS**-Tony Guzak, Tiffin; **OF**-Edwin Kudrycki, Tiffin; Peter Kraus, Fostoria; Stan Platek, Fremont; **C**-Del Wilbur, Findlay; **Util**-Ted Haas, Fremont; **P**-John Brich, Fremont; Frederick Berger, Fostoria; **Manager**-Grover Hartley, Findlay.

BA: Peter Kraus, Fostoria, .372
Runs: Peter Kraus, Fostoria, 100
Hits: Peter Kraus, Fostoria, 137
RBIs: Del Wilber, Findlay, 83
HRs: James "Chappie" Geygan, Fremont, 18
Wins: Glen Fletcher, Fremont/Findlay, 15
SOs: Jack Farmer, Fostoria, 164
Pct: Frederick Berger, Fostoria, .818, 9-2

D Pennsylvania State Association
President: Elmer M. Daily

Standings	W	L	Pct.	GB	Manager
Butler Yankees*(5)	55	43	.561	—	E.L. "Lefty" Jenkins
McKeesport Tubers**	53	43	.552	1	Leo Mackey
Beaver Falls Browns	51	50	.505	5½	Howard Shanks
Greensburg Green Sox	37	60	.381	17½	Ollie Vanek

Playoff: Butler 4 games, McKeesport 1.

All-Star Team: 1B-Hank Sauer, Butler; **2B**-Dan Hayes, Butler; **3B**-Artie Deim, Beaver Falls; **SS**-Frank Wecheck, Greensburg; **OF**-Frank Kalin, McKeesport; John Hyder, Butler; Harold Bush, Greensburg; **C**-Forrest Hunt, Butler; **Util**-William Sheehan, Greensburg; **P**-Justin Fest, McKeesport; Doug Leonardson, Beaver Falls; **Manager**-E.L. "Lefty" Jenkins, Butler.

BA: Hank Sauer, Butler, .350
Runs: John Panek, Beaver Falls, 96
Hits: Hank Sauer, Butler, 135
RBIs: Harold Bush, Greensburg, 85
HRs: Harold Bush, Greensburg, 22
Wins: Justin Fest, McKeesport, 16
SOs: John Kernoski, Butler, 131
ERA: Justin Fest, McKeesport, 3.13

D Texas Valley League
President: Guy F. Airey

Standings	W	L	Pct.	GB	Manager
Corpus Christi Spudders	92	44	.677	—	Rod Whitney
Harlingen Hubs	84	53	.613	8½	Jake Atz
Taft Cardinals	68	67	.504	23½	John Morrow
Refugio Oilers	67	67	.500	24	Carl Littlejohn
McAllen Packers	65	72	.474	27½	Ray Friday
Brownsville Charros	30	103	.226	60½	Ed Konetchy/Brooks Conover

Playoffs: Harlingen 3 games, Taft 0; Corpus Christi 3 games, Refugio 2.
Finals: Harlingen 4 games, Corpus Christi 0.

All-Star Team: 1B-Bill McClaren, Harlingen; **2B**-George Hausman, Corpus Christi; **3B**-Thomas Mays, Harlingen; **SS**-Tommy Woodruff, Corpus Christi; **OF**-Steve Carter, Harlingen; Roger Rotoni, Harlingen; Manuel Cortinas, Corpus Christi; **C**-Walter Kopp, McAllen; **Util**-Tony Swift, Brownsville; **P**-Grover Miller, Brownsville; Gene Hinrichs, Harlingen; **Manager**-Rod Whitney, Corpus Christi.

BA: Manuel Cortinas, Corpus Christi, .380
Runs: George Hausman, Corpus Christi, 157
Hits: Steve Carter, Harlingen, 207
RBIs: Bill McClaren, Harlingen, 151
HRs: Manuel Cortinas, Corpus Christi, 20
    Leo Najo, McAllen, 20
    Bill McClaren, Harlingen, 20
    Kirby Jordan, McAllen, 20
Wins: Gene Hinrichs, Harlingen, 27
SOs: Gene Hinrichs, Harlingen, 223
ERA: Tom Finger, Corpus Christi, 2.75

D West Texas-New Mexico League
President: Milton E. Price

Standings	W	L	Pct.	GB	Manager
Lubbock Hubbers (2)	80	49	.620	—	James "Hack" Miller
Clovis Pioneers	71	58	.550	9	William Ratliff
Midland Cardinals (16)	67	62	.519	13	Fincher Withers
Wink Spudders	63	65	.492	16½	Joe Tate
Big Spring Barons	58	71	.450	22	Charles Barnabee
Hobbs Boosters (4)	48	82	.369	32½	Neal Rabe

Attendance: Lubbock, 32,683; Total, 108,342.

Playoffs: Lubbock 3 games, Wink 0; Clovis 3 games, Midland 1.
Finals: Lubbock 4 games, Clovis 1.

All-Star Team: 1B-Jake Suytar, Midland; **2B**-Robert Decker, Big Spring; **3B**-Purvis Spangler, Wink; **SS**-Joe Gedzius, Lubbock; **OF**-James Morris, Midland; Cecil Smyly, Hobbs; Anthony Bonk, Hobbs; **C**-James "Hack" Miller, Lubbock; **Util**-Clarence Beers, Midland; **P**-Ralph Marshall, Lubbock; Marshall Scott, Hobbs; **Manager**-Joe Tate, Wink.

BA: Cecil Smyly, Hobbs, .367
Runs: Cecil Smyly, Hobbs, 182
Hits: Cecil Smyly, Hobbs, 194
RBIs: Mal Stevens, Lubbock, 132
HRs: Mal Stevens, Lubbock, 31
    Jake Suytar, Midland, 31
Wins: Ernest Nelson, Clovis, 20
SOs: Jerry Blanchard, Lubbock, 265
ERA: Verne "Red" Roberts, Wink, 3.08

Ind Mexican League
President: Ernesto Carmona Verduzco

Standings	W	L	Pct.	GB	Manager
Veracruz Aguila	40	9	.816	—	Agustin Verde
Mexico City Agrario	33	14	.702	6	Chucho Castillo/Horacio Hernandez/
					George Sampson
Tampico Alijadores	32	15	.681	7	Guillermo Ornelas
Cordoba Cafeteros	29	17	.630	9½	Lazaro Penagos/Lazaro Salazar
Nogales Cerveceros	22	27	.449	18	Raymundo Martinez
Santa Rosa Gallos	18	28	.391	20½	Leonardo Olvera
Mexico City Comintra	16	31	.340	23	Manuel Oliveros
Rio Blanco Cidosa	0	49	.000	40	

BA: Martin Dihigo, Veracruz, .387
Hits: Angel Castro, Tampico, 62
RBIs: Angel Castro, Tampico, 40
HRs: Angel Castro, Tampico, 9
Wins: Martin Dihigo, Veracruz, 18
SOs: Martin Dihigo, Veracruz, 184
ERA: Martin Dihigo, Veracruz, 0.90

1938 Interleague Post Season Play

World Series
New York (American) 4 games, Chicago (National) 0

Junior World Series
Kansas City (American Association) 4 games, Newark (International) 3
Total Attendance: 71,813

Dixie Series
Atlanta (Southern Association) 4 games, Beaumont (Texas) 0, one tie
Total Attendance: 25,391

Southern Championship (Little Dixie)
Macon (South Atlantic) 4 games, Mobile (Southeastern) 3

Southeast Championship
Gainesville (Florida State) 4 games, Albany (Georgia-Florida) 1

Class D Interleague Series
Mooresville (North Carolina State) 3 games, Bassett (Bi-State) 1

1938 Major League Farm Systems

American League

1 Boston (8): Minneapolis, Little Rock, Hazleton, Rocky Mount, Clarksdale, Canton, Elizabethton, Crookston.
2 Chicago (7): St. Paul, Dallas, Anniston, Longview, Rayne, DeLand, Lubbock.
3 Cleveland (10): Milwaukee, New Orleans, Spartanburg, Bloomington, Oswego, Springfield (OH), Gainesville, Hopkinsville, Owensboro, Fargo-Moorhead.
4 Detroit (3): Beaumont, Charleston, Hobbs.
5 New York (12): Kansas City, Newark, Binghamton, Norfolk (VA), Augusta, Jackson, Wenatchee, Akron, Joplin, Neosho, Norfolk (NE), Butler.
6 Philadelphia (3): Williamsport, Federalsburg, Lexington (NC).
7 St. Louis (13): Toledo, San Antonio, Meridian, Springfield (IL), Palestine, Johnstown, Easton, Lafayette, Mayfield, Lincoln, Batesville, Tiffin, Findlay.
8 Washington (7): Indianapolis, Chattanooga, Trenton, Charlotte, Salisbury (MD), Sanford, Americus.

National League

9 Boston (4): Hartford, Evansville, Erie, Salisbury (NC).
10 Brooklyn (11): Nashville, Elmira, Winston-Salem, Pensacola, Clinton, Greenwood, Dayton, Tallahassee, Beatrice, Cooleemee, Superior.
11 Chicago (9): Los Angeles, Birmingham, Portsmouth (VA), Moline, Helena, Hot Springs, Ponca City, Greeneville, Eau Claire.
12 Cincinnati (9): Syracuse, Albany (NY), Durham, Columbia, Waterloo, El Dorado, Muskogee, Rogers, Union City.
13 New York (5): Jersey City, Richmond, Ft. Smith, Milford, Blytheville.
14 Philadelphia (2): Montgomery, Centreville.
15 Pittsburgh (5): Louisville, Knoxville, Savannah, Hutchinson, Carthage.
16 St. Louis (27): Columbus (OH), Rochester, Sacramento, Houston, Asheville, Columbus (GA), Mobile, Decatur, Cedar Rapids, Amsterdam, Pine Bluff, Jacksonville (TX), Portsmouth (OH), Springfield (MO), Johnson City, Monett, Cambridge, New Iberia, Daytona Beach, Albany (GA), Paducah, Grand Island, Shelby/Gastonia, Caruthersville, Duluth, Fostoria, Midland.

1938 No-Hitters

Date	Pitcher	Team	League	Opponent	Score
5-8	Jerry Blanchard	Lubbock	W. Texas-N. Mexico	Wink	(7)
5-18	Virgil Trucks	Andalusia	Alabama-Florida	Evergreen	1-0
6-4	Virgil Trucks	Andalusia	Alabama-Florida	Dothan	6-0
6-6	Forrest Brewer	St. Augustine	Florida State	Orlando	3-0
6-11	John Vander Meer	Cincinnati	National	Boston	3-0
6-12	Tom Finger	Corpus Christi	Texas Valley	Harlingen	1-0 (11)
6-13	Clare Bertram	Moline	Three-I	Waterloo	4-0 (7)
6-15	John Vander Meer	Cincinnati	National	Brooklyn	6-0 (C)
7-10	Joe Berry	Los Angeles	Pacific Coast	Oakland	4-0 (7)
7-20	Charlie Suchs	Wilkes-Barre	Eastern	Williamsport	1-0 (7)
7-22	Ralph Marshall	Lubbock	W. Texas-N. Mexico	Hobbs	5-0
7-25	Herman Besse	Greenville	Cotton States	El Dorado	5-0
7-25	Fred Harig	Owensboro	Kitty	Mayfield	4-0
8-5	Eddie Bastien	Waterloo	Three-I	Evansville	1-0
8-10	Merle Settlemire	Sydney	Cape Breton Colliery	Sydney Mines	1-0 (12)
8-11	Ben Kneupper	Corpus Christi	Texas Valley	Refugio	8-0
8-14	Dutch Dietz	Beaumont	Texas	Oklahoma City	6-0 (7)
8-16	Ken Burkhart	New Iberia	Evangeline	Abbeville	1-0
8-21	Ed Schumacher	Alexandria	Evangeline	Opelousas	2-0
8-27	Monte Pearson	New York	American	Cleveland	13-0
8-30	Richard Ward	San Diego	Pacific Coast	Los Angeles	1-0
9-6	Woody Rich	Little Rock	Southern Assoc.	Atlanta	4-0
	Paige Dennis	Thomasville	North Carolina State		

Number in parentheses indicates innings if other than nine; "C" indicates no-hitters in consecutive starts.

THIS DATE IN MINOR LEAGUE HISTORY

January 1, 1938, Three-I League umpire Chester Widerquist lost an inch off the end of his thumb when he attempted to eject a customer from a tavern in Moline, Illinois, where he was tending bar. A patron bit off the end of the finger during a scuffle, and a warrant for disorderly conduct was filed.

April 21, 1938, Virgil Trucks, a 19-year old rookie righthander with Andalusia, fanned 20 batters on opening day in the Alabama-Florida League.

May 6, 1938, Outfielder Bob Seeds of Newark, International League, hit four successive homers plus two singles in six trips to the plate, featuring Newark's 22-9 victory at Buffalo. Seeds drove in 12 runs in the game, played at Offerman Stadium.

May 7, 1938, Newark's Bob Seeds hammered three more consecutive homers in his first three official at bats. In his two-day spree, Seeds had seven homers, 30 total bases and 17 RBIs.

May 18, 1938, In one of the greatest battles ever staged, Virgil Trucks of Andalusia, Alabama-Florida League, won a 1-0 no-hitter over Evergreen, striking out 19 batters. His mound opponent, Francis Manheim, yielded just one safety, a single by Trucks in the ninth inning. Trucks later scored to register the 1-0 triumph.

May 18, 1938, Bill Beams of Reidsville, Bi-State League, literally stole the game from Bassett. He drew a walk in the eleventh inning, then swiped second, third, and home, giving his club a 3-2 verdict.

June 4, 1938, Virgil Trucks of Andalusia, Alabama-Florida League, pitched his second no-hitter of the season, striking out 15 in a 6-0 defeat of Dothan.

June 24, 1938, Newark's 14-game International League winning streak was smashed in a tough 18-inning 3-2 loss in a night game in Syracuse. It was the first game Newark played without the services of Bob Seeds, who had been sold to the New York Giants.

June 24, 1938, Jim Crookston, Grand Island centerfielder and reputedly the fastest runner in the Nebraska State League, stole home twice at Sioux City. The last steal, in the ninth inning, gave Grand Island a 9-8 win.

June 26, 1938, Former major league pilot Rogers Hornsby resigned as coach and pinch-hitter for Baltimore of the International League to move on to Chattanooga and relieve catcher Walter Millies as the manager of the Southern Association club.

July 8, 1938, In the wildest, longest game in Kitty League history, Fulton rallied to score five runs in the 20th inning and beat Paducah 14-9, in a game that started at 8:15 p.m. and ended at 1:45 a.m. on July 9.

July 21, 1938, Linus "Skeeter" Ebnet, 23, shortstop for Winnipeg, Northern League, died in a Winnipeg hospital from being hit by a pitched ball in a game with Grand Forks five days earlier.

July 29, 1938, Mountain State League directors imposed a 60-day suspension and fined Welch business manager Pat Flanagan $100 and manager Eddie Krajnik $50, following the submission of affidavits to the league that the club officials had wagered on the outcome of baseball games.

August 7, 1938, Alex Swails of Muskogee, Western Association, set a record when he issued 32 bases on balls in eight innings of a night game against Ponca City. Ponca City won 16-7 despite stranding 22 baserunners. Ponca City hurler Hub Kittle walked 11, for a total of 43 walks in the game.

August 20, 1938, Andalusia righthander Virgil Trucks fanned 15 Troy batters in an Alabama-Florida League game to increase his season's strikeout total to 413, a record for pitchers for the 60-feet-six-inches distance between mound and plate. Trucks would finish the season with 418 strikeouts in just 272 innings.

August 22, 1938, The Caruthersville-Paragould contest in the Northeast Arkansas League was called after 5-1/2 innings because of a bug storm.

September 8, 1938, Owen "Donie" Bush resigned as manager of Minneapolis, American Association, and purchased an interest in the Louisville club, which he would manage next season. In his six seasons at the helm of the Millers, Bush won three pennants.

1939

American League
President: William Harridge

Standings	W	L	Pct.	GB	Attend.	Manager
New York Yankees	106	45	.702	—	859,785	Joe McCarthy
Boston Red Sox	89	62	.589	17	573,070	Joe Cronin
Cleveland Indians	87	67	.565	20½	563,926	Ossie Vitt
Chicago White Sox	85	69	.552	22½	594,104	Jimmy Dykes
Detroit Tigers	81	73	.526	26½	836,279	Del Baker
Washington Senators	65	87	.428	41½	339,257	Bucky Harris
Philadelphia Athletics	55	97	.362	51½	395,022	Connie Mack
St. Louis Browns	43	111	.279	64½	109,159	Fred Haney

BA: Joe DiMaggio, New York, .381
Runs: Red Rolfe, New York, 139
Hits: Red Rolfe, New York, 213
RBIs: Ted Williams, Boston, 145
HRs: Jimmie Foxx, Boston, 35

Wins: Bob Feller, Cleveland, 24
SOs: Bob Feller, Cleveland, 246
ERA: Lefty Grove, Boston, 2.54
Pct: Lefty Grove, Boston, .789, 15-4

National League
President: Ford Frick

Standings	W	L	Pct.	GB	Attend.	Manager
Cincinnati Reds	97	57	.630	—	981,443	Bill McKechnie
St. Louis Cardinals	92	61	.601	4½	400,245	Ray Blades
Brooklyn Dodgers	84	69	.549	12½	955,668	Leo Durocher
Chicago Cubs	84	70	.545	13	726,663	Gabby Hartnett
New York Giants	77	74	.510	18½	702,457	Bill Terry
Pittsburgh Pirates	68	85	.444	28½	376,734	Pie Traynor
Boston Bees	63	88	.417	32½	285,994	Casey Stengel
Philadelphia Phillies	45	106	.298	50½	277,973	Tommy "Doc" Prothro

BA: John Mize, St. Louis, .349
Runs: Billy Werber, Cincinnati, 115
Hits: Frank McCormick, Cincinnati, 209
RBIs: Frank McCormick, Cincinnati, 128
HRs: John Mize, St. Louis, 28

Wins: Bucky Walters, Cincinnati, 27
SOs: Claude Passeau, Philadelphia/Chicago, 137
ERA: Bucky Walters, Cincinnati, 2.29
Pct: Paul Derringer, Cincinnati, .781, 25-7

AA American Association
President: George Trautman

Standings	W	L	Pct.	GB	Attend.	Manager
Kansas City Blues (5)	107	47	.695	—	269,865	Bill Meyer
Minneapolis Millers	99	55	.643	8	210,082	Tom Sheehan
Indianapolis Indians (12)	82	72	.532	25	129,529	Ray Schalk/Wes Griffin
Louisville Colonels (1)	75	78	.490	31½	245,458	Donie Bush/Bill Burwell
St. Paul Saints (2)	73	81	.474	34	169,168	Babe Ganzel
Milwaukee Brewers (11)	70	83	.458	36½	116,314	Minor Heath
Columbus Senators (16)	62	92	.403	45	74,904	Burt Shotton
Toledo Mud Hens (7)	47	107	.305	60	85,771	Myles Thomas

Playoffs: Louisville 4 games, Minneapolis 1; Indianapolis 4 games, Kansas City 1.
Finals: Louisville 4 games, Indianapolis 1.

Manager of the Year-Bill Meyer, Kansas City.

BA: Gilbert English, St. Paul, .343
Runs: Harvey Walker, Minneapolis, 145
Hits: Ab Wright, Minneapolis, 196
RBIs: Vince DiMaggio, Kansas City, 136

HRs: Vince DiMaggio, Kansas City, 46
Wins: Herb Hash, Minneapolis, 22
SOs: Max Lanier, Columbus, 148
ERA: Marv Breuer, Kansas City, 2.28

AA International League
President: Frank J. Shaughnessy

Standings	W	L	Pct.	GB	Attend.	Manager
Jersey City Giants (13)	89	64	.582	—	378,325	Bert Niehoff
Rochester Red Wings (16)	84	67	.556	4	170,457	Billy Southworth
Buffalo Bisons (3)	82	72	.532	7½	210,424	Steve O'Neill
Newark Bears (5)	82	73	.529	8	176,665	Johnny Neun
Syracuse Chiefs	81	74	.523	9	178,671	Dick Porter
Baltimore Orioles	68	85	.444	21	113,152	Rogers Hornsby
Montreal Royals (10)	64	88	.421	24½	135,733	Burleigh Grimes
Toronto Maple Leafs	63	90	.412	26	119,074	Jack Burns/Tony Lazzeri

Playoffs: Newark defeated Syracuse in a one game playoff for fourth place. Newark 4 games, Jersey City 2; Rochester 4 games, Buffalo 1.
Finals: Rochester 4 games, Newark 3.

MVP-Mickey Witek, Newark.

BA: John Dickshot, Jersey City, .355
Runs: John Tyler, Buffalo, 124
Hits: Mickey Witek, Newark, 204
RBIs: Ollie Carnegie, Buffalo, 112

HRs: Ollie Carnegie, Buffalo, 29
Wins: Silas Johnson, Rochester, 22
SOs: Jack Tising, Baltimore/Syracuse, 144
ERA: Roy Joiner, Jersey City, 2.53

AA Pacific Coast League
President: William C. Tuttle

Standings	W	L	Pct.	GB	Attend.	Manager
Seattle Rainiers	101	73	.580	—	355,792	Jack Lelivelt
San Francisco Seals	97	78	.554	4½	269,616	Lefty O'Doul
Los Angeles Angels (11)	97	79	.551	5	224,045	Truck Hannah
Sacramento Solons (16)	88	88	.500	14	115,002	Bennie Borgmann
San Diego Padres	83	93	.472	19	162,783	Cedric Durst
Hollywood Stars	82	94	.466	20	219,206	Red Killefer
Oakland Oaks	78	98	.443	24	165,000	Johnny Vergez
Portland Beavers	75	98	.434	25½	150,756	Bill Sweeney

Playoffs: Los Angeles 4 games, Seattle 2; Sacramento 4 games, San Francisco 1.
Finals: Sacramento 4 games, Los Angeles 2.

MVP-Dom DiMaggio, San Francisco.

BA: Dom Dallessandro, San Diego, .368
Runs: Dom DiMaggio, San Francisco, 165
Hits: Dom DiMaggio, San Francisco, 239
RBIs: James "Rip" Collins, Los Angeles, 128

HRs: James "Rip" Collins, Los Angeles, 26
Wins: Hal Turpin, Seattle, 23
SOs: Tony Freitas, Sacramento, 172
ERA: Sam Gibson, San Francisco, 2.24

A1 Southern Association
President: Trammell Scott

Standings	W	L	Pct.	GB	Attend.	Manager
Chattanooga Lookouts (8)	85	65	.567	—	133,676	Kiki Cuyler
Memphis Chicks (10)	84	67	.556	1½	90,345	Frank Brazill
Nashville Vols (10)	85	68	.555	1½	124,232	Larry Gilbert
Atlanta Crackers	83	67	.553	2	235,968	Paul Richards
Knoxville Smokies (15)	79	73	.520	7	116,591	Neil Caldwell
Little Rock Travelers (1)	68	83	.450	17½	62,843	George "Specs" Toporcer
Birmingham Barons (12)	64	89	.418	22½	95,381	Dutch Zwilling
New Orleans Pelicans (3)	57	93	.386	28	92,551	Roger Peckinpaugh

Playoffs: Atlanta 3 games, Chattanooga 0; Nashville 3 games, Memphis 0.
Finals: Nashville 4 games, Atlanta 3.

MVP-Herman Besse, Memphis.

BA: Bert Haas, Nashville, .365
Runs: Emil Malho, Atlanta, 122
Hits: Norman Young, Knoxville, 223
RBIs: Norman Young, Knoxville, 137
HRs: Bill Nicholson, Chattanooga, 23

Wins: Ed Heusser, Memphis, 19
Dick Bass, Chattanooga, 19
Dick Lanahan, Chattanooga, 19
SOs: Alpha Brazle, Little Rock, 122
ERA: Dick Lanahan, Chattanooga, 2.95

A1 Texas League
President: J. Alvin Gardner

Standings	W	L	Pct.	GB	Attend.	Manager
Houston Buffaloes (16)	97	63	.606	—	125,364	Eddie Dyer
Dallas Rebels	89	72	.553	8½	167,805	Hap Morse
San Antonio Missions (7)	89	72	.553	8½	116,416	Zach Taylor
Ft. Worth Cats	87	74	.540	10½	94,644	Bob Linton
Shreveport Sports (2)	86	75	.534	11½	143,236	Homer Peel
Tulsa Oilers	78	82	.488	19	81,920	Bruce Connatser/Stanley Schino
Oklahoma City Indians	59	102	.366	38½	63,352	Bruno Haas/Wilcy Moore
Beaumont Exporters (4)	58	103	.360	39½	52,341	Al Vincent

Playoffs: Ft. Worth 3 games, Houston 2; Dallas 3 games, San Antonio 2.
Finals: Ft. Worth 4 games, Dallas 1.

MVP-Nick Cullop, Houston.

BA: Lou Novikoff, Tulsa, .368
Runs: Eddie Lake, Houston, 129
Hits: Paul Easterling, Oklahoma City/Shreveport, 182
John Lucadello, San Antonio, 182
RBIs: Nick Cullop, Houston, 112
John Stoneham, Ft. Worth, 112

HRs: Nick Cullop, Houston, 25
Wins: Ed "Bear Tracks" Greer, Ft. Worth, 22
Murry Dickson, Houston, 22
Emil Bildilli, San Antonio, 22
SOs: Vallie Eaves, Shreveport, 165
ERA: Ed "Bear Tracks" Greer, Ft. Worth, 2.28

A Eastern League
President: Thomas H. Richardson

Standings	W	L	Pct.	GB	Attend.	Manager
Scranton Red Sox (1)	80	60	.571	—	317,249	Nemo Leibold
Elmira Pioneers (10)	75	64	.540	4½	117,796	Clyde Sukeforth
Springfield Nationals (8)	74	66	.529	6	107,972	Spencer Abbott
Albany Senators (12)	72	67	.518	7½	207,385	Rabbit Maranville
Binghamton Triplets (5)	71	69	.507	9	104,377	Bruno Betzel
Williamsport Grays (6)	71	69	.507	9	91,889	Marty McManus
Hartford Bees (9)	58	82	.414	22	53,984	Fresco Thompson
Wilkes-Barre Barons (3)	58	82	.414	22	74,146	Eddie Phillips

*Won first-half   **Won second-half   ***Won both halves
Numbers after nicknames indicate farm system.
Affiliation listed at end of each year.

Playoffs: Scranton 3 games, Springfield 2; Albany 3 games, Elmira 2.
Finals: Scranton 4 games, Albany 1.

All-Star Team: 1B-Tony Lupien, Scranton; 2B-George Fallon, Elmira; 3B-Steve Barath, Albany; SS-Edward Hope, Elmira; OF-George Staller, Elmira; Glenn McQuillen, Williamsport; Jack Graham, Binghamton; C-Milt Gray, Williamsport; Util-Ken Richardson, Williamsport; P-Newton Jacobs, Springfield; Mickey Harris, Scranton; Manager-Spencer Abbott, Springfield.

BA: George Staller, Elmira, .336
Runs: John Burman, Albany, 102
Hits: George Staller, Elmira, 187
RBIs: Al Brancato, Williamsport, 98
HRs: Jack Graham, Binghamton, 29

Wins: Newton Jacobs, Springfield, 18
Rene Monteagudo, Springfield, 18
SOs: Mickey Harris, Scranton, 148
ERA: Xavier Rescigno, Elmira, 2.21

B Piedmont League
President: Ralph Daughton

Standings	W	L	Pct.	GB	Manager
Asheville Tourists (16)	89	55	.618	—	Harold Anderson
Durham Bulls (12)	75	65	.536	12	Oscar Roettger
Rocky Mount Red Sox (1)	70	67	.511	15½	Herb Brett
Richmond Colts	70	71	.496	17½	Lance Richbourg
Portsmouth Cubs (14)	66	71	.482	19½	James Keesey
Norfolk Tars (5)	66	71	.482	19½	Ray White
Charlotte Hornets (8)	68	74	.479	20	Calvin Griffith
Winston-Salem Twins (3)	54	84	.391	32	Charles Clancy

Playoffs: Asheville 3 games, Richmond 0; Rocky Mount 3 games, Durham 1.
Finals: Asheville 4 games, Rocky Mount 2.

All-Star Team: 1B-John Angle, Asheville; 2B-Wayne Blackburn, Durham; 3B-Bob Richards, Asheville; SS-Bill Hart, Asheville; OF-George Ferrell, Richmond; Floyd Yount, Portsmouth; Russ Derry, Norfolk; C-Ken Sears, Norfolk; Util-Gilberto Torres, Charlotte; P-Chuck Hawley, Durham; Max Wilson, Portsmouth; Manager-Harold Anderson, Asheville.

BA: Floyd Yount, Portsmouth, .350
Runs: Russ Derry, Norfolk, 117
Hits: Floyd Yount, Portsmouth, 175
RBIs: George Ferrell, Richmond, 129

HRs: Russ Derry, Norfolk, 40
Wins: Ray Clark, Portsmouth, 20
SOs: Ray Clark, Portsmouth, 185
ERA: Herschel Lyons, Asheville, 1.82

B South Atlantic League
President: Dr. E.M. Wilder

Standings	W	L	Pct.	GB	Manager
Columbus Red Birds (16)	83	55	.601	—	Clay Hopper
Augusta Tigers (5)	83	56	.597	½	Ernie Jenkins
Savannah Indians	80	59	.576	3½	Martin "Chick" Autry
Macon Peaches (10)	71	64	.526	10½	Milt Stock
Greenville Spinners (8)	64	76	.457	20	Alex McColl
Jacksonville Tars	63	75	.457	20	Roy Walker
Columbia Reds (12)	58	81	.417	25½	John Burnett
Spartanburg Spartans (3)	51	87	.370	32	Leon Pettit

Playoffs: Augusta 4 games, Macon 3; Savannah 4 games, Columbus 3.
Finals: Augusta 4 games, Savannah 0.

All-Star Team: 1B-Kenneth Ouzts, Augusta; 2B-Edgar Leip, Greenville; 3B-Felix Rios, Jacksonville; SS-Alfred Anderson, Savannah; OF-Hugh Todd, Jacksonville; William Johnson, Augusta; August Bergamo, Columbus; C-Fermin Guerra, Greenville; Util-Carl Fairly, Macon; P-Leo Twardy, Augusta; Charles Burgess, Savannah; Manager-Martin "Chick" Autry, Savannah.

BA: Hugh Todd, Jacksonville, .384
Runs: James Adlam, Augusta, 130
Hits: Hal Quick, Greenville, 189
RBIs: Hal Quick, Greenville, 106

HRs: Dan Pavlovic, Savannah, 19
Wins: Leo Twardy, Augusta, 21
SOs: Rolland Van Slate, Columbus, 170
ERA: Bill Seinsoth, Columbus, 2.41

B Southeastern League
President: Stuart X. Stephenson

Standings	W	L	Pct.	GB	Attend.	Manager
Pensacola Pilots (14)	87	48	.644	—	70,000	Wally Dashiell
Jackson Senators	78	60	.565	10½		Clarence Blair
Gadsden Pilots (15)	77	66	.538	14		Yam Yaryan
Selma Cloverleafs	68	66	.507	18½		William Bancroft
Anniston Rams (2)	71	70	.504	19	46,000	Pee Wee Wanninger
Montgomery Rebels	60	81	.426	30	70,000	Riggs Stephenson
Mobile Shippers (16)	56	78	.418	30½		Marty Purtell
Meridian Scrappers	55	83	.399	33½		Mel Simons

Playoffs: Pensacola 4 games, Selma 0; Jackson 4 games, Gadsden 1.
Finals: Pensacola 4 games, Jackson 2.

All-Star Team: 1B-Paul Fugit, Jackson; 2B-Norris Simms, Pensacola; 3B-George Jansco, Jackson; SS-Joffre Cross, Mobile; OF-Maurice Jungman, Jackson; Henry "Prince" Oana, Jackson; Grover Resinger, Selma; C-Joe Kracher, Selma; Util-Vernon Boyd, Meridian; P-John Hutchings, Pensacola; Zack Schuessler, Pensacola; Manager-Wally Dashiell, Pensacola.

BA: Bill McGhee, Meridian, .384
Runs: Michael Rocco, Anniston, 127
Hits: George Jansco, Jackson, 192
RBIs: Henry "Prince" Oana, Jackson, 127
HRs: Henry "Prince" Oana, Jackson, 39

Wins: Joseph Roxbury, Jackson, 24
SOs: John Hutchings, Pensacola, 205
ERA: John Hutchings, Pensacola, 1.97
Pct: Joseph Roxbury, Jackson, .828, 24-5

B Three-I League
President: Tom Fairweather

Standings	W	L	Pct.	GB	Attend.	Manager
Cedar Rapids Raiders (3)	73	46	.613	—	56,399	Oliver Marquardt
Evansville Bees (9)	73	48	.603	1	81,371	Bob Coleman
Decatur Commodores (16)	68	51	.571	5	49,710	Tony Kaufman
Springfield Browns (7)	65	55	.542	8½	37,916	Walter Holke
Clinton Giants (13)	63	58	.521	11	41,712	James Ryan
Bloomington Bloomers (11)	49	73	.402	25½	14,005	Mervin Connelly
Moline Plow Boys (11)	49	73	.402	25½	20,911	Michael Gazella
Waterloo Red Hawks (12)	42	78	.350	31½	28,935	Clarence "Cap" Crossley

Playoffs: Springfield 3 games, Evansville 1; Decatur 3 games, Cedar Rapids 1.
Finals: Springfield 3 games, Decatur 2.

All-Star Team: 1B-Eddie Waitkus, Moline; 2B-George Hausmann, Springfield; 3B-Sid Gordon, Clinton; SS-Robert Neighbors, Springfield; OF-Del Jones, Cedar Rapids; Bernard Olsen, Evansville; George Bink, Cedar Rapids; C-James Steiner, Moline; Util-Clarence Levandowski, Moline; P-Joseph Callahan, Evansville; Ray Campbell, Moline; Manager-Bob Coleman, Evansville.

BA: Del Jones, Cedar Rapids, .362
Runs: Del Jones, Cedar Rapids, 120
Hits: Del Jones, Cedar Rapids, 168
RBIs: George Bink, Cedar Rapids, 116

HRs: Fred Stroble, Springfield, 21
Wins: Joseph Callahan, Evansville, 19
SOs: Mike Noymick, Cedar Rapids, 181
ERA: Joseph Callahan, Evansville, 1.86

B Western International League
President: F.H. Knickerbocker

Standings	W	L	Pct.	GB	Manager
Wenatchee Chiefs (5)	86	57	.601	—	Glenn Wright
Tacoma Tigers	78	63	.553	7	Harold Rhyne
Vancouver Capilanos	76	63	.547	8	John Kerr
Spokane Hawks	75	69	.521	11½	Bernie DeViveiros
Yakima Pippins	72	73	.497	15	Raymond Jacobs
Bellingham Chinooks	40	102	.282	45½	Ken Penner

Attendance: Spokane, 222,106.

Playoffs: Tacoma 3 games, Spokane 1; Wenatchee 3 games, Vancouver 0.
Finals: Tacoma 4 games, Wenatchee 2.

All-Star Team: 1B-Robert Garretson, Tacoma; 2B-John Stamper, Yakima; 3B-Wellington Quinn, Vancouver; SS-Bill Skelley, Wenatchee; OF-Lloyd Christopher, Wenatchee; Dwight Aden, Spokane; Roswell Edy, Vancouver; C-Neal Clifford, Tacoma; Util-Charles Petersen, Yakima; P-John Pintar, Wenatchee; Albert Gerhauser, Wenatchee; Manager-Glenn Wright, Wenatchee.

BA: Bill Skelley, Wenatchee, .366
Runs: Bill Skelley, Wenatchee, 133
Hits: Bill Skelley, Wenatchee, 208
RBIs: Lloyd Christopher, Wenatchee, 131
HRs: Morrison Abbott, Tacoma, 37

Wins: Hub Kittle, Yakima, 20
SOs: Floyd Isekite, Tacoma, 219
ERA: Floyd Isekite, Tacoma, 3.29
Ray Medeghini, Tacoma, 3.29

C Canadian-American League
President: Rev. Harold J. Martin

Standings	W	L	Pct.	GB	Attend.	Manager
Amsterdam Rugmakers (5)	81	41	.664	—	39,346	Eddie Sawyer
Oswego Netherlands (8)	69	53	.566	12	25,448	Art Funk
Rome Colonels	68	54	.557	13	57,654	Admiral Martin
Cornwall Maple Leafs	62	56	.525	17	24,285	Steve Yerkes/Emil Graff
Ogdensburg Colts	60	58	.508	19	19,849	Knotty Lee
Ottawa Senators	55	69	.444	27	33,993	Wally Schang
Gloversville-Johnstown Glovers (10)	46	77	.374	35½	25,485	Elmer Yoter
Utica Braves (9)	45	78	.366	36½	105,394	Amby McConnell

Playoffs: Rome 4 games, Cornwall 0; Amsterdam 4 games, Oswego 2.
Finals: Rome 3 games, Amsterdam 2.

All-Star Team: 1B-Cleo Diehl, Amsterdam; 2B-Frank Skaff, Oswego; 3B-Oscar Fleishman, Oswego; SS-Art Funk, Oswego; OF-James Conlon, Oswego; Billy Southworth, Jr., Rome; Eddie Sawyer, Amsterdam; C-Myron Williams, Rome; Util-Ken Hill, Rome; P-Harry Kuntsahian, Oswego; Eugene Davis, Ottawa; Manager-Admiral Martin, Rome.

BA: Eddie Sawyer, Amsterdam, .369
Runs: Henry Hoysradt, Amsterdam, 106
Hits: Eddie Sawyer, Amsterdam, 169
RBIs: Eddie Sawyer, Amsterdam, 103

HRs: John Lehman, Gloversville-Johnstown, 22
Wins: Kenneth Tashian, Oswego, 20
SOs: Leo Pukas, Ogdensburg, 214
ERA: John Cahill, Utica, 2.27

C Cape Breton Colliery League
President: Judge A.D. Campbell

Standings	W	L	Pct.	GB	Manager
Sydney Ramblers	36	20	.643	—	Merle Settlemire/Al Smith
New Waterford Dodgers	31	25	.554	5	Charles Brucato
Glace Bay Miners	26	25	.510	7½	Ray Moore
Sydney Mines Steel Citians	14	37	.275	19½	Fred Loftus/Billy Marshall

Playoff: New Waterford 2 games, Glace Bay 1.

Finals: Sydney 4 games, New Waterford 0.

BA: Abe Abramowitz, Sydney, .325
Runs: Gerard Kiley, Sydney, 40
Walter Bracken, New Waterford, 40
Hits: Charles Brucato, New Waterford, 71
RBIs: Abe Abramowitz, Sydney, 42

HRs: Lester Crabb, Glace Bay, 9
Wins: Bernie Pearlman, Sydney, 11
Phil Mooney, Sydney, 11
SOs: Bernie Pearlman, Sydney, 105
ERA: Bernie Pearlman, Sydney, 1.62

C Cotton States League
President: Judge Emmet Harty

Standings	W	L	Pct.	GB	Attend.	Manager
Monroe White Sox	92	46	.667	—	51,945	Doug Taitt
Clarksdale Red Sox (1)	77	63	.550	16	56,284	Leroy "Cowboy" Jones
Greenwood Crackers	71	63	.530	19	41,873	Cecil "Dusty" Rhodes
Hot Springs Bathers (4)	71	67	.514	21	33,810	Conrad Fisher
Greenville Buckshots (10)	61	75	.449	30	30,958	James Powell
El Dorado Lions (12)	59	75	.440	31	32,291	Frank O'Rourke
Pine Bluff Judges (10)	57	76	.429	32½	23,555	Jimmie Sherlin/Andy Cohen
Helena Seaporters (12)	58	81	.417	34½	19,986	Oliver "Buster" Blakeney

Playoffs: Hot Springs 3 games, Monroe 2; Greenwood 3 games, Clarksdale 1.
Finals: Greenwood 4 games, Hot Springs 1.

All-Star Team: 1B-Murrell Jones, Monroe; 2B-Joe Wessing, Hot Springs; 3B-Guy Pruitt, Monroe; SS-John Conway, Monroe; OF-Steve Carter, Hot Springs; Andy Gilbert, Clarksdale; John Rowe, Helena; C-Frank Krole, Clarksdale; Util-Gerard Lipscomb, Greenwood; P-Earl Harrist, El Dorado; Kelton Maxfield, Monroe; **Manager**-Doug Taitt, Monroe.

BA: Steve Carter, Hot Springs, .369
Runs: Andy Gilbert, Clarksdale, 136
Hits: John Rowe, Helena, 202
RBIs: Steve Carter, Hot Springs, 132

HRs: Al Gardella, Hot Springs, 32
Wins: John Yelovic, Monroe, 21
SOs: Earl Harrist, El Dorado, 223
ERA: James Hogan, Helena, 3.14

C East Texas League
President: C.P. Mosley

Standings	W	L	Pct.	GB	Manager
Henderson Oilers (4)	85	55	.607	—	Jake Atz, Sr.
Kilgore Boomers (16)	80	59	.576	4½	Jimmy Dalrymple
Palestine Pals	76	63	.547	8½	Ray Flood/Jack Calvey
Marshall Tigers	72	68	.514	13	Cal Cowman/Hub Northen/Gabby Lusk/ Guy Sturdy
Tyler Trojans (3)	70	69	.504	14½	Bobby Goff
Texarkana Liners	64	75	.460	20½	Eph Lobaugh
Longview Cannibals/ White Sox (2)	59	79	.428	25	Jack Fitzpatrick
Jacksonville Jax	51	89	.364	34	Jimmy Zinn/Sam Hancock/Lee Stebbins/ Hal Grant/Roxy Middleton

Total Attendance: 227,000.

Playoffs: Henderson 4 games, Marshall 3; Kilgore 4 games, Palestine 1.
Finals: Kilgore 4 games, Henderson 0.

All-Star Team: 1B-George Sturdivant, Henderson; 2B-John Zapor, Henderson; 3B-Al Costello, Palestine; SS-Damon Phillips, Henderson; OF-Gilbert Turner, Marshall; Ed Knoblauch, Kilgore; John Simontacchi, Marshall; C-Lou Kahn, Palestine; Util-Vance Scrivener Randolph, Kilgore; P-Steve Rachunok, Henderson; Gene Hinrichs, Henderson; **Manager**-Jake Atz, Sr., Henderson.

BA: Lou Kahn, Palestine, .346
Runs: Ed Knoblauch, Kilgore, 125
Hits: Ed Knoblauch, Kilgore, 189
RBIs: Gilbert Turner, Marshall, 112

HRs: Gilbert Turner, Marshall, 26
Wins: Steve Rachunok, Henderson, 22
SOs: Bill Roberson, Tyler, 222
ERA: Ed Lopat, Longview, 2.11

C Interstate League
President: Harold G. Hoffman

Standings	W	L	Pct.	GB	Manager
Allentown Dukes (9)	54	48	.529	—	Pete Weimer/George Hennessey/ Louis Parisse
Sunbury Senators	51	51	.500	3	Bill Kerstetter
Trenton Senators	51	51	.500	3	Goose Goslin
Hazleton Mountaineers	48	54	.471	6	Harvey Hiller/Frank DeManicor

Attendance: Trenton, 60,000; Sunbury, 25,000.

Playoff: Sunbury defeated Trenton in a one game playoff for second place.
Finals: Allentown 4 games, Sunbury 3.

All-Star Team: 1B-David Kelly, Sunbury; 2B-Charles Budd, Trenton; 3B-William Long, Hazleton; SS-Michael Simko, Sunbury; OF-Bob Braner, Allentown; Woody Wheaton, Hazleton; Don Dorney, Allentown; C-Joseph Antolick, Allentown; Util-Julius Horvath, Hazleton; P-George Hennessey, Allentown; Joe Fryer, Allentown; **Manager**-Goose Goslin, Trenton.

BA: David Kelly, Sunbury, .404
Runs: Woody Wheaton, Hazleton, 98
Hits: David Kelly, Sunbury, 163
RBIs: David Kelly, Sunbury, 86

HRs: David Kelly, Sunbury, 14
Wins: Mike Koons, Hazleton, 16
SOs: Joe Fryer, Allentown, 159
ERA: Russ Bailey, Trenton, 3.11

C Middle Atlantic League
President: Elmer M. Daily

Standings	W	L	Pct.	GB	Manager
Canton Terriers (1)	77	52	.597	—	Floyd Patterson
Charleston Senators (9)	70	60	.538	7½	Edward Hall
Akron Yankees (5)	69	61	.531	8½	Horace "Pip" Koehler
Springfield Indians (3)	66	64	.508	11½	Earl Wolgamot
Portsmouth Red Birds (16)	61	69	.469	16½	Joe Davis
Dayton Wings (10)	60	69	.465	17	Dudley Lee/Andy Cohen
Youngstown Browns (7)	60	70	.462	17½	Bill Urbanski
Erie Sailors (12)	55	73	.430	21½	Jocko Munch

Playoffs: Canton 3 games, Akron 1; Springfield 3 games, Charleston 1.
Finals: Canton 4 games, Springfield 1.

All-Star Team: 1B-Edward Murphy, Portsmouth; 2B-Archie Horne, Portsmouth; 3B-Laney McConnell, Erie; SS-Ed Pellagrini, Canton; OF-Stanley Hoyinski, Charleston; Peter Kraus, Youngstown; Paul O'Dea, Springfield; C-Stew Hofferth, Dayton; Util-Horace "Pip" Koehler, Akron; P-Robert Waugh, Akron; Al Hodkey, Canton; **Manager**-Edward Hall, Charleston.

BA: Edward Murphy, Portsmouth, .375
Runs: Frank Genovese, Canton, 113
Hits: Peter Kraus, Youngstown, 172
RBIs: John Lazor, Canton, 103

HRs: Edward Murphy, Portsmouth, 22
Wins: Robert Waugh, Akron, 20
SOs: Max Surkont, Portsmouth, 193
ERA: Joe Davis, Portsmouth, 2.49

C Pioneer League
President: Jack Halliwell

Standings	W	L	Pct.	GB	Manager
Twin Falls Cowboys	72	52	.581	—	Eddie Leishman/Wes Schulmerich/ Charles Wry
Pocatello Cardinals (16)	68	56	.548	4	Tony Robello
Boise Pilots	62	62	.500	10	Andy Harrington
Salt Lake City Bees	59	65	.476	13	Eddie Mulligan
Ogden Reds (12)	58	66	.468	14	Bill McCorry
Lewiston Indians	53	71	.427	19	Herb Sanders

Total Attendance: 447,000.

Playoffs: None.

All-Star Team: 1B-Tony Robello, Pocatello; 2B-Ernest Bishop, Twin Falls; 3B-Chester Rosenlund, Ogden; SS-Jack Charles Murphy, Pocatello; OF-Mike Reser, Lewiston; Jay Kirke, Jr., Pocatello; Pete Hughes, Ogden; C-Joe McNamee, Twin Falls; Util-Joe Serpa, Ogden; P-Charles Wry, Twin Falls; Jack Andrews, Salt Lake City; **Manager**-Eddie Mulligan, Salt Lake City.

BA: Pete Hughes, Ogden, .409
Runs: Tony Robello, Pocatello, 168
Hits: Tony Robello, Pocatello, 205
RBIs: Tony Robello, Pocatello, 179
HRs: Tony Robello, Pocatello, 58

Wins: William Schubel, Twin Falls, 19
Charles Wry, Twin Falls, 19
SOs: Harold Erickson, Lewiston, 193
ERA: Robert Costello, Ogden, 3.68
Pct: Charles Wry, Twin Falls, .731, 19-7

C Western Association
President: Tom Fairweather

Standings	W	L	Pct.	GB	Attend.	Manager
Ft. Smith Giants (13)	83	50	.624	—	88,000	Herschel Bobo
Joplin Miners (5)	81	56	.591	4	49,869	Claude Jonnard
Springfield Cardinals (16)	78	60	.565	7½	64,380	George Silvey
Topeka Owls (7)	72	65	.526	13	85,500	William Wilson
St. Joseph Angels (11)	66	72	.478	19½	30,716	Goldie Holt
Muskogee Reds (12)	60	76	.441	24½	36,226	Lester "Pat" Patterson
Salina Millers	55	79	.410	28½	41,725	Riley Parker
Hutchinson Pirates (15)	49	86	.363	35	34,672	Jimmy Jordan

Playoffs: Springfield 3 games, Ft. Smith 1; Topeka 3 games, Joplin 2.
Finals: Springfield 3 games, Topeka 2.

All-Star Team: 1B-Butch Morgan, Muskogee; 2B-Jimmy Jordan, Hutchinson; 3B-Harry Goorabian, Topeka; SS-Harry "Peanuts" Lowrey, St. Joseph; OF-Jack Tighe, Joplin; Richard Lang, Springfield; Albert White, Topeka; C-James Sheehan, Ft. Smith; Util-Lloyd Rigby, Salina; P-Charley Wensloff, Joplin; Steve Tramback, Ft. Smith; **Manager**-William Wilson, Topeka.

BA: Jimmy Jordan, Hutchinson, .348
Runs: Albert White, Topeka, 139
Hits: Clarence Springer, Topeka, 187
RBIs: Butch Morgan, Muskogee, 146
HRs: Harry Goorabian, Topeka, 38

Wins: Charley Wensloff, Joplin, 26
Maurice Newlin, Topeka, 26
SOs: Paul Erickson, St. Joseph, 198
Pct: Charley Wensloff, Joplin, .867, 26-4

D Alabama-Florida League
President: Charles T. Laney

Standings	W	L	Pct.	GB	Manager
Dothan Browns	74	54	.578	—	Ernie Wingard
Tallassee Indians	73	56	.566	1½	Rosy Gilhousen
Andalusia Rams	70	59	.543	4½	Bruner Nix
Panama City Pelicans	63	64	.496	10½	Max Rosenfeld
Troy Trojans (3)	62	68	.477	13	Holt "Cat" Milner
Greenville Lions (2)	44	85	.341	30½	Paul Kardow

Playoffs: Tallassee 3 games, Panama City 2, one tie; Andalusia 3 games, Dothan 2.
Finals: Tallassee 4 games, Andalusia 3.

All-Star Team: 1B-Holt "Cat" Milner, Troy; **2B**-Tom Kane, Tallassee; **3B**-Woodrow Davis, Panama City; **SS**-James Cox, Dothan; **OF**-Rosy Gilhousen, Tallassee; Gordon Goodell, Tallassee; Paul Armstrong, Andalusia; **C**-Malcolm DeWeese, Tallassee; **Util**-Elmer Bohannon, Troy; **P**-Charleston Jones, Dothan; Jacques Weston, Andalusia; **Manager**-Ernie Wingard, Dothan.

BA: Holt "Cat" Milner, Troy, .381	**HRs:** Bruce Middlebrooks, Troy, 20
Runs: James Cox, Dothan, 126	**Wins:** Charleston Jones, Dothan, 20
Hits: Ernie Wingard, Dothan, 180	**SOs:** Pershing Henderson, Troy, 175
RBIs: Ernie Wingard, Dothan, 137	**ERA:** Charleston Jones, Dothan, 2.52

D Appalachian League
President: Ray Ryan

Standings	W	L	Pct.	GB	Manager
Elizabethton Betsy Red Sox (1) ..	71	48	.597	—	Hobe Brummitt
Kingsport Cherokees	70	49	.588	1	Jerry Witner/Claude Trivette
Johnson City Cardinals (16)	69	51	.575	2½	Ollie Vanek
Greeneville Burley Cubs (3) ..	65	54	.546	6	Sam Alexander
Pennington Gap Bears (7)..	52	66	.441	18½	Art Hauger
Newport Canners (5)	30	89	.252	41	Pete Doyle/Bob O'Brien/Ken Mackes

Playoffs: Elizabethton 2 games, Greeneville 1; Kingsport 2 games, Johnson City 1.
Finals: Elizabethton 3 games, Kingsport 1.

All-Star Team: 1B-Leo "Muscle" Shoals, Johnson City; **2B**-Burton Hodge, Elizabethton; **3B**-Don Cross, Elizabethton; **SS**-Cornell Kohlmeyer, Pennington Gap; **OF**-Claude Trivette, Kingsport; Mike Surgent, Pennington Gap; Emil Kreshka, Kingsport; **C**-Dick Bouknight, Johnson City; **Util**-Charles Heffner, Kingsport; **P**-Paul Onkotz, Kingsport; Dick Douthat, Greeneville; **Manager**-Sam Alexander, Greeneville.

BA: Leo "Muscle" Shoals, Johnson City, .365	**HRs:** Leo "Muscle" Shoals, Johnson City, 16
Runs: Emil Kreshka, Kingsport, 106	**Wins:** Ed Rosenbaum, Elizabethton, 21
Hits: Emil Kreshka, Kingsport, 169	**SOs:** Norman Shope, Elizabethton, 154
RBIs: Dick Poydock, Kingsport, 97	**ERA:** Anderson Bush, Greeneville, 2.14

D Arizona-Texas League
President: Dr. R.E. Soners

Standings	W	L	Pct.	GB	Manager
Bisbee Bees**(11)..............	72	57	.558	—	Carl Dittmar
Albuquerque Cardinals*(16)..	70	60	.538	2½	Bill DeLancey
El Paso Texans (5)............	68	62	523	4½	Ted Mayer
Tucson Cowboys	49	80	.380	23	Bill Salkeld/Mike Simon

Attendance: Albuquerque, 100,000; Total, 200,000.

Playoff: Albuquerque 4 games, Bisbee 2.

All-Star Team: 1B-Roy Myers, Bisbee; **2B**-Sam Arico, Bisbee; **3B**-Willie Reyes, Albuquerque; **SS**-Len Ratto, El Paso; **OF**-Bob Joratz, Albuquerque; Donald White, Albuquerque; Joe LaPlana, Bisbee; **C**-Bill Salkeld, Tucson; **Util**-Shaun Denniston, El Paso; **P**-Eddie King, Bisbee; Jack Hawkins, El Paso; **Manager**-Bill DeLancey, Albuquerque.

BA: Bob Joratz, Albuquerque, .348	**HRs:** Al Montgomery, Bisbee, 17
Runs: Bob Joratz, Albuquerque, 126	**Wins:** Eddie King, Bisbee, 25
Hits: Dale Gill, Bisbee, 182	**SOs:** Jack Hawkins, El Paso, 257
RBIs: Willie Reyes, Albuquerque, 124	**ERA:** Ned Rogers, El Paso, 2.20

D Arkansas-Missouri League
President: Robert J. Henry

Standings	W	L	Pct.	GB	Manager
Fayetteville Angels***(7) ..	79	42	.653	—	Frank Oceak
Carthage Pirates (15)	67	54	.554	12	Adolph Arlitt
Neosho Yankees (5)............	65	61	.516	16½	Dennis Burns
Monett Red Birds (16)........	35	89	.282	45½	Freddie Hawn

Playoff: Carthage 4 games, Fayetteville 1.

All-Star Team: 1B-Adolph Arlitt, Carthage; **2B**-Frank Oceak, Fayetteville; **3B**-Grant Harris, Carthage; **SS**-Ed Checkley, Fayetteville; **OF**-Ansel Owen, Neosho; Bill Sarver, Neosho; Harvey Beaster, Carthage; **C**-Ralph Houk, Neosho; **Util**-Clarence Collins, Fayetteville; **P**-George Bender, Fayetteville; Francis Henry, Monett; **Manager**-Dennis Burns, Neosho.

BA: Adolph Arlitt, Carthage, .358	**HRs:** Steve Greble, Neosho, 24
Runs: Steve Greble, Neosho, 129	**Wins:** George Bender, Fayetteville, 20
Hits: Harvey Beaster, Carthage, 171	**SOs:** George Bender, Fayetteville, 208
RBIs: Harvey Beaster, Carthage, 106	**ERA:** George Bender, Fayetteville, 2.35

D Bi-State League
President: Joseph Garrett

Standings	W	L	Pct.	GB	Manager
Danville-Schoolfield Leafs (1)	70	44	.614	—	Emile Barnes
Leaksville-Spray-Draper Triplets (3)	67	48	.583	3½	Arnold Anderson
Bassett Furnituremakers (12)..	60	51	.541	8½	Walter Novak

Standings	W	L	Pct.	GB	Manager
Martinsville Manufacturers (16).	61	52	.540	8½	Jim Poole
Mayodan Millers (14)........	58	57	.504	12½	Harry Daughtry
Reidsville Luckies (10).......	48	65	.425	21½	William Clark
South Boston Wrappers......	46	65	.414	22½	Dixie Parker
Mt. Airy Graniteers.............	42	70	.375	27	Guy Lacy

Playoffs: Leaksville-Spray-Draper 4 games, Martinsville 1; Danville-Schoolfield 4 games, Bassett 3.
Finals: Danville-Schoolfield 4 games, Leaksville-Spray-Draper 2.

All-Star Team: 1B-Richard Bohl, South Boston; **2B**-Jim Gruzdis, Leaksville-Spray-Draper; **3B**-Emmitt Johnson, Leaksville-Spray-Draper; **SS**-Richard Culler, Reidsville; **OF**-Joseph Zentara, Bassett; James Payne, Leaksville-Spray-Draper; Sam Gentile, Danville-Schoolfield; **C**-Frank Warren, Bassett; **Util**-Don Prather, South Boston; **P**-Raymond Poat, Leaksville-Spray-Draper; George Kadis, Danville-Schoolfield; **Manager**-Walter Novak, Bassett.

BA: Sam Gentile, Danville-Schoolfield, .392	**RBIs:** James Payne, Leaksville-Spray-Draper, 126
Runs: Jim Gruzdis, Leaksville-Spray-Draper, 145	**HRs:** Amerigo Scagliarini, Mayodan, 27
Hits: Sam Gentile, Danville-Schoolfield, 199	**Wins:** Joseph Weir, Danville-Schoolfield, 19
	SOs: George Kadis, Danville-Schoolfield, 199
	ERA: Frank Hoerst, Mayodan, 2.82

D Coastal Plain League
Presidents: J.B. Eure/Ray Goodmon

Standings	W	L	Pct.	GB	Manager
Greenville Greenies (8)	74	48	.607	—	Rube Wilson
Goldsboro Goldbugs..........	69	53	.566	5	Mule Shirley
Williamston Martins..........	65	57	.533	9	Paul O'Malley
Kinston Eagles..................	65	59	.524	10	Fred "Snake" Henry/Ray Lucas/Bill Herring
New Bern Bears................	62	59	.512	11½	Doc Smith
Wilson Tobs....................	64	61	.512	11½	Frank Rodgers
Snow Hill Billies	56	64	.467	17	D.C. "Peahead" Walker
Tarboro Serpents/Goobers..	36	90	.286	40	Guy Schatzer/Fred Neisler/Eddie Stumpf

Playoffs: Kinston 4 games, Greenville 2; Williamston 4 games, Goldsboro 1.
Finals: Williamston 4 games, Kinston 1.

All-Star Team: 1B-Harry Soufas, Snow Hill; **2B**-Harry Christopher, Greenville; **3B**-Tony Maisano, Snow Hill; **SS**-Clarence Allen, Greenville; **OF**-Claude Capps, Goldsboro; Uriah Norwood, New Bern; Luis Olmo, Wilson; **C**-Jesse Overton, Goldsboro; **Util**-Sid Stringfellow, Kinston; **P**-Harry Swain, Williamston; Don King, Greenville; **Manager**-Rube Wilson, Greenville.

BA: Uriah Norwood, New Bern, .336	**RBIs:** Joe Bistroff, Snow Hill, 108
Runs: Claude Capps, Goldsboro, 99	**HRs:** Joe Bistroff, Snow Hill, 32
Hits: Ed Black, Greenville, 151	**Wins:** Bill Herring, Kinston, 22
Harry Soufas, Snow Hill, 151	**ERA:** Don King, Greenville, 1.25
Charles Whitaker, Snow Hill, 151	**SO:** Harry Swain, Williamston, 186

D Eastern Shore League
President: Harry S. Russell

Standings	W	L	Pct.	GB	Attend.	Manager
Federalsburg A's (6)..........	83	38	.686	—	27,000	Sam Holbrook
Cambridge Cardinals (16) ..	68	51	.571	14	34,000	Fred Lucas
Dover Orioles	62	57	.521	20	23,500	Wes Kingdon/Walter Millies
Centreville Colts (1)	62	60	.508	21½	21,000	John Clark
Salisbury Senators (8)........	59	59	.500	22½	23,000	Vic Keen/Spud Nachand
Easton Yankees (5)............	51	68	.429	31	32,000	Ray Powell
Milford Giants (13)............	49	69	.416	32½	19,000	Earl Smith/Val Picinich
Pocomoke City Red Sox	43	75	.364	38½	12,000	Jake Flowers

Playoffs: Cambridge 3 games, Centreville 0; Dover 3 games, Federalsburg 0.
Finals: Cambridge 4 games, Dover 2.

All-Star Team: 1B-Irving Kolberg, Federalsburg; **2B**-Herb Freeman, Centreville; **3B**-Henry Schluter, Dover; **SS**-Alex Monchak, Dover; **OF**-Martin Steinman, Milford; James Johnson, Centreville; Ron Northey, Federalsburg; **C**-Sam Holbrook, Federalsburg; **Util**-Robert Maier, Salisbury; **P**-Les Hinckle, Federalsburg; William McLaughlin, Cambridge; **Manager**-Sam Holbrook, Federalsburg.

BA: Martin Steinman, Milford, .378	**HRs:** Henry Schluter, Dover, 29
Runs: Irving Kolberg, Federalsburg, 111	**Wins:** Les Hinckle, Federalsburg, 27
Hits: Francis Walsh, Centreville, 163	**SOs:** Les Hinckle, Federalsburg, 309
RBIs: Francis Walsh, Centreville, 129	**ERA:** Les Hinckle, Federalsburg, 2.49

D Evangeline League
President: A. Wilmont Dalferes

Standings	W	L	Pct.	GB	Manager
Alexandria Aces	82	56	.594	—	Art Phelan
Lafayette White Sox (7)	75	63	.543	7	Rod Whitney
Jeanerette Blues	73	62	.541	7½	Harry Strohm
New Iberia Cardinals (16) ..	72	64	.519	10½	Jimmie Sanders
Rayne Rice Birds	68	68	.500	13	Charlie Engle
Abbeville A's (6).............	65	70	.481	15½	Carlos Moore
Lake Charles Skippers	59	75	.440	21	Joe Bratcher
Opelousas Indians (3)	51	84	.378	29½	Joe Woodard

Playoffs: New Iberia 4 games, Alexandria 1; Lafayette 4 games, Jeanerette 1.
Finals: Lafayette 4 games, New Iberia 3.

All-Star Team: 1B-Jerry Witte, Lafayette; **2B**-John Taylor, Abbeville; **3B**-Edgar Busch, Lafayette; **SS**-Robert Ludwig, Opelousas; **OF**-Gordon Donaldson, Alexandria; Robert Patrick, Alexandria; Anse Moore, Alexandria; **C**-Dennis Gleason, New Iberia; **Util**-J.R. Corbitt, Lake Charles; **P**-Ed Head, Abbeville; Walter Navie, Rayne; **Manager**-Harry Strohm, Jeanerette.

BA: Jerry Witte, Lafayette, .354	**HRs:** Joe Yourkovich, Rayne, 18
Runs: Robert Patrick, Alexandria, 111	**Wins:** Max Fugerson, Abbeville, 22
Hits: Jerry Witte, Lafayette, 184	**SOs:** Walter Navie, Rayne, 223
RBIs: Jerry Witte, Lafayette, 134	**ERA:** Max Fugerson, Abbeville, 2.04

D Florida State League
President: Henry Gray

Standings	W	L	Pct.	GB	Manager
Sanford Lookouts (8)	98	35	.737	—	Dale Alexander
Daytona Beach Islanders (10)	87	48	.644	12	Tommy West
Leesburg Anglers	72	65	.526	28	Nellie Leach
DeLand Red Hats	69	69	.500	31½	Spec Meadows/Don McShane
St. Augustine Saints	68	70	.493	32½	Alan Mobley
Gainesville G-Men	61	77	.442	39½	Don McShane/Ike Livingston
Orlando Senators (8)	54	82	.397	45½	John Ganzel
Palatka Azaleas	36	99	.267	63	Bill Leitz/Sam "Cowboy" Jones

Attendance: DeLand, 30,651.

Playoffs: Sanford 3 games, DeLand 2; Daytona Beach 3 games, Leesburg 0.
Finals: Sanford 4 games, Daytona Beach 3.

All-Star Team: 1B-Walton McMullen, Gainesville; **2B**-Lyle Judy, St. Augustine; **3B**-Lowell Barnett, Sanford; **SS**-Gene Geary, DeLand; **OF**-Al Smathers, DeLand; Joe Niedson, Daytona Beach; Wilmer Skeen, Sanford; **C**-Tommy West, Daytona Beach; **Util**-Ike Livingston, Gainesville; **P**-Sylvester Donnelly, Daytona Beach; Milt Haefner, DeLand; **Manager**-Alan Mobley, St. Augustine.

BA: Tommy West, Daytona Beach, .382	**HRs:** Joe Niedson, Daytona Beach, 11
Runs: Bill Rabe, Daytona Beach, 120	**Wins:** Sid Hudson, Sanford, 24
Hits: Tommy West, Daytona Beach, 186	**SOs:** Sid Hudson, Sanford, 192
Al Smathers, DeLand, 186	**ERA:** Sid Hudson, Sanford, 1.79
RBIs: Al Smathers, DeLand, 134	

D Georgia-Florida League
President: A.D. "Doc" Walker

Standings	W	L	Pct.	GB	Manager
Albany Cardinals (16)	80	53	.602	—	Johnny Keane
Valdosta Trojans (15)	73	63	.537	8½	Bill Morrall
Tallahassee Capitols (3)	69	66	.511	12	Ralph McAdams
Waycross Bears	70	68	.507	12½	Albert Leitz
Moultrie Packers (14)	68	67	.504	13	Joe Halden
Thomasville Orioles	64	72	.491	17½	Cy Morgan
Americus Pioneers (10)	63	76	.471	20	Joe Sims
Cordele Bees	58	80	.453	24½	Harry Ris

Attendance: Waycross, 85,566.

Playoffs: Valdosta 3 games, Waycross 2; Albany 3 games, Tallahassee 1.
Finals: Albany 4 games, Valdosta 0.

All-Star Team: 1B-Cecil "Turkey" Tyson, Tallahassee; **2B**-E. Vandergrift, Thomasville; **3B**-Carl Bethman, Moultrie; **SS**-Lou Lucas, Albany; **OF**-Edgar Hartness, Americus; Casey Kimbrell, Tallahassee; Eddie Lukon, Valdosta; **C**-Albert Leitz, Waycross; **Util**-Pat Dove, Thomasville; **P**-Vernon Horn, Albany; Weldon West, Americus; **Manager**-Cy Morgan, Thomasville.

BA: Edgar Hartness, Americus, .356	**HRs:** Carl Bethman, Moultrie, 9
Runs: Frank Pelat, Moultrie, 113	**Wins:** Lloyd Gross, Moultrie, 22
Hits: Edgar Hartness, Americus, 175	**SOs:** Weldon West, Americus, 245
Carl Bethman, Moultrie, 175	**ERA:** Fred Schmidt, Albany, 1.81
RBIs: Carl Bethman, Moultrie, 111	

D Kitty League
President: B.F. Howard

Standings	W	L	Pct.	GB	Manager
Mayfield Browns (7)	76	49	.608	—	Benny Tate
Bowling Green Barons	75	51	.595	1½	Rip Fanning
Owensboro Oilers (9)	75	51	.595	1½	Hugh Wise
Jackson Generals	67	59	.532	9½	Vincent "Moon" Mullen
Hopkinsville Hoppers (11)	57	68	.456	19	Harry Griswold
Paducah Indians (10)	57	69	.452	19½	Ben Tincup
Fulton Tigers (4)	52	74	.413	24½	Charles Eckert
Union City Greyhounds (16)	44	82	.349	32½	Lee Johnson

Playoffs: Mayfield 3 games, Jackson 2; Bowling Green 3 games, Owensboro 0.
Finals: Bowling Green 4 games, Mayfield 2.

All-Star Team: 1B-Eddie O'Connell, Owensboro; **2B**-Clint Andercek, Bowling Green; **3B**-Don DeVault, Owensboro; **SS**-Vern Stephens, Mayfield; **OF**-Joe Morjoseph, Mayfield; Carl Alto, Hopkinsville; Jack DeVincenzi, Owensboro; **C**-Harry Griswold, Hopkinsville; **Util**-Vincent "Moon" Mullen, Jackson; **P**-Howard Schumacher, Owensboro; Chauncey Scott, Union City; **Manager**-Charles Eckert, Fulton.

BA: Vern Stephens, Mayfield, .361	**HRs:** John Newman, Owensboro, 33
Runs: Joe Morjoseph, Mayfield, 120	**Wins:** Elmer Haas, Bowling Green, 25
Hits: Stan Stencel, Hopkinsville, 184	**SOs:** Chauncey Scott, Union City, 213
RBIs: Vern Stephens, Mayfield, 123	**ERA:** William Scott, Mayfield, 2.31

D Mountain State League
President: Ray Ryan

Standings	W	L	Pct.	GB	Manager
Williamson Red Birds (16)	76	51	.598	—	Harrison Wickel
Welch Miners	72	57	.558	5	Sam Gray
Huntington Boosters (10)	66	61	.520	10	Ellis "Mike" Powers
Bluefield Blue-Greys	65	64	.504	12	Vic Sorrell
Logan Indians (3)	55	75	.423	22½	Eddie Hock
Ashland Colonels	52	78	.400	25½	Harold Conn/Ray French

Attendance: Bluefield, 70,000.

Playoffs: Williamson 2 games, Huntington 1; Bluefield 2 games, Welch 0.
Finals: Bluefield 3 games, Williamson 1.

All-Star Team: 1B-John Streza, Williamson; **2B**-Alfred Norman Beals, Welch; **3B**-Thad Cash, Bluefield; **SS**-Harrison Wickel, Williamson; **OF**-Lewis D'Antoni, Bluefield; Gordon Duff, Welch; Walter Sessi, Williamson; **C**-Sam Hayden, Logan; **Util**-Joseph Bezdek, Ashland; **P**-John Patterson, Huntington; Russell Meers, Huntington; **Manager**-Ellis "Mike" Powers, Huntington.

BA: Bill Shewey, Williamson, .376	**HRs:** Edison Guinter, Logan, 26
Runs: John Streza, Williamson, 127	**Wins:** Howard Smith, Williamson, 19
Hits: John Streza, Williamson, 185	**SOs:** Russell Meers, Huntington, 297
RBIs: Harrison Wickel, Williamson, 142	**ERA:** Sam Gray, Welch, 3.03

D North Carolina State League
President: C.M. Llewellyn

Standings	W	L	Pct.	GB	Attend.	Manager
Mooresville Moors	71	38	.651	—	20,093	Johnny Hicks
Lexington Indians (6)	64	46	.582	7½	51,205	Joe Byrd
Concord Weavers	60	50	.545	11½	41,458	Gerald Fitzgerald
Thomasville Tommies	58	52	.527	13½	60,560	Jimmy Maus
Salisbury Giants (13)	56	54	.509	15½	44,173	Dick Luckey
Cooleemee Cools	49	62	.441	23	17,185	Otis "Blackie" Carter
Kannapolis Towelers	46	65	.414	26	51,336	Phil Lundern
Landis Sens	37	74	.333	35	19,343	Ginger Watts

Playoffs: Mooresville 3 games, Concord 1; Thomasville 3 games, Lexington 2.
Finals: Mooresville 4 games, Thomasville 1.

All-Star Team: 1B-Ted Mueller, Thomasville; **2B**-Ulmont Baker, Concord; **3B**-George Motto, Cooleemee; **SS**-Webster Templeton, Mooresville; **OF**-William Carrier, Mooresville; Claude Wilborn, Cooleemee; Borden Helms, Salisbury; **C**-John Pare, Concord; **Util**-Harvey Black, Mooresville; **P**-Ray Lindsay, Thomasville; Clyde Teague, Mooresville; **Manager**-Gerald Fitzgerald, Concord.

BA: Ted Mueller, Thomasville, .391	**HRs:** James Hamblen, Salisbury, 17
Runs: Borden Helms, Salisbury, 100	**Wins:** Richard Robinson, Mooresville, 23
Webster Templeton, Mooresville, 100	**SOs:** Ray Lindsay, Thomasville, 237
Hits: Ted Mueller, Thomasville, 161	**ERA:** Ray Lindsay, Thomasville, 1.89
RBIs: William Carrier, Mooresville, 92	

D Northeast Arkansas League
President: Joseph R. Bertig

Standings	W	L	Pct.	GB	Manager
Caruthersville Pilots*** (16)	79	39	.669	—	Joseph "Bunny" Simmons
Paragould Broncos (7)	63	57	.525	17	Elmer Kirchoff
Newport Tigers (4)	61	60	.504	19½	Clarence Harris
Jonesboro White Sox (2)	38	85	.309	43½	Dutch Welch

Playoffs: None.

All-Star Team: 1B-Louis Leiter, Jonesboro; **2B**-Robert Stanton, Caruthersville; **3B**-Lou Miller, Paragould; **SS**-John Dantonio, Caruthersville; **OF**-Stan Bazan, Jonesboro; Ray Zimmerman, Caruthersville; Edward Filo, Caruthersville; **C**-Frank Grube, Jonesboro; **Util**-Elmer Kirchoff, Paragould; **P**-Johnny Sain, Newport; Edward Hughes, Newport; **Manager**-Joseph "Bunny" Simmons, Caruthersville.

BA: Robert Stanton, Caruthersville, .340	**HRs:** Joe Rayne, Paragould, 23
Runs: Thomas Woodruff, Paragould, 115	**Wins:** Milton Lowery, Caruthersville, 20
Hits: Elmer Kirchoff, Paragould, 153	**SOs:** Clarence "Hooks" Iott, Paragould, 215
RBIs: Robert Stanton, Caruthersville, 93	**ERA:** Charles Fichter, Caruthersville, 2.14

D Northern League
President: Herman D. White

Standings	W	L	Pct.	GB	Manager
Winnipeg Maroons	72	46	.610	—	Joe Mowry
Duluth Dukes (16)	71	46	.607	½	Dutch Dorman

Fargo-Moorhead Twins (3) 66 48 .579 4 Jack Knight
Eau Claire Bears (11) .... 56 60 .483 15 Ivy Griffin
Superior Blues (10).............. 54 59 .478 15½ George "Red" Treadwell
Wausau Lumberjacks .... 54 62 .466 17 Wally Gilbert
Grand Forks Chiefs (2)...... 49 68 .419 22½ Johnny Mostil
Crookston Pirates............... 43 76 .361 29½ Phil Todt

Playoffs: Eau Claire 4 games, Duluth 2; Winnipeg 4 games, Fargo-Moorhead 3.
Finals: Winnipeg 4 games, Eau Claire 1.

All-Star Team: 1B-Hugh Gustafson, Winnipeg; **2B**-Walter Kordenbrock, Fargo-Moorhead; **3B**-Robert Schmidt, Duluth; **SS**-Harry Semczak, Fargo-Moorhead; **OF**-Marion Ciborowski, Superior; James Cookson, Duluth; William Barnacle, Winnipeg; **C**-Vincent Castino, Eau Claire/Grand Forks; **Util**-Winfred Hansch, Winnipeg; **P**-Jack Dawson, Fargo-Moorhead; Joe Hatten, Crookston; **Manager**-George "Red" Treadwell, Superior.

BA: Robert Schmidt, Duluth, .441
Runs: Robert Schmidt, Duluth, 114
Hits: Robert Schmidt, Duluth, 194
RBIs: Robert Schmidt, Duluth, 133
HRs: Robert Schmidt, Duluth, 31
Wins: Galen Shupe, Winnipeg, 18
SOs: Joe Hatten, Crookston, 299
ERA: Robert Haas, Fargo-Moorhead, 2.57

D Ohio State League
President: Paul H. Shank

Standings	W	L	Pct.	GB	Manager
Findlay Oilers	68	62	.523	—	Grover Hartley
Fremont Green Sox.............	66	63	.512	1½	James "Chappie" Geygan
Fostoria Red Birds (16)	66	63	.512	1½	Jack Farmer
Lima Pandas	64	66	.492	4	Bill Ward
Tiffin Mud Hens (4)	64	66	.492	4	Jim Lawrence
Mansfield Braves (3)	61	69	.469	7	Ray French

Attendance: Fremont, 25,000.

Playoffs: Lima defeated Tiffin in a one game playoff for fourth place. Fremont was awarded second place for playoff purposes by a coin toss. Findlay 2 games, Fostoria 0; Lima 2 games, Fremont 1.
Finals: Lima 4 games, Findlay 3.

BA: Hank Edwards, Mansfield, .395
Runs: Hank Edwards, Mansfield, 135
Hits: Hank Edwards, Mansfield, 209
RBIs: Del Wilber, Findlay, 145
HRs: Hubert Wooten, Lima, 18
Hank Edwards, Mansfield, 18
Wins: Glen Fletcher, Findlay, 22
SOs: Frederick Berger, Fostoria, 231
Pct: Edward Evans, Lima, .846, 11-2

D Pennsylvania State Association
President: Elmer M. Daily

Standings	W	L	Pct.	GB	Manager
Butler Yankees (5)..............	67	43	.609	—	Thomas Kain
Washington Red Birds (16)	64	45	.587	2½	Bob Scheffing
Beaver Falls Bees (7)..........	58	52	.527	9	Ralph Goldsmith
Johnstown Johnnies (14)	50	60	.455	17	Dick Goldberg
McKeesport Little Pirates (15)	49	61	.445	18	Leo Mackey/Joe Agee
Greensburg Senators (8).....	41	68	.376	25½	George Mucci

Attendance: Butler, 45,000.

Playoffs: Butler 3 games, Beaver Falls 1; Washington 3 games, Johnstown 2.
Finals: Washington 3 games, Butler 0.

All-Star Team: 1B-Bob Scheffing, Washington; **2B**-Orval Cott, Washington; **3B**-Bernard Dunn, Beaver Falls; **SS**-Charles Gillespie, Johnstown; **OF**-Arnold Evans, Butler; Leonard Fresh, Washington; Charlie Jamin, Butler; **C**-Ted Bosciak, Butler; **Util**-Tony Venzon, Greensburg; **P**-Wilson Koewing, Washington; Earl Jones, Beaver Falls; **Manager**-Thomas Kain, Butler.

BA: Charlie Jamin, Butler, .367
Runs: Arnold Evans, Butler, 103
Hits: Arnold Evans, Butler, 151
RBIs: Bob Scheffing, Washington, 96
HRs: Dick Sisler, Washington, 16
Wins: Karl Drews, Butler, 16
SOs: Earl Jones, Beaver Falls, 205
ERA: Doyle Mills, Washington, 2.32

D PONY League
President: Robert C. Stedler

Standings	W	L	Pct.	GB	Manager
Olean Oilers (10)	65	38	.631	—	Jake Pitler
Hamilton Red Wings (16)...	61	44	.581	5	Don Hurst
Bradford Bees (9)	59	43	.578	5½	John Rosar
Batavia Clippers	48	54	.471	16½	William Buckley
Niagara Falls Rainbows (3)	44	59	.427	21	Tim Murchison
Jamestown Jaguars (15)......	32	71	.311	33	Louis "Mickey" LaLange

Total Attendance: 267,212.

Playoffs: Hamilton 3 games, Batavia 2, one tie; Olean 3 games, Bradford 1.
Finals: Olean 4 games, Hamilton 2.

All-Star Team: 1B-Charles Lamendola, Olean; **2B**-George Sandford, Batavia; **3B**-Robert Blanchard, Bradford; **SS**-Stanley Rojek, Olean; **OF**-Arthur Strott, Niagara Falls; Harold Gold, Olean; Henry Redmond, Hamilton; **C**-Mike Sandlock, Bradford; **Util**-James McKenna,

Hamilton; **P**-Hayden Shupe, Olean; George Dockins, Hamilton; **Manager**-Jake Pitler, Olean.

BA: Henry Redmond, Hamilton, .397
Runs: William Moore, Olean, 110
Hits: Henry Redmond, Hamilton, 166
RBIs: Charles Lamendola, Olean, 85
HRs: Arthur Strott, Niagara Falls, 17
Wins: Hayden Shupe, Olean, 17
SOs: Hayden Shupe, Olean, 170
ERA: Norman Russell, Hamilton, 2.63
Pct: George Dockins, Hamilton, .750, 15-5

D Tar Heel League
President: M.C. Campbell

Standings	W	L	Pct.	GB	Manager
Gastonia Cardinals (16)......	72	36	.667	—	Al Unser
Lenoir Indians....................	61	46	.570	10½	Clarence Roper
Statesville Owls	56	51	.523	15½	Stuffy McCrone
Shelby Nationals (8)	50	59	.459	22½	Edward Montague
Hickory Rebels	48	62	.436	25	Louis Viau
Newton-Conover Twins	36	69	.343	34½	Mac Arnette

Attendance: Statesville, 74,440.

Playoffs: Gastonia 3 games, Shelby 1; Statesville 3 games, Lenoir 0, one tie.
Finals: Gastonia 4 games, Statesville 3.

All-Star Team: 1B-Michael Natisin, Gastonia; **2B**-James Guinn, Shelby; **3B**-Henry Weiting, Lenoir; **SS**-Joe Zanolli, Statesville; **OF**-Hooper Triplett, Gastonia; Cleston Ray, Statesville; Norman Harris, Hickory; **C**-Marvin Felderman, Lenoir; **Util**-Edwin Martin, Shelby; **P**-Miles Gardner, Gastonia; William Skinner, Hickory; **Manager**-Al Unser, Gastonia.

BA: Hooper Triplett, Gastonia, .391
Runs: Birch Douglas, Lenoir, 127
Hits: James Guinn, Shelby, 161
RBIs: Hooper Triplett, Gastonia, 115
HRs: Hooper Triplett, Gastonia, 27
Wins: Ralph Fox, Newton-Conover/
Statesville, 17
Miles Gardner, Gastonia, 17
SOs: William Skinner, Hickory, 212
ERA: Witt Guise, Lenoir, 2.82

D Virginia League
President: Ray Ryan

Standings	W	L	Pct.	GB	Manager
Harrisonburg Turks............	61	47	.565	—	Hank Hulvey
Lynchburg Grays	55	51	.519	5	Al Weisman
Staunton Presidents............	51	56	.477	9½	Jimmy Bair
Salem-Roanoke Friends......	47	60	.439	13½	Bob Schleicher

Playoff: Lynchburg 1 game, Staunton 0.
Finals: Harrisonburg 3 games, Lynchburg 0.

All-Star Team: 1B-Kenneth Moore, Salem-Roanoke; **2B**-Henry Schenz, Salem-Roanoke; **3B**-William Sheridan, Staunton; **SS**-Steve Sloboda, Staunton; **OF**-Russ Mincy, Salem-Roanoke; Warren Huffman, Staunton; Lewis Utz, Staunton; **C**-Fenton Beaman, Harrisonburg; **Util**-John Fesh, Lynchburg/Harrisonburg; **P**-Paul Crain, Lynchburg; Ernie Utz, Harrisonburg; **Manager**-Hank Hulvey, Harrisonburg.

BA: Warren Huffman, Staunton, .415
Runs: Russ Mincy, Salem-Roanoke, 92
Hits: Nicholas Rhabe, Lynchburg/
Harrisonburg, 156
RBIs: Kenneth Moore, Salem-Roanoke, 95
HRs: Louis Cipalla, Harrisonburg/
Lynchburg, 10
Wins: Vincent Polumbo, Salem-Roanoke, 18
SOs: Ernie Utz, Harrisonburg, 183
ERA: Michael Marko, Staunton, 2.52

D West Texas-New Mexico League
President: Milton E. Price

Standings	W	L	Pct.	GB	Attend.	Manager
Lubbock Hubbers***(2).....	90	48	.652	—	50,000	Francis "Salty" Parker
Pampa Plainsmen...............	78	59	.569	11½	35,000	Grover Seitz
Big Spring Barons (5).........	74	64	.536	16	31,000	Tony Rego
Lamesa Lobos....................	65	73	.471	25		Joe Tate
Midland Cowboys	62	75	.453	27½		Jimmy Kerr
Clovis Pioneers	60	73	.451	27½		William "Dick" Ratliff
Abilene Apaches/						
Borger Gassers#...............	61	76	.445	28½		F.K. Withers
Amarillo Gold Sox.............	57	79	.419	32	51,190	Neal Rabe

#Abilene (4-4 in second half) moved to Borger July 9.
Total Attendance: 273,374.

Playoffs: Lubbock 3 games, Big Spring 0; Pampa 3 games, Lamesa 2.
Finals: Lubbock 4 games, Pampa 1.

All-Star Team: 1B-Malone Sanders, Amarillo; **2B**-Bob Decker, Big Spring; **3B**-William Capps, Big Spring; **SS**-Francis "Salty" Parker, Lubbock; **OF**-Gordon Nell, Pampa; Grover Seitz, Pampa; Pat Stasey, Big Spring; **C**-James Miller, Lubbock; **Util**-Joseph Piet, Midland; **P**-Lee Harris, Lubbock; Bus Dorman, Amarillo; **Manager**-Joe Tate, Lamesa.

BA: Gordon Nell, Pampa, .392
Runs: Gordon Nell, Pampa, 152
Hits: Gordon Nell, Pampa, 207
RBIs: Gordon Nell, Pampa, 189
HRs: Gordon Nell, Pampa, 44
Wins: Jodie Marek, Big Spring, 23
SOs: Howard Parks, Abilene/Borger, 202
ERA: Lee Harris, Lubbock, 2.97
Pct: Lee Harris, Lubbock, .818, 18-4

D Western League
President: J. Roy Carter

Standings	W	L	Pct.	GB	Manager
Norfolk Elks (5)	75	44	.630	—	Elmer "Doc" Bennett
Sioux Falls Canaries (11)	66	52	.559	8½	Ralph Brandon
Sioux City Cowboys (4)	63	52	.548	10	Pete Monahan
Lincoln Links (7)	64	55	.538	11	Francis "Pug" Griffin
Mitchell Kernels	49	69	.415	25½	O.C. "Red" Davis
Worthington Cardinals (16)	36	81	.308	38	Joe McDermott

Playoffs: Sioux City 3 games, Norfolk 2; Lincoln 3 games, Sioux Falls 2.
Finals: Sioux City 4 games, Lincoln 2.

All-Star Team: 1B-Pete Monahan, Sioux City; **2B**-Wendell Finders, Norfolk; **3B**-Ted Kakaloris, Lincoln; **SS**-Floyd McDaniel, Lincoln; **OF**-Ed Wernet, Sioux Falls; William Morgan, Norfolk; Hans Krueger, Lincoln; **C**-Karl Hower, Norfolk; **Util**-Gottlieb Leipelt, Mitchell; **P**-John Miller, Lincoln; Leonard Bobeck, Norfolk; **Manager**-Elmer "Doc" Bennett, Norfolk.

BA: Howard Conners, Sioux Falls, .365   **HRs:** William Morgan, Norfolk, 17
Runs: Bob Dillinger, Lincoln, 139   **Wins:** John Miller, Lincoln, 21
Hits: Wendell Finders, Norfolk, 167   **SOs:** John Miller, Lincoln, 208
RBIs: Ted Kakaloris, Lincoln, 114   **ERA:** Lawrence Kempe, Sioux Falls, 3.02

Ind Mexican League

Standings	W	L	Pct.	GB	Manager
Cordoba Cafeteros	46	12	.793	—	Lazaro Salazar
Veracruz Aguila	37	21	.638	9	Agustin Verde
Tampico Alijadores	30	25	.545	14½	Leonardo Alanis
Anahuac Indios	31	28	.525	15½	Chucho Castillo/George Sampson
Monterrey Carta Blanca	31	29	.517	16	Guillermo Ornelas/Gaudencio Guerra
Mexico City Comintra	16	41	.281	29½	Manuel Oliveros
Santa Rosa Gallos	11	46	.193	34½	Leonardo Olvera

BA: Lazaro Salazar, Cordoba, .374   **Wins:** Lazaro Salazar, Cordoba, 16
Hits: Agustin Bejerano, Cordoba, 81   Barney Brown, Veracruz, 16
RBIs: Angel Castro, Tampico, 50   **SOs:** Martin Dihigo, Veracruz, 202
HRs: Angel Castro, Tampico, 9   **ERA:** Raymond Taylor, Cordoba, 1.19

1939 Interleague Post Season Play

World Series
New York (American) 4 games, Cincinnati (National) 0

Junior World Series
Louisville (American Association) 4 games, Rochester (International) 3
Total Attendance: 62,687

Dixie Series
Ft. Worth (Texas) 4 games, Nashville (Southern Association) 3
Total Attendance: 34,488

Southern Championship (Little Dixie)
Pensacola (Southeastern) 4 games, Augusta (South Atlantic) 2

Southeast Championship
Sanford (Florida State) 4 games, Albany (Georgia-Florida) 1

Class D Interleague Series
Mooresville (North Carolina State) 4 games, Gastonia (Tar Heel) 3

Class D Interleague Series
Bluefield (Mountain State) 3 games, Harrisonburg (Virginia) 2

1939 Major League Farm Systems

American League

1. Boston (9): Louisville, Little Rock, Scranton, Rocky Mount, Clarksdale, Canton, Elizabethton, Danville-Schoolfield, Centreville.
2. Chicago (8): St. Paul, Shreveport, Anniston, Longview, Greenville (AL), Jonesboro, Grand Forks, Lubbock.
3. Cleveland (17): Buffalo, New Orleans, Wilkes-Barre, Winston-Salem, Spartanburg, Cedar Rapids, Tyler, Springfield (OH), Troy, Greeneville, Leaksville-Spray-Draper, Opelousas, Tallahassee, Logan, Fargo-Moorhead, Mansfield, Niagara Falls.
4. Detroit (7): Beaumont, Hot Springs, Henderson, Fulton, Newport, Tiffin, Sioux City.
5. New York (16): Kansas City, Newark, Binghamton, Norfolk (VA), Augusta, Wenatchee, Amsterdam, Akron, Joplin, Newport, El Paso, Neosho, Easton, Butler, Big Spring, Norfolk (NE).
6. Philadelphia (4): Williamsport, Federalsburg, Abbeville, Lexington.
7. St. Louis (12): Toledo, San Antonio, Springfield (IL), Youngstown, Topeka, Pennington Gap, Fayetteville, Lafayette, Mayfield, Paragould, Beaver Falls, Lincoln.
8. Washington (11): Chattanooga, Springfield (MA), Charlotte, Greenville (SC), Oswego, Greenville (NC), Salisbury (MD), Sanford, Orlando, Greensburg, Shelby.

National League

9. Boston (7): Hartford, Evansville, Utica, Allentown, Charleston, Owensboro, Bradford.
10. Brooklyn (16): Montreal, Nashville, Memphis, Elmira, Macon, Gloversville-Johnstown, Greenville (MS), Pine Bluff, Dayton, Reidsville, Daytona Beach, Americus, Paducah, Huntington, Superior, Olean.
11. Chicago (9): Milwaukee, Los Angeles, Moline, Bloomington, St. Joseph, Bisbee, Hopkinsville, Eau Claire, Sioux Falls.
12. Cincinnati (12): Indianapolis, Birmingham, Albany (NY), Durham, Columbia, Waterloo, El Dorado, Helena, Erie, Ogden, Muskogee, Bassett.
13. New York (5): Jersey City, Clinton, Ft. Smith, Milford, Salisbury (NC).
14. Philadelphia (5): Portsmouth (VA), Pensacola, Mayodan, Moultrie, Johnstown.
15. Pittsburgh (7): Knoxville, Gadsden, Hutchinson, Carthage, Valdosta, McKeesport, Jamestown.
16. St. Louis (28): Columbus (OH), Rochester, Sacramento, Houston, Asheville, Columbus (GA), Mobile, Decatur, Kilgore, Portsmouth (OH), Pocatello, Springfield (MO), Johnson City, Albuquerque, Monett, Martinsville, Cambridge, New Iberia, Albany (GA), Union City, Williamson, Caruthersville, Duluth, Fostoria, Washington, Hamilton, Gastonia, Worthington.

1939 No-Hitters

Date	Pitcher	Team	League	Opponent	Score
4-21	Frank Dasso	Little Rock	Southern Assoc.	Memphis	7-0
5-9	Dick Lanahan	Chattanooga	Southern Assoc.	Little Rock	4-0
5-16	Willie Weir	Toronto	International	Baltimore	8-0
6-7	Steve Rachunok	Henderson	East Texas	Palestine	1-0
6-8	Gerald Delion	Palestine	East Texas	Tyler	2-1
6-17	George Shoenecker	Grand Forks	Northern	Crookston	1-0 (11)
6-30	Al Smith	Sydney	Cape Breton Colliery	Glace Bay	3-0
7-1	William Pavlige	Jackson	Kitty	Hopkinsville	5-0
7-1	Frank Hudson	Palatka	Florida State	Gainesville	1-0
7-18	Ernie White	Houston	Texas	Ft. Worth	2-0
7-24	Early Wynn	Charlotte	Piedmont	Asheville	1-2
8-1	Ray Ross	Lexington	N. Carolina State	Salisbury	5-0
8-1	Bill Seinsoth	Columbus	South Atlantic	Augusta	1-2 (13)
8-2	Alfred Jarlett	Rocky Mount	Piedmont	Norfolk	1-0 (16)
8-13	Floyd Bevens	Wenatchee	Western International	Bellingham	4-1
8-18	Luther Smith	Hickory	Tar Heel	Gastonia	0-2 (8)
8-18	Charles Burgess	Savannah	South Atlantic	Spartanburg	4-0 (7)
8-23	Bill Caplinger	Albuquerque	Arizona-Texas	El Paso	10-0
9-20	Floyd Bevens	Wenatchee	Western International	Tacoma	3-0 (PO)

Number in parentheses indicates innings if other than nine; "PO" indicates playoff game.

THIS DATE IN MINOR LEAGUE HISTORY

April 18, 1939, Seventeen-year-old lefthander Hal Newhouser made his Organized Ball debut for Alexandria, Evangeline League, and registered a 5-2 victory over Lafayette, allowing but three hits and striking out 13.

April 19, 1939, A low attendance record was set at Columbus, Ohio when only 39 paid customers saw Kansas City defeat Columbus 5-3 in near-freezing weather.

April 20, 1939, The largest crowd in minor league history to date, 45,112 fans at Jersey City, International League, saw the home team lose to Buffalo 3-2.

April 21, 1939, A crowd of 10,000 fans turned out at Los Angeles to see the Angels tie the Pacific Coast League record of 19 straight victories by blanking San Diego 7-0. The mark was originally set by Seattle in 1903. Los Angeles' streak would end the following day with a 12-6 loss to San Diego.

May 2, 1939, Wallace Montgomery, a 32-year-old truck driver, was killed in Hot Springs when he fell 15 feet off the top of the right field fence at Ban Johnson field, breaking his neck. He was watching the Cotton States League game between Hot Springs and Monroe when he became excited over a Bathers rally.

May 4, 1939, Phil Weintraub of Minneapolis, American Association, cracked a double, triple and two home runs, giving him 22 hits (11 for extra bases) in his last 34 at bats for an average of .647 in a span of 10 games.

May 5, 1939, Led by manager Joe Mowry, who hit four doubles in four trips and drove in five runs, Winnipeg, Northern League, defeated Fargo-Moorhead 9-1 in the season opener before 4,000 fans in Fargo.

May 10, 1939, Outfielder Ed Stewart of Vancouver, Western International League, knocked himself unconscious when he swung and missed at a pitch and hit himself in the head with his bat.

May 22, 1939, Manager Fred "Snake" Henry of Kinston, Coastal Plain League, was suspended for 120 days by National Association President Bramham for an attack on an umpire.

June 17, 1939, Fire destroyed El Toro Park, home of the Piedmont League's Durham Bulls.

July 12, 1939, Coaker Triplett of Columbus, American Association, stole second, third and home successively against St. Paul.

August 4, 1939, The largest night crowd in Kansas City history, 24,894 fans, saw the Blues defeat Minneapolis as Vince DiMaggio hit his 37th and 38th home runs.

August 5, 1939, At a Celebration of Baseball Day at the Golden Gate Exposition, Joe Sprinz, veteran catcher for the Pacific Coast League's San Francisco Seals, suffered a compound jaw fracture, the loss of eight teeth and lacerations of both lips when he attempted to catch a ball dropped 800 feet from a blimp.

August 15, 1939, Millard "Dixie" Howell of Wilkes-Barre, Eastern League, struck out 20 batters in a night game at Binghamton. Wilkes-Barre had only one assist in the contest.

September 4, 1939, First sacker Walter Alston of Columbus, South Atlantic League, played his last 60 games of the season without making an error. His streak began on July 5.

September 15, 1939, Pete Gray, one-armed outfielder with the Bary Parkways of the semi-pro Metropolitan Baseball Association of New York, signed with the Hazleton Mountaineers of the Interstate League. Gray boasted a .632 batting mark in the Metropolitan League.

November 13, 1939, Famed Western story writer William C. Tuttle was re-elected president of the Pacific Coast League.

December 5, 1939, The term of National Association President William G. Bramham was extended for four years. His annual salary was increased by $5,000, making the yearly stipend $25,000.

SPRING TRAINING 1939

AMERICAN LEAGUE

CLUBS	AT	MAIL ADDRESS	DATES
BOSTON	Sarasota, Fla.	Hotel Sarasota Terrace	3/1–3/30
CHICAGO	Pasadena, Ca.	Green Hotel	2/26–4/1
CLEVELAND	New Orleans, La.	Hotel Roosevelt	3/1–4/9
DETROIT	Lakeland, Fla.	Hotel Lakeland Terrace	2/27–4/7
NEW YORK	St. Petersburg, Fla.	Suwanee Hotel	2/27–3/30
PHILADELPHIA	Lake Charles, La.	Majestic Hotel	3/1–3/30
ST. LOUIS	San Antonio, Tex.	Gunter Hotel	3/1–4/9
WASHINGTON	Orlando, Fla.	Angebilt Hotel	3/1–4/8

NATIONAL LEAGUE

BOSTON	Bradenton, Fla.	Manatee River Hotel	2/28–4/6
BROOKLYN	Clearwater, Fla.	Fort Harrison Hotel	3/1–4/6
CHICAGO	Avalon Catalina Is., Ca.	St. Catherine Hotel	2/23–3/16
CHICAGO	Los Angeles, Ca.	Biltmore Hotel	3/17–3/31
CINCINNATI	Tampa, Fla.	Floridian Hotel	2/26–4/2
NEW YORK	Hot Springs, Ark.	Hotel Majestic	2/21–3/4
NEW YORK	Baton Rouge, La.	Hotel Heidelberg	3/4–4/9
PHILADELPHIA	New Braunfels, Tex.	Hotel Faust	3/1–4/3
PITTSBURGH	San Bernardino, Ca.	California Hotel	3/2–3/17
ST. LOUIS	St. Petersburg, Fla.	Hotel Detroit	3/2–3/29

AMERICAN ASSOCIATION

COLUMBUS	Winter Haven, Fla.	Lake Region Hotel	3/15–4/10
INDIANAPOLIS	Bartow, Fla.	Oakes Hotel	3/13–4/8
KANSAS CITY	Haines City, Fla.	Polk Hotel	3/7–4/10
LOUISVILLE	Arcadia, Fla.	Arcadia House	3/5–4/10
MILWAUKEE	Ocala, Fla.	Harrington Hall Hotel	3/12–4/9
MINNEAPOLIS	Daytona Beach, Fla.		3/12–4/3
ST. PAUL	Tarpon Springs, Fla.	Hotel Arcade	3/10–3/31
TOLEDO	Harlington, Tex.	Rees-Wil-Mond Hotel	3/6–4/7

INTERNATIONAL LEAGUE

BALTIMORE	Daytona Beach, Fla.	Hotel Riveria	3/19–4/13
BUFFALO	Plant City, Fla.	Plant Hotel	3/15–4/15
JERSEY CITY	Baton Rouge, La.	Hotel King	3/1–4/9
MONTREAL	Lake Wales, Fla.	Walesbilt Hotel	3/15–4/13
NEWARK	Sebring, Fla.	Sebring Hotel	3/10–4/10
ROCHESTER	Winter Garden, Fla.	Edgewater Hotel	3/20–4/17
SYRACUSE	Camden, S.C.	The Court Inn	3/15–4/15
TORONTO	Avon Park, Fla.	Jacaranda Hotel	3/15–4/11

PACIFIC COAST LEAGUE

HOLLYWOOD	Elsinore, Ca.	Amesbury Hotel	2/26–3/12
HOLLYWOOD	Ventura, Ca.	Ventura and La Barr Hotels	3/13–3/31
LOS ANGELES	Ontario, Ca.	Casa Blanca Hotel	2/27–3/30
OAKLAND	Visalia, Ca.	Hotel Johnson	2/23–3/30
PORTLAND	Fullerton, Ca.	California Hotel	2/24–3/25
SACRAMENTO	Riverside, Ca.	New Reynolds Hotel	2/27–3/28
SAN DIEGO	El Centro, Ca.	Barbara Worth Hotel	3/1–4/1
SAN FRANCISCO	Hanford, Ca.	Hotel Whilton	3/2–3/23
SEATTLE	Anaheim, Ca.	Valencia Hotel	2/22–3/29

SOUTHERN ASSOCIATION

ATLANTA	Savannah, Ga.	Savannah Hotel	3/5–3/31
BIRMINGHAM	At home		3/6–4/13
CHATTANOOGA	Sanford, Fla.	Mayfair Hotel	3/12–4/4
KNOXVILLE	Valdosta, Ga.	Hotel Valdese	3/20–4/6
LITTLE ROCK	At home		3/8–4/13
MEMPHIS	deLand, Fla.	Hotel Putnam	3/13–4/2
NASHVILLE	Monroe, La.	Monroe Hotel	3/6–4/4
NEW ORLEANS	At home		3/1–4/13

TEXAS LEAGUE

BEAUMONT	At home		3/6–4/12
FORT WORTH	Orange, Tex.	General Delivery	3/6–3/31
FORT WORTH	At home		4/1–4/12
HOUSTON	At home		3/13–4/12
OKLAHOMA CITY	San Benito, Tex.	Stonewall Jackson Hotel	3/6–4/3
SAN ANTONIO	Brownsville, Tex.	El Jardin Hotel	3/6–4/9
SHREVEPORT	At home		3/6–4/12
TULSA	McAllen, Tex.	Casa De Palmas Hotel	3/6–4/3

EASTERN LEAGUE

ALBANY			4/1–4/23
BINGHAMTON	Ware Shoals, S.C.	Ware Shoals Inn	3/30–4/20
ELMIRA	Macon, Ga.	Lanier Hotel	4/3–4/16
HARTFORD	Charleston, W.Va.	Kanahwa Park	4/1–4/24
SCRANTON	Wilmington, N.C.		4/3–4/23
SPRINGFIELD	Greenville, S.C.	Hotel Greenville	4/1–4/23
WILKES-BARRE	Suffolk, Va.	Nasemond Hotel	4/2–4/21
WILLIAMSPORT	Tarboro, N.C.	Hotel Tarboro	3/20–4/23

1940

American League
President: William Harridge

Standings	W	L	Pct.	GB	Attend.	Manager
Detroit Tigers	90	64	.584	—	1,112,693	Del Baker
Cleveland Indians	89	65	.578	1	902,576	Ossie Vitt
New York Yankees	88	66	.571	2	988,975	Joe McCarthy
Boston Red Sox	82	72	.532	8	716,234	Joe Cronin
Chicago White Sox	82	72	.532	8	660,336	Jimmy Dykes
St. Louis Browns	67	87	.435	23	239,591	Fred Haney
Washington Senators	64	90	.416	26	381,241	Bucky Harris
Philadelphia Athletics	54	100	.351	36	432,145	Connie Mack

BA: Joe DiMaggio, New York, .352
Runs: Ted Williams, Boston, 134
Hits: Rip Radcliff, St. Louis, 200
  Doc Cramer, Boston, 200
  Barney McCosky, Detroit, 200

RBIs: Hank Greenberg, Detroit, 150
HRs: Hank Greenberg, Detroit, 41
Wins: Bob Feller, Cleveland, 27
SOs: Bob Feller, Cleveland, 261
ERA: Bob Feller, Cleveland, 2.61
Pct: Schoolboy Rowe, Detroit, .842, 16-3

National League
President: Ford Frick

Standings	W	L	Pct.	GB	Attend.	Manager
Cincinnati Reds	100	53	.654	—	850,180	Bill McKechnie
Brooklyn Dodgers	88	65	.575	12	975,978	Leo Durocher
St. Louis Cardinals	84	69	.549	16	324,078	Ray Blades/Mike Gonzalez/ Billy Southworth
Pittsburgh Pirates	78	76	.506	22½	507,934	Frank Frisch
Chicago Cubs	75	79	.487	25½	534,878	Gabby Hartnett
New York Giants	72	80	.474	27½	747,852	Bill Terry
Boston Bees	65	87	.428	34½	241,616	Casey Stengel
Philadelphia Phillies	50	103	.327	50	207,177	Tommy "Doc" Prothro

BA: Deb Garms, Pittsburgh, .355
Runs: Arky Vaughan, Pittsburgh, 113
Hits: Frank McCormick, Cincinnati, 191
  Stan Hack, Chicago, 191
RBIs: John Mize, St. Louis, 137

HRs: John Mize, St. Louis, 43
Wins: Bucky Walters, Cincinnati, 22
SOs: Kirby Higbe, Philadelphia, 137
ERA: Bucky Walters, Cincinnati, 2.48
Pct: Bob Fitzsimmons, Brooklyn, .889, 16-2

AA American Association
President: George Trautman

Standings	W	L	Pct.	GB	Attend.	Manager
Kansas City Blues (5)	95	57	.625	—	203,354	Bill Meyer
Columbus Red Birds (16)	90	60	.600	4	121,680	Burt Shotton
Minneapolis Millers	86	59	.593	5½	155,523	Tom Sheehan
Louisville Colonels (1)	75	75	.500	19	206,529	Bill Burwell
St. Paul Saints (2)	69	79	.466	24	112,278	Babe Ganzel
Indianapolis Indians (12)	62	84	.425	30	97,859	Wes Griffin/Jewell Ens
Toledo Mud Hens (7)	59	90	.396	34½	86,067	James Taylor
Milwaukee Brewers	58	90	.392	35	72,489	Minor Heath/Ray Schalk

Playoffs: Louisville 4 games, Columbus 2; Kansas City 4 games, Minneapolis 2.
Finals: Louisville 4 games, Kansas City 2.

Sporting News Player of the Year-Phil Rizzuto, Kansas City.

BA: Ab Wright, Minneapolis, .369
Runs: Roberto Estalella, Minneapolis, 147
Hits: Frenchy Bordagaray, Kansas City, 214
RBIs: Ab Wright, Minneapolis, 159
HRs: Ab Wright, Minneapolis, 39

Wins: Bob Logan, Indianapolis, 18
  Johnny Lindell, Kansas City, 18
SOs: Frank Melton, Columbus, 142
ERA: Ernie White, Columbus, 2.25

AA International League
President: Frank J. Shaughnessy

Standings	W	L	Pct.	GB	Attend.	Manager
Rochester Red Wings (16)	96	61	.611	—	150,143	Billy Southworth/Estel Crabtree/ Mike Ryba/Tony Kaufmann
Newark Bears (5)	95	65	.594	2½	164,116	Johnny Neun
Jersey City Giants (13)	81	78	.509	16	228,361	Bert Niehoff
Baltimore Orioles (14)	81	79	.506	16½	119,095	Alphonse "Tommy" Thomas
Montreal Royals (10)	80	80	.500	17½	158,799	Clyde Sukeforth
Buffalo Bisons	76	83	.478	21	111,922	Steve O'Neill
Syracuse Chiefs (15)	71	90	.441	27	118,244	Dick Porter
Toronto Maple Leafs (6)	57	101	.361	39½	67,123	Tony Lazzeri

Playoffs: Newark 4 games, Jersey City 0; Baltimore 4 games, Rochester 2.
Finals: Newark 4 games, Baltimore 3.

MVP-Mike Ryba, Rochester.

BA: Murray Howell, Baltimore, .359
Runs: Tommy Holmes, Newark, 126
Hits: Tommy Holmes, Newark, 211
RBIs: Nick Etten, Baltimore, 128

HRs: Bill Nagel, Baltimore, 37
Wins: Mike Ryba, Rochester, 24
SOs: George Washburn, Newark, 145
ERA: Hal White, Buffalo, 2.43

AA Pacific Coast League
President: William C. Tuttle

Standings	W	L	Pct.	GB	Attend.	Manager
Seattle Rainiers	112	66	.629	—	295,820	Jack Lelivelt
Los Angeles Angels (11)	102	75	.576	9½	186,184	Arnold "Jigger" Statz
Oakland Oaks	94	84	.528	18	223,222	Johnny Vergez
San Diego Padres	92	85	.520	19½	173,393	Cedric Durst
Sacramento Solons (16)	90	88	.506	22	97,233	Bennie Borgmann
Hollywood Stars	84	94	.472	28	192,025	Bill Sweeney
San Francisco Seals	81	97	.455	31	221,801	Lefty O'Doul
Portland Beavers	56	122	.315	56	92,338	Johnny Frederick

Playoffs: Seattle 4 games, Oakland 1; Los Angeles 4 games, San Diego 3.
Finals: Seattle 4 games, Los Angeles 1.

MVP-George Archie, Seattle.

BA: Lou Novikoff, Los Angeles, .363
Runs: Lou Novikoff, Los Angeles, 147
Hits: Lou Novikoff, Los Angeles, 259
RBIs: Lou Novikoff, Los Angeles, 171

HRs: Lou Novikoff, Los Angeles, 41
Wins: Dick "Kewpie" Barrett, Seattle, 24
SOs: Dick "Kewpie" Barrett, Seattle, 164
ERA: Jack Salveson, Oakland, 2.30

A1 Southern Association
President: Trammell Scott

Standings	W	L	Pct.	GB	Attend.	Manager
Nashville Vols (10)	101	47	.682	—	133,602	Larry Gilbert
Atlanta Crackers	93	58	.616	9½	196,793	Paul Richards
Memphis Chicks	79	72	.523	23½	61,144	Truck Hannah
Chattanooga Lookouts (8)	73	79	.480	30	75,104	Kiki Cuyler
New Orleans Pelicans (16)	71	80	.470	31½	68,326	Harold Anderson
Birmingham Barons (12)	70	81	.464	32½	74,271	Ira Smith
Little Rock Travelers	59	90	.396	42½	44,475	Herb Brett
Knoxville Smokies (13)	57	96	.373	46½	68,782	Neil Caldwell/Fred Lindstrom

Playoffs: Nashville 3 games, Chattanooga 0; Atlanta 3 games, Memphis 2.
Finals: Nashville 4 games, Atlanta 2.

MVP-Charley George, Nashville; Emil Malho, Atlanta.

BA: Mike Dejan, Chattanooga/ Birmingham, .371
Runs: Emil Malho, Atlanta, 144
Hits: Arnold Moser, Atlanta, 216
RBIs: Gus Dugas, Nashville, 118
  Willard Marshall, Atlanta, 118
  Bob Boken, Nashville, 118

HRs: Guy Dugas, Nashville, 22
  Dutch Meyer, Knoxville, 22
Wins: Boots Poffenberger, Nashville, 26
SOs: Ace Adams, Nashville, 122
ERA: Louis Polli, Chattanooga, 3.00

A1 Texas League
President: J. Alvin Gardner

Standings	W	L	Pct.	GB	Attend.	Manager
Houston Buffaloes (16)	105	56	.652	—	90,872	Eddie Dyer
San Antonio Missions (7)	89	72	.553	16	97,575	Marty McManus
Beaumont Exporters (4)	88	72	.550	16½	49,499	Al Vincent
Oklahoma City Indians	82	78	.513	22½	71,545	Jim Keesey/Rogers Hornsby
Tulsa Oilers (11)	76	82	.481	27½	74,393	Roy Johnson
Dallas Rebels	75	83	.475	28½	83,846	Hal Lee
Shreveport Sports	72	88	.450	32½	71,815	Homer Peel/Hub Northen
Ft. Worth Cats	52	108	.325	52½	43,561	Bob Linton

Playoffs: Houston 3 games, Oklahoma City 1; Beaumont 3 games, San Antonio 0, one tie.
Finals: Houston 4 games, Beaumont 1.

MVP-Bob Muncrief, San Antonio.

BA: Gordy Donaldson, Tulsa, .319
Runs: Danny Murtaugh, Houston, 106
Hits: Eddie Waitkus, Tulsa, 192
RBIs: Vern Stephens, San Antonio, 97

HRs: Carl Jorgensen, Oklahoma City/ San Antonio, 23
Wins: Maury Newlin, San Antonio, 23
SOs: Bob Uhle, Dallas, 205
ERA: Sam Nahem, Houston, 1.65

*Won first-half   **Won second-half   ***Won both halves
Numbers after nicknames indicate farm system.
Affiliation listed at end of each year.

A Eastern League
President: Thomas H. Richardson

Standings	W	L	Pct.	GB	Attend.	Manager
Scranton Red Sox (1)	79	60	.568	—	232,266	Nemo Leibold
Binghamton Triplets (5)	77	62	.554	2	95,308	Bruno Betzel
Hartford Bees (9)	72	66	.522	6½	75,399	Jack Onslow
Albany Senators (15)	70	70	.500	9½	152,957	George "Specs" Toporcer
Springfield Nationals	68	69	.496	10	64,509	Spencer Abbott
Elmira Pioneers (10)	67	72	.482	12	60,066	Bill Killefer
Williamsport Grays (6)	60	74	.448	16½	57,260	Fresco Thompson
Wilkes-Barre Barons (3)	56	76	.424	19½	45,956	Earl Wolgamot

Playoffs: Binghamton 3 games, Albany 1; Hartford 3 games, Scranton 1.
Finals: Binghamton 4 games, Hartford 1.

All-Star Team: 1B-Al Flair, Scranton; **2B**-Maurice Jacobs, Elmira; **3B**-Pete Suder, Binghamton; **SS**-Hal Quick, Springfield; **OF**-Kermit Lewis, Albany; Danny Litwhiler, Wilkes-Barre; John Lazor, Scranton; **C**-Mickey Livingston, Springfield; **Util**-Bill Jackson, Hartford; P-Owen Sheetz, Scranton; Virgil Brown, Albany; **MVP**-Pete Suder, Binghamton; **Manager**-Bruno Betzel, Binghamton.

BA: Kermit Lewis, Albany, .325
Runs: Kermit Lewis, Albany, 86
Hits: Pete Suder, Binghamton, 172
RBIs: Bill Sodd, Albany, 88
HRs: Jack Graham, Binghamton, 20
Wins: Virgil Brown, Albany, 22
SOs: Millard Howell, Wilkes-Barre, 137
ERA: Mickey Harris, Scranton, 2.25

B Interstate League
President: Harold G. Hoffman

Standings	W	L	Pct.	GB	Manager
Reading Chicks	76	52	.594	—	Tom Oliver
Wilmington Blue Rocks (6)	68	52	.567	4	Charles "Chief" Bender/Charlie Berry
Trenton Senators	69	54	.561	4½	Goose Goslin
Hazleton Mountaineers/ Lancaster Red Roses#	62	56	.525	9	Cy Perkins
Harrisburg Senators (15)	60	62	.492	13	Les Bell
Sunbury Indians	58	64	.475	15	Dutch Dorman
York Bees (9)	57	68	.456	17½	Rudy Hulswitt
Allentown Wings (16)	40	82	.328	33	Val Picinich/Bobby Barr

#Hazleton (19-17) moved to Lancaster June 12, first home game June 15.
Attendance: Sunbury, 36,000.

Playoffs: Reading 3 games, Trenton 0; Lancaster 3 games, Wilmington 1.
Finals: Lancaster 4 games, Reading 1.

All-Star Team: 1B-Arnold Greene, Harrisburg; **2B**-Lyle Judy, Reading; **3B**-Bill Homan, Allentown/Harrisburg; **SS**-Billy Cox, Harrisburg; **OF**-Elmer Valo, Wilmington; Tom Oliver, Reading; Robert Hamilton, Reading; **C**-Walter Klimczak, Wilmington; **Util**-Frank Colman, Wilmington; **P**-George Hennessey, Trenton; Fred Archer, Hazleton/Lancaster; **Manager**-Tom Oliver, Reading.

BA: Elmer Valo, Wilmington, .364
Runs: Lyle Judy, Reading, 107
Hits: Elmer Valo, Wilmington, 159
RBIs: Harold Nerino, Sunbury, 96
Charles Lamendola, Allentown/ Reading, 96
HRs: Arnold Greene, Harrisburg, 21
Wins: George Hennessey, Trenton, 18
SOs: James Kerr, Harrisburg, 156
ERA: Fred Kiebler, Reading, 2.44

B Piedmont League
President: Ralph Daughton

Standings	W	L	Pct.	GB	Manager
Richmond Colts (13)	77	59	.566	—	Eddie Phillips
Asheville Tourists (16)	75	60	.556	1½	Tommy West
Rocky Mount Red Sox (1)	75	61	.551	2	Heinie Manush
Durham Bulls (10)	73	62	.541	3½	Oscar Roettger
Charlotte Hornets (8)	68	65	.511	7½	Calvin Griffith
Norfolk Tars (5)	66	71	.482	11½	Ray White
Portsmouth Cubs (14)	59	78	.431	18½	Ray Brubaker/Arthur "Cowboy" McHenry
Winston-Salem Twins	48	85	.361	27½	Eddie Moore/Ray Brubaker

Playoffs: Rocky Mount 4 games, Asheville 2; Durham 4 games, Richmond 3.
Finals: Durham 4 games, Rocky Mount 2.

All-Star Team: 1B-Len Prout, Richmond; **2B**-Snuffy Stirnweiss, Norfolk; **3B**-Joe Bestudik, Durham; **SS**-Johnny Pesky, Rocky Mount; **OF**-Walter Schuerbaum, Asheville; James Maynard, Richmond; Irving Plummer, Rocky Mount; **C**-Richard Hahn, Charlotte; **Util**-Gilberto Torres, Charlotte; **P**-Ken Burkhart, Asheville; Max Wilson, Portsmouth; **Manager**-Oscar Roettger, Durham.

BA: James Maynard, Richmond, .337
Runs: Lawrence Kinzer, Richmond, 115
Hits: Johnny Pesky, Rocky Mount, 187
RBIs: Len Prout, Richmond, 103
HRs: James Maynard, Richmond, 30
Wins: Ken Burkhart, Asheville, 20
Max Wilson, Portsmouth, 20
Lynn Watkins, Richmond, 20
SOs: Ken Burkhart, Asheville, 145
ERA: Barney DeForge, Durham, 2.40

B Quebec Provinical League
President: Jean Barrette

Standings	W	L	Pct.	GB	Manager
St. Hyacinthe Saints	48	30	.615	—	Mel Simons
Quebec Athletics	44	35	.557	4½	Del Bissonette
Granby Red Socks	42	37	.532	6½	Glenn Larsen
Trois Rivieres Renards	37	43	.463	12	Wally Schang
Sherbrooke Braves@	25	31	.446	NA	Doc Gautreau/George Klivok
Drummondville Tigers#	6	26	.188	NA	Charles Small

#Drummondville disbanded July 8.
@Sherbrooke disbanded August 1.

Playoffs: Trois Rivieres 1 game, St. Hyacinthe 0 (St. Hyacinthe forfeited due to prolonged weather delay); Granby 3 games, Quebec 2.
Finals: Trois Rivieres 4 games, Granby 1.

All-Star Team: 1B-James Walsh, Granby; **2B**-Tony DiNubilo, Trois Rivieres; **3B**-Arnold Banta, St. Hyacinthe; **SS**-Edward Albertson, Sherbrooke/Granby; **OF**-Edwin Martin, Trois Rivieres; Joseph Cicero, St. Hyacinthe; Stanley Platek, St. Hyacinthe; **C**-Arthur Galen, Sherbrooke/Trois Rivieres; **Util**-Paul Martin, Trois Rivieres; **P**-Bruno Shedis, St. Hyacinthe; Bill Yocke, Quebec; **Manager**-Del Bissonette, Quebec.

BA: George Andrews, St. Hyacinthe, .339
Runs: Joseph Dooley, Quebec, 64
Hits: Stanley Platek, St. Hyacinthe, 105
RBIs: James Walsh, Granby, 63
HRs: James Walsh, Granby, 17
Wins: Bruno Shedis, St. Hyacinthe, 18
SOs: Bill Yocke, Quebec, 127
ERA: Lou Lepine, Quebec, 1.67

B South Atlantic League
President: Dr. E.M. Wilder

Standings	W	L	Pct.	GB	Manager
Savannah Indians	94	56	.627	—	Martin "Chick" Autry
Columbus Red Birds (16)	88	63	.583	6½	Clay Hopper
Macon Peaches (10)	84	67	.556	10½	Milt Stock
Greenville Spinners (8)	77	72	.517	16½	Alex McColl/Gus Brittain
Augusta Tigers (5)	77	73	.513	17	Phil Page
Columbia Reds (12)	74	77	.490	20½	Clarence "Cap" Crossley
Jacksonville Tars	64	88	.421	31	Bill Steinecke/Nelson Leach
Spartanburg Spartans/ Charleston Rebels#	44	106	.293	50	Cecil Rhodes

#Spartanburg (28-58) moved to Charleston July 15, first home game July 24.

Playoffs: Columbus 4 games, Greenville 0; Macon 4 games, Savannah 2.
Finals: Columbus 4 games, Macon 2.

All-Star Team: 1B-Ray Sanders, Columbus; **2B**-Cecil Rhodes, Spartanburg/Charleston; **3B**-William Johnson, Augusta; **SS**-Eddie Stanky, Macon; **OF**-Hooper Triplett, Columbus; Garrett McBryde, Spartanburg/Charleston; Art Rebel, Augusta; **C**-Herb Crompton, Savannah; **Util**-Robert Winters, Columbia; **P**-James Davis, Augusta; Robert Chipman, Savannah; **Manager**-Martin "Chick" Autry, Savannah.

BA: Hooper Triplett, Columbus, .369
Runs: Ed Knoblauch, Columbus, 135
Hits: Harry Ashworth, Augusta, 206
RBIs: Ray Sanders, Columbus, 152
HRs: Beverly Ferrell, Greenville, 21
Wins: James Davis, Augusta, 23
SOs: Fred Martin, Columbus, 208
ERA: Witt Guise, Columbia, 2.16

B Southeastern League
President: Stuart X. Stephenson

Standings	W	L	Pct.	GB	Manager
Jackson Senators	89	58	.605	—	Clarence Blair
Pensacola Fliers (14)	89	60	.597	1	Wally Dashiell
Mobile Shippers (16)	72	72	.500	15½	Johnny Keane
Selma Cloverleafs (8)	72	77	.483	18	Wes Kingdon
Montgomery Rebels	70	76	.479	18½	Ernie Wingard
Gadsden Pilots (15)	69	81	.460	21½	Billy Bancroft
Meridian Bears	64	80	.444	23½	Clarence Mitchell/Bernie DeViveiros
Anniston Rams (10)	61	82	.427	26	Bill Rodda

Playoffs: Jackson 4 games, Selma 1; Pensacola 4 games, Mobile 3.
Finals: Jackson 4 games, Pensacola 1.

All-Star Team: 1B-Paul Fugit, Jackson; **2B**-Marion "Bill" Adair, Montgomery; **3B**-Grover Resinger, Selma; **SS**-Les floyd, Pensacola; **OF**-Bill Endicott, Mobile; Thomas McBride, Jackson; Frank Kalin, Jackson; **C**-Donald Vettoriel, Jackson; **Util**-Tom Cafego, Montgomery; **P**-Roy Walker, Montgomery; Frank Hoerst, Pensacola; **Manager**-Wally Dashiell, Pensacola.

BA: Ted Mueller, Selma, .346
Runs: Marion "Bill" Adair, Montgomery, 113
Hits: Thomas McBride, Jackson, 194
RBIs: Marion "Bill" Adair, Montgomery, 113
HRs: Norman DeWeese, Pensacola, 22
Wins: Roy Walker, Montgomery, 22
SOs: Ewald Pyle, Meridian, 180
ERA: Gordon Maltzberger, Jackson, 2.20

B Three-I League
President: Tom Fairweather

Standings	W	L	Pct.	GB	Attend.	Manager
Cedar Rapids Raiders (3)	74	51	.592	—	46,475	Oliver Marquardt
Decatur Commodores (16)	73	52	.584	1	37,667	Tony Kaufmann/ Robert Morrow/Lou Scoffic
Springfield Browns (7)	73	53	.579	1½	56,569	Arthur Scharein
Evansville Bees (9)	68	55	.553	5	60,815	Bob Coleman
Clinton Giants (13)@	62	57	.521	9	40,277	John Billings
Madison Blues	61	62	.496	12	36,740	Mervin Connelly

	W	L	Pct.	GB		
Moline Plow Boys (11)	46	78	.471	27½	13,639	Michael Gazella
Waterloo Hawks (2)	36	85	.298	36	23,441	John Fitzpatrick/
						Frederick Bedore

Playoffs: Cedar Rapids 3 games, Springfield 0; Decatur 3 games, Evansville 2.
Finals: Cedar Rapids 3 games, Decatur 1.

All-Star Team: 1B-Robert Hershey, Cedar Rapids; **2B**-Albert Roberge, Evansville; **3B**-Alex Pecora, Clinton; **SS**-Stanley Galle, Madison; **OF**-Lou Scoffic, Decatur; Clarence Bray, Evansville; Charles Workman, Cedar Rapids; **C**-Alvin Montgomery, Moline; **Util**-Steve Tramback, Clinton; **P**-Max Surkont, Decatur; Mike Kash (Kaiserski), Madison; **Manager**-Arthur Scharein, Springfield.

BA: Lou Scoffic, Decatur, .358
Runs: Charles Workman, Cedar Rapids, 108
Hits: Lou Scoffic, Decatur, 164
RBIs: Don Manno, Evansville, 113

HRs: Charles Workman, Cedar Rapids, 29
Wins: Mike Kash (Kaiserski), Madison, 20
SOs: Max Surkont, Decatur, 212
ERA: Max Surkont, Decatur, 2.50

B Western International League
President: Judge Stanley A. Webster

Standings	W	L	Pct.	GB	Manager
Spokane Indians	84	59	.587	—	Eddie Leishman
Yakima Pippins	79	67	.541	6½	Goldie Holt
Vancouver Capilanos	72	71	.503	12	James Crandall
Tacoma Tigers	72	72	.500	12½	Hal Rhyne/Bob Garretson
Salem Senators	69	77	.473	16½	John "Bunny" Griffiths
Wenatchee Chiefs (5)	59	89	.399	27½	Johnny Kerr/Frank Morehouse

Playoffs: Spokane 2 games, Vancouver 0; Tacoma 2 games, Yakima 1.
Finals: Tacoma 3 games, Spokane 2.

All-Star Team: 1B-William Reese, Yakima; **2B**-John Stamper, Yakima; **3B**-Henry Martinez, Spokane; **SS**-Ned Stickle, Spokane; **OF**-Tony Firpo, Tacoma; Ralph Samhammer, Vancouver; Smead Jolley, Spokane; **C**-Roy Younker, Yakima; **Util**-Bill Harris, Salem; **P**-George Windsor, Spokane; Floyd Isekite, Tacoma; **Manager**-Goldie Holt, Yakima.

BA: Smead Jolley, Spokane, .373
Runs: Ralph Samhammer, Vancouver, 151
Hits: Smead Jolley, Spokane, 224
RBIs: Smead Jolley, Spokane, 181
HRs: Tommy Lloyd, Vancouver, 28

Wins: George Windsor, Spokane, 20
Bernard Brewer, Salem, 20
SOs: Floyd Isekite, Tacoma, 225
ERA: Hub Kittle, Yakima, 2.95

C Arizona-Texas League
President: Dr. R.E. Soners

Standings	W	L	Pct.	GB	Attend.	Manager
Tucson Cowboys**(12)	64	59	.520	—	43,000	Lester "Pat" Patterson
El Paso Texans*(3)	64	60	.516	½		Elmer "Spec" Williamson
Albuquerque Cardinals (16)	60	64	.484	4½		Jack Farmer
Bisbee Bees	58	63	.479	5	23,766	Carl Dittmar

Playoff: El Paso 4 games, Tucson 3.

All-Star Team: 1B-Robert Tucker, Tucson; **2B**-Elwood Curtis, Albuquerque; **3B**-Harry Clements, Tucson; **SS**-Burman Bare, Tucson; **OF**-Elmer Olsen, Tucson; Fay Starr, Bisbee; Joe Brovia, El Paso; **C**-Frank Morris, El Paso; **Util**-Elmer "Spec" Williamson, El Paso; **P**-Bob Raines, El Paso; John Brysch, El Paso; Frank Totaro, Bisbee; **Manager**-Carl Dittmar, Bisbee.

BA: Joe Brovia, El Paso, .383
Runs: Elwood Curtis, Albuquerque, 118
Hits: Harry Clements, Tucson, 175
RBIs: Joe Brovia, El Paso, 103
HRs: Joe Skeber, El Paso, 10
Wins: Bob Raines, El Paso, 18
SOs: Frank Totaro, Bisbee, 251
ERA: Luther French, Albuquerque, 3.50

C Canadian-American League
President: Rev. Harold J. Martin

Standings	W	L	Pct.	GB	Attend.	Manager
Ottawa-Ogdensburg Senators#(14)	84	39	.683	—	29,373	Cy Morgan
Gloversville-Johnstown Glovers (15)	72	53	.576	13	39,613	Buster Blakeney
Amsterdam Rugmakers (5)	70	53	.569	14	41,051	Eddie Sawyer
Utica Braves	69	56	.552	16	89,669	Lefty Jenkins
Oneonta Indians	62	63	.496	23	39,851	Leon Riley
Oswego Netherlands	58	63	.479	25	16,478	Art Funk
Rome Colonels	50	73	.407	34	36,395	Admiral Martin
Auburn Colts	28	93	.231	55	10,040	Knotty Lee

#Ottawa played half of its schedule in Ogdensburg, New York.

Playoffs: Gloversville-Johnstown 4 games, Utica 1; Amsterdam 4 games, Ottawa-Ogdensburg 1.
Finals: Amsterdam 3 games, Gloversville-Johnstown 2.

All-Star Team: 1B-Conrad Wotjkowiak, Oswego; **2B**-Harry Marnie, Ottawa-Ogdensburg; **3B**-Paul Badgett, Amsterdam; **SS**-George Jumonvillo, Ottawa-Ogdensburg; **OF**-Barney Hearn, Gloversville-Johnstown; Leon Riley, Oneonta; Eddie Sawyer, Amsterdam; **C**-Homer Howell, Ottawa-Ogdensburg; **Util**-Albert Zachary, Utica; **P**-Bethel Rhem,

Gloversville-Johnstown; Eugene Davis, Ottawa-Ogdensburg; **Manager**-Cy Morgan, Ottawa-Ogdensburg.

BA: John Lehman, Gloversville-Johnstown, .353
Runs: Paul Badgett, Amsterdam, 120
Hits: Barney Hearn, Gloversville-Johnstown, 169
RBIs: Paul Badgett, Amsterdam, 119
HRs: Paul Badgett, Amsterdam, 31

Wins: Paul Masterson, Ottawa-Ogdensburg, 19
Bethel Rhem, Gloversville-Johnstown, 19
SOs: Leo Pukas, Auburn/Utica, 165
ERA: Eugene Davis, Ottawa-Ogdensburg, 2.48

C Cotton States League
President: Judge Emmet Harty

Standings	W	L	Pct.	GB	Manager
Monroe White Sox	82	45	.646	—	Doug Taitt
El Dorado Lions	78	57	.578	8	Guy Sturdy
Helena Seaporters	71	60	.542	13	John "Bud" Clancy
Greenville Buckshots	70	69	.504	18	Andrew Reese
Hot Springs Bathers (4)	67	71	.486	20½	Cecil Coombs
Clarksdale Red Sox	61	75	.449	25½	Leroy "Cowboy" Jones
Greenwood Choctaws	58	76	.433	27½	L.B. Jones/Gerald Lipscomb, Jr.
Pine Bluff Judges	49	83	.371	35½	W.R. "Red" Rollings

Playoffs: Monroe 3 games, Greenville 1; El Dorado 3 games, Helena 1.
Finals: Monroe 4 games, El Dorado 1.

All-Star Team: 1B-Monte Clancy, Helena; **2B**-Burton Hodge, Greenville; **3B**-Dexter Savage, Helena; **SS**-Ed Zydowski, Hot Springs; **OF**-Jack Grantham, Clarksdale; Clark Hack (Hackbarth), El Dorado; Allen Zarilla, Helena; **C**-Robert Schang, Monroe; **Util**-Gerald Lipscomb, Greenwood; **P**-Lloyd Finck, Helena; Tom Perry, Monroe; **Manager**-Doug Taitt, Monroe.

BA: Thurman Tucker, Clarksdale, .390
Runs: Monte Duncan, Hot Springs, 127
Hits: Jack Grantham, Clarksdale, 194
RBIs: Ed Zydowski, Hot Springs, 157

HRs: Ed Zydowski, Hot Springs, 25
Monte Duncan, Hot Springs, 25
Wins: Tom Perry, Monroe, 21
SOs: Carl Wentz, El Dorado, 238
ERA: Edward Smith, Greenville, 2.96

C East Texas League
President: C.P. Mosley

Standings	W	L	Pct.	GB	Manager
Longview Texans (2, 16)	79	53	.598	—	Tex Jeanes/Al Costello
Henderson Oilers (4)	79	55	.590	1	Jake Atz, Sr.
Tyler Trojans (7)	79	56	.585	1½	Bobby Goff/Sam Hancock
Marshall Tigers	67	64	.511	11½	Francis "Salty" Parker
Kilgore Boomers (16)	55	78	.414	24½	Jimmy Dalrymple
Texarkana Liners	47	87	.351	33	Abe Miller/Clair Bates
Palestine Pals#(7)	25	20	.556	NA	Elmer Kirchoff
Jacksonville Jax#	14	32	.304	NA	Cecil "Stormy" Davis/Walt Bohl

#Palestine and Jacksonville disbanded June 5.

Playoffs: Marshall 3 games, Henderson 2; Tyler 3 games, Longview 2.
Finals: Tyler 4 games, Marshall 3.

All-Star Team: 1B-Henry Becker, Longview; **2B**-Ford Mullen, Henderson; **3B**-Sam Hancock, Tyler; **SS**-Francis "Salty" Parker, Marshall; **OF**-Tom Jordan, Marshall; Walter Dieffenbach, Kilgore; Nick Gregory, Tyler; **C**-Joe Eratt, Henderson; **Util**-George Kovach, Palestine/Tyler; **P**-Grover Miller, Tyler; Ado Severi, Kilgore; **Manager**-Jake Atz, Sr., Henderson.

BA: Francis "Salty" Parker, Marshall, .349
Runs: Bill Binstrup, Tyler, 120
Hits: George Kovach, Palestine/Tyler, 175
RBIs: George Kovach, Palestine/Tyler, 108
HRs: Tom Jordan, Marshall, 19
Wins: Pat Beasley, Longview, 20
SOs: Bob Gillespie, Henderson, 224
ERA: Pat Beasley, Longview, 2.33

C Michigan State League
President: Thomas J. Halligan

Standings	W	L	Pct.	GB	Manager
Flint Gems (3)	67	41	.620	—	Jack Knight
Saginaw Athletics	53	48	.525	10½	Dallas Avery/Henry Camilli
St. Joseph Autos	52	51	.505	12½	Conrad Fisher/Elmer Kirchoff
Grand Rapids Dodgers (10)	50	56	.472	16	Burleigh Grimes
Muskegon Reds (4)	49	57	.462	17	Jack Tighe
Lansing Lancers (16)	44	62	.415	22	Jess Altenburg

Playoffs: Saginaw 3 games, Grand Rapids 1; St. Joseph 3 games, Flint 2.
Finals: Cancelled due to inclement weather.

All-Star Team: 1B-Elmer Sidlo, Flint; **2B**-Joe Wessing, Muskegon; **3B**-Dick Shoff, Flint; **SS**-Tom Woodruff, St. Joseph; **OF**-Bill Fuchs, Saginaw; Ralph Brande, Grand Rapids; Norman Petersen, Lansing; **C**-Jack Tighe, Muskegon; **Util**-Frank Gunkel, Saginaw; **P**-Larry Gardner, Lansing; Vernon Kohler, Flint; **Manager**-Jack Knight, Flint.

BA: Robert Ogle, Grand Rapids, .374
Runs: Elmer Sidlo, Flint, 109
Hits: Robert Ogle, Grand Rapids, 171
RBIs: Jerry Burmeister, Lansing, 86
HRs: Joe Wojey, Grand Rapids, 20

Wins: Vernon Kohler, Flint, 18
SOs: Reb Wright, Saginaw, 159
ERA: Clarence Gann, Muskegon, 2.80
Pct: Herb Norquist, St. Joseph, .846, 11-2

C Middle Atlantic League
President: Elmer M. Daily

Standings	W	L	Pct.	GB	Manager
Akron Yankees (5).............	73	54	.575	—	Horace "Pip" Koehler
Charleston Senators (3)	64	62	.508	8½	Ed Hall
Youngstown Browns (7).....	62	62	.500	9½	Rodney Whitney
Dayton Wings (10)	60	65	.480	12	Andy Cohen
Canton Terriers (1)	58	65	.472	13	Floyd Patterson
Portsmouth Red Birds (16).	59	68	.465	14	Fred Dorman/Walter Alston

Playoffs: Akron 3 games, Youngstown 2; Dayton 3 games, Charleston 1.
Finals: Akron 3 games, Dayton 2.

All-Star Team: 1B-Jerry Witte, Youngstown; **2B**-Bob Dillinger, Youngstown; **3B**-J. Schmidt, Portsmouth; **SS**-Stanley Rojek, Dayton; **OF**-Henry Meyer, Dayton; Albert White, Youngstown; Butch Nieman, Canton; **C**-Lou Kahn, Charleston; **Util**-Horace "Pip" Koehler, Akron; **P**-Steve Mlinsarik, Charleston; Clem Dreisewerd, Portsmouth; **Manager**-Ed Hall, Charleston.

BA: Edward Tighe, Akron, .325
Runs: Tony Sams, Akron, 109
  Bob Dillinger, Youngstown, 109
Hits: Tony Sams, Akron, 163
  Bob Dillinger, Youngstown, 163
RBIs: Jerry Witte, Youngstown, 124
HRs: Walter Alston, Portsmouth, 28
Wins: Clem Dreisewerd, Portsmouth, 23
SOs: Mel Queen, Akron, 202
ERA: Bob Haas, Charleston, 2.25

C Pioneer League
President: Jack Halliwell

Standings	W	L	Pct.	GB	Attend.	Manager
Salt Lake City Bees	79	51	.608	—	179,180	Tony Robello
Boise Pilots	66	63	.512	12½	94,350	Andy Harrington
Idaho Falls Russets (5)	65	65	.500	14	70,400	Ted Mayer
Ogden Reds (12).................	64	66	.492	15	61,795	Bill McCorry
Pocatello Cardinals (16)	62	68	.477	17	60,295	Ken Penner
Twin Falls Cowboys...........	53	76	.411	25½	39,807	Frank Tobin/Ray Jacobs

Playoffs: Ogden 2 games, Salt Lake City 0; Boise 2 games, Idaho Falls 1.
Finals: Ogden 3 games, Boise 0.

All-Star Team: 1B-Walter Lowe, Boise; **2B**-Albert Steele, Salt Lake City; **3B**-Ray Perry, Salt Lake City; **SS**-Dale Laybourne, Ogden; **OF**-Robert Joratz, Pocatello; Joe Egnatic, Boise; Pete Hughes, Ogden/Twin Falls; **C**-Roy Partee, Salt Lake City; **Util**-Elden Lorenzen, Boise; **P**-Larry Jansen, Salt Lake City; Melvin Ristau, Salt Lake City; **Manager**-Tony Robello, Salt Lake City.

BA: Bobby Adams, Ogden, .356
Runs: Joe Egnatic, Boise, 119
Hits: Walter Lowe, Boise, 171
RBIs: Walter Lowe, Boise, 121
HRs: Tony Robello, Salt Lake City, 22
Wins: Bill Caplinger, Pocatello, 21
SOs: Bill Caplinger, Pocatello, 265
ERA: Larry Jansen, Salt Lake City, 2.19
Pct: Larry Jansen, Salt Lake City, .741, 20-7

C Western Association
President: Tom Fairweather

Standings	W	L	Pct.	GB	Attend.	Manager
Muskogee Reds..................	90	49	.647	—	44,095	Jack Mealey
Topeka Owls (7).................	73	60	.578	14	95,000	William Wilson/Pete Monahan
Ft. Smith Giants (13)	70	63	.526	17		Herschel Bobo
St. Joseph Saints (11)........	69	63	.522	17½		Keith Frazier
Joplin Miners (5)	68	64	.515	18½		Paul O'Malley
Salina Millers	60	75	.441	28		Jack Calvey
Springfield Cardinals (16)..	56	76	.424	30½	35,800	George Silvey/Ollie Vanek
Hutchinson Pirates (15).......	50	86	.372	38½		Jimmy Jordan/Adolph Arlitt

Playoffs: St. Joseph 3 games, Topeka 1; Ft. Smith 3 games, Muskogee 0.
Finals: St. Joseph 3 games, Ft. Smith 0.

MVP-Henry Mestnik, Muskogee.

BA: Frank Houska, St. Joseph, .379
Runs: Erwin Paul, Muskogee, 152
Hits: Erwin Paul, Muskogee, 200
RBIs: Glenn Peters, Muskogee, 135
HRs: Glenn Peters, Muskogee, 24
Wins: Henry Mestnik, Muskogee, 24
SOs: Stan Zetusky, Hutchinson, 209
ERA: Joe Malman, Topeka, 2.69

D Alabama State League
President: Charles T. Laney

Standings	W	L	Pct.	GB	Manager
Tallassee Indians.................	84	45	.651	—	Steve Bysco
Greenville Lions (10)..........	71	59	.546	13½	Dick Luckey
Dothan Browns...................	67	62	.519	17	Holt "Cat" Milner
Troy Trojans (12)................	66	63	.512	18	Enis Johnson/Harold Fehrenbacher
Brewton Millers	51	79	.392	33½	Yam Yaryan
Andalusia Rams.................	49	80	.380	35	Bruner Nix/Oscar Mosley

Playoffs: Greenville 3 games, Troy 2; Dothan 3 games, Tallassee 2.
Finals: Dothan 4 games, Greenville 2.

All-Star Team: 1B-Gilbert Leatherwood, Brewton; **2B**-William Hodgins, Troy; **3B**-James Persons, Tallassee; **SS**-Ray Quimby, Brewton; **OF**-Oscar Martin, Tallassee; Gordon Goodell, Tallassee; John Ostrowski, Troy; **C**-Emory Lindsey, Tallassee; **Util**-Malvern Morgan, Tallassee; **P**-Steve Bysco, Tallassee; John Travis, Greenville; **Manager**-Yam Yaryan, Brewton.

BA: Emory Lindsey, Tallassee, .350
Runs: Felix Jurwiak, Dothan, 121
Hits: James Persons, Tallassee, 172
RBIs: John Ostrowski, Troy, 120
HRs: Gordon Goodell, Tallassee, 31
Wins: John Travis, Greenville, 20
  Steve Bysco, Tallassee, 20
SOs: Royce Lint, Andalusia, 166
ERA: John Travis, Greenville, 3.18

D Appalachian League
President: J. Ross Edgemon

Standings	W	L	Pct.	GB	Manager
Elizabethton Betsy Red Sox**(1)................	84	33	.718	—	Hobe Brummitt
Johnson City Cardinals*(16) .	84	34	.712	½	Ollie Vanek/George Silvey
Kingsport Cherokees	56	61	.470	28	Claude Trivette
Bristol Twins	54	60	.474	28½	Larry Merville/Tim Murchison/Lance Richbourg
Newport Canners (8)	56	63	.471	29	Jerry Witner/John "Red" Marian
Greeneville Burley Cubs (11).	55	63	.466	29½	Sam Alexander/Hubert Stolpher
Pennington Gap Miners (7)	50	64	.439	32½	Art Hauger/Jim Rollins
Erwin Mountaineers	27	88	.235	56	Tilly Walker/Bill Dubbs

Playoffs: Elizabethton 2 games, Kingsport 0; Johnson City 2 games, Bristol 0; Greeneville 2 games, Newport 1; Johnson City 2 games, Greeneville 1.
Finals: Johnson City 3 games, Elizabethton 0.

All-Star Team: 1B-Robert Williams, Elizabethton; **2B**-Lou Rochelli, Elizabethton; **3B**-George Torres, Newport; **SS**-Herb Stein, Erwin; **OF**-Greyson Davis, Greeneville; C.A. Whaley, Elizabethton; Lew Flick, Elizabethton; **C**-Dick Bouknight, Johnson City; **Util**-John Heffner, Kingsport; **P**-Arthur Richard Cyrulewski, Johnson City; Arthur Boyes, Elizabethton; **Manager**-Hobe Brummitt, Elizabethton.

BA: Dick Bouknight, Johnson City, .376
Runs: Lew Flick, Elizabethton, 124
Hits: Lew Flick, Elizabethton, 181
RBIs: Robert Williams, Elizabethton, 125
HRs: Robert Williams, Elizabethton, 19
Wins: Frank Radler, Elizabethton, 23
SOs: Anderson Bush, Bristol, 199
ERA: Arthur Boyes, Elizabethton, 2.86

D Arkansas-Missouri League
President: Robert J. Henry

Standings	W	L	Pct.	GB	Manager
Carthage Pirates (15)	37	18	.673	—	Adolph Arlitt
Neosho Yankees (5).............	27	29	.482	10½	Ed Grayson
Fayetteville Angels (10)	21	29	.420	13½	Howard "Ducky" Holmes
Siloam Springs Cardinals (16).	21	30	.412	14	Herb Moore

The league disbanded July 1.

BA: Charles Fash, Fayetteville, .356
Runs: Charles Gibson, Carthage, 55
Hits: Charles Gibson, Carthage, 71
RBIs: Adolph Arlitt, Carthage, 59
HRs: Adolph Arlitt, Carthage, 12
Wins: Teddy Greble, Neosho, 9
  Bob Playfair, Carthage, 9
  Joe Prylich, Fayetteville, 9
SOs: Walt Nasalik, Neosho
Pct: Jim Obenour, Carthage, .857, 6-1

D Bi-State League
President: Joseph Garrett

Standings	W	L	Pct.	GB	Manager
Bassett Furnituremakers (10)...	73	44	.624	—	Einar Sorenson
Martinsville Manufacturers (14)	68	49	.581	5	Harry Daughtry
Mt. Airy Graniteers.............	63	56	.529	11	Walter Novak
Danville-Schoolfield Leafs (1)	59	58	.504	14	Emile Barnes
South Boston Wrappers......	56	60	.483	16½	Jack Crosswhite/H.A. Mobley
Leaksville-Draper-Spray Triplets	56	63	.471	18	Arnold Anderson
Mayodan Millers.................	53	66	.445	21	Pete Siciliano
Reidsville Luckies	43	75	.364	30½	Jim Callahan/Jim Gruzdis

Playoffs: Martinsville 4 games, Danville 2; Bassett 4 games, Mt. Airy 1.
Finals: Martinsville 4 games, Bassett 3.

All-Star Team: 1B-Richard Bohl, South Boston; **2B**-Jim Gruzdis, Reidsville; **3B**-Emmitt Johnson, Leaksville-Draper-Spray; **SS**-Noel Casbier, Bassett; **OF**-Dan Amaral, Mayodan; Walter Stewart, South Boston; Clyde Vollmer, Bassett; **C**-Luther Hendrix, Danville-Schoolfield; **Util**-James McDuffy, Danville-Schoolfield; **P**-Paige Dennis, Reidsville/Mt. Airy; Roy Peeler, Bassett; **Manager**-Walter Novak, Mt. Airy.

BA: Dan Amaral, Mayodan, .387
Runs: Alex Johnson, Mayodan, 119
Hits: Alex Johnson, Mayodan, 178
RBIs: Clyde Vollmer, Bassett, 117
HRs: Orville Nesselrode, South Boston, 25
Wins: Roy Peeler, Bassett, 17
  Flory Wojcik, Bassett, 17
SOs: Paige Dennis, Reidsville/Mt. Airy, 187
ERA: Flory Wojcik, Bassett, 2.95

D Coastal Plain League
President: Ray Goodmon

Standings	W	L	Pct.	GB	Manager
Wilson Tobs......................	77	49	.611	—	Frank Rodgers
Tarboro Cubs.....................	72	51	.585	3½	Arthur "Cowboy" McHenry/Wes Ratteree
Goldsboro Goldbugs...........	66	58	.532	10	Mac Arnette
Kinston Eagles	63	60	.516	12½	Denny Sothern/William Aerette

Snow Hill Billies .... 62 64 .492 15   Dwight Wall
New Bern Bears.................. 58 67 .464 18½ Guy Shatzer/Gene McCarty
Greenville Greenies .... 53 71 .427 23   Rube Wilson
Williamston Martins........... 47 78 .376 29½ Dixie Parker/Harry Swain

Playoffs: Kinston 4 games, Wilson 3; Tarboro 4 games, Goldsboro 1.
Finals: Tarboro 4 games, Kinston 2.

All-Star Team: 1B-Phil Morris, Wilson; **2B**-Harry Schenz, Tarboro; **3B**-Floyd Harper, New Bern; **SS**-Walter Rabb, Snow Hill; **OF**-Earl Carnahan, Wilson; Arthur "Cowboy" McHenry, Tarboro; Roy Kennedy, Kinston; **C**-Norm McCaskill, Snow Hill; **Util**-Sid Stringfellow, Kinston; **P**-Fred Caligiuri, Greenville; Joe Talley, Wilson; **Manager**-Frank Rodgers, Wilson.

BA: Earl Carnahan, Wilson, .354
Runs: Charles Metelski, Tarboro, 115
Hits: Phil Morris, Wilson, 185
RBIs: Earl Carnahan, Wilson, 119
HRs: Luis Olmo, Wilson, 18
Wins: Walter Wilson, Goldsboro, 21
SOs: Harry Swain, Williamston, 215
ERA: Bill Zinser, Kinston, 2.08

D Eastern Shore League
President: Harry S. Russell

Standings	W	L	Pct.	GB	Manager
Dover Orioles (14).............	72	48	.600	—	John Clark
Centreville Red Sox (1)......	68	48	.586	2	Ed Walls
Milford Giants (13)............	72	52	.581	2	Clarence "Bubber" Jonnard
Salisbury Cardinals (8).......	65	58	.528	8½	Gus Brittain/Ed Kobesky
Federalsburg A's (6)..........	57	67	.460	17	Sam Nisonoff/Don Maynard
Cambridge Canners (16).....	52	67	.437	19½	Hugh Poland
Easton Yankees (5)............	48	69	.410	22½	Ray Powell
Pocomoke City Chicks	50	75	.400	24½	John Whalen

Playoffs: Milford 3 games, Dover 2; Salisbury 3 games, Centreville 2.
Finals: Salisbury 4 games, Milford 2.

All-Star Team: 1B-Paul Swoboda, Dover; **2B**-Paul Gaulin, Dover; **3B**-Harold Harrigan, Milford; **SS**-Louis Lowe, Milford; **OF**-Lloyd Rice, Federalsburg; Victor Weiss, Pocomoke City; Randall Phillips, Dover; **C**-John Clark, Dover; **Util**-Bobby Maier, Salisbury; **P**-Jorge Comellas, Salisbury; John Thompson, Centreville; **Manager**-John Clark, Dover.

BA: Lloyd Rice, Federalsburg, .363
Runs: Paul Gaulin, Dover, 102
Hits: Bobby Maier, Salisbury, 146
RBIs: Fred Lutz, Easton, 81
HRs: Ed Kobesky, Salisbury, 18
Wins: Jorge Comellas, Salisbury, 21
SOs: John Thompson, Centreville, 268
ERA: John Thompson, Centreville, 1.56

D Evangeline League
President: A. Wilmont Dalferes

Standings	W	L	Pct.	GB	Manager
Lake Charles Skippers........	86	49	.634	—	Otis Brannon
Alexandria Aces	84	54	.609	3½	Carl Kott
Lafayette White Sox (7)	77	55	.583	7½	Harry Strohm
New Iberia Cardinals	78	57	.578	8	Jimmie Sanders
Port Arthur Tarpons...........	63	71	.470	22½	Ray Flood/Louis Viau
Opelousas Indians..............	59	75	.440	26½	Conrad Flippen
Houma Buccaneers/					
Natchez Pilgrims#..........	51	79	.392	32½	Carlos Moore
Rayne Rice Birds (2, 10)	37	95	.280	47½	Art Bartelli

#Houma moved to Natchez June 27.
Attendance: Lake Charles, 49,230.

Playoffs: New Iberia 4 games, Lake Charles 1; Alexandria 4 games, Lafayette 2.
Finals: Alexandria 4 games, New Iberia 0.

All-Star Team: 1B-Joe Yourkovick, Opelousas; **2B**-Danny Menendez, Opelousas; **3B**-Carl Kott, Alexandria; **SS**-Paul Moore, Lake Charles; **OF**-Ray Parrott, Lafayette; Anse Moore, Alexandria; Woody Fair, New Iberia; **C**-Bobby Birchfield, Port Arthur; **Util**-Conrad Flippen, Lake Charles; **P**-Sam Eaton, Alexandria; William Ratteree, Port Arthur; **Manager**-Harry Strohm, Lafayette.

BA: Harry Strohm, Lafayette, .361
Runs: Fred Hancock, Lake Charles, 122
Hits: Ken Grosse, Lafayette, 188
RBIs: Woody Fair, New Iberia, 125
HRs: Woody Fair, New Iberia, 24
Wins: Gordon Pixley, New Iberia, 26
SOs: Sam Eaton, Alexandria, 256
ERA: Sam Eaton, Alexandria, 1.77

D Florida East Coast League
President: Judge Gordon Lynn

Standings	W	L	Pct.	GB	Manager
Ft. Lauderdale Tarpons (15) ..	69	40	.623	—	Herb Thomas
Hollywood Chiefs	62	47	.569	7	Jiggs Donahue
Miami Beach Tigers	60	51	.541	10	Fred Heimach
West Palm Beach Indians ...	52	60	.464	18½	Cecil Downs/Joe Murff
Ft. Pierce Bombers	49	65	.430	22½	Lance Richbourg
Miami Wahoos	42	71	.372	29	Max Carey

Playoffs: Ft. Lauderdale 3 games, West Palm Beach 1; Miami Beach 3 games, Hollywood 0.
Finals: Ft. Lauderdale 4 games, Miami Beach 1.

All-Star Team: 1B-Jack Westley, Ft. Lauderdale/Hollywood; **2B**-Herb Thomas, Ft. Lauderdale; **3B**-Ted Mueller, Ft. Lauderdale; **SS**-Tommy O'Rourke, West Palm Beach; **OF**-Max Rosenfeld, Miami Beach; Bill Baker, Ft. Lauderdale; William Hooks, West Palm Beach; **C**-John Dillon, Hollywood; **Util**-Thomas Cornish, Miami; **P**-Theron Thomasello, Ft. Pierce; Chet Covington, Hollywood; **Manager**-Jiggs Donahue, Hollywood.

BA: Jack Westley, Ft. Lauderdale/Hollywood, .377
Runs: Jack Westley, Ft. Lauderdale/Hollywood, 96
Hits: Pecky Engel, West Palm Beach/Ft. Pierce, 158
RBIs: Jack Westley, Ft. Lauderdale/Hollywood, 98
HRs: Jack Westley, Ft. Lauderdale/Hollywood, 11
Oliver Kelly, Miami, 11
Dale Lynch, Miami Beach, 11
Wins: Chet Covington, Hollywood, 21
SOs: Chet Covington, Hollywood, 212
ERA: Gene Beardon, Miami Beach, 1.63

D Florida State League
President: Henry Gray

Standings	W	L	Pct.	GB	Manager
Daytona Beach Islanders (16) .	86	53	.619	—	Dickie Kerr
Sanford Seminoles	84	55	.604	2	Lynn Campbell
St. Augustine Saints...........	72	68	.514	14½	Alan Mobley/Guy Miller
Orlando Senators (8)..........	71	69	.507	15½	John Ganzel
DeLand Red Hats (8)..........	69	71	.493	17½	Bill Rodgers
Leesburg Anglers..............	62	77	.446	24	Emil Yde
Ocala Yearlings	57	82	.410	29	Wilbur Good, Sr./Gibbs Miller
Gainesville G-Men	57	83	.407	29½	Frank Lariscy/Eddie Moore

Playoffs: Sanford 3 games, St. Augustine 0; Orlando 3 games, Daytona Beach 1.
Finals: Orlando 4 games, Sanford 0.

All-Star Team: 1B-Bill Davis, DeLand; **2B**-Henry Wayton, Daytona Beach; **3B**-Raymond Goolsby, St. Augustine; **SS**-Lou Klein, Daytona Beach; **OF**-Leslie Voshell, Leesburg; Ralph Hyder, Sanford; Wilmer Skeen, Sanford; **C**-Manuel Onis, Orlando; **Util**-Buddy Lake, St. Augustine; **P**-Richard Hearn, St. Augustine; Stan Musial, Daytona Beach; **Manager**-Dickie Kerr, Daytona Beach.

BA: Buddy Lake, St. Augustine, .352
Runs: Ralph Hyder, Sanford, 126
Hits: Ralph Hyder, Sanford, 196
RBIs: Jim Pruitt, Gainesville, 98
HRs: Jim Pruitt, Gainesville, 10
Wins: Harrell Toenes, DeLand, 26
SOs: Richard Hearn, St. Augustine, 305
ERA: J.D. Creel, Daytona Beach, 1.50

D Georgia-Florida League
President: A.D. "Doc" Walker

Standings	W	L	Pct.	GB	Manager
Waycross Bears	93	45	.674	—	Albert Leitz
Thomasville Tourists (8)	81	58	.583	12½	Dale Alexander
Valdosta Trojans................	76	61	.555	16½	Bill Morrell
Albany Cardinals (16).........	77	63	.550	17	Joe Cusick
Americus Pioneers (10)......	67	72	.482	26½	Bernie DeViveiros/Stewart Hofferth
Tallahassee Capitols	64	75	.461	29½	Harold Schultz
Cordele Bees....................	49	89	.355	44	William Taylor
Moultrie Packers (14).........	47	91	.340	46	Joe Holden/George Jacobs

Playoffs: Waycross 3 games, Valdosta 0; Thomasville 3 games, Albany 2.
Finals: Waycross 4 games, Thomasville 1.

All-Star Team: 1B-Eddie Hoffman, Americus; **2B**-Ed Kaczak, Valdosta; **3B**-Cy Lowrey, Tallahassee; **SS**-Charlie Brewster, Waycross; **OF**-Pershing Thomassie, Waycross; Ervin Dusak, Albany; Charles Farrar, Waycross; **C**-Albert Leitz, Waycross; **Util**-Pat Dove, Thomasville; **P**-Elmer Rummans, Valdosta; Ellwood Lawson, Waycross; **Manager**-Dale Alexander, Thomasville.

BA: Sherwood McKenzie, Thomasville, .378
Runs: Russell Leach, Albany, 131
Hits: Ralph Ellis, Thomasville, 203
RBIs: Charles Farrar, Waycross, 131
HRs: Dale Alexander, Thomasville, 14
Wins: Ellwood Lawson, Waycross, 26
SOs: Stan Ferens, Albany, 253
ERA: Elmer Rummans, Valdosta, 2.19

D Kitty League
President: B.F. Howard

Standings	W	L	Pct.	GB	Manager
Bowling Green Barons**(10)..	75	50	.600	—	Ellis "Mike" Powers
Paducah Indians................	75	51	.595	½	Rip Fanning
Owensboro Oilers (9).........	69	57	.532	6½	Hugh Wise/Harold Sueme
Jackson Generals*	66	58	.516	8½	Mickey O'Neil
Mayfield Browns (7)	65	61	.516	10½	Benny Tate
Union City Greyhounds (16)	60	65	.480	15	Charles Manning/Charles Martin
Fulton Tigers (4)...............	56	70	.444	19½	Jim Poole
Hopkinsville Hoppers	35	89	.282	39½	Dutch Welch

Playoff: Jackson 4 games, Bowling Green 3.

All-Star Team: 1B-Frank McElyea, Owensboro; **2B**-Joe Lehan, Bowling Green; **SS**-Len Novak, Owensboro; **OF**-James Cookson, union City; Edward Urban, Owensboro; Joe Polcha, Jackson; **C**-Lem Stewart, Paducah; **P**-Leon Baiser, Paducah; Elmer Haas, Bowling Green; **Util**-Vincent "Moon" Mullen, Fulton; **Manager**-Ellis "Mike" Powers, Bowling Green.

BA: Frank McElyea, Owensboro, .400
Runs: Frank McElyea, Owensboro, 125
Hits: Frank McElyea, Owensboro, 208
RBIs: Ellis "Mike" Powers,
Bowling Green, 155

HRs: Edward Urban, Owensboro, 34
Wins: Elmer Haas, Bowling Green, 23
SOs: Ellis Kinder, Jackson, 307
ERA: Ellis Kinder, Jackson, 2.38

D Mountain State League
President: Ray Ryan

Standings	W	L	Pct.	GB	Manager
Williamson Red Birds (16).	76	45	.628	—	Harrison Wickel
Logan Indians	75	51	.595	3½	Eddie Hock
Bluefield Blue-Greys	65	51	.560	8½	Vic Sorrell
Welch Miners	63	62	.504	15	Byron "Tex" Stuart/Roy Hall
Ashland Colonels	55	71	.437	23½	Tom Thevenow/Ray French
Huntington Aces	33	87	.275	42½	Pee Wee Wanninger/Russ Young/ Ezra Midkiff

Playoffs: Logan 2 games, Welch 0; Williamson 2 games, Bluefield 0.
Finals: Williamson 3 games, Logan 1.

All-Star Team: 1B-Clarence "Buck" Etchison, Welch; **2B**-Pat Capri, Williamson; **3B**-Joe Bezdek, Ashland; **SS**-Harold Kase, Logan; **OF**-Bill Shewey, Williamson; Stan Wentzel, Logan; Pete Mihalic, Bluefield; **C**-Byron "Tex" Stuart, Welch; **Util**-Marvin Lorenz, Bluefield; **P**-Ernest Peters, Williamson; Jake Schoettle, Huntington; **Manager**-Eddie Hock, Logan.

BA: Worthington Day, Ashland, .363
Runs: Bill Shewey, Williamson, 134
Hits: Worthington Day, Ashland, 178
Tennis Mounts, Logan, 178
RBIs: Clarence "Buck" Etchison, Welch, 132

HRs: Stan Wentzel, Logan, 26
Wins: Harold Sharp, Williamson, 18
Joe Pennington, Logan, 18
SOs: Vern Bickford, Welch, 163
ERA: Tom Triner, Welch, 2.76

D North Carolina State League
President: C.M. Llewellyn

Standings	W	L	Pct.	GB	Manager
Kannapolis Towelers	67	45	.598	—	Stumpy Culbreth/Joe Palmisano
Salisbury Giants (13)	64	46	.582	2	Johnny Heving
Lexington Indians	64	48	.571	3	Reece Harris/Lester Smith
Mooresville Moors	60	51	.541	6½	Johnny Hicks
Concord Weavers	58	54	.518	9	Gerald Fitzgerald
Thomasville Tommies (3)	56	54	.509	10	Jimmy Maus
Landis Dodgers (10)	49	63	.438	18	Otis "Blackie" Carter
Cooleemee Cards (16)	27	84	.243	39½	Boyce Morrow/Dutch Dorman

Playoffs: Mooresville 3 games, Salisbury 0; Lexington 3 games, Kannapolis 0.
Finals: Lexington 4 games, Mooresville 1.

All-Star Team: 1B-Michael Schemer, Salisbury; **2B**-Stahle Brown, Concord; **3B**-Ulmont Baker, Concord; **SS**-Lester Smith, Lexington; **OF**-Roy Pinkston, Landis/Lexington; Norman Small, Mooresville; William Carrier, Kannapolis; **C**-Jimmy Maus, Thomasville; **Util**-Harvey Black, Kannapolis/Mooresville; **P**-Ray Lindsay, Thomasville; John Tansey, Salisbury; **Manager**-Johnny Hicks, Mooresville.

BA: Roy Pinkston, Landis/Lexington, .383
Runs: Lew Davis, Kannapolis, 100
Hits: Michael Schemer, Salisbury, 156
RBIs: Norman Small, Mooresville, 115

HRs: Norman Small, Mooresville, 25
Wins: Ray Lindsay, Thomasville, 20
SOs: Ray Lindsay, Thomasville, 269
ERA: James White, Kannapolis, 1.85

D Northeast Arkansas League
President: Joseph R. Bertig

Standings	W	L	Pct.	GB	Attend.	Manager
Paragould Browns**(7)	73	48	.603	—	14,775	Tom Greenwade
Jonesboro White Sox*(2)	67	54	.554	6	21,131	Johnny Mostil
Newport Dodgers (10)	56	68	.452	18½	10,184	Cliff Greer/Paul Chervinko
Caruthersville/ Batesville Pilots#(16)	47	73	.392	25½	8,961	Ernest Stefani

#Caruthersville moved to Batesville July 7 at the start of the second half.

Playoff: Paragould 3 games, Jonesboro 0.

All-Star Team: 1B-Henry Arft, Paragould; **2B**-Gus Albright, Paragould; **3B**-Ernest Stefani, Carutherville/Batesville; **SS**-Jerry Nemitz, Paragould; **OF**-Doc O'Neill, Jonesboro; William Mitterman, Jonesboro; John Snyder, Newport; **C**-James Van Wey, Paragould; **Util**-Chandler Duncan, Newport; **P**-Edward Nolden, Jonesboro; John Menley, Paragould; **Manager**-Johnny Mostil, Jonesboro.

BA: Joe Marco, Paragould, .334
Runs: Jerry Nemitz, Paragould, 106
Hits: Joe Marco, Paragould, 166
RBIs: Doc O'Neill, Jonesboro, 111

HRs: Doc O'Neill, Jonesboro, 20
Wins: Al LaMacchia, Paragould, 16
SOs: Henry Hanson, Newport, 192
ERA: Melvin Gordon, Newport, 2.52

D Northern League
President: Herman D. White

Standings	W	L	Pct.	GB	Manager
Grand Forks Chiefs (2)	79	44	.642	—	Pop Williams
Winnipeg Maroons	65	51	.560	10½	Joe Mowry

Superior Blues (10)	63	52	.548	12	James "Chappie" Geygan
Wausau Timberjacks (14)	64	56	.533	13½	Wally Gilbert
Duluth Dukes (16)	61	59	.508	16½	Joe Davis
Fargo-Moorhead Twins (3)	50	67	.427	26	Chester Bujace/Wes Griffith
Crookston Pirates	49	74	.398	30	Fred Neisler
Eau Claire Bears	42	70	.375	31½	Ivy Griffin

Playoffs: Winnipeg 4 games, Wausau 0; Grand Forks 4 games, Superior 3.
Finals: Grand Forks 4 games, Winnipeg 2.

All-Star Team: 1B-Herbert Wilson, Duluth; **2B**-Frank Danneker, Winnipeg; **3B**-John Blatnik, Fargo-Moorhead; **SS**-Robert Mason, Crookston; **OF**-Joe Mowry, Winnipeg; Paul Welch, Fargo-Moorhead; Chet Cichosz, Wausau; **C**-Herman Bauer, Grand Forks; **Util**-Donald Turck, Crookston; **P**-Robert Peterson, Winnipeg; Dwain Sloat, Grand Forks; **Manager**-James "Chappie" Geygan, Superior.

BA: Chet Cichosz, Wausau, .403
Runs: Robert Decker, Wausau, 121
Hits: Joe Mowry, Winnipeg, 177
RBIs: Joe Mowry, Winnipeg, 125
HRs: Austin Knickerbocker, Wausau, 22

Wins: Hugh Orphan, Wausau, 19
SOs: Hugh Orphan, Wausau, 304
ERA: Danny Horton, Grand Forks, 1.29
Pct: Danny Horton, Grand Forks, .833, 10-2

D Ohio State League
President: Paul H. Shank

Standings	W	L	Pct.	GB	Manager
Lima Pandas	85	34	.714	—	Merle Settlemire
Findlay Oilers	70	46	.603	13½	Grover Hartley/George Ruley
Mansfield Braves (3)	59	59	.500	25½	Dewey Strong
Tiffin Mud Hens	50	64	.429	32½	Myles Thomas
Fostoria Red Birds (16)	44	73	.376	40	Bobby Jones
Fremont Green Sox	43	75	.364	41½	Ray Caldwell/Garland Sewell

Playoffs: Lima 3 games, Mansfield 0; Findlay 3 games, Tiffin 1.
Finals: Lima 4 games, Findlay 2.

All-Star Team: 1B-John Cindric, Lima; **2B**-Jack Cassini, Tiffin; **3B**-Harlan Kiersey, Lima; **SS**-Ray Kozak, Lima; **OF**-Gene Woodling, Mansfield; Bobby Jones, Fostoria; Stanley Mazgay, Findlay; **C**-Ralph Weigel, Lima; **Util**-Ted Haas, Fremont/Lima; **P**-Walter McHugh, Tiffin; Frank Biscan, Lima; **Manager**-Merle Settlemire, Lima.

BA: Gene Woodling, Mansfield, .398
Runs: John Cindric, Lima, 141
Hits: Stanley Mazgay, Findlay, 175
RBIs: John Cindric, Lima, 150

HRs: John Cindric, Lima, 39
Wins: Frank Biscan, Lima, 26
SOs: Frank Biscan, Lima, 243
Pct: Merle Settlemire, Lima, 1.000, 15-0

D Pennsylvania State Association
President: Elmer M. Daily

Standings	W	L	Pct.	GB	Manager
Johnstown Johnnies (10)	65	44	.596	—	George "Red" Treadwell
Butler Yankees (5)	65	44	.596	—	Thomas Kain
Beaver Falls Browns	52	56	.481	12½	Frank Oceak
McKeesport Little Braves/ Oil City Oilers#(15)	51	57	.471	13½	Elmer Klump
Washington Red Birds (16)	49	59	.454	15½	James "Bunny" Simmons
Warren Redskins (3)	42	64	.396	21½	William Rhiel

#McKeesport (24-26) moved to Oil City July 1.

Playoffs: Johnstown defeated Butler 9-7 in a one game playoff for first place. Butler 3 games, Oil City 1; Beaver Falls 3 games, Johnstown 1.
Finals: Butler 3 games, Beaver Falls 0.

All-Star Team: 1B-Joe Collins, Butler; **2B**-Frank Oceak, Beaver Falls; **3B**-Larry Hartman, Butler; **SS**-Robert Ramazzotti, Johnstown; **OF**-Nick Orange, Johnstown; Joe Smith, Johnstown; Steve Greble, Butler; **C**-Elmer Klump, McKeesport/Oil City; **Util**-George Jenkins, Washington; **P**-Ralph Ifft, Beaver Falls; Bill Sample, Johnstown; **Manager**-George "Red" Treadwell, Johnstown.

BA: Nick Orange, Johnstown, .353
Runs: Steve Greble, Butler, 111
Hits: Robert Ramazzotti, Johnstown, 143
RBIs: Steve Greble, Butler, 100

HRs: Steve Greble, Butler, 22
Wins: Bill Sample, Johnstown, 20
SOs: Bill Sample, Johnstown, 206
ERA: Ralph Ifft, Beaver Falls, 2.01

D PONY League
President: Robert C. Stedler

Standings	W	L	Pct.	GB	Manager
Olean Oilers (10)	65	39	.625	—	Jake Pitler
Batavia Clippers	58	48	.547	8	Jack Sanford
London Pirates (15)	48	54	.417	16	Louis "Mickey" LaLange/James Jordan
Hamilton Red Wings (16)	47	53	.470	16	Fred Lucas
Niagara Falls Rainbows/ Jamestown Falcons#	48	55	.466	16½	Joe O'Rourke/Joe Savant
Bradford Bees (9)	44	61	.419	21½	Eddie Onslow/Vic George

#Niagara Falls (22-30) moved to Jamestown July 13, first home game July 19.
Attendance: London, 44,376; Total, 278,514.

Playoffs: Olean 3 games, Hamilton 1; Batavia 3 games, London 2.

Finals: Olean 4 games, Batavia 2.

All-Star Team: 1B-Herb Fash, Olean; **2B**-Bill Burich, Olean; **3B**-Donald Richmond, Batavia; **SS**-Tom Kister, Bradford; **OF**-Lawrence Mancini, Olean; Wesley Cox, London; Henry Redmond, Hamilton; **C**-Warren Robinson, Hamilton; **Util**-Everett Johnston, Hamilton; **P**-John Castoldi, Batavia; Tom Hamill, Olean; **Manager**-Jake Pitler, Olean.

BA: Ed Howard, Batavia, .372
Runs: George Higgins, Olean, 110
  Warren Auchenbach, Hamilton, 110
Hits: Lawrence Mancini, Olean, 174
RBIs: Lawrence Mancini, Olean, 109
HRs: Lawrence Mancini, Olean, 25

Wins: John Castoldi, Batavia, 18
SOs: Richard Schmidt, Olean/
  Niagara Falls/Jamestown, 173
ERA: John Castoldi, Batavia, 2.84
Pct: John Castoldi, Batavia, .720, 18-7

D Tar Heel League
President: M.C. Campbell

Standings	W	L	Pct.	GB	Manager
Statesville Owls	73	37	.664	—	Clarence "Stuffy" McCrone
Gastonia Cardinals (16)	64	44	.593	8	Milt Bocek
Hickory Rebels	54	52	.509	17	Woodrow Traylor
Lenoir Reds (12)	53	55	.491	19	Ray Rice
Newton-Conover Twins#	27	45	.375	NA	Art Hauger/Herman Watts
Shelby Colonels#(8)	16	54	.229	NA	Lou Haneles/Art Patchin

#Newton-Conover and Shelby disbanded July 19.

Playoffs: Hickory 3 games, Gastonia 0; Statesville 3 games, Lenoir 2.
Finals: Statesville 4 games, Hickory 1.

All-Star Team: 1B-Clarence "Stuffy" McCrone, Statesville; **2B**-Bill Huffstetler, Statesville; **3B**-George Motto, Statesville; **SS**-Henry Dvorak, Hickory; **OF**-James Miller, Statesville; Frank Shoue, Lenoir; Milt Bocek, Gastonia; **C**-Ray Rice, Lenoir; **Util**-Copeland Goss, Hickory; **P**-Price Ferguson, Statesville; Herman Drefs, Statesville; **Manager**-Clarence "Stuffy" McCrone, Statesville.

BA: Milt Bocek, Gastonia, .364
Runs: Milt Bocek, Gastonia, 98
Hits: Milt Bocek, Gastonia, 157
RBIs: Milt Bocek, Gastonia, 109

HRs: Robert Traylor, Hickory, 16
  Frank Shoue, Lenoir, 16
Wins: Herman Drefs, Statesville, 17
SOs: Frank Motley, Newton-Conover/
  Gastonia, 174
ERA: Robert Bailey, Lenoir, 1.99

D Virginia League
President: Ray Ryan

Standings	W	L	Pct.	GB	Manager
Lynchburg Senators	70	45	.609	—	Guy Lacy
Harrisonburg Turks	61	56	.521	10	Hank Hulvey
Salem-Roanoke Friends (3)	55	62	.470	16	Eli Harris/Andy Anderson
Staunton Presidents	46	69	.400	24	Vernon Brandes/John Brennan

Playoff: Harrisonburg 2 games, Salem-Roanoke 1.
Finals: Lynchburg 3 games, Harrisonburg 2.

All-Star Team: 1B-John Brennan, Staunton; **2B**-Henry Loman, Harrisonburg; **3B**-Mike Winseck, Lynchburg; **SS**-Robert Schibi, Salem-Roanoke; **OF**-William Booker, Lynchburg; Crawford Howard, Lynchburg; Royce Watson, Lynchburg; **C**-Robert Kubicek, Lynchburg; **Util**-Julian Harrington, Lynchburg; **P**-Forrest Zeiger, Staunton; Dick Tate, Lynchburg; **Manager**-Guy Lacy, Lynchburg.

BA: Henry Loman, Harrisonburg, .322
Runs: Glen Adkins, Harrisonburg, 119
Hits: Glen Adkins, Harrisonburg, 149
RBIs: Joe Kruppa, Salem-Roanoke, 91

HRs: Crawford Howard, Lynchburg, 16
Wins: Dick Tate, Lynchburg, 17
SOs: Ed Haswell, Lynchburg, 162
ERA: Lewis Utz, Harrisonburg, 2.87

D West Texas-New Mexico League
President: Milton E. Price

Standings	W	L	Pct.	GB	Manager
Pampa Oilers	83	56	.601	—	Grover Seitz
Amarillo Gold Sox	82	58	.586	1½	Claude Jonnard
Lubbock Hubbers (2)	81	59	.579	2½	Charlie Engle
Borger Gassers	79	60	.568	4	Pete Susko/Gordon Neil
Lamesa Lobos	71	69	.507	12½	Joe Tate
Midland Cowboys	59	81	.421	24½	Sammy Hale
Clovis Pioneers	58	80	.420	24½	Howard Taylor
Big Spring Barons/					
Odessa Oilers#	45	95	.321	38½	Tony Rego/Stanley Bolton

#Big Spring (27-37) moved to Odessa June 20.
Attendance: Amarillo, 62,890; Total, 240,679.

Playoffs: Borger 3 games, Pampa 0; Lubbock 3 games, Amarillo 0.

Finals: Borger 4 games, Lubbock 3.

All-Star Team: 1B-Murl Prather, Pampa; **2B**-Steve Niedziela, Lubbock; **3B**-Jodie Beeler, Lamesa; **SS**-Larry Gilchrist, Borger; **OF**-Gordon Nell, Borger; Grover Seitz, Pampa; Edwin Schweda, Lubbock; **C**-Bill Ratliff, Amarillo; **Util**-Sammy Hale, Midland; **P**-Lloyd Patterson, Lamesa; Rex Dilbeck, Pampa; **Manager**-Claude Jonnard, Amarillo.

BA: Edwin Schweda, Lubbock, .422
Runs: Grover Seitz, Pampa, 163
Hits: Wiliam Scopetone, Big Spring/
  Borger, 217
RBIs: Gordon Nell, Borger, 175
HRs: Gordon Nell, Borger, 40

Wins: Rex Dilbeck, Pampa, 23
  James Ramsdell, Big Spring/
  Odessa, 23
SOs: Russell Crider, Amarillo, 266
ERA: Pat Ralsh, Lubbock, 3.25
Pct: Pat Ralsh, Lubbock, .833, 20-4

D Western League
President: J. Roy Carter

Standings	W	L	Pct.	GB	Manager
Norfolk Yankees (5)	73	39	.652	—	Elmer "Doc" Bennett
Sioux Falls Canaries	59	58	.504	16½	Robert Fenner
Worthington Cardinals (16)	50	59	.459	21½	Ray Martin/George Payne
Sioux City Soos/					
Mitchell Kernels#	44	70	.386	30	Jimmy Zinn/Ed Grayston

#Sioux City moved to Mitchell July 24.
The league played four quarters. Norfolk won the first, second, and fourth quarters, while Sioux Falls won the third quarter.

Playoff: Sioux Falls 4 games, Norfolk 2.

All-Star Team: 1B-Fred Schenk, Norfolk; **2B**-William Baker, Norfolk; **3B**-Mike Portner, Norfolk; **SS**-Lester Hackett, Worthington; **OF**-Russell Burns, Norfolk; Tony Koenig, Sioux Falls; John Lucas, Worthington; **C**-Harry Heslet, Norfolk; **Util**-Albert Dudas, Worthington; **P**-Ralph Scheef, Worthington; Joe Riss, Sioux Falls; **Manager**-Elmer "Doc" Bennett, Norfolk.

BA: John Lucas, Worthington, .356
Runs: Robert Duby, Norfolk, 112
Hits: Leo Bohanan, Sioux Falls, 158
RBIs: Fred Schenk, Norfolk, 97

HRs: Russell Burns, Norfolk, 17
Wins: Frank Wagner, Sioux Falls, 17
SOs: Frank Wagner, Sioux Falls, 193
ERA: Fred Whalen, Norfolk, 1.36

D Wisconsin State League
President: Herman D. White

Standings	W	L	Pct.	GB	Manager
La Crosse Blackhawks	76	37	.672	—	Ed Konetchy
Fond du Lac Panthers	64	49	.575	12	Harry Rice
Wisconsin Rapids					
White Sox (2)	54	61	.469	23	Frank Parenti
Sheboygan Indians	54	63	.461	24	Joe Hauser
Green Bay Blue Jays	52	65	.444	26	Otto Bluege
Appleton Papermakers	42	67	.385	32	Eddie Dancisak

Playoffs: La Crosse 3 games, Wisconsin Rapids 0; Fond du Lac 3 games, Sheboygan 2.
Finals: La Crosse 4 games, Fond du Lac 0.

All-Star Team: 1B-Murphy Malattia, Appleton; **2B**-John Schroeder, La Crosse; **3B**-Charles Herich, Sheboygan; **SS**-Gordon Foth, Fond du Lac; **OF**-Maxi Muhr, Wisconsin Rapids; James McCarthy, Fond du Lac; Rudy Novak, Green Bay; **C**-Frank Cominsky, Wisconsin Rapids; **Util**-Leo Feret, Green Bay; **P**-Merv Henley, La Crosse; Lawrence Johnson, La Crosse; **Manager**-Harry Rice, Fond du Lac.

BA: Rudy Novak, Green Bay, .368
Runs: Murphy Malattia, Appleton, 98
  Joe Gasper, Sheboygan, 98
Hits: Joe Gasper, Sheboygan, 142
RBIs: Rudy Novak, Green Bay, 94

HRs: Rudy Novak, Green Bay, 20
Wins: Merv Henley, La Crosse, 20
SOs: Merv Henley, La Crosse, 148
ERA: Merv Henley, La Crosse, 1.81

Ind Mexican League
President: Ernesto Carmona Verduzco

Standings	W	L	Pct.	GB	Manager
Veracruz Azules	61	30	.670	—	Martin Dihigo
Mexico City Diablos Rojos	57	38	.633	6	Ernesto Carmona
Monterrey Industriales	52	41	.559	9	Jose Luis Gomez
Tampico Alijadores	46	41	.529	13	Guillermo Ornelas
Torreon Algodoneros	45	41	.523	13½	Matanzas Valdez/Chester Williams
Nuevo Laredo Tecolotes	30	48	.448	24½	Stanley Pintorell
Chihuahua Dorados	14	67	.173	42	Sergio Correa

BA: James "Cool Papa" Bell, Torreon, .437
Hits: James "Cool Papa" Bell, Torreon, 167
RBIs: James "Cool Papa" Bell, Torreon, 79
HRs: James "Cool Papa" Bell, Torreon, 12

Wins: Bill Jefferson, Monterrey, 22
SOs: Edward Porter, Nuevo Laredo, 232
ERA: Ramon Bragana, Veracruz, 2.58

1940 Interleague Post Season Play

World Series
Cincinnati (National) 4 games, Detroit (American) 3

Junior World Series
Newark (International) 4 games, Louisville (American Association) 2
Total Attendance: 45,894

Dixie Series
Nashville (Southern Association) 4 games, Houston (Texas) 1
Total Attendance: 23,108

Little Dixie Championship
Columbus (South Atlantic) 4 games, Jackson (Southeastern) 1

Southeast Championship
Waycross (Georgia-Florida) 4 games, Orlando (Florida State) 2
Waycross (Georgia-Florida) 4 games, Ft. Lauderdale (Florida East Coast) 1

Class D Interleague Series
Lynchburg (Virginia) 4 games, Williamson (Mountain State) 3

Class D Interleague Series
Lynchburg (Virginia) 2 games, Tarboro (Coastal Plain) 1

Class D Interleague Series
Statesville (Tar Heel) 4 games, Lexington (North Carolina State) 2

1940 Major League Farm Systems

American League

1 Boston (7): Louisville, Scranton, Rocky Mount, Canton, Elizabethton, Danville-Schoolfield, Centreville.
2 Chicago (8): St. Paul, Waterloo, Longview, Rayne, Jonesboro, Grand Forks, Lubbock, Wisconsin Rapids.
3 Cleveland (10): Wilkes-Barre, Cedar Rapids, El Paso, Flint, Charleston (WV), Thomasville (NC), Fargo-Moorhead, Mansfield, Warren, Salem-Roanoke.
4 Detroit (5): Beaumont, Hot Springs, Henderson, Muskegon, Fulton.
5 New York (14): Kansas City, Newark, Binghamton, Norfolk (VA), Augusta, Wenatchee, Amsterdam, Akron, Idaho Falls, Joplin, Neosho, Easton, Butler, Norfolk (NE).
6 Philadelphia (4): Toronto, Williamsport, Wilmington, Federalsburg.
7 St. Louis (11): Toledo, San Antonio, Springfield (IL), Tyler, Palestine, Youngstown, Topeka, Pennington Gap, Lafayette, Mayfield, Paragould.
8 Washington (10): Chattanooga, Charlotte, Greenville (SC), Selma, Newport (TN), Salisbury (MD), Orlando, DeLand, Thomasville (GA), Shelby.

National League

9 Boston (5): Hartford, York, Evansville, Owensboro, Bradford.
10 Brooklyn (19): Montreal, Nashville, Elmira, Durham, Macon, Anniston, Grand Rapids, Dayton, Greenville (AL), Fayetteville, Bassett, Rayne, Americus, Bowling Green, Landis, Newport (AR), Superior, Johnstown, Olean.
11 Chicago (5): Los Angeles, Tulsa, Moline, St. Joseph (MO), Greeneville.
12 Cincinnati (7): Indianapolis, Birmingham, Columbia, Tucson, Ogden, Troy, Lenoir.
13 New York (7): Jersey City, Knoxville, Richmond, Clinton, Ft. Smith, Milford, Salisbury (NC).
14 Philadelphia (8): Baltimore, Portsmouth (VA), Pensacola, Ottawa-Ogdensburg, Martinsville, Dover, Moultrie, Wausau.
15 Pittsburgh (10): Syracuse, Albany (NY), Harrisburg, Gadsden, Gloversville-Johnstown, Hutchinson, Carthage, Ft. Lauderdale, McKeesport/Oil City, London.
16 St. Louis (32): Columbus (OH), Rochester, Sacramento, New Orleans, Houston, Allentown, Asheville, Columbus (GA), Mobile, Decatur, Albuquerque, Longview, Kilgore, Lansing, Portsmouth (OH), Pocatello, Springfield (MO), Johnson City, Siloam Springs, Cambridge, Daytona Beach, Albany (GA), Union City, Williamson, Cooleemee, Caruthersville/Batesville, Duluth, Fostoria, Washington, Hamilton, Gastonia, Worthington.

1940 No-Hitters

Date	Pitcher	Team	League	Opponent	Score
4-16	Bob Feller	Cleveland	American	Chicago	1-0
4-30	Tex Carleton	Brooklyn	National	Cincinnati	3-0
5-9	Buddy Blessie	Lafayette	Evangeline	Alexandria	9-2
5-12	Leslie Dunkle	Scranton	Eastern	Hartford	3-0 (7)
5-25	Wendell Davis	Gainesville	Florida State	DeLand	4-1
5-26	Virgil Trucks	Beaumont	Texas	Tulsa	9-0 (7)
5-27	Don Parker	Tarboro	Coastal Plain	Williamston	11-1
5-28	Joe Murray	Easton	Eastern Shore	Federalsburg	1-1 (6)
6-2	Charlie Fuchs	Oklahoma City	Texas	San Antonio	5-0 (7)
6-9	Walt Nasalik	Neosho	Arkansas-Missouri	Fayetteville	0-1 (7)
6-14	Clarence Anderson	Shelby	Tar Heel	Lenoir	2-0
6-15	Pete Rehcamp	Lenoir	Tar Heel	Shelby	2-0
6-16	Don Ryan	Gainesville	Florida State	Ocala	10-0
6-19	James Bivin	Richmond	Piedmont	Durham	1-0
7-2	Don Kepler	Sunbury	Interstate	York	6-0 (7)
7-10	Eddie Harper	DeLand	Florida State	Leesburg	3-1
7-12	Howard Simon	Tarboro	Coastal Plain	Greenville	2-0
7-12	Walt Balash	Niagara Falls	PONY	London	6-0
7-15	Blix Donnelly	Springfield	Western Assoc.	Joplin	14-0
7-16	Norman Brown	Rocky Mount	Piedmont	Portsmouth	3-0
7-20	Karl Wolfberger	Grand Forks	Northern	Superior	3-0
7-20	Johnny Morabito	Centreville	Eastern Shore	Easton	9-0
7-23	Del Leslie	Fargo-Moorhead	Northern	Eau Claire	3-0 (7)
8-3	John Tansey	Salisbury	N. Carolina State	Kannapolis	0-1
8-7	Andy Rose	London	PONY	Bradford	14-0
8-10	Paul Onkotz	Kingsport	Appalachian	Erwin	10-0
8-20	Eli Hodkey	Canton	Middle Atlantic	Charleston	4-1 (7)
8-21	George Branfield/ Lou Lepine	Quebec	Quebec Provincial	St. Hyacinthe	6-3
8-21	Bill Beattie	Harrisonburg	Virginia	Staunton	3-0 (7)
8-22	Les Mueller	Beaumont	Texas	Dallas	1-0
8-30	James White	Kannapolis	N. Carolina State	Mooresville	1-0
9-2	Joe Shroba	Duluth	Northern	Superior	4-0
9-12	Steve Wilski	Gloversville-Johnstown	Canadian-American	Amsterdam	5-0 (P, PO)

Number in parentheses indicates innings if other than nine; "P" indicates perfect game; "PO" indicates playoff game.

THIS DATE IN MINOR LEAGUE HISTORY

May 26, 1940, Virgil Trucks of Beaumont, Texas League, hurled the third no-hitter of his career in Organized Ball, a seven-inning 9-0 win over Tulsa.

June 30, 1940, Young pitcher Johnny Sain, one of 91 Detroit farmhands granted free agency by Commissioner Landis, was signed by Nashville of the Southern Association.

July 4, 1940, Outfielder Albert "Ab" Wright of Minneapolis, American Association, smashed four home runs and a triple in a game at St. Paul. Minneapolis set a league record with eight home runs in the game.

July 12, 1940, Kansas City's Stanley "Frenchy" Bordagaray hit safely for the 13th consecutive time, setting an all-time American Association record. The streak began on July 9.

August 11, 1940, Pitcher Stan Musial of Daytona Beach, Florida State League, who played centerfield when not on the mound, landed on his left shoulder while making a shoestring catch, ending his hurling career. The injury proved to be a blessing in disguise for the 19-year-old, who became a full-time outfielder the following year.

August 12, 1940, Ernest Lawrence Theyer, author of the poem, "Casey at the Bat," died in Santa Barbara, California, at the age of 77.

August 15, 1940, Veteran Buffalo hurler Earl Cook became the fourth pitcher in International League history to throw a double shutout when he beat Jersey City, 2-0 and 2-0. Cook would throw a third straight shutout in his next start, a two-hitter against Syracuse four days later.

September 11, 1940, Nashville's George Jeffcoat set an all-time Southern Association record for strikeouts in a game when he whiffed 18 in a playoff game against Chattanooga.

September 12, 1940, Gloversville-Johnstown's Steve Wilski pitched a perfect game against Amsterdam in the Canadian-American League's final playoff series.

September 19, 1940, Fire destroyed Dallas' Texas League ballpark.

1941

American League
President: William Harridge

Standings	W	L	Pct.	GB	Attend.	Manager
New York Yankees...........	101	53	.656	—	964,722	Joe McCarthy
Boston Red Sox	84	70	.545	17	718,497	Joe Cronin
Chicago White Sox	77	77	.500	24	677,077	Jimmy Dykes
Cleveland Indians	75	79	.487	26	745,948	Roger Peckinpaugh
Detroit Tigers....................	75	79	.487	26	684,915	Del Baker
St. Louis Browns	70	84	.455	31	176,240	Fred Haney/Luke Sewell
Washington Senators	70	84	.455	31	415,663	Bucky Harris
Philadelphia Athletics........	64	90	.416	37	528,894	Connie Mack

BA: Ted Williams, Boston, .406
Runs: Ted Williams, Boston, 135
Hits: Cecil Travis, Washington, 218
RBIs: Joe DiMaggio, New York, 125
HRs: Ted Williams, Boston, 37

Wins: Bob Feller, Cleveland, 25
SOs: Bob Feller, Cleveland, 260
ERA: Thornton Lee, Chicago, 2.37
Pct: Lefty Gomez, New York, .750, 15-5

National League
President: Ford Frick

Standings	W	L	Pct.	GB	Attend.	Manager
Brooklyn Dodgers............	100	54	.649	—	1,214,910	Leo Durocher
St. Louis Cardinals	97	56	.634	2½	633,645	Billy Southworth
Cincinnati Reds..................	88	66	.571	12	643,513	Bill McKechnie
Pittsburgh Pirates..............	81	73	.526	19	482,241	Frank Frisch
New York Giants	74	79	.484	25½	763,098	Bill Terry
Chicago Cubs....................	70	84	.455	30	545,159	Jimmie Wilson
Boston Braves	62	92	.403	38	263,680	Casey Stengel
Philadelphia Phillies	43	111	.279	57	231,401	Tommy "Doc" Prothro

BA: Pete Reiser, Brooklyn, .343
Runs: Pete Reiser, Brooklyn, 117
Hits: Stan Hack, Chicago, 186
RBIs: Dolph Camilli, Brooklyn, 120
HRs: Dolph Camilli, Brooklyn, 34

Wins: Kirby Higbe, Brooklyn, 22
Whitlow Wyatt, Brooklyn, 22
SOs: Johnny Vander Meer, Cincinnati, 202
ERA: Elmer Riddle, Cincinnati, 2.24
Pct: Elmer Riddle, Cincinnati, .826, 19-4

AA American Association
President: George Trautman

Standings	W	L	Pct.	GB	Attend.	Manager
Columbus Red Birds (16)...	95	58	.621	—	159,534	Burt Shotton
Louisville Colonels (1).......	87	66	.569	8	274,805	Bill Burwell
Kansas City Blues (5)........	85	69	.552	10½	137,820	Bill Meyer
Minneapolis Millers............	83	70	.542	12	118,707	Tom Sheehan
Toledo Mud Hens (7).........	82	72	.532	13½	114,823	James Taylor/Fred Haney
Indianapolis Indians (12)...	65	88	.425	30	88,840	Wade Killefer
St. Paul Saints (2)	61	92	.399	34	75,178	Ralph Kress
Milwaukee Brewers...........	55	98	.359	40	87,353	Bill Killefer/Charlie Grimm

Playoffs: Columbus 4 games, Kansas City 2; Louisville 4 games, Minneapolis 2.
Finals: Columbus 4 games, Louisville 1.

Sporting News Manager of the Year-Burt Shotton, Columbus.

BA: Lou Novikoff, Milwaukee, .370
Runs: Ray Sanders, Columbus, 119
Hits: Glenn McQuillen, Toledo, 192
RBIs: Bert Haas, Columbus, 131

HRs: Ab Wright, Minneapolis, 26
Wins: Murry Dickson, Columbus, 21
SOs: Murry Dickson, Columbus, 153
ERA: John Grodzicki, Columbus, 2.58

AA International League
President: Frank J. Shaughnessy

Standings	W	L	Pct.	GB	Attend.	Manager
Newark Bears (5).............	100	54	.649	—	191,250	Johnny Neun
Montreal Royals (10)..........	90	64	.584	10	182,024	Clyde Sukeforth
Buffalo Bisons (4)	88	65	.575	11½	219,542	Al Vincent
Rochester Red Wings (16)..	84	68	.553	15	148,694	Tony Kaufmann
Jersey City Giants (13)	74	76	.493	24	184,665	Tony Cuccinello
Syracuse Chiefs	70	83	.458	29½	109,002	Benny Borgmann
Baltimore Orioles	58	94	.382	41	110,401	Alphonse "Tommy" Thomas
Toronto Maple Leafs (6).....	47	107	.305	53	57,815	Lena Blackburn

Playoffs: Newark 4 games, Rochester 1; Montreal 4 games, Buffalo 3.
Finals: Montreal 4 games, Newark 3.

MVP-Fred Hutchinson, Buffalo.

BA: Gene Corbett, Baltimore/Newark, .306
Runs: Frank Kelleher, Newark, 106
Hits: Tommy Holmes, Newark, 190
RBIs: Frank Kelleher, Newark, 125

HRs: Frank Kelleher, Newark, 37
Wins: Fred Hutchinson, Buffalo, 26
SOs: Virgil Trucks, Buffalo, 204
ERA: Johnny Lindell, Newark, 2.05

AA Pacific Coast League
President: William C. Tuttle

Standings	W	L	Pct.	GB	Attend.	Manager
Seattle Rainiers	104	70	.598	—	273,855	Bill Skiff
Sacramento Solons (16)....	102	75	.576	3½	165,527	Pepper Martin
San Diego Padres..............	101	76	.571	4½	176,331	Cedric Durst
Hollywood Stars (13)........	85	91	.483	20	199,769	Bill Sweeney
San Francisco Seals	81	95	.460	24	243,144	Lefty O'Doul
Oakland Oaks	81	95	.460	24	145,161	John Vergez
Los Angeles Angels (11)....	72	98	.424	30	162,881	Arnold "Jigger" Statz
Portland Beavers................	71	97	.423	30	112,984	Ossie Vitt

Playoffs: Seattle 4 games, Hollywood 3; Sacramento 4 games, San Diego 0.
Finals: Seattle 4 games, Sacramento 3.

MVP-Yank Terry, San Diego.

BA: John Moore, Los Angeles, .331
Runs: Ferris Fain, San Francisco, 122
Hits: Froilan Fernandez, San Francisco, 231
RBIs: Froilan Fernandez, San Francisco, 129

HRs: Ted Norbert, Portland, 20
Wins: Yank Terry, San Diego, 26
SOs: Yank Terry, San Diego, 172
ERA: Yank Terry, San Diego, 2.31

A1 Southern Association
President: Trammell Scott

Standings	W	L	Pct.	GB	Attend.	Manager
Atlanta Crackers	99	55	.643	—	206,477	Paul Richards
Nashville Vols	83	70	.542	15½	97,282	Larry Gilbert
New Orleans Pelicans (16).	78	75	.510	20½	69,665	Ray Blades
Chattanooga Lookouts (8)..	78	76	.506	21	62,418	Kiki Cuyler
Birmingham Barons (12)....	73	79	.480	25	82,748	Oscar Roettger
Little Rock Travelers	71	82	.464	27½	38,727	Bert Niehoff
Memphis Chicks	69	85	.448	30	54,430	Truck Hannah
Knoxville Smokies (10)......	62	91	.405	36½	71,921	Fred Lindstrom

Playoffs: Atlanta 3 games, Chattanooga 1; Nashville 3 games, New Orleans 1.
Finals: Nashville 4 games, Atlanta 3.

MVP-Les Burge, Atlanta.

BA: Les Fleming, Nashville, .414
Runs: Cully Rikard, Memphis, 131
Hits: Cully Rikard, Memphis, 217
RBIs: Les Burge, Atlanta, 146
HRs: Les Burge, Atlanta, 38

Wins: Ed Heusser, Atlanta, 20
Frank Veverka, Memphis, 20
Charles "Red" Barrett, Birmingham, 20
SOs: Russ Meers, Nashville, 161
ERA: Emil Lochbaum, Atlanta, 2.74

A1 Texas League
President: J. Alvin Gardner

Standings	W	L	Pct.	GB	Attend.	Manager
Houston Buffaloes (16)	103	50	.673	—	60,800	Eddie Dyer
Tulsa Oilers (11)................	86	66	.566	16½	73,840	Roy Johnson
Shreveport Sports	80	71	.530	22	79,665	Francis "Salty" Parker
Dallas Rebels....................	80	74	.519	23½	72,950	Wally Dashiell
Ft. Worth Cats....................	78	76	.506	25½	52,055	Bob Linton
Oklahoma City Indians (3).	69	85	.448	34½	37,306	Rogers Hornsby/Homer Peel
Beaumont Exporters (4)......	58	94	.382	44½	25,561	Gordon Hinkle
San Antonio Missions (7)...	58	96	.377	45½	34,010	Marty McManus

Playoffs: Tulsa 3 games, Shreveport 1; Dallas 3 games, Houston 1.
Finals: Dallas 4 games, Tulsa 2.

MVP-Rip Russell, Tulsa.

BA: Grey Clarke, Dallas, .361
Runs: Harold Epps, Houston, 106
Hits: Vern Washington, Shreveport, 181
RBIs: Bill Norman, Houston, 107

HRs: Murrell Jones, Shreveport, 24
Wins: Fred Martin, Houston, 23
SOs: Howie Pollet, Houston, 151
ERA: Howie Pollet, Houston, 1.16

A Eastern League
President: Thomas H. Richardson

Standings	W	L	Pct.	GB	Attend.	Manager
Wilkes-Barre Barons (3).....	87	51	.630	—	116,228	Earl Wolgamot
Williamsport Grays (6).......	82	55	.599	4½	111,734	Spencer Abbott
Elmira Pioneers (4)............	71	67	.514	16	124,384	Ray Brubaker
Scranton Red Sox (1).........	71	68	.511	16½	171,042	Nemo Leibold
Binghamton Triplets (5).....	68	69	.497	18½	61,300	Phil Page
Albany Senators (15).........	66	73	.475	21½	90,741	George "Specs" Toporcer
Hartford Bees (9)	54	81	.400	31½	66,529	Jack Onslow
Springfield Nationals.........	50	85	.370	35½	47,506	Rabbit Maranville

*Won first-half   **Won second-half   ***Won both halves
Numbers after nicknames indicate farm system.
Affiliation listed at end of each year.

322

Playoffs: Elmira 3 games, Wilkes-Barre 0, one tie; Williamsport 3 games, Scranton 0.
Finals: Elmira 4 games, Williamsport 3.

BA: Frank Madura, Elmira, .321
Runs: Bob Lemon, Wilkes-Barre, 109
Hits: Bob Lemon, Wilkes-Barre, 169
Don Richmond, Williamsport, 169
RBIs: Ron Northey, Williamsport, 89

HRs: Larry Barton, Wilkes-Barre, 17
Wins: Red Embree, Wilkes-Barre, 21
SOs: Red Embree, Wilkes-Barre, 213
ERA: Red Embree, Wilkes-Barre, 1.69

B Interstate League
President: Arthur H. Ehlers

Standings	W	L	Pct.	GB	Manager
Harrisburg Senators (15)	81	43	.653	—	Les Bell
Hagerstown Owls (4)	75	48	.610	5½	Dutch Dorman
Reading Brooks (10)	74	51	.592	7½	Fresco Thompson
Trenton Senators	68	57	.544	13½	Goose Goslin/Gerald Hannahoe
Wilmington Blue Rocks (6)	64	62	.508	18	Tom Oliver
Allentown Wings (14)	48	77	.384	33½	Cy Morgan/Jimmy DeShong
Bridgeport Bees (9)	47	79	.373	35	Rudy Hulswitt
Lancaster Red Roses	43	83	.341	39	Billy Rogell/Jimmy Archer

Playoffs: Trenton 3 games, Hagerstown 0; Harrisburg 3 games, Reading 1.
Finals: Harrisburg 4 games, Trenton 3.

All-Star Team: 1B-Tim Murphy, Allentown; 2B-Bill Burich, Allentown; 3B-Leighton Kimball, Reading; SS-Billy Cox, Harrisburg; OF-Elmer Valo, Wilmington; Felix Mackiewicz, Wilmington; Emil Brinsky, Hagerstown; C-Paul Chervinko, Reading; Util-Milt Stroner, Wilmington; P-Fred Caligiuri, Wilmington; Dick Mulligan, Trenton; Manager-Dutch Dorman, Hagerstown.

BA: Billy Cox, Harrisburg, .363
Runs: William Luzansky, Harrisburg, 121
Hits: Billy Cox, Harrisburg, 180
RBIs: Emil Brinsky, Hagerstown, 104
Edward Murphy, Allentown, 104

HRs: Edward Murphy, Allentown, 23
Wins: Anderson Bush, Hagerstown, 20
SOs: Anderson Bush, Hagerstown, 171
ERA: Anderson Bush, Hagerstown, 1.61

B Piedmont League
President: Ralph Daughton

Standings	W	L	Pct.	GB	Manager
Durham Bulls (10)	84	53	.613	—	Bruno Betzel
Portsmouth Cubs (11)	75	65	.536	10½	Don Curry
Greensboro Red Sox (1)	71	66	.518	13	Heinie Manush
Norfolk Tars (5)	71	68	.511	14	Eddie Sawyer
Richmond Colts	67	71	.486	17½	Eddie Phillips
Charlotte Hornets (8)	65	70	.481	18	Calvin Griffith
Asheville Tourists (16)	64	76	.457	21½	Nick Cullop
Winston-Salem Twins (4)	54	82	.397	29½	Jake Atz

Playoffs: Greensboro 4 games, Portsmouth 2; Durham 4 games, Norfolk 1.
Finals: Durham 4 games, Greensboro 0.

All-Star Team: 1B-Herb Scheffler, Greensboro; 2B-John Burman, Durham; 3B-Robert Ramazzotti, Durham; SS-Stanley Rojek, Durham; OF-Luis Olmo, Richmond; Bill Shewey, Asheville; Roberto Ortiz, Charlotte; C-Bill Steinecke, Portsmouth; Util-Emil Verban, Asheville; P-Ed Albosta, Durham; Max Wilson, Portsmouth; Manager-Bruno Betzel, Durham.

BA: John Burman, Durham, .327
Runs: Bill Shewey, Asheville, 107
Hits: John Burman, Durham, 162
RBIs: Luis Olmo, Richmond, 89
Paul Bruno, Durham, 89

HRs: Luis Olmo, Richmond, 13
Wins: James Bivin, Charlotte, 20
SOs: Jack Kraus, Durham, 169
ERA: Ed Albosta, Durham, 1.73

B South Atlantic League
President: Dr. E.M. Wilder

Standings	W	L	Pct.	GB	Manager
Macon Peaches (11)	90	50	.643	—	Milt Stock
Columbia Reds (12)	89	51	.636	1	Clarence "Cap" Crossley
Columbus Red Birds (16)	68	69	.496	20½	Clay Hopper
Augusta Tigers (5)	64	74	.464	25	Ernie Jenkins/Arky Briggs
Jacksonville Tars	63	75	.457	26	Nellie Leach/Babe Ganzel
Charleston Rebels	61	76	.445	27½	Cecil Rhodes
Greenville Spinners (8)	60	77	.438	28½	Gus Brittain/George Nix
Savannah Indians	57	80	.416	31½	Martin "Chick" Autry

Playoffs: Macon 4 games, Columbus 0; Columbia 4 games, Augusta 1.
Finals: Columbia 4 games, Macon 2.

All-Star Team: 1B-Lon Goldstein, Columbia; 2B-Cy Block, Macon; 3B-Nick Polly, Columbia; SS-Eddie Stanky, Macon; OF-Jack Barnes, Charleston; Ed Knoblauch, Columbus; Arnie Traxler, Augusta; C-Floyd Beal, Columbus; Util-Stan Sonnier, Jacksonville; P-Frank Marino, Macon; Stan Ferens, Columbus; Manager-Milt Stock, Macon.

BA: Cy Block, Macon, .357
Runs: Ed Knoblauch, Columbus, 114
Hits: Robert Adams, Columbia, 195
RBIs: Cy Block, Macon, 112

HRs: James Walsh, Jacksonville, 17
Clyde Vollmer, Columbia, 17
Wins: Stan West, Macon, 23
SOs: Lee Anthony, Jacksonville, 202
ERA: Frank Marino, Macon, 2.16
Pct: Frank Marino, Macon, .950, 19-1

B Southeastern League
President: Stuart X. Stephenson

Standings	W	L	Pct.	GB	Manager
Mobile Shippers (16)	88	47	.652	—	Tommy West
Selma Cloverleafs (8)	80	57	.584	9	Dale Alexander
Jackson Senators	77	65	.542	14½	Clarence Blair
Pensacola Pilots	75	67	.528	16½	Frank Kitchens
Montgomery Rebels	66	62	.514	18½	Neil Caldwell/Pee Wee Wanninger
Meridian Eagles (7)	65	74	.468	25	Benny Tate
Anniston Rams	64	76	.457	26½	Dick Porter
Gadsden Pilots#	37	104	.262	54	Babe Ganzel/Andy Reese

#Gadsden became a road team July 8.

Playoffs: Jackson 4 games, Selma 1; Mobile 4 games, Pensacola 0.
Finals: Mobile 4 games, Jackson 0.

All-Star Team: 1B-Ted Mueller, Selma; 2B-Benny Hassler, Selma; 3B-Gene Nance, Meridian; SS-Guy Miller, Meridian; OF-Ralph Ellis, Selma; Paul Armstrong, Montgomery; James Russell, Meridian; C-Dee Moore, Anniston; Util-Pat Dove, Selma; P-Norman Russell, Mobile; George Dockins, Mobile; Manager-Tommy West, Mobile.

BA: Gene Nance, Meridian, .386
Runs: James Russell, Meridian, 112
Hits: Paul Armstrong, Montgomery, 199
RBIs: Fred Stroble, Meridian, 115

HRs: Fred Stroble, Meridian, 25
Wins: Rae Scarborough, Selma, 21
SOs: Rae Scarborough, Selma, 220
ERA: George Dockins, Mobile, 2.05

B Three-I League
President: Tom Fairweather

Standings	W	L	Pct.	GB	Attend.	Manager
Evansville Bees (9)	80	45	.640	—	69,156	Bob Coleman
Cedar Rapids Raiders (3)	72	49	.595	6	40,323	Oliver Marquardt
Decatur Commodores (16)	67	56	.545	12	38,485	Dibrell Williams
Springfield Browns (7)	65	59	.524	14½	41,194	Arthur Scharein
Waterloo Hawks (2)	59	65	.476	20½	55,456	Louis Brower/Johnny Mostil
Clinton Giants (13)	57	68	.456	23	25,861	John Billings
Madison Blues	52	71	.423	27	28,434	Ivy Griffin
Moline Plow Boys	43	82	.344	37	16,534	Joseph Mowry

Playoffs: Decatur 3 games, Evansville 2; Cedar Rapids 3 games, Springfield 1.
Finals: Cedar Rapids 3 games, Decatur 2.

All-Star Team: 1B-Norman Jaeger, Clinton; 2B-Dibrell Williams, Decatur; 3B-Joe Gulledge, Evansville; SS-Floyd Baker, Springfield; OF-Chester Clemens, Evansville; Henry Edwards, Cedar Rapids; Joseph Mowry, Moline; C-Sigmund Broskie, Evansville; Util-Frank Hargrove, Moline; P-John Clay, Decatur; Warren Spahn, Evansville; Manager-Bob Coleman, Evansville.

BA: Henry Edwards, Cedar Rapids, .364
Runs: Henry Edwards, Cedar Rapids, 101
Delbert Jones, Cedar Rapids, 101
Hits: Henry Edwards, Cedar Rapids, 172
RBIs: Henry Edwards, Cedar Rapids, 113

HRs: Henry Edwards, Cedar Rapids, 23
Wins: Warren Spahn, Evansville, 19
SOs: John Clay, Decatur, 204
ERA: Warren Spahn, Evansville, 1.83

B Western International League
President: Robert A. Abel

Standings	W	L	Pct.	GB	Manager
Spokane Indians	89	44	.603	—	Raymond Jacobs
Vancouver Capilanos	73	64	.533	18	Don Osborne
Yakima Pippins	70	64	.522	19½	Goldie Holt
Salem Senators	63	69	.477	25½	John "Bunny" Griffiths
Tacoma Tigers	58	76	.433	31½	Horace "Pip" Koehler
Wenatchee Chiefs	51	87	.370	40½	Ted Mayer

Playoff: All-Stars 4 games, Spokane 1.

All-Star Team: 1B-William Reese, Yakima; 2B-Henry Martinez, Spokane; 3B-Ray Orteig, Vancouver; SS-Joe Gedzius, Spokane; OF-Levi McCormack, Spokane; William Johnson, Yakima; Smead Jolley, Spokane/Vancouver; C-Bill Beard, Spokane; Util-Roy Younker, Yakima; P-Don Osborn, Vancouver; Roy Helser, Salem; Manager-Goldie Holt, Yakima.

BA: Smead Jolley, Spokane/Vancouver, .345
Runs: Pete Hughes, Spokane, 139
Hits: Levi McCormack, Spokane, 191
RBIs: Smead Jolley, Spokane/Vancouver, 128
HRs: Pete Hughes, Spokane, 34

BBs: Pete Hughes, Spokane, 156
Wins: Robert Kinnaman, Spokane, 22
SOs: Charles Eisenmann, Yakima, 204
ERA: Don Osborn, Vancouver, 2.74

C Arizona-Texas League
President: Dr. R.E. Soners

Standings	W	L	Pct.	GB	Manager
Tucson Cowboys***(12)	86	46	.652	—	Lester "Pat" Patterson
Albuquerque Cardinals	63	65	.492	21	Jimmy Zinn
El Paso Texans	61	71	.462	25	Elmer "Spec" Williamson
Bisbee Bees (11)	51	79	.392	34	Carl Dittmar

Playoffs: None.

All-Star Team: 1B-Warren Williams, Bisbee; 2B-Jodie Beeler, Tucson; 3B-Harry

Clements, Tucson; **SS**-James Estrada, Albuquerque; **OF**-Clarence Maddern, Bisbee; Paul Dyke, Albuquerque; Allan Lawrence, Tucson; **C**-George Galios, El Paso; **Util**-Elmer "Spec" Williamson, El Paso; **P**-John Hetki, Albuquerque; George Burpo, Tucson; **Manager**-Elmer "Spec" Williamson, El Paso.

BA: Burl Horton, El Paso, .375
Runs: Doug Smith, Tucson, 147
Hits: Burl Horton, El Paso, 216
RBIs: Clarence Maddern, Bisbee, 129

HRs: Doug Smith, Tucson, 15
Wins: Harry Parks, Albuquerque, 24
SOs: Marino Pieretti, El Paso, 237
ERA: Lee Porterfield, Tucson, 3.01

C California League
President: W.R. "Bill" Schroeder

Standings	W	L	Pct.	GB	Manager
Fresno Cardinals (16)	90	50	.643	—	George Silvey
Santa Barbara Saints (10)	83	56	.597	6½	John "Bud" Clancy
Bakersfield Badgers	73	67	.521	17	Frank Morehouse/Les Powers
Stockton Fliers (11)	70	70	.500	20	Keith Frazier
Anaheim Aces	55	82	.401	33½	Joe Huarte/Charley Smith
Merced Bears	50	87	.365	38½	Bob Gibson
San Bernardino Stars#(13)	43	28	.606	NA	Jack Rothrock
Riverside Reds#(12)	24	48	.333	NA	Elnar Sorensen

#San Bernardino and Riverside disbanded June 29.

Playoffs: Fresno 3 games, Stockton 1; Santa Barbara 3 games, Bakersfield 1.
Finals: Santa Barbara 4 games, Fresno 1.

All-Star Team: 1B-John "Bud" Clancy, Santa Barbara; **2B**-William Hebert, Merced; **3B**-John Jorgenson, Santa Barbara; **SS**-Ray Tran, Anaheim; **OF**-Dick Adams, Fresno; Keith Frazier, Stockton; Charles Strada, Stockton; **C**-Frank Kappelman, Santa Barbara; **Util**-Edward Wheeler, Bakersfield; **P**-Manuel Perez, San Bernardino/Santa Barbara; Chet Johnson, Bakersfield; **Manager**-John "Bud" Clancy, Santa Barbara.

BA: John "Bud" Clancy, Santa Barbara, .344
Runs: Dick Adams, Fresno, 112
Hits: John Jorgenson, Santa Barbara, 184
RBIs: Mel Serafini, Fresno, 125
HRs: Mel Serafini, Fresno, 20

Wins: Manuel Perez, San Bernardino/Santa Barbara, 24; Warren Sandel, Fresno, 24
SOs: Chet Johnson, Bakersfield, 213
ERA: Manuel Perez, San Bernardino/Santa Barbara, 1.86

C Canadian-American League
President: Rev. Harold J. Martin

Standings	W	L	Pct.	GB	Attend.	Manager
Oneonta Indians (1)	78	46	.629	—	46,951	Emil Barnes
Amsterdam Rugmakers (5)	68	54	.557	9	37,738	Paul O'Malley
Rome Colonels	66	58	.532	12	42,828	Leon Riley
Pittsfield Electrics	62	59	.512	14½	32,239	Arthur Funk
Trois Rivieres Renards	63	60	.512	14½	36,143	Wally Schang/Charles Small
Quebec Athletics (10)	57	67	.460	21	47,179	Del Bissonette/Roland Gladu
Gloversville-Johnstown Glovers (15)	54	70	.435	24	34,495	Oliver Blakeney
Utica Braves (4)	45	79	.363	33	51,000	Frank Zubik

Playoffs: Oneonta 4 games, Rome 2; Pittsfield 4 games, Amsterdam 3.
Finals: Oneonta 4 games, Pittsfield 2.

All-Star Team: 1B-Bass Clifton, Rome; **2B**-Lloyd Moore, Pittsfield; **3B**-Bill Sinram, Amsterdam; **SS**-Arthur Funk, Pittsfield; **OF**-Austin Knickerbocker, Oneonta; Frank Genovese, Oneonta; Leon Riley, Rome; **C**-Edward McGah, Oneonta; **Util**-Roland Gladu, Quebec; **P**-John Robinson, Amsterdam; Walter Duda, Pittsfield; **Manager**-Arthur Funk, Pittsfield.

BA: Austin Knickerbocker, Oneonta, .406
Runs: Frank Genovese, Oneonta, 145
Hits: Austin Knickerbocker, Oneonta, 202
RBIs: Austin Knickerbocker, Oneonta, 135
HRs: Leon Riley, Rome, 32

Wins: John Robinson, Amsterdam, 22; Thomas Fine, Oneonta, 22
SOs: Thomas Fine, Oneonta, 185
ERA: John Robinson, Amsterdam, 2.85

C Cotton States League
President: Judge Emmet Harty

Standings	W	L	Pct.	GB	Manager
Monroe White Sox	83	55	.601	—	Doug Taitt
Hot Springs Bathers	77	60	.562	5½	Ellis "Mike" Powers
Greenville Buckshots	76	63	.547	7½	Dave Coble
Vicksburg Hill Billies	76	64	.543	8	Rip Fanning/Al Baker
Helena Seaporters	72	66	.522	11	Jimmy Adair
Texarkana Twins (4)	65	73	.471	18	Wally Kopp/Jake Atz, Jr.
El Dorado Oilers	54	82	.397	28	Ray Rice/Guy Sturdy/Sam Hancock
Clarksdale Ginners/ Marshall Tigers#	48	88	.353	34	Leroy "Cowboy" Jones/Guy Sturdy

#Clarksdale (33-47) moved to Marshall July 10.

Playoffs: Vicksburg 3 games, Monroe 2; Hot Springs 3 games, Greenville 0.
Finals: Hot Springs 4 games, Vicksburg 0.

All-Star Team: 1B-Mervin Connors, Texarkana; **2B**-Roy Marion, Hot Springs; **3B**-Clarence Collins, Helena; **SS**-Jim Lucas, Helena; **OF**-Roy Bueschen, Greenville; Dave Philley, Monroe; Ben "Rosie" Cantrell, Helena; **C**-David Coble, Greenville; **Util**-Robert

Hill, Monroe; **P**-Stanley Todd, Greenville; Charles Pescod, Hot Springs; **Manager**-Ellis "Mike" Powers, Hot Springs.

BA: Roy Bueschen, Greenville, .370
Runs: Colman Powell, Hot Springs, 137
Hits: Roy Marion, Hot Springs, 207
RBIs: Ellis "Mike" Powers, Hot Springs, 137
HRs: Mervin Connors, Texarkana, 29
Wins: Alfred Kelley, Vicksburg, 22
SOs: Bill Reeder, Monroe, 189
ERA: Charles Pescod, Hot Springs, 3.00

C Michigan State League
President: Thomas J. Halligan

Standings	W	L	Pct.	GB	Manager
Flint Arrows***(3)	70	38	.648	—	Jack Knight
St. Joseph Autos	64	50	.561	9	Elmer Kirchoff
Grand Rapids Colts (10)	59	55	.518	14	Charles Lucas
Muskegon Reds (4)	61	57	.517	14	Jack Tighe
Saginaw White Sox (2)	51	62	.451	21½	Bill Prince/Walden McMullen
Lansing Senators	35	78	.310	37½	Danny Taylor/Russell Wein

Playoffs: None.

All-Star Team: 1B-Sheriff Robinson, Lansing; **2B**-Adam Bengoechea, Muskegon; **3B**-Carl Fiore, Flint; **SS**-John Lipon, Muskegon; **OF**-Stanley Platek, Saginaw; Gordon Goodell, Flint; Norman Snyder, St. Joseph; **C**-Jack Tighe, Muskegon; **Util**-Charles Moore, Lansing; **P**-Steve Gromek, Flint; Thomas Hamill, Grand Rapids; **Manager**-Jack Knight, Flint.

BA: Gene Woodling, Flint, .394
Runs: John Lipon, Muskegon, 126
Hits: John Lipon, Muskegon, 176
RBIs: John Lipon, Muskegon, 115; Norman Snyder, St. Joseph, 115
HRs: John Lipon, Muskegon, 35
Wins: Franklin Schulz, Flint, 17
SOs: Thomas Hamill, Grand Rapids, 188
ERA: Steve Gromek, Flint, 2.90

C Middle Atlantic League
President: Elmer M. Daily

Standings	W	L	Pct.	GB	Manager
Akron Yankees (5)	77	48	.616	—	Ralph Boyle
Erie Sailors	75	51	.595	2½	Kerby Farrell
Canton Terriers (1)	71	54	.568	6	Floyd Patterson
Springfield Cardinals (16)	69	57	.548	8½	Walter Alston
Charleston Senators (3)	58	59	.496	15	Ed Hall
Dayton Ducks (10)	50	75	.400	27	Howard "Ducky" Holmes/William McWilliams
Youngstown Browns (7)	49	75	.395	27½	Joe Bilgere/Len Schulte
Zanesville Cubs (11)	43	73	.371	29½	Jackie Warner

Playoffs: Erie 3 games, Springfield 0; Canton 3 games, Akron 2.
Finals: Erie 4 games, Canton 1.

All-Star Team: 1B-Walter Alston, Springfield; **2B**-Mike Portner, Akron; **3B**-Bill Mongiello, Erie; **SS**-Robert Collette, Springfield; **OF**-Robert Jones, Youngstown; Como Cotelle, Dayton/Erie; Borden Helms, Zanesville; **C**-Gus Niarhos, Akron; **Util**-George Verbeck, Akron; **P**-Lou Lucier, Canton; William Baker, Akron; **Manager**-Ralph Boyle, Akron.

BA: Como Cotelle, Dayton/Erie, .367
Runs: Walter Alston, Springfield, 88
Hits: Como Cotelle, Dayton/Erie, 150
RBIs: Walter Alston, Springfield, 102
HRs: Walter Alston, Springfield, 25
Wins: Lou Lucier, Canton, 23
SOs: Lou Lucier, Canton, 199
ERA: Lou Lucier, Canton, 1.51

C Northern League
President: Herman D. White

Standings	W	L	Pct.	GB	Manager
Wausau Lumberjacks (14)	71	40	.640	—	Wally Gilbert
Grand Forks Chiefs (2)	64	48	.571	7½	Larry Bettencourt
Duluth Dukes (16)	63	48	.568	8	Joe Davis
Eau Claire Bears	60	52	.536	11½	Wilfred "Rosy" Ryan
Superior Blues	55	59	.482	17½	Art Hauger
Fargo-Moorhead Twins	48	69	.410	26	Wes Griffin/Mike Blazo
Crookston Pirates	46	68	.404	26½	Ade Stemig
Winnipeg Maroons	44	67	.396	27	Fred "Pap" Williams

Playoffs: Eau Claire 4 games, Grand Forks 1; Duluth 4 games, Wausau 1.
Finals: Eau Claire 4 games, Duluth 3.

All-Star Team: 1B-Richard Rome, Wausau; **2B**-Adrian Thompson, Duluth; **3B**-James Grant, Grand Forks; **SS**-Arthur Tourangeau, Wausau; **OF**-Chet Cichosz, Wausau; Robert Decker, Superior; Larry Bettencourt, Grand Forks; **C**-Wes Westrum, Eau Claire; **Util**-Don Turck, Crookston; **P**-Hugh Orphan, Wausau; Morrie Martin, Grand Forks; **Manager**-Wally Gilbert, Wausau.

BA: Larry Bettencourt, Grand Forks, .366
Runs: Glenn Crawford, Duluth, 109
Hits: James Grant, Grand Forks, 155
RBIs: Larry Bettencourt, Grand Forks, 133
HRs: Larry Bettencourt, Grand Forks, 31
Wins: Hugh Orphan, Wausau, 21
SOs: Leonard Perme, Superior, 216
ERA: Morrie Martin, Grand Forks, 2.05

C Pioneer League
President: J.P. Halliwell

Standings	W	L	Pct.	GB	Manager
Boise Pilots	81	49	.623	—	James Keesey
Ogden Reds (12)	76	51	.598	3½	Bill McCorry

Standings	W	L	Pct.	GB	Manager
Salt Lake City Bees	68	60	.531	12	Tony Robello
Pocatello Cardinals (16)	64	66	.492	17	Bill DeLancey
Idaho Falls Russets (5)	58	70	.453	22	Bob Coltrin/Eddie Marshall
Twin Falls Cowboys	39	90	.302	41½	Andy Harrington

Playoffs: Boise 2 games, Pocatello 0; Ogden 2 games, Salt Lake City 0.
Finals: Ogden 3 games, Boise 1.

All-Star Team: 1B-Tom Canavan, Ogden; **2B**-Jack Radtke, Boise; **3B**-Mike Winseck, Ogden; **SS**-Mervin Bensmiller, Pocatello; **OF**-Charles Henson, Salt Lake City; Joe Egnatic, Boise; Frank Baumholtz, Ogden; **C**-Clifford Barker, Boise; **Util**-Jack Hatchett, Salt Lake City; **P**-Gerry Staley, Boise; Ken Polivka, Ogden; **Manager**-Bill McCorry, Ogden.

BA: Charles Henson, Salt Lake City, .339
Runs: Mervin Bensmiller, Pocatello, 127
Hits: Charles Henson, Salt Lake City, 170
RBIs: Willie Enos, Salt Lake City, 120
HRs: Joe Egnatic, Boise, 15

Wins: Gerry Staley, Boise, 22
SOs: Jack Hawkins, Idaho Falls, 246
ERA: Clayton Lambert, Ogden, 2.21
Pct: Clayton Lambert, Ogden, .778, 21-6

C Virginia League
President: Ray Ryan

Standings	W	L	Pct.	GB	Manager
Petersburg Rebels	66	53	.555	—	Clarence Pickrel/George "Possum" Whitted
Salem-Roanoke Friends	64	55	.538	2	Vernon Mackie
Lynchburg Senators	62	56	.525	3½	Guy Lacy
Harrisonburg Turks	62	56	.525	3½	Vernon Brandes/Vance Dinges
Newport News Pilots (6)	58	58	.500	6½	Charles "Chief" Bender
Staunton Presidents	42	76	.356	23½	Hank Hulvey/Gus Tebell

Playoffs: Lynchburg 3 games, Petersburg 0; Salem-Roanoke 3 games, Harrisonburg 2.
Finals: Salem-Roanoke 3 games, Lynchburg 2.

All-Star Team: 1B-Ben Drake, Newport News; **2B**-William McCann, Petersburg; **3B**-Glen Adkins, Harrisonburg; **SS**-Noel Casbier, Salem-Roanoke; **OF**-William Booker, Lynchburg; Carl Shawver, Salem-Roanoke; Royce Watson, Lynchburg; **C**-Vernon Mackie, Salem-Roanoke; **Util**-Francis Archer, Salem-Roanoke; **P**-Toy Bowen, Salem-Roanoke; Dick Tate, Lynchburg; **Manager**-Vernon Mackie, Salem-Roanoke.

BA: Vernon Mackie, Salem-Roanoke, .355
Runs: Royce Watson, Lynchburg, 125
Hits: Nicholas Rhabe, Petersburg/ Harrisonburg, 164
RBIs: Ben Drake, Newport News, 117

HRs: Noel Casbier, Salem-Roanoke, 21
Wins: Toy Bowen, Salem-Roanoke, 17
SOs: Ed Haswell, Lynchburg, 226
ERA: Don Black, Petersburg, 2.34

C Western Association
President: Tom Fairweather

Standings	W	L	Pct.	GB	Manager
Joplin Miners (5)	93	41	.694	—	Elmer "Doc" Bennett
Springfield Cardinals (16)	92	43	.682	1½	Ollie Vanek
Topeka Owls	75	58	.564	17½	William Wilson
Ft. Smith Giants (13)	73	60	.549	19½	Herschel Bobo
Muskogee Reds (11)	64	69	.481	28½	Jack Mealey
Hutchinson Pirates (15)	53	81	.396	40	John Gooch
Salina Millers (3)	46	88	.343	47	Russ Rollings/Jimmy Payton/ Jack Fitzpatrick
St. Joseph Ponies/ Carthage Browns#(7)	40	96	.394	54	Walter Holke/Gus Albright

#St. Joseph (10-22) moved to Carthage June 3, first home game June 10.

Playoffs: Ft. Smith 3 games, Springfield 1; Joplin 3 games, Topeka 1.
Finals: Joplin 3 games, Ft. Smith 0.

All-Star Team: 1B-Melvin Hicks, Muskogee; **2B**-Jerry Crosby, Muskogee; **3B**-Ed Bockman, Joplin; **SS**-Frank Mabrey, Joplin; **OF**-Roy Broome, Springfield; Ray Baker, Topeka; Stan Musial, Springfield; **C**-Frank Mancuso, Carthage; **Util**-James Van Wey, Carthage; **P**-Blix Donnelly, Springfield; Cliff Hopkins, Springfield; **Manager**-William Wilson, Topeka.

BA: Ed Yarmul, Hutchinson, .356
Runs: Michael Schemer, Ft. Smith, 125
Hits: Harold Olt, Springfield, 177
RBIs: Clarence Springer, Topeka, 127

HRs: Stan Musial, Springfield, 26
Wins: Blix Donnelly, Springfield, 28
SOs: Blix Donnelly, Springfield, 304
ERA: Blix Donnelly, Springfield, 2.26

D Alabama State League
President: J. Eric Ballard

Standings	W	L	Pct.	GB	Manager
Dothan Browns	79	40	.664	—	Holt "Cat" Milner
Tallassee Indians (4)	75	45	.625	4½	Steve Bysco
Andalusia Rams	60	60	.500	19½	Ralph McAdams
Brewton Millers	49	68	.419	29	Lee Head
Troy Dodgers/ Tuskegee Airmen#(10)	48	71	.403	31	Orace Powers
Greenville Lions	45	72	.385	33	Ernie Wingard/Herbert Thomas

#Troy (37-50) moved to Tuskegee July 31.

Playoffs: Dothan 3 games, Andalusia 1, Tallassee 3 games, Brewton 1.
Finals: Dothan 4 games, Tallassee 1.

All-Star Team: 1B-Gilbert Leatherwood, Andalusia; **2B**-Wilburn Downs, Tallassee; **3B**-Marion Johnson, Dothan; **SS**-Luther Gunnells, Dothan; **OF**-Forrest Austin, Tallassee; Ray Knowles, Tallassee; Bob Madison, Andalusia; **C**-Ralph McAdams, Andalusia; **Util**-Malvern Morgan, Tallassee; **P**-Joe Rivers, Dothan; William Whatling, Andalusia; **Manager**-Holt "Cat" Milner, Dothan.

BA: Luther Gunnells, Dothan, .395
Runs: Luther Gunnells, Dothan, 143
Hits: Ray Knowles, Tallassee, 199
RBIs: Forrest Austin, Tallassee, 149

HRs: Forrest Austin, Tallassee, 32
Wins: Joe Rivers, Dothan, 20
SOs: Francis Mannheim, Tallassee, 184
ERA: Cyril Moore, Tallassee, 2.84

D Appalachian League
President: J. Ross Edgemon

Standings	W	L	Pct.	GB	Manager
Elizabethton Betsy Red Sox**(10)	73	45	.619	—	Hobe Brummitt
Bristol Twins	72	45	.615	½	George Hackett/Lee Sherrill
Newport Canners	66	52	.559	7	Red Marion
Johnson City Cardinals*(16)	63	57	.525	11	Johnny Morrow/Harold Michel
Greeneville Burley Cubs	43	75	.364	30	Eddie Krajnik/Hubert Stolper
Kingsport Cherokees	37	80	.316	35½	Dixie Parker/Jerry Witner

Playoffs: Elizabethton 3 games, Newport 2; Johnson City 3 games, Bristol 2.
Finals: Elizabethton 3 games, Johnson City 0.

All-Star Team: 1B-Richard Connell, Johnson City; **2B**-Oscar McClure, Bristol; **3B**-Thad Cash, Elizabethton; **SS**-Alfred Livingston, Newport; **OF**-Lew Flick, Elizabethton; Joseph Molina, Johnson City; Harold Martin, Greeneville; **C**-Harold Michel, Johnson City; **Util**-Andy Seminick, Elizabethton; **P**-Lee Sherrill, Bristol; James Mooney, Johnson City; **Manager**-Red Marion, Newport.

BA: Lew Flick, Elizabethton, .418
Runs: Lew Flick, Elizabethton, 127
Hits: Lew Flick, Elizabethton, 210
RBIs: Lew Flick, Elizabethton, 116
  Harold Michel, Johnson City, 116

HRs: Harold Martin, Greeneville, 19
Wins: Hank Dorin, Elizabethton, 19
SOs: Walter Bass, Elizabethton, 148
ERA: Lee Sherrill, Bristol, 2.13

D Bi-State League
President: J.P. Welles

Standings	W	L	Pct.	GB	Manager
Leaksville-Draper-Spray Triplets	64	46	.582	—	Tim Murchison/Wes Ferrell
Martinsville Manufacturers (14)	63	49	.563	2	George Ferrell
Danville-Schoolfield Leafs (1)	64	50	.561	2	Elmer Yoter
Sanford Spinners	58	54	.518	7	Zeb Harrington
Mt. Airy Graniteers	42	70	.375	23	Jimmy Maus
Mayodan Millers#	25	47	.347	NA	Taylor Sanford

#Mayodan disbanded July 18.

Playoffs: Sanford 4 games, Martinsville 3, one tie; Danville-Schoolfield 4 games, Leaksville-Draper-Spray 1.
Finals: Sanford 4 games, Danville-Schoolfield 2.

All-Star Team: 1B-Bernardo Fernandez, Leaksville-Draper-Spray; **2B**-Daniel Reynolds, Martinsville; **3B**-Richard Kalal, Danville-Schoolfield; **SS**-Walter "Teapot" Frye, Martinsville; **OF**-Tom Burnette, Martinsville; James Payne, Leaksville-Draper-Spray; Albert Behrends, Martinsville; **C**-J.B. Ruark, Sanford; **Util**-Ned Butcher, Sanford; **P**-Roy Boles, Mt. Airy; George Bortz, Sanford; **Manager**-George Ferrell, Martinsville.

BA: Albert Behrends, Martinsville, .378
Runs: Richard Kalal, Danville-Schoolfield, 119
Hits: Albert Behrends, Martinsville, 171
RBIs: Tom Burnette, Martinsville, 114
  George Ferrell, Martinsville, 114

HRs: Tom Burnette, Martinsville, 29
Wins: Dave Odom, Sanford, 16
  Charles Cuellar, Leaksville-Draper-Spray, 16
SOs: Dave Odom, Sanford, 190
Pct: Roy Boles, Mt. Airy, .714, 10-4

D Coastal Plain League
President: Ray Goodmon

Standings	W	L	Pct.	GB	Manager
Wilson Tobs	87	30	.744	—	Bill Herring
Greenville Greenies	64	54	.542	23½	Rube Wilson
New Bern Bears	61	57	.517	26½	Doc Smith/Jake Wade
Rocky Mount Leafs	59	59	.500	28½	Norm McCaskill/Gus Brittain
Goldsboro Goldbugs	58	61	.487	30	Mac Arnette/Dave McKinney/ Arthur "Cowboy" McHenry
Williamston Martins	56	61	.479	31	Frank Rodgers
Tarboro Orioles	44	72	.379	42½	Thomas "Poke" Whalen
Kinston Eagles	42	77	.353	46	Arthur "Cowboy" McHenry/Joe DeMasi

Playoffs: Wilson 4 games, Rocky Mount 1; Greenville 4 games, New Bern 2.
Finals: Wilson 4 games, Greenville 2.

All-Star Team: 1B-Phil Morris, Wilson; **2B**-Irv Dickens, Wilson; **3B**-Bill Upchurch, Kinston; **SS**-W.E. "Pete" Stuart, Wilson; **OF**-Earl Carnahan, Wilson; Dowd Averette, New Bern; Jack Clifton, Goldsboro; **C**-Charlie Wilcox, Williamston; **Util**-Dick Hoyle, Wilson; **P**-Peter Kunis, Williamston; Joe Talley, Wilson; **Manager**-Frank Rodgers, Williamston.

BA: Earl Carnahan, Wilson, .370
Runs: Irv Dickens, Wilson, 114
Hits: Earl Carnahan, Wilson, 176
RBIs: Lyle Thompson, New Bern, 111

HRs: Fred Eason, Wilson, 18
Wins: Monk Webb, Wilson, 23
SOs: Julio Acosta, Goldsboro, 199
ERA: Joe Talley, Wilson, 1.93

D Eastern Shore League
President: Harry S. Russell

Standings	W	L	Pct.	GB	Manager
Milford Giants (13)	66	42	.611	—	Hal Gruber
Cambridge Canners (16)	61	45	.575	4	Everett Johnston
Easton Yankees (5)	57	53	.518	10	Dal Warren
Centreville Red Sox (1)	54	52	.509	11	Ed Walls/Eddie Popowski
Salisbury Cardinals	51	59	.464	16	John Wedemeyer/Bob Maier
Federalsburg A's (6)	35	73	.324	31	Joe O'Rourke

Playoffs: Milford 3 games, Centreville 0; Easton 3 games, Cambridge 0.
Finals: Easton 4 games, Milford 3.

All-Star Team: 1B-Walter Mahoney, Salisbury; **2B-**William Morrison, Cambridge; **3B-**Alvin Kaiser, Cambridge; **SS-**Hal Gruber, Milford; **OF-**Tommy Koval, Cambridge; Charles Price, Milford; Art Flesland, Milford; **C-**James McDuffie, Centreville; **Util-**Walter Forwood, Federalsburg; **P-**Oliver Holmes, Easton; Bill Boland, Milford; **Manager-**Dal Warren, Easton.

BA: Gordon McKinnon, Milford, .344
Runs: Gordon McKinnon, Milford, 98
Hits: Art Flesland, Milford, 157
RBIs: Art Gunning, Milford, 67

HRs: Tommy Koval, Cambridge, 16
Wins: Bill Boland, Milford, 20
SOs: Chris Hayden, Milford, 188
ERA: Joe Ostrowski, Centreville, 1.71

D Evangeline League
President: A. Wilmont Dalferes

Standings	W	L	Pct.	GB	Manager
New Iberia Cardinals	88	42	.677	—	Johnny Keane
Port Arthur Tarpons	78	50	.609	9	Harry Strohm
Alexandria Aces	77	54	.588	11½	Conrad Flippen
Lafayette White Sox (7)	67	67	.500	23	Bobby Goff
Lake Charles Skippers (11)	64	69	.481	25½	Jimmy Lawrence/Ben Meyer
Opelousas Indians	60	69	.465	27½	Eldon Breese
Natchez Pilgrims	49	83	.371	40	Harold Salmon/Copeland Goss
Rayne Rice Birds#	20	69	.225	NA	Lee Stebbins/Leo Norris

#Rayne disbanded July 23.
Attendance: Lake Charles, 27,000.

Playoffs: New Iberia 4 games, Lafayette 0; Alexandria 4 games, Port Arthur 1.
Finals: New Iberia 4 games, Alexandria 3.

All-Star Team: 1B-Phil Wells, Opelousas; **2B-**Fred Barocco, New Iberia; **3B-**John Rigdon, Alexandria; **SS-**William Spears, Opelousas; **OF-**Glenn Dale Murray, Opelousas; Woody Fair, New Iberia; Bob Stoner, Lafayette; **C-**Walter Novick, New Iberia; **Util-**Fred Chumley, Lake Charles; **P-**Alfred Hardouin, Port Arthur; Thomas Finger, Lafayette; **Manager-**Eldon Breese, Opelousas.

BA: Fred Barocco, New Iberia, .372
Runs: Fred Barocco, New Iberia, 116
Hits: Gene Hodge, Lake Charles, 173
RBIs: Woody Fair, New Iberia, 113
HRs: Woody Fair, New Iberia, 13

Wins: Alfred Hardouin, Port Arthur, 21
   James Noblett, New Iberia, 21
SOs: Thomas Finger, Lafayette, 192
ERA: Edward Puck, New Iberia, 1.77

D Florida East Coast League
President: J.B. Lemon

Standings	W	L	Pct.	GB	Manager
West Palm Beach Indians	84	55	.604	—	Harry Hughes
Miami Beach Flamingos	81	58	.583	3	Max Rosenfeld
Ft. Pierce Bombers	75	64	.540	9	Jim Poole
Ft. Lauderdale Tarpons	66	73	.475	18	Herb Thomas/Buster Kinard
Miami Wahoos	63	76	.453	21	Archie Martin
Cocoa Fliers	48	91	.345	36	Jesse Cleveland/Bill Doak

Playoffs: Miami Beach 3 games, Ft. Pierce 1; West Palm Beach 3 games, Ft. Lauderdale 2.
Finals: Miami Beach 4 games, West Palm Beach 2.

All-Star Team: 1B-Harry Hughes, West Palm Beach; **2B-**Edmund Arthur, Miami Beach; **3B-**C.H. Henderson, West Palm Beach; **SS-**William Miller, Miami Beach; **OF-**William Chute, West Palm Beach; Buster Kinard, Ft. Lauderdale; Jack Troupe, Miami; **C-**Joe Murff, Ft. Pierce; **Util-**Truck Melvin, West Palm Beach; **P-**Gibbs Miller, Ft. Lauderdale; Gene Beardon, Miami Beach; **Manager-**Max Rosenfeld, Miami Beach.

BA: John Douglas, Miami, .385
Runs: John Douglas, Miami, 111
Hits: Buster Kinard, Ft. Lauderdale, 210
RBIs: Buster Kinard, Ft. Lauderdale, 123

HRs: Joe Murff, Ft. Pierce, 21
Wins: Gibbs Miller, Ft. Lauderdale, 23
SOs: Milt Rosenstein, Miami Beach, 238
ERA: Chet Covington, Ft. Pierce, 1.90

D Florida State League
President: Henry Gray

Standings	W	L	Pct.	GB	Manager
St. Augustine Saints	83	43	.659	—	Jerry Tiemann
DeLand Red Hats	78	47	.624	4½	Wes Trammell
Orlando Senators (8)	72	53	.576	10½	Carl Weigel
Leesburg Anglers	63	66	.488	21½	Wilbur Good, Jr.
Daytona Beach Islanders (16)	57	70	.449	26½	James "Bunny" Simmons
Gainesville G-Men	55	75	.423	30	Eddie Martin
Ocala Yearlings	49	78	.386	34½	Alan Mobley/Tom Smith
Sanford Seminoles#	20	45	.308	NA	Joe Whitlock/Charles Girk

#Sanford disbanded June 25.

Playoffs: DeLand 3 games, Orlando 0; Leesburg 3 games, St. Augustine 1.
Finals: Leesburg 4 games, DeLand 1.

All-Star Team: 1B-Jerry Tiemann, St. Augustine; **2B-**Mike Conroy, Leesburg; **3B-**Hal Lee, Orlando; **SS-**J.C. Williams, Orlando; **OF-**Paul Varner, St. Augustine; John Danyo, DeLand; Clarence Groat, Leesburg; **C-**Russell Goff, St. Augustine; **Util-**Erby Carroll, Daytona Beach; **P-**Charles Kane, St. Augustine; Edward Harper, DeLand; **Manager-**Jerry Tiemann, St. Augustine.

BA: Mike Conroy, Leesburg, .362
Runs: Clarence Groat, Leesburg, 126
Hits: Lawrence Womack, Orlando, 154
RBIs: John Lavelle, Orlando, 94

HRs: Fauline Kirkland, Ocala/Gainesville, 11
Wins: Fred Swindells, Orlando, 23
SOs: Tom Smith, Ocala, 196
ERA: Wallace McCormack,
   St. Augustine, 1.81

D Georgia-Florida League
President: A.D. "Doc" Walker

Standings	W	L	Pct.	GB	Manager
Albany Cardinals (16)	88	48	.647	—	Joe Cusick
Valdosta Trojans (10)	85	51	.625	3	Stu Hoffreth
Waycross Bears	84	54	.609	5	Albert Leitz
Thomasville Lookouts (8)	69	67	.507	19	Bill Rodgers/Kip Sauerbrun
Moultrie Packers (15)	62	74	.456	26	Adolph Arlitt
Americus Pioneers	56	81	.409	32½	Dick Luckey
Cordele Reds (12)	51	81	.386	35	Bill Morrell
Tallahassee Capitols	47	86	.353	39½	Lance Richbourg

Playoffs: Albany 3 games, Waycross 0; Thomasville 3 games, Valdosta 1.
Finals: Thomasville 4 games, Waycross 3.

All-Star Team: 1B-Russell Leach, Albany; **2B-**Edward Kazak, Albany; **3B-**Pete Castiglione, Moultrie; **SS-**John Sullivan, Thomasville; **OF-**Roland LeBlanc, Albany; Lou Roede, Thomasville; Marion Ciborowski, Valdosta; **C-**Albert Leitz, Waycross; **Util-**Francis McVay, Thomasville; **P-**Melvin Gordon, Valdosta; Earl McGowin, Waycross; **Manager-**Stu Hoffreth, Valdosta.

BA: Edward Kazak, Albany, .378
Runs: Edward Kazak, Albany, 133
Hits: Edward Kazak, Albany, 221
RBIs: Russell Leach, Albany, 117

HRs: Joe Bob Mitchell, Cordele, 12
Wins: Irwin Peterman, Albany, 23
SOs: Joe Rodney, Tallahassee, 220
ERA: Kip Sauerbrun, Moultrie, 1.39

D Kitty League
President: Shelby Peace

Standings	W	L	Pct.	GB	Manager
Jackson Generals	84	43	.661	—	Mickey O'Neil
Hopkinsville Hoppers	69	57	.548	14½	Chet Wilburn
Fulton Tigers (4)	68	59	.535	16	Vincent "Moon" Mullen
Mayfield Browns (7)	64	63	.504	20	Mickey Hornsby
Union City Greyhounds (16)	62	64	.492	21½	Charles Martin/Fred Hawn
Owensboro Oilers (1)	58	68	.460	25½	Hugh Wise
Bowling Green Barons	55	71	.437	28½	Otto Bluege/Mel Simons
Paducah Indians	46	81	.362	38	Mel Simons/Floyd Perryman

Playoffs: Hopkinsville 3 games, Fulton 2; Mayfield 3 games, Jackson 1.
Finals: Mayfield 4 games, Hopkinsville 1.

All-Star Team: 1B-Murphy Malattia, Bowling Green; **2B-**Joe Reese, Fulton; **3B-**Vincent "Moon" Mullen, Fulton; **SS-**Wallace Noon, Jackson; **OF-**Norman Litzinger, Mayfield; Eddie Urbon, Owensboro; Al Cuozzo, Jackson; **C-**Paul Kluk, Owensboro; **Util-**Chet Wilburn, Hopkinsville; **P-**Carl Gaiser, Jackson; Arnold Heft, Owensboro; **Manager-**Mickey O'Neil, Jackson.

BA: Mel Simons, Paducah/
   Bowling Green, .386
Runs: Norman Litzinger, Mayfield, 130
Hits: Norman Litzinger, Mayfield, 188
RBIs: Ray Coleman, Mayfield, 122

HRs: Melvin Merkle, Jackson, 30
Wins: Carl Gaiser, Jackson, 26
SOs: Arnold Heft, Owensboro, 264
ERA: Donald Bakkelund, Union City, 2.12

D Mountain State League
President: Ray Ryan

Standings	W	L	Pct.	GB	Manager
Logan Indians	80	48	.625	—	Eddie Hock
Williamson Red Birds (16)	77	50	.606	2½	Harrison Wickel
Bluefield Blue-Greys	64	61	.512	14½	Bill Averett
Welch Miners	64	62	.508	15	Fred Neisler
Ashland Colonels	53	76	.411	27½	Ray French/Charley Carman
Huntington Aces	43	84	.339	36½	Fred Blake/Robert Larsen

Playoffs: Logan 2 games, Bluefield 1; Welch 2 games, Williamson 0.
Finals: Logan 4 games, Welch 1.

All-Star Team: 1B-Tennis Mounts, Logan; 2B-Leon Tioga, Welch; 3B-Paul Atwater, Williamson; SS-Harrison Wickel, Williamson; OF-Dick Williams, Bluefield; Edison Guinther, Ashland; Oliver Bass, Bluefield; C-Charley Carman, Ashland; Util-Cliff Burkhart, Williamson; P-Tom Triner, Welch; Joe Pennington, Logan; Manager-Eddie Hock, Logan.

BA: Don Smith, Huntington, .406
Runs: Ray King, Williamson, 132
Hits: Don Smith, Huntington, 191
RBIs: Harrison Wickel, Williamson, 147

HRs: Tennis Mounts, Logan, 24
Wins: Joe Pennington, Logan, 21
SOs: Joe Pennington, Logan, 229
ERA: Ed Burtschy, Ashland, 2.46

D North Carolina State League
President: C.M. Llewellyn

Standings	W	L	Pct.	GB	Manager
Kannapolis Towelers	70	30	.700	—	Joe Palmisano
Salisbury Giants (13)	62	38	.620	8	Johnny Heving
Mooresville Moors	57	43	.570	13	Ginger Watts
Thomasville Tommies (3)	56	44	.560	14	Jim Gruzdis
Concord Weavers	51	49	.510	19	Ulmont Baker
Lexington Indians	47	53	.470	23	Lester Smith
Landis Senators	29	71	.290	41	Stuffy McCrone/Red Brandes
Cooleemee Cards (16)	28	72	.280	42	Fred Hawn/Charles Martin

Playoffs: Mooresville 3 games, Kannapolis 1; Salisbury 3 games, Thomasville 2.
Finals: Salisbury 4 games, Mooresville 3.

All-Star Team: 1B-Woodrow Traylor, Kannapolis; 2B-Fletcher Heath, Kannapolis; 3B-Harold Harrigan, Salisbury; SS-Glenn Vaughn, Kannapolis; OF-Dan Amaral, Thomasville; Norman Small, Mooresville; William Carrier, Kannapolis; C-James Gladd, Salisbury; Util-Vincent Russello, Concord; P-James White, Kannapolis; Richard Robinson, Mooresville; Manager-Joe Palmisano, Kannapolis.

BA: Harold Harrigan, Salisbury, .359
Runs: Lewis Davis, Kannapolis, 102
Hits: Roy Nichols, Salisbury, 134
RBIs: William Carrier, Kannapolis, 88

HRs: Harold Harrigan, Salisbury, 26
Wins: James White, Kannapolis, 20
SOs: James White, Kannapolis, 192
ERA: Merle Muhl, Cooleemee, 2.17

D Northeast Arkansas League
President: Joseph Bertig

Standings	W	L	Pct.	GB	Manager
Newport Dodgers***(10)	71	46	.607	—	Merle Settlemire
Batesville Pilots (16)	65	56	.537	8	Ernest Stefani/Jim Winford
Jonesboro White Sox (2)	53	66	.445	19	Johnny Mostil/William Prince
Paragould Browns (7)	48	69	.410	23	Sam Hancock/Gus Albright

Playoffs: None.

All-Star Team: 1B-Oscar Humphries, Batesville; 2B-Gus Albright, Paragould; 3B-George Kell, Newport; SS-Bill Adams, Batesville; OF-Charles Pittman, Batesville; John Snyder, Newport; Boris Martin, Paragould; C-John Joyce, Batesville; Util-Sam Shotwell, Batesville; P-Carl Keeter, Newport; Clarence "Hooks" Iott, Paragould; Manager-Merle Settlemire, Newport.

BA: Boris Martin, Paragould, .353
Runs: Cliff Pemberton, Newport, 88
Hits: George Kell, Newport, 143
RBIs: John Joyce, Batesville, 100

HRs: John Joyce, Batesville, 15
Wins: Carl Keeter, Newport, 21
SOs: Joe Coveleskie, Paragould, 267
ERA: Carl Keeter, Newport, 1.76

D Ohio State League
President: Joe Donnelly

Standings	W	L	Pct.	GB	Manager
Fremont Green Sox***	69	34	.670	—	James "Chappie" Geygan
Mansfield Braves (3)	67	40	.626	4	Alex Clowson
Tiffin Mud Hens	50	55	.476	20	Charles LeCrone/Harry Taylor
Fostoria Red Birds (16)	49	57	.462	21½	Lee Ellison/Charles Cronin
Lima Pandas	43	64	.402	28	Otis Brannon/Rex Settlemire
Findlay Browns	37	65	.363	31½	Grover Hartley

Playoffs: None.

All-Star Team: 1B-Fred Gerken, Fremont; 2B-Harry Stephenson, Findlay; 3B-C.E. Hubbard, Lima; SS-R.V. Ankrum, Mansfield; OF-Albert Gerlach, Tiffin; Eugene Kavanaugh, Lima; Lester Pruett, Fostoria; C-William Campau, Tiffin; Util-John Cindric, Lima; P-J.G. Stasaitis, Fremont; Lloyd Fisher, Fremont; Manager-James "Chappie" Geygan, Fremont.

BA: Albert Gerlach, Tiffin, .340
Lester Pruett, Fostoria, .340
Runs: Fred Gerken, Fremont, 98
Hits: Albert Gerlach, Tiffin, 137

RBIs: Henry Miesle, Fremont, 86
HRs: Ed Mutryn, Mansfield, 22
Wins: J.G. Stasaitis, Fremont, 19
SOs: Don Bayliss, Tiffin, 198
Pct: Lloyd Fisher, Fremont, .857, 18-3

D Pennsylvania State Association
President: Elmer M. Daily

Standings	W	L	Pct.	GB	Manager
Johnstown Johnnies (10)	70	39	.642	—	George "Red" Treadwell
Butler Yankees (5)	63	47	.573	7½	Thomas Kain
Washington Red Birds (16)	53	56	.486	17	Herbert Moore
Oil City Oilers (15)	53	57	.482	17½	George Norton
Warren Buckeyes	46	62	.426	23½	Alex McColl
Beaver Falls Bees	42	66	.384	27½	Glen Schaeffer

Playoffs: Washington 3 games, Johnstown 0; Butler 3 games, Oil City 2.
Finals: Butler 3 games, Washington 1.

All-Star Team: 1B-Vincent Shupe, Johnstown; 2B-Nick DeLuca, Beaver Falls; 3B-Floyd Peters, Oil City; SS-Raymond Scott, Warren; OF-Elmer Durrett, Johnstown; Sam Masserini, Butler; Howard Murdeski, Johnstown; C-William Johnson, Johnstown; Util-Glen Schaeffer, Beaver Falls; P-Joe Smolko, Johnstown; Victor Lombardi, Johnstown; Manager-George "Red" Treadwell, Johnstown.

BA: T.A. Hawke, Butler, .365
Runs: Howard Murdeski, Johnstown, 129
Hits: Floyd Peters, Oil City, 166
Raymond Scott, Warren, 166
RBIs: Howard Murdeski, Johnstown, 139

HRs: Howard Murdeski, Johnstown, 38
Wins: Joe Smolko, Johnstown, 20
SOs: Joe Smolko, Johnstown, 220
ERA: Joe Smolko, Johnstown, 3.08

D PONY League
President: Robert C. Stedler

Standings	W	L	Pct.	GB	Manager
Jamestown Falcons (4)	68	42	.618	—	Greg Mulleavy
Bradford Bees (9)	60	50	.549	8	Del Bissonette
Batavia Clippers	54	54	.500	13	Eddie Howard
Hamilton Red Wings (16)	50	57	.467	16½	Roy Pfleger
Olean Oilers (10)	48	61	.440	19½	Jake Pitler
London Pirates (15)	47	63	.431	21	Jimmy Jordan

Attendance: Jamestown, 122,801; London, 41,318; Total, 355,548.

Playoffs: Hamilton 3 games, Jamestown 2; Bradford 3 games, Batavia 2.
Finals: Bradford 4 games, Hamilton 1.

All-Star Team: 1B-Frank Heller, Jamestown; 2B-Greg Mulleavy, Jamestown; 3B-Robert Barnhart, London; SS-John O'Neil, Jamestown; OF-John Newman, Jamestown; Gene Nafie, Bradford; Gene Hermanski, Olean; C-George Zimmerman, Olean; Util-Paul Schrock, London; P-Joseph Belforti, Bradford; Paul Wargo, Hamilton; Manager-Greg Mulleavy, Jamestown.

BA: John Newman, Jamestown, .358
Runs: John Newman, Jamestown, 112
Hits: Frank Heller, Jamestown, 145
RBIs: John Newman, Jamestown, 96
HRs: John Newman, Jamestown, 29

Wins: Joseph Belforti, Bradford, 17
SOs: George Carlenos, London, 181
ERA: John Mikan, Hamilton, 2.48
Pct: Peter Angell, Jamestown, .824, 14-3

D West Texas-New Mexico League
President: Milton E. Price

Standings	W	L	Pct.	GB	Manager
Big Spring Bombers (10)	91	45	.669	—	Joe Tate
Borger Gassers	89	47	.654	2	Gordon Nell
Clovis Pioneers	76	58	.567	14	Howard Taylor/Grover Seitz
Amarillo Gold Sox	72	64	.529	19	Claude Jonnard
Lubbock Hubbers (2)	61	78	.439	31½	Charlie Engle
Lamesa Lobos	59	80	.424	33½	Sam Scaling
Pampa Oilers	55	79	.410	35	Dutch Prather/Sammy Hale
Wichita Falls Spudders (12)	43	95	.312	49	Sammy Hale/Neal Rabe

Attendance: Amarillo, 42,421; Total, 183,395.

Playoffs: Big Spring 3 games, Amarillo 0; Clovis 3 games, Borger 2.
Finals: Clovis 4 games, Big Spring 3.

All-Star Team: 1B-Paul Schoendienst, Clovis; 2B-Hugh Willingham, Borger; 3B-Stewart Williams, Borger; SS-Larry Gilchrist, Borger; OF-Homer Matney, Pampa; Gordon Nell, Borger; Frank Hargrove, Amarillo; C-William DeCarlo, Amarillo; Util-Stubby Greer, Big Spring; P-Udell Moore, Borger; Raymond Lucas, Wichita Falls; Manager-Joe Tate, Big Spring.

BA: Frank Hargrove, Amarillo, .388
Runs: James Haney, Big Spring, 143
Hits: Stewart Williams, Borger, 210
RBIs: Dutch Prather, Pampa/Amarillo, 142
HRs: Gordon Nell, Borger, 28

Wins: James Ramsdell, Big Spring, 25
SOs: Russell Crider, Amarillo, 232
ERA: John McParland, Pampa, 2.03
Pct: Udell Moore, Borger, .824, 14-3

D Western League
President: J. Roy Carter

Standings	W	L	Pct.	GB	Manager
Norfolk Yankees (5)	64	44	.593	—	Ray Powell
Cheyenne Indians	59	44	.573	2½	John Kerr
Sioux City Soos (16)	54	56	.491	11	Richard Tichacek
Pueblo Rollers (7)	52	54	.491	11	Francis "Pug" Griffin
Sioux Falls Canaries	51	56	.477	12½	Robert Fenner/Tony Koenig
Denver Bears	42	68	.382	23	Coburn Jones

1941

Playoffs: Norfolk 3 games, Sioux City 2; Pueblo 3 games, Cheyenne 2.
Finals: Pueblo 3 games, Norfolk 2.

All-Star Team: 1B-Bernard Steele, Pueblo; **2B-**John Kerr, Cheyenne; **3B-**Jerry Jordan, Cheyenne; **SS-**Maurice McKnight, Cheyenne; **OF-**Orin Crider, Sioux City; Frank Bocek, Norfolk; Albert Dudas, Sioux City; **C-**Vern Hoscheit, Norfolk; **Util-**Francis Tichacek, Sioux City; **P-**Lyle Fritsch, Sioux City; George Milstead, Cheyenne; **Manager-**Ray Powell, Norfolk.

BA: Bernard Steele, Pueblo, .383
Runs: Bernard Steele, Pueblo, 88
Hits: Bernard Steele, Pueblo, 158
RBIs: Frank Bocek, Norfolk, 92

HRs: Mel Bergman, Cheyenne, 10
Wins: George Milstead, Cheyenne, 19
SOs: Robert Bergen, Pueblo, 183
ERA: Frank Wagner, Sioux Falls, 2.15

D Wisconsin State League

President: Herman D. White

Standings	W	L	Pct.	GB	Manager
Green Bay Blue Sox	76	35	.685	—	Red Smith
La Crosse Blackhawks	69	41	.627	6½	Ed Konetchy
Appleton Papermakers (3)	65	44	.596	10	Ed Dancisak
Sheboygan Indians	65	45	.591	10½	Joe Hauser
Wisconsin Rapids					
White Sox (2)	47	63	.427	28½	Frank Parenti
Fond du Lac Panthers	46	64	.418	29½	Harry Rice
Janesville Cubs (11)	38	72	.345	37½	Ed Stumpf
Oshkosh Giants	33	75	.306	41½	Fred Schulte

Playoffs: Sheboygan 3 games, La Crosse 1; Green Bay 2 games, Appleton 0, when rain forced postponement, last game played September 6.
Finals: Sheboygan was awarded the championship when Green Bay forfeited September 9.

All-Star Team: 1B-Gilbert Neuman, La Crosse; **2B-**Clyde Lorenz, Wisconsin Rapids; **3B-**Joe Janet, Green Bay; **SS-**Gus Gregory, Appleton; **OF-**Ordie Timm, Green Bay; Harold Schadt, La Crosse; Pat Seerey, Appleton; **C-**Frank Cominsky, Wisconsin Rapids; **Util-**Donald Opperman, Fond du Lac; **P-**Delmar Marquardt, Fond du Lac; Eugene Joselane, Janesville; **Manager-**Red Smith, Green Bay.

BA: Adolph Krauss, Sheboygan, .366
Runs: Harold Schadt, La Crosse, 112
Hits: Richard Ronovsky, Green Bay, 153
RBIs: Pat Seerey, Appleton, 117
HRs: Pat Seerey, Appleton, 31

Wins: Dan Schoenborn, La Crosse, 18
SOs: Jerome Crowley, Green Bay, 242
ERA: Delmar Marquardt, Fond du Lac, 2.29
WPs: Max Patkin, Wisconsin Rapids, 13

Ind Mexican League

President: Lic. Mario Loastoa

Standings	W	L	Pct.	GB	Manager
Veracruz Azules	67	35	.657	—	Lazaro Salazar
Mexico City Diablos Rojos	52	47	.525	13½	Ernesto Carmona
Tampico Alijadores	52	49	.515	14½	Guillermo Ornelas
Torreon Algodoneros	45	56	.446	21½	Baldomero Almada/Manolo Fortes/ Martin Dihigo
Veracruz Aguila	44	57	.436	22½	Sergio Correa
Monterrey Industriales	43	59	.422	24	Jose Luis Gomez

BA: Burnis Wright, Mexico City, .390
Hits: Silvio Garcia, Mexico City, 159
RBIs: Josh Gibson, Veracruz Azules, 124
HRs: Josh Gibson, Veracruz Azules, 33

Wins: Theolic Smith, Mexico City, 16
Nate Moreland, Tampico, 16
Barney Brown, Veracruz Azules, 16
SOs: Edward Porter, Mexico City, 133
ERA: Jesus Valenzuela, Tampico, 3.12

1941 Interleague Post Season Play

World Series
New York (American) 4 games, Brooklyn (National) 1

Junior World Series
Columbus (American Association) 4 games, Montreal (International) 2
Total Attendance: 57,424

Dixie Series
Nashville (Southern Association) 4 games, Dallas (Texas) 0
Total Attendance: 24,009

Little Dixie Series
Macon (South Atlantic) 4 games, Mobile (Southeastern) 0

Class D Interleague Series
Thomasville (Georgia-Florida) 4 games, Leesburg (Florida State) 3

Class C vs. Class D
Salem-Roanoke (Virginia) 4 games, Logan (Mountain State) 3

1941 Major League Farm Systems

American League

1 Boston (8): Louisville, Scranton, Greensboro, Oneonta, Canton, Danville-Schoolfield, Centreville, Owensboro.
2 Chicago (7): St. Paul, Waterloo, Saginaw, Grand Forks, Jonesboro, Lubbock, Wisconsin Rapids.
3 Cleveland (10): Oklahoma City, Wilkes-Barre, Cedar Rapids, Flint, Charleston (WV), Salina, Thomasville (NC), Mansfield, Appleton.
4 Detroit (11): Buffalo, Beaumont, Elmira, Hagerstown, Winston-Salem, Utica, Texarkana, Muskegon, Tallassee, Jamestown, Fulton.
5 New York (12): Kansas City, Newark, Binghamton, Norfolk (VA), Augusta, Akron, Idaho Falls, Amsterdam, Joplin, Easton, Butler, Norfolk (NE).
6 Philadelphia (5): Toronto, Williamsport, Wilmington, Newport News, Federalsburg.
7 St. Louis (10): Toledo, San Antonio, Meridian, Springfield (IL), Youngstown, St. Joseph/Carthage, Lafayette, Mayfield, Paragould, Pueblo.
8 Washington (6): Chattanooga, Charlotte, Greenville (SC), Selma, Orlando, Thomasville (GA).

National League

9 Boston (4): Hartford, Bridgeport, Evansville, Bradford.
10 Brooklyn (15): Montreal, Knoxville, Reading, Durham, Santa Barbara, Quebec, Grand Rapids, Dayton, Troy/Tuskegee, Elizabethton, Valdosta, Newport (AR), Johnstown, Olean, Big Spring.
11 Chicago (10): Los Angeles, Tulsa, Portsmouth, Macon, Bisbee, Stockton, Zanesville, Muskogee, Lake Charles, Janesville.
12 Cincinnati (8): Indianapolis, Birmingham, Columbia, Tucson, Riverside, Ogden, Cordele, Wichita Falls.
13 New York (7): Jersey City, Hollywood, Clinton, San Bernardino, Ft. Smith, Milford, Salisbury (NC).
14 Philadelphia (3): Allentown, Wausau, Martinsville.
15 Pittsburgh (7): Albany (NY), Harrisburg, Gloversville-Johnstown, Hutchinson, Moultrie, Oil City, London.
16 St. Louis (26): Columbus (OH), Rochester, Sacramento, New Orleans, Houston, Asheville, Columbus (GA), Mobile, Decatur, Fresno, Springfield (OH), Duluth, Pocatello, Springfield (MO), Johnson City, Cambridge, Daytona Beach, Albany (GA), Union City, Williamson, Cooleemee, Batesville, Fostoria, Washington, Hamilton, Sioux City.

1941 No-Hitters

Date	Pitcher	Team	League	Opponent	Score
4-20	Willis Hudlin	Little Rock	Southern Assoc.	New Orleans	4-0 (7)
4-25	Howie Pollet	Houston	Texas	Shreveport	7-0
4-28	Harden Cathey	Charlotte	Piedmont	Winston-Salem	8-0
5-18	Lucien Gouvernal	Rayne	Evangeline	Opelousas	8-0
5-18	Bob Perry	Cheyenne	Western	Sioux Falls	2-0
5-21	Robert Bergen	Pueblo	Western	Norfolk	3-0 (7)
5-30	Arthur Olsen	Pittsfield	Canadian-American	Trois Rivieres	15-0 (7)
5-31	Virgil Trucks	Buffalo	International	Montreal	0-1 (10)
6-5	Russell Crider	Amarillo	W. Texas-N. Mexico	Big Spring	6-0 (7)
6-7	Charles Conklin	Santa Barbara	California	Anaheim	4-0
6-16	Jack Hartz	Waycross	Georgia-Florida	Thomasville	9-0
6-20	Herb Karpel	Binghamton	Eastern	Elmira	2-0
7-4	Robert Brooks	Mayfield	Kitty	Paducah	5-0
7-9	Red LaFlamme	Albany	Eastern	Hartford	3-0 (7)
7-13	Charley Whelchel	Big Spring	W. Texas-N. Mexico	Pampa	2-0 (P, 11)
7-16	Jim Cleghorn	Denver	Western	Sioux City	0-1
7-22	Don Black	Petersburg	Virginia	Staunton	1-0
7-27	Wayne Johnson	Newport	Northeast Arkansas	Batesville	18-0
7-27	Carl Keeter	Newport	Northeast Arkansas	Paragould	1-0 (7)
8-1	Jack Kraus	Durham	Piedmont	Greensboro	6-0
8-2	Tony Foti	Lexington	North Carolina State	Concord	
8-3	Neil Saulia	Ft. Smith	Western Assoc.	Topeka	1-0 (7)
8-5	James Schantel	Fargo-Moorhead	Northern	Grand Forks	10-0
8-6	Carl Keeter	Newport	Northeast Arkansas	Jonesboro	15-0 (7)
8-7	Joe Wood	Scranton	Eastern	Albany	5-0
8-7	Joe Page	Augusta	South Atlantic	Savannah	4-0
8-17	Joe Mitchell	Columbia	South Atlantic	Charleston	3-0 (6)
8-17	George Kunz	Oshkosh	Wisconsin State	Janesville	1-0
8-18	John Moore	Gainesville	Florida State	Ocala	5-0
8-20	Matt Surkont	Rochester	International	Jersey City	1-0 (7)
8-21	Bit Beebe	Ft. Pierce	Florida East Coast	Ft. Lauderdale	7-0
8-24	Jean-Pierre Roy	Trois Rivieres	Canadian-American	Amsterdam	5-0 (7)
8-26	Frank Mottley	Duluth	Northern	Grand Forks	7-0 (7)
8-27	Reggie Grabowski	Albany	Eastern	Syracuse	2-0 (7)
8-30	Lon Warneke	St. Louis	National	Cincinnati	2-0
9-3	Jim Heist/				
	Dale Gentil	Greensboro	Piedmont	Asheville	3-0 (7)
9-6	Richard Robinson	Mooresville	N. Carolina State	Salisbury	5-0 (PO)

Number in parentheses indicates innings if other than nine; "P" indicates perfect game; "PO" indicates playoff game.

THIS DATE IN MINOR LEAGUE HISTORY

January 11, 1941, Rogers Hornsby was re-hired as manager of Oklahoma City in the Texas League.

April 17, 1941, A record minor league attendance of 56,391 paid at Jersey City for the Rochester-Jersey City opener in the International League.

April 23, 1941, Ralph Kiner made his Organized Ball debut with Albany of the Eastern League as an 18-year-old rookie in a game against Binghamton.

May 31, 1941, Virgil Trucks of Buffalo, International League, pitched no-hit ball for 9-1/3 innings against Montreal and Ed Head, but lost the game 1-0. Alex Kampouris singled over shortstop with two outs in the tenth inning and later scored. It was Trucks' fourth no-hit feat in his five minor league campaigns.

June 7, 1941, Edwin "Alabama" Pitts died in Morganton, North Carolina, of knife wounds suffered in a roadside tavern altercation. His entry into the game after having been paroled from Sing Sing prison in 1935 aroused a storm of controversy that was settled by a ruling from Commissioner Landis that allowed him to play in Organized Ball.

June 18, 1941, Clarence "Hooks" Iott struck out 25 in a nine-inning game while hurling Paragould to a two-hit 4-2 victory over Batesville in the Northeast Arkansas League.

June 21, 1941, Bill Veeck purchased the Milwaukee Brewers of the American Association.

June 23, 1941, Rogers Hornsby resigned as manager of Oklahoma City.

July 13, 1941, Charley Whelchel of Big Spring, West Texas-New Mexico League, hurled an eleven inning no-hitter for a 2-0 victory over Pampa. He pitched perfect ball over the first nine frames.

July 15, 1941, Clarence "Hooks" Iott, pitching for Paragould, Northeast Arkansas League, struck out 30 batters in a 16-inning night game at Newport. The game ended in a 1-1 tie. The 30 strikeouts set an all-time single game record for Organized Ball.

July 19, 1941, Vic Lombardi of Johnstown, Pennsylvania State Association, fanned 19 Beaver Falls batters in a nine-inning game. Five days later, the southpaw struck out 19 Butler hitters, for a total of 38 strikeouts in 18 innings.

August 12, 1941, Allie Reynolds, son of a Nazarene preacher in Oklahoma, pitching for Cedar Rapids, Three-I League, struck out 17 in defeating Madison 5-2.

August 16, 1941, Gene Stockdale of Oil City, Pennsylvania State Association, fanned 23 Johnstown batters in a nine-inning game, 19 of them on swinging third strikes.

September 1, 1941, Longtime minor league manager and player Jim Poole, 46, managing Ft. Pierce in the Florida East Coast League, played with his two sons on his club.

September 2, 1941, National Association President Bramham suspended Frederick Showmaker of Oil City, Pennsylvania State Association, for one year on the charge of spitting tobacco juice in the face of Joe Szarfaro, official scorer and sportswriter for the Oil City Blizzard.

September 5, 1941, The one-year suspension of Eddie Mayo of Los Angeles, Pacific Coast League, for allegedly spitting in the face of umpire Ray Snyder, was lifted by the National Association Executive Committee. They refused to rescind the ban on pitcher Julio Bonetti of the same club, who had been placed on the ineligible list for alleged association with gamblers.

September 13, 1941, Paul Richards was signed by Atlanta, Southern Association, to manage the Crackers for a fifth season in 1942.

SPRING TRAINING 1942

AMERICAN LEAGUE

CLUBS	AT	MAIL ADDRESS	DATES
BOSTON	Sarasota, Fla.	Sarasota Terrace Hotel	2/26–3/31
CHICAGO	Pasadena, Ca.	Green Hotel	2/27–3/30
CLEVELAND	Clearwater, Fla.	Fort Harrison Hotel	2/23–3/28
DETROIT	Lakeland, Fla.	Lakeland Terrace Hotel	2/22–4/6
NEW YORK	St. Petersburg, Fla.	Suwanee Hotel	2/22–3/30
PHILADELPHIA	Anaheim, Ca.	Angelina Hotel	2/23–3/25
ST. LOUIS	Deland, Fla.	Putnam Hotel	3/2–4/6
WASHINGTON	Orlando, Fla.	Angebilt Hotel	2/22–4/5

NATIONAL LEAGUE

CLUBS	AT	MAIL ADDRESS	DATES
BOSTON	Sanford, Fla.	Mayfair Hotel	3/3–4/6
BROOKLYN	Havana, Cuba	Hotel Nacional de Cuba	2/19–3/10
BROOKLYN	Daytona Beach, Fla.	El Cotes Manor	3/11–4/3
CHICAGO	Avalon Catalina Is., Ca.	St. Catherine Hotel	2/21–3/12
CHICAGO	Los Angeles, Ca.	Biltmore Hotel	3/13–3/31
CINCINNATI	Tampa, Fla.	Floridian Hotel	2/20–3/30
NEW YORK	Miami, Fla.	Miami Biltmore Hotel	2/16–3/28
PHILADELPHIA	Miami Beach, Fla.	Albion Hotel	3/1–3/31
PITTSBURGH	El Centro, Ca.	Barbara Worth Hotel	2/24–3/5
PITTSBURGH	San Bernardino, Ca.	California Hotel	3/5–3/25
ST. LOUIS	St. Petersburg, Fla.	Bainbridge Hotel	2/23–4/6

AMERICAN ASSOCIATION

CLUBS	AT	MAIL ADDRESS	DATES
COLUMBUS	Lake Worth, Fla.	Florida Hotel	3/10–4/13
INDIANAPOLIS	Cocoa, Fla.	Indian River Hotel	3/9–4/14
KANSAS CITY	Lake Wales, Fla.	Walesbilt Hotel	3/6–4/8
LOUISVILLE	Bradenton, Fla.	Dixie Grande House	3/11–4/13
MILWAUKEE	Ocala, Fla.	Harrington Hall Hotel	3/10–4/13
MINNEAPOLIS	New Braunfels, Tex.	Faust Hotel	3/10–4/6
ST. PAUL	Leesburg, Fla.	Magnolia Hotel	3/12–4/10
TOLEDO	San Antonio, Tex.	Plaza Hotel	3/12–4/10

INTERNATIONAL LEAGUE

CLUBS	AT	MAIL ADDRESS	DATES
BALTIMORE	Hollywood, Fla.	Villa Hermosa	3/8–4/9
BUFFALO	Fort Pierce, Fla.	New Fort Pierce Hotel	3/9–4/12
JERSEY CITY	Jacksonville, Fla.	Mayflower Hotel	3/5–4/8
MONTREAL	Daytona Beach, Fla.	Osceola Hotel	3/14–4/10
NEWARK	Sebring, Fla.	Sebring Hotel	3/10–4/4
ROCHESTER	West Palm Beach, Fla.	Monterey Hotel	3/10–4/12
SYRACUSE	Fort Lauderdale, Fla.	Tropical Hotel	3/10–4/13
TORONTO	Camden, S.C.	Court Inn	3/16–4/10

PACIFIC COAST LEAGUE

CLUBS	AT	MAIL ADDRESS	DATES
HOLLYWOOD	Riverside, Ca.	Tetley Hotel	2/22–3/29
LOS ANGELES	Ontario, Ca.	Casa Blanca Hotel	2/23–3/28
OAKLAND	Napa, Ca.	Plaza Hotel	3/1–4/1
PORTLAND	San Jose, Ca.	Sainte Claire Hotel	2/25–3/31
SACRAMENTO	Fullerton, Ca.	California Hotel	3/2–3/31
SAN DIEGO	El Centro, Ca.	Barbara Worth Hotel	2/21–3/27
SAN FRANCISCO	Boyes Springs, Ca.	Sonoma Mission Inn	3/2–4/1
SEATTLE	San Fernando, Ca.	Porter Hotel	2/16–3/30

SOUTHERN ASSOCIATION

CLUBS	AT	MAIL ADDRESS	DATES
ATLANTA	St. Augustine	Beach Hotel	3/1–3/27
BIRMINGHAM	Palatka, Fla.	Travelers Hotel	3/6–4/3
CHATTANOOGA	Winter Garden, Fla.	Edgewater Hotel	3/15
KNOXVILLE	Tallahassee, Fla.	Cherokee Hotel	3/10–4/8
LITTLE ROCK	Little Rock, Ark.	114 E. 2nd Street	3/9–4/13
MEMPHIS	Bartow, Fla.	New Oaks Hotel	3/10–4/10
NASHVILLE	Baton Rouge, La.	King Hotel	3/5–3/31
NEW ORLEANS	New Orleans, La.	Pelican Stadium	3/2–4/10

TEXAS LEAGUE

CLUBS	AT	MAIL ADDRESS	DATES
BEAUMONT	Lakeland, Fla.	Lakeland Terrace	3/2–4/2
DALLAS	Dallas, Tex.	Rebel Field	3/12–4/12
FORT WORTH	Fort Worth, Tex.	P.O. Box 405	3/12–4/12
HOUSTON	Houston, Tex.	Buffalo Stadium	3/12–4/11
OKLAHOMA CITY	Tyler, Tex.	Blackstone Hotel	3/15–4/11
SAN ANTONIO			
SHREVEPORT	Shreveport, La.	P.O. Box 1462	3/15–4/11
TULSA	Ocala, Fla.	Hoffman Hotel	3/8–4/7

EASTERN LEAGUE

CLUBS	AT	MAIL ADDRESS	DATES
ALBANY	Barnwell, S.C.		4/1–4/22
BINGHAMTON	Edenton, N.C.	Joseph Hewes Hotel	3/28–4/27
ELMIRA	Tarboro, N.C.	Tarboro Hotel	4/1–4/20
HARTFORD	Greenville, N.C.	Proctor Hotel	4/1–4/27
SCRANTON	Bennettsville, S.C.		3/25–4/23
SPRINGFIELD	Mexico City, Mex.	Galveston Hotel	3/1–3/20
WILKES-BARRE	Sumter, S.C.	Claremont Hotel	3/30–4/23
WILLIAMSPORT	Raeford, N.C.	Raeford Hotel	3/29–4/24

THE WAR YEARS: 1942 - 1945

*O*n Dec. 5, 1941, the annual meeting of the National Association, held in Jacksonville, ended with much optimism for the future of the minor leagues. Two days later Japan attacked Pearl Harbor. For the next four years, minor league baseball would struggle to stay alive.

Forty-one leagues had finished the season. In 1942, 31 leagues started the season, but it became apparent that business was not as usual. On May 14 the Florida State League folded, and the Evangeline, Kitty, West Texas-New Mexico and California Leagues quickly followed. Able-bodied athletes were being called into military service, wartime restrictions made the operation of minor league franchises difficult. Gasoline rationing affected teams that traveled by bus. Curtailed railroad transportation hurt other ballclubs. Night baseball was limited by government moves to conserve electric power, and there was some discontinuation of night baseball in coastal cities with blackout restrictions. Fans found it difficult to get to games and wartime shift work cut out other fans from attending. President Franklin Roosevelt had given a green light for baseball, but the war proved difficult for most leagues.

By 1943, nine leagues in 62 cities completed the season. Many teams were composed of players either too old or too young for military service. Some players had received 4-F deferments, while others worked day jobs in defense-related industries, enabling them to continue playing baseball.

The class E Twin Ports League was formed in Duluth, Minn., and Superior, Wis., in 1943. Making use of players who worked in the war-vital shipyards and iron ore industry along Lake Superior, the league lasted just 19 games before it folded. The 1944 season saw one-armed Pete Gray hit .333 for Memphis and *The Sporting News* minor league player of the year was 40-year-old former major leaguer Rip Collins, who hit .389 for Albany, N.Y.

Ten leagues operated that year as the Ohio State League started back up, and in 1945, two North Carolina circuits, the Carolina and North Carolina State Leagues, commenced operations. With the war ending in the summer of 1945, the minor leagues would begin an explosion and the face of minor league baseball would change again.

Bramham's health declined during the war. He managed to withstand a strong challenge to his presidency in 1943 from Frank Shaughnessy of the International League. Shaughnessy came to the annual convention with six of the nine leagues ready to vote for him as president. Bramham ruled that 15 leagues that had suspended operations for the war could vote. Not surprisingly, those 15 leagues voted for Bramham. With much animosity, he was re-elected to another five-year term.

1942

American League
President: William Harridge

Standings	W	L	Pct.	GB	Attend.	Manager
New York Yankees..........	103	51	.669	—	922,011	Joe McCarthy
Boston Red Sox	93	59	.612	9	730,340	Joe Cronin
St. Louis Browns	82	69	.543	19½	255,617	Luke Sewell
Cleveland Indians	75	79	.487	28	459,447	Lou Boudreau
Detroit Tigers.....................	73	81	.474	30	580,087	Del Baker
Chicago White Sox	66	82	.446	34	425,734	Jimmy Dykes
Washington Senators	62	89	.411	39½	403,493	Bucky Harris
Philadelphia Athletics.........	55	99	.357	48	423,487	Connie Mack

BA: Ted Williams, Boston, .356
Runs: Ted Williams, Boston, 141
Hits: Johnny Pesky, Boston, 205
RBIs: Ted Williams, Boston, 137
HRs: Ted Williams, Boston, 36
Wins: Tex Hughson, Boston, 22
SOs: Bobo Newsom, Washington, 113
    Tex Hughson, Boston, 113
ERA: Ted Lyons, Chicago, 2.10
Pct: Tiny Bonham, New York, .808, 21-5

National League
President: Ford Frick

Standings	W	L	Pct.	GB	Attend.	Manager
St. Louis Cardinals	106	48	.688	—	553,552	Billy Southworth
Brooklyn Dodgers..............	104	50	.675	2	1,037,765	Leo Durocher
New York Giants	85	67	.559	20	779,621	Mel Ott
Cincinnati Reds..................	76	76	.500	29	427,031	Bill McKechnie
Pittsburgh Pirates..............	66	81	.449	36½	448,897	Frank Frisch
Chicago Cubs....................	68	86	.442	38	590,972	Jimmie Wilson
Boston Braves....................	59	89	.399	44	285,332	Casey Stengel
Philadelphia Phillies	42	109	.278	62½	230,183	Hans Lobert

BA: Ernie Lombardi, Boston, .330
Runs: Mel Ott, New York, 118
Hits: Enos Slaughter, St. Louis, 188
RBIs: John Mize, New York, 110
HRs: Mel Ott, New York, 30
Wins: Mort Cooper, St. Louis, 22
SOs: Johnny Vander Meer, Cincinnati, 186
ERA: Mort Cooper, St. Louis, 1.78
Pct: Larry French, Brooklyn, .789, 15-4

AA American Association
President: George Trautman

Standings	W	L	Pct.	GB	Attend.	Manager
Kansas City Blues (5)........	84	69	.549	—	113,372	Johnny Neun
Milwaukee Brewers............	81	69	.540	1½	217,966	Charlie Grimm
Columbus Red Birds (16)..	82	72	.532	2½	162,629	Eddie Dyer
Toledo Mud Hens (7)........	78	73	.517	5	110,164	Fred Haney
Louisville Colonels (1).........	78	76	.506	6½	159,448	Bill Burwell
Indianapolis Indians..........	76	78	.494	8½	186,447	Gabby Hartnett
Minneapolis Millers............	76	78	.494	8½	112,304	Tom Sheehan
St. Paul Saints (2)	57	97	.370	27½	73,990	Truck Hannah/Bob Tarlton

Playoffs: Columbus 4 games, Kansas City 3; Toledo 4 games, Milwaukee 2.
Finals: Columbus 4 games, Toledo 0.

All-Star Team: 1B-John McCarthy, Indianapolis; **2B**-Frank Drews, St. Paul; **3B**-Joe Bestudik, Indianapolis; **SS**-Gene Geary, Minneapolis; **OF**-Eric Tipton, Kansas City; Joe Vosmik, Minneapolis; Wayne Blackburn, Indianapolis; Bill Norman, Milwaukee; Chester Moran, Louisville; **C**-Kenneth Sears, Kansas City; George Lacy, Louisville; Tom Heath, Columbus; **Util**-Ralph Kress, Louisville; George Myatt, Columbus; Mark Christman, Toledo; **P**-Charles Wensloff, Kansas City; George Munger, Columbus; Harry Brecheen, Columbus; Milton Haefner, Minneapolis; **MVP**-Eddie Stanky, Milwaukee; **Pitcher of the Year**-Harry Brecheen, Columbus; **Manager**-Bill Burwell, Louisville.

BA: Eddie Stanky, Milwaukee, .342
Runs: Eddie Stanky, Milwaukee, 124
Hits: Hal Peck, Milwaukee, 189
RBIs: John McCarthy, Indianapolis, 113
HRs: Bill Norman, Milwaukee, 24
Wins: Charles Wensloff, Kansas City, 21
SOs: Harry Brecheen, Columbus, 156
ERA: Harry Brecheen, Columbus, 2.09

AA International League
President: Frank J. Shaughnessy

Standings	W	L	Pct.	GB	Attend.	Manager
Newark Bears (5)..............	92	61	.601	—	112,402	Bill Meyer
Montreal Royals (10)..........	82	71	.536	10	183,841	Clyde Sukeforth
Syracuse Chiefs (12).........	78	74	.513	13½	164,466	Jewel Ens
Jersey City Giants (13).......	77	75	.507	14½	195,912	Frank Snyder
Baltimore Orioles (3)..........	75	77	.493	16½	184,376	Alphonse "Tommy" Thomas
Toronto Maple Leafs (6, 15)....	74	79	.484	18	178,327	Burleigh Grimes
Buffalo Bisons (4)	73	80	.477	19	130,071	Al Vincent
Rochester Red Wings (16)..	59	93	.388	32½	72,891	Tony Kaufmann/Estel Crabtree/Ray Hayworth

Playoffs: Syracuse defeated Jersey City in a one game playoff for third place. Jersey City 4 games, Newark 2; Syracuse 4 games, Montreal 1.
Finals: Syracuse 4 games, Jersey City 0.

MVP-Charles "Red" Barrett, Syracuse.

BA: Hank Majeski, Newark, .345
Runs: Gene Moore, Montreal, 114
Hits: Hank Majeski, Newark, 198
RBIs: Hank Majeski, Newark, 121
HRs: Les Burge, Montreal, 28
Wins: Charles "Red" Barrett, Syracuse, 20
SOs: Jack Hallett, Toronto, 187
ERA: Ray Coombs, Jersey City, 1.99

AA Pacific Coast League
President: William C. Tuttle

Standings	W	L	Pct.	GB	Attend.	Manager
Sacramento Solons (16)....	105	73	.590	—	144,057	Pepper Martin
Los Angeles Angels (11)..	104	74	.584	1	271,169	Arnold "Jigger" Statz
Seattle Rainiers	96	82	.539	9	250,779	Bill Skiff
San Diego Padres..............	91	87	.511	14	169,334	Cedric Durst
San Francisco Seals (10)....	88	90	.490	17	202,772	Lefty O'Doul
Oakland Oaks	85	92	.480	19½	144,705	John Vergez
Hollywood Stars	75	103	.421	30	225,987	Ossie Vitt
Portland Beavers	67	110	.379	37½	104,474	Frank Brazill

Playoffs: Seattle 4 games, Sacramento 1; Los Angeles 4 games, San Diego 3.
Finals: Seattle 4 games, Los Angeles 2.

MVP-Ray Mueller, Sacramento.

BA: Ted Norbert, Portland, .378
Runs: Eddie Lake, Sacramento, 118
Hits: Eddie Waitkus, Los Angeles, 235
RBIs: Kermit Lewis, San Francisco, 115
HRs: Ted Norbert, Portland, 28
Wins: Dick "Kewpie" Barrett, Seattle, 27
SOs: Dick "Kewpie" Barrett, Seattle, 178
ERA: Dick "Kewpie" Barrett, Seattle, 1.72

A1 Southern Association
President: Trammell Scott

Standings	W	L	Pct.	GB	Attend.	Manager
Little Rock Travelers	87	59	.596	—	98,461	Willis Hudlin
Nashville Vols	85	66	.563	4½	96,934	Larry Gilbert
Birmingham Barons (12)....	79	73	.520	11	113,937	Johnny Riddle
New Orleans Pelicans (16).	77	73	.513	12	110,401	Pat Ankenman
Atlanta Crackers	76	78	.494	15	134,005	Paul Richards
Memphis Chicks	72	80	.474	18	85,659	Tommy "Doc" Prothro
Chattanooga Lookouts (8)..	66	86	.434	24	57,353	Sparky Olson
Knoxville Smokies	61	88	.409	27½	46,635	Bert Niehoff

Playoffs: Nashville 3 games, Birmingham 1; Little Rock 3 games, New Orleans 1.
Finals: Nashville 4 games, Little Rock 0.

All-Star Team: 1B-Jim Shilling, Nashville; **2B**-Roy Schalk, Little Rock; **3B**-Charley English, Nashville; **SS**-William Hart, New Orleans; **OF**-Guy Dugas, Nashville; Thomas McBride, Little Rock; Mike Dejan, Birmingham; Murray Howell, Knoxville; **C**-Jerry Burmeister, New Orleans; Fermin Guerra, Chattanooga; **P**-Vito Tamulis, Nashville; Bill Seinsoth, New Orleans; James Trexler, Little Rock; Lewis Carpenter, Memphis; Ed Heusser, Birmingham; **MVP**-Roy Schalk, Little Rock.

BA: Charley English, Nashville, .341
Runs: Johnny Milhalic, Nashville, 124
Hits: Charley English, Nashville, 201
RBIs: Charley English, Nashville, 139
HRs: Chuck Workman, Nashville, 29
Wins: Bill Seinsoth, Nashville, 24
SOs: George Jeffcoat, Nashville, 146
ERA: Bill Kennedy, Chattanooga, 2.43

A1 Texas League
President: J. Alvin Gardner

Standings	W	L	Pct.	GB	Attend.	Manager
Beaumont Exporters (4)......	89	58	.615	—	71,275	Steve O'Neill
Shreveport Sports	83	61	.576	4½	78,468	Francis "Salty" Parker
Ft. Worth Cats....................	84	68	.559	7½	87,869	Rogers Hornsby
San Antonio Missions (7)...	80	68	.546	9½	66,792	Ralph Winegarner
Houston Buffaloes (16)	81	70	.536	10	52,692	Clay Hopper
Tulsa Oilers (11).................	76	75	.533	15	59,176	Roy Johnson
Oklahoma City Indians (13)..	58	95	.379	34	36,786	Homer Peel/Jimmy Payton/John Kroner/Clay Touchstone
Dallas Rebels	48	104	.314	43½	37,107	Wally Dashiell

Playoffs: Beaumont 4 games, San Antonio 2; Shreveport 4 games, Ft. Worth 3.
Finals: Shreveport 4 games, Beaumont 3.

MVP-Dick Wakefield, Beaumont.

*Won first-half   **Won second-half   ***Won both halves
Numbers after nicknames indicate farm system.
Affiliation listed at end of each year.

BA: Dick Wakefield, Beaumont, .345
Runs: Thurman Tucker, Ft. Worth, 116
Hits: Dick Wakefield, Beaumont, 192
RBIs: Mervyn Connors, Ft. Worth, 101

HRs: Mervyn Connors, Ft. Worth, 27
Wins: Earl Caldwell, Ft. Worth, 21
SOs: Ralph Hamner, Shreveport, 148
ERA: John Whitehead, Houston, 1.20

A Eastern League
President: Thomas H. Richardson

Standings	W	L	Pct.	GB	Attend.	Manager
Albany Senators (15)	84	56	.600	—	188,359	James "Rip" Collins
Scranton Red Sox (1)	83	57	.593	1	150,839	Nemo Leibold
Binghamton Triplets (5)	80	60	.571	4	103,528	Eddie Sawyer
Wilkes-Barre Barons (3)	79	61	.564	5	76,219	Earl Wolgamot
Williamsport Grays (6)	76	63	.547	7½	71,316	Spencer Abbott
Elmira Pioneers (4)	62	77	.446	21½	61,035	Ray Brubaker
Hartford Bees (9)	62	78	.443	22	68,842	Del Bissonette
Springfield Rifles	33	107	.236	51	27,552	Les Bell

Playoffs: Scranton 3 games, Wilkes-Barre 0; Binghamton 3 games, Albany 2.
Finals: Scranton 4 games, Binghamton 1.

BA: Steve Souchock, Binghamton, .315
Runs: Steve Souchock, Binghamton, 94
Hits: Irvin Hall, Williamsport, 158
RBIs: Steve Souchock, Binghamton, 91

HRs: Ralph Kiner, Albany, 14
Wins: Xavier Rescigno, Albany, 23
SOs: Allie Reynolds, Wilkes-Barre, 193
ERA: Allie Reynolds, Wilkes-Barre, 1.56

B Interstate League
President: Arthur H. Ehlers

Standings	W	L	Pct.	GB	Manager
Hagerstown Owls (4)	80	57	.584	—	Dutch Dorman
Wilmington Blue Rocks (6)	79	57	.581	½	Herb Brett
Harrisburg Senators (15)	69	68	.504	11	Danny Taylor
Allentown Wings (16)	68	69	.496	12	Benny Borgmann
Lancaster Red Roses	59	78	.431	21	Tom Oliver
Trenton Senators (14)	56	82	.406	24½	Lefty Lloyd/Jack Casey/Tony Rensa

Playoffs: Hagerstown 3 games, Harrisburg 1; Wilmington 3 games, Allentown 1.
Finals: Wilmington 4 games, Hagerstown 1.

BA: Edward LaVigne, Allentown, .319
Runs: Thomas Koval, Allentown, 90
Hits: Edward LaVigne, Allentown, 159
RBIs: Edward LaVigne, Allentown, 95

HRs: Thomas Koval, Allentown, 27
Wins: Freddy Schmidt, Allentown, 19
SOs: Alfred Jarlett, Harrisburg, 148
ERA: Royce Lint, Harrisburg, 1.44

B Piedmont League
President: Ralph Daughton

Standings	W	L	Pct.	GB	Manager
Greensboro Red Sox (1)	78	53	.595	—	Heinie Manush
Portsmouth Cubs (11)	80	55	.593	—	Tony Lazzeri
Richmond Colts	74	60	.552	5½	Ben Chapman
Charlotte Hornets (8)	70	62	.530	8½	Harry Smythe
Durham Bulls (10)	65	70	.481	15	Bruno Betzel
Asheville Tourists (16)	61	77	.442	20½	Bill DeLancey
Norfolk Tars (5)	57	79	.419	23½	Buzz Boyle
Winston-Salem Twins (4)	52	81	.391	27	Jack Tighe/Al Unser

Playoffs: Greensboro 4 games, Charlotte 0; Portsmouth 4 games, Richmond 3.
Finals: Greensboro 4 games, Portsmouth 2.

BA: Luis Olmo, Richmond, .337
Runs: Luis Olmo, Richmond, 89
Hits: Luis Olmo, Richmond, 170
RBIs: Luis Olmo, Richmond, 92

HRs: Luis Olmo, Richmond, 10
      Jim Mathews, Winston-Salem, 10
Wins: Joe Ostrowski, Greensboro, 21
SOs: Woody Johnson, Portsmouth, 167
ERA: Walter Dubiel, Norfolk, 1.62

B South Atlantic League
President: Dr. E.M. Wilder

Standings	W	L	Pct.	GB	Manager
Charleston Rebels	85	52	.620	—	Cecil Rhodes
Macon Peaches (11)	81	57	.587	4½	Milt Stock
Jacksonville Tars (13)	75	59	.560	8½	Babe Ganzel
Columbia Reds (12)	66	68	.493	17½	Clarence "Cap" Crossley
Savannah Indians	66	72	.478	19½	Martin "Chick" Autry
Greenville Spinners	61	74	.452	23	Eddie Phillips
Columbus Red Birds (16)	58	80	.420	27½	Harrison Wickel
Augusta Tigers (5)	54	84	.391	31½	Alton Biggs/Wally Schang

Playoffs: Charleston 4 games, Jacksonville 1; Macon 4 games, Columbia 1.
Finals: Macon 4 games, Charleston 2.

All-Star Team: 1B-Roy Zimmerman, Greenville; **2B**-James Martin, Columbia; **3B**-Alexander Pecora, Jacksonville; **SS**-Harold Blackstock, Savannah; **OF**-Hugh Todd, Jacksonville; Vic Bradford, Jacksonville; Jack Barnes, Savannah; **C**-James Pruett, Savannah; **Util**-Alton Biggs, Augusta; **P**-Mack Stewart, Charleston; Adrian Zabala, Jacksonville; **Manager**-Milt Stock, Macon.

BA: Vic Bradford, Jacksonville, .342
Runs: Vic Bradford, Jacksonville, 113
Hits: Vic Bradford, Jacksonville, 187
RBIs: Vic Bradford, Jacksonville, 107
      Hugh Todd, Jacksonville, 107

HRs: Vic Bradford, Jacksonville, 13
Wins: Mack Stewart, Charleston, 24
SOs: William Ayers, Savannah, 143
ERA: Jake Levy, Macon, 1.85

B Southeastern League
President: Pat Moulton

Standings	W	L	Pct.	GB	Manager
Montgomery Rebels	95	50	.655	—	William Cronin
Mobile Shippers (16)	80	60	.571	12½	Tommy West/Adel White
Jackson Senators	72	69	.511	21	Harry Taylor
Anniston Rams	67	76	.489	27	Dee Moore/Merritt Cain
Pensacola Fliers	59	84	.413	35	Buster Chatham/Jake Baker
Meridian Eagles	55	89	.382	39½	Rip Fanning/Andrew Reese

Playoffs: Montgomery 4 games, Anniston 1; Jackson 4 games, Mobile 1.
Finals: Montgomery 4 games, Jackson 2.

BA: A.C. Phillips, Mobile, .348
Runs: Paul Armstrong, Montgomery, 111
      Marion DeJarnett, Meridian, 111
Hits: Paul Armstrong, Montgomery, 189
RBIs: Hugh Holliday, Anniston/
      Montgomery, 114

HRs: Al Simononis, Mobile, 18
Wins: James McClure, Jackson, 20
      Roy Walker, Montgomery, 20
SOs: James McClure, Jackson, 152
ERA: James McClure, Jackson, 2.03

B Three-I League
President: Tom Fairweather

Standings	W	L	Pct.	GB	Manager
Cedar Rapids Raiders (3)	74	43	.632	—	Oliver Marquardt
Springfield Browns (7)	67	48	.583	6	James Adair
Evansville Bees (9)	65	54	.546	10	Bob Coleman
Madison Blues (11)	55	62	.470	19	Walter Millies
Waterloo Hawks (2)	47	71	.398	27½	Johnny Mostil
Decatur Commodores (16)	45	75	.375	30½	Adel White/Tony Kaufman

Playoffs: Cedar Rapids 3 games, Evansville 2, Madison 3 games, Springfield 1.
Finals: Cedar Rapids 3 games, Madison 0.

BA: Mizzell Platt, Madison, .395
Runs: Blas Monaco, Cedar Rapids, 95
Hits: Robert "Ducky" Detweiler,
      Evansville, 149
RBIs: Pat Seerey, Cedar Rapids, 91

HRs: Pat Seerey, Cedar Rapids, 33
Wins: Bryan Stephens, Cedar Rapids, 20
SOs: Leonard Perme, Waterloo, 204
ERA: John Pavlick, Springfield, 2.96

B Western International League
President: Robert B. Abel

Standings	W	L	Pct.	GB	Manager
Vancouver Capilanos (11)	82	56	.594	—	Don Osborn
Tacoma Tigers	77	64	.546	6½	Horace "Pip" Koehler
Salem Senators	60	74	.448	20	Charles Peterson
Spokane Indians	58	83	.411	25½	Raymond Jacobs

Playoffs: None.

BA: Jack Richards, Salem, .351
Runs: Art Lilly, Tacoma, 100
Hits: Clarence Maddern, Vancouver, 178
RBIs: Vic Buccola, Spokane, 97

HRs: Murray Abbott, Vancouver, 17
Wins: Don Osborn, Vancouver, 22
SOs: Chet Johnson, Tacoma, 177
ERA: Don Osborn, Vancouver, 1.63

C California League
President: W.R. "Bill" Schroeder

Standings	W	L	Pct.	GB	Manager
Santa Barbara Saints (10)	43	24	.642	—	John "Bud" Clancy
San Jose Owls	35	32	.552	8	Goldie Holt
Fresno Cardinals (16)	34	33	.507	9	Lou Scoffic
Bakersfield Badgers	22	45	.338	21	Jack Colbern

The league suspended operations June 28.

All-Star Team: 1B-John "Bud" Clancy, Santa Barbara; **2B**-Hayden Greer, Santa Barbara; **3B**-Phil Salstrom, San Jose; **SS**-James Estrada, Santa Barbara; **OF**-Salvador Taormina, San Jose; Lou Scoffic, Fresno; Ed Harrison, San Jose; **C**-Jerry Gardner, Fresno; **P**-Walter Olson, Santa Barbara.

BA: Salvador Taormina, San Jose, .357
Runs: Hayden Greer, Santa Barbara, 60
Hits: Charles Sylvester, Santa Barbara, 93
RBIs: Charles Sylvester, Santa Barbara, 48
      James Warner, Fresno, 48

HRs: Ed Nulty, Santa Barbara, 10
Wins: Don Belton, San Jose, 11
      Brad Trine, Fresno, 11
SOs: Vic Lombardi, Santa Barbara, 114
ERA: Rex Cecil, Bakersfield, 2.09

C Canadian-American League
President: Rev. Harold J. Martin

Standings	W	L	Pct.	GB	Attend.	Manager
Amsterdam Rugmakers (5)	77	46	.626	—	36,627	Paul O'Malley/Shakey Cain
Gloversville-Johnstown Glovers (7)	67	54	.554	9	46,957	Billy Hornsby

	W	L	Pct.	GB		Manager
Utica Braves	66	54	.550	9½	83,443	Red Marion
Oneonta Indians (1)	68	56	.548	9½	34,411	Emil Barnes
Pittsfield Electrics (4)	63	62	.504	15	34,411	Shano Collins/Rabbit Moore/ Vincent "Moon" Mullen
Trois Rivieres Renards	56	66	.459	20½	30,766	Justin Keenoy/Admiral Martin/ George O'Neil
Quebec Athletics	55	67	.451	21½	46,569	Mel Simons/Roland Gladu/ Charlie Small
Rome Colonels (14)	38	85	.309	39	19,819	John "Bunny" Griffiths/ Phil Clark

Playoffs: Amsterdam 4 games, Gloversville-Johnstown 3; Oneonta 4 games, Utica 1.
Finals: Oneonta 4 games, Amsterdam 3.

BA: Reggie Otero, Utica, .364
Runs: Lloyd Moore, Pittsfield, 106
Hits: Costic Navrocki, Pittsfield, 173
RBIs: Costic Navrocki, Pittsfield, 104

HRs: Joe Morjoseph, Gloversville-Johnstown, 20
Wins: Jodie Phipps, Utica, 20
SOs: Earl Jones, Gloversville-Johnstown, 222
ERA: Ernest Thomasson, Pittsfield, 2.62

C Middle Atlantic League
President: Elmer M. Daily

Standings	W	L	Pct.	GB	Manager
Charleston Senators (3)	75	51	.595	—	Jack Knight
Dayton Ducks (10)	74	53	.583	1½	Paul Chervinko/Howard "Ducky" Holmes
Canton Terriers (1)	68	61	.527	8½	Floyd Patterson
Erie Sailors	63	65	.492	13	Kerby Farrell
Springfield Cardinals (16)	59	71	.454	18	Walter Alston
Zanesville Cubs (11)	46	84	.354	31	Jackie Warner

Attendance: Charleston, 110,000

Playoffs: Canton 3 games, Charleston 0; Erie 3 games, Dayton 2.
Finals: Erie 4 games, Canton 0.

BA: Como Cotelle, Erie, .327
Runs: Sam Gentile, Canton, 79
Hits: Sam Gentile, Canton, 149
RBIs: Walter Alston, Springfield, 90

HRs: Walter Alston, Springfield, 12
Wins: Bob Kuzava, Charleston, 21
SOs: Jack Clifton, Canton, 170
ERA: A. Reichert, Dayton, 1.50

C Mountain State League
President: Robert T. Caldwell

Standings	W	L	Pct.	GB	Manager
Huntington Jewels (7)	82	42	.661	—	Charles Lucas/Arthur Scharein
Welch Miners (9)	67	55	.549	14	Don Manno
Williamson Red Birds (16)	66	58	.532	16	Ollie Vanek
Ashland Colonels (11)	60	67	.472	23½	Eddie Hock
Bluefield Blue-Greys	55	69	.443	27	John Gooch
Logan Indians	40	79	.335	39½	Grover Hartley/Charles Hoffman

Playoffs: Ashland 2 games, Williamson 0; Huntington 2 games, Welch 1.
Finals: Ashland 4 games, Huntington 1.

BA: Don Manno, Welch, .381
Runs: Don Manno, Welch, 136
Hits: Don Manno, Welch, 174
RBIs: Kenneth Wood, Welch, 126
HRs: Don Manno, Welch, 34

Wins: Robert Peterson, Huntington, 17
    Robert Raney, Huntington, 17
SOs: Robert Raney, Huntington, 146
Pct: Robert Peterson, Huntington, .810, 17-4

C Northern League
President: Herman D. White

Standings	W	L	Pct.	GB	Manager
Eau Claire Bears	81	41	.664	—	Wilfred "Rosy" Ryan
Winnipeg Maroons	74	38	.661	5	Ivy Griffin
Wausau Timberjacks (3)	67	56	.545	12½	Wally Gilbert
Sioux Falls Canaries	57	60	.487	19½	Joe Bosse
Superior Blues (2)	58	62	.483	20	Art Haugher
Duluth Dukes (16)	56	69	.448	24½	Eddie Malone
Fargo-Moorhead Twins	54	68	.443	25	Mike Blazo/Ben Tincup
Grand Forks Chiefs (2)	31	84	.270	46½	Bruno Haas

Playoffs: Wausau 4 games, Eau Claire 1; Winnipeg 2 games, Sioux Falls 2. Wausau disbanded September 13 and the Winnipeg-Sioux Falls series was extended for the finals.
Finals: Winnipeg 5 games, Sioux Falls 4.

BA: Herb Conyers, Wausau, .362
Runs: Edmund Mutryn, Wausau, 113
Hits: Herb Conyers, Wausau, 158
RBIs: Edmund Mutryn, Wausau, 137

HRs: Edmund Mutryn, Wausau, 31
Wins: Vern Johnson, Eau Claire, 18
SOs: J.R. Hanna, Duluth, 223
ERA: Robert Peterson, Winnipeg, 2.33

C Pioneer League
President: J.P. Halliwell

Standings	W	L	Pct.	GB	Manager
Pocatello Cardinals*(16)	72	46	.610	—	Nick Cullop
Boise Pilots**	68	51	.571	4½	Jim Keesey
Idaho Falls Russets	60	60	.500	13	Lou Garland
Salt Lake City Bees	55	63	.466	17	Andy Harrington
Twin Falls Cowboys	51	67	.432	21	Tony Robello
Ogden Reds (12)	50	69	.420	22½	Bill McCorry

Playoff: Pocatello 4 games, Boise 3.

BA: Willie Enos, Salt Lake City, .340
Runs: George Valine, Pocatello, 115
Hits: Al Korhonen, Boise, 165
RBIs: Willie Enos, Salt Lake City, 105
HRs: Tony Robello, Twin Falls, 20

Wins: Frank Lamanske, Boise, 23
SOs: Manuel Vargas, Pocatello, 199
ERA: John Hetki, Ogden, 2.24
Pct: Frank Lamanske, Boise, .742, 23-8

C Virginia League
President: C.R. Williams

Standings	W	L	Pct.	GB	Manager
Pulaski Counts	79	47	.627	—	Jack Crosswhite
Lynchburg Senators	74	51	.592	4½	Wes Farrell
Petersburg Rebels	74	52	.587	5	Steve Mizerak
Newport News Builders (6)	62	67	.483	18½	Harry Chozen
Salem-Roanoke Friends	59	69	.461	21	Vernon Mackie
Staunton Presidents	32	94	.254	47	Taylor Sanford

Playoffs: Lynchburg 4 games, Newport News 2; Pulaski 4 games, Petersburg 2.
Finals: Pulaski 4 games, Lynchburg 2.

BA: Wes Ferrell, Lynchburg, .361
Runs: Ray Rudisill, Pulaski, 108
Hits: James Blair, Petersburg, 167
RBIs: James Blair, Petersburg, 103

HRs: Wes Ferrell, Lynchburg, 31
Wins: Everett Fagan, Pulaski, 20
SOs: Ed Haswell, Lynchburg, 212
ERA: Ted Garbee, Lynchburg, 1.97

C Western Association
President: Tom Fairweather

Standings	W	L	Pct.	GB	Manager
Topeka Owls**	80	53	.602	—	William Wilson
Muskogee Reds	76	58	.567	4½	Jack Mealey
Ft. Smith Giants*(13)	68	63	.519	11	Fred Lindstrom
Springfield Cardinals (16)	62	70	.470	17½	Clifton "Runt" Marr
Joplin Miners (5)	59	75	.440	21½	Elmer "Doc" Bennett
Hutchinson Pirates (15)	50	76	.397	26½	Walter Holke

Playoff: Ft. Smith 4 games, Topeka 3.

BA: Harry Heslet, Joplin, .343
Runs: Harry Clements, Muskogee, 104
Hits: Harry Clements, Muskogee, 188
RBIs: Mal Stevens, Muskogee, 93

HRs: Mal Stevens, Muskogee, 20
Wins: Roy "Tex" Sanner, Topeka, 20
SOs: Roy "Tex" Sanner, Topeka, 204
Pct: Frank Tincup, Topeka, .783, 18-5

D Appalachian League
President: J. Ross Edgemon

Standings	W	L	Pct.	GB	Manager
Bristol Twins***(13)	71	36	.664	—	Hal Gruber
Elizabethton Betsy Red Sox	60	47	.565	11	Hobe Brummitt
Kingsport Dodgers (10)	55	51	.519	15½	Merle Settlemire
Johnson City Cardinals (16)	42	67	.385	30	Mercer Harris
Newport Canners@(8)	19	28	.404	NA	Red Lucas
Greeneville Burley Cubs#(9)	9	27	.250	NA	Dale Alexander

#Greeneville disbanded June 14.
@Newport disbanded June 26.

Playoffs: Bristol 2 games, Kingsport 1; Elizabethton 2 games, Johnson City 1.
Finals: Bristol 2 games, Elizabethton 0.

All-Star Team: 1B-Edward Zebro, Kingsport; **2B**-Oscar McClure, Bristol; **3B**-Mercer Harris, Johnson City; **SS**-Hal Gruber, Bristol; **OF**-Lew Flick, Elizabethton; Maurice Cook, Bristol; Jack DiGraziano, Bristol; **C**-Andy Seminick, Elizabethton; **Util**-Stanford Wolfson, Johnson City; **P**-Forrest Zeiger, Bristol; Paul Minner, Elizabethton; **Manager**-Hal Gruber, Bristol.

BA: Lew Flick, Elizabethton, .339
Runs: Jack DiGraziano, Bristol, 79
Hits: Lew Flick, Elizabethton, 143
RBIs: Jack DiGraziano, Bristol, 79

HRs: Andy Seminick, Elizabethton, 15
Wins: Paul Minner, Elizabethton, 18
SOs: C.R. Larimer, Elizabethton, 144
ERA: Paul Minner, Elizabethton, 1.41

D Bi-State League
President: Dr. T.S. Wilson

Standings	W	L	Pct.	GB	Manager
Wilson Tobs	69	53	.566	—	Bill Herring
Sanford Spinners	62	59	.512	6½	Frank Rodgers
Rocky Mount Rocks	63	60	.512	6½	George Ferrell
Burlington Bees	62	62	.500	8	Rube Wilson
Leaksville-Draper-Spray Triplets	57	66	.463	12½	Cecil "Zip" Payne
Danville-Schoolfield Leafs (1)	54	67	.446	14½	Elmer Yoter

Playoffs: Rocky Mount 4 games, Wilson 3; Sanford 4 games, Burlington 1.
Finals: Rocky Mount 4 games, Sanford 1.

BA: Richard Hoyle, Wilson, .338
Runs: Richard Hoyle, Wilson, 108
Hits: George Biershenk, Rocky Mount, 151
RBIs: George Ferrell, Rocky Mount, 105
HRs: Harry Soufas, Rocky Mount, 29

Wins: Charles Cuellar, Leaksville-Draper-Spray, 22
SOs: Charles Cuellar, Leaksville-Draper-Spray, 204
ERA: Charles Cuellar, Leaksville-Draper-Spray, 1.67

BA: Everett Johnston, Union City, .388
Runs: Jack McQuiellen, Hopkinsville, 52
Lloyd Maloney, Jackson, 52
Hits: Robert Churchill, Bowling Green, 66
RBIs: Ernie Ankrom, Jackson, 54

HRs: Robert Churchill, Bowling Green, 9
Tony Kvedar, Hopkinsville, 9
Wins: Vernon Curtis, Hopkinsville, 10
Edward Hoffman, Bowling Green, 10
SOs: Vernon Curtis, Hopkinsville, 139
ERA: Lloyd Fisher, Fulton, 0.78

D Evangeline League
President: A. Wilmont Dalferes

Standings	W	L	Pct.	GB	Manager
Natchez Giants	29	10	.744	—	Herschel Bobo
Alexandria Aces	22	17	.564	7	Conrad Flippen
Port Arthur Tarpons	18	22	.450	11½	Harry Strohm/Carl Kott
Lake Charles Skippers	16	22	.421	12½	Joe Bratcher
Lafayette White Sox#	15	16	.484	NA	Carl Kott
New Iberia Cardinals#	9	22	.290	NA	Woody Fair

#Lafayette and New Iberia disbanded May 22.
The league disbanded May 30.

BA: Gene Hodge, Lake Charles, .377
Runs: George Bennington, Natchez, 34
David Sarver, Port Arthur, 34
Hits: Gene Hodge, Lake Charles, 61
RBIs: Paul Moore, Lake Charles, 25

HRs: Clary Hack, Port Arthur, 3
Wins: Cy Carbon, Natchez, 9
SOs: Cy Carbon, Natchez, 65
Pct: Cy Carbon, Natchez, 1.000, 9-0

D Florida East Coast League
President: J.B. Lemon

Standings	W	L	Pct.	GB	Manager
Orlando Nationals	19	9	.679	—	Robert Overstreet
Miami Beach Flamingos	17	10	.630	1½	Max Rosenfield
DeLand Red Hats	13	13	.500	5	Bill Cates
Ft. Pierce Bombers	12	14	.462	6	Russ Maxcy
Miami Seminoles	12	15	.444	6½	Harry Hughes
West Palm Beach Indians	9	18	.333	9½	Al Reitz
Ft. Lauderdale Tarpons@	4	3	.571	NA	Herb Thomas
Cocoa Fliers#	0	4	.000	NA	Burl Munsell

#Cocoa disbanded April 21.
@Ft. Lauderdale disbanded April 25.
The league disbanded May 14.

BA: Bill Hansen, Ft. Pierce, .370
Runs: John Morris, Orlando, 27
Hits: Jim Milner, Miami Beach, 38
RBIs: William Tracy, DeLand, 23

HRs: Fred Leonhardt, DeLand, 2
Pete Burnette, West Palm Beach, 2
Armando Dominguez, Orlando, 2
Wins: Ellaire "Larry" Baldwin, Miami, 6
SOs: Scott Carey, Orlando, 45
ERA: Willard Eckenroth, DeLand, 1.65

D Georgia-Florida League
President: W.T. Anderson

Standings	W	L	Pct.	GB	Manager
Valdosta Trojans (10)	81	45	.643	—	Stewart Hofferth/Clancy Odell
Waycross Bears	72	54	.571	9	Al Leitz
Moultrie Packers (15)	72	54	.571	9	F.M. McVay
Dothan Browns (7)	64	62	.508	17	Holt "Cat" Milner
Tallahassee Capitols	62	64	.492	19	Will Good
Albany Cardinals (16)	56	70	.444	25	Joe Cusick
Americus Pioneers (11)	49	77	.389	32	Jerry Tiemann
Cordele Reds (12)	48	78	.381	33	Frank O'Rourke

Playoffs: Waycross defeated Moultrie in one game playoff for second place. Waycross 3 games, Dothan 0; Valdosta 3 games, Moultrie 1.
Finals: Waycross 4 games, Valdosta 1.

BA: Steve Summerhill, Valdosta, .350
Runs: Chuck Diering, Albany, 102
Hits: Steve Summerhill, Valdosta, 165
RBIs: Dave Pluss, Valdosta, 105
HRs: Dave Pluss, Valdosta, 9

Wins: Paul Wright, Moultrie, 20
William Kirksey, Tallahassee, 20
SOs: Omar "Turk" Lown, Valdosta, 204
ERA: Kip Sauerbrun, Moultrie, 1.83

D Kitty League
President: Shelby Peace

Standings	W	L	Pct.	GB	Manager
Fulton Tigers (4)	30	14	.682	—	Vincent "Moon" Mullen
Bowling Green Barons	31	15	.674	—	Ellis "Mike" Powers
Jackson Generals	29	19	.604	3	Mickey O'Neil
Hopkinsville Hoppers	23	23	.500	8	Mel Ivy
Owensboro Oilers (1)	16	32	.333	16	Wally Schang
Union City Greyhounds (16)	9	35	.205	21	Everett Johnston

The league disbanded June 19.

D North Carolina State League
President: C.M. Llewellyn

Standings	W	L	Pct.	GB	Manager
Concord Weavers	64	34	.653	—	Herman Watts
Mooresville Moors	61	39	.610	4	John Hicks
Thomasville Tommies (3)	61	39	.610	4	Jim Gruzdis/Woody Mabry
Landis Senators	59	39	.602	5	Reid Gowan/H.M. Christopher
Lexington Indians	55	44	.556	9½	Baxter Jordan
Statesville Owls	48	51	.485	16½	Jim Poole
Salisbury Giants (13)	29	69	.296	35	John Heving
Hickory Rebels	18	80	.184	46	Charles "Bud" Shaney

Playoffs: Mooresville was awarded second place by a coin toss. Thomasville 3 games, Concord 1; Landis 3 games, Mooresville 0.
Finals: Thomasville 4 games, Landis 3.

BA: Jim Gruzdis, Thomasville, .418
Runs: Willard Mauney, Concord, 98
Hits: Norman Small, Mooresville, 144
RBIs: Norman Small, Mooresville, 107

HRs: Norman Small, Mooresville, 32
Wins: Herman Drefs, Concord, 23
SOs: Harry Jordan, Mooresville, 175
ERA: Woodrow Crowson, Thomasville, 1.60

D Pennsylvania State Association
President: Elmer M. Daily

Standings	W	L	Pct.	GB	Manager
Butler Yankees**(5)	69	41	.627	—	Dallas Warren
Johnstown Johnnies*(10)	65	49	.570	6	Jay Kirke, Jr.
Oil City Oilers (15)	48	63	.432	21½	Frank Oceak
Washington Red Birds (16)	42	71	.372	28½	George Jenkins/Moose Fralick

Playoffs: Washington 3 games, Oil City 0; Butler 3 games, Johnstown 1.
Finals: Butler 3 games, Washington 2.

BA: Dallas Warren, Butler, .359
Runs: Al Gionfriddo, Oil City, 112
Hits: J.L. Jerina, Butler, 151
RBIs: J.L. Jerina, Butler, 106
HRs: Don Bollweg, Washington, 25

Wins: M.R. Santora, Johnstown, 18
Richard Starr, Butler, 18
SOs: Henry Koch, Washington, 172
ERA: Henry Koch, Washington, 3.24

D PONY League
President: Robert C. Stedler

Standings	W	L	Pct.	GB	Attend.	Manager
Jamestown Falcons (4)	84	41	.672	—	143,016	Greg Mulleavy
Olean Oilers (10)	82	42	.661	1½	38,231	Jake Pitler
Batavia Clippers (3)	72	53	.576	12	38,014	Jack Sanford
Hornell Pirates (15)	65	60	.520	19	49,107	Thomas "Poke" Whalen/Leo Mackey
Wellsville Yankees (5)	65	60	.520	19	30,675	Walt VanGrofski
Bradford Bees (9)	56	68	.452	27½	34,486	Jack Burns
Lockport White Sox (2)	39	85	.315	44½	40,019	Joe Martin/William Prince
Hamilton Red Wings (16)	36	90	.286	48½	34,130	Roy Pfleger/Ken Blackman/Joe Sugden

Playoffs: Hornell defeated Wellsville in a one game playoff for fourth place. Jamestown 3 games, Hornell 0; Olean 3 games, Batavia 0.
Finals: Jamestown 4 games, Olean 2.

BA: John Newman, Jamestown, .353
Runs: Pat McNair, Jamestown, 124
Hits: George Lerchen, Jamestown, 167
RBIs: Connie Creedon, Bradford, 119
HRs: John Newman, Jamestown, 27

Wins: Charlie Schupp, Jamestown, 24
SOs: John "Bubber" Moore, Wellsville, 258
ERA: Charlie Schupp, Jamestown, 2.34
Pct: Charlie Schupp, Jamestown, .774, 24-7

D West Texas-New Mexico League
President: Milton E. Price

Standings	W	L	Pct.	GB	Manager
Clovis Pioneers*	52	19	.732	—	Grover Seitz
Lamesa Dodgers (10)	43	27	.614	8½	Joe Tate
Amarillo Gold Sox	38	29	.567	12	Claude Jonnard
Pampa Oilers	36	32	.529	14½	William Ratliff
Borger Gassers	33	39	.458	19½	Hugh Willingham
Lubbock Hubbers**	30	42	.417	22½	Monty Stratton
Albuquerque Dukes@	25	30	.455	NA	Dixie Howell/E. Miller
Wichita Falls Spudders/ Big Spring Pirates#	8	47	.145	NA	George Milstead

#Wichita Falls (4-14) moved to Big Spring May 22. The franchise was turned back to the league about June 13. The team played only road games and went by "Pirates". The Pirates withdrew June 20.

1942

@Albuquerque withdrew June 23.
The league disbanded July 5.
Attendance: Amarillo, 14,027; Total, 67,399.

BA: Frank Warren, Borger, .402
Runs: Leroy Koenig, Lubbock, 88
Hits: Vincent Castino, Lubbock, 106
RBIs: Frank Hargrove, Amarillo, 84
HRs: Frank Hargrove, Amarillo, 22

Wins: Kenneth Wyatt, Clovis, 17
SOs: Kenneth Wyatt, Clovis, 129
ERA: Kenneth Wyatt, Clovis, 2.09
Pct: Kenneth Wyatt, Clovis, 1.000, 17-0

D Wisconsin State League
President: Herman D. White

Standings	W	L	Pct.	GB	Manager
Sheboygan Indians	73	35	.676	—	Joe Hauser
Green Bay Bluejays	74	37	.667	½	Dick Smith
Fond du Lac Panthers (5)	53	49	.520	17	Ray Powell
Appleton Papermakers (3)	49	54	.476	21½	Ed Dancisak/Dutch Zwilling
Janesville Cubs (11)	51	58	.468	22½	Ed Stumpf
Oshkosh Giants (13)	48	59	.449	24½	Fred Schulte
Wisconsin Rapids White Sox (2)	42	63	.400	29½	Frank Parenti/Roger Reinhart
La Crosse Blackhawks (16)	36	71	.336	36½	Ed Konetchy/Lou Scoffic

Playoffs: Sheboygan 3 games, Fond du Lac 2; Green Bay 3 games, Appleton 2.
Finals: Sheboygan 4 games, Green Bay 2.

BA: William Deininger, Sheboygan, .396
Runs: William Deininger, Sheboygan, 99
Hits: William Deininger, Sheboygan, 149
RBIs: Ordie Timm, Green Bay, 110

HRs: Clifford Aberson, Janesville, 22
Wins: Giles Knowles, Sheboygan, 21
SOs: Giles Knowles, Sheboygan, 261
ERA: Don Opperman, Fond du Lac, 2.20

Ind Mexican League
President: Alejandro Aguilar Reyes

Standings	W	L	Pct.	GB	Manager
Torreon Algodoneros	48	40	.545	—	Martin Dihigo
Monterrey Industriales	46	41	.529	1½	Lazaro Salazar
Tampico Alijadores	44	40	.524	2	Manuel Arroyo
Puebla Angeles	42	45	.483	5½	Jose Luis Gomez/Guillermo Ornelas
Mexico City Diablos Rojos	40	47	.460	7½	Ernesto Carmona
Veracruz Azules	39	46	.459	7½	Agustin Bejerano

BA: Monte Irvin, Veracruz, .397
Hits: Carlos Colas, Torreon, 128
RBIs: Silvio Garcia, Mexico City, 83
HRs: Monte Irvin, Veracruz, 20

Wins: Jesus Valenzuela, Tampico, 25
SOs: Martin Dihigo, Torreon, 211
ERA: Martin Dihigo, Torreon, 2.53

1942 Interleague Post Season Play

World Series
St. Louis (National) 4 games, New York (American) 1

Junior World Series
Columbus (American Association) 4 games, Syracuse (International) 1
Total Attendance: 21,229

Dixie Series
Nashville (Southern Association) 4 games, Shreveport (Texas) 2
Total Attendance: 23,534

1942 Major League Farm Systems

American League

1 Boston (7): Louisville, Scranton, Greensboro, Oneonta, Canton, Danville-Schoolfield, Owensboro.
2 Chicago (6): St. Paul, Waterloo, Grand Forks, Superior, Lockport, Wisconsin Rapids.
3 Cleveland (8): Baltimore, Wilkes-Barre, Cedar Rapids, Charleston (WV), Wausau, Thomasville, Batavia, Appleton.
4 Detroit (8): Buffalo, Beaumont, Elmira, Hagerstown, Winston-Salem, Pittsfield, Fulton, Jamestown.
5 New York (10): Kansas City, Newark, Binghamton, Norfolk, Augusta, Amsterdam, Joplin, Butler, Wellsville, Fond du Lac.
6 Philadelphia (4): Toronto, Williamsport, Wilmington, Newport News.
7 St. Louis (6): Toledo, San Antonio, Springfield (IL), Gloversville-Johnstown, Huntington, Dothan.
8 Washington (3): Chattanooga, Charlotte, Newport.

National League

9 Boston (5): Hartford, Evansville, Welch, Greeneville, Bradford.
10 Brooklyn (10): Montreal, San Francisco, Durham, Santa Barbara, Dayton, Kingsport, Valdosta, Johnstown, Olean, Lamesa.
11 Chicago (10): Los Angeles, Tulsa, Portsmouth, Macon, Madison, Vancouver, Zanesville, Ashland, Americus, Janesville.
12 Cincinnati (5): Syracuse, Birmingham, Columbia, Ogden, Cordele.
13 New York (7): Jersey City, Oklahoma City, Jacksonville, Ft. Smith, Bristol, Salisbury, Oshkosh.
14 Philadelphia (2): Trenton, Rome.
15 Pittsburgh (7): Toronto, Albany (NY), Harrisburg, Hutchinson, Moultrie, Oil City, Hornell.
16 St. Louis (22): Columbus (OH), Rochester, Sacramento, New Orleans, Houston, Allentown, Asheville, Columbus (GA), Mobile, Decatur, Fresno, Springfield (OH), Williamson, Duluth, Pocatello, Springfield (MO), Johnson City, Albany (GA), Union City, Washington, Hamilton, La Crosse.

1942 No-Hitters

Date	Pitcher	Team	League	Opponent	Score
4-12	Harold Turpin	Seattle	Pacific Coast	San Diego	2-0
4-25	Robert Vales	Mobile	Southeastern	Pensacola	
5-17	Tony Jeli	Twin Falls	Pioneer	Pocatello	4-2
5-26	Joe Feria	Twin Falls	Pioneer	Salt Lake City	3-0 (6)
6-3	Joe Nelson	Norfolk	Piedmont	Richmond	0-1
6-3	James Voiselle	Newport News	Virginia	Staunton	0-2 (10)
6-9	Boyd Tepler	Janesville	Wisconsin State	La Crosse	11-1
6-9	Eddie Opalach	Appleton	Wisconsin State	Wisconsin Rapids	1-0 (8)
6-9	E.M. McGlothin	Elizabethton	Appalachian	Newport	2-0
6-15	Hubert Urban	Kingsport	Appalachian	Johnson City	9-1
6-17	George Kunz	Oshkosh	Wisconsin State	Janesville	1-0
7-5	Henry "Prince" Oana	Ft. Worth	Texas	Dallas	6-0
7-8	Doyle Lade	Shreveport	Texas	San Antonio	1-0
7-12	Walter Dubiel	Norfolk	Piedmont	Durham	3-0 (7)
7-19	John McPartland	Dallas	Texas	Shreveport	3-0 (10)
7-25	Hank Behrman	Durham	Piedmont	Asheville	9-0
7-28	Lou Bevil	Chattanooga	Southern Assoc.	Atlanta	3-0 (7)
8-4	Jack Robinson	Binghamton	Eastern	Wilkes-Barre	7-0 (7)
8-4	Don Black	Petersburg	Virginia	Pulaski	4-0
8-9	Roy "Tex" Sanner	Topeka	Western Assoc.	Joplin	9-0 (7)
8-11	Joe Berry	Tulsa	Texas	Oklahoma City	1-0
8-21	Jack Clifton	Burlington	Bi-State	Danville-Schoolfield	
8-24	Jack Casey	Trenton	Interstate	Hagerstown	2-3
8-26	Bill Koy	Wilson	Bi-State	Leaksville-Spray-Draper	
8-27	Eddie Opalach	Appleton	Wisconsin State	Oshkosh	7-2 (7)
9-1	Allie Reynolds	Wilkes-Barre	Eastern	Elmira	0-1 (11)
9-3	Earl Jones	Gloversville-Johnstown	Canadian-American	Rome	7-0

Number in parentheses indicates innings if other than nine.

THIS DATE IN MINOR LEAGUE HISTORY

April 16, 1942, International League openers attracted 77,222 paid admissions, led by a turnout of 55,218 in Jersey City.

April 29, 1942, The Eastern League opened the season with four 1-0 games. Wilkes-Barre, Elmira, Hartford, and Binghamton were the winners.

September 3, 1942, Southpaw Earl Jones of Gloversville-Johnstown, Canadian-American League, hurled one of the greatest games in league history. Pitching at Berkshire Park, Jones not only no-hit Rome, but he also smashed the strikeout record with 22 whiffs. Fans carried Jones from the mound and took up a collection for him, netting $70.

October 31, 1942, Billy Hebert, former second baseman/outfielder for Oakland, Pacific Coast League, became the first professional baseball player to lose his life in World War II. Hebert was killed at Henderson Field, Guadalcanal, in the Solomons.

November 12, 1942, Former major league pitcher Wes Ferrell, manager of Lynchburg, Virginia League, drew a 60 day suspension from the president of the National Association for taking his team off the field during a playoff game and for abuse of the umpire.

December 20, 1942, Major Trammell Scott, retiring president of the Southern Association, was found dead from a self-inflicted gunshot wound near Newton, Georgia, after leaving on a turkey hunt.

1943

American League
President: William Harridge

Standings	W	L	Pct.	GB	Attend.	Manager
New York Yankees............	98	56	.636	—	618,330	Joe McCarthy
Washington Senators	84	69	.549	13½	574,694	Ossie Bluege
Cleveland Indians	82	71	.536	15½	438,894	Lou Boudreau
Chicago White Sox	82	72	.532	16	508,962	Jimmy Dykes
Detroit Tigers....................	78	76	.506	20	606,287	Steve O'Neill
St. Louis Browns	72	80	.474	25	214,392	Luke Sewell
Boston Red Sox	68	84	.447	29	358,275	Joe Cronin
Philadelphia Athletics.........	49	105	.318	49	376,735	Connie Mack

BA: Luke Appling, Chicago, .328
Runs: George Case, Washington, 102
Hits: Dick Wakefield, Detroit, 200
RBIs: Rudy York, Detroit, 118
HRs: Rudy York, Detroit, 34

Wins: Spud Chandler, New York, 20
Dizzy Trout, Detroit, 20
SOs: Allie Reynolds, Cleveland, 151
ERA: Spud Chandler, New York, 1.64
Pct: Spud Chandler, New York, .833, 20-4

National League
President: Ford Frick

Standings	W	L	Pct.	GB	Attend.	Manager
St. Louis Cardinals	105	49	.682	—	517,135	Billy Southworth
Cincinnati Reds..................	87	67	.565	18	379,122	Bill McKechnie
Brooklyn Dodgers..............	81	72	.529	23½	661,739	Leo Durocher
Pittsburgh Pirates..............	80	74	.519	25	498,740	Frank Frisch
Chicago Cubs.....................	74	79	.484	30½	508,247	Jimmie Wilson
Boston Braves	68	85	.444	36½	271,289	Casey Stengel/Bob Coleman
Philadelphia Blue Jays.......	64	90	.416	41	466,975	Bucky Harris/
						Freddie Fitzsimmons
New York Giants	55	98	.359	49½	466,095	Mel Ott

BA: Stan Musial, St. Louis, .357
Runs: Arky Vaughan, Brooklyn, 112
Hits: Stan Musial, St. Louis, 220
RBIs: Bill Nicholson, Chicago, 128
HRs: Bill Nicholson, Chicago, 29

Wins: Elmer Riddle, Cincinnati, 21
Mort Cooper, St. Louis, 21
Rip Sewell, Pittsburgh, 21
SOs: John Vander Meer, Cincinnati, 174
ERA: Howie Pollet, St. Louis, 1.75
Pct: Mort Cooper, St. Louis, .724, 21-8

AA American Association
President: George Trautman

Standings	W	L	Pct.	GB	Attend.	Manager
Milwaukee Brewers............	90	61	.596	—	286,979	Charlie Grimm
Indianapolis Indians (12)....	85	67	.559	5½	215,278	Donie Bush
Columbus Red Birds (16)....	84	67	.556	6	111,398	Nick Cullop
Toledo Mud Hens (7).........	76	76	.500	14½	102,621	Jacques Fournier
Louisville Colonels (1)	70	81	.464	20	142,580	Bill Burwell
Minneapolis Millers............	67	84	.444	23	90,904	Tom Sheehan
Kansas City Blues (5).........	67	85	.441	23½	76,010	Johnny Neun
St. Paul Saints	67	85	.441	23½	82,116	Francis "Salty" Parker

Playoffs: Columbus 3 games, Milwaukee 1; Indianapolis 3 games, Toledo 2.
Finals: Columbus 3 games, Indianapolis 0.

Sporting News Manager of the Year-Nick Cullop, Columbus.

BA: Grey Clarke, Milwaukee, .346
Runs: Wayne Blackburn, Indianapolis, 114
Hits: Tony York, Milwaukee, 187
RBIs: Ted Norbert, Milwaukee, 117

HRs: Ted Norbert, Milwaukee, 25
Wins: James Trexler, Indianapolis, 19
SOs: Preacher Roe, Columbus, 136
ERA: James Trexler, Indianapolis, 2.14

AA International League
President: Frank J. Shaughnessy

Standings	W	L	Pct.	GB	Attend.	Manager
Toronto Maple Leafs (15)...	95	57	.625	—	185,456	Burleigh Grimes
Newark Bears (5)...............	85	68	.556	10½	75,206	Bill Meyer
Syracuse Chiefs (12)..........	82	71	.536	13½	129,494	Jewel Ens
Montreal Royals (10)..........	76	76	.500	19	206,507	Fresco Thompson
Rochester Red Wings (16)..	74	78	.487	21	101,382	Pepper Martin
Baltimore Orioles (3)..........	73	81	.474	23	175,760	Alphonse "Tommy" Thomas
Buffalo Bisons (4)	66	87	.431	29½	135,651	Greg Mulleavy
Jersey City Giants (13)	60	93	.392	35½	111,913	Gabby Hartnett

Playoffs: Toronto 4 games, Montreal 0; Syracuse 4 games, Newark 2.
Finals: Syracuse 4 games, Toronto 2.

MVP-Red Schoendienst, Rochester.

BA: Red Schoendienst, Rochester, .337
Runs: Frank Zak, Toronto, 101
Hits: Red Schoendienst, Rochester, 187
RBIs: George Staller, Baltimore, 98

HRs: Ed Kobesky, Buffalo, 18
Wins: Ed Elieman, Baltimore, 23
SOs: Steve Gromek, Baltimore, 188
ERA: Louis Polli, Jersey City, 1.85

AA Pacific Coast League
President: William C. Tuttle

Standings	W	L	Pct.	GB	Attend.	Manager
Los Angeles Angels (11)..	110	45	.710	—	236,642	Bill Sweeney
San Francisco Seals	89	66	.574	21	202,532	Lefty O'Doul
Seattle Rainiers	85	70	.548	25	143,447	Bill Sisler
Portland Beavers...............	79	76	.510	31	124,790	Merv Shea
Hollywood Stars	73	82	.471	37	151,035	Charlie Root
Oakland Oaks	73	82	.471	37	100,493	John Vergez
San Diego Padres	70	85	.455	40	126,576	Cedric Durst/George Detore
Sacramento Solons (16)......	41	114	.265	69	31,694	Ken Penner

Playoffs: Seattle 4 games, Los Angeles 0; San Francisco 4 games, Portland 2.
Finals: San Francisco 4 games, Seattle 2.

MVP-Andy Pafko, Los Angeles.

BA: Andy Pafko, Los Angeles, .356
Runs: Bill Schuster, Los Angeles, 117
Hits: Andy Pafko, Los Angeles, 215
RBIs: Andy Pafko, Los Angeles, 118

HRs: John Ostrowski, Los Angeles, 21
Wins: Red Lynn, Los Angeles, 21
SOs: Frank Dasso, San Diego, 154
ERA: Alpha Brazle, Sacramento, 1.69

A1 Southern Association
President: Billy Evans

Standings	W	L	Pct.	GB	Attend.	Manager
Nashville Vols*	83	55	.601	—	76,570	Larry Gilbert
New Orleans Pelicans**(10) ...	78	58	.573	4	101,600	Ray Blades
Little Rock Travelers	78	62	.557	8½	86,949	Buck Fausett
Chattanooga Lookouts/						
Montgomery Rebels#(8)..	69	70	.496	17	55,724	Sparky Olson
Knoxville Smokies	65	71	.478	19½	73,649	Buddy Lewis
Birmingham Barons (12)....	63	76	.453	20½	87,448	Johnny Riddle
Atlanta Crackers	60	79	.432	23½	124,057	Al Leitz/Harry Hughes
Memphis Chicks	56	81	.409	26½	84,965	Tommy "Doc" Prothro

#Chattanooga moved to Montgomery July 11, first home game July 25.

Playoff: Nashville 4 games, New Orleans 1.

BA: Ed Sauer, Nashville, .368
Runs: Ed Sauer, Nashville, 113
Hits: Buck Fausett, Little Rock, 205
RBIs: Mel Hicks, Nashville, 107

HRs: Cecil "Dynamite" Dunn, Knoxville, 19
Wins: Jess Danna, New Orleans, 22
SOs: Weldon West, Memphis, 134
ERA: Ed Lopat, Little Rock, 3.05

A Eastern League
President: Thomas H. Richardson

Standings	W	L	Pct.	GB	Attend.	Manager
Scranton Red Sox (1).........	87	51	.630	—	93,319	Nemo Leibold
Elmira Pioneers (6)............	79	60	.568	8½	66,717	Ray Brubaker
Hartford Bees (9)..............	77	59	.566	9	54,854	Del Bissonette
Wilkes-Barre Barons (3).....	77	61	.559	10	57,604	Tony Lazzeri
Albany Senators (15)..........	74	65	.532	13½	80,218	James "Rip" Collins
Binghamton Triplets (5)	74	66	.529	14	45,306	Eddie Sawyer
Springfield Rifles (13)........	46	88	.343	39	28,118	Spencer Abbott
Utica Braves (14)...............	37	101	.268	50	50,058	Wally Schang

Playoffs: Scranton 3 games, Hartford 1; Elmira 3 games, Wilkes-Barre 2.
Finals: Elmira 4 games, Scranton 2, one tie.

BA: Gene Woodling, Wilkes-Barre, .344
Runs: Clarence Etchison, Hartford, 109
Hits: Don Smith, Elmira, 181
RBIs: Tom Neill, Hartford, 91

HRs: Bill Nagel, Albany, 10
Wins: Chet Covington, Scranton, 21
SOs: Chet Covington, Scranton, 187
ERA: Chet Covington, Scranton, 1.51

B Interstate League
President: Arthur H. Ehlers

Standings	W	L	Pct.	GB	Manager
Lancaster Red Roses...........	83	55	.601	—	Elwood Wheaton
Hagerstown Owls (4)...........	83	57	.593	1	Eddie Phillips/Bobby Maier
Wilmington Blue Rocks (6) ..	77	61	.562	6	Dutch Dorman
York White Roses (15).......	73	66	.525	10½	John "Bunny" Griffiths
Trenton Packers (14)	64	73	.467	18½	George Ferrell
Allentown Wings (16)	35	103	.254	48	Barney Roth/Herb Brett/Thomas Koval

*Won first-half   **Won second-half   ***Won both halves
Numbers after nicknames indicate farm system.
Affiliation listed at end of year.

337

Playoffs: Lancaster 3 games, Wilmington 2; York 3 games, Hagerstown 1.
Finals: Lancaster 4 games, York 3.

BA: George Kell, Lancaster, .396
Runs: George Kell, Lancaster, 120
Hits: George Kell, Lancaster, 220
RBIs: William Burgo, Wilmington, 127
HRs: William Burgo, Wilmington, 20

Wins: Fred Clemence, York, 20
Charles Miller, Hagerstown, 20
Stephen Gerkin, Lancaster, 20
SOs: Tal Abernathy, Wilmington, 198
ERA: Norman Shope, Hagerstown/York, 2.65

B Piedmont League
President: Ralph Daughton

Standings	W	L	Pct.	GB	Manager
Portsmouth Cubs (11)	90	40	.692	—	Milt Stock
Richmond Colts	72	57	.558	17½	Larry Kinzer
Norfolk Tars (5)	66	63	.512	23½	Thomas Kain
Roanoke Red Sox (1)	62	68	.477	28	Heinie Manush
Lynchburg Cardinals (16)	54	74	.422	35	Ollie Vanek
Durham Bulls (10)	44	86	.338	46	Bruno Betzel

Playoffs: Portsmouth 4 games, Roanoke 1; Norfolk 4 games, Richmond 0.
Finals: Norfolk 4 games, Portsmouth 2.

BA: Tony Castano, Richmond, .333
Runs: William Glover, Lynchburg, 83
Hits: Wilmer Skeen, Portsmouth, 172
RBIs: Wilmer Skeen, Portsmouth, 71

HRs: Jack Phillips, Norfolk, 8
Wins: Irv Stein, Portsmouth, 24
SOs: Julio Acosta, Richmond, 208
ERA: Garland Braxton, Norfolk, 0.74

D Appalachian League
President: J. Ross Edgemon

Standings	W	L	Pct.	GB	Manager
Bristol Twins***(13)	74	35	.679	—	Hal Gruber
Kingsport Cherokees (8)	55	53	.509	18½	Neal Millard/Beattie Feathers
Erwin Aces (11)	53	53	.500	19½	Jim Poole
Johnson City Cardinals (16)	36	77	.319	40	Ken Blackman

Playoffs: Bristol 3 games, Kingsport 0; Erwin 3 games, Johnson City 1.
Finals: Erwin 4 games, Bristol 3.

All-Star Team: 1B-Perry Roberts, Kingsport; 2B-Oscar McClure, Bristol; 3B-Robert Cummins, Kingsport; SS-Hal Gruber, Bristol; OF-Lee Schulte, Bristol; John Sinnott, Kingsport; C-John Pramesa, Bristol; Util-Don Fitzpatrick, Kingsport; P-Reid Gowan, Erwin; Richard Hoover, Bristol; Manager-Hal Gruber, Bristol.

BA: Hal Gruber, Bristol, .369
Runs: Zelig Fruman, Erwin, 87
Hits: John Pramesa, Bristol, 143
RBIs: John Pramesa, Bristol, 91
HRs: Beattie Feathers, Kingsport, 9

Wins: Wayne Morris, Bristol, 13
Gene Mote, Kingsport/Erwin, 13
SOs: Bob "Sugar" Cain, Bristol, 101
Pct: Richard Hoover, Bristol, .917, 11-1

D PONY League
President: Robert C. Stedler

Standings	W	L	Pct.	GB	Attend.	Manager
Lockport Cubs (11)	65	45	.591	—	48,475	Roy Johnson
Hornell Maples (15)	60	50	.545	5	35,524	Frank Oceak

	58	51	.532	6½		
Wellsville Yankees (5)	58	51	.532	6½		Herb Brett/Sol Mishkin
Jamestown Falcons (16)	54	56	.491	11	67,738	Jack Sanford
Batavia Clippers (3)	49	61	.445	16	27,625	Earl Wolgamot
Olean Oilers (10)	43	66	.394	21½	23,288	Jake Pitler

Playoffs: Wellsville 3 games, Hornell 1; Jamestown 3 games, Lockport 0.
Finals: Wellsville 4 games, Jamestown 3.

BA: Benjamin Visan, Batavia, .369
Runs: Otis Davis, Jamestown, 116
Ray Sowins, Lockport, 116
Hits: Otis Davis, Jamestown, 156
RBIs: Ernest Hrovatic, Jamestown, 96

HRs: Carl Petroziello, Hornell, 11
Wins: Pete Gebrian, Hornell, 16
SOs: Boyd Tepler, Lockport, 254
ERA: Pete Gebrian, Hornell, 2.20
Pct: Pete Gebrian, Hornell, .842, 16-3

E Twin Ports League
President: Frank Wade

Standings	W	L	Pct.	GB	Manager
Superior Bays	11	7	.611	—	George "Red" Treadwell/John Schroeder
Duluth Marine Iron	9	7	.563	1	Wally Gilbert
Duluth Dukes	9	10	.474	2½	Bud McPherson
Duluth Heralds	5	10	.333	4½	Frank Summers

The league disbanded July 13.

BA: Wally Gilbert, Marine Iron, .456
Runs: John Schroeder, Superior, 21
Hits: John Schroeder, Superior, 27
RBIs: John Schroeder, Superior, 23

HRs: Joe Shonts, Heralds, 1
John Norlander, Dukes, 1
Wins: Ed Anderson, Marine Iron, 4
Bob Connolly, Superior, 4
SOs: Verl Westergard, Superior, 56
ERA: Verl Westergard, Superior, 2.25

Ind Mexican League
President: Crl. Octavio Ruedo Magro

Standings	W	L	Pct.	GB	Manager
Monterrey Industriales	53	37	.589	—	Lazaro Salazar
Torreon Algodoneros	51	36	.586	½	Martin Dihigo
Puebla Angeles	44	43	.506	7½	Eugenio Morin
Tampico Alijadores	41	48	.461	11½	William Wells/Santos Amaro
Veracruz Azules	39	51	.433	14	Gustavo Buenrostro/Horacio Hernandez
Mexico City Diablos Rojos	38	51	.427	14½	Jose Luis Gomez

BA: Burnis Wright, Mexico City, 366
Hits: Ray Dandridge, Veracruz, 131
RBIs: Burnis Wright, Mexico City, 70
Ray Dandridge, Veracruz, 70

HRs: Burnis Wright, Mexico City, 13
Wins: Daniel Rios, Monterrey, 20
SOs: Martin Dihigo, Torreon, 134
ERA: Vidal Lopez, Monterrey, 2.08

1943 Interleague Post Season Play

World Series
New York (American) 4 games, St. Louis (National) 1

Junior World Series
Columbus (American Association) 4 games, Syracuse (International) 1
Total Attendance: 30,578

1943 Major League Farm Systems

American League
1. Boston (3): Louisville, Scranton, Roanoke.
3. Cleveland (3): Baltimore, Wilkes-Barre, Batavia.
4. Detroit (2): Buffalo, Hagerstown.
5. New York (5): Kansas City, Newark, Binghamton, Norfolk, Wellsville.
6. Philadelphia (2): Elmira, Wilmington.
7. St. Louis (1): Toledo.
8. Washington (2): Chattanooga/Montgomery, Kingsport.

National League
9. Boston (1): Hartford.
10. Brooklyn (4): Montreal, New Orleans, Durham, Olean.
11. Chicago (4): Los Angeles, Portsmouth, Erwin, Lockport.
12. Cincinnati (3): Indianapolis, Syracuse, Birmingham.
13. New York (3): Jersey City, Springfield, Bristol.
14. Philadelphia (2): Utica, Trenton.
15. Pittsburgh (4): Toronto, Albany, York, Hornell.
16. St. Louis (7): Columbus, Rochester, Sacramento, Allentown, Lynchburg, Johnson City, Jamestown.

1943 No-Hitters

Date	Pitcher	Team	League	Opponent	Score
4-25	Rufus Gentry	Buffalo	International	Newark	1-0 (11)
5-23	Chet Covington	Scranton	Eastern	Springfield	6-0 (P)
5-31	Henry Pippen	Oakland	Pacific Coast	Sacramento	10-0 (P, 7)
6-5	Julio Acosta	Richmond	Piedmont	Portsmouth	8-0
6-10	Bob Williams	New Orleans	Southern Assoc.	Chattanooga	5-0 (7)
6-16	Bob Vetter	Jamestown	PONY	Batavia	9-0
7-22	Bob "Sugar" Cain	Bristol	Appalachian	Johnson City	3-0
8-12	Bill Sucky	Norfolk	Piedmont	Durham	1-0 (7)
8-14	Charley Haag	Binghamton	Eastern	Albany	2-0
8-17	Blix Donnelly	Rochester	International	Jersey City	4-0
9-6	Tom Ananicz	Toronto	International	Buffalo	1-0 (7)
9-11	Jack Kramer	Toledo	American Assoc.	Louisville	5-0
9-15	Walter Dubiel	Newark	International	Syracuse	3-0 (7)
	Stephen Gerkin	Lancaster	Interstate		(7)

Number in parentheses indicates innings if other than nine; "P" indicates perfect game.

THIS DATE IN MINOR LEAGUE HISTORY

April 23, 1943, Toronto and Baltimore played a 21-inning 2-2 tie in the International League.

May 4, 1943, Johnson City and Erwin staged a wild Appalachian League opener, the former club pounding out 21 hits to win 27-11. The Cardinals scored 11 runs in the first and eight in the fourth.

May 5, 1943, Tony Lazzeri made his debut as manager for Wilkes-Barre of the Eastern League. The ex-Yankee played second base as his club beat Scranton 2-0 in the Barons' home opener, before 3,041 cash customers. Lazzeri was reported to be drawing down $1,200 a month from the Cleveland organization.

May 5, 1943, Erwin, Appalachian League, which lost its opener to Johnson City 27-11 the previous day, beat the Cardinals by the same score. In its next game, Erwin scored an 11-10 win over Bristol, for a total of 49 runs scored in three games.

May 8, 1943, Bill Norman hit three consecutive home runs as Milwaukee, American Association, combed four St. Paul pitchers for 24 hits, including seven home runs, five doubles, and 12 singles for 50 total bases, breaking the old league record of 49. Milwaukee overwhelmed the Saints 20-0 in the morning game. Norman added two singles for a 5-for-5 performance and scored five runs. Club President Bill "Sport Shirt" Veeck announced that the Brewers would play other morning games in the future for the benefit of war workers. Free milk, doughnuts and coffee were distributed by ushers garbed in gaudy nightshirts. The game drew about 1,500, many of whom were women war workers attired in slacks.

May 19, 1943, Los Angeles won its 20th consecutive game (one tie not included) in the Pacific Coast League, defeating Hollywood 4-1.

May 23, 1943, Chet Covington, 28-year-old southpaw with Scranton, Eastern League, hurled a 6-0 perfect game against Springfield, in which only four balls were hit to the outfield. Scranton also took the nightcap of the doubleheader before 3,819 at Scranton, to boost its winning streak to ten.

May 30, 1943, Chet Covington of Scranton, Eastern League, notched his fourth straight shutout in a 15-inning 1-0 thriller over Hal Kleine of Wilkes-Barre. During this streak, Covington pitched 49 consecutive scoreless innings.

May 30, 1943, Play in the four-club Twin Ports League, the only loop ever to file under the "E" classification with the National Association, began with Marine Iron defeating the Duluth Dukes 7-2 and Superior edging the Heralds 3-2. The majority of the players were employed in war plants and shipyards.

June 3, 1943, Pete Gray, one-armed outfield wizard with Memphis, Southern Association, had four hits in five at bats.

June 3, 1943, Scranton's winning streak was halted at 17 games, a new Eastern League record, when Hartford slashed out a 7-3 decision.

June 4, 1943, Schoolmaster Jim Konstanty of Syracuse, International League, limited Jersey City to one hit, a Texas League single, yet lost 1-0. He walked four batters in the seventh frame to force in the lone run of the game.

June 6, 1943, Pitcher Bill Herring of Portland, Pacific Coast League, suffered a head injury when part of the dugout caved in on him.

June 9, 1943, Stephen Gromek of Baltimore, International League, pitched an 18-inning scoreless tie against Rochester before the game was called due to rain.

June 16, 1943, In his first start of the season, 56-year-old Thomas "Lefty" George of York, Interstate League, pitched a three-hit shutout against Lancaster. Lancaster's George Kell had his 32-game hitting streak snapped by the ancient southpaw.

July 28, 1943, Olean, PONY League, scored 30 runs against Wellsville.

August 1, 1943, Norfolk's Lawrence "Yogi" Berra drove in 23 runs in a two-day slugging spree in the Piedmont League. On the first day, Berra had two singles, two doubles, and two homers and knocked in 13 tallies. The next day, he bagged 10 RBIs with a single, two doubles and a homer.

August 25, 1943, Little Rock set a Southern Association record by making 32 hits in a nine-inning game.

September 15, 1943, Bill Sarni, age 15, caught 33 games for Los Angeles of the Pacific Coast League.

Milwaukee's Borchert Field was home of the Milwaukee Brewers of the American Association from 1902 through 1952. The capacity was listed at 10,000.

1944

American League
President: William Harridge

Standings	W	L	Pct.	GB	Attend.	Manager
St. Louis Browns	89	65	.578	—	508,644	Luke Sewell
Detroit Tigers	88	66	.571	1	923,176	Steve O'Neill
New York Yankees	83	71	.539	6	789,995	Joe McCarthy
Boston Red Sox	77	77	.500	12	506,975	Joe Cronin
Cleveland Indians	72	82	.468	17	475,272	Lou Boudreau
Philadelphia Athletics	72	82	.468	17	505,322	Connie Mack
Chicago White Sox	71	83	.461	18	563,539	Jimmy Dykes
Washington Senators	64	90	.416	25	525,235	Ossie Bluege

BA: Lou Boudreau, Cleveland, .327
Runs: Snuffy Stirnweiss, New York, 125
Hits: Snuffy Stirnweiss, New York, 205
RBIs: Vern Stephens, St. Louis, 109
HRs: Nick Etten, New York, 22
Wins: Hal Newhouser, Detroit, 29
SOs: Hal Newhouser, Detroit, 187
ERA: Dizzy Trout, Detroit, 2.12
Pct: Tex Hughson, Boston, .783, 18-5

National League
President: Ford Frick

Standings	W	L	Pct.	GB	Attend.	Manager
St. Louis Cardinals	105	49	.682	—	461,968	Billy Southworth
Pittsburgh Pirates	90	63	.588	14½	604,278	Frank Frisch
Cincinnati Reds	89	65	.578	16	409,567	Bill McKechnie
Chicago Cubs	75	79	.487	30	640,110	Jimmie Wilson/Roy Johnson/ Charlie Grimm
New York Giants	67	87	.435	38	674,483	Mel Ott
Boston Braves	65	89	.422	40	208,691	Bob Coleman
Brooklyn Dodgers	63	91	.409	42	605,905	Leo Durocher
Philadelphia Blue Jays	61	92	.399	43½	369,586	Freddie Fitzsimmons

BA: Dixie Walker, Brooklyn, .357
Runs: Bill Nicholson, Chicago, 116
Hits: Phil Cavarretta, Chicago, 197
Stan Musial, St. Louis, 197
RBIs: Bill Nicholson, Chicago, 122
HRs: Bill Nicholson, Chicago, 33
Wins: Bucky Walters, Cincinnati, 23
SOs: Bill Voiselle, New York, 161
ERA: Ed Heusser, Cincinnati, 2.38
Pct: Ted Wilks, St. Louis, .810, 17-4

AA American Association
President: George Trautman

Standings	W	L	Pct.	GB	Attend.	Manager
Milwaukee Brewers	102	51	.667	—	235,840	Charlie Grimm/Casey Stengel
Toledo Mud Hens (7)	95	58	.621	7	198,870	Ollie Marquardt
Louisville Colonels (1)	85	63	.574	14½	224,035	Bill Burwell/Nemo Leibold
St. Paul Saints (10)	85	66	.563	16	116,315	Ray Blades
Columbus Red Birds (16)	86	67	.562	16	140,995	Nick Cullop
Indianapolis Indians	57	93	.380	43½	121,100	Donie Bush/Bernard Kelly
Minneapolis Millers	54	97	.358	47	82,759	Rosy Ryan
Kansas City Blues (5)	41	110	.272	60	37,199	Jack Saltzgaver

Playoffs: Louisville 4 games, Milwaukee 2; St. Paul 4 games, Toledo 3.
Finals: Louisville 4 games, St. Paul 0.

BA: John Wyrostek, Columbus, .358
Runs: Hal Peck, Milwaukee, 140
Hits: Hal Peck, Milwaukee, 200
RBIs: Nick Polly, Louisville, 120
HRs: Babe Barna, Minneapolis, 24
Wins: James Wilson, Louisville, 19
Earl Caldwell, Milwaukee, 19
SOs: James Wilson, Louisville, 147
ERA: Mel Deutsch, Louisville, 2.47

AA International League
President: Frank J. Shaughnessy

Standings	W	L	Pct.	GB	Attend.	Manager
Baltimore Orioles (3)	84	68	.553	—	349,778	Alphonse "Tommy" Thomas
Newark Bears (5)	85	69	.552	—	152,897	Bill Meyer
Toronto Maple Leafs (15)	79	74	.516	5½	165,685	Burleigh Grimes
Buffalo Bisons (4)	78	76	.506	7	198,907	Bucky Harris
Jersey City Giants (13)	74	79	.484	10½	205,683	Gabby Hartnett
Montreal Royals (10)	73	80	.477	11½	207,603	Bruno Betzel
Rochester Red Wings (16)	71	82	.464	13½	101,163	Ken Penner
Syracuse Chiefs (12)	68	84	.447	16	93,641	Jewel Ens

Playoffs: Baltimore 4 games, Buffalo 3; Newark 4 games, Toronto 0.
Finals: Baltimore 4 games, Newark 3.

MVP-Howie Moss, Baltimore.

BA: Mayo Smith, Buffalo, .340
Runs: Blas Monaco, Baltimore, 135
Hits: Howie Moss, Baltimore, 178
RBIs: Howie Moss, Baltimore, 141
HRs: Howie Moss, Baltimore, 27
Wins: Red Embree, Baltimore, 19
SOs: Red Embree, Baltimore, 225
ERA: Woodrow Crowson, Toronto, 2.41

AA Pacific Coast League
President: Clarence H. Rowland

Standings	W	L	Pct.	GB	Attend.	Manager
Los Angeles Angels (11)	99	70	.586	—	362,677	Bill Sweeney
Portland Beavers	87	82	.515	12	270,835	Marv Owen
San Francisco Seals	86	83	.509	13	316,044	Lefty O'Doul
Oakland Oaks	86	83	.509	13	295,613	Dolph Camilli
Seattle Rainiers	84	85	.497	15	339,588	Bill Skiff
Hollywood Stars	83	86	.491	16	322,959	Charlie Root
Sacramento Solons (16)	76	93	.450	23	199,808	Earl Sheely
San Diego Padres	75	94	.444	24	246,150	George Detore

Playoffs: Los Angeles 4 games, Portland 2; San Francisco 4 games, Oakland 1.
Finals: San Francisco 4 games, Los Angeles 3.

MVP-Les Scarsella, Oakland.

BA: Les Scarsella, Oakland, .329
Runs: Cecil Garriott, Los Angeles, 148
Hits: Les Scarsella, Oakland, 196
RBIs: Francis Kelleher, Hollywood, 121
HRs: Francis Kelleher, Hollywood, 29
Wins: Marino Pieretti, Portland, 26
SOs: Frank Dasso, San Diego, 253
ERA: Clem Dreisewerd, Sacramento, 1.61

A1 Southern Association
President: Billy Evans

Standings	W	L	Pct.	GB	Attend.	Manager
Atlanta Crackers	86	53	.619	—	225,380	Tommy "Doc" Prothro
Memphis Chicks*	84	55	.609	2	162,824	Kiki Cuyler
Nashville Vols**(11)	79	61	.564	7½	129,316	Larry Gilbert
Little Rock Travelers	66	72	.478	19½	68,126	Bob Seeds
Birmingham Barons (12)	64	75	.460	22	96,891	Johnny Riddle/Ted Petosky
Knoxville Smokies/ Mobile Bears#	63	74	.459	22	115,434	Buddy Lewis
Chattanooga Lookouts (8)	57	83	.409	29½	63,678	Andy Moore
New Orleans Pelicans (10)	57	83	.409	29½	102,267	Fresco Thompson

#Knoxville (31-36) moved to Mobile July 5 after the first half, first home game July 14.

Playoff: Nashville 4 games, Memphis 3.

BA: Rene Monteagudo, Chattanooga, .370
Runs: Billy Goodman, Atlanta, 122
Hits: Lindsay Deal, Atlanta, 190
RBIs: Lindsay Deal, Atlanta, 124
HRs: Mel Hicks, Nashville, 16
Wins: Ellis Kinder, Memphis, 19
Howie Fox, Birmingham, 19
SOs: Boyd Tepler, Nashville, 147
ERA: Howie Fox, Birmingham, 2.71

A Eastern League
President: Thomas H. Richardson

Standings	W	L	Pct.	GB	Attend.	Manager
Hartford Laurels (9)	99	38	.723	—	116,265	Del Bissonette
Albany Senators (15)	91	47	.659	8½	132,250	James "Rip" Collins
Utica Blue Sox (14)	69	69	.500	30½	86,802	Eddie Sawyer
Binghamton Triplets (5)	64	71	.474	34	52,661	Gene Martin
Williamsport Grays (8)	64	75	.460	36	63,574	Ray Kolp
Elmira Pioneers (6)	58	80	.420	41½	55,661	Al Todd
Scranton Miners (1)	56	83	.403	44	58,343	Heinie Manush
Wilkes-Barre Barons (3)	51	89	.364	49½	33,035	Jack Sanford

Playoffs: Binghamton 3 games, Albany 0; Utica 3 games, Hartford 2.
Finals: Binghamton 4 games, Utica 2.

BA: James "Rip" Collins, Albany, .396
Runs: Al Gionfriddo, Albany, 130
Hits: Vince Shupe, Hartford, 187
RBIs: Vic Barnhart, Albany, 115
HRs: Stan Wentzel, Hartford, 9
3B: Al Gionfriddo, Albany, 28
Wins: Leonard Gilmore, Albany, 21
SOs: John Moore, Binghamton, 186
ERA: Peter Naktenis, Hartford, 1.93

B Interstate League
President: Arthur H. Ehlers

Standings	W	L	Pct.	GB	Manager
Allentown Cardinals (16)	77	62	.554	—	Ollie Vanek
Wilmington Blue Rocks (14)	74	64	.536	2½	Dutch Dorman/Ray Brubaker
York White Roses (15)	69	68	.504	7	John "Bunny" Griffiths
Lancaster Red Roses (6)	66	72	.478	10½	Lena Blackburn
Hagerstown Owls (4)	65	73	.471	11½	Herb Brett
Trenton Packers (10)	63	75	.457	13½	Joe Bird/Walter Alston

Total Attendance: 486,604.

Playoffs: Lancaster 3 games, Wilmington 0; Allentown 3 games, York 1.
Finals: Lancaster 4 games, Allentown 2.

*Won first-half   **Won second-half   ***Won both halves
Numbers after nicknames indicate farm system.
Affiliation listed at end of each year.

BA: Ira Houck, Lancaster, .356
Runs: Clark Henry, York, 120
Hits: Ira Houck, Lancaster, 190
RBIs: Lloyd Randol, York, 117

HRs: John Cappa, Allentown, 30
Wins: Norman Shope, York, 20
SOs: Norman Shope, York, 239
ERA: Harold Kelleher, Trenton, 2.53

B Piedmont League
President: Ralph Daughton

Standings	W	L	Pct.	GB	Manager
Lynchburg Cardinals (16)...	80	60	.571	—	George Ferrell
Portsmouth Cubs (11).........	72	67	.518	7½	Bill Steinecke/Jimmie Foxx
Norfolk Tars (5)..................	72	68	.514	8	Garland Braxton
Richmond Colts (13)	67	72	.482	12½	Ben Chapman/Taylor Sanford
Roanoke Red Sox (1).........	66	73	.475	13½	Eddie Popowski
Newport News Dodgers (10)...	61	78	.439	18½	Jake Pitler

Total Attendance: 450,000.

Playoffs: Portsmouth 4 games, Norfolk 3; Lynchburg 4 games, Richmond 2, one tie.
Finals: Lynchburg 4 games, Portsmouth 3.

BA: Cecil "Zip" Payne, Lynchburg, .340
Runs: Bruce Smith, Lynchburg, 90
Hits: Cecil "Zip" Payne, Lynchburg, 181
RBIs: Cecil "Zip" Payne, Lynchburg, 99
HRs: Duke Snider, Newport News, 9

Wins: Al Gettel, Norfolk, 17
       Henry Koch, Lynchburg, 17
SOs: Al Gettel, Norfolk, 232
ERA: Pedro Jiminez, Portsmouth, 1.51

D Appalachian League
President: Charles T. Herndon

Standings	W	L	Pct.	GB	Manager
Kingsport Cherokees	65	48	.575	—	Hobe Brummitt/Jim "Lefty" Akard
Bristol Twins (13)..............	54	53	.505	8	Hal Gruber
Johnson City Cardinals (16) .	56	56	.500	8½	George Smith
Erwin Cubs (11).................	45	63	.417	17½	Jim Poole

Total Attendance: 125,000.

Playoffs: Kingsport 3 games, Johnson City 1; Bristol 3 games, Erwin 1.
Finals: Kingsport 3 games, Bristol 1.

All-Star Team: 1B-Earl York, Erwin; 2B-George Boniface, Johnson City; 3B-William Cannon, Bristol; SS-Bernard Creger, Johnson City; OF-Tony Matarazzo, Bristol; Gil Coan, Kingsport; C-William Clausen, Bristol; Util-Don Fitzpatrick, Kingsport; P-Harold Breeding, Bristol; Bill Bustle, Erwin; Manager-Hal Gruber, Bristol.

BA: Ray Stokes, Kingsport, .351
Runs: Orbie Brewer, Erwin, 97
Hits: Ray Stokes, Kingsport, 148
RBIs: Ray Stokes, Kingsport, 81

HRs: Gil Coan, Kingsport, 13
Wins: Harold Breeding, Bristol, 14
SOs: Harold Breeding, Bristol, 180
ERA: Jim "Lefty" Akard, Kingsport, 2.24

D Ohio State League
President: Joe Donnelly

Standings	W	L	Pct.	GB	Manager
Springfield Giants (13)	76	54	.585	—	Earl Wolgamot
Newark Moundsmen (7).....	71	58	.550	4½	Clay Bryant
Middletown Red Sox (1)	66	61	.520	8½	Emil Barnes
Lima Red Birds (16)..........	65	62	.512	9½	Clifton "Runt" Marr/Jack Norris
Zanesville Dodgers (10)	58	71	.450	17½	Jack Knight
Marion Diggers (11)	50	80	.385	26	Grover Hartley

Total Attendance: 280,000.

Playoffs: Newark 3 games, Lima 1; Middletown 3 games, Springfield 2.
Finals: Newark 4 games, Middletown 2.

BA: Luke Majorki, Newark, .355
Runs: Neal Reside, Lima, 120
Hits: Neal Reside, Lima, 173
RBIs: Harvey Zernia, Lima, 114

HRs: Eddie Volan, Newark, 20
Wins: Ned Garver, Newark, 21
SOs: Ned Garver, Newark, 221
ERA: Ned Garver, Newark, 1.21

D PONY League
President: Robert C. Stedler

Standings	W	L	Pct.	GB	Attend.	Manager
Lockport Cubs (11)............	76	49	.608	—	54,265	Greg Mulleavy
Jamestown Falcons (4)	70	54	.565	5½	82,601	Ollie Carnegie
Batavia Clippers (3)...........	70	55	.560	6	36,628	Jack Tighe
Hornell Maples (15)...........	62	61	.504	13	31,798	Charles "Dutch" Schesler/Frank Parenti/John Morrow
Erie Sailors (13)................	61	63	.492	14½	96,658	Bill Harris
Olean Oilers (10)	57	66	.463	18	37,605	John Fitzpatrick
Wellsville Yankees (5)	51	73	.411	24½	25,842	Sol Mishkin
Bradford Blue Wings (14)..	48	74	.393	26½	44,915	Ray Brubaker/Ken Blackman

Playoffs: Lockport 3 games, Hornell 0; Jamestown 3 games, Batavia 0.
Finals: Jamestown 4 games, Lockport 0.

BA: John Gwosden, Hornell, .338
Runs: Glen Brundis, Erie, 106
Hits: Robert Rothel, Batavia, 164
RBIs: Steve Kromoko, Batavia, 93
HRs: George Shuba, Olean, 14

Wins: Phil Poole, Lockport, 22
SOs: Victor Trahd, Lockport, 162
ERA: Frank Maloney, Batavia, 1.91
Pct: Victor Trahd, Lockport, .800, 16-4

Ind Mexican League
President: Crl. Octavio Ruedo Magro

Standings	W	L	Pct.	GB	Manager
Veracruz Azules	52	37	.584	—	Rogers Hornsby/Ramon Bragana
Monterrey Industriales........	50	39	.562	2	Lazaro Salazar
Puebla Angeles	49	39	.557	2½	Eugenio Morin
Nuevo Laredo Tecolotes.....	47	42	.528	5	Martin Dihigo
Tampico Alijadores	40	47	.460	11	Porfirio Martinez/Manuel Arroyo
Mexico City Diablos Rojos	28	62	.311	24½	Ernesto Carmona

BA: Alberto Hernandez, Puebla, .395
Hits: Alberto Hernandez, Puebla, 131
RBIs: Salvador Hernandez, Veracruz, 97
HRs: Salvador Hernandez, Veracruz, 13

Wins: Ramon Bragana, Veracruz, 30
SOs: Ramon Bragana, Veracruz, 144
ERA: Adrian Zavala, Puebla, 2.74

1944 Interleague Post Season Play

World Series
St. Louis (National) 4 games, St. Louis (American) 2

Junior World Series
Baltimore (International) 4 games, Louisville (American Association) 2
Total Attendance: 129,618

1944 Major League Farm Systems

American League
1 Boston (4): Louisville, Scranton, Roanoke, Middletown.
3 Cleveland (3): Baltimore, Wilkes-Barre, Batavia.
4 Detroit (3): Buffalo, Hagerstown, Jamestown.
5 New York (5): Kansas City, Newark (NJ), Binghamton, Norfolk, Wellsville.
6 Philadelphia (2): Elmira, Lancaster.
7 St. Louis (2): Toledo, Newark (OH).
8 Washington (2): Chattanooga, Williamsport.

National League
9 Boston (1): Hartford.
10 Brooklyn (7): St. Paul, Montreal, New Orleans, Trenton, Newport News, Zanesville, Olean.
11 Chicago (6): Los Angeles, Nashville, Portsmouth, Erwin, Marion, Lockport.
12 Cincinnati (2): Syracuse, Birmingham.
13 New York (5): Jersey City, Richmond, Bristol, Springfield, Erie.
14 Philadelphia (3): Utica, Wilmington, Bradford.
15 Pittsburgh (4): Toronto, Albany, York, Hornell.
16 St. Louis (7): Columbus, Rochester, Sacramento, Allentown, Lynchburg, Johnson City, Lima.

1944 No-Hitters

Date	Pitcher	Team	League	Opponent	Score
4-27	Jim Tobin	Boston	National	Brooklyn	2-0
5-7	Jorge Comellas	Los Angeles	Pacific Coast	San Francisco	2-0 (7)
5-15	Clyde Shoun	Cincinnati	National	Boston	1-0
6-3	Boyd Tepler	Lockport	PONY	Hornell	
6-20	Buck Tanner	Newport News	Piedmont	Richmond	2-0
6-25	Harold Kelleher	Trenton	Interstate	York	6-0 (7)
7-18	Stanley West	Baltimore	International	Jersey City	5-0
7-19	Manuel Salvo	Oakland	Pacific Coast	Sacramento	2-0
7-19	Ned Garver	Newark	Ohio State	Marion	10-0
7-29	John Orphal	Birmingham	Southern Assoc.	New Orleans	24-1
8-8	Horace Lisenbee	Syracuse	International	Montreal	8-0 (7)
8-13	Don Schuchmann	Johnson City	Appalachian	Kingsport	2-0 (7)
9-1	Paul Travieso	Marion	Ohio State	Middletown	1-0 (P, 7)
9-2	George Kaufman	Newark	Ohio State	Zanesville	4-0 (7)

Number in parentheses indicates innings if other than nine; "P" indicates perfect game.

THIS DATE IN MINOR LEAGUE HISTORY

April 8, 1944, The Pacific Coast League season opened. It was one of just ten National Association leagues scheduled to operate.

May 5, 1944, Casey Stengel replaced Charlie Grimm as manager of Milwaukee, American Association. Grimm moved up to the Chicago Cubs.

May 23, 1944, Milwaukee, American Association, set a new league scoring record by trouncing Toledo 28-0.

June 15, 1944, What was believed to be an Organized Ball record was set at Bristol, Tennessee, when Mario Picone, a 17-year-old Giants farmhand, pitching for Bristol, Appalachian League, fanned 28 batters in a 19-inning, 3-2 victory over Johnson City.

July 4, 1944, The Baltimore Orioles, International League, were forced to go on the road for ten days when fire caused $150,000 in damage to Oriole Park.

July 16, 1944, Hartford scored 18 runs in one inning of a 28-3 battering of Wilkes-Barre in an Eastern League game.

July 19, 1944, Ned Garver of Newark, Ohio State League, won a 10-0 no-hitter over Marion. He faced just 28 batters, as shortstop Chet Conn's failure to hold Joe Bellamy's sharp liner after leaping to spear the ball cost Garver a perfect game.

August 20, 1944, Last-place Syracuse upset Newark twice in a season-ending twin-bill, giving the International League regular season flag to Baltimore by a margin of just .0007 over Newark. Newark had climbed from last place on July 6 to the top rung, nearly duplicating the feat of the Miracle Boston Braves of 1914.

September 24, 1944, A crowd of 32,913 turned out for a semi-final game between Baltimore and Buffalo in the International League Shaughnessy Playoffs. The game was played at Baltimore's Memorial Stadium, a football facility that was converted for baseball after Oriole Park burned in July.

October 9, 1944, Baltimore and Louisville, playing in the Junior World Series, attracted a record-breaking crowd of 52,833 fans to Baltimore's Memorial Stadium.

SPRING TRAINING 1945

AMERICAN LEAGUE

CLUBS	AT	MAIL ADDRESS	DATES
BOSTON	Pleasantville, N.J.	The Claridge, Atlantic City	3/15–4/5
CHICAGO	Terre Haute, Ind.	Terre Haute House	3/11–4/10
CLEVELAND	Lafayette, Ind.	Fowler Hotel	3/12–4/6
DETROIT	Evansville, Ind.	McCurdy Hotel	3/15–4/16
NEW YORK	Atlantic City, N.Y.	Senator Hotel	3/11–4/12
PHILADELPHIA	Frederick, Md.	Francis Scott Key Hotel	3/15–4/14
ST. LOUIS	Cape Girardeau, Mo.	Hotel Marquette	3/12–4/6
WASHINGTON	College Park, Md.	University of Maryland	3/7–4/15

NATIONAL LEAGUE

BOSTON	Washington, D.C.	Georgetown University	3/12–4/15
BROOKLYN	Bear Mountain, N.Y.	Bear Mountain Inn	3/15–4/12
CHICAGO	French Lick, Ind.	French Lick Springs Hotel	3/8–4/11
CINCINNATI	Bloomington, Ind.	Hotel Graham	3/12–4/6
NEW YORK	Lakewood, N.J.	Rockefeller Mansion	3/11–4/13
PHILADELPHIA	Wilmington, Del.	Hotel Darling	3/14–4/14
PITTSBURGH	Muncie, Ind.	Hotel Roberts	3/16–4/13
ST. LOUIS	Cairo, Il.	Hotel Cairo	3/15–4/6

AMERICAN ASSOCIATION

COLUMBUS	Oxford, Ohio	Miami University	3/19–4/16
INDIANAPOLIS	Bloomington, Ind.	Hotel Graham	3/15–4/13
KANSAS CITY	Bartlesville, Ok.	Hotel Burlingame	3/27–4/16
LOUISVILLE	Louisville, Ky.	Kentucky Hotel	3/20–4/16
MILWAUKEE	Waukesha, Wis.	Avalon Hotel	
MINNEAPOLIS	Eau Claire, Wis.	Eau Claire Hotel	3/28–4/17
ST. PAUL	Independence, Kan.	Booth Hotel	3/15–4/15
TOLEDO	Cape Girardeau, Mo.	Hotel Idan-Ha	3/12–4/12

INTERNATIONAL LEAGUE

BALTIMORE	Baltimore, Md.	The Stadium	3/15–4/19
BUFFALO	Hershey, Pa.	Community Inn	3/24–4/14
JERSEY CITY	Lakewood, N.J.	Hartnett Hall	3/19–4/18
MONTREAL	Bear Mountain, N.Y.	Bear Mountain Inn	3/15–4/14
NEWARK	Plainfield, N.J.	Park Hotel	3/28–4/15
ROCHESTER	Oxford, Ohio	Miami University	3/19–4/17
SYRACUSE	Bedford, Ind.	Hotel Greystone	3/24–4/3
SYRACUSE	Bloomington, Ind.	Hotel Graham	4/4–4/13
TORONTO	Hagerstown, Md.	Alexander Hotel	3/24

PACIFIC COAST LEAGUE

HOLLYWOOD	Ontario, Ca.		2/26–3/28
LOS ANGELES	Anaheim, Ca.	Elks Club	2/26–3/30
OAKLAND	Boyes Springs, Ca.		2/26–3/28
PORTLAND	San Jose, Ca.	Sainte Claire Hotel	2/26–3/31
SACRAMENTO	Richardson Springs, Ca.		3/1–3/30
SACRAMENTO	Sacramento, Ca.	Doubleday Park	
SAN DIEGO	El Centro, Ca.	Barbara Worth Hotel	2/25–3/23
SAN FRANCISCO	San Francisco, Ca.	Seals' Stadium	2/26–3/30
SEATTLE	San Fernando, Ca.	Porter Hotel	2/26–3/28

SOUTHERN ASSOCIATION

ATLANTA	Atlanta, Ga.	650 Ponce de Leon Ave. N.E.	3/28–4/26
BIRMINGHAM	Birmingham, Ala.	Rickwood Field	4/1–4/27
CHATTANOOGA	Chattanooga, Tenn.	Hotel Key	4/1–4/27
LITTLE ROCK	Little Rock, Ark.	P.O. Box 1148	4/1–4/27
MEMPHIS	Memphis, Tenn.	Russwood Park	4/1–4/27
MOBILE			
NASHVILLE	Statesville, N.C.	Vance Hotel	3/27–4/24
NEW ORLEANS	New Orleans, La.	Pelican Stadium	4/2–4/27

EASTERN LEAGUE

ALBANY	Albany, N.Y.	Hawkins Stadium	4/7
BINGHAMTON	Binghamton, N.Y.	Arlington Hotel	4/16–5/3
ELMIRA			
HARTFORD			4/9–5/2
SCRANTON	Emmittsburg, Md.		
UTICA	Wilmington, Del.	Hotel Darling	4/9–4/28
WILKES-BARRE			
WILLIAMSPORT	College Park, Md.		4/15–5/1

1945

American League
President: William Harridge

Standings	W	L	Pct.	GB	Attend.	Manager
Detroit Tigers	88	65	.575	—	1,280,341	Steve O'Neill
Washington Senators	87	67	.565	1½	652,660	Ossie Bluege
St. Louis Browns	81	70	.536	6	482,986	Luke Sewell
New York Yankees	81	71	.533	6½	881,845	Joe McCarthy
Cleveland Indians	73	72	.503	11	558,182	Lou Boudreau
Chicago White Sox	71	78	.477	15	657,981	Jimmy Dykes
Boston Red Sox	71	83	.461	17½	603,794	Joe Cronin
Philadelphia Athletics	52	98	.347	34½	462,631	Connie Mack

BA: Snuffy Stirnweiss, New York, .309
Runs: Snuffy Stirnweiss, New York, 107
Hits: Snuffy Stirnweiss, New York, 195
RBIs: Nick Etten, New York, 111
HRs: Vern Stephens, St. Louis, 24

Wins: Hal Newhouser, Detroit, 25
SOs: Hal Newhouser, Detroit, 212
ERA: Hal Newhouser, Detroit, 1.81
Pct: Hal Newhouser, Detroit, .735, 25-9

National League
President: Ford Frick

Standings	W	L	Pct.	GB	Attend.	Manager
Chicago Cubs	98	56	.636	—	1,036,386	Charlie Grimm
St. Louis Cardinals	95	59	.617	3	594,630	Billy Southworth
Brooklyn Dodgers	87	67	.565	11	1,059,220	Leo Durocher
Pittsburgh Pirates	82	72	.532	16	604,694	Frank Frisch
New York Giants	78	74	.513	19	1,016,468	Mel Ott
Boston Braves	67	85	.441	30	374,691	Bob Coleman/Del Bissonette
Cincinnati Reds	61	93	.396	37	290,070	Bill McKechnie
Philadelphia Phillies	46	108	.299	52	285,057	Freddie Fitzsimmons/Ben Chapman

BA: Phil Cavarretta, Chicago, .355
Runs: Eddie Stanky, Brooklyn, 128
Hits: Tommy Holmes, Boston, 224
RBIs: Dixie Walker, Brooklyn, 124
HRs: Tommy Holmes, Boston, 28

Wins: Charles "Red" Barrett, Boston/St. Louis, 23
SOs: Preacher Roe, Pittsburgh, 148
ERA: Hank Borowy, Chicago, 2.13
Pct: Ken Burkhart, St. Louis, .704, 19-8

AA American Association
President: George Trautman

Standings	W	L	Pct.	GB	Attend.	Manager
Milwaukee Brewers	93	61	.604	—	249,819	Nick Cullop
Indianapolis Indians	90	63	.592	2½	229,145	Bill Burwell
Louisville Colonels (1)	84	70	.545	10	265,083	Nemo Leibold
St. Paul Saints (10)	75	76	.497	16½	187,780	Ray Blades
Minneapolis Millers	72	81	.471	20½	122,376	Rosy Ryan
Toledo Mud Hens (7)	69	84	.451	23½	146,638	Ollie Marquardt
Kansas City Blues (5)	65	86	.430	26½	92,853	Casey Stengel
Columbus Red Birds (16)	63	90	.412	29½	87,248	Charley Root

Playoffs: Louisville 4 games, Milwaukee 2; St. Paul 4 games, Indianapolis 2.
Finals: Louisville 4 games, St. Paul 2.

All-Star Team: 1B-Paul Schoendienst, St. Paul; **2B**-Frank Danneker, Minneapolis; **3B**-Gene Nance, Milwaukee; **SS**-Frank Zak, Kansas City; **OF**-Lew Flick, Milwaukee; Stan Wentzel, Indianapolis; Fred Reinhart, Toledo; Frank Genovese, Louisville; Art Rebel, Columbus; **C**-George Savino, Minneapolis; Joe Stephenson, Milwaukee; Bob Brady, Indianapolis; **Util**-Gil English, Indianapolis; Byron LaForest, Louisville; **P**-Owen Sheetz, Milwaukee; Floyd Speer, Milwaukee; James Wallace, Indianapolis; Ed Wright, Indianapolis; Claude Weaver, St. Paul; Charley Root, Columbus.

BA: Lew Flick, Milwaukee, .374
Runs: Henry Nowak, Minneapolis, 110
Hits: Lew Flick, Milwaukee, 215
RBIs: Gene Nance, Milwaukee, 106

HRs: Babe Barna, Minneapolis, 25
Wins: Owen Sheetz, Milwaukee, 19
SOs: Tom Sunkel, St. Paul, 134
ERA: James Wallace, Indianapolis, 1.83

AA International League
President: Frank J. Shaughnessy

Standings	W	L	Pct.	GB	Attend.	Manager
Montreal Royals (10)	95	58	.621	—	338,409	Bruno Betzel
Newark Bears (5)	89	64	.582	6	135,000	Bill Meyer
Toronto Maple Leafs (6)	85	67	.559	9½	205,011	Harry Davis
Baltimore Orioles (3)	80	73	.523	15	291,962	Alphonse "Tommy" Thomas
Jersey City Giants (13)	71	82	.464	24	189,933	Gabby Hartnett
Buffalo Bisons (4)	64	89	.418	31	129,463	Bucky Harris
Syracuse Chiefs (12)	64	89	.418	31	87,858	Jewel Ens
Rochester Red Wings (16)	64	90	.416	31½	77,600	Burleigh Grimes

Playoffs: Montreal 4 games, Baltimore 3; Newark 4 games, Toronto 2.
Finals: Newark 4 games, Montreal 3.

*Won first-half **Won second-half ***Won both halves
Numbers after nicknames indicate farm system.
Affiliation listed at end of each year.

MVP-Sherm Lollar, Baltimore.

BA: Sherm Lollar, Baltimore, .364
Runs: Roland Gladu, Montreal, 126
Hits: Roland Gladu, Montreal, 204
Walter Cazen, Syracuse, 204
RBIs: Frank Skaff, Baltimore, 126

HRs: Frank Skaff, Baltimore, 38
Wins: Jean-Pierre Roy, Montreal, 25
SOs: Jean-Pierre Roy, Montreal, 139
ERA: Lester Webber, Montreal, 1.88

AA Pacific Coast League
President: Clarence H. Rowland

Standings	W	L	Pct.	GB	Attend.	Manager
Portland Beavers	112	68	.622	—	382,187	Marv Owen
Seattle Rainiers	105	78	.574	8½	434,133	Bill Skiff
Sacramento Solons	95	85	.528	17	310,741	Earl Sheely
San Francisco Seals (13)	96	87	.525	17½	423,858	Lefty O'Doul
Oakland Oaks	90	93	.492	23½	346,178	Dolph Camilli/Bill Raimondi
San Diego Padres	82	101	.448	31½	346,057	Pepper Martin
Los Angeles Angels (11)	77	107	.415	37	349,917	Bill Sweeney
Hollywood Stars (15)	73	110	.399	40½	325,895	Buck Fausett

Playoffs: Seattle 4 games, Portland 3; San Francisco 4 games, Sacramento 3.
Finals: San Francisco 4 games, Seattle 2.

MVP-Robert Joyce, San Francisco.

BA: Jo Jo White, Sacramento, .355
Runs: Jo Jo White, Sacramento, 162
Hits: Jo Jo White, Sacramento, 244
RBIs: Louis Vezilich, San Diego, 110
HRs: Ted Norbert, Seattle, 23

Wins: Robert Joyce, San Francisco, 31
SOs: Vallie Eaves, San Diego, 187
ERA: Robert Joyce, San Francisco, 2.17
CGs: Robert Joyce, San Francisco, 35

A1 Southern Association
President: Billy Evans

Standings	W	L	Pct.	GB	Attend.	Manager
Atlanta Crackers	94	46	.671	—	251,694	Kiki Cuyler
Chattanooga Lookouts (8)	85	55	.607	9	145,430	Bert Niehoff
Mobile Bears (10)	74	65	.532	19½	124,594	Clay Hopper
New Orleans Pelicans	73	67	.521	21	142,444	Fresco Thompson
Memphis Chicks	68	72	.486	26	231,152	Tommy "Doc" Prothro
Birmingham Barons (12)	58	82	.414	36	98,767	Frank Snyder
Nashville Vols (11)	55	84	.396	38½	83,014	Larry Gilbert
Little Rock Travelers	52	88	.371	42	62,766	Willis Hudlin

Playoffs: New Orleans 4 games, Atlanta 1; Mobile 4 games, Chattanooga 2.
Finals: Mobile 4 games, New Orleans 1.

BA: Gil Coan, Chattanooga, .372
Runs: Ted Cieslak, Atlanta, 127
Hits: Gil Coan, Chattanooga, 201
RBIs: Ted Cieslak, Atlanta, 120
HRs: Gil Coan, Chattanooga, 16

3B: Gil Coan, Chattanooga, 28
Wins: Lewis Carpenter, Atlanta, 22
SOs: Al Triechel, Little Rock, 207
ERA: Lewis Carpenter, Atlanta, 1.82
Pct: Larry Brunke, Chattanooga, .938, 15-1

A Eastern League
President: Thomas H. Richardson

Standings	W	L	Pct.	GB	Attend.	Manager
Utica Blue Sox (14)	83	52	.615	—	99,731	Eddie Sawyer
Wilkes-Barre Barons (3)	78	59	.569	6	87,696	Dick Porter/Mike McNally
Albany Senators (15)	79	61	.564	6½	123,981	James "Rip" Collins
Hartford Bees (9)	68	67	.504	15	97,557	Merle Settlemire
Scranton Miners (1)	67	69	.493	16½	76,183	Elmer Yoter
Elmira Pioneers (7)	64	73	.467	20	85,164	Jimmy Adair
Binghamton Triplets (5)	56	81	.409	28	52,555	Bill Cronin
Williamsport Grays (8)	52	85	.380	32	51,440	Ray Kolp

Playoffs: Albany 4 games, Utica 2; Wilkes-Barre 4 games, Hartford 2.
Finals: Albany 4 games, Wilkes-Barre 3.

BA: John Mayhew, Albany, .322
Runs: John Ward, Wilkes-Barre, 101
Hits: Don Fitzpatrick, Elmira, 165
RBIs: Aurelio Fernandez, Williamsport, 82

HRs: John Mihalik, Wilkes-Barre, 7
Wins: Fred Clemence, Albany, 23
SOs: Charles Ripple, Utica, 193
ERA: Frank Martin, Utica, 1.60

B Interstate League
President: Arthur H. Ehlers

Standings	W	L	Pct.	GB	Manager
Lancaster Red Roses (6)	87	52	.626	—	Lena Blackburn
Wilmington Blue Rocks (14)	81	57	.587	5½	Ray Brubaker/Cy Morgan
Trenton Spartans (10)	70	69	.504	17	Walter Alston

343

Allentown Cardinals (16) ... 68 71 .489 19 Ollie Vanek
Hagerstown Owls (11)........ 61 77 .442 25½ Mickey Balla/Dutch Dorman
York White Roses (15)....... 49 90 .353 38 John "Bunny" Griffiths

Attendance: Lancaster, 86,755; Total, 330,854.

Playoffs: Lancaster 4 games, Trenton 3; Allentown 4 games, Wilmington 3.
Finals: Lancaster 4 games, Allentown 0.

BA: Lloyd Randol, York, .343
Runs: Nellie Fox, Lancaster, 128
Hits: Nellie Fox, Lancaster, 180
RBIs: Maurice Santomauro, Trenton, 117
HRs: Rolland Seitz, Allentown, 21
Wins: George Estock, Wilmington, 22
SOs: Lester Studener, Trenton, 191
ERA: Harold Kelleher, Trenton, 2.58

B Piedmont League
President: Ralph Daughton

Standings	W	L	Pct.	GB	Manager
Norfolk Tars (5)................	83	57	.593	—	Garland Braxton
Richmond Colts (13)..........	76	60	.559	5	Frank Rodgers
Newport News Dodgers (10)..	69	69	.500	13	Jake Pitler
Portsmouth Cubs (11)........	67	69	.493	14	Ival Goodman
Roanoke Red Sox (1)..........	67	71	.486	15	Eddie Popowski
Lynchburg Cardinals (16)...	52	88	.371	31	George Ferrell/Cecil "Zip" Payne

Attendance: Norfolk, 152,433; Total, 595,000.

Playoffs: Portsmouth 4 games, Norfolk 3; Richmond 4 games, Newport News 0.
Finals: Portsmouth 4 games, Richmond 0.

BA: William West, Richmond, .373
Runs: William West, Richmond, 117
Hits: William West, Richmond, 193
RBIs: William West, Richmond, 101
HRs: Wayne Maxey, Lynchburg, 12
    Elwood Grantham, Portsmouth, 12
Wins: Mario Picone, Richmond, 19
SOs: Mario Picone, Richmond, 202
ERA: Bill Houtz, Norfolk, 1.23

C Carolina League
President: Dr. Thomas S. Wilson

Standings	W	L	Pct.	GB	Attend.	Manager
Danville Leafs (13)............	94	44	.681	—	75,000	Herb Brett
Raleigh Capitals (12)..........	78	60	.565	16	82,000	Charlie Carroll
Martinsville Athletics (6)....	69	67	.507	24	37,000	Heinie Manush
Burlington Bees	67	70	.489	26½	50,000	Tom Greenwade/Cy Perkins/ Rudy Wilson
Leaksville-Draper-Spray Triplets (11)	66	70	.485	27	30,000	Jackie Warner
Winston-Salem Cardinals (16)	61	76	.445	32½	68,000	George Smith/George Ferrell
Durham Bulls (1)	59	77	.434	34	72,000	Floyd Patterson
Greensboro Patriots (14).....	53	83	.394	40	52,000	Wes Ferrell/Charlie Burgess/ Charlie Eatman/Johnny Allen

Playoffs: Raleigh 4 games, Burlington 3; Danville 4 games, Martinsville 2.
Finals: Danville 4 games, Raleigh 1.

All-Star Team: 1B-Jerome Gutt, Martinsville; 2B-August Granzig, Leaksville-Draper-Spray; 3B-Richard Mayers, Burlington; SS-Jaime Almendro, Danville; OF-Rudolph Adkins, Martinsville; John Carenbauer, Danville; Glenn Brundis, Danville; C-Joe Borich, Winston-Salem; Util-Paul Ellington, Raleigh; P-Art Fowler, Danville; Bill Bustle, Leaksville-Draper-Spray; Manager-Herb Brett, Danville.

BA: Glenn Brundis, Danville, .366
Runs: Jaime Almendro, Danville, 139
Hits: Glenn Brundis, Danville, 193
    Jaime Almendro, Danville, 193
RBIs: John Carenbauer, Danville, 121
HRs: August Granzig, Leaksville-Draper-Spray, 12
    Tommy Kirk, Martinsville, 12
    Jerome Gutt, Martinsville, 12
    Maurice Abrams, Martinsville, 12
Wins: Art Fowler, Danville, 23
SOs: Charles Gooding, Winston-Salem, 230
ERA: Charlie Timm, Raleigh, 2.36

D Appalachian League
President: Carl A. Jones

Standings	W	L	Pct.	GB	Attend.	Manager
Kingsport Dodgers..............	73	36	.670	—	28,788	Hobe Brummitt
Bristol Twins (13)..............	63	45	.583	9½	31,406	Hal Gruber
Johnson City Cardinals (16) ..	40	65	.381	31	17,905	Fred Hawn/Clifton "Runt" Marr
Elizabethton Betsy Cubs (11)..	38	68	.358	33½	16,430	William Kelly

Playoffs: Kingsport 3 games, Johnson City 0; Bristol 3 games, Elizabethton 1.
Finals: Kingsport 4 games, Bristol 2.

All-Star Team: 1B-Arden McCaskey, Bristol; 2B-Jackson Hollis, Kingsport; 3B-Billy Gardner, Bristol; SS-Emil Stoecker, Bristol; OF-Sal Zunno, Bristol; Walter Rasmussen, Elizabethton; Ken Guettler, Kingsport; Util-Sidney Langston, Johnson City; P-Harold Jackson, Kingsport; Jim "Lefty" Akard, Kingsport; Manager-Hal Gruber, Bristol.

BA: Arden McCaskey, Bristol, .375
Runs: Emil Stoecker, Bristol, 87
Hits: Arden McCaskey, Bristol, 164
RBIs: Perry Roberts, Kingsport, 100
HRs: Ken Guettler, Kingsport, 13
Wins: Harold Jackson, Kingsport, 19
SOs: Harold Jackson, Kingsport, 207
ERA: Jim "Lefty" Akard, Kingsport, 1.70

D North Carolina State League
President: C.M. Llewellyn

Standings	W	L	Pct.	GB	Manager
Hickory Rebels (13)............	80	34	.702	—	Herschel Bobo
Lexington Indians (6)	69	46	.600	11½	Jim Maus
Landis Millers....................	65	46	.586	13½	Ed Cross
Salisbury Pirates (15).........	59	55	.518	21	Tuck McWilliams
Statesville Cubs (11)...........	53	58	.477	25½	Jim Poole
Mooresville Braves (9)........	51	61	.455	28	Jack Quinlan
Thomasville Tommies (10)	40	72	.357	39	Red Kaiser/Rex Bowen
Concord Weavers (14)........	34	79	.301	45½	John "Hank" Lehman

Total Attendance: 250,000.

Playoffs: Landis 4 games, Hickory 3; Lexington 4 games, Salisbury 1.
Finals: Landis 4 games, Lexington 2.

BA: Lee Cox, Lexington, .367
Runs: John Allen, Hickory, 140
Hits: Stephen Lesigonich, Salisbury, 153
RBIs: Phil Alotta, Hickory, 109
HRs: Stephen Lesigonich, Salisbury, 10
Wins: Forrest Thompson, Mooresville, 24
SOs: Forrest Thompson, Mooresville, 278
ERA: Forrest Thompson, Mooresville, 2.13

D Ohio State League
President: Frank M. Colley

Standings	W	L	Pct.	GB	Attend.	Manager
Middletown Rockets...........	89	50	.640	—	27,399	Ivy Griffin
Zanesville Dodgers (10)	74	66	.529	15½	55,308	Jack Knight/Morris Mikesell/ Ray Hayworth/Eric McNair/ Clay Bryant
Lima Reds (12)	72	68	.514	17½	38,159	Clarence "Cap" Crossley
Springfield Giants (13)........	64	75	.460	25	43,583	Earl Wolgamot
Marion Cardinals (16)	62	77	.446	27	53,210	Grover Hartley/Wally Schang
Newark Moundsmen (7).....	57	82	.410	32	49,045	Mickey O'Neil

Playoffs: Middletown 4 games, Springfield 2; Zanesville 4 games, Lima 2.
Finals: Zanesville 3 games, Middletown 2.

BA: Albert Kaiser, Newark, .368
Runs: William Scott, Middletown, 113
Hits: Albert Kaiser, Newark, 171
RBIs: Troy Bolick, Springfield, 103
HRs: Albert Kaiser, Newark, 12
Wins: Raymond Janikowski, Middletown, 25
SOs: Raymond Janikowski, Middletown, 274
ERA: Raymond Janikowski, Middletown, 1.71

D PONY League
President: Robert C. Stedler

Standings	W	L	Pct.	GB	Attend.	Manager
Batavia Clippers (3)............	84	40	.677	—	44,569	Jack Tighe
Jamestown Falcons (4)	75	51	.595	10	78,524	Jim Levey
Lockport White Socks	73	52	.584	11½	42,014	Greg Mulleavy/Bill Pringle
Bradford Blue Wings (14)....	70	55	.560	14½	49,532	Leon Riley
Wellsville Yankees (5)	57	68	.456	27½	28,000	Bob Crow/Sol Mishkin
Hornell Pirates (15)	55	71	.437	30	28,600	John Morrow/Fred Herring
Erie Sailors (13)	46	77	.374	37½	62,516	Bill Harris
Olean Oilers (10)	40	86	.317	45	24,780	John Fitzpatrick

Playoffs: Batavia 3 games, Bradford 1; Lockport 3 games, Jamestown 1.
Finals: Batavia 4 games, Lockport 3.

BA: Barney Hearn, Jamestown, .352
Runs: George Gasdaska, Bradford, 133
Hits: Ken Humphrey, Jamestown, 165
RBIs: Carl Sawatski, Bradford, 111
HRs: Carl Sawatski, Bradford, 13
    Leon Riley, Bradford, 13
Wins: Leon Titus, Bradford, 19
SOs: Joseph Menarchek, Hornell, 248
ERA: Richard Palmisiano, Batavia, 1.40
Pct: Richard Palmisiano, Batavia, .842, 16-3

Ind Mexican League
President: Crl. Octavio Ruedo Magro

Standings	W	L	Pct.	GB	Manager
Tampico Alijadores	52	38	.578	—	Armando Marsans
Nuevo Laredo Tecolotes.......	48	42	.533	4	Felix Arguelles
Monterrey Industriales........	48	42	.533	4	Lazaro Salazar
Mexico City Diablos Rojos	44	46	.498	8	Ernesto Carmona
Veracruz Azules	42	48	.467	10	Ramon Bragana
Puebla Angeles	36	54	.400	16	Julio Rojo

BA: Claro Duany, Monterrey, .375
Hits: Claro Duany, Monterrey, 140
RBIs: Claro Duany, Monterrey, 100
HRs: Roberto Ortiz, Mexico City, 26
Wins: Agapito Mayor, Nuevo Laredo, 23
SOs: Agapito Mayor, Nuevo Laredo, 156
ERA: Juan Guerrero, Nuevo Laredo, 2.87

1945 Interleague Post Season Play

World Series
Detroit (American) 4 games, Chicago (National) 3

Junior World Series
Louisville (American Association) 4 games, Newark (International) 2
Total Attendance: 57,544

1945 Major League Farm Systems

American League

1 Boston (4): Louisville, Scranton, Roanoke, Durham.
3 Cleveland (3): Baltimore, Wilkes-Barre, Batavia.
4 Detroit (2): Buffalo, Jamestown.
5 New York (5): Kansas City, Newark (NJ), Binghamton, Norfolk, Wellsville.
6 Philadelphia (4): Toronto, Lancaster, Martinsville, Lexington.
7 St. Louis (3): Toledo, Elmira, Newark (OH).
8 Washington (2): Chattanooga, Williamsport.

National League

9 Boston (2): Hartford, Mooresville.
10 Brooklyn (8): St. Paul, Montreal, Mobile, Trenton, Newport News, Olean, Thomasville, Zanesville.
11 Chicago (7): Los Angeles, Nashville, Hagerstown, Portsmouth, Leaksville-Spray-Draper, Elizabethton, Statesville.
12 Cincinnati (4): Syracuse, Birmingham, Raleigh, Lima.
13 New York (8): Jersey City, San Francisco, Richmond, Danville, Bristol, Springfield, Erie, Hickory.
14 Philadelphia (5): Utica, Wilmington, Greensboro, Bradford, Concord.
15 Pittsburgh (5): Hollywood, Albany, York, Hornell, Salisbury.
16 St. Louis (7): Columbus, Rochester, Allentown, Lynchburg, Winston-Salem, Johnson City, Marion.

1945 No-Hitters

Date	Pitcher	Team	League	Opponent	Score
5-15	Pete Naktenis	Hartford	Eastern	Binghamton	6-0
5-17	Ed Wright	Indianapolis	American Assoc.	Kansas City	2-0
5-25	Harold Jackson	Kingsport	Appalachian	Bristol	3-0 (5)
6-3	Pete Mazar	Columbus	American Assoc.	Kansas City	4-0
6-20	Art Houtteman	Buffalo	International	Jersey City	0-2 (8)
7-3	Ralph McCabe	Wilkes-Barre	Eastern	Binghamton	10-0
7-10	Ray Moring	Thomasville	N. Carolina State	Hickory	5-0 (7)
7-12	Fred Chumley	Scranton	Eastern	Albany	(7)
7-16	Claude Crocker	Burlington	Carolina	Greensboro	0-1
7-17	Fred Gehrt	Marion	Ohio State	Springfield	11-0 (7)
7-26	Don Thompson	Louisville	American Assoc.	Indianapolis	8-0
7-30	Larry Belz	Statesville	N. Carolina State	Mooresville	3-0
8-11	Duke Makosky	Hickory	N. Carolina State	Thomasville	4-0
8-13	Raymond Janikowski	Middletown	Ohio State	Zanesville	2-0 (7)
8-23	Dwight Wilkerson	Landis	N. Carolina State	Salisbury	
9-3	Louis Polli	Jersey City	International	Newark	11-0
9-6	Charles Gooding	Winston-Salem	Carolina	Raleigh	5-0 (7)
9-9	Dick Fowler	Philadelphia	American	St. Louis	1-0

Number in parentheses indicates innings if other than nine.

THIS DATE IN MINOR LEAGUE HISTORY

April 26, 1945, The Carolina League began its first season in Organized Ball.

May 14, 1945, Byron Laforest went 6-for-6 for Louisville, American Association.

August 17, 1945, Bob Kuhlman of Elizabethton set an Appalachian League record when he set down 21 Johnson City batters on strikes in nine innings.

August 21, 1945, Syracuse, International League, played its eighth consecutive doubleheader in as many days. The Chiefs won five of the 16 games.

August 25, 1945, York, Interstate League, broke a 15-game losing streak with a win over Lancaster.

August 25, 1945, Former major league infielder Eric McNair, manager of Zanesville, Ohio State League, was suspended for 138 scheduled playing days during the 1945-46 seasons. McNair was charged with assaulting umpire Green during a game at Middletown August 17.

August 26, 1945, In a wild slugfest at Baltimore, International League, the Orioles defeated Syracuse 20-18, despite being outhit 23-22. Six Baltimore hitters had three safeties apiece.

August 27, 1945, After having hit safely in 38 consecutive games, Gil Coan of Chattanooga, Southern Association, had his streak ended by Mobile pitching.

August 30, 1945, Charlie Timm, veteran righthander for Raleigh, Carolina League, set a league record by striking out 20 Martinsville batters. He yielded eight hits in the 7-3 victory.

September 2, 1945, Robert Joyce won his 30th game of the season for San Francisco, Pacific Coast League, when he hung up a 4-1 victory at Los Angeles.

September 3, 1945, Shortstop Wild Bill Hart of St. Paul, American Association, cracked four successive home runs, batting in nine runs against Minneapolis. Hart's feat tied the league record set by Dale Alexander of Kansas City on June 14, 1935 and again by Ab Wright of Minneapolis on July 4, 1940. Teammate Otho Nitcholas, ancient curveballer, went 5-for-5 and hurled St. Paul to the 16-1 win.

September 5, 1945, Louisville receiver Jack Aragon, who had suffered a broken leg August 5, was presented with a washtub filled with 50,000 pennies from Louisville fans. Radio broadcaster Don Hill started the fund for Aragon, who was still disabled by the fracture.

September 6, 1945, With his 28th triple of the season, Chattanooga's Gil Coan shattered a Southern Association record as the Lookouts swamped Birmingham 14-4. Three players, Ike Boone (New Orleans, 1921), Elliott Bigelow (Chattanooga, 1925), and Danny Taylor (Memphis, 1927), held the previous mark of 27 triples.

September 6, 1945, Smoke from a smoldering city dump nearby interrupted the Syracuse-Jersey City contest for a full hour at Syracuse.

September 9, 1945, Completing the season without a miscue over the 154-game schedule, fleet-footed Louisville centerfielder Frank Genovese established an all-time American Association record. He also had a string of 227 consecutive league games and 515 chances without an error. His last miscue had come on July 8, 1944. Genovese played in every game, missing only nine innings.

September 11, 1945, San Francisco pitcher Robert Joyce was extended to 15 innings by Hollywood for his 31st conquest of the season, a 5-4 win. Joyce had a 1.95 ERA over his first 303 innings.

October, 1945, Casey Stengel signed to manage Oakland, Pacific Coast League, at a reported salary of $12,000. Stengel had managed Kansas City in 1945 and Milwaukee in 1944.

October 23, 1945, Jackie Robinson, a former UCLA football star who played shortstop for the Kansas City Monarchs of the Negro League, signed a contract to play for Montreal of the International League, a Brooklyn farm club. The signing thus broke the color barrier which had existed in Organized Ball since the 1880's.

October 26, 1945, Bill Veeck sold his controlling interest in the Milwaukee Brewers to a Chicago attorney for a reported $150,000. Veeck had been in charge of the American Association club since June 23, 1941. The illness of his wife Ellen and the condition of his right leg, injured while he served with the Marine Corps in the South Pacific, prompted Veeck to sell the team.

December 2, 1945, Bert Humphries, 35, a minor league pitcher with a 3-3 record for Syracuse in 1945, began his duties as pastor of the Trinity Congregational Church in East Orange, New Jersey. Humphries, formerly in the Yankees farm system, quit the game for the pulpit. As a minister, he officiated at the wedding of Bob Shawkey, former Yankee and his former manager with Newark, International League.

THE GOLDEN AGE: 1946 - 1951

*T*he war was over, the servicemen were home and it was time to rediscover America. The country boomed, and both major and minor league baseball were caught up in a wave of confidence and expansion that swept the country.

In 1946, more than thirty-two million fans attended minor league games, up from less than ten million the year before. In 1947, 1948 and 1949, the totals climbed to more than 40 million. The jump in number of leagues was just as significant. In 1945 a dozen leagues operated. In 1946 there were 41, then 58 in 1948, and it topped out at 59 leagues in 438 cities in 1949.

With the death of Bramham in 1947, the National Association elected George Trautman, former head of the American Association, as its new president. Trautman encouraged semipro and textile leagues to join his organization. In retrospect, many towns that were not big enough to support minor league baseball were brought into its fold, but at the time, the confidence of baseball was supreme. Who was to say that towns of two thousand could not support professional baseball?

The years following World War II were a heady time for minor league baseball. There was little competition other than movies for the entertainment dollar, and the United States was emerging as an affluent nation. Night baseball had been introduced during the Depression, but in the 1930s there was little disposable income to spend on baseball. After the war, servicemen were home with money in their pockets, and the nation's economy was booming. People had money to spend for leisure and what better place than the ballpark. Minor league baseball did not realize that soon would be available other options for the entertainment dollar.

In 1950, minor league baseball started to fall. Fifty-eight leagues still operated, but attendance fell to 34,735,907, a drop of more than 7 million. The next year, 50 leagues operated with attendance at just over 27 million.

The United States entered the Korean War in June, 1950. As always, war signaled a downturn in the minor leagues. The 1952 season saw the National Association published *The Story of Minor League Baseball*, a 740-page history. The book explained the drop with this statement: "The decline in the number of leagues is easily explained by the fact that hundreds of players were going into the service, and that there was a feeling of uncertainty across the nation concerning the imminence of all-out war." But this time war was not the only cause of the decline, and the minors would begin a 25 year downward spiral that many believed would end minor league baseball in most U.S. cities.

1946

American League
President: William Harridge

Standings	W	L	Pct.	GB	Attend.	Manager
Boston Red Sox	104	50	.675	—	1,416,944	Joe Cronin
Detroit Tigers.....................	92	62	.597	12	1,722,590	Steve O'Neill
New York Yankees............	87	67	.565	17	2,265,512	Joe McCarthy/Bill Dickey/ Johnny Neun
Washington Senators	76	78	.494	28	1,027,216	Ossie Bluege
Chicago White Sox	74	80	.481	30	983,403	Jimmy Dykes/Ted Lyons
Cleveland Indians	68	86	.442	36	1,057,289	Lou Boudreau
St. Louis Browns	66	88	.429	38	526,435	Luke Sewell/Zack Taylor
Philadelphia Athletics........	49	105	.318	55	621,793	Connie Mack

BA: Mickey Vernon, Washington, .353
Runs: Ted Williams, Boston, 142
Hits: Johnny Pesky, Boston, 208
RBIs: Hank Greenberg, Detroit, 127
HRs: Hank Greenberg, Detroit, 44

Wins: Hal Newhouser, Detroit, 26
   Bob Feller, Cleveland, 26
SOs: Bob Feller, Cleveland, 348
ERA: Hal Newhouser, Detroit, 1.94
Pct: Boo Ferriss, Boston, .806, 25-6

National League
President: Ford Frick

Standings	W	L	Pct.	GB	Attend.	Manager
St. Louis Cardinals	98	58	.628	—	1,061,807	Eddie Dyer
Brooklyn Dodgers..............	96	60	.615	2	1,796,824	Leo Durocher
Chicago Cubs.....................	82	71	.536	14½	1,342,970	Charlie Grimm
Boston Braves.....................	81	72	.529	15½	969,673	Billy Southworth
Philadelphia Phillies	69	85	.448	28	749,962	Ben Chapman
Cincinnati Reds...................	67	87	.435	30	715,751	Bill McKechnie/Hank Gowdy
Pittsburgh Pirates	63	91	.409	34	749,962	Frank Frisch/Spud Davis
New York Giants	61	93	.396	36	1,219,873	Mel Ott

Playoff: St. Louis 2 games, Brooklyn 0.

BA: Stan Musial, St. Louis, .365
Runs: Stan Musial, St. Louis, 124
Hits: Stan Musial, St. Louis, 228
RBIs: Enos Slaughter, St. Louis, 130
HRs: Ralph Kiner, Pittsburgh, 23

Wins: Howie Pollet, St. Louis, 21
SOs: John Schmitz, Chicago, 135
ERA: Howie Pollet, St. Louis, 2.10
Pct: Murry Dickson, St. Louis, .714, 15-6

AAA American Association
President: Roy Hamey

Standings	W	L	Pct.	GB	Attend.	Manager
Louisville Colonels (1)	92	61	.601	—	355,241	Nemo Leibold/Fred Walters
Indianapolis Indians (9)......	88	65	.575	4	317,223	Bill Burwell
St. Paul Saints (10)	80	71	.530	11	289,544	Ray Blades
Minneapolis Millers (13)....	76	75	.503	15	242,603	Zeke Bonura/Rosy Ryan/ Tom Sheehan
Milwaukee Brewers (2)	70	78	.473	19½	257,694	Nick Cullop
Toledo Mud Hens (7)	69	84	.451	23	234,062	Don Gutteridge/George Detore
Kansas City Blues (5).........	67	82	.450	23	222,259	Bill Meyer/Burleigh Grimes
Columbus Red Birds (16)....	64	90	.416	28½	102,127	Charley Root

Playoffs: Louisville 4 games, St. Paul 1; Indianapolis 4 games, Minneapolis 3.
Finals: Louisville 4 games, Indianapolis 0.

MVP-Jerry Witte, Toledo.

BA: Sibby Sisti, Indianapolis, .343
Runs: Babe Barna, Minneapolis, 122
Hits: Sibby Sisti, Indianapolis, 203
RBIs: John McCarthy, Minneapolis, 122
HRs: Jerry Witte, Toledo, 46

Wins: Fred Sanford, Toledo, 15
   Harry Taylor, St. Paul, 15
   Ewald Pyle, Milwaukee, 15
SOs: Fred Sanford, Toledo, 154
ERA: Al Widmar, Louisville, 2.43

AAA International League
President: Frank J. Shaughnessy

Standings	W	L	Pct.	GB	Attend.	Manager
Montreal Royals (10)........	100	54	.649	—	412,744	Clay Hopper
Syracuse Chiefs (12)..........	81	72	.529	18½	237,235	Jewel Ens
Baltimore Orioles (3)........	81	73	.526	19	620,726	Alphonse "Tommy" Thomas
Newark Bears (5)...............	80	74	.519	20	264,758	George Selkirk
Buffalo Bisons (4)	78	75	.510	21½	293,813	Gabby Hartnett
Toronto Maple Leafs (6).....	71	82	.464	28½	182,193	Harry Davis
Rochester Red Wings (16)..	65	87	.428	34	172,125	Burleigh Grimes/ Benny Borgmann
Jersey City Giants (13)	57	96	.373	42½	200,096	Bruno Betzel

Playoffs: Baltimore defeated Newark in a one game playoff for third place. Montreal 4 games, Newark 2; Syracuse 4 games, Baltimore 2.
Finals: Montreal 4 games, Syracuse 1.

MVP-Eddie Robinson, Baltimore.

*Won first-half   **Won second-half   ***Won both halves
Numbers after nicknames indicate farm system.
Affiliation listed at end of each year.

BA: Jackie Robinson, Montreal, .349
Runs: Jackie Robinson, Montreal, 113
   Clarence Campbell, Baltimore, 113
Hits: Bobby Brown, Newark, 174
   Danny Murtaugh, Rochester, 174
RBIs: Eddie Robinson, Baltimore, 123

HRs: Howie Moss, Baltimore, 38
Wins: Steve Nagy, Montreal, 17
   Jim Prendergast, Syracuse, 17
SOs: Art Houtteman, Buffalo, 147
ERA: Herb Karpel, Newark, 2.41

AAA Pacific Coast League
President: Clarence H. Rowland

Standings	W	L	Pct.	GB	Attend.	Manager
San Francisco Seals	115	68	.628	—	670,563	Lefty O'Doul
Oakland Oaks	111	72	.607	4	634,311	Casey Stengel
Hollywood Stars (15)........	95	88	.519	20	513,056	Buck Fausett/Jimmy Dykes
Los Angeles Angels (11)....	94	89	.514	21	501,259	Bill Sweeney
Sacramento Solons	94	92	.505	22½	349,839	Earl Sheely
San Diego Padres..............	78	108	.419	38½	291,004	Pepper Martin/Jim Brillheart
Portland Beavers................	74	109	.404	41	314,133	Marv Owen
Seattle Rainiers (9)	74	109	.404	41	444,551	Bill Skiff/Jo Jo White

Playoffs: San Francisco 4 games, Hollywood 0; Oakland 4 games, Los Angeles 3.
Finals: San Francisco 4 games, Oakland 2.

MVP-Les Scarsella, Oakland.

BA: Harvey Storey, Los Angeles/Portland, .326
Runs: Ferris Fain, San Francisco, 117
Hits: William Ramsey, Seattle/ Sacramento, 219
RBIs: Ferris Fain, San Francisco, 112

HRs: Lloyd Christopher, Los Angeles, 26
Wins: Larry Jansen, San Francisco, 30
SOs: Ed Erautt, Hollywood, 234
ERA: Larry Jansen, San Francisco, 1.57

AA Southern Association
President: Billy Evans

Standings	W	L	Pct.	GB	Attend.	Manager
Atlanta Crackers	96	58	.623	—	395,699	Kiki Cuyler
Memphis Chicks	90	63	.588	5½	275,034	Tommy "Doc" Prothro
Chattanooga Lookouts (8) ..	79	73	.520	16	209,598	Bert Niehoff
New Orleans Pelicans (1) ...	75	77	.493	20	329,071	John Peacock
Nashville Vols (11)............	75	78	.490	20½	213,284	Larry Gilbert
Mobile Bears (10)...............	75	78	.490	20½	137,136	Al Todd
Birmingham Barons (15)....	68	84	.447	27	157,823	Frank Snyder
Little Rock Travelers (2) ...	52	99	.344	42½	113,671	Willis Hudlin

Playoffs: Atlanta 4 games, New Orleans 3; Memphis 4 games, Chattanooga 2, one tie.
Finals: Atlanta 4 games, Memphis 3.

BA: Tom Neill, Birmingham, .374
Runs: Lloyd Gearhart, Atlanta, 139
Hits: Tom Neill, Birmingham, 207
RBIs: Tom Neill, Birmingham, 124

HRs: Ted Pawelek, Nashville, 15
Wins: Earl McGowan, Atlanta, 22
SOs: Robert McCall, Nashville, 179
ERA: William Ayers, Atlanta, 1.95

AA Texas League
President: J. Alvin Gardner

Standings	W	L	Pct.	GB	Attend.	Manager
Ft. Worth Cats (10)	101	53	.656	—	272,659	Ray Hayworth
Dallas Rebels (4)	91	63	.591	10	279,049	Al Vincent
San Antonio Missions (7)...	87	65	.572	13	295,103	James Adair
Tulsa Oilers (11)................	84	69	.549	16½	152,493	Gus Mancuso
Beaumont Exporters (5)......	70	83	.458	30½	146,735	Jim Turner
Houston Buffaloes (16).......	64	89	.418	36½	161,421	Johnny Keane
Shreveport Sports (2)..........	61	92	.399	39½	164,421	Francis "Salty" Parker/ Hub Northen
Oklahoma City Indians (3) .	54	98	.355	46	120,384	Roy Schalk

Playoffs: Ft. Worth 4 games, Tulsa 0; Dallas 4 games, San Antonio 1.
Finals: Dallas 4 games, Ft. Worth 1.

MVP-Henry Schenz, Tulsa; **Pitcher of the Year**-Henry "Prince" Oana, Dallas.

BA: Dale Mitchell, Oklahoma City, .337
Runs: Henry Schenz, Tulsa, 102
Hits: Clarence Maddern, Tulsa, 184
RBIs: Bob Moyer, Dallas, 102

HRs: Bob Moyer, Dallas, 24
Wins: Henry "Prince" Oana, Dallas, 24
SOs: John Van Cuyk, Ft. Worth, 207
ERA: John Van Cuyk, Ft. Worth, 1.42

A Eastern League
President: Thomas H. Richardson

Standings	W	L	Pct.	GB	Attend.	Manager
Scranton Red Sox (1)..........	96	43	.691	—	181,302	Elmer Yoter
Albany Senators (15)..........	78	62	.557	18½	166,252	James "Rip" Collins
Wilkes-Barre Barons (3).....	76	62	.551	19½	131,529	Dick Porter

Hartford Bees (9)	71	67	.514	24½	140,249	Dutch Dorman
Elmira Pioneers (7)	65	72	.474	30	98,521	Ralph Winegarner
Williamsport Grays (4)	59	80	.424	37	71,514	Nig Lipscomb/Harry Davis
Utica Blue Sox (14)	59	80	.424	37	93,822	Eddie Sawyer
Binghamton Triplets (5)	51	89	.364	45½	85,480	Garland Braxton/Lefty Gomez

Playoffs: Scranton 4 games, Wilkes-Barre 0; Hartford 4 games, Albany 2.
Finals: Scranton 4 games, Hartford 1.

All-Star Team: 1B-Len Kensecke, Scranton; **2B**-Al Kozar, Scranton; **3B**-Vic Barnhart, Albany; **SS**-Carl Cox, Albany; **OF**-Joe Frazier, Wilkes-Barre; Sam Mele, Scranton; Don Manno, Hartford; **C**-Tex Aulds, Scranton; **Util**-Ray Uniak, Binghamton; Nick Picciuto, Utica; **P**-Tom Fine, Scranton; Bob Kuzava, Wilkes-Barre; **MVP**-Tom Fine, Scranton; **Manager**-Elmer Yoter, Scranton.

BA: Sam Mele, Scranton, .342
Runs: Robert Wilson, Wilkes-Barre, 103
Hits: Robert Wilson, Wilkes-Barre, 157
RBIs: Don Manno, Hartford, 97
HRs: Don Manno, Hartford, 12
Nick Picciuto, Utica, 12
Wins: Tom Fine, Scranton, 23
SOs: Bob Kuzava, Wilkes-Barre, 207
ERA: Mel Parnell, Scranton, 1.30

A South Atlantic League

President: Dr. E.M. Wilder

Standings	W	L	Pct.	GB	Manager
Columbus Cardinals (16)	79	60	.568	—	Kemp Wicker
Columbia Reds (12)	79	61	.564	½	Keith Molesworth
Greenville Spinners (2)	76	62	.551	2½	Ivy Griffin
Augusta Tigers (5)	76	63	.547	3	Dibrell Williams
Charleston Rebels	65	75	.464	14½	Martin "Chick" Autry
Jacksonville Tars (13)	65	75	.464	14½	John Hudson
Macon Peaches (11)	61	79	.436	18½	Al Leitz/Bob Lamotte
Savannah Indians (6)	55	81	.404	22½	Al Bender/Lena Blackburne

Playoffs: Augusta 4 games, Columbus 1; Columbia 4 games, Greenville 2.
Finals: Augusta 4 games, Columbia 0.

All-Star Team: 1B-Harry Ashworth, Augusta; **2B**-Ed Kazak, Columbus; **3B**-Cliff Perez, Augusta; **SS**-Alfred Livingston, Charleston; **OF**-Bob Churchill, Greenville; Frank Baumholtz, Columbia; Ted Kluszewski, Columbia; **C**-Jack Warren, Columbia; **Util**-Frank Dunlap, Macon; **P**-Sheldon Jones, Jacksonville; Matthew Nolan, Greenville; **Manager**-Kemp Wicker, Columbus.

BA: Ted Kluszewski, Columbia, .352
Runs: Frank Bocek, Augusta, 103
Hits: Frank Baumholtz, Columbia, 162
Frank Bocek, Augusta, 162
RBIs: Roy Broome, Columbus, 99
HRs: Robert Erps, Columbus, 16
Wins: Richard Starr, Augusta, 19
Sheldon Jones, Jacksonville, 19
SOs: Richard Starr, Augusta, 233
ERA: Richard Starr, Augusta, 2.07

B Interstate League

President: J. Vincent Jamison, Jr.

Standings	W	L	Pct.	GB	Manager
Wilmington Blue Rocks (14)	87	53	.621	—	Jack Saltzgaver
Harrisburg Senators (3)	76	64	.543	11	Les Bell
Hagerstown Owls (11)	74	65	.532	12½	John "Bunny" Griffiths
Allentown Cardinals (16)	69	70	.496	17½	Ollie Vanek
York White Roses (15)	68	70	.493	18	Walter Beck
Sunbury Yankees (5)	67	73	.479	20	Walt VanGrofski
Trenton Giants (13)	60	78	.435	26	Earl Wolgamot
Lancaster Red Roses (6)	55	83	.399	31	Tom Oliver

Attendance: Sunbury, 101,897.

Playoffs: Wilmington 4 games, Hagerstown 3; Harrisburg 4 games, Allentown 1.
Finals: Harrisburg 4 games, Wilmington 1.

BA: William Marks, Allentown, .372
Runs: Richard Burgett, Allentown, 128
Hits: John Blatnik, Harrisburg, 189
RBIs: Ed Sanicki, Wilmington, 144
HRs: Ed Sanicki, Wilmington, 30
Wins: John Szajna, Sunbury, 19
SOs: John Mackinson, Sunbury, 181
ERA: George Copeland, Wilmington, 2.76

B Mexican National League

President: Fernando N. Moldanado

Standings	W	L	Pct.	GB	Manager
Juarez Indios	23	21	.523	—	Guillermo Ornelas
Chihuahua Dorados	23	21	.523	—	Luis Sansirena
Saltillo Peroneros	23	22	.511	½	Agustin Verde
El Paso Texans	18	27	.400	5½	Andy Cohen
Mexico City Aztecs#	16	13	.551	NA	Zenon Ochoa
Torreon-Gomez Palacio Laguneros#	14	13	.519	NA	Reynaldo Cordeiro

#Mexico City and Torreon-Gomez Palacio dropped out April 27 because of pressure from the independent Mexican League.
The league withdrew from Organized Ball May 27.

B New England League

President: Claude B. Davidson

Standings	W	L	Pct.	GB	Manager
Lynn Red Sox (1)	82	40	.672	—	Thomas Kennedy
Nashua Dodgers (10)	80	41	.661	1½	Walter Alston
Manchester Giants (13)	75	45	.625	6	Hal Gruber
Pawtucket Slaters (9)	70	54	.565	13	Hugh Wise
Lawrence Millionaires	65	53	.551	15	George Kissell
Providence Chiefs	64	60	.516	19	Art Mahan
Fall River Indians	30	94	.242	53	Jack Burns
Portland Gulls	20	99	.168	60½	Ray Jordan

Playoffs: Lynn 3 games, Manchester 0; Nashua 3 games, Pawtucket 0.
Finals: Nashua 4 games, Lynn 2.

All-Star Team: 1B-Robert Sperry, Lynn; **2B**-Lawrence "Crash" Davis, Lawrence; **3B**-Alexander Suss, Providence; **SS**-James Coughlin, Pawtucket; **OF**-Lucien Belanger, Lawrence; Maurice "Mo" Mozzali, Manchester; Clinton Dahlberg, Manchester; **C**-Roy Campanella, Nashua; **Util**-Charles Maloney, Pawtucket; **P**-Walker Cress, Lynn; George Kadis, Lawrence; **Manager**-Walter Alston, Nashua.

BA: Maurice "Mo" Mozzali, Manchester, .356
Runs: Robert Sperry, Lynn, 109
Hits: Robert Sperry, Lynn, 175
RBIs: Maurice "Mo" Mozzali, Manchester, 118
HRs: Lucien Belanger, Lawrence, 22
Wins: Walker Cress, Lynn, 19
SOs: Walker Cress, Lynn, 174
ERA: Walker Cress, Lynn, 1.98

B Piedmont League

President: Richard A. Carrington

Standings	W	L	Pct.	GB	Manager
Roanoke Red Sox (1)	89	51	.636	—	Eddie Popowski
Portsmouth Cubs (11)	83	57	.593	6	Eugene Hassan/Ace Parker
Newport News Dodgers (10)	76	64	.543	13	John Fitzpatrick
Norfolk Tars (5)	71	69	.507	18	Thomas Kain
Richmond Colts (13)	60	80	.429	29	Ray Berres
Lynchburg Cardinals (16)	41	99	.293	48	Wes Ferrell

Playoffs: Newport News 4 games, Portsmouth 0; Roanoke 4 games, Norfolk 2.
Finals: Newport News 4 games, Roanoke 2, one tie.

BA: Ace Parker, Portsmouth, .331
Runs: Paul Varner, Portsmouth, 93
Hits: Virgil Stallcup, Roanoke, 164
RBIs: Virgil Stallcup, Roanoke, 93
HRs: Chuck Connors, Newport News, 17
Wins: Jack Clifton, Roanoke, 20
SOs: Wayne Johnson, Newport News, 193
ERA: Dalbert Bechtol, Roanoke, 2.03

B Southeastern League

President: Stuart X. Stephenson

Standings	W	L	Pct.	GB	Attend.	Manager
Pensacola Fliers (8)	85	48	.639	—	111,325	Bill McGhee
Anniston Rams (15)	81	59	.579	7½	98,836	Tommy West
Vicksburg Billies	70	63	.526	15	59,074	Louis Blair
Montgomery Rebels	66	70	.485	20½	101,776	Gus Brittain/Joe Cavosie/ Frank Skaff
Jackson Senators (9)	64	71	.474	22	64,108	Travis Jackson
Gadsden Pilots	60	76	.441	26½	93,315	Dave Coble
Selma Cloverleafs (15)	60	77	.438	27	43,070	Frank Oceak
Meridian Peps (10)	56	78	.418	29½	59,487	Walter Tauscher/Fred Williams

Playoffs: Vicksburg 4 games, Pensacola 2; Anniston 4 games, Montgomery 2.
Finals: Anniston 4 games, Vicksburg 3.

All-Star Team: 1B-Bill McGhee, Pensacola; **2B**-Robert Fletcher, Pensacola; **3B**-Grover Resinger, Vicksburg; **SS**-Pete Castiglione, Selma; **OF**-Nesbit Wilson, Anniston; Grover Bowers, Gadsden; Joe Cavosie, Montgomery; **C**-Dale Lenn, Gadsden; **Util**-Norbert Barker, Vicksburg; **P**-Everett Hill, Anniston; Robert Tart, Pensacola; **Manager**-Travis Jackson, Jackson.

BA: Bill McGhee, Pensacola, .349
Runs: Garrett McBryde, Pensacola, 108
Hits: Roy Pinkston, Gadsden, 186
RBIs: Roy Pinkston, Gadsden, 145
HRs: Roy Pinkston, Gadsden, 33
Wins: Everett Hill, Anniston, 17
Vernon Horn, Vicksburg, 17
Ralph Hendrix, Pensacola, 17
SOs: Richard Piatnek, Selma, 160
ERA: Everett Hill, Anniston, 2.40

B Three-I League

President: Tom Fairweather

Standings	W	L	Pct.	GB	Manager
Davenport Cubs (11)	76	44	.618	—	William Kelly
Danville Dodgers (10)	76	44	.618	—	Jake Pitler/Paul Chervinko
Evansville Braves (9)	68	51	.571	7½	Bob Coleman
Terre Haute Phillies (14)	63	60	.512	14½	Ray Brubaker
Waterloo White Hawks (2)	62	63	.496	16½	Johnny Mostil
Springfield Browns (7)	58	67	.464	20½	Tony Robello
Decatur Commodores (16)	43	72	.374	30½	Harrison Wickel
Quincy Gems (5)	37	82	.311	38½	Edward Marleau/Cedric Durst

Attendance: Waterloo, 89,825.

Playoffs: Davenport defeated Danville in a one game playoff for first place. Evansville 3 games, Davenport 1; Terre Haute 3 games, Danville 1.
Finals: Evansville 3 games, Terre Haute 0.

All-Star Team: 1B-Frank McElyea, Evansville; **2B**-Edward Bachmann, Springfield; **3B**-James Lucas, Springfield; **SS**-James Ackeret, Terre Haute; **OF**-Andrew Skurski, Waterloo; Cal Abrams, Danville; Hank Bauer, Quincy; **C**-Albert "Rube" Walker, Davenport; **Util**-Robert Peterson, Davenport; **P**-Jean Davison, Davenport; William Linderman, Terre Haute; **Manager**-Bob Coleman, Evansville.

BA: Albert "Rube" Walker, Davenport, .354
Runs: Richard Welker, Terre Haute, 105
Hits: Cal Abrams, Danville, 146
RBIs: Bill Sanders, Terre Haute, 96
HRs: Bill Sanders, Terre Haute, 14
 Jim Christie, Terre Haute, 14

Wins: Bob Kohout, Danville, 14
 Ken Manus, Waterloo, 14
 Charles Shipman, Evansville, 14
SOs: Ray Shore, Springfield, 157
ERA: Jean Davison, Davenport, 2.18

B Tri-State League
President: C.M. Llewellyn

Standings	W	L	Pct.	GB	Manager
Charlotte Hornets (8)	93	46	.669	—	Spencer Abbott
Asheville Tourists (10)	83	57	.593	10½	William Sayles
Knoxville Smokies	73	67	.521	20½	Dale Alexander
Shelby Cubs (11)	59	81	.421	34½	Ray Green
Anderson A's (13)	59	81	.421	34½	Clyde McDowell
Spartanburg Spartans (7)	52	87	.374	41	Francis Kappelman

Attendance: Charlotte, 111,000.

Playoffs: Shelby defeated Anderson in a one game playoff for fourth place. Knoxville 4 games, Asheville 1; Charlotte 4 games, Shelby 2.
Finals: Charlotte 4 games, Knoxville 3.

All-Star Team: 1B-Carl Miller, Charlotte; **2B**-Lawrence Womack, Charlotte; **3B**-Robert Morem, Charlotte; **SS**-Veo Story, Asheville; **OF**-William Sayles, Asheville, Alex Kvasnak, Charlotte, D.C. "Pud" Miller, Spartanburg; **C**-Dick Bouknight, Asheville; **Util**-Herschel Held, Anderson; **P**-John Dixon, Charlotte; Porter Witt, Knoxville; **Manager**-William Sayles, Asheville.

BA: Dick Bouknight, Asheville, .367
Runs: Alex Kvasnak, Charlotte, 101
Hits: Fred Marsh, Knoxville, 180
RBIs: William Sayles, Asheville, 105

HRs: D.C. "Pud" Miller, Spartanburg, 19
Wins: John Dixon, Charlotte, 19
SOs: Ralph Germano, Spartanburg, 179
ERA: Alex Zukowski, Charlotte, 1.41

B Western International League
President: Robert B. Abel

Standings	W	L	Pct.	GB	Manager
Wenatchee Chiefs	89	54	.622	—	Buddy Ryan
Salem Senators	79	63	.556	9½	Leo Edwards
Bremerton Bluejackets	73	63	.537	12½	Sam Gibson
Tacoma Tigers (11)	76	67	.531	13	Luther Harvel
Yakima Stars (15)	71	69	.507	16½	Spencer Harris
Vancouver Capilanos (9)	65	71	.478	20½	Syl Johnson/Ed Carnett
Spokane Indians	54	78	.409	29½	Glenn Wright/Ben Geraghty
Victoria Athletics	49	91	.350	38½	Laurel Harney

Attendance: Salem, 103,000; Wenatchee, 94,471; Total, 780,443.

Playoffs: None

BA: Glenn Stetter, Wenatchee, .366
Runs: William Barisoff, Bremerton, 133
Hits: Bill Garbe, Yakima, 191
RBIs: William Barisoff, Bremerton, 155
 Dick Adams, Wenatchee, 155

HRs: William Barisoff, Bremerton, 40
Wins: Clarence Federmeyer, Bremerton, 21
SOs: Robert Jansen, Victoria, 296
ERA: Carl Gunnarson, Salem, 3.31

C Border League
President: John G. Ward

Standings	W	L	Pct.	GB	Attend.	Manager
Auburn Cayugas	72	44	.621	—	48,683	Barney Hearn
Watertown Athletics	69	51	.575	5	53,605	Jim Scott
Kingston Ponies (6)	58	55	.513	12½	60,957	Ben Lady
Granby Red Sox	54	60	.474	17	31,159	Bill Sisler/Hal Cleves
Ogdensburg Maples	50	68	.424	23	28,395	Bob Dill
Sherbrooke Canadians	46	71	.393	26½	25,576	George Smith/Dutch Proecher

Playoffs: Kingston 3 games, Auburn 1; Watertown 3 games, Granby 1.
Finals: Watertown 4 games, Kingston 2.

BA: Bob Dill, Ogdensburg, .397
Hits: James Heximer, Kingston, 156
RBIs: Bob Dill, Ogdensburg, 118
HRs: Bob Dill, Ogdensburg, 20

Wins: Arnold Jarrell, Kingston, 21
SOs: Peter Karpuk, Kingston, 175
ERA: Arnold Jarrell, Kingston, 2.30

C California League
President: W.R. "Bill" Schroeder

Standings	W	L	Pct.	GB	Attend.	Manager
Stockton Ports	78	52	.600	—	94,706	Tony Governor/Harry Gooarian
Santa Barbara Dodgers (10)	74	56	.569	4	82,406	Jack Knight/Jack Mele
Bakersfield Indians (3)	72	58	.534	6	79,416	Martin Metrovich/Tony Governor
Modesto Reds	69	61	.531	9	46,584	Rupert "Tommy" Thompson
Fresno Cardinals (16)	58	72	.446	20	59,185	Ev Johnson/Paul Bowa
Visalia Cubs (11)	39	91	.300	39	47,113	Bob Schang/Pete Beiden

Playoffs: Stockton 3 games, Bakersfield 2; Modesto 3 games, Santa Barbara 2.
Finals: Stockton 4 games, Modesto 0.

All-Star Team: 1B-Frank Hecklinger, Visalia; **2B**-Edward Samcoff, Stockton; **3B**-Harry Gooarian, Stockton; **SS**-Tom Glaviano, Fresno; **OF**-Alfonso Prieto, Bakersfield; Irv Noren, Santa Barbara; Rupert "Tommy" Thompson, Modesto; Clarence Russell, Bakersfield; **C**-Jack Mele, Santa Barbara; Bob Schang, Visalia/Stockton; **Util**-Theodore Harder, Fresno; **P**-Mike Garcia, Bakersfield; Don Belton, Stockton.

BA: Alfonso Prieto, Bakersfield, .380
Runs: Tom Glaviano, Fresno, 142
Hits: Irv Noren, Santa Barbara, 188
RBIs: Irv Noren, Santa Barbara, 129

HRs: Harry Gooarian, Stockton, 24
Wins: Don Belton, Stockton, 23
SOs: Mike Garcia, Bakersfield, 186
ERA: Mike Garcia, Bakersfield, 2.56

C Canadian-American League
President: Albert E. Houghton

Standings	W	L	Pct.	GB	Attend.	Manager
Trois Rivieres Royals (10)	72	49	.595	—	72,097	Frenchy Bordagaray
Pittsfield Electrics (3)	69	47	.595	½	64,913	Tony Rensa
Rome Colonels (4)	72	52	.581	1½	58,371	Woody Wheaton
Oneonta Red Sox (1)	68	54	.557	4½	56,381	Red Marion
Amsterdam Rugmakers (5).	61	58	.513	10	78,915	Sol Mishkin
Gloversville-Johnstown Glovers (7)	53	67	.442	18½	50,436	Ben Huffman
Schenectady Blue Jays (14)	45	75	.375	26½	53,239	Bill Cronin
Quebec Alouettes (11)	41	79	.342	30½	65,557	Joe Segrue/Tim Murchison/John Intlekofer

Playoffs: Trois Rivieres 4 games, Rome 3; Pittsfield 4 games, Oneonta 3.
Finals: Trois Rivieres 4 games, Pittsfield 1.

BA: Frenchy Bordagaray, Trois Rivieres, .363
Runs: Bunny Mick, Amsterdam, 115
Hits: John Greenwald, Rome, 145
RBIs: Al Rosen, Pittsfield, 86
HRs: Al Rosen, Pittsfield, 15

Wins: Stewart Mackie, Trois Rivieres, 18
SOs: Harry Pilarski, Oneonta, 159
ERA: Louis Palmisiano, Pittsfield, 2.67
Pct: Roy Partlow, Trois Rivieres, .909, 10-1

C Carolina League
President: Dr. Thomas S. Wilson

Standings	W	L	Pct.	GB	Attend.	Manager
Greensboro Patriots	85	57	.599	—	171,801	George Granger
Raleigh Capitals (9)	80	62	.563	5	145,021	Charles Carroll/Ray Thomas
Durham Bulls (1)	80	62	.563	5	151,392	Floyd Patterson
Burlington Bees	69	71	.493	15	103,000	Steve Bysco
Winston-Salem Cardinals (16)	68	72	.486	16	127,000	Cecil "Zip" Payne
Martinsville Athletics (6)	67	75	.472	18	66,000	Cliff Bolton
Danville Leafs (13)	60	82	.423	25	110,000	Herb Brett
Leaksville-Draper-Spray Triplets	57	85	.401	28	67,000	Mickey O'Neil

Playoffs: Durham 4 games, Greensboro 2; Raleigh 4 games, Burlington 2.
Finals: Raleigh 4 games, Durham 2.

All-Star Team: 1B-Jim Blair, Burlington; **2B**-Lee Mohr, Durham; **3B**-Bill Hockenbury, Martinsville; **SS**-Hillard Nance, Martinsville; **OF**-Woody Fair, Durham; Tom Wright, Durham; Gus Zernial, Burlington; **C**-Milton Welch, Durham; **Util**-Nig Lipscomb, Greensboro; **P**-Frank Paulin, Leaksville-Draper-Spray; Willard Speaks, Greensboro; **Manager**-Floyd Patterson, Durham.

BA: Tom Wright, Durham, .380
Runs: Woody Fair, Durham, 161
Hits: Tom Wright, Durham, 200
RBIs: Woody Fair, Durham, 161
HRs: Gus Zernial, Burlington, 41
2B: Woody Fair, Durham, 51

Wins: Roy Pinyoun, Raleigh, 19
 Frank Paulin, Leaksville-Draper-Spray, 19
SOs: Frank Paulin, Leaksville-Draper-Spray, 220
ERA: Harold "Skinny" Brown, Durham, 2.42

C East Texas League
President: J. Walter Morris

Standings	W	L	Pct.	GB	Manager
Henderson Oilers	83	56	.597	—	Ray Honeycutt
Texarkana Bears (2)	81	58	.582	2	Gabby Lusk/Joe Kracher
Tyler Trojans	76	63	.547	7	Doug Taitt/Dutch Prather
Greenville Majors	71	67	.514	11½	Sal Gliatto/Alex Hooks
Sherman Twins	70	70	.500	13½	Guy Sturdy
Paris Red Peppers (7)	68	72	.486	15½	Homer Peel
Jacksonville Jax	60	78	.435	22½	Lloyd "Rabbit" Rigby
Lufkin Foresters	47	92	.338	36	Hank Doty/Mike "Gus" Mistovich

Total Attendance: 700,000.

Playoffs: Texarkana 4 games, Tyler 1; Henderson 4 games, Greenville 3.
Finals: Henderson 4 games, Texarkana 2.

BA: Don Stokes, Tyler/Sherman, .361
Runs: Gene Olive, Henderson, 128
Hits: Gene Olive, Henderson, 211
RBIs: Paul Martin, Henderson, 127

HRs: Frank Sacka, Paris, 30
Wins: Elton Davis, Henderson, 26
SOs: Louis Christy, Tyler/Henderson, 190
ERA: Elton Davis, Henderson, 2.31

C Florida International League
President: Wayne Allen

Standings	W	L	Pct.	GB	Manager
Havana Cubans#	76	41	.650	—	Oscar Rodriguez
Tampa Smokers	76	55	.580	7	Vin Grannell/Frank Pare
Miami Beach Flamingos (9)	64	64	.500	17½	Max Rosenfeld
West Palm Beach Indians	58	64	.475	20½	Herb Thomas
Lakeland Pilots	53	74	.417	28	Ray Hunt/Bill Purrin
Miami Sun Sox	53	82	.393	32	Paul Waner

#Havana lost 17 wins due to using an excessive number of class men.
Attendance: Havana, 202,875.

Playoffs: Tampa 3 games, Miami Beach 0; West Palm Beach 3 games, Havana 2.
Finals: Tampa 4 games, West Palm Beach 2.

BA: Ralph Brown, Tampa, .381
Runs: Ralph Brown, Tampa, 110
Hits: Ralph Brown, Tampa, 195
RBIs: Ben Fernandez, Tampa, 79
HRs: Armando Valdes, Havana/West Palm Beach, 7
Wins: Chet Covington, Tampa, 28
SOs: Chet Covington, Tampa, 260
ERA: Chet Covington, Tampa, 1.66

C Middle Atlantic League
President: Elmer M. Daily

Standings	W	L	Pct.	GB	Manager
Erie Sailors (13)	91	39	.700	—	Steve Mizerak
Butler Yankees (5)	78	52	.600	13	Milt Rosner
Youngstown Gremlins	67	62	.519	23½	Paul Birch
Niagara Falls Frontiers	64	66	.492	27	George Proechel/Bill Mongiello
Johnstown Johnnies (10)	49	80	.388	41½	Cyril Pfeifer
Oil City Oilers (15)	40	90	.308	51	Charles Muse/Charlie Harig

Playoffs: Erie 3 games, Youngstown 1; Niagara Falls 3 games, Butler 1.
Finals: Erie 4 games, Niagara Falls 3.

All-Star Team: 1B-Harry Anderson, Butler; 2B-William Nickols, Erie; 3B-Don Brennan, Erie; SS-Robert Gardner, Youngstown; OF-Bill Behie, Butler; Gerald Scalla, Erie; William Harnick, Niagara Falls; C-William Lance, Erie; Util-Arthur Frantz, Niagara Falls; P-John Uber, Erie; Joseph Och, Butler; Manager-Steve Mizerak, Erie.

BA: Cyril Pfeifer, Johnstown, .344
Runs: Victor Fucci, Butler, 101
Hits: Harry Anderson, Butler, 159
RBIs: Bill Behie, Butler, 87
HRs: Maurice Cunningham, Butler/Youngstown, 14
Wins: John Uber, Erie, 18
SOs: John Uber, Erie, 192
ERA: George Bamberger, Erie, 1.35
Sam Webb, Erie, 18

C Northern League
President: Herman D. White

Standings	W	L	Pct.	GB	Manager
St. Cloud Rox (13)	73	31	.702	—	Walter Kopp
Fargo-Moorhead Twins	63	41	.606	10	Bruno Haas
Superior Blues (2)	59	52	.532	17½	Fred Hensley/George "Red" Treadwell
Eau Claire Bears	56	52	.519	19	Joe Skurski
Aberdeen Pheasants (7)	57	53	.518	19	Gus Albright
Grand Forks Chiefs (10)	50	56	.472	24	Glenn Chapman/Ray Blaemire
Sioux Falls Canaries	41	68	.376	34½	Lynn King
Duluth Dukes (16)	30	76	.283	44	Mercer Harris/Gene Sak

Playoffs: Fargo-Moorhead 4 games, Eau Claire 3; St. Cloud 4 games, Superior 2.
Finals: St. Cloud 4 games, Fargo-Moorhead 1.

BA: Ken Staples, Grand Forks, .382
Runs: Ernie Davis, Grand Forks, 98
Hits: Ernie Davis, Grand Forks, 145
RBIs: Edward Gittens, St. Cloud, 99
HRs: Anthony Jaros, St. Cloud, 14
Wins: Bob Haas, Fargo-Moorhead, 19
SOs: Bob Haas, Fargo-Moorhead, 193
ERA: Bob Haas, Fargo-Moorhead, 2.20

C Pioneer League
President: Jack P. Halliwell

Standings	W	L	Pct.	GB	Attend.	Manager
Salt Lake City Bees**	76	54	.585	—	205,861	Joe Orengo
Twin Falls Cowboys*(5)	72	56	.563	3	80,636	Earl Bolyard
Ogden Reds (12)	68	59	.535	6½	103,922	Jim Kelsey
Pocatello Cardinals (16)	64	63	.504	10½	56,057	Bill Brenzel
Idaho Falls Russets	53	76	.411	22½	64,780	Ed Leishman
Boise Pilots	52	77	.403	23½	62,495	Walt Lohe

Playoffs: Twin Falls defeated Salt Lake City in a one game playoff for the first half championship. Salt Lake City 4 games, Twin Falls 2.

BA: Charles Henson, Salt Lake City, .363
Runs: Charles Henson, Salt Lake City, 117
Hits: Charles Henson, Salt Lake City, 191
RBIs: Harry Heslet, Twin Falls, 124
HRs: Harry Heslet, Twin Falls, 29
Wins: Harry Perkowski, Ogden, 23
SOs: Robert Chesnes, Salt Lake City, 278
ERA: Robert Chesnes, Salt Lake City, 1.52
Pct: Harry Perkowski, Ogden, .793, 23-6

C West Texas-New Mexico League
President: Milton E. Price

Standings	W	L	Pct.	GB	Manager
Abilene Blue Sox (10)	97	40	.708	—	Hayden Greer
Pampa Oilers	92	46	.667	5½	Grover Seitz
Amarillo Gold Sox	93	47	.664	5½	Bob Seeds
Lubbock Hubbers (4)	71	70	.504	28	Jim Miller
Borger Gassers	66	72	.478	31½	Ted Clawitter
Albuquerque Dukes	55	85	.393	43½	Jimmy Zinn
Clovis Pioneers (3)	47	93	.336	51½	Hal Webb
Lamesa Lobos	36	104	.257	62½	George Sturdivant

Attendance: Amarillo, 114,813; Total, 658,796.

Playoffs: Lubbock 4 games, Abilene 1; Pampa 4 games, Amarillo 2.
Finals: Pampa 4 games, Lubbock 2.

All-Star Team: 1B-Gordon Goldsberry, Albuquerque; 2B-Vurdon Gilchrist, Borger; 3B-Leo Thomas, Abilene; SS-Hayden Greer, Abilene; OF-Bill Scopetone, Amarillo; Richard Woldt, Clovis; Bob Crues, Amarillo; C-Ted Clawitter, Borger; Util-Danny Ozark, Abilene; P-William Evans, Amarillo; William Garland, Pampa; Manager-Grover Seitz, Pampa.

BA: Vurdon Gilchrist, Borger, .376
Runs: Vurdon Gilchrist, Borger, 176
Hits: Hayden Greer, Abilene, 202
RBIs: Gordon Nell, Borger, 175
HRs: Joe Bauman, Amarillo, 48
3B: Gordon Goldsberry, Albuquerque, 21
Wins: William Evans, Amarillo, 26
SOs: William Evans, Amarillo, 297
ERA: John Hall, Abilene, 2.45
Pct: Joe Tysko, Abilene, .867, 13-2

C Western Association
President: Tom Fairweather

Standings	W	L	Pct.	GB	Attend.	Manager
Leavenworth Braves (9)	76	57	.571	—	56,176	Charles Carmen
Hutchinson Cubs**(11)	73	56	.566	1	55,868	Dickie Kerr
St. Joseph Cardinals (16)	75	62	.547	3	74,018	Robert Stanton
Muskogee Reds (4)	75	64	.540	4	79,494	Ray Baker
Ft. Smith Giants*(13)	67	63	.515	7½	70,414	Hugh Willingham
Joplin Miners (5)	61	73	.455	15½	90,363	Jim Acton
Topeka Owls	53	79	.402	22½	123,119	Ray Murphy
Salina Blue Jays (14)	51	77	.398	22½	44,050	Edwin Walls

Playoff: Hutchinson 4 games, Ft. Smith 2.

All-Star Team: 1B-Rocky Nelson, St. Joseph; 2B-Joseph Damato, Hutchinson; 3B-Jim Dyck, Joplin; SS-Willard Elliott, Leavenworth; OF-Al Lawrence, Muskogee; Bob Coleman, Ft. Smith; Byron Watkins, Topeka; C-Earl Skaggs, Joplin; Util-Dale Hackett, Joplin; P-Anthony Jacobs, Hutchinson; Lewis Hester, Topeka; Manager-Dickie Kerr, Hutchinson.

BA: Jim Dyck, Joplin, .364
Runs: Frank Celona, St. Joseph, 101
Hits: Byron Watkins, Topeka, 176
RBIs: Jim Dyck, Joplin, 104
HRs: Peter Deem, Muskogee, 18
3B: Rocky Nelson, St. Joseph, 23
Wins: Ralph Rosengarten, Leavenworth, 22
SOs: William Washburn, Salina, 242
ERA: Winlow Johnson, Topeka, 2.22

D Alabama State League
President: Jack Hovater

Standings	W	L	Pct.	GB	Manager
Dothan Browns	72	58	.554	—	Frank Martin
Geneva Red Birds (1)	69	61	.531	3	Charles Holly
Greenville Lions	67	62	.519	4½	Dan Miller/William Anderson
Brewton Millers (2)	63	65	.492	8	Ben Catchings
Troy Trojans	60	68	.469	11	Norman DeWeese
Ozark Eagles	55	72	.433	15½	Ray Knapp/Dick Coffman

Playoffs: Geneva 3 games, Brewton 1; Greenville 3 games, Dothan 1.
Finals: Geneva 3 games, Greenville 1.

BA: Emil Bozick, Troy, .354
Runs: Melvin Schwab, Ozark, 128
Hits: Emil Bozick, Troy, 178
RBIs: Harold Walther, Greenville/Geneva, 124
HRs: Harold Walther, Greenville/Geneva, 17
Melvin Schwab, Ozark, 17
Wins: James Atkins, Geneva, 20
Max Peterson, Greenville, 20
SOs: Carl Johnson, Dothan, 271
ERA: Carl Johnson, Dothan, 2.46

D Appalachian League
President: Carl A. Jones

Standings	W	L	Pct.	GB	Attend.	Manager
New River Rebels#(2)	83	40	.675	—	39,037	Jack Crosswhite
Bristol Twins (13)	72	51	.585	11	68,504	Don Cross
Elizabethton Betsy Cubs (11)	68	57	.544	16	37,660	Lou Bekeza
Pulaski Counts	65	58	.528	18	49,198	Ray Rudisill
Johnson City Cardinals (16)	64	60	.516	19½	47,052	Specs Garbee
Kingsport Cherokees (8)	55	70	.440	29	47,459	Hobe Brummitt/Russell "Red" Mincy
Bluefield Blue-Grays (9)	52	72	.419	31½	53,669	Walter DeFreitas/Bud Clancy
Welch Miners	33	84	.282	47	40,648	Steve Sefcik/George Smiley/Jim McNeish

#represented Narrows-Pearisburg, Virginia.

Playoffs: Elizabethton 3 games, Bristol 0; New River 3 games, Pulaski 2.
Finals: New River 4 games, Elizabethton 2.

All-Star Team: 1B-Thomas Zikmund, Bluefield; **2B**-Charles Pepio, Bristol; **3B**-John Knox, Elizabethton; **SS**-Emil Stoecker, Bluefield; **OF**-John Kruckman, New River; Russell "Red" Mincy, Pulaski/Kingsport; **C**-Jack Crosswhite, New River; **Util**-Lou Bekeza, Elizabethton; **P**-Shannon Hardwick, New River; Paul LaPalme, Bristol; **Manager**-Don Cross, Bristol.

BA: Russell "Red" Mincy, Pulaski/Kingsport, .396
Runs: Ray Rudisill, Pulaski, 169
Hits: Russell "Red" Mincy, Pulaski/Kingsport, 179

RBIs: Russell "Red" Mincy, Pulaski/Kingsport, 136
HRs: Leo "Muscle" Shoals, Kingsport, 21
Wins: Paul LaPalme, Bristol, 20
SOs: Melvin Nee, Kingsport, 203
ERA: Bob Hoch, Johnson City, 2.39

D Blue Ridge League
President: Joe Ryan

Standings	W	L	Pct.	GB	Manager
Salem Friends/ Lenoir Red Sox#	71	35	.670	—	Vernon Mackey/Noel Casbier
Mt. Airy Graniteers	59	45	.567	11	Edwin Morgan
Radford Rockets	53	55	.491	19	Ed Martin
Galax Leafs	30	78	.278	42	Rex Phipps

#Salem (20-8) moved to Lenoir June 25.

Playoffs: None

All-Star Team: 1B-Edwin Morgan, Mt. Airy/Galax; **2B**-Einar Sorenson, Mt. Airy/Galax; **3B**-Richard Kalal, Salem/Lenoir; **SS**-Noel Casbier, Salem/Lenoir; **OF**-Laddie Paul, Galax; Doug Clarke, Mt. Airy/Galax; Edward Wayne, Salem/Lenoir; **C**-Serge Schuster, Salem/Lenoir; **Util**-Michael Brelich, Radford; **P**-Edward Wallace, Salem/Lenoir; Norman Southard, Galax; **Manager**-Noel Casbier, Salem/Lenoir.

BA: Edward Wayne, Salem/Lenoir, .403
Runs: Richard Kalal, Salem/Lenoir, 127
Hits: Edwin Morgan, Mt. Airy/Galax, 155
RBIs: Edwin Morgan, Mt. Airy/Galax, 127
HRs: Edwin Morgan, Mt. Airy/Galax, 16

Wins: Harry Cohick, Radford, 16
 Earl Price, Salem/Lenoir, 16
SOs: Edward Wallace, Salem/Lenoir, 148
ERA: Richard Cooper, Salem/Lenoir, 3.09

D Coastal Plain League
President: Ray Goodmon

Standings	W	L	Pct.	GB	Attend.	Manager
Rocky Mount Rocks	74	51	.592	—	104,218	Harry Soufas
Kinston Eagles	67	56	.545	6	54,120	Frank Rodgers
Wilson Tobs	67	57	.540	6½	108,229	Irv Dickens
Goldsboro Goldbugs	64	60	.516	9½	92,123	Bill Herring
Tarboro Tars (1)	61	65	.484	13½	46,679	Michael Kardish/Bull Hamons
Greenville Greenies	58	67	.464	16	62,359	Horace Payne
New Bern Bears	57	68	.456	17	90,485	Adel White
Fayetteville Cubs (11)	51	75	.405	23½	77,007	John Intlekofer/Don Anderson

Playoffs: Rocky Mount 4 games, Goldsboro 1; Kinston 4 games, Wilson 3.
Finals: Rocky Mount 4 games, Kinston 2.

All-Star Team: 1B-Vern Shetler, New Bern; **2B**-Irv Dickens, Wilson; **3B**-Ed Bauer, Wilson; **SS**-Ray Carlson, Greenville; **OF**-Verne Blackwell, Greenville; John Wolfe, Wilson; Ed Musial, Fayetteville; **C**-Charles Munday, Rocky Mount; **Util**-Grover Fowler, Rocky Mount; **P**-Bill Kennedy, Rocky Mount; **Manager**-Bill Herring, Goldsboro.

BA: Vern Shetler, New Bern, .362
Runs: John Wolfe, Wilson, 123
Hits: Ray Carlson, Greenville, 158
RBIs: Verne Blackwell, Greenville, 114

HRs: Charles Munday, Rocky Mount, 21
Wins: Bill Kennedy, Rocky Mount, 28
SOs: Bill Kennedy, Rocky Mount, 456
ERA: Bill Kennedy, Rocky Mount, 1.03

D Eastern Shore League
President: J. Thomas Kibler

Standings	W	L	Pct.	GB	Manager
Centreville Orioles (3)	88	37	.704	—	Jim McLeod
Milford Red Sox (1)	77	49	.611	11½	Walter Millies
Dover Phillies (14)	68	57	.544	20	Hank Lehman
Salisbury Cardinals (16)	61	64	.488	27	Harold Contini
Easton Yankees (5)	59	66	.472	29	Jack Farmer
Seaford Eagles	58	68	.460	30½	Walter Youse/Joe Becker
Cambridge Dodgers (10)	53	73	.421	35½	Jimmy Cooney/Barney DeForge
Federalsburg A's (6)	37	87	.298	50½	Lew Krausse

Playoffs: Centreville 4 games, Dover 3; Milford 4 games, Salisbury 2.
Finals: Centreville 4 games, Milford 1.

All-Star Team: 1B-Irvin Schupp, Centreville; **2B**-Ray Nadel, Milford; **3B**-Stephen Nemeth, Milford; **SS**-Grady Wilson, Milford; **OF**-Nick Malfara, Centreville; Jimmy Stevens, Centreville; Don Marshall, Dover; **C**-John Martin, Easton; **Util**-Goldsboro Tyler, Cambridge; **P**-Mike Gast, Centreville; Jean Bournot, Cambridge; **Manager**-Walter Millies, Centreville.

BA: Sid Langston, Salisbury, .353
Runs: Jimmy Stevens, Centreville, 132
Hits: Fred Pacitto, Centreville, 164
RBIs: Don Marshall, Dover, 110
HRs: Don Marshall, Dover, 29

Wins: Richard Waldt, Centreville, 17
 Stanley Coulling, Centreville, 17
SOs: Mike Gast, Centreville, 182
ERA: Barney DeForge, Cambridge, 2.48

D Evangeline League
President: J. Walter Morris

Standings	W	L	Pct.	GB	Manager
Houma Indians	92	39	.702	—	Babe Benning/Paul Fugit
Natchez Giants	87	46	.654	6	Merle Coleman
Abbeville Athletics	82	48	.631	9½	Harry Strohm
Alexandria Aces (2)	67	67	.500	26½	Carl Kott
New Iberia Cardinals (1)	53	79	.402	39½	Aaron Ward
Thibodaux Giants	53	80	.398	40	Bob Mosel
Baton Rouge Red Sticks	50	82	.379	42½	Irvin Stein
Hammond Berries	44	87	.336	48	Joe Valenti

Total Attendance: 757,000.

Playoffs: Houma 4 games, Alexandria 1; Abbeville 4 games, Natchez 3.
Finals: Houma 4 games, Abbeville 1.

BA: Michael Conroy, Houma, .372
Runs: Michael Conroy, Houma, 140
Hits: Michael Conroy, Houma, 194
RBIs: Paul Fugit, Houma, 130

HRs: Irving Clement, Hammond/Abbeville, 25
Wins: Bill Thomas, Houma, 35
SOs: Nat Lowe, Abbeville, 215
ERA: Nat Lowe, Abbeville, 2.03

D Florida State League
President: Al Combs

Standings	W	L	Pct.	GB	Attend.	Manager
Orlando Senators (8)	94	44	.681	—	52,669	Ted Majeski
Sanford Celeryfeds	81	57	.587	7	58,671	Edward Levy
St. Augustine Saints	75	62	.547	12½	64,112	Bill Steinecke
DeLand Red Hats	68	68	.500	19	37,009	William Fuchs
Leesburg Anglers	63	71	.470	23	42,271	Bill Good
Palatka Azaleas	62	75	.453	26½	45,133	Myril Hoag
Daytona Beach Islanders (10)	58	73	.443	29	34,562	Jason Sosh
Gainesville G-Men	42	93	.311	47	41,049	Richard Bass

Playoffs: Orlando 4 games, DeLand 2; Sanford 4 games, St. Augustine 3.
Finals: Orlando 4 games, Sanford 3.

All-Star Team: 1B-Joe Eaton, Gainesville; **2B**-Lyle Judy, St. Augustine; **3B**-Jack Wilkes, St. Augustine; **SS**-Will Good, Jr., Leesburg; **OF**-Buddy Lake, Sanford; Myril Hoag, Palatka; Walter Harrington, DeLand; **C**-Bill Steinecke, St. Augustine; **Util**-William Fuchs, DeLand; **P**-Robert Kennington, DeLand; Scott Carey, Orlando; **Manager**-Edward Levy, Sanford.

BA: Myril Hoag, Palatka, .342
Runs: Jay Stebbins, Leesburg, 118
Hits: Buddy Lake, Sanford, 175
RBIs: Buddy Lake, Sanford, 140

HRs: Myril Hoag, Palatka, 8
 William Fuchs, DeLand, 8
 Ken Hill, Gainesville, 8
Wins: Scott Carey, Orlando, 22
 Howard Martin, Orlando, 22
SOs: Scott Carey, Orlando, 244
ERA: Jodie Howington, Sanford, 2.03

D Georgia-Alabama League
President: Carl W. East

Standings	W	L	Pct.	GB	Manager
Carrollton Hornets	75	55	.577	—	Luther Gunnells
Valley Rebels#	72	58	.554	3	Holt "Cat" Milner
Tallassee Indians (15)	71	59	.546	4	John Heving
Newnan Brownies	68	62	.523	7	George Nix/Lloyd Brown
La Grange Troupers	59	71	.454	16	Newton Parker/Jake Daniels
Opelika Owls	45	85	.346	30	Jimmy Hitchcock/Zack Sensussler

#represented Valley-Lanett (AL)-West Point (GA).

Playoffs: Tallassee 3 games, Carrollton 2; Valley 3 games, Newnan 2.
Finals: Tallassee 3 games, Valley 2.

BA: Luther Gunnells, Carrollton, .381
Runs: Jake Daniels, Valley/La Grange, 118
Hits: Jake Daniels, Valley/La Grange, 159
RBIs: Jake Daniels, Valley/La Grange, 122

HRs: Jake Daniels, Valley/La Grange, 30
Wins: John Johnson, Newnan, 20
SOs: John Johnson, Newnan, 138
ERA: Lloyd Brown, Newnan, 2.17

D Georgia-Florida League
President: W.T. Anderson

Standings	W	L	Pct.	GB	Attend.	Manager
Americus Phillies (14)	87	37	.702	—	73,126	Jack Sanford
Moultrie Packers	76	47	.618	10½	96,556	Jim Poole/Edward Parsons
Waycross Bears	75	50	.600	12½	66,902	LeGrant Scott
Valdosta Dodgers (10)	64	61	.512	23½	55,683	Bill Welp
Tallahassee Pirates (15)	63	62	.504	24½	55,193	Arthur Doll
Albany Cardinals (16)	54	71	.432	33½	70,178	Herb Moore
Thomasville Tigers	45	80	.360	42½	51,679	Vincent "Moon" Mullen
Cordele White Sox (2)	35	91	.278	53	44,923	Joe Holden

Playoffs: Americus 3 games, Waycross 2; Moultrie 3 games, Valdosta 1.
Finals: Moultrie 4 games, Americus 3.

All-Star Team: 1B-Bill Glynn, Americus; **2B**-Warren Brooks, Moultrie; **3B**-Walt Rogers, Valdosta; **SS**-Mike Romello, Americus; **OF**-Joe Angeli, Tallahassee; Joe Moody, Waycross; James McCarnes, Waycross; **C**-Norman Wilson, Waycross; **Util**-Hal Haddican, Tallahassee; **P**-

Lee Holloman, Moultrie; Guinn Gronic, Waycross; **Manager**-Jack Sanford, Americus.

BA: LeGrant Scott, Waycross, .368
Runs: James McCarnes, Waycross, 111
Hits: James McCarnes, Waycross, 169
RBIs: Ken Rhyne, Moultrie, 129

HRs: Ken Rhyne, Moultrie, 22
Wins: John Asmer, Americus, 24
SOs: Gaylor Lemish, Moultrie, 278
ERA: Herbert Moore, Albany, 1.44

D Kansas-Oklahoma-Missouri League
President: E.L. Dale

Standings	W	L	Pct.	GB	Manager
Chanute Athletics	68	53	.562	—	Goldie Howard
Miami Indians (10)	69	54	.561	—	Guy Froman
Iola Cubs (11)	63	57	.525	4½	Al Reitz
Pittsburg Browns (7)	61	59	.508	6½	Jim Crandall
Carthage Cardinals (16)	54	66	.450	13½	Adolph Arlitt
Bartlesville Oilers (15)	47	73	.392	20½	Claude Willoughby

Playoffs: Iola 3 games, Miami 2; Chanute 3 games, Pittsburg 2.
Finals: Iola 3 games, Chanute 3, called off due to rain and lack of available grounds.

All-Star Team: 1B-Adolph Arlitt, Carthage; **2B**-Newt Keithley, Miami; **3B**-Ken Aubrey, Iola; **SS**-Richard Bulkley, Chanute; **OF**-Larry Singleton, Iola; Joseph Pollock, Miami; Don Lenhardt, Pittsburg; **C**-Dave Dennis, Miami; **Util**-Jack Bumgarner, Bartlesville; **P**-Ross Grimsley, Chanute; Oscar Walterman, Carthage; **Manager**-Goldie Howard, Chanute.

BA: Newt Keithley, Miami, .346
Runs: Richard Bulkley, Chanute, 111
Hits: Newt Keithley, Miami, 167
RBIs: Adolph Arlitt, Carthage, 82
HRs: Larry Singleton, Iola, 10

Wins: Ross Grimsley, Chanute, 18
Oscar Walterman, Carthage, 18
SOs: Ross Grimsley, Chanute, 295
ERA: Ross Grimsley, Chanute, 1.93

D Kitty League
President: Shelby Peace

Standings	W	L	Pct.	GB	Manager
Owensboro Oilers (9)	83	39	.680	—	Earle Browne
Hopkinsville Hoppers (11)	73	53	.579	12	Calvin Chapman
Fulton Bulldogs	69	56	.552	15½	Hugh Holliday
Mayfield Clothiers (7)	64	59	.520	19½	Eddie O'Connell
Clarksville Owls	58	67	.464	26½	Dick Luckey
Madisonville Miners (2)	53	71	.427	31	Frank Zubik
Union City Greyhounds	52	72	.419	32	Johnny Gill
Cairo Egyptians	45	80	.360	39½	Frank Piet

Playoffs: Owensboro 3 games, Mayfield 1; Fulton 3 games, Hopkinsville 1.
Finals: Owensboro 4 games, Fulton 3.

All-Star Team: 1B-Homer Johnston, Cairo; **2B**-Elmer Gray, Fulton; **3B**-Floyd Fogg, Hopkinsville; **SS**-Harold Boguskie, Hopkinsville; **OF**-Paul Zubak, Mayfield; Juan Kuester, Owensboro; Wally Berger, Owensboro; **C**-Frank Zubik, Madisonville; **Util**-Dan Verderbar, Union City; **P**-James Burns, Hopkinsville; Robert Schultz, Fulton; **Manager**-Earle Browne, Owensboro.

BA: Earle Browne, Owensboro, .429
Runs: Ray Fletcher, Owensboro, 126
Hits: Harold Boguskie, Hopkinsville, 190
RBIs: Ray Fletcher, Owensboro, 140

HRs: Ray Fletcher, Owensboro, 32
Wins: Donald McLeland, Mayfield, 20
SOs: Robert Schultz, Fulton, 361
ERA: George Buickel, Owensboro, 2.58

D North Atlantic League
President: Ernest C. Landgraf

Standings	W	L	Pct.	GB	Attend.	Manager
Peekskill Highlanders (13)	82	32	.719	—	51,200	Tony Ravish
Nazareth Cement Dusters	78	40	.661	6	31,465	
Stroudsburg Poconos	72	47	.605	12½	44,236	Joe Antolick
Carbondale Pioneers	69	48	.590	14½	62,617	Pat Colgan
Nyack Rockies	67	53	.558	18	37,551	Emil Schwab
Bloomingdale Troopers	41	78	.345	43½	15,560	Mickey Weintraub
Mahanoy City Bluebirds	30	79	.275	49½	19,261	George "Bulk" Boyle/Charlie Dulan
Newburgh/Walden Hummingbirds#	27	89	.233	56	10,051	Frank Novosel/Lou Haneles

#Newburgh (4-5) moved to Walden May 23.

Playoffs: Peekskill 4 games, Stroudsburg 2; Carbondale 4 games, Nazareth 1.
Finals: Peekskill 4 games, Carbondale 3.

BA: Walter Forwood, Carbondale, .406
Runs: Alex Garbowski, Nyack, 124
Hits: Walter Forwood, Carbondale, 170
Alex Garbowski, Nyack, 170
RBIs: Alex Garbowski, Nyack, 105

HRs: Alex Garbowski, Nyack, 12
Wins: William John, Peekskill, 20
SOs: William John, Peekskill, 189
ERA: John Jaust, Stroudsburg, 1.66
Pct: Tony Napoles, Peekskill, 1.000, 18-0

D North Carolina State League
President: C.M. Llewellyn

Standings	W	L	Pct.	GB	Manager
Concord Weavers	77	34	.694	—	Herman "Ginger" Watts
Landis Millers	62	50	.554	15½	Ed "Red" Cross
Thomasville Dodgers (10)	58	52	.527	18½	John Carey/Jay Kirke, Jr.
Mooresville Moors	57	52	.523	19	Bob Crow/Norman Small
Salisbury Pirates (15)	58	54	.518	19½	Walt McWilliams

Hickory Rebels (13)	55	56	.495	22	Sam Bell
Statesville Cubs (11)	41	69	.373	35½	Rube Wilson
Lexington A's (6)	34	75	.312	42	James Maus

Playoffs: Concord 4 games, Thomasville 0; Mooresville 4 games, Landis 3.
Finals: Mooresville 4 games, Concord 2.

All-Star Team: 1B-James Milner, Mooresville; **2B**-Sam Bell, Hickory; **3B**-Hal Harrigan, Salisbury; **SS**-Walter Fiala, Thomasville; **OF**-Phillip Cardinale, Thomasville; Norman Small, Mooresville; Willard Mauney, Concord; **C**-George Bradshaw, Landis; **Util**-Lewis Davis, Concord; **P**-Robert Ennis, Concord; Lacy James, Concord; **Manager**-Jay Kirke, Jr., Thomasville.

BA: Walter Fiala, Thomasville, .352
Runs: Norman Small, Mooresville, 100
Hits: Lewis Davis, Concord, 140
RBIs: Ken Howard, Hickory, 86
HRs: Norman Small, Mooresville, 18
Wins: Lacy James, Concord, 22
SOs: Lacy James, Concord, 247
ERA: Robert Ennis, Concord, 1.05

D Ohio State League
President: Frank Colley

Standings	W	L	Pct.	GB	Manager
Springfield Giants (13)	82	57	.590	—	Don Ramsey
Zanesville Dodgers (10)	78	60	.565	3½	Clay Bryant
Richmond Roses (9)	76	63	.547	6	Merle Settlemire
Newark Moundsmen (7)	74	65	.532	8	Bob Boken
Lima Terriers (2)	67	71	.486	14½	Charlie Moore
Marion Cardinals (16)	63	76	.453	19	Walter Schang/Robert Kline
Dayton Indians (3)	58	79	.423	23	Frank Parenti/Ival Goodman
Middletown Rockets (12)	56	83	.403	26	Mike Blazo

Playoffs: Zanesville 4 games, Richmond 0; Springfield 4 games, Newark 2.
Finals: Zanesville 4 games, Springfield 2.

All-Star Team: 1B-John Joslin, Richmond; **2B**-Paul Fouts, Dayton; **3B**-Joe DeStefano, Zanesville; **SS**-Frank Lanzetti, Springfield; **OF**-Peter Shurman, Middletown; Maynard DeWitt, Zanesville; Wayne Reside, Lima/Springfield; **C**-John Pluchino, Springfield; **Util**-Ed Ott, Zanesville; **P**-Hardy Holt, Zanesville; Ewen Bryden, Springfield; **Manager**-Clay Bryant, Zanesville.

BA: Maynard DeWitt, Zanesville, .351
Runs: Maynard DeWitt, Zanesville, 151
Hits: Maynard DeWitt, Zanesville, 187
RBIs: Wayne Reside, Lima/Springfield, 118
HRs: Wayne Reside, Lima/Springfield, 21
SBs: Maynard DeWitt, Zanesville, 110
Wins: Hardy Holt, Zanesville, 23
SOs: Merlin Williams, Lima, 275
ERA: Ewen Bryden, Springfield, 2.14

D PONY League
President: Robert C. Stedler

Standings	W	L	Pct.	GB	Attend.	Manager
Jamestown Falcons (4)	84	41	.667	—	112,371	Marv Olson
Batavia Clippers (3)	84	41	.667	—	67,680	Jack Tighe
Olean Oilers (10)	69	56	.552	15	66,179	Greg Mulleavy
Bradford Blue Wings (14)	58	66	.468	25½	58,235	Leon Riley
Hamilton Cardinals (16)	53	73	.421	31½	65,206	John Newman
Wellsville Yankees (5)	52	72	.419	31½	38,014	Joe Abreu
Lockport Cubs	51	73	.411	32½	43,678	James Moody
Hornell Pirates (15)	48	77	.384	36	49,236	Louis Briganti/Phil Seghi

Playoffs: Jamestown defeated Batavia 6-2 in a one game playoff for first place. Jamestown 4 games, Bradford 3; Batavia 4 games, Olean 3.
Finals: Batavia 4 games, Jamestown 2.

All-Star Team: 1B-Dick Kryhoski, Wellsville; **2B**-Joe Abreu, Wellsville; **3B**-Orval Cott, Jamestown; **SS**-Charles Koshorek, Jamestown; **OF**-Ken Humphrey, Jamestown; George Lerchen, Jamestown; Dick Kokos, Batavia; **C**-Charles Chian, Olean; **Util**-Stephen Kromko, Batavia; **P**-Bill Koszarek, Bradford; Jim Dimitriadis, Jamestown; **Manager**-Greg Mulleavy, Olean.

BA: Joe Abreu, Wellsville, .352
Runs: Dick Kokos, Batavia, 118
Hits: Dick Kokos, Batavia, 166
RBIs: Dick Kokos, Batavia, 114
HRs: Dick Kokos, Batavia, 21
Joe Abreu, Wellsville, 21
Wins: Bill Koszarek, Bradford, 18
SOs: Alfred Gavey, Hamilton, 181
ERA: Jim Dimitriadis, Jamestown, 2.03
Pct: Jim Dimitriadis, Jamestown, .850, 17-3

D Tobacco State League
President: J.E.L. Wade

Standings	W	L	Pct.	GB	Manager
Sanford Spinners	71	48	.597	—	Gaither Riley/Zeb Harrington
Clinton Blues	70	48	.593	½	Willie Duke/Van Lingle Mungo
Smithfield-Selma Leafs	58	62	.483	13½	Mike Balla
Angier-Fuquay Springs Bulls	57	62	.479	14	Paul Dunlap/Gaither Riley
Wilmington Pirates	52	66	.441	18½	Stan Katkaveck/Gus Brittain
Dunn-Erwin Twins	48	70	.407	22½	James Guinn/Alton Stephenson/Dwight Law

Attendance: Wilmington, 57,615; Dunn-Erwin, 47,174.

Playoffs: Angier-Fuquay Springs 4 games, Sanford 2; Clinton 4 games, Smithfield 1.
Finals: Angier-Fuquay Springs 4 games, Clinton 3.

All-Star Team: 1B-Phalti Shoffner, Sanford; **2B**-Mike Balla, Smithfield-Selma; **3B**-Lonnie Smith, Clinton; **SS**-Andrew Cullen, Wilmington; **OF**-Willie Duke, Clinton; Edward Bass, Dunn-Erwin; Orville Nesselrode, Sanford; **C**-William Campau, Clinton; **Util**-William

Ratteree, Angier-Fuquay Springs; **P**-Robert Keane, Clinton; George Bortz, Sanford; **Manager**-Zeb Harrington, Sanford.

BA: Willie Duke, Clinton, .393
Runs: Lonnie Smith, Clinton, 117
Hits: Leo Niezgoda, Smithfield-Selma, 173
RBIs: Orville Nesselrode, Sanford, 150
HRs: Orville Nesselrode, Sanford, 30
Wins: Robert Keane, Clinton, 23
SOs: George Bortz, Sanford, 193
Pct: Robert Keane, Clinton, .852, 23-4

D Wisconsin State League
President: Herman D. White

Standings	W	L	Pct.	GB	Attend.	Manager
Green Bay Bluejays (14)	76	36	.679	—	75,657	Harry Griswold
Oshkosh Giants (13)	66	42	.611	8	83,100	Ray Lucas
Fond du Lac Panthers (5)	62	48	.564	13	84,601	James Adlam
Wisconsin Rapids White Sox (2)	54	54	.500	20	59,951	Charles Engle
Appleton Papermakers (3)	47	60	.439	26½	65,535	Ray Powell
Janesville Bears (11)	44	64	.407	30	32,738	Quinto Valentino
Sheboygan Indians	44	66	.400	31	34,401	Joe Hauser
Wausau Lumberjacks	43	66	.394	31½	58,300	Fred Schulte

Playoffs: None

BA: James Adlam, Fond du Lac, .375
Runs: Wade Tate, Appleton, 118
Hits: Saul Israel, Fond du Lac, 135
RBIs: Saul Israel, Fond du Lac, 96
HRs: Elwood Grantham, Janesville, 20
Wins: Maynard Park, Green Bay, 18
John Perkovich, Wisconsin Rapids, 18
SOs: John Perkovich, Wisconsin Rapids, 229
ERA: Al Esqueda, Oshkosh, 2.22

Ind Mexican League
President: Jorge Pasquel

Standings	W	L	Pct.	GB	Manager
Tampico Alijadores	56	41	.577	—	Armando Marsans
Mexico City Diablos Rojos	55	42	.567	1	Ernesto Carmona
Puebla Angeles	52	46	.531	4½	Dolf Luque
Torreon Algodoneros	50	47	.515	6	Martin Dihigo
Monterrey Industriales	48	49	.495	8	Lazaro Salazar
Nuevo Laredo Tecolotes	48	50	.490	8½	Ezequiel Cruz/James Steiner
Veracruz Azules	41	57	.418	15½	Ramon Bragana/Mickey Owen/Jose Luis Gomez/Jorge Pasquel
San Luis Potosi Tuneros	40	58	.408	16½	Felix Arguelles/Jorge Comellas/Antonio Rodriguez

BA: Claro Duany, Monterrey, .364
Hits: Napoleon Reyes, Puebla, 140
RBIs: Roberto Ortiz, Mexico City, 108
HRs: Roberto Ortiz, Mexico City, 25
Wins: Sal Maglie, Puebla, 20
Agapito Mayor, Nuevo Laredo, 20
SOs: Booker McDaniels, San Luis Potosi, 171
ERA: Max Lanier, Veracruz, 1.93

1946 Interleague Post Season Play

World Series
St. Louis (National) 4 games, Boston (American) 3

Junior World Series
Montreal (International) 4 games, Louisville (American Association) 2
Total Attendance: 90,968

Dixie Series
Dallas (Texas) 4 games, Atlanta (Southern Association) 0
Total Attendance: 33,134

Southeastern Championship
Orlando (Florida State) 4 games, Moultrie (Georgia-Florida) 0

Texas Class C Championship Series
Pampa (West Texas-New Mexico) 4 games, Henderson (East Texas) 0

Class D Series
Tallassee (Georgia-Alabama) 4 games, Geneva (Alabama State) 0

1946 Major League Farm Systems

American League

1. Boston (11): Louisville, New Orleans, Scranton, Lynn, Roanoke, Oneonta, Durham, Geneva, Tarboro, Milford, New Iberia.
2. Chicago (14): Milwaukee, Little Rock, Shreveport, Greenville (SC), Waterloo, Texarkana, Superior, Brewton, New River, Alexandria, Cordele, Madisonville, Lima, Wisconsin Rapids.
3. Cleveland (11): Baltimore, Oklahoma City, Wilkes-Barre, Harrisburg, Bakersfield, Pittsfield, Clovis, Centreville, Dayton, Batavia, Appleton.
4. Detroit (7): Buffalo, Dallas, Williamsport, Rome, Lubbock, Muskogee, Jamestown.
5. New York (15): Kansas City, Newark (NJ), Beaumont, Binghamton, Augusta, Sunbury, Norfolk, Quincy, Amsterdam, Butler, Twin Falls, Joplin, Easton, Wellsville, Fond du Lac.
6. Philadelphia (7): Toronto, Savannah, Lancaster, Kingston, Martinsville, Federalsburg, Lexington.
7. St. Louis (11): Toledo, San Antonio, Elmira, Springfield (IL), Spartanburg, Gloversville-Johnstown, Paris, Aberdeen, Pittsburg, Mayfield, Newark (OH).
8. Washington (5): Chattanooga, Pensacola, Charlotte, Kingsport, Orlando.

National League

9. Boston (13): Indianapolis, Seattle, Hartford, Pawtucket, Jackson, Evansville, Vancouver, Raleigh, Miami Beach, Leavenworth, Bluefield, Owensboro, Richmond (IN).
10. Brooklyn (21): St. Paul, Montreal, Mobile, Ft. Worth, Nashua, Newport News, Meridian, Danville (IL), Asheville, Santa Barbara, Trois Rivieres, Johnstown, Grand Forks, Abilene, Cambridge, Daytona Beach, Valdosta, Miami (OK), Thomasville (NC), Zanesville, Olean.
11. Chicago (18): Los Angeles, Nashville, Tulsa, Macon, Hagerstown, Portsmouth, Davenport, Shelby, Tacoma, Visalia, Quebec, Hutchinson, Elizabethton, Hopkinsville, Fayetteville, Iola, Statesville, Janesville.
12. Cincinnati (4): Syracuse, Columbia, Ogden, Middletown.
13. New York (16): Minneapolis, Jersey City, Jacksonville (FL), Trenton, Manchester, Richmond (VA), Anderson, Danville, Erie, St. Cloud, Ft. Smith, Bristol, Peekskill, Hickory, Springfield (OH), Oshkosh.
14. Philadelphia (9): Utica, Wilmington (DE), Terre Haute, Schenectady, Salina, Dover, Americus, Bradford, Green Bay.
15. Pittsburgh (13): Hollywood, Birmingham, Albany (NY), York, Anniston, Selma, Yakima, Oil City, Tallassee, Tallahassee, Bartlesville, Salisbury (NC), Hornell.
16. St. Louis (18): Columbus (OH), Rochester, Houston, Columbus (GA), Allentown, Lynchburg, Decatur, Fresno, Winston-Salem, Duluth, Pocatello, St. Joseph, Johnson City, Salisbury (MD), Albany (GA), Carthage, Marion, Hamilton.

1946 No-Hitters

Date	Pitcher	Team	League	Opponent	Score
4-4	Joe Demoran	Seattle	Pacific Coast	Los Angeles	3-0
4-21	Ad Liska	Portland	Pacific Coast	Hollywood	1-0 (7)
4-23	Ed Head	Brooklyn	National	Boston	5-0
4-26	William Fuchs	DeLand	Florida State	St. Augustine	5-6
4-30	Bob Feller	Cleveland	American	New York	1-0
4-30	Earl Harrist	Syracuse	International	Buffalo	5-0
5-5	Jim Parton	Zanesville	Ohio State	Lima	5-0 (7)
5-8	Jim Arnold	Twin Falls	Pioneer	Pocatello	4-0
5-12	Randle Smith	Savannah	South Atlantic	Columbus	2-0
5-12	Fernando Rodriguez	Havana	Fla. International	Miami	4-0 (7)
5-13	John Joust	Stroudsburg	North Atlantic	Bloomingdale	7-0
5-14	Gaylor Lemish	Moultrie	Georgia-Florida	Albany	1-0
5-20	Bill Porter	Joplin	Western Assoc.	St. Joseph	10-0
5-21	Steve Rushnock	Erie	Middle Atlantic	Youngstown	2-0
5-22	Nick Saulia	Manchester	New England	Fall River	2-1
5-26	Walker Cress	Lynn	New England	Nashua	4-0
5-30	Cy Greenlaw	Tacoma	W. International	Yakima	3-0 (7)
5-30	Roy Bridges	Manchester	New England	Pawtucket	4-0
5-31	Garth Mann	Sacramento	Pacific Coast	Seattle	6-0
6-2	Carl Kettles	Sanford	Florida State	Gainesville	
6-4	Fran Smith	Lockport	PONY	Hornell	9-0
6-5	Richard Piatnek	Selma	Southeastern	Jackson	5-1
6-10	Whitey Konikowski	Trenton	Interstate	Harrisburg	4-0 (7)
6-15	Red Earey	Hickory	N. Carolina State	Landis	0-1
6-18	John Conant	Idaho Falls	Pioneer	Boise	4-0
6-28	Carl Sculte	Newark	Ohio State	Richmond	7-0 (7)
7-3	Earl Dothager	Shreveport	Texas	Houston	1-0 (7)
7-4	Ed Leiker	Pampa	W. Texas-N. Mexico	Lamesa	12-0
7-7	Red Benton	Wilson	Coastal Plain	Kinston	3-0 (7)
7-12	Roy Hardee	Angier-Fuquay Springs	Tobacco State	Clinton	12-0
7-14	Maury McDermott	Scranton	Eastern	Albany	8-0
7-18	Al Esqueda	Oshkosh	Wisconsin State	Wausau	2-0 (7)
7-19	Rex Heinze	Green Bay	Wisconsin State	Janesville	5-0
7-21	Francis Moore	Brewton	Alabama State	Geneva	6-0 (7)
7-26	Len Seamon	Granby	Border	Ogdensburg	6-0
7-29	Earl Harrist	Syracuse	International	Toronto	5-0
8-2	Jim Maloney	Butler	Middle Atlantic	Erie	2-0
8-4	Ted Novak	Grand Forks	Northern	Duluth	3-0
8-6	Johnny Eiser	Mayfield	Kitty	Hopkinsville	6-0 (P, 7)
8-6	Dick Mitchell	Joplin	Western Assoc.	Leavenworth	2-1
8-7	Gene Shirk	Carbondale	North Atlantic	Stroudsburg	1-0 (7)
8-11	Herbert Moore	Albany	Georgia-Florida	Moultrie	1-0
8-16	Al Comotti	Thomasville	Georgia-Florida	Albany	6-0
8-17	George Koval	DeLand	Florida State	Gainesville	7-0 (7)
8-18	Abe Coffman	Topeka	Western Assoc.	Leavenworth	5-0
8-21	Robert Schultz	Fulton	Kitty	Union City	5-0
8-23	Johnny Warsaw/ Charley Goforth	Portsmouth	Piedmont	Lynchburg	1-0
8-23	George Raetz	Nyack	North Atlantic	Walden	13-0
8-27	Lester Willis	Memphis	Southern Assoc.	Atlanta	3-0
8-29	Walt Doherty	Dover	Eastern Shore	Salisbury	1-0 (8)
9-3	Carl Carter	Jacksonville	East Texas	Lufkin	0-1 (7)
9-10	Jim House	Angier-Fuquay Springs	Tobacco State	Sanford	3-0 (PO)
9-12	Tom Sunkel	St. Paul	American Assoc.	Louisville	3-0 (PO)

Number in parentheses indicates innings if other than nine; "P" indicates perfect game; "PO" indicates playoff game.

THIS DATE IN MINOR LEAGUE HISTORY

February, 1946, San Francisco, Pacific Coast League, held spring training in Hawaii. Players arrived from California by boat.

March 14, 1946, The new Class B Mexican National League became the first circuit in Organized Ball to launch the 1946 season.

April 18, 1946, Jackie Robinson, second baseman for Montreal, International League, and the first Negro to play in Organized Ball in this century, made a sparkling debut as the Royals humbled Jersey City 14-1. After grounding out in his first at bat, Robinson collected four straight hits, including a two-run home run, his first hit. Robinson also stole two bases and scored four times.

April 23, 1946, Second baseman Eddie Kazak, hospitalized for 16 months when wounded in the invasion of Normandy, broke into the Columbus, South Atlantic League, lineup for the first time and performed spectacularly with his bat. He blasted two homers in an 8-run eighth inning and added a single and a double in five tries. He also stole home in the fourth frame.

April 27, 1946, Brewton defeated Ozark 30-29 in a four hour, 18 minute Alabama State League game. Ten pitchers, six from Brewton, were used, and they walked 46 batters, threw six wild pitches, hit four batters and gave up 35 hits. Brewton scored three runs in the last of the ninth to win.

April 29, 1946, Pete Gray, one-armed outfielder with the St. Louis Browns last season, signed with Toledo, American Association, after a lengthy holdout.

May 3, 1946, First baseman Ken Rhyne of Moultrie, Georgia-Florida League, hit four home runs in a game against Thomasville. He drove in nine runs to lead his team to a 12-2 victory.

May 3, 1946, Rookie Greg "Lefty" Parente of Cordele, Georgia-Florida League, whiffed 23 in beating Tallahasee 16-2.

May 7, 1946, Walter Cazen, who stole 74 bases in 1945 for Syracuse, International League, died of tuberculosis at the Niagara County Sanitorium in Lockport, New York, at age 33.

May 8, 1946, Erv Palica of Asheville, Tri-State League, made eight errors in 18 chances in one game at shortstop. Asheville defeated Anderson, however, 8-7 in ten innings as Palica drove in the winning run. Soon thereafter, Palica was shifted to the mound and subsequently won 15 games.

May 8, 1946, Catcher Roy Campanella made his Organized Ball debut with Nashua, New England League, and had three hits in four trips, a two-run homer and two singles.

May 17, 1946, Charlotte, Tri-State League, ballpark was damaged by a tornado which struck about 30 minutes before game time. No injuries occurred.

May 24, 1946, Leo E. "Frisco" Edwards, 45, an umpire who doffed the blue to become a successful manager, died of a heart attack in Bremerton, Washington. Edwards piloted Vancouver, Western International League, to 13 straight victories.

May 27, 1946, The Mexican National League withdrew from Organized Ball due to pressure from the Pasquels' Mexican League which forced the withdrawal of Mexico City and Torreon. Internal feuds and financial difficulties also contributed to the move.

June 8, 1946, In the highest score in West Texas-New Mexico league history, Amarillo defeated Lamesa 32-0.

June 11, 1946, Bill Kennedy of Rocky Mount, Coastal Plain League, fanned 25 Goldsboro batters to run his season strikeout total to 176 in just 87 innings.

June 24, 1946, Nine members of the Spokane, Western International League, club lost their lives and the driver and six other players were injured when their bus careened off a narrow road in the Cascade Mountains. The accident occurred along the Snoqualmie Pass highway at the 3,400-foot level in a drizzling rain. Eight players were killed instantly and the ninth, Chris Hartje, died several days later. The bus, carrying 15 players, was en route to Bremerton, Washington.

July 14, 1946, Maury McDermott, 17-year-old Scranton lefty, hurled an 8-0 no-hit game against Albany.

July 14, 1946, Chet Covington notched his 20th victory of the season when he turned back Lakeland, Florida International League, 8-5, extending the Tampa Smokers' string of wins to 13 in a row.

July 17, 1946, Harry "Nemo" Leibold, manager of Louisville, American Association, was suspended for the balance of the season by minor league President Bramham for assaulting the umpire during the Milwaukee-Louisville doubleheader the previous day.

July 17, 1946, Manager/catcher Hal "Moe" Cleves of Granby, Border League, hit three homers in one game against Odgensburg. Cleves, only 20, was the youngest manager in Organized Ball.

July 19, 1946, Player/manager Bob Crow of Mooresville, North Carolina State

League, was suspended for one year after a run-in with umpire Bob Weaver at Hickory. Crow was also fined $100.

July 26, 1946, Ike Seone, catcher for Orlando, Florida State League, was suspended for the balance of the season for assaulting an umpire.

July 30, 1946, San Francisco drew 23,603 paid spectators for a single game with Oakland, a Pacific Coast League record.

July 31, 1946, The suspension of Louisville manager Harry "Nemo" Leibold was cut to 45 days.

August 8, 1946, First baseman Eddie Robinson, Baltimore, International League, lined into a triple play for the second time this season.

August 9, 1946, Going 5-for-5 in each game August 8-9, after two hits in his last times at bat in the previous contest, outfielder Ralph Brown, Tampa, Florida State League, registered 12 successive safeties to establish a league record and tie the mark of Pinky Higgins in the Majors. Brown hit safely 13 times out of 14 during the series with Lakeland, and over a stretch of four games made 15 hits in 18 trips. Brown, 23, was a Yankee farmhand and was in his first year of pro ball.

August 11, 1946, First baseman Chuck Connors paced Newport News to a 19-11 Piedmont League victory over Lynchburg with three homers - two in one inning - plus a double and a single in a 5-for-5 performance.

August 11, 1946, Buzz Arlett, former Oakland star, was given a plaque from the Helms Athletic Foundation establishing him in the Pacific Coast League's Hall of Fame.

August 11, 1946, Hooper Triplett, 26-year-old Columbus, South Atlantic League, outfielder, was fined $500 and suspended indefinitely for betting $20 on the Columbia team in the game of August 3. Triplett was a younger brother of Coaker Triplett, Buffalo flychaser and formerly with the Cardinals and Phillies. Hooper won the South Atlantic League batting chamionship in 1940 with a .369 mark. He was batting .314 this season.

August 12, 1946, Jack Doyle, rookie righthander for Tulsa, Texas League, broke his arm in a pre-game warmup when he cut loose with a fast pitch that snapped his arm above the wrist.

August 13, 1946, 17-game winning streak of Tom Fine ended when Wilkes-Barre slaughtered the Eastern League Scranton Miners 15-1. The defeat was the first for Fine in three months and put his season mark at 18-2.

August 13, 1946, Van Lingle Mungo, manager of Clinton, Tobacco State League, was suspended for the balance of the season and Gus Brittain, Wilmington pilot, was put on the ineligible list as a result of near-riots at Wilmington.

August 14, 1946, Steve Bilko of Salisbury, Eastern Shore League, rapped two grand slams and a single, driving in 9 tallies as the Cardinals lambasted Easton 16-1.

August 16, 1946, The first 30-game winner of the season in Organized Ball and the first in the history of the Evangeline League was 38-year-old Bill Thomas of Houma, who reached that figure with a 6-4 victory over Thibodaux. Thomas had lost 8 games.

August 20, 1946, Rookie Bill Rose, Fond du Lac, Wisconsin State League, lost to last-place Wausau 6-4 after having won 16 consecutive games. Rose, however, finished the season with a mark of 17-1. The loss was Rose's first after winning his first 16 games during his first season in Organized Ball, a remarkable feat.

August 20, 1946, The string of shutout innings for Gaspar Del Monte, 19-year-old Cuban righthander of Charlotte, Tri-State League, ended at 35 in a game with Knoxville.

August 20, 1946, Bill Kennedy of Rocky Mount, Coastal Plain League, just missed by one Organized Ball's all-time strikeout record when he fanned 22 Tarboro batters in hurling a 1-hit, 2-0 victory. The 22 whiffs brought his season's total to 417. Virgil Trucks set the record of 418 with Andalusia, Alabama-Florida League, in 1938.

August 21, 1946, Outfielder Hooper Triplett, Columbus, South Atlantic League, who was fined $500 and suspended indefinitely by the league for allegedly betting against his club, was placed on the permanent ineligible list of Organized Ball by President W.G. Bramham of the National Association.

August 21, 1946, Clarence Gann, sensational righthander for Shreveport, Texas League, was knocked out of the box by Ft. Worth after having hurled 37-1/3 consecutive scoreless innings. The League record of 41 was set by H.I. Guyn with Waco in 1907. Earl Caldwell, with the Chicago White Sox this year, had 40 consecutive scoreless rounds in 1941.

August 21, 1946, Pitcher Bob Schultz of Fulton, Kitty League, hurled a 5-0 nine-inning no-hitter against Union City, and struck out 18 to increase his all-time league record to 330, 27 above the former mark of 303 set by Ellis Kinder of Jackson in 1934.

August 21, 1946, John Johnson of Newnan, Georgia-Alabama League, turned in an iron-man performance, shutting out league-leading Valley in both ends of a double-

1946

header, 1-0 and 7-0. He gave up 10 hits, six in the first game.

August 21, 1946, Harry Amato, star outfielder with Salisbury, North Carolina State League, was banned for the balance of the season for a run-in with an umpire during a game with Concord.

August 22, 1946, Third baseman Pete Spatafore of Abilene, West Texas-New Mexico League, drew seven free passes in the Blue Sox' 22-2 victory over Lamesa.

August 22, 1946, Only three hits were made in the Chanute-Miami game in the KOM League, won by Chanute 1-0. Ross Grimsley of the winners allowed one hit - a single in the ninth - and fanned 13.

August 23, 1946, Pitcher Willis Dudley of DeLand, Florida State League, was suspended 180 days for assaulting the umpire during a game on July 31 at Sanford, Florida.

August 25, 1946, The Montreal Royals clinched their second straight International League pennant. Newark trailed by 19 games in the runner-up spot. It was the second earliest pennant-clinching date for 154 games in the circuit. Newark sewed up the 1937 flag on August 23 after 131 games.

August 27, 1946, Lester "Wimpy" Willis, veteran lefty for Memphis, Southern Association, who recently hurled four consecutive shutouts, pitched a no-hit game against Atlanta, winning 3-0. Willis lost a perfect game when the Chicks' second baseman made an error in the ninth.

August 28, 1946, Jorge Pasquel, president of the Mexican League, barred the Nuevo Laredo club from signing Hooper Triplett, recently ousted by Organized Ball on a charge of betting against his own club, Columbus of the South Atlantic League.

August 29, 1946, Second baseman Jake Pullens of Topeka, Western Association, participated in a triple play against Muskogee in the first inning in which he received credit for all three putouts, getting the first on a force play and the other two during rundowns.

August 29, 1946, Mrs. Christian Hartje, widow of one of the nine Spokane, Western International League, players killed in a bus accident on June 24, was awarded $17,500 and her unborn child $500 under a settlement with the Washington Motor Company.

August 30, 1946, In his first appearance after a beaning which sidelined him for two weeks, Dick Kryhoski, first baseman with Wellsville, PONY League, delivered three home runs and a single, good for nine RBIs. The ribbies accounted for all of his club's runs in the 10-9, 12-inning loss to Olean.

August 31, 1946, Bill Evans of Amarillo, West Texas-New Mexico League, gained his 26th win of the season, a new mark for the league, in beating Borger 4-2.

September 1, 1946, Bill Kennedy of Rocky Mount, Coastal Plain League, fanned 15 in his final game of the year, increasing his new Organized Ball strikeout record to 456. Kennedy hurled 280 innings and posted a 28-3 mark and an era of 1.03.

September 1, 1946, Harry Perkowski of Ogden, Pioneer League, hurled his 15th consecutive win and fourth straight shutout to beat Pocatello 8-0.

September 2, 1946, Newark rapped 22 hits to beat Jersey City 21-5. Larry "Yogi" Berra, rookie catcher, belted his 13th and 14th homers.

September 2, 1946, Chet Covington of Tampa, Florida International League, registered his 28th victory when he beat Lakeland, 5-4, in ten innings.

September 3, 1946, Harold "Skinny" Brown of Durham, Carolina League, posted his 15th consecutive victory, defeating Burlington 10-7. Brown finshed the season with a

batting average of .352 and a pitching record of 15-5.

September 3, 1946, Bill Thomas of Houma, Evangeline League, won his 34th game of the year by defeating Alexandria 20-4.

September 5, 1946, Infielder Mike Gabriel of Kingston, Border League, was suspended for 180 days for attacking an umpire.

September 6, 1946, A new Eastern League winning percentage record for pitchers was established when Tom Fine, 28-year-old Scranton righthander, turned in his 23rd victory against only three setbacks in sidelining Utica 7-1. The win boosted Fine's percentage to its final mark of .885.

September 8, 1946, Crowning his spectacular 1946 debut in Organized Ball, Jackie Robinson, second baseman for Montreal, captured the International League batting title with a .349 average in 124 games. The Royals ended the season in first place, 18-1/2 games ahead of runner-up Syracuse. Robinson also led International League second basemen in fielding, making only 10 errors for a mark of .985.

September 8, 1946, Jerry Witte of Toledo, who was judged both the American Association's outstanding rookie and MVP of 1946, closed the season in a blaze of glory when he bashed two home runs to raise his season total to 46.

September 8, 1946, Monty Stratton, former Chicago White Sox hurler, made a strong pitching comeback this season, despite the handicap of an artificial leg, posting 18 victories against 8 losses for Sherman in the East Texas League. Stratton lost a leg as the result of a hunting accident in 1938.

September 9, 1946, Outfielder Gaither Riley if Dunn-Erwin, Tobacco State League, was placed on Organized Ball's ineligible list for assaulting an umpire on August 28.

September 9, 1946, Maynard DeWitt of Zanesville, Ohio State League, ended the season with 110 stolen bases. DeWitt, a pitcher turned outfielder, also led the league in batting at .351.

September 12, 1946, Tom Sunkel, 34-year-old ex-Cardinals portsider, hurled a no-hitter as St. Paul defeated Louisville 3-0 in an American Association playoff game. Sunkel was blind in one eye.

September 17, 1946, Tony Napoles of Peekskill annexed his fourth playoff victory in a relief role, his 22nd win without defeat this season in the North Atlantic League. Napoles, a 150-pound Cuban righthander, won 18 straight without a loss in the regular season.

September 19, 1946, Pitcher Larry Jansen won his 30th game of the season for San Francisco, Pacific Coast League. Jansen finished the campaign with a 30-6 mark, leading the circuit in victories, percentage, .833, and ERA, 1.57.

October, 1946, Although one of the club's stockholders, Paul Waner was relieved as manager of the Miami Sun Sox of the Florida International League.

October, 1946, The widowed mother and the brother and sister of Victor Picetti, one of the nine Spokane players killed in a bus accident the previous June, were awarded $27,000 in an adjustment of a claim against the Washington Motor Coach Company.

December 4, 1946, President William G. Bramham, president of the minor leagues for past 14 years, retired from the position and was succeeded by George Trautman, Detroit executive vice-president.

December 21, 1946, Fifteen checks totaling $114,805.25 were mailed to the dependents of nine Spokane players killed and to six others injured in the tragic bus accident that all but wiped out the Spokane, Western International League, club on June 24.

1947

American League
President: William Harridge

Standings	W	L	Pct.	GB	Attend.	Manager
New York Yankees............	97	57	.630	—	2,178,937	Bucky Harris
Detroit Tigers....................	85	69	.552	12	1,398,093	Steve O'Neill
Boston Red Sox	83	71	.539	14	1,427,315	Joe Cronin
Cleveland Indians	80	74	.519	17	1,521,978	Lou Boudreau
Philadelphia Athletics	78	76	.506	19	911,566	Connie Mack
Chicago White Sox	70	84	.455	27	876,948	Ted Lyons
Washington Senators	64	90	.416	33	850,758	Ossie Bluege
St. Louis Browns	59	95	.383	38	320,474	Muddy Ruel

BA: Ted Williams, Boston, .343
Runs: Ted Williams, Boston, 125
Hits: Johnny Pesky, Boston, 207
RBIs: Ted Williams, Boston, 114
HRs: Ted Williams, Boston, 32

Wins: Bob Feller, Cleveland, 20
SOs: Bob Feller, Cleveland, 196
ERA: Spud Chandler, New York, 2.46
Pct: Allie Reynolds, New York, .704, 19-8

National League
President: Ford Frick

Standings	W	L	Pct.	GB	Attend.	Manager
Brooklyn Dodgers............	94	60	.610	—	1,807,526	Clyde Sukeforth/Burt Shotton
St. Louis Cardinals	89	65	.578	5	1,247,913	Eddie Dyer
Boston Braves....................	86	68	.558	8	1,277,361	Billy Southworth
New York Giants	81	73	.526	13	1,600,793	Mel Ott
Cincinnati Reds..................	73	81	.474	21	899,975	Johnny Neun
Chicago Cubs	69	85	.448	25	1,364,039	Charlie Grimm
Philadelphia Phillies	62	92	.403	32	907,332	Ben Chapman
Pittsburgh Pirates	62	92	.403	32	1,283,531	Billy Herman/Bill Burwell

BA: Harry Walker, St. Louis/Philadelphia, .363
Runs: Johnny Mize, New York, 137
Hits: Tommy Holmes, Boston, 191
RBIs: Johnny Mize, New York, 138

HRs: Ralph Kiner, Pittsburgh, 51
Johnny Mize, New York, 51
Wins: Ewell Blackwell, Cincinnati, 22
SOs: Ewell Blackwell, Cincinnati, 193
ERA: Warren Spahn, Boston, 2.33
Pct: Larry Jansen, New York, .808, 21-5

AAA American Association
President: Frank C. Lane

Standings	W	L	Pct.	GB	Attend.	Manager
Kansas City Blues (5).........	93	60	.608	—	379,063	Bill Meyer
Louisville Colonels (1)........	85	68	.556	8	339,872	Nemo Leibold
Milwaukee Brewers (9)	79	75	.513	14½	298,041	Nick Cullop
Minneapolis Millers (13)....	77	77	.500	16½	273,253	Tom Sheehan
Columbus Red Birds (16)....	76	78	.494	17½	157,837	Harold Anderson
Indianapolis Indians (15)....	74	79	.484	19	316,539	Jimmy Brown
St. Paul Saints (10)	69	85	.454	24½	222,331	Herman Franks/Curt Davis
Toledo Mud Hens (7)	61	92	.399	32	169,525	Frank Snyder

Playoffs: Milwaukee 4 games, Kansas City 2; Louisville 4 games, Minneapolis 3.
Finals: Milwaukee 4 games, Louisville 3.

All-Star Team: 1B-Paul Campbell, Louisville; **2B**-Danny Murtaugh, Milwaukee; **3B**-Don Lang, Columbus; **SS**-Alvin Dark, Milwaukee; **OF**-Cliff Mapes, Kansas City; Ed Stewart, Kansas City; Hank Bauer, Kansas City; Eric Tipton, St. Paul; Al Roberge, Milwaukee; **C**-Wes Westrum, Minneapolis; Gus Niarhos, Kansas City; John Riddle, Indianapolis; **Util**-Bobby Rhawn, Minneapolis; **P**-Charley Stanceu, Columbus; Chuck Koney, Louisville; Fred Bradley, Kansas City; Frank Hiller, Kansas City; Clem Dreisewerd, Louisville; Phil Haugstad, St. Paul; Glenn Elliott, Milwaukee; **MVP**-Steve Gerkin, Minneapolis; **Manager**-Nemo Leibold, Louisville.

BA: Heinz Becker, Milwaukee, .363
Runs: Alvin Dark, Milwaukee, 121
Hits: John Douglas, St. Paul, 195
RBIs: Cliff Mapes, Kansas City, 117

HRs: Carden Gillenwater, Milwaukee, 23
Wins: Clem Dreisewerd, Louisville, 18
SOs: Phil Haugstad, St. Paul, 145
ERA: Clem Dreisewerd, Louisville, 2.15

AAA International League
President: Frank J. Shaughnessy

Standings	W	L	Pct.	GB	Attend.	Manager
Jersey City Giants (13)	94	60	.610	—	337,531	Bruno Betzel
Montreal Royals (10)..........	93	60	.608	½	442,485	Clay Hopper
Syracuse Chiefs (12)...........	88	65	.575	5½	288,141	Jewel Ens
Buffalo Bisons (4)	77	75	.507	16	267,012	Paul Richards
Rochester Red Wings (16)..	68	86	.442	26	226,821	Cedric Durst
Newark Bears (5)...............	65	89	.422	29	181,897	George Selkirk
Baltimore Orioles (3).........	65	89	.422	29	358,182	Alphonse "Tommy" Thomas
Toronto Maple Leafs (1)....	64	90	.416	30	171,730	Elmer Yoter

Playoffs: Buffalo 4 games, Jersey City 0; Syracuse 4 games, Montreal 0.
Finals: Syracuse 4 games, Buffalo 3.

All-Star Team: 1B-Ed Stevens, Montreal; **2B**-Burgess Whitehead, Jersey City; **3B**-Oscar Grimes, Toronto; **SS**-Virgil Stallcup, Jersey City; **OF**-Hank Sauer, Syracuse; Dutch Mele, Syracuse; Howie Moss, Baltimore; **C**-Roy Campanella, Montreal; **P**-Ed Heusser, Montreal; Bob Kuzava, Baltimore.

BA: Vernal Jones, Rochester, .337
Runs: Hank Sauer, Syracuse, 130
Hits: Hank Sauer, Syracuse, 182
RBIs: Hank Sauer, Syracuse, 141

HRs: Howie Moss, Baltimore, 53
Wins: Jim Prendergast, Syracuse, 20
SOs: Jack Banta, Montreal, 199
ERA: Luke Hamlin, Toronto, 2.22

AAA Pacific Coast League
President: Clarence H. Rowland

Standings	W	L	Pct.	GB	Attend.	Manager
Los Angeles Angels (11)..	106	81	.567	—	622,485	William Kelly
San Francisco Seals	105	82	.561	1	640,643	Lefty O'Doul
Portland Beavers................	97	89	.522	8½	421,137	Jim Turner
Oakland Oaks	96	90	.516	9½	590,327	Casey Stengel
Seattle Rainiers	91	95	.489	14½	548,308	Jo Jo White
Hollywood Stars (2)...........	88	98	.473	17½	500,607	Jimmie Dykes
Sacramento Solons	83	103	.446	22½	390,914	Dick Bartel
San Diego Padres...............	79	107	.425	26½	353,951	James "Rip" Collins

Playoffs: Los Angeles 4 games, Portland 1; Oakland 4 games, San Francisco 1.
Finals: Los Angeles 4 games, Oakland 1.

All-Star Team: 1B-Tony Lupien, Hollywood; **2B**-Dario Lodigiani, Oakland; **3B**-Johnny Ostrowski, Los Angeles; **SS**-Ron Nicely, San Francisco; **OF**-Max West, San Diego; Cecil Garriott, Los Angeles; Neill Sheridan, San Francisco; **C**-Ed Fitzgerald, Sacramento; **Util**-Hillis Layne, Seattle; Francis Kelleher, Hollywood; **P**-Bob Chesnes, San Francisco; Cliff Chambers, Los Angeles; **MVP**-Tony Lupien, Hollywood; **Manager**-Lefty O'Doul, San Francisco.

BA: Hillis Layne, Seattle, .367
Runs: Tony Lupien, Hollywood, 147
Hits: Tony Lupien, Hollywood, 237
RBIs: Max West, San Diego, 124

HRs: Max West, San Diego, 43
Wins: Cliff Chambers, Los Angeles, 24
SOs: Cliff Chambers, Los Angeles, 175
ERA: Bob Chesnes, San Francisco, 2.32

AA Southern Association
President: Charles A. Hurth

Standings	W	L	Pct.	GB	Attend.	Manager
Mobile Bears (10)...............	94	59	.614	—	237,322	Alfred Todd
New Orleans Pelicans (1)...	93	59	.612	½	400,036	Fred Walters
Nashville Vols (11).............	80	73	.523	14	251,336	Larry Gilbert
Chattanooga Lookouts (8)..	79	75	.513	15½	202,973	Bert Niehoff
Atlanta Crackers	73	78	.483	20	404,584	Kiki Cuyler
Birmingham Barons (6).......	73	80	.477	21	323,309	Dick Porter
Memphis Chicks	69	85	.448	25½	246,215	Tommy "Doc" Prothro
Little Rock Travelers (9)	51	103	.331	43½	114,569	Bill Dickey

Playoffs: Mobile 4 games, Chattanooga 0; Nashville 4 games, New Orleans 1.
Finals: Mobile 4 games, Nashville 2.

All-Star Team: 1B-Albert Flair, New Orleans; **2B**-Al Kozar, New Orleans; **3B**-Mickey Rutner, Birmingham; **SS**-Hal Quick, Nashville; **OF**-Hal Jeffcoat, Nashville; Cal Abrams, Mobile; Tom Wright, New Orleans; Gil Coan, Chattanooga; **C**-Cliff Dapper, Mobile; Fred Walters, New Orleans; Albert "Rube" Walker, Nashville; **Util**-Charley Tripp, Atlanta; Seymour Block, Nashville; **P**-Bob Hall, Mobile; Roy Boles, Mobile; Bill Kennedy, Chattanooga; Walker Cress, New Orleans; Ben Wade, Nashville; Forrest Thompson, Atlanta.

BA: Ted Kluszewski, Memphis, .377
Runs: Cal Abrams, Mobile, 134
Hits: Hal Jeffcoat, Nashville, 218
RBIs: Albert Flair, New Orleans, 128
HRs: Albert Flair, New Orleans, 24

2B: Seymour Block, Nashville, 50
Wins: Bill Kennedy, Chattanooga, 20
SOs: Ben Wade, Nashville, 145
ERA: Bob Hall, Mobile, 2.80

AA Texas League
President: J. Alvin Gardner

Standings	W	L	Pct.	GB	Attend.	Manager
Houston Buffaloes (16)	96	58	.623	—	382,275	Johnny Keane
Ft. Worth Cats (10)..............	95	58	.621	½	337,738	Les Burge
Dallas Rebels (4)	79	74	.516	16½	321,793	Al Vincent
Tulsa Oilers (11).................	79	75	.513	17	195,218	Gus Mancuso
Shreveport Sports	75	79	.487	21	198,834	Francis "Salty" Parker
Oklahoma City Indians (3)..	71	83	.461	25	244,835	Roy Schalk/Pat Ankenman
San Antonio Missions (7)...	60	94	.390	36	152,605	James Adair/Marc Carrola
Beaumont Exporters (5)......	60	94	.390	36	114,883	Goldie Holt

Playoffs: Houston 4 games, Tulsa 0; Dallas 4 games, Ft. Worth 3.
Finals: Houston 4 games, Dallas 2.

MVP-Al Rosen, Oklahoma City; **Pitcher of the Year**-Clarence Beers, Houston.

*Won first-half   **Won second-half   ***Won both halves
Numbers after nicknames indicate farm system.
Affiliation listed at end of each year.

357

BA: Al Rosen, Oklahoma City, .349
Runs: Jack Cassini, Tulsa, 116
Hits: Al Rosen, Oklahoma City, 186
RBIs: Al Rosen, Oklahoma City, 141

HRs: Nick Gregory, Shreveport, 28
Wins: Clarence Beers, Houston, 25
SOs: Dwain Sloat, Ft. Worth, 162
ERA: Dwain Sloat, Ft. Worth, 1.99

A Eastern League
President: Thomas H. Richardson

Standings	W	L	Pct.	GB	Attend.	Manager
Utica Blue Sox (14)	90	48	.652	—	110,786	Eddie Sawyer
Albany Senators (15)	80	58	.580	10	184,055	Pinky May
Wilkes-Barre Barons (3)	80	60	.571	11	125,288	Bill Norman
Scranton Red Sox (1)	78	62	.557	13	162,813	Eddie Popowski
Williamsport Tigers (4)	66	74	.471	25	87,011	George Detore
Hartford Chiefs (9)	58	82	.414	33	92,397	Dutch Dorman
Elmira Pioneers (7)	54	86	.386	37	73,007	Ralph Winegarner
Binghamton Triplets (5)	52	88	.371	39	110,277	Lefty Gomez

Playoffs: Utica 4 games, Wilkes-Barre 2; Albany 4 games, Scranton 3.
Finals: Utica 4 games, Albany 3.

All-Star Team: 1B-Frank Heller, Williamsport; **2B**-Ralph Caballero, Utica; **3B**-Pinky May, Albany; **SS**-Granny Hamner, Utica; **OF**-Richie Ashburn, Utica; Johnny Groth, Williamsport; Ken Wood, Elmira; **C**-Stan Lopata, Utica; **Util**-Harry Heslet, Binghamton; **P**-Mike Garcia, Wilkes-Barre; Dick Koecher, Utica; **Manager**-Eddie Sawyer, Utica.

BA: Joe Tipton, Wilkes-Barre, .375
Runs: Richie Ashburn, Utica, 128
Hits: Richie Ashburn, Utica, 194
RBIs: Frank Heller, Williamsport, 98
HRs: Harry Heslet, Binghamton, 24

Wins: Mike Garcia, Wilkes-Barre, 17
    Dick Koecher, Utica, 17
SOs: Mickey McDermott, Scranton, 136
ERA: Bill Kennedy, Scranton, 2.62

A South Atlantic League
President: Earl Blue

Standings	W	L	Pct.	GB	Attend.	Manager
Columbus Cardinals (16)	88	65	.575	—	134,305	Kemp Wicker
Savannah Indians (6)	85	66	.563	2	192,975	Tom Oliver/James Adair
Charleston Rebels (1)	83	69	.546	4½	184,851	Martin "Chick" Autry
Augusta Tigers (5)	81	69	.540	5½	130,000	Dibrell Williams/Bill Cooper
Greenville Spinners (10)	77	77	.500	11½	130,205	Frenchy Bordagaray/
						Pepper Martin
Macon Peaches (11)	70	82	.461	17½	132,996	Ray Hayworth
Jacksonville Tars (13)	66	87	.431	22	104,824	John Hudson
Columbia Reds (12)	59	94	.386	29	97,445	Gerald Walker

Playoffs: Augusta 4 games, Columbus 2; Savannah 4 games, Charleston 3.
Finals: Savannah 4 games, Augusta 1.

All-Star Team: 1B-Don Bollweg, Columbus; **2B**-Clarence Difani, Augusta; **3B**-Bill Hockenbury, Savannah; **SS**-Mickey Livingston, Charleston; **OF**-Don Mueller, Jacksonville; Ralph Brown, Augusta; Walter Schuerbaum, Augusta; **C**-Lester Fusselman, Columbus; **Util**-Richard Kaess, Macon; Bob Churchill, Greenville; **P**-Lou Brissie, Savannah; Tom Poholsky, Columbus; **Manager**-Kemp Wicker, Columbus.

BA: Ralph Brown, Augusta, .356
Runs: Ralph Brown, Augusta, 117
Hits: Ralph Brown, Augusta, 228
RBIs: Walter Schuerbaum, Augusta, 118

HRs: Lloyd Lowe, Columbus, 19
    Bill Hockenbury, Savannah, 19
3B: Edward Mutryn, Savannah, 24
Wins: Lou Brissie, Savannah, 23
SOs: Lou Brissie, Savannah, 278
ERA: Lou Brissie, Savannah, 1.91

A Western League
President: Senator Edwin C. Johnson

Standings	W	L	Pct.	GB	Attend.	Manager
Sioux City Soos (13)	81	49	.623	—	113,036	Joe Becker
Des Moines Bruins (11)	75	52	.591	4½	152,027	James Keesey
Pueblo Dodgers (10)	70	58	.547	10	80,163	Walter Alston
Omaha Cardinals (16)	67	62	.519	13½	138,308	Ollie Vanek
Denver Bears (5)	54	75	.419	26½	124,923	Marty McManus
Lincoln Athletics (6)	38	89	.299	41½	43,464	Herman Schulte/Tom Oliver

Playoffs: Sioux City 3 games, Omaha 1; Pueblo 3 games, Des Moines 1.
Finals: Pueblo 4 games, Sioux City 1.

All-Star Team: 1B-Preston Ward, Pueblo; **2B**-Eddie Kazak, Omaha; **3B**-Les Peden, Des Moines; **SS**-Ray Carlson, Sioux City; **OF**-Michael Conroy, Omaha; Carmen Mauro, Des Moines; Reggie Clarkson, Pueblo; **C**-John Bucha, Omaha; **Util**-Ray Henningsen, Omaha; Russ Burns, Des Moines; **P**-Sam Webb, Sioux City; Herb Chmiel, Des Moines; **Manager**-Joe Becker, Sioux City.

BA: Edmund Lewinski, Omaha, .346
Runs: Preston Ward, Pueblo, 120
Hits: Michael Conroy, Omaha, 190
RBIs: Preston Ward, Pueblo, 121

HRs: Tony Jaros, Sioux City, 24
Wins: Sam Webb, Sioux City, 19
SOs: Charles Bishop, Omaha, 133
ERA: Herb Chmiel, Des Moines, 2.23

B Big State League
President: J. Walter Morris

Standings	W	L	Pct.	GB	Attend.	Manager
Texarkana Bears	101	53	.656	—	140,333	Vern Washington
Greenville Majors	100	54	.649	1	154,356	Harry Davis, Jr.
Wichita Falls Spudders	92	61	.601	8½	92,553	Bobby Goff
Paris Red Peppers	80	74	.519	21	112,449	Lloyd "Rabbit" Rigby
Sherman-Denison Twins	69	85	.448	32	81,550	Guy Sturdy/Bill Atwood
Gainesville Owls	65	87	.428	35	60,971	Leroy Gilchrist
Austin Pioneers	55	99	.357	46	106,099	Beau Bell
Waco Dons	52	101	.340	48½	52,577	John "Red" Barkley

Playoffs: Texarkana 4 games, Paris 0; Wichita Falls 4 games, Greenville 2.
Finals: Texarkana 4 games, Wichita Falls 2.

BA: Vern Washington, Texarkana, .404
Runs: Buck Frierson, Sherman-Denison, 188
Hits: Buck Frierson, Sherman-Denison, 248
RBIs: Buck Frierson, Sherman-Denison, 197
HRs: Buck Frierson, Sherman-Denison, 58

TBs: Buck Frierson, Sherman-Denison, 470
Wins: Vallie Eaves, Texarkana, 25
SOs: Nat Love, Greenville, 192
ERA: Jimmy Walkup, Paris, 3.72

B Colonial League
President: Ken Strong

Standings	W	L	Pct.	GB	Attend.	Manager
Waterbury Timers	83	38	.686	—	33,946	James Acton
Poughkeepsie Giants	66	50	.569	14½	43,403	Eric McNair
Stamford Bombers	67	61	.523	19½	28,697	Zeke Bonura
New London Raiders	50	67	.427	31	27,431	Edward Butka
Port Chester Clippers	51	71	.418	32½	18,898	Alfred Barillari
Bridgeport Bees	46	76	.377	37½	28,320	Carmen Brunetto

Playoffs: Stamford 4 games, Waterbury 3; New London 4 games, Poughkeepsie 3.
Finals: Stamford 4 games, New London 1.

All-Star Team: 1B-Zeke Bonura, Stamford; **2B**-James Hanlon, Waterbury; **3B**-Vito DeVito, Stamford; **SS**-Pedro Gomez, New London; **OF**-Dan Perlmutter, Stamford; Connie Creedon, Port Chester; Frank Lamanna, Waterbury; Robert Sherwood, Bridgeport; **C**-James Acton, Waterbury; Max Goldsmith, New London; **Util**-Chuck Quimby, Poughkeepsie; **P**-Mike Kash (Kaiserski), Waterbury; Sidney Schacht, Stamford; Richard Welteroth, Poughkeepsie; **Manager**-Eric McNair, Poughkeepsie.

BA: Connie Creedon, Port Chester, .395
Runs: Vito DeVito, Stamford, 128
Hits: Connie Creedon, Port Chester, 153
RBIs: Frank Lamanna, Waterbury, 123
HRs: Frank Lamanna, Waterbury, 21

Wins: Mike Kash (Kaiserski), Waterbury, 20
SOs: Sidney Schacht, Stamford, 180
ERA: Joe Murray, Port Chester/ Bridgeport, 2.34

B Interstate League
President: Gerald P. Nugent

Standings	W	L	Pct.	GB	Attend.	Manager
Trenton Giants (13)	88	50	.638	—	99,115	Tommy Heath
Wilmington Blue Rocks (14)	79	60	.568	9½	123,491	Jack Saltzgaver
Allentown Cardinals (16)	71	67	.514	17	85,922	Specs Garbee/Bennie Borgmann
Harrisburg Senators (3)	71	69	.507	18	89,197	Les Bell
York White Roses (15)	67	70	.489	20½	108,285	Edward Turchin
Lancaster Red Roses (6)	64	73	.467	23½	74,677	Charles English/Clayton Sheedy
Hagerstown Owls (4)	62	75	.453	25½	65,177	John "Bunny" Griffiths
Sunbury Yankees (5)	51	89	.364	38	89,024	Walt VanGrofski

Playoffs: Allentown 4 games, Trenton 2; Wilmington 4 games, Harrisburg 1.
Finals: Wilmington 4 games, Allentown 3.

All-Star Team: 1B-Herb Conyers, Harrisburg; **2B**-Don Dwyer, York; **3B**-Richard Dresser, Hagerstown; **SS**-Grady Wilson, Allentown; **OF**-Steve Filipowicz, Sunbury; Harold Bamberger, Trenton; Ed Sanicki, Wilmington; **C**-Walter Novick, Lancaster; **Util**-Bill Jennings, Trenton; Tom Burgess, Allentown; **P**-Andy Tomasic, Trenton; Curt Simmons, Wilmington; **Manager**-Les Bell, Harrisburg.

BA: Herb Conyers, Harrisburg, .357
Runs: Ed Sanicki, Wilmington, 127
Hits: Herb Conyers, Harrisburg, 194
RBIs: Robert McLean, Allentown, 125
HRs: Ed Sanicki, Wilmington, 37

3B: Harold Bamberger, Trenton, 24
Wins: Andy Tomasic, Trenton, 18
SOs: Andy Tomasic, Trenton, 278
ERA: Andy Tomasic, Trenton, 2.48

B New England League
President: Claude B. Davidson

Standings	W	L	Pct.	GB	Attend.	Manager
Lynn Red Sox (1)	86	38	.694	—	60,458	Mike Ryba
Nashua Dodgers (10)	82	44	.651	5	70,813	John Dantonio
Manchester Giants (13)	74	50	.597	12	48,877	Hal Gruber
Pawtucket Slaters (9)	65	60	.597	21½	92,787	Pete Fox
Providence Chiefs (12)	57	66	.403	28½	32,203	Ralph Boyle
Fall River Indians (2)	49	76	.392	37½	57,468	Joe Holden
Portland Pilots	45	80	.360	41½	75,083	Del Bissonette
Lawrence Millionaires/ Lowell Orphans#	40	84	.323	46	32,582	George Kissell

#Lawrence (29-38) moved to Lowell July 15, first home game July 18.

Playoffs: Manchester 3 games, Lynn 2; Nashua 3 games, Pawtucket 1.
Finals: Nashua 4 games, Manchester 2.

All-Star Team: 1B-Ralph Atkins, Lynn; **2B**-Lawrence "Crash" Davis, Pawtucket; **3B**-

Walter Rogers, Nashua; **SS**-Harry Donabedian, Providence; **OF**-Edward Lynk, Lynn; Edward Yaeger, Nashua; Clifford Blake, Portland; **C**-John Pramesa, Manchester; **Util**-Mylon Vukmire, Manchester; George Kissell, Lawrence/Lowell; Arnold Banta, Lynn; Peter Shurman, Providence; **P**-Don Newcombe, Nashua; George Kadis, Pawtucket; **Manager**-Pete Fox, Pawtucket.

BA: Clifford Blake, Portland, .343
Runs: James Shirley, Lynn, 109
  Ralph Atkins, Lynn, 109
Hits: Clifford Blake, Portland, 171
RBIs: Clifford Blake, Portland, 109

HRs: Ralph Atkins, Lynn, 25
Wins: Don Newcombe, Nashua, 19
SOs: Don Newcombe, Nashua, 186
ERA: Salvatore Frederico, Manchester, 2.37

B Piedmont League
President: Richard A. Carrington

Standings	W	L	Pct.	GB	Attend.	Manager
Roanoke Red Sox (1)	90	49	.647	—	121,175	Pinky Higgins
Norfolk Tars (5)	69	70	.496	21	136,026	Buddy Hassett
Portsmouth Cubs (11)	69	71	.493	21½	154,026	Gene Hasson
Richmond Colts (13)	68	71	.489	22	173,879	Bob Latshaw
Lynchburg Cardinals (16)	63	76	.453	27	104,200	Jack McLain/Vernon Mackie
Newport News Dodgers (10)	59	81	.421	31½	85,189	John Fitzpatrick

Playoffs: Roanoke 4 games, Richmond 1; Norfolk 4 games, Portsmouth 0.
Finals: Roanoke 4 games, Norfolk 3.

All-Star Team: 1B-Dee Fondy, Newport News; **2B**-Johnny Sehrt, Roanoke; **3B**-Roy Allen, Roanoke; **SS**-Bud Hardin, Richmond; **OF**-George Wilson, Roanoke; Lou Columbo, Newport News; Bob Addis, Norfolk; **C**-Bob Scherbarth, Roanoke; Pete Lembo, Newport News; **Util**-Ace Parker, Portsmouth; **P**-John McCall, Roanoke; Bob Porterfield, Norfolk; Sol Coleman, Roanoke.

BA: Rocky Nelson, Lynchburg, .371
Runs: George Wilson, Roanoke, 124
Hits: George Wilson, Roanoke, 206
RBIs: George Wilson, Roanoke, 136

HRs: Leonard Morrison, Richmond, 20
  Vern Shetler, Portsmouth, 20
Wins: Hal "Skinny" Brown, Roanoke, 19
SOs: Bob Porterfield, Norfolk, 208
ERA: Elmer Stepanofsky, Norfolk, 2.35

B Southeastern League
President: Stuart X. Stephenson

Standings	W	L	Pct.	GB	Attend.	Manager
Jackson Senators (9)	77	62	.554	—	117,030	Willis Hudlin
Gadsden Pilots	75	65	.536	2½	112,960	Bill McGhee
Montgomery Rebels (4)	74	65	.532	3	145,458	Frank Skaff
Pensacola Fliers	75	68	.524	4	117,696	Grover Resinger/ Rudy Laskowski
Vicksburg Billies	74	69	.517	5	99,512	Buddy Blair
Meridian Peps (3)	67	73	.479	10½	60,617	Roxie Lawson
Selma Cloverleafs (15)	64	76	.457	13½	60,431	Carl Fischer/Walter Beck
Anniston Rams	56	84	.400	21½	73,874	Tommy West

Playoffs: Pensacola defeated Vicksburg 2 games to 1 in a playoff for fourth place. Montgomery 4 games, Jackson 3; Gadsden 4 games, Pensacola 1.
Finals: Montgomery 4 games, Gadsden 3.

All-Star Team: 1B-Dee Grose, Jackson; **2B**-Bill Johnson, Gadsden; **3B**-Billy Seal, Vicksburg; **SS**-Pete Spatafore, Meridian; **OF**-Bill Martin, Montgomery; Grover Bowers, Gadsden; Nesbit Wilson, Pensacola; **C**-Duke Doolittle, Jackson; **Util**-Oscar Khederian, Jackson; Tom Saffell, Selma; **P**-Woody Rich, Anniston; Chet Covington, Montgomery; **Manager**-Willis Hudlin, Jackson.

BA: Grover Bowers, Gadsden, .375
Runs: Grover Bowers, Gadsden, 132
Hits: Grover Bowers, Gadsden, 210
RBIs: Nesbit Wilson, Pensacola, 129

HRs: Bill Johnson, Gadsden, 27
Wins: Wendell Davis, Meridian, 21
SOs: Woody Rich, Anniston, 197
ERA: Edward Oliver, Pensacola, 2.94

B Three-I League
President: Tom Fairweather

Standings	W	L	Pct.	GB	Attend.	Manager
Danville Dodgers (10)	79	47	.627	—	63,926	Paul Chervinko
Terre Haute Phillies (14)	74	51	.592	4½	133,654	Ray Brubaker/ Whitey Gluchoski/Jack Sanford
Springfield Browns (7)	71	55	.563	8	58,009	Bennie Huffman
Waterloo Hawks (2)	71	55	.563	8	174,064	Johnny Mostil/Jack Onslow
Evansville Braves (9)	70	55	.560	8½	133,163	Bob Coleman
Davenport Cubs (11)	55	70	.440	23½	50,846	Dickie Kerr/Morris Arnovich
Quincy Gems (5)	50	75	.400	28½	100,096	James Adlam
Decatur Commodores (16)	31	93	.250	47	33,069	Gene Corbett

Playoffs: Springfield defeated Waterloo in a playoff for third place. Danville 3 games, Springfield 2; Waterloo 3 games, Terre Haute 0.
Finals: Waterloo 4 games, Danville 1.

All-Star Team: 1B-Hank Arft, Springfield; **2B**-Owen Friend, Springfield; **3B**-Ed Ehlers, Quincy; **SS**-Willie Jones, Terre Haute; **OF**-Bernie Zender, Danville; Bob Riga, Springfield; Gerald Scala, Waterloo; **C**-Joe Stephenson, Waterloo; **Util**-Johnny Logan, Evansville; Bill McCawley, Decatur; **P**-Ken Olson, Danville; Stan Partenheimer, Springfield; **Manager**-Paul Chervinko, Danville.

BA: Hank Arft, Springfield, .364
Runs: Gerald Scala, Waterloo, 116
Hits: Gerald Scala, Waterloo, 163
RBIs: Ray Fletcher, Evansville, 115

HRs: Ed Ehlers, Quincy, 22
Wins: Ken Olson, Danville, 22
SOs: John Perkovich, Waterloo, 207
ERA: John Perkovich, Waterloo, 2.50

B Tri-State League
President: C.M. Llewellyn

Standings	W	L	Pct.	GB	Attend.	Manager
Spartanburg Peaches (3)	88	51	.633	—	157,435	Kerby Farrell
Anderson Rebels	84	55	.604	4	150,290	Bob Richards
Knoxville Smokies	73	67	.521	15½	101,189	Dale Alexander
Charlotte Hornets (8)	72	68	.514	16½	116,729	Spencer Abbott/Cal Ermer
Rock Hill Chiefs	68	71	.489	20	91,042	Dan Carnevale
Asheville Tourists (10)	65	74	.468	23	123,897	William Sayles
Fayetteville Cubs (11)	61	78	.439	27	63,081	Clyde McDowell
Reidsville Luckies	45	92	.328	42	59,403	Lee Gamble

Playoffs: Charlotte 4 games, Spartanburg 1; Anderson 4 games, Knoxville 2.
Finals: Charlotte 4 games, Anderson 3.

All-Star Team: 1B-Harold Kollar, Knoxville; **2B**-Fred Barocco, Anderson; **3B**-George Motto, Reidsville; **SS**-Sam Meeks, Charlotte; **OF**-Al Simononis, Anderson; Rip Russell, Spartanburg; William Sayles, Asheville; **C**-Smoky Burgess, Fayetteville; Len Okrie, Fayetteville; **Util**-Cal Ermer, Charlotte; Pete Milne, Spartanburg; **P**-James Kleckley, Spartanburg; Robert Callan, Charlotte; Edward Craft, Anderson; Ralph Holland, Spartanburg; **Manager**-Kerby Farrell, Spartanburg.

BA: Smoky Burgess, Fayetteville, .387
Runs: Fred Barocco, Anderson, 123
Hits: Sam Meeks, Charlotte, 191
RBIs: Al Simonisis, Anderson, 132

HRs: Al Simonisis, Anderson, 27
Wins: James Kleckley, Spartanburg, 20
SOs: Edward Craft, Anderson, 185
ERA: Robert Callan, Charlotte, 3.08

B Western International League
President: Robert B. Abel

Standings	W	L	Pct.	GB	Attend.	Manager
Vancouver Capilanos	86	66	.566	—	119,303	Bill Brenner
Spokane Indians (10)	87	67	.565	—	287,185	Ben Geraghty
Bremerton Bluejackets	86	68	.558	1	86,522	Alan Strange
Salem Senators	80	68	.541	4	98,247	Jack Wilson
Victoria Athletics (5)	80	72	.526	6	129,862	Ted Norbert
Tacoma Tigers (11)	72	81	.471	14½	113,783	Red Harwel
Wenatchee Chiefs	59	92	.391	26½	72,487	Buddy Ryan
Yakima Stars	59	95	.383	28	86,004	Harland Clift

Playoffs: None.

All-Star Team: 1B-Jack Harshman, Victoria; Herb Gorman, Spokane; **2B**-Art Lilly, Yakima; **3B**-Bobby Morgan, Spokane; **SS**-Clarence Hicks, Spokane; **OF**-Frank Mullens, Vancouver; Edward Murphy, Bremerton; Bill White, Victoria; **C**-Earl Kuper, Tacoma; **Util**-Robert Hedington, Tacoma; Glenn Stetter, Tacoma; **P**-Bob Costello, Spokane; Wandell Mosser, Salem; **Manager**-Jack Wilson, Salem.

BA: Earl Kuper, Tacoma, .389
Runs: Art Lilly, Yakima, 141
Hits: Leon Mohr, Vancouver, 216
RBIs: Jack Harshman, Victoria, 142
HRs: Jack Harshman, Victoria, 36

Wins: James Hedgecock, Vancouver, 21
  Bob Costello, Spokane, 21
SOs: Bill Woop, Victoria, 252
ERA: Joe Sullivan, Bremerton, 2.68

C Arizona-Texas League
President: G.R. Michaels

Standings	W	L	Pct.	GB	Attend.	Manager
Phoenix Senators	82	51	.617	—	55,452	Alton Biggs
Tucson Cowboys**(3)	80	52	.606	1½	63,580	Joe Vosmik
Bisbee Yanks (5)	74	59	.556	8	33,686	Charlie Metro
Juarez Indians*/ Mesa Orphans#	61	69	.469	19½	27,153	Manuel Fortes
Globe-Miami Browns (7)	53	77	.408	27½	60,669	Lloyd Brown
El Paso Texans	44	86	.338	36½	39,996	Syd Cohen

#Juarez disbanded June 22 after winning the first half and was replaced by Mesa June 27.

Playoffs: Tucson 2 games, Bisbee 0; Globe-Miami 2 games, Phoenix 0.
Finals: Globe-Miami 3 games, Tucson 2.

All-Star Team: 1B-Nick Sunseri, Tucson; **2B**-Bob Keeler, Bisbee; **3B**-Billy Martin, Phoenix; **SS**-Joe DeMaestri, El Paso; **OF**-John Ringler, Globe-Miami; Pete Hughes, Phoenix; Frank Finnegan, Bisbee; **C**-Clint Courtney, Bisbee; **Util**-Alton Biggs, Phoenix; Ray Conroy, Tucson; **P**-John Conant, Phoenix; Don Cantrell, Phoenix; Syd Cohen, El Paso; **Manager**-Joe Vosmik, Tucson.

BA: Billy Martin, Phoenix, .392
Runs: Pete Hughes, Phoenix, 180
Hits: Billy Martin, Phoenix, 230
RBIs: Billy Martin, Phoenix, 174
HRs: Pete Hughes, Phoenix, 38

BBs: Pete Hughes, Phoenix, 193
Wins: John Conant, Phoenix, 19
SOs: Lloyd Brown, Globe-Miami, 167
ERA: Syd Cohen, El Paso, 3.38

C Border League
President: John G. Ward

Standings	W	L	Pct.	GB	Attend.	Manager
Ottawa Nationals	82	42	.661	—	62,607	Paul Dean
Watertown Athletics	70	54	.565	12	53,600	Bob Shawkey
Auburn Cayugas	66	60	.524	17	59,637	Barney Hearn
Ogdensburg Maples	61	65	.484	22	63,486	Steve Yerkes
Kingston Ponies	49	77	.389	34	52,268	Ben Lady
Geneva Red Birds	46	76	.377	35	57,308	Charles Small

Playoffs: Ottawa 4 games, Auburn 0; Ogdensburg 4 games, Watertown 3.
Finals: Ottawa 4 games, Ogdensburg 2.

All-Star Team: 1B-Fred Gerken, Watertown; **2B**-Bill Metzig, Ottawa; **3B**-Johnny Russian, Ottawa; **SS**-Bob Harmon, Auburn; **OF**-Barney Hearn, Auburn; Buddy Heximer, Kingston; Anthony Gudaitis, Ogdensburg; **C**-Al Grefe, Ottawa; **Util**-Bob Sanborn, Ottawa; **P**-Charles Schupp, Ottawa; Frank Fanovich, Watertown; **Manager**-Paul Dean, Ottawa.

BA: Barney Hearn, Auburn, .361
Runs: Anthony Gudaitis, Ogdensburg, 122
Hits: Fred Gerken, Watertown, 172
RBIs: Donald Phelps, Geneva, 103
HRs: Donald Phelps, Geneva, 25
Anthony Gudaitis, Ogdensburg, 25
Wins: Frank Fanovich, Watertown, 16
Arnold Jarrell, Kingston, 16
Charles Schupp, Ottawa, 16
Nick Butcher, Ottawa, 16
SOs: Frank Fanovich, Watertown, 182
ERA: Frank Fanovich, Watertown, 2.41

C California League
President: W.R. "Bill" Schroeder

Standings	W	L	Pct.	GB	Attend.	Manager
Stockton Ports	95	45	.679	—	154,547	John Babich
Visalia Cubs (11)	79	61	.564	16	104,311	John Intlekofer
San Jose Red Sox (1)	79	61	.564	16	92,634	Marv Owen
Santa Barbara Dodgers (10)	73	67	.521	22	92,541	Ray Hathaway
Bakersfield Indians (3)	66	74	.471	29	115,400	Tony Governor
Ventura Yankees (5)	58	82	.414	37	64,511	Mike Gazella/John Sturm
Fresno Cardinals (16)	58	82	.414	37	79,050	Frank Demaree/ William Harris/ Charles Baron(ovic)/ William Brenzel
Modesto Reds	52	88	.371	43	49,863	Harry Green

Playoffs: Visalia defeated San Jose in a one game playoff for second place. Stockton 3 games, San Jose 0; Santa Barbara 3 games, Visalia 0.
Finals: Stockton 4 games, Santa Barbara 3.

All-Star Team: 1B-Ed Lenn, San Jose; **2B**-Edward Samcoff, Stockton; **3B**-Bert Bonomi, Fresno; **SS**-Don Alfrano, Visalia; **OF**-Ralph Samhammer, Ventura; James Trew, Visalia; Louis Vezilich, Fresno; **C**-Lilio Marcucci, Stockton; Arnold Riesgo, San Jose; **Util**-Harry Clements, Stockton; Willie Enos, Modesto; **P**-Ray Hathaway, Santa Barbara; Don Belton, Stockton; Lloyd Hittle, Stockton.

BA: Richard Cole, Fresno, .386
Runs: James Trew, Visalia, 134
Hits: Ed Lenn, San Jose, 204
RBIs: Louis Vezilich, Fresno, 141
HRs: Willie Enos, Modesto, 30
Wins: Don Belton, Stockton, 21
SOs: John Hoffman, Visalia, 263
ERA: Lloyd Hittle, Stockton, 2.24

C Canadian-American League
President: Rev. Harold J. Martin

Standings	W	L	Pct.	GB	Attend.	Manager
Schenectady Blue Jays (14)	86	51	.628	—	146,227	Leon Riley
Gloversville-Johnstown Glovers (7)	74	65	.532	13	75,279	Stan "Packy" Rogers
Amsterdam Rugmakers (5)	73	67	.521	14½	88,876	Sol Mishkin
Oneonta Red Sox (1)	70	67	.511	16	53,608	Red Marion
Pittsfield Electrics (3)	71	69	.507	16½	67,644	Tony Rensa
Trois Rivieres Royals (10)	65	69	.485	19½	59,961	Lou Rochelli
Rome Colonels (4)	67	72	.482	20	58,463	Ed Boland/Adam Bengoechea
Quebec Alouettes	45	91	.331	40½	85,572	Buck Desorey/Tony Ravish

Playoffs: Schenectady 4 games, Amsterdam 3; Gloversville-Johnstown 4 games, Oneonta 1.
Finals: Schenectady 4 games, Gloversville-Johnstown 1.

All-Star Team: 1B-Michael Genevrino, Schenectady; **2B**-Charles Dykes, Schenectady; **3B**-Stan "Packy" Rogers, Gloversville-Johnstown; **SS**-Lou Rochelli, Trois Rivieres; **OF**-Benjamin Gregg, Schenectady; Malcolm "Bunny" Mick, Amsterdam; John Lorenz, Schenectady; **C**-Stephen Salata, Oneonta; **Util**-Fred Campbell, Gloversville-Johnstown; **P**-Charles Baker, Schenectady; Irving Medlinger, Oneonta; **Manager**-Leon Riley, Schenectady.

BA: Malcolm "Bunny" Mick, Amsterdam, .356
Runs: Robert Watson, Schenectady, 117
Hits: Benjamin Gregg, Schenectady, 174
RBIs: Benjamin Gregg, Schenectady, 117
HRs: Benjamin Gregg, Schenectady, 15
Wins: Kenneth Rogers, Amsterdam, 18
SOs: Irving Medlinger, Oneonta, 182
ERA: Joseph Milians, Schenectady, 1.98

C Carolina League
President: Dr. Thomas S. Wilson

Standings	W	L	Pct.	GB	Attend.	Manager
Burlington Bees	87	55	.613	—	140,138	Buddy Bates
Winston-Salem Cardinals (16)	85	57	.599	2	223,507	Cecil "Zip" Payne
Raleigh Capitals	81	60	.574	5½	150,110	Ray Thomas
Durham Bulls	70	71	.496	16½	152,095	Willie Duke
Greensboro Patriots	65	75	.464	21	147,128	Charlie Carroll/Rene Desorcy
Danville Leafs (13)	65	77	.458	22	105,700	Herb Brett/Eugene Petty
Leaksville-Draper-Spray Triplets	59	82	.418	27½	54,000	George Granger
Martinsville Athletics (6)	53	88	.376	33½	51,000	Joe Glenn/Woody Wheaton

Playoffs: Durham 4 games, Winston-Salem 2; Raleigh 4 games, Burlington 3.
Finals: Raleigh 4 games, Durham 2.

All-Star Team: 1B-Cecil "Turkey" Tyson, Durham; **2B**-Jim Burns, Greensboro/Burlington; **3B**-Bill Nagel, Leaksville-Draper-Spray/Raleigh; **SS**-Walter "Teapot" Frye, Leaksville-Draper-Spray; **OF**-Willie Duke, Durham; Buddy Bates, Burlington; Emile Showfety, Burlington/Greensboro; **C**-Harry Sullivan, Raleigh; **Util**-Claude Swiggett, Burlington; Harvey Haddix, Winston-Salem; **Manager**-Buddy Bates, Burlington.

BA: Harry Sullivan, Raleigh, .391
Runs: Cecil "Turkey" Tyson, Durham, 138
Hits: Harry Sullivan, Raleigh, 200
RBIs: Bill Nagel, Leaksville-Draper-Spray/Raleigh, 128
HRs: Eugene Petty, Danville, 31
Wins: Ken Deal, Burlington, 23
SOs: Ken Deal, Burlington, 275
ERA: Harvey Haddix, Winston-Salem, 1.90

C Central Association
President: Frank Hearn

Standings	W	L	Pct.	GB	Attend.	Manager
Clinton Cubs (11)	73	51	.589	—	59,553	Robert Peterson
Hannibal Pilots (7)	69	56	.552	4½	40,490	Herb Nordquist
Rockford Rox (12)	68	57	.544	5½	67,938	Cyril Pfeifer
Keokuk Pirates (15)	61	64	.488	12½	44,332	Frank Oceak
Burlington Indians (3)	52	72	.419	21	37,138	Paul O'Dea
Moline A's (6)	51	74	.408	22½	27,479	Elwood Wheaton

Playoffs: Clinton 3 games, Rockford 2; Hannibal 3 games, Keokuk 1.
Finals: Clinton 4 games, Hannibal 1.

All-Star Team: 1B-Joe Lutz, Hannibal; **2B**-Charles Balogh, Clinton; **3B**-Joseph Ruddy, Clinton; **SS**-George Lebedz, Moline; **OF**-Roy Sievers, Hannibal; Edward Wiltsee, Clinton; Frank Pawelek, Rockford; **C**-Bernard Westerkamp, Rockford; Paul Wittingham, Keokuk; **Util**-Fred Marsh, Burlington; Ralph Matzer, Moline; Bill Cross, Hannibal; Matt Zelinsky, Moline; Peter Mish, Burlington; Gene DeAngelis, Clinton; **P**-Stanley Wnetrzak, Clinton; Charles Funk, Hannibal; **Manager**-Robert Peterson, Clinton.

BA: Edward Wiltsee, Clinton, .387
Runs: Roy Sievers, Hannibal, 121
Hits: Roy Sievers, Hannibal, 159
RBIs: Roy Sievers, Hannibal, 141
HRs: Roy Sievers, Hannibal, 34
Wins: Charles Funk, Hannibal, 19
SOs: Charles Funk, Hannibal, 145
ERA: Stanley Wnetrzak, Clinton, 1.72

C Cotton States League
President: James Griffith

Standings	W	L	Pct.	GB	Attend.	Manager
Greenwood Dodgers (10)	92	38	.708	—	68,746	James Bivin
Greenville Bucks	84	46	.646	8	53,887	Harry Chozen
El Dorado Oilers	61	69	.469	31	42,957	James Cookson
Clarksdale Planters	59	71	.454	33	50,136	Calvin Chapman
Hot Springs Bathers	49	81	.377	43	41,818	Joe Santomauro
Helena Seaporters	45	85	.346	47	24,510	Herschel Bobo

Playoffs: Greenwood 3 games, Clarksdale 1; Greenville 3 games, El Dorado 2.
Finals: Greenwood 4 games, Greenville 3.

BA: Ernest Davis, El Dorado, .340
Runs: Robert Lee, Greenwood, 102
Paul Mauldin, Clarksdale, 102
H.G. Talbert, Helena, 102
Hits: Paul Mauldin, Clarksdale, 166
RBIs: Floyd Fogg, Clarksdale, 112
HRs: Floyd Fogg, Clarksdale, 27
Wins: Leslie Edwards, Greenville, 21
Russ Oppliger, Greenwood, 21
SOs: Bob Schultz, Greenville, 274
ERA: Billy Briggs, Greenville, 1.93

C Florida International League
President: Wayne Allen

Standings	W	L	Pct.	GB	Attend.	Manager
Havana Cubans (8)	105	45	.700	—	264,813	Oscar Rodriguez
Tampa Smokers	104	48	.684	2	130,242	Tony Cuccinello
Miami Beach Flamingos	88	65	.575	18½	89,000	Al Leitz
Miami Tourists	74	77	.490	31½	132,429	Dave Coble/Charles Baron(ovic)
St. Petersburg Saints	71	80	.470	34½	114,927	Jimmie Foxx/Lou Finney
West Palm Beach Indians	68	86	.442	39	60,473	Harry Hughes
Lakeland Pilots	50	101	.331	55½	41,926	Bill Perrin
Ft. Lauderdale Braves (9)	48	106	.312	59	53,403	Jimmy Zinn/Walter Kopp

Playoffs: Havana 3 games, Miami 2; Tampa 3 games, Miami Beach 0.
Finals: Havana 4 games, Tampa 0.

All-Star Team: 1B-B.E. Fernandez, Tampa; **2B**-George Bucci, St. Petersburg; **3B**-Glenn Adkins, West Palm Beach; **SS**-E.M. "Bitsy" Mott, Tampa; **OF**-Perry Murphy, Tampa; Robert Ned Harris, West Palm Beach; Oscar Garmendia, Miami Beach; **C**-Stanley Andrews, St. Petersburg; Manuel Fernandez, Tampa; **Util**-George Biershenk, Lakeland; **P**-Catayo Gonzalez, Tampa; Melvin Nee, Miami; Milford Howard, Lakeland; Octavio Rubert, West Palm Beach; Harold Graham, Miami Beach; **Manager**-Al Leitz, Miami Beach.

BA: Lamar Murphy, Tampa, .354
Runs: E.M. "Bitsy" Mott, Tampa, 124
Hits: Manuel Hidalgo, Havana, 200
RBIs: Robert Ned Harris, West Palm Beach, 120

HRs: Robert Ned Harris, West Palm Beach, 34
Wins: Connie Marrero, Havana, 25
SOs: Connie Marrero, Havana, 251
ERA: Connie Marrero, Havana, 1.66

C Lone Star League
President: Fred Nicholson

Standings	W	L	Pct.	GB	Attend.	Manager
Kilgore Drillers	78	60	.565	—	71,685	Joe Kracher
Longview Texans	78	61	.561	½	73,134	Jess Landrum
Marshall Comets	76	63	.547	2½	51,494	Jerry Feille/Paul Kardow
Tyler Trojans (12)	76	64	.543	3	64,810	James "Hack" Miller
Jacksonville Jax (3)	73	67	.521	6	37,817	Lynville "Watty" Watkins
Lufkin Foresters	72	68	.514	7	42,692	Dixie Parsons
Henderson Oilers	65	72	.474	12½	50,000	Ray Honeycutt
Bryan Bombers	38	101	.273	40½	36,817	Mike "Gus" Mistovich/Harry Logan/Joe Moore

Playoffs: Kilgore 4 games, Tyler 0; Marshall 4 games, Longview 1.
Finals: Kilgore 4 games, Marshall 2.

All-Star Team: 1B-Bob Marquis, Lufkin; Mervin Connors, Longview; **2B**-Wendell Finders, Longview; **3B**-Ruether Jones, Tyler; **SS**-Connie Bean, Jacksonville; **OF**-James "Lew" Morton, Henderson; John Stone, Henderson; Marshall Brown, Kilgore; **C**-Joe Kracher, Kilgore; **Util**-Al Kubski, Marshall; Stan Bartkowski, Kilgore; **P**-Robert Ross, Kilgore; Danny Rowland, Jacksonville; **Manager**-Dixie Parsons, Lufkin.

BA: John Stone, Henderson, .396
Runs: James "Lew" Morton, Henderson, 145
Bob Marquis, Lufkin, 145
Hits: John Stone, Henderson, 224
RBIs: John Stone, Henderson, 185

HRs: John Stone, Henderson, 32
Wins: J.C. Henson, Jacksonville, 21
Robert Ross, Kilgore, 21
SOs: Okie Flowers, Longview, 218
ERA: Frank Martin, Longview, 2.55

C Middle Atlantic League
President: Elmer M. Daily

Standings	W	L	Pct.	GB	Attend.	Manager
Vandergrift Pioneers (14)	76	46	.623	—	87,000	Floyd Patterson
Niagara Falls Frontiers (6)	68	55	.553	8½	48,000	Steve Mizerak
Erie Sailors (13)	68	56	.548	9	107,000	Don Cross
Butler Yankees (5)	62	62	.500	15	56,000	Dallas Warner
Oil City Refiners (2)	61	63	.492	16	57,000	Charles Engle
Youngstown Colts	55	68	.447	21½	52,000	Charles Harig
Uniontown Coal Barons (15)	53	72	.424	24½	75,000	Alexander Stutzke
Johnstown Johnnies (10)	52	73	.416	25½	101,000	Jay Kirke, Jr.

Playoffs: Vandergrift 3 games, Erie 0; Butler 3 games, Niagara Falls 2.
Finals: Vandergrift 4 games, Butler 0.

BA: Alex Garbowski, Vandergrift, .396
Runs: Bob Reash, Oil City, 115
Keith Peloe, Niagara Falls, 115
Hits: Bob Reash, Oil City, 183
RBIs: John Merson, Uniontown, 107

HRs: Maurice Cunningham, Youngstown, 26
Wins: Egon Feuker, Erie, 18
SOs: Stan Fain, Uniontown, 165
ERA: Egon Feuker, Erie, 2.81

C Northern League
President: Herman D. White

Standings	W	L	Pct.	GB	Attend.	Manager
Aberdeen Pheasants (7)	82	36	.695	—	90,156	Don Heffner
Sioux Falls Canaries (11)	75	43	.636	7	116,683	Jim Oglesby
Fargo-Moorhead Twins (15)	70	49	.588	12½	106,662	Bruno Haas
Duluth Dukes (16)	60	55	.522	20½	102,639	Paul Bowa
Eau Claire Bears (9)	62	57	.521	20½	77,638	Hugh Wise
Superior Blues (2)	46	68	.404	34	68,762	George "Red" Treadwell
St. Cloud Rox	48	71	.403	34½	42,471	Dave Bancroft
Grand Forks Chiefs	28	92	.233	55	42,071	Claude Jonnard

Playoffs: Aberdeen 3 games, Fargo-Moorhead 2, one forfeit; Sioux Falls 3 games, Duluth 1.
Finals: Sioux Falls 4 games, Aberdeen 2.

BA: Andrew Piesek, Aberdeen, .375
Runs: Andrew Piesek, Aberdeen, 119
Hits: Andrew Piesek, Aberdeen, 178
RBIs: William Wright, Aberdeen, 99

HRs: Harold Schadt, St. Cloud, 19
Wins: Bob Haas, Fargo-Moorhead, 17
SOs: Cloyd Boyer, Duluth, 239
ERA: Frank Smrekar, Duluth, 2.21

C Pioneer League
President: Jack P. Halliwell

Standings	W	L	Pct.	GB	Attend.	Manager
Salt Lake City Bees*	81	57	.587	—	146,187	Rupert "Tommy" Thompson
Twin Falls Cowboys**(5)	77	60	.562	3½	99,153	Earl Bolyard
Ogden Reds (12)	77	61	.558	4	82,056	Horace "Pip" Koehler
Boise Pilots	67	70	.489	13½	110,203	Walter Lowe
Idaho Falls Russets	66	71	.482	14½	72,416	Rosy Gilhousen
Pocatello Cardinals (16)	45	94	.324	36½	41,493	James Tyack

Playoff: Twin Falls 4 games, Salt Lake City 1.

All-Star Team: 1B-Walter Lowe, Boise; **2B**-Jack Radtke, Twin Falls; **3B**-Lou Tamone,

Boise; **SS**-Bobby Thomson, Pocatello; **OF**-Dale Markert, Idaho Falls; George Leyrer, Twin Falls; Charles Balassi, Twin Falls; **C**-Harold Danielson, Twin Falls; **Util**-Gordon Evans, Idaho Falls; Earl Silverthorn, Idaho Falls; **P**-Robert Drilling, Salt Lake City; Walter Eads, Twin Falls; **Manager**-Earl Bolyard, Twin Falls.

BA: Tom O'Laughlin, Pocatello, .360
Runs: George Leyrer, Twin Falls, 163
Hits: Earl Silverthorn, Idaho Falls, 190
RBIs: Walter Lowe, Boise, 157
HRs: Walter Lowe, Boise, 22

Wins: Robert Drilling, Salt Lake City, 23
SOs: James Zavitka, Ogden, 193
ERA: Robert Drilling, Salt Lake City, 2.68
Pct: Robert Drilling, Salt Lake City, .821, 23-5

C Sunset League
President: W.R. "Bill" Schroeder

Standings	W	L	Pct.	GB	Attend.	Manager
Riverside Dons**(15)	80	60	.571	—	45,477	Norman DeWeese/Jack Rothrock
Anaheim Valencias*	79	61	.564	1	16,452	Jack Rothrock/Jerry Gardner
Las Vegas Wranglers (9)	73	67	.521	7	44,574	Newell Kimball
Reno Silver Sox (13)	69	69	.500	10	22,866	Thomas Lloyd
Ontario Orioles	64	75	.460	15½	23,932	Hal Spindel
El Centro Imperials	53	86	.381	26½	45,429	Bob Boken/Ray Viers

Playoffs: Riverside 3 games, Las Vegas 0; Anaheim 3 games, Ontario 0.
Finals: Anaheim 4 games, Riverside 1.

All-Star Team: 1B-Don Cena, Riverside; **2B**-Gene Gaviglio, Anaheim; **3B**-Dick Schattinger, Riverside; **SS**-Bud Dawson, Anaheim; **OF**-Paul Zaby, Las Vegas; Calvin Felix, Las Vegas; Phil Alotta, Reno; **C**-Tom Lloyd, Riverside; Dan Reagan, Ontario; **Util**-Ray Viers, El Centro; Bob Jaderlund, El Centro; **P**-Clarence Jaime, Ontario; Robert Mineo, Riverside; Glenn Lierman, Anaheim; Nate Moreland, El Centro.

BA: Paul Zaby, Las Vegas, .401
Runs: Calvin Felix, Las Vegas, 173
Hits: Calvin Felix, Las Vegas, 236
RBIs: Calvin Felix, Las Vegas, 182
HRs: Calvin Felix, Las Vegas, 52

TBs: Calvin Felix, Las Vegas, 443
Wins: Clarence Jaime, Ontario, 22
SOs: Don Robertson, Reno, 242
ERA: Robert Masters, Riverside, 3.55

C West Texas-New Mexico League
President: Milton E. Price

Standings	W	L	Pct.	GB	Attend.	Manager
Lubbock Hubbers (4)	99	41	.707	—	117,621	Jackie Sullivan
Amarillo Gold Sox (9)	85	55	.607	14	105,224	Harry Lamprich
Albuquerque Dukes	74	64	.536	24	101,623	Buck Fausett
Lamesa Lobos	72	67	.518	26½	66,232	George Sturdivant
Pampa Oilers	67	72	.482	31½	56,262	Grover Seitz
Borger Gassers	61	79	.436	38	72,911	Gordon Nell/Stu Williams
Abilene Blue Sox (10)	58	81	.417	40½	55,426	Hayden Greer/Art Bowland
Clovis Pioneers	41	98	.295	57½	44,602	Joe Dotlich/Jack Riley/John Bottarini

Playoffs: Lubbock 4 games, Lamesa 0; Amarillo 4 games, Albuquerque 2.
Finals: Lubbock 4 games, Amarillo 2.

All-Star Team: 1B-George Sturdivant, Lamesa; **2B**-Jackie Sullivan, Lubbock; **3B**-Buck Fausett, Albuquerque; **SS**-Bill Serena, Lubbock; **OF**-Art Bowland, Abilene; Leon Cato, Borger; Bob Crues, Amarillo; **C**-Don Moore, Albuquerque; **Util**-Hayden Greer, Abilene; Alfred Duarte, Amarillo; **P**-Paul Hinrichs, Lubbock; William "Lefty" Jones, Lamesa; William "Lefty" Lonergan, Amarillo; **Manager**-Grover Seitz, Pampa.

BA: Leon Cato, Borger, .410
Runs: Bill Serena, Lubbock, 183
Hits: Leon Cato, Borger, 229
RBIs: Bill Serena, Lubbock, 190
HRs: Bill Serena, Lubbock, 57

Wins: William "Lefty" Jones, Lamesa, 24
SOs: William "Lefty" Lonergan, Amarillo, 218
ERA: Paul Hinrichs, Lubbock, 3.34
Pct: William "Lefty" Jones, Lamesa, .857, 24-4

C Western Association
President: Tom Fairweather

Standings	W	L	Pct.	GB	Attend.	Manager
Salina Blue Jays (14)	85	53	.616	—	60,369	Edward Walls
Topeka Owls	83	55	.601	2	113,529	Winlow Johnson
Muskogee Reds (7)	75	64	.540	10½	78,511	Ray Baker
St. Joseph Cardinals (16)	72	67	.518	13½	88,000	Robert Stanton
Joplin Miners (5)	67	73	.479	19	70,535	Jimmy McLeod
Hutchinson Cubs (11)	63	76	.453	22½	51,813	Morris Arnovich/Dickie Kerr
Ft. Smith Giants (13)	59	78	.431	25½	52,215	Earl Wolgamot
Leavenworth Braves (9)	50	88	.362	35	28,459	Joe Bowman

Playoffs: St. Joseph 3 games, Topeka 2; Muskogee 3 games, Salina 2.
Finals: St. Joseph 4 games, Muskogee 3.

All-Star Team: 1B-John Davenport, Salina; **2B**-John Bulkley, Topeka; **3B**-Bill Cloude, St. Joseph; **SS**-John Picchiotti, Hutchinson; **OF**-Lloyd Long, Salina; Butch Nieman, Topeka; Mike Scire, Hutchinson; **C**-Mel Brookey, Salina; **Util**-Jay Sousley, Joplin; Denny Aeschliman, Hutchinson; **P**-Lee Dodson, Topeka; Ross Grimsley, Topeka; **Manager**-Edward Walls, Salina.

BA: Jay Sousley, Joplin, .351
Runs: Butch Nieman, Topeka, 135
Hits: Kelly Wingo, Muskogee, 187
RBIs: Butch Nieman, Topeka, 114

HRs: Butch Nieman, Topeka, 29
Wins: Arthur Hartley, Salina, 22
SOs: Ross Grimsley, Topeka, 262
ERA: Lee Dodson, Topeka, 2.37

D Alabama State League
President: Jack Hovater

Standings	W	L	Pct.	GB	Attend.	Manager
Greenville Lions	90	48	.652	—	40,000	Sam Demma
Brewton Millers (8)	78	59	.569	11½	42,000	Norman Veazey
Enterprise Boll Weevils......	77	61	.558	13	53,000	Ben Catchings
Dothan Browns	69	70	.496	21½	50,000	Frank Martin
Andalusia Arrows	67	71	.486	23	62,000	Bob Engle
Ozark Eagles	65	74	.468	25½	45,000	Dolly Lambert
Troy Trojans (4)................	58	80	.420	32	37,000	Bob Benish
Geneva Red Birds	49	90	.353	41½	35,000	James Francoline/
						Francis Welker

Playoffs: Greenville 4 games, Enterprise 3; Brewton 4 games, Dothan 3.
Finals: Greenville 4 games, Brewton 3.

All-Star Team: 1B-Bob Engle, Andalusia; **2B**-Ben Catchings, Enterprise; **3B**-Walter Quimby, Dothan; **SS**-Bernard Donner, Andalusia; **OF**-Manuel Russo, Andalusia; Robert Sprentall, Troy; Emil Bozick, Troy; James Gilbert, Troy; **C**-Emory Lindsey, Dothan; Clyde McAllister, Geneva; **Util**-Doyle Nunnally, Geneva; **P**-Joe Beaugez, Brewton; Henry Delay, Brewton; Marcus Davis, Dothan; Claude Medlin, Geneva; **Manager**-Norman Veazey, Brewton.

BA: Perry Roberts, Greenville, .389
Runs: Ben Catchings, Enterprise, 126
Hits: Perry Roberts, Greenville, 228
RBIs: Perry Roberts, Greenville, 152
HRs: Andy Archipoli, Ozark, 24
Wins: Max Peterson, Greenville, 27
SOs: Max Peterson, Greenville, 266
ERA: Max Peterson, Greenville, 2.02

D Appalachian League
President: Carl A. Jones

Standings	W	L	Pct.	GB	Attend.	Manager
Pulaski Counts (10)	79	43	.648	—	49,472	Larry Kinzer
Bluefield Blue-Grays (9)	69	57	.548	12	86,303	George Lacy
New River Rebels	64	60	.516	16	39,596	Jack Crosswhite
Bristol Twins (13)..............	64	62	.508	17	68,381	Charlie Fox
Elizabethton Betsy Cubs (11)..	62	64	.492	19	38,947	Lou Bekeza
Kingsport Cherokees (8).....	54	65	.454	23½	45,792	Dick Bass
Johnson City Cardinals (16)....	54	70	.435	26	47,054	Bob Kline
Welch Miners (6)...............	49	74	.398	30½	38,345	Walter Youse/Joe Bird

Playoffs: Pulaski 3 games, Bristol 2; New River 3 games, Bluefield 1.
Finals: New River 4 games, Pulaski 2.

All-Star Team: 1B-Leo "Muscle" Shoals, Kingsport; **2B**-Augie Messuri, Elizabethton; **3B**-Art Oliver, Bristol; **SS**-Harry Musselman, Bristol; **OF**-Ray Rudisill, Pulaski; Homer Moore, Bluefield; Ralph Davis, New River; **C**-Charlie Fox, Bristol; Rollie Leveille, Pulaski; Frank Baldwin, Bluefield; **Util**-Lou Bekeza, Elizabethton; Jim Morgan, Kingsport; **P**-William Arrildt, Pulaski; Deon Lampros, Bristol; **Manager**-Jack Crosswhite, New River.

BA: Leo "Muscle" Shoals, Kingsport, .387
Runs: Ray Rudisill, Pulaski, 162
Hits: Charles Frey, Johnson City, 176
RBIs: Ralph Davis, New River, 139
HRs: Leo "Muscle" Shoals, Kingsport, 32
Wins: William Arrildt, Pulaski, 19
SOs: Deon Lampros, Bristol, 181
ERA: Charley Allen, Kingsport, 2.80

D Blue Ridge League
President: Stanley F. Radke

Standings	W	L	Pct.	GB	Attend.	Manager
Galax Leafs**	74	47	.612	—	27,330	Edwin Morgan
Mt. Airy Graniteers*	72	52	.581	3½	23,483	Alfred Dean
Radford Rockets	49	66	.426	22	29,422	Eddie Guinther/Sam Gibson
Lenoir Red Sox	43	73	.371	28½	25,592	Noel Casbier

Playoffs: Galax 3 games, Radford 1; Lenoir 3 games, Mt. Airy 1.
Finals: Galax 4 games, Lenoir 3.

All-Star Team: 1B-Edwin Morgan, Galax; **2B**-Wayne Stewart, Lenoir; **3B**-Eddie Cousins, Mt. Airy; **SS**-Ray Mize, Radford; **OF**-Hal Livingston, Radford; Nick Ciani, Lenoir; Zaven Arakelian, Galax; **C**-Bruce Ohlinger, Lenoir; **Util**-Noel Casbier, Lenoir; **P**-Eurice "Pete" Treece, Mt. Airy; Sidney Weinbach, Galax; **Manager**-Edwin Morgan, Galax.

BA: Edwin Morgan, Galax, .375
Runs: Edwin Morgan, Galax, 117
Hits: Sam Moir, Mt. Airy, 151
RBIs: Edwin Morgan, Galax, 103
HRs: Noel Casbier, Lenoir, 12
Wins: Eurice "Pete" Treece, Mt. Airy, 20
SOs: Eurice "Pete" Treece, Mt. Airy, 234
ERA: Sidney Weinbach, Galax, 2.99

D Coastal Plain League
President: Ray Goodmon

Standings	W	L	Pct.	GB	Attend.	Manager
Wilson Tobs	79	61	.564	—	138,548	Max Wilson
Kinston Eagles	74	65	.532	4½	68,986	Steve Collins
Tarboro Tars	74	66	.529	5	75,281	Bull Hamons
New Bern Bears	73	66	.525	5½	104,426	Jake Daniel/Harry Soufas/
						Tom Murray/Worlise Knowles
Goldsboro Goldbugs	72	67	.518	6½	88,707	Bill Herring
Rocky Mount Leafs	68	71	.489	10½	100,794	Charlie Mundy
Roanoke Rapids Blue Jays .	60	80	.429	19	115,837	Stuart Martin
Greenville Greenies	58	82	.414	21	66,316	Johnny Pare/Larry Baldwin/
						Odie Timm

Playoffs: Wilson 4 games, New Bern 1; Kinston 4 games, Tarboro 2.

Finals: Kinston 4 games, Wilson 2.

All-Star Team: 1B-Harry Soufas, New Bern; **2B**-Steve Collins, Kinston; **3B**-Stuart Martin, Roanoke Rapids; **SS**-Frank Tepedino, Kinston; **OF**-Herbert May, Rocky Mount; LeRoy Kennedy, Tarboro; Bob Cohen, Kinston; **C**-Charles Settle, New Bern; **Util**-David Fowler, Rocky Mount; **P**-Sam McLawhorne, Kinston; Eddie Neville, Tarboro; **Manager**-Bill Herring, Goldsboro.

BA: LeRoy Kennedy, Tarboro, .381
Runs: Sal Zunno, New Bern, 133
Hits: Herbert May, Rocky Mount, 190
RBIs: Harry Soufas, New Bern, 122
HRs: Harry Soufas, New Bern, 25
Wins: Eddie Neville, Tarboro, 28
SOs: Sam McLawhorne, Kinston, 238
ERA: Bill Herring, Goldsboro, 1.79

D Eastern Shore League
President: J. Thomas Kibler

Standings	W	L	Pct.	GB	Attend.	Manager
Cambridge Dodgers (10)	91	34	.728	—	62,118	Roy Nichols
Seaford Eagles (13)	74	49	.602	16	54,637	Bob Westfall
Dover Phillies (14)............	68	56	.548	22½	33,676	Dick Carter
Federalsburg A's (6)	62	63	.496	29	29,781	Pep Rambert
Milford Red Sox (1)	62	64	.492	29½	29,581	Walter Millies
Rehoboth Beach Pirates (15)...	49	75	.395	41	30,521	Gordon McKinnon/Doug Peden
Easton Yankees (5)............	48	78	.381	43½	42,618	Joe Antolick
Salisbury Cardinals (16).....	45	80	.360	46	51,739	Harold Contini

Playoffs: Cambridge 4 games, Dover 3; Seaford 4 games, Federalsburg 0.
Finals: Seaford 4 games, Cambridge 3.

All-Star Team: 1B-Pep Rambert, Federalsburg; **2B**-Fred Shipman, Seaford; **3B**-Roy Nichols, Cambridge; **SS**-Bob Westfall, Seaford; **OF**-Robert "Ducky" Detweiler, Federalsburg; Al Deluca, Seaford; Don Thompson, Milford; **C**-Charley Thompson, Cambridge; **P**-Harry "Duke" Makosky, Seaford; Chris Van Cuyk, Cambridge; **Manager**-Walter Millies, Milford.

BA: Pep Rambert, Federalsburg, .376
Runs: Bob Stramm, Cambridge, 129
Hits: Tim Thompson, Cambridge, 162
Bob Stramm, Cambridge, 162
RBIs: Robert "Ducky" Detweiler, Federalsburg, 133
HRs: Robert "Ducky" Detweiler, Federalsburg, 29
Wins: Chris Van Cuyk, Cambridge, 25
SOs: Chris Van Cuyk, Cambridge, 279
ERA: Chris Van Cuyk, Cambridge, 1.93
Pct: Chris Van Cuyk, Cambridge, .926, 25-2

D Evangeline League
President: J. Walter Morris

Standings	W	L	Pct.	GB	Attend.	Manager
Alexandria Aces	79	53	.598	—	149,899	Art Phelan/Harry Strohm
Thibodaux Giants	76	52	.594	1	103,471	Sidney Gautreaux
New Iberia Cardinals	76	58	.567	4	90,620	Harry Strohm/Vern Thoele
Hammond Berries	73	60	.549	6½	59,126	Babe Benning/Paul Bruno
Houma Indians..................	63	76	.453	19½	100,934	Copeland Gloss/
						George Washburn
Natchez Giants..................	58	76	.433	22	43,346	Barney DeForge
Baton Rouge Red Sticks (7)	54	79	.406	25½	90,832	Graham Moore
Abbeville Athletics	53	78	.405	25½	52,036	Merle Coleman

Playoffs: Hammond 4 games, Alexandria 1; Thibodaux 4 games, New Iberia 2.
Finals: Hammond 4 games, Thibodaux 0.

All-Star Team: 1B-Paul Bruno, Hammond; **2B**-Harry Strohm, New Iberia/Alexandria; **3B**-Allen Cross, Alexandria; **SS**-Jack Hodge, Baton Rouge; **OF**-Alvin Auchon, Abbeville; Stanley Ray, Thibodaux; Robert Masser, Baton Rouge; **C**-Walter Sierotko, Natchez; Sidney Gautreaux, Thibodaux; **Util**-Jack Kelly, Natchez; Bob Gales, Houma; **P**-Joseph Bouchoux, Thibodaux; Warren Kanagy, Thibodaux; Fred Baczewski, Alexandria; **Manager**-Art Phelan, Alexandria.

BA: Alvin Auchon, Abbeville, .351
Runs: Bob Gales, Houma, 138
Hits: George Sopko, New Iberia, 180
RBIs: Dan Seiler, Houma, 115
HRs: Dan Seiler, Houma, 22
Wins: Paul Bruno, Hammond, 25
SOs: Paul Bruno, Hammond, 260
ERA: Paul Bruno, Hammond, 1.96

D Florida State League
President: Al Combs

Standings	W	L	Pct.	GB	Attend.	Manager
St. Augustine Saints...........	85	51	.625	—	76,735	Don Anderson
Gainesville G-Men	80	57	.584	5½	89,763	Myril Hoag
DeLand Red Hats...............	80	58	.580	6	60,033	Bill Steinecke
Orlando Senators (8)..........	71	67	.514	15	49,581	Lou Bevil
Sanford Seminoles	69	66	.511	15½	55,610	B.D. Lake/Don Murray/
						John Krider
Palatka Azaleas.................	64	75	.460	22½	45,997	John Toncoff
Leesburg Pirates (15).........	54	81	.400	30½	42,610	Bill Good
Daytona Beach Islanders	42	90	.318	41	51,661	Grover Hartley/Max Samuels

Playoffs: St. Augustine 4 games, Orlando 1; Gainesville 4 games, DeLand 3.
Finals: Gainesville 4 games, St. Augustine 3.

All-Star Team: 1B-Mario Perez, DeLand; **2B**-Lyle Judy, St. Augustine; **3B**-Jack Wilkes, St. Augustine; **SS**-Bill Good, Leesburg; **OF**-Myril Hoag, Gainesville; Desmond Solter, Leesburg; Douglass Johnson, Leesburg; **C**-John Toncoff, Palatka; **Util**-John Theobold, Palatka/St. Augustine; **P**-George Fultz, Gainesville; Tommy Hyde, Orlando; **Manager**-Bill Steinecke, DeLand.

BA: Myril Hoag, Gainesville, .350
Runs: Lyle Judy, St. Augustine, 98
Hits: Ben Thorpe, Gainesville, 153
RBIs: David Bride, Sanford, 99

HRs: Ben Thorpe, Gainesville, 10
Wins: George Fultz, Gainesville, 23
SOs: Juan Perez, DeLand, 244
ERA: Myril Hoag, Gainesville, 1.82

D Georgia-Alabama League
President: Arthur R. Decatur

Standings	W	L	Pct.	GB	Attend.	Manager
Carrollton Hornets	75	49	.605	—	52,245	Charles Roberts
Opelika Owls	76	50	.603	—	65,173	Luther Gunnells
Valley Rebels	75	51	.595	1	79,829	Arthur Luce
Newnan Brownies	72	53	.576	3½	80,600	Joe Abreu/Ed Westbrook
Tallassee Indians	62	63	.496	13½	44,693	John Hill
Griffin Pimientos	53	68	.438	20½	66,142	Adel White
La Grange Troupers	46	78	.371	29	55,746	Carl East/Howard Ermisch
Alexander City Millers	39	86	.312	36½	34,462	Doug Taitt

Playoffs: Valley 3 games, Carrollton 1; Opelika 3 games, Newnan 1.
Finals: Valley 4 games, Opelika 2.

All-Star Team: 1B-Donald Stoyle, Newnan; **2B**-Joe Chambers, Valley; **3B**-Harold Blackstock, Griffin; **SS**-Charles Roberts, Carrollton; **OF**-Earl Edwards, Valley; Ted Browning, Newnan; Ken Guettler, Griffin; **C**-Charles Danna, Valley; Jim Hill, Carrollton; **Util**-Herbert Marshall, Carrollton; Claude Shoemake, Newnan; **P**-William Webb, Carrollton; Jesse Danna, Valley.

BA: Charles Roberts, Carrollton, .385
Runs: Ted Browning, Newnan, 122
Hits: Malvern Morgan, Valley, 184
RBIs: Ken Guettler, Griffin, 103

HRs: Ken Guettler, Griffin, 25
Wins: Paul Brock, Newnan, 23
SOs: Paul Brock, Newnan, 220
ERA: Jesse Danna, Valley, 2.15

D Georgia-Florida League
President: W.T. Anderson

Standings	W	L	Pct.	GB	Attend.	Manager
Moultrie Packers	85	53	.616	—	89,757	Buster Kinard/Jim Poole
Waycross Bears	79	59	.572	6	72,255	LeGrant Scott
Tallahassee Pirates (15)	80	60	.571	6	81,235	Phil Seghi
Albany Cardinals (16)	78	62	.557	8	86,451	Mickey Katkaveck
Thomasville Tigers (4)	68	69	.498	16½	54,502	Vincent "Moon" Mullen
Americus Phillies (14)	65	74	.468	20½	54,062	Jack Sanford/Lew Krausse
Valdosta Dodgers (10)	54	84	.391	31	61,727	Hugh Holliday
Cordele Indians (3)	45	93	.326	40	41,892	Mercer Harris

Playoffs: Moultrie 3 games, Albany 0; Tallahassee 3 games, Waycross 2.
Finals: Moultrie 4 games, Tallahassee 2.

All-Star Team: 1B-Lamar Weeks, Thomasville; **2B**-David Williams, Waycross; **3B**-Elmer Schoendienst, Albany; **SS**-Emil Rey, Valdosta; **OF**-John Ewaniak, Albany; Elmer Anjeski, Tallahassee; Crasford Howard, Americus; **C**-Pat Tomkinson, Valdosta; **Util**-Billy Dwyer, Waycross; Bill LaFrance, Moultrie; **P**-Bob Galey, Waycross; Jack Frisinger, Albany; **Manager**-LeGrant Scott, Waycross.

BA: Ray Walters, Americus, .343
Runs: David Williams, Waycross, 147
Hits: John Grice, Thomasville, 182
RBIs: Ken Rhyne, Moultrie, 141

HRs: Ken Rhyne, Moultrie, 24
Wins: Ray Burnette, Americus, 21
SOs: Jack Frisinger, Albany, 274
ERA: Jack Frisinger, Albany, 2.18

D Illinois State League
President: Howard V. Millard

Standings	W	L	Pct.	GB	Attend.	Manager
Belleville Stags***(7)	75	37	.670	—	18,539	Walter DeFreitas
Centralia Cubs (11)	60	52	.536	15	35,000	Chuck Hawley
Marion Indians	55	56	.495	19½	36,705	Melvin Ivy
West Frankfort Cardinals (16)	52	60	.464	23	43,004	Everett Johnston
Mt. Vernon Braves	49	63	.438	26	38,330	Otto Huber
Mattoon Indians	41	64	.390	30½	25,671	Frank Parenti

Playoffs: None.

All-Star Team: 1B-Clarence Schambon, Belleville; **2B**-Bob Cherek, Belleville; **3B**-Billy Klaus, Centralia; **SS**-William Queen, Mt. Vernon; **OF**-Eldon "Rip" Repulski, West Frankfort; William Hornsby, Mattoon; Omer Tolson, Belleville; **C**-James Cupp, West Frankfort; Socrates Anthony, Belleville; **Util**-Chet McDowell, Marion; John Osborne, Mattoon; **P**-Robert Freels, Belleville; Don Liddle, Mt. Vernon; **Manager**-Walter DeFreitas, Belleville.

BA: Billy Klaus, Centralia, .341
Runs: Weldon Idol, Belleville, 90
  Bob Cherek, Belleville, 90
Hits: Billy Klaus, Centralia, 147
RBIs: Billy Klaus, Centralia, 84

HRs: Eldon "Rip" Repulski, West Frankfort, 10
Wins: Robert Freels, Belleville, 19
SOs: Don Liddle, Mt. Vernon, 190
ERA: Ken Wild, West Frankfort, 1.73

D Kansas-Oklahoma-Missouri League
President: E.L. Dale

Standings	W	L	Pct.	GB	Attend.	Manager
Miami Owls	76	49	.608	—	53,119	Bill Davis
Iola Cubs (11)	69	54	.561	6	39,862	Al Reitz
Pittsburg Browns (7)	69	54	.561	6	59,435	James Crandall
Bartlesville Oilers (15)	68	56	.548	7½	64,074	Edward Marleau

Carthage Cardinals (16)	66	59	.528	10	42,838	Woody Fair
Ponca City Dodgers (10)	61	62	.496	14	55,554	Boyd Bartley
Chanute Athletics	44	80	.355	31½	34,758	Dave Dennis/Charles Baty
Independence Yankees (5)	41	80	.339	33	22,460	Frank Howard

Playoffs: Miami 3 games, Bartlesville 1; Iola 3 games, Pittsburg 1.
Finals: Miami 4 games, Iola 1.

All-Star Team: 1B-Walter Snider, Miami; **2B**-Ralph Rutherford, Carthage; **3B**-Ken Aubrey, Iola; **SS**-Jim Baxes, Ponca City; **OF**-R.T. "Dixie" Upright, Bartlesville; Albert Solenberger, Bartlesville; Loren Packard, Miami; **C**-Jim Jansen, Miami; **P**-Carroll Dial, Bartlesville; Jim Post, Pittsburg; **Manager**-James Crandall, Pittsburg.

BA: Loren Packard, Miami, .364
Runs: Albert Solenberger, Bartlesville, 131
Hits: Loren Packard, Miami, 185
RBIs: Loren Packard, Miami, 124

HRs: Jim Baxes, Ponca City, 20
Wins: Carroll Dial, Bartlesville, 22
SOs: James Morris, Miami, 240
ERA: Carroll Dial, Bartlesville, 3.32

D Kitty League
President: Shelby Peace

Standings	W	L	Pct.	GB	Attend.	Manager
Owensboro Oilers (9)	77	48	.616	—	83,743	Earle Browne
Mayfield Clothiers (7)	72	52	.581	4½	47,795	Shan Deniston
Hopkinsville Hoppers	69	56	.552	8	37,885	Frank Scalzi
Madisonville Miners (2)	69	56	.552	8	47,227	Frank Zubik
Fulton Chicks	68	57	.544	9	36,123	John Gill
Cairo Egyptians	53	73	.421	24½	21,282	Ray Clonts
Union City Greyhounds (3)	51	74	.408	26	58,280	Steve Bysco
Clarksville Colts	40	83	.325	36	28,750	Harley Boss

Playoffs: Hopkinsville 3 games, Owensboro 2; Madisonville 3 games, Mayfield 1.
Finals: Hopkinsville 4 games, Madisonville 1.

All-Star Team: 1B-Lawson Williams, Mayfield; **2B**-Jerry Majercik, Union City; **3B**-Bob Proulx, Madisonville; **SS**-Frank Scalzi, Hopkinsville; **OF**-Joe Richardson, Hopkinsville; Richard Szpond, Madisonville; Sonny Grasso, Owensboro; **C**-Jose Perez, Owensboro; **Util**-Kenneth Hahn, Cairo; Carroll Peterson, Fulton; **P**-William Bordt, Mayfield; Joseph Dworak, Mayfield; **Manager**-Earle Browne, Owensboro.

BA: Earle Browne, Owensboro, .424
Runs: Bob Proulx, Madisonville, 126
Hits: Jerry Majercik, Union City, 176
RBIs: Richard Szpond, Madisonville, 128

HRs: Joe Richardson, Hopkinsville, 18
Wins: William Bordt, Mayfield, 21
SOs: John Hobbs, Cairo, 236
ERA: Joseph Dworak, Mayfield, 2.69

D Longhorn League
President: Howard Green

Standings	W	L	Pct.	GB	Attend.	Manager
Big Spring Broncs	81	48	.628	—	43,153	Pat Stasey
Midland Indians	75	55	.577	6½	34,013	Harold Webb
Ballinger Cats	68	62	.523	13½	42,662	Stuart Williams
Sweetwater Sports	63	67	.485	18½	31,631	Rowland Murphy
Odessa Oilers	60	70	.462	21½	38,415	Howard McFarland
Vernon Dusters	42	87	.326	39	30,758	Carl Kott

Playoffs: Big Spring 4 games, Sweetwater 3; Ballinger 4 games, Midland 3.
Finals: Ballinger 4 games, Big Spring 2.

All-Star Team: 1B-Joe Dotlich, Sweetwater; **2B**-Jake McClain, Big Spring; **3B**-Orlando Moreno, Big Spring; **SS**-Roy McMillan, Ballinger; **OF**-Bob Cowsar, Sweetwater; Harvel Jakes, Odessa; Pat Stasey, Big Spring; **C**-Armando Traspuesto, Big Spring; **Util**-Rex Pearce, Odessa; Ronald Murphy, Sweetwater; **P**-Jose Cendan, Big Spring; Ernie Nelson, Midland; **Manager**-Stuart Williams, Ballinger.

BA: James Prince, Midland, .429
Runs: Orlando Moreno, Big Spring, 186
Hits: Pat Stasey, Big Spring, 209
  Bob Cowsar, Sweetwater, 209
RBIs: Bob Cowsar, Sweetwater, 176

HRs: Bob Cowsar, Sweetwater, 37
Wins: Jose Cendan, Big Spring, 24
SOs: Lee Roy Jones, Ballinger, 249
ERA: Ernie Nelson, Midland, 3.87

D North Atlantic League
President: Ernest C. Landgraf

Standings	W	L	Pct.	GB	Attend.	Manager
Kingston Dodgers (10)	81	48	.628	—	33,000	George Scherger/George Pratt
Carbondale Pioneers (14)	77	52	.597	4	85,500	Pat Colgan
Peekskill Highlanders (13)	69	64	.519	14	23,300	Al Gardella
Mahanoy City Bluebirds	67	65	.508	15½	51,000	Clarence "Buck" Etchison
Nazareth Tigers (4)	64	66	.492	17½	31,000	John Mueller
Stroudsburg Poconos (5)	57	69	.452	22½	40,200	Jack Farmer
Bloomingdale Troopers (9)	57	74	.435	25	29,100	Butch Scinski
Nyack Rockies (6)	49	83	.371	33½	26,000	Emil Schwab

Playoffs: Peekskill 4 games, Kingston 1; Carbondale 4 games, Mahanoy City 3.
Finals: Carbondale 4 games, Peekskill 1.

BA: John Medica, Mahanoy City, .362
Runs: Anthony Ciori, Mahanoy City, 132
Hits: Howard Gutshall, Nazareth, 182
RBIs: Clarence "Buck" Etchison, Mahanoy City, 163

HRs: Carl Sawatski, Bloomingdale, 34
3B: Walter Kowalski, Kingston, 24
Wins: Anton Gilbert, Kingston, 18
SOs: Joseph Sebir, Stroudsburg, 237
ERA: Henry Neighbors, Kingston, 2.23

D North Carolina State League
President: R.A. Collier

Standings	W	L	Pct.	GB	Attend.	Manager
Mooresville Moors	68	43	.613	—	39,091	Norman Small
Salisbury Pirates (15)........	63	47	.573	4½	60,126	Edgar Leip
Hickory Rebels (13)...........	61	49	.555	6½	54,533	Sam Bell
Lexington Indians (6)	57	53	.518	10½	49,044	Homer Lee Cox
Thomasville Dodgers (10)..	54	56	.491	13½	57,341	George Pratt/George Scherger
Landis Millers....................	51	60	.459	17	22,596	Herman "Ginger" Watts
Concord Weavers	48	63	.432	20	28,045	Nig Lipscomb
Statesville Owls	40	71	.360	28	46,231	Tuck McWilliams

Playoffs: Mooresville 4 games, Hickory 3; Lexington 4 games, Salisbury 3.
Finals: Mooresville 4 games, Lexington 3.

All-Star Team: 1B-Charles Knight, Hickory; **2B**-Edgar Leip, Salisbury; **3B**-Hal Harrigan, Salisbury; **SS**-Bob Brown, Hickory; **OF**-James Miller, Landis; Norman Small, Mooresville; James Thomas, Hickory; **C**-Richard Teed, Thomasville; **Util**-George Wright, Landis; Fred Leonard, Thomasville; **P**-Hoyt Wilhelm, Mooresville; Ray Kalkowski, Salisbury; **Manager**-Sam Bell, Hickory.

BA: James Miller, Landis, .402
Runs: Charles Knight, Hickory, 107
Hits: James Miller, Landis, 170
James Thomas, Hickory, 170
RBIs: James Thomas, Hickory, 131

HRs: James Thomas, Hickory, 31
Norman Small, Mooresville, 31
Wins: Hoyt Wilhelm, Mooresville, 20
SOs: Edmund Beaumier, Landis, 228
ERA: Furman Taylor, Concord, 2.43

D Ohio State League
President: Frank M. Colley

Standings	W	L	Pct.	GB	Attend.	Manager
Zanesville Dodgers (10)	89	50	.640	—	102,250	Clay Bryant
Marion Cardinals (11)........	79	60	.568	10	92,088	Nelson Burbrink
Muncie Reds (12)	75	62	.547	13	51,834	Mike Blazo
Springfield Giants (13).......	73	65	.529	15½	72,462	Don Ramsey
Richmond Roses (9)	62	72	.463	24½	53,050	Rex Carr
Dayton Indians (3).............	62	73	.459	25	65,420	Ival Goodman
Newark Moundsmen (7).....	64	76	.457	25½	58,935	Eddie Dancisak
Lima Terriers (2)	47	93	.336	42½	56,466	Merle Settlemire

Playoffs: Zanesville 4 games, Springfield 2; Marion 4 games, Muncie 1.
Finals: Zanesville 4 games, Marion 2.

All-Star Team: 1B-Johnny Batt, Newark; **2B**-Marty Sebastian, Dayton; **3B**-Robert Verrier, Richmond; **SS**-Maurice Mikesell, Zanesville; **OF**-William Scally, Springfield; Dwight Maxhimer, Marion; Bob Bartholomew, Zanesville; **C**-Nelson Burbrink, Marion; **P**-Tony West, Springfield; Sanford Lambert, Zanesville; **Manager**-Clay Bryant, Zanesville.

BA: Nelson Burbrink, Marion, .378
Runs: Robert Verrier, Richmond, 127
Hits: Jack Maisch, Lima, 194
RBIs: Edward Fowler, Newark, 119
William Scally, Springfield, 119

HRs: Bob Montag, Muncie, 14
Wins: Sanford Lambert, Zanesville, 23
SOs: Sanford Lambert, Zanesville, 232
ERA: Edward Post, Muncie, 2.02

D PONY League
President: Robert C. Stedler

Standings	W	L	Pct.	GB	Attend.	Manager
Jamestown Falcons (4)	87	39	.690	—	95,623	Marvin Olson
Bradford Blue Wings (14)..	69	55	.557	17	70,129	George Savino
Olean Oilers (10)	66	58	.532	20	62,634	Greg Mulleavy
Wellsville Nitros (1)	64	59	.520	21½	54,442	Tom Carey
Lockport Reds (12)............	61	62	.496	24½	48,268	Cecil Scheffel
Batavia Clippers (3)...........	60	63	.488	25½	55,865	Jack Tighe
Hamilton Cardinals (16).....	49	76	.392	37½	70,608	John Newman
Hornell Pirates (15)	40	84	.323	46	35,886	Art Doll

Playoffs: Jamestown 4 games, Wellsville 1; Olean 4 games, Bradford 1.
Finals: Jamestown 4 games, Olean 2.

All-Star Team: 1B-Doc Alexson, Jamestown; **2B**-Hyman Prosk, Olean; **3B**-Orval Cott, Lockport; **SS**-Fred Folkes, Wellsville; **OF**-Charley Maxwell, Wellsville; Jim Pokel, Bradford; Ted Bartz, Jamestown; **C**-Cecil Scheffel, Lockport; **P**-Theodore Wyberanec, Jamestown; Dick Littlefield, Wellsville.

BA: Doc Alexson, Jamestown, .338
Runs: Ed Trojanowski, Bradford, 125
Hits: Doc Alexson, Jamestown, 163
RBIs: Jim Pokel, Bradford, 125
HRs: Jim Pokel, Bradford, 28

Wins: Thaddeus Kapuscinski, Jamestown, 16
SOs: Vance Stine, Hamilton, 194
ERA: Dick Littlefield, Wellsville, 1.97
Pct: Dick Littlefield, Wellsville, .765, 13-4

D Sooner State League
President: Jack Mealey

Standings	W	L	Pct.	GB	Attend.	Manager
Lawton Giants....................	98	42	.700	—	24,248	Lou Brower
Ada Herefords (7)..............	86	51	.628	10½	41,872	Ucal Clanton
McAlester Rockets	73	67	.521	25	43,657	William Nebroak
Ardmore Indians (3)	72	67	.518	25½	27,943	Dutch Prather
Seminole Oilers	48	90	.348	49	30,003	Hugh Willingham
Duncan Cementers	39	99	.283	58	8,220	Otto Utt

Playoffs: Ardmore 3 games, Lawton 2; McAlester 3 games, Ada 2.
Finals: McAlester 4 games, Ardmore 1.

All-Star Team: 1B-Melvin Blaylock, Lawton; **2B**-Morris Card, Ardmore; **3B**-A.B. Everett, McAlester; **SS**-Jack Baumer, Seminole; **OF**-Russell Hawley, McAlester; Leo Pasciak, Lawton; Howard Weeks, Lawton; **C**-Hosea Pfeiffer, McAlester; **Util**-Ted Drakos, Lawton; Paul Richardville, Ada; **P**-Forest Smith, Ada; Elmer Jeter, Seminole; **Manager**-Lou Brower, Lawton.

BA: Russell Hawley, McAlester, .382
Runs: Robert Andrlik, Ardmore, 158
Hits: A.B. Everett, McAlester, 188
RBIs: Paul Richardville, Ada, 111

HRs: Howard Weeks, Lawton, 11
Paul Richardville, Ada, 11
Wins: Forest Smith, Ada, 23
SOs: William Donaghey, Ada, 244
ERA: Forest Smith, Ada, 2.00

D Tobacco State League
President: Arthur T. Moore

Standings	W	L	Pct.	GB	Attend.	Manager
Sanford Spinners................	86	39	.688	—	37,517	Zeb Harrington
Lumberton Cubs (11)..........	71	49	.592	12½	50,758	Charles "Red" Lucas
Wilmington Pirates	68	57	.544	18	63,219	Nate Andrews
Dunn-Erwin Twins	62	62	.500	23½	49,262	Jack Bell/Bill Auerette
Warsaw Red Sox	59	64	.480	26	36,865	James Milner
Clinton Blues	56	67	.455	29	36,778	Robert Hall/Van Lingle Mungo/Survern Wright
Red Springs Red Robins (6) ..	47	78	.480	39	21,000	Red Norris
Smithfield-Selma Leafs	46	79	.368	40	28,847	Mickey Balla/Joe Eonta

Playoffs: Sanford 4 games, Wilmington 3; Lumberton 4 games, Dunn-Erwin 1.
Finals: Sanford 4 games, Lumberton 3.

All-Star Team: 1B-Elmer Marx, Lumberton; **2B**-James Guinn, Sanford; **3B**-Edmond Kukulka, Clinton; **SS**-Pete Howard, Smithfield-Selma; **OF**-Carl McQuillen, Dunn-Erwin; James Wilson, Sanford; Orville Nesselrode, Sanford; **C**-Bruce Hedrick, Sanford; **Util**-Mickey Balla, Dunn-Erwin; Andrew Scrobola, Wilmington; **P**-Robert Spicer, Lumberton; Lewis Cheshire, Wilmington; **Manager**-Charles "Red" Lucas, Lumberton.

BA: James Wilson, Sanford, .385
Runs: James Wilson, Sanford, 133
Hits: James Wilson, Sanford, 205
RBIs: Orville Nesselrode, Sanford, 166

HRs: Orville Nesselrode, Sanford, 32
Wins: Lewis Cheshire, Wilmington, 19
SOs: Carl Johnson, Warsaw, 225
ERA: John McFadden, Sanford, 2.44

D Wisconsin State League
President: Herman D. White

Standings	W	L	Pct.	GB	Attend.	Manager
Sheboygan Indians..............	82	40	.672	—	47,462	Joe Hauser
Janesville Cubs (11)...........	66	54	.550	15	46,353	Frank Piet
Oshkosh Giants (13)	60	59	.504	20½	75,028	Ray Lucas
Wausau Lumberjacks (7)....	62	62	.500	21	86,722	Joe Skurski
Appleton Papermakers (14)	61	61	.500	21	91,401	Andy Lotchick/Whitey Gluchoski
Green Bay Bluejays (3)	58	62	.483	23	65,946	Harry Griswold
Fond du Lac Panthers (5)....	58	67	.464	25½	86,417	James Adlam
Wisconsin Rapids White Sox (2).................	41	83	.331	42	38,616	Tony Parisse

Playoffs: None

All-Star Team: 1B-Don Reidle, Appleton; **2B**-John Imbra, Janesville; **3B**-Stan Jok, Oshkosh; **SS**-Fred Gutherz, Oshkosh; **OF**-Peter Brozovich, Oshkosh; Joe Malsam, Fond du Lac; Bob Sullivan, Green Bay; Anthony Costa, Wausau; **C**-John Schimenz, Appleton; Arnie Mazurek, Green Bay; **Util**-Tom Bartos, Sheboygan; Gene Daniel, Sheboygan; **P**-William Eggert, Sheboygan; Ben Sadusky, Janesville; Pete Leonetti, Fond du Lac; Bruce Johann, Wisconsin Rapids; **Manager**-Harry Griswold, Green Bay.

BA: James Adlam, Fond du Lac, .429
Runs: Melvin Welch, Green Bay, 133
Hits: Anthony Costa, Wausau, 161
RBIs: Peter Brozovich, Oshkosh, 112

HRs: James Adlam, Fond du Lac, 20
Wins: William Eggert, Sheboygan, 23
SOs: Sam Brewer, Oshkosh, 256
ERA: William Eggert, Sheboygan, 2.82

Ind Mexican League
President: Jorge Pasquel

Standings	W	L	Pct.	GB	Manager
Monterrey Industriales........	70	47	.598	—	Lazaro Salazar
Mexico City Diablos Rojos	65	54	.546	6	Ray Dandridge
Puebla Angeles	63	56	.529	8	Dolf Luque
Tampico Alijadores	53	65	.449	17½	Armando Marsans/Santos Amaro
San Luis Potosi Tuneros	52	66	.441	18½	Martin Dihigo/Julio Rojo/Tomas de la Cruz
Veracruz Azules	52	67	.437	19	Jose Luis Gomez/James Steiner

BA: Roberto Avila, Puebla, .346
Hits: Ray Dandridge, Mexico City, 169
RBIs: Alejandro Crespo, Puebla, 96
HRs: Roberto Ortiz, Mexico City, 22

Wins: Theolic Smith, Mexico City, 22
SOs: Booker McDaniels, Veracruz, 127
ERA: Santiago Ulrich, Tampico, 2.64

1947 Interleague Post Season Play

World Series
New York (American) 4 games, Brooklyn (National) 3

Junior World Series
Milwaukee (American Association) 4 games, Syracuse (International) 3
Total Attendance: 64,306

Dixie Series
Houston (Texas) 4 games, Mobile (Southern Association) 2
Total Attendance: 44,794

Southern Championship
Moultrie (Georgia-Florida) 4 games, Gainesville (Florida State) 3

Class C Championship of Texas
Lubbock (West Texas-New Mexico) 4 games, Kilgore (Lone Star) 1

Sunshine Series
Stockton (California) 4 games, Riverside (Sunset) 0

1947 Major League Farm Systems

American League

1 Boston (10): Louisville, Toronto, New Orleans, Scranton, Lynn, Roanoke, San Jose, Oneonta, Milford, Wellsville.
2 Chicago (8): Hollywood, Fall River, Waterloo, Oil City, Superior, Madisonville, Lima, Wisconsin Rapids.
3 Cleveland (17): Baltimore, Oklahoma City, Wilkes-Barre, Harrisburg, Meridian, Spartanburg, Tucson, Bakersfield, Pittsfield, Burlington (IA), Jacksonville (TX), Cordele, Union City, Dayton, Batavia, Ardmore, Green Bay.
4 Detroit (11): Buffalo, Dallas, Williamsport, Hagerstown, Montgomery, Rome, Lubbock, Troy, Thomasville (GA), Nazareth, Jamestown.
5 New York (20): Kansas City, Newark (NJ), Beaumont, Binghamton, Augusta, Denver, Sunbury, Norfolk, Quincy, Victoria, Bisbee, Ventura, Amsterdam, Butler, Twin Falls, Joplin, Easton, Independence, Stroudsburg, Fond du Lac.
6 Philadelphia (12): Birmingham, Savannah, Lincoln, Lancaster, Martinsville, Moline, Niagara Falls, Welch, Federalsburg, Nyack, Lexington, Red Springs.
7 St. Louis (16): Toledo, San Antonio, Elmira, Springfield (IL), Globe-Miami, Gloversville-Johnstown, Hannibal, Aberdeen, Muskogee, Baton Rouge, Belleville, Pittsburg, Mayfield, Newark (OH), Ada, Wausau.
8 Washington (6): Chattanooga, Charlotte, Havana, Brewton, Kingsport, Orlando.

National League

9 Boston (15): Milwaukee, Little Rock, Hartford, Pawtucket, Jackson, Evansville, Ft. Lauderdale, Eau Claire, Las Vegas, Amarillo, Leavenworth, Bluefield, Owensboro, Bloomingdale, Richmond (IN).
10 Brooklyn (24): St. Paul, Montreal, Mobile, Ft. Worth, Greenville (SC), Pueblo, Nashua, Newport News, Danville, Asheville, Spokane, Santa Barbara, Trois Rivieres, Greenwood, Johnstown, Cambridge, Valdosta, Ponca City, Kingston (NY), Olean, Thomasville (NC), Zanesville.
11 Chicago (19): Los Angeles, Nashville, Tulsa, Macon, Des Moines, Portsmouth, Davenport, Fayetteville, Tacoma, Visalia, Clinton (IA), Sioux Falls, Hutchinson, Elizabethton, Centralia, Iola, Marion, Lumberton, Janesville.
12 Cincinnati (8): Syracuse, Columbia, Providence, Rockford, Ogden, Tyler, Muncie, Lockport.
13 New York (17): Minneapolis, Jersey City, Jacksonville (FL), Sioux City, Trenton, Manchester, Richmond (VA), Danville, Erie, Reno, Ft. Smith, Bristol, Seaford, Peekskill, Hickory, Springfield (OH), Oshkosh.
14 Philadelphia (11): Utica, Wilmington (DE), Terre Haute, Schenectady, Vandergrift, Salina, Dover, Americus, Carbondale, Bradford, Appleton.
15 Pittsburgh (14): Indianapolis, Albany (NY), York, Selma, Keokuk, Uniontown, Fargo-Moorhead, Riverside, Rehoboth Beach, Leesburg, Tallahassee, Bartlesville, Salisbury (NC), Hornell.
16 St. Louis (19): Columbus (OH), Rochester, Houston, Columbus (GA), Omaha, Allentown, Lynchburg, Decatur, Fresno, Winston-Salem, Duluth, Pocatello, St. Joseph, Johnson City, Salisbury (MD), Albany (GA), West Frankfort, Carthage, Hamilton.

1947 No-Hitters

Date	Pitcher	Team	League	Opponent	Score
4-20	Tommy Bridges	Portland	Pacific Coast	San Francisco	2-0
4-24	Eulis Rossen	Lubbock	W. Texas-N. Mexico	Clovis	11-0 (7)
4-27	Melvin Nee	Miami	Fla. International	Miami Beach	4-0 (P)
4-30	Paul McGlothin	Clarksdale	Cotton States	Helena	10-1
4-30	James Morris	Miami	KOM	Carthage	12-0
4-30	Robert Brake	Milford	Eastern Shore	Dover	8-0
5-3	Edwin Wissman	Valley	Georgia-Alabama	Carrollton	12-0
5-4	Juan Perez	DeLand	Florida State	Daytona Beach	4-0 (P, 7)
5-8	John Hoffman	Visalia	California	Santa Barbara	4-2
5-12	Walt Graham	Schenectady	Canadian-American	Gloversville-Johnstown	4-0 (7)
5-18	Don Otten	Valdosta	Georgia-Florida	Albany	2-0
5-21	Jack McKinney	Beaumont	Texas	Shreveport	6-0
5-25	Robert Knaub	Elizabethton	Appalachian	Kingsport	5-3 (5)
5-28	Al Comotti	Providence	New England	Lynn	3-0 (7)
6-5	Frank Mediamolle	Houma	Evangeline	Alexandria	4-0
6-6	Bill Woolard	Newark	Ohio State	Muncie	8-0
6-8	Bob Kuhlman	Des Moines	Western	Sioux City	1-0
6-18	Ewell Blackwell	Cincinnati	National	Boston	6-0
6-19	Joseph Sebir	Stroudsburg	North Atlantic	Mahanoy City	10-0
6-21	Stan Stenoff	Kingston	Border	Auburn	8-0
6-22	Roger Binn	Auburn	Border	Kingston	9-1
6-23	Bill Hogue	Dallas	Texas	Beaumont	4-0
6-24	Charlie Mize	Ada	Sooner State	McAlester	1-0 (7)
6-26	Carl DeRose	Kansas City	American Assoc.	Minneapolis	5-0 (P)
7-6	Sam Eatock	Wausau	Wisconsin State	Green Bay	0-1 (10)
7-10	Don Black	Cleveland	American	Philadelphia	3-0
7-12	Connie Marrero	Havana	Fla. International	Tampa	7-0
7-15	Len Seamon	Ottawa	Border	Geneva	8-0
7-15	Joe Alamo	Greenville	Coastal Plain	Tarboro	3-1 (7)
7-22	Ray Minor	Elmira	Eastern	Williamsport	3-2 (7)
7-13	Walter Wilson	Mahanoy City	North Atlantic	Bloomingdale	14-0 (7)
7-22	Bob Galey	Waycross	Georgia-Florida	Valdosta	15-0
7-23	Charlie Cuellar	Tampa	Fla. International	Havana	5-0
7-28	John Rutherford	Olean	PONY	Lockport	2-0 (7)
8-3	Shelby Kinney	Atlanta	Southern Assoc.	New Orleans	5-0 (7)
8-3	Dwain Sloat	Ft. Worth	Texas	Tulsa	1-0
8-3	Pete Leonetti	Fond du Lac	Wisconsin State	Wisconsin Rapids	11-2
8-11	Harvey Haddix	Winston-Salem	Carolina	Danville	6-0 (7)
8-17	Bill Donovan	Amsterdam	Canadian-American	Trois Rivieres	5-0 (7)
8-18	Mel Heiner	St. Augustine	Florida State	Daytona Beach	2-0 (7)
8-18	Bill Regan	La Grange	Georgia-Alabama	Alexander City	5-0 (7)
8-20	Lyman Linde	Oklahoma City	Texas	Shreveport	10-0
8-21	Al Henencheck	Raleigh	Carolina	Greensboro	13-0
8-21	Bill Connelly	Savannah	South Atlantic	Jacksonville	1-0
8-24	Ray Moore	Greenwood	Cotton States	Clarksdale	7-0 (7)
8-24	Eddie Willshaw	Bartlesville	KOM	Iola	8-0
8-27	Ken Fremming	Jamestown	PONY	Wellsville	7-2
9-3	Bill McCahan	Philadelphia	American	Washington	3-0
9-10	Chris Haughey	St. Joseph	Western Assoc.	Topeka	11-0
9-17	Max Wilson	Wilson	Coastal Plain	Kinston	1-0 (PO)

Number in parentheses indicates innings if other than nine; "P" indicates perfect game; "PO" indicates playoff game.

THIS DATE IN MINOR LEAGUE HISTORY

January 11, 1947, Minor league pitcher Leon J. Balser was killed when he was crushed between two railroad cars while working as a switchman for the Nickel Plate Railroad in Cleveland, Ohio. Balser, 28, had a 16-9 record for Greenville of the South Atlantic League during the 1946 season.

January 18, 1947, Bill Dickey, former great catcher of the New York Yankees, signed as player-manager of Little Rock of the Southern League.

January 22, 1947, Portland, Pacific Coast League, purchased former big league outfielder Bob Johnson from Milwaukee, American Association. The Beavers, who had a tie-up with the New York Yankees, also had previously signed Tom Bridges, ex-Tiger hurler. Jim Turner, former Braves and Yankees pitcher, was the team's manager.

January 25, 1947, Five players were placed on Organized Ball's ineligible list following investigation of alleged gambling reports in the Evangeline League by Judge W.G. Bramham, retiring president of the National Association. The quintet included manager Paul Fugit, Alvin Kaiser, Leonard Pecou and Bill Thomas of the Houma team and Don Vettorel of Abbeville.

January 31, 1947, After 52 years as a player, manager and executive, Mike Kelley officially ended his connection with the game, retiring as president of the American Association's Minneapolis Millers. Kelley, 71, had been president of the Millers since 1924. He sold the club to the New York Giants.

February 18, 1947, The San Francisco Seals, under manager Lefty O'Doul, began spring training at Hana, Maui, Hawaii. Their camp was located in a remote tropical hideout between the beach and the jungle at the foot of Mt. Haleakala, the largest inactive volcano in the world. The town of Hana had a population of 500 and was 90 miles across the crater from Honolulu.

March 4, 1947, Lefty O'Doul, manager for San Francisco, Pacific Coast League, marked his 50th birthday by saving the life of a drowning sportswriter.

April 17, 1947, Sal Maglie, former New York Giants righthander with Puebla in the outlaw Mexican League, held first-place Monterrey to one hit, winning 3-0.

April 18, 1947, Tony Freitas, 39-year-old Sacramento southpaw, earned his 200th victory in the Pacific Coast League.

April 20, 1947, In the first game of Organized Ball ever played in Nevada, the Reno Silver Sox of the Sunset League walloped the Anaheim Valencias 11-3 in the season opener at Reno. The 2,000 fans on hand saw a triple play in the sixth inning.

May 1, 1947, Denver, Western League, returned to Organized Ball after a 15-year absence. The Bears won over Lincoln, 11-5, before 4,669 fans.

May 2, 1947, In the Sunset League, Las Vegas hit ten home runs in defeating Ontario 30-5, with first baseman Kenneth Myers clouting a pair of grand slams and pitcher Ned Klingensmith another in the 16-run third inning. In addition to his two grand slams, Myers hit two other homers for a total of four, plus a single, and drove in 12 runs.

May 3, 1947, Ray Brubaker, 51, manager of Terre Haute, Three-I League, died of a heart attack in the dugout at Waterloo, Iowa.

May 4, 1947, Russell Kerns, playing his first day as a shortstop for Macon, South Atlantic League, made an unassisted triple play against Columbia.

May 8, 1947, Jimmie Foxx, who hit 534 home runs during his major league career, hung up his spikes after 24 years in Organized Ball. Foxx was the manager of St. Petersburg in the Florida International League.

May 13, 1947, The Salt Lake City Bees came close to an Organized Ball record when they scored 18 times in the sixth inning of their 19-12 victory over Idaho Falls in the Pioneer League. Nineteen runs had been scored twice in the Texas League, by Ft. Worth, June 29, 1896, and by Waco, August 6, 1930.

May 17, 1947, Manager Paul Bruno of Hammond, who alternated as pitcher and first baseman, established the unique record of relieving three times in one game, returning to first base when not on the mound. At this time, Bruno topped the Evangeline League in batting with a .425 average and boasted a record of nine wins and no losses, all in relief, to also lead his league in pitching.

June 4, 1947, Outfielder Marion Allen McElreath of Muskogee, Western Association, was placed on the permanent ineligibility list by president George Trautman of the National Association, following charges of attempting to induce a fellow player to "throw" a game, of wagering on games, and of not putting forth his best efforts on the field. McElreath, 32, broke into Organized Ball in 1931. He hit .367 in 25 games this season.

June 13, 1947, A doubleheader at Kansas City, American Association, was postponed because of cold weather.

June 21, 1947, Spencer Abbott, 69-year-old manager of Charlotte, Tri-State League, retired as a manager, ending a career in the minors as a manager and player dating back to 1898.

June 26, 1947, Carl DeRose of Kansas City, American Association, righthander who hadn't hurled for a month, and suffering from a sore arm which pained him with every pitch, tossed a perfect game masterpiece against Minneapolis at Blues Stadium, Kansas City. Facing only 27 batters, DeRose threw 93 pitches in his 5-0 victory, for the first perfect game in American Association history. DeRose was able to make only two other mound appearances during the remainder of the season.

July 5, 1947, A Lone Star League game at Bryan, Texas, was delayed in the fifth inning when a snake wandered into right field.

July 8, 1947, Judge William G. Bramham, former president of the minor leagues, died in Durham, North Carolina, at age 73.

July 10, 1947, James "Stormy" Davis, 20-year-old outfielder of Ballinger, Longhorn League, died in a Sweetwater, Texas, hospital from a blow received on the head in a game on July 3. Davis was struck in the head by a pitched ball in a game between Ballinger and Sweetwater. He had a .303 average in 48 games with 17 home runs and 64 RBIs.

July 13, 1947, Stanley "Frenchy" Bordagaray, manager of Greenville, South Atlantic League, who formerly played with the Cardinals, Dodgers, Reds and Yankees, was fined $50 and suspended 60 days for assaulting an umpire.

July 15, 1947, Myril Hoag, former New York Yankees outfielder who finished his 14-year big league career with Cleveland in 1945, was leading the Florida State League in hitting with .355 and topped the league's hurlers with a 11-2 record. He was player-manager of the Gainesville club.

July 21, 1947, Former Cardinals star John "Pepper" Martin succeeded the suspended Frenchy Bordagaray as manager of Greenville in South Atlantic League.

July 21, 1947, Ken Strong, president of the Colonial League, signed his ninth one-year contract with the New York Giants of the National Football League. Ken was the club's leading scorer in 1946.

July 28, 1947, Early postponements and a freak of the schedule combined to force Sioux City and Lincoln to meet 13 straight times.

August 10, 1947, Moses Yellowhorse, Pawnee Indian who pitched for Pittsburgh during the 1920s, was named to the KOM League umpiring staff. Yellowhorse had been groundskeeper for the Ponca City club this season, and earlier in the year served as substitute umpire.

August 14, 1947, Woodrow Crowson, 28-year-old Greensboro pitcher, was killed when the team's bus collided with a watermelon-loaded truck owned by Van Lingle Mungo, former big league pitcher, en route home from Martinsville after a Carolina League game. Crowson appeared in one game for the Philadelphia A's in 1945.

August 17, 1947, Buck Frierson of Sherman-Denison, Big State League, hit three homers to drive in eight runs as the Twins beat Waco 16-14. Monty Stratton, one-legged pitcher, went the route for Waco, being found for 20 hits.

September 1, 1947, After playing 123 games without being shut out, Evansville of the Three-I League was blanked twice in a doubleheader by Terre Haute on the final day of the season. The double zeros not only spoiled an unblemished record, but also knocked the Braves out of the first division and a place in the playoffs. Terre Haute broke the league's attendance record with a turnout of 10,600 for the twinbill.

September 2, 1947, James Slowrey, Jr., 22, regular shortstop for Wisconsin Rapids of the Wisconsin State League, died in Columbus, Wisconsin, of injuries suffered in an auto accident.

September 4, 1947, Al Simoninis of Anderson, Tri-State League, stole home for the 14th time of the season.

September 5, 1947, Pete Hughes closed the season with Phoenix in the Arizona-Texas League with 193 bases on balls for the year, believed to be an all-time Organized Ball record. He scored 180 runs on only 164 hits, 36 doubles, 8 triples and 38 homers, drove in 167 tallies and batted .371.

September 7, 1947, Minneapolis hurler Steve Gerkin worked in his 83rd game, an all-time Organized Ball record, to close the American Association season. Gerkin also pitched in three games washed out by rain. He started only three contests and had no complete games. Gerkin won 10 games and lost two, best in the American Association, and was named the circuit's Most Valuable Player. He was with the Philadelphia A's in 1945 and posted an 0-12 record.

September 20, 1947, Bill Serena hit 70 homers for Lubbock of the West Texas-New Mexico League. He slugged 57 homers in regular season play and an additional 13 circuit clouts in 14 September playoff games.

December 17, 1947, Tommy "Doc" Prothro, retiring manager and part owner of the Memphis Southern Association club, was sued for $100,000 in Memphis by Mrs. Ann Gorin Prothro, a daughter-in-law, charging Prothro and his wife with alienation of the affections of Tommy Prothro, their son.

1948

American League
President: William Harridge

Standings	W	L	Pct.	GB	Attend.	Manager
Cleveland Indians	97	58	.626	—	2,620,627	Lou Boudreau
Boston Red Sox	96	59	.619	1	1,558,798	Joe McCarthy
New York Yankees.............	94	60	.610	2½	2,373,901	Bucky Harris
Philadelphia Athletics........	84	70	.545	12½	945,076	Connie Mack
Detroit Tigers	78	76	.506	18½	1,743,035	Steve O'Neill
St. Louis Browns	59	94	.386	37	335,564	Zack Taylor
Washington Senators	56	97	.366	40	795,254	Joe Kuhel
Chicago White Sox............	51	101	.336	44½	777,844	Ted Lyons

Playoff: Cleveland defeated Boston 8-3 in a one game playoff.

BA: Ted Williams, Boston, .369
Runs: Tommy Henrich, New York, 138
Hits: Bob Dillinger, St. Louis, 207
RBIs: Joe DiMaggio, New York, 155
HRs: Joe DiMaggio, New York, 39

Wins: Hal Newhouser, Detroit, 21
SOs: Bob Feller, Cleveland, 164
ERA: Gene Bearden, Cleveland, 2.43
Pct: Jack Kramer, Boston, .783, 18-5

National League
President: Ford Frick

Standings	W	L	Pct.	GB	Attend.	Manager
Boston Braves....................	91	62	.595	—	1,455,439	Billy Southworth
St. Louis Cardinals	85	69	.552	6½	1,111,440	Eddie Dyer
Brooklyn Dodgers..............	84	70	.545	7½	1,398,967	Leo Durocher/Ray Blades/ Burt Shotton
Pittsburgh Pirates..............	83	71	.539	8½	1,517,021	Bill Meyer
New York Giants	78	76	.506	13½	1,459,269	Mel Ott/Leo Durocher
Philadelphia Phillies	66	88	.429	25½	767,429	Ben Chapman/Dusty Cooke/ Eddie Sawyer
Cincinnati Reds..................	64	89	.418	27	823,386	Johnny Neun/Bucky Walters
Chicago Cubs.....................	64	90	.416	27½	1,237,792	Charlie Grimm

BA: Stan Musial, St. Louis, .376
Runs: Stan Musial, St. Louis, 135
Hits: Stan Musial, St. Louis, 230
RBIs: Stan Musial, St. Louis, 131

HRs: Ralph Kiner, Pittsburgh, 40
  Johnny Mize, New York, 40
Wins: Johnny Sain, Boston, 24
SOs: Harry Brecheen, St. Louis, 149
ERA: Harry Brecheen, St. Louis, 2.24
Pct: Harry Brecheen, St. Louis, .741, 20-7

AAA American Association
President: Frank Lane

Standings	W	L	Pct.	GB	Attend.	Manager
Indianapolis Indians (15)..	100	54	.649	—	494,455	Al Lopez
Milwaukee Brewers (9)	89	65	.576	11	364,510	Nick Cullop
St. Paul Saints (10)	86	68	.558	14	320,483	Walter Alston
Columbus Red Birds (16)....	81	73	.526	19	216,388	Harold Anderson
Minneapolis Millers (13)....	77	77	.500	23	274,890	Frank Shellenback/Billy Herman
Kansas City Blues (5).........	64	88	.421	35	236,487	Dick Bartell
Toledo Mud Hens (7)	61	91	.401	38	114,310	George Detore
Louisville Colonels (1).......	56	98	.364	44	204,320	Nemo Leibold/Owen Scheetz

Playoffs: St. Paul 4 games, Indianapolis 2; Columbus 4 games, Milwaukee 3.
Finals: St. Paul 4 games, Columbus 3.

All-Star Team: **1B**-Les Fleming, Indianapolis; **2B**-Jack Cassini, Indianapolis; **3B**-Al Rosen, Kansas City; **SS**-Pete Castiglione, Indianapolis; **OF**-Marv Rickert, Milwaukee; Jim Gleeson, Milwaukee; Ted Beard, Indianapolis; Eric Tipton, St. Paul; **C**-Ralph Houk, Kansas City; Earl Turner, Indianapolis; **Util**-Damon Phillips, Milwaukee; **P**-Bob Malloy, Indianapolis; Jim Bagby, Indianapolis; Al Epperly, Milwaukee; Harvey Haddix, Columbus; **MVP**-Les Fleming, Indianapolis.

BA: Glenn McQuillen, Toledo, .329
Runs: Ted Beard, Indianapolis, 131
Hits: Froilan Fernandez, Milwaukee, 183
RBIs: Les Fleming, Indianapolis, 143

HRs: Mike Natisin, Columbus, 30
Wins: Bob Malloy, Indianapolis, 21
SOs: John McCall, Louisville, 149
ERA: Glenn Elliott, Milwaukee, 3.76

AAA International League
President: Frank J. Shaughnessy

Standings	W	L	Pct.	GB	Attend.	Manager
Montreal Royals (10)..........	94	59	.614	—	477,638	Clay Hopper
Newark Bears (5)...............	80	72	.526	13½	170,506	Bill Skiff
Syracuse Chiefs (12)..........	77	73	.513	15½	202,253	Jewel Ens
Rochester Red Wings (16)...	78	75	.510	16	304,896	Cedric Durst
Toronto Maple Leafs (14)...	78	76	.506	16½	291,977	Eddie Sawyer/Dick Porter
Buffalo Bisons (4)	71	80	.470	22	264,107	Paul Richards
Jersey City Giants (13).......	69	83	.454	24½	185,560	Bruno Betzel
Baltimore Orioles (3).........	59	88	.401	32	163,312	Alphonse "Tommy" Thomas

Playoffs: Montreal 4 games, Rochester 3; Syracuse 4 games, Newark 3.
Finals: Montreal 4 games, Syracuse 1.

All-Star Team: **1B**-Rocky Nelson, Rochester; **2B**-James Bloodworth, Montreal; **3B**-Edward Jones, Toronto; **SS**-Robert Morgan, Montreal; **OF**-John Groth, Buffalo; Chet Laabs, Buffalo; Clyde Vollmer, Syracuse; **C**-Ken Silvestri, Newark; **P**-Jack Banta, Montreal; Frank Fanovich, Syracuse; **Manager**-Clay Hopper, Montreal.

BA: Coaker Triplett, Buffalo, .353
Runs: John Groth, Buffalo, 124
Hits: John Groth, Buffalo, 199
RBIs: Ed Sanicki, Toronto, 107
HRs: Howie Moss, Baltimore, 33

Wins: Jack Banta, Montreal, 19
  Bill Reeder, Rochester, 19
SOs: Jack Banta, Montreal, 193
ERA: Bob Porterfield, Newark, 2.17

AAA Pacific Coast League
President: Clarence H. Rowland

Standings	W	L	Pct.	GB	Attend.	Manager
Oakland Oaks	114	74	.606	—	552,072	Casey Stengel
San Francisco Seals	112	76	.596	2	606,563	Lefty O'Doul
Los Angeles Angels (11)..	102	86	.543	12	576,372	William Kelly
Seattle Rainiers (4)	93	95	.495	21	452,448	Jo Jo White
Portland Beavers..............	89	99	.473	25	339,758	Jim Turner
Hollywood Stars (2)...........	84	104	.447	30	416,725	Jimmy Dykes/Lou Stringer/ George "Mule" Haas
San Diego Padres	83	105	.441	31	424,200	James "Rip" Collins/ Jack Brillheart
Sacramento Solons	75	113	.399	39	293,028	Joe Orengo

Playoffs: Oakland 4 games, Los Angeles 2; Seattle 4 games, San Francisco 1.
Finals: Oakland 4 games, Seattle 1.

MVP-Jack Graham, San Diego.

BA: Gene Woodling, San Francisco, .385
Runs: Dain Clay, San Diego, 133
Hits: Gus Zernial, Hollywood, 237
RBIs: Gus Zernial, Hollywood, 156

HRs: Jack Graham, San Diego, 48
Wins: Japhet "Red" Lynn, Los Angeles, 19
SOs: Con Dempsey, San Francisco, 171
ERA: Con Dempsey, San Francisco, 2.10

AA Southern Association
President: Charles A. Hurth

Standings	W	L	Pct.	GB	Attend.	Manager
Nashville Vols (11)............	95	58	.621	—	269,893	Larry Gilbert
Memphis Chicks (2)	92	61	.601	3	361,174	Jack Onslow
Birmingham Barons (1)......	84	69	.549	11	445,926	Fred Walters
Mobile Bears (10)..............	75	75	.500	18½	167,733	Alfred Todd
New Orleans Pelicans (15).	70	83	.458	25	234,772	Jimmy Brown
Atlanta Crackers	69	83	.448	26½	300,380	Kiki Cuyler
Little Rock Travelers (4)....	67	83	.447	26½	125,931	Jack Saltzgaver
Chattanooga Lookouts (8)..	58	96	.377	37½	141,059	George Myatt

Playoffs: Nashville 4 games, Mobile 3; Birmingham 4 games, Memphis 2.
Finals: Birmingham 4 games, Nashville 2.

All-Star Team: **1B**-Walt Dropo, Birmingham; **IF**-Oliver Kelly, Memphis; Hal Quick, Nashville; Mickey Rutner, Birmingham; Bobby Mavis, Little Rock; **OF**-Grover Bowers, Memphis; Charley Gilbert, Nashville; Tommy O'Brien, Birmingham; Chuck Workman, Nashville; **C**-Joe Astroth, Memphis; Sam Calderone, Mobile; Joe Erautt, Little Rock; **Util**-John Rizzo, Chattanooga; **P**-Norman Brown, Atlanta; Charles Eisenman, Memphis; Kenneth Olson, Mobile; Russ Oppliger, Mobile; Leo Twardy, Nashville; Ben Wade, Nashville.

BA: Smoky Burgess, Nashville, .386
Runs: Charley Gilbert, Nashville, 178
Hits: Tommy O'Brien, Birmingham, 206
RBIs: Chuck Workman, Nashville, 182
HRs: Chuck Workman, Nashville, 52

Wins: Norman Brown, Atlanta, 22
SOs: John Perkovich, Memphis, 153
ERA: Mike Palm, Birmingham, 2.20
Pct: Roman Brunswick, Memphis, 1.000, 12-0

AA Texas League
President: J. Alvin Gardner

Standings	W	L	Pct.	GB	Attend.	Manager
Ft. Worth Cats (10)............	92	61	.601	—	354,288	Les Burge/George Dockins/ Bobby Bragan
Tulsa Oilers (12)................	91	63	.591	1½	223,569	Al Vincent
Houston Buffaloes (16)	82	71	.536	10	401,383	Johnny Keane
Shreveport Sports	76	77	.497	16	195,616	Francis "Salty" Parker
San Antonio Missions (7)...	75	76	.497	16	263,959	Gus Mancuso
Oklahoma City Indians (3).	70	84	.455	22½	187,763	Pat Ankenman
Dallas Eagles	64	89	.418	28	262,533	James Adair/Les Burge
Beaumont Exporters (5)......	61	90	.404	30	151,932	Martin "Chick" Autry

---

*Won first-half   **Won second-half   ***Won both halves
Numbers after nicknames indicate farm system.
Affiliation listed at end of each year.

367

Playoffs: Ft. Worth 4 games, Shreveport 2; Tulsa 4 games, Houston 2.
Finals: Ft. Worth 4 games, Tulsa 2, one tie.

All-Star Team: 1B-Red Kress, Tulsa; **2B**-Bill Sommers, San Antonio; **3B**-Billy Capps, Tulsa; **SS**-Ray Boone, Oklahoma City; **OF**-Irv Noren, Ft. Worth; Pete Lewis, Oklahoma City; Russell Burns, Tulsa; **C**-Bobby Bragan, Ft. Worth; Al Unser, Tulsa; **Util**-Fred Marsh, Oklahoma City; Tom Tatum, Tulsa; **P**-Harry Perkowski, Tulsa; Bud Lively, Tulsa; Mike Garcia, Oklahoma City; Bob Austin, Ft. Worth; Cloyd Boyer, Houston; **MVP**-Irv Noren, Ft. Worth; **Pitcher of the Year**-Harry Perkowski, Tulsa.

BA: Tom Tatum, Tulsa, .333
Runs: John Lane, Tulsa, 115
Hits: Dee Fondy, Ft. Worth, 193
RBIs: Russell Burns, Tulsa, 113
HRs: Russell Burns, Tulsa, 26
Wins: Harry Perkowski, Tulsa, 22
SOs: Cloyd Boyer, Houston, 188
ERA: Bud Byerly, Houston/Tulsa, 2.20

A Central League
President: T.J. Halligan

Standings	W	L	Pct.	GB	Attend.	Manager
Flint Arrows (4)	89	49	.645	—	120,573	Jack Tighe
Dayton Indians (3)	84	55	.604	5½	157,837	Joe Vosmik
Muskegon Clippers (2)	73	66	.525	16½	80,390	Bennie Huffman
Fort Wayne Generals (15)	64	76	.457	26	32,988	Walter Beck
Saginaw Bears	55	85	.393	35	70,333	Robert Finley
Grand Rapids Jets	52	86	.377	37	46,058	Milton Galatzer/Jack Knight

Playoffs: Fort Wayne 3 games, Flint 2; Dayton 3 games, Muskegon 1.
Finals: Dayton 4 games, Fort Wayne 2.

BA: Herb Conyers, Dayton, .354
Runs: Dick Lane, Muskegon, 121
Hits: Louis Farotto, Saginaw, 185
RBIs: Homer Johnson, Muskegon, 109
HRs: Joe Morjoseph, Dayton, 31
Wins: Charles Sipple, Dayton, 18
SOs: William Evans, Muskegon, 187
ERA: Alex Nedelco, Flint, 2.08

A Eastern League
President: Thomas H. Richardson

Standings	W	L	Pct.	GB	Attend.	Manager
Scranton Red Sox (1)	89	51	.636	—	165,215	Mike Ryba
Albany Senators (15)	86	54	.614	3	210,804	Pinky May
Utica Blue Sox (13)	83	56	.597	5½	118,695	Dick Porter/Pat Colgan
Hartford Chiefs (9)	74	67	.525	15½	122,563	Earle Browne
Williamsport Tigers (4)	73	68	.518	16½	102,714	Gene Desautels
Binghamton Triplets (5)	58	82	.414	31	109,515	Buddy Hassett
Elmira Pioneers (7)	49	91	.350	40	68,235	Stan "Packy" Rogers
Wilkes-Barre Barons (3)	48	91	.345	40½	55,184	Bill Norman

Playoffs: Hartford defeated Williamsport in a one game playoff for fourth place. Scranton 4 games, Utica 1; Albany 4 games, Hartford 3.
Finals: Scranton 4 games, Albany 0.

All-Star Team: 1B-Billy Glynn, Utica; **2B**-Fred Lanifero, Albany; **3B**-Bruce Blanchard, Williamsport; **SS**-Frank Staucet, Albany; **OF**-Don Manno, Albany; Dick Welker, Utica; Ken Humphrey, Williamsport; **C**-Joe Ginsberg, Williamsport; **Util**-Frank Bocek, Binghamton; **P**-Lou Kretlow, Williamsport; Dick Koecher, Utica; **Manager**-Mike Ryba, Scranton.

BA: Bruce Blanchard, Williamsport, .327
Runs: Alex Garbowski, Utica, 100
Hits: Fred Lanifero, Albany, 169
RBIs: Jim Piersall, Scranton, 92
HRs: Homer Moore, Hartford, 20
Wins: Lou Kretlow, Williamsport, 21
SOs: Lou Kretlow, Williamsport, 219
ERA: Max Peterson, Utica, 2.03

A South Atlantic League
President: Earl Blue

Standings	W	L	Pct.	GB	Attend.	Manager
Charleston Rebels	87	65	.572	—	171,096	Herb Crompton
Macon Peaches (11)	86	68	.558	2	181,049	Don Osborn
Greenville Spinners (10)	84	69	.549	3½	122,287	Greg Mulleavy
Columbia Reds (12)	79	72	.523	7½	110,853	Gerald Walker
Jacksonville Tars (13)	78	75	.510	9½	141,198	John Hudson
Columbus Cardinals (16)	65	83	.439	20	93,193	Kemp Wicker
Augusta Tigers (5)	64	87	.424	22½	104,755	Bill Cooper/Mike Garbark/Ernie Jenkins
Savannah Indians (6)	63	87	.420	23	107,168	Eric McNair

Playoffs: Columbia 4 games, Charleston 3; Greenville 4 games, Macon 3.
Finals: Greenville 4 games, Columbia 1.

All-Star Team: 1B-Bennie Taylor, Greenville; **2B**-Roy Marion, Charleston; **3B**-Danny O'Connell, Greenville; **SS**-Bobby Wilkins, Charleston; **OF**-Harold Summers, Augusta; Lloyd Merriman, Columbia; Dick Burgett, Columbus; **C**-Herb Crompton, Charleston; **Util**-Gene Herbert, Augusta; Frank Dunlap, Macon; **P**-Don Osborn, Macon; James Parton, Charleston; **Manager**-Gerald Walker, Columbia.

BA: Harold Summers, Augusta, .331
Runs: Lloyd Merriman, Columbia, 120
Hits: Roy Marion, Charleston, 197
RBIs: Harold Summers, Augusta, 115
HRs: Harold Summers, Augusta, 28
Wins: Frank Smith, Columbia, 21
SOs: Edward Burtschy, Savannah, 178
ERA: Alfred Boresh, Columbia, 2.13

A Western League
President: Senator Edwin C. Johnson

Standings	W	L	Pct.	GB	Attend.	Manager
Des Moines Bruins (11)	76	64	.543	—	232,038	Stan Hack
Denver Bears	70	67	.511	4½	283,377	Mike Gazella
Lincoln Athletics (6)	69	68	.504	5½	127,046	James DeShong
Sioux City Soos (13)	69	68	.504	5½	112,381	Joe Becker
Pueblo Dodgers (10)	69	70	.496	6½	116,304	John Fitzpatrick
Omaha Cardinals (16)	62	78	.443	14	147,130	Ollie Vanek

Playoffs: Lincoln defeated Sioux City 6-0 in a one game playoff for third place. Lincoln 3 games, Des Moines 2; Sioux City 3 games, Denver 2.
Finals: Sioux City 4 games, Lincoln 2.

All-Star Team: 1B-Herb Gorman, Pueblo; **2B**-Nellie Fox, Lincoln; **3B**-Ransom Jackson, Des Moines; **SS**-George Genovese, Denver; **OF**-Larry Miggins, Omaha; Billy Pavlik, Sioux City; Leon "Red" Treadway, Des Moines; **C**-Carl Sawatski, Des Moines; **Util**-Bob Wellman, Lincoln; Ed Martin, Sioux City; **P**-Omar "Turk" Lown, Pueblo; Bobby Shantz, Lincoln; **Manager**-Mike Gazella, Denver.

BA: Leon "Red" Treadway, Des Moines, .352
Runs: George Genovese, Denver, 119
Hits: Nellie Fox, Lincoln, 179
RBIs: Harold "Tookie" Gilbert, Sioux City, 114
HRs: Carl Sawatski, Des Moines, 29
Wins: Bobby Shantz, Lincoln, 18
SOs: Bobby Shantz, Lincoln, 212
ERA: Tony Jacobs, Des Moines, 2.72

B Big State League
President: J. Walter Morris

Standings	W	L	Pct.	GB	Attend.	Manager
Sherman-Denison Twins (8)	94	51	.648	—	117,046	Jose Rodriguez
Wichita Falls Spudders (7)	84	62	.575	10½	130,138	Marcus Carrola
Waco Pirates (15)	82	64	.562	12½	82,762	Buster Chatham
Austin Pioneers	79	67	.541	15½	163,666	Henry "Prince" Oana
Gainesville Owls	69	77	.473	25½	80,479	Babe Peebles/Jackie Reid
Paris Rockets	62	85	.422	33	72,636	Homer Peel
Texarkana Bears	60	83	.420	33	70,508	Vern Washington/Edward Borom
Greenville Majors	52	93	.359	42	67,334	Buddy Hancken/Nat Love

Playoffs: Sherman-Denison 4 games, Austin 1; Wichita Falls 4 games, Waco 0.
Finals: Sherman-Denison 4 games, Wichita Falls 3.

BA: Vern Washington, Texarkana, .384
Runs: Donald Cena, Waco, 142
Hits: Paul Brotherton, Wichita Falls, 218
RBIs: Jack Bradsher, Wichita Falls, 152
HRs: Albert McCarty, Wichita Falls, 32
2B: Lon Goldstein, Gainesville, 58
Wins: Thomas Finger, Wichita Falls, 21
SOs: Glenn Blackwood, Greenville/Wichita Falls, 176
ERA: Rafael Rivas, Sherman-Denison, 2.33

B Colonial League
President: John A. Scalzi, Jr.

Standings	W	L	Pct.	GB	Attend.	Manager
Port Chester Clippers (7)	86	53	.619	—	32,198	Al Barillari
Poughkeepsie Chiefs	76	61	.555	9	38,573	Steve Mizerak
Waterbury Timers	65	68	.489	18	40,988	Mike Kash (Kaiserski)
New Brunswick/Kingston Hubs#	61	71	.462	21½	36,397	Ed Kobesky
Bridgeport Bees (8)	61	72	.459	22	38,049	Glenn Snyder/Buddy Hall
Stamford Pioneers	54	78	.409	28½	25,640	Zeke Bonura

#New Brunswick (29-35) moved to Kingston July 10.

Playoffs: Port Chester 4 games, Waterbury 1; Poughkeepsie 4 games, Kingston 1.
Finals: Port Chester 4 games, Poughkeepsie 1.

All-Star Team: 1B-Leo Eastham, Waterbury; **2B**-John Miggins, Port Chester; **3B**-Charles Quimby, Poughkeepsie; **SS**-Gary Ruttkay, Port Chester; **OF**-Joseph DeToia, Poughkeepsie; Joe Mellendick, Port Chester; Aldo Casadei, Waterbury; **C**-Max Goldsmith, New Brunswick/Kingston; John Pluchino, Port Chester; **P**-Paul Wargo, Port Chester; Guy Coleman, Port Chester; Pete Kowalchyk, Waterbury.

BA: Ed Kobesky, New Brunswick/Kingston, .390
Runs: Joseph DeToia, Poughkeepsie, 116
Hits: Joseph DeToia, Poughkeepsie, 157; Aldo Casadei, Waterbury, 157
RBIs: Joseph DeToia, Poughkeepsie, 96
HRs: Zeke Bonura, Stamford, 23
Wins: Guy Coleman, Port Chester, 17
SOs: Paul Wargo, Port Chester, 158
ERA: Sidney Schacht, Stamford, 2.09

B Interstate League
President: Gerald P. Nugent

Standings	W	L	Pct.	GB	Attend.	Manager
Wilmington Blue Rocks (14)	82	56	.594	—	102,197	Jack Sanford
Trenton Giants (13)	83	57	.593	—	97,389	Tommy Heath
York White Roses (15)	77	62	.554	5½	126,679	Frank Oceak
Sunbury Reds (12)	74	64	.536	8	114,726	Joe Buzas
Allentown Cardinals (16)	73	65	.529	9	102,471	Al Hollingsworth
Harrisburg Senators (3)	64	76	.457	19	68,270	Les Bell
Hagerstown Owls (4)	53	87	.379	30	49,248	Pep Rambert/Gene Crumling/Bennie Culp
Lancaster Red Roses (10)	50	89	.360	32½	65,734	Dibrell Williams/Jack Knight

Playoffs: York 4 games, Wilmington 1; Trenton 4 games, Sunbury 3.
Finals: Trenton 4 games, York 0.

All-Star Team: **1B**-William Plate, York; **2B**-John Merson, York; **3B**-Stan Jok, Trenton; **SS**-George D'Addario, Hagerstown; **OF**-Steve Filipowicz, Sunbury; Harold Sanders, Harrisburg; Jess Levan, Wilmington; **C**-Larry Ciaffone, Allentown; **Util**-John Werner, Wilmington; **P**-Leon Griffeth, Lancaster; Don Robertson, Trenton; **Manager**-Tommy Heath, Trenton.

BA: Larry Ciaffone, Allentown, .373
Runs: Michael Goliat, Wilmington, 123
Hits: Steve Filipowicz, Sunbury, 187
RBIs: Steve Filipowicz, Sunbury, 134
HRs: Maurice Cunningham, Trenton, 25
Wins: Don Robertson, Trenton, 19
SOs: Leon Griffeth, Lancaster, 168
ERA: Robin Roberts, Wilmington, 2.06

B New England League

President: Claude B. Davidson

Standings	W	L	Pct.	GB	Attend.	Manager
Lynn Red Sox (1)	85	40	.680	—	49,088	Eddie Popowski
Nashua Dodgers (10)	84	41	.672	1	63,382	Al Campanis
Portland Pilots (14)	78	47	.624	7	117,606	Del Bissonette
Pawtucket Slaters (9)	61	64	.488	24	60,432	Hugh Wise
Manchester Yankees (5)	58	68	.460	27½	50,664	Thomas Padden
Springfield Cubs (11)	52	74	.413	33½	95,406	Robert Peterson
Providence Grays	45	80	.360	40	28,170	Frank Archer/Donald Burke
Fall River Indians (2)	38	87	.304	47	22,589	Frank Zubik/Luke Urban

Playoffs: Lynn 3 games, Portland 2; Nashua 3 games, Pawtucket 0.
Finals: Nashua 4 games, Lynn 1.

All-Star Team: **1B**-Dale Long, Lynn; **2B**-Fran King, Providence; **3B**-Fred Hatfield, Lynn; **SS**-Frank Verdi, Manchester; **OF**-Ted DelGuercio, Lynn; Ted Bartz (Barczuk), Nashua; Jim Pokel, Portland; **C**-Jim Argeros, Lynn; **P**-Dan Bankhead, Nashua; Harry Schaeffer, Manchester; **Manager**-Del Bissonette, Portland.

BA: Ted Bartz (Barczuk), Nashua, .334
Runs: Ted Bartz (Barczuk), Nashua, 115
Hits: Ted Bartz (Barczuk), Nashua, 167
RBIs: Dale Long, Lynn, 119
HRs: Jim Pokel, Portland, 30
Wins: Dan Bankhead, Nashua, 20
SOs: Dan Bankhead, Nashua, 243
ERA: Harry Schaeffer, Manchester, 2.33

B Piedmont League

President: Richard A. Carrington, Jr.

Standings	W	L	Pct.	GB	Attend.	Manager
Lynchburg Cardinals (16)	80	58	.580	—	137,883	Vernon Mackie
Newport News Dodgers (10)	72	67	.518	8½	111,720	Roy Schalk
Portsmouth Cubs	71	69	.507	10	108,591	Ace Parker
Roanoke Red Sox (1)	65	73	.471	15	80,355	Pinky Higgins
Norfolk Tars (5)	65	75	.464	16	104,742	Earl Bolyard
Richmond Colts (13)	64	75	.460	16½	157,758	Charles George

Playoffs: Lynchburg 4 games, Roanoke 3; Newport News 4 games, Portsmouth 3.
Finals: Newport News 4 games, Lynchburg 0.

All-Star Team: **1B**-Reggie Otero, Portsmouth; **2B**-Art Lilly, Richmond; **3B**-Warren Patterson, Newport News; **SS**-Rocky Krsnich, Norfolk; **OF**-Lewis Davis, Richmond; Bill Boyce, Roanoke; Art Schult, Norfolk; **C**-Harry Land, Portsmouth; **P**-William Eggert, Newport News; Whitey Ford, Norfolk; **Manager**-Vernon Mackie, Lynchburg.

BA: Steve Bilko, Lynchburg, .333
Runs: Bill Spaeter, Roanoke, 100
Hits: Art Schult, Norfolk, 159
RBIs: Bill Boyce, Roanoke, 99
HRs: Steve Bilko, Lynchburg, 20
Wins: William Eggert, Newport News, 19
SOs: Whitey Ford, Norfolk, 171
ERA: Lou Ciola, Portsmouth, 1.69

B Southeastern League

President: Stuart X. Stephenson

Standings	W	L	Pct.	GB	Attend.	Manager
Montgomery Rebels	86	53	.619	—	111,657	Frank Skaff
Vicksburg Billies	77	63	.550	9½	88,047	Buddy Blair
Anniston Rams	75	63	.543	10½	79,464	Charles Baron(ovic)
Jackson Senators (9)	74	65	.532	12	141,493	Willis Hudlin
Pensacola Fliers	71	67	.514	14½	93,734	Otto Denning/Wally Dashiell/ Clyde McDowell
Meridian Peps (3)	63	77	.450	23½	62,808	Ben Geraghty/Jack Maupin
Gadsden Pilots (8)	59	81	.421	27½	64,635	Bill McGhee/Harry Davis
Selma Cloverleafs (11)	52	88	.371	34½	38,776	Morris Arnovich

Playoffs: Montgomery 4 games, Anniston 3; Jackson 4 games, Vicksburg 3.
Finals: Montgomery 4 games, Jackson 1.

All-Star Team: **1B**-Walter Lance, Meridian; Deo Grose, Jackson; **2B**-David Williams, Pensacola; **3B**-Billy Seal, Vicksburg; **SS**-Jack Maupin, Meridian; **OF**-Ken Guettler, Montgomery/Gadsden; Banks McDowell, Jackson; Charles Woodall, Pensacola; **C**-Walt Linden, Jackson; **Util**-Bill Adair, Jackson; Bob Talbot, Selma; **P**-Zennie Britt, Jackson; Woody Rich, Anniston; Fred Baczewski, Anniston; **Manager**-Charles Baron(ovic), Anniston.

BA: Thomas Davis, Jackson, .341
Runs: David Williams, Pensacola, 119
Hits: Lew Flick, Jackson, 190
RBIs: Thomas Davis, Jackson, 125
HRs: Ken Guettler, Montgomery/Gadsden, 24
Wins: Zennie Britt, Jackson, 21
SOs: Woody Rich, Anniston, 196
ERA: Woody Rich, Anniston, 2.48

B Three-I League

President: Tom Fairweather

Standings	W	L	Pct.	GB	Attend.	Manager
Quincy Gems (5)	81	45	.643	—	124,053	James Adlam
Danville Dodgers (10)	72	51	.585	7½	62,284	Paul Chervinko
Evansville Braves (9)	67	54	.554	11½	101,652	Bob Coleman
Terre Haute Phillies (14)	65	57	.533	14	130,009	Pat Colgan/Dale Jones
Waterloo White Hawks (2)	63	61	.508	17	170,018	Pete Fox
Springfield Browns (7)	56	67	.455	23½	54,463	Henry Helf/Irvin Hall
Decatur Commies (11)	50	75	.400	30½	44,943	Red Lucas/Nelson Burbrink
Davenport Pirates (15)	41	85	.325	40	45,711	Ival Goodman

Playoffs: Terre Haute 3 games, Danville 2; Evansville 3 games, Quincy 2.
Finals: Evansville 4 games, Terre Haute 0.

All-Star Team: **1B**-Earl York, Decatur; **2B**-James Adlam, Quincy; **3B**-Don Lenhardt, Springfield; **SS**-Gerald Snyder, Quincy; **OF**-Robert Marquis, Quincy; John Novosel, Springfield; Joseph Tesauro, Terre Haute; **C**-Frank Baldwin, Evansville; **Util**-Joseph Van Hooreweghe, Danville; Maynard DeWitt, Danville; **P**-Glenn Thompson, Evansville; Marvin Rotblatt, Waterloo; **Manager**-Paul Chervinko, Danville.

BA: John Novosel, Springfield, .339
Runs: Robert Marquis, Quincy, 108
Hits: Robert Marquis, Quincy, 164
RBIs: Keith Thomas, Quincy, 99
HRs: John Novosel, Springfield, 22
Don Lenhardt, Springfield, 22
Wins: Art Bohman, Quincy, 16
Lew Burdette, Quincy, 16
SOs: Glenn Thompson, Evansville, 230
ERA: David Thieke, Danville, 1.81

B Tri-State League

President: C.M. Llewellyn

Standings	W	L	Pct.	GB	Attend.	Manager
Asheville Tourists (10)	95	51	.651	—	122,693	Clay Bryant
Anderson Rebels (15)	77	68	.531	17½	103,180	Bob Richards
Rock Hill Chiefs	76	70	.521	19	85,621	Edwin Freed/Dick Bouknight
Fayetteville Cubs (11)	73	71	.507	21	76,956	Frank Scalzi
Charlotte Hornets (8)	72	74	.493	23	122,211	Joe Bowman
Knoxville Smokies (13)	71	76	.483	24½	95,164	Dale Alexander/David Garcia
Spartanburg Peaches (3)	68	77	.469	26½	98,993	Kerby Farrell
Florence Steelers	50	95	.345	44½	72,569	George Motto/James Martin

Playoffs: Rock Hill 3 games, Asheville 1; Fayetteville 3 games, Anderson 1.
Finals: Fayetteville 4 games, Rock Hill 1.

All-Star Team: **1B**-Ray Hickernell, Asheville; **2B**-Forrest "Spook" Jacobs, Asheville; **3B**-Floyd Fogg, Fayetteville; **SS**-Russell Rose, Asheville; **OF**-Ralph Rowe, Rock Hill; Robert Churchill, Knoxville; Norman Koney, Asheville; Oscar Garmendia, Florence; **C**-Les Peden, Fayetteville; **P**-Lacy James, Rock Hill; Joseph Landrum, Asheville; **Manager**-Clay Bryant, Asheville.

BA: Robert Churchill, Knoxville, .406
Runs: Norman Koney, Asheville, 145
Hits: Robert Churchill, Knoxville, 230
RBIs: Floyd Fogg, Fayetteville, 144
HRs: Len Cross, Spartanburg, 29
3B: Robert Churchill, Knoxville, 28
Wins: Arthur "Red" Dwyer, Rock Hill, 22
SOs: Lacy James, Rock Hill, 213
ERA: Joseph Landrum, Asheville, 2.77

B Western International League

President: Robert B. Abel

Standings	W	L	Pct.	GB	Attend.	Manager
Spokane Indians	102	64	.614	—	216,074	Buddy Ryan/Dolph Camilli
Bremerton Bluejackets	95	62	.605	2½	75,195	Alan Strange
Victoria Athletics (5)	93	68	.578	6½	143,081	Ted Norbert
Tacoma Tigers	84	73	.535	13½	96,200	Jack Brillheart/Earl Kuper
Vancouver Capilanos	67	80	.456	25½	116,722	Bill Brenner
Salem Senators	73	88	.453	26½	77,659	Jack Wilson
Wenatchee Chiefs	69	91	.431	30	81,880	Chuck Cronin
Yakima Packers	52	109	.323	47½	73,600	Vernon Johnson/Hub Kittle

Playoffs: None.

All-Star Team: **1B**-Vic Buccola, Victoria; **2B**-Eddie Samcoff, Bremerton; **3B**-Babe Jensen, Victoria; **SS**-Leo Thomas, Spokane; **OF**-Archie Wilson, Victoria; William Wilson, Wenatchee; Dick Sinovic, Salem; **C**-Jack Warren, Vancouver; **P**-Joe Blankenship, Victoria; Frank Nelson, Spokane; Lloyd Hittle, Bremerton; **Manager**-Alan Strange, Bremerton.

BA: Archie Wilson, Victoria, .369
Runs: Archie Wilson, Victoria, 137
Hits: Archie Wilson, Victoria, 244
RBIs: Archie Wilson, Victoria, 132
HRs: William Wilson, Wenatchee, 33
TBs: Archie Wilson, Victoria, 408
Wins: Joe Blankenship, Victoria, 25
SOs: Lloyd Hittle, Bremerton, 201
ERA: Lloyd Hittle, Bremerton, 2.29

C Arizona-Texas League

President: Riney B. Salmon

Standings	W	L	Pct.	GB	Attend.	Manager
Globe-Miami Browns (7)	80	60	.571	—	75,001	Don Heffner
Tucson Cowboys (3)	78	62	.557	2	79,327	Lloyd Brown
El Paso Texans (1)	74	66	.529	6	73,766	Walter Millies
Juarez Indios	74	66	.529	6	52,525	Manuel Fortes/ Francisco Barradas
Phoenix Senators	67	73	.479	13	79,821	Alton Biggs
Bisbee-Douglas Miners (5)	47	93	.336	33	43,610	Mel Steiner/ Mitchell Chetkovich

1948

Playoffs: El Paso defeated Juarez in a one game playoff for third place. Globe-Miami 4 games, El Paso 2; Juarez 4 games, Tucson 1.
Finals: Globe-Miami 4 games, Juarez 3.

BA: Gene Lillard, Phoenix, .364
Runs: Dick Sabatini, Phoenix, 145
Hits: Ramon Vargas, Tucson, 197
RBIs: Daniel Baich, Globe-Miami, 152
HRs: Daniel Baich, Globe-Miami, 27
BBs: Pete Hughes, Phoenix, 207

Wins: Thomas Radcliff, El Paso, 17
Alwin Aguilar, Tucson, 17
William Abernathie, Tucson, 17
SOs: Edward Graham, Phoenix, 178
ERA: Lloyd Brown, Tucson, 3.01

C Border League
President: John G. Ward

Standings	W	L	Pct.	GB	Attend.	Manager
Ottawa Senators	79	48	.622	—	76,299	Bill Metzig
Geneva Robins	72	54	.571	6½	66,149	Charles Small
Ogdensburg Maples (13)	69	60	.535	11	60,116	Russ Wein
Watertown Athletics	63	65	.492	16½	65,590	Fred Gerken
Kingston Ponies (9)	49	76	.392	29	40,656	Ben Lady
Auburn Cayugas (1)	49	78	.386	30	43,102	Barney Hearn

Playoffs: Ogdensburg 4 games, Ottawa 1; Watertown 4 games, Geneva 3.
Finals: Ogdensburg 4 games, Watertown 0.

BA: Garland Lawing, Ogdensburg, .379
Runs: Garland Lawing, Ogdensburg, 112
Hits: Garland Lawing, Ogdensburg, 164
RBIs: Garland Lawing, Ogdensburg, 122
HRs: Bill Reardon, Kingston, 24

Wins: Leonard Seamon, Ottawa, 21
Arthur Cook, Kingston, 21
SOs: William Gates, Watertown, 232
ERA: Leonard Seamon, Ottawa, 2.00

C California League
President: Wiley K. Peterson

Standings	W	L	Pct.	GB	Attend.	Manager
Fresno Cardinals (16)	85	55	.607	—	127,545	Stan Benjamin
Ventura Yankees (5)	80	60	.571	5	74,036	Edward Kearse
Santa Barbara Dodgers (10)	74	66	.529	11	79,685	Chester Kehn
Stockton Ports	72	68	.514	13	145,804	Vince DiMaggio
Modesto Reds (7)	70	70	.500	15	102,923	William Jackson
Bakersfield Indians (3)	70	70	.500	15	102,705	Harry Griswold
San Jose Red Sox (1)	64	76	.457	21	100,009	Marv Owen
Visalia Cubs (11)	45	95	.321	40	53,748	John Intlekofer/ Arnold "Jigger" Statz/ Don Anderson

Playoffs: Santa Barbara 3 games, Fresno 2; Stockton 3 games, Ventura 0.
Finals: Santa Barbara 4 games, Stockton 3.

All-Star Team: 1B-Bob White, Ventura; **2B**-Howard Phillips, Fresno; **3B**-Gene Valla, Ventura; **SS**-Fred Monge, Santa Barbara; **OF**-Rip Repulski, Fresno; Vince DiMaggio, Stockton; Stan Benjamin, Fresno; **C**-Joe Borich, Bakersfield; **Util**-Ernie Sierra, San Jose; Dick Williams, Santa Barbara; **P**-Will Boemler, Ventura; Walter Olsen, Santa Barbara.

BA: Harold Cox, Bakersfield, .345
Runs: Howard Phillips, Fresno, 126
Hits: Harry Clements, Stockton, 186
RBIs: Rip Repulski, Fresno, 125
HRs: Vince DiMaggio, Stockton, 30
Wins: Frank Meagher, Santa Barbara, 18
SOs: Walter Olsen, Santa Barbara, 246
ERA: Walter Olsen, Santa Barbara, 2.16

C Canadian-American League
President: Albert E. Houghton

Standings	W	L	Pct.	GB	Attend.	Manager
Rome Colonels (4)	79	57	.581	—	75,103	Clyde Smoll
Trois Rivieres Royals (10)	78	60	.565	2	80,747	Ed Head
Oneonta Red Sox (1)	72	65	.526	7½	51,204	Red Marion
Pittsfield Electrics (3)	69	67	.507	10	52,986	Gene Hasson
Schenectady Blue Jays (14)	69	68	.504	10½	146,421	Leon Riley
Gloversville-Johnstown Glovers (7)	68	69	.496	11½	61,736	Jim McDonnell
Amsterdam Rugmakers (5)	57	80	.416	22½	90,790	Jim McLeod
Quebec Alouettes (13)	56	82	.406	24	144,156	Tony Ravish/Bernie Woycik

Playoffs: Oneonta 4 games, Rome 3; Pittsfield 4 games, Trois Rivieres 1.
Finals: Oneonta 4 games, Pittsfield 1.

All-Star Team: 1B-Gene Hasson, Pittsfield; **2B**-Robert Mays, Rome; **3B**-James Robinson, Gloversville-Johnstown; **SS**-Alfred Speranza, Schenectady; **OF**-William Booker, Rome; Walt Kowalski, Trois Rivieres; Calvin Burlingame, Oneonta; **C**-Stephen Salata, Oneonta; **Util**-Louis Palmisiano, Pittsfield; **P**-Robert Brake, Oneonta; William Mosser, Trois Rivieres; **Manager**-Red Marion, Oneonta.

BA: Gene Hasson, Pittsfield, .368
Runs: Bill Staker, Gloversville-Johnstown, 107
Hits: Walt Kowalski, Trois Rivieres, 163
RBIs: Gene Hasson, Pittsfield, 106
HRs: Gene Hasson, Pittsfield, 27
Wins: Lynn Lovenguth, Rome, 21
SOs: Duke Markell, Schenectady, 280
ERA: Charles LeBrun, Oneonta, 2.55

C Carolina League
President: Carroll T. Brown

Standings	W	L	Pct.	GB	Attend.	Manager
Raleigh Capitals	84	58	.592	—	125,000	Bill Nagel/Glen Lockamy
Martinsville Athletics (6)	81	61	.570	3	59,481	Edwin Morgan
Burlington Bees	80	62	.563	4	101,000	Buddy Bates
Danville Leafs	77	64	.546	6½	104,000	Bob Latshaw/Woody Fair
Winston-Salem Cardinals (16)	76	65	.539	7½	141,664	Cecil "Zip" Payne
Durham Bulls (4)	63	79	.444	21	95,291	Willie Duke
Reidsville Luckies	57	85	.401	27	71,509	Barney DeForge/ Tal Abernathy/Bill Nagel
Greensboro Patriots	49	93	.345	35	80,000	Rip Radcliff

Playoffs: Burlington 4 games, Raleigh 2; Martinsville 4 games, Danville 1.
Finals: Martinsville 4 games, Burlington 2.

All-Star Team: 1B-Edwin Morgan, Martinsville; **2B**-Lawrence "Crash" Davis, Durham; **3B**-George Wright, Martinsville; **SS**-Walter "Teapot" Frye, Winston-Salem; **OF**-Russell Sullivan, Danville; Buddy Bates, Burlington; Emil Showfety, Greensboro; **C**-Joe Krazter, Martinsville; **Util**-Claude Swiggett, Burlington; **P**-Al Henencheck, Raleigh; Lewis Hester, Reidsville; **MVP**-Lewis Hester, Reidsville; **Manager**-Buddy Bates, Burlington.

BA: Edwin Morgan, Martinsville, .373
Runs: George Wright, Martinsville, 145
Hits: Emil Showfety, Greensboro, 191
RBIs: Russell Sullivan, Danville, 129
HRs: Russell Sullivan, Danville, 35
2B: Lawrence "Crash" Davis, Durham, 50
Wins: Lewis Hester, Reidsville, 25
SOs: Jack Frisinger, Winston-Salem, 234
ERA: Al Henencheck, Raleigh, 2.24

C Central Association
President: Frank Hearn

Standings	W	L	Pct.	GB	Attend.	Manager
Clinton Cubs (11)	79	47	.627	—	53,133	Nelson Burbrink/Lee Eilbracht
Burlington Indians (3)	68	62	.523	13	70,359	Paul O'Dea/Oscar Melillo/ Bruno Haas
Hannibal Pilots (7)	67	62	.519	13½	41,124	Walter DeFreitas
Keokuk Pirates (15)	61	67	.477	19	54,694	Phil Seghi
Rockford Rox (12)	56	72	.438	24	43,133	Cyril Pfeifer/Paul O'Dea
Moline/Kewanee A's#(6)	53	74	.417	26½	38,088	Joe Glenn

#Moline (17-25) moved to Kewanee June 18, first home game June 29.

Playoffs: Clinton 4 games, Burlington 2; Keokuk 4 games, Hannibal 1.
Finals: Clinton 4 games, Keokuk 0.

All-Star Team: 1B-C.W. Shambon, Hannibal; **2B**-Charles Wood, Rockford; **3B**-Weldon Idol, Hannibal; **SS**-Bill Klaus, Clinton; **OF**-Fred Storck, Burlington; Dwight Maxhimer, Clinton; Gus Bell, Keokuk; **C**-Wilmer Schantz, Moline/Kewanee; **Util**-George Gatto, Clinton; Michael Lutz, Burlington; **P**-Ronald McLeland, Hannibal; Calvin Howe, Clinton.

BA: Gus Bell, Keokuk, .319
Runs: Elzer Marx, Clinton, 108
Hits: Bill Klaus, Clinton, 167
RBIs: Dwight Maxhimer, Clinton, 105
HRs: John Tanner, Keokuk, 23
Wins: Ronald McLeland, Hannibal, 18
Calvin Howe, Clinton, 18
SOs: Wesley Carr, Clinton, 163
Merrill Merkle, Hannibal, 163
ERA: Ronald McLeland, Hannibal, 2.39

C Cotton States League
President: James Griffith

Standings	W	L	Pct.	GB	Attend.	Manager
Greenwood Dodgers (10)	92	44	.676	—	48,847	James Bivin
Clarksdale Planters	85	53	.616	8	63,883	Chet Morgan
Hot Springs Bathers (2)	82	56	.594	11	83,425	Joe Holden/George Sobek
Natchez Indians	74	64	.536	19	38,069	Joe Rullo
Greenville Bucks	65	73	.471	28	53,499	Lindsay Deal/Wes Livengood
Helena Seaporters	54	82	.397	38	31,292	Woody Johnson/ Tince Leonard/Michael Sertich
Pine Bluff Cardinals	50	87	.365	42½	58,342	Arthur Nelson/John George
El Dorado Oilers	48	91	.345	45½	36,273	Howard Roberts

Playoffs: Greenwood 3 games, Natchez 0; Hot Springs 3 games, Clarksdale 0.
Finals: Hot Springs 4 games, Greenwood 3.

BA: Herb Adams, Hot Springs, .375
Runs: Herb Adams, Hot Springs, 123
Hits: Herb Adams, Hot Springs, 223
RBIs: Jack Parks, Natchez, 96
HRs: Jack Parks, Natchez, 22
Wins: Bob Upton, Clarksdale, 21
SOs: Eddie Albrecht, Pine Bluff, 195
ERA: Labe Dean, Greenwood, 1.34

C Florida International League
President: Wayne Allen

Standings	W	L	Pct.	GB	Attend.	Manager
Havana Cubans (8)	97	57	.630	—	205,967	Oscar Rodriguez
Tampa Smokers	84	67	.556	11½	101,257	Joe Abreu/Jack Russell
Lakeland Pilots	82	72	.532	15	57,752	Bill Perrin/Charles Aleno
St. Petersburg Saints	78	73	.517	17½	137,947	Lou Finney
Miami Tourists	75	78	.490	21½	107,268	Howard Ermisch/Bill Perrin
West Palm Beach Indians	70	83	.458	26½	73,443	Rudy Laskowski/ Michael Schemer
Miami Beach Flamingos	69	82	.457	26½	78,742	Harry Chozen/Sindo Valle
Ft. Lauderdale Braves	55	98	.359	41½	58,588	Walter Kopp/Ted Madjeski/ Charles Miller

Playoffs: Havana 3 games, Lakeland 0; Tampa 3 games, St. Petersburg 2.
Finals: Havana 4 games, Tampa 3.

All-Star Team: 1B-Bernardo Fernandez, Tampa; **2B**-Francisco Gallardo, Havana; **3B**-

Howard Ermisch, Miami; **SS**-Gilberto Torres, Havana; **OF**-Louis Vezilich, Tampa; Antonio Zardon, Havana; Eddie Wayne, Miami Beach; **C**-Emilio Cabrera, Tampa; **Util**-George Biershenk, Lakeland; Perry Murphy, Tampa; **P**-Antonio Lorenzo, Havana; Harold Schacker, St. Petersburg; Connie Marrero, Havana; Leo Goicoechea, St. Petersburg; William Stanton, Miami; Harold Graham, Ft. Lauderdale; Octavio Rubert, Tampa.

BA: Louis Vezilich, Tampa, .356
Runs: Byron Bridgers, Miami, 119
Hits: Bryan Howell, Lakeland, 190
RBIs: Frederick Bell, St. Petersburg, 111

HRs: Bernardo Fernandez, Tampa, 28
Wins: Antonio Lorenzo, Havana, 23
SOs: Antonio Lorenzo, Havana, 275
ERA: Connie Marrero, Havana, 1.67

C Lone Star League
President: Fred Nicholson

Standings	W	L	Pct.	GB	Attend.	Manager
Kilgore Drillers	94	44	.681	—	67,255	Joe Kracher
Longview Texans (5)	89	50	.640	5½	65,033	Dixie Parsons
Tyler Trojans (12)	77	63	.550	18	67,101	James "Hack" Miller
Henderson Oilers (8)	69	70	.496	25½	48,116	Guy Sturdy/John Stone/Mel Hicks
Bryan Bombers	66	74	.471	29	43,513	Jess Landrum
Gladewater Bears	59	81	.421	36	48,056	Jimmy Dalrymple/Arthur Nelson
Marshall Tigers	55	83	.399	39	38,940	Harry Davis/Morris "Red" Jones
Lufkin Foresters	48	92	.343	47	46,037	Morris "Red" Jones/Stan Bartkowski/Fred Millican

Playoffs: Kilgore 4 games, Henderson 3; Longview 4 games, Tyler 3.
Finals: Kilgore 4 games, Longview 0.

All-Star Team: 1B-Stan Goletz, Bryan; **2B**-John Parino, Longview; **3B**-Al Kubski, Longview; **SS**-Robert Cullins, Gladewater; **OF**-Oscar Engel, Kilgore; John Stone, Henderson; Marshall Brown, Kilgore; **C**-Joe Kracher, Kilgore; **Util**-Reuther Jones, Tyler; Stan Bartkowski, Lufkin; James McCarnes, Longview; **P**-Ralph Pate, Longview; Jay Blomer, Henderson; **Manager**-Dixie Parsons, Longview; Joe Kracher, Kilgore.

BA: Joe Kracher, Kilgore, .433
Runs: Al Kubski, Longview, 140
Hits: Allen Cross, Kilgore, 193
RBIs: John Stone, Henderson, 146

HRs: John Stone, Henderson, 23
Wins: Ralph Pate, Longview, 23
SOs: Willis Chamness, Kilgore, 162
ERA: Otho Nitcholas, Tyler, 1.97

C Middle Atlantic League
President: Elmer M. Daily

Standings	W	L	Pct.	GB	Attend.	Manager
Vandergrift Pioneers (14)	86	39	.688	—	51,367	Floyd Patterson/Lew Krausse
Erie Sailors (13)	80	44	.645	5½	105,562	Don Ramsay
Uniontown Coal Barons (15)	77	49	.611	9½	82,147	Bill Mongiello
Johnstown Johnnies (10)	67	57	.540	18½	102,365	Roy Nichols
Butler Yankees (5)	61	64	.488	25	41,586	Jack Farmer
Oil City Refiners (2)	50	76	.397	36½	47,682	Ray Dahlstrom/Otto Denning
New Castle Chiefs	43	83	.341	43½	42,297	Robert Crow/Frank Pytlak/Carl Miller
Youngstown Colts	37	89	.294	49½	41,123	Bud Ott/Lewis Richardson

Playoffs: Vandergrift 3 games, Uniontown 1; Erie 3 games, Johnstown 1.
Finals: Erie 4 games, Vandergrift 1.

All-Star Team: 1B-Robert Mitchell, Johnstown; **2B**-George Gasdaska, Vandergrift; **3B**-Rocky Tedesco, Vandergrift; **OF**-Art Seguso, Butler; William Henry, Erie; William Hudacek, Uniontown; **C**-Lamar Dorton, Uniontown; **Util**-Charles Hood, Vandergrift; **P**-Hugh Oser, Erie; George Heller, Vandergrift; **Manager**-Don Ramsay, Erie.

BA: Art Seguso, Butler, .357
Runs: Robert Hill, Vandergrift, 120
Hits: Rocky Tedesco, Vandergrift, 178
RBIs: Art Seguso, Butler, 146

HRs: Earl Littenberger, Vandergrift, 26
Wins: George Heller, Vandergrift, 20
SOs: George Heller, Vandergrift, 161
ERA: Walter Cox, Erie, 2.71

C Northern League
President: Herman D. White

Standings	W	L	Pct.	GB	Attend.	Manager
Grand Forks Chiefs (5)	80	39	.672	—	71,139	Gordon Hinkle
St. Cloud Rox (13)	78	40	.661	1½	66,389	Charlie Fox
Eau Claire Bears (9)	66	55	.545	15	87,600	Andy Cohen
Aberdeen Pheasants (7)	64	59	.520	18	85,942	James Crandall
Duluth Dukes (16)	53	61	.465	24½	97,527	George "Red" Treadwell/Theodore Madjeski
Superior Blues (2)	54	67	.446	27	62,109	Johnny Mostil
Sioux Falls Canaries (11)	45	75	.375	35½	63,700	Jim Oglesby
Fargo-Moorhead Twins (15)	41	85	.325	42½	75,485	Bruno Haas/Ralph DiLullo

Playoffs: Grand Forks 3 games, Eau Claire 0; Aberdeen 3 games, St. Cloud 0.
Finals: Grand Forks 4 games, Aberdeen 0.

All-Star Team: 1B-Joe Patanelli, Superior; **2B**-Wally Reed, Grand Forks; **3B**-Elmer Schoendienst, Duluth; **SS**-Herman Rhodes, Superior; **OF**-Bill Polubiatka, Sioux Falls; Frank Marchie, Grand Forks; Cart Howerton, Aberdeen; Rance Pless, St. Cloud; **C**-Ray Katt, St. Cloud; Bernard Gerl, Duluth; **Util**-Herman Rhodes, Superior; **P**-Milton Goemer, Grand Forks; Bob Vogeltanz, Duluth; Jim Post, Aberdeen; **Manager**-Andy Cohen, Eau Claire.

BA: Frank McArthur, St. Cloud, .379
Runs: Ted Drakos, St. Cloud, 107
Hits: Frank McArthur, St. Cloud, 176
RBIs: Omer Tolson, Aberdeen, 106

HRs: Harry Hannebrink, Eau Claire, 16
William Schumm, Grand Forks, 16
Wins: Milton Goemer, Grand Forks, 25
SOs: Charles Henry, Eau Claire, 184
ERA: Milton Goemer, Grand Forks, 1.71

C Pioneer League
President: Jack P. Halliwell

Standings	W	L	Pct.	GB	Attend.	Manager
Pocatello Cardinals (16)	77	49	.611	—	88,193	Roland LeBlanc
Twin Falls Cowboys (5)	75	51	.595	2	111,467	Charlie Metro
Idaho Falls Russets (10)	73	53	.579	4	81,157	Jay Kirke, Jr./Lewis Garland
Ogden Reds (12)	61	65	.484	16	93,665	Horace "Pip" Koehler/Bobby Mattick
Salt Lake City Bees	60	65	.480	16½	143,411	Rupert "Tommy" Thompson
Boise Pilots	58	68	.460	19	82,269	Walter Lowe
Great Falls Electrics	51	75	.405	26	84,647	Rich Gyselman
Billings Mustangs	48	77	.384	28½	117,873	Charles Root

Playoffs: Pocatello 3 games, Idaho Falls 1; Twin Falls 3 games, Ogden 0.
Finals: Twin Falls 4 games, Pocatello 2.

All-Star Team: 1B-Ed Mickelson, Pocatello; **2B**-Gil McDougald, Twin Falls; **3B**-Reno Cheso, Salt Lake City; **SS**-Lester Barnes, Billings; **OF**-Albert Neal, Pocatello; Earl Silverthorn, Idaho Falls; Roy Keating, Great Falls; **C**-Hal Danielson, Twin Falls; **P**-William Franks, Boise; Ken Lehman, Idaho Falls; Dale Maycock, Twin Falls.

BA: Albert Neal, Pocatello, .390
Runs: Raymond Sowins, Pocatello, 154
Hits: Albert Neal, Pocatello, 202
RBIs: Albert Neal, Pocatello, 151
HRs: Albert Neal, Pocatello, 25

Wins: William Franks, Boise, 23
SOs: William Franks, Boise, 194
ERA: Melvin Waters, Idaho Falls, 3.15
Pct: Melvin Waters, Idaho Falls, .750, 21-7

C Sunset League
President: Leslie Powers

Standings	W	L	Pct.	GB	Attend.	Manager
Mexicali Aguilas	81	59	.579	—	68,567	Dominic Castro/Dick Wilson
Las Vegas Wranglers	78	62	.557	3	41,748	Ken Meyers
Reno Silver Sox (13)	77	63	.550	4	34,325	Thomas Lloyd
Riverside Rubes	74	66	.529	7	52,199	George Caster/Henry Bartolomei
El Centro Imperials	67	73	.479	14	42,221	Ray Viers
Anaheim/San Bernardino Valencias#	43	97	.307	38	21,760	Jerry Gardner/Bob Williams

#Anaheim (13-42) moved to San Bernardino June 25, first home game June 29.

Playoffs: Reno 3 games, Mexicali 0; Las Vegas 3 games, Riverside 1.
Finals: Reno 3 games, Las Vegas 2.

All-Star Team: 1B-Marty Krug, Las Vegas; **2B**-Henry Bartolomei, Riverside; **3B**-Frank Stinson, El Centro; **SS**-Bud Dawson, Las Vegas; **SS**-Morrie Serrano, Reno/Mexicali; **OF**-Don Jameson, Riverside; Robert Balcena, Mexicali; Marcial Garcia, Mexicali; **C**-Dick Wilson, Mexicali; **Util**-Gerald Waitman, Riverside; **P**-Elmer Corwin, Reno; Robert Schulte, Riverside; Erwin Coutts, Mexicali; **Manager**-Ken Meyers, Las Vegas; Dick Wilson, Mexicali.

BA: Robert Balcena, Mexicali, .369
Runs: Don Barclay, Reno, 171
Hits: Don Jameson, Riverside, 202
RBIs: Dick Wilson, Mexicali, 188

HRs: Dick Wilson, Mexicali, 42
Wins: Elmer Corwin, Reno, 26
SOs: Robert Schulte, Riverside, 276
ERA: Manuel Echeverria, Mexicali, 2.83

C West Texas-New Mexico League
President: Milton E. Price

Standings	W	L	Pct.	GB	Attend.	Manager
Albuquerque Dukes	88	52	.629	—	116,930	Herschel Martin
Amarillo Gold Sox	84	56	.600	4	102,313	Buck Fausett
Lubbock Hubbers	81	59	.579	7	102,445	Jackie Sullivan
Pampa Oilers	77	61	.558	10	71,677	Grover Seitz
Abilene Blue Sox (10)	62	78	.443	26	51,048	Art Bowland/Otis Davis
Clovis Pioneers	61	77	.442	26	48,736	John Bottarini/Clarence Novotney
Borger Gassers	60	78	.435	27	72,499	Edwin Carnett
Lamesa Lobos	44	96	.314	44	34,363	George Sturdivant/Tony Fiarito/Walter Buckel

Playoffs: Pampa 4 games, Albuquerque 2; Amarillo 4 games, Lubbock 2.
Finals: Amarillo 4 games, Pampa 1.

BA: Herschel Martin, Albuquerque, .425
Runs: Bob Crues, Amarillo, 185
Hits: Ron Bowen, Albuquerque, 234
RBIs: Bob Crues, Amarillo, 254
HRs: Bob Crues, Amarillo, 69
2B: Herschel Martin, Albuquerque, 61

TBs: Bob Crues, Amarillo, 479
Wins: Frank Shone, Albuquerque, 21
Joe Budny, Amarillo, 21
SOs: Frank Shone, Albuquerque, 223
ERA: Frank Shone, Albuquerque, 3.85
Pct: Royce Mills, Lubbock, .842, 16-3

C Western Association
President: Tom Fairweather

Standings	W	L	Pct.	GB	Attend.	Manager
St. Joseph Cardinals (16)	90	48	.652	—	129,230	Harold Olt
Ft. Smith Giants (13)	82	58	.586	9	66,720	Jack Aragon

	W	L	Pct.	GB	Attend.	Manager
Joplin Miners (5)	75	57	.568	12	72,006	John Sturm
Topeka Owls	70	66	.515	19	95,722	Winlow Johnson/Butch Nieman
Muskogee Reds (7)	61	70	.466	25½	62,472	Ray Baker
Leavenworth Braves (9)	62	75	.453	27½	40,639	Dutch Hoffman
Salina Blue Jays (14)	58	80	.420	32	41,850	Vance Dinges
Hutchinson/						
Springfield Cubs#(11)	43	87	.331	43	39,251	Frank Piet

#Hutchinson (25-52) moved to Springfield July 21, first home game July 27.

Playoffs: Topeka 3 games, Ft. Smith 1; St. Joseph 3 games, Joplin 2.
Finals: St. Joseph 4 games, Topeka 2.

All-Star Team: 1B-John Sturm, Joplin; **2B**-Jim Herbison, St. Joseph; **3B**-Guilford Dickens, Ft. Smith; **SS**-Bill Cope, Joplin; **OF**-Sid Langston, St. Joseph; Butch Nieman, Topeka; Roy Samson, Leavenworth; **C**-Del Crandall, Leavenworth; **P**-Bill Freese, Joplin; Jack Collum, St. Joseph; **Manager**-Harold Olt, St. Joseph.

BA: John Sturm, Joplin, .360
Runs: Butch Nieman, Topeka, 135
Hits: Harold Olt, St. Joseph, 171
RBIs: Butch Nieman, Topeka, 146
HRs: Butch Nieman, Topeka, 34
Wins: Jack Collum, St. Joseph, 24
SOs: Winlow Johnson, Topeka, 187
ERA: Jack Collum, St. Joseph, 2.47

D Alabama State League
President: Jack Hovater

Standings	W	L	Pct.	GB	Attend.	Manager
Troy Tigers (4)	83	41	.669	—	40,242	Bob Benish
Greenville Pirates (15)	80	46	.635	4	30,424	Walter Tauscher
Dothan Browns	64	62	.508	20	57,638	Holt "Cat" Milner
Ozark Eagles	61	65	.484	23	36,500	Frank Martin
Brewton Millers	58	68	.460	26	29,227	Joseph Beaugez/Bill McGhee
Enterprise Boll Weevils	57	67	.460	26	39,416	Dolly Lambert/Richard Bixby
Geneva Red Birds	54	72	.429	30	36,781	Harold Ferenbacher
Andalusia Arrows	45	81	.357	39	40,000	John George/Charles Wilcox

Playoffs: Dothan 4 games, Troy 2; Greenville 4 games, Ozark 3.
Finals: Dothan 4 games, Greenville 0.

BA: Bill McGhee, Brewton, .356
Runs: John Burns, Greenville, 108
Hits: Bill Godwin, Ozark, 157
RBIs: Glen Lindermuth, Greenville, 107
HRs: John Powell, Andalusia, 17
Wins: Frank Hill, Dothan, 22
SOs: Frank Hill, Dothan, 209
ERA: Richard Gilkerson, Troy, 1.69

D Appalachian League
President: Chauncey De Vault

Standings	W	L	Pct.	GB	Attend.	Manager
Pulaski Counts (10)	85	40	.680	—	46,405	George Pfister
Welch Miners (6)	70	53	.569	14	52,838	Elwood Wheaton
Bluefield Blue-Grays (9)	68	52	.567	14½	83,208	George Lacy
Johnson City Cardinals (16)	67	56	.545	17	51,846	Ted Garbee
Elizabethton Betsy Cubs (11)	64	61	.512	21	29,967	Adolph Matulis
Bristol Twins (13)	49	72	.405	34	46,397	Rufus Jackson/Dale Alexander
New River Rebels	48	76	.387	36½	26,655	Jack Crosswhite
Kingsport Cherokees (2)	42	83	.336	43	33,138	Russell "Red" Mincy/Phil DeMasi/John Russ

Playoffs: Pulaski 3 games, Johnson City 0; Bluefield 3 games, Welch 0.
Finals: Pulaski 4 games, Bluefield 1.

BA: Norm Postolese, Pulaski, .380
Runs: Norm Postolese, Pulaski, 154
Hits: Norm Postolese, Pulaski, 175
RBIs: Lawrence Pennell, Bluefield, 139
HRs: James Dickey, Johnson City, 22
Wins: Calvin Barnes, Welch, 20
SOs: Joe May, Pulaski, 205
ERA: Ted Garbee, Johnson City, 2.41

D Blue Ridge League
Presidents: Stanley F. Radke, Judge E.C. Bivins

Standings	W	L	Pct.	GB	Attend.	Manager
Galax Leafs	75	48	.610	—	24,985	Harold Kase
North Wilkesboro Flashers	72	54	.571	4½	36,575	Henry Loman
Radford Rockets	68	55	.553	7	23,845	Ray Rudisill
Mt. Airy Graniteers	65	58	.528	10	16,327	Noel Casbier
Wytheville Pioneers	47	74	.388	27	43,046	Mickey Weintraub/Frank Subb
Leaksville-Draper-Spray/						
Abingdon Triplets#	43	81	.347	32½	16,624	Bernard Loman/Joseph Santomauro

#Leaksville-Draper-Spray moved to Abingdon June 18.

Playoffs: Galax 3 games, Radford 0; Mt. Airy 3 games, North Wilkesboro 1.
Finals: Mt. Airy 4 games, Galax 3.

All-Star Team: 1B-Frank Subb, Wytheville; **2B**-Henry Loman, North Wilkesboro; **3B**-Doug Shores, North Wilkesboro; **SS**-Joe Tagliarino, North Wilkesboro; **OF**-Clifton Haywood, Radford; Kenneth Howard, North Wilkesboro; Richard Stockton, Wytheville; **C**-Michael Brelich, North Wilkesboro; Allen Yearick, Mt. Airy; **P**-Eurice "Pete" Treece, Mt. Airy; John Moore, Radford; Lawrence Wilson, Radford; Joseph Santomauro, Leaksville-Draper-Spray/Abingdon; Samuel Gibson, North Wilkesboro; Amado Diaz, Wytheville; **Manager**-Ray Rudisill, Radford.

BA: Noel Casbier, Mt. Airy, .378
Runs: Clifton Haywood, Radford, 109
Hits: Clifton Haywood, Radford, 175
RBIs: Jasper Holt, Mt. Airy, 100
HRs: Bill Akins, Mt. Airy, 13
Wins: Cecil Warren, Galax, 21
SOs: John Moore, Radford, 193
ERA: George Greene, Leaksville-Spray-Draper/Abingdon, 1.56

D Coastal Plain League
President: Ray Goodmon

Standings	W	L	Pct.	GB	Attend.	Manager
Tarboro Tars	87	53	.621	—	67,767	Bull Hamons
Kinston Eagles	80	59	.576	6½	76,770	Steve Collins
Goldsboro Goldbugs	79	61	.564	8	81,499	Bill Herring
Rocky Mount Leafs	78	61	.561	8½	94,811	Cecil "Turkey" Tyson
New Bern Bears	69	70	.496	17½	69,548	Harry Soufas/Tal Abernathy/Winston Palmer
Wilson Tobs	61	79	.436	26	95,238	Max Wilson/Irv Dickens/Bob Latshaw
Roanoke Rapids Jays	54	86	.386	33	87,187	Stuart Martin
Greenville Greenies	50	89	.360	36½	60,938	Bill Phebus/Bob Cohen/Kelly Kee

Playoffs: Tarboro 4 games, Rocky Mount 2; Kinston 4 games, Goldsboro 3.
Finals: Tarboro 4 games, Kinston 1.

All-Star Team: 1B-Jack Hussey, Goldsboro; **2B**-Steve Collins, Kinston; **3B**-Pete Peters, Kinston; **SS**-Ken Andrews, Tarboro; **OF**-John Hanley, Rocky Mount; Ray Komanecky, Tarboro; Clyde Whitener, Goldsboro; **C**-Dave Fowler, Rocky Mount; **Util**-Ralph Caldwell, Tarboro; **P**-Bill See, Tarboro; Harry Helmer, Rocky Mount; **Manager**-Bill Herring, Goldsboro; Bull Hamons, Tarboro.

BA: Valentine Gonzalez, Roanoke Rapids, .383
Runs: Grover Fowler, Rocky Mount, 138
Hits: Quentin Martin, Rocky Mount, 207
RBIs: Ray Komanecky, Tarboro, 137
HRs: John Hanley, Rocky Mount, 35
Wins: Horace "Red" Benton, Rocky Mount, 28
SOs: Harry Helmer, Rocky Mount, 268
ERA: Bill Herring, Goldsboro, 2.60

D Eastern Shore League
President: Dallas Culver

Standings	W	L	Pct.	GB	Attend.	Manager
Salisbury Cardinals (16)	89	32	.736	—	59,164	Gene Corbett
Milford Red Sox (1)	81	43	.653	9½	21,947	Clay Sheedy
Easton Yankees (5)	71	50	.587	18	37,780	Dallas Warren
Cambridge Dodgers (10)	65	61	.516	26½	31,737	Bob Vickery/Stewart Hofferth
Rehoboth Beach Pirates (15)	60	65	.480	31	21,845	Doug Peden
Seaford Eagles (13)	56	70	.444	35½	31,850	Bob Westfall/Harry Seibold
Federalsburg A's (6)	49	76	.392	42	22,901	Bob "Ducky" Detweiler
Dover Phillies (14)	26	100	.206	65½	10,079	Guy Glaser/Grover Wearshing

Playoffs: Teams played a round-robin series: Cambridge (4-2), Milford (4-3), Easton (3-4), and Salisbury (2-4).
Finals: Milford 4 games, Cambridge 1.

All-Star Team: 1B-Norm Zauchin, Milford; **2B**-Donald Davis, Salisbury; **3B**-Miguel Rivers, Salisbury; **SS**-Bob Koppenhauer, Salisbury; **OF**-Ray Jablonski, Milford; Donald Maxa, Easton; Crawford Davidson, Easton; **C**-Stewart Hofferth, Cambridge; **Util**-Bob "Ducky" Detweiler, Federalsburg; **P**-Ed Black, Salisbury; Paul Perry, Milford; **Manager**-Gene Corbett, Salisbury.

BA: Donald Maxa, Easton, .382
Runs: Norm Zauchin, Milford, 126
Hits: Ray Jablonski, Milford, 172
RBIs: Norm Zauchin, Milford, 138
HRs: Norm Zauchin, Milford, 33
Wins: John Andre, Seaford, 21
SOs: John Andre, Seaford, 228
ERA: Ed Black, Salisbury, 2.23

D Evangeline League
President: J. Walter Morris

Standings	W	L	Pct.	GB	Attend.	Manager
Houma Indians	81	55	.596	—	96,744	George Washburn
Hammond Berries	79	58	.577	2½	62,346	Paul Bruno
Thibodaux Giants	75	62	.547	6½	90,158	Sidney Gautreaux
Baton Rouge Red Sticks (14)	72	65	.526	9½	116,939	Richard Carter
New Iberia Pelicans (15)	70	69	.504	12½	72,658	George Stumpf
Alexandria Aces	68	70	.493	14	127,178	Art Phelan/Chester Juckno
Abbeville Athletics	53	82	.393	27½	53,873	Dick Burkhardt/Billy Cox/Morris Jones/Joe Winfield
Lafayette Bulls	49	86	.363	31½	63,258	Harry Strohm

Playoffs: Houma 1 game, Baton Rouge 1; Hammond 2 games, Thibodaux 2, both series cancelled due to bad weather.

BA: Roy "Tex" Sanner, Houma, .386
Runs: Robert Batten, Baton Rouge, 128
Hits: Bobby Greene, Alexandria, 193
RBIs: Roy "Tex" Sanner, Houma, 126
HRs: Roy "Tex" Sanner, Houma, 34
Wins: Paul Bruno, Hammond, 22
SOs: Eugene Thompson, Houma, 259
ERA: James Bradshaw, Baton Rouge, 2.37
Pct: Roy "Tex" Sanner, Houma, .913, 21-2

D Far West League
President: Jerry Donovan

Standings	W	L	Pct.	GB	Attend.	Manager
Oroville Red Sox (1)	67	51	.568	—	13,350	Nino Bongiovanni
Medford Dodgers (10)	66	56	.541	3	29,811	Larry Shepard
Klamath Falls Gems (14)	67	58	.536	3½	36,828	Joe Gantenbein
Santa Rosa Pirates (15)	63	59	.516	6	20,880	Dan Reagan
Willows Cardinals (16)	62	63	.496	8½	21,314	James Tyack/Bill Krueger
Redding Browns (7)	61	62	.496	8½	36,164	Ray Perry
Marysville Braves (9)	59	63	.484	10	20,741	Edward Wheeler/
						James Keller/Spencer Harris
Pittsburg/						
Roseville Diamonds#(13)	38	71	.349	24½	11,054	Gus Suhr/Arnold Rose/
						Bill Shewey

#Pittsburg (31-48) moved to Roseville July 30, first home game August 5.

Playoffs: Klamath Falls 3 games, Oroville 1; Santa Rosa 3 games, Medford 1.
Finals: Santa Rosa 4 games, Klamath Falls 3.

BA: Ray Perry, Redding, .411
Runs: Don Taylor, Medford, 139
Hits: Ray Perry, Redding, 179
RBIs: Ray Perry, Redding, 163
HRs: Ray Perry, Redding, 36
Wins: Larry Shepard, Medford, 22
SOs: Jules Hudson, Oroville, 237
ERA: Ronald Lee, Medford, 2.53

D Florida State League
President: A.S. Herlong

Standings	W	L	Pct.	GB	Attend.	Manager
Orlando Senators (8)	90	50	.643	—	61,509	Lou Bevil
Daytona Beach Islanders	85	53	.616	4	70,119	Sam Demma
Gainesville G-Men	77	63	.550	13	79,241	Myril Hoag
Sanford Giants (13)	74	64	.536	15	49,341	Hal Gruber
St. Augustine Saints (11)	71	69	.507	19	53,866	Don Anderson/John Sebastian
Leesburg Pirates (15)	60	77	.438	28½	38,335	Edgar Leip
DeLand Red Hats	50	90	.357	40	37,871	Joseph Vitter/David Bride
Palatka Azaleas	48	89	.350	40½	33,085	Ray Ryan/Charles Bowles/
						Ben Geraghty

Playoffs: Sanford 3 games, Orlando 1; Daytona Beach 3 games, Gainesville 1.
Finals: Daytona Beach 4 games, Sanford 2.

All-Star Team: 1B-Ray Rosenkranz, Sanford; **2B**-Charles Heinbaugh, Orlando; **3B**-Robert Ruker, Daytona Beach; **SS**-John Sebastian, St. Augustine; **OF**-John Garrison, Orlando; Joe Zander, Daytona Beach; Alvin Pirtle, Gainesville; **C**-John Toncoff, Daytona Beach; **Util**-Buddy Lake, Sanford; **P**-Elvin Stabelfeld, Daytona Beach; Myril Hoag, Gainesville; Don Coker, Gainesville; Ralph Woolford, Leesburg; **Manager**-Hal Gruber, Sanford.

BA: Charles Heinbaugh, Orlando, .338
Runs: Charles Heinbaugh, Orlando, 129
Hits: Charles Heinbaugh, Orlando, 182
RBIs: John Garrison, Orlando, 133
HRs: Ralph Bartolozzi, Leesburg, 17
Wins: Elvin Stabelfeld, Daytona Beach, 28
SOs: Joe Cleary, Gainesville, 257
ERA: Myril Hoag, Gainesville, 1.32

D Georgia State League
President: Joseph W. Matt, Jr.

Standings	W	L	Pct.	GB	Attend.	Manager
Sparta Saints	81	37	.686	—	27,191	Woodrow Bottoms
Baxley Red Sox	66	54	.550	16	24,901	Bud Metheny
Fitzgerald Pioneers	65	55	.542	17	44,877	Bill Good
Eastman Dodgers	58	61	.487	23½	43,891	Charles Farrar/John Pare
Vidalia-Lyons Twins	54	66	.446	28	31,580	Merritt Cain/Truman Connell
Douglas Rebels	34	85	.292	47½	34,709	Bill Barnes/John Humphries/
						Emil Ray

Playoffs: Sparta 3 games, Eastman 2; Fitzgerald 3 games, Baxley 1.
Finals: Fitzgerald 4 games, Sparta 3.

BA: Woodrow Bottoms, Sparta, .375
Runs: Charles Ridgeway, Fitzgerald, 106
Hits: Truman Connell, Vidalia-Lyons, 146
RBIs: Alan Swygert, Sparta, 88
HRs: Truman Connell, Vidalia-Lyons, 11
Wins: Paul Brock, Sparta, 21
SOs: Paul Brock, Sparta, 270
ERA: Jim Harden, Eastman, 1.36

D Georgia-Alabama League
President: Arthur R. Decatur

Standings	W	L	Pct.	GB	Attend.	Manager
Valley Rebels (1)	75	51	.595	—	60,163	Jesse Danna
Carrollton Hornets	73	53	.579	2	53,000	Charles Roberts/Oliver Hill
Newnan Brownies	68	58	.540	7	65,257	Norman Veazey
Alexander City Millers	63	63	.500	12	44,053	Ben Catchings/
						Marvin Chappell/
						Luther Gunnells
Opelika Owls	62	64	.492	13	59,000	Luther Gunnells/James Ball
Griffin Pimientos (7)	55	71	.437	20	63,672	Adel White/Paul Campbell
La Grange Troupers (5)	54	72	.429	21	53,589	James Acton
Tallassee Indians (16)	54	72	.429	21	34,696	Hugh East/Robert Comiskey

Playoffs: Valley 3 games, Newnan 1; Carrollton 3 games, Alexander City 2.
Finals: Valley 4 games, Carrollton 0.

BA: Fred Campbell, Griffin, .357
Runs: Robert Edwards, Valley, 114
Hits: George Bailey, Opelika, 174
RBIs: Fred Campbell, Griffin, 105
HRs: James Acton, La Grange, 14
Wins: William Kallaher, Opelika, 23
Eugene Doerflinger, Carrollton, 23
SOs: Eugene Doerflinger, Carrollton, 233
ERA: Leon Lindsey, Alexander City, 2.00

D Georgia-Florida League
President: W.T. Anderson

Standings	W	L	Pct.	GB	Attend.	Manager
Waycross Bears	85	55	.607	—	65,397	Mickey Katkaveck
Valdosta Dodgers (10)	81	58	.583	3½	71,507	Lou Rochelli
Albany Cardinals (16)	71	69	.507	14	61,971	Bob Stanton
Tallahassee Pirates (15)	70	69	.504	14½	63,625	Jack Rothrock
Moultrie Athletics (6)	69	71	.493	16	48,962	Joe Antolick
Thomasville Tigers (4)	68	71	.489	16½	54,894	Bob Engle
Cordele Indians (3)	64	76	.457	21	40,946	Hal Lee
Americus Phillies (14)	50	89	.360	34½	34,333	LeGrant Scott/Eddie Murphy

Playoffs: Waycross 3 games, Tallahassee 1; Albany 3 games, Valdosta 1.
Finals: Waycross 4 games, Albany 0.

All-Star Team: 1B-Robert Tripp, Americus; **2B**-Howard Henkel, Thomasville; **3B**-Santo Luberto, Valdosta; **SS**-Charles Brewster, Waycross; **OF**-Rocco Ippolito, Moultrie; Frank Thomas, Tallahassee; Joe Kwiatkowski, Valdosta; Norris Strickland, Cordele; **C**-Robert Attaway, Albany; Orville Stammen, Valdosta; **Util**-Donald Gross, Waycross; **P**-Ernest Funk, Thomasville; Donald Stephens, Albany; Raymond Seidel, Waycross; George Yebernetsky, Tallahassee; **Manager**-Mickey Katkaveck, Waycross.

BA: Joe Kwiatkowski, Valdosta, .371
Runs: George Fisher, Waycross, 123
Hits: Howard Henkel, Thomasville, 189
RBIs: Frank Thomas, Tallahassee, 132
HRs: Ken Rhyne, Moultrie, 27
Wins: Raymond Seidel, Waycross, 23
SOs: Donald Stephens, Albany, 221
ERA: Donald Stephens, Albany, 2.27

D Illinois State League
President: Howard V. Millard

Standings	W	L	Pct.	GB	Attend.	Manager
West Frankfort Cardinals (16)	85	35	.708	—	36,656	Harold Contini
Mattoon Indians (3)	75	44	.630	9½	34,754	Chuck Hawley
Marion Indians	53	66	.445	31½	13,697	Melvin Ivy
Mt. Vernon Braves (9)	52	66	.441	32	11,364	Frank Crespi
Belleville Stags (7)	51	67	.432	33	6,085	Gerald Nemitz/Shan Deniston
Centralia Cubs (11)	41	79	.342	44	18,211	Willard Sellergren/
						Claude Passeau

Playoffs: West Frankfort 3 games, Marion 1; Mattoon 3 games, Mt. Vernon 2.
Finals: West Frankfort 3 games, Mattoon 0.

BA: Richard Martz, Marion, .361
Runs: William Broukal, Mattoon, 103
Hits: Don Hazelton, Mt. Vernon, 150
RBIs: Frank Porreca, West Frankfort, 94
HRs: Paul Deters, Marion, 8
Wins: Floyd Melliere, West Frankfort, 21
SOs: Mike Blyzka, Belleville, 192
ERA: Floyd Melliere, West Frankfort, 1.77

D Kansas-Oklahoma-Missouri League
President: E.L. Dale

Standings	W	L	Pct.	GB	Attend.	Manager
Ponca City Dodgers (10)	79	47	.627	—	78,305	Boyd Bartley
Independence Yankees (5)	74	46	.617	2	46,270	Frank Howard/
						Burleigh Grimes/Bones Sanders
Bartlesville Pirates (15)	71	52	.577	6½	64,090	Edward Marleau
Pittsburg Browns (7)	60	60	.500	16	53,743	Shan Deniston/Donald Smith
Miami Owls	58	66	.468	20	33,716	Arthur Priebe/James Hansen
Carthage Cardinals (16)	51	67	.432	24	36,525	Alvin Kluttz
Iola Indians	51	72	.415	26½	42,770	Al Reitz
Chanute Giants (13)	44	78	.361	33	32,561	Alfred Smith

Playoffs: Pittsburg 3 games, Ponca City 2; Independence 3 games, Bartlesville 2.
Finals: Independence 4 games, Pittsburg 1.

All-Star Team: 1B-Henry Wlodarczyk, Carthage; **2B**-Jim Finigan, Independence; **3B**-Leroy Haines, Bartlesville; **SS**-Merle Hughes, Pittsburg; **OF**-Charles Stumborg, Pittsburg; Al Solenberger, Bartlesville; Skip Baas, Pittsburg; **C**-Leon Irwin, Ponca City; Ray Haley, Independence; **Util**-Nick Ananias, Independence; **P**-Joseph Tufteland, Ponca City; Bill Pierro, Bartlesville; Nicholas Najjar, Bartlesville; Bill Buck, Carthage; **Manager**-Bones Sanders, Independence; Boyd Bartley, Ponca City.

BA: William Fox, Chanute, .327
Runs: Louis Godla, Bartlesville, 83
Hits: Al Solenberger, Bartlesville, 134
RBIs: Charles Stumborg, Pittsburg, 78
HRs: Charles Stumborg, Pittsburg, 13
Joseph Beran, Ponca City, 13
Wins: Harland Coffman, Independence, 18
Louis Michels, Independence, 18
Joseph Tufteland, Ponca City, 18
SOs: Bill Pierro, Bartlesville, 300
ERA: Harland Coffman, Independence, 1.94

D Kitty League
President: Shelby Peace

Standings	W	L	Pct.	GB	Attend.	Manager
Hopkinsville Hoppers	85	41	.675	—	49,102	Vito Tamulis
Union City Greyhounds (3)	79	46	.632	5½	57,830	Tony Rensa

1948

	W	L	Pct.	GB	Attend.	Manager
Owensboro Oilers (9)	74	50	.597	10	83,452	Rex Carr
Madisonville Miners (2)	67	55	.549	16	47,245	George Mathauser/ Conrad Juelke/Robert Balance
Fulton Chicks (8)	57	68	.456	27½	28,049	Fred Biggs/Bud Burns/ Ivan Kuester
Clarksville Colts	49	77	.389	36	28,651	Horace Lisenbee/ Stanley Andrews
Cairo Egyptians (10)	44	81	.352	40½	22,226	Hugh Holliday/Norbert Hall
Mayfield Clothiers (7)	43	80	.350	40½	34,772	Michael Sertich/Ken Jungels/ Pete Peterson

Playoffs: Madisonville 3 games, Hopkinsville 2; Union City 3 games, Owensboro 2.
Finals: Union City 4 games, Madisonville 0.

BA: Lester Severin, Cairo, .381
Runs: John Kall, Hopkinsville, 139
Hits: Lester Severin, Cairo, 181
RBIs: Bud Hutson, Union City, 129
HRs: John Kall, Hopkinsville, 23
Wins: Clarence Neuman, Union City, 18
SOs: Donald Schmudlach, Madisonville, 237
ERA: Vito Tamulis, Hopkinsville, 2.32

D Longhorn League
President: Howard Green

Standings	W	L	Pct.	GB	Attend.	Manager
Big Spring Broncs (8)	84	53	.613	—	59,503	Pat Stasey
Odessa Oilers	81	58	.583	4	61,193	Bill Davis/Merle Coleman
Midland Indians	79	60	.568	6	51,865	Harold Webb
Vernon Dusters	76	64	.543	9½	50,250	Lloyd Rigby
Ballinger Cats (12)	68	71	.489	17	34,413	Bill Atwood
Sweetwater Sports	64	76	.457	21½	35,425	Clarence Gann
San Angelo Colts	63	77	.450	22½	29,145	Pepper Martin/Alvin Leedy
Del Rio Cowboys	42	98	.300	43½	13,425	John Zanet/Bill Lacy/ Sam Harshaney

Playoffs: Vernon 4 games, Big Spring 2; Midland 4 games, Odessa 0.
Finals: Midland 4 games, Vernon 3.

All-Star Team: 1B-Cotton McCaskey, Vernon; **2B-**Lupo Gonzales, Vernon; **3B-**Leon Brinkopf, Odessa; **SS-**Clyde Perry, Midland; **OF-**Roberto Fernandez, Big Spring; George Caloia, Del Rio; Pat Stasey, Big Spring; **C-**Morris Cowser, Vernon; **Util-**Kenneth Peacock, Sweetwater; Stuart Williams, Ballinger; **P-**Jimmy Perez, Big Spring; Gerald Fahr, Vernon.

BA: Pat Stasey, Big Spring, .389
Runs: Wilfred Rheingans, Odessa, 134
Hits: Roberto Fernandez, Big Spring, 203
RBIs: Kenneth Peacock, Sweetwater, 162
HRs: Kenneth Peacock, Sweetwater, 34
Wins: Edward Jacome, Vernon, 22
SOs: William Gann, Sweetwater, 207
ERA: Gerald Fahr, Vernon, 1.96

D Mountain States League
President: Virgil Q. Wacks

Standings	W	L	Pct.	GB	Attend.	Manager
Morristown Red Sox	70	46	.603	—	37,744	James Grigg
Oak Ridge/Hazard Bombers#	65	43	.602	4	22,533	Hobe Brummitt
Pennington Gap Miners	59	54	.522	9½	14,988	Joseph Santomauro/ Buford Rhea
Newport Canners	58	59	.496	12½	30,054	Michael Bala/Cy Whaley
Harlan Smokies	56	63	.471	15½	46,187	Bill Sisler/Frank Wilson/ Michael Goda
Jenkins Cavaliers	35	78	.310	33½	23,276	Ray Russell/Jackson Bell/ Brent Mays

#Oak Ridge (24-11) moved to Hazard June 10, first home game June 12.

Playoffs: Morristown 3 games, Newport 2; Hazard 3 games, Pennington Gap 0.
Finals: Morristown 3 games, Hazard 2.

All-Star Team: 1B-Jacob Stirn, Morristown; **2B-**Alberto Costa, Morristown; **3B-**Ned Cooper, Pennington Gap; **3B-**Clarence Peace, Harlan; **SS-**Robert Grose, Pennington Gap; **OF-**Bill Halstead, Pennington Gap; Sam Hancock, Jenkins; George Sifft, Newport; Ralph Painter, Harlan; **C-**James Grigg, Morristown; **P-**Porter Witt, Morristown; Richard Clark, Newport; Brenton Mays, Jenkins; Charles McGee, Pennington Gap; Frank Wilson, Harlan; Walter Wenclewicz, Harlan.

BA: Cy Whaley, Newport, .382
Runs: Eduardo DeHogues, Morristown, 109
Hits: Eduardo DeHogues, Morristown, 145
RBIs: Jacob Stirn, Morristown, 101
HRs: Jacob Stirn, Morristown, 12
Eduardo DeHogues, Morristown, 12
Wins: Richard Clark, Newport, 20
SOs: Dennis Reeder, Oak Ridge/Hazard, 196
ERA: Dennis Reeder, Oak Ridge/Hazard, 2.20

D North Atlantic League
President: Ernest C. Landgraf

Standings	W	L	Pct.	GB	Attend.	Manager
Peekskill Highlanders (7)	84	49	.632	—	42,023	Al Gardella
Carbondale Pioneers (14)	80	49	.620	2	83,485	Dan Carnevale
Bloomingdale Troopers (3)	77	52	.597	5	23,355	Jim Jefferis/Stephen Kuk
Mahanoy City Brewers	79	54	.594	5	53,052	Clarence "Buck" Etchison
Stroudsburg Poconos	72	59	.550	11	51,919	Frank Radler
Nazareth Barons	52	72	.419	27½	22,985	Bill Burich
Nyack Rockies	46	82	.359	35½	22,048	Roland Sabatini/Robert Davis
Lansdale Dukes	28	101	.217	54	14,100	Lawrence Glick/William Leary/ Whitey Mellor

Playoffs: Peekskill 4 games, Bloomingdale 3; Carbondale 4 games, Mahanoy City 3.
Finals: Carbondale 4 games, Peekskill 0.

BA: Dan Carnevale, Carbondale, .380
Runs: Martin Todd, Peekskill, 140
Hits: Martin Todd, Peekskill, 176
RBIs: Peter Benanta, Mahanoy City, 117
HRs: Dan Carnevale, Carbondale, 20
Wins: Frank Radler, Stroudsburg, 20
SOs: Frank Radler, Stroudsburg, 201
ERA: Frank Radler, Stroudsburg, 2.18

D North Carolina State League
President: R.A. Collier

Standings	W	L	Pct.	GB	Attend.	Manager
High Point- Thomasville Hi-Toms (9)	67	43	.609	—	100,227	Jim Gruzdis
Statesville Owls	63	47	.573	4	68,832	Tuck McWilliams
Hickory Rebels (13)	61	49	.555	6	43,998	Sam Bell
Lexington Indians (6)	59	50	.541	7½	48,829	Homer Lee Cox
Mooresville Moors	57	52	.523	9½	33,569	Norman Small
Salisbury Pirates (15)	51	53	.490	13	48,462	Arthur Doll
Concord Weavers	44	62	.415	21	26,146	Jim Mills
Albemarle Rockets	32	78	.291	35	28,025	Stanley Brown/James Miller/ George Motto

Playoffs: Hickory 4 games, High Point-Thomasville 3; Statesville 4 games, Lexington 1.
Finals: Statesville 4 games, Hickory 3.

All-Star Team: 1B-George Edwards, Statesville; **2B-**Charles Raeshe, Statesville; **3B-**Eddie Walczak, Mooresville; **SS-**Brooks Harrington, Mooresville; **OF-**Ross Morrow, Mooresville; Otis Stephens, Hickory; Cecil Lawing, Statesville; **C-**Red Lane, Statesville; Tom Hackett, Hickory; **Util-**John Lybrand, Hi-Toms; Owen Linn, Hickory; **P-**William Miller, Statesville; Frank Smith, Statesville; Charlie Cudd, Concord; Jim Hopper, Mooresville.

BA: Jim Gruzdis, Hi-Toms, .388
Runs: Owen Linn, Hickory, 107
Hits: Henry Hampton, Lexington, 175
RBIs: Norman Small, Mooresville, 130
HRs: Norman Small, Mooresville, 33
Harold Harrigan, Salisbury, 33
Wins: Alfred Jarlett, Hi-Toms, 27
SOs: William Miller, Statesville, 249
ERA: Plaskie McCree, Lexington, 2.82

D Ohio-Indiana League
President: Frank M. Colley

Standings	W	L	Pct.	GB	Attend.	Manager
Zanesville Dodgers (10)	82	57	.590	—	64,594	Ray Hathaway
Portsmouth A's (6)	82	58	.586	½	73,533	George Staller
Muncie Reds (12)	80	59	.576	2	50,925	Mike Blazo
Springfield Giants (13)	66	74	.471	16½	67,558	Robert Roth/Rufus Jackson
Newark Yankees (5)	65	74	.468	17	70,604	Robert Dill/Sol Mishkin
Richmond Braves (9)	64	75	.460	18	58,039	Ollie Byers
Marion Cubs (11)	62	78	.443	20½	60,009	Lou Bekeza/Francis Kristie
Lima Terriers (2)	57	83	.407	25½	45,952	Charles Engle

Playoffs: Zanesville 4 games, Springfield 0; Muncie 4 games, Portsmouth 0.
Finals: Zanesville 4 games, Muncie 2.

All-Star Team: 1B-John Pulcini, Zanesville; **2B-**Frank Major, Portsmouth; **3B-**Bob Ford, Muncie; **SS-**Joe Eshoo, Newark; **OF-**George Staller, Portsmouth; Ray Berns, Springfield; Carl Raucher, Lima; **C-**Rudy Antonetz, Zanesville; Bob Nieman, Muncie; Dan Mathews, Springfield; **Util-**Carl Hosler, Springfield; Robert Huddleston, Lima; **P-**Ray Trava, Muncie; Joe Greco, Springfield; Lawrence Miller, Muncie; Ray Hathaway, Zanesville; Nicholas Alivojvodic, Marion; **Manager-**Mike Blazo, Muncie; Ollie Byers, Richmond.

BA: Bob Nieman, Muncie, .367
Runs: Robert Huddleston, Lima, 144
Hits: Bob Nieman, Muncie, 186
RBIs: Bob Nieman, Muncie, 131
HRs: Bob Nieman, Muncie, 23
Wins: Ray Hathaway, Zanesville, 23
SOs: Nick Alivojvodic, Marion, 255
ERA: Ray Hathaway, Zanesville, 2.82

D PONY League
President: Vincent M. McNamara

Standings	W	L	Pct.	GB	Attend.	Manager
Lockport Reds (12)	76	50	.603	—	63,889	Cecil Scheffel
Jamestown Falcons (4)	74	52	.587	2	84,928	Marvin Olson
Hamilton Red Birds (16)	73	52	.584	2½	122,725	George Kissell
Bradford Blue Wings (14)	66	61	.520	10½	50,159	George Savino
Batavia Clippers (3)	65	62	.512	11½	55,438	George Susce
Wellsville Red Sox (1)	60	64	.484	15	45,853	Tom Carey
Olean Oilers (10)	60	66	.476	16	41,363	George Scherger
Hornell Maple Leafs	29	96	.232	46½	40,282	Russell Kerns

Playoffs: Bradford defeated Batavia 10-0 in a one game playoff for fourth place. Lockport 4 games, Bradford 2; Jamestown 4 games, Hamilton 1.
Finals: Lockport 4 games, Jamestown 1.

BA: Pat Haggerty, Jamestown, .369
Runs: Howard Gutshall, Jamestown, 111
Hits: Howard Gutshall, Jamestown, 171
RBIs: Howard Gutshall, Jamestown, 108
HRs: Joe Fromuth, Wellsville, 18
Wins: Robert Christophel, Lockport, 25
SOs: Gerald Kleinsmith, Jamestown, 258
ERA: Charles McCombie, Hamilton, 2.42
Pct: Richard England, Bradford, .789, 15-4

D Sooner State League
President: Jack Mealey

Standings	W	L	Pct.	GB	Attend.	Manager
McAlester Rockets (5)	91	47	.659	—	63,060	Vern Hoscheit
Lawton Giants (13)	77	59	.566	13	33,861	Lou Brower
Seminole Oilers (2)	75	62	.547	15½	40,053	Hugh Willingham
Chickasha Chiefs	73	63	.537	17	35,640	Ray Honeycutt
Ada Herefords (7)	63	76	.453	28½	27,050	Ucal Clanton
Ardmore Indians (3)	60	78	.435	31	37,944	Donald Smith/Jim Cooke
Pauls Valley Raiders	56	81	.409	34½	27,071	Dutch Prather/Jinx Poindexter
Duncan Cementers	54	83	.394	36½	27,066	Jess Welch/Otto Utt

Playoffs: McAlester 3 games, Chickasha 1; Seminole 3 games, Lawton 2.
Finals: Seminole 4 games, McAlester 2.

All-Star Team: 1B-Cromer Smotherman, McAlester; **2B**-Al Billingsley, McAlester; **3B**-Thomas Marino, Lawton; **SS**-Bob Hyatt, Pauls Valley; **OF**-Howard Martin, McAlester; Gene Creekmore, Seminole; Howard Weeks, Lawton; **C**-Vern Hoscheit, McAlester; Alva Blackaby, Chickasha; **Util**-Frisco Roberts, Duncan; **P**-Victor Stryska, Chickasha; Kenneth Skidmore, Seminole; **Manager**-Vern Hoscheit, McAlester.

BA: Cromer Smotherman, McAlester, .347
Runs: Bob Hyatt, Pauls Valley, 122
Hits: Al Billingsley, McAlester, 190
RBIs: Howard Martin, McAlester, 122
HRs: Howard Martin, McAlester, 19
Wins: Bob Giddings, Lawton, 25
SOs: Tom Kruta, Ardmore, 186
ERA: Buddy Yount, McAlester, 2.11
Pct: Buddy Yount, McAlester, .944, 17-1

D Tobacco State League
President: Arthur T. Moore

Standings	W	L	Pct.	GB	Attend.	Manager
Sanford Spinners	80	56	.588	—	29,374	Zeb Harrington
Wilmington Pirates	76	62	.551	5	77,842	Jim Staton
Red Springs Red Robins (6)	75	62	.547	5½	28,410	Red Norris
Smithfield-Selma Leafs	73	65	.529	8	36,552	Sam Narron/Virgil Payne
Warsaw Red Sox	71	67	.514	10	32,482	Sam Gibson/Verne Blackwell
Clinton Blues (4)	70	67	.511	10½	39,498	Marvin Lorenz
Lumberton Cubs (11)	55	81	.404	25	38,772	Charlie Jamin
Dunn-Erwin Twins	49	89	.355	32	26,475	Carl McQuillen/Babe Bost/Gaither Riley

Playoffs: Sanford 4 games, Smithfield-Selma 1; Red Springs 4 games, Wilmington 3.
Finals: Red Springs 4 games, Sanford 1.

All-Star Team: 1B-Joe Mangini, Red Springs; **2B**-Edward Hardisky, Wilmington; **3B**-Curtis Lowry, Clinton; **SS**-Robert Keane, Sanford; **OF**-Tom Clayton, Red Springs; William Benton, Wilmington; Orville Nesselrode, Sanford; **C**-Bruce Hedrick, Sanford; **Util**-Virgil Payne, Smithfield-Selma; Andrew Scrobola, Warsaw; **P**-John Cheshire, Wilmington; John McFadden, Sanford; **Manager**-Red Norris, Red Springs.

BA: Hargrove Davis, Wilmington, .366
Runs: James Wilson, Sanford, 145
Hits: James Wilson, Sanford, 212
RBIs: Orville Nesselrode, Sanford, 159
HRs: Orville Nesselrode, Sanford, 27
Wins: Aaron Osofsky, Smithfield-Selma, 24
SOs: John Cheshire, Wilmington, 258
ERA: John Cheshire, Wilmington, 2.35

D Virginia League
President: Robert S. Brenaman

Standings	W	L	Pct.	GB	Attend.	Manager
Suffolk Goobers	83	52	.615	—	60,873	Bill Steinecke
Blackstone Barristers (5)	78	62	.557	7½	37,632	Paul Badgett
Franklin Cubs	76	64	.543	9½	54,687	John Zontini
Petersburg Generals	73	62	.541	10	116,062	Paul Varner
Emporia Nationals (8)	63	74	.460	21	33,415	Morris "Smut" Aderholt
Lawrenceville Cardinals (16)	39	98	.285	45	21,104	Robert Comiskey/George Shearin/John Pruett

Playoffs: Petersburg 4 games, Suffolk 2; Blackstone 4 games, Franklin 0.
Finals: Blackstone 4 games, Petersburg 3.

All-Star Team: 1B-Vern Shetler, Franklin; **2B**-Paul Badgett, Blackstone; **3B**-Art Jacobs, Franklin; **SS**-Paul Varner, Petersburg; **OF**-Morris "Smut" Aderholt, Emporia; John Zontini, Franklin; Joe Pendleton, Emporia; **C**-Gordon Knisely, Franklin; William Horne, Emporia; **P**-Al Tefft, Blackstone; George Blair, Petersburg; Cecil Hutson, Suffolk.

BA: Morris "Smut" Aderholt, Emporia, .394
Runs: Art Jacobs, Franklin, 147
Hits: Morris "Smut" Aderholt, Emporia, 185
RBIs: Vern Shetler, Franklin, 150
HRs: Morris "Smut" Aderholt, Emporia, 31
Wins: Cecil Hutson, Suffolk, 23
George Blair, Petersburg, 23
SOs: George Blair, Petersburg, 212
ERA: Al Tefft, Blackstone, 1.57
Pct: Al Tefft, Blackstone, .952, 20-1

D Western Carolina League
President: John H. Moss

Standings	W	L	Pct.	GB	Attend.	Manager
Lincolnton Cardinals	69	41	.627	—	39,954	Fred Withers/Russell "Red" Mincy
Newton-Conover Twins	67	43	.609	2	57,465	Edwin Yount
Morganton Aggies	54	53	.505	13½	65,791	Les McGarity/Homer Daugherty/Wayne Stewart/Boger McGimsey
Forest City Owls	55	56	.495	14½	48,845	Jess Hill/Gene Hollifield
Shelby Farmers	54	55	.495	14½	49,613	Rube Wilson
Marion Marauders	49	54	.476	16½	47,234	Wes Ferrell
Lenoir Red Sox	49	61	.445	20	38,710	Jack McLain/Claude Jonnard
Hendersonville Skylarks	36	70	.340	31	35,768	Charles Munday

Playoffs: Shelby refused to play off the fourth place tie and it was awarded to Forest City. Lincolnton 4 games, Morganton 2; Newton-Conover 4 games, Forest City 2.
Finals: Lincolnton 4 games, Newton-Conover 3.

All-Star Team: 1B-Roger McKee, Shelby; **2B**-Harold Holt, Marion; **3B**-Robert Featherstone, Lenoir; **SS**-Harry Hendershot, Hendersonville; **OF**-Carl Schardt, Lenoir; Leonard Morrison, Shelby; Wes Ferrell, Marion; **C**-Edwin Yount, Newton-Conover; Fred Parnell, Morganton; **Util**-Bealus Smalley, Forest City; Ray Yow, Marion; **P**-Ray Lindsey, Newton-Conover; Myron Bourdette, Shelby; William Haynes, Forest City; Boger McGimsey, Morganton; Leland Jaynes, Morganton; **Manager**-Rube Wilson, Shelby.

BA: Wes Ferrell, Marion, .425
Runs: Edwin Yount, Newton-Conover, 139
Hits: Edwin Yount, Newton-Conover, 169
RBIs: Edwin Yount, Newton-Conover, 140
HRs: Edwin Yount, Newton-Conover, 43
Wins: Ray Lindsey, Newton-Conover, 21
SOs: Ray Lindsey, Newton-Conover, 255
ERA: Boger McGimsey, Morganton, 2.76

D Wisconsin State League
President: Judge Arold F. Murphy

Standings	W	L	Pct.	GB	Attend.	Manager
Sheboygan Indians (10)	85	40	.680	—	59,199	Joe Hauser
Wisconsin Rapids White Sox (2)	75	51	.595	10½	81,128	Frank Parenti/Frank Demaree/Johnny Kerr
Wausau Lumberjacks (7)	71	55	.563	14½	87,143	Joe Skurski
Fond du Lac Panthers (5)	68	57	.544	17	94,665	Fred Collins
Green Bay Bluejays (3)	57	68	.456	28	64,862	Roxie Lawson/Walter Laskowski/Joe Dotlich
Oshkosh Giants (13)	51	74	.408	34	64,625	Ray Lucas
Appleton Papermakers (14)	48	77	.384	37	69,971	Whitey Gluchoski
Janesville Cubs (11)	46	79	.368	39	31,985	Frank Kristie/Lou Bekeza

All-Star Team: 1B-Fred Collins, Fond du Lac; **2B**-Len Heinbigner, Oshkosh; **3B**-Robert Kurtz, Wausau; **SS**-Ralph Loschen, Sheboygan; **OF**-Charles Huwer, Green Bay; Earl "Jug" Girard, Green Bay; Walt Moryn, Sheboygan; **C**-Jim Schymanski, Wisconsin Rapids; Arnold Fischer, Green Bay; **P**-Lowell Grosskopf, Sheboygan; Bill Fischer, Wisconsin Rapids; Edward Lubanski, Wausau; Bill Allen, Sheboygan; Dean Wall, Janesville; **Manager**-Johnny Kerr, Wisconsin Rapids.

BA: Eugene Thomas, Wisconsin Rapids, .360
Runs: Walt Moryn, Sheboygan, 138
Hits: Joe Barracato, Sheboygan, 167
RBIs: Robert Kurtz, Wausau, 132
HRs: Fred Collins, Fond du Lac, 32
Wins: Lowell Grosskopf, Sheboygan, 23
Edward Lubanski, Wausau, 23
SOs: Lowell Grosskopf, Sheboygan, 236
ERA: Ted Shandor, Wisconsin Rapids, 2.62

Ind Mexican League
President: Jorge Pasquel

Standings	W	L	Pct.	GB	Manager
Monterrey Industriales	50	35	.588	—	Lazaro Salazar
Puebla Angeles	47	38	.553	3	Napoleon Reyes
Mexico City Diablos Rojos	44	44	.500	7½	Manuel Arroyo
Veracruz Azules	43	43	.500	7½	Dolf Luque
Tampico Alijadores#	34	33	.507	NA	Jose Luis Gomez
San Luis Potosi Tuneros#	21	46	.312	NA	Hector Leal/Rene Monteagudo/Julio Rojo

#Tampico and San Luis Potosi disbanded.

BA: Ray Dandridge, Veracruz, .369
Hits: Ray Dandridge, Veracruz, 136
RBIs: Roberto Ortiz, Mexico City, 74
HRs: Roberto Ortiz, Mexico City, 19
Wins: Alejandro Carrasquel, Monterrey, 18
SOs: Agapito Mayor, Mexico City, 92
ERA: Guillermo Lopez, Puebla, 2.37

Ind Provincial League
President: Albert Molini

Standings	W	L	Pct.	GB	Manager
Sherbrooke Athletiques	61	37	.622	—	Gene Oliver/Roland Gladu
St. Jean Braves	56	44	.560	6	
St. Hyacinthe Saints	54	46	.540	8	Paul Martin
Granby Red Sox	48	50	.490	13	Armand Proulx
Drummondville Cubs	39	58	.402	21½	
Farnham Pirates	36	59	.379	23½	

BA: Connie Creedon, St. Hyacinthe, .406
Hits: Roland Gladu, Sherbrooke, 116
RBIs: Eugene Nance, St. Hyacinthe, 98
HRs: Buzz Clarkson, St. Jean, 29
Wins: Jean-Pierre Roy, St. Jean, 19

1948 Interleague Post Season Play

World Series
Cleveland (American) 4 games, Boston (National) 2

Junior World Series
Montreal (International) 4 games, St. Paul (American Association) 1
Total Attendance: 54,933

Dixie Series
Birmingham (Southern Association) 4 games, Ft. Worth (Texas) 1
Total Attendance: 56,245

Southeastern Championship
Waycross (Georgia-Florida) 4 games, Daytona Beach (Florida State) 0

Class C Championship of Texas
Amarillo (West Texas-New Mexico) 4 games, Kilgore (Lone Star) 2

1948 Major League Farm Systems

American League

1 Boston (13): Louisville, Birmingham, Scranton, Lynn, Roanoke, El Paso, Auburn, San Jose, Oneonta, Milford, Oroville, Valley, Wellsville.
2 Chicago (13): Hollywood, Memphis, Muskegon, Fall River, Waterloo, Hot Springs, Oil City, Superior, Kingsport, Madisonville, Lima, Seminole, Wisconsin Rapids.
3 Cleveland (18): Baltimore, Oklahoma City, Dayton, Wilkes-Barre, Harrisburg, Meridian, Spartanburg, Tucson, Bakersfield, Pittsfield, Burlington (IA), Cordele, Mattoon, Union City, Bloomingdale, Batavia, Ardmore, Green Bay.
4 Detroit (12): Buffalo, Seattle, Little Rock, Flint, Williamsport, Hagerstown, Rome, Durham, Troy, Thomasville GA, Jamestown, Clinton (NC).
5 New York (24): Kansas City, Newark (NJ), Beaumont, Binghamton, Augusta, Manchester, Norfolk, Quincy, Victoria, Bisbee-Douglas, Ventura, Amsterdam, Longview, Butler, Grand Forks, Twin Falls, Joplin, Easton, La Grange, Independence, Newark (OH), McAlester, Blackstone, Fond du Lac.
6 Philadelphia (10): Savannah, Lincoln, Martinsville, Moline/Kewanee, Welch, Federalsburg, Moultrie, Lexington, Portsmouth (OH), Red Springs.
7 St. Louis (20): Toledo, San Antonio, Elmira, Wichita Falls, Port Chester, Springfield (IL), Globe-Miami, Modesto, Gloversville-Johnstown, Hannibal, Aberdeen, Muskogee, Redding, Griffin, Belleville, Pittsburg (KS), Mayfield, Peekskill, Ada, Wausau.
8 Washington (11): Chattanooga, Sherman-Denison, Bridgeport, Gadsden, Charlotte, Havana, Henderson, Orlando, Fulton, Big Spring, Emporia.

National League

9 Boston (14): Milwaukee, Hartford, Pawtucket, Jackson, Evansville, Kingston (ONT), Eau Claire, Leavenworth, Bluefield, Marysville, Mt. Vernon, Owensboro, High Point-Thomasville, Richmond (IN).
10 Brooklyn (26): St. Paul, Montreal, Mobile, Ft. Worth, Greenville (SC), Pueblo, Lancaster, Nashua, Newport News, Danville (IL), Asheville, Santa Barbara, Trois Rivieres, Greenwood, Johnstown (PA), Idaho Falls, Abilene, Cambridge, Medford, Valdosta, Ponca City, Cairo, Zanesville, Olean, Sheboygan.
11 Chicago (18): Los Angeles, Nashville, Macon, Des Moines, Springfield (MA), Selma, Decatur, Fayetteville, Visalia, Clinton (IA), Sioux Falls, Hutchinson/Springfield (MO), Elizabethton, St. Augustine, Centralia, Marion (OH), Lumberton, Janesville.
12 Cincinnati (10): Syracuse, Tulsa, Columbia, Sunbury, Rockford, Tyler, Ogden, Ballinger, Muncie, Lockport.
13 New York (22): Minneapolis, Jersey City, Jacksonville (FL), Sioux City, Trenton, Richmond (VA), Knoxville, Ogdensburg, Quebec, Erie, St. Cloud, Reno, Ft. Smith, Bristol, Seaford, Pittsburg (CA)/Roseville, Sanford (FL), Chanute, Hickory, Springfield (OH), Lawton, Oshkosh.
14 Philadelphia (15): Toronto, Utica, Wilmington (DE), Portland (ME), Terre Haute, Schenectady, Vandergrift, Salina, Dover, Baton Rouge, Klamath Falls, Americus, Carbondale, Bradford, Appleton.
15 Pittsburgh (19): Indianapolis, New Orleans, Fort Wayne, Albany (NY), Waco, York, Davenport, Anderson, Keokuk, Uniontown, Fargo-Moorhead, Greenville (AL), Rehoboth Beach, New Iberia, Santa Rosa, Leesburg, Tallahassee, Bartlesville, Salisbury (NC).
16 St. Louis (21): Columbus (OH), Rochester, Houston, Columbus (GA), Omaha, Allentown, Lynchburg, Fresno, Winston-Salem, Duluth, Pocatello, St. Joseph, Johnson City, Salisbury (MD), Willows, Tallasee, Albany (GA), West Frankfort, Carthage, Hamilton, Lawrenceville.

1948 No-Hitters

Date	Pitcher	Team	League	Opponent	Score
4-15	Donald Stephens	Albany	Georgia-Florida	Moultrie	10-0
5-1	Charley Hiden	Emporia	Virginia	Lawrenceville	13-0
5-1	Rex Benton	Martinsville	Carolina	Greensboro	5-1
5-3	John Porter	Bristol	Appalachian	Kingsport	6-0
5-5	Herb Hamilt	Marysville	Far West	Pittsburg	14-1
5-5	Garth Mann	Shreveport	Texas	Dallas	4-0 (6)
5-10	William Haynes	Forest City	Western Carolina	Lenoir	7-0
5-16	Dick "Kewpie" Barrett	Seattle	Pacific Coast	Sacramento	3-0 (P, 7)
5-17	Jim Lamay	Idaho Falls	Pioneer	Pocatello	6-0
5-24	Lou Kretlow	Williamsport	Eastern	Binghamton	12-1 (7)
5-28	Vic Johnson	Oklahoma City	Texas	Ft. Worth	4-0 (7)
6-2	Pete Giordano	Nashua	New England	Portland	1-0 (7)
6-8	George Bird	Bridgeport	Colonial	Stamford	1-0 (7)
6-10	Monte Kennedy	Minneapolis	American Assoc.	Louisville	14-0
6-15	Frank McVickers	Warsaw	Tobacco State	Smithfield-Selma	4-1
6-14	Oscar Judd	Toronto	International	Syracuse	7-0 (7)
6-18	Ernie Sawyer	New Bern	Coastal Plain	Rocky Mount	1-0 (11)
6-22	Eurice "Pete" Treece	Mt. Airy	Blue Ridge	Abingdon	5-0 (7)
6-23	Johnny Taylor	Tallassee	Georgia-Alabama	Alexander City	1-0 (11)
6-24	Charles Bowles	Palatka	Florida State	DeLand	3-0
6-29	Lowell Grosskopf	Sheboygan	Wisconsin State	Appleton	4-0 (7)
6-30	Bob Lemon	Cleveland	American	Detroit	2-0
7-2	Alex Kellner	Savannah	South Atlantic	Macon	1-0 (7)
7-4	Frank Totaro	Stockton	California	Visalia	18-0
7-4	Chuck Hagy	Springfield	Ohio-Indiana	Portsmouth	1-0 (7)
7-6	Hal Sontag/				
	Johnny Lopeman	Klamath Falls	Far West	Marysville	7-2
7-7	Dick Rozek	Wilkes-Barre	Eastern	Elmira	2-1
7-7	Dick Strahs	Hot Springs	Cotton States	Pine Bluff	2-0 (P)
7-13	Harvey Vice	Ada	Sooner State	Lawton	0-1
7-15	Lowell Grosskopf	Sheboygan	Wisconsin State	Green Bay	8-0 (7)
7-24	Buddy Lake	Sanford	Florida State	DeLand	6-0 (P)
7-25	Dan Bankhead	Nashua	New England	Springfield	13-1 (7)
7-31	Carl Kolosna	Portland	New England	Lynn	5-0 (7)
8-1	Buck Ross	Toledo	American Assoc.	Minneapolis	1-0 (7)
8-1	Dave Latter/				
	Tom Gorman	Binghamton	Eastern	Elmira	3-4 (7)
8-4	Walt Dixon	Florence	Tri-State	Anderson	2-1 (7)
8-6	Dan Bennett	Pulaski	Appalachian	Bristol	2-0 (7)
8-6	Marvin Rotblatt	Waterloo	Three-I	Terre Haute	3-2
8-6	Bill Kean	Zanesville	Ohio-Indiana	Portsmouth	4-0
8-7	Toby Tobias	Grand Forks	Northern	Eau Claire	1-0
8-7	Walter Wilson	Amsterdam	Canadian-American	Schenectady	1-0
8-12	Myril Hoag	Gainesville	Florida State	St. Augustine	3-0
8-14	Don Newcombe	Montreal	International	Toronto	8-0 (7)
8-16	Ed Black	Salisbury	Eastern Shore	Milford	4-0
8-16	Gene Kern	Cambridge	Eastern Shore	Federalsburg	12-0
8-16	Bill Revels	Carrollton	Georgia-Alabama	Valley	0-1 (7)
8-16	Bob Purkey	Greenville	Alabama State	Dothan	8-0
8-17	Toby Tobias	Grand Forks	Northern	Duluth	10-0
8-19	Ed Santuli	Rehoboth Beach	Eastern Shore	Federalsburg	10-0
8-21	Bob Hingst	Kingston	Border	Auburn	10-0
8-23	Joe Dolan	North Wilkesboro	Blue Ridge	Abingdon	8-0 (7)
8-23	Jim Brosnan	Fayetteville	Tri-State	Rock Hill	1-0 (7)
8-27	Hank Weaver	Hammond	Evangeline	New Iberia	6-0
8-28	Charles McCombie	Hamilton	PONY	Bradford	6-0
8-28	Aaron Osofsky	Smithfield-Selma	Tobacco State	Lumberton	1-0
8-31	Joe Payne	Dayton	Central	Saginaw	11-0
8-31	Lou Blackmore	Wellsville	PONY	Lockport	3-7 (11)
8-31	Gerald Kleinsmith	Jamestown	PONY	Hamilton	15-0
9-1	Bob Cruze	Thomasville	Georgia-Florida	Tallahassee	4-0 (7)
9-4	Ken Vangilder	St. Cloud	Northern	Superior	1-0 (10)
9-4	Cecil Warren	Galax	Blue Ridge	Abingdon	1-0
9-4	Hal Ensley	Muncie	Ohio-Indiana	Richmond	7-1
9-4	Frank Childs	Montgomery	Southeastern	Anniston	7-0 (PO)
9-8	Pat McGlothin	St. Paul	American Assoc.	Milwaukee	7-0
9-9	Rex Barney	Brooklyn	National	New York	2-0
9-16	Maury McDermott	Scranton	Eastern	Utica	8-0 (PO)
9-20	Billy Gates	Watertown	Border	Ogdensburg	0-1 (PO, 10)

Number in parentheses indicates innings if other than nine; "P" indicates perfect game; "PO" indicates playoff game.

THIS DATE IN MINOR LEAGUE HISTORY

February 17, 1948, Dale Lenn, catcher last season with Baltimore, International League, drowned in Clark Fork River, near Huron, Montana, when his boat overturned.

March 10, 1948, The 58th minor league to operate in 1948, the Georgia State League, was formally admitted to membership in the National Association by President George Trautman. The organization gave the National Association a total of 438 clubs.

April 6, 1948, Dick "Kewpie" Barrett of Seattle, Pacific Coast League, earned his 200th league victory. Barrett now had a record of 316 victories and 281 losses in Organized Ball in a career which began in 1925.

April 16, 1948, A record crowd of 21,812 at Ponce de Leon Park in Atlanta, Southern Association, attended the opener between the Crackers and Birmingham. Radio comedians Bud Abbott and Lou Costello staged a 15-minute skit at home plate before the game.

April 19, 1948, Stuart Martin, manager for Roanoke Rapids, Coastal Plain League, was sidelined for 60 days when struck in the head by a pitched ball in an exhibition game. The former Cardinal outfielder was hit with a ball thrown by Ed "Whitey" Ford, young southpaw with Norfolk of the Piedmont League.

April 27, 1948, Robin Roberts, who received $25,000 from the Phillies to sign a contract with Wilmington, Interstate League, following his graduation from Michigan State University, hurled a 19-1 win, striking out 17 Harrisburg batters. The game was the first for Roberts in Organized Ball.

April 28, 1948, Pete Gray, one-armed outfielder who played a wartime season with the St. Louis Browns, joined Elmira in the Eastern League after a year's absence from the game. Gray played semi-pro ball in 1947.

April 29, 1948, Outfielder Hank Savage of Griffin, Georgia-Alabama League, stole home twice in the Pimientos' nine-run eighth inning of their 16-4 win over Alexander City.

May 8, 1948, A game between Reno and Mexicali in Sunset League was postponed when the Silver Sox were stopped at the border and refused admittance. Immigration trouble was cleared up the next day and the series got underway.

May 11, 1948, Robert Osgood, a 19-year-old catcher with Marion, Ohio-Indiana League, died of a heart attack in Richmond, Indiana, after collapsing in the dugout during pre-game practice.

May 16, 1948, Pete Gray, one-armed outfielder who played with the Browns during the war, staged a comeback attempt with Elmira, the Browns' Eastern League farm club. Starting a game for the first time, Gray gave the Sunday crowd of 6,500 a show, getting two singles, twice stealing second, going from first to home on a double, and scoring the winning run. (He batted .290 for the 1948 season while appearing in 82 games.)

May 31, 1948, Fanning 25 batters and singling home the deciding run, Schenectady southpaw Tom Lasorda went the route against Amsterdam to win a 6-5, 15-inning Canadian-American League game.

June 1, 1948, Barney DeForge, pitcher-manager for Reidsville, Carolina League, and Ed Weingarten, official of Florence, Tri-State League, and Leaksville-Spray-Draper, Blue Ridge League, were barred from baseball for life on charges of bribery, gambling and game throwing. DeForge admitted issuing bases on balls in a relief role in order to assure defeat of his team by at least three runs and confirmed he received $300 from a gambler after the game. W.C. McWaters, a Clover, South Carolina, auto dealer, was also indicted later by a civil court. Weingarten died July 9, 1948.

June 8, 1948, Harold Hartung, 22-year-old third baseman signed to play with New Castle, Middle Atlantic League, suffered lacerations and a skull fracture from a fall from a third-story window at his home in Ravenna, Ohio. The youth crashed through his bedroom window and fell to the sidewalk. He apparently had been sleep walking, hospital officials said.

June 20, 1948, A new reason for postponing a game developed at Vernon, Texas, when the Del Rio-Vernon Longhorn League contest was called off because of travel fatigue.

June 24, 1948, Paul Murrell, 13-year-old Salisbury batboy, was ejected from an Eastern Shore League game for umpire heckling.

July 11, 1948, Edmonds Field, home of the Sacramento Solons, Pacific Coast League, was destroyed by fire, believed caused by a carelessly dropped cigarette. As a result of the disaster, the Solons finished the campaign on the road.

July 24, 1948, Five members of the Duluth, Northern League, club and the truck driver were killed and 13 players injured in a bus-truck crash near St. Paul.

August 1, 1948, The game at Asheville, North Carolina, was postponed and three other scheduled Tri-State League games were transferred to Charlotte due to the polio epidemic.

August 3, 1948, Billy Gates pulled an "iron man" performance for Watertown Border League as he started and completed both ends of a doubleheader against Kingston, winning 16-1 and 7-0 with 21 strikeouts in 16 innings.

August 11, 1948, Tony Freitas, 40-year-old lefthander with Sacramento, Pacific Coast League, notched his 220th PCL triumph, a 3-1 win over Dick "Kewpie" Barrett of Seattle, who had 211 wins in the league.

August 14, 1948, Henderson Park in the Lone Star League was destroyed by fire. In same loop, Tyler had lost its stands to a fire on the night of August 5.

August 20, 1948, Only 23 fans turned out on a rainy night to see Lansdale split a North Atlantic League doubleheader with Peekskill.

August 29, 1948, Ed Musial, first baseman with Stamford, Colonial League, and brother of the Cardinals' Stan Musial, made seven hits in nine trips in a doubleheader with Poughkeepsie, including going 5-for-5 in the nightcap and scoring five runs. In the first game Musial tallied from second base on a fly to centerfield and in the second contest stole home in the ninth inning.

August 29, 1948, After almost 50 years in Organized Ball, Charles H. Graham, president of the San Francisco Seals, died at age 70. Graham sold many stars to the Majors, including Lefty O'Doul, Lefty Gomez, Paul Waner, Earl Averill and many others. He had a brief trial with Red Sox as a catcher in 1906.

September 3, 1948, Al Tefft, Yankee farmhand with Blackstone, Virginia League, won his 20th straight game against only one defeat. Tefft lost his only game of the season in relief, 9-8 to Franklin on June 5, when a teammate committed an error. He was released as a third baseman in mid-May of this year by the Cardinals organization.

September 3, 1948, Denver set a Western League attendance record with a crowd of 12,752.

September 5, 1948, Outfielder Bob Crues of Amarillo, West Texas-New Mexico League, hit two home runs against Lubbock to give him 69 for the season, tying the all-time Organized Ball record set by Joe Hauser, Minneapolis, American Association, in 1933. With two games in which to break the record, Crues failed to connect for a circuit drive, but finished the season hitting .404 with 254 RBIs and an .848 slugging average. Crues broke into Organized Ball as a pitcher in 1939 and in 1940 went 20-5 for Lamesa and Borger. An arm injury cut short his hill career.

September 6, 1948, Forty-year-old Wes Ferrell, former A.L. pitcher who managed Marion of the Western Carolina League this season, won the circuit's batting championship with a lofty average of .425. Ferell, who hurled for Cleveland, Washington, Boston, and New York, collected 162 hits, including 24 homers, 14 triples, and 30 doubles in 381 times at bat and drove in 119 runs. He played in the outfield in most games.

September 8, 1948, Larry Gilbert, who managed New Orleans and Nashville in the Southern Association for 25 years and who won eight championships, announced his retirement as a pilot. Gilbert, one of the most widely-known men in the minor leagues, skippered six consecutive playoff titles for Nashville from 1939 through 1944.

September 10, 1948, Albert "Dutch" Mele, former Syracuse, International League, outfielder, was awarded $10,000 in a lawsuit against the F & M Schaffer Brewing Company of New York City, for negligence and improper bottling, following the explosion of a beer bottle last February 15 at his tavern in Oak Tree, New Jersey, resulting in a piece of glass piercing his left eye.

September 19, 1948, The Mexican League folded, five weeks ahead of schedule, as the season was to have run to October 24. Losses over a three-year period were put at 2,500,000 pesos.

October 14, 1948, Leonard "Lefty" Seamon, 22, who won 21 games and lost 4 for Ottawa of the Border League this year, died in an Ottawa hospital following a month-long confinement for the removal of a chest tumor.

October 21, 1948, Barney DeForge, former manager and pitcher of the Reidsville, Carolina League club, was sentenced to one year in prison in a Winston-Salem, North Carolina, Superior Court after pleading guilty to a charge of conspiracy and bribery in connection with a Carolina League game the past summer. Two Clover, South Carolina, used car dealers, W.C. McWaters and Tommy Phillips, were acquitted on the same charges. A fourth defendant, a former official of the Florence, Tri-State League, and Leaksville-Spray-Draper, Blue Ridge League clubs, had died last summer.

October 28, 1948, The Pascual family gave up control of the Mexican League.

November 28, 1948, The Venezuelan Winter League resumed play after a week's interruption because of a revolution.

November 30, 1948, The Negro National League, organized in 1920, dissolved after 29 years.

1949

American League
President: William Harridge

Standings	W	L	Pct.	GB	Attend.	Manager
New York Yankees............	97	57	.630	—	2,283,676	Casey Stengel
Boston Red Sox	96	58	.623	1	1,596,650	Joe McCarthy
Cleveland Indians	89	65	.578	8	2,233,771	Lou Boudreau
Detroit Tigers....................	87	67	.565	10	1,821,204	Red Rolfe
Philadelphia Athletics	81	73	.526	16	816,514	Connie Mack
Chicago White Sox	63	91	.409	34	937,151	Jack Onslow
St. Louis Browns	53	101	.344	44	270,936	Zack Taylor
Washington Senators	50	104	.325	47	770,745	Joe Kuhel

BA: George Kell, Detroit, .343
Runs: Ted Williams, Boston, 150
Hits: Dale Mitchell, Cleveland, 203
RBIs: Ted Williams, Boston, 159
Vern Stephens, Boston, 159

HRs: Ted Williams, Boston, 43
Wins: Mel Parnell, Boston, 25
SOs: Virgil Trucks, Detroit, 153
ERA: Mel Parnell, Boston, 2.77
Pct: Ellis Kinder, Boston, .793, 23-6

National League
President: Ford Frick

Standings	W	L	Pct.	GB	Attend.	Manager
Brooklyn Dodgers.............	97	57	.630	—	1,633,747	Burt Shotton
St. Louis Cardinals	96	58	.623	1	1,430,676	Eddie Dyer
Philadelphia Phillies	81	73	.526	16	819,698	Eddie Sawyer
Boston Braves....................	75	79	.487	22	1,081,795	Billy Southworth
New York Giants	73	81	.474	24	1,218,446	Leo Durocher
Pittsburgh Pirates	71	83	.461	26	1,449,435	Bill Meyer
Cincinnati Reds..................	62	92	.403	35	707,782	Bucky Walters/Luke Sewell
Chicago Cubs.....................	61	93	.396	36	1,143,139	Charlie Grimm/Frank Frisch

BA: Jackie Robinson, Brooklyn, .342
Runs: Pee Wee Reese, Brooklyn, 132
Hits: Stan Musial, St. Louis, 207
RBIs: Ralph Kiner, Pittsburgh, 127
HRs: Ralph Kiner, Pittsburgh, 54

Wins: Warren Spahn, Boston, 21
SOs: Warren Spahn, Boston, 151
ERA: Dave Koslo, New York, 2.50
Pct: Preacher Roe, Brooklyn, .714, 15-6

AAA American Association
President: Bruce Dudley

Standings	W	L	Pct.	GB	Attend.	Manager
St. Paul Saints (10)	93	60	.608	—	352,911	Walter Alston
Indianapolis Indians (15)...	93	61	.604	½	413,973	Al Lopez
Milwaukee Brewers (9)	76	76	.500	16½	266,061	Nick Cullop
Minneapolis Millers (13)....	74	78	.487	18½	247,637	Thomas Heath
Kansas City Blues (5).........	71	80	.470	21	216,754	Bill Skiff
Louisville Colonels (1).......	70	83	.458	23	227,758	Fred Walters/Mike Ryba
Columbus Red Birds (16)....	70	83	.458	23	170,464	Harold Anderson
Toledo Mud Hens (4)	64	90	.416	29½	103,712	Eddie Mayo

Playoffs: Milwaukee 4 games, St. Paul 3; Indianapolis 4 games, Minneapolis 3.
Finals: Indianapolis 4 games, Milwaukee 2.

All-Star Team: 1B-Joe Collins, Kansas City; **2B-**Hank Schenz, St. Paul; **3B-**Froilan Fernandez, Indianapolis; **SS-**Buddy Hicks, St. Paul; **OF-**Eric Tipton, St. Paul; Bill Howerton, Columbus; Tom Wright, Louisville; **C-**Ferrell Anderson, St. Paul; **P-**Mel Queen, Indianapolis; Harvey Haddix, Columbus; **MVP-**Froilan Fernandez, Indianapolis.

BA: Tom Wright, Louisville, .368
Runs: Jack Harshman, Minneapolis, 121
Hits: Roy Hartsfield, Milwaukee, 203
RBIs: Froilan Fernandez, Indianapolis, 128
HRs: Chuck Workman, Minneapolis, 41

Wins: Mel Queen, Indianapolis, 22
Phil Haugstad, St. Paul, 22
SOs: Mel Queen, Indianapolis, 178
ERA: Mel Queen, Indianapolis, 2.57

AAA International League
President: Frank J. Shaughnessy

Standings	W	L	Pct.	GB	Attend.	Manager
Buffalo Bisons (4)	90	64	.584	—	383,943	Paul Richards
Rochester Red Wings (16)..	85	67	.559	4	443,536	Johnny Keane
Montreal Royals (10)..........	84	70	.545	6	473,798	Clay Hopper
Jersey City Giants (13)	83	71	.539	7	174,314	Joseph Becker
Toronto Maple Leafs (14)...	80	72	.526	9	364,962	Del Bissonette
Syracuse Chiefs (12)..........	73	80	.477	16½	190,255	Jewel Ens
Baltimore Orioles (7)..........	63	91	.409	27	203,823	Alphonse "Tommy" Thomas/Jack Dunn III
Newark Bears (5)................	55	98	.359	34½	88,170	Buddy Hassett

Playoffs: Buffalo 4 games, Jersey City 1; Montreal 4 games, Rochester 0.
Finals: Montreal 4 games, Buffalo 1.

All-Star Team: 1B-Steve Bilko, Rochester; **2B-**Pete Pavlick, Jersey City; **3B-**Gene Markland, Buffalo; **SS-**Bobby Morgan, Montreal; **OF-**Russ Derry, Rochester; Sam Jethroe, Montreal; Ken Wood, Baltimore; **C-**John Bucha, Rochester; **P-**Al Widmar, Baltimore; Jocko Thompson, Toronto; **MVP-**Bobby Morgan, Montreal.

BA: Bobby Morgan, Montreal, .337
Runs: Sam Jethroe, Montreal, 154
Hits: Sam Jethroe, Montreal, 207
RBIs: Steve Bilko, Rochester, 125
HRs: Russ Derry, Rochester, 42

3B: Sam Jethroe, Montreal, 19
SBs: Sam Jethroe, Montreal, 89
Wins: Al Widmar, Baltimore, 22
SOs: Dan Bankhead, Montreal, 176
ERA: Bubba Church, Toronto, 2.35

AAA Pacific Coast League
President: Clarence H. Rowland

Standings	W	L	Pct.	GB	Attend.	Manager
Hollywood Stars (10)........	109	78	.583	—	502,445	Fred Haney
Oakland Oaks	104	83	.556	5	534,711	Chuck Dressen
Sacramento Solons	102	85	.545	7	447,556	Del Baker
San Diego Padres (3)	96	92	.510	13½	493,780	Bucky Harris
Seattle Rainiers	95	93	.508	14½	545,434	Jo Jo White/William Lawrence
Portland Beavers...............	85	102	.454	24	378,892	Bill Sweeney
San Francisco Seals	84	103	.449	25	447,022	Lefty O'Doul
Los Angeles Angels (11)....	74	113	.395	35	402,089	William Kelly

Playoffs: Hollywood 4 games, Sacramento 1; San Diego 4 games, Oakland 3.
Finals: Hollywood 4 games, San Diego 2.

All-Star Team: 1B-Chuck Stevens, Hollywood; **2B-**Gene Handley, Hollywood; **3B-**Jim Baxes, Hollywood; **SS-**Artie Wilson, San Diego/Oakland; **OF-**Clarence Maddern, Los Angeles; Irv Noren, Hollywood; Max West, San Diego; **C-**Bill Raimondi, Sacramento; **P-**Ken Holcombe, Sacramento; Roy Helser, Portland; **MVP-**Irv Noren, Hollywood.

BA: Artie Wilson, San Diego/Oakland, .348
Runs: Max West, San Diego, 166
Hits: Albert White, Sacramento, 244
RBIs: Max West, San Diego, 166
HRs: Max West, San Diego, 48
BBs: Max West, San Diego, 201

Wins: Harold Saltzman, Portland, 23
Guy Fletcher, Seattle, 23
George Woods, Hollywood, 23
SOs: Cornelius Dempsey, San Francisco, 164
ERA: Willard Ramsdell, Hollywood, 2.60

AA Southern Association
President: Charles A. Hurth

Standings	W	L	Pct.	GB	Attend.	Manager
Nashville Vols (11)............	95	57	.625	—	228,034	Rollie Hemsley
Birmingham Barons (1)......	91	62	.595	4½	421,305	Pinky Higgins
Mobile Bears (10)..............	82	69	.543	12½	152,117	Paul Chervinko
New Orleans Pelicans (15)..	77	75	.507	18	248,304	Hugh Luby
Atlanta Crackers	71	82	.464	24½	370,361	Cliff Dapper
Little Rock Travelers (4)	69	85	.448	27	153,812	Jack Saltzgaver
Memphis Chicks (2)	65	88	.425	30½	218,172	Alfred Todd
Chattanooga Lookouts (8)...	60	92	.395	35	155,468	George Myatt/Fred Walters

Playoffs: Nashville 4 games, New Orleans 2; Mobile 4 games, Birmingham 1.
Finals: Nashville 4 games, Mobile 2.

All-Star Team: 1B-Harold "Tookie" Gilbert, Nashville; **2B-**Dave Williams, Atlanta; **3B-**Fred Hatfield, Birmingham; **SS-**Russ Rose, Mobile; **OF-**Bob Borkowski, Nashville; Norman Koney, Birmingham; George Shuba, Mobile; **C-**Carl Sawatski, Nashville; **P-**Bill MacDonald, New Orleans; Pete Mallory, Nashville; Jim Davis, Birmingham.

BA: Bob Borkowski, Nashville, .376
Runs: Harold "Tookie" Gilbert, Nashville, 146
Hits: Harold "Tookie" Gilbert, Nashville, 197
RBIs: Carl Sawatski, Nashville, 153

HRs: Carl Sawatski, Nashville, 45
Wins: Pete Mallory, Nashville, 20
SOs: Bobo Newsom, Chattanooga, 141
ERA: Jim Suchecki, Birmingham, 2.77

AA Texas League
President: J. Alvin Gardner

Standings	W	L	Pct.	GB	Attend.	Manager
Ft. Worth Cats (10)..........	100	54	.649	—	265,982	Bobby Bragan
Tulsa Oilers (12)................	90	64	.584	10	221,176	Al Vincent
Oklahoma City Indians (3) .	81	72	.529	18½	287,858	Joe Vosmik
Shreveport Sports	80	74	.519	20	222,331	Francis "Salty" Parker
Dallas Eagles	76	77	.497	23½	404,851	James Adair/Bobby Goff
San Antonio Missions (7)...	70	83	.458	29½	225,500	Gus Mancuso
Houston Buffaloes (16)	60	91	.397	38½	263,965	Del Wilber
Beaumont Exporters (5)......	55	97	.362	44	116,264	Martin "Chick" Autry

Playoffs: Ft. Worth 4 games, Shreveport 1; Tulsa 4 games, Oklahoma City 2.
Finals: Tulsa 4 games, Ft. Worth 3.

All-Star Team: 1B-Herb Conyers, Oklahoma City; **2B-**Solly Hemus, Houston; **3B-**Bill Serena, Dallas; **SS-**Chico Carrasquel, Ft. Worth; **OF-**Milt Nielsen, Oklahoma City; Ben

*Won first-half   **Won second-half   ***Won both halves
Numbers after nicknames indicate farm system.
Affiliation listed at end of each year.

Guintini, Dallas; Russell Burns, Tulsa; **C**-Ray Murray, Oklahoma City; **P**-Joe Landrum, Ft. Worth; Albert Olsen, Oklahoma City; **MVP**-Herb Conyers, Oklahoma City; **Pitcher of the Year**-Joe Landrum, Ft. Worth.

BA: Herb Conyers, Oklahoma City, .355
Runs: Milt Nielsen, Oklahoma City, 139
Hits: Herb Conyers, Oklahoma City, 214
RBIs: Russell Burns, Tulsa, 153
HRs: Jerry Witte, Dallas, 50
Wins: Joe Landrum, Ft. Worth, 19
SOs: Dick Rozek, Oklahoma City, 145
ERA: Carl Erskine, Ft. Worth, 2.07

A Central League
President: T.J. Halligan

Standings	W	L	Pct.	GB	Attend.	Manager
Dayton Indians (3)	80	57	.584	—	103,519	Oscar Melillo
Flint Arrows (4)	77	62	.554	4	86,451	Jack Tighe
Grand Rapids Jets	70	66	.515	9½	62,982	Jack Knight
Charleston Senators (12)	67	68	.496	12	183,352	Joe Beggs
Muskegon Clippers (2)	60	79	.432	21	46,560	Red Ruffing
Saginaw Bears	58	80	.420	22½	74,934	Robert Finley

Playoffs: Charleston 3 games, Dayton 1; Grand Rapids 3 games, Flint 2.
Finals: Grand Rapids 4 games, Charleston 2.

All-Star Team: 1B-Sheriff Robinson, Grand Rapids; **2B**-Bob Ankrum, Dayton; **3B**-Oscar Khederian, Saginaw; **SS**-Clem Koshorek, Flint; **OF**-Stuart Locklin, Dayton; Bill Higdon, Muskegon; Conrad Juelke, Muskegon; **C**-Dee Moore, Saginaw; **P**-Charles Sipple, Dayton; Joe Nuxhall, Charleston.

BA: Bill Higdon, Muskegon, .330
Runs: Sheriff Robinson, Grand Rapids, 91
Hits: Stuart Locklin, Dayton, 169
RBIs: Ron Bowen, Saginaw, 123
HRs: Ron Bowen, Saginaw, 25
Wins: Charles Sipple, Dayton, 19
SOs: Jose Santiago, Dayton, 233
ERA: Ernie Funk, Flint, 2.13

A Eastern League
President: Thomas H. Richardson

Standings	W	L	Pct.	GB	Attend.	Manager
Albany Senators (15)	93	47	.664	—	198,256	Pinky May
Scranton Red Sox (1)	79	61	.564	14	131,875	Mike Ryba/Jack Burns
Wilkes-Barre Indians (3)	77	63	.550	16	112,566	Bill Norman
Binghamton Triplets (5)	70	70	.500	23	182,778	George Selkirk
Hartford Chiefs (9)	66	74	.471	27	138,306	Earle Brown/James "Rip" Collins
Williamsport Tigers (4)	66	74	.471	27	91,848	Gene Desautels
Elmira Pioneers (7)	58	82	.414	35	88,471	Donald Heffner/John Tobin/ Salvador Madrid
Utica Blue Sox (14)	51	89	.364	42	72,689	Pat Colgan

Playoffs: Wilkes-Barre 4 games, Albany 0; Binghamton 4 games, Scranton 0.
Finals: Binghamton 4 games, Wilkes-Barre 3.

All-Star Team: 1B-Henry Ertman, Hartford; **2B**-Bill Reed, Hartford; **3B**-Herschel Held, Albany; **SS**-Frank Staucet, Albany; **OF**-Ted DelGuercio, Scranton; Harry Simpson, Wilkes-Barre; Gus Bell, Albany; **C**-Frank Baldwin, Hartford; **P**-Orie Arntzen, Albany; Whitey Ford, Binghamton.

BA: Bill Reed, Hartford, .338
Runs: Harry Simpson, Wilkes-Barre, 125
Hits: Gus Bell, Albany, 174
RBIs: Harry Simpson, Wilkes-Barre, 120
HRs: Harry Simpson, Wilkes-Barre, 31
Wins: Orie Arntzen, Albany, 25
SOs: Bob Raney, Elmira, 191
ERA: Whitey Ford, Binghamton, 1.61

A South Atlantic League
President: Earl Blue

Standings	W	L	Pct.	GB	Attend.	Manager
Macon Peaches (11)	96	58	.623	—	212,416	Don Osborn
Savannah Indians (6)	84	68	.553	11	150,109	Frank Skaff
Greenville Spinners (10)	82	72	.532	14	104,505	Clay Bryant
Columbus Cardinals (16)	80	73	.523	15½	105,394	Kemp Wicker
Jacksonville Tars (13)	73	81	.474	23	110,007	Jack Aragon
Augusta Tigers (5)	69	83	.454	26	110,179	Alton Biggs/James Pruett
Charleston Rebels (2)	68	83	.450	26½	94,816	Herb Crompton/Albert Fisher
Columbia Reds (12)	59	93	.388	36	100,572	Gerald Walker

Playoffs: Macon 4 games, Columbus 3; Greenville 4 games, Savannah 3.
Finals: Macon 4 games, Greenville 1.

All-Star Team: 1B-Earl York, Columbia; **2B**-Cal Ermer, Savannah; **3B**-Fred Postolese, Greenville; **SS**-Roy Peterson, Macon; **OF**-Lou Colombo, Columbus; Bill Benton, Savannah; Bill Lutes, Jacksonville; **C**-Ray Cash, Macon; **P**-Robert Spicer, Macon; Ivan Johannes, Columbia.

BA: Bill Lutes, Jacksonville, .313
Runs: Gene Faszholz, Columbus, 109
Hits: Gene Faszholz, Columbus, 179
RBIs: Roy Peterson, Macon, 100
HRs: Ray Cash, Macon, 19
Wins: Jim Atchley, Macon, 20
Alfred Burch, Savannah, 20
Robert Spicer, Macon, 20
John Faszholz, Columbus, 20
SOs: Ray Moore, Greenville, 229
ERA: Sandy Silverstein, Savannah, 2.10
Pct: Alfred Burch, Savannah, .769, 20-6
Robert Spicer, Macon, .769, 20-6

A Western League
President: Senator Edwin C. Johnson

Standings	W	L	Pct.	GB	Attend.	Manager
Lincoln Athletics (6)	74	64	.536	—	149,159	James DeShong
Denver Bears (9)	71	68	.511	3½	463,039	Mike Gazella/William DeCarlo/ Earle Browne
Pueblo Dodgers (10)	71	68	.511	3½	138,726	Ray Hathaway
Des Moines Bruins (11)	70	70	.500	5	210,204	Stan Hack
Omaha Cardinals (16)	68	71	.489	6½	277,370	Cedric Durst
Sioux City Soos (13)	63	76	.453	11½	125,356	Don Ramsay

Playoffs: Denver defeated Pueblo 5-3 in a one game playoff for second place. Des Moines 3 games, Lincoln 1; Pueblo 3 games, Denver 1.
Finals: Pueblo 4 games, Des Moines 3.

All-Star Team: 1B-Lou Limmer, Lincoln; **2B**-Joe Torpey, Pueblo; **3B**-Stan Jok, Sioux City; **SS**-Bob Stewart, Lincoln; **OF**-Rocco Ippolito, Lincoln; Bob Jaderland, Denver; Vic Marasco, Pueblo; **C**-Walter Linden, Denver; **P**-Ernie Johnson, Denver; Ken Lehman, Pueblo.

BA: Vic Marasco, Pueblo, .330
Runs: James Williams, Pueblo, 126
Hits: Fred Richards, Des Moines, 178
RBIs: Vic Marasco, Pueblo, 121
HRs: Lou Limmer, Lincoln, 29
Wins: Elvin Stabelfeld, Des Moines, 17
Lynn Lovenguth, Lincoln, 17
Walter Cox, Sioux City, 17
SOs: Ken Lehman, Pueblo, 203
ERA: George Uhle, Denver, 2.25

B Big State League
President: J. Walter Morris

Standings	W	L	Pct.	GB	Attend.	Manager
Wichita Falls Spudders (7)	90	58	.608	—	128,400	Jack Bradsher
Texarkana Bears	86	61	.585	3½	96,522	George Archie
Austin Pioneers	86	62	.581	4	188,193	Henry "Prince" Oana
Waco Pirates (15)	76	72	.514	14	95,825	Buddy Hancken
Sherman-Denison Twins	70	78	.473	20	77,474	Lindsay Brown/Pete Appleton
Greenville Majors	66	82	.446	24	58,500	John "Red" Davis
Gainesville Owls	59	89	.399	31	66,544	Ray Taylor/Lon Goldstein
Temple Eagles	58	89	.395	31½	72,624	Barney White/Homer Peel

Playoffs: Waco 4 games, Wichita Falls 2; Texarkana 4 games, Austin 1.
Finals: Waco 4 games, Texarkana 1.

All-Star Team: 1B-George Archie, Texarkana; **2B**-Gerald McNair, Wichita Falls; **3B**-Cecil McClung, Wichita Falls; **SS**-Fred Campbell, Austin; **OF**-Frank Carswell, Texarkana; Dean Stafford, Sherman-Denison; Emery Hresko, Austin; **C**-Frank Saucier, Wichita Falls; **P**-Bill Pierro, Waco; Agapito Mayor, Sherman-Denison.

BA: Frank Saucier, Wichita Falls, .446
Runs: Al McCarty, Wichita Falls, 132
Hits: Frank Carswell, Texarkana, 229
RBIs: Frank Carswell, Texarkana, 145
HRs: Conklyn Meriwether, Greenville, 27
Wins: Elwood Moore, Austin, 20
Sidney Peterson, Wichita Falls, 20
George Estock, Austin, 20
SOs: Bill Pierro, Waco, 275
ERA: John Whitehead, Sherman-Denison, 2.73

B Carolina League
President: Glenn E. "Ted" Mann

Standings	W	L	Pct.	GB	Attend.	Manager
Danville Leafs	86	57	.601	—	84,471	Woody Fair
Winston-Salem Cardinals (16)	84	61	.579	3	153,110	Willie Duke/George Ferrell/ Rolland LeBlanc
Raleigh Capitals	76	68	.528	10½	94,348	Glen Lockamy/Charles Cronin
Burlington Bees	72	72	.500	14½	83,150	Buddy Bates/Herb Crompton
Greensboro Patriots	72	73	.497	15	147,501	Wes Ferrell/Fred Vaughn/ Buddy Bates
Durham Bulls (4)	70	72	.493	15½	118,356	Ace Parker
Reidsville Luckies	63	80	.441	23	76,114	John George/George Souter/ Harry Hatch/Cecil "Zip" Payne
Martinsville Athletics (6)	52	92	.361	34½	32,489	George Staller

Playoffs: Burlington 4 games, Danville 2; Raleigh 4 games, Winston-Salem 0.
Finals: Burlington 4 games, Raleigh 3.

All-Star Team: 1B-Leo "Muscle" Shoals, Reidsville; **2B**-Mike Hafenecker, Burlington; **3B**-Don Siegert, Raleigh; **SS**-Walter "Teapot" Frye, Winston-Salem; **OF**-Carl Linhart, Durham; Dick Sipek, Reidsville; William Brown, Danville; **C**-Hugh Taylor, Danville; **P**-Pete Angell, Danville; Mike Forline, Reidsville; Adam Twarkins, Danville; **MVP**-Leo "Muscle" Shoals, Reidsville; **Manager**-Ace Parker, Durham.

BA: William Brown, Danville, .361
Runs: Leo "Muscle" Shoals, Reidsville, 131
Hits: William Brown, Danville, 199
RBIs: Leo "Muscle" Shoals, Reidsville, 137
HRs: Leo "Muscle" Shoals, Reidsville, 55
Wins: Eddie Neville, Durham, 25
SOs: Adam Twarkins, Danville, 240
ERA: Adam Twarkins, Danville, 2.07

B Colonial League
President: John A. Scalzi, Jr.

Standings	W	L	Pct.	GB	Attend.	Manager
Bristol Owls	82	47	.636	—	62,485	Al Barillari/Joseph O'Connell
Stamford Pioneers	74	52	.587	6½	31,092	Joe Glenn/Herb Stein
Bridgeport Bees	73	54	.575	8	37,309	Ollie Ryers/James Paules/ Jimmie Foxx/Thomas Downey
Waterbury Timers	62	63	.496	18	39,857	Bert Shepard/Leo Eastham

| Poughkeepsie Chiefs | 45 | 78 | .366 | 34 | 25,123 | Woody Williams/ Elmer Weingartner/ Gabriel Mauro |
| Kingston Colonials | 39 | 81 | .325 | 38½ | 29,231 | Julius Laviano/Emil Gall |

Playoffs: Bristol 4 games, Waterbury 1; Bridgeport 4 games, Stamford 3.
Finals: Bristol 2 games, Bridgeport 1.

All-Star Team: 1B-Leo Eastham, Waterbury; **2B**-George Handy, Bridgeport; **3B**-Joseph O'Connell, Bristol; **SS**-Carlos Santiago, Stamford; **OF**-James Callahan, Stamford; Carlos Bernier, Bristol; Joe Koproski, Stamford; Don Perlmutter, Kingston; **C**-Roger LaFrance, Bristol; **P**-Edward Hrabcsak, Stamford; Hamilton Graham, Bridgeport; Joe Linskey, Bridgeport.

BA: Leo Eastham, Waterbury, .349
Runs: Carlos Bernier, Bristol, 136
Hits: George Handy, Bridgeport, 183
RBIs: James Callahan, Stamford, 107
James Paules, Bridgeport, 107
HRs: Leo Eastham, Waterbury, 26
SBs: Carlos Bernier, Bristol, 89
Wins: Emil Moscowitz, Stamford, 19
Phillip Frick, Bridgeport, 19
Edward Hrabcsak, Stamford, 19
SOs: Edward Hrabcsak, Stamford, 234
ERA: Emil Moscowitz, Stamford, 2.01

B Florida International League
President: Phil O'Connell

Standings	W	L	Pct.	GB	Attend.	Manager
Havana Cubanos (8)	95	57	.625	—	226,293	Oscar Rodriguez
Miami Sun Sox (10)	87	62	.584	6½	170,466	Pepper Martin
Miami Beach Flamingos	81	70	.536	13½	90,682	Joe Medwick
Tampa Smokers	81	72	.529	14½	105,949	Travis Jackson/Wes Ferrell
West Palm Beach Indians	74	78	.487	21	81,132	Lou Finney
Ft. Lauderdale Braves	65	88	.425	30½	66,544	Charles Aleno
St. Petersburg Saints (3)	62	86	.419	31	108,397	Myril Hoag/Harry Sullivan/ John Beazley/Dick Porter
Lakeland Pilots	60	92	.395	35	50,108	John Rizzo

Playoffs: Havana 3 games, Miami Beach 2; Tampa 3 games, Miami 1.
Finals: Tampa 4 games, Havana 0.

All-Star Team: 1B-Benny Fernandez, Tampa; **2B**-August Rose, Miami; **3B**-Gil Torres, Havana; **SS**-Manuel Hidalgo, Havana; **OF**-Bryan Howell, Lakeland; Charles Rotzell, Miami Beach; Dick Haviland, Miami; Michael Conroy, Miami Beach; **C**-Stan Andrews, West Palm Beach; **P**-Connie Marrero, Havana; Joe Murray, West Palm Beach.

BA: Michael Conroy, Miami Beach, .359
Runs: Carlos DeSouza, Tampa, 116
Hits: Ted Cieslak, Ft. Lauderdale, 196
RBIs: Art Rebel, Tampa, 115
HRs: Charles Aleno, Ft. Lauderdale, 31
Wins: Connie Marrero, Havana, 25
SOs: Connie Marrero, Havana, 167
ERA: Chet Covington, Tampa, 1.46

B Interstate League
President: Gerald P. Nugent

Standings	W	L	Pct.	GB	Attend.	Manager
Allentown Cardinals (16)	87	52	.626	—	100,788	Al Hollingsworth
Wilmington Blue Rocks (14)	75	62	.547	11	52,427	Jack Sanford
Harrisburg Senators (3)	74	64	.536	12½	80,896	Les Bell
Trenton Giants (13)	73	66	.525	14	67,604	Hugh Poland
Lancaster Red Roses (10)	71	68	.511	16	85,796	Al Campanis
York White Roses (15)	66	72	.478	20½	93,034	Frank Oceak
Sunbury Reds (12)	59	81	.421	28½	69,746	Joe Buzas
Hagerstown Owls (8)	49	89	.355	37½	34,762	Woody Wheaton

Playoffs: Harrisburg 4 games, Allentown 2; Trenton 4 games, Wilmington 2.
Finals: Trenton 4 games, Harrisburg 3.

All-Star Team: 1B-Harvey Zernia, Allentown; **2B**-Doug Hansen, Harrisburg; **3B**-Ray Rambin, Trenton; **SS**-Harry Malmberg, Harrisburg; **OF**-Jim Lemon, Harrisburg; Tom Westcott, Allentown; Bill Ripken, Lancaster; Larry Ciaffone, Allentown; **C**-Ed Oswald, Wilmington; **P**-John Brittin, Wilmington; Bob Hoch, Allentown.

BA: William Henry, Trenton, .333
Runs: Don Collins, Lancaster, 107
Hits: William Henry, Trenton, 178
RBIs: Maurice Cunningham, Trenton, 101
Jim Lemon, Harrisburg, 101
HRs: Jim Lemon, Harrisburg, 27
Wins: John Brittin, Wilmington, 21
SOs: George Dries, Allentown, 181
ERA: Don Robertson, Trenton, 1.90

B New England League
President: Claude B. Davidson

Standings	W	L	Pct.	GB	Attend.	Manager
Pawtucket Slaters**(9)	83	43	.659	—	68,767	James "Rip" Collins/ Dutch Dorman/Earle Browne
Nashua Dodgers*(10)	71	52	.577	10½	38,979	Greg Mulleavy
Portland Pilots (14)	66	57	.537	15½	83,100	Skeeter Newsome
Springfield Cubs (11)	57	64	.471	23½	102,387	Robert Peterson
Fall River Indians@(2)	27	42	.391	NA	18,191	Dick Porter
Manchester Yankees@(5)	28	44	.389	NA	30,391	Walter Berger
Lynn Tigers@(4)	29	47	.382	NA	12,882	Thomas Kennedy/Charles Webb
Providence Grays#	18	30	.375	NA	7,305	Frank Pytlak/Joseph Pullano

#Providence disbanded June 20.
@Manchester, Lynn and Fall River disbanded July 19.

Playoff: Springfield 2 games, Pawtucket 0.
Finals: Portland 4 games, Springfield 3.

All-Star Team: 1B-George Crowe, Pawtucket; **2B**-Joseph Mayer, Portland; **3B**-Walter Derucki, Portland; **SS**-Billy Hunter, Nashua; **OF**-Dusty Rhodes, Springfield; Norman Postolese, Nashua; Bob Montag, Pawtucket; **C**-Raymond Fletcher, Pawtucket; **P**-William Jankowski, Portland; Ralph Albers, Pawtucket.

BA: Bob Montag, Pawtucket, .423
Runs: Bob Montag, Pawtucket, 139
Hits: Bob Montag, Pawtucket, 192
RBIs: George Crowe, Pawtucket, 106
HRs: Bob Montag, Pawtucket, 21
Wins: Ralph Albers, Pawtucket, 14
SOs: Wesley Carr, Springfield, 130
ERA: Marion Fricano, Nashua, 1.48

B Piedmont League
President: Richard A. Carrington, Jr.

Standings	W	L	Pct.	GB	Attend.	Manager
Lynchburg Cardinals (16)	77	62	.554	—	121,177	Pug Griffin/Vernon Mackie
Portsmouth Cubs	74	66	.529	3½	124,630	Frank Scalzi
Richmond Colts (13)	71	68	.511	6	177,354	Vince Smith
Roanoke Red Sox (1)	71	69	.507	6½	138,968	Red Marion
Norfolk Tars (5)	68	72	.486	9½	140,553	Earl Bolyard/Frank Novosel
Newport News Dodgers (10)	58	82	.414	19½	101,708	Roy Schalk

Playoffs: Lynchburg 4 games, Roanoke 3; Portsmouth 4 games, Richmond 2.
Finals: Lynchburg 4 games, Portsmouth 2.

All-Star Team: 1B-Reggie Otero, Portsmouth; **2B**-Howard Phillips, Lynchburg; **3B**-Russ Kerns, Portsmouth; **SS**-Milt Bolling, Roanoke; **OF**-Ralph Davis, Richmond; Charlie Maxwell, Roanoke; Arthur Metheny, Portsmouth; **C**-Pete Daley, Roanoke; **P**-Angelo Nardella, Portsmouth; Ronnie Lee, Newport News.

BA: Charlie Maxwell, Roanoke, .345
Runs: Robert Edwards, Roanoke, 118
Hits: Charlie Maxwell, Roanoke, 164
RBIs: Charlie Maxwell, Roanoke, 112
HRs: Charlie Maxwell, Roanoke, 29
Wins: Angelo Nardella, Portsmouth, 20
SOs: Paul Perry, Roanoke, 192
ERA: Joseph Baker, Portsmouth, 2.20

B Southeastern League
President: Stuart X. Stephenson

Standings	W	L	Pct.	GB	Attend.	Manager
Pensacola Fliers	98	42	.700	—	88,595	Bill Herring
Meridian Millers	80	57	.584	16½	76,387	Jack Maupin
Jackson Senators (9)	72	62	.537	23	129,140	Willis Hudlin
Vicksburg Billies	68	66	.507	27	53,033	Buddy Blair
Montgomery Rebels	65	73	.471	32	77,099	George "Mule" Haas
Anniston Rams	64	74	.464	33	40,640	Charles Baron(ovic)/Perry Crosby
Selma Cloverleafs (11)	59	76	.437	36½	46,526	Leo Twardy/Joseph Szuch
Gadsden Chiefs	39	95	.291	56	52,166	Ben Chapman

Playoffs: Pensacola 4 games, Jackson 0; Vicksburg 4 games, Meridian 3.
Finals: Pensacola 4 games, Vicksburg 1.

All-Star Team: 1B-Dallas Womack, Jackson; **2B**-Jack Hollis, Pensacola; **3B**-John Tayoan, Anniston; **SS**-Jack Maupin, Meridian; **OF**-John Liptak, Selma; Ed Kosan, Selma; Harold Summers, Meridian; **C**-Bill Lewis, Jackson; **P**-Ambrose Palica, Meridian.

BA: Harold Summers, Meridian, .344
Runs: Jack Maupin, Meridian, 95
Hits: Nesbit Wilson, Pensacola, 165
RBIs: Harold Summers, Meridian, 95
HRs: Harold Summers, Meridian, 19
Wins: Ambrose Palica, Meridian, 23
SOs: Charles Henry, Jackson, 180
ERA: Joe Ed Kirkland, Pensacola, 1.62

B Three-I League
President: Tom Fairweather

Standings	W	L	Pct.	GB	Attend.	Manager
Evansville Braves (9)	74	51	.592	—	145,657	Bob Coleman
Waterloo White Hawks (2)	70	56	.556	4½	146,421	Bennie Huffman/ Frederick Shaffer
Terre Haute Phillies (14)	69	56	.552	5	122,493	Leon Riley
Davenport Pirates (15)	67	59	.532	7½	133,505	Bill Burwell
Quincy Gems (5)	59	67	.468	15½	85,130	James Adlam
Decatur Cubs (11)	55	70	.440	19	51,147	Morris Arnovich
Danville Dodgers (10)	55	70	.440	19	49,605	Lou Rochelli
Springfield Browns (7)	53	73	.421	21½	48,952	James Crandall

Playoffs: Evansville 3 games, Terre Haute 2; Davenport 3 games, Waterloo 2.
Finals: Davenport 3 games, Evansville 0.

All-Star Team: 1B-Al Grunwald, Davenport; **2B**-Herman Rhodes, Waterloo; **3B**-Ford Jordan, Evansville; **SS**-Harry Hanebrink, Evansville; **OF**-John Novosel, Springfield; Jim Busby, Waterloo; Ed McGhee, Waterloo; **C**-Melvin Brookey, Terre Haute; **P**-Bob Miller, Terre Haute; Jack Brunner, Waterloo.

BA: Emil Tellinger, Quincy, .322
Runs: Herman Rhodes, Waterloo, 86
Hits: Robert Anderlik, Decatur, 140
RBIs: Ed McGhee, Waterloo, 88
HRs: Emil Tellinger, Quincy, 15
Lloyd Lowe, Decatur, 15
Wins: Bob Miller, Terre Haute, 19
SOs: Paul Stuffell, Terre Haute, 288
ERA: William Koszarek, Terre Haute, 1.97

B Tri-State League
President: C.M. Llewellyn

Standings	W	L	Pct.	GB	Attend.	Manager
Florence Steelers	87	59	.596	—	60,124	James Martin
Spartanburg Peaches (3)	81	60	.574	3½	128,490	Kerby Farrell
Asheville Tourists (10)	76	71	.517	11½	105,899	Ed Head
Rock Hill Chiefs	71	70	.504	13½	98,237	Dick Bouknight
Knoxville Smokies (13)	72	73	.497	14½	94,809	Frank Genovese
Sumter Chicks	65	80	.448	21½	55,309	Wes Livengood/Glenn Schaeffer
Charlotte Hornets (8)	62	80	.437	23	94,276	Clyde McDowell
Anderson Rebels	62	83	.428	24½	85,760	Bob Richards

Playoffs: Florence 3 games, Rock Hill 2; Spartanburg 3 games, Asheville 1.
Finals: Florence 4 games, Spartanburg 2.

All-Star Team: 1B-John Streza, Florence; **2B**-Sid Zomlefer, Spartanburg; **3B**-Harold Harrigan, Anderson; **SS**-Ziggy Jasinski, Knoxville; **OF**-Alexander Driskill, Asheville; Robert Knight, Knoxville; Jim Fridley, Spartanburg; **C**-Phil Tomkinson, Knoxville; **P**-Survern Wright, Rock Hill; Al Aber, Spartanburg.

BA: Robert Churchill, Rock Hill, .360
Runs: Harold Harrigan, Anderson, 118
Hits: Alexander Driskill, Asheville, 172
RBIs: Harold Harrigan, Anderson, 121
HRs: Harold Harrigan, Anderson, 43
Wins: Melvin Fisher, Florence, 27
SOs: John Fitzgerald, Florence, 166
ERA: Survern Wright, Rock Hill, 1.86

B Western International League
President: Robert B. Abel

Standings	W	L	Pct.	GB	Attend.	Manager
Yakima Bears	99	51	.660	—	133,917	Joe Orengo
Vancouver Capilanos	91	57	.615	7	137,611	Bill Brenner
Spokane Indians	78	71	.523	20½	186,648	Jack Brillheart
Wenatchee Chiefs	77	73	.513	22	68,668	Charles Petersen
Victoria Athletics (5)	68	84	.447	32	114,544	Ted Norbert/Earl Bolyard
Salem Senators	64	87	.424	35½	67,495	Bill Beard
Tacoma Tigers	63	88	.417	36½	49,673	Bob Johnson
Bremerton Bluejackets	60	89	.403	38½	35,440	Alan Strange

Playoffs: Yakima 3 games, Spokane 1; Vancouver 3 games, Wenatchee 1.
Finals: Vancouver 3 games, Yakima 0.

All-Star Team: 1B-Larry Barton, Spokane; **2B**-Gil McDougald, Victoria; **3B**-Ted Jennings, Yakima; **SS**-Richard Briskey, Yakima; **OF**-James Warner, Wenatchee; Dick Sinovic, Vancouver; Edo Vanni, Yakima; **C**-Jack Parks, Spokane; **P**-John Marshall, Bremerton; James Propst, Victoria.

BA: Clint Cameron, Wenatchee, .380
Runs: James Warner, Wenatchee, 152
Hits: James Robinson, Vancouver, 221
RBIs: Larry Barton, Spokane, 132
HRs: James Warner, Wenatchee, 43
Wins: John Marshall, Bremerton, 22; Robert Snyder, Vancouver, 22
SOs: James Propst, Victoria, 192
ERA: Dewey Soriano, Yakima, 2.30

C Arizona-Texas League
President: Riney B. Salmon

Standings	W	L	Pct.	GB	Attend.	Manager
Phoenix Senators	94	55	.631	—	126,347	Don Trower
Juarez Indios	92	58	.613	2½	85,769	Hector Leal/Victor Canales
Tucson Cowboys (3)	74	76	.493	20½	53,771	Gene Lillard
El Paso Texans	67	83	.447	27½	107,778	Syd Cohen
Bisbee-Douglas Copper Kings	66	83	.443	28	60,149	Elmer Williamson/Paul Jones/Buck Elliott
Globe-Miami Browns (7)	56	94	.373	38½	60,394	Frank Volpi/Edward Dancisak

Playoffs: Phoenix 4 games, Tucson 2; El Paso 4 games, Juarez 2.
Finals: El Paso 4 games, Phoenix 2.

All-Star Team: 1B-Nick Sunseri, Tucson; **2B**-Vinicio Garcia, Juarez; **3B**-Lou Tamone, El Paso; **SS**-Mike Baxes, Phoenix; **OF**-Dick Steinhauer, Phoenix; Gene Clough, Bisbee-Douglas; Jim Thomas, Globe-Miami; **C**-Lee Smith, Tucson; **P**-Edward Graham, Phoenix; Memo Luna, Juarez.

BA: Vinicio Garcia, Juarez, .377
Runs: Vinicio Garcia, Juarez, 170
Hits: Vinicio Garcia, Juarez, 227
RBIs: Dick Steinhauer, Phoenix, 151
HRs: Gene Clough, Bisbee-Douglas, 37
BBs: Gene Lillard, Tucson, 154
Wins: Edward Graham, Phoenix, 24
SOs: William Abernathie, Tucson, 220
ERA: Richard Drilling, Phoenix, 2.55

C Border League
President: John G. Ward

Standings	W	L	Pct.	GB	Attend.	Manager
Geneva Robins (10)	81	49	.623	—	67,259	Charles Small
Ottawa Senators	74	55	.574	6½	78,577	Bill Metzig
Ogdensburg Maples	70	60	.538	11	58,749	Russ Wein
Auburn Cayugas	67	62	.519	13½	55,634	Barney Hearn
Watertown Athletics	58	71	.450	22½	61,026	Frank Heller
Kingston Ponies	38	91	.295	42½	38,671	Zeke Bonura/Harold Leach

Playoffs: Geneva 4 games, Ogdensburg 3; Auburn 4 games, Ottawa 3.

Finals: Geneva 4 games, Auburn 2.

All-Star Team: 1B-Frank Heller, Watertown; **2B**-Bill Metzig, Ottawa; **3B**-Steve Nemeth, Auburn; **SS**-Peter Karpuk, Ottawa; **OF**-William Scally, Ogdensburg; Tony Romeo, Geneva; Doug Harvey, Ottawa; **C**-Bill Kivett, Ottawa; **P**-Walter Balash, Ottawa; Bob Gates, Auburn.

BA: Doug Harvey, Ottawa, .351
Runs: Doug Harvey, Ottawa, 121
Hits: William Scally, Ogdensburg, 177
RBIs: Doug Harvey, Ottawa, 109
HRs: Pete Kousagen, Geneva, 22
Wins: Donald Bryant, Ogdensburg, 20
SOs: Bill Forst, Geneva, 170
ERA: Robert Sundstrom, Geneva, 2.29

C California League
President: Jerry Donovan

Standings	W	L	Pct.	GB	Attend.	Manager
Bakersfield Indians (3)	85	54	.612	—	140,389	Harry Griswold
Fresno Cardinals (16)	83	57	.593	2½	145,946	Frenchy Uhalt
Ventura Yankees (5)	80	60	.571	5½	53,071	Bones Sanders
San Jose Red Sox (1)	76	64	.543	9½	113,358	Marv Owen
Santa Barbara Dodgers (10)	75	65	.536	10½	72,244	Chester Kehn
Stockton Ports (2)	64	76	.457	21½	130,849	Nino Bongiovanni
Modesto Reds (15)	54	85	.388	31	78,469	William Jackson/Max Macon
Visalia Cubs (11)	42	98	.300	43½	55,614	Leon "Red" Treadway/Arnold "Jigger" Statz/Claude Passeau

Playoffs: Ventura 3 games, Bakersfield 2; San Jose 3 games, Fresno 0.
Finals: San Jose 4 games, Ventura 1.

All-Star Team: 1B-Norm Zauchin, San Jose; **2B**-Ed Barbarito, Ventura; **3B**-Harry Clements, Stockton; **SS**-Bob Thomson, Fresno; **OF**-Bill Garbe, Fresno; Jess Pike, Bakersfield; Tommy Perez, Visalia; **C**-Dick Wilson, Visalia; **P**-Earl Escalante, Bakersfield; Fred Hahn, Fresno; Warren Sandel, Stockton.

BA: Max Macon, Modesto, .383
Runs: Jess Pike, Bakersfield, 167
Hits: Wellington Quinn, Bakersfield, 196
RBIs: Jess Pike, Bakersfield, 156
HRs: Jess Pike, Bakersfield, 37
BBs: Jess Pike, Bakersfield, 194
Wins: Earl Escalante, Bakersfield, 28
SOs: Armand Castro, Modesto, 237
ERA: Drexel Waters, Santa Barbara, 2.54

C Canadian-American League
President: Albert E. Houghton

Standings	W	L	Pct.	GB	Attend.	Manager
Quebec Braves	90	48	.652	—	176,779	Frank McCormick
Oneonta Red Sox (1)	75	62	.547	14½	63,217	Eddie Popowski
Trois Rivieres Royals (10)	75	64	.540	15½	76,672	George Scherger
Pittsfield Indians (3)	74	65	.532	16½	56,674	Gene Hasson
Amsterdam Rugmakers (5)	67	71	.486	23	83,449	Mayo Smith
Gloversville-Johnstown Glovers (7)	65	74	.468	25½	83,638	James Cullinane
Schenectady Blue Jays (14)	58	80	.420	32	115,966	Richard Carter
Rome Colonels (4)	48	88	.353	41	40,331	Clyde Smoll

Playoffs: Quebec 4 games, Trois Rivieres 0; Oneonta 4 games, Pittsfield 2.
Finals: Quebec 4 games, Oneonta 0.

All-Star Team: 1B-Keith Little, Rome; **2B**-Julio Ondani, Oneonta; **3B**-Frank Malzone, Oneonta; **SS**-George Clark, Trois Rivieres; **OF**-Garland Lawing, Quebec; LeRoy Smith, Oneonta; Charles Huwer, Pittsfield; **C**-Steve Salata, Oneonta; **P**-Harold Erickson, Quebec; John O'Donnell, Gloversville-Johnstown.

BA: Peter Elko, Quebec, .348
Runs: Garland Lawing, Quebec, 129
Hits: Frank Malzone, Oneonta, 178
RBIs: Vernon Shetler, Quebec, 133
HRs: Donald Marshall, Schenectady, 27
Wins: Harold Erickson, Quebec, 21
SOs: Harold Erickson, Quebec, 206
ERA: John Masuga, Pittsfield, 2.20

C Central Association
President: Lee A. Thomas

Standings	W	L	Pct.	GB	Attend.	Manager
Burlington Indians (3)	81	48	.628	—	57,915	Lloyd Brown
Keokuk Pirates (15)	74	54	.578	6½	38,931	Charles Hargreaves
Kewanee A's (6)	68	60	.531	12½	29,482	Harold Hoffman
Cedar Rapids Rockets	63	67	.485	18½	84,185	Stan "Packy" Rogers
Clinton Steers (11)	61	65	.484	18½	35,764	Adolph Matulis/Joe Blake
Rockford Rox (12)	38	91	.295	43	19,304	Robert Dill/Fred Lietz

Playoffs: Cedar Rapids 3 games, Burlington 0; Kewanee 3 games, Keokuk 0.
Finals: Kewanee 4 games, Cedar Rapids 2.

All-Star Team: 1B-Joe Macko, Burlington; **2B**-George Sopko, Keokuk; **3B**-Duke Bowman, Burlington; **SS**-Eddie Wopinek, Keokuk; **OF**-Rudy Halabuk, Kewanee; Lloyd Foster, Rockford; Jimmy King, Keokuk; **C**-Harry Minor, Keokuk; **P**-Gene Bussman, Keokuk; John Graney, Clinton.

BA: Harry Minor, Keokuk, .350
Runs: George Sopko, Keokuk, 120
Hits: John Miller, Kewanee, 158
RBIs: John Tanner, Cedar Rapids, 121
HRs: John Tanner, Cedar Rapids, 37
Wins: Walter Rush, Burlington, 16
SOs: John Graney, Clinton, 164
ERA: Harry Pritts, Keokuk, 1.32

C Cotton States League
President: Al Haraway

Standings	W	L	Pct.	GB	Attend.	Manager
Greenwood Dodgers (10) ...	84	56	.600	—	53,228	James Bivin
El Dorado Oilers	80	59	.576	3½	56,780	James McClure
Natchez Indians	73	66	.533	10½	35,168	Joe Rullo
Pine Bluff Cardinals (7)......	72	66	.522	11	82,442	Harry Chozen
Greenville Bucks	72	67	.518	11½	60,371	James Acton
Hot Springs Bathers (2)	64	75	.460	19½	48,563	Pete Fox/Glen Stewart
Clarksdale Planters	58	80	.420	25	56,363	Ernest Davis/Chet Morgan/ Clint Dahlberg
Helena Seaporters	53	87	.378	31	34,468	Ray Baker/John McPherson/ Bob Benish

Playoffs: Natchez 4 games, El Dorado 3; Pine Bluff 4 games, Greenwood 2.
Finals: Natchez 4 games, Pine Bluff 1.

All-Star Team: 1B-Ed Sudol, El Dorado; **2B**-Dominick Chiola, El Dorado; Joe Rullo, Natchez; **3B**-Francis McCluskey, Greenwood; **SS**-Jim Morgan, El Dorado; **OF**-Richard Anderson, Hot Springs; Harvill Jakes, El Dorado; Ben Cantrell, Pine Bluff; **C**-Othur Pardue, El Dorado; **P**-Eddie Albrecht, Pine Bluff; Fred Waters, Greenwood.

BA: Harold Seawright, Greenville, .325
Runs: Ed Sudol, El Dorado, 106
Hits: Harold Seawright, Greenville, 172
RBIs: Harold Seawright, Greenville, 108
HRs: Dan Phalen, Hot Springs, 22
Wins: Eddie Albrecht, Pine Bluff, 29
SOs: Eddie Albrecht, Pine Bluff, 389
ERA: Stan Poloczyk, Greenwood, 1.82

C East Texas League
President: J. Walter Morris

Standings	W	L	Pct.	GB	Attend.	Manager
Longview Texans	89	51	.636	—	63,103	Dixie Parsons
Gladewater Bears...............	87	53	.621	2	50,328	Hal Van Pelt
Paris Panthers	75	62	.547	12½	66,509	Jimmy Walkup
Kilgore Drillers.................	75	65	.536	14	52,701	Joe Kracher
Marshall Browns (7)..........	69	68	.504	18½	60,585	Walter DeFreitas
Tyler Trojans (12)..............	62	78	.443	27	56,064	Carl McNabb/Mel Hicks
Henderson Oilers	51	88	.367	37½	34,500	Mel Hicks/George Milstead
Bryan Bombers..................	48	91	.345	40½	40,000	Felix Penso/Stan Goletz

Playoffs: Kilgore 4 games, Longview 3; Gladewater 4 games, Paris 3.
Finals: Gladewater 4 games, Kilgore 0.

All-Star Team: 1B-Merv Connors, Kilgore; **2B**-Dutch Meyer, Gladewater; **3B**-Al Kubski, Longview; **SS**-Clyde Perry, Gladewater; **OF**-Jim Morton, Longview; John Stone, Henderson; Vern Washington, Gladewater; **C**-El Tappe, Henderson; **P**-George Yanen, Paris; James Upchurch, Marshall.

BA: Vern Washington, Gladewater, .387
Runs: Al Kubski, Longview, 132
Hits: John Stone, Henderson, 199
RBIs: Glenn Burns, Longview, 136
HRs: Nick Gregory, Kilgore, 23
Wins: George Yanen, Paris, 22
SOs: James Upchurch, Marshall, 210
ERA: Rafael Rivas, Gladewater, 2.09

C Evangeline League
President: Edmond L. Deramee

Standings	W	L	Pct.	GB	Attend.	Manager
Houma Indians..................	81	58	.586	—	73,853	George Washburn
Lafayette Bulls..................	79	60	.568	2	73,753	Harry Strohm
Hammond Berries	76	63	.547	5	51,071	Paul Bruno
Alexandria Aces................	75	65	.536	6½	107,597	Merle Coleman/Art Phelan
Abbeville Athletics	68	68	.500	11½	48,780	Nat Love
Thibodaux Giants	64	74	.464	16½	71,450	Wilfred Theard/Gus Ploger
New Iberia Cardinals.........	61	79	.429	20½	64,728	Sidney Gautreaux
Baton Rouge Red Sticks.....	50	87	.365	30	53,889	Anthony DiBartolo/ Edward Borom

Playoffs: Alexandria 4 games, Houma 1; Hammond 4 games, Lafayette 1.
Finals: Hammond 4 games, Alexandria 2.

All-Star Team: 1B-Robert Belford, Alexandria; **2B**-Freddie Barocco, Hammond; **3B**-Vincent Liberto, Abbeville; **SS**-Charles Adams, Hammond; **OF**-Robert Dunn, Hammond; Bobby Gales, Abbeville; Chester Juckno, Alexandria; **C**-Ray Smith, Alexandria; **P**-Tom Spears, Lafayette; Eusebio Perez, Abbeville.

BA: Sidney Gautreaux, New Iberia, .335
Runs: Gipson Gayle, New Iberia, 112
Charles Wilcox, Hammond, 112
Hits: Robert Dunn, Hammond, 165
RBIs: Mike Ryan, Houma, 108
HRs: Robert Dunn, Hammond, 30
Wins: Herman Gilreath, Houma, 22
SOs: Eusebio Perez, Abbeville, 180
ERA: Tom Spears, Lafayette, 1.04

C Middle Atlantic League
President: Elmer M. Daily

Standings	W	L	Pct.	GB	Attend.	Manager
Erie Sailors**(13)............	85	53	.616	—	101,038	Pete Pavich
Johnstown Johnnies*(10) ...	84	55	.604	1½	105,776	Roy Nichols
Youngstown Athletics (6)...	74	62	.544	10	62,667	Edwin Morgan
Oil City Refiners (2)...........	67	69	.493	17	55,316	Otto Denning
Butler Tigers (4)	66	72	.478	19	40,221	Robert Engle/Walter Beck
Vandergrift Pioneers (14)...	63	72	.467	20½	40,523	George Savino
Uniontown Coal Barons (15)...	55	83	.398	30	38,037	Wes Griffin
New Castle Nats (8)..........	54	82	.397	30	28,233	Bill Mongiello

Playoff: Erie 4 games, Johnstown 3.

All-Star Team: 1B-Ed Kestler, Erie; **2B**-Bill Palumbo, Johnstown; **3B**-Bob Gardner, Youngstown; **SS**-Charles Wilhelm, Youngstown; **OF**-Chuck Harig, Youngstown; John Moore, Oil City; Robert Betz, Youngstown; **C**-Joe Lonnett, Vandergrift; **P**-John Kucab, Youngstown; Murray Richardson, Johnstown.

BA: Robert Betz, Youngstown, .345
Runs: Charles Wilhelm, Youngstown, 145
Hits: Charles Wilhelm, Youngstown, 181
Robert Betz, Youngstown, 181
RBIs: Robert Betz, Youngstown, 135
HRs: Joseph Beran, Youngstown, 36
Wins: John Kucab, Youngstown, 21
SOs: Franklin Wagner, New Castle, 206
ERA: Franklin Wagner, New Castle, 3.20

C Northern League
President: Herman D. White

Standings	W	L	Pct.	GB	Attend.	Manager
Eau Claire Bears (9)	71	52	.577	—	100,996	Andy Cohen
Aberdeen Pheasants (7)	71	54	.568	1	85,624	Irvin Hall
St. Cloud Rox (13).............	65	59	.524	6½	65,015	Charlie Fox
Superior Blues (2).............	64	62	.508	8½	76,417	George Sobek
Duluth Dukes (16).............	60	66	.476	12½	107,548	Theodore Madjeski/ Russell Rolandson
Sioux Falls Canaries (11) ...	58	67	.464	14	87,823	Irvin Fortune/Lee Eilbracht
Fargo-Moorhead Twins	56	70	.444	16½	87,931	Art Doll
Grand Forks Chiefs (5).......	55	70	.440	17	49,757	Ed Kearse/Joe McDermott/ Wally Berger

Playoffs: Eau Claire 3 games, St. Cloud 1; Aberdeen 3 games, Superior 1.
Finals: Aberdeen 4 games, Eau Claire 1.

All-Star Team: 1B-Bill Staker, Aberdeen; **2B**-Irvin Hall, Aberdeen; **3B**-Robert Ries, Eau Claire; **SS**-Fred McAlister, Duluth; **OF**-Pete Brozovich, St. Cloud; John Kropf, St. Cloud; Ted Lotz, Sioux Falls; **C**-Tommy Venn, Fargo-Moorhead; **P**-Bob Turley, Aberdeen; Neil Lettau, Grand Forks.

BA: Irvin Hall, Aberdeen, .342
Runs: Robert Coats, Sioux Falls, 107
Hits: Robert Ries, Eau Claire, 175
RBIs: Bernard Kozub, Sioux Falls, 96
HRs: George DiPillo, Fargo-Moorhead, 16
Wins: Bob Turley, Aberdeen, 23
SOs: Bob Turley, Aberdeen, 205
ERA: George Yorke, Eau Claire, 2.06

C Pioneer League
President: Jack P. Halliwell

Standings	W	L	Pct.	GB	Attend.	Manager
Twin Falls Cowboys (5)	78	47	.624	—	108,523	Charlie Metro
Billings Mustangs (10)	77	48	.616	1	174,080	Larry Shepard
Pocatello Cardinals (16).....	75	51	.595	3½	87,352	Walter Lowe
Salt Lake City Bees	73	53	.579	5½	151,563	Rupert "Tommy" Thompson
Great Falls Selectrics	62	62	.500	15½	129,640	Joe Bowman
Ogden Reds (12)................	58	68	.460	20½	66,192	Herman Schulte
Boise Pilots	47	77	.379	30½	71,850	William Stenger/ Gordon Williamson
Idaho Falls Russets (13)	31	95	.246	47½	41,195	John Babich/Louis Garland/ Frank Gabler

Playoffs: Pocatello 2 games, Twin Falls 0; Billings 2 games, Salt Lake City 0.
Finals: Pocatello 3 games, Billings 2.

All-Star Team: 1B-Sven "Red" Jessen, Twin Falls; **2B**-Dom Barczewski, Pocatello; **3B**-Billy Ford, Ogden; **SS**-Ted Lewandowski, Pocatello; **OF**-Simon Koerner, Great Falls; George Caloia, Billings; Bill Renna, Twin Falls; **C**-Richard Morgan, Pocatello; **P**-Richard Larner, Salt Lake City; Otto Schroeder, Twin Falls.

BA: John Temple, Ogden, .400
Runs: Dom Barczewski, Pocatello, 135
Hits: John Temple, Ogden, 200
RBIs: Charles Williams, Pocatello, 120
HRs: Bill Renna, Twin Falls, 21
Wins: Larry Shepard, Billings, 21
SOs: Otto Schroeder, Twin Falls, 172
ERA: Richard Larner, Salt Lake City, 3.00
Pct: Larry Shepard, Billings, .778, 21-6

C Sunset League
President: Leslie Powers

Standings	W	L	Pct.	GB	Attend.	Manager
Las Vegas Wranglers..........	88	38	.698	—	61,050	Ken Meyers
Mexicali Aguilas................	79	47	.627	9	59,810	Ed Wheeler
San Bernardino Pioneers ...	62	64	.492	26	35,871	Jack Rothrock
Porterville Packers	61	65	.484	27	66,280	Thomas Lloyd
El Centro Imperials............	59	66	.472	28½	34,957	Ray Viers/Frank Stinson
Salinas/Tijuana Colts#(7) ...	58	68	.460	30	39,701	Bruce Ogrodowski
Reno Silver Sox (13)	49	75	.395	38	37,780	Lilio Marcucci
Riverside Dons	46	79	.368	41½	32,450	Don Jameson

#Salinas moved to Tijuana August 5.

Playoffs: None.

All-Star Team: 1B-Frank Stinson, El Centro; **2B**-Stan Gray, San Bernardino; **3B**-Hank Bartolomei, Las Vegas; **SS**-Bud Dawson, San Bernardino; **OF**-Forrest "Frosty" Kennedy, Riverside; Bob Balcena, Mexicali; Pete Hughes, Las Vegas; **C**-John Albini, Las Vegas; **P**-Erwin Coutts, Mexicali; Warren Kanagy, Riverside/San Bernardino.

BA: Forrest "Frosty" Kennedy, Riverside, .411
Runs: Pete Hughes, Las Vegas, 156
Hits: Forrest "Frosty" Kennedy, Riverside, 194
RBIs: Bob Balcena, Mexicali, 132
HRs: Pete Hughes, Las Vegas, 24

BBs: Pete Hughes, Las Vegas, 210
Wins: Eugene Roenspie, San Bernardino, 20
SOs: Warren Kanagy, Riverside/
San Bernardino, 210
ERA: Erwin Coutts, Mexicali, 2.69

C West Texas-New Mexico League
President: Milton E. Price

Standings	W	L	Pct.	GB	Attend.	Manager
Albuquerque Dukes	83	56	.597	—	107,911	Herschel Martin
Abilene Blue Sox	73	66	.527	10	100,609	Hayden Greer
Amarillo Gold Sox	73	66	.527	10	111,487	Jess Landrum/Buck Fausett
Lamesa Lobos	72	66	.522	10½	76,627	Jay Haney
Pampa Oilers	70	70	.500	13½	57,280	Grover Seitz
Lubbock Hubbers	70	70	.500	13½	97,855	Jackie Sullivan
Borger Gassers	63	75	.457	19½	74,999	Edwin Carnett/Kenneth Sears
Clovis Pioneers	52	87	.374	31	47,697	Paul Dean

Playoffs: Albuquerque 4 games, Lamesa 3; Amarillo 4 games, Abilene 0.
Finals: Albuquerque 4 games, Amarillo 1.

All-Star Team: 1B-Jim Prince, Lubbock; **2B**-Jackie Sullivan, Lubbock; **3B**-Len Attyd, Albuquerque; **SS**-Hayden Greer, Abilene; **OF**-D.C. "Pud" Miller, Lamesa; Herschel Martin, Albuquerque; Roberto Fernandez, Abilene; **C**-Les Mulcahy, Albuquerque; **P**-Frank Shone, Albuquerque; Don Ferrarese, Albuquerque; Roy Parker, Pampa.

BA: Roberto Fernandez, Abilene, .408
Runs: Jerry Folkman, Amarillo, 135
Hits: Roberto Fernandez, Abilene, 241
RBIs: Isaac Palmer, Clovis, 148
HRs: D.C. "Pud" Miller, Lamesa, 52
2B: Roberto Fernandez, Abilene, 56

3B: Cliff McClain, Albuquerque, 21
Wins: Roy Parker, Pampa, 23
SOs: Roy Parker, Pampa, 235
ERA: Rene Vega, Abilene, 2.95
Pct: Jack Gutierrez, Lamesa, .818, 18-4

C Western Association
President: Tom Fairweather

Standings	W	L	Pct.	GB	Attend.	Manager
St. Joseph Cardinals (16)	96	42	.696	—	126,301	Harold Olt
Ft. Smith Giants (13)	86	54	.614	11	62,534	Harold Kollar
Joplin Miners (5)	80	58	.580	16	67,434	John Sturm
Topeka Owls	77	61	.558	19	116,136	Butch Nieman
Muskogee Reds (7)	77	62	.554	19½	84,903	Heinie Mueller
Salina Blue Jays (14)	69	69	.500	27	50,145	Joseph Gantenbein
Hutchinson Elks	41	93	.306	53	65,755	Russell Schon/ Howard McCormick/Burl Storie
Leavenworth Braves	25	112	.182	70½	33,132	William Cronin/Fido Murphy/ Red Harvel

Playoffs: Topeka 3 games, St. Joseph 2; Joplin 3 games, Ft. Smith 0.
Finals: Joplin 4 games, Topeka 2.

All-Star Team: 1B-Harold Kollar, Ft. Smith; **2B**-Jim Finigan, Joplin; **3B**-Olin Martin, Joplin; **SS**-Ed Waytula, Salina; **OF**-Jim Neufeldt, St. Joseph; Butch Nieman, Topeka; Bob Masser, Muskogee; **C**-Ken Morgan, St. Joseph; **P**-Nick Huck, St. Joseph; Dennis Jent, Joplin.

BA: Olin Martin, Joplin, .355
Runs: Harvey Gentry, Ft. Smith, 125
Hits: Jim Finigan, Joplin, 180
RBIs: Butch Nieman, Topeka, 110

HRs: Butch Nieman, Topeka, 26
Wins: Bill Bagwell, Joplin, 20
SOs: Dennis Jent, Joplin, 214
ERA: Nick Huck, St. Joseph, 2.25

D Alabama State League
President: Charles T. Laney

Standings	W	L	Pct.	GB	Attend.	Manager
Greenville Pirates (15)	83	44	.654	—	23,443	Walter Tauscher
Ozark Eagles	82	45	.646	1	25,804	George Hennessey
Enterprise Boll Weevils	63	61	.508	18½	30,603	Russell Taylor
Andalusia Arrows	59	65	.476	22½	39,958	Manuel Russo/Robert Engle
Dothan Browns	57	68	.456	25	32,471	Joe Cavosie/James Coller/ Dan Long
Geneva Red Birds	56	69	.448	26	23,775	Carl Wollgast
Brewton Millers	51	73	.411	30½	25,533	Joseph Szuch/Norman Veazey
Troy Tigers (4)	49	75	.395	32½	18,323	Holt "Cat" Milner

Playoffs: Greenville 4 games, Enterprise 1; Andalusia 4 games, Ozark 1.
Finals: Andalusia 4 games, Greenville 1.

All-Star Team: 1B-John Beasley, Enterprise; **2B**-Roy LeFevre, Greenville; **3B**-Dick Smith, Greenville; **SS**-Bobby Clark, Ozark; **OF**-Dan Kravitz, Greenville; George Hughes, Ozark; Alvin Hope, Brewton; **C**-Louis Jones, Ozark; **P**-Harry Weakley, Greenville; Spencer Davis, Ozark.

BA: Roy LeFevre, Greenville, .321
Runs: George Hughes, Ozark, 114
Hits: Roy LeFevre, Greenville, 151
RBIs: Doug Walker, Ozark, 107

HRs: Tom McBride, Geneva/Ozark, 15
Wins: Carl Wollgast, Geneva, 22
SOs: Spencer Davis, Ozark, 220
ERA: Carl Wollgast, Geneva, 1.89

D Appalachian League
President: Chauncey De Vault

Standings	W	L	Pct.	GB	Attend.	Manager
Bluefield Blue-Grays (9)	88	34	.721	—	116,572	Ernie White
Pulaski Counts (10)	80	38	.678	6	45,580	George Pfister
Bristol Twins (13)	76	41	.650	9½	66,536	Ben Geraghty
Johnson City Cardinals (16)	59	63	.484	29	40,280	Ben Catchings
New River Rebels	52	69	.430	35½	29,476	Jack Crosswhite
Welch Miners (6)	48	73	.397	39½	41,092	William Hoffner/Mike Kreshka
Elizabethton Betsy Local	40	76	.345	45	27,265	Charles Munday/Andy Belcik/ Julian Morgan
Kingsport Cherokees	35	84	.294	51½	23,967	Irvine Jeffries/Alvin Kluttz

Playoffs: Bluefield 2 games, Johnson City 0; Bristol 2 games, Pulaski 1.
Finals: Bluefield 3 games, Bristol 0.

All-Star Team: 1B-Edwin Heap, Bluefield; **2B**-Dave Little, Pulaski; **3B**-Joe Roddin, Bluefield; **SS**-Bob Farrick, Pulaski; **OF**-John Karpinski, Bluefield; Nick Romeo, Bristol; William Kerr, Pulaski; **C**-Cannie Forsyth, Bristol; **P**-Clifford Littledove, Bristol; James Pope, Bluefield.

BA: William Kerr, Pulaski, .401
Runs: Nick Romeo, Bristol, 151
Hits: Edwin Heap, Bluefield, 190
RBIs: John Karpinski, Bluefield, 137

HRs: John Karpinski, Bluefield, 20
Wins: Clifford Littledove, Bristol, 18
SOs: Robert Hartig, Elizabethton, 200
ERA: Clifford Littledove, Bristol, 2.66

D Blue Ridge League
President: Judge E.C. Bivins

Standings	W	L	Pct.	GB	Attend.	Manager
Mt. Airy Graniteers	68	58	.540	—	36,230	Frank Essic/Phil Lundeen/ Eurice "Pete" Treece/ Okey Flowers
Galax Leafs	66	61	.520	2½	24,353	Stephen Sloboda/Bob Latshaw
Wytheville Statesmen	65	61	.516	3	19,753	Frank Subb
North Wilkesboro Flashers	62	62	.500	5	31,814	Thomas Daddino/ Henry Loman/Bernard Keating
Elkin Blanketeers	62	65	.488	6½	33,000	Tige Harris
Radford Rockets	55	71	.437	13	26,407	Bob Thompson/Frank Cirelli/ Garland Braxton

Playoffs: Wytheville 4 games, Mt. Airy 2; North Wilkesboro 4 games, Galax 2.
Finals: North Wilkesboro 4 games, Wytheville 1.

All-Star Team: 1B-Bob Latshaw, Galax; **2B**-Pat Poscitelli, North Wilkesboro; **3B**-Doug Shores, North Wilkesboro; **SS**-Joe Tagliarino, Galax; Bob Winkelspecht, North Wilkesboro; **OF**-Henry Brown, Elkin; William Akins, Mt. Airy; Jasper Holt, Mt. Airy; **C**-Tommy Thompson, Wytheville; **P**-Eurice "Pete" Treece, Mt. Airy; Bob Masinick, Galax.

BA: Michael Brelich, Wytheville/Mt. Airy, .333
Runs: Robert Horan, Galax, 92
Hits: Don Lavigne, Wytheville, 151
RBIs: Jasper Holt, Mt. Airy, 94

HRs: Lloyd Wilcox, Radford, 15
Wins: Eurice "Pete" Treece, Mt. Airy, 21
SOs: Eurice "Pete" Treece, Mt. Airy, 229
ERA: John Moore, Radford, 2.11

D Coastal Plain League
President: Ray Goodmon

Standings	W	L	Pct.	GB	Attend.	Manager
Rocky Mount Leafs	79	60	.568	—	80,786	Quentin Martin/ Horace "Red" Benton
Kinston Eagles	74	64	.536	4½	88,814	Steve Collins
New Bern Bears	73	66	.525	6	72,291	Bull Hamons
Greenville Greenies	71	67	.514	7½	72,420	Fred Williams
Goldsboro Goldbugs	68	68	.500	9½	71,690	Steve Mizerak/Max Wilson
Tarboro Athletics (6)	68	68	.500	9½	41,212	Joe Antolick
Roanoke Rapids Jays	60	78	.435	18½	68,247	Russell Meers/Glen Lockamy
Wilson Tobs	57	79	.419	20½	71,413	Ross Morrow

Playoffs: Greenville 4 games, Rocky Mount 2; Kinston 4 games, New Bern 2.
Finals: Greenville 4 games, Kinston 2.

All-Star Team: 1B-Fred Williams, Greenville; **2B**-Irv Dickens, Wilson; **3B**-Robert Johnson, Rocky Mount; **SS**-John Tepedino, Greenville; Al Rhem, Wilson; **OF**-William Mauney, Greenville; Charles Sedor, Rocky Mount; Clyde Whitener, Goldsboro; **C**-Quentin Martin, Rocky Mount; **P**-Claude Voiselle, Kinston; Vincent Gohl, Tarboro.

BA: Clyde Whitener, Goldsboro, .355
Runs: John Tepedino, Greenville, 132
Hits: Clyde Whitener, Goldsboro, 194
RBIs: Fred Williams, Greenville, 122

HRs: Quentin Martin, Rocky Mount, 27
Wins: William Padgett, New Bern, 22
SOs: Robert Mangum, Goldsboro, 248
ERA: Vincent Gohl, Tarboro, 1.27

D Eastern Shore League
President: Fred Lucas

Standings	W	L	Pct.	GB	Attend.	Manager
Easton Yankees (5)	68	52	.567	—	38,651	Jack Farmer
Federalsburg Feds	63	56	.529	4½	30,139	Carl McQuillen
Salisbury Cardinals (16)	60	59	.504	7½	39,063	Gene Corbett
Rehoboth Beach Sea Hawks	56	63	.471	11½	22,358	William Sisler/John Watson
Seaford Eagles (14)	56	64	.467	12	35,519	Paul Galin
Cambridge Dodgers (10)	55	64	.462	12½	29,434	Merle Strachan

Playoffs: Teams played a round-robin series: Federalsburg (4-1), Rehoboth Beach (4-2), Easton (2-4), Salisbury (1-4).
Finals: Rehoboth Beach 4 games, Federalsburg 3.

All-Star Team: 1B-Gene Corbett, Salisbury; **2B**-Bob "Ducky" Detweiler, Federalsburg; **3B**-Hank Parker, Cambridge; **SS**-Bob Westfall, Federalsburg; **OF**-Ronnie Berger, Salisbury; Dom Bertocci, Cambridge; Gordon Bragg, Easton; **C**-Andy Anderson, Easton; **P**-George McPhail, Seaford; Andy Schultz, Salisbury.

BA: Gordon Bragg, Easton, .362
Runs: Bob Westfall, Federalsburg, 126
Hits: Bob Westfall, Federalsburg, 158
RBIs: Bob Westfall, Federalsburg, 113
HRs: Bob Westfall, Federalsburg, 19
Wins: Babe Pinelli, Rehoboth Beach, 18
SOs: John Andre, Rehoboth Beach, 240
ERA: Duke Markell, Seaford, 2.17

D Far West League
President: Jerry Donovan

Standings	W	L	Pct.	GB	Attend.	Manager
Pittsburg Diamonds	84	43	.661	—	33,951	Vince DiMaggio
Klamath Falls Gems (14)	78	46	.629	4½	58,474	Hub Kittle
Willows Cardinals (16)	68	58	.540	15½	24,918	Bert Bonomi/Fred Fass
Redding Browns (7)	63	64	.496	21	35,178	Ray Perry
Marysville Braves (9)	59	66	.472	24	16,784	Rex Carr
Medford Nuggets	39	84	.317	43	34,689	Dan Reagan
Santa Rosa Cats@	43	49	.467	NA	12,849	Joe Abreu/Alvin Kruk/ Lembert Serpa/Louis Vezilich
Vallejo Chiefs#	34	58	.370	NA	5,999	Louis Vezilich

#Vallejo disbanded July 31.
@Santa Rosa disbanded August 4.

Playoffs: Pittsburg 3 games, Willows 2; Redding 3 games, Klamath Falls 2.
Finals: Pittsburg 4 games, Redding 3.

All-Star Team: 1B-Bill Ashley, Marysville; **2B**-Don Davis, Willows; **3B**-Glenn Gorbous, Medford; **SS**-Morrie Nordell, Klamath Falls; **OF**-Gene Mitzel, Willows; Theodore Hesse, Klamath Falls; Willie Enos, Pittsburg; **C**-Milt Martin, Pittsburg; **P**-Blair Simpson, Pittsburg; James Howard, Redding; Niles Jordan, Klamath Falls.

BA: Louis Vezilich, Vallejo/Santa Rosa, .406
Runs: Ray Perry, Redding, 135
    Theodore Hesse, Klamath Falls, 135
Hits: Theodore Hesse, Klamath Falls, 188
RBIs: Ray Perry, Redding, 155
HRs: Ray Perry, Redding, 45
Wins: William Carr, Pittsburg, 21
SOs: James Howard, Redding, 226
ERA: William Carr, Pittsburg, 3.28

D Florida State League
President: Jim Butler

Standings	W	L	Pct.	GB	Attend.	Manager
Gainesville G-Men	87	50	.635	—	84,718	Vern Dozier
Daytona Beach Islanders	79	56	.585	7	73,756	Sam Demma
St. Augustine Saints (11)	75	60	.556	11	55,797	Frank Piet
Palatka Azaleas	76	62	.551	11½	59,500	Julian Morgan/E.M. "Bitsy" Mott
Sanford Giants (13)	74	63	.540	13	44,603	Hal Gruber
DeLand Red Hats	64	70	.478	21½	42,950	Bill Perrin
Orlando Senators (8)	51	85	.375	35½	42,425	Ralph Dulaney/Walter Zurowski/ George Myatt
Leesburg Dodgers	37	97	.276	48½	49,958	Lou Haneles/Julian Acosta/ Luke Hamlin

Playoffs: Palatka 4 games, Gainesville 3; St. Augustine 4 games, Daytona Beach 3.
Finals: St. Augustine 4 games, Palatka 1.

All-Star Team: 1B-LaVerne Mayer, Palatka; **2B**-Mel Kerestes, Orlando; **3B**-Jim Jones, Sanford; **SS**-Gus Montalbane, Daytona Beach; **OF**-Herb McLeod, Palatka; Manuel Rivera, Gainesville; Al Pirtle, Gainesville; **C**-Ray Dunne, DeLand; **P**-Stan Karpinski, St. Augustine; Chet Covington, Palatka.

BA: Al Pirtle, Gainesville, .383
Runs: Manuel Rivera, Gainesville, 142
Hits: Al Pirtle, Gainesville, 187
RBIs: Al Pirtle, Gainesville, 110
HRs: Lou Bevil, Daytona Beach, 18
Wins: Stan Karpinski, St. Augustine, 29
SOs: Myril Hoag, Gainesville, 280
ERA: Stan Karpinski, St. Augustine, 1.56

D Georgia State League
President: Joseph W. Matt, Jr.

Standings	W	L	Pct.	GB	Attend.	Manager
Eastman Dodgers	86	51	.628	—	43,691	Edgar Hartness
Douglas Trojans	77	62	.554	10	45,403	David Coble
Tifton Blue Sox	74	63	.540	12	53,846	Charles Farrar
Vidalia-Lyons Twins	72	65	.526	14	45,463	Michael Rossi/Julian Morgan/ Joe Santomauro
Sparta Saints	69	68	.504	17	33,436	Woodrow Bottoms/J.B. Ruark
Dublin Green Sox	63	75	.457	23½	62,049	Bill Phebus/Bill Davis/ Joseph Chambers
Baxley-Hazlehurst Red Socks	57	81	.413	29½	29,257	Mike Milosevich/Ray Baker
Fitzgerald Pioneers	52	85	.386	34	38,736	Bill Good/Charles DiCola/ John Pawlick

Playoffs: Vidalia-Lyons 3 games, Eastman 2; Tifton 3 games, Douglas 2.
Finals: Tifton 4 games, Vidalia-Lyons 2.

All-Star Team: 1B-Edgar Hartness, Eastman; **2B**-Orestes Pereda, Douglas; **3B**-Jack Collins, Sparta; **SS**-Emil Rey, Douglas; **OF**-Russell "Red" Mincy, Douglas; Pete Gula, Sparta; Don Ricketson, Vidalia-Lyons; **C**-Fred Tschudin, Douglas; **P**-Jim Harden, Eastman; George Cook, Sparta.

BA: James Stoyle, Sparta, .400
Runs: James Martin, Douglas, 130
Hits: James Stoyle, Sparta, 191
RBIs: Edgar Hartness, Eastman, 136
HRs: Ralph Burgamy, Eastman/Dublin, 28
Wins: Mike Rossi, Vidalia-Lyons, 25
SOs: Noel Oquendo, Fitzgerald, 224
ERA: Jim Harden, Eastman, 2.61

D Georgia-Alabama League
President: Arthur R. Decatur

Standings	W	L	Pct.	GB	Attend.	Manager
Newnan Brownies	74	52	.587	—	56,976	Bob Schmidt
Alexander City Millers	69	57	.548	5	37,373	Charles Roberts
Tallassee Cardinals (16)	66	60	.524	8	43,364	Robert Comiskey/ William Blackwell
La Grange Troupers (5)	65	61	.516	9	59,952	Bill Cooper
Valley Rebels (1)	62	64	.492	12	52,859	Jesse Danna/Malvern Morgan/ Woodrow Bottoms
Opelika Owls	62	64	.492	12	44,885	James Ball
Carrollton Hornets	56	70	.444	18	36,029	William Seal/William Rucker
Griffin Pimientos	50	76	.397	24	47,825	Clarence "Buck" Etchison/ Rudy York/Lew Sanders/ Sam Gibson

Playoffs: Newnan 3 games, Tallassee 2; Alexander City 3 games, La Grange 1.
Finals: Alexander City 4 games, Newnan 2.

All-Star Team: 1B-Alton McAfee, Newnan; **2B**-John Heusman, Alexander City; **3B**-Carl Franson, Newnan; **SS**-John Millard, Newnan; **OF**-Bert Hudson, Opelika; James Ball, Opelika; Joel Chapman, Valley; **C**-Bob Rinker, Griffin; **P**-Marvin Chappell, Alexander City; Ralph Clements, Tallassee.

BA: Joel Chapman, Valley, .351
Runs: John Heusman, Alexander City, 108
Hits: J.W. Spruil, Valley, 153
RBIs: Robert Schmidt, Newnan, 108
HRs: Carl Franson, Newnan, 28
Wins: John McFadden, Newnan, 21
SOs: John McFadden, Newnan, 180
ERA: Elmer Wallace, Newnan, 2.02

D Georgia-Florida League
President: W.T. Anderson

Standings	W	L	Pct.	GB	Attend.	Manager
Albany Cardinals (16)	96	42	.696	—	93,096	Sheldon "Chief" Bender
Valdosta Dodgers (10)	86	54	.614	11	51,105	Doc Alexson
Waycross Bears	83	56	.597	13½	54,508	Mickey Katkaveck
Americus Phillies (14)	71	67	.514	25	46,906	Eddie Murphy
Thomasville Tigers (4)	60	80	.429	37	44,072	Ralph DiLullo
Moultrie Athletics (6)	56	82	.406	40	28,911	Bill Peterman
Cordele Indians (3)	54	85	.388	42½	40,198	Hal Lee
Tallahassee Pirates (15)	49	89	.355	47	48,079	Norman Veazey/Bob Shawkey/ John Heving/Gene Cabaniss

Playoffs: Albany 3 games, Americus 1; Waycross 3 games, Valdosta 0.
Finals: Waycross 4 games, Albany 1.

All-Star Team: 1B-Neal Hartweck, Albany; **2B**-Edward Trojanowski, Americus; **3B**-Hal Grote, Valdosta; **SS**-Whitey Koppenhaver, Albany; **OF**-Gene Dopperschmidt, Valdosta; Dick Jones, Valdosta; Russell Rac, Albany; **C**-Vic Comolli, Americus; **P**-Morris Frank, Albany; Art Ceccarelli, Valdosta.

BA: Delton Childs, Albany, .343
Runs: Edward Trojanowski, Americus, 141
Hits: John Philips, Thomasville, 192
RBIs: Russell Rac, Albany, 134
HRs: Harold Shiles, Waycross, 21
Wins: Morris Frank, Albany, 22
SOs: Art Ceccarelli, Valdosta, 294
ERA: Morris Frank, Albany, 1.94

D Kansas-Oklahoma-Missouri League
President: E.L. Dale

Standings	W	L	Pct.	GB	Attend.	Manager
Independence Yankees (5)	71	53	.573	—	46,607	Harry Craft
Bartlesville Pirates (15)	71	55	.563	1	51,000	Tedd Gullic
Iola Indians (3)	70	55	.560	1½	49,491	Winlow Johnson
Ponca City Dodgers (10)	66	59	.528	5½	62,082	Boyd Bartley
Chanute Athletics	65	60	.520	6½	39,228	James Hansen/Charles Bates
Carthage Cubs (11)	62	64	.492	10	38,028	Don Anderson
Miami Owls	56	69	.448	15½	32,887	Omar Lane
Pittsburg Browns (7)	39	85	.315	32	39,755	Albert Barkus/Olan Smith

Playoffs: Independence 3 games, Ponca City 1; Iola 3 games, Bartlesville 1.
Finals: Independence 3 games, Iola 0.

All-Star Team: 1B-Bob Speake, Carthage; **2B**-Gene Castiglione, Ponca City; **3B**-Lou Skizas, Independence; **SS**-Kent Pflasterer, Chanute; **OF**-Harold Neighbors, Bartlesville; Dick Getter, Iola; James Bello, Independence; **C**-Dean Manns, Carthage; **P**-Woody Wuethrich, Carthage; Conrad Swensson, Ponca City.

BA: Richard Drury, Bartlesville, .317
Runs: Charles Weber, Independence, 98
Hits: James Bello, Independence, 156
RBIs: Harry Bright, Miami, 96

HRs: Bob Speake, Carthage, 14
Wins: Vernon Thies, Chanute, 18
SOs: Bob Weisler, Independence, 240
ERA: Conrad Swensson, Ponca City, 1.69

D Kitty League
President: Shelby Peace

Standings	W	L	Pct.	GB	Attend.	Manager
Owensboro Oilers (9)	82	40	.672	—	67,700	Bill Adair
Cairo Dodgers (10)	74	51	.592	9½	31,563	William Hart
Hopkinsville Hoppers	68	56	.548	15	31,090	John Mueller
Madisonville Miners (2)	67	57	.540	16	36,760	Joe DeMasi
Union City Greyhounds (3)	65	60	.520	18½	43,978	Tony Rensa/Rudy York
Fulton Railroaders (8)	62	61	.504	20½	34,363	Ivan Kuester
Clarksville Colts	40	85	.320	43½	25,250	Horace Lisenbee
Mayfield Clothiers (7)	38	86	.306	45	23,244	Bill Enos

Playoffs: Madisonville 3 games, Owensboro 0; Cairo 3 games, Hopkinsville 2.
Finals: Madisonville 2 games, Cairo 1, series cut short by bad weather.

All-Star Team: 1B-Don Hazelton, Owensboro; **2B**-Bill Adair, Owensboro; **3B**-Raymond Cattaneo, Owensboro; **SS**-Buddy Afremow, Hopkinsville; **OF**-Maurice Partain, Clarksville; John Mueller, Hopkinsville; Joe DeMasi, Madisonville; **C**-Jack Litzenfelner, Cairo; **P**-Harley Grossman, Fulton; Ray Crone, Owensboro; Joseph Linn, Union City.

BA: William Hart, Cairo, .404
Runs: Don Hazelton, Owensboro, 116
Hits: Joe DeMasi, Madisonville, 163
RBIs: Joe DeMasi, Madisonville, 133

HRs: Bill Adair, Owensboro, 23
Wins: Harley Grossman, Fulton, 19
SOs: Fred Wagner, Owensboro, 184
ERA: Joseph Linn, Union City, 2.28

D Longhorn League
President: Hal Sayles

Standings	W	L	Pct.	GB	Attend.	Manager
Big Spring Broncs	94	45	.676	—	58,559	Pat Stasey
Midland Indians	74	66	.529	20½	52,078	Harold Webb
Vernon Dusters	72	66	.522	21½	50,386	Robert Huntley
San Angelo Colts	69	68	.504	24	83,245	Sam Harshaney
Odessa Oilers	66	74	.471	28½	60,426	Alex Monchak
Ballinger Cats	64	76	.457	30½	44,815	Charles English/Stuart Williams/Lindsay Brown
Sweetwater Swatters	60	79	.432	34	33,770	Richard Gyselman/Kermit Lewis
Roswell Rockets	57	82	.410	37	43,584	Bob Crues/Potsy Allen

Playoffs: Big Spring 4 games, San Angelo 0; Midland 4 games, Vernon 1.
Finals: Big Spring 4 games, Midland 0.

All-Star Team: 1B-Wayne Batson, Odessa; **2B**-Alex Monchak, Odessa; **3B**-Carlos Pascual, Big Spring; **SS**-Eduardo Vasquez, Big Spring; **OF**-Harry Scherting, Vernon; Stuart Williams, Ballinger; Pat Stasey, Big Spring; **C**-Frank Mormino, Odessa; **P**-Humberto Garcia, Big Spring; Julio Ramos, Big Spring.

BA: Pat Stasey, Big Spring, .376
Runs: Alex Monchak, Odessa, 147
Hits: Carlos Pascual, Big Spring, 188
Harry Scherting, Vernon, 188
RBIs: Frank Mormino, Odessa, 140

HRs: Alex Monchak, Odessa, 35
Wins: Julio Ramos, Big Spring, 22
SOs: Julio Ramos, Big Spring, 262
ERA: Humberto Garcia, Big Spring, 1.77

D Mississippi-Ohio Valley League
President: C.C. "Dutch" Hoffman

Standings	W	L	Pct.	GB	Attend.	Manager
Centralia Cubs	74	44	.627	—	35,000	Lou Bekeza
West Frankfort Cardinals (16)	71	49	.592	4	24,140	Robert Stanton
Mattoon Indians	62	56	.525	12	38,325	Chuck Hawley
Paducah Chiefs	54	65	.454	20½	54,859	Carroll Peterson/Edwin Kearse
Mt. Vernon Kings	53	67	.442	22	36,240	Robert Shreve/William Trotter
Belleville Stags (5)	43	76	.361	31½	13,500	Les Mueller/Joe Yurkovich/Addie Nesbit/Malcolm "Bunny" Mick

Playoffs: Mattoon 3 games, Centralia 0; Paducah 3 games, West Frankfort 0.
Finals: Paducah 4 games, Mattoon 3.

All-Star Team: 1B-George Murphy, Mattoon; **2B**-Roger DallaBetta, Centralia; **3B**-George Gatto, Centralia; **SS**-Donald Breidenbach, Mattoon; **OF**-Donald Wagner, Mt. Vernon; Richard Martz, Paducah; James Nelms, Mt. Vernon; **C**-Socrates Anthony, Belleville; **P**-Joseph Prucha, Centralia; Joseph Mattis, Mattoon.

BA: Malcolm "Bunny" Mick, Belleville, .354
Runs: Ev Joyner, West Frankfort, 104
Hits: Ev Joyner, West Frankfort, 170
RBIs: Richard Martz, Paducah, 100

HRs: Arthur Oliver, Paducah, 17
Wins: Joseph Prucha, Centralia, 19
SOs: Joseph Mattis, Mattoon, 166
ERA: Dick Loeser, West Frankfort, 2.22

D Mountain States League
President: Virgil Q. Wacks

Standings	W	L	Pct.	GB	Attend.	Manager
Harlan Smokies	83	41	.669	—	49,615	George Motto
Morristown Red Sox	72	52	.581	11	44,362	James Grigg
Middlesboro Athletics	69	56	.552	14½	25,833	Hobe Brummitt/Ted Russ/James Burns
Jenkins Cavaliers	63	61	.508	20	19,654	Joe Vitter
Pennington Gap Miners	62	63	.496	21½	14,820	Lew Flick/Burgess Wolfenbarger
Newport Canners	59	66	.472	24½	14,148	Cy Whaley
Big Stone Gap Rebels	55	70	.440	28½	37,751	Rudolph Parsons/Dale Markert/Fred Marsh
Hazard Bombers	35	89	.282	48	23,543	Fred Marsh/George Mitrus/Hobe Brummitt

Playoffs: Harlan 3 games, Middlesboro 1; Morristown 3 games, Jenkins 2.
Finals: Harlan 3 games, Morristown 2.

All-Star Team: 1B-Kelly Lunn, Pennington Gap; **2B**-Alberto Costa, Morristown; **3B**-Edward Cousins, Harlan; **SS**-Phil Lewandowski, Hazard; **OF**-Lew Flick, Pennington Gap; Andy Fronduto, Jenkins; Cy Whaley, Newport; **C**-Charles McCormick, Harlan; **P**-Frank Wilson, Harlan; Porter Witt, Morristown.

BA: Kelly Lunn, Pennington Gap, .358
Runs: Robert Grose, Pennington Gap, 127
Hits: Kelly Lunn, Pennington Gap, 179
RBIs: Kelly Lunn, Pennington Gap, 126

HRs: Jack Hall, Jenkins, 18
Wins: Frank Wilson, Harlan, 27
SOs: Frank Wilson, Harlan, 176
ERA: Frank Wilson, Harlan, 2.77

D North Atlantic League
President: Ernest C. Landgraf

Standings	W	L	Pct.	GB	Attend.	Manager
Stroudsburg Poconos (3)	101	36	.737	—	39,890	Frank Radler
Lebanon Chix (16)	80	56	.588	20½	33,000	Harold Contini
Mahanoy City Brewers	71	63	.530	28½	35,000	Michael Coons
Peekskill Highlanders	64	75	.460	38	27,300	Al Gardella
Carbondale Pioneer Blues (14)	63	76	.453	39	28,000	Bernard Lutz
Bangor Pickers	59	75	.440	40½	27,112	Bill Long
Hazleton Mountaineers	53	76	.411	44	34,003	Joe Langworthy/Earl Stack/Armond Cardoni
Nazareth Barons	52	86	.377	49½	17,716	Richard Errickson/Charles Heath

Playoffs: Stroudsburg 4 games, Mahanoy City 3; Peekskill 4 games, Lebanon 1.
Finals: Stroudsburg 4 games, Peekskill 2.

All-Star Team: 1B-Harry Warner, Stroudsburg; **2B**-Tom Ambrose, Mahanoy City; **3B**-Stan Pawloski, Stroudsburg; Joe Penczak, Peekskill; **SS**-Dom Dellarocca, Stroudsburg; **OF**-Mickey Finn, Stroudsburg; J.C. Dunn, Lebanon; Jack Rothenhausler, Stroudsburg; **C**-Ellsworth Dean, Carbondale; Marty Powers, Peekskill; **P**-Dale Melms, Stroudsburg; Edward Varhely, Stroudsburg.

BA: J.C. Dunn, Lebanon, .384
Runs: J.C. Dunn, Lebanon, 141
Hits: J.C. Dunn, Lebanon, 216
RBIs: J.C. Dunn, Lebanon, 137

HRs: Alphonse Baselici, Lebanon, 18
Charles McLean, Lebanon, 18
Wins: Edward Varhely, Stroudsburg, 20
SOs: Richard Umberger, Lebanon, 174
ERA: Frank Radler, Stroudsburg, 1.59

D North Carolina State League
President: Frank Spencer

Standings	W	L	Pct.	GB	Attend.	Manager
High Point-Thomasville Hi-Toms (9)	90	34	.726	—	95,792	Jim Gruzdis
Mooresville Moors	72	52	.581	18	37,414	Jim Mills
Landis Spinners	69	53	.566	20	24,806	Fred Chapman
Lexington Indians (6)	60	64	.484	30	28,996	Archie Templeton/Walt VanGrofski
Statesville Owls	53	71	.427	37	49,856	Tuck McWilliams
Concord Nationals (8)	50	72	.410	39	29,640	James Calleran
Hickory Rebels (13)	50	74	.403	40	34,042	Owen Linn/Richard Jackson & James Proctor/Charles Bowles
Salisbury Pirates (15)	49	73	.402	40	45,840	John Corriden/George O'Neil

Playoffs: High Point-Thomasville 4 games, Landis 1; Lexington 4 games, Mooresville 0.
Finals: High Point-Thomasville 4 games, Lexington 3.

All-Star Team: 1B-Charley Knight, Mooresville; Herman Niehaus, Hi-Toms; **2B**-Vann Harrington, Hi-Toms; **3B**-Fred Chapman, Landis; **SS**-Robert Deese, Landis; **OF**-Owen Linn, Hickory; Norman Small, Mooresville; Jim Mills, Mooresville; **C**-Cliff Bolton, Hi-Toms; **P**-Harold Wood, Lexington; Frank Smith, Statesville.

BA: Cliff Bolton, Hi-Toms, .399
Runs: Clarence Williams, Hi-Toms, 133
Hits: Fred Chapman, Landis, 169
Vann Harrington, Hi-Toms, 169
George Bradshaw, Statesville, 169
RBIs: Norman Small, Mooresville, 152

HRs: Norman Small, Mooresville, 41
Wins: Lynn Southworth, Hi-Toms, 21
Lester Bringle, Mooresville, 21
SOs: Harold Wood, Lexington, 204
ERA: Ernie Johnson, Statesville, 2.04
Pct: Lynn Southworth, Hi-Toms, .955, 21-1

D Ohio-Indiana League
President: Frank M. Colley

Standings	W	L	Pct.	GB	Attend.	Manager
Portsmouth A's (6)	81	58	.583	—	61,106	Homer Lee Cox
Springfield Giants (13)	77	63	.550	4½	67,568	Anthony Ravish
Muncie Reds (12)	75	63	.543	5½	49,004	Mike Blazo

	W	L	Pct.	GB	Attend.	Manager
Marion Red Sox (1)	73	64	.533	7	57,113	Walter Millies
Zanesville Indians (3)	69	67	.507	10½	58,034	Pat McLaughlin
Newark Yankees (5)	65	72	.474	15	62,321	James McLend
Richmond Tigers	65	73	.471	15½	44,346	Cyril Pfeifer/Kenneth Holtcamp
Lima Chiefs	46	91	.336	34	31,298	Grover Hartley/George Kinnamon

Playoffs: Marion 3 games, Portsmouth 1; Muncie 3 games, Springfield 1.
Finals: Marion 4 games, Muncie 3.

All-Star Team: 1B-Robert Diedrick, Lima; **2B**-Louis Ruehl, Muncie; **3B**-Edward Ralston, Muncie; **SS**-Milton Kress, Springfield; **OF**-Forrest Rende, Portsmouth; Joseph Beleta, Lima; Robert Brigham, Marion; Ralph Lucas, Springfield; **C**-Ben Haddix, Springfield; **P**-Allen Romberger, Portsmouth; Neilan Smith, Marion.

BA: Ralph Lucas, Springfield, .347
Runs: Wayne Yoder, Springfield, 121
Hits: Anthony Yula, Portsmouth, 166
RBIs: Ralph Lucas, Springfield, 103
HRs: Forrest Rende, Portsmouth, 25
Wins: Clark Mains, Springfield, 20
SOs: Charles Hagy, Springfield, 194
ERA: Ewen Bryden, Portsmouth, 1.82

D PONY League
President: Vincent M. McNamara

Standings	W	L	Pct.	GB	Attend.	Manager
Bradford Blue Wings (14)	80	46	.635	—	78,139	Dan Carnevale
Jamestown Falcons (4)	78	48	.619	2	110,690	Marvin Olson
Hamilton Cardinals (16)	75	50	.600	4½	137,340	George Kissell
Batavia Clippers (3)	66	60	.524	14	54,325	Ed Kobesky
Hornell Maple Leafs (1)	62	64	.492	18	85,926	Marius Russo
Lockport Reds (12)	58	68	.460	22	47,336	Cecil Scheffel
Wellsville Nitros	45	81	.357	35	48,253	Tom Kister/Jim Wasdell
Olean Oilers (7)	39	86	.312	40½	40,264	Shan Deniston/Lawrence Mancini

Playoffs: Bradford 4 games, Batavia 3; Hamilton 4 games, Jamestown 1.
Finals: Bradford 4 games, Hamilton 1.

All-Star Team: 1B-Bill Spangler, Bradford; Frank Seastrand, Wellsville; **2B**-Bruno Casanova, Hamilton; **3B**-Orval Cott, Lockport; **SS**-Dan Carnevale, Bradford; **OF**-Carmen Links, Batavia; Al Gilbert, Jamestown; George Schachle, Hamilton; **C**-Harry Psutka, Jamestown; **P**-John Gilbert, Hornell; William Furlong, Jamestown.

BA: Ed Kobesky, Batavia, .390
Runs: Emil Carlini, Bradford, 127
Hits: Dan Carnevale, Bradford, 192
RBIs: Dan Carnevale, Bradford, 126
HRs: Carmen Links, Batavia, 24
Wins: Willard Schmidt, Hamilton, 22
SOs: John Gilbert, Hornell, 191
ERA: William Furlong, Jamestown, 1.89
Pct: William Furlong, Jamestown, .762, 16-5

D Rio Grande Valley League
President: William R. Byrd

Standings	W	L	Pct.	GB	Attend.	Manager
Corpus Christi Aces	89	51	.686	—	97,192	William Gann
Laredo Apaches	80	60	.571	9	47,857	William Cearley/Ishmael Montalvo
Brownsville Charros	75	65	.536	14	51,416	Joseph King
McAllen Giants	70	68	.507	18	22,598	Frank Matthews/Philip Kuykendall
Del Rio Cowboys	58	80	.420	30	32,323	Boyd SoRelle
Donna/Robstown Cardinals#	45	93	.326	43	19,753	Russell Frisch/Charles Engle/Mimi Cavazos

#Donna moved to Robstown June 6.

Playoffs: Corpus Christi 4 games, McAllen 0; Brownsville 4 games, Laredo 2.
Finals: Corpus Christi 4 games, Brownsville 0.

All-Star Team: 1B-Bernard Pardue, Corpus Christi; **2B**-Mike Boettcher, Brownsville; **3B**-Frank McAlexander, Corpus Christi; **SS**-Eloy Barrera, Laredo; **OF**-William Cearley, Laredo; Lloyd Pearson, Corpus Christi; Dave Fairman, Del Rio; **C**-Jack Trench, Corpus Christi; **P**-Edward Arthur, McAllen; George Davis, Corpus Christi.

BA: Joseph King, Brownsville, .354
Runs: Lloyd Pearson, Corpus Christi, 140
Hits: Bernard Pardue, Corpus Christi, 205
RBIs: Donald Petschow, Brownsville, 146
HRs: Donald Petschow, Brownsville, 28
Wins: Gilberto Garza, Laredo, 21
SOs: Edward Arthur, McAllen, 178
ERA: Robert Wiltse, Brownsville, 2.08

D Sooner State League
President: Jack Mealey

Standings	W	L	Pct.	GB	Attend.	Manager
Pauls Valley Raiders	88	52	.629	—	61,085	Clarence Phillips
Lawton Giants (13)	87	52	.626	½	45,501	Lou Brower
Chickasha Chiefs	78	61	.561	9½	59,306	Ray Honeycutt
Ada Herefords (7)	69	70	.497	18½	33,525	Bill Krueger
Duncan Uttmen	65	74	.468	22½	36,678	Edward Marleau/James Skidgel/Hosea Pfeiffer
McAlester Rockets (5)	58	82	.414	30	56,733	Vern Hoscheit
Ardmore Indians	57	81	.413	30	43,348	Dutch Prather/James Skidgel
Seminole Oilers (2)	54	84	.391	33	33,258	Hugh Willingham/Paul Schoendienst

Playoffs: Pauls Valley 3 games, Ada 2; Lawton 3 games, Chickasha 0.
Finals: Lawton 4 games, Pauls Valley 1.

All-Star Team: 1B-Dick Vonder Haar, Lawton; **2B**-Bob King, Ada; **3B**-Pete Runnels, Chickasha; **SS**-Daryl Spencer, Pauls Valley; **OF**-Gene Creekmore, Seminole; Joe Nodar, Ardmore; Andy Teter, Pauls Valley; Dick Bornholdt, Lawton; **C**-Vern Hoscheit, McAlester; **P**-Jim Melton, Pauls Valley; Joseph Micciche, Lawton.

BA: Pete Runnels, Chickasha, .372
Runs: Kelly Wingo, Chickasha, 123
Hits: Pete Runnels, Chickasha, 188
RBIs: A.B. Pearson, Pauls Valley, 123
HRs: Daryl Spencer, Pauls Valley, 23
Bill Milligan, Ada, 23
Wins: Jim Melton, Pauls Valley, 23
SOs: Joseph Micciche, Lawton, 297
ERA: James Spencer, Lawton, 1.96
Pct: Joseph Micciche, Lawton, .769, 20-6

D Tobacco State League
President: Arthur T. Moore

Standings	W	L	Pct.	GB	Attend.	Manager
Dunn-Erwin Twins	81	54	.600	—	39,335	Jim Staton
Red Springs Red Robins (6)	76	59	.563	5	33,303	Red Norris
Lumberton Auctioneers (11)	75	61	.551	6½	60,038	Charles Lucas/James Guinn
Sanford Spinners	71	62	.530	9	36,046	Zeb Harrington
Smithfield-Selma Leafs	70	65	.519	11	41,618	Virgil Payne/Claude Weaver/Paul Kluk
Fayetteville Scotties	61	76	.445	21	56,999	Cecil "Zip" Payne/Joe Roseberry/Nicholas Rhabe/John Helms
Clinton Sampson Blues	60	78	.435	22½	37,496	Marvin Lorenz
Wilmington Pirates	49	88	.358	33	49,009	Ab Tiedemann/John Edens/Gus Brittain/Hargrove Davis

Playoffs: Dunn-Erwin 4 games, Lumberton 1; Red Springs 4 games, Sanford 2.
Finals: Red Springs 4 games, Dunn-Erwin 1.

All-Star Team: 1B-Marvin Lorenz, Clinton; **2B**-James Guinn, Lumberton; **3B**-Henry Miller, Dunn-Erwin; **SS**-Thomas Campbell, Red Springs; **OF**-John Richards, Dunn-Erwin; William Bohlender, Lumberton; Hargrove Davis, Wilmington; **C**-Steve Marko, Dunn-Erwin; **P**-Clarence Condit, Dunn-Erwin; Gordon McDonald, Lumberton.

BA: Joe Roseberry, Fayetteville, .409
Runs: Granville Denning, Dunn-Erwin, 118
Nicholas Purchia, Clinton, 118
Hits: Granville Denning, Dunn-Erwin, 185
RBIs: Granville Denning, Dunn-Erwin, 119
HRs: Joseph Stern, Clinton/Lumberton, 15
John Helms, Fayetteville, 15
Wins: Clarence Condit, Dunn-Erwin, 20
SOs: Clarence Condit, Dunn-Erwin, 264
ERA: Leslie Price, Clinton, 2.19

D Virginia League
President: Robert S. Brenaman

Standings	W	L	Pct.	GB	Attend.	Manager
Franklin Kildees	80	48	.625	—	54,282	George Lacy
Petersburg Generals	72	54	.571	7	76,000	Paul Varner
Emporia Nationals (8)	67	55	.549	10	29,050	Morris "Smut" Aderholt
Suffolk Goobers	57	65	.467	20	41,381	Bill Steinecke/Paul Badgett
Hopewell Blue Sox	52	75	.409	27½	39,600	Joe Mills
Lawrenceville Robins	45	76	.372	31½	29,000	Garland Braxton/James Myers/Glenn Titus/Claude Weaver/Walter Wholey

Playoffs: Franklin 4 games, Suffolk 1; Petersburg 4 games, Emporia 3.
Finals: Petersburg 4 games, Franklin 2.

All-Star Team: 1B-Sil DiMenna, Petersburg; **2B**-Walter Wholey, Lawrenceville; **3B**-Paul Varner, Petersburg; **SS**-Desmond Charouhas, Emporia; **OF**-John Garrison, Emporia; John Zontini, Franklin; Morris "Smut" Aderholt, Emporia; **C**-Ted Jones, Hopewell; **P**-Arnold Atkins, Franklin; Joe Hash, Suffolk.

BA: Paul Varner, Petersburg, .355
Runs: John Cornwell, Franklin, 129
Hits: James Gillette, Franklin, 181
RBIs: James Gillette, Franklin, 118
HRs: John Garrison, Emporia, 25
Wins: Arnold Atkins, Franklin, 21
SOs: Arnold Atkins, Franklin, 204
ERA: Arnold Atkins, Franklin, 2.70

D Western Carolina League
President: Cloyd A. Hager

Standings	W	L	Pct.	GB	Attend.	Manager
Newton-Conover Twins	72	36	.667	—	82,481	Edwin Yount
Lincolnton Cardinals	69	41	.627	4	66,766	Carl Miller
Rutherford County Owls# (11)	64	45	.587	8½	52,382	Sam Gibson/Rube Wilson
Morganton Aggies	58	49	.542	13½	60,107	Sam Bell
Lenoir Red Sox (13)	57	50	.533	14½	43,666	Claude Jonnard
Marion Marauders	40	62	.392	29	37,387	John Lanning/Jack Triplett
Shelby Farmers	40	68	.370	32	37,341	Joseph Borich/Harold Dedmon/Walt Dixon
Hendersonville Skylarks	29	78	.269	42½	31,235	Rube Wilson/Raymond Hunt

#represented Spindale, North Carolina.

Playoffs: Rutherford County 4 games, Newton-Conover 2; Morganton 4 games, Lincolnton 3.
Finals: Rutherford County 4 games, Morganton 1.

All-Star Team: 1B-Carl Miller, Lincolnton; **2B-**Bus Huffstetler, Lincolnton; **3B-**Bobby Caldwell, Lincolnton; **SS-**Noel Casbier, Lenoir; **OF-**Tom Cumby, Marion; Elmer Roberts, Morganton; Ralph Dixon, Rutherford County; **C-**Edwin Yount, Newton-Conover; **P-**Ray Lindsey, Newton-Conover; Bill Haynes, Rutherford County.

BA: Carl Miller, Lincolnton, .404	**HRs:** Carl Miller, Lincolnton, 22
Runs: Carl Miller, Lincolnton, 125	**Wins:** Lelon Jaynes, Morganton, 19
Hits: Carl Miller, Lincolnton, 159	**SOs:** Lelon Jaynes, Morganton, 202
RBIs: Robert McGimsey, Morganton, 118	**ERA:** Walter Lentz, Lenoir, 3.03

D Wisconsin State League
President: Judge Arold F. Murphy

Standings	W	L	Pct.	GB	Attend.	Manager
Oshkosh Giants (13)	72	49	.595	—	115,956	David Garcia
Green Bay Bluejays (3)	71	55	.563	3½	105,765	Phil Seghi
Sheboygan Indians (10)	67	56	.545	6	58,730	Joe Hauser
Wisconsin Rapids White Sox (2)	64	58	.525	8½	52,828	Glen Stewart/George Mitro
Fond du Lac Panthers (5)	59	63	.484	13½	78,103	Fred Collins
Appleton Papermakers (14)	57	69	.452	17½	92,938	Frederick Clemence
Wausau Lumberjacks (7)	54	69	.439	19	55,418	Joe Skurski
Janesville Cubs (11)	50	75	.400	24	68,768	Jim Oglesby/Michael Frederick/Adolph Matulis

Playoffs: None.

All-Star Team: 1B-Robert Myers, Oshkosh; **2B-**Stan Gorecki, Green Bay; **3B-**Earl "Jug" Girard, Green Bay; **SS-**Edward Sterger, Sheboygan; **OF-**Ted Steggeman, Fond du Lac; Joe Biancalana, Appleton; Jack Ramm, Wausau; **C-**Harry Fredericks, Appleton; Ron Neff, Oshkosh; **P-**Rudy Yandoli, Oshkosh; Bill Allen, Sheboygan.

BA: Earl "Jug" Girard, Green Bay, .367	**HRs:** Edward Fenelon, Sheboygan, 18
Runs: Robert Myers, Oshkosh, 103	**Wins:** Bill Allen, Sheboygan, 18
Hits: Kenneth McCormick, Fond du Lac, 155	Rudy Yandoli, Oshkosh, 18
RBIs: Ken Landenberger, Wisconsin Rapids, 129	**SOs:** Bill Allen, Sheboygan, 242
	ERA: Jennins Norman, Oshkosh, 2.03

Ind Mexican League
President: Dr. Eduardo Quijano Pitman

Standings	W	L	Pct.	GB	Manager
Monterrey Sultanes*	52	33	.612	—	Lazaro Salazar
Torreon Algodoneros**	49	36	.576	3	Memo Garibay
Jalisco Charros	43	41	.512	8½	Manuel Arroyo/Alberto Romo Chavez
Veracruz Azules	42	42	.500	9½	Salvador Hernandez
Mexico City Diablos Rojos	41	43	.488	10½	Napoleon Reyes/Raymond Brown
San Luis Potosi Tuneros	41	44	.482	11	Jose Luis Gomez
Veracruz Aguila	39	45	.464	12½	Eustaquio Martinez
Nuevo Laredo Tecolotes	31	53	.369	20½	Agustin Bejerano/James Steiner

Playoff: Monterrey 4 games, Torreon 0.

BA: Adolfo Cabrera, Jalisco, .379	**Wins:** Daniel Rios, Monterrey, 21
Hits: Dilio Rodriguez, Torreon, 132	**SOs:** Wilfredo Salas, Torreon, 158
RBIs: Jesus Diaz, Torreon, 83	**ERA:** Alfonso Ramirez, Mexico City, 2.35
HRs: Jesus Diaz, Torreon, 13	

Ind Provincial League
President: Albert Molini

Standings	W	L	Pct.	GB	Manager
Drummondville Cubs	63	34	.650	—	Max Lanier/Stan Beard
Granby Red Sox	55	42	.567	8	Gene Oliver
Sherbrooke Athletiques	53	47	.530	11½	Roland Gladu
St. Jean Braves	45	53	.459	18½	Don Savage/Red Hayworth
Farnham Pirates	43	55	.439	20½	Vern Thoele
St. Hyacinthe Saints	36	64	.360	28½	Paul Martin/Del Friar

BA: Al Armour, Farnham, .342	**HRs:** Quincy Barbee, St. Jean, 23
Hits: Sylvio Garcia, Sherbrooke, 126	**Wins:** Sal Maglie, Drummondville, 18
RBIs: Claro Duany, Sherbrooke, 99	

1949 Interleague Post Season Play

World Series
New York (American) 4 games, Brooklyn (National) 1

Junior World Series
Indianapolis (American Association) 4 games, Montreal (International) 2
Total Attendance: 64,799

Dixie Series
Nashville (Southern Association) 4 games, Tulsa (Texas) 3
Total Attendance: 35,265

Little Dixie Series
Gladewater (East Texas) 4 games, Hammond (Evangeline) 0

Class B Florida Series
Pensacola (Southeastern) 4 games, Tampa (Florida International) 2

Class D Series
Waycross (Georgia-Florida) 4 games, Alexander City (Georgia-Alabama) 1

Class D Texas Series
Corpus Christi (Rio Grande Valley) 4 games, Big Spring (Longhorn) 1

1949 Major League Farm Systems

American League

1 Boston (9): Louisville, Birmingham, Scranton, Roanoke, San Jose, Oneonta, Valley, Marion (OH), Hornell.

2 Chicago (11): Memphis, Muskegon, Charleston (SC), Waterloo, Stockton, Hot Springs, Oil City, Superior, Madisonville, Seminole, Wisconsin Rapids.

3 Cleveland (17): San Diego, Oklahoma City, Dayton, Wilkes-Barre, St. Petersburg, Spartanburg, Tucson, Bakersfield, Pittsfield, Burlington (IA), Cordele, Iola, Union City, Stroudsburg, Zanesville, Batavia, Green Bay.

4 Detroit (12): Toledo, Buffalo, Little Rock, Flint, Williamsport, Durham, Lynn, Rome, Butler, Troy, Thomasville (GA), Jamestown.

5 New York (21): Kansas City, Newark (NJ), Beaumont, Binghamton, Augusta, Manchester, Norfolk, Quincy, Victoria, Ventura, Amsterdam, Grand Forks, Twin Falls, Joplin, Easton, La Grange, Independence, Belleville, Newark (OH), McAlester, Fond du Lac.

6 Philadelphia (11): Savannah, Lincoln, Martinsville, Kewanee, Youngstown, Welch, Tarboro, Moultrie, Lexington, Portsmouth (OH), Red Springs.

7 St. Louis (18): Baltimore, San Antonio, Elmira, Wichita Falls, Springfield (IL), Globe-Miami, Gloversville-Johnstown, Pine Bluff, Marshall, Aberdeen, Salinas/Tijuana, Muskogee, Redding, Pittsburg (KS), Mayfield, Olean, Ada, Wausau.

8 Washington (9): Chattanooga, Havana, Hagerstown, Charlotte, New Castle, Orlando, Fulton, Concord, Emporia.

National League

9 Boston (11): Milwaukee, Hartford, Denver, Pawtucket, Jackson, Evansville, Eau Claire, Bluefield, Marysville, Owensboro, High Point-Thomasville.

10 Brooklyn (25): St. Paul, Montreal, Hollywood, Mobile, Ft. Worth, Greenville (SC), Pueblo, Miami (FL), Lancaster, Nashua, Newport News, Danville (IL), Asheville, Geneva (NY), Santa Barbara, Trois Rivieres, Greenwood, Johnstown, Billings, Pulaski, Cambridge, Valdosta, Ponca City, Cairo, Sheboygan.

11 Chicago (15): Los Angeles, Nashville, Macon, Des Moines, Springfield (MA), Selma, Decatur, Visalia, Clinton, Sioux Falls, St. Augustine, Carthage, Lumberton, Rutherford County, Janesville.

12 Cincinnati (10): Syracuse, Tulsa, Charleston (WV), Columbia, Sunbury, Rockford, Tyler, Ogden, Muncie, Lockport.

13 New York (19): Minneapolis, Jersey City, Jacksonville, Sioux City, Trenton, Richmond (VA), Knoxville, Erie, St. Cloud, Idaho Falls, Reno, Ft. Smith, Bristol (VA), Sanford (FL), Hickory, Springfield (OH), Lawton, Lenoir, Oshkosh.

14 Philadelphia (14): Toronto, Utica, Wilmington (DE), Portland (ME), Terre Haute, Schenectady, Vandergrift, Salina, Seaford, Klamath Falls, Americus, Carbondale, Bradford, Appleton.

15 Pittsburgh (13): Indianapolis, New Orleans, Albany (NY), Waco, York, Davenport, Modesto, Keokuk, Uniontown, Greenville (AL), Tallahassee, Bartlesville, Salisbury (NC).

16 St. Louis (20): Columbus (OH), Rochester, Houston, Columbus (GA), Omaha, Winston-Salem, Allentown, Lynchburg, Fresno, Duluth, Pocatello, St. Joseph, Johnson City, Salisbury (MD), Willows, Tallassee, Albany (GA), West Frankfort, Lebanon, Hamilton.

1949 No-Hitters

Date	Pitcher	Team	League	Opponent	Score
4-18	Roger Wright	Tampa	Fla. International	St. Petersburg	7-0
4-24	Lauren Monroe	Stockton	California	Modesto	5-1 (7)
5-4	Clifford Littledove	Bristol	Appalachian	Bluefield	
5-6	Rollie Schuster	Scranton	Eastern	Williamsport	3-0 (5)
5-7	Biggie Moran	Poughkeepsie	Colonial	Waterbury	4-0
5-7	Tony West	Trenton	Interstate	Sunbury	11-0
5-10	Don Rexford	Lima	Ohio-Indiana	Muncie	3-2
5-13	John Andre	Rehoboth Beach	Eastern Shore	Seaford	4-0
5-15	Bob Schultz	Nazareth	North Atlantic	Stroudsburg	7-0 (7)
5-28	Wilfred Roca	Havana	Fla. International	West Palm Beach	4-0
6-1	Bill Loes	Nashua	New England	Fall River	2-0
6-10	Buck Thiel	Hartford	Eastern	Elmira	(7)
6-17	Bobby Coburn	Morristown	Mountain States	Big Stone Gap	8-0 (7)
6-18	Herm Miller	Duluth	Northern	St. Cloud	4-0 (7)
6-19	Bill Allen	Sheboygan	Wisconsin State	Janesville	9-0
6-23	Emory Hewlett	Baton Rouge	Evangeline	New Iberia	3-0 (P, 7)
6-24	Tom Spears	Lafayette	Evangeline	Houma	4-0
6-26	Don Harris	Aberdeen	Northern	Fargo-Moorhead	3-1 (6)
6-28	Jim Morris	St. Joseph	Western Assoc.	Hutchinson	9-0
6-29	Tom Pullig	Greenville	Big State	Sherman-Denison	3-0 (P, 7)
7-4	John Masuga	Pittsfield	Canadian-American	Schenectady	8-0
7-5	Alex Gounaris	La Grange	Georgia-Alabama	Griffin	5-0 (7)
7-8	Clarence "Hooks" Iott	Beaumont	Texas	Shreveport	2-0
7-10	Erwin Coutts	Mexicali	Sunset	San Bernardino	7-0
7-12	Hugh Sooter	Anniston	Southeastern	Montgomery	
7-13	Paul Billet	Lebanon	North Atlantic	Nazareth	9-0
7-13	Lefty Aguila	Tucson	Arizona-Texas	Bisbee-Douglas	3-0
7-15	Alex Gounaris	La Grange	Georgia-Alabama	Griffin	(7)
7-16	Mike Rossi	Vidalia-Lyons	Georgia State	Tifton	2-0 (7)
7-19	Ivan Johannes	Columbia	South Atlantic	Charleston	2-0
7-21	Joe Reedy	Roanoke	Piedmont	Richmond	8-0
7-21	J.D. Davis	Mt. Airy	Blue Ridge	Radford	8-1
7-23	Charlie Rose	Sanford	Florida State	DeLand	1-0 (7)
7-23	George Vinston	Newark	Ohio-Indiana	Marion	3-0 (7)
7-24	Armand Castro	Modesto	California	Stockton	1-0 (7)
7-25	Bert Heffernan	Pensacola	Southeastern	Montgomery	6-0 (P)
7-25	Hank Dlugokecki	Greenville	Cotton States	Helena	1-0
7-26	Earl Dothager	Alexandria	Evangeline	Baton Rouge	6-0
7-28	Stan Couling	Montgomery	Southeastern	Meridian	3-0 (7)
7-30	Richard Umberger	Lebanon	North Atlantic	Peekskill	7-0 (5)
8-3	Joe Mallot	Lafayette	Evangeline	Alexandria	9-0 (7)
8-4	Walter Nothe	Toledo	American Assoc.	Minneapolis	2-0 (8)
8-7	Richard Umberger	Lebanon	North Atlantic	Hazleton	5-0 (7)
8-8	Dick Rozek	Oklahoma City	Texas	San Antonio	2-1 (7)
8-9	Eddie Beach	Valley	Georgia-Alabama	Carrollton	4-0 (7)
8-10	Chino Melendez	El Paso	Arizona-Texas	Tucson	12-0 (7)
8-11	Jess Bramlett	Houma	Evangeline	Hammond	3-0 (7)
8-12	Bill Forst	Geneva	Border	Kingston	5-0 (7)
8-12	Herm Wollitz	Burlington	Central Assoc.	Cedar Rapids	1-0
8-15	Manuel Echeverria	Mexicali	Sunset	Las Vegas	7-1
8-16	Elvin Stabelfeld	Des Moines	Western	Pueblo	7-0
8-17	Jim Wilson	Buffalo	International	Jersey City	5-0 (7)
8-18	Dinty Moore	Austin	Big State	Greenville	5-1
8-23	Nick Huck	St. Joseph	Western Assoc.	Leavenworth	12-0
8-25	Mike McCarron	Peekskill	North Atlantic	Stroudsburg	1-0
8-25	Marvin Chappell	Alexander City	Georgia-Alabama	La Grange	7-0 (7)
8-27	Harry Penton	Moultrie	Georgia-Florida	Waycross	18-0
8-28	Roy Welmaker	Wilkes-Barre	Eastern	Williamsport	3-0
8-30	Tom Williams	Galax	Blue Ridge	North Wilkesboro	2-0
8-30	Herb Preul	Greenville	Cotton States	Natchez	3-0 (7)
8-31	Dick McCoy	Ponca City	KOM	Pittsburg	4-0
8-31	Omar "Turk" Lown	Ft. Worth	Texas	Tulsa	14-0
9-1	Jim Barr	Dunn-Erwin	Tobacco State	Sanford	4-1
9-2	Jack Elkins	Zanesville	Ohio-Indiana	Marion	2-0
9-2	Herm Doering	Sheboygan	Wisconsin State	Appleton	5-1
9-6	Morris Fisher	Muncie	Ohio-Indiana	Richmond	6-0 (7)
9-6	Bill Connelly	Toledo	American Assoc.	Louisville	5-0

Number in parentheses indicates innings if other than nine; "P" indicates perfect game.

THIS DATE IN MINOR LEAGUE HISTORY

April 17, 1949, Colorful Louis "Bobo" Newsom, 41-year-old righthander who won 205 games in the major leagues and two World Series decisions, returned to the minor leagues for the first time since 1933, after signing with Chattanooga of the Southern Association. Bobo was pounded by Nashville in his debut and lost 7-1.

April 28, 1949, Pete Gray, one-armed Dallas flyhawk, collected four singles in six trips, drove in a run, scored two himself and stole a base in a Texas League contest.

May 15, 1949, The San Diego at Los Angeles doubleheader in the Pacific Coast League drew 23,090 in paid attendance.

June 14, 1949, Mickey Mantle received his pro baptism with Independence of the Kansas-Oklahoma-Missouri League in a game at Chanute, Kansas. In four times at bat he delivered two hits and scored three times as his team romped to a 12-2 victory. Mantle went on to hit .313 for the season, finishing only four points behind the league leader.

June 23, 1949, Bob Montag of Pawtucket, New England League, made his 100th hit of the season in 198 times at bat for a .505 batting average. He finished with a mark of .423.

June 27, 1949, One-armed outfielder Pete Gray, 32, was released by Dallas, Texas League, and retired from the game. Gray had played in 44 games, batted 56 times, scored 18 runs and made 12 hits, including two doubles, for a batting average of .214. He batted in only five tallies. Gray's refusal to transfer to the Class C Gladewater club resulted in his release, and the outfielder resumed the operation of a billiard hall he owned in Nanticoke, Pennsylvania.

June 29, 1949, Gunplay added excitement to the Interstate League doubleheader at Hagerstown, when a stadium guard fired two shots in the general direction of a fan, whom the guard had ejected from the stadium on the charge of pocketing foul and stray balls. Owner Oren Sterling stated that 96 balls were lost that night. To add to his woes, the Owls lost both games to Allentown.

July 24, 1949, A free-for-all fight, involving players, spectators, umpires and police, was brought to a sudden halt at Cedar Rapids, Iowa, during the Cedar Rapids-Kewanee game in the Central Association, when the public address operator, Bob Hahn, inserted a platter with the National Anthem and turned up the volume. That brought everyone to attention, and when the music had ceased, tempers had cooled off.

July 28, 1949, Umpire Steamboat Johnson, rounding out his 30th year as a Southern Association arbiter, was honored in New Orleans on Steamboat Johnson Night.

August 6, 1949, Earl Mann headed a syndicate that purchased the Atlanta Crackers, Southern Association, from the Coca-Cola Company for $700,000.

August 14, 1949, Games have been called for a variety of reasons, but the Sumter, Tri-State League, club came up with a new one. Because of the lofty position of the mercury, the contest with Rock Hill promised to bring few to the park, so the club's officials announced: "Game postponed because of terrific heat."

August 25, 1949, Leonard Pecou and Bill Thomas, two of the five players placed on the ineligible list in connection with the alleged throwing of games in the Evangeline League during the season of 1946, were restored to good standing by president George Trautman of the National Association.

August 28, 1949, Mickey Mantle of Independence, Kansas-Oklahoma-Missouri League, received credit for a homer when his long fly ball struck outfielder Bill Hornsby, son of the immortal Rajah, on the head and knocked him out.

August 28, 1949, Bobo Newsom, given a "day" at Chattanooga, Southern Association, attended by 5,215 fans, was ejected from the game in the seventh inning after a run-in with the umpire.

August 30, 1949, D.C. "Pud" Miller of Lamesa followed his four homers in one game the previous night with two more to run his total for the year to 50, despite having missed the first 31 contests of the season.

August 31, 1949, The Miami Sun Sox, Florida International League, dedicated their new stadium before 13,007 fans.

September 1, 1949, Pepper Martin, former Cardinals star and current manager of the Miami Sun Sox, was suspended for the balance of the season and fined $100 by the Florida International League president, for using his hands to choke umpire Clem Camia in a rhubarb at Havana.

September 2, 1949, Playing with both wrists taped after what sheriff's deputies termed a suicide attempt during a domestic squabble the previous night, Forrest "Frosty" Kennedy, Riverside outfielder and the Sunset League's leading hitter, cracked out two hits in five trips against San Bernardino.

September 7, 1949, A Class A record crowd of 18,253 overflowed the Denver, Western League, park to see the Bears wind up the season. The club's total attendance for 62 regular season home dates was 463,039, despite the Bears being in the cellar for two months.

October 12, 1949, Manager Lefty O'Doul and his touring troupe of San Francisco Seals arrived in Tokyo for an exhibition series that drew in excess of 500,000 Japanese fans.

November 11, 1949, The National Association announced a record minor league attendance of 41,872,762 for 59 leagues in 1949. The Western League made the biggest increase, 345,000 fans.

1950

American League
President: William Harridge

Standings	W	L	Pct.	GB	Attend.	Manager
New York Yankees............	98	56	.636	—	2,081,380	Casey Stengel
Detroit Tigers....................	95	59	.617	3	1,951,474	Red Rolfe
Boston Red Sox	94	60	.610	4	1,344,080	Joe McCarthy/Steve O'Neill
Cleveland Indians	92	62	.597	6	1,727,464	Lou Boudreau
Washington Senators	67	87	.435	31	699,697	Bucky Harris
Chicago White Sox	60	94	.390	38	781,330	Jack Onslow/Red Corriden
St. Louis Browns	58	96	.377	40	247,131	Zack Taylor
Philadelphia Athletics.........	52	102	.338	46	309,805	Connie Mack

BA: Billy Goodman, Boston, .354
Runs: Dom DiMaggio, Boston, 131
Hits: George Kell, Detroit, 218
RBIs: Walt Dropo, Boston, 144
    Vern Stephens, Boston, 144

HRs: Al Rosen, Cleveland, 37
Wins: Bob Lemon, Cleveland, 23
SOs: Bob Lemon, Cleveland, 170
ERA: Early Wynn, Cleveland, 3.20
Pct: Vic Raschi, New York, .724, 21-8

National League
President: Ford Frick

Standings	W	L	Pct.	GB	Attend.	Manager
Philadelphia Phillies	91	63	.591	—	1,217,035	Eddie Sawyer
Brooklyn Dodgers..............	89	65	.578	2	1,185,896	Burt Shotton
New York Giants	86	68	.558	5	1,008,878	Leo Durocher
Boston Braves	83	71	.539	8	944,391	Billy Southworth
St. Louis Cardinals	78	75	.510	12½	1,093,411	Eddie Dyer
Cincinnati Reds.................	66	87	.431	24½	538,794	Luke Sewell
Chicago Cubs....................	64	89	.418	26½	1,165,944	Frank Frisch
Pittsburgh Pirates	57	96	.373	33½	1,166,267	Bill Meyer

BA: Stan Musial, St. Louis, .346
Runs: Earl Torgeson, Boston, 120
Hits: Duke Snider, Brooklyn, 199
RBIs: Del Ennis, Philadelphia, 126
HRs: Ralph Kiner, Pittsburgh, 47

Wins: Warren Spahn, Boston, 21
SOs: Warren Spahn, Boston, 191
ERA: Jim Hearn, St. Louis/New York, 2.49
Pct: Sal Maglie, New York, .818, 18-4

AAA American Association
President: Bruce Dudley

Standings	W	L	Pct.	GB	Attend.	Manager
Minneapolis Millers (13)....	90	64	.584	—	238,285	Thomas Heath
Indianapolis Indians (15)....	85	67	.559	4	294,451	Al Lopez
Columbus Red Birds (16)....	84	69	.549	5½	170,950	Rollie Hemsley
St. Paul Saints (10)	83	69	.546	6	200,149	Clay Hopper
Louisville Colonels (1)........	82	71	.536	7½	219,429	Mike Ryba
Milwaukee Brewers (9)	68	85	.444	21½	145,868	Bob Coleman
Toledo Mud Hens (4)	65	87	.428	24	88,393	Eddie Mayo
Kansas City Blues (5).........	54	99	.353	35½	147,320	Joe Kuhel

Playoffs: Columbus 4 games, Minneapolis 2; Indianapolis 4 games, St. Paul 0.
Finals: Columbus 4 games, Indianapolis 3.

All-Star Team: 1B-Lou Limmer, St. Paul; **2B**-Solly Hemus, Columbus; **3B**-Ray Dandridge, Minneapolis; **SS**-Jim Pendleton, St. Paul; **OF**-Bob Addis, Milwaukee; Taft Wright, Louisville; Bert Haas, Minneapolis; Tom Saffell, Indianapolis; **C**-Eddie FitzGerald, Indianapolis; Bill Sarni, Columbus; **Util**-Mel Hoderlein, Louisville; **P**-Harvey Haddix, Columbus; Dixie Howell, Minneapolis; Phil Haugstad, St. Paul; Bob Alexander, Louisville; **MVP**-Ray Dandridge, Minneapolis.

BA: Bob Addis, Milwaukee, .323
Runs: Davey Williams, Minneapolis, 113
Hits: Ray Dandridge, Minneapolis, 195
RBIs: Lou Limmer, St. Paul, 111
HRs: Lou Limmer, St. Paul, 29
Wins: Harvey Haddix, Columbus, 18
SOs: Harvey Haddix, Columbus, 160
ERA: Harvey Haddix, Columbus, 2.70

AAA International League
President: Frank J. Shaughnessy

Standings	W	L	Pct.	GB	Attend.	Manager
Rochester Red Wings (16)..	92	59	.609	—	320,067	Johnny Keane
Montreal Royals (10)..........	86	67	.562	7	391,001	Walter Alston
Baltimore Orioles (7).........	85	68	.556	8	317,534	Nick Cullop
Jersey City Giants (13)	81	70	.536	11	63,191	Joseph Becker
Springfield Cubs (11)	74	78	.487	18½	201,217	Stan Hack
Syracuse Chiefs (12)..........	74	79	.484	19	106,939	Bruno Betzel
Toronto Maple Leafs (14)....	60	90	.400	31½	226,951	Jack Sanford
Buffalo Bisons (6)	56	97	.366	37	96,236	Frank Skaff/Ray Schalk

Playoffs: Rochester 4 games, Jersey City 2; Baltimore 4 games, Montreal 3.
Finals: Baltimore 4 games, Rochester 2.

MVP-Tom Poholsky, Rochester.

BA: Don Richmond, Rochester, .333
Runs: Don Richmond, Rochester, 126
Hits: Don Richmond, Rochester, 191
RBIs: Russ Derry, Rochester, 102

HRs: Russ Derry, Rochester, 30
    Chet Laabs, Toronto/Jersey City, 30
Wins: Tom Poholsky, Rochester, 18
SOs: Roger Bowman, Jersey City, 181
ERA: Tom Poholsky, Rochester, 2.17

AAA Pacific Coast League
President: Clarence H. Rowland

Standings	W	L	Pct.	GB	Attend.	Manager
Oakland Oaks	118	82	.590	—	491,732	Chuck Dressen
San Diego Padres (3)	114	86	.570	4	439,646	Del Baker
Hollywood Stars (10)........	104	96	.520	14	422,389	Fred Haney
Portland Beavers	101	99	.505	17	348,938	Bill Sweeney
San Francisco Seals	100	100	.500	18	377,274	Lefty O'Doul
Seattle Rainiers	96	104	.480	22	492,647	Paul Richards
Los Angeles Angels (11)	86	114	.430	32	320,757	William Kelly
Sacramento Solons (2)........	81	119	.405	37	279,335	Red Kress/Joseph Marty

Playoffs: None.

MVP-George Metkovich, Oakland.

BA: Frank Baumholtz, Los Angeles, .379
Runs: Artie Wilson, Oakland, 168
Hits: Artie Wilson, Oakland, 264
RBIs: Harry Simpson, San Diego, 156
HRs: Francis Kelleher, Hollywood, 40
Wins: James Wilson, Seattle, 24
SOs: James Wilson, Seattle, 228
ERA: Jack Salveson, Hollywood, 2.84

AA Southern Association
President: Charles A. Hurth

Standings	W	L	Pct.	GB	Attend.	Manager
Atlanta Crackers (9)............	92	59	.609	—	395,696	Dixie Walker
Birmingham Barons (1)......	87	62	.584	4	372,089	Pinky Higgins
Nashville Vols (11).............	86	64	.573	5½	188,541	Don Osborn
Memphis Chicks (2)	81	70	.536	11	242,460	Alfred Todd
New Orleans Pelicans (15).	71	79	.473	20½	203,445	Hugh Luby/Bill Burwell
Mobile Bears (10).............	70	79	.470	21	112,972	Paul Chervinko
Chattanooga Lookouts (8) ..	59	89	.399	31½	132,102	Fred Walters
Little Rock Travelers (4)	52	96	.351	38½	82,742	Jack Saltzgaver

Playoffs: Atlanta 4 games, Memphis 0; Nashville 4 games, Birmingham 1.
Finals: Nashville 4 games, Atlanta 1.

All-Star Team: 1B-Nick Etten, Memphis; **2B**-Ellis Clary, Atlanta; **3B**-Fred Hatfield, Birmingham; Ed Mathews, Atlanta; **SS**-Gene Verble, Atlanta; **OF**-Bill Wilson, Memphis; Pat Haggerty, Little Rock; Bill Higdon, Memphis; Tom Neill, Nashville; **C**-Ebba St. Claire, Atlanta; Carl Sawatski, Nashville; Andy Fleitas, Chattanooga; Dick Krsnich, Memphis; **P**-Marvin Rotblatt, Memphis; Leo Goicoechea, Memphis; Dick Littlefield, Birmingham; Dave "Boo" Ferriss, Birmingham; Bob Schultz, Nashville; Art Fowler, Atlanta.

BA: Pat Haggerty, Little Rock, .346
Runs: Gene Verble, Atlanta, 118
Hits: Benjamin Thorpe, Atlanta, 195
RBIs: Bill Wilson, Memphis, 125
HRs: Bill Wilson, Memphis, 36
Wins: Bob Schultz, Nashville, 25
SOs: Marvin Rotblatt, Memphis, 203
ERA: Marvin Rotblatt, Memphis, 2.67

AA Texas League
President: J. Alvin Gardner

Standings	W	L	Pct.	GB	Attend.	Manager
Beaumont Roughnecks (5) .	91	62	.595	—	170,536	Rogers Hornsby
Ft. Worth Cats (10).............	88	64	.579	2½	233,789	Bobby Bragan
Tulsa Oilers (12)...............	83	69	.546	7½	184,677	Al Vincent
San Antonio Missions (7)...	79	75	.513	12½	180,580	Don Heffner
Dallas Eagles	74	78	.487	16½	317,592	Charlie Grimm
Oklahoma City Indians (3).	72	79	.477	18	187,991	Joe Vosmik/Hank Gowdy/ Thomas Reis
Shreveport Sports	63	91	.409	28½	117,854	Francis "Salty" Parker
Houston Buffaloes (16)	61	93	.396	30½	255,809	Kemp Wicker/Benny Borgmann

Playoffs: San Antonio 4 games, Beaumont 0; Tulsa 4 games, Ft. Worth 0, one tie.
Finals: San Antonio 4 games, Tulsa 2.

BA: Frank Saucier, San Antonio, .343
Runs: Robert Marquis, Beaumont, 124
Hits: Gil McDougald, Beaumont, 187
RBIs: Jim Lemon, Oklahoma City, 119
HRs: Jim Lemon, Oklahoma City, 39
Wins: James Blackburn, Tulsa, 21
    Wayne McLeland, Dallas, 21
    Ernie Nevel, Beaumont, 21
SOs: Joe Presko, Houston, 165
ERA: John Rutherford, Ft. Worth, 2.21

A Central League
President: T.J. Halligan

Standings	W	L	Pct.	GB	Attend.	Manager
Flint Arrows (4)	80	53	.602	—	67,954	Gene Desautels
Muskegon Clippers (5)	75	64	.540	8	51,054	Robert Finley

*Won first-half   **Won second-half   ***Won both halves
Numbers after nicknames indicate farm system.
Affiliation listed at end of year.

389

Dayton Indians (3) .... 69 63 .523 10½ 45,849 Dolph Camilli
Grand Rapids Jets (11) .... 64 68 .485 15½ 54,741 Jack Knight
Charleston Senators (12) .... 58 73 .443 21 112,946 Joe Beggs
Saginaw Bears .... 56 81 .365 26 39,895 Henry Camelli

Playoffs: Flint 3 games, Grand Rapids 1; Muskegon 3 games, Dayton 2.
Finals: Flint 4 games, Muskegon 1.

All-Star Team: 1B-Keith Little, Flint; **2B**-Loren Babe, Muskegon; **3B**-Dave Jaska, Flint; **SS**-Clem Koshorek, Flint; **OF**-Ed Krage, Muskegon; John Phillips, Flint; Joe Rowell, Dayton; **C**-Robert O'Neal, Muskegon; **P**-Ernie Funk, Flint; Frank Logue, Muskegon; William Houtz, Muskegon.

BA: Joe Rowell, Dayton, .344
Runs: Louis Urcho, Muskegon, 112
Hits: Ron Bowen, Muskegon, 169
RBIs: Ron Bowen, Muskegon, 128
HRs: Ron Bowen, Muskegon, 28
Wins: Ernie Funk, Flint, 22
SOs: William Abernathie, Dayton, 171
ERA: Jimmy Wallace, Saginaw, 2.05

A Eastern League
President: Thomas H. Richardson

Standings	W	L	Pct.	GB	Attend.	Manager
Wilkes-Barre Barons (3)	90	48	.652	—	110,472	Bill Norman
Binghamton Triplets (5)	81	58	.583	9½	161,338	George Selkirk
Hartford Chiefs (9)	80	59	.576	10½	84,159	James "Rip" Collins
Albany Senators (15)	66	73	.475	24½	91,477	Pinky May
Utica Blue Sox (14)	64	73	.467	25½	57,139	Leon Riley
Williamsport Grays (4)	61	77	.442	29	76,703	Jack Tighe
Elmira Pioneers (10)	58	81	.417	32½	87,517	Greg Mulleavy/George Fallon
Scranton Miners (1)	54	85	.388	36½	43,773	Jack Burns

Playoffs: Wilkes-Barre 4 games, Hartford 2; Binghamton 4 games, Albany 1.
Finals: Wilkes-Barre 4 games, Binghamton 1.

All-Star Team: 1B-George Crowe, Hartford; **2B**-Doug Hansen, Wilkes-Barre; **3B**-Walt Derucki, Utica; **SS**-Jim Brideweser, Binghamton; **OF**-Russ Sullivan, Williamsport; Clark Henry, Albany; Art Schult, Binghamton; **C**-Dick Kinaman, Wilkes-Barre; **P**-Bob Chakales, Wilkes-Barre; Pete Fox, Hartford.

BA: George Crowe, Hartford, .353
Runs: George Crowe, Hartford, 122
Hits: George Crowe, Hartford, 185
RBIs: Dale Long, Binghamton, 130
HRs: Dale Long, Binghamton, 27
Wins: William Freese, Binghamton, 19
SOs: Sam Jones, Wilkes-Barre, 169
ERA: Bob Chakales, Wilkes-Barre, 2.04

A South Atlantic League
President: Earl Blue

Standings	W	L	Pct.	GB	Attend.	Manager
Macon Peaches	90	63	.588	—	134,680	Ivy Griffin
Savannah Indians (6)	83	70	.542	7	101,331	Red Norris
Columbia Reds (12)	83	70	.542	7	103,278	Gerald Walker
Charleston Rebels (15)	79	72	.523	10	86,063	Rip Sewell
Columbus Cardinals (16)	78	73	.517	11	88,101	Harold Anderson
Greenville Spinners (10)	68	85	.444	22	54,785	Oscar Grimes
Augusta Tigers (8)	66	87	.431	24	64,303	Pete Appleton
Jacksonville Tars (13)	63	90	.412	27	88,667	Hal Gruber/Dale Alexander

Playoffs: Macon 3 games, Charleston 2; Columbia 3 games, Savannah 2.
Finals: Macon 4 games, Columbia 0.

All-Star Team: 1B-James Dickey, Columbus; **2B**-Glenn Crawford, Augusta; **3B**-Edwin Allegar, Jacksonville; **SS**-Johnny Temple, Columbia; **OF**-Lewis Davis, Macon; Rip Repulski, Columbus; Bob "Hurricane" Hazle, Columbia; **C**-Joe Stringfellow, Savannah; **Util**-Gus Gregory, Macon; John Fiscalini, Charleston; **P**-Stan Karpinski, Macon; Moe Savransky, Columbia; **Manager**-Gerald Walker, Columbia.

BA: Pete Kraus, Charleston, .323
Runs: Gus Gregory, Macon, 116
Hits: Gus Gregory, Macon, 186
RBIs: Lewis Davis, Macon, 119
HRs: James Dickey, Columbus, 20
Wins: Stan Karpinski, Macon, 20
SOs: Robert Garber, Charleston, 205
ERA: Moe Savransky, Columbia, 2.25
Pct: George Dries, Columbus, .737, 14-5

A Western League
President: Senator Edwin C. Johnson

Standings	W	L	Pct.	GB	Attend.	Manager
Omaha Cardinals (16)	96	58	.623	—	218,393	Al Hollingsworth
Sioux City Soos (13)	89	65	.578	7	143,237	Hugh Poland
Des Moines Bruins (11)	84	70	.545	12	147,549	Charlie Root
Wichita Indians (7)	77	77	.500	19	126,729	Joe Schultz
Denver Bears (9)	75	79	.487	21	379,180	Earle Browne
Colorado Springs Sky Sox (2)	72	82	.468	24	107,264	Buddy Hassett
Lincoln Athletics (6)	69	85	.448	27	68,884	James DeShong
Pueblo Dodgers (10)	54	100	.351	42	91,299	Ray Hathaway

Playoffs: Wichita 3 games, Omaha 0; Sioux City 3 games, Des Moines 2.
Finals: Sioux City 3 games, Wichita 1.

All-Star Team: 1B-Harvey Zernia, Omaha; **2B**-Eddie Samcoff, Sioux City; **3B**-Pete Grammas, Colorado Springs; **SS**-Fred McAlister, Omaha; **OF**-Bill Taylor, Sioux City; Tom Whisenant, Denver; Bob Balcena, Wichita; Pat Seerey, Colorado Springs; **C**-Nick Adzick, Omaha; Bruce McWhorter, Denver; **P**-Robert Mahoney, Omaha; Octavio Rubert, Omaha; John O'Donnell, Wichita; Mason Bowes, Lincoln.

BA: Bill Taylor, Sioux City, .346
Runs: Danny Holden, Denver, 131
Hits: Chuck Tanner, Denver, 195
RBIs: Tom Whisenant, Denver, 119
HRs: Pat Seerey, Colorado Springs, 44
Wins: Robert Mahoney, Omaha, 20
SOs: Robert Mahoney, Omaha, 162
ERA: Vern Fear, Des Moines, 2.83

B Big State League
President: J. Walter Morris

Standings	W	L	Pct.	GB	Attend.	Manager
Texarkana Bears	93	51	.646	—	83,604	George Archie
Gainesville Owls	82	63	.566	11½	56,890	James Adair
Wichita Falls Spudders (7)	80	66	.548	14	103,439	James "Hack" Miller
Temple Eagles	74	70	.514	19	105,081	Lou Finney
Greenville Majors	75	71	.514	19	50,511	Bill Gann
Waco Pirates (15)	72	76	.486	23	85,173	Buddy Hancken
Sherman-Denison Twins	54	91	.372	39½	48,762	Homer Peel
Austin Pioneers	52	94	.356	42	116,941	Henry "Prince" Oana/David Sarver

Playoffs: Texarkana 4 games, Temple 2; Greenville 4 games, Wichita Falls 2.
Finals: Texarkana 4 games, Greenville 2.

BA: Frank Carswell, Texarkana, .400
Runs: Lou Fitzgerald, Texarkana, 138
Hits: James Basso, Temple, 213
RBIs: Milan Vucelich, Texarkana, 144
HRs: John Powers, Waco, 39
Wins: Junior Bunch, Temple, 19
SOs: Jodie Phipps, Texarkana, 173
ERA: Carmen Ferullo, Wichita Falls, 2.89

B Carolina League
President: Glenn E. "Ted" Mann

Standings	W	L	Pct.	GB	Attend.	Manager
Winston-Salem Cardinals (16)	106	47	.693	—	172,895	George Kissell
Danville Leafs	87	66	.569	19	85,323	Ben Chapman
Burlington Bees	83	70	.542	23	82,834	Herb Crompton
Reidsville Luckies	82	72	.532	24½	87,490	Herb Brett
Greensboro Patriots	78	74	.513	27½	132,554	Buddy Bates
Durham Bulls (4)	73	79	.480	32½	80,834	Ace Parker
Raleigh Capitals	55	97	.362	50½	52,721	Wes Livengood
Fayetteville Athletics (6)	47	106	.307	59	63,400	George "Mule" Haas/Tom Oliver

Playoffs: Winston-Salem 3 games, Reidsville 2; Burlington 3 games, Danville 1.
Finals: Winston-Salem 4 games, Burlington 1.

All-Star Team: 1B-Neil Hartwick, Winston-Salem; **2B**-Fred Vaughn, Greensboro; **3B**-Bucky Jacobs, Danville; **SS**-Mike Romelio, Danville; **OF**-Russell Rac, Winston-Salem; Bill Evans, Burlington; Buster Maynard, Burlington; **C**-Al Spaziano, Burlington; **Util**-Claude Swiggett, Greensboro; **P**-Woody Rich, Greensboro; Wilmer "Vinegar Bend" Mizell, Winston-Salem; **MVP**-Bill Evans, Burlington; **Manager**-George Kissell, Winston-Salem.

BA: Bill Evans, Burlington, .338
Runs: John Huesman, Winston-Salem, 116
Hits: Bill Evans, Burlington, 207
RBIs: Woody Fair, Danville, 103
HRs: Fred Vaughn, Greensboro, 27
Wins: Lee Peterson, Winston-Salem, 21; Pete Angell, Danville, 21
SOs: Wilmer "Vinegar Bend" Mizell, Winston-Salem, 227
ERA: Woody Rich, Greensboro, 2.41

B Colonial League
President: John A. Scalzi, Jr.

Standings	W	L	Pct.	GB	Manager
Poughkeepsie Chiefs	43	26	.623	—	Robert Doyle
Kingston Colonials	39	28	.582	3	Emil Gall
Bristol Owls	36	31	.537	6	Al Barillari
Torrington Braves	33	32	.507	8	Merle Strachan
Waterbury Timers	23	39	.371	16½	John Morris/Charles Bowles
Bridgeport Bees	23	41	.359	17½	Bud Stapleton/Frank Silva

The league disbanded July 16.

BA: Saturnino Escalera, Bristol, .389
Runs: Carlos Bernier, Bristol, 67
Hits: Saturnino Escalera, Bristol, 93
RBIs: John Sinnott, Poughkeepsie, 53
HRs: Carlos Santiago, Poughkeepsie, 11
Wins: Emil Moscowitz, Poughkeepsie, 12
SOs: Emil Moscowitz, Poughkeepsie, 102; Robert Doyle, Poughkeepsie, 102
ERA: Emil Moscowitz, Poughkeepsie, 1.51

B Florida International League
President: Phil O'Connell

Standings	W	L	Pct.	GB	Attend.	Manager
Havana Cubanos (8)	101	49	.673	—	168,419	Oscar Rodriguez
Miami Sun Sox (10)	98	55	.641	4½	160,450	Pepper Martin
Tampa Smokers	85	60	.586	13½	80,626	Art Rebel
Miami Beach Flamingos	77	72	.517	23½	47,278	Jerry Crosby/Jimmy Outlaw
Ft. Lauderdale Braves	70	80	.467	31	60,919	Charles Aleno
West Palm Beach Indians (6)	67	85	.441	35	57,078	Clyde Smoll/Rudy Laskowski
Lakeland Pilots	57	93	.380	44	42,588	Charles Cuellar/William Ankoviak
St. Petersburg Saints	43	104	.293	56½	77,115	Dick Porter/Leon Cato/James Pruett/Roxie Humberson

Playoffs: Havana 3 games, Tampa 0; Miami 3 games, Miami Beach 0.
Finals: Miami 4 games, Havana 1.

All-Star Team: 1B-William Ankoviak, Lakeland; **2B**-Carlos DeSouza, Tampa; **3B**-Charles Aleno, Ft. Lauderdale; **SS**-Jasper Spears, Tampa; **OF**-Charles Rotzell, Miami Beach; Edward Wayne, Tampa; Mike Conroy, Miami Beach; **C**-Warren Patterson, Miami; **P**-William Padgett, Tampa; Ernesto Morilla, Miami Beach; Labe Dean, Miami; Chet Covington, Ft. Lauderdale; Joe Murray, West Palm Beach.

BA: Charles Aleno, Ft. Lauderdale, .314
Runs: Manuel Hidalgo, Havana, 106
Hits: Manuel Hidalgo, Havana, 188
RBIs: Jack Tanner, Lakeland/
  Ft. Lauderdale, 101

HRs: Jack Tanner, Lakeland/
  Ft. Lauderdale, 27
Wins: Labe Dean, Miami, 24
SOs: Antonio Lorenzo, Havana, 177
ERA: Julio Moreno, Havana, 1.47

B Interstate League
President: Gerald P. Nugent

Standings	W	L	Pct.	GB	Attend.	Manager
Wilmington Blue Rocks (14)...	82	56	.594	—	37,550	Skeeter Newsome
Hagerstown Braves (9)	75	60	.556	5½	84,350	Dutch Dorman
Harrisburg Senators (3)	77	62	.554	5½	51,707	Les Bell
Trenton Giants (13)	73	65	.529	9	48,354	Frank Genovese
Allentown Cardinals (16)...	70	67	.511	11½	48,144	Gene Corbett
York White Roses (15)	65	73	.471	17	54,067	Frank Oceak
Lancaster Red Roses (10)..	56	82	.406	26	32,684	Ed Head
Sunbury Athletics (6)	53	86	.381	29½	53,049	George Staller

Playoffs: Wilmington 4 games, Harrisburg 3; Hagerstown 4 games, Trenton 1.
Finals: Wilmington 4 games, Hagerstown 1.

All-Star Team: 1B-Robert Myers, Trenton; **2B**-Lamar Newsome, Wilmington; **3B**-Dick Young, Wilmington; **SS**-Thomas Korczowski, Trenton; **OF**-Danny Schell, Wilmington; Jesse Levan, Hagerstown; Willie Mays, Trenton; **C**-Louis Heyman, Wilmington; **P**-Leo Christante, Wilmington; Al Bennett, Hagerstown; Joe Micciche, Trenton; William Stratton, York.

BA: Jesse Levan, Hagerstown, .334
Runs: Dick Young, Wilmington, 101
Hits: Jesse Levan, Hagerstown, 171
  Danny Schell, Wilmington, 171
RBIs: Danny Schell, Wilmington, 104

HRs: Frederick Marolewski, Allentown, 24
Wins: Leo Christante, Wilmington, 18
SOs: Willard Schmidt, Allentown, 172
ERA: William Stratton, York, 2.27

B Piedmont League
President: Richard A. Carrington, Jr.

Standings	W	L	Pct.	GB	Attend.	Manager
Portsmouth Cubs	83	54	.606	—	106,898	Frank Scalzi
Roanoke Red Sox (1)	81	58	.583	3	108,987	Red Marion
Lynchburg Cardinals (16)...	76	61	.555	7	91,839	Whitey Kurowski
Richmond Colts (13)	63	76	.453	21	104,687	Vince Smith
Norfolk Tars (5)	58	82	.414	26½	93,793	Frank Novosel
Newport News Dodgers (10)	55	85	.393	29½	67,363	Al Campanis/Bud Metheny

Playoffs: Portsmouth 4 games, Richmond 0; Roanoke 4 games, Lynchburg 1.
Finals: Roanoke 4 games, Portsmouth 3.

East All-Star Team: 1B-Reggie Otero, Portsmouth; **2B**-William Palumbo, Newport News; **3B**-Robert Kehoe, Newport News; **SS**-Dan Lynch, Portsmouth; **OF**-Leon "Red" Treadway, Portsmouth; Crawford Davidson, Norfolk; Robert Broome, Portsmouth; **C**-George Menard, Norfolk; **Util**-Jack Wilkinson, Norfolk; Daniel Keith, Newport News; Allen Winters, Newport News; **P**-Al Cicotte, Norfolk; Earl Mossor, Portsmouth; Ed Roebuck, Newport News; Donald Otten, Newport News; **Manager**-Frank Scalzi, Portsmouth.

BA: Daniel Keith, Newport News, .357
Runs: George Contratto, Roanoke, 104
Hits: Leon "Red" Treadway, Portsmouth, 177
RBIs: Julio Ondani, Roanoke, 89
HRs: Robert Mosakoski, Roanoke, 23

Wins: Earl Mossor, Portsmouth, 20
  John Hartsell, Roanoke, 20
SOs: Duke Markell, Portsmouth, 219
ERA: John Ahern, Roanoke, 1.61

B Southeastern League
President: Stuart X. Stephenson

Standings	W	L	Pct.	GB	Attend.	Manager
Pensacola Fliers	82	52	.612	—	64,965	George Dozier
Meridian Millers	78	52	.600	2	71,264	Jack Maupin
Montgomery Rebels (16)....	77	54	.588	3½	72,593	Charlie Metro
Jackson Senators (9)	73	55	.570	6	101,805	Willis Hudlin
Vicksburg Hill Billies (13).	63	63	.500	15	44,038	Buddy Blair
Selma Cloverleafs	43	87	.331	37	40,581	Bert Niehoff
Gadsden Pilots@	50	51	.495	NA	50,411	Bill McGhee
Anniston Rams#	21	73	.223	NA	22,466	Charles Letchas/Lou Bevil/ Dick Wentworth

#Anniston disbanded July 25.
@Gadsden disbanded August 1.

Playoffs: Pensacola 4 games, Montgomery 2; Meridian 4 games, Jackson 3.
Finals: Pensacola 4 games, Meridian 1.

All-Star Team: 1B-Ed Mickelson, Montgomery; **2B**-Frank DiPrima, Montgomery; **3B**-Billy Seal, Gadsden; **SS**-Ralph Frank, Montgomery; **OF**-Nesbit Wilson, Pensacola; Art Seguso, Meridian; Ray Poole, Vicksburg; **C**-Del Friar, Selma; **P**-Andrew Elko, Pensacola; Antonio Palica, Meridian; George Yorke, Jackson; Hamilton Graham, Montgomery.

BA: Nesbit Wilson, Pensacola, .355
Runs: James Rivera, Pensacola, 139
  Frank DiPrima, Montgomery, 139
Hits: Ray Williams, Pensacola, 192
RBIs: Nesbit Wilson, Pensacola, 163

HRs: Nesbit Wilson, Pensacola, 35
Wins: Andrew Elko, Pensacola, 22
SOs: Donald Kohler, Selma, 141
ERA: Homer Spragins, Gadsden, 2.11

B Three-I League
President: Tom Fairweather

Standings	W	L	Pct.	GB	Attend.	Manager
Terre Haute Phillies (14)	78	48	.619	—	111,228	Dan Carnevale
Danville Dodgers (10)	74	52	.587	4	51,616	James Bivin
Waterloo White Hawks (2).	70	56	.556	8	119,244	Otto Denning
Quincy Gems (5)	64	60	.516	13	53,322	James Adlam
Cedar Rapids Indians (3)....	59	67	.468	19	85,038	Bill Jurges
Evansville Braves (9)	56	70	.444	22	102,865	Ernie White
Decatur Commodores (11) .	52	74	.413	26	35,516	Morris Arnovich
Davenport Quads	49	75	.395	28	90,584	Gene Hasson

Playoffs: Terre Haute 3 games, Quincy 0; Danville 3 games, Waterloo 0.
Finals: Terre Haute 3 games, Danville 1.

All-Star Team: 1B-Bill Boudreau, Danville; **2B**-Burt Stone, Evansville; **3B**-Jerome Stoutland, Quincy; **SS**-Bill Cope, Quincy; **OF**-Frank Marchio, Quincy; Jim King, Cedar Rapids; Jim Watson, Terre Haute; **C**-Bob Wilson, Waterloo; **P**-Bill Bagwell, Quincy; Ray Peters, Cedar Rapids; Jacob Schmitt, Terre Haute; Niles Jordan, Terre Haute; **Manager**-Dan Carnevale, Terre Haute.

BA: Jim King, Cedar Rapids, .332
Runs: Jack Lillis, Danville, 110
Hits: Frank Marchio, Quincy, 162
RBIs: Frank Marchio, Quincy, 112

HRs: Allen Thomas, Waterloo, 25
Wins: Jacob Schmitt, Terre Haute, 21
SOs: Niles Jordan, Terre Haute, 206
ERA: Niles Jordan, Terre Haute, 2.35

B Tri-State League
President: C.M. Llewellyn

Standings	W	L	Pct.	GB	Attend.	Manager
Knoxville Smokies (13)	89	58	.605	—	150,396	Jack Aragon
Asheville Tourists (10)	83	62	.572	5	111,177	Clay Bryant
Spartanburg Peaches (3)	80	63	.559	7	103,056	Kerby Farrell
Rock Hill Chiefs (11)	73	69	.514	13½	66,589	Dick Bouknight
Charlotte Hornets (8)	72	73	.497	16	104,598	Rabbitt McDowell/ Joseph Bird
Anderson Rebels	65	79	.451	22½	75,881	Bob Richards
Florence Steelers	63	83	.432	25½	34,991	James Martin
Sumter Chicks	53	91	.368	34½	30,324	Alton Biggs/Vance Carlson

Playoffs: Rock Hill 3 games, Knoxville 0; Asheville 3 games, Spartanburg 0.
Finals: Rock Hill 4 games, Asheville 3.

All-Star Team: 1B-Donald Stafford, Charlotte; **2B**-James Martin, Florence; **3B**-Frank Colasinki, Sumter; **SS**-Dominic Della Rocca, Spartanburg; **OF**-Albert Neal, Knoxville; Harvey Gentry, Knoxville; Ralph Rowe, Rock Hill; Robert Churchill, Anderson; **C**-Frank Sacka, Anderson; Omer Ehlers, Asheville; **Util**-William Kearns, Asheville; **P**-Hugh Oser, Knoxville; John Carmichael, Spartanburg; William Samson, Asheville; William Mosser, Asheville; **Manager**-Jack Aragon, Knoxville.

BA: Robert Churchill, Anderson, .356
Runs: Harvey Gentry, Knoxville, 116
Hits: Frank Dunlap, Sumter, 170
  James Martin, Florence, 170
RBIs: Albert Neal, Knoxville, 146

HRs: Albert Neal, Knoxville, 33
Wins: Dale Fisher, Knoxville, 19
  John Carmichael, Spartanburg, 19
SOs: Dale Fisher, Knoxville, 202
ERA: William Samson, Asheville, 1.93

B Western International League
President: Robert B. Abel

Standings	W	L	Pct.	GB	Attend.	Manager
Yakima Bears	92	58	.613	—	117,790	Joe Orengo
Tacoma Tigers (3)	90	58	.608	1	85,777	Jack Brillheart
Tri-City Braves#	83	66	.557	8½	91,797	Charles Petersen
Wenatchee Chiefs	80	70	.533	12	105,501	Rupert "Tommy" Thompson
Victoria Athletics	66	84	.440	26	110,317	Marty Krug
Vancouver Capilanos	64	82	.438	26	97,276	Bill Brenner
Spokane Indians	63	85	.426	28	116,503	Alan Strange
Salem Senators	57	92	.383	34½	56,935	Ad Liska

#represented Kennewick, Richland and Pasco Washington.

All-Star Team: 1B-Wellington Quinn, Tacoma; **2B**-Ron Gifford, Tacoma; **3B**-Dan Fracchia, Wenatchee; **SS**-Carl "Buddy" Peterson, Tri-City; **OF**-Richard Greco, Tacoma; Gene Thompson, Victoria; James Warner, Tri-City; **C**-Joe Rossi, Spokane; **P**-John Marshall, Victoria; Robert Kerrigan, Tacoma.

BA: Glenn Stetter, Tacoma/Spokane, .369
Runs: James Warner, Tri-City, 143
Hits: Richard Greco, Tacoma, 203
RBIs: Richard Greco, Tacoma, 154

HRs: Richard Greco, Tacoma, 36
Wins: Robert Kerrigan, Tacoma, 26
SOs: Lloyd Dickey, Yakima, 224
ERA: Thomas Kipp, Tacoma, 2.76

C Arizona-Texas League
President: Riney B. Salmon

Standings	W	L	Pct.	GB	Attend.	Manager
Juarez Indios	93	55	.628	—	69,738	Syd Cohen
El Paso Texans	92	58	.613	2	100,212	Art Lilly
Phoenix Senators	82	68	.547	12	104,137	Don Trower
Bisbee-Douglas Copper Kings (10)	69	79	.466	24	68,651	Buck Elliott
Tucson Cowboys (3)	64	86	.427	30	61,254	Henry Leiber
Globe-Miami Browns	48	102	.320	46	47,388	Thornton Lee

Playoffs: Phoenix 4 games, Juarez 2; El Paso 4 games, Bisbee-Douglas 1.
Finals: El Paso 4 games, Phoenix 2.

BA: Art Lilly, El Paso, .386
Runs: Alfredo Perez, Tucson, 172
Hits: Dick Zwaing, Tucson, 221
RBIs: Irv Noren, Phoenix, 169
Don Mason, El Paso, 169
HRs: Hector Lara, El Paso, 28
Wins: Jesus Valenzuela, Juarez, 25
Hector Anzamar, Juarez, 25
SOs: Jesus Valenzuela, Juarez, 256
ERA: Jesus Valenzuela, Juarez, 3.47

C Border League
President: John G. Ward

Standings	W	L	Pct.	GB	Attend.	Manager
Ottawa Nationals	75	53	.586	—	97,091	Bill Metzig
Ogdensburg Maples	74	54	.578	1	55,291	Russ Wein
Kingston Ponies	68	60	.531	7	52,453	Barney Hearn
Watertown Athletics	60	68	.469	15	65,329	Frank Heller
Geneva Robins	56	71	.441	18½	42,353	Charles Small/Clyde Theriault
Auburn Cayugas	50	77	.394	24½	41,755	Bill Sisler/Tom Accardo/William Gates

Playoffs: Ottawa 4 games, Kingston 1; Ogdensburg 4 games, Watertown 1.
Finals: Ogdensburg 4 games, Ottawa 2.

All-Star Team: 1B-Frank Heller, Watertown; **2B**-Bill Metzig, Ottawa; **3B**-Johnny Russian, Ottawa; **SS**-Joe Camacho, Ogdensburg; **OF**-Peter Kousagan, Geneva; Stu Erickson, Auburn; Howie Weeks, Ogdensburg; **C**-Dave Abramson, Watertown; John Sosh, Ogdensburg; **P**-Harry Pilarski, Kingston; Norm Gosselin, Geneva; Joseph Greco, Ogdensburg; Jerry Daly, Watertown.

BA: John Sosh, Ogdensburg, .348
Runs: Peter Karpuk, Ottawa, 111
Hits: Irvin Schupp, Ogdensburg, 173
RBIs: Peter Kousagan, Geneva, 125
HRs: Peter Kousagan, Geneva, 31
Wins: Harry Pilarski, Kingston, 19
Norm Gosselin, Geneva, 19
SOs: Joseph Greco, Ogdensburg, 204
ERA: Edward Flanagan, Ottawa, 1.96

C California League
President: Jerry Donovan

Standings	W	L	Pct.	GB	Attend.	Manager
Ventura Braves (9)	85	55	.607	—	65,680	Gene Lillard
Modesto Reds (15)	82	58	.586	3	100,554	Marcus Carrola
Stockton Ports	79	61	.564	6	117,552	Harry Clements
San Jose Red Sox (1)	78	62	.557	7	100,302	Marv Owen
Visalia Cubs (11)	65	75	.464	20	71,083	James Acton
Bakersfield Indians (3)	61	79	.436	24	83,006	Harry Griswold
Fresno Cardinals (16)	58	82	.414	27	98,675	Roland LeBlanc
Santa Barbara Dodgers (10)	52	88	.371	33	42,997	Bill Hart

Playoffs: Modesto 3 games, San Jose 1; Stockton 3 games, Ventura 2.
Finals: Modesto 4 games, Stockton 1.

All-Star Team: 1B-Dick Wilson, Modesto; **2B**-Gene Lillard, Ventura; **3B**-Michael Durock, San Jose; **SS**-Robert Stevens, Stockton; **OF**-Earl Smith, Modesto; Eugene Faszholz, Fresno; D. Lee Kast, Ventura; **C**-Roland LeBlanc, Fresno; **P**-John Walsh, Ventura; John Guldborg, Stockton; Tony Freitas, Modesto; Warren Sandel, Fresno.

BA: James Acton, Visalia, .355
Runs: Jess Pike, Modesto, 122
Hits: Earl Smith, Modesto, 167
RBIs: Dick Wilson, Modesto, 154
HRs: Dick Wilson, Modesto, 30
Wins: John Guldborg, Stockton, 22
SOs: Gordon Jones, Fresno, 200
ERA: Tony Freitas, Modesto, 2.56

C Canadian-American League
President: Albert E. Houghton

Standings	W	L	Pct.	GB	Attend.	Manager
Quebec Braves	97	40	.708	—	123,352	George McQuinn
Schenectady Blue Jays (14)	88	46	.657	7½	76,853	Richard Carter
Oneonta Red Sox (1)	86	52	.623	11½	45,911	Eddie Popowski
Amsterdam Rugmakers (5)	72	65	.526	25	49,026	Mayo Smith
Gloversville-Johnstown Glovers	57	81	.413	40½	48,448	James Cullinane
Rome Colonels	51	86	.372	46	34,535	William Gates/Bill Booker/Emil Gall
Pittsfield Indians (3)	49	86	.363	47	28,668	Lloyd Brown
Trois Rivieres Royals (10)	46	90	.338	50½	46,339	George Scherger

Playoffs: Quebec 4 games, Oneonta 1; Amsterdam 4 games, Schenectady 2.
Finals: Quebec 4 games, Amsterdam 0.

All-Star Team: 1B-Spencer Robbins, Schenectady; **2B**-Edward Barbarito, Amsterdam; **3B**-William Sinram, Quebec; **SS**-Michael Turturro, Gloversville-Johnstown; **OF**-Garland Lawing, Quebec; Royce Watson, Schenectady; Joseph DeToia, Oneonta; **C**-Gus Triandos, Amsterdam; **P**-Fred Belinsky, Quebec; Harold Erickson, Quebec; John Nansteel, Quebec; Harry Wilson, Gloversville-Johnstown.

BA: Garland Lawing, Quebec, .346
Runs: Louis Palmisiano, Quebec, 130
Hits: Harold Buckwalter, Oneonta, 165
RBIs: Garland Lawing, Quebec, 141
HRs: Garland Lawing, Quebec, 19
Wins: Fred Belinsky, Quebec, 22
SOs: Harold Erickson, Quebec, 205
ERA: Harold Erickson, Quebec, 2.40

C Cotton States League
President: Al Haraway

Standings	W	L	Pct.	GB	Attend.	Manager
Pine Bluff Judges (7)	84	54	.609	—	94,902	Harry Chozen
Monroe Sports	81	56	.591	2½	80,814	Al Mazar
Hot Springs Bathers (2)	77	60	.562	6½	61,153	John Antonelli
Natchez Indians	78	61	.561	6½	44,310	Richard Adkins
Greenwood Dodgers (10)	69	69	.500	15	35,140	Lou Rochelli
Greenville Bucks	63	75	.457	21	45,885	Joe Rullo
Clarksdale Planters	62	76	.449	22	47,340	Chet Morgan
El Dorado Oilers	38	101	.273	46½	25,703	Roy Schalk

Playoffs: Hot Springs 4 games, Monroe 2; Natchez 4 games, Pine Bluff 1.
Finals: Hot Springs 4 games, Natchez 3.

All-Star Team: 1B-Dan Phalen, Pine Bluff; **2B**-Harry Schwegman, Pine Bluff; **3B**-George Ruzina, Natchez; **SS**-Alex Cosmidis, Hot Springs; **OF**-Ben Cantrell, Pine Bluff; Jim Gilbert, Natchez; Jack Ramm, Pine Bluff; **C**-Lou Landini, Greenwood; **P**-Cliff Coggin, Monroe; Adam Stempkowski, Pine Bluff; Dan Caccavo, Hot Springs; John Miskulin, Natchez.

BA: Ben Cantrell, Pine Bluff, .363
Runs: Harry Schwegman, Pine Bluff, 150
Hits: Ben Cantrell, Pine Bluff, 189
RBIs: Ben Cantrell, Pine Bluff, 144
HRs: Richard Atkins, Natchez, 25
Wins: Cliff Coggin, Monroe, 21
SOs: Ryne Duren, Pine Bluff, 233
ERA: Ronald Lurk, Monroe, 1.55

C East Texas League
President: J. Walter Morris

Standings	W	L	Pct.	GB	Attend.	Manager
Gladewater Bears	92	45	.672	—	27,789	Dutch Meyer/Hal Van Pelt
Marshall Browns (7)	88	46	.657	2½	47,254	Bruce Ogrodowski
Kilgore Drillers	78	59	.569	14	37,742	Al Kubski
Longview Texans	67	67	.500	23½	41,146	Dixie Parsons
Tyler Trojans	60	78	.435	32½	54,778	Otho Nitcholas/Stan Goletz/Joe Kracher
Henderson Oilers	60	79	.432	33	23,384	Burl Storie/John Stone/Bill Sinton
Paris Panthers#	30	59	.337	NA	30,600	Jimmy Walkup/Joe Weeks
Bryan Sports#	23	65	.261	NA	26,050	Bones Sanders

#Paris and Bryan disbanded July 20.

Playoffs: Longview 4 games, Gladewater 3; Marshall 4 games, Kilgore 1.
Finals: Marshall 4 games, Longview 1.

BA: Lambert Meyer, Gladewater, .375
Runs: Hal Van Pelt, Gladewater, 130
Hits: Jack Jones, Longview, 168
RBIs: Jack Jones, Longview, 128
HRs: Jack Jones, Longview, 26
Mervin Connors, Kilgore, 26
Wins: Darwin Dobbs, Tyler, 21
SOs: John Fine, Longview, 178
ERA: Howard Waters, Marshall, 1.87

C Evangeline League
President: Edmond L. Deramee

Standings	W	L	Pct.	GB	Attend.	Manager
Lafayette Bulls	86	53	.619	—	78,854	Harry Strohm
Baton Rouge Red Sticks	82	58	.586	4½	106,345	Paul Bruno
Thibodaux Giants	71	63	.530	12½	64,301	Art Kowalski
Hammond Berries	71	65	.522	13½	38,500	Joe Kracher/Joe Powers
Alexandria Aces	71	67	.514	14½	81,381	Roy Lee Smith
New Iberia Rebels	66	73	.475	20	84,235	Sidney Gautreaux
Houma Indians	53	84	.387	32	43,283	George Washburn
Abbeville Athletics	50	87	.365	35	22,811	Greek George/Lloyd Harrington/Wilfred Theard/Glenn Murray/Joe Demoran

Playoffs: Hammond 4 games, Lafayette 1; Baton Rouge 4 games, Thibodaux 2.
Finals: Baton Rouge 4 games, Hammond 0.

BA: Charles Williams, Thibodaux, .381
Runs: Earl Bossenberry, New Iberia, 139
Hits: Charles Williams, Thibodaux, 218
RBIs: Charles Williams, Thibodaux, 150
HRs: Ray Dunn, Hammond, 39
Wins: Marshall O'Coine, Thibodaux, 24
SOs: Marshall O'Coine, Thibodaux, 208
ERA: Tom Spears, Lafayette, 2.60

C Gulf Coast League
President: Howard Green

Standings	W	L	Pct.	GB	Attend.	Manager
Crowley Millers	90	56	.616	—	79,640	John George
Galveston White Caps	80	68	.541	11	89,592	Ben Phillips
Jacksonville Jax	79	68	.537	11½	36,029	Charles Baron(ovic)

Standings	W	L	Pct.	GB	Attend.	Manager
Lufkin/Leesville Angels# ...	75	70	.517	14½	26,456	Carl Carter
Lake Charles Lakers	59	88	.401	31½	78,441	George Milstead/Woodie Head/ Bill Elliott/Bill Monahan
Port Arthur Seahawks	58	91	.389	33½	66,861	Jesse Landrum/Bill Wilson/ Charles Harper

#Lufkin (43-51) moved to Leesville July 15.

Playoffs: Crowley 4 games, Leesville 2; Jacksonville 4 games, Galveston 1.
Finals: Jacksonville 4 games, Crowley 2.

All-Star Team: 1B-Charles Baron(ovic), Jacksonville; **2B**-Ray Smerek, Crowley; **3B**-Alois Turk, Crowley; **SS**-Emilio Mozo, Jacksonville; **OF**-Art Edinger, Jacksonville; Jim Sinovich, Jacksonville; Al Kaiser, Lufkin/Leesville; **C**-Floyd Economides, Jacksonville; **P**-G.T. Walters, Crowley; Bob Upton, Jacksonville; Jim Hogan, Jacksonville; Charles Davis, Lufkin/Leesville.

BA: Art Edinger, Jacksonville, .378
Runs: Alois Turk, Crowley, 126
Hits: Art Edinger, Jacksonville, 212
RBIs: Charles Harper, Port Arthur, 126

HRs: Conklyn Meriwether, Lake Charles, 24
Charles Harper, Port Arthur, 24
Wins: G.T. Walters, Crowley, 30
SOs: Bob Upton, Jacksonville, 346
ERA: Ramon Roger, Galveston, 2.51

C Middle Atlantic League
President: Elmer M. Daily

Standings	W	L	Pct.	GB	Attend.	Manager
Oil City Refiners.................	70	44	.617	—	39,267	James Davis
Butler Tigers (4)	67	49	.578	4	31,816	Marvin Olson
Erie Sailors (13).................	63	52	.548	7½	54,850	Pete Pavich
New Castle Nats (8)............	64	54	.542	8	31,082	Charles Cronin
Youngstown Athletics (6).....	51	61	.455	18	14,003	Clarence "Buck" Etchison
Niagara Falls Citizens	48	69	.410	23½	50,224	Michael Ulisney/Walter Chipple
Johnstown Johnnies	45	69	.395	25	43,387	Roy Nichols
Vandergrift Pioneers#(14)..	31	41	.431	NA	13,493	Don Hasenmayer

#Vandergrift disbanded July 20.

Playoffs: Oil City 3 games, Erie 0; Butler 3 games, New Castle 2.
Finals: Butler 4 games, Oil City 3.

All-Star Team: 1B-Edward Kestler, Erie; **2B**-William Paolisso, Youngstown; **3B**-Henry DiJohnson, Niagara Falls; **SS**-George Eikenberg, New Castle; **OF**-John Golich, Erie; Robert Huddleston, Oil City; Joseph Adcock, Butler; Larry Rush, Oil City; **C**-William Horne, New Castle; **Util**-Roy Nichols, Johnstown; **P**-Paul Foytack, Butler; Don Olexio, Butler; **Manager**-Jim Davis, Oil City.

BA: Robert Huddleston, Oil City, .364
Runs: Milton Kress, Erie, 116
Hits: Tom Falk, Butler, 148
RBIs: Clarence "Buck" Etchison, Youngstown, 115

HRs: Harvey Roop, Vandergrift, 21
Wins: Paul Foytack, Butler, 18
SOs: Paul Foytack, Butler, 219
ERA: Paul Foytack, Butler, 2.78

C Northern League
President: Herman D. White

Standings	W	L	Pct.	GB	Attend.	Manager
St. Cloud Rox (13).............	72	51	.585	—	63,385	Charlie Fox
Eau Claire Bears (9)	73	53	.579	½	86,169	Andy Cohen
Sioux Falls Canaries (11) ...	70	55	.560	3	94,001	Lee Eilbracht
Superior Blues (2).............	68	57	.544	5	67,702	Bennie Huffman/Red Kress
Aberdeen Pheasants (7)......	62	57	.521	8	61,208	Irvin Hall
Grand Forks Chiefs (5).......	52	73	.416	21	41,976	Jack Farmer/Cedric Durst
Duluth Dukes (16)	50	73	.407	22	66,208	Russell Rolandson
Fargo-Moorhead Twins	49	77	.389	24½	74,157	Art Doll

Playoffs: Sioux Falls 3 games, St. Cloud 0; Superior 3 games, Eau Claire 1.
Finals: Sioux Falls 4 games, Superior 1.

All-Star Team: 1B-Ken Landenberger, Superior; **2B**-Wally Reed, Grand Forks; **3B**-Charles Weymann, St. Cloud; **SS**-Ted Sterger, Sioux Falls; **OF**-Bill Bruton, Eau Claire; Dick Bornholt, St. Cloud; Clair Bailey, Aberdeen; Richard Anderson, Superior; **C**-Tex Hough, Eau Claire; **P**-Raymond Kirchoff, St. Cloud; Ronald Ploetz, Superior; **Manager**-Andy Cohen, Eau Claire.

BA: Richard Anderson, Superior, .345
Runs: Bill Bruton, Eau Claire, 126
Hits: Bill Bruton, Eau Claire, 157
RBIs: Ken Landenberger, Superior, 104

HRs: Howard Boles, Sioux Falls, 22
Wins: Raymond Kirchoff, St. Cloud, 19
SOs: John Virkstis, Superior, 235
ERA: Robert Hartig, Sioux Falls, 2.44

C Pioneer League
President: Jack P. Halliwell

Standings	W	L	Pct.	GB	Attend.	Manager
Pocatello Cardinals (16)	80	46	.635	—	77,265	Larry Barton
Twin Falls Cowboys (5)	76	50	.603	4	76,618	Wally Berger
Billings Mustangs (10)	72	54	.571	8	136,489	Larry Shepard
Great Falls Selectrics	68	57	.544	11½	127,434	Joe Bowman/John Angelone
Ogden Reds (12)................	58	68	.460	22	77,980	Cecil Scheffel
Salt Lake City Bees	55	70	.440	24½	105,750	Earl Bolyard/Robert White
Boise Pilots	50	74	.403	29	62,545	Ford Mullen
Idaho Falls Russets (13)	43	83	.341	37	47,229	Lilio Marcucci

Playoffs: Billings 2 games, Pocatello 0; Twin Falls 2 games, Great Falls 1.
Finals: Billings 3 games, Twin Falls 0.

All-Star Team: 1B-Sven "Red" Jessen, Twin Falls; **2B**-Billy Rice, Pocatello; **3B**-Ray Posipanka, Twin Falls; **SS**-John Angelone, Great Falls; **OF**-Dick Cordell, Pocatello; Eddie Moore, Billings; Bob Van Eman, Salt Lake City; **C**-Lilio Marcucci, Idaho Falls; **P**-Ivan Abromowitz, Twin Falls; Cliff Ross, Ogden.

BA: Bob Van Eman, Salt Lake City, .368
Runs: Ernest Schuerman, Pocatello, 134
Hits: Ed Moore, Billings, 166
RBIs: William Pinckard, Billings, 135
Dick Cordell, Pocatello, 135
HRs: Ray Posipanka, Twin Falls, 32

Wins: Larry Shepard, Billings, 22
Ivan Abromowitz, Twin Falls, 22
SOs: Ivan Abromowitz, Twin Falls, 198
Cliff Ross, Ogden, 198
ERA: Larry Shepard, Billings, 2.54
Pct: Ivan Abromowitz, Twin Falls, .786, 22-6
Larry Shepard, Billings, .786, 22-6

C Provincial League
President: Albert Molini

Standings	W	L	Pct.	GB	Attend.	Manager
St. Jean Braves..................	58	49	.542	—	86,268	Steve Mizerak
Sherbrooke Les Athletiques.....	57	51	.528	1½	95,053	Roland Gladu
Farnham Pirates	55	52	.514	3	62,151	Stan "Packy" Rogers
Drummondville Cubs	53	52	.505	4	110,350	Fido Murphy/John White/ Stanislaus Breard
St. Hyacinthe Saints...........	52	55	.486	6	89,521	Jay Kirke, Jr.
Granby Red Sox	45	61	.425	12½	82,512	Bob Latshaw/Bud Kimball

Playoffs: St. Jean 4 games, Farnham 1; Sherbrooke 4 games, Drummondville 2.
Finals: St. Jean 4 games, Sherbrooke 3.

BA: Silvio Garcia, Sherbrooke, .365
Runs: Joseph Scott, Farnham, 89
Hits: Silvio Garcia, Sherbrooke, 150
RBIs: Silvio Garcia, Sherbrooke, 116
HRs: Silvio Garcia, Sherbrooke, 21

Wins: Louis Shapiro, Sherbrooke, 18
SOs: Fred Luciano, Drummondville, 140
Ruben Gomez, St. Jean, 140
ERA: Melvin Nee, St. Hyacinthe, 1.69

C Rio Grande Valley League
President: William R. Byrd

Standings	W	L	Pct.	GB	Attend.	Manager
Harlingen Capitols.............	86	62	.581	—	80,001	Sam Harshaney
Laredo Apaches	84	62	.575	1	57,948	Leo Najo/Jack Smith/ Manuel Salvatierra
Corpus Christi Aces............	79	64	.552	4½	68,313	John "Red" Davis
Brownsville Charros	80	67	.544	5½	56,146	Joseph King
Del Rio Cowboys	76	69	.524	8	30,568	Robert Hamric
McAllen Giants	42	102	.292	42	32,473	Boyd SoRelle/Philip Kuykendall
Robstown Rebels@	13	18	.419	NA	6,637	Fabian Kowalik
Donna-Weslaco Twins#	4	20	.167	NA	3,008	G.C. "Baldy" Quinn

#Donna-Weslaco disbanded May 4.
@Robstown disbanded May 13.

Playoffs: Harlingen 4 games, Brownsville 2; Corpus Christi 4 games, Laredo 1.
Finals: Corpus Christi 4 games, Harlingen 1.

All-Star Team: 1B-Hal Jackson, Del Rio; **2B**-John "Red" Davis, Corpus Christi; **3B**-Eddie Rzendzian, Brownsville; **SS**-Juan Perez, Brownsville; **OF**-Manuel Salvatierra, Laredo; Lloyd Pearson, Corpus Christi; Jesse McClain, Harlingen; **C**-Frank Mormino, Del Rio; **P**-Bob Covington, Harlingen; William Guthrie, Harlingen; Richard Midkiff, Del Rio; Julio Moreno, Del Rio.

BA: Lloyd Pearson, Corpus Christi, .383
Runs: Joseph Koppe, Corpus Christi, 181
Hits: Lloyd Pearson, Corpus Christi, 207
Jesse McClain, Harlingen, 207
RBIs: Jesse McClain, Harlingen, 173

HRs: Jesse McClain, Harlingen, 53
Wins: Richard Midkiff, Del Rio, 22
SOs: William Guthrie, Harlingen, 195
ERA: Richard Midkiff, Del Rio, 3.77

C Sunset League
President: Leslie Powers

Standings	W	L	Pct.	GB	Attend.	Manager
Mexicali Eagles	98	47	.676	—	80,871	Dolf Luque
El Centro Imperials.............	85	58	.595	12	46,380	Ken Meyers
Las Vegas Wranglers	76	69	.524	22	39,415	Ed Wheeler
Riverside Rubes	73	72	.503	23	49,270	Ray Viers
Tijuana Potros...................	70	77	.476	29	39,250	Zenon Ochoa/ Enrique Fernandez/Butch Moran
San Bernardino Pioneers	65	80	.448	33	28,250	Frank Demaree/Gerald Waltman
Yuma Panthers..................	62	83	.428	36	50,101	Butch Moran/Frank Gabler
Porterville Packers.............	52	95	.354	47	50,213	Thomas Lloyd/William Harris/ Joseph Gonzales

Playoffs: Mexicali 2 games, Las Vegas 1; El Centro 2 games, Riverside 0.
Finals: El Centro 2 games, Mexicali 1.

All-Star Team: 1B-Virgilio Arteaga, Mexicali; **2B**-Tony Villa, Riverside; **3B**-Blas Guzman, Mexicali; **SS**-Robert Strader, El Centro; Manuel Serrano, Mexicali; **OF**-Pete Hughes, El Centro; Felipe Montemayor, Mexicali; Guido Falappino, Tijuana; **C**-Rube Johnson, Las Vegas; **P**-Manuel Echeverria, Mexicali; Bob Shore, Las Vegas; George Pain, Riverside; Charles Gowett, El Centro.

BA: Pete Hughes, El Centro, .393
Runs: Manuel Serrano, Mexicali, 153
Hits: Blas Guzman, Mexicali, 216
RBIs: Blas Guzman, Mexicali, 138
HRs: Ron Johnson, Las Vegas, 26

Wins: Manuel Echeverria, Mexicali, 28
SOs: Manuel Echeverria, Mexicali, 333
ERA: Manuel Echeverria, Mexicali, 2.74
IP: Manuel Echeverria, Mexicali, 328

C West Texas-New Mexico League
President: Milton E. Price

Standings	W	L	Pct.	GB	Attend.	Manager
Pampa Oilers	92	53	.634	—	59,670	Grover Seitz
Albuquerque Dukes	89	58	.605	4	85,605	Herschel Martin
Lubbock Hubbers	80	63	.559	11	109,129	Jackie Sullivan
Lamesa Lobos	79	63	.556	11½	87,438	Jay Haney/Jodie Beeler
Borger Gassers	71	73	.493	20½	66,610	Mickey Burnett
Amarillo Gold Sox	59	82	.418	31	65,633	Harry Davis/Pete Knapp/ Crawford Howard
Clovis Pioneers (11)	53	90	.371	38	45,301	Paul Dean/Harold Hoffman/ Ray Bauer/Charles Bushong
Abilene Blue Sox	51	92	.357	40	57,755	Hayden Greer

Playoffs: Lamesa 4 games, Pampa 3; Albuquerque 4 games, Lubbock 1.
Finals: Albuquerque 4 games, Lamesa 1, one tie.

All-Star Team: 1B-Doug Lewis, Amarillo; 2B-Jackie Sullivan, Lubbock; 3B-Billy Capps, Lamesa; SS-Jodie Beeler, Lamesa; OF-Crawford Howard, Amarillo; Herschel Martin, Albuquerque; Joe Fortin, Pampa; C-Mike Dooley, Lubbock; P-Don Cantrell, Albuquerque; Roy Parker, Pampa.

BA: Harry Bright, Clovis, .413
Runs: Lyle Palmer, Albuquerque, 164
Hits: Joe Fortin, Pampa, 236
RBIs: Joe Fortin, Pampa, 171
HRs: Crawford Howard, Amarillo, 37

Wins: Roy Parker, Pampa, 27
SOs: Roy Parker, Pampa, 256
ERA: Eddie Carnett, Borger, 3.15
Pct: Don Cantrell, Albuquerque, .769, 20-6
   Royce Mills, Lubbock, .769, 10-3

C Western Association
President: Howard Goetz

Standings	W	L	Pct.	GB	Attend.	Manager
Joplin Miners (5)	90	46	.663	—	58,644	Harry Craft
Hutchinson Elks (15)	77	60	.562	13½	91,500	Wes Griffin
Springfield Cubs (11)	74	61	.548	15½	34,860	Robert Peterson
Enid Giants (13)	71	63	.530	18	40,713	Harold Kollar
St. Joseph Cardinals (16)	67	69	.493	23	71,312	Harold Olt
Topeka Owls	58	81	.427	33½	106,250	Butch Nieman
Muskogee Reds	52	79	.397	35½	52,126	Heinie Mueller
Salina Blue Jays (14)	53	83	.390	37	44,773	John Davenport

Playoffs: Springfield 3 games, Joplin 1; Hutchinson 3 games, Enid 1.
Finals: Hutchinson 4 games, Springfield 0.

All-Star Team: 1B-Harold Kollar, Enid; 2B-Frank Santora, Muskogee; 3B-Harold Olt, St. Joseph; SS-Mickey Mantle, Joplin; OF-Pete Maropis, Hutchinson; Butch Nieman, Topeka; Ace Adamewicz, St. Joseph; C-Harry Chiti, Springfield; P-Max DeCamp, Hutchinson; Paul Pawli, Salina; Frank Simanovsky, Joplin; Bob Wiesler, Joplin; Manager-Harry Craft, Joplin.

BA: Mickey Mantle, Joplin, .383
Runs: Mickey Mantle, Joplin, 141
Hits: Mickey Mantle, Joplin, 199
RBIs: Butch Nieman, Topeka, 149

HRs: Butch Nieman, Topeka, 28
Wins: Frank Simanovsky, Joplin, 21
SOs: Bob Wiesler, Joplin, 277
ERA: Bob Wiesler, Joplin, 2.35

D Alabama State League
President: Charles T. Laney

Standings	W	L	Pct.	GB	Attend.	Manager
Enterprise Boll Weevils	76	49	.608	—	23,269	Paul O'Dea
Dothan Browns	72	53	.576	4	51,665	Clarence Hodge
Headland Dixie Runners	68	56	.548	7½	27,121	John McPherson
Greenville Pirates (15)	65	61	.516	11½	17,106	Mickey O'Neil
Andalusia Arrows	63	62	.504	13	43,163	James Ball
Brewton Millers	54	72	.429	22½	24,397	Holt "Cat" Milner/ Cotton McCaskey/Sam Demma
Geneva Red Birds (16)	52	73	.416	24	14,194	John Grodzicki/Robert Comiskey
Ozark Eagles	51	75	.405	25½	17,799	Julian Morgan

Playoffs: Headland 4 games, Enterprise 3; Dothan 4 games, Greenville 2.
Finals: Dothan 4 games, Headland 1.

BA: John McPherson, Headland, .405
Runs: Joe Harper, Headland, 138
Hits: John McPherson, Headland, 197
RBIs: John McPherson, Headland, 132

HRs: Lamar Bowden, Dothan, 15
Wins: David Hataway, Andalusia, 23
SOs: Thomas Stone, Headland, 246
ERA: James Pomykala, Greenville, 2.195

D Appalachian League
President: Chauncey De Vault

Standings	W	L	Pct.	GB	Attend.	Manager
Bluefield Blue-Grays***(9)	80	40	.667	—	61,158	Bill Adair
Bristol Twins (13)	74	47	.612	6½	42,301	Ben Geraghty
Johnson City Cardinals (16)	73	48	.603	7½	51,258	Ben Catchings
Elizabethton Betsy Local	72	52	.581	10	36,318	Jack Crosswhite
Pulaski Counts	66	51	.564	12½	36,410	Bob Westfall

Welch Miners (6)	46	76	.377	35	34,000	Edwin Morgan/Woody Wheaton
Kingsport Cherokees	42	75	.359	36½	38,023	Hobe Brummitt
New River Rebels	31	95	.246	52	24,000	Floyd Brooks/Worlise Knowles

Playoff: Bristol 3 games, Bluefield 0.

BA: Bob Boring, Elizabethton, .388
Runs: Vince LaSala, Bristol, 116
Hits: Billy Queen, Bluefield, 159
RBIs: Louis Dolci, Welch, 124

HRs: Bob Boring, Elizabethton, 26
Wins: Doug Clark, Elizabethton, 27
SOs: Doug Clark, Elizabethton, 228
ERA: Doug Clark, Elizabethton, 2.41

D Blue Ridge League
President: John B. Spiers

Standings	W	L	Pct.	GB	Attend.	Manager
Elkin Blanketeers	82	32	.719	—	21,578	Tige Harris
Mt. Airy Graniteers	71	48	.596	13½	16,306	Cecil "Zip" Payne/Joe Roseberry
Galax Leafs (13)	68	50	.576	16	15,813	James Grigg
Radford Rockets	52	70	.426	34	20,500	Garland Braxton/Stephen Sloboda
Wytheville/Bassett Statesmen#	39	74	.345	42½	22,183	Richard Hartnett
North Wilkesboro Flashers	40	78	.339	44	23,118	Bernard Loman/Henry Loman

#Wytheville moved to Bassett July 27 due to a polio outbreak.

Playoffs: Elkin 3 games, Galax 0; Mt. Airy 3 games, Radford 1.
Finals: Mt. Airy 4 games, Elkin 0.

BA: Henry Brown, Elkin, .379
Runs: Bob Withrow, Elkin, 104
   Bob Horan, Galax, 104
Hits: Bob Horan, Galax, 153
RBIs: Henry Brown, Elkin, 87

HRs: Bob Horan, Galax, 14
Wins: Mitchell Mozejko, Galax, 18
SOs: James Jones, Mt. Airy, 160
ERA: Gary Thornburg, North Wilkesboro, 2.27

D Coastal Plain League
President: Ray H. Goodmon

Standings	W	L	Pct.	GB	Attend.	Manager
Roanoke Rapids Jays	80	58	.580	—	80,665	Glen Lockamy/Walt McJunkin
Rocky Mount Leafs	73	65	.525	7	62,027	Horace "Red" Benton
New Bern Bears	71	67	.514	9	63,486	Harry Land
Kinston Eagles (1)	70	68	.507	10	51,794	Walter Millies
Wilson Tobs	68	70	.493	12	84,159	Bill Herring
Greenville Robins	67	70	.489	12½	49,140	Randy Heflin
Tarboro Athletics (6)	67	71	.486	13	36,467	Joe Antolick
Goldsboro Cardinals (16)	56	83	.403	24½	35,719	James Herbison

Playoffs: Kinston 4 games, Roanoke Rapids 0; New Bern 4 games, Rocky Mount 2.
Finals: New Bern 4 games, Kinston 0.

All-Star Team: 1B-Harry Soufas, New Bern; 2B-Irv Dickens, Wilson; 3B-Leo Katkaveck, Roanoke Rapids; SS-Ken Aspromonte, Kinston; OF-Walt McJunkin, Roanoke Rapids; Paul Strausser, Greenville; Billy Johnson, Goldsboro; Ed Christoff, New Bern; C-Enid Drake, Tarboro; Util-Quentin Martin, Rocky Mount; P-Alton Brown, Roanoke Rapids; Fred Pittman, Wilson; Leo Groeschen, Kinston; Bobby Slaybaugh, Goldsboro; Manager-Joe Antolick, Tarboro.

BA: Quentin Martin, Rocky Mount, .351
Runs: Dallas Orf, Tarboro, 110
Hits: Quentin Martin, Rocky Mount, 171
RBIs: Warriner Bass, Roanoke Rapids, 148

HRs: William Smith, Goldsboro, 24
Wins: Alton Brown, Roanoke Rapids, 28
SOs: Alton Brown, Roanoke Rapids, 204
ERA: Leo Groeschen, Kinston, 1.74

D Far West League
President: Jerry Donovan

Standings	W	L	Pct.	GB	Attend.	Manager
Klamath Falls Gems (14)	87	52	.626	—	62,078	Hub Kittle
Redding Browns (7)	86	54	.614	1½	47,235	Ray Perry
Reno Silver Sox	75	63	.543	11½	46,899	Joe Borich
Medford Rogues (13)	69	70	.497	18	37,293	Thomas Nelson/Wilfred Jonas
Pittsburg Diamonds	67	73	.479	20½	22,179	Vince DiMaggio
Eugene Larks	62	77	.446	25	46,487	Louis Vezilich
Marysville Peaches	56	82	.406	30½	14,146	Bert Kenmuir/Charles Welchel
Willows Cardinals (16)	54	85	.388	33	17,128	Ray Malgradi

Playoffs: Klamath Falls 3 games, Reno 2; Redding 3 games, Medford 0.
Finals: Redding 3 games, Klamath Falls 1.

All-Star Team: 1B-Jack Cooney, Medford; 2B-Wayne Peterson, Klamath Falls; 3B-Ray Perry, Redding; SS-Al Sahlberg, Klamath Falls; OF-Russ Rosburg, Redding; Chet Ashman, Klamath Falls; Vince DiMaggio, Pittsburg; C-George Triandos, Klamath Falls; P-Clyde DeWitt, Klamath Falls; Charles Closs, Reno; Andrew Sierra, Klamath Falls; Pat Monahan, Reno.

BA: Joe Borich, Reno, .387
Runs: Ray Perry, Redding, 162
Hits: George Triandos, Klamath Falls, 183
RBIs: Ray Perry, Redding, 170

HRs: Ray Perry, Redding, 44
Wins: Andrew Sierra, Klamath Falls, 22
SOs: Andrew Sierra, Klamath Falls, 258
ERA: Eugene Valentine, Pittsburg, 1.82

D Florida State League
President: Earle M. Bussey

Standings	W	L	Pct.	GB	Attend.	Manager
Orlando Senators (8)	88	52	.629	—	47,346	Cal Ermer
Daytona Beach Islanders (3)	87	52	.626	½	73,260	Red Ruffing

	W	L	Pct.	GB	Attend.	Manager
DeLand Red Hats	82	57	.590	5½	38,469	Bill Perrin
Gainesville G-Men	77	63	.550	11	47,900	Lou Kahn/Charles Brewster
Sanford Giants (13)	71	68	.511	16½	34,719	Ed Levy
St. Augustine Saints	57	83	.407	31	27,796	Ernest Jenkins/Lyle Judy/ Charles Starasta
Leesburg Packers	54	84	.391	33	30,302	Frank Piet/Floyd Clift/ Bill Steinecke
Palatka Azaleas	41	98	.295	46½	22,481	E.M. "Bitsy" Mott/Robert Rucker

Playoffs: Gainesville 4 games, Orlando 1; DeLand 4 games, Daytona Beach 0.
Finals: DeLand 4 games, Gainesville 1.

All-Star Team: 1B-Ed Levy, Sanford; **2B**-Mel Kerestes, Orlando; **3B**-Cal Ermer, Orlando; **SS**-Charles Brewster, Gainesville; **OF**-Herbert McLeod, DeLand; Bruce Barmes, Orlando; Richard Stellern, Daytona Beach; **C**-Ray Dunne, DeLand; **P**-George Erath, St. Augustine; Henry Bruder, Orlando; Ed Brooklyn, Orlando; Peter Nicolis, DeLand.

BA: Bruce Barmes, Orlando, .372
Runs: Richard Stellern, Daytona Beach, 146
Hits: Bruce Barmes, Orlando, 217
RBIs: Al Pirtle, Gainesville, 124
HRs: Ed Levy, Sanford, 33
Wins: Charles Tedesco, Sanford, 19
SOs: Clyde Stevens, Sanford, 186
ERA: Bill Glessner, Daytona Beach, 1.61

D Georgia State League
President: Earl Blue

Standings	W	L	Pct.	GB	Attend.	Manager
Dublin Green Sox	84	56	.600	—	50,160	Edward Wissman/Parnell Ruark/ William Seal
Douglas Trojans	78	60	.565	5	32,590	David Coble/Fred Tschudin
Eastman Dodgers	79	61	.564	5	35,000	Edgar Hartness
Fitzgerald Pioneers	73	66	.525	10½	42,227	Ray Harrell
Jesup Bees	69	69	.500	14	23,893	Herb Stein
Tifton Blue Sox	69	70	.496	14½	54,784	William Barnes/David Coble
Vidalia-Lyons Twins	56	83	.403	29½	30,350	Mike Kreshka/James Smith
Baxley-Hazlehurst Red Sox	48	91	.345	35½	25,000	Bill Enos

Playoffs: Dublin 3 games, Fitzgerald 2; Eastman 3 games, Douglas 1.
Finals: Eastman 4 games, Dublin 3.

All-Star Team: 1B-Edgar Hartness, Eastman; **2B**-Charles Ridgeway, Fitzgerald; **3B**-James Smith, Vidalia-Lyons; **SS**-Lewis Hallford, Jesup; **OF**-Parnell Ruark, Dublin; Bill Crago, Fitzgerald; John Tidwell, Dublin; **C**-Fred Tschudin, Douglas; **Util**-Wilbur Caldwell, Eastman; Don Lewis, Baxley-Hazlehurst; **P**-Clarence Richardson, Eastman; Charles Smalley, Dublin; **Manager**-Ray Harrell, Fitzgerald.

BA: Edgar Hartness, Eastman, .400
Runs: Edgar Hartness, Eastman, 137
Hits: Edgar Hartness, Eastman, 201
RBIs: Edgar Hartness, Eastman, 134
HRs: Parnell Ruark, Dublin, 39
Wins: Charles Smalley, Dublin, 23
SOs: Charles Smalley, Dublin, 237
ERA: Charles Smalley, Dublin, 2.46

D Georgia-Alabama League
President: Arthur R. Decatur

Standings	W	L	Pct.	GB	Attend.	Manager
La Grange Troupers (5)	73	48	.603	—	53,781	Bill Cooper
Alexander City Millers	73	53	.579	2½	36,546	Charles Roberts
Carrollton Hornets	66	57	.537	8	26,365	Herb Marshall
Newnan Brownies	62	60	.508	11½	37,215	Bob Schmidt
Valley Rebels	58	65	.472	16	31,619	Myril Hoag/Jake Daniel
Griffin Tigers	57	64	.471	16	37,167	Adel White/Jack Bearden
Opelika Owls	52	72	.419	22½	36,912	Woodrow Bottoms/ Don Bailey/Wheeler Flemming
Rome Red Sox (8)	49	71	.408	23½	30,482	Norman Veazey/John Stowe/ Myril Hoag

Playoffs: La Grange 2 games, Carrollton 0; Alexander City 2 games, Newnan 0.
Finals: La Grange 3 games, Alexander City 2.

All-Star Team: 1B-James Stoyle, Griffin; **2B**-Joe Schmidt, Newnan; **3B**-Leon Carter, La Grange; **SS**-George Noga, Griffin; **OF**-Jack Bearden, Griffin; George Hughes, Valley; Earl Cooper, La Grange; **C**-Eugene Solt, Carrollton; James Durkin, La Grange; **Util**-Billy Rigdon, Opelika; David Krings, La Grange; Lee Lindsley, Alexander City; Bill Bustle, Newnan; Edward Bobowski, Carrollton.

BA: Eugene Solt, Carrollton, .365
Runs: Fred DeSouza, Carrollton, 149
Hits: Eugene Solt, Carrollton, 168
RBIs: Eugene Solt, Carrollton, 151
HRs: Eugene Solt, Carrollton, 38
Wins: Don Bessent, La Grange, 22
SOs: Don Bessent, La Grange, 229
ERA: Don Bessent, La Grange, 2.33

D Georgia-Florida League
President: W.T. Anderson

Standings	W	L	Pct.	GB	Attend.	Manager
Albany Cardinals (16)	83	57	.592	—	62,950	Sheldon "Chief" Bender
Valdosta Dodgers (10)	81	56	.591	½	56,089	Stan Wasiak
Tallahassee Pirates (15)	77	58	.570	3½	55,475	Walter Tauscher
Americus Phillies (14)	70	67	.510	11½	38,939	Eddie Murphy
Moultrie Cubs (11)	71	69	.507	12	48,458	Steve Collins/James Trew
Waycross Bears	57	81	.413	25	43,638	Don Manno/Charles Webb
Cordele A's (6)	55	80	.407	25½	32,655	Bill Peterman
Thomasville Tigers (4)	55	81	.404	26	27,760	Bob Benish

Playoffs: Americus 4 games, Albany 1; Tallahassee 4 games, Valdosta 3.
Finals: Tallahassee 4 games, Americus 1.

All-Star Team: 1B-J.W. Spruill, Cordele; **2B**-Everett Kell, Cordele; **3B**-Richard Smith, Tallahassee; **SS**-Mike Korcheck, Valdosta; Fred Ryan, Albany; **OF**-Charles Coles, Valdosta; Paul Smith, Tallahassee; Ralph Lageman, Albany; **C**-Richard Lindermuth, Tallahassee; **P**-Eftimeo Talas, Tallahassee; Julian Joyner, Albany; Leroy Pounds, Albany; Wes Breschini, Thomasville.

BA: Charles Coles, Valdosta, .355
Runs: Hubert Rose, Moultrie, 145
Hits: Paul Smith, Tallahassee, 196
RBIs: Harold Ivy, Moultrie, 131
HRs: Robert Fulton, Thomasville, 15
Wins: John Hushbeck, Americus, 22
SOs: William Currie, Waycross, 240
ERA: Leroy Pounds, Albany, 2.56

D Kansas-Oklahoma-Missouri League
President: E.L. Dale

Standings	W	L	Pct.	GB	Attend.	Manager
Ponca City Dodgers (10)	80	42	.656	—	63,313	Boyd Bartley
Bartlesville Pirates (15)	73	48	.603	6½	56,250	Tedd Gullic
Carthage Cubs (11)	75	50	.600	6½	29,080	Don Anderson
Pittsburg Browns (7)	71	52	.577	9½	43,953	Olan Smith/James Crandall
Miami Eagles	62	60	.508	18	27,548	Jack Hodge/Jim Oglesby/ Pug Griffin
Independence Yankees (5)	60	66	.476	22	38,274	Malcolm "Bunny" Mick/ Bones Sanders
Iola Indians	35	84	.294	43½	23,872	Winlow Johnson
Chanute Athletics	35	89	.282	46	21,372	Charles Bates/Thomas Imfeld/ Charles Hostetler

Playoffs: Ponca City 3 games, Pittsburg 2; Bartlesville 3 games, Carthage 1.
Finals: Ponca City 3 games, Bartlesville 1.

All-Star Team: 1B-Loren Doll, Ponca City; **2B**-Don Hunter, Ponca City; Jim McHugh, Miami; **3B**-John LaPorta, Carthage; **SS**-Ray Khoury, Iola; **OF**-Stan Gwinn, Ponca City; Jim Pisoni, Pittsburg; Leo Kedzierski, Iola; **C**-Dean Manns, Carthage; **P**-Tom Vines, Carthage; Donald McKeon, Miami; Conrad Swensson, Ponca City; Don Brate, Ponca City.

BA: Stan Gwinn, Ponca City, .320
Runs: Jim Pisoni, Pittsburg, 115
Hits: Don Hunter, Ponca City, 152
Loren Doll, Ponca City, 152
RBIs: Harold Neighbors, Bartlesville, 107
HRs: Willard Davis, Ponca City, 21
Wins: Tom Vines, Carthage, 17
Donald McKeon, Miami, 17
SOs: Tom Vines, Carthage, 234
ERA: David Elliot, Bartlesville, 2.04

D Kitty League
President: Shelby Peace

Standings	W	L	Pct.	GB	Attend.	Manager
Mayfield Clothiers (15)	73	45	.609	—	30,224	Jerry Gardner
Fulton Railroaders (8)	69	50	.580	4½	27,404	Ivan Kuester
Jackson Generals	68	52	.567	6	30,078	Glenn Stewart
Owensboro Oilers (9)	64	51	.557	7½	44,869	Travis Jackson
Madisonville Miners (2)	63	51	.553	8	30,275	George Mitro/Skeeter Webb
Hopkinsville Hoppers	60	60	.500	14	27,504	Joe DeMasi
Union City Greyhounds	43	72	.374	28½	30,144	John Mueller
Cairo Dodgers	26	85	.234	43½	8,485	Harold Seawright/Paul Box

Playoffs: Mayfield 3 games, Owensboro 2; Fulton 3 games, Jackson 2.
Finals: Mayfield 1 game, Fulton 0, series cancelled by bad weather.

All-Star Team: 1B-Ned Waldrop, Fulton; **2B**-Joe Urso, Union City; **3B**-Al Ware, Madisonville; **SS**-Ed Milecevich, Owensboro; **OF**-Joe Andrews, Owensboro; John Mueller, Union City; Ivan Kuester, Fulton; **C**-Glenn Stewart, Jackson; **P**-Ed Wilson, Madisonville; Don McMahon, Owensboro; Dick McIntyre, Mayfield; Everett McCray, Owensboro.

BA: Joe Andrews, Owensboro, .373
Runs: Maurice Partain, Jackson, 113
Hits: Ned Waldrop, Fulton, 150
RBIs: Ned Waldrop, Fulton, 130
HRs: Ned Waldrop, Fulton, 28
Wins: Don McMahon, Owensboro, 20
SOs: Don McMahon, Owensboro, 143
ERA: Don McMahon, Owensboro, 2.72

D Longhorn League
President: Hal Sayles

Standings	W	L	Pct.	GB	Attend.	Manager
Odessa Oilers	97	55	.638	—	73,226	Alex Monchak
Roswell Rockets	89	62	.589	7½	82,671	Tom Jordan
Big Spring Broncs	84	68	.553	13	49,302	Pat Stasey
Vernon Dusters	83	70	.542	14½	46,099	Joe Berry
San Angelo Colts	82	71	.536	15½	97,936	James McClure
Sweetwater Swatters	68	84	.447	29	39,773	John Bottarini/Dominic Chiola
Midland Indians	66	87	.431	31½	47,042	Harold Webb
Ballinger Cats	39	111	.260	57	27,902	Dutch Funderburk/Larry Gilchrist

Playoffs: Odessa 4 games, Vernon 1; Big Spring 4 games, Roswell 0.
Finals: Odessa 4 games, Big Spring 3.

All-Star Team: 1B-Jim Prince, Midland; **2B**-Alex Monchak, Odessa; Dominic Chiola, Sweetwater; **3B**-Carlos Pascual, Big Spring; **SS**-Stanley Hughes, Midland; **OF**-Pat Stasey, Big Spring; Stu Williams, Ballinger; Bill Clearley, Odessa; **C**-Tom Jordan, Roswell; **P**-Billy Russell, Vernon; Ernie Nelson, Midland/Vernon.

BA: Tom Jordan, Roswell, .391
Runs: Leo Eastham, Odessa, 166
Hits: Tom Jordan, Roswell, 216
RBIs: Tom Jordan, Roswell, 180
HRs: Tom Jordan, Roswell, 44
Wins: Billy Russell, Vernon, 25
SOs: Ray Hill, Roswell, 195
ERA: James McClure, San Angelo, 2.54

D Mississippi-Ohio Valley League

President: C.C. "Dutch" Hoffman

Standings	W	L	Pct.	GB	Attend.	Manager
Centralia Sterlings	83	40	.675	—	35,767	Lou Bekeza
West Frankfort Cardinals (16)	72	47	.605	9	20,910	Robert Stanton
Mattoon Indians	71	47	.602	9½	27,982	Chuck Hawley
Paducah Chiefs	67	55	.549	15½	47,297	Walter DeFreitas
Springfield Giants	60	59	.504	21	21,126	Herman Schulte/Von Price
Paris Lakers	43	75	.364	37½	24,089	Earl Skaggs/Von Price/ John Morris
Vincennes Citizens	43	76	.361	38	18,977	Melvin Ivy/Andrew Smith
Mt. Vernon Kings	37	77	.325	41½	28,431	Benny Meyer/Robert Schlemmer

Playoffs: Centralia 3 games, Mattoon 1; Paducah 3 games, West Frankfort 0.
Finals: Cancelled due to bad weather and military call-ups.

All-Star Team: 1B-George Murphy, Mattoon; **2B**-Roger DallaBetta, Centralia; **3B**-Mike Krsnich, Paris; **SS**-Harold Loughary, Paducah; **OF**-James Belz, West Frankfort; Bob Brummer, Mattoon; Jim Frey, Paducah; **C**-Steve Karas, Paducah; **P**-Bob Randant, Centralia; Barry Dosser, Paducah; Gene Pisarski, Centralia; William Ecklund, Centralia.

BA: James Belz, West Frankfort, .349
Runs: James Belz, West Frankfort, 133
Hits: James Belz, West Frankfort, 154
RBIs: Lou Bekeza, Centralia, 120
HRs: Kenneth Dickens, Vincennes, 21
Wins: Gene Pisarski, Centralia, 22
SOs: William Ecklund, Centralia, 174
ERA: Gene Pisarski, Centralia, 2.06

D Mountain States League

President: Virgil Q. Wacks

Standings	W	L	Pct.	GB	Attend.	Manager
Harlan Smokies	81	44	.648	—	41,707	Rex Carr
Hazard Bombers (10)	76	49	.608	5	55,184	Max Macon
Big Stone Gap Rebels	75	51	.595	6½	38,878	Jack Rothrock
Middlesboro Athletics	59	67	.468	22½	20,248	James Burns
Jenkins Cavaliers	58	66	.468	22½	13,880	Bob Bowman/Wayne Stewart/ Bill Scopetone
Morristown Red Sox	56	67	.455	24	30,448	Fred Hartman/Pinky Doyle
Newport Canners	51	74	.408	30	20,920	Robert Mitchell/Matthew Zidich
Pennington Gap Miners	44	82	.349	37½	11,164	Lew Flick/Michael Brelich/ Vince Pankovits

Playoffs: Harlan 3 games, Big Stone Gap 1; Middlesboro 3 games, Hazard 0.
Finals: Harlan 3 games, Middlesboro 0.

BA: Max Macon, Hazard, .392
Runs: Joe Christian, Harlan, 127
Hits: Joe Christian, Harlan, 173
RBIs: Joe Riola, Morristown, 130
HRs: Joe Christian, Harlan, 27
Wins: Nick Bunato, Middlesboro, 22
SOs: Nick Bunato, Middlesboro, 132
ERA: Michael Hudak, Big Stone Gap, 2.89

D North Atlantic League

President: Ernest C. Landgraf

Standings	W	L	Pct.	GB	Attend.	Manager
Lebanon Chix (16)	87	46	.654	—	18,916	Harold Contini
Stroudsburg Poconos	80	50	.615	5½	23,160	Frank Radler
Carbondale Pioneers (14)	76	55	.580	10	37,548	Joe Glenn
Hazleton Dodgers (10)	71	58	.550	14	42,102	George Pfister
Berwick Slaters	64	65	.496	21	15,489	Louis Hummel/Michael Koons
Bangor Bangors	65	71	.478	23½	15,302	Al Gardella
Mahanoy City Brewers	48	88	.353	40½	14,550	Joseph Santomauro/ Richard Dresser
Nazareth Barons	35	90	.280	48	8,567	Ivan Fortune

Playoffs: Lebanon 4 games, Carbondale 3; Stroudsburg 4 games, Hazleton 1.
Finals: Lebanon 3 games, Stroudsburg 2, series stopped by bad weather.

BA: George Pfister, Hazleton, .334
Runs: Gerald Manguson, Bangor, 107
Hits: Ralph Guyton, Hazleton, 162
RBIs: George Rhoads, Carbondale, 100
HRs: Chester Krajeski, Stroudsburg, 13
Wins: Frank Radler, Stroudsburg, 21
SOs: Gerald Mertz, Lebanon, 186
ERA: Frank Radler, Stroudsburg, 1.81

D North Carolina State League

President: Robert A. Collier

Standings	W	L	Pct.	GB	Attend.	Manager
Salisbury Pirates (15)	68	44	.607	—	65,766	George Detore
Mooresville Moors	64	47	.577	3½	32,798	Jim Mills
Landis Spinners	63	49	.563	5	31,816	Fred Chapman
High Point-Thomasville Hi-Toms	61	50	.550	6½	68,986	Jim Gruzdis
Statesville Owls	59	53	.527	9	50,222	George Bradshaw
Lexington A's (6)	49	62	.441	18½	36,402	Homer Lee Cox
Concord Nationals (8)	44	68	.393	24	22,558	George Lacy/ Thomas Hockenbury/ Ginger Watts
Hickory Rebels	38	73	.342	29½	36,816	Charles Bowles/ D.C. "Pud" Miller

Playoffs: Landis 4 games, Salisbury 2; High Point-Thomasville 4 games, Mooresville 2.
Finals: Landis 4 games, High Point-Thomasville 3.

All-Star Team: 1B-Ken Rhyne, Statesville; **2B**-Fred Daniels, Statesville; **3B**-John Lybrand, Hi-Toms; **SS**-John Richardson, Salisbury; **OF**-D.C. "Pud" Miller, Hickory; Norman Small, Mooresville; Owen Linn, Landis; **C**-Clifton Bolton, Hi-Toms; **P**-Alfred Jarlett, Hi-Toms; Ernie Johnson, Statesville.

BA: D.C. "Pud" Miller, Hickory, .369
Runs: Charles Petters, Hi-Toms, 113
Hits: Ken Rhyne, Statesville, 151
George Hott, Salisbury, 151
John Lybrand, Hi-Toms, 151
RBIs: Ken Rhyne, Statesville, 119
HRs: Norman Small, Mooresville, 32
Ken Rhyne, Statesville, 32
Wins: Charles Moore, Landis, 20
Ernie Johnson, Statesville, 20
SOs: John Shofer, Hickory, 276
ERA: Alfred Jarlett, Hi-Toms, 2.63

D Ohio-Indiana League

President: Frank M. Colley

Standings	W	L	Pct.	GB	Attend.	Manager
Marion Red Sox (1)	91	49	.650	—	41,002	George Susce/Elmer Yoter
Newark Yankees (5)	89	49	.645	1	41,126	William Holm
Richmond Tigers (4)	80	58	.580	10	45,302	Ralph DiLullo/Kenneth Holtcamp
Springfield Giants (13)	72	64	.529	17	37,619	Andy Gilbert
Muncie Reds (12)	73	65	.529	17	39,354	Mike Blazo
Lima Phillies (14)	52	85	.380	37½	24,627	Frank McCormick
Portsmouth A's (6)	46	89	.341	42½	21,685	Walter VanGrofski
Zanesville Indians (3)	46	90	.328	43	22,888	J. Knowles Piercey

Playoffs: Marion 3 games, Springfield 1; Newark 3 games, Richmond 2.
Finals: Marion 4 games, Newark 0.

BA: James Engleman, Newark, .373
Runs: Keith Jones, Richmond, 140
Hits: James Engleman, Newark, 208
RBIs: Edwin Bryan, Marion, 134
HRs: Andy Gilbert, Springfield, 37
Wins: Theodore Birkeland, Springfield, 24
SOs: Louis Job, Newark, 228
ERA: Daniel Searle, Richmond, 2.12

D PONY League

President: Vincent M. McNamara

Standings	W	L	Pct.	GB	Attend.	Manager
Hornell Dodgers (10)	81	43	.653	—	97,563	Doc Alexson
Olean Oilers	71	54	.568	10½	59,811	Len Schulte
Hamilton Cardinals (16)	68	57	.544	13½	92,673	Vedie Himsl
Bradford Phillies (14)	63	62	.504	18½	38,785	Barney Lutz
Batavia Clippers (3)	61	64	.488	20½	38,785	Ed Kobesky
Jamestown Falcons (4)	60	64	.484	21	60,790	Bob Shawkey
Wellsville Senators (8)	50	75	.400	31½	35,874	Jim Wasdell/Bill Mongiello
Lockport Reds (12)	45	80	.360	36½	28,513	Cyril Pfeifer

Playoffs: Hornell 4 games, Bradford 0; Olean 4 games, Hamilton 2.
Finals: Olean 4 games, Hornell 3.

All-Star Team: 1B-Doc Alexson, Hornell; **2B**-Chuck Harmon, Olean; **3B**-Len Schulte, Olean; **SS**-Don Zimmer, Hornell; **OF**-Oscar Sierra, Hornell; Robert Aiello, Batavia; Barney Lutz, Bradford; **C**-James Tuite, Hornell; Joseph Ossola, Hamilton; **P**-Ralph Butler, Hornell; Thomas Keating, Hamilton; El Roy Face, Bradford; Edwin Williams, Olean.

BA: Oscar Sierra, Hornell, .422
Runs: Don Zimmer, Hornell, 146
Hits: Chuck Harmon, Olean, 206
RBIs: Chuck Harmon, Olean, 139
HRs: Don Zimmer, Hornell, 23
Wins: Ralph Butler, Hornell, 23
SOs: Ralph Butler, Hornell, 175
ERA: El Roy Face, Bradford, 2.58
Pct: El Roy Face, Bradford, .783, 18-5

D Sooner State League

President: Jack Mealey

Standings	W	L	Pct.	GB	Attend.	Manager
Ada Herefords (7)	96	41	.701	—	31,981	Bill Krueger
McAlester Rockets (5)	92	48	.657	5½	58,048	Vern Hoscheit
Chickasha Chiefs	80	59	.575	17	43,759	Ray Honeycutt
Ardmore Indians	75	65	.536	22½	44,454	Bennie Warren
Pauls Valley Raiders	68	72	.486	29½	25,848	Clarence Phillips/Joseph Jacobs
Seminole Ironmen	55	83	.399	41½	21,366	Kelly Wingo/Lloyd Giger/ Dennis Rackley
Duncan Uttmen/ Shawnee Hawks#	51	85	.375	44½	15,950	Hosea Pfeiffer/Dutch Prather/ Kelly Wingo
Lawton Giants (13)	37	101	.268	59½	31,817	Lou Brower

#Duncan moved to Shawnee August 18.

Playoffs: Ardmore 3 games, Ada 2; McAlester 3 games, Chickasha 0.
Finals: McAlester 4 games, Ardmore 2.

All-Star Team: 1B-Donald Davenport, Ada; **2B**-Don Leppart, McAlester; **3B**-Bill Krueger, Ada; **SS**-Andrew Durika, Pauls Valley; **OF**-Clinton Weaver, McAlester; Whitey Herzog, McAlester; Stephen Molinari, Ada; **C**-Vern Hoscheit, McAlester; **Util**-William Milligan, Ada; **P**-Jack Urban, McAlester; William Donaghey, Ada; **Manager**-Bennie Warren, Ardmore.

BA: Clinton Weaver, McAlester, .378
Runs: Ron Jackson, Ada, 154
Hits: Jack Taylor, McAlester, 212
RBIs: Stephen Molinari, Ada, 162
HRs: Stephen Molinari, Ada, 39

Wins: William Donaghey, Ada, 26
SOs: Jack Urban, McAlester, 279
ERA: Jack Urban, McAlester, 2.15
Pct: William Donaghey, Ada, .839, 26-5

D Tobacco State League
President: Arthur T. Moore

Standings	W	L	Pct.	GB	Attend.	Manager
Lumberton Auctioneers	92	43	.682	—	42,796	John Streza
Sanford Spinners................	90	44	.672	1½	19,686	Zeb Harrington
Red Springs Red Robins (6)	68	61	.527	21	26,198	Bob "Ducky" Detweiler
Rockingham Eagles	63	69	.477	27½	31,806	Jack Bell/Cecil "Turkey" Tyson
Clinton Sampson Blues	61	72	.459	30	29,060	Alvin Kluttz/Nicholas Rhabe/ Marvin Lorenz
Wilmington Pirates (12)	56	75	.427	34	35,950	Bull Hamons/Red Teague/ Steve Collins
Whiteville Tobs	39	92	.298	51	20,839	Jim Staton
Smithfield-Selma Leafs#	49	62	.441	NA	19,369	Marvin Lorenz

#Smithfield-Selma disbanded August 16.

Playoffs: Rockingham 4 games, Lumberton 2; Sanford 4 games, Red Springs 0.
Finals: Rockingham 4 games, Sanford 3.

All-Star Team: 1B-Marvin Lorenz, Smithfield-Selma/Clinton; **2B**-Nicholas Purchia, Clinton; **3B**-John Edens, Wilmington; **SS**-Mike Milosevich, Lumberton; **OF**-James Francoline, Lumberton; Granville Denning, Whiteville; Herb May, Sanford; **C**-James Petit, Sanford; **Util**-Bob "Ducky" Detweiler, Red Springs; Bill Kay, Clinton; **P**-Hoyt Clegg, Sanford; Bill Bernier, Lumberton; John Lagan, Lumberton; George Vereault, Red Springs; **Manager**-Zeb Harrington, Sanford.

BA: Granville Denning, Whiteville, .374
Runs: Pierre Ethier, Lumberton, 146
Hits: Granville Denning, Whiteville, 176
RBIs: Mike Milosevich, Lumberton, 121

HRs: Mike Milosevich, Lumberton, 14
Wins: Hoyt Clegg, Sanford, 24
SOs: Richard Causey, Sanford, 148
ERA: Clayton Andrews, Sanford, 2.63

D Virginia League
President: Robert S. Brenaman

Standings	W	L	Pct.	GB	Attend.	Manager
Emporia Nationals (8)	71	57	.555	—	26,380	Morris "Smut" Aderholt
Petersburg Generals...........	69	61	.531	3	43,508	Paul Varner
Elizabeth City Albemarles..	68	61	.527	3½	35,000	Paul Crawford
Hopewell Blue Sox	65	65	.500	7	29,320	Herbert Moore
Franklin Kildees	65	65	.500	7	30,249	Paul Badgett
Suffolk Goobers.................	50	79	.388	21½	28,638	Buster Kinard

Playoffs: Hopewell defeated Franklin by forfeit for fourth place. Emporia 4 games, Hopewell 1; Petersburg 4 games, Elizabeth City 2.
Finals: Emporia 4 games, Petersburg 2.

All-Star Team: 1B-Gordon Giebel, Suffolk; **2B**-Walter Wholey, Petersburg; **3B**-Raymond Urban, Hopewell; **SS**-Clyde Reinert, Suffolk; **OF**-Bob Harkins, Franklin; Kenneth Hatcher, Petersburg; Tom Higgins, Elizabeth City; **C**-Paul Crawford, Elizabeth City; **Util**-Paul Badgett, Franklin; **P**-Raymond Zbiciak, Suffolk; Edmond McCloskey, Petersburg; Bob Gibbons, Hopewell.

BA: Paul Varner, Petersburg, .335
Runs: LeRoy Dietzel, Emporia, 121
Hits: John Garrison, Emporia, 170
RBIs: Kenneth Hatcher, Petersburg, 120
HRs: Kenneth Hatcher, Petersburg, 32

Wins: Vernon Holland, Franklin, 20
Melvin Doxtator, Emporia, 20
SOs: Herman Dowdy, Elizabeth City, 176
ERA: Eugene Hoberg, Franklin, 2.50

D Western Carolina League
President: Cloyd A. Hager

Standings	W	L	Pct.	GB	Attend.	Manager
Newton-Conover Twins	69	41	.627	—	58,310	Edwin Yount
Lenoir Red Sox (13)	67	40	.626	½	42,996	Claude Jonnard
Rutherford County Owls (11)..	57	53	.518	12	37,511	Rube Wilson
Marion Marauders	56	54	.509	13	45,379	Russell "Red" Mincy
Morganton Aggies	54	57	.486	15½	45,026	Sam Bell/Homer Daugherty/ Jim Poole
Lincolnton Cardinals	49	61	.445	20	48,711	Hugh Rudisill/Nathaniel Dodgin
Shelby Farmers.................	47	63	.427	22	36,962	Walt Dixon
Gastonia Browns................	40	70	.364	29	39,846	Noel Casbier/Tuck McWilliams

Playoffs: Newton-Conover 4 games, Rutherford County 2; Lenoir 4 games, Marion 3.
Finals: Lenoir 4 games, Newton-Conover 3.

All-Star Team: 1B-Carl Butler, Rutherford County; **2B**-Bob Beal, Marion; **3B**-Tom Marino, Lenoir; **SS**-Nathaniel Dodgin, Lincolnton; **OF**-Robert Featherstone, Lenoir; James Wood, Morganton; George Rose, Lincolnton; **C**-Milton Narron, Lenoir; **Util**-Russell "Red" Mincy, Marion; **P**-Rudy Yandoli, Lenoir; John White, Newton-Conover; Bill Haynes, Marion; **Manager**-Edwin Yount, Newton-Conover.

BA: Russell "Red" Mincy, Marion, .421
Runs: Bobby Brown, Lenoir, 135
Hits: Russell "Red" Mincy, Marion, 161
RBIs: George Rose, Lincolnton, 120

HRs: Robert Featherstone, Lenoir, 27
Wins: John White, Newton-Conover, 21
SOs: Carl Brown, Shelby, 236
ERA: John White, Newton-Conover, 3.05

D Wisconsin State League
President: Judge Arold F. Murphy

Standings	W	L	Pct.	GB	Attend.	Manager
Oshkosh Giants (13)	74	49	.602	—	69,653	David Garcia
Sheboygan Indians (10).......	71	53	.573	3½	48,449	Joe Hauser
Janesville Cubs (11)............	70	54	.565	4½	78,099	Adolph Matulis
Fond du Lac Panthers (5)....	65	57	.533	8½	59,110	Wayne Tucker
Green Bay Bluejays (3)	63	62	.504	12	79,688	Phil Seghi
Wisconsin Rapids White Sox (2)................	59	64	.480	15	48,524	John Kerr/Joseph Holden
Appleton Papermakers (7)..	58	66	.468	16½	80,381	Joe Skurski
Wausau Lumberjacks	33	88	.273	40	33,312	Bruno Haas

Playoffs: Oshkosh 3 games, Fond du Lac 1; Janesville 3 games, Sheboygan 2.
Finals: Oshkosh 4 games, Janesville 2.

All-Star Team: 1B-Jack Hasten, Janesville; **2B**-Walter Gilbo, Wausau; **3B**-Sam David, Appleton; **SS**-Delmar Russell, Wisconsin Rapids; **OF**-Sam Palamara, Wisconsin Rapids; Raymond Shearer, Sheboygan; Robert Pascal, Oshkosh; **C**-Wilburn Jenkins, Oshkosh; **P**-Harold Hurn, Appleton; Merlin Nehring, Fond du Lac; Joe Margoneri, Oshkosh.

BA: Wilburn Jenkins, Oshkosh, .354
Runs: Rodney Graber, Green Bay, 124
Hits: Wilburn Jenkins, Oshkosh, 156
RBIs: Raymond Shearer, Sheboygan, 137

HRs: Raymond Shearer, Sheboygan, 30
Wins: Joe Margoneri, Oshkosh, 23
SOs: Joe Margoneri, Oshkosh, 288
ERA: Adolph Matulis, Janesville, 1.85

Ind Mexican League
President: Dr. Eduardo Quijano Pitman

Standings	W	L	Pct.	GB	Manager
Jalisco Charros**	50	34	.595	—	Quincey Trouppe
Torreon Algodoneros*	48	36	.571	2	Memo Garibay
Monterrey Sultanes............	47	37	.560	3	Lazaro Salazar
Veracruz Aguila.................	45	39	.536	5	Martin Dihigo
San Luis Potosi Tuneros.....	43	41	.512	7	Jose Luis Gomez
Mexico City Diablos Rojos	38	46	.452	12	Manuel Oliveros/Ernesto Carmona
Veracruz Azules	34	50	.405	16	Ramon Bragana
Nuevo Laredo Tecolotes.....	31	53	.369	19	Guillermo Ornelas

Playoff: Torreon 4 games, Jalisco 2.

BA: Lorenzo Cabrera, Mexico City, .354
Hits: Mario Ariosa, Veracruz Aguila, 119
RBIs: Angel Castro, Veracruz Azules, 68
HRs: Angel Castro, Veracruz Azules, 10
Jesus Diaz, Torreon, 10

Wins: Tomas Arroyo, Torreon, 18
Guillermo Lopez, Veracruz Aguila, 18
SOs: Barney Brown, Torreon, 157
ERA: Pedro Antunez, Nuevo Laredo, 1.87

1950 Interleague Post Season Play

World Series
New York (American) 4 games, Philadelphia (National) 0

Junior World Series
Columbus (American Association) 4 games, Baltimore (International) 1
Total Attendance: 67,205

Dixie Series
San Antonio (Texas) 4 games, Nashville (Southern Association) 3
Total Attendance: 37,296

Little Dixie Series
Corpus Christi (Rio Grande Valley) 4 games, Jacksonville (Gulf Coast) 3

Border Series
Juarez (Arizona-Texas) 5 games, Mexicali (Sunset) 5

1950 Major League Farm Systems

American League

1 Boston (8): Louisville, Birmingham, Scranton, Roanoke, San Jose, Oneonta, Kinston, Marion.
2 Chicago (8): Sacramento, Memphis, Colorado Springs, Waterloo, Hot Springs, Superior, Madisonville, Wisconsin Rapids.
3 Cleveland (15): San Diego, Oklahoma City, Dayton, Wilkes-Barre, Harrisburg, Cedar Rapids, Spartanburg, Tacoma, Tucson, Bakersfield, Pittsfield, Daytona Beach, Zanesville, Batavia, Green Bay.
4 Detroit (9): Toledo, Little Rock, Flint, Williamsport, Durham, Butler, Thomasville, Richmond (IN), Jamestown.
5 New York (15): Kansas City, Beaumont, Muskegon, Binghamton, Norfolk, Quincy, Amsterdam, Grand Forks, Twin Falls, Joplin, La Grange, Independence, Newark, McAlester, Fond du Lac.
6 Philadelphia (13): Buffalo, Savannah, Lincoln, Fayetteville, West Palm Beach, Sunbury, Youngstown, Welch, Tarboro, Cordele, Lexington, Portsmouth, Red Springs.
7 St. Louis (11): Baltimore, San Antonio, Wichita, Wichita Falls, Pine Bluff, Marshall, Aberdeen, Redding, Pittsburg, Ada, Appleton.
8 Washington (11): Chattanooga, Augusta, Havana, Charlotte, New Castle, Orlando, Rome (GA), Fulton, Concord, Wellsville, Emporia.

National League

9 Boston (11): Milwaukee, Atlanta, Hartford, Denver, Hagerstown, Jackson, Evansville, Ventura, Eau Claire, Bluefield, Owensboro.
10 Brooklyn (24): St. Paul, Montreal, Hollywood, Mobile, Ft. Worth, Elmira, Greenville (SC), Pueblo, Miami (FL), Lancaster, Newport News, Danville (IL), Asheville, Bisbee-Douglas, Santa Barbara, Trois Rivieres, Greenwood, Billings, Valdosta, Ponca City, Hazard, Hazleton, Hornell, Sheboygan.
11 Chicago (15): Springfield (MA), Los Angeles, Nashville, Grand Rapids, Des Moines, Decatur, Rock Hill, Visalia, Sioux Falls, Clovis, Springfield (MO), Moultrie, Carthage, Rutherford County, Janesville.
12 Cincinnati (8): Syracuse, Tulsa, Charleston (WV), Columbia, Ogden, Muncie, Lockport, Wilmington (NC).
13 New York (20): Minneapolis, Jersey City, Jacksonville (FL), Sioux City, Trenton, Richmond (VA), Vicksburg, Knoxville, Erie, St. Cloud, Idaho Falls, Enid, Bristol (VA), Galax, Medford, Sanford (FL), Springfield (OH), Lawton, Lenoir, Oshkosh.
14 Philadelphia (12): Toronto, Utica, Wilmington (DE), Terre Haute, Schenectady, Vandergrift, Salina, Klamath Falls, Americus, Carbondale, Lima, Bradford.
15 Pittsburgh (13): Indianapolis, New Orleans, Albany (NY), Charleston (SC), Waco, York, Modesto, Hutchinson, Greenville (AL), Tallahassee, Bartlesville, Mayfield, Salisbury.
16 St. Louis (21): Columbus (OH), Rochester, Houston, Columbus (GA), Omaha, Winston-Salem, Allentown, Lynchburg, Montgomery, Fresno, Duluth, Pocatello, St. Joseph, Geneva (AL), Johnson City, Goldsboro, Willows, Albany (GA), West Frankfort, Lebanon, Hamilton.

1950 No-Hitters

Date	Pitcher	Team	League	Opponent	Score
4-30	Robert Swanson	Baton Rouge	Evangeline	New Iberia	2-0 (7)
5-3	Bob Snyder/				
	Norman Wielansky	Marshall	East Texas	Tyler	4-3
5-4	Alex Gounaris/				
	Julius Moore	Norfolk	Piedmont	Newport News	1-0
5-5	James Waugh	Pittsburg	KOM	Independence	12-5
5-7	Alf Porto	Toronto	International	Newark	5-0 (7)
5-12	Jack Gilbert	St. Augustine	Florida State	Leesburg	1-0 (7)
5-12	William Tanner	Ft. Lauderdale	Florida Int'l	Miami Beach	2-0 (11)
5-15	Hall	Sherbrooke	Provincial	Drummondville	3-0
5-16	George Nicholas	Vancouver	Western Int'l	Spokane	7-0
5-18	Bill Conroy	Hi-Toms	N. Carolina State	Concord	15-0
5-23	Lauren Monroe	Stockton	California	Fresno	5-2
5-30	Alfred Jarlett	Hi-Toms	N. Carolina State	Lexington	1-0 (7)
5-30	Gene Stemm	Stroudsburg	North Atlantic	Lebanon	0-1
5-31	James Pomykala	Greenville	Alabama State	Geneva	12-0 (P)
6-10	Prosper Boutet	Terre Haute	Three-I	Davenport	1-0 (7)
6-11	James Zundel/				
	John McCarthy	Las Vegas	Sunset	El Centro	7-1 (7)
6-17	Reid Lemly	Salisbury	N. Carolina State	Concord	18-0
6-23	Jose Aguiar	Newport	Mountain States	Big Stone Gap	7-0
6-24	Tom Dunovant	Harlan	Mountain States	Newport	7-0
6-27	Marlin Stuart	Toledo	American Assoc.	Indianapolis	1-0 (P)
6-27	Bob Alexander	Louisville	American Assoc.	Milwaukee	5-0
6-30	Ernest Nelson	Midland	Longhorn	Vernon	3-0
6-30	Clarence Richardson	Eastman	Georgia State	Douglas	5-0
7-1	Bill DuFour	Wisconsin Rapids	Wisconsin State	Sheboygan	13-0
7-4	Moe Savransky	Columbia	South Atlantic	Savannah	7-0 (7)
7-8	Gene Pisarski	Centralia	Miss.-Ohio Valley	West Frankfort	6-0
7-8	Len Perme	Durham	Carolina	Greensboro	2-1 (7)
7-11	Joe Micciche	Trenton	Interstate	Harrisburg	9-0
7-12	Al Cicotte	Norfolk	Piedmont	Newport News	4-1
7-12	Nat Love	Lafayette	Evangeline	Alexandria	4-0
7-12	John Gerace	Lumberton	Tobacco State	Red Springs	5-0
7-13	Bill Sweatt	Newnan	Georgia-Alabama	Alexander City	6-0
7-13	John Pollock	Enterprise	Alabama State	Ozark	14-0
7-13	John Lifsey	Hammond	Evangeline	Houma	4-1
7-14	Harry Clark	Dothan	Alabama State	Enterprise	2-0 (P)
7-14	Bob Cruze	Durham	Carolina	Fayetteville	1-0
7-16	Ramon Garcia	Havana	Florida Int'l	West Palm Beach	1-0 (7)
7-16	Richard Crichton	Grand Forks	Northern	St. Cloud	2-0 (7)
7-18	John Mikan	Burlington	Carolina	Raleigh	1-0
7-20	Fred Belinsky	Quebec	Canadian-American	Pittsfield	8-1
7-20	Dick Fortune	Jamestown	PONY	Lockport	2-0
7-21	Bob Friend	Waco	Big State	Wichita Falls	10-0
7-21	Vern Fear	Des Moines	Western	Denver	5-0 (7)
7-22	Wes Breschini	Thomasville	Georgia-Florida	Albany	2-1
7-23	Melvin Nee	St. Hyacinthe	Provincial	St. Jean	0-1
7-27	Kirby Higbe	Minneapolis	American Assoc.	Columbus	3-1 (7)
7-29	Bob Alexander	Louisville	American Assoc.	Milwaukee	5-0
7-29	Alois Zilian	Greensboro	Carolina	Reidsville	7-0 (7)
8-1	Norman Stephens	Clarksdale	Cotton States	Pine Bluff	1-0 (7)
8-3	Wes Livengood	Raleigh	Carolina	Burlington	6-0 (7)
8-4	James Younger	Quebec	Canadian-American	Schenectady	3-0 (7)
8-6	Jake Wade	Buffalo	International	Syracuse	2-0 (7)
8-7	Cliff Ross	Ogden	Pioneer	Boise	2-1
8-10	Bill Sheckler	Wausau	Wisconsin State	Oshkosh	2-1
8-10	Dixie Howell	Minneapolis	American Assoc.	Columbus	6-0
8-11	Vern Bickford	Boston	National	Brooklyn	7-0
8-12	Pat McGlothin	Ft. Worth	Texas	Shreveport	2-1
8-12	John Francis	Seminole	Sooner State	Lawton	4-0
8-13	Joe Budny	Texarkana	Big State	Gainesville	14-0
8-13	George New	Terre Haute	Three-I	Evansville	3-0
8-16	Gene Pereya	Greensboro	Carolina	Fayetteville	6-0 (7)
8-18	Aldon Wilkie	Victoria	Western Int'l	Vancouver	1-0
8-19	Cliff Ross	Ogden	Pioneer	Great Falls	4-0
8-19	Jose Aguiar	Newport	Mountain States	Morristown	9-0
8-21	Bob Easterbrook	Trenton	Interstate	Harrisburg	1-0
8-25	Tony Segzda	York	Interstate	Sunbury	6-0
8-25	Don Stephens	Omaha	Western	Denver	5-0
8-25	Higgins Duncan	Douglas	Georgia State	Fitzgerald	4-0 (P)
8-31	Leonard Koenen	Daytona Beach	Florida State	Palatka	6-0
9-4	Tom Jones	Clinton	Tobacco State	Wilmington	3-0 (7)
9-4	Don Bessent	La Grange	Georgia-Alabama	Carrollton	14-0 (PO)
9-4	Howard Sutherland	Charlotte	Tri-State	Rock Hill	0-1
9-5	Charles Menke	Knoxville	Tri-State	Florence	1-0
9-7	Don Bryant	Ottawa	Border	Geneva	4-0 (7)
9-7	Billy Russell	Vernon	Longhorn	San Angelo	4-0 (7)
9-11	Robert Smith	Ogdensburg	Border	Watertown	2-0 (PO)

Number in parentheses indicates innings if other than nine; "P" indicates perfect game; "PO" indicates playoff game.

THIS DATE IN MINOR LEAGUE HISTORY

January 6, 1950, Charlie Grimm resigned as vice-president of the Cubs to accept a managerial post with the Dallas Eagles, Texas League, at a record-breaking salary of $90,000 for three years.

January 14, 1950, Verle Penney, 41-year-old Portland, Oregon trucking contractor, was arrested in Hollywood, California, for assault with intent to murder Tommy Bridges, former Detroit pitcher, now with San Francisco, Pacific Coast League. The contractor, who filed a $20,000 alienation of affections suit against the pitcher, was arrested during an affray on the street involving the two men and Penney's former wife. The Penneys were married in 1929 and divorced in August 1949.

February 4, 1950, The International League announced the transfer of the Newark franchise to Springfield, Massachusetts. It was the first club change in the International League in 13 years.

April 1, 1950, The Hollywood Stars, Pacific Coast League, appeared on the playing field in shorts, marking the first time such attire had been worn in a regular Organized Ball contest. The idea originated with Fred Haney, manager of the Hollywood club.

April 11, 1950, With nine immortal baseball players as a special attraction, Dallas, Texas League, lost to Tulsa 10-3 in the season opener before a crowd of 53,578 in the Cotton Bowl at Dallas. The attendance set an all-time record for actual attendance in a season opener. Jersey City, International League, drew 56,391 for a game in 1941.

April 11, 1950, Joseph Becker, Jr., of Duluth, Northern League, son of the manager of the Jersey City club, International League, who lost four fingers from his left hand and suffered a fractured leg and other injuries in the collision of the Duluth team bus with a truck near St. Paul, Minnesota on July 24, 1948, settled out of court for $68,000.

April 15, 1950, Ralph Fraser and Bert Roseberry of Emporia, Virginia League, were killed when their auto crashed into the rear of a truck near Emporia, Virginia. Fraser was the son of the late Ralph "Chick" Fraser, former major league catcher and outfielder who died in Washington, D.C. in April 1948.

April 26, 1950, Bill McMahon, who signed a $10,000 bonus contract with Oneonta, Canadian-American League, while digging graves in a cemetery, made his pro debut with a victory over Trois Rivieres, yielding only two hits, fanning five and walking eight.

April 27, 1950, Lenoir, Western Carolina League, set a league record when they defeated Rutherford 33-9, on 18 hits off six pitchers. 16 errors aided in the loss.

April 28, 1950, Catcher Jim Martin of Pampa, West Texas-New Mexico League, was knocked unconscious when hit by lightning in a game at Abilene, Texas. Martin suffered from nothing more than shock and was back in uniform the next evening. The bolt knocked Martin's mask 20 feet past the pitcher's mound.

May 5, 1950, Outfielder Dick McNemer of Welch, Appalachian League, hit a pair of successive grand slams in the sixth and seventh innings and Guy Morton struck out 16 Johnson City batters for an 11-2 victory.

May, 1950, Tony Freitas, 43-year-old southpaw, was given his release by Sacramento, Pacific Coast League, Freitas closed out a 16-year tenure in the loop with 228 wins against 165 losses. He was in Solon regalia all of those years except for part of 1933.

May 10, 1950, Winless since their home opener on April 18, Little Rock broke a 33-year-old Southern Association record by dropping a 7-1 decision to Nashville for their 21st consecutive defeat. The Travelers had lost 24 of their first 25 games.

June 4, 1950, Righthander Babe Salerno of Marion, Ohio-Indiana League, was charged with 18 earned runs when he gave up 19 hits, walked 10, hit a batter and made three wild pitches in an 18-0 Newark victory.

June 9, 1950, Dick Littlefield, southpaw for Birmingham, Southern Association, tied a loop mark by whiffing eight of the first nine Memphis batters in the game, including seven in succession. The crowd of 16,249 at Birmingham set the all-time record for Rickwood Field.

June 9, 1950, In his last four games, Pete Hughes of El Centro, Sunset League, had walked nine times and made nine hits, including four home runs, in 18 consecutive trips to the plate.

June 9, 1950, Frank Saucier was honored as the batting king of the minor leagues of 1949 at a ceremony in San Antonio, Texas. Saucier batted .446 for Wichita Falls in the Big State League in 1949 to win the sterling silver Louisville Slugger bat presented by the Hillerich & Bradsby Co., bat manufacturers. Saucier was with San Antonio, Texas League, this year.

June 17, 1950, Monty Stratton, who returned to Organized Ball after a three-year absence, went the route to defeat Austin 11-6 in his first appearance for Greenville, Big State League. The former Chicago White Sox ace, who lost a leg in a hunting accident in 1938, gave up 11 hits.

June 19, 1950, The smallest crowd in Utica history, 146 paid, saw the Blue Sox roar back to win the Eastern League game 12-11, after spotting Williamsport a nine run lead in the first inning.

June 24, 1950, Willie Mays made his Organized Ball debut with Trenton, Interstate League, a New York Giants farm team. Willie went hitless but beat out two infield hits the next day.

June 28, 1950, Willie Mays hit his first Organized Ball homer, a grand slam, as Trenton, Interstate League, beat Sunbury 21-8.

July 16, 1950, The Class B Colonial League closed up shop when five of the six clubs voted to pay off all obligations and discontinue play immediately. Poor patronage, attributed primarily to unusually bad weather and the proximity of telecasts and radio broadcasts of Major League games, was the reason given for the action.

July 18, 1950, Tony Freitas, who formerly hurled for the Philadelphia A's and Cincinnati Reds, posted the 300th victory of his 20-year Organized Ball career when he turned in a sparkling relief job to lead Modesto, California League, to an 8-5 triumph over Visalia in 15 innings.

July 24, 1950, Billy Hoeft, 17-year-old southpaw from Oshkosh, Wisconsin, came within one strikeout of tying the Ohio-Indiana League record when he fanned 18 in hurling Richmond to a 15-1 victory over Marion.

July 27, 1950, Wytheville, Blue Ridge League, suspended play for the balance of the season due to a severe polio epidemic in that city. The count was 88 cases, including 11 deaths. The vacancy in the league was filled by Bassett, Virginia.

July 31, 1950, Robert Larkin, pitcher for Ottawa, Border League, was killed and four of his teammates injured when their automobile collided with a two-ton Army truck near Watertown, New York.

August 1, 1950, The owners of the Ft. Lauderdale club, Florida International League, were recently unsuccessful in signing a female player, Dorothy Kamenshek, a 26-year-old star first baseman for the Rockford Peaches. The president of the All-American Girls Baseball League refused to approve the sale.

August 4, 1950, Tossing firecrackers at passing automobiles cost pitcher Bill Hoeft and outfielder Keith Jones, both of Richmond, Ohio-Indiana League, $20 each in a city court at Richmond, Indiana. They had been arrested the week before by a detective sergeant at whose automobile they had thrown one of the firecrackers.

August 8, 1950, After wearing the new-style shorts for two games, Abilene, West Texas-New Mexico League, abandoned the garb because of mosquitoes.

August 14, 1950, Monty Stratton made his final 1950 Organized Ball effort for Brownsville, Rio Grande Valley League, defeating Del Rio 10-2 for a perfect 4-0 record for the season. The one-legged pitcher allowed only six hits, walked one and made one of the 12 hits collected by his team.

August 18, 1950, The Miami Sun Sox, Florida International League, were believed to have set an Organized Ball record when they defeated St. Petersburg 8-3 to sweep the 22-game season series with the Saints.

August 21, 1950, In one of the most beautiful ceremonies in Organized Ball history, four Ft. Worth players were married in new million-dollar LaGrave Field before 9,817 fans. The players were Joe Torpey, Russ Rose, Don Hoak and John Rutherford. Three of the new bridegrooms played in the Ft. Worth-Oklahoma City contest after the ceremonies, won by Ft. Worth 6-4.

August 21, 1950, Pennington Gap, Mountain States League, broke a 23-game losing streak with a 7-6 win over Newport.

August 23, 1950, A 59-year-old "rookie" broke into the Georgia-Alabama League when Charlie Milner, a former semi-pro star celebrating his birthday, signed with the Valley Rebels. He hurled four innings and gave up four singles and one run.

August 26, 1950, Jack Harshman, who clouted 40 homers for Minneapolis, American Association, last season, and who failed to make the grade as a first sacker with Jacksonville, South Atlantic League, switched to the mound and came through with a four-hit 5-2 victory over Augusta.

August 29, 1950, Managers Walter DeFreitas of Paducah and Lou Bekeza of Centralia engaged in a milking contest before a Mississippi-Ohio Valley League game at Paducah, and DeFreitas not only lost, but was unable to play that evening because the cow kicked him on the shins.

September 1, 1950, Tony Freitas, 42-year-old veteran southpaw with Modesto, California League, joined the ranks of the 20-game winners with a 4-3 decision over Fresno.

September 4, 1950, First baseman Dick Wilson of Modesto, California League, cracked out successive grand slams in the third and fourth innings of the season's finale with Stockton.

September 4, 1950, A member of the Joplin Miners was batting king of the Western Association for the fifth straight season, as Mickey Mantle, an 18-year-old switch-hitter, maintained the string with an official mark of .383.

September 10, 1950, Pat Haggerty of Little Rock, Southern Association, made six hits in eight trips on closing day including four successive safe bunts in the twinbill nightcap, to win the batting championship by four-tenths of one point, .3464 to .3460.

December 10, 1950, The Jersey City franchise in the International League moved to Ottawa, Canada for 1951.

December 12, 1950, Mel Ott signed a two-year contract to manage Oakland in the Pacific Coast League.

1951

American League
President: William Harridge

Standings	W	L	Pct.	GB	Attend.	Manager
New York Yankees	98	56	.636	—	1,950,107	Casey Stengel
Cleveland Indians	93	61	.604	5	1,704,984	Al Lopez
Boston Red Sox	87	67	.565	11	1,312,282	Steve O'Neill
Chicago White Sox	81	73	.526	17	1,328,234	Paul Richards
Detroit Tigers	73	81	.474	25	1,132,641	Red Rolfe
Philadelphia Athletics	70	84	.455	28	466,469	Jimmy Dykes
Washington Senators	62	92	.403	36	695,187	Bucky Harris
St. Louis Browns	52	102	.338	46	293,790	Zack Taylor

BA: Ferris Fain, Philadelphia, .344
Runs: Dom DiMaggio, Boston, 113
Hits: George Kell, Detroit, 191
RBIs: Gus Zernial, Chicago/Philadelphia, 129
HRs: Gus Zernial, Chicago/Philadelphia, 33
Wins: Bob Feller, Cleveland, 22
SOs: Vic Raschi, New York, 164
ERA: Saul Rogovin, Detroit/Chicago, 2.78
Pct: Bob Feller, Cleveland, .733, 22-8

National League
Presidents: Ford Frick/Warren C. Giles

Standings	W	L	Pct.	GB	Attend.	Manager
New York Giants	98	59	.624	—	1,059,539	Leo Durocher
Brooklyn Dodgers	97	60	.618	1	1,282,628	Chuck Dressen
St. Louis Cardinals	81	73	.526	15½	1,013,429	Marty Marion
Boston Braves	76	78	.494	20½	487,475	Billy Southworth/Tommy Holmes
Philadelphia Phillies	73	81	.474	23½	937,658	Eddie Sawyer
Cincinnati Reds	68	86	.442	28½	588,268	Luke Sewell
Pittsburgh Pirates	64	90	.416	32½	980,590	Bill Meyer
Chicago Cubs	62	92	.403	34½	894,415	Frank Frisch/Phil Cavarretta

Playoff: New York 2 games, Brooklyn 1.

BA: Stan Musial, St. Louis, .355
Runs: Stan Musial, St. Louis, 124
Ralph Kiner, Pittsburgh, 124
Hits: Richie Ashburn, Philadelphia, 221
RBIs: Monte Irvin, New York, 121
HRs: Ralph Kiner, Pittsburgh, 42
Wins: Sal Maglie, New York, 23
Larry Jansen, New York, 23
SOs: Warren Spahn, Boston, 164
Don Newcombe, Brooklyn, 164
ERA: Chet Nichols, Boston, 2.88
Pct: Preacher Roe, Brooklyn, .880, 22-3

AAA American Association
President: Bruce Dudley

Standings	W	L	Pct.	GB	Attend.	Manager
Milwaukee Brewers (9)	94	57	.623	—	245,066	Charlie Grimm
St. Paul Saints (10)	85	66	.563	9	171,999	Clay Hopper
Kansas City Blues (5)	81	70	.536	13	242,118	George Selkirk
Louisville Colonels (1)	80	73	.523	15	148,101	Pinky Higgins
Minneapolis Millers (13)	77	75	.507	17½	143,279	Thomas Heath
Toledo Mud Hens (4)	70	82	.481	24½	99,932	Jack Tighe
Indianapolis Indians (15)	68	84	.447	26½	181,241	Don Gutteridge
Columbus Red Birds (16)	53	101	.344	42½	102,320	Harry Walker

Playoffs: Milwaukee 4 games, Kansas City 1; St. Paul 4 games, Louisville 1.
Finals: Milwaukee 4 games, St. Paul 2.

All-Star Team: 1B-George Crowe, Milwaukee; **2B**-William Reed, Milwaukee; **3B**-Billy Klaus, Milwaukee; **SS**-Allen Richter, Louisville; **OF**-Bob Cerv, Kansas City; Harry Walker, Columbus; Taft Wright, Louisville; James Basso, Milwaukee; **C**-Al Unser, Milwaukee; Ray Katt, Minneapolis; **Util**-Mel Hoderlein, Louisville; **P**-Ernie Johnson, Milwaukee; Murray Wall, Milwaukee; John Rutherford, St. Paul; James Atkins, Louisville; **MVP**-Al Unser, Milwaukee.

BA: Harry Walker, Columbus, .393
Runs: Jim Pendleton, St. Paul, 116
Hits: George Crowe, Milwaukee, 189
RBIs: George Crowe, Milwaukee, 119
HRs: Harold Gilbert, Minneapolis, 29
Wins: James Atkins, Louisville, 18
SOs: Bob Wiesler, Kansas City, 162
ERA: Ernie Johnson, Milwaukee, 2.62

AAA International League
President: Frank J. Shaughnessy

Standings	W	L	Pct.	GB	Attend.	Manager
Montreal Royals (10)	95	59	.617	—	391,107	Walter Alston
Rochester Red Wings (16)	83	69	.546	11	252,538	Johnny Keane
Syracuse Chiefs	82	71	.536	12½	150,219	Bruno Betzel
Buffalo Bisons	79	75	.513	16	141,593	George "Specs" Toporcer/Coaker Triplett
Toronto Maple Leafs (7)	77	76	.505	17½	296,847	Joseph Becker
Baltimore Orioles (14)	69	82	.457	24½	158,013	Nick Cullop
Ottawa Giants (13)	62	88	.413	31	117,411	Hugh Poland
Springfield Cubs (11)	63	90	.412	31½	105,052	William Kelly

Playoffs: Montreal 4 games, Buffalo 0; Syracuse 4 games, Rochester 1.

Finals: Montreal 4 games, Syracuse 1.

All-Star Team: 1B-Ed Shokes, Syracuse; **2B**-Junior Gilliam, Montreal; **3B**-Hector Rodriguez, Montreal; **SS**-Bobby Morgan, Montreal; **OF**-Archie Wilson, Buffalo; Marv Rickert, Baltimore; Wally Post, Buffalo; **C**-John Bucha, Rochester; **P**-Rudy Minarcin, Buffalo; Chris Van Cuyk, Montreal; **MVP**-Archie Wilson, Buffalo; **Manager**-George "Specs" Toporcer, Buffalo.

BA: Don Richmond, Rochester, .350
Runs: Junior Gilliam, Montreal, 117
Hits: Archie Wilson, Buffalo, 191
RBIs: Archie Wilson, Buffalo, 112
HRs: Marv Rickert, Baltimore, 35
Wins: John Hetki, Toronto, 19
SOs: Bill Miller, Syracuse, 131
ERA: Alex Konikowski, Ottawa, 2.59

AAA Pacific Coast League
President: Clarence H. Rowland

Standings	W	L	Pct.	GB	Attend.	Manager
Seattle Rainiers	99	68	.593	—	465,727	Rogers Hornsby
Hollywood Stars (15)	93	74	.557	6	287,977	Fred Haney
Los Angeles Angels (11)	86	81	.515	13	328,294	Stan Hack
Portland Beavers	83	85	.494	16½	304,152	Bill Sweeney
Oakland Oaks	80	88	.476	19½	193,822	Mel Ott
San Diego Padres (3)	79	88	.473	20	217,102	Del Baker
Sacramento Solons (2)	75	92	.449	24	285,874	Joe Gordon
San Francisco Seals (5)	74	93	.443	25	199,083	Lefty O'Doul

Playoffs: Seattle 2 games, Los Angeles 1; Hollywood 2 games, Portland 0.
Finals: Seattle 3 games, Hollywood 2.

MVP-Jim Rivera, Seattle.

BA: Jim Rivera, Seattle, .352
Runs: Jim Rivera, Seattle, 135
Hits: Jim Rivera, Seattle, 231
RBIs: Joe Gordon, Sacramento, 136
HRs: Joe Gordon, Sacramento, 43
Wins: Marv Grissom, Seattle, 20
William Ayers, Oakland, 20
SOs: Sam Jones, San Diego, 246
ERA: James Davis, Seattle, 2.44

AA Southern Association
President: Charles A. Hurth

Standings	W	L	Pct.	GB	Attend.	Manager
Little Rock Travelers (4)	93	60	.608	—	225,780	Gene Desautels
Birmingham Barons (1)	83	71	.539	10½	297,366	Red Marion
Mobile Bears (10)	80	74	.519	13½	132,789	Paul Chervinko
Memphis Chicks (2)	79	75	.513	14½	208,061	Luke Appling
Nashville Vols (11)	78	76	.506	15½	136,008	Don Osborn
Atlanta Crackers (9)	76	78	.494	17½	274,293	Dixie Walker/Whitlow Wyatt
New Orleans Pelicans (15)	64	90	.418	29½	127,304	Rip Sewell
Chattanooga Lookouts (8)	62	91	.405	31	132,820	Jack Onslow

Playoffs: Little Rock 4 games, Memphis 2; Birmingham 4 games, Mobile 0.
Finals: Birmingham 4 games, Little Rock 0.

All-Star Team: 1B-Larry DiPippo, Birmingham; **2B**-Dale Lynch, Birmingham; **3B**-Bob Ludwig, Nashville; **SS**-Clem Koshorek, Little Rock; **OF**-Hal Simpson, Little Rock; George Wilson, Birmingham; Jim Piersall, Birmingham; Frank Thomas, New Orleans; **C**-Willie Mathis, Birmingham; Lawrence Ciesielski, Little Rock; Bob Brady, Nashville; **Util**-Jack Dittmer, Atlanta; James Cronin, Little Rock; **P**-Milo Johnson, Little Rock; Howard Anderson, Atlanta; Ralph Brickner, Birmingham; James Atchley, Nashville; Bob Cruze, Little Rock; Robert McCall, Little Rock.

BA: Babe Barna, Nashville, .358
Runs: Hal Simpson, Little Rock, 121
Hits: Bob Ludwig, Nashville, 213
RBIs: Walt Moryn, Mobile, 148
HRs: Jack Harshman, Nashville, 47
Wins: Al Yaylian, Little Rock, 16
Frank Biscan, Memphis, 16
Bobo Newsom, Birmingham, 16
Robert McCall, Little Rock, 16
Tom Lakos, Mobile, 16
SOs: Dick Littlefield, Memphis, 195
ERA: Frank Biscan, Memphis, 2.55

AA Texas League
President: J. Alvin Gardner

Standings	W	L	Pct.	GB	Attend.	Manager
Houston Buffaloes (16)	99	61	.619	—	333,201	Al Hollingsworth
San Antonio Missions (7)	86	75	.534	13½	180,577	Jo Jo White
Dallas Eagles (3)	85	75	.531	14	228,263	Dutch Meyer
Beaumont Roughnecks (5)	84	77	.522	15½	109,893	Harry Craft
Ft. Worth Cats (10)	84	77	.522	15½	160,276	Bobby Bragan
Oklahoma City Indians (2)	75	86	.466	24½	109,181	Tom Tatum
Tulsa Oilers (12)	67	94	.416	32½	147,907	Al Vincent
Shreveport Sports	63	98	.391	36½	76,073	Francis "Salty" Parker

Playoffs: Houston 4 games, Beaumont 2; San Antonio 4 games, Dallas 3.

*Won first-half   **Won second-half   ***Won both halves
Numbers after nicknames indicate farm system.
Affiliation listed at end of each year.

400

Finals: Houston 4 games, San Antonio 0.

BA: Bob Nieman, Tulsa/Oklahoma City, .324
Runs: Bob Balcena, San Antonio, 114
Hits: Johnny Temple, Tulsa, 180
RBIs: Jim Dyck, San Antonio, 127
HRs: Jerry Witte, Houston, 38

Wins: Al Papai, Houston, 23
SOs: Wilmer "Vinegar Bend" Mizell, Houston, 257
ERA: Tom Gorman, Beaumont, 1.94

A Central League
President: T.J. Halligan

Standings	W	L	Pct.	GB	Attend.	Manager
Dayton Indians (7)	87	50	.635	—	62,787	James Crandall
Muskegon Reds (5)	86	54	.614	2½	44,773	Jimmy Gleeson
Saginaw Jacks	79	58	.577	8	61,923	Bert Niehoff
Charleston Senators (12)	69	70	.496	19	102,684	Ernie White
Grand Rapids Jets (11)	53	82	.393	33	21,230	Jack Knight/Sheriff Robinson
Flint Arrows	38	98	.279	48½	25,900	Steve Bysco

All-Star Team: 1B-Cyril Pfeifer, Charleston; **2B**-Ed Bachmann, Saginaw; **3B**-Oscar Khederian, Saginaw; **SS**-Bud Thomas, Muskegon; **OF**-Frank Scarpace, Dayton; Yogi Giammarco, Saginaw; Saturnino Escalera, Muskegon; Ed Krage, Muskegon; **C**-James Robertson, Muskegon; **Util**-Ted Bell, Muskegon; **P**-Frank Barnes, Muskegon; James Freels, Dayton; Max Sumwalt, Charleston; George Piktuzis, Grand Rapids.

BA: Jim Greengrass, Muskegon, .379
Runs: Ed Krage, Muskegon, 128
Hits: Oscar Khederian, Saginaw, 185
RBIs: Ed Krage, Muskegon, 114
Ron Bowen, Muskegon, 114

HRs: Ed Krage, Muskegon, 31
Wins: Emil Patrick, Muskegon, 20
SOs: Ryne Duren, Dayton, 238
ERA: Calvin Howe, Grand Rapids, 2.33

A Eastern League
President: Thomas H. Richardson

Standings	W	L	Pct.	GB	Attend.	Manager
Wilkes-Barre Indians (3)	85	54	.612	—	74,548	Bill Norman
Scranton Red Sox (1)	77	60	.562	7	64,188	Jack Burns
Elmira Pioneers (10)	74	64	.536	10½	126,188	George Fallon
Hartford Chiefs (9)	75	65	.536	10½	106,801	Tommy Holmes/Travis Jackson
Schenectady Blue Jays (14)	73	66	.525	12	93,559	Leon Riley
Binghamton Triplets (8)	69	69	.500	15½	90,757	Bill Skiff
Williamsport Tigers (4)	55	84	.396	30	62,739	Schoolboy Rowe
Albany Senators	46	92	.333	38½	57,277	Pinky May

Playoffs: Elmira 4 games, Wilkes-Barre 3; Scranton 4 games, Hartford 0.
Finals: Scranton 4 games, Elmira 0.

All-Star Team: 1B-Dick Gernert, Scranton; **2B**-Dick Young, Schenectady; **3B**-Bob Wilson, Elmira; **SS**-Don Zimmer, Elmira; **OF**-Bob DiPietro, Scranton; Dave Pope, Wilkes-Barre; Eulas Hutson, Wilkes-Barre; **C**-Sam White, Scranton; **P**-Gene Conley, Hartford; Bill George, Schenectady.

BA: Bob Verrier, Hartford, .323
Runs: Dave Pope, Wilkes-Barre, 113
Hits: Dick Young, Schenectady, 166
RBIs: Eulas Hutson, Wilkes-Barre, 117

HRs: Eulas Hutson, Wilkes-Barre, 24
Clint Weaver, Binghamton, 24
Wins: Jose Santiago, Wilkes-Barre, 21
SOs: Paul Stuffel, Schenectady, 183
ERA: Jose Santiago, Wilkes-Barre, 1.59

A South Atlantic League
President: Earl Blue

Standings	W	L	Pct.	GB	Attend.	Manager
Montgomery Rebels	85	55	.607	—	114,849	Charlie Metro
Jacksonville Tars (13)	79	58	.577	4½	111,409	Ben Geraghty
Macon Peaches	75	63	.543	9	96,553	Edgar Hartness
Charleston Rebels (15)	75	65	.536	10	87,275	Frank Oceak
Columbus Cardinals (16)	68	71	.489	16½	79,106	Harold Anderson
Savannah Indians (6)	64	74	.464	20	80,063	George Staller
Augusta Tigers	62	76	.449	22	57,094	Ivy Griffin
Columbia Reds (12)	46	92	.333	38	52,483	Buddy Hancken

Playoffs: Montgomery 3 games, Charleston 2; Jacksonville 3 games, Macon 2.
Finals: Montgomery 4 games, Jacksonville 0.

All-Star Team: 1B-James Dickey, Columbus; **2B**-Everett Kell, Savannah; **3B**-Rance Pless, Jacksonville; **SS**-Donald Boring, Jacksonville; **OF**-Richard Greco, Montgomery; Banks McDowell, Montgomery; Len Morrison, Montgomery; Robert Betz, Savannah; **C**-Lou Kahn, Columbus; **Util**-Richard Smith, Charleston; **P**-James Bryant, Columbus; Vince DiLorenzo, Jacksonville; **Manager**-Charlie Metro, Montgomery.

BA: Lou Kahn, Columbus, .351
Runs: Banks McDowell, Montgomery, 121
Hits: Rance Pless, Jacksonville, 185
RBIs: William Johnson, Montgomery, 107
HRs: Richard Greco, Montgomery, 33

Wins: Vince DiLorenzo, Jacksonville, 22
SOs: Harry Byrd, Savannah, 180
ERA: Stan West, Macon, 2.31
Pct: Vince DiLorenzo, Jacksonville, .733, 22-8

A Western League
President: Senator Edwin C. Johnson

Standings	W	L	Pct.	GB	Attend.	Manager
Omaha Cardinals (16)	90	64	.584	—	162,247	George Kissell
Denver Bears (9)	88	66	.571	2	424,065	Andy Cohen
Wichita Indians (3)	84	68	.553	5	122,060	Joe Schultz
Sioux City Soos (13)	77	71	.520	10	104,247	Frank Genovese
Des Moines Bruins (11)	73	78	.483	15½	94,137	Alfred Todd
Pueblo Dodgers (10)	74	80	.481	16	104,254	James Bivin
Colorado Springs Sky Sox (2)	64	87	.424	24½	107,320	Skeeter Webb/Otto Denning
Lincoln Athletics (6)	57	93	.380	31	37,123	Frank Skaff

Playoffs: Sioux City 3 games, Omaha 1; Denver 3 games, Wichita 1.
Finals: Sioux City 3 games, Denver 1.

All-Star Team: 1B-Joe Macko, Wichita; **2B**-Ron Samford, Sioux City; **3B**-George Freese, Pueblo; **SS**-Gus Gregory, Denver; **OF**-Russell Rac, Omaha; Bob Anderlik, Des Moines; Bill Bruton, Denver; **C**-Harry Chiti, Des Moines; **P**-El Roy Face, Pueblo; Jack Shirley, Omaha; Mason Bowes, Lincoln; Rafael Rivas, Denver; **Manager**-Joe Schultz, Wichita.

BA: George Freese, Pueblo, .338
Runs: Ron Samford, Sioux City, 108
Hits: George Freese, Pueblo, 183
RBIs: George Freese, Pueblo, 106

HRs: Howard Boles, Des Moines/Denver, 32
Wins: El Roy Face, Pueblo, 23
SOs: Willard Schmidt, Omaha, 202
ERA: Willard Schmidt, Omaha, 2.11

B Big State League
President: Howard Green

Standings	W	L	Pct.	GB	Attend.	Manager
Gainesville Owls	89	58	.605	—	50,771	Hal Van Pelt
Temple Eagles	88	60	.595	1½	112,022	Bill Herring/Jack Bradsher
Sherman-Denison Twins	79	68	.537	10	60,059	Billy Capps
Austin Pioneers	75	72	.510	14	147,461	Tom Jordan
Waco Pirates (15)	75	73	.507	14½	61,371	Walter Tauscher
Texarkana Bears	71	77	.480	18½	57,640	Henry "Prince" Oana/Jodie Phipps/Gabby Lusk
Wichita Falls Spudders (7)	66	82	.446	23½	73,415	Bruce Ogrodowski/Cecil McClung
Tyler East Texans	47	100	.320	42	41,541	Harold Epps/Joe Kracher/Gale Pringle

Playoffs: Gainesville 4 games, Austin 2; Sherman-Denison 4 games, Temple 1.
Finals: Gainesville 4 games, Sherman-Denison 1.

All-Star Team: 1B-Les Goldstein, Temple; **2B**-Ross Passineau, Waco; **3B**-Billy Capps, Sherman-Denison; **SS**-Al Joe Hunt, Gainesville; **OF**-Dean Stafford, Sherman-Denison; Joe Szekely, Texarkana; Frederick Bell, Temple; **C**-Tom Jordan, Austin; **P**-George O'Donnell, Waco; Bud Lively, Sherman-Denison; Lee Roy Jones, Austin; Junior Bunch, Temple.

BA: Les Goldstein, Temple, .376
Runs: Bobby Phillips, Wichita Falls, 128
Hits: Frederick Bell, Temple, 216
RBIs: Dean Stafford, Sherman-Denison, 151
HRs: Dean Stafford, Sherman-Denison, 32

Wins: Lee Roy Jones, Austin, 22
George O'Donnell, Waco, 22
SOs: Robert Upton, Gainesville, 209
ERA: Robert Upton, Gainesville, 2.54

B Carolina League
President: Glenn E. "Ted" Mann

Standings	W	L	Pct.	GB	Attend.	Manager
Durham Bulls (4)	84	56	.600	—	93,766	Ace Parker
Winston-Salem Cardinals (16)	81	58	.583	2½	100,988	Harold Olt
Raleigh Capitals	78	62	.557	6	80,976	Joe Medwick
Reidsville Luckies	76	64	.543	8	61,841	Herb Brett
Greensboro Patriots (11)	67	73	.479	17	67,953	Robert Peterson
Danville Leafs	66	73	.475	17½	68,031	Bob Latshaw
Fayetteville Athletics (6)	59	79	.428	24	55,760	Red Norris
Burlington Bees (15)	47	93	.336	37	42,685	Red Barrett/Mike Kash (Kaiserski)

Playoffs: Winston-Salem 4 games, Raleigh 0; Reidsville 4 games, Durham 1.
Finals: Winston-Salem 4 games, Reidsville 1.

All-Star Team: 1B-Joe Cunningham, Winston-Salem; **2B**-Bill Romano, Greensboro; **3B**-Ray Jablonski, Winston-Salem; **SS**-Henry Navarro, Durham; **OF**-Carl Miller, Reidsville; Dick Sipek, Reidsville; Jack Baumgartner, Durham; **C**-Dick Rand, Winston-Salem; **P**-Mike Forline, Reidsville; James Lewey, Winston-Salem; Bill Bustle, Danville; Dennis Reeder, Winston-Salem; **MVP**-Ray Jablonski, Winston-Salem; **Manager**-Ace Parker, Durham.

BA: Ray Jablonski, Winston-Salem, .363
Runs: Henry Navarro, Durham, 116
Hits: Ray Jablonski, Winston-Salem, 200
RBIs: Ray Jablonski, Winston-Salem, 127

HRs: Ray Jablonski, Winston-Salem, 28
Carl Miller, Reidsville, 28
Wins: Mike Forline, Reidsville, 21
SOs: Dennis Reeder, Winston-Salem, 155
ERA: James Lewey, Winston-Salem, 2.64

B Florida International League
President: Phil O'Connell

Standings	W	L	Pct.	GB	Attend.	Manager
Tampa Smokers	90	50	.643	—	92,449	Ben Chapman
St. Petersburg Saints	83	56	.597	6½	139,464	Art Rebel
Miami Sun Sox (10)	77	61	.558	12	128,107	Pepper Martin
Lakeland Patriots	71	68	.511	18½	81,878	Roy Hughes
Havana Cubanos (8)	68	71	.489	21½	83,051	Dolf Luque
Miami Beach Flamingos	74	74	.471	24	42,194	George Dozier
West Palm Beach Indians	64	75	.460	25½	64,425	Rudy Laskowski/Herschel Held
Ft. Lauderdale Braves	38	102	.271	52	32,739	Lloyd Brown/Ed Goostree/Charles Aleno

Playoffs: St. Petersburg 3 games, Lakeland 2; Miami 3 games, Tampa 1.
Finals: St. Petersburg 4 games, Miami 0.

BA: Ted Cieslak, Lakeland, .332
Runs: Carlos Bernier, Tampa, 124
Hits: Forest Smith, West Palm Beach, 162
RBIs: Earle Brucker, Miami, 90
HRs: Jack Tanner, Ft. Lauderdale, 19

Wins: Woody Rich, St. Petersburg, 25
SOs: Clarence "Hooks" Iott, St. Petersburg, 273
ERA: Clarence "Hooks" Iott, St. Petersburg, 2.00

B Gulf Coast League
President: Howard Green

Standings	W	L	Pct.	GB	Attend.	Manager
Corpus Christi Aces	98	56	.636	—	89,632	John "Red" Davis
Harlingen Capitols	86	68	.559	12	65,762	Sam Harshaney/Earl Caldwell/ Keith Carpenter
Brownsville Charros	79	74	.516	18½	46,360	Jesse Landrum
Laredo Apaches	75	79	.487	23	48,049	Julian Morgan/Marty Errante/ Boyd SoRelle
Galveston White Caps	71	83	.461	27	63,037	Harry Gumbert
Texas City Texans	70	84	.455	28	46,617	Rollie Hemsley/William Rogers
Port Arthur Seahawks	69	84	.451	28½	79,601	Charles Baron(ovic)/Carl Carter
Lake Charles Lakers	66	86	.434	31	67,468	Harry Chozen

Playoffs: Corpus Christi 4 games, Laredo 2; Brownsville 4 games, Harlingen 2.
Finals: Brownsville 4 games, Corpus Christi 3.

All-Star Team: 1B-Bob Moyer, Corpus Christi; **2B**-Jorge Lopez, Laredo; **3B**-Bob Hedington, Brownsville; **SS**-Joe Koppe, Corpus Christi; **OF**-Fred Schroeder, Texas City; Gene Depperschmidt, Port Arthur; Manuel Salvatierra, Corpus Christi; **C**-Jack Trench, Corpus Christi; **P**-Bud Chipman, Port Arthur; Jesus Valenzuela, Corpus Christi; Bill Creech, Port Arthur; Danny Parra, Laredo.

BA: Stan Goletz, Brownsville, .378
Runs: Stan Goletz, Brownsville, 137
Hits: Stan Goletz, Brownsville, 207
RBIs: Bob Moyer, Corpus Christi, 164

HRs: Stan Goletz, Brownsville, 37
Bob Moyer, Corpus Christi, 37
Wins: Bud Chipman, Port Arthur, 22
SOs: Ramon Salgado, Texas City, 270
ERA: Earl Caldwell, Harlingen, 2.21

B Interstate League
President: Gerald P. Nugent

Standings	W	L	Pct.	GB	Attend.	Manager
Hagerstown Braves (9)	94	46	.671	—	67,452	Dutch Dorman
Allentown Cardinals (16)	91	47	.659	2	71,822	Whitey Kurowski
Wilmington Blue Rocks (14)	83	52	.615	8½	43,135	Dan Carnevale
Sunbury Giants (13)	73	65	.529	20	43,050	Charlie Fox
Lancaster Red Roses (10)	71	67	.514	22	46,821	Ed Head
Harrisburg Senators (3)	55	84	.398	38½	40,619	Les Bell/Harold Cox
York White Roses	51	88	.367	42½	40,740	Joe Bowman/Edmund Waleski/ Eugene Crumling
Salisbury Athletics (6)	33	102	.244	58½	22,528	John "Bunny" Griffiths

Playoffs: Wilmington 4 games, Hagerstown 1; Sunbury 4 games, Allentown 1.
Finals: Wilmington 4 games, Sunbury 0.

All-Star Team: 1B-Bill Smith, Hagerstown; **2B**-Charley Neal, Lancaster; **3B**-Robert Louis, Lancaster; **SS**-Thomas Lind, Hagerstown; **OF**-Charles Hood, Wilmington; Harold Cox, Harrisburg; William Killinger, Allentown; **C**-James Solt, Hagerstown; **P**-Anderson Bush, Hagerstown; Daniel Lewandowski, Allentown; Niles Jordan, Wilmington; Joe Margoneri, Sunbury.

BA: Bill Smith, Hagerstown, .373
Runs: Charley Neal, Lancaster, 114
Hits: Everett Joyner, Allentown, 175
RBIs: Pete Perini, Hagerstown, 91

HRs: Harold Cox, Harrisburg, 20
Wins: Daniel Lewandowski, Allentown, 24
SOs: Joe Margoneri, Sunbury, 212
ERA: Ralph Beard, Allentown, 1.69

B Piedmont League
President: Frank L. Summers

Standings	W	L	Pct.	GB	Attend.	Manager
Norfolk Tars (5)	81	58	.583	—	104,914	Mayo Smith
Richmond Colts	77	63	.550	4½	97,761	Billy Herman/Roy Allen
Newport News Dodgers (10)	75	66	.532	7	85,732	Clay Bryant
Portsmouth Cubs	74	67	.525	8	92,997	Reggie Otero
Lynchburg Cardinals (16)	64	75	.460	17	62,218	Frank Scalzi
Roanoke Ro-Sox (1)	49	91	.350	32½	58,697	Walter Millies

Playoffs: Norfolk 4 games, Portsmouth 1; Richmond 4 games, Newport News 2.
Finals: Norfolk 4 games, Richmond 2.

All-Star Team: 1B-Reggie Otero, Portsmouth; **2B**-Francisco Gallardo, Portsmouth; **3B**-Leon Carter, Norfolk; **SS**-Jasper Spears, Norfolk; **OF**-Ken Guettler, Portsmouth; Bert Hamric, Newport News; Charles Coles, Newport News; **C**-Ronald Curnan, Lynchburg; **P**-Albert Bennett, Newport News; Jim Barnhardt, Portsmouth; Wade Browning, Richmond; Dewey Wilkins, Richmond.

BA: Bill Skowron, Norfolk, .334
Runs: Ken Guettler, Portsmouth, 114
Hits: Charles Coles, Newport News, 165
RBIs: Ken Guettler, Portsmouth, 116

HRs: Ken Guettler, Portsmouth, 30
Wins: Floyd Melliere, Lynchburg, 21
SOs: John Gray, Norfolk, 192
ERA: Jim Barnhardt, Portsmouth, 2.53

B Three-I League
President: Vern McMillan

Standings	W	L	Pct.	GB	Attend.	Manager
Terre Haute Phillies (14)	75	55	.577	—	81,511	Skeeter Newsome
Evansville Braves (9)	69	60	.535	5½	101,254	Bob Coleman
Quincy Gems (5)	65	65	.500	10	62,503	Dutch Zwilling
Cedar Rapids Indians (3)	64	66	.492	11	92,102	Kerby Farrell
Waterloo White Hawks (2)	60	69	.466	14½	79,687	Otto Denning/Edward Taylor/ Skeeter Webb
Davenport Tigers (4)	56	74	.431	19	100,328	Marv Olson

Playoffs: Quincy 3 games, Terre Haute 1; Cedar Rapids 3 games, Evansville 2.
Finals: Quincy 3 games, Cedar Rapids 2.

All-Star Team: 1B-Thomas Kelly, Quincy; **2B**-Stan Pawloski, Cedar Rapids; James Deery, Terre Haute; **3B**-Ed Barbarito, Quincy; James Command, Terre Haute; **SS**-Melvin Cooper, Evansville; Gail Larson, Davenport; **OF**-Jim Frey, Evansville; Bill Renna, Quincy; Andrew Baud, Waterloo; James Watson, Terre Haute; **C**-Louis Heyman, Terre Haute; J.W. Porter, Waterloo; **Util**-Robert Erps, Davenport; **P**-Bob Coleman, Cedar Rapids; Daniel Ramer, Terre Haute; Jack Urban, Quincy; Richard Hoeksama, Davenport; Alfred Dumouchelle, Evansville; **Manager**-Bob Coleman, Evansville.

BA: James Command, Terre Haute, .328
Runs: James Deery, Terre Haute, 103
Hits: James Command, Terre Haute, 166
RBIs: Robert Erps, Davenport, 97
HRs: Bill Renna, Quincy, 26

Wins: Alfred Dumouchelle, Evansville, 17
Jack Urban, Quincy, 17
Bob Coleman, Cedar Rapids, 17
SOs: Jack Urban, Quincy, 164
ERA: Ben Johnson, Evansville, 2.47

B Tri-State League
President: Robert E. Hipps

Standings	W	L	Pct.	GB	Attend.	Manager
Charlotte Hornets (8)	100	40	.714	—	112,061	Cal Ermer
Asheville Tourists (10)	85	55	.607	15	71,948	Ray Hathaway
Rock Hill Chiefs (11)	84	55	.604	15½	71,301	Dick Bouknight
Spartanburg Peaches (3)	73	67	.521	27	67,135	Harry Griswold
Knoxville Smokies (15)	60	79	.432	39½	55,142	Jack Aragon
Anderson Rebels (7)	59	80	.424	40½	67,047	Len Schulte/Hillis Layne
Greenwood Tigers	56	81	.409	42½	48,111	Walt Dixon/Michael Garbark
Greenville Spinners	38	98	.279	60	37,564	Vance Carlson/David Burke/ Macklin Stewart

Playoffs: Spartanburg 3 games, Charlotte 1; Asheville 3 games, Rock Hill 2.
Finals: Spartanburg 4 games, Asheville 0.

All-Star Team: 1B-Dean Padgett, Rock Hill; **2B**-Al Denson, Anderson; **3B**-Claude Siple, Asheville; **SS**-Chris Kitsos, Asheville; **OF**-Albert Neal, Spartanburg; Francisco Campos, Charlotte; Dusty Rhodes, Rock Hill; Bill Kerr, Asheville; **C**-Dick Bouknight, Rock Hill; **Util**-Hank Nasternak, Rock Hill; **P**-Dave Hillman, Asheville; Jim Cater, Asheville; **Manager**-Cal Ermer, Charlotte; Ray Hathaway, Asheville.

BA: Francisco Campos, Charlotte, .368
Runs: Chris Kitsos, Asheville, 134
Hits: Dusty Rhodes, Rock Hill, 182
RBIs: Albert Neal, Spartanburg, 154

HRs: Albert Neal, Spartanburg, 44
Wins: Ralph Butler, Asheville, 21
SOs: Dave Hillman, Rock Hill, 203
ERA: Ralph Butler, Asheville, 2.68

B Western International League
President: Robert B. Abel

Standings	W	L	Pct.	GB	Attend.	Manager
Spokane Indians	93	49	.655	—	145,739	Alan Strange
Vancouver Capilanos	94	51	.648	½	164,026	Bill Schuster
Salem Senators	74	68	.521	19	109,976	Hugh Luby
Wenatchee Chiefs	68	75	.476	25½	64,482	Rupert "Tommy" Thompson
Yakima Bears	63	80	.441	30½	60,018	Bill Brenner
Tacoma Tigers	63	82	.434	31½	42,463	Jack Brillheart
Victoria Athletics	62	83	.428	32½	69,850	Dick "Kewpie" Barrett/ Robert Sturgeon
Tri-City Braves (16)	58	87	.400	36½	64,599	Charles Petersen

Playoffs: None.

All-Star Team: 1B-James Wert, Spokane; **2B**-James Brown, Spokane; **3B**-Ken Richardson, Spokane; **SS**-Carl "Buddy" Peterson, Tri-City; **OF**-Dick Sinovic, Vancouver; Edward Murphy, Spokane; Wilbert Hafey, Wenatchee; **C**-John Ritchey, Vancouver; **P**-Robert Snyder, Vancouver; Tom Breisinger, Wenatchee.

BA: John Ritchey, Vancouver, .346
Runs: Edward Murphy, Spokane, 124
Hits: Edo Vanni, Spokane, 195
RBIs: James Wert, Spokane, 122

HRs: Wilbert Hafey, Wenatchee, 24
Wins: Robert Snyder, Vancouver, 27
SOs: Tom Breisinger, Wenatchee, 210
ERA: Sol DeGeorge, Salem, 2.57

C Border League
President: John G. Ward

Standings	W	L	Pct.	GB	Attend.	Manager
Kingston Ponies	38	25	.603	—	13,862	Barney Hearn
Ogdensburg Maples	29	35	.453	9½	13,978	John Sosh/Irvin Schupp
Cornwall Canadians#	29	18	.617	NA	4,892	Bill Metzig
Auburn Falcons@	26	26	.500	NA	13,826	William Gates
Watertown Athletics@	22	30	.423	NA	18,055	Bob Shawkey
Geneva Robins#	20	30	.400	NA	12,405	Humberto Baez

#Cornwall and Geneva disbanded June 26.
@Auburn and Watertown disbanded July 1.
The league disbanded July 16 (last game played on July 10).

BA: Bob Masterson, Auburn, .394
Runs: Pedro Arroyo, Kingston, 53
Hits: Pedro Arroyo, Kingston, 79
RBIs: Olav Kollevoll, Ogdensburg, 57

HRs: Olav Kollevoll, Ogdensburg, 12
John Sosh, Ogdensburg, 12
Wins: Gideon Applegate, Kingston, 10
SOs: William Gates, Auburn, 94
ERA: Gideon Applegate, Kingston, 2.85

C California League
President: Jerry Donovan

Standings	W	L	Pct.	GB	Attend.	Manager
Santa Barbara Dodgers (10)	88	59	.599	—	61,948	Bill Hart
San Jose Red Sox (1)	80	67	.544	8	86,244	Marv Owen
Stockton Ports	79	68	.537	9	99,825	Harry Clements
Visalia Cubs (11)	76	71	.517	12	88,845	James Trew/Cecil Garriott
Modesto Reds (15)	74	73	.503	14	103,187	Tony Freitas
Ventura Braves (9)	72	75	.490	16	50,713	Gene Lillard
Fresno Cardinals (16)	61	86	.415	27	97,967	Larry Barton
Bakersfield Indians (3)	58	89	.395	30	67,680	Wellington Quinn

Playoffs: Santa Barbara 3 games, Stockton 1; Visalia 3 games, San Jose 1.
Finals: Santa Barbara 4 games, Visalia 1.

All-Star Team: 1B-Dick Wilson, Modesto; **2B**-Bobby Dallas, Santa Barbara; **3B**-Lee Walls, Modesto; **SS**-Wally Lammers, Fresno; **OF**-Ed Sobczak, San Jose; James Warner, Modesto; Jim King, Fresno; **C**-Joe Borich, Bakersfield; **P**-Tony Freitas, Modesto; Frank White, Santa Barbara; Stan McWilliams, San Jose; Harry Wilson, Stockton.

BA: Dick Wilson, Modesto, .371
Runs: James Warner, Modesto, 145
Hits: Dick Wilson, Modesto, 205
RBIs: William Gabler, Santa Barbara, 153

HRs: Dick Wilson, Modesto, 40
Wins: Tony Freitas, Modesto, 25
SOs: Frank Dasso, Modesto, 210
ERA: Stan McWilliams, San Jose, 2.55

C Canadian-American League
President: Albert E. Houghton

Standings	W	L	Pct.	GB	Attend.	Manager
Oneonta Red Sox***(1)	83	34	.709	—	32,503	Owen Scheetz
Pittsfield Phillies (14)	72	42	.632	9½	39,820	Richard Carter
Amsterdam Rugmakers (5)	62	56	.525	21½	30,837	Frank Novosel
Gloversville-Johnstown Glovers	52	61	.460	29	36,807	Al Barillari
Rome Colonels (6)	46	71	.393	37	23,454	Clarence "Buck" Etchison
Kingston Colonials	33	84	.282	50	16,961	Henry Camelli/Joel Kern/ John Sosh

Playoffs: Oneonta 3 games, Amsterdam 1; Gloversville-Johnstown 3 games, Pittsfield 2.
Finals: Oneonta 3 games, Gloversville-Johnstown 1.

All-Star Team: 1B-John Jones, Amsterdam; **2B**-Robert Guttilla, Oneonta; **3B**-Arthur Getgen, Oneonta; **SS**-Charles Ruddock, Pittsfield; **OF**-John Minarcin, Oneonta; William McMillan, Gloversville-Johnstown; William Casanova, Amsterdam; Arnold Spence, Oneonta; **C**-Bernard Vogt, Gloversville-Johnstown; **Util**-Dick Karl, Oneonta; **P**-George McPhail, Pittsfield; George Uhaze, Oneonta; Paul Wargo, Gloversville-Johnstown; Allen Leech, Pittsfield; **Manager**-Owen Scheetz, Oneonta.

BA: William McMillan, Gloversville-Johnstown, .377
Runs: William Casanova, Amsterdam, 121
Hits: William Casanova, Amsterdam, 155
RBIs: John Jones, Amsterdam, 127

HRs: John Jones, Amsterdam, 18
Wins: George McPhail, Pittsfield, 24
SOs: Robert Jeffries, Pittsfield, 140
ERA: George Uhaze, Oneonta, 1.64

C Cotton States League
President: Al Haraway

Standings	W	L	Pct.	GB	Attend.	Manager
Monroe Sports	89	51	.636	—	70,262	Al Mazar
Greenwood Dodgers (10)	83	57	.593	6	44,051	Lou Rochelli
Pine Bluff Judges (7)	82	58	.586	7	63,218	Bob Richards
Natchez Indians	79	61	.564	10	57,844	Jorge Torres
El Dorado Oilers	77	62	.554	11½	63,009	Bill McGhee
Hot Springs Bathers (2)	53	86	.381	35½	40,564	Rex Carr
Clarksburg Planters	53	87	.379	36	31,050	James Pruett/Herschel Bobo/ Rudy Regelsky/Joseph Kopach
Greenville Bucks	43	97	.307	46	26,082	Alton Biggs/Lawrence Bucynski

Playoffs: Natchez 4 games, Monroe 3; Pine Bluff 4 games, Greenwood 3.
Finals: Natchez 4 games, Pine Bluff 1.

All-Star Team: 1B-Bill Jones, Natchez; **2B**-Melvin Nunes, El Dorado; **3B**-Peter Konyar, Pine Bluff; **SS**-Carl Tumlinson, Greenwood; **OF**-Fred Boiko, Pine Bluff; James Gilbert, Natchez; Bob Greene, Monroe; **C**-Dick Anderson, Monroe; **P**-Billy Muffett, Monroe; Vachel Perkins, Pine Bluff; Robert Wiltse, Greenville; Fred Waters, Greenwood.

BA: James Gilbert, Natchez, .352
Runs: Fred Boiko, Pine Bluff, 125
Hits: Fred Boiko, Pine Bluff, 182
RBIs: Steve Molinari, Pine Bluff, 106
HRs: Peter Konyar, Pine Bluff, 27

Wins: Billy Muffett, Monroe, 22
Vachel Perkins, Pine Bluff, 22
SOs: Bud Black, Pine Bluff, 171
ERA: Billy Muffett, Monroe, 2.25

C Evangeline League
President: Edmond L. Deramee

Standings	W	L	Pct.	GB	Attend.	Manager
Thibodaux Giants	75	61	.551	—	63,560	William Adams
New Iberia Pelicans	76	64	.543	1	105,077	Randy Heflin
Hammond Berries	73	64	.533	2½	28,230	Joe Powers
Baton Rouge Red Sticks	72	66	.522	4	66,438	George Washburn
Crowley Millers	70	70	.500	7	100,595	John George
Alexandria Aces	68	71	.489	8½	60,621	Otho Nitcholas
Houma Indians	60	78	.435	16	32,716	Sidney Gautreaux
Lafayette Bulls	60	80	.429	17	46,782	Rudy Briner

Playoffs: Baton Rouge 4 games, Thibodaux 2; Hammond 4 games, New Iberia 3.
Finals: Hammond 4 games, Baton Rouge 2.

BA: Bill Radulovich, Baton Rouge, .409
Runs: Fred Barocco, Hammond, 147
Hits: Harry Elliott, Alexandria, 221
RBIs: Bob Akenhead, Hammond, 153

HRs: Remy LeBlanc, New Iberia, 42
Wins: Jack Cardey, Hammond, 25
SOs: Roy Price, Houma, 344
ERA: Jack Cardey, Hammond, 2.67

C Longhorn League
President: Hal Sayles

Standings	W	L	Pct.	GB	Attend.	Manager
San Angelo Colts	93	47	.664	—	115,818	Dutch Funderburk
Big Spring Broncs	82	57	.590	10½	43,370	Pat Stasey
Roswell Rockets	79	61	.564	14	65,361	Alex Monchak
Odessa Oilers	76	63	.547	16½	58,825	Jackie Sullivan/Robert Martin
Midland Indians	69	70	.497	23½	52,797	Harold Webb/Zeke Bonura
Vernon Dusters	67	71	.486	25	36,686	Joe Berry/Homer Matney
Sweetwater Swatters	46	93	.331	46½	32,430	Earl Harriman/Warren Sliter/ Joe Bratcher/Julian Morgan/ Julian Pressley
Artesia Drillers	45	95	.321	48	34,545	Hayden Greer

Playoffs: Odessa 4 games, San Angelo 1; Roswell 4 games, Big Spring 2.
Finals: Odessa 4 games, Roswell 2.

All-Star Team: 1B-Wayne Wallace, San Angelo; **2B**-Alex Monchak, Roswell; **3B**-John Tayoan, San Angelo; **SS**-Stanley Hughes, Midland; **OF**-Bob West, Roswell; Wilber Cearley, Roswell; Pat Stasey, Big Spring; **C**-Kenneth Jones, Midland; **P**-Dean Franks, Roswell; Marshall Epperson, Vernon.

BA: Pat Stasey, Big Spring, .387
Runs: Leo Eastham, Odessa, 157
Hits: John Tayoan, San Angelo, 209
RBIs: Wilber Cearley, Roswell, 141

HRs: Wayne Wallace, San Angelo, 36
Wins: Dean Franks, Roswell, 30
SOs: Marshall Epperson, Vernon, 167
ERA: Mike Fornieles, Big Spring, 2.85

C Middle Atlantic League
President: Elmer M. Daily

Standings	W	L	Pct.	GB	Attend.	Manager
Erie Sailors*(8)	85	40	.680	—	45,892	Pete Appleton
Niagara Falls Citizens**(**)	74	47	.612	9	44,000	James Davis
New Castle Indians	61	58	.513	21	42,000	Albert Milnar
Lockport Locks	65	63	.508	21½	24,375	Bill Mongiello/Glenn Gardner
Butler Tigers (15)	48	74	.352	35½	31,000	Norman Gerdeman/ William Allen/Red Barrett
Youngstown/Oil City A's#	24	75	.242	NA	14,988	Michael Garbark/Rudy York

#Youngstown moved to Oil City June 2; Oil City disbanded August 6.

Playoff: Niagara Falls 4 games, Erie 2.

All-Star Team: 1B-Stan Machinsky, Butler; **2B**-William Paolisso, Lockport/Oil City; **3B**-Eli Russo, Erie; **SS**-Lou Ciccone, Niagara Falls; **OF**-Walter Kowalski, New Castle; Jack Byers, Erie; Henry DiJohnson, Niagara Falls; Walter Chipple, Lockport; **C**-Orlando Echevarria, Erie; **Util**-Charles Harig, New Castle/Oil City; **P**-Kenneth Yount, Niagara Falls; Dean Stone, Erie; **Manager**-Pete Appleton, Erie; James Davis, Niagara Falls.

BA: Walter Kowalski, New Castle, .375
Runs: Walter Kowalski, New Castle, 134
Jack Byers, Erie, 134
Hits: Walter Kowalski, New Castle, 169
RBIs: Walter Kowalski, New Castle, 134

HRs: Rudy York, New Castle/Oil City, 34
Wins: Kenneth Yount, Niagara Falls, 20
SOs: Frank Zeisz, Niagara Falls, 153
ERA: Kenneth Yount, Niagara Falls, 2.84

C Northern League
President: Herman D. White

Standings	W	L	Pct.	GB	Attend.	Manager
Eau Claire Bears (9)	77	44	.636	—	69,015	Bill Adair
St. Cloud Rox (13)	64	55	.538	12	44,507	Harold Kollar
Superior Blues (2)	61	59	.508	15½	49,703	Buster Mills
Grand Forks Chiefs (14)	64	62	.508	15½	64,132	Eddie Murphy
Aberdeen Pheasants (7)	61	60	.504	16	62,203	Joe King/Jim Post/ Bruce Ogrodowski
Fargo-Moorhead Twins	59	65	.476	19½	104,077	Emil Gall
Duluth Dukes	54	66	.450	22½	47,755	Orie Arntzen/Ken Blackman
Sioux Falls Canaries (11)	46	75	.380	31	50,466	Lee Eilbracht/Richard Lloyd

Playoffs: Eau Claire 1 game, Superior 1 (Eau Claire won after five successive rain postponements and Superior conceded the series); Grand Forks 3 games, St. Cloud 2.

Finals: Grand Forks 2 games, Eau Claire 0.

All-Star Team: 1B-Dan Phalen, Superior; **2B**-Francis King, Grand Forks; **3B**-David Rush, Aberdeen; **SS**-Robert Harmon, Fargo-Moorhead; **OF**-Horace Garner, Eau Claire; Robert Pascal, St. Cloud; Terry Thomas, Superior; **C**-Cannie Forsyth, St. Cloud; **P**-Arthur Webb, St. Cloud; John Brandreth, Eau Claire; Carlton Post, Aberdeen; Robert Simpson, Superior.

BA: Horace Garner, Eau Claire, .359
Runs: Mervin Holbeck, Superior, 115
    Vincent LaSala, St. Cloud, 115
Hits: Dan Phalen, Superior, 154
RBIs: Rufus Crawford, Aberdeen, 111

HRs: Rufus Crawford, Aberdeen, 23
Wins: Arthur Vicital, Fargo-Moorhead, 20
SOs: Charles Locke, Aberdeen, 215
ERA: James Brown, Grand Forks, 2.54

C Pioneer League
President: Jack P. Halliwell

Standings	W	L	Pct.	GB	Attend.	Manager
Salt Lake City Bees (14)	84	52	.618	—	134,737	Hub Kittle
Ogden Reds (12)	78	61	.561	7½	62,211	Cecil Scheffel
Great Falls Electrics	76	60	.559	8	102,182	Buck Elliott
Twin Falls Cowboys (5)	71	68	.511	14½	48,040	Donald Trower
Idaho Falls Russets (13)	69	70	.496	16½	55,174	Sven "Red" Jessen
Billings Mustangs (10)	65	70	.481	18½	92,142	Larry Shepard
Pocatello Cardinals (16)	56	81	.409	28½	40,293	Norman Shope/Robert Comiskey
Boise Pilots	51	88	.387	34½	37,663	Thomas Lloyd/Frank Gregory

Playoffs: Great Falls 2 games, Salt Lake City 0; Twin Falls 2 games, Ogden 1.
Finals: Great Falls 3 games, Twin Falls 2.

All-Star Team: 1B-Sven "Red" Jessen, Idaho Falls; **2B**-Gordon Hernandez, Salt Lake City; **3B**-Nick Ananias, Pocatello; **SS**-Chico Fernandez, Billings; **OF**-Ron Harrison, Ogden; Bill Van Heuit, Pocatello; Vern Campbell, Twin Falls; **C**-George Triandos, Salt Lake City; **P**-Lawrence Manier, Great Falls; James Russell, Twin Falls.

BA: Vern Campbell, Twin Falls, .335
Runs: Olney Patterson, Idaho Falls, 135
Hits: Bryce Carmichael, Pocatello, 169
RBIs: Ron Harrison, Ogden, 134
HRs: Ron Harrison, Ogden, 24

BBs: Olney Patterson, Idaho Falls, 194
Wins: Lawrence Manier, Great Falls, 26
SOs: James Russell, Twin Falls, 296
ERA: Burton Barkelew, Salt Lake City, 2.13
Pct: Lawrence Manier, Great Falls, .788, 26-7

C Provincial League
President: Albert Molini

Standings	W	L	Pct.	GB	Attend.	Manager
Sherbrooke Les Athletiques	73	50	.593	—	100,933	Roland Gladu
Granby Red Sox	74	51	.592	—	76,823	Oscar Major/Bud Kimball/ Vernon Thoele
Drummondville Cubs	71	49	.591	½	87,615	Stanislaus Breard
Quebec Braves (9)	65	58	.528	8	103,712	George McQuinn
St. Hyacinthe Saints	55	67	.451	17½	57,476	Bull Hamons/Henry Camelli
St. Jean Braves	52	68	.423	19½	48,500	Steve Mizerak
Farnham Pirates	52	71	.423	21	33,519	Sam Bankhead
Trois Rivieres Royals	48	76	.387	25½	69,139	Al Gardella/Del Bissonette

Playoffs: Sherbrooke 4 games, Drummondville 2; Quebec 4 games, Granby 0.
Finals: Sherbrooke 4 games, Quebec 1.

BA: Joseph Montiero, Granby, .353
Runs: John Davis, Drummondville, 106
Hits: Joseph Montiero, Granby, 171
RBIs: Frank Gravino, St. Jean, 123
HRs: Frank Gravino, St. Jean, 42
Wins: John Andre, Granby, 20
SOs: Connie Johnson, St. Hyacinthe, 172
ERA: Carlton Willey, Quebec, 1.95

C Southwest International League
President: Leslie E. Powers
(The Arizona-Texas League combined with the Sunset League to form the Southwest International League.)

Standings	W	L	Pct.	GB	Attend.	Manager
El Paso Texans	88	56	.611	—	104,061	Art Lilly
Juarez Indios	87	57	.604	1	68,000	Victor Manuel Canajes/ Red Kress
Phoenix Senators**	83	61	.576	5	65,320	Wayne Tucker
Mexicali Eagles*	81	63	.563	7	88,426	Virgilio Arteaga/Dee Moore
Las Vegas Wranglers	72	71	.503	15½	48,000	Newell Kimball
Tucson Cowboys	68	75	.476	19½	62,841	Ken Meyers/Bud Dawson
Tijuana Potros	65	79	.451	23	55,000	Luis Montes de Oca/ Enrique Fernandez
Bisbee-Douglas Copper Kings (10)	64	80	.444	24	57,786	Syd Cohen
El Centro Imperials	59	85	.410	29	23,847	Red Kress/Bud Beringhele
Yuma Panthers	52	92	.361	36	50,557	Ray Viers/Don Jameson

Playoff: Mexicali 4 games, Phoenix 1.

All-Star Team: 1B-Len Noren, Phoenix; **2B**-Art Lilly, El Paso; **3B**-Pingua Canales, Juarez; **SS**-Hector Mayer, El Paso; **OF**-Ramon Vargas, Juarez/El Paso; Johnnie Moore, El Centro; Herman Lewis, Phoenix; **C**-Tommy Lloyd, Las Vegas; **P**-Bill Stites, El Paso; Tony Ponce, Phoenix; Manuel Morales, Bisbee-Douglas; Wenceslao Gonzalez, Juarez; Memo Luna, Tijuana.

BA: Ramon Vargas, Juarez/El Paso, .377
Runs: Eduardo Cruz, Juarez, 135
Hits: Ramon Vargas, Juarez/El Paso, 229
RBIs: Ramon Vargas, Juarez/El Paso, 149
HRs: Herman Lewis, Phoenix, 23
Wins: Wenceslao Gonzalez, Juarez, 32
SOs: Memo Luna, Tijuana, 318
ERA: Memo Luna, Tijuana, 2.52
CGs: Tony Ponce, Phoenix, 38

C West Texas-New Mexico League
President: Milton E. Price

Standings	W	L	Pct.	GB	Attend.	Manager
Abilene Blue Sox	90	51	.638	—	94,945	James "Hack" Miller
Albuquerque Dukes	82	60	.577	8½	93,177	Herschel Martin
Lamesa Lobos	81	61	.570	9½	59,283	Jay Haney
Lubbock Hubbers	80	61	.567	10	112,046	Don Moore/Al Kubski
Amarillo Gold Sox	67	74	.472	23	65,124	Buck Fausett/Les Mulcahy/ Pat McLaughlin
Pampa Oilers	64	77	.451	26	37,515	Grover Seitz/Virgil Richardson
Borger Gassers	54	87	.383	36	34,491	Edwin Carnett/Lloyd Brown
Clovis Pioneers (11)	47	94	.333	43	37,169	Charles Bushong/Grover Seitz

Playoffs: Abilene 4 games, Lubbock 3; Lamesa 4 games, Albuquerque 2.
Finals: Abilene 4 games, Lamesa 1.

All-Star Team: 1B-Earl Hochstatter, Lubbock; **2B**-Frank Murray, Amarillo; **3B**-Al Kubski, Lubbock; **SS**-Charles Schmidt, Abilene; **OF**-Glenn Burns, Lamesa; Thomas Howard, Amarillo; Don Stokes, Lamesa; **C**-Arthur Bowland, Abilene; **P**-Edward Arthur, Lamesa; John "Monk" Webb, Amarillo; **Manager**-James "Hack" Miller, Abilene.

BA: Glenn Burns, Lamesa, .392
Runs: Pedro Santiago, Lamesa, 163
Hits: Glenn Burns, Lamesa, 230
RBIs: Glenn Burns, Lamesa, 197
HRs: Les Mulcahy, Amarillo, 35

2Bs: Don Stokes, Lamesa, 59
Wins: Edward Arthur, Lamesa, 27
SOs: Carroll "Red" Dial, Pampa, 174
ERA: Jesse Priest, Albuquerque, 3.15
Pct: Jesse Priest, Albuquerque, .826, 19-4

C Western Association
President: Howard Goetz

Standings	W	L	Pct.	GB	Attend.	Manager
Topeka Owls (11)	74	44	.627	—	89,474	Butch Nieman
Joplin Miners (5)	77	48	.616	½	46,921	William Holm
St. Joseph Cardinals (16)	69	51	.575	6	47,133	Gene Corbett
Salina Blue Jays (14)	63	58	.521	12½	47,550	Floyd Patterson
Muskogee Giants (13)	61	63	.492	16	56,032	Harold Bamberger
Hutchinson Elks (15)	57	66	.463	19½	73,720	Wes Griffin
Enid Buffalos	45	79	.363	32	39,584	Ray Honeycutt
Ft. Smith Indians (3)	43	80	.350	33½	48,545	Paul O'Dea

Playoffs: None (cancelled due to floods).

All-Star Team: 1B-John Cooney, Muskogee; **2B**-Mike Morongiello, Joplin; **3B**-Harry Bright, Topeka; **SS**-Wally Habel, Salina; **OF**-Dick Tettelbach, Joplin; Solly Drake, Topeka; Bill Beery, Topeka; **C**-Joe Breidt, Salina; **P**-Merlin Nehring, Joplin; Jack Dunn, Topeka; Gene Snyder, Salina; Fred Sherkel, Joplin.

BA: John Cooney, Muskogee, .344
Runs: Dick Tettelbach, Joplin, 128
Hits: John Cooney, Muskogee, 175

RBIs: Eugene Barth, St. Joseph, 103
    Robert Williams, Hutchinson, 103
HRs: Butch Nieman, Topeka, 28
Wins: Merlin Nehring, Joplin, 20
SOs: Walter Montgomery, St. Joseph, 230
ERA: Harry Wise, Topeka, 2.61

D Alabama-Florida League
President: G.D. Halstead

Standings	W	L	Pct.	GB	Attend.	Manager
Headland Dixie Runners	84	36	.700	—	13,675	Bubba Ball
Ozark Eagles	72	45	.615	10½	15,983	Chase Riddle/Walter Jones
Tallahassee Citizens	65	52	.556	17½	31,051	Charles Quimby
Dothan Browns	50	69	.420	33½	45,101	Emory Lindsey/Holt "Cat" Milner
Enterprise Boll Weevils	44	76	.367	40	14,500	Richard Hahn/James Guinn/ Irvin Fortune/Bill Brightwell
Panama City Fliers	41	78	.345	42½	40,116	Roxie Humberson/Phillip Noto/ Bill Herring

Playoffs: Tallahassee 4 games, Headland 3; Dothan 4 games, Ozark 1.
Finals: Dothan 4 games, Tallahassee 2.

All-Star Team: 1B-Charles Quimby, Tallahassee; **2B**-Herbert Marshall, Headland; **3B**-Jim Colley, Dothan; **SS**-George Wehymer, Tallahassee; **OF**-John McPherson, Headland; Wilmer Lee Chappell, Tallahassee; Morris Johnson, Dothan; **C**-Thomas Vonn, Tallahassee; Phillip Noto, Panama City; **P**-Tommy Stone, Headland; Dario Jiminez, Tallahassee; William Williams, Headland; Lorenzo Joe Hinchman, Enterprise; Richard York, Dothan.

BA: Charles Quimby, Tallahassee, .404
Runs: Al Rivenbark, Headland, 127
Hits: Al Rivenbark, Headland, 169
RBIs: John McPherson, Headland, 130
HRs: Charles Quimby, Tallahassee, 13

Wins: Harry Clifton, Headland, 22
    Tommy Stone, Headland, 22
SOs: Harry Clifton, Headland, 245
Pct: Harry Clifton, Headland, .786, 22-6

D Appalachian League
President: Chauncey De Vault

Standings	W	L	Pct.	GB	Attend.	Manager
Kingsport Cherokees	85	44	.659	—	65,646	Jack Crosswhite
Bluefield Blue-Grays (9)	69	59	.539	15½	45,464	Travis Jackson/Xavier Rescigno
Johnson City Cardinals (16)	64	65	.496	21	40,919	Ben Catchings
Elizabethton Phils (14)	57	70	.449	27	28,369	John Davenport/Donald Marshall
Bristol Twins (13)	56	73	.434	29	41,146	Russell Wein
Welch Miners (12)	54	74	.422	30½	33,265	Mike Blazo

Playoffs: Kingsport 2 games, Elizabethton 0; Bluefield 2 games, Johnson City 1.

Finals: Kingsport 3 games, Bluefield 2.

BA: Leo "Muscle" Shoals, Kingsport, .383
Runs: Bob Westfall, Kingsport, 140
Hits: Lantz Blaney, Bluefield, 184
RBIs: Leo "Muscle" Shoals, Kingsport, 129
HRs: Leo "Muscle" Shoals, Kingsport, 30

Wins: Jesse James, Kingsport, 23
Gary Blaylock, Johnson City, 23
SOs: Gary Blaylock, Johnson City, 248
ERA: Jesse James, Kingsport, 1.91

D Coastal Plain League
President: Ray H. Goodmon

Standings	W	L	Pct.	GB	Attend.	Manager
Kinston Eagles..................	79	47	.627	—	41,516	Wes Livengood
New Bern Bears	72	54	.571	7	45,388	Harry Land
Goldsboro Cardinals (16) ...	70	55	.550	8½	36,529	George Ferrell
Wilson Tobs.......................	69	57	.548	10	54,753	Joe Antolick/Alfred Rehm
Roanoke Rapids Jays (8)	59	66	.472	19½	34,132	Morris "Smut" Aderholt
Rocky Mount Leafs	39	86	.312	39½	27,753	Jim Mills/Bull Hamons/
						Horace "Red" Benton
Tarboro A's#......................	13	22	.371	NA	6,431	Joe Rullo
Greenville Robins#.............	10	24	.294	NA	5,932	John Streza

#Tarboro and Greenville disbanded June 6.

Playoffs: Wilson 4 games, Kinston 2; New Bern 4 games, Goldsboro 2.
Finals: New Bern 4 games, Wilson 3.

All-Star Team: 1B-Gene Stewart, New Bern; **2B**-John Russo, New Bern; **3B**-Frank Tepedino, New Bern; **SS**-Mel Kerestes, Roanoke Rapids; **OF**-Jim McComas, Wilson; John Garrison, Roanoke Rapids; Shamrock Denning, Goldsboro; **C**-Dave Fowler, Rocky Mount; **P**-Alexander Zych, Kinston; Fred Pittman, Wilson; Bucky Stewart, New Bern; Robert Slaybaugh, Goldsboro; **Manager**-Wes Livengood, Kinston.

BA: Gerald Thomas, Goldsboro, .343
Runs: Bob Horan, Kinston, 109
Hits: Gerald Thomas, Goldsboro, 175
RBIs: Jim McComas, Wilson, 95

HRs: Jim McComas, Wilson, 20
Wins: Alexander Zych, Kinston, 22
SOs: Robert Slaybaugh, Goldsboro, 223
ERA: Bucky Stewart, New Bern, 1.16

D Far West League
President: Jerry Donovan

Standings	W	L	Pct.	GB	Attend.	Manager
Redding Browns**(7).........	76	55	.580	—	37,660	Ray Perry
Klamath Falls Gems*(14)...	74	54	.578	½	41,115	Bill DeCarlo
Reno Silver Sox	52	65	.444	17	36,461	Cotton Pippen
Eugene Larks (15)	51	70	.421	20	54,482	Duster Mails/George Matile/
						Cliff Dapper
Medford Rogues	47	67	.412	20½	34,337	Frank Lucchesi
Pittsburg Diamonds#	29	18	.617	NA	4,925	Vince DiMaggio

#Pittsburg disbanded June 14.

Playoff: Klamath Falls 3 games, Redding 0.

All-Star Team: 1B-Ellis Daugherty, Reno; **2B**-Hank Moreno, Redding; **3B**-Stan Roseboro, Klamath Falls; **SS**-Dick Zaccarelli, Reno; **OF**-Frank Lucchesi, Medford; Claude Buckley, Eugene; Bernie Anderson, Redding; **C**-Bill DeCarlo, Klamath Falls; **P**-Gordon Tench, Redding; Jim Foster, Klamath Falls; Ray O'Connor, Eugene; Lavere Herrmann, Medford.

BA: Stan Roseboro, Klamath Falls, .409
Runs: Bernie Anderson, Redding, 135
Hits: Bill Stumpus, Klamath Falls, 171
RBIs: Ray Perry, Redding, 128

HRs: Ray Perry, Redding, 18
Wins: Gordon Tench, Redding, 16
SOs: Ransom Rolfe, Redding, 178
ERA: Lavere Herrmann, Medford, 4.03

D Florida State League
President: John Krider

Standings	W	L	Pct.	GB	Attend.	Manager
DeLand Red Hats...............	90	50	.643	—	32,347	Frank Radler
Orlando Senators (8).........	81	59	.579	9	43,205	Ed Levy
Palatka Azaleas	80	59	.576	9½	46,146	Bill Steinecke
Leesburg Packers...............	71	69	.507	19	37,843	Floyd Clift/Mickey Burnett
Sanford Giants (13)	67	70	.489	21½	19,289	Richard Klaus
Daytona Beach Islanders (3)....	62	78	.443	28	45,100	Mike Tresh
Gainesville G-Men	57	81	.413	32	30,968	Charles Brewster/Myril Hoag
Cocoa Indians	49	91	.350	41	24,393	Carl Kettles/Lee Hipp/
						Sam Demma/Harry Murdock

Playoffs: DeLand 4 games, Leesburg 3; Palatka 4 games, Orlando 2.
Finals: DeLand 4 games, Palatka 0.

All-Star Team: 1B-Joe Altobelli, Daytona Beach; **2B**-Lyle Judy, Palatka; **3B**-George Barrow, DeLand; **SS**-Lyle Luttrell, Orlando; **OF**-Mike Kassabian, Palatka; Gene Oravetz, Orlando; Rocky Colavito, Daytona Beach; **C**-Ray Dunne, DeLand; **Util**-Ora Burnett, Leesburg; **P**-John Jansce, DeLand; Mike Dzingelowski, Orlando; **Manager**-Bill Steinecke, Palatka.

BA: Gene Oravetz, Orlando, .364
Runs: Gene Oravetz, Orlando, 122
Hits: Bob Truss, Daytona Beach, 208
RBIs: Al Pirtle, DeLand/Gainesville, 119

HRs: Eldon Pichan, Palatka, 23
Rocky Colavito, Daytona Beach, 23
Wins: John Jansce, DeLand, 26
SOs: James Coppock, Daytona Beach, 176
ERA: Walter Jasinski, DeLand, 1.70

D Georgia State League
President: J.T. Morris

Standings	W	L	Pct.	GB	Attend.	Manager
Jesup Bees.........................	86	43	.667	—	23,931	James Stoyle
Dublin Green Sox	78	50	.609	7½	40,166	Parnell Ruark/William Kushta
Eastman Dodgers................	76	54	.585	10½	22,736	Pep Rambert
Douglas Trojans.................	62	68	.477	24½	21,839	Witt Guise
Hazlehurst-Baxley Red Sox..	52	77	.403	34	24,120	William Kushta/Al Faehr
Fitzgerald Pioneers	34	96	.262	52½	26,247	John Duncan/Bill McGhee/
						J.B. Ruark/Charles Ridgeway

Playoffs: Eastman 4 games, Dublin 2; Douglas 4 games, Jesup 0.
Finals: Douglas 4 games, Eastman 3.

BA: Alvin Jenkins, Jesup, .376
Runs: Alvin Jenkins, Jesup, 135
Hits: Alvin Jenkins, Jesup, 207
RBIs: Parnell Ruark, Dublin, 140

HRs: Parnell Ruark, Dublin, 32
Wins: Don Rudolph, Jesup, 28
SOs: Don Rudolph, Jesup, 148
ERA: Witt Guise, Douglas, 2.16

D Georgia-Alabama League
President: Arthur R. Decatur

Standings	W	L	Pct.	GB	Attend.	Manager
La Grange Troupers**(5)...	67	47	.588	—	33,734	Bill Cooper
Valley Rebels....................	64	52	.552	4	37,515	Gabby Grant
Rome Red Sox	58	57	.504	9½	41,000	Leon Culberson
Griffin Pimientos*	58	58	.500	10	24,804	Michael Conte/Fred Campbell/
						Jack Bearden
Alexander City Millers@ ...	33	45	.423	NA	19,737	Sam Demma/William Brown
Opelika Owls#...................	23	44	.343	NA	18,000	Wheeler Flemming/Don Bailey

#Opelika disbanded July 1.
@Alexander City disbanded July 15.

All-Star Team: 1B-Johnny Stowe, Rome; **2B**-Joe Campbell, Griffin; **3B**-Bill Godwin, Opelika; **SS**-Fred Campbell, Griffin; **OF**-Claude Shoemake, Rome; George Hughes, Valley; Jack Bearden, Griffin; **C**-Roy Drews, Griffin; **P**-Charles Harrison, La Grange; Marvin Chappell, La Grange; Joe McManus, Rome; Richard Lazicky, Valley.

BA: Joe Campbell, Griffin, .379
Runs: Fred Campbell, Griffin, 111
Hits: Claude Shoemake, Rome, 171
RBIs: Claude Shoemake, Rome, 135

HRs: Claude Shoemake, Rome, 26
Wins: Marvin Chappell, La Grange, 21
SOs: Marvin Chappell, La Grange, 120
ERA: Joseph Pennington, Valley, 2.45

D Georgia-Florida League
President: W.T. Anderson

Standings	W	L	Pct.	GB	Attend.	Manager
Valdosta Dodgers (10)........	81	45	.643	—	51,546	Stan Wasiak
Albany Cardinals (16)	76	50	.603	5	45,694	Sheldon "Chief" Bender
Waycross Bears	70	55	.560	10½	54,448	Fred Williams
Tifton Blue Sox	62	63	.496	18½	48,472	Fred Tschudin
Brunswick Pirates (15)	60	66	.476	21	46,522	Mickey O'Neill
Americus Rebels................	55	70	.440	25½	38,047	Mike Milosevich
Moultrie To-baks................	52	74	.413	29	40,910	Jim Poole
Cordele A's (6)..................	46	79	.368	34½	25,857	Bob "Ducky" Detweiler/
						James DeShong

Playoffs: Tifton 4 games, Valdosta 1; Waycross 4 games, Albany 0.
Finals: Waycross 4 games, Tifton 1.

All-Star Team: 1B-George Kendall, Valdosta; **2B**-Charles Webb, Waycross; **3B**-Richard Gray, Valdosta; **SS**-Jack Caro, Waycross; **OF**-John Tidwell, Tifton; James Daley, Albany; Denver Rikard, Albany; Glenn Eury, Moultrie; **C**-Charles Bledsoe, Waycross; Alphonse Giordano, Valdosta; **P**-Robert Betancourt, Tifton; Harry Raulerson, Waycross; Philip Clark, Albany; Ottis Jacobs, Tifton; William Harris, Valdosta; Robert Hoffman, Valdosta; **Manager**-Stan Wasiak, Valdosta.

BA: Wendell Davis, Moultrie, .344
Runs: Richard Gray, Valdosta, 118
Hits: Wendell Davis, Moultrie, 160
RBIs: William Murphy, Albany, 100

HRs: Glenn Eury, Moultrie, 29
Wins: Harry Raulerson, Waycross, 22
SOs: Robert Betancourt, Tifton, 201
ERA: Harry Raulerson, Waycross, 1.99

D Kansas-Oklahoma-Missouri League
President: E.L. Dale

Standings	W	L	Pct.	GB	Attend.	Manager
Ponca City Dodgers (10)	85	39	.686	—	44,960	George Scherger
Bartlesville Pirates (15)	77	45	.631	7	34,296	Tedd Gullic
Miami Eagles....................	67	55	.549	17	23,500	Pug Griffin/Thomas Warren
Carthage Cubs (11).............	60	65	.480	25½	20,022	Don Anderson/Al Reitz
Pittsburg Brownies (7)........	41	80	.339	42½	22,534	Bill Enos
Iola Indians	38	84	.311	46	16,981	Forrest Crawford/Al Reitz/
						Mason Pool/Floyd Temple

Playoffs: Carthage 3 games, Ponca City 2; Miami 3 games, Bartlesville 1.
Finals: Carthage 3 games, Miami 0.

All-Star Team: 1B-Stan Santo, Ponca City; **2B**-E.C. Leslie, Bartlesville; **3B**-Morris Mack, Ponca City; **SS**-Len Bourdet, Carthage; **SS**-Jack Dolan, Ponca City; **OF**-Brandy Davis, Bartlesville; Jack Denison, Ponca City; Robert Ottesen, Pittsburg; **C**-Delbert Gay, Miami;

P-Ron Kline, Bartlesville; Joe Stanka, Ponca City; Dick Wiegand, Ponca City; George Garrison, Miami.

BA: Jack Denison, Ponca City, .365
Runs: Jack Denison, Ponca City, 133
Hits: Jack Denison, Ponca City, 167
RBIs: Robert Ottesen, Pittsburg, 89

HRs: Brandy Davis, Bartlesville, 13
Bill Phillips, Bartlesville, 13
Wins: Ron Kline, Bartlesville, 18
Donald Cochran, Bartlesville, 18
SOs: Ron Kline, Bartlesville, 208
ERA: John Mudd, Carthage, 2.12

D Kitty League
President: Shelby Peace

Standings	W	L	Pct.	GB	Attend.	Manager
Fulton Railroaders (8)	73	46	.613	—	30,513	Sam Lamatina
Owensboro Oilers	71	48	.597	2	56,180	Wayne Blackburn
Mayfield Clothiers (15)	66	53	.555	7	27,432	Jerry Gardner
Paducah Chiefs	64	55	.538	9	49,446	Robert Stanton
Jackson Generals	59	61	.492	14½	24,961	Glenn Stewart
Union City Greyhounds	57	63	.475	16½	33,652	Charles Moore/ Curtis Englebright/Jay Stasko
Madisonville Miners (2)	46	73	.387	27	20,835	Burl Storie
Hopkinsville Hoppers	41	78	.345	32	24,122	Steve Carter/Vito Tamulis

Playoffs: Fulton 3 games, Paducah 2; Owensboro 3 games, Mayfield 1.
Finals: Fulton 4 games, Owensboro 0.

All-Star Team: 1B-Ned Waldrop, Fulton; **2B**-Milt McEneny, Fulton; **3B**-Curtis Englebright, Union City; **SS**-Billy Joe Forrest, Fulton; **OF**-Harold Seawright, Jackson; Joe Duhem, Mayfield; Howard Weeks, Fulton; **C**-Jack Hall, Owensboro; **P**-William Howard, Paducah; Walter Bryja, Fulton; Scott Keeney, Mayfield; Cal Bowen, Owensboro.

BA: Wayne Blackburn, Owensboro, .364
Runs: Wayne Blackburn, Owensboro, 116
Hits: Harold Seawright, Jackson, 161
RBIs: Harold Seawright, Jackson, 122

HRs: Joe Duhem, Mayfield, 18
Wins: Walter Bryja, Fulton, 24
SOs: Scott Keeney, Mayfield, 212
ERA: William Howard, Paducah, 1.29

D Mississippi-Ohio Valley League
President: C.C. "Dutch" Hoffman

Standings	W	L	Pct.	GB	Attend.	Manager
Paris Lakers***	84	36	.700	—	51,331	Tom Sunkel
Centralia Zeros	69	51	.575	15	38,554	Lou Bekeza
Mt. Vernon Kings	60	59	.504	23½	39,665	Chuck Hawley/Charles Popovich
Danville Dans	51	67	.432	32	24,775	Frank Piet/Everett Hall
Mattoon Indians	49	69	.415	34	28,442	Melvin Ivy
Vincennes Velvets	43	74	.368	39½	25,652	George Kromer/Robert Signaigo

Playoffs: Mt. Vernon 2 games, Centralia 0; Danville 2 games, Paris 1.
Finals: Danville 2 games, Mt. Vernon 0.

All-Star Team: 1B-Clint McCord, Paris; **2B**-Sonny Hancks, Mattoon; **3B**-Mike Krsnich, Paris; **SS**-Oscar Solorzano, Mt. Vernon; **OF**-Everett Hall, Danville; Walter Dunkovich, Mattoon; Quincy Smith, Paris; **C**-Lowell Black, Paris; **P**-Lee Tunnison, Centralia; Ken Grubb, Paris; Richard Collins, Danville; Orville Mehringer, Vincennes.

BA: Clint McCord, Paris, .363
Runs: Clint McCord, Paris, 132
Hits: Clint McCord, Paris, 173
RBIs: James Given, Mt. Vernon, 119

HRs: Lou Bekeza, Centralia, 16
Clint McCord, Paris, 16
Wins: Lee Tunnison, Centralia, 20
SOs: Lee Tunnison, Centralia, 170
ERA: Lee Tunnison, Centralia, 3.12

D Mountain States League
President: Virgil Q. Wacks

Standings	W	L	Pct.	GB	Attend.	Manager
Hazard Bombers (10)	93	33	.738	—	35,129	Max Macon
Morristown Red Sox	86	39	.688	6½	22,184	James Burns
Harlan Smokies	82	43	.656	10½	35,657	Bones Sanders/John Streza
Middlesboro Athletics	59	66	.472	33½	19,228	Ted Russ/George Kennis
Pennington Gap Miners	54	71	.432	38½	14,994	Vince Pankovits
Norton Braves	53	72	.424	39½	12,314	Bob Bowman/George Sifft/ George Motto
Big Stone Gap Rebels	49	75	.395	43	13,737	Herman Schulte/Lew Flick
Jenkins Cavaliers	24	101	.192	68½	12,250	James Grigg/Thomas McBride

Playoffs: Hazard 3 games, Harlan 0; Morristown 3 games, Middlesboro 1.
Finals: Hazard 3 games, Morristown 0.

All-Star Team: 1B-Orville Kitts, Morristown; **2B**-Mark Muslin, Harlan; **3B**-Ken Pack, Morristown; **SS**-Bill Geier, Harlan; **OF**-Lew Flick, Big Stone Gap; Barry Cox, Harlan; Len Feriancek, Pennington Gap; **C**-Earl Motsinger, Big Stone Gap; **P**-Carl Legursky, Harlan; Rafael Codinachs, Middlesboro; Bob Hathaway, Big Stone Gap; Frank Wilson, Harlan.

BA: Orville Kitts, Morristown, .424
Runs: Max Macon, Hazard, 139
Hits: Len Feriancek, Pennington Gap, 216
RBIs: Max Macon, Hazard, 148

HRs: Bill Halstead, Pennington Gap, 34
Wins: Dan Hayling, Hazard, 24
SOs: Johnny Podres, Hazard, 228
ERA: Johnny Podres, Hazard, 1.67

D North Carolina State League
President: Walter H. Woodson, Jr.

Standings	W	L	Pct.	GB	Attend.	Manager
High Point- Thomasville Hi-Toms (1)	90	36	.714	—	52,187	Jim Gruzdis
Hickory Rebels	72	54	.571	18	53,662	D.C. "Pud" Miller
Landis Spinners/ Elkin Blanketeers#	67	59	.532	23	22,780	Fred Chapman
Statesville Owls	62	64	.492	28	46,021	Kenneth Rhyne/Len Cross
Lexington Indians (6)	61	65	.484	29	35,033	Harold Harrigan/ Gray Hampton/Robert Deese
Concord Sports	56	70	.444	34	22,236	Ginger Watts/Harry Bell
Mooresville Moors	55	71	.437	35	18,666	Tuck McWilliams/Jim Mills
Salisbury Pirates (15)	41	85	.325	49	14,964	George Detore

#Landis moved to Elkin July 18.

Playoffs: High Point-Thomasville 4 games, Elkin 1; Statesville 4 games, Hickory 0.
Finals: High Point-Thomasville 4 games, Statesville 0.

All-Star Team: 1B-Jack Gibson, Lexington; **2B**-Gray Hampton, Lexington; **3B**-Bill Cayavec, Salisbury; **SS**-Hilliard Nance, Hi-Toms; **OF**-Gene Corso, Salisbury; Gene Stephens, Hi-Toms; Tom Umphlett, Hi-Toms; Poke Linn, Landis/Elkin; **C**-Bill Poole, Lexington; Cliff Bolton, Hi-Toms; **P**-Pete Morant, Landis/Elkin; Plaskie McCree, Lexington; Ron Necciai, Salisbury; Red Hamilton, Hi-Toms.

BA: D.C. "Pud" Miller, Hickory, .425
Runs: Hilliard Nance, Hi-Toms, 128
Hits: John Lybrand, Hi-Toms, 189
RBIs: D.C. "Pud" Miller, Hickory, 136

HRs: D.C. "Pud" Miller, Hickory, 40
Wins: Roy Boles, Hickory, 23
SOs: Ernie Johnson, Statesville, 223
ERA: Tom Brewer, Hi-Toms, 2.25

D Ohio-Indiana League
President: Frank M. Colley

Standings	W	L	Pct.	GB	Attend.	Manager
Marion Red Sox**(1)	91	37	.711	—	24,710	Elmer Yoter
Springfield Giants (13)	61	67	.477	30	45,862	Andy Gilbert
Richmond Tigers (4)	53	74	.417	37½	20,004	Ralph DiLullo
Lima Phillies (14)	41	86	.323	49½	33,440	Barney Lutz
Newark Yankees*#(5)	49	31	.613	NA	33,960	Malcolm "Bunny" Mick

#Newark won the first half, which ended June 28, then withdrew July 17. The second half was restarted.

Playoff: Marion 4 games, Springfield 0.

All-Star Team: 1B-Ed Sadowski, Marion; **2B**-James Evanik, Marion; **3B**-Charles Lavene, Marion; **SS**-Joseph "Peppy" LaMonica, Marion; **OF**-Andy Gilbert, Springfield; Marv Stendel, Marion; Emil Carlini, Lima; **C**-Maxlee Ross, Marion; **P**-Richard Brodowski, Marion; Danny Banaszak, Springfield; Richard Tarys, Marion; Burton Ostby, Richmond.

BA: Andy Gilbert, Springfield, .381
Runs: Marv Stendel, Marion, 158
Hits: Marv Stendel, Marion, 185
RBIs: Marv Stendel, Marion, 125

HRs: Maxlee Ross, Marion, 20
Wins: Richard Tarys, Marion, 22
SOs: Richard Brodowski, Marion, 212
ERA: Richard Brodowski, Marion, 2.60

D PONY League
President: Vincent M. McNamara

Standings	W	L	Pct.	GB	Attend.	Manager
Olean Oilers	79	48	.622	—	56,095	Orval Cott
Jamestown Falcons (4)	78	49	.614	1	73,699	Tony Lupien
Hornell Dodgers (10)	71	55	.564	7½	74,086	Doc Alexson
Hamilton Cardinals (16)	66	60	.524	12½	62,000	Vedie Himsl
Bradford Phillies (14)	64	62	.508	14½	34,519	Frank McCormick/John Davenport
Wellsville Rockets	53	73	.421	25½	47,082	Walter VanGrofski
Batavia Clippers (3)	49	77	.389	29½	29,525	Ed Kobesky/Joe Vosmik
Corning Athletics (6)	45	81	.357	33½	34,155	Irvin Hall

Playoffs: Olean defeated Jamestown 6-1 in a one game playoff for first place. Olean 4 games, Hamilton 3; Hornell 4 games, Jamestown 1.
Finals: Hornell 4 games, Olean 3.

All-Star Team: 1B-Paul Owens, Olean; **2B**-Frank Bolling, Jamestown; **3B**-Paul Farrell, Bradford; **SS**-Ray Reed, Wellsville; **OF**-Stan Anderson, Olean; William Hudacsek, Wellsville; Emil Karlik, Jamestown; **C**-Gilbert Shirk, Hornell; Carroll Anstaett, Olean; **P**-Jim Stump, Jamestown; Douglas Gostlin, Hornell; Milton Bayne, Hamilton; Robert Shutt, Bradford.

BA: Paul Owens, Olean, .407
Runs: Stan Anderson, Olean, 134
Hits: Paul Owens, Olean, 187
RBIs: Charles Harmon, Olean, 143
HRs: Ray Reed, Wellsville, 27

Wins: Douglas Gostlin, Hornell, 17
Ed Williams, Olean, 17
John Gates, Olean, 17
SOs: Karl Spooner, Hornell, 200
ERA: Jim Stump, Jamestown, 1.93
Pct: Jim Stump, Jamestown, .824, 14-3

D Sooner State League
President: Jack Mealey

Standings	W	L	Pct.	GB	Attend.	Manager
Ardmore Indians	99	40	.712	—	40,742	Bennie Warren
Shawnee Hawks	96	44	.686	3½	44,428	Lou Fitzgerald

McAlester Rockets (5)........ 91 48 .655 8 42,028 Vern Hoscheit
Pauls Valley Raiders........... 90 50 .643 9½ 27,580 Lou Brower
Ada Herefords (7)............... 54 86 .386 45½ 12,779 Stanley Galle
Chickasha Chiefs .... 46 94 .329 53½ 21,107 Kelly Wingo/Jerry Jackson/
Ivan Wilkerson/Chet Bryan/
William Reyes

Lawton Giants (13) .... 46 94 .329 53½ 17,252 Ray Baker
Seminole Ironmen................ 37 103 .264 62½ 16,915 James "Rip" Collins/
Dutch Prather

Playoffs: Ardmore 3 games, Pauls Valley 0; McAlester 3 games, Shawnee 0.
Finals: McAlester 4 games, Ardmore 2.

All-Star Team: 1B-Edwin Graham Dickson, McAlester; **2B**-Manuel Temes, Ardmore; **3B**-Lou Fitzgerald, Shawnee; **SS**-Doyle Chadwick, McAlester; **SS**-Claude Barcelo, Shawnee; **OF**-Dan Toma, Pauls Valley; Joe Nodar, Ardmore; J.J. Burris, McAlester; **C**-Bennie Warren, Ardmore; **Util**-James Dionisotis, Pauls Valley; **P**-Dee Sanders, McAlester; Ken Hemphill, Pauls Valley; Armin Somonte, Ardmore; Andrew Pane, Pauls Valley.

BA: Lou Fitzgerald, Shawnee, .379
Runs: Joe Nodar, Ardmore, 179
Hits: Dan Toma, Pauls Valley, 195
   Manuel Temes, Ardmore, 195
RBIs: Glenn Snyder, Ardmore, 155
   Manuel Temes, Ardmore, 155

HRs: Dan Demby, Pauls Valley, 30
   Donnie Williamson, Pauls Valley, 30
Wins: Dee Sanders, McAlester, 27
   Ken Hemphill, Pauls Valley, 27
SOs: Armin Somonte, Ardmore, 341
ERA: Dee Sanders, McAlester, 1.67
Pct: Dee Sanders, McAlester, .871, 27-4

D Virginia League
President: Benjamin L. Campbell

Standings	W	L	Pct.	GB	Attend.	Manager
Colonial Heights-Petersburg Generals.........	80	39	.672	—	35,146	Cecil "Turkey" Tyson
Elizabeth City Albemarles..	67	50	.573	12	34,301	Paul Crawford
Edenton Colonials...............	63	55	.534	16½	28,528	Gashouse Parker
Suffolk Goobers..................	56	62	.475	23½	26,000	Leon "Red" Treadway
Franklin Kildees	49	70	.412	31	18,299	Carl McQuillen/Awood Holland
Emporia Rebels..................	39	78	.333	40	12,000	Joe Mills/Harold Martin

Playoffs: Colonial Heights-Petersburg 4 games, Suffolk 1; Elizabeth City 4 games, Edenton 3.
Finals: Elizabeth City 4 games, Colonial Heights-Petersburg 1.

All-Star Team: 1B-William Parker, Edenton; **2B**-Frank Sangalli, Colonial Heights-Petersburg; **3B**-Horace Inge, Colonial Heights-Petersburg; **SS**-St. Pierre Howard, Elizabeth City; **OF**-Kenneth Hatcher, Colonial Heights-Petersburg; Donald Warfield, Elizabeth City; Buster Kinard, Suffolk; **C**-Paul Crawford, Elizabeth City; **P**-John Brockwell, Colonial Heights-Petersburg; John Raines, Edenton; William Garthwaite, Colonial Heights-Petersburg; Charles Hagy, Elizabeth City.

BA: Buster Kinard, Suffolk, .378
Runs: Kenneth Hatcher, Colonial Heights-Petersburg, 109
Hits: Buster Kinard, Suffolk, 156
RBIs: Kenneth Hatcher, Colonial Heights-Petersburg, 121

HRs: Kenneth Hatcher, Colonial Heights-Petersburg, 34
Wins: John Brockwell, Colonial Heights-Petersburg, 25
SOs: John Brockwell, Colonial Heights-Petersburg, 164
ERA: John Brockwell, Colonial Heights-Petersburg, 2.05

D Western Carolina League
President: P.W. Deaton

Standings	W	L	Pct.	GB	Attend.	Manager
Morganton Aggies	71	39	.645	—	49,265	George Bradshaw
Shelby Farmers	67	44	.604	4½	39,582	David Coble
Lincolnton Cardinals	67	45	.598	5	42,145	Bob Beal
Newton-Conover Twins	63	48	.568	8½	31,625	Edwin Yount
Rutherford County Owls (11)..	62	48	.564	9	32,428	Rube Wilson
Marion Marauders	58	52	.527	13	31,037	Russell "Red" Mincy
Lenoir Red Sox (13)	40	70	.364	31	17,736	Claude Jonnard/Okey Flowers/John Olsen
Granite Falls Graniteers	14	96	.127	57	11,500	Charles Bowles/Ralph Barnardini/Fred Dale/Wallace Carpenter/Robert Pugh

Playoffs: Morganton 4 games, Lincolnton 3; Shelby 4 games, Newton-Conover 2.

Finals: Shelby 4 games, Morganton 3.

All-Star Team: 1B-Donald Stafford, Newton-Conover; **2B**-Daniel Reynolds, Shelby; **3B**-Bob Beal, Lincolnton; **SS**-Robert Peters, Lincolnton; **OF**-Jack Triplett, Marion; Robert Featherstone, Lenoir; Henry Miller, Shelby; **C**-Bill Bowles, Shelby; **P**-George Long, Rutherford County; William Roland, Lincolnton; Norman Reinhardt, Newton-Conover.

BA: Henry Miller, Shelby, .387
Runs: Charles Ballard, Shelby, 137
Hits: Henry Miller, Shelby, 179
   Robert Peters, Lincolnton, 179
RBIs: Edward Bass, Shelby, 157

HRs: Bordie Waddle, Morganton, 24
Wins: Eurice "Pete" Treece, Morganton, 25
SOs: Eurice "Pete" Treece, Morganton, 264
ERA: George Long, Rutherford County, 2.12

D Wisconsin State League
President: Judge Arold F. Murphy

Standings	W	L	Pct.	GB	Attend.	Manager
Sheboygan Indians (10)......	76	43	.639	—	36,509	Joe Hauser
Oshkosh Giants (13)	65	55	.542	11½	40,566	David Garcia
Green Bay Bluejays (3)	64	57	.529	13	57,843	Phil Seghi
Wisconsin Rapids Sox (2) ..	60	58	.508	15½	33,001	Ira Hutchinson
Fond du Lac Panthers (5)....	59	61	.492	17½	43,097	James Adlam
Wausau Lumberjacks (4).....	57	62	.479	19	38,791	Bob Benish
Janesville Cubs (11)............	56	64	.467	20½	62,982	Adolph Matulis
Appleton Papermakers (7)..	43	80	.350	35	54,179	Joe Skurski/Paul Erickson

Playoffs: None.

All-Star Team: 1B-Bob Johnson, Fond du Lac; **2B**-Emil Piscopo, Wisconsin Rapids; **3B**-Tom Murphy, Sheboygan; **SS**-Earl Willis, Oshkosh; **OF**-John Gierek, Fond du Lac; Vern Grace, Green Bay; Chuck Oertel, Appleton; **C**-Stan Grossman, Oshkosh; **P**-John Wilson, Wausau; Bill Eckland, Appleton; Tony DeVelis, Sheboygan; Ed Poquette, Green Bay; **Manager**-James Adlam, Fond du Lac.

BA: David Garcia, Oshkosh, .369
Runs: Earl Willis, Oshkosh, 121
Hits: David Garcia, Oshkosh, 157
RBIs: David Garcia, Oshkosh, 127

HRs: David Garcia, Oshkosh, 23
Wins: Walter Yowell, Wisconsin Rapids, 18
SOs: Earl McClellan, Sheboygan, 216
ERA: Walter Yowell, Wisconsin Rapids, 1.90

Ind Mexican League
President: Dr. Eduardo Quijano Pitman

Standings	W	L	Pct.	GB	Manager
Veracruz Azules**	49	35	.583	—	Angel Castro
Monterrey Sultanes.............	46	38	.548	3	Lazaro Salazar/Daniel Rios
Torreon Algodoneros..........	45	39	.536	4	Memo Garibay
Veracruz Aguila..................	43	41	.512	6	Santos Amaro
San Luis Potosi Tuneros* ..	42	42	.500	7	Jose Luis Gomez
Jalisco Charros	40	44	.476	9	Quincey Trouppe
Mexico City Diablos Rojos	37	47	.440	12	Ernesto Carmona/Burnis Wright/Marvin Williams/Basilio Rosell
Nuevo Laredo Tecolotes.....	34	50	.369	15	Salvador Hernandez/Ismael Montalvo/Ezequiel Cruz

Playoff: Veracruz Azules 4 games, San Luis Potosi 1.

BA: Angel Castro, Veracruz Azules, .354
Hits: Angel Castro, Veracruz Azules, 118
RBIs: Angel Castro, Veracruz Azules, 79
   Rene Gonzalez, San Luis Potosi, 79

HRs: Angel Castro, Veracruz Azules, 22
Wins: James LaMarque, Mexico City, 19
SOs: Lino Donoso, Veracruz Aguila, 197
ERA: Lino Donoso, Veracruz Aguila, 2.55

1951 Interleague Post Season Play

World Series
New York (American) 4 games, New York (National) 2

Junior World Series
Milwaukee (American Association) 4 games, Montreal (International) 2
Total Attendance: 59,216

Dixie Series
Birmingham (Southern Association) 4 games, Houston (Texas) 2
Total Attendance: 67,605

1951 Major League Farm Systems

American League

1. Boston (8): Louisville, Birmingham, Scranton, Roanoke, San Jose, Oneonta, High Point-Thomasville, Marion.
2. Chicago (8): Sacramento, Memphis, Colorado Springs, Waterloo, Hot Springs, Superior, Madisonville, Wisconsin Rapids.
3. Cleveland (12): San Diego, Dallas, Wilkes-Barre, Wichita, Harrisburg, Cedar Rapids, Spartanburg, Bakersfield, Ft. Smith, Daytona Beach, Batavia, Green Bay.
4. Detroit (8): Toledo, Little Rock, Williamsport, Durham, Davenport, Richmond (IN), Jamestown, Wausau.
5. New York (14): Kansas City, San Francisco, Beaumont, Muskegon, Binghamton, Norfolk, Quincy, Amsterdam, Twin Falls, Joplin, La Grange, Newark, McAlester, Fond du Lac.
6. Philadelphia (8): Savannah, Lincoln, Fayetteville, Salisbury (MD), Rome (NY), Cordele, Lexington, Corning.
7. St. Louis (11): Toronto, San Antonio, Dayton, Wichita Falls, Anderson, Pine Bluff, Aberdeen, Redding, Pittsburg (KS), Ada, Appleton.
8. Washington (7): Chattanooga, Havana, Charlotte, Erie, Roanoke Rapids, Orlando, Fulton.

National League

9. Boston (10): Milwaukee, Atlanta, Hartford, Denver, Hagerstown, Evansville, Ventura, Eau Claire, Quebec, Bluefield.
10. Brooklyn (19): St. Paul, Montreal, Mobile, Ft. Worth, Elmira, Pueblo, Miami (FL), Lancaster, Newport News, Asheville, Santa Barbara, Greenwood (MS), Billings, Bisbee-Douglas, Valdosta, Ponca City, Hazard, Hornell, Sheboygan.
11. Chicago (14): Springfield (MA), Los Angeles, Nashville, Grand Rapids, Des Moines, Greensboro, Rock Hill, Visalia, Sioux Falls, Clovis, Topeka, Carthage, Rutherford County, Janesville.
12. Cincinnati (5): Tulsa, Charleston (WV), Columbia, Ogden, Welch.
13. New York (15): Minneapolis, Ottawa, Jacksonville, Sioux City, Sunbury, Knoxville, St. Cloud, Idaho Falls, Muskogee, Bristol, Sanford, Springfield (OH), Lawton, Lenoir, Oshkosh.
14. Philadelphia (12): Baltimore, Schenectady, Wilmington, Terre Haute, Pittsfield, Grand Forks, Salt Lake City, Salina, Elizabethton, Klamath Falls, Lima, Bradford.
15. Pittsburgh (14): Indianapolis, Hollywood, New Orleans, Charleston (SC), Waco, Burlington, Modesto, Butler, Hutchinson, Eugene, Brunswick, Bartlesville, Mayfield, Salisbury (NC).
16. St. Louis (16): Columbus (OH), Rochester, Houston, Columbus (GA), Omaha, Winston-Salem, Allentown, Lynchburg, Tri-City, Fresno, Pocatello, St. Joseph, Johnson City, Goldsboro, Albany (GA), Hamilton.

1951 No-Hitters

Date	Pitcher	Team	League	Opponent	Score
4-20	Hugh Lott/				
	Vachel Perkins	Pine Bluff	Cotton States	Hot Springs	6-2
4-21	Norman Morton	New Orleans	Southern Assoc.	Little Rock	1-0 (5)
4-28	Keith Kelley	Lancaster	Interstate	Wilmington	10-0
4-29	Juan Ravello	Hazard	Mountain States	Harlan	10-0
5-6	Cliff Chambers	Pittsburgh	National	Boston	3-0
5-10	Darvin Chrisco	Monroe	Cotton States	Hot Springs	5-0
5-15	Karl Spooner	Hornell	PONY	Bradford	15-1
5-18	David Charles	Burlington	Carolina	Greensboro	3-0 (7)
5-20	Robert Umfleet	Goldsboro	Coastal Plain	Wilson	1-0 (7)
5-20	Rudy Lorona	Artesia	Longhorn	San Angelo	6-0
5-26	Robert Betancourt	Tifton	Georgia-Florida	Americus	4-1
5-27	Paul Calvert	Seattle	Pacific Coast	Sacramento	4-0
5-28	Dave Hillman	Rock Hill	Tri-State	Greenwood	9-0 (P, 7)
6-4	Paul Stuffel	Schenectady	Eastern	Elmira	6-3
6-7	Harry Clifton	Headland	Alabama-Florida	Panama City	19-2
6-8	John Murff	Texas City	Gulf Coast	Harlingen	6-0
6-9	William Howard	Paducah	Kitty	Fulton	0-1 (10)
6-13	Fred Pittman	Wilson	Coastal Plain	Rocky Mount	2-0
6-14	Ron Kline	Bartlesville	KOM	Pittsburg	5-1
6-14	Robert Ennis	Richmond	Piedmont	Lynchburg	6-0
6-14	William Minton	Salisbury	Interstate	Harrisburg	0-2
6-15	Thomas Herrin	Scranton	Eastern	Elmira	5-0 (7)
6-17	George Bamberger	Ottawa	International	Toronto	1-0
6-17	Ed Poquette	Green Bay	Wisconsin State	Sheboygan	4-0 (7)
6-18	Vern Edmunds	Yuma	Southwest Int'l	Bisbee-Douglas	7-2
6-19	Mike Bycofsky	Welch	Appalachian	Bristol	7-1
6-20	Gene Black	Valley	Georgia-Alabama	La Grange	4-0
6-21	Richard Midkiff	Brownsville	Gulf Coast	Port Arthur	1-0
6-24	Tom Fine	San Antonio	Texas	Tulsa	2-0 (7)
6-25	Ted Morris	Olean	PONY	Hornell	6-0
6-26	Bob Harrison	Flint	Central	Grand Rapids	0-2 (12)
7-1	Bob Feller	Cleveland	American	Detroit	2-1
7-1	Glenn Hittner	Ventura	California	Stockton	0-1 (6)
7-2	Andrew Pane	Pauls Valley	Sooner State	Lawton	5-0
7-2	Ralph Romero	Salt Lake City	Pioneer	Ogden	5-0
7-2	Dick Fiedler	Quincy	Three-I	Evansville	5-0
7-3	George Vidal	Hammond	Evangeline	New Iberia	9-0
7-4	Thomas Warren	Miami	KOM	Iola	1-0 (7)
7-6	Pat McCullough	Lockport	Middle Atlantic	Oil City	6-0
7-7	Jack Cardey	Hammond	Evangeline	Crowley	9-1
7-7	Robert Stowe	Greenville	Tri-State	Greenwood	6-0 (7)
7-12	Allie Reynolds	New York	American	Cleveland	1-0
7-17	Alois Zilian	Lakeland	Florida Int'l	West Palm Beach	9-1 (8)
7-18	Tom Casagrande	Wilmington	Interstate	York	0-1 (10)
7-20	Taylor Phillips	Waycross	Georgia-Florida	Moultrie	11-0
7-21	Umberto Flammini	Nashville	Southern Assoc.	Atlanta	2-0
7-21	Burton Barkelew	Salt Lake City	Pioneer	Great Falls	7-0 (7)
7-22	Tom Simpson	Buffalo	International	Toronto	3-0 (7)
7-27	Leon Foulk	Des Moines	Western	Denver	5-0
7-28	Ernest Nichols	Lancaster	Interstate	Salisbury	6-2
7-30	Fred Hengeveld	Mooreshie	N. Carolina State	Lexington	0-1
7-31	Albert McKinney	New Bern	Coastal Plain	Wilson	6-0 (7)
8-2	Vern Williamson	Little Rock	Southern Assoc.	Birmingham	2-0 (7)
8-4	Marvin Williams	Billings	Pioneer	Boise	3-0
8-4	George Uhaze	Oneonta	Canadian-American	Pittsfield	7-0 (7)
8-4	Gene Bone	Johnson City	Appalachian	Elizabethton	5-0 (7)
8-5	Basil Mitchell	Goldsboro	Coastal Plain	Roanoke Rapids	6-0
8-8	Armin Somonte	Ardmore	Sooner State	Lawton	18-0
8-12	Don Shaffer	Valdosta	Georgia-Florida	Americus	1-0 (6)
8-12	Ken Kimball	Idaho Falls	Pioneer	Great Falls	3-0 (P)
8-14	William Roland	Lincolnton	Western Carolina	Granite Falls	10-0
8-16	Buck Thiel	Milwaukee	American Assoc.	Toledo	5-0 (7)
8-18	William Talbot	Dothan	Alabama-Florida	Panama City	7-0
8-19	Oliverio Ortiz	Juarez	Southwest Int'l	El Centro	2-0
8-20	Jack Heinen	San Jose	California	Stockton	1-0
8-20	Tom Casagrande	Wilmington	Interstate	Harrisburg	4-0 (7)
8-23	Jim Barnhardt	Portsmouth	Piedmont	Richmond	8-0
8-24	Robert Reich	Muskogee	Western Assoc.	Enid	6-0
8-24	Rudy Dillard	Valdosta	Georgia-Florida	Americus	2-1
8-24	Bucky Stewart	New Bern	Coastal Plain	Wilson	1-0
8-26#	Ramon Salgado	Texas City	Gulf Coast	Harlingen	1-0 (7)
9-1	William Wolf	Appleton	Wisconsin State	Oshkosh	1-0 (7)
9-2	Larry Schadel	Billings	Pioneer	Great Falls	2-0
9-4	Marvin Deal	Colonial Heights-Petersburg	Virginia	Suffolk	12-0 (PO)
9-4	Stanley Burat	Mt. Vernon	Miss.-Ohio Valley	Centralia	10-0 (PO)
9-7	Warren Hacker	Los Angeles	Pacific Coast	Seattle	4-0
9-28	Allie Reynolds	New York	American	Boston	8-0

#Started on 8-26, ended by curfew, and finished 8-27 in the afternoon.

Number in parentheses indicates innings if other than nine; "P" indicates perfect game; "PO" indicates playoff game.

THIS DATE IN MINOR LEAGUE HISTORY

January 25, 1951, Tom Fairweather, one-time head of three minor leagues at the same time, who had been associated with the game as an executive as early as 1907, died at his farm near Des Moines, Iowa. One of the patriarchs of the minors, Fairweather long was a power in the councils of the National Association and the shaping of its policies.

February 20, 1951, Harry S. "Steamboat" Johnson, colorful minor league umpire who handled an indicator for 31 years, including 27 seasons in the Southern Association, died in Memphis, Tennessee, at age 66.

March 17, 1951, Sam Bankhead, brother of pitcher Dan Bankhead of the Dodgers, became the first black to manage a club in Organized Ball, when he signed to pilot Farnham of the Provincial League. Bankhead, a shortstop, was slated to be a playing manager.

April 22, 1951, Oscar "Ox" Eckhardt, 49, who averaged .366 at bat in 13 seasons (1928-1940) in the majors and minors, died at Yorktown, Texas, of a heart attack. Although not a slugger, making only 67 home runs out of a total of 2,783 hits, Eckhardt compiled some fantastic batting marks despite awkward form at the plate. He was a lefthanded hitter, yet most of his drives went into left field. Ox had big league trials with the Boston Braves and Brooklyn, but was unable to untrack himself in the majors as a batter or fielder. Eckhardt hit .414 in 1933 with Mission in the Pacific Coast League and .399 in 1935. His averages during his stay with Mission from 1932 to 1935 were .371, .414, .378 and .399. In 1935, Ox beat out Joe DiMaggio for the Pacific Coast League batting championship by one point, bunting safely twice in the final doubleheader although he had bunted only once before in five years, to win the title. He won five batting titles in his career.

April 24, 1951, Kyle Rote, former All-American football star at Southern Methodist University, bonus choice of the New York Giants of the NFL, made his baseball debut with Corpus Christi of the Class B Gulf Coast League. Two nights later, Rote pounded three home runs in a game against Galveston. In his 22 games with the

Aces, outfielder Rote made 23 hits, including seven round-trippers, and drove in 13 runs. He turned in his uniform on May 23 to report to the football training camp of the Giants.

May 8, 1951, OF Bobby Cherry of Salt Lake City, Pioneer League, banged into the fence so hard while chasing a drive by Dick Small of Billings, that his arm slipped through a crack and he was stuck with the ball lying only four feet away, resulting in an inside-the-park homer for Small.

May 13, 1951, Rex Barney, recently assigned to Ft. Worth, Texas League, by Brooklyn to gain control, lost his first start, 6-2 to Houston, and walked a record 16 batters in 7-2/3 innings.

May 13, 1951, Willie Mays, young flychaser, enjoyed one of the most productive two weeks at bat ever experienced in Organized Ball during Minneapolis' first homestand. In 14 games, the Millers rookie tagged opposing pitchers for 34 hits in 56 at bats, a .607 pace.

May 23, 1951, Rex Barney of Ft. Worth, Texas League, walked seven batters in 1-2/3 frames, making the former Brooklyn righthander's record with the Cats 30 walks, 12 hits and 16 runs in 12-1/3 innings.

May 29, 1951, Suffolk, Virginia League, put 19 batters on base but failed to score in losing to Colonial Heights-Petersburg, 11-0. William Garthwaite allowed eight hits, walked eight and hit one, but struck out only three, and there were two errors. Three double plays helped to end the scoring threats.

June 2, 1951, Tarboro, Coastal Plain League, scored 24 times in one inning, the fifth, to wallop Wilson 31-4. Shortstop Bill Carr collected eight total bases in the big round with a homer and two doubles. 25 men batted before the first out was made. The A's made 17 hits for 35 total bases in the frame as 29 men batted. Carr appeared four times, getting a walk in addition to his three hits. Wilson employed seven pitchers in the big frame.

June 10, 1951, Ottis Johnson of Dothan, Alabama-Florida League, one of the leading hitters in the Class D circuit, died of a fractured skull received eight days earlier when hit by a pitched ball thrown by southpaw Harry Clifton of Headland. Johnson was hitting at a .393 clip and had blasted 10 homers. He was 24 years old, married and the father of one child. His death was the first in Organized Ball resulting from a pitched ball since Ballinger outfielder James "Stormy" Davis died of injuries from a pitch that struck him July 3, 1947, in a game with Sweetwater.

June 11, 1951, Manager Elmer Yoter of Marion, Ohio-Indiana League, was suspended indefinitely for allegedly instructing his team to stall and "for turning the game into a travesty." Newark won 32-6. It was claimed that the Sox deliberately dropped flies and fumbled easy grounders.

June 16, 1951, A lightning bolt killed Andy Strong, 23-year-old Crowley outfielder, in an Evangeline League game at Alexandria, Louisiana. Strong had taken his position in center field during the last half of the sixth inning when the bolt struck, killing him instantly. None of the other players were injured. A mild-appearing summer thundercloud hung over Bringhurst Field as the game began, but there was no threat of a storm.

June 25, 1951, Roy Price, veteran southpaw of Houma, Evangeline League, turned in one of the best strikeout performances in the history of Organized Ball, when he whiffed 23 Lafayette batters in nine innings, while walking eight and allowing five hits in an 8-1 victory. On June 17, Price had fanned 23 Hammond batters in 14 frames.

June 29, 1951, Dick Conway, hard-hitting 19-year-old catcher of Twin Falls, Pioneer League, died on the playing field at Ogden, Utah, after being struck over the heart by a thrown ball during a warmup session.

July 4, 1951, McAlester hurler Dee Sanders set a Sooner State League record when he gave up his first walk in 75-1/3 innings in a game with Ada. It may be the all-time Organized Ball record.

July 7, 1951, Emmett Ashford, the first black umpire in Organized Ball, broke in on the Southwest International League staff, working behind the plate for the game between Yuma and Mexicali.

July 8, 1951, Floods in Kansas virtually put the Western Association out of business. Parks at Topeka and Salina were under 10 feet of water and some of the teams were marooned and unable to get to their destinations.

July 16, 1951, The Class C Border League collapsed, leaving 49 circuits operating under the NA banner.

July 22, 1951, Midland's Longhorn League game at Vernon was postponed because of the heat, with temperature readings of 104 degrees.

July 22, 1951, A Sunday afternoon Billings-Twin Falls game in the Pioneer League was postponed because of 100-degree heat at Billings, Montana.

July 25, 1951, Five of the six umpires of the Alabama-Florida League staff resigned in a dispute with league president G.D. Halstead. The arbiters quit when Halstead failed to comply immediately with their demand for the suspension of Chase Riddle, Ozark player-manager, and Bob Odenheimer, Dothan catcher.

July 26, 1951, Granite Falls ended a 26-game losing streak in the Western Carolina League by defeating Marion 5-4. The Class D club's skein of reverses was far from the minor league record of 38 straight defeats, set by Muskogee in the old Southwestern League in 1923.

August 1, 1951, The 31-year Organized Ball career of George "Specs" Toporcer, the first major league infielder to wear glasses, ended when an eye ailment forced him to quit as manager of the Buffalo International League club. Toporcer became blind when treatments failed to save his sight.

August 3, 1951, The grandstands, portions of the bleachers and equipment of the local club and of the visiting Grand Forks Chiefs were destroyed by an early morning fire at the Aberdeen, Northern League, park. Damage was estimated at $150,000.

August 13, 1951, Pitcher-manager Tony Freitas, former Major Leaguer approaching his 44th birthday, became a 20-game winner for Modesto, California League, by defeating Santa Barbara 12-1.

August 19, 1951, Wenceslao Gonzalez of Juarez, Southwest International League, became the first pitcher in Organized Ball to win 30 games this season when he blanked El Centro 2-0.

August 20, 1951, Billy Cesta, popular 31-year-old Houston shortstop, was sidelined for the balance of the season after being stricken with polio.

August 26, 1951, Although Norton won from Hazard by the top-heavy score of 25-4, scoring 11 runs in the fourth inning, the Mountain States League game was completed in one hour and 50 minutes.

August 27, 1951, The PONY League game in Olean between the Oilers and Batavia was disrupted by a skunk who wouldn't be chased by either the players or the umpires. The contest, after a long delay, was completed before virtually empty stands.

September 1, 1951, Earl Caldwell, 46-year-old righthander, rapped a single, double and homer as he pitched Harlingen, Gulf Coast League, to a 14-5 win over Brownsville for his 19th victory of the season.

September 1, 1951, Tony Ponce of Phoenix, Southwest International League, was believed to have established a modern Organized Ball record by pitching his 38th consecutive game of the season without relief. Ponce marked up his 25th win of the year compared to 16 losses, when he defeated Yuma 4-2. He hurled 38 complete games. (Glenn Liebhardt had 45 complete games in 1906 for Memphis, 40 successive, while compiling a 35-11 record.)

September 1, 1951, Granite Falls, Western Carolina League, winding up the season with a 5-4 loss, suffered its 33rd successive defeat. The club previously had lost 26 in a row before starting the record string and dropped 59 of its last 60 games. Granite Falls won only 14 games and lost 96 for a percentage of .127, finishing 57 games behind Morganton in a 110-game schedule.

September 9, 1951, Nashville first baseman Jack Harshman set an all-time Southern Association record on the final day of the season when he smashed his sixth home run with the bases full, one over Carl Sawatski's previous mark, set with Nashville in 1949. Harshman finished with 47 round-trippers, leading the league, and he batted in more runs (141) than the number of hits he collected (136).

September 20, 1951, Lefty O'Doul retired as manager of the San Francisco Seals of the Pacific Coast League after 17 seasons at the helm.

November 19, 1951, Lefty O'Doul's barnstorming Americans closed their triumphant tour of Japan, the U.S. team winning 13, losing one and tying two.

November 29, 1951, Lefty O'Doul, who managed San Francisco, Pacific Coast League, for 17 years, was recently signed as pilot of the San Diego Padres.

December 18, 1951, Spencer Abbott, 74, who was connected with the game since 1898 as a player, manager, umpire and scout until retiring in 1950 because of illness, died in Washington, D.C.

THE DECLINE: 1952 - 1962

*N*o one really expected the minors to continue at the postwar heights. Fifty-nine leagues and 400-plus cities were too many. Yet it was impossible to foresee that within a decade more than 300 cities would lose their minor league clubs. Those that held on barely clung to existence. Experts predicted the total demise of minor league baseball.

Forty-three leagues started the 1952 season. By 1956 the number was down to 27, and by 1959 there were only 21. The minors thought they knew the culprit. During the boom years of the late 1940s, TV was just beginning, and other than the World Series, virtually no games were televised. There was very little national radio. This was changing and minor league owners loudly protested that the unrestricted telecasting and broadcasting of major league games into minor league markets were killing their game.

But the amount of major league games available during the decline in the 1950s was minimal with only the Saturday afternoon Game of the Week telecast, plus the radio Game of the Day.

Major league attendance was also slipping, but the big leagues had a solution for weak franchises: move to the good minor league towns. In 1953 the Boston Braves moved to Milwaukee and had phenomenal success. In 1954 the St. Louis Browns took Baltimore, and 1955 saw the Philadelphia A's in Kansas City. With the move of the Dodgers and Giants to the West Coast in 1958, three PCL clubs - Hollywood, Los Angeles and San Francisco - had to find new homes.

Much of baseball's decline was not of its own making but rather a mirror of change within the nation. Baseball was no longer a priority. Television boomed, but it was not baseball on TV that was keeping the fans at home. For an evening's entertainment a family could watch "Milton Berle," "I Love Lucy" and a dozen other shows. Earlier, people were looking for a way out of hot, stuffy houses; now with air conditioning there was no need to leave home. Families were moving to the suburbs and the ballpark was no longer just around the corner. The sudden death playoff between the Baltimore Colts and New York Giants in 1958 signaled the rise of professional football and baseball was to take a back seat to the new glamorous TV sport.

The minors also had themselves to blame. Many of the ballparks, built as WPA projects during the Depression or hastily constructed after the war, were deteriorating. They were no longer attractive places to spend an evening. Clubs had little money for fix up and local governments, which had earlier embraced stadiums as civic gathering places, allocated very little for improvements. Many stadiums were torn down..

The major leagues were worried also. Their source of talent for over 50 years was drying up. Something needed to be done. Football and basketball used colleges as a talent pool, but college baseball could not be counted on to supply the players. At a meeting on Aug. 2, 1956, commissioner Ford Frick appointed a "Save the Minors" committee. In 1957 $500,000 was appropriated to create a stabilization fund, with the primary goal to help teams in the lower minors.

The Professional Baseball Fund continued for the next three years, but it was not enough. In 1959 it was discontinued, and in its place the Player Development and Promotion program was instituted, financed with $1 million dollars from the big leagues. The minors had requested 50 percent of the big leagues' TV revenue, and were turned down. Instead, the major leagues voted to pay each club for finishing the season, ranging from $22,500 for Triple A clubs down to $3,000 for class D clubs.

The decline continued. Now Triple A and Double A teams were having difficulty. The cream of the cities had been taken by major league moves and expansion was in the offing. With Branch Rickey's plan for a new major league, the Continental League, more Triple A and Double A cities were talking big league baseball, further hurting the credibility of the minor league product. The Southern Association which in 1949 drew nearly two million fans drew only 614,000 in 1959. Two years later the league folded.

By 1962 it was clear that the two previous efforts had failed. On May 18, 1962, the major leagues unanimously passed the Player Development Plan. Major League baseball guaranteed that at least a hundred minor league clubs would survive. The classifications of B, C and D were abolished and replaced with Class A. The Eastern, South Atlantic and Texas Leagues became Class AA, and two Triple-A leagues remained. Twenty clubs at both the Triple-A and Double-A were guaranteed, and 60 clubs were assured at the A and rookie levels. The big leagues agreed to pay all salaries above $800 per month in Triple-A; all but $150 per month in Double-A salaries; and Class A teams had to pitch in $50 per month per player. The minor leagues were now the wards of the big leagues.

1952

American League
President: William Harridge

Standings	W	L	Pct.	GB	Attend.	Manager
New York Yankees............	95	59	.617	—	1,629,665	Casey Stengel
Cleveland Indians	93	61	.604	2	1,444,607	Al Lopez
Chicago White Sox............	81	73	.526	14	1,231,675	Paul Richards
Philadelphia Athletics.........	79	75	.513	16	627,100	Jimmy Dykes
Washington Senators	78	76	.506	17	699,457	Bucky Harris
Boston Red Sox	76	78	.494	19	1,115,750	Lou Boudreau
St. Louis Browns	64	90	.416	31	518,796	Rogers Hornsby/Marty Marion
Detroit Tigers....................	50	104	.325	45	1,026,846	Red Rolfe/Fred Hutchinson

BA: Ferris Fain, Philadelphia, .327
Runs: Larry Doby, Cleveland, 104
Hits: Nellie Fox, Chicago, 192
RBIs: Al Rosen, Cleveland, 105
HRs: Larry Doby, Cleveland, 32

Wins: Bobby Shantz, Philadelphia, 24
SOs: Allie Reynolds, New York, 160
ERA: Allie Reynolds, New York, 2.06
Pct: Bobby Shantz, Philadelphia, .774, 24-7

National League
President: Warren C. Giles

Standings	W	L	Pct.	GB	Attend.	Manager
Brooklyn Dodgers...............	96	57	.627	—	1,088,704	Chuck Dressen
New York Giants	92	62	.597	4½	984,940	Leo Durocher
St. Louis Cardinals	88	66	.571	8½	913,113	Eddie Stanky
Philadelphia Phillies	87	67	.565	9½	755,417	Eddie Sawyer/Steve O'Neill
Chicago Cubs.....................	77	77	.500	19½	1,024,836	Phil Cavarretta
Cincinnati Reds..................	69	85	.448	27½	604,197	Luke Sewell/Earle Brucker/ Rogers Hornsby
Boston Braves.....................	64	89	.418	32	281,278	Tommy Holmes/Charlie Grimm
Pittsburgh Pirates	42	112	.273	54½	686,673	Bill Meyer

BA: Stan Musial, St. Louis, .336
Runs: Solly Hemus, St. Louis, 105
Stan Musial, St. Louis, 105
Hits: Stan Musial, St. Louis, 194
RBIs: Hank Sauer, Chicago, 121

HRs: Ralph Kiner, Pittsburgh, 37
Hank Sauer, Chicago, 37
Wins: Robin Roberts, Philadelphia, 28
SOs: Warren Spahn, Boston, 183
ERA: Hoyt Wilhelm, New York, 2.43
Pct: Hoyt Wilhelm, New York, .833, 15-3

(Open) Pacific Coast League
President: Clarence H. Rowland

Standings	W	L	Pct.	GB	Attend.	Manager
Hollywood Stars (15)........	109	71	.606	—	311,043	Fred Haney
Oakland Oaks	104	76	.578	5	234,952	Mel Ott
Seattle Rainiers	96	84	.533	13	287,333	Bill Sweeney
Portland Beavers...............	92	88	.511	17	322,736	Clay Hopper
San Diego Padres	88	92	.489	21	290,456	Lefty O'Doul
Los Angeles Angels (11)....	87	93	.483	22	359,161	Stan Hack
San Francisco Seals	78	102	.433	31	198,778	Tommy Heath
Sacramento Solons	66	114	.367	43	159,776	Joe Gordon

MVP-Johnny Lindell, Hollywood.

BA: Bob Boyd, Seattle, .320
Runs: Carlos Bernier, Hollywood, 105
Hits: Artie Wilson, Seattle, 216
RBIs: Harold Gilbert, Oakland, 118

HRs: Max West, Los Angeles, 35
Wins: Johnny Lindell, Hollywood, 24
SOs: Johnny Lindell, Hollywood, 190
ERA: Red Adams, Portland, 2.17

AAA American Association
President: Bruce Dudley

Standings	W	L	Pct.	GB	Attend.	Manager
Milwaukee Brewers (9)	101	53	.656	—	195,839	Charlie Grimm/Red Smith/ Bucky Walters
Kansas City Blues (5).........	89	65	.578	12	243,974	George Selkirk
St. Paul Saints (10)	80	74	.519	21	125,769	Clay Bryant
Minneapolis Millers (13)....	79	75	.513	22	120,185	Frank Genovese
Louisville Colonels (1)......	77	77	.500	24	132,626	Pinky Higgins
Indianapolis Indians (3)......	75	79	.487	26	165,220	Gene Desautels
Columbus Red Birds (16)...	68	85	.444	32½	78,132	Johnny Keane
Toledo Mud Hens/ Charleston Senators#.......	46	107	.301	54½	164,641	Rollie Hemsley

#Toledo moved to Charleston June 23.

Playoffs: Milwaukee 4 games, St. Paul 0; Kansas City 4 games, Minneapolis 1.
Finals: Kansas City 4 games, Milwaukee 3.

All-Star Team: 1B-Don Bollweg, Kansas City; **2B**-Jack Cassini, St Paul; **3B**-Robert Wilson, St Paul; **SS**-Daryl Spencer, Minneapolis; **OF**-Bill Skowron, Kansas City; Bill Renna, Kansas City; Clint Hartung, Minneapolis; Dave Pope, Indianapolis; **C**-Ray Katt,

Minneapolis; Roy Partee, Kansas City; **Util**-Vic Power, Kansas City; **P**-Eddie Erautt, Kansas City; Edward Cereghino, Kansas City; Stu Miller, Columbus; Don Liddle, Milwaukee; **MVP**-Don Bollweg, Kansas City.

BA: Dave Pope, Indianapolis, .352
Runs: Billy Bruton, Milwaukee, 130
Hits: Billy Bruton, Milwaukee, 211
RBIs: Bill Skowron, Kansas City, 134

HRs: Bill Skowron, Kansas City, 31
Wins: Eddie Erautt, Kansas City, 21
SOs: Don Liddle, Milwaukee, 159
ERA: Don Liddle, Milwaukee, 2.70

AAA International League
President: Frank J. Shaughnessy

Standings	W	L	Pct.	GB	Attend.	Manager
Montreal Royals (10).........	95	56	.629	—	313,160	Walter Alston
Syracuse Chiefs	88	66	.571	8½	141,751	Bruno Betzel
Rochester Red Wings (16)..	80	74	.519	16½	232,271	Harry Walker
Toronto Maple Leafs (7)...	78	76	.506	18½	446,040	Joseph Becker/Burleigh Grimes
Buffalo Bisons (4)	71	83	.461	25½	152,137	Jack Tighe/Schoolboy Rowe
Baltimore Orioles (14)......	70	84	.455	26½	153,828	Don Heffner
Ottawa Athletics (6)...........	65	85	.433	29½	153,152	Frank Skaff
Springfield Cubs (11)	65	88	.425	31	107,675	William Kelly

Playoffs: Montreal 4 games, Toronto 3; Rochester 4 games, Syracuse 0.
Finals: Rochester 4 games, Montreal 2.

All-Star Team: 1B-Ed Stevens, Toronto; **2B**-Junior Gilliam, Montreal; **3B**-Don Richmond, Rochester; **SS**-Jim Pendleton, Montreal; **OF**-Carmen Mauro, Montreal; Harry Walker, Rochester; Roy Weatherly, Baltimore; **C**-Tim Thompson, Montreal; **P**-Bob Keegan, Syracuse; Mal Mallette, Montreal; **MVP**-Junior Gilliam, Montreal.

BA: Frank Carswell, Buffalo, .344
Runs: Junior Gilliam, Montreal, 111
Hits: Don Richmond, Rochester, 190
RBIs: Ed Stevens, Toronto, 113
HRs: Frank Carswell, Buffalo, 30

Wins: Bob Keegan, Syracuse, 20
Charles Bishop, Ottawa, 20
SOs: Duke Markell, Toronto, 120
ERA: Marion Fricano, Ottawa, 2.26

AA Southern Association
President: Charles A. Hurth

Standings	W	L	Pct.	GB	Attend.	Manager
Chattanooga Lookouts (8) ..	86	66	.566	—	252,703	Cal Ermer
Atlanta Crackers (9)...........	82	72	.532	5	232,994	Dixie Walker
Mobile Bears (10)..............	80	73	.523	6½	158,989	Ed Head
Memphis Chicks (2)	81	74	.522	6½	174,830	Luke Appling
New Orleans Pelicans (15).	80	75	.516	7½	232,043	Danny Murtaugh
Nashville Vols (13)............	73	79	.480	13	113,193	Hugh Poland
Little Rock Travelers (4)	68	85	.444	18½	121,482	Willis Hudlin
Birmingham Barons (1)......	64	90	.416	23	177,898	Al Vincent/Red Mathis

Playoffs: Memphis defeated New Orleans 3-2 in a one game playoff for fourth place. Memphis 4 games, Chattanooga 0; Mobile 4 games, Atlanta 2.
Finals: Memphis 4 games, Mobile 2, one tie.

All-Star Team: 1B-Norm Larker, Mobile; **2B**-Forrest "Spook" Jacobs, Mobile; **3B**-Rance Pless, Nashville; **SS**-Don Zimmer, Mobile; **OF**-Frank Thomas, New Orleans; Dusty Rhodes, Nashville; Bill Antonello, Nashville; Paul Smith, New Orleans; Charles Coles, Mobile; **C**-Jack Paepke, New Orleans; Ralph Novotney, Nashville; Dick Teed, Mobile; **Util**-Ellis Clary, Chattanooga; **P**-Norman Morton, New Orleans; Woody Rich, Memphis; John Dixon, Chattanooga; Peter Modica, Nashville; Al Sima, Chattanooga; Robert Ludwick, Mobile.

BA: Rance Pless, Nashville, .364
Runs: Frank Thomas, New Orleans, 112
Hits: Rance Pless, Nashville, 196
RBIs: Frank Thomas, New Orleans, 131
HRs: Frank Thomas, New Orleans, 35

SBs: Don Nicholas, Memphis, 84
Wins: Al Sima, Chattanooga, 24
SOs: Al Worthington, Nashville, 152
ERA: Wade Browning, Mobile, 2.90

AA Texas League
President: J. Alvin Gardner

Standings	W	L	Pct.	GB	Attend.	Manager
Dallas Eagles (3)................	92	69	.571	—	266,532	Dutch Meyer
Ft. Worth Cats (10)............	86	75	.534	6	180,559	Bobby Bragan
Shreveport Sports	84	77	.522	8	153,127	Mickey Livingston
Oklahoma City Indians........	82	79	.509	10	146,972	Tom Tatum
San Antonio Missions (7)...	79	82	.491	13	110,001	Jo Jo White
Tulsa Oilers (12)................	78	83	.484	14	155,064	Joe Schultz
Beaumont Roughnecks (5) .	77	84	.478	15	101,717	Harry Craft
Houston Buffalos (16)	66	95	.419	26	195,246	Al Hollingsworth

Playoffs: Oklahoma City 4 games, Dallas 2; Shreveport 4 games, Ft. Worth 0.
Finals: Shreveport 4 games, Oklahoma City 1.

*Won first-half **Won second-half ***Won both halves
Numbers after nicknames indicate farm system.
Affiliation listed at end of year.

412

BA: Grant Dunlap, Shreveport, .333
Runs: Joe Koppe, Shreveport, 99
Hits: Harry Elliott, Shreveport, 204
RBIs: Russ Burns, Oklahoma City, 120

HRs: Harry Heslet, San Antonio, 31
Wins: Dave Hoskins, Dallas, 22
SOs: John Gray, Beaumont, 151
ERA: Joe Landrum, Ft. Worth, 1.94

A Eastern League
President: Thomas H. Richardson

Standings	W	L	Pct.	GB	Attend.	Manager
Albany Senators (1)	82	54	.603	—	101,498	Jack Burns
Binghamton Triplets (5)	77	60	.562	5½	79,902	Jimmy Gleeson
Reading Indians (3)	75	63	.543	8	97,757	Kerby Farrell
Schenectady Blue Jays (14)	73	65	.529	10	81,912	Dan Carnevale
Elmira Pioneers (10)	72	68	.514	12	93,637	George Fallon
Scranton Miners (7)	66	73	.475	17½	64,221	Zack Taylor
Hartford Chiefs (9)	59	79	.428	24	36,281	Del Bissonette
Williamsport Tigers (4)	48	90	.348	35	52,737	Paul Campbell

Playoffs: Reading 4 games, Albany 1; Binghamton 4 games, Schenectady 3.
Finals: Binghamton 4 games, Reading 1.

All-Star Team: 1B-Paul Campbell, Williamsport; **2B-**Stanley Pawloski, Reading; **3B-**Frank Verdi, Binghamton; **3B-**Herbert Rossman, Albany; **SS-**Ted Kazanski, Schenectady; **OF-**Mike Lutz, Reading; Bill Smith, Hartford; Rufus "Jake" Crawford, Scranton; **C-**Jim Robertson, Binghamton; **P-**Charles Haag, Albany; Roberto Vargas, Reading; **Manager-**Jack Burns, Albany.

BA: Mike Lutz, Reading, .321
Runs: Arnold Spence, Albany, 89
Hits: Bill Smith, Hartford, 153
RBIs: Rufus "Jake" Crawford, Scranton, 93
　　Mike Lutz, Reading, 93

HRs: Rufus "Jake" Crawford, Scranton, 27
Wins: Charles Haag, Albany, 18
　　George Uhaze, Albany, 18
SOs: Ron Mrozinski, Schenectady, 148
ERA: George Uhaze, Albany, 2.13

A South Atlantic League
President: Earl Blue

Standings	W	L	Pct.	GB	Attend.	Manager
Columbia Reds (12)	100	54	.649	—	110,012	Ernie White
Columbus Cardinals (16)	87	67	.565	13	86,671	Sheldon "Chief" Bender
Montgomery Grays	86	68	.558	14	85,152	Charlie Metro
Macon Peaches (11)	83	71	.539	17	75,963	Edgar Hartness
Charleston Rebels (15)	78	75	.510	21½	70,175	Frank Oceak
Savannah Indians (6)	74	79	.484	25½	78,289	George Staller
Jacksonville Tars (13)	69	85	.448	31	60,409	Ben Geraghty
Augusta Tigers	38	116	.247	62	42,628	Bob Latshaw/Burl Storie/ Walter Snider/Charles Marshall

Playoffs: Macon 3 games, Columbia 0; Montgomery 3 games, Columbus 2.
Finals: Montgomery 4 games, Macon 2.

All-Star Team: 1B-Tom Hamilton, Savannah; **2B-**Frank DiPrima, Macon; **3B-**Robert Hyatt, Charleston; **SS-**John Berdella, Columbia; **OF-**Dick Greco, Montgomery; Leonard Morrison, Montgomery; Gilbert Daley, Columbus; Tom Burgess, Columbus; **C-**Ronald "Mike" Curnan, Columbus; **Util-**Bobby Ross Howard, Macon; **P-**Barney Martin, Columbia; Dennis Reeder, Columbus; **Manager-**Ernie White, Columbia.

BA: Tom Hamilton, Savannah, .343
Runs: Robert Wilson, Columbia, 112
Hits: Tom Hamilton, Savannah, 196
RBIs: Dick Greco, Montgomery, 135
HRs: Dick Greco, Montgomery, 24

Wins: Barney Martin, Columbia, 23
SOs: Barney Martin, Columbia, 174
ERA: George Dries, Charleston, 1.93
Pct: Dennis Reeder, Columbus, .769, 20-6

A Western League
President: Senator Edwin C. Johnson

Standings	W	L	Pct.	GB	Attend.	Manager
Denver Bears (15)	88	66	.571	—	461,419	Andy Cohen
Colorado Springs Sky Sox (2)	87	67	.565	1	170,041	Don Gutteridge
Omaha Cardinals (16)	86	68	.558	2	137,378	George Kissell
Sioux City (13)	83	71	.539	5	103,004	Ray Mueller
Pueblo Dodgers (10)	81	73	.526	7	122,746	William McCahan
Wichita Indians (3)	67	87	.435	21	116,703	Ralph Winegarner
Lincoln Athletics (6)	67	87	.435	21	61,483	Les Bell
Des Moines Bruins (11)	57	97	.370	31	62,597	Harry Strohm

Playoffs: Denver 3 games, Sioux City 1; Omaha 3 games, Colorado Springs 1.
Finals: Denver 3 games, Omaha 0.

All-Star Team: 1B-Ken Landenberger, Colorado Springs; **2B-**Earl Weaver, Omaha; **3B-**Chico Ibanez, Sioux City; **SS-**Sherwin Dixon, Omaha; **OF-**Bill Pinckard, Denver; Norman Postolese, Pueblo; Raymond Berns, Sioux City; **C-**Sam Hairston, Colorado Springs; **P-**Connie Johnson, Colorado Springs; Alberto Osorio, Denver; Edward Hrabcsak, Lincoln; Marvin Williams, Pueblo.

BA: Ed Phillips, Omaha, .320
Runs: Ken Landenberger, Colorado Springs, 112
Hits: Ken Landenberger, Colorado Springs, 183

RBIs: Ken Landenberger, Colorado Springs, 133
HRs: Bill Pinckard, Denver, 35
Wins: Alberto Osorio, Denver, 20
SOs: Connie Johnson, Colorado Springs, 233
ERA: Jim Singleton, Sioux City, 2.73

A Western International League
President: Robert B. Abel

Standings	W	L	Pct.	GB	Attend.	Manager
Victoria Tyees	94	55	.631	—	105,948	Cecil Garriott
Spokane Indians	91	64	.587	6	104,500	Don Osborn
Vancouver Capilanos	72	69	.511	18	119,533	Bill Schuster/Edo Vanni
Salem Senators	74	78	.487	21½	83,047	Hugh Luby
Yakima Bears	73	79	.480	22½	64,044	Dario Lodigiani
Lewiston Broncs	71	82	.464	25	62,366	Bill Brenner
Tri-City Braves (14)	67	79	.459	25½	54,022	Charlie Gassaway
Wenatchee Chiefs	58	94	.382	37½	52,660	Richard Adams

Playoffs: None.

All-Star Team: 1B-Richard Adams, Wenatchee; **2B-**Hugh Luby, Salem; **3B-**Dario Lodigiani, Yakima; **SS-**Jim Clark, Victoria; **OF-**Cecil Garriott, Victoria; Edward Murphy, Spokane; Melvin Wasley, Spokane; **C-**John Ritchey, Vancouver; **P-**Robert Greenwood, Tri-City; Ben Lorino, Victoria.

BA: Walt Pocekay, Wenatchee, .352
Runs: Milton Smith, Lewiston, 126
Hits: Walt Pocekay, Wenatchee, 203
RBIs: Granville Gladstone, Victoria, 126
HRs: Cecil Garriott, Victoria, 17
Wins: Ben Lorino, Victoria, 24
SOs: Jehosie Heard, Victoria, 216
ERA: Cal McIrvin, Victoria, 2.28

B Big State League
President: Howard Green

Standings	W	L	Pct.	GB	Attend.	Manager
Temple Eagles	85	62	.578	—	101,906	Francis "Salty" Parker
Tyler East Texans	84	63	.571	1	73,337	Billy Capps
Texarkana Bears	82	65	.558	3	79,275	Tony York
Austin Pioneers	81	66	.551	4	149,601	Tom Jordan
Paris Indians	79	68	.537	6	77,761	John "Red" Davis
Wichita Falls Spudders (9)	77	70	.524	8	95,240	Frank Mancuso
Longview Cherokees	71	76	.483	14	59,913	Clemens Hausmann/ Lou Fitzgerald
Waco Pirates (15)	29	118	.197	56	32,966	Tedd Gullic

Playoffs: Austin 4 games, Temple 1; Tyler 4 games, Texarkana 2.
Finals: Tyler 4 games, Austin 0.

All-Star Team: 1B-Leslie Goldstein, Temple; **2B-**Frank Murray, Wichita Falls; **3B-**James Kirby, Paris; **SS-**Bob Mainzer, Wichita Falls; **OF-**Buck Frierson, Paris; Dean Stafford, Paris/Tyler; Roy "Tex" Sanner, Texarkana; **C-**Tom Jordan, Austin; **P-**Billy Joe Waters, Paris; Gale Pringle, Tyler; Dale Myrland, Temple; Leon Taylor, Waco.

BA: Bob Van Eman, Wichita Falls, .387
Runs: Billy Queen, Wichita Falls, 157
Hits: Buck Frierson, Paris, 222
RBIs: Roy "Tex" Sanner, Texarkana, 165
HRs: Dean Stafford, Paris/Tyler, 47

2Bs: Buck Frierson, Paris, 52
Wins: John Andre, Austin, 25
SOs: Gale Pringle, Tyler, 164
ERA: Gale Pringle, Tyler, 2.93

B Carolina League
President: Glenn E. "Ted" Mann

Standings	W	L	Pct.	GB	Attend.	Manager
Raleigh Capitals	79	57	.581	—	76,566	Herb Brett
Durham Bulls (4)	76	59	.563	2½	68,422	Ace Parker
Winston-Salem Cardinals (16)	74	63	.540	5½	60,118	Harold Olt/James Brown
Reidsville Luckies	74	64	.536	6	59,014	Ralph Hodgin
Greensboro Patriots (11)	70	64	.522	8	74,563	Kemp Wicker
Danville Leafs (8)	65	74	.468	15½	63,721	Morris "Smut" Aderholt
Fayetteville Athletics (6)	63	73	.463	16	58,203	Bob "Ducky" Detweiler/ Red Norris
Burlington-Graham Pirates (15)	45	92	.328	34½	42,236	Jerry Gardner

Playoffs: Reidsville 3 games, Raleigh 0; Durham 3 games, Winston-Salem 0.
Finals: Reidsville 4 games, Durham 0.

All-Star Team: 1B-Paul Owens, Winston-Salem; **2B-**Lawrence "Crash" Davis, Raleigh; **3B-**Arthur "Bucky" Jacobs, Raleigh; **SS-**Jimmy Edwards, Fayetteville; **OF-**Charles King, Durham; Emil Karlik, Durham; Joseph Pancoe, Reidsville; **C-**Ralph Caldwell, Durham; **Util-**Walter "Teapot" Frye, Reidsville; Bob Riga, Greensboro; **P-**Len Matarazzo, Fayetteville; Lee Peterson, Winston-Salem; Michael Forline, Reidsville; Al Cleary, Raleigh; Eddie Neville, Durham; Luke Dawson, Durham; **MVP-**Len Matarazzo, Fayetteville; **Manager-**Herb Brett, Raleigh.

BA: Emil Karlik, Durham, .347
Runs: Luis Morales, Danville, 110
Hits: Charles King, Durham, 186
RBIs: Paul Owens, Winston-Salem, 105
　　Dale Powell, Danville, 105
HRs: Dale Powell, Danville, 25
Wins: Len Matarazzo, Fayetteville, 22
SOs: Ron Necciai, Burlington-Graham, 172
ERA: Eddie Neville, Durham, 1.72

B Florida International League
President: Henry S. Baynard

Standings	W	L	Pct.	GB	Attend.	Manager
Miami Sun Sox (10)	104	48	.684	—	121,203	Max Macon
Miami Beach Flamingos	103	49	.678	1	57,533	Pepper Martin
Tampa Smokers	85	68	.556	19½	75,608	Joe Medwick/Oscar Rodriguez
St. Petersburg Saints	84	70	.545	21	91,390	Gerald Dozier/Herschel Held/ Bill Herring

Havana Cubanos (8) .... 76 77 .497 28½ 81,463 Fermin Guerra
West Palm Beach Indians ... 68 85 .444 36½ 60,725 William Holm/Charles Harris
Lakeland Pilots .... 51 103 .331 54 43,909 Rip Sewell/Buddy Bates
Ft. Lauderdale Braves/
   Key West Conchs# ...... 40 111 .265 63½ 44,482 Barney Lutz

#Ft. Lauderdale was taken over by the league June 1, then moved to Key West June 20.

Playoffs: Miami 3 games, Tampa 2; Miami Beach 3 games, St. Petersburg 2.
Finals: Miami 4 games, Miami Beach 3.

BA: Jesse Levan, Miami Beach, .334
Runs: Hiram Gonzales, Tampa, 93
    Jesse Levan, Miami Beach, 93
Hits: Jesse Levan, Miami Beach, 192
RBIs: Jesse Levan, Miami Beach, 87

HRs: Nesbit Wilson, St. Petersburg, 15
Wins: William Harris, Miami, 25
SOs: Clarence "Hooks" Iott,
    St. Petersburg, 210
ERA: William Harris, Miami, 0.83

B Gulf Coast League
President: Howard Green

Standings	W	L	Pct.	GB	Attend.	Manager
Port Arthur Seahawks	89	65	.578	—	86,240	Carl Carter
Corpus Christi Aces	80	73	.523	8½	73,687	Tom Pullig
Harlingen Capitols	80	73	.523	8½	79,985	Bob Hamric
Galveston White Caps	80	74	.519	9	61,824	Stan Goletz/Harry Gumbert
Laredo Apaches	76	77	.497	12½	48,254	Joe King
Brownsville Charros	76	77	.497	12½	69,991	Richard Midkiff/
						Richard Gosselin
Lake Charles Lakers	69	85	.448	20	82,270	Sidney Gautreaux/Joe Kracher
Texas City Texans	64	90	.416	25	44,001	Bones Sanders/Derrast Williams
						& Zane Skinner

Playoffs: Port Arthur 4 games, Galveston 2; Harlingen 4 games, Corpus Christi 3.
Finals: Harlingen 4 games, Port Arthur 1.

All-Star Team: 1B-Bill Radulovich, Port Arthur; **2B**-Septine Baron, Port Arthur; **3B**-Jorge Lopez, Laredo; **SS**-William McCloskey, Laredo; **OF**-Walt Sessi, Brownsville; Hardie Nettles, Lake Charles; Warren Schroeder, Texas City; **C**-Robert Bareford, Port Arthur; **P**-Earl Caldwell, Harlingen; Ray Contreras, Galveston; Albert Point, Corpus Christi; Danny Parra, Corpus Christi.

BA: Bill Radulovich, Port Arthur, .389
Runs: Walt Sessi, Brownsville, 148
Hits: Bill Radulovich, Port Arthur, 212
RBIs: Walt Sessi, Brownsville, 179

HRs: Walt Sessi, Brownsville, 45
Wins: Ray Contreras, Galveston, 22
SOs: Bill Guthrie, Harlingen, 166
ERA: Earl Caldwell, Harlingen, 2.73

B Interstate League
President: Gerald P. Nugent

Standings	W	L	Pct.	GB	Attend.	Manager
Hagerstown Braves (9)	85	48	.639	—	48,367	Dutch Dorman
Allentown Cardinals (16)	82	57	.590	6	49,707	Whitey Kurowski
York White Roses (7)	74	62	.544	12½	78,707	James Crandall
Lancaster Red Roses (10) ...	75	65	.536	13½	41,913	James Bivin
Wilmington Blue Rocks (14) ...	72	66	.522	15½	24,526	Leon Riley
Salisbury Reds (12)	65	73	.471	22½	44,479	Mike Blazo/Dick Porter
Sunbury Giants (13)	53	87	.379	35½	31,575	Frank Scalzi/James Reggio
Harrisburg Senators (6)	46	94	.329	42½	30,592	Clarence "Buck" Etchison/
						Woody Wheaton

Playoffs: Hagerstown 4 games, York 0; Lancaster 4 games, Allentown 1.
Finals: Hagerstown 4 games, Lancaster 2.

All-Star Team: 1B-Clarence Riddle, Hagerstown; **2B**-Elbert Israel, Harrisburg; **3B**-Clarence Moore, Lancaster; **SS**-Joe Tedesco, Lancaster; **OF**-Joseph Christian, Hagerstown; Elmer Westfall, Salisbury; Juan Senties, York; **C**-Jack Tanner, Salisbury; **P**-Robert Giggie, Hagerstown; Eugene Swinger, Allentown; Robert Hoch, Allentown; Harry Wilson, York.

BA: Elbert Israel, Harrisburg, .318
Runs: Robert Jaderlund, Hagerstown, 113
Hits: Clarence Moore, Lancaster, 166
RBIs: Clarence Riddle, Hagerstown, 93
HRs: Louis Heyman, Wilmington, 30

Wins: Harry Wilson, York, 18
    Robert Giggie, Hagerstown, 18
    Douglas Gostlin, Lancaster, 18
SOs: Gene Snyder, Wilmington, 208
ERA: Robert Hoch, Allentown, 1.78

B Piedmont League
President: Frank L. Summers

Standings	W	L	Pct.	GB	Attend.	Manager
Norfolk Tars***(5)	96	36	.727	—	79,085	Mayo Smith
Portsmouth Cubs	71	64	.526	26½	56,683	Reggie Otero
Richmond Colts	69	66	.511	28½	76,914	Tom O'Connell
Lynchburg Cardinals (16) ...	64	66	.492	31	50,958	James Brown/Harold Olt
Roanoke Ro-Sox (1)	59	74	.444	37½	42,789	Owen Scheetz
Newport News Dodgers (10) ...	41	94	.304	56½	28,085	Ray Hathaway

Playoffs: Richmond 4 games, Norfolk 1; Portsmouth 4 games, Lynchburg 2.
Finals: Richmond 4 games, Portsmouth 1.

All-Star Team: 1B-William Gabler, Newport News; **2B**-Garvin Hamner, Richmond; **3B**-Leon Carter, Norfolk; **SS**-John Hunton, Norfolk; **OF**-Dick Tettelbach, Norfolk; Ken Guettler, Portsmouth; Crawford Davidson, Lynchburg; **C**-Isaac Seoane, Portsmouth; **P**-Charles LeBrun, Norfolk; John Kucks, Norfolk; Dewey Wilkins, Richmond.

BA: Ken Guettler, Portsmouth, .334
Runs: Bill Casanova, Norfolk, 108
Hits: Leon Carter, Norfolk, 168
RBIs: Ken Guettler, Portsmouth, 104

HRs: Ken Guettler, Portsmouth, 28
Wins: Charles LeBrun, Norfolk, 23
SOs: Dewey Wilkins, Richmond, 169
ERA: Charles LeBrun, Norfolk, 1.87

B Three-I League
President: Hal Totten

Standings	W	L	Pct.	GB	Attend.	Manager
Evansville Braves (9)	74	47	.612	—	124,381	Bob Coleman
Terre Haute Phillies (14)	75	49	.605	½	63,267	Skeeter Newsome
Burlington Flints (12)	64	60	.516	11½	57,259	Len Schulte
Waterloo White Hawks (2) ...	65	61	.515	11½	75,071	Skeeter Webb
Keokuk Kernels	56	66	.459	18½	64,931	Rudy Laskowski
Davenport Tigers (4)	54	69	.439	21	71,989	Marv Owen
Quincy Gems (5)	54	72	.429	22½	45,541	Paul Chervinko
Cedar Rapids Indians (3)	53	71	.427	22½	94,428	Jim Bloodworth

Playoffs: Evansville 3 games, Burlington 2; Terre Haute 3 games, Waterloo 0.
Finals: Terre Haute 3 games, Evansville 1.

All-Star Team: 1B-Marv Throneberry, Quincy; **2B**-Gerald Claycomb, Terre Haute; **3B**-Chuck Harmon, Burlington; **SS**-Felix Mantilla, Evansville; **OF**-Horace Garner, Evansville; Art Pennington, Keokuk; Robert Erps, Waterloo; **C**-Dutch Dotterer, Burlington; **P**-Dan Ramer, Terre Haute; George Yorke, Evansville; Herbert Agase, Terre Haute; Bud Daley, Cedar Rapids.

BA: Art Pennington, Keokuk, .349
Runs: Art Pennington, Keokuk, 126
Hits: Chuck Harmon, Burlington, 153
RBIs: Horace Garner, Evansville, 107

HRs: Robert Erps, Waterloo, 27
Wins: George Yorke, Evansville, 17
SOs: Bud Daley, Cedar Rapids, 198
ERA: Gerald Speck, Waterloo, 2.44

B Tri-State League
President: Robert E. Hipps

Standings	W	L	Pct.	GB	Attend.	Manager
Gastonia Rockets (2)	89	50	.640	—	94,788	Hal Van Pelt
Charlotte Hornets (8)	87	51	.630	1½	96,738	Ivan Kuester
Spartanburg Peaches (3)	83	55	.601	5½	67,577	Pinky May
Anderson Rebels (7)	67	72	.482	22	80,979	George Hausmann
Asheville Tourists (5)	65	75	.464	24½	48,039	William Hart/George Tesnow
Greenville Spinners	63	76	.453	26	64,704	Ralph DiLullo
Knoxville Smokies (13)	52	88	.371	37½	50,638	Jack Aragon/Fred Gerken
Rock Hill Chiefs	49	88	.358	39	52,528	Harry Land/Leon Culberson

Playoffs: Spartanburg 3 games, Gastonia 2; Charlotte 3 games, Anderson 1.
Finals: Charlotte 4 games, Spartanburg 1.

All-Star Team: 1B-Leo "Muscle" Shoals, Rock Hill; **2B**-George Hausmann, Anderson; **3B**-Juan Perez, Anderson; **SS**-Alex Cosmidis, Gastonia; **OF**-Bruce Barmes, Charlotte; Carl Powis, Anderson; Fred Leonard, Gastonia; **C**-Arnold Davis, Gastonia; **Util**-Phil Qualben, Spartanburg; Richard Honacki, Anderson; **P**-William Upton, Spartanburg; Murphy Murszewski, Spartanburg.

BA: Bruce Barmes, Charlotte, .360
Runs: Alex Cosmidis, Gastonia, 122
Hits: Bruce Barmes, Charlotte, 182
RBIs: Carl Powis, Anderson, 116

HRs: Juan Perez, Anderson, 27
Wins: William Upton, Spartanburg, 21
SOs: Murphy Murszewski, Spartanburg, 239
ERA: Bob Danielson, Charlotte, 2.62

C Arizona-Texas League
President: G.R. Sloane

Standings	W	L	Pct.	GB	Attend.	Manager
Juarez Indios	84	55	.604	—	64,870	Manuel Fortes
El Paso Texans	79	61	.564	5½	83,373	Art Lilly
Phoenix Senators	78	62	.557	6½	64,410	Jeep Trower
Tucson Cowboys	61	78	.439	23	68,500	Don Jameson
Bisbee-Douglas						
Copper Kings	60	80	.429	24½	56,206	Syd Cohen
Chihuahua Dorados	57	83	.407	27½	130,329	Domingo Santana/
						Marvin Williams

Playoffs: None.

BA: Marvin Williams, Chihuahua, .401
Runs: Felipe Hernandez, Juarez, 144
Hits: Dick Steinhauer, Phoenix, 233
RBIs: Ramon Vargas, El Paso, 143

HRs: Marvin Williams, Chihuahua, 45
Wins: Wenceslao Gonzalez, Juarez, 25
SOs: Wenceslao Gonzalez, Juarez, 222
ERA: Donald Cantrell, Phoenix, 3.64

C California League
President: Jerry Donovan

Standings	W	L	Pct.	GB	Attend.	Manager
Fresno Cardinals (16)	88	52	.629	—	120,524	Roland LeBlanc
Santa Barbara Dodgers (10) ...	74	66	.529	14	36,259	George Scherger
San Jose Red Sox (1)	74	66	.529	14	62,953	Red Marion
Visalia Cubs (11)	72	68	.514	16	83,399	Larry Barton
Bakersfield Indians (3)	70	70	.500	18	83,480	Gene Lillard
Modesto Reds (15)	67	73	.479	21	74,155	Buck Elliott/Clinton Cameron
Stockton Ports (7)	59	81	.421	29	56,855	Harry Clements/Tony Freitas
Ventura Braves (9)	56	84	.400	32	30,320	Robert Sturgeon/Jose Perez

Playoffs: Fresno 3 games, Santa Barbara 1; San Jose 3 games, Visalia 1.
Finals: Fresno 4 games, San Jose 2.

All-Star Team: 1B-Jose Perez, Ventura; **2B**-Carl "Buddy" Jones, Visalia; **3B**-Harry Clements, Stockton; **SS**-Alan Grandcolas, Fresno; **OF**-Ben Downs, Fresno; Nathaniel Peeples, Santa Barbara; Napoleon Gulley, Visalia; **C**-Roland LeBlanc, Fresno; **P**-Larry Jackson, Fresno; Robert Crane, Visalia; Jake Abbott, Santa Barbara; Tony Stathos, Fresno.

BA: Alan Grandcolas, Fresno, .347
Runs: David Cunningham, Visalia, 132
Hits: Alan Grandcolas, Fresno, 191
RBIs: Ben Downs, Fresno, 154
HRs: Ben Downs, Fresno, 34
Wins: Larry Jackson, Fresno, 28
SOs: Larry Jackson, Fresno, 351
ERA: Jake Abbott, Santa Barbara, 2.26

C Cotton States League
President: Al Haraway

Standings	W	L	Pct.	GB	Attend.	Manager
Meridian Millers	78	48	.619	—	61,487	Thomas Davis
Natchez Indians	73	53	.579	5	50,345	Homer Ray Wilson/ Troy Mitchell
Greenwood Dodgers (10)	70	56	.556	8	52,067	Stan Wasiak
Monroe Sports	66	60	.524	12	59,128	Charles Harrington
El Dorado Oilers	65	61	.516	13	65,909	James Morgan/Ray Perry
Pine Bluff Judges (7)	62	64	.492	16	45,749	Hillis Layne
Greenville Bucks	47	79	.373	31	37,918	Harry Chozen
Hot Springs Bathers	43	83	.341	35	37,796	Bob Benish/James Hogan

Playoffs: Meridian 4 games, Monroe 2; Natchez 4 games, Greenwood 2.
Finals: Meridian 4 games, Natchez 3.

BA: Don Allen, Natchez, .335
Runs: Gene Pompelia, Meridian, 102
Hits: John Jones, Monroe, 163
RBIs: John Jones, Monroe, 91
HRs: Ray Perry, El Dorado, 15
Wins: Bob Harrison, Meridian, 24
SOs: John Forizs, Greenwood, 252
ERA: Bob Harrison, Meridian, 1.82

C Evangeline League
President: Edmond L. Deramee

Standings	W	L	Pct.	GB	Attend.	Manager
Crowley Millers	81	59	.579	—	110,814	John George
Thibodaux Giants	75	63	.543	5	52,727	William Adams
Baton Rouge Red Sticks	76	64	.542	5	80,613	Buddy Hancken
Lafayette Bulls	74	65	.532	6½	78,706	Joe Powers
New Iberia Pelicans	72	68	.514	9	74,794	Randy Heflin
Abbeville Athletics	62	78	.443	19	64,650	Nathaniel Love/Marvin Holleman
Houma Indians	58	79	.423	21½	25,821	Woodie Head/Robert Gales
Alexandria Aces	59	81	.421	22	66,196	Buddy Blair/George Washburn

Playoffs: Crowley 4 games, Lafayette 0; Baton Rouge 4 games, Thibodaux 3.
Finals: Crowley 4 games, Baton Rouge 0.

All-Star Team: 1B-Conklyn Meriwether, Crowley; **2B**-Fred Barocco, Lafayette; **3B**-Fred DeSousa, Lafayette; **SS**-John Millard, New Iberia; **OF**-Art Edinger, Crowley; Robert Troyer, New Iberia; James Moore, Crowley; **C**-Robert Thompson, New Iberia; George John, Lafayette; **Util**-Alvin Lichtenstein, Lafayette; Anthony Helbig, Abbeville; **P**-Marvin Holleman, Abbeville; William Sterling, Crowley; Hugh Blanton, Crowley; John Richard, Lafayette; Leverette Spencer, New Iberia; **Manager**-John George, Crowley.

BA: William Lynn, Alexandria, .386
Runs: Art Edinger, Crowley, 141
Hits: William Lynn, Alexandria, 209
RBIs: Fred DeSousa, Lafayette, 130
HRs: Conklyn Meriwether, Crowley, 33
Wins: Hugh Blanton, Crowley, 21
SOs: Leverette Spencer, New Iberia, 248
ERA: Marvin Holleman, Abbeville, 2.46

C Longhorn League
President: Hal Sayles

Standings	W	L	Pct.	GB	Attend.	Manager
Odessa Oilers	87	53	.621	—	72,665	Robert Martin
Big Spring Broncs	86	54	.614	1	49,652	Pat Stasey
Midland Indians	85	55	.607	2	64,188	Zeke Bonura/Jay Haney
Artesia Drillers	75	65	.536	12	42,972	Earl Perry
Roswell Rockets	65	75	.464	22	52,583	Alex Monchak
San Angelo Colts	65	75	.464	22	76,892	Mark Christman
Sweetwater Braves	52	88	.371	35	37,060	Alex Carrasquel/John Morris
Vernon Dusters	45	95	.321	42	30,105	Chester Fowler/ Albert Richardson/ Pat McLaughlin

Playoffs: Odessa 4 games, Artesia 1; Midland 4 games, Big Spring 0.
Finals: Midland 4 games, Odessa 2.

All-Star Team: 1B-Joe Bauman, Artesia; **2B**-John Tayoan, San Angelo; **3B**-Witty Quintana, Big Spring; **SS**-Hayden Greer, Roswell; **OF**-Roman Loyko, Odessa; Leo Eastham, Odessa; Charles Buck, Sweetwater; **C**-Rudolph Briner, Artesia; **P**-Keith Nicolls, Midland; Gilberto Guerra, Big Spring; Evelio Ortega, Odessa; Lloyd Wallis, Vernon.

BA: Charles Buck, Sweetwater, .382
Runs: Leo Eastham, Odessa, 157
Hits: Charles Buck, Sweetwater, 210
RBIs: Joe Bauman, Artesia, 157
HRs: Joe Bauman, Artesia, 50
Wins: Gilberto Guerra, Big Spring, 26
SOs: Gilberto Guerra, Big Spring, 225
ERA: Israel Ten, Midland, 2.51

C Northern League
President: Herman D. White

Standings	W	L	Pct.	GB	Attend.	Manager
Superior Blues (2)	81	42	.659	—	65,282	Walter Millies
Sioux Falls Canaries (11)	73	48	.603	7	87,149	Al Kubski
Eau Claire Bears (9)	72	53	.576	10	61,429	Bill Adair
Duluth Dukes	63	59	.516	17½	62,907	James Trew/Ken Blackman
Aberdeen Pheasants (7)	63	62	.504	19	87,897	Bruce Ogrodowski
St. Cloud Rox (13)	60	64	.484	21½	45,612	Charlie Fox
Fargo-Moorhead Twins	44	80	.355	37½	71,624	Nick Cullop/Bob Harmon/ Danny Litwhiler
Grand Forks Chiefs (14)	38	86	.306	43½	32,059	Eddie Murphy

Playoffs: Superior 2 games, Eau Claire 1; Sioux Falls 2 games, Duluth 1.
Finals: Superior 3 games, Sioux Falls 0.

All-Star Team: 1B-Dan Phalen, Superior; **2B**-Dick Lloyd, Sioux Falls; **3B**-Jose Bustamente, Superior; **SS**-Henry Aaron, Eau Claire; **OF**-Joe Caffie, Duluth; Frank Gravino, Fargo-Moorhead; Wes Covington, Eau Claire; **C**-Donald Biebel, Sioux Falls; **P**-Don Elston, Sioux Falls; Alfredo Ibanez, Superior; Rueben Stohs, Fargo-Moorhead; William Conroy, Eau Claire.

BA: Joe Caffie, Duluth, .342
Runs: Joe Caffie, Duluth, 105
Hits: Joe Caffie, Duluth, 171
RBIs: Frank Gravino, Fargo-Moorhead, 108
HRs: Frank Gravino, Fargo-Moorhead, 32
Wins: Don Elston, Sioux Falls, 18
  Alfredo Ibanez, Superior, 18
SOs: Gideon Applegate, Superior, 188
ERA: Don Elston, Sioux Falls, 1.85

C Pioneer League
President: Jack P. Halliwell

Standings	W	L	Pct.	GB	Attend.	Manager
Pocatello Bannocks (7)	78	53	.595	—	64,793	Ed Fernandes
Idaho Falls Russets	75	56	.573	3	58,643	Sven "Red" Jessen
Billings Mustangs (15)	73	59	.553	5½	142,208	Cliff Dapper
Great Falls Electrics (10)	67	64	.511	11	118,029	Lou Rochelli
Boise Yankees (5)	63	69	.477	15½	68,469	Wayne Tucker
Salt Lake City Bees (14)	60	71	.458	18	93,920	Hub Kittle
Magic Valley Cowboys#	55	77	.417	23½	63,773	Tommy Thompson
Ogden Reds (12)	55	77	.417	23½	54,686	Dee Moore

#represented Twin Falls, Idaho.

Playoffs: Pocatello 2 games, Billings 1; Idaho Falls 2 games, Great Falls 0.
Finals: Idaho Falls 3 games, Pocatello 0.

All-Star Team: 1B-Sven "Red" Jessen, Idaho Falls; **2B**-Gordon Hernandez, Salt Lake City; **3B**-Steve Mesner, Ogden; **SS**-Ernie Sierra, Pocatello; **OF**-Dick Stuart, Billings; Willie Tasby, Pocatello; Dick Smith, Great Falls; **C**-Cliff Dapper, Billings; **P**-Ken Kimball, Idaho Falls; Nicolas Genesta, Billings.

BA: Steve Mesner, Ogden, .343
Runs: Dick Stuart, Billings, 115
Hits: Steve Mesner, Ogden, 161
  Dick Stuart, Billings, 161
  Earl Silverthorn, Great Falls, 161
RBIs: Dick Stuart, Billings, 121
HRs: Dick Stuart, Billings, 31
Wins: Ken Kimball, Idaho Falls, 26
SOs: Ken Kimball, Idaho Falls, 203
ERA: Nicolas Genesta, Billings, 1.58

C Provincial League
President: Albert Molini

Standings	W	L	Pct.	GB	Attend.	Manager
St. Hyacinthe A's (6)	79	49	.617	—	60,147	John Sosh
Quebec Braves (9)	78	51	.605	1½	111,800	George McQuinn
St. Jean Canadians (15)	63	66	.488	16½	61,899	Gordon Maltzberger
Trois Rivieres Yankees	59	68	.465	19½	85,526	Frank Novosel
Drummondville Cubs (8)	57	68	.456	20½	40,192	Herb Crompton
Granby Phillies (14)	45	79	.363	32	31,554	Al Barillari

Playoffs: St. Hyacinthe 4 games, St. Jean 3; Quebec 4 games, Trois Rivieres 3.
Finals: Quebec 4 games, St. Hyacinthe 3.

BA: Al Pinkston, St. Hyacinthe, .360
Runs: Hector Lopez, St. Hyacinthe, 115
Hits: Fred Pacitto, Trois Rivieres, 176
RBIs: Al Pinkston, St. Hyacinthe, 121
HRs: Al Pinkston, St. Hyacinthe, 30
Wins: John Wingo, Trois Rivieres, 16
  Stan Wotychowicz, St. Hyacinthe, 16
  Thomas Smith, Drummondville, 16
  Robert Trice, St. Hyacinthe, 16
SOs: Robert Long, St. Jean, 179
ERA: Marco Mainini, Trois Rivieres, 2.61

C Southwest International League
President: Harry Ledell

Standings	W	L	Pct.	GB	Attend.	Manager
Tijuana Potros	80	56	.588	—	45,000	Fernando Paredes
Mexicali Eagles	74	57	.565	3½	35,239	Dolf Luque/Virgilio Arteaga
Las Vegas Wranglers	70	66	.515	10	53,200	William DeCarlo
Yuma Panthers	62	68	.477	15	52,280	Lou Bekeza
Porterville Comets#	39	59	.398	NA	32,000	Chet Brewer
El Centro Imps@	28	47	.373	NA	12,000	Bud Beringhele/Frank Gabler/ Henry Savin

#Franchise started the season as Riverside-Ensenada, became Riverside-Porterville, moved to Porterville April 25, then disbanded August 1.
@El Centro disbanded July 13.

All-Star Team: 1B-Tom Alston, Porterville; Lou Bekeza, Yuma; **2B**-Terrence Carroll, Yuma; **3B**-John Malgarini, El Centro/Porterville; **SS**-Romualdo Urias, Tijuana; **OF**-Pete Hughes, Tijuana; Lester Witherspoon, Porterville; Segundo Crespo, Tijuana; **C**-William DeCarlo, Las Vegas; **P**-Silverio Rodriguez, Mexicali; Jose Rayle, Tijuana; Forrest Orrell, Tijuana.

BA: Pete Hughes, Tijuana, .366
Walter Tyler, Porterville/Yuma, .366
Runs: Joe Clardy, Las Vegas, 142
Hits: Joe Clardy, Las Vegas, 202
RBIs: Pete Hughes, Tijuana, 131
HRs: Pete Hughes, Tijuana, 28
Refugio Bernal, Mexicali, 28
BBs: Pete Hughes, Tijuana, 180
Wins: Amador Guzman, Mexicali, 22
SOs: Silverio Rodriguez, Mexicali, 209
ERA: Forrest Orrell, Tijuana, 2.01
Pct: Forrest Orrell, Tijuana, .875, 21-3

C West Texas-New Mexico League

President: Ray Winkler

Standings	W	L	Pct.	GB	Attend.	Manager
Clovis Pioneers	94	47	.667	—	42,747	Grover Seitz
Albuquerque Dukes	77	65	.542	17½	85,125	Buck Fausett
Amarillo Gold Sox	70	70	.500	23½	82,630	Pat McLaughlin/ John "Monk" Webb/Ted Clawitter
Borger Gassers	70	70	.500	23½	48,789	Lloyd Brown
Lamesa Lobos	69	73	.486	25½	41,541	Jay Haney/Jackie Sullivan
Lubbock Hubbers	63	79	.444	31½	90,360	Isaac Palmer
Pampa Oilers	62	80	.437	32½	38,023	Jake Phillips
Abilene Blue Sox	60	81	.426	34	64,492	James "Hack" Miller/ Otho Nitcholas

Playoffs: Amarillo 4 games, Clovis 1; Borger 4 games, Albuquerque 2.
Finals: Amarillo 4 games, Borger 0.

All-Star Team: 1B-Mervin Connors, Amarillo; **2B**-Clifford Pemberton, Clovis; **3B**-John Bruzga, Amarillo; **SS**-Clyde Perry, Amarillo; **OF**-James Eldridge, Borger; Francis Rice, Clovis; Don Stokes, Lamesa; **C**-Lester Mulcahy, Amarillo; **P**-Carroll "Red" Dial, Clovis; Jesse Priest, Albuquerque; Ed Flanagan, Borger/Albuquerque; Joe Hinchman, Albuquerque.

BA: Pat Lorenzo, Lamesa/Borger, .416
Runs: Francis Rice, Clovis, 151
Hits: Don Stokes, Lamesa, 211
RBIs: Joe Fortin, Lamesa, 142
HRs: Mervin Connors, Amarillo, 47
2Bs: Isaac Palmer, Lubbock, 62
Wins: Carroll "Red" Dial, Clovis, 27
SOs: Juan Montero, Pampa/Lubbock, 183
ERA: Jim Cain, Borger, 2.94
Pct: Melvin Kramer, Clovis, .846, 11-2

C Western Association

President: Howard Goetz

Standings	W	L	Pct.	GB	Attend.	Manager
Joplin Miners**(5)	87	52	.626	—	49,511	Vern Hoscheit
Muskogee Giants*(13)	73	66	.525	14	61,391	Andy Gilbert
Hutchinson Elks (15)	70	66	.515	15½	78,713	Wes Griffin
Topeka Owls (11)	63	76	.453	24	64,967	Adolph Matulis/Jack Dean
Salina Blue Jays (14)	61	77	.442	25½	35,984	Floyd Patterson
Ft. Smith Indians (3)	60	77	.438	26	46,520	Harry Griswold

Playoff: Joplin 4 games, Muskogee 0.

All-Star Team: 1B-Andy Gilbert, Muskogee; **2B**-Jack Varnado, Muskogee; **3B**-Arnold Green, Topeka; **SS**-Ernesto Blanco, Ft. Smith; **OF**-Jack Lewis, Muskogee; Norm Siebern, Joplin; Bobby Prescott, Hutchinson; **C**-Johnny Blanchard, Joplin; **P**-Frank Lucas, Joplin; John Brown, Hutchinson; Edward Smrekar, Salina; Gerald Schultz, Muskogee.

BA: Andy Gilbert, Muskogee, .357
Runs: Norm Siebern, Joplin, 115
Mel Collins, Muskogee, 115
Hits: Jack Lewis, Muskogee, 156
RBIs: Johnny Blanchard, Joplin, 112
HRs: Johnny Blanchard, Joplin, 30
Wins: Frank Lucas, Joplin, 24
SOs: John Brown, Hutchinson, 209
ERA: Willard Ford, Joplin, 2.12

D Alabama-Florida League

President: C.C. Hodge

Standings	W	L	Pct.	GB	Attend.	Manager
Ozark Eagles	77	37	.675	—	24,670	Chase Riddle
Eufaula Millers	67	51	.568	12	26,480	Arkie Walls/Robert Murphy/ Dutch Konemann/ Blackie Connell
Dothan Browns	59	56	.514	18½	33,650	Parks York/Holt "Cat" Milner
Panama City Fliers	60	57	.513	18½	45,358	Bill Herring/Carl Walker/ John McPherson
Headland Dixie Runners	51	66	.436	27½	13,820	Walt Dixon/Hugh Kirkland
Enterprise/Graceville Boll Weevils#	33	80	.292	43½	17,720	Shorty Marshall/Red Glover/ Joe Boehmer/Ed Mitchell/ Carl Walker

#Enterprise moved to Graceville July 5.

Playoffs: Ozark 4 games, Dothan 1; Panama City 4 games, Eufaula 1.
Finals: Ozark 4 games, Panama City 1.

All-Star Team: 1B-Lewis Letlow, Eufaula; **2B**-Robert Phillips, Panama City; **3B**-William Buchanan, Eufaula; **SS**-Ralph Prince, Eufaula; **OF**-J.G. "Jake" Moore, Dothan; Roberto Gonzalez, Panama City; Joe Clark, Ozark; **C**-Chase Riddle, Ozark; **P**-Russell Harris, Ozark; Gene Summerlin, Panama City; Walter Collins, Dothan; J.G. "Jake" Moore, Dothan.

BA: J.G. "Jake" Moore, Dothan, .358
Runs: Lewis Letlow, Eufaula, 114
Hits: Roberto Gonzalez, Panama City, 160
RBIs: Roberto Gonzalez, Panama City, 115
HRs: William Buchanan, Eufaula, 24
Wins: Russell Harris, Ozark, 27
SOs: Russell Harris, Ozark, 243
ERA: Russell Harris, Ozark, 2.83

D Appalachian League

President: Chauncey De Vault

Standings	W	L	Pct.	GB	Attend.	Manager
Johnson City Cardinals (16)	69	47	.595	—	49,550	James Hercinger
Bristol Twins (15)	60	57	.513	9½	45,702	George Detore
Welch Miners (9)	59	57	.509	10	34,662	Jack Crosswhite
Pulaski Phillies (14)	57	60	.487	12½	37,256	Al Gardella
Bluefield Blue-Grays	52	64	.448	17	38,469	Joe Beggs
Kingsport Cherokees (13)	52	64	.448	17	24,121	Harold Kollar

Playoffs: Pulaski 2 games, Johnson City 1; Welch 2 games, Bristol 0.
Finals: Welch 3 games, Pulaski 1.

BA: Andy Lee, Johnson City, .373
Runs: Harold Kollar, Kingsport, 112
Hits: James Partin, Bluefield/Welch, 161
RBIs: Harold Kollar, Kingsport, 112
HRs: Harold Kollar, Kingsport, 21
Wins: John Kazmerowicz, Pulaski, 17
SOs: John Kazmerowicz, Pulaski, 204
ERA: Bill Bell, Bristol, 2.09

D Coastal Plain League

President: Ray H. Goodmon

Standings	W	L	Pct.	GB	Attend.	Manager
Kinston Eagles (4)	76	47	.608	—	43,301	Wayne Blackburn
Wilson Tobs	71	51	.582	4½	57,565	Jake McComas/Alfred Rehm
Edenton Colonials	69	55	.557	7½	24,420	Vernon Mustian/Tom Inge/ Gashouse Parker
Goldsboro Jets (16)	63	59	.516	12½	35,365	Wes Livengood
Roanoke Rapids Jays (8)	63	61	.508	13½	36,830	Pete Appleton
Rocky Mount Leafs	59	63	.484	16½	40,629	Paul Badgett/Quentin Martin/ Cecil "Turkey" Tyson/ Wiley Warren
Tarboro Tars	49	71	.408	25½	28,439	Bill Long
New Bern Bears	40	83	.325	36	29,056	Larry Dempsey/John Pavlich/ Steve Collins

Playoffs: Goldsboro 4 games, Kinston 3; Edenton 4 games, Wilson 0.
Finals: Edenton 4 games, Goldsboro 1.

All-Star Team: 1B-Robert Hepler, New Bern; **2B**-Oscar Barham, Rocky Mount; **3B**-Gene Hassell, Wilson; **SS**-Joseph Gauci, Kinston; **OF**-Sam Stell, Tarboro; Tom Leonard, Goldsboro; Hilliary "Moe" Evans, Edenton; **C**-Woodrow Wrenn, Wilson; **P**-John Raines, Edenton; Richard McCleney, Wilson; Gene Host, Kinston; John Kovalchick, Rocky Mount.

BA: Tom Leonard, Goldsboro, .375
Runs: Cecil Fogleman, Tarboro, 101
Hits: Bill Wollet, Roanoke Rapids, 151
RBIs: Sam Stell, Tarboro, 77
HRs: Wade Martin, Rocky Mount, 11
Wins: John Raines, Edenton, 26
Gene Host, Kinston, 26
SOs: Ted Abernathy, Roanoke Rapids, 293
ERA: Rodney Heath, Rocky Mount, 1.27
ShO: John Perry, Goldsboro, 10

D Florida State League

President: John Krider

Standings	W	L	Pct.	GB	Attend.	Manager
DeLand Red Hats***	95	40	.704	—	28,195	Charles Brewster
Jacksonville Beach Sea Birds	80	56	.588	15½	23,210	Leon "Red" Treadway
Palatka Azaleas	78	59	.569	18	31,486	Bill Steinecke
Daytona Beach Islanders (3)	77	59	.566	18½	58,305	Red Kress
Orlando Senators (8)	68	67	.504	27	34,836	Ed Levy
Sanford Seminole Blues	64	70	.478	30½	38,360	Charles Aleno
Leesburg Packers	52	84	.382	43½	17,653	Walter Chipple/Don Anderson/ John Pawlick/Bob Latshaw
Cocoa Indians	40	93	.301	54	19,815	Pep Rambert/James Balogh
Gainesville G-Men#	24	23	.511	NA	9,623	Don Anderson
St. Augustine Saints#	10	37	.213	NA	6,909	Bert Shepard/Bob Rucker/ Stan Karpinski

#Gainesville and St. Augustine disbanded June 2.

Playoffs: Daytona Beach 2 games, DeLand 0; Palatka 2 games, Jacksonville Beach 0.
Finals: Palatka 3 games, Daytona Beach 1.

All-Star Team: 1B-Perry Roberts, DeLand; **2B**-Charles Brewster, DeLand; **3B**-Jesse Cade, DeLand; **SS**-William Mostransky, DeLand; **OF**-Howard Tesnow, Daytona Beach; Kenneth Braeseke, DeLand; Leon "Red" Treadway, Jacksonville Beach; **C**-Raymond Dunne, DeLand; **Util**-Robert Rucker, Daytona Beach; **P**-Tom Mills, Jacksonville Beach; Joe Frank Pennington, Palatka.

BA: Jesse Cade, DeLand, .382
Runs: Jesse Cade, DeLand, 150
Hits: Jesse Cade, DeLand, 202
RBIs: Charles Aleno, Sanford, 131
HRs: Charles Aleno, Sanford, 25
Wins: Tom Mills, Jacksonville Beach, 27
SOs: Richard Wenger, Daytona Beach, 203
ERA: Perry Roberts, DeLand, 1.94

D Georgia State League
President: Bill Estroff

Standings	W	L	Pct.	GB	Attend.	Manager
Eastman Dodgers	75	49	.605	—	32,600	Robert Reid
Hazlehurst-Baxley Cardinals (16)	72	52	.581	3	27,586	Arnold Riesgo
Vidalia Indians	66	58	.532	9	37,485	Bull Hamons
Douglas Trojans	64	61	.512	11½	27,532	Van Davis
Statesboro Pilots	59	65	.476	16	32,146	Charles Quimby
Fitzgerald Pioneers	56	70	.444	20	33,172	Ace Adams/Charles Ridgeway
Dublin Green Sox (12)	55	71	.437	21	34,334	Cyril Pfeifer/George Hearn/ Jack Bearden
Jesup Bees	52	73	.416	23½	16,657	James Stoyle/Nig Warren

Playoffs: Douglas 4 games, Eastman 2; Vidalia 4 games, Hazlehurst-Baxley 2.
Finals: Vidalia 4 games, Douglas 2.

All-Star Team: 1B-Jim Beavers, Hazlehurst-Baxley; **2B**-Charles Ridgeway, Fitzgerald; **3B**-Charles Quimby, Statesboro; **SS**-Frank Tepedino, Vidalia; **OF**-Bill McGhee, Hazlehurst-Baxley; Raymond Nichting, Fitzgerald; Jim Burns, Vidalia; **C**-Arnold Riesgo, Hazlehurst-Baxley; **P**-Noel Oquendo, Dublin; Phil Gilbert, Eastman; Walter Bauman, Hazlehurst-Baxley; Jerry Jones, Douglas.

BA: Jim Beavers, Hazlehurst-Baxley, .363
Runs: Jim Beavers, Hazlehurst-Baxley, 119
Hits: Jim Beavers, Hazlehurst-Baxley, 191
RBIs: Jim Burns, Vidalia, 155
HRs: Charles Quimby, Statesboro, 31

Wins: Noel Oquendo, Dublin, 20
    Walter Bauman, Hazlehurst-Baxley, 20
SOs: Noel Oquendo, Dublin, 245
ERA: James Harp, Eastman, 2.40

D Georgia-Florida League
President: W.T. Anderson

Standings	W	L	Pct.	GB	Attend.	Manager
Valdosta Dodgers (10)	81	58	.583	—	47,127	John Angelone
Albany Cardinals (16)	81	59	.579	½	63,244	Gene Corbett
Waycross Bears	80	59	.576	1	53,428	Fred Williams
Tifton Blue Sox	78	61	.561	3	37,805	Greek George/ Edmond Dickerman/ Parnell Ruark
Cordele A's (6)	66	73	.475	15	32,549	Norm Wilson
Thomasville Tomcats	66	74	.471	15½	45,651	Frank Lucchesi
Brunswick Pirates (15)	62	78	.443	19½	50,605	Mickey O'Neil/George Pratt/ George Kinnamon
Moultrie Giants (13)	44	96	.314	37½	33,083	Richard Klaus

Playoffs: Valdosta defeated Waycross 1-0 in a one game playoff for first place. Tifton 4 games, Valdosta 0; Albany 4 games, Waycross 2.
Finals: Albany 4 games, Tifton 0.

All-Star Team: 1B-Walter Shannon, Albany; **2B**-Paul DeMont, Cordele; **3B**-Walter Bremer, Waycross; **SS**-Gerald Schypinski, Cordele; **OF**-Denver Rikard, Albany; Jack Denison, Valdosta; Donovan Day, Cordele; Robert Murphy, Albany; **C**-Paul Emmes, Thomasville; Clair Troxell, Albany; **P**-Fred Green, Brunswick; Taylor Phillips, Waycross; Donald Shaffer, Valdosta; Julian Joyner, Albany; Antonio Sarmiento, Tifton; **Manager**-Fred Williams, Waycross.

BA: Ken Robinett, Thomasville, .352
Runs: Sam Goody, Albany, 95
Hits: Ken Robinett, Thomasville, 176
RBIs: Denver Rikard, Albany, 111
HRs: Parnell Ruark, Tifton, 19

Wins: Donald Shaffer, Valdosta, 25
SOs: Taylor Phillips, Waycross, 265
    Fred Green, Brunswick, 265
ERA: Antonio Sarmiento, Tifton, 1.26

D Kansas-Oklahoma-Missouri League
President: E.L. Dale

Standings	W	L	Pct.	GB	Attend.	Manager
Iola Indians	79	47	.627	—	42,327	Floyd Temple/Woody Fair
Miami Eagles (14)	67	57	.540	11	43,008	John Davenport
Ponca City Dodgers (10)	68	58	.540	11	55,726	Boyd Bartley
Bartlesville/Pittsburg Pirates# (15)	59	65	.476	19	34,267	Herschel Martin/Edward Hayes
Blackwell Cubs (11)	57	69	.452	22	51,000	Al Reitz
Independence Browns (7)	46	80	.365	33	39,487	Fred Collins

#Bartlesville moved to Pittsburg July 7.

Playoffs: Ponca City 1 game, Iola 0; Miami 1 game, Pittsburg 0.
Finals: Miami 2 games, Ponca City 0.

All-Star Team: 1B-Elbert Jarvis, Ponca City; **2B**-James McHugh, Miami; **3B**-Woody Fair, Iola; **SS**-Paul Weeks, Iola; **OF**-John Vossen, Miami; Don Stewart, Ponca City; Donald Geresy, Blackwell; **C**-Edward Sack, Miami; **P**-Jim Owens, Iola; Joe Vilk, Iola; William Wigle, Iola; Sylvester Zacher, Ponca City; Andy Varga, Blackwell.

BA: John Vossen, Miami, .335
Runs: Paul Weeks, Iola, 128
Hits: Gaspar del Toro, Iola, 155
RBIs: John Davenport, Miami, 116
HRs: Don Ervin, Miami, 24

Wins: Joe Vilk, Iola, 26
SOs: Jim Owens, Miami, 300
ERA: Jim Owens, Miami, 1.76

D Kitty League
President: Shelby Peace

Standings	W	L	Pct.	GB	Attend.	Manager
Fulton Lookouts (8)	82	37	.689	—	29,744	Sam Lamatina
Paducah Chiefs (16)	67	53	.558	15½	49,027	Robert Stanton/Gregory Masson
Madisonville Miners (2)	65	55	.542	17½	20,818	Sheriff Robinson
Union City Greyhounds	63	56	.529	19	27,230	Frank Radler
Owensboro Oilers	55	65	.458	27½	44,674	D.C. "Pud" Miller/ Moose Shetler
Hopkinsville Hoppers	50	70	.417	32½	19,129	Larry Brunke
Jackson Generals	48	71	.403	34	27,647	Vince Pankovits/ Dominic Italiano/Mickey O'Neil
Mayfield Clothiers (15)	47	70	.402	34	35,480	Red Barrett

Playoffs: Union City 3 games, Fulton 2; Madisonville 3 games, Paducah 1.
Finals: Madisonville 3 games, Union City 0.

All-Star Team: 1B-William Forbes, Hopkinsville; **2B**-Julius Stasko, Union City; **3B**-Howard Harkins, Owensboro; **SS**-Kenneth Meyer, Mayfield; **OF**-John Rothenhausler, Union City; Joseph Segrest, Paducah; Arthur Sabulsky, Hopkinsville; **C**-Robert Rand, Paducah; Jack Hall, Owensboro; **P**-Harold McGahey, Madisonville; Donnie Ford, Paducah; Melvin Rainey, Madisonville; Michael Conovan, Jackson.

BA: Howard Weeks, Fulton, .370
Runs: Harley Pierce, Fulton, 120
Hits: J.T. Jaynes, Owensboro/Union City, 166
RBIs: John Rothenhausler, Union City, 138
HRs: Jack Hall, Owensboro, 21
Wins: Alvin Brown, Fulton, 25
SOs: Michael Conovan, Jackson, 345
ERA: Walter Dypko, Paducah, 2.17

D Mississippi-Ohio Valley League
President: C.C. "Dutch" Hoffman

Standings	W	L	Pct.	GB	Attend.	Manager
Danville Dans*(9)	87	40	.685	—	75,898	Virl Minnis
Paris Lakers**	85	42	.669	2	36,606	Tom Sunkel
Decatur Commodores	73	52	.584	13	94,300	Julian Acosta
Hannibal Stags	70	57	.551	17	36,616	Walter DeFreitas
Mt. Vernon Kings	55	67	.451	29½	34,752	James Granneman/ Stanley Sadich/Frank Brookman
Vincennes Velvets/ Canton Citizens#	54	70	.435	31½	25,654	Chuck Hawley/Robert Sisk
Centralia Zeros	41	83	.331	44½	28,755	Charles Starasta/John Streza
Mattoon Indians (12)	35	89	.282	50½	49,316	Walter Dunkovich/ Charles Popovich/ Robert Carson

#Vincennes moved to Canton June 7.

Playoffs: Hannibal 3 games, Danville 1; Decatur 3 games, Paris 2.
Finals: Decatur 3 games, Hannibal 1.

All-Star Team: 1B-Clint McCord, Paris; **2B**-Virl Minnis, Danville; **3B**-Doyle Chadwick, Paris; **SS**-Gonzalo Chenard, Decatur; **OF**-Quincy Smith, Paris; Carlos Paula, Decatur; Jim Zapp, Paris; **C**-Arley Patino, Mt. Vernon; **P**-Ken Gohn, Danville; Armando Diaz, Hannibal; Amacio Ferro, Hannibal; James Paolo, Paris.

BA: Clint McCord, Paris, .392
Runs: Quincy Smith, Paris, 124
Hits: Clint McCord, Paris, 189
RBIs: Jim Zapp, Paris, 136
HRs: Jim Zapp, Paris, 20
Wins: Ken Gohn, Danville, 22
SOs: Amacio Ferro, Hannibal, 183
ERA: Ken Gohn, Danville, 1.58

D Mountain States League
President: Virgil Q. Wacks

Standings	W	L	Pct.	GB	Attend.	Manager
Hazard Bombers (10)	87	32	.731	—	14,600	Mervin Dornburg
Harlan Smokies (9)	73	45	.619	13½	32,579	Rex Carr
Morristown Red Sox	61	58	.513	26	10,597	James Burns
Big Stone Gap Rebels (13)	57	60	.487	29	11,161	Len Cross
Middlesboro Athletics	47	72	.395	40	15,364	Leon Culberson/Red Goff/ Joe McManus
Norton Braves	30	88	.254	56½	10,025	George Motto/Bill Fitchko/ Mark Muslin

Playoffs: Morristown 3 games, Hazard 1; Harlan 3 games, Big Stone Gap 2.
Finals: Harlan 3 games, Morristown 0.

BA: Orville Kitts, Morristown, .372
Runs: Ken Johnson, Hazard, 146
Hits: Len Cross, Big Stone Gap, 138
    Joe McManus, Middlesboro, 138
RBIs: Len Cross, Big Stone Gap, 125
HRs: Len Cross, Big Stone Gap, 40
Wins: Michael DelPiano, Harlan, 22
SOs: Michael DelPiano, Harlan, 144
ERA: Rafael Codinachs, Middlesboro, 2.78

D North Carolina State League
President: Walter H. Woodson, Jr.

Standings	W	L	Pct.	GB	Attend.	Manager
High Point-Thomasville Hi-Toms (1)	74	33	.692	—	17,345	Jim Gruzdis
Mooresville Moors	70	39	.642	5	18,241	Jim Mills
Salisbury Pirates	64	43	.598	10	31,920	Don Padgett

Elkin Blanketeers................ 45 64 .413 30   16,322 Wayne Harris
Statesville Owls (13) .... 41 68 .376 34   16,913 Ed Sokol/Robert Deese
Lexington Indians (6) .... 30 77 .280 44   16,720 Robert Deese/
                                                           Bob "Ducky" Detweiler/
                                                           Carl Campbell/Cliff Bolton

Playoffs: Salisbury 4 games, High Point-Thomasville 0; Mooresville 4 games, Elkin 1.
Finals: Mooresville 4 games, Salisbury 3.

BA: Don Stafford, Salisbury, .408 | **HRs:** Glenn Eury, Salisbury, 27
Runs: Henry Hampton, Salisbury, 111 | **Wins:** Roy Matthews, Salisbury, 20
Hits: Don Stafford, Salisbury, 160 | **SOs:** Jack Swift, Elkin, 283
RBIs: John Lybrand, Hi-Toms, 102 | **ERA:** Jack Swift, Elkin, 2.31

D PONY League
President: Vincent M. McNamara

Standings	W	L	Pct.	GB	Attend.	Manager
Hamilton Cardinals (16)	83	43	.659	—	82,286	Hal Contini
Jamestown Falcons (4)	81	45	.643	2	56,408	Tony Lupien
Olean Yankees (5)	70	55	.560	12½	31,850	Malcolm "Bunny" Mick
Hornell Dodgers (10).........	69	56	.552	13½	50,965	Doc Alexson
Batavia Clippers (15)..........	57	68	.456	25½	31,227	George Genovese
Corning Athletics (6)	53	71	.427	29	32,511	Joe Rullo
Bradford Phillies (14)	51	73	.411	31	27,228	Richard Carter
Wellsville Rockets (7)	36	89	.288	46½	27,289	Eugene Crumling/Rocco Sgro

Playoffs: Hornell 4 games, Hamilton 1; Jamestown 4 games, Olean 0.
Finals: Jamestown 4 games, Hornell 0.

All-Star Team: 1B-Tony Lupien, Jamestown; **2B**-Maury Wills, Hornell; **3B**-Alton Miller, Hamilton; **SS**-Richard Lisiecki, Jamestown; **OF**-Mike Trapani, Hamilton; Tom McDonald, Olean; Maurice Galand, Hornell; **C**-Charlie Lau, Jamestown; **P**-Bob Umfleet, Hamilton; Jerald Davie, Jamestown; George William Glendenning, Bradford; Jim Coates, Olean.

BA: Howard Jennings, Batavia, .373 | **Wins:** Bob Umfleet, Hamilton, 23
Runs: Maury Wills, Hornell, 108 | **SOs:** Jim Coates, Olean, 223
Hits: Maury Wills, Hornell, 160 | **ERA:** Bob Umfleet, Hamilton, 1.60
RBIs: Tom McDonald, Olean, 111 | **Pct:** Bob Umfleet, Hamilton, .852, 23-4
HRs: Tom McDonald, Olean, 20

D Sooner State League
President: Ucal Clanton

Standings	W	L	Pct.	GB	Attend.	Manager
McAlester Rockets (5)........	87	53	.621	—	52,395	Bill Cope
Pauls Valley Raiders (13) ...	80	59	.576	6½	34,500	Lou Brower
Chickasha Chiefs	78	62	.557	9	27,494	Ray Taylor
Shawnee Hawks	73	67	.521	14	44,680	Lou Fitzgerald/James Jolly
Sherman Twins	72	68	.514	15	19,815	Bennie Warren
Lawton Reds (12)	63	77	.450	24	52,807	Tuck McWilliams
Ada Herefords (7)...............	57	82	.410	29½	38,387	Bill Enos/Virl Loman/Jim England
Ardmore Indians	49	91	.350	38	24,362	Jackie Sullivan/Royce Mills/
						Hugh Willingham/
						Clyde Baldwin/Julian Morgan

Playoffs: McAlester 3 games, Shawnee 1; Pauls Valley 3 games, Chickasha 1.
Finals: McAlester 4 games, Pauls Valley 3.

All-Star Team: 1B-Don Williamson, Pauls Valley; **2B**-Blas Fernandez, Sherman; **3B**-Hector Bonet, Sherman; **SS**-Dale Harbaugh, McAlester; **OF**-Bob Hertel, McAlester; Vincent Downs, Lawton; Richard Sobeck, Ada; **C**-Bennie Warren, Sherman; **C**-Harold Long, Jr., Shawnee; **Util**-Raymond Maurer, Pauls Valley; **P**-Charles Seymour, McAlester; Charlie Rabe, Lawton.

BA: Ray Taylor, Chickasha, .365 | **HRs:** Bob Hertel, McAlester, 22
Runs: Vincent Downs, Lawton, 142 | Don Williamson, Pauls Valley, 22
Hits: Jim England, Ada, 198 | **Wins:** Charles Seymour, McAlester, 25
RBIs: Don Williamson, Pauls Valley, 148 | **SOs:** Charles Seymour, McAlester, 292
| **ERA:** Charles Seymour, McAlester, 1.91
| **Pct:** Charles Seymour, McAlester, .806, 25-6

D Western Carolina League
President: T. Earl Franklin

Standings	W	L	Pct.	GB	Attend.	Manager
Lincolnton Cardinals	72	39	.649	—	30,503	Bob Beal
Shelby Farmers	71	39	.645	½	31,598	David Coble
Marion Marauders	58	50	.537	12½	26,353	Gabby Grant/William Smith/
						Franklin Robinson
Rutherford County Owls	46	58	.442	22½	20,687	Cliff Bolton/William Greene

Hickory Rebels (11)........... 28 79 .262 42   14,729 Norman Small/Edwin Yount/
                                                          Charles Bowles
Morganton Aggies#.............. 41 51 .446 NA   18,124 George Bradshaw/
                                                          Eurice "Pete" Treece

#Morganton withdrew August 3.

Playoffs: Lincolnton 4 games, Marion 1; Shelby 4 games, Rutherford County 0.
Finals: Shelby 4 games, Lincolnton 3.

All-Star Team: 1B-Billy Reid Smith, Marion; **2B**-Bobby Davis, Marion; **3B**-Carroll Wright, Lincolnton; **SS**-John McAnulty, Morganton; **OF**-William McKenney, Morganton; Jack Triplett, Rutherford County; George Rose, Lincolnton; **P**-Harold Griggs, Hickory; William Barkley, Lincolnton; Eurice "Pete" Treece, Morganton; August Begemann, Marion; Norman Reinhardt, Rutherford County.

BA: Charles Ballard, Shelby, .352 | **HRs:** Ken Paschal, Rutherford County, 19
Runs: Tom Centeno, Lincolnton, 117 | **Wins:** Joe Sheppard, Shelby, 24
Hits: Carroll Wright, Lincolnton, 155 | **SOs:** Harold Griggs, Hickory, 195
RBIs: George Rose, Lincolnton, 107 | **ERA:** Joe Sheppard, Shelby, 2.31

D Wisconsin State League
President: Dan G. Cisco

Standings	W	L	Pct.	GB	Attend.	Manager
Sheboygan Indians (10)......	76	47	.618	—	33,387	Joe Hauser
Wausau Lumberjacks (4)....	64	57	.529	11	39,775	Mike Tresh
Oshkosh Giants (13)	63	58	.521	12	41,899	David Garcia
Appleton Papermakers (9)..	63	60	.512	13	71,999	Travis Jackson
Green Bay Bluejays (3)	64	61	.512	13	52,920	Phil Seghi
Wisconsin Rapids White Sox (2).................	60	60	.500	14½	43,911	Ira Hutchinson
Janesville Cubs (11).........	54	66	.450	20½	42,060	Harry Bright
Fond du Lac Panthers (5)....	43	78	.355	32	31,374	James Adlam/John Wilkinson

Playoffs: None.

All-Star Team: 1B-Dick Patton, Wisconsin Rapids; **2B**-Melvin Lightner, Wisconsin Rapids; **3B**-Jim Landis, Wisconsin Rapids; **SS**-Ralph Manfredi, Sheboygan; **OF**-Jesse Bucy, Wausau; Gordon Windhorn, Oshkosh; Pedro Almenares, Sheboygan; Gerald Sheehan, Janesville; **C**-John Sass, Wausau; **P**-Dick Grabowski, Appleton; Conrad Grob, Sheboygan; Walter Seward, Green Bay; John Gebhard, Fond du Lac.

BA: Sidney Ford, Wausau, .344 | **HRs:** Paul Bentley, Oshkosh, 21
Runs: Melvin Lightner, Wisconsin Rapids, 125 | **Wins:** Conrad Grob, Sheboygan, 24
Hits: Dick Patton, Wisconsin Rapids, 155 | **SOs:** Dick Grabowski, Appleton, 292
RBIs: Harry Bright, Janesville, 101 | **ERA:** Lawrence Donovan, Wausau, 2.17

Ind Mexican League
President: Dr. Eduardo Quijano Pitman

Standings	W	L	Pct.	GB	Manager
Veracruz Aguila	57	33	.633	—	Santos Amaro
Torreon Algodoneros..........	48	42	.528	9	Memo Garibay
Jalisco Charros...................	46	44	.511	11	Ramon Bragana/Jesus Diaz
San Luis Potosi Tuneros/ Mexico City Diablos Rojos#	45	45	.500	12	Rafael Pedrozo/Angel Castro
Nuevo Laredo Tecolotes.....	38	52	.422	19	Ezequiel Cruz/Agustin Bejerano/
					Roberto Ortiz
Monterrey Sultanes..............	36	54	.400	21	Lazaro Salazar

#San Luis Potosi (9-6) moved to Mexico City April 24.

BA: Rene Gonzalez, Veracruz, .370 | **Wins:** Guillermo Lopez, Veracruz, 19
Hits: Mario Ariosa, Veracruz, 132 | **SOs:** Lino Donoso, Veracruz, 235
RBIs: Rene Gonzalez, Veracruz, 84 | **ERA:** Vicente Torres, Monterrey, 2.43
HRs: Rene Gonzalez, Veracruz, 21

1952 Interleague Post Season Play

World Series
New York (American) 4 games, Brooklyn (National) 3

Junior World Series
Rochester (International) 4 games, Kansas City (American Association) 3
Total Attendance: 67,892

Dixie Series
Memphis (Southern Association) 4 games, Shreveport (Texas) 2
Total Attendance: 41,384

1952 Major League Farm Systems

American League

1 Boston (6): Louisville, Birmingham, Albany (NY), Roanoke, San Jose, High Point-Thomasville.
2 Chicago (7): Memphis, Colorado Springs, Waterloo, Gastonia, Superior, Madisonville, Wisconsin Rapids.
3 Cleveland (10): Indianapolis, Dallas, Reading, Wichita, Cedar Rapids, Spartanburg, Bakersfield, Ft. Smith, Daytona Beach, Green Bay.
4 Detroit (8): Buffalo, Little Rock, Williamsport, Durham, Davenport, Kinston, Jamestown, Wausau.
5 New York (10): Kansas City, Beaumont, Binghamton, Norfolk, Quincy, Boise, Joplin, Olean, McAlester, Fond du Lac.
6 Philadelphia (9): Ottawa, Savannah, Lincoln, Fayetteville, Harrisburg, St. Hyacinthe, Cordele, Lexington, Corning.
7 St. Louis (12): Toronto, San Antonio, Scranton, York, Anderson, Stockton, Pine Bluff, Aberdeen, Pocatello, Independence, Wellsville, Ada.
8 Washington (8): Chattanooga, Danville (VA), Havana, Charlotte, Drummondville, Roanoke Rapids, Orlando, Fulton.

National League

9 Boston (13): Milwaukee, Atlanta, Hartford, Wichita Falls, Hagerstown, Evansville, Ventura, Eau Claire, Quebec, Welch, Danville (IL), Harlan, Appleton.
10 Brooklyn (17): St. Paul, Montreal, Mobile, Ft. Worth, Elmira, Pueblo, Miami (FL), Lancaster, Newport News, Santa Barbara, Greenwood, Great Falls, Valdosta, Ponca City, Hazard, Hornell, Sheboygan.
11 Chicago (11): Springfield, Los Angeles, Macon, Des Moines, Greensboro, Visalia, Sioux Falls, Topeka, Blackwell, Hickory, Janesville.
12 Cincinnati (8): Tulsa, Columbia, Salisbury (MD), Burlington (IA), Ogden, Dublin, Mattoon, Lawton.
13 New York (14): Minneapolis, Nashville, Jacksonville, Sioux City, Sunbury, Knoxville, St. Cloud, Muskogee, Kingsport, Moultrie, Big Stone Gap, Statesville, Pauls Valley, Oshkosh.
14 Philadelphia (12): Baltimore, Schenectady, Tri-City, Wilmington, Terre Haute, Grand Forks, Salt Lake City, Granby, Salina, Pulaski, Miami (OK), Bradford.
15 Pittsburgh (15): Hollywood, New Orleans, Charleston (SC), Denver, Waco, Burlington-Graham, Modesto, Billings, St. Jean, Hutchinson, Bristol, Brunswick, Bartlesville/Pittsburg, Mayfield, Batavia.
16 St. Louis (15): Columbus (OH), Rochester, Houston, Columbus (GA), Omaha, Winston-Salem, Allentown, Lynchburg, Fresno, Johnson City, Goldsboro, Hazlehurst-Baxley, Albany (GA), Paducah, Hamilton.

1952 No-Hitters

Date	Pitcher	Team	League	Opponent	Score
4-24	Mason Bowes	Lincoln	Western	Omaha	3-0
4-24	Elmer Singleton	San Francisco	Pacific Coast	Sacramento	0-1 (12)
4-26	Joe Angel	Jacksonville Beach	Florida State	St. Augustine	16-0
4-30	Jack Bruner	Wichita	Western	Lincoln	7-0
5-1	Harold Gregg	Oakland	Pacific Coast	Portland	3-0 (7)
5-2	John Brown	Hutchinson	Western Assoc.	Salina	3-0
5-9	Clarence "Hooks" Iott	St. Petersburg	Florida Int'l	Ft. Lauderdale	5-0
5-12	Phil Gilbert	Eastman	Georgia State	Fitzgerald	3-0
5-12	Wallace Sinner	Billings	Pioneer	Boise	7-0
5-13	Ron Necciai	Bristol	Appalachian	Welch	7-0
5-15	Virgil Trucks	Detroit	American	Washington	1-0
5-15	John Brkich/ Nathan Feldman	Boise	Pioneer	Magic Valley	5-2 (5)
5-17	John Kenny	Greenville	Cotton States	Monroe	1-0
5-18	Gideon Applegate	Superior	Northern	Sioux Falls	3-0
5-22	Bill Herman	Jacksonville Beach	Florida State	Leesburg	4-0
5-22	Bill Bell	Bristol	Appalachian	Kingsport	1-0
5-23	John Briggs	Idaho Falls	Pioneer	Pocatello	8-0
5-24	Charles Bishop	Ottawa	International	Syracuse	1-0
5-24	Wilbur Striker	Green Bay	Wisconsin State	Appleton	8-0
5-25	Dick Lesch	Oshkosh	Wisconsin State	Sheboygan	2-1
5-26	Bill Bell	Bristol	Appalachian	Bluefield	4-0 (C)
5-28	Dean Stone	Charlotte	Tri-State	Gastonia	8-0
5-31	Ed Garrett	Decatur	Miss.-Ohio Valley	Mt. Vernon	5-1
6-5	Bob Beresford	Harrisburg	Interstate	Wilmington	1-0
6-6	El Roy Face	Ft. Worth	Texas	Houston	3-0 (10)
6-8	Wayne McLeland	Buffalo	International	Ottawa	4-0 (7)
6-12	McPherson Crum	Canton	Miss.-Ohio Valley	Hannibal	3-0
6-16	Gideon Applegate	Superior	Northern	St. Cloud	9-0 (7)
6-16	Tony DeVelis	Ponca City	KOM	Iola	8-0
6-17	Don Terwedow	Valdosta	Georgia-Florida	Moultrie	7-0
6-19	Carl Erskine	Brooklyn	National	Chicago	5-0
6-19	Marvin Hatcher	Monroe	Cotton States	Greenwood	5-0
6-24	Charlie Rabe	Lawton	Sooner State	Ardmore	2-0
6-25	John Wingo	Trois Rivieres	Provincial	Granby	11-0 (8)
6-28	Doug McDermid/ Fred Plushanski	Vidalia	Georgia State	Eastman	4-2
6-29	Gene Derwinski	Appleton	Wisconsin State	Oshkosh	1-0 (7)
7-1	Bill Wakely	Trois Rivieres	Provincial	Quebec	7-0 (7)
7-1	Bill Chambers	Portsmouth	Piedmont	Newport News	3-0
7-3	Mario Picone	Sioux City	Western	Des Moines	3-0
7-3	Roger Bowman	Oakland	Pacific Coast	Hollywood	5-0
7-4	Tom Mills	Jacksonville Beach	Florida State	Cocoa	4-0
7-4	Walter Bauman	Hazlehurst-Baxley	Georgia State	Fitzgerald	14-0
7-8	Lee Griffeth	Elmira	Eastern	Binghamton	0-2 (10)
7-10	Gilberto Torres	Miami	Florida Int'l	West Palm Beach	1-0
7-12	Wilson Parsons	Norfolk	Piedmont	Richmond	1-0
7-13	Walter Evans	Yuma	Southwest Int'l	Porterville	9-2 (7)
7-15	John Vander Meer	Tulsa	Texas	Shreveport	12-0
7-22	Jim Barnhardt	Portsmouth	Piedmont	Roanoke	5-1
7-26	Victor Vick/ Cameron Lewis	Oshkosh	Wisconsin State	Fond du Lac	1-0 (8)
7-27	Dick Strahs	Colorado Springs	Western	Lincoln	3-0 (7)
7-27	Ken Yount	Augusta	South Atlantic	Savannah	3-0 (5)
7-31	Bob Curtis	Waco	Big State	Tyler	2-1
8-3	Stan Wotychowicz	St. Hyacinthe	Provincial	Granby	6-0
8-4	Frank Sulkowski	West Palm Beach	Florida Int'l	Lakeland	5-0 (7)
8-6	Douglas Gostlin	Lancaster	Interstate	Sunbury	1-0
8-6	Walter Nothe	Miami Beach	Florida Int'l	Miami	0-1 (10)
8-12	J. Ford Smith	Phoenix	Arizona-Texas	Juarez	4-0
8-13	Don Elston	Sioux Falls	Northern	Grand Forks	5-0 (7)
8-15	Dick Marlowe	Buffalo	International	Baltimore	2-0 (P)
8-18	Robert Rauber	Hamilton	PONY	Olean	1-0
8-19	Lee Griffeth	Elmira	Eastern	Hartford	1-0 (10)
8-19	Stan Johnson	Norfolk	Piedmont	Roanoke	1-0 (5)
8-20	Frank Etchberger	Bradford	PONY	Batavia	1-0
8-20	Jim Mitchell	Batavia	PONY	Bradford	0-1
8-21	Vallie Eaves	Meridian	Cotton States	Natchez	3-0
8-25	Virgil Trucks	Detroit	American	New York	1-0
8-25	Bill Bell	Bristol	Appalachian	Bluefield	4-0 (7)
8-26	Frank Ramsey	Bristol	Appalachian	Bluefield	1-0
8-28	Gordon Roach	Eau Claire	Northern	Aberdeen	10-1 (7)
8-28	Robert Smith	Roanoke	Piedmont	Newport News	3-0 (7)
8-29	Dick Grabowski	Appleton	Wisconsin State	Oshkosh	2-0
9-1	Hank Aguirre	Bakersfield	California	Ventura	11-0 (7)
9-4	Bob Danielson	Charlotte	Tri-State	Anderson	1-0 (PO)
9-5	Jack Collum	Rochester	International	Ottawa	9-0
9-7	Dean Stone	Charlotte	Tri-State	Anderson	5-0 (PO)
9-7	Ernest Nevel	Kansas City	American Assoc.	Minneapolis	3-0 (7)
9-10	Jehosie Heard	Victoria	Western Int'l	Lewiston	11-2
9-11	Gene Staton	Salisbury	N. Carolina State	Mooresville	5-2 (PO)

Number in parentheses indicates innings if other than nine; "P" indicates perfect game; "PO" indicates playoff game; "C" indicates no-hitters in consecutive starts.

THIS DATE IN MINOR LEAGUE HISTORY

February 15, 1952, The first black umpire in Organized Ball, Emmett L. Ashford, signed to work in the Class C Southwest International League.

April 21, 1952, Sheldon "Larry" Lejeune, an outfielder whose record of throwing a ball 426 feet, 9-1/2 inches on October 8, 1910, had never been surpassed by a player in Organized Ball, died in Eloise, Michigan. Lejeune was a member of the Evansville club of the Central League at the time he set the record, while competing in a field meet at Cincinnati. The previous mark of 400 feet, 7 inches was set by Jack Hatfield of the New York Mutuals at Union Park, Brooklyn, October 15, 1872.

April 29, 1952, Ageless Earl Caldwell made his first start of the Gulf Coast League season and hurled the Harlingen Capitols to a four-hit, 5-1 victory over Lake Charles. Caldwell, who observed his 47th birthday on April 9, now had 27 years in the game, having started his Organized Ball career in 1926 with Temple of the Texas

Association. Last year Caldwell led the Gulf Coast League in ERA with a 2.21 mark.

April 29, 1952, Ft. Lauderdale, after losing its first 29 games to set a Florida International League record, won its initial decision of the season with a 7-4 win over West Palm Beach.

May 2, 1952, Ron Necciai of Bristol, Appalachian League, struck out 20 Kingsport batters, one shy of the loop record. He allowed only two hits in a 4-0 shutout.

May 3, 1952, Two umpires, armed with bats, killed a cottonwood moccasin in the outfield at Crowley, Evangeline League, during a game with Houma.

May 13, 1952, Ron Necciai of Bristol, Appalachian League, hurled a no-hitter over Welch, West Virginia, and fanned a fantastic 27 batters. Ironically, one batter was retired on a ground out. Necciai set down 27 on strikes because his catcher missed a third strike and he fanned four in that frame. Necciai joined the Pittsburgh Pirates during the latter part of the 1952 season and compiled a 1-6 record. His arm went dead the following spring and he quit baseball at that time, though he made a brief comeback attempt with Hollywood of the Pacific Coast League in 1955.

May 21, 1952, Bristol righthander Ron Necciai continued his sensational strikeout performance when he whiffed 24 Kingsport batters in an Appalachian League victory. It was Necciai's final appearance in a Bristol uniform before being reassigned by the parent Pittsburgh Pirates to Burlington-Graham in the Class B Carolina League. Necciai started four games for Bristol, winning them all, and appeared twice in relief roles. In his debut he struck out 20 and followed this with 19 more in his second effort. He set down 27 on strikes on May 13, for an Organized Ball record. Four days before his triumph over Kingsport he struck out eight in 2-2/3 innings against Johnson City. He fanned five in the eighth frame when two batters reached base as the catcher dropped the ball.

May 25, 1952, Jack Salveson of San Diego, now 38 and playing his 21st year in Organized Ball, notched his 200th Pacific Coast League victory, a record matched by only ten others in the history of the loop. The 200-game winners were: Frank Shellenback, 295; Spider Baum, 261; Harry Krause, 249; Dick "Kewpie" Barrett, 234; Otis Crandall, 230; Tony Freitas, 228; Sad Sam Gibson, 227; Herman Pillette, 220; Cack Henley, 215; Rudy Kallio, 208; and Salveson, 200.

May 26, 1952, Bill Bell, 18-year-old righthander from Goldsboro, North Carolina, notched his second consecutive no-hit game for Bristol while beating Bluefield 4-0 in an Appalachian League game. He struck out 20. On May 22, Bell threw his first no-hitter, blanking Kingsport 1-0, striking out 17. Bell's feat was the first recorded since Johnny Vander Meer turned the trick in 1938 for the Cincinnati Reds, and was believed to have been the first in the minor leagues since 1901, when Clarence Wright of Dayton hurled successive no-hitters against Columbus and Grand Rapids. Bell now had three victories for Bristol, and had allowed only one run and five hits while striking out 58. In his first start, he beat Bluefield 13-1 and struck out 20.

June 13, 1952, Superior, Northern League, suffered its first loss in 18 games on the road this season, losing to Duluth 2-1 in a contest called after six innings, following four interruptions because of fog.

June 15, 1952, Two were killed and 60 injured when a portion of the old wooden grandstand collapsed twenty minutes before game time at Parque Delta, Mexico City, where the Mexican League games were played.

June 21, 1952, The Harrisburg club of the Interstate League signed Mrs. Eleanor Engle, an attractive 24-year-old, as a player. Mrs. Engle took the field the next day and worked out at shortstop before Harrisburg's game with Lancaster. The 132-pound stenographer scooped up a few grounders and took a turn at bat in the practice session, but did not play. President George Trautman of the National Association immediately voided the contract and barred any minor league club from signing women players.

June 29, 1952, Bobby Slaybaugh, who suffered the loss of an eye during spring training with the St. Louis Cardinals, made his first start of the season for Omaha, Western League, and came through with a sparkling four-hit 1-0 win over Des Moines.

July 3, 1952, Froggie Betcher rapped a home run for Cordele, the first round-tripper of the season in 73 games for the Georgia-Florida League club. (It was Cordele's only homer of their 139-game season.)

July 4, 1952, One of the game's rarities, an ambidextrous pitcher, turned up in a Longhorn League game at Roswell. Rudie Malone, normally a righthander, switched to pitching lefthanded in an attempt to stop Joe Bauman, Artesia's lefthanded slugging star. Malone held Bauman to a single in two trips, but, pitching righthanded to the other hitters in the Artesia lineup, he was driven from the mound in the fourth and charged with a 12-8 defeat.

July 6, 1952, Marv Throneberry of Quincy, 18-year-old bonus first sacker of the New York Yankees, doubled into a double play during a Three-I League game with Cedar Rapids. Two base runners were caught at home on Throneberry's drive.

July 11, 1952, Herb Score, $60,000 bonus pitcher, received a rough reception in his Organized Ball debut against Milwaukee. The Indianapolis, American Association, southpaw gave up three runs in the fourth inning and was chased during a seven-run fifth as the Brewers handed him a 12-0 setback.

July 15, 1952, Two members of the Monterrey club of the Mexican League, pitchers Vicente Torrez and Adolfo Garcia, were killed and ten others injured as the team's chartered bus had a head-on crash with a grain truck en route to Mexico City.

July 17, 1952, Jim Piersall, zany Birmingham outfielder recently sent down by the Red Sox, was handed a three-day suspension by the Southern Association president after having been tossed out of a game the previous night for the fourth time in less than three weeks with the Barons. Piersall had reportedly run up a long distance telephone bill of $106 during the club's four-day stay in New Orleans earlier this month.

July 19, 1952, Fitzgerald's use of a 12-year-old black batboy in a Georgia State League game at Statesboro not only broke the color line in the Class D circuit, but it also cost an umpire his job and resulted in the suspension of a manager.

August 4, 1952, Tony Ponce of Phoenix, Arizona-Texas League, made five hits in five trips at bat in posting a 12-3 win over Bisbee-Douglas.

August 12, 1952, The Ft. Worth-Beaumont game at Beaumont, Texas League, was interrupted by seagulls landing on the field. The gulls harassed the players for several minutes before finally settling down in deep center field to watch the game.

August 21, 1952, Chet Covington, appearing with his 22nd club since breaking into Organized Ball in 1939, hurled Greensboro, Carolina League, to a 9-1 victory over Danville. The 41-year-old lefty was acquired from Lakeland, Florida International League.

August 22, 1952, Sam Lynn Park, home of the Bakersfield team in the California League, escaped the earthquake that caused millions of dollars of damage to the business district of that city.

August 25, 1952, Bill Bell of Bristol, Appalachian League, hurled his third no-hit game of the season when he blanked Bluefield 4-0 in a seven-inning game. Earlier in the season, Bell hurled two straight no-hitters, beating Kingsport 1-0 on May 22, and coming back four nights later with a 4-0 decision over Bluefield.

August 29, 1952, Durham, Carolina League, defeated Greensboro 1-0 in 18 innings. Eddie Neville went the distance for the winners, scattering nine hits and scoring the game's only run in the final frame.

August 30, 1952, Hickory, Western Carolina League, which had lost 20 straight games, closed the season without any further losses as the result of a 1-1 tie in a nine-inning game stopped by rain and a washout of the final scheduled contest on August 31.

August 31, 1952, Tony Freitas, 44-year-old pitcher with Stockton, California League, who hurled for the Athletics in 1932 and 1933 and for the Reds from 1934 to 1936, turned in his 18th win of the season by defeating San Jose.

September 1, 1952, Earl Caldwell, 47-year-old righthander, captured his 20th victory for Harlingen, Gulf Coast League, when he beat Brownsville 6-2.

September 7, 1952, Larry Lejeune's distance-throwing record, which had stood for 42 years, was broken by Chattanooga outfielder Don Grate, when he heaved a ball 434 feet, one inch at Engel Stadium in Chattanooga. The former record by a professional ball player was 426 feet, 9-1/2 inches set by Lejeune at Cincinnati, October 8, 1910. Grate, a former All-American basketball player at Ohio State University, was signed by the Philadelphia Phillies as a pitcher in 1945. He switched to the outfield in 1951 with Chattanooga.

November 4, 1952, John Leonard "Pepper" Martin, the old Wild Horse of the Osage, hung up his spikes in order to don a deputy sheriff's badge in McAlester, Oklahoma. Martin managed Miami Beach in the Florida International League the past season.

December 6, 1952, David Johnson, a 21-year-old Cardinals farmhand who played with Omaha, Houston and Columbus the past season as an outfielder, was fatally wounded in a deer hunting accident near Pineville, Missouri.

1953

American League
President: William Harridge

Standings	W	L	Pct.	GB	Attend.	Manager
New York Yankees............	99	52	.656	—	1,537,811	Casey Stengel
Cleveland Indians	92	62	.597	8½	1,069,176	Al Lopez
Chicago White Sox............	89	65	.578	11½	1,191,353	Paul Richards
Boston Red Sox	84	69	.549	16	1,026,133	Lou Boudreau
Washington Senators	76	76	.500	23½	595,594	Bucky Harris
Detroit Tigers....................	60	94	.390	40½	884,658	Fred Hutchinson
Philadelphia Athletics.........	59	95	.383	41½	362,113	Jimmy Dykes
St. Louis Browns	54	100	.351	46½	297,238	Marty Marion

BA: Mickey Vernon, Washington, .337
Runs: Al Rosen, Cleveland, 115
Hits: Harvey Kuenn, Detroit, 209
RBIs: Al Rosen, Cleveland, 145
HRs: Al Rosen, Cleveland, 43

Wins: Bob Porterfield, Washington, 22
SOs: Billy Pierce, Chicago, 186
ERA: Eddie Lopat, New York, 2.42
Pct: Eddie Lopat, New York, .800, 16-4

National League
President: Warren C. Giles

Standings	W	L	Pct.	GB	Attend.	Manager
Brooklyn Dodgers............	105	49	.682	—	1,163,419	Chuck Dressen
Milwaukee Braves	92	62	.597	13	1,826,397	Charlie Grimm
Philadelphia Phillies	83	71	.539	22	853,644	Steve O'Neill
St. Louis Cardinals	83	71	.539	22	880,242	Eddie Stanky
New York Giants	70	84	.455	35	811,518	Leo Durocher
Cincinnati Reds.................	68	86	.442	37	548,086	Rogers Hornsby/Buster Mills
Chicago Cubs....................	65	89	.422	40	763,658	Phil Cavarretta
Pittsburgh Pirates................	50	104	.325	55	572,757	Fred Haney

BA: Carl Furillo, Brooklyn, .344
Runs: Duke Snider, Brooklyn, 132
Hits: Richie Ashburn, Philadelphia, 205
RBIs: Roy Campanella, Brooklyn, 142
HRs: Ed Mathews, Milwaukee, 47

Wins: Warren Spahn, Milwaukee, 23
Robin Roberts, Philadelphia, 23
SOs: Robin Roberts, Philadelphia, 198
ERA: Warren Spahn, Milwaukee, 2.10
Pct: Carl Erskine, Brooklyn, .769, 20-6

(Open) Pacific Coast League
President: Clarence H. Rowland

Standings	W	L	Pct.	GB	Attend.	Manager
Hollywood Stars	106	74	.589	—	274,522	Bobby Bragan
Seattle Rainiers	98	82	.544	8	224,562	Bill Sweeney
Los Angeles Angels (10)	93	87	.517	13	363,818	Stan Hack
Portland Beavers................	92	88	.511	14	236,762	Clay Hopper
San Francisco Seals	91	89	.506	15	175,459	Tommy Heath
San Diego Padres	88	92	.489	18	168,617	Lefty O'Doul
Oakland Oaks	77	103	.428	29	135,784	Augie Galan
Sacramento Solons	75	105	.417	31	180,271	Gene Desautels

All-Star Team: 1B-Fred Richards, Los Angeles; **2B**-Artie Wilson, Seattle; **3B**-Leo Thomas, Seattle; **SS**-Gene Baker, Los Angeles; **OF**-Bobby Usher, Los Angeles; Dale Long, Hollywood; Jack Tobin, Seattle; **C**-Raymond Orteig, Seattle; **Util**-Jack Phillips, Hollywood; **P**-Allen Gettel, Oakland; George O'Donnell, Hollywood; Royce Lint, Portland; **MVP**-Dale Long, Hollywood; **Manager**-Bobby Bragan.

BA: Bob Dillinger, Sacramento, .366
Runs: Jack Tobin, Seattle, 116
Hits: Bob Dillinger, Sacramento, 236
RBIs: Dale Long, Hollywood, 116

HRs: Dale Long, Hollywood, 35
Wins: Allen Gettel, Oakland, 24
SOs: Joe Hatten, Los Angeles, 152
ERA: Memo Luna, San Diego, 2.67

AAA American Association
Presidents: Bruce Dudley/Edward S. Doherty

Standings	W	L	Pct.	GB	Attend.	Manager
Toledo Mud Hens (12)	90	64	.584	—	343,614	Tommy Holmes/George Selkirk
Kansas City Blues (5)...........	88	66	.571	2	247,556	Harry Craft
Louisville Colonels (1).......	84	70	.545	6	177,080	Pinky Higgins
Indianapolis Indians (3)......	82	72	.532	8	206,786	Birdie Tebbetts
Minneapolis Millers (13)....	76	78	.494	14	128,630	Frank Genovese/Fred Fitzsimmons
St. Paul Saints (9)	72	82	.468	18	139,348	Clay Bryant
Columbus Red Birds (16)....	64	90	.416	26	84,995	Johnny Keane
Charleston Senators (2)	60	94	.390	30	178,377	Joe Becker

Playoffs: Toledo 4 games, Louisville 3; Kansas City 4 games, Indianapolis 2.
Finals: Kansas City 4 games, Toledo 3.

All-Star Team: 1B-Maurice "Mo" Mozzali, Columbus; **2B**-Jack Cassini, St. Paul; **3B**-Rance Pless, Minneapolis; **SS**-Alex Grammas, Kansas City; **OF**-Sam Jethroe, Toledo; Vic Power, Kansas City; Wally Post, Indianapolis; Charley Maxwell, Louisville; **C**-Ray Katt, Minneapolis; Bill Sarni, Columbus; **P**-Gene Conley, Toledo; Edward Blake, Indianapolis; Frank Baumann, Louisville; Dick Tomanek, Indianapolis; **MVP**-Gene Conley, Toledo; **Manager**-George Selkirk, Toledo.

BA: Vic Power, Kansas City, .349
Runs: Sam Jethroe, Toledo, 137
Hits: Vic Power, Kansas City, 217
RBIs: Wally Post, Indianapolis, 120

HRs: George Wilson, Minneapolis, 34
Wins: Gene Conley, Toledo, 23
SOs: Gene Conley, Toledo, 211
ERA: Gene Conley, Toledo, 2.90

AAA International League
President: Frank J. Shaughnessy

Standings	W	L	Pct.	GB	Attend.	Manager
Rochester Red Wings (16)..	97	57	.630	—	252,467	Harry Walker
Montreal Royals (9)............	89	63	.586	7	285,552	Walter Alston
Buffalo Bisons (4)	87	65	.572	9	268,086	Jack Tighe
Baltimore Orioles (14).......	82	72	.532	15	207,182	Don Heffner
Toronto Maple Leafs	78	76	.506	19	382,432	Burleigh Grimes
Ottawa Athletics (6)..........	71	83	.461	26	149,219	Frank Skaff
Syracuse Chiefs	58	95	.379	38½	83,992	Bruno Betzel
Springfield Cubs (10)	51	102	.333	45½	85,281	Bruce Edwards/John Sheehan

Playoffs: Rochester 4 games, Baltimore 3; Montreal 4 games, Buffalo 2.
Finals: Montreal 4 games, Rochester 0.

All-Star Team: 1B-Rocky Nelson, Montreal; **2B**-Louis Ortiz, Rochester; **3B**-Hector Rodriguez, Syracuse; **SS**-Clarence "Buddy" Hicks, Buffalo; **OF**-Sandy Amoros, Montreal; Tom Burgess, Rochester; Frank Carswell, Buffalo; **C**-Charles Thompson, Montreal; **P**-Bob Trice, Ottawa; Tom Lasorda, Montreal; **MVP**-Rocky Nelson, Montreal; **Pitcher of the Year**-Bob Trice, Ottawa; **Manager**-Harry Walker, Rochester.

BA: Sandy Amoros, Montreal, .353
Runs: Sandy Amoros, Montreal, 128
Hits: Sandy Amoros, Montreal, 190
RBIs: Rocky Nelson, Montreal, 136

HRs: John Wallaesa, Springfield/Buffalo, 36
Wins: Bob Trice, Ottawa, 21
SOs: Don Johnson, Toronto, 156
ERA: Don Johnson, Toronto, 2.67

AA Southern Association
President: Charles A. Hurth

Standings	W	L	Pct.	GB	Attend.	Manager
Memphis Chicks (2)	87	67	.565	—	202,577	Luke Appling
Nashville Vols (13).............	85	69	.552	2	149,578	Hugh Poland
Atlanta Crackers (12)..........	84	70	.545	3	290,510	Gene Mauch
Birmingham Barons (5)......	78	76	.506	9	207,612	Mayo Smith
New Orleans Pelicans (15) ..	76	78	.494	11	123,905	Danny Murtaugh
Chattanooga Lookouts (8) ..	73	81	.474	14	172,042	Cal Ermer
Mobile Bears (9)	66	87	.431	20½	77,621	Ed Head
Little Rock Travelers (4)	66	87	.431	20½	104,081	Paul Campbell

Playoffs: Birmingham 4 games, Memphis 1; Nashville 4 games, Atlanta 2.
Finals: Nashville 4 games, Birmingham 1.

All-Star Team: 1B-Gus Triandos, Birmingham; **2B**-Harry Bright, Memphis; **3B**-Bob Boring, Nashville; **SS**-Dick Smith, New Orleans; **OF**-Roy Shearer, Mobile; Norm Siebern, Birmingham; Bill Wilson, Memphis; Dick Sinovic, Atlanta; William Kerr, Mobile; **C**-Hal Smith, Birmingham; Ralph Novotney, Nashville; Jack Parks, Atlanta; **Util**-David Jaska, Little Rock; **P**-Dick Strahs, Memphis; Tom Fine, Memphis; John Kucab, Birmingham; Jack Harshman, Nashville; Len Yochim, New Orleans; Taylor Phillips, Atlanta.

BA: Bill Taylor, Nashville, .350
Runs: Bob Boring, Nashville, 108
Hits: Dick Sinovic, Atlanta, 201
RBIs: Dick Sinovic, Atlanta, 126

HRs: Bill Wilson, Memphis, 34
Wins: Jack Harshman, Nashville, 23
SOs: Jim Constable, Nashville, 183
ERA: Art Fowler, Atlanta, 3.03

AA Texas League
President: J. Alvin Gardner

Standings	W	L	Pct.	GB	Attend.	Manager
Dallas Eagles	88	66	.571	—	207,676	Dutch Meyer
Tulsa Oilers (11).................	83	71	.539	5	154,683	Joe Schultz
Ft. Worth Cats (9)..............	82	72	.532	6	136,524	Max Macon
Oklahoma City Indians.......	80	74	.519	8	133,064	Tom Tatum
Shreveport Sports	79	75	.513	9	155,424	Mickey Livingston
Houston Buffalos (16)........	72	82	.468	16	203,543	Al Hollingsworth/Dixie Walker
San Antonio Missions (7)...	67	87	.435	21	98,711	James Crandall/Bill Norman
Beaumont Exporters	65	89	.422	23	102,802	Al Vincent

Playoffs: Dallas 4 games, Oklahoma City 3; Tulsa 4 games, Ft. Worth 2.
Finals: Dallas 4 games, Tulsa 1.

MVP-Joe Frazier, Oklahoma City; **Pitcher of the Year**-Don Fracchia, Beaumont.

BA: Joe Frazier, Oklahoma City, .332
Runs: Joe Frazier, Oklahoma City, 109
Hits: Vinicio Garcia, Shreveport, 183
RBIs: Russ Burns, Oklahoma City, 124

HRs: Harry Heslet, Shreveport, 41
Wins: Red Murff, Dallas, 17
SOs: Ryne Duren, San Antonio, 212
ERA: Floyd Wooldridge, Houston, 2.20

*Won first-half   **Won second-half   ***Won both halves
Numbers after nicknames indicate farm system.
Affiliation listed at end of year.

A Eastern League
President: Thomas H. Richardson

Standings	W	L	Pct.	GB	Attend.	Manager
Reading Indians (3)	101	47	.682	—	106,368	Kerby Farrell
Binghamton Triplets (5)	96	55	.636	6½	89,301	Phil Page
Schenectady Blue Jays (14)	86	65	.570	16½	66,320	Skeeter Newsome
Albany Senators (1)	78	74	.513	25	80,267	Jack Burns/Elmer Yoter
Elmira Pioneers (9)	70	80	.467	32	59,918	Albert Brancato
Williamsport Athletics (6)	65	85	.433	37	64,572	George Staller
Wilkes-Barre Barons	54	95	.362	47½	89,773	Danny Litwhiler
Scranton Miners (8)	51	100	.338	51½	62,266	Morris "Smut" Aderholt

Playoffs: Reading 4 games, Schenectady 2; Binghamton 4 games, Albany 1.
Finals: Binghamton 4 games, Reading 2.

All-Star Team: 1B-Joe Altobelli, Reading; **2B**-James Cleverly, Reading; **3B**-Jim Finigan, Binghamton; **SS**-Tom Korczowski, Wilkes-Barre; **OF**-Danny Schell, Schenectady; Rocky Colavito, Reading; James Engleman, Binghamton; **C**-Kenneth Worley, Elmira; **C**-Charles Saverine, Schenectady; **P**-Wally Burnette, Binghamton; Steve Kraly, Binghamton.

BA: Danny Schell, Schenectady, .333
Runs: James Cleverly, Reading, 112
Hits: Danny Schell, Schenectady, 185
RBIs: Rocky Colavito, Reading, 121
HRs: Rocky Colavito, Reading, 28
Wins: Wally Burnette, Binghamton, 23
SOs: John Meyer, Schenectady, 226
ERA: Steve Kraly, Binghamton, 2.08

A South Atlantic League
President: Dick Butler

Standings	W	L	Pct.	GB	Attend.	Manager
Jacksonville Braves (12)	93	44	.679	—	142,721	Ben Geraghty
Columbia Reds (11)	92	48	.657	2½	97,234	Ernie White
Columbus Cardinals (16)	67	70	.489	26	75,801	Sheldon "Chief" Bender
Savannah Indians (6)	68	73	.482	27	84,142	Les Bell
Macon Peaches (10)	67	74	.475	28	64,452	Frank Kerr
Augusta Rams	65	74	.468	29	96,776	Lou Fitzgerald/Robert Wilkins
Charleston Rebels (15)	55	84	.396	39	55,837	Frank Oceak/Norman Shope/ Larry Shepard
Montgomery Grays (4)	50	90	.357	44½	64,279	Charlie Metro

Playoffs: Jacksonville 3 games, Savannah 1; Columbia 3 games, Columbus 0.
Finals: Columbia 4 games, Jacksonville 3.

All-Star Team: 1B-Joe Andrews, Jacksonville; **2B**-Hank Aaron, Jacksonville; **3B**-Robert Hyatt, Columbus; **SS**-Felix Mantilla, Jacksonville; **OF**-Everett Joyner, Columbus; Ted Delguercio, Charleston; Omer Tolson, Augusta; **C**-Harry Minor, Savannah; **Util**-Tom Giordano, Savannah; Lewis Davis, Columbia; **P**-Clarence Zieser, Columbia; Larry Lasalle, Jacksonville; **Manager**-Ben Geraghty, Jacksonville.

BA: Hank Aaron, Jacksonville, .362
Runs: Hank Aaron, Jacksonville, 115
Hits: Hank Aaron, Jacksonville, 208
RBIs: Hank Aaron, Jacksonville, 125
HRs: Tom Giordano, Savannah, 24
Wins: Larry Lasalle, Jacksonville, 19
Ray Crone, Jacksonville, 19
SOs: Larry Lasalle, Jacksonville, 185
ERA: Corky Valentine, Columbia, 2.11

A Western League
President: Senator Edwin C. Johnson

Standings	W	L	Pct.	GB	Attend.	Manager
Colorado Springs Sky Sox (2)	95	59	.617	—	141,117	Don Gutteridge
Denver Bears (15)	94	60	.610	1	322,128	Andy Cohen
Pueblo Dodgers (9)	78	77	.503	17½	103,878	George Pfister
Des Moines Bruins (10)	77	78	.497	18½	98,972	Kemp Wicker/Bruce Edwards
Omaha Cardinals (16)	74	80	.481	21	115,512	George Kissell
Lincoln Chiefs (12)	71	83	.461	24	87,615	Lou Finney/Walter Linden
Sioux City Soos (13)	70	84	.455	25	45,412	Ray Mueller
Wichita Indians (7)	58	96	.377	37	68,683	George Hausmann/Mark Christman

Playoffs: Des Moines 3 games, Colorado Springs 1; Denver 3 games, Pueblo 0.
Finals: Des Moines 3 games, Denver 1.

All-Star Team: 1B-Jim Gentile, Pueblo; **2B**-Curt Roberts, Denver; **3B**-Bob Ries, Denver; **SS**-Clyde Perry, Colorado Springs; **OF**-Glen Gorbous, Pueblo; Jim Landis, Colorado Springs; Russell Rac, Omaha; Orinthal Anderson, Denver; **C**-Sam Hairston, Colorado Springs; Jack Shepard, Denver; **Util**-William Ley, Colorado Springs; **P**-Norman Brown, Lincoln; Nelson King, Sioux City; Jake Thies, Denver; Robert Zick, Des Moines; Joe Stupak, Sioux City; Karl Spooner, Pueblo; **Manager**-Don Gutteridge, Colorado Springs.

BA: Kent Pflasterer, Pueblo, .350
Runs: Len Johnston, Colorado Springs, 133
Hits: Glen Gorbous, Pueblo, 204
RBIs: Jerry Crosby, Colorado Springs, 115
HRs: Jim Gentile, Pueblo, 34
Wins: Norman Brown, Lincoln, 21
SOs: Karl Spooner, Pueblo, 198
ERA: Walt Montgomery, Omaha, 2.43
Jake Thies, Denver, 2.43

A Western International League
President: Robert P. Brown

Standings	W	L	Pct.	GB	Attend.	Manager
Lewiston Broncs (7)	78	55	.586	—	81,914	Bill Brenner
Salem Senators*	79	58	.577	1	81,305	Hugh Luby
Edmonton Eskimos	79	61	.564	2½	92,758	Bob Sturgeon
Vancouver Capilanos	77	64	.546	5	75,877	Harvey Storey
Spokane Indians**(14)	75	67	.528	7½	80,873	Don Osborn
Yakima Bears	70	74	.486	13½	59,100	Dario Lodigiani/Walt Novick
Calgary Stampeders	59	75	.440	19½	40,106	Gene Lillard
Tri-City Braves	59	77	.434	20½	70,638	Edo Vanni
Wenatchee Chiefs	59	80	.424	22	64,036	Myron McCormick
Victoria Tyees	57	81	.413	23½	55,352	Cecil Garriott

Playoff: Spokane 4 games, Salem 2.

All-Star Team: 1B-John Weaver, Edmonton; Leonard Noren, Yakima; **2B**-Leonard Tran, Tri-City; **3B**-Harvey Storey, Vancouver; **SS**-Gene Tanselli, Salem; **OF**-Bob Wellman, Yakima; Stan Palys, Spokane; Granville Gladstone, Victoria; James Deyo, Salem; **C**-Jack Warren, Tri-City; **P**-John Conant, Edmonton; Gene Roenspie, Salem; Jack Spring, Spokane; Arthur Worth, Spokane.

BA: Jack Warren, Tri-City, .354
Runs: Charles Mead, Calgary, 124
Hits: Leonard Noren, Yakima, 187
RBIs: Charles Mead, Calgary, 116
HRs: Charles Mead, Calgary, 31
Wins: John Conant, Edmonton, 24
SOs: John Maryhall, Lewiston, 165
ERA: Pete Hernandez, Vancouver, 3.06

B Big State League
President: Howard Green

Standings	W	L	Pct.	GB	Attend.	Manager
Wichita Falls Spudders (12)	85	58	.594	—	71,247	Whitey Wietelmann
Tyler East Texans	81	63	.563	4½	50,273	Billy Capps
Texarkana Bears	78	68	.534	8½	89,604	Chuck Hawley
Waco/Longview Pirates#(15)	77	68	.531	9	32,646	Buster Chatham
Temple Eagles	72	73	.497	14	66,341	Francis "Salty" Parker/ Len Goldstein
Greenville/Bryan Majors@	70	77	.476	17	30,051	Jimmy Adair/Clyde McDowell
Austin Pioneers	69	77	.473	17½	73,229	Al Unser
Paris Indians	48	96	.333	37½	40,658	John "Red" Davis

#Waco (16-17) moved to Longview May 22 after a tornado destroyed Katy Park in Waco.
@Greenville (39-28) moved to Bryan June 25.

Playoffs: Wichita Falls 4 games, Longview 0; Tyler 4 games, Texarkana 1.
Finals: Wichita Falls 4 games, Tyler 3.

All-Star Team: 1B-William Ankoviak, Texarkana; **2B**-John Lucadello, Wichita Falls; **3B**-Oran Davis, Texarkana; **SS**-Everett Hall, Wichita Falls; **OF**-Albert Neil, Wichita Falls; James Kirby, Tyler; Jacques Monette, Waco/Longview; **C**-Humberto Marti, Wichita Falls; **P**-Noel Oquendo, Wichita Falls; Gale Pringle, Tyler; Fred Green, Waco/Longview; Pat Scantlebury, Texarkana.

BA: Albert Neil, Wichita Falls, .356
Runs: Albert Neil, Wichita Falls, 126
Hits: Albert Neil, Wichita Falls, 185
RBIs: Albert Neil, Wichita Falls, 137
HRs: Albert Neil, Wichita Falls, 39
Wins: Pat Scantlebury, Texarkana, 24
SOs: Pat Scantlebury, Texarkana, 177
ERA: Jodie Phipps, Greenville/Bryan, 2.19

B Carolina League
President: Glenn E. "Ted" Mann

Standings	W	L	Pct.	GB	Attend.	Manager
Raleigh Capitals	83	57	.593	—	75,130	Herb Brett
Danville Leafs (13)	79	59	.572	3	84,494	Andy Gilbert
Burlington-Graham Pirates (15)	75	65	.536	8	71,708	Stan Wentzel
Reidsville Luckies	73	66	.525	9½	61,377	Ralph Hodgin
Greensboro Patriots (1)	70	70	.500	13	68,549	Eddie Popowski
Winston-Salem Cardinals (16)	69	70	.496	13½	53,700	James Brown
Durham Bulls (4)	64	75	.460	18½	53,823	Marv Owen
Fayetteville Highlanders (6)	44	95	.317	38½	40,090	Clarence "Buck" Etchison/ Bill Bergeron/Bob Eiziminger/ Kemp Wicker

Playoffs: Danville 3 games, Burlington-Graham 1; Reidsville 3 games, Raleigh 2.
Finals: Danville 4 games, Reidsville 2.

All-Star Team: 1B-Bill Radulovich, Durham; **2B**-Joe Rovner, Danville; **3B**-Bobby Caldwell, Danville; **SS**-Don Buddin, Greensboro; **OF**-Jack Hussey, Raleigh; John Mitchell, Reidsville; Bob Honor, Burlington-Graham; **C**-Ed Sadowski, Greensboro; Bill Robertson, Fayetteville; **Util**-Jimmy Edwards, Raleigh; Rudy Tanner, Raleigh; **P**-Ramon Monzant, Danville; Eddie Neville, Durham; **MVP**-Ramon Monzant, Danville; **Manager**-Herb Brett, Raleigh.

BA: Bill Radulovich, Durham, .349
Runs: George Hott, Burlington-Graham, 104
Hits: John Mitchell, Reidsville, 184
RBIs: Don Buddin, Greensboro, 123
HRs: Jack Hussey, Raleigh, 29
Wins: Ramon Monzant, Danville, 23
SOs: Ramon Monzant, Danville, 232
ERA: Duane Wilson, Greensboro, 2.21

B Florida International League
President: Phil O'Connell

Standings	W	L	Pct.	GB	Attend.	Manager
Ft. Lauderdale Lions***	92	46	.667	—	61,330	Pepper Martin
Miami Sun Sox (9)	76	58	.567	14	67,572	Doc Alexson
St. Petersburg Saints	72	62	.537	18	33,385	Bill Herring/William Seal
Havana Cubanos	63	69	.477	26	23,460	Armando Marsans
West Palm Beach Indians	57	80	.416	34½	52,077	Whitey Platt/Charles Harris
Tampa Smokers	46	91	.336	45½	39,234	Ben Chapman/Art Rebel

Playoffs: Ft. Lauderdale 3 games, Havana 1; St. Petersburg 3 games, Miami 0.
Finals: Ft. Lauderdale 4 games, St. Petersburg 2.

BA: James Ray Williams, Ft. Lauderdale, .336
Runs: John Davis, Ft. Lauderdale, 117
Hits: Jesse Levan, Ft. Lauderdale, 175
RBIs: John Davis, Ft. Lauderdale, 136
HRs: John Davis, Ft. Lauderdale, 35

Wins: Charles Harris, West Palm Beach, 18
    Winston Brown, Ft. Lauderdale, 18
SOs: Winston Brown, Ft. Lauderdale, 151
ERA: Clarence "Hooks" Iott,
    St. Petersburg, 1.99

B Gulf Coast League
President: Guy Airey

Standings	W	L	Pct.	GB	Attend.	Manager
Galveston White Caps	94	48	.662	—	52,763	Barney White
Texas City Texans	87	57	.604	8	36,354	Bones Sanders
Harlingen Capitals	77	69	.527	19	53,649	Bob Hamric
Laredo Apaches	71	76	.483	25½	42,347	Speedy Montalvo/ Procopio Herrera
Brownsville Charros	69	78	.469	27½	44,266	Hayden Greer/Walter Sessi/ Sam Harshaney
Port Arthur Seahawks	67	80	.456	29½	48,805	Carl Carter
Corpus Christi Aces	61	83	.424	34	53,489	Jack Trench/George Fisher
Lake Charles Lakers	54	89	.378	40½	52,669	Buddy Hancken

Playoffs: Galveston 4 games, Laredo 1; Texas City 4 games, Harlingen 3.
Finals: Texas City 4 games, Galveston 2.

All-Star Team: 1B-Stan Goletz, Galveston; **2B**-Manuel Perez, Texas City; **3B**-Jorge Lopez, Harlingen; **SS**-Charles Schmidt, Galveston; **OF**-Juan Senties, Laredo; Delton Childs, Texas City; Warren Schroeder, Port Arthur; **C**-Henry Robinson, Galveston; **P**-Bill Bagwell, Texas City; Vallie Eaves, Brownsville; Tillman Conovan, Galveston; James Price, Harlingen.

BA: Juan Senties, Laredo, .379
Runs: Ron Gifford, Corpus Christi, 135
Hits: Juan Senties, Laredo, 211
RBIs: Henry Robinson, Galveston, 130

HRs: Henry Robinson, Galveston, 29
Wins: Bill Bagwell, Texas City, 26
SOs: Tillman Conovan, Galveston, 212
ERA: James Price, Harlingen, 1.93

B Piedmont League
President: Frank L. Summers

Standings	W	L	Pct.	GB	Attend.	Manager
Norfolk Tars (5)	81	51	.614	—	69,119	Mickey Owen
Hagerstown Braves (12)	78	53	.595	2½	57,246	Dutch Dorman/Jimmy Zinn/ Billy Jurges
Newport News Dodgers (9)	80	56	.588	3	90,000	Stan Wasiak
Portsmouth Merrimacs	72	63	.533	10½	64,000	Bob Ankrum
York White Roses (7)	59	70	.457	20½	58,500	Mark Christman/Bill Enos/ George Hausmann
Lynchburg Cardinals (16)	55	77	.417	26	37,000	Richard Landis/John Sullivan
Richmond Colts	45	86	.344	35½	40,000	Charles Letchas
Roanoke Ro-Sox#(1)	39	53	.424	NA	39,302	Elmer Yoter

#Roanoke disbanded July 24.

Playoffs: Norfolk 4 games, Portsmouth 1; Newport News 4 games, Hagerstown 0.
Finals: Norfolk 4 games, Newport News 1.

All-Star Team: 1B-Wayne Wallace, Lynchburg; **2B**-Charlie Neal, Newport News; **3B**-Joe Blake, Hagerstown; **SS**-Bob Lillis, Newport News; **OF**-Jerry Lynch, Norfolk; Joe Durham, York; Ken Guettler, Portsmouth; **C**-Ted Laguna, Hagerstown; **Util IF**-Raymond Lindquist, York; **Util OF**-Joseph Monteiro, Richmond; **P**-Lloyd Merritt, Norfolk; Tom Horton, Hagerstown; Emerson Unzicker, Newport News; **MVP**-Jerry Lynch, Norfolk; **Manager**-Stan Wasiak, Newport News.

BA: Jerry Lynch, Norfolk, .333
Runs: Bob Lillis, Newport News, 102
Hits: Jerry Lynch, Norfolk, 180
RBIs: Jerry Lynch, Norfolk, 133

HRs: Ken Guettler, Portsmouth, 30
Wins: Lloyd Merritt, Norfolk, 20
SOs: Wilson Parsons, Norfolk, 169
ERA: Wilson Parsons, Norfolk, 2.04

B Three-I League
President: Hal Totten

Standings	W	L	Pct.	GB	Attend.	Manager
Terre Haute Phillies (14)	76	52	.594	—	64,428	Hub Kittle
Quincy Gems (5)	70	58	.547	6	75,363	Vern Hoscheit
Evansville Braves (12)	70	59	.543	6½	88,438	Bob Coleman
Waterloo White Hawks (2)	69	60	.535	7½	93,153	Zack Taylor
Peoria Chiefs (3)	63	65	.492	13	124,866	Whitey Kurowski
Cedar Rapids Indians (10)	63	65	.492	13	93,501	Al Kubski/William Prince
Keokuk Kernels	53	75	.414	23	76,405	Rudy Laskowski
Burlington Flints (11)	49	79	.383	27	49,370	John Vander Meer

Playoffs: Evansville 3 games, Terre Haute 2; Quincy 3 games, Waterloo 1.
Finals: Quincy 3 games, Evansville 0.

All-Star Team: 1B-Dan Phelan, Waterloo; **2B**-Ben Tompkins, Terre Haute; **3B**-Ed Barbarito, Quincy; **SS**-Woody Held, Quincy; **OF**-John Herman, Peoria; Frank Tanana, Peoria; Joseph Podoley, Terre Haute; **C**-Louis Heyman, Terre Haute; **P**-Jim Owens, Terre Haute; John Anderson, Terre Haute; Seth Morehead, Terre Haute; Walter Seward, Peoria.

BA: Bob Coats, Cedar Rapids, .327
Runs: James Fishback, Peoria, 107
Hits: Bob Coats, Cedar Rapids, 162
    Ed Barbarito, Quincy, 162
RBIs: Ed Barbarito, Quincy, 127

HRs: Marv Throneberry, Quincy, 30
Wins: Jim Owens, Terre Haute, 22
SOs: Seth Morehead, Terre Haute, 206
ERA: Joe Stanka, Cedar Rapids, 2.35

B Tri-State League
President: Robert E. Hipps

Standings	W	L	Pct.	GB	Attend.	Manager
Spartanburg Peaches (3)	96	54	.640	—	71,264	Jim Bloodworth
Asheville Tourists (9)	83	67	.553	13	64,186	Ray Hathaway
Charlotte Hornets (8)	74	71	.510	19½	59,630	Pete Appleton
Anderson Rebels (7)	75	74	.503	20½	78,944	Hillis Layne
Gastonia Rockets	66	81	.449	28½	69,052	Hal Van Pelt
Rock Hill Chiefs	51	98	.342	44½	63,542	James Burns/Fred Hartman/ Tom O'Connell

Playoffs: Charlotte 3 games, Spartanburg 0; Anderson 3 games, Asheville 1.
Finals: Charlotte 3 games, Anderson 0.

All-Star Team: 1B-Philip Qualben, Spartanburg; **2B**-Lamar Bowden, Spartanburg; **3B**-Jack Falls, Gastonia; **SS**-William Kallas, Rock Hill; **OF**-Joe Fuller, Spartanburg; James Finn, Spartanburg; Karol Kwak, Anderson; **C**-Joe Pignatano, Asheville; **Util**-Pompeyo Davalillo, Charlotte; **P**-Eugene Law, Spartanburg; Fred Kipp, Asheville; **Manager**-Jim Bloodworth, Spartanburg; Ray Hathaway, Asheville.

BA: Karol Kwak, Anderson, .359
Runs: Joe Fuller, Spartanburg, 134
Hits: Joe Fuller, Spartanburg, 228
RBIs: James Finn, Spartanburg, 140

HRs: Lamar Bowden, Spartanburg, 26
Wins: Eugene Law, Spartanburg, 24
SOs: Harry Beitsuss, Charlotte, 189
ERA: Fred Kipp, Asheville, 2.23

C Arizona-Texas League
President: G.R. Sloane

Standings	W	L	Pct.	GB	Attend.	Manager
Tucson Cowboys	90	49	.647	—	92,157	Don Jameson
Mexicali Eagles	77	62	.554	13	68,719	Art Lilly
Juarez Indios	74	65	.532	16	46,800	Manuel Fortes/Pingua Canales
El Paso Texans	60	80	.429	30½	52,501	Diamond Cecil
Bisbee-Douglas Copper Kings	59	80	.424	31	44,650	Syd Cohen
Phoenix Senators	58	82	.414	32½	49,270	Buck Elliott

All-Star Team: 1B-Manuel Magallon, Bisbee-Douglas; **2B**-Moises Camacho, Mexicali; **3B**-Victor Canales, Juarez; **SS**-Joe Joshua, Tucson; **OF**-Lloyd Jenney, Tucson; Gordon Windhorn, Phoenix; Eduardo Cruz, Juarez; **C**-Ernest Choukalos, Tucson; **P**-Wenceslao Gonzalez, Juarez; Marcelino Solis, El Paso; LeRoy "Corky" Reddell, Tucson; Don Cantrell, Phoenix.

BA: Edwin Roberts, Tucson, .392
Runs: Joe Joshua, Tucson, 164
Hits: Roberto Canales, Juarez, 208
RBIs: Lloyd Jenney, Tucson, 152

HRs: Charles Lundgren, Tucson, 34
Wins: LeRoy "Corky" Reddell, Tucson, 29
SOs: Wenceslao Gonzalez, Juarez, 276
ERA: LeRoy "Corky" Reddell, Tucson, 2.64

C California League
President: Jerry Donovan

Standings	W	L	Pct.	GB	Attend.	Manager
San Jose Red Sox (1)	93	47	.664	—	74,492	Red Marion/Joe Stephenson
Bakersfield Indians (4)	75	65	.536	18	100,008	Ray Perry
Santa Barbara Dodgers (9)	74	66	.529	19	29,007	George Scherger
Stockton Ports (10)	72	68	.514	21	63,257	William Salkeld
Visalia Stars	67	73	.479	26	53,396	Jerry Gardner
Fresno Cardinals (16)	64	77	.454	29½	71,313	Roland LeBlanc
Modesto Reds (12)	64	77	.454	29½	58,094	Guy Fletcher
Ventura Oilers	52	88	.371	41	30,632	Jose Perez/Dario Lodigiani

Playoffs: San Jose 3 games, Santa Barbara 0; Stockton 3 games, Bakersfield 0.
Finals: San Jose 4 games, Stockton 2.

All-Star Team: 1B-John O'Keefe, Visalia; **2B**-Leo Alarid, San Jose; **3B**-Ray Perry, Bakersfield; **SS**-George "Sparky" Anderson, Santa Barbara; **OF**-Edward Sobczak, San Jose; Marty Keough, San Jose; Jose Perez, Ventura; **C**-Roland LeBlanc, Fresno; **Util IF**-Albert Karan, Santa Barbara; **Util OF**-Albie Pearson, San Jose; **P**-Truman "Tex" Clevenger, San Jose; Clair Parkin, San Jose; Tony Freitas, Stockton; Edwin Mayer, San Jose.

BA: Jose Perez, Ventura, .373
Runs: Ray Perry, Bakersfield, 120
Hits: James O'Brien, Stockton, 181
RBIs: Edward Sobczak, San Jose, 142
HRs: Ray Perry, Bakersfield, 36

Wins: Tony Freitas, Stockton, 22
SOs: Clair Parkin, San Jose, 192
ERA: Truman "Tex" Clevenger,
    San Jose, 1.51

C Cotton States League
President: Al Haraway

Standings	W	L	Pct.	GB	Attend.	Manager
Meridian Millers	79	46	.632	—	59,514	Thomas Davis
El Dorado Oilers	67	59	.532	12½	47,938	Bill Adair
Pine Bluff Judges (7)	65	60	.520	14	43,276	Frank Lucchesi
Jackson Senators (4)	63	61	.508	15½	43,805	Marland Doolittle
Hot Springs Bathers	63	61	.508	15½	43,360	Vern Shetler
Greenville Buckshots	63	62	.504	16	51,090	Harold Martin/Chester Morgan/ William Vaughn
Natchez Indians	50	75	.400	29	20,424	Wayne Tucker
Monroe Sports	50	76	.397	29½	40,918	Charles Harrington

Playoffs: Jackson defeated Hot Springs 6-2 in a one game playoff for fourth place.
Meridian 4 games, Jackson 2; El Dorado 4 games, Pine Bluff 0.
Finals: Meridian 4 games, El Dorado 0.

1953

All-Star Team: 1B-Patrick O'Keefe, El Dorado; **2B**-Hugh Glaze, Meridian; **3B**-Ray Posipanka, Greenville; **SS**-Adolph Regelsky, Meridian; **OF**-Louis Schaufele, Jackson; Harold Martin, Hot Springs; Eugene Pompelia, Meridian; **C**-William Lewis, Meridian; **P**-Bob Harrison, Meridian; Tom Pollet, Greenville; Robert Brown, El Dorado; Charles Lindquist, Greenville; **Manager**-Bill Adair, El Dorado.

BA: Hugh Glaze, Meridian, .355
Runs: Harold Martin, Hot Springs, 127
Hits: Harold Martin, Hot Springs, 169
RBIs: Harold Martin, Hot Springs, 111

HRs: Harold Martin, Hot Springs, 41
Wins: Bob Harrison, Meridian, 19
SOs: Bob Harrison, Meridian, 172
ERA: Bob Harrison, Meridian, 2.15

C Evangeline League
President: Edmond L. Deramee

Standings	W	L	Pct.	GB	Attend.	Manager
Crowley Millers	84	54	.609	—	100,239	Tony York
Thibodaux Giants	71	67	.514	13	31,745	William Adams
Baton Rouge Red Sticks	69	69	.500	15	53,670	Bill Spears
Lafayette Bulls	68	69	.496	15½	62,525	Earl Caldwell, Sr.
Alexandria Aces	68	69	.496	15½	66,819	Harry Strohm
New Iberia Cardinals	52	84	.382	31	53,407	Art Visconti/John Millard/ Joseph Powers

Playoffs: Lafayette defeated Alexandria 8-1 in a one game playoff for fourth place. Lafayette 4 games, Crowley 2; Thibodaux 4 games, Baton Rouge 3.
Finals: Thibodaux 4 games, Lafayette 1.

BA: Mauro Iacovello, Thibodaux, .347
Runs: Fred Barocco, Lafayette, 130
Hits: Juan Izaguirre, Crowley, 187
RBIs: Conklyn Meriwether, Crowley, 134

HRs: Conklyn Meriwether, Crowley, 42
Wins: Marvin Holleman, Crowley, 24
SOs: John Lagan, New Iberia, 162
ERA: Earl Caldwell, Sr., Lafayette, 2.07

C Longhorn League
President: Hal Sayles

Standings	W	L	Pct.	GB	Attend.	Manager
Carlsbad Potashers	80	52	.606	—	83,462	Pat McLaughlin
San Angelo Colts	77	52	.597	1½	68,146	Rudy Briner
Midland Indians	73	58	.557	6½	52,035	Jay Haney
Artesia Drillers	72	62	.537	9	40,042	Earl Perry/Joe Bauman
Roswell Rockets	60	70	.462	19	35,459	Pat Stasey
Odessa Oilers	53	78	.405	26½	41,931	Robert Martin
Big Spring Broncs@	35	57	.380	NA	24,809	James "Hack" Miller/ Joseph Niedson
Lamesa Lobos/ Winters-Ballinger Eagles#	10	31	.244	NA	8,314	Harold Webb

#Lamesa moved to Winters-Ballinger June 3, then disbanded June 7.
@Big Spring disbanded July 31.

Playoffs: Carlsbad 4 games, Artesia 3; Midland 4 games, San Angelo 3.
Finals: Carlsbad 4 games, Midland 2.

All-Star Team: 1B-Joe Bauman, Artesia; **2B**-Ossie Alvarez, Roswell; **3B**-Julio de la Torre, Midland; **SS**-Stanley "Scooter" Hughes, Midland; **OF**-Glenn Burns, San Angelo; Buddy Grimes, Roswell; Elias Osorio, Carlsbad; **C**-Les Mulcahy, Artesia; **P**-Leonard Ruyle, Artesia; Gilberto Guerra, San Angelo; Marshall Epperson, Carlsbad; Robert Gregg, San Angelo.

BA: Isaiah Jackson, Carlsbad, .388
Runs: Joe Bauman, Artesia, 135
Hits: Isaiah Jackson, Carlsbad, 190
RBIs: Les Mulcahy, Artesia, 143
HRs: Joe Bauman, Artesia, 53

TBs: Joe Bauman, Artesia, 376
Wins: Audie Malone, Carlsbad, 25
SOs: Marshall Epperson, Carlsbad, 214
ERA: Mario Saldana, San Angelo, 3.46

C Northern League
President: Herman D. White

Standings	W	L	Pct.	GB	Attend.	Manager
Fargo-Moorhead Twins (3)	86	39	.688	—	108,210	Zeke Bonura/Santo Luberto
Duluth Dukes	73	52	.584	13	106,383	Alfred Todd
St. Cloud Rox (13)	66	59	.528	20	61,425	Charlie Fox
Aberdeen Pheasants (7)	60	63	.488	25	54,532	Barney Lutz
Sioux Falls Canaries (10)	59	65	.476	26½	51,251	Dale Lynch
Grand Forks Chiefs	55	70	.440	31	52,063	Carl Hosler/Frank Calo
Superior Blues	51	74	.408	35	33,859	Bob Latshaw
Eau Claire Bears (12)	49	77	.389	37½	35,853	Rex Carr

Playoffs: Fargo-Moorhead 2 games, St. Cloud 0; Duluth 2 games, Aberdeen 0.
Finals: Fargo-Moorhead 3 games, Duluth 2.

All-Star Team: 1B-Tito Francona, Aberdeen; **2B**-Santo Luberto, Fargo-Moorhead; **3B**-John Morse, Fargo-Moorhead; **SS**-Blas Fernandez, Sioux Falls; **OF**-Frank Gravino, Fargo-Moorhead; Jerald MacKay, Sioux City; Horace Greenwood, Duluth; **C**-Bernard Gerl, Duluth; **P**-Raymond Seif, Fargo-Moorhead; Raymond Coombs, Sioux Falls; Burton Ostby, Grand Forks; John Fitzgerald, St. Cloud.

BA: Santo Luberto, Fargo-Moorhead, .361
Runs: Joe Camacho, Fargo-Moorhead, 139
Hits: Horace Greenwood, Duluth, 176
RBIs: Frank Gravino, Fargo-Moorhead, 174
HRs: Frank Gravino, Fargo-Moorhead, 52

Wins: Raymond Seif, Fargo-Moorhead, 20
Donald Nace, Fargo-Moorhead, 20
SOs: Raymond Seif, Fargo-Moorhead, 163
ERA: Raymond Seif, Fargo-Moorhead, 2.52

C Pioneer League
President: Claude Engberg

Standings	W	L	Pct.	GB	Attend.	Manager
Ogden Reds (11)	89	42	.679	—	63,251	Earle Brucker
Great Falls Electrics (9)	77	54	.588	12	109,455	Lou Rochelli
Billings Mustangs (15)	71	60	.542	18	105,369	Cliff Dapper
Salt Lake City Bees (14)	69	62	.527	20	93,161	Eddie Murphy/Charlie Gassaway
Idaho Falls Russets	68	64	.515	21½	52,083	Sven "Red" Jessen
Boise Yankees (5)	63	68	.481	26	44,098	Tedd Gullic
Magic Valley Cowboys	48	83	.366	41	46,179	Dolph Camilli
Pocatello Bannocks (7)	40	92	.303	49½	39,202	Herschel Martin/Butch Moran

Playoffs: Salt Lake City 2 games, Ogden 0; Great Falls 2 games, Billings 0.
Finals: Salt Lake City 3 games, Great Falls 0.

All-Star Team: 1B-John Moskus, Salt Lake City; **2B**-Stanley Miller, Billings; **3B**-John Hack, Idaho Falls; **SS**-Lazaro Terry, Ogden; **OF**-Oscar Sardinas, Great Falls; Pedro Almenares, Great Falls; Frank Robinson, Ogden; **C**-Ellsworth Dean, Salt Lake City; **P**-Reno Barbisan, Idaho Falls; Clyde DeWitt, Salt Lake City; Carl Wells, Ogden; Allen Flaugher, Ogden.

BA: Oscar Sardinas, Great Falls, .416
Runs: Michael Witwicki, Great Falls, 132
Hits: Oscar Sardinas, Great Falls, 194
RBIs: John Moskus, Salt Lake City, 117
HRs: John Moskus, Salt Lake City, 28

Wins: Clyde DeWitt, Salt Lake City, 19
Carl Wells, Ogden, 19
SOs: Thomas Puehl, Great Falls, 176
ERA: Allen Flaugher, Ogden, 2.35

C Provincial League
President: Albert Molini

Standings	W	L	Pct.	GB	Attend.	Manager
Sherbrooke Indians (3)	84	41	.672	—	58,288	Pinky May
Granby Phillies (14)	72	52	.581	11½	46,935	Al Barillari
Quebec Braves (12)	71	52	.577	12	115,943	George McQuinn
Thetford Mines Mineurs (7)	59	65	.476	24½	72,530	Bill Krueger
Trois Rivieres Yankees	58	65	.472	25	73,982	Frank Novosel
St. Jean Canadians (15)	57	65	.467	25½	39,607	George Genovese
St. Hyacinthe A's (6)	49	73	.402	33½	30,501	John Sosh/Joseph Rullo
Drummondville Royals	42	79	.347	40	35,202	Al Gionfriddo/Joseph Oliffe

Playoffs: Quebec 4 games, Sherbrooke 1; Granby 4 games, Thetford Mines 2.
Finals: Quebec 4 games, Granby 3.

BA: John Waters, Sherbrooke, .348
Runs: David Mann, Thetford Mines, 114
Hits: John Waters, Sherbrooke, 182
RBIs: John Werner, Quebec, 118
HRs: Robert Diers, Sherbrooke, 26

Wins: William Diemer, Thetford Mines, 20
Michael Munsinger, St. Hyacinthe, 20
SOs: Marco Mainini, Trois Rivieres, 194
ERA: Alfred Dumouchelle, Quebec, 2.29

C West Texas-New Mexico League
President: Hal Sayles

Standings	W	L	Pct.	GB	Attend.	Manager
Albuquerque Dukes	87	55	.613	—	92,605	Tom Jordan
Clovis Pioneers	79	61	.564	7	44,115	Grover Seitz
Plainview Ponies	80	62	.563	7	79,780	Jackie Sullivan
Lubbock Hubbers	80	62	.563	7	83,782	Bill Metzig
Pampa Oilers	77	65	.542	10	50,618	Ted Pawelek
Amarillo Gold Sox	71	71	.500	16	59,379	Jim Matthews
Borger Gassers	49	93	.345	38	35,335	Lloyd Brown/Herschel Martin
Abilene Blue Sox	43	97	.307	43	44,148	Herschel Martin/Isaac Palmer

Playoffs: Albuquerque 4 games, Lubbock 2; Clovis 4 games, Plainview 2.
Finals: Albuquerque 4 games, Clovis 3.

All-Star Team: 1B-Doug Lewis, Pampa; **2B**-Forrest "Frosty" Kennedy, Plainview; **3B**-John Bruzga, Amarillo; **SS**-Robert Brown, Plainview; **OF**-Roberto Fernandez, Lubbock; Roy Woldt, Pampa; Don Stokes, Plainview; **C**-Frank Benitez, Clovis; Isaac Palmer, Abilene; **Util**-Joe Valdivielso, Lubbock; James Eldridge, Borger; **P**-Carroll "Red" Dial, Clovis; Charles Garmon, Lubbock; Joe Hinchman, Albuquerque; Eddie Locke, Amarillo; Sam Williams, Pampa.

BA: Don Stokes, Plainview, .426
Runs: Roy Parker, Clovis, 177
Hits: Don Stokes, Plainview, 242
RBIs: Don Stokes, Plainview, 174
HRs: Jim Matthews, Amarillo, 50

2B: Doug Lewis, Pampa, 66
Wins: Carroll "Red" Dial, Clovis, 28
SOs: Jack Venable, Amarillo, 295
ERA: Grover Blacksher, Albuquerque, 2.84
Pct: George Socha, Albuquerque, 1.000, 14-0

C Western Association
President: George Barr

Standings	W	L	Pct.	GB	Attend.	Manager
St. Joseph Cardinals (16)	83	57	.593	—	58,647	Harold Olt
Hutchinson Elks (15)	80	60	.571	3	87,718	Wes Griffin
Topeka Owls (2)	78	62	.557	5	81,450	Ira Hutchinson
Joplin Miners (5)	71	68	.511	11½	41,006	Malcolm "Bunny" Mick
Muskogee Giants (13)	57	81	.413	25	41,749	Harold Kollar
Ft. Smith-Van Buren Twins	49	90	.353	33½	30,901	Edwin Walls/Edwin Dickson

Playoffs: St. Joseph 3 games, Joplin 0; Hutchinson 3 games, Topeka 0.
Finals: Hutchinson 4 games, St. Joseph 1.

All-Star Team: 1B-Ellis Daugherty, Topeka; **2B**-Sam Goody, St. Joseph; **3B**-Harold Olt, St. Joseph; **SS**-Gordon Figard, Hutchinson; **OF**-Joseph Beran, Hutchinson; Glenn Zimmerman, St. Joseph; Daniel Toma, Muskogee; **C**-Jay Drake, St. Joseph; **P**-Rogers Fister, St. Joseph; John Dean, Topeka; Roger Sawyer, Hutchinson; Edward Donnelly, St. Joseph.

BA: Daniel Toma, Muskogee, .313
Runs: Lamar Moore, Hutchinson, 115
Hits: Daniel Toma, Muskogee, 152
RBIs: Joseph Beran, Hutchinson, 118

HRs: Joseph Beran, Hutchinson, 37
Wins: Roger Sawyer, Hutchinson, 22
SOs: Rogers Fister, St. Joseph, 239
ERA: Roger Sawyer, Hutchinson, 1.99

D Alabama-Florida League
President: C.C. Hodge

Standings	W	L	Pct.	GB	Attend.	Manager
Panama City Fliers.............	69	47	.595	—	43,150	Chase Riddle
Graceville Oilers................	64	53	.547	5½	35,687	Holt "Cat" Milner
Dothan Rebels (16).............	59	58	.504	10½	35,799	Homer Ray Wilson
Andalusia Arrows	56	60	.483	13	20,981	Julius McDougald
Ft. Walton Beach Jets	54	63	.462	15½	16,801	Charles Quimby/ Ralph Hendrix/John Streza
Eufaula Millers	48	69	.410	21½	19,265	Blackie Connell/ Bill Buchanan/Dutch Konemann

Playoffs: Dothan 4 games, Panama City 3; Graceville 4 games, Andalusia 1.
Finals: Dothan 4 games, Graceville 2.

All-Star Team: 1B-Charles Quimby, Ft. Walton Beach/Graceville; **2B**-Homer Ray Wilson, Dothan; **3B**-Edward Richardson, Panama City; **SS**-David Garcia, Dothan; **OF**-Julius Sheridan, Andalusia; Roy Sinquefield, Andalusia; Charles Goca, Panama City; **C**-Chase Riddle, Panama City; **P**-Nick Berbesia, Graceville; Spencer Davis, Dothan.

BA: Chase Riddle, Panama City, .411
Runs: Chase Riddle, Panama City, 131
Hits: Chase Riddle, Panama City, 179
RBIs: Chase Riddle, Panama City, 125

HRs: Charles Quimby, Ft. Walton Beach/Graceville, 27
Wins: Spencer Davis, Dothan, 22
SOs: Spencer Davis, Dothan, 196
ERA: Spencer Davis, Dothan, 1.21

D Appalachian League
President: Chauncey De Vault

Standings	W	L	Pct.	GB	Attend.	Manager
Johnson City Cardinals**(16).	84	43	.661	—	48,846	James Hercinger
Welch Miners*(6)...............	82	43	.656	1	41,150	Jack Crosswhite
Pulaski Phillies (14)...........	66	59	.528	17	24,400	Al Gardella
Bristol Twins (15)...............	54	72	.429	29½	34,810	George Detore
Wytheville Statesmen (7) ...	48	78	.381	35½	28,250	John O'Donnell
Bluefield Blue-Grays (8)	43	82	.344	40	33,569	Ivan Kuester

Playoff: Welch 3 games, Johnson City 0.

BA: Ernie Boushy, Welch, .349
Runs: Grady Chavis, Johnson City, 120
Hits: Ernie Boushy, Welch, 169
RBIs: Ray Carr, Welch, 124

HRs: Dick Stanton, Johnson City, 27
Wins: Paul Johnston, Welch, 18
SOs: Walter DeLotelle, Bristol, 161
ERA: Billy Joe Bowman, Johnson City, 2.10

D Florida State League
President: Jack Dempsey

Standings	W	L	Pct.	GB	Attend.	Manager
Daytona Beach Islanders*(3) ..	86	49	.637	—	65,353	Ed Levy
DeLand Red Hats**	78	56	.528	7½	23,100	Ray Dunne
Cocoa Indians	78	59	.569	9	23,824	Carvel "Bama" Rowell
Sanford Cardinals (16)........	66	63	.512	17	37,378	J.C. Dunn
Jacksonville Beach Sea Birds ..	68	65	.511	17	17,785	Leon "Red" Treadway
Leesburg Lakers	56	77	.421	29	17,000	Red Dulaney/Francis Barrett
Orlando Senators (8)...........	54	75	.419	29	24,579	Don Ford/Les Filkins
Palatka Azaleas/ Lakeland Pilots#	47	89	.346	39½	28,506	Charles Baird/Peter Kantor/ Paul Crawford/Charles Aleno

#Palatka (13-22) moved to Lakeland May 15.

Playoff: Daytona Beach 3 games, DeLand 1.

All-Star Team: 1B-Ed Levy, Daytona Beach; **2B**-Carvel "Bama" Rowell, Cocoa; **3B**-Jesse "Jack" Cade, DeLand; **SS**-John Skorupski, Daytona Beach; **OF**-Jack Leonard, Sanford; Leon "Red" Treadway, Jacksonville Beach; Richard Baller, Daytona Beach; **C**-Arthur Pardue, Daytona Beach; **Util**-J.C. Dunn, Sanford; **P**-Joe Angel, Jacksonville Beach; Howard Wise, Orlando; **Manager**-Carvel "Bama" Rowell, Cocoa.

BA: Jack Leonard, Sanford, .380
Runs: Richard Baller, Daytona Beach, 139
Hits: Jack Leonard, Sanford, 191
RBIs: Carvel "Bama" Rowell, Cocoa, 127

HRs: J.C. Dunn, Sanford, 20
Wins: Joe Angel, Jacksonville Beach, 28
SOs: Bobby Locke, Daytona Beach, 247
ERA: James Vickery, DeLand, 2.23

D Georgia State League
President: Bill Estroff

Standings	W	L	Pct.	GB	Attend.	Manager
Hazlehurst-Baxley Cardinals (16)	84	41	.672	—	19,101	Arnold Riesgo
Jesup Bees.......................	78	46	.629	5½	20,629	Bill Steinecke
Eastman Dodgers................	77	49	.611	7½	29,232	Robert Reid

Douglas Trojans................	76	50	.603	8½	26,613	Charles Bledsoe
Statesboro Pilots	49	77	.389	35½	38,431	Red Thrasher/Jack Hines
Sandersville Wacos (12).....	48	77	.384	36	33,895	Gabby Grant/Parnell Ruark/ Luscius Morgan/Julian Morgan
Dublin Irish (15)	47	78	.376	37	25,394	John George/Frank Oceak
Vidalia Indians..................	41	82	.333	42	28,665	Bull Hamons/Jake Daniel/ Donald Cross

Playoffs: Hazlehurst-Baxley 4 games, Douglas 1; Eastman 4 games, Jesup 0.
Finals: Hazlehurst-Baxley 4 games, Eastman 3.

All-Star Team: 1B-Vaughn Dyer, Statesboro; **2B**-Samuel Hernandez, Statesboro; **3B**-Ray Herrera, Hazlehurst-Baxley; **SS**-Eli Maricich, Eastman; **OF**-James Sosebee, Jesup; Bob Zuccarini, Hazlehurst-Baxley; James "Pete" Caudle, Eastman; **C**-Raymond Warzyniak, Eastman; **P**-Fred Huthmaker, Hazlehurst-Baxley; James Harp, Eastman; Milan Cop, Hazlehurst-Baxley; Don Quinn, Douglas.

BA: Parnell Ruark, Sandersville/Dublin, .372
Runs: Bob Zuccarini, Hazlehurst-Baxley, 131
Hits: James Sosebee, Jesup, 186
RBIs: Van Davis, Douglas, 159
HRs: Van Davis, Douglas, 44

Wins: Fred Huthmaker, Hazlehurst-Baxley, 19
SOs: Charles Ready, Jesup, 161
ERA: Carlos Lopez, Statesboro, 2.37

D Georgia-Florida League
President: W.T. Anderson

Standings	W	L	Pct.	GB	Attend.	Manager
Thomasville Dodgers (9)......	90	47	.657	—	41,223	John Angelone
Brunswick Pirates (15).........	85	54	.612	6	47,077	Jack Paepke
Tifton Blue Sox	84	55	.604	7	31,260	Edgar Hartness
Albany Cardinals (16)	82	56	.594	8½	51,870	Russ McGovern
Fitzgerald Pioneers (11)......	62	77	.446	29	39,264	Robert Carson/Charles Ridgeway/ Bull Hamons
Waycross Bears	59	78	.431	31	27,994	Morton Smith/Al Aucoin
Valdosta Browns (7)...........	55	81	.404	34½	42,353	Rollie Stuckmeyer/Gil Torres
Cordele A's (6)	35	104	.252	56	17,705	Joseph Rullo/Lewis Richardson

Playoffs: Thomasville 4 games, Albany 2; Brunswick 4 games, Tifton 0.
Finals: Brunswick 4 games, Thomasville 3.

All-Star Team: 1B-Franklin Van Burkleo, Brunswick; **2B**-Ken Hilyer, Albany; **3B**-Tom Burcham, Jr., Valdosta; **SS**-Gene Freese, Brunswick; **OF**-Ultus Alvarez, Thomasville; Heaford McKinney, Albany; Larry Hampshire, Thomasville; Larry Burford, Valdosta; Edgar Sinquefield, Brunswick; **C**-Robert Rand, Albany; William Dixon, Thomasville; **P**-James Carter, Tifton; James Nisewonger, Brunswick; Robert Koczwara, Thomasville; Donald Kildoo, Brunswick; George Wasconis, Thomasville; **Manager**-John Angelone, Thomasville.

BA: Ken Hilyer, Albany, .334
Runs: Russ McGovern, Albany, 133
Hits: Ken Hilyer, Albany, 171
RBIs: Ultus Alvarez, Thomasville, 123

HRs: Jack Paepke, Brunswick, 21
Wins: James Carter, Tifton, 21
SOs: James Carter, Tifton, 251
ERA: James Nisewonger, Brunswick, 1.98

D Kitty League
President: Shelby Peace

Standings	W	L	Pct.	GB	Attend.	Manager
Fulton Lookouts (8)	70	50	.583	—	27,473	Sam Lamatina
Madisonville Miners (2)	67	53	.558	3	37,324	Sheriff Robinson
Paducah Chiefs (16)...........	67	53	.558	3	53,607	Lee Peterson
Hopkinsville Hoppers (6) ...	59	60	.496	10½	32,192	Norman Wilson/Edward Wright
Mayfield Clothiers (13).......	58	61	.487	11½	24,553	Austin Knickerbocker
Jackson Generals (11)........	58	62	.483	12	17,601	Mickey O'Neil
Union City Dodgers (9)	51	69	.425	19	33,392	Earl Naylor
Owensboro Oilers (5)	49	71	.408	21	64,375	Marvin Crater

Playoffs: Fulton 2 games, Hopkinsville 1; Paducah 2 games, Madisonville 0.
Finals: Paducah 3 games, Fulton 0.

All-Star Team: 1B-Ned Waldrop, Fulton; **2B**-Peter Aviotti, Paducah; **3B**-Howard Warrell, Hopkinsville; **SS**-Glenn Young, Paducah; **OF**-Hal Crotts, Hopkinsville; William Sells, Mayfield; Howard Weeks, Fulton; **C**-Bill Wilhelm, Paducah; **P**-Ronald Foster, Fulton; Rodriguez Arias, Madisonville; **Manager**-Mickey O'Neil, Jackson.

BA: Howard Weeks, Fulton, .373
Runs: Howard Warrell, Hopkinsville, 113 William Kasper, Hopkinsville, 113
Hits: William Sells, Mayfield, 157
RBIs: Howard Warrell, Hopkinsville, 129

HRs: Austin Knickerbocker, Mayfield, 26 Howard Warrell, Hopkinsville, 26
Wins: Ronald Foster, Fulton, 21
SOs: Rodriguez Arias, Madisonville, 247
ERA: Lee Peterson, Paducah, 2.69

D Mississippi-Ohio Valley League
President: C.C. "Dutch" Hoffman

Standings	W	L	Pct.	GB	Attend.	Manager
Decatur Commodores	68	50	.576	—	96,337	Ray Taylor
Paris Lakers	66	53	.555	2½	35,000	Tom Sunkel
Mattoon Phillies (14)..........	64	56	.533	5	61,000	James Deery
Hannibal Cardinals (16)......	55	62	.470	12½	35,200	Tince Leonard
Mt. Vernon Kings	55	64	.462	13½	31,600	Robert Schmidt
Danville Dans (2)...............	48	71	.403	20½	62,700	Virl Minnis

Playoffs: Decatur 3 games, Hannibal 0; Paris 3 games, Mattoon 0.
Finals: Decatur 3 games, Paris 2.

BA: Robert Schmidt, Mt. Vernon, .358
Runs: Gonzalo Chenard, Decatur, 105
Hits: James Partin, Danville, 167
RBIs: James Freeman, Decatur, 106
HRs: Kenneth Payne, Paris, 16

Wins: Juan Garcia, Decatur, 18
    Tince Leonard, Hannibal, 18
SOs: Dennis Hamilton, Mattoon, 195
ERA: William Bright, Mattoon, 2.51

D Mountain States League
President: Virgil Q. Wacks

Standings	W	L	Pct.	GB	Attend.	Manager
Maryville-Alcoa Twins.......	78	46	.629	—	25,000	Jim Poole
Knoxville Smokies	70	55	.560	8½	36,255	Vince Pankovits
Kingsport Cherokees	69	56	.552	9½	46,717	Leo "Muscle" Shoals
Morristown Red Sox...........	64	62	.508	15	37,384	Napoleon Reyes
Norton Braves....................	63	63	.500	16	21,873	Walt Dixon
Big Stone Gap Rebels.........	55	70	.440	23½	8,230	Kelly Lunn
Harlan Smokies..................	53	72	.424	25½	20,630	Clifford Melton/Barry Cox/ James Grigg
Middlesboro Athletics	48	76	.387	30	12,600	Julian Morgan/Ben Pardue

Playoffs: Maryville-Alcoa 3 games, Kingsport 2; Knoxville 3 games, Morristown 1.
Finals: Knoxville 3 games, Maryville-Alcoa 1.

BA: Leo "Muscle" Shoals, Kingsport, .427
Runs: Hugh Hamil, Maryville-Alcoa, 165
Hits: Walt Dixon, Norton, 197
RBIs: Willie Kirkland, Maryville-Alcoa, 164
HRs: Walt Dixon, Norton, 37

Wins: James Tugerson, Knoxville, 29
SOs: James Tugerson, Knoxville, 286
ERA: Raymond Johnston,
    Maryville-Alcoa, 1.90

D PONY League
President: Vincent M. McNamara

Standings	W	L	Pct.	GB	Attend.	Manager
Jamestown Falcons (4)	88	37	.704	—	49,023	Dan Carnevale
Hornell Dodgers (9)...........	70	56	.556	18½	38,293	Mervin Dornburg/Jack Banta
Hamilton Cardinals (16).....	69	57	.548	19½	53,291	Hal Contini
Bradford Phillies (14)........	66	60	.524	22½	29,181	John Davenport
Olean Yankees (5).............	63	61	.508	24½	27,139	Bill Davis/Walter Lance
Wellsville Braves (12)........	59	67	.468	29½	44,509	Ted Sepkowski
Batavia Clippers (15).........	46	78	.371	41½	25,813	George Kinnamon
Corning Independents.........	40	85	.320	48	24,076	Tony Lupien/Paul O'Dea

Playoffs: Jamestown 3 games, Bradford 0; Hamilton 3 games, Hornell 0.
Finals: Jamestown 4 games, Hamilton 1.

All-Star Team: 1B-Ken Walters, Jamestown; 2B-Robert Taylor, Jamestown; 3B-Pablo Rivera, Olean; SS-Frank McElroy, Jamestown; OF-John Maggio, Bradford; Robert Kosis, Hamilton; George Alusik, Jamestown; C-John Turk, Bradford; P-Vince Trakan, Jamestown; George Player, Wellsville; Richard McClenney, Bradford; Robert Rauber, Hamilton.

BA: George Alusik, Jamestown, .372
Runs: Pablo Rivera, Olean, 118
    Frank McElroy, Jamestown, 118
Hits: John Maggio, Bradford, 184
RBIs: Ted Sepkowski, Wellsville, 145

HRs: Ted Sepkowski, Wellsville, 37
Wins: Vince Trakan, Jamestown, 19
SOs: George Player, Wellsville, 179
ERA: Vince Trakan, Jamestown, 2.51

D Sooner State League
President: Ucal Clanton

Standings	W	L	Pct.	GB	Attend.	Manager
Ardmore Cardinals (16)......	91	46	.664	—	43,000	Bennie Warren
Shawnee Hawks (9)............	86	53	.619	6	39,441	Boyd Bartley
Ada Herefords (7)...............	84	54	.609	7½	36,128	Lou Brower
McAlester Rockets (5)........	83	56	.597	9	40,485	Bill Cope
Pauls Valley Raiders (13)...	63	74	.460	28	18,453	Richard Klaus
Sherman-Denison Twins	61	77	.442	30½	18,784	Red McCarty
Lawton Reds (11)...............	47	89	.346	43½	18,029	Tuck McWilliams
Gainesville Owls (10)........	36	102	.261	55½	20,523	James Grigg/Ernest Shadid/ Jesse Landrum

Playoffs: McAlester 3 games, Ardmore 1; Ada 3 games, Shawnee 1.
Finals: McAlester 4 games, Ada 1.

All-Star Team: 1B-Don Williamson, Pauls Valley; 2B-Floyd Robinson, Sherman-Denison; 3B-Ronald Slawski, Ada; SS-Donald McGregor, Ada; OF-Russ Snyder, McAlester; Jackie Brandt, Ardmore; Al Viotta, Ardmore; C-Albert Stieglitz, Pauls Valley; John Gannon, Lawton; Util-George Blash, Ada; P-Donald Huffman, Shawnee; J.L. Rhodes, Ada; Manager-Bennie Warren, Ardmore.

BA: Russ Snyder, McAlester, .432
Runs: Al Viotta, Ardmore, 159
Hits: Russ Snyder, McAlester, 240
RBIs: Al Viotta, Ardmore, 161
HRs: Ronald Slawski, Ada, 31

Wins: J.L. Rhodes, Ada, 21
SOs: Donald Huffman, Shawnee, 250
ERA: James Peterson, Shawnee, 1.94
Pct: Robert Shipman, McAlester, .813, 13-3

D Tar Heel League
President: Walter H. Woodson, Jr.

Standings	W	L	Pct.	GB	Attend.	Manager
Marion Marauders	74	35	.679	—	35,322	Bob Beal
Forest City Owls.................	72	40	.643	3½	48,812	Len Cross/Boger McGimsey
Shelby Clippers..................	60	49	.550	14	19,247	David Coble

Lexington Indians..............	59	54	.522	17	39,453	Alex Monchak
Mooresville Moors	58	55	.513	18	19,413	Jim Mills
Lincolnton Cardinals/						
Statesville Sports@..........	47	64	.423	28	27,866	Burl Storie/Hugh Rudisill/ Junior Dodgin/Charley Knight
Hickory Rebels (10)...........	46	66	.411	29½	22,742	William Parker
Salisbury Rocots (1)	44	67	.396	31	21,690	Franklin Robinson
High Point-Thomasville						
Hi-Toms#......................	13	28	.317	NA	5,862	Jim Gruzdis/John Lybrand
Statesville Blues#..............	13	28	.317	NA	20,925	Fred Chapman/Charley Knight

#High Point-Thomasville and Statesville disbanded June 11.
@Lincolnton moved to Statesville July 12.

Playoffs: Marion 4 games, Shelby 2; Lexington 4 games, Forest City 2.
Finals: Lexington 4 games, Marion 2.

All-Star Team: 1B-Don Stafford, Hi-Toms/Lexington; 2B-Howard Henkle, Lincolnton/Statesville; 3B-John Harrington, Forest City; SS-Robert Cross, Forest City; OF-Norman Small, Mooresville; Russell "Red" Mincy, Shelby; George Rose, Forest City; C-George Oates, Forest City; Allen Baker, Salisbury; Util-Giles Setzer, Hickory; Bill Hare, Forest City; P-Butler Jones, Salisbury; Eli Grba, Salisbury; Efird Gwaltney, Lincolnton/Statesville; Fred Hengeveld, Mooresville; Jose Nakamura, Shelby; William Forgay, Lexington; Manager-Len Cross, Forest City.

BA: Don Stafford, Hi-Toms/Lexington, .374
Runs: Carl Miller, Marion, 129
Hits: Bob Barker, Marion, 166
RBIs: Don Stafford, Hi-Toms/Lexington, 124

HRs: Carl Miller, Marion, 21
Wins: Kelly Jack Swift, Marion, 30
SOs: Kelly Jack Swift, Marion, 321
ERA: Jose Nakamura, Shelby, 2.40

D Wisconsin State League
President: Duane F. Bowman

Standings	W	L	Pct.	GB	Attend.	Manager
Green Bay Bluejays*(3)	80	42	.656	—	71,013	Phil Seghi
Wausau Lumberjacks**(4)..	76	49	.608	5½	37,138	Wayne Blackburn
Sheboygan Indians (9)........	71	52	.577	9½	33,387	Joe Hauser
Fond du Lac Panthers	68	55	.553	12½	54,286	Joe Consoli
Oshkosh Giants (13)..........	57	66	.463	23½	31,746	David Garcia
Wisconsin Rapids						
White Sox (2).................	53	70	.431	27½	37,066	Walter Millies
Appleton Papermakers (12)	43	77	.358	36	40,591	Travis Jackson
Janesville Cubs (10)...........	43	80	.350	37½	27,544	Robert Dant

Playoff games included in final standings.

Playoff: Green Bay 2 games, Wausau 0.

All-Star Team: 1B-William Adelhelm, Sheboygan; 2B-Roger Vander Wyst, Appleton; 3B-Joseph Tuminelli, Fond du Lac; SS-Pedro Ballester, Fond du Lac; OF-John Olczak, Janesville; Allan Shinn, Sheboygan; Bernie Mateosky, Wausau; C-Leonard Jackson, Janesville; P-Edward Knapp, Sheboygan; James Spear, Janesville; Chester Vincent, Oshkosh; Robert Laskowski, Fond du Lac.

BA: Joseph Tuminelli, Fond du Lac, .390
Runs: Joseph Tuminelli, Fond du Lac, 123
Hits: Joseph Tuminelli, Fond du Lac, 170
RBIs: Joseph Tuminelli, Fond du Lac, 148

HRs: Joseph Tuminelli, Fond du Lac, 28
Wins: Mel Heim, Green Bay, 19
SOs: Chester Vincent, Oshkosh, 203
ERA: Mel Heim, Green Bay, 2.14

Ind Mexican League
President: Arnulfo T. Canales

Standings	W	L	Pct.	GB	Manager
Nuevo Laredo Tecolotes.....	43	33	.566	—	Dolf Luque
Monterrey Sultanes.............	40	35	.533	2½	Lazaro Salazar
Veracruz Aguila	37	35	.514	4	Santos Amaro
Mexico City Diablos Rojos	32	39	.451	8½	Jose Luis Gomez
Anahuac Indios#.................	29	31	.487	NA	Jesus Diaz
Torreon Algodoneros#........	27	33	.450	NA	Memo Garibay

#Anahuac and Torreon withdrew.

BA: Rene Gonzalez, Veracruz, .343
Hits: Barney Serrell, Nuevo Laredo, 109
RBIs: Rene Gonzalez, Veracruz, 63
HRs: Hector Lara, Nuevo Laredo, 13

Wins: Juan Crespo, Mexico City, 18
    Jesus Moreno, Nuevo Laredo, 18
SOs: Lino Donoso, Veracruz, 160
ERA: Jesus Moreno, Nuevo Laredo, 1.75

1953 Interleague Post Season Play

World Series
New York (American) 4 games, Brooklyn (National) 2

Junior World Series
Montreal (International) 4 games, Kansas City (American Association) 1
Total Attendance: 27,869

Dixie Series
Dallas (Texas) 4 games, Nashville (Southern Association) 2
Total Attendance: 35,710

1953 Major League Farm Systems

American League

1 Boston (6): Louisville, Albany (NY), Greensboro, Roanoke, San Jose, Salisbury.
2 Chicago (8): Charleston (WV), Memphis, Colorado Springs, Waterloo, Topeka, Madisonville, Danville (IL), Wisconsin Rapids.
3 Cleveland (8): Indianapolis, Reading, Peoria, Spartanburg, Fargo-Moorhead, Sherbrooke, Daytona Beach, Green Bay.
4 Detroit (8): Buffalo, Little Rock, Montgomery, Durham, Bakersfield, Jackson, Jamestown, Wausau.
5 New York (10): Kansas City, Birmingham, Binghamton, Norfolk, Quincy, Boise, Joplin, Owensboro, Olean, McAlester.
6 Philadelphia (8): Ottawa, Williamsport, Savannah, Fayetteville, St. Hyacinthe, Welch, Cordele, Hopkinsville.
7 St. Louis (12): San Antonio, Wichita, Lewiston, York, Anderson, Pine Bluff, Aberdeen, Pocatello, Thetford Mines, Wytheville, Valdosta, Ada.
8 Washington (6): Chattanooga, Scranton, Charlotte, Bluefield, Orlando, Fulton.

National League

9 Brooklyn (16): St. Paul, Montreal, Mobile, Ft. Worth, Elmira, Pueblo, Miami, Newport News, Asheville, Santa Barbara, Great Falls, Thomasville, Union City, Hornell, Shawnee, Sheboygan.
10 Chicago (10): Springfield, Los Angeles, Macon, Des Moines, Cedar Rapids, Stockton, Sioux Falls, Gainesville, Hickory, Janesville.
11 Cincinnati (7): Tulsa, Columbia, Burlington, Ogden, Fitzgerald, Jackson, Lawton.
12 Milwaukee (13): Toledo, Atlanta, Jacksonville, Lincoln, Wichita Falls, Hagerstown, Evansville, Modesto, Eau Claire, Quebec, Sandersville, Wellsville, Appleton.
13 New York (9): Minneapolis, Nashville, Sioux City, Danville, St. Cloud, Muskogee, Mayfield, Pauls Valley, Oshkosh.
14 Philadelphia (9): Baltimore, Schenectady, Spokane, Terre Haute, Salt Lake City, Granby, Pulaski, Mattoon, Bradford.
15 Pittsburgh (7): New Orleans, Charleston (SC), Denver, Waco/Longview, Burlington-Graham, Billings, St. Jean, Hutchinson, Bristol, Dublin, Brunswick, Batavia.
16 St. Louis (18): Columbus (OH), Rochester, Houston, Columbus (GA), Omaha, Winston-Salem, Lynchburg, Fresno, St. Joseph, Dothan, Johnson City, Sanford, Hazlehurst-Baxley, Albany (GA), Paducah, Hannibal, Hamilton, Ardmore.

1953 No-Hitters

Date	Pitcher	Team	League	Opponent	Score
4-27	Billy Beane	Burlington-Graham	Carolina	Raleigh	4-2
5-2	Dan Stupur/				
	Jim Melton	Ft. Worth	Texas	Beaumont	7-2 (7)
5-5	Ray Parker	Thibodaux	Evangeline	Lafayette	5-0
5-6	Bobo Holloman	St. Louis	American	Philadelphia	6-0
5-20	Thomas Jones	Asheville	Tri-State	Rock Hill	2-0 (7)
5-20	Hamilton Graham	Portsmouth	Piedmont	Hagerstown	8-0
5-24	Ted Schriener/				
	George Compton	Welch	Appalachian	Bristol	2-1 (7)
5-25	Joseph Emery	Wausau	Wisconsin State	Wisconsin Rapids	1-0 (7)
5-29	Billy Joe Davidson	Reading	Eastern	Williamsport	3-0
6-1	Charles Craig	Odessa	Longhorn	Big Spring	11-0
6-7	Joe Hatten	Los Angeles	Pacific Coast	San Diego	6-0 (7)
6-9	Don Quinn	Douglas	Georgia State	Jesup	4-1
6-10	Art Bielefeld	Stockton	California	San Jose	0-1
6-13	George Aitken	Tucson	Arizona-Texas	Bisbee-Douglas	13-2
6-13	Reeve Watkins	Stockton	California	Modesto	1-0
6-14	Bill Harris	Mobile	Southern Assoc.	Memphis	1-0 (P, 7)
6-15	Joseph Pipak	Greenville	Big State	Austin	2-0
6-15	Gene Wolfe	Ft. Walton Beach	Alabama-Florida	Dothan	3-0
6-19	Norman Bell	Lincoln	Western	Des Moines	1-0 (7)
6-21	Bob Spry	Pulaski	Appalachian	Bristol	9-0
6-22	Clarence "Hooks" Iott	St. Petersburg	Florida Int'l	Tampa	7-0 (7)
6-28	James Kelly	Drummondville	Provincial	St. Jean	15-1 (7)
7-1	Ryne Duren	San Antonio	Texas	Beaumont	4-1 (7)
7-4	Red Munger	Hollywood	Pacific Coast	Sacramento	1-0 (7)
7-17	Ed Hughes	Baton Rouge	Evangeline	Crowley	5-1
7-18	Bill Johnson	Madisonville	Kitty	Mayfield	4-0 (7)
7-20	George Wasconis	Thomasville	Georgia-Florida	Valdosta	1-0 (7)
7-23	Earl Walton	Bluefield	Appalachian	Bristol	7-0 (7)
7-27	Ray Britt	Jacksonville Beach	Florida State	Cocoa	4-0
7-28	Karl Spooner	Pueblo	Western	Denver	2-0
7-29	Howard Anderson	Dallas	Texas	San Antonio	5-0 (7)
7-29	McKinley Mosley	Newport News	Piedmont	Portsmouth	8-0
8-5	Roy Moore	Ardmore	Sooner State	Sherman-Denison	7-3
8-5	James Lilly	Ft. Smith-Van Buren	Western Assoc.	St. Joseph	2-0 (7)
8-6	Duke Markell	Syracuse	International	Toronto	4-1 (7)
8-8	Courtney Stempel	Savannah	South Atlantic	Columbus	14-0
8-10	Dave Hillman	Springfield	International	Toronto	5-0
8-11	Marshall Long	St. Petersburg	Florida Int'l	Ft. Lauderdale	6-0 (7)
8-11	Clarence Marshall	Vancouver	Western Int'l	Salem	12-1
8-11	Art Hartley	Syracuse	International	Montreal	4-1 (7)
8-11	James Vickery	DeLand	Florida State	Jacksonville Beach	1-0
8-14	Vanoide Fletcher	Vancouver	Western Int'l	Yakima	2-0 (7)
8-14	Ramiro Cuevas	Nuevo Laredo	Mexican	Mexico City	1-0 (P)
8-19	John Stasney	Sherman-Denison	Sooner State	McAlester	2-1
8-21	Ted Koenigsmark	Valdosta	Georgia-Florida	Cordele	10-0
8-22	Roman Bartkowski	Monroe	Cotton States	Natchez	4-0
8-25	James Atkins	Oakland	Pacific Coast	San Francisco	2-0 (7)
8-30	Jodie Howington	Harlingen	Gulf Coast	Laredo	1-2 (7)
9-5	Bill Butler	Lewiston	Western Int'l	Spokane	4-0 (P)
9-7	Eurice "Pete" Treece	Charlotte	Tri-State	Gastonia	5-0
9-9	Frank Lary	Buffalo	International	Ottawa	5-0 (7)
9-12	Charles Locke	Wichita	Western	Sioux City	6-1

Number in parentheses indicates innings if other than nine; "P" indicates perfect game.

THIS DATE IN MINOR LEAGUE HISTORY

January 3, 1953, Charles Workman, former outfielder-third baseman with the Indians, Braves and Pirates, who set a Southern Association record of 52 home runs in 1948, died in Kansas City at the age of 37. Death was caused by internal hemorrhages resulting from an ulcer.

February 13, 1953, Chuck Connors, colorful first baseman for Los Angeles, Pacific Coast League, and formerly with the Chicago Cubs and Brooklyn Dodgers, announced he was retiring from the game to enter the movies. He played his first movie role in January 1952, for MGM in "Pat and Mike." His current role is "Zulu Sea" at Warner Brothers.

April 5, 1953, Herbert Gorman, 28-year-old outfielder with San Diego, Pacific Coast League, was stricken with a heart attack during the game with Hollywood at San Diego and died en route to the hospital.

April 18, 1953, Only 30 fans braved 40-degree temperatures to watch Tyler defeat Austin 5-2 in a Big State League game at Tyler, Texas.

April 20, 1953, Jerry Crosby, 33-year-old third baseman for Colorado Springs, Western League, belted four consecutive home runs as the Sky Sox defeated Pueblo 20-16. He also had a single for 17 total bases. Crosby hit his first four-bagger righthanded and the last three batting lefthanded. His circuit clouts came in successive innings, the fourth, fifth, sixth and seventh.

May 6, 1953, A crowd of 10,213, one of the largest opening day turnouts ever to witness a Class C League game, jammed Barnett Field in Fargo, North Dakota, to see the Fargo-Moorhead Twins launch their Northern League campaign with a 12-3 victory over Sioux Falls.

May 11, 1953, Bad weather, which already had hit the game hard this spring with rain, snow and frigid temperatures, dealt its worst blow to the Big State League club in Waco with a tornado that wrecked Katy Park and left the Pittsburgh farm club homeless. The tornado caused the death of more than 100 in Waco.

May 22, 1953, The Waco club, Big State League, made homeless when a tornado destroyed Katy Park, was transferred to Longview, Texas.

July 7, 1953, Pueblo lefty Karl Spooner, who set a postwar Western League record on June 22 when he whiffed 18 Wichita batters, set 16 Des Moines swatsmiths down on strikes while winning 3-1. The 16 whiffs increased Spooner's record to 63 in his last 39 innings.

August 11, 1953, Monty Stratton, whose Major League pitching career was cut short when he lost his right leg in a hunting accident in 1938, failed in his second brief comeback attempt in 1953. Out of Organized Ball since 1950, the former White Sox hurler had signed with Greenville, Big State League, but was released after one appearance. Stratton was signed by Sherman-Denison, Sooner State League, later in the season as a gate attraction. Pitching eight innings, Stratton lost 7-4 when Gainesville rallied for four runs in the eighth.

August 23, 1953, Outfielder Don Grate of Chattanooga, Southern Association, broke his own world record for a baseball throw during a field meet at Chattanooga, tossing a ball 443 feet, 3-1/2 inches from a running start. Grate set the previous record of 434 feet, one inch the previous September.

September 13, 1953, Tony Ponce, 32-year-old Mexican who joined San Francisco, Pacific Coast League, from the Class C Ventura club in the California League during the final week of August, won his eighth straight game without a loss in the last 17 days of the season. Knuckleballer Ponce had posted a 15-20 record for last-place Ventura.

December 10, 1953, After pitching 23 seasons in the majors and minors, Tony Freitas requested his release from the Stockton club of the California League and notified the club he was retiring from the game. He won 22 games and lost nine with Stockton the past season and had an 18-13 record in 1952. Tony posted 25 victories in the majors, 228 in the Pacific Coast League and 85 in the California League.

1954

American League
President: William Harridge

Standings	W	L	Pct.	GB	Attend.	Manager
Cleveland Indians	111	43	.721	—	1,335,472	Al Lopez
New York Yankees...........	103	51	.669	8	1,475,171	Casey Stengel
Chicago White Sox.............	94	60	.610	17	1,231,629	Paul Richards/Marty Marion
Boston Red Sox	69	85	.448	42	931,127	Lou Boudreau
Detroit Tigers....................	68	86	.442	43	1,079,847	Fred Hutchinson
Washington Senators	66	88	.429	45	503,542	Bucky Harris
Baltimore Orioles	54	100	.351	57	1,060,910	Jimmy Dykes
Philadelphia Athletics.........	51	103	.331	60	304,666	Eddie Joost

BA: Bobby Avila, Cleveland, .341
Runs: Mickey Mantle, New York, 129
Hits: Nellie Fox, Chicago, 201
　　　Harvey Kuenn, Detroit, 201
RBIs: Larry Doby, Cleveland, 126
HRs: Larry Doby, Cleveland, 32

Wins: Bob Lemon, Cleveland, 23
　　　Early Wynn, Cleveland, 23
SOs: Bob Turley, Baltimore, 185
ERA: Mike Garcia, Cleveland, 2.64
Pct: Sandy Consuegra, Chicago, .842, 16-3

National League
President: Warren C. Giles

Standings	W	L	Pct.	GB	Attend.	Manager
New York Giants	97	57	.630	—	1,155,067	Leo Durocher
Brooklyn Dodgers	92	62	.597	5	1,020,531	Walter Alston
Milwaukee Braves	89	65	.578	8	2,131,388	Charlie Grimm
Philadelphia Phillies	75	79	.487	22	738,991	Steve O'Neill/Terry Moore
Cincinnati Reds..................	74	80	.481	23	704,167	Birdie Tebbetts
St. Louis Cardinals	72	82	.468	25	1,039,698	Eddie Stanky
Chicago Cubs	64	90	.416	33	748,183	Stan Hack
Pittsburgh Pirates	53	101	.344	44	475,494	Fred Haney

BA: Willie Mays, New York, .345
Runs: Duke Snider, Brooklyn, 120
　　　Stan Musial, St. Louis, 120
Hits: Don Mueller, New York, 212
RBIs: Ted Kluszewski, Cincinnati, 141

HRs: Ted Kluszewski, Cincinnati, 49
Wins: Robin Roberts, Philadelphia, 23
SOs: Robin Roberts, Philadelphia, 185
ERA: Johnny Antonelli, New York, 2.30
Pct: Johnny Antonelli, New York, .750, 21-7

(Open) Pacific Coast League
President: Clarence H. Rowland

Standings	W	L	Pct.	GB	Attend.	Manager
San Diego Padres..............	102	67	.604	—	292,487	Lefty O'Doul
Hollywood Stars (15)........	101	68	.598	1	269,385	Bobby Bragan
Oakland Oaks	85	82	.509	16	201,922	Chuck Dressen
San Francisco Seals	84	84	.500	17½	298,908	Tommy Heath
Seattle Rainiers	77	85	.475	21½	151,071	Jerry Priddy
Los Angeles Angels (10)....	73	92	.442	27	238,567	Bill Sweeney
Sacramento Solons	73	94	.437	28	186,245	Gene Desautels/Tony Freitas
Portland Beavers................	71	94	.430	29	135,058	Clay Hopper

Playoffs: San Diego defeated Hollywood 7-2 in a one game playoff for first place. Oakland 2 games, San Diego 0; San Francisco 2 games, Hollywood 1.
Finals: Oakland 3 games, San Francisco 0.

All-Star Team: 1B-Jim Marshall, Oakland; **2B**-Al Federoff, San Diego; **3B**-Jack Phillips, Hollywood; **SS**-Dick Smith, Hollywood; **OF**-Harry Elliott, San Diego; Tom Saffell, Hollywood; Earl Rapp, San Diego; **C**-Raymond Orteig, Seattle; Leonard Neal, Oakland; **P**-Tommy Byrne, Seattle; Bill Wight, San Diego; Lino Donoso, Hollywood; **MVP**-Jack Phillips, Hollywood.

BA: Harry Elliott, San Diego, .350
Runs: Al Federoff, San Diego, 110
Hits: Harry Elliott, San Diego, 224
RBIs: Jim Marshall, Oakland, 123

HRs: Jim Marshall, Oakland, 31
Wins: Roger Bowman, Hollywood, 22
SOs: Tommy Byrne, Seattle, 199
ERA: Bill Wight, San Diego, 1.93

AAA American Association
President: Edward S. Doherty

Standings	W	L	Pct.	GB	Attend.	Manager
Indianapolis Indians (4)......	95	57	.625	—	282,979	Kerby Farrell
Louisville Colonels (2).......	85	68	.556	10½	141,353	Pinky Higgins
Minneapolis Millers (13)....	78	73	.517	16½	128,187	Bill Rigney
Columbus Red Birds (16)....	77	76	.503	18½	110,696	Johnny Keane
St. Paul Saints (9)............	75	78	.490	20½	134,006	Clay Bryant
Toledo Mud Hens (12)	74	80	.481	22	156,989	George Selkirk
Kansas City Blues (6)........	68	85	.444	27½	141,905	Harry Craft
Charleston Senators (3)	59	94	.386	36½	129,748	Joe Becker

Playoffs: Indianapolis 4 games, Minneapolis 2; Louisville 4 games, Columbus 3.
Finals: Louisville 4 games, Indianapolis 1.

All-Star Team: 1B-Maurice "Mo" Mozzali, Columbus; George Crowe, Toledo; **2B**-Harry Malmberg, Indianapolis; **3B**-Kal Segrist, Kansas City; Rance Pless, Minneapolis; **SS**-Billy Klaus, Minneapolis; **OF**-Marty Keough, Louisville; Bert Hamric, St. Paul; Rocky Colavito, Indianapolis; Eulas Hutson, St. Paul; **C**-Hank Foiles, Indianapolis; Hal Smith, Columbus; Pete Daley, Louisville; **Util**-Owen Friend, Indianapolis; **P**-Ivan DeLock, Louisville; Bob Darnell, St. Paul; Wade Browning, St. Paul; Herb Score, Indianapolis; Sam Jones, Indianapolis; John Kucab, Kansas City; Charles Gorin, Toledo; **MVP**-Herb Score, Indianapolis; **Manager**-Kerby Farrell, Indianapolis.

BA: Hal Smith, Columbus, .350
Runs: George Wilson, Minneapolis, 110
　　　Billy Klaus, Minneapolis, 110
Hits: George Crowe, Toledo, 197
RBIs: George Crowe, Toledo, 128

HRs: Rocky Colavito, Indianapolis, 38
Wins: Herb Score, Indianapolis, 22
SOs: Herb Score, Indianapolis, 330
ERA: Herb Score, Indianapolis, 2.62

AAA International League
President: Frank J. Shaughnessy

Standings	W	L	Pct.	GB	Attend.	Manager
Toronto Maple Leafs	97	57	.630	—	408,876	Luke Sewell
Montreal Royals (9)...........	88	66	.571	9	195,896	Max Macon
Rochester Red Wings (16)..	86	68	.558	11	195,141	Harry Walker
Syracuse Chiefs (14)...........	79	76	.510	18½	121,652	Skeeter Newsome
Havana Sugar Kings	78	77	.503	19½	295,453	Reggie Otero
Buffalo Bisons	71	83	.461	26	120,621	Bill Hitchcock
Richmond Virginians.........	60	94	.390	37	223,981	Luke Appling
Ottawa Athletics (7)...........	58	96	.377	39	93,982	Les Bell/Taft Wright

Playoffs: Syracuse 4 games, Toronto 2; Montreal 4 games, Rochester 2.
Finals: Syracuse 4 games, Montreal 3.

All-Star Team: 1B-Rocky Nelson, Montreal; **2B**-Louis Ortiz, Rochester; **3B**-Loren Babe, Toronto; **SS**-Humberto Fernandez, Montreal; **OF**-Bill Virdon, Rochester; Joe Taylor, Ottawa; Sam Jethroe, Toronto; **C**-Elston Howard, Toronto; **P**-John Faszholz, Rochester; Ken Lehman, Montreal; **MVP**-Elston Howard, Toronto; **Pitcher of the Year**-Tony Jacobs, Rochester.

BA: Bill Virdon, Rochester, .333
Runs: Sam Jethroe, Toronto, 113
Hits: Sam Jethroe, Toronto, 181
RBIs: Ed Stevens, Toronto, 113
HRs: Rocky Nelson, Montreal, 31

Wins: Ken Lehman, Montreal, 18
　　　Ed Roebuck, Montreal, 18
　　　John Faszholz, Rochester, 18
SOs: Bob Meyer, Syracuse, 173
ERA: Jim Owens, Syracuse, 2.87

AA Southern Association
President: Charles A. Hurth

Standings	W	L	Pct.	GB	Attend.	Manager
Atlanta Crackers (12)..........	94	60	.610	—	312,259	Whitlow Wyatt
New Orleans Pelicans (15) .	92	62	.597	2	206,305	Danny Murtaugh
Birmingham Barons (6)......	81	70	.536	11½	186,310	Mayo Smith
Memphis Chicks (3)	80	74	.519	14	108,898	Don Gutteridge
Chattanooga Lookouts (8) ..	75	76	.497	17½	149,453	Cal Ermer
Little Rock Travelers (5)....	64	90	.416	30	74,449	Bill Norman/Stubby Overmire/Pat Mullin
Nashville Vols (13).............	64	90	.416	30	89,470	Hugh Poland
Mobile Bears (9)................	63	91	.409	31	87,191	Stan Wasiak/Greg Mulleavy

Playoffs: Atlanta 4 games, Memphis 2; New Orleans 4 games, Birmingham 2.
Finals: Atlanta 4 games, New Orleans 1.

All-Star Team: 1B-Frank Torre, Atlanta; **2B**-Gene Freese, New Orleans; **3B**-Herbie Plews, Birmingham; **SS**-John Kline, Birmingham; **OF**-Bob Lennon, Nashville; Richard Tettlebach, Birmingham; Bob Montag, Atlanta; Eric Rodin, Nashville; Pete Whisenant, Atlanta; **C**-Lou Berberet, Birmingham; Frank Sacka, Chattanooga; James Solt, Atlanta; **Util**-Don Leppert, Birmingham; **P**-Leo Cristante, Atlanta; James Pearce, Chattanooga; Billy Currie, Chattanooga; Bill Harris, Mobile; Bob Schultz, New Orleans; David Benedict, Birmingham.

BA: Bob Lennon, Nashville, .345
Runs: Bob Lennon, Nashville, 139
Hits: Bob Lennon, Nashville, 210
RBIs: Bob Lennon, Nashville, 161

HRs: Bob Lennon, Nashville, 64
Wins: Leo Cristante, Atlanta, 24
SOs: Joe Margoneri, Nashville, 184
ERA: Nelson King, New Orleans, 2.25

AA Texas League
President: John L. Reeves

Standings	W	L	Pct.	GB	Attend.	Manager
Shreveport Sports	90	71	.559	—	142,970	Mel McGaha
Houston Buffalos (16)........	89	72	.553	1	310,531	Dixie Walker
Oklahoma City Indians	87	74	.540	3	101,938	Tom Tatum
Ft. Worth Cats (9)..............	81	80	.503	9	122,274	Al Vincent
San Antonio Missions (1)...	78	83	.484	12	149,065	Don Heffner
Tulsa Oilers (11)................	78	83	.484	12	104,378	Joe Schultz
Beaumont Exporters (10)...	77	84	.478	13	100,008	Les Fleming/Mickey Livingston
Dallas Eagles	64	97	.398	26	134,955	Dutch Meyer/Les Fleming

*Won first-half　**Won second-half　***Won both halves
Numbers after nicknames indicate farm system.
Affiliation listed at end of each year.

428

Playoffs: Ft. Worth 4 games, Shreveport 1; Houston 4 games, Oklahoma City 1.
Finals: Houston 4 games, Ft. Worth 1.

MVP-Frank Kellert, San Antonio; **Pitcher of the Year**-John Andre, Shreveport.

BA: Les Fleming, Beaumont/Dallas, .358	**HRs:** Buzz Clarkson, Dallas, 42
Runs: Everett Joyner, Shreveport, 121	**Wins:** Karl Spooner, Ft. Worth, 21
Jim Neufeldt, Oklahoma City, 121	John Andre, Shreveport, 21
Hits: Everett Joyner, Shreveport, 213	**SOs:** Karl Spooner, Ft. Worth, 262
RBIs: Frank Kellert, San Antonio, 146	**ERA:** Bob Smith, Shreveport, 2.89

A Eastern League
President: Thomas H. Richardson

Standings	W	L	Pct.	GB	Attend.	Manager
Wilkes-Barre Barons (5)	80	59	.576	—	96,599	Dan Carnevale
Elmira Pioneers (9)	77	63	.550	3½	77,467	Tommy Holmes
Albany Senators (2)	75	64	.540	5	72,985	Jack Burns
Reading Indians (4)	71	69	.507	9½	76,076	Pinky May
Binghamton Triplets (6)	70	70	.500	10½	49,221	Phil Page
Allentown Cardinals (16)	66	74	.471	14½	69,686	Dutch Dorman/Harold Olt
Williamsport Grays (15)	63	77	.450	17½	73,974	Larry Shepard
Schenectady Blue Jays (14)	57	83	.407	23½	45,529	George Stirnweiss/Lew Krausse

Playoffs: Albany 4 games, Wilkes-Barre 2; Reading 4 games, Elmira 0.
Finals: Albany 4 games, Reading 1.

All-Star Team: 1B-Fred Koenig, Allentown; **2B**-Bobby Richardson, Binghamton; **3B**-Clyde Parris, Elmira; **SS**-Sherwin Dixon, Allentown; **OF**-Fred Flemming, Wilkes-Barre; Joe Belcastro, Albany; Stan Palys, Schenectady; **C**-Joe Pignatano, Elmira; **P**-Al Schroll, Albany; James Stump, Wilkes-Barre; Clifford Ross, Schenectady; Hank Aguirre, Reading.

BA: Clyde Parris, Elmira, .313	**Wins:** Al Schroll, Albany, 16
Runs: Roy LaFevre, Williamsport, 92	James Stump, Wilkes-Barre, 16
Hits: Bobby Richardson, Binghamton, 171	**SOs:** Seth Morehead, Schenectady, 207
RBIs: Clyde Parris, Elmira, 90	**ERA:** Al Schroll, Albany, 2.07
HRs: George Wopinek, Williamsport, 16	

A South Atlantic League
President: Dick Butler

Standings	W	L	Pct.	GB	Attend.	Manager
Jacksonville Braves (12)	83	57	.593	—	119,454	Ben Geraghty
Savannah Athletics (7)	80	60	.571	3	82,232	Clyde Kluttz
Macon Peaches (10)	78	61	.561	4½	74,469	Nick Cullop
Columbia Reds (11)	77	62	.554	5½	75,108	Ernie White
Montgomery Rebels	68	72	.486	15	84,006	Marv Olson
Charlotte Hornets (8)	62	77	.446	20½	92,641	Pete Appleton/Ellis Clary
Augusta Rams	58	82	.414	25	93,091	Al Unser/John Liptak/El Tappe
Columbus Cardinals (16)	51	86	.372	30½	37,245	George Kissell

Playoffs: Jacksonville 3 games, Columbia 1; Savannah 3 games, Macon 0.
Finals: Savannah 4 games, Jacksonville 3.

All-Star Team: 1B-Clarence Riddle, Jacksonville; **2B**-Everett Kell, Savannah; **3B**-Elbert Israel, Savannah; **SS**-Ted Lewandowski, Macon; **OF**-Frank Robinson, Columbia; Jim Frey, Jacksonville; Al Pinkston, Savannah; **C**-Mike Roarke, Jacksonville; **Util**-Lyle Luttrell, Charlotte; Joseph Fuller, Montgomery; **P**-Humberto Robinson, Jacksonville; Calvin Howe, Macon; **Manager**-Clyde Kluttz, Savannah.

BA: Al Pinkston, Savannah, .360	**HRs:** Clarence Riddle, Jacksonville, 28
Runs: Frank Robinson, Columbia, 112	Jim Dickey, Macon, 28
Hits: Al Pinkston, Savannah, 180	**Wins:** Humberto Robinson, Jacksonville, 23
RBIs: Clarence Riddle, Jacksonville, 112	**SOs:** Humberto Robinson, Jacksonville, 243
	ERA: Humberto Robinson, Jacksonville, 2.41

A Western League
President: Governor Edwin C. Johnson

Standings	W	L	Pct.	GB	Attend.	Manager
Denver Bears (15)	94	56	.627	—	232,686	Andy Cohen
Des Moines Bruins (10)	88	66	.571	8	113,691	Les Peden
Omaha Cardinals (16)	83	68	.550	11½	150,131	Ferrell Anderson
Pueblo Dodgers (9)	79	74	.516	16½	80,768	Goldie Holt
Sioux City Soos (13)	78	75	.510	17½	69,333	David Garcia
Wichita Indians (14)	76	77	.497	19½	87,854	Herb Brett/Les Layton
Lincoln Chiefs (12)	62	88	.413	32	80,660	Whitey Wietelman/Red McQuillen
Colorado Springs Sky Sox (3)	48	104	.316	47	59,606	Mickey Livingston/Ed Stewart/Alvin Jacinto

Playoffs: Denver 3 games, Pueblo 1; Des Moines 3 games, Omaha 1.
Finals: Des Moines 3 games, Denver 1.

All-Star Team: 1B-Bill White, Sioux City; **2B**-Earl Weaver, Denver; **3B**-Joe Kirrene, Colorado Springs; **SS**-Edward Winceniak, Des Moines; **OF**-Jim King, Omaha; Ted Delguercio, Wichita; Bobby Prescott, Denver; **C**-Les Peden, Des Moines; **P**-Bob Garber, Denver; Hy Cohen, Des Moines; Mel Heim, Omaha; John O'Donnell, Wichita.

BA: Joe Kirrene, Colorado Springs, .343	**HRs:** Bill White, Sioux City, 30
Runs: Bobby Prescott, Denver, 137	**SBs:** Bill White, Sioux City, 40
Hits: Reno DeBenedetti, Denver, 183	**Wins:** Bob Clear, Omaha, 20
Bill White, Sioux City, 183	**SOs:** Bob Garber, Denver, 173
RBIs: Rocco Ippolito, Denver, 131	**ERA:** Hy Cohen, Des Moines, 1.88

A Western International League
President: Robert B. Abel

Standings	W	L	Pct.	GB	Attend.	Manager
Vancouver Capilanos*	74	49	.602	—	55,217	Bill Brenner
Yakima Bears	80	57	.584	1	66,571	Lou Stringer
Lewiston Broncs**(1)	77	61	.558	4½	74,258	Larry Barton
Salem Senators (14)	71	66	.518	10	48,438	Harvey Storey/Hugh Luby
Edmonton Eskimos	62	63	.496	13	67,746	Bob Sturgeon
Tri-City Braves	56	81	.409	25	57,625	Edo Vanni
Wenatchee Chiefs	54	80	.403	25½	49,615	George Kelly
Spokane Indians#	30	24	.556	NA	17,940	Don Osborn
Victoria Tyees@	43	57	.430	NA	28,561	Don Pries
Calgary Stampeders#	19	28	.404	NA	9,745	Gene Lillard

#Spokane and Calgary disbanded June 21.
@Victoria disbanded August 2. The league named a special team to play the clubs next scheduled to meet Victoria. These games counted in the standings. The special team went 1-8.

Playoff: Vancouver 4 games, Lewiston 0.

All-Star Team: 1B-Harry Warner, Salem; **2B**-Marvin Williams, Vancouver; **3B**-Harvey Storey, Salem/Lewiston; **SS**-James Clark, Vancouver; **OF**-Alfred Heist, Lewiston; Byron Charlton, Vancouver; Edward Murphy, Spokane/Vancouver; **C**-Lonnie Summers, Yakima; **P**-Bill Brenner, Vancouver; Al Yaylian, Lewiston; Jonathan Briggs, Salem.

BA: Marvin Williams, Vancouver, .360	**HRs:** Bob Wellman, Vancouver, 21
Runs: Alfred Heist, Lewiston, 136	Don Hunter, Calgary/Lewiston, 21
Hits: Byron Charlton, Vancouver, 183	**Wins:** Bill Brenner, Vancouver, 21
RBIs: Bob Wellman, Vancouver, 108	**SOs:** Jonathan Briggs, Salem, 233
	ERA: Jonathan Briggs, Salem, 2.50

B Big State League
President: Howard Green

Standings	W	L	Pct.	GB	Attend.	Manager
Waco Pirates (15)	105	42	.714	—	79,201	Jack Paepke
Tyler Tigers	92	55	.626	13	56,361	Francis "Salty" Parker
Corpus Christi Clippers (12)	87	60	.592	18	97,255	Billy Capps
Austin Pioneers	79	67	.541	25½	85,119	George Hausmann
Galveston White Caps	73	73	.500	31½	34,205	Chase Riddle/Sheriff Robinson
Bryan/Del Rio Indians#	53	93	.363	51½	34,217	Ray Taylor/Al LaMacchia/Chuck Hawley
Harlingen Capitals	53	94	.361	52	47,825	Earl Caldwell/Sam Harshaney
Temple Eagles	44	102	.301	60½	31,673	Fred Martin/Fred Campbell/Robert Moyer

#Bryan moved to Del Rio July 28.

Playoffs: Waco 4 games, Austin 2; Corpus Christi 4 games, Tyler 1.
Finals: Waco 4 games, Corpus Christi 3.

All-Star Team: 1B-Keith Little, Galveston; **2B**-Rex Babcock, Waco; **3B**-Oran Davis, Tyler; **SS**-Roberto Sanchez, Waco; **OF**-Roman Mejias, Waco; Jack Falls, Waco; Hardie Nettles, Austin; **C**-Troy Mitchell, Tyler; **P**-Gale Pringle, Tyler; James Vitter, Corpus Christi; Richard Roberson, Austin; Donald Kildoo, Waco.

BA: Dean Stafford, Galveston/ Corpus Christi, .362	**RBIs:** Dean Stafford, Galveston/ Corpus Christi, 171
Runs: John Wilkinson, Temple/ Corpus Christi, 151	**HRs:** Dean Stafford, Galveston/ Corpus Christi, 38
Hits: Dean Stafford, Galveston/ Corpus Christi, 212	**Wins:** James Vitter, Corpus Christi, 23
	SOs: Gale Pringle, Tyler, 212
	ERA: Gale Pringle, Tyler, 2.58

B Carolina League
President: Glenn E. "Ted" Mann

Standings	W	L	Pct.	GB	Attend.	Manager
Fayetteville Highlanders	86	51	.628	—	84,304	Hugo Taylor/Aaron Robinson
Burlington-Graham Pirates (15)	82	56	.594	4½	59,923	Stan Wentzel
Greensboro Patriots (2)	79	59	.572	7½	81,607	Eddie Popowski
Durham Bulls (5)	70	68	.507	16½	49,398	Charlie Metro
Danville Leafs (5)	70	69	.504	17	49,863	Andy Gilbert
High Point-Thomasville Hi-Toms (11)	66	73	.475	21	65,403	Tom Reis/Don Padgett/Fred Lanifero
Reidsville Luckies	56	83	.403	31	28,321	Fred Harrington
Winston-Salem Twins	44	94	.319	42½	44,380	Ralph Hodgin/Herb Brett

Playoffs: Fayetteville 3 games, Durham 1; Burlington-Graham 3 games, Greensboro 2.
Finals: Fayetteville 4 games, Burlington-Graham 1.

All-Star Team: 1B-Jim Pokel, Fayetteville; **2B**-Jake Charvat, Greensboro; **3B**-Gene Hassell, Burlington-Graham; **SS**-John Pfeiffer, Greensboro; **OF**-Jack Hussey, Fayetteville; Dewey Benson, Fayetteville; George Bullard, Durham; **C**-Guy Morton, Greensboro; Peter Naton, Fayetteville; **Util**-Mel Collins, Danville; Bill Evans, Reidsville; **P**-Harry Gilbert, Burlington-Graham; Bob Cruze, Durham; **MVP**-Guy Morton, Greensboro; **Manager**-Stan Wentzel, Burlington-Graham.

BA: Guy Morton, Greensboro, .348
Runs: Bob Lyons, Fayetteville, 108
Hits: Steve Demeter, Durham, 169
RBIs: Guy Morton, Greensboro, 120
HRs: Jim Pokel, Fayetteville, 38

Wins: Bob Cruze, Durham, 19
Curt Barclay, Danville, 19
SOs: Don Schultz, Burlington-Graham, 178
ERA: John Patula, Greensboro, 1.58

B Florida International League
President: Dale Miller

Standings	W	L	Pct.	GB	Attend.	Manager
St. Petersburg Saints	64	37	.634	—	30,759	Rudy Laskowski
Miami Beach/						
Greater Miami Flamingos@	63	39	.618	1½	14,407	Pepper Martin
West Palm Beach Indians	47	51	.480	15½	23,247	Gil Torres
Tallahassee Rebels	22	76	.224	40½	12,151	John George/
						Conklyn Meriwether/
						Marland Doolittle/Gene Harvey/
						Charles Cuellar
Miami Sun Sox#(9)	13	12	.520	NA	1,773	Doc Alexson
Tampa Smokers#	17	11	.607	NA	6,134	Art Rebel

#Tampa and Miami disbanded May 5.
@Miami Beach moved to Miami May 22.
The league disbanded July 27.

BA: Jesse Levan, Miami Beach/
Greater Miami, .348
Runs: Nesbit Wilson, St. Petersburg, 96
Hits: Jesse Levan, Miami Beach/
Greater Miami, 130
RBIs: Nesbit Wilson, St. Petersburg, 109

HRs: Jesse Levan, Miami Beach/
Greater Miami, 23
Wins: Stan Milankovich, St. Petersburg, 18
SOs: Robert Hines, Miami Beach/
Greater Miami, 95
ERA: William Tosheff, Tampa/
St. Petersburg, 2.61

B Piedmont League
President: Frank L. Summers

Standings	W	L	Pct.	GB	Attend.	Manager
Norfolk Tars (6)	87	53	.621	—	129,918	Frank Scalzi
Newport News Dodgers (9)	76	63	.547	10½	51,123	George Scherger
York White Roses (1)	72	67	.518	14½	68,023	George Staller
Portsmouth Merrimacs	71	69	.507	16	44,506	Alex Monchak/Pepper Martin
Hagerstown Packets (8)	66	74	.471	21	50,174	Paul Campbell/Zeke Bonura
Lynchburg Cardinals (16)	63	77	.450	24	34,614	Roland LeBlanc
Lancaster Red Roses (7)	62	78	.443	25	56,000	Kemp Wicker/Lena Blackburne/
						Buddy Walker
Colonial Heights-Petersburg Colts (11)	62	78	.443	25	44,127	John Vander Meer

Playoffs: Portsmouth 4 games, Norfolk 2; Newport News 4 games, York 0.
Finals: Newport News 4 games, Portsmouth 3.

All-Star Team: 1B-Daniel Keith, Norfolk; 2B-Tom Giuliano, Lancaster; 3B-Harold Treinen, Colonial Heights-Petersburg; SS-Stan Rosenzweig, Norfolk; OF-William Schimchak, Colonial Heights-Petersburg; Edward Stockton, Lynchburg; Charles Peete, Portsmouth; C-Roland LeBlanc, Lynchburg; P-Al Bennett, Hagerstown; Kenneth Beardslee, Norfolk; Eugene Weglarz, York; Lloyd Carden, Portsmouth.

BA: William Schimchak,
Colonial Heights-Petersburg, .336
Runs: Stan Rosenzweig, Norfolk, 116
Hits: Charles Peete, Portsmouth, 170
RBIs: Willie Tasby, York, 121

HRs: Willie Tasby, York, 27
Wins: Paul Doughty, Norfolk, 17
SOs: Al Bennett, Hagerstown, 162
ERA: Al Bennett, Hagerstown, 2.35

B Three-I League
President: Hal Totten

Standings	W	L	Pct.	GB	Attend.	Manager
Evansville Braves (12)	81	54	.600	—	71,691	Bob Coleman
Keokuk Kernels (4)	78	58	.574	3½	49,957	Jo Jo White
Peoria Chiefs (16)	73	63	.537	8½	78,497	Whitey Kurowski
Quincy Gems (6)	71	64	.526	10	54,168	Vern Hoscheit
Waterloo White Hawks (3)	66	69	.489	15	51,600	Walter Millies
Cedar Rapids Indians (10)	63	72	.467	18	60,605	William Prince
Terre Haute Phillies (14)	60	76	.441	21½	37,104	Hub Kittle
Burlington Bees	50	86	.368	31½	37,010	James Crandall

Playoffs: Peoria 3 games, Evansville 1; Quincy 3 games, Keokuk 1.
Finals: Quincy 3 games, Peoria 0.

All-Star Team: 1B-Eugene Faszholz, Peoria; 2B-Bobby Malkmus, Evansville; 3B-Ed Barbarito, Quincy; SS-Robert Shawver, Peoria; OF-Roger Maris, Keokuk; Tom Gott, Quincy; Larry Novak, Terre Haute; C-Earl Battey, Waterloo; P-Stan Pitula, Keokuk; Danny Osinski, Keokuk; Jack McMahan, Quincy; James O'Reilly, Quincy.

BA: Tom Gott, Quincy, .348
Runs: Ed Barbarito, Quincy, 121
Hits: Tom Gott, Quincy, 168
RBIs: Bob Kosis, Peoria, 121

HRs: Ed Barbarito, Quincy, 35
Wins: Stan Pitula, Keokuk, 20
SOs: Stan Pitula, Keokuk, 179
ERA: Ray Ripplemeyer, Evansville, 2.91

B Tri-State League
President: Robert E. Hipps

Standings	W	L	Pct.	GB	Attend.	Manager
Asheville Tourists (9)	86	54	.614	—	65,436	Ray Hathaway
Knoxville Smokies	72	66	.522	13	77,975	Pat McGlothin/Lewis Davis
Greenville Spinners	68	72	.486	18	89,595	George Bradshaw/
						Dickson Hendley
Spartanburg Peaches (4)	66	72	.478	19	34,918	Jim Bloodworth
Rock Hill Chiefs (8)	65	75	.464	21	59,180	Sam Lamatina/Mel Kerestes/
						Jacob Early
Anderson Rebels (1)	61	79	.436	25	43,381	Virgil Stallcup/Fred Boiko/
						Robert Knoke

Playoffs: Asheville 3 games, Greenville 2; Knoxville 3 games, Spartanburg 2.
Finals: Knoxville 3 games, Asheville 1.

All-Star Team: 1B-Fred Boiko, Anderson; 2B-Robert Parker, Asheville; 3B-Thomas Marino, Greenville; SS-Jasper Spears, Asheville; OF-Omer Tolson, Rock Hill; Albert Neil, Knoxville; Gordon Coleman, Spartanburg; C-Kenneth Worley, Asheville; Util-Mel Kerestes, Rock Hill; Oscar Sierra, Asheville; George Bradshaw, Greenville/Knoxville; P-Lester Fessette, Asheville; Ralph Mauriello, Asheville; Eurice "Pete" Treece, Rock Hill; Freddy Rodriguez, Greenville.

BA: Omer Tolson, Rock Hill, .347
Runs: Jasper Spears, Asheville, 120
Hits: Jasper Spears, Asheville, 188
RBIs: Oscar Sierra, Asheville, 104

HRs: Albert Neil, Knoxville, 22
Wins: Eurice "Pete" Treece, Rock Hill, 26
SOs: Freddy Rodriguez, Greenville, 221
ERA: Joseph Pipak, Knoxville, 2.78

C Arizona-Texas League
President: E.T. "Tim" Cusick

Standings	W	L	Pct.	GB	Attend.	Manager
Phoenix Stars	93	47	.664	—	114,450	Jerry Gardner
Mexicali Eagles (16)	92	48	.657	1	92,377	Art Lilly
Cananea Mineros	69	71	.493	24	85,053	Memo Garibay
El Paso Texans	69	71	.493	24	63,401	Syd Cohen
Tucson Cowboys	64	76	.457	29	60,735	Don Jameson
Nogales Yaquis	61	79	.436	32	98,092	Manuel Fortes/Virgilio Arteaga
Bisbee-Douglas Copper Kings	57	83	.407	36	45,031	Edwin Roberts/Ron Smith
Juarez Indians	55	85	.393	38	69,365	Enrique Fernandez

Playoffs: None.

BA: Leo Rodriguez, Cananea, .430
Runs: Ken Toothman, Phoenix, 193
Hits: Leo Rodriguez, Cananea, 259
RBIs: Earl Smith, Phoenix, 195
HRs: Claudio Solano, Cananea, 47

TBs: Claudio Solano, Cananea, 394
Wins: Nathaniel Moreland, Mexicali, 22
SOs: Richard Schroyer, Phoenix, 196
ERA: Fernando Ramirez, Mexicali, 3.51

C California League
President: Jerry Donovan

Standings	W	L	Pct.	GB	Attend.	Manager
Modesto Reds (6)	88	52	.623	—	102,888	Jack Graham/Jerry Crosby
Bakersfield Indians (9)	80	60	.571	8	73,660	Ray Perry
Stockton Ports (10)	80	60	.571	8	85,475	Gene Handley
San Jose Red Sox (2)	78	62	.557	10	67,968	Red Marion
Fresno Cardinals (16)	73	67	.521	15	51,678	James Hercinger
Channel Cities Oilers#	68	72	.486	20	40,763	Dario Lodigiani
Salinas Packers	56	84	.400	32	40,790	John O'Neil/George Genovese
Visalia Cubs	37	103	.264	51	29,689	Larry Flynn/Robert Hughes/
						Larry Powell

#represented Ventura and Santa Barbara, California..

Playoffs: Modesto 3 games, Stockton 0; San Jose 3 games, Bakersfield 1.
Finals: Modesto 4 games, San Jose 1.

All-Star Team: 1B-Jose Perez, Channel Cities; 2B-Renaldo Camacho, Fresno; 3B-Ray Perry, Bakersfield; SS-Charles Bell, Modesto; OF-James Keating, Modesto; Joe Brunacki, Fresno; Donald Musto, Bakersfield; C-Franklin Kerr, Modesto; Util-John Smith, San Jose; P-Robert Thorpe, Stockton; Rene Valdes, Bakersfield; Rick Botelho, Modesto; Marshall Epperson, Visalia.

BA: Joe Brunacki, Fresno, .344
Runs: Ray Perry, Bakersfield, 142
Hits: Bobby Smith, Fresno, 179
RBIs: Nick Ananias, Bakersfield, 139

HRs: Ray Perry, Bakersfield, 37
Wins: Robert Thorpe, Stockton, 28
SOs: Rick Botelho, Modesto, 234
ERA: Robert Thorpe, Stockton, 2.28

C Cotton States League
President: Judge Emmet Harty

Standings	W	L	Pct.	GB	Attend.	Manager
Greenville Tigers (5)	80	39	.672	—	48,372	Willis Hudlin
El Dorado Oilers	79	39	.669	½	36,115	Bill Adair
Meridian Millers	62	56	.525	17½	33,598	Thomas Davis
Monroe Sports	53	67	.442	27½	30,961	Ed Head
Pine Bluff Judges (1)	47	71	.398	32½	24,196	Frank Lucchesi/Bill Enos
Hot Springs Bathers (16)	35	84	.294	45	24,245	Paul Dean/Louis Lucas

Playoffs: Greenville 4 games, Monroe 1; El Dorado 4 games, Meridian 3.
Finals: El Dorado 4 games, Greenville 2.

BA: Frank Walenga, El Dorado, .382
Runs: Banks McDowell, Greenville, 121
Hits: Frank Walenga, El Dorado, 174
RBIs: Frank Walenga, El Dorado, 125
HRs: Pelham Austin, El Dorado, 28

Wins: Roy Jayne, Meridian, 20
 Robert Brown, El Dorado, 20
SOs: Bill Halley, Monroe, 176
ERA: Jerry Dean, Greenville, 1.80

C Evangeline League
President: Edmond L. Deramee

Standings	W	L	Pct.	GB	Attend.	Manager
New Iberia Pelicans	85	55	.607	—	87,350	William Adams
Port Arthur Sea Hawks	83	57	.593	2	46,512	Lou Fitzgerald
Crowley Millers	77	63	.550	8	65,099	Tony York
Lake Charles Lakers	67	72	.482	17½	71,555	Pop Faucett
Baton Rouge Red Sticks	66	74	.471	19	57,189	Joe Powers/Bill Spears
Alexandria Aces	65	74	.468	19½	51,793	Harry Strohm
Texas City/Thibodaux Pilots#	61	79	.436	24	28,523	Bones Sanders/Bill Dossey
Lafayette Oilers	55	85	.393	30	74,882	Bob Hedington

#Texas City moved to Thibodaux June 17.

Playoffs: New Iberia 4 games, Lake Charles 2; Crowley 4 games, Port Arthur 2.
Finals: New Iberia 4 games, Crowley 3.

All-Star Team: 1B-Ed Stutsman, Lafayette; **2B**-Victor Colo, Alexandria; **3B**-J.J. Gonzales, Baton Rouge; **SS**-Juan Alvarez, Lafayette; **OF**-Joe Nodar, Texas City/Thibodaux; Bill Lynn, Alexandria; Roger McKee, Baton Rouge; **C**-Royce McElroy, Lafayette; Jack Hall, Alexandria; **Util**-Rac Slider, Alexandria; Jose Garcia, Baton Rouge; **P**-John Laliberte, Alexandria; John Richard, Lafayette; Antonio Sosa, Lafayette; Lucio Alvarez, Baton Rouge; Carmine Donato, Texas City/Thibodaux; **Manager**-Harry Strohm, Alexandria.

BA: Bill Dossey, Texas City/Thibodaux, .410
Runs: Remy LeBlanc, New Iberia, 146
Hits: Bill Lynn, Alexandria, 211
RBIs: Roy "Tex" Sanner, Port Arthur, 141

HRs: Remy LeBlanc, New Iberia, 42
Wins: Fidel Alvarez, Port Arthur, 24
SOs: Rene Vega, Port Arthur, 207
ERA: John Laliberte, Alexandria, 2.99

C Longhorn League
President: Harry A. James

Standings	W	L	Pct.	GB	Attend.	Manager
Artesia Numexers	92	46	.667	—	54,450	John Gibson/Jimmy Adair
Roswell Rockets	87	51	.630	5	53,280	Pat Stasey
Carlsbad Potashers	87	52	.626	5½	60,963	Pat McLaughlin
Midland Indians	80	59	.576	12½	43,109	Rudy Briner
Big Spring Broncs	70	65	.519	20½	42,078	Robert Martin
Odessa Oilers	54	82	.397	37	26,281	Jack Knight/Everett Batson
San Angelo Colts	53	86	.381	39½	72,727	Hillis Layne
Wichita Falls/ Sweetwater Spudders#(8)	27	109	.199	64	20,101	Red McCarty

#Wichita Falls moved to Sweetwater May 6.

Playoffs: Artesia 4 games, Midland 2; Carlsbad 4 games, Roswell 2.
Finals: Artesia 4 games, Carlsbad 2.

BA: Joe Bauman, Roswell, .400
Runs: Joe Bauman, Roswell, 188
Hits: Isaiah Jackson, Carlsbad, 215
RBIs: Joe Bauman, Roswell, 224
HRs: Joe Bauman, Roswell, 72

TBs: Joe Bauman, Roswell, 456
Wins: Robert Weaver, Carlsbad, 21
SOs: Julio Ramos, Sweetwater/Midland, 222
ERA: Bartolo DiMaggio, Artesia, 3.60

C Mountain States League
President: Virgil Q. Wacks

Standings	W	L	Pct.	GB	Attend.	Manager
Middlesboro Athletics***	48	34	.585	—	9,031	Walt Dixon
Harlan Smokies	39	33	.542	4	10,000	Bill Steinecke
Kingsport Cherokees	41	40	.506	6½	33,000	Leo "Muscle" Shoals
Oak Ridge Pioneers	35	43	.449	11	18,286	Bert Niehoff
Morristown Red Sox#	7	7	.500	NA		Napoleon Reyes
Lexington Colts+	30	36	.455	NA	4,000	Zeke Bonura
Maryville-Alcoa/ Morristown Twins@(11)	29	36	.446	NA	9,559	Tuck McWilliams

#Morristown disbanded May 15.
@Maryville-Alcoa moved to Morristown June 19, then disbanded July 7.
+Lexington disbanded July 7.
The league disbanded July 20.

BA: Ray Adams, Oak Ridge, .352
Runs: Aldo Salvent, Kingsport, 84
Hits: Ray Adams, Oak Ridge, 112
RBIs: Walt Dixon, Middlesboro, 80

HRs: Leo "Muscle" Shoals, Kingsport, 18
Wins: Norman Hughes, Harlan, 16
SOs: Norman Hughes, Harlan, 85
ERA: Ray Johnston, Oak Ridge, 2.28

C Northern League
President: Herman D. White

Standings	W	L	Pct.	GB	Attend.	Manager
Fargo-Moorhead Twins (4)	85	55	.607	—	88,160	Phil Seghi
St. Cloud Rox (13)	76	54	.585	4	56,383	Charlie Fox
Winnipeg Goldeyes (16)	73	60	.549	8½	100,458	Mickey O'Neil
Eau Claire Braves (12)	71	63	.530	11	45,952	Charlie Root

Duluth Dukes (11)	67	70	.489	16½	91,096	Oscar Khederian/ Richard Wade/Danny Litwhiler
Superior Blues	63	70	.474	18½	37,185	Walt Novick
Aberdeen Pheasants (1)	60	75	.444	22½	62,503	Barney Lutz
Grand Forks Chiefs	43	91	.321	39	36,534	Virl Minnis/Frank Calo/ Frank Major

Playoffs: Fargo-Moorhead 2 games, Winnipeg 1; Eau Claire 2 games, St. Cloud 1.
Finals: Fargo-Moorhead 3 games, Eau Claire 0.

All-Star Team: 1B-David Roberts, Aberdeen; **2B**-John Wigley, St. Cloud; **3B**-John Goryl, Eau Claire; **SS**-William Hain, Aberdeen; **OF**-Jesse Rogers, St. Cloud; Frank Gravino, Fargo-Moorhead; Richard Anderson, Superior; **C**-Kenneth Bawek, Duluth; **P**-Leverette Spencer, Winnipeg; William Smith, Winnipeg.

BA: Willie Kirkland, St. Cloud, .360
Runs: Frank Gravino, Fargo-Moorhead, 128
Hits: Richard Anderson, Superior, 174
 Horace Greenwood, Duluth, 174
RBIs: Frank Gravino, Fargo-Moorhead, 158

HRs: Frank Gravino, Fargo-Moorhead, 56
Wins: Jim "Mudcat" Grant, Fargo-Moorhead, 21
SOs: Georges Maranda, Eau Claire, 179
ERA: Ron Mahrt, St. Cloud, 2.84

C Pioneer League
President: Claude Engberg

Standings	W	L	Pct.	GB	Attend.	Manager
Salt Lake City Bees (14)	78	53	.595	—	128,001	Charlie Gassaway
Billings Mustangs (15)	76	56	.576	2½	118,998	Cliff Dapper
Idaho Falls Russets (5)	74	58	.561	4½	49,105	Bob Mavis
Great Falls Electrics (9)	70	62	.530	8½	80,713	Lou Rochelli
Magic Valley Cowboys (10)	67	65	.508	11½	66,952	Everett Robinson
Ogden Reds (11)	61	71	.462	17½	45,884	Earle Brucker
Pocatello Bannocks	54	78	.409	24½	48,452	Butch Moran/Ernest Schuerman
Boise Pilots	47	84	.359	31	31,836	Edward Fernandez

Playoffs: Salt Lake City 2 games, Idaho Falls 1; Great Falls 2 games, Billings 1.
Finals: Great Falls 3 games, Salt Lake City 2.

All-Star Team: 1B-William Newkirk, Ogden; **2B**-Walter Carmichael, Pocatello; **3B**-Tom Sarna, Idaho Falls; **SS**-Pablo Bernard, Billings; **OF**-Bernie Mateosky, Idaho Falls; Edgar Sinquefield, Billings; Donald Cameron, Pocatello; **C**-John Turk, Salt Lake City; **P**-Kenneth Hommel, Ogden; Burton Barkelew, Salt Lake City; William Francis, Boise; Charles Jorgenson, Magic Valley.

BA: Tom Sarna, Idaho Falls, .372
Runs: Bob Lemmel, Magic Valley, 135
Hits: Clarence Moore, Great Falls, 198
RBIs: Bernie Mateosky, Idaho Falls, 140
HRs: Bernie Mateosky, Idaho Falls, 27

Wins: Kenneth Hommel, Ogden, 17
 Dwight Stoddard, Magic Valley, 17
 Louis Shade, Salt Lake City, 17
 Richard Armbruster, Idaho Falls, 17
SOs: Kenneth Hommel, Ogden, 277
ERA: Kenneth Hommel, Ogden, 3.10

C Provincial League
President: Albert Molini

Standings	W	L	Pct.	GB	Attend.	Manager
Quebec Braves (12)	80	48	.625	—	105,269	George McQuinn
Sherbrooke Indians (4)	76	53	.589	4½	44,541	Mark Wylie
Trois Rivieres Phillies (14)	73	57	.562	8	64,902	Al Barillari/George Stirnweiss
Drummondville A's (7)	60	69	.465	20½	36,302	Henry Biasatti
St. Jean Canadians (15)	53	73	.421	26	35,222	George Detore/Steve Mizerak
Thetford Mines Mineurs (1)	43	85	.336	37	47,334	Bill Krueger

Playoffs: Quebec 4 games, Trois Rivieres 3; Drummondville 4 games, Sherbrooke 3.
Finals: Quebec 4 games, Drummondville 2.

All-Star Team: 1B-Robert Stephens, Sherbrooke; **2B**-Michael Fandozzi, Quebec; **3B**-David Kiley, Trois Rivieres; **SS**-Julio Palazzini, Quebec; **OF**-William Stuifbergen, Drummondville; David Shea, Drummondville; Bill Williamson, Sherbrooke; **C**-Edward Stack, Trois Rivieres; **P**-Paul Bletz, Trois Rivieres; Matt Peoplis, Quebec; **Manager**-George McQuinn, Quebec.

BA: Michael Fandozzi, Quebec, .331
Runs: Michael Fandozzi, Quebec, 110
Hits: Michael Fandozzi, Quebec, 173
RBIs: Bill Williamson, Sherbrooke, 118
 William Stuifbergen, Drummondville, 118

HRs: Bill Williamson, Sherbrooke, 27
Wins: John Luthern, Sherbrooke, 20
SOs: Matt Peoplis, Quebec, 220
ERA: Matt Peoplis, Quebec, 2.34

C West Texas-New Mexico League
President: Hal Sayles

Standings	W	L	Pct.	GB	Attend.	Manager
Pampa Oilers	81	54	.600	—	34,594	Doug Lewis/Herschel Martin
Clovis Pioneers	79	53	.598	½	51,927	Grover Seitz
Amarillo Gold Sox	71	63	.530	9½	51,800	Ted Clawitter/Frank Kempa
Abilene Blue Sox	65	70	.481	16	77,668	Jay Haney
Albuquerque Dukes	62	74	.456	19½	83,446	Tom Jordan
Plainview Ponies	60	73	.451	20	56,071	Jackie Sullivan
Lubbock Hubbers	58	75	.436	22	75,515	Japhet "Red" Lynn/Bill Metzig/ Frank Benites
Borger Gassers#	36	50	.419	NA	22,500	Herschel Martin/Tommy Warren

#Borger disbanded July 16.

Playoffs: Pampa 4 games, Abilene 2; Clovis 4 games, Amarillo 3.
Finals: Pampa 4 games, Clovis 2.

All-Star Team: 1B-Doug Lewis, Pampa; **2B**-Robert Westfall, Albuquerque; **3B**-Curt Hardaway, Pampa; **SS**-Gilberto Valentin, Albuquerque; **OF**-Don Stokes, Plainview; Peter Trabucco, Clovis; Roberto Fernandez, Lubbock; **C**-Isaac Palmer, Pampa; **P**-Carroll "Red" Dial, Clovis; John Isenhart, Lubbock; Jonas Gaines, Pampa; Ernesto Clark, Pampa.

BA: Don Stokes, Plainview, .405
Runs: Curt Hardaway, Pampa, 152
Hits: Don Stokes, Plainview, 207
RBIs: Glenn Burns, Abilene, 137
HRs: Forrest "Frosty" Kennedy, Amarillo, 35
Wins: Carroll "Red" Dial, Clovis, 28
SOs: Ernesto Clark, Pampa, 234
    Carroll "Red" Dial, Clovis, 234
ERA: John Isenhart, Lubbock, 1.81

C Western Association
President: George Barr

Standings	W	L	Pct.	GB	Attend.	Manager
Topeka Owls (3)	87	51	.630	—	58,671	Ira Hutchinson
Muskogee Giants (13)	85	54	.612	2½	44,193	John Davenport
St. Joseph Saints (6)	82	57	.590	5½	41,035	William Cope
Blackwell Broncos (10)	79	61	.564	9	39,637	Joe Consoli/Al Kubski
Hutchinson Elks (15)	72	67	.518	15½	70,196	George Genovese/Larry Dorton
Ponca City Jets	62	76	.449	25	33,902	Edwin Carnett
Joplin Cardinals (16)	50	89	.360	37½	32,890	William Kelly
Iola Indians	39	101	.279	49	25,791	Willard Ramsdell/ Ralph Kennedy

Playoffs: Blackwell 3 games, Topeka 0; St. Joseph 3 games, Muskogee 2.
Finals: Blackwell 4 games, St. Joseph 1.

All-Star Team: 1B-Al Kubski, Blackwell; **2B**-Tom Watson, Hutchinson; **3B**-Ray Posipanka, Topeka; **SS**-Fritz Brickell, St. Joseph; **OF**-Reginald Gerald, Hutchinson; Walter Fishburn, Muskogee; James Eldridge, Ponca City; **C**-Charles Schaffernoth, Topeka; **P**-Robert Lowe, Topeka; Malcolm Landry, Muskogee.

BA: Ray Posipanka, Topeka, .338
Runs: David Wondra, Blackwell, 138
Hits: Tom Watson, Hutchinson, 182
RBIs: Al Kubski, Blackwell, 144
HRs: Al Kubski, Blackwell, 37
Wins: Robert Lowe, Topeka, 21
SOs: Harold Woods, Hutchinson, 207
ERA: Robert Lowe, Topeka, 2.84

D Alabama-Florida League
President: C.C. Hodge

Standings	W	L	Pct.	GB	Attend.	Manager
Dothan Rebels (16)	72	53	.576	—	38,050	Homer Ray Wilson
Andalusia-Opp Indians	71	55	.563	1½	26,925	Bull Hamons/Frank Tepedino
Ft. Walton Beach Jets (11)	68	57	.544	4	14,510	John Streza
Graceville Oilers	63	62	.504	9	42,260	Holt "Cat" Milner/Marcus Davis
Crestview Braves	55	69	.444	16½	16,565	Pappy Williams
Panama City Fliers	46	79	.368	26	20,055	Roy Sinquefield/ George Marquette/ Raymond Yochim

Playoffs: Dothan 4 games, Ft. Walton Beach 2; Graceville 4 games, Andalusia-Opp 2.
Finals: Graceville 4 games, Dothan 3.

All-Star Team: 1B-John Streza, Ft. Walton Beach; **2B**-Homer Ray Wilson, Dothan; **3B**-Frank Mirielli, Ft. Walton Beach; **SS**-Frank Tepedino, Andalusia-Opp; **OF**-Neal Cobb, Crestview; James Burns, Andalusia-Opp; Richard Hicks, Ft. Walton Beach; **C**-Tommy Patton, Dothan; **P**-Nicolas Berbesia, Graceville; Charles Vowels, Dothan; Spencer Davis, Dothan; Ronald Sturgill, Ft. Walton Beach.

BA: Neal Cobb, Crestview, .432
Runs: Frank Tepedino, Andalusia-Opp, 149
Hits: Neal Cobb, Crestview, 188
RBIs: James Burns, Andalusia-Opp, 143
HRs: John Streza, Ft. Walton Beach, 31
Wins: Spencer Davis, Dothan, 23
SOs: Spencer Davis, Dothan, 196
ERA: Spencer Davis, Dothan, 2.83

D Appalachian League
President: Chauncey De Vault

Standings	W	L	Pct.	GB	Attend.	Manager
Bluefield Blue-Grays (2)	70	43	.619	—	45,667	Len Okrie
Pulaski Phillies (14)	67	46	.593	3	19,890	George Triandos
Bristol Twins (6)	65	51	.560	6½	55,703	Walter Lance
Welch Miners (7)	59	54	.522	11	25,086	Jack Crosswhite
Johnson City Cardinals (16)	49	70	.412	24	22,553	Lee Peterson/Harold Contini
Wytheville Statesmen (1)	36	82	.305	36½	20,289	Joseph Murray/Bill Enos/ James Cisternelli

Playoffs: Bluefield 2 games, Welch 0; Pulaski 2 games, Bristol 0.
Finals: Bluefield 3 games, Pulaski 0.

All-Star Team: 1B-Walter Lance, Bristol; **2B**-William Whiteko, Pulaski; **3B**-Richard Stanton, Johnson City; **SS**-James Mahoney, Bluefield; **OF**-Marshall "Buster" Radebach, Bluefield; George Pfister, Wytheville; Carl Chianese, Welch; **C**-George Triandos, Pulaski; Bob Walsh, Bluefield; **Util**-Andy Madalone, Bluefield; Alfred Davis, Johnson City; Bob Quinn, Pulaski; **P**-Dick Morgan, Bluefield; Don Cardwell, Pulaski; Ken McBride, Bluefield; Jerome Kucharski, Pulaski.

BA: Walter Lance, Bristol, .361
Runs: James Mahoney, Bluefield, 101
Hits: Walter Lance, Bristol, 153
RBIs: Walter Lance, Bristol, 103
HRs: Bob Quinn, Pulaski, 26
Wins: Dick Morgan, Bluefield, 21
SOs: Jerome Kucharski, Pulaski, 208
ERA: Don Cardwell, Pulaski, 1.91

D Florida State League
President: John Krider

Standings	W	L	Pct.	GB	Attend.	Manager
Orlando C.B.s (8)	79	61	.564	—	57,309	Tom O'Brien
DeLand Red Hats	77	62	.554	1½	23,738	James Forbes/ Carvel "Bama" Rowell
Jacksonville Beach Sea Birds*(4)	76	63	.547	2½	22,660	Spud Chandler
Lakeland Pilots**	71	67	.514	7	41,808	James Bello/Rip Sewell
Cocoa Indians	60	76	.441	17	32,427	Carvel "Bama" Rowell/ Bill Steinecke
Daytona Beach Islanders (16)	52	86	.377	26	38,709	Ed Levy

Playoff: Lakeland 3 games, Jacksonville Beach 2.

BA: Russ Nixon, Jacksonville Beach, .387
Runs: Jesse Cade, DeLand, 118
Hits: Don Bratley, Daytona Beach, 201
RBIs: Gail Penza, DeLand, 110
HRs: Herman Niehaus, Lakeland, 23
Wins: John Blodgett, DeLand, 23
SOs: Ray Konkoleski, Jacksonville Beach, 228
ERA: Carmelo Ruiz, DeLand, 2.23

D Georgia State League
President: Bill Estroff

Standings	W	L	Pct.	GB	Attend.	Manager
Vidalia Indians	85	44	.659	—	53,334	James Beavers
Douglas Trojans (11)	85	45	.654	½	35,589	Charles Bledsoe
Dublin Irish (15)	82	48	.631	3½	57,945	George Kinnamon
Statesboro Pilots	57	73	.438	28½	18,532	Jack Hines
Hazlehurst-Baxley Cardinals (16)	47	82	.364	38	18,121	Arnold Riesgo/Bill McGhee
Sandersville Wacos	33	97	.254	52½	25,600	Stan West/David Madison

Playoffs: Vidalia 4 games, Statesboro 2; Douglas 4 games, Dublin 3.
Finals: Vidalia 4 games, Douglas 0.

All-Star Team: 1B-Van Davis, Douglas; **2B**-Lester Crouch, Douglas; **3B**-Dennis Meekins, Dublin; **SS**-Belasco Bossard, Douglas; **OF**-Bobby Driggers, Vidalia; Drew Gilbert, Douglas; James Warren, Statesboro; **C**-Bryan Hinson, Vidalia; **P**-Phil Gilbert, Vidalia; Jimmie Hiland, Hazlehurst-Baxley; Bill Green, Douglas; Donald Vaughan, Vidalia.

BA: Belasco Bossard, Douglas, .360
Runs: Sam Buell, Dublin, 150
Hits: Drew Gilbert, Douglas, 173
RBIs: Van Davis, Douglas, 135
HRs: Van Davis, Douglas, 31
Wins: Phil Gilbert, Vidalia, 22
SOs: Jimmie Hiland, Hazlehurst-Baxley, 247
ERA: Phil Gilbert, Vidalia, 2.23

D Georgia-Florida League
President: W.T. Anderson

Standings	W	L	Pct.	GB	Attend.	Manager
Brunswick Pirates (15)	88	52	.629	—	54,475	Frank Oceak
Fitzgerald Redlegs (11)	80	59	.576	7½	38,652	Leon "Red" Treadway
Albany Cardinals (16)	73	65	.529	14	47,092	Russ McGovern
Waycross Bears	68	67	.504	17½	36,854	Paul Eames
Valdosta Tigers (5)	68	70	.493	19	52,911	Marv Owen/Stan Wasiak
Thomasville Dodgers (9)	64	71	.474	21½	36,079	Boyd Bartley/John Angelone
Tifton Indians (4)	60	80	.429	28	30,143	Edgar Hartness
Americus-Cordele Orioles (1)	51	88	.367	36½	26,136	Cliff Melton/Jack Landis

Playoffs: Brunswick 4 games, Waycross 1; Fitzgerald 4 games, Albany 1.
Finals: Fitzgerald 3 games, Brunswick 2, rainouts forced cancellation of the series. No champion was declared.

All-Star Team: 1B-Chuck Buheller, Brunswick; **2B**-Adrian Rechichar, Brunswick; **3B**-Robert Stewart, Valdosta; **SS**-Philip Shartzer, Fitzgerald; **OF**-Kelvin Roberts, Tifton; Floyd Faust, Brunswick; Samuel Farless, Brunswick; Van Hill, Fitzgerald; **C**-Don Williams, Thomasville; Kenneth Retzer, Tifton; **Util**-Charles Brockwell, Brunswick; **P**-Charles Douglas, Brunswick; William Knox, Albany; Earl Gearhart, Fitzgerald; Ronald Gray, Brunswick; **Manager**-Leon "Red" Treadway, Fitzgerald.

BA: Edgar Hartness, Tifton, .364
Runs: Floyd Faust, Brunswick, 143
Hits: Chuck Buheller, Brunswick, 184
RBIs: Bill Thompson, Fitzgerald, 131
HRs: Chuck Buheller, Brunswick, 19
    Larry Spinner, Tifton, 19
Wins: Charles Douglas, Brunswick, 27
SOs: Charles Douglas, Brunswick, 273
ERA: William Knox, Albany, 1.80

D Kitty League
President: Shelby Peace

Standings	W	L	Pct.	GB	Attend.	Manager
Union City Dodgers*(9)	76	40	.655	—	36,000	Earl Naylor
Fulton Lookouts (8)	69	47	.595	7	24,555	Russell "Red" Mincy
Owensboro Oilers (6)	65	49	.570	10	39,290	Marvin Crater
Mayfield Clothiers (13)	64	52	.552	12	26,099	John "Red" Davis
Madisonville Miners**(3)	61	52	.540	13½	31,097	Robert Latshaw/William Close
Hopkinsville Hoppers (7)	58	59	.496	18½	31,504	Edward Wright/Bearl Brooks/ Richards Ramsey

Paducah Chiefs (16)............	45	67	.402	29	32,222	Horace Contina/Lee Peterson
Central City Reds#..............	13	44	.228	NA	15,203	Joe Richardson/Hayden Ray
Jackson Generals#	1	44	.022	NA	3,700	Louis Lucas

#Jackson disbanded June 1, after losing 26 straight games. Central City started the second half on July 5.

Playoff: Union City 4 games, Madisonville 2.

All-Star Team: 1B-Allan Shinn, Union City; 2B-Bearl Brooks, Hopkinsville; 3B-Norman Abrams, Hopkinsville; SS-William Pass, Madisonville; OF-Joseph Moran, Mayfield; Frank Layana, Madisonville; Edwin Allen, Union City; C-Marvin Crater, Owensboro; P-Rene Masip, Union City; Dominick Maisano, Owensboro; Charles Templeton, Union City; Edward Dick, Owensboro.

BA: Allan Shinn, Union City, .391	**HRs:** Ned Waldrop, Fulton, 22
Runs: Ned Waldrop, Fulton, 114	**Wins:** Rene Masip, Union City, 18
Hits: William Pass, Madisonville, 162	**SOs:** James Major, Union City, 174
RBIs: Ned Waldrop, Fulton, 159	**ERA:** Charles Templeton, Union City, 2.13

D Mississippi-Ohio Valley League
President: C.C. "Dutch" Hoffman

Standings	W	L	Pct.	GB	Attend.	Manager
Decatur Commodores	74	52	.587	—	38,776	John Lucadello
Danville Dans (13)..............	66	59	.528	7½	39,992	Richard Klaus
Clinton Pirates (15)............	63	59	.516	9	74,768	Robert Clark
Dubuque Packers (3)	62	61	.504	10½	65,993	Jack Conway
Mattoon Phillies (14)..........	62	64	.492	12	48,422	Carl Bush/Don Osborn
Paris Lakers	58	68	.460	16	39,103	Tom Sunkel
Hannibal Cardinals (16)......	58	68	.460	16	33,065	J.C. Dunn
Mt. Vernon Kings	57	69	.452	17	27,584	Lou Bekeza

Playoffs: Clinton 2 games, Decatur 0; Danville 2 games, Dubuque 1.
Finals: Danville 3 games, Clinton 0.

All-Star Team: 1B-Donald Strickland, Dubuque; 2B-Robert Loftin, Danville; 3B-Arthur Burnett, Hannibal; SS-Manuel Valdez, Decatur; OF-Richard Lombardi, Dubuque; John Wrye, Clinton; Leon Wagner, Danville; C-Charles Starasta, Mt. Vernon; P-David Jiminez, Clinton; John Bumgarner, Decatur; Kenneth Anderson, Danville; Luis Herrera, Decatur.

BA: John Lucadello, Decatur, .362	**HRs:** J.C. Dunn, Hannibal, 26
Runs: Leon Wagner, Danville, 108	**Wins:** John Bumgarner, Decatur, 22
Hits: Leon Wagner, Danville, 160	**SOs:** David Jiminez, Clinton, 249
RBIs: Joseph Schmidt, Paris, 125	**ERA:** John Bumgarner, Decatur, 2.67

D PONY League
President: Vincent M. McNamara

Standings	W	L	Pct.	GB	Attend.	Manager
Corning Red Sox (2)..........	77	47	.621	—	61,582	Sheriff Robinson
Jamestown Falcons (5)	78	48	.619	—	86,460	Danny Litwhiler/Wayne Blackburn
Wellsville Braves (12).........	69	56	.552	8½	37,392	Ted Sepkowski
Hornell Dodgers (9)...........	65	60	.520	12½	37,519	John Angelone/Doc Alexson
Bradford Phillies (14)	61	65	.484	17	49,944	James Deery
Hamilton Cardinals (16)......	61	65	.484	17	41,379	James Brown
Olean Giants (13)................	46	80	.365	32	19,203	Austin Knickerbocker/ Frank Genovese
Erie Sailors (8)....................	45	81	.357	33	42,502	Tom O'Connell/ Napoleon Reyes/Thomas Milich/ Joe Consoli

Playoffs: Corning 3 games, Hornell 0; Jamestown 3 games, Wellsville 0.
Finals: Corning 4 games, Jamestown 1.

All-Star Team: 1B-Hollis Powell, Jamestown; 2B-Robert Yoder, Hornell; 3B-Ted Sepkowski, Wellsville; SS-Raymond Reed, Wellsville; OF-Harold Gruner, Corning; Charles Soraci, Hornell; Arthur Remsa, Hamilton; C-Ronald Witucki, Jamestown; P-Robert Harrell, Bradford; Thomas Van Remmen, Jamestown; Marty Kutyna, Hamilton; Eli Grba, Corning.

BA: Robert Yoder, Hornell, .398	**Wins:** Marty Kutyna, Hamilton, 17
Runs: Robert Yoder, Hornell, 130	Robert Stragier, Wellsville, 17
Hits: Robert Yoder, Hornell, 201	**SOs:** Eli Grba, Corning, 209
RBIs: Ted Sepkowski, Wellsville, 144	**ERA:** Bob Mische, Jamestown, 3.30
HRs: Ted Sepkowski, Wellsville, 45	**Pct:** Bob Mische, Jamestown, .727, 16-6

D Sooner State League
President: Ucal Clanton

Standings	W	L	Pct.	GB	Attend.	Manager
Shawnee Hawks (9)	92	48	.657	—	42,189	Jack Banta
Lawton Braves (12)	81	58	.583	10½	47,431	Travis Jackson
McAlester Rockets (6)........	76	64	.543	16	53,410	Malcolm "Bunny" Mick
Ardmore Cardinals (16)......	72	67	.518	19½	31,090	Bennie Warren/Frank Mancuso
Gainesville Owls (10).........	72	68	.514	20	14,385	Richard Rigazio
Ada Herefords/Cementers (1)...	64	76	.457	28	28,482	Lou Brower/John Densmore
Seminole Oilers	61	79	.436	31	16,840	Tom Warren/Ray Taylor
Pauls Valley Raiders...........	41	99	.293	51	29,468	Lloyd Pearson/Bennie Warren

Playoffs: Ardmore 3 games, Shawnee 2; Lawton 3 games, McAlester 2.
Finals: Lawton 4 games, Ardmore 0.

All-Star Team: 1B-Robert White, Ardmore; 2B-Billie Davidson, Shawnee; 3B-Ray Mitchell, Shawnee; SS-Don LeJohn, Shawnee; OF-Carl Hrovatic, Lawton; Gene Green, Ardmore; Eddie Haas, Gainesville; C-Leonard Jackson, Gainesville; Frank Ricco, McAlester; Util-Walter Massefski, Gainesville/Ada; P-Wendell Doss, Lawton; Joe Roberson, Shawnee; **Manager**-Travis Jackson, Lawton.

BA: Ray Mitchell, Shawnee, .371	**HRs:** Gene Green, Ardmore, 34
Runs: Louis Fox, Shawnee, 139	**Wins:** Wendell Doss, Lawton, 24
Hits: Louis Fox, Shawnee, 193	**SOs:** Joe Roberson, Shawnee, 225
RBIs: Jim Humbert, Shawnee, 136	**ERA:** Joe Roberson, Shawnee, 2.52

D Tar Heel League
President: Lawson Brown

Standings	W	L	Pct.	GB	Attend.	Manager
Hickory Rebels (10)...........	34	18	.654	—	8,598	Charles Teague
Marion Marauders (1).........	26	26	.500	8	8,203	Bob Knoke
Forest City Owls	24	24	.500	8	8,147	Woody Rich/Richard McKeithan
Shelby Clippers (13)..........	16	32	.333	16	12,000	Harold Kollar

The league disbanded June 21.

BA: Mike Yaremchuk, Hickory, .376	**HRs:** Joe Cristello, Forest City, 5
Runs: Lou McCotter, Hickory, 52	Harold Kollar, Shelby, 5
Hits: Mike Yaremchuk, Hickory, 74	**Wins:** Russell Wingo, Hickory, 11
RBIs: Mike Yaremchuk, Hickory, 45	**SOs:** John Cathey, Forest City, 95
	ERA: Leo Davis, Hickory, 1.82

Ind Mexican League
President: Arnulfo T. Canales

Standings	W	L	Pct.	GB	Manager
Nuevo Laredo Tecolotes.....	56	24	.700	—	Dolf Luque
Yucatan Leones	47	32	.595	8½	Oscar Garmendia/Mario Collazo
Monterrey Sultanes............	41	38	.519	14½	Lazaro Salazar
Veracruz Aguila.................	39	40	.494	16½	Santos Amaro
Mexico City Azul	30	50	.375	26	Agustin Bejerano
Mexico City Diablos Rojos	25	54	.316	30½	Ramon Bragana/Luis Montes de Oca

BA: Rene Gonzalez, Veracruz, .359	**Wins:** Tomas Arroyo, Nuevo Laredo, 15
Hits: Barney Serrell, Nuevo Laredo, 126	**SOs:** Raul Galata, Veracruz, 118
RBIs: Fernando Pedrozo, Nuevo Laredo, 80	**ERA:** Humberto Garcia, Yucatan, 2.29
HRs: Rene Gonzalez, Veracruz, 21	

1954 Interleague Post Season Play

World Series
New York (National) 4 games, Cleveland (American) 0

Junior World Series
Louisville (American Association) 4 games, Syracuse (International) 2
Total Attendance: 38,360

Dixie Series
Atlanta (Southern Association) 4 games, Houston (Texas) 3
Total Attendance: 73,633

1954 Major League Farm Systems

American League

1 Baltimore (12): San Antonio, Wichita, Lewiston, York, Anderson, Pine Bluff, Aberdeen, Thetford Mines, Wytheville, Americus-Cordele, Ada, Marion.
2 Boston (6): Louisville, Albany (NY), Greensboro, San Jose, Bluefield, Corning.
3 Chicago (7): Charleston, Memphis, Colorado Springs, Waterloo, Topeka, Madisonville, Dubuque.
4 Cleveland (8): Indianapolis, Reading, Keokuk, Spartanburg, Fargo-Moorhead, Sherbrooke, Jacksonville Beach, Tifton.
5 Detroit (8): Buffalo, Little Rock, Wilkes-Barre, Durham, Greenville (MS), Idaho Falls, Valdosta, Jamestown.
6 New York (10): Kansas City, Birmingham, Binghamton, Norfolk, Quincy, Modesto, St. Joseph, Bristol, Owensboro, McAlester.
7 Philadelphia (6): Ottawa, Savannah, Lancaster, Drummondville, Welch, Hopkinsville.
8 Washington (8): Chattanooga, Charlotte, Hagerstown, Rock Hill, Wichita Falls/Sweetwater, Orlando, Fulton, Erie.

National League

9 Brooklyn (15): St. Paul, Montreal, Mobile, Ft. Worth, Elmira, Pueblo, Miami, Newport News, Asheville, Bakersfield, Great Falls, Thomasville, Union City, Hornell, Shawnee.
10 Chicago (10): Los Angeles, Beaumont, Macon, Des Moines, Cedar Rapids, Stockton, Magic Valley, Blackwell, Gainesville, Hickory.
11 Cincinnati (10): Tulsa, Columbia, High Point-Thomasville, Colonial Heights-Petersburg, Maryville-Alcoa/Morristown, Duluth, Ogden, Ft. Walton Beach, Douglas, Fitzgerald.
12 Milwaukee (10): Toledo, Atlanta, Jacksonville, Lincoln, Corpus Christi, Evansville, Eau Claire, Quebec, Wellsville, Lawton.
13 New York (10): Minneapolis, Nashville, Sioux City, Danville (VA), St. Cloud, Muskogee, Mayfield, Danville (IL), Olean, Shelby.
14 Philadelphia (9): Syracuse, Schenectady, Salem, Terre Haute, Salt Lake City, Trois Rivieres, Pulaski, Mattoon, Bradford.
15 Pittsburgh (12): Hollywood, New Orleans, Williamsport, Denver, Waco, Burlington-Graham, Billings, St. Jean, Hutchinson, Dublin, Brunswick, Clinton.
16 St. Louis (22): Columbus (OH), Rochester, Houston, Allentown, Columbus (GA), Omaha, Lynchburg, Peoria, Mexicali, Fresno, Hot Springs, Winnipeg, Joplin, Dothan, Johnson City, Daytona Beach, Hazlehurst-Baxley, Albany (GA), Paducah, Hannibal, Hamilton, Ardmore.

1954 No-Hitters

Date	Pitcher	Team	League	Opponent	Score
4-22	John Scroggs	Waycross	Georgia-Florida	Thomasville	3-0
4-26	Leo Dansby	Colonial Heights-Petersburg	Piedmont	York	0-1 (10)
5-2	Austin McDonald	Andalusia-Opp	Alabama-Florida	Dothan	1-0
5-9	George Starrette	Reidsville	Carolina	Danville	1-0
5-10	Bill Washburn	Winston-Salem	Carolina	Hi-Toms	4-0
5-26	Joe Roberson	Shawnee	Sooner State	Pauls Valley	9-1
6-4	Don Schultz	Burlington-Graham	Carolina	Durham	4-0
6-5	Dominick Zanni	Sioux City	Western	Denver	3-0
6-9	Ralph Romero	Spokane	Western Int'l	Victoria	8-0
6-9	Tom McMullen	Thomasville	Georgia-Florida	Americus-Cordele	8-1
6-11	Earl Hunsinger	Pulaski	Appalachian	Johnson City	11-0
6-12	Jim Wilson	Milwaukee	National	Philadelphia	2-0
6-19	Bill Barkley	Charlotte	South Atlantic	Augusta	2-0 (7)
6-22	Eugene Weglarz	York	Piedmont	Hagerstown	1-0 (7)
6-23	Tony Sarmiento	Tifton	Georgia-Florida	Americus-Cordele	10-0 (7)
6-27	Terry Kniffen	Bakersfield	California	Salinas	3-1
6-29	Chester Dickey	Grand Forks	Northern	St. Cloud	2-0 (7)
7-15	Ray Konkoleski	Jacksonville Beach	Florida State	Cocoa	3-0
7-16	Myron Garland	Andalusia-Opp	Alabama-Florida	Dothan	3-0 (7)
7-28	John Bumgarner	Decatur	Miss.-Ohio Valley	Clinton	1-0
8-1	Gale Pringle	Tyler	Big State	Temple	1-0 (P, 7)
8-3	Bubba Church	Los Angeles	Pacific Coast	Portland	3-0
8-4	Winston Brown	Portsmouth	Piedmont	Norfolk	5-2
8-4	John Blodgett	DeLand	Florida State	Daytona Beach	3-1
8-7	Kriesler Speas	Johnson City	Appalachian	Welch	5-0 (7)
8-11	Luis Arroyo	Houston	Texas	Dallas	4-0
8-17	Robert Alexander	Portland	Pacific Coast	Oakland	3-0 (7)
8-19	John O'Neill	Waycross	Georgia-Florida	Tifton	4-0
8-20	Evelio Hernandez	Roswell	Longhorn	Odessa	6-0
8-20	Ray Crone	Toledo	American Assoc.	St. Paul	3-0 (7)
8-22	Jack Urban	Birmingham	Southern Assoc.	New Orleans	0-0 (7)
8-24	Tom Cronin	Mattoon	Miss.-Ohio Valley	Hannibal	2-0 (7)
9-10	Orinthal Anderson	Lincoln	Western	Omaha	0-1 (7)
9-12	Roger Bowman	Hollywood	Pacific Coast	Portland	10-0 (P, 7)

Number in parentheses indicates innings if other than nine; "P" indicates perfect game.

THIS DATE IN MINOR LEAGUE HISTORY

April 24, 1954, A youngster who bought a ticket to get into the park, then asked for a tryout and was signed just an hour before game time, made one of the most dramatic debuts in South Atlantic League history at Columbus, Georgia. Joe Carolan, a 21-year-old outfielder from Detroit, blasted a grand slam for the Columbus Cardinals on his first trip to the plate.

May 10, 1954, Seven members of the Decatur, Mississippi-Ohio Valley League, club had a close brush with death by carbon monoxide poisoning in a bus carrying them to Decatur after a night game in Danville. They were found overcome by gas fumes when a stop was made in Decatur to let out six of the players. Three players were carried from the bus unconscious and four others became ill after getting out. All were taken to a hospital where they were revived and later released.

May 17, 1954, Five members of the Abilene, West Texas-New Mexico League, team were hospitalized in the second case within a week of carbon monoxide poisoning from gas fumes suffered by players traveling by bus.

May 18, 1954, Vern Kennedy, 47-year-old relief hurler of the Beaumont club of the Texas League, quit the Exporters for personal reasons. The ex-major leaguer, who broke into Organized Ball in 1930, had worked in 16 of the Exporters' 40 games, compiling a 3-4 record.

May 21, 1954, Veteran Los Angeles outfielder Max West walloped home run number 300 of his 17-year Organized Ball career against Seattle. All but 77 of his 300 homers were hit in the Pacific Coast League.

May 31, 1954, Jackson lost its 26th consecutive game in the Kitty League, bowing to Madisonville in the afternoon game of a day-night doubleheader. The Generals ended their losing streak by winning the evening tilt 10-2, before a crowd of only 64. The following day, the Jackson club disbanded. One of the club's losses (the 18th) was a forfeit, being unable to appear for their game due to bus trouble.

June 21, 1954, The four-team Class D Tar Heel League, the smallest circuit in Organized Ball, disbanded when Shelby was forced to quit because of financial difficulties. The loop was the first to fail to finish out a season since the Border League disbanded in July 1951.

June 27, 1954, Angered at umpires' decisions, Japanese fans rioted at two professional games in Osaka, tossing bottles and fists, smashing seats and breaking windows. More than 400 police were called out to quell one riot that did not end until after midnight.

July 2, 1954, Raymond "Mac" Smith, catcher for Hagerstown, Piedmont League, collapsed and died on the field a few minutes after hitting a single in the fifth inning during a game with Portsmouth at Hagerstown. Doctors stated his death was caused by malaria and complications.

July 22, 1954, The Arizona-Texas League came up with a new reason for postponing a game: bad roads. Rain almost completely washed out the road to Cananea, Mexico, making it impossible for Tucson to get through to fill a date with the Mineros.

August 1, 1954, A 29-year career in Organized Ball came to a close when Earl Caldwell, former major league hurler, hung up his glove after winning his 354st game. Called to the mound in a relief role for Corpus Christi in the fourth inning of a Big State League game with Del Rio, the 48-year-old veteran blanked the Indians on four hits in six innings and was credited with a 14-8 victory, his 12th of the season against only four defeats. He also began a 10-run Clipper rally in the fourth inning by leading off with a single.He won 33 games and lost 43 in the majors.

September 5, 1954, Joe Bauman of Roswell, Longhorn League, smashed three homers in a doubleheader for a season total of 72 to set a new all-time Organized Ball record. The 6'5", 245-pounder, 32 years of age, hit 50 homers for Artesia in 1952 and last season collected 53 for a three-year total of 175.

September 6, 1954, Slugger Bob Lennon of Nashville, Southern Association, hit three homers in a Labor Day doubleheader, winding up the season with 64 round-trippers.

September 10, 1954, Despite losing 2-1 to St. Paul in his last appearance of the season, Herb Score, Indianapolis, American Association, finished with a record of 22-5 and struck out 330 batters in 251 innings.

September 12, 1954, Robert Thorpe, 19-year-old Stockton righthander, tied the California League record for most victories when he won his 28th game of the season by defeating Modesto 6-4. Thorpe ended the campaign with a 28-4 ledger, had 32 complete games in 33 starts and finished the season with a string of 30 complete contests.

1955

American League
President: William Harridge

Standings	W	L	Pct.	GB	Attend.	Manager
New York Yankees............	96	58	.623	—	1,490,138	Casey Stengel
Cleveland Indians..............	93	61	.604	3	1,221,780	Al Lopez
Chicago White Sox............	91	63	.591	5	1,175,684	Marty Marion
Boston Red Sox	84	70	.545	12	1,203,200	Pinky Higgins
Detroit Tigers....................	79	75	.513	17	1,181,838	Bucky Harris
Kansas City Athletics	63	91	.409	33	1,393,054	Lou Boudreau
Baltimore Orioles	57	97	.370	39	852,039	Paul Richards
Washington Senators	53	101	.344	43	425,238	Chuck Dressen

BA: Al Kaline, Detroit, .340
Runs: Al Smith, Cleveland, 123
Hits: Al Kaline, Detroit, 200
RBIs: Ray Boone, Detroit, 116
  Jackie Jensen, Boston, 116
HRs: Mickey Mantle, New York, 37

Wins: Whitey Ford, New York, 18
  Bob Lemon, Cleveland, 18
  Frank Sullivan, Boston, 18
SOs: Herb Score, Cleveland, 245
ERA: Billy Pierce, Chicago, 1.97
Pct: Tommy Byrne, New York, .762, 16-5

National League
President: Warren C. Giles

Standings	W	L	Pct.	GB	Attend.	Manager
Brooklyn Dodgers..............	98	55	.641	—	1,033,589	Walter Alston
Milwaukee Braves	85	69	.552	13½	2,005,836	Charlie Grimm
New York Giants	80	74	.519	18½	824,112	Leo Durocher
Philadelphia Phillies	77	77	.500	21½	922,886	Mayo Smith
Cincinnati Reds..................	75	79	.487	23½	693,662	Birdie Tebbetts
Chicago Cubs....................	72	81	.471	26	875,800	Stan Hack
St. Louis Cardinals	68	86	.442	30½	849,130	Eddie Stanky/Harry Walker
Pittsburgh Pirates	60	94	.390	38½	469,397	Fred Haney

BA: Richie Ashburn, Philadelphia, .338
Runs: Duke Snider, Brooklyn, 126
Hits: Ted Kluszewski, Cincinnati, 192
RBIs: Duke Snider, Brooklyn, 136
HRs: Willie Mays, New York, 51

Wins: Robin Roberts, Philadelphia, 23
SOs: Sad Sam Jones, Chicago, 198
ERA: Bob Friend, Pittsburgh, 2.83
Pct: Don Newcombe, Brooklyn, .800, 20-5

(Open) Pacific Coast League
President: Claire V. Goodwin

Standings	W	L	Pct.	GB	Attend.	Manager
Seattle Rainiers	95	77	.552	—	342,101	Fred Hutchinson
San Diego Padres................	92	80	.535	3	226,005	Bob Elliott
Hollywood Stars (15)..........	91	81	.529	4	248,528	Bobby Bragan
Los Angeles Angels (10)......	91	81	.529	4	291,732	Bill Sweeney/Jack Warner/ Bob Scheffing
Portland Beavers................	86	86	.500	9	199,238	Clay Hopper
San Francisco Seals	80	92	.465	15	161,570	Tommy Heath
Oakland Oaks	77	95	.448	18	141,397	Lefty O'Doul
Sacramento Solons	76	96	.442	19	163,578	Tony Freitas

Playoffs: None.

All-Star Team: 1B-Steve Bilko, Los Angeles; **2B**-Curt Roberts, Hollywood; **3B**-Harry Bright, Sacramento; **SS**-Carl "Buddy" Peterson, San Diego; **OF**-George Metkovich, Oakland; Earl Rapp, San Diego; Bobby Del Greco, Hollywood; **C**-Joe Ginsberg, Seattle; **P**-Bud Daley, Sacramento; George "Red" Munger, Hollywood; **MVP**-Steve Bilko, Los Angeles.

BA: George Metkovich, Oakland, .335
Runs: Earl Rapp, San Diego, 109
Hits: Vern Jones, Sacramento, 206
RBIs: Earl Rapp, San Diego, 133

HRs: Steve Bilko, Los Angeles, 37
Wins: George "Red" Munger, Hollywood, 23
SOs: Bob Garber, Hollywood, 199
ERA: George "Red" Munger, Hollywood, 1.85

AAA American Association
President: Edward S. Doherty

Standings	W	L	Pct.	GB	Attend.	Manager
Minneapolis Millers (13)....	92	62	.597	—	177,307	Bill Rigney
Omaha Cardinals (16)........	84	70	.545	8	316,012	Johnny Keane
Denver Bears (7)................	83	71	.539	9	426,248	Ralph Houk
Louisville Colonels (2)........	83	71	.539	9	139,948	Red Marion
Toledo Mud Hens (12)	81	73	.526	11	187,911	George Selkirk
St. Paul Saints (9)..............	75	78	.490	16½	118,318	Max Macon
Indianapolis Indians (4)......	67	86	.438	24½	129,517	Kerby Farrell
Charleston Senators	50	104	.325	42	108,431	Danny Murtaugh/Vern Rapp

Playoffs: Minneapolis 4 games, Denver 0; Omaha 4 games, Louisville 3.
Finals: Minneapolis 4 games, Omaha 0.

All-Star Team: 1B-Frank Torre, Toledo; Maurice "Mo" Mozzali, Omaha; **2B**-Don Blasingame, Omaha; **3B**-Frank Malzone, Louisville; **SS**-Jasper Spears, St. Paul; Bill Harrell, Indianapolis; **OF**-Bob Lennon, Minneapolis; George Wilson, Minneapolis; Jim Dyck, Indianapolis; Marty Keough, Louisville; **C**-Darrell Johnson, Denver; Carl Sawatski, Minneapolis; Haywood Sullivan, Louisville; **Util IF**-Rance Pless, Minneapolis; Bill Gardner, Minneapolis; **P**-Ross Grimsley, Charleston/Omaha; Bob Trowbridge, Toledo; Stu Miller, Omaha; Al Worthington, Minneapolis; Joe Margoneri, Minneapolis; **MVP**-Rance Pless, Minneapolis; **Manager**-Bill Rigney, Minneapolis.

BA: Rance Pless, Minneapolis, .337
Runs: Rance Pless, Minneapolis, 116
Hits: Rance Pless, Minneapolis, 200
RBIs: Marv Throneberry, Denver, 117

HRs: Marv Throneberry, Denver, 36
Wins: Al Worthington, Minneapolis, 19
SOs: Jerry Casale, Louisville, 186
ERA: Willard Schmidt, Omaha, 2.56

AAA International League
President: Frank J. Shaughnessy

Standings	W	L	Pct.	GB	Attend.	Manager
Montreal Royals (9)............	95	59	.619	—	205,134	Greg Mulleavy
Toronto Maple Leafs	94	59	.614	½	350,742	Luke Sewell
Havana Sugar Kings (11) ...	87	66	.569	7½	313,232	Reggie Otero
Rochester Red Wings (16)..	76	77	.497	18½	150,061	Harry Walker/Lou Kahn/ Dixie Walker
Syracuse Chiefs (14)...........	74	79	.484	20½	85,191	Skeeter Newsome
Buffalo Bisons (5)	65	89	.422	30	120,490	Dan Carnevale
Columbus Jets (6)..............	64	89	.418	30½	202,854	Nick Cullop
Richmond Virginians...........	58	95	.379	36½	126,607	Luke Appling

Playoffs: Rochester 4 games, Montreal 1; Toronto 4 games, Havana 1.
Finals: Rochester 4 games, Toronto 0.

All-Star Team: 1B-Rocky Nelson, Montreal; **2B**-Forrest "Spook" Jacobs, Columbus; **3B**-Steve Demeter, Buffalo; **SS**-Hector Rodriguez, Toronto; **OF**-Archie Wilson, Toronto; Gino Cimoli, Montreal; Jackie Brandt, Rochester; **C**-Ken Lehman, Montreal; Jack Crimian, Toronto; **MVP**-Rocky Nelson, Montreal; **Pitcher of the Year**-Jack Crimian, Toronto; **Manager**-Reggie Otero, Havana.

BA: Rocky Nelson, Montreal, .364
Runs: Rocky Nelson, Montreal, 118
Hits: Bob Wilson, Montreal, 190
RBIs: Rocky Nelson, Montreal, 130

HRs: Rocky Nelson, Montreal, 37
Wins: Ken Lehman, Montreal, 22
SOs: Jim Owens, Syracuse, 161
ERA: Jack Crimian, Toronto, 2.10

AA Mexican League
President: Arnulfo T. Canales

Standings	W	L	Pct.	GB	Attend.	Manager
Mexico City Tigres.............	53	47	.530	—	200,802	George Genovese
Nuevo Laredo Tecolotes.....	53	47	.530	—	97,547	Dolf Luque
Mexico City Diablos Rojos	52	48	.520	1	261,809	Gilberto Torres/Mario Diaz
Veracruz Aguila.................	52	48	.520	1	92,115	Santos Amaro
Monterrey Sultanes	46	54	.460	7	111,079	Epitacio Torres
Yucatan Leones	44	56	.440	9	167,443	Fermin Guerra/Gilberto Garza

Playoff: MC Tigres 2 games, Nuevo Laredo 0.

All-Star Team: 1B-Alonso Perry, MC Diablos Rojos; **2B**-Felipe Hernandez, MC Diablos Rojos; **3B**-Leo Rodriguez, MC Tigres; **SS**-Guillermo Alvarez, Veracruz; **OF**-Fernando Diaz Pedrozo, Nuevo Laredo; Gail Henley, MC Tigres; Paul Pettit, MC Tigres; **C**-Leon Kellman, Nuevo Laredo; **C**-Mario Diaz, MC Diablos Rojos; **P**-Fred Waters, MC Tigres; Vicente Lopez, MC Diablos Rojos.

BA: Leo Rodriguez, MC Tigres, .385
Runs: Roy Parker, MC Diablos Rojos, 90
Hits: Felipe Hernandez, MC Diablos Rojos, 157
RBIs: Alonso Perry, MC Diablos Rojos, 122

HRs: Mario Ariosa, Veracruz, 22
Wins: Fred Waters, MC Tigres, 18
SOs: Fred Waters, MC Tigres, 126
ERA: Fred Waters, MC Tigres, 2.06

AA Southern Association
President: Charles A. Hurth

Standings	W	L	Pct.	GB	Attend.	Manager
Memphis Chicks (3)	90	63	.588	—	134,823	Jack Cassini/Ted Lyons
Birmingham Barons (7)......	88	65	.575	2	201,570	Phil Page
Chattanooga Lookouts (8)..	80	74	.519	10½	160,009	Cal Ermer
Mobile Bears (9)................	79	75	.513	11½	94,214	Clay Bryant
Nashville Vols (11).............	77	74	.510	12	116,952	Joe Schultz
New Orleans Pelicans (15).	76	75	.503	13	128,993	Andy Cohen
Atlanta Crackers (12).........	70	84	.455	20½	239,037	George McQuinn/ Marvin Rackley/Clyde King
Little Rock Travelers (5)	52	102	.338	38½	51,514	Bobby Mavis/Steve Souchock

Playoffs: Mobile 4 games, Memphis 3; Birmingham 4 games, Chattanooga 2.
Finals: Mobile 4 games, Birmingham 2.

*Won first-half **Won second-half ***Won both halves
Numbers after nicknames indicate farm system.
Affiliation listed at end of each year.

435

1955

All-Star Team: 1B-Bob Skinner, New Orleans; **2B**-Charles Williams, Nashville; **3B**-Leon Carter, Birmingham; **SS**-Jerry Lumpe, Birmingham; **OF**-Edward White, Memphis; Bob Martyn, Birmingham; Ben Downs, Nashville; Jim Lemon, Chattanooga; Bob "Hurricane" Hazle, Nashville; **C**-Cal Neeman, Birmingham; Danny Kravitz, New Orleans; Joe Tipton, Memphis; **Util IF**-Frank DiPrima, Atlanta; **P**-Ralph Mauriello, Mobile; John Wingo, Birmingham; Bill George, Atlanta; Donald Gross, Nashville; Hal Griggs, Chattanooga.

BA: Charles Williams, Nashville, .368
Runs: Bob "Hurricane" Hazle, Nashville, 114
Hits: Charles Williams, Nashville, 211
RBIs: Jim Lemon, Chattanooga, 109
Jim Gentile, Mobile, 109

HRs: Bob "Hurricane" Hazle, Nashville, 29
Wins: Jerry Dahlke, Memphis, 19
SOs: Gene Host, Little Rock, 184
ERA: Ralph Mauriello, Mobile, 2.76

AA Texas League
President: Dick Butler

Standings	W	L	Pct.	GB	Attend.	Manager
Dallas Eagles (13)	93	67	.581	—	297,596	John "Red" Davis
San Antonio Missions (1)	93	68	.578	½	150,861	Don Heffner
Shreveport Sports	87	74	.540	6½	94,036	Mel McGaha
Houston Buffalos (16)	86	75	.534	7½	224,651	Mike Ryba
Tulsa Oilers (4)	86	75	.534	7½	143,692	Dutch Meyer/Henry Schenz
Ft. Worth Cats (9)	77	84	.478	16½	107,959	Tommy Holmes
Oklahoma City Indians	70	90	.438	23	70,173	Tom Tatum/Rudy Laskowski
Beaumont Exporters (12)	51	110	.317	42½	60,375	Mickey Livingston

Playoffs: Houston 4 games, Dallas 2; Shreveport 4 games, San Antonio 2.
Finals: Shreveport 4 games, Houston 3.

All-Star Team: 1B-Bob Boyd, Houston; **2B**-George "Sparky" Anderson, Ft. Worth; **3B**-Ossie Virgil, Dallas; **SS**-Joe Koppe, Shreveport; **OF**-Dick Williams, Ft. Worth; Ed Knoblauch, Beaumont/Dallas; Pidge Browne, Shreveport; **C**-Ray Murray, Dallas; **P**-Red Murff, Dallas; **MVP**-Ray Murray, Dallas; **Pitcher of the Year**-Red Murff, Dallas; **Manager**-John "Red" Davis, Dallas.

BA: Ed Knoblauch, Beaumont/Dallas, .327
Runs: Joe Koppe, Shreveport, 118
Hits: Bob Boyd, Houston, 197
RBIs: Jim Pisoni, San Antonio, 118

HRs: Pidge Browne, Shreveport, 33
Wins: Red Murff, Dallas, 27
SOs: Pete Burnside, Dallas, 235
ERA: Red Murff, Dallas, 1.99

A Eastern League
President: Thomas H. Richardson

Standings	W	L	Pct.	GB	Attend.	Manager
Reading Indians (4)	84	53	.613	—	99,412	Jo Jo White
Allentown Cardinals (16)	78	60	.565	6½	78,382	Harold Olt
Binghamton Triplets (7)	75	62	.547	9	89,529	George Stirnweiss
Schenectady Blue Jays (14)	74	64	.536	10½	73,585	Don Osborn
Williamsport Grays (15)	71	66	.518	13	98,827	Larry Shepard
Wilkes-Barre Barons/						
Johnstown Johnnies#(13)	59	78	.431	25	81,721	Mike McCormick
Elmira Pioneers (9)	56	83	.403	29	59,276	Ray Hathaway
Albany Senators	53	84	.387	31	52,752	Bert Haas

#Wilkes-Barre moved to Johnstown July 1.

Playoffs: Schenectady 3 games, Reading 1; Allentown 3 games, Binghamton 1.
Finals: Allentown 3 games, Schenectady 2.

All-Star Team: 1B-Neal Hertweck, Allentown; **2B**-Martin Devlin, Elmira; **3B**-Milt Graff, Williamsport; **SS**-Richard Barone, Williamsport; **OF**-Roger Maris, Reading; Sam Suplizio, Binghamton; John "Zeke" Bella, Binghamton; **C**-John Blanchard, Binghamton; William Onuska, Williamsport; **P**-Jim Singleton, Wilkes-Barre/Johnstown; Don Minnick, Reading.

BA: John "Zeke" Bella, Binghamton, .371
Runs: John Huesman, Allentown, 116
Hits: Jack Reed, Binghamton, 172
RBIs: Neal Hertweck, Allentown, 112
HRs: John Blanchard, Binghamton, 34

Wins: Don Minnick, Reading, 20
SOs: Jim Coates, Binghamton, 186
ERA: Jim Singleton, Wilkes-Barre/Johnstown, 2.42

A South Atlantic League
President: Bill Terry

Standings	W	L	Pct.	GB	Attend.	Manager
Columbia Reds (11)	89	51	.636	—	83,339	Ernie White
Jacksonville Braves (12)	79	61	.564	10	124,211	Ben Geraghty
Augusta Tigers (5)	76	64	.543	13	96,322	Charlie Metro
Montgomery Rebels (2)	75	64	.540	13½	58,665	Eddie Popowski/Fred Maguire
Macon Peaches (10)	67	73	.479	22	71,652	Pepper Martin/Ivy Griffin
Savannah Athletics (6)	61	79	.436	28	47,863	Clyde Kluttz
Columbus Cardinals (16)	58	81	.417	30½	46,800	Andy Anderson
Charlotte Hornets (8)	54	86	.386	35	87,788	Jim Bloodworth

Playoffs: Augusta 1 game, Columbia 0; Montgomery 1 game, Jacksonville 0.
Finals: Augusta 2 games, Montgomery 1.

All-Star Team: 1B-John Jones, Macon; **2B**-Jimmy Bragan, Columbia; **3B**-Tom Sarna, Augusta; **SS**-Al Facchini, Jacksonville; **OF**-George Toepfer, Montgomery; Al Spangler, Jacksonville; Horace Garner, Jacksonville; **C**-Bill Robertson, Savannah; **Util IF**-Matt Sczesny, Montgomery; **Util OF**-Albie Pearson, Montgomery; **P**-Charlie Rabe, Columbia; Paul Cave, Jacksonville.

BA: Wes Covington, Jacksonville, .326
Runs: Ultus Alvarez, Columbia, 102
Hits: George Toepfer, Montgomery, 180
RBIs: Bill Thompson, Columbia, 94
Larry "Bo" Osborne, Augusta, 94

HRs: Wiley Williams, Savannah/ Jacksonville, 28
Wins: Charlie Rabe, Columbia, 21
SOs: Charlie Rabe, Columbia, 219
ERA: Charlie Rabe, Columbia, 2.01

A Western League
President: Governor Edwin C. Johnson

Standings	W	L	Pct.	GB	Attend.	Manager
Colorado Springs Sky Sox (3)	81	69	.540	—	87,527	John Conway
Pueblo Dodgers (9)	79	71	.527	2	73,941	Goldie Holt
Wichita Indians (1)	78	73	.517	3½	94,862	Buddy Bates
Des Moines Bruins (10)	77	74	.510	4½	88,181	Les Peden/Pepper Martin
Sioux City Soos (13)	69	81	.460	12	62,902	John Davenport
Lincoln Chiefs (15)	67	83	.447	14	90,024	Bill Burwell

Playoffs: Wichita defeated Des Moines 21-3 in a one game playoff for third place. Des Moines 3 games, Colorado Springs 1; Wichita 3 games, Pueblo 2.
Finals: Wichita 3 games, Des Moines 0.

All-Star Team: 1B-Ken Landenberger, Colorado Springs; **2B**-Robert McKee, Des Moines; **3B**-Ed Barbarito, Wichita; **SS**-Clarence Moore, Pueblo; **OF**-Willie Kirkland, Sioux City; Domenick DiTusa, Colorado Springs; Francis Rice, Lincoln; **C**-Sam Hairston, Colorado Springs; Miguel Gaspar, Wichita; **P**-Andrew Pane, Sioux City; Bob Harrison, Wichita.

BA: Sam Hairston, Colorado Springs, .350
Runs: Willie Kirkland, Sioux City, 117
Hits: Clarence Moore, Pueblo, 194
RBIs: Ron Cooper, Colorado Springs, 117

HRs: Willie Kirkland, Sioux City, 40
Wins: Joe Stanka, Des Moines, 17
SOs: Bob Harrison, Wichita, 270
ERA: Dick Hall, Lincoln, 2.24

B Big State League
President: Howard Green

Standings	W	L	Pct.	GB	Attend.	Manager
Corpus Christi Clippers***(12)	93	48	.660	—	102,788	Connie Ryan
Waco Pirates (15)	74	69	.517	20	53,961	Stan Wentzel
Texas City Texans	71	67	.514	20½	35,402	Bones Sanders
Port Arthur Sea Hawks	64	74	.464	27½	71,063	Lou Fitzgerald/Earl Perry/ Jack Bumgarner
Harlingen Capitols	65	79	.451	29½	55,418	Ford Garrison
Austin Pioneers	58	85	.406	36	50,536	George Hausmann
Tyler Tigers@	36	37	.493	NA	26,443	Jodie Phipps
Galveston White Caps#	28	30	.483	NA	19,600	Jodie Beeler

#Galveston disbanded June 12.
@Tyler disbanded July 1.

Playoffs: Corpus Christi 4 games, Port Arthur 1; Waco 4 games, Texas City 3.
Finals: Corpus Christi 4 games, Waco 0.

All-Star Team: 1B-Keith Little, Corpus Christi; **2B**-Ed Charles, Corpus Christi; **3B**-Jack Bloomfield, Harlingen; **SS**-Jack Wilkinson, Corpus Christi; **OF**-Lynn Vandehey, Texas City; Junior Griffith, Texas City; Dean Stafford, Corpus Christi; **C**-John Faucett, Texas City; Kenneth Jones, Austin; **P**-Alvin Jackson, Waco; Elmer Toth, Texas City.

BA: Lynn Vandehey, Texas City, .377
Runs: Ed Charles, Corpus Christi, 135
Hits: Lynn Vandehey, Texas City, 195
RBIs: Dean Stafford, Corpus Christi, 159

HRs: Keith Little, Corpus Christi, 47
Wins: Rene Vega, Corpus Christi, 28
SOs: Donald Rowe, Waco, 226
ERA: Rene Vega, Corpus Christi, 2.69

B Carolina League
President: Glenn E. "Ted" Mann

Standings	W	L	Pct.	GB	Attend.	Manager
High Point-Thomasville Hi-Toms (11)	80	58	.580	—	67,003	James Brown
Danville Leafs (13)	73	64	.533	6½	78,341	Andy Gilbert
Fayetteville Highlanders (1)	70	67	.511	9½	52,236	Aaron Robinson/Jack McKeon/ Jack Sanford
Durham Bulls (5)	69	69	.500	11	40,965	Frank Skaff
Reidsville Phillies (14)	68	70	.493	12	38,181	Charlie Gassaway
Greensboro Patriots (2)	66	72	.478	14	58,282	Elmer Yoter
Winston-Salem Twins (7)	65	73	.471	15	45,944	Ken Silvestri/Aaron Robinson
Burlington-Graham Pirates (15)	60	78	.435	20	33,605	Larry Dorton

Playoffs: Danville 4 games, Fayetteville 1; High Point-Thomasville 4 games, Durham 3.
Finals: Danville 4 games, High Point-Thomasville 2.

All-Star Team: 1B-Hal Holland, Danville; **2B**-Bob Beier, Danville; **2B**-Bill Ford, Hi-Toms; **3B**-Arthur "Bucky" Jacobs, Fayetteville; **SS**-Mel Collins, Danville; **OF**-Dan Morejon, Hi-Toms; Al Viotta, Fayetteville; Dick McCarthy, Greensboro; **C**-Charlie Lau, Durham; Larry Dorton, Burlington-Graham; **Util IF**-Fred Harrington, Hi-Toms; **Util OF**-Joe Cristello, Fayetteville; **P**-Woody Rich, Hi-Toms; Jack Taylor, Hi-Toms; John Fitzgerald, Danville; Malcolm Simmons, Durham; **MVP**-Dan Morejon, Hi-Toms; **Manager**-James Brown, Hi-Toms.

BA: Dan Morejon, Hi-Toms, .324
Runs: Peppy LaMonica, Greensboro, 111
Hits: Dick McCarthy, Greensboro, 172
RBIs: Hal Holland, Danville, 121

HRs: Hal Holland, Danville, 31
Wins: Woody Rich, Hi-Toms, 19
SOs: John Fitzgerald, Danville, 233
ERA: Jack Taylor, Hi-Toms, 1.78

B Northwest League
President: Arthur H. Pohlman

Standings	W	L	Pct.	GB	Attend.	Manager
Eugene Emeralds**	79	45	.637	—	76,823	Cliff Dapper
Salem Senators*	75	54	.581	6½	66,441	Hugh Luby
Wenatchee Chiefs	71	54	.568	8½	79,421	Edo Vanni
Tri-City Braves	66	63	.512	15½	49,296	Don Pries
Yakima Bears	59	69	.461	22	36,314	Hub Kittle
Lewiston Broncs	47	79	.373	33	43,278	Hillis Layne
Spokane Indians	47	80	.370	33½	44,015	Eddie Lake

Playoff: Eugene 4 games, Salem 2.

All-Star Team: 1B-Carl Porter, Spokane; **2B**-Joe Jacobs, Lewiston; **3B**-Tom Agosta, Salem; **SS**-Gene Tanselli, Salem; **OF**-Duane Helbig, Tri-City; Herman Lewis, Yakima; Napoleon Gulley, Spokane; **C**-Robert Duretto, Wenatchee; **Util**-William Preston, Eugene; Melvin Krause, Salem; **P**-Gene Hayden, Wenatchee; George Storti, Eugene.

BA: Hillis Layne, Lewiston, .391
Runs: Robert Duretto, Wenatchee, 123
Hits: Napoleon Gulley, Spokane, 173
Tom Agosta, Salem, 173
RBIs: Robert Duretto, Wenatchee, 143

HRs: Robert Duretto, Wenatchee, 27
Wins: Robert Roberts, Wenatchee, 21
SOs: Gene Hayden, Wenatchee, 166
ERA: George Storti, Eugene, 2.26

B Piedmont League
President: Benjamin L. Campbell

Standings	W	L	Pct.	GB	Attend.	Manager
Newport News Dodgers (9)	77	52	.597	—	68,596	George Scherger
Lancaster Red Roses (6)	72	54	.571	3½	60,845	Henry Biasatti
York White Roses (1)	64	65	.496	13	62,581	George Staller
Portsmouth Merrimacs	64	66	.492	13½	36,702	Ken Guettler
Lynchburg Cardinals (16)	64	67	.489	14	64,741	George Kissell
Hagerstown Packets (8)	58	65	.472	16	53,025	John Welaj
Sunbury Red Legs (11)	47	80	.370	29	45,000	Virgil Stallcup/Dutch Dorman
Norfolk Tars#(7)	37	34	.521	NA	30,000	Al Evans/Alton Brown/Bill Herring

#Norfolk disbanded July 14.

Playoffs: Portsmouth 3 games, Newport News 1; Lancaster 3 games, York 1.
Finals: Lancaster 3 games, Portsmouth 2.

BA: Robert Phillips, Sunbury, .347
Runs: Crawford Davidson, Hagerstown, 103
Hits: Crawford Davidson, Hagerstown, 164
RBIs: Ken Guettler, Portsmouth, 113

HRs: Ken Guettler, Portsmouth, 41
Wins: Charles Schassler, Newport News, 19
SOs: Stan Williams, Newport News, 301
ERA: Stan Williams, Newport News, 2.42

B Three-I League
President: Hal Totten

Standings	W	L	Pct.	GB	Attend.	Manager
Keokuk Kernels (4)	92	34	.730	—	39,179	Pinky May
Waterloo White Hawks (3)	70	56	.556	22	71,864	Dutch Dorman/Willard Marshall
Peoria Chiefs (16)	63	63	.500	29	62,347	Whitey Kurowski
Burlington Bees (10)	62	64	.492	30	91,946	Harold Meek
Evansville Braves (12)	60	66	.476	32	47,414	Bob Coleman
Terre Haute Tigers (5)	56	70	.444	36	50,334	Stubby Overmire
Quincy Gems (7)	52	74	.413	40	39,081	Vern Hoscheit
Cedar Rapids Raiders (9)	49	77	.389	43	58,611	Ray Perry

Playoffs: Keokuk 3 games, Peoria 0; Burlington 3 games, Waterloo 1.
Finals: Keokuk 3 games, Burlington 1.

All-Star Team: 1B-Donald Voigt, Burlington; **2B**-Grover "Deacon" Jones, Waterloo; **3B**-Robert Sagers, Waterloo; **SS**-Tony Kubek, Quincy; **OF**-Gordy Coleman, Burlington; Bob Will, Burlington; Gene Green, Peoria; **C**-John Romano, Waterloo; Russ Nixon, Keokuk; **Util**-Enrique Izquierdo, Keokuk; **P**-Norman Rehm, Evansville; Donald Swanson, Burlington; Barry Latman, Waterloo; William Roland, Evansville; **MVP**-John Romano, Waterloo; **Manager**-Pinky May, Keokuk.

BA: Russ Nixon, Keokuk, .385
Runs: John Romano, Waterloo, 108
Hits: Tony Kubek, Quincy, 157
RBIs: John Romano, Waterloo, 124

HRs: John Romano, Waterloo, 38
Wins: Jim "Mudcat" Grant, Keokuk, 19
SOs: Bob Yanen, Keokuk, 177
ERA: Bill Dailey, Keokuk, 2.52

B Tri-State League
President: Robert E. Hipps

Standings	W	L	Pct.	GB	Attend.	Manager
Spartanburg Peaches**(4)	74	44	.627	—	35,925	Spud Chandler
Greenville Spinners*	60	55	.522	12½	50,813	Earl Wooten
Asheville Tourists (9)	53	63	.457	20	53,200	Earl Naylor
Rock Hill Chiefs (8)	45	70	.391	27½	33,847	Buster Boguskie/Frank Colasinski/Eurice "Pete" Treece

Playoff: Spartanburg 3 games, Greenville 0.

BA: Robert Jarvis, Spartanburg, .361
Runs: Paul Jones, Spartanburg, 106
Hits: Robert Jarvis, Spartanburg, 157
RBIs: William Kallas, Spartanburg, 86
Ed Serrano, Asheville, 86

HRs: Paul Jones, Spartanburg, 18
Wins: Eurice "Pete" Treece, Rock Hill, 17
SOs: Freddy Rodriguez, Greenville, 211
ERA: Freddy Rodriguez, Greenville, 2.12

B West Texas-New Mexico League
President: Hal Sayles

Standings	W	L	Pct.	GB	Attend.	Manager
Amarillo Gold Sox	80	60	.571	—	132,128	Red McQuillen/Buck Fausett/Taft Wright
Albuquerque Dukes	79	60	.568	½	78,432	Eddie Bockman
Pampa Oilers	75	64	.540	4½	65,931	Grover Seitz
Plainview Ponies	73	67	.521	7	63,269	Jackie Sullivan/Jodie Beeler
Abilene Blue Sox	69	71	.493	11	125,714	Bob Westfall/Jay Haney
Clovis Pioneers	68	72	.486	12	64,017	Frank Benites
Lubbock Hubbers	59	81	.421	21	58,555	Mike Curnan/Bob Scott
El Paso Texans	56	84	.400	24	71,771	Syd Cohen/James Mangan

Playoffs: Amarillo 4 games, Plainview 2; Pampa 4 games, Albuquerque 2.
Finals: Pampa 4 games, Amarillo 1.

All-Star Team: 1B-Robert Pascal, Abilene; **2B**-Robert Scott, Lubbock; **3B**-Eddie Bockman, Albuquerque; **SS**-Gilberto Valentin, Albuquerque; **OF**-Len Attyd, Amarillo; Don Stokes, Plainview; Taft Wright, Amarillo; **C**-Isaac Palmer, Plainview; Ernie Choukalos, Albuquerque; **P**-Kenneth Yoke, El Paso; Ted Shandor, Albuquerque.

BA: Isaac Palmer, Plainview, .406
Runs: Karl Heron, Amarillo, 141
Hits: Isaac Palmer, Plainview, 228
RBIs: Lincoln Boyd, Clovis, 157

HRs: Lincoln Boyd, Clovis, 44
Wins: Ted Shandor, Albuquerque, 23
SOs: Jack Venable, Pampa, 204
ERA: Carroll "Red" Dial, Pampa, 3.55

C Arizona-Mexico League
President: E.T. "Tim" Cusick

Standings	W	L	Pct.	GB	Attend.	Manager
Cananea Mineros	86	53	.619	—	213,074	Memo Garibay
Yuma Sun Sox	83	57	.593	3½	79,083	Whitey Wietelmann
Phoenix Stars (15)	80	59	.576	6	74,185	Jerry Gardner
Mexicali Eagles (16)	78	62	.557	8½	59,787	Art Lilly
Tucson Cowboys	66	74	.471	20½	70,973	Don Jameson
Bisbee-Douglas Copper Kings	63	77	.450	23½	45,567	Everett Robinson
Globe-Miami Miners	51	87	.370	34½	33,886	Del Ballinger/Corky Reddell/Vern Campbell
Nogales Yaquis	49	87	.360	35½	74,145	Virgilio Arteaga/Eddie Aros/Guillermo Nunez/Carlos Galina

Playoffs: None.

BA: Moises Camacho, Mexicali, .363
Runs: Ellis Burton, Phoenix, 140
Ruben Amaro, Mexicali, 140
Hits: Humberto Barbon, Nogales/Yuma, 202
RBIs: Claudio Solano, Cananea, 164

HRs: Humberto Barbon, Nogales/Yuma, 38
Wins: James Peete, Tucson, 24
Olaf Nelson, Phoenix, 24
SOs: James Peete, Tucson, 322
ERA: Fernando Ramirez, Mexicali, 2.95

C California League
President: Jerry Donovan

Standings	W	L	Pct.	GB	Attend.	Manager
Fresno Cardinals**(16)	104	43	.707	—	65,592	Roland LeBlanc
San Jose Red Sox (2)	98	48	.671	5½	59,024	Sheriff Robinson
Stockton Ports*	94	53	.639	10	80,437	Roy Partee
Modesto Reds (7)	76	71	.517	28	57,548	Jerry Crosby
Bakersfield Indians (9)	61	85	.418	42½	44,789	Doc Alexson
Salinas Packers (15)	60	86	.411	43½	41,352	Buck Elliott/Jack Paepke
Visalia Cubs	53	94	.361	51	36,212	Dee Moore
Channel Cities Oilers/Reno Silver Sox#	40	106	.274	63½	30,554	Leonard Noren

#Channel Cities moved to Reno July 1.

Playoff: Fresno 3 games, Stockton 1.

All-Star Team: 1B-Russ Rosburg, Modesto; **2B**-James Coughtry, San Jose; **3B**-Ben Valenzuela, Fresno; **SS**-Pumpsie Green, Stockton; **OF**-Donald Moitoza, Stockton; Bobby Gene Smith, Fresno; Al Gionfriddo, Visalia; **C**-Roland LeBlanc, Fresno; **Util**-Jerry Crosby, Modesto; **P**-Ted Wills, San Jose; Charlie Beamon, Stockton; Ronald May, Salinas; Glen Stabelfeld, Fresno; **Manager**-Roland LeBlanc, Fresno.

BA: Bobby Gene Smith, Fresno, .370
Runs: Ben Valenzuela, Fresno, 151
Melvin Nelson, Fresno, 151
Hits: Ben Valenzuela, Fresno, 209
RBIs: Bobby Gene Smith, Fresno, 141

HRs: Russ Rosburg, Modesto, 33
Wins: Glen Stabelfeld, Fresno, 24
SOs: Tom Hughes, Fresno, 273
ERA: Charlie Beamon, Stockton, 1.36

C Cotton States League
President: Judge Emmet Harty

Standings	W	L	Pct.	GB	Attend.	Manager
Monroe Sports***(7)	76	41	.650	—	57,704	Ed Head
El Dorado Oilers (13)	70	50	.583	7½	40,512	Francis "Salty" Parker
Pine Bluff Judges/						
Meridian Millers#(1)	59	56	.513	16	37,959	Robert Knoke/Merrill Smith
Hot Springs Bathers (6)	57	62	.479	20	25,550	Joe Lutz/Mickey O'Neil
Greenville Bucks (5)	49	69	.415	27½	30,641	Willis Hudlin/Luther Tucker/
						Banks McDowell/Dan Ryan
Vicksburg Hill Billies (10)	43	76	.361	34	35,995	Pap Williams

#Pine Bluff moved to Meridan June 16.

Playoffs: Monroe 4 games, Hot Springs 0; El Dorado 4 games, Meridian 1.
Finals: Monroe 4 games, El Dorado 3.

All-Star Team: 1B-Marshall Gilbert, Monroe; **2B**-Bob Maness, Monroe; **3B**-Jim Davenport, El Dorado; **SS**-Jose Pagan, El Dorado; **SS**-Kenneth Kortum, Hot Springs; **OF**-George Blash, Meridian; Banks McDowell, Greenville; Roy Mantle, Monroe; **C**-Wallace Widholm, Vicksburg; **P**-Edward Dick, Monroe; Richard Maibauer, El Dorado.

BA: Jim Davenport, El Dorado, .363
Runs: Bob Maness, Monroe, 109
Hits: Jim Davenport, El Dorado, 147
Bob Maness, Monroe, 147
RBIs: Marshall Gilbert, Monroe, 101

HRs: Marshall Gilbert, Monroe, 19
Wins: Richard Maibauer, El Dorado, 17
SOs: Richard Maibauer, El Dorado, 197
ERA: Edward Dick, Monroe, 1.77

C Evangeline League
President: Edmond L. Deramee

Standings	W	L	Pct.	GB	Attend.	Manager
New Iberia Pelicans*	77	62	.554	—	41,794	Red Smith
Lafayette Oilers**(10)	77	63	.550	½	57,082	Lou Klein
Alexandria Aces	74	65	.532	3	37,977	A.B. Cross
Baton Rouge Red Sticks	73	66	.525	4	56,603	Bill Dossey
Crowley Millers	65	75	.464	12½	45,130	Marvin Holleman
Lake Charles Lakers	52	87	.374	25	33,881	Joe Powers/Jackie Bales/
						Buster Boguskie/Sam Tarleton/
						Herman Brown

Playoffs: Lafayette 4 games, New Iberia 2; Alexandria 4 games, Baton Rouge 1.
Finals: Lafayette 4 games, Alexandria 2.

All-Star Team: 1B-Ben Dye, New Iberia; **2B**-Alvin Seegar, Lafayette; **3B**-Lou Klein, Lafayette; **SS**-Lawrence Koppe, Alexandria; **OF**-James Moore, Crowley; William Lynn, Alexandria; Tom Nerad, Lafayette; **C**-Richard Tindall, Lafayette; Red Smith, New Iberia; **P**-Donald Robinson, Baton Rouge; John Fuller, Alexandria; **Manager**-Lou Klein, Lafayette.

BA: James Moore, Crowley, .354
Runs: Jose Garcia, Baton Rouge, 117
Hits: William Lynn, Alexandria, 196
RBIs: Tom Nerad, Lafayette, 103
HRs: Tom Nerad, Lafayette, 26

Wins: Terrance Fox, New Iberia, 21
John Fuller, Alexandria, 21
SOs: Mario Cardenas, New Iberia, 205
ERA: Donald Robinson, Baton Rouge, 1.56

C Longhorn League
President: J.C. Cunningham

Standings	W	L	Pct.	GB	Attend.	Manager
San Angelo Colts	85	55	.607	—	62,446	Pat McLaughlin
Roswell Rockets	79	56	.585	3½	39,911	Hayden Greer
Artesia Numexers	80	57	.584	3½	28,880	Tom Jordan
Carlsbad Potashers	72	67	.518	12½	46,152	Thurman Tucker
Midland Indians	67	72	.482	17½	62,602	Billy Capps
Hobbs Sports	62	77	.446	22½	46,101	Pat Stasey
Big Spring Cosden Cops	57	83	.407	28	27,918	Robert Martin
Odessa Eagles	51	86	.372	32½	34,574	Tony York

Playoffs: San Angelo 4 games, Carlsbad 1; Roswell 4 games, Artesia 3.
Finals: San Angelo 4 games, Roswell 0.

All-Star Team: 1B-Elias Osorio, San Angelo; **2B**-Oswaldo Alvarez, Hobbs; **3B**-Carroll "Tex" Gholson, Carlsbad; **SS**-Eny Wilcox, Midland; **OF**-Jimmy Bawcom, Artesia; Duane White, Roswell; E.L. "Jeff" Adams, Roswell; **C**-Art Bowland, San Angelo; Bob Boyd, Artesia; **Util**-Tom Jordan, Artesia; **P**-Marshall Epperson, San Angelo; Harry Young, Artesia.

BA: Tom Jordan, Artesia, .407
Runs: Elias Osorio, San Angelo, 142
Hits: Tom Jordan, Artesia, 221
RBIs: Tom Jordan, Artesia, 159
HRs: Joe Bauman, Roswell, 46

2B: Tom Jordan, Artesia, 69
Wins: Evelio Hernandez, Hobbs, 23
SOs: Evelio Hernandez, Hobbs, 227
ERA: Robert Swanson, Midland, 3.04

C Northern League
President: Herman D. White

Standings	W	L	Pct.	GB	Attend.	Manager
Eau Claire Braves (12)	81	43	.653	—	65,074	Joe Just
St. Cloud Rox (13)	78	47	.624	3½	47,170	Charlie Fox
Winnipeg Goldeyes (16)	70	56	.556	12	84,668	Al Kubski
Aberdeen Pheasants (1)	70	56	.556	12	75,401	Bill Krueger
Fargo-Moorhead Twins (4)	61	64	.488	20½	56,244	Phil Seghi/Paul O'Dea
Superior Blues (3)	55	68	.447	25½	36,695	Walt Novick
Duluth Dukes (11)	45	80	.360	36½	50,503	Leon "Red" Treadway/
						James Crandall
Grand Forks Chiefs	39	85	.315	42	38,419	Johnny Hopp/Joe McDermott/
						Ray Fletcher

Playoffs: Eau Claire 2 games, Aberdeen 1; St. Cloud 2 games, Winnipeg 0.
Finals: St. Cloud 3 games, Eau Claire 1.

All-Star Team: 1B-Edward Kopacz, St. Cloud; **2B**-John Stratton, Eau Claire; **3B**-Henry Moreno, Aberdeen; **SS**-Andre Rodgers, St. Cloud; **OF**-Theodore Dargie, Fargo-Moorhead; Leon Wagner, St. Cloud; Richard Phillips, Eau Claire; **C**-Kenneth Retzer, Fargo-Moorhead; Roger Jongewaard, Eau Claire; **P**-Clifford Savage, Winnipeg; Merlin Beatty, Fargo-Moorhead.

BA: Andre Rodgers, St. Cloud, .387
Runs: Andre Rodgers, St. Cloud, 133
Hits: Andre Rodgers, St. Cloud, 175
RBIs: Leon Wagner, St. Cloud, 127

HRs: Leon Wagner, St. Cloud, 29
Wins: Frank Funk, St. Cloud, 18
SOs: Tom Richards, Superior, 208
ERA: Robert Bennett, Superior, 2.51

C Pioneer League
President: Claude Engberg

Standings	W	L	Pct.	GB	Attend.	Manager
Boise Braves (12)	77	54	.588	—	85,534	Lou Stringer
Great Falls Electrics (9)	74	58	.561	3½	78,362	Lou Rochelli
Pocatello Bannocks	72	59	.550	5	48,685	Frank Lucchesi
Magic Valley Cowboys (10)	64	67	.489	13	59,972	Edward McDade
Billings Mustangs (15)	64	68	.485	13½	82,495	Jack Paepke/Buck Elliott
Salt Lake City Bees (14)	61	70	.466	16	89,040	Don Sturgeon/Sven "Red" Jessen
Idaho Falls Russets (5)	60	72	.455	17½	31,464	Patrick Mullin
Ogden Reds (11)	54	78	.409	23½	41,737	James Crandall/
						Leon "Red" Treadway

Playoffs: Magic Valley 2 games, Boise 1; Pocatello 2 games, Great Falls 1.
Finals: Magic Valley 3 games, Pocatello 2.

All-Star Team: 1B-Daniel Lobitz, Magic Valley; **2B**-Dolson Ayers, Salt Lake City; **3B**-Don LeJohn, Great Falls; **SS**-Robert King, Boise; **OF**-Arnold Hallgren, Boise; Dick Stuart, Billings; Drew Gilbert, Ogden; **C**-Tommie Roberson, Pocatello; **P**-Bob Shaffer, Magic Valley; James Espinola, Boise.

BA: Arnold Hallgren, Boise, .348
Runs: Jess Duran, Pocatello, 126
Hits: Arnold Hallgren, Boise, 171
RBIs: Arnold Hallgren, Boise, 139

HRs: Dick Stuart, Billings, 32
Wins: Bob Shaffer, Magic Valley, 17
SOs: James Lee, Pocatello, 223
ERA: William Dunn, Billings, 2.31

C Provincial League
President: Albert Molini

Standings	W	L	Pct.	GB	Attend.	Manager
St. Jean Canadians (15)	86	44	.662	—	45,000	Steve Mizerak/Fred Luciano
Quebec Braves (12)	81	49	.623	5	101,695	Sibby Sisti
Burlington A's (6)	65	64	.504	20½	51,267	Vincent Plumbo
Trois Rivieres Phillies (14)	62	68	.477	24	47,873	Al Barillari
Sherbrooke Indians (4)	53	76	.411	32½	38,509	Edgar Hartness
Thetford Mines Mineurs (1)	42	88	.323	44	35,556	Barney Lutz

Playoffs: Burlington 4 games, St. Jean 1; Quebec 4 games, Trois Rivieres 2.
Finals: Quebec 4 games, Burlington 1.

All-Star Team: 1B-Ray Barker, Thetford Mines; **2B**-Michael Fandozzi, Quebec; **3B**-Francis Klamp, St. Jean; **SS**-Walter Hardy, St. Jean; **OF**-John Wrye, St. Jean; Frank Washington, St. Jean; Bill Robertson, Quebec; **C**-Vincent Plumbo, Burlington; Valmy Thomas, St. Jean; **P**-Jack Hale, Burlington; Ramon Salgado, St. Jean.

BA: Bill Robertson, Quebec, .342
Runs: Bill Causion, St. Jean, 105
Hits: Bill Robertson, Quebec, 173
RBIs: Bill Robertson, Quebec, 108
HRs: Bill Causion, St. Jean, 24

Wins: Jack Hale, Burlington, 17
Dean Lakatosh, St. Jean, 17
SOs: Richard Mitchener, Sherbrooke, 171
ERA: Ramon Salgado, St. Jean, 2.21

D Alabama-Florida League
President: Sam C. Smith

Standings	W	L	Pct.	GB	Attend.	Manager
Panama City Fliers (5)	73	47	.608	—	36,104	Bill Adair
Ft. Walton Beach Jets (11)	70	50	.583	3	19,680	John Streza/C.C. Hodge
Dothan Cardinals (16)	65	54	.546	7½	34,056	Chase Riddle
Crestview Braves	54	66	.450	19	15,362	Nesbit Wilson
Graceville Oilers	50	69	.420	22½	27,876	Marcus Davis
Donalsonville Indians	47	73	.392	26	24,196	Charles Grant

Playoffs: Panama City 4 games, Dothan 2; Crestview 4 games, Ft. Walton Beach 1.
Finals: Panama City 3 games, Crestview 1.

All-Star Team: 1B-John Streza, Ft. Walton Beach; **2B**-Charles Grant, Donalsonville; **3B**-Richard Johnson, Panama City; **SS**-Albert Morris, Dothan; **OF**-Jimmie Cantrell, Dothan; Barton Dupon, Panama City; Nesbit Wilson, Crestview; **C**-Chase Riddle, Dothan; Jack Feller, Panama City; **P**-Dizzy Dean Higgenbotham, Ft. Walton Beach; Jeff Wadkins, Crestview.

BA: Nesbit Wilson, Crestview, .403
Runs: Charles Tulner, Ft. Walton Beach, 129
Hits: Jimmie Cantrell, Dothan, 164
RBIs: Charles Tulner, Ft. Walton Beach, 114
HRs: Charles Grant, Donalsonville, 37

Wins: Jeff Wadkins, Crestview, 20
SOs: Dizzy Dean Higgenbotham, Ft. Walton Beach, 240
ERA: Renaldo Alonzo, Ft. Walton Beach, 2.96

D Appalachian League
President: Chauncey De Vault

Standings	W	L	Pct.	GB	Attend.	Manager
Salem Rebels	84	38	.689	—	31,213	Jack Crosswhite
Johnson City Cardinals (16)	74	51	.592	11½	29,919	Virgil Wallace
Bristol Twins (7).................	63	61	.508	22	32,587	David Madison
Kingsport Cherokees	64	62	.508	22	20,328	Leo "Muscle" Shoals
Wytheville Statesmen.........	58	68	.460	28	22,505	Bull Hamons/Frank Tepedino
Bluefield Blue-Grays (2)	55	67	.451	29	29,914	Len Okrie
Pulaski Phillies (14)...........	53	72	.424	32½	18,386	Eddie Murphy
Welch Miners/Marion A's#(6)	45	77	.369	39	24,104	Herb Mancini

#Welch moved to Marion July 14.

Playoffs: Salem 2 games, Kingsport 0; Johnson City 2 games, Bristol 1.
Finals: Salem and Johnson City were declared co-champions when bad weather forced cancellation of the final series.

All-Star Team: 1B-Arthur Oody, Welch/Marion; **2B**-Chester Boak, Salem; **3B**-Stanley Anderson, Wytheville; **SS**-Ronald Percise, Pulaski; **OF**-Lu Clinton, Bluefield; Allen Barbee, Salem; Chuck Weatherspoon, Salem; Ronald Glasgow, Welch/Marion; **C**-Joe Theis, Bluefield; **P**-Ben Swaringen, Salem; Rudy Tanner, Bluefield.

BA: Grady Chavis, Johnson City, .377
Runs: Charles Sedor, Salem, 116
Chester Boak, Salem, 116
Hits: Chester Boak, Salem, 163
RBIs: Leo "Muscle" Shoals, Kingsport, 134

HRs: Leo "Muscle" Shoals, Kingsport, 33
Michael Coppola, Wytheville, 33
Wins: Paul Johnston, Salem, 20
SOs: Howie Nunn, Johnson City, 249
ERA: Bill Wing, Bluefield/Salem, 2.79

D Florida State League
President: John Krider

Standings	W	L	Pct.	GB	Attend.	Manager
Orlando C.B.s***(8)..........	92	48	.657	—	46,370	Tom O'Brien
Daytona Beach Islanders	77	63	.550	15	45,959	John Vander Meer
Cocoa Indians	75	64	.540	16½	34,808	Gaspar Del Monte/Doug Williams
Gainesville G-Men..............	72	68	.514	20	46,761	Ralph Dulaney
West Palm Beach Indians (12)	71	68	.511	20½	35,583	Bill Steinecke
Sanford Cardinals (16)........	61	79	.436	31	35,301	Dan Keith/Mario Mauriello
Lakeland Pilots	57	81	.413	34	28,130	Jim Turner
St. Petersburg Saints..........	51	85	.375	39	45,964	Art Rebel/Clarence "Hooks" Iott/Gaspar Del Monte

Playoffs: None.

All-Star Team: 1B-Dan Keith, Sanford/Daytona Beach; **2B**-Edward Houseknecht, Orlando; **3B**-Bill Wyatt, Gainesville; **SS**-Dave Drapp, Orlando; **OF**-Thurman Terrell, Sanford; Inocencio Rodriguez, Cocoa; Charlie "Dike" Wilson, Orlando; **C**-Doug Williams, Cocoa; John Cuesta, St. Petersburg; **P**-John Valmas, Orlando; John Herlihy, Cocoa; Rolando Ortega, Gainesville.

BA: Dan Keith, Sanford/Daytona Beach, .400
Runs: Dave Drapp, Orlando, 132
Hits: Dan Keith, Sanford/Daytona Beach, 199
RBIs: Dan Keith, Sanford/Daytona Beach, 122
HRs: Inocencio Rodriguez, Cocoa, 20

Wins: Rolando Ortega, Gainesville, 25
John Valmas, Orlando, 25
SOs: John Ivory Smith, Daytona Beach, 320
ERA: William Boyette, West Palm Beach, 1.91

D Georgia State League
President: W.H. Lovett

Standings	W	L	Pct.	GB	Attend.	Manager
Douglas Trojans (11)..........	62	46	.574	—	32,925	Bob Wellman
Sandersville Giants (13)	56	51	.523	5½	31,005	Pete Pavlick
Hazlehurst-Baxley Cardinals (16)............	57	53	.518	6	10,397	Sam Goodsoozian
Vidalia Indians (4).............	56	54	.509	7	24,251	Ed Levy
Dublin Irish (15)	49	61	.445	14	16,997	George Kinnamon
Statesboro Pilots#..............	25	40	.385	NA	8,750	James Sosebee/Gerald Peters

#Statesboro withdrew July 1.

Playoffs: Douglas 3 games, Vidalia 1; Sandersville 3 games, Hazlehurst-Baxley 1.
Finals: Douglas 3 games, Sandersville 3, rain forced postponement of the series. The teams were declared co-champions.

BA: Jack Elias, Sandersville, .332
Runs: Felix Torres, Douglas, 101
Hits: Bob Wilson, Vidalia, 132
RBIs: Willie McCovey, Sandersville, 113
HRs: Bob Wellman, Douglas, 21
Wins: Leo Quatro, Sandersville, 15
SOs: Victor Davis, Sandersville, 189
ERA: Richard Welage, Douglas, 2.36

D Georgia-Florida League
President: W.T. Anderson

Standings	W	L	Pct.	GB	Attend.	Manager
Brunswick Pirates (15)	87	52	.626	—	41,743	Frank Oceak
Albany Cardinals (16)	85	55	.607	2½	50,115	J.C. Dunn
Waycross Bears	72	65	.526	14	46,266	James Deery/Walter Widmayer
Valdosta Tigers (5).............	68	70	.493	18½	51,543	Stan Wasiak
Thomasville Dodgers (9)......	66	72	.478	20½	30,274	Pete Reiser
Cordele Orioles (1)	63	74	.460	23	31,221	Lloyd Brown/Max Carey
Tifton Blue Sox	59	80	.424	28	38,363	Paul Eames
Moultrie Redlegs (11).........	53	85	.384	33½	30,451	Ken Polivka

Playoffs: Brunswick 3 games, Valdosta 2; Waycross 3 games, Albany 0.
Finals: Brunswick 1 game, Waycross 1, bad weather terminated the series.

All-Star Team: 1B-Earl Fackler, Brunswick; **2B**-Galen Williams, Albany; **3B**-William Robertson, Brunswick; **SS**-Marv Breeding, Cordele; **OF**-Warren Wilson, Brunswick; Wayne Davis, Albany; Phillip Condu, Moultrie; Dick Lubinski, Cordele; **C**-Joseph Canuso, Brunswick; William Thompson, Albany; **Util IF**-Paul DeMont, Cordele; **P**-William Lackey, Albany; Jim Duffalo, Brunswick; David Scranton, Waycross; Robert Sedlak, Thomasville; **Manager**-Frank Oceak, Brunswick.

BA: Warren Wilson, Brunswick, .349
Runs: Warren Wilson, Brunswick, 125
Hits: Warren Wilson, Brunswick, 175
RBIs: J.C. Dunn, Albany, 125
HRs: Wayne Davis, Albany, 20
Dick Lubinski, Cordele, 20
Wins: William Lackey, Albany, 22
SOs: William Lackey, Albany, 222
ERA: Robert Sedlak, Thomasville, 1.53

D Kitty League
President: Shelby Peace

Standings	W	L	Pct.	GB	Attend.	Manager
Paducah Chiefs (16)...........	64	39	.621	—	35,850	Homer Ray Wilson
Mayfield Clothiers (13)	65	43	.602	1½	24,500	David Garcia
Owensboro Oilers (7)	53	56	.486	14	26,412	Walter Lance/Ken Silvestri
Union City Dodgers (9)........	50	57	.467	16	17,040	Joe Hauser
Fulton Lookouts (8)...........	43	66	.394	24	11,035	Ned Waldrop/Sam Lamatina/Mel Simons/Robert Harmon
Madisonville Miners#(3)....	23	37	.383	NA	5,350	William Close

#Madisonville disbanded July 7.

Playoffs: Paducah was declared champion by default when other clubs refused to take part in playoffs.

All-Star Team: 1B-Edward Russell, Mayfield; **2B**-Charles Burris, Fulton; **3B**-Fred Studstill, Mayfield; **SS**-Ed Herstek, Mayfield; **OF**-Eugene Conquy, Union City; Robert Thomas, Fulton; Joseph Cintron, Owensboro; Benjamin Bland, Union City; **C**-Leland Browning, Fulton; Paul Stammen, Union City; **Util**-Russell Serzen, Owensboro; **P**-Vernon White, Mayfield; Joe Shipley, Mayfield; William Liberto, Union City; David Palmer, Owensboro; **Manager**-David Garcia, Mayfield.

BA: Ed Herstek, Mayfield, .359
Runs: Fred Studstill, Mayfield, 111
Hits: Fred Studstill, Mayfield, 150
RBIs: Edward Russell, Mayfield, 114
HRs: Paul Bentley, Mayfield, 24
Wins: Thomas Baker, Paducah, 16
SOs: Joe Shipley, Mayfield, 174
ERA: Darold Satchell, Paducah, 2.85

D Mississippi-Ohio Valley League
President: C.C. "Dutch" Hoffman

Standings	W	L	Pct.	GB	Attend.	Manager
Dubuque Packers (3)	74	52	.587	—	94,925	Ira Hutchinson
Mattoon Phillies (14).........	68	57	.544	5½	51,277	Burl Storie
Clinton Pirates (15)...........	68	57	.544	5½	57,683	Robert Clark
Kokomo Giants..................	64	62	.508	10	45,289	Walt Dixon/Jack Milaskey
Lafayette Chiefs (4)............	63	63	.500	11	61,287	Mark Wylie
Decatur Commodores (16) .	62	64	.492	12	54,260	Al Unser
Paris Lakers (10)................	62	64	.492	12	30,245	Richard Rigazio
Hannibal Citizens	42	84	.333	32	40,977	James Granneman/Allan Shinn

Playoffs: Dubuque 2 games, Clinton 0; Mattoon 2 games, Kokomo 0.
Finals: Dubuque 3 games, Mattoon 0.

All-Star Team: 1B-Richard Patton, Dubuque; **2B**-Billy Wilgus, Clinton; **3B**-Orlando Cepeda, Kokomo; **SS**-Lawrence Cutler, Dubuque; **OF**-Jimmy Lynn, Dubuque; Edward Jones, Decatur; Thomas Paddock, Paris; **C**-Jimmie Coker, Mattoon; Larry Smith, Decatur; **P**-Fritz Ackley, Dubuque; John Dewald, Mattoon; Ronald Hagler, Hannibal; Richard Ghelfi, Decatur; **Util**-Daniel Brown, Paris.

BA: Orlando Cepeda, Kokomo, .393
Runs: Jimmy Lynn, Dubuque, 121
Hits: Jimmy Lynn, Dubuque, 180
RBIs: Jimmy Lynn, Dubuque, 121
HRs: Walt Dixon, Kokomo, 24
Wins: Allen Evans, Kokomo, 21
SOs: Benjamin Rich, Clinton, 199
ERA: Dave Wegerek, Lafayette, 2.59

D PONY League
President: Vincent M. McNamara

Standings	W	L	Pct.	GB	Attend.	Manager
Hamilton Cardinals (16)......	82	43	.656	—	53,989	Eddie Lyons
Bradford Phillies (14).........	74	51	.592	8	35,979	Lew Krausse/Pat Colgan
Corning Red Sox (2)...........	69	57	.548	13½	42,919	Glenn Wright
Wellsville Braves (12).........	68	58	.540	14½	45,799	Alex Monchak
Erie Senators (8)...............	66	60	.524	16½	53,151	Ted Sepkowski
Hornell Dodgers (9)............	50	76	.397	32½	27,314	Boyd Bartley
Jamestown Falcons (5)	48	78	.381	34½	32,700	Tony Lupien
Olean Oilers......................	46	80	.365	36½	47,189	Paul Owens

Playoffs: Hamilton 2 games, Wellsville 1; Corning 2 games, Bradford 1.
Finals: Hamilton 3 games, Corning 0.

All-Star Team: 1B-Paul Owens, Olean; **2B**-Eddie Lyons, Hamilton; **3B**-Arthur Burnett, Hamilton; **SS**-Don Carter, Wellsville; **OF**-Don Landrum, Bradford; Tom Keane, Bradford; Dale Bennetch, Bradford; **C**-Bob Walsh, Corning; William Brown, Hamilton; **P**-Gary Geiger, Hamilton; Don Nottebart, Wellsville.

1955

BA: Fran Boniar, Hornell, .435
Runs: Tom Keane, Bradford, 115
Hits: John Schaive, Erie, 178
RBIs: Eddie Lyons, Hamilton, 115
HRs: Dale Bennetch, Bradford, 19

Wins: Gary Geiger, Hamilton, 20
    Henry Bolinda, Bradford, 20
SOs: Gary Geiger, Hamilton, 177
ERA: Garland Shifflett, Erie, 1.95

BA: Harold Gordon, Seminole, .345
Runs: William Caye, Muskogee, 117
Hits: Walter Massefski, Paris, 178
RBIs: Walter Massefski, Paris, 107

HRs: James Brown, Ardmore, 21
Wins: Bobby Dudley, Lawton, 23
SOs: Dale Hendrickson, Lawton, 256
ERA: Dale Hendrickson, Lawton, 1.26

D Sooner State League
President: Ucal Clanton

Standings	W	L	Pct.	GB	Attend.	Manager
Lawton Braves (12)	95	44	.683	—	45,554	Travis Jackson
Shawnee Hawks (9)	77	61	.558	17½	37,817	Jack Banta
Muskogee Giants (13)	74	66	.529	21½	47,485	Richard Klaus
Paris Orioles (1)	68	69	.496	26	44,805	Jimmy Adair
Ardmore Cardinals (16)	65	75	.464	30½	33,731	Frank Mancuso
McAlester Rockets (7)	65	75	.464	30½	47,295	Marvin Crater
Gainesville Owls/						
Ponca City Cubs#(10)	56	83	.403	39	29,169	Edwin Carnett
Seminole Oilers (6)	56	83	.403	39	26,775	Charles Hopkins/Al Evans

#Gainesville moved to Ponca City May 19.

Playoffs: Lawton 3 games, Paris 1; Muskogee 3 games, Shawnee 2.
Finals: Lawton 4 games, Muskogee 2.

1955 Interleague Post Season Play

World Series
Brooklyn (National) 4 games, New York (American) 3

Junior World Series
Minneapolis (American Association) 4 games, Rochester (International) 3
Total Attendance: 52,926

Dixie Series
Mobile (Southern Association) 4 games, Shreveport (Texas) 0
Total Attendance: 22,726

Little Dixie Series
Corpus Christi (Big State) 4 games, Pampa (West Texas-New Mexico) 0
Total Attendance: 7,128

1955 Major League Farm Systems

American League

1. Baltimore (9): San Antonio, Wichita, Fayetteville, York, Pine Bluff/Meridian, Aberdeen, Thetford Mines, Cordele, Paris.
2. Boston (6): Louisville, Montgomery, Greensboro, San Jose, Bluefield, Corning.
3. Chicago (6): Memphis, Colorado Springs, Waterloo, Superior, Madisonville, Dubuque.
4. Cleveland (9): Indianapolis, Tulsa, Reading, Keokuk, Spartanburg, Fargo-Moorhead, Sherbrooke, Vidalia, Lafayette (IN).
5. Detroit (10): Buffalo, Little Rock, Augusta, Durham, Terre Haute, Greenville (MS), Idaho Falls, Panama City, Valdosta, Jamestown.
6. Kansas City (7): Columbus (OH), Savannah, Lancaster, Hot Springs, Burlington (VT), Welch/Marion, Seminole.
7. New York (11): Denver, Birmingham, Binghamton, Winston-Salem, Norfolk, Quincy, Modesto, Monroe, Bristol, Owensboro, McAlester.
8. Washington (7): Chattanooga, Charlotte, Hagerstown, Rock Hill, Orlando, Fulton, Erie.

National League

9. Brooklyn (15): St. Paul, Montreal, Mobile, Ft. Worth, Elmira, Pueblo, Newport News, Cedar Rapids, Asheville, Bakersfield, Great Falls, Thomasville, Union City, Hornell, Shawnee.
10. Chicago (9): Los Angeles, Macon, Des Moines, Burlington (IA), Vicksburg, Lafayette (LA), Magic Valley, Paris, Gainesville/Ponca City.
11. Cincinnati (10): Havana, Nashville, Columbia, High Point-Thomasville, Sunbury, Duluth, Ogden, Ft. Walton Beach, Douglas, Moultrie.
12. Milwaukee (12): Toledo, Atlanta, Beaumont, Jacksonville, Corpus Christi, Evansville, Eau Claire, Boise, Quebec, West Palm Beach, Wellsville, Lawton.
13. New York (10): Minneapolis, Dallas, Wilkes-Barre/Johnstown, Sioux City, Danville, El Dorado, St. Cloud, Sandersville, Mayfield, Muskogee.
14. Philadelphia (8): Syracuse, Schenectady, Reidsville, Salt Lake City, Trois Rivieres, Pulaski, Mattoon, Bradford.
15. Pittsburgh (13): Hollywood, New Orleans, Williamsport, Lincoln, Waco, Burlington-Graham, Phoenix, Salinas, Billings, St. Jean, Dublin, Brunswick, Clinton.
16. St. Louis (19): Omaha, Rochester, Houston, Allentown, Columbus (GA), Lynchburg, Peoria, Mexicali, Fresno, Winnipeg, Dothan, Johnson City, Sanford, Hazlehurst-Baxley, Albany (GA), Paducah, Decatur, Hamilton, Ardmore.

1955 No-Hitters

Date	Pitcher	Team	League	Opponent	Score
4-21	Robert Spier	Thomasville	Georgia-Florida	Waycross	6-0
4-28	Bill Dietrich	Monroe	Cotton States	Greenville	5-2
4-29	Duke Markell	Rochester	International	Columbus	9-0
4-30	Pete Spasoff	Macon	South Atlantic	Savannah	4-0
5-10	Alex Perinis	Brunswick	Georgia-Florida	Cordele	1-0
5-11	Melvin Held	San Antonio	Texas	Ft. Worth	0-0 (5)
5-12	Sam Jones	Chicago	National	Pittsburgh	4-0
5-15	John Schieffer	Albany	Georgia-Florida	Moultrie	6-0 (5)
5-17	Bill McNeil	Panama City	Alabama-Florida	Graceville	9-0
5-23	John Husich	Moultrie	Georgia-Florida	Tifton	9-1
5-25	Ramon Salgado	St. Jean	Provincial	Burlington	4-0 (7)
5-27	Charles Kolakowski	Spartanburg	Tri-State	Asheville	5-4
5-29	John Zarcone	St. Cloud	Northern	Aberdeen	13-0
6-9	Gary Geiger	Hamilton	PONY	Erie	5-0
6-15	Frank Childers	Channel Cities	California	Visalia	2-1 (7)
6-15	Frank Barnes	Oklahoma City	Texas	Shreveport	1-0
6-16	Freddy Rodriguez	Greenville	Tri-State	Rock Hill	5-0
6-17	Jack Kralick	Madisonville	Kitty	Union City	1-0 (7)
6-19	Hugh Sooter	Houston	Texas	Oklahoma City	1-0 (7)
7-7	Jeff Wadkins	Crestview	Alabama-Florida	Dothan	2-0
7-11	Bill Drummond/Bob Shipman/				
	Bob Wiltse	All-Stars	Cotton States	El Dorado	2-0
7-21	George Piktuzis	Los Angeles	Pacific Coast	San Francisco	2-1
7-24	Elmer Singleton	Seattle	Pacific Coast	San Diego	2-0 (7)
7-24	Robert Roberts	Wenatchee	Northwest	Eugene	1-0 (7)
7-26	Bobby Millard	Ponca City	Sooner State	McAlester	6-0 (7)
7-26	Odell Martin	Sunbury	Piedmont	Hagerstown	11-1
7-26	Chris Van Cuyk	Oakland	Pacific Coast	Los Angeles	2-0 (7)
7-27	Frank Funk	St. Cloud	Northern	Superior	1-0 (P, 7)
7-28	Hugh Coy/				
	Clyde Thompson	Dothan	Alabama-Florida	Crestview	4-5 (10)
7-28	Rudy Tanner	Bluefield	Appalachian	Bristol	8-0
7-29	Charles Kolakowski	Spartanburg	Tri-State	Asheville	5-1
8-1	James Bronstad	Monroe	Cotton States	Meridian	5-1
8-1	Robert Theiss	Quebec	Provincial	Trois Rivieres	4-0 (7)
8-6	Leo Quatro	Sandersville	Georgia State	Hazlehurst-Baxley	1-0
8-8	Marcus Davis	Graceville	Alabama-Florida	Dothan	4-0 (7)
8-9	Richard Lessman	Hannibal	Miss.-Ohio Valley	Lafayette	1-0 (7)
8-9	Bob Miller	Augusta	South Atlantic	Jacksonville	1-0 (7)
8-13	Jaime Ochoa	MC Tigres	Mexican	Veracruz	15-0 (7)
8-14	Bartolo DiMaggio	Oklahoma City	Texas	San Antonio	1-0 (8)
8-14	Dick Hoover	Columbus	International	Richmond	10-0 (7)
8-17	Troy Herriage	Montgomery	South Atlantic	Charlotte	4-0 (7)
8-17	Marvin Williams	Schenectady	Eastern	Elmira	2-0
8-17	Cedric Wolfman	Muskogee	Sooner State	Ponca City	9-2
8-17	Juan Izaguirre	Crowley	Evangeline	New Iberia	1-0 (7)
8-18	Ken Lehman	Montreal	International	Columbus	3-0 (P, 7)
8-19	John Rieder	Magic Valley	Pioneer	Idaho Falls	6-0
8-21	Jim Davis	Burlington	Provincial	Trois Rivieres	4-0 (7)
8-31	Don Ferrarese	San Antonio	Texas	Beaumont	3-1 (7)
9-1	Jim Hemric	Johnson City	Appalachian	Bristol	2-0 (PO)
9-1	Miguel Sotelo	Cananea	Arizona-Mexico	Phoenix	6-0
9-12	Billy Muffett	Shreveport	Texas	San Antonio	10-0 (PO)
9-14	Bob Harrison	Wichita	Western	Des Moines	2-0 (PO)

Number in parentheses indicates innings if other than nine; "P" indicates perfect game; "PO" indicates playoff game.

THIS DATE IN MINOR LEAGUE HISTORY

January 7, 1955, Columbus, Ohio remained in Organized Ball when a civic group purchased the International League's Ottawa franchise from the Athletics and then bought Redbird Stadium from the Cardinals.

January 21, 1955, The Mexican League was admitted to the National Association as a Class AA circuit.

January 29, 1955, Neal Cobb, 28-year-old outfielder-first baseman for Crestview, Alabama-Florida League, won the 1954 batting championship of the minor leagues with a .432 mark, the National Association announced in Columbus, Ohio. Cobb, who batted lefthanded and threw right, played in 115 games, had 124 RBIs, scored 108 runs and had 188 hits in 435 trips to the plate. Cobb, married with one child, was the police chief of Crestview, Florida, during the winter.

April 23, 1955, Dust storms caused the postponement of three games in the Longhorn League, at Hobbs, Midland and Big Spring. Also postponed were Sooner State League games in Muskogee and Seminole.

April 26, 1955, Lake Charles, Evangeline League, won its first game of the season after having lost 14 straight, defeating Baton Rouge 14-1.

May 1, 1955, After sending up a succession of eight "pinch-hitters" for one batter, manager Bobby Bragan of Hollywood drew the criticism of fans and scribes for "bush tactics" in the twinbill opener against Los Angeles. Bragan later was fined $50 by the Pacific Coast League president.

May 4, 1955, Steve Bilko, former Cardinal and Cub first baseman with Los Angeles, Pacific Coast League, hit a 552-foot home run at Oakland. Outfielder Roy Carlyle had hit a 618-foot blast in 1929 in the same park.

May 12, 1955, Thirteen fans were in Southside Park at the completion of a three-hour, 53-minute game in which Winston-Salem, Carolina League, walloped Burlington-Graham 29-4. The Twins pounded out 26 hits and scored 13 runs in the fourth frame of a contest played during threatening weather. A crowd of 311 was in the stands at the start of the game.

May 13, 1955, Righthander John Ivory Smith of Daytona Beach, Florida State League, came within one of the league's strikeout record when he fanned 19 while hurling a one-hitter to defeat Lakeland 10-1.

May 24, 1955, A concrete wall at Jennings Stadium, home of the Augusta club in the South Atlantic League, collapsed during a windstorm, killing two boys and a man outside the park. The accident occurred during the fifth inning of a game with Montgomery.

May 25, 1955, Ron Necciai, who once amazed the baseball world by striking out 27 batters in a nine-inning game, announced his retirement. Necciai, who was on the staff of Waco, Big State League, a Pittsburgh farm team, said he was quitting because of the reoccurrence of an arm injury. Out of the game last year, he started this season with Hollywood, Pacific Coast League. He won one game for Waco before he hung up his glove.

May 31, 1955, Stan Williams, 18-year-old Newport News righthander, equalled a Piedmont League record set by Johnny Vander Meer in 1937 when he struck out 20 batters in a 5-2 victory over Lynchburg. He allowed only one hit, a two-run homer by the Lynchburg pitcher.

June 6, 1955, Michael Joseph "Mike" Kelley, former owner of the Minneapolis Millers and one of the founders of the American Association in 1902, died in Minneapolis at age 79. Kelley was active in Organized Ball as a player, manager and club owner for 52 years.

June 12, 1955, Larry Segovia's display of temper almost washed out a West Texas-New Mexico League game at Albuquerque. When the Dukes' outfielder was called out on strikes against Amarillo, he kicked a water fountain near his club's bench. The boot was solid enough to break the pipe at the base of the fountain. A 60-foot geyser of water shot into the air, soaking the first row customers and scattering Albuquerque players. It took three minutes for the groundskeepers to shut off the water, a valuable commodity in that area.

June 25, 1955, Two rookie pitchers for Syracuse, International League, Dick Farrell and Seth Morehead, were charged with third degree assault on Normile Hannon, sportswriter for the Syracuse Post-Standard, in a downtown grill. Hannon suffered a broken nose and lacerations during the altercation. The two hurlers were regarded as promising prospects in the Philadelphia Phillies organization.

June 28, 1955, Charles "Spider" Baum, former president of the San Diego club and one of the all-time pitching greats in the Pacific Coast League, died in Renton, Washington at age 73. Baum, a righthander, won 262 games in the PCL, a record that stood for a number of years until it was topped by Frank Shellenback, whose mark of 295 was still on the books. Once known as "the Matty of the Minors," Baum's favorite pitch was a spitball.

July 1, 1955, The Mexico City Tigres, Mexican League, blanked the Mexico City Diablos Rojos for their 14th consecutive victory. The contest attracted 20,000 to Social Security Stadium.

July 1, 1955, Outfielder Omer Tolson of Norfolk, Piedmont League, was suspended for the balance of the season on charges of striking an umpire. Tolson, who won the Tri-State League batting championship with a .347 average while with Rock Hill last season, was charged with striking umpire Earl Mohr in the mouth during a game at York on June 26, following a dispute over a called strike.

July 4, 1955, Righthander Jim "Mudcat" Grant of Keokuk, Three-I League, not only hurled a three-hitter in a 12-2 victory over Cedar Rapids, but blasted three homers and drove in seven runs. The four-baggers came in consecutive innings, the sixth, seventh and eighth.

July 7, 1955, Earl Averill, 24-year-old Nashville catcher and son of Howard Earl Averill, the former Cleveland outfielder, hit three consecutive home runs and two doubles to set a new Southern Association mark for total bases with 16. The old record of 15 was set by Jim Poole of Nashville on June 14, 1930.

July 17, 1955, Seattle, Pacific Coast League, put an end to the 19-game winning streak of Charlie Beamon, rookie pitcher recently called up from Stockton, California League, by beating the 20-year-old righthander 4-2 in his second start with Oakland. The youngster had won 16 straight for Stockton this year plus his last two decisions with Wenatchee, Western International League, last year.

July 19, 1955, Before a record all-star crowd of 19,830, Chattanooga slugger Jim Lemon pounded four homers, accounting for seven runs as the Southern Association All-Stars defeated the league-leading Birmingham Barons 10-5. The game was played in Birmingham.

August 3, 1955, John Romano, who had hit one home run a night for nine consecutive nights, was stopped on the streak by Peoria, failing to rap one over the wall in Waterloo's 18-2 victory in the Three-I League. Romano missed in only one game of a doubleheader during the nine-game stretch, but still had a string of seven games in which he hit at least one homer.

August 4, 1955, For the second time this season, three runs scored on a sacrifice fly in the Appalachian League. Wytheville had the bases loaded in the sixth inning against Bristol when Joe Oxendine drove a long fly to center field. Jimmy Flanagan, racing back, made a leaping catch but crashed into a stone wall surrounding the park. He fell stunned at the base of the barrier, and before left fielder Bill McGuchin could recover the ball from Flanagan's glove, all three Wytheville runners had tagged up and scored.

August 10, 1955, Alex Cosmidis' record skein of errorless play came to an end when the Dallas, Texas League, second sacker booted an easy grounder in a game with Beaumont. Cosmidis had fielded flawlessly for 62 games and 311 chances without a miscue. Dallas' Red Murff posted his tenth shutout of the season, winning a stirring 12-inning, 1-0 pitchers' battle from the Exporters.

August 18, 1955, Woody Rich, veteran righthander with High Point-Thomasville, Carolina League, racked up his 14th consecutive triumph in a 4-3 victory over Durham.

August 20, 1955, Nashville catcher Earl Averill was named as a defendant in a $50,000 damage suit following a brawl in Chattanooga, in which Averill broke the jaw of Chattanooga's Lyle Luttrell with a right-handed haymaker. Averill was arrested on the scene, released later under $500 bond, suspended for 10 days and fined $50 by the Southern Association president. He was served with papers to appear in court on September 5.

August 26, 1955, Daytona Beach righthander John Ivory Smith whiffed 11 Lakeland batters to set a new season strikeout record in the Florida State League. Smith broke the old mark of 305, set in 1939 by Dick Hearn of St. Augustine. Smith finished the season with a total of 320 strikeouts.

December 10, 1955, Hamilton of the Class D PONY League announced that the club would be operated by two young women in 1956, Jean Marini, 21, of Hamilton, and Carroll Jean Hodge, 22, of Winston-Salem. Miss Marini, secretary of the club, took over majority stock interest the previous week from Alex Brown and John Mooradian of Hamilton. Miss Marini's uncle, Amilio Latti, was to act as president while Miss Hodge, business manager at Winston-Salem, Carolina League, last season, was to serve as General Manager.

December 20, 1955, The Syracuse franchise of the International League was sold to Sid Salomon and Elliott Stein, who moved the club to Miami, Florida.

1956

American League
President: William Harridge

Standings	W	L	Pct.	GB	Attend.	Manager
New York Yankees	97	57	.630	—	1,491,784	Casey Stengel
Cleveland Indians	88	66	.571	9	865,467	Al Lopez
Chicago White Sox	85	69	.552	12	1,000,090	Marty Marion
Boston Red Sox	84	70	.545	13	1,137,158	Pinky Higgins
Detroit Tigers	82	72	.532	15	1,051,182	Bucky Harris
Baltimore Orioles	69	85	.448	28	901,201	Paul Richards
Washington Senators	59	95	.383	38	431,647	Chuck Dressen
Kansas City Athletics	52	102	.338	45	1,015,154	Lou Boudreau

BA: Mickey Mantle, New York, .353
Runs: Mickey Mantle, New York, 132
Hits: Harvey Kuenn, Detroit, 196
RBIs: Mickey Mantle, New York, 130
HRs: Mickey Mantle, New York, 52

Wins: Frank Lary, Detroit, 21
SOs: Herb Score, Cleveland, 263
ERA: Whitey Ford, New York, 2.47
Pct: Whitey Ford, New York, .760, 19-6

National League
President: Warren C. Giles

Standings	W	L	Pct.	GB	Attend.	Manager
Brooklyn Dodgers	93	61	.604	—	1,213,562	Walter Alston
Milwaukee Braves	92	62	.597	1	2,046,331	Charlie Grimm/Fred Haney
Cincinnati Reds	91	63	.591	2	1,125,928	Birdie Tebbetts
St. Louis Cardinals	76	78	.494	17	1,029,773	Fred Hutchinson
Philadelphia Phillies	71	83	.461	22	934,798	Mayo Smith
New York Giants	67	87	.435	26	629,179	Bill Rigney
Pittsburgh Pirates	66	88	.429	27	949,878	Bobby Bragan
Chicago Cubs	60	94	.390	33	720,118	Stan Hack

BA: Hank Aaron, Milwaukee, .328
Runs: Frank Robinson, Cincinnati, 122
Hits: Hank Aaron, Milwaukee, 200
RBIs: Stan Musial, St. Louis, 109
HRs: Duke Snider, Brooklyn, 43

Wins: Don Newcombe, Brooklyn, 27
SOs: Sad Sam Jones, Chicago, 176
ERA: Lew Burdette, Milwaukee, 2.70
Pct: Don Newcombe, Brooklyn, .794, 27-7

(Open) Pacific Coast League
President: Leslie M. O'Connor

Standings	W	L	Pct.	GB	Attend.	Manager
Los Angeles Angels (10)	107	61	.637	—	271,982	Bob Scheffing
Seattle Rainiers (11)	91	77	.542	16	256,625	Luke Sewell/Bill Brenner
Portland Beavers (9)	86	82	.512	21	305,729	Tommy Holmes/Bill Sweeney
Hollywood Stars (15)	85	83	.506	22	165,517	Clay Hopper
Sacramento Solons	84	84	.500	23	157,134	Tommy Heath
San Francisco Seals (2)	77	88	.467	28½	183,241	Eddie Joost/Joe Gordon
San Diego Padres	72	96	.429	35	141,405	Bob Elliott
Vancouver Mounties (1)	67	98	.406	38½	152,893	Lefty O'Doul

Playoffs: None.

All-Star Team: 1B-Steve Bilko, Los Angeles; **2B**-Gene Mauch, Los Angeles; **3B**-George Risley, Sacramento; **SS**-Jack Littrell, Portland; **OF**-Bobby Usher, San Diego; Bob Speake, Los Angeles; Jim Bolger, Los Angeles; Luis Marquez, Portland; **C**-El Tappe, Los Angeles; Haywood Sullivan, San Francisco; **Util**-Lorenzo "Piper" Davis, Los Angeles; **P**-Darius Hillman, Los Angeles; Rene Valdes, Portland; Elmer Singleton, Seattle; **MVP**-Steve Bilko, Los Angeles.

BA: Steve Bilko, Los Angeles, .360
Runs: Steve Bilko, Los Angeles, 163
Hits: Steve Bilko, Los Angeles, 215
RBIs: Steve Bilko, Los Angeles, 164

HRs: Steve Bilko, Los Angeles, 55
Wins: Rene Valdes, Portland, 22
SOs: Dick Drott, Los Angeles, 184
ERA: Elmer Singleton, Seattle, 2.55

AAA American Association
President: Edward S. Doherty

Standings	W	L	Pct.	GB	Attend.	Manager
Indianapolis Indians (4)	92	62	.597	—	231,189	Kerby Farrell
Denver Bears (7)	87	67	.565	5	368,305	Ralph Houk
Omaha Cardinals (16)	82	71	.536	9½	212,859	Johnny Keane
Minneapolis Millers (13)	78	75	.510	13½	318,326	Eddie Stanky
St. Paul Saints (9)	75	78	.490	16½	102,004	Max Macon
Charleston Senators (5)	74	79	.484	17½	150,318	Charlie Metro/Frank Skaff
Wichita Braves (12)	65	88	.425	26½	109,207	George Selkirk
Louisville Colonels (8)	60	93	.392	31½	78,842	Red Marion/Max Carey

Playoffs: Indianapolis 4 games, Minneapolis 3; Denver 4 games, Omaha 2.
Finals: Indianapolis 4 games, Denver 0.

All-Star Team: 1B-Marv Throneberry, Denver; **2B**-Bobby Richardson, Denver; **3B**-Woody Held, Denver; **SS**-Tony Kubek, Denver; **OF**-Charlie Peete, Omaha; Willie Kirkland, Minneapolis; Bob Martyn, Denver; Danny Schell, Omaha; **C**-Darrell Johnson, Denver; John Bucha, St. Paul; Wilburn Jenkins, Minneapolis; **Util**-Harry Hanebrink,

Wichita; Bill Harrell, Indianapolis; **P**-Tom Cheney, Omaha; Jim DePalo, Denver; Jim Bunning, Charleston; Ted Abernathy, Louisville; John Jancse, St. Paul; Ralph Terry, Denver; **MVP**-Marv Throneberry, Denver; **Manager**-Kerby Farrell, Indianapolis.

BA: Charlie Peete, Omaha, .350
Runs: Marv Throneberry, Denver, 123
Hits: Bob Martyn, Denver, 183
RBIs: Marv Throneberry, Denver, 145
HRs: Marv Throneberry, Denver, 42

Wins: Curt Barclay, Minneapolis, 15
  Stan Pitula, Indianapolis, 15
SOs: Ted Abernathy, Louisville, 212
ERA: John Gray, Indianapolis, 2.72

AAA International League
President: Frank J. Shaughnessy

Standings	W	L	Pct.	GB	Attend.	Manager
Toronto Maple Leafs	86	66	.566	—	315,161	Bruno Betzel
Rochester Red Wings (16)	83	67	.553	2	179,739	Dixie Walker
Miami Marlins (14)	80	71	.530	5½	288,582	Don Osborn
Montreal Royals (9)	80	72	.526	6	191,624	Greg Mulleavy
Richmond Virginians (7)	74	79	.484	12½	214,533	Ed Lopat
Havana Sugar Kings (11)	72	82	.468	15	220,357	Reggie Otero/Napoleon Reyes
Columbus Red Birds (6)	69	84	.451	17½	163,128	Nick Cullop
Buffalo Bisons	64	87	.424	21½	186,811	Phil Cavarretta

Playoffs: Toronto 4 games, Montreal 1; Rochester 4 games, Miami 1.
Finals: Rochester 4 games, Toronto 3.

All-Star Team: 1B-Ed Bouchee, Miami; **2B**-Mike Goliat, Toronto; **3B**-Clyde Parris, Montreal; **SS**-Eddie Kasko, Rochester; **OF**-Cal Abrams, Miami; Bob Wilson, Montreal; Archie Wilson, Toronto; **C**-Carl Sawatski, Toronto; **P**-Fred Kipp, Montreal; Lynn Lovenguth, Toronto; **MVP**-Mike Goliat, Toronto; **Pitcher of the Year**-Lynn Lovenguth, Toronto; **Manager**-Don Osborn, Miami.

BA: Clyde Parris, Montreal, .320
Runs: Sam Jethroe, Toronto, 105
Hits: Len Johnston, Richmond, 182
RBIs: Luke Easter, Buffalo, 106

HRs: Luke Easter, Buffalo, 35
Wins: Lynn Lovenguth, Toronto, 24
SOs: Seth Morehead, Miami, 168
ERA: Ed Blake, Toronto, 2.61

AA Mexican League
President: Federico Miranda

Standings	W	L	Pct.	GB	Attend.	Manager
Mexico City Diablos Rojos	83	37	.692	—	178,235	Lazaro Salazar
Mexico City Tigres	73	45	.619	9	197,883	George Genovese
Yucatan Leones	55	63	.466	27	115,818	Dolf Luque
Veracruz Aguila	54	66	.450	29	209,615	Santos Amaro/Martin Dihigo
Monterrey Sultanes	51	69	.425	32	164,213	Epitacio Torres
Nuevo Laredo Tecolotes	42	78	.350	41	85,658	Antonio Castano/Leon Kellman/Ramon Bragana

Playoffs: None.

All-Star Team: 1B-Alonso Perry, MC Diablos Rojos; **2B**-Barney Serrell, Nuevo Laredo; **3B**-Leonardo Rodriguez, MC Tigres; **SS**-Hector Mayer, MC Diablos Rojos; **OF**-Fernando Pedrozo, MC Diablos Rojos; Alejandro Moreno, MC Tigres; Felipe Angel Montemayor, MC Tigres; **C**-Leon Kellman, Nuevo Laredo; Guillermo Vento, Monterrey; **P**-Rafael Rivas, MC Diablos Rojos; Francisco Ramirez, MC Diablos Rojos.

BA: Alonso Perry, MC Diablos Rojos, .392
Runs: Alonso Perry, MC Diablos Rojos, 103
Hits: Alonso Perry, MC Diablos Rojos, 177
RBIs: Alonso Perry, MC Diablos Rojos, 118
HRs: Alonso Perry, MC Diablos Rojos, 28

Wins: Francisco Ramirez, MC Diablos Rojos, 20
SOs: Francisco Ramirez, MC Diablos Rojos, 148
ERA: Francisco Ramirez, MC Diablos Rojos, 2.25

AA Southern Association
President: Charles A. Hurth

Standings	W	L	Pct.	GB	Attend.	Manager
Atlanta Crackers (12)	89	65	.578	—	265,578	Clyde King
Memphis Chicks (3)	82	72	.532	7	163,832	Jack Cassini/Don Griffin
Mobile Bears (4)	82	73	.529	7½	81,727	Jo Jo White
Birmingham Barons (7)	81	74	.523	8½	194,997	Phil Page
New Orleans Pelicans (15)	79	75	.513	10	96,753	Andy Cohen
Chattanooga Lookouts (8)	76	78	.494	13	99,091	Cal Ermer
Nashville Vols (11)	75	79	.487	14	115,049	Ernie White
Little Rock Travelers/ Montgomery Rebels#	53	101	.344	36	71,104	Steve Souchock

#Little Rock moved to Montgomery July 14.

Playoffs: Atlanta 4 games, Birmingham 0; Memphis 4 games, Mobile 3.
Finals: Atlanta 4 games, Memphis 3.

*Won first-half **Won second-half ***Won both halves
Numbers after nicknames indicate farm system.
Affiliation listed at end of each year.

All-Star Team: 1B-Clarence Riddle, Atlanta; **2B**-Milt Graff, Birmingham; **3B**-Tom Brown, Nashville; **SS**-Lyle Luttrell, Chattanooga; **OF**-Guilford Dickens, Memphis; Emil Panko, New Orleans; Johnny Powers, New Orleans; Harold Grote, Birmingham; **C**-John Blanchard, Birmingham; Bob Oldis, Chattanooga; Dick Brown, Mobile; **Util**-Larry Taylor, Nashville; **P**-John Gebhard, Birmingham; Corky Valentine, Atlanta; Al Papai, Memphis; John Wingo, Birmingham; John Brechin, Nashville.

BA: Stan Roseboro, Chattanooga, .340　　**HRs:** Johnny Powers, New Orleans, 39
Runs: Johnny Powers, New Orleans, 131　**Wins:** Al Papai, Memphis, 20
Hits: Milt Graff, Birmingham, 207　　**SOs:** Bob Kelly, Nashville, 180
RBIs: Gordy Coleman, Mobile, 118　　**ERA:** Bill Dailey, Mobile, 3.18

AA Texas League
President: Dick Butler

Standings	W	L	Pct.	GB	Attend.	Manager
Houston Buffalos (16)	96	58	.623	—	232,696	Harry Walker
Dallas Eagles (13)	94	60	.610	2	165,052	John "Red" Davis
Ft. Worth Cats (9)	84	70	.545	12	138,905	Clay Bryant
Tulsa Oilers (10)	77	77	.500	19	153,612	Al Widmar
San Antonio Missions (1)	76	78	.494	20	100,001	Joe Schultz
Austin Senators (12)	72	82	.468	24	129,722	Connie Ryan
Shreveport Sports	69	85	.448	27	88,943	Mel McGaha
Oklahoma City Indians (2)	48	106	.312	48	50,113	Rudy Laskowski/Ray Cash/ Jodie Beeler

Playoffs: Houston 4 games, Tulsa 1; Dallas 4 games, Ft. Worth 0.
Finals: Houston 4 games, Dallas 1.

All-Star Team: 1B-Prentice Browne, Houston; **2B**-Howard Phillips, Houston; **3B**-Dick Gray, Ft. Worth; **SS**-Andre Rodgers, Dallas; **OF**-Everett Joyner, Shreveport; Don Demeter, Ft. Worth; Ken Guettler, Shreveport; **C**-Robert Schmidt, Dallas; **P**-Bert Thiel, Dallas; **MVP**-Ken Guettler, Shreveport; **Pitcher of the Year**-Bert Thiel, Dallas; **Manager**-John "Red" Davis, Dallas.

BA: Albie Pearson, Oklahoma City, .371　　**RBIs:** Ken Guettler, Shreveport, 143
Runs: Ken Guettler, Shreveport, 115　　**HRs:** Ken Guettler, Shreveport, 62
　　Don Demeter, Ft. Worth, 115　　**Wins:** Bob Mabe, Houston, 21
　　Dick Gray, Ft. Worth, 115　　**SOs:** Bob Mabe, Houston, 195
Hits: Everett Joyner, Shreveport, 201　　**ERA:** Freddy Rodriguez, Dallas, 2.33

A Eastern League
President: Thomas H. Richardson

Standings	W	L	Pct.	GB	Attend.	Manager
Schenectady Blue Jays (14)	84	54	.609	—	66,458	Dick Carter
Binghamton Triplets (7)	81	58	.583	3½	77,317	Freddie Fitzsimmons
Reading Indians (16)	80	59	.576	4½	102,418	Don Heffner
Allentown Cardinals (16)	70	67	.511	13½	77,144	Roland LeBlanc
Syracuse Chiefs (5)	62	77	.446	22½	53,431	Red McQuillen/Joe Torpey/ Frank Calo
Albany Senators (2)	61	77	.442	23	62,932	Sheriff Robinson
Williamsport Grays (15)	60	78	.435	24	78,853	John Fitzpatrick
Johnstown Johnnies (13)	55	83	.399	29	57,851	Andy Gilbert/Frank Genovese

Playoffs: Schenectady 3 games, Allentown 0; Reading 3 games, Binghamton 0.
Finals: Schenectady 3 games, Reading 0.

All-Star Team: 1B-Tony Bartirome, Williamsport; **2B**-Moises Camacho, Allentown; **3B**-Dick Sanders, Binghamton; **SS**-Pumpsie Green, Albany; **OF**-Gerald Thomas, Allentown; Don Landrum, Schenectady; Marvin Melton, Johnstown; **C**-Lamar North, Binghamton; Richard Czekaj, Allentown; **P**-Richard Bunker, Schenectady; Bobby Locke, Reading.

BA: Tony Bartirome, Williamsport, .305　　**HRs:** Andy Rellick, Reading/Schenectady, 22
Runs: Dick Sanders, Binghamton, 101　　**Wins:** Bobby Locke, Reading, 18
Hits: Ramon Conde, Johnstown, 155　　**SOs:** Gary Bell, Reading, 192
　　Russ Snyder, Binghamton, 155　　**ERA:** Vic Lapiner, Reading, 1.96
RBIs: Dick Sanders, Binghamton, 95

A South Atlantic League
President: Bill Terry

Standings	W	L	Pct.	GB	Attend.	Manager
Jacksonville Braves (12)	87	53	.621	—	129,047	Ben Geraghty
Charlotte Hornets (8)	79	61	.564	8	108,255	Rollie Hemsley
Columbus Foxes (1)	79	61	.564	8	101,120	Skeeter Newsome
Augusta Tigers (5)	74	66	.529	13	65,610	Frank Skaff/Willis Hudlin/ Bill Norman
Macon Dodgers (9)	64	76	.457	23	70,305	Goldie Holt
Columbia Gems (6)	64	76	.457	23	49,604	Hank Biasatti
Savannah Redlegs (11)	60	80	.429	27	46,292	James Brown
Montgomery Rebels/ Knoxville Smokies#	53	87	.379	34	80,394	Dick Bartell/Earl Weaver

#Montgomery moved to Knoxville June 18.

Playoffs: Jacksonville 1 game, Charlotte 0; Columbus 1 game, Augusta 0.
Finals: Jacksonville 2 games, Columbus 0.

All-Star Team: 1B-Larry "Bo" Osborne, Augusta; **2B**-Marv Breeding, Columbus; **3B**-Joseph Pahr, Columbia; **3B**-Ed Barbarito, Jacksonville; **SS**-Elio Chacon, Savannah; **OF**-Fleming "Junior" Reedy, Columbia; Len Green, Columbus; Glenn Zimmerman, Charlotte; **C**-Bill Robertson, Columbia; **Util**-Rudy Tanner, Knoxville; John Glenn, Macon; **P**-Juan

Pizarro, Jacksonville; Bobby Lee Bown, Charlotte; John Tsitouris, Augusta; Roger Wright, Macon; **MVP**-Juan Pizarro, Jacksonville; **Manager**-Ben Geraghty, Jacksonville.

BA: Len Green, Columbus, .318　　**HRs:** Ed Barbarito, Jacksonville, 27
Runs: Len Green, Columbus, 92　　**Wins:** Juan Pizarro, Jacksonville, 23
Hits: Joseph Pahr, Columbia, 159　　**SOs:** Juan Pizarro, Jacksonville, 318
RBIs: Ed Barbarito, Jacksonville, 99　　**ERA:** John Tsitouris, Augusta, 1.51

A Western League
President: O'Neal M. Hobbs

Standings	W	L	Pct.	GB	Attend.	Manager
Amarillo Gold Sox**	87	52	.626	—	77,628	Charles Stevens
Lincoln Chiefs*(15)	84	54	.609	2½	92,554	Larry Shepard
Des Moines Bruins (10)	72	67	.518	15	67,973	Lou Klein
Topeka Hawks (12)	70	68	.507	16½	103,938	Buddy Bates
Pueblo Dodgers (9)	68	70	.493	18½	51,496	Ray Hathaway
Colorado Springs Sky Sox (3)	62	72	.478	20½	59,282	Jack Conway
Albuquerque Dukes (13)	59	81	.421	28½	94,176	Bob Swift
Sioux City Soos (16)	49	91	.350	38½	40,734	Harold Olt/Bob Clear

Playoff: Lincoln 4 games, Amarillo 1.

All-Star Team: 1B-Ken Landenberger, Sioux City; **2B**-Ken Toothman, Lincoln; **3B**-Don Russell, Pueblo; **SS**-Maury Wills, Pueblo; **OF**-Art Cuitti, Amarillo; Eddie Haas, Des Moines; Dick Stuart, Lincoln; **C**-Sammy Taylor, Topeka; Kenneth Worley, Pueblo; **P**-Marshall Bridges, Topeka; Reggie Lee, Albuquerque; Bennie Daniels, Lincoln; Michael Coen, Amarillo.

BA: Art Cuitti, Amarillo, .364　　**HRs:** Dick Stuart, Lincoln, 66
Runs: Art Cuitti, Amarillo, 132　　**Wins:** Marshall Bridges, Topeka, 18
Hits: Lynn Vandehey, Albuquerque, 197　**SOs:** Marshall Bridges, Topeka, 213
RBIs: Dick Stuart, Lincoln, 158　　**ERA:** John O'Donnell, Topeka, 3.32

B Big State League
President: Hal Sayles

Standings	W	L	Pct.	GB	Attend.	Manager
Corpus Christi Clippers (12)	83	57	.593	—	112,625	Sibby Sisti
Port Arthur Sea Hawks (16)	78	62	.557	5	57,117	Lloyd Gearhart/Al Barillari
Waco Pirates (15)	78	62	.557	5	39,096	Monty Basgall
Wichita Falls Spudders (9)	76	64	.543	7	60,891	Danny Ozark
Abilene Blue Sox (6)	73	67	.521	10	83,700	Al Evans
Lubbock Hubbers/ Texas City Texans @(1)	59	81	.421	24	53,900	Bill Krueger/Jay Haney
Beaumont Exporters#(16)	57	83	.407	26	35,000	Ford Garrison
Victoria Eagles	56	84	.400	27	35,639	James Basso/Lou Fitzgerald/ Hayden Greer

#Beaumont moved to Texas City July 2, then returned to Beaumont July 8.
@Lubbock moved to Texas City July 8.

Playoffs: Corpus Christi 4 games, Wichita Falls 1; Port Arthur 4 games, Waco 3.
Finals: Port Arthur 4 games, Corpus Christi 3.

All-Star Team: 1B-Danny Ozark, Wichita Falls; **2B**-Ken Hilyer, Beaumont; **3B**-Don LeJohn, Wichita Falls; **SS**-Julio Palazzini, Port Arthur; **OF**-James Kirby, Port Arthur; Joe Christian, Corpus Christi; Bill Lajoie, Texas City; **C**-Dan Gatta, Wichita Falls; Victor Comolli, Port Arthur; **P**-Ben Swaringen, Abilene; Roy "Tex" Sanner, Port Arthur; James Hardison, Waco; Herman Greene, Corpus Christi; **Player of the Year**-Joe Christian, Corpus Christi; **Manager**-Monty Basgall, Waco.

BA: James Kirby, Port Arthur, .358　　**Wins:** Leverette Spencer, Port Arthur, 21
Runs: Joe Christian, Corpus Christi, 119　　Ramon Salgado, Waco, 21
Hits: James Kirby, Port Arthur, 190　　Herman Greene, Corpus Christi, 21
RBIs: Joe Christian, Corpus Christi, 142　**SOs:** Evans Killeen, Abilene, 236
HRs: Danny Ozark, Wichita Falls, 32　　**ERA:** Leverette Spencer, Port Arthur, 2.37
　　Rudolph Mayling, Abilene, 32

B Carolina League
President: Glenn E. "Ted" Mann

Standings	W	L	Pct.	GB	Attend.	Manager
High Point-Thomasville Hi-Toms (11)	91	63	.591	—	64,625	Bert Haas
Durham Bulls (5)	84	69	.549	6½	41,934	Johnny Pesky
Danville Leafs (13)	83	69	.546	7	75,688	Francis "Salty" Parker
Fayetteville Highlanders (4)	78	71	.523	10½	49,212	Dutch Meyer
Greensboro Patriots (2)	75	79	.467	16	39,738	Eddie Popowski
Wilson Tobs (14)	72	79	.477	17½	80,409	Charlie Gassaway
Kinston Eagles (15)	66	87	.431	24½	37,834	Jack Paepke/Tex Taylor
Winston-Salem Twins (7)	59	91	.398	30	81,117	George Hausmann/Lee Peterson

Playoffs: Fayetteville 3 games, High Point-Thomasville 0; Danville 3 games, Durham 1.
Finals: Fayetteville 4 games, Danville 2.

All-Star Team: 1B-Willie McCovey, Danville; **2B**-Billy Joe Ford, Hi-Toms; **3B**-Doug Hubacek, Greensboro; **SS**-John Pfeiffer, Greensboro; **OF**-Leon Wagner, Danville; Curt Flood, Hi-Toms, Carl Long, Kinston; **C**-Jim Coker, Wilson; **Util**-Don Montgomery, Fayetteville; Curt Hardaway, Winston-Salem; **P**-Jack Taylor, Hi-Toms, Larry Dresen, Fayetteville; Orlando Pena, Hi-Toms, Pinky Wilson, Fayetteville; **MVP**-Curt Flood, Hi-Toms; **Manager**-Johnny Pesky, Durham.

BA: Curt Flood, Hi-Toms, .340
Runs: Curt Flood, Hi-Toms, 133
Hits: Curt Flood, Hi-Toms, 190
    George Contratto, Greensboro, 190
RBIs: Leon Wagner, Danville, 166

HRs: Leon Wagner, Danville, 51
Wins: Jack Taylor, Hi-Toms, 22
SOs: Earl Hunsinger, Wilson, 232
ERA: Cleo Lewright, Kinston, 2.38

B Northwest League
President: James M. Fleishman

Standings	W	L	Pct.	GB	Attend.	Manager
Yakima Bears***	86	45	.656	—	66,370	Hub Kittle
Lewiston Broncs	72	59	.550	14	53,472	Hillis Layne
Salem Senators	64	68	.485	22½	66,629	Hugh Luby
Eugene Emeralds	63	67	.485	22½	83,745	Cliff Dapper
Wenatchee Chiefs	60	72	.455	26½	59,155	Edo Vanni
Tri-City Braves	59	72	.450	27	78,761	Don Pries
Spokane Indians	56	77	.421	31	68,371	Joseph Rossi

Playoffs: None.

All-Star Team: 1B-Roy Nixon, Yakima; **2B**-Ron Jackson, Spokane; **3B**-Hillis Layne, Lewiston; **SS**-Elwayne Wilcox, Yakima; **OF**-Chuck Essegian, Salem; Lawrence Segovia, Wenatchee; Herman Lewis, Yakima; **C**-Joe Rossi, Spokane; **Util**-Daniel Holden, Tri-City; Vince Moreci, Yakima; **P**-Jerry Cade, Salem; Richard Young, Yakima; **Manager**-Hugh Luby, Salem.

BA: Chuck Essegian, Salem, .366
Runs: Vince Moreci, Yakima, 126
Hits: Herman Lewis, Yakima, 187
RBIs: Herman Lewis, Yakima, 140

HRs: Vince Moreci, Yakima, 36
Wins: Richard Young, Yakima, 22
SOs: Jerry Cade, Salem, 212
ERA: Andrew George, Salem, 2.70

B Southwestern League
President: W.J. Green

Standings	W	L	Pct.	GB	Attend.	Manager
Hobbs Sports (8)	90	52	.634	—	44,206	Pat Stasey
El Paso Texans	85	59	.590	6	51,386	Pat McLaughlin/Art Lilly
Pampa Oilers	80	60	.571	9	42,150	Grover Seitz/Allen Cross
San Angelo Colts	78	65	.545	12½	47,296	Art Bowland
Plainview Ponies	76	68	.528	15	43,892	Jodie Beeler/Frank Tornay
Ballinger Westerners	73	69	.514	17	24,614	Tony York
Carlsbad Potashers	70	74	.486	21	51,165	Thurman Tucker
Midland Indians	63	81	.438	28	77,601	Everett Robinson/Rudy Briner/ Juan Izaguirre
Roswell Rockets	53	90	.371	37½	18,367	Tom Jordan/Halbert Simpson
Clovis Pioneers (11)	45	95	.321	44	41,125	Frank Benites/Red McQuillen/ Roy Parker

Playoffs: San Angelo 4 games, Hobbs 3; El Paso 4 games, Pampa 0.
Finals: El Paso 4 games, San Angelo 1.

BA: Len Tucker, Pampa, .404
Runs: Len Tucker, Pampa, 181
Hits: Roberto Fernandez, Roswell, 231
RBIs: Forrest "Frosty" Kennedy, Plainview, 184
HRs: Forrest "Frosty" Kennedy, Plainview, 60

2Bs: Roberto Fernandez, Roswell, 64
Wins: Bill Bagwell, San Angelo, 23
SOs: Jodie Phipps, San Angelo, 242
ERA: James Grimm, Hobbs, 3.11

B Three-I League
President: Hal Totten

Standings	W	L	Pct.	GB	Attend.	Manager
Evansville Braves***(12)	84	36	.700	—	60,910	Bob Coleman
Waterloo White Hawks (3)	62	56	.525	21	46,119	Ira Hutchinson
Keokuk Kernels (4)	60	59	.504	23½	47,440	Pinky May
Peoria Chiefs (16)	58	58	.500	24	54,359	George Kissell
Quincy Gems (7)	56	64	.467	28	35,308	Vern Hoscheit
Burlington Bees (10)	46	75	.380	38½	68,260	Ed McDade
Cedar Rapids Raiders (9)	44	76	.367	40	47,352	George Scherger
Terre Haute Tigers#(5)	40	26	.606	NA	23,368	Bill Norman/Charlie Metro

#Terre Haute disbanded July 3.

Playoffs: None.

All-Star Team: 1B-Billy Smith, Evansville; **2B**-Clyde McNeal, Cedar Rapids; **3B**-James Vandewettering, Keokuk; **SS**-Lyle Krall, Peoria; **OF**-Norm Cash, Waterloo; Lee Maye, Evansville; Horace Garner, Evansville; **C**-Arlan Barber, Keokuk; Roger Jongewaard, Evansville; **Util**-Richard Windle, Quincy; **P**-Ernest Craumer, Keokuk; Dale Hendrickson, Evansville; Don Nottebart, Evansville; Glen Rosenbaum, Waterloo; **MVP**-Don Nottebart, Evansville; **Manager**-Ira Hutchinson, Waterloo.

BA: Horace Garner, Evansville, .354
Runs: Lee Maye, Evansville, 103
Hits: Lee Maye, Evansville, 159
RBIs: Lee Maye, Evansville, 99
HRs: Clyde McNeal, Cedar Rapids, 27
Wins: Don Nottebart, Evansville, 18
SOs: Dave Wegereck, Keokuk, 158
ERA: Don Nottebart, Evansville, 2.24

C Arizona-Mexico League
President: E.T. "Tim" Cusick

Standings	W	L	Pct.	GB	Attend.	Manager
Cananea Mineros*	75	56	.573	—	134,723	Memo Garibay
Douglas Copper Kings (15)	73	58	.557	2	42,059	Jerry Gardner
Nogales Diablos Rojos	71	59	.546	3½	60,000	Carlos Galina
Phoenix Stars (1)	70	59	.543	4	60,017	Billy Capps
Yuma Sun Sox**(11)	66	65	.504	9	35,076	Whitey Wietelmann/Bill Harris
Mexicali Eagles (16)	63	65	.492	10½	74,417	Larry Barton/Artie Wilson
Tucson Cowboys	57	71	.445	16½	40,000	Don Jameson
Tijuana Potros#	17	59	.224	NA	30,000	Virgilio Arteaga

#Tijuana disbanded June 28.

Playoff: Cananea 3 games, Yuma 0.

BA: Walter Tyler, Yuma, .392
Runs: Claudio Solano, Cananea, 147
Hits: Walter Tyler, Yuma, 208
RBIs: Claudio Solano, Cananea, 174
HRs: Claudio Solano, Cananea, 45

Wins: James Johnson, Phoenix, 19
    Amador Guzman, Nogales, 19
    P.A. Perez, Cananea, 19
SOs: John Ivory Smith, Tucson, 217
ERA: Forrest Orrell, Tijuana/Mexicali, 2.70

C California League
President: Edward J. Mulligan

Standings	W	L	Pct.	GB	Attend.	Manager
Fresno Cardinals (16)	91	49	.650	—	62,954	Eddie Lyons
Stockton Senators	83	57	.593	8	52,570	Roy Partee
San Jose JoSox	79	61	.564	12	41,176	Dick Whitman
Reno Silver Sox (9)	73	67	.521	18	41,886	Ray Perry
Visalia Cubs	67	73	.479	24	37,110	Eddie Bockman
Modesto Reds (7)	66	74	.471	25	36,807	Albert Lyons
Salinas Packers (12)	53	87	.379	38	33,630	Eddie Lake
Bakersfield Boosters (14)	48	92	.343	43	25,085	Art Lilly/Dick Wilson

Playoffs: Fresno 2 games, San Jose 0; Stockton 2 games, Reno 1.
Finals: Fresno 3 games, Stockton 1.

All-Star Team: 1B-Dick Wilson, Bakersfield; **2B**-Eddie Lyons, Fresno; **3B**-Antonio Conde Alomar, Fresno; **SS**-Bob Reasonover, Reno; **OF**-Bud Heslet, Visalia; Richard Greco, Modesto; Dick Whitman, San Jose; **C**-Wilbert Tiesiera, Salinas; **Util**-Edward Lake, Salinas; **P**-Donald Orwiler, Modesto; David Jordan, Stockton; Peter Hernandez, Visalia; Alvin Spearman, Stockton; **MVP**-Dick Whitman, San Jose; **Rookie of the Year**-Nelson Chittum, Fresno; **Manager**-Eddie Lyons, Fresno.

BA: Dick Whitman, San Jose, .391
Runs: Bud Heslet, Visalia, 147
Hits: Richard Greco, Modesto, 192
RBIs: Bud Heslet, Visalia, 172

HRs: Bud Heslet, Visalia, 51
Wins: Peter Hernandez, Visalia, 24
SOs: David Jordan, Stockton, 227
ERA: Alvin Spearman, Stockton, 2.62

C Central Mexican League
President: Anuar Canavati

Standings	W	L	Pct.	GB	Attend.	Manager
Saltillo Saraperos	58	41	.589	—	86,735	Augustin Bejerano
Chihuahua Dorados	58	42	.580	½	89,275	Manuel Arroyo
Ciudad Juarez Indios	48	52	.480	10½	103,721	Manuel Fortes/Syd Cohen
Fresnillo Mineros	47	53	.470	11½	61,436	Eduardo Reyes/Jose Gutierrez/ Jesus Diaz
Durango Alacranes	45	54	.455	13	84,441	Salvador Sahuayo/ Adolfo Cabrera
Aguascalientes Rieleros	43	57	.430	15½	63,042	Martin Dihigo/Armando Flores

Playoffs: None.

All-Star Team: 1B-Pedro Ramirez, Saltillo; **2B**-Ramon Mendoza, Saltillo; **3B**-Joseph Joshua, Ciudad Juarez; **SS**-Gilberto Villarreal, Chihuahua; **OF**-Juan Hernandez, Durango; William "Burnis" Wright, Aguascalientes; Juan Rodriguez, Durango; **C**-Jose Luis St. Claire, Saltillo; Jose Sosa, Durango; **P**-Marcelino Solis, Saltillo; Marte de Alejandro, Chihuahua.

BA: Juan Hernandez, Durango, .365
Runs: Juan Hernandez, Durango, 103
Hits: Gilberto Villarreal, Chihuahua, 143
RBIs: Pedro Ramirez, Saltillo, 108

HRs: Blas Guzman, Fresnillo, 28
    Lupe Pedroza, Fresnillo, 28
Wins: Marte de Alejandro, Chihuahua, 18
SOs: Marte de Alejandro, Chihuahua, 129
ERA: Aurelio Espericueto, Aguascalientes, 3.29

C Evangeline League
President: Ray Mullins

Standings	W	L	Pct.	GB	Attend.	Manager
Lafayette Oilers (10)	78	49	.614	—	30,596	Ken Raffensberger
Thibodaux Senators (8)	66	56	.541	9½	61,000	Bill Dossey
Crowley Millers (6)	63	60	.512	13	37,265	Vincent Plumbo
Lake Charles Giants (13)	62	62	.500	14½	48,482	Mike McCormick
Alexandria Aces	55	67	.451	20½	48,049	Red Smith
Monroe Sports (7)	54	68	.443	21½	25,831	Ed Head
Baton Rouge Rebels	53	70	.431	23	42,000	Robert Reid/James Smith
New Iberia Indians#	15	14	.517	NA	11,252	Al Barillari

#New Iberia disbanded May 19.

Playoffs: Lafayette 4 games, Lake Charles 1; Thibodaux 4 games, Crowley 1.
Finals: Cancelled due to lack of interest.

BA: Jose Garcia Cruz, Baton Rouge, .329
Runs: Doug Kassay, Thibodaux, 99
Hits: Jose Garcia Cruz, Baton Rouge, 152
RBIs: Grady Watts, Thibodaux, 99

HRs: Eugene Johnson, Lake Charles, 20
Wins: David Gerard, Lafayette, 18
SOs: Andrew Yetsko, Lake Charles, 242
ERA: Dave Stenhouse, Lafayette, 1.92

C Northern League
President: Herman D. White

Standings	W	L	Pct.	GB	Attend.	Manager
Eau Claire Braves (12)	70	52	.574	—	36,650	Joe Just
Winnipeg Goldeyes (16)	63	55	.534	5	64,459	Vern Benson
Duluth-Superior						
White Sox (3)	63	56	.529	5½	41,533	Joe Hauser
Aberdeen Pheasants (1)	64	61	.512	7½	60,673	George Staller
Wausau Lumberjacks (11)	61	63	.492	10	28,510	John Streza
St. Cloud Rox (13)	61	64	.488	10½	31,964	Charlie Fox
Grand Forks Chiefs (15)	59	65	.476	12	37,573	Al Kubski
Fargo-Moorhead Twins (4)	49	74	.398	21½	37,120	Tom Oliver

Playoffs: Duluth-Superior 1 game, Eau Claire 0; Aberdeen 1 game, Winnipeg 0.
Finals: Duluth-Superior 2 games, Aberdeen 0.

All-Star Team: 1B-Orlando Cepeda, St. Cloud; **2B**-Robert MacConnell, Eau Claire; **3B**-Martin Rosell, Wausau; **SS**-Daryl Robertson, St. Cloud; **OF**-Richard Lombardi, Duluth-Superior; Inocencio Rodriguez, St. Cloud; Pedro Cardenal, Winnipeg; **C**-Jesse Gonder, Wausau; Bob Rikard, Winnipeg; **P**-Jack Kralick, Duluth-Superior; Elliott Coleman, Aberdeen.

BA: Orlando Cepeda, St. Cloud, .355
Runs: Elder White, Grand Forks, 109
Hits: Orlando Cepeda, St. Cloud, 177
RBIs: Orlando Cepeda, St. Cloud, 112
HRs: Orlando Cepeda, St. Cloud, 26
Wins: Ron Piche, Eau Claire, 16
SOs: Wes Stock, Aberdeen, 182
ERA: Ed Szyczewski, Duluth-Superior, 2.19

C Pioneer League
President: Claude Engberg

Standings	W	L	Pct.	GB	Attend.	Manager
Boise Braves (12)	74	58	.561	—	87,732	Mickey Livingston/ George McQuinn
Billings Mustangs (15)	70	62	.530	4	75,887	Buck Elliott
Salt Lake City Bees (14)	70	62	.530	4	103,307	Frank Lucchesi
Idaho Falls Russets (5)	69	63	.523	5	39,497	Stan Wasiak/Charlie Metro
Magic Valley Cowboys (10)	69	63	.523	5	48,723	Al Zarilla/Bill Raimondi
Great Falls Electrics (9)	64	68	.485	10	74,469	Lou Rochelli
Missoula Timberjacks	61	71	.462	13	59,049	Jack McKeon
Pocatello Bannocks (6)	51	81	.386	23	43,474	Joe Lutz/Lou Stringer

Playoffs: None.

All-Star Team: 1B-Robert Pascal, Magic Valley; **2B**-Ellis Burton, Billings; **3B**-Bob Johnson, Idaho Falls; **SS**-Robert King, Boise; **OF**-Duane Hermon, Magic Valley; Mike Coppola, Pocatello; Jackie Lee Lundquist, Salt Lake City; **C**-Samuel Mauney, Magic Valley; Charles Brockell, Billings; **P**-Tommy Hull, Billings; John Buzhardt, Magic Valley.

BA: Robert Pascal, Magic Valley, .364
Runs: Duane Hermon, Magic Valley, 134
Hits: Bob Johnson, Idaho Falls, 198
RBIs: Robert Pascal, Magic Valley, 137
HRs: Mike Coppola, Pocatello, 28
Wins: Tommy Hull, Billings, 22
SOs: Dallas Green, Salt Lake City, 226
ERA: Tommy Hull, Billings, 2.41

D Alabama-Florida League
President: Sam C. Smith

Standings	W	L	Pct.	GB	Attend.	Manager
Graceville Oilers	69	49	.585	—	21,584	Wayland Goza
Donalsonville Seminoles	68	49	.581	½	22,089	Nesbit Wilson
Ft. Walton Beach Jets (8)	63	55	.534	6	14,550	Bill Brightwell
Dothan Cardinals (16)	58	59	.496	10½	16,600	Whitey Reis
Crestview Braves (10)	51	69	.425	19	8,100	Walt Dixon
Panama City Fliers (5)	45	73	.381	24	19,923	Al Lakeman

Playoffs: Ft. Walton Beach 3 games, Graceville 1; Donalsonville 3 games, Dothan 2.
Finals: Donalsonville 4 games, Ft. Walton Beach 2.

All-Star Team: 1B-Nesbit Wilson, Donalsonville; **2B**-Charles Grant, Graceville; **3B**-Whitey Ries, Dothan; **SS**-Nicholas Aloisi, Dothan; **OF**-Edward Napoleon, Dothan; John Wyatt, Ft. Walton Beach; Byrd Whigham, Graceville; **C**-James Crawford, Ft. Walton Beach; Charles Staniland, Dothan; **P**-Robert Hoffman, Donalsonville; Thomas Fitzgerald, Donalsonville.

BA: Charles Grant, Graceville, .356
Runs: Nesbit Wilson, Donalsonville, 133
Hits: Charles Grant, Graceville, 154
RBIs: Nesbit Wilson, Donalsonville, 125
HRs: Nesbit Wilson, Donalsonville, 40
Wins: Alex Gargiulo, Graceville, 17
SOs: Thomas Fitzgerald, Donalsonville, 206
ERA: Rene Nodarse, Ft. Walton Beach, 2.26

D Florida State League
President: John Krider

Standings	W	L	Pct.	GB	Attend.	Manager
Cocoa Indians***(13)	90	50	.643	—	28,237	Buddy Kerr
Gainesville G-Men (16)	81	56	.591	7½	30,408	Homer Ray Wilson
West Palm Beach						
Sun Chiefs (11)	81	58	.583	8½	45,936	Walt Novick
Daytona Beach Islanders (4)	72	65	.526	16½	34,168	Henry Majeski
Palatka Tigers (5)	59	80	.424	30½	36,704	Ralph Hodgin/Charles Baird
St. Petersburg Saints (7)	59	81	.421	31	49,230	Ken Silvestri
Leesburg Braves (12)	58	82	.414	32	22,971	Tom Giordano
Orlando Seratomas	55	83	.399	34	24,758	Taft Wright/Gerald Walker

Playoffs: None.

All-Star Team: 1B-Gene Cockrell, Cocoa; **2B**-Cookie Rojas, West Palm Beach; **3B**-Dave Bristol, West Palm Beach; **SS**-Thomas Wright, Cocoa; **OF**-David Dillard, Daytona Beach; Felipe Alou, Cocoa; Walter Bennett, Daytona Beach; **C**-William Johnson, St. Petersburg; **Util**-William Close, West Palm Beach; **P**-Michael Marinko, Leesburg; Robert Dunn, West Palm Beach; David Tyriver, Daytona Beach; Julio Navarro, Cocoa; **Manager**-Buddy Kerr, Cocoa.

BA: Felipe Alou, Cocoa, .380
Runs: Charles Matthews, Daytona Beach, 114
Hits: David Dillard, Daytona Beach, 191
RBIs: David Dillard, Daytona Beach, 127
HRs: Gene Cockrell, Cocoa, 22
German Pizzaro, Gainesville, 22
Wins: Julio Navarro, Cocoa, 24
SOs: Julio Navarro, Cocoa, 216
ERA: Julio Navarro, Cocoa, 2.16

D Georgia State League
President: Oswald Hadden

Standings	W	L	Pct.	GB	Attend.	Manager
Douglas Reds***(11)	77	43	.642	—	32,316	John Vander Meer
Sandersville Giants (13)	70	50	.583	7	31,287	Pete Pavlick
Vidalia Indians (4)	63	57	.525	14	17,273	Mark Wylie
Thomson Orioles (1)	61	59	.508	16	40,849	Lloyd Brown/Enid Drake
Hazlehurst-Baxley Tigers (5)	49	71	.408	28	9,565	Wayne Wallace/Stan Wasiak
Dublin Irish (15)	40	80	.333	37	20,577	Bobby Clark/Wilbur Caldwell/ Wayne Wallace

Playoffs: Douglas 3 games, Vidalia 2; Sandersville 3 games, Thomson 2.
Finals: Douglas 3 games, Sandersville 1.

BA: Frank Reveira, Sandersville, .332
Runs: Pete Pavlick, Sandersville, 95
Dan Sarver, Sandersville, 95
Hits: Daniel Almeida, Vidalia, 145
RBIs: Al Milley, Sandersville, 103
HRs: Al Milley, Sandersville, 21
Wins: Gilbert Bassetti, Sandersville, 21
SOs: Dick Stigman, Vidalia, 263
ERA: Dick Stigman, Vidalia, 1.44

D Georgia-Florida League
President: W.T. Anderson

Standings	W	L	Pct.	GB	Attend.	Manager
Valdosta Tigers (5)	94	45	.676	—	43,088	Bill Adair
Waycross Braves (12)	79	59	.572	14½	32,300	James Deery
Tifton Phillies (14)	70	66	.515	22½	20,794	Wes Griffin/Edward Miller
Albany Cardinals (16)	70	68	.507	23½	26,949	Chase Riddle
Moultrie Reds (11)	68	71	.489	26	29,211	Bob Wellman
Thomasville Dodgers (9)	63	76	.453	31	21,697	Rudy Rufer/George Pfister
Brunswick Pirates (15)	62	76	.449	31½	30,714	Frank Oceak
Fitzgerald A's (6)	47	92	.338	47	17,723	Leon "Red" Treadway

Playoffs: None.

All-Star Team: 1B-Fred Hopke, Tifton; **2B**-Ronald Welch, Valdosta; **3B**-James Cross, Valdosta; **SS**-William Ryckman, Valdosta; **OF**-Jim Hickman, Albany; Barton Dupon, Valdosta; Arvie Pilgrim, Waycross; John Lowery, Waycross; **C**-Ray Engel, Waycross; Donald Whitcomb, Brunswick; **Util**-Francis Sisolak, Brunswick; **P**-Benny Rich, Brunswick; Richard Scott, Thomasville; David Scranton, Waycross; Kenneth Sheppard, Valdosta; **Manager**-Bill Adair, Valdosta.

BA: Chase Riddle, Albany, .353
Runs: Chase Riddle, Albany, 115
Hits: Bob Wellman, Moultrie, 165
RBIs: Chase Riddle, Albany, 142
HRs: Bob Wellman, Moultrie, 30
Wins: Lawrence Kendig, Albany, 20
William McNeil, Valdosta, 20
SOs: Kenneth Sheppard, Valdosta, 271
ERA: Richard Scott, Thomasville, 212

D Midwest League
President: C.C. "Dutch" Hoffman

Standings	W	L	Pct.	GB	Attend.	Manager
Paris Lakers*(10)	73	52	.584	—	60,350	Marty Purtell
Lafayette Red Sox (2)	69	56	.552	4	42,821	Len Okrie
Dubuque Packers**(3)	66	57	.537	6	92,364	George Noga
Clinton Pirates (15)	63	60	.512	9	60,544	Stan Wentzel
Decatur Commodores (14)	62	64	.492	11½	64,263	Al Unser
Mattoon Phillies (16)	61	65	.484	12½	35,144	Benedict Zientara
Michigan City						
White Caps (13)	55	71	.437	18½	48,765	Allan Shinn
Kokomo Dodgers (9)	51	75	.405	22½	49,437	Pete Reiser

Playoffs: Dubuque 2 games, Clinton 0; Paris 2 games, Lafayette 0.
Finals: Paris 3 games, Dubuque 1.

All-Star Team: 1B-John Kreuter, Paris; **2B**-Grover "Deacon" Jones, Dubuque; **3B**-Carroll "Tex" Gholson, Paris; **SS**-Dale DeSilva, Lafayette; **OF**-Eddie Logan, Mattoon; Lee Handley, Paris; Donald Miles, Kokomo; **C**-Joe Theis, Lafayette; Jimmie Schaffer, Decatur; **P**-Charles Smith, Lafayette; Arturo Miro, Clinton; Joseph Schaffernoth, Paris; William Rouse, Dubuque; Charles Alsop, Michigan City; **MVP**-Grover "Deacon" Jones, Dubuque; **Manager**-Len Okrie, Lafayette.

BA: Grover "Deacon" Jones, Dubuque, .409
Runs: Eddie Logan, Mattoon, 131
Hits: Eddie Logan, Mattoon, 203
RBIs: Grover "Deacon" Jones, Dubuque, 120
HRs: Carroll "Tex" Gholson, Paris, 30
Wins: Arturo Miro, Clinton, 22
SOs: Charles Smith, Lafayette, 263
ERA: Charles Alsop, Michigan City, 2.64

D Nebraska State League
President: Mike Hollinger

Standings	W	L	Pct.	GB	Attend.	Manager
Lexington Red Sox (2)	41	22	.651	—	28,393	Danny Doyle
Grand Island Athletics (6)	35	28	.556	6	30,915	Art Mazmanian
Kearney Yankees (7)	35	28	.556	6	30,943	Randy Gumpert
McCook Braves (12)	35	28	.556	6	32,224	Bill Steinecke
Superior Senators (8)	34	29	.540	7	22,860	Charles Ray Baker
Holdrege White Sox (3)	33	30	.524	8	24,326	Frank Scalzi
North Platte Indians (4)	24	39	.381	17	28,578	Spencer Harris
Hastings Giants (13)	15	48	.238	26	28,713	Gene Thompson

Playoffs: None.

All-Star Team: 1B-Jimmie Hall, Superior; 2B-Thomas Plath, Holdrege; 3B-Jay Ward, Kearney; SS-James Knerr, Lexington; OF-Deron Johnson, Kearney; Roy Scercy, Grand Island; Claude Horn, Grand Island; C-Edward Stogoski, Superior; John Sweazy, Lexington; P-Gary Peters, Holdrege; Ted Ellis, Lexington.

BA: Bill Fries, Kearney, .394
Runs: Deron Johnson, Kearney, 70
Hits: Jimmie Hall, Superior, 87
RBIs: Deron Johnson, Kearney, 78
HRs: Deron Johnson, Kearney, 24
Wins: Ted Ellis, Lexington, 11
Richard Allen, McCook, 11
SOs: Gary Peters, Holdrege, 142
ERA: Ted Ellis, Lexington, 1.76

D PONY League
President: Vincent M. McNamara

Standings	W	L	Pct.	GB	Attend.	Manager
Wellsville Braves (12)	74	46	.617	—	30,470	Alex Monchak
Corning Red Sox (2)	68	55	.553	7½	33,450	Elmer Yoter
Olean Oilers (14)	65	58	.528	10½	27,281	Paul Owens
Hornell Dodgers (9)	57	58	.496	14½	20,334	Boyd Bartley/Charlie Gelbert
Jamestown Falcons (5)	52	62	.456	19	19,757	Pat Mullin/Don Lund/Wayne Blackburn
Erie Senators (8)	45	74	.378	28½	28,223	John Welaj
Hamilton Red Wings#	6	8	.429	NA	1,200	Cart Howerton
Bradford Yankees#(7)	3	9	.250	NA	1,258	Randy Gumpert

#Hamilton and Bradford disbanded May 18.

Playoffs: Wellsville 2 games, Hornell 1; Olean 2 games, Corning 1.
Finals: Wellsville 3 games, Olean 2.

All-Star Team: 1B-Paul Owens, Olean; 2B-Joey Lawrence, Hornell; 3B-Sheldon Brodsky, Hornell; SS-Juan Guzman, Wellsville; OF-Gustave Sancimino, Hornell; Glenn Owens, Olean; George Lewis, Corning; C-Wendell Antoine, Jamestown; Sidney Goldfader, Wellsville; P-

Robert Milo, Olean; Antonio Diaz, Wellsville; **Manager**-Alex Monchak, Wellsville.

BA: Paul Owens, Olean, .368
Runs: Lou Vassie, Olean, 116
Hits: Glenn Owens, Olean, 155
RBIs: Jim Hubbard, Erie, 109
HRs: George Lewis, Corning, 32
Wins: Robert Milo, Olean, 20
SOs: Martin Stabiner, Hornell, 216
ERA: Keith Nicolls, Wellsville, 1.76

D Sooner State League
President: George Barr

Standings	W	L	Pct.	GB	Attend.	Manager
Ardmore Cardinals (16)	83	56	.597	—	47,110	J.C. Dunn
Lawton Braves (12)	80	60	.571	3½	30,550	Travis Jackson
Seminole Oilers (6)	74	66	.529	9½	31,249	Burl Storie
Paris Orioles (1)	72	67	.518	11	37,764	Barney Lutz
Ponca City Cubs (10)	70	70	.500	13½	20,674	Don Biebel
Muskogee Giants (13)	63	76	.453	20	37,983	Richard Klaus
McAlester Rockets (7)	60	79	.432	23	32,302	Marvin Crater
Shawnee Hawks (9)	56	84	.400	27½	24,872	Jack Banta

Playoffs: Ardmore 3 games, Paris 2; Seminole 3 games, Lawton 1.
Finals: Seminole 4 games, Ardmore 3.

All-Star Team: 1B-Anthony Lembo, Shawnee; Douglas Smith, Lawton; 2B-Peter Aviotti, Ardmore; Jim Burton, Paris; Daniel Staniec, Lawton; 3B-Phil Jantze, Ardmore; SS-Gary Anderson, Lawton; OF-Gene Oliver, Ardmore; Russell Gragg, Ponca City; Richard Lubinski, Paris; C-Anthony Cannizzo, Seminole; William Gilmore, Lawton; P-John Bartek, Ardmore; Rolf Scheel, Paris.

BA: Russell Gragg, Ponca City, .352
Runs: Robert Stangel, Ardmore, 132
Hits: Russell Gragg, Ponca City, 183
RBIs: J.C. Dunn, Ardmore, 134
HRs: Gene Oliver, Ardmore, 39
Wins: John Bartek, Ardmore, 21
SOs: Vincent Kilpela, Ardmore, 276
ERA: Michael Mazzamorra, Seminole, 2.28

1956 Interleague Post Season Play

World Series
New York (American) 4 games, Brooklyn (National) 3

Junior World Series
Indianapolis (American Association) 4 games, Rochester (International) 0
Total Attendance: 36,517

Dixie Series
Houston (Texas) 4 games, Atlanta (Southern Association) 2
Total Attendance: 38,582

1956 Major League Farm Systems

American League

1 Baltimore (8): Vancouver, San Antonio, Columbus (GA), Lubbock/Texas City, Phoenix, Aberdeen, Thomson, Paris.
2 Boston (7): San Francisco, Oklahoma City, Albany (NY), Greensboro, Lafayette (IN), Lexington, Corning.
3 Chicago (6): Memphis, Colorado Springs, Waterloo, Duluth-Superior, Dubuque, Holdrege.
4 Cleveland (9): Indianapolis, Mobile, Reading, Fayetteville, Keokuk, Fargo-Moorhead, Daytona Beach, Vidalia, North Platte.
5 Detroit (11): Charleston, Syracuse, Augusta, Durham, Terre Haute, Idaho Falls, Panama City, Palatka, Hazlehurst-Baxley, Valdosta, Jamestown.
6 Kansas City (8): Columbus (OH), Columbia, Abilene, Crowley, Pocatello, Fitzgerald, Grand Island, Seminole.
7 New York (12): Denver, Richmond, Birmingham, Binghamton, Winston-Salem, Quincy, Modesto, Monroe, St. Petersburg, Kearney, Bradford, McAlester.
8 Washington (8): Louisville, Chattanooga, Charlotte, Hobbs, Thibodaux, Ft. Walton Beach, Superior, Erie.

National League

9 Brooklyn (14): Portland, St. Paul, Montreal, Ft. Worth, Macon, Pueblo, Wichita Falls, Cedar Rapids, Reno, Great Falls, Thomasville, Kokomo, Hornell, Shawnee.
10 Chicago (9): Los Angeles, Tulsa, Des Moines, Burlington, Lafayette (LA), Magic Valley, Crestview, Paris, Ponca City.
11 Cincinnati (11): Seattle, Havana, Nashville, Savannah, High Point-Thomasville, Clovis, Yuma, Wausau, West Palm Beach, Douglas (GA), Moultrie.
12 Milwaukee (15): Wichita, Atlanta, Austin, Jacksonville, Topeka, Corpus Christi, Evansville, Salinas, Eau Claire, Boise, Leesburg, Waycross, McCook, Wellsville, Lawton.
13 New York (12): Minneapolis, Dallas, Johnstown, Albuquerque, Danville, Lake Charles, St. Cloud, Cocoa, Sandersville, Michigan City, Hastings, Muskogee.
14 Philadelphia (8): Miami, Schenectady, Wilson, Bakersfield, Salt Lake City, Tifton, Decatur, Olean.
15 Pittsburgh (12): Hollywood, New Orleans, Williamsport, Lincoln, Waco, Kinston, Douglas (AZ), Grand Forks, Billings, Dublin, Brunswick, Clinton.
16 St. Louis (15): Omaha, Rochester, Houston, Allentown, Sioux City, Beaumont, Peoria, Mexicali, Fresno, Winnipeg, Dothan, Gainesville, Albany (GA), Mattoon, Ardmore.

1956 No-Hitters

Date	Pitcher	Team	League	Opponent	Score
5-7	Jere Hill	Albany	Georgia-Florida	Thomasville	2-1
5-12	Carl Erskine	Brooklyn	National	New York	3-0
5-18	Ted Stone	Greensboro	Carolina	Kinston	5-0 (7)
5-26	Johnny Klippstein/Hershell Freeman/Joe Black	Cincinnati	National	Milwaukee	1-2
6-2	Hank Szostak	Fitzgerald	Georgia-Florida	Brunswick	3-0 (P, 7)
6-5	Don Johnson	Toronto	International	Columbus	2-0 (7)
6-5	Richard Atkinson	Sioux City	Western	Topeka	2-0
6-7	Ed Gunning	Thomson	Georgia State	Hazlehurst-Baxley	14-2
6-13	Lou Hribar/Will Hunter	Wichita Falls	Big State	Victoria	3-0
6-16	Lynn Lovenguth	Toronto	International	Richmond	8-0
6-19	Albert Wilson	Danville	Carolina	Kinston	2-0 (7)
6-25	George Brunet	Crowley	Evangeline	Alexandria	3-0
7-11	Cliff Adams	Panama City	Alabama-Florida	Crestview	6-0
7-13	Ed Hobaugh	Waterloo	Three-I	Burlington	11-0
7-14	Mel Parnell	Boston	American	Chicago	4-0
7-14	Theodore Herrera	Yakima	Northwest	Spokane	11-0 (7)
7-16	Mike Wallace	Mattoon	Midwest	Clinton	6-0 (7)
7-22	John Lutz	Eau Claire	Northern	Winnipeg	5-0 (7)
7-25	John Herbert	Erie	PONY	Hornell	7-0 (P)
8-4	Jim Cahoon	Waycross	Georgia-Florida	Moultrie	2-0
8-4	Herman Brown	Charlotte	South Atlantic	Augusta	5-0
8-7	Jim Allison	Thomson	Georgia State	Douglas	9-0
8-8	Jack Kralick	Duluth-Superior	Northern	Fargo-Moorhead	5-0 (7)
8-9	Donald Rowe	Lincoln	Western	Amarillo	1-0 (7)
8-12	Bennie Daniels	Lincoln	Western	Amarillo	0-1
8-14	Lewis Glidewell	Dubuque	Midwest	Kokomo	5-0
8-21	Philip Mudrock	Kearney	Nebraska State	North Platte	11-0
8-23	Will Souillard	Waycross	Georgia-Florida	Fitzgerald	6-0
8-30	Ken McBride	Greensboro	Carolina	Fayetteville	6-0
9-1	Zack Monroe	Binghamton	Eastern	Syracuse	6-0 (7)
9-1	Henry Bolinda	Schenectady	Eastern	Albany	1-0
9-4	Arlen Downs	Yakima	Northwest	Eugene	1-0 (7)
9-25	Sal Maglie	Brooklyn	National	Philadelphia	5-0
10-8	Don Larsen	New York	American	Brooklyn (Nat'l)	2-0 (P, PO)

Number in parentheses indicates innings if other than nine; "P" indicates perfect game; "PO" indicates playoff game.

THIS DATE IN MINOR LEAGUE HISTORY

April 21, 1956, Juan Pizarro, who fanned 14 in six innings in his Organized Ball debut four days previously, turned in an even more spectacular performance in his second start with Jacksonville, South Atlantic League. He struck out 21 and allowed only four hits in a 12-inning, 1-0 victory over Charlotte. The hard-throwing lefty walked only one. The fastballer's 21 strikeouts gave him a total of 38 for 18 innings in his first two Organized Ball games. Pizarro, a batboy in the Puerto Rican League two years ago, received a reported $35,000 to sign with the Milwaukee Braves last winter.

April 22, 1956, The ageless Satchel Paige made his debut with Miami, International League, in a relief role against Rochester in the second game of a doubleheader. The twinbill lasted seven hours and 36 minutes, the first game going 18 innings and the second seven.

April 24, 1956, Minneapolis, American Association, opened its new stadium in suburban Bloomington before 18,366 paid customers. Wichita won the game 5-3.

April 27, 1956, Augusta, South Atlantic League, defeated Montgomery 6-4 in 20 innings. The number of innings played tied the league record. It was the third 20-inning game in loop history.

April 27, 1956, Rookie Nashville southpaw Rick Botelho, who had marked his Southern Association debut with a three-hit, 12-strikeout shutout two weeks earlier, used his bat to achieve individual heroics. He collected six straight hits, including two homers, and drove in eight runs to pace a 31-hit attack with which the Vols slaughtered Mobile 23-6. Botelho's feats had never been equalled by a Southern Association pitcher.

April 29, 1956, Satchel Paige, who joined the Miami Marlins of the International League at the start of the season after only four days of training, added another chapter to his amazing diamond record, chalking up a four-hit, 3-0 shutout over Montreal in his first start. The contest was a seven-inning affair.

April 29, 1956, Robert Finch, 71, director of public relations of the National Association, died in Columbus, Ohio. He was one of the three authors of "The Story of Minor League Baseball," a 444-page volume which traced the growth of the minor leagues and was a comprehensive record of the years between 1901 and 1952. Co-authors were L.H. Addington of Durham, North Carolina, and the late Ben M. Morgan.

April 30, 1956, Outfielder Linc Boyd of Clovis, Southwestern League, hammered out two grand slams, a two-run triple and a single, good for 11 RBIs, to enable the Pioneers to defeat El Paso 17-12.

May 1, 1956, Kinston, Carolina League, recorded the fifth highest scoring total in league history in a 27-1 rout of Greensboro. The record was 35, set by Durham against Leaksville-Spray-Draper in 1947. The Eagles crossed the plate five times in the first inning and held an 18-1 lead after four frames. They collected 23 hits and were aided by seven Patriot errors.

May 3, 1956, Unusual names and spellings have always proved troublesome for official scorers, but Big State League scribes had a headache over the common name of Smith at a game at Lubbock, Texas. There were five Smiths in the box score when Beaumont and Lubbock clashed, three of whom were named George Smith.

May 4, 1956, Eight homers were clubbed in Cananea's bandbox park as the Mineros beat Phoenix 17-12 in an Arizona-Mexico League encounter, for a total of 19 in two successive games. Cananea outfielder Claudio Solano, who hit a pair of round-trippers the day before against Douglas, came up with three more against Phoenix for a total of five in two games. Cananea set a loop mark by stealing 10 bases as another feature of the victory.

May 5, 1956, Johnny Wartelle of Paris, Sooner State League, set a loop record by striking out 22 in an 8-4 victory over Seminole. The former high was 20, set by Leonard Fassler of Lawton in 1950. In his next start, on May 10, southpaw Wartelle whiffed 16 more but lost 4-2 to Ardmore.

May 6, 1956, Earl Hersh of Wichita, American Association, smashed a tremendous 503-foot home run in a game with St. Paul at Wichita. The blow came in the seventh frame in the second game of a doubleheader.

May 15, 1956, The efforts of two young women, secretary Jean Marini, 21, and general manager Carroll Jean Hodge, 22, to operate the Hamilton Red Wings on an independent basis ended in failure, when the franchise was returned to the PONY League.

May 15, 1956, Al Weygandt of Topeka, Western League, belted two more homers in two official at bats at Albuquerque for total of 10 round-trippers in a span of four games. On the club's next stop in Pueblo, Weygandt hit four more circuit smashes, giving him 14 home runs, 30 RBIs and 21 hits in 37 tries for the 10-game road trip. He also scored 21 runs.

May 17, 1956, With the gate affected by a combination of 35-degree weather and the knowledge that Hamilton was about to drop out of the PONY League, only 63 fans showed up for the Red Wings' game with Hornell.

May 25, 1956, Third baseman Tommy Brown of Nashville, Southern League, set a probable Organized Ball record when he reached base for the 20th consecutive time. The string included ten hits and ten walks.

May 27, 1956, Southpaw Tony Komisar of Leesburg, Florida State League, relieving with the bases full and none out in the final frame of a seven-inning game, made one pitch, which was hit into a triple play.

June 8, 1956, Joe Bauman, who set an all-time record for Organized Ball when he hit 72 home runs in 1954, hung up his spikes because of an old ankle injury.

June 26, 1956, Dick Stuart of Lincoln, Western League, connected for his 23rd homer in his last 28 games and number 40 for the season, in a game against Albuquerque.

July 1, 1956, Rocky Colavito, touted as probably the strongest throwing outfielder in the game, twice failed in attempts to break the Organized Ball long distance throwing record at San Diego. The Cleveland-owned flyhawk heaved one throw 435 feet, 10 inches from the plate over the centerfield wall at Lane Field, but fell slightly more than seven feet short of the record of 443 feet, 3-1/2 inches set by Don Grate at Chattanooga, Southern Association, on August 23, 1953.

July 14, 1956, Manager Danny Ozark of Wichita Falls, Big State League, blasted four home runs for six RBIs while pacing the Spudders to a 7-3 triumph over Beaumont.

August 7, 1956, The largest crowd in minor league history, 57,713, saw 50-year-old Satchel Paige of Miami, International League, beat Columbus in a contest played in the Orange Bowl.

August 13, 1956, Ageless righthander Satchel Paige of Miami, International League, pitched a seven-inning one-hitter to blank Rochester 4-0. The victory boosted Paige's season mark to 10-3 and lowered his ERA to 1.50.

August 26, 1956, Ken Guettler of Shreveport, Texas League, walloped his 60th home run in a game with Ft. Worth, becoming only the ninth player in Organized Ball history to reach the 60 mark.

August 27, 1956, Second baseman Curt Roberts of Columbus, International League, slammed four consecutive homers in a seven-inning game with Havana. His third homer was an inside-the-park drive. Roberts had six RBIs in the game. He hit only eight dingers for the season.

August 27, 1956, Outfielder Don Grate of Minneapolis, American Association, broke his own long-distance throwing record with a heave of 445 feet, one inch at Metropolitan Stadium, Minneapolis.

August 28, 1956, A chartered bus carrying the Albuquerque Dukes overturned near Walsenburg, Colorado, injuring 19 players and complicating the Western League clubs' personnel and schedule problems for the balance of the season, which was slated to end September 3. Two of the players suffered serious injuries which put them out for the rest of the season and the others, including manager Bob Swift, sustained minor cuts or bruises or were shaken up.

September 2, 1956, Arturo Miro of Clinton, Midwest League, who won 19 straight games in the regular season, saw his streak broken by Dubuque with an 8-2 loss in the league playoffs.

September 3, 1956, Dick Stuart, Lincoln outfielder-first baseman, smashed his 66th home run on the final day of the Western League regular season in a game with Topeka. Only three other players were ahead of the Californian on the all-time single-season homer list: Joe Bauman, Bob Crues and Joe Hauser.

September 6, 1956, First baseman Forrest "Frosty" Kennedy of Plainview, Southwestern League, became the tenth player in Organized Ball to slam as many as 60 homers in one campaign when he connected against San Angelo on the final day of the season. Kennedy batted in 184 runs in 144 games.

1957

American League
President: William Harridge

Standings	W	L	Pct.	GB	Attend.	Manager
New York Yankees............	98	56	.636	—	1,497,134	Casey Stengel
Chicago White Sox............	90	64	.584	8	1,135,668	Al Lopez
Boston Red Sox	82	72	.532	16	1,181,087	Pinky Higgins
Detroit Tigers....................	78	76	.506	20	1,272,346	Jack Tighe
Baltimore Orioles	76	76	.500	21	1,029,581	Paul Richards
Cleveland Indians	76	77	.497	21½	722,256	Kerby Farrell
Kansas City Athletics	59	94	.386	38½	901,067	Lou Boudreau/Harry Craft
Washington Senators	55	99	.357	43	457,079	Chuck Dressen/Cookie Lavagetto

BA: Ted Williams, Boston, .388
Runs: Mickey Mantle, New York, 121
Hits: Nellie Fox, Chicago, 196
RBIs: Roy Sievers, Washington, 114
HRs: Roy Sievers, Washington, 42

Wins: Jim Bunning, Detroit, 20
  Billy Pierce, Chicago, 20
SOs: Early Wynn, Cleveland, 184
ERA: Bobby Shantz, New York, 2.45
Pct: Dick Donovan, Chicago, .727, 16-6

National League
President: Warren C. Giles

Standings	W	L	Pct.	GB	Attend.	Manager
Milwaukee Braves	95	59	.617	—	2,215,404	Fred Haney
St. Louis Cardinals	87	67	.565	8	1,183,575	Fred Hutchinson
Brooklyn Dodgers...............	84	70	.545	11	1,028,258	Walter Alston
Cincinnati Reds...................	80	74	.519	15	1,070,850	Birdie Tebbetts
Philadelphia Phillies	77	77	.500	18	1,146,230	Mayo Smith
New York Giants	69	85	.448	26	653,923	Bill Rigney
Chicago Cubs.....................	62	92	.403	33	670,629	Bob Scheffing
Pittsburgh Pirates	62	92	.403	33	850,732	Bobby Bragan/Danny Murtaugh

BA: Stan Musial, St. Louis, .351
Runs: Hank Aaron, Milwaukee, 118
Hits: Red Schoendienst, New York/
  Milwaukee, 200
RBIs: Hank Aaron, Milwaukee, 132

HRs: Hank Aaron, Milwaukee, 44
Wins: Warren Spahn, Milwaukee, 21
SOs: Jack Sanford, Philadelphia, 188
ERA: Johnny Podres, Brooklyn, 2.66
Pct: Bob Buhl, Milwaukee, .720, 18-7

(Open) Pacific Coast League
President: Leslie M. O'Connor

Standings	W	L	Pct.	GB	Attend.	Manager
San Francisco Seals (2).....	101	67	.601	—	284,532	Joe Gordon
Vancouver Mounties (1).....	97	70	.581	3½	306,145	Charlie Metro
Hollywood Stars (15)..........	94	74	.560	7	198,012	Clyde King
San Diego Padres (4).........	89	79	.530	12	178,179	Bob Elliott/George Metkovich
Seattle Rainiers (11)	87	80	.521	13½	199,327	Lefty O'Doul
Los Angeles Angels (9)......	80	88	.476	21	220,547	Clay Bryant
Sacramento Solons	63	105	.375	38	113,955	Tommy Heath
Portland Beavers (10)	60	108	.357	41	208,196	Bill Sweeney/Frank Carswell/ Bill Posedel

Playoffs: None.

All-Star Team: 1B-Steve Bilko, Los Angeles; 2B-Ken Aspromonte, San Francisco; 3B-Jim Baumer, Hollywood; SS-Carl "Buddy" Peterson, Vancouver; OF-Bill Renna, San Francisco; Lennie Green, Vancouver; Joe Taylor, Seattle; C-Bill Hall, Hollywood; P-Morrie Martin, Vancouver; Leo Kiely, San Francisco; Jim "Mudcat" Grant, San Diego; George Witt, Hollywood; MVP-Steve Bilko, Los Angeles.

BA: Ken Aspromonte, San Francisco, .334
Runs: Steve Bilko, Los Angeles, 111
Hits: Jim Marshall, Vancouver, 188
RBIs: Steve Bilko, Los Angeles, 140

HRs: Steve Bilko, Los Angeles, 56
Wins: Leo Kiely, San Francisco, 21
SOs: Jim "Mudcat" Grant, San Diego, 178
ERA: Morrie Martin, Vancouver, 1.90

AAA American Association
President: Edward S. Doherty

Standings	W	L	Pct.	GB	Attend.	Manager
Wichita Braves (12)............	93	61	.604	—	145,028	Ben Geraghty
Denver Bears (7)................	90	64	.584	3	305,625	Ralph Houk
Minneapolis Millers (13)....	85	69	.552	8	256,113	John "Red" Davis
St. Paul Saints (9)	82	72	.532	11	202,260	Max Macon
Omaha Cardinals (16)........	76	78	.494	17	177,066	Johnny Keane
Indianapolis Indians (3)......	74	80	.481	19	159,947	Andy Cohen
Charleston Senators (5)	67	87	.435	26	124,144	Frank Skaff/Don Griffin/ Bill Norman
Louisville Colonels.............	49	105	.318	44	135,978	Dutch Meyer

Playoffs: St. Paul 4 games, Wichita 1; Denver 4 games, Minneapolis 0.
Finals: Denver 4 games, St. Paul 2.

All-Star Team: 1B-Ron Jackson, Indianapolis; 2B-Curt Roberts, Denver; 3B-Dick Gray, St. Paul; SS-Eddie Bressoud, Minneapolis; OF-Norm Siebern, Denver; Don Demeter, St. Paul; OF-Archie Wilson, Charleston; Ray Shearer, Wichita; C-Robert Schmidt, Minneapolis; Bob Oldis, Denver; P-Carlton Willey, Wichita; Frank Barnes, Omaha; Stan Williams, St. Paul; Pete Burnside, Minneapolis; MVP-Carlton Willey, Wichita; Manager-Ben Geraghty, Wichita.

BA: Norm Siebern, Denver, .349
Runs: Norm Siebern, Denver, 124
Hits: Norm Siebern, Denver, 191
RBIs: Marv Throneberry, Denver, 124

HRs: Marv Throneberry, Denver, 40
Wins: Carlton Willey, Wichita, 21
SOs: Stan Williams, St. Paul, 223
ERA: Frank Barnes, Omaha, 2.41

AAA International League
President: Frank J. Shaughnessy

Standings	W	L	Pct.	GB	Attend.	Manager
Toronto Maple Leafs	88	65	.575	—	342,597	Dixie Walker
Buffalo Bisons (6)	88	66	.571	½	386,071	Phil Cavarretta
Richmond Virginians (7)....	81	73	.526	7½	258,861	Ed Lopat
Miami Marlins (14)............	75	78	.490	13	181,651	Don Osborn
Rochester Red Wings (16)..	74	80	.481	14½	258,778	Cot Deal
Havana Sugar Kings (11) ...	72	82	.468	16½	84,320	Napoleon Reyes
Columbus Red Birds (15)...	69	85	.448	19½	180,418	Frank Oceak
Montreal Royals (9)...........	68	86	.442	20½	176,137	Greg Mulleavy/Al Campanis/ Al Ronning/Tommy Holmes

Playoffs: Miami 4 games, Toronto 2; Buffalo 4 games, Richmond 2.
Finals: Buffalo 4 games, Miami 1.

All-Star Team: 1B-Luke Easter, Buffalo; 2B-Mike Goliat, Toronto; 3B-Forest Smith, Miami; SS-Mike Baxes, Buffalo; OF-John Powers, Columbus; Don Landrum, Miami; Joe Caffie, Buffalo; C-Harry Chiti, Richmond; P-Walt Craddock, Buffalo; Jim Coates, Richmond; MVP-Mike Baxes, Buffalo; Pitcher of the Year-Don Johnson, Toronto; Manager-Phil Cavarretta, Buffalo.

BA: Joe Caffie, Buffalo, .330
Runs: Mike Baxes, Buffalo, 101
Hits: Mike Baxes, Buffalo, 179
RBIs: Luke Easter, Buffalo, 128
HRs: Luke Easter, Buffalo, 40

Wins: Walt Craddock, Buffalo, 18
  Humberto Robinson, Toronto, 18
SOs: Jim Coates, Richmond, 161
ERA: Mike Cuellar, Havana, 2.44

AA Mexican League
President: Federico Miranda

Standings	W	L	Pct.	GB	Attend.	Manager
Yucatan Leones	68	52	.567	—	246,864	Oscar Rodriguez
Mexico City Diablos Rojos ...	66	54	.550	2	340,180	Lazaro Salazar/Preston Gomez
Mexico City Tigres	63	57	.525	5	258,964	George Genovese
Monterrey Sultanes............	60	60	.500	8	193,325	Reggie Otero
Nuevo Laredo Tecolotes.....	56	64	.467	12	93,865	Memo Garibay
Veracruz Aguila.................	47	73	.392	21	168,296	Martin Dihigo

Playoffs: MC Tigres 4 games, Yucatan 2; MC Diablos Rojos 4 games, Monterrey 0.
Finals: MC Diablos Rojos 4 games, MC Tigres 3.

All-Star Team: 1B-Alonso Perry, MC Diablos Rojos; 2B-Aldo Salvent, Veracruz; 3B-Jose Guerrero, Monterrey; SS-Hector Mayer, MC Diablos Rojos; OF-Fernando Pedrozo, MC Diablos Rojos; Oscar Sardinas, Monterrey; Orlando Leroux, Yucatan; C-Earl Taborn, Nuevo Laredo; Leon Kellman, Yucatan; P-Lino Donoso, MC Tigres; Gilberto Guerra, MC Diablos Rojos.

BA: Aldo Salvent, Veracruz, .359
Runs: Alonso Perry, MC Diablos Rojos, 96
Hits: Alonso Perry, MC Diablos Rojos, 164
RBIs: Alonso Perry, MC Diablos Rojos, 107

HRs: Earl Taborn, Nuevo Laredo, 27
Wins: Eddie Locke, Monterrey, 18
SOs: Julian Ladera, Yucatan, 136
ERA: Eddie Locke, Monterrey, 3.20

AA Southern Association
President: Charles A. Hurth

Standings	W	L	Pct.	GB	Attend.	Manager
Atlanta Crackers (12)..........	87	67	.565	—	256,876	Buddy Bates
Memphis Chicks (10)	86	67	.562	½	125,085	Lou Klein
Nashville Vols (11)............	83	69	.546	3	152,203	Dick Sisler
Chattanooga Lookouts (8) ..	83	70	.542	3½	130,417	Cal Ermer
Mobile Bears (4)................	75	78	.490	11½	71,522	Don Heffner
Birmingham Barons (5)......	74	79	.484	12½	133,913	Johnny Pesky
Little Rock Travelers (6)	64	88	.421	22	75,181	Al Evans
New Orleans Pelicans (7) ...	60	94	.390	27	67,287	Peanuts Lowrey

Playoffs: Atlanta 4 games, Chattanooga 2; Nashville 4 games, Memphis 2.
Finals: Atlanta 4 games, Nashville 0.

All-Star Team: 1B-Dick Sisler, Nashville; 2B-Stan Roseboro, Chattanooga; 3B-Harmon Killebrew, Chattanooga; SS-Phil Shartzer, Nashville; OF-Stan Palys, Nashville; Bob Coats, Memphis; Donald Nicholas, Nashville; C-Dutch Dotterer, Nashville; Sammy Taylor, Atlanta; Guy Morton, Chattanooga; Util-Joe Morgan, Atlanta; Util OF-Eric Rodin, Little Rock; Vern Morgan, Chattanooga; P-George Brunet, Little Rock; Gerald Davis, Nashville; Bob Kelly, Nashville; Don Minnick, Chattanooga; Gary Bell, Mobile; Hal Griggs, Chattanooga.

*Won first-half   **Won second-half   ***Won both halves
Numbers after nicknames indicate farm system.
Affiliation listed at end of each year.

448

BA: Stan Palys, Nashville, .359
Runs: Stan Palys, Nashville, 116
Hits: Bob Coats, Memphis, 184
RBIs: Jesse Levan, Chattanooga, 114

HRs: Harmon Killebrew, Chattanooga, 29
Wins: Bob Kelly, Nashville, 24
SOs: George Brunet, Little Rock, 235
ERA: Hy Cohen, Memphis, 2.72

AA Texas League
President: Dick Butler

Standings	W	L	Pct.	GB	Attend.	Manager
Dallas Eagles (13).............	102	52	.662	—	123,561	Francis "Salty" Parker
Houston Buffalos (16)........	97	57	.630	5	152,914	Harry Walker
San Antonio Missions (1)...	76	78	.494	26	93,661	Joe Schultz
Tulsa Oilers (14).................	75	79	.487	27	127,465	Al Widmar
Austin Senators (12)...........	71	83	.461	31	96,879	Sibby Sisti
Ft. Worth Cats (10).............	70	84	.455	32	75,188	Lee Handley
Oklahoma City Indians (2).	66	88	.429	36	51,128	Sheriff Robinson
Shreveport Sports	59	95	.383	43	40,919	Mel McGaha

Playoffs: Dallas 4 games, Tulsa 2; Houston 4 games, San Antonio 3.
Finals: Houston 4 games, Dallas 3.

All-Star Team: 1B-Willie McCovey, Dallas; **2B**-Alex Cosmidis, Dallas; **3B**-Benjamin Valenzuela, Houston; **SS**-Bobby Winkles, Tulsa; **OF**-Jim Frey, Tulsa; Donald Taussig, Dallas; Dick Sinovic, Austin; **C**-Nelson Burbrink, Houston; **P**-Tom Bowers, Dallas; **MVP**-Jim Frey, Tulsa; **Pitcher of the Year**-Tom Bowers, Dallas; **Manager**-Francis "Salty" Parker, Dallas.

BA: Jim Frey, Tulsa, .336
Runs: Jim Frey, Tulsa, 102
Hits: Jim Frey, Tulsa, 198
RBIs: Spence Robbins, Oklahoma City, 95

HRs: Keith Little, Houston, 30
Wins: Tom Bowers, Dallas, 20
SOs: Larry Sherry, Ft. Worth, 146
ERA: Murray Wall, Dallas, 1.79

A Eastern League
President: Thomas H. Richardson

Standings	W	L	Pct.	GB	Attend.	Manager
Binghamton Triplets (7)	85	55	.607	—	94,492	Steve Souchock
Schenectady Blue Jays (14)..	83	57	.593	2	59,522	Dick Carter
Reading Indians (4)	74	66	.529	11	95,528	Jo Jo White
Albany Senators (2).............	66	73	.475	18½	50,956	Eddie Popowski
Syracuse/Allentown Chiefs# ..	56	84	.400	29	68,110	Frank Calo
Springfield Giants (13)	55	84	.396	29½	133,140	Mike McCormick/Ray Murray

#Syracuse moved to Allentown July 13.

Playoffs: Albany 3 games, Binghamton 2; Reading 3 games, Schenectady 0.
Finals: Reading 3 games, Albany 1.

All-Star Team: 1B-Matthew Daskalakis, Albany; **2B**-Bob Deakin, Binghamton; **3B**-Ramon Conde, Springfield; **SS**-Paul Jones, Reading; **OF**-Deron Johnson, Binghamton; Felipe Alou, Springfield; Dave Mann, Reading; **C**-Frank Biskup, Reading; Lamar North, Binghamton; **P**-Ed Dick, Binghamton; Leverette Spencer, Allentown.

BA: Dick McCarthy, Albany, .327
Runs: Deron Johnson, Binghamton, 103
Hits: Dave Mann, Reading, 156
RBIs: Frank Leja, Binghamton, 117

HRs: Deron Johnson, Binghamton, 26
Wins: Ed Dick, Binghamton, 18
SOs: Ed Dick, Binghamton, 204
ERA: Bill Slack, Albany, 2.24

A South Atlantic League
President: Bill Terry

Standings	W	L	Pct.	GB	Attend.	Manager
Augusta Tigers (5)..............	98	56	.636	—	71,253	Bill Adair
Charlotte Hornets (8).........	86	67	.562	11½	87,962	Gene Verble
Savannah Redlegs (11).......	81	72	.529	16½	84,838	James Brown
Knoxville Smokies (1)........	81	73	.526	17	97,751	George Staller
Columbus Foxes (16)..........	81	73	.526	17	68,193	Skeeter Newsome
Jacksonville Braves (12).....	76	78	.494	22	67,184	Mickey Owen/Grady Wilson/ Joe Just
Columbia Gems (6)	59	95	.383	39	39,536	Ernie White
Macon Dodgers (9).............	53	101	.344	45	47,902	Goldie Holt

Playoffs: Augusta 2 games, Savannah 0; Charlotte 2 games, Knoxville 0.
Finals: Charlotte 2 games, Augusta 1.

All-Star Team: 1B-Ray Barker, Knoxville; **2B**-Ed Charles, Savannah; **3B**-Curt Flood, Savannah; **SS**-Gene Verble, Charlotte; **OF**-Bernie Mateosky, Augusta; Tom St. John, Savannah; Drew Gilbert, Savannah; **C**-Joseph Montalvo, Charlotte; **Util**-Kent Hadley, Augusta; George Alusik, Augusta; **P**-Jerry Cade, Macon; Ron Rozman, Augusta; **MVP**-Bernie Mateosky, Augusta; **Manager**-Bill Adair, Augusta.

BA: Tom St. John, Savannah, .326
Runs: Curt Flood, Savannah, 98
Hits: Ray Barker, Knoxville, 174
RBIs: Ray Barker, Knoxville, 97
HRs: Jacques Monette, Knoxville/ Jacksonville, 25

Wins: Matt Saban, Charlotte, 16
Angel Oliva, Charlotte, 16
Federico Olivo, Jacksonville, 16
SOs: Bill Smith, Columbus, 196
ERA: Ron Rozman, Augusta, 1.64

A Western League
President: O'Neal M. Hobbs

Standings	W	L	Pct.	GB	Attend.	Manager
Lincoln Chiefs (15)............	98	56	.636	—	100,190	Larry Shepard
Amarillo Gold Sox..............	97	57	.630	1	102,210	Eddie Bockman

	87	64	.576	9½	88,014	Red Smith/Bill Dossey
Topeka Hawks (12)	87	64	.576	9½	88,014	Red Smith/Bill Dossey
Sioux City Soos	71	82	.464	26½	46,851	Ken Landenberger
Colorado Springs Sky Sox (3).	68	86	.442	30	45,184	Ira Hutchinson
Albuquerque Dukes.............	66	88	.429	32	92,236	Nick Cullop/Hal Toso
Pueblo Dodgers (9).............	66	88	.429	32	40,887	Ray Hathaway
Des Moines Demons (10)...	60	92	.395	37	79,965	Lou Stringer/Herschel Martin

Playoffs: None.

All-Star Team: 1B-Bob Pascal, Des Moines; **2B**-Chuck Cottier, Topeka; **3B**-Mike Krsnich, Topeka; **SS**-Ray Webster, Amarillo; **OF**-Leonard Williams, Topeka; Chuck Coles, Albuquerque; Al Pinkston, Amarillo; **C**-Clay Dalrymple, Amarillo; **Util**-Jim McDaniel, Topeka; Gene Sheets, Colorado Springs; **P**-Kenneth Yoke, Amarillo; Joe Gibbon, Lincoln; John Stadnicki, Topeka; Hugh Blanton, Amarillo; **Manager**-Eddie Bockman, Amarillo.

BA: Sammy Miley, Lincoln, .374
Runs: Ray Webster, Amarillo, 136
Hits: Chuck Coles, Albuquerque, 208
RBIs: Al Pinkston, Amarillo, 133

HRs: Leonard Williams, Topeka, 43
Wins: John Stadnicki, Topeka, 23
SOs: Dave Stenhouse, Des Moines, 184
ERA: Hugh Blanton, Amarillo, 2.86

B Big State League
President: Hal Sayles

Standings	W	L	Pct.	GB	Attend.	Manager
Victoria Rosebuds**(9)......	75	49	.605	—	42,378	Lou Rochelli
Corpus Christi Clippers*(15)...	69	58	.543	7½	56,871	Joe Just/Jack Wilkinson
Beaumont Pirates (12)........	61	63	.492	14	56,342	Monty Basgall
Abilene Blue Sox (6)..........	61	66	.480	15½	29,995	Burl Storie
Port Arthur/ Temple Redlegs@(11).....	48	56	.462	NA	25,484	Al Barillari
Wichita Falls Spudders#.......	4	26	.133	NA	2,558	Jack Wilkinson/Jodie Beeler

#Wichita Falls disbanded May 23.
@Port Arthur moved to Temple May 30; Temple disbanded August 20.

Playoff: Victoria 4 games, Corpus Christi 1.

All-Star Team: 1B-Tony Washington, Beaumont; **2B**-Don Domenichelli, Victoria; **3B**-William Robertson, Victoria; **SS**-Gilberto Valentin, Abilene; **OF**-Don Miles, Victoria; Chuck Buheller, Beaumont; Nate Peeples, Corpus Christi; **C**-Ronald Henry, Victoria; Dan Gatta, Victoria; **P**-Roy "Tex" Sanner, Victoria; John Bober, Abilene; Chris Nicolosi, Victoria; Dave Wickersham, Beaumont; **MVP**-Don Miles, Victoria; **Manager**-Monty Basgall, Beaumont.

BA: Tony Washington, Beaumont, .356
Runs: Nate Peeples, Corpus Christi, 116
Hits: Tony Washington, Beaumont, 179
RBIs: Nate Peeples, Corpus Christi, 99

HRs: Don Miles, Victoria, 28
Wins: Chris Nicolosi, Victoria, 21
SOs: Chris Nicolosi, Victoria, 208
ERA: Dave Wickersham, Beaumont, 1.95

B Carolina League
President: J.C. "Bill" Jessup

Standings	W	L	Pct.	GB	Attend.	Manager
Durham Bulls*(5)...............	79	61	.564	—	46,848	Bob Mavis
High Point-Thomasville Hi-Toms**(14)	79	61	.564	—	46,755	Frank Lucchesi
Greensboro Patriots (2).......	76	64	.543	3	49,798	Len Okrie
Winston-Salem Red Birds (16)	72	68	.514	7	101,000	George Kissell
Danville Leafs (13).............	63	77	.450	16	61,987	Dave Garcia/Mike McCormick
Kinston Eagles/ Wilson Tobs#(8).............	51	89	.364	28	51,500	Pete Suder

#Kinston moved to Wilson May 11.

Playoff: Durham 4 games, High Point-Thomasville 3.

All-Star Team: 1B-Inocencio Rodriguez, Danville; **2B**-Billy Joe Ford, Hi-Toms; **3B**-Leroy Bradley, Greensboro; **SS**-Frank Kostro, Durham; **OF**-Fred Van Dusen, Hi-Toms; Bob Perry, Danville; Bubba Morton, Durham; **C**-Dick Harris, Hi-Toms; Jack Feller, Durham; **Util**-Fred Harrington, Hi-Toms; Gene Oliver, Winston-Salem; **P**-Reggie Lee, Danville; David Reed, Durham; Arthur Hirst, Hi-Toms; George Moton, Winston-Salem; Bill Lore, Greensboro; **MVP**-Fred Van Dusen, Hi-Toms; **Manager**-Bob Mavis, Durham.

BA: Eddie Logan, Hi-Toms, .327
Runs: Inocencio Rodriguez, Danville, 109
Hits: Frank Kostro, Durham, 167
RBIs: Inocencio Rodriguez, Danville, 114

HRs: Gene Oliver, Winston-Salem, 30
Bob Perry, Danville, 30
Wins: George Moton, Winston-Salem, 18
SOs: David Reed, Durham, 200
ERA: David Reed, Durham, 2.04

B Northwest League
President: James M. Fleishman

Standings	W	L	Pct.	GB	Attend.	Manager
Eugene Emeralds*	77	58	.570	—	78,639	Hugh Luby
Wenatchee Chiefs**(11).....	77	59	.566	½	59,773	Don Lundberg/Bert Haas
Yakima Bears	69	66	.511	8	56,718	Hub Kittle
Salem Senators	69	67	.507	8½	63,029	Bill Brenner
Lewiston Broncs (14).........	58	78	.426	19½	47,102	Hillis Layne
Tri-City Braves	57	79	.419	20½	54,761	Don Pries

Playoffs: Wenatchee 4 games, Eugene 3.

All-Star Team: 1B-Herbert Anderson, Wenatchee/Yakima; **2B**-Ellis Burton, Tri-City; **3B**-Hillis Layne, Lewiston; **SS**-John Keller, Eugene; **OF**-Donald Frailey, Eugene; John Dunn, Salem; Herman Lewis, Yakima; **C**-Don Lundberg, Wenatchee; **Util**-Melvin Krause, Eugene; Daniel Holden, Eugene; **P**-James Bailey, Wenatchee; Charles Lybeck, Salem; **Manager**-Hugh Luby, Eugene.

BA: Karl Kuehl, Salem, .347
Runs: Joe Jacobs, Lewiston, 114
Hits: Carl Porter, Tri-City, 165
RBIs: Herman Lewis, Yakima, 114

HRs: Ellis Burton, Tri-City, 23
Wins: Ollie Brantley, Eugene, 22
SOs: Tom Gibson, Wenatchee/Salem, 186
ERA: James Bailey, Wenatchee, 1.92

B Southwestern League
President: W.J. Green

Standings	W	L	Pct.	GB	Attend.	Manager
Hobbs Sports	73	52	.584	—	21,840	Thurman Tucker
Ballinger Westerners	69	56	.552	4	16,542	Tony York
Carlsbad Potashers	65	54	.546	5	29,769	Jodie Phipps
Midland/Lamesa Indians$(8)	45	79	.363	27½	19,212	John Welaj/Hank O'Neal
Clovis Redlegs@(11)	36	12	.750	NA	3,405	Bert Haas
El Paso Texans+	33	45	.423	NA	13,260	James Basso
Pampa Oilers/						
San Angelo Colts#+	32	44	.421	NA	8,916	Allen Cross
Plainview Ponies@	16	27	.372	NA	5,321	Art Bowland

#Pampa moved to San Angelo May 16.
@Clovis and Plainview disbanded June 16.
+El Paso and San Angelo disbanded July 17.
$Midland moved to Lamesa August 1.

Playoffs: None.

BA: John Spicuzza, Hobbs, .388
Runs: Raymond Patterson, Carlsbad, 125
Hits: John Spicuzza, Hobbs, 193
RBIs: John Spicuzza, Hobbs, 130
HRs: Raymond Patterson, Carlsbad, 34

Wins: Robert Leach, Ballinger, 19
Eugene Lippold, Ballinger, 19
SOs: Eugene Lippold, Ballinger, 179
ERA: Manuel Fierro, Hobbs, 2.94

B Three-I League
President: Hal Totten

Standings	W	L	Pct.	GB	Attend.	Manager
Evansville Braves (12)	81	49	.623	—	54,295	Bob Coleman
Peoria Chiefs (7)	80	49	.620	½	54,737	Vern Hoscheit
Davenport DavSox (3)	65	65	.500	16	79,478	Frank Scalzi
Burlington Bees (10)	57	71	.445	23	58,771	Ken Raffensberger
Keokuk Kernels (4)	55	74	.426	25½	35,028	Pinky May
Cedar Rapids Raiders (9)	49	79	.383	31	54,717	Danny Ozark

Playoffs: None.

All-Star Team: 1B-Billy Smith, Evansville; **2B**-Anthony Asaro, Peoria; **3B**-George Holder, Evansville; **SS**-William Davidson, Peoria; **OF**-Ray Reed, Evansville; Jim McAnany, Davenport; Horace Garner, Evansville; **C**-Jim Koranda, Cedar Rapids; Tom Tarrantino, Peoria; **Util**-Rod Kanehl, Peoria; **P**-Henry Hemmerly, Evansville; Peter Olsen, Keokuk; Don Nichols, Peoria; Noel Mickelson, Evansville; **MVP**-Don Nichols, Peoria; **Rookie of the Year**-William Davidson, Peoria; **Manager**-Vern Hoscheit, Peoria.

BA: Horace Garner, Evansville, .334
Runs: Billy Smith, Evansville, 107
Hits: George Holder, Evansville, 148
RBIs: Horace Garner, Evansville, 100
HRs: Jim Koranda, Cedar Rapids, 31
Wins: Don Nichols, Peoria, 20
SOs: Hal Trosky, Jr., Davenport, 204
ERA: Don Nichols, Peoria, 2.09

C Arizona-Mexico League
President: Charles S. Hollinger

Standings	W	L	Pct.	GB	Attend.	Manager
Phoenix Stars***(1)	89	48	.650	—	76,063	Bob Hooper
Cananea Mineros	76	56	.576	10½	103,571	Claudio Solano/Daniel Rios
Douglas Copper Kings (15)	68	69	.496	21	27,949	Bob Clear
Las Vegas Wranglers	62	74	.456	26½	35,804	Red Marion
Tucson Cowboys	62	77	.446	28	28,157	Don Jameson/Ernest Choukalos
Mexicali Eagles#	51	84	.378	37	54,591	Artie Wilson/Manuel Magallon

#Mexicali disbanded September 6 and forfeited 10 remaining games.

Playoffs: None.

BA: Claudio Solano, Cananea, .402
Runs: Barry Shetrone, Phoenix, 151
Hits: Barry Shetrone, Phoenix, 199
RBIs: Claudio Solano, Cananea, 159
HRs: Claudio Solano, Cananea, 41
Wins: Candido Andrade, Tucson, 20
Bob Clear, Douglas, 20
SOs: Candido Andrade, Tucson, 260
ERA: Donald Bruns, Phoenix, 3.59

C California League
President: Edward J. Mulligan

Standings	W	L	Pct.	GB	Attend.	Manager
Visalia Redlegs***(11)	84	51	.622	—	52,470	Bruce Edwards
Reno Silver Sox (9)	79	59	.572	6½	56,702	Ray Perry
Modesto Reds (7)	75	65	.536	11½	40,008	Damon Phillips
Salinas Packers (12)	68	67	.504	16	40,876	Leo Thomas/Bill Krueger
San Jose JoSox (15)	67	68	.496	17	36,003	Dick Whitman
Bakersfield Bears (10)	64	75	.460	22	54,962	Dick Wilson/Babe Herman
Stockton Ports	61	79	.436	25½	41,683	Roy Partee
Fresno Sun Sox	52	86	.377	33½	30,412	Roland LeBlanc

Playoffs: Reno 2 games, Visalia 0; Salinas 2 games, Modesto 1.
Finals: Salinas 3 games, Reno 1.

All-Star Team: 1B-Jerome Stack, Visalia; **2B**-Damon Phillips, Modesto; **3B**-Ray Perry, Reno; **SS**-James Dougherty, San Jose; **OF**-Fran Boniar, Reno; Vada Pinson, Visalia; Thomas Humber, Reno; **C**-William Gilmore, Salinas; **P**-Bill Dial, San Jose; Robert Giallombardo, Reno; Pete Hernandez, Visalia; William Cornell, Modesto; **MVP**-Vada Pinson, Visalia; **Rookie of the Year**-John Callison, Bakersfield; **Manager**-Roy Partee, Stockton.

BA: Fran Boniar, Reno, .436
Runs: Vada Pinson, Visalia, 165
Hits: Vada Pinson, Visalia, 209
RBIs: Fran Boniar, Reno, 138
HRs: Dick Wilson, Bakersfield, 27
Wins: Pete Hernandez, Visalia, 25
SOs: Charles Drummond, Stockton, 251
ERA: Bill Dial, San Jose, 2.12

C Central Mexican League
President: Anuar Canavati

Standings	W	L	Pct.	GB	Attend.	Manager
Chihuahua Dorados	62	38	.620	—	67,896	Manuel Arroyo
Saltillo Saraperos	55	45	.550	7	58,194	Domingo Santana/ Jose Luis St. Claire/ Gustavo Bello
Durango-Laguna Alacranes	52	48	.520	10	86,538	Virgilio Arteaga
Ciudad Juarez Indios	49	51	.490	13	66,305	Syd Cohen/Jesus Diaz
Fresnillo Rojos	43	55	.439	18	59,094	Preston Gomez/ Augustin Bejerano/ Jose Luis Garcia/Bill Wright
Aguascalientes Tigres	37	61	.378	24	42,946	Armando Flores/Chile Gomez

Playoffs: None.

All-Star Team: 1B-Pedro Ramirez, Saltillo; **2B**-Juan Arias, Fresnillo; **3B**-Rogelio Vargas, Fresnillo; **SS**-Gilberto Villarreal, Chihuahua; **OF**-Silvio Meza, Saltillo; Francisco Jaime, Saltillo; Norlden Williams, Chihuahua; **C**-Jose Luis St. Claire, Saltillo; Mario Flores, Durango-Laguna; **P**-Marcelino Solis, Saltillo; Ruben Rendon, Chihuahua.

BA: Juan Arias, Fresnillo, .420
Runs: Luis Casablanca, Chihuahua, 105
Hits: Silvio Meza, Saltillo, 153
RBIs: Silvio Meza, Saltillo, 122
HRs: Juan Hernandez, Durango-Laguna, 27
Wins: Pete Hernandez, Visalia, 17
SOs: Antonio Dicochea, Chihuahua, 157
ERA: Jaime Ochoa, Aguascalientes, 3.78

C Evangeline League
President: Ray Mullins

Standings	W	L	Pct.	GB	Attend.	Manager
Alexandria Aces**(7)	68	43	.613	—	52,937	Ken Silvestri
Crowley Millers (6)	63	47	.573	4½	17,779	Everett Robinson
Thibodaux Senators	45	66	.405	23	28,653	Bill Dossey/Henry Robinson
Lake Charles Giants	43	67	.391	24½	15,589	Whitey McDowell
Lafayette Oilers*#(10)	36	21	.632	NA	9,567	Walt Dixon
Baton Rouge Rebels#	24	35	.407	NA	8,297	John Streza

#Baton Rouge and Lafayette disbanded June 20.

Playoffs: None.

All-Star Team: 1B-Joe McElroy, Lake Charles; **2B**-Dave "Red" Irby, Alexandria; **3B**-Henry MacKenzie, Crowley; **SS**-Joseph Mueller, Lake Charles; **OF**-Claude Horn, Crowley; James Nisewonger, Thibodaux; Jack Davis, Alexandria; **C**-Aaron Silvera, Crowley; **P**-Bob Riesener, Alexandria; Donald Gorrondona, Lake Charles.

BA: Claude Horn, Crowley, .349
Runs: Dave "Red" Irby, Alexandria, 98
Hits: Joe McElroy, Lake Charles, 141
RBIs: Joe McElroy, Lake Charles, 92
HRs: Dave "Red" Irby, Alexandria, 26
Wins: Bob Riesener, Alexandria, 20
SOs: Donald Gorrondona, Lake Charles, 161
ERA: Bob Riesener, Alexandria, 2.16
Pct: Bob Riesener, Alexandria, 1.000, 20-0

C Northern League
President: Herman D. White

Standings	W	L	Pct.	GB	Attend.	Manager
Duluth-Superior White Sox*(3)	73	52	.584	—	70,423	Joe Hauser
Winnipeg Goldeyes**(16)	69	53	.566	2½	86,214	Vern Benson
Eau Claire Braves (12)	70	55	.560	3	34,703	Gordon Maltzberger
Fargo-Moorhead Twins (4)	65	57	.533	6½	52,819	Frank Tornay/Ken Blackman
St. Cloud Rox (13)	59	63	.484	12½	31,991	Pete Pavlick
Wausau Lumberjacks (11)	52	69	.430	19	19,044	Walt Novick
Aberdeen Pheasants (1)	51	70	.421	20	47,312	Billy Capps/Barney Lutz
Grand Forks Chiefs (15)	52	72	.419	20½	33,808	Al Kubski/Jack Paepke

Playoff: Winnipeg 2 games, Duluth-Superior 1.

All-Star Team: 1B-Walt Matthews, Winnipeg; **2B**-Charles Lehmann, Duluth-Superior; **3B**-Gene Elliott, Fargo-Moorhead; **SS**-Juan Guzman, Eau Claire; **OF**-Richard Lombardi, Duluth-Superior; Don Brown, Winnipeg; James Miller, St. Cloud; Sam Hill, Duluth-Superior; **C**-Donald Whitcomb, Grand Forks; Alberto Alvarez, Wausau; **P**-Joe Hoerner, Duluth-Superior; David Tyriver, Fargo-Moorhead.

BA: Richard Lombardi, Duluth-Superior, .327
Runs: Don Brown, Winnipeg, 98
Hits: Don Brown, Winnipeg, 152
RBIs: Walt Matthews, Winnipeg, 100

HRs: Harry Huber, Fargo-Moorhead, 22
Wins: Harold Byfuss, Winnipeg, 17
SOs: Robert Dennison, St. Cloud, 161
ERA: Richard Sovde, St. Cloud, 1.95

C Pioneer League
President: Claude Engberg

Standings	W	L	Pct.	GB	Attend.	Manager
Billings Mustangs**(16)	79	47	.627	—	83,233	Eddie Lyons
Idaho Falls Russets (5)	73	53	.579	6	42,801	Al Lakeman
Pocatello Athletics (6)	64	62	.508	15	36,035	Vincent Plumbo
Missoula Timberjacks (8)...	62	64	.492	17	47,052	Jack McKeon
Salt Lake City Bees*(14)...	61	64	.488	17½	80,095	Cliff Dapper
Magic Valley Cowboys (10)....	60	66	.476	19	36,274	Burdette Thurlby/Walt Dixon
Boise Braves (12)	56	70	.444	23	61,052	George McQuinn
Great Falls Dodgers (9)	48	77	.384	30½	47,091	Jack Banta

Playoff: Billings 3 games, Salt Lake City 2.

All-Star Team: 1B-Fred Hopke, Salt Lake City; **2B**-Lou Vassie, Salt Lake City; **3B**-Bob Sadowski, Billings; **SS**-Donald Dantoni, Missoula; **OF**-Duke Carmel, Billings; Robert Jacoby, Boise; Jackson Queen, Idaho Falls; **C**-Anthony Canizzo, Pocatello; **P**-Ernest Evans, Billings; Richard Schultz, Missoula.

BA: Richard Greco, Missoula, .364
Runs: Duke Carmel, Billings, 118
Lou Vassie, Salt Lake City, 118
Hits: Glen Plaster, Great Falls, 177
RBIs: Duke Carmel, Billings, 121

HRs: Richard Greco, Missoula, 30
Wins: Richard Schultz, Missoula, 21
SOs: Winston Brown, Boise, 217
ERA: Ernest Evans, Billings, 2.95

D Alabama-Florida League
President: Sam C. Smith

Standings	W	L	Pct.	GB	Attend.	Manager
Montgomery Rebels (5)......	68	52	.567	—	28,298	Stubby Overmire
Graceville Oilers (11)	66	54	.550	2	23,098	Bob Wellman/Charles Grant
Panama City Fliers..............	59	61	.492	9	21,876	James Deery
Ft. Walton Beach Jets (8) ...	56	64	.467	12	15,557	Neal Cobb
Pensacola Dons....................	56	64	.467	12	43,882	Lou Fitzgerald/Rex Ford
Selma Cloverleafs (13)	55	65	.458	13	24,234	Buddy Kerr

Playoffs: Panama City 4 games, Montgomery 3; Graceville 4 games, Ft. Walton Beach 2.
Finals: Graceville 3 games, Panama City 3, teams were declared co-champions when bad weather cancelled the last game.

All-Star Team: 1B-Bob Wellman, Graceville; **2B**-James Deery, Panama City; **3B**-Charles Strange, Montgomery; **SS**-Norman Manning, Montgomery; **OF**-Al Jakubowski, Graceville; Bob Zuccarini, Pensacola; Henry Marockie, Ft. Walton Beach; **C**-James Hay, Panama City; William Maupin, Montgomery; **P**-Robert "Bo" Belinsky, Pensacola; Bill Beck, Graceville.

BA: Bob Zuccarini, Pensacola, .352
Runs: Bob Zuccarini, Pensacola, 111
Hits: Al Jakubowski, Graceville, 163
RBIs: Bob Wellman, Graceville, 113
HRs: Bob Wellman, Graceville, 30

Wins: Bill Kakuske, Graceville, 19
Bill Beck, Graceville, 19
SOs: Bill Kakuske, Graceville, 205
ERA: Bill Kakuske, Graceville, 2.26

D Appalachian League
President: Chauncey De Vault

Standings	W	L	Pct.	GB	Attend.	Manager
Bluefield Dodgers (9)	47	20	.701	—	17,264	Jimmy Bragan
Johnson City Phillies (14)..	46	23	.667	2	20,712	Ben Taylor
Salem Rebels (15)...............	38	30	.559	9½	18,007	Larry Dorton
Wytheville Cardinals (16) ..	32	38	.457	16½	26,027	John Grodzicki
Pulaski Cubs (10)................	23	47	.329	25½	10,321	Vedie Himsl/Jim Bottomley/Rube Wilson/Burdette Thurly
Kingsport Orioles (1)..........	21	49	.300	27½	13,519	Enid Drake

Playoffs: None.

All-Star Team: 1B-Jim Nidds, Johnson City; **2B**-James Hatfield, Johnson City; **3B**-Anthony Nicotera, Salem; **3B**-Dick Shepler, Johnson City; **SS**-Bobby Wine, Johnson City; **OF**-Ronald Zander, Kingsport; Ken Fisher, Pulaski; Al Fantuzzi, Bluefield; **C**-Duane Emaar, Salem; **Util**-Frank Burgey, Bluefield; Felix Pizarro, Salem; **P**-Jack Hamilton, Wytheville; Tom Donovan, Bluefield; **Manager**-John Grodzicki, Wytheville.

BA: Al Fantuzzi, Bluefield, .377
Runs: Andy Cockrell, Salem, 68
Mike Ricigliano, Bluefield, 68
Hits: Ken Fisher, Pulaski, 93
RBIs: Duane Emaar, Salem, 82

HRs: Ken Clark, Wytheville, 11
Wins: Jim Duckworth, Bluefield, 10
SOs: Tom Donovan, Bluefield, 141
ERA: Bob George, Johnson City, 2.31

D Florida State League
President: John Krider

Standings	W	L	Pct.	GB	Attend.	Manager
Tampa Tarpons**(14)	84	54	.609	—	46,601	Charlie Gassaway
Daytona Beach Islanders (16)..	84	56	.600	1	44,897	Homer Ray Wilson
Palatka Redlegs*(11).........	78	62	.557	7	32,944	John Vander Meer
St. Petersburg Saints (7)	72	67	.518	12½	55,588	Nesbit Wilson
Leesburg Braves (12)..........	64	75	.460	20½	25,254	Tom Giordano
Cocoa Indians (4)................	62	76	.449	22	26,560	Henry Majeski/Jim Gruzdis
Gainesville G-Men	60	78	.435	24	22,052	Red Dulaney
Orlando Flyers (5)	51	87	.370	33	26,581	Marland Doolittle/John Rose

Playoff: Tampa 3 games, Palatka 1.

All-Star Team: 1B-Nesbit Wilson, St. Petersburg; **2B**-Homer Ray Wilson, Daytona Beach; **3B**-Robert Whitekiller, Daytona Beach; **SS**-Neal Skeeters, Palatka; **OF**-Larry Helms, Palatka; Dario Rubensteing, Tampa; Tony Curry, Tampa; **C**-Charles Fields, Tampa; **Util**-Chuck Hiller, Cocoa; **P**-Harry Coe, Tampa; Julio Guerra, Cocoa; **Manager**-John Vander Meer, Palatka.

BA: Nesbit Wilson, St. Petersburg, .373
Runs: Neal Skeeters, Palatka, 111
Hits: Nesbit Wilson, St. Petersburg, 192
RBIs: Larry Helms, Palatka, 112
HRs: German Pizzaro, Gainesville, 16

Wins: Harry Coe, Tampa, 26
Julio Guerra, Cocoa, 26
SOs: Julio Guerra, Cocoa, 308
ERA: Harry Coe, Tampa, 1.37

D Georgia-Florida League
President: W.T. Anderson

Standings	W	L	Pct.	GB	Attend.	Manager
Albany Cardinals**(16)	84	55	.604	—	38,174	Chase Riddle
Valdosta Dodgers*(5).........	77	62	.554	7	35,910	Stan Wasiak
Thomasville Tigers (9)	71	68	.511	13	25,438	Rudy Rufer/Leon Hamilton/Roger Wright
Fitzgerald Orioles (1)..........	65	74	.468	19	18,046	Earl Weaver
Moultrie/ Brunswick Phillies#(14) ..	62	77	.446	22	28,987	Ben Zientara
Waycross Braves (12).........	58	81	.417	26	27,226	Michael Fandozzi

#Moultrie moved to Brunswick June 1.

Playoff: Albany 3 games, Valdosta 2.

All-Star Team: 1B-Michael Stopchuck, Brunswick; **2B**-Albert Morris, Albany; **3B**-James Cross, Valdosta; **SS**-George Scott, Thomasville; **OF**-Jim Hickman, Albany; Ronald Rossi, Thomasville; Danny Briner, Valdosta; Donald Brown, Albany; **C**-Jack Bowen, Valdosta; William DeGraaf, Albany; **Util**-Ronald Sockman, Fitzgerald; **P**-Fred Gladding, Valdosta; Siebert Scott, Thomasville; Clarence Ingram, Albany; William Fincher, Fitzgerald; **Manager**-Chase Riddle, Albany.

BA: Michael Fandozzi, Waycross, .422
Runs: Bob Burright, Thomasville, 115
Hits: Michael Fandozzi, Waycross, 189
RBIs: Jim Hickman, Albany, 113

HRs: Jim Hickman, Albany, 26
Wins: Siebert Scott, Thomasville, 20
SOs: Richard Sheldon, Valdosta, 213
ERA: Fred Gladding, Valdosta, 2.12

D Midwest League
President: C.C. "Dutch" Hoffman

Standings	W	L	Pct.	GB	Attend.	Manager
Kokomo Dodgers (9)	77	50	.606	—	53,690	Pete Reiser
Decatur Commodores*(16) ..	76	51	.598	1	52,660	Al Unser
Dubuque Packers (3)	73	51	.589	2½	91,647	George Noga
Michigan City White Caps (13)..............	68	57	.544	8	25,484	Richie Klaus
Clinton Pirates**(15).........	56	68	.452	19½	70,597	Stan Wentzel
Lafayette Red Sox (2).........	55	67	.451	19½	32,667	Ken Deal
Paris Lakers (10).................	51	73	.411	24½	28,000	Verlon Walker
Mattoon Athletics (6)..........	43	82	.344	33	22,000	Lew Krausse

Playoffs: Clinton 2 games, Dubuque 0; Decatur 2 games, Kokomo 0.
Finals: Decatur 2 games, Clinton 0.

All-Star Team: 1B-Tom Harkness, Kokomo; **2B**-Galen Williams, Decatur; **3B**-John Riley, Clinton; **SS**-Eugene Klyczek, Dubuque; **OF**-Donald Gordon, Dubuque; Thomas Paddock, Paris; Tommy Davis, Kokomo; **C**-Charles Staniland, Decatur; John Orsino, Michigan City; **Util**-Lawrence Cutler, Clinton; Manny Mota, Michigan City; **P**-William Rouse, Dubuque; Dick Lines, Clinton; Emerson Unzicker, Kokomo; William Garcia, Decatur.

BA: Tommy Davis, Kokomo, .357
Runs: Tommy Davis, Kokomo, 115
Hits: Tommy Davis, Kokomo, 185
RBIs: Donald Gordon, Dubuque, 116

HRs: Donald Gordon, Dubuque, 22
Wins: Emerson Unzicker, Kokomo, 20
SOs: Harold Morris, Mattoon, 202
ERA: Dick Lines, Clinton, 1.80

D Nebraska State League
President: Mike Hollinger

Standings	W	L	Pct.	GB	Attend.	Manager
Grand Island Athletics (6) ..	33	22	.600	—	26,982	Art Mazmanian
Holdrege White Sox (3).......	33	23	.589	½	21,581	Frank Parenti
Lexington Red Sox (2)	33	23	.589	½	24,218	Jack Kaiser
Kearney Yankees (7)	30	26	.536	3½	23,349	Randy Gumpert
Hastings Giants (13)	29	26	.527	4	21,863	Leo Schrall
McCook Braves (12)	27	29	.482	6½	25,844	Bill Steinecke
Superior Senators (8)	27	29	.482	6½	19,796	Charles Ray Baker
North Platte Indians (4)	11	45	.196	22½	21,207	Rudy York

All-Star Team: 1B-Milt Campo, Kearney; **2B**-Tony Christopher, Holdrege; **3B**-James Wasem, Holdrege; **SS**-Phil Linz, Kearney; **OF**-Jackie Creed, Lexington; Robert Boyd,

1957

Superior; James McClain, Hastings; **C**-Tony DeGennaro, Grand Island; **P**-Phil Groth, Holdrege; Wayne Coughtry, Lexington.

BA: James Wasem, Holdrege, .366
Runs: Don Bonomini, Holdrege, 58
Hits: Jackie Creed, Lexington, 71
RBIs: Milt Campo, Kearney, 59

HRs: Milt Campo, Kearney, 17
Wins: Wayne Coughtry, Lexington, 11
SOs: Leonardo Ferguson, Kearney, 149
ERA: Leonardo Ferguson, Kearney, 1.68

D New York-Pennsylvania League
President: Vincent M. McNamara

Standings	W	L	Pct.	GB	Attend.	Manager
Wellsville Braves (12)	74	43	.632	—	28,299	Alex Monchak
Erie Sailors (5)	70	47	.598	4	54,923	Charles Kress
Corning Red Sox (2)	65	52	.556	9	38,526	Elmer Yoter
Batavia Indians (4)	58	59	.496	16	31,617	Don Richmond
Olean Oilers (14)	52	65	.444	22	28,045	Paul Owens
Elmira Pioneers (8)	51	66	.436	23	40,203	Bill Brightwell
Bradford Beagles/ Hornell Redlegs#(11)	43	74	.368	31	14,963	Chip Shapiro/Earl Johnson/ Dave Bristol
Jamestown Falcons@(15)	28	35	.444	NA	15,027	Jack Paepke

#Bradford disbanded May 23 and was replaced by Hornell May 28.
@Jamestown disbanded June 25.

Playoffs: Batavia 2 games, Wellsville 1; Erie 2 games, Corning 1.
Finals: Erie 3 games, Batavia 1.

All-Star Team: 1B-Ken Kraynak, Batavia; **2B**-Joaquin Perez, Wellsville; **3B**-Thaddeus Brzenk, Erie; **SS**-Yogi Hergenrader, Corning; **OF**-Ray Withrow, Wellsville; Joseph Edgeley, Wellsville; Norman Bernard, Corning; **C**-Robert Rodgers, Erie; Stephen Herschner, Olean; **P**-Richard Griffith, Elmira; Luis DeLeon, Wellsville.

BA: Paul Owens, Olean, .407
Runs: Norman Bernard, Corning, 104
Hits: Ken Kraynak, Batavia, 157
RBIs: Richard Seelinger, Wellsville, 100
HRs: Tony Gonzales, Hornell, 22

Wins: Luis DeLeon, Wellsville, 17
    Gerald Lis, Batavia, 17
SOs: Richard Griffith, Elmira, 174
ERA: Luis DeLeon, Wellsville, 2.36

D Sooner State League
President: George Barr

Standings	W	L	Pct.	GB	Attend.	Manager
Paris Orioles (1)	74	51	.592	—	33,953	Barney Lutz/Billy Capps
Ardmore Cardinals (16)	74	52	.587	½	36,201	J.C. Dunn/Mike Ryba
Muskogee Giants (13)	71	55	.563	3½	21,253	Andy Gilbert
Shawnee Hawks (9)	64	62	.508	10½	22,301	Edward Serrano
Greenville Majors (7)	62	63	.496	12	23,066	Thomas Gott
Lawton Braves (12)	59	66	.472	15	15,605	Travis Jackson
Ponca City Cubs (10)	52	74	.413	22½	21,253	Don Biebel
Seminole Oilers (6)	46	79	.368	28	17,379	Lee Anthony

Playoffs: Paris 3 games, Shawnee 1; Ardmore 3 games, Muskogee 0.
Finals: Ardmore 4 games, Paris 0.

All-Star Team: 1B-William Rozich, Paris; **2B**-Bobby Knoop, Lawton; **3B**-Jim McKnight, Ardmore; **SS**-Ainsworth Yeomans, Muskogee; **OF**-Johnny Weekly, Muskogee; Billy Leon Williams, Ponca City; Bob Beattie, Paris; **C**-Wade Arnold, Shawnee; Richard Muffick, Greenville; **P**-Steve Barber, Paris; William Corrigan, Seminole; Harold DeMars, Lawton; Gerald Keller, Ardmore.

BA: Jim McKnight, Ardmore, .340
Runs: Dick Simpson, Paris, 116
Hits: Dick Simpson, Paris, 163
RBIs: Jim McKnight, Ardmore, 112

HRs: Bob Beattie, Paris, 25
Wins: Jack Curtis, Ponca City, 18
SOs: Jack Curtis, Ponca City, 219
ERA: John Jeanes, Paris, 2.41

1957 Interleague Post Season Play

World Series
Milwaukee (National) 4 games, New York (American) 3

Junior World Series
Denver (American Association) 4 games, Buffalo (International) 1
Total Attendance: 51,245

Dixie Series
Houston (Texas) 4 games, Atlanta (Southern Association) 2
Total Attendance: 20,120

1957 Major League Farm Systems

American League

1 Baltimore (8): Vancouver, San Antonio, Knoxville, Phoenix, Aberdeen, Kingsport, Fitzgerald, Paris.
2 Boston (7): San Francisco, Oklahoma City, Albany (NY), Greensboro, Lafayette (IN), Lexington, Corning.
3 Chicago (6): Indianapolis, Colorado Springs, Davenport, Duluth-Superior, Dubuque, Holdrege.
4 Cleveland (8): San Diego, Mobile, Reading, Keokuk, Fargo-Moorhead, Cocoa, North Platte, Batavia.
5 Detroit (9): Charleston, Birmingham, Augusta, Durham, Idaho Falls, Montgomery, Orlando, Valdosta, Erie.
6 Kansas City (9): Buffalo, Little Rock, Columbia, Abilene, Crowley, Pocatello, Mattoon, Grand Island, Seminole.
7 New York (10): Denver, Richmond, New Orleans, Binghamton, Peoria, Modesto, Alexandria, St. Petersburg, Kearney, Greenville (TX).
8 Washington (8): Chattanooga, Charlotte, Kinston/Wilson, Midland/Lamesa, Missoula, Ft. Walton Beach, Superior (NE), Elmira.

National League

9 Brooklyn (13): Los Angeles, St. Paul, Montreal, Macon, Pueblo, Victoria, Cedar Rapids, Reno, Great Falls, Bluefield, Thomasville, Kokomo, Shawnee.
10 Chicago (11): Portland, Memphis, Ft. Worth, Des Moines, Burlington, Bakersfield, Lafayette (LA), Magic Valley, Pulaski, Paris, Ponca City.
11 Cincinnati (12): Seattle, Havana, Nashville, Savannah, Port Arthur/Temple, Wenatchee, Clovis, Visalia, Wausau, Graceville, Palatka, Bradford/Hornell.
12 Milwaukee (15): Wichita, Atlanta, Austin, Jacksonville, Topeka, Beaumont, Evansville, Salinas, Eau Claire, Boise, Leesburg, Waycross, McCook, Wellsville, Lawton.
13 New York (9): Minneapolis, Dallas, Springfield, Danville, St. Cloud, Selma, Michigan City, Hastings, Muskogee.
14 Philadelphia (10): Miami, Tulsa, Schenectady, High Point-Thomasville, Lewiston, Salt Lake City, Johnson City, Tampa, Moultrie/Brunswick, Olean.
15 Pittsburgh (10): Hollywood, Columbus (OH), Lincoln, Corpus Christi, Douglas, San Jose, Grand Forks, Salem (VA), Clinton, Jamestown.
16 St. Louis (12): Omaha, Rochester, Houston, Columbus (GA), Winston-Salem, Winnipeg, Billings, Wytheville, Daytona Beach, Albany (GA), Decatur, Ardmore.

1957 No-Hitters

Date	Pitcher	Team	League	Opponent	Score
4-16	Stu Miller	Minneapolis	American Assoc.	Indianapolis	1-0 (6)
4-22	Bob Quinn	Danville	Carolina	Greensboro	7-2 (6)
5-2	Carl Thomas	Mobile	Southern Assoc.	Atlanta	2-0 (5)
5-3	David Tyriver	Fargo-Moorhead	Northern	Winnipeg	2-0
5-5	Fred Hoffman	Waycross	Georgia-Florida	Moultrie	1-0 (8)
5-12	Luis DeLeon	Wellsville	New York-Penn.	Elmira	4-1
5-16	Mauro Contreras	Ciudad Juarez	Central Mexican	Fresnillo	4-0
5-17	Fred Haddix	Corning	New York-Penn.	Wellsville	2-0 (6)
5-26	Peter Rubenacker	Thibodaux	Evangeline	Baton Rouge	2-0
5-26	Joe McClain/Bill Smith/ Dick Niesyto	Columbus	South Atlantic	Savannah	4-2 (7)
6-7	Albert McKinney/ Joe Hoerner	Duluth-Superior	Northern	Winnipeg	14-0
6-9	Martin Stabiner	Macon	South Atlantic	Columbus	1-0
6-10	Charles Smith	Greensboro	Carolina	Durham	2-0
6-10	Jose Lizondro	Dubuque	Midwest	Decatur	5-0 (5)
6-10	Donald McGue	Tampa	Florida State	Orlando	1-2 (7)
6-13	Andre Pleau	Orlando	Florida State	Daytona Beach	5-1 (7)
6-15	Vern Kindsfather	Salem	Northwest	Eugene	3-0 (P, 7)
6-19	Winston Brown	Boise	Pioneer	Billings	1-0 (7)
6-23	Ryne Duren	Denver	American Assoc.	Louisville	3-0 (7)
6-23	Jaime Ochoa	Aguascalientes	Central Mexican	Fresnillo	1-0 (7)
6-25	Frank Baumann	Oklahoma City	Texas	Ft. Worth	1-0
7-1	Murray Wall	Dallas	Texas	Ft. Worth	0-1
7-14	Gary Bell	Mobile	Southern Assoc.	Little Rock	4-0
8-7	Ivor Mink	Cedar Rapids	Three-I	Keokuk	2-0 (7)
8-8	Jack Hamilton	Wytheville	Appalachian	Kingsport	5-0 (7)
8-10	Les Temple	Graceville	Alabama-Florida	Panama City	7-0 (7)
8-12	Bobby Bolin	Michigan City	Midwest	Dubuque	11-0 (7)
8-15	Tom Butters	Eau Claire	Northern	Fargo-Moorhead	0-1 (7)
8-16	Ross Carter	Paris	Midwest	Michigan City	12-0
8-18	Kenneth Rollins	Paris	Midwest	Michigan City	12-0
8-20	Bob Keegan	Chicago	American	Washington	6-0
8-20	Dick Lines	Clinton	Midwest	Decatur	6-0 (7)
8-22	Vince DiGiulio/ Gene Cochran	Seminole	Sooner State	Greenville	3-2 (7)
8-30	Harry Coe	Tampa	Florida State	Orlando	2-0
9-2	Charles Wrinn	Jacksonville	South Atlantic	Columbus	10-0

Number in parentheses indicates innings if other than nine; "P" indicates perfect game.

THIS DATE IN MINOR LEAGUE HISTORY

May 6, 1957, Michigan City, Midwest League, scored 13 runs in the fifth to wallop Clinton 15-3.

May 9, 1957, Phoenix, Arizona-Mexico League, blanked Mexicali 29-0.

May 10, 1957, Topeka, Western League, established a new league record by smashing 10 straight hits in the eighth inning against Albuquerque in a 16-5 victory. The Hawks scored seven runs in the eighth and nine in the ninth.

May 19, 1957, Carlsbad, Southwestern League, outslugged Midland 26-22 in a 12-inning game. Catcher Ed Schlitz of Midland collected seven hits in eight trips.

May 23, 1957, Southpaw Jack O'Donnell of Atlanta, Southern League, won his fourth game in as many nights, all against Mobile.

May 23, 1957, Stockton, California League, committed 10 errors in a 10-2 loss to Salinas. Two nights earlier they had been charged with eight miscues in a 9-3 setback to Salinas.

May 23, 1957, Five flingers for Olean, New York-Pennsylvania League, passed 20 batters in a 13-5 loss to Elmira.

May 26, 1957, Cananea, Arizona-Mexico League, scored 17 runs in the seventh inning and swamped Douglas 30-9.

May 26, 1957, Las Vegas, Arizona-Mexico League, made 13 errors in a 12-6 loss to Douglas.

May 27, 1957, Three hurlers for Jamestown, New York-Pennsylvania League, hurlers issued 21 walks in a 16-6 loss to Wellsville, one shy of the league mark.

May 31, 1957, Jim Fitzgerald of Wellsville, New York-Pennsylvania League, scored seven runs in a 22-1 rout of Elmira.

June 1, 1957, Schenectady, Eastern League, scored 13 runs in the first inning and defeated Syracuse 18-7.

June 4, 1957, Roy Stotler of Jamestown, New York-Pennsylvania League, stole home in the 17th inning to give the Falcons a 2-1 victory over Corning in the third longest game in the league's 19-year history.

June 6, 1957, Stockton, California League, achieved the rarity of going through an inning without an official time at bat, although they scored a run. Manager Roy Partee, leading off the third inning, walked and Buck Kahler was hit by a pitch. Charlie Drummond moved the runners along with a sacrifice bunt. Bob Schurr then hit a sacrifice fly, scoring Partee; Kahler attempted to take third on the play but was thrown out to retire the side.

June 13, 1957, Outfielder Barry Shetrone of Phoenix, Arizona-Mexico League, was collared by Cananea after having hit safely in 33 straight games.

June 13, 1957, Jose "Diablo" Nunez, Fresnillo, Central Mexican League, smashed four consecutive home runs, plus a double, driving in ten runs in a game against Durango-Laguna. Fresnillo won the contest 23-7.

June 16, 1957, Catcher Dick Banes hit two homers and batted in seven runs in one inning and had ten runs batted in total as Cocoa, Florida State League, beat Orlando 27-1.

June 22, 1957, Los Angeles, Pacific Coast League, unloaded nine homers to bury Sacramento 22-5. Five circuit drives came in one inning.

June 22, 1957, Wendell Doss of Topeka, Western League, hurled nine no-hit innings and retired 25 consecutive batters over one stretch in a relief role, as the Hawks defeated Albuquerque 4-1 in 12 frames.

June 22, 1957, Stan Silcott of Corpus Christi, Big State League, won his 13th straight game.

June 26, 1957, Arnie Atkins of Birmingham, Southern League, retired 31 consecutive batters in a relief role in a 13-inning game with Mobile.

July 2, 1957, Mike Sinclair of Salem, Appalachian League, struck out 21 in a 7-3 win over Kingsport.

July 3, 1957, Don Gaffney, a 19-year-old catcher from Baltimore, made a resounding debut with Hornell, New York-Pennsylvania League, when he hit a grand slam on his first trip to the plate in Organized Ball.

July 9, 1957, The Salt Lake City Bees, Pioneer League, lost to Idaho Falls 8-0, after 14 straight victories.

July 9, 1957, Len Briles of Kearney, Nebraska State League, fanned 21 batters in a 9-4 victory over North Platte.

July 13, 1957, St. Cloud, Northern League, committed seven errors in one inning in a 13-0 loss to Eau Claire.

July 28, 1957, Wellsville, New York-Pennsylvania League, made seven home runs in walloping Hornell 28-7.

July 29, 1957, Wellsville, New York-Pennsylvania League, scored 11 runs in the sixth inning to outslug Olean 19-18, extending its winning streak to 14 consecutive games.

August 1, 1957, Glen Gorbous, former Reds and Phillies outfielder now with Omaha, American Association, heaved a baseball 445 feet, ten inches, setting a new world's record. The former mark was set on August 27, 1956, by Minneapolis outfielder Don Grate.

August 4, 1957, Mike Baxes of Buffalo, International League, hit two grand slams plus a double and a single for ten runs batted in during a 20-1 victory over Havana.

August 6, 1957, Walt Tyler, outfielder-first baseman with Tucson, Arizona-Mexico League, was collared by Cananea after having hit in 36 straight games.

August 11, 1957, Don Nichols, Peoria, Three-I League, won his 20th game of the season, all in relief, against only three losses.

August 13, 1957, First basemen Ken Kraynak made six hits and scored six runs in six at bats as Batavia battered Erie 22-1 in the New York-Pennsylvania League. Bill Palka, a teammate, took RBI honors with eight on two homers, a triple and two singles.

August 17, 1957, Steve Dalkowski, lefty with Kingsport, Appalachian League, walked 21 and made six wild pitches in a 9-7 loss to Wytheville.

August 18, 1957, Outfielder Fran Boniar of Reno, California League, 1955's champion batter of the minors with Hornell, PONY League, boosted his average to .437 with nine hits in a three-game series with Stockton.

August 21, 1957, Bob Riesener of Alexandria, Evangeline League, finished the season with an all-time Organized Ball record of 20 victories and no defeats.

August 24, 1957, Bob Riesener, who posted a 20-0 record with Alexandria in the Evangeline League this season, saw his perfect mark shattered in his Southern League debut with New Orleans, being shelled for a 12-6 defeat to Mobile.

August 24, 1957, Jack Shaw of Wytheville, Appalachian League, fanned 20 in a 12-4 win over Johnson City.

August 30, 1957, Lefty Harry Coe of Tampa, Florida State League, hurled a no-hit, 18-strikeout, 2-0 victory over Orlando to finish the season with a mound record of 26-3.

August 31, 1957, Ron Rozman of Augusta, South Atlantic League, lost to Charlotte 3-0, after having won 14 consecutive games. Rozman posted a season record of 15-1.

August 31, 1957, Steve Dalkowski of Kingsport, Appalachian League, struck out 24 and walked 18 in a Dr. Jekyll-and-Mr. Hyde performance and defeated Bluefield 7-5.

September 6, 1957, Steve Bilko of Los Angeles hit his 56th homer of the season. The big slugger failed to connect in his last eleven games and thus fell four short of Tony Lazzeri's Pacific Coast League record. Bilko had hit 55 homers in 1956 for a two-year total of 111.

September 7, 1957, Don Nichols gained his 22nd relief triumph of the season, 20 with Peoria, Three-I League, and two with Binghamton, Eastern League. His overall season mark was 22-3. He started no games during the season.

September 8, 1957, The Southern League's Atlanta Crackers won their 16th championship, a minor league record.

September 8, 1957, Lefty Leo Kiely of San Francisco, Pacific Coast League, gained his 20th relief victory of the season.

September 8, 1957, Fran Boniar of Reno, California League, ended the season with a batting average of .436 to win the championship of the minors for the second time in three years.

September 11, 1957, Colorado Springs, Western League, overcame a 13-run deficit to win a seven-inning game from Albuquerque, 17-16. The Sky Sox tallied 12 runs in the sixth inning.

December 2, 1957, The Pacific Coast League accepted $900,000 in indemnity, to be paid over three years, for the invasion of its territory by the Dodgers and Giants. In the realignment of the league, the Los Angeles franchise shifted to Spokane, San Francisco moved to Phoenix, and the Hollywood franchise was sold to Salt Lake City.

1958

American League
President: William Harridge

Standings	W	L	Pct.	GB	Attend.	Manager
New York Yankees	92	62	.597	—	1,428,438	Casey Stengel
Chicago White Sox	82	72	.532	10	797,451	Al Lopez
Boston Red Sox	79	75	.513	13	1,077,047	Pinky Higgins
Cleveland Indians	77	76	.503	14½	663,805	Bobby Bragan/Joe Gordon
Detroit Tigers	77	77	.500	15	1,098,924	Jack Tighe/Bill Norman
Baltimore Orioles	74	79	.484	17½	829,991	Paul Richards
Kansas City Athletics	73	81	.474	19	925,090	Harry Craft
Washington Senators	61	93	.396	31	475,288	Cookie Lavagetto

BA: Ted Williams, Boston, .328
Runs: Mickey Mantle, New York, 127
Hits: Nellie Fox, Chicago, 187
RBIs: Jackie Jensen, Boston, 122
HRs: Mickey Mantle, New York, 42

Wins: Bob Turley, New York, 21
SOs: Early Wynn, Chicago, 179
ERA: Whitey Ford, New York, 2.01
Pct: Bob Turley, New York, .750, 21-7
Saves: Ryne Duren, New York, 20

National League
President: Warren C. Giles

Standings	W	L	Pct.	GB	Attend.	Manager
Milwaukee Braves	92	62	.597	—	1,971,101	Fred Haney
Pittsburgh Pirates	84	70	.545	8	1,311,988	Danny Murtaugh
San Francisco Giants	80	74	.519	12	1,272,625	Bill Rigney
Cincinnati Reds	76	78	.494	16	788,582	Birdie Tebbetts/Jimmy Dykes
Chicago Cubs	72	82	.468	20	979,904	Bob Scheffing
St. Louis Cardinals	72	82	.468	20	1,063,730	Fred Hutchinson/Stan Hack
Los Angeles Dodgers	71	83	.461	21	1,845,556	Walter Alston
Philadelphia Phillies	69	85	.448	23	931,110	Mayo Smith/Eddie Sawyer

BA: Richie Ashburn, Philadelphia, .350
Runs: Willie Mays, San Francisco, 121
Hits: Richie Ashburn, Philadelphia, 215
RBIs: Ernie Banks, Chicago, 129
HRs: Ernie Banks, Chicago, 47
Wins: Bob Friend, Pittsburgh, 22
 Warren Spahn, Milwaukee, 22

SOs: Sad Sam Jones, St. Louis, 225
ERA: Stu Miller, San Francisco, 2.47
Pct: Warren Spahn, Milwaukee, .667, 22-11
 Lew Burdette, Milwaukee, .667, 20-10
Saves: Elroy Face, Pittsburgh, 20

AAA American Association
President: Edward S. Doherty

Standings	W	L	Pct.	GB	Attend.	Manager
Charleston Senators (5)	89	62	.589	—	162,914	Bill Norman/Bill Adair
Wichita Braves (12)	83	71	.539	7½	101,371	Ben Geraghty
Minneapolis Millers (2)	82	71	.536	8	152,533	Gene Mauch
Denver Bears (7)	78	71	.523	10	228,262	Andy Cohen
Omaha Cardinals (15)	80	74	.519	10½	157,715	Johnny Keane
Indianapolis Indians (3)	72	82	.468	18½	162,565	Walker Cooper
St. Paul Saints (11)	70	84	.455	20½	132,120	Max Macon
Louisville Colonels (1)	56	95	.371	33	96,883	Del Wilber

Playoffs: Minneapolis 4 games, Wichita 2; Denver 4 games, Charleston 3.
Finals: Minneapolis 4 games, Denver 0.

All-Star Team: 1B-Zeke Bella, Denver; **2B**-Wayne Terwilliger, Charleston; **3B**-Ben Valenzuela, Omaha; **SS**-Bob Lillis, St. Paul; **OF**-Bobby Gene Smith, Omaha; Bob Wilson, St. Paul; Willie Tasby, Louisville; John Callison, Indianapolis; **C**-John Blanchard, Denver; Ed Sadowski, Minneapolis; John Romano, Indianapolis; **P**-Juan Pizarro, Wichita; John Gabler, Denver; Jerry Davie, Charleston; Bob Mabe, Omaha; Barry Latman, Indianapolis; Ted Bowsfield, Minneapolis; **Util**-Pumpsie Green, Minneapolis; **MVP**-Wayne Terwilliger, Charleston; **Manager**-Gene Mauch, Minneapolis.

BA: Gordon Windhorn, Denver, .328
Runs: Wayne Terwilliger, Charleston, 103
Hits: Willie Tasby, Louisville, 174
RBIs: Earl Hersh, Wichita, 98

HRs: John Callison, Indianapolis, 29
Wins: John Gabler, Denver, 19
SOs: Bob Blaylock, Omaha, 193
ERA: Jerry Davie, Charleston, 2.45

AAA International League
President: Frank J. Shaughnessy

Standings	W	L	Pct.	GB	Attend.	Manager
Montreal Royals (11)	90	63	.588	—	213,475	Clay Bryant
Toronto Maple Leafs (1)	87	65	.572	2½	281,971	Dixie Walker
Rochester Red Wings (15)	77	75	.507	12½	272,675	Cot Deal
Columbus Red Birds (14)	77	77	.500	13½	196,644	Clyde King
Miami Marlins (13)	75	78	.490	15	161,042	Kerby Farrell
Richmond Virginians (7)	71	82	.464	19	160,633	Ed Lopat
Buffalo Bisons (6)	69	83	.454	20½	286,480	Phil Cavarretta
Havana Sugar Kings (10)	65	88	.425	25	178,340	Napoleon Reyes/Tony Pacheco

Playoffs: Montreal 4 games, Columbus 3; Toronto 4 games, Rochester 1.
Finals: Montreal 4 games, Toronto 1.

All-Star Team: 1B-Rocky Nelson, Toronto; **2B**-George "Sparky" Anderson, Montreal; **3B**-Forest Smith, Miami; **SS**-Elio Chacon, Havana; **OF**-Solly Drake, Montreal; Jim Pendleton, Columbus; Deron Johnson, Richmond; **C**-Tim Thompson, Toronto; **P**-Tom Lasorda, Montreal; Ben Daniels, Columbus; **MVP**-Rocky Nelson, Toronto; **Pitcher of the Year**-Tom Lasorda, Montreal; **Manager**-Clay Bryant, Montreal.

BA: Rocky Nelson, Toronto, .326
Runs: Solly Drake, Montreal, 105
Hits: Solly Drake, Montreal, 183
RBIs: Rocky Nelson, Toronto, 120

HRs: Rocky Nelson, Toronto, 43
Wins: Tom Lasorda, Montreal, 18
SOs: Cal Browning, Rochester, 173
ERA: Bob Tiefenauer, Toronto, 1.89

AAA Pacific Coast League
President: Leslie M. O'Connor

Standings	W	L	Pct.	GB	Attend.	Manager
Phoenix Giants (16)	89	65	.578	—	122,748	Red Davis
San Diego Padres (4)	84	69	.549	4½	233,691	George Metkovich
Vancouver Mounties (1)	79	73	.520	9	245,590	Charlie Metro
Portland Beavers (9)	78	76	.506	11	179,100	Tom Heath/Larry Jansen
Salt Lake City Bees (14)	77	77	.500	12	217,448	Larry Shepard
Sacramento Solons	71	83	.461	18	95,251	Sibby Sisti
Spokane Indians (11)	68	85	.444	20½	270,297	Goldie Holt/Bobby Bragan
Seattle Rainiers (10)	68	86	.442	21	142,499	Connie Ryan

Playoffs: None.

All-Star Team: 1B-Willie McCovey, Phoenix; Nippy Jones, Sacramento; **2B**-Jack Dittmer, Phoenix; **2B**-Tony Roig, Spokane; **3B**-George Freese, Portland; **SS**-Andre Rodgers, Phoenix; **OF**-James McDaniel, Salt Lake City; Vada Pinson, Seattle; Dave Pope, San Diego; **C**-Earl Averill, San Diego; **P**-Marshall Bridges, Sacramento; George Bamberger, Vancouver; **MVP**-Earl Averill, San Diego.

BA: Andre Rodgers, Phoenix, .354
Runs: Carlos Bernier, Salt Lake City, 121
Hits: Carlos Bernier, Salt Lake City, 181
RBIs: James McDaniel, Salt Lake City, 100
 Dusty Rhodes, Phoenix, 100

HRs: James McDaniel, Salt Lake City, 37
Wins: Marshall Bridges, Sacramento, 16
 Art Fowler, Seattle/Spokane, 16
SOs: Marshall Bridges, Sacramento, 205
ERA: George Bamberger, Vancouver, 2.45

AA Mexican League
President: Federico Miranda

Standings	W	L	Pct.	GB	Attend.	Manager
Nuevo Laredo Tecolotes	75	45	.625	—	113,994	Jose Ramos
Mexico City Diablos Rojos	65	55	.542	10	207,255	Preston Gomez/Luis Montes de Oca
Yucatan Leones	60	60	.500	15	108,933	Oscar Rodriguez/Willie Alvarez
Monterrey Sultanes	56	64	.467	19	146,558	Reggie Otero/Ray Garza
Mexico City Tigres	52	68	.433	23	179,370	George Genovese
Poza Rica Petroleros	52	68	.433	23	354,413	Jesus Valenzuela/Pepe Bache

Playoffs: None.

All-Star Team: 1B-Alonso Perry, MC Diablos Rojos; **2B**-Moi Camacho, Nuevo Laredo; **3B**-Luis Garcia, Poza Rica; **SS**-Pablo Bernard, Nuevo Laredo; **OF**-Herminio Cortes, Nuevo Laredo; Eddie Moore, Monterrey; Orlando Leroux, Yucatan; **C**-Ramon Rodriguez, Poza Rica; Earl Taborn, Nuevo Laredo; **P**-Juan Piedra, Yucatan; Julio Moreno, Nuevo Laredo; **Manager**-Jose Ramos, Nuevo Laredo.

BA: Pablo Bernard, Nuevo Laredo, .371
Runs: Pablo Bernard, Nuevo Laredo, 106
Hits: Pablo Bernard, Nuevo Laredo, 182
RBIs: Herminio Cortes, Nuevo Laredo, 98

HRs: Eddie Moore, Monterrey, 32
Wins: Eddie Locke, Monterrey, 18
SOs: Juan Piedra, Yucatan, 159
ERA: Julio Moreno, Nuevo Laredo, 2.70

AA Southern Association
President: Charles A. Hurth

Standings	W	L	Pct.	GB	Attend.	Manager
Birmingham Barons (5)	91	62	.595	—	184,682	Cal Ermer
Mobile Bears (4)	84	68	.553	6½	81,593	Mel McGaha
Atlanta Crackers (12)	84	70	.545	7½	178,791	Buddy Bates
Chattanooga Lookouts (8)	77	76	.503	14	86,328	Red Marion
Nashville Vols (10)	76	78	.494	15½	92,199	Dick Sisler
Little Rock Travelers (6)	74	80	.481	17½	67,810	Les Peden
Memphis Chicks (2)	69	84	.451	22	62,403	Sheriff Robinson
New Orleans Pelicans (7)	57	94	.377	33	50,369	Charlie Silvera/Ray Yochim

Playoffs: Mobile 4 games, Atlanta 0; Birmingham 4 games, Chattanooga 1.
Finals: Birmingham 4 games, Mobile 1.

All-Star Team: 1B-Charles Coles, Nashville; **2B**-Chuck Cottier, Atlanta; **3B**-Samuel Meeks, Atlanta; **SS**-Dick Phillips, Atlanta; **OF**-Jim Fridley, Nashville; Drew Gilbert, Nashville; Bob Thorpe, Birmingham; Don Dillard, Mobile; **C**-Les Peden, Little Rock; Ebba St. Claire, Atlanta; **Util IF**-Shep Frazier, Memphis; Lamar North, New Orleans; **P**-Bob Hartman, Memphis; Jim O'Toole, Nashville; Wilbur Striker, Mobile; Joe Grzenda, Birmingham; Dick Stigman, Mobile; Bill Slack, Memphis; William DuFour, Chattanooga.

*Won first-half **Won second-half ***Won both halves
Numbers after nicknames indicate farm system.
Affiliation listed at end of year.

BA: Jim Fridley, Nashville, .348
Runs: John Reed, New Orleans, 120
Hits: John Reed, New Orleans, 198
RBIs: Charles Coles, Nashville, 107
HRs: Kent Hadley, Little Rock, 34

Wins: Bill Harrington, Birmingham, 20
Bob Hartman, Atlanta, 20
Jim O'Toole, Nashville, 20
SOs: Joe Grzenda, Birmingham, 189
Jim O'Toole, Nashville, 189
ERA: Bob Davis, Little Rock, 2.17

AA Texas League
President: Dick Butler

Standings	W	L	Pct.	GB	Attend.	Manager
Ft. Worth Cats (9)	89	64	.582	—	81,611	Lou Klein
Houston Buffs (15)	79	74	.516	10	121,234	Harry Walker
Corpus Christi Giants (16)	77	75	.507	11½	87,774	Ray Murray
Austin Senators (12)	77	76	.503	12	117,829	Peanuts Lowrey
Dallas Rangers	76	77	.497	13	116,085	David Williams/ George Schepps/Fred Martin
San Antonio Missions (1)	74	79	.484	15	101,305	Grady Hatton
Tulsa Oilers (13)	71	81	.467	17½	110,759	Al Widmar/Jim Fanning
Victoria Rosebuds (11)	68	85	.444	21	79,464	Lou Rochelli

Playoffs: Austin 4 games, Ft. Worth 0; Corpus Christi 4 games, Houston 1.
Finals: Corpus Christi 4 games, Austin 3.

All-Star Team: 1B-Bill Gabler, Ft. Worth; **2B**-Jerry Kindall, Ft. Worth; **3B**-Joe Macko, Ft. Worth; **SS**-Rick Herscher, Austin; **OF**-Don Miles, Victoria; Eric Rodin, Corpus Christi; Mike Lutz, Corpus Christi; **C**-Ray Murray, Corpus Christi; **P**-Joe Kotrany, Dallas; **MVP**-Mike Lutz, Corpus Christi; **Pitcher of the Year**-Joe Kotrany, Dallas; **Manager**-Harry Walker, Houston.

BA: Eric Rodin, Corpus Christi, .320
Runs: Mike Lutz, Corpus Christi, 114
Hits: Eric Rodin, Corpus Christi, 171
Mike Lutz, Corpus Christi, 171
RBIs: Mike Lutz, Corpus Christi, 111

HRs: Mike Lutz, Corpus Christi, 39
Wins: Joe Kotrany, Dallas, 19
SOs: Jim Tugerson, Dallas, 195
ERA: Don Erickson, Tulsa, 2.96

A Eastern League
President: Thomas H. Richardson

North Standings	W	L	Pct.	GB	Attend.	Manager
Springfield Giants (16)	68	65	.511	—	84,974	Andy Gilbert
Williamsport Grays**(13)	67	65	.508	½	75,867	Dick Carter
Binghamton Triplets*(7)	66	68	.493	2½	62,357	Steve Souchock
Albany Senators (6)	57	70	.449	8	43,385	Alfred Evans

South Standings	W	L	Pct.	GB	Attend.	Manager
Lancaster Red Roses**(5)	75	57	.568	—	81,932	Johnny Pesky
Reading Indians (4)	75	58	.564	½	70,722	Clyde McCullough
York White Roses*(15)	68	61	.527	5½	76,139	Joe Schultz
Allentown Red Sox (2)	51	83	.381	25	47,795	Eddie Popowski

Playoffs: Lancaster 3 games, York 1; Binghamton 3 games, Williamsport 0.
Finals: Binghamton 3 games, Lancaster 2.

All-Star Team: 1B-Walt Matthews, York; **2B**-Steve Jankowski, Reading; **3B**-Jose Pagan, Springfield; **SS**-Chico Valentin, Albany; **OF**-John Easton, Williamsport; Dave Mann, Reading; Paul Leslie, York; **C**-Roger McCardell, Springfield; Don Gile, Allentown; **Util IF**-Cooter Jones, Reading; **Util OF**-Dale Bennetch, Williamsport; **P**-Ed Drapcho, Reading; Bill Stafford, Binghamton.

BA: John Easton, Williamsport, .321
Runs: Dave Mann, Reading, 110
Hits: Charlie Dees, Springfield, 158
RBIs: Dale Bennetch, Williamsport, 102

HRs: Don Gile, Albany, 23
Wins: Gordon Seyfried, Lancaster, 17
SOs: Julio Navarro, Springfield, 142
ERA: Bill Stafford, Binghamton, 2.25

A South Atlantic League
President: Sam Wolfson

Standings	W	L	Pct.	GB	Attend.	Manager
Augusta Tigers (5)	77	63	.550	—	62,695	Bill Adair/Stan Charnofsky/ Wayne Blackburn
Jacksonville Braves (12)	76	64	.543	1	78,686	Joe Just/Chuck Buheller
Macon Dodgers (11)	70	70	.500	7	86,830	Danny Ozark
Charlotte Hornets (8)	69	71	.497	8	58,758	Gene Verble
Knoxville Smokies (1)	67	73	.479	10	64,552	George Staller
Savannah Redlegs (10)	61	79	.436	16	68,437	Bob Wellman

Playoffs: Macon 1 game, Augusta 0; Jacksonville 1 game, Charlotte 0.
Finals: Macon 2 games, Jacksonville 0.

All-Star Team: 1B-Bill Thompson, Jacksonville; **2B**-Cookie Rojas, Savannah; **3B**-Leo Burke, Knoxville; **SS**-Leo Cardenas, Savannah; **OF**-George Alusik, Augusta; Charles Soraci, Macon; Chuck Buheller, Jacksonville; **C**-Jack Feller, Augusta; **P**-Roberto Vargas, Macon; Jerry Walker, Knoxville.

BA: George Alusik, Augusta, .325
Runs: Leo Burke, Knoxville, 95
Hits: Charles Soraci, Macon, 170
RBIs: George Alusik, Augusta, 88
Harry Warner, Charlotte, 88

HRs: Carl Warwick, Macon, 22
Wins: Jerry Walker, Knoxville, 18
SOs: Chuck Estrada, Knoxville, 181
ERA: Ross Carter, Jacksonville, 2.19

A Western League
President: O'Neal M. Hobbs

Standings	W	L	Pct.	GB	Attend.	Manager
Colorado Springs Sky Sox (3)	87	60	.592	—	61,091	Frank Scalzi
Amarillo Gold Sox	84	63	.571	3	85,931	Eddie Bockman/Gale Pringle
Lincoln Chiefs (14)	75	71	.514	11½	67,604	Monty Basgall
Pueblo Dodgers (9)	73	74	.497	14	39,179	Ray Mueller
Albuquerque Dukes (10)	71	75	.486	15½	81,702	Jimmy Brown
Sioux City Soos	69	77	.473	17½	55,951	Rocky Tedesco/Ted Shandor
Topeka Hawks (12)	65	82	.442	22	43,686	George McQuinn
Des Moines Bruins (11)	61	83	.424	24½	35,039	Roy Hartsfield

Playoffs: None.

All-Star Team: 1B-R.T. Upright, Amarillo; **2B**-Gerald Streeter, Amarillo; **3B**-Daniel Lynk, Sioux City; **SS**-Don Prohovich, Colorado Springs; **OF**-Jim McAnany, Colorado Springs; Stan Johnson, Colorado Springs; Bill Hicks, Colorado Springs; **C**-Ron Henry, Topeka; Charles Stanidald, Sioux City; **P**-Al Jackson, Lincoln; Dick Lines, Lincoln; Pedro Carrillo, Albuquerque; Hugh Blanton, Amarillo.

BA: Jim McAnany, Colorado Springs, .400
Runs: Stan Johnson, Colorado Springs, 120
Hits: Stan Johnson, Colorado Springs, 204
Al Pinkston, Amarillo, 204
RBIs: Al Pinkston, Amarillo, 126

HRs: Daniel Lynk, Sioux City, 37
Wins: Hugh Blanton, Amarillo, 20
SOs: Pedro Carrillo, Albuquerque, 177
Hal DeMars, Topeka, 177
ERA: Al Jackson, Lincoln, 2.07

B Carolina League
President: J.C. "Bill" Jessup

Standings	W	L	Pct.	GB	Attend.	Manager
Danville Leafs (16)	80	59	.575	—	58,306	Bob Hofman
High Point-Thomasville Hi-Toms (13)	76	63	.547	4	40,175	Frank Lucchesi
Greensboro Yankees (7)	75	64	.540	5	64,874	Vern Hoscheit
Burlington Indians (4)	70	67	.511	9	40,978	Pinky May
Winston-Salem Red Birds (15)	69	68	.504	10	90,151	Vern Benson
Raleigh Capitals (2)	63	73	.463	15½	42,089	Len Okrie
Wilson Tobs (1)	60	78	.435	19½	56,163	Bob Hooper/Barney Lutz
Durham Bulls (5)	58	79	.423	21	31,218	Charles Kress

Playoffs: Burlington 2 games, Danville 1; Greensboro 2 games, High Point-Thomasville 1.
Finals: Burlington 2 games, Greensboro 1.

All-Star Team: 1B-Jim Johnston, Greensboro; **2B**-Gene Elliott, Burlington; **3B**-Joe Theis, Raleigh; **SS**-Ron Kabbes, Winston-Salem; **OF**-Jackie Davis, Hi-Toms; Fred Valentine, Wilson; Manny Mota, Danville; **C**-Bob Tillman, Raleigh; Jack Bowen, Durham; **Util**-Bert Barth, Wilson; Robin Coffman, Danville; **P**-Jack Taylor, Hi-Toms; Roland Passaro, Winston-Salem; Chris Short, Hi-Toms; Don Hyman, Danville; **MVP**-Fred Valentine, Wilson; **Manager**-Vern Hoscheit, Greensboro; Pinky May, Burlington.

BA: Fred Valentine, Wilson, .319
Runs: Tony Curry, Hi-Toms, 106
Hits: Tony Curry, Hi-Toms, 168
RBIs: Al Milley, Danville, 97

HRs: Bert Barth, Wilson, 25
Jackie Davis, Hi-Toms, 25
Wins: Jack Taylor, Hi-Toms, 19
SOs: Eugene Snyder, Hi-Toms, 234
ERA: Johnny Aehl, Durham, 1.86

B Northwest League
President: James M. Fleishman

Standings	W	L	Pct.	GB	Attend.	Manager
Lewiston Broncs*	80	56	.588	—	64,976	Hillis Layne
Wenatchee Chiefs (10)	76	60	.559	4	57,074	Bert Haas
Yakima Bears**(12)	76	60	.559	4	64,974	Hub Kittle
Eugene Emeralds	66	69	.489	13½	83,879	Hugh Luby
Tri-City Braves (14)	62	73	.459	17½	45,283	Ray Hathway
Salem Senators	47	89	.346	33	47,756	Don Lundberg/ Vern Kindsfather

Playoff: Yakima 4 games, Lewiston 1.

All-Star Team: 1B-Bruce McIntosh, Lewiston; **2B**-Maurice Lerner, Yakima; **3B**-Hillis Layne, Lewiston; **SS**-Reggie Hamilton, Tri-City; **OF**-Elio Toboso, Wenatchee; Photios Anthony, Salem; Arnie Hallgren, Lewiston; **C**-John McNamara, Lewiston; **P**-Ted Kambour, Yakima; Thornton Kipper, Lewiston.

BA: Arnold Hallgren, Lewiston, .349
Runs: Bruce McIntosh, Lewiston, 111
Hits: Bruce McIntosh, Lewiston, 174
RBIs: Larry Helms, Wenatchee, 116

HRs: Larry Helms, Wenatchee, 26
Wins: Thornton Kipper, Lewiston, 23
SOs: Thornton Kipper, Lewiston, 193
ERA: Thornton Kipper, Lewiston, 2.71

B Three-I League
President: Hal Totten

Standings	W	L	Pct.	GB	Attend.	Manager
Cedar Rapids Braves**(12)	77	53	.592	—	81,437	Alex Monchak
Davenport DavSox*(3)	71	58	.550	5½	61,522	Ira Hutchinson
Green Bay Bluejays (11)	65	64	.504	11½	63,782	Pete Reiser
Burlington Bees (9)	62	67	.481	14½	51,632	Walt Dixon
Rochester/Winona A's#(6)	57	73	.438	20	39,589	Burl Storie/Lew Krausse
Fox Cities Foxes@(8)	56	73	.434	20½	58,602	Pete Suder

#Rochester (20-37) moved to Winona June 29.
@represented Appleton, Wisconsin.

Playoff: Cedar Rapids 3 games, Davenport 2.

All-Star Team: 1B-Don Mincher, Davenport; **2B**-Bobby Knoop, Cedar Rapids; **3B**-Bob Sagers, Davenport; **SS**-Harry Wallace, Green Bay; **OF**-Frank Howard, Green Bay; Richard Lombardi, Davenport; Lee Handley, Burlington; **C**-Chuck Lindstrom, Davenport; Gordon Massa, Burlington; **P**-Bill Hamilton, Cedar Rapids; Charles Hendley, Cedar Rapids; Bill Rouse, Davenport; Robert Sedlak, Green Bay; **MVP**-Frank Howard, Green Bay; **Manager**-Ira Hutchinson, Davenport.

BA: Carlos Pascual, Fox Cities, .372
Runs: Frank Howard, Green Bay, 104
Hits: Bob Sagers, Davenport, 180
RBIs: Frank Howard, Green Bay, 119
HRs: Frank Howard, Green Bay, 37

Wins: Bill Hamilton, Cedar Rapids, 15
Ed Rakow, Green Bay, 15
Robert Sedlak, Green Bay, 15
SOs: Stan Horvatin, Rochester/Winona, 210
ERA: Bill Hamilton, Cedar Rapids, 2.18

C Arizona-Mexico League
President: Charles S. Hollinger

Standings	W	L	Pct.	GB	Attend.	Manager
Douglas Copper Kings (14) ..	68	52	.567	—	25,315	Bob Clear
Tucson Cowboys	66	54	.550	2	42,257	Harry Dunlop
Nogales Mineros................	59	59	.500	8	48,887	Memo Garibay
Chihuahua Dorados	56	62	.475	11	59,917	Leonel Aldama
Juarez Indios	55	64	.462	12½	59,847	Epitacio Torres
						Barney Serrell/Pedro Ramirez
Mexicali Aguilas................	53	66	.445	14½	55,649	Felipe Hernandez

Playoffs: None.

BA: Jose Medrano, Mexicali, .385
Runs: Jose Podilla, Nogales, 136
Hits: Jose Medrano, Mexicali, 173
RBIs: Jose Echeverria, Chihuahua, 126

HRs: Jose Echeverria, Chihuahua, 35
Wins: Jose Ibarra, Chihuahua, 19
SOs: Manual Estrada, Nogales, 244
ERA: Kermit Kowalk, Tucson, 3.04

C California League
President: Edward J. Mulligan

Standings	W	L	Pct.	GB	Attend.	Manager
Fresno Giants*(16)	85	55	.607	—	54,534	Mike McCormick
Bakersfield Bears**(13)....	84	55	.604	½	66,785	Paul Owens
Stockton Ports (15)	70	68	.507	14	25,991	Don Pries
Visalia Redlegs (10)	69	69	.500	15	39,669	Bruce Edwards/
						Bobby Mattick/Larry Taylor
Modesto Reds (7)...............	69	70	.497	15½	40,760	Damon Phillips
Reno Silver Sox (11)	68	69	.497	15½	35,245	Ray Perry
San Jose Pirates/						
Las Vegas Wranglers#(14)	54	81	.400	28½	23,845	Jack Paepke
Salinas Packers (12)...........	53	85	.384	31	21,258	Victor Marasco/Al Forthmann

#San Jose moved to Las Vegas May 26.

Playoffs: Fresno 2 games, Stockton 1; Visalia 2 games, Bakersfield 1.
Finals: Fresno 3 games, Visalia 1.

All-Star Team: 1B-Richard Beall, Visalia; **2B**-John Scramaglia, Fresno; **3B**-Tom Dotterer, Visalia; **SS**-Bobby Wine, Bakersfield; **OF**-Barton Dupon, Bakersfield; Willard Fox, Reno; Carlos Dore, Stockton; Tom Johnson, Visalia; **C**-Neil Wilson, Fresno; **Util IF**-Thomas Humber, Reno; **P**-Alvin Spearman, Stockton; Dale Zeigler, Modesto; Bob Gontkosky, Bakersfield; Len Fergunson, Modesto; Frederick Rick, Las Vegas; **MVP**-O'Neil Wilson, Fresno; **Manager**-Paul Owens, Bakersfield.

BA: O'Neil Wilson, Fresno, .349
Runs: Bob Farley, Fresno, 128
Hits: O'Neil Wilson, Fresno, 191
RBIs: Barton Dupon, Bakersfield, 136

HRs: Barton Dupon, Bakersfield, 40
Wins: Len Fergunson, Modesto, 23
SOs: Len Fergunson, Modesto, 302
ERA: Alvin Spearman, Stockton, 2.60

C Northern League
President: Peter Bradbury

Standings	W	L	Pct.	GB	Attend.	Manager
St. Cloud Rox (16)...............	72	50	.590	—	33,902	Richard Klaus
Fargo-Moorhead Twins (7)	72	51	.585	½	52,942	Ken Silvestri
Winnipeg Goldeyes (15)....	65	53	.551	5	90,998	Al Unser
Minot Mallards (4)............	67	55	.549	5	34,355	Ken Landenberger
Eau Claire Braves (12)	65	56	.537	6½	30,032	Gordon Maltzberger
Duluth-Superior White Sox (3)	55	67	.451	17	39,780	Joe Hauser/George Sobek
Grand Forks Chiefs (14).....	51	68	.429	19½	28,961	James Adlam
Aberdeen Pheasants (1)	39	86	.312	34½	36,599	Barney Lutz/Billy DeMars

Playoffs: St. Cloud 1 game, Winnipeg 0; Fargo-Moorhead 1 game, Minot 0.
Finals: Fargo-Moorhead 2 games, St. Cloud 1.

All-Star Team: 1B-Joe Martin, Duluth-Superior; **2B**-Don Brummer, Fargo-Moorhead; **3B**-Julio Gotay, Winnipeg; **SS**-Mike de la Hoz, Minot; **OF**-Matty Alou, St. Cloud; Manny Jiminez, Eau Claire; Will Williams, Minot; **C**-John Orsino, St. Cloud; Jim Schaffer, Winnipeg; **P**-Bo Belinsky, Aberdeen; Gary Willison, Winnipeg.

BA: Manny Jiminez, Eau Claire, .340
Runs: Don Brummer, Fargo-Moorhead, 119
Hits: Joe Martin, Duluth-Superior, 153
RBIs: Glen Merklen, Fargo-Moorhead, 104

HRs: Julio Gotay, Winnipeg, 24
Wins: Gary Willison, Winnipeg, 19
SOs: Bo Belinsky, Aberdeen, 184
ERA: Bo Belinsky, Aberdeen, 2.24

C Pioneer League
President: Claude Engberg

Standings	W	L	Pct.	GB	Attend.	Manager
Boise Braves**(12)	76	54	.585	—	72,038	Billy Smith
Missoula Timberjacks (8)...	70	59	.543	5½	63,138	Jack McKeon
Pocatello Athletics (6)......	70	63	.526	7½	39,521	Bill Capps

Idaho Falls Russets (5)	65	66	.496	11½	37,580	Al Lakeman
Great Falls Electrics*(11)...	63	70	.474	14½	51,540	Stan Wasiak
Magic Valley Cowboys (9)..	58	74	.439	19	33,666	Dick Wilson
Billings Mustangs (15)	56	72	.438	19	47,256	Chase Riddle

Playoff: Boise 3 games, Great Falls 2.

All-Star Team: 1B-Norm Shill, Pocatello; **2B**-Lou Klimchock, Pocatello; **3B**-Tom Brown, Boise; **SS**-Alex George, Pocatello; **OF**-Chuck Weatherspoon, Missoula; Bill DiCrosta, Billings; Jackson Queen, Idaho Falls; **C**-Doug Camilli, Great Falls; Bob Uecker, Boise; **Util**-Frank Franchi, Idaho Falls; **P**-Don Orwiller, Missoula; Jim Kaat, Missoula; Charles Herzberger, Twin Falls; Charles Holmes, Boise; **Manager**-Jack McKeon, Missoula.

BA: Lou Klimchock, Pocatello, .389
Runs: Lou Klimchock, Pocatello, 123
Hits: Lou Klimchock, Pocatello, 197
RBIs: Aurelio Ala, Pocatello, 118

HRs: Chuck Weatherspoon, Missoula, 35
Wins: William Holmes, Boise, 17
SOs: Jim Kaat, Missoula, 245
ERA: Jim Kaat, Missoula, 2.99

D Alabama-Florida League
President: Sam C. Smith

Standings	W	L	Pct.	GB	Attend.	Manager
Selma Cloverleafs (6)	71	49	.592	—	31,786	Tom Giordano
Columbus Foxes (11)..........	74	52	.587	—	32,689	Brandy Davis
Pensacola Dons (1)	67	55	.549	5	52,989	Lou Fitzgerald
Dothan Cardinals (15)	68	57	.544	5½	31,482	J.C. Dunn
Montgomery Rebels (5).......	61	61	.516	9	24,700	Schoolboy Rowe/Neil Berry
Graceville Oilers (10)	58	65	.472	14½	11,771	Michael Fandozzi
Ft. Walton Beach Jets (8) ...	53	72	.424	20½	12,447	Nesbit Wilson/Vince Magi
Panama City Fliers (16)......	39	84	.317	33½	15,721	Bill Brightwell/
						Charles Clark/
						Joe Tipton/Charles Grant

Playoffs: Selma 3 games, Pensacola 2; Dothan 3 games, Columbus 1.
Finals: Dothan 4 games, Selma 1.

All-Star Team: 1B-Leo Smith, Montgomery; **2B**-Francis Traill, Selma; **3B**-Charlie Strange, Montgomery; **SS**-Al Caesar, Columbus; **OF**-Brandy Davis, Columbus; Nesbit Wilson, Ft. Walton Beach/Pensacola; Teo Acosta, Dothan; **C**-Bob Catton, Columbus; Ray Oliver, Dothan; **P**-Tom Kelleher, Selma; Paul Underwood, Graceville.

BA: Nesbit Wilson, Ft. Walton Beach/Pensacola, .396
Runs: Nesbit Wilson, Ft. Walton Beach/Pensacola, 102
Hits: Teo Acosta, Dothan, 163
RBIs: Nesbit Wilson, Ft. Walton Beach/Pensacola, 106

HRs: Nesbit Wilson, Ft. Walton Beach/Pensacola, 24
Wins: Tom Kelleher, Selma, 20
James Lehew, Pensacola, 20
SOs: Paul Underwood, Graceville, 215
ERA: Frank Roland, Selma, 2.10

D Appalachian League
President: Chauncey De Vault

Standings	W	L	Pct.	GB	Attend.	Manager
Johnson City Phillies (13)...	47	24	.662	—	14,286	Eddie Lyons
Wytheville Cardinals (15) ..	44	28	.611	3½	26,198	Whitey Kurowski
Salem Rebels (14)..............	42	29	.592	5	21,351	Larry Dorton
Pulaski Cubs (9).................	24	46	.343	22½	8,991	Herschel Martin
Bluefield Orioles (1)...........	21	51	.292	26½	11,732	Barney Lutz
						Fred Hofman/Bob Hooper

Playoffs: None.

All-Star Team: 1B-Charles Leonard, Salem; **2B**-George Williams, Johnson City; **3B**-Bill Schnellbacker, Wytheville; **SS**-Danny Cater, Johnson City; **OF**-Dan Branson, Wytheville; Frank Coimbre, Salem; Dan Casteen, Johnson City; **C**-Jesus McFarlane, Salem; **P**-Bill Hofmeister, Johnson City; Jack Pregenzer, Salem; **Rookie of the Year**-Danny Cater, Johnson City; **Manager**-Whitey Kurowski, Wytheville.

BA: George Williams, Johnson City, .361
Runs: Danny Cater, Johnson City, 70
Hits: Danny Cater, Johnson City, 90
RBIs: Danny Cater, Johnson City, 68

HRs: Danny Cater, Johnson City, 14
Wins: Bill Hofmeister, Johnson City, 11
SOs: Buster Narum, Bluefield, 115
ERA: Dennis Bennett, Johnson City, 1.5

D Florida State League
President: Julian Jackson

Standings	W	L	Pct.	GB	Attend.	Manager
St. Petersburg Saints***(7) .	101	42	.706	—	73,798	Tom Hamilton
Daytona Beach Islanders (15) .	79	58	.577	19	31,049	Ray Wilson
Palatka Redlegs (10)...........	76	65	.539	24	19,031	John Vander Meer
Tampa Tarpons (13)	74	69	.518	27	42,683	Charles Gassaway
Cocoa Indians (4)..............	64	78	.451	36½	16,563	Paul O'Dea
Orlando Flyers	51	88	.367	48	17,615	Charles Grant/Ty Braziel
Gainesville G-Men (8)........	47	92	.338	52	18,600	Buddy Leftridge/Red Dulaney

Playoffs: None.

All-Star Team: 1B-German Pizzaro, Gainesville/Tampa; **2B**-Pedro Gonzales, St. Petersburg; **3B**-George Banks, St. Petersburg; **SS**-Tom Tresh, St. Petersburg; **OF**-Jim Niemann, Palatka; Clarence Bartunek, Cocoa; Art Pennington, St. Petersburg; **C**-Charles Jennings, Daytona Beach; **Util**-Jesus Torres, Daytona Beach; **P**-Jorge Talavera, Daytona Beach; Jim Horsford, St. Petersburg; **Manager**-John Vander Meer, Palatka.

BA: Jim Niemann, Palatka, .340
Runs: Pedro Gonzales, St. Petersburg, 117
Hits: Pedro Gonzales, St. Petersburg, 162
RBIs: George Banks, St. Petersburg, 113
HRs: German Pizzaro,
    Gainesville/Tampa, 25

Wins: Jim Horsford, St. Petersburg, 18
    Bob Cruze, Tampa, 18
    Jorge Talavera, Daytona Beach, 18
    Harry Coe, Tampa, 18
SOs: Harry Coe, Tampa, 194
ERA: Jim Horsford, St. Petersburg, 1.93

D Georgia-Florida League
President: W.T. Anderson

Standings	W	L	Pct.	GB	Attend.	Manager
Albany Cardinals**(15)	86	41	.677	—	42,828	Mo Mozzali
Valdosta Dodgers*(5)	75	52	.591	11	38,582	Stubby Overmire
Dublin Orioles (1)	72	56	.563	14½	31,704	Earl Weaver
Brunswick Phillies (13)	64	64	.500	22½	45,157	Cart Howerton
Waycross Braves (12)	47	80	.370	39	26,512	Everett Robinson
Thomasville Tigers (11)	38	89	.299	48	17,451	Rudy Rufer/Sam Suplizio

Playoff: Valdosta 3 games, Albany 1.

All-Star Team: 1B-David Bedner, Dublin; **2B**-Jim Hatfield, Waycross; **3B**-John Simicich, Brunswick; **SS**-Dick McAuliffe, Valdosta; **OF**-Bob Boyer, Albany; Tom Shannon, Albany; Michael Stopchuck, Brunswick; Don Ewin, Dublin; **C**-William Morton, Albany; Charles Julian, Thomasville; **P**-Cecil Butler, Waycross; Ronald Pearson, Dublin; Warren Roddenberry, Albany; Joel McDaniel, Valdosta; **Manager**-Mo Mozzali, Albany.

BA: John Simicich, Brunswick, .358
Runs: Samuel Hernandez, Albany, 118
Hits: John Simicich, Brunswick, 156
RBIs: Bob Boyer, Albany, 121

HRs: Bob Boyer, Albany, 32
Wins: George Werley, Dublin, 16
SOs: Joe Pokorny, Burnswick, 177
ERA: Eugene Burroughs, Valdosta, 1.66

D Midwest League
President: C.C. "Dutch" Hoffman

Standings	W	L	Pct.	GB	Attend.	Manager
Kokomo Dodgers (11)	68	51	.571	—	35,638	Edward Serrano
Michigan City White Caps*(16)	69	54	.556	1½	30,562	Buddy Kerr
Waterloo Hawks**(2)	66	55	.545	3	62,500	Ken Deal
Paris Lakers (9)	64	61	.512	7	45,674	Verlon Walker
Keokuk Cardinals (15)	62	60	.508	7½	41,133	Frank Calo
Dubuque Packers (3)	59	63	.484	10½	93,070	Frank Parenti
Decatur Commodores (5)	59	66	.472	12	40,047	Frank Carswell
Clinton Pirates (14)	44	80	.355	26½	59,678	Stan Wentzel/Walt Millies

Playoff: Waterloo 3 games, Michigan City 2.

All-Star Team: 1B-Fred Whitfield, Keokuk; **2B**-Tony Christopher, Dubuque; **3B**-Nap Savinson, Kokomo; **SS**-Don Williams, Kokomo; **OF**-Larry Elliott, Clinton; Gustave Sancimino, Kokomo; Lou Johnson, Paris; **C**-Bob Smith, Clinton; Jim Napier, Dubuque; **Util IF**-Chico Fernandez, Decatur; **Util OF**-Seymour Bonem, Keokuk; **P**-Bob Butterfield, Kokomo; Harvey Branch, Paris; Barney Kunert, Clinton; Juan Marichal, Michigan City; Hal Kolstad, Waterloo; **Player of the Year**-Gus Sancimino, Kokomo; **Rookie of the Year**-Juan Marichal, Michigan City; **Manager**-Buddy Kerr, Michigan City.

BA: Lou Johnson, Paris, .365
Runs: Lou Johnson, Paris, 103
    Bob Newman, Dubuque, 103
Hits: Seymour Bonem, Keokuk, 162
RBIs: Fred Whitfield, Keokuk, 118

HRs: Gustave Sancimino, Kokomo, 29
Wins: Juan Marichal, Michigan City, 21
SOs: Hal Kolstad, Waterloo, 250
ERA: Juan Marichal, Michigan City, 1.87

D Nebraska State League
President: Mike Hollinger

Standings	W	L	Pct.	GB	Attend.	Manager
North Platte Indians (4)	41	22	.651	—	18,766	Mark Wylie
McCook Braves (12)	40	23	.635	1	17,372	Bill Steinecke
Grand Island Athletics (6)	33	30	.524	8	18,762	Art Mazmanian
Kearney Yankees (7)	33	30	.524	8	14,147	Randy Gumpert
Lexington Red Sox (2)	30	33	.476	11	12,838	Jack Kaiser
Holdrege White Sox (3)	29	34	.460	12	11,565	George Noga
Hastings Giants (16)	24	39	.381	17	11,522	Leo Schrall
Superior Senators (8)	22	41	.349	19	8,953	Hal Keller

Playoffs: None.

All-Star Team: 1B-Keith Williams, North Platte; **2B**-Joe Teague, North Platte; **3B**-Ron Debus, Grand Island; **SS**-Larry Bulla, North Platte; **OF**-Ed Gary, Kearney; Kent Hathaway, North Platte; Hugh Mendez, McCook; **C**-Robert Biedermann, McCook; Ron Staples, Lexington; **P**-Tom Gensauer, North Platte; Ceferino Foy, McCook.

BA: Ron Debus, Grand Island, .393
Runs: Larry Bulla, North Platte, 68
Hits: Gerry McNertney, Holdrege, 84
RBIs: Keith Williams, North Platte, 72
HRs: Keith Williams, North Platte, 12

Wins: Ceferino Foy, McCook, 10
    Larry Gansauer, North Platte, 10
SOs: Bill Spanswick, Lexington, 142
ERA: Larry Del Margo, Kearney, 2.25

D New York-Pennsylvania League
President: Vincent M. McNamara

Standings	W	L	Pct.	GB	Attend.	Manager
Wellsville Braves (12)	70	56	.556	—	24,970	Harry Minor
Geneva Redlegs (10)	69	57	.548	1	39,745	Dave Bristol
Olean Oilers (13)	67	57	.540	2	22,973	Ben Zientara
Auburn Yankees (7)	67	58	.536	2½	46,216	Tom Gott
Corning Red Sox (2)	64	61	.512	5½	25,986	Elmer Yoter
Batavia Indians (4)	60	65	.480	9½	33,158	Don Richmond
Erie Sailors (5)	53	72	.424	16½	24,310	Steve Gromek
Elmira Pioneers (8)	50	74	.403	19	32,980	Mel Kerestes/Packy Rogers

Playoffs: Wellsville 2 games, Auburn 1; Geneva 2 games, Olean 0.
Finals: Geneva 3 games, Wellsville 0.

All-Star Team: 1B-Harold Jones, Batavia; **2B**-William Wyatt, Batavia; **3B**-Ray Greisheimer, Geneva; **SS**-Zoilo Versalles, Elmira; **OF**-Ray Withrow, Wellsville; Marcial Allen, Wellsville; Harry Panaro, Geneva; **C**-Merritt Ranew, Wellsville; William Maupin, Erie; **P**-Bob Risenhoover, Geneva; Wallace Bush, Geneva.

BA: Nate Dickerson, Olean, .338
Runs: Charles Bergdoll, Wellsville, 104
    Ray Withrow, Wellsville, 104
Hits: Harold Jones, Batavia, 160
RBIs: Ray Withrow, Wellsville, 142

HRs: Ray Withrow, Wellsville, 32
Wins: Bob Risenhoover, Geneva, 20
SOs: Bob Risenhoover, Geneva, 236
ERA: Ed Banach, Wellsville, 1.92
Pct: Ed Banach, Wellsville, .929, 13-1

D Sophomore League
President: Grady Terry

East Standings	W	L	Pct.	GB	Attend.	Manager
Midland Braves (12)	72	48	.600	—	28,210	Travis Jackson/Earl Halstead/Ernie White
San Angelo Pirates (14)	61	59	.509	11	27,881	Al Kubski
Plainview Athletics (6)	50	70	.417	22	21,640	Vincent Plumbo

West Standings	W	L	Pct.	GB	Attend.	Manager
Artesia Giants (16)	63	57	.527	—	15,431	Jodie Phipps
Hobbs Cardinals (15)	59	61	.492	4	18,301	Wayne Wallace
Carlsbad Potashers (9)	55	65	.458	8	21,820	Tony York

Playoff: Midland 3 games, Artesia 1.

BA: Jim Smith, Hobbs, .372
Runs: Duncan Campbell, San Angelo, 116
    Gary Krupsky, Artesia, 116
Hits: James McClain, Artesia, 161
RBIs: Craig Sorensen, Carlsbad, 114

HRs: Kenneth Clark, Hobbs, 27
Wins: John Aherns, Hobbs, 18
SOs: Ervin Moore, Plainview, 175
ERA: Leslie Bass, Midland, 3.47

1958 Interleague Post Season Play

World Series
New York (American) 4 games, Milwaukee (National) 3

Junior World Series
Minneapolis (American Association) 4 games, Montreal (International) 0
Total Attendance: 25,774

Dixie Series
Birmingham (Southern Association) 4 games, Corpus Christi (Texas) 2
Total Attendance: 18,219

1958 Major League Farm Systems

American League

1. Baltimore (9): Louisville, Vancouver, San Antonio, Knoxville, Wilson, Aberdeen, Pensacola, Bluefield, Dublin.
2. Boston (7): Minneapolis, Memphis, Allentown, Raleigh, Waterloo, Lexington, Corning.
3. Chicago (6): Indianapolis, Colorado Springs, Davenport, Duluth-Superior, Dubuque, Holdrege.
4. Cleveland (8): San Diego, Mobile, Reading, Burlington (NC), Minot, Cocoa, North Platte.
5. Detroit (10): Charleston, Birmingham, Lancaster, Augusta, Durham, Idaho Falls, Montgomery, Valdosta, Decatur, Erie.
6. Kansas City (8): Buffalo, Little Rock, Albany (NY), Rochester (MN)/Winona, Pocatello, Selma, Grand Island, Batavia, Plainview.
7. New York (10): Denver, Richmond, New Orleans, Binghamton, Greensboro, Modesto, Fargo-Moorhead, St. Petersburg, Kearney, Auburn.
8. Washington (8): Chattanooga, Charlotte, Fox Cities, Missoula, Ft. Walton Beach, Gainesville, Superior (NE), Elmira.

National League

9. Chicago (8): Portland, Ft. Worth, Pueblo, Burlington (IA), Magic Valley, Pulaski, Paris, Carlsbad.
10. Cincinnati (10): Seattle, Havana, Nashville, Savannah, Albuquerque, Wenatchee, Visalia, Graceville, Palatka, Geneva.
11. Los Angeles (12): St. Paul, Montreal, Spokane, Victoria, Macon, Des Moines, Green Bay, Reno, Great Falls, Columbus (GA), Thomasville, Kokomo.
12. Milwaukee (14): Wichita, Atlanta, Austin, Jacksonville, Topeka, Yakima, Cedar Rapids, Salinas, Eau Claire, Boise, Waycross, McCook, Wellsville, Midland.
13. Philadelphia (9): Miami, Tulsa, Williamsport, High Point-Thomasville, Bakersfield, Johnson City, Tampa, Brunswick, Olean.
14. Pittsburgh (10): Columbus (OH), Salt Lake City, Lincoln, Tri-City, Douglas, San Jose/Las Vegas, Grand Forks, Salem (VA), Clinton, San Angelo.
15. St. Louis (14): Omaha, Rochester (NY), Houston, York, Winston-Salem, Stockton, Winnipeg, Billings, Dothan, Wytheville, Daytona Beach, Albany (GA), Keokuk, Hobbs.
16. San Francisco (10): Phoenix, Corpus Christi, Springfield, Danville, Fresno, St. Cloud, Panama City, Michigan City, Hastings, Artesia.

1958 No-Hitters

Date	Pitcher	Team	League	Opponent	Score
4-27	Richard Hanlon	Spokane	Pacific Coast	Vancouver	1-0 (7)
5-16	James Conrad	Dubuque	Midwest	Clinton	2-0
5-19	Scott Breeden	Kokomo	Midwest	Keokuk	3-0 (7)
5-22	Carlton Willey	Wichita	American Assoc.	Louisville	6-0
5-24	John Aehl	Durham	Carolina	Greensboro	2-0 (7)
5-25	Joe Laughlin	Montgomery	Alabama-Florida	Pensacola	6-0
5-25	Fred Gladding	Augusta	South Atlantic	Macon	7-0 (7)
5-25	Ted Kambour	Yakima	Northwest	Salem	1-0 (P, 7)
5-27	Arthur Henriksen	St. Petersburg	Florida State	Daytona Beach	2-1 (7)
5-30	Charles Drummond	Yakima	Northwest	Lewiston	2-0 (7)
5-31	Charles Fowler	Corpus Christi	Texas	Austin	1-0
6-7	Richard Moavero	Ft. Walton Beach	Alabama-Florida	Dothan	2-0
6-10	Sam McIntrye	Billings	Pioneer	Missoula	6-0 (7)
6-14	Joseph Drotar	Tri-City	Northwest	Wenatchee	6-0 (7)
6-15	Hal Trosky, Jr.	Colorado Springs	Western	Des Moines	6-0
6-17	Cubert Smith	Erie	New York-Penn.	Auburn	1-0 (7)
6-20	Dave Stenhouse	Pueblo	Western	Topeka	5-0
6-22	Bud Watkins	Sacramento	Pacific Coast	Phoenix	0-4 (8)
6-29	Robert Daniels	Salem	Appalachian	Bluefield	2-0
6-30	Octavio Acosta	Grand Forks	Northern	Winnipeg	12-1
6-30	Angelo Cundari/ Orlando Valdes	Superior	Nebraska State	Hastings	3-0
7-9	Evans Killen/ Don Williams	Albany	Eastern	Allentown	3-0 (7)
7-10	Thomas Gansauer	North Platte	Nebraska State	Superior	7-0
7-20	Jim Bunning	Detroit	American	Boston	3-0
7-23	Bill Williams	Columbus	Alabama-Florida	Panama City	3-0 (7)
7-29	John Flachman	Palatka	Florida State	St. Petersburg	5-0 (7)
8-3	Gerald Fields	Decatur	Midwest	Clinton	5-0
8-4	Frank Barnes	Omaha	American Assoc.	Louisville	3-0
8-5	Paul Underwood	Graceville	Alabama-Florida	Pensacola	6-0 (7)
8-6	William Fazekas/ Billy Carter	Cocoa	Florida State	Tampa	5-2 (7)
8-13	Theron Reeves	Carlsbad	Sophomore	San Angelo	3-1 (7)
8-17	Rudolfo Arias	Havana	International	Rochester	7-0 (7)
8-18	Gale Peregrin	Palatka	Florida State	Tampa	2-0 (7)
8-23	Bob Paffel	Lancaster	Eastern	Springfield	2-0 (7)
8-27	Ben Tench	Raleigh	Carolina	Burlington	2-0 (7)
9-1	John B. Swango	Fargo-Moorhead	Northern	Minot	8-0
9-20	Hoyt Wilhelm	Baltimore	American	New York	1-0

Number in parentheses indicates innings if other than nine; "P" indicates perfect game.

THIS DATE IN MINOR LEAGUE HISTORY

January 10, 1958, Angel Castro, first baseman, Mazatlan, Mexican Pacific Coast League, hit three homers and drove in 11 runs as Mazatlan defeated Navajoa-Guaymas, 26-10.

March 26, 1958, Clarence "Big Boy" Kraft, one of the most powerful hitters in minor league history, died in Fort Worth, Texas at age 70. In 1924, Kraft hit 55 home runs and batted in 196 runs for Ft. Worth of the Texas League.

May 6, 1958, Midland, Sophomore League, counted 15 runs in the second inning to whip Plainview, 19-9.

May 8, 1958, Charlie Bergdell hit three successive homers and a double, and Marcial Allen smashed three triples for Wellsville, New York-Penn League, as the Braves rapped Auburn.

May 9, 1958, Wellsville, New York-Penn League, lost the nightcap of a twin-bill to Auburn, 5-1, for their first loss of the year after nine straight victories. Wellsville hurlers went the route in seven consecutive games.

May 10, 1958, Pedro Perez, 18-year-old Cuban righthander with Wellsville, New York-Penn League, pitched his third consecutive nine-inning shutout in defeating Batavia, 10-0. Perez' scoreless streak ended at 30 consecutive innings May 17.

May 18, 1958, Paris, Midwest League, outslugged Dubuque 30-17.

May 19, 1958, Aberdeen, Northern League, ended an 18-game losing streak, beating Duluth-Superior 3-0.

May 19, 1958, The Arizona-Mexico League standings showed a rarity when it read all six clubs tied for first place with identical 9-9 records.

May 21, 1958, Pocatello, Pioneer League, defeated Magic Valley 25-20.

May 22, 1958, Clinton, Midwest League, made twelve errors in a 10-6 loss to Michigan City.

May 28, 1958, Luke Easter, Buffalo, International League, hit a 520-foot home run against Havana.

May 29, 1958, Carlos Bernier, Salt Lake City, Pacific Coast League, was stopped after hitting safely in 35 straight games.

June 2, 1958, Dubuque, Midwest League, lost to Michigan City, 6-4, after 15 straight wins.

June 18, 1958, Jim McAnany, Colorado Springs, Western League, outfielder, knocked in 10 runs in the Sky Sox' 17-15 win over Sioux City.

June 23, 1958, George Boehler, righthanded pitcher who won 38 games for Tulsa, Western League, in 1922, died in Lawrenceburg, Indiana at age 66. Boehler was a 20-game winner seven times in his minor league career and finished with 248 life-time wins.

June 30, 1958, Tampa scored 15 runs in the second inning to trounce Orlando, 32-1, in the Florida State League.

July 2, 1958, Seven pitchers walked 29 batters as Olean, New York-Penn League, defeated Batavia, 11-10. Four Batavia hurlers gave up 16 of the free passes.

July 11, 1958, Kenny Kuhn, Burlington, Carolina League, made twelve consecutive hits in a two-day span.

July 13, 1958, Pocatello, Pioneer League, hit eight homers in a 25-4 win over Great Falls.

July 16, 1958, Haven Schmidt, Albuquerque, Sophomore League, a 6'4", 220-pound catcher, blasted the longest foul ball ever hit and taped against Amarillo righthander Jim Johnson. The ball left the field two feet outside the foul marker and was taped at 560 feet by a sportswriter.

July 20, 1958, Salt Lake City, Pacific Coast League, scored 14 times in the second inning and beat San Diego 19-5.

July 21, 1958, Greensboro, Carolina League, smashed eight homers to slaughter Danville, 21-9.

July 23, 1958, Valdosta, Georgia-Florida League, scored 16 runs in one inning to win a 20-16 slugfest from Thomasville.

July 24, 1958, Fargo-Moorhead, Northern League, scored 13 runs in one inning to wallop St. Cloud, 16-7.

July 25, 1958, Kearney, Nebraska State League, made twelve errors in an 18-16 loss to McCook.

July 27, 1958, Al Spearman, 27-year-old righthander with Stockton, California League, turned in his 20th straight complete game in 20 starts this season, defeating Bakersfield, 12-2. Pitching the distance was nothing unusual for Spearman, who had done it 55 times in 58 starts in the last three years. Spearman increased his string to 21 straight befored being recalled by Rochester, International League, August 8. The recall, however, was cancelled by National Association rules, and he was returned to Stockton after only one day in Rochester.

August 1, 1958, Isaac "Ike" Boone, 61, who compiled an all-time career record average of .370 in 14 seasons in the minor leagues, and in addition posted a creditable .319 mark in the majors with the Giants, Red Sox, White Sox and Dodgers, died in Northport, Alabama.

August 6, 1958, Jacksonville, Sally League, lost to Savannah 14-5 after winning 15 straight games.

August 9, 1958, Ollie Brantley, Colorado Springs, Western League, righthander retired 26 consecutive batters in a relief role in an 18-inning game with Topeka.

August 14, 1958, George Bamberger, Vancouver, Pacific Coast League, righthander, increased his string of walkless innings to 68-2/3.

August 14, 1958, Al Spearman, returning to Stockton, California League, after his recall to Rochester, International League, was cancelled by the National Association, posted his 22nd complete game of the season, defeating Modesto 14-0.

August 19, 1958, A home run feat never accomplished before in Organized Baseball was recorded when every member of the Douglas Copper Kings contributed one home run in a 22-8 rout of Chihuahua in an Arizona-Mexico League game. In addition to the nine homers, the Copper Kings collected 14 other hits.

August 19, 1958, Dubuque, Midwest League, smashed nine homers while bombarding Paris 25-3.

August 20, 1958, Binghamton, Eastern League, ended a 17-game losing steak, beating York 4-2.

August 21, 1958, Bill Spanswick, Lexington, Nebraska State League, lefty, struck out 22 while pitching a one-hit, 13-0 victory over Superior. Earlier in the season, Spanswick whiffed 24 in a 14-inning game.

August 23, 1958, Elmira, New York-Penn League, made 11 errors but defeated Geneva, 8-7.

August 24, 1958, McCook, Nebraska State League, lost to Grand Island, 3-2, after 18 straight wins.

September 2, 1958, Southpaw Harvey Branch, Paris, Midwest League, struck out 21 in a 4-1 victory over Clinton.

September 8, 1958, Glenn "Rocky" Nelson, veteran first baseman, Toronto, International League, won the triple crown for the second time. Nelson also accomplished the feat in 1955.

1959

American League
Presidents: William Harridge/Joseph E. Cronin

Standings	W	L	Pct.	GB	Attend.	Manager
Chicago White Sox	94	60	.610	—	1,423,144	Al Lopez
Cleveland Indians	89	65	.578	5	1,497,976	Joe Gordon
New York Yankees	79	75	.513	15	1,552,030	Casey Stengel
Detroit Tigers	76	78	.494	18	1,221,221	Bill Norman/Jimmy Dykes
Boston Red Sox	75	79	.487	19	984,102	Pinky Higgins/Rudy York/
						Bill Jurges
Baltimore Orioles	74	80	.481	20	891,926	Paul Richards
Kansas City Athletics	66	88	.429	28	963,683	Harry Craft
Washington Senators	63	91	.409	31	615,372	Cookie Lavagetto

BA: Harvey Kuenn, Detroit, .353
Runs: Eddie Yost, Detroit, 115
Hits: Harvey Kuenn, Detroit, 198
RBIs: Jackie Jensen, Boston, 112
HRs: Rocky Colavito, Cleveland, 42
    Harmon Killebrew, Washington, 42

Wins: Early Wynn, Chicago, 22
ERA: Hoyt Wilhelm, Baltimore, 2.19
SOs: Jim Bunning, Detroit, 201
Pct: Bob Shaw, Chicago, .750, 18-6

National League
President: Warren C. Giles

Standings	W	L	Pct.	GB	Attend.	Manager
Los Angeles Dodgers	88	68	.564	—	2,071,045	Walter Alston
Milwaukee Braves	86	70	.551	2	1,749,112	Fred Haney
San Francisco Giants	83	71	.539	4	1,422,130	Bill Rigney
Pittsburgh Pirates	78	76	.506	9	1,359,917	Danny Murtaugh
Chicago Cubs	74	80	.481	13	858,255	Bob Scheffing
Cincinnati Reds	74	80	.481	13	801,298	Mayo Smith/Fred Hutchinson
St. Louis Cardinals	71	83	.461	16	929,953	Solly Hemus
Philadelphia Phillies	64	90	.416	23	802,815	Eddie Sawyer

Playoff: Los Angeles 2 games, Milwaukee 0.

BA: Hank Aaron, Milwaukee, .355
Runs: Vada Pinson, Cincinnati, 131
Hits: Hank Aaron, Milwaukee, 223
RBIs: Ernie Banks, Chicago, 143
HRs: Ed Mathews, Milwaukee, 46

Wins: Lew Burdette, Milwaukee, 21
    Sad Sam Jones, San Francisco, 21
    Warren Spahn, Milwaukee, 21
SOs: Don Drysdale, Los Angeles, 242
ERA: Sad Sam Jones, San Francisco, 2.83
Pct: Elroy Face, Pittsburgh, .947, 18-1

AAA American Association
President: Edward S. Doherty

East Standings	W	L	Pct.	GB	Attend.	Manager
Louisville Colonels (12)	97	65	.599	—	222,854	Ben Geraghty
Minneapolis Millers (2)	95	67	.586	2	160,167	Gene Mauch
Indianapolis Indians (3)	86	76	.531	11	249,384	Walker Cooper
St. Paul Saints (11)	81	81	.500	16	116,574	Max Macon
Charleston Senators (5)	77	84	.478	19½	102,774	Bill Adair

West Standings	W	L	Pct.	GB	Attend.	Manager
Omaha Cardinals (15)	83	78	.516	—	116,088	Joe Schultz
Ft. Worth Cats (9)	81	81	.500	2½	97,315	Louis Klein
Denver Bears	76	86	.469	7½	161,127	Stan Hack
Dallas Rangers	75	87	.463	8½	130,334	Fred Martin/Jim Fanning
Houston Buffs	58	104	.358	25½	120,474	Rube Walker/Del Wilber

Playoffs: Ft. Worth 4 games, Louisville 0; Minneapolis 4 games, Omaha 2.
Finals: Minneapolis 4 games, Ft. Worth 3.

All-Star Team: 1B-Jim Gentile, St. Paul; **2B**-Pumpsie Green, Minneapolis; **3B**-Steve Demeter, Charleston; **SS**-Ray Bellino, Ft. Worth; **OF**-Bob Will, Ft. Worth; Lee Maye, Louisville; Chuck Tanner, Minneapolis; Lu Clinton, Minneapolis; **C**-Bob Oldis, Denver; Camillo Carreon, Indianapolis; Chris Cannizzaro, Omaha; **Util**-Ossie Virgil, Charleston; **P**-George Maranda, Louisville; Earl Wilson, Minneapolis; Jack Spring, Dallas; Carl Thomas, Indianapolis; Ed Donnelly, Denver; Dean Stone, Omaha; Don Lee, Charleston; **MVP**-Bob Will, Ft. Worth; **Manager**-Gene Mauch, Minneapolis.

BA: Luis Marquez, Dallas, .345
Runs: Bob Will, Ft. Worth, 101
Hits: Bob Will, Ft. Worth, 203
RBIs: Ron Jackson, Indianapolis, 99
HRs: Ron Jackson, Indianapolis, 30

Wins: George Maranda, Louisville, 18
    Don Nottebart, Louisville, 18
SOs: Bob Bruce, Charleston, 177
ERA: Marion Fricano, Dallas, 2.02

AAA International League
President: Frank J. Shaughnessy

Standings	W	L	Pct.	GB	Attend.	Manager
Buffalo Bisons (13)	89	64	.582	—	413,263	Kerby Farrell
Columbus Jets (14)	84	70	.545	5½	204,157	Cal Ermer
Havana Sugar Kings (10)	80	73	.523	9	200,094	Preston Gomez
Richmond Virginians (7)	76	78	.494	13½	220,198	Steve Souchock
Rochester Red Wings (15)	74	80	.481	15½	256,286	Cot Deal/Clyde King
Montreal Royals (11)	72	82	.468	17½	136,340	Clay Bryant
Miami Marlins (1)	71	83	.461	18½	140,384	Pepper Martin
Toronto Maple Leafs	69	85	.448	20½	207,505	Dixie Walker

Playoffs: Richmond 4 games, Buffalo 1; Havana 4 games, Columbus 0.
Finals: Havana 4 games, Richmond 2.

All-Star Team: 1B-Frank Herrera, Buffalo; **2B**-Curt Roberts, Montreal; **3B**-Forest Smith, Miami; **SS**-Ruben Amaro, Buffalo; **OF**-Bobby Del Greco, Buffalo; Sandy Amoros, Montreal; Charlie James, Rochester; **C**-Jimmie Coker, Buffalo; **P**-Bill Short, Richmond; Ted Wieand, Havana; **MVP**-Frank Herrera, Buffalo; **Pitcher of the Year**-Bill Short, Richmond; **Manager**-Clay Bryant, Montreal.

BA: Frank Herrera, Buffalo, .329
Runs: Bobby Del Greco, Buffalo, 109
Hits: Frank Herrera, Buffalo, 187
RBIs: Frank Herrera, Buffalo, 128

HRs: Frank Herrera, Buffalo, 37
Wins: Bob Keegan, Rochester, 18
SOs: Joe Gibbon, Columbus, 152
ERA: Artie Kay, Miami, 2.08

AAA Pacific Coast League
President: Leslie M. O'Connor

Standings	W	L	Pct.	GB	Attend.	Manager
Salt Lake City Bees (14)	85	69	.552	—	195,350	Larry Shepard
Vancouver Mounties (1)	82	69	.543	1½	238,970	Charlie Metro
San Diego Padres (4)	78	75	.510	6½	166,741	George Metkovich
Sacramento Solons (12)	78	76	.506	7	186,238	Bob Elliott
Spokane Indians (11)	77	77	.500	8	245,012	Bobby Bragan
Portland Beavers (6)	75	77	.493	9	225,257	Tom Heath
Seattle Rainiers (10)	74	80	.481	11	172,725	Fred Hutchinson/Alan Strange
Phoenix Giants (16)	64	90	.416	21	79,106	John "Red" Davis

Playoffs: None.

All-Star Team: 1B-Steve Bilko, Spokane; **2B**-Jim Baumer, Salt Lake City; **3B**-George Freese, Portland; **SS**-Bob Lillis, Spokane; **OF**-Sam Miley, Salt Lake City; Tommy Davis, Spokane; Joe Taylor, Vancouver; **C**-Hal Bevan, Seattle; Al Jones, San Diego; **P**-Jake Striker, San Diego; Dick Hall, Salt Lake City; **MVP**-Dick Hall, Salt Lake City.

BA: Tommy Davis, Spokane, .345
Runs: Ken Toothman, Salt Lake City, 94
Hits: Tommy Davis, Spokane, 211
RBIs: Steve Bilko, Spokane, 92
    Willie McCovey, Phoenix, 92

HRs: Willie McCovey, Phoenix, 29
Wins: Dick Hall, Salt Lake City, 18
SOs: Dick Stigman, San Diego, 181
ERA: Dick Hall, Salt Lake City, 1.87

AA Mexican League
President: Carlos Rubio

Standings	W	L	Pct.	GB	Attend.	Manager
Poza Rica Petroleros	84	62	.575	—	272,324	Pepe Bache/Luis Garcia
Nuevo Laredo Tecolotes	78	68	.534	6	93,602	Cheo Ramos/
						Agustin Bejerano
Mexico City Diablos Rojos	74	72	.507	10	204,308	Luis Montes De Oca/
						Memo Garibay
Monterrey Sultanes	70	74	.486	13	145,055	Ray Garza
Veracruz Aguilas	67	78	.462	16	142,554	Willie Alvarez/Pilo Gaspar
Mexico City Tigres	39	104	.273	43½	97,107	Santos Amaro/Memo Garibay/
						Virgilio Arteaga

Each team played 36 games with Texas League teams which counted in the standings. The combined leagues were known as the Pan American Association.

Playoffs: MC Diablos Rojos 2 games, Poza Rica 1; Nuevo Laredo 2 games, Monterrey 0.
Finals: MC Diablos Rojos 3 games, Nuevo Laredo 2.

All-Star Team: 1B-Marvin Williams, MC Diablos Rojos; **2B**-Moises Camacho, Nuevo Laredo; **3B**-Luis Garcia, Poza Rica; **SS**-Hector Mayer, MC Diablos Rojos; **OF**-Al Pinkston, MC Diablos Rojos; Jose Garcia, Veracruz; Aldo Salvent, Poza Rica; **C**-Ramon Rodriguez, Poza Rica; Miguel Gaspar, Veracruz; **P**-Roberto Vargas, Poza Rica; Eddie Locke, Monterrey.

BA: Al Pinkston, MC Diablos Rojos, .369
Runs: Al Pinkston, MC Diablos Rojos, 114
Hits: Al Pinkston, MC Diablos Rojos, 197
RBIs: Marvin Williams, MC Tigres, 109
HRs: Aldo Salvent, Poza Rica, 29
    Marvin Williams, MC Tigres, 29

Wins: Eddie Locke, Monterrey, 21
    Diomedes Olivo, Poza Rica, 21
SOs: Diomedes Olivo, Poza Rica, 233
ERA: Roberto Vargas, Poza Rica, 2.55

AA Southern Association
President: Charles A. Hurth

Standings	W	L	Pct.	GB	Attend.	Manager
Birmingham Barons*(5)	92	61	.601	—	120,618	Skeeter Newsome
Mobile Bears**(4)	89	63	.586	2½	64,309	Mel McGaha
Nashville Vols (10)	84	64	.568	5½	129,125	Dick Sisler

*Won first-half   **Won second-half   ***Won both halves
Numbers after nicknames indicate farm system.
Affiliation listed at end of year.

	W	L	Pct.	GB	Attend.	Manager
Memphis Chicks	76	77	.497	16	49,682	Luke Appling
Shreveport Sports (6)	75	79	.487	17½	47,636	Les Peden
New Orleans Pelicans	68	81	.456	22	71,577	Mel Parnell
Chattanooga Lookouts (8)	67	86	.438	25	60,128	Red Marion
Atlanta Crackers (12)	56	96	.368	35½	71,139	Buddy Bates/Bob Montag

Playoff: Mobile 4 games, Birmingham 1.

All-Star Team: 1B-Jay Cooke, Birmingham; Gordon Coleman, Mobile; **2B**-Lou Klimchock, Shreveport; **3B**-Bob Johnson, Birmingham; **SS**-Phil Shartzer, Nashville; **OF**-Ultus Alvarez, Nashville; Crawford Davidson, Nashville; Emerit Lindbeck, Atlanta; Don Saner, New Orleans; George Alusik, Birmingham; **C**-Eddie Irons, Nashville; Les Peden, Shreveport; Frank Baldwin, New Orleans; **Util IF**-George Holder, Atlanta; **P**-Wyman Carey, Birmingham; Don Bradey, New Orleans; Thomas Gibson, Nashville; Wayne Hawkins, Mobile; Carl Mathias, Mobile; Ray Rippelmeyer, Atlanta.

BA: Gordy Coleman, Mobile, .353
Runs: John Water, Mobile, 103
Hits: Lou Klimchock, Shreveport, 192
RBIs: Gordy Coleman, Mobile, 110

HRs: Gordy Coleman, Mobile, 30
Wins: Don Bradey, New Orleans, 19
SOs: Carl Mathias, Mobile, 183
ERA: Bill Dailey, Mobile, 2.41

AA Texas League
President: Dick Butler

Standings	W	L	Pct.	GB	Attend.	Manager
Victoria Rosebuds (11)	86	60	.589	—	86,040	Pete Reiser
Austin Senators (12)	80	66	.548	6	101,847	Ernie White
Tulsa Oilers (15)	77	67	.535	8	118,409	Vern Benson
San Antonio Missions (9)	75	70	.517	10½	111,487	Grady Hatton
Amarillo Gold Sox (1)	75	71	.514	11	80,154	Bernard Lutz/George Staller
Corpus Christi Giants (16)	66	79	.455	19½	61,501	Ray Murray

Each team played 36 games with Mexican League teams which counted in the standings. The combined leagues were known as the Pan American Association.

Playoffs: San Antonio 2 games, Victoria 0; Austin 2 games, Tulsa 1.
Finals: Austin 3 games, San Antonio 0.

All-Star Team: 1B-Duke Carmel, Tulsa; **2B**-Jim McKnight, Tulsa; **3B**-Ray Conde, Victoria; **SS**-Julio Gotay, Tulsa; **OF**-Al Nagel, Amarillo; Carl Warwick, Victoria; Lee Handley, San Antonio; **C**-Ray Murray, Corpus Christi; **P**-Carroll Beringer, Victoria; **MVP**-Carl Warwick, Victoria; **Pitcher of the Year**-Carroll Beringer, Victoria; **Manager**-Pete Reiser, Victoria.

BA: Al Nagel, Amarillo, .344
Runs: Carl Warwick, Victoria, 129
Hits: Howie Bedell, Austin, 194
RBIs: Al Nagel, Amarillo, 123

HRs: Carl Warwick, Victoria, 35
Wins: Carroll Beringer, Victoria, 19
SOs: Charles Gorin, Austin, 143
ERA: Bobby Hendley, Austin, 2.96

A Eastern League
President: Thomas H. Richardson

Standings	W	L	Pct.	GB	Attend.	Manager
Springfield Giants (16)	85	55	.607	—	110,499	Andy Gilbert
Allentown Red Sox (2)	82	59	.582	3½	84,430	Sheriff Robinson
Williamsport Grays (13)	81	60	.574	4½	91,819	Frank Lucchesi
Binghamton Triplets (7)	71	68	.511	13½	60,499	Charles Silvera
Reading Indians (4)	71	69	.507	14	81,311	Al Hollingsworth
York White Roses (15)	59	81	.421	26	48,449	Mike Ryba/Eddie Lyons
Lancaster Red Roses (9)	57	83	.407	28	49,073	Nick Cullop
Albany Senators (6)	54	85	.388	30½	45,446	Alfred Evans

Playoffs: Springfield 3 games, Binghamton 0; Williamsport 3 games, Allentown 0.
Finals: Springfield 3 games, Williamsport 1.

All-Star Team: 1B-Fred Hopke, Williamsport; **2B**-Wilbur Johnson, Williamsport; **3B**-James Woods, Lancaster; **SS**-Mike de la Hoz, Reading; **OF**-Tony Curry, Williamsport; Dave Mann, Reading; Lou Jackson, Lancaster; Tom Haller, Springfield; **Util IF**-Chico Valentin, Albany; **Util OF**-Bill Kern, Albany; **P**-Julius Grant, Reading; Juan Marichal, Springfield.

BA: Lou Jackson, Lancaster, .339
Runs: Tony Curry, Williamsport, 108
Hits: Tony Curry, Williamsport, 178
RBIs: Fred Hopke, Williamsport, 130

HRs: Jackie Davis, Williamsport, 33
Wins: Juan Marichal, Springfield, 18
SOs: Juan Marichal, Springfield, 208
ERA: Juan Marichal, Springfield, 2.39

A South Atlantic League
President: Sam C. Smith, Jr.

Standings	W	L	Pct.	GB	Attend.	Manager
Knoxville Smokies (5)	78	62	.557	—	108,633	Johnny Pesky
Charlotte Hornets (8)	75	65	.536	3	106,287	Gene Verble
Charleston ChaSox (3)	71	69	.507	7	85,689	Skeeter Scalzi
Columbus/ Gastonia Pirates#(14)	70	69	.504	7½	78,489	Ray Hathaway
Asheville Tourists (13)	70	70	.500	8	113,001	Clyde McCullough
Savannah Reds (10)	67	73	.479	11	54,212	Bob Wellman/Jack Cassini
Jacksonville Braves (12)	65	75	.464	13	80,019	Sibby Sisti
Macon Dodgers (11)	63	76	.453	14½	64,663	Danny Ozark

#Columbus moved to Gastonia July 6.

Playoffs: Charleston 3 games, Knoxville 2; Gastonia 3 games, Charlotte 2.
Finals: Gastonia 3 games, Charleston 0.

All-Star Team: 1B-Nate Dickerson, Asheville; **2B**-Willie Menendez, Columbus/Gastonia; **3B**-Clifford Cook, Savannah; **SS**-Juan Guzman, Jacksonville; **OF**-Sheldon Brodsky, Macon; Manny Jimenez, Jacksonville; Sandy Valdespino, Charlotte; **C**-Bob Rogers, Knoxville; Sam Hairston, Charleston; **P**-Ralph Lumenti, Charlotte; Jim Proctor, Knoxville.

BA: Nate Dickerson, Asheville, .362
Runs: Harry Warner, Charlotte, 95
Hits: Tom St. John, Savannah, 148
RBIs: Cliff Cook, Savannah, 100

HRs: Cliff Cook, Savannah, 32
Wins: Byron "Jack" Taylor, Asheville, 18
SOs: Roy Daviault, Macon, 169
ERA: Jim Proctor, Knoxville, 2.19

B Carolina League
President: J.C. "Bill" Jessup

Standings	W	L	Pct.	GB	Attend.	Manager
Raleigh Capitals (2)	78	52	.600	—	51,278	Ken Deal
Wilson Tobs (14)	71	58	.550	6½	54,922	Harding Peterson/Don Osborn
Durham Bulls (5)	70	60	.538	8	32,039	Frank Skaff
Winston-Salem Red Birds (15)	67	62	.519	10½	77,157	Al Unser
Greensboro Yankees (7)	54	76	.415	24	39,408	Vern Hoscheit
Burlington Indians (4)	49	81	.377	29	67,874	Pinky May

Playoffs: Wilson 3 games, Durham 0; Raleigh 2 games, Winston-Salem 0 (series reduced to best of 3 because of rain).
Finals: Wilson 4 games, Raleigh 0.

All-Star Team: 1B-Fred Whitfield, Winston-Salem; **2B**-Carl Yastrzemski, Raleigh; **3B**-Mike White, Burlington; **SS**-Dick McAuliffe, Durham; **OF**-Tom Agosta, Raleigh; Danny Briner, Durham; George Watts, Wilson; **C**-Joe Theis, Raleigh; Harding Peterson, Wilson; **Util**-Yogi Hergenrader, Raleigh; **P**-Bob Veale, Wilson; Bill Spanswick, Raleigh; Frank Carpin, Greensboro; Warren Hodgdon, Raleigh; **MVP**-Carl Yastrzemski, Raleigh; **Manager**-Ken Deal, Raleigh;

BA: Carl Yastrzemski, Raleigh, .377
Runs: Don Lock, Greensboro, 102
Hits: Carl Yastrzemski, Raleigh, 170
RBIs: Don Lock, Greensboro, 122
HRs: Don Lock, Greensboro, 30

Wins: Bill Spanswick, Raleigh, 15
    Don Dobrino, Wilson, 15
SOs: Bob Veale, Wilson, 187
ERA: Bill Spanswick, Raleigh, 2.49

B Northwest League
President: James M. Fleishman

Standings	W	L	Pct.	GB	Attend.	Manager
Lewiston Broncs	75	66	.532	—	55,996	John McNamara
Wenatchee Chiefs	74	67	.525	1	43,978	Dick Wilson
Salem Senators*	73	67	.521	1½	66,607	Karl Kuehl
Yakima Bears**(12)	70	69	.504	4	43,895	Hub Kittle
Eugene Emeralds (16)	68	71	.489	6	67,386	Roy Partee
Tri-City Braves	60	80	.429	14½	46,751	Jack Lohrke/Dan Holden

Playoff: Yakima 4 games, Salem 1.

All-Star Team: 1B-Dick Wilson, Wenatchee; **2B**-Chuck Hiller, Eugene; **3B**-Rocky Columbo, Yakima; **SS**-Sal Ferrera, Lewiston; **OF**-Gerald Mason, Wenatchee; Walter O'Neil, Yakima; Joe Wilson, Salem; **C**-John McNamara, Lewiston; **Util IF**-Mel Krause, Eugene; **Util OF**-Layton Ducote, Wenatchee; **P**-Jack Curtis, Wenatchee; Bobby Bolin, Eugene; **Manager**-Dick Wilson, Wenatchee.

BA: Gerald Mason, Wenatchee, .356
Runs: Allison Owen, Wenatchee, 104
Hits: Chuck Hiller, Eugene, 166
RBIs: Walter O'Neil, Yakima, 100

HRs: Joe Wilson, Salem, 30
Wins: Roger Clapp, Yakima, 21
SOs: Bobby Bolin, Eugene, 271
ERA: Roger Clapp, Yakima, 2.48

B Three-I League
President: Hal Totten

Standings	W	L	Pct.	GB	Attend.	Manager
Des Moines Demons**(13)	78	48	.619	—	86,923	Charlie Kress
Green Bay Bluejays**(11)	74	51	.592	3½	41,107	Stan Wasiak
Topeka Hawks (10)	69	56	.552	8½	59,803	John Vander Meer
Fox Cities Foxes (8)	59	67	.468	19	51,004	Jack McKeon
Lincoln Chiefs (3)	58	68	.460	20	44,783	Ira Hutchinson
Sioux City Soos (6)	58	68	.460	20	38,332	Bill Capps
Burlington Bees (9)	54	72	.429	24	53,536	Ray Mueller
Cedar Rapids Braves (12)	53	73	.421	25	70,039	Alex Monchak

Playoff: Green Bay 3 games, Des Moines 1.

All-Star Team: 1B-Cal Emery, Des Moines; **2B**-Robert Parker, Green Bay; **3B**-George Scott, Green Bay; **SS**-Zoilo Versalles, Fox Cities; **OF**-James Lynn, Lincoln; Tom McDonald, Sioux City; Bill McGuckin, Des Moines; **C**-Al Kenders, Des Moines; **Util**-Chuck Weatherspoon, Fox Cities; **P**-Pete Richert, Green Bay; Henry Hemmerly, Cedar Rapids; Barton Dziadek, Topeka; Fred Bruckbauer, Fox Cities; **MVP**-Cal Emery, Des Moines; **Outstanding Rookie**-Fred Bruckbauer, Fox Cities; **Manager**-Charlie Kress, Des Moines.

BA: Hernan Vila, Fox Cities, .330
Runs: Cal Emery, Des Moines, 107
    Dick Howser, Sioux City, 107
Hits: George Scott, Green Bay, 155
RBIs: Cal Emery, Des Moines, 129

HRs: Cal Emery, Des Moines, 27
Wins: Barton Dziadek, Topeka, 15
SOs: Larry Maxie, Cedar Rapids, 187
ERA: Jim Brewer, Burlington, 2.67

C California League
President: Edward J. Mulligan

Standings	W	L	Pct.	GB	Attend.	Manager
Modesto Reds**(7)	86	55	.610	—	44,464	Hal Charnofsky
Reno Silver Sox (11)	81	58	.583	4	46,358	Ray Perry
Stockton Ports (1)	76	63	.547	9	34,426	Billy DeMars
Bakersfield Bears*(13)	70	71	.496	16	56,346	Paul Owens
Visalia Redlegs (10)	63	77	.450	22½	30,500	Dave Bristol
Fresno Giants (16)	44	96	.314	41½	38,556	Myron McCormick

Playoff: Modesto 4 games, Bakersfield 2.

All-Star Team: 1B-Jerome Stack, Fresno; **2B**-Dave Bristol, Visalia; **3B**-Hal Charnofsky, Modesto; **SS**-Chico Ruiz, Visalia; **OF**-Willie Davis, Reno; Ron Wiley, Bakersfield; Rich Barry, Modesto; **C**-John Edwards, Visalia; **Util**-Chuck Strange, Fresno; **P**-Ken Page, Reno; Horace Denny, Stockton; Hal Reniff, Modesto; Hugh Hendry, Modesto; **MVP**-Willie Davis, Reno; **Rookie of the Year**-Willie Davis, Reno; **Manager**-Hal Charnofsky, Modesto.

BA: Willie Davis, Reno, .365
Runs: Willie Davis, Reno, 135
Hits: Willie Davis, Reno, 187
RBIs: Ron Wiley, Bakersfield, 125
HRs: Rich Barry, Modesto, 37
Wins: Hal Reniff, Modesto, 21
SOs: Paul Underwood, Visalia, 193
ERA: George Gaffney, Stockton, 2.49

C Northern League
President: Peter Bradbury

Standings	W	L	Pct.	GB	Attend.	Manager
Winnipeg Goldeyes (15)	80	41	.661	—	79,847	Chase Riddle
Aberdeen Pheasants (1)	69	55	.556	12½	63,111	Earl Weaver
Fargo-Moorhead Twins (7)	64	59	.520	17	46,146	Dee Phillips
Minot Mallards (4)	63	60	.512	18	29,337	Ken Landenberger
Duluth-Superior Dukes (3)	61	61	.500	19½	35,966	George Noga
Grand Forks Chiefs (14)	57	68	.456	25	29,267	James Adlam
Eau Claire Braves (12)	55	68	.447	26	35,895	Travis Jackson/ Robert Dudley/ Gordon Maltzberger
St. Cloud Rox (16)	43	80	.350	38	22,595	Richard Klaus

Playoffs: Winnipeg 1 game, Fargo-Moorhead 0; Aberdeen 1 game, Minot 0.
Finals: Winnipeg 2 games, Aberdeen 1.

All-Star Team: 1B-Harold Jones, Minot; **2B**-Fabio Fiallo, Fargo-Moorhead; **3B**-Emile Fiore, St. Cloud; **SS**-Chico Suarez, Winnipeg; **OF**-Manly Johnston, Duluth-Superior; Chuck Hinton, Aberdeen; Rogers Robinson, Winnipeg; **C**-Roberto Herrera, Winnipeg; Jim Napier, Duluth-Superior; **P**-Tim Lane, St. Cloud; Bill Carpenter, Winnipeg.

BA: Chuck Hinton, Aberdeen, .358
Runs: Bill Wyatt, Minot, 118
Hits: Chuck Hinton, Aberdeen, 178
RBIs: Harold Jones, Minot, 127
HRs: Harold Jones, Minot, 35
Dave Nicholson, Aberdeen, 35
Wins: Bill Carpenter, Winnipeg, 19
SOs: Robert Leopold, Aberdeen, 174
ERA: Bill Carpenter, Winnipeg, 1.59

C Pioneer League
President: Claude Engberg

Standings	W	L	Pct.	GB	Attend.	Manager
Boise Braves (12)	81	47	.633	—	54,029	Billy Smith
Billings Mustangs (15)	68	62	.523	14	44,817	Whitey Kurowski
Idaho Falls Russets (14)	64	65	.496	17½	30,219	Bob Clear
Great Falls Electrics (11)	60	70	.462	22	33,990	Brandy Davis
Pocatello Athletics (6)	58	70	.453	23	27,423	Tom Giordano
Missoula Timberjacks (8)	56	73	.434	25½	25,935	Ralph Rowe

Playoffs: Idaho Falls 2 games, Boise 0; Billings 2 games, Great Falls 1.
Finals: Billings 3 games, Idaho Falls 1.

All-Star Team: 1B-Donn Clendenon, Idaho Falls; **2B**-Mike Castanon, Great Falls; **3B**-Minnie Mendoza, Missoula; **SS**-Roberto Sanchez, Idaho Falls; **OF**-Ronald Hogg, Pocatello; Kerry Buckner, Boise; Eddie Reed, Great Falls; **C**-James Hay, Boise; James Campbell, Idaho Falls; **Util**-Richard Rogers, Billings; **P**-Leslie Bass, Boise; Bill Kunkel, Great Falls; John Tupper, Pocatello; Bruce Haroldson, Billings.

BA: Billy Smith, Boise, .390
Runs: Domingo Carrasquel, Great Falls, 134
Hits: Minnie Mendoza, Missoula, 174
RBIs: Eddie Reed, Great Falls, 103
Bruno Terilli, Boise, 103
HRs: Jim Campbell, Idaho Falls, 24
Bruno Terilli, Boise, 24
Wins: Leslie Bass, Boise, 21
SOs: Leslie Bass, Boise, 214
ERA: Bob Clear, Idaho Falls, 2.81

D Alabama-Florida League
President: William Moore

Standings	W	L	Pct.	GB	Attend.	Manager
Montgomery Rebels (5)	77	42	.647	—	36,199	Frank Carswell
Selma Cloverleafs (4)	73	46	.613	4	26,633	John Lipon
Dothan Cardinals (15)	58	61	.487	19	39,015	J.C. Dunn
Pensacola Dons (1)	51	66	.436	25	30,227	Lou Fitzgerald
Ft. Walton Beach Jets (8)	50	70	.417	27½	13,456	Vince Magi
Panama City Fliers (11)	47	71	.398	29½	10,422	Al Ronning

Playoffs: Dothan 3 games, Montgomery 2; Selma 3 games, Pensacola 0.
Finals: Selma 4 games, Dothan 1.

All-Star Team: 1B-Keith Williams, Selma; **2B**-Legrant Scott, Montgomery; **3B**-Max Alvis, Selma; **SS**-Larry Brown, Selma; **OF**-Teo Acosta, Dothan; Jim Bethea, Montgomery; Peter Walski, Montgomery; **C**-Howard "Doc" Edwards, Selma; Robert Koehl, Montgomery; **P**-Jorge Rapado, Dothan; Joseph Kaiser, Ft. Walton Beach.

BA: Keith Williams, Selma, .341
Runs: Legrant Scott, Montgomery, 129
Hits: Keith Williams, Selma, 156
RBIs: Jim Bethea, Montgomery, 99
HRs: Jim Bethea, Montgomery, 21
Peter Walski, Montgomery, 21
Wins: Joe Kaiser, Ft. Walton Beach, 16
SOs: Dick Egan, Montgomery, 201
ERA: Jorge Rapado, Dothan, 2.25

D Appalachian League
President: Chauncey De Vault

Standings	W	L	Pct.	GB	Attend.	Manager
Morristown Cubs (9)	41	27	.603	—	26,681	Red Hayworth
Salem Rebels (14)	38	29	.567	2½	36,128	Larry Dorton
Johnson City Phillies (13)	36	31	.537	4½	17,751	Eddie Lyons
Bluefield Orioles (1)	37	32	.536	4½	19,628	Bob Hooper
Wytheville Cardinals (15)	29	37	.439	11	20,553	Don Pries
Lynchburg Senators (8)	22	47	.319	19½	11,795	Chick Payne

Playoffs: None.

All-Star Team: 1B-Rich Marks, Salem; **2B**-John Carey, Salem; **3B**-Bertrand Gladney, Morristown; **SS**-Bob Saverine, Bluefield; **OF**-John "Boog" Powell, Bluefield; Larry Daniels, Johnson City; Art Blunt, Salem; **C**-Ed Cannon, Salem; Jim Saul, Wytheville; **P**-Gary Aldrich, Salem; Arne Thorsland, Bluefield; **Rookie of the Year**-Arne Thorsland, Bluefield; Bob Saverine, Bluefield; **Manager**-Red Hayworth, Morristown.

BA: Bob Saverine, Bluefield, .353
Runs: Bob Saverine, Bluefield, 70
Hits: Bob Saverine, Bluefield, 89
RBIs: Bertrand Gladney, Morristown, 68
HRs: Larry Daniels, Johnson City, 18
Wins: Arthur Thompson, Morristown, 13
SOs: Arne Thorsland, Bluefield, 180
ERA: Arne Thorsland, Bluefield, 2.93

D Florida State League
President: Julian Jackson

Standings	W	L	Pct.	GB	Attend.	Manager
Tampa Tarpons*(13)	78	55	.587	—	89,068	Charles Gassaway
St. Petersburg Saints**(7)	79	57	.581	½	119,424	Tom Hamilton
Palatka Redlegs (10)	74	62	.544	5½	27,989	Scooter Koshorek/ Tony Pacheco
Daytona Beach Islanders (15)	71	63	.530	7½	33,777	Ray Wilson
Orlando Dodgers (11)	69	70	.497	12	27,633	Martin Devlin
Sanford Greyhounds (8)	33	97	.253	43½	21,828	Packy Rogers/Ed Barbarito/ Joe Abernethy

Playoff: St. Petersburg 4 games, Tampa 2.

All-Star Team: 1B-Tom Hamilton, St. Petersburg; **2B**-Ray Wilson, Daytona Beach; **3B**-Don Keller, St. Petersburg; **SS**-Joe Curtin, Orlando; **OF**-Gerald Reimer, Tampa; Mario Zambrano, Palatka; Elvio Jiminez, St. Petersburg; **C**-Clarence "Choo Choo" Coleman, Orlando; **Util**-Von McDaniel, Daytona Beach; **P**-Vic Davalillo, Palatka; Gilberto Clark, Palatka; **Manager**-Ray Wilson, Daytona Beach.

BA: Tom Hamilton, St. Petersburg, .387
Runs: Horace Clarke, St. Petersburg, 115
Hits: Elvio Jiminez, St. Petersburg, 181
RBIs: John Moskus, Tampa, 110
HRs: Tom Hamilton, St. Petersburg, 20
Wins: Gilberto Clark, Palatka, 22
SOs: Gilberto Clark, Palatka, 213
ERA: Vic Davalillo, Palatka, 2.45

D Midwest League
President: C.C. "Dutch" Hoffman

Standings	W	L	Pct.	GB	Attend.	Manager
Waterloo Hawks***(2)	76	48	.613	—	67,260	Elmer Yoter
Clinton Pirates (3)	71	52	.577	4½	82,773	John Hutchings
Decatur Commodores (15)	63	61	.508	13	75,834	Stubby Overmire
Keokuk Cardinals (5)	62	60	.508	13	39,045	Frank Calo
Kokomo Dodgers (11)	60	65	.480	16½	44,721	Edward Serrano
Paris Lakers (9)	57	68	.456	19½	33,209	Verlon Walker
Dubuque Packers (14)	56	68	.452	20	97,220	Walter Millies/John Armstrong/ Syd Thrift/Al Kubski
Michigan City White Caps (16)	51	74	.408	25½	28,775	Buddy Kerr

Playoffs: None.

All-Star Team: 1B-Gary Dobereiner, Keokuk; **2B**-Julio Duran, Clinton; **3B**-Frank Jaciuk, Decatur; **SS**-Rich Johnson, Waterloo; **OF**-Stan Schultz, Kokomo; Donald Branson, Keokuk; Bo Toft, Waterloo; **C**-Bill Smith, Clinton; **Util IF**-Dale Reichert, Kokomo; **Util OF**-Jorge Aguiles Gomez, Kokomo; **P**-Al Madigan, Clinton; Morris Steevens, Paris; Joe McDaniel, Decatur; Galen Cisco, Waterloo; **Player of the Year**-Joel McDaniel, Decatur; **Rookie of the Year**-Dale Reichert, Kokomo; **Manager**-Stubby Overmire, Decatur.

BA: Donald Branson, Keokuk, .336
Runs: Jose Tartabull, Michigan City, 106
Hits: Gary Dobereiner, Keokuk, 148
RBIs: Dale Reichert, Kokomo, 116
HRs: Dale Reichert, Kokomo, 30
Wins: Joel McDaniel, Decatur, 22
SOs: Joel McDaniel, Decatur, 212
ERA: Galen Cisco, Waterloo, 2.23

D Nebraska State League
President: Mike Hollinger

Standings	W	L	Pct.	GB	Attend.	Manager
McCook Braves (12)	43	19	.694	—	19,788	Bill Steinecke
Holdrege White Sox (3)	39	23	.629	4	11,963	Frank Parenti
Grand Island Athletics (6)	32	30	.516	11	16,716	Art Mazmanian
Kearney Yankees (7)	27	35	.435	16	13,141	Jimmy Gleeson
Hastings Giants (16)	23	39	.371	20	10,235	Leo Schrall
North Platte Indians (4)	22	40	.355	21	14,275	Mark Wylie

Playoffs: None.

All-Star Team: 1B-Frank Saia, McCook; **2B**-William Fontana, Grand Island; **3B**-Woody Huyke, Hastings; **SS**-Ike Futch, Kearney; **OF**-Jim Hicks, Holdrege; Fred Loesekam, Holdrege; Bill Stevens, McCook; **C**-Boyd Coffie, Kearney; Robert Barton, Hastings; **P**-Dennis Overby, McCook; Paul Chenger, McCook.

BA: Ike Futch, Kearney, .319
Runs: Frank Saia, McCook, 63
Hits: Woody Huyke, Hastings, 71
RBIs: Boyd Coffie, Kearney, 63
HRs: Woody Huyke, Hastings, 12
Wins: Anthony Filicchia, Grand Island, 11
SOs: Dennis Overby, McCook, 136
ERA: Paul Chenger, McCook, 2.13

D New York-Pennsylvania League
President: Vincent M. McNamara

Standings	W	L	Pct.	GB	Attend.	Manager
Wellsville Braves (12)	80	46	.635	—	25,659	Harry Minor
Geneva Redlegs (10)	72	52	.581	7	29,130	Reno DeBenedetti
Elmira Pioneers (13)	67	57	.540	12	39,867	Andy Seminick
Corning Cor-Sox (2)	63	62	.504	16½	32,429	Len Okrie
Auburn Yankees (7)	58	67	.464	21½	34,139	Bob Bauer
Olean Athletics (6)	57	69	.452	23	21,414	William Robertson
Batavia Indians (4)	54	71	.432	25½	24,185	Paul O'Dea
Erie Sailors (5)	49	76	.392	30½	24,158	Al Lakeman/Pat Mullin

Playoffs: Wellsville 2 games, Corning 0; Elmira 2 games, Geneva 0.
Finals: Wellsville 3 games, Elmira 2.

All-Star Team: 1B-Robert Lawrence, Corning; **2B**-Mario Diaz, Wellsville; **3B**-Lee Elia, Elmira; **SS**-Amado Samuel, Wellsville; **OF**-Marcial Allen, Wellsville; Willard Hamill, Corning; Harry Panaro, Geneva; **C**-John Sullivan, Erie; Howard McGaughey, Wellsville; **P**-Stanley Jones, Geneva; Robert Baillargeon, Elmira; Ben Griggs, Wellsville; James King, Wellsville.

BA: Marcial Allen, Wellsville, .356
Runs: Gus Gill, Geneva, 104
Hits: Marcial Allen, Wellsville, 164
RBIs: Marcial Allen, Wellsville, 92
  Willard Hamill, Corning, 92
HRs: Bob Bauer, Auburn, 22
Wins: Ben Griggs, Wellsville, 21
SOs: Ben Griggs, Wellsville, 175
ERA: Dick Dumas, Auburn, 2.22

D Sophomore League
President: Grady Terry

North Standings	W	L	Pct.	GB	Attend.	Manager
Carlsbad Potashers (9)	72	54	.571	—	30,733	Walter Dixon
Hobbs Cardinals (15)	70	54	.565	1	23,703	Thurman Tucker
Plainview Athletics (6)	60	65	.480	11½	12,329	Bob Hofman
Artesia Giants (16)	50	75	.400	21½	15,249	Jodie Phipps

South Standings	W	L	Pct.	GB	Attend.	Manager
Alpine Cowboys (2)	88	34	.721	—	22,630	Eddie Popowski
Midland Braves (12)	56	70	.444	34	17,106	James Brown
Odessa Dodgers (11)	54	69	.439	34½	30,459	Roy Hartsfield
San Angelo/ Roswell Pirates#(14)	48	77	.384	41½	17,346	Al Kubski/ Joe Bauman/Walter Millies

#San Angelo moved to Roswell June 9.

Playoffs: Alpine 2 games, Hobbs 0; Carlsbad 2 games, Midland 0.
Finals: Alpine 2 games, Carlsbad 0.

BA: Emiliano Telleria, San Angelo/Roswell, .358
Runs: Bob Stotsky, Alpine, 132
Hits: Bob Stotsky, Alpine, 156
RBIs: Bob Caruthers, Plainview, 119
HRs: Gilbert Carter, Carlsbad, 34
Wins: Don Schwall, Alpine, 23
SOs: Terry Barber, Odessa, 214
ERA: Jack Warner, Carlsbad, 2.41

1959 Interleague Post Season Play

World Series
Los Angeles (National) 4 games, Chicago (American) 2

Junior World Series
Havana (International) 4 games, Minneapolis (American Association) 3
Total Attendance: 103,808

Pan-American Series
Austin (Texas) 4 games, Mexico City Diablos Rojos (Mexican) 1
Total Attendance: 29,166

1959 Major League Farm Systems

American League
1 Baltimore (7): Miami, Vancouver, Amarillo, Stockton, Aberdeen, Pensacola, Bluefield.
2 Boston (6): Minneapolis, Allentown, Raleigh, Waterloo, Corning, Alpine.
3 Chicago (6): Indianapolis, Charleston (SC), Lincoln, Duluth-Superior, Clinton, Holdrege.
4 Cleveland (8): San Diego, Mobile, Reading, Burlington (NC), Minot, Selma, North Platte, Batavia.
5 Detroit (7): Charleston (WV), Birmingham, Knoxville, Durham, Montgomery, Keokuk, Erie.
6 Kansas City (8): Portland, Shreveport, Albany, Sioux City, Pocatello, Grand Island, Olean, Plainview.
7 New York (8): Richmond, Binghamton, Greensboro, Modesto, Fargo-Moorhead, St. Petersburg, Kearney, Auburn.
8 Washington (7): Chattanooga, Charlotte, Fox Cities, Missoula, Ft. Walton Beach, Lynchburg, Sanford.

National League
9 Chicago (7): Ft. Worth, San Antonio, Lancaster, Burlington (IA), Morristown, Paris, Carlsbad.
10 Cincinnati (8): Havana, Seattle, Nashville, Savannah, Topeka, Visalia, Palatka, Geneva.
11 Los Angeles (12): St. Paul, Montreal, Spokane, Victoria, Macon, Green Bay, Reno, Great Falls, Panama City, Orlando, Kokomo, Odessa.
12 Milwaukee (12): Louisville, Sacramento, Atlanta, Austin, Jacksonville, Yakima, Cedar Rapids, Eau Claire, Boise, McCook, Wellsville, Midland.
13 Philadelphia (8): Buffalo, Williamsport, Asheville, Des Moines, Bakersfield, Johnson City, Tampa, Elmira.
14 Pittsburgh (9): Columbus (OH), Salt Lake City, Columbus (GA)/Gastonia, Wilson, Grand Forks, Idaho Falls, Salem (VA), Dubuque, San Angelo/Roswell.
15 St. Louis (12): Omaha, Rochester, Tulsa, York, Winston-Salem, Winnipeg, Billings, Dothan, Wytheville, Daytona Beach, Decatur, Hobbs.
16 San Francisco (9): Phoenix, Corpus Christi, Springfield, Eugene, Fresno, St. Cloud, Michigan City, Hastings, Artesia.

1959 No-Hitters

Date	Pitcher	Team	League	Opponent	Score
4-29	Carroll Dial	Columbus	South Atlantic	Charleston	5-0 (5)
5-3	Michael Urrizola	Bakersfield	California	Fresno	13-0
5-7	Russell Heman	San Diego	Pacific Coast	Vancouver	2-0
5-13	George Perez	Salt Lake City	Pacific Coast	Sacramento	7-0
5-17	Steve Dalkowski	Aberdeen	Northern	Grand Forks	6-0
5-17	Ron Vingle	Burlington	Three-I	Topeka	3-0
5-19	Larry Foster	Durham	Carolina	Greensboro	3-0
5-26	Harvey Haddix	Pittsburgh	National	Milwaukee	0-1 (P, 12)
5-26	Dick Stigman	San Diego	Pacific Coast	Salt Lake City	1-0 (10)
6-2	Thomas Fisher	Clinton	Midwest	Paris	3-0
6-6	Bob Baillargeon	Elmira	New York-Penn.	Geneva	4-0 (7)
6-8	Raphael Lumenti	Charlotte	South Atlantic	Savannah	3-0
6-10	Art Mehuron	Billings	Pioneer	Great Falls	5-0 (7)
6-11	Ron Bloodworth	Lincoln	Three-I	Green Bay	3-0 (P)
6-16	Juan Pizarro	Louisville	American Assoc.	Charleston	1-0
6-20	Winston Brown	Sacramento	Pacific Coast	Vancouver	10-0
6-26	Don Kildoo	New Orleans	Southern Assoc.	Birmingham	5-0
6-29	Carlos Mendez	Lynchburg	Appalachian	Johnson City	0-2
7-3	Dennis Ballard	Auburn	New York-Penn.	Geneva	12-0
7-3	Jim Weaver	Burlington	Carolina	Durham	3-1
7-17	Ron Woods	Holdrege	Nebraska State	Kearney	4-0 (7)
7-23	Bob Veale	Wilson	Carolina	Raleigh	2-0
7-24	Gary Peters	Indianapolis	American Assoc.	Minneapolis	5-0
7-29	Jim Little	Roswell	Sophomore	Plainview	8-0 (7)
8-3	Robert Gordon	Selma	Alabama-Florida	Pensacola	6-0 (7)
8-3	Gary Kroll	Johnson City	Appalachian	Lynchburg	9-0
8-12	Horace Womack	Fargo-Moorhead	Northern	Minot	4-0 (7)
8-15	Joe McCauley	Bluefield	Appalachian	Salem	4-0 (7)
8-18	Mark Freeman	Seattle	Pacific Coast	Vancouver	3-0
8-20	Gerald Fosnow	Selma	Alabama-Florida	Pensacola	5-0 (PO)
8-21	Greg Jancich	Visalia	California	Bakersfield	9-0
8-23	Bobby Bolin	Eugene	Northwest	Lewiston	13-0 (7)
8-27	Marcel Guilbault	Orlando	Florida State	Daytona Beach	3-0 (7)
9-20	Charles Gorin	Austin	Texas	MC Diablos Rojos	2-0 (PO)

Number in parentheses indicates innings pitched if other than nine; "P" indicates perfect game; "PO" indicates playoff game.

THIS DATE IN MINOR LEAGUE HISTORY

January 24, 1959, George Payne, 64, who won 348 games in his 26-year career in minor league ball, died at Long Beach, California. Payne was one of the best control pitchers in the game, averaging 1.5 walks per nine-inning game for his career.

April 25, 1959, Scoring eight runs in the first inning before a batter was retired, Auburn, New York-Penn League, stepped off to a rousing start in the season with a 16-7 victory over Geneva.

May 1, 1959, Al Spearman, Houston, American Association, was replaced in the eighth inning in a game with St. Paul. It was the first time Spearman had filed to finish a game in 33 consecutive starts, dating back to late 1957. Spearman, who had finished three earlier starting assignments this season, went the route in each of 28 starts for Stockton, California League, last year. In 1957, he went all the way in all but two of 19 openings, while in '56 he turned in 16 consecutive victories and wound up at 18-3 with Stockton. That year he was around at the finish of 18 of 19 starts.

May 7, 1959, Corning, New York-Penn League, came up with 10 runs in one inning in a wild-scoring victory over Olean, 25-10. Going to the other extreme, in another meeting the following night, Corning was held to two hits and lost to Olean, 1-0.

May 8, 1959, Nashville, Southern League, trailing 7-0 going into the final frame, exploded nine successive hits to score eight runs and top Memphis, 8-7.

May 10, 1959, Erie, New York-Penn League, apparently trounced, 12-1, after six innings, scored six runs in the seventh, two in the eighth and then won with a five-run rally after two were out in the ninth to defeat Elmira, 14-13.

May 26, 1959, Dick Stigman, San Diego, Pacific Coast League, southpaw, pitched 10 2/3 innings of no-hit ball against Salt Lake City but relief hurler received credit for the 15-inning, 1-0, thriller. Stigman yielded singles in the 11th and 12th frames before going out for pich hitter.

May 28, 1959, Former pitcher Kenneth Penner, 63, who won 330 games in the minor leagues from 1913 to 1943, died at Sacramento, California.

June 8, 1959, Frank Howard, Victoria, Texas League, slammed three consecutive three-run homers and batted in 10 runs in the Rosebud's 19-4 rout of Austin.

June 9, 1959, Frank Heulsman, star minor league outfielder from 1897 to 1916, died at Afton, Missouri, at age 80. Huelsman batted over .400 three times in his 17-year career in the minors. He won five batting titles and compiled a lifetime batting average of .342.

June 10, 1959, Olean broke the New York-Penn League record with nine doubles while taking a 17-6 decision from Batavia.

June 10, 1959, Auburn, New York-Penn League, collected only three hits but capitalized on 15 walks to defeat Elmira, 6-5.

June 13, 1959, Bobby Lee Smith, handyman with Clinton, Midwest League, belted four homers and drove in 10 runs to lead his club to a 20-12 victory over Dubuque.

June 13, 1959, Raleigh, Carolina League, lost to Wilson after 15 straight victories.

June 17, 1959, Tippy Johnson, Wellsville, New York-Penn League, outfielder, hit two homers in the fourth inning in a game with Auburn.

June 17, 1959, Bob Lawrence, Corning, New York-Penn League, first baseman drove in six runs with a pair of bases-loaded doubles to feature a 12-1 trouncing of Batavia.

June 18, 1959, Tommy Wells, one of Reno's flingers in a wild game with Stockton, California League, hit three successive batters in the third inning with pitched balls.

June 19, 1959, Dennis Mendyk, former Michigan State football star, smashed two homers in one inning for Erie, New York-Penn League, as the Sailors trounced Auburn, 18-5. Mendyk homered to lead off the second inning and then connected again with two men on base to climax an eight-run outburst.

June 19, 1959, The Alpine Cowboys, Sophmore League, lost to Plainview after winning 15 straight games.

June 19, 1959, Johnnie Seale, Paris, Midwest League, struck out 20 in a 17-5 win over Dubuque.

June 30, 1959, Three Modesto, California League, pitchers struck out 20 in the first nine innings of an overtime game with Stockton. Although four more Ports went down in extra innings, Stockton won in the 14th, 12-11.

July 6, 1959, Kenneth Ryback, 20-year-old pitcher in Philadelphia Phillies farm system, drowned in Saginaw Bay near Bay City, Michigan, while skin diving. He had been home on leave of absence from Elmira, New York-Penn League, for dental work at the time of his death.

July 7, 1959, Bob Bolin, Eugene, set a Northwest League record when he fanned 22 in blanking Salem, 2-0.

July 10, 1959, Missoula, Pioneer League, scored 13 runs in the first inning and defeated Great Falls, 26-13.

July 10, 1959, Bob Kaczynski, Auburn, New York-Penn League, outfielder, hit two consecutive grand-slam homers against Erie, first and third innings, to give the Yankees a 9-0 victory. Other players with two grandslams in one game in the loop were John Newman of Jamestown in 1941, Barney Hearn of Auburn in 1944, and Jim Hercinger of Hamilton in 1948.

July 16, 1959, Robert "Bob" Coleman, 69, who managed in the minors for 35 years, most of it in the Three-I League between 1919 and 1957, died in Boston, Massachusetts. Coleman won 2,496, the record in the minor leagues.

July 18, 1959, Lynchburg, Appalachian League, defeated Bluefield, 11-4, after 17 straight losses.

July 22, 1959, After hitting at least one homer in 42 consecutive home games. Phoenix, Pacific Coast League, was stopped by Lefty George Brunet of Portland.

July 30, 1959, Wellsville, New York-Penn League, hit five homers in battering Elmira, 22-4.

August 3, 1959, Knute Westergreen, Alpine, Sophmore League, third sacker, smashed three homers and drove in 10 runs when the Cowboys outsluffed Midland, 19-14.

August 8, 1959, Austin, Texas League, mound corps posted its fifth consecutive shutout.

August 11, 1959, Gil Carter, outfielder with Carlsbad, Sophmore League, smashed one of the longest home runs in the game's history, estimated to have carried over 650 feet on the fly.

August 12, 1959, In the Alabama-Florida League, Montgomery lost to Panama City, 7-5, after 15 straight victories.

August 14, 1959, Arne Thorsland, Bluefield, Appalachian League, whiffed 23 in a 4-2 victory over Johnson City.

August 18, 1959, Catcher Jim Carver, Stockton, California League, hit four doubles, but the Ports lost to Fresno, 16-14, in a wind-blown, dusty marathon.

August 20, 1959, Four Fresno, California League, flingers issued a total of 38 bases on balls - 17 on the 19th, 21 on the 20th - in 14-5 and 14-2 losses to Stockton, August 19-20.

August 21, 1959, Wellsville won its fourth straight pennant in the New York-Penn League.

August 30, 1959, Mobile, Southern League, lost to Shreveport, 5-3, after winning 14 consecutive games.

August 30, 1959, Carl Yaztrzemski, Raleigh, Carolina League, 20 years old, playing in his first pro season, batted .377 to win the batting title. He had 100 RBIs in 120 games.

1960

American League
President: Joseph E. Cronin

Standings	W	L	Pct.	GB	Attend.	Manager
New York Yankees	97	57	.630	—	1,627,349	Casey Stengel
Baltimore Orioles	89	65	.578	8	1,187,849	Paul Richards
Chicago White Sox	87	67	.565	10	1,644,460	Al Lopez
Cleveland Indians	76	78	.494	21	950,985	Joe Gordon/ Jo Jo White/Jimmy Dykes
Washington Senators	73	81	.474	24	743,404	Cookie Lavagetto
Detroit Tigers	71	83	.461	26	1,167,669	Jimmy Dykes/ Billy Hitchcock/Joe Gordon
Boston Red Sox	65	89	.422	32	1,129,866	Bill Jurges/Del Baker/ Pinky Higgins
Kansas City Athletics	58	96	.377	39	774,944	Bob Elliott

BA: Pete Runnels, Boston, .320
Runs: Mickey Mantle, New York, 119
Hits: Minnie Minoso, Chicago, 184
RBIs: Roger Maris, New York, 112
HRs: Mickey Mantle, New York, 40

Wins: Jim Perry, Cleveland, 18
  Chuck Estrada, Baltimore, 18
SOs: Jim Bunning, Detroit, 201
ERA: Joe Baumann, Chicago, 2.67
Pct: Jim Perry, Cleveland, .643, 18-10
Games: Mike Fornieles, Boston, 70

National League
President: Warren C. Giles

Standings	W	L	Pct.	GB	Attend.	Manager
Pittsburgh Pirates	95	59	.617	—	1,705,828	Danny Murtaugh
Milwaukee Braves	88	66	.571	7	1,497,799	Chuck Dressen
St. Louis Cardinals	86	68	.558	9	1,096,632	Solly Hemus
Los Angeles Dodgers	82	72	.532	13	2,253,887	Walter Alston
San Francisco Giants	79	75	.513	16	1,795,356	Bill Rigney
Cincinnati Reds	67	87	.435	28	663,486	Fred Hutchinson
Chicago Cubs	60	94	.390	35	809,770	Charlie Grimm Lou Boudreau
Philadelphia Phillies	59	95	.383	36	862,205	Eddie Sawyer Andy Cohen/Gene Mauch

BA: Dick Groat, Pittsburgh, .325
Runs: Billy Bruton, Milwaukee, 112
Hits: Willie Mays, San Francisco, 190
RBIs: Hank Aaron, Milwaukee, 126
HRs: Ernie Banks, Chicago, 41
Wins: Ernie Broglio, St. Louis, 21
  Warren Spahn, Milwaukee, 21

SOs: Don Drysdale, Los Angeles, 246
ERA: Mike McCormick, San Francisco, 2.70
Pct: Ernie Broglio, St. Louis, .700, 21-9
Saves: Lindy McDaniel, St. Louis, 26

AAA American Association
President: Edward S. Doherty, Jr.

Standings	W	L	Pct.	GB	Attend.	Manager
Denver Bears (5)	88	66	.571	—	269,783	Charlie Metro
Louisville Colonels (12)	85	68	.556	2½	139,028	Ben Geraghty/Bill Adair
Houston Buffs (9)	83	71	.539	5	118,584	Enos Slaughter
St. Paul Saints (11)	83	71	.539	5	119,926	Danny Ozark
Minneapolis Millers (2)	82	72	.532	6	115,702	Eddie Popowski
Charleston Senators (8)	65	88	.425	22½	95,976	Del Wilber
Indianapolis Indians (13)	65	89	.422	23	162,123	John Hutchings/Ted Beard
Dallas-Ft. Worth Rangers (6)	64	90	.416	24	113,849	Jim Fanning

Playoffs: Denver 4 games, Houston 3; Louisville 4 games, St. Paul 2.
Finals: Louisville 4 games, Denver 2.

All-Star Team: 1B-Larry "Bo" Osborne, Denver; **2B**-John Schaive, Charleston; **3B**-Steve Boros, Denver; **SS**-Zoilo Versalles, Charleston; **OF**-Billy Williams, Houston; Lee Maye, Louisville; Carl Warwick, St. Paul; Jim McDaniel, Denver; **C**-Mike Roarke, Denver; Bob Taylor, Louisville; Bob Tillman, Minneapolis; **P**-Carroll Beringer, St. Paul; Jim Brewer, Houston; Al Lary, Houston; Mel Wright, Dallas-Ft. Worth; Phil Regan, Denver; Art Fowler, St. Paul; **MVP**-Steve Boros, Denver; **Manager**-Bill Adair, Louisville.

BA: Larry "Bo" Osborne, Denver, .342
Runs: Steve Boros, Denver, 128
Hits: Carl Yastrzemski, Minneapolis, 193
RBIs: Steve Boros, Denver, 119
  Larry "Bo" Osborne, Denver, 119

HRs: Larry "Bo" Osborne, Denver, 34
Wins: Jim Golden, St. Paul, 20
SOs: Dick Tomanek, Dallas-Ft. Worth, 172
ERA: Jim Golden, St. Paul, 2.32

AAA International League
President: Frank J. Shaughnessy

Standings	W	L	Pct.	GB	Attend.	Manager
Toronto Maple Leafs (4)	100	54	.649	—	203,700	Mel McGaha
Richmond Virginians (7)	82	70	.539	17	188,129	Steve Souchock
Rochester Red Wings (15)	81	73	.526	19	219,008	Clyde King
Buffalo Bisons (13)	78	75	.510	21½	278,352	Kerby Farrell
Havana Sugar Kings/ Jersey City Jerseys#(10)	76	77	.497	23½	121,755	Tony Castano/ Napoleon Reyes
Columbus Jets (14)	69	84	.451	30½	136,195	Cal Ermer
Miami Marlins (1)	65	88	.425	34½	109,890	Al Vincent
Montreal Royals (11)	62	92	.403	38	111,991	Clay Bryant

#Havana moved to Jersey City July 13.

Playoffs: Toronto 4 games, Buffalo 0; Rochester 4 games, Richmond 1.
Finals: Toronto 4 games, Rochester 1.

All-Star Team: 1B-Joe Altobelli, Montreal; **2B**-George "Sparky" Anderson, Toronto; **3B**-Billy Harrell, Rochester; **SS**-Jerry Adair, Miami; **OF**-Jim Pendleton, Havana/Jersey City; Don Landrum, Buffalo; Jim King, Toronto; **C**-Jesse Gonder, Richmond; **P**-Al Cicotte, Toronto; Robert W. Smith, Toronto; **MVP**-Jim King, Toronto; **Pitcher of the Year**-Al Cicotte, Toronto.

BA: Jim Frey, Rochester, .317
Runs: Don Landrum, Buffalo, 112
Hits: Don Landrum, Buffalo, 178
  Jim Pendleton, Havana/Jersey City, 178
RBIs: Joe Altobelli, Montreal, 105

HRs: Joe Altobelli, Montreal, 31
Wins: Al Cicotte, Toronto, 16
SOs: Al Cicotte, Toronto, 158
ERA: Al Cicotte, Toronto, 1.79

AAA Pacific Coast League
President: Dewey Soriano

Standings	W	L	Pct.	GB	Attend.	Manager
Spokane Indians (11)	92	61	.601	—	261,858	Preston Gomez
Tacoma Giants (16)	81	73	.526	11½	270,024	John "Red" Davis
Salt Lake City Bees (14)	80	73	.523	12	140,073	Larry Shepard
Seattle Rainiers (10)	77	75	.507	14½	163,997	Dick Sisler
San Diego Padres (3)	77	75	.507	14½	120,848	George Metkovich/ Jimmy Reese
Sacramento Solons (12)	73	81	.474	19½	117,506	Ernie White
Vancouver Mounties (1)	68	84	.447	23½	144,278	George Staller
Portland Beavers	64	90	.416	28½	116,130	Tom Heath

Playoffs: None.

All-Star Team: 1B-R.C. Stevens, Salt Lake City; **2B**-Jim Baumer, Salt Lake City; **3B**-Harry Bright, Salt Lake City; **SS**-Charlie Smith, Spokane; **OF**-Ron Fairly, Spokane; Willie Davis, Spokane; Stan Johnson, San Diego; **C**-Tom Haller, Tacoma; Hal Bevan, Seattle; **P**-Chet Nichols, Vancouver; Eddie Fisher, Tacoma; **MVP**-Willie Davis, Spokane.

BA: Willie Davis, Spokane, .346
Runs: Willie Davis, Spokane, 126
Hits: Willie Davis, Spokane, 216
RBIs: Harry Bright, Salt Lake City, 119

HRs: R.C. Stevens, Salt Lake City, 37
Wins: Chet Nichols, Vancouver, 18
SOs: Noel Mickelsen, Portland, 156
ERA: Don Rudolph, Seattle, 2.42

AA Mexican League
President: Eduardo Orvananos

Standings	W	L	Pct.	GB	Attend.	Manager
Mexico City Tigres	77	66	.538	—	266,139	Memo Garibay
Veracruz Aguilas	71	74	.490	7	228,784	Santos Amaro
Mexico City Diablos Rojos	69	77	.473	9½	318,797	Chile Gomez/Chero Mayer
Poza Rica Petroleros	65	78	.455	12	279,554	Dan Rios/Ben Lopez
Monterrey Sultanes	66	79	.455	12	110,180	Manuel Arroyo
Puebla Pericos	63	80	.441	14	112,957	Jesus Diaz/Julio Moreno

Each team played 36 games with Texas League teams which counted in the standings. The combined leagues were known as the Pan American Association.

Playoffs: None.

All-Star Team: 1B-Jose Echeverria, MC Tigres; **2B**-Vinicio Garcia, Monterrey; **3B**-Miguel Fernandez, Veracruz; **SS**-Carlos Ramirez, MC Tigres; **OF**-Al Pinkston, MC Diablos Rojos; Aldo Salvent, Poza Rica; Juan Delis, Monterrey; **C**-Oscar Rodriguez, Puebla; Miguel Gaspar, Veracruz; **P**-Silvio Castellanos, Veracruz; Luis Tiant, MC Tigres.

BA: Al Pinkston, MC Diablos Rojos, .397
Runs: Bobby Avila, MC Tigres, 125
Hits: Al Pinkston, MC Diablos Rojos, 225
RBIs: Al Pinkston, MC Diablos Rojos, 144
HRs: Aldo Salvent, Poza Rica, 36

Wins: Francisco Ramirez, MC Diablos Rojos, 17
  Luis Tiant, MC Tigres, 17
  Silvio Castellanos, Veracruz, 17
SOs: Silvio Castellanos, Veracruz, 122
ERA: Silvio Castellanos, Veracruz, 3.24

AA Southern Association
President: Hal Totten

Standings	W	L	Pct.	GB	Attend.	Manager
Atlanta Crackers (11)	87	67	.565	—	154,143	Rube Walker
Shreveport Sports (6)	86	67	.562	½	53,498	Les Peden
Little Rock Travelers	82	69	.543	3½	179,471	Fred Hatfield
Birmingham Barons (5)	83	70	.542	3½	119,140	Skeeter Newsome
Mobile Bears (4)	79	72	.523	6½	67,846	Al Hollingsworth/John Lipon
Nashville Vols (10)	71	82	.464	15½	99,721	Jim Turner

*Won first-half   **Won second-half   ***Won both halves
Numbers after nicknames indicate farm system.
Affiliation listed at end of each year.

Memphis Chicks (15) .... 59 87 .404 24   48,487   Joe Schultz
Chattanooga Lookouts (13) 60 93 .392 26½   58,010   Forrest "Spook" Jacobs

Playoffs: None.

All-Star Team: 1B-Tim Harkness, Atlanta; **2B**-Chet Boak, Shreveport; **3B**-Don LeJohn, Atlanta; **SS**-Dick Tracewski, Atlanta; **OF**-Stan Palys, Birmingham; Leo Posada, Shreveport; Jim Koranda, Atlanta; Ernie Oravetz, Chattanooga; Bob Thorpe, Little Rock; **C**-John Edwards, Nashville; Doug Camilli, Atlanta; Les Peden, Shreveport; **Util IF**-Al Grandcolas, Chattanooga; **P**-Pete Richert, Atlanta; Ron Nischwitz, Birmingham; Bob Allen, Mobile; Bob Milo, Chattanooga; Charles Ready, Little Rock; Don Bradey, Little Rock; **MVP**-Stan Palys, Birmingham; **Rookie of the Year**-Pete Richert, Atlanta.

BA: Stan Palys, Birmingham, .370
Runs: Jay Hankins, Shreveport, 116
Hits: Stan Palys, Birmingham, 200
RBIs: Leo Posada, Shreveport, 122
HRs: Jim McManus, Shreveport, 32
Wins: Pete Richert, Atlanta, 19
SOs: Pete Richert, Atlanta, 251
ERA: Ron Nischwitz, Birmingham, 2.31

AA Texas League
President: Dick Butler

Standings	W	L	Pct.	GB	Attend.	Manager
Rio Grande Valley Giants# (16).	85	59	.590	—	75,291	Ray Murray
San Antonio Missions (9) ...	77	68	.531	8½	106,273	Grady Hatton/Lou Klein
Tulsa Oilers (15)	76	68	.528	9	111,835	Vern Benson
Victoria Rosebuds (5)	77	69	.527	9	69,760	Johnny Pesky
Austin Senators (12)	73	71	.507	12	73,605	Alex Monchak
Amarillo Gold Sox (7)	68	78	.466	18	52,783	Jimmy Gleeson

Each team played 36 games with Mexican League teams which counted in the standings. The combined leagues were known as the Pan American Association.
#represented Harlingen, Texas.

Playoffs: Victoria 3 games, Rio Grande Valley 0; Tulsa 3 games, San Antonio 1.
Finals: Tulsa 3 games, Victoria 0.

All-Star Team: 1B-Fred Whitfield, Tulsa; **2B**-Chuck Hiller, Rio Grande Valley; **3B**-Kal Segrist, Victoria; **SS**-J.C. Hartman, San Antonio; **OF**-Layton Ducote, San Antonio; Manny Mota, Rio Grande Valley; Jim Hickman, Tulsa; **C**-John Orsino, Rio Grande Valley; **P**-Jack Curtis, San Antonio; **MVP**-Chuck Hiller, Rio Grande Valley; **Pitcher of the Year**-Jack Curtis, San Antonio; **Manager**-Ray Murray, Rio Grande Valley.

BA: Chuck Hiller, Rio Grande Valley, .334
Runs: Art Burnett, Tulsa, 111
Hits: Chuck Hiller, Rio Grande Valley, 187
RBIs: Harry Watts, Tulsa, 99
HRs: Layton Ducote, San Antonio, 32
Wins: Jack Curtis, San Antonio, 19
SOs: Denny Lemaster, Austin, 181
ERA: Gaylord Perry, Rio Grande Valley, 2.83

A Eastern League
President: Thomas H. Richardson

Standings	W	L	Pct.	GB	Attend.	Manager
Williamsport Grays (13)	76	62	.551	—	100,298	Frank Lucchesi
Binghamton Triplets (7)	70	69	.504	6½	71,671	Damon Phillips
Springfield Giants (16)	69	70	.496	7½	66,857	Andy Gilbert
Reading Indians (4)	69	71	.493	8	75,777	Ray Mueller
Allentown Red Sox (2).......	67	72	.482	9½	51,654	Sheriff Robinson
Lancaster Red Roses (9).....	66	73	.475	10½	82,895	Phil Cavarretta

Playoffs: Williamsport 2 games, Reading 0; Springfield 2 games, Binghamton 1.
Finals: Williamsport 1 game, Springfield 0, when rain hit. Co-champions were declared.

All-Star Team: 1B-Bud Zipfel, Binghamton; **2B**-Pedro Gonzalez, Binghamton; **3B**-Don Eaddy, Lancaster; **SS**-Larry Brown, Reading; **OF**-Don Lock, Binghamton; John Herrnstein, Williamsport; Bill Williams, Reading; **C**-Dick Harris, Williamsport; Tim Talton, Springfield; **P**-Julius Grant, Reading; Jim Duffalo, Springfield; **Manager**-Frank Lucchesi, Williamsport.

BA: Pedro Gonzalez, Binghamton, .327
Runs: Harold Jones, Reading, 107
Hits: Pedro Gonzalez, Binghamton, 179
RBIs: Don Lock, Binghamton, 117
HRs: Don Lock, Binghamton, 35
Wins: Jim Duffalo, Springfield, 16
Robert Heffner, Allentown, 16
SOs: Clark Johnson, Springfield, 169
ERA: Jim Duffalo, Springfield, 2.63

A South Atlantic League
President: Sam C. Smith, Jr.

Standings	W	L	Pct.	GB	Attend.	Manager
Columbia Reds (10)...........	83	56	.597	—	47,626	Max Macon
Charlotte Hornets (8)	79	61	.564	4½	87,432	Gene Verble
Savannah Pirates (14)	78	61	.561	5	63,957	Ray Hathaway
Knoxville Smokies (5)........	71	67	.514	11½	84,072	Frank Skaff
Jacksonville Braves (12).....	70	69	.504	13	60,451	Red Murff
Asheville Tourists (13)	62	77	.446	21	73,276	Charlie Kress
Charleston White Sox (3) ...	59	80	.424	24	43,461	Skeeter Scalzi/Benny Huffman/Bob Kuzava
Macon Dodgers (11)	54	85	.388	29	30,919	Ray Perry

Playoffs: Savannah 3 games, Columbia 1; Knoxville 3 games, Charlotte 1.
Finals: Savannah 3 games, Knoxville 0.

All-Star Team: 1B-Leo Smith Jr., Knoxville; **2B**-Bobby Case, Charleston; **3B**-Ed Sada, Savannah; **SS**-Chico Ruiz, Columbia; **OF**-Purnal Goldy, Knoxville; Donn Clendenon, Savannah; Lamar Jacobs, Charlotte; **C**-Guy Lavalliere, Charlotte; **Util IF**-Dick McAuliffe, Knoxville; **Util OF**-Len Gabrielson, Jacksonville; Ernie Rodriguez, Macon; **P**-Charlie Rabe, Columbia; Ken Hunt, Columbia.

BA: Purnal Goldy, Knoxville, .342
Runs: Dick McAuliffe, Knoxville, 109
Hits: Purnal Goldy, Knoxville, 186
RBIs: Leo Smith, Jr., Knoxville, 111
HRs: Donn Clendenon, Savannah, 28
Wins: Ken Hunt, Columbia, 16
SOs: Ken Hunt, Columbia, 221
ERA: Charlie Rabe, Columbia, 2.39

B Carolina League
President: J.C. "Bill" Jessup

Standings	W	L	Pct.	GB	Attend.	Manager
Greensboro Yankees*(7).....	84	55	.604	—	97,594	Hal Charnofsky
Wilson Tobs (8)	73	65	.529	10½	45,447	Jack McKeon
Raleigh Capitals (2)	70	65	.507	12	30,505	Ken Deal
Burlington Indians**(4).....	67	73	.479	17½	44,159	Pinky May
Winston-Salem Red Birds (15)..	61	76	.445	22	76,888	Chase Riddle
Durham Bulls (5)	57	78	.422	25	30,005	Stubby Overmire

Playoff: Greensboro 4 games, Burlington 1.

All-Star Team: 1B-Gene Davis, Wilson; **2B**-Joe Teague, Burlington; **3B**-Ed Olivares, Winston-Salem; **SS**-Phil Linz, Greensboro; **OF**-Mitchell June, Burlington; Fred Carpenter, Greensboro; Juan Visteur, Wilson; Andy Kosco, Durham; **C**-John Sullivan, Durham; Bob Rikard, Wilson; **Util**-Jim Burton, Wilson; **P**-Lee Stange, Wilson; Jim Bouton, Greensboro; Johnny Seale, Durham; Joe Kaiser, Wilson; **MVP**-Ed Olivares, Winston-Salem; **Manager**-Pinky May, Burlington.

BA: Phil Linz, Greensboro, .321
Runs: Jim Orton, Greensboro, 101
Hits: Phil Linz, Greensboro, 162
RBIs: Ed Olivares, Winston-Salem, 125
HRs: Ed Olivares, Winston-Salem, 35
Wins: Lee Stange, Wilson, 20
SOs: Johnny Seale, Durham, 197
ERA: Jim Bouton, Greensboro, 2.73

B Northwest League
President: James M. Fleishman

Standings	W	L	Pct.	GB	Attend.	Manager
Yakima Bears***(12).........	85	57	.599	—	60,166	Buddy Hicks
Tri-City Braves (1)	81	60	.574	3½	80,063	Whitey McDowell
Lewiston Broncs (6)	78	63	.553	6½	39,396	John McNamara
Eugene Emeralds (16)	74	67	.525	10½	60,542	Richard Klaus
Salem Senators	56	86	.394	29	43,231	Karl Kuehl
Wenatchee Chiefs...............	50	91	.355	34½	32,974	Dick Wilson/Owen Friend

Playoffs: None.

All-Star Team: 1B-Len Tucker, Yakima; **2B**-Ray Tabacchi, Lewiston; **3B**-Edmund Zander, Yakima; **SS**-Denis Menke, Yakima; **OF**-Jose Tartabull, Eugene; Lorne Johnson, Yakima; Walter O'Neil, Tri-City; **C**-Merritt Ranew, Yakima; Harry Dunlop, Tri-City; **P**-John Stokoe, Yakima; Frederick Rick, Tri-City; **Manager**-John McNamara, Lewiston.

BA: Tom Agosta, Tri-City, .384
Runs: Len Tucker, Yakima, 126
Hits: Jose Tartabull, Eugene, 178
RBIs: Edmund Zander, Yakima, 122
HRs: Robert Nelson, Tri-City, 29
Wins: Frederick Rick, Tri-City, 20
SOs: Frederick Rick, Tri-City, 176
ERA: Don Tarlton, Tri-City, 2.98

B Three-I League
President: Vern Hoscheit

Standings	W	L	Pct.	GB	Attend.	Manager
Fox Cities Foxes (1)	82	56	.594	—	61,062	Earl Weaver
Lincoln Chiefs (3)...............	71	66	.518	10½	45,170	Ira Hutchinson
Sioux City Soos (6)............	71	68	.511	11½	41,385	Bob Hofman
Cedar Rapids Braves (12)....	71	69	.507	12	62,358	James Brown
Burlington Bees (14)	66	74	.471	17	51,988	Pete Peterson
Green Bay Dodgers (11)......	65	73	.471	17	29,940	Stan Wasiak
Des Moines Demons (13).....	64	74	.464	18	53,828	Andy Seminick
Topeka Reds (10)...............	64	74	.464	18	36,365	John Vander Meer

Playoffs: None.

All-Star Team: 1B-Gerry Reimer, Des Moines; **2B**-George Williams, Des Moines; **3B**-Pete Ward, Fox Cities; **SS**-Al Weis, Lincoln; **OF**-Don Buford, Lincoln; Ed Napoleon, Burlington; Billy Joe Dashner, Topeka; **C**-Cal Ripken, Fox Cities; **P**-Pat Gillick, Fox Cities; Dick Warren, Green Bay; Ron Woods, Lincoln; Hank Fischer, Cedar Rapids; **Manager**-Bob Hofman, Sioux City.

BA: Pete Ward, Fox Cities, .345
Runs: Frank Montgomery, Fox Cities, 111
Hits: Gerry Reimer, Des Moines, 179
RBIs: Billy Joe Dashner, Topeka, 108
HRs: Billy Joe Dashner, Topeka, 23
Manly Johnston, Lincoln, 23
Wins: Ron Woods, Lincoln, 17
SOs: Hank Fischer, Cedar Rapids, 217
ERA: Hank Fischer, Cedar Rapids, 2.01

C California League
President: Edward J. Mulligan

Standings	W	L	Pct.	GB	Attend.	Manager
Reno Silver Sox***(11)	89	51	.636	—	37,762	Tom Saffell
Fresno Giants (16)	75	65	.536	14	53,242	Buddy Kerr
Bakersfield Bears (13)........	74	66	.529	15	44,069	Lou Kahn
Stockton Ports (1)	66	74	.471	23	14,375	Billy DeMars
Modesto Reds (7)...............	61	78	.439	27½	30,007	Tom Hamilton
Visalia Athletics (6)	54	85	.388	34½	27,728	Bill Capps/Art Mazmanian/Bill Robertson

Playoffs: None.

All-Star Team: 1B-Richard Edwards, Bakersfield; **2B**-Ike Futch, Modesto; **3B**-Ricardo Joseph, Fresno; **SS**-Joseph Curtin, Reno; **OF**-Elvio Jimenez, Modesto; Chuck Hinton, Stockton; Lowell Barnhart, Reno; **C**-Frank Zupo, Stockton; **Util IF**-Lionel Rodgers, Fresno; **Util OF**-Al Ferrara, Reno; **P**-Robert Arrighi, Reno; Thad Tillotson, Reno; Bob Lasko, Modesto; Gary Kroll, Bakersfield; **MVP**-Robert Arrighi, Reno; **Rookie of the Year**-Thad Tillotson, Reno; **Manager**-Billy DeMars, Stockton.

BA: Chuck Hinton, Stockton, .369
Runs: Lowell Barnhart, Reno, 116
    Al Ferrara, Reno, 116
Hits: Al Ferrara, Reno, 185
RBIs: Lowell Barnhart, Reno, 109

HRs: Richard Edwards, Bakersfield, 22
Wins: Thad Tillotson, Reno, 19
SOs: Gary Kroll, Bakersfield, 309
ERA: John Hogg, Bakersfield, 2.59

C Northern League
President: Herman D. White

Standings	W	L	Pct.	GB	Attend.	Manager
Winnipeg Goldeyes (15).....	72	51	.585	—	83,014	Whitey Kurowski
Duluth-Superior Dukes (5).	70	51	.579	1	51,301	Frank Carswell
Aberdeen Pheasants (1)	63	61	.508	9½	45,321	Lou Fitzgerald
Minot Mallards (4)..............	62	62	.500	10½	25,376	Walter Novick
Grand Forks Chiefs (14).....	61	62	.496	11	32,602	Bob Clear
Fargo-Moorhead Twins (7)	58	66	.468	14½	27,443	John Fitzpatrick
Eau Claire Braves (12)	58	66	.468	14½	37,831	Bill Steinecke
St. Cloud Rox (9)................	49	74	.398	23	31,380	Fred Martin

Playoffs: Winnipeg 1 game, Aberdeen 0; Duluth-Superior 1 game, Minot 0.
Finals: Winnipeg 2 games, Duluth-Superior 0.

All-Star Team: 1B-Roger Morgan, Eau Claire; **2B**-Al Muench, Grand Forks; **3B**-Max Alvis, Minot; **SS**-Horace Clarke, Fargo-Moorhead; **OF**-Joe Patterson, Winnipeg; John Lewis, Winnipeg; Gates Brown, Duluth-Superior; **C**-Joe Torre, Eau Claire; Elmo Plaskett, Grand Forks; **P**-Basil Curry, St. Cloud; Larry West, Grand Forks.

BA: Joe Torre, Eau Claire, .344
Runs: Joe Patterson, Winnipeg, 113
Hits: Max Alvis, Minot, 147
RBIs: Johnny Lewis, Winnipeg, 104
HRs: Johnny Lewis, Winnipeg, 23

Wins: Bob Clear, Grand Forks, 21
SOs: Bob Clear, Grand Forks, 183
    Harry Fanok, Winnipeg, 183
ERA: Alejandro Castro, Aberdeen, 2.13

C Pioneer League
President: Claude Engberg

Standings	W	L	Pct.	GB	Attend.	Manager
Idaho Falls Russets**(3)	81	49	.623	—	31,271	Peanuts Lowrey/George Noga
Boise Braves*(12)	78	52	.557	3	36,885	Billy Smith
Billings Mustangs (15)	65	65	.500	16	39,123	Ray Wilson
Missoula Timberjacks (10).	58	71	.450	22½	32,677	Rocky Tedesco
Great Falls Electrics (11)....	55	75	.440	26	34,106	Spider Jorgensen
Pocatello Giants (16)	52	77	.403	28½	28,909	Mike McCormick

Playoff: Boise 3 games, Idaho Falls 0.

All-Star Team: 1B-Gerald McNertney, Idaho Falls; **2B**-Cesar Tovar, Missoula; **3B**-Chico Salmon, Pocatello; **SS**-Bill Lucas, Boise; **OF**-Ray Reed, Boise; Fred Loesekam, Idaho Falls; Bill Shepherd, Missoula; **C**-Milo Fuller, Pocatello; Tony Cannizzo, Missoula; **P**-Robert Radovich, Great Falls; David Eilers, Boise; Fred Talbot, Idaho Falls; Lou Vickery, Billings.

BA: Teo Acosta, Billings/Missoula, .369
Runs: Bill Lucas, Boise, 128
Hits: Ruthford Salmon, Pocatello, 182
RBIs: Ray Reed, Boise, 134
HRs: Ray Reed, Boise, 37
Wins: Fred Talbot, Idaho Falls, 16
SOs: Roberto Barbosa, Boise, 202
ERA: David Eilers, Boise, 3.46

D Alabama-Florida League
President: William Moore

Standings	W	L	Pct.	GB	Attend.	Manager
Panama City Fliers (11)......	74	44	.627	—	25,770	Roy Hartsfield
Selma Cloverleafs (4)	58	57	.504	14½	25,317	Ken Landenberger/ Joe Morlan/Paul O'Dea
Pensacola Angels (3)	59	60	.496	15½	24,301	J.C. Dunn
Ft. Walton Beach Jets (8) ...	56	60	.483	17	15,284	Ralph Rowe
Dothan Cardinals (15)	56	63	.471	18½	35,202	Fred McAlister
Montgomery Rebels (5).......	50	69	.420	24½	22,621	Al Lakeman

Playoffs: Pensacola 3 games, Panama City 2; Selma 3 games, Ft. Walton Beach 0.
Finals: Pensacola 3 games, Selma 1.

All-Star Team: 1B-Joe Abdella, Selma; **2B**-Weldon Bowlin, Dothan; **3B**-Carlos Pascual, Ft. Walton Beach; **SS**-Bob Sloan, Panama City; **OF**-Jose Villar, Selma; Vic Pagel, Panama City; Jim Barbieri, Panama City; **C**-Bill Kelso, Panama City; Duke Sims, Selma; **P**-William Kalmes, Panama City; George Miller, Ft. Walton Beach.

BA: Carlos Pascual, Ft. Walton Beach, .325
Runs: Jose Villar, Selma, 87
Hits: Bob Sloan, Panama City, 138
RBIs: Carlos Pascual, Ft. Walton Beach, 82
HRs: Jose Villar, Selma, 23
Wins: Peter Pekich, Selma, 17
SOs: William Kalmes, Panama City, 239
ERA: Bruce Griewe, Panama City, 1.84

D Appalachian League
President: Chauncey De Vault

Standings	W	L	Pct.	GB	Attend.	Manager
Wytheville Senators (8)......	43	27	.614	—	24,350	Adelbert "Red" Norwood
Kingsport Pirates (14).........	37	31	.544	5	29,252	James Gibbons
Bluefield Orioles (1)	35	32	.522	6½	14,236	Bernard Lutz

Morristown Cubs (9)	32	35	.478	9½	13,777	Melvin Cooper
Johnson City Phillies (13)...	29	40	.420	13½	10,355	Ben Tompkins
Salem Rebels (16)..............	28	39	.418	13½	38,929	Jodie Phipps

Playoffs: None.

All-Star Team: 1B-Phil Barth, Bluefield; **2B**-Bill Sorrell, Johnson City; **2B**-Francis Pittaro, Wytheville; **3B**-Norm Housley, Kingsport; **SS**-LeRoy Hock, Wytheville; **OF**-Joy Gritts, Wytheville; Kenny Faulkner, Morristown; Sam Bowens, Bluefield; **C**-Randy Hundley, Salem; **P**-Vern Merrick, Wytheville; John Ellen, Bluefield; **Rookie of the Year**-LeRoy Hock, Wytheville; **Manager**-Adelbert "Red" Norwood, Wytheville.

BA: Jose Lezcano, Kingsport, .335
Runs: Gerald Cassidy, Wytheville, 65
Hits: Ken Faulkner, Morristown, 82
RBIs: Joy Gritts, Wytheville, 60
HRs: Joy Gritts, Wytheville, 24
Wins: Tim Pelczynski, Bluefield, 8
SOs: John Ellen, Bluefield, 137
ERA: Vern Merrick, Wytheville, 2.59

D Florida State League
Presidents: Julian Jackson/Herbert C. Smith

Standings	W	L	Pct.	GB	Attend.	Manager
Lakeland Indians*(4)..........	82	48	.631	—	26,522	John Lipon/Charlie Gassaway
Palatka Redlegs**(10)........	81	56	.591	4½	17,330	Dave Bristol
Sanford Greyhounds (6)	77	60	.562	8½	15,633	Bill Robertson/ Jack Sanford/Lloyd Brown
Tampa Tarpons (13)	68	67	.504	16½	76,616	Wilbur Johnson
Daytona Beach Islanders (15)..	66	69	.489	18½	28,166	Frank Calo
Orlando Dodgers (11)..........	58	77	.430	26½	15,916	Brandy Davis
St. Petersburg Saints (7)	55	83	.399	31	60,003	Stan Charnofsky/ Randy Gumpert
Leesburg Orioles (1)...........	53	80	.398	30½	16,541	Bob Hooper

Playoff: Palatka 3 games, Lakeland 1.

All-Star Team: 1B-Ken Harrelson, Sanford; **2B**-Dave Bristol, Palatka; **3B**-Charlie Green, Tampa; **SS**-Tommy Helms, Palatka; **OF**-Bolivar Hinojosa, Sanford; Pat Sisk, Sanford; Miles McWilliams, Palatka; **C**-Bob Perez, Sanford; Pat Corrales, Tampa; **Util IF**-Luis Alcarez, Orlando; **Util OF**-Julian Vicente, St. Petersburg; **P**-Bob Golick, Sanford; Sam Thompson, Palatka; Jim Dunlap, Leesburg; Marcelino Lopez, Tampa.

BA: Santiago Rosario, Daytona Beach, .319
Runs: Tommy Helms, Palatka, 119
Hits: Tommy Helms, Palatka, 171
RBIs: Miles McWilliams, Palatka, 113
HRs: Miles McWilliams, Palatka, 15
    Dave Bristol, Palatka, 15
Wins: Ken Sanders, Sanford, 19
SOs: Marcelino Lopez, Tampa, 231
ERA: Ted Davidson, Palatka, 2.35

D Mexican Center League
President: Eduardo Orvananos

Standings	W	L	Pct.	GB	Attend.	Manager
Salamanca Petroleros..........	57	41	.582	—	27,708	Walter Graham
Celaya Cajeteros	54	45	.545	3½	17,110	Augustin Bejerano
Leon Diablos Rojos	50	48	.510	7	55,537	Luis Montes de Oca
Aguascalientes Tigres.........	47	51	.480	10	15,350	Jesus Robles/Carlos Galina
San Luis Potosi Tuneros	47	52	.475	10½	44,535	Domingo Santana
Guanajuato Tuzos	41	59	.410	17	29,625	Mario Flores/Fernando Garcia

Playoffs: None.

All-Star Team: 1B-Ildefonso Ruiz, San Luis Potosi; **2B**-Genaro Puente, San Luis Potosi; **3B**-Rogelio Jimenez, Salamanca; **SS**-Abundio Hernandez, Aguascalientes; **OF**-Saul Villegas, Salamanca; Roberto Moreno, Guanajuato; Luis Hernandez, Guanajuato; **C**-Eloy Gutierrez, Guanajuato; Alfonso Ibarra, San Luis Potosi; **P**-Adolfo Flores, Celaya; Gregorio Polo, Aguascalientes.

BA: Luis Hernandez, Guanajuato, .404
Runs: Saul Villegas, Salamanca, 105
Hits: Eloy Gutierrez, Guanajuato, 128
RBIs: Saul Villegas, Salamanca, 105
HRs: Saul Villegas, Salamanca, 23
Wins: Emilio Chavez, Salamanca, 17
SOs: Jose Soto, Salamanca, 146
ERA: Rafael Rodriguez, Leon, 1.44

D Midwest League
President: C.C. "Dutch" Hoffman

Standings	W	L	Pct.	GB	Attend.	Manager
Waterloo Hawks***(2)........	81	43	.653	—	58,579	Matt Sczesny
Dubuque Packers (14)	66	56	.541	14	58,452	James Adlam
Clinton C-Sox (3)	61	56	.521	16½	54,000	George Noga/Frank Parenti
Kokomo Dodgers (11)..........	63	59	.516	17	40,560	Al Ronning
Davenport Braves (12)........	55	65	.458	24	58,987	Travis Jackson
Quincy Giants (16)	55	66	.455	24½	32,542	Sam Calderone
Keokuk Cardinals (15)........	53	69	.434	27	38,427	Al Unser
Decatur Commodores (5) ...	51	71	.418	29	53,531	Al Federoff

Playoffs: None.

All-Star Team: 1B-John Mason, Keokuk; **2B**-Julio Linares, Quincy; **3B**-Joe DeCandido, Waterloo; **SS**-Karl Frantz, Davenport; **OF**-Art Blunt, Dubuque; Wayne McDonald, Davenport; Al Ramirez, Dubuque; **C**-Hector Valle, Kokomo; Arch Skeen, Waterloo; **Util IF**-John Ryan, Decatur; **Util OF**-James Springborn, Quincy; **P**-Bob Sprout, Decatur; Scot Seger, Clinton; Tom Haake, Dubuque; Gale Dennis, Waterloo; **Player of the Year**-Tom Haake, Dubuque; **Rookie of the Year**-Bob Sprout, Decatur; **Manager**-Matt Sczesny, Waterloo.

BA: Julio Linares, Quincy, .324
Runs: Art Blunt, Dubuque, 99
Hits: Julio Linares, Quincy, 149
RBIs: Art Blunt, Dubuque, 92

HRs: Art Blunt, Dubuque, 26
Wins: Tom Haake, Dubuque, 19
SOs: Bob Sprout, Decatur, 264
ERA: Tom Haake, Dubuque, 2.52

D New York-Pennsylvania League
President: Vincent M. McNamara

Standings	W	L	Pct.	GB	Attend.	Manager
Erie Senators (8)	83	46	.643	—	32,733	Harry Warner
Wellsville Braves (12)	69	60	.535	14	21,806	Harry Minor
Auburn Yankees (7)	65	63	.508	17½	40,220	Bob Bauer
Corning Red Sox (2)	60	69	.465	23	25,292	Len Okrie
Elmira Pioneers (13)	56	74	.431	27½	30,704	Jack Phillips
Geneva Redlegs (10)	54	75	.419	29	20,897	Reno DeBenedetti/
						Jack Cassini

Playoffs: Erie 2 games, Corning 0; Wellsville 2 games, Auburn 1.
Finals: Wellsville 2 games, Erie 1, when rain postponed the series.

All-Star Team: 1B-William Halter, Corning; **2B**-David Sanchez, Erie; **3B**-Gene Domzalski, Auburn; **SS**-Loevel Vento, Erie; **OF**-Kenneth Roesler, Wellsville; Art Shamsky, Geneva; Pablo Mitchell, Erie; **C**-Peter Cronin, Corning; Walter James, Auburn; Frank Franchi, Erie; **P**-Joel Kiger, Erie; Roland Sheldon, Auburn; Bruce Brubaker, Wellsville; William Jones, Erie; **Manager**-Harry Warner, Erie.

BA: Pablo Mitchell, Erie, .348
Runs: Ronnie Retton, Auburn, 136
Hits: Pablo Mitchell, Erie, 157
RBIs: Gene Domzalski, Auburn, 104

HRs: Lary Daniels, Elmira, 22
Wins: William Jones, Erie, 20
SOs: William Jones, Erie, 196
ERA: Norm Forsythe, Elmira, 2.52

D Sophomore League
Presidents: Grady Terry/C.F. Montgomery

Standings	W	L	Pct.	GB	Attend.	Manager
Alpine Cowboys*(2)	76	52	.594	—	14,771	Dick Kinaman
Hobbs Pirates**(14)	70	58	.547	6	16,002	Al Kubski
Carlsbad Potashers (9)	66	64	.508	11	16,346	Verlon Walker
Artesia Giants (16)	62	68	.477	15	10,485	George Genovese
Albuquerque Dukes (6)	57	72	.442	19½	44,526	Bert Thiel
Odessa Dodgers (11)	57	74	.435	20½	16,182	Edward Serrano

Playoff: Hobbs 2 games, Alpine 1.

All-Star Team: 1B-Tommy Rinks, Hobbs; **2B**-Hector Martinez, Albuquerque; **3B**-Michael Imbiani, Alpine; **SS**-Gil Garrido, Artesia; **OF**-Jesus Alou, Artesia; Dick McLaughlin, Odessa; Lewis Bishop, Carlsbad; **C**-William Bevels, Odessa; Dave Massarelli, Hobbs; **P**-Frank Bork, Hobbs; Rodger Irvine, Hobbs.

BA: Gil Garrido, Artesia, .362
Runs: Roberto Pena, Hobbs, 121
Hits: Jesus Alou, Artesia, 188
RBIs: Dick McLaughlin, Odessa, 109

HRs: Lewis Bishop, Carlsbad, 23
Wins: Ken Whitmore, Hobbs, 16
SOs: Jose Santiago, Albuquerque, 217
ERA: Jose Santiago, Albuquerque, 3.30

D Western Carolina League
President: John H. Moss

Standings	W	L	Pct.	GB	Attend.	Manager
Lexington Indians	70	29	.707	—	41,437	Jack Hale
Salisbury Braves	65	35	.650	5½	31,041	Larry Taylor
Hickory Rebels	53	44	.546	16	14,503	Joe Abernethy/Marc Hoy
Newton-Conover Twins	47	52	.475	23	16,052	John Isaac
Shelby Colonels	42	53	.442	26	14,103	George Wilson
Rutherford County Owls	43	57	.430	27½	16,167	Jim Poole/Ray Walsh/ Len Jackson
Statesville Owls	38	62	.380	32½	30,229	Jake Early/Gail Thomas/ Paul Fouts
Gastonia Rippers	36	62	.367	33½	16,456	Billy Queen/Jack Falls

Playoffs: Hickory 2 games, Lexington 1; Salisbury 2 games, Newton-Conover 1.
Finals: Salisbury 3 games, Hickory 2.

All-Star Team: 1B-Roy Scercy, Salisbury; **2B**-Jack Turney, Salisbury; **3B**-Charlie Forte, Lexington; **SS**-Don Killian, Shelby; **OF**-Jack Falls, Gastonia; Lanier Robinson, Shelby; Herb Burnette, Lexington; **C**-Gary Cowan, Rutherford County; Jim Burnette, Newton-Conover; **P**-John Isaac, Newton-Conover; Danny Hayling, Hickory.

BA: Jack Turney, Salisbury, .362
Runs: Norman Smith, Lexington, 83
Hits: Jack Turney, Salisbury, 144
RBIs: Paul Roberts, Salisbury, 91

HRs: Paul Roberts, Salisbury, 23
Wins: Danny Hayling, Hickory, 22
SOs: John Isaac, Newton-Conover, 177
ERA: Bill Bethea, Lexington, 1.35

1960 Interleague Post Season Play

World Series
Pittsburgh (National) 4 games, New York (American) 3

Junior World Series
Louisville (American Association) 4 games, Toronto (International) 2
Total Attendance: 41,358

Pan-American Series
Tulsa (Texas) 4 games, Mexico City Tigres (Mexican) 1
Total Attendance: 14,916

1960 Major League Farm Systems

American League
1 Baltimore (8): Miami, Vancouver, Tri-City, Fox Cities, Stockton, Aberdeen, Bluefield, Leesburg.
2 Boston (6): Minneapolis, Allentown, Raleigh, Waterloo, Corning, Alpine.
3 Chicago (6): Seattle, Charleston (SC), Lincoln, Idaho Falls, Pensacola, Clinton.
4 Cleveland (7): Toronto, Mobile, Reading, Burlington (NC), Minot, Selma, Lakeland.
5 Detroit (8): Denver, Birmingham, Victoria, Knoxville, Durham, Duluth-Superior, Montgomery, Decatur.
6 Kansas City (7): Dallas-Ft. Worth, Shreveport, Lewiston, Sioux City, Visalia, Sanford, Albuquerque.
7 New York (8): Richmond, Amarillo, Binghamton, Greensboro, Modesto, Fargo-Moorhead, St. Petersburg, Auburn.
8 Washington (6): Charleston (WV), Charlotte, Wilson, Ft. Walton Beach, Wytheville, Erie.

National League
9 Chicago (6): Houston, San Antonio, Lancaster, St. Cloud, Morristown, Carlsbad.
10 Cincinnati (8): Havana/Jersey City, San Diego, Nashville, Columbia, Topeka, Missoula, Palatka, Geneva.
11 Los Angeles (12): St. Paul, Montreal, Spokane, Atlanta, Macon, Green Bay, Reno, Great Falls, Panama City, Orlando, Kokomo, Odessa.
12 Milwaukee (10): Louisville, Sacramento, Austin, Jacksonville, Yakima, Cedar Rapids, Eau Claire, Boise, Davenport, Wellsville.
13 Philadelphia (10): Indianapolis, Buffalo, Chattanooga, Williamsport, Asheville, Des Moines, Bakersfield, Johnson City, Tampa, Elmira.
14 Pittsburgh (8): Columbus, Salt Lake City, Savannah, Burlington (IA), Grand Forks, Kingsport, Dubuque, Hobbs.
15 St. Louis (9): Rochester, Memphis, Tulsa, Winston-Salem, Winnipeg, Billings, Dothan, Daytona Beach, Keokuk.
16 San Francisco (9): Tacoma, Rio Grande Valley, Springfield, Eugene, Fresno, Pocatello, Salem (VA), Quincy, Artesia.

1960 No-Hitters

Date	Pitcher	Team	League	Opponent	Score
4-24	Joe Bonikowski	Wilson	Carolina	Greensboro	6-0
5-3	Michael Mattiace	Palatka	Florida State	Daytona Beach	4-0
5-4	Andre Bessette	Des Moines	Three-I	Lincoln	5-0
5-12	Michael Mattiace	Palatka	Florida State	Tampa	20-0
5-15	Don Cardwell	Chicago	National	St. Louis	4-0
5-20	Gary Kroll	Bakersfield	California	Visalia	1-0
5-24	Ralph Lumenti	Charleston	American Assoc.	Louisville	2-0 (6)
5-25	James Schamp	Lakeland	Florida State	St. Petersburg	9-0
5-30	Howie Koplitz	Louisville	American Assoc.	Indianapolis	2-0 (7)
6-13	Jose Santiago	Albuquerque	Sophomore	Hobbs	2-0
6-15	Jerry Alford	Aberdeen	Northern	Eau Claire	7-0
6-16	Frank Funk	Toronto	International	Havana	1-0 (7)
6-19	Scott Seger	Clinton	Midwest	Quincy	3-0 (7)
6-24	Lowell Bussler	Quincy	Midwest	Kokomo	3-0 (7)
7-10	John Kirby	Macon	South Atlantic	Jacksonville	0-0 (5)
7-10	John Kerrigan	Des Moines	Three-I	Cedar Rapids	8-1
7-20	Bill Kirk	Lancaster	Eastern	Binghamton	1-0 (7)
7-20	Kermit Doub	Salisbury	Western Carolina	Statesville	8-0 (7)
7-27	Pedro Perez	Waterloo	Midwest	Quincy	1-0 (7)
7-29	John Kerrigan	Des Moines	Three-I	Lincoln	1-3
7-31	Dennis O'Melia	Missoula	Pioneer	Billings	2-0
8-3	Ronald Visheau/ Paul McKenzie	Daytona Beach	Florida State	Tampa	4-3 (7)
8-9	Ignacio Martinez	Artesia	Sophomore	Albuquerque	5-0
8-10	Jim Dunlap	Leesburg	Florida State	Lakeland	9-0
8-18	Lew Burdette	Milwaukee	National	Philadelphia	1-0
8-18	Bob Sprout	Decatur	Midwest	Waterloo	3-0
8-19	Tom Hughes	Tulsa	Texas	Rio Grande Valley	4-0
8-25	Conrad Gasper	Odessa	Sophomore	Albuquerque	14-0 (7)
8-28	Jack McCracken	Williamsport	Eastern		(7)
9-2	Dick Sherrow	Wellsville	New York-Penn.	Geneva	9-0 (7)
9-3	Al Cicotte	Toronto	International	Montreal	1-0 (11)
9-3	Hugo Rios	Leon	Mexican Center	Salamanca	1-0 (7)
9-5	Warren Hodgdon	Raleigh	Carolina	Greensboro	6-0 (7)
9-11	Doug Gallagher	Knoxville	South Atlantic	Charlotte	3-0 (PO)
9-16	Warren Spahn	Milwaukee	National	Philadelphia	4-0

Number in parentheses indicates innings if other than nine; "PO" indicates playoff game.

THIS DATE IN MINOR LEAGUE HISTORY

April 29, 1960, In the longest game in Texas League history, Rio Grande Valley defeated San Antonio 4-2 in 24 innings.

April 30, 1960, Herman "Old Folks" Pillette, 64, who pitched a record 23 years in one minor league, the Pacific Coast League, died in Sacramento, California. Pillette won 264 games in the minors, plus 34 in the majors in a 29-year career from 1917 to 1945.

May 3, 1960, Yakima, Northwest League, defeated Salem, 28-0.

May 8, 1960, In the Mexican League, the Mexico City Diablos Rojos outlasted Poza Rica, 24-20.

May 12, 1960, Michael Mattiace, rookie righthander with Palatka, Florida State League, hurled his second no-hitter of the season, posting two gems in his first four starts in Organized Baseball.

May 15, 1960, Shortstop Bill Lucas, Boise, Pioneer League, brother-in-law of Milwaukee's Henry Aaron, smashed three homers, a double and a single for ten RBIs in his club's 19-9 pasting of Pocatello.

May 21, 1960, After winning 14 successive games, Lakeland, Florida State League, lost to Palatka, 9-3.

June 1, 1960, Pete Pekich, Selma, Alabama-Florida League, fanned 20 in a 9-3 victory over Montgomery.

July 4, 1960, Dick Creighton, Wytheville, Appalachian League, fanned 21 while defeating Bluefield 8-1.

July 17, 1960, In the Mexican Center League, Aguascalientes defeated Leon, 5-4, in 27 innings. Pitcher Hugo Rios went the entire route for Leon.

August 12, 1960, Charleston, American Association, ended a 16-game losing streak by beating Minneapolis 6-3.

August 18, 1960, Bob Sproul, lefthander with Decatur, Midwest League, hurled a no-hitter and set a loop record with 22 strikeouts in a 3-0 victory over Waterloo.

August 25, 1960, Albuquerque, Sophomore League, stroked 24 hits, 17 for extra bases, in the Dukes' 27-3 win over Odessa.

August 26, 1960, Tom Haake, Dubuque, Midwest League, pitched his fifth one-hitter of the season.

September 3, 1960, Al Cicotte, Toronto, International League, pitched an 11-inning no-hit game to defeat Montreal 1-0. Cicotte ended the season by yielding no earned runs in 56 straight innings.

September 6, 1960, Willie Davis, Spokane, Pacific Coast League, banged his 26th triple of the season.

September 11, 1960, The Mexico City Tigres, Mexican League, scored 13 times in the eighth to defeat the Mexico City Reds, 18-8.

November 11, 1960, The financially strapped Memphis Chicks bowed out of the Southern Association after 60 years as a charter member.

December 17, 1960, Hawaii replaced the defunct Sacramento club in the Pacific Coast League.

SPRING TRAINING 1960

AMERICAN LEAGUE

CLUBS	AT	MAIL ADDRESS	DATES
BALTIMORE	Miami, Fla.	McAllister Hotel	2/27–4/14
BOSTON	Scottsdale, Ariz.	Safari Hotel	2/25–4/8
CHICAGO	Sarasota, Fla.	Terrace Hotel	2/29–4/15
CLEVELAND	Tucson, Ariz.	Santa Rita Hotel	3/1–4/8
DETROIT	Lakeland, Fla.	Tigertown	2/21–4/18
KANSAS CITY	West Palm Beach, Fla.	Hotel George Washington	2/28–4/17
NEW YORK	St. Petersburg, Fla.	Soreno Hotel	2/24–4/13
WASHINGTON	Orlando, Fla.	Hotel Cherry Plaza	2/26–4/16

NATIONAL LEAGUE

CHICAGO	Mesa, Ariz.	Maricopa Inn	2/22–4/8
CINCINNATI	Tampa, Fla.	Floridan Hotel	2/27–4/4
LOS ANGELES	Vero Beach, Fla.	Dodgertown	2/22–4/4
MILWAUKEE	Bradenton, Fla.	Manatee River Hotel	2/25–4/3
PHILADELPHIA	Clearwater, Fla.	Fort Harrison Hotel	2/24–4/1
PITTSBURGH	Fort Myers, Fla.	Bradford Hotel	2/24–4/10
ST. LOUIS	St. Petersburg, Fla.	Riviera Hotel	2/25–4/4
SAN FRANCISCO	Phoenix, Ariz.	Adams Hotel	3/1–4/7

AMERICAN ASSOCIATION

CHARLESTON			
DALLAS	Pompano Beach, Fla.	Gulfstream Apartments	3/15–4/14
DENVER	Lakeland, Fla.		
HOUSTON	Mesa, Ariz.	Cubs Camp	3/20–4/14
INDIANAPOLIS			
LOUISVILLE	Bradenton, Fla.	Dixie Grande Hotel	3/12–4/12
MINNEAPOLIS	Deland, Fla.	Dixie Motor Lodge	3/15–4/13
ST. PAUL	Vero Beach, Fla.	Dodgertown	3/15–4/15

INTERNATIONAL LEAGUE

BUFFALO	Dunedin, Fla.	Fenway Hotel	3/20–4/18
COLUMBUS	Jacksonville Beach, Fla.	Sea Ranch Hotel	3/20–4/10
HAVANA	Moron, Cuba	Hotel Santiago-Habana	3/25–4/19
MIAMI			
MONTREAL	Vero Beach, Fla.	Dodgertown	3/14–4/5
RICHMOND	Lake Wales, Fla.	Hotel Walesbilt	3/14–4/13
ROCHESTER	Homestead, Fla.	Cardinal Base	3/6–4/19
TORONTO	Daytona Beach, Fla.	Indianville	3/12–4/17

PACIFIC COAST LEAGUE

PORTLAND	Ontario, Ca.	Hotel Orange	3/14–4/12
SACRAMENTO	San Bernardino, Ca.	Mission Court Hotel	3/14
SALT LAKE CITY	Jacksonville Beach, Fla.	Sea Ranch Hotel	3/12–4/10
SAN DIEGO	Indio, Ca.	Hacienda Motel	3/14–4/14
SEATTLE	Palm Springs, Ca.	The Pueblo	3/16–4/14
SPOKANE	Vero Beach, Fla.	Dodgertown	3/12–4/12
TACOMA	Sanford, Fla.	Mayfair Inn	3/22–4/12
VANCOUVER	Yuma, Ariz.	Wash-Yuma Motel	3/14–4/12

SOUTHERN ASSOCIATION

ATLANTA	Vero Beach, Fla.	Dodgertown	3/15–4/14
BIRMINGHAM	Auburndale, Fla.	Chandler's Rainbow Motel	3/8–4/7
CHATTANOOGA			
MEMPHIS	Homestead, Fla.	Cardinal Base	3/6–4/13
MOBILE	Daytona Beach, Fla.	Indianville	3/13–4/14
NASHVILLE	Tampa, Fla.	Hillsboro Hotel	3/11–4/8
NEW ORLEANS			
SHREVEPORT	Haines City, Fla.	Haines City Motor Court	3/15

TEXAS LEAGUE

AMARILLO	Bartow, Fla.	Oakes Hotel	3/15–4/10
AUSTIN	Waycross, Ga.	Milwaukee Camp	3/14–4/1
AUSTIN	Jacksonville, Fla.	Ambassador Hotel	4/4–4/10
CORPUS CHRISTI			
SAN ANTONIO	Mesa, Ariz.	Cubs Camp	3/20–4/12
TULSA	Homestead, Fla.	Cardinal Base	3/6–4/12
VICTORIA	Lakeland, Fla.	Tigertown	3/8–4/10

EASTERN LEAGUE

ALBANY			
ALLENTOWN	Ocala, Fla.	Hotel Marion	3/10–4/16
BINGHAMTON	Bartow, Fla.	Hotel Oaks	3/21–4/17
LANCASTER	Mesa, Ariz.	Cubs Camp	3/20–4/20
READING	Daytona Beach, Fla.	Indianville	3/21–4/19
SPRINGFIELD	Sanford, Fla.	Giants Training Base	3/15–4/15
WILLIAMSPORT	Plant City, Fla.	Hotel Plant	3/21–4/17
YORK			

SOUTH ATLANTIC LEAGUE

ASHEVILLE	Plant City, Fla.	Hotel Plant	3/21–4/17
CHARLOTTE	Fernandina Beach, Fla.	Keystone Hotel	3/10–4/15
COLUMBIA	Tampa, Fla.	Hotel Hillsboro	3/22–4/14
JACKSONVILLE	Waycross, Ga.	Milwaukee Camp	3/13–4/10
KNOXVILLE	Lakeland, Fla.	Tigertown	3/15–4/15
MACON	Vero Beach, Fla.	Dodgertown	3/15–4/16
SAVANNAH	Jacksonville Beach, Fla.	Box 2000	3/21–4/17

1961

American League
President: Joseph E. Cronin

Standings	W	L	Pct.	GB	Attend.	Manager
New York Yankees	109	53	.673	—	1,747,725	Ralph Houk
Detroit Tigers	101	61	.623	8	1,600,710	Bob Scheffing
Baltimore Orioles	95	67	.586	14	951,089	Paul Richards/Luman Harris
Chicago White Sox	86	76	.531	23	1,146,019	Al Lopez
Cleveland Indians	78	83	.484	30½	725,547	Jimmy Dykes/Mel Harder
Boston Red Sox	76	86	.469	33	850,589	Pinky Higgins
Minnesota Twins	70	90	.438	38	1,256,723	Cookie Lavagetto/Sam Mele
Los Angeles Angels	70	91	.435	38½	603,510	Bill Rigney
Washington Senators	61	100	.379	47½	597,287	Mickey Vernon
Kansas City Athletics	61	100	.379	47½	683,817	Joe Gordon/Hank Bauer

BA: Norm Cash, Detroit, .361
Runs: Mickey Mantle, New York, 132
Roger Maris, New York, 132
Hits: Norm Cash, Detroit, 193
RBIs: Roger Maris, New York, 142
HRs: Roger Maris, New York, 61

Wins: Whitey Ford, New York, 25
SOs: Camilo Pascual, Minnesota, 221
ERA: Dick Donovan, Washington, 2.40
Pct: Whitey Ford, New York, .862, 25-4
Saves: Luis Arroyo, New York, 29

National League
President: Warren C. Giles

Standings	W	L	Pct.	GB	Attend.	Manager
Cincinnati Reds	93	61	.604	—	1,117,603	Fred Hutchinson
Los Angeles Dodgers	89	65	.578	4	1,804,250	Walter Alston
San Francisco Giants	85	69	.552	8	1,390,679	Alvin Dark
Milwaukee Braves	83	71	.539	10	1,101,441	Chuck Dressen/Birdie Tebbetts
St. Louis Cardinals	80	74	.519	13	885,305	Solly Hemus/Johnny Keane
Pittsburgh Pirates	75	79	.487	18	1,199,128	Danny Murtaugh
Chicago Cubs	64	90	.416	29	673,057	El Tappe/Vedie Himsl/Harry Craft/Lou Klein
Philadelphia Phillies	47	107	.305	46	590,039	Gene Mauch

BA: Roberto Clemente, Pittsburgh, .351
Runs: Willie Mays, San Francisco, 129
Hits: Vada Pinson, Cincinnati, 208
RBIs: Orlando Cepeda, San Francisco, 142
HRs: Orlando Cepeda, San Francisco, 46
Wins: Joey Jay, Cincinnati, 21
Warren Spahn, Milwaukee, 21

SOs: Sandy Koufax, Los Angeles, 269
ERA: Warren Spahn, Milwaukee, 3.02
Pct: Johnny Podres, Los Angeles, .783, 18-5
Saves: Stu Miller, San Francisco, 17
Elroy Face, Pittsburgh, 17

AAA American Association
President: James Burris

Standings	W	L	Pct.	GB	Attend.	Manager
Indianapolis Indians (12)	86	64	.573	—	179,423	Cot Deal
Louisville Colonels (15)	80	70	.533	6	119,808	Ben Geraghty
Denver Bears (5)	75	73	.507	10	142,746	Charlie Metro
Houston Buffs (11)	73	77	.487	13	120,104	Grady Hatton/Fred Martin/Lou Klein/Harry Craft
Dallas-Ft. Worth Rangers (7)	72	77	.483	13½	105,933	Walker Cooper
Omaha Dodgers (14)	62	87	.416	23½	120,690	Danny Ozark

Playoffs: Houston 4 games, Indianapolis 1; Louisville 4 games, Denver 3.
Finals: Louisville 4 games, Houston 2.

All-Star Team: 1B-Bud Zipfel, Houston; **2B-**Jim Baumer, Denver; **3B-**Cliff Cook, Indianapolis; **SS-**Jim Fregosi, Dallas-Ft. Worth; **OF-**Jim McDaniel, Denver; Bill Lajoie, Omaha; George Alusik, Denver; **C-**J.W. Porter, Denver; Bob Rodgers, Dallas-Ft. Worth; Don Pavletich, Indianapolis; Ted Kazanski, Dallas-Ft. Worth; **Util-**J.C. Hartman, Houston; **P-**Claude Osteen, Indianapolis; Hugh Pepper, Dallas-Ft. Worth; Jack Waters, Houston; Jack Spring, Dallas-Ft. Worth; Gordon Seyfried, Denver; Don Rudolph, Indianapolis; Will Hunter, Omaha; **MVP-**Cliff Cook, Indianapolis; **Manager-**Charlie Metro, Denver.

BA: Don Wert, Denver, .328
Runs: Cliff Cook, Indianapolis, 102
Hits: Howie Bedell, Louisville, 194
RBIs: Cliff Cook, Indianapolis, 119
HRs: Cliff Cook, Indianapolis, 32
Wins: Don Rudolph, Indianapolis, 18
SOs: Charlie Spell, Omaha, 164
ERA: Federico Olivo, Louisville, 2.66

AAA International League
President: Thomas H. Richardson

Standings	W	L	Pct.	GB	Attend.	Manager
Columbus Jets (18)	92	62	.597	—	187,471	Larry Shepard
San Juan/Charleston Marlins# (19)	88	66	.571	4	107,344	Joe Schultz
Buffalo Bisons (17)	85	67	.559	6	259,724	Kerby Farrell
Rochester Red Wings (1)	77	78	.497	15½	219,944	Clyde King
Toronto Maple Leafs (6)	76	79	.490	16½	150,960	John Lipon/Tim Thompson
Richmond Virginians (9)	71	83	.4610	21	131,232	Cal Ermer
Jersey City Jerseys (12)	70	82	.461	21	61,940	Napoleon Reyes
Syracuse Chiefs (8)	56	98	.364	36	126,016	Gene Verble/Frank Verdi

*Won first-half   **Won second-half   ***Won both halves
Numbers after nicknames indicate farm system.
Affiliation listed at end of each year.

#San Juan moved to Charleston May 19.

Playoffs: Rochester 4 games, Columbus 1; Buffalo 4 games, Charleston 0.
Finals: Buffalo 4 games, Rochester 1.

All-Star Team: 1B-Donn Clendenon, Columbus; **2B-**Julio Gotay, San Juan/Charleston; **3B-**Felix Torres, Buffalo; **SS-**Tom Tresh, Richmond; **OF-**Ted Savage, Buffalo; Boog Powell, Rochester; Roman Mejias, Columbus; **C-**Bob Oldis, Columbus; **P-**Ray Washburn, San Juan/Charleston; Bob Veale, Columbus; **MVP-**Ted Savage, Buffalo; **Pitcher of the Year-**Diomedes Olivo, Columbus; **Manager-**Larry Shepard, Columbus.

BA: Ted Savage, Buffalo, .325
Runs: Ted Savage, Buffalo, 111
Hits: Ted Savage, Buffalo, 178
RBIs: Frank Leja, Richmond/Syracuse, 98
HRs: Boog Powell, Rochester, 32
Wins: Ray Washburn, San Juan/Charleston, 16
SOs: Bob Veale, Columbus, 208
ERA: Ray Washburn, San Juan/Charleston, 2.34

AAA Pacific Coast League
President: Dewey Soriano

Standings	W	L	Pct.	GB	Attend.	Manager
Tacoma Giants (20)	97	57	.630	—	243,790	John "Red" Davis
Vancouver Mounties (15)	87	67	.565	10	200,143	Billy Hitchcock
Seattle Rainiers (2)	86	68	.558	11	174,889	Johnny Pesky
San Diego Padres (3)	72	82	.468	25	172,521	Jimmy Reese/Whitey Wietelmann/Bill Norman
Portland Beavers (19)	71	83	.461	26	132,834	Vern Benson/Ray Katt
Hawaii Islanders# (6)	68	86	.442	29	165,786	Tommy Heath/Bill Werle
Spokane Indians (14)	68	86	.442	29	153,393	Preston Gomez
Salt Lake City Bees (4)	67	87	.435	30	106,454	Herman Franks/Fred Fitzsimmons

#represented Honolulu, Hawaii.

Playoffs: None

All-Star Team: 1B-Gene Oliver, Portland; **2B-**Chuck Hiller, Tacoma; **3B-**Ed Charles, Vancouver; **SS-**Denis Menke, Vancouver; **OF-**Al Luplow, Salt Lake City; Howie Goss, Vancouver; Lou Clinton, Seattle; **C-**Howard "Doc" Edwards, Salt Lake City; Ken Retzer, San Diego; **P-**Ron Herbel, Tacoma; Ron Piche, Vancouver; **MVP-**Dick Phillips, Tacoma; **Manager-**John "Red" Davis, Tacoma.

BA: Carlos Bernier, Hawaii, .351
Runs: Ed Charles, Vancouver, 114
Hits: Ed Charles, Vancouver, 181
RBIs: Harry Simpson, San Diego, 105
HRs: Gene Oliver, Portland, 36
Wins: Ron Herbel, Tacoma, 16
Gaylord Perry, Tacoma, 16
SOs: Sam McDowell, Salt Lake City, 156
ERA: Ron Piche, Vancouver, 2.26

AA Mexican League
President: Eduardo Orvananos

Standings	W	L	Pct.	GB	Attend.	Manager
Veracruz Aguilas	77	57	.575	—	205,937	Santos Amaro
Puebla Pericos	73	61	.545	4	194,181	Luis Montes de Oca
Poza Rica Petroleros	61	72	.459	15½	203,305	Bernardo Lopez
Monterrey Sultanes	59	73	.447	17	152,776	Bert Haas
Mexico City Diablos Rojos	59	75	.440	18	285,301	Hector Mayer/Wilfredo Calvino
Mexico City Tigres	48	86	.358	29	204,423	Memo Garibay

Each team played 24 games with Texas League teams which counted in the standings. The combined leagues were known as the Pan American Association.

Playoffs: None.

All-Star Team: 1B-Jose Guerrero, Puebla; **2B-**Vinicio Garcia, Monterrey; **3B-**Louis B. Garcia, Poza Rica; **SS-**Jorge Fitch, Puebla; **OF-**Asdrubal Baro, Veracruz; Juan Delis, Monterrey; Al Pinkston, Veracruz; **C-**Miguel Gaspar, Veracruz; Alberto Palafox, MC Diablos Rojos; **P-**Julio Moreno, Puebla, Ramon Arano, Veracruz; **Manager-**Memo Garibay, MC Tigres.

BA: Al Pinkston, Veracruz, .374
Runs: Asdrubal Baro, Veracruz, 108
Hits: Pedro Cardenal, Puebla, 175
RBIs: Witremundo Quintana, Veracruz, 89
HRs: Witremundo Quintana, Veracruz, 23
Wins: Silvio Castellanos, Veracruz, 14
SOs: Juan Piedra, Monterrey, 171
ERA: Julio Moreno, Pueblo, 3.01

AA Southern Association
President: Hal Totten

Standings	W	L	Pct.	GB	Attend.	Manager
Chattanooga Lookouts (17)	90	62	.592	—	107,419	Frank Lucchesi
Birmingham Barons (5)	89	63	.586	1	112,217	Frank Skaff
Little Rock Travelers (1)	80	73	.523	10½	136,316	Fred Hatfield

	W	L	Pct.	GB	Attend.	Manager
Atlanta Crackers (14)	77	74	.510	12½	59,061	Rube Walker
Macon Peaches	75	79	.487	16	91,136	Max Macon/Gerald Snyder
Nashville Vols (8)	69	83	.454	21	64,460	Spencer Robbins
Shreveport Sports (6)	69	84	.451	21½	28,349	Les Peden
Mobile Bears (16)	61	92	.399	29½	48,843	Ernie White

Playoffs: None.

All-Star Team: 1B-Don Saner, Little Rock; **2B**-Legrant Scott, Birmingham; **3B**-Wayne Graham, Chattanooga; **SS**-Arnaldo Suarez, Macon; **OF**-Stan Palys, Birmingham; Joe Christian, Nashville; John Herrnstein, Chattanooga; Gerald Reimer, Chattanooga; Al Ferrara, Atlanta; **C**-Lou Holdener, Mobile; Mike Brumley, Atlanta; John Sullivan, Birmingham; **Util IF**-Norm Gigon, Chattanooga; **P**-Howie Koplitz, Birmingham; John Boozer, Chattanooga; Charlie Rabe, Macon; Al Koch, Birmingham; Dale Willis, Shreveport; Jack Smith, Atlanta; Douglas Gallagher, Birmingham; **MVP**-Howie Koplitz, Birmingham; **Rookie of the Year**-John Boozer, Chattanooga; **Manager**-Frank Lucchesi, Chattanooga.

BA: Don Saner, Little Rock, .349
Runs: Legrant Scott, Birmingham, 128
Hits: Wayne Graham, Chattanooga, 199
RBIs: Stan Palys, Birmingham, 114
HRs: Bill Gabler, Macon, 30
Wins: Howie Koplitz, Birmingham, 23
SOs: Bo Belinsky, Little Rock, 182
ERA: Jack Smith, Atlanta, 2.09

AA Texas League
President: Dick Butler

Standings	W	L	Pct.	GB	Attend.	Manager
Amarillo Gold Sox (9)	90	50	.643	—	85,406	Sheriff Robinson/ Steve Souchock
Tulsa Oilers (19)	83	55	.601	6	130,443	Whitey Kurowski
San Antonio Missions (11)	74	65	.532	15½	91,493	James "Rip" Collins/Harry Craft/ Bobby Adams/Rube Walker
Austin Senators (15)	69	71	.493	21	68,761	Bill Adair
Rio Grande Valley/ Victoria Giants@(20)/ Victoria	69	71	.493	21	43,184	Ray Murray
Ardmore Rosebuds#(1)	57	83	.407	33	48,894	George Staller

Each team played 24 games with Mexican League teams. The combined leagues were known as the Pan American Association.
#Victoria moved to Ardmore May 27.
@Rio Grande Valley moved to Victoria June 10.

Playoffs: Austin defeated Victoria 4-3 to decide fourth place. Austin 3 games, Amarillo 2; San Antonio 3 games, Tulsa 1.
Finals: San Antonio 3 games, Austin 0.

All-Star Team: 1B-Tommie Aaron, Austin; **2B**-Jack Damaska, Tulsa; **3B**-Mike Mathiesen, Amarillo; **SS**-Phil Linz, Amarillo; **OF**-Dick Berardino, Amarillo; Jose Tartabull, Rio Grande Valley/Victoria; Johnny Lewis, Tulsa; Joe Pepitone, Rio Grande Valley/Victoria; **C**-Tim Talton, Rio Grande Valley/Victoria; **Util**-Charlie Strange, Victoria/Ardmore; **P**-Larry Maxie, Austin; Hal Stowe, Amarillo; **MVP**-Phil Linz, Amarillo; **Pitcher of the Year**-Larry Maxie, Austin.

BA: Phil Linz, Amarillo, .349
Runs: Jose Tartabull, Rio Grande Valley/Victoria, 103
Hits: Don Brummer, Amarillo, 174
RBIs: Dick Berardino, Amarillo, 93
HRs: Craig Sorenson, San Antonio, 27
Wins: Paul Toth, Tulsa, 18
SOs: Harry Fanok, Tulsa, 158
ERA: Larry Maxie, Austin, 2.08

A Eastern League
President: A. Rankin Johnson

Standings	W	L	Pct.	GB	Attend.	Manager
Springfield Giants (20)	85	54	.612	—	77,893	Andy Gilbert
Williamsport Grays (17)	79	61	.564	6½	79,183	Andy Seminick
Binghamton Triplets (9)	75	64	.540	10	62,283	Jimmy Gleeson
Johnstown Red Sox (2)	61	79	.436	24½	58,179	Eddie Popowski
Lancaster Red Roses (19)	60	80	.429	25½	51,311	Chase Riddle
Reading Indians (4)	59	81	.421	26½	53,283	Ray Mueller

Playoffs: None.

All-Star Team: 1B-Charley Keller, Binghamton; **2B**-Lou Vassie, Williamsport; **3B**-George Banks, Binghamton; **SS**-Tony Martinez, Reading; **OF**-Jim O'Rourke, Lancaster; Bob Stotsky, Johnstown; Keith Williams, Reading; **C**-Archie Skeen, Johnstown; Larry Cutright, Williamsport; **Util**-Danny Cater, Williamsport; **P**-Jerry Thomas, Springfield; Marcelino Lopez, Williamsport; **Manager**-Andy Gilbert, Springfield.

BA: Charley Keller, Binghamton, .349
Runs: Alan Moran, Johnstown, 118
Hits: Danny Cater, Williamsport, 193
RBIs: George Banks, Binghamton, 108
HRs: George Banks, Binghamton, 30
Wins: Gerry Thomas, Springfield, 20
SOs: Gerry Thomas, Springfield, 214
ERA: Gerry Thomas, Springfield, 2.40

A South Atlantic League
President: Sam C. Smith

Standings	W	L	Pct.	GB	Attend.	Manager
Asheville Tourists (18)	87	50	.635	—	97,065	Ray Hathaway
Knoxville Smokies (5)	75	64	.540	13	66,312	Frank Carswell
Greenville Spinners (14)	72	66	.522	15½	100,168	Roy Hartsfield
Columbia Reds (12)	70	65	.519	16	25,998	Ted Beard/Hershell Freeman
Charleston White Sox (3)	70	68	.507	17½	40,600	Ira Hutchinson

	W	L	Pct.	GB	Attend.	Manager
Portsmouth-Norfolk Tides (6)	66	72	.478	21½	87,158	Granny Hamner
Charlotte Hornets (8)	61	79	.436	27½	50,033	Ellis Clary
Jacksonville Jets (13)	51	88	.367	37	25,156	Tom Saffell/Dixie Howell

Playoffs: None.

All-Star Team: 1B-Bill Roman, Knoxville; **2B**-Bobby Klaus, Columbia; **3B**-Duncan Campbell, Asheville; **SS**-Nestor Velazquez, Charlotte; **OF**-Jess Queen, Knoxville; Gary Rushing, Asheville; Teo Acosta, Columbia; **C**-Jesus McFarlane, Asheville; **Util**-Jose Cesar, Greenville; **P**-Jim Hardison, Asheville; Jon Willhite, Greenville; **MVP**-Gary Rushing, Asheville; **Manager**-Ray Hathaway, Asheville.

BA: Teo Acosta, Columbia, .343
Runs: Gary Rushing, Asheville, 108
Hits: Teo Acosta, Columbia, 167
 William Roman, Knoxville, 167
RBIs: Gary Rushing, Asheville, 99
HRs: Gary Rushing, Asheville, 25
Wins: Byron "Jack" Taylor, Charlotte, 17
SOs: Nick Willhite, Greenville, 161
ERA: Nick Willhite, Greenville, 1.80

B Carolina League
President: J.C. "Bill" Jessup

Standings	W	L	Pct.	GB	Attend.	Manager
Wilson Tobs***(8)	83	56	.597	—	37,893	Jack McKeon
Burlington Indians (4)	71	66	.518	11	32,405	Bill Herring/Walter Novick
Greensboro Yankees (9)	70	68	.507	12½	61,017	Wayne Terwilliger
Winston-Salem Red Sox (2)	68	72	.486	15½	70,236	Elmer Yoter/Matt Sczesny
Durham Bulls (5)	65	73	.471	17½	33,235	Al Lakeman
Raleigh Capitals (16)	58	80	.420	24½	36,480	Enos Slaughter

Playoffs: None.

All-Star Team: 1B-Chuck Reidell, Greensboro; **2B**-Rufus Anderson, Durham; **3B**-Gene Domzalski, Greensboro; **SS**-Orlando Martinez, Wilson; **OF**-Chuck Weatherspoon, Wilson; Gates Brown, Durham; Dean Robbins, Winston-Salem; Ron Solomini, Greensboro; **C**-Joe McCabe, Wilson; Duke Sims, Burlington; **Util**-Ron Retton, Greensboro; **P**-Bill MacLeod, Winston-Salem; Al Eisele, Burlington; Dick Klunder, Durham; Norm Forsythe, Greensboro; **MVP**-Chuck Weatherspoon, Wilson; **Manager**-Jack McKeon, Wilson.

BA: Bill Brown, Durham, .324
Runs: Chuck Weatherspoon, Wilson, 121
Hits: Ike Futch, Greensboro, 164
RBIs: Chuck Weatherspoon, Wilson, 123
HRs: Chuck Weatherspoon, Wilson, 31
Wins: Bill MacLeod, Winston-Salem, 15
 Bill Jones, Wilson, 15
 Edward Merritt, Greensboro, 15
 Al Eisele, Burlington, 15
SOs: Bill MacLeod, Winston-Salem, 208
ERA: Bill MacLeod, Winston-Salem, 2.31

B Northwest League
President: James M. Fleishman

Standings	W	L	Pct.	GB	Attend.	Manager
Lewiston Broncs*(6)	84	56	.600	—	49,602	John McNamara
Yakima Bears**(15)	79	60	.568	4½	42,806	Buddy Hicks
Salem Dodgers (14)	74	66	.529	10	72,703	Stan Wasiak
Eugene Emeralds (20)	69	70	.497	14½	53,046	Richard Klaus
Wenatchee Chiefs (11)	63	76	.453	20½	31,338	Rube Walker/Vedie Himsl/ Richard Cole/Bobby Adams
Tri-City Atoms (1)	49	90	.353	34½	37,817	Whitey McDowell/ Billy DeMars

Playoff: Lewiston 4 games, Yakima 1.

All-Star Team: 1B-Mo Morhardt, Wenatchee; **2B**-Ossie Chavarria, Lewiston; **3B**-Dick Green, Lewiston; **SS**-Michael Sinnerud, Yakima; **OF**-Jesus Alou, Eugene; Dick Bogard, Salem; Jim Barbieri, Salem; **C**-Bob Barton, Eugene; John McNamara, Lewiston; Bill Bryan, Lewiston; **P**-Larry Danforth, Lewiston; Lazaro Gomez, Eugene; **Manager**-John McNamara, Lewiston.

BA: Mo Morhardt, Wenatchee, .339
Runs: Jim Barbieri, Salem, 102
 Ossie Chavarria, Lewiston, 102
Hits: Jesus Alou, Eugene, 174
RBIs: Eddie Kopacz, Salem, 112
HRs: Raynor Youngdahl, Tri-City, 28
Wins: Larry Danforth, Lewiston, 20
SOs: Larry Danforth, Lewiston, 180
ERA: Larry Danforth, Lewiston, 2.41

B Three-I League
President: Vern Hoscheit

Standings	W	L	Pct.	GB	Attend.	Manager
Topeka Reds (12)	79	50	.612	—	56,384	Dave Bristol
Cedar Rapids Braves (15)	73	57	.562	6½	69,617	James Brown
Lincoln Chiefs (3)	68	62	.523	11½	42,866	George Noga
Fox Cities Foxes (1)	67	62	.519	12	47,552	Earl Weaver
Burlington Bees (18)	65	65	.500	14½	36,798	Pete Peterson
Des Moines Demons (17)	37	93	.285	42½	33,337	Charlie Kress

Playoffs: None.

All-Star Team: 1B-Paul Snyder, Cedar Rapids; **2B**-Tommy Harper, Topeka; **3B**-Dayton Orsburn, Lincoln; **SS**-Roberto Pena, Burlington; **OF**-Sam Bowens, Fox Cities; Barry Morgan, Cedar Rapids; Joseph Trenary, Cedar Rapids; **C**-Pat Corrales, Des Moines; **Util**-Ron Brand, Burlington; **P**-Bill Holmes, Cedar Rapids; Bob Locker, Lincoln; Richard Kelley, Cedar Rapids; Dave McNally, Fox Cities; **Manager**-Dave Bristol, Topeka.

BA: Dick Haines, Des Moines, .355
Runs: Tommy Harper, Topeka, 131
Hits: Paul Snyder, Cedar Rapids, 153
RBIs: Miles McWilliams, Topeka, 102

HRs: Barry Morgan, Cedar Rapids, 23
Wins: Bill Holmes, Cedar Rapids, 18
SOs: Bob Locker, Lincoln, 215
ERA: Bill Holmes, Cedar Rapids, 2.21

C California League
President: Edward J. Mulligan

Standings	W	L	Pct.	GB	Attend.	Manager
Reno Silver Sox***(14)	97	43	.693	—	43,573	Roy Smalley
Bakersfield Bears (17)........	82	58	.586	15	45,992	Lou Kahn
Fresno Giants (20)	68	72	.486	29	34,904	Salvador Taormina
Visalia Athletics (6)...........	60	79	.432	36½	19,509	Bob Hofman
Modesto Reds (9)...............	57	82	.410	39½	15,865	Vern Rapp
Stockton Ports (1)	54	84	.391	42	11,660	Harry Dunlop

Playoffs: None.

All-Star Team: 1B-Dick Nen, Reno; **2B-**Louis Ertle, Reno; **3B-**Jim Ray Hart, Fresno; **SS-**Don Williams, Reno; **OF-**John Upham, Bakersfield; Jerry Kushner, Fresno; Ken Harrelson, Visalia; **C-**Hector Valle, Reno; **P-**Natividad Martinez, Stockton; Joe Moeller, Reno; Bruce Gardner, Reno; John Hogg, Bakersfield; **MVP-**Don Williams, Reno; **Rookie of the Year-**Dick Nen, Reno; **Manager-**Lou Kahn, Bakersfield.

BA: Don Williams, Reno, .363
Runs: Don Williams, Reno, 132
Hits: Don Williams, Reno, 197
RBIs: Dick Nen, Reno, 144

HRs: Dick Nen, Reno, 32
Wins: Bruce Gardner, Reno, 20
SOs: Jose Santiago, Visalia, 218
ERA: Bruce Gardner, Reno, 2.82

C Mexican Center League
President: Eduardo Orvananos

Standings	W	L	Pct.	GB	Attend.	Manager
Aguascalientes Tigres.........	68	52	.567	—	22,527	Jesus Robles
Celaya Cajeteros	66	54	.550	2	15,904	Ciro Soto/Nazario Moreno
Leon Aguilas.....................	63	56	.529	4½	36,291	Felipe Hernandez/ Manuel Arroyo
San Luis Potosi Tuneros	56	64	.467	12	61,274	Domingo Santana
Guanajuato Tuzos	54	66	.450	14	32,775	Gustavo Bello
Salamanca Petroleros..........	52	67	.437	15½	24,269	Walter Graham

All-Star Team: 1B-Alejandro Flores, Salamanca; **2B-**Gabriel Heredia, Aguascalientes; **3B-**Jorge Calvo, Guanajuato; **SS-**Fernando Remes, Aguascalientes; **OF-**Eladio Urias, Celaya; Luis Hernandez, Aguascalientes; Humberto Ayala, Leon; **C-**Alfonso Ibarra, San Luis Potosi; Jesus Contreras, Celaya; **P-**Cesar Gutierrez, Aguascalientes; Adolfo Flores, Celaya; **Manager-**Walter Graham, Salamanca.

BA: Jorge Calvo, Guanajuato, .368
Runs: Lorenzo Lopez, Guanajuato, 117
Hits: Alejandrino Cuevas, San Luis Potosi, 157
RBIs: Jorge Calvo, Guanajuato, 130

HRs: Jorge Calvo, Guanajuato, 29
Wins: Cesar Gutierrez, Aguascalientes, 21
SOs: Cesar Gutierrez, Aguascalientes, 190
ERA: Nicolas Garcia, Celaya, 2.52

C Northern League
President: Herman D. White

Standings	W	L	Pct.	GB	Attend.	Manager
Duluth-Superior Dukes (5) ...	76	52	.594	—	47,163	Bob Swift
Aberdeen Pheasants (1)	74	54	.578	2	34,136	Lou Fitzgerald
St. Cloud Rox (11).............	73	54	.575	2½	24,320	Joe Macko
Grand Forks Chiefs (18)......	60	66	.476	15	29,352	Bob Clear
Eau Claire Braves (15)	52	78	.400	25	26,480	Jim Fanning
Winnipeg Goldeyes (19).....	46	77	.374	27½	45,874	Grover Resinger/Owen Friend

Playoffs: St. Cloud 1 game, Duluth-Superior 0; Aberdeen 1 game, Grand Forks 0.
Finals: Aberdeen 2 games, St. Cloud 0.

All-Star Team: 1B-Bert Barth, Aberdeen; **2B-**Al Baker, Duluth-Superior; **3B-**Ron Campbell, St. Cloud; **SS-**Jose Martinez, Grand Forks; **OF-**Lou Brock, St. Cloud; Don Branson, Aberdeen; Pat Owens, Grand Forks; Carlos Dore, Winnipeg; **C-**Dave Massarelli, Aberdeen; Pat Foley, Winnipeg; **P-**Tom Timmerman, Duluth-Superior; Darold Knowles, Aberdeen; **Manager-**Bob Swift, Duluth-Superior.

BA: Lou Brock, St. Cloud, .361
Runs: Lou Brock, St. Cloud, 117
Hits: Lou Brock, St. Cloud, 181
RBIs: Bert Barth, Aberdeen, 99
HRs: Patrick Owens, Grand Forks, 24

Wins: Tom Timmerman, Duluth-Superior, 15
SOs: Darold Knowles, Aberdeen, 183
ERA: Ceferino Foy, Eau Claire, 2.03

C Pioneer League
President: Claude Engberg

Standings	W	L	Pct.	GB	Attend.	Manager
Boise Braves*(15)	72	55	.567	—	41,797	Gordon Maltzberger
Great Falls Electrics**(14).	72	58	.554	1½	59,406	Al Ronning
Idaho Falls Russets (3)	67	63	.515	6½	29,576	Herman Reich/George Sobek
Magic Valley Cowboys (17)....	64	66	.492	9½	61,405	Jack Phillips
Pocatello Bannocks (6, 20) ...	57	72	.442	16	32,099	Bert Thiel
Billings Mustangs (19)	55	73	.430	17½	36,613	Owen Friend/Grover Resinger

Playoff: Great Falls 3 games, Boise 1.

All-Star Team: 1B-Costen Shockley, Magic Valley; **2B-**Douglas Clayton, Boise; **3B-**James Shinn, Great Falls; **SS-**Domingo Carrasquel, Great Falls; **OF-**Bobby Sanders, Magic Valley; Eugene Duffy, Idaho Falls; Eddie Reed, Great Falls; Otto Knowles, Billings; **C-**Everett Krug, Billings; Victor Baron, Magic Valley; **Util-**Jose Valladares, Idaho Falls; **P-**Jim Ward, Great Falls; William Ryan, Boise; Joel Gibson, Magic Valley; Robert Wasko, Great Falls; **Manager-**Al Ronning, Great Falls.

BA: Domingo Carrasquel, Great Falls, .361
Runs: Domingo Carrasquel, Great Falls, 115
Hits: Domingo Carrasquel, Great Falls, 182
RBIs: Bobby Sanders, Magic Valley, 118

HRs: Bobby Sanders, Magic Valley, 40
Wins: Jim Ward, Great Falls, 20
SOs: Jim Ward, Great Falls, 219
ERA: Richard Scarbrough, Great Falls, 3.39

D Alabama-Florida League
President: William Moore

Standings	W	L	Pct.	GB	Attend.	Manager
Selma Cloverleafs***(4)	76	43	.639	—	21,760	Walter Novick/Joe Morlan
Pensacola Senators (10)......	70	47	.598	5	46,993	Archie Wilson
Ft. Walton Beach Jets (8) ...	61	55	.526	13½	15,603	Vern Morgan
Montgomery Rebels (5)......	56	62	.475	19½	21,600	Gail Henley
Panama City Fliers (14)......	55	64	.462	21	24,167	George Scherger
Dothan Phillies (17)...........	35	82	.299	40	7,963	Bob Wellman

Playoffs: None.

All-Star Team: 1B-Bob Loftin, Panama City; **2B-**John Erickson, Ft. Walton Beach; **3B-**Gary Dempsey, Panama City; **SS-**John Kennedy, Pensacola; **OF-**Mickey Strickland, Panama City; Braxton Bailey, Panama City; John Schoenberger, Pensacola; **C-**Lance Nichols, Panama City; **P-**Tom Young, Panama City; Fred Waters, Pensacola; **Manager-**Archie Wilson, Pensacola.

BA: Braxton Bailey, Panama City, .356
Runs: Horace Strickland, Panama City, 103
Hits: Alf Sommerstad, Ft. Walton Beach, 146
RBIs: Bob Loftin, Panama City, 91

HRs: Pedro Fernandez, Ft. Walton Beach, 20
Wins: David Seeman, Selma, 17
SOs: Fred Waters, Pensacola, 197
ERA: Tom Young, Panama City, 1.95

D Appalachian League
President: Chauncey De Vault

Standings	W	L	Pct.	GB	Attend.	Manager
Middlesboro Senators (10) ..	39	27	.591	—	16,751	Lewis Morton
Wytheville Twins (8)..........	38	29	.567	1½	16,930	Red Norwood
Harlan Smokies (3, 9)........	35	34	.507	5½	19,466	Frank Parenti & Ed Lyons
Bluefield Orioles (1)	34	34	.500	6	19,066	Dee Phillips/Walt Youse/ Joe Cursick/Buddy Bates
Morristown Cubs (11)	34	36	.486	7	11,772	John Fitzpatrick
Kingsport Pirates (18)........	31	35	.470	8	19,815	James Gibbons
Salem Rebels (20).............	31	35	.470	8	34,125	Jodie Phipps
Johnson City Cardinals (19)..	26	38	.406	12	13,336	Edward Lyons/George Kissell/ Charles Frey/Mo Mozzali/ John Grodzicki

Playoffs: None.

All-Star Team: 1B-Dick Hickerson, Bluefield; **2B-**Bill Oplinger, Bluefield; **3B-**Dave Wissman, Kingsport; **SS-**Stan Majesky, Middlesboro; **OF-**Tony Oliva, Wytheville; Wally Cockrell, Salem; Bob Michael, Morristown; **C-**Dan Hagan, Wytheville; **P-**Lynn Bridwell, Wytheville; Carlos Medrano, Middlesboro; **Rookie of the Year-**Tony Oliva, Wytheville; **Manager-**Lewis Morton, Middlesboro.

BA: Tony Oliva, Wytheville, .410
Runs: David Wissman, Kingsport, 72
Hits: Tony Oliva, Wytheville, 102
RBIs: Tony Oliva, Wytheville, 81

HRs: Jim Winn, Harlan, 14
Wins: Carlos Medrano, Middlesboro, 11
SOs: Mike Degerick, Harlan, 113
ERA: Leroy Heiser, Middlesboro, 2.19

D Florida State League
President: William McKechnie Jr.

Standings	W	L	Pct.	GB	Attend.	Manager
Tampa Tarpons*(12)	90	44	.672	—	32,027	John Vander Meer
Sarasota Sun Sox**(6)........	79	60	.568	13½	30,164	Bill Robertson
St. Petersburg Saints (9)	67	75	.472	27	53,330	Bob Bauer
Orlando Dodgers (9).........	66	74	.471	27	13,554	Edward Serrano
Daytona Beach Islanders (3)..	63	71	.470	27	29,490	Ray Wilson
Palatka Redlegs (15)..........	61	78	.439	31½	21,682	Michael Fandozzi
Leesburg Orioles (1)...........	56	80	.412	35	10,605	Billy DeMars/Cal Ripken, Sr./ Ray Scarborough

Playoff: Tampa 3 games, Sarasota 2.

All-Star Team: 1B-William Meyer, St. Petersburg; **2B-**Pete Rose, Tampa; **3B-**Jim Livesey, Leesburg; **SS-**Ted Kubiak, Sarasota; **OF-**Lawson Mitchell, Daytona Beach; Fleming Reedy, Sarasota; Norman Shuey, Tampa; **C-**Pedro Martinez, Tampa; **Util-**Ronald Paiva, Palatka; **P-**Dan Neville, Tampa; Pete Cianfione, Orlando; **Manager-**Bill Robertson, Sarasota.

BA: Jim Livesey, Leesburg, .339
Runs: Fleming Reedy, Sarasota, 107
Hits: Pete Rose, Tampa, 160
RBIs: Paul Catto, Palatka, 93
HRs: Paul Catto, Palatka, 12

3B: Pete Rose, Tampa, 30
Wins: Ron Banovic, Sarasota, 18
Pete Cianfione, Tampa, 18
SOs: Jim Farland, Orlando, 206
ERA: Dan Neville, Tampa, 1.94

D Midwest League
President: C.C. "Dutch" Hoffman

Standings	W	L	Pct.	GB	Attend.	Manager
Waterloo Hawks*(2)	75	51	.595	—	70,025	Matt Sczesny/Bill Slack
Clinton C-Sox (3)	69	56	.552	5½	57,162	Richard Kinaman
Quad Cities Braves#(15)	68	56	.548	6	74,617	Alex Monchak
Quincy Giants**(20)	67	59	.532	8	26,094	Buddy Kerr
Dubuque Packers (4)	64	61	.512	10½	67,864	Pinky May
Decatur Commodores (5)	57	65	.467	16	65,094	John Groth
Kokomo Dodgers (14)	55	65	.458	17	30,041	Don Domenichelli
Keokuk Cardinals (19)	40	82	.328	33	25,064	Al Unser

#represented Davenport-Bettendorf (IA)-Moline-Rock Island (IL).

Playoff: Quincy 3 games, Waterloo 2.

All-Star Team: 1B-Antulio Martinez, Quincy; **2B**-Larry Rojas, Dubuque; **3B**-Pete Jernigan, Waterloo; **SS**-John Butler, Dubuque; **OF**-Ken Berry, Clinton; Tom Richards, Kokomo; Hector Cardenas, Dubuque; **C**-Ron Staples, Waterloo; Doyle Wagner, Quad Cities; **Util IF**-Dick Krotz, Kokomo; **Util OF**-Bill Dixon, Quincy; **P**-Steve Busby, Waterloo; Dennis Ribant, Quad Cities; Bob House, Clinton; Tom Newton, Quad Cities; **Player of the Year**-Hector Cardenas, Dubuque; **Rookie of the Year**-Dennis Ribant, Quad Cities; **Manager**-Buddy Kerr, Quincy.

BA: Antulio Martinez, Quincy, .368
Runs: Bob Lawrence, Waterloo, 113
Hits: Antulio Martinez, Quincy, 166
RBIs: Bob Lawrence, Waterloo, 127

HRs: Bob Lawrence, Waterloo, 30
Wins: Steve Busby, Waterloo, 21
SOs: Steve Busby, Waterloo, 237
ERA: Dennis Ribant, Quad Cities, 1.86

D New York-Pennsylvania League
President: Vincent M. McNamara

Standings	W	L	Pct.	GB	Attend.	Manager
Geneva Redlegs (12)	77	48	.616	—	32,505	Karl Kuehl
Erie Sailors (8)	68	57	.544	9	19,583	Harry Warner
Batavia Pirates (18)	65	59	.524	11½	32,211	James Adlam/Gene Baker
Olean Red Sox (2)	64	61	.512	13	40,380	Harold Holland
Elmira Pioneers (17)	61	63	.492	15½	30,416	Wilbur Johnson
Jamestown Tigers (5)	58	68	.460	19½	65,402	Al Federoff
Wellsville Braves (15)	55	71	.437	22½	17,385	Bill Steinecke
Auburn Yankees (9)	52	73	.416	25	33,216	Loren Babe

Playoffs: Olean 2 games, Geneva 1; Batavia 2 games, Erie 1.
Finals: Olean 2 games, Batavia 0.

All-Star Team: 1B-Humberto Sama, Erie; **2B**-Cesar Tovar, Geneva; **3B**-Tony Perez, Geneva; **SS**-Teofilo James, Wellsville; **OF**-Leon Douglas, Wellsville; Art Blunt, Batavia; Arthur Jasinski, Jamestown; **C**-Larry Baughman, Elmira; **P**-Jim Hannan, Olean; Gary Aldrich, Batavia; **Manager**-Karl Kuehl, Geneva.

BA: Tony Perez, Geneva, .348
Runs: Cesar Tovar, Geneva, 134
Hits: Tony Perez, Geneva, 160
RBIs: Tony Perez, Geneva, 132
HRs: Roberto Sanchez, Batavia, 36

SBs: Cesar Tovar, Geneva, 88
Wins: Jim Hannan, Olean, 17
SOs: Jim Hannan, Olean, 254
ERA: John Morris, Elmira, 2.02

D Sophomore League
President: C.F. Montgomery

Standings	W	L	Pct.	GB	Attend.	Manager
Hobbs Pirates*(18)	77	48	.616	—	15,482	Al Kubski
El Paso Sun Kings (20)	73	57	.562	6½	79,115	George Genovese
Albuquerque Dukes**(6)	64	63	.504	14	50,760	Grady Wilson
Alpine Cowboys (2)	62	63	.496	15	9,392	Mel Parnell
Carlsbad Potashers (11)	56	71	.441	22	14,974	Lou Klein/Walt Dixon
Artesia Dodgers (14)	48	78	.381	29½	9,724	John "Spider" Jorgensen

Playoff: Hobbs 3 games, Albuquerque 0.

All-Star Team: 1B-Jose Calero, El Paso; **2B**-Luis Alcarez, Artesia; **3B**-Jose Cardenal, El Paso; **SS**-Gene Michael, Hobbs; **OF**-Tommie Martz, Hobbs; Luis Rodriguez, Albuquerque; Bob Chance, El Paso; **C**-Dick Dietz, El Paso; Ron Thompson, Alpine; **P**-Jim Little, Hobbs; Aurelio Monteagudo, Albuquerque; **Manager**-Al Kubski, Hobbs.

BA: Tommie Martz, Hobbs, .387
Runs: Jose Cardenal, El Paso, 159
Hits: Jose Calero, El Paso, 180
RBIs: Mike Maloney, Albuquerque, 109

HRs: Jose Cardenal, El Paso, 35
Wins: Jim Little, Hobbs, 17
SOs: Fred Hatter, Alpine, 201
ERA: John Drysdale, Artesia, 3.32

D Western Carolina League
President: John H. Moss

Standings	W	L	Pct.	GB	Attend.	Manager
Salisbury Braves**(13)	64	38	.627	—	29,981	Alex Cosmidis
Statesville Owls*(7)	63	39	.618	1	34,954	George Wilson
Lexington Indians (16)	51	53	.490	14	27,777	Jack Hale
Shelby Colonels (18)	51	55	.481	15	11,587	Aaron Robinson/James Adlam
Belmont Chiefs (20)	39	61	.390	24	10,081	Jim Poole/Whitey Ries/ Max Lanier
Newton-Conover Twins (15)	36	58	.383	24	17,822	Joe Abernethy

Playoffs: Shelby 2 games, Salisbury 0; Lexington 2 games, Statesville 0.
Finals: Shelby 2 games, Lexington 1.

All-Star Team: 1B-Aaron Pointer, Salisbury; **2B**-Buddy Cia, Belmont; **3B**-Jerry Autry, Shelby; **SS**-Lee Hyman, Salisbury; **OF**-Ron Henson, Lexington; Richard Simpson, Statesville; Dick Loughridge, Salisbury; **C**-Bob Worthington, Lexington; Jack Hiatt, Statesville; **P**-Phil Andress, Shelby; George Conrad, Statesville; **MVP**-Aaron Pointer, Salisbury; **Outstanding Prospect**-Richard Simpson, Statesville; **Outstanding Pitcher**-George Conrad, Statesville; **Manager**-Alex Cosmidis, Salisbury.

BA: Aaron Pointer, Salisbury, .402
Runs: Aaron Pointer, Salisbury, 117
Hits: Aaron Pointer, Salisbury, 129
RBIs: Tommy Murray, Salisbury, 83

HRs: Richard Simpson, Statesville, 15
Wins: Phil Andress, Shelby, 13
SOs: George Conrad, Statesville, 172
ERA: George Conrad, Statesville, 3.21

1961 Interleague Post Season Play

World Series
New York (American) 4 games, Cincinnati (National) 1

Junior World Series
Buffalo (International) 4 games, Louisville (American Association) 0
Total Attendance: 37,462

Pan-American Series
San Antonio (Texas) 4 games, Veracruz (Mexican) 2
Total Attendance: 10,252
The series was originally scheduled to be played entirely in San Antonio with each team alternating as home team, but Hurricane Carla caused postponements and finally, the transfer of the games to Veracruz.

1961 Major League Farm Systems

American League

1 Baltimore (9): Rochester, Little Rock, Victoria/Ardmore, Tri-City, Fox Cities, Stockton, Aberdeen, Bluefield, Leesburg.
2 Boston (6): Seattle, Johnstown, Winston-Salem, Waterloo, Olean, Alpine.
3 Chicago (7): San Diego, Charleston (SC), Lincoln, Idaho Falls, Harlan, Clinton, Daytona Beach.
4 Cleveland (5): Salt Lake City, Reading, Burlington (NC), Selma, Dubuque.
5 Detroit (8): Denver, Birmingham, Knoxville, Durham, Duluth-Superior, Montgomery, Decatur, Jamestown.
6 Kansas City (8): Hawaii, Shreveport, Portsmouth-Norfolk, Lewiston, Visalia, Pocatello, Sarasota, Albuquerque.
7 Los Angeles (2): Dallas-Ft. Worth, Statesville.
8 Minnesota (7): Syracuse, Nashville, Charlotte, Wilson, Ft. Walton Beach, Wytheville, Erie.
9 New York (8): Richmond, Amarillo, Binghamton, Greensboro, Modesto, Harlan, St. Petersburg, Auburn.
10 Washington (2): Pensacola, Middlesboro.

National League

11 Chicago (6): Houston, San Antonio, Wenatchee, St. Cloud, Morristown, Carlsbad.
12 Cincinnati (6): Indianapolis, Jersey City, Columbia, Topeka, Tampa, Geneva.
13 Houston (2): Jacksonville, Salisbury.
14 Los Angeles (11): Omaha, Spokane, Atlanta, Greenville, Salem (OR), Reno, Great Falls, Panama City, Orlando, Kokomo, Artesia.
15 Milwaukee (11): Louisville, Vancouver, Austin, Yakima, Cedar Rapids, Eau Claire, Boise, Palatka, Quad Cities, Wellsville, Newton-Conover.
16 New York (3): Mobile, Raleigh, Lexington.
17 Philadelphia (8): Buffalo, Chattanooga, Williamsport, Des Moines, Bakersfield, Magic Valley, Dothan, Elmira.
18 Pittsburgh (8): Columbus, Asheville, Burlington (IA), Grand Forks, Kingsport, Batavia, Hobbs, Shelby.
19 St. Louis (8): San Juan/Charleston (WV), Portland, Tulsa, Lancaster, Winnipeg, Billings, Johnson City, Keokuk.
20 San Francisco (10): Tacoma, Rio Grande Valley/Victoria, Springfield, Eugene, Fresno, Pocatello, Salem (VA), Quincy, El Paso, Belmont.

1961 No-Hitters

Date	Pitcher	Team	League	Opponent	Score
4-28	Warren Spahn	Milwaukee	National	San Francisco	1-0
5-10	Joe Durelli	Elmira	New York-Penn.	Erie	2-0
5-17	John Bauer	Daytona Beach	Florida State	St. Petersburg	1-6 (8)
5-24	Robert Olson	Leesburg	Florida State	Orlando	0-1 (7)
5-27	Jim Duckworth	Columbia	South Atlantic	Charleston	0-1 (10)
5-27	Benjamin Griggs	Jacksonville	South Atlantic	Greenville	0-1 (12)
6-3	Fred Wolff	Olean	New York-Penn.	Batavia	2-0
6-4	Mickey Lolich/David Reed/				
	Ross Grimsley	Knoxville	South Atlantic	Asheville	3-4
6-11	Gerald Thomas	Springfield	Eastern	Johnstown	1-0 (7)
6-14	Larry Maxie	Austin	Texas	Victoria	2-0
6-15	Bob Miller	Dubuque	Midwest	Quincy	12-0 (7)
6-20	Vern Orndorff	Decatur	Midwest	Clinton	3-0 (P, 7)
6-25	Tommy Jones	Visalia	California	Bakersfield	3-0
6-27	John Flavin	Topeka	Three-I	Fox Cities	12-0 (7)
6-28	Mike McCarthy	Daytona Beach	Florida State	Leesburg	2-0 (P, 7)
6-30	Howie Koplitz	Birmingham	Southern Assoc.	Mobile	10-0
7-1	Rip Coleman	Toronto	International	Richmond	3-0 (7)
7-1	Dennis Ribant	Quad Cities	Midwest	Clinton	1-0 (P)
7-4	Art Quirk	Rochester	International	Syracuse	5-0 (7)
7-9	Franklin Hodges	St. Cloud	Northern	Aberdeen	1-0 (7)
7-9	Tom Burrell/				
	Paul Chuma	Modesto	California	Fresno	6-3 (7)
7-14	Roman Ramos	Poza Rica	Mexican	Austin	11-0
7-15	Larry Shuck	Johnson City	Appalachian	Wytheville	5-0
7-15	Larry Maxie	Austin	Texas	Poza Rica	5-0
7-27	Sam McDowell	Salt Lake City	Pacific Coast	Spokane	1-0 (7)
8-1	Rodger Irvine	Burlington	Three-I	Des Moines	7-1
8-4	Bob Locker	Lincoln	Three-I	Cedar Rapids	6-0
8-5	Dale Willis	Shreveport	Southern Assoc.	Macon	6-1 (7)
8-13	Mike Thornton	Geneva	New York-Penn.	Olean	8-1 (7)
8-14	Tracy Rivers	Raleigh	Carolina	Greensboro	7-0 (7)
8-18	Wayne Schurr	Victoria	Texas	San Antonio	1-0
8-25	Mike Degerick	Harlan	Appalachian	Morristown	3-0 (P, 7)
8-26	Alan Flitcraft	Statesville	Western Carolina	Newton-Conover	7-0 (7)
8-26	Al Worthington	San Diego	Pacific Coast	Hawaii	5-0
8-27	Larry Miller	Greenville	South Atlantic	Jacksonville	1-0 (7)
8-28	Jack McCracken	Williamsport	Eastern	Lancaster	2-0 (7)
9-2	Ron Woods	Charleston	South Atlantic	Greenville	7-0 (P, 7)
9-3	John Hanes	Pocatello	Pioneer	Magic Valley	6-0

Number in parentheses indicates innings if other than nine; "P" indicates perfect game.

THIS DATE IN MINOR LEAGUE HISTORY

January 26, 1961, George "Hoggy" Hogriever, 91, who established a minor league career record by stealing at least 947 bases, died in Appleton, Wisconsin. Hogriever played from 1889 to 1912, stroking 2,868 hits in 2,614 games for a batting mark of .295. He was an outfielder, but also played in the infield and a few games behind the plate.

April 20, 1961, Organized Baseball made an auspicious debut in Honolulu with the Hawaiian Islanders of the Pacific Coast League edging the Vancouver Mounties 4-3, before a turnout of 6,041 paid.

May 1, 1961, Winnipeg, Northern League, scored 13 runs in the eighth to beat Eau Claire 23-9.

May 2, 1961, Chuck Weatherspoon hit two grand slams in successive innings for Wilson of the Carolina League.

May 3, 1961, Ellis Burton, Toronto, International League, hit two homers in one inning, one batting righthanded with the bases full and one batting lefthanded with one on.

May 22, 1961, Belmont, Western Carolina League, defeated Lexington 6-4 to snap a 17-game losing streak.

May 29, 1961, Outfielder Alfred Nagel, Ardmore, hit four home runs in a Texas League game.

June 23, 1961, After hitting safely in 43 straight games, outfielder Howie Bedell, Louisville, American Association, had his streak stopped by a pair of Dallas-Ft. Worth lefties.

June 25, 1961, Don DiChiara, Batavia, New York-Penn League, hit four consecutive homers against Jamestown. He had only five RBIs in the contest, and his club lost 14-9.

August 7, 1961, Morristown, Appalachian League, scored 15 runs in one inning in a 21-0 victory over Harlan.

August 11, 1961, The Vancouver Mounties, Pacific Coast League, pilfered nine bases in one inning against Salt Lake City. The Mounties pulled two triple steals in the frame, in which they scored five times.

August 16, 1961, Joe Christian, Nashville, Southern Association, collected four doubles and a triple in a game with Macon.

August 16, 1961, Outfielder Chuck Weatherspoon, Wilson, Carolina League, hit his seventh grand slam of the season.

August 20, 1961, Tacoma, Pacific Coast League, lost a doubleheader to Portland after winning 16 consecutive games.

August 30, 1961, Winnipeg's consecutive loss streak extended to 17 in a row with a Northern League doubleheader setback to Duluth-Superior.

August 30, 1961, St. Cloud, Northern League, lost to Grand Forks, 6-4, after 16 straight wins.

November 4, 1961, Ernest "Kid" Mohler, who set a career record for games played at second base, despite being a lefthanded thrower, died in San Francisco at the age of 87. Mohler played from 1891 to 1914.

1962

American League
President: Joseph E. Cronin

Standings	W	L	Pct.	GB	Attend.	Manager
New York Yankees	96	66	.593	—	1,493,574	Ralph Houk
Minnesota Twins	91	71	.562	5	1,433,116	Sam Mele
Los Angeles Angels	86	76	.531	10	1,144,063	Bill Rigney
Detroit Tigers	85	76	.528	10½	1,207,881	Bob Scheffing
Chicago White Sox	85	77	.525	11	1,131,562	Al Lopez
Cleveland Indians	80	82	.494	16	716,076	Mel McGaha/Mel Harder
Baltimore Orioles	77	85	.475	19	790,254	Billy Hitchcock
Boston Red Sox	76	84	.475	20	733,080	Pinky Higgins
Kansas City Athletics	72	90	.444	24	635,675	Hank Bauer
Washington Senators	60	101	.373	35½	729,775	Mickey Vernon

BA: Pete Runnels, Boston, .326
Runs: Albie Pearson, Los Angeles, 115
Hits: Bobby Richardson, New York, 209
RBIs: Harmon Killebrew, Minnesota, 126
HRs: Harmon Killebrew, Minnesota, 48

Wins: Ralph Terry, New York, 23
SOs: Camilo Pascual, Minnesota, 206
ERA: Hank Aguirre, Detroit, 2.21
Pct: Ray Herbert, Chicago, .690, 20-9
Saves: Dick Radatz, Boston, 24

National League
President: Warren C. Giles

Standings	W	L	Pct.	GB	Attend.	Manager
San Francisco Giants	103	62	.624	—	1,592,594	Alvin Dark
Los Angeles Dodgers	102	63	.618	1	2,755,184	Walter Alston
Cincinnati Reds	98	64	.605	3½	982,095	Fred Hutchinson
Pittsburgh Pirates	93	68	.578	8	1,090,648	Danny Murtaugh
Milwaukee Braves	86	76	.531	15½	766,921	Birdie Tebbetts
St. Louis Cardinals	84	78	.519	17½	953,895	Johnny Keane
Philadelphia Phillies	81	80	.503	20	762,034	Gene Mauch
Houston Colt .45s	64	96	.400	36½	924,456	Harry Craft
Chicago Cubs	59	103	.364	42½	609,802	El Tappe/Lou Klein/Charlie Metro
New York Mets	40	120	.250	60½	922,530	Casey Stengel

Playoff: San Francisco 2 games, Los Angeles 1.

BA: Tommy Davis, Los Angeles, .346
Runs: Frank Robinson, Cincinnati, 134
Hits: Tommy Davis, Los Angeles, 230
RBIs: Tommy Davis, Los Angeles, 153
HRs: Willie Mays, San Francisco, 49

Wins: Don Drysdale, Los Angeles, 25
SOs: Don Drysdale, Los Angeles, 232
ERA: Sandy Koufax, Los Angeles, 2.54
Pct: Bob Purkey, Cincinnati, .821, 23-5
Saves: Elroy Face, Pittsburgh, 28

AAA American Association
President: James Burris

Standings	W	L	Pct.	GB	Attend.	Manager
Indianapolis Indians (3)	89	58	.605	—	148,626	Luke Appling
Omaha Dodgers (14)	79	68	.537	10	109,851	Danny Ozark
Denver Bears (5)	79	71	.527	11½	165,614	Frank Skaff
Louisville Colonels (15)	71	75	.486	17½	70,550	Jack Tighe
Oklahoma City 89ers (13)	66	81	.449	23	184,683	Connie Ryan
Dallas-Ft. Worth Rangers (7, 17)	59	90	.396	31	80,034	Dick Littlefield/Ray Murray

Playoffs: Louisville 3 games, Indianapolis 0; Denver 3 games, Omaha 1.
Finals: Louisville 4 games, Denver 2.

All-Star Team: 1B-Tom McCraw, Indianapolis; **2B**-Leo Burke, Dallas-Ft. Worth; **3B**-Wayne Graham, Dallas-Ft. Worth; **SS**-Al Weis, Indianapolis; **OF**-Jim Koranda, Indianapolis; David Roberts, Oklahoma City; Ellis Burton, Louisville; Jackson Queen, Denver; **C**-Mike Brumley, Denver; Bill Freehan, Denver; **Util**-Frank Kostro, Denver; **P**-Jack Smith, Omaha; Conrad Grob, Louisville; Jon Wilhite, Omaha; Frank Kreutzer, Indianapolis; **MVP**-Jack Smith, Omaha; **Manager**-Luke Appling, Indianapolis; Danny Ozark, Omaha.

BA: Tom McCraw, Indianapolis, .326
Runs: Jackson Queen, Denver, 98
Hits: Wayne Graham, Dallas-Ft. Worth, 187
RBIs: Jim Koranda, Indianapolis, 103

HRs: Leo Burke, Dallas-Ft. Worth, 27
Wins: Nick Wilhite, Omaha, 18
SOs: Frederico Olivo, Louisville, 151
ERA: Conrad Grob, Louisville, 2.86

AAA International League
President: Thomas H. Richardson

Standings	W	L	Pct.	GB	Attend.	Manager
Jacksonville Suns (4)	94	60	.610	—	229,579	Ben Geraghty
Toronto Maple Leafs (15)	91	62	.595	2½	193,656	Chuck Dressen
Atlanta Crackers (19)	83	71	.539	11	167,275	Joe Schultz
Rochester Red Wings (1)	82	72	.532	12	272,178	Clyde King
Columbus Jets (18)	80	74	.519	14	191,730	Larry Shepard
Buffalo Bisons (17)	73	80	.477	20½	214,134	Kerby Farrell
Richmond Virginians (9)	59	95	.383	35	101,853	Sheriff Robinson
Syracuse Chiefs (10, 16)	53	101	.344	41	103,191	Frank Verdi/John Vander Meer

Playoffs: Jacksonville 4 games, Rochester 3, Atlanta 4 games, Toronto 2.
Finals: Atlanta 4 games, Jacksonville 3.

All-Star Team: 1B-Frank "Pancho" Herrera, Buffalo; **2B**-Phil Gagliano, Atlanta; **3B**-Bob Bailey, Columbus; **SS**-Tony Martinez, Jacksonville; **OF**-Vic Davalillo, Jacksonville; Pete Ward, Rochester; Neil Chrisley, Toronto; **C**-Harry Chiti, Jacksonville; **P**-Joe Schaffernoth, Jacksonville; Jim Constable, Toronto; **MVP**-Tony Martinez, Jacksonville; **Pitcher of the Year**-Joe Schaffernoth, Jacksonville; **Manager**-Ben Geraghty, Jacksonville.

BA: Vic Davalillo, Jacksonville, .346
Runs: Pete Ward, Rochester, 114
Hits: Vic Davalillo, Jacksonville, 200
RBIs: Bob Bailey, Columbus, 108
   Frank "Pancho" Herrera, Buffalo, 108

HRs: Frank "Pancho" Herrera, Buffalo, 32
Wins: Joe Schaffernoth, Jacksonville, 18
SOs: Harry Fanok, Atlanta, 192
ERA: Jim Constable, Toronto, 2.56

AAA Pacific Coast League
President: Dewey Soriano

Standings	W	L	Pct.	GB	Attend.	Manager
San Diego Padres (12)	93	61	.604	—	211,514	Don Heffner
Salt Lake City Bees (4, 11)	81	73	.526	12	122,619	Bob Kennedy
Tacoma Giants (20)	81	73	.526	12	168,600	John "Red" Davis
Seattle Rainiers (2)	76	74	.507	15	136,156	Johnny Pesky
Hawaii Islanders (7)	77	76	.503	15½	149,737	Irv Noren
Portland Beavers (6)	74	80	.481	19	98,525	Les Peden
Vancouver Mounties (8)	72	79	.477	19½	88,075	Jack McKeon
Spokane Indians (14)	58	96	.377	35	80,519	Preston Gomez

Playoffs: None.

All-Star Team: 1B-Rogelio Alvarez, San Diego; **2B**-Nate Oliver, Spokane; **3B**-Tommy Harper, San Diego; **SS**-Chico Ruiz, San Diego; **OF**-Ken Walters, San Diego; Stan Palys, Hawaii; Walter Bond, Salt Lake City; **C**-Jesse Gonder, San Diego; **P**-John Tsitouris, San Diego; Dick Egan, Hawaii; **MVP**-Jesse Gonder, San Diego; **Manager**-Don Heffner, San Diego.

BA: Jesse Gonder, San Diego, .342
Runs: Tommy Harper, San Diego, 120
Hits: Max Alvis, Salt Lake City, 189
RBIs: Jesse Gonder, San Diego, 116

HRs: Stan Palys, Hawaii, 33
Wins: Dick Egan, Hawaii, 17
SOs: Dick Egan, Hawaii, 201
ERA: Gaylord Perry, Tacoma, 2.48

AA Mexican League
President: Antonio Ramirez Muro

Standings	W	L	Pct.	GB	Attend.	Manager
Monterrey Sultanes	77	53	.592	—	239,479	Clemente Carreras
Veracruz Aguilas	69	61	.531	8	139,388	Santos Amaro
Mexico City Diablos Rojos	67	63	.515	10	349,753	Wilfredo Calvino/Manuel Arroyo
Puebla Pericos	64	66	.492	13	127,985	Luis Montes de Oca/Jose Guerrero
Mexico City Tigres	62	68	.477	15	260,544	Memo Garibay
Poza Rica Petroleros	51	79	.392	26	305,864	Jose Bache/Walter Graham/Bernardo Lopez

Playoffs: None.

All-Star Team: 1B-Alonzo Perry, Monterrey; **2B**-Vinicio Garcia, Monterrey; **3B**-Luis Garcia, Poza Rica; **SS**-Leo Rodriguez, MC Diablos Rojos; **OF**-Hector Espino, Monterrey; Ruben Esquivias, MC Tigres; Al Pinkston, Veracruz; **C**-Jaime Corella, Monterrey; Miguel Gaspar, Veracruz; **P**-Ramon Arano, Veracruz; Aaron Flores, MC Diablos Rojos; **Manager**-Clemente Carreras, Monterrey.

BA: Al Pinkston, Veracruz, .381
Runs: Hector Espino, Monterrey, 106
Hits: Vinicio Garcia, Monterrey, 172
   Al Pinkston, Veracruz, 172
RBIs: Hector Espino, Monterrey, 105
   Alonzo Perry, Monterrey, 105

HRs: Ron Camacho, Puebla, 25
Wins: Arturo Cacheux, MC Tigres, 18
   Francisco Ramirez, Monterrey, 18
SOs: Mike Cuellar, Monterrey, 124
ERA: Ramon Arano, Veracruz, 2.60

AA Texas League
President: Dick Butler

Standings	W	L	Pct.	GB	Attend.	Manager
El Paso Sun Kings (20)	80	60	.571	—	148,649	George Genovese
Tulsa Oilers (19)	77	63	.550	3	182,895	Whitey Kurowski
Albuquerque Dukes (6)	70	70	.500	10	133,076	Bob Hofman
Austin Senators (15)	69	71	.493	11	41,057	Jimmy Brown
San Antonio Missions (11)	68	72	.486	12	101,917	Walt Dixon
Amarillo Gold Sox (9)	56	84	.400	24	52,257	Rube Walker

Playoffs: Austin 3 games, El Paso 2; Tulsa 3, Albuquerque 0.
Finals: Tulsa 3 games, Austin 1.

All-Star Team: 1B-Charlie Dees, El Paso; Paul Snyder, Austin; **2B**-Jerry Robinson, El Paso; **3B**-Don Eaddy, San Antonio; **SS**-Cap Peterson, El Paso; **OF**-Corky Withrow, Austin;

*Won first-half **Won second-half ***Won both halves
Numbers after nicknames indicate farm system.
Affiliation listed at end of each year.

Joe Patterson, Tulsa; Jesus Alou, El Paso; Jim Small, Albuquerque; **C**-Tim Talton, El Paso; **Util**-Clyde Bloomfield, Tulsa; **P**-Lazaro Gomez, El Paso; Gordy Richardson, Tulsa; **MVP**-Cap Peterson, El Paso; **Pitcher of the Year**-Gordy Richardson, Tulsa.

BA: Charlie Dees, El Paso, .348
Runs: Cap Peterson, El Paso, 128
Hits: Charlie Dees, El Paso, 179
RBIs: Cap Peterson, El Paso, 130

HRs: Jerry Robinson, El Paso, 36
Wins: Jose Santiago, Albuquerque, 16
SOs: Harvey Branch, San Antonio, 216
ERA: Gordy Richardson, Tulsa, 3.18

A Eastern League
President: A. Rankin Johnson

Standings	W	L	Pct.	GB	Attend.	Manager
Williamsport Grays (17)	83	57	.593	—	77,595	Frank Lucchesi
Elmira Pioneers (1)	72	68	.514	11	83,328	Earl Weaver
York White Roses (2)	70	70	.500	13	57,113	Mel Parnell
Springfield Giants (20)	68	72	.486	15	78,375	Andy Gilbert
Charleston Indians (4)	67	73	.479	16	53,935	John Lipon
Binghamton Triplets (6)	60	80	.429	23	71,810	Granny Hamner/ Dan Carnevale

Playoffs: Williamsport 2 games, Springfield 1; Elmira 2 games, York 1.
Finals: Elmira 3 games, Williamsport 1.

All-Star Team: 1B-Ken Harrelson, Binghamton; **2B**-Bobby Sanders, Williamsport; **3B**-Jim Ray Hart, Springfield; **SS**-Dalton Jones, York; **OF**-Richie Allen, Williamsport; Ray Youngdahl, Elmira; Jerry Griffin, Williamsport; **C**-Duke Sims, Charleston; Bob Barton, Springfield; **P**-Dave McNally, Elmira; Herm Starrette, Elmira; **Manager**-Frank Lucchesi, Williamsport.

BA: Jim Ray Hart, Springfield, .337
Runs: Bobby Sanders, Williamsport, 98
Hits: Jim Ray Hart, Springfield, 182
RBIs: Ken Harrelson, Binghamton, 138

HRs: Ken Harrelson, Binghamton, 38
Wins: Paul Seitz, Binghamton, 16
SOs: Bob Heffner, York, 234
ERA: Granny Hamner, Binghamton, 2.03

A South Atlantic League
President: Sam C. Smith, Jr.

Standings	W	L	Pct.	GB	Attend.	Manager
Savannah/Lynchburg White Sox#(3)	92	47	.662	—	77,180	Les Moss
Knoxville Smokies (5)	86	54	.614	6½	90,089	Frank Carswell
Macon Peaches (12)	80	59	.576	12	100,297	Dave Bristol
Asheville Tourists (18)	70	70	.500	22½	78,559	Ray Hathaway
Greenville Spinners (14)	65	75	.464	27½	59,024	Roy Hartsfield
Augusta Yankees (9)	57	83	.407	35½	39,476	Ernie White
Portsmouth-Norfolk Tides (19)	55	85	.393	37½	48,560	Chase Riddle
Charlotte Hornets (8)	54	86	.386	38½	50,712	Spencer Robbins

#Savannah moved to Lynchburg on August 26 because of racial conflicts.

Playoffs: Macon 3 games, Lynchburg 0; Knoxville 3 games, Asheville 1.
Finals: Macon 3 games, Knoxville 1.

All-Star Team: 1B-Grover "Deacon" Jones, Savannah/Lynchburg; **2B**-Pete Rose, Macon; **3B**-Don Buford, Savannah/Lynchburg; **SS**-Tommy Helms, Macon; **OF**-Ronnie Cox, Portsmouth; Elmo Plaskett, Asheville; Tony Oliva, Charlotte; **C**-J.C. Martin, Savannah/Lynchburg; John Sullivan, Knoxville; **P**-Camilo Estevis, Greenville; Marv Mecklenburg, Portsmouth; **Manager**-Frank Carswell, Knoxville.

BA: Elmo Plaskett, Asheville, .349
Runs: Pete Rose, Macon, 136
Hits: Tommy Helms, Macon, 195
RBIs: Grover "Deacon" Jones, Savannah/Lynchburg, 101

HRs: Dick Means, Charlotte/Asheville, 36
BBs: Ronnie Retton, Augusta, 114
Wins: Camilo Estevis, Greenville, 18
SOs: Leo Marentette, Knoxville, 205
ERA: Dick Lines, Asheville, 2.11

B Carolina League
President: J.C. "Bill" Jessup

Standings	W	L	Pct.	GB	Attend.	Manager
Durham Bulls (13)	89	51	.636	—	71,050	Lou Fitzgerald
Kinston Eagles (18)	83	57	.593	6	141,227	Pete Peterson
Winston-Salem Red Sox (2)	76	64	.543	13	75,038	Eddie Popowski/Mace Brown
Burlington Indians (4)	66	74	.471	23	30,226	Gene Verble
Wilson Tobs (8)	65	75	.464	24	40,669	Harry Warner
Greensboro Yankees (9)	65	75	.464	24	38,109	Vern Rapp/Steve Souchock
Rocky Mount Leafs (12)	60	80	.429	29	53,651	Hershell Freeman/ Jack Cassini
Raleigh Capitals (10)	56	84	.400	33	29,552	Archie Wilson

Playoffs: Durham 2 games, Burlington 0; Kinston 2 games, Winston-Salem 1.
Finals: Kinston 4 games, Durham 3.

All-Star Team: 1B-Rusty Staub, Durham; **2B**-Cesar Tovar, Rocky Mount; **3B**-Tony Perez, Rocky Mount; **SS**-Rico Petrocelli, Winston-Salem; **OF**-Ron Flender, Rocky Mount; Ronnie Davis, Durham; Ed Napoleon, Kinston; Jim Gosger, Winston-Salem; Bert Barth, Rocky Mount; **C**-Buddy Booker, Burlington; Clint Courtney, Durham; **Util**-Glenn Vaughan, Durham; **P**-Steve Blass, Kinston; Wally Wolf, Durham; Mel Stottlemyre, Greensboro; Frank Bork, Kinston; Jimmy Roland, Wilson; **MVP**-Rusty Staub, Durham; **Manager**-Lou Fitzgerald, Durham.

BA: Cesar Tovar, Rocky Mount, .329
Runs: Cesar Tovar, Rocky Mount, 115
Rusty Staub, Durham, 115
Hits: Cesar Tovar, Rocky Mount, 168
Ron Flender, Rocky Mount, 168

RBIs: Bert Barth, Rocky Mount, 136
HRs: Bert Barth, Rocky Mount, 33
Wins: Frank Bork, Kinston, 19
SOs: Steve Blass, Kinston, 209
ERA: Steve Blass, Kinston, 1.97

B Northwest League
President: James Fleishman

Standings	W	L	Pct.	GB	Attend.	Manager
Tri-City Braves**	78	62	.557	—	68,399	Tom Heath
Salem Dodgers (14)	74	67	.525	4½	56,857	Stan Wasiak
Wenatchee Chiefs*(11)	72	69	.511	6½	36,619	Joe Macko
Yakima Bears (15)	69	71	.493	9	35,059	Buddy Hicks
Lewiston Broncs (6)	66	75	.468	12½	36,123	John McNamara
Eugene Emeralds (20)	63	78	.447	15½	46,067	Bud Byerly

Playoff: Wenatchee 4 games, Tri-City 2.

All-Star Team: 1B-Gary Johnson, Tri-City; **2B**-Rafael Gomez, Yakima; **3B**-Ronald Campbell, Wenatchee; **SS**-Walt Hriniak, Yakima; **OF**-Nelson Mathews, Wenatchee; Emiliano Telleria, Tri-City; Ethan Blackaby, Yakima; **C**-Rico Carty, Yakima; John McNamara, Lewiston; **P**-Larry Staab, Salem; Ed Nottle, Tri-City; **Manager**-John McNamara, Lewiston.

BA: Gary Johnson, Tri-City, .341
Runs: Ethan Blackaby, Yakima, 108
Hits: Gary Johnson, Tri-City, 178
RBIs: Gary Johnson, Tri-City, 103
HRs: Billy Cowan, Wenatchee, 24

Wins: Darrell Peters, Salem, 15
Art Thompson, Wenatchee, 15
SOs: Bruce Brubaker, Yakima, 209
Matt Gayeski, Eugene, 209
ERA: Bill Ballou, Wenatchee, 3.41

C California League
President: Edward J. Mulligan

Standings	W	L	Pct.	GB	Attend.	Manager
San Jose Bees*(7)	78	58	.574	—	62,695	Red Marion
Modesto Colts (13)	75	65	.536	5	34,762	Fred Hatfield
Stockton Ports (1)	70	68	.507	9	29,613	Harry Dunlop
Reno Silver Sox**(14)	70	68	.507	9	22,819	Roy Macko
Santa Barbara Rancheros (16)	68	72	.486	12	25,861	Gene Lillard
Bakersfield Bears (17)	67	72	.482	12½	40,405	Bob Wellman
Fresno Giants (20)	67	72	.482	12½	34,883	Salvador Taormina
Visalia White Sox (3)	60	80	.429	20	28,545	Dick Kinaman

Playoff: San Jose 4 games, Reno 3.

All-Star Team: 1B-Bill Haas, Reno; **2B**-Jim Lefebvre, Reno; **3B**-Fred Studstill, Stockton; **SS**-Hal Lanier, Fresno; **OF**-Grimm Mason, Santa Barbara; Larry Daniels, Bakersfield; Dick Simpson, San Jose; Dennis Marquardt, Reno; **C**-Bob Rikard, Santa Barbara; John Bateman, Modesto; **Util**-Dale Rohde, Visalia; **P**-Jose Lizondro, Visalia; Darold Knowles, Stockton; Pat Rogan, San Jose; Mike Urrizola, Bakersfield; **MVP**-Bill Haas, Reno; **Rookie of the Year**-Bill Haas, Reno; **Manager**-Roy Smalley, Reno.

BA: Bill Haas, Reno, .368
Runs: Larry Ramsey, Reno, 141
Hits: Bill Haas, Reno, 204
RBIs: Bill Haas, Reno, 144
HRs: Larry Daniels, Bakersfield, 44

Wins: Fred Newman, San Jose, 15
Mike Urrizola, Bakersfield, 15
SOs: Norman Koch, Reno, 244
ERA: Darold Knowles, Stockton, 2.29

C Mexican Center League
President: Antonio Ramirez (Muro)

Standings	W	L	Pct.	GB	Attend.	Manager
Fresnillo Rojos	70	49	.588	—	37,000	Manuel Arroyo/Tony Castano
Aguascalientes Tigres	66	54	.550	4½	35,794	Bill Wright/Jesus Robles
Leon Diablos Verdes	64	56	.533	6½	55,641	Daniel Rios
San Luis Potosi Tuneros	56	64	.467	14½	68,624	Domingo Santana
Guanajuato Tuzos	54	66	.450	16½	50,924	Ramiro Caballero
Salamanca Petroleros	49	70	.412	21	35,956	Bernardo Lopez

Playoffs: None

All-Star Team: 1B-Ramiro Caballero, Guanajuato; **2B**-Rogelio Vargas, Leon; **SS**-Jose Maria Murillo, Guanajuato; **3B**-Manuel Salinas, Fresnillo; **OF**-Servando Gonzalez, Leon; Miguel Angel Gutierrez, San Luis Potosi; Gonzalo Villalobos, Guanajuato; **C**-Rogelio Jimenez, Salamanca; Alfonso Ibarra, Leon; **P**-Ricardo Vazquez, Leon; Alfredo Ortiz, Fresnillo; **Manager**-Tony Castano, Fresnillo.

BA: Ramiro Caballero, Guanajuato, .414
Runs: Enrique Garcia, San Luis Potosi, 127
Hits: Ramiro Caballero, Guanajuato, 175
RBIs: Ramiro Caballero, Guanajuato, 170

HRs: Ramiro Caballero, Guanajuato, 59
Wins: Pedro Ortiz, San Luis Potosi, 19
SOs: Pedro Ortiz, San Luis Potosi, 145
ERA: Ricardo Vazquez, Leon, 2.38

C Northern League
President: Brooks Baukol

Standings	W	L	Pct.	GB	Attend.	Manager
Grand Forks Chiefs (18)	72	52	.581	—	37,309	Tom Saffell
Duluth-Superior Dukes (5)	69	55	.556	3	35,083	Al Lakeman
Eau Claire Braves (15)	65	59	.524	7	20,906	Jim Fanning
Aberdeen Pheasants (1)	64	60	.516	8	39,101	Billy DeMars

	W	L	Pct.	GB	Attend.	Manager
St. Cloud Rox (11)	61	63	.492	11	25,169	George Freese
Bismarck-Mandan Pards (8)	60	62	.492	11	37,786	Vernon Morgan
Winnipeg Goldeyes (19)	59	63	.484	12	83,645	Fred Koenig
Minot Mallards (6)	44	80	.355	28	41,052	Grady Wilson

Playoffs: Eau Claire 1 game, Grand Forks 0; Aberdeen 1 game, Duluth-Superior 0.
Finals: Eau Claire 2 games, Aberdeen 0.

All-Star Team: 1B-Mike Derrick, Grand Forks; **2B**-Willard Oplinger, Aberdeen; **3B**-Dave Wissman, Grand Forks; **SS**-Teo James, Eau Claire; **OF**-Curt Motton, St. Cloud; Mickey Stanley, Duluth-Superior; Lorne Johnson, Eau Claire; Vic Ramirez, Grand Forks; **C**-Jim Price, Grand Forks; Ray Oliver, Winnipeg; **P**-Troy Giles, Grand Forks; Tom Hilgendorf, Winnipeg; **Manager**-Tom Saffell, Grand Forks.

BA: Donald Wallace, Aberdeen, .324
Runs: Vic Ramirez, Grand Forks, 102
Hits: Russ Penny, Bismarck-Mandan, 146
RBIs: Lorne Johnson, Eau Claire, 80

HRs: Mack Kuykendall, St. Cloud, 18
Wins: Troy Giles, Grand Forks, 18
SOs: Tom Phoebus, Aberdeen, 195
ERA: Troy Giles, Grand Forks, 1.72

C Pioneer League
President: Claude Engberg

Standings	W	L	Pct.	GB	Attend.	Manager
Billings Mustangs**(19)	81	48	.628	—	45,720	Grover Resinger
Boise Braves*(15)	69	62	.527	13	28,352	Al Unser
Magic Valley Cowboys (17)	64	65	.496	17	49,297	Jack Phillips
Pocatello Chiefs (2)	63	66	.488	18	16,092	Bill Slack
Great Falls Electrics (14)	60	70	.462	21½	36,010	Al Ronning
Idaho Falls Yankees (9)	52	78	.400	29½	21,312	Loren Babe

Playoff: Billings 3 games, Boise 0.

All-Star Team: 1B-Harold Allen, Magic Valley; **2B**-Derrell Griffith, Great Falls; **3B**-Jim Livesey, Great Falls; **SS**-Sandy Alomar, Boise; **OF**-Adolfo Phillips, Magic Valley; Felix DeLeon, Billings; Marcial Allen, Boise; **C**-Ferdinand Walters, Magic Valley; Tom Kowalowski, Idaho Falls; **Util IF**-Jerry Funk, Pocatello; **Util OF**-Jim Horsford, Idaho Falls; **P**-Robert Radovich, Great Falls; Fred Ballard, Billings; Gerald Wild, Billings; James Handrahan, Boise; **Manager**-Jack Phillips, Magic Valley.

BA: Harold Allen, Magic Valley, .346
Runs: Adolfo Phillips, Magic Valley, 135
Hits: Harold Allen, Magic Valley, 176
Sandy Alomar, Boise, 176
RBIs: Harold Allen, Magic Valley, 140

HRs: Harold Allen, Magic Valley, 37
Felix DeLeon, Billings, 37
Wins: Clay Carroll, Boise, 14
SOs: James Handrahan, Boise, 241
ERA: Gerald Wild, Billings, 2.69

D Alabama-Florida League
President: William Moore

Standings	W	L	Pct.	GB	Attend.	Manager
Pensacola Senators (10)	79	38	.675	—	25,201	Wayne Terwilliger
Ft. Walton Beach Jets (8)	58	61	.487	22	16,313	Ralph Rowe
Dothan Phillies (17)	57	62	.479	23	18,500	Wilbur Johnson
Selma Cloverleafs (4)	55	63	.466	24½	16,589	Pinky May
Ozark/Andalusia Dodgers#(14)	54	66	.450	26½	15,183	George Scherger
Montgomery Rebels (5)	53	66	.445	27	20,617	John Groth

#Ozark moved to Andalusia July 10.

Playoffs: Pensacola 2 games, Dothan 0; Selma 2 games, Ft. Walton Beach 0.
Finals: Selma 3 games, Pensacola 1.

All-Star Team: 1B-Carlos Pascual, Ft. Walton Beach; **2B**-Bill Timberlake, Pensacola; **3B**-Gary Dempsey, Ozark/Andalusia; **SS**-Frank Caradonna, Pensacola; **OF**-Nelson Gardner, Dothan; Lou Abrahams, Pensacola; Dick DeLong, Montgomery; **C**-Walt Dobrzykowski, Selma; **P**-Charles Herzberger, Dothan; Fred Waters, Pensacola; **Manager**-Wayne Terwilliger, Pensacola.

BA: Carlos Pascual, Ft. Walton, .339
Runs: Mike Holodick, Montgomery, 118
Hits: Carlos Pascual, Ft. Walton, 147
RBIs: Carlos Pascual, Ft. Walton, 103

HRs: Nelson Gardner, Dothan, 22
Wins: Charles Herzberger, Dothan, 15
SOs: Robert Baird, Pensacola, 207
ERA: Fred Waters, Pensacola, 1.42

D Appalachian League
President: Chauncey De Vault

Standings	W	L	Pct.	GB	Attend.	Manager
Bluefield Orioles (1)	47	23	.671	—	24,157	Billy Hunter
Wytheville Twins (8)	40	30	.571	7	20,426	Red Norwood
Middlesboro Senators (10)	35	34	.507	11½	14,523	Lewis Morton
Kingsport Pirates (18)	31	38	.449	15½	19,946	Al Kubski
Salem Rebels (20)	31	39	.443	16	40,913	Alex Cosmidis
Harlan Smokies (3, 9)	25	45	.357	22	16,056	George Sobek/Lamar North

Playoffs: None.

All-Star Team: 1B-Allen Feldhaus, Middlesboro; **2B**-Wayne Edwards, Bluefield; **3B**-Jack Jaciak, Harlan; **SS**-Mark Belanger, Bluefield; **OF**-Jerry Pritchett, Wytheville; John Riddle, Bluefield; Dave May, Salem; Louis Delis, Middlesboro; Charles Aikens, Bluefield; **C**-George Farson, Bluefield; **Util**-Tom Solters, Wytheville; **P**-Bill Larkin, Bluefield; Geoff Maloney, Wytheville; Dick Sorenson, Wytheville; **Rookie of the Year**-Jerry Pritchett, Wytheville; **Manager**-Billy Hunter, Bluefield.

BA: Dave May, Salem, .379
Runs: Wayne Edwards, Bluefield, 70
Hits: Jerry Pritchett, Wytheville, 86
RBIs: Jerry Pritchett, Wytheville, 66
HRs: John Riddle, Bluefield, 16

Wins: Ron Kopp, Bluefield, 8
Geoff Maloney, Wytheville, 8
Tom Fisher, Bluefield, 8
SOs: Gene Ross, Kingsport, 113
ERA: Ron Kopp, Bluefield, 2.96

D Florida State League
President: William B. McKechnie Jr.

Standings	W	L	Pct.	GB	Attend.	Manager
Ft. Lauderdale Yankees**(9)	71	50	.587	—	49,349	Bob Bauer
Sarasota Sun Sox*(3)	69	51	.575	1½	39,917	George Noga
Tampa Tarpons (12)	66	54	.550	4½	55,015	John Vander Meer/ Hershell Freeman
Miami Marlins (17)	67	57	.540	5½	90,887	Andy Seminick
Daytona Beach Islanders (6)	61	61	.500	10½	34,547	Bill Robertson
St. Petersburg Saints (14)	54	66	.450	16½	63,842	Spider Jorgensen
Lakeland Giants (20)	49	66	.426	19	28,343	Bert Haas/Max Lanier
Palatka Cubs (11)	45	77	.369	26½	28,037	Hal Jeffcoat/Bobby Adams/ Rip Collins/Rube Walker

Playoff: Ft. Lauderdale 3 games, Sarasota 0.

All-Star Team: 1B-Mike Hegan, Ft. Lauderdale; **2B**-Tito Fuentes, Lakeland; Reinold Garcia, Miami; **3B**-Jim Wynn, Tampa; **SS**-Len Boehmer, Tampa; **OF**-Bryce Smith, Daytona Beach; Art Lopez, Ft. Lauderdale; William Evans, Sarasota; Alex Johnson, Miami; **C**-Ed Barberie, Sarasota; **P**-John Zahn, Sarasota; Stephen Dillon, Ft. Lauderdale; **Manager**-George Noga, Sarasota; Andy Seminick, Miami.

BA: Alex Johnson, Miami, .313
Runs: Cleo James, St. Petersburg, 98
Hits: Cleo James, St. Petersburg, 143
RBIs: Jim Wynn, Tampa, 81

HRs: Jim Wynn, Tampa, 14
Wins: Ed Stein, Tampa, 16
SOs: John Zahn, Sarasota, 255
ERA: Nicky Curtis, Daytona Beach, 2.13

D Georgia-Florida League
President: Larry Brumitt

Standings	W	L	Pct.	GB	Attend.	Manager
Thomasville Tigers (5)	76	41	.650	—	18,610	Gail Henley
Dublin Braves (15)	68	50	.576	8½	19,582	Bill Steinecke
Brunswick Cardinals (19)	47	70	.462	29	36,123	Owen Friend
Moultrie Colt .22s (13)	44	74	.373	32½	18,560	James Walton

Playoffs: None.

All-Star Team: 1B-Steve Jacobus, Moultrie; **2B**-Jack Newcomer, Brunswick; **3B**-Glen Clark, Dublin; **SS**-John Matchick, Brunswick; **OF**-Dick Anderson, Dublin; Chuck Staub, Moultrie; Al Peterkin, Moultrie; **C**-Butch Troy, Moultrie; Warren Barty, Brunswick; **P**-Dick Hagen, Dublin; Jim Holbrook, Moultrie; **Manager**-Bill Steinecke, Dublin.

BA: Ken Schultz, Thomasville, .291
Runs: Manuel Samuel, Dublin, 100
Hits: Manuel Samuel, Dublin, 124
RBIs: George Campbell, Thomasville, 75
HRs: Glen Clark, Dublin, 26

Wins: Alex Pietrewicz, Dublin, 14
Charles Haygood, Thomasville, 14
SOs: Alex Pietrewicz, Dublin, 175
ERA: Charles Haygood, Thomasville, 2.08

D Midwest League
President: C.C. "Dutch" Hoffman

Standings	W	L	Pct.	GB	Attend.	Manager
Waterloo Hawks**(2)	73	50	.593	—	57,054	Matt Sczesny
Dubuque Packers*(4)	71	52	.577	2	57,510	Walter Novick
Quad Cities Angels (7)	71	54	.568	3	75,568	John Fitzpatrick
Quincy Jets (16)	68	57	.544	6	52,788	Ken Deal
Keokuk/Midwest Dodgers#(14)	67	57	.540	6½	28,787	Ed Serrano
Clinton C-Sox (3)	63	62	.504	11	53,855	Ira Hutchinson
Appleton Foxes (1)	61	63	.492	12½	41,323	Cal Ripken, Sr.
Cedar Rapids Red Raiders (15)	58	66	.468	15½	61,696	Ken Blackman
Burlington Bees (18)	44	79	.358	29	33,037	James Adlam
Decatur Commodores (20)	42	78	.350	29½	71,461	Richard Klaus

#Keokuk surrendered its franchise to the league August 7. The club played its remaining games in Dubuque and was renamed Midwest Dodgers.

Playoff: Dubuque 3 games, Waterloo 1.

All-Star Team: 1B-Tony Torchia, Keokuk/Midwest; **2B**-Bob Kilpatrick, Clinton; **3B**-Orlando Centelles, Dubuque; **SS**-Bob Litchfield, Appleton; **OF**-Vince Ferguson, Cedar Rapids; Ed Crawford, Quad Cities; Felix Pizarro, Burlington; **C**-Milt Swift, Cedar Rapids; William Sebera, Keokuk/Midwest; **P**-Art Seifert, Dubuque; Ernie Kumerow, Waterloo; Barry Shollenberger, Waterloo; Jim McGlothlin, Quad Cities; **Player of the Year**-Tony Torchia, Keokuk/Midwest; **Rookie of the Year**-Barry Shollenberger, Waterloo; **Manager**-Cal Ripken, Sr., Appleton.

BA: Tony Torchia, Keokuk/Midwest, .324
Runs: Paul Schaal, Quad Cities, 109
Hits: Tony Torchia, Keokuk/Midwest, 161
RBIs: Tony Torchia, Keokuk/Midwest, 94

HRs: John Price, Decatur, 27
Wins: Paul Deem, Quincy, 18
SOs: Barry Shollenberger, Waterloo, 226
ERA: Tony Komisar, Cedar Rapids, 2.10

D New York-Pennsylvania League
President: Vincent M. McNamara

Standings	W	L	Pct.	GB	Attend.	Manager
Jamestown Tigers (5)..........	69	50	.580	—	68,632	Stubby Overmire
Erie Sailors (8)....................	68	51	.571	1	33,766	Frank Franchi
Olean Red Sox (2)	62	57	.521	7	11,104	Harold Holland
Auburn Mets (16)	62	57	.521	7	43,128	Richard Cole
Batavia Pirates (18)	51	67	.432	17½	29,237	Bob Clear
Geneva Redlegs (12)	44	74	.373	24½	22,882	Karl Kuehl

Playoffs: Auburn 2 games, Jamestown 0; Olean 2 games, Erie 0.
Finals: Auburn 2 games, Olean 0.

All-Star Team: 1B-Bob Guindon, Olean; **2B**-Hilario Rojas, Jamestown; **3B**-Thomas Schroeder, Jamestown; **SS**-Rigoberto Mena, Jamestown; **OF**-Brant Alyea, Geneva; Ted Uhlaender, Erie; Dick Bazinet, Auburn; **C**-Jerry May, Batavia; Donald Bryant, Jamestown; **P**-Malcolm Warren, Auburn; Michael Fedak, Jamestown; Jim Merritt, Erie; Robert Schmidt, Jamestown; **Manager**-Stubby Overmire, Jamestown.

BA: Ted Uhlaender, Erie, .342
Runs: Dick Bazinet, Auburn, 113
Hits: Rigoberto Mena, Jamestown, 154
RBIs: Bob Guindon, Olean, 121
HRs: Bob Guindon, Olean, 37

Wins: Jim Merritt, Erie, 19
SOs: Jim Merritt, Erie, 249
ERA: Garry Roggenburk, Erie, 2.07
Pct: Garry Roggenburk, Erie, .765, 13-4

D Western Carolina League
President: John H. Moss

Standings	W	L	Pct.	GB	Attend.	Manager
Statesville Owls***	62	36	.633	—	28,723	Jack Hale/Bobby Bralley
Salisbury Braves (16)	52	44	.542	9	23,461	Harvey Stratton
Newton-Conover Twins	42	57	.424	20½	10,452	Henry Nichols
Shelby Colonels.................	40	59	.404	22½	14,743	Joe Abernethy/Cloyd Boyer

Playoffs: None.

All-Star Team: 1B-Charles Truesdell, Statesville; **2B**-Mickey Campbell, Shelby; **3B**-Jack Sargent, Statesville; **SS**-John Pavlus, Salisbury; **OF**-J.C. Snead, Statesville; Carmen Iannaccone, Salisbury; Steve Whitaker, Shelby; **C**-Dave Partrick, Salisbury; Bob Weaver, Salisbury; **P**-George Bechtold, Shelby; Robert Kenny, Statesville; **MVP**-Charles Truesdell, Statesville; **Most Outstanding Player**-John Pavlus, Salisbury; **Most Outstanding Pitcher**-Robert Kenny, Statesville; **Manager**-Bobby Bralley, Statesville.

BA: Charles Truesdell, Statesville, .344
Runs: J.C. Snead, Statesville, 75
Hits: Charles Truesdell, Statesville, 111
RBIs: Henry Nichols, Newton-Conover, 66

HRs: Frank Petrellis, Shelby, 9
J.C. Snead, Statesville, 9
Steve Whitaker, Shelby, 9
Wins: Robert Kenny, Statesville, 16
SOs: Nick DeMatteis, Statesville, 161
ERA: Robert Kenny, Statesville, 2.21

1962 Interleague Post Season Play

World Series
New York (American) 4 games, San Francisco (National) 3

1962 Major League Farm Systems

American League
1. Baltimore (6): Rochester, Elmira, Stockton, Aberdeen, Bluefield, Appleton.
2. Boston (6): Seattle, York, Winston-Salem, Pocatello, Waterloo, Olean.
3. Chicago (6): Indianapolis, Savannah/Lynchburg, Visalia, Harlan, Sarasota, Clinton.
4. Cleveland (6): Jacksonville, Salt Lake City, Charleston, Burlington (NC), Selma, Dubuque.
5. Detroit (6): Denver, Knoxville, Duluth-Superior, Montgomery, Thomasville, Jamestown.
6. Kansas City (6): Portland, Albuquerque, Binghamton, Lewiston, Minot, Daytona Beach.
7. Los Angeles (4): Dallas-Ft. Worth, Hawaii, San Jose, Quad Cities.
8. Minnesota (7): Vancouver, Charlotte, Wilson, Bismarck-Mandan, Ft. Walton Beach, Wytheville, Erie.
9. New York (7): Richmond, Amarillo, Augusta, Greensboro, Idaho Falls, Harlan, Ft. Lauderdale.
10. Washington (4): Syracuse, Raleigh, Pensacola, Middlesboro.

National League
11. Chicago (5): Salt Lake City, San Antonio, Wenatchee, St. Cloud, Palatka.
12. Cincinnati (5): San Diego, Macon, Rocky Mount, Tampa, Geneva.
13. Houston (4): Oklahoma City, Durham, Modesto, Moultrie.
14. Los Angeles (9): Omaha, Spokane, Greenville, Salem (OR), Reno, Great Falls, Ozark/Andalusia, St. Petersburg, Keokuk/Midwest.
15. Milwaukee (8): Louisville, Toronto, Austin, Yakima, Eau Claire, Boise, Dublin, Cedar Rapids.
16. New York (5): Syracuse, Santa Barbara, Quincy, Auburn, Salisbury.
17. Philadelphia (7): Dallas-Ft. Worth, Buffalo, Williamsport, Bakersfield, Magic Valley, Dothan, Miami.
18. Pittsburgh (7): Columbus, Asheville, Kinston, Grand Forks, Kingsport, Burlington (IA), Batavia.
19. St. Louis (6): Atlanta, Tulsa, Portsmouth-Norfolk, Winnipeg, Billings, Brunswick.
20. San Francisco (8): Tacoma, El Paso, Springfield, Eugene, Fresno, Salem (VA), Lakeland, Decatur.

1962 No-Hitters

Date	Pitcher	Team	League	Opponent	Score
4-26	Garnet Steubing	Boise	Pioneer	Magic Valley	10-0
5-4	Joe Carboni	Rocky Mount	Carolina	Wilson	10-0
5-5	Bo Belinsky	Los Angeles	American	Baltimore	2-0
5-6	Vincent Scales	Quad Cities	Midwest	Clinton	2-0
5-12	Al Downing	Richmond	International	Syracuse	4-0
5-13	Matthew Gayeski	Eugene	Northwest	Wenatchee	3-0
6-15	Darold Knowles	Stockton	California	San Jose	0-3 (6)
6-19	Richard Beck	Idaho Falls	Pioneer	Boise	4-0 (7)
6-26	Earl Wilson	Boston	American	Los Angeles	2-0
6-28	Denny McLain	Harlan	Appalachian	Salem	9-0
6-30	Sandy Koufax	Los Angeles	National	New York	5-0
7-1	Pete Cimino	Wilson	Carolina	Winston-Salem	1-0
7-3	Duane Richards	Macon	South Atlantic	Portsmouth-Norfolk	4-0
7-5	Gerard Merz	Rocky Mount	Carolina	Kinston	0-1 (8)
7-12	Mark Clarke	Aberdeen	Northern	Grand Forks	0-1
7-28	Barry Miller	Dublin	Georgia-Florida	Thomasville	2-0 (5)
7-28	Juan Gomez	Raleigh	Carolina	Greensboro	16-0
7-31	Dick Estelle	Eugene	Northwest	Salem	6-0 (7)
8-1	Bill Monbouquette	Boston	American	Chicago	1-0
8-8	John Gregory	Duluth-Superior	Northern	Bismarck-Mandan	2-0 (7)
8-12	Tony Komisar	Cedar Rapids	Midwest	Clinton	8-0
8-14	Charles Ling	Burlington	Midwest	Keokuk	6-0
8-14	Sammy Ellis	San Diego	Pacific Coast	Tacoma	4-0
8-14	John Stolarchuk	Salisbury	Western Carolina	Newton-Conover	2-0 (5)
8-22	Patrick House	Boise	Pioneer	Magic Valley	3-0 (7)
8-26	Jack Kralick	Minnesota	American	Kansas City	1-0
8-26	Dick LeMay	Tacoma	Pacific Coast	Vancouver	4-0 (7)
8-31	Weldon Mauldin	Tulsa	Texas	Amarillo	3-0 (7)

Number in parentheses indicates innings if other than nine.

THIS DATE IN MINOR LEAGUE HISTORY

January 7, 1962, The Three-I League disbanded. The 61-year-old circuit was the oldest Class B league in Organized Baseball.

April 21, 1962, Jim Gosger, playing in only his third game in Organized Baseball, set a Carolina League record by driving in ten runs to pace Winston-Salem to a 15-3 victory over Rocky Mount.

April 23, 1962, Shortstop Ernesto De La Osa, Miami, in his first game in Organized Baseball, executed an unassisted triple play in a game with Ft. Lauderdale in the opening of the Florida State League season.

April 24, 1962, Macon, South Atlantic League, swamped Greenville, 32-5.

June, 8, 1962, Bob Guindon, Olean, New York-Penn League, crashed three homers in a game for the second time in three days.

June 14, 1962, Aguascalientes, Mexican Center League, belted ten homers in one game but lost to Guanajuato, 17-15.

June 28, 1962, Denny McLain, Harlan, Appalachian League, fanned 17 and pitched a no-hit game to defeat Salem, 3-0, in his first pro contest.

June 29, 1962, Jesus Alou, El Paso, Texas League, outfielder, was handcuffed by Austin after hitting safely in 48 of his last 49 games. He had batting streaks of 23 and 25 games.

August 10, 1962, Bob Veale, Columbus southpaw, set an International League record when he struck out 22 in nine innings at Buffalo. Columbus won the game, 6-5, in 12 innings. Veale did not get the win, as he was removed for a pinch-hitter in the tenth.

August 13, 1962, Dagoberto "Bert" Campaneris, Daytona Beach, Florida State League, pitched both right and lefthanded in a two-inning relief stint.

August 20, 1962, Charlie Dees, El Paso, Texas League, hit four homers as the Sun Kings clobbered Amarillo, 11-3.

November 29, 1962, The International League and Pacific Coast League absorbed the American Association and became ten-club circuits.

THE SUBSISTENCE YEARS: 1963 - 1977

*T*he face of minor league baseball was changed in 1963. Gone were hundreds of cities that had been part of Organized Baseball little more than a decade before. Gone were Class B, C and D. And, after 61 continuous years of operation, the American Association was gone, the first Triple-A league to fold.

The Association, down to five clubs, could not find a sixth working agreement for the 1963 season. The five remaining teams merged with the International and Pacific Coast leagues. The key to survival in minor league baseball was no longer winning games and drawing fans. It was now tied to having a Player Development Contract - the PDC - the agreement that paid most of the bills.

With the demise of the Georgia-Florida League after the 1963 season, the minors were down to 15 U.S leagues. The Mexican and Mexican Center Leagues were members of the National Association, but were not part of the player-development program and continued to operate independently. The minor leagues did stabilize and of the leagues that started in 1964, the only failure during the next 30 years was the Northern League which folded after the 1971 season. There were alterations, but the major leagues kept their promise to see that at least 100 teams survived.

By the mid-1960s the Vietnam War was having an effect on manpower in the minor leagues. During the conflict, young men could receive deferments as long as they remained in college. In the past, a minor league contract had been the signal to drop out of school, but the unpopular Vietnam War kept many ball players in school. The major leagues did not want to see a good prospect lose two years or, perhaps, pay a greater price in the service. They now encouraged prospects to remain in school.

The result was leagues that operated during summer vacation. In 1963 there was only one league, the Appalachian League, that played a short season, lasting from June through August. The Pioneer League, in 1964, became a Rookie League with a short schedule. A new classification, Short Season Class A, was instituted in 1965 so that the Northern League could get players with more experience who had to remain in school. In 1966 the Northwest League went short season, and in 1967 the New York-Penn League followed suit. These were also cold weather leagues where April and May playing dates proved difficult. For most of these leagues short season was a way to survive. With the big leagues guaranteeing that a PDC was tied to going short season, there was little incentive to resist.

During this period, the major leagues also instituted complex leagues, the Gulf Coast League, Sarasota Rookie League and others. No admission was charged and no fans attended. It was a new method of player development: giving instruction in daytime leagues with no fans, press or long bus rides. Minor leaguers protested that players should be trained in front of fans, but the complex leagues soon were an integral part of the player development system.

The 1960s saw few bright spots in minor league baseball. A few clubs, such as Rochester, N.Y., and Hawaii, had consistent fan bases year after year, but for most franchises survival was the only success. Expansion of the major leagues in 1969 brought a few new working agreements, and the American Association was revived in 1969. As the Vietnam War dragged on with protests in the streets and on college campuses baseball struggled.

George Trautman died in 1963, and his longtime assistant, Phil Piton, was elected President of the National Association. Piton retired after the 1971 season. Piton's successor, Hank Peters, was a longtime major league farm director. His election, strongly supported by the major leagues, emphasized the control of the majors. Peters worked to stabilize the weaker leagues, but he returned to the major leagues in 1975 and was replaced by Bobby Bragan, president of the Texas League and a former big league player and manager.

The changes in the presidency of the National Association had little effect on the health of the minors, which was terrible. By 1975 the Carolina and Western Carolinas leagues were down to four teams each and began an interlocking schedule. The Northwest League survived with teams attempting the old independent route. Portland, Ore., a former PCL, enjoyed remarkable success as a short season independent but few willingly followed this route.

Promotions, giveaways and free tickets were the norm in the minors as clubs tried to pull anybody to the park. A new breed of minor league operators was coming to the fore as the men who had run clubs in the 1940s and '50s retired or left the game. Sports administration programs in colleges were beginning, and young general managers were starting to join the sport. The country was starting to change. The cyclical nature of minor league baseball was to show itself in another upswing.

1963

American League
President: Joseph E. Cronin

Standings	W	L	Pct.	GB	Attend.	Manager
New York Yankees	104	57	.646	—	1,308,920	Ralph Houk
Chicago White Sox	94	68	.580	10½	1,158,848	Al Lopez
Minnesota Twins	91	70	.565	13	1,406,652	Sam Mele
Baltimore Orioles	86	76	.531	18½	774,343	Billy Hitchcock
Cleveland Indians	79	83	.488	25½	562,507	Birdie Tebbetts
Detroit Tigers	79	83	.488	25½	821,952	Bob Scheffing/Chuck Dressen
Boston Red Sox	76	85	.472	28	942,642	Johnny Pesky
Kansas City Athletics	73	89	.451	31½	762,364	Ed Lopat
Los Angeles Angels	70	91	.435	34	821,015	Bill Rigney
Washington Senators	56	106	.346	48½	535,604	Mickey Vernon/ Eddie Yost/Gil Hodges

BA: Carl Yastrzemski, Boston, .321
Runs: Bob Allison, Minnesota, 99
Hits: Carl Yastrzemski, Boston, 183
RBIs: Dick Stuart, Boston, 118
HRs: Harmon Killebrew, Minnesota, 45

Wins: Whitey Ford, New York, 24
SOs: Camilo Pascual, Minnesota, 202
ERA: Gary Peters, Chicago, 2.33
Pct: Whitey Ford, New York, .774, 24-7
Saves: Stu Miller, Baltimore, 27

National League
President: Warren C. Giles

Standings	W	L	Pct.	GB	Attend.	Manager
Los Angeles Dodgers	99	63	.611	—	2,538,602	Walter Alston
St. Louis Cardinals	93	69	.574	6	1,170,546	Johnny Keane
San Francisco Giants	88	74	.543	11	1,571,306	Alvin Dark
Philadelphia Phillies	87	75	.537	12	907,141	Gene Mauch
Cincinnati Reds	86	76	.531	13	858,805	Fred Hutchinson
Milwaukee Braves	84	78	.519	15	773,018	Bobby Bragan
Chicago Cubs	82	80	.506	17	979,551	Bob Kennedy
Pittsburgh Pirates	74	88	.457	25	783,648	Danny Murtaugh
Houston Colt .45s	66	96	.407	33	719,502	Harry Craft
New York Mets	51	111	.315	48	1,080,108	Casey Stengel

BA: Tommy Davis, Los Angeles, .326
Runs: Hank Aaron, Milwaukee, 121
Hits: Vada Pinson, Cincinnati, 204
RBIs: Hank Aaron, Milwaukee, 130
HRs: Hank Aaron, Milwaukee, 44
  Willie McCovey, San Francisco, 44

Wins: Sandy Koufax, Los Angeles, 25
  Juan Marichal, San Francisco, 25
SOs: Sandy Koufax, Los Angeles, 306
ERA: Sandy Koufax, Los Angeles, 1.88
Pct: Ron Perranoski, Los Angeles, .842, 16-3
Saves: Lindy McDaniel, Chicago, 22

AAA International League
President: Thomas H. Richardson

North Standings	W	L	Pct.	GB	Attend.	Manager
Syracuse Chiefs (5)	80	70	.533	—	165,611	Bob Swift/Frank Carswell
Toronto Maple Leafs (15)	76	75	.503	4½	119,596	Bill Adair
Rochester Red Wings (1)	75	76	.497	5½	271,968	Darrell Johnson
Buffalo Bisons (16)	74	77	.490	6½	136,020	Kerby Farrell
Richmond Virginians (9)	66	81	.449	12½	155,772	Preston Gomez

South Standings	W	L	Pct.	GB	Attend.	Manager
Indianapolis Indians (3)	86	67	.562	—	174,558	Rollie Hemsley
Atlanta Crackers (19)	85	68	.556	1	170,677	Harry Walker
Arkansas Travelers#(17)	78	73	.517	7	141,287	Frank Lucchesi
Columbus Jets (18)	75	73	.507	8½	167,121	Lawrence Shepard
Jacksonville Suns (4)	56	91	.381	27	95,265	Ben Geraghty/Casey Wise

#represented Little Rock, Arkansas.

Playoffs: Indianapolis defeated Atlanta 1-0 in a one-game playoff for first place. Indianapolis 4 games, Syracuse 1; Atlanta 4 games, Toronto 0.
Finals: Indianapolis 4 games, Atlanta 2.

All-Star Team: 1B-Grover "Deacon" Jones, Indianapolis; **2B**-Pedro Gonzalez, Richmond; **3B**-Don Buford, Indianapolis; **SS**-Jerry Buchek, Atlanta; **OF**-Richie Allen, Arkansas; Lou Jackson, Toronto; Bob Burda, Columbus; **C**-Jim Coker, Toronto; **P**-Fritz Ackley, Indianapolis; Willie Smith, Syracuse; **MVP**-Don Buford, Indianapolis; **Pitcher of the Year**-Fritz Ackley, Indianapolis; **Manager**-Harry Walker, Atlanta.

BA: Don Buford, Indianapolis, .336
Runs: Don Buford, Indianapolis, 114
Hits: Don Buford, Indianapolis, 206
RBIs: Richie Allen, Arkansas, 97

HRs: Richie Allen, Arkansas, 33
Wins: Fritz Ackley, Indianapolis, 18
SOs: Frank Kreutzer, Indianapolis, 157
ERA: Fritz Ackley, Indianapolis, 2.76

AAA Pacific Coast League
President: Dewey Soriano

North Standings	W	L	Pct.	GB	Attend.	Manager
Spokane Indians (14)	98	60	.620	—	170,808	Danny Ozark
Hawaii Islanders (7)	81	77	.513	17	236,848	Irv Noren
Tacoma Giants (20)	79	79	.500	19	146,050	Andy Gilbert
Portland Beavers (6)	73	84	.465	24½	87,438	Les Peden/Dan Carnevale
Seattle Rainiers (2)	68	90	.430	30	132,769	Mel Parnell

South Standings	W	L	Pct.	GB	Attend.	Manager
Oklahoma City 89ers (13)	84	74	.532	—	185,108	Grady Hatton
San Diego Padres (12)	83	74	.529	½	202,765	Don Heffner
Dallas-Ft. Worth Rangers (8)	79	79	.500	5	118,350	Jack McKeon
Salt Lake City Bees (11)	73	85	.462	11	108,405	El Tappe
Denver Bears (15)	71	87	.449	13	112,118	Jack Tighe

Playoff: Oklahoma City 4 games, Spokane 3.

All-Star Team: 1B-Deron Johnson, San Diego; **2B**-Bob Klaus, San Diego; **3B**-Chico Ruiz, San Diego; **SS**-Gil Garrido, Tacoma; **OF**-Jesus Alou, Tacoma; Billy Cowan, Salt Lake City; Chico Salmon, Denver; **C**-Mike Brumley, Spokane; Jim Saul, San Diego; **P**-Howie Reed, Spokane; Bill Spanswick, Seattle; **MVP**-Billy Cowan, Salt Lake City; **Manager**-Danny Ozark, Spokane.

BA: Chico Salmon, Denver, .325
Runs: Cesar Tovar, Dallas-Ft. Worth, 115
Hits: Jesus Alou, Tacoma, 210
RBIs: Billy Cowan, Salt Lake City, 120

HRs: Deron Johnson, San Diego, 33
Wins: Howie Reed, Spokane, 19
SOs: Bill Spanswick, Seattle, 209
ERA: Sammy Ellis, San Diego, 2.62

AA Eastern League
President: A. Rankin Johnson

Standings	W	L	Pct.	GB	Attend.	Manager
Charleston Indians (4)	83	57	.593	—	52,468	John Lipon
Elmira Pioneers (1)	76	64	.543	7	74,811	Earl Weaver
Springfield Giants (20)	72	68	.514	11	76,376	Buddy Kerr
Binghamton Triplets (6)	65	75	.464	18	47,465	John McNamara
York White Roses (10)	63	77	.450	20	42,827	Danny O'Connell/ John Schiave
Reading Red Sox (2)	61	79	.436	22	46,541	Eddie Popowski

Playoffs: None.

All-Star Team: 1B-Bob Chance, Charleston; **2B**-Don Wallace, Elmira; **3B**-Mickey McGuire, Elmira; **SS**-Rico Petrocelli, Reading; **OF**-Bob Stotsky, Reading; Jim Liggett, Elmira; Tony Curry, Charleston; **C**-Duke Sims, Charleston; Frank Zupo, York; **P**-Frank Linzy, Springfield; Darold Knowles, Elmira; **Manager**-John Lipon, Charleston.

BA: Bob Chance, Charleston, .343
Runs: Tony Curry, Charleston, 81
Hits: Hal Lanier, Springfield, 163
RBIs: Bob Chance, Charleston, 114
HRs: Bob Chance, Charleston, 26

Wins: Darold Knowles, Elmira, 16
  Frank Linzy, Springfield, 16
SOs: Fred Norman, Binghamton, 258
ERA: Frank Linzy, Springfield, 1.55

AA Mexican League
President: Antonio Ramirez Muro

Standings	W	L	Pct.	GB	Attend.	Manager
Puebla Pericos	80	52	.606	—	201,280	Tony Castano
Mexico City Diablos Rojos	71	61	.538	9	388,014	Tomas Herrera
Monterrey Sultanes	70	62	.530	10	166,449	Clemente Carreras
Mexico City Tigres	66	66	.500	14	335,955	Memo Garibay/ Jose Luis Garcia
Poza Rica Petroleros	66	66	.500	14	436,018	Manuel Arroyo/David Garcia
Veracruz Aguilas	56	76	.424	24	107,210	Santos Amaro
Reynosa Broncs	53	79	.402	27	159,500	Ray Garza

Playoffs: None.

All-Star Team: 1B-Ron Camacho, Puebla; **2B**-Vinicio Garcia, Monterrey; **3B**-Leonardo Rodriguez, MC Diablos Rojos; **SS**-Jorge Fitch, Puebla; **OF**-Hector Espino, Monterrey; Angel Scull, Poza Rica; Al Pinkston, Veracruz; **C**-Rodolfo Sandoval, Puebla; Jaime Corella, Monterrey; **P**-Miguel Sotelo, Puebla; Arturo Cacheux, MC Tigres; **Manager**-Tony Castano, Puebla.

BA: Vinicio Garcia, Monterrey, .368
Runs: Ron Camacho, Puebla, 107
  Vinicio Garcia, Monterrey, 107
Hits: Alfredo Rios, Monterrey, 185
RBIs: Ron Camacho, Puebla, 108

HRs: Ron Camacho, Puebla, 39
Wins: Miguel Sotelo, Puebla, 24
SOs: Miguel Sotelo, Puebla, 208
ERA: Arturo Cacheux, MC Tigres, 2.69

AA South Atlantic League
President: Sam C. Smith, Jr.

Standings	W	L	Pct.	GB	Attend.	Manager
Macon Peaches (12)	81	59	.579	—	60,253	Dave Bristol
Asheville Tourists (18)	79	61	.564	2	71,845	Ray Hathaway
Lynchburg White Sox**(3)	79	61	.564	2	74,980	Les Moss
Augusta Yankees*(9)	75	63	.543	5	41,813	Rube Walker
Knoxville Smokies (5)	71	68	.511	9½	43,894	Frank Carswell/Frank Skaff
Chattanooga Lookouts (17)	62	78	.443	19	58,402	Jack Phillips
Charlotte Hornets (8)	58	82	.414	23	46,065	Al Evans
Nashville Vols (7)	53	86	.381	27½	54,564	John Fitzpatrick

*Won first-half   **Won second-half   ***Won both halves
Numbers after nicknames indicate farm system.
Affiliation listed at end of each year.

Playoff: Augusta 3 games, Lynchburg 2.

All-Star Team: 1B-Charles Leonard, Asheville; **2B**-Ike Futch, Augusta; **3B**-Tony Perez, Macon; **SS**-Marv Staehle, Nashville; **OF**-Jim Hicks, Macon/Lynchburg; Willie Horton, Knoxville; Jim Northrup, Knoxville; **C**-Pat Corrales, Chattanooga; John Griffin, Lynchburg; **P**-Troy Giles, Asheville; Charlie Rabe, Macon; **Manager**-Les Moss, Lynchburg.

BA: Marv Staehle, Nashville, .337
Runs: Jim Hicks, Macon/Lynchburg, 90
    Adolfo Phillips, Chattanooga, 90
Hits: Ike Futch, Augusta, 177
RBIs: Jim Hicks, Macon/Lynchburg, 83

HRs: Jim Hicks, Macon/Lynchburg, 21
    Fred Loesekam, Lynchburg, 21
Wins: Fred Talbot, Lynchburg, 18
    Troy Giles, Asheville, 18
SOs: Troy Giles, Asheville, 159
ERA: Tom Richards, Lynchburg, 2.22

AA Texas League
President: Dick Butler

Standings	W	L	Pct.	GB	Attend.	Manager
San Antonio Bullets (13)	79	61	.564	—	84,965	Lou Fitzgerald
Austin Senators (15)	75	65	.536	4	58,384	Jimmy Brown
Tulsa Oilers (19)	74	66	.529	5	200,557	Grover Resinger
El Paso Sun Kings (20)	68	72	.489	11	111,954	George Genovese
Albuquerque Dukes (14)	67	73	.479	12	75,973	Clay Bryant
Amarillo Gold Sox (11)	57	83	.407	22	58,119	Joe Macko

Playoffs: Tulsa 3 games, Austin 0; San Antonio 3 games, El Paso 2.
Finals: Tulsa 3 games, San Antonio 1.

All-Star Team: 1B-George Kopacz, Austin; **2B**-Mike White, San Antonio; **3B**-Derrell Griffith, Albuquerque; **SS**-Sandy Alomar, Austin; **OF**-Jim Beauchamp, Tulsa; Dick Dietz, El Paso; Arlo Engel, El Paso; Jose Cardenal, El Paso; Rico Carty, Austin; **C**-Randy Hundley, El Paso; **Util**-Ron Campbell, Amarillo; **P**-Camilo Estevis, Albuquerque; Joe Hoerner, San Antonio; **MVP**-Jim Beauchamp, Tulsa; **Pitcher of the Year**-Camilo Estevis, Albuquerque.

BA: Dick Dietz, El Paso, .354
Runs: Dick Dietz, El Paso, 128
Hits: George Kopacz, Austin, 180
RBIs: Arlo Engel, El Paso, 126

HRs: Arlo Engel, El Paso, 41
Wins: Camilo Estevis, Albuquerque, 16
SOs: Camilo Estevis, Albuquerque, 196
ERA: Sterling Slaughter, Amarillo, 3.00

A California League
President: Edward J. Mulligan

Standings	W	L	Pct.	GB	Attend.	Manager
Stockton Ports**(1)	87	52	.626	—	42,506	Harry Dunlop
Bakersfield Bears (17)	78	62	.557	9½	40,776	Bob Wellman
Fresno Giants (20)	73	67	.521	14½	34,192	Bill Werle
Modesto Colts*(13)	72	68	.514	15½	22,266	Dave Philley
Reno Silver Sox (18)	71	69	.507	16½	17,182	Tom Saffell
Santa Barbara Rancheros (14)	67	72	.482	20	11,608	James Williams
San Jose Bees (7)	62	78	.443	25½	42,677	Red Marion
Salinas Mets (16)	49	91	.350	38½	18,891	Ken Deal

Playoff: Stockton 2 games, Modesto 0.

All-Star Team: 1B-Len Tucker, Modesto; **2B**-Joe Nichols, Stockton; **3B**-Paul Schaal, San Jose; **SS**-Damaso Blanco, Fresno; **OF**-Jose Vidal, Reno; Paul Blair, Stockton; Jim Perkins, Bakersfield; **C**-Fred Walters, Bakersfield; **Util**-Harry Land, Reno; **P**-Bob Olson, Stockton; Wally Bunker, Stockton; Dick Selma, Salinas; Bill Boehlert, Santa Barbara; **MVP**-Jose Vidal, Reno; **Rookie of the Year**-Dick Selma, Salinas; **Manager**-Harry Dunlop, Stockton.

BA: Jose Vidal, Reno, .340
Runs: Damaso Blanco, Fresno, 127
Hits: Damaso Blanco, Fresno, 187
RBIs: Jose Vidal, Reno, 162

HRs: Jose Vidal, Reno, 40
Wins: Bob Olson, Stockton, 19
SOs: Dick Selma, Salinas, 221
ERA: Dick Selma, Salinas, 2.58

A Carolina League
President: J.C. "Bill" Jessup

East Standings	W	L	Pct.	GB	Attend.	Manager
Kinston Eagles (18)	77	66	.538	—	119,346	Pete Peterson
Wilson Tobs (8)	77	67	.535	½	44,789	Ralph Rowe
Rocky Mount Leafs (12)	72	72	.500	5½	53,023	John "Red" Davis
Portsmouth Tides	65	79	.451	12½	63,468	Allen Jones
Peninsula Senators# (10)	58	86	.403	19½	50,171	Archie Wilson

West Standings	W	L	Pct.	GB	Attend.	Manager
Greensboro Yankees (9)	85	59	.590	—	44,556	Frank Verdi
Durham Bulls (13)	78	65	.545	6½	47,453	Billy Goodman
Burlington Indians (4)	77	66	.538	7½	62,704	Patrick Colgan
Winston-Salem Red Sox (2)	67	76	.469	17½	43,481	Matt Sczesny/Bill Slack
Raleigh Mets (16)	62	82	.431	23	34,309	Clyde McCullough/Tommy Byrne

#represented Newport News-Hampton, Virginia.

Playoffs: Wilson 3 games, Kinston 0; Greensboro 3 games, Durham 2.
Finals: Wilson 2 games, Greensboro 1.

All-Star Team: 1B-Luke Vasser, Wilson; **2B**-Roy White, Greensboro; **3B**-Ron Clark, Wilson; **SS**-Len Boehmer, Rocky Mount; **OF**-Don Bosch, Kinston; Joe Wilson, Kinston; Lou Piniella, Peninsula; Walt Matthews, Durham; **C**-Jim Price, Kinston; Tom Kowalowski,

Greensboro; **Util**-Gene Michael, Kinston, **P**-Sherman "Roadblock" Jones, Raleigh; Chuck Kovach, Burlington; George Pressley, Burlington; Gerald Merz, Rocky Mount; **MVP**-Jim Price, Kinston; **Manager**-Patrick Colgan, Burlington.

BA: Don Bosch, Kinston, .332
Runs: Roy White, Greensboro, 117
Hits: Don Bosch, Kinston, 189
RBIs: Jim Price, Kinston, 109
HRs: Walt Matthews, Durham, 30

Wins: Chuck Kovach, Burlington, 17
    Gerald Merz, Rocky Mount, 17
SOs: Luis Tiant, Burlington, 207
ERA: Sherman "Roadblock" Jones, Raleigh, 2.10

A Florida State League
President: J. Roy Stockton

Standings	W	L	Pct.	GB	Attend.	Manager
Sarasota Sun Sox***(3)	80	42	.656	—	48,136	Ira Hutchinson
St. Petersburg Saints (14)	64	57	.529	15½	68,218	Roy Hartsfield
Orlando Twins (8)	64	59	.520	16½	33,404	Harry Warner
Ft. Lauderdale Yankees (9)	60	60	.500	19	28,222	Pinky May/Steve Souchock/Cloyd Boyer
Lakeland Tigers (5)	60	61	.496	19½	14,027	Gail Henley
Miami Marlins (17)	58	65	.472	22½	75,349	Andy Seminick
Daytona Beach Islanders (6)	51	71	.418	29	22,343	Bob Hofman
Tampa Tarpons (12)	49	71	.408	30	29,938	Hershell Freeman

Playoffs: None.

BA: Ramon Webster, Daytona Beach, .333
Runs: John Mustion, Miami, 85
Hits: John Mustion, Miami, 143
RBIs: Terry Bartholme, Orlando, 84

HRs: Rich Littleton, Sarasota, 12
Wins: Henry Harden, St. Petersburg, 22
SOs: Richard Gardner, Orlando, 213
ERA: Gil Downs, Sarasota, 1.38

A Georgia-Florida League
President: Larry Brumitt

Standings	W	L	Pct.	GB	Attend.	Manager
Thomasville Tigers (5)	65	54	.546	—	7,342	Al Federoff
Moultrie Colt .22s (13)	62	54	.534	1½	11,401	James Walton
Waycross Braves (15)	56	63	.471	9	21,560	Bill Steinecke
Brunswick Cardinals (19)	52	64	.448	11½	9,363	George Kissell

Playoffs: None.

All-Star Team: 1B-Hal Breeden, Waycross; **2B**-Jimmy Glover, Thomasville; **3B**-Ray Ferrand, Moultrie; **SS**-Dennis Willett, Moultrie; **OF**-Bill Robinson, Waycross; John Bly, Thomasville; Oliverio Sparks, Moultrie; **C**-Jim Green, Moultrie; Bruce Nichols, Thomasville; **P**-Carl Elmstrom, Waycross; Jim Tuholski, Thomasville; **Manager**-Bill Steinecke, Waycross.

BA: Hal Breeden, Waycross, .330
Runs: Dennis Willett, Moultrie, 73
Hits: Bill Robinson, Waycross, 132
RBIs: Hal Breeden, Waycross, 64

HRs: Charlie Murray, Moultrie, 15
Wins: Robert Laton, Thomasville, 12
SOs: Carl Elmstrom, Waycross, 138
ERA: Carl Elmstrom, Waycross, 1.66

A Mexican Center League
President: Antonio Ramirez (Muro)

Standings	W	L	Pct.	GB	Attend.	Manager
Guanajuato Tuzos	69	41	.627	—	45,000	Domingo Santana
Aguascalientes Tigres	58	50	.537	10	41,613	Camilo Varona/Daniel Rios
Leon Diablos Verdes	57	54	.514	12½	29,356	Luis Montes de Oca
San Luis Potosi Reds	47	65	.420	23	59,985	Felipe Hernandez
San Luis Potosi Indians	45	66	.405	24½	60,521	Barney Serrell/Alfonso Pena

Playoffs: None.

All-Star Team: 1B-Jose Angel Guerrero, SLP Reds; **2B**-Armando de Leon, Guanajuato; **3B**-Ernesto Cruz, Aguascalientes; **SS**-Isidoro Sainz, Leon; **OF**-Eladio Urias, SLP Reds; Heriberto Vargas, Guanajuato; Miguel Angel Gutierrez, SLP Indians; **C**-Alfonso Ibarra, Leon; Lorenzo Ramirez, SLP Reds; **P**-Horacio Solano, Aguascalientes; Justino Hernandez, Guanajuato; **Manager**-Domingo Santana, Guanajuato.

BA: Armando de Leon, Guanajuato, .379
Runs: Eladio Urias, SLP Reds, 108
Hits: Eladio Urias, SLP Reds, 145
RBIs: Heriberto Vargas, Guanajuato, 96
HRs: Heriberto Vargas, Guanajuato, 24

Wins: Homero Gonzalez, Leon, 16
SOs: Homero Gonzalez, Leon, 141
ERA: Horacio Solano, Aguascalientes, 2.50

A Midwest League
President: Walter C. Wagner

Standings	W	L	Pct.	GB	Attend.	Manager
Clinton C-Sox***(3)	83	41	.669	—	76,185	Don Bacon
Burlington Bees (6)	72	52	.581	11	70,902	Grady Wilson
Quad Cities Angels (7)	66	57	.537	16½	90,668	Chuck Tanner
Decatur Commodores (20)	62	61	.508	20½	68,812	Richard Klaus
Wisconsin Rapids Senators (10)	58	62	.483	23	62,621	Wayne Terwilliger
Waterloo Hawks (2)	58	66	.468	25	49,175	Len Okrie
Cedar Rapids Red Raiders (12)	56	65	.463	25½	61,585	Mike Ryba
Fox Cities Foxes (1)	55	65	.458	26	45,644	Billy DeMars
Quincy Jets (16)	56	68	.452	27	26,572	Sheriff Robinson/Walter Millies
Dubuque Packers (4)	47	76	.382	35½	77,130	Walter Novick

Playoffs: None.

All-Star Team: 1B-Tony Horton, Waterloo; **2B**-Tito Fuentes, Decatur; **3B**-Tommie Reynolds, Burlington; **SS**-Agustin Enriquez, Burlington; **OF**-Ed Stroud, Clinton; Dennis Meyers, Quad Cities; Brennan Asplen, Wisconsin Rapids; **C**-James Lang, Quincy; **P**-Jerome Rozmus, Clinton; Donald McNeal, Clinton; **Manager**-Don Bacon, Clinton.

BA: Tommie Reynolds, Burlington, .332
Runs: Ed Stroud, Clinton, 116
Hits: Chris Coletta, Waterloo, 148
RBIs: Tommie Reynolds, Burlington, 88
Tony Horton, Waterloo, 88

HRs: Lincoln Curtis, Cedar Rapids, 28
Wins: Ken Turner, Quad Cities, 18
SOs: Nicholas DeMatteis, Decatur, 237
ERA: Jerome Rozmus, Clinton, 1.44

A New York-Pennsylvania League
President: Vincent M. McNamara

Standings	W	L	Pct.	GB	Attend.	Manager
Auburn Mets (16)	76	54	.585	—	41,770	Richard Cole
Wellsville Red Sox (2)	73	57	.562	3	18,844	Bill Slack/Matt Sczesny
Batavia Pirates (18)	63	67	.485	13	28,967	Buddy Hancken
Jamestown Tigers (5)	62	68	.477	14	31,360	Stubby Overmire/John O'Neil/Max Macon/Fred Hatfield
Geneva Senators (10)	59	71	.454	17	16,923	Owen Friend
Erie Sailors (8)	57	73	.438	19	29,775	Frank Franchi

Playoffs: Batavia 2 games, Auburn 0; Jamestown 2 games, Wellsville 0.
Finals: Batavia 2 games, Jamestown 1.

All-Star Team: 1B-Bob Lawrence, Wellsville; **2B**-Michael Holodick, Jamestown; **3B**-George Scott, Wellsville; **SS**-John Pavlus, Auburn; **OF**-Dick Bazinet, Auburn; Louis Abrahams, Geneva; Tony Conigliaro, Wellsville; **C**-Carl Taylor, Batavia; Paul Casanova, Geneva; **P**-Bob Lee, Batavia; George Angel, Geneva; Ronald Locke, Auburn; Robert Kenny, Geneva; **Manager**-Richard Cole, Auburn.

BA: Michael Holodick, Jamestown, .327
Runs: Michael Holodick, Jamestown, 105
Dick Bazinet, Auburn, 105
Hits: Michael Holodick, Jamestown, 178
RBIs: John Maddox, Wellsville, 101

HRs: Byron Browne, Batavia, 32
Wins: Bob Lee, Batavia, 20
SOs: George Angel, Geneva, 250
ERA: Bob Lee, Batavia, 1.70
Pct: Bob Lee, Batavia, .909, 20-2

A Northern League
President: Brooks Baukol

Standings	W	L	Pct.	GB	Attend.	Manager
Duluth-Superior Dukes (5)	77	43	.642	—	42,082	Bob Mavis
Aberdeen Pheasants (1)	65	55	.542	12	39,949	Cal Ripken, Sr.
Bismarck-Mandan Pards (8)	56	63	.471	20½	31,769	Vern Morgan
Winnipeg Goldeyes (19)	55	64	.462	21½	61,377	Fred Koenig
Grand Forks Chiefs (4)	54	64	.458	22	18,336	Ray Dabek
St. Cloud Rox (11)	51	69	.425	26	31,665	Walt Dixon

Baukol Playoffs: Grand Forks 17-11, Duluth-Superior 18-12, Aberdeen 17-13, St. Cloud 16-14, Winnipeg 11-18, Bismarck-Mandan 9-20. (Baukol Playoffs based on last 30 days of season.)

All-Star Team: 1B-Jim Rouse, Aberdeen; **2B**-Marty Richardson, Duluth-Superior; **3B**-Bob Pfeil, St. Cloud; **SS**-Nellie Cochran, Aberdeen; **OF**-Jim Rooker, Duluth-Superior; Jose Villar, Grand Forks; Bill Hess, Bismarck-Mandan; Paul Pavelko, Duluth-Superior; Bobby Dews, Winnipeg; John Scruggs, Aberdeen; **C**-John Felske, St. Cloud; Ray Fulk, Duluth-Superior; **P**-Rudy May, Bismarck-Mandan; Denny McLain, Duluth-Superior; Bill Harvey, St. Cloud; Fred Herrmann, Winnipeg; **Manager**-Vern Morgan, Bismarck-Mandan.

BA: Jim Rouse, Aberdeen, .332
Runs: Jose Villar, Grand Forks, 91
Hits: Jim Rouse, Aberdeen, 143
RBIs: Jim Rouse, Aberdeen, 80

HRs: Jim Rouse, Aberdeen, 27
Wins: Bob Casburn, Grand Forks, 15
SOs: Pat Jarvis, Duluth-Superior, 185
ERA: Peter Craig, Duluth-Superior, 2.51

A Northwest League
President: James M. Fleishman

Standings	W	L	Pct.	GB	Attend.	Manager
Yakima Bears**(15)	84	56	.600	—	40,628	Buddy Hicks
Salem Dodgers (14)	81	59	.579	3	57,037	Stan Wasiak
Lewiston Broncs*(6)	77	63	.550	7	46,002	Robbie Robertson
Tri-City Angels (7)	65	75	.464	19	60,123	Tom Heath
Wenatchee Chiefs (11)	63	77	.450	21	32,799	George Freese
Eugene Ems (3)	50	90	.357	34	51,007	George Noga/George Sobek

Playoff: Yakima 3 games, Lewiston 1.

All-Star Team: 1B-Danny Kern, Yakima; **2B**-Jim Lefebvre, Salem; **3B**-Ernie Foli, Tri-City; **SS**-Ted Kubiak, Lewiston; **OF**-Phil Borders, Wenatchee; Vic Pagel, Salem; Lorne Johnson, Yakima; **C**-Butler Powell, Yakima; **P**-David Eilers, Yakima; Terry Barber, Salem; **Manager**-Robbie Robertson, Lewiston.

BA: Lorne Johnson, Yakima, .327
Runs: Weldon Bowlin, Lewiston, 102
Hits: Glenn Beckert, Wenatchee, 161
RBIs: Danny Kern, Yakima, 101

HRs: Danny Kern, Yakima, 24
Wins: Ron Herr, Yakima, 16
SOs: Gene Brabender, Salem, 223
ERA: Terry Barber, Salem, 2.58

A Pioneer League
President: Claude Engberg

Standings	W	L	Pct.	GB	Attend.	Manager
Magic Valley Cowboys**(17)	84	44	.656	—	61,500	Moose Johnson
Idaho Falls Yankees*(9)	77	49	.611	6	51,474	Loren Babe
Great Falls Electrics (14)	69	59	.539	15	42,708	Al Ronning
Billings Mustangs (19)	61	66	.480	22½	44,048	Ron Plaza
Boise Braves (15)	48	82	.369	37	39,204	Billy Smith
Pocatello Chiefs (11)	44	83	.346	39½	27,822	Frank Calo

Playoffs: Idaho Falls 2 games, Magic Valley 0; Billings 2 games, Great Falls 0.
Finals: Idaho Falls 2 games, Billings 1.

All-Star Team: 1B-Mike Hegan, Idaho Falls; **2B**-Louis Ertle, Great Falls; **3B**-Bobby Cox, Great Falls; **SS**-Joe Palma, Idaho Falls; **OF**-Alex Johnson, Magic Valley; Fred Woessner, Great Falls; Gene Kerns, Magic Valley; **C**-James Fox, Idaho Falls; Spencer Scott, Pocatello; **Util IF**-Nolan Campbell, Magic Valley; **Util OF**-LeRoy Reams, Idaho Falls; **P**-Bob Cerone, Idaho Falls; George Bechtold, Idaho Falls; O'Dell Deloney, Magic Valley; Ronald Cayll, Billings; **Manager**-Loren Babe, Idaho Falls.

BA: Gene Kerns, Magic Valley, .349
Runs: Mike Hegan, Idaho Falls, 123
Hits: Glenn Clark, Boise, 160
RBIs: Alex Johnson, Magic Valley, 128
HRs: Alex Johnson, Magic Valley, 35

Wins: Bob Cerone, Idaho Falls, 16
Jeff James, Magic Valley, 16
O'Dell Deloney, Magic Valley, 16
SOs: Jeff James, Magic Valley, 218
ERA: George Bechtold, Idaho Falls, 3.07

A Western Carolinas League
President: John H. Moss

Standings	W	L	Pct.	GB	Attend.	Manager
Gastonia Pirates (18)	73	52	.584	—	37,103	Bob Clear
Salisbury Dodgers**(14)	73	53	.579	½	38,857	George Scherger
Spartanburg Phillies (17)	66	58	.532	6½	94,012	Lou Kahn
Lexington Giants (20)	64	60	.516	8½	62,402	Max Lanier
Rock Hill Wrens (x)	63	63	.500	10½	48,746	Wes Ferrell
Greenville Braves*(15)	59	65	.476	13½	42,002	Jim Fanning/Paul Snyder
Statesville Owls (x)	52	73	.416	21	38,587	Bobby Bralley/Norman Small
Shelby Colonels (9)	48	74	.393	23½	34,324	Bill Shantz

Playoff: Greenville 2 games, Salisbury 0.

All-Star Team: 1B-Jerry Orlandini, Salisbury; **2B**-Joe Magliarditi, Lexington; **3B**-Gary Dempsey, Salisbury; **SS**-Cesar Gutierrez, Lexington; **OF**-John May, Greenville; George Lott, Gastonia; Fred Mason, Spartanburg; **C**-Larry Fidalgo, Gastonia; Dave McDonald, Shelby/Statesville; **P**-Mike Szemplenski, Statesville; Glen Davis, Salisbury; **MVP**-Larry Fidalgo, Gastonia; **Most Outstanding Player**-John May, Greenville; **Most Outstanding Pitcher**-Mike Szemplenski, Statesville; **Manager**-Bob Clear, Gastonia; George Scherger, Salisbury.

BA: John May, Greenville, .333
Runs: Mike Dobbins, Salisbury, 102
Hits: John May, Greenville, 146
RBIs: Levi Brown, Greenville, 91
HRs: Dave McDonald, Shelby/Statesville, 21

Wins: Jim Shellenback, Gastonia, 17
Glen Davis, Salisbury, 17
SOs: Mike Szemplenski, Statesville, 313
ERA: Dave Roberts, Spartanburg, 1.79

R Appalachian League
President: Chauncey De Vault

Standings	W	L	Pct.	GB	Attend.	Manager
Bluefield Orioles (1)	45	24	.652	—	20,652	Billy Hunter
Salem Rebels (20)	36	34	.514	9½	34,001	Alex Cosmidis
Wytheville Twins (8)	35	35	.500	10½	14,802	Red Norwood
Kingsport Pirates (18)	31	37	.456	13½	12,852	Al Kubski
Middlesboro Cubsox (3, 11)	31	37	.456	13½	13,052	Rip Collins/Hugh Mulcahy/George Noga
Harlan Yankees (9)	28	39	.418	16	13,134	Gary Blaylock

Playoffs: None.

BA: George Shuford, Bluefield, .364
Runs: William McAdams, Bluefield, 63
Hits: George Shuford, Bluefield, 84
RBIs: Hector Soto, Salem, 61

HRs: Chuck Howard, Kingsport, 11
Matt Szykowny, Wytheville, 11
Wins: Keith Sieck, Middlesboro, 8
SOs: Keith Sieck, Middlesboro, 133
ERA: Brian Holler, Bluefield, 2.41

1963 Interleague Post Season Play

World Series
Los Angeles (National) 4 games, New York (American) 0

1963 Major League Farm Systems

American League

1 Baltimore (6): Rochester, Elmira, Stockton, Fox Cities, Aberdeen, Bluefield.
2 Boston (5): Seattle, Reading, Winston-Salem, Waterloo, Wellsville.
3 Chicago (6): Indianapolis, Lynchburg, Sarasota, Clinton, Eugene, Middlesboro.
4 Cleveland (5): Jacksonville, Charleston, Burlington (NC), Dubuque, Grand Forks.
5 Detroit (6): Syracuse, Knoxville, Lakeland, Thomasville, Jamestown, Duluth-Superior.
6 Kansas City (5): Portland, Binghamton, Daytona Beach, Burlington (IA), Lewiston.
7 Los Angeles (5): Hawaii, Nashville, San Jose, Quad Cities, Tri-City.
8 Minnesota (5): Dallas-Ft. Worth, Charlotte, Wilson, Orlando, Erie, Bismarck-Mandan, Wytheville.
9 New York (7): Richmond, Augusta, Greensboro, Ft. Lauderdale, Idaho Falls, Shelby, Harlan.
10 Washington (4): York, Peninsula, Wisconsin Rapids, Geneva.

National League

11 Chicago (6): Salt Lake City, Amarillo, St. Cloud, Wenatchee, Pocatello, Middlesboro.
12 Cincinnati (5): San Diego, Macon, Rocky Mount, Tampa, Cedar Rapids.
13 Houston (5): Oklahoma City, San Antonio, Modesto, Durham, Moultrie.
14 Los Angeles (7): Spokane, Albuquerque, Santa Barbara, St. Petersburg, Salem (OR), Great Falls, Salisbury.
15 Milwaukee (7): Toronto, Denver, Austin, Waycross, Yakima, Boise, Greenville.
16 New York (5): Buffalo, Salinas, Raleigh, Quincy, Auburn.
17 Philadelphia (6): Arkansas, Chattanooga, Bakersfield, Miami, Magic Valley, Spartanburg.
18 Pittsburgh (7): Columbus, Asheville, Reno, Kinston, Batavia, Gastonia, Kingsport.
19 St. Louis (5): Atlanta, Tulsa, Brunswick, Winnipeg, Billings.
20 San Francisco (7): Tacoma, Springfield, El Paso, Fresno, Decatur, Lexington, Salem (VA).

Co-op (x): Rock Hill, Statesville.

1963 No-Hitters

Date	Pitcher	Team	League	Opponent	Score
4-19	Bob Bishop	Springfield	Eastern	Reading	2-0
4-29	Michael Mattiace	Macon	South Atlantic	Nashville	9-0 (7)
5-7	Luis Tiant	Burlington	Carolina	Winston-Salem	4-0
5-8	Jimmy Davis	Salisbury	W. Carolinas	Rock Hill	4-0
5-11	Sandy Koufax	Los Angeles	National	San Francisco	8-0
5-13	Ernest Milius	Rock Hill	W. Carolinas	Spartanburg	0-2
5-14	Glen Davis	Salisbury	W. Carolinas	Lexington	0-1 (8)
5-17	Don Nottebart	Houston	National	Philadelphia	4-1
5-23	Bill Dawson	Clinton	Midwest	Fox Cities	10-0 (7)
5-28	Howard Stethers	Aberdeen	Northern	Grand Forks	6-0 (7)
6-1	Cliff Davis	San Antonio	Texas	El Paso	5-0 (7)
6-7	Jerome Hummitzach	Austin	Texas	Tulsa	2-0 (7)
6-9	Nat Martinez	Rochester	International	Jacksonville	5-0 (7)
6-15	Juan Marichal	San Francisco	National	Houston	1-0
6-20	Gilbert Downs	Sarasota	Florida State	Ft. Lauderdale	5-0 (7)
6-22	Orl. Marentette	Knoxville	South Atlantic	Charlotte	3-0 (7)
6-30	Johnny Ellen	Stockton	California	Bakersfield	5-0 (7)
7-4	Bill Smith	Little Rock	International	Indianapolis	4-0 (7)
7-6	Bob Radovich	Spokane	Pacific Coast	Hawaii	18-0
7-17	Ed Kikla	Nashville	South Atlantic	Augusta	8-0 (7)
7-18	Henry Harden	St. Petersburg	Florida State	Tampa	1-0
7-22	Diomedes Olivo	Atlanta	International	Toronto	1-0 (7)
7-25	Jay Dahl	Moultrie	Georgia-Florida	Brunswick	0-1
8-2	Jack Spurgin	Greensboro	Carolina	Winston-Salem	1-0
8-13	Ollie Brown	Decatur	Midwest	Wisconsin Rapids	8-0
8-23	Gerald Nelson	Oklahoma City	Pacific Coast	Salt Lake City	9-1
8-26	Lyndon Kurt	Tidewater	Carolina	Kinston	0-1 (12)
8-29	Dave Leonhard	Aberdeen	Northern	Winnipeg	5-0 (7)
9-1	Gerald Thomas	Tacoma	Pacific Coast	Denver	1-0 (7)
9-8	Jack Spurgin/ Teddy Dillard	Greensboro	Carolina	Durham	(PO)

Number in parentheses indicates innings if other than nine; "PO" indicates playoff game.

THIS DATE IN MINOR LEAGUE HISTORY

February 10, 1963, Anthony "Bunny" Brief, former first baseman/outfielder who won seven minor league home run titles and who set an American Association mark which still stands when he batted in 191 runs for the Kansas City Blues in 1921, died in Milwaukee at age 70.

May 2, 1963, Veteran Pancho Ramirez, Veracruz, Mexican League, extended his streak of innings without a walk to 60 in a 3-1 win over Monterrey.

May 17, 1963, Wellsville, New York-Penn League, had eight homers in a 13-11 victory over Erie.

May 17, 1963, Joe Wooten, Oklahoma City, Pacific Coast League, rapped seven successive hits in a 13-inning game with Denver. Wooten had six singles and a double in a 7-for-7 performance.

May 28, 1963, Ken Ramsey, Statesville, Western Carolinas League, fanned 21 in a 7-1 win over Shelby.

June 1, 1963, Salt Lake City, Pacific Coast League, ended a 16-game losing streak by defeating Seattle, 3-2.

June 16, 1963, Jim Rouse, Aberdeen first baseman, turned an unassisted triple play against Duluth-Superior in a Northern League game.

June 17, 1963, Jerry Newman, Erie, New York-Penn League, retired 29 batters in a row in one stretch and struck out 23 in a 13-inning, 3-2 victory over Batavia.

July 2, 1963, Boise, Pioneer League, ended a 19-game losing streak by downing Billings, 10-6.

July 5, 1963, Decatur, Midwest League, scored 15 runs in the first inning to best Quad City, 16-3.

August 11, 1963, Paul Alspach, Auburn, New York-Penn League, righthander, fanned 24 in a 1-0 victory over Batavia.

August 16, 1963, Andy Darriault, pitching for Batavia, New York-Penn League, whiffed 20 batters in posting a 3-1 victory over Erie.

August 24, 1963, Bob Lee, Batavia, New York-Penn League, chalked up his 16th consecutive victory in beating Geneva, 5-1. Lee would win 18 successive games and finish the season with a 20-2 mark.

November 25, 1963, James "Rube" Parnham, 67, who set the International League record for the most consecutive games won in one season, died in McKeesport, Pennsylvania. Parnham, a righthander, set the mark in 1923 by winning 20 games in a row, 33 overall, for the Baltimore Orioles. He lost seven times that year.

1964

American League
President: Joseph E. Cronin

Standings	W	L	Pct.	GB	Attend.	Manager
New York Yankees	99	63	.611	—	1,305,638	Yogi Berra
Chicago White Sox	98	64	.605	1	1,250,053	Al Lopez
Baltimore Orioles	97	65	.599	2	1,116,215	Hank Bauer
Detroit Tigers	85	77	.525	14	816,139	Chuck Dressen
Los Angeles Angels	82	80	.506	17	760,439	Bill Rigney
Cleveland Indians	79	83	.488	20	653,293	George Strickland/Birdie Tebbetts
Minnesota Twins	79	83	.488	20	1,207,514	Sam Mele
Boston Red Sox	72	90	.444	27	883,276	Johnny Pesky/Billy Herman
Washington Senators	62	100	.383	37	600,106	Gil Hodges
Kansas City Athletics	57	105	.352	42	642,478	Ed Lopat/Mel McGaha

BA: Tony Oliva, Minnesota, .323
Runs: Tony Oliva, Minnesota, 109
Hits: Tony Oliva, Minnesota, 217
RBIs: Brooks Robinson, Baltimore, 118
HRs: Harmon Killebrew, Minnesota, 49

Wins: Gary Peters, Chicago, 20
Dean Chance, Los Angeles, 20
SOs: Al Downing, New York, 217
ERA: Dean Chance, Los Angeles, 1.65
Pct: Wally Bunker, Baltimore, .792, 19-5
Saves: Dick Radatz, Boston, 29

National League
President: Warren C. Giles

Standings	W	L	Pct.	GB	Attend.	Manager
St. Louis Cardinals	93	69	.574	—	1,143,294	Johnny Keane
Cincinnati Reds	92	70	.568	1	862,466	Fred Hutchinson/Dick Sisler
Philadelphia Phillies	92	70	.568	1	1,425,891	Gene Mauch
San Francisco Giants	90	72	.556	3	1,504,364	Alvin Dark
Milwaukee Braves	88	74	.543	5	910,911	Bobby Bragan
Los Angeles Dodgers	80	82	.494	13	2,228,751	Walter Alston
Pittsburgh Pirates	80	82	.494	13	759,496	Danny Murtaugh
Chicago Cubs	76	86	.469	17	751,647	Bob Kennedy
Houston Colt .45s	66	96	.407	27	725,773	Harry Craft/Luman Harris
New York Mets	53	109	.327	40	1,732,597	Casey Stengel

BA: Roberto Clemente, Pittsburgh, .339
Runs: Dick Allen, Philadelphia, 125
Hits: Roberto Clemente, Pittsburgh, 211
Curt Flood, St. Louis, 211
RBIs: Ken Boyer, St. Louis, 119
HRs: Willie Mays, San Francisco, 47

Wins: Larry Jackson, Chicago, 24
SOs: Bob Veale, Pittsburgh, 250
ERA: Sandy Koufax, Los Angeles, 1.74
Pct: Sandy Koufax, Los Angeles, .792, 19-5
Saves: Hal Woodeshick, Houston, 23

AAA International League
President: Thomas H. Richardson

Standings	W	L	Pct.	GB	Attend.	Manager
Jacksonville Suns (19)	89	62	.589	—	169,045	Harry Walker
Syracuse Chiefs (5)	88	66	.571	2½	189,098	Frank Carswell
Buffalo Bisons (16)	80	69	.537	8	160,804	Whitey Kurowski
Rochester Red Wings (1)	82	72	.532	8½	272,091	Darrell Johnson
Toronto Maple Leafs (10, 15)	80	72	.526	9½	144,785	Sparky Anderson
Columbus Jets (18)	68	85	.444	22	134,448	Larry Shepard
Richmond Virginians (9)	65	88	.425	25	141,191	Preston Gomez
Atlanta Crackers (8)	55	93	.372	32½	68,537	Jack McKeon/Pete Appleton

Playoffs: Rochester 4 games, Jacksonville 0; Syracuse 4 games, Buffalo 3.
Finals: Rochester 4 games, Syracuse 2.

All-Star Team: 1B-Duke Carmel, Buffalo; **2B**-Jack Damaska, Jacksonville; **3B**-Joe Morgan, Jacksonville; **SS**-Ray Oyler, Syracuse; **OF**-Jim Northrup, Syracuse; Mack Jones, Syracuse; Sandy Valdespino, Atlanta; **C**-Ron Brand, Columbus; **P**-Mel Stottlemyre, Richmond; Jim Merritt, Atlanta; **MVP**-Joe Morgan, Jacksonville; **Pitcher of the Year**-Mel Stottlemyre, Richmond; **Manager**-Harry Walker, Jacksonville.

BA: Sandy Valdespino, Atlanta, .337
Runs: Mack Jones, Syracuse, 109
Hits: Sandy Valdespino, Atlanta, 179
RBIs: Mack Jones, Syracuse, 102

HRs: Mack Jones, Syracuse, 39
Wins: Bruce Brubaker, Syracuse, 15
SOs: Jim Merritt, Atlanta, 174
ERA: Bruce Brubaker, Syracuse, 2.63

AAA Pacific Coast League
President: Dewey Soriano

East Standings	W	L	Pct.	GB	Attend.	Manager
Arkansas Travelers (17)	95	61	.609	—	132,170	Frank Lucchesi
Indianapolis Indians (3)	89	69	.563	7	151,493	Les Moss
Oklahoma City 89ers (13)	88	70	.537	8	187,948	Grady Hatton
Denver Bears (15)	80	78	.508	16	139,200	Bill Adair
Salt Lake City Bees (11)	58	98	.372	37	89,789	Vedie Himsl
Dallas Rangers (6)	53	104	.338	42½	39,391	John McNamara

West Standings	W	L	Pct.	GB	Attend.	Manager
San Diego Padres (12)	91	67	.576	—	196,293	Dave Bristol
Portland Beavers (4)	90	68	.570	1	207,848	John Lipon
Spokane Indians (14)	85	73	.538	6	139,370	Danny Ozark
Seattle Rainiers (2)	81	75	.519	9	136,525	Edo Vanni
Tacoma Giants (20)	73	82	.471	16½	126,192	Charley Fox
Hawaii Islanders (7)	60	98	.380	31	154,827	Bob Lemon

Playoff: San Diego 4 games, Arkansas 3.

All-Star Team: 1B-Costen Shockley, Arkansas; **2B**-Gus Gil, San Diego; **3B**-Lou Klimchock, Denver; **SS**-Tommy Helms, San Diego; **OF**-Alex Johnson, Arkansas; Adolfo Phillips, Arkansas; Lou Johnson, Spokane; **C**-Pat Corrales, Arkansas; Jim Coker, Denver; **P**-Luis Tiant, Portland; Wilbur Wood, Seattle; Ken Rowe, Spokane; **MVP**-Tony Perez, San Diego; **Manager**-Frank Lucchesi, Arkansas.

BA: Lou Klimchock, Denver, .334
Runs: Tommie Aaron, Denver, 103
Hits: Lou Johnson, Spokane, 193
RBIs: Lou Klimchock, Denver, 112
Costen Shockley, Arkansas, 112

HRs: Costen Shockley, Arkansas, 36
Wins: Bob Locker, Indianapolis, 16
Ken Rowe, Spokane, 16
SOs: Albert Stanek, Tacoma, 220
ERA: Bruce Howard, Indianapolis, 2.20

AA Eastern League
President: A. Rankin Johnson

Standings	W	L	Pct.	GB	Attend.	Manager
Elmira Pioneers (1)	82	58	.586	—	65,528	Earl Weaver
Reading Red Sox (2)	80	60	.571	2	51,200	Eddie Popowski
Springfield Giants (20)	77	63	.550	5	63,221	Andy Gilbert
Charleston Indians (4)	70	70	.500	12	45,422	Bob Nieman
Williamsport Mets (16)	56	84	.400	26	51,002	Ernie White
York White Roses (10)	55	85	.393	27	35,540	Jim Lemon

Playoffs: None.

All-Star Team: 1B-Tony Horton, Reading; **2B**-Johnny Parker, Charleston; **3B**-Frank Johnson, Springfield; **SS**-Mike Andrews, Reading; **OF**-Paul Blair, Elmira; Jim McClain, Springfield; Ron Swoboda, Williamsport; **C**-Andy Etchebarren, Elmira; Mike Ryan, Reading; **P**-Frank Bertaina, Elmira; Tom Arruda, Springfield; **Manager**-Earl Weaver, Elmira.

BA: Paul Blair, Elmira, .311
Runs: Jim McClain, Springfield, 96
Hits: Jim McClain, Springfield, 155
RBIs: Jose Calero, Springfield, 86
HRs: Bobby Sanders, Williamsport, 15

Wins: Tom Arruda, Springfield, 16
Fran Kasheta, Springfield, 16
SOs: Tom Arruda, Springfield, 178
ERA: Joe Overton, Springfield, 1.72

AA Mexican League
President: Antonio Ramirez Muro

Standings	W	L	Pct.	GB	Attend.	Manager
Mexico City Diablos Rojos	82	58	.586	—	464,689	Tomas Herrera
Puebla Pericos	79	61	.564	3	181,018	Tony Castano
Veracruz Aguilas	78	62	.557	4	237,705	Wilfredo Calvino
Mexico City Tigres	76	63	.547	5½	312,359	Jose Luis Garcia
Poza Rica Petroleros	70	70	.500	12	362,298	Memo Garibay
Monterrey Sultanes	66	74	.471	16	188,058	Clemente Carrera
Reynosa Broncs	61	79	.436	21	180,402	Ray Garza/Santos Amaro
Jalisco Charros	47	92	.338	34½	232,896	Jim Rivera

Playoffs: None.

All-Star Team: 1B-Hector Espino, Monterrey; **2B**-Moises Camacho, Puebla; **3B**-Leonardo Rodriguez, MC Diablos Rojos; **SS**-Jorge Fitch, Puebla; **OF**-Miguel Fernandez, MC Diablos Rojos; Angel Scull, Poza Rica; Al Pinkston, Veracruz; **C**-Rene Friol, Veracruz; Eloy Gutierrez, MC Tigres; **P**-Alberto Osorio, Veracruz; Andres Ayon, Puebla; **Manager**-Wilfredo Calvino, Veracruz.

BA: Hector Espino, Monterrey, .371
Runs: Hector Espino, Monterrey, 118
Hits: Alfredo Rios, Monterrey, 189
RBIs: George Prescott, Poza Rica, 123

HRs: Hector Espino, Monterrey, 46
Wins: Miguel Sotelo, Puebla, 17
SOs: Jose Ramon Lopez, Monterrey, 213
ERA: Alberto Osorio, Veracruz, 2.56

AA Southern League
President: Sam C. Smith

Standings	W	L	Pct.	GB	Attend.	Manager
Lynchburg White Sox (3)	81	59	.579	—	78,157	George Noga
Birmingham Barons (6)	80	60	.571	1	95,703	Haywood Sullivan
Macon Peaches (12)	75	65	.536	6	60,097	John "Red" Davis
Charlotte Hornets (8)	73	67	.521	8	59,886	Alfred Evans
Knoxville Smokies (5)	67	73	.479	14	41,803	Bobby Mavis
Chattanooga Lookouts (17)	65	74	.468	15½	40,331	Andy Seminick
Columbus Yankees (9)	65	74	.468	15½	67,117	Rube Walker
Asheville Tourists (18)	52	86	.377	28	41,086	Ray Hathaway/Bob Clear

*Won first-half   **Won second-half   ***Won both halves
Numbers after nicknames indicate farm system.
Affiliation listed at end of each year.

484

Playoffs: None.

All-Star Team: 1B-Lee May, Macon; **2B**-Len Boehmer, Macon; **3B**-Dick Kenworthy, Lynchburg; **SS**-Bert Campaneris, Birmingham; **OF**-George Spriggs, Asheville; Mickey Stanley, Knoxville; Tommy Reynolds, Birmingham; **C**-Jim Napier, Lynchburg; Bill Madden, Columbus; **P**-Manly Johnston, Lynchburg; Paul Lindblad, Birmingham; **Manager**-George Noga, Lynchburg.

BA: Len Boehmer, Macon, .329
Runs: Dick Kenworthy, Lynchburg, 99
Hits: Dick Kenworthy, Lynchburg, 174
RBIs: Lee May, Macon, 110
HRs: Dick Kenworthy, Lynchburg, 29
Wins: Manly Johnston, Lynchburg, 20
SOs: David Galligan, Macon, 168
ERA: Manly Johnston, Lynchburg, 2.46

AA Texas League
President: James H. Burris

Standings	W	L	Pct.	GB	Attend.	Manager
San Antonio Bullets (13)	85	55	.670	—	85,808	Lou Fitzgerald
Tulsa Oilers (19)	79	61	.564	6	200,430	Grover Resinger
Albuquerque Dukes (14)	75	65	.536	10	85,597	Clay Bryant
El Paso Sun Kings (20)	67	73	.479	18	90,244	Dave Garcia
Austin Senators (15)	63	77	.450	22	49,877	Buddy Hicks
Ft. Worth Cats (11)	51	89	.364	34	93,574	Alex Grammas

Playoffs: San Antonio 3 games, El Paso 1; Tulsa 3 games, Albuquerque 2.
Finals: San Antonio 3 games, Tulsa 1.

All-Star Team: 1B-Mel Corbo, Albuquerque; Larry "Moose" Stubing, El Paso; **2B**-Joe Morgan, San Antonio; **3B**-Don LeJohn, Albuquerque; **SS**-Sonny Jackson, San Antonio; **OF**-Braxton Bailey, Albuquerque; Bobby Tolan, Tulsa; Joe Patterson, Tulsa; Leo Posada, San Antonio; Ellis Burton, Ft. Worth; **C**-Hector Valle, Albuquerque; Butler Powell, Austin; Clint Courtney, San Antonio; **Util**-Chuck Harrison, San Antonio; **P**-Chris Zachary, San Antonio; Don Bradey, San Antonio; Jim Ward, Albuquerque; Nellie Briles, Tulsa; Paul Doyle, El Paso; Pat House, Austin; **MVP**-Joe Morgan, San Antonio; **Pitcher of the Year**-Chris Zachary, San Antonio; **Manager**-Grover Resinger, Tulsa.

BA: Mel Corbo, Albuquerque, .339
Runs: Joe Patterson, Tulsa, 116
Hits: Braxton Bailey, Albuquerque, 174
RBIs: Larry "Moose" Stubing, El Paso, 120
HRs: Chuck Harrison, San Antonio, 40
Wins: Jim Ward, Albuquerque, 17
SOs: Jim Ward, Albuquerque, 224
Charles Spell, Albuquerque, 224
ERA: Dick Burwell, Ft. Worth, 2.55

A California League
President: Edward J. Mulligan

Standings	W	L	Pct.	GB	Attend.	Manager
Fresno Giants***(20)	86	53	.619	—	34,203	Bill Werle
Salinas Mets (16)	79	59	.572	6½	16,009	Kerby Farrell
San Jose Bees (7)	73	67	.521	13½	40,185	Rocky Bridges
Stockton Ports (1)	69	70	.496	17	28,265	Harry Dunlop
Santa Barbara Dodgers (14)	68	71	.489	18	13,408	Al Ronning
Reno Silver Sox (18)	66	71	.482	19	15,178	Tom Saffell/Harvey Koepf
Modesto Colts (13)	58	81	.417	28	16,849	Chuck Churn
Bakersfield Bears (17)	56	83	.403	30	26,725	Moose Johnson

Playoffs: None.

All-Star Team: 1B-Dave Allen, Salinas; **2B**-John Reed, Stockton; **3B**-Bob Mitchell, San Jose; **SS**-Butch Land, Reno; **OF**-Ollie Brown, Fresno; Bob Taylor, Fresno; Hal Green, San Jose; **C**-Larry Fidalgo, Reno; **P**-Masanori Murakami, Fresno; Pedro Reinoso, Fresno; Ed Barnowski, Stockton; Bob Parker, Salinas; **MVP**-Ollie Brown, Fresno; **Rookie of the Year**-Masanori Murakami, Fresno; **Manager**-Bill Werle, Fresno.

BA: Bob Taylor, Fresno, .364
Runs: Ollie Brown, Fresno, 111
Hits: Bob Taylor, Fresno, 188
RBIs: Ollie Brown, Fresno, 133
HRs: Ollie Brown, Fresno, 40
Wins: Pedro Reinoso, Fresno, 18
SOs: Ed Barnowski, Stockton, 321
ERA: Ed Barnowski, Stockton, 1.95

A Carolina League
President: J.C. "Bill" Jessup

East Standings	W	L	Pct.	GB	Attend.	Manager
Kinston Eagles (18)	79	59	.572	—	101,915	Pete Peterson
Portsmouth Tides (3)	75	63	.543	4	83,255	Allen Jones
Peninsula Grays (12)	61	76	.445	17½	38,020	Jack Cassini
Rocky Mount Senators (10)	61	77	.442	18	55,561	Owen Friend
Wilson Tobs (8)	57	82	.410	22½	24,599	Ralph Rowe

West Standings	W	L	Pct.	GB	Attend.	Manager
Winston-Salem Red Sox (2)	82	57	.590	—	55,361	Bill Slack
Greensboro Yankees (9)	76	61	.555	5	58,528	Loren Babe
Raleigh Cards (19)	76	62	.551	5½	52,620	George Kissell
Burlington Indians (4)	68	70	.493	13½	48,003	Bill Herring
Durham Bulls (13)	54	82	.397	26½	30,631	Billy Goodman/Walt Matthews

Playoffs: Winston-Salem 2 games, Greensboro 0; Portsmouth 2 games, Kinston 0.
Finals: Winston-Salem 2 games, Portsmouth 0.

All-Star Team: 1B-Ron Durham, Burlington; **2B**-Stan Swanson, Peninsula; **3B**-Jose "Coco" Laboy, Raleigh; **SS**-Chet Trail, Greensboro; **OF**-Steve Whitaker, Greensboro; Michael Page, Winston-Salem; Sam Parrilla, Burlington; Ed Stroud, Portsmouth; **C**-Jim French, Rocky Mount; Tommy Smith, Raleigh; **Util**-Bill Tarrolly, Wilson; **P**-Casey Cox, Rocky Mount; Don Hagen, Raleigh; Mario Pagano, Winston-Salem; Chuck Holle, Wilson; **MVP**-Ed Stroud, Portsmouth; **Manager**-Bill Slack, Winston-Salem.

BA: Michael Page, Winston-Salem, .344
Runs: Ed Stroud, Portsmouth, 108
Hits: Ed Stroud, Portsmouth, 167
RBIs: Steve Whitaker, Greensboro, 100
HRs: Edwin Chasteen, Raleigh, 28
Wins: Don Hagen, Raleigh, 16
SOs: Don Hagen, Raleigh, 202
ERA: Tom Moser, Burlington, 2.47

A Florida State League
President: George MacDonald, Sr.

Standings	W	L	Pct.	GB	Attend.	Manager
St. Petersburg Saints**(14)	83	55	.601	—	75,780	Roy Hartsfield
Ft. Lauderdale Yankees*(9)	81	59	.579	3	40,069	Frank Verdi
Lakeland Tigers (5)	67	69	.493	15	15,935	Al Federoff
Tampa Tarpons (12)	68	71	.489	15½	58,759	Pinky May
Daytona Beach Islanders (6)	63	71	.470	18	18,755	Grady Wilson/Bill Posedel/Lew Krausse
Sarasota Sun Sox (3)	63	71	.470	18	36,521	Ira Hutchinson
Miami Marlins (17)	64	75	.460	19½	103,687	Bobby Morgan
Orlando Twins (8)	60	78	.435	23	32,923	Harry Warner

Playoff: Ft. Lauderdale 3 games, St. Petersburg 1.

All-Star Team: 1B-Don Pepper, Lakeland; **2B**-Rufus Anderson, Lakeland; **3B**-Stan Bledsoe, Daytona Beach; **SS**-Haley Young, Sarasota; **OF**-Alan Lewis, Daytona Beach; Bill Voss, Lakeland; Angie Galasso, Miami; **C**-Joe Cherry, Sarasota; Jake Martinez, Tampa; **P**-Bud Scherman, Orlando; Dave Morgan, St. Petersburg; **Manager**-Roy Hartsfield, St. Petersburg.

BA: Mike Ferraro, Ft. Lauderdale, .317
Runs: Willie Mobley, Ft. Lauderdale, 107
Hits: Mike Ferraro, Ft. Lauderdale, 158
RBIs: Mike Ferraro, Ft. Lauderdale, 77
HRs: Don Pepper, Lakeland, 11
Wins: Jim Smith, Ft. Lauderdale, 17
SOs: Tom Frondorf, Tampa, 167
ERA: Jim Smith, Ft. Lauderdale, 1.38

A Mexican Center League
President: Antonio Ramirez (Muro)

Standings	W	L	Pct.	GB	Attend.	Manager
Leon Broncos	75	44	.630	—	53,638	Santos Amaro/Dan Bankhead
Guanajuato Tuzos	67	52	.563	8	50,000	Domingo Santana
San Luis Potosi Reds	62	58	.517	13½	59,633	Manuel Arroyo/Andres Tanaka
Salamanca Tigres	60	60	.500	15½	44,143	Pompeyo Davalillo
Saltillo Sultanes	58	62	.483	17½	33,439	Avelino Canizares
Fresnillo Charros	37	83	.308	38½	31,868	Felipe Hernandez

Playoffs: None.

All-Star Team: 1B-Ramiro Caballero, Leon; **2B**-Jose Garibay, Leon; **3B**-Alfonso Preciado, Guanajuato; **SS**-Francisco Rodriguez, Salamanca; **OF**-Jorge Negrete, Salamanca; Juan Rodriguez, Guanajuato; Jose Angel Guerrero, Fresnillo; **C**-Sergio Gonzalez, Salamanca; Sergio Aguirre, Saltillo; **P**-Exiquio Colis, San Luis Potosi; Margarito Flores, San Luis Potosi; **Manager**-Dan Bankhead, Leon.

BA: Ramiro Caballero, Leon, .380
Runs: Ramiro Caballero, Leon, 135
Hits: Ramiro Caballero, Leon, 175
RBIs: Ramiro Caballero, Leon, 145
HRs: Ramiro Caballero, Leon, 35
Wins: Rosario Valdez, Salamanca, 14
SOs: Rosario Valdez, Salamanca, 195
ERA: Exiquio Colis, San Luis Potosi, 2.71

A Mexican Southeast League
President: Antonio Ramirez (Muro)

Standings	W	L	Pct.	GB	Attend.	Manager
Tabasco Plataneros*	52	35	.598	—	107,579	Corito Varona
Campeche Pirates**	50	38	.568	2½	90,456	Hector Rodriguez
Yucatan Venados	43	46	.483	10	87,612	Leonel Aldama
Puerto Mexico Portenos	32	58	.356	21½	41,603	Jesus Diaz/Ray Garza/Mauro Ramirez

Playoff: Tabasco 4 games, Campeche 2.

All-Star Team: 1B-Celso Oviedo, Puerto Mexico; **2B**-Manuel Lopez, Campeche; **3B**-Benjamin Reyes, Campeche; **SS**-Benjamin Cerda, Tabasco; **OF**-Luis Casablanca, Yucatan; Asdrubal Baro, Campeche; Earl Wood, Yucatan; **C**-Tomas Martell, Campeche; Hector Arellano, Yucatan; **P**-Jose Leyva, Tabasco; Alfonso Cisneros, Tabasco; **Manager**-Corito Varona, Tabasco.

BA: Manuel Lopez, Campeche, .339
Runs: Enrique Garcia, Yucatan, 68
Hits: Manuel Lopez, Campeche, 117
RBIs: Tomas Martell, Campeche, 66
HRs: Celso Oviedo, Puerto Mexico, 15
Wins: Jose Leyva, Tabasco, 14
SOs: Raul Galata, Puerto Mexico, 119
ERA: Jose Leyva, Tabasco, 2.01

A Midwest League
President: Walter C. Wagner

Standings	W	L	Pct.	GB	Attend.	Manager
Fox Cities Foxes**(1)	81	43	.653	—	45,557	Billy DeMars
Clinton C-Sox*(3)	77	48	.616	4½	73,812	Don Bacon/Hugh Mulcahy
Quad Cities Angels (7)	62	56	.525	16	108,129	Chuck Tanner
Burlington Bees (6)	63	59	.516	17	64,491	Robbie Robertson
Waterloo Hawks (2)	65	61	.516	17	50,821	Matt Sczesny
Decatur Commodores (20)	61	63	.492	20	83,043	Richard Klaus
Dubuque Packers (4)	59	63	.484	21	63,234	Walter Novick
Cedar Rapids Red Raiders (12)	51	69	.425	28	58,873	Rollie Hemsley
Wisconsin Rapids Twins (8)	50	71	.413	29½	67,330	Joe Clinton
Quincy Gems	42	78	.350	37	39,338	Jim Finigan/Les Peden

Playoff: Fox Cities 1 game, Clinton 0.

BA: Dave May, Fox Cities, .368
Runs: Dave May, Fox Cities, 111
    Eusebio Rosas, Burlington, 111
Hits: Dave May, Fox Cities, 166
RBIs: Clarence Stanley, Decatur, 93

HRs: Rene Lachemann, Burlington, 24
Wins: Michael Carubia, Quad Cities, 15
SOs: Joseph McKirahan, Decatur, 208
ERA: Michael Carubia, Quad Cities, 1.69

A New York-Pennsylvania League
President: Vincent M. McNamara

Standings	W	L	Pct.	GB	Attend.	Manager
Auburn Mets (16)	79	48	.622	—	50,163	Clyde McCullough
Geneva Senators (10).........	79	51	.608	1½	23,406	Wayne Terwilliger
Wellsville Red Sox (2)	70	60	.538	10½	20,083	Larry Thomas
Jamestown Tigers (5).........	68	60	.531	11½	34,121	Jack Phillips
Binghamton Triplets (15) ...	58	71	.450	22	38,901	Andy Pafko and Paul Snyder
Batavia Pirates (18)	33	97	.245	47½	24,920	Gene Baker

Playoff: Auburn 4 games, Geneva 2.

All-Star Team: 1B-Jim Mooring, Jamestown; **2B**-Richard Haymore, Auburn; **3B**-Juan Munoz, Geneva; **SS**-John Pavlus, Auburn; **OF**-Mike Lum, Binghamton; John May, Binghamton; Bill Schlesinger, Wellsville; Danny Napoleon, Auburn; **C**-Paul Casanova, Geneva; Gerald Moses, Wellsville; **Util**-Anthony Alello, Wellsville; Dick Bazinet, Auburn; **P**-Dick Nold, Geneva; Jack Nutter, Jamestown; Bill Craft, Auburn; Michael Blue, Geneva; **Manager**-Clyde McCullough, Auburn.

BA: Wenton "Bill" Etheridge, Binghamton, .365
Runs: Danny Napoleon, Auburn, 129
    Bill Schlesinger, Wellsville, 129
Hits: Danny Napoleon, Auburn, 175
RBIs: Danny Napoleon, Auburn, 134

HRs: Bill Schlesinger, Wellsville, 37
Wins: Dick Nold, Geneva, 20
SOs: Dick Nold, Geneva, 274
ERA: Bill Craft, Auburn, 3.28
Pct: Bill Craft, Auburn, .750, 15-5

A Northern League
President: Brooks Baukol

Standings	W	L	Pct.	GB	Attend.	Manager
Aberdeen Pheasants (1)	80	37	.684	—	46,397	Cal Ripken, Sr.
Grand Forks Chiefs (14).....	69	50	.580	12	34,654	James Williams
Duluth-Superior Dukes (5) ...	61	55	.526	18½	30,830	Gail Henley
Winnipeg Goldeyes (19)......	52	65	.444	28	85,425	Ron Plaza
St. Cloud Rox (11).............	54	68	.443	28½	34,574	Walt Dixon
Bismarck-Mandan Pards (8) ..	39	80	.328	42	19,332	Vern Morgan

Baukol Playoffs: Aberdeen 19-10, Duluth-Superior 15-10, Grand Forks 15-13, St. Cloud 15-18, Bismarck-Mandan 13-18, Winnipeg 11-19. (Baukol Playoffs based on last 30 days of season.)

All-Star Team: 1B-Michael Fiore, Aberdeen; **2B**-Mickey Dobbins, Grand Forks; **3B**-Nellie Cochran, Aberdeen; **SS**-Mark Belanger, Aberdeen; **OF**-John Scruggs, Aberdeen; Felix de Leon, Winnipeg; Mickey Strickland, Grand Forks; Tom Richards, Grand Forks; **C**-George Farson, Aberdeen; Jim Procopio, St. Cloud; **P**-Chuck Lauritson, Grand Forks; William Hall, Grand Forks; Dave Boswell, Bismarck-Mandan; Ed Watt, Aberdeen; **Manager**-Vern Morgan, Bismarck-Mandan; Cal Ripken, Sr., Aberdeen; James Williams, Grand Forks.

BA: Andy Kosco, Duluth-Superior/Bismarck-Mandan, .346
Runs: Michael Fiore, Aberdeen, 88
Hits: Andy Kosco, Duluth-Superior/Bismarck-Mandan, 153
RBIs: Andy Kosco, Duluth-Superior/Bismarck-Mandan, 97

HRs: Andy Kosco, Duluth-Superior/Bismarck-Mandan, 28
Wins: Dave Leonhard, Aberdeen, 16
SOs: Dave Boswell, Bismarck-Mandan, 173
ERA: William Hall, Grand Forks, 1.71

A Northwest League
President: James Fleishman

Standings	W	L	Pct.	GB	Attend.	Manager
Salem Dodgers (14)............	78	62	.557	—	51,914	Stan Wasiak
Eugene Emeralds*(17)	77	63	.550	1	65,884	Bob Wellman
Yakima Bears**(15)..........	72	68	.514	6	39,300	Hub Kittle
Lewiston Broncs (6)	70	70	.500	8	34,608	Bob Hofman
Tri-City Angels (7)	66	74	.471	12	51,220	Tom Heath
Wenatchee Chiefs (11)	57	83	.407	21	24,529	Joe Macko

Playoff: Yakima 3 games, Eugene 0.

All-Star Team: 1B-Dick McLaughlin, Salem; **2B**-Rafael Gomez, Yakima; **3B**-Winston Llenas, Tri-City; **SS**-John Donaldson, Lewiston; **OF**-Clarence Jones, Salem; Bill Robinson, Yakima; Jack Warner, Tri-City; **C**-Jim Campanis, Salem; Del Bates, Tri-City; **P**-Bill Edgerton, Lewiston; Philip Brown, Salem; **Manager**-Stan Wasiak, Salem.

BA: Bill Robinson, Yakima, .348
Runs: Clarence Jones, Salem, 114
Hits: Clarence Jones, Salem, 168
    Winston Llenas, Tri-City, 168
RBIs: Clarence Jones, Salem, 120

HRs: John Warner, Tri-City, 37
Wins: Philip Brown, Salem, 17
SOs: Gene Garnell, Yakima, 199
ERA: Gene Garnell, Yakima, 3.02

A Western Carolinas League
President: John H. Moss

Standings	W	L	Pct.	GB	Attend.	Manager
Salisbury Dodgers**(14)....	77	51	.602	—	35,705	George Scherger
Rock Hill Cardinals*(19)....	76	51	.598	½	54,441	Hal Smith
Lexington Giants (20).........	71	54	.568	4½	52,008	Max Lanier
Greenville Braves (15)........	63	63	.500	13	26,007	Bill Steinecke/Jimmy Brown
Gastonia Pirates (18)	60	68	.469	17	38,319	Bob Clear/Ray Hathaway
Shelby Yankees (9)...........	59	68	.465	17½	34,620	Gary Blaylock
Statesville Colts (2, 13).......	52	70	.426	22	26,324	Dave Philley/Rudy York
Spartanburg Phillies (17)....	47	80	.370	29½	46,115	Dick Teed

Playoff: Salisbury 2 games, Rock Hill 1.

All-Star Team: 1B-Gary Holman, Salisbury; **2B**-Richard Schmidt, Salisbury; **3B**-Murray Cook, Gastonia; **SS**-Jose Herrera, Statesville; **OF**-Roy Foster, Gastonia; Bill Parlier, Salisbury; John Jones, Greenville; **C**-Gary Stone, Rock Hill; Raymond Johnson, Salisbury; **P**-Rich Licklider, Lexington; John Purdin, Salisbury; **MVP**-Richard Schmidt, Salisbury; **Most Outstanding Player**-Bill Parlier, Salisbury; **Most Outstanding Pitcher**-Rich Licklider, Lexington; **Manager**-George Scherger, Salisbury.

BA: Richard Schmidt, Salisbury, .306
Runs: Richard Schmidt, Salisbury, 86
Hits: Murray Cook, Gastonia, 132
RBIs: Roy Foster, Gastonia, 72

HRs: Bill Parlier, Salisbury, 20
Wins: Rich Licklider, Lexington, 16
SOs: Herman Alvarez, Lexington, 243
ERA: Rich Licklider, Lexington, 1.52

R Appalachian League
President: Chauncey De Vault

Standings	W	L	Pct.	GB	Attend.	Manager
Johnson City Yankees (9)...	47	24	.662	—	14,258	Lamar North
Wytheville Athletics (6)	38	33	.535	9	17,120	Gus Niarhos
Salem Pirates (18)..............	30	41	.426	17	36,184	George Detore
Bluefield Orioles (1)..........	27	44	.380	20	15,144	Jim Frey

Playoffs: None.

All-Star Team: 1B-Larry Elsasser, Wytheville; **2B**-Ken Gay, Bluefield; Dave Trulock, Johnson City; **3B**-Bobby Christian, Johnson City; **SS**-Bobby Murcer, Johnson City; **OF**-Ross Moschitto, Johnson City; James Walrath, Johnson City; Jim Heilman, Salem; **C**-Ellie Rodriguez, Wytheville; **Util IF**-Terry Tewell, Johnson City; **Util OF**-Gary Fancher, Bluefield; **P**-Perry Pappas, Johnson City; Frank DeVivo, Johnson City; **Rookie of the Year**-Ross Moschitto, Johnson City; **Manager**-Lamar North, Johnson City.

BA: James Walrath, Johnson City, .354
Runs: Ross Moschitto, Johnson City, 72
Hits: John Jeter, Salem, 88
RBIs: James Walrath, Johnson City, 84

HRs: Ross Moschitto, Johnson City, 20
Wins: Frank DeVivo, Johnson City, 11
SOs: Frank DeVivo, Johnson City, 123
ERA: Frank DeVivo, Johnson City, 2.83

R Cocoa Rookie League

Standings	W	L	Pct.	GB	Manager
Melbourne Twins (8)	34	18	.654	—	Fred Waters
Florida Mets (16)	28	22	.560	5	Ken Deal
Cocoa Colts (13)................	23	29	.442	11	Dave Philley
Cocoa Tigers (5)	17	33	.340	16	Harold Daugherty

All games played at Cocoa, Florida.
Total Attendance: 1,683.

Playoffs: None.

BA: Lawrence Seneta, Tigers, .383
Runs: Jim Bachus, Twins, 44
Hits: Lawrence Seneta, Tigers, 52
RBIs: Albert Yates, Mets, 31

HRs: Albert Yates, Mets, 2
    John Agnetti, Mets, 2
    Gerald Lyscio, Twins, 2
Wins: Gerald Lyscio, Twins, 7
SOs: Claude Melton, Twins, 63
ERA: Claude Melton, Twins, 1.22

R Pioneer League
President: Claude Engberg

Standings	W	L	Pct.	GB	Attend.	Manager
Treasure Valley Cubs#(11)....	40	25	.615	—	19,095	George Freese
Magic Valley Cowboys (20)..	33	32	.508	7	26,126	Rex Carr
Pocatello Chiefs (14).........	30	36	.455	10½	13,058	Ernie Rodriguez
Idaho Falls Angels (7)	28	38	.424	12½	17,706	John Fitzpatrick

#represented Caldwell, Idaho.

Playoffs: None.

BA: Juan Joa, Magic Valley, .311
Runs: Juan Joa, Magic Valley, 59
Hits: Juan Joa, Magic Valley, 74
RBIs: John Allison, Pocatello, 52
HRs: Johnny Smith, Pocatello, 12

Wins: Joe Robinson, Pocatello, 8
    Jorge Rubio, Idaho Falls, 8
SOs: Dennis Daboll, Pocatello, 131
ERA: Paul Symeon, Treasure Valley, 2.13

R Sarasota Rookie League

Standings	W	L	Pct.	GB	Manager
Braves (15)	36	23	.610	—	Paul Snyder
Cardinals (19)	30	30	.500	6½	Fred Koenig
White Sox (3)	29	31	.483	7½	Frank Parenti
Yankees (9)	24	35	.407	12	Bill Shantz

All games played at Sarasota, Florida.

All-Star Team: 1B-Wenlyn Lindeman, White Sox; **2B**-Henry Kress, Cardinals; **3B**-Oscar Boultinghouse, Cardinals; **SS**-James Vickers, White Sox; **OF**-Randall Hoxie, White Sox; Milton Menton, Braves; Jacob Burroughs, Cardinals; **C**-Larry Snyder, Braves; **Util IF**-Clarence Warmsley, Yankees; **Util OF**-Jim Ridley, Braves; **P**-Ken Murphy, Braves; Alex

Bonci, Braves; **MVP**-Leora Montgomery, Braves.

BA: Milton Menton, Braves, .311
Runs: Leora Montgomery, Braves, 34
Hits: Milton Menton, Braves, 61
RBIs: Milton Menton, Braves, 25
HRs: Michael Mantsch, Braves, 3

Wins: Alex Bonci, Braves, 7
Robert DuGuid, Braves, 7
Ken Murphy, Braves, 7
SOs: Tom Rowe, White Sox, 72
ERA: Alex Bonci, Braves, 1.00

1964 Interleague Post Season Play

World Series
St. Louis (National) 4 games, New York (American) 3

1964 Major League Farm Systems

American League

1 Baltimore (6): Rochester, Elmira, Stockton, Fox Cities, Aberdeen, Bluefield.
2 Boston (6): Seattle, Reading, Winston-Salem, Waterloo, Wellsville, Statesville.
3 Chicago (6): Indianapolis, Lynchburg, Portsmouth, Sarasota, Clinton, Sarasota Rookie.
4 Cleveland (4): Portland, Charleston, Burlington (NC), Dubuque.
5 Detroit (6): Syracuse, Knoxville, Lakeland, Jamestown, Duluth-Superior, Cocoa.
6 Kansas City (6): Dallas, Birmingham, Daytona Beach, Burlington (IA), Lewiston, Wytheville.
7 Los Angeles (5): Hawaii, San Jose, Quad Cities, Tri-City, Idaho Falls.
8 Minnesota (7): Atlanta, Charlotte, Wilson, Orlando, Wisconsin Rapids, Bismarck-Mandan, Melbourne.
9 New York (7): Richmond, Columbus (GA), Greensboro, Ft. Lauderdale, Shelby, Johnson City, Sarasota Rookie.
10 Washington (4): Toronto, York, Rocky Mount, Geneva.

National League

11 Chicago (5): Salt Lake City, Ft. Worth, St. Cloud, Wenatchee, Treasure Valley.
12 Cincinnati (5): San Diego, Macon, Peninsula, Tampa, Cedar Rapids.
13 Houston (6): Oklahoma City, San Antonio, Modesto, Durham, Statesville, Cocoa.
14 Los Angeles (8): Spokane, Albuquerque, Santa Barbara, St. Petersburg, Grand Forks, Salem (OR), Salisbury, Pocatello.
15 Milwaukee (7): Toronto, Denver, Austin, Binghamton, Yakima, Greenville, Sarasota Rookie.
16 New York (5): Buffalo, Williamsport, Salinas, Auburn, Florida (Cocoa).
17 Philadelphia (6): Arkansas, Chattanooga, Bakersfield, Miami, Eugene, Spartanburg.
18 Pittsburgh (7): Columbus (OH), Asheville, Reno, Kinston, Batavia, Gastonia, Salem (VA).
19 St. Louis (6): Jacksonville, Tulsa, Raleigh, Winnipeg, Rock Hill, Sarasota Rookie.
20 San Francisco (7): Tacoma, Springfield, El Paso, Fresno, Decatur, Lexington, Magic Valley.

1964 No-Hitters

Date	Pitcher	Team	League	Opponent	Score
4-23	Ken T. Johnson	Houston	National	Cincinnati	0-1
4-23	Bill Singer	Spokane	Pacific Coast	Dallas	3-0 (7)
5-3	Doug Gallagher	Knoxville	Southern	Asheville	3-0 (7)
5-6	Sam McDowell	Portland	Pacific Coast	Salt Lake City	8-0
5-6	Francis Smith	Charleston	Eastern	Elmira	6-1
5-14	Gilbert Downs/ Charley Payne	Greensboro	Carolina	Wilson	2-0 (7)
5-21	Phil Massicotte	Daytona Beach	Florida State	Miami	3-0
5-30	Kent Thaxton/ Bob Saterfield	Statesville	W. Carolinas	Shelby	1-0 (7)
6-2	Bob Proctor	Salisbury	W. Carolinas	Spartanburg	3-0 (7)
6-3	Darrell Clark	Duluth-Superior	Northern	Bismarck-Mandan	2-0
6-4	Sandy Koufax	Los Angeles	National	Philadelphia	3-0
6-4	Ed Barnowski	Stockton	California	Salinas	3-2 (10)
6-17	Bobby Aldridge	Lexington	W. Carolinas	Gastonia	6-0 (7)
6-19	Jim Palmer	Aberdeen	Northern	Duluth-Superior	8-0
6-21	Jim Bunning	Philadelphia	National	New York	6-0 (P)
6-22	Dick Estelle	Tacoma	Pacific Coast	Denver	2-0
6-22	Gilbert Blanco	Ft. Lauderdale	Florida State	Orlando	1-0 (7)
6-23	Norbert Rodgers	Clinton	Midwest	Quincy	2-0 (7)
6-24	Jay Hook	Denver	Pacific Coast	Tacoma	1-2 (10)
6-30	Carl Nelson	Williamsport	Eastern	York	2-0 (7)
7-3	Joel Gibson	Arkansas	Pacific Coast	Dallas	4-0
7-3	Tug McGraw	Mets	Cocoa Rookie	Colts	4-0 (7)
7-4	Gerald Lyscio/ Claude Melton	Twins	Cocoa Rookie	Tigers	2-0 (7)
7-9	Rich Masterman	Winnipeg	Northern	St. Cloud	2-0 (7)
7-11	Bob Baird/ Carlos Medrano	York	Eastern	Springfield	0-1 (7)
7-16	Nick DeMatteis	El Paso	Texas	Tulsa	1-0
7-24	Leo Newton	Rock Hill	W. Carolinas	Lexington	3-0 (7)
7-26	John Miller	Rochester	International	Columbus	2-0 (7)
7-27	Ron Morris/ Tom Rowe	White Sox	Sarasota Rookie	Braves	0-1
7-29	Ross Mersinger	Gastonia	W. Carolinas	Greenville	5-0 (5)
8-3	Ray Miller	Lexington	W. Carolinas	Statesville	0-0 (8)
8-8	John Purdin	Salisbury	W. Carolinas	Lexington	1-0 (P,7)
8-14	Ken Murphy	Braves	Sarasota Rookie	White Sox	1-0
8-14	Bill Palko/ Dave Morgan	St. Petersburg	Florida State	Sarasota	1-0
8-18	Robert Richmond	Miami	Florida State	Daytona Beach	5-0 (7)
8-18	Leroy Heiser	Rocky Mount	Carolina	Burlington	5-0 (7)
8-25	Lawrence Yellen	Oklahoma City	Pacific Coast	Indianapolis	0-0 (5)
8-29	Raymond Newman	Lakeland	Florida State	Miami	10-1 (7)
8-30	Ed Barnowski	Stockton	California	Reno	3-0 (7)
8-30	Claude Melton/ Gerald Lyscio	Twins	Cocoa Rookie	Colts	2-1 (5)
9-5	Steve Cosgrove	Elmira	Eastern	York	6-0
9-8	Mike Daniel	St. Petersburg	Florida State	Ft. Lauderdale	0-1 (PO,8)
9-9	Morris Steevens	Arkansas	Pacific Coast	Dallas	3-0

Number in parentheses indicates innings if other than nine; "P" indicates perfect game; "PO" indicates playoff game.

THIS DATE IN MINOR LEAGUE HISTORY

May 9, 1964, Ed Barnowski, Stockton, California League, whiffed 20 in a 5-1 victory over Santa Barbara.

May 12, 1964, Steve Caria, Fox Cities, Midwest League, whiffed 20 batters, including nine in a row, in a 6-3 win over Quincy.

May 15, 1964, Jack Nutter, Jamestown, New York-Penn League, righthander, struck out 20 in a 7-4 triumph over Wellsville.

May 16, 1964, Indianapolis, Pacific Coast League, scored 15 runs in the first inning to whip Seattle, 18-0.

May 16, 1964, Russell "Buzz" Arlett, one of the minor league's greatest sluggers, died in Minneapolis at the age of 65. A pitcher when he broke in with Oakland in 1918, Arlett shifted to the outfield after hurting his arm. He posted 108 victories with Oakland, including 29 in 1920, and posted a batting average of .341 in the minors. He hit four home runs in one game twice during the 1932 season for Baltimore of the International League. He slammed 54 circuit drives that year. Arlett hit 432 homers in the minor leagues.

May 20, 1964, Larry Dewey, Salinas, California League, rookie, struck out 20, including ten in a row, in eight innings as his team topped Santa Barbara, 4-1.

May 27, 1964, Dave Turnbull, El Paso, Texas League, relieving in the second inning, retired 23 consecutive batters, all that he faced, to lock up a 6-1 victory over Austin.

May 29, 1964, Mike Kekich, St. Petersburg, Florida State League, equalled a minor league record set by Ron Necciai in 1952 by striking out eleven straight Miami batters.

June 28, 1964, Reno, California League, scored 16 runs in the first frame to rout Modesto, 17-0.

June, 1964, Luis Tiant, Portland, Pacific Coast League, was called up by the Cleveland Indians. He sported a gaudy 15-1 for the Beavers. He would win 10 games in the American League for a 25-5 mark for the combined season.

July 4, 1964, Rick Bazinet, Auburn, New York-Penn League, outfielder, batted in ten tallies in his club's 23-12 victory over Geneva. Bazinet hit three homers and a double.

July 6, 1964, Angry Tomas Herrera, manager of the Mexico City Reds, Mexican League, sent ten pinch-hitters to the plate during a 6-2 loss to Reynosa.

September 12, 1964, Ken Rowe, Spokane's relief hurler, pitched in his 88th game of the season in the final contest of the Pacific Coast League season.

December 15, 1964, Paul Wachtel, 71, pitcher who had six 20-game winning seasons and who posted 317 victories in the minor leagues, died in San Antonio. Wachtel, a righthander, won 20 or more games six times in seven seasons for Fort Worth, Texas League, from 1919 to 1925.

1965

American League
President: Joseph E. Cronin

Standings	W	L	Pct.	GB	Attend.	Manager
Minnesota Twins	102	60	.630	—	1,463,258	Sam Mele
Chicago White Sox	95	67	.586	7	1,130,519	Al Lopez
Baltimore Orioles	94	68	.580	8	781,649	Hank Bauer
Detroit Tigers	89	73	.549	13	1,029,645	Bob Swift/Chuck Dressen
Cleveland Indians	87	75	.537	15	934,786	Birdie Tebbetts
New York Yankees	77	85	.475	25	1,213,552	Johnny Keane
California Angels	75	87	.463	27	566,727	Bill Rigney
Washington Senators	70	92	.432	32	560,083	Gil Hodges
Boston Red Sox	62	100	.383	40	652,201	Billy Herman
Kansas City Athletics	59	103	.364	43	528,344	Mel McGaha/Haywood Sullivan

BA: Tony Oliva, Minnesota, .321
Runs: Zoilo Versalles, Minnesota, 26
Hits: Tony Oliva, Minnesota, 185
RBIs: Rocky Colavito, Cleveland, 108
HRs: Tony Conigliaro, Boston, 32

Wins: Mudcat Grant, Minnesota, 21
SOs: Sam McDowell, Cleveland, 325
ERA: Sam McDowell, Cleveland, 2.18
Pct: Mudcat Grant, Minnesota, .750, 21-7
Saves: Ron Kline, Washington, 29

National League
President: Warren C. Giles

Standings	W	L	Pct.	GB	Attend.	Manager
Los Angeles Dodgers	97	65	.599	—	2,553,577	Walter Alston
San Francisco Giants	95	67	.586	2	1,546,075	Herman Franks
Pittsburgh Pirates	90	72	.556	7	909,279	Harry Walker
Cincinnati Reds	89	73	.549	8	1,047,824	Dick Sisler
Milwaukee Braves	86	76	.531	11	555,584	Bobby Bragan
Philadelphia Phillies	85	76	.528	11½	1,166,376	Gene Mauch
St. Louis Cardinals	80	81	.497	16½	1,241,201	Red Schoendienst
Chicago Cubs	72	90	.444	25	641,361	Bob Kennedy/Lou Klein
Houston Astros	65	97	.401	32	2,151,470	Luman Harris
New York Mets	50	112	.309	47	1,768,389	Casey Stengel/Wes Westrum

BA: Roberto Clemente, Pittsburgh, .329
Runs: Tommy Harper, Cincinnati, 126
Hits: Pete Rose, Cincinnati, 209
RBIs: Deron Johnson, Cincinnati, 130
HRs: Willie Mays, San Francisco, 52

Wins: Sandy Koufax, Los Angeles, 26
SOs: Sandy Koufax, Los Angeles, 382
ERA: Sandy Koufax, Los Angeles, 2.04
Pct: Sandy Koufax, Los Angeles, .765, 26-8
Saves: Ted Abernathy, Chicago, 31

AAA International League
President: Thomas H. Richardson

Standings	W	L	Pct.	GB	Attend.	Manager
Columbus Jets (18)	85	61	.582	—	197,680	Lawrence Shepard
Atlanta Crackers (15)	83	64	.565	2½	151,614	Bill Adair
Toronto Maple Leafs (2)	81	64	.556	3½	118,310	Dick Williams
Syracuse Chiefs (6)	74	73	.503	11½	139,223	Frank Carswell
Rochester Red Wings (1)	73	74	.497	12½	222,588	Darrell Johnson
Jacksonville Suns (19)	71	76	.483	14½	111,283	Grover Resinger
Toledo Mud Hens (9)	68	78	.466	17	92,984	Frank Verdi
Buffalo Bisons (16)	51	96	.347	34½	97,695	Sheriff Robinson/Kerby Farrell

Playoffs: Columbus 4 games, Syracuse 2; Toronto 4 games, Atlanta 0.
Finals: Toronto 4 games, Columbus 1.

All-Star Team: **1B-**Frank Herrera, Columbus; **2B-**Jack Damaska, Columbus; **3B-**Joe Foy, Toronto; **SS-**Ernie Brown, Atlanta; **OF-**Mickey Stanley, Syracuse; George Kernek, Jacksonville; Bobby Tolan, Jacksonville; **C-**Bob Barton, Atlanta; **P-**Jack Lamabe, Toronto; Dick LeMay, Jacksonville; **MVP-**Joe Foy, Toronto; **Pitcher of the Year-**Sam Jones, Columbus; **Manager-**Lawrence Shepard, Columbus.

BA: Joe Foy, Toronto, .302
Runs: Bob Saverine, Rochester, 91
Hits: Steve Demeter, Rochester, 165
RBIs: Steve Demeter, Rochester, 90

HRs: Frank Herrera, Columbus, 21
Wins: Dick LeMay, Jacksonville, 17
SOs: Frank Bertaina, Rochester, 188
ERA: Jack Hamilton, Syracuse, 2.42

AAA Pacific Coast League
President: Dewey Soriano

East Standings	W	L	Pct.	GB	Attend.	Manager
Oklahoma City 89ers (13)	91	54	.628	—	218,129	Grady Hatton
Denver Bears (8)	83	62	.572	8	187,518	Cal Ermer
San Diego Padres (12)	70	78	.473	22½	164,017	Dave Bristol
Indianapolis Indians (4)	70	78	.473	22½	159,502	George Noga
Arkansas Travelers (17)	67	79	.459	24½	77,570	Frank Lucchesi
Salt Lake City Bees (11)	56	91	.381	36	98,951	Stan Hack

West Standings	W	L	Pct.	GB	Attend.	Manager
Portland Beavers (5)	81	67	.547	—	172,291	John Lipon
Seattle Angels (3)	79	69	.534	2	144,029	Bob Lemon
Vancouver Mounties (7)	77	69	.527	3	124,048	Haywood Sullivan/Bob Hofman
Hawaii Islanders (10)	75	72	.510	5½	174,699	George Case
Tacoma Giants (20)	75	72	.510	5½	119,762	Bill Werle
Spokane Indians (14)	57	90	.388	23½	78,384	Bill Brenzel/Duke Snider/Pete Reiser

Playoff: Oklahoma City 4 games, Portland 1.

All-Star Team: **1B-**Lee May, San Diego; Bill Davis, Portland; **2B-**Ernie Fazio, Oklahoma City; **3B-**George Banks, Portland; **SS-**Sonny Jackson, Oklahoma City; **OF-**Andy Kosco, Denver; Ted Uhlaender, Denver; Dave Roberts, Oklahoma City; **C-**John Bateman, Oklahoma City; **P-**Tom Kelley, Portland; Jim Merritt, Denver; **MVP-**Dave Roberts, Oklahoma City; **Manager-**Grady Hatton, Oklahoma City.

BA: Ted Uhlaender, Denver, .340
Runs: Fred Valentine, Hawaii, 116
Hits: Sonny Jackson, Oklahoma City, 193
RBIs: Andy Kosco, Denver, 116
HRs: Dave Roberts, Oklahoma City, 38

Wins: Bill Hands, Spokane, 17
Chris Zachary, Oklahoma City, 17
SOs: Tom Kelley, Portland, 190
ERA: Bill Hands, Tacoma, 2.19

AA Eastern League
President: A. Rankin Johnson

Standings	W	L	Pct.	GB	Attend.	Manager
Pittsfield Red Sox (2)	85	55	.607	—	79,001	Eddie Popowski
Elmira Pioneers (1)	83	55	.601	1	67,075	Earl Weaver
York White Roses (10)	67	72	.482	17½	53,345	Billy Klaus
Williamsport Mets (16)	67	73	.479	18	65,189	Kerby Farrell/Bunky Warren
Springfield Giants (20)	63	77	.450	22	61,545	Andy Gilbert
Reading Indians (5)	53	86	.381	31½	40,594	Whitey Kurowski

Playoffs: None.

All-Star Team: **1B-**John Riddle, Elmira; **2B-**Johnny Parker, Reading; **3B-**George Scott, Pittsfield; **SS-**Mark Belanger, Elmira; **OF-**Chris Coletta, Pittsfield; Hank Allen, York; Howie Bedell, York; **C-**Owen Johnson, Pittsfield; Jim French, York; **P-**Bill MacLeod, Pittsfield; Tom Arruda, Springfield; **Manager-**Eddie Popowski, Pittsfield.

BA: George Scott, Pittsfield, .319
Runs: Chris Coletta, Pittsfield, 92
Hits: George Scott, Pittsfield, 167
RBIs: George Scott, Pittsfield, 94

HRs: George Scott, Pittsfield, 25
Wins: Dave Leonhard, Elmira, 20
SOs: Dave Leonhard, Elmira, 209
ERA: Tom Arruda, Springfield, 1.88

AA Mexican League
President: Antonio Ramirez Muro

Standings	W	L	Pct.	GB	Attend.	Manager
Mexico City Tigres	82	57	.590	—	441,885	Jose Luis Garcia
Puebla Pericos	78	61	.561	4	163,002	Tony Castano
Jalisco Charros	71	68	.511	11	287,866	Memo Garibay
Monterrey Sultanes	68	72	.486	14½	219,002	Vinicio Garcia
Mexico City Diablos Rojos	66	74	.471	16½	350,660	Tomas Herrera
Veracruz Aguila	65	75	.464	17½	153,239	Wilfredo Calvino
Reynosa Broncs	64	75	.460	18	153,276	Alberto Palafox
Poza Rica Petroleros	64	76	.457	18½	265,889	Guillermo Frayde

Playoffs: None.

All-Star Team: **1B-**George Prescott, Poza Rica; **2B-**Moises Camacho, Puebla; **3B-**Armando Murillo, MC Tigres; **SS-**Fernando Remes, MC Tigres; **OF-**Minnie Minoso, Jalisco; Emilio Sosa, Poza Rica; Jaime Fabela, Jalisco; **C-**Elrod Hendricks, Jalisco; Roberto Herrera, Reynosa; **P-**Frank Barnes, Reynosa; Minnie Rojas, Jalisco; **Manager-**Jose Luis Garcia, MC Tigres.

BA: Emilio Sosa, Poza Rica, .368
Runs: Minnie Minoso, Jalisco, 106
Hits: Emilio Sosa, Poza Rica, 193
RBIs: Jaime Fabela, Jalisco, 109

HRs: George Prescott, Poza Rica, 39
Wins: Minnie Rojas, Jalisco, 21
SOs: Jose Ramon Lopez, Monterrey, 201
ERA: Frank Barnes, Reynosa, 1.58

AA Southern League
President: Sam C. Smith

Standings	W	L	Pct.	GB	Attend.	Manager
Columbus Yankees (9)	79	59	.572	—	72,732	Loren Babe
Asheville Tourists (18)	80	60	.571	—	68,490	Pete Peterson
Lynchburg White Sox (4)	75	64	.540	4½	54,619	Gordon Maltzberger
Knoxville Smokies (12)	73	66	.525	6½	35,449	John "Red" Davis
Charlotte Hornets (8)	72	68	.514	8	52,966	Alfred Evans
Montgomery Rebels (6)	63	74	.460	15½	42,129	Wayne Blackburn
Chattanooga Lookouts (17)	60	80	.429	20	25,707	Andy Seminick
Birmingham Barons (7)	54	85	.388	25½	28,001	John McNamara

Playoffs: None.

All-Star Team: **1B-**Charles Leonard, Asheville; **2B-**Roy White, Columbus; **3B-**Ron Clark, Charlotte; **SS-**Minnie Mendoza, Charlotte; **OF-**Gerald Reimer, Knoxville; Bill Voss,

*Won first-half   **Won second-half   ***Won both halves
Numbers after nicknames indicate farm system.
Affiliation listed at end of year.

488

Lynchburg; Tom Umphlett, Charlotte; **C**-Duane Josephson, Lynchburg; Orlando McFarlane, Asheville; **P**-Rich Beck, Columbus; Luke Walker, Asheville; **Manager**-Loren Babe, Columbus.

BA: Gerald Reimer, Knoxville, .310
Runs: Roy White, Columbus, 103
Hits: Roy White, Columbus, 168
RBIs: Charles Leonard, Asheville, 78
HRs: Orlando McFarlane, Asheville, 22

Wins: Tom Frondorf, Knoxville, 16
  Milt Osteen, Knoxville, 16
SOs: Luke Walker, Asheville, 197
ERA: Luke Walker, Asheville, 2.26

AA Texas League
Presidents: James H. Burris/Hugh J. Finnerty

East Standings	W	L	Pct.	GB	Attend.	Manager
Tulsa Oilers (19)	81	60	.574	—	215,423	Vern Rapp
Dallas-Ft. Worth Spurs (11)	80	61	.567	1	329,294	Whitey Lockman
Austin Braves (15)	70	70	.500	10½	76,587	Buddy Hicks

West Standings	W	L	Pct.	GB	Attend.	Manager
Albuquerque Dodgers (14)	77	63	.550	—	83,280	Roy Hartsfield
Amarillo Sonics (13)	60	80	.429	17	80,608	Lou Fitzgerald
El Paso Sun Kings (3)	53	87	.379	24	75,655	Chuck Tanner

Playoff: Tulsa defeated Dallas-Ft. Worth in a one game playoff to win the East Division.
Finals: Albuquerque 3 games, Tulsa 1.

All-Star Team: 1B-Clarence Jones, Albuquerque; **2B**-Don Williams, Albuquerque; **3B**-Mike Sinnerud, Austin; **SS**-Roberto Pena, Dallas-Ft. Worth; **OF**-Vince Ferguson, Austin; Don Young, Dallas-Ft. Worth; Leo Posada, Amarillo; Walt Williams, Tulsa; **C**-Dave Pavlesic, Tulsa; **Util**-Dick McLaughlin, Albuquerque; **P**-Larry Jaster, Tulsa; Herb Hippauf, Austin; Ken Nixon, Austin; **MVP**-Leo Posada, Amarillo; **Pitcher of the Year**-Ken Nixon, Austin; **Manager**-Whitey Lockman, Dallas-Ft. Worth.

BA: Dave Pavlesic, Tulsa, .344
Runs: Walt Williams, Tulsa, 106
Hits: Walt Williams, Tulsa, 189
RBIs: Leo Posada, Amarillo, 107
HRs: Leo Posada, Amarillo, 26

Wins: Ken Nixon, Austin, 19
SOs: Larry Jaster, Tulsa, 219
ERA: Chuck Hartenstein,
  Dallas-Ft. Worth, 2.18

A California League
President: Edward J. Mulligan

Standings	W	L	Pct.	GB	Attend.	Manager
Stockton Ports** (1)	83	57	.593	—	27,774	Harry Malmberg
San Jose Bees* (3)	72	68	.514	11	34,517	Rocky Bridges
Fresno Giants (20)	70	69	.504	12½	22,362	Ed FitzGerald
Salinas Indians (5)	67	72	.482	15½	8,828	Phil Cavarretta
Bakersfield Bears (17)	66	74	.471	17	23,234	Dick Teed
Santa Barbara Dodgers (14)	61	79	.436	22	12,121	Norm Sherry

Playoff: Stockton 2 games, San Jose 0.

All-Star Team: 1B-Mike Epstein, Stockton; **2B**-Bob Powell, Fresno; **3B**-Bobby Etheridge, Fresno; **SS**-Bob Holbert, Fresno; **OF**-Gary Fancher, Stockton; Jim Fairey, Santa Barbara; Rick Scheinblum, Salinas; **C**-George Pena, San Jose; **P**-Joe DeLuise, Stockton; Bob Patrylo, Stockton; Jack Nutter, Bakersfield; Huey Howden, Salinas; **Manager**-Harry Malmberg, Stockton.

BA: Mike Epstein, Stockton, .338
Runs: Angelo Galasso, Bakersfield, 113
Hits: Bobby Etheridge, Fresno, 176
RBIs: Bobby Etheridge, Fresno, 107

HRs: Mike Epstein, Stockton, 30
Wins: Jack Nutter, Bakersfield, 16
SOs: Jack Nutter, Bakersfield, 223
ERA: George Sherrod, San Jose, 2.81

A Carolina League
President: J.C. "Bill" Jessup

East Standings	W	L	Pct.	GB	Attend.	Manager
Peninsula Grays (12)	86	58	.597	—	102,424	Jack Cassini/Pinky May
Portsmouth Tides (4)	76	68	.528	10	61,667	Allen Jones
Kinston Eagles (18)	72	71	.503	13½	90,274	Bob Clear
Wilson Tobs (8)	68	75	.476	17½	26,850	Vern Morgan
Rocky Mount Leafs (6)	62	82	.431	24	41,798	Al Lakeman

West Standings	W	L	Pct.	GB	Attend.	Manager
Durham Bulls (13)	83	60	.580	—	34,956	Dave Philley
Greensboro Yankees (9)	79	65	.549	4½	86,423	Lamar North
Winston-Salem Red Sox (2)	65	79	.451	18½	43,921	Bill Slack
Raleigh Cardinals (19)	64	79	.448	19	36,221	Ray Hathaway
Burlington Senators (10)	63	81	.438	20½	36,391	Owen Friend

Playoffs: Portsmouth 2 games, Peninsula 1; Durham 2 games, Greensboro 1.
Finals: Portsmouth 2 games, Durham 0.

All-Star Team: 1B-Mike Derrick, Kinston; **2B**-Jose Herrera, Durham; **3B**-Ron Boyer, Greensboro; **SS**-Bobby Murcer, Greensboro; **OF**-Ed Stroud, Portsmouth; Teo Acosta, Peninsula; Mike Maloney, Burlington; **C**-Paul Casanova, Burlington; Ellie Rodriguez, Greensboro; **Util**-Tony Torchia, Winston-Salem; Felix DeLeon, Raleigh; **P**-Dock Ellis, Kinston; Marv Dutt, Durham; Jim Morio, Peninsula; Jack DiLauro, Rocky Mount; **MVP**-Bobby Murcer, Greensboro; **Manager**-Pinky May, Peninsula.

BA: Ed Stroud, Portsmouth, .341
Runs: Sam Thompson, Peninsula, 121
Hits: Teo Acosta, Peninsula, 167
RBIs: Mike Derrick, Kinston, 103
HRs: Mike Derrick, Kinston, 28

Wins: Jim Morio, Peninsula, 16
  Wayne McAlpin, Wilson, 16
SOs: Ernest Barron, Wilson, 183
ERA: Dock Ellis, Kinston, 1.98

A Florida State League
President: George MacDonald, Sr.

Standings	W	L	Pct.	GB	Attend.	Manager
Ft. Lauderdale Yankees*** (9)	87	51	.630	—	50,897	Jack Reed
Sarasota Sun Sox (4)	85	53	.616	2	26,999	Don Bacon
Orlando Twins (8)	77	57	.575	8	42,143	Harry Warner
St. Petersburg Saints (14)	68	69	.496	18½	65,650	George Scherger
Tampa Tarpons (12)	67	69	.493	19	61,316	Pinky May/Jack Cassini
Daytona Beach Islanders (6)	67	74	.475	21½	19,165	Al Federoff
Miami Marlins (17)	67	75	.472	22	71,964	Bobby Morgan
West Palm Beach Braves (15)	59	73	.447	25	27,514	Andy Pafko
Leesburg Athletics (7)	53	80	.398	31½	12,746	Tony Frulio
Cocoa Astros (13)	52	81	.391	32½	14,707	Billy Goodman

Playoffs: None.

All-Star Team: 1B-Grover "Deacon" Jones, Sarasota; **2B**-Rod Carew, Orlando; **3B**-Joe Lis, Miami; **SS**-Rick Renick, Orlando; **OF**-Al Lewis, Leesburg; Guy Rose, St. Petersburg; Harvey Yancey, Tampa; **C**-Gail Hopkins, Sarasota; **P**-Gary Schlieve, Miami; John Schroeppel, Ft. Lauderdale; **Util**-Dick Severson, Sarasota; **Manager**-Jack Reed, Ft. Lauderdale.

BA: Harvey Yancey, Tampa, .305
Runs: Harvey Yancey, Tampa, 78
Hits: Dick Severson, Sarasota, 142
RBIs: Bill McNulty, Leesburg, 62
HRs: Roy Bethell, Cocoa, 9

Wins: Larry Whitley, Orlando, 18
SOs: Gerald Schroeppel, Sarasota, 226
ERA: Earl Willoughby,
  Ft. Lauderdale, 0.90

A Mexican Center League
President: Antonio Ramirez (Muro)

Standings	W	L	Pct.	GB	Attend.	Manager
San Luis Potosi Reds	88	51	.633	—	76,651	Hector Rodriguez
Leon Diablos Verdes	81	58	.583	7	61,319	Dan Bankhead
Guanajuato Tuzos	80	59	.576	8	58,543	Domingo Santana
Durango Alacranes	66	72	.478	21½	64,332	Regino Garcia/ Francisco Martinez
Zacatecas Pericos	63	76	.453	25	40,720	Jesus Chanquilon
Fresnillo Mineros	62	77	.446	26	26,962	Felipe Hernandez
Aguascalientes Tigres	61	78	.439	27	46,019	Santos Amaro/Bill Wright
Salamanca Tigres	55	85	.393	33½	20,119	Enrique Fernandez/ Ricardo Garza

Playoffs: None.

All-Star Team: 1B-Ramiro Caballero, Leon; **2B**-Javier Hernandez, Fresnillo; **3B**-Fernando Castro, Zacatecas; **SS**-Ruben Hernandez, Zacatecas; **OF**-Alfonso Preciado, Guanajuato; Roberto Espinosa, Zacatecas; Luis Peralta, San Luis Potosi; **C**-Luis Esma, Zacatecas; Gregorio Ayala, Leon; **P**-Raul Gamez, San Luis Potosi; Luciano Ortega, Guanajuato; **Manager**-Hector Rodriguez, San Luis Potosi.

BA: Alfonso Preciado, Guanajuato, .423
Runs: Javier Hernandez de la F., Guanajuato, 139
Hits: Alfonso Preciado, Guanajuato, 224
RBIs: Alfonso Preciado, Guanajuato, 147

HRs: Ramiro Caballero, Leon, 34
Wins: Raul Gamez, San Luis Potosi, 20
SOs: Raul Gamez, San Luis Potosi, 234
ERA: Raul Gamez, San Luis Potosi, 2.63

A Mexican Southeast League
President: Antonio Ramirez (Muro)

Standings	W	L	Pct.	GB	Attend.	Manager
Tabasco Plataneros*	52	38	.578	—	111,435	Pompeyo Davalillo
Campeche Pirates**	49	38	.563	1½	106,078	Mauro Contreras
Yucatan Venados	38	49	.437	12½	100,782	Leonel Aldama
Puerto Mexico Portenos	38	52	.422	14	79,032	Alfonso Pena/Marcos Cobos

Playoff: Campeche 4 games, Tabasco 1.

All-Star Team: 1B-Celso Oviedo, Puerto Mexico; **2B**-Hilario Pena, Campeche; **3B**-Hector Sanudo, Campeche; **SS**-Domingo Carrasquel, Campeche; **OF**-Rafael Alomar, Campeche; Luis Zayas, Campeche; Ramiro Rubio, Tabasco; **C**-Angel Montano, Campeche; Marcos Cobos, Puerto Mexico; **P**-Concepcion Cruz, Campeche; Jose Leyva, Tabasco; **Manager**-Pompeyo Davalillo, Tabasco.

BA: Rafael Alomar, Campeche, .362
Runs: Domingo Carrasquel, Campeche, 74
Hits: Rafael Alomar, Campeche, 123
RBIs: Hector Sanudo, Campeche, 66

HRs: Hector Sanudo, Campeche, 16
Wins: Jose Leyva, Tabasco, 12
SOs: Jose Leyva, Tabasco, 99
ERA: Concepcion Cruz, Campeche, 2.18

A Midwest League
President: Jim Gruenwald

Standings	W	L	Pct.	GB	Attend.	Manager
Burlington Bees*** (7)	82	40	.672	—	60,925	Gus Niarhos
Quincy Cubs (11)	69	50	.580	11½	43,254	Walt Dixon
Cedar Rapids Cardinals (19)	62	52	.544	16	62,115	Ron Plaza
Waterloo Hawks (2)	63	55	.534	17	39,708	Larry Thomas
Decatur Commodores (20)	60	60	.500	21	47,265	Richard Klaus
Wisconsin Rapids Twins (8)	60	61	.496	21½	53,462	Ray Bellino/Pete Appleton
Fox Cities Foxes (1)	55	63	.466	25	45,443	Billy DeMars
Quad Cities Angels (3)	53	70	.442	29½	80,391	Harry Dunlop/Ken Blackman
Dubuque Packers (5)	47	73	.392	34	36,785	Elmer Valo
Clinton C-Sox (4)	45	72	.378	34½	37,919	Ira Hutchinson

Playoffs: None.

All-Star Team: 1B-Randall Schwartz, Burlington; **2B**-Frank Ferro, Decatur; **3B**-Sal Bando, Burlington; **SS**-Jim Williams, Waterloo; **OF**-Curt Motton, Fox Cities; Daniel DiPace, Wisconsin Rapids; John Oster, Wisconsin Rapids; **C**-Fred Velasquez, Burlington; **Util**-Harold Wade, Waterloo; **P**-Danny Morris, Wisconsin Rapids; Gordon Riese, Burlington; **Manager**-Gus Niarhos, Burlington.

BA: Daniel DiPace, Wisconsin Rapids, .333
Runs: Randall Schwartz, Burlington, 94
Hits: Daniel DiPace, Wisconsin Rapids, 132
RBIs: John Oster, Wisconsin Rapids, 94

HRs: Randall Schwartz, Burlington, 29
Wins: Danny Morris, Wisconsin Rapids, 16
SOs: Danny Morris, Wisconsin Rapids, 274
ERA: Tony Pierce, Burlington, 1.84

A New York-Pennsylvania League
President: Vincent M. McNamara

Standings	W	L	Pct.	GB	Attend.	Manager
Binghamton Triplets***(9)	81	45	.643	—	75,753	Gary Blaylock
Auburn Mets (16)	73	55	.570	9	40,944	Clyde McCullough
Geneva Senators (10)	65	61	.516	16	19,218	Wayne Terwilliger
Wellsville Red Sox (2)	62	64	.492	19	16,145	Matt Sczesny
Batavia Pirates (18)	47	75	.385	32	30,096	Tom Saffell
Jamestown Tigers (6)	47	75	.385	32	31,613	Gail Henley

Playoffs: None.

All-Star Team: 1B-William Contreras, Auburn; **2B**-David Truelock, Binghamton; **3B**-Donato Fazio, Wellsville; **SS**-Jerry Kenney, Binghamton; **OF**-Richard Smith, Geneva; William Murphy, Binghamton; Bruce Fitzpatrick, Auburn; **C**-Greg Goossen, Auburn; Carl Solarek, Jamestown; **Util OF**-John Sanders, Wellsville; **Util IF**-Harvey Mattingly, Geneva; **P**-Bill Denehy, Auburn; Louis Romanucci, Binghamton; Bill Hepler, Geneva; Robert Parchem, Geneva; **Manager**-Clyde McCullough, Auburn.

BA: Richard Smith, Geneva, .331
Runs: Dave Truelock, Binghamton, 96
Hits: Richard Smith, Geneva, 158
RBIs: Richard Smith, Geneva, 109
HRs: Lewis Dorsch, Wellsville, 29

Wins: Bill Denehy, Auburn, 13
Paul Alspach, Auburn, 13
Bill Hepler, Geneva, 13
SOs: George Robinson, Wellsville, 221
ERA: Louis Romanucci, Binghamton, 2.53

A Northern League
President: Roland E. Parcel

Standings	W	L	Pct.	GB	Attend.	Manager
St. Cloud Rox (8)	43	23	.652	—	22,446	Jim Rantz
Duluth-Superior Dukes (6, 11)	31	35	.470	12	13,860	Doc Daugherty
Huron Phillies (17)	31	35	.470	12	44,001	Joe Lonnett
Aberdeen Pheasants (1)	27	39	.409	16	23,525	Ray Rippelmeyer

Playoffs: None.

BA: Chris Barkulis, Duluth-Superior, .335
Runs: Louis Smith, St. Cloud, 56
Hits: Chris Barkulis, Duluth-Superior, 84
RBIs: Bob Brooks, St. Cloud, 46

HRs: Bob Brooks, St. Cloud, 8
Nathaniel King, St. Cloud, 8
Wins: Bob Gebhard, St. Cloud, 11
SOs: Ron Keller, St. Cloud, 132
ERA: Billy Champion, Huron, 1.20

A Northwest League
President: James Fleishman

Standings	W	L	Pct.	GB	Attend.	Manager
Lewiston Broncs*(7)	86	53	.619	—	52,547	Bob Hofman/Bill Posedel/Al Ronning
Tri-City Atoms**(1)	81	58	.583	5	42,856	Cal Ripken, Sr.
Eugene Emeralds (17)	71	65	.522	13½	45,098	Bob Wellman
Wenatchee Chiefs (11)	66	70	.485	18½	24,568	Les Peden
Yakima Braves (15)	62	77	.446	24	36,050	Hub Kittle
Salem Dodgers (14)	47	90	.343	38	43,585	Stan Wasiak

Playoff: Tri-City 3 games, Lewiston 0.

All-Star Team: 1B-Michael Fiore, Tri-City; **2B**-Felix Millan, Yakima; **3B**-Bill Southworth, Yakima; **SS**-Bob Floyd, Tri-City; **OF**-Arlie Burge, Lewiston; Dave May, Tri-City; Herman Rathman, Tri-City; **C**-Jim Procopio, Wenatchee; George Farson, Tri-City; **P**-Sam Cook, Wenatchee; Larry Loughlin, Eugene; **Manager**-Cal Ripken, Sr., Tri-City.

BA: Arlie Burge, Lewiston, .354
Runs: Dave May, Tri-City, 129
Hits: Dave May, Tri-City, 173
RBIs: Michael Fiore, Tri-City, 106

HRs: Herman Rathman, Tri-City, 31
Wins: Sam Cook, Wenatchee, 15
SOs: Jim Nash, Lewiston, 190
ERA: Larry Loughlin, Eugene, 2.12

A Western Carolinas League
President: John H. Moss

Standings	W	L	Pct.	GB	Attend.	Manager
Salisbury Astros*(13)	70	48	.593	—	27,855	Chuck Churn
Thomasville Hi-Toms (8)	73	52	.584	½	71,256	Ralph Rowe
Gastonia Pirates (18)	70	54	.565	3	45,879	Clyde Sukeforth/Donald Osborn
Lexington Giants (20)	62	54	.534	7	54,566	Max Lanier
Rock Hill Cardinals**(19)	59	63	.484	13	28,079	Sparky Anderson

Shelby Rebels (7)	55	68	.447	17½	22,876	Wes Ferrell/Jim Williams
Spartanburg Phillies (17)	54	68	.443	18	114,796	Wilbur Johnson
Greenville Mets (16)	44	80	.355	29	30,250	Ken Deal

Playoff: Rock Hill 2 games, Salisbury 0.

All-Star Team: 1B-Ossie Blanco, Lexington; **2B**-Robert Clifton, Shelby; **3B**-Bob Robertson, Gastonia; **SS**-Cesar Gutierrez, Lexington; **OF**-Edmondo Moxey, Salisbury; Ben Bracy, Rock Hill; **C**-Kenneth Jensen, Shelby; Gary Cunning, Spartanburg; **P**-Roger Brown, Gastonia; Richard Sommer, Thomasville; **MVP**-Bob Robertson, Gastonia; **Most Outstanding Prospect**-Bobby Bonds, Lexington; **Most Outstanding Pitcher**-Richard Sommer, Thomasville; **Manager**-Clyde Sukeforth, Gastonia.

BA: Edmondo Moxey, Salisbury, .345
Runs: Bobby Bonds, Lexington, 103
Hits: Al Oliver, Gastonia, 159
RBIs: Bob Robertson, Gastonia, 98

HRs: Bob Robertson, Gastonia, 32
Wins: Felix Roque, Rock Hill, 18
SOs: Richard Sommer, Thomasville, 199
ERA: Sal Campisi, Rock Hill, 1.95

R Appalachian League
President: Chauncey De Vault

Standings	W	L	Pct.	GB	Attend.	Manager
Salem Rebels (18)	43	27	.614	—	44,254	George Detore
Wytheville Senators (10)	38	31	.551	4½	18,394	Lee Anthony
Marion Mets (16)	37	33	.529	6	29,868	Pete Pavlick
Harlan Red Sox (2)	33	37	.471	10	23,190	Rac Slider
Bluefield Orioles (1)	31	38	.449	11½	21,512	Jim Frey
Johnson City Yankees (9)	27	43	.386	16	21,844	Bob Bauer

Playoffs: None.

All-Star Team: 1B-Bob Weigle, Wytheville; **2B**-Luther Quinn, Salem; **3B**-Bob Jones, Bluefield; **SS**-Don Money, Salem; **OF**-Gregory Sims, Salem; Jim Clark, Wytheville; Tom Porter, Johnson City; **C**-Jerry Branch, Salem; David Coleman, Bluefield; **P**-Scott McDonald, Bluefield; Roger Hayward, Salem; Arvell Boyett, Harlan; Alan Closter, Johnson City; **Rookie of the Year**-Dick Hense, Wytheville; Luther Quinn, Salem; **Manager**-George Detore, Salem.

BA: Bob Weigle, Wytheville, .363
Runs: Wayne Dickerson, Salem, 63
Hits: Luther Quinn, Salem, 90
RBIs: Luther Quinn, Salem, 64

HRs: Dick Hense, Wytheville, 20
Wins: Marvin Tidd, Wytheville, 9
SOs: John Silva, Harlan, 145
ERA: Arvell Boyett, Harlan, 2.74

R Florida Rookie League
President: George MacDonald, Sr.

Standings	W	L	Pct.	GB	Manager
Astros (13)	36	21	.632	—	Joe Frazier
Braves (15)	34	25	.576	3	Paul Snyder
Twins (8)	32	28	.533	5½	Fred Water
White Sox (4)	29	28	.509	7	Frank Parenti
Cardinals (19)	27	31	.466	9½	George Kissell
Yankees (9)	17	42	.288	20	Chuck Boone

All games played at Sarasota and Bradenton, Florida.

Playoffs: None

All-Star Team: 1B-Terrence Milani, Cardinals; **2B**-Roger Sugimoto, Twins, Van Kelly, Braves; **3B**-Rusty Riley, Braves; **SS**-James Maness, White Sox; **OF**-Gene Noble, Astros; Ronald Lolich, White Sox; James Alvey, Yankees; **C**-Bill Plummer, Cardinals; **P**-Louis Fiore, Cardinals; Chuck Vaughan, Braves; **Util**-Gary Schmidt, White Sox; **Manager**-Paul Snyder, Braves.

BA: James Alvey, Yankees, .371
Runs: Danny Loftin, Twins, 43
Hits: James Alvey, Yankees, 63
RBIs: Terry Graham, Twins, 39

HRs: Larry Hall, Astros, 3
Wins: Dan Eggart, Twins, 10
SOs: Charles Vaughan, Braves, 71
ERA: Louis McKown, Astros, 1.77

R Pioneer League
President: Claude Engberg

Standings	W	L	Pct.	GB	Attend.	Manager
Treasure Valley Cubs (11)	35	31	.530	—	19,545	George Freese
Magic Valley Cowboys (20)	33	33	.500	2	20,012	Dick Wilson
Pocatello Chiefs (14)	33	33	.500	2	8,692	Tom Lasorda
Idaho Falls Angels (3)	31	35	.470	4	15,197	Fred Koenig

Playoffs: None.

BA: Don Anderson, Idaho Falls, .378
Runs: Don Anderson, Idaho Falls, 58
Hits: Don Anderson, Idaho Falls, 88
RBIs: Buddy Hollowell, Pocatello, 56

HRs: Gary Cortopassi, Treasure Valley, 15
Wins: Walter Peterson, Pocatello, 10
SOs: Walter Peterson, Pocatello, 129
ERA: Billy Patrick, Magic Valley, 2.54

1965 Interleague Post Season Play

World Series
Los Angeles (National) 4 games, Minnesota (American) 3

1965 Major League Farm Systems

American League

1 Baltimore (7): Rochester, Elmira, Stockton, Fox Cities, Aberdeen, Tri-City, Bluefield.
2 Boston (6): Toronto, Pittsfield, Winston-Salem, Waterloo, Wellsville, Harlan.
3 California (5): Seattle, El Paso, San Jose, Quad Cities, Idaho Falls.
4 Chicago (6): Indianapolis, Lynchburg, Portsmouth, Sarasota, Clinton, Florida Rookie.
5 Cleveland (4): Portland, Reading, Salinas, Dubuque.
6 Detroit (6): Syracuse, Montgomery, Rocky Mount, Daytona Beach, Jamestown, Duluth-Superior.
7 Kansas City (6): Vancouver, Birmingham, Leesburg, Burlington (IA), Lewiston, Shelby.
8 Minnesota (8): Denver, Charlotte, Wilson, Orlando, Wisconsin Rapids, St. Cloud, Thomasville, Florida Rookie.
9 New York (7): Toledo, Columbus (GA), Greensboro, Ft. Lauderdale, Binghamton, Johnson City, Florida Rookie.
10 Washington (5): Hawaii, York, Burlington (NC), Geneva, Wytheville.

National League

11 Chicago (6): Salt Lake City, Dallas-Ft. Worth, Quincy, Duluth-Superior, Wenatchee, Treasure Valley.
12 Cincinnati (4): San Diego, Knoxville, Peninsula, Tampa.
13 Houston (6): Oklahoma City, Amarillo, Durham, Cocoa, Salisbury, Florida Rookie.
14 Los Angeles (6): Spokane, Albuquerque, Santa Barbara, St. Petersburg, Salem (OR), Pocatello.
15 Milwaukee (5): Atlanta, Austin, West Palm Beach, Yakima, Florida Rookie.
16 New York (5): Buffalo, Williamsport, Auburn, Greenville, Marion.
17 Philadelphia (7): Arkansas, Chattanooga, Bakersfield, Miami, Huron, Eugene, Spartanburg.
18 Pittsburgh (6): Columbus (OH), Asheville, Kinston, Batavia, Gastonia, Salem (VA).
19 St. Louis (6): Jacksonville, Tulsa, Raleigh, Cedar Rapids, Rock Hill, Florida Rookie.
20 San Francisco (6): Tacoma, Springfield, Fresno, Decatur, Lexington, Magic Valley.

1965 No-Hitters

Date	Pitcher	Team	League	Opponent	Score
4-21	Bill Henry	Greensboro	Carolina	Wilson	3-0 (7)
4-24	Ed Watt	Elmira	Eastern	Williamsport	4-0
4-27	William Seifert/Gus Marco/Robert Hoy Charles Kuhn	Daytona Beach	Florida State	Miami	4-3 (7)
4-29	Paul Seitz	Birmingham	Southern	Chattanooga	2-0 (7)
5-6	Ed Watt	Elmira	Eastern	Reading	5-0
5-6	Don Pierce	Burlington	Midwest	Fox Cities	4-0
5-11	Dick Estelle	Tacoma	Pacific Coast	Hawaii	6-0
5-29	Tom Kelley	Portland	Pacific Coast	Spokane	5-0
5-30	Chris Heintz/ Dave Langrock	Quincy	Midwest	Fox Cities	0-1 (7)
5-30	Darrel Bunge	Waterloo	Midwest	Wisconsin Rapids	7-0
6-6	Ernest Abels	Wellsville	New York-Penn.	Jamestown	3-0
6-14	Jim Maloney	Cincinnati	National	New York	0-1 (10)
6-15	Michael Wegener	Miami	Florida State	Daytona Beach	2-0
6-29	George Bosworth	Burlington	Midwest	Cedar Rapids	3-0
6-30	Mike Jurewicz	Columbus	Southern	Charlotte	2-0 (7)
7-4	Pete Mikkelsen	Toledo	International	Atlanta	5-0
7-9	Simon Betacourt	Fresnillo	Mexican Center	Aguascalientes	4-0 (7)
7-11	Jon Robisch	Wenatchee	Northwest	Eugene	7-0 (7)
7-16	Juan Quintana	Durham	Carolina	Raleigh	1-0 (7)
7-19	John Rawls	Bluefield	Appalachian	Marion	7-0 (7)
7-19	Bob Schmidt	Williamsport	Eastern	Springfield	4-0 (7)
7-22	Emman. Fitzgerald	Fox Cities	Midwest	Quincy	4-0 (7)
7-23	Drannon Guinn	West Palm Beach	Florida State	Daytona Beach	8-0 (7)
7-24	Michael Kilkenny	Daytona Beach	Florida State	Tampa	4-0
7-27	Ed Barnowski	Elmira	Eastern	Reading	2-0
8-11	Bill Whitby	Charlotte	Southern	Asheville	5-0
8-13	Rich Beck	Columbus	Southern	Lynchburg	2-0 (7)
8-15	Ray Goodwin	Huron	Northern	Duluth-Superior	0-1 (10)
8-17	Ron Keller	St. Cloud	Northern	Aberdeen	3-1 (7)
8-17	Larry Maxie	Atlanta	International	Toledo	1-0 (7)
8-19	Jim Maloney	Cincinnati	National	Chicago	1-0 (10)
8-22	Andy Shirrel	Fresno	California	Stockton	1-0 (7)
8-27	Bob Settle	Salem	Appalachian	Bluefield	5-0 (7)
8-28	Chuck Dobson	Lewiston	Northwest	Salem	4-3
9-9	Sandy Koufax	Los Angeles	National	Chicago	1-0 (P)
9-16	Dave Morehead	Boston	American	Cleveland	2-0

Number in parentheses indicates innings if other than nine; "P" indicates perfect game.

THIS DATE IN MINOR LEAGUE HISTORY

February 17, 1965, Larry Gilbert, 73, who fashioned one of the greatest managerial records in minor league history, leading his teams to nine Southern Association championships, died in New Orleans.

April 16, 1965, Austin, Texas League, scored 13 runs in the second inning to drub Dallas-Ft. Worth, 17-1, in Austin's season opener.

April 23, 1965, Dick Joyce, Lewiston, Northwest League, lefty, made a spectacular Organized Baseball debut when the ex-Holy Cross collegian whiffed the first nine men to face him and finished with 17 strikeouts in a 7-2 victory over Salem.

May 8, 1965, Elmira, Eastern League, defeated Springfield 2-1 in 27 innings, the longest game by innings in the history of Organized Baseball.

May 9, 1965, Jim Ellis, Quincy, Midwest League, allowed only one hit in a 25-0 victory over Dubuque and smashed three home runs, a double and a single in six at bats.

May 22, 1965, After 15 successive victories, Thomasville, Western Carolinas League, lost to Shelby, 9-5.

June 4, 1965, Cecil Robinson, Wellsville, New York-Penn League, struck out 20 but lost to Auburn, 3-2.

June 17, 1965, In the longest game in the 77-year history of the Texas League, Austin defeated Dallas-Ft. Worth 2-1 in 25 innings.

July 19, 1965, Cedar Rapids, Midwest League, defeated Fox Cities for its 17th straight victory.

July 28, 1965, Pitcher Danny Morris, Wisconsin Rapids, Midwest League, fanned 21 in a 5-1 success over Clinton.

July 30, 1965, Spokane, Pacific Coast League, greeted Moe Drabowski, Vancouver pitcher, with five straight doubles in the first inning that resulted in three runs and an eventual 8-5 victory.

August 2, 1965, Amarillo, Texas League, ended a string of 58 scoreless innings in a game with Tulsa. The Sonics absorbed six straight shutouts during the streak.

August 28, 1965, Salem, Appalachian League, scored 13 runs in the first inning and defeated Bluefield, 15-4.

1966

American League
President: Joseph E. Cronin

Standings	W	L	Pct.	GB	Attend.	Manager
Baltimore Orioles	97	63	.606	—	1,203,366	Hank Bauer
Minnesota Twins	89	73	.549	9	1,259,374	Sam Mele
Detroit Tigers	88	74	.543	10	1,124,293	Chuck Dressen/ Bob Swift/Frank Skaff
Chicago White Sox	83	79	.512	15	990,016	Eddie Stanky
Cleveland Indians	81	81	.500	17	903,359	Birdie Tebbetts/ George Strickland
California Angels	80	82	.494	18	1,400,321	Bill Rigney
Kansas City Athletics	74	86	.463	23	773,929	Alvin Dark
Washington Senators	71	88	.447	25½	576,260	Gil Hodges
Boston Red Sox	72	90	.444	26	811,172	Billy Herman/Pete Runnels
New York Yankees	70	89	.440	26½	1,124,648	Johnny Keane/Ralph Houk

BA: Frank Robinson, Baltimore, .316
Runs: Frank Robinson, Baltimore, 122
Hits: Tony Oliva, Minnesota, 191
RBIs: Frank Robinson, Baltimore, 122
HRs: Frank Robinson, Baltimore, 49

Wins: Jim Kaat, Minnesota, 25
SOs: Sam McDowell, Cleveland, 225
ERA: Gary Peters, Chicago, 1.98
Pct: Sonny Siebert, Cleveland, .667, 16-8
Saves: Jack Aker, Kansas City, 32

National League
President: Warren C. Giles

Standings	W	L	Pct.	GB	Attend.	Manager
Los Angeles Dodgers	95	67	.586	—	2,617,029	Walter Alston
San Francisco Giants	93	68	.578	1½	1,657,192	Herman Franks
Pittsburgh Pirates	92	70	.568	3	1,196,618	Harry Walker
Philadelphia Phillies	87	75	.537	8	1,108,201	Gene Mauch
Atlanta Braves	85	77	.525	10	1,539,801	Bobby Bragan/ Billy Hitchcock
St. Louis Cardinals	83	79	.512	12	1,712,980	Red Schoendienst
Cincinnati Reds	76	84	.475	18	742,958	Don Heffner/Dave Bristol
Houston Astros	72	90	.444	23	1,872,108	Grady Hatton
New York Mets	66	95	.410	28½	1,932,693	Wes Westrum
Chicago Cubs	59	103	.364	36	635,891	Leo Durocher

BA: Matty Alou, Pittsburgh, .342
Runs: Felipe Alou, Atlanta, 122
Hits: Felipe Alou, Atlanta, 218
RBIs: Hank Aaron, Atlanta, 127
HRs: Hank Aaron, Atlanta, 44
Wins: Sandy Koufax, Los Angeles, 27

SOs: Sandy Koufax, Los Angeles, 317
ERA: Sandy Koufax, Los Angeles, 1.73
Pct: Juan Marichal, San Francisco, .806, 25-6
Saves: Phil Regan, Los Angeles, 21

AAA International League
President: George H. Sisler, Jr.

Standings	W	L	Pct.	GB	Attend.	Manager
Rochester Red Wings (1)	83	64	.565	—	273,247	Earl Weaver
Columbus Jets (18)	82	65	.558	1	193,881	Lawrence Shepard
Toronto Maple Leafs (2)	82	65	.558	1	96,918	Dick Williams
Richmond Braves (11)	75	72	.510	8	234,005	Bill Adair
Buffalo Bisons (13)	72	74	.493	10½	126,914	John "Red" Davis
Toledo Mud Hens (9)	71	75	.486	11½	124,048	Loren Babe
Jacksonville Suns (16)	68	79	.463	15	93,374	Solly Hemus
Syracuse Chiefs (6)	54	93	.367	29	106,298	Frank Carswell

Playoffs: Richmond 3 games, Rochester 1; Toronto 3 games, Columbus 2.
Finals: Toronto 4 games, Richmond 1.

All-Star Team: 1B-Mike Epstein, Rochester; 2B-Jack Damaska, Columbus; 3B-Steve Demeter, Rochester; SS-Mark Belanger, Rochester; OF-Reggie Smith, Toronto; Don Bosch, Columbus; Bill Robinson, Richmond; C-Frank Fernandez, Toledo; Jim Price, Columbus; P-Gary Waslewski, Toronto; Wilbur Wood, Columbus; Jackie Moore, Syracuse; MVP-Mike Epstein, Rochester; Pitcher of the Year-Gary Waslewski, Toronto; Manager-Dick Williams, Toronto.

BA: Reggie Smith, Toronto, .320
Runs: Mike Andrews, Toronto, 97
Hits: Steve Demeter, Rochester, 166
RBIs: Mike Epstein, Rochester, 102

HRs: Mike Epstein, Rochester, 29
Wins: Gary Waslewski, Toronto, 18
SOs: Tom Phoebus, Rochester, 208
ERA: Wilbur Wood, Columbus, 2.41

AAA Pacific Coast League
President: Dewey Soriano

East Standings	W	L	Pct.	GB	Attend.	Manager
Tulsa Oilers (19)	85	62	.578	—	158,595	Charlie Metro
Phoenix Giants (20)	81	67	.547	4½	152,508	Bill Werle
Indianapolis Indians (4)	80	68	.541	5½	183,682	Les Moss
Denver Bears (8)	79	68	.537	6	182,041	Cal Ermer
San Diego Padres (17)	72	75	.490	13	173,607	Frank Lucchesi
Oklahoma City 89ers (14)	59	89	.399	26½	97,761	Mel McGaha

(West Standings)

West Standings	W	L	Pct.	GB	Attend.	Manager
Seattle Angels (3)	83	65	.561	—	163,319	Bob Lemon
Vancouver Mounties (7)	77	71	.520	6	121,482	Mickey Vernon
Spokane Indians (15)	75	73	.507	8	100,468	Roy Hartsfield
Portland Beavers (5)	69	79	.466	14	118,024	John Lipon
Hawaii Islanders (10)	63	84	.429	19½	191,367	George Case
Tacoma Cubs (12)	63	85	.426	20	104,719	Les Peden

Playoff: Seattle 4 games, Tulsa 3.

All-Star Team: 1B-Chuck Vinson, Seattle; 2B-Marv Staehle, Indianapolis; 3B-Dick Kenworthy, Indianapolis; SS-Bob Schroder, Phoenix; OF-Walt Williams, Tulsa; Ted Savage, Tulsa; Rick Reese, Denver; C-Duane Josephson, Indianapolis; Dave Ricketts, Tulsa; Util-John Werhas, Spokane; Frank Johnson, Phoenix; P-Jimmy Ollom, Denver; Bob Heffner, Portland; Ron Willis, Indianapolis; Bill Kelso, Seattle; MVP-Duane Josephson, Indianapolis; Manager-Bob Lemon, Seattle.

BA: Walt Williams, Tulsa, .330
Runs: Walt Williams, Tulsa, 107
Hits: Walt Williams, Tulsa, 193
RBIs: Ron Clark, Denver, 94
Dick Kenworthy, Indianapolis, 94

HRs: Tommy Murray, Oklahoma City, 26
Wins: Jimmy Ollom, Denver, 20
SOs: Bill Singer, Spokane, 217
ERA: Bill Fischer, Indianapolis, 2.35

AA Eastern League
President: A. Rankin Johnson

Standings	W	L	Pct.	GB	Attend.	Manager
Elmira Pioneers (1)	88	51	.633	—	65,771	Darrell Johnson
Pawtucket Indians (5)	68	71	.489	20	74,479	Clay Bryant
Pittsfield Red Sox (2)	68	71	.489	20	51,113	Eddie Popowski
Williamsport Mets (16)	68	72	.486	20½	61,873	Bill Virdon
Waterbury Giants (20)	64	76	.457	24½	80,042	Andy Gilbert
York White Roses (10)	62	77	.446	26	42,588	Billy Klaus

Playoffs: None.

All-Star Team: 1B-Tony Torchia, Pittsfield; 2B-Dave Nelson, Pawtucket; 3B-Frank Peters, Elmira; SS-Kevin Collins, Williamsport; OF-Howie Bedell, York; Curt Motton, Elmira; Robert Taylor, Waterbury; C-Lloyd Flodin, Williamsport; Jerry Moses, Pittsfield; P-Fred Beene, Elmira; Tom Fisher, Elmira; Manager-Darrell Johnson, Elmira.

BA: Howie Bedell, York, .322
Runs: Bernie Smith, Williamsport, 87
Hits: Robert Taylor, Waterbury, 150
RBIs: Tony Torchia, Pittsfield, 83

HRs: Hank McGraw, Williamsport/Elmira, 12
Wins: Jerry Hudgins, Pittsfield, 15
SOs: Tom Fisher, Elmira, 142
ERA: Tom Fisher, Elmira, 1.88

AA Mexican League
President: Antonio Ramirez Muro

Standings	W	L	Pct.	GB	Attend.	Manager
Monterrey Sultanes	79	61	.564	—	319,216	Wilfredo Calvino
Mexico City Tigres*	78	62	.557	1	387,520	Jose Luis Garcia/ Ricardo Garza
Mexico City Diablos Rojos**	74	66	.529	5	445,664	Tomas Herrera
Puebla Pericos	73	66	.525	5½	184,809	Roberto Avila
Veracruz Aguila	72	67	.518	6½	143,199	Vinicio Garcia
Jalisco Charros	69	70	.496	9½	280,126	Memo Garibay
Poza Rica Petroleros	61	79	.436	18	234,611	Tony Castano
Reynosa Broncs	52	87	.374	26½	119,845	Alberto Palafox/ John Schaive/Dan Bankhead

Playoff: MC Tigres 4 games, MC Diablos Rojos 2.

All-Star Team: 1B-Hector Espino, Monterrey; 2B-Arnoldo Castro MC Tigres; 3B-Armando Murillo, MC Tigres; SS-Rigoberto Mena, Monterrey; OF-Emilio Sosa, Poza Rica; Ramon Montoya, MC Diablos Rojos; Manuel Ponce, MC Tigres; C-Elrod Hendricks, Jalisco; Miguel Gaspar, Veracruz/MC Diablos Rojos; P-Vicente Romo, MC Tigres; Felipe Leal, MC Diablos Rojos; Manager-Vinicio Garcia, Veracruz.

BA: Hector Espino, Monterrey, .369
Runs: Ron Camacho, Puebla, 109
Hits: Oscar Rodriguez, Puebla, 165
RBIs: George Prescott, Poza Rica, 122

HRs: George Prescott, Poza Rica, 41
Wins: Julious Grant, Monterrey, 20
SOs: Jose Ramon Lopez, Monterrey, 309
ERA: Waldo Velo, Jalisco, 2.01

AA Southern League
President: Sam C. Smith

Standings	W	L	Pct.	GB	Attend.	Manager
Mobile Athletics (7)	88	52	.629	—	52,631	John McNamara
Asheville Tourists (18)	78	61	.561	9½	51,704	Pete Peterson
Evansville White Sox (4)	68	72	.486	20	69,697	George Noga
Macon Peaches (17)	67	73	.479	21	45,011	Andy Seminick
Montgomery Rebels (6)	66	72	.478	21	32,246	Wayne Blackburn
Charlotte Hornets (8)	64	74	.464	23	33,943	Harry Warner
Columbus Yankees (9)	63	76	.453	24½	48,847	Jack Reed
Knoxville Smokies (13)	61	75	.449	25	28,101	Jack Cassini

*Won first-half   **Won second-half   ***Won both halves
Numbers after nicknames indicate farm system.
Affiliation listed at end of year.

492

Playoffs: None

All-Star Team: 1B-Charles Leonard, Asheville; **2B**-Ron Theobald, Charlotte; **3B**-Bob Robertson, Asheville; **SS**-Jerry Kenney, Columbus; **OF**-John Fenderson, Knoxville; Rick Monday, Mobile; Pat Kelly, Charlotte; **C**-Rene Lachemann, Mobile; Carl Taylor, Asheville; **P**-Jim Nash, Mobile; Bill Edgerton, Mobile; **Manager**-John McNamara, Mobile.

BA: John Fenderson, Knoxville, .324
Runs: Sam Thompson, Knoxville, 114
Hits: Sam Thompson, Knoxville, 166
RBIs: Bob Robertson, Asheville, 99
HRs: Bob Robertson, Asheville, 32
Wins: Bill Edgerton, Mobile, 17
SOs: George Korince, Montgomery, 183
ERA: Dave Roberts, Asheville, 2.61

AA Texas League
President: Hugh J. Finnerty

Standings	W	L	Pct.	GB	Attend.	Manager
Arkansas Travelers (19)	81	59	.579	—	108,288	Vern Rapp
Amarillo Sonics (14)	77	63	.550	4	78,656	Buddy Hancken
Albuquerque Dodgers (15)	74	66	.529	7	82,083	Bob Kennedy
Austin Braves (11)	67	73	.479	14	54,104	Hub Kittle
El Paso Sun Kings (3)	62	78	.443	19	62,192	Chuck Tanner
Dallas-Ft. Worth Spurs (12)	59	81	.421	22	271,367	Stan Hack/Pete Reiser/ Lou Klein

Playoffs: Austin 2 games, Arkansas 1; Albuquerque 2 games, Amarillo 1.
Finals: Austin 1 game, Albuquerque 0, series called on account of rain.

All-Star Team: 1B-Tom Hutton, Albuquerque; **2B**-Roy Majtyka, Arkansas; **3B**-Doug Rader, Amarillo; **SS**-Steve Huntz, Arkansas; **OF**-Don Davis, Amarillo; Floyd Wicker, Arkansas; Jim Fairey, Albuquerque; Willie Crawford, Albuquerque; Don Wilkinson, El Paso; **C**-Dan Breeden, Arkansas; **Util**-Winston Llenas, El Paso; **P**-Fred Norman, Dallas-Ft. Worth; Don Wilson, Amarillo; **MVP**-Tom Hutton, Albuquerque; **Pitcher of the Year**-Fred Norman, Dallas-Ft. Worth; **Manager**-Vern Rapp, Arkansas.

BA: Tom Hutton, Albuquerque, .340
Runs: Willie Crawford, Albuquerque, 94
Hits: Doug Rader, Amarillo, 153
RBIs: Tom Hutton, Albuquerque, 81; George Pena, El Paso, 81
HRs: Winston Llenas, El Paso, 25; Larry "Moose" Stubing, Arkansas, 25
Wins: Bill Larkin, Albuquerque, 20
SOs: Fred Norman, Dallas-Ft. Worth, 198
ERA: Pat House, Austin, 2.13

A California League
President: Edward J. Mulligan

Standings	W	L	Pct.	GB	Attend.	Manager
Modesto Reds***(7)	88	53	.624	—	57,846	Gus Niarhos
San Jose Bees (3)	77	64	.546	11	70,964	Rocky Bridges
Fresno Giants (20)	74	66	.529	13½	54,630	Ed FitzGerald
Reno Silver Sox (5)	69	71	.493	18½	29,342	Phil Cavarretta
Santa Barbara Dodgers (15)	69	71	.493	18½	30,582	Norm Sherry
Bakersfield Bears (17)	68	72	.486	19½	29,650	Dick Teed
Lodi Crushers (12)	59	81	.421	28½	56,221	Don Elston/Ray Perry
Stockton Ports (1)	57	83	.407	30½	20,808	Harry Malmberg

Playoff: Modesto defeated San Jose in a one game playoff for the first half championship.

All-Star Team: 1B-DeGold Francis, Fresno; **2B**-Dan Greenfield, Modesto; **3B**-Ed Bays, Reno, Alan Gallagher, Fresno; **SS**-Cesar Gutierrez, Fresno; **OF**-Bobby Mitchell, San Jose; Larry Wilson, Modesto; Merv Rettenmund, Stockton; **C**-Dave Duncan, Modesto; **Util**-Bruce Hix, Fresno; **P**-Rollie Fingers, Modesto; Stanley Jones, Modesto; Dan Keller, San Jose; Harold Jeffcoat, Fresno; **MVP**-Dave Duncan, Modesto; **Rookie of the Year**-Jarvis Tatum, San Jose; **Manager**-Gus Niarhos, Modesto.

BA: Dan Greenfield, Modesto, .339
Runs: Dan Greenfield, Modesto, 111
Hits: Jarvis Tatum, San Jose, 168; Ed Bays, Reno, 168
RBIs: Larry Wilson, Modesto, 117
HRs: David Duncan, Modesto, 46
Wins: Greg Conger, Modesto, 16; John Fouse, Reno, 16; Richard Armstrong, Santa Barbara, 16
SOs: Richard Armstrong, Santa Barbara, 186
ERA: Greg Conger, Modesto, 2.73

A Carolina League
President: J.C. "Bill" Jessup

East Standings	W	L	Pct.	GB	Attend.	Manager
Kinston Eagles (11)	76	63	.547	—	68,757	Andy Pafko
Rocky Mount Leafs (6)	72	63	.533	2	34,004	Al Federoff
Wilson Tobs (8)	72	65	.526	3	23,501	Vern Morgan
Peninsula Grays (13)	63	75	.457	12½	74,366	Pinky May
Portsmouth Tides (17)	58	81	.417	18	42,182	Bobby Morgan/Lou Kahn

West Standings	W	L	Pct.	GB	Attend.	Manager
Winston-Salem Red Sox (2)	82	58	.586	—	80,024	Bill Slack
Burlington Senators (10)	76	62	.551	5	22,041	Wayne Terwilliger
Raleigh Pirates (18)	71	66	.518	9½	25,562	Joe Morgan
Lynchburg White Sox (4)	64	75	.460	17½	33,805	Ira Hutchinson
Greensboro Yankees (9)	64	76	.457	18	43,204	Gary Blaylock
Durham Bulls (14)	62	76	.449	19	32,023	Chuck Churn

Playoffs: Rocky Mount 2 games, Kinston 0; Winston-Salem 2 games, Burlington 0.
Finals: Rocky Mount 2 games, Winston-Salem 0.

All-Star Team: 1B-Jose Calero, Winston-Salem; **2B**-Rod Carew, Wilson; **3B**-Juan Guzman, Kinston; **SS**-Al Cambero, Kinston; **OF**-Jerry Dorsch, Winston-Salem; Barry Morgan, Kinston; Richard Billings, Burlington; **C**-Johnny Bench, Peninsula; Manny Sanguillen, Raleigh; **Util**-Al Oliver, Raleigh; Richard Smith, Burlington; **P**-Robbie Snow, Winston-Salem; Dick Drago, Rocky Mount; Dan Lazar, Lynchburg; Francis Pollard, Portsmouth; **MVP**-Robbie Snow, Winston-Salem; **Manager**-Joe Morgan, Raleigh.

BA: Jose Calero, Winston-Salem, .330
Runs: Al Cambero, Kinston, 115
Hits: Al Cambero, Kinston, 170
RBIs: Barry Morgan, Kinston, 104
HRs: Barry Morgan, Kinston, 28
Wins: Robbie Snow, Winston-Salem, 20
SOs: Wally Wolf, Peninsula, 185
ERA: Robbie Snow, Winston-Salem, 1.75

A Florida State League
President: George MacDonald, Sr.

Standings	W	L	Pct.	GB	Attend.	Manager
St. Petersburg Cards**(19)	91	45	.669	—	69,644	Sparky Anderson
Leesburg Athletics*(7)	87	44	.664	1½	30,567	James Williams
Cocoa Astros (14)	81	55	.596	10	10,286	Joe Frazier
Miami Marlins (1)	75	63	.543	17	74,078	Billy DeMars
Orlando Twins (8)	71	68	.511	21½	40,229	John Goryl
Daytona Beach Islanders (6)	71	70	.504	22½	19,190	Gail Henley
Ft. Lauderdale Yankees (9)	63	75	.457	29	37,313	Lamar North
Deerfield Beach/ Winter Haven Sun Sox#(4)	55	83	.399	37	14,448	Don Bacon/Bruce Andrew
West Palm Beach Braves (11)	45	89	.336	45	16,437	Buddy Hicks
Tampa Tarpons (13)	47	94	.333	46½	39,882	Lou Fitzgerald

#Deerfield Beach moved to Winter Haven June 27.

Playoff: Leesburg 3 games, St. Petersburg 2.

All-Star Team: 1B-Dick Hickerson, Miami; **2B**-Bruce Andrew, Deerfield Beach/Winter Haven; **3B**-Steve Hertz, Cocoa; **SS**-Tim Marting, Daytona Beach; **OF**-Ernie Davis, St. Petersburg; Archie Wade, St. Petersburg; Fred Rico, Miami; Frank Tepedino, Miami; **C**-Bob Watson, Cocoa; Fred Velazquez, Leesburg; **P**-Paul Gilliford, Miami; Tony King, West Palm Beach; **Manager**-Sparky Anderson, St. Petersburg.

BA: Bruce Andrew, Deerfield Beach/Winter Haven, .329
Runs: Allen Lewis, Leesburg, 92
Hits: Allen Lewis, Leesburg, 156
RBIs: Charles Robinson, Leesburg, 78
HRs: Charles Robinson, Leesburg, 13
SBs: Allen Lewis, Leesburg, 116
Wins: Lloyd Fourroux, Miami, 17
SOs: Lloyd Fourroux, Miami, 183
ERA: Paul Gilliford, Miami, 1.27

A Mexican Center League
President: Antonio Ramirez (Muro)

Standings	W	L	Pct.	GB	Attend.	Manager
San Luis Potosi Rojos**	85	53	.616	—	36,933	Humberto Ayala
Guanajuato Tuzos*	77	57	.575	6	37,924	Domingo Santana
Aguascalientes Broncos	73	61	.545	10	54,004	Guillermo Frayde
Zacatecas Pericos	73	64	.533	11½	35,095	Jesus Diaz/Leonel Aldama
Durango Alacranes	67	69	.493	17	75,946	Francisco Martinez
Fresnillo Mineros	61	76	.445	23½	23,710	Oswaldo Alvarez/ Marco Manzo
Morelia Tigres	59	77	.434	25	23,997	Arturo Cacheux/Jesus Robles
Leon Diablos Verdes	49	87	.360	35	30,836	Angel Castro/Jose Guerrero Guadalupe Pedroza/

Playoff: Guanajuato 4 games, San Luis Potosi 1.

All-Star Team: 1B-Heriberto Vargas, Guanajuato; **2B**-Gabriel Lugo, Fresnillo; **3B**-Adam Contreras, Morelia; **SS**-Ruben Hurtado, Aguascalientes; **OF**-Mauro Rocha, Guanajuato; Alejandro Zazueta, Aguascalientes; Antonio Rubio, San Luis Potosi; **C**-Pedro Hernandez, Guanajuato; Jose Jesus Hernandez, Zacatecas; **P**-Raul Salazar, San Luis Potosi; Gustavo Guerrero, Aguascalientes; **Manager**-Domingo Santana, Guanajuato.

BA: Heriberto Vargas, Guanajuato, .445
Runs: Heriberto Vargas, Guanajuato, 168
Hits: Pedro Hernandez, Guanajuato, 221
RBIs: Heriberto Vargas, Guanajuato, 174
HRs: Heriberto Vargas, Guanajuato, 55
Wins: Gustavo Guerrero, Aguascalientes, 20; Abelardo Vega, San Luis Potosi, 20
SOs: Abelardo Vega, San Luis Potosi, 183
ERA: Raul Salazar, San Luis Potosi, 3.99

A Mexican Southeast League
President: Dr. Fernando Canton Franco

Standings	W	L	Pct.	GB	Attend.	Manager
Campeche Pirates**	67	45	.598	—	77,634	Ricardo Garza/ Jose Luis Garcia/ David Garcia
Tabasco Plataneros	63	46	.578	2½	39,771	Hector Rodriguez
Yucatan Venados	60	52	.536	7	88,447	Leonel Aldama/ Alberto Palafox/ Ernesto Garcia
Puerto Mexico Portenos*	53	56	.486	12½	45,940	Claudio Solano
Orizaba Cervaceros	33	77	.300	33	18,070	Felipe Hernandez

Playoff: Puerto Mexico 4 games, Campeche 3.

All-Star Team: 1B-Celso Oviedo, Puerto Mexico; **2B**-Jesus Leal, Puerto Mexico; **3B**-Celerino Sanchez, Campeche; **SS**-Victor Osuna, Yucatan; **OF**-Miguel Gutierrez, Yucatan; Ernesto Cruz, Campeche; Ricardo Nevarez, Puerto Mexico; **C**-Marcos Cobos, Mexico; Alberto Palafox, Yucatan; **P**-Eusebio Elizalde, Campeche; Ruben Soqui, Tabasco; **Manager**-Claudio Solano, Puerto Mexico.

BA: Celerino Sanchez, Campeche, .448
Runs: Maximo Garcia, Campeche, 75
Hits: Celerino Sanchez, Campeche, 160
RBIs: Celerino Sanchez, Campeche, 82
HRs: Celso Oviedo, Puerto Mexico, 17

Wins: Eusebio Elizalde, Campeche, 13
Juan Hernandez, Yucatan, 13
Miguel Pereira, Campeche, 13
SOs: Fernando Turrent, Yucatan, 138
ERA: Eusebio Elizalde, Campeche, 1.08

A Midwest League
President: James Doster

Standings	W	L	Pct.	GB	Attend.	Manager
Cedar Rapids Cardinals**(19) ...	81	40	.669	—	67,625	Ron Plaza
Fox Cities Foxes*(4)	77	47	.621	5½	57,496	Stan Wasiak
Burlington Bees (7)	77	48	.616	6	55,023	Al Ronning
Quad Cities Angels (3)	63	61	.508	19½	67,387	Harry Dunlop
Quincy Cubs (12)	61	63	.492	21½	36,165	Walt Dixon
Wisconsin Rapids Twins (8)..	59	63	.484	22½	37,245	Ray Bellino
Waterloo Hawks (2)............	56	68	.452	26½	37,613	Dave Philley
Decatur Commodores (20) ...	49	76	.392	34	50,572	Richard Klaus
Clinton Pilots (18)	48	76	.387	34½	34,804	Frank Oceak
Dubuque Packers (5)	44	73	.376	35	33,705	Elmer Valo

Playoff: Fox Cities 2 games, Cedar Rapids 1.

All-Star Team: 1B-Bill Johns, Quincy; **2B**-Doug Griffin, Quad Cities; **3B**-Bill McNulty, Burlington; **SS**-Neil McPhee, Wisconsin Rapids; **OF**-Tom Simon, Quincy; Jim Clark, Burlington; Zelman Jack, Clinton; **C**-Tim Young, Decatur; Tim Murtaugh, Clinton; **Util**-Paul Alderette, Quad Cities; Jose Arcia, Cedar Rapids; **P**-Vern Geishert, Quad Cities; Jess Huggins, Decatur; **Manager**-Al Ronning, Burlington.

BA: Grover "Deacon" Jones,
Fox Cities, .353
Runs: Neil McPhee, Wisconsin Rapids, 87
Hits: Bob Clifton, Burlington, 144
RBIs: Grover "Deacon" Jones, Fox Cities, 80

HRs: Graig Nettles, Wisconsin Rapids, 28
Wins: Fred Rath, Fox Cities, 17
SOs: Michael Abarbanel, Fox Cities, 206
ERA: Vern Geishert, Quad Cities, 1.13

A New York-Pennsylvania League
President: Vincent M. McNamara

Standings	W	L	Pct.	GB	Attend.	Manager
Auburn Mets*(16)	80	49	.620	—	35,933	Clyde McCullough
Jamestown Dodgers (15)......	70	55	.560	8	29,743	Bill Berrier
Binghamton Triplets**(9) ..	67	58	.536	11	51,126	Frank Verdi
Oneonta Red Sox (2)	65	59	.524	12½	24,425	Matt Sczesny
Batavia Trojans (x)	58	63	.479	18	31,279	Max Lanier
Geneva Senators (10)..........	34	90	.274	43½	13,529	Gordon MacKenzie

Playoff: Auburn 2 games, Binghamton 0.

All-Star Team: 1B-Amos Otis, Oneonta; **2B**-David Casey, Oneonta; **3B**-Edward Gagle, Auburn; **SS**-Warren Miller, Geneva/Oneonta; **OF**-Cito Gaston, Batavia; James Dix, Auburn; David McCammon, Jamestown; Ivey Armstrong, Jamestown; **C**-Dick Howard, Auburn; Louis Howell, Binghamton; **Util**-Frederick Moulder, Jamestown; **P**-Alan Schmelz, Auburn; Gerald Wild, Auburn; Jerry Koosman, Auburn; John Radosevich, Jamestown; **Manager**-Clyde McCullough, Auburn; Max Lanier, Batavia.

BA: David McCammon, Jamestown, .335
Runs: John Gonsalves, Auburn, 98
Hits: Joseph Moock, Auburn, 146
RBIs: Cito Gaston, Batavia, 104

HRs: Cito Gaston, Batavia, 28
Wins: Mickey Scott, Binghamton, 15
SOs: Mickey Scott, Binghamton, 190
ERA: Jerry Koosman, Auburn, 1.38

A Northern League
President: Roland E. Parcel

Standings	W	L	Pct.	GB	Attend.	Manager
St. Cloud Rox (8)...............	49	18	.731	—	22,292	Ken Staples
Aberdeen Pheasants (1)......	47	22	.681	3	24,767	Cal Ripken, Sr.
Huron Phillies (17)	32	35	.478	17	35,110	Joe Lonnett
Duluth-Superior Dukes (12)..	29	36	.446	19	10,937	LaVern Grace
Sioux Falls Packers (13).....	26	41	.388	23	25,125	James Snyder
Bismarck-Mandan Pards (14)..	16	47	.254	31	6,988	Tony Pacheco

Playoffs: None.

BA: James Williams, Aberdeen, .360
Runs: James Williams, Aberdeen, 63
Hits: James Williams, Aberdeen, 102
RBIs: Roger Freed, Aberdeen, 58
HRs: Roger Freed, Aberdeen, 13

Wins: Michael Colin, St. Cloud, 10
Louis Stephen, St. Cloud, 10
SOs: Robert Castiglione, St. Cloud, 174
ERA: Gaston Holland, Huron, 1.15

A Northwest League
President: James Fleishman

Standings	W	L	Pct.	GB	Attend.	Manager
Tri-City Atoms (15)...........	57	27	.679	—	29,402	Duke Snider
Eugene Emeralds (17, 19) ..	44	40	.524	13	28,409	Hugh Luby
Yakima Braves (11)...........	39	44	.470	17½	13,262	Eddie Haas
Lewiston Broncs (7)	27	56	.325	29½	18,797	Grady Wilson

Playoffs: None.

All-Star Team: 1B-Doug Pautz, Eugene; **2B**-Billy Grabarkewitz, Tri-City; **3B**-Bob Young, Eugene; **SS**-Tony Canzano, Tri-City; **OF**-Roger Nelson, Eugene; Oscar Brown, Yakima; Roy Gleason, Tri-City; Terry Heizenrader, Tri-City; **C**-Ted Sizemore, Tri-City; **P**-Bob Baird, Tri-City; Mike Mathwig, Tri-City; **Util**-Larry Vlasin, Lewiston; **Manager**-Duke Snider, Tri-City.

BA: Oscar Brown, Yakima, .346
Runs: Billy Grabarkewitz, Tri-City, 62
Hits: Doug Pautz, Eugene, 96
RBIs: Doug Pautz, Eugene, 53
HRs: Roy Gleason, Tri-City, 16

Wins: Ray Lamb, Tri-City, 12
Albert Choate, Tri-City, 12
SOs: Ray Lamb, Tri-City, 143
ERA: Bob Baird, Tri-City, 1.36

A Western Carolinas League
President: John H. Moss

Standings	W	L	Pct.	GB	Attend.	Manager
Spartanburg Phillies***(17) ..	91	35	.722	—	173,010	Bob Wellman
Greenville Mets (16)...........	86	40	.683	5	59,078	Pete Pavlick
Thomasville Hi-Toms (8) ...	71	52	.577	18½	30,940	Ralph Rowe
Gastonia Pirates (18)	67	57	.540	23	39,344	Bob Clear
Rock Hill Cardinals (19).....	58	68	.460	33	43,100	Jack Krol
Salisbury Astros (14)	44	77	.364	44½	23,737	Walt Matthews
Statesville Tigers (6)..........	42	81	.341	47½	25,424	Al Lakeman/George Spencer
Lexington Giants (20).........	37	86	.301	52½	30,004	Alex Cosmidis/Dennis Sommers

Playoffs: None.

All-Star Team: 1B-Mike Mitchell, Greenville; **2B**-Denny Doyle, Spartanburg; **3B**-Luis Lagunas, Thomasville; **SS**-Pablo Cruz, Gastonia; **OF**-Gil Torres, Spartanburg; Danny Loftin, Thomasville; Charlie Howard, Gastonia; **C**-Wayne Martin, Spartanburg; John Francis, Salisbury; **P**-Nolan Ryan, Greenville; John Penn, Spartanburg; **MVP**-Luis Lagunas, Thomasville; **Most Outstanding Prospect**-Nolan Ryan, Greenville; **Most Outstanding Pitcher**-Nolan Ryan, Greenville; **Manager**-Bob Wellman, Spartanburg.

BA: Gil Torres, Spartanburg, .365
Runs: Louis Smith, Thomasville, 98
Hits: Denny Doyle, Spartanburg, 153
RBIs: Luis Lagunas, Thomasville, 106

HRs: Luis Lagunas, Thomasville, 35
Wins: Nolan Ryan, Greenville, 17
SOs: Nolan Ryan, Greenville, 272
ERA: John Penn, Spartanburg, 2.21

R Appalachian League
President: Chauncey De Vault

Standings	W	L	Pct.	GB	Attend.	Manager
Marion Mets (16)...............	43	26	.623	—	24,457	Carl "Buddy" Peterson
Johnson City Yankees (9)...	41	30	.577	3	22,355	Bob Bauer
Bluefield Orioles (1)..........	38	33	.535	6	30,847	Joe Altobelli
Covington Red Sox (2).......	28	43	.394	16	34,622	Rac Slider
Salem Rebels (18)..............	25	43	.368	17½	34,884	George Detore

Playoffs: None.

All-Star Team: 1B-Mike Jorgensen, Marion; **2B**-Ed Mello, Covington; **3B**-Ingram Haley, Johnson City; **SS**-Paul Flesner, Bluefield; **OF**-Julio Morales, Marion; Alonzo Harris, Bluefield; Earl Hash, Johnson City; **C**-Dave May, Bluefield; **P**-Vaughn Kovach, Bluefield; Doug Watkins, Salem; **Rookie of the Year**-Julio Morales, Marion; **Manager**-Buddy Peterson, Marion.

BA: Jerald Albin, Johnson City, .302
Runs: Ed Mello, Covington, 56
Hits: Gene Clines, Salem, 63
RBIs: Paul Flesner, Bluefield, 43
Jim Zgorzelski, Covington, 43

HRs: Earl Hash, Johnson City, 9
Wins: Ed Lindblad, Marion, 10
SOs: Steve Blateric, Covington, 95
ERA: Vaughn Kovach, Bluefield, 2.57

R Gulf Coast League
President: George MacDonald, Sr.

Standings	W	L	Pct.	GB	Manager
Yankees (9)........................	32	16	.667	—	Dick Berardino
Braves (11)	27	21	.563	5	Tom Saffell
Twins (8)...........................	24	24	.500	8	Fred Waters
Cardinals (19)	20	28	.417	12	George Kissell
White Sox (4).....................	17	31	.354	15	Frank Parenti

All games played at Sarasota, Florida.

Playoffs: None.

All-Star Team: 1B-Tony Solaita, Yankees; **2B**-Frank DaVanon, Cardinals; **3B**-Ralph Wells, Braves; **SS**-Jim Kennedy, Yankees; **OF**-Joe Pactwa, Yankees; Herman Hill, Twins; Chuck Chase, Twins; Fred Winston, Yankees; **C**-Steve Mezich, Yankees; Chuck Walke, Braves; **Util**-Fred Brown, Yankees; **P**-Joe Atilee, Cardinals; Tom Hall, Twins; **Manager**-Tom Saffell, Braves.

BA: Tony Solaita, Yankees, .324
Runs: Joe Pactwa, Yankees, 37
Hits: Wayne Dees, Cardinals, 48
RBIs: Tony Solaita, Yankees, 40
HRs: Fred Winston, Yankees, 5

Wins: Tom Hall, Twins, 6
Wenty Ford, Braves, 6
SOs: Tom Hall, Twins, 100
ERA: Eugene Damron, Braves, 1.88

R Pioneer League
President: Ben Jewell

Standings	W	L	Pct.	GB	Attend.	Manager
Ogden Dodgers (15)	39	27	.591	—	33,822	Tom Lasorda
Treasure Valley Cubs (12)..	36	30	.545	3	20,266	George Freese
Idaho Falls Angels (3)	29	37	.439	10	23,350	Tom Morgan/Alex Monchak/Joe Gordon/John Fitzpatrick
Magic Valley Cowboys (20) ...	28	38	.424	11	11,776	Harvey Koepf

Playoffs: None.

All-Star Team: 1B-Paul Campbell, Idaho Falls; **2B-**Richard Thompson, Ogden; **3B-**Robert Harvey, Ogden; **SS-**Frederick Rodriguez, Treasure Valley; **OF-**Jay Reed, Magic Valley; John Wyatt, Ogden; Gorrell Stinson, Ogden; **C-**Randy Brown, Idaho Falls; John Harrell, Magic Valley; **Util-**Don DeSousa, Magic Valley; Jack Intlekofer, Idaho Falls; **P-**Robert Reynolds, Magic Valley; Archie Reynolds, Treasure Valley; Dennis James, Ogden; Dean Burk, Treasure Valley; **Manager-**George Freese, Treasure Valley.

BA: Richard Thompson, Ogden, .322
Runs: Frederick Rodriguez, Treasure Valley, 68
Hits: Richard Thompson, Ogden, 89
RBIs: Paul Campbell, Idaho Falls, 60
HRs: Frederick Rodriguez, Treasure Valley, 11
Paul Campbell, Idaho Falls, 11

Wins: Dean Burk, Treasure Valley, 9
Larry Hutton, Ogden, 9
Alonso Olivares, Idaho Falls, 9
Archie Reynolds, Treasure Valley, 9
SOs: Robert Reynolds, Magic Valley, 147
ERA: Dennis James, Ogden, 1.75

1966 Interleague Post Season Play

World Series
Baltimore (American) 4 games, Los Angeles (National) 0

1966 Major League Farm Systems

American League

1 Baltimore (6): Rochester, Elmira, Stockton, Miami, Aberdeen, Bluefield.
2 Boston (6): Toronto, Pittsfield, Winston-Salem, Waterloo, Oneonta, Covington.
3 California (5): Seattle, El Paso, San Jose, Quad Cities, Idaho Falls.
4 Chicago (6): Indianapolis, Evansville, Lynchburg, Deerfield Beach/Winter Haven, Fox Cities, Gulf Coast.
5 Cleveland (4): Portland, Pawtucket, Reno, Dubuque.
6 Detroit (5): Syracuse, Montgomery, Rocky Mount, Daytona Beach, Statesville.
7 Kansas City (6): Vancouver, Mobile, Modesto, Leesburg, Burlington (IA), Lewiston.
8 Minnesota (8): Denver, Charlotte, Wilson, Orlando, Wisconsin Rapids, St. Cloud, Thomasville, Gulf Coast.
9 New York (7): Toledo, Columbus (GA), Greensboro, Ft. Lauderdale, Binghamton, Johnson City, Gulf Coast.
10 Washington (4): Hawaii, York, Burlington (NC), Geneva.

National League

11 Atlanta (6): Richmond, Austin, Kinston, West Palm Beach, Yakima, Gulf Coast.
12 Chicago (6): Tacoma, Dallas-Ft. Worth, Lodi, Quincy, Duluth-Superior, Treasure Valley.
13 Cincinnati (5): Buffalo, Knoxville, Peninsula, Tampa, Sioux Falls.
14 Houston (6): Oklahoma City, Amarillo, Durham, Cocoa, Bismarck-Mandan, Salisbury.
15 Los Angeles (6): Spokane, Albuquerque, Santa Barbara, Jamestown, Tri-City, Ogden.
16 New York (5): Jacksonville, Williamsport, Auburn, Greenville, Marion.
17 Philadelphia (7): San Diego, Macon, Bakersfield, Portsmouth, Huron, Eugene, Spartanburg.
18 Pittsburgh (6): Columbus (OH), Asheville, Raleigh, Clinton, Gastonia, Salem.
19 St. Louis (7): Tulsa, Arkansas, St. Petersburg, Cedar Rapids, Eugene, Rock Hill, Gulf Coast.
20 San Francisco (6): Phoenix, Waterbury, Fresno, Decatur, Lexington, Magic Valley.
Co-op(x): Batavia.

1966 No-Hitters

Date	Pitcher	Team	League	Opponent	Score
4-19	Juan Quintana	Durham	Carolina	Peninsula	8-0
4-28	Curtis Sauer	Wilson	Carolina	Greensboro	2-0 (7)
5-2	Phil Knuckles	St. Petersburg	Florida State	Orlando	1-0 (7)
5-2	Stan Robinson	Cocoa	Florida State	Tampa	5-2 (7)
5-6	David Lowery	Orlando	Florida State	Cocoa	6-1 (7)
5-6	Vern Geishert	Quad Cities	Midwest	Appleton	7-0
5-15	Dick Drago	Rocky Mount	Carolina	Greensboro	5-0 (7)
5-15	Darrell Clark	Rocky Mount	Carolina	Greensboro	2-0 (7)
5-18	Jim Hardin	Elmira	Eastern	Williamsport	4-1 (6)
5-27	Enrique Rojo	Campeche	Mexican S.E.	Orizaba	3-0
5-28	Michael Abarbanel	Fox Cities	Midwest	Wisconsin Rapids	9-1
5-29	Dick Mergler	Raleigh	Carolina	Lynchburg	3-0
6-1	Don Loun	York	Eastern	Williamsport	3-2 (7)
6-7	Jesse Huggins	Decatur	Midwest	Wisconsin Rapids	1-0 (7)
6-9	Mack Gendreau	Spartanburg	W. Carolinas	Statesville	6-0 (7)
6-10	Sonny Siebert	Cleveland	American	Washington	2-0
6-11	Conrad Noessel	Kinston	Carolina	Tidewater	5-0 (7)
6-15	Manuel Lugo	Fresnillo	Mexican Center	Durango	4-0
6-24	Andres Ayon	Puebla	Mexican	Jalisco	7-0
6-30	Bill Butler	Rocky Mount	Carolina	Raleigh	0-1 (8)
6-30	Steve Miller	Salisbury	W. Carolinas	Lexington	6-1
7-4	Steve Jones	Evansville	Southern	Columbus	1-0
7-7	Dennis Palazzo	New York	Gulf Coast	Minnesota	5-0
7-8	Bill Burbach	Greensboro	Carolina	Lynchburg	3-1 (10)
7-8	George Wolger	Aberdeen	Northern	Huron	1-0
7-9	Joe Borowy	Orlando	Florida State	Winter Haven	2-0 (7)
7-15	Richard Johnson/ Thomas Beck	Huron	Northern	Bismarck-Mandan	15-0
7-17	Jim Wingate	Pawtucket	Eastern	Waterbury	5-0
7-17	Stan Bahnsen	Syracuse	International	Richmond	1-0 (7)
7-22	John Silva	Oneonta	New York-Penn.	Auburn	1-0 (7)
7-28	Larry Tolliver	Lexington	W. Carolinas	Salisbury	2-3 (8)
7-28	Dave Vineyard	Rochester	International	Toledo	1-0
7-28	Tony King	West Palm Beach	Florida State	Orlando	3-0 (7)
8-4	Steve Blateric	Covington	Appalachian	Salem	4-0 (7)
8-9	Neil Boyle	Duluth-Superior	Northern	Sioux Falls	0-1 (8)
8-10	William Matusz/ Ron Herr	West Palm Beach	Florida State	Tampa	9-0
8-10	Evelio Hernandez	Monterrey	Mexican	Puebla	2-0 (7)
8-10	Bruce Von Hoff	Durham	Carolina	Rocky Mount	5-1
8-12	Bob Simmons	Minnesota	Gulf Coast	New York	3-1 (7)
8-15	Tom Phoebus	Rochester	International	Buffalo	1-0 (7)
8-16	Al Santorini	Austin	Texas	El Paso	2-1 (7)
8-23	Don Lohse	Leesburg	Florida State	Winter Haven	2-0 (7)
8-25	John Rawls	Miami	Florida State	Orlando	1-0 (7)
8-27	Paul Gilliford	Miami	Florida State	Daytona Beach	1-0
9-2	Ken Reynolds	Huron	Northern	Sioux Falls	3-0 (7)

Number in parentheses indicates innings if other than nine.

THIS DATE IN MINOR LEAGUE HISTORY

May 3, 1966, George Prescott, Poza Rica, Mexican League, slugger, hit three homers and drove in ten runs as the Oilers trounced Veracruz, 19-5.

May 15, 1966, Dick Drago and Darrell Clark pitched back-to-back no-hit games for Rocky Mount, Carolina League, to win a twin bill from Greensboro, 5-0 and 2-0. Both games lasted seven innings.

May 21, 1966, St. Petersburg, Florida State League, lost a 1-0 decision to Cocoa after winning 22 consecutive games. The streak was the eighth longest in minor league history.

May 22, 1966, Art Groza, Burlington, Midwest League, pitcher, struck out ten straight Dubuque batters, but lost, 3-2.

May 31, 1966, Guanajuato, Mexican Center League, amassed 33 hits to defeat Fresnillo 36-15, in a game shortened to eight innings by darkness. Miguel Escanilla went 7-for-7 for the winners.

June 11, 1966, Nolan Ryan, rookie righthander, Greenville, Western Carolinas League, struck out 19 in a four-hit, 8-0 win over Statesville.

June 14, 1966, Miami defeated St. Petersburg 4-3 in a Florida State League contest which lasted 29 innings, the longest game in the history of Organized Baseball.

June 26, 1966, Kinston, Carolina League, tallied 14 runs in the fifth inning and coasted to a 16-1 victory over Rocky Mount.

July 1, 1966, Tampa, Florida State League, ended a 50-inning scoreless string in a game with Miami.

July 16, 1966, Actress Mamie Van Doren, playing the baseball wife, watched her husband, Lee Meyers, pitch for Lodi in the California League.

August 5, 1966, Reggie Jackson, Modesto, California League, hit three homers in a game with Reno.

August 12, 1966, Spartanburg, Western Carolinas League, extended their winning streak to 25 straight, two shy of the all-time mark, with a doubleheader sweep over Lexington. (The streak ended August 13 with a 12-inning loss to Greenville.)

August 18, 1966, Dick Barnes, Waterloo, Midwest League, fanned nine consecutive Fox Cities batters in a relief role.

August 21, 1966, After 14 consecutive victories, Gary Puttman, Greenville, Western Carolinas League, lost his first game of the season, 12-8, to Thomasville.

August 31, 1966, In the longest game in California League history, Reno edged Lodi 6-5 in 23 innings.

October 30, 1966, "Kewpie" Dick Barrett, 60, who won 325 minor league games, plus 34 in the Majors, died in Seattle. Barrett won 20 or more games seven times in eight seasons with Seattle of the Pacific Coast League between 1935 and 1942, pitching the Rainiers to three consecutive pennants.

1967

American League
President: Joseph E. Cronin

Standings	W	L	Pct.	GB	Attend.	Manager
Boston Red Sox	92	70	.568	—	1,727,832	Dick Williams
Detroit Tigers....................	91	71	.562	1	1,447,143	Mayo Smith
Minnesota Twins	91	71	.562	1	1,483,547	Sam Mele/Cal Ermer
Chicago White Sox	89	73	.549	3	985,634	Eddie Stanky
California Angels..............	84	77	.522	7½	1,317,713	Bill Rigney
Baltimore Orioles	76	85	.472	15½	955,053	Hank Bauer
Washington Senators	76	85	.472	15½	770,868	Gil Hodges
Cleveland Indians	75	87	.463	17	662,980	Joe Adcock
New York Yankees.............	72	90	.444	20	1,259,514	Ralph Houk
Kansas City Athletics	62	99	.385	29½	726,639	Alvin Dark/Luke Appling

BA: Carl Yastrzemski, Boston, .326
Runs: Carl Yastrzemski, Boston, 112
Hits: Carl Yastrzemski, Boston, 189
RBIs: Carl Yastrzemski, Boston, 121
HRs: Carl Yastrzemski, Boston, 44
    Harmon Killebrew, Minnesota, 44

Wins: Jim Lonborg, Boston, 22
    Earl Wilson, Detroit, 22
SOs: Jim Lonborg, Boston, 246
ERA: Joel Horlen, Chicago, 2.06
Pct: Joel Horlen, Chicago, .731, 19-7
Saves: Minnie Rojas, California, 27

National League
President: Warren C. Giles

Standings	W	L	Pct.	GB	Attend.	Manager
St. Louis Cardinals	101	60	.627	—	2,090,145	Red Schoendienst
San Francisco Giants	91	71	.562	10½	1,242,480	Herman Franks
Chicago Cubs....................	87	74	.540	14	977,226	Leo Durocher
Cincinnati Reds.................	87	75	.537	14½	958,300	Dave Bristol
Philadelphia Phillies	82	80	.506	19½	828,888	Gene Mauch
Pittsburgh Pirates..............	81	81	.500	20½	907,012	Harry Walker/
						Danny Murtaugh
Atlanta Braves	77	85	.475	24½	1,389,222	Billy Hitchcock/Ken Silvestri
Los Angeles Dodgers..........	73	89	.451	28½	1,664,362	Walter Alston
Houston Astros	69	93	.426	32½	1,348,303	Grady Hatton
New York Mets	61	101	.377	40½	1,565,492	Wes Westrum/
						Francis "Salty" Parker

BA: Roberto Clemente, Pittsburgh, .357
Runs: Lou Brock, St. Louis, 113
    Hank Aaron, Atlanta, 113
Hits: Roberto Clemente, Pittsburgh, 209
RBIs: Orlando Cepeda, St. Louis, 111
HRs: Hank Aaron, Atlanta, 39

Wins: Mike McCormick, San Francisco, 22
SOs: Jim Bunning, Philadelphia, 253
ERA: Phil Niekro, Atlanta, 1.87
Pct: Dick Hughes, St. Louis, .727, 16-6
Saves: Ted Abernathy, Cincinnati, 28

AAA International League
President: George H. Sisler, Jr.

Standings	W	L	Pct.	GB	Attend.	Manager
Richmond Braves (11)........	81	60	.574	—	264,814	Luman Harris
Rochester Red Wings (1)....	80	61	.567	1	303,500	Earl Weaver
Toledo Mud Hens (6)	73	66	.525	7	94,308	Jack Tighe
Columbus Jets (18)............	69	71	.493	11½	148,365	Pete Peterson
Jacksonville Suns (16)........	66	73	.475	14	64,705	Bill Virdon
Toronto Maple Leafs (2).....	64	75	.460	16	67,216	Eddie Kasko
Buffalo Bisons (13)............	63	76	.453	17	105,516	Lou Fitzgerald/Don Zimmer
Syracuse Chiefs (9)............	63	77	.450	17½	152,781	Gary Blaylock

Playoffs: Toledo 3 games, Richmond 2; Columbus 3 games, Rochester 1.
Finals: Toledo 4 games, Columbus 1.

All-Star Team: 1B-Jim Beauchamp, Richmond; **2B**-Felix Millan, Richmond; **3B**-Steve Demeter, Richmond; **SS**-Bobby Matchick, Toledo; **OF**-Curt Motton, Rochester; Tommie Aaron, Richmond; **C**-Elvio Jimenez, Columbus; **P**-Dave Leonhard, Rochester; Ron Reed, Richmond; Bill Short, Columbus; **MVP**-Tommie Aaron, Richmond; **Pitcher of the Year**-Dave Leonhard, Rochester; **Manager**-Jack Tighe, Toledo.

BA: Elvio Jimenez, Columbus, .340
Runs: Wayne Comer, Toledo, 86
Hits: Elvio Jimenez, Columbus, 164
RBIs: Curt Motton, Rochester, 70

HRs: Jim Beauchamp, Richmond, 25
Wins: Dave Leonhard, Rochester, 15
SOs: Jerry Koosman, Jacksonville, 183
ERA: Tug McGraw, Jacksonville, 1.99

AAA Mexican League
President: Antonio Ramirez Muro

Standings	W	L	Pct.	GB	Attend.	Manager
Jalisco Charros..................	85	55	.607	—	373,219	Memo Garibay
Reynosa Broncs	80	60	.571	5	203,904	Luis Arroyo
Mexico City Diablos Rojos	76	63	.547	8½	536,743	Tomas Herrera
Veracruz Aguila	71	69	.507	14	143,373	Vinicio Garcia
Poza Rica Petroleros	65	75	.464	20	247,227	Winston Brown
Mexico City Tigres	64	75	.460	20½	260,289	Ricardo Garza
Monterrey Sultanes............	60	80	.429	25	262,281	Wilfredo Calvino
Puebla Pericos...................	57	81	.413	27	132,210	Jose Garcia

Playoffs: None.

All-Star Team: 1B-Hector Espino, Monterrey; **2B**-Arnoldo Castro, MC Tigres; **3B**-Winston Llenas, Jalisco; **SS**-Roberto Mendez, Jalisco; **OF**-Danny Morejon, Reynosa; Jose Rodriguez, Jalisco; Ramiro Rubio, MC Tigres; **C**-Elrod Hendricks, Jalisco; **P**-Andres Ayon, Jalisco; Alfredo Ortiz, MC Diablos Rojos; **Manager**-Memo Garibay, Jalisco.

BA: Hector Espino, Monterrey, .379
Runs: Elrod Hendricks, Jalisco, 124
Hits: Emilio Sosa, Poza Rica, 184
RBIs: Winston Llenas, Jalisco, 113

HRs: Elrod Hendricks, Jalisco, 41
Wins: Andres Ayon, Jalisco, 25
SOs: Francisco Maytorena, Reynosa, 175
ERA: Juan Suby, Jalisco, 2.36

AAA Pacific Coast League
President: Dewey Soriano

East Standings	W	L	Pct.	GB	Attend.	Manager
San Diego Padres (17)........	85	63	.574	—	250,537	Bob Skinner
Indianapolis Indians (4)......	76	71	.517	8½	162,636	Don Gutteridge
Phoenix Giants (20)............	75	72	.510	9½	122,747	Bill Werle
Oklahoma City 89ers (14)..	74	74	.500	11	128,553	Mel McGaha
Denver Bears (8)................	69	76	.476	14½	169,442	Cal Ermer/John Goryl
Tulsa Oilers (19)................	65	79	.451	18	120,357	Warren Spahn

West Standings	W	L	Pct.	GB	Attend.	Manager
Spokane Indians (15)........	80	68	.541	—	140,658	Roy Hartsfield
Portland Beavers (5)	79	69	.534	1	202,507	John Lipon
Vancouver Mounties (7)......	77	69	.527	2	143,541	Mickey Vernon
Tacoma Cubs (12)	73	75	.493	7	132,697	Whitey Lockman
Seattle Angels (3)	69	79	.466	11	130,862	Chuck Tanner
Hawaii Islanders (10).........	60	87	.408	19½	218,983	Wayne Terwilliger

Playoff: San Diego 4 games, Spokane 2.

All-Star Team: 1B-Jim Hicks, Indianapolis; **2B**-Bobby Klaus, San Diego; **3B**-Ricardo Joseph, San Diego; **SS**-Cesar Gutierrez, Phoenix; **OF**-Willie Kirkland, Hawaii; Ivan Murrell, Oklahoma City; Robert Raudman, Tacoma; **C**-Don Bryant, Phoenix; Bob Barton, Tacoma; **P**-Howie Reed, Oklahoma City; Jim Weaver, Oklahoma City; **MVP**-Ricardo Joseph, San Diego; **Manager**-John Lipon, Portland.

BA: Cesar Gutierrez, Phoenix, .322
Runs: Jim Hicks, Indianapolis, 87
Hits: Frank Coggins, Hawaii, 168
RBIs: Willie Kirkland, Hawaii, 97

HRs: Willie Kirkland, Hawaii, 34
Wins: Howie Reed, Oklahoma City, 19
SOs: Rich Robertson, Phoenix, 184
ERA: Bobby Locke, Seattle, 2.22

AA Eastern League
President: A. Rankin Johnson

East Standings	W	L	Pct.	GB	Attend.	Manager
Binghamton Triplets (9)	82	58	.586	—	52,538	Jack Reed
Pittsfield Red Sox (2)	75	62	.547	5½	40,420	Billy Gardner
Waterbury Giants (20).......	71	69	.507	11	50,744	Andy Gilbert
Pawtucket Indians (5)........	67	71	.486	14	61,401	John "Red" Davis

West Standings	W	L	Pct.	GB	Attend.	Manager
Elmira Pioneers (1)............	74	65	.532	—	55,189	Billy DeMars
Williamsport Mets (16)	73	66	.525	1	55,704	Roy Sievers
Reading Phillies (17)	70	69	.504	4	85,559	Frank Lucchesi
York White Roses (10).......	43	95	.312	30½	27,826	Billy Klaus/George Case

Playoff: Binghamton 3 games, Elmira 1.

All-Star Team: 1B-Dave McDonald, Binghamton; **2B**-Don Mason, Waterbury; **3B**-Billy Scripture, Elmira; **SS**-Damaso Blanco, Waterbury; **OF**-Bill Schlesinger, Pittsfield; Bernie Smith, Williamsport; Merv Rettenmund, Elmira; **C**-Gerald Moses, Pittsfield; Fran Healy, Pawtucket; **P**-Ken Brett, Pittsfield; Jim Horsford, Binghamton; **MVP**-Bernie Smith, Williamsport; **Manager**-Jack Reed, Binghamton.

BA: Bernie Smith, Williamsport, .306
Runs: Bobby Mitchell, Pittsfield, 74
Hits: Bobby Mitchell, Pittsfield, 141
    Bill Schlesinger, Pittsfield, 141
    Howie Bedell, Reading, 141

RBIs: Bill Schlesinger, Pittsfield, 81
HRs: Bill Schlesinger, Pittsfield, 21
Wins: Gary Girouard, Binghamton, 14
SOs: Alan Schmelz, Williamsport, 181
ERA: Jim McAndrew, Williamsport, 1.47

AA Southern League
President: Sam C. Smith

Standings	W	L	Pct.	GB	Attend.	Manager
Birmingham A's (7)...........	84	55	.604	—	53,075	John McNamara
Montgomery Rebels (6)......	80	58	.580	3½	39,579	Frank Carswell
Evansville White Sox (4)....	76	63	.547	8	54,020	George Noga

*Won first-half **Won second-half ***Won both halves
Numbers after nicknames indicate farm system.
Affiliation listed at end of each year.

496

	W	L	Pct.	GB	Attend.	
Charlotte Hornets (8)	75	65	.536	9½	41,844	Harry Warner
Macon Peaches (18)	55	85	.393	29½	30,658	Don Osborne/Frank Oceak
Knoxville Smokies (13)	47	91	.341	36½	21,390	Don Zimmer/Lou Fitzgerald

Playoffs: None.

All-Star Team: 1B-Joe Rudi, Birmingham; **2B**-Bob Christian, Montgomery; **3B**-Graig Nettles, Charlotte; **SS**-Minnie Mendoza, Charlotte; **OF**-Reggie Jackson, Birmingham; Dan DiPace, Charlotte; Stan Wojcik, Birmingham; **C**-Carl Taylor, Macon; Dave Duncan, Birmingham; **P**-Les Cain, Montgomery; George Lauzerique, Birmingham; **Manager**-Frank Carswell, Montgomery.

BA: Minnie Mendoza, Charlotte, .297
Runs: Reggie Jackson, Birmingham, 84
Hits: Minnie Mendoza, Charlotte, 157
RBIs: Barry Morgan, Montgomery, 87
HRs: Rogelio Alvarez, Knoxville/Evansville, 19
Graig Nettles, Charlotte, 19
Wins: Dick Drago, Montgomery, 15
SOs: Dick Drago, Montgomery, 134
ERA: George Lauzerique, Birmingham, 2.299

AA Texas League
President: Hugh J. Finnerty

Standings	W	L	Pct.	GB	Attend.	Manager
Albuquerque Dodgers (15)	78	62	.557	—	73,283	Duke Snider
Amarillo Sonics (14)	75	65	.539	3	74,024	Buddy Hancken
El Paso Sun Kings (3)	73	67	.521	5	76,935	Rocky Bridges
Austin Braves (11)	69	71	.493	9	61,509	Hub Kittle
Arkansas Travelers (19)	63	77	.450	15	77,824	Vern Rapp
Dallas-Ft. Worth Spurs (12)	62	78	.443	16	246,315	Jo Jo White

Playoffs: None.

All-Star Team: 1B-Jim Spencer, El Paso; **2B**-Luis Alcaraz, Albuquerque; **3B**-Bill Sudakis, Albuquerque; **SS**-Don Williams, Albuquerque; **OF**-Nate Colbert, Amarillo; Adrian Garrett, Austin; Cito Gaston, Austin; Willie Crawford, Albuquerque; **C**-Tom Egan, El Paso; **Util**-Mike Sinnerud, Amarillo; **P**-John Duffie, Albuquerque; Mike Kekich, Albuquerque; **MVP**-Nate Colbert, Amarillo; **Pitcher of the Year**-John Duffie, Albuquerque; **Manager**-Buddy Hancken, Amarillo.

BA: Luis Alcaraz, Albuquerque, .328
Runs: Willie Crawford, Albuquerque, 93
Hits: Luis Alcaraz, Albuquerque, 156
RBIs: Joe Hague, Arkansas, 95
HRs: Nate Colbert, Amarillo, 28
Wins: John Duffie, Albuquerque, 16
SOs: Ed Everitt, Albuquerque, 200
ERA: Sal Campisi, Arkansas, 2.26

A California League
President: Edward J. Mulligan

Standings	W	L	Pct.	GB	Attend.	Manager
San Jose Bees*(3)	86	52	.623	—	60,902	Harry Dunlop
Modesto Reds**(19)	79	61	.564	8	36,453	Sparky Anderson
Santa Barbara Dodgers (15)	77	63	.550	10	15,479	Norm Sherry
Bakersfield Bears (17)	70	68	.507	16	27,426	Nolan Campbell
Fresno Giants (20)	67	72	.482	19½	35,727	David Garcia
Lodi Crushers (12)	63	77	.450	24	71,818	Walt Dixon
Stockton Ports (15)	58	81	.417	28½	20,003	Harry Malmberg
Reno Silver Sox (5)	56	82	.406	30	17,007	Phil Cavarretta

Playoff: San Jose 2 games, Modesto 0.

All-Star Team: 1B-James Mallon, Fresno; **2B**-John Marsden, Fresno; **3B**-Joe Lis, Bakersfield; **SS**-Bill Grabarkewitz, Santa Barbara; **OF**-Steve Hovley, San Jose; Leron Lee, Modesto; Michael Christino, Modesto; **C**-John Hairston, Lodi; **Util**-Buddy Hollowell, Santa Barbara; **P**-Pat Bayless, Bakersfield; Tom Jones, Reno; Charley Hough, Santa Barbara; Phil Knuckles, Modesto; **MVP**-Leron Lee, Modesto; **Manager**-Harry Dunlop, San Jose.

BA: Phil Mastagni, Stockton, .308
Runs: Bill Grabarkewitz, Santa Barbara, 122
Hits: James Mallon, Fresno, 159
RBIs: Joe Lis, Bakersfield, 90
HRs: Joe Lis, Bakersfield, 33
Wins: Pat Bayless, Bakersfield, 18
SOs: Pat Bayless, Bakersfield, 217
ERA: Ken Tatum, San Jose, 2.12

A Carolina League
President: J.C. "Bill" Jessup

East Standings	W	L	Pct.	GB	Attend.	Manager
Raleigh Pirates (18)	77	65	.542	—	45,344	Joe Morgan
Peninsula Grays (7)	74	64	.536	1	89,857	Gus Niarhos
Rocky Mount Leafs (6)	74	68	.521	3	33,666	Al Federoff
Portsmouth Tides (17)	70	68	.507	5	53,097	Bob Wellman
Wilson Tobs (8)	61	72	.459	11½	20,108	Vern Morgan
Kinston Eagles (11)	60	75	.444	13½	61,905	Andy Pafko

West Standings	W	L	Pct.	GB	Attend.	Manager
Durham Bulls (16)	74	64	.536	—	24,210	Clyde McCullough
Winston-Salem Red Sox (2)	69	68	.504	4½	45,665	Bill Slack
Burlington Senators (10)	70	69	.504	4½	24,785	Len Johnston
Lynchburg White Sox (4)	68	68	.500	5	38,970	Stan Wasiak
Greensboro Yankees (9)	66	72	.478	8	54,680	Bob Bauer
Asheville Tourists (14)	64	74	.464	10	34,279	Chuck Churn

Playoffs: East - Portsmouth 1 game, Peninsula 0; Raleigh 1 game, Rocky Mount 0; Portsmouth 2 games, Raleigh 0. West - Durham 1 game, Burlington 0; Lynchburg 1 game, Winston-Salem 0; Durham 2 games, Lynchburg 0.

Finals: Durham 2 games, Portsmouth 1.

All-Star Team: 1B-Ron Allen, Portsmouth; **2B**-Bobby Heise, Durham; **3B**-Duncan Campbell, Raleigh; **SS**-Don Money, Raleigh; **OF**-Danny Walton, Asheville; Larry Hisle, Portsmouth; Jim Holt, Peninsula; **C**-Hal King, Asheville; **P**-Harold Clem, Raleigh; Gary Jones, Greensboro; **MVP**-Don Money, Raleigh; **Manager**-Clyde McCullough, Durham.

BA: Van Kelly, Kinston, .323
Runs: Danny Greenfield, Peninsula, 93
Hits: Van Kelly, Kinston, 161
RBIs: Ron Allen, Portsmouth, 100
HRs: Hal King, Asheville, 30
Wins: Harold Clem, Raleigh, 15
Gary Jones, Greensboro, 15
Mike Daniel, Asheville, 15
Jon Warden, Rocky Mount, 15
SOs: Mark Schaeffer, Winston-Salem, 226
ERA: Harold Clem, Raleigh, 1.64

A Florida State League
President: George MacDonald, Sr.

East Standings	W	L	Pct.	GB	Attend.	Manager
Orlando Twins***(8)	88	50	.638	—	51,753	Ralph Rowe
Ft. Lauderdale Yankees (9)	69	69	.500	19	38,302	Billy Shantz
Miami Marlins (1)	65	76	.461	24½	72,581	Cal Ripken, Sr.
W. Palm Beach Braves (11)	51	81	.386	34	19,733	Eddie Haas
Cocoa Astros (14)	49	84	.368	36½	5,553	Walt Matthews

West Standings	W	L	Pct.	GB	Attend.	Manager
St. Petersburg Cards***(19)	96	43	.691	—	74,889	Ron Plaza
Winter Haven Mets (16)	94	46	.671	2½	27,401	Pete Pavlick
Leesburg Athletics (7)	64	71	.474	30	24,161	Jim Williams
Tampa Tarpons (13)	55	71	.437	34½	33,636	George Scherger
Lakeland Tigers (6)	50	90	.357	46½	8,590	Frank Overmire

Playoff: St. Petersburg 3 games, Orlando 1.

All-Star Team: 1B-Mike Jorgensen, Winter Haven; **2B**-Roberto Diaz, St. Petersburg; **3B**-Bobbye Beckner, Orlando; **SS**-Roger Sugimoto, Orlando; **OF**-Joe Keough, Leesburg; Herman Hill, Orlando; Charles Stewart, St. Petersburg; **C**-Johnny Oates, Miami; **P**-Charles Murray, Orlando; Ron Paul, Winter Haven; **Manager**-Ron Plaza, St. Petersburg.

BA: Charles Stewart, St. Petersburg, .296
Runs: Charles Stewart, St. Petersburg, 97
Hits: Joe Keough, Leesburg, 149
RBIs: Joe Keough, Leesburg, 80
HRs: Joe Keough, Leesburg, 18
Wins: Charles Murray, Orlando, 17
SOs: Charles Murray, Orlando, 206
ERA: Brian Clark, Ft. Lauderdale, 1.50

A Mexican Center League
President: Antonio Ramirez Muro

Standings	W	L	Pct.	GB	Attend.	Manager
Leon Bravos	84	55	.604	—	53,093	Mario Ariosa
Saltillo Saraperos	83	55	.601	½	46,545	Jesus Robles/ Hector Rodriguez
Fresnillo Mineros	83	56	.597	1	42,366	Marco Manzo
Zacatecas Pericos	78	62	.557	6½	55,093	Leonel Aldama
Tampico Pirates	74	64	.536	9½	109,801	Humberto Ayala/ Eusebio Perez/Manuel Estrada
Guanajuato Tuzos	55	84	.396	29	24,821	Domingo Santana
Aguascalientes Broncos	53	84	.387	30	25,395	Dan Bankhead/ Nazario Moreno
Durango Alacranes	45	95	.321	39½	27,635	Epitacio Torres

Playoffs: None.

All-Star Team: 1B-Juan Martinez, Guanajuato; **2B**-Roberto Castellon, Fresnillo; **3B**-Adan Contreras, Saltillo; **SS**-Antelmo Bonilla, Zacatecas; **OF**-Juan Rodriguez, Aguascalientes; J. Manuel Gutierrez, Leon; Jesus Nieblas, Tampico; **C**-Juan Ortigosa, Guanajuato; Luis Peralta, Saltillo; **P**-Maximo Leon, Fresnillo; Rigoberto Lopez, Tampico; **Manager**-Mario Ariosa, Leon.

BA: Juan Martinez, Guanajuato, .392
Runs: Felix Alanis, Guanajuato, 111
Hits: Juan Martinez, Guanajuato, 190
RBIs: Jose Romellon, Zacatecas, 136
HRs: Felix Alanis, Guanajuato, 26
Wins: O. Jose Luis Delgado, Saltillo, 17
SOs: Joel Navarro, Aguascalientes, 133
ERA: Rigoberto Lopez, Tampico, 2.73

A Mexican Southeast League
President: Dr. Fernando Canton Franco

Standings	W	L	Pct.	GB	Attend.	Manager
Campeche Pirates	64	41	.610	—	132,157	David Garcia
Yucatan Venados	59	48	.551	6	113,868	Ben Valenzuela
Carmen Camaroneros	54	51	.514	10	67,859	Guillermo Frayde
Las Choapas Diablos Rojos	54	52	.509	10½	36,258	Andres Tanaka
Puerto Mexico Portenos	54	53	.505	11	41,174	Claudio Solano
Tabasco Cattlemen	46	60	.434	18½	34,014	Jose Landeros
Orizaba Charros	40	66	.377	24½	15,532	Minnie Minoso

Playoffs: Campeche 2 games, Las Choapas 1; Carmen 2 games, Yucatan 0.
Finals: Campeche 4 games, Carmen 1.

All-Star Team: 1B-Felipe Montemayor, Campeche; **2B**-Hilario Pena, Campeche; **3B**-Juan Velez, Yucatan; **SS**-Juan Manuel Salinas, Yucatan; **OF**-Alfredo Palomino, Carmen; Nicolas Vasquez, Las Choapas; Miguel Gutierrez, Yucatan; **C**-Lucas Bouye, Campeche; Jesus Hernandez, Yucatan; **P**-David Lopez, Carmen; Raul Cano, Las Choapas; **Manager**-David Garcia, Campeche.

BA: Hilario Pena, Campeche, .394
Runs: Reggie Grenald, Puerto Mexico, 86
Hits: Hilario Pena, Campeche, 159
RBIs: Humberto Guerrero, Campeche, 79

HRs: Celso Oviedo, Puerto Mexico, 21
Wins: William de Jesus, Campeche, 17
SOs: David Jimenez, Carmen/Tabasco, 167
ERA: David Lopez, Carmen, 1.81

A Midwest League
President: James Doster

Standings	W	L	Pct.	GB	Attend.	Manager
Appleton Foxes (4)	71	46	.607	—	48,186	Alex Cosmidis
Wisconsin Rapids Twins (8)	70	46	.603	½	31,823	Ray Bellino
Quad City Angels (3)	69	51	.579	3½	53,213	Fred Koenig
Decatur Commodores (20)	62	58	.517	10½	37,730	Dennis Sommers
Burlington Bees (7)	56	59	.487	14	38,137	Al Ronning
Quincy Cubs (12)	58	63	.479	15	32,393	Harry Bright
Waterloo Hawks (2)	56	65	.463	17	36,158	Rac Slider
Cedar Rapids Cardinals (19)	53	67	.442	19½	50,215	Jack Krol
Clinton Pilots (18)	51	69	.425	21½	42,026	Bob Clear
Dubuque Packers (15)	49	71	.408	23½	33,737	Bill Berrier

Playoff: Appleton 2 games, Wisconsin Rapids 0.

All-Star Team: 1B-Joe Dodder, Dubuque; **2B**-Roy Radmaker, Appleton; **3B**-Bruce Davis, Quad City; **SS**-Rafael Robles, Decatur; **OF**-Charlie Manuel, Wisconsin Rapids; Carlos May, Appleton; Richard White, Decatur; Jose Ortiz, Appleton; **C**-John Harrell, Decatur; Wilbert Hammond, Clinton; Charles Brinkman, Appleton; **Util**-James Gruber, Waterloo; **P**-Al Fitzmorris, Appleton; John Lamb, Clinton; Tom Hall, Wisconsin Rapids; Gerald Lyscio, Wisconsin Rapids; James Moyer, Decatur; Raul Medrano, Burlington; Charles Schoene, Cedar Rapids; Jesus Hernaiz, Quincy; Raymond Jarvis, Waterloo; Steve Kealey, Quad City; **Manager**-Alex Cosmidis, Appleton.

BA: Charlie Manuel, Wisconsin Rapids, .313
Runs: Charlie Manuel, Wisconsin Rapids, 76
Hits: Jose Ortiz, Appleton, 129
RBIs: Charlie Manuel, Wisconsin Rapids, 70
James Williams, Quincy, 70

HRs: James Williams, Quincy, 17
Wins: Robert DeLong, Decatur, 15
Raymond Jarvis, Waterloo, 15
Gerald Lyscio, Wisconsin Rapids, 15
SOs: Robert DeLong, Decatur, 191
ERA: Robert DeLong, Decatur, 1.97

A New York-Pennsylvania League
President: Vincent M. McNamara

Standings	W	L	Pct.	GB	Attend.	Manager
Auburn Twins (8)	52	26	.667	—	26,991	Tommy Umphlett
Batavia Trojans (17)	41	36	.532	10½	26,908	Max Lanier
Oneonta Yankees (9)	40	39	.506	12½	18,524	Frank Verdi
Jamestown Braves (11)	39	41	.488	14	21,152	Harry Dorish
Geneva Senators (10)	37	42	.468	15½	11,612	Gordie MacKenzie
Erie Tigers (6)	26	51	.338	25½	9,988	Ed Lyons

Playoffs: None.

All-Star Team: 1B-William Hahn, Auburn; **2B**-Paul Mankowski, Auburn; **3B**-Danny Monzon, Auburn; **SS**-Steve Richman, Auburn; **OF**-Andrew Finlay, Jamestown; Charles Lelas, Oneonta; Tommy Cole, Auburn; Harry Wright, Batavia; **C**-Chet Bergalowski, Jamestown; Gabe Puniska, Geneva; **Util**-Bob Churchich, Jamestown; **P**-Paul Epperson, Auburn; Gary Timberlake, Oneonta; Larry Mischik, Geneva; Danny LeBright, Batavia; **Manager**-Tommy Umphlett, Auburn.

BA: Tommy Cole, Auburn, .389
Runs: Danny Monzon, Auburn, 82
Hits: Tommy Cole, Auburn, 96
RBIs: Tommy Cole, Auburn, 66
Danny Monzon, Auburn, 66

HRs: Charles Lelas, Oneonta, 12
Wins: Paul Epperson, Auburn, 11
Mike Colin, Auburn, 11
SOs: Paul Epperson, Auburn, 132
ERA: Larry Herring, Geneva, 1.65

A Northern League
President: Roland E. Parcel

Standings	W	L	Pct.	GB	Attend.	Manager
St. Cloud Rox (8)	44	26	.629	—	23,250	Ken Staples
Mankato Mets (16)	37	33	.529	7	12,415	Carl "Buddy" Peterson
Sioux Falls Packers (13)	35	33	.515	8	33,480	Jim Snyder
Aberdeen Pheasants (1)	34	36	.486	10	18,555	Owen Friend
Duluth-Superior Dukes (4, 12)	30	39	.435	13½	14,902	Ira Hutchinson
Huron Phillies (17)	27	40	.403	15½	40,242	Joe Lonnett

Playoffs: None.

All-Star Team: 1B-Tom Robson, Mankato; **2B**-John Cox, Duluth-Superior; **3B**-Steve Brye, St. Cloud; **SS**-Tom Silicato, Huron; **OF**-Roger Freed, Aberdeen; Ron Markowski, Duluth-Superior; Ray Starnes, Huron; **C**-Elby Bushong, Duluth-Superior; **P**-Stephen Blateric, Sioux Falls; Terry Parks, Mankato; **Manager**-Carl "Buddy" Peterson, Mankato.

BA: Ray Starnes, Huron, .348
Runs: Steve Brye, St. Cloud, 59
Hits: Steve Brye, St. Cloud, 82
RBIs: Gary Reierson, St. Cloud, 59

HRs: Steve Brye, St. Cloud, 13
Roger Freed, Aberdeen, 13
Wins: Steve Christopher, St. Cloud, 12
SOs: Stephen Blateric, Sioux Falls, 118
ERA: Terry Parks, Mankato, 1.92

A Northwest League
President: Hugh Luby

Standings	W	L	Pct.	GB	Attend.	Manager
Medford Giants (20)	51	33	.607	—	43,478	Tony Eichelberger
Eugene Emeralds (17)	50	34	.595	1	31,249	Bobby Malkmus
Tri-City Atoms (15)	37	47	.440	14	22,421	Don LeJohn
Lewiston Broncs (19)	30	54	.357	21	17,583	Ray Hathaway

Playoffs: None.

All-Star Team: 1B-Nick Van Lue, Eugene; **2B**-Robert Leatherwood, Eugene; **3B**-Noel Finley, Medford; **SS**-Alfonso Mairena, Lewiston; **OF**-Jim Magnuson, Eugene; Von Joshua, Tri-City; Gary York, Medford; **C**-John Martinez, Eugene; Jerry Muse, Medford; **P**-Wayne Swango, Eugene; Dale Spier, Medford; **Manager**-Bobby Malkmus, Eugene.

BA: Von Joshua, Tri-City, .363
Runs: Jim Magnuson, Eugene, 73
Hits: Von Joshua, Tri-City, 97
RBIs: Nick Van Lue, Eugene, 77

HRs: Nick Van Lue, Eugene, 16
Wins: Wayne Swango, Eugene, 12
SOs: Wayne Swango, Eugene, 133
ERA: Wayne Swango, Eugene, 0.88

A Western Carolinas League
President: John H. Moss

Standings	W	L	Pct.	GB	Attend.	Manager
Spartanburg Phillies***(17)	80	43	.650	—	141,680	Dick Teed
Gastonia Pirates (18)	61	59	.508	17½	33,483	Don Leppert
Greenville Red Sox (2)	59	61	.492	19½	43,053	Matt Sczesny
Statesville Tigers (6)	59	62	.488	20	17,473	Len Okrie
Lexington Braves (11)	55	63	.466	22½	49,012	Buddy Hicks
Rock Hill Indians (5)	46	72	.390	31½	19,812	Pinky May

Playoffs: None.

All-Star Team: 1B-Pat Dennebaum, Lexington; **2B**-Larry Calton, Statesville; **3B**-Victor Ramirez, Gastonia; **SS**-Dave Cash, Gastonia; **OF**-Patrick Skrable, Spartanburg; Jim Walker, Greenville; John Jeter, Gastonia; **C**-Walter Czopczyc, Lexington; **P**-John Parker, Spartanburg; Ken Reynolds, Spartanburg; **Manager**-Dick Teed, Spartanburg.

BA: Dave Cash, Gastonia, .335
Runs: John Jagutis, Spartanburg, 95
Hits: Dave Cash, Gastonia, 148
RBIs: Paul Dennebaum, Lexington, 83

HRs: John Jeter, Gastonia, 18
Wins: Joe Brauer, Statesville, 17
John Parker, Spartanburg, 17
SOs: Ken Reynolds, Spartanburg, 215
ERA: John Parker, Spartanburg, 1.78

R Appalachian League
President: Chauncey De Vault

Standings	W	L	Pct.	GB	Attend.	Manager
Bluefield Orioles (1)	42	25	.627	—	34,119	Joe Altobelli
Marion Mets (16)	37	27	.578	3½	24,042	Birdie Tebbetts
Johnson City Yankees (9)	35	30	.538	6	14,012	Dick Berardino
Covington Astros (14)	29	35	.453	11½	31,322	Tony Pacheco
Salem Pirates (18)	28	38	.424	13½	34,822	Bob Pritchard
Wytheville Reds (13)	24	40	.375	16½	14,345	Scott Breeden

Playoffs: None.

BA: Don Baylor, Bluefield, .346
Runs: Ron Blomberg, Johnson City, 51
Hits: Don Baylor, Bluefield, 85
RBIs: Ron Blomberg, Johnson City, 55
Jim Plant, Marion, 55
HRs: Richie Zisk, Salem, 16

Wins: Jesse Hudson, Marion, 7
David Tomlin, Wytheville, 7
Russ Seals, Marion, 7
Charles Hopkins, Johnson City, 7
Winston Presley, Bluefield, 7
SOs: Jesse Hudson, Marion, 84
ERA: Jesse Hudson, Marion, 2.07

R Gulf Coast League
President: George MacDonald, Sr.

Standings	W	L	Pct.	GB	Manager
Athletics (7)	35	22	.614	—	Connie Ryan
Indians (5)	30	29	.508	6	Gordon Seyfried
Twins (8)	29	29	.500	6½	Fred Waters
White Sox (4)	27	29	.482	7½	Bruce Andrew
Braves (11)	27	32	.458	9	Tom Saffell
Cardinals (19)	25	32	.439	10	George Kissell

Games played at Sarasota and Bradenton, Florida.
Total Attendance: 10,103.

Playoffs: None.

All-Star Team: 1B-Leahman Stanley, Twins; **2B**-Steve Braun, Twins; **3B**-Bobby Jones, Twins; **SS**-Ron Hart, Indians; **OF**-Bob Storm, Twins; Richard Kissell, Cardinals; Clarence Stoner, Athletics; **C**-Jose Cotto, Cardinals; **P**-Dave Goltz, Twins; Ron Butterfield, Indians; **Manager**-Fred Waters, Twins.

BA: Phil Trombino, Cardinals, .331
Runs: Edward Southard, Indians, 41
Hits: Edward Southard, Indians, 61
RBIs: Joe Fanning, Braves, 29

HRs: Bob Storm, Twins, 7
Wins: Dave Goltz, Twins, 6
Ron Butterfield, Indians, 6
SOs: Ron Butterfield, Indians, 64
ERA: Dave Goltz, Twins, 2.00

R Pioneer League
President: Ben Jewell

Standings	W	L	Pct.	GB	Attend.	Manager
Ogden Dodgers (15)	41	25	.621	—	28,706	Tom Lasorda
Caldwell Cubs (12)	40	26	.606	1	24,064	George Freese
Idaho Falls Angels (3)	26	40	.394	15	27,932	Tom Sommers
Salt Lake City Giants (20)	25	41	.379	16	53,653	Harvey Koepf

Playoffs: None.

All-Star Team: 1B-Tom Whelan, Caldwell; **2B**-Vann Fixico, Salt Lake City; **3B**-Robert Hughes, Ogden; **SS**-Tom Krawczyk, Caldwell; **OF**-Bill Rainer, Ogden; Romel Canada, Ogden; Gary Pinnow, Salt Lake City; **C**-Randy Bobb, Caldwell; **Util**-Ron Estes, Ogden; Larry McFarlin, Idaho Falls; **P**-Larry Burchart, Ogden; Jim Johnson, Salt Lake City; Darcy Fast, Caldwell; Terry Bongiovanni, Caldwell; **Manager**-Tom Lasorda, Ogden.

BA: Gary Pinnow, Salt Lake City, .338
Runs: Ron Estes, Ogden, 59
Hits: Bill Rainer, Ogden, 84
RBIs: Charles Oakes, Idaho Falls, 50

HRs: John Lung, Caldwell, 7
Wins: Larry Burchart, Ogden, 9
SOs: Darcy Fast, Caldwell, 137
ERA: Craig Baker, Idaho Falls, 1.82

1967 Interleague Post Season Play

World Series
St. Louis (National) 4 games, Boston (American) 3

Dixie Series
Birmingham (Southern Association) 4 games, Albuquerque (Texas) 2
Total Attendance: 14,940

1967 Major League Farm Systems

American League
1 Baltimore (6): Rochester, Elmira, Stockton, Miami, Aberdeen, Bluefield.
2 Boston (5): Toronto, Pittsfield, Winston-Salem, Waterloo, Greenville.
3 California (5): Seattle, El Paso, San Jose, Quad City, Idaho Falls.
4 Chicago (6): Indianapolis, Evansville, Lynchburg, Appleton, Duluth-Superior, Gulf Coast.
5 Cleveland (5): Portland, Pawtucket, Reno, Rock Hill, Gulf Coast.
6 Detroit (6): Toledo, Montgomery, Rocky Mount, Lakeland, Erie, Statesville.
7 Kansas City (6): Vancouver, Birmingham, Peninsula, Leesburg, Burlington (IA), Gulf Coast.
8 Minnesota (8): Denver, Charlotte, Wilson, Orlando, Wisconsin Rapids, Auburn, St. Cloud, Gulf Coast.
9 New York (6): Syracuse, Binghamton, Greensboro, Ft. Lauderdale, Oneonta, Johnson City.
10 Washington (4): Hawaii, York, Burlington (NC), Geneva.

National League
11 Atlanta (7): Richmond, Austin, Kinston, West Palm Beach, Jamestown, Lexington, Gulf Coast.
12 Chicago (6): Tacoma, Dallas-Ft. Worth, Lodi, Quincy, Duluth-Superior, Caldwell.
13 Cincinnati (5): Buffalo, Knoxville, Tampa, Sioux Falls, Wytheville.
14 Houston (5): Oklahoma City, Amarillo, Asheville, Cocoa, Covington.
15 Los Angeles (6): Spokane, Albuquerque, Santa Barbara, Dubuque, Tri-City, Ogden.
16 New York (6): Jacksonville, Williamsport, Durham, Winter Haven, Mankato, Marion.
17 Philadelphia (8): San Diego, Reading, Bakersfield, Portsmouth, Batavia, Huron, Eugene, Spartanburg.
18 Pittsburgh (6): Columbus, Macon, Raleigh, Clinton, Gastonia, Salem.
19 St. Louis (7): Tulsa, Arkansas, Modesto, St. Petersburg, Cedar Rapids, Lewiston, Gulf Coast.
20 San Francisco (6): Phoenix, Waterbury, Fresno, Decatur, Medford, Salt Lake City.

1967 No-Hitters

Date	Pitcher	Team	League	Opponent	Score
4-14	James Britton	Austin	Texas	Arkansas	3-0
4-23	Robert Sturges	Macon	Southern	Evansville	0-0 (5)
4-25	Rick Young	Lakeland	Florida State	Winter Haven	1-0 (10)
4-25	Paul Campbell	Elmira	Eastern	York	3-0 (7)
4-30	Steve Barber/ Stu Miller	Baltimore	American	Detroit	1-2
5-13	Felipe Leal	El Paso	Texas	Albuquerque	8-0
5-13	Larry Tolliver	Waterbury	Eastern	York	6-0
5-21	Pat Bayless	Bakersfield	California	Reno	5-0 (7)
5-22	Robert Hall	Tampa	Florida State	West Palm Beach	4-0
5-23	Ron Locke	Williamsport	Eastern	Pawtucket	7-0
5-23	Dave Vineyard	Toronto	International	Rochester	2-1
5-29	Gilberto Castro	Saltillo	Mexican Center	Durango	3-0
6-1	Wenty Ford	West Palm Beach	Florida State	Ft. Lauderdale	1-0 (P)
6-11	John Lamb	Clinton	Midwest	Quad City	3-0 (7)
6-12	Roger Harrington	Lexington	W. Carolinas	Rock Hill	1-0 (7)
6-18	Don Wilson	Houston	National	Atlanta	2-0
6-22	Joe Barnett	Clinton	Midwest	Quincy	2-0 (7)
6-23	James Horsford	Binghamton	Eastern	Pittsfield	2-0 (7)
6-24	Bill Hepler	Williamsport	Eastern	Elmira	0-1 (6)
6-30	Lowell Palmer	Tidewater	Carolina	Kinston	7-0
7-4	Ralph Custer	Portland	Pacific Coast	Denver	1-0 (7)
7-4	Robert Patrylo	Miami	Florida State	St. Petersburg	4-0 (7)
7-6	George Lauzerique	Birmingham	Southern	Evansville	1-0 (7)
7-8	Dennis Saunders	Statesville	W. Carolinas	Rock Hill	6-1 (5)
7-9	Stan Bahnsen	Syracuse	International	Buffalo	8-0 (P, 7)
7-12	Homera Mendia	Campeche	Mexican S.E.	Yucatan	6-0
7-22	Bill Burbach	Binghamton	Eastern	Williamsport	3-0 (7)
7-22	Leslie Cain	Montgomery	Southern	Birmingham	2-0
7-25	Steve Arlin	Reading	Eastern	York	9-2 (7)
7-31	Milciades Olivo	Birmingham	Southern	Evansville	2-0 (7)
8-5	Charles Thompson	St. Petersburg	Florida State	Tampa	1-0 (7)
8-7	Dennis Musgraves	Durham	Carolina	Kinston	5-0 (5)
8-9	Louis Stephen/ Mike Mathwig	Santa Barbara	California	Stockton	7-0
8-16	Alan Foster	Spokane	Pacific Coast	Seattle	1-0 (7)
8-17	Robert Ware	Lakeland	Florida State	Miami	1-0 (7)
8-18	James Merrick	Orlando	Florida State	Ft. Lauderdale	1-0
8-25	Dean Chance	Minnesota	American	Cleveland	2-1
8-25	Bob Guindon	Pittsfield	Eastern	York	5-0 (7)
8-25	Bill Laxton	Clinton	Midwest	Waterloo	2-1 (7)
8-26	Benjamin Proulx	Twins	Gulf Coast	Athletics	5-0 (7)
8-30	Billy Farmer	Pittsfield	Eastern	Elmira	2-0 (7)
9-1	Alan Foster	Spokane	Pacific Coast	Seattle	1-0
9-10	Joel Horlen	Chicago	American	Detroit	6-0

Number in parentheses indicates innings if other than nine; "P" indicates perfect game.

THIS DATE IN MINOR LEAGUE HISTORY

April 21, 1967, Austin, Texas League, scored 13 runs in the sixth frame to beat Albuquerque 13-5.

April 22, 1967, Frederick "Fritz" Maisel, star third baseman for Jack Dunn's famed Baltimore Orioles, rated one of minor league baseball's greatest teams, that won seven consecutive International League pennants from 1919 through 1925, died in Baltimore at age 77. Maisel compiled a batting average of .303 in his minor league career from 1910 to 1928.

April 25, 1967, In his first pro start, Rick Young, Lakeland, Florida State League, pitched 10-1/2 innings before allowing a hit in a 12-inning, 1-0 victory over Winter Haven. The lefty gave up only one safety, a single, struck out eleven and walked two.

June 1, 1967, Percival "Wenty" Ford, West Palm Beach, Florida State League, pitched a perfect nine-inning game to defeat Ft. Lauderdale 1-0.

June 17, 1967, Robin Roberts' career, which reached its height with six consecutive seasons of 20 or more victories for the Phillies, came to an end with a 5-3 record for Reading in the Eastern League.

July 19, 1967, Jerry Cram, St. Cloud, Northern League, struck out nine consecutive batters in a relief role against Duluth-Superior.

July 23, 1967, Three San Jose, California League, hurlers recorded 28 strikeouts in a 3-1, 15-inning loss to Bakersfield.

July 25, 1967, Puebla, Mexican League, hit eight triples, including four in one inning, in a 14-9 win over Monterrey.

August 8, 1967, West Palm Beach, Florida State League, defeated Leesburg 3-2 in 25 innings.

August 9, 1967, Raleigh, Carolina League, reeled off seven double plays in a seven-inning game while winning 6-0 over Burlington.

August 13, 1967, Medford, Northwest League, completed a four-game sweep over Lewiston, winning the contests, 18-2, 8-3, 16-2 and 19-6. Medford had three big innings during the set, scoring 15 runs in one frame, 12 in another and banging across 10 in the first inning of the finale.

August 25, 1967, Righthander Maurice Ozier, Wilson, Carolina League, struck out the first nine Peninsula batters to face him in a seven-inning game.

August 28, 1967, Righthander Dick Such, York, Eastern League, was handed his 16th straight defeat of the season and finished the campaign with a record of 0-16.

September 6, 1967, Dave Leonhard, Rochester, International League, finished the season with a 15-3 record to give him a four-year record of 60-19.

1968

American League
President: Joseph E. Cronin

Standings	W	L	Pct.	GB	Attend.	Manager
Detroit Tigers	103	59	.636	—	2,031,847	Mayo Smith
Baltimore Orioles	91	71	.562	12	943,977	Hank Bauer/Earl Weaver
Cleveland Indians	86	75	.534	16½	857,994	Alvin Dark
Boston Red Sox	86	76	.531	17	1,940,788	Dick Williams
New York Yankees	83	79	.512	20	1,185,666	Ralph Houk
Oakland Athletics	82	80	.506	21	837,466	Bob Kennedy
Minnesota Twins	79	83	.488	24	1,143,257	Cal Ermer
California Angels	67	95	.414	36	1,025,956	Bill Rigney
Chicago White Sox	67	95	.414	36	803,775	Eddie Stanky/ Les Moss/Al Lopez
Washington Senators	65	96	.404	37½	546,661	Jim Lemon

BA: Carl Yastrzemski, Boston, .301
Runs: Dick McAuliffe, Detroit, 95
Hits: Bert Campaneris, Oakland, 177
RBIs: Ken Harrelson, Boston, 109
HRs: Frank Howard, Washington, 44
Wins: Denny McLain, Detroit, 31
SOs: Sam McDowell, Cleveland, 283
ERA: Luis Tiant, Cleveland, 1.60
Pct: Denny McLain, Detroit, .838, 31-6
Saves: Al Worthington, Washington, 18

National League
President: Warren C. Giles

Standings	W	L	Pct.	GB	Attend.	Manager
St. Louis Cardinals	97	65	.599	—	2,011,167	Red Schoendienst
San Francisco Giants	88	74	.543	9	837,220	Herman Franks
Chicago Cubs	84	78	.519	13	1,043,409	Leo Durocher
Cincinnati Reds	83	79	.512	14	733,354	Dave Bristol
Atlanta Braves	81	81	.500	16	1,126,540	Luman Harris
Pittsburgh Pirates	80	82	.494	17	693,485	Larry Shephard
Los Angeles Dodgers	76	86	.469	21	1,581,093	Walter Alston
Philadelphia Phillies	76	86	.469	21	664,546	Gene Mauch/ George Myatt/Bob Skinner
New York Mets	73	89	.451	24	1,781,657	Gil Hodges
Houston Astros	72	90	.444	25	1,312,887	Grady Hatton/Harry Walker

BA: Pete Rose, Cincinnati, .335
Runs: Glen Beckert, Chicago, 98
Hits: Felipe Alou, Atlanta, 210
 Pete Rose, Cincinnati, 210
RBIs: Willie McCovey, San Francisco, 105
HRs: Willie McCovey, San Francisco, 36
Wins: Juan Marichal, San Francisco, 26
SOs: Bob Gibson, St. Louis, 268
ERA: Bob Gibson, St. Louis, 1.12
Pct: Steve Blass, Pittsburgh, .750, 18-6
Saves: Phil Regan, Los Angeles/Chicago, 25

AAA International League
President: George H. Sisler, Jr.

Standings	W	L	Pct.	GB	Attend.	Manager
Toledo Mud Hens (6)	83	64	.565	—	113,098	Jack Tighe
Columbus Jets (20)	82	64	.562	½	178,003	Johnny Pesky
Rochester Red Wings (1)	77	69	.527	5½	243,498	Billy DeMars
Jacksonville Suns (18)	75	71	.514	7½	83,950	Clyde McCullough
Syracuse Chiefs (9)	72	75	.490	11	150,455	Gary Blaylock/Frank Verdi
Louisville Colonels (2)	72	75	.490	11	244,018	Eddie Kasko
Buffalo Bisons (12)	66	81	.449	17	109,749	Wayne Terwilliger
Richmond Braves (13)	59	87	.404	23½	151,617	Eddie Haas

Playoffs: Jacksonville 3 games, Toledo 1; Columbus 3 games, Rochester 2.
Finals: Jacksonville 4 games, Columbus 0.

All-Star Team: 1B-Al Oliver, Columbus; **2B**-David Campbell, Toledo; **3B**-Mike Ferraro, Syracuse; **SS**-Gil Garrido, Richmond; **OF**-Merv Rettenmund, Rochester; Robert Christian, Toledo; Amos Otis, Jacksonville; **C**-Manny Sanguillen, Columbus; **P**-Mike Marshall, Toledo; Dave Roberts, Columbus; **MVP**-Merv Rettenmund, Rochester; **Pitcher of the Year**-Dave Roberts, Columbus; **Manager**-Jack Tighe, Toledo.

BA: Merv Rettenmund, Rochester, .331
Runs: Merv Rettenmund, Rochester, 104
Hits: Elvio Jimenez, Columbus, 157
 Bobby Pfeil, Jacksonville, 157
RBIs: Dave Nicholson, Richmond, 86
HRs: Dave Nicholson, Richmond, 34
Wins: Dave Roberts, Columbus, 18
SOs: Jim Rooker, Toledo, 206
ERA: Galen Cisco, Louisville, 2.21

AAA Mexican League
President: Antonio Ramirez Muro

Standings	W	L	Pct.	GB	Attend.	Manager
Mexico City Diablos Rojos	82	58	.586	—	480,068	Tomas Herrera
Veracruz Aguila	79	60	.568	2½	143,805	Vinicio Garcia
Jalisco Charros	77	63	.550	5	202,398	Memo Garibay
Puebla Pericos	72	68	.514	10	183,659	Tony Castano
Reynosa Broncs	69	71	.493	13	129,628	Luis Arroyo
Mexico City Tigres	62	78	.443	20	280,306	Jose Garcia
Poza Rica Petroleros	60	79	.432	21½	200,507	Winston Brown/ Ricardo Garza
Monterrey Sultanes	58	82	.414	24	279,482	Willie Miranda

Playoffs: None.

All-Star Team: 1B-Hector Espino, Monterrey; **2B**-Bernardo Calvo, Veracruz; **3B**-Roberto Ortiz, Veracruz; **SS**-Ramon Hernandez, MC Diablos Rojos; **OF**-Angel Macias, Reynosa; Ramon Montoya, MC Diablos Rojos; Hector Zamudio, MC Tigres; **C**-Manuel Antonio Diaz, Poza Rica; Gregorio Luque, MC Tigres; **P**-Jim Horsford, Reynosa; Celso Contreras, Veracruz; **Manager**-Tomas Herrera, MC Diablos Rojos.

BA: Hector Espino, Monterrey, .365
Runs: Marcelo Juarez, Veracruz, 92
Hits: Manuel Antonio Diaz, Poza Rica, 173
RBIs: George Prescott, Poza Rica, 84
HRs: Hector Espino, MC Diablos Rojos, 27
Wins: Jim Horsford, Reynosa, 20
SOs: Jim Horsford, Reynosa, 212
ERA: Jim Horsford, Reynosa, 1.59

AAA Pacific Coast League
President: Dewey Soriano

East Standings	W	L	Pct.	GB	Attend.	Manager
Tulsa Oilers (21)	95	53	.642	—	196,115	Warren Spahn
San Diego Padres (19)	76	70	.521	18	203,369	Bob Skinner/Bobby Klaus
Phoenix Giants (22)	76	71	.517	18½	113,517	Clyde King
Denver Bears (8)	73	72	.503	20½	187,159	John Goryl/Billy Martin
Indianapolis Indians (15)	66	78	.458	27	136,818	Don Zimmer
Oklahoma City 89ers (16)	61	84	.421	32½	113,056	Cot Deal

West Standings	W	L	Pct.	GB	Attend.	Manager
Spokane Indians (17)	85	60	.586	—	121,178	Roy Hartsfield
Hawaii Islanders (4)	78	69	.531	8	255,569	Bill Adair
Portland Beavers (5)	72	72	.500	12½	110,426	John "Red" Davis
Seattle Angels (3)	71	76	.483	15	155,090	Joe Adcock
Tacoma Cubs (14)	65	83	.439	21½	79,897	Whitey Lockman
Vancouver Mounties (10)	58	88	.397	27½	82,028	Mickey Vernon

Playoff: Tulsa 4 games, Spokane 1.

All-Star Team: 1B-Joe Hague, Tulsa; **2B**-Hal McRae, Indianapolis; **3B**-Graig Nettles, Denver; **SS**-Don Money, San Diego; **OF**-Jim Hicks, Tulsa; Billy Cowan, San Diego; Lou Piniella, Portland; **C**-Ray Fosse, Portland; Dan Breeden, Tulsa; **P**-Rich Robertson, Phoenix; Dick LeMay, Tulsa; **MVP**-Jim Hicks, Tulsa; **Manager**-Warren Spahn, Tulsa.

BA: Jim Hicks, Tulsa, .366
Runs: Jim Hicks, Tulsa, 100
Hits: Billy Cowan, San Diego, 158
 Cesar Gutierrez, Phoenix, 158
RBIs: Jose Laboy, Tulsa, 100
HRs: Clarence Jones, Tacoma, 24
Wins: Jerry Crider, Denver, 18
 Rich Robertson, Phoenix, 18
 Chuck Taylor, Tulsa, 18
SOs: Rich Robertson, Phoenix, 216
ERA: Pete Mikkelson, Tulsa, 1.91

AA Eastern League
President: A. Rankin Johnson

Standings	W	L	Pct.	GB	Attend.	Manager
Pittsfield Red Sox (2)	84	55	.604	—	48,067	Billy Gardner
Reading Phillies (19)	81	59	.579	3½	107,168	Frank Lucchesi
Elmira Pioneers (1)	77	63	.550	7½	54,998	Cal Ripken, Sr.
Binghamton Triplets (9)	67	72	.482	17	47,834	Frank Verdi/Cloyd Boyer/ Jim Gleeson
York Pirates (20)	58	82	.414	26½	42,005	Joe Morgan
Waterbury Indians (5)	52	88	.371	32½	40,205	Phil Cavarretta/Ray Mueller

Playoffs: Pittsfield 2 games, Elmira 0; Reading 2 games, Binghamton 0.
Finals: Reading 3 games, Pittsfield 1.

All-Star Team: 1B-James Campbell, Elmira; **2B**-Denny Doyle, Reading; **3B**-Carmen Fanzone, Pittsfield; **SS**-Luis Alvarado, Pittsfield; **OF**-Tony Torchia, Pittsfield; Alfredo Rico, Elmira; Howie Bedell, Reading; **C**-David Watkins, Reading; Thurman Munson, Binghamton; **P**-Dick Baney, Pittsfield; Gary Jones, Binghamton; **MVP**-Carmen Fanzone, Pittsfield; **Manager**-Billy Gardner, Pittsfield.

BA: Tony Torchia, Pittsfield, .294
Runs: Carmen Fanzone, Pittsfield, 71
Hits: Luis Alvarado, Pittsfield, 125
RBIs: Carmen Fanzone, Pittsfield, 75
HRs: Carmen Fanzone, Pittsfield, 17
Wins: Dick Baney, Pittsfield, 14
 Gene Rounsaville, Reading, 14
SOs: Mike Hedlund, Waterbury, 149
ERA: Silvano Quezada, York, 1.34

AA Southern League
President: Sam C. Smith

Standings	W	L	Pct.	GB	Attend.	Manager
Asheville Tourists (15)	86	54	.614	—	43,324	Sparky Anderson
Montgomery Rebels (6)	80	57	.584	4½	59,243	Frank Carswell
Charlotte Hornets (8)	72	68	.514	14	89,898	Harry Warner
Birmingham A's (10)	66	74	.471	20	46,356	Gus Niarhos
Savannah Senators (12)	57	79	.419	27	50,639	Buddy Hicks
Evansville White Sox (4)	55	84	.396	30½	35,027	Stan Wasiak/Gary Johnson

Playoffs: None.

All-Star Team: 1B-Archie Moore, Asheville; **2B**-Darrel Chaney, Asheville; **3B**-Minnie Mendoza, Charlotte; **SS**-Richard McKinney, Evansville; **OF**-Arlie Burge, Asheville;

*Won first-half **Won second-half ***Won both halves
Numbers after nicknames indicate farm system.
Affiliation listed at end of each year.

Charlie Manuel, Charlotte; Wayne Redmond, Montgomery; C-Fred Kendall, Asheville; P-Grover Powell, Asheville; James Brown, Montgomery; **Manager**-Sparky Anderson, Asheville.

BA: Arlie Burge, Asheville, .317
Runs: Paul Pavelko, Montgomery, 93
Hits: Minnie Mendoza, Charlotte, 165
RBIs: Barry Morgan, Montgomery, 91

HRs: Wayne Redmond, Montgomery, 26
Wins: Grover Powell, Asheville, 16
SOs: George Korince, Montgomery, 146
ERA: Grover Powell, Asheville, 2.54

AA Texas League
President: Hugh J. Finnerty

East Standings	W	L	Pct.	GB	Attend.	Manager
Arkansas Travelers (21)	82	58	.586	—	101,531	Vern Rapp
Shreveport Braves (13)	78	62	.557	4	67,671	Charlie Lau
Memphis Blues (18)	67	69	.493	13	141,418	Roy Sievers
Dallas-Ft. Worth Spurs (16)	60	79	.432	21½	215,756	Hub Kittle

West Standings	W	L	Pct.	GB	Attend.	Manager
El Paso Sun Kings (3)	77	60	.562	—	78,137	Chuck Tanner
Albuquerque Dodgers (17)	70	69	.504	8	100,093	Roger Craig
Amarillo Giants (22)	67	71	.486	10½	54,261	Andy Gilbert
San Antonio Missions (14)	53	86	.381	25	40,069	Harry Bright

Playoff: El Paso 3 games, Arkansas 1.

All-Star Team: 1B-Jim Spencer, El Paso; **2B**-John Sipin, Arkansas; **3B**-Bill Sudakis, Albuquerque; **SS**-Billy Grabarkewitz, Albuquerque; **OF**-Bob Taylor, Amarillo; Rod Gaspar, Memphis; Boots Day, Arkansas; Jarvis Tatum, El Paso; **C**-Walt Hriniak, Shreveport; **Util**-Jim Barfield, Albuquerque; **P**-Santiago Guzman, Arkansas; Rich Folkers, Memphis; **MVP**-Jim Spencer, El Paso; Bill Sudakis, Albuquerque; **Pitcher of the Year**-Santiago Guzman, Arkansas; **Manager**-Chuck Tanner, El Paso.

BA: Bob Taylor, Amarillo, .321
Runs: Jim Spencer, El Paso, 85
  Tomas Silverio, El Paso, 85
Hits: Rod Gaspar, Memphis, 160
RBIs: Jim Spencer, El Paso, 96
HRs: Jim Spencer, El Paso, 28

Wins: Joe DiFabio, Arkansas, 13
  Rich Folkers, Memphis, 13
  Carl Morton, Shreveport, 13
  Santiago Guzman, Arkansas, 13
  Archie Reynolds, San Antonio, 13
  Phil Knuckles, Arkansas, 13
SOs: Paul Doyle, Dallas-Ft. Worth, 149
ERA: Joe DiFabio, Arkansas, 2.17

A California League
President: Edward J. Mulligan

Standings	W	L	Pct.	GB	Attend.	Manager
San Jose Bees*(3)	80	60	.571	—	67,119	Harry Dunlop/Del Rice
Fresno Giants**(22)	79	60	.568	½	51,810	David Garcia
Lodi Crushers (14)	75	65	.536	5	41,776	Jim Marshall/Al Heist
Modesto Reds (21)	69	71	.493	11	56,511	Joe Cunningham
Reno Silver Sox (5)	67	72	.482	12½	26,337	Clay Bryant
Stockton Ports (1)	67	73	.479	13	10,633	Joe Altobelli
Bakersfield Dodgers (17)	61	79	.436	19	25,488	Don Williams
Visalia Mets (18)	61	79	.436	19	36,848	Roy McMillan

Playoff: Fresno 2 games, San Jose 1.

All-Star Team: 1B-Tom Robson, Visalia; **2B**-Bob Fenwick, Fresno; **3B**-John Lung, Lodi; **SS**-Bruce Christensen, San Jose; **OF**-Joe Patterson, Modesto; Don Baylor, Stockton; Roger Freed, Modesto; **C**-Ted Simmons, Modesto; **P**-Jophery Brown, Lodi; Ray Miller, Reno; James Moyer, Fresno; Joe Henderson, San Jose; **MVP**-Ted Simmons, Modesto; **Manager**-Del Rice, San Jose; David Garcia, Fresno.

BA: Ted Simmons, Modesto, .331
Runs: Joe Patterson, Modesto, 121
Hits: Joe Patterson, Modesto, 169
RBIs: Ted Simmons, Modesto, 117
HRs: Tom Robson, Visalia, 35
Wins: Jophery Brown, Lodi 18
  James Moyer, Fresno, 18
SOs: James Moyer, Fresno, 269
ERA: Tim Griffin, Stockton, 2.15

A Carolina League
President: J.C. "Bill" Jessup

East Standings	W	L	Pct.	GB	Attend.	Manager
Raleigh-Durham Mets (18)	83	56	.597	—	48,532	Pete Pavlick
Portsmouth Tides (19)	80	60	.571	3½	50,014	Bob Wellman
Peninsula Grays (10)	75	65	.536	8½	74,978	Jimmie Williams
Wilson Tobs (8)	71	68	.511	12	22,811	Vern Morgan
Rocky Mount Leafs (6)	70	70	.500	13½	30,792	Al Federoff
Kinston Eagles (9)	62	75	.453	20	55,516	Bob Bauer

West Standings	W	L	Pct.	GB	Attend.	Manager
Salem Rebels (20)	85	55	.607	—	64,532	Don Hoak
High Point-Thomasville Hi-Toms (x)	69	71	.493	16	42,574	Jack McKeon
Lynchburg White Sox (4)	68	72	.486	17	45,771	Alex Cosmidis
Greensboro Patriots (16)	61	79	.436	24	26,465	Brandy Davis
Winston-Salem Red Sox (2)	56	81	.409	27½	46,239	Bill Slack
Burlington Senators (12)	56	84	.400	29	20,806	Len Johnston

Playoffs: East - Raleigh-Durham 1 game, Peninsula 0; Wilson 1 game, Portsmouth 0; Raleigh-Durham 2 games, Wilson 1. West - Hi-Toms 1 game, Greensboro 0; Lynchburg 1 game, Salem 0; Hi-Toms 2 games, Lynchburg 0.
Finals: Hi-Toms 2 games, Raleigh-Durham 0.

All-Star Team: 1B-Tony Solaita, Hi-Toms; **2B**-Dave Cash, Salem; **3B**-Joe Lis,

---

Portsmouth; **SS**-Frank Baker, Kinston; **OF**-Wilbert Hammond, Salem; John Jeter, Salem; Robert Brooks, Peninsula; Carlos May, Lynchburg; **C**-Gene Tenace, Peninsula; **Util**-Jack Lind, Greensboro; **P**-Robert Settle, Salem; Jon Matlack, Raleigh-Durham; **MVP**-Tony Solaita, Hi-Toms; **Manager**-Don Hoak, Salem.

BA: Carlos May, Lynchburg, .330
Runs: Lee Green, Hi-Toms, 106
Hits: John Jeter, Salem, 156
RBIs: Tony Solaita, Hi-Toms, 122
HRs: Tony Solaita, Hi-Toms, 49

Wins: Jerry Cram, Wilson, 16
  Charlie Hudson, Raleigh-Durham, 16
  Ed Smith, Lynchburg, 16
SOs: Al Fitzmorris, Lynchburg, 214
ERA: Billy Champion, Portsmouth, 2.03

A Florida State League
President: George MacDonald, Sr.

East Standings	W	L	Pct.	GB	Attend.	Manager
Miami Marlins (1)	87	55	.613	—	85,572	Harry Malmberg
Cocoa Astros (16)	74	65	.532	11½	28,923	Tony Pacheco/Leo Posada
Daytona Beach Dodgers (17)	73	70	.510	14½	60,186	Bill Berrier
Ft. Lauderdale Yankees (9)	62	75	.453	22½	29,108	Billy Shantz
W. Palm Beach Braves (13)	59	77	.434	25	13,387	Andy Pafko

West Standings	W	L	Pct.	GB	Attend.	Manager
Orlando Twins (8)	81	59	.613	—	54,166	Ralph Rowe
St. Petersburg Cardinals (21)	80	63	.559	2½	73,047	Ron Plaza
Tampa Tarpons (15)	74	62	.544	5	45,359	George Scherger
Lakeland Tigers (6)	58	81	.417	22½	8,335	Len Okrie
Leesburg Athletics (10)	51	92	.357	31½	8,214	Al Ronning

Playoffs: Miami 2 games, St. Petersburg 1; Orlando 2 games, Cocoa 0.
Finals: Orlando 2 games, Miami 1.

All-Star Team: 1B-Larry Johnson, Miami; **2B**-Stan Martin, Miami; **3B**-Alfonso Mairena, St. Petersburg; **SS**-Eric Soderholm, Orlando; **OF**-Al Crawford, Tampa; Ike Blessitt, Lakeland; Robert Alexander, Orlando; **C**-Cliff Johnson, Cocoa; Lee Robinson, Orlando; **P**-Michael Willis, Tampa; Reggie Cleveland, St. Petersburg; **Manager**-George Scherger, Tampa.

BA: Stan Martin, Miami, .303
Runs: Ike Blessitt, Lakeland, 76
Hits: Larry Johnson, Miami, 135
RBIs: Larry Johnson, Miami, 74
HRs: Nathaniel King, Orlando, 16
Wins: Reggie Cleveland, St. Petersburg, 15
SOs: Michael Willis, Tampa, 174
ERA: Joe DeLuise, Daytona Beach, 1.94

A Mexican Center League
President: Antonio Ramirez Muro

Standings	W	L	Pct.	GB	Attend.	Manager
Saltillo Saraperos	81	44	.648	—	38,671	Hector Rodriguez
Ciudad Madero Bravos	76	49	.608	5	109,128	Leonel Aldama
Torreon	71	53	.573	9½	12,642	Pedro Gonzalez
Tampico Pirates	71	55	.563	10½	52,743	Tony Gonzalez
Nuevo Laredo Tecolotes	56	68	.452	24½	19,272	Miguel Sotelo
Fresnillo Mineros	55	70	.440	26	25,963	Ben Reyes
Leon Aguiluchos	50	75	.400	31	26,948	Abril McDillon
Zacatecas Petroleros	40	86	.317	41½	38,894	Domingo Gonzalez/ Arturo Cacheux

Playoffs: None.

All-Star Team: 1B-Jose Romellon, Ciudad Madero; **2B**-Miguel DeLeon, Nuevo Laredo; **3B**-Adal Contreras, Saltillo; **SS**-Guillermo Murrillo, Torreon; **OF**-Jose Mora, Saltillo; L. Jose Luis Delgado, Torreon; Alejandro Robles, Tampico; **C**-Gerardo Gutierrez, Saltillo; Ayala, Ciudad Madero; **P**-O. Jose Luis Delgado, Saltillo; Enrique Icedo, Saltillo; **Manager**-Hector Rodriguez, Saltillo.

BA: Guillermo Murillo, Torreon, .347
Runs: Jose Romellon, Ciudad Madero, 115
Hits: Guillermo Murillo, Torreon, 172
RBIs: Jose Romellon, Ciudad Madero, 125
HRs: Jose Romellon, Ciudad Madero, 40
Wins: O. Jose Luis Delgado, Saltillo, 20
SOs: Enrique Icedo, Saltillo, 181
ERA: Enrique Icedo, Saltillo, 2.53

A Mexican Northern League
President: Horacio Lopez

Standings	W	L	Pct.	GB	Attend.	Manager
Ensenada Tigres	62	40	.608	—	42,135	Jesus Robles
Nogales Internacionales	60	40	.600	1	12,933	Ernesto Gracia
Mexicali Aguilas	56	45	.554	5½	37,583	Ramon Sandoval
San Luis Rio Colorado Algodoneros	52	50	.510	10	24,724	Marco Antonio Manzo

Played an interlocking schedule with the Mexican Rookie League.

Playoffs: None.

All-Star Team: 1B-Marcos Aguilar, San Luis Rio Colorado; **2B**-Eduardo Cruz, Nogales; **3B**-Fortino Morales, Ensenada; **SS**-Hector Huerta, Ensenada; **OF**-Fernando Castro, Mexicali; Pedro Lozano, San Luis Rio Colorado; Octavio Orozco, Nogales; **C**-Edgardo Tiburcio, Mexicali; Luis Peralta, Ensenada; **P**-Alberto Villa, San Luis Rio Colorado; Alfredo Meza, Ensenada; **Manager**-Jesus Robles, Ensenada.

BA: Fernando Castro, Mexicali, .349
Runs: Fernando Castro, Mexicali, 77
Hits: Hector Huerta, Ensenada, 135
RBIs: Hector Escamilla, Ensenada, 66
HRs: Pedro Lozano, San Luis Rio Colorado, 12
Wins: Alberto Villa, San Luis Rio Colorado, 15
  Raymundo Parra, Mexicali, 15
SOs: Raymundo Parra, Mexicali, 168
ERA: Cruz Ruvalcaba, Nogales, 1.41

A Mexican Southeast League
President: Fernando Canton

Standings	W	L	Pct.	GB	Attend.	Manager
Campeche Pirates	57	33	.633	—	56,568	David Garcia
Carmen Camaroneros	59	35	.628	—	74,503	Rosendo del Rio
Puerto Mexico Portenos	57	36	.613	1½	61,813	Minnie Minoso
Yucatan Venados	53	42	.558	6½	108,893	Ben Valenzuela
Las Choapas Diablos Rojos	40	48	.455	16	29,071	Andres Tanaka
Minatitlan Petroleros	34	59	.366	24½	30,028	Jose Echevarria
Tabasco Cattlemen	21	68	.236	35½	61,774	Dave Jimenez

Playoff: Carmen 3 games, Puerto Mexico 2.
Finals: Carmen 4 games, Campeche 3.

All-Star Team: 1B-Humberto Guerrero, Campeche; **2B**-Narciso Ruiz, Campeche; **3B**-Antonio Fuentes, Minatitlan; **SS**-Francisco Conkle, Campeche; **OF**-Juan Menchaca, Puerto Mexico; Miguel Gutierrez, Yucatan; Adan Contreras, Campeche; **C**-Lucas Bouye, Campeche; **P**-Manuel Uriarte, Puerto Mexico; Pablo Montes de Oca, Campeche; **Manager**-Rosendo Del Rio, Carmen.

BA: Lucas Bouye, Campeche, .370
Runs: Gabriel Lugo, Puerto Mexico, 64
Hits: Gabriel Lugo, Puerto Mexico, 118
Juan Menchaca, Puerto Mexico, 118
RBIs: Art Bernal, Carmen, 80
HRs: Francisco "Pancho" Herrera, Carmen, 22
Wins: Pablo Montes de Oca, Campeche, 21
SOs: Julio Imbert, Yucatan, 155
ERA: Pablo Montes de Oca, Campeche, 1.53

A Midwest League
President: James Doster

Standings	W	L	Pct.	GB	Attend.	Manager
Decatur Commodores**(22)	69	48	.590	—	51,789	Denny Sommers
Quad City Angels*(3)	65	50	.565	3	63,233	Fred Koenig/Tom Morgan
Cedar Rapids Cardinals (21)	63	53	.543	5½	52,109	Jack Krol
Wisconsin Rapids Twins (8)	62	57	.521	8	33,176	Ray Bellino/Tom Umphlett
Quincy Cubs (14)	59	59	.500	10½	27,055	Walt Dixon
Appleton Foxes (4)	57	61	.483	12½	45,436	Gary Johnson/Stan Wasiak
Dubuque Royals (7)	54	61	.470	14	49,411	Max Lanier/Paul Pettit
Waterloo Hawks (9)	53	60	.469	14	30,484	Rac Slider
Clinton Pilots (20)	54	67	.446	17	49,148	Bob Clear
Burlington Bees (10)	48	68	.414	20½	40,097	Jim Hughes

Playoff: Quad City 2 games, Decatur 1.

All-Star Team: 1B-Peter Middlekauff, Dubuque; **2B**-Roberto Diaz, Cedar Rapids; **3B**-George Gove, Wisconsin Rapids; **SS**-Jesus Aristimuno, Decatur; **OF**-Luis Melendez, Cedar Rapids; George Hendrick, Burlington; Lorenzo Lanier, Clinton; **C**-Robert Bonalewicz, Cedar Rapids; Robert Mewes, Dubuque; **P**-Steve Sibley, Decatur; Robert Bellemare, Dubuque; **Manager**-Jack Krol, Cedar Rapids.

BA: George Hendrick, Burlington, .327
Runs: Lorenzo Lanier, Clinton, 99
Hits: Lorenzo Lanier, Clinton, 132
RBIs: Roe Skidmore, Decatur, 94
HRs: Roe Skidmore, Decatur, 27
Wins: Alec Distaso, Quincy, 13
SOs: Vida Blue, Burlington, 231
ERA: Steve Sibley, Decatur, 2.01

A New York-Pennsylvania League
President: Vincent M. McNamara

Standings	W	L	Pct.	GB	Attend.	Manager
Auburn Twins (8)	49	27	.645	—	25,053	Boyd Coffie
Oneonta Yankees (9)	43	34	.558	6½	18,510	Jerry Walker
Williamsport Astros (x)	40	35	.533	8½	28,562	Dick Bogard
Newark Co-Pilots (11)	38	36	.514	10	20,121	Sibby Sisti
Batavia Trojans (6)	37	38	.493	11½	25,084	Bob Dustal
Geneva Senators (12)	37	39	.487	12	16,204	Joe Marchese
Jamestown Falcons (2)	31	44	.413	17½	15,120	Jackie Moore
Corning Royals (7)	27	49	.355	22	19,685	Bo Osborne

Playoffs: Auburn 1 game, Williamsport 0; Oneonta 1 game, Newark 0.
Finals: Oneonta 1 game, Auburn 0.

All-Star Team: 1B-Robert Welz, Batavia; **2B**-Jerry Terrell, Auburn; **3B**-Jerry Merlet, Geneva; **SS**-Manuel Crespo, Jamestown; **OF**-Tommy Lolos, Auburn; Cliff Foster, Auburn; Tom Kelly, Newark; Oscar Brown, Williamsport; **C**-John Dempsey, Auburn; Michael Murray, Batavia; **Util**-Bruce Davis, Williamsport; **P**-Jeff Vollweiler, Geneva; Stephen Luebber, Auburn; Russ Rothermel, Williamsport; Ray DeRiggi, Oneonta; Paul Splittorff, Corning; **Manager**-Boyd Coffie, Auburn.

BA: Jerry Merlet, Geneva, .353
Runs: Cliff Foster, Auburn, 66
Hits: Manuel Crespo, Jamestown, 95
RBIs: Clarence Vaughns, Newark, 73
HRs: Tommy Lolos, Auburn, 14
Wins: Stephen Cushmore, Batavia, 11
SOs: Paul Splittorff, Corning, 136
Jeff Vollweiler, Geneva, 136
ERA: Guy Hansen, Oneonta, 1.67

A Northern League
President: Roland E. Parcel

Standings	W	L	Pct.	GB	Attend.	Manager
St. Cloud Rox (8)	43	27	.614	—	24,709	Carroll Hardy
Mankato Mets (18)	42	27	.609	½	8,056	Joe Frazier
Sioux Falls Packers (15)	41	29	.586	2	36,838	Jim Snyder
Duluth-Superior Dukes (4)	31	39	.443	12	12,955	Bruce Andrew
Huron Phillies (19)	26	43	.377	16½	17,554	Dallas Green
Aberdeen Pheasants (1)	26	44	.371	17	15,517	Bill Werle

Playoffs: None.

BA: Richard Barnes, Sioux Falls, .330
Runs: James Nettles, St. Cloud, 50
Hits: Alex Rowell, St. Cloud, 78
RBIs: Bobby Jones, St. Cloud, 43
Greg Luzinski, Huron, 43
HRs: Greg Luzinski, Huron, 13
Wins: Thomas Ferraro, St. Cloud, 11
SOs: David Goltz, St. Cloud, 122
ERA: Allan Clements, Mankato, 1.42

A Northwest League
President: Hugh Luby

Standings	W	L	Pct.	GB	Attend.	Manager
Tri-City Atoms (17)	45	30	.600	—	19,356	Don LeJohn
Eugene Emeralds (19)	41	32	.562	3	22,169	Nolan Campbell
Medford Giants (22)	34	43	.442	12	20,585	Harvey Koepf
Lewiston Broncs (21)	30	45	.400	15	19,818	Roy Majtyka

Playoffs: None.

All-Star Team: 1B-Andre Thornton, Eugene; **2B**-Patrick Locanto, Eugene; **3B**-Ron Cey, Tri-City; **SS**-Lucky Thompson, Lewiston; **OF**-Bill Brooks, Lewiston; George Foster, Medford; Joe Ferguson, Tri-City; **C**-Stephen Krines, Tri-City; **Util**-Reid Braden, Eugene; **P**-Richard Dorsch, Tri-City; Ronald Henson, Eugene; **Manager**-Don LeJohn, Tri-City.

BA: Bill Brooks, Lewiston, .311
Runs: Bob Buckner, Tri-City, 54
Hits: Fredrick Grooms, Lewiston, 82
RBIs: Ron Cey, Tri-City, 62
HRs: Joe Ferguson, Tri-City, 12
Wins: James Alviso, Eugene, 9
Richard Dorsch, Tri-City, 9
SOs: Bob Snyder, Eugene, 120
ERA: Mark Ballinger, Eugene, 2.79

A Western Carolinas League
President: John H. Moss

Standings	W	L	Pct.	GB	Attend.	Manager
Greenwood Braves**(13)	73	51	.589	—	62,033	Lou Fitzgerald
Spartanburg Phillies*(19)	71	54	.568	2½	112,789	Bobby Malkmus
Greenville Red Sox (2)	68	54	.557	4	59,368	Matt Sczesny
Gastonia Pirates (20)	68	55	.553	4½	32,960	Frank Oceak
Rock Hill Indians (5)	54	67	.446	17½	23,176	Pinky May
Salisbury Senators (12)	34	87	.281	37½	24,072	Billy Klaus

Playoff: Greenwood 2 games, Spartanburg 1.

All-Star Team: 1B-Nick Van Lue, Spartanburg; **2B**-Brian Murphy, Gastonia; **3B**-Alberto Cambero, Greenwood; **SS**-Kris Krebs, Greenville; **OF**-Zelman Jack, Gastonia; Roger Nelson, Spartanburg; Jim Breazeale, Greenwood; **C**-Vic Correll, Rock Hill; Bob Didier, Greenwood; **P**-Gordon Knutson, Spartanburg; Ray Allen, Greenwood; **Manager**-Lou Fitzgerald, Greenwood.

BA: Zelman Jack, Gastonia, .326
Runs: Zelman Jack, Gastonia, 84
Hits: Zelman Jack, Gastonia, 142
RBIs: Jim Breazeale, Greenwood, 88
HRs: Zelman Jack, Gastonia, 24
Wins: Dave Warmbrod, Gastonia, 12
SOs: Michael Thompson, Salisbury, 136
ERA: Dave Warmbrod, Gastonia, 2.27

R Appalachian League
President: Chauncey De Vault

Standings	W	L	Pct.	GB	Attend.	Manager
Marion Mets (18)	42	30	.583	—	16,203	Lloyd Gearhart
Covington Astros (16)	39	32	.549	2½	21,906	Tony Pacheco
Johnson City Yankees (9)	39	32	.549	2½	10,657	Gene Hassell
Bluefield Orioles (1)	23	49	.319	19	14,405	Ken Rowe

Playoffs: None.

All-Star Team: 1B-Larry Mansfield, Covington; **2B**-Don McLaughlin, Covington; **3B**-Jeff Turner, Johnson City; **SS**-Tim Foli, Marion; **OF**-Richard Chiles, Covington; Ed Watts, Bluefield; John Milner, Marion; Javier Andino, Bluefield; **C**-Graig Kogut, Johnson City; **P**-Bruce Olson, Johnson City; Alonzo Ramirez, Johnson City; Eugene Zawatski, Marion; **Manager**-Gene Hassell, Johnson City.

BA: Javier Andino, Bluefield, .353
Runs: Ed Watts, Bluefield, 64
Hits: Javier Andino, Bluefield, 90
RBIs: Larry Mansfield, Covington, 62
HRs: Larry Mansfield, Covington, 18
Wins: Bruce Olson, Johnson City, 8
SOs: Walter Harris, Covington, 107
ERA: Bruce Olson, Johnson City, 1.84

R Gulf Coast League
President: George MacDonald, Sr.

Standings	W	L	Pct.	GB	Manager
Athletics (10)	39	21	.650	—	Billy Herman
Cardinals (21)	34	27	.557	5½	George Kissell/Ray Hathaway
Indians (33)	33	27	.550	6	Ken Aspromonte
Twins (8)	32	27	.542	6½	Fred Waters
Reds (15)	28	33	.459	11½	Bill Lajoie
Pirates (20)	27	33	.450	12	Buddy Pritchard
Tigers (6)	27	36	.429	13½	Wayne Blackburn
White Sox (4)	21	37	.362	17	Tom Saffell

Games played at Sarasota and Bradenton, Florida.
Total Attendance: 12,579.

Playoffs: None.

All-Star Team: 1B-Michael Brooks, Twins; **2B**-Danny Covert, Indians; **3B**-Michael Cavanaugh, Twins; **SS**-Craig Carter, Tigers; **OF**-Jose Stennett, Twins; Joe Bowen, White

Sox; Stephen Jones, Pirates; **C**-Gary Lear, Indians; Milt May, Pirates; **P**-Jerry Killian, Tigers; Ron Oglesby, Twins; **Manager**-Fred Waters, Twins.

BA: Joe Bowen, White Sox, .338
Runs: Jose Stennett, Twins, 46
Hits: Jose Stennett, Twins, 74
RBIs: Jose Stennett, Twins, 40
HRs: Michael Holbrook, Twins, 8

Wins: William Ingram, Athletics, 8
Ron Oglesby, Twins, 8
David Sells, Pirates, 8
SOs: John Hefferon, Athletics, 80
John Howell, Indians, 80
ERA: John Hefferon, Athletics, 1.67

R Mexican Rookie League
President: Horacio Lopez

Standings	W	L	Pct.	GB	Attend.	Manager
Caborca Tigres	55	40	.570	—	14,805	Sergio Gonzalez
Empalme Rieleros	43	52	.453	12	3,279	Mauro Ruiz
Agua Prieta Charros	33	62	.347	22	12,202	Zenon Ochoa
Cananea Mineros	30	64	.319	24½	4,462	Alfonso Ibarra

Played an interlocking schedule with the Mexican Northern League.

Playoffs: None.

All-Star Team: 1B-Carlos Garza, Caborca; **2B**-Jorge Solano, Empalme; **3B**-Mario Valenzuela, Caborca; **SS**-Jose Valdez, Caborca; **OF**-Rogelio Montoya, Agua Prieta; Leonardo Gallegos, Cananea; Armando Lara, Caborca; **C**-Rogelio Carmona, Caborca; Sergio Cota, Empalme; **P**-Ramon Reynoso, Caborca; Javier Martinez, Empalme; **Manager**-Sergio Gonzalez, Caborca.

BA: Jose Valdez, Caborca, .356
Runs: Marcelino Montoya, Agua Prieta, 72
Hits: Jose Valdez, Caborca, 105
RBIs: Marcelino Montoya, Agua Prieta, 74

HRs: Marcelino Montoya, Agua Prieta, 18
Wins: Ramon Reynoso, Caborca, 16
SOs: Ramon Reynoso, Caborca, 163
ERA: Ramon Reynoso, Caborca, 1.24

R Pioneer League
President: Ben Jewell

Standings	W	L	Pct.	GB	Attend.	Manager
Ogden Dodgers (17)	39	25	.609	—	33,523	Tom Lasorda
Idaho Falls Angels (3)	38	25	.603	½	26,056	Tom Sommers/ Eddie Bressoud
Caldwell Cubs (14)	33	30	.524	5½	22,462	George Freese
Magic Valley Cowboys (13)	30	31	.492	7½	10,064	Connie Ryan
Salt Lake City Giants (22)	16	45	.262	21½	54,195	Ray Malgradi

Playoffs: None.

All-Star Team: 1B-Bill Buckner, Ogden; **2B**-Matt Alexander, Ogden; **3B**-Steve Garvey, Ogden; **SS**-Edward Goodson, Salt Lake City; **OF**-Bobby Valentine, Ogden; Larry LaGarde, Magic Valley; Damon Howell, Idaho Falls; **C**-Patrick Burke, Ogden; Randall Niles, Idaho Falls; **Util**-James Cesario, Idaho Falls; Curtis Moore, Magic Valley; **P**-Sandy Vance, Ogden; Dennis Taylor, Caldwell; D. Bingham, Salt Lake City; Bruce Ellingsen, Ogden; **Manager**-Tom Lasorda, Ogden.

BA: Bill Buckner, Ogden, .344
Runs: Bobby Valentine, Ogden, 62
Hits: Bill Buckner, Ogden, 88
RBIs: Steve Garvey, Ogden, 59

HRs: Steve Garvey, Ogden, 20
Wins: Sandy Vance, Ogden, 14
SOs: Sandy Vance, Ogden, 150
ERA: Bruce Ellingsen, Ogden, 1.43

1968 Interleague Post Season Play

World Series
Detroit (American) 4 games, St. Louis (National) 3

1968 Major League Farm Systems

American League
1 Baltimore (6): Rochester, Elmira, Stockton, Miami, Aberdeen, Bluefield.
2 Boston (6): Louisville, Pittsfield, Winston-Salem, Waterloo, Greenville, Jamestown.
3 California (5): Seattle, El Paso, San Jose, Quad City, Idaho Falls.
4 Chicago (6): Hawaii, Evansville, Lynchburg, Appleton, Duluth-Superior, Gulf Coast.
5 Cleveland (5): Portland, Waterbury, Reno, Rock Hill, Gulf Coast.
6 Detroit (5): Toledo, Montgomery, Rocky Mount, Lakeland, Batavia.
7 Kansas City (2): Dubuque, Corning.
8 Minnesota (8): Denver, Charlotte, Wilson, Orlando, Wisconsin Rapids, Auburn, St. Cloud, Gulf Coast.
9 New York (6): Syracuse, Binghamton, Kinston, Ft. Lauderdale, Oneonta, Johnson City.
10 Oakland (6): Vancouver, Birmingham, Peninsula, Leesburg, Burlington (IA), Gulf Coast.
11 Seattle (1): Newark.
12 Washington (5): Buffalo, Savannah, Burlington (NC), Geneva, Salisbury.

National League
13 Atlanta (5): Richmond, Shreveport, West Palm Beach, Greenwood, Magic Valley.
14 Chicago (5): Tacoma, San Antonio, Lodi, Quincy, Caldwell.
15 Cincinnati (5): Indianapolis, Asheville, Tampa, Sioux Falls, Gulf Coast.
16 Houston (5): Oklahoma City, Dallas-Ft. Worth, Greensboro, Cocoa, Covington.
17 Los Angeles (6): Spokane, Albuquerque, Bakersfield, Daytona Beach, Tri-City, Ogden.
18 New York (6): Jacksonville, Memphis, Visalia, Raleigh-Durham, Mankato, Marion.
19 Philadelphia (6): San Diego, Reading, Portsmouth, Huron, Eugene, Spartanburg.
20 Pittsburgh (6): Columbus, York, Salem, Clinton, Gastonia, Gulf Coast.
21 St. Louis (7): Tulsa, Arkansas, Modesto, St. Petersburg, Cedar Rapids, Lewiston, Gulf Coast.
22 San Francisco (6): Phoenix, Amarillo, Fresno, Decatur, Medford, Salt Lake City.

Co-op (x): High Point-Thomasville, Williamsport.

1968 No-Hitters

Date	Pitcher	Team	League	Opponent	Score
3-25	Javier Herrera/ Jorge Espinoso	Torreon	Mexican Center	Tampico	5-0
4-23	Israel Buentello	Nuevo Laredo	Mexican Center	Tampico	2-1
4-23	Victor Agundez	Puerto Mexico	Mexican S.E.	Tabasco	4-0
4-27	Tom Phoebus	Baltimore	American	Boston	6-0
4-30	Alberto Joachin	Carmen	Mexican S.E.	Tabasco	3-0
5-2	Dick Armstrong	Albuquerque	Texas	Dallas-Ft. Worth	10-0
5-8	Catfish Hunter	Oakland	American	Minnesota	4-0 (P)
5-13	Javier Martinez	Empalme	Mexican Rookie	Caborca	1-0
5-13	Larry Bohannon	Orlando	Florida State	Leesburg	3-0 (P)
5-15	Jorge Villa	San Luis Rio Colo.	Mexican Northern	Ensenada	7-0
5-24	Alfredo Meza	Ensenada	Mexican Northern	Empalme	7-0
5-24	Bob Watkins	Dallas-Ft. Worth	Texas	Memphis	2-0
5-25	Pablo Torrealba	Greenwood	W. Carolinas	Salisbury	6-0 (7)
5-26	Luis Penalver	Dallas-Ft. Worth	Texas	Memphis	3-0 (7)
5-29	Sergio Murillo	Torreon	Mexican Center	Leon	2-0
6-5	Dean Burk	San Antonio	Texas	Albuquerque	1-0 (7)
6-6	Alberto Villa	San Luis Rio Colo.	Mexican Northern	Empalme	4-0
6-15	Paul Strauch	Gastonia	W. Carolinas	Salisbury	5-0 (7)
6-19	Vida Blue	Burlington	Midwest	Appleton	4-0 (7)
6-23	Robert Meyer	Vancouver	Pacific Coast	Hawaii	6-0
6-23	Bob Snyder	Eugene	Northwest	Medford	3-0
6-28	Richard Dorsch	Tri-City	Northwest	Medford	8-0
6-29	Paul Doyle	Dallas-Ft. Worth	Texas	El Paso	4-0
6-29	Concepcion Munoz	Minatitlan	Mexican S.E.	Las Choapas	2-0 (7)
6-30	Geoff Zahn	Daytona Beach	Florida State	St. Petersburg	0-1
7-7	James Brown	Montgomery	Southern	Charlotte	2-0 (7)
7-7	Michael Price	Bakersfield	California	Lodi	0-1 (7)
7-9	Silvano Quezada	York	Eastern	Elmira	2-0
7-14	Enrique Icedo	Saltillo	Mexican Center	Zacatecas	2-0
7-17	Edward Phillips	Winston-Salem	Carolina	Rocky Mount	3-0 (P)
7-18	Carlos Uacanga	Fresnillo	Mexican Center	Torreon	6-0 (7)
7-20	Jim Britton/ Jim Sanders	Shreveport	Texas	San Antonio	1-0
7-21	Steve Renko	Memphis	Texas	Albuquerque	1-0 (7)
7-25	James Brown	Montgomery	Southern	Birmingham	3-0
7-28	Edmund Mantie	Salt Lake City	Pioneer	Ogden	3-0 (7)
7-29	George Culver	Cincinnati	National	Philadelphia	6-1
7-30	Michael Cichon/ Thomas Hroncich	Minnesota	Gulf Coast	St. Louis	0-4 (7)
8-11	Dan Roberts	Daytona Beach	Florida State	Ft. Lauderdale	1-0 (7)
8-14	Ed Silverman	West Palm Beach	Florida State	St. Petersburg	4-0 (7)
8-18	Bo Belinsky	Hawaii	Pacific Coast	Tacoma	1-0
8-22	Lloyd Allen	Idaho Falls	Pioneer	Magic Valley	1-0 (7)
9-3	Howie Reed	Oklahoma City	Pacific Coast	Indianapolis	1-0 (7)
9-17	Gaylord Perry	San Francisco	National	St. Louis	1-0
9-18	Ray Washburn	St. Louis	National	San Francisco	2-0

Number in parentheses indicates innings if other than nine; "P" indicates perfect game.

THIS DATE IN MINOR LEAGUE HISTORY

March 24, 1968, Ovid Nicholson, 79, who stole an incredible 111 bases in only 123 games with Frankfort, Blue Grass League, in 1912, died at Salem, Indiana.

April 28, 1968, After 16 straight losses, Leesburg, Florida State League, finally posted its first 1968 victory, a 6-2 decision over Cocoa.

May 2, 1968, Jose Cruz, Modesto, California League, went 6-for-6, giving the outfielder ten consecutive hits in two days.

May 6, 1968, Cedar Rapids, Midwest League, made twelve errors, including seven in one inning, in a 21-4 loss to Wisconsin Rapids.

May 11, 1968, James "Danny" Boone, who with his brother, Isaac "Ike" Boone, ranks among the all-time leaders in batting average, died at Tuscaloosa, Alabama, at age 73. Danny compiled a batting mark of .356 in his 14-year career in the minors, won four batting titles, and in 1928 hit .419 with High Point of the Piedmont League. Ike set the minor league career record with a batting average of .370.

May 26, 1968, Walt "No-Neck" Williams, Hawaii, Pacific Coast League, was stopped after making 11 straight hits.

June 30, 1968, St. Petersburg, Florida State League, had only one hit in a 1-0, 15-inning loss to Daytona Beach.

July 22, 1968, Fresno defeated Modesto 22-19 in a California League game.

Modesto scored 12 runs in the third and Fresno tallied 10 in the sixth frame.

July 24, 1968, After 13 straight victories, Marion, Appalachian League, was upended by Johnson City, 9-7.

July 24, 1968, Twenty-two Dubuque, Midwest League, batters struck out, but the Packers beat Quad City 3-2.

July 28, 1968, Montgomery, Southern League, lost to Savannah 8-7 after winning 16 straight games.

August 4, 1968, Jim Horsford, Reynosa, Mexican League, pitched his fifth successive shutout. His scoreless string would end at 51 innings three days later.

August 13, 1968, Tug McGraw, Jacksonville, International League, went 5-for-5 at the plate (four singles and a homer) and pitched the Suns to a 14-1 win over Buffalo.

August 31, 1968, Judson "Jay" Kirke, 80, one of the minor leagues' greatest hitters and a baseball legend in his time, died in New Orleans. Kirke, a first baseman, had 3,165 hits in his 20 years in the minors for a batting average of .316. He also hit .301 in 320 major league games. In 1921, he had 282 hits for Louisville and won the American Association batting crown with an average of .386.

September 6, 1968, The first three El Paso batters hit home runs in the opening inning in a Texas League playoff game against Arkansas.

MINOR LEAGUE CONSECUTIVE WINS

WINS	TEAM	LEAGUE	YEAR
29	Salt Lake City	Pioneer	1987
26	Des Moines	Western	1896
27	Baltimore	International	1921
27	Corsicana	Texas	1902
26	Peekskill	North Atlantic	1946
26	Stockton	California	1947
25	Charlotte	North Carolina	1902
25	Wilkes-Barre	New York State	1912
25	Spartanburg	Western Carolinas	1966
25	Des Moines	Northwestern	1886
25	Wichita Falls	Texas	1922
25	Baltimore	International	1920
24	Jersey City	Eastern	1903
23	Johnson City	Appalachian	1986
22	Des Moines	Western Assoc.	1896
22	Austin	Texas	1911
22	St. Petersburg	Florida State	1966
21	Aguila	Mexican	1939
21	Rocky Mount	Piedmont	1938
21	Lancaster	Atlantic	1897
21	Milwaukee	American Assoc.	1926
20	Los Angeles	Pacific Coast	1943
20	Elizabethton	Appalachian	1990
20	Alexandria	Evangeline	1940
20	Erie	Middle Atlantic	1951
19	Wichita	Western	1921
19	Joplin	Western Assoc.	1910
19	Seattle	Pacific Coast	1903
19	Enid	Western Assoc.	1922
19	Lethbridge	Pioneer	1980
19	Rochester	International	1953
19	Los Angeles	Pacific Coast	1939
19	Toronto	International	1919
19	Birmingham	Southern Assoc.	1927
18	Memphis	Southern Assoc.	1928
18	New Orleans	Southern Assoc.	1936
18	Harrisburg	Tri-State	1907
18	Seattle	Northwestern	1915
18	McCook	Nebraska	1959
18	Ponca City	Sooner	1951
17	Des Moines	Western Assoc.	1893
17	Fitchburg	New England	1915
17	Pawtucket	New England	1947
17	Scranton	Eastern	1943
17	Cedar Rapids	Midwest	1965
17	Salem	Appalachian	1955
17	Lynn	New England	1947
17	Dallas	Texas	1956
17	Shawnee	Sooner	1954

1969

American League
President: Joseph E. Cronin

East Standings	W	L	Pct.	GB	Attend.	Manager
Baltimore Orioles	109	53	.673	—	1,062,069	Earl Weaver
Detroit Tigers....................	90	72	.566	19	1,577,481	Mayo Smith
Boston Red Sox	87	75	.537	22	1,833,246	Dick Williams/
						Eddie Popowski
Washington Senators	86	76	.531	23	918,106	Ted Williams
New York Yankees.............	80	81	.497	28½	1,067,996	Ralph Houk
Cleveland Indians	62	99	.358	46½	619,970	Alvin Dark

West Standings	W	L	Pct.	GB	Attend.	Manager
Minnesota Twins	97	65	.599	—	1,349,328	Billy Martin
Oakland Athletics	88	74	.543	9	778,232	Hank Bauer/John McNamara
California Angels	71	91	.438	26	758,388	Bill Rigney/Lefty Phillips
Kansas City Royals............	69	93	.426	28	902,414	Joe Gordon
Chicago White Sox	68	94	.420	29	589,546	Al Lopez/Don Gutteridge
Seattle Pilots	64	98	.395	33	677,944	Joe Schultz

Playoff: Baltimore 3 games, Minnesota 0.

BA: Rod Carew, Minnesota, .332
Runs: Reggie Jackson, Oakland, 123
Hits: Tony Oliva, Minnesota, 197
RBIs: Harmon Killebrew, Minnesota, 140
HRs: Harmon Killebrew, Minnesota, 49

Wins: Denny McLain, Detroit, 24
SOs: Sam McDowell, Cleveland, 279
ERA: Dick Bosman, Washington, 2.19
Pct: Jim Palmer, Baltimore, .800, 16-4
Saves: Ron Perranoski, Minnesota, 31

National League
President: Warren C. Giles

East Standings	W	L	Pct.	GB	Attend.	Manager
New York Mets	100	62	.617	—	2,175,373	Gil Hodges
Chicago Cubs....................	92	70	.568	8	1,674,993	Leo Durocher
Pittsburgh Pirates................	88	74	.543	12	769,369	Larry Shephard/
						Alex Grammas
St. Louis Cardinals	87	75	.537	13	1,682,783	Red Schoendienst
Philadelphia Phillies	63	99	.389	37	519,414	Bob Skinner/George Myatt
Montreal Expos..................	52	110	.321	48	1,212,608	Gene Mauch

West Standings	W	L	Pct.	GB	Attend.	Manager
Atlanta Braves	93	69	.574	—	1,458,320	Luman Harris
San Francisco Giants	90	72	.556	3	873,603	Clyde King
Cincinnati Reds.................	89	73	.549	4	987,991	Dave Bristol
Los Angeles Dodgers	85	77	.525	8	1,784,527	Walter Alston
Houston Astros	81	81	.500	12	1,442,995	Harry Walker
San Diego Padres................	52	110	.321	41	512,970	Preston Gomez

Playoff: New York 3 games, Atlanta 0.

BA: Pete Rose, Cincinnati, .348
Runs: Bobby Bonds, San Francisco, 120
Pete Rose, Cincinnati, 120
Hits: Matty Alou, Pittsburgh, 231
RBIs: Willie McCovey, San Francisco, 126
HRs: Willie McCovey, San Francisco, 45

Wins: Tom Seaver, New York, 25
SOs: Ferguson Jenkins, Chicago, 273
ERA: Juan Marichal, San Francisco, 2.10
Pct: Tom Seaver, New York, .781, 25-7
Saves: Fred Gladding, Houston, 29

AAA American Association
President: Allie Reynolds

Standings	W	L	Pct.	GB	Attend.	Manager
Omaha Royals (7).............	85	55	.607	—	177,619	Jack McKeon
Tulsa Oilers (22)................	79	61	.564	6	166,023	Warren Spahn
Indianapolis Indians (15)........	74	66	.529	11	130,485	Vern Rapp
Iowa Oaks#(10)	62	78	.443	23	129,432	Jimy Williams
Oklahoma City 89ers (16)..	62	78	.443	23	103,759	Cot Deal
Denver Bears (8)................	58	82	.414	27	175,229	Don Heffner

#represented Des Moines, Iowa.

Playoffs: None.

All-Star Team: 1B-John Mayberry, Oklahoma City; **2B**-Luis Alcaraz, Omaha; **3B**-Minnie Mendoza, Denver; **SS**-James Driscoll, Iowa; **OF**-Bernie Carbo, Indianapolis; Danny Walton, Oklahoma City; George Spriggs, Omaha; **C**-Ted Simmons, Tulsa; **P**-Chris Zachary, Omaha; Billy Short, Indianapolis; **MVP**-Bernie Carbo, Indianapolis; **Pitcher of the Year**-Sal Campisi, Tulsa; **Manager**-Jack McKeon, Omaha.

BA: Bernie Carbo, Indianapolis, .359
Runs: George Spriggs, Omaha, 103
Hits: Minnie Mendoza, Denver, 194
RBIs: Danny Walton, Oklahoma City, 119

HRs: Danny Walton, Oklahoma City, 25
Wins: Sal Campisi, Tulsa, 13
Jerry Reuss, Tulsa, 13
SOs: Jerry Reuss, Tulsa, 151
ERA: Ron Cook, Oklahoma City, 3.11

AAA International League
President: George H. Sisler, Jr.

Standings	W	L	Pct.	GB	Attend.	Manager
Tidewater Tides#(19)	76	59	.563	—	67,292	Clyde McCullough
Louisville Colonels (2)	77	63	.550	1½	162,935	Eddie Kasko
Syracuse Chiefs (9)............	75	65	.536	3½	124,663	Frank Verdi
Columbus Jets (21)	74	66	.529	4½	153,802	Don Hoak
Rochester Red Wings (1)....	71	69	.507	7½	267,987	Cal Ripken, Sr.
Toledo Mud Hens (6)	68	72	.486	10½	100,493	Jack Tighe
Buffalo Bisons (12)	58	78	.426	18½	77,808	Hector Lopez
Richmond Braves (13)........	56	83	.403	22	80,477	Mickey Vernon

#represented Norfolk, Virginia.

Playoffs: Columbus 3 games, Tidewater 1; Syracuse 3 games, Louisville 2.
Finals: Syracuse 4 games, Columbus 1.

All-Star Team: 1B-Bob Robertson, Columbus; **2B**-Dave Cash, Columbus; **3B**-Mike Ferraro, Rochester; **SS**-Luis Alvarado, Louisville; **OF**-Ralph Garr, Richmond; Terry Crowley, Rochester; Roy Foster, Tidewater; **C**-Bob Montgomery, Louisville; **P**-Ron Klimkowski, Syracuse; Jon Matlack, Tidewater; **MVP**-Luis Alvarado, Louisville; **Pitcher of the Year**-Ron Klimkowski, Syracuse; **Manager**-Clyde McCullough, Tidewater.

BA: Ralph Garr, Richmond, .329
Runs: Luis Alvarado, Louisville, 89
Hits: Luis Alvarado, Louisville, 166
RBIs: Roy Foster, Tidewater, 92
HRs: Bob Robertson, Columbus, 34

Wins: Gerard Janeski, Louisville, 15
Fred Beene, Rochester, 15
Ron Klimkowski, Syracuse, 15
SOs: Mike Adamson, Rochester, 133
ERA: Ron Klimkowski, Syracuse, 2.18

AAA Mexican League
President: Antonio Ramirez Muro

Standings	W	L	Pct.	GB	Attend.	Manager
Reynosa Broncs	91	63	.591	—	207,429	Miguel Sotelo
Monterrey Sultanes.............	88	66	.571	3	417,182	Jaime Corella/Arturo Narvaez/
						Rodolfo Alvarado/
						Manuel Magallon
Jalisco Charros..................	82	70	.539	8	218,068	Memo Garibay
Veracruz Aguila.................	81	73	.526	10	145,995	Vinicio Garcia
Mexico City Diablos Rojos ...	74	80	.481	17	428,548	Tomas Herrera
Puebla Pericos....................	72	82	.468	19	123,216	Tony Castano
Poza Rica Petroleros...........	66	87	.431	24½	187,354	Ricardo Garza
Mexico City Tigres.............	60	93	.392	30½	246,033	Jose Garcia

Playoffs: None.

All-Star Team: 1B-Ron Camacho, Puebla; **2B**-Bernardo Calvo, Veracruz; **3B**-Luis Lagunas, Jalisco; **SS**-Rigoberto Mena, Monterrey; **OF**-Ramon Montoya, MC Diablos Rojos; Nicolas Vazquez, MC Diablos Rojos/Aguascalientes; Angel Macias, Reynosa; **C**-Rodolfo Sandoval, Reynosa; Manuel Diaz, Poza Rica; **P**-Salvador Sanchez, Reynosa; Jose Pena, Reynosa; **Manager**-Miguel Sotelo, Reynosa.

BA: Teo Acosta, Puebla, .354
Runs: Hector Espino, MC Diablos Rojos, 101
Hits: Teo Acosta, Puebla, 189
RBIs: Ron Camacho, Puebla, 116

HRs: Hector Espino, MC Diablos Rojos, 37
Wins: Alfredo Ortiz, MC Diablos Rojos, 23
SOs: Jim Horsford, Monterrey, 199
ERA: Salvador Sanchez, Reynosa, 1.84

AAA Pacific Coast League
President: William B. McKechnie, Jr.

North Standings	W	L	Pct.	GB	Attend.	Manager
Tacoma Cubs (14)	86	60	.589	—	114,931	Whitey Lockman
Spokane Indians (17)........	71	73	.493	14	115,633	Tom Lasorda
Vancouver Mounties (11, 18)..	71	73	.493	14	62,666	Bob Lemon
Portland Beavers (5)	57	89	.390	29	107,423	John "Red" Davis

South Standings	W	L	Pct.	GB	Attend.	Manager
Eugene Emeralds (20)........	88	58	.603	—	152,256	Frank Lucchesi
Phoenix Giants (24)...........	75	71	.514	13	117,385	Charlie Fox
Hawaii Islanders (3)............	74	72	.507	14	280,477	Chuck Tanner
Tucson Toros (4)	60	86	.411	28	105,207	Bill Adair

Playoff: Tacoma 3 games, Eugene 2.

All-Star Team: 1B-Roe Skidmore, Tacoma; **2B**-Denny Doyle, Eugene; **3B**-John Werhas, Hawaii; **SS**-Larry Bowa, Eugene; **OF**-Angel Bravo, Tucson; Tom Silverio, Hawaii; John Matias, Tucson; **C**-Jimmie Schaffer, Spokane; **P**-Archie Reynolds, Tacoma; Dennis Bennett, Hawaii; **MVP**-Denny Doyle, Eugene; **Manager**-Whitey Lockman, Tacoma.

BA: Angel Bravo, Tucson, .342
Runs: Cleo James, Spokane, 93
Hits: Denny Doyle, Eugene, 182
RBIs: John Werhas, Hawaii, 90
HRs: Russ Nagelson, Portland, 23

Wins: Dennis Bennett, Hawaii, 13
Bob Garibaldi, Phoenix, 13
Jeff James, Eugene, 13
Fred Norman, Spokane, 13
Larry Staab, Spokane, 13
SOs: Jeff James, Eugene, 155
ERA: Jim Colburn, Tacoma, 2.28

*Won first-half **Won second-half ***Won both halves
Numbers after nicknames indicate farm system.
Affiliation listed at end of each year.

505

AA Eastern League
President: Thomas H. Richardson

Standings	W	L	Pct.	GB	Attend.	Manager
York Pirates (21)	89	50	.640	—	52,934	Joe Morgan
Reading Phillies (20)	81	59	.579	8½	69,350	Bob Wellman
Elmira Pioneers (7, 23)	70	71	.496	20	52,471	Harry Bright
Pittsfield Red Sox (2)	68	72	.486	21½	79,642	Billy Gardner
Manchester Yankees (9)	64	75	.460	25	91,165	Jerry Walker
Waterbury Indians (5).........	48	93	.340	42	37,371	Clay Bryant

Playoffs: Cancelled with Elmira 1 game, Reading 0; Pittsfield 1 game, York 0.

All-Star Team: 1B-Ron Allen, Reading; **2B**-Pat Locanto, Reading; **3B**-Edward Gagle, Manchester; **SS**-Pablo Cruz, York; **OF**-Bob Kelly, Reading; Ron Blomberg, Manchester; Angel Mangual, York; **C**-Fred Kendall, Elmira; Carlton Fisk, Pittsfield; **P**-Ken Reynolds, Reading; Art Dawson, Manchester; **MVP**-Angel Mangual, York; **Manager**-Joe Morgan, York.

BA: Bob Kelly, Reading, .323		**Wins:** Jack Nutter, Reading, 16	
Runs: Ron Allen, Reading, 91		Ken Reynolds, Reading, 16	
Hits: Angel Mangual, York, 159		**SOs:** Ken Reynolds, Reading, 180	
RBIs: Angel Mangual, York, 102		**ERA:** Lyn Fitzer, York, 2.03	
HRs: Angel Mangual, York, 26			

AA Southern League
President: Sam C. Smith

Standings	W	L	Pct.	GB	Attend.	Manager
Charlotte Hornets (8)	81	59	.579	—	146,141	Ralph Rowe
Birmingham A's (10)............	78	62	.557	3	51,574	Gus Niarhos
Asheville Tourists (15)	69	69	.500	11	34,912	Alex Cosmidis
Columbus White Sox (4)	65	75	.464	16	23,714	Gary Johnson
Montgomery Rebels (6)........	62	73	.459	16½	45,265	Frank Carswell
Savannah Senators (12, 16) ..	59	76	.437	19½	31,910	Hub Kittle

Playoffs: None.

All-Star Team: 1B-Don Anderson, Asheville; **2B**-Joe Sparks, Columbus; **3B**-Kurt Bevacqua, Asheville; **SS**-Danny Thompson, Charlotte; Don Anderson, Birmingham; **OF**-Robert Brooks, Birmingham; Tom Simon, Savannah; Al Crawford, Asheville; **C**-Gene Tenace, Birmingham; Doug Adams, Columbus; **P**-Bill Zepp, Charlotte; Jack Jenkins, Savannah; **Manager**-Ralph Rowe, Charlotte.

BA: Don Anderson, Asheville, .324		**HRs:** Robert Brooks, Birmingham, 23	
Runs: Robert Brooks, Birmingham, 102		**Wins:** Bill Zepp, Charlotte, 15	
Hits: Gonzalo Marquez, Birmingham, 159		**SOs:** Paul Coleman, Montgomery, 153	
RBIs: Don Anderson, Asheville, 100		**ERA:** LaDon Boyd, Birmingham, 2.19	
Robert Brooks, Birmingham, 100			

AA Texas League
President: Bobby Bragan

East Standings	W	L	Pct.	GB	Attend.	Manager
Memphis Blues (19)	66	65	.504	—	107,288	Pete Pavlick/John Antonelli
Arkansas Travelers (22)	66	69	.489	2	89,321	Ray Hathaway
Shreveport Braves (13)........	61	75	.449	7½	50,223	Lou Fitzgerald
San Antonio Missions (14) ..	51	81	.386	15½	38,024	Jim Marshall

West Standings	W	L	Pct.	GB	Attend.	Manager
Amarillo Giants (24)...........	80	55	.585	—	68,045	Andy Gilbert
Dallas-Ft. Worth Spurs (1) ..	75	58	.564	4	235,827	Joe Altobelli
El Paso Sun Kings (3)........	71	65	.522	9½	62,869	Del Rice
Albuquerque Dodgers (17) ...	67	69	.493	13½	176,671	Del Crandall

Playoff: Memphis 3 games, Amarillo 0.

MVP-Larry Johnson, Dallas-Ft. Worth and Bobby Grich, Dallas-Ft. Worth; **Pitcher of the Year**-Bill Frost, Amarillo; **Manager**-Joe Altobelli, Dallas-Ft. Worth.

BA: Larry Johnson, Dallas-Ft. Worth, .337		**RBIs:** Carlos Trevino, El Paso, 92	
Runs: Damaso Blanco, Amarillo, 90		**HRs:** Adrian Garrett, San Antonio, 24	
Hits: Damaso Blanco, Amarillo, 164		**Wins:** Bill Frost, Amarillo, 16	
Carlos Trevino, El Paso, 164		**SOs:** Jim Strickland, Albuquerque, 137	
		ERA: Ramon Hernandez, Arkansas, 2.40	

A California League
President: Edward J. Mulligan

Standings	W	L	Pct.	GB	Attend.	Manager
Stockton Ports*(1)	81	59	.579	—	27,906	Bill Werle
Visalia Mets**(19)	80	60	.571	1	49,192	Roy McMillan/
						Chuck Estrada/Harry Minor
Fresno Giants (24)	72	68	.514	9	58,570	Dennis Sommers
Reno Silver Sox (5)	72	68	.514	9	36,970	Ken Aspromonte
San Jose Bees (3)	68	72	.486	13	59,210	Tom Morgan/Eddie Bressoud
Bakersfield Dodgers (17)....	67	73	.479	14	64,377	Don LeJohn
Modesto Reds (22)..............	63	77	.450	18	35,165	Joe Cunningham
Lodi Crushers (10)..............	57	83	.407	24	37,827	Billy Klaus/Eli Grba

Playoff: Stockton 2 games, Visalia 1.

All-Star Team: 1B-Mike Carruthers, Reno; **2B**-Ed Southard, Reno; **3B**-Terry Dailey, Visalia; **SS**-Junior Kennedy, Stockton; **OF**-George Foster, Fresno; John Milner, Visalia; Pete Watts, Stockton; **C**-Sergio Robles, Bakersfield; **Util**-Terry DeWald, Visalia; **P**-Bill Kirkpatrick, Stockton; Jim Willoughby, Fresno; Dick Tidrow, Reno; Cory Wilshusen, Stockton; **MVP**-Junior Kennedy, Stockton; **Manager**-Bill Werle, Stockton.

BA: Mike Carruthers, Reno, .353		**HRs:** Ernie Davis, Modesto, 27	
Runs: Ed Southard, Reno, 93		**Wins:** Bill Kirkpatrick, Stockton, 16	
Hits: Carlos Castanon, Fresno, 162		**SOs:** Ron Zuber, Reno, 230	
RBIs: Paul Alderete, San Jose, 93		**ERA:** Bill Kirkpatrick, Stockton, 1.96	

A Carolina League
President: J.C. "Bill" Jessup

East Standings	W	L	Pct.	GB	Attend.	Manager
Rocky Mount Leafs (6).......	82	62	.569	—	41,957	Al Federoff
Raleigh-Durham Phillies (20)..	79	62	.560	1½	50,564	Nolan Campbell
Kinston Eagles (9)	74	68	.521	7	46,323	Gene Hassell
Peninsula Astros (16)...........	67	76	.469	14½	60,414	Tony Pacheco
Red Springs Twins (8).........	57	84	.404	23½	40,332	Tom Umphlett

West Standings	W	L	Pct.	GB	Attend.	Manager
Salem Rebels (21)...............	78	66	.542	—	63,248	Chuck Hiller
Winston-Salem Red Sox (2)....	77	67	.535	1	66,710	Matt Sczesny
Burlington Senators (12)	71	71	.500	6	20,550	Buddy Hicks/Bill Haywood
High Point-						
Thomasville Royals (7)........	69	74	.483	8½	44,472	Harry Malmberg
Lynchburg White Sox (4)...	60	84	.417	18	42,286	Stan Wasiak

Playoffs: East - Peninsula 2 games, Rocky Mount 0; Raleigh-Durham 2 games, Kinston 0; Raleigh-Durham 2 games, Peninsula 1. West - Burlington 2 games, Winston-Salem 1; Salem 2 games, High Point-Thomasville 0; Burlington 2 games, Salem 0.
Finals: Raleigh-Durham 2 games, Burlington 1.

All-Star Team: 1B-Greg Luzinski, Raleigh-Durham; **2B**-Tom Grayson, Rocky Mount; **3B**-Luther Quinn, Salem; **SS**-Mario Guerrero, Kinston; **OF**-Mel Civil, Salem; Sam Parrilla, Raleigh-Durham; Ron Lolich, Lynchburg; **C**-Tim Hosley, Rocky Mount; Art Kusnyer, Lynchburg; **P**-John Penn, Raleigh-Durham; Gordon Knutson, Raleigh-Durham; **MVP**-Luther Quinn, Salem; **Manager**-Al Federoff, Rocky Mount.

BA: Ken Huebner, Hi-Toms, .324		**Wins:** John Penn, Raleigh-Durham, 15	
Runs: Rusty Torres, Kinston, 96		**SOs:** Mike Garman, Winston-Salem, 183	
Hits: Mel Civil, Salem, 166		John Penn, Raleigh-Durham, 183	
RBIs: Greg Luzinski, Raleigh-Durham, 92		**ERA:** Gordon Knutson, Raleigh-Durham, 1.90	
HRs: Greg Luzinski, Raleigh-Durham, 31			

A Florida State League
President: George MacDonald, Sr.

Central Standings	W	L	Pct.	GB	Attend.	Manager
Orlando Twins (8)	80	52	.606	—	60,888	Harry Warner
Winter Haven Red Sox (2) ...	76	53	.589	2½	17,876	Rac Slider
Tampa Tarpons (15)	65	67	.492	15	38,367	Bunky Warren
Lakeland Tigers (6)	63	68	.481	16½	8,667	Len Okrie
Daytona Beach Dodgers (17)..	62	71	.466	18½	46,974	Bob Shaw
St. Petersburg Cardinals (22) ..	54	76	.415	25	69,400	Jack Krol

South Standings	W	L	Pct.	GB	Attend.	Manager
Miami Marlins (1)	80	52	.606	—	77,354	Woody Smith
Ft. Lauderdale Yankees (9).....	68	55	.553	7½	40,590	Billy Shantz
Key West Padres (23)........	67	63	.515	12	42,829	Don Zimmer
Pompano Beach Mets (19)...	67	63	.515	12	7,234	Joe Frazier
W. Palm Beach Expos (18)..	56	73	.434	22½	30,473	Ed Sadowski
Cocoa Astros (16)..............	42	87	.326	36½	24,010	Leo Posada

Playoff: Miami 4 games, Orlando 1.

All-Star Team: 1B-John Young, Lakeland; **2B**-Martin Barski, Lakeland; **3B**-Buddy Nelson, Orlando; **SS**-Juan Beniquez, Winter Haven; **OF**-Danny Godby, Tampa; Lew Beasley, Miami; Ray Shoup, Orlando; **C**-Joe Ferguson, Daytona Beach; **P**-Rogelio Moret, Winter Haven; Lawrence Gowell, Ft. Lauderdale; **MVP**-John Young, Lakeland; **Manager**-Harry Warner, Orlando.

BA: John Young, Lakeland, .325		**HRs:** Wayne Dees, St. Petersburg, 14	
Runs: Don Sheppard, Key West, 85		**Wins:** Lawrence Gowell, Ft. Lauderdale, 16	
Hits: Danny Godby, Tampa, 155		**SOs:** Lawrence Gowell, Ft. Lauderdale, 217	
RBIs: Ron Downing, Daytona Beach, 78		**ERA:** John Montague, Miami, 1.53	

A Mexican Center League
President: Antonio Ramirez Muro

Standings	W	L	Pct.	GB	Attend.	Manager
San Luis Potosi Charros* ...	81	45	.643	—	39,361	Ben Reyes
Ciudad Madero Bravos	70	55	.560	10½	106,143	Leonel Aldama
Zacatecas Petroleros**	77	48	.616	3½	39,634	Arturo Cacheux
Ciudad Mante Broncos	68	58	.540	13	58,513	Domingo Santana
Tampico Algodoneros	60	66	.476	21	39,415	Andres Tanaka
Saltillo Saraperos	53	72	.424	27½	10,753	Pedro Gonzalez
Leon Little Aguila	48	77	.384	32½	21,906	Hector Rodriguez
Aguascalientes Tigres.........	45	81	.357	36	41,089	Jesus Robles

Playoff: San Luis Potosi 4 games, Zacatecas 1.

BA: Antonio Fuentes, Zacatecas, .352		**HRs:** Juan Martinez, Zacatecas, 20	
Runs: Jesus Paredes, Ciudad Madero, 83		**Wins:** Luis Mere, Ciudad Madero, 17	
Miguel Suarez, Tampico, 83		**SOs:** Saul Montoya, Tampico, 186	
Hits: Guillermo Garcia, Aguascalientes, 154		**ERA:** Saul Montoya, Tampico, 1.65	
RBIs: Juan Martinez, Zacatecas, 104			

A Mexican Northern League
President: Horatio Lopez

Standings	W	L	Pct.	GB	Manager
Nogales	57	33	.633	—	Ernesto Garcia
San Luis Rio Colorado	48	42	.533	9	Javier Espinoza
Puerto Penasco	46	44	.511	11	Jesus Bustamante
Ensenada	46	44	.511	11	Guillermo Frayde
Mexicali	44	46	.489	13	Mauro Ruiz
Caborca	29	61	.322	28	Sergio Gonzalez

Total Attendance: 145,244.

Playoffs: None.

All-Star Team: 1B-Humberto Villa, Nogales; **2B**-Eduardo Cruz, Nogales; **3B**-Gilberto Morales, Puerto Penasco; **SS**-Ernesto Corella, Nogales; **OF**-Romulo Munoz, Ensenada; Jesus Sommers, Puerto Penasco; Pedro Lozano, San Luis Rio Colorado; **C**-Porfirio Ruiz, Nogales; Gregorio Ayala, Mexicali; **P**-Alberto Villa, San Luis Rio Colorado; Armando Mora, Caborca; **Manager**-Ernesto Garcia, Nogales.

BA: Romulo Munoz, Ensenada, .359
Runs: Hector Escamilla, Ensenada, 72
　Jesus Sommers, Puerto Penasco, 72
Hits: Jesus Sommers, Puerto Penasco, 118
RBIs: Pedro Lozano, San Luis Rio Colorado, 71
　Romulo Munoz, Ensenada, 71

HRs: Romulo Munoz, Ensenada, 23
Wins: Alberto Villa, San Luis Rio Colorado, 14
SOs: Alberto Villa, San Luis Rio Colorado, 137
ERA: Armando Mora, Caborca, 1.71

A Mexican Southeast League
President: Fernando Canton

Standings	W	L	Pct.	GB	Attend.	Manager
Campeche Shrimpers	75	46	.620	—	48,383	David Garcia
Las Choapas/ Minatitlan Diablos Rojos#	62	58	.517	12½	46,533	Jose Guerrero
Yucatan Stags	60	59	.504	14	79,390	Rene Friol
Puerto Mexico Charros	56	59	.487	16	55,414	Minnie Minoso
Carmen Camaroneros	55	61	.470	17½	54,144	Francisco "Pancho" Herrera
Tabasco Plataneros	46	71	.393	27	57,838	Ben Valenzuela

#Las Choapas moved to Minatitlan May 16.

Playoff: Campeche 4 games, Minatitlan 3.

All-Star Team: 1B-Francisco "Pancho" Herrera, Carmen; **2B**-Armando Barajas, Las Choapas/Minatitlan; **3B**-Hector Sanudo, Yucatan; **SS**-Carlos Casas, Carmen; **OF**-Arturo Bernal, Carmen; Antonio Burgos, Yucatan; Jesus Contreras, Puerto Mexico; **C**-Sergio Aguirre, Campeche; Anselmo Armenta, Carmen; **P**-Julio Imbert, Yucatan; Antonio Franco, Campeche; **Manager**-Jose Guerrero, Las Choapas/Minatitlan.

BA: Arturo Bernal, Carmen, .356
Runs: Lucas Buye, Campeche, 88
Hits: Arturo Bernal, Carmen, 165
RBIs: Francisco "Pancho" Herrera, Carmen, 106

HRs: Francisco "Pancho" Herrera, Carmen, 39
Wins: Julio Imbert, Yucatan, 22
SOs: Julio Imbert, Yucatan, 170
ERA: Julio Imbert, Yucatan, 1.68

A Midwest League
President: James Doster

Standings	W	L	Pct.	GB	Attend.	Manager
Appleton Foxes***(4)	84	41	.672	—	67,028	Tom Saffell
Clinton Pilots (11)	72	51	.585	11	59,430	Sibby Sisti/Karl Kuehl/ Tom Giordano
Quincy Cubs (14)	64	55	.538	17	27,717	Walt Dixon
Quad City Angels (3)	64	57	.529	18	62,026	Fred Koenig
Burlington Bees (10)	58	66	.468	25½	31,190	Roy Sievers
Decatur Commodores (24)	53	66	.455	28	33,160	Frank Funk
Cedar Rapids Cardinals (22)	55	68	.447	28	34,101	Roy Majtyka
Waterloo Hawks (7)	52	72	.419	31½	30,267	Rollie Hemsley
Wisconsin Rapids Twins (8)	49	75	.395	34½	22,541	Tom Videtich

Playoffs: None.

All-Star Team: 1B-Jerry Feldman, Quad City; **2B**-Samuel Lovelace, Burlington; **3B**-Gary Holland, Clinton; **SS**-Matthew Moschetti, Quad City; **OF**-Gary Matthews, Decatur; Jose Stennett, Wisconsin Rapids; Donald Cunningan, Quad City; **C**-Gregory Howell, Appleton; Francis Kimball, Clinton; **P**-Don Eddy, Appleton; Jesse Hill, Quincy; **Manager**-Tom Saffell, Appleton.

BA: Ted Parks, Waterloo, .307
Runs: Jerry Feldman, Quad City, 83
Hits: Ted Parks, Waterloo, 178
RBIs: William Parker, Quad City, 67
　Nick Van Lue, Waterloo, 67

HRs: Chris Barkulis, Quincy, 18
　Robert Wissler, Wisconsin Rapids, 18
Wins: Don Eddy, Appleton, 18
SOs: Bart Johnson, Appleton, 200
ERA: Don Eddy, Appleton, 1.81

A New York-Pennsylvania League
President: Vincent M. McNamara

Standings	W	L	Pct.	GB	Attend.	Manager
Oneonta Yankees (9)	52	27	.662	—	20,859	George Case
Batavia Trojans (6)	42	33	.560	8	45,239	Bob Dustal
Newark Co-Pilots (11)	42	34	.553	8½	20,499	Earl Torgeson
Williamsport Astros (16)	39	36	.520	11	41,581	Billy Smith
Corning Royals (7)	35	42	.455	16	13,599	Carl "Buddy" Peterson
Jamestown Falcons (2)	33	41	.446	16½	13,049	Jackie Moore
Auburn Twins (8)	31	42	.425	18	20,997	Steve Thornton
Geneva Pirates (21)	27	46	.355	22	14,696	Bob Clear

Playoffs: None.

All-Star Team: 1B-Jim Wosman, Batavia; **2B**-Keith Sonnichen, Auburn; **3B**-Steve Smith, Batavia; **SS**-Paul Berreta, Oneonta; **OF**-Curt Suchan, Jamestown; Ed Waters, Oneonta; Bob Storm, Auburn; Jose Alcaide, Newark; **C**-Jim Deidel, Oneonta; Pete Duhamel, Newark; **Util**-Richard Walls, Batavia; **P**-Tom Lehman, Williamsport; Bob Strampe, Batavia; Ron Thomas, Batavia; Bill Olsen, Oneonta; **Manager**-George Case, Oneonta.

BA: David Schmidt, Auburn, .349
Runs: Richard Walls, Batavia, 67
Hits: David Schmidt, Auburn, 95
RBIs: Bob Storm, Auburn, 57
HRs: Larry Mansfield, Williamsport, 21

Wins: Bob Strampe, Batavia, 10
　Joe Jabar, Newark, 10
SOs: Bob Strampe, Batavia, 138
ERA: Jerry Bell, Newark, 2.18

A Northern League
President: Roland E. Parcel

Standings	W	L	Pct.	GB	Attend.	Manager
Duluth-Superior Dukes (4)	46	23	.667	—	16,145	Pel Austin
Sioux Falls Packers (16)	45	25	.643	1½	33,767	Jim Snyder
St. Cloud Rox (8)	33	37	.471	13½	21,550	Jim Merrick
Huron Cubs (15)	31	39	.443	15½	23,879	Mel Wright
Aberdeen Pheasants (1)	28	42	.400	18½	15,546	Ken Rowe
Winnipeg Goldeyes (7)	26	43	.377	20	18,077	John Jorgensen

Playoffs: None.

BA: Jim Mueller, Duluth-Superior, .351
Runs: Jim Mueller, Duluth-Superior, 52
Hits: Jim Mueller, Duluth-Superior, 104
RBIs: Jim Brunette, Huron, 47
　Ron Davini, Duluth-Superior, 47

HRs: Kent Burkick, Sioux Falls, 10
　Tom Dittmar, Sioux Falls, 10
Wins: Steve Spanich, Duluth-Superior, 10
SOs: Gerald Christman, St. Cloud, 120
ERA: Don Gullett, Sioux Falls, 1.96

A Northwest League
President: John Carbray

Standings	W	L	Pct.	GB	Attend.	Manager
Rogue Valley Dodgers#(17)	50	29	.633	—	23,696	Bill Berrier
Tri-City A's (10)	41	38	.519	9	28,586	Billy Herman
Walla Walla Bears (20)	37	42	.468	13	27,882	Howie Bedell
Lewiston Broncs (22)	30	49	.380	20	21,494	Bobby Dews

#represented Medford, Oregon.

Playoffs: None.

All-Star Team: 1B-Edward Goldstone, Walla Walla; **2B**-Tommy Thompson, Lewiston; **3B**-Bob Buckner, Rogue Valley; **SS**-Tommy Sandt, Tri-City; Ed Crosby, Lewiston; **OF**-James Cardasis, Rogue Valley; Robert Long, Rogue Valley; Stephen Cooley, Tri-City; **C**-James Dietz, Walla Walla; **Util**-Stephen Krines, Rogue Valley; **P**-Don Stanhouse, Tri-City; Ted Gilje, Rogue Valley; **Manager**-Bill Berrier, Rogue Valley.

BA: Bob Buckner, Rogue Valley, .348
Runs: Tommy Sandt, Tri-City, 63
Hits: Tommy Thompson, Lewiston, 84
RBIs: Stephen Cooley, Tri-City, 62

HRs: Bruce Hotchkiss, Walla Walla, 12
Wins: Albert Dawson, Rogue Valley, 10
SOs: Don Stanhouse, Tri-City, 88
ERA: Craig Scramuzzo, Walla Walla, 2.33

A Western Carolinas League
President: John H. Moss

Standings	W	L	Pct.	GB	Attend.	Manager
Greenwood Braves*(13)	69	55	.556	—	47,204	Eddie Haas
Gastonia Pirates (21)	67	58	.536	2½	37,227	Frank Oceak
Statesville/Monroe Indians#(5)	61	63	.492	8	27,570	Pinky May
Shelby Senators**(12)	61	63	.492	8	31,563	Joe Klein
Spartanburg Phillies (20)	58	65	.472	10½	32,735	Bobby Malkmus
Greenville Red Sox (2)	56	68	.452	13	52,991	Bill Slack

#Statesville moved to Monroe June 20.

Playoff: Greenwood 2 games, Shelby 1.

All-Star Team: 1B-Earl Williams, Greenwood; **2B**-Dick Bechetel, Shelby; **3B**-John Lyles, Gastonia; **SS**-Eulises Urrieta, Spartanburg; **OF**-Ed Blackman, Gastonia; Steve Coley, Greenville; Dalton Renfroe, Shelby; **C**-Rich Stelmaszek, Shelby; **P**-Tom Dettore, Gastonia; Jim Britton, Greenwood; **Manager**-Eddie Haas, Greenwood.

BA: Earl Williams, Greenwood, .340
Runs: Edward Mello, Greenville, 89
Hits: Dalton Renfroe, Shelby, 132
RBIs: Dalton Renfroe, Shelby, 113

HRs: Earl Williams, Greenwood, 33
Wins: Jimmy Blackmon, Shelby, 15
SOs: John Curtis, Greenville, 158
ERA: Tom Dettore, Gastonia, 1.91

R Appalachian League
President: Chauncey De Vault

North Standings	W	L	Pct.	GB	Attend.	Manager
Pulaski Phillies (20)	38	29	.567	—	22,151	Dallas Green
Bluefield Orioles (1)	33	36	.4782	6	23,153	Jackie Ferrell
Covington Astros (16)	32	35	.4776	6	19,382	Dick Bogard
Wytheville Senators (12)	31	35	.470	6½	15,721	Dick Gernert

South Standings

South Standings	W	L	Pct.	GB	Attend.	Manager
Marion Mets (19)	37	32	.536	—	15,555	Jack Cassini
Johnson City Yankees (9)	37	32	.536	—	12,751	Bill Monbouquette
Bristol Tigers (6)	34	34	.500	2½	22,119	Bill Lajoie
Kingsport Royals (7)	29	38	.433	7	7,931	Red Norwood

Playoffs: None.

All-Star Team: 1B-Enos Cabell, Bluefield; **2B**-Fred Frazier, Johnson City; **3B**-Terry Clapp, Bluefield; **SS**-Nelson Pichardo, Marion; Stan Papi, Covington; **OF**-Jeff Burroughs, Wytheville; Bob Cole, Bristol; Larry Fritz, Marion; **C**-Joe Nolan, Marion; **P**-Bob Wiltshire, Pulaski; Mike Wallace, Pulaski; **Manager**-Bill Lajoie, Bristol; Dallas Green, Pulaski.

BA: Tom O'Connor, Johnson City, .375　**HRs:** Larry Fritz, Marion, 13
Runs: Enos Cabell, Bluefield, 62　**Wins:** Bob Wiltshire, Pulaski, 8
Hits: Enos Cabell, Bluefield, 86　**SOs:** Mike Wallace, Pulaski, 123
RBIs: Larry Fritz, Marion, 66　**ERA:** Tom Pratt, Kingsport, 2.67

R Gulf Coast League
President: George MacDonald, Sr.

Standings	W	L	Pct.	GB	Manager
Expos (18)	31	22	.585	—	J.W. Porter
Indians (5)	30	23	.566	1	Joe Lutz
Reds (15)	30	24	.556	1½	George Scherger
Pirates (21)	28	26	.519	3½	Buddy Pritchard
White Sox (4)	26	27	.491	5	Bruce Andrew
Twins (8)	21	32	.396	10	Fred Waters
Cardinals (22)	21	33	.389	10½	Tom Burgess

Games played at Sarasota and Bradenton, Florida.
Total Attendance: 8,817.

Playoffs: None.
All-Star Team: 1B-Ray Johnson, Indians; **2B**-Buddy Bell, Indians; **3B**-Ron McDonald, Twins; **SS**-Robert Welsh, Reds; **OF**-Wayne Danson, Indians; Ted Nicholson, White Sox; Gary Isakson, White Sox; Willie Javier, Expos; **C**-Terry Humphrey, Expos; Kala Kaaihue, Pirates; **Util**-John Nixon, Cardinals; **P**-John Howell, Indians; Balor Moore, Expos; Rick Derrickson, Indians; Dennis Slagle, Pirates; **Manager**-Tom Burgess, Cardinals.

BA: Ray Johnson, Indians, .304　**HRs:** Russ Bodkin, Cardinals, 4
Runs: Tim Mappin, Twins, 32　　Ronald McDonald, Twins, 4
Hits: Ray Johnson, Indians, 55　　Mike Poepping, Twins, 4
RBIs: Doug Heykens, Reds, 30　**Wins:** Clarence Cooper, Reds, 8
　　SOs: Balor Moore, Expos, 91
　　ERA: Balor Moore, Expos, 0.27

R Pioneer League
President: Ben Jewell

Standings	W	L	Pct.	GB	Attend.	Manager
Ogden Dodgers (17)	44	27	.620	—	32,124	Ray Malgradi
Great Falls Giants (24)	40	31	.563	4	12,835	Harvey Koepf
Magic Valley Cowboys (13)	39	33	.542	5½	11,227	Connie Ryan
Salt Lake City Bees (23)	38	33	.535	6	76,789	David Garcia
Caldwell Cubs (14)	33	39	.458	11½	17,819	George Freese
Idaho Falls Angels (3)	30	42	.417	14½	18,205	Norm Sherry
Billings Mustangs (11)	26	45	.366	18	11,626	Bobby Mavis/Ronald LeBlanc

Playoffs: None.

All-Star Team: 1B-Randy Elliott, Salt Lake City; **2B**-Pedro Garcia, Billings; **3B**-Lee Lacy, Ogden; **SS**-Rudy Meoli, Idaho Falls; **OF**-Mickey Rivers, Magic Valley; Phil Zahn, Billings; Royle Stillman, Ogden; **C**-Terry McDermott, Ogden; Jose Salado, Billings; **Util**-Steve Collette, Caldwell; Horace Speed, Great Falls; **P**-Richard Zinniger, Salt Lake City; Bob O'Brien, Ogden; **Manager**-Ray Malgradi, Ogden.

BA: Gilbert Vidrio, Salt Lake City, .354　**HRs:** Pedro Garcia, Billings, 10
Runs: Sam Houston, Magic Valley, 76　**Wins:** Richard Zinniger, Salt Lake City, 13
Hits: Bobby Randall, Ogden, 90　**SOs:** Bob O'Brien, Ogden, 186
RBIs: Bill North, Caldwell, 42　**ERA:** John Sielicki, Great Falls, 1.15

1969 Interleague Post Season Play

World Series
New York (National) 4 games, Baltimore (American) 1

1969 Major League Farm Systems

American League

1　Baltimore (6): Rochester, Dallas-Ft. Worth, Stockton, Miami, Aberdeen, Bluefield.
2　Boston (6): Louisville, Pittsfield, Winston-Salem, Winter Haven, Jamestown, Greenville.
3　California (5): Hawaii, El Paso, San Jose, Quad City, Idaho Falls.
4　Chicago (6): Tucson, Columbus, Lynchburg, Appleton, Duluth-Superior, Gulf Coast.
5　Cleveland (5): Portland, Waterbury, Reno, Statesville/Monroe, Gulf Coast.
6　Detroit (6): Toledo, Montgomery, Rocky Mount, Lakeland, Batavia, Bristol.
7　Kansas City (7): Omaha, Elmira, High Point-Thomasville, Waterloo, Corning, Winnipeg, Kingsport.
8　Minnesota (8): Denver, Charlotte, Red Springs, Orlando, Wisconsin Rapids, Auburn, St. Cloud, Gulf Coast.
9　New York (6): Syracuse, Manchester, Kinston, Ft. Lauderdale, Oneonta, Johnson City.
10　Oakland (5): Iowa, Birmingham, Lodi, Burlington (IA), Tri-City.
11　Seattle (4): Vancouver, Clinton, Newark, Billings.
12　Washington (5): Buffalo, Savannah, Burlington (NC), Shelby, Wytheville.

National League

13　Atlanta (4): Richmond, Shreveport, Greenwood, Magic Valley.
14　Chicago (4): Tacoma, San Antonio, Quincy, Caldwell.
15　Cincinnati (5): Indianapolis, Asheville, Tampa, Huron, Gulf Coast.
16　Houston (7): Oklahoma City, Savannah, Peninsula, Cocoa, Williamsport, Sioux Falls, Covington.
17　Los Angeles (6): Spokane, Albuquerque, Bakersfield, Daytona Beach, Rogue Valley, Ogden.
18　Montreal (3): Vancouver, West Palm Beach, Gulf Coast.
19　New York (5): Tidewater, Memphis, Visalia, Pompano Beach, Marion.
20　Philadelphia (6): Eugene, Reading, Raleigh-Durham, Walla Walla, Spartanburg, Pulaski.
21　Pittsburgh (6): Columbus, York, Salem, Geneva, Gastonia, Gulf Coast.
22　St. Louis (7): Tulsa, Arkansas, Modesto, St. Petersburg, Cedar Rapids, Lewiston, Gulf Coast.
23　San Diego (3): Elmira, Key West, Salt Lake City.
24　San Francisco (5): Phoenix, Amarillo, Fresno, Decatur, Great Falls.

1969 No-Hitters

Date	Pitcher	Team	League	Opponent	Score
4-17	Bill Stoneman	Montreal	National	Philadelphia	7-0
4-20	Leslie Rohr	Memphis	Texas	San Antonio	8-0 (7)
4-30	Jim Maloney	Cincinnati	National	Houston	10-0
5-1	Don Wilson	Houston	National	Cincinnati	4-0
5-4	Gordon Knutson/Ed Cecil	Raleigh-Durham	Carolina	Lynchburg	0-1 (10)
5-4	Marcos Gil	Aguascalientes	Mexican Center	Ciudad Mante	1-0
5-4	Marcelino Lopez	Rochester	International	Richmond	5-1 (7)
5-8	Scipio Spinks	Oklahoma City	American Assoc.	Omaha	1-2 (6)
5-12	John Major	Lodi	California	Stockton	1-0
5-13	Gary Washington	Pittsfield	Eastern	Manchester	0-3
5-23	Paul Edmondson	Columbus	Southern	Montgomery	3-0 (7)
5-24	Aurelio Lopez	Minatitlan	Mexican S.E.	Carmen	1-0
6-1	Ed Maras	Stockton	California	Fresno	2-0 (7)
6-7	Bill Kirkpatrick	Stockton	California	Lodi	1-0 (7)
6-7	Charles Bowlby	Cedar Rapids	Midwest	Decatur	3-0 (10)
6-16	James Minshall	Salem	Carolina	Hi-Toms	4-0
6-30	Lucio Carrillo	Campeche	Mexican S.E.	Yucatan	0-0 (5)
7-5	Gonzalo Meza	San Luis Rio Colo.	Mexican Northern	Caborca	1-0 (P)
7-6	Abel Armas	Ciudad Mante	Mexican Center	Saltillo	5-0 (P)
7-7	Eduardo Acosta	Rogue Valley	Northwest	Walla Walla	6-0 (P, 7)
7-15	Frederick Cambria	York	Eastern	Waterbury	5-0 (P, 7)
7-20	Monty McMillan	San Jose	California	Reno	1-0 (7)
7-21	Danny Osborn	Tampa	Florida State	Cocoa	1-0
7-26	John Gregory	Montgomery	Southern	Savannah	6-0 (7)
7-27	Travis King	Daytona Beach	Florida State	Key West	4-0
7-27	James Keenan	Shelby	W. Carolinas	Gastonia	8-0
7-31	Richard Zinniger	Salt Lake City	Pioneer	Great Falls	3-1 (7)
8-7	John Preston	Salt Lake City	Pioneer	Idaho Falls	7-0
8-12	Mike Corkins	Elmira	Eastern	Manchester	2-0
8-13	Jim Palmer	Baltimore	American	Oakland	8-0
8-15	Gary Lavelle	Decatur	Midwest	Clinton	4-0 (7)
8-15	Miguel Puente	Amarillo	Texas	Shreveport	3-0
8-16	Dan Roberts	Rogue Valley	Northwest	Lewiston	2-0 (7)
8-17	Ramon Hernandez	Arkansas	Texas	El Paso	2-0 (7)
8-18	Balor Moore	West Palm Beach	Florida State	Key West	1-0 (7)
8-18	Nils Lambert/Ron Thornes	Batavia	New York-Penn	Geneva	3-0 (7)
8-19	Ken Holtzman	Chicago	National	Atlanta	3-0
8-20	James Koering	Wisconsin Rapids	Midwest	Waterloo	3-0 (7)
8-22	Ron Crook	Asheville	Southern	Savannah	3-0 (7)
8-28	Mike Baldwin	Lynchburg	Carolina	Red Springs	2-0
9-20	Bob Moose	Pittsburgh	National	New York	4-0

Number in parentheses indicates innings if other than nine; "P" indicates perfect game.

THIS DATE IN MINOR LEAGUE HISTORY

April 18, 1969, The American Association returned to play after a six year absence.

May 16, 1969, Outfielder Jackie Mountain, Pittsfield, Eastern League, cracked five consecutive doubles in his club's 14-2 victory over Waterbury.

May 20, 1969, El Paso, Texas League, posted its fifth straight shutout and ran the Sun Kings' string of consecutive scoreless innings to 52. El Paso's Bobby Trivon was stopped after hitting in 37 consecutive games.

July 1, 1969, First baseman George Kalafatis, Montgomery, Southern League, set a league record with four home runs in one game.

July 10, 1969, Winston Llenas, Hawaii, Pacific Coast League, made his tenth successive hit.

July 16, 1969, Red Springs of the Carolina League, a town with a population of 4,037, drew 4,157 fans for a game with Lynchburg.

July 17, 1969, Catcher Hank Izquierdo of Oklahoma City, American Association, was suspended for the rest of the season after being involved in a bat swinging incident with catcher Ted Simmons of Tulsa.

July 19, 1969, Buffalo's game at War Memorial Stadium was postponed, even though the sun was shining. Players refused to play after the clubhouse was broken into the night before and a gang robbed them at knifepoint. Most of Buffalo's home games were played in Niagara Falls in 1969.

August 1, 1969, National Association President Phil Piton rejected the umpiring contract of Mrs. Bernice Gera in her attempt to become the first female umpire in Organized Baseball.

August 9, 1969, Savannah manager Hub Kittle became the oldest pitcher in Southern League history. The 53-year-old took the mound to help a pitching shortage on his staff. He pitched an inning and two thirds and gave up one earned run.

August 10, 1969, After 51-2/3 scoreless innings, Lakeland, Florida State League, broke a dry spell with three runs to take a 3-2 win from St. Petersburg.

August 17, 1969, Frank Shellenback, player, manager, coach and scout in Organized Ball for more than 50 years, died in Newton, Massachusetts at age 70. Shellenback, a spitball pitcher, hurled for various clubs in the Pacific Coast League from 1920 through 1938, winning 295 games. He won 15 straight games in 1933 and 33 of 34 over the 1930-1931 seasons. He won 315 games in the minors and eleven in the majors. Shellenback was also a good batter, hitting 63 home runs and compiling a .271 batting average as a pitcher/pinch hitter.

October 24, 1969, Jack Bentley, 74, one of the minor leagues' greatest players, died in Olney, Maryland. Bentley posted a batting average in the minors of .354 and won 80 games against only 29 defeats as a pitcher. In 1921, Bentley, playing first base and outfield, batted .412 to win the International League batting championship and led in pitching percentage with a mound mark of 12-1.

December 7, 1969, Frank "Lefty" O'Doul, 72, two-time National League batting champion who managed in the Pacific Coast League for more than two decades, including 17 years with the San Francisco Seals, died in San Francisco.

MINOR LEAGUE CONSECUTIVE LOSSES

LOSSES	TEAM	LEAGUE	YEAR
38	Muskogee	Southwestern	1923
33	Granite Falls	Western Carolinas	1951
32	Reading	International	1927
32	Gainesville	Florida State	1946
28	Winston-Salem	Piedmont	1937
31	Austin	Texas	1914
28	Paducah	Kitty	1922
27	Meridian	Cotton States	1913
26	Granite Falls	Western Carolina	1951
26	Reading	International	1932
26	Jackson	Kitty	1954
23	Pennington Gap	Mountain States	1950
23	Reading	International	1926
23	Leavenworth	Western Assoc.	1949
22	Bakersfield	California	1996
22	Bryan	East Texas	1950
22	Scranton	New York State	1917
22	Leavenworth	Western Assoc.	1949
22	Charleston, S.C.	Western Carolinas	1975
22	Peninsula	Carolina	1991
21	Grand Forks	Northern	1947
21	Augusta	South Atlantic	1952
21	Aguila	Mexican	1986
21	Norton	Mountain States	1952
21	Syracuse	International	1953
21	Little Rock	Southern Assoc.	1950
20	Fresno	California	1988
20	Hickory	Western Carolina	1952
20	Mobile	Southern Assoc.	1917
20	Nogales	Arizona-Mexico	1955
20	Springfield	International	1951
19	Medicine Hat	Pioneer	1980
19	Wilkes-Barre	Eastern	1948
19	Boise	Pioneer	1963
19	Fayetteville	Carolina	1950
19	Lake Charles	Gulf Coast	1953
19	Waco	Big State	1952
18	Pueblo	Western	1950
18	Rocky Mount	Carolina	1980
18	St. Petersburg	Florida Int'l	1950
18	Newport News	Virginia	1913
18	Kingston	Canadian-American	1951
18	Geneva	New York-Penn	1988

1970

American League
President: Joseph E. Cronin

East Standings	W	L	Pct.	GB	Attend.	Manager
Baltimore Orioles	108	54	.667	—	1,057,069	Earl Weaver
New York Yankees	93	69	.574	15	1,136,879	Ralph Houk
Boston Red Sox	87	75	.537	21	1,595,278	Eddie Kasko
Detroit Tigers....................	79	83	.488	29	1,501,293	Mayo Smith
Cleveland Indians	76	86	.469	32	729,752	Alvin Dark
Washington Senators	70	92	.432	38	824,789	Ted Williams

West Standings	W	L	Pct.	GB	Attend.	Manager
Minnesota Twins	98	64	.605	—	1,261,887	Bill Rigney
Oakland Athletics	89	73	.549	9	778,355	John McNamara
California Angels	86	76	.531	12	1,077,741	Lefty Phillips
Kansas City Royals	65	97	.401	33	693,047	Charlie Metro/Bob Lemon
Milwaukee Brewers	65	97	.401	33	933,690	Dave Bristol
Chicago White Sox............	56	106	.346	42	495,355	Don Gutteridge/ Bill Adair/Chuck Tanner

Playoff: Baltimore 3 games, Minnesota 0.

BA: Alex Johnson, California, .329
Runs: Carl Yastrzemski, Boston, 125
Hits: Tony Oliva, Minnesota, 204
RBIs: Frank Howard, Washington, 126
HRs: Frank Howard, Washington, 44

Wins: Dave McNally, Baltimore, 24
Jim Perry, Minnesota, 24
Mike Cuellar, Baltimore, 24
SOs: Sam McDowell, Cleveland, 304
ERA: Diego Segui, Oakland, 2.56
Pct: Mike Cuellar, Baltimore, .750, 24-8
Saves: Ron Perranoski, Minnesota, 34

National League
President: Charles S. Feeney

East Standings	W	L	Pct.	GB	Attend.	Manager
Pittsburgh Pirates...............	89	73	.549	—	1,341,947	Danny Murtaugh
Chicago Cubs....................	84	78	.519	5	1,642,705	Leo Durocher
New York Mets	83	79	.512	6	2,697,479	Gil Hodges
St. Louis Cardinals	76	86	.469	13	1,629,736	Red Schoendienst
Philadelphia Phillies...........	73	88	.453	15½	708,247	Frank Lucchesi
Montreal Expos..................	73	89	.451	16	1,424,683	Gene Mauch

West Standings	W	L	Pct.	GB	Attend.	Manager
Cincinnati Reds.................	102	60	.630	—	1,803,568	Sparky Anderson
Los Angeles Dodgers	87	74	.540	14½	1,697,142	Walter Alston
San Francisco Giants	86	76	.531	16	740,720	Clyde King/Charlie Fox
Houston Astros	79	83	.488	23	1,253,444	Harry Walker
Atlanta Braves	76	86	.469	26	1,078,848	Luman Harris
San Diego Padres...............	63	99	.389	39	643,679	Preston Gomez

Playoff: Cincinnati 3 games, Pittsburgh 0.

BA: Rico Carty, Atlanta, .366
Runs: Billy Williams, Chicago, 137
Hits: Pete Rose, Cincinnati, 205
Billy Williams, Chicago, 205
RBIs: Johnny Bench, Cincinnati, 148
HRs: Johnny Bench, Cincinnati, 45

Wins: Gaylord Perry, San Francisco, 23
Bob Gibson, St. Louis, 23
SOs: Tom Seaver, New York, 283
ERA: Tom Seaver, New York, 2.81
Pct: Bob Gibson, St. Louis, .767, 23-7
Saves: Wayne Granger, Cincinnati, 35

AAA American Association
President: Allie Reynolds

East Standings	W	L	Pct.	GB	Attend.	Manager
Omaha Royals (7)............	73	65	.529	—	196,096	Jack McKeon
Iowa Oaks (11)	70	68	.507	3	133,929	Sherman Lollar
Indianapolis Indians (15)....	71	69	.507	3	150,807	Vern Rapp
Evansville Triplets (9)	67	71	.486	6	130,809	Ralph Rowe

West Standings	W	L	Pct.	GB	Attend.	Manager
Denver Bears (12)..............	70	69	.504	—	175,746	Whitey Kurowski/ Dick Gernert
Tulsa Oilers (22)	70	70	.500	½	151,258	Warren Spahn
Oklahoma City 89ers (16) ..	68	71	.489	2	157,728	Hub Kittle
Wichita Aeros (5)	67	73	.479	3½	256,824	Ken Aspromonte

Playoff: Omaha 4 games, Denver 1.

All-Star Team: 1B-Gonzalo Marquez, Iowa; **2B**-Jim Glover, Evansville; **3B**-Kurt Bevacqua, Indianapolis; **SS**-Danny Thompson, Evansville; **OF**-Richie Scheinblum, Wichita; Bill McNulty, Iowa; Luis Melendez, Tulsa; Cesar Cedeno, Oklahoma City; **C**-Gene Tenace, Iowa; Ken Suarez, Wichita; **Util**-Lou Camilli, Wichita; **P**-Vida Blue, Iowa; Ross Grimsley, Indianapolis; Cisco Carlos, Denver; Paul Splittorff, Omaha; **MVP**-George Spriggs, Omaha; **Pitcher of the Year**-Milt Wilcox, Indianapolis; **Manager**-Jack McKeon, Omaha.

BA: Chris Chambliss, Wichita, .342
Runs: Richie Scheinblum, Wichita, 79
Hits: Richie Scheinblum, Wichita, 155
Luis Melendez, Tulsa, 155
RBIs: Richie Scheinblum, Wichita, 84

HRs: Cotton Nash, Evansville, 33
Wins: Francisco Carlos, Denver, 13
SOs: Vida Blue, Iowa, 165
ERA: Ross Grimsley, Indianapolis, 2.73

AAA International League
President: George H. Sisler, Jr.

Standings	W	L	Pct.	GB	Attend.	Manager
Syracuse Chiefs (10)...........	84	56	.600	—	221,376	Frank Verdi
Columbus Jets (21)	81	59	.579	3	140,700	Joe Morgan
Rochester Red Wings (1)......	76	64	.543	8	323,743	Cal Ripken, Sr.
Tidewater Tides (19)	74	66	.529	10	142,290	Chuck Hiller
Richmond Braves (13).........	73	67	.521	11	120,928	Mickey Vernon
Louisville Colonels (2).......	69	71	.493	15	136,439	Billy Gardner
Buffalo Bisons/ Winnipeg Whips#(18)	52	88	.371	32	89,901	Clyde McCullough
Toledo Mud Hens (6)	51	89	.364	33	86,428	Frank Carswell

#Buffalo moved to Winnipeg June 11.

Playoffs: Syracuse 3 games, Tidewater 0; Columbus 3 games, Rochester 2.
Finals: Syracuse 3 games, Columbus 1.

All-Star Team: 1B-George Kopacz, Columbus; **2B**-Len Boehmer, Syracuse; **3B**-Mike Ferraro, Rochester; **SS**-Frank Baker, Syracuse; **OF**-Roger Freed, Rochester; Don Baylor, Rochester; Ralph Garr, Richmond; **C**-Bob Montgomery, Louisville; **P**-Hal Reniff, Syracuse; Ernest McNally, Winnipeg; **MVP**-George Kopacz, Columbus; Roger Freed, Rochester; **Pitcher of the Year**-Bob Gardner, Syracuse; **Manager**-Frank Verdi, Syracuse.

BA: Ralph Garr, Richmond, .386
Runs: Don Baylor, Rochester, 127
Hits: Roger Freed, Rochester, 168
RBIs: Roger Freed, Rochester, 130

HRs: Hal Breeden, Richmond, 37
Wins: Rob Gardner, Syracuse, 16
SOs: Ernest McAnally, Winnipeg, 176
ERA: Rob Gardner, Syracuse, 2.53

AAA Mexican League
President: Antonio Ramirez Muro

North Standings	W	L	Pct.	GB	Attend.	Manager
Mexico City Diablos Rojos	91	59	.607	—	275,815	Jose Guerrero
Reynosa Broncs	76	72	.513	14	123,239	Miguel Sotelo
Union Laguna Algodoneros#...	68	82	.453	23	211,879	Minnie Minoso
Monterrey Sultanes.............	67	81	.453	23	244,594	Vinicio Garcia/ Rodolfo Alvarado
Saltillo Saraperos	67	83	.447	24	256,595	Tomas Herrera/ Andres Tanaka

South Standings	W	L	Pct.	GB	Attend.	Manager
Veracruz Aguila..................	87	63	.580	—	122,663	Enrique Izquierdo
Jalisco Charros...................	83	66	.557	3½	170,055	Memo Garibay
Yucatan Leones	77	73	.513	10	130,369	Tony Castano/Luis Esma
Mexico City Tigres.............	73	74	.497	12½	200,936	Jose Luis Garcia
Poza Rica Petroleros...........	57	93	.380	30	143,398	David Garcia

#represented Gomez Palacio and Torreon, Mexico.

Playoff: Veracruz 4 games, MC Diablos Rojos 2.

All-Star Team: 1B-Francisco Campos, Jalisco; **2B**-Francisco Chavez, Veracruz; **3B**-Celerino Sanchez, MC Tigres; **SS**-Francisco Rodriguez, Veracruz; **OF**-Francisco Garcia, Union Laguna; Emilio Sosa, Veracruz; Ramon Montoya, MC Diablos Rojos; **C**-Francisco Estrada, MC Diablos Rojos; Gregorio Luque, MC Tigres; **P**-Blas Mazon, Veracruz; Alfredo Mariscal, Yucatan; **Manager**-Enrique Izquierdo, Veracruz.

BA: Francisco Campos, Jalisco, .358
Runs: Francisco Garcia, Union Laguna, 120
Hits: Francisco Garcia, Union Laguna, 185
RBIs: Ildefonso Ruiz, Union Laguna, 99

HRs: Rogelio Alvarez, Veracruz, 33
Wins: Alfredo Mariscal, Yucatan, 21
SOs: Felipe Leal, MC Diablos Rojos, 170
ERA: Alfredo Mariscal, Yucatan, 1.85

AAA Pacific Coast League
President: William B. McKechnie, Jr.

North Standings	W	L	Pct.	GB	Attend.	Manager
Spokane Indians (17).........	94	52	.644	—	151,394	Tom Lasorda
Portland Beavers (8)...........	68	78	.466	26	119,906	Al Federoff
Eugene Emeralds (20)	66	80	.452	28	101,142	Bob Wellman/Lou Kahn
Tacoma Cubs (14)	45	98	.315	47½	137,891	Whitey Lockman

South Standings	W	L	Pct.	GB	Attend.	Manager
Hawaii Islanders (3)...........	98	48	.671	—	467,217	Chuck Tanner
Phoenix Giants (24)...........	85	61	.582	13	122,213	Charley Fox/ Bob Garibaldi/Hank Sauer
Tucson Toros (4)	81	65	.555	17	164,072	Gordon Maltzberger
Salt Lake City Bees (23).....	44	99	.308	52½	100,373	Don Zimmer

Playoff: Spokane 4 games, Hawaii 0.

*Won first-half   **Won second-half   ***Won both halves
Numbers after nicknames indicate farm system.
Affiliation listed at end of each year.

510

All-Star Team: 1B-Tom Hutton, Spokane; **2B**-Doug Griffin, Hawaii; **3B**-Steve Garvey, Spokane; **SS**-Bobby Valentine, Spokane; **OF**-Joe Lis, Eugene; Winston Llenas, Hawaii; Bill Buckner, Spokane; **C**-John Felske, Portland; **P**-Bob Garibaldi, Phoenix; Bob O'Brien, Spokane; **MVP**-Bobby Valentine, Spokane; **Manager**-Tom Lasorda, Spokane; Chuck Tanner, Hawaii.

BA: Bobby Valentine, Spokane, .340
Runs: Bobby Valentine, Spokane, 122
Hits: Bobby Valentine, Spokane, 211
RBIs: Winston Llenas, Hawaii, 108
HRs: Joe Lis, Eugene, 36
Wins: Dennis Bennett, Hawaii, 18
Jerry Stephenson, Spokane, 18
SOs: Darrell Brandon, Tucson, 167
ERA: Jerry Stephenson, Spokane, 2.82

AA Eastern League
President: Thomas H. Richardson

Standings	W	L	Pct.	GB	Attend.	Manager
Waterbury Pirates (21)	79	62	.560	—	70,031	John "Red" Davis
Reading Phillies (20)	78	63	.553	1	96,684	Andy Seminick
Pittsfield Senators (12)	72	66	.522	5½	49,875	Dick Gernert/Joe Klein
Pawtucket Red Sox (2)	68	70	.493	9½	105,027	Matt Sczesny
Manchester Yankees (10)	66	73	.475	12	36,928	Gene Hassell
Elmira Pioneers (7, 23)	55	84	.396	23	51,907	Harry Malmberg

Playoffs: None.

All-Star Team: 1B-Greg Luzinski, Reading; **2B**-Buddy Hunter, Pawtucket; **3B**-Luther Quinn, Waterbury; **SS**-Toby Harrah, Pittsfield; **OF**-Dennis Baldridge, Manchester; Gene Clines, Waterbury; Mel Civil, Waterbury; **C**-Rich Stelmaszek, Pittsfield; **P**-Bill Gogolewski, Pittsfield; John Curtis, Pawtucket; **MVP**-Greg Luzinski, Reading; **Manager**-John "Red" Davis, Waterbury.

BA: Greg Luzinski, Reading, .325
Runs: Greg Luzinski, Reading, 94
Hits: Ken Huebner, Elmira, 156
RBIs: Greg Luzinski, Reading, 120
HRs: Richie Zisk, Waterbury, 34
Wins: Bill Gogolewski, Pittsfield, 14
Bob Terlecki, Reading, 14
SOs: Bill Gogolewski, Pittsfield, 146
ERA: Dave Bennett, Waterbury, 2.22

AA Southern League
President: Sam C. Smith

Standings	W	L	Pct.	GB	Attend.	Manager
Columbus Astros (16)	78	59	.569	—	40,758	Jim Williams
Montgomery Rebels (6)	79	60	.568	—	57,631	Stubby Overmire
Birmingham A's (11)	73	65	.529	5½	39,787	Phil Cavarretta
Savannah Indians (5)	71	67	.514	7½	33,854	Ray Hathaway
Jacksonville Suns (8, 18)	67	70	.489	11	64,722	Gus Niarhos
Charlotte Hornets (9)	66	73	.475	13	57,107	Harry Warner/Pete Appleton
Mobile White Sox (4)	59	78	.431	19	35,775	Tom Saffell/Larry Sherry
Asheville Tourists (15)	59	80	.424	20	28,720	Jim Snyder

Playoffs: None.

All-Star Team: 1B-John Dolinsek, Columbus; **2B**-Hagen Anderson, Montgomery; **3B**-Gomer Hodge, Savannah; **SS**-Ray Busse, Columbus; **OF**-Jim Covington, Jacksonville; Jim Clark, Birmingham; Steve Brye, Charlotte; **C**-Rick Dempsey, Charlotte; Bill Ferguson, Asheville; **P**-Chuck Swanson, Montgomery; Lerrin LaGrow, Montgomery; **Manager**-Jim Williams, Columbus.

BA: Steve Brye, Charlotte, .307
Runs: Gomer Hodge, Savannah, 72
Fred Smith, Savannah, 72
Hits: Danny Monzon, Charlotte, 149
RBIs: Jim Clark, Birmingham, 73
Reggie Sanders, Birmingham, 73
HRs: Jim Covington, Jacksonville, 21
Wins: Ken Forsch, Columbus, 13
Bill Gilbreath, Montgomery, 13
SOs: Bill Gilbreath, Montgomery, 192
ERA: David Hartman, Jacksonville, 2.01

AA Texas League
President: Bobby Bragan

East Standings	W	L	Pct.	GB	Attend.	Manager
Memphis Blues (19)	69	67	.507	—	107,584	Johnny Antonelli
Arkansas Travelers (22)	67	67	.500	1	119,554	Ken Boyer
San Antonio Missions (14)	67	69	.493	2	44,271	Jim Marshall
Shreveport Braves (13)	58	76	.433	10	42,807	Lou Fitzgerald/Clint Courtney

West Standings	W	L	Pct.	GB	Attend.	Manager
Albuquerque Dodgers (17)	83	52	.615	—	177,747	Del Crandall
El Paso Sun Kings (3)	77	59	.566	6½	37,337	Del Rice
Dallas-Ft. Worth Spurs (1)	63	73	.463	20½	182,743	Joe Altobelli
Amarillo Giants (24)	57	78	.433	26	58,027	Andy Gilbert

Playoff: Albuquerque 3 games, Memphis 1.

All-Star Team: 1B-John Milner, Memphis; **2B**-Larry Eckenrode, Albuquerque; **3B**-Ron Cey, Albuquerque; **SS**-Chris Speier, Amarillo; **OF**-Mickey Rivers, El Paso; Bob Gallagher, Albuquerque; Jose Cruz, Arkansas; Adrian Garrett, San Antonio; **C**-Joe Ferguson, Albuquerque; Skip Jutze, Arkansas; **P**-Jim Flynn, Albuquerque; Bruce Ellingsen, Albuquerque; Lloyd Allen, El Paso; Andy Hassler, El Paso; Charlie Williams, Memphis; Pat Jacquez, San Antonio; Dyar Miller, Dallas-Ft. Worth; **MVP**-Mickey Rivers, El Paso; **Pitcher of the Year**-Jim Flynn, Albuquerque; **Manager**-Del Crandall, Albuquerque.

BA: Mickey Rivers, El Paso, .343
Runs: Mickey Rivers, El Paso, 99
Hits: Mickey Rivers, El Paso, 154
Chico Diaz, Memphis, 154
RBIs: Chico Diaz, Memphis, 102
HRs: Adrian Garrett, San Antonio, 29
Wins: Jim Flynn, Albuquerque, 19
SOs: Randy Cohen, Dallas-Ft. Worth, 151
ERA: George Manz, Dallas-Ft. Worth, 1.99

A California League
President: Edward J. Mulligan

Standings	W	L	Pct.	GB	Attend.	Manager
Bakersfield Dodgers***(17)	93	46	.669	—	88,784	Don LeJohn
Reno Silver Sox (5)	79	61	.564	14½	29,887	Pinky May
San Jose Bees (7)	77	63	.550	16½	71,303	Carl "Buddy" Peterson
Modesto Reds (22)	76	64	.543	17½	57,332	Jack Krol
Fresno Giants (24)	71	68	.511	22	54,872	Dennis Sommers
Visalia Mets (19)	66	74	.471	27½	42,344	Joe Frazier
Stockton Ports (1)	54	86	.386	39½	46,167	Bill Werle
Lodi Padres (23)	43	97	.307	50½	18,285	Sonny Ruberto/Ken Bracey

Playoffs: None.

All-Star Team: 1B-Ed Goodson, Fresno; **2B**-Jim Timmons, Visalia; **3B**-Bob Cummings, Bakersfield; **SS**-Lee Lacy, Bakersfield; **OF**-Paul Johnson, Bakersfield; Jorge Roque, Modesto; George Kazmarek, Visalia; **C**-Jake Brown, Fresno; **Util**-Royle Stillman, Bakersfield; **P**-Doug Rau, Bakersfield; Albert Dawson, Bakersfield; **MVP**-Paul Johnson, Bakersfield; **Manager**-Don LeJohn, Bakersfield.

BA: Paul Johnson, Bakersfield, .350
Runs: Jorge Roque, Modesto, 101
Hits: Jorge Roque, Modesto, 96
RBIs: George Greer, Modesto, 96
HRs: Larry Fritz, Visalia, 24
Wins: Albert Dawson, Bakersfield, 17
SOs: Albert Dawson, Bakersfield, 244
ERA: Albert Dawson, Bakersfield, 2.47

A Carolina League
President: Wallace McKenna

Standings	W	L	Pct.	GB	Attend.	Manager
Winston-Salem Red Sox*(2)	79	58	.577	—	36,923	Bill Slack
Raleigh-Durham Triangles (x)	77	63	.550	3½	56,138	Cliff Davis
Burlington Senators**(12)	72	65	.526	7	33,046	Joe Klein/Whitey Kurowski
Kinston Eagles (10)	72	65	.526	7	49,949	Alex Cosmidis
Rocky Mount Leafs (7)	70	68	.507	9½	34,062	Max Lanier
Peninsula Phillies (20)	67	72	.482	13	65,114	Nolan Campbell
Salem Rebels (21)	60	80	.429	20½	50,076	Billy Klaus
Lynchburg Twins (9)	57	83	.407	23½	42,949	Tom Umphlett/Spencer Robbins

Playoff: Winston-Salem 2 games, Burlington 0.

All-Star Team: 1B-Mike Anderson, Peninsula; **2B**-Bob Adams, Rocky Mount; Fred Frazier, Kinston; **3B**-Steve Braun, Lynchburg; **SS**-Juan Beniquez, Winston-Salem; **OF**-Dave Moates, Burlington; Rennie Stennett, Salem; Bob Storm, Lynchburg; **C**-Cliff Johnson, Raleigh-Durham; **P**-Bill Olsen, Kinston; Lynn McGlothen, Winston-Salem; **MVP**-Cliff Johnson, Raleigh-Durham; **Manager**-Cliff Davis, Raleigh-Durham.

BA: Rennie Stennett, Salem, .326
Runs: Fred Frazier, Kinston, 92
Hits: Rennie Stennett, Salem, 176
RBIs: Cliff Johnson, Raleigh-Durham, 91
HRs: Cliff Johnson, Raleigh-Durham, 27
Wins: Lynn McGlothen, Winston-Salem, 15
SOs: Lynn McGlothen, Winston-Salem, 202
ERA: Danny Bootcheck, Rocky Mount, 1.92

A Florida State League
President: George MacDonald, Sr.

East Standings	W	L	Pct.	GB	Attend.	Manager
Miami Marlins (1)	88	45	.662	—	74,235	Woody Smith
West Palm Beach Expos (18)	79	50	.612	7	50,620	J.W. Porter
Daytona Beach Dodgers (17)	76	55	.580	11	31,371	Stan Wasiak
Pompano Beach Mets (19)	58	70	.453	27½	14,759	Gordon McKenzie
Ft. Lauderdale Yankees (10)	59	76	.424	31½	51,063	Lamar North
Cocoa Astros (16)	43	84	.339	42	22,166	Tony Pacheco

West Standings	W	L	Pct.	GB	Attend.	Manager
St. Petersburg Cardinals (22)	78	52	.600	—	104,485	Joe Cunningham
Lakeland Tigers (6)	69	62	.527	10½	15,524	Dick Tracewski
Tampa Tarpons (15)	64	68	.485	15	32,408	Dick Kennedy
Winter Haven Red Sox (2)	61	71	.462	18	15,684	John K. Butler
Orlando Twins (9)	59	74	.444	20½	51,931	Jackie Ferrell
DeLand Sun Caps (x)	55	77	.417	24	16,357	Bunky Warren

Playoffs: Miami 2 games, Lakeland 0; St. Petersburg 2 games, West Palm Beach 1.
Finals: Miami 2 games, St. Petersburg 0.

All-Star Team: 1B-Joe Staton, Lakeland; **2B**-Ken Stroman, Winter Haven; **3B**-Ken Reitz, St. Petersburg; **SS**-Robert Garcia, Orlando; **OF**-Russ Calderella, St. Petersburg; Angel Mangual, Winter Haven; Mike Reinbach, Miami; **C**-Terry McDermott, Daytona Beach; **P**-Michael Hebert, Miami; Stephen Luebber, Orlando; **MVP**-Michael Hebert, Miami; **Manager**-Dick Tracewski, Lakeland.

BA: Joe Staton, Lakeland, .346
Runs: John Gamble, Daytona Beach, 99
Hits: Joe Staton, Lakeland, 169
RBIs: Lee Robinson, Daytona Beach, 86
HRs: Moe Hill, Orlando, 22
Wins: Michael Hebert, Miami, 21
SOs: Stephen Luebber, Orlando, 172
ERA: Michael Hebert, Miami, 1.44

A Mexican Center League
President: Antonio Ramirez Muro

Standings	W	L	Pct.	GB	Attend.	Manager
Ciudad Madero Bravos***	79	44	.642	—	98,857	Rene Friol
Tampico Algodoneros	69	56	.552	11	25,034	Francisco Martinez
San Luis Potosi Charros	66	60	.524	14½	19,542	Ben Reyes
Ciudad Mante Broncos	62	61	.504	17	37,767	Agustin Enriquez
Monterrey Indios	60	64	.484	19½	20,605	Javier Espinosa
Zacatecas Petroleros	57	67	.460	22½	18,088	Jose Villegas
Aguascalientes Tigres	55	70	.440	25	24,011	Jesus Valenzuela
Leon Little Aguila	49	75	.395	30½	10,290	Hector Rodriguez

Playoffs: None.

All-Star Team: 1B-Juan Martinez, Zacatecas; **2B**-Bulmaro Garcia, Ciudad Mante; **3B**-Eugenio Guerra, San Luis Potosi; **SS**-Valencian Vega, Ciudad Madero; **OF**-Miguel Suarez, Tampico; Alberto Rendon, Ciudad Madero; Victor Sauceda, San Luis Potosi; **C**-Rafael Mendivil, Tampico; Magdaleno Feliciano, Aguascalientes; **P**-Porfirio Salomon, Ciudad Mante; Javier Reyes, San Luis Potosi; **Manager**-Rene Friol, Ciudad Madero.

BA: Miguel Suarez, Tampico, .393
Runs: Alberto Rendon, Ciudad Mante, 120
Hits: Miguel Suarez, Tampico, 181
RBIs: Juan Martinez, Ciudad Mante, 117
HRs: Trinidad Cardona, Ciudad Madero, 29
Wins: Javier Reyes, San Luis Potosi, 17
SOs: Rosario Reyes, Ciudad Madero, 147
ERA: Porfirio Salomon, Ciudad Mante, 1.78

A Mexican Southeast League
President: Fernando Canton

Standings	W	L	Pct.	GB	Attend.	Manager
Campeche Pirates**	64	38	.627	—	35,959	Mario Pelaez
Puerto Mexico Charros*	59	43	.578	5	9,503	Felipe Hernandez
Carmen Camoneros	48	58	.453	18	31,311	Leonel Aldama
Tabasco Plataneros	37	69	.349	29	11,803	Luis Montes de Oca

Playoff: Puerto Mexico 4 games, Campeche 0.

All-Star Team: 1B-Jaime Lopez, Puerto Mexico; **2B**-Teodoro Flores, Puerto Mexico; **3B**-Carlos Osuna, Puerto Mexico; **SS**-Francisco Conkle, Campeche; **OF**-Luis Peralta, Campeche; David Ochoa, Puerto Mexico; Mario Salazar, Puerto Mexico; **C**-Arturo Orozco, Campeche; Alfonso Jackson, Puerto Mexico; **P**-Leonardo Ferguson, Campeche; Roberto Ruiz, Tabasco; **Manager**-Mario Pelaez, Campeche.

BA: Francisco Conkle, Campeche, .356
Runs: Luis Peralta, Campeche, 62
Hits: Francisco Conkle, Campeche, 114
RBIs: Luis Peralta, Campeche, 65
HRs: Luis Peralta, Campeche, 14
Wins: Leonardo Ferguson, Campeche, 13
SOs: Leonardo Ferguson, Campeche, 128
ERA: Leonardo Ferguson, Campeche, 1.82

A Midwest League
President: James Doster

Standings	W	L	Pct.	GB	Attend.	Manager
Quincy Cubs (14)	68	45	.602	—	46,932	Walt Dixon
Quad Cities Angels (3)	68	53	.562	4	70,089	Mike Stubbins
Decatur Commodores (24)	63	56	.529	8	47,633	Frank Funk
Danville Warriors (x)	64	59	.520	9	67,091	Bob Bauer
Appleton Foxes (4)	64	60	.516	9½	83,818	Ira Hutchinson
Wisconsin Rapids Twins (9)	59	60	.496	12	45,579	John Goryl
Cedar Rapids Cardinals (22)	57	64	.471	15	42,724	Roy Majtyka
Clinton Pilots (8)	57	67	.460	16½	59,610	Earl Torgeson
Burlington Bees (11)	56	68	.452	17½	35,017	Roy Sievers
Waterloo Royals (7)	49	73	.402	23½	33,541	Steve Boros

Playoff: Quincy 2 games, Quad Cities 0.

All-Star Team: 1B-Cecil Cooper, Danville; **2B**-Sam Ashford, Quad Cities; **3B**-Walter Ransom, Danville; **SS**-Bob Hansen, Clinton; **OF**-Wilber Howard, Clinton; Joseph Bowen, Danville; Roger Cain, Burlington; **C**-Ron Davini, Appleton; Gene Dusan, Burlington; Andriano Rodriguez, Decatur; **P**-Ron Jones, Quincy; Joe Stover, Quincy; **Manager**-Bob Bauer, Danville.

BA: Cecil Cooper, Danville, .336
Runs: Walter Ransom, Danville, 91
Hits: Wilber Howard, Clinton, 142
RBIs: Joseph Bowen, Danville, 83
HRs: Roger Cain, Burlington, 23
Wins: John Conzatti, Clinton, 12
Arnold Johannes, Wisconsin Rapids, 12
Jerry Bell, Clinton, 12
Larry Gonsalves, Decatur, 12
Steve Hardin, Wisconsin Rapids, 12
SOs: Steve Hardin, Wisconsin Rapids, 161
ERA: Doug Bird, Waterloo, 1.84

A New York-Pennsylvania League
President: Vincent M. McNamara

Standings	W	L	Pct.	GB	Attend.	Manager
Auburn Twins (9)	43	26	.623	—	32,383	Boyd Coffie
Oneonta Yankees (10)	41	28	.594	2	23,015	George Case
Batavia Trojans (6)	37	32	.536	6	50,977	Joe Lewis
Newark Co-Pilots (8)	36	33	.522	7	20,988	Sandy Johnson
Geneva Senators (12)	33	35	.485	9½	21,466	Bill Haywood
Jamestown Falcons (2)	30	40	.429	13½	25,260	Jackie Jensen
Niagara Falls Pirates (21)	28	40	.412	14½	60,962	Irv Noren
Williamsport Astros (16)	28	42	.400	15½	43,599	Dick Bogard

Playoffs: None.

All-Star Team: 1B-Martin Cott, Williamsport; **2B**-Don Blood, Auburn; **3B**-Pat O'Keefe, Williamsport; **SS**-Pedro Garcia, Newark; **OF**-John Sinclair, Jamestown; Lambert Ford, Williamsport; Jackson Miller, Auburn; Brian Lambe, Batavia; **C**-Jack Walsh, Newark; Tom Smithson, Auburn; **P**-Mark Wiley, Auburn; Bill Leinheiser, Newark; Art DeFilippis, Geneva; Henry LaRose, Jamestown; **Manager**-Boyd Coffie, Auburn.

BA: Lambert Ford, Williamsport, .368
Runs: Tom O'Connor, Oneonta, 56
Hits: Lambert Ford, Williamsport, 88
Jackson Miller, Auburn, 88
RBIs: Martin Cott, Williamsport, 52
HRs: Pedro Garcia, Newark, 14
Wins: Mark Wiley, Auburn, 10
SOs: Mark Wiley, Auburn, 144
ERA: Bill Leinheiser, Newark, 1.01
Pct: Bill Leinheiser, Newark, .818, 9-2

A Northern League
President: Roland E. Parcel

Standings	W	L	Pct.	GB	Attend.	Manager
Duluth-Superior Dukes (4)	48	21	.696	—	22,747	Joe Sparks
Huron Cubs (15)	37	31	.544	10½	23,997	George Freese
Aberdeen Pheasants (1)	36	33	.522	12	20,880	Ken Rowe
Watertown Expos (18)	32	38	.457	16½	14,475	Bobby Malkmus
St. Cloud Rox (9)	31	39	.443	17½	27,581	Jim Merrick
Sioux Falls Packers (16)	24	46	.343	24½	21,477	Russ Nixon

Playoffs: None.

BA: Steve Houck, Duluth-Superior, .365
Runs: Dan Rourke, Duluth-Superior, 74
Hits: Steve Angelo, Watertown, 86
RBIs: Jim Stafford, Aberdeen, 56
HRs: Jim Stafford, Aberdeen, 17
Wins: Louis Billmeier, Duluth-Superior, 11
SOs: Louis Billmeier, Duluth-Superior, 112
ERA: Paul Sullivan, Watertown, 1.99

A Northwest League
President: John Carbray

North Standings	W	L	Pct.	GB	Attend.	Manager
Lewiston Broncs (22)	43	37	.538	—	22,395	Fred Hatfield
Walla Walla Phillies (20)	39	41	.488	4	32,043	Garry Powel
Tri-City Padres (23)	38	42	.475	5	30,320	Marty Keough

South Standings	W	L	Pct.	GB	Attend.	Manager
Coos Bay-North Bend A's (11)	45	35	.563	—	14,817	Harry Bright
Bend Rainbows (3)	39	41	.488	6	21,677	Charlie Silvera
Medford Dodgers (17)	36	44	.450	9	19,687	Bill Berrier

Playoffs: None.

All-Star Team: 1B-Bob Beall, Walla Walla; **2B**-Jim Van Wyck, Bend; **3B**-Dan Joost, Coos Bay-North Bend; **SS**-Dave Ristig, Medford; **OF**-Lloyd Hutchinson, Walla Walla; Phil Bushman, Bend; Doug Hunt, Tri-City; **C**-Mike Ivie, Tri-City; Stephen Krines, Medford; **P**-Dan Spillner, Tri-City; Greg Millikan, Lewiston; **Manager**-Fred Hatfield, Lewiston.

BA: Bob Beall, Walla Walla, .389
Runs: Bob Beall, Walla Walla, 81
Hits: Bob Beall, Walla Walla, 102
RBIs: Alan Wise, Bend, 65
HRs: Dale Sanner, Coos Bay-North Bend, 14
Blas Santana, Walla Walla, 14
Lloyd Hutchinson, Walla Walla, 14
Wins: Ed Cecil, Bend, 10
Wayne Sinclair, Coos Bay-North Bend, 10
SOs: Richard Brown, Tri-City, 120
ERA: Ron Hall, Medford, 3.03

A Western Carolinas League
President: John H. Moss

Standings	W	L	Pct.	GB	Attend.	Manager
Greenville Red Sox***(2)	77	52	.597	—	46,245	Rac Slider
Greenwood Braves (13)	70	60	.538	7½	48,648	Eddie Haas
Spartanburg Phillies (20)	64	64	.500	12½	29,743	Howie Bedell
Sumter Indians (5)	61	68	.473	16	33,196	Len Johnston
Anderson Senators (12)	61	69	.469	16½	184,212	Frank Gable
Gastonia Pirates (21)	55	75	.423	22½	27,381	Ed Hobaugh

Playoffs: None.

All-Star Team: 1B-Danny Covert, Sumter; **2B**-Jerry Coker, Spartanburg; **3B**-George Hodge, Spartanburg; **SS**-Frank Taveras, Gastonia; **OF**-Nelson Garcia, Spartanburg; James Bottoms, Anderson; Allan Matson, Spartanburg; **C**-Bill Hancock, Anderson; Dan Benoit, Spartanburg; **Util**-Larvell Blanks, Greenwood; Roy Gibson, Anderson; **P**-Paul Sparkman, Greenville; Brad Gratz, Gastonia; **Manager**-Rac Slider, Greenville.

BA: George Hodge, Spartanburg, .357
Runs: James Bottoms, Anderson, 104
Hits: George Hodge, Spartanburg, 144
RBIs: LaMar Davis, Anderson, 88
HRs: Roy Gibson, Anderson, 18
Wins: Paul Sparkman, Greenville, 16
SOs: Brad Gratz, Gastonia, 160
ERA: Brad Gratz, Gastonia, 2.26

R Appalachian League
President: Chauncey De Vault

Standings	W	L	Pct.	GB	Attend.	Manager
Bluefield Orioles (1)	38	21	.551	—	19,306	Ray Malgradi
Covington Astros (16)	32	24	.571	4½	20,870	Dick Smith
Johnson City Yankees (10)	28	27	.509	8	14,199	Jerry Walker
Pulaski Phillies (20)	27	28	.491	9	16,699	Brandy Davis
Bristol Tigers (6)	26	31	.456	11	15,520	Al Lakeman
Kingsport Royals (7)	26	33	.441	12	22,572	Owen Friend
Marion Mets (19)	23	36	.390	15	10,786	Terry Christman

Playoffs: None.

All-Star Team: 1B-Stan Jackson, Kingsport; **2B**-Joel Serna, Covington; **3B**-Otto Velez, Johnson City; **SS**-Doug DeCinces, Bluefield; **OF**-Greg Gross, Covington; Terry Jones, Bluefield; Ken Bennett, Johnson City; **C**-Jim Essian, Pulaski; **P**-Fred Holdsworth, Bristol; Dave Cheadle, Johnson City; **Manager**-Ray Malgradi, Bluefield.

BA: Otto Velez, Johnson City, .369
Runs: Otto Velez, Johnson City, 49
Hits: Greg Gross, Covington, 83
RBIs: Otto Velez, Johnson City, 44
Tom Hallums, Marion, 44
HRs: Tom Hallums, Marion, 14
Wins: Herbie Hutson, Bluefield, 9
SOs: Don Stratton, Covington, 107
ERA: Fred Holdsworth, Bristol, 1.31

R Gulf Coast League
President: George MacDonald, Sr.

Standings	W	L	Pct.	GB	Manager
White Sox (4)	36	24	.600	—	Joe Jones
Expos (18)	36	27	.571	1½	Ed Sadowski
Indians (5)	34	26	.567	2	Joe Lutz
Twins (9)	34	29	.549	3½	Fred Waters
Cardinals (22)	32	28	.533	4	Tom Burgess
Reds (15)	25	35	.417	11	Ron Plaza
Tourists (21)	26	37	.413	11½	Ed Napoleon
Pirates (21)	23	40	.365	14½	Dick Cole

Games played at Sarasota and Bradenton, Florida.
Total Attendance: 8,772.

Playoffs: None.

BA: Mark Carlson, Twins, .359
Runs: Burnel Flowers, Indians, 55
Hits: Mark Carlson, Twins, 78
RBIs: Jeff Newman, Indians, 53

HRs: Bob Gorinski, Twins, 6
  Dave Parker, Pirates, 6
  Jeff Newman, Indians, 6
Wins: Harold McClain, White Sox, 10
SOs: Harold McClain, White Sox, 108
ERA: Harold McClain, White Sox, 1.27

R Pioneer League
President: Claude Engberg

Standings	W	L	Pct.	GB	Attend.	Manager
Idaho Falls Angels (3)	44	26	.629	—	39,361	Bob Clear
Ogden Dodgers (17)	43	27	.614	1	33,369	Buddy Hollowell
Magic Valley Cowboys (13)	41	29	.586	3	17,657	Paul Snyder
Billings Mustangs (7)	37	33	.529	7	21,007	Dave Pavlesic
Caldwell Cubs (14)	23	47	.329	21	15,670	Sparky Davis
Great Falls Giants (24)	22	48	.314	22	20,217	Harvey Koepf

Playoffs: None.

All-Star Team: 1B-Frank Ortenzio, Billings; **2B**-Elmer Mixon, Ogden; **3B**-Marc Mengo, Magic Valley; **SS**-Gary Granville, Idaho Falls; **OF**-Morris Nettles, Idaho Falls; Al Cowens, Billings; Joe Daniels, Ogden; **C**-James Smith, Billings; Ray Lombardo, Great Falls; **P**-Richard Lange, Idaho Falls; Bruce Raible, Ogden.

BA: Morris Nettles, Idaho Falls, .369
Runs: Elmer Mixon, Ogden, 70
Hits: Gary Granville, Idaho Falls, 88
  Elmer Mixon, Ogden, 88
RBIs: Marc Mengo, Magic Valley, 60

HRs: Marc Mengo, Magic Valley, 12
Wins: Richard Lange, Idaho Falls, 13
SOs: Richard Lange, Idaho Falls, 151
ERA: Richard Lange, Idaho Falls, 1.95

1970 Interleague Post Season Play

World Series
Baltimore (American) 4 games, Cincinnati (National) 1

Junior World Series
Syracuse (International) 4 games, Omaha (American Association) 1
Total Attendance: 20,427

1970 Major League Farm Systems

American League
1 Baltimore (6): Rochester, Dallas-Ft. Worth, Stockton, Miami, Aberdeen, Bluefield.
2 Boston (6): Louisville, Pawtucket, Winston-Salem, Winter Haven, Jamestown, Greenville.
3 California (5): Hawaii, El Paso, Quad Cities, Bend, Idaho Falls.
4 Chicago (5): Tucson, Mobile, Appleton, Duluth-Superior, Gulf Coast.
5 Cleveland (5): Wichita, Savannah, Reno, Sumter, Gulf Coast.
6 Detroit (6): Toledo, Montgomery, Rocky Mount, Lakeland, Batavia, Bristol.
7 Kansas City (6): Omaha, Elmira, San Jose, Waterloo, Kingsport, Billings.
8 Milwaukee (4): Portland, Jacksonville, Clinton, Newark.
9 Minnesota (8): Evansville, Charlotte, Lynchburg, Orlando, Wisconsin Rapids, Auburn, St. Cloud, Gulf Coast.
10 New York (6): Syracuse, Manchester, Kinston, Ft. Lauderdale, Oneonta, Johnson City.
11 Oakland (4): Iowa, Birmingham, Burlington (IA), Coos Bay-North Bend.
12 Washington (5): Denver, Pittsfield, Burlington (NC), Geneva, Anderson.

National League
13 Atlanta (4): Richmond, Shreveport, Greenwood, Magic Valley.
14 Chicago (4): Tacoma, San Antonio, Quincy, Caldwell.
15 Cincinnati (5): Indianapolis, Asheville, Tampa, Huron, Gulf Coast.
16 Houston (6): Oklahoma City, Columbus, Cocoa, Williamsport, Sioux Falls, Covington.
17 Los Angeles (5): Spokane, Albuquerque, Daytona Beach, Medford, Ogden.
18 Montreal (5): Buffalo/Winnipeg, Jacksonville, West Palm Beach, Watertown, Gulf Coast.
19 New York (5): Tidewater, Memphis, Visalia, Pompano Beach, Marion.
20 Philadelphia (6): Eugene, Reading, Peninsula, Walla Walla, Spartanburg, Pulaski.
21 Pittsburgh (6): Columbus, Waterbury, Salem, Niagara Falls, Gastonia, Gulf Coast.
22 St. Louis (7): Tulsa, Arkansas, Modesto, St. Petersburg, Cedar Rapids, Lewiston, Gulf Coast.
23 San Diego (4): Salt Lake City, Elmira, Lodi, Tri-City.
24 San Francisco (5): Phoenix, Amarillo, Fresno, Decatur, Great Falls.

Co-op (x): DeLand, Raleigh-Durham, Danville.

1970 No-Hitters

Date	Pitcher	Team	League	Opponent	Score
5-9	Dyar Miller	Dallas-Ft. Worth	Texas	Amarillo	10-0 (7)
5-11	Bill Olsen	Kinston	Carolina	Burlington	2-0
5-24	Saul Montoya	Campeche	Mexican S.E.	Tabasco	5-0
5-29	Mike Whitson	Pittsfield	Eastern	Waterbury	4-0 (7)
6-1	Wallace Smallwood	Burlington	Carolina	Salem	5-0 (7)
6-11	Mike Jackson	Eugene	Pacific Coast	Tucson	5-0 (7)
6-11	Leonardo Ferguson	Campeche	Mexican S.E.	Puerto Mexico	2-0 (P, 7)
6-12	Dock Ellis	Pittsburgh	National	San Diego	2-0
6-14	Robert Elliott	Kinston	Carolina	Lynchburg	5-0 (7)
6-26	Brad Roker/Mike Ward/				
	Miguel Sosa	Kingsport	Appalachian	Bristol	1-2
6-28	Don Leshnock	Rocky Mount	Carolina	Peninsula	4-0
7-2	Larry Kleem/Dennis Kline/				
	Robert Williams	West Palm Beach	Florida State	Pompano Beach	5-2 (7)
7-3	Clyde Wright	California	American	Oakland	4-0
7-4	Milt Wilcox	Indianapolis	American Assoc.	Evansville	2-0 (7)
7-11	Jose Ramon Lopez	Monterrey	Mexican	Jalisco	1-0 (7)
7-17	Wayne Retig/				
	Frederick Seibly	Tri-City	Northwest	Bend	0-2 (7)
7-19	Mark Ballinger	Reno	California	San Jose	4-0 (7)
7-20	Bill Singer	Los Angeles	National	Philadelphia	5-0
7-23	Charles Arrendale	Niagara Falls	New York-Penn.	Newark	1-0
7-29	Hector Madrigal	Poza Rica	Mexican	Jalisco	2-0
8-4	Larry McDowell	Albuquerque	Texas	Amarillo	12-0
8-5	Robert Gorski	Gastonia	W. Carolinas	Greenwood	4-0 (7)
8-7	John Canzalti	Clinton	Midwest	Quad Cities	2-0 (6)
8-11	Randy Pugh	Marion	Appalachian	Kingsport	12-0 (7)
8-14	Chuck Swanson	Montgomery	Southern	Savannah	3-0 (P)
8-24	Billy Farmer	Louisville	International	Toledo	8-0 (7)
8-26	Bill Martin	Pulaski	Appalachian	Kingsport	4-1 (7)
8-28	James Horschi	Expos	Gulf Coast	Pirates	6-0 (7)
8-28	Milt Kelly	Orlando	Florida State	DeLand	2-0 (7)
8-28	James Richards	Cocoa	Florida State	Daytona Beach	2-0 (7)
9-7	Ron Schueler	Shreveport	Texas	San Antonio	2-0
9-21	Vida Blue	Oakland	American	Minnesota	6-0

Number in parentheses indicates innings if other than nine; "P" indicates perfect game.

THIS DATE IN MINOR LEAGUE HISTORY

March 19, 1970, Negro League baseball historian Normal "Tweed" Webb organized the Oldtime Negro Baseball Players Association to aid black ex-baseball players.

April 16, 1970, James "Rip" Collins, 65, a member of the St. Louis Cardinals' famous Gas House Gang during the early 1930s, and who compiled a .331 batting average in his 15 years in the minors, died in New Haven, New York. Serving as player-manager for the Albany Eastern League club in 1944, Collins won the batting title with a .396 mark, leading all of Organized Ball in hitting.

April 25, 1970, El Paso, Texas League, scored one run in each of ten innings to beat Shreveport 10-9.

June 11, 1970, After 93 seasons of baseball, Buffalo, International League, lost its franchise as the club moved to Winnipeg.

July 30, 1970, Righthander Bruce Kison, Waterbury, Eastern League, hit seven Pittsfield batters with pitches before being removed in the sixth inning.

August 12, 1970, Ronnie Comacho, Yucatan, Mexican League, smashed his 300th career home run.

September 30, 1970, Lou Novikoff, 54, former slugging outfielder in the minor and major leagues, died in South Gate, California. "The Mad Russian" had his greatest season in 1940 with Los Angeles, leading the Pacific Coast League in homers (41), RBIs (171), and batting (.363).

1971

American League
President: Joseph E. Cronin

East Standings	W	L	Pct.	GB	Attend.	Manager
Baltimore Orioles	101	57	.639	—	1,023,037	Earl Weaver
Detroit Tigers	91	71	.562	12	1,591,073	Billy Martin
Boston Red Sox	85	77	.525	18	1,678,732	Eddie Kasko
New York Yankees	82	80	.506	21	1,070,771	Ralph Houk
Washington Senators	63	96	.396	38½	655,156	Ted Williams
Cleveland Indians	60	102	.370	43	591,361	Alvin Dark/John Lipon

West Standings	W	L	Pct.	GB	Attend.	Manager
Oakland Athletics	101	60	.627	—	914,993	Dick Williams
Kansas City Royals	85	76	.528	16	910,784	Bob Lemon
Chicago White Sox	79	83	.488	22½	833,891	Chuck Tanner
California Angels	76	86	.469	25½	926,373	Lefty Phillips
Minnesota Twins	74	86	.463	26½	940,858	Bill Rigney
Milwaukee Brewers	69	92	.429	32	731,531	Dave Bristol

Playoff: Baltimore 3 games, Oakland 0.

BA: Tony Oliva, Minnesota, .337
Runs: Don Buford, Baltimore, 99
Hits: Cesar Tovar, Minnesota, 204
RBIs: Harmon Killebrew, Minnesota, 119
HRs: Bill Melton, Chicago, 33

Wins: Mickey Lolich, Detroit, 25
SOs: Mickey Lolich, Detroit, 308
ERA: Vida Blue, Oakland, 1.82
Pct: Dave McNally, Baltimore, .808, 21-5
Saves: Ken Sanders, Milwaukee, 31

National League
President: Charles S. Feeney

East Standings	W	L	Pct.	GB	Attend.	Manager
Pittsburgh Pirates	97	65	.599	—	1,501,132	Danny Murtaugh
St. Louis Cardinals	90	72	.556	7	1,604,671	Red Schoendienst
Chicago Cubs	83	79	.512	14	1,653,007	Leo Durocher
New York Mets	83	79	.512	14	2,266,680	Gil Hodges
Montreal Expos	71	90	.441	25½	1,290,963	Gene Mauch
Philadelphia Phillies	67	95	.414	30	1,511,223	Frank Lucchesi

West Standings	W	L	Pct.	GB	Attend.	Manager
San Francisco Giants	90	72	.556	—	1,106,043	Charlie Fox
Los Angeles Dodgers	89	73	.549	1	2,064,594	Walter Alston
Atlanta Braves	82	80	.506	8	1,006,320	Luman Harris
Cincinnati Reds	79	83	.488	11	1,501,122	Sparky Anderson
Houston Astros	79	83	.488	11	1,261,589	Harry Walker
San Diego Padres	61	100	.379	28½	557,513	Preston Gomez

Playoff: Pittsburgh 3 games, San Francisco 1.

BA: Joe Torre, St. Louis, .363
Runs: Lou Brock, St. Louis, 126
Hits: Joe Torre, St. Louis, 230
RBIs: Joe Torre, St. Louis, 137
HRs: Willie Stargell, Pittsburgh, 48

Wins: Ferguson Jenkins, Chicago, 24
SOs: Tom Seaver, New York, 289
ERA: Tom Seaver, New York, 1.76
Pct: Don Gullett, Cincinnati, .727, 16-6
Saves: Dave Giusti, Pittsburgh, 30

AAA American Association
President: Allie Reynolds

East Standings	W	L	Pct.	GB	Attend.	Manager
Indianapolis Indians (15)	84	55	.604	—	156,668	Vern Rapp
Iowa Oaks (11)	71	69	.507	13½	130,336	Sherman Lollar
Omaha Royals (7)	69	70	.496	15	175,462	Jack McKeon
Evansville Triplets (8)	60	78	.435	23½	107,818	Del Crandall

West Standings	W	L	Pct.	GB	Attend.	Manager
Denver Bears (12)	73	67	.521	—	313,912	Del Wilber
Oklahoma City 89ers (16)	71	69	.507	3	329,513	Jimy Williams
Wichita Aeros (5)	66	74	.471	7	280,320	Ken Aspromonte
Tulsa Oilers (22)	64	76	.457	9	186,414	Warren Spahn/Gary Geiger

Playoff: Denver 4 games, Indianapolis 3.

All-Star Team: 1B-Bill McNulty, Iowa; **2B**-James Driscoll, Iowa/Denver; **3B**-Buddy Bell, Wichita; **SS**-Ray Busse, Oklahoma City; **OF**-Richie Scheinblum, Denver; Fred Rico, Tulsa; Keith Lampard, Oklahoma City; **C**-Bill Plummer, Indianapolis; Buck Martinez, Omaha; **P**-J.R. Richard, Oklahoma City; Milt Wilcox, Indianapolis; **MVP**-Richie Scheinblum, Denver; **Pitcher of the Year**-Garland Shifflet, Denver; **Manager**-Vern Rapp, Indianapolis.

BA: Richie Scheinblum, Denver, .388
Runs: Fred Rico, Tulsa, 87
Hits: Fred Rico, Tulsa, 150
RBIs: Richie Scheinblum, Denver 108

HRs: Bill McNulty, Iowa, 27
Wins: Richard Estelle, Evansville, 13
SOs: J.R. Richard, Oklahoma City, 202
ERA: J.R. Richard, Oklahoma City, 2.45

AAA International League
President: George H. Sisler, Jr.

Standings	W	L	Pct.	GB	Attend.	Manager
Rochester Red Wings (1)	86	54	.614	—	361,701	Joe Altobelli
Tidewater Tides (19)	79	61	.564	7	134,894	Hank Bauer
Charleston Charlies (21)	78	62	.557	8	131,359	Joe Morgan
Syracuse Chiefs (10)	73	67	.521	13	208,892	Loren Babe
Louisville Colonels (2)	71	69	.507	15	110,814	Darrell Johnson
Richmond Braves (13)	69	71	.493	17	112,675	Clyde King
Toledo Mud Hens (6)	60	80	.429	26	88,438	Mike Roarke
Winnipeg Whips (18)	44	96	.314	42	95,954	Clyde McCullough/ Jimmy Bragan

Playoffs: Tidewater 3 games, Charleston 0; Rochester 3 games, Syracuse 1.
Finals: Rochester 3 games, Tidewater 2.

All-Star Team: 1B-Dave McDonald, Winnipeg; **2B**-Rennie Stennett, Charleston; **3B**-Len Boehmer, Syracuse; **SS**-Bobby Grich, Rochester; **OF**-Leroy Stanton, Tidewater; Don Baylor, Rochester; John Jeter, Charleston; **C**-George Pena, Syracuse; **P**-Roric Harrison, Rochester, Brent Strom, Tidewater; **MVP**-Bobby Grich, Rochester; **Pitcher of the Year**-Roric Harrison, Rochester; **Manager**-Joe Altobelli, Rochester.

BA: Bobby Grich, Rochester, .336
Runs: Bobby Grich, Rochester, 124
Hits: John Jeter, Charleston, 168
RBIs: Richie Zisk, Charleston, 109
HRs: Bobby Grich, Rochester, 32

Wins: Roric Harrison, Rochester, 15
Jim Bibby, Tidewater, 15
SOs: Roric Harrison, Rochester, 182
ERA: Buzz Capra, Tidewater, 2.19

AAA Mexican League
President: Antonio Ramirez Muro

North Standings	W	L	Pct.	GB	Attend.	Manager
Saltillo Saraperos	86	59	.593	—	255,739	Tomas Herrera/ Andres Tanaka
Monterrey Sultanes	83	63	.568	3½	273,559	Manuel Magallon
Tampico Stevedores	79	65	.549	6½	150,508	Miguel Sotelo
Union Laguna Algodoneros	72	76	.486	15½	230,277	Minnie Minoso
Sabinas Piratas	62	83	.428	24	99,445	Vinicio Garcia/ Roberto Montelongo/ Andres Ayon/Manuel Lopez/ Jesus Moreno/Ruben Gomez/ Alfonso Preciado
Reynosa Broncs	47	100	.320	40	86,533	Ron Camacho

South Standings	W	L	Pct.	GB	Attend.	Manager
Jalisco Charros	82	65	.558	—	158,485	Ben Reyes
Mexico City Diablos Rojos	81	65	.555	½	352,730	Jose Guerrero
Mexico City Tigres	80	67	.544	2	232,835	Jose Luis Garcia
Yucatan Leones	71	75	.486	10½	102,950	Leonel Aldama
Veracruz Aguila	70	75	.483	11	88,961	Tony Castano/ Enrique Izquierdo
Poza Rica Petroleros	61	81	.430	18½	186,024	David Garcia/ Moises Camacho

Playoff: Jalisco 4 games, Saltillo 3.

All-Star Team: 1B-Hector Espino, Tampico; **2B**-Gabriel Lugo, Saltillo; **3B**-Celerino Sanchez, MC Tigres; **SS**-Guadalupe Chavez, Saltillo; **OF**-Teo Acosta, Yucatan; Miguel Suarez, MC Diablos Rojos; Marcelo Juarez, Saltillo; Bill Parlier, Jalisco; **C**-Gregorio Luque, Saltillo; Roberto Herrera, Yucatan; **P**-Andres Ayon, Sabinas/Saltillo; Jose Soto, Saltillo; **Manager**-Ben Reyes, Jalisco.

BA: Teo Acosta, Yucatan, .392
Runs: Jose Manuel Ortiz, Monterrey, 98
Hits: Miguel Suarez, MC Diablos Rojos, 188
RBIs: Victor Torres, Monterrey, 107
HRs: Humberto Garcia, Tampico, 23

Wins: Ernesto Gonzalez, Tampico, 22
Juan Suby, MC Tigres, 22
SOs: Felipe Leal, Saltillo, 223
ERA: Andres Ayon, Sabinas/Saltillo, 1.22

AAA Pacific Coast League
President: William B. McKechnie, Jr.

North Standings	W	L	Pct.	GB	Attend.	Manager
Tacoma Cubs (14)	78	65	.545	—	152,732	Jim Marshall
Portland Beavers (9)	71	71	.500	6½	105,565	Ralph Rowe
Spokane Indians (17)	69	76	.476	10	137,553	Tom Lasorda
Eugene Emeralds (20)	66	79	.455	13	86,843	Andy Seminick

South Standings	W	L	Pct.	GB	Attend.	Manager
Salt Lake City Angels (3)	78	68	.534	—	152,160	Del Rice
Phoenix Giants (24)	74	70	.514	3	123,199	Jim Davenport
Hawaii Islanders (23)	73	73	.500	5	375,957	Bill Adair
Tucson Toros (4)	69	76	.476	8½	166,879	Gordon Maltzberger

Playoff: Salt Lake City 3 games, Tacoma 1.

---

*Won first-half **Won second-half ***Won both halves
Numbers after nicknames indicate farm system.
Affiliation listed at end of year.

All-Star Team: 1B-Tom Hutton, Spokane; **2B**-Bill Parker, Salt Lake City; **3B**-Ron Cey, Spokane; **SS**-Steve Huntz, Tacoma; **OF**-Mike Anderson, Eugene; Adrian Garrett, Tacoma; Tom Paciorek, Spokane; **C**-Art Kusnyer, Salt Lake City; Dave Rader, Phoenix; **P**-Roberto Rodriguez, Tacoma; Jim Willoughby, Phoenix; **MVP**-Tom Hutton, Spokane; **Manager**-Del Rice, Salt Lake City.

BA: Tom Hutton, Spokane, .352
Runs: Tom Hutton, Spokane, 117
Hits: Tom Hutton, Spokane, 190
RBIs: Ron Cey, Spokane, 123

HRs: Adrian Garrett, Tacoma, 43
Wins: Dick Woodson, Portland, 16
SOs: Dick Woodson, Portland, 163
ERA: Jerry Crider, Hawaii, 3.29

AA Eastern League
President: Roy Jackson

American Standings	W	L	Pct.	GB	Attend.	Manager
Elmira Royals (7)	78	61	.561	—	52,949	Harry Malmberg
Pittsfield Senators (12)	68	69	.496	9	49,770	Joe Klein
Pawtucket Red Sox (2)	63	76	.453	15	75,159	Billy Gardner
Manchester Yankees (10)	61	75	.449	15½	28,981	Mickey Vernon

National Standings	W	L	Pct.	GB	Attend.	Manager
Trois Rivieres Aigles (15)	78	59	.569	—	109,346	Jim Snyder
Reading Phillies (20)	72	67	.518	7	78,737	Nolan Campbell
Waterbury Pirates (21)	68	70	.493	10½	64,568	John "Red" Davis
Quebec Carnavals (18)	64	75	.460	15	99,688	Gus Niarhos

Playoff: Elmira 3 games, Trois Rivieres 1.

All-Star Team: 1B-Andre Thornton, Reading; **2B**-Joe Lovitto, Pittsfield; **3B**-Gary Sanserino, Elmira; **SS**-Joe Frias, Quebec; **OF**-Gene Locklear, Trois Rivieres; Jose Mangual, Quebec; Don Carson, Manchester; **C**-Bill Fahey, Pittsfield; **P**-Mike Ruddell, Trois Rivieres; Craig Skok, Pawtucket; **MVP**-Gene Locklear, Trois Rivieres; **Manager**-Jim Snyder, Trois Rivieres.

BA: Gene Locklear, Trois Rivieres, .323
Runs: Jose Mangual, Quebec, 80
Hits: Richard Guarnera, Pittsfield, 132
RBIs: Al Thompson, Pittsfield, 92

HRs: Al Thompson, Pittsfield, 27
Wins: Steve Blateric, Trois Rivieres, 14
SOs: Mike Ruddell, Trois Rivieres, 186
ERA: Bob Terlecki, Reading, 2.30

AA Southern League (Dixie Association)
President: Sam C. Smith

Standings	W	L	Pct.	GB	Attend.	Manager
Charlotte Hornets (9)	92	50	.648	—	69,132	Harry Warner
Asheville Tourists (4)	90	51	.638	1½	46,976	Larry Sherry
Montgomery Rebels (6)	73	69	.514	19	45,110	Dick Tracewski
Jacksonville Suns (5)	63	77	.450	28	58,751	Ray Hathaway
Savannah Braves (13)	57	84	.404	34½	60,712	Eddie Haas
Columbus Astros (16)	51	91	.359	41	19,950	Cliff Davis
Birmingham A's (11)	48	93	.340	43½	33,275	Phil Cavarretta

Played an interlocking schedule with the Texas League known as the Dixie Association.

Playoff: Charlotte 2 games, Asheville 1.

All-Star Team: 1B-Larry Mansfield, Columbus; **2B**-Bobby Marcano, Jacksonville; **3B**-Minnie Mendoza, Charlotte; **SS**-Chuck Miller, Asheville; **OF**-Ken Hottman, Asheville; Greg Gross, Columbus; Bob Storm, Charlotte; Ed Armbrister, Columbus; **C**-David Bike, Montgomery; **Util**-Frank Obregon, Savannah; Ike Blessitt, Montgomery; **P**-Dennis O'Toole, Asheville; Jim MacDonnell, Asheville; **Manager**-Larry Sherry, Asheville.

BA: Minnie Mendoza, Charlotte, .316
Runs: Ken Hottman, Asheville, 99
Hits: Minnie Mendoza, Charlotte, 163
RBIs: Ken Hottman, Asheville, 116
HRs: Ken Hottman, Asheville, 37

Wins: Jim MacDonnell, Asheville, 17
    Dick Rusteck, Charlotte, 17
SOs: Chris Floethe, Birmingham, 225
ERA: Dick Rusteck, Charlotte, 2.40

AA Texas League (Dixie Association)
President: Bobby Bragan

East Standings	W	L	Pct.	GB	Attend.	Manager
Arkansas Travelers (22)	75	64	.540	—	101,000	Jack Krol
Memphis Blues (19)	69	70	.496	6	96,410	Johnny Antonelli
Shreveport Captains (3)	69	73	.486	7½	44,662	Les Moss

West Standings	W	L	Pct.	GB	Attend.	Manager
Amarillo Giants (24)	88	54	.620	—	66,117	Andy Gilbert
Dallas-Ft. Worth Spurs (1)	82	59	.582	5½	213,249	Cal Ripken, Sr.
Albuquerque Dodgers (17)	67	75	.472	21	165,308	Monty Basgall
San Antonio Missions (14)	63	77	.450	24	47,113	Walt Dixon

Played an interlocking schedule with the Southern League known as the Dixie Association.

Playoff: Arkansas 2 games, Amarillo 0.

All-Star Team: 1B-Enos Cabell, Dallas-Ft. Worth; **2B**-Lee Lacy, Albuquerque; **3B**-Rudy Meoli, Shreveport; **SS**-Jim Plant, Memphis; **OF**-Leon Brown, Dallas-Ft. Worth; Billy North, San Antonio; Paul Johnson, Albuquerque; **C**-Steve Yeager, Albuquerque; **Util**-Art Cleary, Amarillo; **P**-Wayne Garland, Dallas-Ft. Worth; Gary Ryerson, Amarillo; **MVP**-Enos Cabell, Dallas-Ft. Worth; **Pitcher of the Year**-Wayne Garland, Dallas-Ft. Worth; **Manager**-Andy Gilbert, Amarillo.

BA: Enos Cabell, Dallas-Ft. Worth, .311
Runs: Billy North, San Antonio, 91
Hits: Enos Cabell, Dallas-Ft. Worth, 162
RBIs: Gary Matthews, Amarillo, 86

HRs: Larry Fritz, Memphis, 20
Wins: Wayne Garland, Dallas-Ft. Worth, 19
SOs: Tommy Moore, Memphis, 160
ERA: Wayne Garland, Dallas-Ft. Worth, 1.71

A California League
President: Edward J. Mulligan

Standings	W	L	Pct.	GB	Attend.	Manager
Modesto Reds (22)	83	56	.597	—	56,267	Roy Majtyka
Visalia Mets** (19)	81	58	.583	2	44,933	Joe Frazier
Fresno Giants* (24)	70	70	.500	13½	69,599	Dennis Sommers
San Jose Bees (7)	70	70	.500	13½	81,663	Carl "Buddy" Peterson
Stockton Ports (1)	67	71	.486	15½	21,335	Ray Malgradi
Lodi Padres (23)	65	74	.468	18	18,907	George Freese
Reno Silver Sox (5)	64	75	.460	19	30,541	Pinky May
Bakersfield Dodgers (17)	56	82	.406	26½	58,872	Don LeJohn

Playoff: Visalia 2 games, Fresno 0.

All-Star Team: 1B-Frank Ortenzio, San Jose; **2B**-Ron Collins, Visalia; **3B**-Steve Ontiveros, Fresno; **SS**-Tim Nordbrook, Stockton; **OF**-Lewis Beasley, Stockton; Garry Maddox, Fresno; George Theodore, Visalia; Burnel Flowers, Reno; **C**-Alan Ashby, Reno; **Util**-Alan Putz, Modesto; **P**-Doug Bird, San Jose; Don Durham, Modesto; Ron Stewart, Visalia; Don Belluomini, Stockton; **MVP**-George Theodore, Visalia; **Manager**-Roy Majtyka, Modesto.

BA: Bill Bright, Modesto, .340
Runs: Burnel Flowers, Reno, 113
Hits: Burnel Flowers, Reno, 175
RBIs: George Theodore, Visalia, 113

HRs: Frank Ortenzio, San Jose, 32
Wins: Doug Bird, San Jose, 15
SOs: Don Durham, Modesto, 202
ERA: Don Durham, Modesto, 2.80

A Carolina League
President: Wallace McKenna

Standings	W	L	Pct.	GB	Attend.	Manager
Peninsula Phillies** (20)	85	53	.616	—	60,286	Howie Bedell
Kinston Eagles* (10)	83	52	.615	½	52,020	Gene Hassell
Lynchburg Twins (9)	68	67	.504	15	38,902	John Goryl
Winston-Salem Red Sox (2)	67	67	.500	15½	34,141	Don Lock
Rocky Mount Leafs (6)	65	69	.485	17½	26,750	Len Okrie
Salem Rebels (21)	65	71	.478	18½	37,872	Tim Murtaugh
Raleigh-Durham Triangles (x)	56	80	.412	27½	40,447	Dick Kennedy
Burlington Senators (12)	54	84	.391	30½	22,247	Whitey Kurowski

Playoff: Peninsula 2 games, Kinston 0.

All-Star Team: 1B-Bob Beall, Peninsula; **2B**-Don Kinzell, Peninsula; **3B**-Art Howe, Salem; **SS**-Sterling Coward, Peninsula; **OF**-Charlie Spikes, Kinston; Marv Lane, Rocky Mount; Richard Giallella, Peninsula; **C**-Jim Essian, Peninsula; **P**-Richard Fusari, Peninsula; Jim Golden, Kinston; **MVP**-Richard Giallella, Peninsula; **Manager**-Gene Hassell, Kinston.

BA: Art Howe, Salem, .348
Runs: Nelson Garcia, Peninsula, 92
Hits: Nelson Garcia, Peninsula, 155
RBIs: Craig Kusick, Lynchburg, 91

HRs: Charley Spikes, Kinston, 22
Wins: Richard Fusari, Peninsula, 19
SOs: Don Schroeder, Kinston, 176
ERA: Richard Fusari, Peninsula, 2.19

A Florida State League
President: George MacDonald, Sr.

East Standings	W	L	Pct.	GB	Attend.	Manager
Miami Orioles (1)	94	47	.667	—	70,887	Woody Smith
Cocoa Astros (16)	80	59	.576	13	24,628	Tony Pacheco
Pompano Beach Mets (19)	70	69	.504	23	23,994	Gordon MacKenzie
Ft. Lauderdale Yankees (10)	71	70	.504	23	33,952	Bobby Cox
West Palm Beach Expos (18)	58	81	.417	35	65,517	Bobby Malkmus
Key West Sun Caps (x)	45	93	.326	47½	44,499	Bob Dustal/Terry Christman

West Standings	W	L	Pct.	GB	Attend.	Manager
Daytona Beach Dodgers (17)	82	58	.586	—	38,934	Stan Wasiak
Tampa Tarpons (15)	79	61	.564	3	46,990	Russ Nixon
St. Petersburg Cardinals (22)	72	69	.511	10½	110,444	Joe Cunningham
Orlando Twins (9)	65	73	.471	16	40,205	Jackie Ferrell
Lakeland Tigers (6)	63	78	.447	19½	4,395	Stubby Overmire
Winter Haven Red Sox (2)	58	79	.423	22½	13,534	John K. Butler

Playoffs: Miami 2 games, Tampa 0; Cocoa 2 games, Daytona Beach 1.
Finals: Miami 2 games, Cocoa 1.

All-Star Team: 1B-Wayne Burney, Daytona Beach; **2B**-Elmer Mixon, Daytona Beach; **3B**-Donnie Collins, Miami; **SS**-Sergio Ferrer, Daytona Beach; **OF**-Jim Fuller, Miami; Mike Easler, Cocoa; Kent Burdick, Tampa; **C**-Fred Senger, Pompano Beach; **Util**-Tommy Cruz, St. Petersburg; Mike Krizmanich, Ft. Lauderdale; **P**-Lance Rautzhan, Daytona Beach; Herbie Hutson, Miami; **MVP**-Jim Fuller, Miami; **Manager**-Stan Wasiak, Daytona Beach.

BA: Donnie Collins, Miami, .330
Runs: Jim Fuller, Miami, 102
Hits: Jim Fuller, Miami, 156
RBIs: Jim Fuller, Miami, 110

HRs: Jim Fuller, Miami, 33
Wins: Herbie Hutson, Miami, 17
SOs: Michael Cosgrove, Cocoa, 231
ERA: Herbie Hutson, Miami, 1.65

A Mexican Center League
President: Antonio Ramirez Muro

Central Standings	W	L	Pct.	GB	Attend.	Manager
San Luis Potosi Tuneros	45	27	.625	—	19,497	Felipe Hernandez
Aguascalientes Tigres	41	30	.577	3½	14,446	Ben Valenzuela
Zacatecas Tuzos	40	32	.556	5	15,993	Hector Villalobos
Leon Bravos	20	50	.286	24	8,937	Guillermo Frayde

Gulf Standings

	W	L	Pct.	GB	Attend.	Manager
Ebano Reds	50	21	.704	—	18,000	Mario Pelaez
Monterrey Indios	39	31	.557	10½	4,553	Javier Espinoza
Ciudad Mante Caneros	26	45	.366	24	13,870	Fidel Alvarez
Ciudad Victoria	23	48	.324	27	15,386	Augustin Enriquez

Playoff: Ebano 3 games, San Luis Potosi 1.

All-Star Team: **1B**-Manuel Parra, San Luis Potosi; **2B**-Jose Valdez, Aguascalientes; **3B**-Santos Lara, Leon; **SS**-Juan Navarrete, Zacatecas; **OF**-Enrique Verdugo, Zacatecas; Felipe Valenzuela, Monterrey; Carlos Lopez, Aguascalientes; Victor Sauceda, San Luis Potosi; **C**-Jose Aguilar, Zacatecas; Luis Peralta, Aguascalientes; **P**-Tomas Armas, San Luis Potosi; Alfonso Bourgette, Ebano; **Manager**-Mario Pelaez, Ebano.

BA: Jorge Orta, San Luis Potosi, .423
Runs: Rodolfo Hernandez, San Luis Potosi, 61
Hits: Juan Navarrete, Zacatecas, 91
RBIs: Rafael Ornelas, Ebano, 62
Manuel Parra, San Luis Potosi, 62
Victor Sauceda, San Luis Potosi, 62

HRs: Manuel Parra, San Luis Potosi, 14
Rafael Ornelas, Ebano, 14
Wins: Enrique Pacheco, Ebano, 12
SOs: Adan Munoz, Ciudad Mante, 73
ERA: Tomas Armas, San Luis Potosi, 2.28

A Midwest League
President: James Doster

North Standings	W	L	Pct.	GB	Attend.	Manager
Appleton Foxes***(4)	79	44	.642	—	83,881	Joe Sparks
Cedar Rapids Cardinals (22)	67	53	.558	11½	51,023	Bobby Dews
Waterloo Royals (7)	55	64	.462	22	35,886	Steve Boros
Clinton Pilots (6)	48	76	.387	31½	19,178	Max Lanier
Wisconsin Rapids Twins (9)	42	78	.350	35½	42,581	Hoss Bowlin

South Standings	W	L	Pct.	GB	Attend.	Manager
Burlington Bees (11)	71	50	.587	—	44,056	Harry Bright
Quad Cities Angels**(3)	68	56	.548	4½	82,467	Mike Stubbins
Danville Warriors*(8)	65	56	.537	6	85,765	Sandy Johnson
Quincy Cubs (14)	61	63	.492	11½	49,131	Dick LeMay
Decatur Commodores (24)	54	70	.435	18½	39,921	Frank Funk

Playoff: Quad Cities 1 game, Danville 0.
Finals: Quad Cities 2 games, Appleton 1.

All-Star Team: **1B**-Keith Lieppman, Burlington; **2B**-Larry Milbourne, Decatur; **3B**-Paul Dade, Quad Cities; **SS**-Tommy Sandt, Burlington; **OF**-Gorman Thomas, Danville; Bob Gorinski, Wisconsin Rapids; Darnell Ford, Burlington; **C**-Tom Lundstedt, Quincy; Bill Fitzgerald, Burlington; **P**-Dennis Myers, Burlington; John D'Acquisto, Decatur; **Manager**-Joe Sparks, Appleton.

BA: Randolph Crews, Quincy, .323
Runs: Dave Lindsey, Danville, 92
Hits: Larry Milbourne, Decatur, 156
RBIs: Lamar Johnson, Appleton, 97

HRs: Gorman Thomas, Danville, 31
Wins: Rich Gossage, Appleton, 18
SOs: John D'Acquisto, Decatur, 244
ERA: Rich Gossage, Appleton, 1.83

A New York-Pennsylvania League
President: Vincent M. McNamara

Standings	W	L	Pct.	GB	Attend.	Manager
Oneonta Yankees (10)	45	23	.662	—	29,726	George Case
Auburn Twins (9)	42	28	.600	4	36,071	Boyd Coffie
Niagara Falls Pirates (21)	37	33	.529	9	56,052	Chuck Cottier/Dick Cole
Newark Co-Pilots (8)	35	35	.500	11	20,393	Al Widmar
Geneva Senators (12)	34	36	.486	12	20,023	Frank Gable
Williamsport Red Sox (2)	30	39	.435	15½	41,875	Dick Berardino
Batavia Trojans (6)	30	40	.429	16	52,909	Joe Lewis
Jamestown Falcons (18)	25	44	.362	20½	12,840	Ed Sadowski

Playoffs: None.

All-Star Team: **1B**-Ron Knaub, Niagara Falls; **2B**-Roger Adams, Oneonta; **3B**-Tom Bianco, Newark; **SS**-Terry Collins, Niagara Falls; **OF**-Jack Maloof, Auburn; Tom O'Connor, Oneonta; James Johnson, Niagara Falls; Tony Scott, Jamestown; **C**-John Hasbrouck, Auburn; Terry Mappin, Batavia; **Util**-Mike Cubbage, Geneva; **P**-George Whileyman, Niagara Falls; Joseph Blake, Oneonta; Stephen Foran, Williamsport; Bill Sheets, Oneonta; David Allen, Auburn; **Manager**-George Case, Oneonta.

BA: Jack Maloof, Auburn, .402
Runs: Jack Maloof, Auburn, 57
Hits: Jack Maloof, Auburn, 103
RBIs: Mike Poepping, Auburn, 57

HRs: Mike Poepping, Auburn, 18
Wins: Stephen Foran, Williamsport, 10
SOs: Stephen Foran, Williamsport, 138
ERA: Stan Thomas, Geneva, 1.63

A Northern League
President: Arthur O. White

Standings	W	L	Pct.	GB	Attend.	Manager
St. Cloud Rox (9)	42	28	.600	—	17,071	Ken Staples
Aberdeen Pheasants (1)	35	36	.493	7½	17,467	Ken Rowe
Sioux Falls Packers (15)	34	37	.479	8½	21,677	Dave Pavlesic
Watertown Expos (18)	30	40	.429	12	8,825	Bob Oldis

Playoffs: None.

BA: Bob Bailor, Aberdeen, .340
Runs: Bob Bailor, Aberdeen, 71
Hits: Bob Bailor, Aberdeen, 91
RBIs: Dennis Silvey, Aberdeen, 71

HRs: Dennis Silvey, Aberdeen, 15
Wins: John Moncler, St. Cloud, 11
SOs: Ken Hansen, Sioux Falls, 135
ERA: Ken Hansen, Sioux Falls, 1.76

A Northwest League
President: John Carbray

North Standings	W	L	Pct.	GB	Attend.	Manager
Tri-City Padres (23)	50	30	.625	—	32,648	Cliff Ditto
Walla Walla Phillies (20)	47	32	.595	2½	32,195	Garry Powel
Lewiston Broncs (x)	28	51	.354	21½	17,121	Jim Brideweser

South Standings	W	L	Pct.	GB	Attend.	Manager
Bend Rainbows (3)	42	36	.538	—	22,049	Edward Cecil
Coos Bay-North Bend A's (11)	36	42	.462	6	11,701	Jim Reinebold
Medford Dodgers (17)	34	46	.425	9	12,930	Bill Berrier

Playoffs: None.

All-Star Team: **1B**-Tom Kostolsky, Medford; **2B**-Kurt Russell, Bend; **3B**-Marc Rhea, Tri-City; **SS**-Victor Diaz, Lewiston; **OF**-Dane Iorg, Walla Walla; Allan Wise, Bend; John Scott, Tri-City; **C**-John Dusenbury, Walla Walla; **P**-John Franklin, Tri-City; Bob Wolf, Coos Bay-North Bend; **Manager**-Cliff Ditto, Tri-City.

BA: Dane Iorg, Walla Walla, .367
Runs: James Hogan, Bend, 74
Hits: John Scott, Tri-City, 109
RBIs: Robert Davis, Tri-City, 83

HRs: Robert Davis, Tri-City, 14
Terry Thompson, Bend, 14
Wins: Bob Wolf, Coos Bay-North Bend, 13
SOs: John Franklin, Tri-City, 134
ERA: Jerry Lewis, Bend, 2.69

A Western Carolinas League
President: John H. Moss

Standings	W	L	Pct.	GB	Attend.	Manager
Greenwood Braves***(13)	85	38	.691	—	45,926	Clint Courtney
Spartanburg Phillies (20)	78	47	.624	8	46,277	Bob Wellman
Greenville Red Sox (2)	62	63	.496	24	41,402	Rac Slider
Anderson Senators (12)	55	66	.455	29	50,412	Frank Gable/Bill Haywood
Sumter Astros (16)	47	80	.370	40	33,706	Jackie Brandt
Monroe Pirates (21)	44	77	.364	40	11,587	Tom Saffell

Playoffs: None.

All-Star Team: **1B**-Bob Jones, Anderson; **2B**-William McMonigle, Spartanburg; **3B**-Blas Santana, Spartanburg; Rod Gilbreath, Greenwood; **SS**-Stu Cann, Greenwood; **OF**-Lloyd Hutchinson, Spartanburg; Rowland Office, Greenwood; Greg Foreman, Greenwood; **C**-Dave Criscione, Anderson; **P**-Sam Phillips, Greenville; Michael Kemp, Anderson; **Manager**-Bob Wellman, Spartanburg.

BA: Steve Gardner, Sumter, .343
Runs: Manuel "Chico" Ruiz, Greenwood, 104
Hits: William McMonigle, Spartanburg, 157
RBIs: Blas Santana, Spartanburg, 93

HRs: Dave Criscione, Anderson, 25
Lloyd Hutchinson, Spartanburg, 25
Wins: Michael Kemp, Anderson, 12
Erskine Thomason, Spartanburg, 12
SOs: Jim Streleski, Sumter, 132
ERA: Michael Martin, Spartanburg, 2.92

R Appalachian League
President: Chauncey De Vault

North Standings	W	L	Pct.	GB	Attend.	Manager
Bluefield Orioles (1)	42	27	.609	—	19,137	Jim Schaeffer
Pulaski Phillies (20)	36	32	.529	5½	18,123	Harry Lloyd
Wytheville Braves (13)	35	34	.507	7	15,036	Paul Snyder
Covington Astros (16)	33	35	.485	8½	25,105	Billy Smith

South Standings	W	L	Pct.	GB	Attend.	Manager
Kingsport Royals (7)	38	30	.559	—	24,538	Owen Friend
Marion Mets (19)	33	35	.485	5	10,545	Chuck Hiller
Bristol Tigers (6)	31	35	.470	6	14,510	Joe Lewis
Johnson City Yankees (10)	24	44	.353	14	21,227	Jerry Walker

Playoffs: None.

All-Star Team: **1B**-Gary Szakacs, Pulaski; **2B**-Steve Bissett, Pulaski; **3B**-Alvin Moore, Wytheville; **SS**-Tom Veryzer, Bristol; **OF**-Terry Whitfield, Johnson City; Art Gardner, Covington; Gil Flores, Bluefield; Charles Smith, Kingsport; **C**-Edward Jordan, Bluefield; **P**-Greg Pavlick, Marion; Paul Siebert, Covington; **Manager**-Jim Schaeffer, Bluefield.

BA: Steve Bissett, Pulaski, .365
Runs: Roger Williams, Wytheville, 47
Hits: Roger Williams, Wytheville, 82
RBIs: Terry Whitfield, Johnson City, 43
HRs: Terry Whitfield, Johnson City, 10

Wins: Greg Pavlick, Marion, 8
Blake Green, Covington, 8
Larry Hendrickson, Wytheville, 8
SOs: Steve Patterson, Bluefield, 112
ERA: Bob Sekel, Bluefield, 1.54

R Gulf Coast League
President: George MacDonald, Sr.

Standings	W	L	Pct.	GB	Manager
Royals (7)	40	13	.755	—	Buzzy Keller
White Sox (4)	30	22	.577	9½	Joe Jones
Indians (5)	28	24	.538	11½	Len Johnston
Reds (15)	23	29	.442	16½	Ron Plaza
Twins (9)	22	30	.423	17½	Fred Waters
Pirates (21)	20	32	.385	19½	Ed Napoleon
Cardinals (22)	20	33	.377	20	Tom Burgess

Games played at Sarasota and Bradenton, Florida.
Total Attendance: 10,818.

Playoffs: None.

National League All-Star Team: **1B**-Monte Bolinger, Cardinals; **2B**-Fausto Sosa, Pirates; **3B**-Bob Borowicz, Reds; **SS**-Gordon Reynolds, Pirates; **OF**-Mark Melanson, Reds; Omar Moreno, Pirates; Jerry Mumphrey, Cardinals; **C**-Juan Lebron, Pirates; Bill Pinkham, Reds; **Util**-Oscar Lewis, Reds; **P**-Art Cover, Reds; Steve Hagen, Pirates; **Manager**-Ron Plaza, Reds.
American League All-Star Team: **1B**-Jim Norris, Indians; **2B**-Mike Buskey, White Sox; **3B**-Ricky Boone, Royals; **SS**-Eric Soderholm, Twins; **OF**-Mark Burris, Twins; Fred Norton, White Sox; Gary Rahe, Royals; **C**-James Johnson, Indians; Ron Washington, Royals; **Util**-Bobby Bridges, White Sox; **P**-Mike Byrne, White Sox; Dennis Queen, Indians; **Manager**-Len Johnston, Indians.

BA: Jim Norris, Indians, .382
Runs: Jim Norris, Indians, 34
Hits: Jim Norris, Indians, 63
RBIs: Dave Revering, Reds, 33

HRs: Dave Revering, Reds, 8
Wins: Bob Gipson, Royals, 7
SOs: Hector Artiles, Reds, 64
ERA: Paul Sands, White Sox, 1.89

R Pioneer League
President: Claude Engberg

Standings	W	L	Pct.	GB	Attend.	Manager
Great Falls Giants (24)	45	25	.643	—	33,230	Dick Wilson
Billings Mustangs (7)	43	27	.614	2	27,017	Gary Blaylock
Idaho Falls Angels (3)	36	34	.514	9	44,899	Bob Clear
Magic Valley Cowboys (x).	36	34	.514	9	26,718	Art Mazmanian
Caldwell Cubs (14).............	28	42	.400	17	13,229	Sparky Davis
Ogden Dodgers (17)	22	48	.314	23	26,335	Buddy Hollowell

Playoffs: None.

All-Star Team: **1B**-Thad Philyaw, Ogden; **2B**-Scott Wolfe, Great Falls; **3B**-Bill Adkison, Great Falls; **SS**-George Brett, Billings; **OF**-John Balaz, Idaho Falls; Dan DeMichele, Caldwell; Steve Stroughter, Great Falls; **C**-Craig Perkins, Billings; Dominic Gaudioso, Magic Valley; **P**-Rex Hudson, Ogden; Frank Reyes, Great Falls; **Manager**-Dick Wilson, Great Falls.

BA: Steve Stroughter, Great Falls, .351
Runs: Steve Staggs, Billings, 72
Hits: David Landress, Billings, 80
RBIs: John Balaz, Idaho Falls, 51
HRs: John Balaz, Idaho Falls, 14

Wins: Frank Reyes, Great Falls. 9
Greg Thayer, Great Falls, 9
SOs: Rex Hudson, Ogden, 110
ERA: James Officer, Idaho Falls, 1.89

1971 Interleague Post Season Play

World Series
Pittsburgh (National) 4 games, Baltimore (American) 3

Junior World Series
Rochester (International) 4 games, Denver (American Association) 3
Total Attendance: 58,838

Dixie Association Championship
Charlotte (Southern) 3 games, Arkansas (Texas) 0

1971 Major League Farm Syatems

American League
1 Baltimore (6): Rochester, Dallas-Ft. Worth, Stockton, Miami, Aberdeen, Bluefield.
2 Boston (6): Louisville, Pawtucket, Winston-Salem, Winter Haven, Williamsport, Greenville.
3 California (5): Salt Lake City, Shreveport, Quad Cities, Bend, Idaho Falls.
4 Chicago (4): Tucson, Asheville, Appleton, Gulf Coast.
5 Cleveland (5): Wichita, Jacksonville, Reno, Sumter, Gulf Coast.
6 Detroit (7): Toledo, Montgomery, Rocky Mount, Lakeland, Clinton, Batavia, Bristol.
7 Kansas City (6): Omaha, San Jose, Waterloo, Kingsport, Elmira, Gulf Coast.
8 Milwaukee (3): Evansville, Danville, Newark.
9 Minnesota (8): Portland, Charlotte, Lynchburg, Orlando, Wisconsin Rapids, Auburn, St. Cloud, Gulf Coast.
10 New York (6): Syracuse, Manchester, Kinston, Ft. Lauderdale, Oneonta, Johnson City.
11 Oakland (4): Iowa, Birmingham, Burlington (IA), Coos Bay-North Bend.
12 Washington (5): Denver, Pittsfield, Burlington (NC), Geneva, Anderson.

National League
13 Atlanta (4): Richmond, Savannah, Greenwood, Wytheville.
14 Chicago (4): Tacoma, San Antonio, Quincy, Caldwell.
15 Cincinnati (5): Indianapolis, Trois Rivieres, Tampa, Sioux Falls, Gulf Coast.
16 Houston (5): Oklahoma City, Columbus, Cocoa, Sumter, Covington.
17 Los Angeles (6): Spokane, Albuquerque, Bakersfield, Daytona Beach, Medford, Ogden.
18 Montreal (5): Winnipeg, Quebec, West Palm Beach, Jamestown, Watertown.
19 New York (5): Tidewater, Memphis, Visalia, Pompano Beach, Marion.
20 Philadelphia (6): Eugene, Reading, Peninsula, Walla Walla, Spartanburg, Pulaski.
21 Pittsburgh (6): Charleston, Waterbury, Salem, Niagara Falls, Monroe, Gulf Coast.
22 St. Louis (6): Tulsa, Arkansas, Modesto, St. Petersburg, Cedar Rapids, Gulf Coast.
23 San Diego (3): Hawaii, Lodi, Tri-City.
24 San Francisco (5): Phoenix, Amarillo, Fresno, Decatur, Great Falls.

Co-op (x): Raleigh-Durham, Key West, Lewiston, Magic Valley.

1971 No-Hitters

Date	Pitcher	Team	League	Opponent	Score
3-24	Francisco Maytorena/Hector Diaz/ Nicolas Garcia	MC Tigres	Mexican	Veracruz	3-0 (P, 7)
4-8	Enrique Icedo/Jose Leyva/ Nicolas Garcia	MC Tigres	Mexican	Poza Rica	3-0 (7)
4-25	Ray O'Neill	Lynchburg	Carolina	Peninsula	7-0 (7)
5-4	Sid Monge	Quad Cities	Midwest	Cedar Rapids	6-0
5-4	Randal Fairbanks	Daytona Beach	Florida State	St. Petersburg	4-1 (7)
5-10	Michael Everett	Waterbury	Eastern	Elmira	5-0 (7)
5-16	Enrique Pacheco	Ebano	Mexican Center	Leon	6-0
5-27	Mickey Pless	Trois Rivieres	Eastern	Pittsfield	2-0 (7)
5-28	Greg Arnold	Rochester	International	Charleston	6-0 (7)
5-29	Jim Kern	Reno	California	San Jose	2-0
5-30	Bill Travers	Danville	Midwest	Quad Cities	16-1
6-3	Ken Holtzman	Chicago	National	Cincinnati	1-0
6-4	Antonio Gallardo	Monterrey	Mexican Center	Ciudad Mante	5-1 (7)
6-5	Fred Norman	Tulsa	American Assoc.	Indianapolis	4-0
6-9	Alejo Ahumada	Tampico	Mexican	Poza Rica	4-0 (7)
6-12	Dennis Yard	Danville	Midwest	Quincy	3-0 (7)
6-14	John Jackson	Trois Rivieres	Eastern	Quebec City	3-0 (7)
6-18	Mike Ruddell	Trois Rivieres	Eastern	Pawtucket	1-0 (11)
6-23	Rick Wise	Philadelphia	National	Cincinnati	4-0
6-25	Tommy Moore	Memphis	Texas	Arkansas	4-0 (7)
7-8	Fred Arroyo	Lakeland	Florida State	W. Palm Beach	5-0 (P, 7)
7-9	Robert Kaiser	Jacksonville	Southern	Montgomery	3-0
7-10	Harold Clem	Asheville	Southern	Savannah	1-0 (7)
7-16	Tim Howard	Kingsport	Appalachian	Johnson City	5-0 (7)
7-26	Pat McKean	Wytheville	Appalachian	Bristol	1-0 (7)
7-30	Mike Ruddell/ Steve Blateric	Trois Rivieres	Eastern	Elmira	3-0 (7)
8-1	Sergio Garcia	Reynosa	Mexican	Saltillo	0-1 (10)
8-1	Danny Fife	Rocky Mount	Carolina	Lynchburg	2-1 (7)
8-3	Richard Burgoon	Pirates	Gulf Coast	Indians	2-0
8-4	John Gaylord	Billings	Pioneer	Magic Valley	6-0
8-4	Tommy Walker	Dallas-Ft. Worth	Texas	Albuquerque	1-0 (15)
8-11	Bert Raschke	Oneonta	New York-Penn.	Newark	5-0 (7)
8-12	Raymond Brown	Billings	Pioneer	Idaho Falls	10-0
8-14	Bob Gibson	St. Louis	National	Pittsburgh	11-0
8-18	Frank Schuster/ Terry Bowman	Twins	Gulf Coast	Indians	7-1
8-19	Rich Hand	Wichita	American Assoc.	Tulsa	3-0
8-19	Marc Bombard	Reds	Gulf Coast	Twins	2-0 (7)
8-22	Leslie Scott	Amarillo	Texas	Dallas-Ft. Worth	5-0 (7)
8-24	Gerald Ginter	Geneva	New York-Penn.	Niagara Falls	3-0 (7)
8-26	Dave Goltz	Lynchburg	Carolina	Burlington	5-0 (7)
8-28	Mike Wallace	Reading	Eastern	Manchester	2-0 (7)
8-29	Pat Darcy	Columbus	Southern	Charlotte	2-0
8-30	John Franklin	Tri-City	Northwest	Medford	2-0 (7)
8-31	Mike Pazik	Syracuse	International	Rochester	5-0
9-5	Daniel Evans	Columbus	Southern	Jacksonville	3-0

Number in parentheses indicates innings if other than nine; "P" indicates perfect game.

THIS DATE IN MINOR LEAGUE HISTORY

March 11, 1971, Clyde Barfoot, 79, pitcher with the St. Louis Cardinals in 1922-23 and Detroit in 1926, died in Highland Park, California. Barfoot pitched for many years in the high minors, winning 26 games for Vernon, Pacific Coast League, in 1925.

April 19, 1971, Sam C. Smith, Jr., 50, president of the Alabama-Florida League from 1954 through 1958, the South Atlantic League from 1959 through 1963 and the Southern League from 1964 until this date, died in Knoxville, Tennessee.

July 17, 1971, Monty Montgomery, Elmira, Eastern League, shut out Pawtucket 4-0, allowing only three hits - all by Cecil Cooper.

August 4, 1971, Righthander Tommy Walker, Dallas-Fort Worth, Texas League,

pitched a 15-inning, 1-0 no-hit victory over Albuquerque. Walker walked just four batters and faced only two over the minimum of 45. The hurler's feat was the 97th, and longest, no-hitter in the 83-year history of the Texas League.

August 13, 1971, Clarence L. "Brick" Laws, 69, president of the Oakland and Vancouver clubs of the Pacific Coast League from 1944 through 1956, died in Monterrey, California.

August 15, 1971, Catcher Steve Turigliatto, Dallas-Ft. Worth, Texas League, hit his first homer of the season, but stumbled and fell on his left arm while running the bases and suffered a broken elbow.

1972

American League
President: Joseph E. Cronin

East Standings	W	L	Pct.	GB	Attend.	Manager
Detroit Tigers	86	70	.551	—	1,892,386	Billy Martin
Boston Red Sox	85	70	.548	½	1,441,718	Eddie Kasko
Baltimore Orioles	80	74	.519	5	899,950	Earl Weaver
New York Yankees	79	76	.510	6½	966,328	Ralph Houk
Cleveland Indians	72	84	.462	14	626,354	Ken Aspromonte
Milwaukee Brewers	65	91	.417	21	600,440	Dave Bristol/ Roy McMillan/Del Crandall

West Standings	W	L	Pct.	GB	Attend.	Manager
Oakland Athletics	93	62	.600	—	921,323	Dick Williams
Chicago White Sox	87	67	.565	5½	1,177,318	Chuck Tanner
Minnesota Twins	77	77	.500	15½	797,901	Bill Rigney/Frank Quilici
Kansas City Royals	76	78	.494	16½	707,656	Bob Lemon
California Angels	75	80	.484	18	744,190	Del Rice
Texas Rangers	54	100	.351	38½	662,974	Ted Williams

Playoffs: Oakland 3 games, Detroit 2.

BA: Rod Carew, Minnesota, .318
Runs: Bobby Murcer, New York, 102
Hits: Joe Rudi, Oakland, 181
RBIs: Dick Allen, Chicago, 113
HRs: Dick Allen, Chicago, 37

Wins: Wilbur Wood, Chicago, 24
Gaylord Perry, Cleveland, 24
SOs: Nolan Ryan, California, 329
ERA: Luis Tiant, Boston, 1.91
Pct: Catfish Hunter, Oakland, .750, 21-7
Saves: Sparky Lyle, New York, 35

National League
President: Charles S. Feeney

East Standings	W	L	Pct.	GB	Attend.	Manager
Pittsburgh Pirates	96	59	.619	—	1,427,460	Bill Virdon
Chicago Cubs	85	70	.548	11	1,299,163	Leo Durocher/ Whitey Lockman
New York Mets	83	73	.532	13½	2,134,185	Yogi Berra
St. Louis Cardinals	75	81	.481	21½	1,196,894	Red Schoendienst
Montreal Expos	70	86	.449	26½	1,142,145	Gene Mauch
Philadelphia Phillies	59	97	.378	37½	1,343,329	Frank Lucchesi/Paul Owens

West Standings	W	L	Pct.	GB	Attend.	Manager
Cincinnati Reds	95	59	.617	—	1,611,459	Sparky Anderson
Houston Astros	84	69	.549	10½	1,469,247	Harry Walker/ Francis "Salty" Parker/ Leo Durocher
Los Angeles Dodgers	85	70	.548	10½	1,860,858	Walter Alston
Atlanta Braves	70	84	.445	25	752,973	Luman Harris/Eddie Mathews
San Francisco Giants	69	86	.445	26½	647,744	Charlie Fox
San Diego Padres	58	95	.379	36½	644,273	Preston Gomez/Don Zimmer

Playoff: Cincinnati 3 games, Pittsburgh 2.

BA: Billy Williams, Chicago, .333
Runs: Joe Morgan, Cincinnati, 122
Hits: Pete Rose, Cincinnati, 198
RBIs: Johnny Bench, Cincinnati, 125
HRs: Johnny Bench, Cincinnati, 40

Wins: Steve Carlton, Philadelphia, 27
SOs: Steve Carlton, Philadelphia, 310
ERA: Steve Carlton, Philadelphia, 1.97
Pct: Gary Nolan, Cincinnati, .750, 15-5
Saves: Clay Carroll, Cincinnati, 37

AAA American Association
President: Joe Ryan

East Standings	W	L	Pct.	GB	Attend.	Manager
Evansville Triplets (8)	83	57	.593	—	147,807	Del Crandall/Mike Roarke
Omaha Royals (7)	71	69	.507	12	180,067	Jack McKeon
Iowa Oaks (11)	62	78	.443	21	89,477	Sherman Lollar
Indianapolis Indians (15)	61	79	.436	22	117,415	Vern Rapp

West Standings	W	L	Pct.	GB	Attend.	Manager
Wichita Aeros (14)	87	53	.621	—	276,451	Jim Marshall
Tulsa Oilers (22)	78	62	.557	9	190,080	Jack Krol
Denver Bears (12)	61	79	.436	26	128,568	Del Wilber
Oklahoma City 89ers (16)	57	83	.407	30	245,009	Tony Pacheco

Playoff: Evansville 3 games, Wichita 0.

All-Star Team: 1B-Bob Hansen, Evansville; 2B-Jim Wohlford, Omaha; 3B-Ken Reitz, Tulsa; SS-Dave Rosello, Wichita; OF-Gene Locklear, Indianapolis; Bob Coluccio, Evansville; Ed Armbrister, Indianapolis; Cleo James, Wichita; C-Skip Jutze, Tulsa; P-Lloyd Gladden, Evansville; Mike Jackson, Omaha; MVP-Patrick Bourque, Wichita; **Pitcher of the Year**-Lloyd Gladden, Evansville; **Manager** -Jim Marshall, Wichita.

BA: Gene Locklear, Indianapolis, .325
Runs: Bob Coluccio, Evansville, 79
Hits: Wilbur Howard, Evansville, 155
RBIs: Roe Skidmore, Indianapolis, 89

HRs: Robert Hansen, Evansville, 25
Wins: Lloyd Gladden, Evansville, 15
SOs: Steve Busby, Omaha, 221
ERA: Joe Decker, Wichita, 2.26

AAA International League
President: George H. Sisler, Jr.

Standings	W	L	Pct.	GB	Attend.	Manager
Louisville Colonels (2)	81	63	.563	—	116,328	Darrell Johnson
Charleston Charlies (21)	80	64	.556	1	109,522	John "Red" Davis
Tidewater Tides (19)	78	65	.545	2½	104,275	Hank Bauer
Rochester Red Wings (1)	76	68	.528	5	296,864	Joe Altobelli
Toledo Mud Hens (6)	75	69	.521	6	100,171	John Lipon
Richmond Braves (13)	65	78	.455	15½	84,231	Clyde King
Syracuse Chiefs (10)	64	80	.444	17	179,075	Frank Verdi
Peninsula Whips (18)	56	88	.389	25	48,681	Bill Adair

Playoffs: Louisville 2 games, Rochester 1; Tidewater 2 games, Charleston 1.
Finals: Tidewater 3 games, Louisville 2.

All-Star Team: 1B-Cecil Cooper, Louisville; 2B-Chuck Goggin, Charleston; 3B-Bobby Matchick, Rochester; SS-Mario Guerrero, Louisville; OF-Richie Zisk, Charleston; Al Bumbry, Rochester; Dwight Evans, Louisville; C-Vic Correll, Louisville; P-Gene Garber, Charleston; Craig Skok, Louisville; MVP-Dwight Evans, Louisville; **Pitcher of the Year**-Gene Garber, Charleston; **Manager**-Hank Bauer, Tidewater.

BA: Al Bumbry, Rochester, .345
Runs: Pepe Mangual, Peninsula, 91
Hits: Cecil Cooper, Louisville, 162
RBIs: Dwight Evans, Louisville, 95

HRs: Richie Zisk, Charleston, 26
Wins: Craig Skok, Louisville, 15
SOs: Jim McKee, Charleston, 159
ERA: Gene Garber, Charleston, 2.26

AAA Mexican League
President: Antonio Ramirez Muro

North Standings	W	L	Pct.	GB	Attend.	Manager
Saltillo Saraperos	89	51	.636	—	146,179	Tomas Herrera
Tampico Stevedores	86	51	.628	1½	303,773	Pedro Gonzalez
Jalisco Charros	77	60	.562	10½	138,828	Ben Reyes/Ossie Alvarez
Sabinas Piratas	62	76	.449	26	114,348	Vinicio Garcia
Reynosa Bravos	62	77	.446	26½	98,229	Ron Camacho/Jorge Fitch
Union Laguna Algodoneros	56	84	.400	33	165,400	Minnie Minoso/Jose Guerrero
Monterrey Sultanes	53	82	.393	33½	142,964	Manuel Magallon/ Rodolfo Alvarado

South Standings	W	L	Pct.	GB	Attend.	Manager
Cordoba Cafeteros	72	61	.541	—	217,604	Mario Pelaez
Mexico City Tigres	73	65	.529	1½	282,619	Jose Luis Garcia/ David Garcia
Puebla Pericos	72	65	.526	2	171,075	Miguel Sotelo/Pedro Ramos
Yucatan Leones	72	66	.522	2½	152,741	Enrique Izquierdo
Mexico City Diablos Rojos	69	71	.493	6½	349,684	Ernesto Garcia/ Wilfredo Calvino
Poza Rica Petroleros	65	70	.481	8	134,215	Moises Camacho
Veracruz Aguila	55	84	.396	20	66,343	Alberto Osorio/ Ben Valenzuela/Mario Ariosa

Playoff: Cordoba 4 games, Saltillo 2.

All-Star Team: 1B-Hector Espino, Tampico; 2B-Gabriel Lugo, Saltillo; 3B-Humberto Garcia, Saltillo; SS-Guadalupe Chavez, Saltillo; OF-Donald Anderson, Jalisco; Marcelo Juarez, Saltillo; Elvio Jimenez, Reynosa; C-Gregorio Luque, Saltillo; Hector Valle, Reynosa; P-Andres Ayon, Saltillo; Alfredo Meza, MC Tigres; **Manager**-Mario Pelaez, Cordoba.

BA: Donald Anderson, Jalisco, .362
Runs: Hector Espino, Tampico, 101
Hits: Roberto Pena, Tampico, 183
RBIs: Gabriel Lugo, Saltillo, 106

HRs: Hector Espino, Tampico, 37
Wins: Andres Ayon, Saltillo, 22
SOs: Alvin Martin, Jalisco, 166
ERA: Alfredo Meza, MC Tigres, 1.83

AAA Pacific Coast League
President: William B. McKechnie, Jr.

East Standings	W	L	Pct.	GB	Attend.	Manager
Albuquerque Dukes (17)	92	56	.622	—	182,044	Tom Lasorda
Phoenix Giants (24)	81	67	.547	11	109,542	Jim Davenport
Salt Lake City Angels (3)	80	68	.541	12	191,577	Les Moss
Tucson Toros (4)	60	88	.405	32	136,050	Larry Sherry

West Standings	W	L	Pct.	GB	Attend.	Manager
Eugene Emeralds (20)	79	69	.534	—	168,094	Andy Seminick
Hawaii Islanders (23)	74	74	.500	5	305,878	Rocky Bridges
Tacoma Twins (9)	65	83	.439	14	180,209	Harry Warner
Portland Beavers (5)	61	87	.412	18	91,907	Ray Hathaway/ Clay Bryant/Dan Carnevale

Playoff: Albuquerque 3 games, Eugene 1.
All-Star Team: 1B-Tom Paciorek, Albuquerque; 2B-Mike Schmidt, Eugene; 3B-Ron Cey, Albuquerque; SS-Craig Robinson, Eugene; OF-Larry Hisle, Albuquerque; Jim Hicks, Hawaii; Gary Matthews, Phoenix; C-Bob Boone, Eugene; Util-Jim Hutto, Salt Lake City; P-Dick Lange, Salt Lake City; Doug Rau, Albuquerque; Aurelio Monteagudo, Hawaii; MVP-Tom Paciorek, Albuquerque; **Manager**-Andy Seminick, Eugene.

*Won first-half   **Won second-half   ***Won both halves
Numbers after nicknames indicate farm system.
Affiliation listed at end of each year.

518

BA: Von Joshua, Albuquerque, .337
Runs: Tom Paciorek, Albuquerque, 125
Hits: Tom Paciorek, Albuquerque, 186
RBIs: Doug Howard, Salt Lake City, 109

HRs: Tom Paciorek, Albuquerque, 27
Wins: Mike Wallace, Eugene, 16
SOs: Steve Luebber, Albuquerque, 199
ERA: Dick Lange, Salt Lake City, 2.97

AA Eastern League
President: Roy Jackson

American Standings	W	L	Pct.	GB	Attend.	Manager
West Haven Yankees (10) ..	84	56	.600	—	102,537	Bobby Cox
Pittsfield Senators (12)	66	73	.475	17½	47,199	Joe Klein
Pawtucket Red Sox (2)	61	79	.436	23	66,650	Don Lock
Elmira Pioneers (5)............	46	91	.336	36½	54,534	Len Johnston

National Standings	W	L	Pct.	GB	Attend.	Manager
Trois Rivieres Aigles (15) ..	76	60	.559	—	119,751	Jim Snyder
Sherbrooke Pirates (21)	77	63	.550	1	66,101	Steve Demeter
Quebec Carnavals (18)	75	64	.540	2½	148,818	Karl Kuehl
Reading Phillies (20)	70	69	.504	7½	65,874	Jim Bunning

Playoff: West Haven 3 games, Trois Rivieres 0.

All-Star Team: 1B-Dan Driessen, Trois Rivieres; **2B**-Thomas Silicato, Reading; **3B**-Fernando Gonzalez, Sherbrooke; **SS**-Larry Lintz, Quebec; **OF**-Charlie Spikes, West Haven; David Augustine, Sherbrooke; Ken Griffey, Trois Rivieres; **C**-Barry Foote, Quebec; **P**-Larry Gowell, West Haven; Will McEnaney, Trois Rivieres; **MVP**-Fernando Gonzalez, Sherbrooke; **Manager**-Karl Kuehl, Quebec.

BA: Fernando Gonzalez, Sherbrooke, .333
Runs: Ken Griffey, Trois Rivieres, 96
Hits: Fernando Gonzalez, Sherbrooke, 172
RBIs: Al Thompson, Pittsfield, 110

HRs: Al Thompson, Pittsfield, 31
Wins: Pete Hamm, Trois Rivieres, 17
SOs: Brad Meyring, Sherbrooke, 181
ERA: Pete Hamm, Trois Rivieres, 2.30

AA Southern League
President: Billy Hitchcock

East Standings	W	L	Pct.	GB	Attend.	Manager
Asheville Orioles (1)	81	58	.583	—	49,745	Cal Ripken, Sr.
Savannah Braves (13)..........	80	59	.576	1	78,147	Clint Courtney
Charlotte Hornets (9)..........	70	70	.500	11½	30,769	John Goryl
Jacksonville Suns (7)..........	64	75	.460	17	47,168	Billy Gardner

West Standings	W	L	Pct.	GB	Attend.	Manager
Montgomery Rebels (6)......	78	61	.561	—	56,249	Fred Hatfield
Knoxville White Sox (4).....	76	64	.543	2½	67,942	Joe Sparks
Columbus Astros (16).........	59	80	.424	19	73,413	Jackie Brandt
Birmingham A's (11)..........	49	90	.353	29	30,841	Phil Cavarretta

Playoff: Montgomery 3 games, Asheville 0.

All-Star Team: 1B-Jack Pierce, Savannah; **2B**-Manuel "Chico" Ruiz, Savannah; **3B**-Rod Gilbreath, Savannah; **SS**-Bucky Dent, Knoxville; **OF**-Mike Reinbach, Asheville; Royle Stillman, Asheville; Marvin Lane, Montgomery; Smokey Robinson, Montgomery; **C**-Gene Lamont, Montgomery; **Util**-Jerry Hairston, Knoxville; **P**-Danny Bootcheck, Montgomery; Bill Campbell, Charlotte; **Manager**-Joe Sparks, Knoxville.

BA: Mike Reinbach, Asheville, .346
Runs: Mike Reinbach, Asheville, 123
Hits: Mike Reinbach, Asheville, 169
RBIs: Mike Reinbach, Asheville, 109

HRs: Mike Reinbach, Asheville, 30
Wins: Paul Mitchell, Asheville, 16
SOs: Bill Campbell, Charlotte, 204
ERA: Danny Vossler, Charlotte, 2.11

AA Texas League
President: Bobby Bragan

East Standings	W	L	Pct.	GB	Attend.	Manager
Alexandria Aces (23)..........	84	56	.600	—	123,325	Duke Snider
Memphis Blues (19)	75	64	.540	8½	113,425	Johnny Antonelli
Arkansas Travelers (22)......	65	74	.468	18½	79,358	Fred Koenig
Shreveport Captains (3)......	64	76	.457	20	34,165	Norm Sherry

West Standings	W	L	Pct.	GB	Attend.	Manager
El Paso Dodgers (17).........	78	62	.557	—	108,158	Monty Basgall
Amarillo Giants (24)..........	71	68	.511	6½	65,560	Dennis Sommers
Midland Cubs (14).............	68	71	.489	9½	71,747	Al Spangler
San Antonio Brewers (8)....	53	87	.379	25	253,139	Mike Roarke/Al Widmar/ Jim Walton

Playoff: El Paso 3 games, Alexandria 0.

All-Star Team: 1B-Mike Ivie, Alexandria; **2B**-Terry Deremer, Memphis; **3B**-John Hilton, Alexandria; **SS**-Milt Ramirez, Arkansas; **OF**-John Grubb, Alexandria; Randy Elliott, Alexandria; Leon Brown, Amarillo; **C**-Terry McDermott, El Paso; Joe Nolan, Memphis; **P**-Dave Freisleben, Alexandria; Frank Riccelli, Amarillo; **MVP**-Randy Elliott, Alexandria; **Pitcher of the Year**-Dave Freisleben, Alexandria; **Manager**-Duke Snider, Alexandria.

BA: Randy Elliott, Alexandria, .335
Runs: Jerry Royster, El Paso, 89
Hits: Leon Brown, Amarillo, 169
RBIs: Randy Elliott, Alexandria, 85

HRs: Gorman Thomas, San Antonio, 26
Wins: Dave Freisleben, Alexandria, 17
SOs: Frank Riccelli, Amarillo, 183
ERA: Dave Freisleben, Alexandria, 2.33

A California League
President: Edward J. Mulligan

Standings	W	L	Pct.	GB	Attend.	Manager
Bakersfield Dodgers*(17)...	88	52	.629	—	53,228	Don LeJohn
Modesto Reds**(22)..........	76	63	.547	11½	57,754	Tom Burgess
San Jose Bees (7)...............	76	64	.543	12	77,581	Harry Malmberg

	W	L	Pct.	GB	Attend.	Manager
Fresno Giants (24)	74	64	.536	13	61,864	Frank Funk
Visalia Mets (19)	73	67	.521	15	43,213	Joe Frazier
Lodi Orions (1)	67	73	.479	21	21,532	Jim Schaffer
Stockton Ports (3)	52	85	.380	34½	22,125	Mike Stubbins
Reno Silver Sox (5)	50	88	.362	37	22,228	Lou Klimchock

Playoff: Modesto 2 games, Bakersfield 0.

All-Star Team: 1B-Skip James, Fresno; **2B**-Bobby Randall, Bakersfield; **3B**-Glenn Monroe, Reno; **SS**-Bob Bailor, Lodi; Sergio Ferrer, Bakersfield; **OF**-Rex Goodson, San Jose; Duane Kuiper, Reno; **C**-Steve Patchin, Bakersfield; **Util**-Duane Kuiper, Reno; **P**-Rick Nitz, Bakersfield; John D'Acquisto, Fresno; Steve Broege, Modesto; Taru Hamaura, Fresno; Jim Officer, Stockton; Cecil Reynolds, Visalia; **MVP**-Skip James, Fresno; **Manager**-Tom Burgess, Modesto.

BA: Glenn Monroe, Reno, .349
Runs: Skip James, Fresno, 111
Hits: Bobby Randall, Bakersfield, 184
RBIs: Skip James, Fresno, 123

HRs: Skip James, Fresno, 32
Wins: Rick Nitz, Bakersfield, 18
SOs: John D'Acquisto, Fresno, 245
ERA: Paul Pelz, San Jose, 2.36

A Carolina League
President: Wallace McKenna

Standings	W	L	Pct.	GB	Attend.	Manager
Salem Pirates**(21)	79	58	.577	—	43,910	Tim Murtaugh
Burlington Rangers*(12)....	77	61	.558	1½	18,222	Frank Gable
Kinston Eagles (10)	73	64	.533	6	31,346	Gene Hassell
Lynchburg Twins (9)..........	70	68	.507	9½	60,282	Kerby Farrell
Winston-Salem Red Sox (2)..	65	74	.468	15	31,156	Rac Slider
Rocky Mount Leafs (6).......	49	88	.358	30	21,242	Len Okrie

Playoff: Salem 2 games, Burlington 1.

All-Star Team: 1B-Ron Mitchell, Salem; **2B**-Mike Cubbage, Burlington; **3B**-Ron Cash, Rocky Mount; **SS**-Marion Prince, Kinston; **OF**-Dave Parker, Salem; Ed Ott, Salem; Mike Krizmanich, Kinston; **C**-Tom Smithson, Lynchburg; **P**-Richard Kemp, Burlington; Doug Bair, Salem; **MVP**-Dave Parker, Salem; **Manager**-Gene Hassell, Kinston.

BA: Dave Parker, Salem, .310
Runs: Dave Parker, Salem, 91
Hits: Dave Parker, Salem, 162
RBIs: Dave Parker, Salem, 101

HRs: Bob Gorinski, Lynchburg, 23
Wins: Jim Minshall, Salem, 16
SOs: Dave Pagan, Kinston, 192
ERA: Dave Pagan, Kinston, 2.53

A Florida State League
Presidents: George MacDonald, Sr., George MacDonald, Jr.

East Standings	W	L	Pct.	GB	Attend.	Manager
Miami Orioles (1)	73	57	.562	—	86,683	Woody Smith
Pompano Beach Mets (19) .	73	59	.553	1	33,507	Gordon MacKenzie
Ft. Lauderdale Yankees (10)..	66	66	.500	8	59,008	Pete Ward
West Palm Beach Expos (18)..	64	65	.496	8½	73,836	Lance Nichols
Cocoa Astros (16)...............	56	72	.438	16	16,385	Jim Williams
Key West Conchs (x)..........	55	76	.420	18½	18,228	Francisco "Pancho" Herrera

West Standings	W	L	Pct.	GB	Attend.	Manager
Daytona Beach Dodgers (17)..	80	52	.606	—	52,331	Stan Wasiak/Bob Shaw
Tampa Tarpons (15)	66	64	.508	13	102,979	Russ Nixon
St. Petersburg Cardinals (22)...	66	66	.500	14	131,063	Roy Majtyka
Orlando Twins (9)	63	68	.481	16½	50,332	Early Wynn
Lakeland Tigers (6)	61	69	.469	18	27,055	Stubby Overmire
Winter Haven Red Sox (2) .	61	70	.466	18½	7,412	John K. Butler

Playoffs: Miami 2 games, Tampa 1; Daytona Beach 2 games, Pompano Beach 0.
Finals: Miami 2 games, Daytona Beach 1.

All-Star Team: 1B-Jack Baker, Winter Haven; **2B**-Dan Beerbower, Miami; **3B**-Phil Mankowski, Lakeland; **SS**-Ivan DeJesus, Daytona Beach; **OF**-George Vazquez, Daytona Beach; Thad Philyaw, Daytona Beach; Jim Rice, Winter Haven; **C**-Kevin Pasley, Daytona Beach; **Util**-John Busco, Pompano Beach; Michael Potter, St. Petersburg; **P**-David Allen, Orlando; Orlando Pena, Miami; **MVP**-Michael Potter, St. Petersburg; **Manager**-Gordon MacKenzie, Pompano Beach.

BA: Thad Philyaw, Daytona Beach, .317
Runs: Jim Rice, Winter Haven, 80
Hits: Jim Rice, Winter Haven, 143
RBIs: Jack Baker, Winter Haven, 89
HRs: Jack Baker, Winter Haven, 27

Wins: Carlos Paz, Key West, 15
Orlando Pena, Miami, 15
SOs: Santo Alcala, Key West, 176
ERA: Dale Harrington, Miami, 1.51

A Mexican Center League
President: Antonio Ramirez Muro

Standings	W	L	Pct.	GB	Attend.	Manager
Ebano Reds*	43	22	.662	—	36,700	Armando Barajas
Aguascalientes Tigres**	43	23	.652	½	24,942	Ben Valenzuela
Monterrey Sultanes	36	26	.581	5½	3,400	Pajayro Narvaez
Durango Algodoneros	34	35	.493	11	32,932	Guillermo Frayde
Naranjos	23	46	.333	22	9,448	Fidel Alvarez
Zacatecas Tuzos	20	47	.299	24	13,818	Felipe Hernandez

Playoff: Aguascalientes 3 games, Ebano 2.

All-Star Team: 1B-Cruz Espinoza, Ebano; **2B**-Augustin Zamudio, Zacatecas; **3B**-Alfredo Zavala, Ebano; **SS**-Victor Escalante, Aguascalientes; **OF**-Victor Perez, Naranjos; Bernardo Martinez, Aguascalientes; Enrique Zamudio, Monterrey; **C**-Bartolo Mojica, Naranjos; Norberto Guillen, Aguascalientes; **P**-Humberto Valenzuela, Ebano; Gustavo Mackliz, Monterrey; **Manager**-Ben Valenzuela, Aguascalientes.

BA: Alfredo Zavala, Ebano, .391
Runs: Alfredo Zavala, Ebano, 57
    Trinidad Aguirre, Ebano, 57
Hits: Alfredo Zavala, Ebano, 92
RBIs: Manuel Parra, Zacatecas, 63

HRs: Manuel Parra, Zacatecas, 15
Wins: Gustavo Mackliz, Monterrey, 12
SOs: Gustavo Mackliz, Monterrey, 82
ERA: Humberto Valenzuela, Ebano, 3.18

A Midwest League
President: James Doster

North Standings	W	L	Pct.	GB	Attend.	Manager
Appleton Foxes**(4)	76	51	.598	—	72,851	Bert Thiel
Waterloo Royals (7)	72	53	.576	3	41,628	Steve Boros
Wisconsin Rapids Twins*(9) ..	70	56	.556	5½	53,639	Jay Ward
Cedar Rapids Cardinals (22)....	51	77	.398	24½	41,528	Gary Geiger
Clinton Pilots (6)	49	77	.389	26½	37,302	Jim Leyland

South Standings	W	L	Pct.	GB	Attend.	Manager
Danville Warriors***(8).....	73	52	.584	—	95,023	Joe Nossek
Quad Cities Angels (3)	69	59	.539	5½	67,108	Dick Kinaman
Burlington Bees (11)	65	63	.508	9½	46,496	Harry Bright
Quincy Cubs (14)..............	61	67	.477	13½	46,446	Dick LeMay
Decatur Commodores (24) .	48	79	.378	26	43,100	Jim McKnight

Playoff: Appleton 1 game, Wisconsin Rapids 0.
Finals: Danville 2 games, Appleton 0.

All-Star Team: 1B-James Cates, Clinton; **2B**-Duane Espy, Danville; **3B**-William Jackson, Waterloo; **SS**-Thomas Smith, Decatur; **OF**-Frankie George, Quad Cities; Ken Dempsey, Wisconsin Rapids; Charles Smith, Waterloo; **C**-Charles Moore, Danville; Michael Uremovich, Wisconsin Rapids; **P**-Carl Austerman, Danville; Fred Bruntrager, Clinton; **Manager**-Joe Nossek, Danville.

BA: Duane Espy, Danville, .340
Runs: Duane Espy, Danville, 85
Hits: Duane Espy, Danville, 160
RBIs: Lamar Johnson, Appleton, 89

HRs: Lamar Johnson, Appleton, 26
Wins: Carl Austerman, Danville, 16
SOs: Mark Littell, Waterloo, 199
ERA: Fred Bruntrager, Clinton, 1.67

A New York-Pennsylvania League
President: Vincent M. McNamara

Standings	W	L	Pct.	GB	Attend.	Manager
Niagara Falls Pirates (21) ...	48	22	.686	—	52,476	Chuck Cottier
Oneonta Yankees (10)	45	25	.643	3	32,429	George Case
Jamestown Falcons (18)	42	28	.600	6	14,398	Walt Hriniak
Auburn Phillies (20)	39	30	.565	8½	44,162	Nolan Campbell
Geneva Senators (12)..........	30	40	.429	18	15,108	Bill Haywood
Batavia Trojans (19)..........	29	40	.420	18½	44,324	Wilbur Huckle
Newark Co-Pilots (8)..........	23	46	.333	24½	14,151	Sandy Johnson
Williamsport Red Sox (2)...	22	47	.319	25½	19,038	Dick Berardino

Playoffs: None.

All-Star Team: 1B-Cannon Smith, Jamestown; **2B**-James Cooper, Oneonta; **3B**-Ronald DeFeo, Auburn; **SS**-Jimmy Sexton, Niagara Falls; **OF**-Kenneth Melvin, Niagara Falls; Omar Moreno, Niagara Falls; Terry Whitfield, Oneonta; **C**-Bill Nahorodny, Auburn; Ernest DiStasi, Batavia; **P**-Scott Larson, Oneonta; Tom Deidel, Newark; **Manager**-Chuck Cottier, Niagara Falls.

BA: Cannon Smith, Jamestown, .319
Runs: Terry Whitfield, Oneonta, 65
Hits: Felix Arce, Jamestown, 79
RBIs: Cannon Smith, Jamestown, 56
HRs: Cannon Smith, Jamestown, 14

Wins: David Fanning, Auburn, 9
    Scott Larson, Oneonta, 9
SOs: David Fanning, Auburn, 128
ERA: Robert Artemenko, Oneonta, 1.52
Pct: Robert Artemenko, Oneonta, .636, 7-4

A Northwest League
President: Bob Freitas

North Standings	W	L	Pct.	GB	Attend.	Manager
Lewiston Broncs (1)	54	26	.675	—	30,041	Bobby Malkmus
Spokane Indians (17)..........	42	36	.538	11	44,876	Bill Berrier
Seattle Rainiers (x)	30	50	.375	24	40,487	Ray Washburn

South Standings	W	L	Pct.	GB	Attend.	Manager
Walla Walla Rainbows#.....	41	39	.513	—	37,604	Jack Spring
Tri-City Padres (23)............	38	42	.475	3	36,919	Cliff Ditto
Coos Bay-North Bend A's (11)..	33	45	.423	7	10,220	Grover Resinger

#Walla Walla was a farm team of Hawaii, Pacific Coast League.

Playoff: Lewiston declared winner under league rules.

All-Star Team: 1B-Timothy Steele, Spokane; **2B**-Kim Andrew, Lewiston; **3B**-Dan Joost, Walla Walla; **SS**-Jim Van Wyck, Walla Walla; **OF**-Jim Buckner, Lewiston; Nathaniel Clayton, Lewiston; Jerry Turner, Tri-City; **C**-Michael Satterlee, Lewiston; **Util**-John Snider, Spokane; Craig Settles, Tri-City; **P**-Pat House, Lewiston; Don Standley, Spokane; **Manager**-Bobby Malkmus, Lewiston.

BA: Jerry Turner, Tri-City, .377
Runs: Jim Buckner, Lewiston, 74
Hits: Jim Buckner, Lewiston, 113
RBIs: Jim Buckner, Lewiston, 62

HRs: Jim Buckner, Lewiston, 17
Wins: Don Standley, Spokane, 10
SOs: David Paynter, Walla Walla, 150
ERA: Don Standley, Spokane, 2.33

A Western Carolinas League
President: John H. Moss

Standings	W	L	Pct.	GB	Attend.	Manager
Spartanburg Phillies*(20)...	89	43	.674	—	57,431	Bob Wellman
Greenville Rangers**(12)...	71	57	.555	16	11,481	Rich Donnelly
Greenwood Braves (13)......	70	61	.534	18½	26,027	Paul Snyder
Gastonia Pirates (21)	60	70	.462	28	44,740	Tom Saffell
Charlotte Twins (9)............	50	79	.388	37½	13,835	Bob Sadowski
Anderson Giants (24)..........	51	81	.386	38	29,409	Max Lanier

Playoff: Spartanburg 2 games, Greenville 1.

All-Star Team: 1B-Ken Caldwell, Greenville; **2B**-Toy McCord, Greenwood; **3B**-Alvin Moore, Greenwood; **SS**-Charles Bordes, Greenville; **OF**-Jerry Martin, Spartanburg; Robert Spinner, Greenville; Gary Boyce, Greenville; **C**-Richard Revta, Greenville; **P**-Don Kreke, Spartanburg; Charles Kniffin, Spartanburg; **Manager**-Rich Donnelly, Greenville.

BA: Charles Bordes, Greenville, .352
Runs: Steve Bissett, Spartanburg, 105
Hits: Jerry Martin, Spartanburg, 162
RBIs: Jerry Martin, Spartanburg, 112

HRs: Ken Caldwell, Greenville, 19
Wins: Don Kreke, Spartanburg, 15
SOs: Louis Lerner, Charlotte, 194
ERA: Charles Kniffin, Spartanburg, 2.11

R Appalachian League
President: Chauncey De Vault

Standings	W	L	Pct.	GB	Attend.	Manager
Bristol Tigers (6)	40	28	.588	—	14,663	Joe Lewis
Covington Astros (16)........	41	29	.586	—	21,260	Billy Smith
Kingsport Royals (7)	38	32	.543	3	35,261	Jay Hankins
Wytheville Braves (13).......	35	30	.538	3½	12,518	Eddie Haas
Bluefield Orioles (1)..........	36	32	.529	4	14,373	George Farson
Johnson City Cardinals (22)....	31	39	.443	10	20,312	Jerry Walker
Pulaski Phillies (20)..........	31	39	.443	10	17,779	Harry Lloyd
Marion Mets (19)................	22	45	.328	17½	7,592	Chuck Hiller

Playoffs: None.

All-Star Team: 1B-Gary Rahe, Kingsport; **2B**-Mike Markl, Covington; Blake Doyle, Bluefield; **3B**-Danny Meyer, Bristol; **SS**-John O'Rear, Bluefield; **OF**-Joe Zdeb, Kingsport; Art James, Bristol; Rocky Skolisky, Pulaski; **C**-Hal Workman, Wytheville; **P**-John Travis, Wytheville; Ken Clay, Johnson City; James Crawford, Covington; **Manager**-Jay Hankins, Kingsport.

BA: Danny Meyer, Bristol, .396
Runs: Joe Zdeb, Kingsport, 57
Hits: Danny Meyer, Bristol, 93
RBIs: Robert Wilson, Johnson City, 60

HRs: Robert Wilson, Johnson City, 16
    David Michalec, Wytheville, 16
Wins: John Travis, Wytheville, 9
SOs: James Crawford, Covington, 123
ERA: James Crawford, Covington, 1.59

R Florida East Coast League

Standings	W	L	Pct.	GB	Manager
Melbourne Reds (15)..........	44	15	.746	—	Dave Pavlesic
Melbourne Twins (9)..........	35	22	.614	8	Fred Waters
Cocoa Astros (16)............	26	30	.464	16½	Leo Posada
Cocoa Expos (18)	9	47	.161	33½	Pat Daugherty

Total Attendance: 966.

Playoffs: None.

BA: Dave Edwards, Twins, .313
Runs: Randy Bass, Twins, 47
Hits: Dave Covert, Reds, 62
RBIs: Randy Bass, Twins, 41
HRs: Randy Bass, Twins, 10

Wins: Kevin Cooney, Twins, 8
    Paul Howlend, Reds, 8
SOs: Gary Myers, Reds, 58
ERA: Forrest Clemmons, Reds, 1.86

R Gulf Coast League
Presidents: George MacDonald Sr., George MacDonald Jr.

Standings	W	L	Pct.	GB	Manager
Cubs (14)	41	22	.651	—	Walt Dixon
Royals (7)	41	22	.651	—	Buzzy Keller
Indians (5)...................	34	26	.567	5½	Pinky May
White Sox (4)...............	34	27	.557	6	Joe Jones
Cardinals (22)	27	32	.458	12	Bobby Dews
Red Birds (22)	23	35	.397	15½	Julio Gotay
Pirates (21)...................	21	39	.350	18½	Ed Napoleon
Reds (15).....................	21	39	.350	18½	Ron Plaza

Games played at Sarasota and Bradenton, Florida.
Total Attendance: 8,306.

Playoffs: None.

All-Star Team: 1B-Robert Polaski, Reds; Rafael Rodriguez, Cubs; **2B**-Steve Temple, Royals; David Embree, Reds; **3B**-Walter Barnes, Cubs; Gary Cleverly, Indians; **SS**-Bruce Beranek, Royals; Sal Butera, White Sox; **OF**-Jerry Mumphrey, Cardinals; Douglas Carvalho, Cubs; Cleo Kilpatrick, White Sox; **C**-Daniel Radison, Cardinals; **Util**-Gary Whaley, White Sox; **P**-Gerard Thomas, Pirates; Edward Joyce, Cardinals; Jeffrey Wehmeier, Cubs; Larry Hubbard, Royals; Michael Gonzalez, Pirates; Peter Dresser, Cubs; Curtis Karpinski, Indians; **Manager**-Walt Dixon, Cubs.

BA: Cleo Kilpatrick, White Sox, .329
Runs: Cleo Kilpatrick, White Sox, 46
Hits: Cleo Kilpatrick, White Sox, 77
RBIs: Cleo Kilpatrick, White Sox, 38
HRs: Cleo Kilpatrick, White Sox, 5

Wins: Donald Oxindine, Royals, 8
SOs: Larry Hubbard, Royals, 90
    Glenn Bryant, White Sox, 90
ERA: Larry Hubbard, Royals, 1.24

BA: Kenzie Davis, Billings, .342
Runs: Kenzie Davis, Billings, 66
Hits: Kenzie Davis, Billings, 92
RBIs: David Cripe, Billings, 43
    Cleo Smith, Ogden, 43
    Randolph Wilson, Idaho Falls, 43

HRs: Randolph Wilson, Idaho Falls, 11
Wins: Roy Branch, Billings, 9
SOs: Barry Bagley, Ogden, 110
ERA: Tom O'Donnell, Great Falls, 1.71

R Pioneer League
President: Claude Engberg

Standings	W	L	Pct.	GB	Attend.	Manager
Billings Mustangs (7)	50	22	.694	—	22,627	Gary Blaylock
Great Falls Giants (24)	36	34	.514	13	23,232	Dick Wilson
Ogden Dodgers (17)	29	41	.414	20	23,440	Gail Henley
Idaho Falls Angels (3)	27	45	.375	23	26,302	Bob Clear

Playoffs: None.

All-Star Team: 1B-Sheldon Mallory, Billings; **2B**-Thaddeus Tassone, Idaho Falls; **3B**-David Cripe, Billings; **SS**-Jamie Quirk, Billings; **OF**-Cleo Smith, Ogden; Kenzie Davis, Billings; David Collins, Idaho Falls; **C**-William Binder, Great Falls; Mike Roberts, Billings; **P**-Roy Branch, Billings; Steven O'Brien, Ogden; **Manager**-Gary Blaylock, Billings.

1972 Interleague Postseason Play

World Series
Oakland (American) 4 games, Cincinnati (National) 3

World Baseball Classic
Elimination Round
Albuquerque (Pacific Coast)	3-1
Tidewater (International)	3-1
Evansville (American Assoc.)	2-2
Caribbean All Stars#	1-3
Hawaii (Host Club)	1-3

#Won a one game playoff to qualify for the sudden death round.

Sudden Death Round
CARIBBEAN ALL STARS	3-0
Albuquerque (Pacific Coast)	0-1
Tidewater (International)	0-1
Evansville (American Assoc.)	0-1

1972 Farm Systems

American League

1 Baltimore (6): Rochester, Asheville, Lodi, Miami, Lewiston, Bluefield.
2 Boston (5): Louisville, Pawtucket, Winston-Salem, Winter Haven, Williamsport.
3 California (5): Salt Lake City, Shreveport, Stockton, Quad Cities, Idaho Falls.
4 Chicago (4): Tucson, Knoxville, Appleton, Gulf Coast.
5 Cleveland (4): Portland, Elmira, Reno, Gulf Coast.
6 Detroit (6): Toledo, Montgomery, Rocky Mount, Lakeland, Clinton, Bristol.
7 Kansas City (7): Omaha, Jacksonville, San Jose, Waterloo, Kingsport, Gulf Coast, Billings.
8 Milwaukee (4): Evansville, San Antonio, Danville, Newark.
9 Minnesota (7): Tacoma, Charlotte, Lynchburg, Orlando, Wisconsin Rapids, Port Charlotte, Florida East Coast.
10 New York (5): Syracuse, West Haven, Kinston, Ft. Lauderdale, Oneonta.
11 Oakland (4): Iowa, Birmingham, Burlington (IA), Coos Bay-North Bend.
12 Texas (5): Denver, Pittsfield, Burlington (NC), Greenville, Geneva.

National League

13 Atlanta (4): Richmond, Savannah, Greenwood, Wytheville.
14 Chicago (4): Wichita, Midland, Quincy, Gulf Coast.
15 Cincinnati (5): Indianapolis, Trois Rivieres, Tampa, Gulf Coast, Florida East Coast.
16 Houston (5): Oklahoma City, Columbus, Cocoa, Covington, Florida East Coast.
17 Los Angeles (6): Albuquerque, El Paso, Bakersfield, Daytona Beach, Spokane, Ogden.
18 Montreal (5): Peninsula, Quebec, West Palm Beach, Jamestown, Florida East Coast.
19 New York (6): Tidewater, Memphis, Visalia, Pompano Beach, Batavia, Marion.
20 Philadelphia (5): Eugene, Reading, Auburn, Spartanburg, Pulaski.
21 Pittsburgh (6): Charleston, Sherbrooke, Salem, Niagara Falls, Gastonia, Gulf Coast.
22 St. Louis (7): Tulsa, Arkansas, Modesto, St. Petersburg, Cedar Rapids, Johnson City, Gulf Coast.
23 San Diego (3): Hawaii, Alexandria, Tri-City.
24 San Francisco (6): Phoenix, Amarillo, Fresno, Decatur, Anderson, Great Falls.

Co-op (x): Key West, Seattle.

1972 No-Hitters

Date	Pitcher	Team	League	Opponent	Score
4-16	Burt Hooton	Chicago	National	Philadelphia	4-0
4-20	Daniel Baker	Greenville	W. Carolinas	Charlotte	7-0
4-22	Steve Paterson	Miami	Florida State	West Palm Beach	1-0 (10)
5-3	Larry Bracco	Clinton	Midwest	Waterloo	0-1 (7)
5-12	Ed Figueroa	Savannah	Southern	Jacksonville	1-0
5-13	Bob Forsch	Arkansas	Texas	Memphis	4-0 (7)
5-14	Blake Green	Cocoa	Florida State	Winter Haven	3-0
5-21	Jackie Stripling	Arkansas	Texas	Midland	3-1
5-22	Carlos Moreno	Monterrey	Mexican	MC Tigres	4-1
5-25	John Pangle	Charlotte	W. Carolinas	Greenwood	4-0
5-30	Jerry Bostic	Greenville	W. Carolinas	Charlotte	2-0 (7)
5-31	Doug Capilla	Decatur	Midwest	Appleton	1-0 (7)
6-4	Daniel Carey	Pompano Beach	Florida State	Cocoa	3-0 (6)
6-15	Wayne McCauley	Appleton	Midwest	Quincy	2-0 (7)
6-20	Marc Bomback	Winter Haven	Florida State	Orlando	1-0 (7)
6-21	John Morlan/				
	DeWayne Mason	Salem	Carolina	Kinston	1-2 (5)
6-25	Frank Schuster	Wisconsin Rapids	Midwest	Burlington	2-0 (7)
6-28	Mike Willis	Bluefield	Appalachian	Pulaski	4-0
6-30	Andres Ayon	Saltillo	Mexican	Monterrey	9-0 (P, 7)
6-30	Rich Hinton	Syracuse	International	Toledo	5-0 (7)
7-2	Mike McCammon	Greenwood	W. Carolinas	Spartanburg	5-0 (7)
7-12	Steve Ayers	Jamestown	New York-Penn.	Batavia	7-0 (7)
7-15	Dennis Leonard	Waterloo	Midwest	Quincy	3-0 (7)
7-15	Lorin Grow	Reds	Florida East Coast	Expos	2-0
7-16	Joe Niekro	Toledo	International	Tidewater	2-0 (P, 7)
7-17	Gary Smith	Miami	Florida State	Key West	2-0 (7)
7-19	Gerard Thomas	Pirates	Gulf Coast	Cubs	0-0 (P, 5)
7-21	Mike Heintz	Tampa	Florida State	Lakeland	0-1 (10)
7-30	Jim Hughes	Lynchburg	Carolina	Rocky Mount	3-0 (P, 7)
7-31	John Kuhnie	Bluefield	Appalachian	Johnson City	5-0 (P, 7)
8-2	Gary Trumbauer	Cedar Rapids	Midwest	Burlington	0-1
8-3	Jim Slaton	Evansville	American Assoc.	Wichita	5-0
8-3	Tom Deidel	Newark	New York-Penn.	Batavia	0-2 (5)
8-3	Gary Martin	Twins	Florida East Coast	Expos	2-0
8-5	Denis McSween	Quebec	Eastern	Pawtucket	4-0 (7)
8-6	Robert Babcock	Quebec	Eastern	Pawtucket	4-0
8-6	Tommy Moore	Tidewater	International	Rochester	2-0 (7)
8-8	Mike Redden	Pirates	Gulf Coast	Cardinals	4-0
8-10	David Moore/				
	Andre Rabouin	Reds	Florida East Coast	Expos	4-1
8-13	Eleno Cuen	Cocoa	Florida State	Orlando	2-0 (7)
8-16	Russ Parker	Anderson	W. Carolinas	Charlotte	4-2 (7)
8-18	James Wells	Twins	Florida East Coast	Expos	9-0 (7)
8-23	Tom Bruno	Waterloo	Midwest	Danville	2-0 (7)
8-25	Tom Murphy	Omaha	American Assoc.	Indianapolis	7-0
8-26	Tim Juran	Batavia	New York-Penn.	Niagara Falls	1-0 (7)
8-26	Robert Eldridge	Elmira	Eastern	Pawtucket	6-0
9-2	Milt Pappas	Chicago	National	San Diego	8-0
9-2	Oscar Zamora	Oklahoma City	American Assoc.	Denver	5-0 (P, 7)
10-2	Bill Stoneman	Montreal	National	New York	7-0

Number in parentheses indicates innings if other than nine; "P" indicates perfect game.

THIS DATE IN MINOR LEAGUE HISTORY

April 11, 1972, Charlotte, N.C., began the season with two minor league teams, one in the Southern League, the other in the Western Carolinas. The following year, the city would be without any minor league baseball.

April 26, 1972, Reading, Eastern League, despite being held to one hit in each of two consecutive games, managed to beat Quebec City both nights, 3-2 and 1-0, April 25 and 26.

April 27, 1972, Reading, Eastern League, committed 10 errors in losing 7-2 to Quebec City.

May 1, 1972, Wichita, American Association, lost to Denver 3-2 after having won 10 straight games.

May 8, 1972, Catcher Tom Harmon, Jacksonville, Southern League, had six hits in a 14-inning game.

May 9, 1972, Arturo Orozco hit two homers in one inning in the Mexico City Diablos Rojos' 21-3 Mexican League romp over Sabinas.

May 11, 1972, Von Joshua, Albuquerque, Pacific Coast League, hit a homer and a triple in one inning against Tacoma to account for five runs batted in.

May 30, 1972, Larry McDermitt, El Paso, Texas League, smashed three home runs and two singles for nine RBIs as his club beat Memphis 12-2.

June 3, 1972, Tom Paciorek, Ron Cey and Steve Huntz hit consecutive home runs for Albuquerque of the Pacific Coast League.

June 3, 1972, Gene Martin hit three homers in one game for Poza Rica, Mexican League.

June 9, 1972, Wayne McCauley, Appleton, Midwest League, struck out nine straight batters in a game with Waterloo, setting a loop mark. McCauley posted 20 strikeouts in the 12-inning contest, but dropped a 2-1 decision.

June 12, 1972, Outfielder John Rolisek, Oklahoma City, American Association, hit two homers in one inning versus Denver.

June 12, 1972, Mike Reinback, Asheville, Southern League, collected six hits in six tries and drove in nine runs to highlight a 17-1 victory over Columbus. Reinback's safeties included two homers (one a grand slam), a double and a triple.

June 15, 1972, Relief pitcher Pablo Torrealba, Savannah, Southern League, was suspended for the rest of the season and fined $250 for striking an umpire across the back with his bat in an outburst of anger during a game with Knoxville.

June 21, 1972, Omaha southpaw Mike Jackson set an American Association record by extending his consecutive scoreless innings pitched streak to 42 before two unearned runs broke the spell in a game with Evansville. The old mark of 41-2/3 frames was set by Frank Barnes of Omaha in June 1957.

June 24, 1972, Bernice Gera, 41, professional baseball's first woman umpire, resigned after working seven innings of a New York-Penn League doubleheader between Geneva and Auburn. Mrs. Gera had fought for six years to crash the gender barrier among umpiring professionals.

July 2, 1972, Sam Ashford of Shreveport, Texas League, had a 24-game hitting streak ended by San Antonio pitchers.

July 5, 1972, San Antonio's Dennis Yard surrendered a leadoff single, then retired the next 27 batters in a 1-0 Texas League win over Alexandria.

July 6, 1972, In the Gulf Coast League, the Pirates, after 11 consecutive defeats, won their first game of the season.

July 7, 1972, After being whitewashed for 41 consecutive innings, Veracruz, Mexican League, scored a run in a 3-1 loss to the Mexico City Tigres. The league mark of 42 innings without a run was set by Poza Rica in 1970.

July 10, 1972, Albuquerque's Charlie Hough relieved twice in one inning in a game with Tacoma. Hough was switched to right field after relieving in the eighth frame and retiring one batter, then was brought back to the mound later in the inning and retired the side with a strikeout.

July 13, 1972, Julio Navarro, winner of 11 consecutive games for the Mexico City Diablos Rojos, Mexican League, had his streak ended by Poza Rica with a 6-1 setback. The league record win streak of 14 in a row was set by Jesus "Choy" Moreno of Nuevo Laredo in 1953.

July 15, 1972, Geneva, New York-Pennsylvania League, buried Williamsport 24-0. The league record for the most lopsided shutout was 25-0, set by Hamilton over London in 1940.

July 16, 1972, Joe Niekro, sent down by the Detroit Tigers the previous day, hurled a seven-inning perfect game for Toledo, International League, in a 2-0 win over Tidewater.

July 16, 1972, Gil Passarello of Kinston set a Carolina League record with 11 assists at second base.

July 16, 1972, Outfielder Romel Canada, Saltillo, equalled a Mexican League record of 10 hits in a row before being stopped by Jalisco. He was only the sixth player in the circuit's history to have a 10-hit streak. Canada made 13 safeties in 15 trips in the four-game series with Jalisco.

July 17, 1972, In the New York-Pennsylvania League, Newark slaughtered Batavia 26-3. The Co-Pilots scored 13 times in the second frame and four Batavia hurlers uncorked 11 wild pitches.

July 18, 1972, Pittsfield, Eastern League, scored 11 runs in the first inning, then called it a night at the plate and coasted to an 11-0 victory over Quebec.

July 21, 1972, Lefty Mike Heintz, Tampa, Florida State League, pitched 9-2/3 innings of hitless ball against Lakeland but wound up losing a 1-0, one-hit decision in 10 frames.

July 21, 1972, Minnie Minoso, 49, hit his 12th homer of the season for Union Laguna of the Mexican League.

July 21, 1972, Taking advantage of a rookie catcher's inexperience, Savannah stole 10 bases for a new Southern League record during a 7-2 victory over Jacksonville.

July 26, 1972, Righthander Jim Bibby, Tulsa, American Association, fanned 16 and blanked Denver 9-0.

July 27, 1972, Wichita, American Association, scored 14 runs (one shy of the league's single inning record set in 1930 by St. Paul and tied in 1936 by Minneapolis) in the second frame and demolished Oklahoma City, 24-8.

July 28, 1972, Jamestown, New York-Pennsylvania League, hit six triples, three by Tony Hewitt, in a 9-8 loss to Oneonta.

July 29, 1972, First baseman Bob Spence of Eugene made 21 putouts in a nine-inning game against Salt Lake City, tying the Pacific Coast League record.

July 31, 1972, Tulsa's Jim Bibby registered 16 strikeouts for the second straight game, in a contest with Iowa.

August 2, 1972, Leonardo Ferguson pitched 12 innings of scoreless relief to receive credit for Yucatan's 3-2 Mexican League victory over the Mexico City Tigres in 18 frames.

August 6, 1972, A Texas League game at Midland was postponed due to a grasshopper plague.

August 13, 1972, In the first tripleheader in Florida State League history, played at Cocoa, Florida, the Astros won all three games from Orlando, 5-0, 2-0, and 4-3. Eleno Cuen, an 18-year-old rookie, hurled a no-hitter in the second tilt. A total of 19-1/2 innings were played.

August 15, 1972, Al Thompson, Pittsfield, Eastern League, made his 10th straight hit in a game with Reading.

August 16, 1972, Alexandria, Texas League, scored 13 times in the fifth inning to humiliate Arkansas 13-0. John Grubb smashed a pair of bases-loaded doubles in the round, driving in six runs.

August 20, 1972, Outfielder Tom Epperly, Lynchburg, Carolina League, struck out seven times in an 18-inning game with Salem. The contest produced 41 strikeouts by six pitchers.

August 23, 1972, Jim Minshall, Salem, Carolina League, won his 15th straight game by stopping Rocky Mount 13-5. Minshall won his last 16 games of the season to finish with a 16-1 record.

August 30, 1972, Frank Ricelli, Amarillo, Texas League, fanned 17 in a 4-3 win over San Antonio.

1973

American League
President: Joseph E. Cronin

East Standings	W	L	Pct.	GB	Attend.	Manager
Baltimore Orioles	97	65	.599	—	958,667	Earl Weaver
Boston Red Sox	89	73	.549	8	1,481,002	Eddie Kasko/Eddie Popowski
Detroit Tigers.....................	85	77	.525	12	1,724,146	Billy Martin/Joe Schultz
New York Yankees............	80	82	.494	17	1,262,103	Ralph Houk
Milwaukee Brewers............	74	88	.457	23	1,092,158	Del Crandall
Cleveland Indians	71	91	.438	26	615,107	Ken Aspromonte

West Standings	W	L	Pct.	GB	Attend.	Manager
Oakland Athletics	94	68	.580	—	1,000,763	Dick Williams
Kansas City Royals............	88	74	.543	6	1,345,341	Jack McKeon
Minnesota Twins	81	81	.500	13	907,499	Frank Quilici
California Angels...............	79	83	.488	15	1,058,206	Bobby Winkles
Chicago White Sox	77	85	.475	17	1,302,527	Chuck Tanner
Texas Rangers....................	57	105	.352	37	686,085	Whitey Herzog/Del Wilber/Billy Martin

Playoff: Oakland 3 games, Baltimore 2.

BA: Rod Carew, Minnesota, .350
Runs: Reggie Jackson, Oakland, 99
Hits: Rod Carew, Minnesota, 203
RBIs: Reggie Jackson, Oakland, 117
HRs: Reggie Jackson, Oakland, 32

Wins: Wilbur Wood, Chicago, 24
SOs: Nolan Ryan, California, 383
ERA: Jim Palmer, Baltimore, 2.40
Pct: Catfish Hunter, Oakland, .808, 21-5
Saves: John Hiller, Detroit, 38

National League
President: Charles S. Feeney

East Standings	W	L	Pct.	GB	Attend.	Manager
New York Mets	82	79	.509	—	1,912,390	Yogi Berra
St. Louis Cardinals	81	81	.500	1½	1,574,046	Red Schoendienst
Pittsburgh Pirates	80	82	.494	2½	1,319,913	Bill Virdon/Danny Murtaugh
Montreal Expos	79	83	.488	3½	1,246,863	Gene Mauch
Chicago Cubs.....................	77	84	.478	5	1,351,705	Whitey Lockman
Philadelphia Phillies	71	91	.438	11½	1,475,934	Danny Ozark

West Standings	W	L	Pct.	GB	Attend.	Manager
Cincinnati Reds..................	99	63	.611	—	2,017,601	Sparky Anderson
Los Angeles Dodgers	95	66	.590	3½	2,136,192	Walter Alston
San Francisco Giants	88	74	.543	11	834,193	Charlie Fox
Houston Astros	82	80	.506	17	1,394,004	Leo Durocher
Atlanta Braves	76	85	.472	22½	800,655	Eddie Mathews
San Diego Padres................	60	102	.370	39	611,826	Don Zimmer

Playoff: New York 3 games, Cincinnati 2.

BA: Pete Rose, Cincinnati, .338
Runs: Bobby Bonds, San Francisco, 131
Hits: Pete Rose, Cincinnati, 230
RBIs: Willie Stargell, Pittsburgh, 119
HRs: Willie Stargell, Pittsburgh, 44

Wins: Ron Bryant, San Francisco, 24
SOs: Tom Seaver, New York, 251
ERA: Tom Seaver, New York, 2.08
Pct: Tommy John, Los Angeles, .696, 16-7
Saves: Mike Marshall, Montreal, 31
Games: Mike Marshall, Montreal, 92

AAA American Association
President: Joe Ryan

East Standings	W	L	Pct.	GB	Attend.	Manager
Iowa Oaks (4)	83	53	.610	—	126,012	Joe Sparks
Indianapolis Indians (15)....	74	62	.544	9	130,477	Vern Rapp
Evansville Triplets (8)	66	70	.485	17	114,113	Mike Roarke
Omaha Royals (7)..............	62	73	.459	20½	136,439	Harry Malmberg

West Standings	W	L	Pct.	GB	Attend.	Manager
Tulsa Oilers (22)................	68	67	.504	—	135,698	Jack Krol
Wichita Aeros (14)	67	68	.496	1	203,791	Jim Marshall
Oklahoma City 89ers (5)	61	74	.452	7	164,579	Frank Lucchesi
Denver Bears (16)..............	61	75	.449	7½	184,279	Jimy Williams

Playoff: Tulsa 4 games, Iowa 3.

All-Star Team: 1B-Roe Skidmore, Indianapolis; **2B**-Gary Sutherland, Denver; **3B**-George Brett, Omaha; **SS**-Bucky Dent, Iowa; **OF**-Jim Dwyer, Tulsa; Greg Gross, Denver; Ken Griffey, Indianapolis; Tommy Smith, Oklahoma City; **C**-Tom Lundstedt, Wichita; Pete Varney, Iowa; **DH**-Cliff Johnson, Denver; **Util**-Dave Rosello, Wichita; **P**-Mark Littell, Omaha; Ken Fraling, Iowa; **MVP**-Cliff Johnson, Denver; **Pitcher of the Year**-Mark Littell, Omaha; **Manager of the Year**-Joe Sparks, Iowa.

BA: Jim Dwyer, Tulsa, .387
Runs: Cliff Johnson, Denver, 105
Hits: Greg Gross, Denver, 174
RBIs: Cliff Johnson, Denver, 117

HRs: Cliff Johnson, Denver, 33
Wins: Mark Littell, Omaha, 16
SOs: Lowell Palmer, Oklahoma City, 203
ERA: Mark Littell, Omaha, 2.51

AAA International League
President: George H. Sisler, Jr.

North Standings	W	L	Pct.	GB	Attend.	Manager
Rochester Red Wings (1)....	79	67	.541	—	302,789	Joe Altobelli
Pawtucket Red Sox (2)	78	68	.534	1	78,592	Darrell Johnson
Syracuse Chiefs (10)...........	76	70	.521	3	180,064	Bobby Cox
Toledo Mud Hens (6)	65	81	.445	14	92,366	John Lipon/Cot Deal

South Standings	W	L	Pct.	GB	Attend.	Manager
Charleston Charlies (21).......	85	60	.586	—	96,883	Joe Morgan
Tidewater Tides (19)........	75	70	.517	10	105,635	Johnny Antonelli
Peninsula Whips (18)..........	72	74	.493	13½	45,354	Bill Adair
Richmond Braves (13)........	53	93	.363	32½	72,156	Bobby Hofman/Clint Courtney

Playoffs: Charleston 3 games, Rochester 0; Pawtucket 3 games, Tidewater 2.
Finals: Pawtucket 3 games, Charleston 2.

All-Star Team: 1B-Cecil Cooper, Pawtucket; **2B**-Jim Cox, Peninsula; **3B**-Doug DeCinces, Rochester; **SS**-Frank Taveras, Charleston; **OF**-Otto Velez, Syracuse; Jim Fuller, Rochester; Dave Parker, Charleston; **C**-Bob Didier, Toledo; Barry Foote, Peninsula; **P**-Dick Pole, Pawtucket; Craig Caskey, Peninsula; **MVP**-Jim Fuller, Rochester; **Pitcher of the Year**-Dick Pole, Pawtucket; **Manager**-Joe Morgan, Charleston.

BA: Juan Beniquez, Pawtucket, .298
Runs: Richard Bladt, Syracuse, 97
Hits: Michael Cummings, Pawtucket, 139
RBIs: Jim Fuller, Rochester, 108

HRs: Jim Fuller, Rochester, 39
Wins: Ed Montague, Peninsula, 15
SOs: Dick Pole, Pawtucket, 158
ERA: Dick Pole, Pawtucket, 2.03

AAA Mexican League
President: Antonio Ramirez Muro

North West Standings	W	L	Pct.	GB	Attend.	Manager
Saltillo Saraperos................	86	45	.656	—	169,059	Andres Tanaka
Union Laguna Algodoneros	65	65	.500	20½	180,392	Jose Guerrero
Ciudad Juarez Indios	55	78	.414	32	173,950	Ben Reyes
Chihuahua Dorados	45	87	.341	41½	174,338	Mauro Ruiz/Mauro Contreras

North East Standings	W	L	Pct.	GB	Attend.	Manager
Tampico Alijadores	74	56	.569	—	218,444	Pedro Gonzalez
Reynosa Bravos	67	66	.504	8½	97,341	Jorge Fitch
Monterrey Sultanes	66	68	.493	10	180,000	Miguel Sotelo
Sabinas Piratas	51	81	.386	24	98,132	Benjamin Valenzuela

South West Standings	W	L	Pct.	GB	Attend.	Manager
Jalisco Charros	79	52	.603	—	187,142	Vinicio Garcia
Poza Rica Petroleros	79	53	.598	½	219,851	Moises Camacho
Puebla Pericos	71	62	.534	9	143,565	Tomas Herrera/Jorge Calvo/Raul Cano
Mexico City Tigres.............	59	72	.450	20	252,306	Jose Luis Garcia

South East Standings	W	L	Pct.	GB	Attend.	Manager
Mexico City Diablos Rojos	79	55	.590	—	434,133	Wilfredo Calvino
Veracruz Aguila.................	66	62	.516	10	100,993	Mario Ariosa/Ron Camacho
Yucatan Leones	60	74	.448	19	79,967	Enrique Izquierdo
Cordoba Cafeteros	53	79	.402	25	160,894	Mario Pelaez

Playoffs: Saltillo 3 games, Reynosa 1; Tampico 3 games, Union Laguna 1; Veracruz 3 games, Jalisco 0; MC Diablos Rojos 3 games, Poza Rica 1. Saltillo 3 games, Tampico 2; MC Diablos Rojos 3 games, Veracruz 1.
Finals: MC Diablos Rojos 4 games, Saltillo 3.

All-Star Team: 1B-Hector Espino, Tampico; **2B**-Gabriel Lugo, Saltillo; **3B**-Ben Cerda, Jalisco; **SS**-Francisco Rodriguez, Aguila; **OF**-Romel Canada, Saltillo; Domingo Cruz, Saltillo; Nicolas Vazquez, Jalisco; **C**-Gregorio Luque, Saltillo; Hector Valle, Reynosa; **P**-Manuel Lugo, Jalisco; Silvano Quezada, Tampico; **Manager**-Wilfredo Calvino, MC Diablos Rojos.

BA: Hector Espino, Tampico, .377
Runs: Tomas Silverio, Tampico, 115
Hits: Domingo Cruz, Saltillo, 173
RBIs: Hector Espino, Tampico, 107

HRs: Romel Canada, Saltillo, 26
Wins: Ed Bauta, Poza Rica, 23
SOs: Jose Pena, Puebla, 195
ERA: Manuel Lugo, Jalisco, 1.60

AAA Pacific Coast League
President: William B. McKechnie, Jr.

East Standings	W	L	Pct.	GB	Attend.	Manager
Tucson Toros (11)	84	60	.583	—	233,004	Sherm Lollar
Salt Lake City Angels (3)...	79	65	.549	5	162,581	Les Moss
Phoenix Giants (24)...........	70	73	.490	13½	115,217	Jim Davenport
Albuquerque Dukes (17)	62	82	.431	22	128,955	Stan Wasiak

West Standings	W	L	Pct.	GB	Attend.	Manager
Spokane Indians (12)..........	81	63	.563	—	122,595	Del Wilber
Hawaii Islanders (23)..........	70	74	.486	11	238,390	Rocky Bridges/Warren Hacker/Roy Hartsfield
Tacoma Twins (9)...............	65	79	.451	16	182,553	Kerby Farrell
Eugene Emeralds (20)	64	79	.448	16½	124,458	Jim Bunning

Playoff: Spokane 3 games, Tucson 0.

*Won first-half   **Won second-half   ***Won both halves
Numbers after nicknames indicate farm system.
Affiliation listed at end of each year.

1973

East All-Star Team: 1B-Doug Howard, Salt Lake City; 2B-Manny Trillo, Tucson; Bill Parker, Salt Lake City; 3B-Jerry Royster, Albuquerque; SS-Steve Huntz, Albuquerque; OF-Jim Fairey, Albuquerque; Bernard Williams, Phoenix; Mickey Rivers, Salt Lake City; Steve Ontiveros, Phoenix; C-Jerald Brown, Phoenix; Larry Haney, Tucson; P-Greg Shanahan, Albuquerque; John D'Acquisto, Phoenix; Glenn Abbott, Tucson.

West All-Star Team: 1B-Craig Kusick, Tacoma; 2B-Bill Madlock, Spokane; 3B-Rick Renick, Tacoma; SS-Craig Robinson, Eugene; OF-Gene Martin, Eugene/Hawaii; Charlie Manuel, Tacoma; Richard Wissel, Eugene; Clarence Vaughns, Eugene; C-Bill Fahey, Spokane; Glenn Borgmann, Tacoma; P-Dave Freisleben, Hawaii; Richard Henninger, Spokane; Earl Stephenson, Eugene.

BA: Steve Ontiveros, Phoenix, .357
Runs: Bill Madlock, Spokane, 119
Hits: Mickey Rivers, Salt Lake City, 187
RBIs: Gene Martin, Eugene/Hawaii, 106

HRs: Gene Martin, Eugene/Hawaii, 31
Wins: Glenn Abbott, Tucson, 18
SOs: Dave Freisleben, Hawaii, 206
ERA: Dave Freisleben, Hawaii, 2.82

AA Eastern League
President: Roy Jackson

American Standings	W	L	Pct.	GB	Attend.	Manager
Pittsfield Rangers (12)	75	61	.551	—	44,333	Joe Klein
West Haven Yankees (10)	72	66	.522	4	75,128	Doc Edwards
Bristol Red Sox (2)	62	77	.446	14½	47,288	Rac Slider
Waterbury Dodgers (17)	59	79	.428	17	73,241	Don LeJohn

National Standings	W	L	Pct.	GB	Attend.	Manager
Reading Phillies (20)	76	62	.551	—	76,651	Cal Emery
Sherbrooke Pirates (21)	76	63	.547	½	70,457	Tim Murtaugh
Trois Rivieres Aigles (15)	67	72	.482	9½	90,565	Jim Snyder
Quebec Carnavals (18)	65	72	.474	10½	116,236	Karl Kuehl

Playoff: Reading 3 games, Pittsfield 1.

All-Star Team: 1B-Tom Robson, Pittsfield; 2B-Mike Cubbage, Pittsfield; 3B-Luther Quinn, Sherbrooke; SS-Mario Mendoza, Sherbrooke; OF-Orlando Alvarez, Waterbury; Dave Arrington, Sherbrooke; Jim Rice, Bristol; C-Jim Essian, Reading; P-Greg Heydeman, Waterbury; Charles Ross, Bristol; MVP-Tom Robson, Pittsfield; Manager-Doc Edwards, West Haven.

BA: Jim Rice, Bristol, .317
Runs: Tom Robson, Pittsfield, 83
Hits: Orlando Alvarez, Waterbury, 139
RBIs: Tom Robson, Pittsfield, 126
HRs: Tom Robson, Pittsfield, 38

Wins: Scott McGregor, West Haven, 12
Joe Pactwa, West Haven, 12
Kent Tekulve, Sherbrooke, 12
Erskine Thomason, Reading, 12
Pat Zachry, Trois Rivieres, 12
SOs: Greg Heydeman, Waterbury, 179
ERA: Joe Pactwa, West Haven, 3.18

AA Southern League
President: Billy Hitchcock

East Standings	W	L	Pct.	GB	Attend.	Manager
Jacksonville Suns (7)	76	60	.559	—	77,766	Billy Gardner
Savannah Braves (13)	71	68	.511	6½	74,318	Clint Courtney/Tommie Aaron
Columbus Astros (16)	69	70	.496	8½	90,017	Wayne Terwilliger
Orlando Twins (9)	65	70	.481	10½	52,162	Harry Warner

West Standings	W	L	Pct.	GB	Attend.	Manager
Montgomery Rebels (6)	80	58	.580	—	46,675	Fred Hatfield
Asheville Orioles (1)	71	69	.507	10	48,254	Cal Ripken, Sr.
Knoxville White Sox (4)	70	69	.504	10½	33,604	Jim Napier
Birmingham A's (11)	50	88	.362	30	21,016	Harry Bright

Playoff: Montgomery 3 games, Jacksonville 1.

All-Star Team: 1B-Joe Staton, Montgomery; 2B-Rob Andrews, Asheville; 3B-Al Cowens, Jacksonville; SS-Bob Bailor, Asheville; OF-Jason Moxey, Columbus; Greg Foreman, Savannah; Ed Palat, Orlando; C-Don Hickey, Asheville; P-Russ Rothermel, Columbus; Doug Konieczny, Columbus; Manager-Billy Gardner, Jacksonville.

BA: Rob Andrews, Asheville, .309
Runs: Rob Andrews, Asheville, 98
Hits: Rob Andrews, Asheville, 167
RBIs: Terry Clapp, Asheville, 98
HRs: Terry Clapp, Asheville, 35
Wins: Joe Henderson, Knoxville, 17
SOs: Doug Konieczny, Columbus, 222
ERA: Russ Rothermel, Columbus, 1.81

AA Texas League
President: Bobby Bragan

East Standings	W	L	Pct.	GB	Attend.	Manager
Memphis Blues (19)	77	61	.558	—	113,863	Joe Frazier
Shreveport Captains (8)	70	68	.507	7	57,243	Gene Freese
Arkansas Travelers (22)	69	71	.493	9	89,302	Tom Burgess
Alexandria Aces (23)	59	77	.434	17	70,507	Jackie Brandt

West Standings	W	L	Pct.	GB	Attend.	Manager
San Antonio Missions (5)	82	57	.590	—	177,197	Tony Pacheco
El Paso Sun Kings (3)	69	71	.493	13½	63,081	Norm Sherry/Moose Stubing
Midland Cubs (14)	64	74	.464	17½	69,277	Al Spangler
Amarillo Giants (24)	64	75	.460	18	49,750	Dennis Sommers

Playoff: Memphis 3 games, San Antonio 2.

All-Star Team: 1B-Tom Hallums, Memphis; 2B-Duane Kuiper, San Antonio; 3B-Ronald Dunn, Midland; SS-Manny Perez, Amarillo; OF-Greg Harts, Memphis; Hector Cruz, Arkansas; Sixto Lezcano, Shreveport; C-Marc Hill, Arkansas; Jeff Newman, San Antonio; DH-Joe Azcue, San Antonio; P-Frank Tanana, El Paso; Tim Juran, Memphis; MVP-Hector

Cruz, Arkansas; **Pitcher of the Year**-Frank Tanana, El Paso; **Manager**-Tony Pacheco, San Antonio.

BA: Morris Nettles, El Paso, .332
Runs: Hector Cruz, Arkansas, 94
Hits: Morris Nettles, El Paso, 156
RBIs: Hector Cruz, Arkansas, 105
HRs: Hector Cruz, Arkansas, 30
Wins: Rick Sawyer, San Antonio, 18
SOs: Frank Tanana, El Paso, 197
ERA: Dan Corder, Midland, 2.32

A California League
President: Edward J. Mulligan

Standings	W	L	Pct.	GB	Attend.	Manager
Lodi Lions*(1)	77	63	.550	—	43,053	Jimmie Schaffer
Salinas Packers (3)	77	63	.550	—	51,477	Jim Saul
San Jose Bees (7)	75	65	.536	2	125,047	Steve Boros
Bakersfield Dodgers**(17)	70	70	.500	7	46,732	George Freese
Reno Silver Sox (5)	70	70	.500	7	29,402	Lou Klimchock
Fresno Giants (24)	69	71	.493	8	58,586	Frank Funk
Visalia Mets (19)	62	78	.443	15	38,719	Nolan Campbell
Modesto Reds (22)	60	80	.429	17	60,300	Bobby Dews

Playoff: Lodi 2 games, Bakersfield 0.

All-Star Team: 1B-Michael Satterlee, Lodi; 2B-Richard Puig, Visalia; 3B-David Cripe, San Jose; SS-Dan Beerbower, Salinas; OF-John Balaz, Salinas; Kenzie Davis, San Jose; Cleo Smith, Bakersfield; C-Glenn Woodruff, Reno; Util-Richard Guerra, Fresno; Gary Rahe, San Jose; P-Larry McCall, Lodi; Anastasio Velazquez, Modesto; Dennis Leonard, San Jose; Curt Isom, San Jose; James Officer, Salinas; MVP-John Balaz, Salinas; Manager-Jimmie Schaffer, Lodi.

BA: David Cripe, San Jose, .310
Runs: Rick Manning, Reno, 101
Hits: Michael Eden, Fresno, 159
RBIs: John Balaz, Salinas, 113
HRs: John Balaz, Salinas, 28
Wins: Dennis Leonard, San Jose, 15
SOs: Curt Isom, San Jose, 227
ERA: Curt Isom, San Jose, 2.42

A Carolina League
President: Wallace McKenna

Standings	W	L	Pct.	GB	Attend.	Manager
Lynchburg Twins*(9)	78	60	.565	—	66,015	Dick Phillips
Winston-Salem Red Sox**(2)	77	62	.554	1½	30,235	Bill Slack
Rocky Mount Phillies (20)	75	65	.536	4	28,389	Bob Wellman
Kinston Eagles (x)	68	69	.496	9½	30,012	Gene Hassell
Salem Pirates (21)	66	72	.478	12	45,915	Steve Demeter
Wilson Pennants (x)	52	88	.371	27	45,132	Ray Hathaway/Don Lock

Playoff: Winston-Salem 3 games, Lynchburg 2.

All-Star Team: 1B-Jim Obradovich, Lynchburg; 2B-Albert Ryan, Winston-Salem; 3B-Richard Oliver, Wilson; SS-Greg Pryor, Rocky Mount; OF-Terry Whitfield, Kinston; Jimmie Collins, Kinston; Omar Moreno, Salem; Bill Thomas, Salem; C-Bill Nahorodny, Rocky Mount; P-Randy Hill, Rocky Mount; Roy Thomas, Rocky Mount; Manager-Dick Phillips, Lynchburg.

BA: Terry Whitfield, Kinston, .335
Runs: Omar Moreno, Salem, 112
Hits: Craig Reynolds, Salem, 160
RBIs: Chuck Erickson, Winston-Salem, 101
HRs: Jim Obradovich, Lynchburg, 18
Terry Whitfield, Kinston, 18
Wins: Bill Stiegemeier, Lynchburg, 15
Roy Thomas, Rocky Mount, 15
SOs: Roy Thomas, Rocky Mount, 193
ERA: Roy Thomas, Rocky Mount, 2.24

A Florida State League
President: George MacDonald, Jr.

North Standings	W	L	Pct.	GB	Attend.	Manager
St. Petersburg Cardinals (22)	84	62	.575	—	145,167	Roy Majtyka
Lakeland Tigers (6)	80	60	.571	1	12,662	Frank "Stubby" Overmire
Daytona Beach Dodgers (17)	71	68	.511	9½	39,168	Bart Shirley
Tampa Tarpons (15)	73	71	.507	10	15,006	Russ Nixon
Winter Haven Red Sox (2)	50	94	.347	33	5,348	Al Lehrer

South Standings	W	L	Pct.	GB	Attend.	Manager
West Palm Beach Expos (18)	80	58	.580	—	69,053	Lance Nichols
Miami Orioles (1)	77	64	.546	4½	39,721	Bobby Malkmus
Ft. Lauderdale Yankees (10)	67	72	.482	13½	46,872	Pete Ward
Key West Conchs (x)	64	78	.451	18	18,019	Woody Smith
Pompano Beach Mets (19)	61	80	.433	20½	14,343	Gordy MacKenzie

Playoffs: St. Petersburg 2 games, Miami 0; West Palm Beach 2 games, Lakeland 1.
Finals: St. Petersburg 2 games, West Palm Beach 0.

All-Star Team: 1B-Wayne Cage, Key West; 2B-Kim Andrew, Miami; 3B-Larry Parrish, West Palm Beach; SS-John Johnson, Key West; OF-Darryl Jones, Ft. Lauderdale; Glenn Burke, Daytona Beach; Dave Edwards, Ft. Lauderdale; C-Bobbie Goodman, West Palm Beach; Dick Bengston, Pompano Beach; P-Larry Payne, Tampa; L. Antonio Gonzalez, St. Petersburg; MVP-Larry Parrish, West Palm Beach; Manager-Frank "Stubby" Overmire, Lakeland.

BA: Kim Andrew, Miami, .336
Runs: Jerry Mumphrey, St. Petersburg, 93
Hits: Jerry Mumphrey, St. Petersburg, 159
RBIs: Wayne Cage, Key West, 82
HRs: Wayne Cage, Key West, 18
Wins: L. Antonio Gonzalez, St. Pete, 15
SOs: L. Antonio Gonzalez, St. Petersburg, 162
ERA: Mike Proly, St. Petersburg, 1.76

A Mexican Center League
President: Antonio Ramirez Muro

Center Standings	W	L	Pct.	GB	Attend.	Manager
Zacatecas Tuzos	49	19	.721	—	17,875	Ossie Alvarez
Ciudad Victoria	33	35	.485	16	13,780	Jesus Valtier
Aguascalientes Tigres	30	40	.429	20	16,157	Alberto Joachin
Durango Alacranes	25	43	.368	24	21,824	Felipe Hernandez

Gulf Standings	W	L	Pct.	GB	Attend.	Manager
Ebano Reds	44	23	.657	—	26,400	Arturo Cacheux
Tamuin	36	34	.514	9½	2,431	Bimbo Villegas
Ciudad Mante Azucareros	31	37	.456	13½	6,496	Jose Guerrero
Naranjos	26	43	.377	19	9,321	Alfonso Preciado

Playoffs: Zacatecas 2 games, Ciudad Victoria 0; Ebano 2 games, Tamuin 1.
Finals: Zacatecas 2 games, Ebano 1.

All-Star Team: 1B-Jose Gutierrez, Aguascalientes; **2B**-Trinidad Aguirre, Ebano; **3B**-Juan Martinez, Ciudad Victoria; **SS**-Julio Esparza, Tamuin; **OF**-Juan Rodriguez, Ebano; Fernando Felix, Durango; Baudel Lopez, Ebano; **C**-Carlos Soto, Ebano; Francisco Pacheco, Zacatecas; **P**-Rodolfo Vallejano, Ciudad Mante; Jesus Gutierrez, Zacatecas; **Manager**-Ossie Alvarez, Zacatecas.

BA: Jose Guerrero, Ciudad Mante, .385
Runs: Miguel Ruiz, Zacatecas, 52
Hits: Fernando Felix, Durango, 101
RBIs: Jose Guerrero, Ciudad Mante, 58
Juan Martinez, Ciudad Victoria, 58
Carlos Soto, Ebano, 58

HRs: Cruz Espinosa, Ebano, 13
Wins: Alfonso Bourguette, Ebano, 11
Rodolfo Vallejano, Ciudad Mante, 11
SOs: Humberto Valenzuela, Ebano, 139
Rodolfo Vallejano, Ciudad Mante, 139
ERA: Rodolfo Vallejano, Ciudad Mante, 1.71

A Midwest League
President: James Doster

North Standings	W	L	Pct.	GB	Attend.	Manager
Clinton Pilots**(6)	73	51	.589	—	37,302	Jim Leyland
Wisconsin Rapids Twins*(9)	68	53	.562	3½	51,869	John Goryl
Waterloo Royals (7)	64	56	.533	7	42,930	Billy Scripture
Cedar Rapids Astros (16)	61	60	.504	10½	53,369	Leo Posada
Appleton Foxes (4)	44	76	.367	27	61,693	Deacon Jones/Bert Thiel

South Standings	W	L	Pct.	GB	Attend.	Manager
Danville Warriors*(8)	66	57	.537	—	83,135	Bernie Smith
Decatur Commodores**(24)	63	62	.504	4	34,385	John Van Ornum
Quincy Cubs (14)	61	64	.488	6	38,570	Walt Dixon
Burlington Bees (11)	54	64	.458	8½	45,801	Rene Lachemann
Quad Cities Angels (3)	55	66	.455	10	58,833	Dick Kinaman

Playoffs: Wisconsin Rapids 2 games, Clinton 0; Danville 2 games, Decatur 0.
Finals: Wisconsin Rapids 2 games, Danville 1.

All-Star Team: 1B-Randy Bass, Wisconsin Rapids; **2B**-Jerry Remy, Quad Cities; **3B**-Chet Lemon, Burlington; **SS**-Michael Coronado, Wisconsin Rapids; **OF**-Lanny Little, Quad Cities; Claudell Washington, Burlington; Gary Alexander, Decatur; **C**-Mike Roberts, Waterloo; Luis Camilo, Decatur; **P**-Stan Butkus, Waterloo; Ed Glynn, Clinton; **Manager**-Bernie Smith, Danville.

BA: Jerry Remy, Quad Cities, .335
Runs: Claudell Washington, Burlington, 92
Hits: Jerry Remy, Quad Cities, 160
RBIs: Chet Lemon, Burlington, 88

HRs: Randy Bass, Wisconsin Rapids, 21
Wins: Jerry Gomez, Waterloo, 14
SOs: Gerald Tyler, Clinton, 168
ERA: Gerald Tyler, Clinton, 2.17

A New York-Pennsylvania League
President: Vincent M. McNamara

Standings	W	L	Pct.	GB	Attend.	Manager
Auburn Phillies (20)	46	23	.667	—	53,044	Harry Lloyd
Oneonta Yankees (10)	44	26	.629	2½	33,006	Hank Majeski
Jamestown Expos (18)	41	28	.594	5	18,437	Walt Hriniak
Geneva Twins (9)	39	29	.574	6½	18,769	Fred Waters
Batavia Trojans (19)	33	36	.478	13	50,375	Wilbur Huckle
Elmira Pioneers (2)	32	37	.464	14	34,121	Dick Berardino
Niagara Falls Pirates (21)	27	43	.386	19½	56,996	Woody Huyke
Newark Co-Pilots (8)	15	55	.214	31½	16,876	Matt Galante

Playoffs: None.

All-Star Team: 1B-Jack Mednick, Elmira; **2B**-Charles Meyers, Elmira; **3B**-Ron Roenicke, Jamestown; **SS**-Robin Yount, Newark; **OF**-Kerry Dineen, Oneonta; Rick Miller, Batavia; John Guarnaccia, Auburn; Joe Poscotty, Niagara Falls; **C**-Tim Grice, Oneonta; Andy Russo, Auburn; Robert Reece, Jamestown; **P**-Ronnie Sims, Elmira; Randy Lerch, Auburn; **Manager**-Harry Lloyd, Auburn.

BA: Kerry Dineen, Oneonta, .352
Runs: Rick Bosetti, Auburn, 68
Hits: Steven Coulson, Oneonta, 95
RBIs: John Guarnaccia, Auburn, 59

HRs: Randy Trapp, Batavia, 12
Wins: Neal Mersch, Oneonta, 11
SOs: Ronnie Sims, Elmira, 129
ERA: Michael Van DeCasteele, Geneva, 0.72

A Northwest League
President: Bob Freitas

East Standings	W	L	Pct.	GB	Attend.	Manager
Walla Walla Padres (23)	51	29	.638	—	33,259	Cliff Ditto
Tri-City Triplets (x)	42	38	.525	9	20,791	Mike Cloutier/Jerry Pomeroy
Lewiston Broncs (11)	26	54	.325	25	19,830	Michael Sgobba

West Standings	W	L	Pct.	GB	Attend.	Manager
Portland Mavericks	45	35	.563	—	80,705	Hank Robinson
Bellingham Dodgers (17)	42	37	.532	2½	38,396	Bill Berrier
Seattle Rainiers (15)	33	46	.418	11½	35,533	Jim Hoff

Playoff: None.

All-Star Team: 1B-Bill Hobbs, Lewiston; **2B**-Ed Cervantes, Tri-City; **3B**-Michael Dupree, Walla Walla; **SS**-Mike Champion, Walla Walla; **OF**-Kent Froede, Tri-City; Bob Cummings, Seattle; Terrence Jones, Portland; **C**-Gerard Stone, Walla Walla; **DH**-Reggie Thomas, Portland; **P**-Joe McIntosh, Walla Walla; Gene Lanthorn, Portland; Mike Allen, Walla Walla.

BA: Michael Dupree, Walla Walla, .351
Runs: Reggie Thomas, Portland, 66
Hits: Michael Dupree, Walla Walla, 102
RBIs: Jose Del Moral, Bellingham, 58

HRs: Gary Walls, Walla Walla, 10
Gerard Stone, Walla Walla, 10
Steve Smith, Tri-City, 10
Wins: Esteban Texidor, Bellingham, 10
SOs: Joe McIntosh, Walla Walla, 117
ERA: Mike Allen, Walla Walla, 1.72

A Western Carolinas League
President: John H. Moss

Standings	W	L	Pct.	GB	Attend.	Manager
Charleston Pirates (21)	72	52	.581	—	92,523	Chuck Cottier
Gastonia Rangers*(12)	74	54	.578	—	18,696	Rich Donnelly
Spartanburg Phillies**(20)	67	61	.523	7	40,189	Howie Bedell
Greenwood Braves (13)	61	66	.480	12½	52,286	Hoyt Wilhelm
Anderson Tigers (6)	54	73	.425	19½	32,284	Len Okrie
Orangeburg Cards (x)	50	72	.410	21	20,837	Jim Piersall

Playoff: Spartanburg 2 games, Gastonia 0.

All-Star Team: 1B-Mike Hargrove, Gastonia; **2B**-Willie Randolph, Charleston; **3B**-Brad Fulk, Gastonia; **SS**-Rick Albert, Greenwood; **OF**-Doug Ault, Gastonia; Daniel Gonzales, Anderson; Rocky Skalisky, Spartanburg; **C**-Natanael Alvarado, Spartanburg; Hal Workman, Greenwood; **P**-Jeff Scott, Gastonia; Tom Underwood, Spartanburg; **Manager**-Rich Donnelly, Gastonia.

BA: Mike Hargrove, Gastonia, .351
Runs: Miguel Dilone, Charleston, 94
Hits: Mike Hargrove, Gastonia, 160
RBIs: Doug Ault, Gastonia, 88
HRs: Doug Ault, Gastonia, 19

Wins: Dave Fanning, Spartanburg, 14
Jeff Scott, Gastonia, 14
SOs: Tom Underwood, Spartanburg, 187
ERA: Tom Underwood, Spartanburg, 2.10

R Appalachian League
President: Chauncey De Vault

Standings	W	L	Pct.	GB	Attend.	Manager
Kingsport Royals (7)	53	17	.757	—	36,249	John Sullivan
Johnson City Yankees (10)	37	31	.544	15	14,029	Steve Hamilton
Wytheville Braves (13)	37	32	.536	15½	12,851	Paul Snyder
Bluefield Orioles (1)	37	33	.529	16	14,590	George Farson
Marion Mets (19)	36	33	.522	16½	10,204	Owen Friend
Pulaski Phillies (20)	32	38	.457	21	12,328	Bob Wren
Bristol Tigers (6)	24	45	.348	28½	14,147	Joe Lewis
Covington Astros (16)	21	48	.304	31½	13,673	Billy Smith

Playoffs: None.

All-Star Team: 1B-Eddie Murray, Bluefield; **2B**-Thomas Butler, Bristol; **3B**-John Ihlenburg, Kingsport; **SS**-U.L. Washington, Kingsport; **OF**-Steve Blomberg, Kingsport; Rodney Lee, Bluefield; John LiBrandi, Kingsport; **C**-Luis Rosado, Marion; **P**-Russell Peach, Bluefield; Willie Clark, Kingsport; Mike Parrott, Bluefield; Francisco Gonzalez, Marion; **Manager**-John Sullivan, Kingsport.

BA: John Shupe, Johnson City, .350
Runs: Steve Blomberg, Kingsport, 61
Hits: John Shupe, Johnson City, 75
Jake Arena, Bluefield, 75
R3Is: John Shupe, Johnson City, 54

HRs: John Shupe, Johnson City, 13
Wins: Willie Clark, Kingsport, 10
SOs: Manuel Seoane, Pulaski, 101
ERA: Willie Clark, Kingsport, 2.02

R Gulf Coast League
President: George MacDonald, Jr.

Standings	W	L	Pct.	GB	Manager
Rangers (12)	41	15	.732	—	Bill Haywood
Indians (5)	32	24	.571	9	Len Johnston
White Sox (4)	29	26	.527	11½	Joe Jones
Red Birds (22)	29	27	.518	12	LeRoy Thomas
Royals (7)	27	28	.491	13½	Buzzy Keller
Cubs (14)	27	28	.491	13½	Q.V. Lowe
Cardinals (22)	25	30	.455	15½	Ken Boyer
Reds (15)	20	32	.385	19	Ron Plaza
Pirates (21)	17	37	.315	23	Ed Napoleon

Games played at Sarasota and Bradenton, Florida.

Playoffs: None.

All-Star Team: 1B-Phillip Bittle, Reds; Hector Eduardo, Cardinals; **2B**-Walter Gaskin, Red Birds; Victor Estrella, Pirates; **3B**-Bill Miller, Pirates; Benny Edelen, Cardinals; **SS**-Richard Shaw, Cardinals; Jamye Peper, Reds; **OF**-Paul Nelson, Pirates; Thurman Smith,

Cardinals; Ken Kral, Cubs; Brad Kesseler, Reds; Marvin Whitehurst, Pirates; David Sandlin, Red Birds; **C**-Dennis Starr, Red Birds; Steve Clancy, Cubs; **P**-Bob Arnold, Cardinals; Dick Kuhn, Reds; Charles Steffen, Pirates; Randy Wiles, Cardinals; Ron Selak, Cardinals; Harold Rasmussen, Cardinals; James Temple, Cubs; Cardell Camper, Red Birds; **Manager**-Ken Boyer, Cardinals.

BA: Larry Foster, White Sox, .382
Runs: Gary Cooper, Rangers, 50
Hits: Curt Minges, White Sox, 59
RBIs: Jonathan Astroth, Rangers, 43
HRs: Hector Eduardo, Cardinals, 6

Wins: Len Barker, Rangers, 7
    Jim McCutchin, Indians, 7
    Barry Smith, White Sox, 7
    James Temple, Cubs, 7
SOs: Mike Krukow, Cubs, 80
ERA: Byron Wilkerson, Cubs, 1.13

R Pioneer League
President: Claude Engberg

Standings	W	L	Pct.	GB	Attend.	Manager
Billings Mustangs (7)	44	26	.629	—	32,345	Gary Blaylock
Ogden Dodgers (17)	37	33	.529	7	19,116	Gail Henley
Great Falls Giants (24)	37	34	.521	7½	26,207	Art Mazmanian
Idaho Falls Angels (3)	23	48	.324	21½	26,027	Bob Clear

Playoffs: None.

All-Star Team: 1B-Craig Barnes, Great Falls; **2B**-Arturo Marin, Great Falls; **3B**-Tony Cabrera, Great Falls; **SS**-Rodney Scott, Billings; **OF**-Bobby Detherage, Ogden; Jack Clark, Great Falls; Ruppert Jones, Billings; **C**-John Fleming, Billings; Ted Farr, Ogden; **P**-Pete Falcone, Great Falls; Bob McClure, Billings; **Manager**-Gary Blaylock, Billings.

BA: Tony Cabrera, Great Falls, .354
Runs: Craig Barnes, Great Falls, 57
Hits: Bobby Detherage, Ogden, 85
RBIs: Bobby Detherage, Ogden, 55

HRs: Philip Robinson, Billings, 10
Wins: Bob McClure, Billings, 10
SOs: Robert Falcon, Billings, 180
ERA: Pete Falcone, Great Falls, 1.50

1973 Interleague Post Season Play

World Series
Oakland (American) 4 games, New York (National) 3

Junior World Series
Pawtucket (International) 4 games, Tulsa (American Association) 1
Total Attendance: 13,235

1973 Major League Farm Systems

American League
1. Baltimore (5): Rochester, Asheville, Lodi, Miami, Bluefield.
2. Boston (5): Pawtucket, Bristol (CT), Winston-Salem, Winter Haven, Elmira.
3. California (5): Salt Lake City, El Paso, Salinas, Quad Cities, Idaho Falls.
4. Chicago (4): Iowa, Knoxville, Appleton, Gulf Coast.
5. Cleveland (4): Oklahoma City, San Antonio, Reno, Gulf Coast.
6. Detroit (6): Toledo, Montgomery, Lakeland, Clinton, Anderson, Bristol (VA).
7. Kansas City (7): Omaha, Jacksonville, San Jose, Waterloo, Kingsport, Billings, Gulf Coast.
8. Milwaukee (4): Evansville, Shreveport, Danville, Newark.
9. Minnesota (5): Tacoma, Orlando, Lynchburg, Wisconsin Rapids, Geneva.
10. New York (5): Syracuse, West Haven, Ft. Lauderdale, Oneonta, Johnson City.
11. Oakland (4): Tucson, Birmingham, Burlington, Lewiston.
12. Texas (4): Spokane, Pittsfield, Gastonia, Gulf Coast.

National League
13. Atlanta (4): Richmond, Savannah, Greenwood, Wytheville.
14. Chicago (4): Wichita, Midland, Quincy, Gulf Coast.
15. Cincinnati (5): Indianapolis, Trois Rivieres, Tampa, Seattle, Gulf Coast.
16. Houston (4): Denver, Columbus, Cedar Rapids, Covington.
17. Los Angeles (6): Albuquerque, Waterbury, Bakersfield, Daytona Beach, Bellingham, Odgen.
18. Montreal (4): Peninsula, Quebec, West Palm Beach, Jamestown.
19. New York (6): Tidewater, Memphis, Visalia, Pompano Beach, Batavia, Marion.
20. Philadelphia (6): Eugene, Reading, Rocky Mount, Spartanburg, Auburn, Pulaski.
21. Pittsburgh (6): Charleston (WV), Sherbrooke, Salem, Charleston (SC), Niagara Falls, Gulf Coast.
22. St. Louis (6): Tulsa, Arkansas, Modesto, St. Petersburg, Gulf Coast Red Birds, Gulf Coast Cardinals.
23. San Diego (3): Hawaii, Alexandria, Walla Walla.
24. San Francisco (5): Phoenix, Amarillo, Fresno, Decatur, Great Falls.

Co-op (x): Kinston, Wilson, Key West, Orangeburg, Tri-City.
Independent: Portland.

1973 No-Hitters

Date	Pitcher	Team	League	Opponent	Score
4-18	Steve Hardin	Wilson	Carolina	Winston-Salem	3-0 (P)
4-26	Dennis Leonard	San Jose	California	Visalia	2-0
4-27	Steve Busby	Kansas City	American	Detroit	3-0
4-27	Cesar Moreno	Ciudad Victoria	Mexican Center	Aguascalientes	3-0
5-1	Ken Fortar	Lakeland	Florida State	Tampa	5-0 (7)
5-1	Robert Perkins	Anderson	W. Carolinas	Charleston	2-1 (8)
5-11	Charles Ross	Bristol	Eastern	Sherbrooke	3-0
5-14	Dennis Malseed	Sherbrooke	Eastern	West Haven	3-0 (7)
5-15	Nolan Ryan	California	American	Kansas City	3-0
5-16	John D'Acquisto	Phoenix	Pacific Coast	Tacoma	7-0 (7)
5-17	John Denny	Arkansas	Texas	Midland	8-1
5-19	John Larkin	Orangeburg	W. Carolinas	Charleston	5-2
5-20	Patrick Tatom	Salinas	California	Reno	0-1 (7)
5-25	Bob Forsch	Tulsa	American Assoc.	Denver	5-0
6-2	Dave Freisleben	Hawaii	Pacific Coast	Albuquerque	1-0 (7)
6-3	L. Antonio Gonzalez	St. Petersburg	Florida State	Winter Haven	1-0 (7)
6-8	Randall Tate	Pompano Beach	Florida State	Ft. Lauderdale	2-0 (7)
6-22	Gene Lanthorn	Portland	Northwest	Walla Walla	4-0 (7)
6-23	Dick Pole	Pawtucket	International	Peninsula	2-0 (7)
6-27	Ed Ricks	Ft. Lauderdale	Florida State	Pompano Beach	2-0 (7)
7-1	Dennis Stegman	Lewiston	Northwest	Walla Walla	4-0 (7)
7-15	Nolan Ryan	California	American	Detroit	6-0
7-18	Gregory Reinecker	Bellingham	Northwest	Portland	5-0
7-20	Jim Bibby	Texas	American	Oakland	6-0
7-25	Robert Dean/ Paulo DeLeon	Cedar Rapids	Midwest	Danville	6-0 (7)
7-25	Rick Jensen	Tampa	Florida State	Miami	1-0 (7)
7-26	Matt Rosiek	Columbus	Southern	Savannah	9-0
8-2	Bill Kouns	Pawtucket	International	Richmond	1-0 (7)
8-2	Douglas Dreier	Seattle	Northwest	Lewiston	6-0
8-4	Robert Lang	Quebec	Eastern	West Haven	3-0
8-5	Phil Niekro	Atlanta	National	San Diego	9-0
8-5	Dave Lemanczyk	Montgomery	Southern	Asheville	3-0
8-14	Fred Anyzeski	Johnson City	Appalachian	Bristol	2-0 (7)
8-18	Mark Klein	Pulaski	Appalachian	Marion	3-1 (7)
8-19	Dennis Malseed	Sherbrooke	Eastern	Pittsfield	6-0
8-20	Jimmie Johnson	Marion	Appalachian	Wytheville	6-0 (5)
8-21	Daniel Boitano	Auburn	New York-Penn.	Elmira	2-0
8-22	David Aloi	Covington	Appalachian	Bristol	6-0
8-24	Brian Sheekey	Anderson	W. Carolinas	Orangeburg	10-0
8-25	Rick Jensen	Tampa	Florida State	Lakeland	3-0 (7)
8-26	Gary Lance	Jacksonville	Southern	Birmingham	3-0
8-28	Raymond Brown	San Jose	California	Modesto	3-0 (P, 7)

Number in parentheses indicates innings if other than nine; "P" indicates perfect game.

THIS DATE IN MINOR LEAGUE HISTORY

April 14, 1973, Columbus and Savannah played a 23-inning game in the Southern League. The game was scheduled as the first game of a doubleheader, but when it ended at 1 a.m., game two was postponed. However, a between games fireworks display went off as scheduled until police arrived.

April 26, 1973, Dennis Leonard, San Jose, California League, retired 27 batters in a row after walking the leadoff batter in a game with Visalia. Leonard posted a 2-0 no-hit victory.

May 3, 1973, Raymond Perry, 52, former infielder who led a minor league in home runs for seven consecutive years, 1948-1954, died in Fremont, California.

May 13, 1973, The Appleton Foxes, Midwest League, defeated Clinton 4-2 after having lost their first 15 games of the season.

June 15, 1973, Tommie Aaron, younger brother of the Braves' Hank Aaron, was appointed manager of Savannah, Southern League, becoming the first black manager of a club in the deep South and the first black manager in a Double A League.

June 19, 1973, Silvano Quezada, Tampico, Mexican League, lost his first game of the season after 16 consecutive victories, bowing 4-1 to the Mexico City Tigres. Quezada finished the season with a record of 22-2.

August 20, 1973, Minnie Minoso, at age 50, completed the Mexican League season with a batting average of .265 in 120 games for Union Laguna. Minoso, an ex-major league star, hit 12 homers and drove in 83 runs.

December 10, 1973, Joseph Riggert, 87, the all-time minor league career leader in triples with 228, died in Kansas City, Missouri. Riggert, an outfielder, had 2,708 hits in his minor league career from 1909 to 1928 for a batting mark of .301.

1974

American League
President: Leland S. MacPhail, Jr.

East Standings	W	L	Pct.	GB	Attend.	Manager
Baltimore Orioles	91	71	.562	—	962,572	Earl Weaver
New York Yankees.............	89	73	.549	2	1,273,075	Bill Virdon
Boston Red Sox	84	78	.519	7	1,556,411	Darrell Johnson
Cleveland Indians	77	85	.475	14	1,114,262	Ken Aspromonte
Milwaukee Brewers.............	76	86	.469	15	955,741	Del Crandall
Detroit Tigers.....................	72	90	.444	19	1,243,080	Ralph Houk

West Standings	W	L	Pct.	GB	Attend.	Manager
Oakland Athletics	90	72	.556	—	845,693	Alvin Dark
Texas Rangers....................	84	76	.525	5	1,193,902	Billy Martin
Minnesota Twins	82	80	.506	8	662,401	Frank Quilici
Chicago White Sox	80	80	.500	9	1,149,596	Chuck Tanner
Kansas City Royals.............	77	85	.475	13	1,173,292	Jack McKeon
California Angels	68	94	.420	22	917,269	Bobby Winkles/Whitey Herzog/ Dick Williams

Playoff: Oakland 3 games, Baltimore 1.

BA: Rod Carew, Minnesota, .364
Runs: Carl Yastrzemski, Boston, 93
Hits: Rod Carew, Minnesota, 218
RBIs: Jeff Burroughs, Texas, 118
HRs: Dick Allen, Chicago, 32

Wins: Catfish Hunter, Oakland, 25
Ferguson Jenkins, Texas, 25
SOs: Nolan Ryan, California, 367
ERA: Catfish Hunter, Oakland, 2.49
Pct: Mike Cuellar, Baltimore, .688, 22-10
Saves: Terry Forster, Chicago, 24

National League
President: Charles S. Feeney

East Standings	W	L	Pct.	GB	Attend.	Manager
Pittsburgh Pirates................	88	74	.543	—	1,110,552	Danny Murtaugh
St. Louis Cardinals	86	75	.534	1½	1,838,413	Red Schoendienst
Philadelphia Phillies	80	82	.494	8	1,808,648	Danny Ozark
Montreal Expos	79	82	.491	8½	1,019,134	Gene Mauch
New York Mets	71	91	.438	17	1,722,209	Yogi Berra
Chicago Cubs......................	66	96	.407	22	1,015,378	Whitey Lockman/ Jim Marshall

West Standings	W	L	Pct.	GB	Attend.	Manager
Los Angeles Dodgers........	102	60	.630	—	2,632,474	Walter Alston
Cincinnati Reds...................	98	64	.605	4	2,164,307	Sparky Anderson
Atlanta Braves	88	74	.543	14	981,085	Eddie Mathews/Clyde King
Houston Astros	81	81	.500	21	1,090,728	Preston Gomez
San Francisco Giants	72	90	.444	30	519,987	Charlie Fox/Wes Westrum
San Diego Padres................	60	102	.370	42	1,075,399	John McNamara

Playoff: Los Angeles 3 games, Pittsburgh 1.

BA: Ralph Garr, Atlanta, .353
Runs: Pete Rose, Cincinnati, 110
Hits: Ralph Garr, Atlanta, 214
RBIs: Johnny Bench, Cincinnati, 129
HRs: Mike Schmidt, Philadelphia, 36

Wins: Phil Niekro, Atlanta, 20
Andy Messersmith, Los Angeles, 20
SOs: Steve Carlton, Philadelphia, 240
ERA: Buzz Capra, Atlanta, 2.28
Pct: Andy Messersmith, L.A., .769, 20-6
Saves: Mike Marshall, Los Angeles, 21
Games: Mike Marshall, Los Angeles, 106

AAA American Association
President: Joe Ryan

East Standings	W	L	Pct.	GB	Attend.	Manager
Indianapolis Indians (15)....	78	57	.578	—	138,717	Vern Rapp
Iowa Oaks (4)	74	62	.544	4½	110,350	Joe Sparks
Evansville Triplets (6)........	68	67	.504	10	104,496	Fred Hatfield
Omaha Royals (7)...............	54	82	.397	24½	120,992	Harry Malmberg

West Standings	W	L	Pct.	GB	Attend.	Manager
Tulsa Oilers (22).................	76	58	.567	—	135,207	Ken Boyer
Wichita Aeros (14)	67	68	.496	9½	185,482	Mike Roarke
Oklahoma City 89ers (5)...	62	73	.459	14½	55,813	John "Red" Davis
Denver Bears (16)...............	62	74	.455	15	159,721	Frank Verdi

Playoff: Tulsa 4 games, Indianapolis 3.

All-Star Team: 1B-Keith Hernandez, Tulsa; **2B**-Duane Kuiper, Oklahoma City; **3B**-Bill Stein, Iowa; **SS**-Doug Flynn, Indianapolis; **OF**-Pete LaCock, Wichita; Tom Spencer, Indianapolis; Dan Godby, Tulsa; **C**-Marc Hill, Tulsa; Skip Jutze, Denver; **DH**-Lamar Johnson, Iowa; **Util**-Danny Meyer, Evansville; **P**-Jim Kern, Oklahoma City; Ray Bare, Tulsa; **MVP**-Pete LaCock, Wichita; **Pitcher of the Year**-Jim Kern, Oklahoma City; **Manager**-Vern Rapp, Indianapolis.

BA: Keith Hernandez, Tulsa, .351
Runs: Bill Stein, Iowa, 107
Hits: Bill Stein, Iowa, 178
RBIs: Lamar Johnson, Iowa, 96

HRs: Adrian Garrett, Wichita, 26
Wins: Jim Kern, Oklahoma City, 17
SOs: Jim Kern, Oklahoma City, 220
ERA: Ray Bare, Tulsa, 2.34

AAA International League
President: George H. Sisler, Jr.

North Standings	W	L	Pct.	GB	Attend.	Manager
Rochester Red Wings (1)....	88	56	.611	—	269,703	Joe Altobelli
Syracuse Chiefs (10).........	74	70	.514	14	174,673	Bobby Cox
Toledo Mud Hens (20)	70	74	.486	18	93,384	Jim Bunning
Pawtucket Red Sox (2)	57	87	.396	31	80,268	Joe Morgan

South Standings	W	L	Pct.	GB	Attend.	Manager
Memphis Blues (18)	87	55	.613	—	132,513	Karl Kuehl
Richmond Braves (13)........	75	65	.536	11	93,679	Clint Courtney
Charleston Charlies (21)....	62	81	.434	25½	92,237	Steve Demeter
Tidewater Tides (19)	57	82	.410	28½	70,813	Johnny Antonelli

Playoffs: Rochester 4 games, Memphis 2; Syracuse 4 games, Richmond 1.
Finals: Rochester 4 games, Syracuse 3.

All-Star Team: 1B-Bob Beall, Richmond; **2B**-Rob Andrews, Rochester; **3B**-Doug DeCinces, Rochester; **SS**-Tim Nordbrook, Rochester; **OF**-Jim Rice, Pawtucket; Fred Lynn, Pawtucket; Jose Mangual, Memphis; **C**-Gary Carter, Memphis; **P**-Bill Kirkpatrick, Rochester; Scott McGregor, Syracuse; **MVP**-Jim Rice, Pawtucket; **Pitcher of the Year**-Scott McGregor, Syracuse; **Manager**-Karl Kuehl, Memphis.

BA: Jim Rice, Pawtucket, .337
Runs: Bob Beall, Richmond, 105
Hits: Rob Andrews, Rochester, 165
RBIs: Jim Rice, Pawtucket, 93

HRs: Jim Rice, Pawtucket, 25
Wins: Bill Kirkpatrick, Rochester, 15
SOs: Jim Burton, Pawtucket, 165
ERA: Larry Gura, Syracuse, 2.14

AAA Mexican League
President: Antonio Ramirez Muro

North West Standings	W	L	Pct.	GB	Attend.	Manager
Saltillo Saraperos................	83	53	.610	—	193,903	Andres Tanaka
Union Laguna Algodoneros	79	57	.581	4	205,570	Jose Guerrero
Chihuahua Dorados	64	71	.474	18½	200,573	Pedro Gonzalez
Ciudad Juarez Indios	60	78	.435	24	165,447	Minnie Mendoza

North East Standings	W	L	Pct.	GB	Attend.	Manager
Tampico Alijadores	66	71	.482	—	185,858	Francisco Herrera
Monterrey Sultanes.............	65	72	.474	1	195,833	Miguel Sotelo
Coahuila Mineros	59	77	.434	6½	202,072	Tomas Herrera
Reynosa Bravos	53	79	.402	10½	61,190	Jorge Fitch

South West Standings	W	L	Pct.	GB	Attend.	Manager
Jalisco Charros...................	84	50	.627	—	152,341	Vinicio Garcia
Puebla Pericos	81	56	.591	4½	143,517	Tony Castano
Poza Rica Petroleros	71	65	.522	14	119,570	Moises Camacho
Mexico City Tigres	56	78	.418	28	253,189	Jose Luis Garcia/ Ron Camacho

South East Standings	W	L	Pct.	GB	Attend.	Manager
Mexico City Diablos Rojos	75	61	.551	—	398,122	Ben Reyes
Cordoba Cafeteros	66	67	.496	7½	286,694	Mario Pelaez/Alberto Joachin
Veracruz Aguila	62	74	.456	13	96,910	Enrique Izquierdo
Yucatan Leones	60	75	.444	14½	169,848	Julian Javier/Mario Pelaez

Playoffs: MC Diablos Rojos 4 games, Puebla 2; Jalisco 4 games, Cordoba 0; Union Laguna 4 games, Tampico 1; Saltillo 4 games, Monterrey 1. MC Diablos Rojos 4 games, Jalisco 2; Union Laguna 4 games, Saltillo 3.
Finals: MC Diablos Rojos 4 games, Union Laguna 0.

All-Star Team: 1B-Hector Espino, Tampico; **2B**-Gabriel Lugo, Saltillo; **3B**-Benjamin Cerda, Jalisco; **SS**-Guadalupe Chavez, Saltillo; **OF**-Ramon Montoya, MC Diablos Rojos; Jorge Roque, Puebla; Miguel Suarez, MC Diablos Rojos; **C**-Sergio Robles, MC Diablos Rojos; **P**-Juan Pizarro, Cordoba; Antonio Pollorena, Union Laguna; **Manager**-Ben Reyes, MC Diablos Rojos.

BA: Teo Acosta, Puebla, .366
Runs: Teo Acosta, Puebla, 93
Hits: Teo Acosta, Puebla, 170
Angel Bravo, Chihuahua/Monterrey, 170
RBIs: Jorge Roque, Puebla, 90

HRs: Byron Browne, Tampico, 32
Wins: Antonio Pollorena, Union Laguna, 25
SOs: Antonio Pollorena, Union Laguna, 183
ERA: Juan Pizarro, Cordoba, 1.57

AAA Pacific Coast League
President: Roy Jackson

East Standings	W	L	Pct.	GB	Attend.	Manager
Albuquerque Dukes (17)	76	66	.535	—	162,856	Stan Wasiak
Phoenix Giants (24)............	75	69	.521	2	158,213	Rocky Bridges
Salt Lake City Angels (3)...	69	73	.486	7	56,883	Norm Sherry
Tucson Toros (11)	65	78	.455	11½	165,221	Sherm Lollar

West Standings	W	L	Pct.	GB	Attend.	Manager
Spokane Indians (12)	78	64	.549	—	79,614	Del Wilber
Tacoma Twins (9)...............	75	66	.532	2½	165,313	Cal Ermer
Hawaii Islanders (23).........	67	77	.465	12	179,633	Roy Hartsfield
Sacramento Solons (8)........	66	78	.458	13	295,831	Bob Lemon

Playoff: Spokane 3 games, Albuquerque 0.

*Won first-half   **Won second-half   ***Won both halves
Numbers after nicknames indicate farm system.
Affiliation listed at end of each year.

527

All-Star Team: 1B-Phil James, Phoenix; **2B-**Bobby Randall, Albuquerque; **3B-**Bill McNulty, Sacramento; Phil Garner, Tucson; **SS-**Ivan DeJesus, Albuquerque; **OF-**Bruce Bochte, Salt Lake City; Dave Moates, Spokane; Charlie Manuel, Albuquerque; **C-**Tim Hosley, Tucson; **DH-**Tom Robson, Spokane; **P-**Rex Hudson, Albuquerque; Rick Waits, Spokane; **MVP-**Tom Robson, Spokane; **Manager-**Rocky Bridges, Phoenix.

BA: Glenn Adams, Phoenix, .352
Runs: Bill McNulty, Sacramento, 135
Hits: Bobby Randall, Albuquerque, 181
RBIs: Bill McNulty, Sacramento, 135
HRs: Bill McNulty, Sacramento, 55
Wins: Rex Hudson, Albuquerque, 16
SOs: Butch Metzger, Phoenix, 148
ERA: Juan Veintidos, Tacoma, 3.67

AA Eastern League
President: P. Patrick McKernan

American Standings	W	L	Pct.	GB	Attend.	Manager
Bristol Red Sox (2)	74	61	.548	—	47,989	Stan Williams
Pittsfield Rangers (12)	69	70	.496	7	29,234	Joe Klein
Waterbury Dodgers (17)	64	72	.471	10½	54,506	Don LeJohn
West Haven Yankees (10)	58	79	.423	17	42,878	Doc Edwards

National Standings	W	L	Pct.	GB	Attend.	Manager
Quebec Carnavals (18)	76	64	.543	—	82,133	Lance Nichols
Thetford Mines Pirates (21)	75	65	.536	1	22,516	Tim Murtaugh
Reading Phillies (20)	69	66	.511	4½	73,509	Bob Wellman
Trois Rivieres Aigles (15)	65	73	.471	10	84,843	Jim Snyder

Playoffs: Thetford Mines 2 games, Bristol 0; Pittsfield 2 games, Quebec 0.
Finals: Thetford Mines 2 games, Pittsfield 0.

All-Star Team: 1B-Jack Baker, Bristol; **2B-**Freddie Andrews, Reading; Willie Randolph, Thetford Mines; **3B-**Larry Parrish, Quebec; **SS-**Roy Smalley, Pittsfield; **OF-**Warren Cromartie, Quebec; Omar Moreno, Thetford Mines; Joe Simpson, Waterbury; **C-**Ken Macha, Thetford Mines; **P-**Steve Barr, Bristol; **MVP-**Ken Macha, Thetford Mines; **Manager-**Stan Williams, Bristol.

BA: Ken Macha, Thetford Mines, .345
Runs: Willie Randolph, Thetford Mines, 103
Hits: Warren Cromartie, Quebec, 162
RBIs: Jack Baker, Bristol, 105
HRs: Jack Baker, Bristol, 27
Wins: Steve Barr, Bristol, 16
SOs: Roy Thomas, Reading, 168
ERA: Denis McSween, Quebec, 1.89

AA Southern League
President: Billy Hitchcock

East Standings	W	L	Pct.	GB	Attend.	Manager
Jacksonville Suns (7)	78	60	.565	—	98,652	Billy Gardner
Orlando Twins (9)	73	61	.545	3	44,952	Dick Phillips
Savannah Braves (13)	73	65	.529	5	77,025	Tommie Aaron
Columbus Astros (16)	65	73	.471	13	106,462	Jimmie Williams

West Standings	W	L	Pct.	GB	Attend.	Manager
Knoxville Knox Sox (4)	72	63	.533	—	52,432	Jim Napier
Asheville Orioles (1)	70	67	.511	3	42,840	Cal Ripken, Sr.
Montgomery Rebels (6)	61	76	.445	12	46,320	Jim Leyland
Birmingham A's (11)	54	81	.400	18	22,897	Harry Bright

Playoff: Knoxville 3 games, Jacksonville 2.

All-Star Team: 1B-Mike Squires, Knoxville; **2B-**Kim Andrew, Asheville; **3B-**Chet Lemon, Birmingham; **SS-**Kiko Garcia, Asheville; **OF-**Nyls Nyman, Knoxville; Claudell Washington, Birmingham; Bob Gorinski, Orlando; **C-**Biff Pocoroba, Savannah; **Util-**Steve Staggs, Jacksonville; **P-**Paul Siebert, Columbus; Leo Williams, Knoxville; **Manager-**Jim Napier, Knoxville.

BA: Nyls Nyman, Knoxville, .325
Runs: Nyls Nyman, Knoxville, 87
Hits: Nyls Nyman, Knoxville, 166
RBIs: Bob Gorinski, Orlando, 100
HRs: Bob Gorinski, Orlando, 23
  Mike Poepping, Orlando, 23
Wins: Paul Siebert, Columbus, 15
  Domingo Figueroa, Savannah, 15
SOs: Mike Stanton, Columbus, 146
ERA: Michael Beard, Savannah, 2.40

AA Texas League
President: Bobby Bragan

East Standings	W	L	Pct.	GB	Attend.	Manager
Victoria Toros (19)	79	57	.581	—	49,020	Joe Frazier
Arkansas Travelers (22)	75	59	.560	3	66,456	Jack Krol
Shreveport Captains (8)	59	79	.428	21	35,503	Gene Freese/Ken McBride
Alexandria Aces (23)	49	85	.366	29	44,083	Jackie Brandt/Ken Bracey

West Standings	W	L	Pct.	GB	Attend.	Manager
El Paso Diablos (3)	76	61	.555	—	112,477	Dave Garcia
Amarillo Giants (24)	69	62	.527	4	45,691	Dennis Sommers
San Antonio Missions (5)	68	64	.515	5½	143,519	Woody Smith
Midland Cubs (14)	65	73	.471	11½	87,870	Walt Dixon

Playoff: Victoria 3 games, El Paso 0.

All-Star Team: 1B-Brock Pemberton, Victoria; **2B-**Jerry Remy, El Paso; **3B-**Randy Trapp, Victoria; **SS-**Mike Miley, El Paso; **OF-**Jerry Turner, Alexandria; Jerry Mumphrey, Arkansas; John Balaz, El Paso; **C-**Mike Minster, Amarillo; **DH-**Wayne Tyrone, Midland; **Util-**Rudy Kinard, Arkansas; **P-**Dennis Eckersley, San Antonio; Randy Wiles, Arkansas; **MVP-**John Balaz, El Paso; **Manager-**Joe Frazier, Victoria.

BA: Dave Collins, El Paso, .352
Runs: John Balaz, El Paso, 100
Hits: John Balaz, El Paso, 177
RBIs: John Balaz, El Paso, 111
HRs: Jerry Tabb, Midland, 29
  Wayne Tyrone, Midland, 29
Wins: Dennis Eckersley, San Antonio, 14
  Sid Monge, El Paso, 14
  Harold Rasmussen, Arkansas, 14
SOs: Dennis Eckersley, San Antonio, 163
ERA: Randy Wiles, Arkansas, 2.56

A California League
President: Edward J. Mulligan

Standings	W	L	Pct.	GB	Attend.	Manager
Fresno Giants*(24)	85	55	.607	—	73,335	John Van Ornum
San Jose Bees**(7)	81	59	.579	4	96,115	Steve Boros
Salinas Packers (3)	78	62	.557	7	41,386	Jim Saul
Modesto Reds (22)	68	72	.486	17	50,218	Roy Thomas
Bakersfield Dodgers (17)	65	75	.464	20	43,294	George Freese
Lodi Orioles (1)	61	79	.436	24	36,170	Jimmie Schaffer
Reno Silver Sox (5)	61	79	.436	24	36,563	Joe Azcue/Del Youngblood
Visalia Mets (19)	61	79	.436	24	41,714	Nolan Campbell

Playoff: Fresno 3 games, San Jose 2.

All-Star Team: 1B-Craig Cacek, Visalia; **2B-**Jose Baez, Bakersfield; **3B-**Jack Clark, Fresno; **SS-**Dave Machemer, Salinas; **OF-**Michael Dimmel, Bakersfield; Paul Husband, Modesto; Sheldon Mallory, San Jose; **C-**Gary Alexander, Fresno; **Util-**Darrel Darrow, Salinas; **P-**Bob Knepper, Fresno; Steve Greenough, Fresno; Lynn McKinney, San Jose; William Rothan, Salinas; **MVP-**Gary Alexander, Fresno; **Manager-**John Van Ornum, Fresno.

BA: Jose Baez, Bakersfield, .330
Runs: Craig Cacek, Visalia, 112
Hits: Jose Baez, Bakersfield, 167
RBIs: Jack Clark, Fresno, 117
HRs: Gary Alexander, Fresno, 27
Wins: Bob Knepper, Fresno, 20
SOs: Bob Knepper, Fresno, 247
ERA: Lynn McKinney, San Jose, 2.23

A Carolina League
President: Wallace McKenna

Standings	W	L	Pct.	GB	Attend.	Manager
Salem Pirates***(21)	87	50	.635	—	41,379	John Lipon
Lynchburg Twins (9)	78	62	.557	10½	48,732	Harry Warner
Winston-Salem Red Sox (2)	76	61	.555	11	33,182	Bill Slack
Rocky Mount Phillies (20)	72	67	.518	16	38,677	Cal Emery
Peninsula Pennants (x)	58	76	.433	27½	36,087	Len Johnston
Kinston Expos (18)	38	93	.290	46	27,342	Jack Damaska

Playoffs: None.

All-Star Team: 1B-Randy Bass, Lynchburg; **2B-**Charley Meyers, Winston-Salem; **3B-**Frank Grundler, Lynchburg; **SS-**Todd Cruz, Rocky Mount; **OF-**Miguel Dilone, Salem; Willie Norwood, Lynchburg; Alfredo Edmead, Salem; **C-**Steve Nicosia, Salem; **P-**Doug Nelson, Salem; Don Aase, Winston-Salem; **MVP-**Miguel Dilone, Salem; **Manager-**John Lipon, Salem.

BA: Frank Grundler, Lynchburg, .335
Runs: Frank Grundler, Lynchburg, 115
Hits: Miguel Dilone, Salem, 177
RBIs: Randy Bass, Lynchburg, 112
HRs: Randy Bass, Lynchburg, 30
Wins: Don Aase, Winston-Salem, 17
SOs: Dan Greenhalgh, Rocky Mount, 177
ERA: Don Aase, Winston-Salem, 2.43

A Florida State League
President: George MacDonald, Jr.

North Standings	W	L	Pct.	GB	Attend.	Manager
Tampa Tarpons (15)	68	64	.515	—	70,004	Russ Nixon
Lakeland Tigers (6)	66	64	.508	1	27,824	Frank "Stubby" Overmire
Winter Haven Red Sox (2)	59	71	.454	8	6,006	Rac Slider
St. Petersburg Cardinals (22)	59	71	.454	8	145,230	Roy Majtyka

South Standings	W	L	Pct.	GB	Attend.	Manager
Ft. Lauderdale Yankees (10)	82	49	.626	—	70,147	Pete Ward
West Palm Beach Expos (18)	79	53	.598	3½	107,790	Gordy MacKenzie
Miami Orioles (1)	74	58	.561	8½	50,194	George Farson
Key West Conchs (14)	37	94	.282	45	17,489	Jack Mull/Q.V. Lowe

Playoffs: West Palm Beach 2 games, Tampa 0; Ft. Lauderdale 2 games, Lakeland 0.
Finals: West Palm Beach 2 games, Ft. Lauderdale 1.

All-Star Team: 1B-Eddie Murray, Miami; **2B-**Richard Cuoco, Miami; **3B-**Ron Roenicke, West Palm Beach; **SS-**Mark Cunningham, West Palm Beach; **OF-**Ron LeFlore, Lakeland; Bob Baldwin, Lakeland; Leonel Carrion, West Palm Beach; **C-**Willie Royster, Miami; Greg Shippy, Lakeland; **Util-**Luis Gonzalez, St. Petersburg; Ernest Rosseau, St. Petersburg; **P-**Joe Keener, West Palm Beach; Gary Christenson, Lakeland; **MVP-**Ron LeFlore, Lakeland; **Manager-**Gordy MacKenzie, West Palm Beach.

BA: Ron LeFlore, Lakeland, .339
Runs: Ron LeFlore, Lakeland, 79
Hits: Bob Baldwin, Lakeland, 150
RBIs: Gary Roenicke, West Palm Beach, 82
HRs: Joe Wallis, Key West, 16
Wins: Joe Keener, West Palm Beach, 16
SOs: Richard Anderson, Ft. Lauderdale, 179
ERA: Antonio Chevez, Miami, 1.57

A Mexican Center League
President: Antonio Ramirez Muro

Center Standings	W	L	Pct.	GB	Attend.	Manager
Durango	52	23	.693	—	18,893	Ossie Alvarez
San Pedro	42	34	.553	10½	18,848	Felipe Hernandez
Aguascalientes Tigres	41	36	.532	12	23,623	Ben Valenzuela
Parras	35	43	.449	18½	20,499	Hector Rodriguez

Gulf Standings	W	L	Pct.	GB	Attend.	Manager
Ciudad Valles Valles	39	37	.513	—	6,800	Juan Hernandez
Ciudad Mante Azucareros	34	42	.447	5	7,425	Ramiro Cuevas
Ciudad Victoria Henequeneros	34	44	.436	6	12,000	Bimbo Villegas
Ebano Rojos	30	48	.385	10	12,300	Arturo Cacheux

Playoffs: Ciudad Valles 2 games, Ciudad Mante 1; Durango 2 games, San Pedro 0.
Finals: Durango 3 games, Ciudad Valles 2.

All-Star Team: 1B-Enrique Jordan, Durango; **2B**-Donaldo Lugo, Parras; **3B**-Nelson Barrera, Ebano; **SS**-Julio Esparza, Ciudad Valles; **OF**-Candy Cardona, Parras; Romulo Munoz, Aguascalientes; Jose Valenzuela, Durango; **C**-Luis Guillermo Gonzalez, San Pedro; Jesus Robles, Ciudad Valles; **P**-Regio Moroyoqui, Ciudad Valles; Mario Valdez, Aguascalientes; **MVP**-Jose Valenzuela, Durango; **Manager**-Ben Valenzuela, Aguascalientes.

BA: Jose Valenzuela, Durango, .384
Runs: Jose Valenzuela, Durango, 64
Hits: Jose Valenzuela, Durango, 108
RBIs: Jose Valenzuela, Durango, 79

HRs: Jose Valenzuela, Durango, 12
Juan Martinez, Ciudad Victoria, 12
Roberto Ornelas, San Pedro, 12
Wins: Eleazar Beltran, Ebano/San Pedro, 13
SOs: Hector Lopez, Aguascalientes, 112
ERA: Regio Moroyoqui, Ciudad Valles, 0.58

A Midwest League
President: Bill Walters

North Standings	W	L	Pct.	GB	Attend.	Manager
Wisconsin Rapids Twins*(9)	80	48	.625	—	69,856	John Goryl
Appleton Foxes**(4)	73	50	.593	4½	69,210	Gordon Lund
Waterloo Royals (7)	68	56	.548	10	71,229	John Sullivan
Cedar Rapids Astros (16)	54	66	.450	22	36,056	Leo Posada
Dubuque Packers (x)	44	78	.361	33	52,394	Bert Thiel

South Standings	W	L	Pct.	GB	Attend.	Manager
Quad Cities Angels*(3)	65	58	.528	—	61,285	Jimy Williams
Danville Warriors**(8)	61	57	.517	1½	58,475	Matt Galante
Burlington Bees (11)	61	59	.508	2½	46,630	Rene Lachemann
Decatur Commodores (24)	55	69	.444	10½	45,550	Bob Hartsfield
Clinton Pilots (6)	52	72	.419	13½	46,587	Len Okrie

Playoffs: Appleton 2 games, Wisconsin Rapids 0; Danville 2 games, Quad Cities 1.
Finals: Danville 2 games, Appleton 1.

All-Star Team: 1B-James Richardson, Danville; **2B**-Doug Clarey, Wisconsin Rapids; **3B**-Larry Wolfe, Wisconsin Rapids; **SS**-Alex Taveras, Cedar Rapids; **OF**-Moe Hill, Wisconsin Rapids; Alvis Woods, Wisconsin Rapids; Alan Newsome, Clinton; **C**-Thomas Mutz, Dubuque; Ernie Young, Decatur; **P**-Jeff Gressick, Waterloo; Michael Van DeCasteele, Wisconsin Rapids; **Manage**-John Goryl, Wisconsin Rapids.

BA: Moe Hill, Wisconsin Rapids, .339
Runs: Gary Ward, Wisconsin Rapids, 104
Hits: Moe Hill, Wisconsin Rapids, 150
RBIs: Moe Hill, Wisconsin Rapids, 113

HRs: Moe Hill, Wisconsin Rapids, 32
Wins: Michael Messman, Wisconsin Rapids, 16
SOs: Lafayette Currence, Danville, 184
ERA: Luis Sanchez, Cedar Rapids, 1.59

A New York-Pennsylvania League
President: Vincent M. McNamara

Standings	W	L	Pct.	GB	Attend.	Manager
Oneonta Yankees (10)	53	16	.768	—	35,836	Mike Ferraro
Auburn Phillies (20)	34	32	.515	17½	46,157	Larry Rojas
Elmira Red Sox (2)	34	35	.493	19	41,347	Dick Berardino
Niagara Falls Pirates (21)	33	36	.478	20	32,299	Ron Brand
Newark Co-Pilots (8)	30	36	.455	21½	15,467	John Felske
Batavia Trojans (19)	20	49	.290	33	38,751	Wilbur Huckle

Playoffs: None.

All-Star Team: 1B-Dave Bergman, Oneonta; **2B**-Michael Edwards, Niagara Falls; **3B**-Pat Peterson, Oneonta; **SS**-Jim Gantner, Newark; **OF**-Marv Thompson, Oneonta; Lonnie Smith, Auburn; Sam Bowen, Elmira; Dale Lydecker, Batavia; **C**-Dennis Werth, Oneonta; Larry Silveira, Auburn; **Util**-Steve Hughes, Niagara Falls; **P**-Greg Diehl, Oneonta; Fred Anyzeski, Oneonta; Rod Scurry, Niagara Falls; Barry Cort, Newark; **Manager**-Mike Ferraro, Oneonta.

BA: Dave Bergman, Oneonta, .348
Runs: Marv Thompson, Oneonta, 62
Hits: Pat Peterson, Oneonta, 88
RBIs: Dennis Werth, Oneonta, 61

HRs: Steve Bowling, Newark, 12
Wins: Fred Anyzeski, Oneonta, 10
SOs: Barry Cort, Newark, 123
ERA: Fred Anyzeski, Oneonta, 1.61

A Northwest League
President: Bob Richmond

East Standings	W	L	Pct.	GB	Attend.	Manager
Eugene Emeralds (x)	48	36	.571	—	48,360	Hugh Luby/Joseph Verbanic
Walla Walla Padres (23)	47	37	.560	1	28,295	Cliff Ditto
Lewiston Broncs (11)	33	51	.393	15	13,872	Bobby Hofman/Carl "Buddy" Peterson
Tri-City Ports	27	57	.321	21	21,611	Carl Thompson

West Standings	W	L	Pct.	GB	Attend.	Manager
Bellingham Dodgers (17)	52	32	.619	—	30,350	Bill Berrier
Portland Mavericks	50	34	.595	2	100,111	Frank Peters
Seattle Rainiers (15)	45	39	.536	7	36,143	Greg Riddoch
New Westminster Frasers	34	50	.405	18	10,599	John Wojcik/Gregory Werdick

Playoff: Eugene 2 games, Bellingham 1.

All-Star Team: 1B-Mark Lucich, Eugene; **2B**-Ed Cervantes, Portland; **3B**-Gene Delyon, Walla Walla; **SS**-Robert Waits, Portland; **OF**-Clifton Holland, Portland; Terrence Jones, Portland; Jeff Leonard, Bellingham; **C**-Bill Hamilton, Walla Walla; **DH**-Dick Meily, Eugene; **P**-Rick Sutcliffe, Bellingham; James Emery, Portland; Guy Todd, Bellingham; Keith Halgerson, Seattle.

BA: Bill Hamilton, Walla Walla, .352
Runs: Reggie Thomas, Portland, 63
Hits: Clifton Holland, Portland, 101
RBIs: Barry Moss, Eugene, 69

HRs: Dick Meily, Eugene, 15
Wins: Guy Todd, Bellingham, 11
SOs: Doug Slocum, Bellingham, 94
ERA: Guy Todd, Bellingham, 1.73

A Western Carolinas League
President: John H. Moss

Standings	W	L	Pct.	GB	Attend.	Manager
Gastonia Rangers***(12)	84	48	.636	—	18,977	Rich Donnelly
Charleston Pirates (21)	71	60	.542	12½	50,011	Larry Sherry
Greenwood Braves (13)	70	63	.526	14½	37,255	Gary Geiger
Orangeburg Dodgers (17)	63	71	.470	22	22,908	Bart Shirley
Anderson Mets (19)	61	72	.459	23½	27,840	Owen Friend
Spartanburg Phillies (20)	49	84	.368	35½	34,752	Howie Bedell

Playoffs: None.

All-Star Team: 1B-Dan Duran, Gastonia; **2B**-Gary Cooper, Gastonia; **3B**-Jose Del Moral, Orangeburg; **SS**-Bill Dancy, Spartanburg; **OF**-John Guarnaccia, Spartanburg; Lee Mazzilli, Anderson; Calvin Smith, Greenwood; **C**-Luis Rosado, Anderson; **Util**-Pat Rockett, Greenwood; **P**-Randy Sealy, Charleston; Willie Hernandez, Spartanburg; **Manager**-Rich Donnelly, Gastonia.

BA: Calvin Smith, Greenwood, .324
Runs: Gary Cooper, Gastonia, 97
Hits: Calvin Smith, Greenwood, 148
RBIs: Dan Duran, Gastonia, 99

HRs: John Guarnaccia, Spartanburg, 28
Wins: Michael Bacsik, Gastonia, 15
SOs: Willie Hernandez, Spartanburg, 179
ERA: Randy Sealy, Charleston, 1.97

R Appalachian League
President: Chauncey De Vault

North Standings	W	L	Pct.	GB	Attend.	Manager
Bristol Tigers (6)	52	17	.754	—	10,822	Joe Lewis
Elizabethton Twins (9)	41	27	.603	10½	17,430	Bob Butler
Johnson City Yankees (10)	31	38	.449	21	16,090	Gene Hassell
Kingsport Braves (13)	31	39	.443	21½	35,841	Hoyt Wilhelm

South Standings	W	L	Pct.	GB	Attend.	Manager
Bluefield Orioles (1)	37	32	.536	—	15,675	Bobby Malkmus
Marion Mets (19)	33	35	.485	3½	10,087	Chuck Hiller
Covington Astros (16)	32	37	.464	5	15,360	Billy Smith
Pulaski Phillies (20)	18	50	.265	18½	10,080	Bob Wren

Playoffs: None.

All-Star Team: 1B-Fay Thompson, Covington; **2B**-Juan Martinez, Bluefield; **3B**-Lance Parrish, Bristol; **SS**-Richard Rickman, Bluefield; **OF**-Fred Swanson, Bristol; Michael Beck, Elizabethton; Joe Cannon, Covington; **C**-Butch Wynegar, Elizabethton; **P**-Bob Sykes, Bristol; Frank Quintero, Elizabethton; **Manager**-Joe Lewis, Bristol.

BA: Butch Wynegar, Elizabethton, .346
Runs: John Butler, Johnson City, 56
Hits: Joe Cannon, Covington, 84
RBIs: Fred Swanson, Bristol, 64

HRs: Fay Thompson, Covington, 19
Wins: Bob Sykes, Bristol, 11
SOs: Michael Darr, Bluefield, 104
ERA: Bob Sykes, Bristol, 1.07

R Gulf Coast League
President: George MacDonald, Jr.

Standings	W	L	Pct.	GB	Manager
Cubs (14)	33	14	.702	—	Jack Mull
Royals Academy (7)	35	16	.686	—	Billy Goodman
Rangers (12)	32	20	.615	3½	Bill Haywood
Royals (7)	29	19	.604	4½	Billy Scripture
Cardinals (22)	27	21	.563	6½	Tom Burgess & Bobby Dews
White Sox (4)	23	26	.469	11	Joe Jones
Expos (18)	21	33	.389	15½	Pat Daugherty
Indians (5)	16	36	.308	19½	Wilfredo Calvino
Pirates (21)	11	42	.208	25	Woody Huyke

Games played at Sarasota and Bradenton, Florida.

Playoffs: None.

BA: Joe Gates, Academy, .379
Runs: Joe Gates, Academy, 54
Hits: Darrell Parker, Academy, 67
RBIs: Darrell Parker, Academy, 38

HRs: Edwin Olszta, White Sox, 4
Wins: Paul Bock, White Sox, 8
SOs: Stephen Hamrick, Cubs, 87
ERA: Stephen Hamrick, Cubs, 0.93

R Pioneer League

President: Claude Engberg

Standings	W	L	Pct.	GB	Attend.	Manager
Idaho Falls Angels (3)	41	31	.569	—	24,496	Larry Himes
Billings Mustangs (15)	35	37	.486	6	30,146	James Hoff
Great Falls Giants (24)	35	37	.486	6	29,877	Art Mazmanian
Ogden Spikers (x)	33	39	.458	8	13,042	Ben Hines

Playoffs: None.

All-Star Team: 1B-Steve Henderson, Billings; **2B**-Julio Cruz, Idaho Falls; **3B**-Mike Grace, Billings; **SS**-Danny Miller, Ogden; **OF**-Bill Taylor, Idaho Falls; Marshall Edwards, Ogden; Joe Zagarino, Great Falls; **C**-Phil Cannuci, Great Falls; **P**-Andrew Castillo, Idaho Falls;

John Roslund, Idaho Falls; Doug Bird, Ogden; John Caneira, Idaho Falls; **Manager**-Larry Himes, Idaho Falls.

BA: Bill Taylor, Idaho Falls, .344
Runs: Steve Henderson, Billings, 60
Hits: Joe Zagarino, Great Falls, 82
RBIs: Steve Henderson, Billings, 44
Bill Taylor, Idaho Falls, 44

HRs: Steve Henderson, Billings, 8
Dan Daniel, Ogden, 8
Wins: John Caneira, Idaho Falls, 10
SOs: Lawrence Groover, Ogden, 117
ERA: John Roslund, Idaho Falls, 1.14

1974 Interleague Post Season Play

World Series
Oakland (American) 4 games, Los Angeles (National) 1

1974 Major League Farm Systems

American League

1 Baltimore (5): Rochester, Asheville, Lodi, Miami, Bluefield.
2 Boston (5): Pawtucket, Bristol (CT), Winston-Salem, Winter Haven, Elmira.
3 California (5): Salt Lake City, El Paso, Salinas, Quad Cities, Idaho Falls.
4 Chicago (4): Iowa, Knoxville, Appleton, Gulf Coast.
5 Cleveland (4): Oklahoma City, San Antonio, Reno, Gulf Coast.
6 Detroit (5): Evansville, Montgomery, Lakeland, Clinton, Bristol (VA).
7 Kansas City (6): Omaha, Jacksonville, San Jose, Waterloo, Gulf Coast Royals, Gulf Coast Royals Academy.
8 Milwaukee (4): Sacramento, Shreveport, Danville, Newark.
9 Minnesota (5): Tacoma, Orlando, Lynchburg, Wisconsin Rapids, Elizabethton.
10 New York (5): Syracuse, West Haven, Ft. Lauderdale, Oneonta, Johnson City.
11 Oakland (4): Tucson, Birmingham, Burlington, Lewiston.
12 Texas (4): Spokane, Pittsfield, Gastonia, Gulf Coast.

National League

13 Atlanta (4): Richmond, Savannah, Greenwood, Kingsport.
14 Chicago (4): Wichita, Midland, Key West, Gulf Coast.
15 Cincinnati (5): Indianapolis, Trois Rivieres, Tampa, Seattle, Billings.
16 Houston (4): Denver, Columbus, Cedar Rapids, Covington.
17 Los Angeles (5): Albuquerque, Waterbury, Bakersfield, Orangeburg, Bellingham.
18 Montreal (5): Memphis, Quebec, Kinston, West Palm Beach, Gulf Coast.
19 New York (6): Tidewater, Victoria, Visalia, Anderson, Batavia, Marion.
20 Philadelphia (6): Toledo, Reading, Rocky Mount, Spartanburg, Auburn, Pulaski.
21 Pittsburgh (6): Charleston (WV), Thetford Mines, Salem, Charleston (SC), Niagara Falls, Gulf Coast.
22 St. Louis (5): Tulsa, Arkansas, Modesto, St. Petersburg, Gulf Coast.
23 San Diego (3): Hawaii, Alexandria, Walla Walla.
24 San Francisco (5): Phoenix, Amarillo, Fresno, Decatur, Great Falls.

Co-op (x): Peninsula, Dubuque, Eugene, Ogden.
Independent: Tri-City, Portland, New Westminster.

1974 No-Hitters

Date	Pitcher	Team	League	Opponent	Score
4-21	Wayne Garland	Rochester	International	Charleston	5-0
4-29	Odell Jones	Thetford Mines	Eastern	Pittsfield	7-0
4-29	Anastacio Velazquez	Veracruz	Mexican	Chihuahua	1-0
5-4	Alfredo Meza	MC Tigres	Mexican	Tampico	3-0
5-14	Jackson Todd	Victoria	Texas	Arkansas	3-0
5-20	Frank Snook	Alexandria	Texas	Victoria	3-0 (7)
5-24	Thomas Carroll	Indianapolis	American Assoc.	Omaha	2-0
6-1	Richard Stumpp	Salinas	California	San Jose	12-0 (7)
6-1	Larry Andersen	San Antonio	Texas	Victoria	6-0
6-7	Hank Webb	Tidewater	International	Rochester	1-0 (7)
6-9	Stan Williams	Bristol	Eastern	Quebec	9-0 (7)
6-12	Jeff Little	Decatur	Midwest	Dubuque	1-0 (7)
6-19	Steve Busby	Kansas City	American	Milwaukee	2-0
7-5	Tom Bruno	Jacksonville	Southern	Columbus	5-0 (7)
7-7	Greg Diehl	Oneonta	New York-Penn.	Newark	9-0 (P)
7-13	William Rothan	Salinas	California	Fresno	8-0
7-14	Ed Kelly	Jalisco	Mexican	Coahuila	3-0
7-19	Dick Bosman	Cleveland	American	Oakland	4-0
7-21	Charles Ross	Pawtucket	International	Rochester	4-0 (7)
7-25	Mickey Mahler	Savannah	Southern	Birmingham	6-0 (7)
7-31	Joe Henderson	Iowa	American Assoc.	Wichita	10-0
8-5	Curran Percival	Bristol	Eastern	Trois Rivieres	5-0 (7)
8-6	Sam Basile	New Westminster	Northwest	Portland	6-0 (7)
8-7	Lou Irwin	Bristol	Appalachian	Marion	2-0 (7)
8-9	Larry Jenson	Tampa	Florida State	Key West	8-0 (7)
8-16	Steve Dunning	Spokane	Pacific Coast	Sacramento	10-0
8-16	Gary Robson	Rochester	International	Charleston	2-0 (P, 7)
8-20	Roy Thomas	Reading	Eastern	West Haven	2-0 (7)
8-21	Lamar Wright	Quad Cities	Midwest	Danville	2-0 (6)
8-22	Jared Garvini	Wisconsin Rapids	Midwest	Waterloo	2-0 (7)
8-25	Jim Wright	Auburn	New York-Penn.	Batavia	5-0 (7)
8-25	Homer Stinson	Iowa	American Assoc.	Indianapolis	7-0
8-30	Mike Ruddell	Trois Rivieres	Eastern	Quebec	1-0
9-28	Nolan Ryan	California	American	Minnesota	4-0

Number in parentheses indicates innings if other than nine; "P" indicates perfect game.

THIS DATE IN MINOR LEAGUE HISTORY

April 17, 1974, Sacramento returned to the Pacific Coast League after a 13-year absence. Because no baseball park was available, the team played in a football facility, Hughes Stadium.

May 13, 1974, Evansville registered 49 total bases in a game against Wichita, four short of the American Association record set in 1953 by Kansas City.

June 4, 1974, Tacoma, Pacific Coast League, hit four successive homers in the ninth inning of a 10-9 victory at Sacramento.

June 24, 1974, Junior Kennedy of Indianapolis tied an American Association record by going 6-for-6.

July 2, 1974, Paul Strand, 80, former star outfielder in the Pacific Coast League in the 1920s, died in Salt Lake City, Utah. Strand had 325 hits and batted .394 for Salt Lake City in 1923.

July 6, 1974, Phoenix, Pacific Coast League, hit ten homers in a 24-4 victory at Sacramento.

August 6, 1974, A total of 14 homers, seven by each club, were hit in Sacramento's 14-10 victory over Tacoma in the Pacific Coast League.

August 20, 1974, A total of 14 home runs were belted, including nine by Sacramento and five by Spokane, in a 17-12 Sacramento victory.

August 22, 1974, Alfredo Edmead, outfielder with Salem of the Carolina League, was killed when he collided with a teammate during a game against Rocky Mount at Salem.

August 31, 1974, Veteran Elmore "Moe" Hill of Wisconsin Rapids won the Midwest League Triple Crown with a .339 average, 32 home runs, and 113 RBIs.

September 5, 1974, Sacramento finished the 144-game Pacific Coast League schedule with 305 homers. The Solons' cozy left field fence was only 233 feet from home plate. Bill McNulty led the Solons with 55 home runs, while Gorman Thomas had 51.

November 25, 1974, Herb Brett, longtime minor league manager and founder of the Carolina League, died at the age of 74.

1975

American League
President: Leland S. MacPhail, Jr.

East Standings	W	L	Pct.	GB	Attend.	Manager
Boston Red Sox	95	65	.594	—	1,748,587	Darrell Johnson
Baltimore Orioles	90	69	.566	4½	1,002,157	Earl Weaver
New York Yankees	83	77	.519	12	1,288,048	Bill Virdon/Billy Martin
Cleveland Indians	79	80	.497	15½	977,039	Frank Robinson
Milwaukee Brewers	68	94	.420	28	1,213,357	Del Crandall/Harvey Kuenn
Detroit Tigers	57	102	.358	37½	1,058,836	Ralph Houk

West Standings	W	L	Pct.	GB	Attend.	Manager
Oakland Athletics	98	64	.605	—	1,075,518	Alvin Dark
Kansas City Royals	91	71	.562	7	1,151,836	Jack McKeon/Whitey Herzog
Texas Rangers	79	83	.488	19	1,127,924	Billy Martin/Frank Lucchesi
Minnesota Twins	76	83	.478	20½	737,156	Frank Quilici
Chicago White Sox	75	86	.466	22½	750,802	Chuck Tanner
California Angels	72	89	.447	25½	1,058,163	Dick Williams

Playoff: Boston 3 games, Oakland 0.

BA: Rod Carew, Minnesota, .359
Runs: Fred Lynn, Boston, 103
Hits: George Brett, Kansas City, 195
RBIs: George Scott, Milwaukee, 109
HRs: Reggie Jackson, Oakland, 36
George Scott, Milwaukee, 36

Wins: Jim Palmer, Baltimore, 23
Catfish Hunter, New York, 23
SOs: Frank Tanana, California, 269
ERA: Jim Palmer, Baltimore, 2.09
Pct: Mike Torrez, Baltimore, .690, 20-9
Saves: Rich "Goose" Gossage, Chicago, 26

National League
President: Charles S. Feeney

East Standings	W	L	Pct.	GB	Attend.	Manager
Pittsburgh Pirates	92	69	.571	—	1,270,018	Danny Murtaugh
Philadelphia Phillies	86	76	.531	6½	1,909,233	Danny Ozark
New York Mets	82	80	.506	10½	1,730,566	Yogi Berra/Roy McMillan
St. Louis Cardinals	82	80	.506	10½	1,695,270	Red Schoendienst
Chicago Cubs	75	87	.463	17½	1,034,819	Jim Marshall
Montreal Expos	75	87	.463	17½	908,292	Gene Mauch

West Standings	W	L	Pct.	GB	Attend.	Manager
Cincinnati Reds	108	54	.667	—	2,315,603	Sparky Anderson
Los Angeles Dodgers	88	74	.543	20	2,539,349	Walter Alston
San Francisco Giants	80	81	.497	27½	522,919	Wes Westrum
San Diego Padres	71	91	.438	37	1,281,747	John McNamara
Atlanta Braves	67	94	.416	40½	534,672	Clyde King/Connie Ryan
Houston Astros	64	97	.398	43½	858,002	Preston Gomez/Bill Virdon

Playoff: Cincinnati 3 games, Pittsburgh 0.

BA: Bill Madlock, Chicago, .354
Runs: Pete Rose, Cincinnati, 112
Hits: Dave Cash, Philadelphia, 213
RBIs: Greg Luzinski, Philadelphia, 120
HRs: Mike Schmidt, Philadelphia, 38
Wins: Tom Seaver, New York, 22

SOs: Tom Seaver, New York, 243
ERA: Randy Jones, San Diego, 2.24
Pct: Don Gullett, Cincinnati, .789, 15-4
Saves: Rawley Eastwick, Cincinnati, 22
Al Hrabosky, St. Louis, 22

AAA American Association
President: Joe Ryan

East Standings	W	L	Pct.	GB	Attend.	Manager
Evansville Triplets (6)	77	59	.566	—	114,985	Fred Hatfield
Indianapolis Indians (15)	71	64	.526	5½	142,953	Vern Rapp
Omaha Royals (7)	67	69	.493	10	107,988	Billy Gardner
Iowa Oaks (16)	56	79	.415	20½	108,165	Joe Sparks

West Standings	W	L	Pct.	GB	Attend.	Manager
Denver Bears (4)	81	55	.596	—	193,571	Loren Babe
Tulsa Oilers (22)	73	63	.537	8	143,131	Ken Boyer
Wichita Aeros (14)	68	68	.500	13	173,504	Mike Roarke
Oklahoma City 89ers (5)	50	86	.368	31	46,752	John "Red" Davis

Playoff: Evansville 4 games, Denver 2.

All-Star Team: 1B-Lamar Johnson, Denver; **2B**-Manuel Estrada, Denver; **3B**-Hector Cruz, Tulsa; **SS**-Dave Rosello, Wichita; **OF**-James Tyrone, Wichita; Tommy Smith, Oklahoma City; Mike Easler, Tulsa; **C**-Jeff Sovern, Denver; John Wathan, Omaha; **Util**-Michael Adams, Wichita; **DH**-Sam Ewing, Denver; **P**-Steve Dunning, Denver; Pat Zachry, Indianapolis; **MVP**-Hector Cruz, Tulsa; **Pitcher of the Year**-Steve Dunning, Denver; **Manager**-Fred Hatfield, Evansville.

BA: Lamar Johnson, Denver, .336
Runs: Michael Adams, Wichita, 104
Hits: Lamar Johnson, Denver, 163
RBIs: Hector Cruz, Tulsa, 116

HRs: Hector Cruz, Tulsa, 29
Wins: Steve Dunning, Denver, 15
SOs: Steve Dunning, Denver, 139
ERA: Pat Zachry, Indianapolis, 2.44

AAA International League
President: George H. Sisler, Jr.

Standings	W	L	Pct.	GB	Attend.	Manager
Tidewater Tides (19)	86	55	.610	—	117,462	Joe Frazier
Rochester Red Wings (1)	85	56	.603	1	326,702	Joe Morgan
Syracuse Chiefs (10)	72	64	.529	11½	193,467	Bobby Cox
Charleston Charlies (21)	72	67	.518	13	79,119	Steve Demeter
Memphis Blues (18)	65	75	.464	20½	75,462	Karl Kuehl
Richmond Braves (13)	62	75	.453	22	68,348	Clint Courtney/Bob Lemon
Toledo Mud Hens (20)	62	78	.443	23½	103,189	Jim Bunning
Pawtucket Red Sox (2)	53	87	.379	32½	118,289	Joe Morgan

Playoffs: Tidewater defeated Rochester 8-0 in a one game playoff for first place. Tidewater 3 games, Charleston 0; Syracuse 3 games, Rochester 1.
Finals: Tidewater 3 games, Syracuse 1.

All-Star Team: 1B-Brock Pemberton, Tidewater; **2B**-Willie Randolph, Charleston; **3B**-Roy Staiger, Tidewater; **SS**-Bob Bailor, Rochester; **OF**-Mike Vail, Tidewater; Ellis Valentine, Memphis; Royle Stillman, Rochester; **C**-Bill Nahorodny, Toledo; **P**-Craig Swan, Tidewater; Mike Flanagan, Rochester; **MVP**-Mike Vail, Tidewater; **Pitcher of the Year**-Craig Swan, Tidewater; **Manager**-Joe Frazier, Tidewater.

BA: Mike Vail, Tidewater, .342
Runs: Ellis Valentine, Memphis, 87
Hits: Ellis Valentine, Memphis, 151
RBIs: Roy Staiger, Tidewater, 81
HRs: Bill Nahorodny, Tidewater, 19

Wins: Mike Willis, Rochester, 14
Odell Jones, Charleston, 14
SOs: Odell Jones, Charleston, 157
ERA: Pablo Torrealba, Richmond, 1.45

AAA Mexican League
President: Antonio Ramirez Muro

North West Standings	W	L	Pct.	GB	Attend.	Manager
Saltillo Saraperos	81	55	.596	—	193,912	David Garcia
Union Laguna Algodoneros	66	70	.493	14	259,511	Jose Guerrero/Manolo Fortes
Chihuahua Dorados	66	69	.489	14½	229,195	Miguel Gaspar
Ciudad Juarez Indios	58	80	.420	24	136,912	Minnie Mendoza

North East Standings	W	L	Pct.	GB	Attend.	Manager
Tampico Alijadores	73	62	.541	—	370,506	Benjamin Valenzuela
Monterrey Sultanes	64	73	.467	10	242,000	Miguel Sotelo
Reynosa Bravos	58	75	.436	14	72,067	Jorge Fitch
Coahuila Mineros	57	77	.425	15½	186,139	Tomas Herrera

South West Standings	W	L	Pct.	GB	Attend.	Manager
Puebla Pericos	80	58	.580	—	188,092	Tony Castano
Jalisco Charros	73	61	.545	5	165,784	Vinicio Garcia
Mexico City Tigres	64	72	.471	15	179,162	Jose Luis Garcia
Aguascalientes Rieleros	51	85	.424	28	274,643	Ron Camacho

South East Standings	W	L	Pct.	GB	Attend.	Manager
Cordoba Cafeteros	87	47	.649	—	311,809	Napoleon Reyes
Mexico City Diablos Rojos	80	57	.584	8½	380,528	Ben Reyes
Poza Rica Petroleros	68	67	.504	19½	206,772	Moises Camacho
Villahermosa Cardenales	56	76	.424	30	162,251	Francisco "Pancho" Herrera/Pedro Ramos

Playoffs: Monterrey 4 games, Saltillo 3; Tampico 4 games, Union Laguna 2; MC Diablos Rojos 4 games, Puebla 2; Cordoba 4 games, Jalisco 3. Cordoba 4 games, MC Diablos Rojos 3; Tampico 4 games, Monterrey 3.
Finals: Tampico 4 games, Cordoba 1.

All-Star Team: 1B-Pat Bourque, MC Diablos Rojos; Hector Espino, Tampico; **2B**-Ramon Hernandez, MC Diablos Rojos; **3B**-Victor Torres, Tampico; **SS**-Antonio Villaescusa, MC Diablos Rojos; **OF**-Andres Mora, Saltillo; Vic Davalillo, Cordoba; Romel Canada, Union Laguna; **C**-Francisco Estrada, Puebla; **DH**-James Dugan, Jalisco; **Util**-Manuel Alvarez, Cordoba; **P**-Jose Pena, Villahermosa; Ricardo Sandate, Poza Rica; **Manager**-Benjamin Valenzuela, Tampico.

BA: Pat Bourque, MC Diablos Rojos, .372
Runs: Angel Bravo, Monterrey/Cordoba, 91
Romel Canada, Union Laguna, 91
Tomas Silverio, Tampico, 91
Hits: Gonzalo Villalobos, Aguascalientes, 187

RBIs: Andres Mora, Saltillo, 109
HRs: Andres Mora, Saltillo, 35
Wins: Jose Pena, Villahermosa, 21
SOs: Jose Pena, Villahermosa, 199
ERA: Ricardo Sandate, Poza Rica, 1.42

AAA Pacific Coast League
President: Roy Jackson

East Standings	W	L	Pct.	GB	Attend.	Manager
Salt Lake City Gulls (3)	80	64	.556	—	122,251	Norm Sherry
Tucson Toros (11)	72	71	.503	7½	170,521	Hank Aguirre
Albuquerque Dukes (17)	71	73	.493	9	157,863	Stan Wasiak
Phoenix Giants (24)	66	77	.462	13½	160,897	Rocky Bridges

West Standings	W	L	Pct.	GB	Attend.	Manager
Hawaii Islanders (23)	88	56	.611	—	213,432	Roy Hartsfield
Tacoma Twins (9)	73	69	.514	14	197,583	Cal Ermer
Spokane Indians (12)	64	78	.451	23	103,803	Del Wilber
Sacramento Solons (8)	59	85	.410	29	252,201	Harry Bright

*Won first-half   **Won second-half   ***Won both halves
Numbers after nicknames indicate farm system.
Affiliation listed at end of each year.

Playoff: Hawaii 4 games, Salt Lake City 2.

All-Star Team: 1B-Tom Robson, Spokane; 2B-Bob Sheldon, Sacramento; 3B-Jerry Royster, Albuquerque; SS-Johnnie LeMaster, Phoenix; OF-David Moates, Spokane; Tommy Cruz, Spokane; John Turner, Hawaii; C-Robert Davis, Hawaii; DH-Charlie Manuel, Albuquerque; P-Gary Ross, Hawaii; Eddie Bane, Tacoma; Manager-Roy Hartsfield, Hawaii.

BA: Jerry Royster, Albuquerque, .333	HRs: Robert Hansen, Sacramento, 29
Runs: Jerry Royster, Albuquerque, 91	Wins: Gary Ross, Hawaii, 16
Hits: John Turner, Hawaii, 176	SOs: Greg Shanahan, Albuquerque, 147
RBIs: Robert Hansen, Sacramento, 102	ERA: Steve Luebber, Tacoma, 2.39

AA Eastern League
President: P. Patrick McKernan

Standings	W	L	Pct.	GB	Attend.	Manager
Reading Phillies*(20)	84	53	.613	—	85,257	Bob Wellman
Bristol Red Sox**(2)	81	57	.587	3½	42,238	Dick McAuliffe/Bill Slack
Waterbury Dodgers (17)	77	59	.566	6½	63,847	Don LeJohn
West Haven Yankees (10)	66	71	.482	18	26,549	Pete Ward
Quebec Carnavals (18)	63	73	.463	20½	55,509	Lance Nichols
Pittsfield Rangers (12)	59	73	.447	22½	34,878	Jackie Moore/Orlando Martinez
Thetford Mines Pirates (8)	59	80	.424	26	16,360	John Felske
Trois Rivieres Aigles (15)	57	80	.416	27	54,436	Jim Snyder/Ron Plaza

Playoff: Bristol 3 games, Reading 0.

All-Star Team: 1B-Dave Bergman, West Haven; 2B-Lenn Sakata, Trois Rivieres; 3B-Butch Hobson, Bristol; SS-Rafael Landestoy, Waterbury; OF-Ron Roenicke, Quebec; Rick Bosetti, Reading; Wendell Alston, West Haven; C-Jack Bastable, Reading; Util-Bump Wills, Pittsfield; P-Randy Lerch, Reading; Tom Farias, Bristol; Doug Heinold, West Haven; Manager-Bob Wellman, Reading.

BA: Dave Bergman, West Haven, .311	HRs: Dick Davis, Thetford Mines, 16
Runs: Wendell Alston, West Haven, 77	Wins: Randy Lerch, Reading, 16
Hits: Bump Wills, Pittsfield, 140	SOs: Richard Anderson, West Haven, 138
RBIs: Gary Roenicke, Quebec, 74	ERA: Tom Farias, Bristol, 1.55

AA Southern League
President: Billy Hitchcock

East Standings	W	L	Pct.	GB	Attend.	Manager
Orlando Twins (9)	81	57	.587	—	44,405	Dick Phillips
Savannah Braves (13)	70	64	.522	9	67,971	Tommie Aaron
Columbus Astros (16)	70	64	.522	9	74,797	Jim Beauchamp
Jacksonville Suns (7)	59	79	.428	22	52,737	Billy Scripture

West Standings	W	L	Pct.	GB	Attend.	Manager
Montgomery Rebels (6)	73	61	.545	—	35,751	Les Moss
Birmingham A's (11)	65	69	.485	8	30,483	Harry Malmberg
Knoxville Knox Sox (4)	63	75	.457	12	43,730	Jim Napier
Asheville Orioles (1)	63	75	.457	12	48,928	Jim Schaffer

Playoff: Montgomery 3 games, Orlando 0.

All-Star Team: 1B-Mike Squires, Knoxville; 2B-Doug Stodgel, Knoxville; 3B-Phil Mankowski, Montgomery; SS-Pat Rockett, Savannah; OF-Alfredo Javier, Columbus; John Valle, Montgomery; Derek Bryant, Birmingham; Chuck Heil, Asheville; C-Freddy Velazquez, Savannah; DH-Jim Obradovich, Orlando; Util-Rob Picciolo, Birmingham; P-Ken Kravec, Knoxville; Bob Maneely, Orlando; Manager-Dick Phillips, Orlando.

BA: Chuck Heil, Asheville, .322	Wins: Ken Kravec, Knoxville, 14
Runs: Calvin Portley, Columbus, 82	Bob Sykes, Montgomery, 14
Hits: Derek Bryant, Birmingham, 147	Bob Maneely, Orlando, 14
RBIs: Jim Obradovich, Orlando, 74	SOs: Joe Sambito, Columbus, 140
HRs: Jim Obradovich, Orlando, 27	ERA: Dan Larson, Columbus, 2.18

AA Texas League
President: Bobby Bragan

East Standings	W	L	Pct.	GB	Attend.	Manager
Lafayette Drillers (24)	72	57	.558	—	72,549	Dennis Sommers
Jackson Mets (19)	65	65	.500	7½	77,046	Johnny Antonelli
Arkansas Travelers (22)	63	72	.467	12	67,473	Roy Majtyka
Alexandria Aces (23)	58	72	.446	14½	47,874	Pat Corrales

West Standings	W	L	Pct.	GB	Attend.	Manager
Midland Cubs (14)	81	53	.604	—	69,678	Doc Edwards
Shreveport Captains (21)	76	52	.594	2	39,088	Tim Murtaugh
El Paso Diablos (3)	62	71	.466	18½	162,399	Jimy Williams
San Antonio Missions (5)	50	85	.370	31½	138,517	Woody Smith

Playoff: Midland 2, Lafayette 2 (Both declared co-champions when rain prevented completion of series).

All-Star Team: 1B-John Young, Arkansas; 2B-Al Montreuil, Midland; 3B-Jack Clark, Lafayette; SS-Garry Templeton, Arkansas; OF-Mike Potter, Arkansas; Tommy Thomas, Shreveport; Carlos Lopez, El Paso; C-Jerry Stone, Alexandria; Steve Nicosia, Shreveport; DH-Gary Alexander, Lafayette; P-Stan Butkus, Arkansas; Frank Riccelli, Lafayette; MVP-Gary Alexander, Lafayette; Manager-Dennis Sommers, Lafayette.

BA: Butch Alberts, El Paso, .342	HRs: Mitchell Page, Shreveport, 23
Runs: Dave Machemer, El Paso, 101	Gary Alexander, Lafayette, 23
Hits: Dave Machemer, El Paso, 153	Jack Clark, Lafayette, 23
RBIs: Mitchell Page, Shreveport, 90	Wins: Tim Jones, Shreveport, 16
	SOs: Frank Panik, El Paso, 126
	ERA: Mike Bruhert, Jackson, 2.62

A California League
President: Edward J. Mulligan

Standings	W	L	Pct.	GB	Attend.	Manager
Reno Silver Sox***(9, 23)	86	54	.614	—	48,314	Harry Warner
Fresno Giants (24)	74	66	.529	12	57,005	John Van Ornum
Lodi Orioles (1)	71	69	.507	15	33,813	Bobby Malkmus
Modesto A's (11)	68	72	.486	18	59,145	Rene Lachemann
Salinas Packers (3)	67	73	.479	19	44,725	Bob Rodgers
Visalia Mets (19)	67	73	.479	19	51,169	Jack Aker
San Jose Bees (5)	67	73	.479	19	88,995	Del Youngblood
Bakersfield Dodgers (17)	60	80	.429	26	34,987	Ron Brand

Playoffs: None.

All-Star Team: 1B-Craig Ryan, Lodi; 2B-Ken Perry, Visalia; 3B-Mark Hance, Bakersfield; SS-Miguel Villaran, Bakersfield; OF-Gene Richards, Reno; Luis Lora, Visalia; C-Butch Wynegar, Reno; Util-Luis Garcia, Visalia; P-Jerry Garvin, Reno; Paul Ausman, Reno; Edward Plank, Fresno; Greg Ward, Lodi; MVP-Gene Richards, Reno; Manager-Harry Warner, Reno.

BA: Gene Richards, Reno, .381	Wins: Jerry Garvin, Reno, 17
Runs: Gene Richards, Reno, 148	Edward Plank, Fresno, 17
Hits: Gene Richards, Reno, 191	SOs: Jerry Garvin, Reno, 129
RBIs: Butch Wynegar, Reno, 112	ERA: Edward Plank, Fresno, 2.26
HRs: Claude Westmoreland, Bakersfield, 20	

A Carolina League
President: Wallace McKenna

Standings	W	L	Pct.	GB	Attend.	Manager
Rocky Mount Phillies***(20)	91	51	.641	—	24,345	Cal Emery
Winston-Salem Red Sox (2)	81	62	.566	10½	38,226	John Kennedy
Salem Pirates (21)	74	66	.529	16	39,007	John Lipon
Lynchburg Rangers (12)	60	78	.435	29	28,527	Wayne Terwilliger

Played an interlocking schedule with the Western Carolinas League.

Playoffs: None.

All-Star Team: 1B-John Poff, Rocky Mount; 2B-Brian Doyle, Lynchburg; Steve Gerlecz, Salem; 3B-Jim Morrison, Rocky Mount; SS-Rick Albert, Lynchburg; OF-Luke Wrenn, Salem; Bobby Thompson, Lynchburg; Rick Berg, Winston-Salem; Alberto Lois, Salem; C-Steve Tarbell, Winston-Salem; P-Larry Bradford, Lynchburg; Rick Jones, Winston-Salem; Warren Brusstar, Rocky Mount; MVP-Luke Wrenn, Salem; Manager-Cal Emery, Rocky Mount.

BA: Ted Cox, Winston-Salem, .305	Wins: Oliver Bell, Rocky Mount, 14
Runs: Jim Morrison, Rocky Mount, 98	Warren Brusstar, Rocky Mount, 14
Hits: Ted Cox, Winston-Salem, 154	Allen Ripley, Winston-Salem, 14
RBIs: Luke Wrenn, Salem, 97	SOs: Burke Suter, Winston-Salem, 150
HRs: Jim Morrison, Rocky Mount, 20	ERA: Frederick Jones, Winston-Salem, 2.11

A Florida State League
President: George MacDonald, Jr.

North Standings	W	L	Pct.	GB	Attend.	Manager
St. Petersburg Cardinals (22)	88	47	.652	—	132,666	Jack Krol
Tampa Tarpons (15)	72	59	.550	14	71,433	Russ Nixon
Winter Haven Red Sox (2)	57	70	.449	27	9,844	Rac Slider
Lakeland Tigers (6)	53	79	.402	33½	22,281	Frank "Stubby" Overmire

South Standings	W	L	Pct.	GB	Attend.	Manager
Miami Orioles (1)	79	57	.581	—	52,106	George Farson
Key West Cubs (14)	65	69	.485	13	18,088	Walt Dixon
Ft. Lauderdale Yankees (10)	61	75	.449	18	43,600	Leo Posada
West Palm Beach Expos (18)	58	77	.430	20½	125,568	Gordy MacKenzie

Playoffs: St. Petersburg 2 games, Key West 1; Tampa 2 games, Miami 0.
Finals: St. Petersburg 3 games, Tampa 2.

All-Star Team: 1B-Tom Chism, Miami; 2B-Tony Bernazard, West Palm Beach; 3B-Martin Parrill, Miami; SS-Garry Templeton, St. Petersburg; OF-Don Whiting, Miami; Earle Chew, Key West; Dan Norman, Tampa; C-Michael Gordon, Key West; Mark Unsoeld, Tampa; Util-Karl Gordon, Key West; Ernie Rosseau, St. Petersburg; P-Alan Viebrock, Tampa; Bill Caudill, St. Petersburg; MVP-Ernie Rosseau, St. Petersburg; Manager-Jack Krol, St. Petersburg.

BA: Tom Chism, Miami, .314	Wins: Bill Caudill, St. Petersburg, 14
Runs: Ernie Rosseau, St. Petersburg, 79	John Urrea, St. Petersburg, 14
Hits: Ernie Rosseau, St. Petersburg, 151	Antonio Chevez, Miami, 14
RBIs: Martin Parrill, Miami, 75	SOs: Bill Caudill, St. Petersburg, 153
HRs: Jerry Fry, West Palm Beach, 14	ERA: Lawrence Bashaw, St. Petersburg, 1.69

A Mexican Center League
President: Antonio Ramirez Muro

Standings	W	L	Pct.	GB	Attend.	Manager
Uriangato	55	14	.797	—	10,254	Domingo Rivera
Cortazar	40	28	.588	14½	7,591	Hector Villalobos
Celaya Cajeteros	36	33	.522	19	4,972	Felipe Hernandez
Guanajuato	32	34	.485	21½	12,481	Juan Hernandez
Lagos de Moreno	31	35	.470	22½	10,391	Arturo Cacheux
Leon	28	39	.418	26	5,754	Minnie Minoso
Acambaro	26	43	.377	29	15,431	Roberto Castellon
Salamanca	23	45	.338	31½	7,638	Bimbo Villegas

Playoffs: Cortazar 3 games, Guanajuato 0; Uriangato 3 games, Celaya 0.
Finals: Uriangato 2 games, Cortazar 2, when rain cancelled the series. Uriangato was declared champion due to higher won-lost percentage.

All-Star Team: 1B-Ignacio Hermida, Guanajuato; **2B-**Jose Hernandez, Leon; **3B-**Jeronimo Ibarra, Acambaro; **SS-**Fernando Elinzondo, Cortazar; **OF-**Clemente Juarez, Guanajuato; Mario Arballo, Uriangato; Jose Luis Quiroz, Leon; **C-**Fernando Camargo, Salamanca; Martin Terrazas, Uriangato; **P-**Alvaro Soto, Cortazar; Rogelio Garcia, Acambaro; **Manager-**Domingo Rivera, Uriangato.

BA: Jose Hernandez, Leon, .372
Runs: Candy Cardona, Cortazar, 59
Hits: Donaldo Lugo, Cortazar, 102
RBIs: Clemente Juarez, Guanajuato, 51
Nelson Barrera, Lagos de Moreno, 51

HRs: Jose Luis Quiroz, Leon, 12
Wins: Rogelio Garcia, Acambaro, 11
SOs: Rogelio Garcia, Acambaro, 100
ERA: Alvaro Soto, Cortazar, 0.63

A Midwest League
President: Bill Walters

North Standings	W	L	Pct.	GB	Attend.	Manager
Waterloo Royals***(7)	93	35	.727	—	91,625	John Sullivan
Wisconsin Rapids Twins (9)	71	58	.550	22½	58,422	John Goryl
Dubuque Packers (16)	58	67	.464	33½	54,371	Bob Cluck
Wausau Mets (19)	51	77	.398	42	63,461	Owen Friend
Appleton Foxes (4)	50	77	.394	42½	45,838	Gordon Lund

South Standings	W	L	Pct.	GB	Attend.	Manager
Quad Cities Angels***(3)	78	47	.624	—	60,840	Bobby Knoop
Clinton Pilots (6)	67	61	.523	12½	41,555	Jim Leyland
Danville Dodgers (17)	65	63	.508	14½	54,057	Bart Shirley
Burlington Bees (8)	64	66	.492	16½	46,948	Matt Galante
Cedar Rapids Giants (24)	41	87	.320	38½	47,251	Bob Hartsfield

Playoff: Waterloo 2 games, Quad Cities 0.

All-Star Team: 1B-Willie Aikens, Quad Cities; Charles Beamon, Waterloo; **2B-**Joe Gates, Waterloo; **3B-**Pedro Guerrero, Danville; **SS-**Mark Wagner, Clinton; **OF-**Willie Wilson, Waterloo; Thad Bosley, Quad Cities; Terry Puhl, Quad Cities; **C-**Terry Bulling, Wisconsin Rapids; **P-**Mitch Bobinger, Danville; Jim Dorsey, Quad Cities; **MVP-**Willie Wilson, Waterloo; **Manager-**John Sullivan, Waterloo.

BA: Pedro Guerrero, Danville, .345
Runs: Joe Gates, Waterloo, 115
Hits: Willie Wilson, Waterloo, 132
RBIs: Willie Aikens, Quad Cities, 91

HRs: Moe Hill, Wisconsin Rapids, 31
Wins: Mitch Bobinger, Danville, 17
SOs: Mitch Bobinger, Danville, 201
ERA: David Aloi, Dubuque, 1.69

A New York-Pennsylvania League
President: Vincent M. McNamara

Standings	W	L	Pct.	GB	Attend.	Manager
Newark Co-Pilots***(8)	47	20	.701	—	18,430	Tony Roig
Elmira Red Sox (2)	38	30	.559	9½	42,546	Dick Berardino
Oneonta Yankees (10)	35	34	.507	13	33,732	Mike Ferraro
Auburn Phillies (20)	31	37	.456	16½	43,765	June Raines
Niagara Falls Pirates (21)	29	40	.420	19	37,145	Glenn Ezell
Batavia Trojans (x)	24	43	.358	23	32,650	Hal White

Playoffs: None.

All-Star Team: 1B-Vaughn Robbins, Niagara Falls; **2B-**Gary LaRocque, Newark; **3B-**Dale Berra, Niagara Falls; **SS-**Ray Hall, Newark; **OF-**Billy Severns, Newark; Greg Anderson, Newark; Nathan Chapman, Oneonta; Charles Pinkney, Batavia; **C-**Terry Bevington, Oneonta; David Schmidt, Elmira; **DH-**Daniel DeBattista, Niagara Falls; **Util-**Mark Saber, Niagara Falls; **P-**William Dick, Newark; Gil Patterson, Oneonta; Richard Waller, Elmira; Jeff Schneider, Auburn; **Manager-**Tony Roig, Newark.

BA: Charles Pinkney, Batavia, .308
Runs: Charles Pinkney, Batavia, 48
Hits: Charles Pinkney, Batavia, 76
RBIs: Dale Berra, Niagara Falls, 49
HRs: Greg Anderson, Newark, 9
Sammie Jones, Batavia, 9

Wins: Walter Bigos, Elmira, 9
William Dick, Newark, 9
SOs: Gil Patterson, Oneonta, 97
ERA: Richard Waller, Elmira, 1.37

A Northwest League
President: Bob Richmond

North Standings	W	L	Pct.	GB	Attend.	Manager
Portland Mavericks	42	35	.545	—	119,253	Frank Peters
Seattle Rainiers	35	44	.443	8	22,686	Ron Gibson/ Doug Peterson/Bill Tsoukalas
Bellingham Dodgers (17)	17	61	.218	25½	21,357	Bill Berrier

South Standings	W	L	Pct.	GB	Attend.	Manager
Eugene Emeralds (15)	54	25	.684	—	64,864	Greg Riddoch
Walla Walla Padres (23)	48	31	.608	6	25,662	Cliff Ditto
Boise A's (11)	39	39	.500	14½	29,286	Tom Trebelhorn

Playoff: Eugene 2 games, Portland 0.

All-Star Team: 1B-Mark Lucich, Eugene; **2B-**Tom Watkins, Eugene; **3B-**John Helfrick, Portland; **SS-**Darrell Woodard, Boise; **OF-**Don Reynolds, Walla Walla; George McPherson, Eugene; Lynn Jones, Eugene; **C-**Rick Sweet, Walla Walla; **DH-**Michael Rodriguez, Boise; Paul Gilmartin, Seattle; **Util-**Steve Collette, Portland; **P-**George Benson, Seattle; Paul Moskau, Eugene; Rick Hicks, Portland; Ron Gill, Walla Walla; **Manager-**Greg Riddoch, Eugene.

BA: Rick Sweet, Walla Walla, .350
Runs: Don Reynolds, Walla Walla, 79
Hits: Tom Watkins, Eugene, 98
RBIs: Rick Sweet, Walla Walla, 66

HRs: Don Reynolds, Walla Walla, 15
Wins: Paul Moskau, Eugene, 10
SOs: Paul Moskau, Eugene, 92
ERA: Paul Moskau, Eugene, 1.50

A Western Carolinas League
President: John H. Moss

Standings	W	L	Pct.	GB	Attend.	Manager
Spartanburg Phillies***(20)	81	59	.579	—	27,336	Lee Elia
Anderson Rangers (12)	67	70	.489	12½	25,591	Rich Donnelly
Greenwood Braves (13)	62	79	.440	19½	23,195	Bobby Dews
Charleston Pirates (21)	45	96	.319	36½	21,693	Mike Ryan

Played an interlocking schedule with the Carolina League.

Playoffs: None.

All-Star Team: 1B-Gary Begnaud, Spartanburg; **2B-**Albert Ryan, Greenwood; **3B-**Jerry Maddox, Greenwood; **SS-**Ike Brookens, Anderson; **OF-**Barry Bonnell, Spartanburg/ Greenwood; Lonnie Smith, Spartanburg; Tony Bernazard, Charleston; **C-**Dale Murphy, Greenwood; **P-**Don Bright, Anderson; John Gibson, Spartanburg; **Manager-**Lee Elia, Spartanburg.

BA: Barry Bonnell, Spartanburg/ Greenwood, .324
Runs: Lonnie Smith, Spartanburg, 114
Hits: Lonnie Smith, Spartanburg, 150
RBIs: Gary Begnaud, Spartanburg, 100

HRs: Gary Begnaud, Spartanburg, 25
Wins: Jim Wright, Spartanburg, 14
SOs: John Gibson, Spartanburg, 143
ERA: Joey McLaughlin, Greenwood, 2.58

R Appalachian League
President: Chauncey De Vault

North Standings	W	L	Pct.	GB	Attend.	Manager
Marion Mets (19)	35	33	.515	—	10,258	Chuck Hiller/Billy Connors
Covington Astros (16)	35	34	.507	½	18,376	Billy Smith
Pulaski Phillies (20)	27	41	.397	8	15,385	Bob Wren
Bluefield Orioles (1)	26	43	.377	9½	17,153	Paul Flesner

South Standings	W	L	Pct.	GB	Attend.	Manager
Johnson City Cardinals (22)	41	27	.603	—	41,896	Tom Burgess
Elizabethton Twins (9)	38	30	.559	3	18,193	Fred Waters
Bristol Tigers (6)	37	31	.544	4	9,999	Joe Lewis
Kingsport Braves (13)	33	33	.500	7	19,672	Gene Hassell

Playoffs: None.

All-Star Team: 1B-Richard Green, Kingsport; **2B-**James Draper, Bristol; **3B-**Sheldon Draimin, Bluefield; **SS-**Mike Ramsey, Johnson City; **OF-**Hosken Powell, Elizabethton; Henry Mays, Johnson City; Bobby G. Smith, Bluefield; **C-**Bruce Bochy, Covington; **P-**Randy Lee, Elizabethton; Len Strelitz, Johnson City; Roy Jackson, Marion; David Ford, Bluefield; Willie Simon, Marion; **Manager-**Tom Burgess, Johnson City.

BA: Bobby G. Smith, Bluefield, .363
Runs: Ken Berger, Pulaski, 58
Henry Mays, Johnson City, 58
Hits: Bobby G. Smith, Bluefield, 94
RBIs: Hosken Powell, Elizabethton, 58

HRs: Marshall Brant, Marion, 13
Wins: Len Strelitz, Johnson City, 9
SOs: Richard Miller, Covington, 88
ERA: Randy Lee, Elizabethton, 2.35

R Gulf Coast League
President: George MacDonald, Jr.

Standings	W	L	Pct.	GB	Manager
Rangers (12)	41	12	.774	—	Joe Klein
Royals (7)	31	18	.633	8	Gary Blaylock
Cubs (14)	30	24	.556	11½	Jack Hiatt
Pirates (21)	23	31	.426	18½	Woody Huyke
White Sox (4)	23	31	.426	18½	Joe Jones
Indians (5)	19	33	.365	21½	Tony Pacheco
Cardinals (22)	17	35	.327	23½	Fred Koenig

Games played at Sarasota and Bradenton, Florida.

Playoffs: None.

All-Star Team: 1B-David Chapman, Rangers; **2B-**Mike Denevi, Royals; **3B-**James Alessio, Cubs; **SS-**Pedro Ithier, Indians; **OF-**Brian Rosinski, Cubs; Clint Hurdle, Royals; Luis Silverio, Royals; **C-**Ron Hill, Cubs; **P-**Randy McMurray, Rangers; Mark Soroko, Rangers; **Manager-**Joe Klein, Rangers.

BA: James Alessio, Cubs, .331
Runs: Ed Miller, Rangers, 47
Hits: Nelson Norman, Pirates, 53
RBIs: Clint Hurdle, Royals, 31
HRs: Luis Silverio, Royals, 5

Wins: Bob Barr, Royals, 6
　　Dave McCarthy, Rangers, 6
　　Randy McMurray, Rangers, 6
　　Mark Soroko, Rangers, 6
SOs: Don Robinson, Pirates, 70
ERA: Harold Kelly, Rangers, 0.88

R Pioneer League
President: Ralph C. Nelles

Standings	W	L	Pct.	GB	Attend.	Manager
Great Falls Giants (24)	41	30	.577	—	30,892	Ernest Rodriguez
Idaho Falls Angels (3)	41	31	.569	½	27,430	Larry Himes
Lethbridge Expos (18)........	35	37	.486	6½	31,719	Van Kelly
Billings Mustangs (15)	26	45	.396	15	30,488	James Hoff

Playoffs: None.

All-Star Team: 1B-George Weicker, Billings; **2B-**Richard Brewster, Idaho Falls; **3B-**Steven Grimes, Great Falls; **SS-**James Anderson, Idaho Falls; **OF-**Andre Dawson, Lethbridge; Andrew Dyes, Lethbridge; James Elrod, Great Falls; **C-**Wayne Cato, Great Falls; **P-**Carlos Perez, Idaho Falls; Gene Schmidt, Great Falls.

BA: Richard Brewster, Idaho Falls, .347
Runs: Richard Brewster, Idaho Falls, 61
Hits: Andre Dawson, Lethbridge, 99
RBIs: Andrew Dyes, Lethbridge, 58

HRs: Andre Dawson, Lethbridge, 13
Wins: Gene Schmidt, Great Falls, 10
SOs: Alan Wirth, Great Falls, 90
ERA: Carlos Perez, Idaho Falls, 1.89

1975 Interleague Post Season Play

World Series
Cincinnati (National) 4 games, Boston (American) 3

Junior World Series
Evansville (American Association) 4 games, Tidewater (International) 1
Total Attendance: 10,186

1975 Major League Farm Systems

American League
1 Baltimore (5): Rochester, Asheville, Lodi, Miami, Bluefield.
2 Boston (5): Pawtucket, Bristol (CT), Winston-Salem, Winter Haven, Elmira.
3 California (5): Salt Lake City, El Paso, Salinas, Quad Cities, Idaho Falls.
4 Chicago (4): Denver, Knoxville, Appleton, Gulf Coast.
5 Cleveland (4): Oklahoma City, San Antonio, San Jose, Gulf Coast.
6 Detroit (5): Evansville, Montgomery, Lakeland, Clinton, Bristol (VA).
7 Kansas City (4): Omaha, Jacksonville, Waterloo, Gulf Coast.
8 Milwaukee (4): Sacramento, Thetford Mines, Burlington, Newark.
9 Minnesota (5): Tacoma, Orlando, Reno, Wisconsin Rapids, Elizabethton.
10 New York (4): Syracuse, West Haven, Ft. Lauderdale, Oneonta.
11 Oakland (4): Tucson, Birmingham, Modesto, Boise.
12 Texas (5): Spokane, Pittsfield, Lynchburg, Anderson, Gulf Coast.

National League
13 Atlanta (4): Richmond, Savannah, Greenwood, Kingsport.
14 Chicago (4): Wichita, Midland, Key West, Gulf Coast.
15 Cincinnati (5): Indianapolis, Trois Rivieres, Tampa, Eugene, Billings.
16 Houston (4): Iowa, Columbus, Dubuque, Covington.
17 Los Angeles (5): Albuquerque, Waterbury, Bakersfield, Danville, Bellingham.
18 Montreal (4): Memphis, Quebec, West Palm Beach, Lethbridge.
19 New York (5): Tidewater, Jackson, Visalia, Wausau, Marion.
20 Philadelphia (6): Toledo, Reading, Rocky Mount, Spartanburg, Auburn, Pulaski.
21 Pittsburgh (6): Charleston (WV), Shreveport, Salem, Charleston (SC), Niagara Falls, Gulf Coast.
22 St. Louis (5): Tulsa, Arkansas, St. Petersburg, Johnson City, Gulf Coast.
23 San Diego (4): Hawaii, Alexandria, Reno, Walla Walla.
24 San Francisco (5): Phoenix, Lafayette, Fresno, Cedar Rapids, Great Falls.

Co-op (x): Batavia.
Independent: Portland, Seattle.

1975 No-Hitters

Date	Pitcher	Team	League	Opponent	Score
5-10	Horacio Pina	Aguascalientes	Mexican	Juarez	1-0 (7)
5-11	Tom McGough	San Antonio	Texas	Shreveport	1-0
5-14	Bill Caudill	St. Petersburg	Florida State	Winter Haven	4-0 (6)
5-19	Gary Ross	Hawaii	Pacific Coast	Salt Lake City	19-0 (P, 5)
5-20	Roger Hambright	Ciudad Juarez	Mexican	Tampico	4-0
5-20	Jim Dorsey	Quad Cities	Midwest	Clinton	4-0 (7)
5-27	Joseph Neal	Salem	Carolina	Anderson	1-0
6-1	Nolan Ryan	California	American	Baltimore	1-0
6-6	Marc Bombard	Tampa	Florida State	Lakeland	1-0 (P)
6-8	Tom Miali	Coahuila	Mexican	Chihuahua	1-0 (7)
6-8	Jim Burton	Pawtucket	International	Tidewater	2-0
6-14	Tom Farias	Bristol	Eastern	Thetford Mines	2-0 (7)
6-20	Wayne Simpson	Toledo	International	Syracuse	3-0 (7)
6-21	Tom Norton	Tacoma	Pacific Coast	Hawaii	1-0
6-30	Dean Olson	Wisconsin Rapids	Midwest	Clinton	6-0
7-4	Dyain Frazier	Salinas	California	San Jose	8-0 (7)
7-6	John Morris	Newark	New York-Penn.	Oneonta	10-0
7-14	Salvatore Ferrara	Billings	Pioneer	Lethbridge	9-0
7-17	Chuck Dobson	Salt Lake City	Pacific Coast	Hawaii	5-0 (7)
7-17	Nestor Espinoza/				
	Ruben Garcia	MC Tigres	Mexican	Puebla	1-0 (5)
7-20	Abelino Pena	Burlington	Midwest	Cedar Rapids	2-0 (P, 7)
7-21	Hector Valenzuela	Coahuila	Mexican	Tampico	3-0
7-24	Dave McCarthy	Rangers	Gulf Coast	White Sox	5-0
7-27	Bernie Plent/				
	Charley Moore	Billings	Pioneer	Great Falls	11-0 (7)
8-11	Rod Scurry/				
	Chet Gunter	Salem	Carolina	Lynchburg	1-2
8-16	Jose Alfaro	Dubuque	Midwest	Cedar Rapids	5-0
8-22	Larry Monroe	Appleton	Midwest	Cedar Rapids	1-0 (7)
8-24	Ed Halicki	San Francisco	National	New York	6-0
8-29	Bill Patten/Harold Kelly/Randy McMurray/Mike Arrington/Pat Moock/				
	Mark Soroko	Rangers	Gulf Coast	White Sox	1-0
9-1	Jeff Little/Steven Greenough/				
	Silvano Quezada	Lafayette	Texas	Jackson	1-0 (7)
9-28	Vida Blue/Glenn Abbott/Paul Lindblad/				
	Rollie Fingers	Oakland	American	California	5-0

Number in parentheses indicates innings if other than nine; "P" indicates perfect game.

THIS DATE IN MINOR LEAGUE HISTORY

January 2, 1975, James Poole, who may have played professional baseball longer than any other person, died in Hickory, North Carolina, at age 79. Poole was an active player for 34 years, starting in 1912 and ending in 1946 when he was 51 years old. The lefthanded slugger hit 50 homers for Nashville, Southern Association, in 1930. Poole was with 30 teams, most of them in the lower minors, and managed more than a dozen of them.

April 14, 1975, Due to the inability to secure major league working agreements, both the Carolina League and the Western Carolinas League opened the season with just four clubs. The two leagues played an interlocking schedule with the faster Carolina League winning the season series, 117 games to 64.

June 10, 1975, Waterloo, Midwest League, defeated Dubuque 3-2, marking the second time this season the Kansas City farm club had posted 13 successive victories. The win was the 26th in the last 27 games for Waterloo and it upped the club's overall record to 41-9, an .820 percentage.

June 11, 1975, Waterloo, Midwest League, lost to Burlington after 14 straight victories.

June 15, 1975, Clint Courtney, manager of Richmond, International League, died of a heart attack in Rochester, New York at age 48.

July 31, 1975, The American Association All-Stars defeated the Chicago White Sox 7-4 before 11,615 fans at Denver.

September 1, 1975, Quebec's Gary Roenicke led the Eastern League in RBIs, but set a league record for fewest RBIs for a league leader as he knocked in 74 runs.

September 2, 1975, Second baseman Luis Alvarado, who played with Oklahoma City and Tulsa, set an American Association fielding record as he made only three errors on the season and finished with a .994 fielding percentage.

September 16, 1975, Evansville defeated Tidewater four games to one in the resumption of the Junior World Series after a one year hiatus.

December 5, 1975, President Bobby Bragan of the Texas League was elected President of the National Association. He succeeded Hank Peters, who had become general manager of the Baltimore Orioles.

1976

American League
President: Leland S. MacPhail, Jr.

East Standings	W	L	Pct.	GB	Attend.	Manager
New York Yankees............	97	62	.610	—	2,012,434	Billy Martin
Baltimore Orioles	88	74	.543	10½	1,058,609	Earl Weaver
Boston Red Sox	83	79	.512	15½	1,895,846	Darrell Johnson/Don Zimmer
Cleveland Indians	81	78	.509	16	948,776	Frank Robinson
Detroit Tigers....................	74	87	.460	24	1,467,020	Ralph Houk
Milwaukee Brewers...........	66	95	.410	32	1,012,164	Alex Grammas

West Standings	W	L	Pct.	GB	Attend.	Manager
Kansas City Royals............	90	72	.556	—	1,680,265	Whitey Herzog
Oakland Athletics	87	74	.540	2½	780,593	Chuck Tanner
Minnesota Twins	85	77	.525	5	715,394	Gene Mauch
California Angels...............	76	86	.469	14	1,006,774	Dick Williams/Norm Sherry
Texas Rangers....................	76	86	.469	14	1,164,982	Frank Lucchesi
Chicago White Sox.............	64	97	.398	25½	914,945	Paul Richards

Playoff: New York 3 games, Kansas City 2.

BA: George Brett, Kansas City, .333
Runs: Roy White, New York, 104
Hits: George Brett, Kansas City, 215
RBIs: Lee May, Baltimore, 109
HRs: Graig Nettles, New York, 32

Wins: Jim Palmer, Baltimore, 22
SOs: Nolan Ryan, California, 327
ERA: Mark Fidrych, Detroit, 2.34
Pct: Bill Campbell, Minnesota, .773, 17-5
Saves: Sparky Lyle, New York, 23

National League
President: Charles S. Feeney

East Standings	W	L	Pct.	GB	Attend.	Manager
Philadelphia Phillies	101	61	.623	—	2,480,150	Danny Ozark
Pittsburgh Pirates.............	92	70	.568	9	1,025,945	Danny Murtaugh
New York Mets	86	76	.531	15	1,468,754	Joe Frazier
Chicago Cubs	75	87	.463	26	1,026,217	Jim Marshall
St. Louis Cardinals	72	90	.444	29	1,207,079	Red Schoendienst
Montreal Expos	55	107	.340	46	646,704	Karl Kuehl/Charlie Fox

West Standings	W	L	Pct.	GB	Attend.	Manager
Cincinnati Reds.................	102	60	.630	—	2,629,708	Sparky Anderson
Los Angeles Dodgers.........	92	70	.568	10	2,386,301	Walter Alston/Tom Lasorda
Houston Astros	80	82	.494	22	886,146	Bill Virdon
San Francisco Giants	74	88	.457	28	626,868	Bill Rigney
San Diego Padres	73	89	.451	29	1,458,478	John McNamara
Atlanta Braves	70	92	.432	32	818,179	Dave Bristol

Playoff: Cincinnati 3 games, Philadelphia 0.

BA: Bill Madlock, Chicago, .339
Runs: Pete Rose, Cincinnati, 130
Hits: Pete Rose, Cincinnati, 215
RBIs: George Foster, Cincinnati, 121
HRs: Mike Schmidt, Philadelphia, 38

Wins: Randy Jones, San Diego, 22
SOs: Tom Seaver, New York, 235
ERA: John Denny, St. Louis, 2.52
Pct: Steve Carlton, Philadelphia, .741, 20-7
Saves: Rawley Eastwick, Cincinnati, 26

AAA American Association
President: Joe Ryan

East Standings	W	L	Pct.	GB	Attend.	Manager
Omaha Royals (7)...............	78	58	.574	—	120,799	Billy Gardner
Iowa Oaks (4)	68	68	.500	10	124,575	Loren Babe
Indianapolis Indians (15)....	62	73	.459	15½	139,615	Jim Snyder
Evansville Triplets (6)	55	81	.404	23	100,696	Fred Hatfield

West Standings	W	L	Pct.	GB	Attend.	Manager
Denver Bears (18)..............	86	50	.632	—	202,444	Vern Rapp
Oklahoma City 89ers (20) ..	72	63	.533	13½	122,287	Jim Bunning
Tulsa Oilers (22)................	65	70	.481	20½	135,474	Ken Boyer
Wichita Aeros (14)	56	79	.415	29½	124,107	Doc Edwards

Playoff: Denver 4 games, Omaha 2.

All-Star Team: 1B-Roger Freed, Denver; 2B-Steve Staggs, Omaha; 3B-Pat Scanlon, Denver; SS-Garry Templeton, Tulsa; OF-Mike Easler, Tulsa; Sam Ewing, Iowa; Warren Cromartie, Denver; Rick Bosetti, Oklahoma City; C-Steve Patchin, Omaha; Bill Nahorodny, Oklahoma City; Util-Rodney Scott, Denver; P-Randy Lerch, Oklahoma City; John Montague, Oklahoma City; MVP-Roger Freed, Denver; Pitcher of the Year-John Montague, Oklahoma City; Manager-Vern Rapp, Denver.

BA: Mike Easler, Tulsa, .352
Runs: Lonnie Smith, Oklahoma City, 93
Hits: Rick Bosetti, Oklahoma City, 154
RBIs: Roger Freed, Denver, 102
HRs: Roger Freed, Denver, 42

Wins: Joe Keener, Denver, 14
John Montague, Oklahoma City, 14
SOs: Randy Lerch, Oklahoma City, 152
ERA: Joe Henderson, Indianapolis, 2.31

AAA International League
President: George H. Sisler, Jr.

Standings	W	L	Pct.	GB	Attend.	Manager
Rochester Red Wings (1)....	88	50	.638	—	258,101	Joe Altobelli
Syracuse Chiefs (10)..........	82	57	.590	6½	187,397	Bobby Cox
Memphis Blues (16)	69	69	.500	19	92,973	Jim Beauchamp
Richmond Braves (13).......	69	71	.493	20	109,636	Jack McKeon
Pawtucket Red Sox (2).......	68	70	.493	20	106,052	Joe Morgan
Charleston Charlies (21)....	62	73	.459	24½	72,543	Tim Murtaugh
Tidewater Tides (19)	60	78	.435	28	106,458	Tom Burgess
Toledo Mud Hens (5)	55	85	.393	34	106,106	Joe Sparks

Playoffs: Syracuse 3 games, Memphis 0; Richmond 3 games, Rochester 1.
Finals: Syracuse 3 games, Richmond 1.

All-Star Team: 1B-Joe Lis, Toledo; 2B-Rich Dauer, Rochester; 3B-Butch Hobson, Pawtucket; SS-Mickey Klutts, Syracuse; OF-Miguel Dilone, Charleston; Terry Whitfield, Syracuse; Omar Moreno, Charleston; C-John Stearns, Tidewater; P-Dennis Martinez, Rochester; Scott McGregor, Rochester; MVP-Rich Dauer, Rochester; Mickey Klutts, Syracuse; Joe Lis, Toledo; Pitcher of the Year-Dennis Martinez, Rochester; Manager-Joe Altobelli, Rochester.

BA: Rich Dauer, Rochester, .336
Runs: Joe Lis, Toledo, 93
Hits: Rich Dauer, Rochester, 176
RBIs: Joe Lis, Toledo, 103

HRs: Jack Baker, Pawtucket, 36
Wins: Dennis Martinez, Rochester, 14
SOs: Dennis Martinez, Rochester, 140
ERA: Dennis Martinez, Rochester, 2.50

AAA Mexican League
President: Antonio Ramirez Muro

North West Standings	W	L	Pct.	GB	Attend.	Manager
Ciudad Juarez Indios	74	61	.548	—	262,535	Jose Guerrero
Union Laguna Algodoneros	75	62	.547	—	192,134	Moises Camacho
Saltillo Saraperos	72	61	.541	1	101,439	Enrique Izquierdo/Gregorio Luque
Chihuahua Dorados	67	68	.496	7	229,155	Miguel Gaspar

North East Standings	W	L	Pct.	GB	Attend.	Manager
Reynosa Bravos	67	68	.496	—	101,828	Jorge Fitch/Marte de Alejandro
Coahuila Mineros	61	66	.480	2	256,459	Wilfredo Calvino
Monterrey Sultanes	59	75	.440	7½	214,636	Miguel Sotelo/Jesus Valtier
Nuevo Laredo Tecolotes ...	54	82	.397	13½	169,504	Vinicio Garcia

South West Standings	W	L	Pct.	GB	Attend.	Manager
Puebla Angeles	80	55	.593	—	213,996	Clemente Carrera
Aguascalientes Rieleros	68	66	.507	11½	305,397	Pompeyo Davalillo
Mexico City Tigres	54	78	.409	24½	178,896	Jose Luis Garcia
Durango Alacranes	54	79	.406	25	143,980	Al Gallagher/Jorge Fitch

South East Standings	W	L	Pct.	GB	Attend.	Manager
Cordoba Cafeteros	78	53	.595	—	225,649	Napoleon Reyes
Mexico City Diablos Rojos	75	63	.543	6½	351,416	Ben Reyes
Poza Rica Petroleros..........	68	67	.504	12	229,029	David Garcia
Tampico Alijadores	66	68	.493	13½	272,287	Ben Valenzuela/Ron Camacho

Playoffs: Ciudad Juarez 4 games, Coahuila 1; Union Laguna 4 games, Reynosa 1; Cordoba 4 games, Aguascalientes 1; MC Diablos Rojos 4 games, Puebla 2. Union Laguna 4 games, Ciudad Juarez 2; MC Diablos Rojos 4 games, Cordoba 2.
Finals: MC Diablos Rojos 4 games, Union Laguna 2.

All-Star Team: 1B-Jack Pierce, Puebla; 2B-Antonio Briones, Ciudad Juarez; 3B-Jose Del Moral, Ciudad Juarez; SS-Antonio Villasecusa, MC Diablos Rojos; OF-Vic Davalillo, Puebla; Lambert Ford, Reynosa; Miguel Suarez, MC Diablos Rojos; C-Francisco Estrada, Puebla; DH-Mike Walseth, Puebla; P-Enrique Romo, MC Diablos Rojos; Antonio Pollorena, Union Laguna; Manager-Jose Guerrero, Ciudad Juarez.

BA: Larry Fritz, Aguascalientes, .355
Runs: Curtis Moore, Chihuahua, 108
Hits: Mike Walseth, Puebla, 171
Miguel Suarez, MC Diablos Rojos, 171
RBIs: Jack Pierce, Puebla, 118

HRs: Jack Pierce, Puebla, 36
Wins: Antonio Pollorena, Union Laguna, 20
Enrique Romo, MC Diablos Rojos, 20
SOs: Enrique Romo, MC Diablos Rojos, 239
ERA: Gary Ryerson, Tampico, 1.52

AAA Pacific Coast League
President: Roy Jackson

East Standings	W	L	Pct.	GB	Attend.	Manager
Salt Lake City Gulls (3)......	90	54	.625	—	239,321	Jimy Williams
Phoenix Giants (24)..........	75	67	.528	14	151,207	Rocky Bridges
Albuquerque Dukes (17)	66	78	.458	24	169,278	Stan Wasiak
Tucson Toros (11)	54	88	.380	35	102,514	Harry Bright/Lee Stange

West Standings	W	L	Pct.	GB	Attend.	Manager
Hawaii Islanders (23).........	77	68	.531	—	306,236	Roy Hartsfield
Tacoma Twins (9)...............	76	69	.524	1	192,758	Cal Ermer
Sacramento Solons (12)......	71	72	.497	5	82,324	Rich Donnelly
Spokane Indians (8)...........	65	78	.455	11	116,646	Frank Howard

*Won first-half   **Won second-half   ***Won both halves
Numbers after nicknames indicate farm system.
Affiliation listed at end of each year.

535

Playoff: Hawaii 3 games, Salt Lake City 2.

All-Star Team: 1B-Doug Ault, Sacramento; 2B-Bump Wills, Sacramento; 3B-Wayne Gross, Tacoma; SS-Johnnie LeMaster, Phoenix; OF-Jack Clark, Phoenix; Pilo Gaspar, Hawaii; Carlos Lopez, Salt Lake City; C-Gary Alexander, Phoenix; DH-Bob Gorinski, Tacoma; P-Mark Wiley, Tacoma; Bob Knepper, Phoenix; Manager of the Year-Jimy Williams, Salt Lake City.

BA: Paul Dade, Salt Lake City, .363	Wins: Dennis Lewallyn, Albuquerque, 15
Runs: Doug Ault, Sacramento, 112	Ed Plank, Phoenix, 15
Hits: Gene Richards, Hawaii, 173	Mark Wiley, Tacoma, 15
RBIs: Bob Gorinski, Tacoma, 110	Gary Wheelock, Salt Lake City, 15
HRs: Bob Gorinski, Tacoma, 28	SOs: Gary Wheelock, Salt Lake City, 138
	ERA: Diego Segui, Hawaii, 3.18

AA Eastern League
President: P. Patrick McKernan

North Standings	W	L	Pct.	GB	Attend.	Manager
Trois Rivieres Aigles (15)	83	55	.601	—	62,655	Roy Majtyka
Quebec Metros (18)	78	59	.569	4½	54,061	Lance Nichols
Berkshire Brewers#(8)	68	68	.500	14	23,561	John Felske
Waterbury Dodgers (17)	62	73	.459	19½	64,912	Don LeJohn

South Standings	W	L	Pct.	GB	Attend.	Manager
West Haven Yankees (10)	80	59	.576	—	28,331	Pete Ward
Bristol Red Sox (2)	74	60	.552	3½	38,637	John Kennedy
Reading Phillies (20)	54	82	.397	24½	71,152	Bob Wellman/ Granny Hamner
Williamsport Tomahawks (5)	48	91	.345	32	53,757	John "Red" Davis

#represented Pittsfield, Massachusetts.

Playoff: West Haven 3 games, Trois Rivieres 0.

All-Star Team: 1B-Pedro Guerrero, Waterbury; 2B-Charles Meyers, Bristol; 3B-Jim Gantner, Berkshire; SS-Ron Oester, Trois Rivieres; OF-Steve Henderson, Trois Rivieres; Richard Berg, Bristol; Larry Murray, West Haven; C-Tim Blackwell, Reading; P-Gerald Hannahs, Quebec; Paul Moskau, Trois Rivieres; MVP-Danny Thomas, Berkshire; Manager-Roy Majtyka, Trois Rivieres.

BA: Danny Thomas, Berkshire, .325	HRs: Danny Thomas, Berkshire, 29
Runs: Larry Murray, West Haven, 92	Wins: Gerald Hannahs, Quebec, 20
Hits: Richard Berg, Bristol, 158	SOs: Gerald Hannahs, Quebec, 126
Steve Henderson, Trois Rivieres, 158	ERA: Paul Moskau, Trois Rivieres, 1.55
RBIs: Danny Thomas, Berkshire, 83	

AA Southern League
President: Billy Hitchcock

East Standings	W	L	Pct.	GB	Attend.	Manager
Orlando Twins**(9)	75	64	.540	—	41,951	Dick Phillips
Charlotte O's*(1)	74	66	.529	1½	113,559	Jim Schaffer
Savannah Braves (13)	69	71	.493	6½	58,361	Tommie Aaron
Jacksonville Suns (7)	66	72	.478	8½	69,343	Billy Scripture

West Standings	W	L	Pct.	GB	Attend.	Manager
Montgomery Rebels**(6)	81	56	.591	—	59,754	Les Moss
Chattanooga Lookouts*(11)	70	68	.507	11½	135,144	Rene Lachemann
Knoxville Knox Sox (4)	61	77	.442	20½	38,046	Gordon Lund
Columbus Astros (16)	58	80	.420	23½	50,171	Leo Posada

Playoffs: Orlando 1 game, Charlotte 0; Montgomery 1 game, Chattanooga 0.
Finals: Montgomery 3 games, Orlando 1.

All-Star Team: 1B-Eddie Murray, Charlotte; 2B-Blake Doyle, Charlotte; 3B-Martin Parrill, Charlotte; SS-Glenn Gulliver, Montgomery; OF-Derek Bryant, Chattanooga; Mark Budaska, Chattanooga; Larry Foster, Knoxville; Joe Cannon, Columbus; C-Dale Murphy, Savannah; DH-Jim Obradovich, Orlando; Util-Ike Brookens, Montgomery; P-Dave Ford, Charlotte; Dennis DeBarr, Montgomery; Manager-Rene Lachemann, Chattanooga.

BA: Larry Foster, Knoxville, .311	HRs: Jim Obradovich, Orlando, 21
Runs: Jim Obradovich, Orlando, 84	Wins: Dave Ford, Charlotte, 17
Hits: Blake Doyle, Charlotte, 158	SOs: Dave Ford, Charlotte, 121
RBIs: Jim Obradovich, Orlando, 68	ERA: Dave Rozema, Montgomery, 1.57

AA Texas League
President: Carl Sawatski

East Standings	W	L	Pct.	GB	Attend.	Manager
Shreveport Captains (21)	70	66	.515	—	47,930	John Lipon
Jackson Mets (19)	69	66	.511	½	86,069	Johnny Antonelli
Arkansas Travelers (22)	59	76	.437	10½	90,255	Jack Krol
Lafayette Drillers (24)	58	76	.433	11	35,808	John Van Ornum

West Standings	W	L	Pct.	GB	Attend.	Manager
Amarillo Gold Sox (23)	81	54	.600	—	76,799	Bob Miller
El Paso Diablos (3)	77	56	.579	3	181,746	Bobby Knoop
San Antonio Missions (12)	63	71	.470	17½	60,122	Orlando Martinez
Midland Cubs (14)	62	74	.456	19½	66,457	Dennis Sommers

Playoff: Amarillo 3 games, Shreveport 2.

All-Star Team: 1B-Willie Aikens, El Paso; 2B-Fred Frazier, El Paso; 3B-Ron Farkas, El Paso; SS-Rance Mulliniks, El Paso; OF-Don Reynolds, Amarillo; Al Lois, Shreveport; Lee Mazzilli, Jackson; C-Rick Bradley, Lafayette; DH-Gene Deylon, Amarillo; P-Jay Dillard, Lafayette;

John Poloni, San Antonio; MVP-Willie Aikens, El Paso; Manager-Bob Miller, Amarillo.

BA: Fred Frazier, El Paso, .363	Wins: Bob Nolan, El Paso, 15
Runs: Willie Aikens, El Paso, 99	John Caneira, El Paso, 15
Hits: Wendell Kim, Lafayette, 164	SOs: Bill Caudill, Arkansas, 140
RBIs: Willie Aikens, El Paso, 117	ERA: Jay Dillard, Lafayette, 2.30
HRs: Willie Aikens, El Paso, 30	

A California League
President: E.W. "Bill" Wickert

Standings	W	L	Pct.	GB	Attend.	Manager
Salinas Angels*(3)	91	49	.650	—	69,887	Del Crandall
Fresno Giants (24)	77	63	.550	14	62,377	Andy Gilbert
Reno Silver Sox**(9, 23)	75	62	.547	14½	38,226	John Goryl
Modesto A's (11)	65	72	.474	24½	48,295	George Farson
Lodi Dodgers (17)	64	76	.457	27	28,886	James Williams
San Jose Bees (5)	45	95	.321	46	98,437	Gomer Hodge

Playoff: Reno 3 games, Salinas 1.

All-Star Team: 1B-Dan Argee, Modesto; 2B-Julio Cruz, Salinas; 3B-Floyd Rayford, Salinas; SS-James Anderson, Salinas; Mike Cash, Fresno; OF-Thad Bosley, Salinas; Tom Bhagwat, Fresno; Hosken Powell, Reno; C-Dan Graham, Reno; P-Ken Califano, Salinas; Monroe Greenfield, Fresno; David Hagman, Modesto; Greg Heydeman, Lodi; MVP-Thad Bosley, Salinas; Manager-Del Crandall, Salinas.

BA: Dan Argee, Modesto, .356	HRs: Dan Graham, Reno, 29
Runs: Hosken Powell, Reno, 118	Wins: Ken Califano, Stockton, 15
Hits: Frank Estes, Reno, 184	SOs: Greg Heydeman, Lodi, 159
RBIs: Dan Graham, Reno, 115	ERA: Monroe Greenfield, Fresno, 2.45

A Carolina League
President: Wallace McKenna

Standings	W	L	Pct.	GB	Attend.	Manager
Winston-Salem Red Sox***(2)	80	57	.584	—	49,314	Tony Torchia
Peninsula Pilots (20)	71	65	.522	8½	41,367	Cal Emery
Salem Pirates (21)	68	69	.496	12	30,387	Steve Demeter
Lynchburg Mets (19)	64	75	.460	17	46,302	Jack Aker

Played an interlocking schedule with the Western Carolinas League.

Playoffs: None.

All-Star Team: 1B-Marshall Brant, Lynchburg; 2B-Dave Lozano, Lynchburg; 3B-Ron Evans, Winston-Salem; SS-Juan Deliza, Salem; Marty Ryczek, Peninsula; OF-Roger Lee Brown, Peninsula; Luis Delgado, Winston-Salem; Ken Huizenga, Winston-Salem; C-Mike O'Berry, Winston-Salem; DH-Paul McClure, Winston-Salem; P-Breen Newcomer, Winston-Salem; Ed Whitson, Salem; MVP-Marshall Brant, Lynchburg; Manager-Tony Torchia, Winston-Salem.

BA: Roger Lee Brown, Peninsula, .349	Wins: Don Fowler, Peninsula, 15
Runs: Dave Lozano, Lynchburg, 89	Ed Whitson, Salem, 15
Hits: Luis Delgado, Winston-Salem, 143	SOs: Ed Whitson, Salem, 186
RBIs: Marshall Brant, Lynchburg, 93	ERA: Peter Manos, Peninsula, 1.16
HRs: Marshall Brant, Lynchburg, 23	

A Florida State League
President: George MacDonald, Jr.

North Standings	W	L	Pct.	GB	Attend.	Manager
Tampa Tarpons (15)	76	60	.559	—	104,021	Ron Brand
Lakeland Tigers (6)	74	64	.536	3	53,397	Jim Leyland
St. Petersburg Cardinals (22)	70	71	.496	8½	70,128	Hal Lanier
Winter Haven Red Sox (2)	65	76	.461	13½	12,480	Rac Slider

South Standings	W	L	Pct.	GB	Attend.	Manager
Miami Orioles (1)	79	63	.556	—	42,672	Len Johnston
Ft. Lauderdale Yankees (10)	77	62	.554	½	52,290	Mike Ferraro
West Palm Beach Expos (18)	63	79	.444	16	127,361	Gordy MacKenzie
Pompano Beach Cubs (14)	56	85	.397	22½	21,590	Jack Hiatt

Playoffs: Lakeland 2 games, Miami 0; Tampa 2 games, Ft. Lauderdale 0.
Finals: Lakeland 2 games, Tampa 0.

All-Star Team: 1B-Tom Chism, Miami; 2B-Tim Ireland, Pompano Beach; 3B-Lou Whitaker, Lakeland; SS-Domingo Ramos, Ft. Lauderdale; OF-William Michael, Lakeland; Marshall Edwards, Miami; Rich Stenholm, Ft. Lauderdale; C-Gregory Shippy, Lakeland; Roberto Ramos, West Palm Beach; Util-Scott Boras, St. Petersburg; Dave Koza, Winter Haven; P-Larry Pekarcik, Tampa; Randy Niemann, Ft. Lauderdale; Ricky Mayo, Miami; John Murphy, Lakeland; MVP-Lou Whitaker, Lakeland; Manager-Ron Brand, Tampa.

BA: Bobby G. Smith, Miami, .324	HRs: Dave Koza, Winter Haven, 18
Runs: Lou Whitaker, Lakeland, 70	Wins: Ricky Mayo, Miami, 15
Hits: Dave Koza, Winter Haven, 141	SOs: Mario Soto, Tampa, 124
RBIs: Dave Koza, Winter Haven, 83	ERA: Win Remmerswaal, Winter Haven, 1.74

A Gulf States League
President: Howard Green

East Standings	W	L	Pct.	GB	Attend.	Manager
Baton Rouge Cougars#***	43	27	.614	—	42,133	Matt Batts
Seguin Toros	29	48	.377	17½	10,106	Jimmy Smith
Beeville Bees	33	53	.384	18	12,580	Bob Leach

West Standings	W	L	Pct.	GB	Attend.	Manager
Corpus Christi Seagulls***	50	27	.649	—	74,280	Leo Mazzone
Victoria Cowboys	43	35	.551	7½	16,886	Kenny Richardson
Rio Grande Valley White Wings@	32	40	.444	14½	15,996	Ted Uhlaender

#Baton Rouge withdrew August 13.
@represented Harlingen, Texas.

Playoff: Seguin 2 games, Beeville 0.
Finals: Corpus Christi 3 games, Seguin 0.

BA: Mike Krizmanich, Corpus Christi, .386
Runs: Steve Greene, Victoria, 77
Hits: Greg "Boomer" Wells, Beeville, 114
RBIs: Jim Capehart, Corpus Christi, 87
HRs: Jim Capehart, Corpus Christi, 16

Wins: Byron McLaughlin, Victoria, 10
Frank Slivinski, Victoria, 10
SOs: Maddison Owens, Corpus Christi, 113
ERA: Thomas Brown, Baton Rouge, 1.51

A Mexican Center League
President: Antonio Ramirez Muro

Standings	W	L	Pct.	GB	Attend.	Manager
Lagos de Moreno	47	20	.701	—	9,288	Domingo Rivera
Guanajuato	34	33	.507	13	7,426	Hugo Rios/Hector Rodriguez
Ciudad Victoria	32	35	.478	15	7,097	Leo Rodriguez
Acambaro	32	36	.471	15½	7,749	Roberto Castellon
Zacatecas	30	37	.448	17	11,300	Felipe Hernandez/Manolo Fortes
Fresnillo	26	40	.394	20½	25,326	Mario Pelaez/Armando Ortiz

Playoffs: None.

All-Star Team: 1B-Olegario Valle, Guanajuato; **2B**-Rigoberto Robles, Guanajuato; **3B**-Roberto Zamora, Lagos de Moreno; **SS**-Vicente Lopez, Ciudad Victoria; **OF**-Ubaldo Guzman, Lagos de Moreno; Miguel Chavarria, Zacatecas; Jaime Rodriguez, Lagos de Moreno; **C**-Roberto Heras, Lagos de Moreno; **P**-Ramon Munguia, Lagos de Moreno; Arturo Casas, Acambaro.

BA: Ubaldo Guzman, Lagos de Moreno, .374
Runs: Ubaldo Guzman, Lagos de Moreno, 55
Hits: Rigoberto Robles, Guanajuato, 101
RBIs: Nelson Barrera, Fresnillo, 63
Roberto Heras, Lagos de Moreno, 63

HRs: Roberto Heras, Lagos de Moreno, 15
Wins: Ramon Munguia, Lagos de Moreno, 10
Arturo Casas, Acambaro, 10
Homero Vazquez, Guanajuato, 10
SOs: Javier Pina, Lagos de Moreno, 111
ERA: Ramon Munguia, Lagos de Moreno, 1.05

A Mexican Pacific League
President: Antonio Ramirez Muro

Standings	W	L	Pct.	GB	Attend.	Manager
Ciudad Obregon Yacquis	28	22	.560	—	15,146	Jim Williams
Navojoa Mayos	26	22	.542	1	14,264	Cesar Gutierrez
Los Mochis Caneros	27	23	.540	1	3,500	
Mazatlan Venados	27	23	.540	1	2,311	Jesus Robles
Guasave Algodoneros	26	24	.520	2	3,965	
Hermosillo Naranjeros	24	25	.490	3½	4,420	
Guaymas Ostioneros	19	28	.404	7½	3,847	Alfred Rios
Guamuchil Tomateros	20	30	.400	8	6,992	

Playoffs: Los Mochis 2 games, Mazatlan 0; Ciudad Obregon 2 games, Navojoa 1.
Finals: Ciudad Obregon 3 games, Los Mochis 2.

BA: Ricardo Vega, Los Mochis, .361
Runs: Ricardo Vega, Los Mochis, 29
Hits: Ricardo Vega, Los Mochis, 57
RBIs: Severo Arandas, Mazatlan, 30
HRs: Oscar Noris, Mazatlan, 6

Wins: Juan Castro, Los Mochis, 9
Jose Lara, Guasave, 9
SOs: Pablo Estrada, Guaymas, 112
ERA: Manuel Olea, Guaymas, 0.64

A Midwest League
President: Bill Walters

North Standings	W	L	Pct.	GB	Attend.	Manager
Waterloo Royals*** (7)	78	52	.600	—	56,390	John Sullivan
Wisconsin Rapids Twins (9)	67	63	.515	11	57,816	Harry Warner
Dubuque Packers (16)	59	71	.454	19	58,437	Robert Cluck
Wausau Mets (19)	56	73	.434	21½	57,797	Bill Monbouquette
Appleton Foxes (4)	56	74	.431	22	55,398	Jim Napier

South Standings	W	L	Pct.	GB	Attend.	Manager
Cedar Rapids Giants* (24)	78	53	.595	—	78,801	Francis "Salty" Parker
Quad Cities Angels** (3)	72	59	.550	6	66,062	Moose Stubing
Burlington Bees (8)	68	61	.527	9	46,675	Matt Galante
Clinton Pilots (x)	59	70	.457	18	35,425	Bob Hartsfield
Danville Dodgers (17)	56	73	.434	21	28,325	Dick McLaughlin

Playoff: Quad Cities 1 game, Cedar Rapids 0.
Finals: Waterloo 2 games, Quad Cities 0.

All-Star Team: 1B-Daniel Garcia, Waterloo; **2B**-Steve Lacy, Waterloo; **3B**-Art Fischetti, Danville; **SS**-Tim Doerr, Clinton; **OF**-Jose Barrios, Cedar Rapids; Darrell Parker, Waterloo; Don Pisker, Quad Cities; Jim Monasterio, Wausau; **C**-Wayne Cato, Cedar Rapids; Terry Bulling, Wisconsin Rapids; **DH**-Moe Hill, Wisconsin Rapids; **P**-John Johnson, Cedar Rapids; Ron Hodges, Cedar Rapids; **MVP**-Wayne Cato, Cedar Rapids; **Manager**-Francis "Salty" Parker, Cedar Rapids.

BA: Don Pisker, Quad Cities, 3.45
Runs: Moe Hill, Wisconsin Rapids, 112
Hits: Art Fischetti, Danville, 144
RBIs: Moe Hill, Wisconsin Rapids, 103
HRs: Moe Hill, Wisconsin Rapids, 30

Wins: Ron Hodges, Cedar Rapids, 14
Dave Steck, Quad Cities, 14
SOs: Ted Barnicle, Cedar Rapids, 160
ERA: Ron Hodges, Cedar Rapids, 1.24

A New York-Pennsylvania League
President: Vincent M. McNamara

Standings	W	L	Pct.	GB	Attend.	Manager
Elmira Red Sox*** (2)	50	20	.714	—	45,045	Dick Berardino
Newark Co-Pilots (8)	46	24	.657	4	12,501	Tony Roig
Niagara Falls Pirates (21)	35	34	.507	14½	45,687	Glenn Ezell
Batavia Trojans (5)	30	40	.429	20	40,716	Jack Cassini
Auburn Phillies (20)	24	45	.348	25½	35,352	Michael Compton
Oneonta Yankees (10)	24	46	.343	26	21,082	Ed Napoleon

Playoffs: None.

All-Star Team: 1B-Gary Holle, Newark; **2B**-David Denton, Elmira; **3B**-Richard Walterhouse, Niagara Falls; **SS**-Garry Pyka, Newark; **OF**-Michael Ongarato, Elmira; Garry Smith, Oneonta; Elijah Bonaparte, Auburn; Richard Howard, Niagara Falls; Jose Oppenheimer, Newark; **C**-Terence Shoebridge, Newark; Mark Thiel, Oneonta; **Util**-Don Hogestyn, Oneonta; **P**-Michael Howard, Elmira; Larry Kienzle, Niagara Falls; Lary Sorensen, Newark; John Teising, Batavia; **Manager**-Dick Berardino, Elmira.

BA: Garry Smith, Oneonta, .391
Runs: Gary Holle, Newark, 70
Hits: Gary Holle, Newark, 81
Michael Ongarato, Elmira, 81
RBIs: Gary Holle, Newark, 77

HRs: Gary Holle, Newark, 19
Wins: Michael Howard, Elmira, 8
SOs: Fred Honeycutt, Niagara Falls, 98
ERA: Danny Parks, Elmira, 2.27

A Northwest League
President: Bob Richmond

North Standings	W	L	Pct.	GB	Attend.	Manager
Portland Mavericks	40	32	.556	—	83,780	Jack Spring
Seattle Rainiers	39	33	.542	1	16,294	Arthur Peterson
Grays Harbor Ports#	26	46	.361	14	28,842	Carl Thompson

South Standings	W	L	Pct.	GB	Attend.	Manager
Walla Walla Padres (23)	46	26	.639	—	28,971	Cliff Ditto
Eugene Emeralds (15)	37	34	.521	8½	48,871	Greg Riddoch
Boise A's (11)	33	38	.465	12½	16,294	Tom Trebelhorn
Bellingham Dodgers (17)	30	42	.417	16	23,225	Bill Berrier

#represented Aberdeen-Hoquiam, Washington.

Playoff: Walla Walla 2 games, Portland 1.

All-Star Team: 1B-George Kaage, Bellingham; **2B**-Steve Collette, Portland; **3B**-Paul O'Neill, Walla Walla; **SS**-Edward Cervantes, Portland; **OF**-Ron McNeely, Boise; Robert Kraft, Seattle; Duane Walker, Eugene; **C**-Doug Wantz, Portland; **DH**-Mike Rodriguez, Boise; **P**-George Benson, Seattle; Scott Brown, Eugene; Barry Biggerstaff, Grays Harbor; Steve Mura, Walla Walla; Bill Joseph, Walla Walla; Mark Lee, Walla Walla; **Manager**-Cliff Ditto, Walla Walla.

BA: Ron McNeely, Boise, .403
Runs: Xavier Dixson, Seattle, 63
Hits: Steve Collette, Portland, 83
RBIs: Broderick Perkins, Walla Walla, 63

HRs: Mike Rodriguez, Boise, 12
Wins: Tom Winkelbauer, Portland, 10
SOs: Barry Biggerstaff, Grays Harbor, 123
ERA: Steve Mura, Walla Walla, 1.37

A Western Carolinas League
President: John H. Moss

Standings	W	L	Pct.	GB	Attend.	Manager
Asheville Tourists* (12)	76	62	.551	—	41,580	Wayne Terwilliger
Greenwood Braves** (13)	75	64	.540	1½	26,380	Gene Hassell
Charleston Patriots (21)	59	80	.424	17½	34,249	Michael Ryan
Spartanburg Phillies (20)	59	80	.424	17½	32,008	Lee Elia

Played an interlocking schedule with the Carolina League.

Playoff: Greenwood 3 games, Asheville 1.

All-Star Team: 1B-Pat Putnam, Asheville; **2B**-Jose Moreno, Spartanburg; **3B**-Dale Berra, Charleston; **SS**-Nelson Norman, Charleston; **OF**-Larry Whisenton, Greenwood; Eddie Miller, Asheville; Phil Convertino, Spartanburg; **C**-Joe Russell, Asheville; **DH**-Daniel DeBattista, Charleston; **Util**-Jim Doherty, Greenwood; Jim Busby, Charleston; **P**-William Free, Greenwood; Lamar "Monk" Jones, Greenwood; Paul Mirabella, Asheville; Carlos Arroyo, Spartanburg; **Manager**-Gene Hassell, Greenwood.

BA: Pat Putnam, Asheville, .361
Runs: LaRue Washington, Asheville, 106
Hits: Pat Putnam, Asheville, 194
RBIs: Pat Putnam, Asheville, 142

HRs: Pat Putnam, Asheville, 24
Wins: Harold Kelly, Asheville, 13
SOs: Paul Mirabella, Asheville, 136
ERA: Harold Kelly, Asheville, 3.02

R Appalachian League
President: Chauncey De Vault

North Standings	W	L	Pct.	GB	Attend.	Manager
Bluefield Orioles (1)	42	28	.600	—	28,487	Ben Hines
Covington Astros (16)	38	32	.543	4	17,400	Julio Linares
Pulaski Phillies (x)	32	38	.457	10	13,340	Art Mazmanian
Marion Mets (19)	28	42	.400	14	7,198	Tom Egan

South Standings

South Standings	W	L	Pct.	GB	Attend.	Manager
Johnson City Cardinals (22) ..	50	20	.714	—	37,569	Buzzy Keller
Bristol Tigers (6)	35	32	.522	13½	32,498	Joe Lewis
Elizabethton Twins (9)	27	43	.386	23	17,031	Fred Waters
Kingsport Braves (13)	25	42	.373	23½	23,742	Bobby Dews

Playoffs: None.

All-Star Team: 1B-Jim Skaalen, Bluefield; **2B**-Harold Witt, Johnson City; **3B**-Phil Klimas, Covington; **SS**-Alan Trammell, Bristol; **OF**-Mark Corey, Bluefield; Vernon Thomas, Bluefield; Bill Bowman, Johnson City; **C**-Reggie Baldwin, Covington; **P**-Clint Thomas, Bluefield; Alan Olmsted, Johnson City; Dennis Miscik, Covington; **Manager**-Buzzy Keller, Johnson City.

BA: Mark Corey, Bluefield, .400
Runs: Mark Corey, Bluefield, 62
Hits: Mark Corey, Bluefield, 114
RBIs: Mark Corey, Bluefield, 59
HRs: Mark Corey, Bluefield, 17
Wins: Clint Thomas, Bluefield, 11
SOs: Pete Torres, Bluefield, 102
ERA: Roger Weaver, Bristol, 1.43

R Gulf Coast League
President: George MacDonald, Jr.

Standings	W	L	Pct.	GB	Manager
Rangers (12)	38	16	.704	—	Joe Klein
Cubs (14)	36	17	.679	1½	Walt Dixon
Royals (7)	29	25	.537	9	Jose Martinez
Cardinals (22)	27	24	.529	9½	Dave Ricketts
White Sox (4).....................	23	30	.434	14½	Joe Jones
Braves (13)	21	32	.396	16½	Chuck Goggin & Pedro Gonzalez
Pirates (21)........................	11	41	.212	26	Woody Huyke

Games played at Sarasota and Bradenton, Florida.

Playoffs: None.

All-Star Team: 1B-Ken Phelps, Royals; Jim Jennings, Rangers; **2B**-Billy Sample, Rangers; Paul Stevens, Royals; **3B**-Eugenio Cotes, Pirates; Felipe Zaya, Cardinals; **SS**-Steve Davis, Cubs; Francis McCann, Royals; **OF**-John Hoscheidt, Royals; Greg Jemison, Rangers; Jared Martin, Cubs; David Long, Braves; Dave Rivera, Rangers; Steve Rackley, Cubs; **C**-William Evers, Cubs; Jim Gaudet, Royals; **P**-Robert Clark, Cubs; Mike Tulacz, White Sox; Richard Couch, Rangers; Ray Searage, White Sox/Cardinals; Danny England, Cubs; Steve Finch, Rangers; Leon Gullette, Braves; Fred Howard, White Sox; **Manager**-Joe Klein, Rangers.

BA: Billy Sample, Rangers, .382
Runs: Greg Jemison, Rangers, 40
Hits: John Hoscheidt, Royals, 59
RBIs: Dave Rivera, Rangers, 40
HRs: Dave Rivera, Rangers, 4
    Darrell Vosejpka, Royals, 4
Wins: Danny England, Cubs, 10
SOs: Fred Howard, White Sox, 76
ERA: Steve Comer, Rangers, 0.90

R Pioneer League
President: Ralph C. Nelles

Standings	W	L	Pct.	GB	Attend.	Manager
Great Falls Giants (24)	41	30	.577	—	34,439	Ernest Rodriguez
Billings Mustangs (15)	36	35	.507	5	34,673	James Hoff
Idaho Falls Angels (3)	36	36	.500	5½	18,769	Larry Himes
Lethbridge Expos (18)........	30	42	.417	11½	19,200	Walt Hriniak

Playoffs: None.

All-Star Team: 1B-Don Lyons, Idaho Falls; **2B**-Joe Strain, Great Falls; **3B**-John Scoras, Lethbridge; **SS**-Craig Hendrickson, Idaho Falls; **OF**-John Sylvester, Great Falls; Eddie Milner, Billings; Paul Herring, Billings; **C**-Doug Simunic, Lethbridge; **P**-Richard Adams, Idaho Falls; Bill Dawley, Billings; Greg Johnson, Idaho Falls; **Manager**-Larry Himes, Idaho Falls.

BA: John Scoras, Lethbridge, .370
Runs: John Sylvester, Great Falls, 66
Hits: John Scoras, Lethbridge, 101
RBIs: John Scoras, Lethbridge, 63
HRs: John Scoras, Lethbridge, 13
Wins: Jim Ball, Idaho Falls, 8
    Larry Frakes, Billings, 8
SOs: Greg Johnson, Idaho Falls, 84
ERA: Larry Frakes, Billings, 1.53

1976 Interleague Post Season Play

World Series
Cincinnati (National) 4 games, New York (American) 0.

1976 Major League Farm Systems

American League

1 Baltimore (4): Rochester, Charlotte, Miami, Bluefield.
2 Boston (4): Pawtucket, Bristol (CT), Winston-Salem, Winter Haven, Elmira.
3 California (5): Salt Lake City, El Paso, Salinas, Quad Cities, Idaho Falls.
4 Chicago (4): Iowa, Knoxville, Appleton, Gulf Coast.
5 Cleveland (4): Toledo, Williamsport, San Jose, Batavia.
6 Detroit (4): Evansville, Montgomery, Lakeland, Bristol (VA).
7 Kansas City (4): Omaha, Jacksonville, Waterloo, Gulf Coast.
8 Milwaukee (4): Spokane, Berkshire, Burlington, Newark.
9 Minnesota (4): Tacoma, Orlando, Reno, Wisconsin Rapids, Elizabethton.
10 New York (4): Syracuse, West Haven, Ft. Lauderdale, Oneonta.
11 Oakland (4): Tucson, Chattanooga, Modesto, Boise.
12 Texas (4): Sacramento, San Antonio, Asheville, Gulf Coast.

National League

13 Atlanta (5): Richmond, Savannah, Greenwood, Kingsport, Gulf Coast.
14 Chicago (4): Wichita, Midland, Pompano Beach, Gulf Coast.
15 Cincinnati (5): Indianapolis, Trois Rivieres, Tampa, Eugene, Billings.
16 Houston (4): Memphis, Columbus, Dubuque, Covington.
17 Los Angeles (4): Albuquerque, Waterbury, Lodi, Bellingham, Danville.
18 Montreal (4): Denver, Quebec, West Palm Beach, Lethbridge.
19 New York (5): Tidewater, Jackson, Lynchburg, Wausau, Marion.
20 Philadelphia (5): Oklahoma City, Reading, Peninsula, Spartanburg, Auburn.
21 Pittsburgh (6): Charleston (WV), Shreveport, Salem, Charleston (SC), Niagara Falls, Gulf Coast.
22 St. Louis (5): Tulsa, Arkansas, St. Petersburg, Johnson City, Gulf Coast.
23 San Diego (4): Hawaii, Amarillo, Reno, Walla Walla.
24 San Francisco (5): Phoenix, Lafayette, Fresno, Cedar Rapids, Great Falls.

Co-op (x): Clinton, Pulaski.
Independent: Portland, Seattle, Grays Harbor, Gulf States League.

1976 No-Hitters

Date	Pitcher	Team	League	Opponent	Score
4-24	Steve Trella	Montgomery	Southern	Jacksonville	1-0 (7)
4-25	Frank Harris	Lakeland	Florida State	St. Petersburg	7-0
5-2	Thomas Baxter	Modesto	California	Salinas	1-0 (7)
5-8	Jesus Reynoso	Fresnillo	Mexican Center	Ciudad Victoria	2-0 (7)
5-16	Jesus Esparza	Lagos de Moreno	Mexican Center	Fresnillo	7-0
5-25	Richard Waller	Winston-Salem	Carolina	Charleston	4-1
5-25	John Montague	Oklahoma City	American Assoc.	Omaha	1-0 (7)
5-30	Rick Langford	Charleston	International	Memphis	11-0
5-31	Don Mraz	Quad Cities	Midwest	Wisconsin Rapids	3-0 (7)
6-2	David Hasbach	Omaha	American Assoc.	Tulsa	4-0 (7)
6-4	Mark Ballinger	Jacksonville	Southern	Columbus	3-0 (7)
6-6	Bob Smith	Rio Grande Valley	Gulf States	Beeville	12-1 (7)
6-8	Bernard Beckman	Midland	Texas	San Antonio	5-0 (7)
6-13	Chris Knapp	Iowa	American Assoc.	Evansville	3-0 (7)
6-24	Sheldon Burnside	Montgomery	Southern	Charlotte	8-0 (7)
6-28	Gilbert Patterson	West Haven	Eastern	Williamsport	1-0
6-29	Ted Barnicle	Cedar Rapids	Midwest	Dubuque	5-0
7-9	Larry Dierker	Houston	National	Montreal	5-0
7-11	Barry Biggerstaff	Grays Harbor	Northwest	Bellingham	8-0
7-11	Mike Guischer	Portland	Northwest	Boise	7-0 (7)
7-11	George Riley	Pompano Beach	Florida State	Ft. Lauderdale	10-0 (7)
7-15	Ed Glynn	Evansville	American Assoc.	Iowa	3-0 (7)
7-18	Don Fowler	Peninsula	Carolina	Lynchburg	3-0
7-20	Sammy Stewart	Miami	Florida State	Winter Haven	1-0 (7)
7-26	Ralph Botting	Quad Cities	Midwest	Wausau	3-0 (7)
7-28	John "Blue Moon" Odom/ Francisco Barrios	Chicago	American	Oakland	6-0
7-30	Larry Kienzle	Niagara Falls	New York-Penn.	Batavia	4-1 (7)
8-1	Hal Dues	West Palm Beach	Florida State	Pompano Beach	2-0 (6)
8-5	Michael Rowland	Lafayette	Texas	Jackson	1-0 (7)
8-9	John Candelaria	Pittsburgh	National	Los Angeles	2-0
8-12	Tom Kibbee	Miami	Florida State	Pompano Beach	1-0 (P, 7)
8-18	Steve Brisbin	Salinas	California	Fresno	2-0 (7)
8-21	Stu Livingstone	Braves	Gulf Coast	Pirates	6-0
8-27	Ray Prince	Royals	Gulf Coast	Braves	1-0
8-28	Terry Jacob	Johnson City	Appalachian	Elizabethton	7-0 (7)
9-29	John Montefusco	San Francisco	National	Atlanta	9-0

Number in parentheses indicates innings if other than nine; "P" indicates perfect game.

THIS DATE IN MINOR LEAGUE HISTORY

April 14, 1976, The Carolina League and Western Carolinas League continued play as four team circuits. In interleague play, the Carolina League would win the season series, 40 games to 23.

April 15, 1976, Chattanooga returned to baseball after a ten year absence. Playing in historic Engel Stadium, the Lookouts would lead the Southern League in attendance with 135,144 fans.

May 30, 1976, Burlington, Midwest League, defeated Waterloo 4-3 in 22 innings.

June 1, 1976, The independent Gulf States League was set to open. With the exception of complex leagues for rookies, it was the first new U.S. league to open since the Western Carolina League joined the National Association in 1960.

June 11, 1976, Chester "Chet" Covington, 65, southpaw pitcher who compiled one of the lowest career ERAs in minor league history (2.57), died in Pembroke, Florida. Covington was named minor league Player of the Year in 1943 when he registered a 21-7 mark for Scranton, Eastern League, with an ERA of 1.51. He pitched a perfect game against Springfield that season. On May 23, 1950, he hurled a 16-inning two-hitter for Ft. Lauderdale, Florida International League, against Lakeland, winning 1-0.

June 19, 1976, Henry "Prince" Oana, longtime minor league player and manager, died in Austin, Texas, at age 68.

August 13, 1976, Baton Rouge of the Gulf States League withdrew from the league. While the team was in first place, there were reports of many unpaid bills.

August 26, 1976, The American Association All-Stars beat the St. Louis Cardinals 3-1 before 6,734 fans at Omaha.

August 31, 1976, Bluefield's Mark Corey won the Triple Crown in the Appalachian League with a phenomenal .400 batting average, 17 home runs and 59 RBIs.

September 2, 1976, Montgomery set a Southern League record by playing their 31st doubleheader of the season. They won 13, lost two, and split 16.

September 2, 1976, Denver's Roger Freed finished the American Association season as the league's home run leader with 42, the most in the league since Marv Throneberry hit 42 for Denver in 1956.

October 4, 1976, Ollie Carnegie, outfielder for Buffalo from 1931 through 1941 and again in 1945, died at age 77. He held the International League record for career home runs with 258.

December 3, 1976, Wallace McKenna, president of the Carolina League since 1970, died in Lynchburg, Virginia, at age 57.

Franklin County Stadium was rebuilt in 1976-77 at a cost of $5 million for the Columbus (OH) Clippers of the International League. Originally constructed in 1931 as Redbird Stadium, the present name is Cooper Stadium.

1977

American League

President: Leland S. MacPhail, Jr.

East Standings	W	L	Pct.	GB	Attend.	Manager
New York Yankees...........	100	62	.617	—	2,103,092	Billy Martin
Baltimore Orioles	97	64	.602	2½	1,195,769	Earl Weaver
Boston Red Sox	97	64	.602	2½	2,074,549	Don Zimmer
Detroit Tigers....................	74	88	.457	26	1,359,856	Ralph Houk
Cleveland Indians	71	90	.441	28½	900,365	Frank Robinson/Jeff Torborg
Milwaukee Brewers	67	95	.414	33	1,114,938	Alex Grammas
Toronto Blue Jays..............	54	107	.335	45½	1,701,052	Roy Hartsfield

West Standings	W	L	Pct.	GB	Attend.	Manager
Kansas City Royals...........	102	60	.630	—	1,852,603	Whitey Herzog
Texas Rangers....................	94	68	.580	8	1,250,722	Frank Lucchesi/Eddie Stanky/ Connie Ryan/Billy Hunter
Chicago White Sox	90	72	.556	12	1,657,135	Bob Lemon
Minnesota Twins	84	77	.522	17½	1,162,727	Gene Mauch
California Angels................	74	88	.457	28	1,432,633	Norm Sherry/Dave Garcia
Seattle Mariners................	64	98	.395	38	1,338,511	Darrell Johnson
Oakland Athletics	63	98	.391	38½	495,599	Jack McKeon/Bobby Winkles

Playoff: New York 3 games, Kansas City 2.

BA: Rod Carew, Minnesota, .388
Runs: Rod Carew, Minnesota, 128
Hits: Rod Carew, Minnesota, 239
RBIs: Larry Hisle, Minnesota, 119
HRs: Jim Rice, Boston, 39

Wins: Jim Palmer, Baltimore, 20
Dave Goltz, Minnesota, 20
Dennis Leonard, Kansas City, 20
SOs: Nolan Ryan, California, 341
ERA: Frank Tanana, California, 2.54
Pct: Paul Splittorff, Kansas City, .727, 16-6
Saves: Bill Campbell, Boston, 31

National League

President: Charles S. Feeney

East Standings	W	L	Pct.	GB	Attend.	Manager
Philadelphia Phillies	101	61	.623	—	2,700,070	Danny Ozark
Pittsburgh Pirates	96	56	.593	5	1,237,349	Chuck Tanner
St. Louis Cardinals	83	79	.512	18	1,659,287	Vern Rapp
Chicago Cubs	81	81	.500	20	1,439,834	Herman Franks
Montreal Expos..................	75	87	.463	26	1,433,757	Dick Williams
New York Mets	64	98	.395	37	1,066,825	Joe Frazier/Joe Torre

West Standings	W	L	Pct.	GB	Attend.	Manager
Los Angeles Dodgers..........	98	64	.605	—	2,955,087	Tom Lasorda
Cincinnati Reds..................	88	74	.543	10	2,519,670	Sparky Anderson
Houston Astros	81	81	.500	17	1,109,560	Bill Virdon
San Francisco Giants	75	87	.463	23	700,056	Joe Altobelli
San Diego Padres...............	69	93	.426	29	1,376,269	John McNamara/ Bob Skinner/Alvin Dark
Atlanta Braves	61	101	.377	37	872,464	Dave Bristol/Ted Turner/ Vern Benson

Playoff: Los Angeles 3 games, Philadelphia 1.

BA: Dave Parker, Pittsburgh, .338
Runs: George Foster, Cincinnati, 124
Hits: Dave Parker, Pittsburgh, 215
RBIs: George Foster, Cincinnati, 149
HRs: George Foster, Cincinnati, 52

Wins: Steve Carlton, Philadelphia, 23
SOs: Phil Niekro, Atlanta, 262
ERA: John Candelaria, Pittsburgh, 2.34
Pct: John Candelaria, Pittsburgh, .800, 20-5
Saves: Rollie Fingers, San Diego, 35

AAA American Association

President: Joe Ryan

East Standings	W	L	Pct.	GB	Attend.	Manager
Omaha Royals (7)..............	76	59	.563	—	149,533	John Sullivan
Indianapolis Indians (17)....	72	64	.529	4½	165,451	Roy Majtyka
Evansville Triplets (6)	65	68	.489	10	110,663	Les Moss
Iowa Oaks (4)	61	75	.449	15½	124,135	Joe Sparks

West Standings	W	L	Pct.	GB	Attend.	Manager
Denver Bears (20)..............	71	65	.522	—	288,167	Jim Marshall
Wichita Aeros (16)	68	64	.515	1	132,488	Harry Dunlop
Oklahoma City 89ers (22) ..	70	66	.515	1	113,243	Cal Ermer/Connie Ryan/ Billy Connors
New Orleans Pelicans (24) .	57	79	.419	14	217,957	Lance Nichols

Playoff: Denver 4 games, Omaha 2.

All-Star Team: 1B-Frank Ortenzio, Denver; **2B**-Freddy Andrews, Oklahoma City; Rudolph Meoli, Indianapolis; **3B**-David Cripe, Omaha; **SS**-Stan Papi, Denver; **OF**-Benny Ayala, New Orleans; Jim Dwyer, Wichita; Clint Hurdle, Omaha; **C**-Lance Parrish, Evansville; Craig Perkins, Omaha; **Util**-Michael Adams, Wichita; **P**-Dennis Lamp, Wichita; Jim Wright, Oklahoma City; **MVP**-Frank Ortenzio, Denver; **Pitcher of the Year**-Jim Wright, Oklahoma City; **Manager**-Jim Marshall, Denver.

BA: Jim Dwyer, Wichita, .332
Runs: Jim Dwyer, Wichita, 113
Hits: Jim Dwyer, Wichita, 154
RBIs: Frank Ortenzio, Denver, 126

HRs: Frank Ortenzio, Denver, 40
Wins: Gary Lance, Omaha, 16
SOs: Larry Landreth, Denver, 134
ERA: John Kucek, Iowa, 2.54

AAA International League

President: Roy Jackson

Standings	W	L	Pct.	GB	Attend.	Manager
Pawtucket Red Sox (2)	80	60	.571	—	70,344	Joe Morgan
Charleston Charlies (18).....	78	62	.557	2	131,418	Jim Beauchamp
Tidewater Tides (21)	73	67	.521	7	135,138	Frank Verdi
Richmond Braves (15)........	71	69	.507	9	185,628	Tommie Aaron
Syracuse Chiefs (10)...........	70	70	.500	10	200,002	Pete Ward
Rochester Red Wings (1).....	67	73	.479	13	245,693	Ken Boyer
Columbus Clippers (23)......	65	75	.464	15	457,251	Tim Murtaugh/John Lipon
Toledo Mud Hens (5)	56	84	.400	24	102,606	Jack Cassini

Playoffs: Pawtucket 3 games, Richmond 1; Charleston 3 games, Tidewater 1.
Finals: Charleston 4 games, Pawtucket 0.

All-Star Team: 1B-Terry Crowley, Rochester; **2B**-Mike Edwards, Columbus; **3B**-Ted Cox, Pawtucket; **SS**-Greg Pryor, Syracuse; **OF**-Joe Cannon, Charleston; Larry Harlow, Rochester; Darryl Jones, Syracuse; **C**-Dale Murphy, Richmond; **P**-Larry McCall, Syracuse; Mickey Mahler, Richmond; **MVP**-Ted Cox, Pawtucket; **Pitcher of the Year**-Mike Parrott, Rochester; **Manager**-Joe Morgan, Pawtucket.

BA: Wayne Harer, Pawtucket, .350
Runs: Pepe Mangual, Tidewater, 95
Hits: Mike Edwards, Columbus, 157
RBIs: Dale Murphy, Richmond, 90

HRs: Terry Crowley, Rochester, 30
Wins: Larry McCall, Syracuse, 16
SOs: Mike Parrott, Rochester, 146
ERA: Tom Dixon, Charleston, 2.25

AAA Mexican League

President: Antonio Ramirez Muro

North West Standings	W	L	Pct.	GB	Attend.	Manager
Saltillo Saraperos..............	84	67	.556	—	223,529	Gregorio Luque
Union Laguna Algodoneros	83	67	.553	½	254,157	Moises Camacho
Ciudad Juarez Indios	81	70	.536	3	298,065	Jose Guerrero
Chihuahua Dorados	62	88	.413	21½	193,185	Miguel Gaspar

North East Standings	W	L	Pct.	GB	Attend.	Manager
Nuevo Laredo Tecolotes.....	77	75	.507	—	241,579	Jorge Calvo/Jorge Fitch
Monterrey Sultanes............	74	77	.490	2½	227,287	Marte de Alejandro
Coahuila Mineros	70	81	.464	6½	194,870	Miguel Sotelo
Tampico Alijadores	57	97	.370	21	171,886	Clemente Carrera/ Ben Valenzuela

South West Standings	W	L	Pct.	GB	Attend.	Manager
Puebla Angeles	96	54	.640	—	214,383	Raul Cano
Durango Alacranes	77	71	.520	18	219,058	Benjamin Cerda
Aguascalientes Rieleros	77	73	.513	19	310,967	Pompeyo Davalillo
Mexico City Tigres	73	77	.487	23	252,737	Jose Luis Garcia/Ron Camacho

South East Standings	W	L	Pct.	GB	Attend.	Manager
Mexico City Diablos Rojos	94	57	.623	—	410,624	Ben Reyes
Cordoba Cafeteros	86	64	.573	7½	180,712	Ramon Arano/Wilfredo Calvino
Poza Rica Petroleros	58	91	.389	35	226,377	George Brunet/David Garcia
Tabasco Plataneros#	56	96	.368	38½	219,773	Napoleon Reyes/Carlos Trevino

#represented Villahermosa, Mexico.

Playoffs: Saltillo 4 games, Monterrey 3; Nuevo Laredo 4 games, Union Laguna 2; Cordoba 4 games, Puebla 3; MC Diablos Rojos 4 games, Durango 1. Nuevo Laredo 4 games, Saltillo 2; MC Diablos Rojos 4 games, Cordoba 0.
Finals: Nuevo Laredo 4 games, MC Diablos Rojos 1.

BA: Vic Davalillo, Aguascalientes, .384
Runs: Ismael Oquendo, Saltillo, 107
Hits: Miguel Suarez, MC Diablos Rojos, 227
RBIs: Reggie Sanders, Durango, 119

HRs: Ismael Oquendo, Saltillo, 34
Wins: Guadalupe Salinas, Union Laguna, 22
SOs: Byron McLaughlin, Nuevo Laredo, 221
ERA: Horacio Pina, Aguascalientes, 1.70

AAA Pacific Coast League

President: Roy Jackson

East Standings	W	L	Pct.	GB	Attend.	Manager
Phoenix Giants (26)............	81	59	.579	—	160,321	Rocky Bridges
Salt Lake City Gulls (3)......	74	65	.532	6½	254,679	Jimy Williams
Tucson Toros (13)	65	73	.471	15	123,520	Rich Donnelly
Albuquerque Dukes (19)	60	78	.435	20	192,355	James B. Williams

West Standings	W	L	Pct.	GB	Attend.	Manager
Hawaii Islanders (25).........	79	67	.541	—	347,931	Dick Phillips
Spokane Indians (8)...........	75	69	.521	3	133,270	John Felske
Tacoma Twins (9)..............	68	75	.476	9½	207,538	Del Wilber/Tom Kelly
San Jose Missions (11)	64	80	.444	14	88,265	Rene Lachemann

*Won first-half   **Won second-half   ***Won both halves
Numbers after nicknames indicate farm system.
Affiliation listed at end of each year.

540

Playoff: Phoenix 3 games, Salt Lake City 2.

All-Star Team: 1B-Philip James, Phoenix; **2B**-Julio Cruz, Hawaii; **3B**-Jim Gantner, Spokane; **SS**-Junior Kennedy, Phoenix; **OF**-Dick Davis, Spokane; Henry Cruz, Albuquerque; Joe Simpson, Albuquerque; **C**-Rick Sweet, Hawaii; **DH**-Danny Walton, Albuquerque; **P**-Mark Wiley, Hawaii; Bill Butler, Tacoma; **Manager**-Rocky Bridges, Phoenix.

BA: Don Cardoza, Albuquerque, .356
Runs: Danny Walton, Albuquerque, 117
Hits: Henry Cruz, Albuquerque, 174
RBIs: Danny Walton, Albuquerque, 122
HRs: Danny Walton, Albuquerque, 42
Wins: Mark Wiley, Hawaii, 16
SOs: Frank Riccelli, Phoenix, 135
ERA: Eddie Bane, Tacoma, 4.14

AA Eastern League
President: P. Patrick McKernan

Can-Am Standings	W	L	Pct.	GB	Attend.	Manager
Trois Rivieres Aigles (17)	76	62	.551	—	52,927	Chuck Goggin
Quebec Metros (20)	65	70	.481	9½	60,524	Doc Edwards
Reading Phillies (22)	63	75	.457	13	57,540	Lee Elia
Jersey City Indians (5)	40	97	.292	35½	60,024	John Orsino

New England Standings	W	L	Pct.	GB	Attend.	Manager
West Haven Yankees (10)	86	52	.623	—	41,072	Mike Ferraro
Waterbury Giants (26)	77	63	.550	10	76,626	Andy Gilbert
Holyoke Millers (8)	73	66	.525	13½	61,171	Matt Galante
Bristol Red Sox (2)	72	67	.518	14½	57,563	John Kennedy

Playoff: West Haven 3 games, Trois Rivieres 0.

All-Star Team: 1B-Harry Spilman, Trois Rivieres; **2B**-Tony Bernazard, Quebec; **3B**-Tim Doerr, Trois Rivieres; **SS**-Santo Domingo, Trois Rivieres; **OF**-Garry Smith, West Haven; Casey Parsons, Waterbury; Gary Purcell, Bristol; Larry Phillips, Holyoke; **C**-Jerry Narron, West Haven; **DH**-George Weiker, Trois Rivieres; **P**-Alan Wirth, Waterbury; Jeff Little, Waterbury; **MVP**-Harry Spilman, Trois Rivieres; **Manager**-Mike Ferraro, West Haven; Andy Gilbert, Waterbury.

BA: Harry Spilman, Trois Rivieres, .373
Runs: Harry Spilman, Trois Rivieres, 94
Hits: Harry Spilman, Trois Rivieres, 184
RBIs: Ike Blessitt, Holyoke, 104
HRs: Gary Holle, Holyoke, 30
Wins: Mark Armstrong, Trois Rivieres, 16
SOs: Alan Wirth, Waterbury, 149
ERA: Roger Slagle, West Haven, 2.81

AA Southern League
President: Billy Hitchcock

East Standings	W	L	Pct.	GB	Attend.	Manager
Orlando Twins (9)	76	61	.555	—	46,113	John Goryl
Savannah Braves*(15)	77	63	.550	½	80,070	Gene Hassell
Jacksonville Suns**(7)	72	66	.522	4½	86,888	Gordy MacKenzie
Charlotte O's (1)	69	71	.493	8½	89,506	Jim Schaffer

West Standings	W	L	Pct.	GB	Attend.	Manager
Montgomery Rebels***(6)	86	51	.628	—	61,738	Ed Brinkman
Chattanooga Lookouts (11)	61	75	.449	24½	92,601	George Farson
Columbus Astros (18)	60	77	.438	26	48,449	Leo Posada
Knoxville Knox Sox (4)	50	87	.365	36	34,938	Jim Napier

Playoff: Jacksonville 2 games, Savannah 1.
Finals: Montgomery 2 games, Jacksonville 0.

All-Star Team: 1B-Tom Chism, Charlotte; **2B**-Lou Whitaker, Montgomery; **3B**-Mike Macha, Charlotte; **SS**-Alan Trammell, Montgomery; **OF**-Mark Corey, Charlotte; Alfredo Javier, Columbus; Mike Gatlin, Orlando; Dave Stegman, Montgomery; **C**-Bruce Benedict, Savannah; **DH**-Fernando Tatis, Columbus; **Util**-Wayne Krenchicki, Charlotte; **P**-Gregory Field, Orlando; Richard Wortham, Knoxville; **Manager**-Ed Brinkman, Montgomery.

BA: Mark Corey, Charlotte, .310
Runs: Lou Whitaker, Montgomery, 81
Hits: Mark Corey, Charlotte, 152
RBIs: Jerry Keller, Savannah, 86
HRs: Tom Chism, Charlotte, 17
Alfredo Javier, Columbus, 17
Jerry Keller, Savannah, 17
Wins: Bryn Smith, Charlotte, 15
SOs: Matt Keough, Chattanooga, 153
ERA: Sammy Stewart, Charlotte, 2.08

AA Texas League
President: Carl Sawatski

East Standings	W	L	Pct.	GB	Attend.	Manager
Tulsa Drillers*(13)	66	62	.516	—	96,045	Orlando Martinez
Arkansas Travelers**(24)	63	67	.485	4	116,695	Buzzy Keller/ Tommy Thompson
Shreveport Captains (23)	62	68	.477	5	44,011	John Lipon/Tim Murtaugh
Jackson Mets (21)	62	68	.477	5	86,742	Bob Wellman

West Standings	W	L	Pct.	GB	Attend.	Manager
El Paso Diablos***(3)	78	52	.600	—	217,346	Buck Rodgers
Midland Cubs (16)	70	60	.538	8	76,461	Jim Saul
San Antonio Dodgers (19)	61	67	.477	16	53,359	Don LeJohn
Amarillo Gold Sox (25)	56	74	.431	22	50,381	David Campbell

Playoff: Arkansas 2 games, Tulsa 0.
Finals: Arkansas 2 games, El Paso 0.

All-Star Team: 1B-Joe Boyland, Shreveport; **2B**-Bob Slater, El Paso; **3B**-Carney Lansford, El Paso; **SS**-Jim Anderson, El Paso; **OF**-Eddie Miller, Tulsa; Karl Pagel, Midland; Gilbert Kubski, El Paso; **C**-Pat Kelly, El Paso; **DH**-Billy Sample, Tulsa; **P**-Danny Darwin, Tulsa; Rick Honeycutt, Shreveport; **MVP**-Karl Pagel, Midland; **Manager**-Buck Rodgers, El Paso.

BA: Tom Smith, El Paso, .366
Runs: Gilbert Kubski, El Paso, 114
Hits: Gilbert Kubski, El Paso, 177
RBIs: Steve Stroughter, El Paso, 116
HRs: Karl Pagel, Midland, 28
Wins: Mike Scott, Jackson, 14
SOs: Juan Berenguer, Jackson, 160
ERA: Rick Honeycutt, Shreveport, 2.47

A California League
President: E.W. "Bill" Wickert

Standings	W	L	Pct.	GB	Attend.	Manager
Fresno Giants (26)	83	57	.593	—	65,533	John Van Ornum
Lodi Dodgers**(19)	81	59	.579	2	38,171	Stan Wasiak
Salinas Angels*(3)	79	61	.564	4	74,457	Moose Stubing
Visalia Oaks (9)	65	75	.464	18	44,747	Roy McMillan
Reno Silver Sox (25)	59	81	.421	24	50,016	Glenn Ezell
Modesto A's (11)	53	87	.379	30	57,865	Tom Trebelhorn

Playoff: Lodi 3 games, Salinas 0.

All-Star Team: 1B-Kelly Snider, Lodi; **2B**-Joe Strain, Fresno; **3B**-Earl Battey, Reno; **SS**-Michael Rex, Fresno; **OF**-Tim Derryberry, Reno; Bill Ewing, Salinas; Rickey Henderson, Modesto; **C**-Stan Cliburn, Salinas; **Util**-Jack Perconte, Lodi; **P**-John Johnson, Fresno; David Mendoza, Fresno; Tom Tellmann, Reno; Richard Sander, Lodi; **MVP**-Kelly Snider, Lodi; **Manager**-Stan Wasiak, Lodi.

BA: Rudy Law, Lodi, .386
Runs: Jack Perconte, Lodi, 132
Hits: Joe Strain, Fresno, 188
RBIs: Kelly Snider, Lodi, 139
HRs: Kelly Snider, Lodi, 36
Wins: David Mendoza, Fresno, 16
SOs: Ted Barnicle, Fresno, 179
ERA: John Johnson, Fresno, 3.38

A Carolina League
President: James B. Mills

Standings	W	L	Pct.	GB	Attend.	Manager
Lynchburg Mets*(21)	78	60	.565	—	55,123	Jack Aker
Peninsula Pilots**(22)	71	67	.514	7	44,032	Jim Snyder
Salem Pirates (23)	66	72	.478	12	32,744	Steve Demeter
Winston-Salem Red Sox (2)	61	77	.442	17	33,652	Tony Torchia

Playoff: Peninsula 3 games, Lynchburg 2.

All-Star Team: 1B-Winston Cole, Salem; **2B**-Luis Aguayo, Peninsula; **3B**-Wade Boggs, Winston-Salem; **SS**-Julio Valdez, Winston-Salem; **OF**-Eugenio Cotes, Salem; Ossie Olivares, Salem; Robert Bryant, Lynchburg; **C**-Alfred "Butch" Benton, Lynchburg; **DH**-John Hughes, Peninsula; **P**-Jeff Schneider, Peninsula; Neil Allen, Lynchburg; **MVP**-Ossie Olivares, Salem; **Manager**-Jack Aker, Lynchburg.

BA: Ossie Olivares, Salem, .370
Runs: Ossie Olivares, Salem, 121
Hits: Ossie Olivares, Salem, 208
RBIs: Eugenio Cotes, Salem, 102
HRs: John Hughes, Peninsula, 22
Wins: Jeff Schneider, Peninsula, 15
SOs: Neil Allen, Lynchburg, 126
ERA: Jeff Schneider, Peninsula, 2.50

A Florida State League
President: George MacDonald, Jr.

North Standings	W	L	Pct.	GB	Attend.	Manager
Lakeland Tigers (6)	85	53	.616	—	60,154	Jim Leyland
St. Petersburg Cardinals (24)	83	56	.597	2½	152,642	Hub Kittle
Winter Haven Red Sox (2)	70	66	.515	14	13,389	Rac Slider
Tampa Tarpons (17)	65	70	.481	18½	92,031	James Hoff
Daytona Beach Islanders (7)	57	77	.425	26	30,011	Jose Martinez

South Standings	W	L	Pct.	GB	Attend.	Manager
West Palm Beach Expos (20)	77	55	.583	—	118,306	Felipe Alou
Miami Orioles (1)	72	66	.522	8	41,605	Len Johnston
Pompano Beach Cubs (16)	72	68	.514	9	30,639	Jack Hiatt
Ft. Lauderdale Yankees (10)	53	80	.398	24½	47,003	Ed Napoleon
Cocoa Astros (18)	46	89	.341	32½	36,473	Jim Johnson

Playoffs: Lakeland 2 games, Miami 0; St. Petersburg 2 games, West Palm Beach 1.
Finals: Lakeland 3 games, St. Petersburg 1.

All-Star Team: 1B-John Scoras, West Palm Beach; **2B**-Tommy Herr, St. Petersburg; **3B**-Julio Perez, West Palm Beach; **SS**-Glenn Hoffman, Winter Haven; **OF**-Dale McMullen, West Palm Beach; David Penniall, St. Petersburg; Eric Grandy, Pompano Beach; **C**-Roberto Ramos, West Palm Beach; Greg Keatley, Pompano Beach; **Util**-Godfrey Evans, West Palm Beach; Marshall Edwards, Miami; **P**-Bill Presley, Miami; John Fulgham, St. Petersburg; Robert Clark, Pompano Beach; Michael Chris, Lakeland; **MVP**-John Scoras, West Palm Beach; **Manager**-Jim Leyland, Lakeland.

BA: Marshall Edwards, Miami, .334
Runs: Tommy Herr, St. Petersburg, 80
Hits: Tommy Herr, St. Petersburg, 156
RBIs: John Scoras, West Palm Beach, 86
HRs: John Scoras, West Palm Beach, 19
Wins: Michael Chris, Lakeland, 18
John Fulgham, St. Petersburg, 18
SOs: John Fulgham, St. Petersburg, 130
ERA: Michael Chris, Lakeland, 2.01

A Lone Star League
President: Vernon L. Harrison

North Standings	W	L	Pct.	GB	Attend.	Manager
Victoria Rosebuds*	38	42	.475	—	14,198	Tom Zimmer
Beeville Blazers	37	43	.463	1	7,150	Bill Bryk
Texas City Stars**	35	41	.461	1	12,305	Al Gallagher

South Standings	W	L	Pct.	GB	Attend.	Manager
Corpus Christi Seagulls***	53	27	.663	—	92,137	Leo Mazzone
Harlingen Suns	40	38	.513	12	68,203	Paul Thomas/ Mike Krizmanich
McAllen Dusters	33	45	.423	19	35,752	Shannon Kelly/Jack Allen

Playoffs: None. Corpus Christi refused to play; Victoria and Texas City cancelled their series for a North Division championship.

BA: Ken Jones, Beeville, .393
Runs: Mike Manderino, Beeville, 76
Hits: Lloyd Thompson, Corpus Christi, 109 Charles Diering, Victoria, 109
RBIs: Jim Rainey, Corpus Christi, 67

HRs: Marc Sinovich, Corpus Christi, 16
Wins: Nick Baltz, Beeville, 12
SOs: Armando Reyes, Corpus Christi, 101
ERA: Armando Reyes, Corpus Christi, 2.59

A Mexican Center League
President: Antonio Ramirez Muro

Central Standings	W	L	Pct.	GB	Attend.	Manager
Teocaltiche	41	23	.641	—	9,392	Eladio Urias/Waldo Velo
Zacatecas	38	30	.559	5	8,601	Felipe Hernandez
Arandas	37	31	.544	6	6,453	Cesar Gutierrez
Guadalajara	35	31	.530	7	4,636	Manuel Fortes
Lagos de Moreno	30	36	.455	12	6,855	Alfonso Pena/Domingo Rivera

Gulf Standings	W	L	Pct.	GB	Attend.	Manager
Ciudad Victoria	45	21	.682	—	9,820	Fidel Flores
Jalisco	32	35	.478	13½	3,859	Ossie Alvarez
Ciudad Mante	27	37	.422	17	2,723	Roberto Palafox
Ebano	27	42	.391	19½	14,690	Ben Valenzuela
Fresnillo	21	47	.309	25	19,904	Mario Pelaez

Playoff: Teocaltiche 4 games, Ciudad Victoria 3.

BA: Raymundo Torres, Jalisco, .421
Runs: Juan Contreras, Zacatecas, 63
Hits: Juan Contreras, Zacatecas, 101
RBIs: Juan Contreras, Zacatecas, 72

HRs: Juan Contreras, Zacatecas, 12
Wins: Cesareo Rodriguez, Teocaltiche, 12
SOs: Ramiro Sauceda, Ciudad Victoria, 90
ERA: Eduardo Silva, Guadalajara, 1.14

A Midwest League
President: Bill Walters

North Standings	W	L	Pct.	GB	Attend.	Manager
Waterloo Indians***(5)	80	58	.580	—	63,101	Woody Smith
Wisconsin Rapids Twins (9)	66	72	.478	14	60,229	Jim Rantz/Carlos Pascual/ Spencer "Red" Robbins
Wausau Mets (21)	55	83	.399	25	61,912	Tom Egan
Appleton Foxes (4)	54	84	.391	26	65,584	Gordon Lund

South Standings	W	L	Pct.	GB	Attend.	Manager
Clinton Dodgers (19)	79	59	.572	—	42,238	Dick McLaughlin
Quad City Angels (3)	75	64	.540	4½	108,662	Chuck Cottier
Cedar Rapids Giants*(26)	74	66	.529	6	96,763	Jack Mull
Burlington Bees**(8)	71	68	.511	8½	49,608	Denis Menke

Playoff: Burlington 1 game, Cedar Rapids 0.
Finals: Burlington 2 games, Waterloo 0.

All-Star Team: 1B-John Harris, Quad City; **2B**-Kelvin Chapman, Wausau; **3B**-Elmer Cardwell, Wausau; **SS**-Paul Molitor, Burlington; **OF**-Scott Moffitt, Quad City; Steve Splitt, Burlington; Mickey Hatcher, Clinton; **C**-Mike Scioscia, Clinton; **P**-Phil Nastu, Cedar Rapids; Dave Stewart, Clinton; **MVP**-Paul Molitor, Burlington; **Manager**-Denis Menke, Burlington.

BA: Elmer Cardwell, Wausau, .332
Runs: Craig Adams, Waterloo, 105
Hits: Jesus Vega, Burlington, 155
RBIs: Moe Hill, Wisconsin Rapids, 112

HRs: Moe Hill, Wisconsin Rapids, 41
Wins: Dave Stewart, Clinton, 17
SOs: Joel Crisler, Quad City, 155
ERA: Phil Nastu, Cedar Rapids, 1.88

A New York-Pennsylvania League
President: Vincent M. McNamara

East Standings	W	L	Pct.	GB	Attend.	Manager
Oneonta Yankees (10)	47	23	.671	—	41,531	Art Mazmanian
Utica Blue Jays (14)	43	28	.606	4½	49,398	Duane Larson
Elmira Pioneer Red Sox (2)	33	36	.478	13½	41,415	Dick Berardino
Little Falls Mets (21)	32	39	.451	15½	34,804	Chris Krug
Auburn Phillies (22)	17	53	.243	30	38,293	Ruben Amaro

West Standings	W	L	Pct.	GB	Attend.	Manager
Batavia Trojans (5)	42	28	.600	—	41,795	Gene Dusan
Newark Co-Pilots (8)	43	29	.597	1	9,892	Dennis Holmberg
Jamestown Expos (20)	35	32	.522	5½	17,938	Pat Daugherty
Geneva Cubs (16)	31	40	.437	11½	25,918	Bob Hartsfield
Niagara Falls Pirates (23)	27	42	.391	14½	35,495	Luther Quinn

Playoff: Oneonta 2 games, Batavia 0.

All-Star Team: 1B-Sal Rende, Batavia; **2B**-Ronald MacDonald, Little Falls; **3B**-James Messmer, Geneva; **SS**-Wally Backman, Little Falls; **OF**-Ken Baker, Oneonta; Benny Lee Lloyd, Oneonta; Samuel Davis, Batavia; Doug McCracken, Geneva; **C**-Bill Foley, Newark; Tim Glass, Batavia; **Util**-Dan Schmitz, Oneonta; **P**-Mike McLeod, Oneonta; Chris Welsh, Oneonta; Ron Driver, Newark; Mark Baum, Elmira; **Manager**-Art Mazmanian, Oneonta.

BA: Sal Rende, Batavia, .356
Runs: Ron Sorey, Utica, 57
Hits: Greg "Boomer" Wells, Utica, 97
RBIs: Greg "Boomer" Wells, Utica, 68

HRs: Tim Glass, Batavia, 21
Wins: Mike McLeod, Oneonta, 9
SOs: Chris Welsh, Oneonta, 125
ERA: Ron Driver, Newark, 1.68

A Northwest League
President: Bob Richmond

Affiliate Standings	W	L	Pct.	GB	Attend.	Manager
Bellingham Mariners (12)	42	26	.618	—	36,730	Bobby Floyd
Walla Walla Padres (25)	41	27	.603	1	27,272	Cliff Ditto
Eugene Emeralds (17)	31	37	.456	11	45,513	John Underwood

Independent Standings	W	L	Pct.	GB	Attend.	Manager
Portland Mavericks	44	22	.667	—	125,300	Steve Collette
Grays Harbor Loggers (x)	22	44	.333	22	10,571	Ralph Dick
Salem Senators	22	46	.324	23	11,860	Carl Thompson

Playoff: Bellingham 2 games, Portland 1.

All-Star Team: 1B-Greg Jackson, Eugene; **2B**-Barry Evans, Walla Walla; **3B**-Tom Kotchman, Eugene; **SS**-Ozzie Smith, Walla Walla; **OF**-Patrick Ingraham, Eugene; Robert Blakley, Walla Walla/Grays Harbor; Dave Henderson, Bellingham; **C**-Tom Johnson, Grays Harbor; Rodolfo Arias, Bellingham; **DH**-Juan Delgado, Grays Harbor; Paul Kirsch, Salem; **P**-Greg Biercevicz, Bellingham; John Dunn, Portland; Joey McLaughlin, Portland; Eric Mustad, Walla Walla; John Yandle, Walla Walla; **Manager**-Bobby Floyd, Bellingham.

BA: Steve Sbragia, Salem, .376
Runs: Ozzie Smith, Walla Walla, 69
Hits: Barry Evans, Walla Walla, 97
RBIs: Barry Evans, Walla Walla, 64

HRs: Dave Henderson, Bellingham, 16 Juan Delgado, Grays Harbor, 16
Wins: Greg Biercevicz, Bellingham, 11
SOs: Greg Biercevicz, Bellingham, 97
ERA: Greg Biercevicz, Bellingham, 0.90

A Western Carolinas League
President: John H. Moss

Standings	W	L	Pct.	GB	Attend.	Manager
Gastonia Cardinals**(24)	82	57	.590	—	34,730	Hal Lanier
Asheville Tourists (13)	81	58	.583	1	43,527	Wayne Terwilliger
Greenwood Braves*(15)	75	64	.540	7	44,842	Bobby Dews
Spartanburg Phillies (22)	67	73	.479	15½	27,381	Mike Compton
Shelby Reds (17)	60	79	.432	22	22,576	Jim Lett
Charleston Patriots (23)	53	87	.379	29½	31,891	Jim Mahoney

Playoff: Gastonia 3 games, Greenwood 1.

All-Star Team: 1B-Jeff Toothman, Gastonia; **2B**-Don Carr, Shelby; **3B**-Wayne Wilkerson, Asheville; **SS**-James Wessinger, Greenwood; **OF**-Greg Jemison, Asheville; David Rivera, Asheville; Gary Cooper, Greenwood; Paul Herring, Shelby; **C**-Ozzie Virgil, Spartanburg; **DH**-Freddie Tisdale, Gastonia; **P**-Michael Griffin, Asheville; Steve Bianchi, Asheville; Dominic Chiti, Greenwood; Glenn Comoletti, Gastonia; **Manager**-Hal Lanier, Gastonia.

BA: David Rivera, Asheville, .346
Runs: Greg Jemison, Asheville, 125
Hits: David Rivera, Asheville, 176
RBIs: David Rivera, Asheville, 118

HRs: David Rivera, Asheville, 26
Wins: Michael Griffin, Asheville, 17
SOs: Michael Griffin, Asheville, 201
ERA: Bruce Berenyi, Shelby, 2.30

R Appalachian League
President: Chauncey De Vault

Standings	W	L	Pct.	GB	Attend.	Manager
Bristol Tigers (6)	43	26	.623	—	27,410	Joe Lewis
Kingsport Braves (15)	43	27	.614	½	22,489	Bob Didier
Johnson City Cardinals (24)	37	33	.529	6½	31,492	Dave Ricketts
Elizabethton Twins (9)	32	38	.457	11½	18,263	Fred Waters
Bluefield Orioles (1)	29	40	.420	14	27,200	Junior Miner
Pulaski Phillies (x)	25	45	.357	18½	9,488	Granny Hamner

Playoffs: None.

All-Star Team: 1B-Danny Logan, Bluefield; **2B**-Tom Mee, Kingsport; **3B**-Lance Hallberg, Elizabethton; **SS**-Larry Randell, Bristol; **OF**-Joe Rothwell, Bristol; Steven Swain, Pulaski; Gene Roof, Johnson City; **C**-Raymond Smith, Elizabethton; **DH**-James McIntyre, Johnson City; **P**-Mark Smith, Bluefield; Mike Rachuba, Bluefield; **Manager**-Joe Lewis, Bristol.

BA: Gene Roof, Johnson City, .368
Runs: Raphael Hampton, Bristol, 55
Hits: Clifton Wilder, Bristol, 90
RBIs: Danny Logan, Bluefield, 56

HRs: Danny Logan, Bluefield, 14 Bruce Tonascia, Kingsport, 14
Wins: Charles Irving, Bristol, 9
SOs: Mark Smith, Bluefield, 89
ERA: Burwell Geiger, Bristol, 2.01

R Gulf Coast League
President: George MacDonald, Jr.

Standings	W	L	Pct.	GB	Manager
White Sox (4)	38	14	.731	—	Joe Jones
Royals (7)	34	19	.642	4½	Billy Scripture
Cubs (16)	30	24	.556	9	Ron Matney
Rangers (13)	27	27	.500	12	Joe Klein
Braves (15)	22	31	.415	16½	Pedro Gonzalez
Astros (18)	22	32	.407	17	Julio Linares
Pirates (23)	22	32	.407	17	Woody Huyke
Expos (20)	19	35	.352	20	Ray Bellino

Games played at Sarasota and Bradenton, Florida.

Playoffs: None.

All-Star Team: 1B-Marty Scott, Rangers; Edward Bahns, White Sox; **2B**-James Campowski, Rangers; Dewey Minton, Cubs; **3B**-George Ramos, Braves; Jose Rodriguez, Pirates; **SS**-Dave Hibner, Rangers; Don Simmons, Expos; **OF**-Dennis Webb, Royals; Michael Cline, Braves; Alan Knicely, Pirates; Ron Carney, Rangers; Phil Westendorf, Royals; Melvin Taylor, Expos; **C**-Randy Rouse, Astros; **Util**-Lorenzo Gray, White Sox; **P**-Richard Barnes, White Sox; Jackie Smith, White Sox; Mike Morley, Royals; Thomas Butler, Cubs; Vince Valentini, Cubs; Marc Gelinas, Pirates; Kevin Rupp, Expos; Steven Nielsen, Rangers; **Manager** -Joe Klein, Rangers.

BA: Dennis Webb, Royals, .374
Runs: Anthony Hill, White Sox, 49
    Rusty Kuntz, White Sox, 49
    Dennis Webb, Royals, 49
Hits: Dennis Webb, Royals, 73

RBIs: Marv Wooten, Royals, 47
HRs: Phil Westendorf, Royals, 8
Wins: Richard Barnes, White Sox, 8
SOs: Richard Barnes, White Sox, 61
ERA: Vince Valentini, Cubs, 0.98

R Pioneer League
President: Ralph C. Nelles

Standings	W	L	Pct.	GB	Attend.	Manager
Lethbridge Dodgers (19)	44	26	.629	—	24,423	Gail Henley
Great Falls Giants (26)	43	27	.614	1	38,920	Ernest Rodriguez
Idaho Falls Angels (3)	36	33	.552	7½	17,436	Larry Himes

Calgary Cardinals (24)........	34	36	.486	10	27,774	Johnny Lewis
Medicine Hat A's (11)........	29	41	.414	15	26,665	Juan Gomez
Billings Mustangs (17)	23	46	.333	20½	25,655	Greg Riddoch

Playoffs: None.

All-Star Team: 1B-Glenn Goya, Great Falls; **2B**-Don LeJohn, Lethbridge; **3B**-Ty Waller, Calgary; **SS**-LeRoy Grossini, Calgary; **OF**-Michael Ventress, Billings; Gregory Ris, Idaho Falls; Jim Bennett, Medicine Hat; **C**-Jesse Baez, Lethbridge; **P**-Rich Dotson, Idaho Falls; Scott Budner, Great Falls; Douglas Neuenschwander, Billings; **Manager**-Ernest Rodriguez, Great Falls.

BA: Jim Reeves, Calgary, .376
Runs: Ty Waller, Calgary, 77
Hits: Ty Waller, Calgary, 96
RBIs: Glenn Goya, Great Falls, 77
    Ty Waller, Calgary, 77

HRs: Michael Zournas, Lethbridge, 21
Wins: Scott Budner, Great Falls, 9
    James Nobles, Lethbridge, 9
SOs: Scott Budner, Great Falls, 121
ERA: Scott Budner, Great Falls, 3.36

1977 Interleague Post Season Play

World Series
New York (American) 4 games, Los Angeles (National) 2

1977 Major League Farm Systems

American League
1 Baltimore (4): Rochester, Charlotte, Miami, Bluefield.
2 Boston (5): Pawtucket, Bristol (CT), Winston-Salem, Winter Haven, Elmira.
3 California (5): Salt Lake City, El Paso, Salinas, Quad City, Idaho Falls.
4 Chicago (4): Iowa, Knoxville, Appleton, Gulf Coast.
5 Cleveland (4): Toledo, Jersey City, Waterloo, Batavia.
6 Detroit (4): Evansville, Montgomery, Lakeland, Bristol (VA).
7 Kansas City (4): Omaha, Jacksonville, Daytona Beach, Gulf Coast.
8 Milwaukee (4): Spokane, Holyoke, Burlington, Newark.
9 Minnesota (5): Tacoma, Orlando, Visalia, Wisconsin Rapids, Elizabethton.
10 New York (4): Syracuse, West Haven, Ft. Lauderdale, Oneonta.
11 Oakland (4): San Jose, Chattanooga, Modesto, Medicine Hat.
12 Seattle (1): Bellingham.
13 Texas (4): Tucson, Tulsa, Asheville, Gulf Coast.
14 Toronto (1): Utica.

National League
15 Atlanta (5): Richmond, Savannah, Greenwood, Kingsport, Gulf Coast.
16 Chicago (5): Wichita, Midland, Pompano Beach, Geneva, Gulf Coast.
17 Cincinnati (6): Indianapolis, Trois Rivieres, Tampa, Shelby, Eugene, Billings.
18 Houston (4): Charleston (WV), Columbus (GA), Cocoa, Gulf Coast.
19 Los Angeles (5): Albuquerque, San Antonio, Lodi, Clinton, Lethbridge.
20 Montreal (5): Denver, Quebec, West Palm Beach, Jamestown, Gulf Coast.
21 New York (5): Tidewater, Jackson, Lynchburg, Wausau, Little Falls.
22 Philadelphia (5): Oklahoma City, Reading, Peninsula, Auburn, Spartanburg.
23 Pittsburgh (6): Columbus (OH), Shreveport, Salem (VA), Charleston (SC), Niagara Falls, Gulf Coast.
24 St. Louis (6): New Orleans, Arkansas, St. Petersburg, Gastonia, Johnson City, Calgary.
25 San Diego (4): Hawaii, Amarillo, Reno, Walla Walla.
26 San Francisco (5): Phoenix, Waterbury, Fresno, Cedar Rapids, Great Falls.

Co-op (x): Grays Harbor, Pulaski.
Independent: Portland, Salem (OR), Lone Star League.

1977 No-Hitters

Date	Pitcher	Team	League	Opponent	Score
4-15	John Pacella	Jackson	Texas	Tulsa	3-0
4-16	Rafael Garcia	Ciudad Juarez	Mexican	Nuevo Laredo	9-1
5-6	Michael Chris	Lakeland	Florida State	St. Petersburg	1-0
5-14	Jim Colborn	Kansas City	American	Texas	6-0
5-26	Arturo Casas	Tampico	Mexican	Cordoba	1-0 (7)
5-29	Dionicio Madrigal	Ebano	Mexican Center	Guadalajara	1-0
5-30	Dennis Eckersley	Cleveland	American	California	1-0
6-1	Mickey Mahler	Richmond	International	Toledo	7-0
6-2	Jeff Grose/Michael Van DeCasteele	Jackson	Texas	Midland	5-0
6-7	Kevin Stephenson	Winston-Salem	Carolina	Salem	2-0 (7)
6-18	Mercedes Esquer	Ciudad Victoria	Mexican Center	Fresnillo	3-0 (P, 7)
6-20	George Brunet	Poza Rica	Mexican	Durango	5-0
7-9	Rafael Garcia	Ciudad Juarez	Mexican	Durango	3-1
7-25	Rod Scurry	Columbus	International	Richmond	2-0 (7)
7-27	Kevin Houston	Astros	Gulf Coast	Expos	3-2 (7)
8-8	Rich Dotson/ George Tucker	Idaho Falls	Pioneer	Billings	7-1
8-14	Mike Tennant	Lodi	California	Fresno	3-0 (7)
8-18	Greg Staffon	Jamestown	New York-Penn.	Elmira	11-3 (7)
8-20	Jeff Jackowiak	Bristol	Appalachian	Bluefield	3-0 (7)
8-27	Nick Baltz	Beeville	Lone Star	Texas City	4-0
8-30	Danny Parks	Winter Haven	Florida State	West Palm Beach	2-0 (7)
9-1	Larry Prewitt	Jackson	Texas	Tulsa	8-1
9-1	Chris Knapp/ Fred Howard	Iowa	American Assoc.	Omaha	8-0
9-22	Bert Blyleven	Texas	American	California	6-0

Number in parentheses indicates innings if other than nine; "P" indicates perfect game.

THIS DATE IN MINOR LEAGUE HISTORY

April 14, 1977, New Orleans returned to professional baseball in the American Association. The Pelicans played their home games in the 62,000 seat Superdome.

April 26, 1977, The Hawaii Islanders drew 25,189 fans for a home game.

June 3, 1977, The Evansville Triplets defeated New Orleans 23-2, making 21 hits for 49 total bases.

June 9, 1977, Randy Bass, Tacoma, Pacific Coast League, ripped four homers in one game.

June 10, 1977, The Lone Star League, formerly the Gulf States League, began its second season.

July 4, 1977, The largest crowd of the season in the National Association, 33,904 fans, attended the game in Honolulu's new Aloha Stadium.

July 14, 1977, Gene Locklear hit four home runs in one game for Columbus in the International League.

July 21, 1977, The Texas Rangers walloped the American Association All-Stars 9-1

before 5,277 fans in New Orleans.

August 17, 1977, First baseman Hector Espino hit 14 home runs for Tampico in the Mexican League, bringing his career total to 435, an all-time minor league record.

September 3, 1977, Japanese slugger Sadaharu Oh walloped his 756th career home run in Tokyo to surpass Hank Aaron's record. Oh was a 37-year-old first baseman.

September 5, 1977, Columbus, International League, ended the season with a total attendance of 457,251 fans. Franklin County Stadium was refurbished for a reported $5 million to bring baseball back to the Ohio city.

November 9, 1977, John Ogden, pitching star for the Baltimore Orioles' seven-time International League champions in the early 1920s, died in Philadelphia at age 80. Ogden posted 31 victories for the Orioles in 1921 and was a 20-game winner six times in eight seasons between 1920 and 1927. He won 213 games in the minors against only 103 defeats for a high winning percentage of .674.

December 25, 1977, Kenneth Guettler, who led a minor league in home runs in eight different years, including the Texas League with a record 62 in 1956, died in Jacksonville, Florida, at age 50.

THE REVIVAL: 1978 - 1991

*I*t is hard to pinpoint the exact time or reasons for the turnaround, but in the 1970s minor league baseball was starting to change. Perhaps it was simply that the long Vietnam nightmare was, over and the country was ready to return to more traditional pursuits. Some said it was the 1975 World Series between the Reds and Red Sox that woke America up to the forgotten joy of the game. Others would say it was a new breed of minor league operators breathing life into the game, but the signs were unmistakable.

In 1977, Columbus, Ohio, without baseball for six years, saw its county government pump more than five million dollars into its old park, refurbishing the stadium and bringing back a team. It was a remarkable sum for a government to spend on a minor league park, but the results were immediate. Seventh place Columbus drew 457,251 fans, a total almost unheard of since the boom days of the late 1940s.

In 1978. a former college baseball coach, Larry Schmittou, brought a Double-A Southern League team to Nashville. He pushed to get a new park built, and the team drew a phenomenal 380,159 fans. The next year, the revival extended to Class A. Greensboro in the Western Carolinas League drew 165,596 fans. In 1982, baseball returned to Louisville. Playing in 33,000 seat Cardinal Stadium, the team drew a minor league-record 868,418 fans, breaking the record of 670,563 set by San Francisco in 1946.

Earlier, cities had been lukewarm to the idea of having a minor league team. Now municipalities embraced the idea and new parks started springing up across the country. During the 1980s nearly 40 new facilities were built, and millions of dollars were pumped into revitalizing old parks.

The apogee was reached in 1988 when the city of Buffalo, trying to lure major league baseball, built forty-five million dollar Pilot Field to house the minor league club. The stadium, seating more than 19,000 fans, with restaurants, skyboxes and facilities better than those of many major league teams, enabled the Bisons to draw more than a million fans for five straight seasons.

Major league baseball also was undergoing a boom and farm systems expanded. Clubs had made do with four minor league affiliates earlier. Now most had six or seven and the expansion at the minor league level saw some leagues grow to 14 teams. Franchise values exploded and by 1991 it was rare for a full season Class A team to sell for less than one million dollars. Triple A franchise values exceeded four million dollars.

In 1978. Johnny Johnson, a career administrator in the commissioner's office, succeeded Bobby Bragan as president of the National Association. Johnson's presidency was concerned primarily with getting the National Association's finances in order. Though his office did not actively push the minors in the resurgence, the stability of the office gave the majors confidence to continue their partnership with the National Association. Johnson died in 1988 and was replaced by his assistant, Sal Artiaga, a former minor league administrator with the Cincinnati Reds.

The resurgence of the minors was not totally welcomed by all at the major league level. The success of minor league operators gave them an independence they had not seen in decades. Demands for winning clubs and shifts in Player Development Contracts by minor league clubs left a disagreeable taste on major league palates. Also, the Player Development Contract had been negotiated when minor league baseball was in dire straits. Now there was success, but the payments from the major league clubs had not lessened. The new breed of major league owners had no ties to the minor league game. These owners had difficulty understanding why they were sending money to the minor leagues.

The renewal of the Professional Baseball Agreement, the document that held the majors and minors together, was normally a rubber stamp vote every five years. In 1990, the major leagues gave the minors indication that the relationship would not remain the same. After bitter negotiations, and with threats from the majors that they would break up the 90-year association by forming their own minor leagues, a new agreement was passed at the 1990 Winter Meetings. New controls were given to the major league office that made many in the minor leagues wary of the future. In the aftermath of the negotiations, Artiaga did not run for re-election at the 1991 meetings. He was succeeded by his assistant, Mike Moore. Minor league baseball was in transition, and there was concern about the future.

1978

American League
President: Leland S. MacPhail, Jr.

East Standings	W	L	Pct.	GB	Attend.	Manager
New York Yankees	100	63	.613	—	2,335,871	Billy Martin/Dick Howser/Bob Lemon
Boston Red Sox	99	64	.607	1	2,320,643	Don Zimmer
Milwaukee Brewers	93	69	.574	6½	1,601,406	George Bamberger
Baltimore Orioles	90	71	.559	9	1,051,724	Earl Weaver
Detroit Tigers	86	76	.531	13½	1,714,893	Ralph Houk
Cleveland Indians	69	90	.434	29	800,584	Jeff Torborg
Toronto Blue Jays	59	102	.366	40	1,562,585	Roy Hartsfield

West Standings	W	L	Pct.	GB	Attend.	Manager
Kansas City Royals	92	70	.568	—	2,255,493	Whitey Herzog
California Angels	87	75	.537	5	1,755,386	Dave Garcia/Jim Fregosi
Texas Rangers	87	75	.537	5	1,447,963	Billy Hunter/Pat Corrales
Minnesota Twins	73	89	.451	19	787,878	Gene Mauch
Chicago White Sox	71	90	.441	20½	1,491,100	Bob Lemon/Larry Doby
Oakland Athletics	69	93	.426	23	526,999	Bobby Winkles/Jack McKeon
Seattle Mariners	56	104	.350	35	877,440	Darrell Johnson

Playoffs: New York defeated Boston in a one game playoff for the East title. New York 3 games, Kansas City 1.

BA: Rod Carew, Minnesota, .333
Runs: Ron LeFlore, Detroit, 126
Hits: Jim Rice, Boston, 213
RBIs: Jim Rice, Boston, 139
HRs: Jim Rice, Boston, 46

Wins: Ron Guidry, New York, 25
SOs: Nolan Ryan, California, 260
ERA: Ron Guidry, New York, 1.74
Pct: Ron Guidry, New York, .893, 25-3
Saves: Rich "Goose" Gossage, New York, 27

National League
President: Charles S. Feeney

East Standings	W	L	Pct.	GB	Attend.	Manager
Philadelphia Phillies	90	72	.556	—	2,583,389	Danny Ozark
Pittsburgh Pirates	88	73	.547	1½	964,106	Chuck Tanner
Chicago Cubs	79	83	.488	11	1,525,311	Herman Franks
Montreal Expos	76	86	.469	14	1,427,007	Dick Williams
St. Louis Cardinals	69	93	.426	21	1,278,215	Vern Rapp/Jack Krol/Ken Boyer
New York Mets	66	96	.407	24	1,007,328	Joe Torre

West Standings	W	L	Pct.	GB	Attend.	Manager
Los Angeles Dodgers	95	67	.586	—	3,347,845	Tom Lasorda
Cincinnati Reds	92	69	.571	2½	2,532,497	Sparky Anderson
San Francisco Giants	89	73	.549	6	1,740,477	Joe Altobelli
San Diego Padres	84	78	.519	11	1,670,107	Roger Craig
Houston Astros	74	88	.457	21	1,126,145	Bill Virdon
Atlanta Braves	69	93	.426	26	904,494	Bobby Cox

Playoff: Los Angeles 3 games, Philadelphia 1.

BA: Dave Parker, Pittsburgh, .334
Runs: Ivan DeJesus, Chicago, 104
Hits: Steve Garvey, Los Angeles, 202
RBIs: George Foster, Cincinnati, 120
HRs: George Foster, Cincinnati, 40
2B: Pete Rose, Cincinnati, 51

Wins: Gaylord Perry, San Diego, 21
SOs: J.R. Richard, Houston, 303
ERA: Craig Swan, New York, 2.43
Pct: Gaylord Perry, San Diego, .778, 21-6
Saves: Rollie Fingers, San Diego, 37

AAA American Association
President: Joe Ryan

East Standings	W	L	Pct.	GB	Attend.	Manager
Indianapolis Indians (17)	78	57	.578	—	165,014	Roy Majtyka
Evansville Triplets (6)	78	58	.574	½	109,106	Les Moss
Springfield Redbirds (24)	70	66	.515	8½	110,301	Jimy Williams
Iowa Oaks (4)	66	70	.485	12½	121,510	Joe Sparks

West Standings	W	L	Pct.	GB	Attend.	Manager
Omaha Royals (7)	66	69	.489	—	139,447	John Sullivan
Denver Bears (20)	64	71	.474	2	261,647	Doc Edwards
Oklahoma City 89ers (22)	62	74	.456	4½	172,996	Mike Ryan
Wichita Aeros (16)	58	77	.430	8	150,840	Harry Dunlop

Playoff: Omaha 4 games, Indianapolis 1.

All-Star Team: 1B-Dane Iorg, Springfield; **2B**-Jerry Manuel, Evansville; **3B**-Harry Spilman, Indianapolis; **SS**-Ron Oester, Indianapolis; **OF**-Kerry Dineen, Oklahoma City; Champ Summers, Indianapolis; Arturo DeFreites, Indianapolis; Jim Lentine, Springfield; **C**-Keith Moreland, Oklahoma City; **Util**-Pete Mackanin, Denver; **P**-Dan Warthen, Oklahoma City; John Kucek, Iowa; **MVP**-Champ Summers, Indianapolis; **Pitcher of the Year**-Dan Warthen, Oklahoma City; **Manager**-Les Moss, Evansville.

BA: Dane Iorg, Springfield, .371
Runs: Tony Bernazard, Denver, 107
Hits: Champ Summers, Indianapolis, 170
RBIs: Champ Summers, Indianapolis, 124
HRs: Champ Summers, Indianapolis, 34

Wins: Sheldon Burnside, Evansville, 14; William Paschall, Omaha, 14
SOs: Dan Warthen, Oklahoma City, 144
ERA: John Kucek, Iowa, 2.46

AAA International League
President: Harold Cooper

Standings	W	L	Pct.	GB	Attend.	Manager
Charleston Charlies (18)	85	55	.607	—	130,653	Jim Beauchamp
Pawtucket Red Sox (2)	81	59	.579	4	123,310	Joe Morgan
Toledo Mud Hens (9)	74	66	.529	11	163,651	Cal Ermer
Richmond Braves (15)	71	68	.511	13½	202,106	Tommie Aaron
Tidewater Tides (21)	69	71	.493	16	116,685	Frank Verdi
Rochester Red Wings (1)	68	72	.486	17	219,814	Ken Boyer/Al Widmar/Frank Robinson
Columbus Clippers (23)	61	78	.439	23½	324,510	John Lipon
Syracuse Chiefs (14)	50	90	.357	35	160,519	Vern Benson

Playoffs: Richmond 3 games, Charleston 1; Pawtucket 3 games, Toledo 2.
Finals: Richmond 4 games, Pawtucket 3.

All-Star Team: 1B-Hank Small, Richmond; **2B**-Glenn Hubbard, Richmond; **3B**-Robert Sperring, Charleston; **SS**-Dale Berra, Columbus; **OF**-Dave Coleman, Pawtucket; Mike Easler, Columbus; Al Woods, Syracuse; **C**-Gary Allenson, Pawtucket; **DH**-Jim Obradovich, Charleston; **P**-Dan Larson, Charleston; John LaRose, Pawtucket; **MVP**-Gary Allenson, Pawtucket; **Pitcher of the Year**-Juan Berenguer, Tidewater; **Manager**-Jim Beauchamp, Charleston.

BA: Mike Easler, Columbus, .330
Runs: Wayne Krenchicki, Rochester, 93
Hits: Keith Drumright, Charleston, 159
RBIs: Hank Small, Richmond, 101
HRs: Hank Small, Richmond, 25

Wins: Dan Larson, Charleston, 14; Gary Wilson, Charleston, 14
SOs: Odell Jones, Columbus, 169
ERA: Frank Riccelli, Charleston, 2.78

AAA Mexican League
President: Antonio Ramirez Muro

North West Standings	W	L	Pct.	GB	Attend.	Manager
Saltillo Saraperos	88	64	.579	—	197,782	Gregorio Luque
Union Laguna Algodoneros	79	72	.523	8½	207,661	Moises Camacho
Ciudad Juarez Indios	69	84	.451	19½	219,244	Jose Guerrero
Chihuahua Dorados	60	89	.403	26½	188,934	Ron Camacho

North East Standings	W	L	Pct.	GB	Attend.	Manager
Monterrey Sultanes	80	73	.523	—	213,550	Marte de Alejandro
Tampico Alijadores	76	78	.494	4½	154,186	Ben Valenzuela
Nuevo Laredo Tecolotes	68	79	.463	9	247,583	Miguel Sotelo/Gerardo Gutierrez
Coahuila Mineros	65	85	.433	13½	166,047	Pompeyo Davalillo

South West Standings	W	L	Pct.	GB	Attend.	Manager
Aguascalientes Rieleros	89	62	.589	—	351,326	Jaime Favela
Durango Alacranes	85	65	.567	3½	230,919	Benjamin Cerda
Puebla Angeles	85	65	.567	3½	187,954	Raul Cano
Mexico City Tigres	65	85	.433	23½	232,059	Mario Saldana/Obed Plascencia

South East Standings	W	L	Pct.	GB	Attend.	Manager
Cordoba Cafeteros	95	50	.655	—	152,763	Winston Llenas
Mexico City Diablos Rojos	70	76	.479	25½	312,709	Ben Reyes
Poza Rica Petroleros	67	84	.444	31	185,150	Luis Arroyo/Emilio Sosa/David Garcia
Tabasco Plataneros	60	90	.400	37½	297,122	Alfredo Ortiz/Von Joshua/Fernando Graham

Playoffs: Cordoba 4 games, Durango 1; Aguascalientes 4 games, MC Diablos Rojos 2; Saltillo 4 games, Tampico 2; Union Laguna 4 games, Monterrey 3. Aguascalientes 4 games, Cordoba 2; Union Laguna 4 games, Saltillo 1.
Finals: Aguascalientes 4 games, Union Laguna 1.

All-Star Team: 1B-Rafael Batista, Cordoba; **2B**-Roberto Mendez, Durango; **3B**-Blas Santana, Union Laguna; **SS**-Francisco Rodriguez, Aguascalientes; **OF**-Jimmie Collins, Chihuahua; Gonzalo Villalobos, Aguascalientes; Romel Canada, Saltillo; **C**-Fernando Camargo, Monterrey; **DH**-Hal King, Saltillo; **P**-Mike Nagy, Tabasco; Tomas Armas, Saltillo; **Manager**-Jamie Favela, Aguascalientes.

BA: Romel Canada, Saltillo, .366
Runs: Romel Canada, Saltillo, 108
Hits: Blas Santana, Union Laguna, 196
RBIs: Hal King, Saltillo, 114

HRs: Hal King, Saltillo, 28
Wins: Jose Pena, Cordoba, 22
SOs: Aurelio Monteagudo, Coahuila, 222
ERA: Mike Nagy, Tabasco, 1.64

AAA Pacific Coast League
President: Roy Jackson

East Standings	W	L	Pct.	GB	Attend.	Manager
Albuquerque Dukes (19)	78	62	.557	—	231,524	Del Crandall
Salt Lake City Gulls (3)	72	65	.526	4½	207,440	Deron Johnson

*Won first-half   **Won second-half   ***Won both halves
Numbers after nicknames indicate farm system.
Affiliation listed at end of each year.

546

	W	L	Pct.	GB	Attend.	Manager
Phoenix Giants (26)	72	68	.514	6	157,044	Rocky Bridges
Tucson Toros (13)	69	71	.493	9	120,744	Rich Donnelly
San Jose Missions (12)	53	87	.379	25	67,037	Rene Lachemann

West Standings	W	L	Pct.	GB	Attend.	Manager
Tacoma Yankees (10)..........	80	57	.584	—	211,030	Mike Ferraro
Portland Beavers (5)...........	76	62	.551	4½	96,395	Gene Dusan
Vancouver Canadians (11) .	74	65	.532	7	123,466	Jim Marshall
Spokane Indians (8)............	64	75	.460	17	101,751	John Felske
Hawaii Islanders (25)..........	56	82	.406	24½	154,477	Dick Phillips

Playoffs: Albuquerque 3 games, Salt Lake City 0; Tacoma and Portland were tied 2 games each when the series was cancelled due to rain. Albuquerque and Tacoma were declared co-champions.

BA: Jeff Leonard, Albuquerque, .365
Runs: Billy Sample, Tucson, 141
Hits: Jeff Leonard, Albuquerque, 183
RBIs: Pedro Guerrero, Albuquerque, 116
HRs: Willie Aikens, Salt Lake City, 29
Wins: Eric Wilkins, Portland, 15
SOs: Steve Mura, Hawaii, 158
ERA: Larry McCall, Tacoma, 2.93

AA Eastern League
President: P. Patrick McKernan

Standings	W	L	Pct.	GB	Attend.	Manager
West Haven Yankees (10)..	82	57	.590	—	46,048	Stump Merrill
Reading Phillies**(22)......	79	57	.581	1½	66,969	Lee Elia
Bristol Red Sox*(2)............	72	66	.522	9½	64,921	Tony Torchia
Waterbury Giants (26).......	65	74	.468	17	46,011	Andy Gilbert
Holyoke Millers (8)	61	76	.445	20	48,565	George Farson
Jersey City A's (11)............	54	83	.394	27	28,969	John Kennedy

Playoff: Bristol 2 games, Reading 0.

All-Star Team: 1B-Jim McDonald, West Haven; **2B**-Michael Rex, Waterbury; **3B**-Neil Rasmussen, Holyoke; **SS**-Mike Henderson, Holyoke; **OF**-Jeff Yurak, Holyoke; Rick Stenholm, West Haven; Nathan Chapman, West Haven; Rickey Henderson, Jersey City; **C**-Mike Heath, West Haven; **DH**-John Hughes, Reading; **Util**-Dennis Sherrill, West Haven; Julio Valdez, Bristol; **P**-Steve Schneck, Bristol; Paul Semall, West Haven; **MVP**-Jeff Yurak, Holyoke; **Manager**-Lee Elia, Reading.

BA: Mike Henderson, Holyoke, .325
Runs: Joe Lefebvre, West Haven, 102
Hits: Jeff Yurak, Holyoke, 154
RBIs: Rick Stenholm, West Haven, 102
HRs: Jeff Yurak, Holyoke, 21
Wins: Paul Semall, West Haven, 17
SOs: Steve Schneck, Bristol, 180
ERA: Steve Schneck, Bristol, 2.15

AA Southern League
President: Billy Hitchcock

East Standings	W	L	Pct.	GB	Attend.	Manager
Orlando Twins*(9)	82	61	.573	—	42,801	John Goryl
Jacksonville Suns (7).........	73	69	.544	8½	86,834	Gordy MacKenzie
Savannah Braves**(15)......	72	72	.500	10½	68,126	Bobby Dews
Columbus Astros (18)........	70	73	.490	12	75,438	James Johnson
Charlotte O's (1)..............	66	78	.458	16½	64,163	Lance Nichols

West Standings	W	L	Pct.	GB	Attend.	Manager
Knoxville Knox Sox***(4)	88	56	.611	—	87,916	Tony LaRussa/Joe Jones
Memphis Chicks (20)	71	73	.493	17	153,686	Felipe Alou
Montgomery Rebels (6).....	67	77	.465	21	41,618	Ed Brinkman
Nashville Sounds (17)	64	77	.454	22½	380,159	Chuck Goggin
Chattanooga Lookouts (5) ..	63	80	.441	24½	53,917	John Orsino/Jimmy Bragan

Playoff: Savannah 2 games, Orlando 1.
Finals: Knoxville 2 games, Savannah 1.

All-Star Team: 1B-Sal Rende, Chattanooga; **2B**-Gene Menees, Nashville; **3B**-Mark Naehring, Knoxville; **SS**-Jim Wessinger, Savannah; **OF**-Eddie Gates, Memphis; Tom Spencer, Knoxville; Altar Greene, Montgomery; **C**-Marv Foley, Knoxville; **DH**-Terry Crowley, Memphis; **Util**-John Castino, Orlando; Michael Wolf, Knoxville; **P**-Bruce Berenyi, Nashville; Randy Niemann, Columbus; **Manager**-Bobby Dews, Savannah.

BA: Joe Gates, Knoxville, .332
Runs: Joe Gates, Knoxville, 85
Hits: Joe Gates, Knoxville, 161
RBIs: Sal Rende, Chattanooga, 87
HRs: Eddie Gates, Memphis, 25
Wins: Terry Sheehan, Orlando, 17
SOs: Jay Howell, Nashville, 173
ERA: Roger Alexander, Savannah, 1.84

AA Texas League
President: Carl Sawatski

East Standings	W	L	Pct.	GB	Attend.	Manager
Arkansas Travelers*(24).....	77	55	.583	—	175,686	Tommy Thompson
Jackson Mets**(21)...........	76	58	.567	2	68,178	Bob Wellman
Tulsa Drillers (13)	57	78	.422	21½	46,098	Marty Martinez
Shreveport Captains (23)....	55	81	.404	24	38,209	Steve Demeter

West Standings	W	L	Pct.	GB	Attend.	Manager
El Paso Diablos***(3).........	80	55	.593	—	251,086	Moose Stubing
San Antonio Dodgers (19)..	79	57	.581	1½	74,420	Don LeJohn
Midland Cubs (16)..............	70	65	.519	10	86,080	Jim Saul
Amarillo Gold Sox (25)......	44	89	.331	35	53,110	Glenn Ezell

Playoff: Jackson 2 games, Arkansas 1.
Finals: El Paso 3 games, Jackson 0.

All-Star Team: 1B-Leon Durham, Arkansas; **2B**-Tommy Herr, Arkansas; **3B**-Mickey Hatcher, San Antonio; **SS**-Steve Macko, Midland; **OF**-Jim Beswick, Amarillo; Bob Clark,

---

El Paso; Mookie Wilson, Jackson; **C**-Terry Kennedy, Arkansas; **DH**-Danny Goodwin, El Paso; **Util**-Kevin Drury, Midland; **P**-Rafael Vazquez, Shreveport; Dave Righetti, Tulsa; Dave Patterson, San Antonio; Kim Seaman, Jackson; **MVP**-Bob Clark, El Paso; **Manager**-Jim Saul, Midland.

BA: Danny Goodwin, El Paso, .360
Runs: Kurt Seibert, Midland, 118
Hits: Steve Macko, Midland, 166
RBIs: Bob Clark, El Paso, 111
HRs: Bob Clark, El Paso, 31
Wins: Jeff Reardon, Jackson, 17
SOs: Dick Sander, San Antonio, 159
ERA: Neil Allen, Jackson, 2.10

A California League
President: E.W. "Bill" Wickert

North Standings	W	L	Pct.	GB	Attend.	Manager
Lodi Dodgers***(19)	85	55	.607	—	41,248	Stan Wasiak
Stockton Mariners (12)......	63	77	.450	22	35,670	Bobby Floyd
Reno Silver Sox (25)	62	78	.443	23	32,570	Eddie Watt
Modesto A's (11)................	61	79	.436	24	55,794	Gaylen Pitts

South Standings	W	L	Pct.	GB	Attend.	Manager
Visalia Oaks***(9).............	97	42	.698	—	52,618	Roy McMillan
Salinas Angels (3).............	84	56	.600	13½	108,453	Chuck Cottier
Fresno Giants (26)	59	80	.424	38	67,683	John Van Ornum
Bakersfield Outlaws	48	92	.343	49½	36,503	George Culver

Playoff: Visalia 3 games, Lodi 2.

All-Star Team: 1B-John Harris, Salinas; **2B**-John Shoemaker, Lodi; **3B**-Mike Zouras, Lodi; **SS**-Don Ruzek, Salinas; **OF**-Steve Douglas, Visalia; Joe Charbonneau, Visalia; Mark Brouhard, Salinas; **C**-Steven Herz, Visalia; **DH**-Steve McManaman, Visalia; Patrick Roy, Fresno; **P**-David Beard, Modesto; Joel Crisler, Salinas; James Lewis, Stockton; Gene Robinson, Visalia; **MVP**-Steve Douglas, Visalia; **Manager**-Stan Wasiak, Lodi.

BA: Joe Charbonneau, Visalia, .350
Runs: Steve Douglas, Visalia, 142
Hits: Steve Douglas, Visalia, 192
RBIs: Steve McManaman, Visalia, 120
HRs: Steve McManaman, Visalia, 29
Wins: Gene Robinson, Visalia, 18
　　　Robert Veselic, Visalia, 18
SOs: James Lewis, Stockton, 189
ERA: James Lewis, Stockton, 2.12

A Carolina League
President: James B. Mills

Standings	W	L	Pct.	GB	Attend.	Manager
Peninsula Pilots**(22)........	90	49	.647	—	34,343	Jim Snyder
Lynchburg Mets*(21)........	72	63	.533	16	56,905	Jack Aker
Salem Pirates (23).............	73	64	.533	16	51,096	Jim Mahoney
Alexandria Dukes	58	75	.436	24	45,220	Les Peden
Kinston Eagles..................	57	77	.425	25½	31,072	Leo Mazzone
Winston-Salem Red Sox (2).	55	77	.417	26½	48,617	Bill Slack

Playoff: Lynchburg 3 games, Peninsula 0.

All-Star Team: 1B-Charles "Chick" Valley, Salem; **2B**-Ron MacDonald, Lynchburg; **3B**-Nicholas Popovich, Peninsula; **SS**-Wally Backman, Lynchburg; **OF**-George Vukovich, Peninsula; Elijah Bonaparte, Peninsula; Mel Barrow, Kinston; Raymond Boyer, Alexandria; **C**-Ozzie Virgil, Peninsula; **DH**-Roger LaFrancois, Winston-Salem; **P**-Tim Costello, Kinston; Henry Mack, Peninsula; **MVP**-Ozzie Virgil, Peninsula; **Manager**-Jack Aker, Lynchburg.

BA: Ron MacDonald, Lynchburg, .325
Runs: George Vukovich, Peninsula, 94
Hits: Ron MacDonald, Lynchburg, 158
RBIs: Ozzie Virgil, Peninsula, 98
HRs: Ozzie Virgil, Peninsula, 29
Wins: Marty Bystrom, Peninsula, 15
　　　Henry Mack, Peninsula, 15
SOs: Marty Bystrom, Peninsula, 159
ERA: Jose Martinez, Peninsula, 2.07

A Florida State League
President: George MacDonald, Jr.

North Standings	W	L	Pct.	GB	Attend.	Manager
St. Petersburg Cardinals*(24)	84	56	.600	—	154,833	Hal Lanier
Winter Haven Red Sox (2) .	82	56	.594	1	13,922	Rac Slider
Lakeland Tigers**(6)	78	60	.565	5	58,067	Jim Leyland
Tampa Tarpons (17)	61	73	.455	20	90,058	Mike Compton
Dunedin Blue Jays (14)	59	83	.415	26	17,165	Denis Menke
Daytona Beach Astros#(18)..	42	93	.311	NA	30,942	Leo Posada/Chuck Sprinkle

South Standings	W	L	Pct.	GB	Attend.	Manager
Miami Orioles**(1)	76	65	.539	—	60,118	Jim Williams
Ft. Lauderdale Yankees (10) ...	74	68	.521	2½	58,266	Doug Holmquist
Ft. Myers Royals*(7)..........	71	66	.518	3	65,574	Gene Lamont
Pompano Beach Cubs (16) ..	72	69	.511	4	24,631	Jack Hiatt
West Palm Beach Expos (20).	67	77	.465	10½	104,236	Larry Bearnarth

#Daytona Beach was in the North Division for the first half and South for the second.

Playoffs: Miami 1 game, Ft. Myers 0; Lakeland 1 game, St. Petersburg 0.
Finals: Miami 2 games, Lakeland 1.

All-Star Team: 1B-Greg "Boomer" Wells, Dunedin; **2B**-Tom Eaton, Miami; **3B**-Francis McCann, Ft. Myers; **SS**-Rafael Santana, Ft. Lauderdale; **OF**-Eddie Milner, Tampa; Paul Householder, Tampa; Anthony Johnson, West Palm Beach; **C**-Patrick Callahan, Ft. Lauderdale; Rich Gedman, Winter Haven; **Util**-Dennis Webb, Ft. Myers; Terry Landrum, St. Petersburg; **P**-Brian Denman, Winter Haven; Bill Gullickson, Ft. Myers; Joe Price, Tampa; Michael Morley, Ft. Myers; **MVP**-Eddie Milner, Tampa; **Manager**-Jim Leyland, Lakeland.

BA: Dennis Webb, Ft. Myers, .324
Runs: Danny Rohn, Pompano Beach, 95
Hits: Dennis Webb, Ft. Myers, 144
Clay Westlake, West Palm Beach, 144
RBIs: Clay Westlake, West Palm Beach, 96
HRs: Fay Thompson, Dunedin, 19
Wins: Brian Denman, Winter Haven, 16
SOs: Larry Jones, Miami, 143
ERA: Scott Brown, Tampa, 1.31

A Mexican Center League

President: Antonio Ramirez Muro

Central Standings	W	L	Pct.	GB	Attend.	Manager
La Barca	34	24	.586	—	9,435	Alfonso Pena
Zacatecas	35	25	.583	—	13,954	Felipe Hernandez
Fresnillo	29	26	.527	3½	25,070	Carlos Pax
Teocaltiche	30	29	.508	4½	10,987	Roberto Castellon
Guanajuato	26	32	.448	8	20,526	Alfredo Preciado
Silao	24	31	.436	8½	15,001	Armando Murillo
Guadalajara	23	34	.404	10½	13,212	Manuel Fortes
Gulf Standings	**W**	**L**	**Pct.**	**GB**	**Attend.**	**Manager**
Matamoros	49	18	.731	—	22,678	Cesar Gutierrez
Ciudad Victoria	48	19	.716	1	14,466	Fidel Flores
Ciudad Valles	33	32	.508	15	14,177	Angel Scull
Cerro Azul	26	31	.456	18	11,332	Eduardo Gavilan
Miguel Aleman	20	42	.323	26½	5,481	Armando Barajas
Diaz Ordaz	15	49	.234	32½	5,396	Norman McRae

Playoff: La Barca 5 games, Matamoros 1.

BA: Angel Ortega, Fresnillo, .408
Runs: Miguel Chavarria, Zacatecas, 71
Hits: Angel Ortega, Fresnillo, 86
RBIs: Angel Ortega, Fresnillo, 54
HRs: Angel Ortega, Fresnillo, 12
Wins: Guillermo Valenzuela, La Barca, 12
SOs: Fernando Valenzuela, Guanajuato, 91
ERA: Federico Longoria, Ciudad Victoria, 0.79

A Midwest League

President: Bill Walters

North Standings	W	L	Pct.	GB	Attend.	Manager
Appleton Foxes*(4)	97	40	.708	—	94,730	Gordon Lund
Waterloo Indians**(5)	91	46	.664	6	66,406	Woody Smith
Wisconsin Rapids Twins (9)	62	76	.449	35½	51,154	Rich Stelmaszek
Wausau Mets (21)	55	81	.404	41½	48,213	Danny Monzon
South Standings	**W**	**L**	**Pct.**	**GB**	**Attend.**	**Manager**
Burlington Bees**(8)	69	69	.500	—	59,218	Lee Sigman
Quad City Angels*(3)	67	70	.489	1½	124,288	Cotton Nash
Clinton Dodgers (19)	53	82	.393	14½	43,921	Dick McLaughlin
Cedar Rapids Giants (26)	53	83	.390	15	67,616	Jack Mull

Playoffs: Burlington 2 games, Quad City 0; Appleton 2 games, Waterloo 0.
Finals: Appleton 2 games, Burlington 1.

All-Star Team: 1B-Daryl Sconiers, Quad City; **2B**-Juan Bonilla, Waterloo; **3B**-Michael Bishop, Quad City; **SS**-Harry Chappas, Appleton; **OF**-Kevin Bass, Burlington; Donald Hubbard, Waterloo; Bobby G. Smith, Burlington; **C**-Bill Foley, Burlington; **DH**-Moe Hill, Wisconsin Rapids; **P**-Brad Havens, Quad City; Russell McDonald, Clinton; Mark Esser, Appleton; Dewey Robinson, Appleton; **MVP**-Bill Foley, Burlington; **Manager**-Gordon Lund, Appleton; Woody Smith, Waterloo.

BA: Bobby G. Smith, Burlington, .336
Runs: Leo Sutherland, Appleton, 100
Hits: Bobby G. Smith, Burlington, 172
RBIs: Brian Harper, Quad City, 101
HRs: Bill Foley, Burlington, 34
Wins: LaMarr Hoyt, Appleton, 18
SOs: Brad Havens, Quad City, 197
ERA: Sam Spence, Waterloo, 2.38

A New York-Pennsylvania League

President: Vincent M. McNamara

Yawkey Standings	W	L	Pct.	GB	Attend.	Manager
Oneonta Yankees (10)	51	19	.729	—	35,222	Art Mazmanian
Utica Blue Jays (14)	37	34	.521	14½	30,638	Duane Larson
Auburn Phillies (x)	32	40	.444	20	47,711	Dick Rockwell
Little Falls Mets (21)	29	42	.408	22½	27,416	Chris Krug
Elmira Red Sox (2)	21	48	.304	29½	31,485	Dick Berardino
Wrigley Standings	**W**	**L**	**Pct.**	**GB**	**Attend.**	**Manager**
Geneva Cubs (16)	51	20	.718	—	30,645	Bob Hartsfield
Jamestown Expos (20)	44	28	.611	7½	30,896	Pat Daugherty
Batavia Trojans (5)	34	38	.472	17½	39,359	Luis Isaac
Niagara Falls Pirates	30	40	.429	20½	20,304	Don Colpoys/Duke McGuire
Newark Co-Pilots (8)	26	46	.361	25½	14,228	Ken Richardson

Playoff: Geneva 2 games, Oneonta 0.

All-Star Team: 1B-Joe Hicks, Geneva; **2B**-Michael Turgeon, Geneva; **3B**-Brian Dayett, Oneonta, James Mitchell, Geneva; **SS**-Rex Hudler, Oneonta; **OF**-Thad Wilborn, Oneonta; Frank Wren, Jamestown; Andre Wood, Utica; Ed Saavedra, Batavia; **C**-Ted May, Geneva; Daniel Plante, Oneonta; **Util**-Thomas Soto, Newark; **P**-Mark Parker, Geneva; William Earley, Geneva; Lou Whetstone, Geneva; Charlie Puleo, Utica; **Manager**-Pat Daugherty, Jamestown.

BA: Michael Turgeon, Geneva, .344
Runs: Mark Gilbert, Geneva, 83
Hits: Michael Turgeon, Geneva, 98
RBIs: Joe Hicks, Geneva, 74
HRs: Thomas Anderson, Batavia, 18
Ted May, Geneva, 18
Wins: Mark Parker, Geneva, 13
SOs: Charlie Puleo, Utica, 125
ERA: Scott Gleckel, Niagara Falls, 2.16

A Northwest League

President: Bob Richmond

North Standings	W	L	Pct.	GB	Attend.	Manager
Grays Harbor Loggers	47	23	.671	—	19,842	Bill Bryk
Walla Walla Padres (25)	45	24	.652	1½	51,488	Cliff Ditto
Bellingham Mariners (12)	41	30	.577	6½	29,739	Bob Didier
Victoria Mussels	29	40	.420	17½	10,103	Jim Chapman
South Standings	**W**	**L**	**Pct.**	**GB**	**Attend.**	**Manager**
Eugene Emeralds (17)	36	34	.514	—	50,505	Greg Riddoch
Bend Timber Hawks (11)	35	37	.486	2	14,420	Ed Nottle
Salem Senators	25	44	.362	10½	8,140	Carl Thompson
Boise Buckskins	23	49	.319	14	23,126	Gerry Craft

Playoff: Grays Harbor 1 game, Eugene 0, series called due to rain and wet grounds. Grays Harbor was declared champion.

All-Star Team: 1B-Emil Drzayich, Boise; **2B**-Jerry Johnson, Walla Walla; **3B**-Jim Gattis, Grays Harbor; **SS**-Mobil Cox, Walla Walla; **OF**-Albert Richmond, Walla Walla; Nick Belmonte, Boise; Paul Stevens, Grays Harbor; **C**-Ray Corbett, Eugene; Darryl Cias, Salem; **DH**-Danny Thomas, Boise; **Util**-Kevin Jacobsen, Eugene; **P**-Jack Hobbs, Bellingham; David Jannusch, Grays Harbor; Dale Mohorcic, Victoria; Randy Miller, Walla Walla; Robert Pietroburgo, Bellingham; **Manager**-Bill Bryk, Grays Harbor.

BA: Danny Thomas, Boise, .359
Runs: Nick Belmonte, Boise, 75
Hits: Nick Belmonte, Boise, 95
RBIs: Albert Richmond, Walla Walla, 60
HRs: Albert Richmond, Walla Walla, 17
Wins: David Jannusch, Grays Harbor, 13
SOs: David Jannusch, Grays Harbor, 131
ERA: Frank Herschy, Grays Harbor, 1.99
Pct: David Jannusch, Grays Harbor, .929, 13-1

A Western Carolinas League

President: John H. Moss

Standings	W	L	Pct.	GB	Attend.	Manager
Greenwood Braves***(15)	82	57	.590	—	42,201	Al Gallagher
Shelby Reds (17)	75	64	.540	7	22,058	Jim Lett
Spartanburg Phillies (22)	73	67	.521	9½	26,721	Ron Clark
Asheville Tourists (13)	73	67	.521	9½	36,517	Wayne Terwilliger
Gastonia Cardinals (24)	69	71	.493	13½	46,326	Buzzy Keller
Charleston Pirates (23)	47	93	.336	35½	19,536	Billy Scripture

Playoffs: None.

All-Star Team: 1B-Jim Barbe, Asheville; **2B**-Steve Curry, Spartanburg; **3B**-Tom Watkins, Shelby; **SS**-Rafael Ramirez, Greenwood; **OF**-Ron Carney, Asheville; Steve Hammond, Greenwood; Bob Porter, Greenwood; Ty Waller, Shelby; **C**-Steve Christmas, Shelby; **DH**-Scott Thayer, Greenwood; Jerry Poston, Gastonia; **Util**-LeRoy Grossini, Gastonia; **P**-Paul Gibson, Shelby; Greg Hughes, Shelby; Mark Mercer, Asheville; Doug Neuenschwander, Shelby; Jerry Reed, Spartanburg; **Manager**-Jim Lett, Shelby.

BA: Steve Hammond, Greenwood, .306
Runs: Jim Barbe, Asheville, 91
Hits: Jim Barbe, Asheville, 143
RBIs: Jim Barbe, Asheville, 99
HRs: Jim Barbe, Asheville, 18
Wins: Scott Munninghoff, Spartanburg, 17
SOs: Chuck Lamson, Asheville, 155
ERA: Greg Hughes, Shelby, 2.14

R Appalachian League

President: Chauncey De Vault

Standings	W	L	Pct.	GB	Attend.	Manager
Elizabethton Twins (9)	41	28	.594	—	22,173	Fred Waters
Johnson City Cardinals (24)	37	33	.529	4½	40,053	Nick Leyva
Bristol Tigers (6)	35	34	.507	6	29,736	Joe Lewis
Paintsville Highlanders	33	36	.478	8	16,098	Ron Mihal
Kingsport Braves (15)	33	37	.471	8½	20,203	Eddie Haas
Bluefield Orioles (1)	29	40	.420	12	28,625	Junior Miner

Playoffs: None.

All-Star Team: 1B-Ron Grout, Elizabethton; **2B**-Everett Smith, Johnson City; **3B**-Bob Boyce, Bluefield; **SS**-Len Faedo, Elizabethton; **OF**-Vince Bienek, Paintsville; Jimmy Hickman, Johnson City; Leo Vargas, Kingsport; **C**-Aurelio Cadahia, Paintsville; **DH**-Victor Rodriguez, Bluefield; **P**-Donald Welchel, Bluefield; Steven Green, Elizabethton; Rubio Malone, Elizabethton; **Manager**-Fred Waters, Elizabethton.

BA: Vince Bienek, Paintsville, .338
Runs: Todd Ervin, Bristol, 52
Hits: Ron Rudd, Kingsport, 85
RBIs: Larry Sheets, Bluefield, 48
HRs: Ron Grout, Elizabethton, 12
Wins: Ken Angulo, Elizabethton, 9
SOs: Ken Angulo, Elizabethton, 97
ERA: Michael Smith, Kingsport, 2.10

R Gulf Coast League

President: George MacDonald, Jr.

Standings	W	L	Pct.	GB	Manager
Rangers (13)	33	22	.600	—	Joe Klein
Royals (7)	31	24	.564	2	Jose Martinez
Cubs (16)	30	24	.556	2½	Randy Hundley
Braves (15)	25	30	.455	8	Pedro Gonzalez
Astros (18)	23	31	.426	9½	Julio Linares
Pirates (23)	21	32	.396	11	Woody Huyke

Games played at Sarasota and Bradenton, Florida.

Playoffs: None.

BA: Timothy Tolman, Astros, .344
Runs: Ray Bresnahan, Royals, 41
Hits: Ray Bresnahan, Royals, 54
RBIs: Terry Bogener, Rangers, 32
HRs: Ira Turner, Royals, 7

Wins: Juan Alduey, Braves, 6
Stephen Hartery, Cubs, 6
Kevin Kirby, Cubs, 6
SOs: Kevin Houston, Astros, 65
ERA: Mike Vickers, Rangers, 1.96

R Pioneer League
President: Ralph C. Nelles

Standings	W	L	Pct.	GB	Attend.	Manager
Billings Mustangs (17)	50	18	.735	—	58,750	Jim Hoff
Idaho Falls Angels (3)	41	27	.594	9	27,033	Reuben Rodriguez
Calgary Cardinals (24)	37	32	.536	13½	25,198	Johnny Lewis
Great Falls Giants (26)	33	34	.493	16½	47,912	Ernest Rodriguez
Lethbridge Dodgers (19)	33	35	.485	17	14,320	Jim Lefebvre
Helena Phillies (22)	30	38	.441	20	25,463	Larry Rojas
Medicine Hat Blue Jays (14)	28	40	.412	22	17,010	John McLaren
Butte Copper Kings (x)	19	47	.288	30	19,469	Tom Zimmer

Playoff: Billings 2 games, Idaho Falls 0.

All-Star Team: 1B-Steven Swain, Butte; **2B**-Gary Redus, Billings; **3B**-German Rivera, Lethbridge; **SS**-William Springman, Idaho Falls; **OF**-Earl Neal, Helena; Bill Barnes, Billings; Lloyd Moseby, Medicine Hat; **C**-Dennis Delany, Calgary; **P**-Steven Skaggs, Billings; Axel Vega, Calgary; Mike Witt, Idaho Falls; **Manager**-Jim Hoff, Billings.

BA: Gary Redus, Billings, .462
Runs: Gary Redus, Billings, 100
Hits: Gary Redus, Billings, 117
RBIs: Bill Barnes, Billings, 76

HRs: Edward Packard, Idaho Falls, 20
Wins: Roberto Alexander, Lethbridge, 9
SOs: Steve Brown, Idaho Falls, 95
ERA: Richard Morgan, Medicine Hat, 1.97

1978 Interleague Post Season Play

World Series
New York (American) 4 games, Los Angeles (National) 2

1978 Major League Farm Systems

American League
1 Baltimore (4): Rochester, Charlotte, Miami, Bluefield.
2 Boston (5): Pawtucket, Bristol (CT), Winston-Salem, Winter Haven, Elmira.
3 California (5): Salt Lake City, El Paso, Salinas, Quad City, Idaho Falls.
4 Chicago (3): Iowa, Knoxville, Appleton.
5 Cleveland (4): Portland, Chattanooga, Waterloo, Batavia.
6 Detroit (4): Evansville, Montgomery, Lakeland, Bristol (VA).
7 Kansas City (4): Omaha, Jacksonville, Ft. Myers, Gulf Coast.
8 Milwaukee (4): Spokane, Holyoke, Burlington, Newark.
9 Minnesota (5): Toledo, Orlando, Visalia, Wisconsin Rapids, Elizabethton.
10 New York (4): Tacoma, West Haven, Ft. Lauderdale, Oneonta.
11 Oakland (4): Vancouver, Jersey City, Modesto, Bend.
12 Seattle (3): San Jose, Stockton, Bellingham.
13 Texas (4): Tucson, Tulsa, Asheville, Gulf Coast.
14 Toronto (4): Syracuse, Dunedin, Utica, Medicine Hat.

National League
15 Atlanta (5): Richmond, Savannah, Greenwood, Kingsport, Gulf Coast.
16 Chicago (5): Wichita, Midland, Pompano Beach, Geneva, Gulf Coast.
17 Cincinnati (6): Indianapolis, Nashville, Tampa, Shelby, Eugene, Billings.
18 Houston (4): Charleston (WV), Columbus (GA), Daytona Beach, Gulf Coast.
19 Los Angeles (5): Albuquerque, San Antonio, Lodi, Clinton, Lethbridge.
20 Montreal (4): Denver, Memphis, West Palm Beach, Jamestown.
21 New York (5): Tidewater, Jackson, Lynchburg, Wausau, Little Falls.
22 Philadelphia (5): Oklahoma City, Reading, Peninsula, Spartanburg, Helena.
23 Pittsburgh (5): Columbus (OH), Shreveport, Salem (VA), Charleston (SC), Gulf Coast.
24 St. Louis (6): Springfield, Arkansas, St. Petersburg, Gastonia, Johnson City, Calgary.
25 San Diego (4): Hawaii, Amarillo, Reno, Walla Walla.
26 San Francisco (5): Phoenix, Waterbury, Fresno, Cedar Rapids, Great Falls.

Co-op (x): Auburn, Butte.
Independent: Bakersfield, Alexandria, Kinston, Niagara Falls, Grays Harbor, Victoria, Salem (OR), Boise, Paintsville.

1978 No-Hitters

Date	Pitcher	Team	League	Opponent	Score
3-28	Arturo Gonzalez	Monterrey	Mexican	Ciudad Juarez	0-0 (10)
4-14	Darrell Jackson	Orlando	Southern	Jacksonville	1-0 (12)
4-16	Bob Forsch	St. Louis	National	Philadelphia	5-0
5-2	Robert Harrison	Arkansas	Texas	Jackson	0-0 (6)
5-15	Russell McDonald	Clinton	Midwest	Wausau	1-0 (7)
5-26	John Kucek	Iowa	American Assoc.	Oklahoma City	6-1
5-26	Silvio Martinez	Springfield	American Assoc.	Omaha	4-0
5-26	Terry Sheehan	Orlando	Southern	Savannah	3-0
6-4	Jean-Pierre LeDuc	Charleston	W. Carolinas	Asheville	9-0 (7)
6-16	Tom Seaver	Cincinnati	National	St. Louis	4-0
6-21	Diego Segui	Cordoba	Mexican	Nuevo Laredo	5-0 (P, 7)
6-23	Rubio Malone	Elizabethton	Appalachian	Johnson City	8-1 (7)
6-26	Jose Alcantara	Ft. Lauderdale	Florida State	Ft. Myers	0-1 (7)
6-28	Arturo Gonzalez	Monterrey	Mexican	Union Laguna	2-0
7-1	Henry Mack	Peninsula	Carolina	Lynchburg	2-3
7-9	Jim Beattie	Tacoma	Pacific Coast	Spokane	2-0 (7)
7-12	Rodney Boxberger	Columbus	Southern	Montgomery	3-0 (7)
7-12	Horacio Pina	Aguascalientes	Mexican	MC Diablos Rojos	3-0 (P)
7-12	Mike Paul	Ciudad Juarez	Mexican	Monterrey	1-0 (7)
7-12	David Andrews/ Mark Deutsch	Cubs	Gulf Coast	Braves	4-0 (7)
7-16	Jim Nobles	Clinton	Midwest	Wisconsin Rapids	7-1 (7)
7-19	Rubio Malone	Elizabethton	Appalachian	Bluefield	6-0
7-28	John Hessler	Astros	Gulf Coast	Royals	2-1 (8)
7-29	Theis Meyer	St. Petersburg	Florida State	Tampa	6-2 (7)
8-3	Robin Fuson	Waterloo	Midwest	Appleton	2-0
8-7	Don Cooper	Ft. Lauderdale	Florida State	Ft. Myers	5-0
8-12	Marty Bystrom	Peninsula	Carolina	Winston-Salem	3-0 (P)
8-14	Rich Aspenleiter	Cubs	Gulf Coast	Braves	8-0 (7)
8-15	Randy Bozeman	Little Falls	New York-Penn.	Batavia	7-0 (7)
8-17	Steven Skaggs	Billings	Pioneer	Calgary	12-0 (7)
8-19	Juan Arias	Shreveport	Texas	Jackson	3-0 (7)
8-20	Mike Finlayson	Memphis	Southern	Montgomery	1-0 (7)
8-26	Bill Klank	Bristol	Appalachian	Bluefield	8-0

Number in parentheses indicates innings if other than nine; "P" indicates perfect game.

THIS DATE IN MINOR LEAGUE HISTORY

March 7, 1978, Steve Bilko, 49, former minor and major league slugger, died in Wilkes-Barre, Pennsylvania. Bilko terrorized Pacific Coast League pitching for several seasons, hitting 55 home runs for Los Angeles in 1956 and 56 in 1957.

April 3, 1978, Raymond French, 81, who played a record 2,736 games at shortstop in the minors, died in Alameda, California. French had 3,254 hits in his 28-year minor league career for a batting average of .267.

April 13, 1978, The Southern League expanded to 10 teams with the addition of Nashville and Memphis.

May 1, 1978, Jim Bouton, former big leaguer and author of the controversial book "Ball Four", began his comeback with Savannah of the Southern League. Bouton, 39 years old and now a knuckleball pitcher, convinced Braves owner Ted Turner to sign him for the comeback attempt.

May 24, 1978, Tampa set a Florida State League record by scoring 18 runs in the fourth inning of a 20-2 victory over Daytona Beach. The Tarpons scored 15 runs before the first putout was made.

June 24, 1978, Mike Bishop, Quad City slugger, hit four home runs in a Midwest League contest.

July 12, 1978, Horacio Pina, Aguascalientes, Mexican League, pitched a perfect game against the Mexico City Diablos Rojos, winning 3-0.

July 16, 1978, Tulsa's Dave Righetti struck out 21 Midland Cubs to break a 69-year-old Texas League record.

September 1, 1978, Billings' Gary Redus finished the Pioneer League season with a league record .462 batting average, 94 points better than the next leading batter.

September 3, 1978, Jim Bouton ended his season with Savannah with a record of 11-9 and a 2.92 ERA. He was then recalled to Atlanta by the parent Braves.

September 3, 1978, Nashville ended its Southern League season, having drawn a league record 380,159 fans.

December 5, 1978, Johnny Johnson was elected President of the National Association. Johnson, a former Yankees farm director, had been working in the commissioner's office for the past eight years.

December 8, 1978, Henry Nicholas "Nick" Cullop, 78, the "Babe Ruth of the Minors," died in Westerville, Ohio. Cullop played for the New York Yankees, Cleveland, Washington, Brooklyn and Cincinnati, but was best remembered for his 1,856 RBIs, more than any other minor leaguer, and 420 minor league home runs. He hit 54 homers for Minneapolis in 1930.

1979

American League
President: Leland S. MacPhail, Jr.

East Standings	W	L	Pct.	GB	Attend.	Manager
Baltimore Orioles	102	57	.642	—	1,681,009	Earl Weaver
Milwaukee Brewers...........	95	66	.590	8	1,918,343	George Bamberger
Boston Red Sox	91	69	.569	11½	2,353,114	Don Zimmer
New York Yankees	89	71	.556	13½	2,537,765	Bob Lemon/Billy Martin
Detroit Tigers....................	85	76	.528	18	1,630,929	Les Moss/Dick Tracewski/
						Sparky Anderson
Cleveland Indians	81	80	.503	22	1,011,644	Jeff Torborg/Dave Garcia
Toronto Blue Jays..............	53	109	.327	50½	1,431,651	Roy Hartsfield

West Standings	W	L	Pct.	GB	Attend.	Manager
California Angels................	88	74	.543	—	2,523,575	Jim Fregosi
Kansas City Royals.............	85	77	.525	3	2,261,845	Whitey Herzog
Texas Rangers....................	83	79	.512	5	1,519,671	Pat Corrales
Minnesota Twins................	82	80	.506	6	1,070,521	Gene Mauch
Chicago White Sox	73	87	.456	14	1,280,702	Don Kessinger/Tony LaRussa
Seattle Mariners.................	67	95	.414	21	844,447	Darrell Johnson
Oakland Athletics	54	108	.333	34	306,763	Jim Marshall

Playoff: Baltimore 3 games, California 1.

BA: Fred Lynn, Boston, .333
Runs: Don Baylor, California, 120
Hits: George Brett, Kansas City, 212
RBIs: Don Baylor, California, 139
HRs: Gorman Thomas, Milwaukee, 45

Wins: Mike Flanagan, Baltimore, 23
SOs: Nolan Ryan, California, 223
ERA: Ron Guidry, New York, 2.78
Pct: Mike Caldwell, Milwaukee, .727, 16-6
Saves: Mike Marshall, Minnesota, 32

National League
President: Charles S. Feeney

East Standings	W	L	Pct.	GB	Attend.	Manager
Pittsburgh Pirates	98	64	.605	—	1,435,454	Chuck Tanner
Montreal Expos..................	95	65	.594	2	2,102,173	Dick Williams
St. Louis Cardinals	86	76	.531	12	1,627,256	Ken Boyer
Philadelphia Phillies	84	78	.519	14	2,775,011	Danny Ozark/Dallas Green
Chicago Cubs.....................	80	82	.494	18	1,648,587	Herman Franks/
						Joey Amalfitano
New York Mets	63	99	.389	35	788,905	Joe Torre

West Standings	W	L	Pct.	GB	Attend.	Manager
Cincinnati Reds..................	90	71	.559	—	2,356,933	John McNamara
Houston Astros	89	73	.549	1½	1,900,312	Bill Virdon
Los Angeles Dodgers..........	79	83	.488	11½	2,860,954	Tom Lasorda
San Francisco Giants	71	91	.438	19½	1,456,967	Joe Altobelli/Dave Bristol
San Diego Padres	68	93	.422	22	1,456,402	Roger Craig
Atlanta Braves	66	94	.413	23½	769,465	Bobby Cox

Playoff: Pittsburgh 3 games, Cincinnati 0.

BA: Keith Hernandez, St. Louis, .344
Runs: Keith Hernandez, St. Louis, 116
Hits: Garry Templeton, St. Louis, 211
RBIs: Dave Winfield, San Diego, 118
HRs: Dave Kingman, Chicago, 48

Wins: Phil Niekro, Atlanta, 21
Joe Niekro, Houston, 21
SOs: J.R. Richard, Houston, 313
ERA: J.R. Richard, Houston, 2.71
Pct: Tom Seaver, Cincinnati, .727, 16-6
Saves: Bruce Sutter, Chicago, 37

AAA American Association
President: Joe Ryan

East Standings	W	L	Pct.	GB	Attend.	Manager
Evansville Triplets (6)	78	58	.574	—	120,265	Jim Leyland
Springfield Redbirds (24) ...	73	63	.537	5	94,910	Hal Lanier
Iowa Oaks (4)	69	67	.507	9	136,138	Tony LaRussa/Joe Sparks
Indianapolis Indians (17)....	67	69	.493	11	166,063	Roy Majtyka

West Standings	W	L	Pct.	GB	Attend.	Manager
Oklahoma City 89ers (22) ..	72	63	.533	—	193,792	Lee Elia
Omaha Royals (7)...............	65	71	.478	7½	157,277	Gordy MacKenzie
Denver Bears (20)..............	62	73	.459	10	335,684	Jack McKeon
Wichita Aeros (16)	57	79	.419	15½	92,611	Jack Hiatt

Playoff: Evansville 4 games, Oklahoma City 2.

All-Star Team: 1B-Randy Bass, Denver; **2B**-Fred Frazier, Iowa; **3B**-Manny Castillo, Springfield; **SS**-Ron Oester, Indianapolis; **OF**-Leon Durham, Springfield; Bob Molinaro, Iowa; Karl Pagel, Wichita; Keith Moreland, Oklahoma City; **C**-Bruce Kimm, Evansville; **Util**-Jim Cox, Denver; **P**-Gary Beare, Oklahoma City; Dewey Robinson, Iowa; **MVP**-Karl Pagel, Wichita; **Pitcher of the Year**-Dewey Robinson, Iowa; **Manager**-Jim Leyland, Evansville.

BA: Keith Smith, Springfield, .350
Runs: Lonnie Smith, Oklahoma City, 106
Hits: Manny Castillo, Springfield, 169
RBIs: Karl Pagel, Wichita, 123

HRs: Karl Pagel, Wichita, 39
Wins: Dewey Robinson, Iowa, 13
SOs: Bruce Berenyi, Indianapolis, 136
ERA: Bruce Berenyi, Indianapolis, 2.82

AAA Inter-American League
President: Roberto Maduro

Standings	W	L	Pct.	GB	Manager
Miami Amigos***	51	21	.708	—	Davey Johnson
Caracas Metropolitanos	37	27	.578	10	Jim Busby
Santo Domingo Azucareros	38	29	.567	10½	Mike Kekich
Maracaibo Petroleros de Zulia.	31	36	.463	17½	Pat Dobson/Gus Gil/Luis Aparicio
Panama Banqueros#	15	36	.294	NA	Chico Salmon/Willie Miranda
Puerto Rico Boricuas#........	16	39	.291	NA	Jose Santiago

#Panama and Puerto Rico disbanded June 17. The league disbanded June 30.
All clubs were unaffiliated.

BA: Jim Tyrone, Miami, .364
Runs: Jim Tyrone, Miami, 50
Hits: Jim Tyrone, Miami, 94
RBIs: Brock Pemberton, Miami, 51

HRs: Wayne Tyrone, Miami, 8
Wins: Mike Wallace, Miami, 11
SOs: Alberto Williams, Panama/Caracas, 52
ERA: Ron Martinez, Miami, 0.89

AAA International League
President: Harold Cooper

Standings	W	L	Pct.	GB	Attend.	Manager
Columbus Clippers (10)......	85	54	.612	—	599,544	Gene Michael
Syracuse Chiefs (14)...........	77	63	.550	8½	176,539	Vern Benson
Richmond Braves (15)........	76	64	.543	9½	159,864	Tom Burgess
Tidewater Tides (21)	73	67	.521	12½	111,570	Frank Verdi
Pawtucket Red Sox (2).......	66	74	.471	19½	147,420	Joe Morgan
Charleston Charlies (18).....	65	74	.468	20	72,609	Jim Beauchamp
Toledo Mud Hens (9)	63	76	.453	22	148,592	Cal Ermer
Rochester Red Wings (1)....	53	86	.381	32	200,013	Doc Edwards

Playoffs: Columbus 3 games, Tidewater 1; Syracuse 3 games, Richmond 2.
Finals: Columbus 4 games, Syracuse 3.

All-Star Team: 1B-Tom Chism, Rochester; **2B**-Roger Holt, Columbus; **3B**-Dave Stapleton, Pawtucket; **SS**-Glenn Hoffman, Pawtucket; **OF**-Roger Brown, Columbus; Mookie Wilson, Tidewater; Sam Bowen, Pawtucket; **C**-Brad Gulden, Columbus; **DH**-Dave Koza, Pawtucket; **P**-Tommy Boggs, Richmond; Rick Anderson, Columbus; **MVP**-Bobby Brown, Columbus; Dave Stapleton, Pawtucket; **Pitcher of the Year**-Rick Anderson, Columbus; **Manager**-Vern Benson, Syracuse.

BA: Garry Hancock, Pawtucket, .325
Runs: Dave Stapleton, Pawtucket, 88
Hits: Dave Stapleton, Pawtucket, 169
RBIs: Sam Bowen, Pawtucket, 75
Jerry Keller, Richmond, 75

HRs: Sam Bowen, Pawtucket, 28
Wins: Bob Kammeyer, Columbus, 16
SOs: Tommy Boggs, Richmond, 138
ERA: Scott Holman, Tidewater, 1.99

AAA Mexican League
President: Antonio Ramirez Muro

North West Standings	W	L	Pct.	GB	Attend.	Manager
Saltillo Saraperos	95	40	.704	—	257,646	Gregorio Luque
Ciudad Juarez Indios	80	53	.602	14	254,439	Jose Guerrero
Union Laguna Algodoneros	66	70	.485	29½	222,839	Moises Camacho
Coahuila Mineros	64	70	.478	30½	142,808	Victor Favela
Chihuahua Dorados	51	78	.395	41	160,609	Mauro Contreras/
						Norman McRae

North East Standings	W	L	Pct.	GB	Attend.	Manager
Nuevo Laredo Tecolotes.....	75	60	.556	—	236,605	Gerardo Gutierrez
Monterrey Sultanes............	66	67	.496	8	163,634	Marte de Alejandro
Tampico Alijadores	59	75	.440	15½	118,268	Felipe Leal/Carlos Trevino
Poza Rica Petroleros	57	74	.435	16	172,225	Emilio Sosa
Leon Bravos	52	82	.388	22½	189,748	Benjamin Valenzuela/
						Eusebio Elizalde/Luis Alcaraz

South West Standings	W	L	Pct.	GB	Attend.	Manager
Puebla Angeles	86	51	.628	—	182,910	Jorge Fitch
Aguascalientes Rieleros......	65	67	.492	18½	233,734	Jaime Favela
Mexico City Tigres	62	73	.459	23	270,085	Domingo Rivera/Jose Luis Garcia
Durango Alacranes	58	74	.439	25½	155,634	Benjamin Cerda
Veracruz Aguila.................	48	85	.361	36	168,524	Ron Camacho/Miguel Sotelo/
						Rolando Camarero

South East Standings	W	L	Pct.	GB	Attend.	Manager
Cordoba Cafeteros	76	56	.576	—	133,959	Winston Llenas
Tabasco Plataneros	73	58	.557	2½	441,835	Raul Cano
Mexico City Diablos Rojos	74	64	.536	5	405,695	Ben Reyes
Coatzacoalcos Azules	66	69	.489	11½	223,883	Miguel Gaspar/Ellie Rodriguez
Yucatan Leones	62	69	.473	13½	453,206	Carlos Paz

Playoffs: Puebla 4 games, Tabasco 0; Cordoba 4 games, Aguascalientes 3; Saltillo 4 games, Monterrey 3; Ciudad Juarez 4 games, Nuevo Laredo 3. Puebla 4 games, Cordoba 1; Ciudad Juarez 4 games, Saltillo 1.
Finals: Puebla 4 games, Ciudad Juarez 3.

*Won first-half   **Won second-half   ***Won both halves
Numbers after nicknames indicate farm system.
Affiliation listed at end of year.

550

All-Star Team: 1B-Earl Williams, Durango; **2B**-Juan Navarrete, Saltillo; **3B**-Blas Santana, Union Laguna; **SS**-Alfonso Jimenez, Puebla; **OF**-Jimmie Collins, Chihuahua; Luis Lora, Puebla; Andres Mora, Saltillo; **C**-Francisco Estrada, Puebla; **DH**-Wenceslao Gonzalez, Chihuahua; **P**-Rafael Garcia, Ciudad Juarez; Ramon Munguia, Puebla; Michael Paul, Ciudad Juarez; **Manager**-Jorge Fitch, Puebla.

BA: Jimmie Collins, Chihuahua, .438
Runs: Juan Navarrete, Saltillo, 110
Hits: Jimmie Collins, Chihuahua, 206
RBIs: Earl Williams, Durango, 112

HRs: Luis Alcaraz, Leon, 24
Ivan Murrell, Puebla, 24
Wins: Miguel Solis, Saltillo, 25
SOs: Rafael Garcia, Ciudad Juarez, 222
ERA: Rafael Garcia, Ciudad Juarez, 1.69

AAA Pacific Coast League
President: Bill Cutler

North Standings	W	L	Pct.	GB	Attend.	Manager
Vancouver Canadians**(8)...	79	68	.537	—	131,367	John Felske
Tacoma Tugs (5).................	74	73	.503	5	181,443	Gene Dusan
Portland Beavers (23).........	73	74	.497	6	159,181	John Lipon
Hawaii Islanders*(25).........	72	76	.486	7½	176,049	Dick Phillips
Spokane Indians (12)...........	68	79	.463	11	217,300	Rene Lachemann

South Standings	W	L	Pct.	GB	Attend.	Manager
Albuquerque Dukes*(19) ...	86	62	.581	—	266,586	Del Crandall
Salt Lake City Gulls**(3)..	80	68	.541	6	214,825	Jimy Williams
Tucson Toros (13)	74	74	.500	12	175,213	Rich Donnelly
Ogden A's (11)	72	75	.490	13½	77,027	Jose Pagan
Phoenix Giants (26)	59	88	.401	26½	162,496	Rocky Bridges

Playoffs: Hawaii 2 games, Vancouver 1; Salt Lake City 2 games, Albuquerque 0.
Finals: Salt Lake City 3 games, Hawaii 0.

All-Star Team: 1B-Craig Cacek, Portland; **2B**-Lenn Sakata, Vancouver; **3B**-Mickey Hatcher, Albuquerque; **SS**-Rance Mulliniks, Salt Lake City; **OF**-Pedro Guerrero, Albuquerque; Bob Clark, Salt Lake City; Chris Bourjos, Phoenix; **C**-Mike Scioscia, Albuquerque; **DH**-Ike Hampton, Salt Lake City; **P**-Mark Bomback, Vancouver; Fred Kuhaulua, Hawaii; **Manager**-Jimy Williams, Salt Lake City.

BA: Mickey Hatcher, Albuquerque, .371
Runs: Pepe Mangual, Salt Lake City, 115
Hits: Craig Cacek, Portland, 180
RBIs: Pedro Guerrero, Albuquerque, 103

HRs: Ike Hampton, Salt Lake City, 30
Wins: Mark Bomback, Vancouver, 22
SOs: Juan Berenguer, Tacoma, 220
ERA: Mark Bomback, Vancouver, 2.56

AA Eastern League
President: P. Patrick McKernan

Standings	W	L	Pct.	GB	Attend.	Manager
West Haven Yankees***(10)	83	56	.597	—	71,302	Stump Merrill
Reading Phillies (22)	77	61	.558	5½	84,200	Jim Snyder
Bristol Red Sox (2).............	73	66	.525	10	66,844	Tony Torchia
Buffalo Bisons (23)	72	67	.518	11	133,148	Steve Demeter
Holyoke Millers (8)	63	76	.453	20	50,207	George Farson
Waterbury A's (11).............	49	91	.350	34½	30,339	Ed Nottle

Playoffs: None.

All-Star Team: 1B-Charles "Chick" Valley, Buffalo; **2B**-Jerry McDonald, Buffalo; **3B**-Wade Boggs, Bristol; **SS**-Thomas Soto, Holyoke; **OF**-Rick Lancellotti, Buffalo; Joe Lefebvre, West Haven; Luis Salazar, Buffalo; George Vukovich, Reading; **C**-Tony Pena, Buffalo; **DH**-Dave Schmidt, Bristol; **Util**-John Loviglio, Reading; **P**-Dave Righetti, West Haven; Bob Walk, Reading; **MVP**-Rick Lancellotti, Buffalo; **Manager**-Stump Merrill, West Haven.

BA: Dave Schmidt, Bristol, .322
Runs: Luis Salazar, Buffalo, 108
Hits: Luis Salazar, Buffalo, 181
RBIs: Rick Lancellotti, Buffalo, 107
Joe Lefebvre, West Haven, 107

HRs: Rick Lancellotti, Buffalo, 41
Wins: Brian Denman, Bristol, 14
Scott Munninghoff, Reading, 14
SOs: Bob Walk, Reading, 135
ERA: Bob Walk, Reading, 2.24

AA Southern League
President: Billy Hitchcock

East Standings	W	L	Pct.	GB	Attend.	Manager
Columbus Astros**(18).....	84	59	.587	—	108,780	Jim Johnson
Charlotte O's*(1)................	73	69	.514	10½	122,336	Jimmy Williams
Jacksonville Suns (7).........	69	72	.489	14	114,546	Joe Jones
Orlando Twins (9)	60	81	.426	23	41,021	Roy McMillan
Savannah Braves (15).........	60	83	.420	24	85,001	Eddie Haas

West Standings	W	L	Pct.	GB	Attend.	Manager
Nashville Sounds**(17)....	83	61	.576	—	515,482	George Scherger
Memphis Chicks*(20)........	82	62	.569	1	226,832	Billy Gardner
Chattanooga Lookouts (5)..	75	69	.521	8	107,780	Woody Smith
Knoxville Knox Sox (4)	65	76	.461	16½	62,876	Gordon Lund
Montgomery Rebels (6)......	62	81	.434	20½	98,487	Denny Sommers

Playoffs: Columbus 2 games, Charlotte 0; Nashville 2 games, Memphis 1.
Finals: Nashville 3 games, Columbus 1.

All-Star Team: 1B-Danny Logan, Charlotte; **2B**-Tim Raines, Memphis; **3B**-Mark Naehring, Knoxville; **SS**-Bob Bonner, Charlotte; **OF**-Joe Charbonneau, Chattanooga; Danny Heep, Columbus; Duane Walker, Nashville; **C**-Alan Knicely, Columbus; **DH**-Dave Hostetler, Memphis; **Util**-Paul Householder, Nashville; Marty Castillo, Montgomery; **P**-Craig Chamberlain, Jacksonville; Geoffrey Combe, Nashville; Bruce Robbins, Montgomery; **Manager**-Jim Johnson, Columbus.

BA: Joe Charbonneau, Chattanooga, .352
Runs: Tim Raines, Memphis, 104
Hits: Danny Heep, Columbus, 171
RBIs: Dave Hostetler, Memphis, 114

HRs: Alan Knicely, Columbus, 33
Wins: Delrick Leatherwood, Columbus, 15
SOs: Robert Veselic, Orlando, 151
ERA: Scott Brown, Nashville, 2.40

AA Texas League
President: Carl Sawatski

East Standings	W	L	Pct.	GB	Attend.	Manager
Arkansas Travelers*(24).....	76	57	.571	—	183,643	Tommy Thompson
Shreveport Captains**(26).	73	62	.541	4	47,333	Andy Gilbert
Jackson Mets (21)...............	70	65	.519	7	68,340	Bob Wellman
Tulsa Drillers (13)	58	75	.436	18	48,844	Jim Schaffer

West Standings	W	L	Pct.	GB	Attend.	Manager
Midland Cubs**(16)...........	76	59	.563	—	89,915	Randy Hundley
San Antonio Dodgers*(19).	69	62	.527	5	63,990	Don LeJohn
El Paso Diablos (3).............	61	75	.449	15½	266,475	Moose Stubing
Amarillo Gold Sox (25)......	54	82	.397	22½	57,667	Glenn Ezell/Rusty Gerhardt

Playoffs: Arkansas 2 games, Shreveport 0; San Antonio 2 games, Midland 1.
Finals: Arkansas 3 games, San Antonio 0.

All-Star Team: 1B-Joe DeSa, Arkansas; **2B**-Tim Flannery, Amarillo; **3B**-Hubie Brooks, Jackson; **SS**-Gary Weiss, San Antonio; **OF**-Mark Brouhard, El Paso; Ron Roenicke, San Antonio; Carlos Lezcano, Midland; **C**-Jody Davis, Jackson; **Util**-Rick Lisi, Tulsa; **DH**-Eric Grandy, Midland; **P**-Chris Davis, Arkansas; Greg Harris, Jackson; Ray Searage, Arkansas; Bob Tufts, Shreveport; **MVP**-Mark Brouhard, El Paso; **Manager**-Andy Gilbert, Shreveport.

BA: Jim Tracy, Midland, .355
Runs: Danny Rohn, Midland, 122
Hits: Mark Brouhard, El Paso, 181
Tim Flannery, Amarillo, 181
RBIs: Mark Brouhard, El Paso, 107

HRs: Mark Brouhard, El Paso, 28
Wins: Bob Tufts, Shreveport, 14
SOs: Scott Budner, Shreveport, 110
Joe Carroll, Amarillo, 110
ERA: Greg Harris, Jackson, 2.26

A California League
President: E.W. "Bill" Wickert

North Standings	W	L	Pct.	GB	Attend.	Manager
Reno Silver Sox (25)	74	67	.525	—	59,422	Eddie Watt
Stockton Ports (8)	73	68	.518	1	25,901	Lee Sigman
Lodi Dodgers (19)	67	72	.482	6	44,102	Stan Wasiak
Modesto A's (11)................	66	74	.471	7½	61,037	Gaylen Pitts
Santa Clara Padres (x)	47	93	.336	26½	19,952	Joe Volpi

South Standings	W	L	Pct.	GB	Attend.	Manager
San Jose Missions (12)	89	51	.636	—	71,320	Bob Didier
Visalia Oaks (9).................	86	54	.614	3	50,199	Tom Kelly
Salinas Angels (3)..............	69	71	.493	20	53,023	Chris Cannizzaro
Fresno Giants (26)	66	73	.475	22½	74,985	Jack Mull
Bakersfield Outlaws	63	77	.450	26	44,546	Ron Mihal

Playoffs: Stockton 2 games, Lodi 0; San Jose 2 games, Visalia 1.
Finals: San Jose 3 games, Stockton 2.

All-Star Team: 1B-Mark Funderburk, Visalia; **2B**-Jerry Lane, Fresno; **3B**-Les Pearsey, Visalia; **SS**-Onix Concepcion, Bakersfield; **OF**-Eddie Brunson, Stockton; Marvin Garrison, Lodi; Dave Henderson, San Jose; Miguel Negron, San Jose; **C**-Aurelio Cadahia, Visalia; **DH**-Mike Marshall, Lodi; **P**-Thomas Biko, Visalia; Steve Green, Visalia; Ron McGee, San Jose; Randy Miller, Reno; Eric Show, Reno; **MVP**-Mike Marshall, Lodi; Les Pearsey, Visalia; **Manager**-Tom Kelly, Visalia.

BA: Mike Marshall, Lodi, .354
Runs: Les Pearsey, Visalia, 111
Hits: Mike Marshall, Lodi, 186
RBIs: Les Pearsey, Visalia, 121

HRs: Mark Funderburk, Visalia, 31
Wins: Steve Green, Visalia, 16
SOs: Dave LaPoint, Stockton, 208
ERA: Steve Brown, Salinas, 2.41

A Carolina League
President: James B. Mills

Standings	W	L	Pct.	GB	Attend.	Manager
Winston-Salem Red Sox***(2)	85	55	.607	—	68,702	Bill Slack
Alexandria Mariners (12) ...	74	62	.544	9	34,614	Bobby Floyd
Peninsula Pilots (22).........	68	68	.500	15	44,050	Ron Clark
Kinston Eagles (14)...........	67	69	.493	16	38,569	Duane Larson
Lynchburg Mets (21)..........	61	73	.455	21	53,400	Jack Aker
Salem Pirates (23)..............	54	82	.397	29	43,036	Jim Mahoney

Playoffs: None.

All-Star Team: 1B-Greg Walker, Peninsula; **2B**-Eduardo Dennis, Kinston; Michael Barnes, Salem; **3B**-Ralph "Rocket" Wheeler, Kinston; **SS**-Ron Gardenhire, Lynchburg; Manuel McDonald, Peninsula; **OF**-Bob Dernier, Peninsula; Reid Nichols, Winston-Salem; Jack Sauer, Winston-Salem; **C**-Pat Kelly, Kinston; Junior Ortiz, Salem; **DH**-Tom Lombarski, Peninsula; **P**-Ernest Gause, Peninsula; Bryan Clark, Alexandria; Thomas Hart, Peninsula; **MVP**-Bob Dernier, Peninsula; **Pitcher of the Year**-Thomas Hart, Peninsula; **Manager**-Bill Slack, Winston-Salem.

BA: Pat Kelly, Kinston, .309
Runs: Reid Nichols, Winston-Salem, 107
Hits: Reid Nichols, Winston-Salem, 156
RBIs: Mike Fitzgerald, Lynchburg, 75
HRs: Gary Pellant, Alexandria, 18

Wins: Bryan Clark, Alexandria, 14
Thomas Hart, Peninsula, 14
SOs: Mike Howard, Winston-Salem, 161
ERA: Thomas Hart, Peninsula, 2.22

A Florida State League
President: George MacDonald, Jr.

North Standings
	W	L	Pct.	GB	Attend.	Manager
Winter Haven Red Sox***(2)	79	58	.577	—	28,022	Rac Slider
Tampa Tarpons (17)	74	60	.552	3½	93,303	Mike Compton
Dunedin Blue Jays (14)	68	69	.496	11	36,676	Denis Menke
St. Petersburg Cardinals (24)	64	71	.474	14	157,669	Sonny Ruberto
Lakeland Tigers (6)	50	87	.365	29	54,017	Fred Hatfield

South Standings
	W	L	Pct.	GB	Attend.	Manager
Ft. Lauderdale Yankees***(10)	92	51	.643	—	76,762	Doug Holmquist
West Palm Beach Expos (20)	79	65	.549	13½	125,213	Larry Bearnarth
Ft. Myers Royals (7)	69	69	.500	20½	59,194	Gene Lamont
Miami Orioles (1)	60	81	.426	31	41,313	Lance Nichols
Daytona Beach Astros (18)	56	80	.412	32½	50,109	Carlos Alfonso

Playoff: Winter Haven 3 games, Ft. Lauderdale 0.

All-Star Team: 1B-Tim Thompson, Dunedin; **2B**-Ray Rivas, St. Petersburg; **3B**-Nick Esasky, Tampa; **SS**-Cal Ripken, Jr., Miami; **OF**-John Denman, Miami; Lee Graham, Winter Haven; Lloyd Moseby, Dunedin; **C**-Stephen Christmas, Tampa; George Bjorkman, St. Petersburg; **DH**-Ron Johnson, Ft. Myers; **Util**-Paul Herring, Tampa; Rafael Santana, Ft. Lauderdale; **P**-Bill Scherrer, Tampa; Brian Ryder, Ft. Lauderdale; Bob Ojeda, Winter Haven; Paul Boris, Ft. Lauderdale; **Manager**-Rac Slider, Winter Haven.

BA: Ray Rivas, St. Petersburg, .334
Runs: Lloyd Moseby, Dunedin, 89
Hits: Lloyd Moseby, Dunedin, 148
RBIs: Steve Balboni, Ft. Lauderdale, 91
HRs: Steve Balboni, Ft. Lauderdale, 26
Wins: Paul Boris, Ft. Lauderdale, 16
  Gary Givens, Winter Haven, 16
SOs: Brian Ryder, Ft. Lauderdale, 156
ERA: Jeffrey Taylor, Ft. Lauderdale, 1.67

A Midwest League
President: Bill Walters

North Standings
	W	L	Pct.	GB	Attend.	Manager
Waterloo Indians*(5)	81	54	.600	—	70,196	Cal Emery
Wausau Timbers**(x)	69	61	.531	9½	43,059	Tom Robson
Appleton Foxes (4)	63	72	.463	18	72,011	Jim Breazeale
Wisconsin Rapids Twins (9)	60	72	.455	19½	41,239	Rich Stelmaszek

South Standings
	W	L	Pct.	GB	Attend.	Manager
Quad City Cubs*(16)	77	56	.579	—	89,256	Jim Napier
Clinton Dodgers**(19)	74	59	.556	3	41,949	Dick McLaughlin
Cedar Rapids Giants (26)	58	78	.426	20½	73,206	Wayne Cato
Burlington Bees (8)	53	83	.390	25½	55,001	Duane Espy

Playoffs: Quad City 2 games, Clinton 1; Waterloo 2 games, Wausau 1.
Finals: Quad City 2 games, Waterloo 1.

All-Star Team: 1B-Thomas Anderson, Waterloo; **2B**-Paul Plinsky, Cedar Rapids; **3B**-Peter Peltz, Waterloo; **SS**-Ivan Mesa, Appleton; **OF**-Dave Stockstill, Wausau; Mark Gilbert, Quad City; Mitch Webster, Clinton; **C**-Bobby Johnson, Wausau; **DH**-David Hudgens, Waterloo; **P**-Randy Clark, Quad City; Doug Jones, Burlington; Kevin Joyce, Clinton; Randy Rambus, Waterloo; Matt Sutherland, Cedar Rapids; **MVP**-Dave Stockstill, Wausau; **Manager**-Tom Robson, Wausau.

BA: Mitch Webster, Clinton, .326
Runs: Paul Plinsky, Cedar Rapids, 98
Hits: Mitch Webster, Clinton, 154
RBIs: Dave Stockstill, Wausau, 101
HRs: Thomas Anderson, Waterloo, 30
Wins: Randy Clark, Quad City, 16
SOs: Thomas Owens, Wausau, 136
ERA: Doug Jones, Burlington, 1.75

A New York-Pennsylvania League
President: Vincent M. McNamara

Yawkey Standings
	W	L	Pct.	GB	Attend.	Manager
Oneonta Yankees (10)	42	26	.618	—	38,446	Art Mazmanian
Elmira Pioneers (2)	34	35	.493	8½	35,071	Dick Berardino
Little Falls Mets (21)	31	39	.443	12	27,873	Matt Galante
Utica Blue Jays (14)	25	41	.379	16	19,100	John McLaren
Auburn Phillies (x)	22	45	.328	19½	37,459	Tom Kotchman

Wrigley Standings
	W	L	Pct.	GB	Attend.	Manager
Geneva Cubs (16)	50	19	.725	—	22,828	Bob Hartsfield
Jamestown Expos (20)	43	27	.614	7½	32,325	Pat Daugherty
Batavia Trojans (5)	37	34	.521	14	41,376	Tom Trebelhorn
Newark Co-Pilots	32	39	.451	19	14,152	Mal Fichman
Niagara Falls Pirates	30	41	.423	21	29,908	Duane Shaffer

Playoff: Oneonta 2 games, Geneva 1.

All-Star Team: 1B-Jack Upton, Geneva; **2B**-Wallace Johnson, Jamestown; **3B**-Glenn Swires, Oneonta; **SS**-Scott Fletcher, Geneva; **OF**-Kalvin Adams, Jamestown; Larry Caprio, Newark; Carmelo Castillo, Batavia; Mel Hall, Geneva; **C**-David Buffamoyer, Oneonta; Marc Siciliano, Little Falls; **DH**-Brian Stemberger, Utica; **Util**-Jeffrey Brown, Niagara Falls; **P**-Robert Blyth, Geneva; Bryan Hardy, Geneva; Stefan Wever, Oneonta; Fred Toliver, Oneonta; **Manager**-Pat Daugherty, Jamestown.

BA: Brian Stemberger, Utica, .359
Runs: Gene Glynn, Jamestown, 71
Hits: Kalvin Adams, Jamestown, 99
RBIs: Kalvin Adams, Jamestown, 69
HRs: Thomas Grant, Geneva, 10
  Randall LaVigne, Geneva, 10
  Tommy Barrett, Geneva, 10
  Edward Petryschuk, Utica, 10
  Jack Upton, Geneva, 10
  Matt Winters, Oneonta, 10
Wins: Fred Toliver, Oneonta, 10
SOs: Bryan Hardy, Geneva, 82
  Bill Sattler, Jamestown, 82
ERA: Stefan Wever, Oneonta, 1.77

A Northwest League
President: Bob Richmond

North Standings
	W	L	Pct.	GB	Attend.	Manager
Walla Walla Padres (25)	40	30	.571	—	20,358	Curt Daniels
Bellingham Mariners (12)	41	31	.569	—	31,741	Jeff Scott
Victoria Mussels	41	31	.569	—	9,073	Bill Bryk
Grays Harbor Mets (21)	19	52	.268	21½	16,665	Danny Monzon

South Standings
	W	L	Pct.	GB	Attend.	Manager
Central Oregon Phillies#(22)	43	28	.606	—	18,610	Tom Harmon
Medford A's (11)	38	33	.535	5	34,656	Rich Morales
Salem Senators	33	39	.458	10½	15,904	Gene Lanthorn
Eugene Emeralds (17)	30	41	.423	13	66,156	Greg Riddoch

#represented Bend, Oregon.

Playoff: Central Oregon 2 games, Walla Walla 1.

All-Star Team: 1B-Emil Drzayich, Victoria; **2B**-Roy Clark, Bellingham; **3B**-John Seefried, Salem; **SS**-Julio Franco, Central Oregon; **OF**-Bobby Garrett, Medford; Ramon Estepa, Bellingham; Aaron Cain, Walla Walla; **C**-Herb Orensky, Central Oregon; **DH**-Doug Lulay, Walla Walla; **Util**-Jim Durrman, Medford; **P**-Michael Barba, Walla Walla; David Froelich, Walla Walla; Ed Koziol, Victoria; Mike Ramsey, Eugene; Mark Runyan, Salem; **Manager**-Tom Harmon, Central Oregon.

BA: Pedro Rabassa, Victoria, .381
Runs: Bobby Garrett, Medford, 66
Hits: Julio Franco, Central Oregon, 98
RBIs: Doug Lulay, Walla Walla, 62
HRs: Julio Franco, Central Oregon, 10
  Jim Durrman, Medford, 10
Wins: Ed Koziol, Victoria, 9
SOs: Ed Koziol, Victoria, 104
ERA: Joe Georger, Bellingham, 2.18

A Western Carolinas League
President: John H. Moss

Standings
	W	L	Pct.	GB	Attend.	Manager
Greenwood Braves*(15)	78	60	.565	—	37,010	Al Gallagher
Asheville Tourists (13)	75	63	.543	3	42,012	Wayne Terwilliger
Spartanburg Phillies**(22)	73	66	.525	5½	28,960	Bill Dancy
Greensboro Hornets (17)	65	71	.478	12	165,596	Jim Lett
Gastonia Cardinals (24)	65	74	.468	13½	58,089	Johnny Lewis
Shelby Pirates (23)	56	78	.418	20	15,570	Tom Zimmer

Playoff: Greenwood 3 games, Spartanburg 1.

All-Star Team: 1B-Hediberto Vargas, Shelby; **2B**-Jeff Doyle, Gastonia; **3B**-Ray Borucki, Spartanburg; **SS**-Albert Hall, Greenwood; **OF**-George Bell, Spartanburg; Ron Rudd, Greenwood; Tony Walker, Greensboro; **C**-Patrick Rubino, Shelby; **DH**-Luis Gonzalez, Asheville; **Util**-Steve Hammond, Greenwood; Walter Pierce, Gastonia; **P**-Mark Davis, Spartanburg; Jamie Farr, Asheville; Lance Gore, Greenwood; Jeff Lahti, Greensboro; **Manager**-Al Gallagher, Greenwood.

BA: Gerald Perry, Greenwood, .333
Runs: Jeff Doyle, Gastonia, 90
Hits: Jeff Doyle, Gastonia, 168
RBIs: George Bell, Spartanburg, 102
HRs: Hediberto Vargas, Shelby, 31
Wins: Jamie Farr, Asheville, 14
SOs: Darren Burroughs, Spartanburg, 180
ERA: Jerry Johnson, Gastonia, 2.65

R Appalachian League
President: Chauncey De Vault

Standings
	W	L	Pct.	GB	Attend.	Manager
Paintsville Yankees (10)	52	13	.800	—	21,214	Bill Livesey
Kingsport Braves (15)	39	31	.557	15½	26,085	Gene Hassell
Elizabethton Twins (9)	37	33	.529	17½	16,660	Fred Waters
Bluefield Orioles (1)	33	35	.485	20½	23,530	Junior Miner
Johnson City Cardinals (24)	25	43	.368	28½	29,591	Nick Leyva
Bristol Tigers (6)	19	50	.275	35	11,555	Joe Lewis

Playoffs: None.

All-Star Team: 1B-Randall Guerra, Paintsville; **2B**-Mike Garcia, Kingsport; **3B**-Otis Nixon, Paintsville; **SS**-Paul Runge, Kingsport; **OF**-David Schuman, Bluefield; Bob Teegarden, Paintsville; Milt Thompson, Kingsport; **C**-Richard Austin, Elizabethton; **DH**-Kevin Miller, Elizabethton; **P**-Pete Filson, Paintsville; Frank Ricci, Paintsville; **Manager**-Bill Livesey, Paintsville.

BA: Kevin Miller, Elizabethton, .336
Runs: Bob Teegarden, Paintsville, 66
Hits: Kevin Miller, Elizabethton, 81
RBIs: Bob Teegarden, Paintsville, 74
  Kevin Miller, Elizabethton, 74
HRs: Harold Williams, Kingsport, 16
Wins: Pete Filson, Paintsville, 9
SOs: Pete Filson, Paintsville, 118
ERA: Pete Filson, Paintsville, 1.68

R Gulf Coast League
President: George MacDonald, Jr.

Standings	W	L	Pct.	GB	Manager
Astros (18)	33	19	.635	—	Julio Linares
Rangers (13)	33	21	.611	1	Andy Hancock
Royals Gold (7)	29	23	.558	4	Jose Martinez
Braves (15)	26	28	.481	8	Pedro Gonzalez
Royals Blue (7)	24	29	.453	9½	Brian Murphy
Pirates (23)	20	32	.385	13	Woody Huyke
Cubs (16)	19	31	.380	13½	Ken Rudolph

Games played at Sarasota and Bradenton, Florida.

Playoffs: None.

BA: Michael Brewer, Royals Gold, .371
Runs: Robin Townley, Royals Gold, 43
Hits: Michael Brewer, Royals Gold, 76
RBIs: Michael Brewer, Royals Gold, 47

HRs: Greg Dikos, Braves, 5
Leon Doak, Royals Gold, 5
Miguel Sosa, Braves, 5
Wins: Doug Welenc, Astros, 7
SOs: Doug Welenc, Astros, 51
ERA: Michael Roberts, Rangers, 0.71

R Pioneer League
President: Ralph C. Nelles

North Standings	W	L	Pct.	GB	Attend.	Manager
Lethbridge Dodgers (19)	38	30	.559	—	20,656	Gail Henley
Calgary Expos (20)	34	36	.486	5	37,552	Bob Bailey

	W	L	Pct.	GB	Attend.	Manager
Great Falls Giants (26)	32	38	.457	7	54,842	Ernest Rodriguez
Medicine Hat Blue Jays (14)	27	42	.391	11½	13,343	Dennis Holmberg
South Standings	W	L	Pct.	GB	Attend.	Manager
Helena Phillies (22)	43	26	.623	—	23,005	Rollie DeArmas
Billings Mustangs (17)	43	26	.623	—	59,880	Jim Hoff
Butte Copper Kings (8)	32	34	.485	9½	28,398	Ken Richardson/Tom Gamboa
Idaho Falls Angels (3)	25	42	.373	17	34,905	Reuben Rodriguez

Helena was awarded first place by virtue of having won the season series with Billings.

Playoff: Lethbridge 2 games, Helena 0.

All-Star Team: 1B-Greg Brock, Lethbridge; **2B-**Julio Paula, Medicine Hat; **3B-**David Perez, Calgary; **SS-**Fred Manrique, Medicine Hat; **OF-**Willie Darkis, Helena, Rob Deer, Great Falls; **Fernando Marin, Calgary; C-**Kurtis Kingsolver, Butte; **P-**Nick Fiorillo, Billings; Richard Rodas, Lethbridge; **Manager-**Gail Henley, Lethbridge.

BA: Joe Bruno, Helena, .385
Runs: Joe Bruno, Helena, 78
Hits: Joe Bruno, Helena, 112
RBIs: Willie Darkis, Helena, 83

HRs: Willie Darkis, Helena, 20
Wins: Richard Rodas, Lethbridge, 12
SOs: Richard Rodas, Lethbridge, 148
ERA: Richard Rodas, Lethbridge, 1.12

1979 Interleague Post Season Play

World Series
Pittsburgh (National) 4 games, Baltimore (American) 3

1979 Major League Farm Systems

American League
1 Baltimore (4): Rochester, Charlotte, Miami, Bluefield.
2 Boston (5): Pawtucket, Bristol (CT), Winston-Salem, Winter Haven, Elmira.
3 California (4): Salt Lake City, El Paso, Salinas, Idaho Falls.
4 Chicago (3): Iowa, Knoxville, Appleton.
5 Cleveland (4): Tacoma, Chattanooga, Waterloo, Batavia.
6 Detroit (4): Evansville, Montgomery, Lakeland, Bristol (VA).
7 Kansas City (5): Omaha, Jacksonville, Ft. Myers, Gulf Coast Blue, Gulf Coast Gold.
8 Milwaukee (5): Vancouver, Holyoke, Stockton, Burlington, Butte.
9 Minnesota (5): Toledo, Orlando, Visalia, Wisconsin Rapids, Elizabethton.
10 New York (5): Columbus (OH), West Haven, Ft. Lauderdale, Oneonta, Paintsville.
11 Oakland (4): Ogden, Waterbury, Modesto, Medford.
12 Seattle (4): Spokane, Alexandria, San Jose, Bellingham.
13 Texas (4): Tucson, Tulsa, Asheville, Gulf Coast.
14 Toronto (5): Syracuse, Dunedin, Kinston, Utica, Medicine Hat.

National League
15 Atlanta (5): Richmond, Savannah, Greenwood, Kingsport, Gulf Coast.
16 Chicago (5): Wichita, Midland, Quad City, Geneva, Gulf Coast.
17 Cincinnati (6): Indianapolis, Nashville, Tampa, Greensboro, Eugene, Billings.
18 Houston (4): Charleston, Columbus (GA), Daytona Beach, Gulf Coast.
19 Los Angeles (5): Albuquerque, San Antonio, Lodi, Clinton, Lethbridge.
20 Montreal (5): Denver, Memphis, West Palm Beach, Jamestown, Calgary.
21 New York (5): Tidewater, Jackson, Lynchburg, Little Falls, Grays Harbor.
22 Philadelphia (6): Oklahoma City, Reading, Peninsula, Spartanburg, Central Oregon, Helena.
23 Pittsburgh (5): Portland, Buffalo, Salem (VA), Shelby, Gulf Coast.
24 St. Louis (5): Springfield, Arkansas, St. Petersburg, Gastonia, Johnson City.
25 San Diego (4): Hawaii, Amarillo, Reno, Walla Walla.
26 San Francisco (5): Phoenix, Shreveport, Fresno, Cedar Rapids, Great Falls.

Co-op (x): Santa Clara, Wausau, Auburn.
Independent: Bakersfield, Newark, Niagara Falls, Victoria, Salem (OR), Inter-American League

---

1979 No-Hitters

Date	Pitcher	Team	League	Opponent	Score
3-25	Miguel Solis/ Manuel Pena	Saltillo	Mexican	Ciudad Juarez	1-0 (7)
3-28	Arturo Gonzalez	Monterrey	Mexican	Ciudad Juarez	0-0 (10)
4-7	Ken Forsch	Houston	National	Atlanta	6-0
4-13	Tomas Armas	Saltillo	Mexican	Monterrey	5-0
5-12	Rick Anderson	Jackson	Texas	Shreveport	8-0
5-19	Aurelio Monteagudo	Coahuila	Mexican	Nuevo Laredo	10-0 (7)
6-2	Thomas Hart	Peninsula	Carolina	Salem	5-0 (P, 7)
6-15	Mike Glinatsis	Shreveport	Texas	Jackson	1-0 (7)
6-22	Len Whitehouse	Tulsa	Texas	Shreveport	2-0 (7)
6-28	Jack O'Connor	West Palm Beach	Florida State	Ft. Myers	1-0
7-1	Jose Ochoa	Tabasco	Mexican	Veracruz	2-0 (5)
7-4	Richard Goulding	San Antonio	Texas	Amarillo	5-0
7-8	Fernando Lopez	Puebla	Mexican	Durango	2-0 (7)
7-11	Luis Leal	Dunedin	Florida State	Tampa	2-0
7-14	Jamie Easterly	Denver	American Assoc.	Iowa	10-0 (P, 7)
7-25	Dave LaPoint	Stockton	California	Reno	4-0
8-7	Pete Filson	Paintsville	Appalachian	Kingsport	10-0 (7)
8-13	Charlie Puleo	Dunedin	Florida State	St. Petersburg	3-0 (7)
8-17	Peter Bonfils	Poza Rica	Mexican	Tampico	2-0 (5)
8-29	Paul Moskau/Davis May/Sheldon Burnside/ Angel Torres	Indianapolis	American Assoc.	Evansville	5-0

Number in parentheses indicates innings if other than nine; "P" indicates perfect game.

THIS DATE IN MINOR LEAGUE HISTORY

March 28, 1979, Luke Easter, great Negro League, American League, and International League first baseman, was shot and killed in Cleveland. He had been to a bank to cash paychecks for fellow employees. He was 63.

April 6, 1979, Rudolph Kallio, 86, who won more than 200 games in the Pacific Coast League and 288 total in his minor league career, died in Newport, Oregon.

April 30, 1979, Gary Pellant, third baseman for Alexandria, Carolina League, accomplished a feat performed only once before in Organized Ball when he hit home runs from each side of the plate in the same inning of a 20-7 victory over Salem. A check of the records showed that former major league outfielder Ellis Burton turned the same trick for Toronto, International League, on May 3, 1961.

June 10, 1979, Stan Wasiak, manager for Lodi, California League, piloted his 2,000th minor league victory, in his 30th year at the helm.

June 17, 1979, Panama and Puerto Rico withdrew from the Inter-American League.

June 30, 1979, The Inter-American League folded. All six clubs lost money as the league was plagued by poor weather and unreliable transportation.

July 9, 1979, First baseman Jose Barrios of Shreveport hit his fifth grand slam of the season. Barrios would not go on to tie the Texas League record of six, set by Roy Ostergard in 1923.

July 15, 1979, Geneva, New York-Pennsylvania League, defeated Utica 29-4. Shortstop Scott Fletcher had seven hits, including four doubles and a home run. Geneva scored 15 of its runs in the ninth inning.

August 17, 1979, Former Atlanta Braves farmhand Jimmie Collins set the Mexican League afire, hitting .438 for the season, 72 points higher than his closest rival.

August 18, 1979, Vancouver's Mark Bomback became the first Triple-A pitcher in 13 years to win 20 games in a season as he beat Ogden 7-2 in the Pacific Coast League. He would finish the season with a 22-7 record.

August 31, 1979, Paintsville of the Appalachian League ended the season with a 52-13 record and an .800 winning percentage. They were 15-1/2 games ahead of second place Kingsport.

September 1, 1979, Rick Lancellotti finished the season with 41 home runs for Buffalo, Eastern League, to tie the league record set in 1930 by Ken Strong of Hazleton.

1980

American League
President: Leland S. MacPhail, Jr.

East Standings
	W	L	Pct.	GB	Attend.	Manager
New York Yankees	103	59	.636	—	2,627,417	Dick Howser
Baltimore Orioles	100	62	.617	3	1,797,438	Earl Weaver
Milwaukee Brewers	86	76	.531	17	1,857,408	Buck Rodgers/
						George Bamberger
Boston Red Sox	83	77	.519	19	1,956,092	Don Zimmer/Johnny Pesky
Detroit Tigers	84	78	.519	19	1,785,293	Sparky Anderson
Cleveland Indians	79	81	.494	23	1,033,827	Dave Garcia
Toronto Blue Jays	67	95	.414	36	1,400,327	Bobby Mattick

West Standings
	W	L	Pct.	GB	Attend.	Manager
Kansas City Royals	97	65	.599	—	2,288,714	Jim Frey
Oakland Athletics	83	79	.512	14	842,259	Billy Martin
Minnesota Twins	77	84	.478	19½	769,206	Gene Mauch/John Goryl
Texas Rangers	76	85	.472	20½	1,198,175	Pat Corrales
Chicago White Sox	70	90	.438	26	1,200,365	Tony LaRussa
California Angels	65	95	.406	31	2,297,327	Jim Fregosi
Seattle Mariners	59	103	.364	38	836,204	Darrell Johnson/Maury Wills

Playoff: Kansas City 3 games, New York 0.

BA: George Brett, Kansas City, .390
Runs: Willie Wilson, Kansas City, 133
Hits: Willie Wilson, Kansas City, 230
RBIs: Cecil Cooper, Milwaukee, 122
HRs: Reggie Jackson, New York, 41
  Ben Oglivie, Milwaukee, 41
Wins: Steve Stone, Baltimore, 25
SOs: Len Barker, Cleveland, 187
ERA: Rudy May, New York, 2.47
Pct: Steve Stone, Baltimore, .781, 25-7
Saves: Dan Quisenberry, Kansas City, 33
  Rich "Goose" Gossage, New York, 33

National League
President: Charles S. Feeney

East Standings
	W	L	Pct.	GB	Attend.	Manager
Philadelphia Phillies	91	71	.562	—	2,651,650	Dallas Green
Montreal Expos	90	72	.556	1	2,208,175	Dick Williams
Pittsburgh Pirates	83	79	.512	8	1,646,757	Chuck Tanner
St. Louis Cardinals	74	88	.457	17	1,385,147	Ken Boyer/Jack Krol/
						Red Schoendienst/
						Whitey Herzog
New York Mets	67	95	.414	24	1,192,073	Joe Torre
Chicago Cubs	64	98	.395	27	1,206,776	Preston Gomez/
						Joey Amalfitano

West Standings
	W	L	Pct.	GB	Attend.	Manager
Houston Astros	93	70	.571	—	2,278,217	Bill Virdon
Los Angeles Dodgers	92	71	.564	1	3,249,287	Tom Lasorda
Cincinnati Reds	89	73	.549	3½	2,022,450	John McNamara
Atlanta Braves	81	80	.503	11	1,048,411	Bobby Cox
San Francisco Giants	75	86	.466	17	1,096,115	Dave Bristol
San Diego Padres	73	89	.451	19½	1,139,026	Jerry Coleman

Playoff: Philadelphia 3 games, Houston 2.

BA: Bill Buckner, Chicago, .324
Runs: Keith Hernandez, St. Louis, 111
Hits: Steve Garvey, Los Angeles, 200
RBIs: Mike Schmidt, Philadelphia, 121
HRs: Mike Schmidt, Philadelphia, 48
Wins: Steve Carlton, Philadelphia, 24
SOs: Steve Carlton, Philadelphia, 286
ERA: Don Sutton, Los Angeles, 2.21
Pct: Jim Bibby, Pittsburgh, .760, 19-6
Saves: Bruce Sutter, Chicago, 28

AAA American Association
President: Joe Ryan

East Standings
	W	L	Pct.	GB	Attend.	Manager
Springfield Redbirds (24)	75	61	.551	—	99,935	Hal Lanier
Evansville Triplets (6)	61	74	.452	13½	106,849	Jim Leyland
Iowa Oaks (4)	59	77	.434	16	126,981	Pete Ward/Sam Ewing
Indianapolis Indians (17)	58	77	.430	16½	180,483	Jim Beauchamp

West Standings
	W	L	Pct.	GB	Attend.	Manager
Denver Bears (20)	92	44	.676	—	565,214	Billy Gardner
Oklahoma City 89ers (22)	70	65	.519	21½	200,938	Jim Snyder
Omaha Royals (7)	66	70	.485	26	159,113	Joe Sparks
Wichita Aeros (16)	61	74	.452	30½	101,108	Jack Hiatt

Playoff: Springfield 4 games, Denver 1.

All-Star Team: 1B-Ken Phelps, Omaha; **2B**-Tim Raines, Denver; **3B**-Tim Wallach, Denver; **SS**-Jerry Manuel, Denver; **OF**-Orlando Gonzalez, Oklahoma City; Art Gardner, Denver; Dan Briggs, Denver; Paul Householder, Indianapolis; **C**-Glenn Borgmann, Iowa; Don McCormack, Oklahoma City; **DH**-Randy Bass, Denver; **Util**-Tim Ireland, Omaha; **P**-Steve Ratzer, Denver; Alan Olmsted, Springfield; **MVP**-Randy Bass, Denver; **Pitcher of the Year**-Steve Ratzer, Denver; **Manager**-Billy Gardner, Denver.

BA: Tim Raines, Denver, .354
Runs: Randy Bass, Denver, 106
Hits: Manny Castillo, Omaha, 173
RBIs: Randy Bass, Denver, 143
HRs: Randy Bass, Denver, 37
Wins: Steve Ratzer, Denver, 15
SOs: Bruce Berenyi, Indianapolis, 121
ERA: Alan Olmsted, Springfield, 2.77

AAA International League
President: Harold Cooper

Standings
	W	L	Pct.	GB	Attend.	Manager
Columbus Clippers (10)	83	57	.593	—	546,074	Joe Altobelli
Toledo Mud Hens (9)	77	63	.550	6	199,602	Cal Ermer
Rochester Red Wings (1)	74	65	.532	8½	292,667	Doc Edwards
Richmond Braves (15)	69	71	.493	14	187,462	Fred Hatfield
Charleston Charlies (13)	67	71	.486	15	118,881	Tom Burgess
Tidewater Tides (21)	67	72	.482	15½	116,756	Frank Verdi
Pawtucket Red Sox (2)	62	77	.446	20½	163,283	Joe Morgan
Syracuse Chiefs (14)	58	81	.417	24½	189,151	Harry Warner

Playoffs: Columbus 3 games, Richmond 2; Toledo 3 games, Rochester 1.
Finals: Columbus 4 games, Toledo 1.

All-Star Team: 1B-Marshall Brant, Columbus; **2B**-Michael Richardt, Charleston; **3B**-Thomas Ashford, Charleston; **SS**-Bob Bonner, Rochester; **OF**-Mookie Wilson, Tidewater; Dave Engle, Toledo; Greg Johnston, Toledo; **C**-Ray Smith, Rochester; **DH**-John Valle, Rochester; **P**-Bob Kammeyer, Columbus; Bob Babcock, Charleston; **MVP**-Marshall Brant, Columbus; **Pitcher of the Year**-Bob Kammeyer, Columbus; **Manager**-Joe Altobelli, Columbus.

BA: Dave Engle, Toledo, .307
Runs: Mookie Wilson, Tidewater, 94
Hits: Mookie Wilson, Tidewater, 152
RBIs: Marshall Brant, Columbus, 92
HRs: Marshall Brant, Columbus, 23
Wins: Bob Kammeyer, Columbus, 15
SOs: Juan Berenguer, Tidewater, 178
ERA: Ken Clay, Columbus, 1.96

AAA Mexican League
President: Antonio Ramirez Muro

North West Standings
	W	L	Pct.	GB	Attend.	Manager
Ciudad Juarez Indios	57	37	.606	—	144,450	Jose Guerrero
Saltillo Saraperos	52	47	.525	7½	170,262	Gregorio Luque
Union Laguna Diablos Blancos	46	51	.474	12½	156,403	Jesus Diaz
Chihuahua Dorados	34	57	.374	21½	128,348	Manuel Magallon
Monclova Acereros	36	61	.371	22½	141,148	Victor Favela

North East Standings
	W	L	Pct.	GB	Attend.	Manager
Aguascalientes Rieleros	61	33	.649	—	132,527	Moises Camacho
Reynosa Broncos	52	46	.531	11	151,766	Winston Llenas
Nuevo Laredo Tecolotes	49	46	.516	12½	120,414	Marte de Alejandro/
						Gerardo Gutierrez
Leon Cachorros	43	53	.448	19	119,427	Mario Saldana
Monterrey Sultanes	37	56	.398	23½	95,621	Hector Valle

South West Standings
	W	L	Pct.	GB	Attend.	Manager
Mexico City Tigres	51	47	.520	—	219,426	Fernando Remes
Veracruz Aguila	48	47	.505	1½	166,109	Miguel Sotelo/Willie Davis
Coatzacoalcos Azules	47	48	.495	2½	160,752	Benjamin Cerda
Tabasco Plataneros	39	54	.419	9½	209,885	Raul Cano/Arnoldo Castro
Toluca Osos Negros	39	55	.415	10	68,689	Carlos Trevino

South East Standings
	W	L	Pct.	GB	Attend.	Manager
Puebla Angeles	63	25	.716	—	128,014	Jorge Fitch/
						Rosendo Dominguez
Yucatan Leones	57	41	.582	11	361,092	Jaime Favela
Mexico City Diablos Rojos	52	40	.565	13	269,177	Benjamin Reyes
Campeche Alacranes	45	43	.511	18	201,705	Jerry Hairston/Arnoldo Castro/
						Alfonso Pena
Poza Rica Petroleros	36	57	.387	29½	132,775	David Garcia

Playoffs: None. Season ended July 3 due to player strike.

BA: Roberto Rodriguez, Union Laguna, .404
Runs: Raul Sanchez, Leon, 77
Hits: Vic Davalillo, Aguascalientes, 143
RBIs: Ivan Murrell, Puebla/Leon, 91
HRs: Ivan Murrell, Puebla/Leon, 32
Wins: Ernesto Escarrega, Puebla, 16
  Pablo Gutierrez, Puebla, 16
SOs: Luis Mercedes Sanchez, Veracruz, 155
ERA: Gilberto Rondon, Yucatan, 1.44

Six teams did not join the player strike and played a 40-game season.

Standings
	W	L	Pct.	GB	Manager
Saltillo Saraperos	28	11	.718	—	Gregorio Luque
Ciudad Juarez Indios	22	15	.595	5	Jose Guerrero
Coatzacoalcos Azules	18	18	.500	8½	Benjamin Cerda
Union Laguna Diablos Blancos	18	19	.486	9	Jesus Diaz
Reynosa Broncos	14	22	.389	12½	Winston Llenas
Mexico City Tigres	11	26	.297	16	Fernando Remes

Playoffs: None.

*Won first-half   **Won second-half   ***Won both halves
Numbers after nicknames indicate farm system.
Affiliation listed at end of each year.

554

BA: Jimmie Collins, Saltillo, .380
Runs: Roberto Rodriguez, Union Laguna, 29
Hits: Jimmie Collins, Saltillo, 52
RBIs: Jimmie Collins, Saltillo, 31
HRs: Jack Pierce, Coatzacoalcos, 7

Wins: Cardell Camper, Saltillo, 8
SOs: Vicente Romo, Coatzacoalcos, 47
Rafael Garcia, Ciudad Juarez, 47
ERA: Angel Hernandez, Saltillo, 1.13

AAA Pacific Coast League
President: Bill Cutler

North Standings	W	L	Pct.	GB	Attend.	Manager
Vancouver Canadians**(8)	79	60	.568	—	150,758	Bob Didier
Hawaii Islanders*(25)	76	65	.539	4	137,777	Doug Rader
Tacoma Tigers (5)	74	74	.500	9½	191,738	Jim Dusan
Portland Beavers (23)	69	76	.476	13	129,814	Jim Mahoney
Spokane Indians (12)	60	80	.429	19½	148,480	Rene Lachemann

South Standings	W	L	Pct.	GB	Attend.	Manager
Tucson Toros*(18)	87	59	.596	—	207,591	Jimmy Johnson
Albuquerque Dukes**(19)	85	62	.578	2½	192,852	Del Crandall
Salt Lake City Gulls (3)	77	65	.542	8	203,346	Moose Stubing
Ogden A's (11)	59	83	.415	26	76,336	Jose Pagan
Phoenix Giants (26)	53	95	.358	35	173,957	Rocky Bridges

Playoffs: Hawaii 2 games, Vancouver 1; Albuquerque 2 games, Tucson 0.
Finals: Albuquerque 3 games, Hawaii 2.

All-Star Team: 1B-Danny Heep, Tucson; **2B**-Jack Perconte, Albuquerque; **3B**-Dave Edler, Spokane; **SS**-Charles Baker, Hawaii; **OF**-Robert Mitchell, Albuquerque; Gary Rajsich, Tucson; Luis Salazar, Portland/Hawaii; **C**-Tony Pena, Portland; **DH**-Gary Gray, Tacoma; **P**-Dennis Lewallyn, Albuquerque; Mickey Mahler, Portland; **MVP**-Dennis Lewallyn, Albuquerque; **Manager**-Jimmy Johnson, Tucson.

BA: Danny Heep, Tucson, .343
Runs: Tack Wilson, Albuquerque, 110
Hits: John Harris, Salt Lake City, 172
RBIs: Alan Knicely, Tucson, 105
HRs: Tim Hosley, Ogden, 26

Wins: Ralph Botting, Salt Lake City, 15
Gerald Hannahs, Albuquerque, 15
Dennis Lewallyn, Albuquerque, 15
Dave Stewart, Albuquerque, 15
SOs: Mickey Mahler, Portland, 140
ERA: Dennis Lewallyn, Albuquerque, 2.13

AA Eastern League
President: P. Patrick McKernan

North Standings	W	L	Pct.	GB	Attend.	Manager
Holyoke Millers**(8)	78	61	.561	—	65,036	Lee Sigman
Buffalo Bisons*(23)	67	70	.489	10	130,674	Steve Demeter
Lynn Sailors (12)	66	71	.482	11	50,786	Bobby Floyd
Glens Falls White Sox (4)	63	74	.460	14	84,472	Mike Pazik

South Standings	W	L	Pct.	GB	Attend.	Manager
Bristol Red Sox (2)	79	60	.568	—	65,991	Tony Torchia
Reading Phillies**(22)	78	61	.561	1	97,235	Ron Clark
Waterbury Reds*(17)	75	64	.540	4	54,807	Mike Compton
West Haven White Caps (11)	47	92	.338	32	30,112	Ed Nottle

Playoffs: Holyoke 2 games, Buffalo 0; Waterbury 2 games, Reading 0.
Finals: Holyoke 2 games, Waterbury 1.

All-Star Team: 1B-Hediberto Vargas, Buffalo; **2B**-Steven Curry, Reading; **3B**-Nick Esasky, Waterbury; **SS**-Ryne Sandberg, Reading; **OF**-Kevin Bass, Holyoke; Bob Dernier, Reading; David Green, Holyoke; Randall Johnson, Glens Falls; **C**-Junior Ortiz, Buffalo; **DH**-Alfredo Torres, Buffalo; Ossie Virgil, Reading; **P**-Mark Davis, Reading; Jose Brito, Waterbury; **MVP**-Mark Davis, Reading; **Manager**-Lee Sigman, Holyoke.

BA: Junior Oritz, Buffalo, .346
Runs: Bob Dernier, Reading, 111
Hits: Junior Ortiz, Buffalo, 178
RBIs: Ossie Virgil, Reading, 104

HRs: Nick Esasky, Waterbury, 30
Wins: Mark Davis, Reading, 19
SOs: Mark Davis, Reading, 185
ERA: Mark Davis, Reading, 2.47

AA Southern League
President: Billy Hitchcock

East Standings	W	L	Pct.	GB	Attend.	Manager
Savannah Braves**(15)	77	67	.535	—	88,326	Eddie Haas
Columbus Astros (18)	76	68	.528	1	123,173	Matt Galante
Charlotte O's*(1)	72	72	.500	5	198,528	Jimmy Williams
Orlando Twins (9)	65	78	.455	11½	49,801	Roy McMillan
Jacksonville Suns (7)	63	81	.438	14	133,218	Gene Lamont

West Standings	W	L	Pct.	GB	Attend.	Manager
Nashville Sounds**(10)	97	46	.678	—	575,676	Stump Merrill
Memphis Chicks*(20)	83	61	.576	14½	322,037	Larry Bearnarth
Montgomery Rebels (6)	68	76	.472	29½	81,168	Roy Majtyka
Chattanooga Lookouts (5)	61	83	.424	36½	132,338	Woody Smith
Knoxville Blue Jays (14)	57	87	.396	40½	56,927	Duane Larson

Playoffs: Charlotte 3 games, Savannah 0; Memphis 3 games, Nashville 1.
Finals: Charlotte 3 games, Memphis 1.

All-Star Team: 1B-Steve Balboni, Nashville; **2B**-Pat Tabler, Nashville; **3B**-Cal Ripken, Jr., Charlotte; **SS**-Onix Concepcion, Jacksonville; **OF**-Drungo Hazewood, Charlotte; Pat Rooney, Memphis; Buck Showalter, Nashville; **C**-Chris Bando, Chattanooga; **DH**-Eddie Gates, Montgomery; **Util**-John Ray, Columbus; **P**-Andy McGaffigan, Nashville; Ron Meredith, Columbus; **Manager**-Stump Merrill, Nashville.

BA: Chris Bando, Chattanooga, .349
Runs: Steve Balboni, Nashville, 101
Hits: Buck Showalter, Nashville, 178
RBIs: Steve Balboni, Nashville, 122

HRs: Steve Balboni, Nashville, 34
Wins: Jim MacDonald, Columbus, 17
SOs: Steve Bedrosian, Savannah, 161
ERA: Andy McGaffigan, Nashville, 2.38

AA Texas League
President: Carl Sawatski

East Standings	W	L	Pct.	GB	Attend.	Manager
Arkansas Travelers (24)	81	55	.596	—	216,592	Sonny Ruberto
Tulsa Drillers (13)	75	61	.551	6	58,020	Wayne Terwilliger
Jackson Mets (21)	74	62	.544	7	98,833	Bob Wellman
Shreveport Captains (26)	49	87	.360	32	40,380	Andy Gilbert

West Standings	W	L	Pct.	GB	Attend.	Manager
Amarillo Gold Sox (25)	77	59	.566	—	70,097	Eddie Watt
San Antonio Dodgers (19)	74	62	.544	3	153,355	Don LeJohn
Midland Cubs (16)	64	72	.471	13	95,820	Randy Hundley/ Les Moss/George Enright
El Paso Diablos (3)	50	86	.368	27	265,062	Jim Saul

Playoffs: Arkansas 2 games, Jackson 0; San Antonio 2 games, Amarillo 0.
Finals: Arkansas 3 games, San Antonio 0.

All-Star Team: 1B-Daryl Sconiers, El Paso; **2B**-Scott Fletcher, Midland; **3B**-Jim Riggleman, Arkansas; **SS**-Wayne Tolleson, Tulsa; **OF**-Mel Barrow, Tulsa; Mike Bishop, El Paso; Tom Brunansky, El Paso; **C/DH**-Frank Hunsaker, Arkansas; **Util**-Phil Klimas, Tulsa; **P**-Daniel Boone, Amarillo; Luis DeLeon, Arkansas; Jerry Don Gleaton, Tulsa; Tim Leary, Jackson; **MVP**-Tim Leary, Jackson; **Manager**-Bob Wellman, Jackson.

BA: Daryl Sconiers, El Paso, .370
Runs: Scott Fletcher, Midland, 111
Hits: Daryl Sconiers, El Paso, 187
RBIs: Mike Bishop, El Paso, 104
HRs: Mike Bishop, El Paso, 33

Wins: Tim Leary, Jackson, 15
Brian Holton, San Antonio, 15
SOs: Fernando Valenzuela, San Antonio, 162
ERA: Billy Joe Edelen, Arkansas, 2.62

A California League
President: E.W. "Bill" Wickert

North Standings	W	L	Pct.	GB	Attend.	Manager
Stockton Ports***(8)	90	51	.638	—	80,790	Tony Muser
Modesto A's (11)	74	65	.532	15	65,614	Keith Lieppman
Reno Silver Sox (25)	75	66	.532	15	50,108	Jack Maloof
Lodi Dodgers (19)	57	83	.407	32½	49,570	Dick McLaughlin
Redwood Pioneers# (x)	55	85	.393	34½	55,686	Barry Woodhead

South Standings	W	L	Pct.	GB	Attend.	Manager
Fresno Giants*(26)	74	66	.529	—	85,929	Jack Mull
San Jose Missions (12)	73	66	.525	½	58,132	Bill Plummer
Visalia Oaks**(9)	71	69	.507	3	39,690	Tom Kelly
Salinas Angels (3)	61	79	.436	13	47,017	Tom Zimmer

#represented Rohnert park, California.

Playoff: Visalia 2 games, Fresno 0.
Finals: Stockton 3 games, Visalia 0.

All-Star Team: 1B-Stan Davis, Stockton; **2B**-Ricky McMullen, Reno; **3B**-Jack Hanley, Redwood; **SS**-John Stevenson, Reno; **OF**-Al Chambers, San Jose; Ramon Estepa, San Jose; Candy Maldonado, Lodi; **C**-James Durman, Modesto; **DH**-James Bennett, Modesto; **P**-Jaime Cocanower, Stockton; Phil Hinrichs, Fresno; Jim Koontz, Stockton; Scott Stranski, San Jose; **MVP**-Jaime Cocanower, Stockton; Candy Maldonado, Lodi; **Manager**-Tom Kelly, Visalia; Jack Mull, Fresno.

BA: Chris Flammang, San Jose, .348
Runs: Bobby Garrett, Modesto, 117
Hits: Ed Irvine, Stockton, 177
RBIs: Candy Maldonado, Lodi, 102
HRs: Greg Brock, Lodi, 29

SBs: Alan Wiggins, Lodi, 120
Wins: Scott Stranski, San Jose, 18
SOs: Brad Havens, Visalia, 179
ERA: Mike Madden, Stockton, 1.95

A Carolina League
President: James B. Mills

North Carolina Standings	W	L	Pct.	GB	Attend.	Manager
Durham Bulls***(15)	84	56	.600	—	175,963	Al Gallagher
Winston-Salem Red Sox (2)	76	64	.543	8	84,645	Buddy Hunter
Kinston Eagles (14)	69	69	.500	14	38,822	Dennis Holmberg
Rocky Mount Pines	24	114	.174	59	26,702	Mal Fichman

Virginia Standings	W	L	Pct.	GB	Attend.	Manager
Peninsula Pilots***(22)	100	40	.714	—	75,874	Bill Dancy
Salem Pirates (23)	79	60	.568	20½	102,456	John Lipon
Lynchburg Mets (21)	71	68	.511	28½	66,207	Jack Aker
Alexandria Dukes	54	86	.386	46	30,140	Mike Toomey

Playoff: Peninsula 3 games, Durham 1.

All-Star Team: 1B-Mike Anicich, Lynchburg; **2B**-Bill Rittweger, Lynchburg; **3B**-Ray Borucki, Peninsula; **SS**-Julio Franco, Peninsula; **OF**-Wilfred Culmer, Peninsula; Joe Bruno, Peninsula; Albert Hall, Durham; **DH**-Rico Colbert, Winston-Salem; **P**-Wally Goff, Winston-Salem; Jay Fredlund, Winston-Salem; **MVP**-Julio Franco, Peninsula; **Pitcher of the Year**-LeRoy Smith, Peninsula; **Manager**-John Lipon, Salem.

BA: Wilfred Culmer, Peninsula, .369
Runs: Wilfred Culmer, Peninsula, 112
Hits: Wilfred Culmer, Peninsula, 184
RBIs: Julio Franco, Peninsula, 99

HRs: Craig Brooks, Winston-Salem, 24
Wins: LeRoy Smith, Peninsula, 17
SOs: Don Carman, Peninsula, 141
ERA: Jim Wright, Peninsula, 1.85

A Florida State League
President: George MacDonald, Jr.

North Standings	W	L	Pct.	GB	Attend.	Manager
Daytona Beach Astros (18)	86	51	.628	—	58,162	Carlos Alfonso
St. Petersburg Cardinals (24)	70	66	.515	15½	124,350	Tommy Thompson
Tampa Tarpons (17)	64	67	.489	19	87,660	George Scherger
Winter Haven Red Sox (2)	60	80	.429	27½	25,771	Rac Slider
Lakeland Tigers (6)	56	77	.421	28	46,001	Eddie Brinkman

South Standings	W	L	Pct.	GB	Attend.	Manager
Ft. Lauderdale Yankees (10)	83	54	.605	—	78,447	Doug Holmquist
Vero Beach Dodgers (19)	82	59	.582	3	80,063	Stan Wasiak
Ft. Myers Royals (7)	66	70	.485	16½	55,927	Brian Murphy
West Palm Beach Expos (20)	64	73	.467	19	118,452	Bob Bailey
Miami Orioles (1)	51	85	.375	31½	44,368	Lance Nichols

Playoffs: Vero Beach 2 games, Daytona Beach 0; Ft. Lauderdale 2 games, St. Petersburg 1.
Finals: Ft. Lauderdale 3 games, Vero Beach 1.

BA: Wallace Johnson, West Palm Beach, .334
Runs: Mark Strucher, Daytona Beach, 88
Hits: Wallace Johnson, West Palm Beach, 163
RBIs: German Rivera, Vero Beach, 80
HRs: Mark Strucher, Daytona Beach, 17
Wins: Gene Nelson, Ft. Lauderdale, 20
SOs: Charles Wickensheimer, Vero Beach, 162
ERA: Mike Dowless, Tampa, 1.68

A Midwest League
President: Bill Walters

North Standings	W	L	Pct.	GB	Attend.	Manager
Waterloo Indians*(5)	86	55	.610	—	72,606	Cal Emery
Appleton Foxes (4)	76	63	.547	9	74,207	Gordon Lund
Wisconsin Rapids Twins**(9)	77	64	.546	9	47,899	Rich Stelmaszek
Wausau Timbers (x)	57	82	.410	28	37,175	Orlando Martinez

South Standings	W	L	Pct.	GB	Attend.	Manager
Quad City Cubs*(16)	74	65	.532	—	103,445	Jim Napier
Burlington Bees**(8)	70	72	.493	5½	51,486	Duane Espy
Clinton Giants (26)	62	59	.440	13	58,723	Wayne Cato
Cedar Rapids Reds (17)	59	81	.421	15½	84,062	Jim Lett

Playoffs: Waterloo 2 games, Wisconsin Rapids 1; Quad City 2 games, Burlington 1.
Finals: Waterloo 2 games, Quad City 1.

All-Star Team: 1B-Greg Walker, Appleton; 2B-Jim Christensen, Wisconsin Rapids; 3B-Von Hayes, Waterloo; SS-Escamillo Viltz, Cedar Rapids; OF-Keith Brown, Appleton; Joe Kubit, Wisconsin Rapids; Stan Levi, Burlington; C-Bob Cummings, Clinton; DH-Ron Kittle, Appleton; P-Carlos Gil, Quad City; Bob Konopa, Wisconsin Rapids; Mike Thompson, Quad City; Dennis Vasquez, Appleton; MVP-Von Hayes, Waterloo; Manager-Rich Stelmaszek, Wisconsin Rapids.

BA: Von Hayes, Waterloo, .329
Runs: Ricky Baker, Waterloo, 108
Hits: Von Hayes, Waterloo, 162
RBIs: Greg Walker, Appleton, 98
HRs: Gary Gaetti, Wisconsin Rapids, 22
Wins: Bob Konopa, Wisconsin Rapids, 17
SOs: Scott Garrelts, Clinton, 159
ERA: Bengie Biggus, Burlington, 2.27

A New York-Pennsylvania League
President: Vincent M. McNamara

East Standings	W	L	Pct.	GB	Attend.	Manager
Oneonta Yankees (10)	49	25	.662	—	35,500	Art Mazmanian
Little Falls Mets (21)	40	33	.548	8½	18,840	Danny Monzon
Elmira Pioneers (2)	39	35	.527	10	56,912	Dick Berardino
Utica Blue Jays (14)	27	44	.380	20½	17,179	Larry Hardy

West Standings	W	L	Pct.	GB	Attend.	Manager
Geneva Cubs (16)	48	26	.649	—	20,970	Bob Hartsfield
Batavia Trojans (5)	31	42	.425	16½	29,670	Rick Colzie
Jamestown Expos (20)	29	42	.408	17½	48,078	Pat Daugherty
Auburn Phillies (x)	29	45	.392	19	9,474	Bill Julio

Playoff: Oneonta 2 games, Geneva 1.

All-Star Team: 1B-Tony Stevens, Elmira; 2B-Ron Oddo, Elmira; 3B-Jeff Reynolds, Oneonta; SS-Dave Hoeksema, Jamestown; OF-Michael Ciampa, Elmira; Roger Frash, Little Falls; James Glenn, Elmira; Roy Johnson, Jamestown; C-Kevin Shannon, Oneonta; Wayne Rohlfing, Geneva; DH-Richard Poe, Little Falls; Util-Luis Guzman, Utica; P-Oil Can Boyd, Elmira; Joe Housey, Geneva; Craig Lefferts, Geneva; Kevin Spicer, Little Falls; Manager-Bob Hartsfield, Geneva.

BA: Roger Frash, Little Falls, .346
Runs: Michael Ciampa, Elmira, 59
Hits: Russ Piggott, Geneva, 85
RBIs: Jeff Reynolds, Oneonta, 56
HRs: Tony Stevens, Elmira, 15
Wins: Joe Housey, Geneva, 10
Kevin Spicer, Little Falls, 10
SOs: Craig Lefferts, Geneva, 99
ERA: Joe Housey, Geneva, 1.50

A Northwest League
President: Bob Richmond

North Standings	W	L	Pct.	GB	Attend.	Manager
Bellingham Mariners (12)	45	25	.643	—	42,292	Jeff Scott
Victoria Mussels (25)	42	28	.600	3	11,127	Jim Gaddis
Walla Walla Padres (25)	35	34	.507	9½	15,118	Curt Daniels
Grays Harbor Loggers	33	36	.478	11½	20,020	Bill Bryk

South Standings	W	L	Pct.	GB	Attend.	Manager
Eugene Emeralds (17)	37	33	.529	—	96,058	Greg Riddoch
Salem Senators	34	36	.486	3	35,268	Randy Lamb
Central Oregon Phillies (22)	31	39	.443	6	28,486	P.J. Carey
Medford A's (11)	22	48	.314	15	27,118	Brad Fischer

Playoff: Bellingham 1 game, Eugene 1, declared co-winners when rain cancelled the rest of the series.

All-Star Team: 1B-Monte McAbee, Central Oregon; 2B-Juan Samuel, Central Oregon; Paul Serna, Bellingham; 3B-Kevin McGann, Bellingham; SS-Rod Murphy, Victoria; OF-Ron Little, Eugene; George Perez, Walla Walla; Crestwell Pratt, Eugene; C-Jerry Willard, Central Oregon; DH-Willie Darkis, Central Oregon; P-Mike Couchee, Grays Harbor; William Johnson, Central Oregon; Ken Klacza, Victoria; Jeff Stottlemyre, Bellingham; Ed Vandeberg, Bellingham; Manager-Jeff Scott, Bellingham.

BA: George Perez, Walla Walla, .377
Runs: Aaron Cain, Grays Harbor, 69
Hits: George Perez, Walla Walla, 93
RBIs: Willie Darkis, Central Oregon, 73
HRs: Willie Darkis, Central Oregon, 25
Wins: Ken Klacza, Victoria, 11
SOs: Brian Duffy, Grays Harbor, 93
ERA: Neil Bryant, Walla Walla, 2.51

A South Atlantic League
President: John H. Moss

North Standings	W	L	Pct.	GB	Attend.	Manager
Greensboro Hornets***(10)	82	57	.590	—	255,130	Bob Schaefer
Gastonia Cardinals (24)	74	66	.529	8½	90,198	Nick Leyva
Asheville Tourists (13)	69	71	.493	13½	49,066	Tom Robson
Shelby Pirates (23)	58	80	.420	23½	15,393	Joe Frisina

South Standings	W	L	Pct.	GB	Attend.	Manager
Charleston Royals***(7)	78	61	.561	—	109,191	Ron Mihal
Spartanburg Phillies (22)	73	65	.529	4½	35,480	Tom Harmon
Anderson Braves (15)	64	76	.457	14½	40,836	Sonny Jackson
Macon Peaches (x)	59	81	.421	19½	56,671	Brock Pemberton/ Brannon Bonifay/Ted Brazell

Playoffs: Greensboro 2 games, Gastonia 1; Charleston 2 games, Spartanburg 1.
Finals: Greensboro 3 games, Charleston 0.

All-Star Team: 1B-Pete O'Brien, Asheville; 2B-Mike Wolters, Gastonia; 3B-Otis Nixon, Greensboro; SS-John Lindsey, Spartanburg; Miguel Sosa, Anderson; OF-Brook Jacoby, Anderson; Don Mattingly, Greensboro; Alejandro Sanchez, Spartanburg; Marvell Wynne, Charleston; C-Don Scott, Asheville; DH-Matt Winters, Greensboro; Util-James Scranton, Charleston; P-Scott Arigoni, Gastonia; Byron Ballard, Greensboro; Matt Guante, Shelby; Brian Murphy, Greensboro; Manager-Bob Schaefer, Greensboro.

BA: Don Mattingly, Greensboro, .358
Runs: Otis Nixon, Greensboro, 124
Hits: Don Mattingly, Greensboro, 177
RBIs: Brook Jacoby, Anderson, 108
HRs: Dave Kable, Gastonia, 26
Wins: Byron Ballard, Greensboro, 17
SOs: Ron Krauss, Charleston, 150
ERA: Ralph Citarella, Gastonia, 1.64

R Appalachian League
President: Paul Fyffe

Standings	W	L	Pct.	GB	Attend.	Manager
Paintsville Yankees (10)	46	24	.657	—	17,404	Mike Easom
Bristol Tigers (6)	36	33	.522	9½	12,300	Tom Kotchman
Kingsport Mets (21)	35	35	.500	11	35,730	Chuck Hiller
Elizabethton Twins (9)	32	36	.471	13	10,974	Fred Waters
Bluefield Orioles (1)	29	39	.426	16	24,413	Grady Little
Johnson City Cardinals (24)	29	40	.420	16½	26,887	Johnny Lewis

Playoffs: None.

All-Star Team: 1B-Ken Foster, Elizabethton; 2B-John Milholland, Paintsville; 3B-Luis Ojeda, Johnson City; SS-Mike Harris, Johnson City; OF-Jim Eisenreich, Elizabethton; John Heller, Kingsport; Matt Vejar, Paintsville; Jeff Williams, Bluefield; C-Emilio Carrasquel, Bristol; DH-Erik Peterson, Paintsville; Util-Larry Pittman, Kingsport; P-John Gaston, Paintsville; Scott Johnson, Bluefield; Manager-Tom Kotchman, Bristol.

BA: Erik Peterson, Paintsville, .379
Runs: Matt Vejar, Paintsville, 59
Hits: Matt Vejar, Paintsville, 91
RBIs: Ken Foster, Elizabethton, 55
HRs: Larry Sheets, Bluefield, 14
Wins: John Gaston, Paintsville, 8
Doug Sisk, Kingsport, 8
Mark Fellows, Bristol, 8
SOs: Mark Fellows, Bristol, 63
ERA: Ben Callahan, Paintsville, 2.38

R Gulf Coast League
President: Thomas J. Saffell

Standings	W	L	Pct.	GB	Manager
Royals Blue (7)	40	23	.635	—	Joe Jones
Astros Blue (18)	38	24	.613	1½	Eric Swanson
Braves (15)	37	25	.597	2½	Pedro Gonzalez
Rangers (13)	35	28	.556	5	Andy Hancock
Astros Orange (18)	34	28	.548	5½	Fernando Tatis
Cubs (16)	33	29	.532	6½	Rich Morales
Yankees (10)	27	35	.435	12½	Carlos Tosca
Pirates (23)	24	39	.381	16	Woody Huyke
Royals Gold (7)	22	40	.355	17½	Roy Tanner
White Sox (4)	22	41	.349	18	Duane Shaffer

Games played at Sarasota and Bradenton, Florida.
Total Attendance: 10,680

Playoffs: None.

All-Star Team: 1B-Charles Barclift, Royals Gold; Wesley Clements, Astros Orange; **2B**-Wade McKinney, Royals Gold; Bill Weems, Astros Blue; **3B**-David Stokes, Rangers; Dennis Cleveland, Astros Blue; **SS**-Gary D'Onofrio, Astros Blue; Mike Morse, White Sox; **OF**-Mark Bonner, Braves; Wallace Davis, Royals Blue; Sergio DeSena, Astros Orange; Cecil Espy, White Sox; Dan O'Regan, Yankees; Marc Thomas, Astros Blue; **C**-Thomas Colburn, Rangers; David Sullivan, Astros Blue; **Util**-Pedro Medina, Yankees; Dale Weaver, Braves; **P**-Junior Cooper, Royals Blue; Roberto Yan, Astros Orange; **Manager**-Joe Jones, Royals Blue.

BA: Marc Thomas, Astros Blue, .338
Runs: Bill Weems, Astros Blue, 52
Hits: Wallace Davis, Royals Blue, 74
RBIs: Tom Johnson, Cubs, 42
HRs: Bert Gjesdal, Yankees, 7

Wins: Junior Cooper, Royals Blue, 8
Bert Johnson, Royals Blue, 8
SOs: Mike Mason, Rangers, 55
ERA: Scott Eichholz, Cubs, 1.15

R Pioneer League
President: Ralph C. Nelles

North Standings	W	L	Pct.	GB	Attend.	Manager
Lethbridge Dodgers (19)	52	18	.743	—	27,044	Gail Henley
Great Falls Giants (26)	49	21	.700	3	68,003	Ernest Rodriguez
Calgary Expos (20).............	23	46	.333	28½	26,317	Steve Boros
Medicine Hat Blue Jays (14)...	16	54	.229	36	15,700	John McLaren

South Standings	W	L	Pct.	GB	Attend.	Manager
Billings Mustangs (17)	44	26	.629	—	58,464	Jim Hoff
Idaho Falls Angels (3)	34	36	.486	10	37,646	Reuben Rodriguez
Helena Phillies (22)	32	38	.457	12	18,888	Rollie DeArmas
Butte Copper Kings (8).......	29	40	.420	14½	29,410	Ken Richardson

Playoff: Lethbridge 2 games, Billings 1.

All-Star Team: 1B-Greg Smith, Lethbridge; **2B**-Randy Ready, Butte; **3B**-Danny Tartabull, Billings; **SS**-Michael Foote, Billings; **OF**-Dion James, Butte; John McGaffey, Idaho Falls; Jessie Reid, Great Falls; **C**-Randy Gomez, Great Falls; **DH**-Audie Cole, Lethbridge; **P**-Mark Dempsey, Great Falls; Tom Layton, Billings; Curtis Reade, Lethbridge; **Manager**-Gail Henley, Lethbridge.

BA: Randy Ready, Butte, .376
Runs: Randy Ready, Butte, 65
Hits: Greg Smith, Lethbridge, 99
RBIs: Gerard Miller, Butte, 67

HRs: Gerard Miller, Butte, 9
Wins: Mark Dempsey, Great Falls, 14
SOs: Charles Jones, Lethbridge, 115
ERA: Mark Dempsey, Great Falls, 1.58

1980 Interleague Post Season Play

World Series
Philadelphia (National) 4 games, Kansas City (American) 2

1980 Major League Farm Systems

American League
1. Baltimore (4): Rochester, Charlotte, Miami, Bluefield.
2. Boston (5): Pawtucket, Bristol (CT), Winston-Salem, Winter Haven, Elmira.
3. California (4): Salt Lake City, El Paso, Salinas, Idaho Falls.
4. Chicago (4): Iowa, Glens Falls, Appleton, Gulf Coast.
5. Cleveland (4): Tacoma, Chattanooga, Waterloo, Batavia.
6. Detroit (4): Evansville, Montgomery, Lakeland, Bristol (VA).
7. Kansas City (6): Omaha, Jacksonville, Ft. Myers, Charleston (SC), Gulf Coast Blue, Gulf Coast Gold.
8. Milwaukee (5): Vancouver, Holyoke, Stockton, Burlington, Butte.
9. Minnesota (5): Toledo, Orlando, Visalia, Wisconsin Rapids, Elizabethton.
10. New York (7): Columbus (OH), Nashville, Ft. Lauderdale, Greensboro, Oneonta, Paintsville, Gulf Coast.
11. Oakland (4): Ogden, West Haven, Modesto, Medford.
12. Seattle (4): Spokane, Lynn, San Jose, Bellingham.
13. Texas (4): Charleston (WV), Tulsa, Asheville, Gulf Coast.
14. Toronto (5): Syracuse, Knoxville, Kinston, Utica, Medicine Hat.

National League
15. Atlanta (5): Richmond, Savannah, Durham, Anderson, Gulf Coast.
16. Chicago (5): Wichita, Midland, Quad City, Geneva, Gulf Coast.
17. Cincinnati (6): Indianapolis, Waterbury, Tampa, Cedar Rapids, Eugene, Billings.
18. Houston (5): Tucson, Columbus (GA), Daytona Beach, Gulf Coast Blue, Gulf Coast Orange.
19. Los Angeles (5): Albuquerque, San Antonio, Lodi, Vero Beach, Lethbridge.
20. Montreal (5): Denver, Memphis, West Palm Beach, Jamestown, Calgary.
21. New York (5): Tidewater, Jackson, Lynchburg, Little Falls, Kingsport.
22. Philadelphia (6): Oklahoma City, Reading, Peninsula, Central Oregon, Spartanburg, Helena.
23. Pittsburgh (5): Portland, Buffalo, Salem (VA), Shelby, Gulf Coast.
24. St. Louis (5): Springfield, Arkansas, St. Petersburg, Gastonia, Johnson City.
25. San Diego (4): Hawaii, Amarillo, Reno, Walla Walla.
26. San Francisco (5): Phoenix, Shreveport, Fresno, Clinton, Great Falls.

Co-op (x): Redwood, Wausau, Auburn, Macon.
Independent: Rocky Mount, Alexandria, Victoria, Grays Harbor, Salem (OR).

1980 No-Hitters

Date	Pitcher	Team	League	Opponent	Score
4-16	Wayne Guinn/Steve Daniels/				
	Mark Moore	Cedar Rapids	Midwest	Quad City	2-0 (11)
4-23	Rick Rhoden	Portland	Pacific Coast	Phoenix	1-0 (7)
4-25	Pete Filson	Greensboro	South Atlantic	Gastonia	4-0 (7)
5-20	Joe Henderson	Coatzacoalcos	Mexican	Monterrey	3-0
5-22	Mike Dowless	Tampa	Florida State	Ft. Myers	4-0 (7)
6-4	Jerry Stovall	Clinton	Midwest	Wausau	2-0 (7)
6-7	Dane Anthony	Waterloo	Midwest	Appleton	3-0 (7)
6-8	Frank DiPino	Holyoke	Eastern	Reading	6-0 (7)
6-24	Brian Snyder	San Jose	California	Modesto	4-0
6-27	Jerry Reuss	Los Angeles	National	San Francisco	8-0
7-3	Kevin Keefe	Albuquerque	Pacific Coast	Tucson	0-1 (8)
7-10	Frank Cutty/				
	Mark Huismann	Royals Blue	Gulf Coast	Astros Blue	4-0
7-16	David LaBounty	Pirates	Gulf Coast	Cubs	2-0
7-27	Matt Sutherland	Fresno	California	Lodi	1-2 (8)
7-28	Rafael Vazquez/				
	Rick Horton	Gastonia	South Atlantic	Charleston	4-0 (7)
7-29	Chris Willsher	Bluefield	Appalachian	Johnson City	13-0 (7)
8-17	Robert Madden/				
	Mark Lemongello	Wichita	American Assoc.	Iowa	5-2
8-21	Michael Otto	Victoria	Northwest	Grays Harbor	3-0 (7)
8-24	Larry McCall	Tacoma	Pacific Coast	Spokane	1-0 (7)
8-26	Larry Williams	Ft. Myers	Florida State	West Palm Beach	5-0
8-29	Rick Behenna	Durham	Carolina	Rocky Mount	8-0

Number in parentheses indicates innings if other than nine.

THIS DATE IN MINOR LEAGUE HISTORY

April 24, 1980, Hector Espino, Union Laguna, set a Mexican League record with eleven consecutive hits in a three-game series against Leon.

June 14, 1980, Spokane, Pacific Coast League, stole ten bases against Vancouver.

June 18, 1980, Tom Brunansky, El Paso, Texas League, hit four consecutive homers and drove in nine runs to lead the Diablos to a 19-9 romp past Midland.

June 18, 1980, Pitcher Tom Lewis, Alexandria, Carolina League, struck out 20 in a 7-1 victory over Winston-Salem.

July 1, 1980, The Reno Silver Sox routed Visalia 25-3 in a California League game. Shortstop John Stevenson collected seven hits for Reno.

July 3, 1980, A newly formed players' union struck, halting Mexican League play. Six teams, not part of the union, continued play with a new 40 game schedule.

July 17, 1980, After hitting in 35 straight games, Spokane's Kim Allen was stopped by Ogden pitcher John Sutton.

July 30, 1980, Lethbridge set a Pioneer League record with its 19th successive victo-ry, defeating Idaho Falls 17-3.

July 30, 1980, In the wildest one-inning scoring spree in American Association history, Evansville erupted for 17 runs in the fourth inning on their way to a 20-3 romp over Iowa.

August 17, 1980, Clarence "Hooks" Iott, great minor league pitcher, died in St. Petersburg, Florida at the age of 60.

August 26, 1980, The Medicine Hat Blue Jays set a Pioneer League record for futility when they lost their 19th successive game. The club would end the season with a 16-54 record.

August 31, 1980, Lodi's Alan Wiggins became the modern stolen base king in the minor leagues as he finished the year with 120 steals in the California League. He broke the old mark of 116 set by Allan Lewis in the Florida State League in 1966. The all-time mark of 124 steals was set by Jim Johnston of San Francisco in the PCL in 1913. Johnston played in 190 games compared to Wiggins' 135.

September 2, 1980, Columbus set a modern International League attendance record by drawing 546,074 fans for the season.

1981

American League

President: Leland S. MacPhail, Jr.

East Standings	W	L	Pct.	GB	Attend.	Manager
Milwaukee Brewers**	62	47	.569	—	874,292	Buck Rodgers
Baltimore Orioles	59	46	.562	1	1,024,247	Earl Weaver
New York Yankees*	59	48	.551	2	1,614,353	Gene Michael/Bob Lemon
Detroit Tigers	60	49	.550	2	1,149,144	Sparky Anderson
Boston Red Sox	59	49	.546	2½	1,060,379	Ralph Houk
Cleveland Indians	52	51	.505	7	661,395	Dave Garcia
Toronto Blue Jays	37	69	.349	23½	755,083	Bobby Mattick

West Standings	W	L	Pct.	GB	Attend.	Manager
Oakland Athletics*	64	45	.587	—	1,304,052	Billy Martin
Texas Rangers	57	48	.543	5	850,076	Don Zimmer
Chicago White Sox	54	52	.509	8½	946,651	Tony LaRussa
Kansas City Royals**	50	53	.485	11	1,279,403	Jim Frey/Dick Howser
California Angels	51	59	.464	13½	1,441,545	Jim Fregosi/Gene Mauch
Seattle Mariners	44	65	.404	20	636,276	Maury Wills/Rene Lachemann
Minnesota Twins	41	68	.376	23	469,090	John Goryl/Billy Gardner

Playoffs: New York 3 games, Milwaukee 2; Oakland 3 games, Kansas City 0.
Finals: New York 3 games, Oakland 0.

BA: Carney Lansford, Boston, .336
Runs: Rickey Henderson, Oakland, 89
Hits: Rickey Henderson, Oakland, 135
RBIs: Eddie Murray, Baltimore, 78
HRs: Tony Armas, Oakland, 22
Dwight Evans, Boston, 22
Bobby Grich, California, 22
Eddie Murray, Baltimore, 22

Wins: Dennis Martinez, Baltimore, 14
Steve McCatty, Oakland, 14
Jack Morris, Detroit, 14
Pete Vuckovich, Milwaukee, 14
SOs: Len Barker, Cleveland, 127
ERA: Steve McCatty, Oakland, 2.32
Pct: Pete Vuckovich, Milwaukee, .778, 14-4
Saves: Rollie Fingers, Milwaukee, 28

National League

President: Charles S. Feeney

East Standings	W	L	Pct.	GB	Attend.	Manager
St. Louis Cardinals	59	43	.578	—	1,010,247	Whitey Herzog
Montreal Expos**	60	48	.556	2	1,534,564	Dick Williams/Jim Fanning
Philadelphia Phillies*	59	48	.551	2½	1,638,752	Dallas Green
Pittsburgh Pirates	46	56	.451	13	541,789	Chuck Tanner
New York Mets	41	62	.398	18½	704,244	Joe Torre
Chicago Cubs	38	65	.369	21½	565,637	Joey Amalfitano

West Standings	W	L	Pct.	GB	Attend.	Manager
Cincinnati Reds	66	42	.611	—	1,093,791	John McNamara
Los Angeles Dodgers*	63	47	.573	4	2,381,292	Tom Lasorda
Houston Astros**	61	49	.555	6	1,321,282	Bill Virdon
San Francisco Giants	56	55	.505	11½	632,274	Frank Robinson
Atlanta Braves	50	56	.472	15	535,418	Bobby Cox
San Diego Padres	41	69	.373	26	519,161	Frank Howard

Playoffs: Montreal 3 games, Philadelphia 2; Los Angeles 3 games, Houston 2.
Finals: Los Angeles 3 games, Montreal 2.

BA: Bill Madlock, Pittsburgh, .341
Runs: Mike Schmidt, Philadelphia, 78
Hits: Pete Rose, Philadelphia, 140
RBIs: Mike Schmidt, Philadelphia, 91
HRs: Mike Schmidt, Philadelphia, 31

Wins: Tom Seaver, Cincinnati, 14
SOs: Fernando Valenzuela, Los Angeles, 180
ERA: Nolan Ryan, Houston, 1.69
Pct: Tom Seaver, Cincinnati, .875, 14-2
Saves: Bruce Sutter, St. Louis, 25

AAA American Association

President: Joe Ryan

East Standings	W	L	Pct.	GB	Attend.	Manager
Evansville Triplets (6)	73	63	.537	—	113,167	Jim Leyland
Springfield Redbirds (24)	66	70	.485	7	120,537	Tommy Thompson
Indianapolis Indians (17)	62	74	.456	11	205,220	Jim Beauchamp
Iowa Oaks (16)	53	82	.393	19½	124,371	Randy Hundley/Roy Hartsfield

West Standings	W	L	Pct.	GB	Attend.	Manager
Omaha Royals (7)	79	57	.581	—	196,924	Joe Sparks
Denver Bears (20)	76	60	.559	3	555,806	Felipe Alou
Oklahoma City 89ers (22)	69	67	.507	10	191,502	Jim Snyder
Wichita Aeros (13)	65	70	.481	13½	122,371	Rich Donnelly

Playoffs: Denver 3 games, Evansville 1; Omaha 3 games, Springfield 2.
Finals: Denver 4 games, Omaha 0.

All-Star Team: 1B-Dave Hostetler, Denver; 2B-Mike Richardt, Wichita; SS-Ryne Sandberg, Oklahoma City; 3B-Manny Castillo, Omaha; OF-Dan Briggs, Denver; Bob Dernier, Oklahoma City; Terry Francona, Denver; Paul Householder, Indianapolis; C-George Bjorkman, Springfield; Dave van Gorder, Indianapolis; DH-Bob Jones, Wichita; Util-Michael Gates, Denver; Len Matuszek, Oklahoma City; P-Mike Jones, Omaha; Dennis

Lewallyn, Wichita; Jeff Schattinger, Omaha; Bryn Smith, Denver; **MVP**-Manny Castillo, Omaha; **Pitcher of the Year**-Bryn Smith, Denver; **Manager**-Joe Sparks, Omaha.

BA: Mike Richardt, Wichita, .354
Runs: Bob Dernier, Oklahoma City, 105
Hits: Manny Castillo, Omaha, 182
RBIs: Dan Briggs, Denver, 110

HRs: George Bjorkman, Springfield, 28
Wins: Bryn Smith, Denver, 15
SOs: Dave LaPoint, Springfield, 128
ERA: Larry Pashnick, Evansville, 2.64

AAA International League

President: Harold Cooper

Standings	W	L	Pct.	GB	Attend.	Manager
Columbus Clippers (10)	88	51	.633	—	527,124	Frank Verdi
Richmond Braves (15)	83	56	.597	5	218,208	Eddie Haas
Tidewater Tides (21)	70	68	.507	17½	135,001	Jack Aker
Rochester Red Wings (1)	69	70	.496	19	349,341	Doc Edwards
Charleston Charlies (5)	67	72	.482	21	99,537	Cal Emery/Frank Lucchesi
Pawtucket Red Sox (2)	67	73	.479	21½	191,859	Joe Morgan
Syracuse Chiefs (14)	60	80	.429	28½	198,097	Bob Humphreys
Toledo Mud Hens (9)	53	87	.379	35½	170,359	Cal Ermer

Playoffs: Richmond 3 games, Tidewater 2; Columbus 3 games, Rochester 2.
Finals: Columbus 2 games, Richmond 1 (shortened due to rain).

All-Star Team: 1B-Greg "Boomer" Wells, Syracuse; 2B-Brian Giles, Tidewater; SS-Andre Robertson, Columbus; 3B-Cal Ripken, Jr., Rochester; OF-Sam Bowen, Pawtucket; Brett Butler, Richmond; Gary Rajsich, Tidewater; DH-Steve Balboni, Columbus; C-Chris Bando, Charleston; P-Dale Murray, Syracuse; Bob Ojeda, Pawtucket; **MVP**-Brett Butler, Richmond; **Pitcher of the Year**-Bob Ojeda, Pawtucket; **Manager**-Eddie Haas, Richmond.

BA: Wade Boggs, Pawtucket, .335
Runs: Brett Butler, Richmond, 93
Hits: Wade Boggs, Pawtucket, 167
RBIs: Steve Balboni, Columbus, 98
HRs: Steve Balboni, Columbus, 33

Wins: Ken Dayley, Richmond, 13
Larry McWilliams, Richmond, 13
SOs: Ken Dayley, Richmond, 162
ERA: Bob Ojeda, Pawtucket, 2.13

AAA Mexican League

President: Antonio Ramirez Muro

North West Standings	W	L	Pct.	GB	Manager
Saltillo Saraperos	72	52	.581	—	Gregorio Luque
Ciudad Juarez Indios	71	57	.556	3	Jose Guerrero
Union Laguna Diablos Blancos	68	58	.540	5	Felipe Hernandez
Chihuahua Dorados	36	90	.286	37	Jesus Diaz

North East Standings	W	L	Pct.	GB	Manager
Nuevo Laredo Tecolotes	75	50	.600	—	Victor Ramirez
Reynosa Broncos	62	64	.492	13½	Benjamin Valenzuela
Monterrey Sultanes	59	68	.461	17½	Hector Valle/Marcelo Juarez
Aguascalientes Rieleros	57	70	.449	19	Moises Camacho

South West Standings	W	L	Pct.	GB	Manager
Mexico City Tigres	65	56	.537	—	Jose Luis Garcia
Coatzacoalcos Azules	62	60	.508	3½	Jose Leyva/Armando Barajas
Tabasco Plataneros	59	59	.500	4½	Ramon Conde/Hugo Rios
Veracruz Aguila	51	73	.411	15½	Lino Donoso

South East Standings	W	L	Pct.	GB	Manager
Mexico City Diablos Rojos	75	47	.615	—	Winston Llenas
Campeche Piratas	71	50	.587	3½	Juan Ramon Bernhardt
Yucatan Leones	72	51	.585	3½	Wilfredo Calvino
Poza Rica Petroleros	38	87	.304	38½	Luis Alcaraz

Playoffs: Campeche 4 games, MC Tigres 1; MC Diablos Rojos 4 games, Coatzacoalcos 1; Reynosa 4 games, Saltillo 0; Nuevo Laredo 4 games, Ciudad Juarez 2. MC Diablos Rojos 4 games, Campeche 3; Reynosa 4 games, Nuevo Laredo 1.
Finals: MC Diablos Rojos 4 games, Reynosa 3.

BA: Willie Norwood, Ciudad Juarez, .365
Runs: Jim Obradovich, Aguascalientes, 84
Hits: Roberto Rodriguez, MC Diablos Rojos, 165
RBIs: Andres Mora, Saltillo, 93

HRs: Andres Mora, Saltillo, 23
Wins: Rafael Garcia, Ciudad Juarez, 20
SOs: Rafael Garcia, Ciudad Juarez, 187
ERA: Vicente Romo, Coatzacoalcos, 1.40

AAA Pacific Coast League

President: Bill Cutler

North Standings	W	L	Pct.	GB	Attend.	Manager
Tacoma Tigers** (11)	78	61	.561	—	244,083	Ed Nottle
Portland Beavers (23)	72	65	.526	5	192,214	Pete Ward
Hawaii Islanders* (25)	72	65	.526	5	157,918	Doug Rader
Edmonton Trappers (4)	62	74	.456	14½	187,501	Gordon Lund
Vancouver Canadians (8)	56	79	.424	18½	127,161	Lee Sigman
Spokane Indians (12)	56	84	.400	22½	227,050	Rene Lachemann

South Standings	W	L	Pct.	GB	Attend.	Manager
Albuquerque Dukes*** (19)	94	38	.712	—	244,464	Del Crandall
Phoenix Giants (26)	69	63	.523	25	240,832	Rocky Bridges

*Won first-half   **Won second-half   ***Won both halves
Numbers after nicknames indicate farm system.
Affiliation listed at end of year.

558

	W	L	Pct.	GB	Attend.	Manager
Salt Lake City Gulls (3)	63	71	.470	32	205,353	Moose Stubing
Tucson Toros (18)	57	82	.410	40½	188,488	Jimmy Johnson

Playoff: Tacoma 2 games, Hawaii 1.
Finals: Albuquerque 3 games, Tacoma 0.

All-Star Team: 1B-Kelvin Moore, Tacoma; **2B**-John Loviglio, Edmonton; **SS**-Jimmy Sexton, Tacoma; **3B**-Larry Rush, Vancouver; **OF**-Michael Davis, Hawaii; Dave Henderson, Spokane; Alan Wiggins, Hawaii; **C**-Robert Kearney, Tacoma; **DH**-Gary Holle, Edmonton; **P**-Richard Barnes, Edmonton; Robert Long, Portland; **MVP**-Mike Marshall, Albuquerque; **Manage**-Ed Nottle, Tacoma.

BA: Mike Marshall, Albuquerque, .373
Runs: Mike Marshall, Albuquerque, 114
Hits: Brian Harper, Salt Lake City, 192
RBIs: Mike Marshall, Albuquerque, 137
HRs: Mike Marshall, Albuquerque, 34
Wins: Ted Power, Albuquerque, 18
SOs: Odell Jones, Portland, 135
ERA: Bob Stoddard, Spokane, 2.90

AA Eastern League
President: P. Patrick McKernan

North Standings	W	L	Pct.	GB	Attend.	Manager
Glens Falls White Sox***(4)	83	52	.615	—	101,567	Jim Mahoney
Holyoke Millers (3)	68	70	.493	16½	80,117	Jim Saul
Lynn Sailors (12)	62	76	.449	22½	38,468	Bobby Floyd
Buffalo Bisons (23)	56	81	.409	28	83,464	John Lipon

South Standings	W	L	Pct.	GB	Attend.	Manager
Bristol Red Sox**(2)	79	58	.577	—	77,066	Tony Torchia
Reading Phillies*(22)	76	63	.547	4	117,050	Ron Clark
West Haven A's (11)	71	67	.514	8½	55,552	Bob Didier
Waterbury Reds (17)	55	83	.399	24½	67,609	George Scherger

Playoff: Bristol 2 games, Reading 0.
Finals: Bristol 3 games, Glens Falls 2.

All-Star Team: 1B-Greg Walker, Glens Falls; **2B**-Tom Lawless, Waterbury; **SS**-Julio Franco, Reading; **3B**-Ed Jurak, Bristol; **OF**-Mike Brown, Holyoke; Luis Rois, Glens Falls; Randy Johnson, Glens Falls; **C**-Miguel Ibarra, Reading; **DH**-Ron Kittle, Glens Falls; **Util**-Joe Bruno, Reading; **P**-Gorman Heimueller, West Haven; Brian Denman, Bristol; **MVP**-Ron Kittle, Glens Falls; **Manager**-Jim Mahoney, Glens Falls.

BA: Ed Jurak, Bristol, .340
Runs: Greg Walker, Glens Falls, 117
Hits: Greg Walker, Glens Falls, 163
RBIs: Ron Kittle, Glens Falls, 103
HRs: Ron Kittle, Glens Falls, 40
Wins: Larry Edwards, Glens Falls, 15
Rick Foley, Holyoke, 15
Tracy Harris, Lynn, 15
Brian Denman, Bristol, 15
SOs: Jerome King, Bristol, 168
ERA: Brian Denman, Bristol, 2.44

AA Southern League
President: Jimmy Bragan

East Standings	W	L	Pct.	GB	Attend.	Manager
Orlando Twins*(9)	79	63	.556	—	69,391	Tom Kelly
Charlotte O's (1)	74	69	.517	5½	204,546	Mark Wiley
Savannah Braves**(15)	70	70	.500	8	104,254	Andy Gilbert
Jacksonville Suns (7)	65	77	.458	14	126,384	Gene Lamont
Columbus Astros (18)	63	78	.447	15½	109,135	Matt Galante

West Standings	W	L	Pct.	GB	Attend.	Manager
Nashville Sounds**(10)	81	62	.566	—	550,676	Stump Merrill
Memphis Chicks*(20)	77	66	.538	4	307,007	Larry Bearnarth
Birmingham Barons (6)	71	70	.504	9	220,219	Roy Majtyka
Chattanooga Lookouts (5)	67	75	.472	13½	149,017	Woody Smith
Knoxville Blue Jays (14)	63	80	.441	18	70,807	Duane Larson/Larry Hardy

Playoffs: Orlando 3 games, Savannah 1; Nashville 3 games, Memphis 0.
Finals: Orlando 3 games, Nashville 1.

All-Star Team: 1B-Mike Laga, Birmingham; **2B**-Kevin Rhomberg, Chattanooga; **SS**-Bryan Little, Memphis; **3B**-Gary Gaetti, Orlando; **OF**-Albert Hall, Savannah; Don Mattingly, Nashville; Randy Bush, Orlando; Willie McGee, Nashville; Larry Ray, Columbus; **C**-Tim Laudner, Orlando; **DH**-Willie Royster, Charlotte; **P**-Tom Gorman, Memphis; James Werly, Nashville; **MVP**-Tim Laudner, Orlando; **Pitcher of the Year**-James Werly, Nashville; **Manager**-Tom Kelly, Orlando.

BA: Kevin Rhomberg, Chattanooga, .366
Runs: Thad Wilborn, Nashville, 106
Hits: Kevin Rhomberg, Chattanooga, 187
RBIs: Larry Ray, Columbus, 107
HRs: Tim Laudner, Orlando, 42
Wins: Craig McMurtry, Savannah, 15
SOs: James Werly, Nashville, 193
ERA: Mark Ross, Columbus, 2.25

AA Texas League
President: Carl Sawatski

East Standings	W	L	Pct.	GB	Attend.	Manager
Tulsa Drillers**(13)	68	65	.511	—	155,845	Tom Burgess
Jackson Mets*(21)	68	66	.507	½	112,511	Davey Johnson
Shreveport Captains (26)	68	67	.504	1	46,930	Jack Mull
Arkansas Travelers (24)	52	83	.394	15½	202,604	Gaylen Pitts

West Standings	W	L	Pct.	GB	Attend.	Manager
San Antonio Dodgers*(19)	76	57	.571	—	134,668	Don LeJohn
Amarillo Gold Sox**(25)	77	59	.566	½	89,476	Eddie Watt
El Paso Diablos (8)	65	69	.458	11½	210,398	Tony Muser
Midland Cubs (16)	62	73	.459	15	105,294	Roy Hartsfield/George Enright

Playoffs: Jackson 2 games, Tulsa 1; San Antonio 2 games, Amarillo 0.
Finals: Jackson 4 games, San Antonio 0.

All-Star Team: 1B-Stan Davis, El Paso; **2B**-Steve Sax, San Antonio; **SS**-Willie Lozado, El Paso; **3B**-Tom O'Malley, Shreveport; **OF**-Mel Hall, Midland; Mark Bradley, San Antonio; Gotay Mills, Arkansas; Dale Holeman, San Antonio; **C**-Ron Tingley, Amarillo; Mike Fitzgerald, Jackson; **DH**-John Evans, El Paso; **Util**-Marty Scott, Tulsa; Dave Sax, San Antonio; **P**-Rich Rodas, San Antonio; Alan Fowlkes, Shreveport; Rick Ownbey, Jackson; John Semprini, Jackson; Mark Dempsey, Shreveport; Tom Niedenfuer, San Antonio; Dave Dravecky, Amarillo; **MVP**-Steve Sax, San Antonio; **Pitcher of the Year**-Alan Fowlkes, Shreveport; **Manager**-Don LeJohn, San Antonio.

BA: Steve Sax, San Antonio, .346
Runs: Mel Hall, Midland, 98
Mark Bradley, San Antonio, 98
Hits: Mel Hall, Midland, 170
RBIs: Stan Davis, El Paso, 109
HRs: Greg Brock, San Antonio, 32
Wins: Dave Dravecky, Amarillo, 15
Walt Terrell, Tulsa, 15
Mark Dempsey, Shreveport, 15
SOs: Alan Fowlkes, Shreveport, 152
ERA: Tim Hamm, Amarillo, 2.27

A California League
President: E.W. "Bill" Wickert

Standings	W	L	Pct.	GB	Attend.	Manager
Visalia Oaks*(9)	87	53	.621	—	44,576	Dick Phillips
Reno Silver Sox**(25)	81	58	.583	5½	100,947	Jack Maloof
Lodi Dodgers (19)	73	67	.521	14	61,271	Terry Collins
Stockton Ports (8)	68	71	.489	18½	106,170	Duane Espy
Modesto A's (11)	67	74	.486	19	65,675	Keith Lieppman
Redwood Pioneers (3)	66	74	.471	21	66,466	Chris Cannizzaro
Fresno Giants (26)	63	77	.450	24	89,666	Wayne Cato
San Jose Missions (x)	53	87	.379	34	99,701	Fred Hatfield

Playoffs: Visalia 2 games, Stockton 1; Lodi 2 games, Reno 1.
Finals: Lodi 3 games, Visalia 2.

All-Star Team: 1B-Kent Hrbek, Visalia; **2B**-James Christensen, Visalia; **SS**-German Rivera, Lodi; **3B**-Harry Francis, Redwood; **OF**-George Hinshaw, Reno; Rob Deer, Fresno; Patrick Casey, Reno; Dion James, Stockton; **C**-Scotti Madison, Visalia; **DH**-Anthony Brewer, Lodi; **P**-Ron Romanick, Redwood; Frank Williams, Fresno; Willie Hardwick, Reno; Paul Voigt, Visalia; Mike Couchee, Reno; **MVP**-Kent Hrbek, Visalia; **Manager**-Terry Collins, Lodi.

BA: Kent Hrbek, Visalia, .379
Runs: Steve Garcia, Reno, 120
Hits: George Hinshaw, Reno, 189
RBIs: George Hinshaw, Reno, 131
HRs: Rob Deer, Fresno, 33
Wins: Paul Voigt, Visalia, 16
SOs: Ron Romanick, Redwood, 178
ERA: Ron Romanick, Redwood, 2.91

A Carolina League
President: James B. Mills

North Standings	W	L	Pct.	GB	Attend.	Manager
Hagerstown Suns*(1)	70	68	.507	—	145,335	Grady Little
Lynchburg Mets (21)	71	69	.507	—	51,960	Gene Dusan
Salem Redbirds**(25)	66	74	.471	5	72,125	Glenn Ezell
Alexandria Dukes (23)	62	75	.453	7½	40,659	Mike Toomey

South Standings	W	L	Pct.	GB	Attend.	Manager
Peninsula Pilots**(22)	71	65	.522	—	66,261	Bill Dancy
Winston-Salem Red Sox (2)	72	67	.518	½	72,132	Buddy Hunter
Kinston Eagles*(14)	72	68	.514	1	40,183	John McLaren
Durham Bulls (15)	70	68	.507	2	151,905	Al Gallagher

Playoffs: Hagerstown 1 game, Salem 0; Peninsula 1 game, Kinston 0.
Finals: Hagerstown 3 games, Peninsula 0.

All-Star Team: 1B-Michael Anicich, Lynchburg; John Schiave, Alexandria; **2B**-Larry Jeltz, Peninsula; **SS**-Tony Fernandez, Kinston; Jose Oquendo, Lynchburg; **3B**-Tom Hayes, Durham; **OF**-Gerald Davis, Salem; Brad Komminsk, Durham; Paul Croft, Hagerstown; **C**-Marc Sullivan, Winston-Salem; **DH**-David Rivera, Hagerstown; **P**-Randy Ford, Kinston; Mike Brown, Winston-Salem; **MVP**-Brad Komminsk, Durham; **Pitcher of the Year**-Mike Brown, Winston-Salem; **Manager**-Grady Little, Hagerstown.

BA: Brad Komminsk, Durham, .322
Runs: Gerald Davis, Salem, 114
Hits: Brad Komminsk, Durham, 148
Ben Perez, Kinston, 148
RBIs: Brad Komminsk, Durham, 104
HRs: Gerald Davis, Salem, 34
Wins: Mike Brown, Winston-Salem, 14
SOs: Jeff Bittiger, Lynchburg, 168
ERA: Mike Brown, Winston-Salem, 1.49

A Florida State League
President: George MacDonald, Jr.

North Standings	W	L	Pct.	GB	Attend.	Manager
Tampa Tarpons*(17)	79	54	.594	—	61,758	Jim Lett
St. Pete Cardinals (24)	69	63	.523	9½	116,477	Nick Leyva
Lakeland Tigers (6)	69	64	.519	10	43,490	Ted Brazell
Daytona Beach Astros**(8)	68	67	.503	12	70,194	Carlos Alfonso
Winter Haven Red Sox (2)	62	77	.446	20	21,133	Rac Slider

South Standings	W	L	Pct.	GB	Attend.	Manager
Ft. Lauderdale Yankees**(10)	81	53	.604	—	56,507	Doug Holmquist
Ft. Myers Royals*(7)	72	58	.554	7	59,150	Brian Murphy
West Palm Beach Expos (20)	65	71	.478	17	165,656	Bob Bailey
Vero Beach Dodgers (19)	63	73	.463	19	91,732	Stan Wasiak
Miami Orioles (1)	44	92	.324	38	46,885	Minnie Mendoza

Playoffs: Daytona 2 games, Tampa 0; Ft. Myers 2 games, Ft. Lauderdale 0.
Finals: Daytona Beach 3 games, Ft. Myers 1.

All-Star Team: 1B-Bob Gerris, Ft. Myers; **2B**-Paul Hundhammer, Winter Haven; **SS**-Julio Beltran, Daytona; **3B**-Danny Tartabull, Tampa; **OF**-Wallace Davis, Ft. Myers; Bruce Fields, Lakeland; Ed Amelung, Vero Beach; Mike Young, Miami; **C**-Joel Pepel, West Palm Beach; Jeff Hall, Winter Haven; **DH**-Mike Brewer, Ft. Myers; **Util**-Rex Hudler, Ft. Lauderdale; **P**-Ken Westray, West Palm Beach; Nick Fiorillo, Tampa; Al Nipper, Winter Haven; Mark Williams, Lakeland; **MVP**-Danny Tartabull, Tampa; **Manager**-Brian Murphy, Ft. Myers.

BA: Danny Tartabull, Tampa, .310
Runs: Wallace Davis, Ft. Myers, 89
Hits: Ed Amelung, Vero Beach, 155
RBIs: Jeff Hall, Winter Haven, 84
　　Mike Brewer, Ft. Myers, 84
HRs: Wes Clements, Daytona Beach, 19
Wins: Ben Callahan, Ft. Lauderdale, 17
SOs: Ken Westray, West Palm Beach, 171
ERA: Al Nipper, Winter Haven, 1.70

A Midwest League
President: Bill Walters

North Standings	W	L	Pct.	GB	Attend.	Manager
Wausau Timbers***(12)	84	48	.636	—	58,116	Bill Plummer
Waterloo Indians (5)	81	55	.596	5	80,355	Gomer Hodge
Wisconsin Rapids Twins (9)	68	65	.511	16½	43,509	Ken Staples
Appleton Foxes (4)	54	80	.403	31	66,780	Sam Ewing

South Standings	W	L	Pct.	GB	Attend.	Manager
Quad City Cubs**(16)	77	58	.570	—	134,142	Rich Morales
Cedar Rapids Reds*(17)	65	68	.489	11	89,824	Randy Davidson
Burlington Bees (8)	54	81	.400	23	63,127	Terry Bevington
Clinton Giants (26)	52	80	.394	23½	67,940	Wendell Kim

Playoffs: Wausau 2 games, Waterloo 1; Quad City 2 games, Cedar Rapids 1.
Finals: Wausau 3 games, Quad City 0.

All-Star Team: 1B-Kenneth Foster, Wisconsin Rapids; **2B**-Harold Reynolds, Wausau; **SS**-Darnell Coles, Wausau; **3B**-Randy Ready, Burlington; **OF**-Henry Cotto, Quad City; Jim Eisenreich, Wisconsin Rapids; Ed Saavedra, Waterloo; **C**-John Fimple, Waterloo; **DH**-Kevin King, Wausau; **P**-Rich Adair, Wausau; Edwin Nunez, Wausau; Conrad Everett, Wisconsin Rapids; **MVP**-Ed Saavedra, Waterloo; **Manager**-Gomer Hodge, Waterloo.

BA: Ed Saavedra, Waterloo, .336
Runs: John Moses, Wausau, 102
Hits: Jim Eisenreich, Wisconsin Rapids, 152
　　Ed Saavedra, Waterloo, 152
RBIs: Glen Walker, Wausau, 111
HRs: Glen Walker, Wausau, 35
Wins: Edwin Nunez, Wausau, 16
SOs: Edwin Nunez, Wausau, 205
ERA: Ken Pryce, Quad City, 1.98

A New York-Pennsylvania League
President: Vincent M. McNamara

East Standings	W	L	Pct.	GB	Attend.	Manager
Oneonta Yankees (10)	48	25	.658	—	39,075	Art Mazmanian
Utica Blue Sox	39	31	.557	7½	19,146	Jim Gattis
Little Falls Mets (21)	31	39	.443	15½	23,516	Gene Dusan
Elmira Suns (2)	25	48	.342	23	49,556	Dick Berardino

West Standings	W	L	Pct.	GB	Attend.	Manager
Jamestown Expos (20)	48	26	.649	—	44,931	Pat Daugherty
Erie Cardinals (24)	44	30	.595	4	76,063	Sonny Ruberto
Geneva Cubs (16)	41	34	.547	7½	24,403	Bob Hartsfield
Batavia Trojans (5)	16	59	.213	32½	24,841	Dave Oliver

Playoff: Oneonta 2 games, Jamestown 1.

All-Star Team: 1B-Rene Marchand, Jamestown; **2B**-John Damon, Jamestown; **SS**-Michael Harris, Erie; **3B**-Bill Lyons, Erie; **OF**-Francisco Batista, Erie; Willie Cooley, Jamestown; Scott Holliday, Little Falls; Randy Washington, Batavia; **C**-Scott Bradley, Oneonta; Robert Gilles, Little Falls; **DH**-David Malpeso, Elmira; **Util**-David Rosenhahn, Geneva; **P**-Phil Deriso, Batavia; Michael Flinn, Utica; John Adams, Erie; Greg Dunn, Erie; **Manager**-Pat Daugherty, Jamestown.

BA: Tom Romano, Utica, .337
Runs: Greg Guin, Erie, 67
Hits: John Damon, Jamestown, 91
RBIs: Bill Lyons, Erie, 65
HRs: Robert Gilles, Little Falls, 19
Wins: Charles Scott, Jamestown, 10
SOs: John Adams, Erie, 107
ERA: Jackie Uhey, Utica, 2.65

A Northwest League
President: Bob Freitas

North Standings	W	L	Pct.	GB	Attend.	Manager
Bellingham Mariners (12)	39	31	.557	—	21,390	Jeff Scott
Bend Phillies (22)	31	39	.443	8	19,719	Bill Bryk
Walla Walla Padres (25)	29	41	.414	10	28,909	P.J. Carey

South Standings	W	L	Pct.	GB	Attend.	Manager
Medford A's (11)	42	28	.600	—	54,243	Brad Fisher
Salem Senators (3)	36	34	.514	6	30,174	Rick Ingalls
Eugene Emeralds (17)	33	37	.471	9	85,073	Greg Riddoch

Playoff: Medford 2 games, Bellingham 1.

All-Star Team: 1B-Brick Smith, Bellingham; **2B**-Dennis Seatts, Eugene; **SS**-Steve Kiefer, Medford; **3B**-Graham Conklin, Bellingham; **OF**-Eric Davis, Eugene; Kevin Coughlin, Medford; Phil Bradley, Bellingham; Ricky Nelson, Bellingham; **C**-William Worden, Salem; Scot Mitchell, Medford; Ricky Wilson, Bellingham; **P**-Brian Hunter, Bend; Mark Langston, Bellingham; **Manager**-Brad Fisher, Medford.

BA: Tony Gwynn, Walla Walla, .331
Runs: Eric Davis, Eugene, 67
Hits: Kevin Coughlin, Medford, 78
RBIs: Graham Conklin, Bellingham, 57
HRs: Graham Conklin, Bellingham, 15
Wins: Robert Vavrock, Medford, 9
SOs: Tim Kammeyer, Salem, 108
ERA: Curt Heidenreich, Eugene, 2.39

A South Atlantic League
President: John H. Moss

North Standings	W	L	Pct.	GB	Attend.	Manager
Greensboro Hornets***(10)	98	43	.695	—	260,340	Bob Schaefer
Asheville Tourists (13)	74	68	.521	24½	70,957	Tom Robson
Spartanburg Traders (22)	71	70	.504	27	43,404	Tom Harmon
Gastonia Cardinals (24)	68	76	.472	31½	80,869	Joe Rigoli
Anderson Braves (15)	57	86	.399	42	34,349	Sonny Jackson

South Standings	W	L	Pct.	GB	Attend.	Manager
Greenwood Pirates***(23)	79	65	.549	—	20,740	Joe Frisina
Charleston Royals (7)	75	67	.528	3	83,934	Rick Mathews
Florence Blue Jays (14)	66	72	.478	10	74,645	Dennis Holmberg
Macon Peaches (6)	62	79	.440	15½	72,557	Tom Kotchman
Shelby Mets (21)	59	83	.415	19	51,324	Danny Monzon

Playoff: Greensboro 3 games, Greenwood 2.

All-Star Team: 1B-Larry Pittman, Shelby; **2B**-Garry Harris, Florence; **SS**-Ralph "Rocket" Wheeler, Florence; Bobby Meacham, Gastonia; **3B**-Jeff Reynolds, Greensboro; **OF**-Joe Orsulak, Greenwood; Jeff Stone, Spartanburg; Danny Murphy, Asheville; **C**-Joel Skinner, Greenwood; **DH**-Matt Winters, Greensboro; **P**-Glenn Ray, Charleston; Chris Green, Greenwood; **MVP**-Danny Murphy, Asheville; Jeff Reynolds, Greensboro; **Pitcher of the Year**-Glenn Ray, Charleston; **Manager**-Bob Schaefer, Greensboro.

BA: Danny Murphy, Asheville, .369
Runs: Jeff Stone, Spartanburg, 108
Hits: Trench Davis, Greenwood, 158
RBIs: Jeff Reynolds, Greensboro, 103
HRs: Tom Dodd, Greensboro, 29
Wins: Kelly Scott, Greensboro, 16
　　Darryl Smith, Asheville, 16
SOs: Tim Wheeler, Greenwood, 166
ERA: Jeff Gladden, Charleston, 2.09

R Appalachian League
President: Paul Fyffe

Standings	W	L	Pct.	GB	Attend.	Manager
Paintsville Yankees (10)	46	24	.657	—	21,520	Mike Easom
Elizabethton Twins (9)	42	28	.600	4	11,932	Fred Waters
Bluefield Orioles (1)	36	34	.514	10	21,525	Lance Nichols
Johnson City Cardinals (24)	36	34	.514	10	32,035	Johnny Lewis
Bristol Tigers (6)	29	41	.414	17	9,486	Joe Lewis
Kingsport Mets (21)	21	49	.300	25	22,630	Al Jackson

Playoffs: None.

All-Star Team: 1B-Orestes Destrade, Paintsville; **2B**-Curtis Ford, Johnson City; **SS**-Steve Lombardozzi, Elizabethton; **3B**-Kevin Mitchell, Kingsport; **OF**-Michael Reddish, Paintsville; Tom Jones, Paintsville; David Hoyt, Elizabethton; **C**-Stanley Haas, Johnson City; **Util**-Mike Williams, Bristol; David Falcone, Bluefield; **P**-Paul Cherry, Johnson City; Danny Cox, Johnson City; **Manager**-Fred Waters, Elizabethton.

BA: Tom Jones, Paintsville, .348
Runs: David Hoyt, Elizabethton, 59
Hits: David Hoyt, Elizabethton, 85
RBIs: Mike Williams, Bristol, 60
HRs: Orestes Destrade, Paintsville, 14
Wins: Paul Cherry, Johnson City, 10
SOs: Danny Cox, Johnson City, 87
ERA: Danny Cox, Johnson City, 2.06

R Gulf Coast League
President: Thomas J. Saffell

Standings	W	L	Pct.	GB	Manager
Royals Gold (7)	44	20	.688	—	Roy Tanner
White Sox (4)	41	23	.641	3	John Boles
Royals Blue (7)	35	28	.556	8½	Joe Jones
Astros Orange (18)	33	28	.541	9½	Lyle Olsen
Pirates (23)	32	28	.533	10	Woody Huyke
Rangers (13)	32	30	.516	11	Andy Hancock
Yankees (10)	30	29	.508	12½	Carlos Tosca
Braves (15)	28	34	.452	15	Pedro Gonzalez
Blue Jays (14)	26	39	.400	18½	Rich Hacker
Cubs (16)	25	38	.397	18½	Hugh Yancy
Padres (25)	25	38	.397	18½	Jim Zarilla
Astros Blue (18)	22	38	.367	20	Eric Swanson

Games played at Sarasota and Bradenton, Florida.

Playoffs: None.

All-Star Team: 1B-Kyle Sanford, Braves; **2B**-Philander Smith, Astros Blue; **SS**-Steven McAllister, Astros Orange; **3B**-Denio Gonzales, Pirates; **OF**-Richard Plautz, Royals Gold; Kevin Buckley, Rangers; Rolund Oruna, Royals Gold; **C**-Mitchell Ashmore, Royals Gold; **P**-Ramon Vargas, Braves; Guillermo Castro, Astros Orange.

BA: Wendell Henderson, Cubs, .356
Runs: Bill Pecota, Royals Blue, 61
Hits: Wendell Henderson, Cubs, 72
RBIs: Tom Thompson, Royals Gold/Blue, 44
HRs: Tom Thompson, Royals Gold/Blue, 10
Wins: Mark Gubicza, Royals Gold, 8
　　John Hardy, White Sox, 8
SOs: John Hardy, White Sox 78
ERA: Ed Reilly, Astros Orange, 1.30

R Pioneer League

President: Ralph C. Nelles

North Standings	W	L	Pct.	GB	Attend.	Manager
Calgary Expos (20)	46	24	.657	—	38,748	Junior Minor
Lethbridge Dodgers (19)	43	27	.614	3	37,361	Gary LaRocque
Medicine Hat Blue Jays (14)	37	33	.529	9	33,109	Wayne Graham
Great Falls Giants (26)	32	38	.457	14	58,179	Ernest Rodriguez

South Standings	W	L	Pct.	GB	Attend.	Manager
Butte Copper Kings (8)	39	31	.557	—	30,519	Ken Richardson
Billings Mustangs (17)	30	40	.429	9	79,018	Jim Hoff
Idaho Falls Angels (3)	27	43	.386	12	33,283	Joe Maddon
Helena Phillies (22)	26	44	.371	13	25,143	Rollie DeArmas

Playoff: Butte 3 games, Calgary 2.

All-Star Team: 1B-Charles Colclough, Billings; **2B**-Norman Carrasco, Idaho Falls; **SS**-Earnest Riles, Butte; **3B**-Tom Fettig, Calgary; **OF**-Eric Peyton, Butte; Glen Stacheit,

Calgary; Herman Lewis, Medicine Hat; **C**-Bill Pinkham, Medicine Hat; **P**-Sid Fernandez, Lethbridge; Barry Branam, Calgary; John Cerutti, Medicine Hat; **Manager**-Gary LaRocque, Lethbridge.

BA: Eric Peyton, Butte, .403
Runs: Eric Peyton, Butte, 64
Hits: Eric Peyton, Butte, 110
RBIs: Eric Peyton, Butte, 65

HRs: Tom Fettig, Calgary, 10
Glen Stacheit, Calgary, 10
Wins: Barry Branam, Calgary, 10
SOs: Sid Fernandez, Lethbridge, 128
ERA: Sid Fernandez, Lethbridge, 1.54

1981 Interleague Post Season Play

World Series
Los Angeles (National) 4 games, New York (American) 2

1981 Major League Farm Systems

American League

1 Baltimore (5): Rochester, Charlotte, Hagerstown, Miami, Bluefield.
2 Boston (5): Pawtucket, Bristol (CT), Winston-Salem, Winter Haven, Elmira.
3 California (5): Salt Lake City, Holyoke, Redwood, Salem (OR), Idaho Falls.
4 Chicago (4): Edmonton, Glens Falls, Appleton, Gulf Coast.
5 Cleveland (4): Charleston (WV), Chattanooga, Waterloo, Batavia.
6 Detroit (5): Evansville, Birmingham, Lakeland, Macon, Bristol (VA).
7 Kansas City (6): Omaha, Jacksonville, Ft. Myers, Charleston (SC), Gulf Coast Blue, Gulf Coast Gold.
8 Milwaukee (5): Vancouver, El Paso, Stockton, Burlington, Butte.
9 Minnesota (5): Toledo, Orlando, Visalia, Wisconsin Rapids, Elizabethton.
10 New York (7): Columbus (OH), Nashville, Ft. Lauderdale, Greensboro, Oneonta, Paintsville, Gulf Coast.
11 Oakland (4): Tacoma, West Haven, Modesto, Medford.
12 Seattle (4): Spokane, Lynn, Wausau, Bellingham.
13 Texas (4): Wichita, Tulsa, Asheville, Gulf Coast.
14 Toronto (6): Syracuse, Knoxville, Kinston, Florence, Medicine Hat, Gulf Coast.

National League

15 Atlanta (5): Richmond, Savannah, Durham, Anderson, Gulf Coast.
16 Chicago (5): Iowa, Midland, Quad City, Geneva, Gulf Coast.
17 Cincinnati (6): Indianapolis, Waterbury, Tampa, Cedar Rapids, Eugene, Billings.
18 Houston (5): Tucson, Columbus (GA), Daytona Beach, Gulf Coast Blue, Gulf Coast Orange.
19 Los Angeles (5): Albuquerque, San Antonio, Lodi, Vero Beach, Lethbridge.
20 Montreal (5): Denver, Memphis, West Palm Beach, Jamestown, Calgary.
21 New York (6): Tidewater, Jackson, Lynchburg, Shelby, Little Falls, Kingsport.
22 Philadelphia (6): Oklahoma City, Reading, Peninsula, Spartanburg, Bend, Helena.
23 Pittsburgh (5): Portland, Buffalo, Alexandria, Greenwood, Gulf Coast.
24 St. Louis (6): Springfield, Arkansas, St. Petersburg, Gastonia, Erie, Johnson City.
25 San Diego (6): Hawaii, Amarillo, Reno, Salem (VA), Walla Walla, Gulf Coast.
26 San Francisco (5): Phoenix, Shreveport, Fresno, Clinton, Great Falls.

Co-op (x): San Jose.
Independent: Utica.

1981 No-Hitters

Date	Pitcher	Team	League	Opponent	Score
3-29	Ramon de los Santos	Union Laguna	Mexican	Chihuahua	4-0
4-12	Rolando Menendez	Saltillo	Mexican	Reynosa	2-0
4-18	Luis Tiant	Portland	Pacific Coast	Spokane	2-0 (7)
4-20	Greg Bangert	Clinton	Midwest	Burlington	4-1 (7)
4-26	Victor Garcia	Nuevo Laredo	Mexican	Ciudad Juarez	1-0 (P)
4-27	Mike Jones	Omaha	American Assoc.	Iowa	2-0
5-10	Charlie Lea	Montreal	National	San Francisco	4-0
5-15	Len Barker	Cleveland	American	Toronto	3-0 (P)
5-16	Jeff Cornell	Jacksonville	Southern	Nashville	4-0
5-17	Rafael Garcia	Ciudad Juarez	Mexican	Coatzacoalcos	3-0
5-25	Gary Beare	Nuevo Laredo	Mexican	MC Diablos Rojos	1-0 (7)
6-2	Billy Smith	Tucson	Pacific Coast	Vancouver	4-0 (P, 6)
6-9	Kelly Scott	Greensboro	South Atlantic	Charleston	3-0 (7)
6-9	Walter Vanderbush	Ft. Myers	Florida State	Daytona Beach	(7)
6-13	George Stablein	Hawaii	Pacific Coast	Tacoma	6-1
6-16	Rene Quinones	Vancouver	Pacific Coast	Edmonton	3-0 (7)
6-17	Derek Botelho	Ft. Myers	Florida State	Miami	8-0 (7)
7-6	Brian Denman	Bristol	Eastern	West Haven	4-1
7-13	Mitchell Cook/ Mark Nowlin	Cubs	Gulf Coast	Braves	3-1
7-22	Thomas Hart	Reading	Eastern	Lynn	3-0 (7)
8-3	Greg Dunn	Erie	New York-Penn.	Batavia	11-1
8-9	Danny Cox	Johnson City	Appalachian	Bristol	11-0
8-11	John Nurthen	Ft. Lauderdale	Florida State	Miami	2-0 (7)
8-12	Michael Tanzi	White Sox	Gulf Coast	Astros Blue	4-0
8-15	Steve Ibarguen	Lynchburg	Carolina	Alexandria	10-0 (P, 6)
8-15	Alan Walker	Anderson	South Atlantic	Florence	5-0 (7)
8-19	Larry Pashnick	Evansville	American Assoc.	Iowa	1-0
8-23	Randy O'Neal	Lakeland	Florida State	Winter Haven	4-0 (7)
8-30	Rick Kranitz	Stockton	California	San Jose	7-0
9-26	Nolan Ryan	Houston	National	Los Angeles	5-0

Number in parentheses indicates innings if other than nine; "P" indicates perfect game.

THIS DATE IN MINOR LEAGUE HISTORY

March 18, 1981, Alfred Pinkston, 64, winner of four consecutive Mexican League batting titles, 1959-1962, died in New Orleans. A member of the Mexican League Hall of Fame, his .372 career batting average is the highest in the loop's history. He also won the batting championship in the Provincial League in 1952.

April 10, 1981, The Texas League opened with Pam Postema as an umpire.

April 13, 1981, In a Texas League game, San Antonio crushed Midland 34-8. Brothers Steve and Dave Sax each had three-run homers in the Dodgers' ten-run seventh inning.

April 18, 1981, Rochester and Pawtucket played the longest game in baseball history Saturday night and Sunday morning, April 18-19 at McCoy Stadium in Pawtucket, Rhode Island. It ended shortly after 4 a.m. in a 2-2, 32-inning tie. The contest was finished June 23, with Pawtucket winning 3-2 in the 33rd frame. The International League game lasted eight hours and seven minutes. A total of 156 baseballs were used.

April 27, 1981, Lakeland, Florida State League, stranded 22 baserunners in an 8-6, nine-inning victory over Vero Beach.

April 29, 1981, George Greco, Winter Haven, Florida State League, issued 16 bases on balls in a two-inning relief job against Tampa. The Tarpons, receiving 22 walks overall, won 18-9.

May 5, 1981, Amarillo's John Alvarez hit three homers and a triple to drive in ten runs and lead the Gold Sox to a 16-8 win over El Paso in the Texas League.

May 17, 1981, Ciudad Juarez righthander Rafael Garcia pitched the third no-hitter of his Mexican League career, blanking Coatzacoalcos 3-0. All three were nine-inning contests.

May 25, 1981, Ft. Lauderdale, Florida State League, defeated Tampa 1-0 in 23 innings. The contest was completed after having been called the night before after 22 frames.

June 6, 1981, Roberto Mendez of Veracruz made his 2,000th hit in the Mexican League.

June 7, 1981, Benjamin Cerda, Veracruz, Mexican League, made his 2,000th hit.

June 8, 1981, Durham, Carolina League, hit eight homers to drub Salem 19-1.

July 2, 1981, A record minor league crowd of 59,691 jammed Denver's Mile High Stadium to watch the Denver Bears of the American Association topple the Omaha Royals 8-3. The throng was attracted in part by a post-game fireworks display.

July 17, 1981, Craig Goodin, Gulf Coast League Rangers second baseman, executed an unassisted triple play against Astros Orange.

July 31, 1981, Bristol, Eastern League, lost 1-0 to Lynn, after having won 13 straight games.

August 21, 1981, Sid Fernandez, young Dodgers farmhand, fanned 21 as Lethbridge, Pioneer League, blanked Helena 6-0. The southpaw allowed only two hits.

1982

American League
President: Leland S. MacPhail, Jr.

East Standings	W	L	Pct.	GB	Attend.	Manager
Milwaukee Brewers	95	67	.586	—	1,978,896	Buck Rodgers/Harvey Kuenn
Baltimore Orioles	94	68	.580	1	1,613,031	Earl Weaver
Boston Red Sox	89	73	.549	6	1,950,124	Ralph Houk
Detroit Tigers	83	79	.512	12	1,636,058	Sparky Anderson
New York Yankees	79	83	.488	16	2,041,219	Bob Lemon/Gene Michael/Clyde King
Cleveland Indians	78	84	.481	17	1,044,021	Dave Garcia
Toronto Blue Jays	78	84	.481	17	1,275,978	Bobby Cox

West Standings	W	L	Pct.	GB	Attend.	Manager
California Angels	93	69	.574	—	2,807,360	Gene Mauch
Kansas City Royals	90	72	.556	3	2,284,464	Dick Howser
Chicago White Sox	87	75	.537	6	1,567,787	Tony LaRussa
Seattle Mariners	76	86	.469	17	1,070,404	Rene Lachemann
Oakland Athletics	68	94	.420	25	1,735,489	Billy Martin
Texas Rangers	64	98	.395	29	1,154,432	Don Zimmer/Darrell Johnson
Minnesota Twins	60	102	.370	33	921,186	Billy Gardner

Playoff: Milwaukee 3 games, California 2.

BA: Willie Wilson, Kansas City, .332
Runs: Paul Molitor, Milwaukee, 136
Hits: Robin Yount, Milwaukee, 210
RBIs: Hal McRae, Kansas City, 133
HRs: Reggie Jackson, California, 39
Gorman Thomas, Milwaukee, 39

Wins: LaMarr Hoyt, Chicago, 19
SOs: Floyd Bannister, Seattle, 209
ERA: Rick Sutcliffe, Cleveland, 2.96
Pct: Jim Palmer, Baltimore, .750, 15-5
Pete Vuckovich, Milwaukee, .750, 18-6
Saves: Dan Quisenberry, Kansas City, 35

National League
President: Charles S. Feeney

East Standings	W	L	Pct.	GB	Attend.	Manager
St. Louis Cardinals	92	70	.568	—	2,111,906	Whitey Herzog
Philadelphia Phillies	89	73	.549	3	2,376,394	Pat Corrales
Montreal Expos	86	76	.531	6	2,318,292	Jim Fanning
Pittsburgh Pirates	84	78	.519	8	1,024,106	Chuck Tanner
Chicago Cubs	73	89	.451	19	1,249,278	Lee Elia
New York Mets	65	97	.401	27	1,323,036	George Bamberger

West Standings	W	L	Pct.	GB	Attend.	Manager
Atlanta Braves	89	73	.549	—	1,801,985	Joe Torre
Los Angeles Dodgers	88	74	.543	1	3,608,881	Tom Lasorda
San Francisco Giants	87	75	.537	2	1,200,948	Frank Robinson
San Diego Padres	81	81	.500	8	1,607,516	Dick Williams
Houston Astros	77	85	.475	12	1,558,555	Bill Virdon/Bob Lillis
Cincinnati Reds	61	101	.377	28	1,326,528	John McNamara/Russ Nixon

Playoff: St. Louis 3 games, Atlanta 0.

BA: Al Oliver, Montreal, .331
Runs: Lonnie Smith, St. Louis, 120
Hits: Al Oliver, Montreal, 204
RBIs: Dale Murphy, Atlanta, 109
Al Oliver, Montreal, 109
HRs: Dave Kingman, New York, 37

Wins: Steve Carlton, Philadelphia, 23
SOs: Steve Carlton, Philadelphia, 286
ERA: Steve Rogers, Montreal, 2.40
Pct: Phil Niekro, Atlanta, .810, 17-4
Saves: Bruce Sutter, St. Louis, 36

AAA American Association
President: Joe Ryan

East Standings	W	L	Pct.	GB	Attend.	Manager
Indianapolis Indians (17)	75	61	.551	—	213,965	George Scherger
Iowa Cubs (16)	73	62	.541	1½	203,169	Jim Napier
Louisville Redbirds (24)	73	62	.541	1½	868,418	Joe Frazier
Evansville Triplets (6)	68	65	.511	5½	118,139	Roy Majtyka

West Standings	W	L	Pct.	GB	Attend.	Manager
Omaha Royals (7)	71	66	.518	—	178,235	Joe Sparks
Wichita Aeros (20)	70	67	.511	1	106,754	Felipe Alou
Denver Bears (13)	68	67	.504	2	537,914	Rich Donnelly
Oklahoma City 89ers (22)	43	91	.321	26½	180,932	Ron Clark/Cot Deal/Tony Taylor

Playoff: Omaha defeated Wichita in a one game playoff for the West Division title.
Finals: Indianapolis 4 games, Omaha 2.

All-Star Team: 1B-Ken Phelps, Wichita; 2B-Tom Lawless, Indianapolis; 3B-Pat Tabler, Iowa; SS-Kelly Paris, Louisville; OF-Mel Hall, Iowa; Roy Johnson, Wichita; Gary Redus, Indianapolis; Bombo Rivera, Omaha; C-Butch Benton, Iowa; Tom Wieghaus, Wichita/Oklahoma City; DH-Mike Calise, Louisville; Util-Jim Anderson, Denver; P-Jay Howell, Iowa; Bob Tufts, Omaha; MVP-Ken Phelps, Wichita; Pitcher of the Year-Jay Howell, Iowa; Manager-Jim Napier, Iowa.

BA: Roy Johnson, Wichita, .367
Runs: Mel Hall, Iowa, 116
Hits: Ron Johnson, Omaha, 166
RBIs: Ken Phelps, Wichita, 141

HRs: Ken Phelps, Wichita, 46
Wins: Ralph Citarella, Louisville, 15
SOs: Mike Smithson, Denver, 144
ERA: Jay Howell, Iowa, 2.36

AAA International League
President: Harold Cooper

Standings	W	L	Pct.	GB	Attend.	Manager
Richmond Braves (15)	82	57	.590	—	257,611	Eddie Haas
Columbus Clippers (10)	79	61	.564	3½	400,899	Frank Verdi
Tidewater Tides (21)	74	63	.540	7	148,271	Jack Aker
Rochester Red Wings (1)	72	68	.514	10½	361,312	Lance Nichols
Pawtucket Red Sox (2)	67	71	.486	14½	204,724	Joe Morgan
Syracuse Chiefs (14)	64	76	.457	18½	184,483	Jim Beauchamp
Toledo Mud Hens (9)	60	80	.429	22½	150,184	Cal Ermer
Charleston Charlies (5)	59	81	.421	23½	145,337	Doc Edwards

Playoffs: Rochester 3 games, Richmond 0; Tidewater 3 games, Columbus 0.
Finals: Tidewater 3 games, Rochester 0.

All-Star Team: 1B-Greg "Boomer" Wells, Toledo; 2B-Marty Barrett, Pawtucket; 3B-Tucker Ashford, Columbus; SS-Tony Fernandez, Syracuse; OF-Don Mattingly, Columbus; Garry Hancock, Pawtucket; John Shelby, Rochester; C-Geno Petralli, Syracuse; DH-Marshall Brant, Columbus; P-Craig McMurtry, Richmond; Curt Kaufman, Columbus; MVP-Tucker Ashford, Columbus; Craig McMurtry, Richmond; Manager-Eddie Haas, Richmond.

BA: Greg "Boomer" Wells, Toledo, .336
Runs: Paul Runge, Richmond, 106
Hits: Greg "Boomer" Wells, Toledo, 182
RBIs: Greg "Boomer" Wells, Toledo, 107

HRs: Steve Balboni, Columbus, 32
Wins: Craig McMurtry, Richmond, 17
SOs: Don Cooper, Toledo, 125
ERA: James Lewis, Columbus, 2.60

AAA Mexican League
Presidents: Roberto Avila Gonzalez/Pedro Treto Cisneros/Roberto Mansur Galan

North East Standings	W	L	Pct.	GB	Attend.	Manager
Nuevo Laredo Tecolotes	78	53	.595	—	190,000	Victor Ramirez
Reynosa Broncos	70	61	.534	8	110,000	Benjamin Valenzuela
Aguascalientes Rieleros	66	63	.512	11	180,000	Moises Camacho
Monterrey Sultanes	48	81	.372	29	90,000	Gregorio Luque

North West Standings	W	L	Pct.	GB	Attend.	Manager
Ciudad Juarez Indios	73	55	.570	—	130,000	Jose Guerrero
Saltillo Saraperos	70	58	.547	3	190,000	Marcelo Juarez/Francisco Perez/Gerardo Gutierrez
Monclova Acereros	62	68	.477	12	140,000	Felipe Hernandez
Chihuahua Dorados	43	87	.331	31	100,000	Arnoldo Castro

South East Standings	W	L	Pct.	GB	Attend.	Manager
Poza Rica Petroleros	81	49	.623	—	240,000	David Garcia
Yucatan Leones	72	56	.563	8	560,000	Wilfredo Calvino/Jose Luis Garcia/Carlos Paz
Mexico City Diablos Rojos	69	61	.531	12	130,000	Winston Llenas
Campeche Piratas	55	70	.440	23½	150,000	Juan Ramon Bernhardt

South West Standings	W	L	Pct.	GB	Attend.	Manager
Coatzacoalcos Azules	73	54	.575	—	182,000	Ben Reyes
Mexico City Tigres	65	63	.508	8½	150,000	Mauro Ruiz/Fernando Remes
Veracruz Aguila	59	69	.461	14½	100,000	Lee Sigman
Tabasco Plataneros	46	82	.359	27½	120,000	Raul Cano

Playoffs: Saltillo 4 games, Nuevo Laredo 1; Ciudad Juarez 4 games, Reynosa 1; MC Tigres 4 games, Poza Rica 1; Coatzacoalcos 4 games, Yucatan 1. Ciudad Juarez 4 games, Saltillo 0; MC Tigres 4 games, Coatzacoalcos 0.
Finals: Ciudad Juarez 4 games, MC Tigres 0.

All-Star Team: 1B-George Scott, Poza Rica; 2B-Juan Navarrete, Saltillo; 3B-Jesus Sommers, Tabasco; SS-Larvell Blanks, Coatzacoalcos; OF-Andres Mora, Saltillo/Nuevo Laredo; Robert Smith, Ciudad Juarez; Andy Dyes, Monclova; C-Porfirio Ruiz, Saltillo; DH-Felipe Lopez Felix, Ciudad Juarez; P-Jesus Hernaiz, Coatzacoalcos; Ricardo Sandate, Poza Rica; Manager-David Garcia, Poza Rica.

BA: Robert Smith, Ciudad Juarez, .357
Runs: Wendell Alston, Coatzacoalcos, 98
Hits: Robert Smith, Ciudad Juarez, 164
RBIs: Andres Mora, Saltillo/Nuevo Laredo, 80

HRs: Andres Mora, Saltillo/Nuevo Laredo, 25
Wins: Andres Mora, Saltillo/Nuevo Laredo, 19
SOs: Santos Alcala, Monterrey, 192
ERA: Ernesto Cordova, Veracruz, 1.58

AAA Pacific Coast League
President: Bill Cutler

North Standings	W	L	Pct.	GB	Attend.	Manager
Tacoma Tigers*(11)	84	59	.587	—	223,289	Ed Nottle
Spokane Indians**(3)	78	65	.545	6	221,526	Moose Stubing
Vancouver Canadians (8)	72	72	.500	12½	158,767	Dick Phillips
Edmonton Trappers (4)	70	74	.486	14½	233,044	Gordon Lund
Portland Beavers (23)	65	79	.451	19½	272,781	Tom Trebelhorn

*Won first-half   **Won second-half   ***Won both halves
Numbers after nickname indicate farm system.
Affiliation listed at end of year.

South Standings	W	L	Pct.	GB	Attend.	Manager
Albuquerque Dukes*(19) ...	85	58	.594	—	290,249	Del Crandall
Salt Lake City Gulls**(12).	73	70	.510	12	255,671	Bobby Floyd
Hawaii Islanders (25)	73	71	.507	12½	136,676	Doug Rader
Tucson Toros (18)	59	83	.415	25½	196,009	Jimmy Johnson
Phoenix Giants (26)	58	86	.403	27½	244,570	Rocky Bridges

Playoffs: Albuquerque 2 games, Salt Lake City 0; Spokane 2 games, Tacoma 1.
Finals: Albuquerque 4 games, Spokane 2.

All-Star Team: 1B-Greg Brock, Albuquerque; **2B**-Bill Doran, Tucson; **3B**-Steve Lubratich, Spokane; **SS**-Don Anderson, Albuquerque; **OF**-Ron Kittle, Edmonton; Gary Gray, Edmonton; Michael Davis, Tacoma; **C**-John Rabb, Phoenix; **DH**-Tack Wilson, Albuquerque; **P**-Steven Baker, Tacoma; Frank DiPino, Vancouver; **MVP**-Ron Kittle, Edmonton; **Manager**-Moose Stubing, Spokane.

BA: Tack Wilson, Albuquerque, .378
Runs: Ron Kittle, Edmonton, 121
Hits: Steve Lubratich, Spokane, 181
RBIs: Ron Kittle, Edmonton, 144
HRs: Ron Kittle, Edmonton, 50
Wins: Odell Jones, Portland, 16
SOs: Odell Jones, Portland, 172
ERA: Chris Codiroli, Tacoma, 1.90

AA Eastern League
President: Charles E. Eshbach

North Standings	W	L	Pct.	GB	Attend.	Manager
Lynn Sailors**(12)	82	57	.590	—	23,791	Mickey Bowers
Glens Falls White Sox*(4) .	77	63	.550	5½	93,428	Jim Mahoney
Holyoke Millers (3)	63	77	.450	19½	54,291	Jack Hiatt
Buffalo Bisons (23)	55	84	.396	27	77,077	Tommy Sandt

South Standings	W	L	Pct.	GB	Attend.	Manager
West Haven A's***(11).......	86	54	.614	—	51,791	Bob Didier
Bristol Red Sox (2)	75	65	.536	11	67,564	Tony Torchia
Reading Phillies (22)	63	75	.457	22	81,875	John Felske
Waterbury Reds (17)	56	82	.406	29	54,757	Jim Lett

Playoff: Lynn 2 games, Glens Falls 0.
Finals: West Haven 3 games, Lynn 0.

All-Star Team: 1B-Reggie Whittemore, Bristol; **2B**-Tim Hulett, Glens Falls; **3B**-William Barnes, Waterbury; **SS**-Jackie Gutierrez, Bristol; **OF**-Jim Bennett, West Haven; John Moses, Lynn; David Yobs, Glens Falls; **C**-Joel Skinner, Glens Falls; **DH**-Alfredo Torres, Buffalo; **P**-Oil Can Boyd, Bristol; Bill Krueger, West Haven; **Manager**-Mickey Bowers, Lynn.

BA: Phil Klimas, Glens Falls, .311
Runs: Tim Hulett, Glens Falls, 113
Hits: Phil Klimas, Glens Falls, 164
RBIs: Jim Bennett, West Haven, 115
HRs: Jim Bennett, West Haven, 29
Wins: John Lackey, Glens Falls, 16
SOs: Oil Can Boyd, Bristol, 191
ERA: Jay Baller, Reading, 2.68

AA Southern League
President: Jimmy Bragan

East Standings	W	L	Pct.	GB	Attend.	Manager
Jacksonville Suns***(7)	83	61	.576	—	125,645	Gene Lamont
Columbus Astros (18)........	74	69	.517	8½	159,266	Matt Galante
Orlando Twins (9)	74	70	.514	9	66,505	Tom Kelly
Savannah Braves (15)........	69	75	.479	14	111,910	Andy Gilbert
Charlotte O's (1).............	66	77	.462	16½	148,973	Mark Wiley

West Standings	W	L	Pct.	GB	Attend.	Manager
Nashville Sounds**(10)	77	67	.535	—	507,907	Johnny Oates
Knoxville Blue Jays*(14)...	73	71	.507	4	84,451	Larry Hardy
Memphis Chicks (20).........	70	74	.486	7	315,628	Rick Renick
Birmingham Barons (6)......	69	74	.483	7½	231,294	Ed Brinkman
Chattanooga Lookouts (5)..	63	80	.441	13½	157,948	Al Gallagher

Playoffs: Jacksonville 3 games, Columbus 1; Nashville 3 games, Knoxville 1.
Finals: Nashville 3 games, Jacksonville 1.

All-Star Team: 1B-Tim Thompson, Knoxville; **2B**-Tim Teufel, Orlando; **3B**-Jeff Reynolds, Nashville/Knoxville; **SS**-Jesus Alfaro, Charlotte; **OF**-Kenneth Baker, Birmingham; Brian Dayett, Nashville; Mike Fuentes, Memphis; **C**-John Mizerock, Columbus; Russell Stephens, Jacksonville; **DH**-Barbaro Garbey, Birmingham; **P**-Stefan Wever, Nashville; Paul Gibson, Birmingham; **Manager**-Gene Lamont, Jacksonville.

BA: Kenneth Baker, Birmingham, .342
Runs: Mike Fuentes, Memphis, 104
Hits: Buck Showalter, Nashville, 152
RBIs: Mike Fuentes, Memphis, 115
HRs: Mike Fuentes, Memphis, 37
Wins: Stefan Wever, Nashville, 16
Clay Christiansen, Nashville, 16
SOs: Stefan Wever, Nashville, 191
ERA: Stefan Wever, Nashville, 2.78

AA Texas League
President: Carl Sawatski

East Standings	W	L	Pct.	GB	Attend.	Manager
Tulsa Drillers**(13)	70	66	.515	—	128,668	Tom Burgess
Jackson Mets*(21).............	68	65	.511	½	103,535	Gene Dusan
Arkansas Travelers (24)	68	68	.500	2	213,566	Gaylen Pitts/Nick Leyva
Shreveport Captains (26)	62	73	.459	7½	46,920	Jack Mull

West Standings	W	L	Pct.	GB	Attend.	Manager
El Paso Diablos**(8)..........	79	60	.559	—	326,084	Tony Muser
Midland Cubs*(16)............	67	66	.504	7½	114,045	Brian Murphy
San Antonio Dodgers (19)..	68	68	.500	8	138,024	Don LeJohn
Amarillo Gold Sox (25)......	61	74	.452	14½	51,812	Glenn Ezell

Playoffs: Tulsa 2 games, Jackson 1; El Paso 2 games, Midland 0.
Finals: Tulsa 3 games, El Paso 0.

All-Star Team: 1B-Kelvin Torve, Shreveport; **2B**-Ron Koenigsfeld, El Paso; **3B**-Randy Ready, El Paso; **SS**-Dan Davidsmeier, El Paso; **OF**-Darryl Strawberry, Jackson; Brian Greer, Amarillo; Tommy Dunbar, Tulsa; **C**-Bill Foley, El Paso; **DH**-Dann Bilardello, San Antonio; **P**-Mike Couchee, Amarillo; Jeff Bittiger, Jackson; Dean Rennicke, San Antonio; Paul Voigt, San Antonio; Kevin Hagen, Arkansas; Mike Brecht, Shreveport; Brad Mengwasser, Tulsa; **MVP**-Darryl Strawberry, Jackson; **Pitcher of the Year**-Jeff Bittiger, Jackson; **Manager**-Tom Burgess, Tulsa.

BA: Randy Ready, El Paso, .375
Runs: Randy Ready, El Paso, 122
Hits: Randy Ready, El Paso, 178
RBIs: Bill Foley, El Paso, 106
HRs: Darryl Strawberry, Jackson, 34
Wins: Brad Mengwasser, Tulsa, 13
Jon Perlman, Midland, 13
Doug Welenc, Midland, 13
SOs: Jeff Bittiger, Jackson, 190
ERA: Doug Sisk, Jackson, 2.67

A California League
President: Joe Gagliardi

North Standings	W	L	Pct.	GB	Attend.	Manager
Modesto A's***(11)...........	94	46	.671	—	83,651	Pete Whisenant
Stockton Ports (8)	81	57	.587	12	117,561	Duane Espy
Reno Padres (25)	70	68	.507	23	54,750	Jack Maloof
Redwood Pioneers (3)	65	75	.464	29	82,119	Chris Cannizzaro
Lodi Dodgers (19)	58	82	.414	36	62,530	Rick Ollar

South Standings	W	L	Pct.	GB	Attend.	Manager
Visalia Oaks***(9)...........	82	58	.586	—	43,845	Phil Roof
Salinas Spurs (16)...........	68	72	.486	14	51,693	Rich Morales
San Jose Expos (20).........	66	74	.471	16	66,221	Tommy Thompson
Bakersfield Mariners (12)..	64	76	.457	18	82,745	Ken Pape
Fresno Giants (26)	50	90	.357	32	77,286	Jim Maloney

Playoff: Modesto 4 games, Visalia 2.

All-Star Team: 1B-Jessie Reid, Fresno; Darryl Stephens, Redwood; **2B**-Ray Etchebarren, Reno; **3B**-Jon Debus, Lodi; **SS**-Ozzie Guillen, Reno; **OF**-Phil Bradley, Bakersfield; Dave Hudgens, Modesto; Ricky Nelson, Bakersfield; **C**-Jeff Reed, Visalia; **DH**-Kevin McReynolds, Reno; **P**-Tim Conroy, Modesto; Mark Ferguson, Modesto; Ron Sylvia, Redwood; Mike Warren, Stockton/Modesto; **MVP**-Kevin McReynolds, Reno; **Manager**-Pete Whisenant, Modesto.

BA: Kevin McReynolds, Reno, .376
Runs: Ozzie Guillen, Reno, 103
Hits: Ozzie Guillen, Reno, 183
RBIs: Ricky Nelson, Bakersfield, 101
HRs: Kevin McReynolds, Reno, 28
Wins: Mike Warren, Stockton/Modesto, 19
SOs: Tim Conroy, Modesto, 184
ERA: Mark Ferguson, Modesto, 1.77

A Carolina League
President: James B. Mills

North Standings	W	L	Pct.	GB	Attend.	Manager
Alexandria Dukes*(23).......	80	54	.597	—	44,306	John Lipon
Hagerstown Suns (1)	71	65	.522	10	135,336	Grady Little
Lynchburg Mets**(21).......	65	71	.478	16	49,539	Danny Monzon
Salem Redbirds (25)	39	101	.279	52½	47,202	Jim Zerilla

South Standings	W	L	Pct.	GB	Attend.	Manager
Peninsula Pilots**(22).......	90	47	.657	—	42,145	Bill Dancy
Durham Bulls*(15)...........	80	56	.588	9½	157,325	Bobby Dews
Kinston Blue Jays (14)	76	59	.563	13	41,861	John McLaren
Winston-Salem Red Sox (2).	45	93	.326	45½	46,430	Rac Slider

Playoffs: Alexandria 1 game, Lynchburg 0; Durham 1 game, Peninsula 0.
Finals: Alexandria 3 games, Durham 0.

All-Star Team: 1B-Keith Hagman, Durham; **2B**-Juan Samuel, Peninsula; **3B**-Pat Dumouchelle, Hagerstown; **SS**-Miguel Sosa, Durham; **OF**-Jeff Stone, Peninsula; Mark Gillaspie, Salem; Joe Orsulak, Alexandria; LaSchelle Tarver, Lynchburg; **C**-David Malpeso, Winston-Salem; **DH**-Rich Renteria, Alexandria; **P**-Chris Green, Alexandria; Frankie Griffin, Peninsula; Charles Hudson, Peninsula; **MVP**-Juan Samuel, Peninsula; **Pitcher of the Year**-Charles Hudson, Peninsula; **Manager**-Bill Dancy, Peninsula.

BA: Rich Renteria, Alexandria, .331
Runs: Juan Samuel, Peninsula, 111
Hits: Rich Renteria, Alexandria, 168
RBIs: Rich Renteria, Alexandria, 100
HRs: David Malpeso, Winston-Salem, 29
Wins: Charles Hudson, Peninsula, 15
Jon McKnight, Kinston, 15
SOs: Tony Ghelfi, Peninsula, 162
ERA: Charles Hudson, Peninsula, 1.85

A Florida State League
President: George MacDonald, Jr.

North Standings	W	L	Pct.	GB	Attend.	Manager
Tampa Tarpons***(17)	71	59	.546	—	61,950	Jim Hoff
St. Petersburg Cardinals (24) ..	69	64	.529	3½	132,629	Nick Leyva
Daytona Beach Astros (18).	66	68	.493	7	97,037	Eric Swanson
Lakeland Tigers (6)	65	68	.489	7½	47,774	Bruce Kimm
Winter Haven Red Sox (2) .	59	74	.444	13½	23,000	Tom Kotchman

South Standings	W	L	Pct.	GB	Attend.	Manager
Ft. Lauderdale Yankees*(10).	82	50	.621	—	62,686	Stump Merrill
Vero Beach Dodgers**(19)	80	53	.602	2½	70,798	Terry Collins
Ft. Myers Royals (7)	69	68	.504	15½	101,597	Rick Mathews
West Palm Beach Expos (20)..	54	80	.403	29	143,840	Junior Minor
Miami Marlins	53	84	.387	31½	44,774	Jose Arcia/ Oscar Zamora/John Tamargo

Playoff: Ft. Lauderdale 2 games, Vero Beach 1.
Finals: Ft. Lauderdale 3 games, Tampa 2.

All-Star Team: 1B-Glenn Davis, Daytona Beach; **2B**-Scott Earl, Lakeland; **3B**-Ken Weislak, West palm Beach; **SS**-Bobby Meachum, St. Petersburg; **OF**-Ty Gainey, Daytona Beach; Eric Bullock, Daytona Beach; Cecil Espy, Vero Beach; **C**-Scott Bradley, Ft. Lauderdale; **DH**-Stu Pederson, Vero Beach; **P**-Bob Tewksbury, Ft. Lauderdale; Sid Fernandez, Vero Beach; Mike Smith, Tampa; Tony Ferrera, Ft. Myers; **Player of the Year**-Sid Fernandez, Vero Beach.

BA: Ty Gainey, Daytona Beach, .341
Runs: Cecil Espy, Vero Beach, 100
Hits: Cecil Espy, Vero Beach, 166
RBIs: Eric Bullock, Daytona Beach, 85
   Larry See, Vero Beach, 85
HRs: Glenn Davis, Daytona Beach, 19
   Mark Strucher, Daytona Beach, 19
Wins: Bob Tewksbury, Ft. Lauderdale, 15
SOs: Sid Fernandez, Vero Beach, 137
ERA: Bob Tewksbury, Ft. Lauderdale, 1.88

A Midwest League
President: Bill Walters

North Standings	W	L	Pct.	GB	Attend.	Manager
Madison Muskies (11)	87	52	.626	—	127,639	Brad Fischer
Appleton Foxes (4)	81	59	.579	6½	81,970	Adrian Garrett
Wisconsin Rapids Twins (9)	56	82	.406	30½	37,748	Ken Staples
Wausau Timbers (12)	55	84	.396	32	43,077	R.J. Harrison

Central Standings	W	L	Pct.	GB	Attend.	Manager
Springfield Cardinals (24)	83	53	.610	—	108,182	Dave Bialas
Beloit Brewers (8)	71	68	.511	13½	81,512	Terry Bevington
Clinton Giants (26)	63	75	.457	21	89,352	Wendell Kim
Danville Suns (3)	57	80	.416	26½	44,105	Gus Gil/Aurelio Monteagudo

South Standings	W	L	Pct.	GB	Attend.	Manager
Quad City Cubs (16)	79	60	.568	—	157,960	George Enright
Waterloo Indians (5)	75	64	.540	4	73,597	Gomer Hodge
Burlington Rangers (13)	63	75	.457	15½	59,292	Marty Scott
Cedar Rapids Reds (17)	61	79	.436	18½	101,096	Randy Davidson

Playoffs: Appleton 2 games, Springfield 0; Madison 2 games, Quad City 0.
Finals: Appleton 2 games, Madison 1.

All-Star Team: 1B-Wendell Henderson, Quad City; **2B**-Norman Carrasco, Danville; **3B**-Donell Nixon, Wausau; Wade Rowdon, Appleton; **SS**-Dick Schofield, Danville; **OF**-Daryl Boston, Appleton; Kevin Buckley, Burlington; Ivan Calderon, Wausau; Jeff Jones, Cedar Rapids; Tom Romano, Madison; **C**-Randy Hunt, Springfield; **DH**-Monte McAbee, Madison; **P**-Mark Grant, Clinton; Mike Tanzi, Appleton; **MVP**-Tom Romano, Madison; **Manager**-George Enright, Quad City.

BA: Dick Schofield, Danville, .360
Runs: Norman Carrasco, Danville, 115
Hits: Francisco Batista, Springfield, 167
RBIs: Alan Hunsinger, Springfield, 102
HRs: Jeff Jones, Cedar Rapids, 42
Wins: Mark Grant, Clinton, 16
SOs: Mark Grant, Clinton, 243
ERA: Mike Tanzi, Appleton, 2.22

A New York-Pennsylvania League
President: Vincent M. McNamara

East Standings	W	L	Pct.	GB	Attend.	Manager
Oneonta Yankees (10)	43	33	.566	—	40,155	Ken Berry
Utica Blue Sox	41	34	.547	1½	34,014	Jim Gattis
Little Falls Mets (21)	38	38	.500	5	21,918	Sam Perlozzo
Auburn Astros (18)	35	39	.473	7	38,075	Bob Hartsfield
Elmira Suns (2)	34	40	.459	8	50,189	Dick Berardino

West Standings	W	L	Pct.	GB	Attend.	Manager
Niagara Falls Sox (4)	42	34	.553	—	29,883	Fred Nelson
Jamestown Expos (20)	36	38	.486	5	38,139	Moby Benedict
Geneva Cubs (16)	36	39	.480	5½	23,341	Tony Franklin
Erie Cardinals (24)	35	38	.479	5½	48,138	Joe Rigoli
Batavia Trojans (5)	33	40	.452	7½	26,378	Dave Oliver

Playoff: Niagara Falls 2 games, Oneonta 1.

All-Star Team: 1B-John Hennell, Utica; **2B**-Jesus Alcala, Oneonta; **3B**-David Cochrane, Little Falls; **SS**-David Clements, Erie; **OF**-Ray Alonzo, Utica; Jason Felice, Little Falls; Ricky Lemon, Jamestown; **C**-Bill Packer, Erie; Hector Rivera, Jamestown; **DH**-Sam Horn, Elmira; **P**-Roy Moretti, Utica; Michael Trujillo, Niagara Falls; Jim Deshaies, Oneonta; Charles Tomaselli, Oneonta; **Manager**-Fred Nelson, Niagara Falls.

BA: Ray Alonzo, Utica, .340
Runs: John Hennell, Utica, 68
Hits: John Hennell, Utica, 91
   Ricky Lemon, Jamestown, 91
RBIs: John Hennell, Utica, 69
HRs: John Hennell, Utica, 23
Wins: Roy Moretti, Utica, 9
SOs: Jim Deshaies, Oneonta, 137
ERA: Mike Hogan, Auburn, 1.82

A Northwest League
President: Bob Freitas

North Standings	W	L	Pct.	GB	Attend.	Manager
Salem Angels (3)	34	36	.486	—	37,392	Joe Maddon
Bellingham Mariners (12)	33	37	.471	1	17,211	Jeff Scott
Walla Walla Padres (25)	32	38	.457	2	18,771	Jim Skaalen

South Standings	W	L	Pct.	GB	Attend.	Manager
Medford A's (11)	53	17	.757	—	58,053	Dennis Rogers
Bend Phillies (22)	30	40	.429	23	28,334	Rollie DeArmas
Eugene Emeralds (17)	28	42	.400	25	55,273	Jim Stewart

Playoff: Salem 2 games, Medford 0.

All-Star Team: 1B-Jim Eppard, Medford; **2B**-Brian Graham, Medford; **3B**-Chris James, Bend; **SS**-Ray Thoma, Medford; **OF**-Tony Laurenzi, Medford; Gregory Key, Salem; Roger Hill, Bellingham; **C**-Terry McGriff, Eugene; **DH**-Phil Strom, Medford; **P**-Eric Barry, Medford; Edward Myers, Medford; **Manager**-Joe Maddon, Salem.

BA: Jim Eppard, Medford, .376
Runs: Mike Madril, Salem, 61
Hits: Jim Eppard, Medford, 91
RBIs: Phil Strom, Medford, 71
HRs: Phil Strom, Medford, 15
Wins: Eric Barry, Medford, 13
SOs: Eric Barry, Medford, 106
ERA: Randy Newman, Bellingham, 1.88

A South Atlantic League
President: John H. Moss

North Standings	W	L	Pct.	GB	Attend.	Manager
Greensboro Hornets***(10)	96	45	.681	—	224,107	Doug Holmquist
Shelby Mets (21)	77	63	.550	18½	11,784	Rick Miller
Spartanburg Traders (22)	69	71	.493	26½	40,288	Tony Taylor/P.J. Carey
Asheville Tourists (18)	65	76	.461	31	55,228	Dave Cripe
Gastonia Cardinals (24)	54	89	.378	43	51,025	Lloyd Merritt

South Standings	W	L	Pct.	GB	Attend.	Manager
Florence Blue Jays**(14)	77	64	.546	—	54,446	Dennis Holmberg
Charleston Royals*(7)	74	66	.529	2½	114,859	Roy Tanner
Anderson Braves (15)	72	70	.507	5½	35,023	Brian Snitker
Macon Peaches (6)	66	72	.478	9½	66,467	Ted Brazell
Greenwood Pirates (23)	52	86	.377	23½	21,019	Joe Frisina

Playoff: Florence 2 games, Charleston 0.
Finals: Greensboro 3 games, Florence 2.

All-Star Team: 1B-Glenn Carpenter, Asheville; **2B**-Edwin Rodriguez, Greensboro; **3B**-Cliff Pastornicky, Charleston; **SS**-Edward Lowry, Spartanburg; **OF**-Mark Carreon, Shelby; Vic Mata, Greensboro; Matt Winters, Greensboro; **C**-Roger Hansen, Charleston; **DH**-Inocencio Guerrero, Anderson; **P**-David Szymczak, Greensboro; Mark Shiflett, Greensboro; **Manager**-Ted Brazell, Macon.

BA: Cliff Pastornicky, Charleston, .343
Runs: Mark Carreon, Shelby, 120
Hits: Cliff Pastornicky, Charleston, 182
RBIs: John Christensen, Shelby, 97
HRs: Randall Braun, Asheville, 23
Wins: Mark Shiflett, Greensboro, 14
   Mark Silva, Greensboro, 14
   David Szymczak, Greensboro, 14
SOs: Devallon Harper, Florence, 196
ERA: Dorn Taylor, Greenwood, 2.30

R Appalachian League
President: Bill Halstead

North Standings	W	L	Pct.	GB	Attend.	Manager
Bluefield Orioles (1)	47	22	.681	—	28,837	John Hart
Paintsville Yankees (10)	43	27	.614	4½	12,973	Mike Notaro
Pulaski Braves (15)	36	33	.522	11	31,009	Rick Albert
Pikeville Brewers (8)	25	42	.373	21	13,441	Tim Nordbrook

South Standings	W	L	Pct.	GB	Attend.	Manager
Johnson City Cardinals (24)	32	35	.478	—	21,619	Rich Hacker
Elizabethton Twins (9)	32	36	.471	½	10,912	Fred Waters
Bristol Tigers (6)	28	36	.438	2½	7,835	Boots Day
Kingsport Mets (21)	28	40	.412	4½	13,522	Ed Olsen

Playoffs: None.

All-Star Team: 1B-Jim Traber, Bluefield; **2B**-Richard Diaz, Kingsport; **3B**-Jeff Doerr, Bluefield; **SS**-Michael Moreno, Elizabethton; **OF**-Stan Javier, Johnson City; Dan Pasqua, Paintsville; Kirby Puckett, Elizabethton; **C**-Tim Wallace, Johnson City; **DH**-Preston Cash, Pulaski; **P**-Dwight Gooden, Kingsport; Tandy Charley, Bluefield; **Manager**-John Hart, Bluefield.

BA: Kirby Puckett, Elizabethton, .382
Runs: Kirby Puckett, Elizabethton, 65
Hits: Kirby Puckett, Elizabethton, 105
RBIs: Dan Pasqua, Paintsville, 63
   Jim Traber, Bluefield, 63
HRs: Dan Pasqua, Paintsville, 16
Wins: John Habyan, Bluefield, 9
   Keith Turnbull, Johnson City, 9
SOs: Randy Myers, Kingsport, 86
   Keith Turnbull, Johnson City, 86
ERA: Jose Ortega, Johnson City, 1.55

R Gulf Coast League
President: Thomas J. Saffell

Standings	W	L	Pct.	GB	Manager
Yankees (10)	42	21	.667	—	Carlos Tosca
White Sox (4)	40	23	.635	2	John Boles
Rangers (13)	36	27	.571	6	Tom Grieve
Braves (15)	32	31	.508	10	Pedro Gonzalez
Blue Jays (14)	30	33	.476	12	Hector Torres
Cubs (16)	30	33	.476	12	Jim Fairey
Padres (25)	29	34	.460	13	Manny Crespo
Royals (7)	28	35	.444	14	Joe Jones
Pirates (23)	27	35	.435	14½	Woody Huyke
Astros (18)	20	42	.323	21½	Jose Tartabull

Games played at Bradenton and Sarasota, Florida.

Playoffs: None.

All-Star Team: 1B-Fred McGriff, Yankees; **2B**-Garry Keeton, White Sox; **3B**-Shawon Dunston, Cubs; **SS**-Jose Rivera, Pirates; **OF**-Willie Broderick, Cubs; Simon Hodge, Astros; David McLaughlin, White Sox; **C**-Ron Karkovice, White Sox; **P**-Rich DeVincenzo, White Sox; Randy Coleman, San Diego; **Manager**-John Boles, White Sox.

BA: David McLaughlin, White Sox, .350
Runs: David McLaughlin, White Sox, 48
Hits: David McLaughlin, White Sox, 83
RBIs: Fred McGriff, Yankees, 41
Darnell Nelson, Yankees, 41

HRs: Fred McGriff, Yankees, 9
Wins: Rich DeVincenzo, White Sox, 9
Daryl Humphrey, Yankees, 9
SOs: Rich DeVincenzo, White Sox, 94
ERA: David Hopkins, Rangers, 1.67

R Pioneer League
President: Ralph C. Nelles

North Standings	W	L	Pct.	GB	Attend.	Manager
Medicine Hat Blue Jays (14)	44	26	.629	—	51,236	Duane Larson
Great Falls Giants (26)	43	27	.614	1	67,044	Ernest Rodriguez
Calgary Expos (20)	25	45	.357	19	25,576	Robert Reece
Lethbridge Dodgers (19)	25	45	.357	19	21,645	Gary LaRocque

South Standings	W	L	Pct.	GB	Attend.	Manager
Idaho Falls A's (11)	42	28	.600	—	22,497	Keith Lieppman
Butte Copper Kings (7)	41	29	.586	1	33,883	Tommy Jones

| Billings Mustangs (17) | 31 | 39 | .443 | 11 | 63,931 | Marc Bombard |
| Helena Phillies (22) | 29 | 41 | .414 | 13 | 14,910 | Ronald Smith |

Playoff: Medicine Hat 3 games, Idaho Falls 1.

All-Star Team: 1B-Joe Citari, Butte; **2B**-Armando Moreno, Calgary; **3B**-Leon Baham, Idaho Falls; **SS**-Kenneth Clayton, Idaho Falls; **OF**-Kal Daniels, Billings; Kash Beauchamp, Medicine Hat; Matt Cimo, Great Falls; **C**-Steven Ramler, Calgary; **P**-Pat Larkin, Great Falls; Lance McCullers, Helena; Daniel Gorden, Medicine Hat; **Manager**-Tommy Jones, Butte.

BA: Jeff Neuzil, Butte, .379
Runs: Joe Citari, Butte, 75
Hits: Leon Baham, Idaho Falls, 102
RBIs: Chris Johnston, Medicine Hat, 77

HRs: Cecil Fielder, Butte, 20
Wins: Keith Gilliam, Medicine Hat, 10
SOs: Tom Browning, Billings, 87
ERA: Todd Fischer, Idaho Falls, 1.12

1982 Interleague Post Season Play

World Series
St. Louis (National) 4 games, Milwaukee (American) 3

1982 Major League Farm Systems

American League
1 Baltimore (4): Rochester, Charlotte, Hagerstown, Bluefield.
2 Boston (5): Pawtucket, Bristol (CT), Winston-Salem, Winter Haven, Elmira.
3 California (5): Spokane, Holyoke, Redwood, Danville, Salem (OR).
4 Chicago (5): Edmonton, Glens Falls, Appleton, Niagara Falls, Gulf Coast
5 Cleveland (4): Charleston (WV), Chattanooga, Waterloo, Batavia.
6 Detroit (5): Evansville, Birmingham, Lakeland, Macon, Bristol (VA).
7 Kansas City (6): Omaha, Jacksonville, Ft. Myers, Charleston (SC), Butte, Gulf Coast.
8 Milwaukee (5): Vancouver, El Paso, Stockton, Beloit, Pikeville.
9 Minnesota (5): Toledo, Orlando, Visalia, Wisconsin Rapids, Elizabethton.
10 New York (7): Columbus (OH), Nashville, Ft. Lauderdale, Greensboro, Oneonta, Paintsville, Gulf Coast.
11 Oakland (5): Tacoma, West Haven, Modesto, Madison, Medford, Idaho Falls.
12 Seattle (5): Salt Lake City, Lynn, Bakersfield, Wausau, Bellingham.
13 Texas (4): Denver, Tulsa, Burlington, Gulf Coast.
14 Toronto (6): Syracuse, Knoxville, Kinston, Florence, Medicine Hat, Gulf Coast.

National League
15 Atlanta (6): Richmond, Savannah, Durham, Anderson, Pulaski, Gulf Coast.
16 Chicago (6): Iowa, Midland, Salinas, Quad City, Geneva, Gulf Coast.
17 Cincinnati (6): Indianapolis, Waterbury, Tampa, Cedar Rapids, Eugene, Billings.
18 Houston (6): Tucson, Columbus (GA), Daytona Beach, Asheville, Auburn, Gulf Coast.
19 Los Angeles (5): Albuquerque, San Antonio, Lodi, Vero Beach, Lethbridge.
20 Montreal (6): Wichita, Memphis, San Jose, West Palm Beach, Jamestown, Calgary.
21 New York (6): Tidewater, Jackson, Lynchburg, Shelby, Little Falls, Kingsport.
22 Philadelphia (6): Oklahoma City, Reading, Peninsula, Spartanburg, Bend, Helena.
23 Pittsburgh (5): Portland, Buffalo, Alexandria, Greenwood, Gulf Coast.
24 St. Louis (7): Louisville, Arkansas, St. Petersburg, Springfield, Gastonia, Erie, Johnson City.
25 San Diego (6): Hawaii, Amarillo, Reno, Salem (VA), Walla Walla, Gulf Coast.
26 San Francisco (5): Phoenix, Shreveport, Fresno, Clinton, Great Falls.

Independent: Miami, Utica.

1982 No-Hitters

Date	Pitcher	Team	League	Opponent	Score
4-24	Sid Fernandez	Vero Beach	Florida State	Winter Haven	5-0
4-27	Ron Romanick	Holyoke	Eastern	Buffalo	1-0
5-6	Herminio Dominguez	Campeche	Mexican	MC Tigres	2-0 (7)
5-6	Tim Kammeyer/				
	Ron Sylvia	Redwood	California	Bakersfield	1-0 (6)
5-9	Brian Brown	Gastonia	South Atlantic	Macon	3-0
5-19	Rafael Garcia	Ciudad Juarez	Mexican	MC Diablos Rojos	2-0 (P, 8)
5-21	Matt West	Savannah	Southern	Jacksonville	0-1
5-24	Jose Rodriguez	Jackson	Texas	San Antonio	5-0
5-23	Bob Kenyon	Vero Beach	Florida State	Ft. Myers	3-0
6-8	Sid Fernandez	Vero Beach	Florida State	Ft. Lauderdale	1-0
7-3	Alvaro Soto	Yucatan	Mexican	Veracruz	2-0 (7)
7-7	Jesse Jefferson	Nuevo Laredo	Mexican	Chihuahua	9-0 (7)
7-15	Jesus Hernaiz	Coatzacoalcos	Mexican	Yucatan	11-0
7-17	Les Straker	Tampa	Florida State	Winter Haven	4-0
7-18	Lenny Garcia	Nuevo Laredo	Mexican	Reynosa	5-0
7-21	Brian Innis	Lodi	California	Visalia	5-0
7-26	Brandon Chesser	West Palm Beach	Florida State	Tampa	3-1 (7)
8-2	Mark Esser/				
	Bill Atkinson	Glens Falls	Eastern	Reading	1-0 (11)
8-6	John Moller	Lakeland	Florida State	Ft. Myers	4-0 (7)
8-8	Tim Henry	Tulsa	Texas	Arkansas	1-0
8-9	Walter Pierce	St. Petersburg	Florida State	Miami	2-0 (7)
8-12	Mark Grant	Clinton	Midwest	Danville	9-0
8-13	Fernando Gonzales	Alexandria	Carolina	Winston-Salem	3-0
8-13	Rick Hatcher	Durham	Carolina	Salem	3-0 (P, 7)
8-17	Rich DeVincenzo	White Sox	Gulf Coast	Braves	3-0 (5)
8-27	Tim Wheeler/Benjamin Wiltbank/				
	Craig Pippin	Buffalo	Eastern	West Haven	1-0 (7)

Number in parentheses indicates innings if other than nine; "P" indicates perfect game.

THIS DATE IN MINOR LEAGUE HISTORY

April 14, 1982, Randy Bush of Toledo, International League, hit a home run at Charleston, West Virginia, that landed on a moving coal train beyond the right field fence. It reportedly traveled 200 miles.

April 17, 1982, Louisville, American Association, returned to baseball after a nine year absence and drew an opening night crowd of 19,632.

April 30, 1982, Durham's Brian Fisher tied a Carolina League record with 20 strike-outs against Salem. He tied another league mark by striking out the first nine batters he faced.

May 1, 1982, The sons of two well-known baseball men were added to the roster of the Anderson Braves of the South Atlantic League. Bill Lucas, Jr., son of the late Atlanta Braves general manager, and Lary Aaron, son of Henry Aaron, spent most of their time on the bench.

May 20, 1982, Slugger Ron Kittle had hit 20 home runs in his first 34 games for Edmonton, Pacific Coast League.

June 11, 1982, Yankees draft pick John Elway reported to Oneonta for an abbreviated New York-Pennsylvania League season. The outfielder would return to Stanford University in August for his final season as quarterback on the football team.

July 3, 1982, The Denver Bears, American Association, broke their own single-game attendance record when they drew 65,666 fans for a Fireworks Night game against Omaha.

August 1, 1982, Mexico City Diablos Rojos righthander Ramon Arano won his 300th Mexican League game. He would finish his 24th pro season with a 9-9 record, running his career mark to 302-216. Arano started his epic career in 1959 with Poza Rica.

August 8, 1982, The Louisville Redbirds, American Association, broke the 36-year-old record for minor league attendance in a season by drawing 19,251 fans, pushing their season total to 681,479. The figure surpassed the previous record of 670,563 set by the San Francisco Seals of the Pacific Coast League in 1946. San Francisco set the record playing a 190-game schedule, while Louisville broke the mark in its 55th home date.

September 13, 1982, Spokane's Pacific Coast League franchise moved to Las Vegas, Nevada, after 24 seasons in the Washington city.

September 14, 1982, The American Association set an all-time season attendance record of 2,407,526. The eight-team league broke its own mark of 2,235,853 set in 1948.

September 15, 1982, Steve Balboni, Columbus, International League, led a minor league in home runs for the fourth consecutive year. He had 32 homers for the Clippers.

1983

American League
President: Leland S. MacPhail, Jr.

East Standings	W	L	Pct.	GB	Attend.	Manager
Baltimore Orioles	98	64	.605	—	2,042,071	Joe Altobelli
Detroit Tigers	92	70	.568	6	1,829,636	Sparky Anderson
New York Yankees	91	71	.562	7	2,257,976	Billy Martin
Toronto Blue Jays	89	73	.537	9	1,930,415	Bobby Cox
Milwaukee Brewers	87	75	.537	11	2,397,131	Harvey Kuenn
Boston Red Sox	78	84	.481	20	1,782,285	Ralph Houk
Cleveland Indians	70	92	.432	28	768,941	Mike Ferraro/Pat Corrales

West Standings	W	L	Pct.	GB	Attend.	Manager
Chicago White Sox	99	63	.611	—	2,132,821	Tony LaRussa
Kansas City Royals	79	83	.488	20	1,963,875	Dick Howser
Texas Rangers	77	85	.475	22	1,363,469	Doug Rader
Oakland Athletics	74	88	.457	25	1,294,941	Steve Boros
California Angels	70	92	.432	29	2,555,016	John McNamara
Minnesota Twins	70	92	.432	29	858,939	Billy Gardner
Seattle Mariners	60	102	.370	39	813,537	Rene Lachemann/Del Crandall

Playoff: Baltimore 3 games, Chicago 1.

BA: Wade Boggs, Boston, .361
Runs: Cal Ripken, Jr., Baltimore, 121
Hits: Cal Ripken, Jr., Baltimore, 211
RBIs: Cecil Cooper, Milwaukee, 126
Jim Rice, Boston, 126
HRs: Jim Rice, Boston, 39

Wins: LaMarr Hoyt, Chicago, 24
SOs: Jack Morris, Detroit, 232
ERA: Rick Honeycutt, Texas, 2.42
Pct: Rich Dotson, Chicago, .759, 22-7
Saves: Dan Quisenberry, Kansas City, 45

National League
President: Charles S. Feeney

East Standings	W	L	Pct.	GB	Attend.	Manager
Philadelphia Phillies	90	72	.556	—	2,128,339	Pat Corrales/Paul Owens
Pittsburgh Pirates	84	78	.519	6	1,225,916	Chuck Tanner
Montreal Expos	82	80	.506	8	2,320,651	Bill Virdon
St. Louis Cardinals	79	83	.488	11	2,317,914	Whitey Herzog
Chicago Cubs	71	91	.438	19	1,479,717	Lee Elia/Charlie Fox
New York Mets	68	94	.420	22	1,112,774	George Bamberger/Frank Howard

West Standings	W	L	Pct.	GB	Attend.	Manager
Los Angeles Dodgers	91	71	.562	—	3,510,313	Tom Lasorda
Atlanta Braves	88	74	.543	3	2,119,938	Joe Torre
Houston Astros	85	77	.525	6	1,351,962	Bob Lillis
San Diego Padres	81	81	.500	10	1,539,815	Dick Williams
San Francisco Giants	79	83	.488	12	1,251,530	Frank Robinson
Cincinnati Reds	74	88	.457	17	1,190,419	Russ Nixon

Playoff: Philadelphia 3 games, Los Angeles 1.

BA: Bill Madlock, Pittsburgh, .323
Runs: Tim Raines, Montreal, 133
Hits: Jose Cruz, Houston, 189
Andre Dawson, Montreal, 189
RBIs: Dale Murphy, Atlanta, 121
HRs: Mike Schmidt, Philadelphia, 40

Wins: John Denny, Philadelphia, 19
SOs: Steve Carlton, Philadelphia, 275
ERA: Atlee Hammaker, San Francisco, 2.25
Pct: John Denny, Philadelphia, .760, 19-6
Saves: Lee Smith, Chicago, 29

AAA American Association
President: Joe Ryan

East Standings	W	L	Pct.	GB	Attend.	Manager
Louisville Redbirds (24)	78	57	.578	—	1,052,438	Jim Fregosi
Iowa Cubs (16)	71	65	.522	7½	255,830	Jim Napier
Indianapolis Indians (17)	64	72	.471	14½	227,595	Roy Hartsfield
Evansville Triplets (6)	61	75	.449	17½	120,703	Gordy MacKenzie

West Standings	W	L	Pct.	GB	Attend.	Manager
Denver Bears (4)	73	61	.545	—	442,870	Jim Mahoney
Oklahoma City 89ers (13)	66	69	.489	7½	226,079	Tom Burgess
Wichita Expos (20)	65	71	.478	9	128,756	Felipe Alou
Omaha Royals (7)	64	72	.471	10	137,545	Joe Sparks

Playoffs: Denver 3 games, Iowa 1; Louisville 3 games, Oklahoma City 2.
Finals: Denver 4 games, Louisville 0.

All-Star Team: 1B-Mike Stenhouse, Wichita; **2B**-Danny Rohn, Iowa; **3B**-Fritz Connally, Iowa; **SS**-Curtis Wilkerson, Oklahoma City; **OF**-Mike Fuentes, Wichita; Dave Stegman, Denver; Joe Carter, Iowa; Dallas Williams, Indianapolis; **C**-Joel Skinner, Denver; **DH**-Bill Nahorodny, Evansville; **Util**-Jeff Doyle, Louisville; **P**-Rich Barnes, Denver; Dan Larson, Iowa; **MVP**-Mike Stenhouse, Wichita; **Pitcher of the Year**-Rich Barnes, Denver; **Manager**-Jim Fregosi, Louisville.

BA: Mike Stenhouse, Wichita, .355
Runs: Mike Fuentes, Wichita, 96
Hits: Dallas Williams, Indianapolis, 168
RBIs: Jim Adducci, Louisville, 101

HRs: Carmelo Martinez, Iowa, 31
Wins: Fernando Arroyo, Denver, 14
SOs: Greg Harris, Indianapolis, 146
ERA: Craig Eaton, Evansville, 2.64

AAA International League
President: Harold Cooper

Standings	W	L	Pct.	GB	Attend.	Manager
Columbus Clippers (10)	83	57	.593	—	367,480	Johnny Oates
Richmond Braves (15)	80	59	.576	2½	293,328	Eddie Haas
Charleston Charlies (5)	74	66	.529	9	103,977	Doc Edwards
Tidewater Tides (21)	71	68	.511	11½	147,584	Davey Johnson
Toledo Mud Hens (9)	68	72	.486	15	164,269	Cal Ermer
Rochester Red Wings (1)	65	75	.464	18	284,046	Lance Nichols
Syracuse Chiefs (14)	61	78	.439	21½	166,030	Jim Beauchamp
Pawtucket Red Sox (2)	56	83	.403	26½	188,186	Tony Torchia

Playoffs: Richmond 3 games, Charleston 0; Tidewater 3 games, Columbus 2.
Finals: Tidewater 3 games, Richmond 1.

All-Star Team: 1B-Gerald Perry, Richmond; **2B**-Tim Teufel, Toledo; **3B**-Brook Jacoby, Richmond; **SS**-Tony Fernandez, Syracuse; **OF**-Brian Dayett, Columbus; Brad Komminsk, Richmond; Otis Nixon, Columbus; **C**-Geno Petralli, Syracuse; **DH**-Karl Pagel, Charleston; **P**-Walt Terrell, Tidewater; Don Cooper, Syracuse; **MVP**-Tim Teufel, Toledo; **Pitcher of the Year**-Walt Terrell, Tidewater; **Manager**-Doc Edwards, Charleston.

BA: Jack Perconte, Charleston, .346
Runs: Otis Nixon, Columbus, 129
Hits: Otis Nixon, Columbus, 162
RBIs: Brian Dayett, Columbus, 108
HRs: Brian Dayett, Columbus, 35

Wins: Mark Bomback, Syracuse, 13
Dennis Rasmussen, Columbus, 13
SOs: Dennis Rasmussen, Columbus, 187
ERA: Tom Brennan, Charleston, 3.31

AAA Mexican League
President: Pedro Treto Cisneros

North Standings	W	L	Pct.	GB	Attend.	Manager
Aguascalientes Rieleros	64	54	.542	—	235,998	Eladio Urias
Ciudad Juarez Indios	62	54	.535	1	156,388	Jose Guerrero
Tampico Astros	57	55	.509	4	178,123	Felipe Hernandez/Roberto Castellon
Saltillo Saraperos	60	58	.508	4	163,760	Cesar Gutierrez/Juan Navarrete
Nuevo Laredo Tecolotes	58	59	.496	5½	154,798	Moises Camacho/Jorge Calvo
Leon Bravos	55	61	.474	8	132,629	Domingo Rivera/Ben Valenzuela
Monterrey Sultanes	50	67	.427	13½	125,315	Mario Pelaez
Monclova Acereros	49	69	.415	15	108,526	Lee Sigman/Adolfo Cabrera

South Standings	W	L	Pct.	GB	Attend.	Manager
Mexico City Diablos Rojos	74	37	.667	—	254,900	Ben Reyes
Campeche Piratas	70	44	.614	5½	287,749	Francisco Estrada
Mexico City Tigres	65	51	.560	11½	216,913	Gregorio Luque/Fernando Remes
Yucatan Leones	60	55	.522	16	400,978	Carlos Paz
Coatzacoalcos Azules	54	63	.462	23	98,306	Ramon Arano
Tabasco Plataneros	53	62	.461	23	176,304	Mario Saldana/Mario Salazar
Veracruz Aguila	51	61	.455	23½	85,650	Jose Luis Garcia
Poza Rica Petroleros	41	73	.360	34½	105,479	David Garcia/Aaron Flores

Playoffs: In an 18-game qualifying series, Campeche, 13-5, won in the South; Ciudad Juarez, 11-7, defeated Saltillo, 11-7, in a one game playoff in the North.
Finals: Campeche 4 games, Ciudad Juarez 3.

BA: Ricardo Duran, Ciudad Juarez, .377
Runs: Ron Arnold, Nuevo Laredo, 92
Hits: Paul Herring, Tabasco, 142
RBIs: Enrique Aguilar, Aguascalientes, 89
HRs: Carlos Soto, Nuevo Laredo, 22

Wins: Teddy Higuera, Ciudad Juarez, 17
Alfonso Pulido, MC Diablos Rojos, 17
SOs: Teddy Higuera, Ciudad Juarez, 165
ERA: Arturo Gonzalez, Monterrey, 1.92

AAA Pacific Coast League
President: Bill Cutler

North Standings	W	L	Pct.	GB	Attend.	Manager
Edmonton Trappers*(3)	75	67	.528	—	224,822	Moose Stubing
Portland Beavers**(22)	75	67	.528	—	283,688	John Felske
Salt Lake City Gulls (12)	67	75	.472	8	280,130	Bobby Floyd
Tacoma Tigers (11)	65	77	.458	10	215,049	Bob Didier
Vancouver Canadians (8)	60	80	.429	14	179,337	Dick Phillips/Tony Muser

South Standings	W	L	Pct.	GB	Attend.	Manager
Albuquerque Dukes**(19)	85	58	.594	—	295,094	Del Crandall/Terry Collins
Las Vegas Stars*(25)	83	60	.580	2	365,848	Harry Dunlop/Bob Cluck
Hawaii Islanders (23)	72	71	.503	13	145,880	Tom Trebelhorn
Tucson Toros (18)	68	74	.479	16½	167,231	Matt Galante
Phoenix Giants (26)	61	82	.427	24	189,713	Jack Mull

*Won first-half   **Won second-half   ***Won both halves
Numbers after nicknames indicate farm system.
Affiliation listed at end of year.

Playoffs: Portland 3 games, Edmonton 1; Albuquerque 3 games, Las Vegas 2.
Finals: Portland 3 games, Albuquerque 0.

All-Star Team: 1B-Sid Bream, Albuquerque; **2B**-Juan Samuel, Portland; **3B**-Randy Ready, Vancouver; **SS**-Dick Schofield, Edmonton; **OF**-Kevin McReynolds, Las Vegas; Mike Brown, Edmonton; Gerald Davis, Las Vegas; **C**-Bill Schroeder, Vancouver; **DH**-Chris Smith, Phoenix; **P**-Jose DeLeon, Hawaii; Rick Rodas, Albuquerque; **MVP**-Kevin McReynolds, Las Vegas; **Manager**-John Felske, Portland.

BA: Chris Smith, Phoenix, .379
Runs: Gary Pettis, Edmonton, 138
Hits: Lemmie Miller, Albuquerque, 180
RBIs: Sid Bream, Albuquerque, 118

HRs: Sid Bream, Albuquerque, 32
Kevin McReynolds, Las Vegas, 32
Wins: Rick Rodas, Albuquerque, 16
SOs: Rick Rodas, Albuquerque, 157
ERA: Jose DeLeon, Hawaii, 3.04

AA Eastern League
President: Charles E. Eshbach

Standings	W	L	Pct.	GB	Attend.	Manager
Reading Phillies (22)	96	44	.686	—	88,484	Bill Dancy
Lynn Pirates (23)	77	62	.554	18½	31,575	Tommy Sandt
Buffalo Bisons (5)	74	65	.532	21½	200,531	Al Gallagher
New Britain Red Sox (2)	72	67	.518	23½	130,433	Rac Slider
Albany-Colonie A's (11)	63	73	.463	31	200,126	Pete Whisenant
Nashua Angels (3)	60	80	.429	36	138,030	Winston Llenas
Waterbury Reds (17)	59	80	.424	36½	55,274	Jim Lett
Glens Falls White Sox (4)	53	83	.390	41	64,562	Adrian Garrett

Playoffs: New Britain 2 games, Reading 1; Lynn 2 games, Buffalo 0.
Finals: New Britain 3 games, Lynn 1.

All-Star Team: 1B-Francisco Melendez, Reading; **2B**-Shanie Dugas, Buffalo; **3B**-Tim Pyznarski, Albany-Colonie; **SS**-Rafael Belliard, Lynn; **OF**-Benny Distefano, Lynn; Tom Romano, Albany-Colonie; Jeff Stone, Reading; **C**-Darren Daulton, Reading; **P**-Curtis Heidenreich, Waterbury; Don Carman, Reading; **MVP**-Jeff Stone, Reading; **Manager**-Bill Dancy, Reading.

BA: Dave Gallagher, Buffalo, .338
Runs: Jeff Stone, Reading, 109
Hits: Tom Romano, Albany-Colonie, 164
RBIs: Jim Wilson, Buffalo, 105
HRs: Willie Darkis, Reading, 31

Wins: Mike Bielecki, Lynn, 15
Jay Davisson, Reading, 15
SOs: Mike Bielecki, Lynn, 143
ERA: Steve Farr, Buffalo, 1.61

AA Southern League
President: Jimmy Bragan

East Standings	W	L	Pct.	GB	Attend.	Manager
Savannah Braves*(15)	81	64	.559	—	66,057	Bobby Dews
Jacksonville Suns**(7)	77	68	.531	4	137,480	Gene Lamont
Charlotte O's (1)	69	77	.473	12½	113,450	Grady Little
Columbus Astros (18)	64	79	.448	16	118,102	Jack Hiatt
Orlando Twins (9)	62	83	.428	19	70,202	Phil Roof

West Standings	W	L	Pct.	GB	Attend.	Manager
Birmingham Barons*(6)	91	54	.628	—	241,253	Roy Majtyka
Nashville Sounds**(10)	88	58	.603	3½	490,002	Doug Holmquist
Chattanooga Lookouts (12)	68	75	.476	22	150,473	Mickey Bowers/Bill Haywood
Knoxville Blue Jays (14)	64	82	.438	27½	107,304	John McLaren
Memphis Chicks (20)	61	85	.418	30½	213,183	Rick Renick

Playoffs: Jacksonville 3 games, Savannah 1; Birmingham 3 games, Nashville 2.
Finals: Birmingham 3 games, Jacksonville 1.

All-Star Team: 1B-Alvin Davis, Chattanooga; **2B**-Vic Rodriguez, Charlotte; **3B**-George Foussianes, Birmingham; **SS**-Douglas Baker, Birmingham; **OF**-Ivan Calderon, Chattanooga; Glenn Davis, Columbus; John Morris, Jacksonville; **C**-Jeff Reed, Orlando; **DH**-Gerry Lomastro, Orlando; **P**-Don Heinkel, Birmingham; Mark Langston, Chattanooga; **Manager**-Roy Majtyka, Birmingham.

BA: Ivan Calderon, Chattanooga, .311
Runs: George Foussianes, Birmingham, 106
Hits: Ivan Calderon, Chattanooga, 170
Vic Rodriguez, Charlotte, 170
RBIs: Miguel Sosa, Savannah, 93
HRs: Larry Sheets, Charlotte, 25
Glenn Davis, Columbus, 25
Wins: Don Heinkel, Birmingham, 19
SOs: Mark Gubicza, Jacksonville, 146
ERA: Roger Mason, Birmingham, 2.06

AA Texas League
President: Carl Sawatski

East Standings	W	L	Pct.	GB	Attend.	Manager
Shreveport Captains (26)	72	64	.529	—	41,963	Duane Espy
Arkansas Travelers**(24)	69	67	.507	3	214,460	Nick Leyva
Jackson Mets*(21)	69	67	.507	3	105,456	Bob Schaefer
Tulsa Drillers (13)	63	73	.463	9	92,347	Marty Scott

West Standings	W	L	Pct.	GB	Attend.	Manager
El Paso Diablos**(8)	74	62	.544	—	282,272	Tony Muser/Lee Sigman
Beaumont Golden Gators*(25)	68	68	.500	6	129,214	Jack Maloof
San Antonio Dodgers (19)	66	70	.485	8	100,283	Terry Collins/Rick Ollar/Dave Wallace
Midland Cubs (16)	63	73	.463	11	124,144	Tommy Harmon

Playoffs: Jackson 2 games, Arkansas 0; Beaumont 2 games, El Paso 1.
Finals: Beaumont 3 games, Jackson 0.

All-Star Team: 1B-Carlos Ponce, El Paso; **2B**-Trey Brooks, Midland; **3B**-Billy Max, El Paso; **SS**-Earnest Riles, El Paso; **OF**-Kevin Buckley, Tulsa; R.J. Reynolds, San Antonio; John Kruk, Beaumont; **C**-John Gibbons, Jackson; **DH**-Mark Gillaspie, Beaumont; **Util**-Steve Buechele, Tulsa; **P**-Joe Georger, Jackson; Sid Fernandez, San Antonio; **MVP**-Mark Gillaspie, Beaumont; **Pitcher of the Year**-Sid Fernandez, San Antonio; **Manager** -Nick Leyva, Arkansas.

BA: Earnest Riles, El Paso, .349
Runs: Billy Hatcher, Midland, 132
Hits: Carlos Ponce, El Paso, 176
RBIs: Mark Gillaspie, Beaumont, 122
HRs: Rob Deer, Shreveport, 35

Wins: Sid Fernandez, San Antonio, 13
Joe Georger, Jackson, 13
SOs: Sid Fernandez, San Antonio, 209
ERA: Sid Fernandez, San Antonio, 2.82

A California League
President: Joe Gagliardi

North Standings	W	L	Pct.	GB	Attend.	Manager
Stockton Ports*(8)	79	59	.572	—	89,701	Terry Bevington
Modesto A's (11)	75	64	.540	4½	76,664	George Mitterwald
Redwood Pioneers**(3)	73	65	.529	6	41,682	Jack Lind
Reno Padres (25)	63	76	.453	16½	62,749	Jim Skaalen
Lodi Dodgers (19)	60	78	.435	19	67,668	Don LeJohn

South Standings	W	L	Pct.	GB	Attend.	Manager
Visalia Oaks***(9)	87	53	.621	—	69,728	Harry Warner
Fresno Giants (26)	78	62	.557	9	87,174	Wendell Kim
Bakersfield Mariners (12)	68	72	.486	19	95,896	Greg Mahlberg
Salinas Spurs (16)	57	83	.407	30	48,850	George Enright
San Jose Bees (x)	56	84	.400	31	51,802	Frank Verdi

Playoff: Redwood 2 games, Stockton 1.
Finals: Redwood 3 games, Visalia 1.

All-Star Team: 1B-Greg Smith, Lodi; **2B**-Matt Sferrazza, Stockton; **3B**-Donell Nixon, Bakersfield; **SS**-Alvaro Espinoza, Visalia; **OF**-Dave Klipstein, Stockton; Kirby Puckett, Visalia; Mike Madril, Redwood; Brian Williams, Lodi; **C**-Matt Nokes, Fresno; **P**-Bill Wegman, Stockton; Tim Meeks, Lodi; Lee Guetterman, Bakersfield; Tim Kammeyer, Redwood; **MVP**-Stan Holmes, Visalia; **Manager**-Harry Warner, Visalia.

BA: Dave Klipstein, Stockton, .341
Runs: Donell Nixon, Bakersfield, 116
Hits: Dave Klipstein, Stockton, 185
RBIs: Stan Holmes, Visalia, 115
HRs: Stan Holmes, Visalia, 37

SBs: Donell Nixon, Bakersfield, 144
Wins: Bill Wegman, Stockton, 16
SOs: Randy Bockus, Fresno, 144
ERA: Bill Wegman, Stockton, 1.30

A Carolina League
President: James B. Mills

North Standings	W	L	Pct.	GB	Attend.	Manager
Lynchburg Mets***(21)	96	43	.691	—	80,104	Sam Perlozzo
Hagerstown Suns (1)	84	52	.618	10½	153,660	John Hart
Alexandria Dukes (23)	69	68	.504	26	41,404	John Lipon
Salem Redbirds (25)	50	89	.360	46	56,451	Steve Smith

South Standings	W	L	Pct.	GB	Attend.	Manager
Winston-Salem Red Sox***(2)	74	66	.529	—	54,803	Bill Slack
Kinston Blue Jays (14)	62	76	.449	11	45,125	Ron Clark/Doug Ault
Durham Bulls (15)	59	78	.431	13½	142,370	Brian Snitker
Peninsula Pilots (22)	58	80	.420	15	34,053	Tony Taylor

Playoff: Lynchburg 3 games, Winston-Salem 0.

All-Star Team: 1B-Sam Nattile, Winston-Salem; **2B**-Fermin Ubri, Lynchburg; **3B**-Jim Opie, Alexandria; **SS**-Mike Mesh, Winston-Salem; **OF**-Lenny Dykstra, Lynchburg; Ken Gerhart, Hagerstown; Mark Carreon, Lynchburg; **C**-Danny Sheaffer, Winston-Salem; **DH**-Dave Cochrane, Lynchburg; **P**-Mike Rochford, Winston-Salem; Dwight Gooden, Lynchburg; **MVP**-Lenny Dykstra, Lynchburg; **Pitcher of the Year**-Dwight Gooden, Lynchburg; **Manager**-Sam Perlozzo, Lynchburg.

BA: Lenny Dykstra, Lynchburg, .358
Runs: Lenny Dykstra, Lynchburg, 132
Hits: Lenny Dykstra, Lynchburg, 188
RBIs: Dave Cochrane, Lynchburg, 102
HRs: Ken Gerhart, Hagerstown, 31
Wins: Dwight Gooden, Lynchburg, 19
SOs: Dwight Gooden, Lynchburg, 300
ERA: Dwight Gooden, Lynchburg, 2.50

A Florida State League
President: George MacDonald, Jr.

North Standings	W	L	Pct.	GB	Attend.	Manager
Daytona Beach Astros***(18)	85	49	.634	—	100,155	Dave Cripe
St. Petersburg Cardinals (24)	70	64	.526	15	150,138	Nick Leyva
Lakeland Tigers (6)	58	72	.446	25	49,220	Ted Brazell
Tampa Tarpons (17)	56	71	.441	25½	64,754	Jim Hoff
Winter Haven Red Sox (2)	49	83	.371	35	24,585	Tom Kotchman

South Standings	W	L	Pct.	GB	Attend.	Manager
Ft. Lauderdale Yankees (10)	77	54	.588	—	45,415	Stump Merrill
Ft. Myers Royals*(7)	74	53	.583	1	124,259	Rick Mathews
West Palm Beach Expos (20)	75	57	.568	2½	147,805	Tommy Thompson
Vero Beach Dodgers**(19)	69	65	.515	9½	77,636	Stan Wasiak
Miami Marlins (25)	44	89	.336	34	40,652	Jim Breazeale

Playoff: Vero Beach 2 games, Ft. Myers 1.
Finals: Vero Beach 3 games, Daytona Beach 2.

All-Star Team: 1B-Glenn Carpenter, Daytona Beach; **2B**-Casey Candaele, West Palm

1983

Beach; **3B**-Tom Barrett, Ft. Lauderdale; **SS**-Brad Luther, St. Petersburg; **OF**-Curtis Burke, Daytona Beach; Orestes Destrade, Ft. Lauderdale; Dan Pasqua, Ft. Lauderdale; **C**-Roger Hansen, Ft. Myers; **DH**-Crestwell Pratt, Tampa; **P**-Jose Rijo, Ft. Lauderdale; Tom Browning, Tampa; Tim Birtsas, Ft. Lauderdale; Bret Saberhagen, Ft. Myers; **Player of the Year**-Jose Rijo, Ft. Lauderdale.

BA: Tommy Barrett, Ft. Lauderdale, .327
Runs: Randy Braun, Daytona Beach, 85
Hits: Tom Francis, Miami, 157
RBIs: Glenn Carpenter, Daytona Beach, 104
HRs: Crestwell Pratt, Tampa, 21
Wins: Jose Rijo, Ft. Lauderdale, 15
SOs: Tim Birtsas, Ft. Lauderdale, 160
ERA: Jose Rijo, Ft. Lauderdale, 1.68

A Midwest League
President: Bill Walters

North Standings	W	L	Pct.	GB	Attend.	Manager
Appleton Foxes (4)	87	50	.635	—	68,751	John Boles
Madison Muskies (11)	71	67	.514	16½	131,646	Brad Fischer
Wisconsin Rapids Twins (9)	71	67	.514	16½	51,717	Charlie Manuel
Wausau Timbers (12)	55	83	.399	34½	50,147	R.J. Harrison

Central Standings	W	L	Pct.	GB	Attend.	Manager
Cedar Rapids Reds (17)	76	64	.543	—	134,328	Bruce Kimm
Waterloo Indians (5)	76	64	.543	—	89,158	Gomer Hodge
Beloit Brewers (8)	66	71	.482	10½	91,448	Tim Nordbrook
Clinton Giants (26)	56	82	.406	19	98,641	Bill Lachemann

South Standings	W	L	Pct.	GB	Attend.	Manager
Springfield Cardinals (24)	80	59	.576	—	144,844	Dave Bialas
Burlington Rangers (13)	71	68	.511	9	49,828	Orlando Gomez
Quad City Cubs (16)	68	71	.489	12	185,677	Larry Cox
Peoria Suns (3)	54	85	.388	26	84,765	Joe Coleman

Playoffs: Appleton 2 games, Waterloo 1; Springfield 2 games, Cedar Rapids 0.
Finals: Appleton 3 games, Springfield 1.

All-Star Team: 1B-Patrick Adams, Appleton; **2B**-Gary Jones, Quad City; **3B**-Billy Joe Robidoux, Beloit; **SS**-Shawon Dunston, Quad City; **OF**-John Cangelosi, Appleton; Curt Ford, Springfield; Javier Ortiz, Burlington; Randy Washington, Waterloo; **C**-Ron Karkovice, Appleton; **DH**-David McLaughlin, Appleton; **P**-Michael Trujillo, Appleton; John Young, Springfield; **MVP**-Curt Ford, Springfield; **Manager**-Gomer Hodge, Waterloo.

BA: Javier Ortiz, Burlington, .352
Runs: Gary Jones, Quad City, 105
Hits: Edwin Tanner, Springfield, 163
RBIs: Curt Ford, Springfield, 91
HRs: Dave Heath, Peoria, 27
Wins: Rich DeVincenzo, Appleton, 18
SOs: Rich DeVincenzo, Appleton, 193
ERA: Barry Bass, Burlington, 1.68

A New York-Pennsylvania League
President: Vincent M. McNamara

East Standings	W	L	Pct.	GB	Attend.	Manager
Utica Blue Sox	48	26	.649	—	42,779	Jim Gattis
Little Falls Mets (21)	48	27	.640	½	29,867	Mike Cubbage
Auburn Astros (18)	43	31	.581	5	55,328	Bob Hartsfield
Elmira Suns (2)	38	36	.514	10	63,382	Dick Berardino
Oneonta Yankees (10)	32	44	.421	17	37,384	Bill Livesey
Watertown Pirates (23)	21	55	.276	28	78,460	Bill Bryk

West Standings	W	L	Pct.	GB	Attend.	Manager
Newark Orioles (1)	48	26	.649	—	25,001	Art Mazmanian
Jamestown Expos (20)	38	36	.514	10	36,109	Moby Benedict
Erie Cardinals (24)	37	38	.493	11½	47,111	Joe Rigoli
Geneva Cubs (16)	33	40	.452	14½	29,542	Tony Franklin
Batavia Trojans (5)	32	43	.427	16½	27,766	Brian Doyle
Niagara Falls Sox (4)	29	45	.392	19	28,301	Fred Nelson

Playoff: Utica 2 games, Newark 1.

All-Star Team: 1B-Rey Martinez, Batavia; **2B**-Rich Mattocks, Oneonta, Batavia; **SS**-Rey Quinones, Elmira; **OF**-George Chadwick, Jamestown; Stanley Jefferson, Little Falls; John Rigos, Erie; Paul Thoutsis, Elmira; **C**-Carl Nichols, Newark; Tom Pagnozzi, Erie; Robbie Wine, Auburn; **DH**-Don Jacoby, Utica; **P**-John Boyles, Little Falls; Jeff Innis, Little Falls; Rich Sauveur, Watertown; Hector Stewart, Elmira; **Manager**-Mike Cubbage, Little Falls.

BA: George Chadwick, Jamestown, .387
Runs: Don Jacoby, Utica, 67
Barry Moss, Utica, 67
Hits: Don Jacoby, Utica, 105
RBIs: Don Jacoby, Utica, 74
HRs: Don Jacoby, Utica, 22
Wins: John Boyles, Little Falls, 12
John Seitz, Utica, 12
Mike Zamba, Utica, 12
SOs: Roy Moretti, Utica, 116
ERA: Mike Friedrich, Auburn, 1.79

A Northwest League
President: Bob Freitas

Washington Standings	W	L	Pct.	GB	Attend.	Manager
Bellingham Mariners (12)	40	28	.588	—	12,944	Jeff Scott
Walla Walla Bears (x)	33	36	.478	7½	9,019	Ron Mihal
Tri-Cities Triplets (13)	33	37	.471	8	48,896	Dave Oliver
Spokane Indians (25)	23	46	.333	17½	40,137	Ed Olsen

Oregon Standings	W	L	Pct.	GB	Attend.	Manager
Medford A's (11)	50	18	.735	—	73,278	Dennis Rogers
Eugene Emeralds (17)	33	34	.493	16½	85,021	Sam Mejias
Bend Phillies (22)	32	37	.464	18½	29,063	Jay Ward
Salem Angels (3)	31	39	.443	20	31,458	Joe Maddon

Playoff: Medford 2 games, Bellingham 0.

All-Star Team: 1B-Jose Tolentino, Medford; **2B**-Keith Thrower, Medford; **3B**-Robert Martinez, Tri-Cities; **SS**-Tony Evans, Eugene; **OF**-Oriol Perez, Bellingham; Larry Beardman, Medford; Mike O'Hara, Salem; **C**-Bill Hance, Tri-Cities; Greg Toler, Eugene; **DH**-Jose Canseco, Medford; **P**-Mike Fulmer, Medford; Mark Bauer, Medford; **Manager**-Dennis Rogers, Medford.

BA: Bill Hance, Tri-Cities, .340
Runs: Brian Guinn, Medford, 61
Hits: Mike O'Hara, Salem, 86
RBIs: Reggie Montgomery, Salem, 47
HRs: Oriol Perez, Bellingham, 15
Wins: Mark Bauer, Medford, 12
SOs: Scott Whaley, Medford, 111
ERA: Mike Spini, Walla Walla, 1.34

A South Atlantic League
President: John H. Moss

North Standings	W	L	Pct.	GB	Attend.	Manager
Gastonia Expos*** (20)	84	59	.587	—	65,094	Junior Miner
Greensboro Hornets (10)	73	71	.507	11½	159,064	Carlos Tosca
Spartanburg Spinners (22)	72	71	.503	12	57,331	Rollie DeArmas
Anderson Braves (15)	64	79	.488	20	34,193	Rick Albert
Asheville Tourists (18)	64	80	.444	20½	70,985	Tom Spencer

South Standings	W	L	Pct.	GB	Attend.	Manager
Columbia Mets*** (21)	88	54	.620	—	107,113	John Tamargo
Florence Blue Jays (14)	71	72	.497	17½	54,779	Dennis Holmberg
Macon Redbirds (24)	71	73	.493	18	37,992	Lloyd Merritt
Greenwood Pirates (23)	66	78	.458	23	8,345	Joe Frisina
Charleston Royals (7)	64	80	.444	25	100,318	Roy Tanner

Playoff: Gastonia 3 games, Columbia 2.

All-Star Team: 1B-Cecil Fielder, Florence; **2B**-Armando Moreno, Gastonia; **3B**-Chris James, Spartanburg; **SS**-Timothy Thiessen, Gastonia; **OF**-Vince Coleman, Macon; Paul Hollins, Columbia; Van Snider, Charleston; **C**-Dave Stenhouse, Florence; **DH**-Keith Hughes, Spartanburg; **P**-Charley Kerfeld, Asheville; Randy Myers, Columbia; Johnny Baldwin, Greensboro; John Mortillaro, Anderson; **Manager**-John Tamargo, Columbia.

BA: Vince Coleman, Macon, .350
Runs: Jose Leiva, Spartanburg, 128
Hits: Steve Springer, Columbus, 165
RBIs: Chris James, Spartanburg, 121
HRs: Tracy Dophied, Asheville, 27
SBs: Vince Coleman, Macon, 145
Wins: Charley Kerfeld, Asheville, 16
SOs: Kevin Brown, Columbia, 221
ERA: Kevin Brown, Columbia, 2.74

R Appalachian League
President: Bill Halstead

Standings	W	L	Pct.	GB	Attend.	Manager
Paintsville Brewers (8)	47	25	.653	—	8,023	Tom Gamboa
Pulaski Braves (15)	46	26	.639	1	15,470	Buddy Bailey
Bristol Tigers (6)	34	38	.472	13	8,217	Boots Day
Pikeville Cubs (16)	33	37	.471	13	4,998	Jim Fairey
Bluefield Orioles (1)	33	38	.465	13½	25,767	Greg Biagini
Johnson City Cardinals (24)	29	43	.403	18	18,420	Rich Hacker
Elizabethton Twins (9)	28	43	.394	18½	9,983	Fred Waters

Playoffs: None.

All-Star Team: 1B-Glenn Harris, Johnson City; **2B**-Jim Walewander, Bristol; **3B**-Kerry Evertt, Paintsville; **SS**-Hector Quinones, Paintsville; **OF**-Glenn Braggs, Paintsville; Chris Baird, Pulaski; **C**-Sal D'Alessandro, Pulaski; **DH**-George Page, Bluefield; **P**-Mark Ciardi, Paintsville; Dan Plesac, Paintsville; **Manager**-Buddy Bailey, Pulaski.

BA: Glenn Braggs, Paintsville, .390
Runs: Glenn Braggs, Paintsville, 65
Hits: Glenn Braggs, Paintsville, 94
RBIs: Glenn Braggs, Paintsville, 74
HRs: Glenn Braggs, Paintsville, 16
Chris Baird, Pulaski, 16
Wins: Dan Plesac, Paintsville, 9
SOs: Dan Plesac, Paintsville, 85
ERA: Jack Hein, Johnson City, 2.53

R Gulf Coast League
President: Thomas J. Saffell

North Standings	W	L	Pct.	GB	Manager
Dodgers (19)	37	23	.617	—	Gary LaRocque
Braves (15)	32	28	.533	5	Pedro Gonzalez
Pirates (23)	28	32	.467	9	Woody Huyke
Blue Jays (14)	15	46	.246	22½	Epy Guerrero

South Standings	W	L	Pct.	GB	Manager
Rangers (13)	40	22	.645	—	Andy Hancock
White Sox (4)	38	24	.613	2	Steve Dillard
Royals (7)	30	31	.492	9½	Joe Jones
Astros (18)	29	32	.475	10½	Jose Tartabull
Mets (21)	24	35	.407	14½	Vern Hoscheit

Games played at Sarasota and Bradenton, Florida.

Playoff: Dodgers 1 game, Rangers 0.

All-Star Team: 1B-Peter Mueller, Astros; **2B**-Juan Picart, Dodgers; **3B**-Dimas Gutierrez, Pirates; **SS**-Martin Blair, Rangers; **OF**-Michael Taylor, White Sox; Gary Thurman, Royals; Fausto Quino, Rangers; **C**-Andrew Hall, Pirates; **P**-Dennis Powell, Dodgers; David Harmon, Rangers; **Manager**-Gary LaRocque, Dodgers.

BA: Peter Mueller, Astros, .376
Runs: Michael Taylor, White Sox, 55
Hits: Peter Mueller, Astros, 79
RBIs: Warren Bachmann, Braves, 47

HRs: Michael Taylor, White Sox, 8
Dimas Gutierrez, Pirates, 8
Wins: Kevin Kristan, White Sox, 9
SOs: Dennis Powell, Dodgers, 103
ERA: Ricky Hester, Rangers, 1.17

R Pioneer League
President: Ralph C. Nelles

North Standings	W	L	Pct.	GB	Attend.	Manager
Calgary Expos (20)	42	28	.600	—	41,333	Ed Creech
Lethbridge Dodgers (19)	39	31	.557	3	24,051	Gail Henley
Great Falls Giants (26)	36	34	.514	6	57,684	Terry Christman
Medicine Hat Blue Jays (14)	33	34	.493	7½	49,811	Duane Larson

South Standings	W	L	Pct.	GB	Attend.	Manager
Billings Mustangs (17)	43	27	.614	—	88,534	Marc Bombard
Butte Copper Kings (7)	41	29	.586	2	28,623	Tommy Jones
Idaho Falls A's (11)	27	40	.403	14½	21,261	Keith Lieppman/Jim Nettles
Helena Phillies (22)	16	54	.229	27	10,694	P.J. Carey

Playoff: Billings 3 games, Calgary 1.

All-Star Team: 1B-Tom Krupa, Calgary; **2B**-Ken Harvey, Lethbridge; **3B**-Mark Van Blaricom, Butte; **SS**-Jeff Hamilton, Lethbridge; **OF**-Scott Loseke, Billings; William Moore, Calgary; Otis Green, Medicine Hat; **C**-Michael Rupp, Calgary; **P**-Hubert Kemp, Billings; Jeffrey Montgomery, Billings; Joaquin Torres, Medicine Hat; **Manager**-Tommy Jones, Butte.

BA: Vic Davila, Butte, .391
Runs: Ken Harvey, Lethbridge, 70
Hits: Vince Beringhele, Lethbridge, 94
Jeff Hamilton, Lethbridge, 94
RBIs: Tom Krupa, Calgary, 70
HRs: Tom Krupa, Calgary, 20

Wins: Peter Grimm, Billings, 9
Hubert Kemp, Billings, 9
Derek Lee, Lethbridge, 9
SOs: Hubert Kemp, Billings, 138
ERA: Hubert Kemp, Billings, 2.21

1983 Interleague Post Season Play

World Series
Baltimore (American) 4 games, Philadelphia (National) 1

AAA World Series
Round Robin (at Louisville)
TIDEWATER (International) 3-1
Portland (Pacific Coast) 2-2
Denver (American Association) 1-3
Total Attendance: 26,914

1983 Major League Farm Systems

American League
1 Baltimore (5): Rochester, Charlotte, Hagerstown, Newark, Bluefield.
2 Boston (5): Pawtucket, New Britain, Winston-Salem, Winter Haven, Elmira.
3 California (5): Edmonton, Nashua, Redwood, Peoria, Salem (OR).
4 Chicago (5): Denver, Glens Falls, Appleton, Niagara Falls, Gulf Coast.
5 Cleveland (4): Charleston (WV), Buffalo, Waterloo, Batavia.
6 Detroit (4): Evansville, Birmingham, Lakeland, Bristol.
7 Kansas City (6): Omaha, Jacksonville, Ft. Myers, Charleston (SC), Butte, Gulf Coast.
8 Milwaukee (5): Vancouver, El Paso, Stockton, Beloit, Paintsville.
9 Minnesota (5): Toledo, Orlando, Visalia, Wisconsin Rapids, Elizabethton.
10 New York (5): Columbus (OH), Nashville, Ft. Lauderdale, Greensboro, Oneonta.
11 Oakland (6): Tacoma, Albany-Colonie, Modesto, Madison, Medford, Idaho Falls.
12 Seattle (5): Salt Lake City, Chattanooga, Bakersfield, Wausau, Bellingham.
13 Texas (5): Oklahoma City, Tulsa, Burlington, Tri-Cities, Gulf Coast.
14 Toronto (6): Syracuse, Knoxville, Kinston, Florence, Medicine Hat, Gulf Coast.

National League
15 Atlanta (6): Richmond, Savannah, Durham, Anderson, Pulaski, Gulf Coast.
16 Chicago (6): Iowa, Midland, Salinas, Quad City, Geneva, Pikeville.
17 Cincinnati (6): Indianapolis, Waterbury, Tampa, Cedar Rapids, Eugene, Billings.
18 Houston (6): Tucson, Columbus (GA), Daytona Beach, Asheville, Auburn, Gulf Coast.
19 Los Angeles (6): Albuquerque, San Antonio, Lodi, Vero Beach, Lethbridge, Gulf Coast.
20 Montreal (6): Wichita, Memphis, West Palm Beach, Gastonia, Jamestown, Calgary.
21 New York (6): Tidewater, Jackson, Lynchburg, Columbia, Little Falls, Gulf Coast.
22 Philadelphia (6): Portland, Reading, Peninsula, Spartanburg, Bend, Helena.
23 Pittsburgh (6): Hawaii, Lynn, Alexandria, Greenwood, Watertown, Gulf Coast.
24 St. Louis (7): Louisville, Arkansas, St. Petersburg, Macon, Springfield, Erie, Johnson City.
25 San Diego (6): Las Vegas, Beaumont, Reno, Salem (VA), Miami, Spokane.
26 San Francisco (5): Phoenix, Shreveport, Fresno, Clinton, Great Falls.

Co-op (x): San Jose, Walla Walla.
Independent: Utica.

1983 No-Hitters

Date	Pitcher	Team	League	Opponent	Score
4-12	Brian Brown/ James Strichek	Macon	South Atlantic	Florence	10-5
4-23	Francisco Cota	Miami	Florida State	Tampa	1-0
4-26	Tim Meeks	Lodi	California	Visalia	3-0
5-4	Richard Wright	Albuquerque	Pacific Coast	Portland	4-2
5-5	David Wilhelmi	Shreveport	Texas	Arkansas	7-0 (P)
5-9	Ramon Bautista	Clinton	Midwest	Appleton	2-0 (7)
5-12	Hector Madrigal	Veracruz	Mexican	Ciudad Juarez	7-0
5-18	Michael Olson	Ft. Myers	Florida State	St. Petersburg	3-0
5-21	John Glidewell	Gastonia	South Atlantic	Greensboro	3-0 (7)
6-5	Mark Ferguson	Albany-Colonie	Eastern	Nashua	9-0
6-7	Rich Doyle	Buffalo	Eastern	Albany-Colonie	6-1 (7)
6-13	Arbrey Lucas	Asheville	South Atlantic	Columbia	1-0
6-28	James Allison/ Dan Lindquist	Tri-Cities	Northwest	Spokane	4-0 (7)
6-28	Louis Marietta	San Jose	California	Visalia	5-0
7-4	Dave Righetti	New York	American	Boston	4-0
7-4	Mike Cunningham	Lodi	California	Redwood	2-0 (7)
7-8	James Allison/ Nick Esposito	Tri-Cities	Northwest	Salem	2-1
7-9	Anthony Ferreira	Jacksonville	Southern	Knoxville	6-0
7-15	Jeff Green/ Steven Cotter	Pulaski	Appalachian	Paintsville	3-1
7-16	Richard Strasser	Asheville	South Atlantic	Anderson	1-0
7-21	Alvaro Soto	Leon	Mexican	Monterrey	5-0 (7)
7-25	Bill Fulton	Oneonta	New York-Penn.	Geneva	1-0
8-3	Randy Ramirez	Bakersfield	California	Stockton	1-0 (P)
8-12	Richard Gaynor	Reading	Eastern	Nashua	6-0
8-17	Martin Schreiber	Pulaski	Appalachian	Elizabethton	5-0
8-20	Scott Garrelts	Phoenix	Pacific Coast	Tacoma	1-0 (7)
8-24	Richard Burke	Royals	Gulf Coast	Dodgers	13-0
8-25	Robert Veselic	Columbus	Southern	Nashville	2-0
9-1	Peter Grimm	Billings	Pioneer	Calgary	5-0 (PO)
9-26	Bob Forsch	St. Louis	National	Montreal	3-0
9-29	Mike Warren	Oakland	American	Chicago	3-0

Number in parentheses indicates innings if other than nine; "P" indicates perfect game; "PO" indicates playoff game.

THIS DATE IN MINOR LEAGUE HISTORY

April 10, 1983, Pam Postema became the first woman to umpire in Triple-A baseball.

April 30, 1983, In a Texas League game at El Paso, the home club defeated Beaumont 35-21 in one of the highest scoring games in minor league history. The contest, which lasted three hours, 39 minutes, produced 56 hits.

June 21, 1983, Author Roger Kahn, who wrote the baseball classic "Boys of Summer", became president of the independent Utica Blue Sox of the New York-Pennsylvania League. He would write a book about the season, titled "Good Enough to Dream".

July 7, 1983, 69-year-old Eddie Popowski, interim manager for Winston-Salem, won his first 12 games with the Red Sox. Manager Bill Slack had taken a leave to be with his ailing mother.

August 25, 1983, The Louisville Redbirds became the first minor league team in baseball history to attract one million fans during a season. The Redbirds reached the mark with two home dates remaining. The club's final attendance was 1,052,438.

August 30, 1983, 18-year old Dwight Gooden of Lynchburg set a new Carolina League record by striking out 300 batters in a season. Ken Deal set the previous mark of 275 for Burlington in 1947. Gooden reached his mark in just 191 innings pitched.

September 1, 1983, Peter Grimm, Billings, tossed the first ever Pioneer League playoff no-hitter as he beat Calgary 5-0. Grimm faced only 27 batters. The only Expos' runner was erased in a fourth inning double play. The righthander fanned 12, including striking out the side in the final stanza.

September 1, 1983, Vince Coleman, Macon, South Atlantic League, set the all-time minor league record with his 145th stolen base of the season. Bakersfield's Donell Nixon finished with 144 steals in the California League.

September 14, 1983, With the Triple-A World Series scheduled to begin in Louisville, the Chicago White Sox recalled six key players from Denver, American Association. Substitutes were summoned from Class AA Glens Falls and Class A Appleton.

1984

American League
President: Dr. Robert W. Brown

East Standings	W	L	Pct.	GB	Attend.	Manager
Detroit Tigers..................	104	58	.642	—	2,704,794	Sparky Anderson
Toronto Blue Jays.............	89	73	.549	15	2,110,009	Bobby Cox
New York Yankees.............	87	75	.537	17	1,821,815	Yogi Berra
Boston Red Sox	86	76	.531	17	1,661,618	Ralph Houk
Baltimore Orioles	85	77	.525	18	2,045,784	Joe Altobelli
Cleveland Indians.............	75	87	.463	28	734,079	Pat Corrales
Milwaukee Brewers...........	67	94	.416	36½	1,608,509	Rene Lachemann

West Standings	W	L	Pct.	GB	Attend.	Manager
Kansas City Royals............	84	78	.519	—	1,810,018	Dick Howser
California Angels...............	81	81	.500	3	2,402,997	John McNamara
Minnesota Twins................	81	81	.500	3	1,598,692	Billy Gardner
Oakland Athletics	77	85	.475	7	1,353,281	Steve Boros/Jackie Moore
Chicago White Sox	74	88	.457	10	2,136,988	Tony LaRussa
Seattle Mariners................	74	88	.457	10	870,372	Del Crandall/Chuck Cottier
Texas Rangers...................	69	92	.429	14½	1,102,471	Doug Rader

Playoff: Detroit 3 games, Kansas City 0.

BA: Don Mattingly, New York, .343
Runs: Dwight Evans, Boston, 121
Hits: Don Mattingly, New York, 207
RBIs: Tony Armas, Boston, 123
HRs: Tony Armas, Boston, 43

Wins: Mike Boddicker, Baltimore, 20
SOs: Mark Langston, Seattle, 204
ERA: Mike Boddicker, Baltimore, 2.79
Pct: Doyle Alexander, Toronto, .739, 17-6
Saves: Dan Quisenberry, Kansas City, 44

National League
President: Charles S. Feeney

East Standings	W	L	Pct.	GB	Attend.	Manager
Chicago Cubs....................	96	65	.596	—	2,107,655	Jim Frey
New York Mets	90	72	.556	6½	1,842,695	Davey Johnson
St. Louis Cardinals	84	78	.519	12½	2,037,448	Whitey Herzog
Philadelphia Phillies	81	81	.500	15½	2,062,693	Paul Owens
Montreal Expos	78	83	.484	18	1,606,531	Bill Virdon/Jim Fanning
Pittsburgh Pirates	75	87	.463	21½	773,500	Chuck Tanner

West Standings	W	L	Pct.	GB	Attend.	Manager
San Diego Padres...............	92	70	.568	—	1,983,904	Dick Williams
Atlanta Braves	80	82	.494	12	1,724,892	Joe Torre
Houston Astros	80	82	.494	12	1,229,862	Bob Lillis
Los Angeles Dodgers..........	79	83	.488	13	3,134,824	Tom Lasorda
Cincinnati Reds.................	70	92	.432	22	1,275,887	Vern Rapp/Pete Rose
San Francisco Giants	66	96	.407	26	1,001,545	Frank Robinson/Danny Ozark

Playoff: San Diego 3 games, Chicago 2.

BA: Tony Gwynn, San Diego, .351
Runs: Ryne Sandberg, Chicago, 114
Hits: Tony Gwynn, San Diego, 213
RBIs: Gary Carter, Montreal, 106
    Mike Schmidt, Philadelphia, 106

HRs: Dale Murphy, Atlanta, 36
    Mike Schmidt, Philadelphia, 36
Wins: Joaquin Andujar, St. Louis, 20
SOs: Dwight Gooden, New York, 276
ERA: Alejandro Pena, Los Angeles, 2.48
Pct: Rick Sutcliffe, Chicago, .941, 16-1
Saves: Bruce Sutter, St. Louis, 45

AAA American Association
President: Joe Ryan

Standings	W	L	Pct.	GB	Attend.	Manager
Indianapolis Indians (20)....	91	63	.591	—	223,262	Buck Rodgers
Iowa Cubs (16).................	80	74	.519	11	275,163	Jim Napier
Denver Bears (4)................	79	75	.513	12	366,262	Vern Law/Adrian Garrett
Louisville Redbirds (24).....	79	76	.510	12½	846,878	Jim Fregosi
Wichita Aeros (17)	78	77	.503	13½	137,018	Gene Dusan
Evansville Triplets (6)........	72	84	.468	19	100,326	Gordy MacKenzie
Oklahoma City 89ers (13) ..	70	84	.455	21	243,423	Tom Burgess/Rusty Gerhardt
Omaha Royals (7)..............	68	86	.442	23	149,369	Gene Lamont

Playoffs: Louisville defeated Wichita in a one game playoff for fourth place. Louisville 4 games, Indianapolis 2; Denver 4 games, Iowa 1.
Finals: Louisville 4 games, Denver 1.

All-Star Team: 1B-Alan Knicely, Wichita; **2B**-Scott Earl, Evansville; **3B**-Jose Castro, Denver; **SS**-Jose Gonzales, Louisville; **OF**-Daryl Boston, Denver; Vince Coleman, Louisville; Tommy Dunbar, Oklahoma City; **C**-Kevin Buckley, Oklahoma City; Russ Stephans, Omaha; **DH**-Gary Rajsich, Louisville; **P**-Dick Grapenthin, Indianapolis; Joe Hesketh, Indianapolis; **MVP**-Alan Knicely, Wichita; **Pitcher of the Year**-Joe Hesketh, Indianapolis; **Manager**-Buck Rodgers, Indianapolis.

BA: Tommy Dunbar, Oklahoma City .337
Runs: Vince Coleman, Louisville, 97
Hits: Alan Knicely, Wichita, 190
RBIs: Alan Knicely, Wichita, 126

HRs: Joe Hicks, Iowa, 37
Wins: Reggie Patterson, Iowa, 14
SOs: Tom Browning, Wichita, 160
ERA: Chris Welsh, Indianapolis, 3.01

AAA International League
President: Harold Cooper

Standings	W	L	Pct.	GB	Attend.	Manager
Columbus Clippers (10)......	82	57	.590	—	520,478	Stump Merrill
Maine Guides#(5)..............	77	59	.566	3½	183,289	Doc Edwards
Toledo Mud Hens (9).........	74	63	.540	7	182,247	Cal Ermer
Pawtucket Red Sox (2)	75	65	.536	7½	198,786	Tony Torchia
Tidewater Tides (21)	71	69	.507	11½	132,260	Bob Schaefer
Richmond Braves (15)........	66	73	.475	16	165,513	Eddie Haas/Bobby Dews
Syracuse Chiefs (14)..........	58	81	.417	24	141,499	Jim Beauchamp
Rochester Red Wings (1)....	52	88	.371	30½	191,607	Frank Verdi

#represented Old Orchard Beach, Maine.

Playoffs: Pawtucket 3 games, Columbus 1; Maine 3 games, Toledo 0.
Finals: Pawtucket 3 games, Maine 2.

All-Star Team: 1B-Dan Briggs, Columbus; **2B**-Rex Hudler, Columbus; **3B**-Steve Lyons, Pawtucket; **SS**-Paul Zuvella, Richmond; **OF**-John Christensen, Tidewater; Milt Thompson, Richmond; Mitch Webster, Syracuse; **C**-Scott Bradley, Columbus; **DH**-Jerry Keller, Syracuse; **P**-Brad Havens, Toledo; Wes Gardner, Tidewater; **MVP**-Scott Bradley, Columbus; **Pitcher of the Year**-Brad Havens, Toledo; **Manager**-Tony Torchia, Pawtucket.

BA: Scott Bradley, Columbus, .335
Runs: Milt Thompson, Richmond, 91
    Chico Walker, Pawtucket, 91
Hits: Scott Bradley, Columbus, 180

RBIs: Scott Bradley, Columbus, 84
    Jim Wilson, Maine, 84
HRs: Jerry Keller, Syracuse, 28
Wins: Gerald Ujdur, Maine, 14
SOs: Brad Havens, Toledo, 169
ERA: Jim Deshaies, Columbus, 2.39

AAA Mexican League
President: Pedro Treto Cisneros

North Standings	W	L	Pct.	GB	Attend.	Manager
Aguascalientes Rieleros......	65	52	.556	—	251,135	Francisco Rodriguez
Nuevo Laredo Tecolotes.....	64	53	.547	1	160,030	Jorge Calvo
Ciudad Juarez Indios	57	55	.509	5½	140,642	Jose Guerrero
Saltillo Saraperos...............	58	58	.500	6½	222,764	Moises Camacho/Juan Navarrete
Tampico Astros..................	54	56	.491	7½	305,297	Gregorio Luque
Monterrey Sultanes............	56	60	.483	8½	136,005	Mario Pelaez
Leon Bravos.....................	53	61	.465	10½	119,734	Marcelo Juarez/Ben Valenzuela
Monclova Acereros............	39	76	.339	25	95,409	Mario Mendoza/Servando Gonzalez/Vinicio Garcia

South Standings	W	L	Pct.	GB	Attend.	Manager
Mexico City Diablos Rojos......	75	41	.647	—	211,084	Ben Reyes
Mexico City Tigres.............	66	44	.600	6	232,664	Fernando Remes
Toluca Truchas	67	49	.578	8	56,839	Francisco Estrada/Max Oliveras
Yucatan Leones.................	65	51	.560	10	515,440	Carlos Paz
Cordoba Cafeteros.............	60	52	.536	13	159,135	Roberto Castellon
Veracruz Aguila.................	55	62	.470	20½	157,758	Jose Luis Garcia/George Scott/Cesar Gutierrez
Tabasco Plataneros	39	68	.364	31½	90,055	Alberto Joachin/Domingo Cruz
Campeche Piratas	37	72	.339	34½	116,660	David Garcia/Jose Dolores Juarez

Playoffs: Aguascalientes 4 games, Saltillo 3; Ciudad Juarez 4 games, Nuevo Laredo 1; Yucatan 4 games, MC Diablos Rojos 0; MC Tigres 4 games, Toluca 2. Ciudad Juarez 4 games, Aguascalientes 3; Yucatan 4 games, MC Tigres 3.
Finals: Yucatan 4 games, Ciudad Juarez 2.

BA: Jimmie Collins, MC Diablos Rojos/Cordoba, .412
Runs: Juan Monasterio, MC Diablos Rojos, 105
    Jesus Rivera, Aguascalientes, 105
Hits: Juan Monasterio, MC Diablos Rojos, 175
RBIs: Ramon Lora, Toluca, 127
HRs: Derek Bryant, Tampico, 41

Wins: Salvador Colorado, Cordoba, 17
    Miguel Solis, Saltillo, 17
    Jesus Rios, MC Tigres, 17
    Luis Fernando Mendez, MC Diablos Rojos, 17
    Jaime Orozco, Toluca, 17
SOs: Jesus Rios, MC Tigres, 194
ERA: Salvador Colorado, Cordoba, 2.20

AAA Pacific Coast League
President: Bill Cutler

North Standings	W	L	Pct.	GB	Attend.	Manager
Salt Lake City Gulls**(12).	74	66	.529	—	167,803	Bobby Floyd
Vancouver Canadians (8) ...	71	71	.500	4	147,599	Tony Muser
Tacoma Tigers (11)............	69	71	.493	5	203,821	Ed Nottle
Edmonton Trappers*(3)......	69	73	.486	6	228,102	Moose Stubing
Portland Beavers (22).........	62	78	.443	12	184,143	Lee Elia

*Won first-half   **Won second-half   ***Won both halves
Numbers after nicknames indicate farm system.
Affiliation listed at end of year.

570

South Standings	W	L	Pct.	GB	Attend.	Manager
Hawaii Islanders**(23)	87	53	.621	—	144,232	Tommy Sandt
Las Vegas Stars*(25)	71	65	.522	14	320,157	Bob Cluck
Tucson Toros (18)	69	71	.493	18	124,232	Matt Galante
Phoenix Giants (26)	69	74	.483	19½	163,843	Jack Mull
Albuquerque Dukes (19)	62	81	.434	26½	244,229	Terry Collins

Playoffs: Hawaii 3 games, Las Vegas 1; Edmonton 3 games, Salt Lake City 2.
Finals: Edmonton 2 games, Hawaii 0.

All-Star Team: 1B-Sid Bream, Albuquerque; **2B**-Harold Reynolds, Salt Lake City; **3B**-Rick Schu, Portland; **SS**-Ozzie Guillen, Las Vegas; **OF**-Alejandro Sanchez, Phoenix; Doug Loman, Vancouver; Tony Brewer, Albuquerque; **C**-Jamie Nelson, Vancouver; **DH**-Rick Lancellotti, Las Vegas; **P**-Mike Bielecki, Hawaii; Alfonso Pulido, Hawaii; **MVP**-Alejandro Sanchez, Phoenix; **Manager**-Tommy Sandt, Hawaii.

BA: Tony Brewer, Albuquerque, .357
Runs: Chris Clark, Edmonton, 104
Hits: Doug Loman, Vancouver, 170
RBIs: Rick Lancellotti, Las Vegas, 131
HRs: Rob Deer, Phoenix, 31
Wins: Mike Bielecki, Hawaii, 19
SOs: Mike Bielecki, Hawaii, 162
ERA: Bob Walk, Hawaii, 2.26

AA Eastern League
President: Charles E. Eshbach

Standings	W	L	Pct.	GB	Attend.	Manager
Albany-Colonie A's (11)	81	57	.587	—	199,534	Keith Lieppman
Glens Falls White Sox (4)	75	63	.543	6	103,225	John Boles
Waterbury Angels (3)	76	64	.543	6	36,323	Winston Llenas
Vermont Reds#(17)	75	65	.536	7	121,102	Jack Lind
Buffalo Bisons (5)	72	67	.518	9½	223,644	Jack Aker
New Britain Red Sox (2)	64	76	.457	18	79,949	Rac Slider
Nashua Pirates (23)	58	82	.414	24	126,263	Bill Scripture
Reading Phillies (22)	56	83	.403	25½	67,333	Bill Dancy

#represented Burlington, Vermont.

Playoffs: Vermont 3 games, Albany-Colonie 0; Waterbury 3 games, Glens Falls 1.
Finals: Vermont 3 games, Waterbury 2.

All-Star Team: 1B-Pat Adams, Glens Falls; **2B**-Norman Carrasco, Waterbury; **3B**-Rick Stromer, Waterbury; **SS**-Jeff Moronko, Buffalo; **OF**-Kal Daniels, Vermont; Don Carter, Buffalo; John Cangelosi, Glens Falls; **C**-Mickey Tettleton, Albany-Colonie; **DH**-Wally Joyner, Waterbury; **P**-Scott Terry, Vermont; Dave Lochner, Vermont; Chuck Dale, New Britain; **MVP**-Pat Adams, Glens Falls; **Manager**-Keith Lieppman, Albany-Colonie.

BA: Thad Reece, Albany-Colonie, .331
Runs: Mike Madril, Waterbury, 95
Hits: Don Carter, Buffalo, 149
RBIs: Pat Adams, Glens Falls, 102
HRs: Pat Adams, Glens Falls, 24
Wins: Tim Lambert, Albany-Colonie, 17
SOs: Bob Bastian, Waterbury, 119
ERA: Scott Terry, Vermont, 1.50

AA Southern League
President: Jimmy Bragan

East Standings	W	L	Pct.	GB	Attend.	Manager
Greenville Braves*(15)	80	61	.567	—	217,096	Bobby Dews/Leo Mazzone
Orlando Twins (9)	79	65	.549	2½	72,258	Charlie Manuel
Jacksonville Suns (20)	76	69	.524	6	97,158	Rick Renick
Charlotte O's**(1)	75	72	.510	8	122,792	Grady Little/John Hart
Columbus Astros (18)	69	71	.493	10½	95,167	Bob Bailey/Jimmy Johnson

West Standings	W	L	Pct.	GB	Attend.	Manager
Nashville Sounds**(10)	74	73	.503	—	372,701	Jim Marshall
Memphis Chicks (7)	71	75	.486	2½	208,851	Rick Mathews
Knoxville Blue Jays*(14)	70	75	.483	3	100,576	John McLaren
Birmingham Barons (6)	66	81	.449	8	175,958	Roy Majtyka
Chattanooga Lookouts (12)	63	81	.439	9½	130,509	Bill Plummer

Playoffs: Charlotte 3 games, Greenville 1; Knoxville 3 games, Nashville 1.
Finals: Charlotte 3 games, Knoxville 0.

All-Star Team: 1B-Andres Galarraga, Jacksonville; **2B**-Mike Sharperson, Knoxville; **3B**-Bill Pecota, Memphis; **SS**-Keith Smith, Nashville; **OF**-Mickey Brantley, Chattanooga; Frank "Doc" Estes, Greenville; Ty Gainey, Columbus; Dan Pasqua, Nashville; **C**-Matt Sinatro, Greenville; **DH**-Stan Holmes, Orlando; **P**-Ken Dixon, Charlotte; Bryan Oelkers, Orlando; **MVP**-Andres Galarraga, Jacksonville; **Pitcher of the Year**-Ken Dixon, Charlotte; **Manager**-Charlie Manuel, Orlando; Rick Renick, Jacksonville.

BA: Frank "Doc" Estes, Greenville, .341
Runs: Mike Cole, Greenville, 105
Hits: Frank "Doc" Estes, Greenville, 174
RBIs: Stan Holmes, Orlando, 101
HRs: Dan Pasqua, Nashville, 33
Wins: Ken Dixon, Charlotte, 16; Bryan Oelkers, Orlando, 16
SOs: Ken Dixon, Charlotte, 211
ERA: Mark Williams, Jacksonville, 2.49

AA Texas League
President: Carl Sawatski

East Standings	W	L	Pct.	GB	Attend.	Manager
Jackson Mets***(21)	83	53	.610	—	119,007	Sam Perlozzo
Tulsa Drillers (13)	62	73	.459	20½	124,160	Orlando Gomez
Arkansas Travelers (24)	62	74	.456	21	212,029	Dave Bialas
Shreveport Captains (26)	59	77	.434	24	42,384	Duane Espy

West Standings	W	L	Pct.	GB	Attend.	Manager
Beaumont Golden Gators***(25)	89	47	.654	—	130,950	Bobby Tolan
El Paso Diablos (8)	72	63	.533	16½	205,196	Terry Bevington
San Antonio Dodgers (19)	64	72	.471	25	125,542	Gary LaRocque
Midland Cubs (16)	52	84	.382	37	101,312	George Enright

Playoff: Jackson 4 games, Beaumont 2.

All-Star Team: 1B-Pat Casey, Beaumont; **2B**-Greg Tabor, Tulsa; **3B**-Dale Sveum, El Paso; **SS**-Shawon Dunston, Midland; **OF**-Ralph Bryant, San Antonio; James Steels, Beaumont; Curt Ford, Arkansas; **C**-Gilberto Reyes, San Antonio; Mark Parent, Beaumont; **DH**-Mark Gillaspie, Beaumont; **Util**-Joe Vavra, San Antonio; **P**-Calvin Schiraldi, Jackson; William Long, Beaumont; Tim Meeks, San Antonio; Pete Kutsukos, Beaumont; Teddy Higuera, El Paso; **MVP**-James Steels, Beaumont; **Pitcher of the Year**-Calvin Schiraldi, Jackson; **Manager**-Sam Perlozzo, Jackson.

BA: James Steels, Beaumont, .340
Runs: Lenny Dykstra, Jackson, 100
Hits: Dale Sveum, El Paso, 172
RBIs: Mark Gillaspie, Beaumont, 87
HRs: Ralph Bryant, San Antonio, 31
Wins: William Long, Beaumont, 14; Tim Meeks, San Antonio, 14; Calvin Schiraldi, Jackson, 14
SOs: John Young, Arkansas, 136
ERA: Teddy Higuera, El Paso, 2.60

A California League
President: Joe Gagliardi

North Standings	W	L	Pct.	GB	Attend.	Manager
Redwood Pioneers**(3)	91	48	.655	—	60,282	Tom Kotchman
Modesto A's*(11)	83	56	.597	8	70,356	George Mitterwald
Reno Padres (25)	65	74	.468	26	75,938	Jim Skaalen
Stockton Mudville Nine (8)	64	75	.460	27	97,005	Tim Nordbrook/Mike Pazik/Andy Etchebarren
Lodi Crushers (16)	58	82	.414	33½	45,027	Junior Kennedy

South Standings	W	L	Pct.	GB	Attend.	Manager
Fresno Giants*(26)	82	58	.586	—	86,711	Wendell Kim
Bakersfield Dodgers**(19)	68	72	.486	14	102,053	Don LeJohn
Salinas Spurs (12)	66	74	.471	16	54,400	R.J. Harrison
Visalia Oaks (9)	66	74	.471	16	65,043	Dave Hilton
San Jose Bees	55	85	.393	27	46,081	Al Gallagher

Playoffs: Modesto 2 games, Redwood 1; Bakersfield 2 games, Fresno 1.
Finals: Modesto 3 games, Bakersfield 1.

All-Star Team: 1B-Mike Aldrete, Fresno; **2B**-Roy Etchebarren, Reno; **3B**-Steve Aragon, Visalia; **SS**-Rickey Coleman, Reno; **OF**-Reggie Montgomery, Redwood; Rock Coyle, Modesto; **C**-Benito Santiago, Reno; **DH**-Glenn Braggs, Stockton; **P**-Bob Kipper, Redwood; Don Timberlake, Redwood; Doug McKenzie, Redwood; Johnny Abrego, Lodi; **MVP**-Glenn Braggs, Stockton; **Pitcher of the Year**-Bob Kipper, Redwood; **Manager**-Tom Kotchman, Redwood.

BA: Rickey Coleman, Reno, .351
Runs: Gary Jones, Lodi, 111
Hits: Rickey Coleman, Reno, 175
RBIs: Mark Bonner, Redwood, 92
HRs: Mark Bonner, Redwood, 20
Wins: Bob Kipper, Redwood, 18
SOs: Randy Newman, Salinas, 169
ERA: Bob Kipper, Redwood, 2.04

A Carolina League
President: John Hopkins

East Standings	W	L	Pct.	GB	Attend.	Manager
Lynchburg Mets***(21)	89	49	.645	—	75,034	Mike Cubbage
Prince William Pirates#(23)	75	65	.536	15	108,818	John Lipon
Salem Redbirds (13)	64	74	.464	25	61,623	Bill Stearns
Hagerstown Suns (1)	60	80	.429	30	114,951	John Hart/Grady Little/Len Johnston

West Standings	W	L	Pct.	GB	Attend.	Manager
Peninsula Pilots**(22)	73	67	.521	—	27,465	Ron Clark
Kinston Blue Jays (14)	71	69	.507	2	61,204	Doug Ault
Durham Bulls*(15)	68	72	.486	5	157,109	Brian Snitker
Winston-Salem Spirits (2)	58	82	.414	15	75,272	Bill Slack

#represented Woodbridge, Virginia.

Playoff: Durham 2 games, Peninsula 0.
Finals: Lynchburg 3 games, Durham 1.

All-Star Team: 1B-Dave Magadan, Lynchburg; **2B**-Bip Roberts, Prince William; **3B**-Kim Christensen, Prince William; **SS**-Rey Quinones, Winston-Salem; **OF**-Kash Beauchamp, Kinston; Stanley Jefferson, Lynchburg; Jason Felice, Lynchburg; **C**-Barry Lyons, Lynchburg; **DH**-Sam Horn, Winston-Salem; **P**-Randy Myers, Lynchburg; Mitch Cook, Lynchburg; **MVP**-Barry Lyons, Lynchburg; **Pitcher of the Year**-Randy Myers, Lynchburg; **Manager**-Mike Cubbage, Lynchburg.

BA: Dave Magadan, Lynchburg, .350
Runs: Stanley Jefferson, Lynchburg, 113
Hits: Bip Roberts, Prince William, 150
RBIs: Randy Day, Peninsula, 103
HRs: Randy Day, Peninsula, 29
Wins: Mitch Cook, Lynchburg, 16
SOs: Mitch Cook, Lynchburg, 178
ERA: Randy Myers, Lynchburg, 2.06

A Florida State League
President: George MacDonald, Jr.

North Standings	W	L	Pct.	GB	Attend.	Manager
Daytona Beach Astros**(18)	82	62	.569	—	102,510	Dave Cripe
Tampa Tarpons*(17)	74	65	.532	5½	62,776	Marc Bombard
St. Petersburg Cardinals (24)	71	73	.493	11	144,692	Jim Riggleman
Winter Haven Red Sox (2)	70	74	.486	12	18,249	Dave Holt
Lakeland Tigers (6)	46	98	.319	36	36,107	Bill Fahey

South Standings

	W	L	Pct.	GB	Attend.	Manager
Ft. Myers Royals*(7)	81	60	.574	—	137,553	Tommy Jones
Vero Beach Dodgers (19)	79	67	.541	4½	81,453	Stan Wasiak
Ft. Lauderdale Yankees**(10)	74	68	.521	7½	50,201	Barry Foote
West Palm Beach Expos (20)	72	72	.500	10½	134,771	Tommy Thompson
Miami Marlins (25)	64	74	.464	15½	38,313	Steve Smith

Playoffs: Ft. Lauderdale 2 games, Ft. Myers 0; Tampa 2 games, Daytona Beach 0.
Finals: Ft. Lauderdale 3 games, Tampa 2.

All-Star Team: 1B-Mike Hocutt, West Palm Beach; **2B**-Chris Cannizzaro, Winter Haven; **3B**-Jeff Hamilton, Vero Beach; **SS**-Nelson Rood, Daytona Beach; **OF**-Bill Moore, West Palm Beach; Mike Ramsey, Vero Beach; Tracy Jones, Tampa; **C**-Robbie Wine, Daytona Beach; **DH**-Dana Williams, Winter Haven; **P**-Billy Hawley, Tampa; Jeff Montgomery, Tampa; John Mitchell, Winter Haven; Mark Heuer, Vero Beach; **MVP**-Bill Moore, West Palm Beach; **Manager**-Barry Foote, Ft. Lauderdale.

BA: Dana Williams, Winter Haven, .327
Runs: Bill Moore, West Palm Beach, 102
Hits: Dana Williams, Winter Haven, 167
RBIs: Mike Hocutt, West Palm Beach, 100

HRs: Bill Moore, West Palm Beach, 22
Wins: Bill Hawley, Tampa, 18
SOs: Eric Plunk, Ft. Lauderdale, 152
ERA: Bill Hawley, Tampa, 1.87

A Midwest League
President: Bill Walters

North Standings

	W	L	Pct.	GB	Attend.	Manager
Appleton Foxes (4)	87	49	.640	—	54,281	Sal Rende
Madison Muskies (11)	77	61	.558	11	118,161	Brad Fischer
Wausau Timbers (12)	70	66	.515	17	50,095	Greg Mahlberg
Kenosha Twins (9)	70	68	.507	18	87,672	Duffy Dyer

Central Standings

	W	L	Pct.	GB	Attend.	Manager
Beloit Brewers (8)	86	53	.619	—	92,474	Tom Gamboa
Cedar Rapids Reds (17)	75	63	.543	10½	134,639	Jim Lett
Waterloo Indians (5)	65	74	.468	21	70,878	Gomer Hodge
Clinton Giants (26)	62	77	.446	24	91,872	Bill Lachemann

South Standings

	W	L	Pct.	GB	Attend.	Manager
Springfield Cardinals (24)	70	69	.504	—	141,321	Joe Rigoli
Peoria Chiefs (3)	66	73	.475	4	116,473	Joe Madden
Burlington Rangers (13)	51	88	.367	19	60,528	Rudy Jaramillo
Quad City Cubs (16)	50	88	.362	19½	124,788	Larry Cox

Playoffs: Springfield 2 games, Beloit 0; Appleton 2 games, Madison 1.
Finals: Appleton 3 games, Springfield 2.

All-Star Team: 1B-Ron Henika, Cedar Rapids; **2B**-Greg Steen, Peoria; **3B**-Bill Merrifield, Peoria; **SS**-Kurt Stillwell, Cedar Rapids; **OF**-Luis Polonia, Madison; Dave Hengel, Wausau; Brian Finley, Beloit; Mark Doran, Peoria; **C**-Tom Pagnozzi, Springfield; **DH**-Joey Meyer, Beloit; **P**-Craig Henderson, Kenosha; Mike Birkbeck, Beloit; Al Candelaria, Clinton; Jim Hickey, Appleton; **MVP**-Joey Meyer, Beloit; **Manager**-Tom Gamboa, Beloit.

BA: Joey Meyer, Beloit, .320
Runs: Brian Finley, Beloit, 113
Hits: Luis Polonia, Madison, 162
RBIs: Joey Meyer, Beloit, 102

HRs: Joey Meyer, Beloit, 30
Wins: Chris Bosio, Beloit, 17
SOs: Mark Ciardi, Beloit, 166
ERA: Bruce Tanner, Appleton, 1.96

A New York-Pennsylvania League
President: Vincent M. McNamara

East Standings

	W	L	Pct.	GB	Attend.	Manager
Little Falls Mets (21)	44	31	.587	—	30,356	Bud Harrelson
Watertown Pirates (23)	39	35	.527	4½	61,563	Bill Bryk
Auburn Astros (18)	38	38	.500	6½	22,392	Bob Hartsfield
Elmira Pioneers (2)	35	38	.479	8	57,448	Dick Berardino
Utica Blue Sox	31	44	.413	13	26,077	Bob McBee
Oneonta Yankees (10)	29	45	.392	14½	33,817	Bill Livesey

West Standings

	W	L	Pct.	GB	Attend.	Manager
Newark Orioles (1)	46	28	.622	—	22,240	Jim Hutto
Erie Cardinals (24)	43	31	.581	3	35,694	Rich Hacker
Batavia Trojans (5)	41	35	.539	6	32,958	Eddie Bane
Geneva Cubs (16)	38	36	.514	8	26,392	Tony Franklin
Niagara Falls Sox (4)	35	40	.467	11½	38,131	Fred Nelson
Jamestown Expos (20)	28	46	.378	18	30,057	Moby Benedict

Playoff: Little Falls 2 games, Newark 1.

All-Star Team: 1B-Chuck Lynn, Newark; **2B**-Paul Daddario, Batavia; **3B**-Kevin Birkover, Jamestown; **SS**-Kevin Elster, Little Falls; **OF**-Jay Buhner, Watertown; Dave Dahse, Newark; Lance Johnson, Erie; Miguel Roman, Batavia; **C**-Butch Garcia, Batavia; Tony DeFrancesco, Elmira; **DH**-Randy Riley, Newark; **P**-Joel Davis, Niagara Falls; Brad Mettler, Elmira; Steve Hill, Erie; Jamie Moyer, Geneva; **Manager**-Bud Harrelson, Little Falls.

BA: Randy Riley, Newark, .351
Runs: Lance Johnson, Erie, 63
Hits: Lance Johnson, Erie, 96
RBIs: Jay Buhner, Watertown, 58
Chuck Lynn, Newark, 58
HRs: Bernardo Brito, Batavia, 19
Wins: David Bear, Utica, 9

Jamie Moyer, Geneva, 9
Brad Mettler, Elmira, 9
Richard Caldwell, Newark, 9
SOs: Jamie Moyer, Geneva, 120
ERA: Todd Simmons, Niagara Falls, 1.29

A Northwest League
President: Bob Freitas

North Standings

	W	L	Pct.	GB	Attend.	Manager
Tri-Cities Triplets (13)	46	28	.622	—	52,042	Marty Scott
Bellingham Mariners (12)	42	32	.568	4	15,812	Gary Pellant
Everett Giants (26)	36	38	.486	10	41,442	Rocky Bridges
Spokane Indians (25)	35	39	.473	11	43,607	Jack Maloof

South Standings

	W	L	Pct.	GB	Attend.	Manager
Medford A's (11)	45	29	.608	—	62,905	Dennis Rogers
Bend Phillies (22)	38	36	.514	7	32,201	Ramon Aviles
Salem Angels (3)	35	39	.473	10	30,800	Larry Patterson
Eugene Emeralds (7)	19	55	.257	26	66,738	Dave Roberts

Playoff: Tri-Cities 1 game, Medford 0.

All-Star Team: 1B-Ron Gideon, Bend; **2B**-Greg Litton, Everett; **3B**-Brad Pounders, Spokane; **SS**-Sergio Perez, Bend; **OF**-Sam Haley, Bellingham; Kevin Bootay, Tri-Cities; Brad Hill, Tri-Cities; **C**-Dan Winters, Medford; **DH**-Robyn Amble, Tri-Cities; **P**-Greg Brake, Medford; Jim Walker, Bellingham; **MVP**-Sam Haley, Bellingham; **Manager**-Marty Scott, Tri-Cities.

BA: Ron King, Tri-Cities, .370
Runs: Kevin Bootay, Tri-Cities, 66
Hits: Sam Haley, Bellingham, 85
Brad Pounders, Spokane, 85
RBIs: Brad Hill, Tri-Cities, 59

HRs: Brad Pounders, Spokane, 10
Wins: Greg Brake, Medford, 12
SOs: Tom Messier, Everett, 116
ERA: Russell Kibler, Medford, 1.74
Pct: Greg Brake, Medford, 1.000, 12-0

A South Atlantic League
President: John H. Moss

North Standings

	W	L	Pct.	GB	Attend.	Manager
Greensboro Hornets*(10)	75	69	.521	—	183,646	Carlos Tosca
Asheville Tourists**(18)	73	70	.510	1½	66,597	Tom Spencer
Spartanburg Suns (22)	70	70	.500	3	40,223	Jay Ward
Gastonia Expos (20)	67	75	.472	7	60,832	Junior Miner
Anderson Braves (15)	61	82	.427	13½	24,935	Rick Albert

South Standings

	W	L	Pct.	GB	Attend.	Manager
Columbia Mets (21)	82	57	.590	—	76,600	Rich Miller
Savannah Cardinals**(24)	78	61	.561	4	37,897	Lloyd Merritt
Charleston Royals*(7)	78	64	.549	5½	117,185	Duane Gustavson
Florence Blue Jays (14)	65	73	.471	16½	44,217	Dennis Holmberg
Macon Pirates (23)	57	85	.401	26½	32,059	Joe Frisina

Playoffs: Asheville 2 games, Greensboro 1; Charleston 2 games, Savannah 1.
Finals: Asheville 3 games, Charleston 0.

All-Star Team: 1B-Andy Lawrence, Columbia; **2B**-Ramon Sambo, Spartanburg; **3B**-Kevin Seitzer, Columbia; **SS**-Manny Lee, Columbia; **OF**-Wayne Dannenberg, Spartanburg; George Chadwick, Gastonia; Dave Dyrek, Asheville; Brad Winkler, Greensboro; **C**-Sal D'Alessandro, Anderson; **DH**-Maurice Ching, Greensboro; **P**-Jeff Hull, Charleston; Cliff Young, Gastonia; Ramon Caraballo, Spartanburg; Joe Klink, Columbia; **MVP**-Kevin Seitzer, Charleston; **Pitcher of the Year**-Ramon Caraballo, Spartanburg; **Manager**-Rich Miller, Columbia.

BA: Manny Lee, Columbia, .329
Runs: Kevin Seitzer, Charleston, 96
Hits: Kevin Seitzer, Charleston, 145
RBIs: Pat Borders, Florence, 85
Kurt Kaull, Savannah, 85
HRs: Wilmer Caraballo, Columbia, 20
John DiGioia, Savannah, 20
Wins: Jeff Hull, Charleston, 16
SOs: Reggie Dobie, Columbia, 128
ERA: Kyle Hartshorn, Columbia, 2.48

R Appalachian League
President: Bill Halstead

North Standings

	W	L	Pct.	GB	Attend.	Manager
Pulaski Braves (15)	37	32	.536	—	17,533	Buddy Bailey
Paintsville Brewers (8)	37	33	.529	½	7,595	Ron Hansen
Pikeville Cubs (16)	34	34	.500	2½	5,511	Jim Fairey
Bluefield Orioles (1)	32	38	.457	5½	25,100	Greg Biagini

South Standings

	W	L	Pct.	GB	Attend.	Manager
Elizabethton Twins (9)	40	29	.580	—	12,063	Fred Waters
Bristol Tigers (6)	37	33	.529	3½	10,114	Hal Dyer
Kingsport Mets (21)	31	38	.449	9	34,007	Dan Radison
Johnson City Cardinals (24)	29	40	.420	11	12,263	Chuck Hiller

Playoff: Elizabethton 1 game, Pulaski 0.

All-Star Team: 1B-Gene Larkin, Elizabethton; **2B**-Bryan House, Pikeville; **3B**-Craig Mills, Bristol; **SS**-Jay Bell, Elizabethton; **OF**-Shawn Abner, Kingsport; Dave Vetsch, Elizabethton; Tim Casey, Paintsville; **C**-Kurt Beamesderfer, Bluefield; **DH**-Mike Fitzgerald, Johnson City; **P**-Alfredo Cardwood, Elizabethton; Tim Rice, Pikeville; **MVP**-Dave Vetsch, Elizabethton; **Manager**-Fred Waters, Elizabethton.

BA: Mike Fitzgerald, Johnson City, .345
Runs: Jerry Mack, Bristol, 56
Hits: Tim Casey, Paintsville, 73
RBIs: Tim Casey, Paintsville, 52
HRs: Tim Casey, Paintsville, 18

Wins: Alan Sadler, Paintsville, 9
SOs: Alfredo Cardwood, Elizabethton, 93
Greg Talamantez, Bluefield, 93
ERA: Alan Sadler, Paintsville, 1.91

R Gulf Coast League
President: Thomas J. Saffell

North Standings	W	L	Pct.	GB	Manager
Rangers (13)	36	27	.571	—	Mike Bucci
Dodgers (19)	34	29	.540	2	Jose Alvarez
Braves (15)	31	32	.492	5	Pedro Gonzalez
Blue Jays (14)	29	34	.460	7	Ramon Webster
Pirates (23)	21	42	.333	15	Woody Huyke

South Standings	W	L	Pct.	GB	Manager
White Sox (4)	41	22	.651	—	Steve Dillard
Astros (18)	36	27	.571	5	Jose Tartabull
Reds (17)	32	31	.508	9	Sam Mejias
Yankees (10)	28	35	.444	13	Jack Gillis
Phillies (22)	27	36	.429	14	Rollie DeArmas

Games played at Sarasota and Bradenton, Florida.

Playoff: Rangers 1 game, White Sox 0.

All-Star Team: 1B-Luis Peraza, White Sox; **2B**-Mark Lemke, Braves; **3B**-Norm Santiago, White Sox; **SS**-Santiago Garcia, Blue Jays; **OF**-Drew Denson, Braves; Jerry Bertolani, White Sox; Tim McMillan, Pirates; **C**-Jorge Alcazar, White Sox; **P**-Jim Filippi, White Sox; Jeff Gray, Phillies; **Manager** -Steve Dillard, White Sox.

BA: Drew Denson, Braves, .322
Runs: Jerry Bertolani, White Sox, 49
Hits: Drew Denson, Braves, 77
RBIs: Drew Denson, Braves, 45
HRs: Drew Denson, Braves, 10; Michael Smiciklas, Braves, 10
Wins: Jim Filippi, White Sox, 10
SOs: Mark Cieslak, Reds, 76
ERA: Jim Filippi, White Sox, 0.61

R Pioneer League
President: Ralph C. Nelles

North Standings	W	L	Pct.	GB	Attend.	Manager
Helena Gold Sox	44	24	.647	—	20,199	Harry Gurley
Great Falls Dodgers (19)	37	31	.544	7	64,309	Kevin Kennedy
Medicine Hat Blue Jays (14)	32	38	.457	13	51,401	Duane Larson
Calgary Expos (20)	28	42	.400	17	32,562	Ed Creech

South Standings	W	L	Pct.	GB	Attend.	Manager
Billings Mustangs (17)	47	21	.691	—	96,670	Larry Barton
Butte Copper Kings (12)	38	32	.543	10	25,766	Manuel Estrada
Idaho Falls A's (11)	27	41	.397	20	18,043	Jim Nettles
Pocatello Gems (x)	23	47	.329	25	26,346	Ron Mihal

Playoff: Helena 3 games, Billings 1.

All-Star Team: 1B-Jack Daugherty, Helena; **2B**-Daniel Clark, Butte; **3B**-Ruben Machado, Billings; **SS**-Brooks Shumake, Billings; **OF**-Darryl Landrum, Medicine Hat; Jonathan Groth, Billings; Evan Evans, Pocatello; **C**-Mark Berry, Billings; **DH**-Edward Jacobo, Great Falls; **P**-Greg Brinkman, Butte; Greg Mayberry, Great Falls; John Dodd, Calgary; **Manager**-Larry Barton, Billings.

BA: Jack Daugherty, Helena, .402
Runs: Jack Daugherty, Helena, 77
Hits: Jack Daugherty, Helena, 104
RBIs: Jack Daugherty, Helena, 82
HRs: Darryl Landrum, Medicine Hat, 17
Wins: Greg Brinkman, Butte, 10
SOs: Greg Mayberry, Great Falls, 89
ERA: Clay Daniel, Billings, 2.56

1984 Interleague Post Season Play

World Series
Detroit (American) 4 games, San Diego (National) 1

1984 Major League Farm Systems

American League
1 Baltimore (5): Rochester, Charlotte, Hagerstown, Newark, Bluefield.
2 Boston (5): Pawtucket, New Britain, Winston-Salem, Winter Haven, Elmira.
3 California (5): Edmonton, Waterbury, Redwood, Peoria, Salem (OR).
4 Chicago (5): Denver, Glens Falls, Appleton, Niagara Falls, Gulf Coast.
5 Cleveland (4): Maine, Buffalo, Waterloo, Batavia.
6 Detroit (4): Evansville, Birmingham, Lakeland, Bristol.
7 Kansas City (5): Omaha, Memphis, Ft. Myers, Charleston, Eugene.
8 Milwaukee (5): Vancouver, El Paso, Stockton, Beloit, Paintsville.
9 Minnesota (5): Toledo, Orlando, Visalia, Kenosha, Elizabethton.
10 New York (6): Columbus (OH), Nashville, Ft. Lauderdale, Greensboro, Oneonta, Gulf Coast.
11 Oakland (6): Tacoma, Albany-Colonie, Modesto, Madison, Medford, Idaho Falls.
12 Seattle (6): Salt Lake City, Chattanooga, Salinas, Wausau, Bellingham, Butte.
13 Texas (6): Oklahoma City, Tulsa, Salem (VA), Burlington (IA), Tri-Cities, Gulf Coast.
14 Toronto (6): Syracuse, Knoxville, Kinston, Florence, Medicine Hat, Gulf Coast.

National League
15 Atlanta (6): Richmond, Greenville, Durham, Anderson, Pulaski, Gulf Coast.
16 Chicago (6): Iowa, Midland, Lodi, Quad City, Geneva, Pikeville.
17 Cincinnati (6): Wichita, Vermont, Tampa, Cedar Rapids, Billings, Gulf Coast.
18 Houston (6): Tucson, Columbus (GA), Daytona Beach, Asheville, Auburn, Gulf Coast.
19 Los Angeles (6): Albuquerque, San Antonio, Bakersfield, Vero Beach, Great Falls, Gulf Coast.
20 Montreal (6): Indianapolis, Jacksonville, West Palm Beach, Gastonia, Jamestown, Calgary.
21 New York (6): Tidewater, Jackson, Lynchburg, Columbia, Little Falls, Kingsport.
22 Philadelphia (6): Portland, Reading, Peninsula, Spartanburg, Bend, Gulf Coast.
23 Pittsburgh (6): Hawaii, Nashua, Prince William, Macon, Watertown, Gulf Coast.
24 St. Louis (7): Louisville, Arkansas, St. Petersburg, Springfield, Savannah, Erie, Johnson City.
25 San Diego (5): Las Vegas, Beaumont, Reno, Miami, Spokane.
26 San Francisco (5): Phoenix, Shreveport, Fresno, Clinton, Everett.

Co-op (x): Pocatello.
Independent: San Jose, Utica, Helena.

1984 No-Hitters

Date	Pitcher	Team	League	Opponent	Score
4-7	Jack Morris	Detroit	American	Chicago	4-0
4-29	Bill Scudder	Bakersfield	California	Reno	1-0
5-4	Jim Deshaies	Nashville	Southern	Columbus	5-1 (7)
5-12	Jesus Rios	MC Tigres	Mexican	Cordoba	2-0
5-24	Brad Arnsberg	Greensboro	South Atlantic	Savannah	5-0
5-26	Juan Eichelberger	Vancouver	Pacific Coast	Portland	2-0 (7)
5-29	Steve Kordish	Tulsa	Texas	Midland	6-0 (7)
5-31	Ed Myers	Albany-Colonie	Eastern	Vermont	2-0 (7)
6-7	Tony Castillo/ Mike Yearout	Florence	South Atlantic	Charleston	4-0
6-9	Chris Martinez	St. Petersburg	Florida State	Lakeland	1-0 (7)
6-10	Bob Kipper	Redwood	California	San Jose	9-0 (7)
6-10	Jairo Valenzuela	Saltillo	Mexican	Cordoba	5-0 (P, 7)
6-12	Andy Rincon	Hawaii	Pacific Coast	Tacoma	3-0
6-15	Ulises Sierra	Reno	California	Modesto	2-0 (7)
6-19	Vance Lovelace/Brian Piper/ Steve Martin	San Antonio	Texas	Beaumont	1-0
7-18	Duane James	Lakeland	Florida State	Daytona Beach	1-0 (7)
7-30	Clay Daniel	Billings	Pioneer	Pocatello	6-1
7-31	Tom Browning	Wichita	American Assoc.	Iowa	2-0 (7)
8-8	John Martin	Springfield	Midwest	Wausau	2-0
8-11	Steve Susce	Nashua	Eastern	Waterbury	4-0 (7)
8-15	Randy Norton	Gastonia	South Atlantic	Anderson	1-0 (7)
8-21	Thomas Epple	St. Petersburg	Florida State	Tampa	4-0
8-21	Reggie Paterson	Iowa	American Assoc.	Omaha	2-0
8-28	David Shipanoff/Mercedes Esquer/ Tim Rodgers	Knoxville	Southern	Charlotte	0-1
9-30	Mike Witt	California	American	Texas	1-0 (P)

Number in parentheses indicates innings if other than nine; "P" indicates perfect game.

THIS DATE IN MINOR LEAGUE HISTORY

April 9, 1984, Greenville, South Carolina returned to Organized Ball in the Southern League, with the opening of a new $3 million stadium.

April 25, 1984, The 1984 Triple-A World Series was cancelled. It was scheduled to take place in Las Vegas in September, but Commissioner Bowie Kuhn objected to the city because of gambling, and no acceptable alternative site was found.

May 18, 1984, Louisville and Evansville combined for an American Association record 17 doubles, breaking a 52-year-old record.

May 27, 1984, Umpire Pam Postema threw 14-year-old Portland batboy Sam Morris out of the game when he refused to retrieve a chair thrown on the field by Portland manager Lee Elia. He was ejected in the 12th inning of a game which Vancouver won 8-7 in 18 innings.

June 21, 1984, Saul Lopez, 19-year-old righthanded pitcher for Macon, South Atlantic League, was arrested for the murder of a woman who lived next door to him in his Macon apartment complex.

July 11, 1984, John "Moose" Clabaugh, slugging outfielder who hit 62 home runs for Tyler, East Texas League, in 1926 and who won four minor league batting titles, died at age 83.

August 13, 1984, Alan Knicely of Wichita went 6-for-6 in an American Association game against Denver.

August 15, 1984, George Brunet, 49-year-old southpaw, pitched in 21 games in the Mexican League, in his 32nd consecutive year in Organized Ball. He won six games, bringing his lifetime total in the majors and the minors to 313 wins. Brunet established a new minor league career strikeout record with 3,175, far more than any other hurler. He pitched 55 shutouts in the Mexican League.

August 15, 1984, Hector Espino played 24 games in the Mexican League, in his 25th and final season. He hit one home run to increase his all-time minor league record to 484 homers.

August 15, 1984, Ramon Arano won 11 games for Veracruz, raising his career win total to 324.

August 16, 1984, Tommie Aaron, one of the first black managers in minor league baseball, and later a coach for the Atlanta Braves, died of leukemia at the age of 45.

August 31, 1984, The Salt Lake City franchise in the Pacific Coast League finished the season in disarray. During the final month of the season, the club lost its electricity, telephone service, and radio broadcasts due to non payment of bills. Checks for players' meal money bounced in two cities. The league had electricity restored so that the Gulls could finish their home games, but during the playoffs, all of their games were played on the road. The team would move to Calgary for the following season.

September 10, 1984, Edmonton won the Pacific Coast League finals over Hawaii, two games to none. Due to a stadium conflict, no games could be played in Hawaii, and with the first two games cancelled by rain, the best-of-five series was shortened to best-of-three.

September 14, 1984, The American Association announced that the Evansville and Wichita franchises had been sold and would be moved to Nashville and Buffalo, respectively.

Buffalo's Pilot Field opened in 1988. The cost was $42 million and that season more than 1 million fans attended American Association games. The current name of the stadium is North AmeriCare Park.

1985

American League
President: Dr. Robert W. Brown

East Standings	W	L	Pct.	GB	Attend.	Manager
Toronto Blue Jays	99	62	.615	—	2,468,925	Bobby Cox
New York Yankees	97	64	.602	2	2,214,587	Yogi Berra/Billy Martin
Detroit Tigers	84	77	.522	15	2,286,609	Sparky Anderson
Baltimore Orioles	83	78	.516	16	2,132,387	Joe Altobelli/Cal Ripken, Sr./ Earl Weaver
Boston Red Sox	81	81	.500	18½	1,786,633	John McNamara
Milwaukee Brewers	71	90	.441	28	1,360,265	George Bamberger
Cleveland Indians	60	102	.370	39½	655,181	Pat Corrales

West Standings	W	L	Pct.	GB	Attend.	Manager
Kansas City Royals	91	71	.562	—	2,162,717	Dick Howser
California Angels	90	72	.556	1	2,567,427	Gene Mauch
Chicago White Sox	85	77	.525	6	1,669,888	Tony LaRussa
Minnesota Twins	77	85	.475	14	1,651,814	Billy Gardner/Ray Miller
Oakland Athletics	77	85	.475	14	1,334,599	Jackie Moore
Seattle Mariners	74	88	.457	17	1,128,696	Chuck Cottier
Texas Rangers	62	99	.385	28½	1,112,497	Doug Rader/Bobby Valentine

Playoff: Kansas City 4 games, Toronto 3.

BA: Wade Boggs, Boston, .368
Runs: Rickey Henderson, New York, 146
Hits: Wade Boggs, Boston, 240
RBIs: Don Mattingly, New York, 145
HRs: Darrell Evans, Detroit, 40

Wins: Ron Guidry, New York, 22
SOs: Bert Blyleven, Cleveland/Minnesota, 206
ERA: Dave Stieb, Toronto, 2.48
Pct: Ron Guidry, New York, .786, 22-6
Saves: Dan Quisenberry, Kansas City, 37

National League
President: Charles S. Feeney

East Standings	W	L	Pct.	GB	Attend.	Manager
St. Louis Cardinals	101	61	.623	—	2,637,563	Whitey Herzog
New York Mets	98	64	.605	3	2,761,601	Davey Johnson
Montreal Expos	84	77	.522	16½	1,502,494	Buck Rodgers
Chicago Cubs	77	84	.478	23½	2,161,534	Jim Frey
Philadelphia Phillies	75	87	.463	26	1,830,350	John Felske
Pittsburgh Pirates	57	104	.354	43½	735,900	Chuck Tanner

West Standings	W	L	Pct.	GB	Attend.	Manager
Los Angeles Dodgers	95	67	.586	—	3,264,593	Tom Lasorda
Cincinnati Reds	89	72	.553	5½	1,834,619	Pete Rose
Houston Astros	83	79	.512	12	1,184,314	Bob Lillis
San Diego Padres	83	79	.512	12	2,210,352	Dick Williams
Atlanta Braves	66	96	.407	29	1,350,137	Eddie Haas/Bobby Wine
San Francisco Giants	62	100	.383	33	818,697	Jim Davenport/Roger Craig

Playoff: St. Louis 4 games, Los Angeles 2.

BA: Willie McGee, St. Louis, .353
Runs: Dale Murphy, Atlanta, 118
Hits: Willie McGee, St. Louis, 216
RBIs: Dave Parker, Cincinnati, 125
HRs: Dale Murphy, Atlanta, 37

Wins: Dwight Gooden, New York, 24
SOs: Dwight Gooden, New York, 268
ERA: Dwight Gooden, New York, 1.53
Pct: Orel Hershiser, Los Angeles, .864, 19-3
Saves: Jeff Reardon, Montreal, 41

AAA American Association
President: Joe Ryan

East Standings	W	L	Pct.	GB	Attend.	Manager
Louisville Redbirds (24)	74	68	.521	—	651,090	Jim Fregosi
Nashville Sounds (6)	71	70	.504	2½	364,225	Lee Walls/Gordy MacKenzie
Buffalo Bisons (4)	66	76	.465	8	362,762	John Boles
Indianapolis Indians (20)	61	81	.430	13	209,041	Felipe Alou

West Standings	W	L	Pct.	GB	Attend.	Manager
Oklahoma City 89ers (13)	79	63	.556	—	364,247	Dave Oliver
Denver Zephyrs (17)	77	65	.542	2	308,268	Gene Dusan
Omaha Royals (7)	73	69	.514	6	175,329	Gene Lamont
Iowa Cubs (16)	66	75	.485	12½	269,513	Larry Cox

Playoff: Louisville 4 games, Oklahoma City 1.

All-Star Team: 1B-Andres Galarraga, Indianapolis; **2B**-Tom Runnells, Denver; **3B**-Steve Buechele, Oklahoma City; **SS**-Wade Rowdon, Denver; **OF**-Darrell Brown, Nashville; Wally Johnson, Indianapolis; Paul O'Neill, Denver; **C**-Scotti Madison, Nashville; Joel Skinner, Buffalo; **DH**-Dave Hostetler, Indianapolis/Iowa; **P**-Mark Huismann, Omaha; Tony Ferreira, Omaha; **MVP**-Steve Buechele, Oklahoma City; **Pitcher of the Year**-Mark Huismann, Omaha; **Manager**-Jim Fregosi, Louisville; Dave Oliver, Oklahoma City.

BA: Scotti Madison, Nashville, .341
Runs: Andres Galarraga, Indianapolis, 75
Hits: Paul O'Neill, Denver, 155
RBIs: Dave Hostetler, Indianapolis/Iowa, 89

HRs: Dave Hostetler, Indianapolis/Iowa, 29
Wins: Bill Long, Buffalo, 13
SOs: Todd Worrell, Louisville, 126
ERA: Steve Farr, Omaha, 2.02

AAA International League
President: Harold Cooper

Standings	W	L	Pct.	GB	Attend.	Manager
Syracuse Chiefs (14)	79	61	.564	—	222,813	Doug Ault
Maine Guides (5)	76	63	.547	2½	135,985	Doc Edwards
Columbus Clippers (10)	75	64	.540	3½	568,735	Doug Holmquist/ Stump Merrill
Tidewater Tides (21)	75	64	.540	3½	153,100	Bob Schaefer
Richmond Braves (15)	75	65	.536	4	379,019	Roy Majtyka
Toledo Mud Hens (9)	71	68	.511	7½	167,787	Cal Ermer
Rochester Red Wings (1)	58	81	.417	20½	208,955	Frank Verdi/Mark Wiley
Pawtucket Red Sox (2)	48	91	.345	30½	166,504	Rac Slider

Playoffs: Columbus 3 games, Syracuse 1; Tidewater 3 games, Maine 2.
Finals: Tidewater 3 games, Columbus 1.

All-Star Team: 1B-Jim Wilson, Maine; **2B**-Juan Bonilla, Columbus; **3B**-Kelly Gruber, Syracuse; **SS**-Kelly Paris, Rochester; **OF**-Dan Pasqua, Columbus; Rick Leach, Syracuse; Billy Beane, Tidewater; **C**-Larry Owen, Richmond; **DH**-Willie Aikens, Syracuse; **P**-Stan Clarke, Syracuse; Tom Henke, Syracuse; **MVP**-Dan Pasqua, Columbus; **Pitcher of the Year**-Tom Henke, Syracuse; **Manager**-Doug Ault, Syracuse.

BA: Juan Bonilla, Columbus, .330
Runs: Mike Sharperson, Syracuse, 86
Hits: Mike Sharperson, Syracuse, 155
RBIs: Jim Wilson, Maine, 101
HRs: Jim Wilson, Maine, 26

Wins: Dennis Burtt, Toledo, 14
Stan Clarke, Syracuse, 14
SOs: Brad Havens, Toledo, 129
ERA: Don Gordon, Syracuse, 2.07

AAA Mexican League
President: Pedro Treto Cisneros

North Standings	W	L	Pct.	GB	Attend.	Manager
Aguascalientes Rieleros	65	58	.528	—	159,610	David Garcia/ Roberto Castellon
Dos Laredos Tecolotes	67	60	.528	—	123,553	Jorge Calvo
Monclova Acereros	64	62	.509	2½	259,724	Vinicio Garcia
Tampico Alijadores	66	64	.508	2½	197,210	Gregorio Luque
Saltillo Saraperos	64	65	.496	4	184,129	Roger Freed/Juan Navarrete
Leon Bravos	60	67	.472	7	107,543	Ben Valenzuela
Union Laguna Algodoneros	61	70	.466	8	132,802	Mario Pelaez/Rodolfo Sandoval/ Gerardo Gutierrez
Monterrey Sultanes	60	69	.465	8	164,067	Jose Guerrero/ Aurelio Rodriguez

South Standings	W	L	Pct.	GB	Attend.	Manager
Mexico City Diablos Rojos	80	52	.606	—	181,628	Ben Reyes/Roberto Castellon
Yucatan Leones	74	49	.602	1½	364,326	Carlos Paz
Mexico City Tigres	72	54	.571	5	181,508	Roberto Mendez
Cordoba Cafeteros	72	55	.567	5½	138,652	Alberto Joachin/Alfredo Ortiz
Puebla Angeles	70	54	.565	6	71,389	Max Olivares
Campeche Piratas	58	60	.492	15	120,618	Francisco Estrada
Tabasco Plataneros	43	83	.341	34	82,624	Javier Espinoza/Hugo Rios
Veracruz Aguila	39	93	.295	41	122,057	Fred Velazquez/ Francisco Rodriguez

Playoffs: Aguascalientes 4 games, Tampico 0; Dos Laredos 4 games, Monclova 0; MC Diablos Rojos 4 games, Cordoba 2; MC Tigres 4 games, Yucatan 2. Dos Laredos 4 games, Aguascalientes 2; MC Diablos Rojos 4 games, MC Tigres 1.
Finals: MC Diablos Rojos 4 games, Dos Laredos 1.

BA: Ossie Olivares, Aguascalientes/Campeche, .397
Runs: Julian Perez, Tampico, 120
Hits: Ossie Olivares, Aguascalientes/Campeche, 175

RBIs: Rich Renteria, MC Tigres, 125
HRs: Andres Mora, Dos Laredos, 41
Wins: Jesus Rios, MC Tigres, 21
SOs: Ramon Serna, Union Laguna, 200
ERA: Jesus Rios, MC Tigres, 2.52

AAA Pacific Coast League
President: Bill Cutler

North Standings	W	L	Pct.	GB	Attend.	Manager
Vancouver Canadians**(8)	79	64	.552	—	199,781	Tom Trebelhorn
Calgary Cannons*(12)	71	70	.504	7	272,322	Bobby Floyd
Portland Beavers (22)	68	74	.479	10½	188,042	Bill Dancy
Edmonton Trappers (3)	66	76	.465	12½	229,112	Winston Llenas
Tacoma Tigers (11)	66	76	.465	12½	208,534	Keith Lieppman

South Standings	W	L	Pct.	GB	Attend.	Manager
Hawaii Islanders*(23)	84	59	.587	—	134,864	Tommy Sandt
Phoenix Giants**(26)	80	62	.563	3½	168,620	Jim Lefebvre
Albuquerque Dukes (19)	67	76	.469	17	252,453	Terry Collins
Tucson Toros (18)	65	75	.464	17½	128,540	Jimmy Johnson
Las Vegas Stars (25)	65	79	.451	19½	313,783	Bob Cluck

Playoffs: Vancouver 3 games, Calgary 0; Phoenix 3 games, Hawaii 0.
Finals: Vancouver 3 games, Phoenix 0.

All-Star Team: 1B-Franklin Stubbs, Albuquerque; **2B**-Mike Woodard, Phoenix; **3B**-Jack Howell, Edmonton; **SS**-Danny Tartabull, Calgary; **OF**-John Moses, Calgary; John Kruk,

*Won first-half **Won second-half ***Won both halves
Numbers after nicknames indicate farm system.
Affiliation listed at end of each year.

575

Las Vegas; Mike Felder, Vancouver; **C**-Mike Diaz, Hawaii; **DH**-Carlos Ponce, Vancouver; **P**-Bob Walk, Hawaii; Tim Conroy, Tacoma; Ray Krawczyk, Hawaii; **MVP**-Danny Tartabull, Calgary; **Manager**-Jim Lefebvre, Phoenix.

BA: John Kruk, Las Vegas, .351
Runs: Tack Wilson, Phoenix, 109
Hits: Mike Woodard, Phoenix, 181
RBIs: Danny Tartabull, Calgary, 109

HRs: Danny Tartabull, Calgary, 43
Wins: Bob Walk, Hawaii, 16
SOs: Jose Rijo, Tacoma, 179
ERA: Bob Walk, Hawaii, 2.65

AA Eastern League
President: Charles E. Eshbach

Standings	W	L	Pct.	GB	Attend.	Manager
Albany-Colonie Yankees (10).	82	57	.590	—	324,003	Barry Foote
Waterbury Indians (5)	75	64	.540	7	37,318	Jack Aker
New Britain Red Sox (2)	75	64	.540	7	90,802	Ed Nottle
Vermont Reds (17)	71	67	.514	10½	90,478	Jack Lind
Glens Falls White Sox (4)	68	71	.489	14	69,260	Steve Dillard
Nashua Pirates (23)	66	73	.475	16	73,867	John Lipon
Pittsfield Cubs (16)	59	79	.428	22½	60,585	Tom Spencer
Reading Phillies (22)	58	79	.423	23	76,819	Tony Taylor

Playoffs: Vermont 3 games, Albany-Colonie 1; New Britain 3 games, Waterbury 1.
Finals: Vermont 3 games, New Britain 1.

All-Star Team: 1B-Russ Morman, Glens Falls; **2B**-Jeff Treadway, Vermont; **3B**-Cory Snyder, Waterbury; **SS**-Mike Brumley, Pittsfield; **OF**-Randy Washington, Waterbury; Dave Clark, Waterbury; Dana Williams, New Britain; **C**-Andy Allanson, Waterbury; **DH**-Orestes Destrade, Albany-Colonie; **P**-Brad Arnsberg, Albany-Colonie; Scott Bailes, Nashua/Waterbury; Barry Jones, Nashua; **MVP**-Cory Snyder, Waterbury; **Pitcher of the Year**-Brad Arnsberg, Albany-Colonie; **Manager**-Barry Foote, Albany-Colonie.

BA: Andy Allanson, Waterbury, .312
Runs: Ken Williams, Glens Falls, 87
Hits: Keith Miller, Reading, 147
RBIs: Cory Snyder, Waterbury, 94
HRs: Cory Snyder, Waterbury, 28

Wins: Brad Arnsberg, Albany-Colonie, 14
    Jeff Sellers, New Britain, 14
SOs: Doug Drabek, Albany-Colonie, 153
ERA: Brad Arnsberg, Albany-Colonie, 1.59

AA Southern League
President: Jimmy Bragan

East Standings	W	L	Pct.	GB	Attend.	Manager
Columbus Astros*(18)	79	65	.549	—	109,603	Carlos Alfonso
Charlotte O's**(1)	78	65	.545	½	104,085	John Hart
Jacksonville Expos (20)	73	70	.510	5½	82,907	Tommy Thompson
Orlando Twins (9)	72	71	.503	6½	62,122	Charlie Manuel
Greenville Braves (15)	70	74	.486	9	214,471	Jim Beauchamp

West Standings	W	L	Pct.	GB	Attend.	Manager
Knoxville Blue Jays**(14)	79	64	.553	—	108,952	John McLaren
Huntsville Stars*(11)	78	66	.542	1½	300,810	Brad Fischer
Chattanooga Lookouts (12)	66	77	.462	13	112,700	Bill Plummer
Memphis Chicks (7)	65	79	.451	14½	200,682	Tommy Jones
Birmingham Barons (6)	57	86	.399	22	140,671	Gordy MacKenzie/ Mark DeJohn/ Frank Franchi/Jerry Grote

Playoffs: Charlotte 3 games, Columbus 1; Huntsville 3 games, Knoxville 1.
Finals: Huntsville 3 games, Charlotte 2.

All-Star Team: 1B-Rob Nelson, Huntsville; **2B**-Brian David, Chattanooga; **3B**-Jim Sherman, Columbus; **SS**-Luis Rivera, Jacksonville; **OF**-Randy Braun, Chattanooga; Bill Moore, Jacksonville; Mark Davidson, Orlando; Jose Canseco, Huntsville; Alexis Marte, Orlando; **C**-Robbie Wine, Columbus; **DH**-Mark Funderburk, Orlando; **P**-John Habyan, Charlotte; Steve Davis, Knoxville; **MVP**-Jose Canseco, Huntsville; **Pitcher of the Year**-Steve Davis, Knoxville; **Manager**-John McLaren, Knoxville; Carlos Alfonso, Columbus.

BA: Bruce Fields, Birmingham, .323
Runs: Alexis Marte, Orlando, 117
Hits: Alexis Marte, Orlando, 171
RBIs: Mark Funderburk, Orlando, 116
HRs: Mark Funderburk, Orlando, 34

Wins: Steve Davis, Knoxville, 17
SOs: Scott Bankhead, Memphis, 128
    John Hoover, Charlotte, 128
ERA: Steve Davis, Knoxville, 2.45

AA Texas League
President: Carl Sawatski

East Standings	W	L	Pct.	GB	Attend.	Manager
Jackson Mets**(21)	73	63	.537	—	132,021	Sam Perlozzo
Shreveport Captains (26)	72	64	.529	1	56,025	Duane Espy
Arkansas Travelers*(24)	64	70	.478	8	207,985	Jim Riggleman
Tulsa Drillers (13)	60	76	.441	13	154,514	Orlando Gomez

West Standings	W	L	Pct.	GB	Attend.	Manager
El Paso Diablos***(8)	86	50	.632	—	245,744	Terry Bevington
Beaumont Golden Gators (25).	69	67	.507	17	108,729	Bobby Tolan
San Antonio Dodgers (19)	59	75	.440	26	106,183	Gary LaRocque
Midland Angels (3)	59	77	.434	27	127,836	Joe Maddon

Playoff: Jackson 2 games, Arkansas 0.
Finals: Jackson 4 games, El Paso 0.

All-Star Team: 1B-Billy Joe Robidoux, El Paso; **2B**-Mark McLemore, Midland; **3B**-Jeff Hamilton, San Antonio; **SS**-Rod Booker, Arkansas; **OF**-Glenn Braggs, El Paso; Johnny Tutt, Beaumont; Jose Gonzalez, San Antonio; **C**-Barry Lyons, Jackson; Benito Santiago, Beaumont; **DH**-Joey Meyer, El Paso; **Util**-Mark Wasinger, Beaumont; **P**-Chris Bosio, El

Paso; Juan Nieves, El Paso; Dan Plesac, El Paso; Terry Mulholland, Shreveport; Scott May, San Antonio; **MVP**-Billy Joe Robidoux, El Paso; **Pitcher of the Year**-Juan Nieves, El Paso; **Manager**-Terry Bevington, El Paso.

BA: Billy Joe Robidoux, El Paso, .342
Runs: Billy Joe Robidoux, El Paso, 111
Hits: Billy Joe Robidoux, El Paso, 176
RBIs: Billy Joe Robidoux, El Paso, 132
HRs: Joey Meyer, El Paso, 37
Wins: Randy Bockus, Shreveport, 14
SOs: Chris Bosio, El Paso, 155
ERA: Randy Bockus, Shreveport, 2.73

A California League
President: Joe Gagliardi

North Standings	W	L	Pct.	GB	Attend.	Manager
Stockton Ports**(8)	82	63	.566	—	69,334	Tom Gamboa
Modesto A's*(11)	76	68	.528	5½	73,661	George Mitterwald
Redwood Pioneers (3)	70	76	.479	12½	25,836	Tom Kotchman
Reno Padres (25)	64	81	.441	18	77,693	Steve Smith
San Jose Bees	55	88	.385	26	53,423	Jethro McIntyre

South Standings	W	L	Pct.	GB	Attend.	Manager
Salinas Spurs*(12)	89	55	.618	—	39,720	R.J. Harrison
Fresno Giants**(26)	84	62	.575	6	83,351	Wendell Kim
Visalia Oaks (9)	66	78	.458	23	74,407	Dan Schmitz
Bakersfield Dodgers (19)	65	80	.448	24½	74,054	Mel Queen

Playoffs: Stockton 3 games, Modesto 1; Fresno 3 games, Salinas 1.
Finals: Fresno 3 games, Stockton 2.

All-Star Team: 1B-Jim Eppard, Modesto; **2B**-Phil Smith, San Jose; **3B**-Mark McGwire, Modesto; **SS**-Brian Guinn, Modesto; **OF**-Mike Jones, Fresno; Bob Loscalzo, Modesto; Mackey Sasser, Fresno; **C**-Jeff Brown, Bakersfield; **DH**-Chris Chapman, Bakersfield; Tim Hill, San Jose; **P**-Charlie Corbell, Fresno; Jeff Parrett, Stockton; Ed Puikunas, Reno; Rick Moore, Salinas; **MVP**-Eric Hardgrave, Reno; **Pitcher of the Year**-Charlie Corbell, Fresno; **Manager**-Wendell Kim, Fresno.

BA: Jim Eppard, Modesto, .345
Runs: William Wrona, Reno, 107
Hits: Jim Eppard, Modesto, 183
RBIs: Gene Larkin, Visalia, 106
    Mark McGwire, Modesto, 106
HRs: Eric Hardgrave, Reno, 24
    Mark McGwire, Modesto, 24
Wins: Charlie Corbell, Fresno, 17
SOs: Dennis Livingston, Bakersfield, 166
ERA: Jeff Parrett, Stockton, 2.75

A Carolina League
President: John Hopkins

North Standings	W	L	Pct.	GB	Attend.	Manager
Lynchburg Mets***(21)	95	45	.679	—	95,657	Mike Cubbage
Salem Redbirds (13)	72	65	.526	21½	71,788	Bill Stearns
Hagerstown Suns (1)	65	72	.474	28½	112,978	Greg Biagini
Prince William Pirates (23)	65	74	.468	29½	127,356	Ed Ott

South Standings	W	L	Pct.	GB	Attend.	Manager
Peninsula Pilots (22)	67	68	.496	—	59,151	Ron Clark
Durham Bulls (15)	66	74	.471	3½	182,720	Harry Bright
Kinston Blue Jays**(14)	64	73	.467	4	74,722	Grady Little
Winston-Salem Spirits*(16)	58	81	.417	11	98,434	Cal Ermer

Playoff: Winston-Salem 2 games, Kinston 0.
Finals: Winston-Salem 3 games, Lynchburg 1.

All-Star Team: 1B-Chris Padget, Hagerstown; **2B**-Jerry Browne, Salem; **3B**-Dimas Gutierrez, Prince William; **SS**-Kevin Elster, Lynchburg; D.L. Smith, Hagerstown; **OF**-Shawn Abner, Lynchburg; Dave Martinez, Winston-Salem; Eric Yelding, Kinston; **C**-Buck Goldthorn, Prince William; **DH**-Jim Dickerson, Winston-Salem; **P**-Kyle Hartshorn, Lynchburg; Shawn Barton, Peninsula; **MVP**-Shawn Abner, Lynchburg; **Pitcher of the Year**-Kyle Hartshorn, Lynchburg; **Manager**-Grady Little, Kinston.

BA: Dave Martinez, Winston-Salem, .342
Runs: Kevin Bootay, Salem, 73
    Jose Leiva, Peninsula, 73
Hits: Shawn Abner, Lynchburg, 163
RBIs: Shawn Abner, Lynchburg, 89
HRs: Jim Dickerson, Winston-Salem, 28
Wins: Kyle Hartshorn, Lynchburg, 17
SOs: Eric Bell, Hagerstown, 162
ERA: Kyle Hartshorn, Lynchburg, 1.69

A Florida State League
President: George MacDonald, Jr.

West Standings	W	L	Pct.	GB	Attend.	Manager
Ft. Myers Royals (7)	82	57	.590	—	46,163	Duane Gustavson
St. Petersburg Cardinals (24)	78	62	.557	4½	136,689	Dave Bialas
Tampa Tarpons (17)	73	62	.541	7	60,764	Marc Bombard
Clearwater Phillies (22)	69	72	.489	14	44,081	Ramon Aviles

South Standings	W	L	Pct.	GB	Attend.	Manager
Ft. Lauderdale Yankees (10)	77	63	.550	—	52,115	Bucky Dent
West Palm Beach Expos (20)	74	66	.529	3	114,659	Junior Minor
Vero Beach Dodgers (19)	67	73	.479	10	81,800	Stan Wasiak
Miami Marlins	58	83	.411	19½	32,321	Tom Burgess/Jim Essian

Central Standings	W	L	Pct.	GB	Attend.	Manager
Osceola Astros#(18)	77	58	.570	—	38,082	Dave Cripe
Winter Haven Red Sox (2)	71	68	.511	8	18,788	Dave Holt
Lakeland Tigers (6)	56	84	.400	23½	50,229	Jerry Grote/Moby Benedict
Daytona Bch. Islanders (1, 13)	53	87	.379	26½	30,736	Jim Hutto

#represented Kissimmee, Florida.

Playoffs: Ft. Lauderdale 2 games, Osceola 1; Ft. Myers 2 games, St. Petersburg 1.
Finals: Ft. Myers 3 games, Ft. Lauderdale 1.

All-Star Team: 1B-Jack Daugherty, West Palm Beach; **2B**-Carson Carroll, Miami; **3B**-Ken Caminiti, Osceola; **SS**-Jody Reed, Winter Haven; **OF**-Pete Camelo, West Palm Beach; Jay Buhner, Ft. Lauderdale; Darren Reed, Ft. Lauderdale; **C**-Marty Pevey, St. Petersburg; Joe Oliver, Tampa; **DH**-Steve DeAngelis, Clearwater; **P**-Scott Young, St. Petersburg; Andy Araujo, Winter Haven; Cliff Young, West Palm Beach; Rob Mallicoat, Osceola; Jeff Gray, Clearwater; Mark Baker, Osceola; **MVP**-Jack Daugherty, West Palm Beach; **Manager**-Dave Bialas, St. Petersburg.

BA: Jody Reed, Winter Haven, .321
Runs: Jody Reed, Winter Haven, 95
Hits: Gary Weinberger, West Palm Beach, 158
RBIs: Jack Daugherty, West Palm Beach, 87
HRs: Steve DeAngelis, Clearwater, 16
Wins: Rob Mallicoat, Osceola, 16
SOs: Rob Mallicoat, Osceola, 158
ERA: Greg Mathews, St. Petersburg, 1.11

A Midwest League
President: Bill Walters

North Standings	W	L	Pct.	GB	Attend.	Manager
Appleton Foxes (4)	85	54	.612	—	76,860	Sal Rende
Kenosha Twins (9)	76	60	.568	6	60,977	Duffy Dyer
Madison Muskies (11)	65	73	.464	19½	110,949	Jim Nettles
Wausau Timbers (12)	52	85	.380	32	50,352	Greg Mahlberg

Central Standings	W	L	Pct.	GB	Attend.	Manager
Beloit Brewers (8)	79	57	.581	—	93,638	Dave Machemer
Cedar Rapids Reds (17)	78	61	.561	2½	155,034	Jay Ward
Clinton Giants (26)	71	69	.507	10	101,499	Tim Blackwell
Waterloo Indians (5)	67	73	.479	14	78,125	Steve Swisher

South Standings	W	L	Pct.	GB	Attend.	Manager
Peoria Chiefs (16)	75	65	.536	—	165,053	Pete Mackanin
Springfield Cardinals (24)	66	74	.471	9	149,069	Lloyd Merritt
Quad City Angels (3)	66	74	.471	9	153,414	Bill Lachemann
Burlington Rangers (13)	50	88	.362	24	64,763	Mike Bucci

Playoffs: Peoria 2 games, Beloit 1; Kenosha 2 games, Appleton 1.
Finals: Kenosha 3 games, Peoria 1.

All-Star Team: 1B-Greg Monda, Cedar Rapids; **2B**-Pete Coachman, Quad City; Bryan House, Peoria; **3B**-Eddie Williams, Cedar Rapids; **SS**-Julius McDougal, Peoria; **OF**-Darryel Walters, Beloit; Tom Thomas, Kenosha; Dante Bichette, Quad City; Troy Thomas, Appleton; Miguel Roman, Waterloo; Oriol Perez, Wausau; **C**-B.J. Surhoff, Beloit; **DH**-Tom Amante, Springfield; **P**-Dan Scarpetta, Beloit; Alan Sontag, Kenosha; Greg Dunn, Springfield; Bill Mendek, Wausau; **MVP**-Eddie Williams, Cedar Rapids; **Manager**-Duffy Dyer, Kenosha.

BA: Henry McCulla, Springfield, .317
Runs: Mike Taylor, Appleton, 107
Hits: Bruce Crabbe, Peoria, 147
RBIs: James Winter, Appleton, 91
HRs: Bernardo Brito, Waterloo, 29
Wins: Keith Silver, Clinton, 17
SOs: Alan Sontag, Kenosha, 213
ERA: Keith Silver, Clinton, 2.24

A New York-Pennsylvania League
President: Leo A. Pinckney

North Standings	W	L	Pct.	GB	Attend.	Manager
Oneonta Yankees (10)	55	23	.705	—	42,372	Buck Showalter
Utica Blue Sox	35	41	.461	19	56,390	Ken Brett
Little Falls Mets (21)	34	41	.453	19½	27,950	Dan Radison
Watertown Pirates (23)	22	54	.289	32	51,840	Woody Hunt

Central Standings	W	L	Pct.	GB	Attend.	Manager
Auburn Astros (18)	47	31	.603	—	23,966	Bob Hartsfield
Geneva Cubs (16)	45	33	.577	2	31,298	Tony Franklin
Newark Orioles (1)	41	36	.532	5½	22,888	Art Mazmanian
Elmira Pioneers (2)	28	49	.364	18½	66,636	Dick Berardino

South Standings	W	L	Pct.	GB	Attend.	Manager
Jamestown Expos (20)	45	33	.577	—	52,576	Ed Creech
Erie Cardinals (24)	44	34	.564	1	48,347	Fred Koenig
Niagara Falls Sox (4)	34	43	.442	10½	31,149	Luis Lagunas
Batavia Trojans (5)	33	45	.423	12	35,581	Eddie Bane

Playoffs: Oneonta 1 game, Geneva 0; Auburn 1 game, Jamestown 0.
Finals: Oneonta 2 games, Auburn 0.

All-Star Team: 1B-Rich Johnson, Auburn; **2B**-Jose Mota, Niagara Falls; **3B**-Scott Shaw, Oneonta; **SS**-Scott Gray, Auburn; **OF**-Doug Dascenzo, Geneva; Dennis Carter, Erie; Luis Medina, Batavia; Andre Tolliver, Niagara Falls; **C**-Jorge Alcazar, Niagara Falls; Geoff Davis, Jamestown; **DH**-Don Levell, Batavia; **P**-Dody Rather, Oneonta; Mike Christopher, Oneonta; Blaise Ilsley, Auburn; Jeff Ballard, Newark; **Manager**-Buck Showalter, Oneonta.

BA: George Flower, Jamestown, .336
Runs: Doug Dascenzo, Geneva, 59
Hits: Andrew Donatelli, Utica, 87
RBIs: Dennis Carter, Erie, 77
HRs: Dennis Carter, Erie, 16
Wins: Jeff Ballard, Newark, 10
Troy Evers, Oneonta, 10
SOs: Bill Cunningham, Jamestown, 116
Blaise Ilsley, Auburn, 116
ERA: Troy Evers, Oneonta, 1.87

A Northwest League
President: Jack Cain

Washington Standings	W	L	Pct.	GB	Attend.	Manager
Everett Giants (26)	40	34	.541	—	53,869	Joe Strain
Bellingham Mariners (12)	39	35	.527	1	18,343	Gary Pellant
Spokane Indians (25)	33	41	.446	7	70,576	Jack Maloof
Tri-Cities Triplets	33	41	.446	7	32,424	Ed Olsen

Oregon Standings	W	L	Pct.	GB	Attend.	Manager
Eugene Emeralds (7)	40	34	.541	—	103,193	Frank Funk
Bend Phillies (22)	39	35	.527	1	30,507	P.J. Carey
Salem Angels (3)	39	35	.527	1	34,450	Bruce Hines
Medford A's (11)	33	41	.446	7	64,720	Grady Fuson

Playoff: Everett 1 game, Eugene 0.

All-Star Team: 1B-Jim McCollom, Salem; **2B**-Julio Alcala, Eugene; **3B**-Dave Cortez, Tri-Cities; **SS**-John Verducci, Everett; **OF**-Ron Jones, Bend; Mike Loggins, Eugene; Jerald Clark, Spokane; **C**-Chris Jelic, Eugene; **DH**-Keith Foley, Tri-Cities; **P**-Randy McCament, Everett; Dave Otto, Medford; **MVP**-Jerald Clark, Spokane; **Manager**-Frank Funk, Eugene.

BA: Keith Foley, Tri-Cities, .376
Runs: Danny Lamar, Tri-Cities, 65
Hits: Danny Lamar, Tri-Cities, 96
RBIs: Danny Lamar, Tri-Cities, 69
HRs: Danny Lamar, Tri-Cities, 17
Wins: Tim Burcham, Salem, 8
Steve McGuire, Salem, 8
Jeff Shaver, Medford, 8
Edwin West, Bellingham, 8
SOs: Tim Burcham, Salem, 91
Wally Whitehurst, Medford, 91
ERA: Clay Parker, Bellingham, 1.55

A South Atlantic League
President: John H. Moss

North Standings	W	L	Pct.	GB	Attend.	Manager
Asheville Tourists (18)	76	62	.551	—	73,888	Fred Hatfield
Greensboro Hornets**(2)	74	63	.540	1½	172,626	Doug Camilli
Sumter Braves*(15)	72	63	.533	2½	36,518	Buddy Bailey
Spartanburg Suns (22)	66	70	.485	9	48,742	Rollie DeArmas
Gastonia Jets	44	93	.321	31½	53,307	Bob McBee

South Standings	W	L	Pct.	GB	Attend.	Manager
Florence Blue Jays**(14)	82	55	.599	—	41,546	Hector Torres
Columbia Mets*(21)	79	57	.581	2½	101,277	Bud Harrelson/Rich Miller
Charleston Rainbows (25)	78	61	.561	5	105,647	Jim Skaalen
Savannah Cardinals (24)	57	78	.422	24	34,287	Gaylen Pitts
Macon Pirates (23)	56	82	.406	26½	39,679	Mike Quade

Playoffs: Florence 2 games, Columbia 0; Greensboro 2 games, Sumter 0.
Finals: Florence 3 games, Greensboro 2.

All-Star Team: 1B-Carey Cheek, Macon; **2B**-Jeff Gardner, Columbia; **3B**-Zolio Sanchez, Columbia; Roberto Zambrano, Greensboro; **SS**-Santiago Garcia, Florence; **OF**-Sil Campusano, Florence; Marcus Lawton, Columbia; Drew Denson, Sumter; Shawn Dantzler, Spartanburg; **C**-Jaime Williams, Asheville; **DH**-Pat Jelks, Greensboro; **P**-Tim Englund, Florence; Mike Miller, Spartanburg; Mike Shelton, Spartanburg; Tom Funk, Asheville; **MVP**-Sil Campusano, Florence; **Manager**-Hector Torres, Florence.

BA: Manuel Jose, Greensboro, .323
Runs: Alan Ashkinazy, Greensboro, 115
Hits: Chris Moritz, Greensboro, 167
RBIs: Angelo Cuevas, Columbia, 101
HRs: Peter Mueller, Asheville, 28
Wins: Tim Englund, Florence, 18
SOs: Tim Englund, Florence, 210
ERA: Tom Glavine, Sumter, 2.35

R Appalachian League
President: Bill Halstead

Standings	W	L	Pct.	GB	Attend.	Manager
Bristol Tigers (6)	44	25	.638	—	10,218	Tom Burgess
Johnson City Cardinals (24)	39	29	.574	4½	12,998	Rich Hacker
Wytheville Cubs (16)	39	31	.557	5½	26,696	Ramon Conde
Bluefield Orioles (1)	36	34	.514	8½	24,511	Mike Verdi
Elizabethton Twins (9)	31	40	.437	14	7,172	Fred Waters
Pulaski Braves (15)	28	40	.412	15½	10,198	Craig Robinson
Kingsport Mets (21)	26	44	.371	18½	20,817	Tucker Ashford

Playoffs: None.

All-Star Team: 1B-Mark McMorris, Wytheville; **2B**-Gator Thiesen, Johnson City; **3B**-Craig Worthington, Bluefield; **SS**-Gregg Jefferies, Kingsport; **OF**-Alex Cole, Johnson City; Tony Hamza, Wytheville; Jaime Archibald, Kingsport; **C**-Dave Liddell, Wytheville; **DH**-Tim Leiper, Bristol; **P**-Barry Hightower, Kingsport; Mike Adams, Elizabethton; **MVP**-Gregg Jefferies, Kingsport; **Manager**-Tom Burgess, Bristol.

BA: Mark McMorris, Wytheville, .370
Runs: Alex Cole, Johnson City, 60
Hits: Mark McMorris, Wytheville, 84
RBIs: Mark McMorris, Wytheville, 53
HRs: Brandon Bailey, Kingsport, 10
Dave Justice, Pulaski, 10
Bob Tomberlin, Pulaski, 10
Wins: Kerry Griffith, Johnson City, 9
Michael York, Bristol, 9
SOs: Les Lancaster, Wytheville, 81
ERA: Mike Adams, Elizabethton, 2.19

R Gulf Coast League
President: Thomas J. Saffell

North Standings	W	L	Pct.	GB	Manager
Rangers (13)	33	29	.532	—	Rudy Jaramillo
Dodgers (19)	28	33	.459	4½	Jose Alvarez
Braves (26)	26	35	.426	6½	Pedro Gonzalez
Blue Jays (14)	23	39	.371	10	Ralph "Rocket" Wheeler
Pirates (23)	15	47	.242	18	Woody Huyke

1985

South Standings	W	L	Pct.	GB	Manager
Yankees (10)	43	18	.705	—	Carlos Tosca
White Sox (4)	40	22	.645	3½	J.C. Martin
Royals (7)	38	24	.613	5½	Joe Jones
Reds (17)	38	24	.613	5½	Sam Mejias
Astros (18)	24	37	.393	19	Julio Linares

Games played at Sarasota and Bradenton, Florida.

Playoff: Yankees and Rangers were rained out. Yankees were declared champions on the basis of overall winning percentage.

All-Star Team: 1B-Isidore Rondon, Reds; **2B**-Rob Lambert, Yankees; **3B**-Domingo Martinez, Blue Jays; **SS**-Francisco Burgos, Rangers; **OF**-Fred Carter, Yankees; Javon Edwards, Dodgers; Ted Higgins, Yankees; **C**-Michael Dotzler, Rangers; **P**-Dan Belinskas, Reds; Phil Dale, Reds; **Manager**-Carlos Tosca, Yankees.

BA: Rob Lambert, Yankees, .350	**Wins:** Wayne Edwards, White Sox, 7
Runs: Rob Lambert, Yankees, 51	Donn Pall, White Sox, 7
Hits: Rob Lambert, Yankees, 79	Dick Sisler, Yankees, 7
RBIs: Ted Higgins, Yankees, 36	**SOs:** Ricky Rojas, Royals, 78
HRs: Jesus Alvarez, White Sox, 5	**ERA:** Alvin West, Rangers, 1.33

R Pioneer League
President: Ralph C. Nelles

North Standings	W	L	Pct.	GB	Attend.	Manager
Great Falls Dodgers (19)	54	16	.771	—	85,193	Kevin Kennedy
Helena Gold Sox (8)	42	26	.618	11	23,276	Michael Easom
Medicine Hat Blue Jays (14)	26	44	.371	28	46,284	Mike Young
Butte Copper Kings (x)	24	45	.348	29½	20,573	Hal Dyer

South Standings	W	L	Pct.	GB	Attend.	Manager
Salt Lake City Trappers	46	24	.657	—	57,683	Jim Gattis
Billings Mustangs (17)	41	27	.603	4	97,773	James Lett
Pocatello Gems (11)	24	45	.348	21½	22,397	Dave Hudgens
Idaho Falls Nuggets	19	49	.279	26	20,647	Ruben Rodriguez

Playoff: Salt Lake City 3 games, Great Falls 2.

All-Star Team: 1B-Marty Brown, Billings; **2B**-Mike Watters, Great Falls; **3B**-Mark Grimes, Salt Lake City; **SS**-Walt Weiss, Pocatello; **OF**-Mike Devereaux, Great Falls; Todd Brown, Helena; Brian Morrison, Medicine Hat; **C**-Greg David, Medicine Hat; **DH**-Joe Shotnick, Salt Lake City; **P**-Fred Farwell, Great Falls; Bill Ray, Great Falls; Ed McCarter, Salt Lake City; **Manager of the Year**-Kevin Kennedy, Great Falls.

BA: Todd Brown, Helena, .447	**Wins:** Fred Farwell, Great Falls, 10
Runs: Mike Devereaux, Great Falls, 73	Bryan Smith, Great Falls, 10
Hits: Mike Devereaux, Great Falls, 103	**SOs:** Ed McCarter, Salt Lake City, 111
RBIs: Mike Devereaux, Great Falls, 67	**ERA:** Rob Lopez, Billings, 1.32
HRs: Peter Callas, Idaho Falls, 11	

1985 Interleague Post Season Play

World Series
Kansas City (American) 4 games, St. Louis (National) 3

1985 Major League Farm Systems

American League

1 Baltimore (6): Rochester, Charlotte, Hagerstown, Daytona Beach, Newark, Bluefield.
2 Boston (5): Pawtucket, New Britain, Winter Haven, Greensboro, Elmira.
3 California (5): Edmonton, Midland, Redwood, Quad City, Salem (OR).
4 Chicago (5): Buffalo, Glens Falls, Appleton, Niagara Falls, Gulf Coast.
5 Cleveland (4): Maine, Waterbury, Waterloo, Batavia.
6 Detroit (4): Nashville, Birmingham, Lakeland, Bristol.
7 Kansas City (5): Omaha, Memphis, Ft. Myers, Eugene, Gulf Coast.
8 Milwaukee (5): Vancouver, El Paso, Stockton, Beloit, Helena.
9 Minnesota (5): Toledo, Orlando, Visalia, Kenosha, Elizabethton.
10 New York (5): Columbus (OH), Albany-Colonie, Ft. Lauderdale, Oneonta, Gulf Coast.
11 Oakland (6): Tacoma, Huntsville, Modesto, Madison, Medford, Pocatello.
12 Seattle (5): Calgary, Chattanooga, Salinas, Wausau, Bellingham.
13 Texas (6): Oklahoma City, Tulsa, Salem (VA), Daytona Beach, Burlington (IA), Gulf Coast.
14 Toronto (6): Syracuse, Knoxville, Kinston, Florence, Medicine Hat, Gulf Coast.

National League

15 Atlanta (6): Richmond, Greenville, Durham, Sumter, Pulaski, Gulf Coast.
16 Chicago (6): Iowa, Pittsfield, Winston-Salem, Peoria, Geneva, Wytheville.
17 Cincinnati (6): Denver, Vermont, Tampa, Cedar Rapids, Billings, Gulf Coast.
18 Houston (6): Tucson, Columbus (GA), Osceola, Asheville, Auburn, Gulf Coast.
19 Los Angeles (6): Albuquerque, San Antonio, Bakersfield, Vero Beach, Great Falls, Gulf Coast.
20 Montreal (4): Indianapolis, Jacksonville, West Palm Beach, Jamestown.
21 New York (6): Tidewater, Jackson, Lynchburg, Columbia, Little Falls, Kingsport.
22 Philadelphia (6): Portland, Reading, Peninsula, Clearwater, Spartanburg, Bend.
23 Pittsburgh (6): Hawaii, Nashua, Prince William, Macon, Watertown, Gulf Coast.
24 St. Louis (7): Louisville, Arkansas, St. Petersburg, Springfield, Savannah, Erie, Johnson City.
25 San Diego (5): Las Vegas, Beaumont, Reno, Charleston, Spokane.
26 San Francisco (5): Phoenix, Shreveport, Fresno, Clinton, Everett.

Co-op (x): Butte.

Independent: San Jose, Miami, Utica, Tri-Cities, Gastonia, Salt Lake City, Idaho Falls.

1985 No-Hitters

Date	Pitcher	Team	League	Opponent	Score
4-14	Herminio Dominguez	Campeche	Mexican	Cordoba	1-0 (P, 7)
4-15	Bill Clossen	Sumter	South Atlantic	Florence	2-0
4-18	Richard Henning/				
	Ed Puikunas	Fresno	California	Bakersfield	5-2
4-25	Eric Sonberg/				
	Steve Martin	Albuquerque	Pacific Coast	Hawaii	7-1
5-2	John Johnson	Hawaii	Pacific Coast	Calgary	5-0
5-13	Scott Elam	Knoxville	Southern	Memphis	2-0
5-13	John Habyan	Charlotte	Southern	Columbus	6-0
5-14	Tim Conroy	Tacoma	Pacific Coast	Tucson	1-0 (7)
5-26	Jose Bautista	Lynchburg	Carolina	Prince William	6-0
5-31	Frank Wills	Calgary	Pacific Coast	Tacoma	1-0 (7)
6-7	Pat Saitta/				
	Richard Moyer	Florence	South Atlantic	Charleston	4-3
6-8	Gary Parmenter	Pittsfield	Eastern	Nashua	6-0
6-8	Carlos Sosa	Tampico	Mexican	Puebla	4-0
6-14	Salvador Colorado	Cordoba	Mexican	Monterrey	4-0 (6)
6-20	Curt Heidenreich	Vermont	Eastern	Pittsfield	2-0 (5)
6-20	Rick Waits	Vancouver	Pacific Coast	Portland	7-0
6-22	Osvaldo Soto	Cedar Rapids	Midwest	Clinton	2-0

Date	Pitcher	Team	League	Opponent	Score
7-1	Keith Swartzlander/				
	Manuel Valenzuela	Pirates	Gulf Coast	Dodgers	6-0
7-2	Bill Fulton	Ft. Lauderdale	Florida State	Lakeland	5-0
7-3	Ernie Bacon	Tampa	Florida State	Miami	1-0
7-17	Brian Kelly	Nashville	American Assoc.	Oklahoma City	6-0
7-17	Barry Wohler	Vero Beach	Florida State	St. Petersburg	1-0
7-22	David West/Richard Rodriguez				
	Doug Barba	Columbia	South Atlantic	Charleston	12-0
7-24	Dody Rather	Oneonta	New York-Penn.	Watertown	6-0
7-25	Robert Link	Waterloo	Midwest	Clinton	10-0
7-25	Gary Eave/				
	Bienvenido Mota	Braves	Gulf Coast	White Sox	8-0 (7)
8-1	Johnny Abrego	Pittsfield	Eastern	Nashua	1-0
8-4	Mike Friedrich	Osceola	Florida State	Lakeland	2-0
8-14	Stephen George	Ft. Lauderdale	Florida State	Miami	6-0 (5)
8-14	David West	Columbia	South Atlantic	Spartanburg	3-0
8-20	Mike Converse	Reds	Gulf Coast	Astros	3-0 (7)
8-27	Richard Stoll	Indianapolis	American Assoc.	Buffalo	3-0 (7)

Number in parentheses indicates innings if other than nine; "P" indicates perfect game.

THIS DATE IN MINOR LEAGUE HISTORY

March 16, 1985, Crockett Park, longtime home of baseball in Charlotte, North Carolina, burned to the ground. Arson was suspected. A temporary facility would be built on the same site.

April 9, 1985, The California League began play with an awkward nine team format.

April 17, 1985, Richmond, International League, opened its new park, The Diamond.

April 22, 1985, Salinas Spurs pitcher Bobby Hinson was struck by a line drive on the right temple. He would remain in critical condition for some time, and doctors advised the pitcher against playing again.

May 20, 1985, Two Modesto players hit for the cycle in the same California League game, Bob Loscalzo and Kevin Stock accomplishing their feats in a 23-4 win over Visalia.

June 20, 1985, Barry Bonds, son of former big leaguer Bobby Bonds, reported to Prince William of the Carolina League after being signed by Pittsburgh. Also in the league was Carl Yastrzemski's son Mike, who was with Durham.

June 26, 1985, Organist Wilbur Snapp was ejected from a Florida State League game for playing "Three Blind Mice" following a disputed call against the home team.

August 15, 1985, Stan Wasiak became the winningest minor league manager when he piloted Vero Beach, Florida State League, to his 2,497th lifetime victory. The triumph surpassed Bob Coleman's mark of 2,496 established from 1919 to 1957. This season was Wasiak's 36th consecutive year as a minor league manager.

August 16, 1985, George Brunet, pitching coach for the Mexico City Tigres, hurled briefly in two Mexican League games, giving him 33 consecutive years of play in Organized Ball.

August 29, 1985, Eleven ex-big leaguers played for Miami of the Florida State League during the season. Mike Torrez, Ed Farmer, and Juan Eichelberger were among the major leaguers to perform for the Marlins, but the independent club still finished in the cellar.

September 2, 1985, Jose Canseco was promoted to Oakland after hitting 36 home runs during the season between Huntsville, Southern League, and Tacoma, Pacific Coast League.

MEXICAN LEAGUE AND OTHER SPANISH NICKNAME TRANSLATIONS

Acereros	Steelers	Guerreros	Warriors
Agrario	Farmers	Indios	Indians
Agricultura	Aggies	Industriales	Industrials
Aguila	Eagle	Laguneros	Lakers
Alacranes	Scorpions	Langosteros	Lobstermen
Algodoneros	Cotton Pickers	Leones	Lions
Alijadores	Stevedores	Metropolitanos	Metropolitans
Amigos	Friends	Mineros	Miners
Angeles	Angels	Olmecas	Olmecas
Angeles Negros	Black Angels	Osos Negros	Black Bears
Astros	Astros	Pericos	Parrots
Azucareros	Sugar Makers	Peroneros	Pear Growers
Azules	Blues	Petroleros	Oilers
Banqueros	Bankers	Piratas	Pirates
Boricuas	Puerto Ricans	Plataneros	Banana Growers
Bravos	Braves	Potros	Colts
Broncos	Broncos	Reales	Royals
Cachorros	Cubs	Rieleros	Railroadmen
Cafeteros	Coffee Growers	Rojos	Reds
Cardenales	Cardinals	Saraperos	Sarape Makers
Cerveceros	Brewers	Sultanes	Sultans
Charros	Cowboys	Tecolotes	Owls
Diablos Blancos	White Devils	Tiburones	Sharks
Diablos Rojos	Red Devils or Reds	Tigres	Tigers
Dorados	Goldens	Transito	Trafficmen
Gallos	Roosters	Truchas	Trout
Ganaderos	Cattlemen	Tuneros	Cactusmen

1986

American League
President: Dr. Robert W. Brown

East Standings	W	L	Pct.	GB	Attend.	Manager
Boston Red Sox	95	66	.590	—	2,147,641	John McNamara
New York Yankees	90	72	.556	5½	2,268,030	Lou Piniella
Detroit Tigers	87	75	.537	8½	1,899,437	Sparky Anderson
Toronto Blue Jays	86	76	.531	9½	2,455,477	Jimy Williams
Cleveland Indians	84	78	.519	11½	1,471,805	Pat Corrales
Milwaukee Brewers	77	84	.478	18	1,265,041	George Bamberger/ Tom Trebelhorn
Baltimore Orioles	73	89	.451	22½	1,973,176	Earl Weaver

West Standings	W	L	Pct.	GB	Attend.	Manager
California Angels	92	70	.568	—	2,655,872	Gene Mauch
Texas Rangers	87	75	.537	5	1,692,002	Bobby Valentine
Kansas City Royals	76	86	.469	16	2,320,794	Dick Howser/Mike Ferraro
Oakland Athletics	76	86	.469	16	1,314,646	Jackie Moore/ Jeff Newman/Tony LaRussa
Chicago White Sox	72	90	.444	20	1,424,313	Tony LaRussa/ Doug Rader/Jim Fregosi
Minnesota Twins	71	91	.438	21	1,255,453	Ray Miller/Tom Kelly
Seattle Mariners	67	95	.414	25	1,029,045	Chuck Cottier/ Marty Martinez/Dick Williams

Playoff: Boston 4 games, California 3.

BA: Wade Boggs, Boston, .357
Runs: Rickey Henderson, New York, 130
Hits: Don Mattingly, New York, 238
RBIs: Joe Carter, Toronto, 121
HRs: Jesse Barfield, Toronto, 40

Wins: Roger Clemens, Boston, 24
SOs: Mark Langston, Seattle, 245
ERA: Roger Clemens, Boston, 2.48
Pct: Roger Clemens, Boston, .857, 24-4
Saves: Dave Righetti, New York, 46

National League
President: Charles S. Feeney

East Standings	W	L	Pct.	GB	Attend.	Manager
New York Mets	108	54	.667	—	2,767,601	Davey Johnson
Philadelphia Phillies	86	75	.534	21½	1,933,335	John Felske
St. Louis Cardinals	79	82	.491	28½	2,471,974	Whitey Herzog
Montreal Expos	78	83	.484	29½	1,128,981	Buck Rodgers
Chicago Cubs	70	90	.438	37	1,859,102	John Frey/ John Vukovich/Gene Michael
Pittsburgh Pirates	64	98	.395	44	1,000,917	Jim Leyland

West Standings	W	L	Pct.	GB	Attend.	Manager
Houston Astros	96	66	.593	—	1,734,276	Hal Lanier
Cincinnati Reds	86	76	.531	10	1,692,432	Pete Rose
San Francisco Giants	83	79	.512	13	1,528,748	Roger Craig
San Diego Padres	74	88	.457	22	1,805,716	Steve Boros
Los Angeles Dodgers	73	89	.451	23	3,023,208	Tom Lasorda
Atlanta Braves	72	89	.447	23½	1,387,181	Chuck Tanner

Playoff: New York 4 games, Houston 2.

BA: Tim Raines, Montreal, .334
Runs: Von Hayes, Philadelphia, 107
Tony Gwynn, San Diego, 107
Hits: Tony Gwynn, San Diego, 211
RBIs: Mike Schmidt, Philadelphia, 119
HRs: Mike Schmidt, Philadelphia, 37

Wins: Fernando Valenzuela, Los Angeles, 21
SOs: Mike Scott, Houston, 306
ERA: Mike Scott, Houston, 2.22
Pct: Bob Ojeda, New York, .783, 18-5
Saves: Todd Worrell, St. Louis, 36

AAA American Association
President: Joe Ryan

East Standings	W	L	Pct.	GB	Attend.	Manager
Indianapolis Indians (20)	80	62	.563	—	220,285	Joe Sparks
Buffalo Bisons (4)	71	71	.500	9	425,113	Jim Marshall
Nashville Sounds (6)	68	74	.479	12	364,614	Leon Roberts
Louisville Redbirds (24)	64	78	.451	16	660,200	Jim Fregosi/Dave Bialas

West Standings	W	L	Pct.	GB	Attend.	Manager
Denver Zephyrs (17)	76	66	.535	—	301,787	Jack Lind
Iowa Cubs (16)	74	68	.521	2	257,986	Larry Cox
Omaha Royals (7)	72	70	.507	4	255,290	John Boles/Frank Funk
Oklahoma City 89ers (13)	63	79	.444	13	282,752	Dave Oliver

Playoff: Indianapolis 4 games, Denver 3.

All-Star Team: 1B-Joe DeSa, Buffalo; **2B**-Casey Candaele, Indianapolis; **3B**-German Rivera, Nashville; **SS**-Barry Larkin, Denver; **OF**-Bruce Fields, Nashville; Kevin Seitzer, Omaha; Bob Brower, Oklahoma City; Daryl Boston, Buffalo; Chico Walker, Iowa; **C**-Terry McGriff, Denver; Mike Stanley, Oklahoma City; **DH**-Lloyd McClendon, Denver; **P**-Al Hargesheimer, Omaha; Pete Filson, Buffalo; **MVP**-Barry Larkin, Denver; **Manager**-Joe Sparks, Indianapolis.

BA: Bruce Fields, Nashville, .368
Runs: Bob Brower, Oklahoma City, 130
Hits: Bob Brower, Oklahoma City, 158
Chico Walker, Iowa, 158
RBIs: Jim Lindeman, Louisville, 96

HRs: Lloyd McClendon, Denver, 24
Wins: Pete Filson, Buffalo, 14
SOs: Jack Lazorko, Nashville, 119
ERA: Pete Filson, Buffalo, 2.27

AAA International League
President: Harold Cooper

Standings	W	L	Pct.	GB	Attend.	Manager
Richmond Braves (15)	80	60	.571	—	381,364	Roy Majtyka
Rochester Red Wings (1)	75	63	.543	4	308,807	John Hart
Pawtucket Red Sox (2)	74	65	.532	5½	186,517	Ed Nottle
Tidewater Tides (21)	74	66	.529	6	171,589	Sam Perlozzo
Syracuse Chiefs (14)	72	67	.518	7½	187,758	Doug Ault
Toledo Mud Hens (9)	62	77	.446	17½	145,909	Charlie Manuel
Columbus Clippers (10)	62	77	.446	17½	548,417	Barry Foote
Maine Guides (5)	58	82	.414	22	105,578	Jim Napier

Playoffs: Richmond 3 games, Tidewater 0; Rochester 3 games, Pawtucket 1.
Finals: Richmond 3 games, Rochester 2.

All-Star Team: 1B-Pat Dodson, Pawtucket; **2B**-Mike Sharperson, Syracuse; **3B**-Dave Magadan, Tidewater; **SS**-Paul Zuvella, Richmond/Columbus; **OF**-Mike Greenwell, Pawtucket; Gerald Perry, Richmond; LaSchelle Tarver, Pawtucket; **C**-Pat Dempsey, Toledo; **DH**-Pete Dalena, Columbus; **P**-John Mitchell, Tidewater; Randy Myers, Tidewater; **MVP**-Pat Dodson, Pawtucket; **Pitcher of the Year**-John Mitchell, Tidewater; **Manager**-John Hart, Rochester.

BA: Andre David, Toledo, .328
Runs: Mike Sharperson, Syracuse, 86
Hits: Mike Sharperson, Syracuse, 150
RBIs: Pat Dodson, Pawtucket, 102
HRs: Ken Gerhart, Rochester, 28

Wins: Charlie Puleo, Richmond, 14
SOs: Charlie Puleo, Richmond, 124
Steve Shields, Richmond, 124
ERA: Doug Jones, Maine, 2.09

AAA Mexican League
President: Pedro Treto Cisneros

North Standings	W	L	Pct.	GB	Attend.	Manager
Monclova Acereros	76	51	.598	—	272,756	Alfredo Rios
Monterrey Sultanes	72	56	.558	4½	184,204	Vinicio Garcia/Miguel Sotelo
Aguascalientes Rieleros	70	56	.556	5½	156,198	Roberto Castellon
Dos Laredos Tecolotes	67	57	.540	7½	135,193	Jorge Calvo/Jose Guerrero
San Luis Potosi Tuneros	66	63	.512	11	186,148	Gregorio Luque
Union Laguna Algodoneros	60	65	.480	15	88,258	Wito Conde/ Gerardo Gutierrez
Leon Bravos	51	75	.405	24½	72,310	Jack Pierce
Saltillo Saraperos	52	78	.400	25½	58,739	Juan Navarrete/ Javier Espinoza/Victor Favela

South Standings	W	L	Pct.	GB	Attend.	Manager
Puebla Angeles	88	41	.682	—	145,951	Rodolfo Sandoval
Mexico City Tigres	75	48	.610	10	164,621	Roberto Mendez
Campeche Piratas	70	57	.551	17	117,834	Francisco Estrada
Mexico City Diablos Rojos	68	60	.531	19½	158,914	Ben Reyes
Yucatan Leones	61	68	.473	27	214,362	Carlos Paz
Cordoba Cafeteros	59	69	.461	28½	74,210	Victor Ramirez
Tabasco Ganaderos	52	74	.413	34½	93,072	Eduardo Gavilan/ Domingo Cruz
Veracruz Aguila	30	98	.234	57½	82,402	Francisco Rodriguez/ Alfredo Ortiz/ Ramon Arano/Jose Leyva

Playoffs: Monclova 4 games, Dos Laredos 2; Monterrey 4 games, Aguascalientes 3; Puebla 4 games, MC Diablos Rojos 2; MC Tigres 4 games, Campeche 2. Monterrey 4 games, Monclova 3; Puebla 4 games, MC Tigres 1.
Finals: Puebla 4 games, Monterrey 1.

BA: Willie Aikens, Puebla, .454
Runs: Nick Castaneda, San Luis Potosi, 141
Hits: Willie Aikens, Puebla, 202
RBIs: Willie Aikens, Puebla, 154
HRs: Jack Pierce, Leon, 54

Wins: Rodolfo Valdez, Campeche, 17
German Jimenez, Puebla, 17
Cecilio Ruiz, Yucatan, 17
SOs: Rafael Garcia, Saltillo, 155
ERA: Barry Bass, Monterrey, 2.03

AAA Pacific Coast League
President: Bill Cutler

North Standings	W	L	Pct.	GB	Attend.	Manager
Vancouver Canadians***(8)	85	53	.616	—	231,819	Terry Bevington
Tacoma Tigers (11)	72	72	.500	16	247,098	Keith Lieppman
Edmonton Trappers (3)	68	73	.482	18½	229,682	Winston Llenas
Portland Beavers (22)	68	73	.482	18½	138,677	Bill Dancy
Calgary Cannons (12)	66	77	.462	21½	288,197	Bill Plummer

*Won first-half   **Won second-half   ***Won both halves
Numbers after nicknames indicate farm system.
Affiliation listed at end of each year.

580

South Standings	W	L	Pct.	GB	Attend.	Manager
Phoenix Firebirds*(26)	81	61	.570	—	161,583	Jim Lefebvre
Las Vegas Stars**(25)	80	62	.563	1	291,060	Larry Bowa
Tucson Toros (18)	71	72	.497	10½	116,117	Carlos Alfonso
Hawaii Islanders (23)	65	79	.451	17	84,613	Tommy Sandt
Albuquerque Dukes (19)	54	88	.380	27	235,737	Terry Collins

Playoffs: Las Vegas 3 games, Phoenix 2; Vancouver 3 games, Tacoma 0.
Finals: Las Vegas 3 games, Vancouver 2.

All-Star Team: 1B-Tim Pyznarski, Las Vegas; **2B**-Greg Legg, Portland; **3B**-Randy Johnson, Phoenix; **SS**-Gus Polidor, Edmonton; **OF**-Glenn Braggs, Vancouver; Mickey Brantley, Calgary; Ty Gainey, Tucson; **C**-B.J. Surhoff, Vancouver; **DH**-Mark Ryal, Edmonton; **P**-Mark Grant, Phoenix; Bob Patterson, Hawaii; Chris Bosio, Vancouver; **MVP**-Tim Pyznarski, Las Vegas; **Manager**-Jim Lefebvre, Phoenix.

BA: Ty Gainey, Tucson, .351
Runs: Mickey Brantley, Calgary, 104
Hits: Luis Polonia, Tacoma, 165
RBIs: Tim Pyznarski, Las Vegas, 119
HRs: Rick Lancellotti, Phoenix, 31
Wins: Mark Grant, Phoenix, 14
SOs: Bob Patterson, Hawaii, 137
ERA: Dave Johnson, Hawaii, 3.17

AA Eastern League
President: Charles E. Eshbach

Standings	W	L	Pct.	GB	Attend.	Manager
Reading Phillies (22)	77	59	.566	—	83,506	George Culver
Vermont Reds (17)	77	62	.554	1½	77,959	Jay Ward
Pittsfield Cubs (16)	76	64	.543	3	47,709	Tom Spencer
Glens Falls Tigers (6)	67	71	.486	11	70,020	Bob Schaefer
Waterbury Indians (5)	66	73	.475	12½	37,267	Orlando Gomez
Albany-Colonie Yankees (10)	65	74	.468	13½	316,034	Jim Saul
New Britain Red Sox (2)	64	73	.467	13½	81,617	Tony Torchia
Nashua Pirates (23)	62	78	.443	17	78,103	Dennis Rogers

Playoffs: Vermont 3 games, Pittsfield 2; Reading 3 games, Glens Falls 1.
Finals: Vermont 3 games, Reading 2.

All-Star Team: 1B-Phil Stephenson, Pittsfield; **2B**-Jose Lind, Nashua; **3B**-Len Harris, Vermont; **SS**-Paul Noce, Pittsfield; **OF**-Dan Boever, Vermont; Jim Olander, Reading; Rafael Palmeiro, Pittsfield; **C**-Rey Palacios, Glens Falls; **DH**-Bernardo Brito, Waterbury; **P**-Jim Neidlinger, Nashua; Steve Searcy, Glens Falls; Jeff Gray, Vermont; **MVP**-Rafael Palmeiro, Pittsfield; **Pitcher of the Year**-Jim Neidlinger, Nashua; **Manager**-Bob Schaefer, Glens Falls.

BA: Jim Olander, Reading, .325
Runs: Paul Noce, Pittsfield, 87
Hits: Rafael Palmeiro, Pittsfield, 156
RBIs: Rafael Palmeiro, Pittsfield, 95
HRs: Bernardo Brito, Waterbury, 18
Wins: Jeff Gray, Vermont, 14
SOs: Steve Searcy, Glens Falls, 139
ERA: Jim Neidlinger, Nashua, 2.42

AA Southern League
President: Jimmy Bragan

East Standings	W	L	Pct.	GB	Attend.	Manager
Jacksonville Expos*(20)	75	68	.524	—	164,772	Tommy Thompson
Greenville Braves (15)	73	71	.507	2½	203,647	Jim Beauchamp
Columbus Astros**(18)	70	70	.500	3½	134,964	Dave Cripe/Gary Tuck
Charlotte O's (1)	71	73	.493	4½	106,426	Greg Biagini
Orlando Twins (9)	70	73	.490	5	75,728	George Mitterwald

West Standings	W	L	Pct.	GB	Attend.	Manager
Huntsville Stars*(11)	78	63	.553	—	263,198	Brad Fischer
Knoxville Blue Jays**(14)	74	70	.514	5½	109,731	Larry Hardy
Birmingham Barons (4)	70	73	.490	9	175,932	Tom Haller/Bob Bailey
Memphis Chicks (7)	69	75	.479	10½	252,036	Tommy Jones
Chattanooga Lookouts (12)	64	78	.451	14½	118,684	R.J. Harrison

Playoffs: Columbus 3 games, Jacksonville 1; Huntsville 3 games, Knoxville 1.
Finals: Columbus 3 games, Huntsville 1.

All-Star Team: 1B-Brick Smith, Chattanooga; **2B**-Billy Ripken, Charlotte; **3B**-Jeff Reynolds, Jacksonville; **SS**-Brian Guinn, Huntsville; **OF**-Glenallen Hill, Knoxville; Alonzo Powell, Jacksonville; Larry Ray, Columbus; Gary Thurman, Memphis; **C**-Terry Steinbach, Huntsville; **DH**-Tom Dodd, Charlotte; **P**-Tony Kelley, Columbus; Tom Glavine, Greenville; Paul Schneider, Chattanooga; **MVP**-Terry Steinbach, Huntsville; **Manager**-Gary Tuck, Columbus.

BA: Brick Smith, Chattanooga, .344
Runs: Gary Jones, Huntsville, 116
Hits: Gene Larkin, Orlando, 170
  Jose Tolentino, Huntsville, 170
RBIs: Terry Steinbach, Huntsville, 132
HRs: Glenallen Hill, Knoxville, 31
Wins: Tony Kelley, Columbus, 14
SOs: Terry Taylor, Chattanooga, 164
ERA: Eric Bell, Charlotte, 3.05

AA Texas League
President: Carl Sawatski

East Standings	W	L	Pct.	GB	Attend.	Manager
Shreveport Captains**(26)	80	56	.588	—	183,560	Wendell Kim
Jackson Mets*(21)	72	63	.533	7½	118,894	Mike Cubbage
Arkansas Travelers (24)	67	67	.500	13	222,613	Jim Riggleman
Tulsa Drillers (13)	49	85	.366	30	162,529	Bill Stearns

West Standings	W	L	Pct.	GB	Attend.	Manager
El Paso Diablos***(8)	85	50	.630	—	210,261	Duffy Dyer
San Antonio Dodgers (19)	64	71	.474	21	122,261	Gary LaRocque
Midland Angels (3)	62	71	.466	22	129,674	Joe Maddon
Beaumont Golden Gators (25)	60	76	.441	25½	101,060	Steve Smith

Playoff: Jackson 2 games, Shreveport 1.
Finals: El Paso 4 games, Jackson 0.

All-Star Team: 1B-Steve Stanicek, El Paso; **2B**-Keith Miller, Jackson; **3B**-Tracy Woodson, San Antonio; **SS**-Kevin Elster, Jackson; **OF**-Alan Cartwright, El Paso; Mike Devereaux, San Antonio; Shane Mack, Beaumont; **C**-Charlie O'Brien, El Paso; Mackey Sasser, Shreveport; **DH**-Kevin King, Midland; **Util**-Eddie Tanner, Arkansas; **P**-Charlie Corbell, Shreveport; George Ferran, Shreveport; Shawn Hillegas, Jackson; Dan Scarpetta, El Paso; Jeff Innis, Jackson; **MVP**-Steve Stanicek, El Paso; **Pitcher of the Year**-George Ferran, Shreveport; **Manager**-Wendell Kim, Shreveport.

BA: Steve Stanicek, El Paso, .343
Runs: Steve Stanicek, El Paso, 116
Hits: Steve Stanicek, El Paso, 167
RBIs: Jason Felice, Jackson, 97
  Jesus Alfrero, El Paso, 97
HRs: Kevin King, Midland, 30
Wins: George Ferran, Shreveport, 16
SOs: George Ferran, Shreveport, 147
ERA: George Ferran, Shreveport, 2.29

A California League
President: Joe Gagliardi

North Standings	W	L	Pct.	GB	Attend.	Manager
Stockton Ports (8)	83	59	.585	—	56,129	Dave Machemer
Salinas Spurs (12)	77	65	.542	6	47,737	Greg Mahlberg
Reno Padres (25)	73	69	.514	10	81,397	Jim Skaalen
Modesto A's (11)	69	73	.486	14	72,757	Tommie Reynolds
San Jose Bees	65	77	.458	18	87,235	Harry Steve/Mike Verdi

South Standings	W	L	Pct.	GB	Attend.	Manager
Palm Springs Angels (3)	87	55	.613	—	47,547	Tom Kotchman
Visalia Oaks (9)	75	67	.528	12	72,962	Dan Schmitz
Ventura County Gulls (14)	75	67	.528	12	38,868	Glenn Ezell
Fresno Giants (26)	66	76	.465	21	100,348	Tim Blackwell
Bakersfield Dodgers (19)	40	102	.282	47	78,635	Don LeJohn

Playoffs: Stockton 3 games, Salinas 0; Visalia 3 games, Palm Springs 1.
Finals: Stockton 3 games, Visalia 0.

North All-Star Team: 1B-Brad Pounders, Reno; **2B**-Norio Tanabe, San Jose; **3B**-Joe Mitchell, Stockton; **SS**-Joe Xavier, Modesto; **OF**-Todd Brown, Stockton; Felix Jose, Modesto; Jerald Clark, Reno; **C**-Bill McGuire, Salinas; **DH**-Ty Brilinski, Modesto; **P**-Ed Puig, Reno.

South All-Star Team: 1B-Ty Van Burkleo, Palm Springs; **2B**-Ted Holcomb, Bakersfield; **3B**-Ty Dabney, Fresno; **SS**-Tony Perezchica, Fresno; **OF**-Geronimo Berroa, Ventura County; Tom Thomas, Visalia; T.J. McDonald, Fresno; **C**-Greg Myers, Ventura County; **DH**-Mike Burke, Bakersfield; **P**-Willie Fraser, Palm Springs; **MVP**-Ty Dabney, Fresno; **Pitcher of the Year**-Jeff Peterek, Stockton; **Manager**-Tom Kotchman, Palm Springs.

BA: Roberto Alomar, Reno, .346
Runs: Tom Schwarz, Visalia, 102
Hits: Norio Tanabe, San Jose, 166
RBIs: Ty Van Burkleo, Palm Springs, 108
HRs: Brad Pounders, Reno, 35
Wins: Jeff Peterek, Stockton, 15
SOs: Dennis Cook, Fresno, 173
ERA: Mike Christ, Salinas, 2.69

A Carolina League
President: John Hopkins

North Standings	W	L	Pct.	GB	Attend.	Manager
Hagerstown Suns***(1)	91	48	.655	—	144,161	Bob Molinaro
Lynchburg Mets (21)	75	65	.514	16½	87,930	Bobby Floyd
Prince William Pirates (23)	67	72	.482	24	117,000	Rocky Bridges
Salem Redbirds (13)	45	93	.326	45½	87,047	Mike Bucci

South Standings	W	L	Pct.	GB	Attend.	Manager
Winston-Salem Spirits***(16)	82	56	.594	—	136,841	Jim Essian
Durham Bulls (15)	72	68	.514	11	197,125	Buddy Bailey
Peninsula White Sox (4)	60	74	.484	20	75,928	Bob Bailey/Duke Sims
Kinston Eagles	60	76	.441	21	48,845	Dave Trembley

Playoff: Winston-Salem 3 games, Hagerstown 1.

All-Star Team: 1B-Lance Belen, Prince William; **2B**-Pete Stanicek, Hagerstown; **3B**-Craig Worthington, Hagerstown; **SS**-Gregg Jefferies, Lynchburg; **OF**-Doug Dascenzo, Winston-Salem; Sherwin Clintje, Hagerstown; Ron Scheer, Peninsula; **C**-Hector Villanueva, Winston-Salem; **DH**-Gene Gentile, Kinston; **Util**-Ron Gant, Durham; **P**-Dave Pavlas, Winston-Salem; Rob Russell, Prince William; **MVP**-Gregg Jefferies, Lynchburg; **Pitcher of the Year**-Dave Pavlas, Winston-Salem; **Manager**-Jim Essian, Winston-Salem.

BA: Gregg Jefferies, Lynchburg, .354
Runs: Marcus Lawton, Lynchburg, 118
Hits: Doug Dascenzo, Winston-Salem, 178
RBIs: Craig Worthington, Hagerstown, 105
HRs: Ron Gant, Durham, 26
Wins: Martin Reed, Kinston, 16
SOs: Chris Ritter, Prince William, 149
ERA: Jeff Ballard, Hagerstown, 1.85

A Florida State League
President: George MacDonald, Jr.

West Standings	W	L	Pct.	GB	Attend.	Manager
St. Petersburg Cardinals (24)	88	48	.647	—	126,242	Dave Bialas/Marty Mason/Mike Jorgensen
Tampa Tarpons (17)	79	57	.581	9	57,930	Marc Bombard
Clearwater Phillies (22)	63	74	.460	25½	53,824	Ron Clark
Ft. Myers Royals (7)	50	85	.370	37½	42,083	Duane Gustavson

South Standings	W	L	Pct.	GB	Attend.	Manager
West Palm Beach Expos (20)	80	55	.593	—	97,481	Felipe Alou
Ft. Lauderdale Yankees (10)	80	59	.576	2	43,316	Bucky Dent

| Miami Marlins | 74 | 66 | .529 | 8½ | 35,569 | Fred Hatfield/Max Oliveras |
| Vero Beach Dodgers (19)... | 68 | 70 | .493 | 13½ | 81,919 | Stan Wasiak |

Central Standings	W	L	Pct.	GB	Attend.	Manager
Winter Haven Red Sox (2) .	80	47	.630	—	21,486	Dave Holt
Osceola Astros (18)	59	78	.431	26	36,135	Tom Wiedenbauer
Lakeland Tigers (6)	54	79	.406	29	53,147	Tom Burgess
Daytona Beach Islanders (13)..	40	97	.292	45	42,774	Chino Cadahia

Playoffs: West Palm Beach 2 games, Winter Haven 0; St. Petersburg 2 games, Tampa 1.
Finals: St. Petersburg 3 games, West Palm Beach 1.

All-Star Team: 1B-Ron Johns, St. Petersburg; **2B-**Jim Reboulet, St. Petersburg; **3B-**Chris Alvarez, Ft. Lauderdale; **SS-**Esteban Beltre, West Palm Beach; **OF-**Brady Anderson, Winter Haven; Ron Jones, Clearwater; Jimmy Fortenberry, Clearwater; Chris Morgan, Lakeland; **C-None; DH-**Tary Scott, Winter Haven; **P-**Rob Lopez, Tampa; Dody Rather, Osceola; Jeff Fassero, St. Petersburg; Joel Lono, Tampa; Gary Wayne, West Palm Beach; Ray Perkins, Miami; **MVP-**Ron Jones, Clearwater; **Manager-**Dave Holt, Winter Haven.

BA: Ron Jones, Clearwater, .371
Runs: Greg Lotzar, Winter Haven, 94
Hits: Ron Jones, Clearwater, 153
  James St. Laurent, Daytona Beach, 153
RBIs: Tary Scott, Winter Haven, 93
HRs: Jimmy Fortenberry, Clearwater, 18
Wins: Sergio Valdez, West Palm Beach, 16
SOs: Dody Rather, Osceola, 151
ERA: Rob Lopez, Tampa, 1.92

A Midwest League
President: Ed Larson

North East Standings	W	L	Pct.	GB	Attend.	Manager
Madison Muskies (11)	86	54	.614	—	118,310	Jim Nettles
Wausau Timbers (12)	73	66	.525	12½	59,634	Bobby Cuellar
Appleton Foxes (4)	56	83	.403	29½	60,001	Duke Sims/Rico Petrocelli
Kenosha Twins (9)	46	92	.333	39	57,495	Don Leppert

Central Standings	W	L	Pct.	GB	Attend.	Manager
Waterloo Indians (5)	78	62	.557	—	80,124	Steve Swisher
Beloit Brewers (8)	70	69	.504	7½	101,127	Gomer Hodge
Cedar Rapids Reds (17)	70	70	.500	8	131,534	Gene Dusan/Paul Kirsch
Clinton Giants (26)	63	76	.453	14½	100,326	Jack Mull

South Standings	W	L	Pct.	GB	Attend.	Manager
Springfield Cardinals (24) ..	87	53	.621	—	151,815	Gaylen Pitts
Peoria Chiefs (16)	77	63	.550	10	179,183	Pete Mackanin
Burlington Expos (20)	69	71	.493	18	68,457	J.R. Miner
Quad City Angels (3)	62	78	.443	25	116,062	Bill Lachemann

Playoffs: Waterloo 2 games, Madison 0; Peoria 2 games, Springfield 0.
Finals: Waterloo 3 games, Peoria 0.

All-Star Team: 1B-Mark Grace, Peoria; **2B-**Mark Howie, Madison; **3B-**Marty Brown, Cedar Rapids; **SS-**Walt Weiss, Madison; **OF-**Luis Medina, Waterloo; Dwight Smith, Peoria; Bob Simonson, Beloit; **C-**Mike Fox, Springfield; **DH-**Mike Fitzgerald, Springfield; **P-**Dave Otto, Madison; Jeff Oyster, Springfield; Paul Wilmet, Springfield; Tim O'Connor, Kenosha; **MVP-**Luis Medina, Waterloo; **Manager-**Gaylen Pitts, Springfield.

BA: Mark Grace, Peoria, .342
Runs: Luis Medina, Waterloo, 107
Hits: Luis Medina, Waterloo, 160
RBIs: Luis Medina, Waterloo, 110
HRs: Luis Medina, Waterloo, 35
Wins: Jeff Oyster, Springfield, 17
SOs: Steve Gasser, Kenosha, 225
ERA: Greg Simpson, Cedar Rapids, 1.81

A New York-Pennsylvania League
President: Leo A. Pinckney

Yawkey Standings	W	L	Pct.	GB	Attend.	Manager
Oneonta Yankees (10)	59	18	.766	—	49,611	Buck Showalter
Little Falls Mets (21)	36	40	.474	22½	40,557	Rich Miller
Watertown Pirates (23)	30	48	.385	29½	35,480	Ed Ott
Utica Blue Sox (22)	26	52	.333	33½	29,950	Tony Taylor

Wrigley Standings	W	L	Pct.	GB	Attend.	Manager
St. Catharines Blue Jays (14)...	48	28	.632	—	42,125	Cloyd Boyer
Erie Cardinals (24)	37	40	.481	11½	49,411	Joe Rigoli
Batavia Trojans (5)	30	45	.400	17½	34,765	Tom Chandler
Jamestown Expos (20)	30	46	.395	18	37,009	Gene Glynn

McNamara Standings	W	L	Pct.	GB	Attend.	Manager
Auburn Astros (18)	44	32	.579	—	24,249	Keith Bodie
Newark Orioles (1)	41	37	.526	4	17,199	Art Mazmanian
Elmira Pioneers (2)	39	36	.520	4½	71,463	Bill Limoncelli
Geneva Cubs (16)	40	38	.513	5	22,851	Jay Loviglio

Playoffs: Newark 1 game, Oneonta 0; St. Catharines 1 game, Auburn 0.
Finals: St. Catharines 2 games, Newark 1.

All-Star Team: 1B-Hal Morris, Oneonta; **2B-**Oscar Escobar, St. Catharines; **3B-**Carey Nemeth, Erie; **SS-**Ben Figueroa, Erie; **OF-**Barry Shifflett, St. Catharines; Tom Baine, Erie; Ced Landrum, Geneva; **C-**Todd Zeile, Erie; Fritz Polka, Little Falls; **DH-**Frank Bellino, Newark; **P-**Alan Koonce, Newark; Dean Wilkins, Oneonta; Ken Patterson, Oneonta; Joel Estes, Auburn; **Manager-**Cloyd Boyer, St. Catharines.

BA: Tom Hinzo, Batavia, .333
Runs: Tom Baine, Erie, 55
Hits: Oscar Escobar, St. Catharines, 100
RBIs: Todd Zeile, Erie, 63
HRs: Julian Yan, St. Catharines, 15
Wins: Blaine Beatty, Newark, 11
SOs: Joe Skalski, Batavia, 130
ERA: Ken Patterson, Oneonta, 1.35

A Northwest League
President: Jack Cain

Washington Standings	W	L	Pct.	GB	Attend.	Manager
Bellingham Mariners (12) ..	45	29	.608	—	14,916	Sal Rende
Everett Giants (26)	40	34	.541	5	51,131	Joe Strain
Spokane Indians (25)	39	35	.527	6	102,826	Rob Picciolo
Tri-Cities Triplets (x)	25	49	.338	20	30,605	Pat Murphy

Oregon Standings	W	L	Pct.	GB	Attend.	Manager
Eugene Emeralds (7)	45	29	.608	—	116,286	Ed Napoleon
Medford A's (11)	43	31	.581	2	70,590	Dave Hudgens
Salem Angels (3)	38	36	.514	7	37,279	Bruce Hines
Bend Phillies (22)	21	53	.284	24	29,766	Ed Pebley

Playoff: Bellingham 1 game, Eugene 0.

All-Star Team: 1B-Nathan Oglesbee, Eugene; **2B-**John Toal, Everett; **3B-**Anthony Pellegrino, Spokane; **SS-**Tom LeVasseur, Spokane; **OF-**Lee Stevens, Salem; Drew Stratton, Medford; Dave Nash, Everett; **C-**Mike Knapp, Salem; **DH-**Carlos Escalera, Eugene; **P-**Gary Blouin, Eugene; Jim Pena, Everett; **MVP-**Dave Nash, Everett; **Manager-**Sal Rende, Bellingham.

BA: Tom LeVasseur, Spokane, .372
Runs: Brian McRae, Eugene, 66
Hits: Carlos Escalera, Eugene, 98
RBIs: Carlos Escalera, Eugene, 69
HRs: John Jaha, Tri-Cities, 15
Wins: Jim Pena, Everett, 10
SOs: Jim Pena, Everett, 92
ERA: Rich DeLucia, Bellingham, 1.70

A South Atlantic League
President: John H. Moss

North Standings	W	L	Pct.	GB	Attend.	Manager
Asheville Tourists***(18) ..	90	50	.643	—	101,962	Ken Bolek
Sumter Braves (15)	77	60	.562	11½	45,290	Brian Snitker
Greensboro Hornets (2)	75	63	.543	14	180,715	Doug Camilli
Gastonia Tigers (6)	59	80	.424	30½	79,029	John Lipon
Spartanburg Phillies (22)	40	95	.296	47½	16,833	Rollie DeArmas

South Standings	W	L	Pct.	GB	Attend.	Manager
Columbia Mets***(21)	90	42	.682	—	106,403	Tucker Ashford
Savannah Cardinals (24)....	75	60	.556	16½	44,787	Mark DeJohn
Charleston Rainbows (25) ..	63	69	.477	27	131,696	Pat Kelly
Florence Blue Jays (14)	56	76	.424	34	36,010	Hector Torres
Macon Pirates (23)	54	84	.391	39	37,816	Mike Quade

Playoff: Columbia 3 games, Asheville 1.

All-Star Team: 1B-Rich Johnson, Asheville; **2B-**Dave Gelatt, Columbia; **3B-**Carlo Colombino, Asheville; **SS-**Juan Villanueva, Columbia; **OF-**Cameron Drew, Asheville; Carlos Quintana, Greensboro; Alan Hayden, Columbia; **C-**Dan Walters, Asheville; **DH-**Paul Thoutsis, Greensboro; **P-**Kevin Armstrong, Columbia; Rob Livchak, Asheville; **MVP-**Cameron Drew, Asheville; **Pitcher of the Year-**Blaise Ilsley, Asheville; **Manager-**Tucker Ashford, Columbia.

BA: Carlo Colombino, Asheville, .339
Runs: Scott Markley, Asheville, 113
Hits: Scott Markley, Asheville, 147
RBIs: Cameron Drew, Asheville, 117
HRs: Cameron Drew, Asheville, 26
Wins: Kevin Armstrong, Columbia, 17
SOs: Brian Givens, Columbia, 189
ERA: Blaise Ilsley, Asheville, 1.95

R Appalachian League
President: Bill Halstead

North Standings	W	L	Pct.	GB	Attend.	Manager
Pulaski Braves (15)	41	25	.621	—	14,040	Grady Little
Bluefield Orioles (1)	39	29	.574	3	33,888	Glenn Gulliver
Burlington Indians (5)	36	31	.537	5½	62,701	Glenn Adams
Wytheville Cubs (16)	22	46	.324	20	18,014	Tony Franklin

South Standings	W	L	Pct.	GB	Attend.	Manager
Johnson City Cardinals (24)..	44	22	.667	—	23,965	Dan Radison
Elizabethton Twins (9)	37	31	.544	8	10,338	Fred Waters
Bristol Tigers (6)	35	34	.507	10½	15,040	Tom Gamboa
Kingsport Mets (21)	16	52	.235	29	30,425	Chuck Hiller

Playoff: Pulaski 2 games, Johnson City 1.

All-Star Team: 1B-Chris Hoiles, Bristol; **2B-**Geronimo Pena, Johnson City; **3B-**Pat Austin, Bristol; **SS-**Scott Leius, Elizabethton; **OF-**Jerome Walton, Wytheville; Vince Kindred, Johnson City; Ken Adderly, Bluefield; **C-**Brian Deak, Pulaski; **DH-**Scott Johnson, Burlington; **P-**Dave Osteen, Johnson City; Dave Sala, Johnson City; **MVP-**Brian Deak, Pulaski; **Manager-**Dan Radison, Johnson City.

BA: Phil Clark, Bristol, .352
Runs: Geronimo Pena, Johnson City, 55
Hits: Phil Clark, Bristol, 82
RBIs: Chris Hoiles, Bristol, 57
HRs: Scott Johnson, Burlington, 14
Wins: Mark Gilles, Burlington, 9
  Toby Nivens, Elizabethton, 9
  Dave Osteen, Johnson City, 9
  Dave Sala, Johnson City, 9
SOs: Jim LeMasters, Pulaski, 85
ERA: John Stewart, Pulaski, 2.25

R Gulf Coast League
President: Thomas J. Saffell

North Standings	W	L	Pct.	GB	Manager
Dodgers (19)	33	28	.541	—	Jose Alvarez
Expos (20)	33	29	.532	½	Mike Easom
Rangers (13)	31	31	.500	2½	Rudy Jaramillo

	W	L	Pct.	GB		Manager
Braves (15)	29	34	.460	5		Pedro Gonzalez
Pirates (23)	24	39	.381	10		Woody Huyke

South Standings	W	L	Pct.	GB	Manager
Reds (17)	34	28	.548	—	Sam Mejias
Astros (18)	34	29	.540	½	Julio Linares
Yankees (10)	33	29	.532	1	Fred Ferreira
White Sox (4)	31	32	.492	3½	Steve Dillard
Royals (7)	30	33	.476	4½	Luis Silverio

Games played at Sarasota and Bradenton, Florida.

Playoff: Dodgers 1 game, Reds 0.

All-Star Team: 1B-John Joslyn, Royals; **2B**-Ed Renteria, Astros; **3B**-Hensley Meulens, Yankees; **SS**-Hector Vargas, Yankees; **OF**-Dan Arendas, Yankees; Sean Ross, Braves; Bernie Williams, Yankees; **C**-Carlos Gonzalez, Royals; **P**-Sam August, Astros; Jose Tapia, Dodgers; **Manager**-Sam Mejias, Reds.

BA: John Joslyn, Royals, .339
Runs: Bernie Williams, Yankees, 45
Hits: Amilcar Valdez, Dodgers, 69
RBIs: Eduardo Gonzalez, Yankees, 48

HRs: Eduardo Gonzalez, Yankees, 9
Wins: Carl Thomas, Dodgers, 8
SOs: Carl Thomas, Dodgers, 77
ERA: Wayne Rosenthal, Rangers, 0.73

R Pioneer League
President: Ralph C. Nelles

Standings	W	L	Pct.	GB	Attend.	Manager
Salt Lake City Trappers	45	25	.643	—	108,721	John Freitas/Ruben Rodriguez
Great Falls Dodgers (19)	40	30	.571	5	75,228	Kevin Kennedy

	W	L	Pct.	GB	Attend.	Manager
Helena Gold Sox (8)	38	32	.543	7	22,566	Dave Huppert
Idaho Falls Braves (15)	32	38	.457	13	43,507	Rod Gilbreath
Billings Mustangs (17)	31	39	.443	14	95,234	Jeff Cox
Medicine Hat Blue Jays (14)	24	46	.343	21	30,671	Dennis Holmberg

Playoff: Salt Lake City 3 games, Great Falls 1.

All-Star Team: 1B-James Kating, Great Falls; **2B**-Keith Lockhart, Billings; **3B**-Robert Tinkey, Salt Lake City; **SS**-Gary Sheffield, Helena; **OF**-Jeff Weiss, Idaho Falls; Joe Kesselmark, Great Falls; Darryl Hamilton, Helena; **C**-Adam Brown, Great Falls; **DH**-Matt Huff, Salt Lake City; **P**-Doug Vontz, Salt Lake City; Mike Kolovitz, Salt Lake City; Joe Lazor, Billings; **Manager**-Rod Gilbreath, Idaho Falls.

BA: Darryl Hamilton, Helena, .391
Runs: Darryl Hamilton, Helena, 72
Hits: Darryl Hamilton, Helena, 97
    Joe Kesselmark, Great Falls, 97
RBIs: Gary Sheffield, Helena, 71

HRs: Greg Vaughn, Helena, 16
    Jeff Weiss, Idaho Falls, 16
Wins: Mike Kolovitz, Salt Lake City, 8
    Doug Vontz, Salt Lake City, 8
SOs: Mike Pitz, Great Falls, 111
ERA: Joe Lazor, Billings, 1.61

1986 Interleague Post Season Play

World Series
New York (National) 4 games, Boston (American) 3

1986 Major League Farm Systems

American League
1 Baltimore (5): Rochester, Charlotte, Hagerstown, Newark, Bluefield.
2 Boston (5): Pawtucket, New Britain, Winter Haven, Greensboro, Elmira.
3 California (5): Edmonton, Midland, Palm Springs, Quad City, Salem (OR).
4 Chicago (5): Buffalo, Birmingham, Peninsula, Appleton, Gulf Coast.
5 Cleveland (5): Maine, Waterbury, Waterloo, Batavia, Burlington (NC).
6 Detroit (5): Nashville, Glens Falls, Lakeland, Gastonia, Bristol.
7 Kansas City (5): Omaha, Memphis, Ft. Myers, Eugene, Gulf Coast.
8 Milwaukee (5): Vancouver, El Paso, Stockton, Beloit, Helena.
9 Minnesota (5): Toledo, Orlando, Visalia, Kenosha, Elizabethton.
10 New York (5): Columbus (OH), Albany-Colonie, Ft. Lauderdale, Oneonta, Gulf Coast.
11 Oakland (5): Tacoma, Huntsville, Modesto, Madison, Medford.
12 Seattle (5): Calgary, Chattanooga, Salinas, Wausau, Bellingham.
13 Texas (5): Oklahoma City, Tulsa, Salem (VA), Daytona Beach, Gulf Coast.
14 Toronto (6): Syracuse, Knoxville, Ventura County, Florence, St. Catharines, Medicine Hat.

National League
15 Atlanta (7): Richmond, Greenville, Durham, Sumter, Pulaski, Idaho Falls, Gulf Coast.
16 Chicago (6): Iowa, Pittsfield, Winston-Salem, Peoria, Geneva, Wytheville.
17 Cincinnati (6): Denver, Vermont, Tampa, Cedar Rapids, Billings, Gulf Coast.
18 Houston (6): Tucson, Columbus (GA), Osceola, Asheville, Auburn, Gulf Coast.
19 Los Angeles (6): Albuquerque, San Antonio, Bakersfield, Vero Beach, Great Falls, Gulf Coast.
20 Montreal (6): Indianapolis, Jacksonville, West Palm Beach, Burlington (IA), Jamestown, Gulf Coast.
21 New York (6): Tidewater, Jackson, Lynchburg, Columbia, Little Falls, Kingsport.
22 Philadelphia (6): Portland, Reading, Clearwater, Spartanburg, Bend, Utica.
23 Pittsburgh (6): Hawaii, Nashua, Prince William, Macon, Watertown, Gulf Coast.
24 St. Louis (7): Louisville, Arkansas, St. Petersburg, Springfield, Savannah, Erie, Johnson City.
25 San Diego (5): Las Vegas, Beaumont, Reno, Charleston, Spokane.
26 San Francisco (5): Phoenix, Shreveport, Fresno, Clinton, Everett.

Co-op (x): Tri-Cities.
Independent: San Jose, Kinston, Miami, Salt Lake City.

1986 No-Hitters

Date	Pitcher	Team	League	Opponent	Score
5-4	Kenneth Angulo	Yucatan	Mexican	MC Tigres	8-0 (7)
5-25	Herminio Dominguez	Campeche	Mexican	Veracruz	12-0 (7)
5-26	John Stein	Appleton	Midwest	Beloit	5-0
6-6	Mike Converse	Cedar Rapids	Midwest	Beloit	2-0
6-8	Troy McKay	Jacksonville	Southern	Chattanooga	0-0
6-14	Dan Gabriele	Greensboro	South Atlantic	Gastonia	4-0
7-1	Jim Neidlinger	Nashua	Eastern	Glens Falls	2-0
7-2	Mitch McKelvey	Memphis	Southern	Columbus	16-0
7-17	Rich DeLucia	Bellingham	Northwest	Everett	1-0 (7)
7-23	Doug Cinnella	Newark	New York-Penn.	Oneonta	1-0
8-2	Rudy Seanez	Burlington	Appalachian	Pulaski	4-0
8-2	Zach Crouch	Winter Haven	Florida State	Miami	4-0
8-3	Doug Cinnella	Newark	New York-Penn.	Auburn	3-0
8-4	Rick DePastino	Medicine Hat	Pioneer	Salt Lake City	2-0 (7)
8-13	Wes Langley/ Kevin Nelson	Dodgers	Gulf Coast	Braves	5-0
8-16	Don Cooper/ Colin McLaughlin	Syracuse	International	Richmond	4-0
8-19	Enrique Burgos/ Bill Shanks	Ventura County	California	Visalia	2-0
8-21	Barry Hightower	Columbia	South Atlantic	Savannah	10-2
8-27	Bill Cooper	Glens Falls	Eastern	Nashua	4-0
8-31	Kevin Towers	Charleston	South Atlantic	Savannah	4-0
9-19	Joe Cowley	Chicago	American	California	7-1
9-25	Mike Scott	Houston	National	San Francisco	2-0

Number in parentheses indicates innings if other than nine.

THIS DATE IN MINOR LEAGUE HISTORY

February 10, 1986, Midwest League President Bill Walters died after suffering a heart attack. He had been league president for 13 years.

April 10, 1986, Spartanburg, South Atlantic League, did not open the season as scheduled due to legal problems concerning the ownership of the franchise. A court order kept the team from playing until April 12.

April 11, 1986, Ventura returned to the California League, but the team would play all home games during the day at Ventura College because no lighted facility was available in the city. The college park sat only 1,400 and no beer could be served.

April 28, 1986, The South Atlantic League took control of the Spartanburg franchise, revoking the membership of the previous owners.

May 22, 1986, Hawaii defeated Phoenix 31-5 in a Pacific Coast League game. The Islanders scored 14 runs in the ninth inning.

June 1, 1986, Roberto Clemente, Jr. retired from Charleston of the South Atlantic League. He had hit .229 in 31 games.

June 21, 1986, Heisman Trophy winner Bo Jackson, signed by the Kansas City Royals for a substantial bonus, made his debut before over 7,000 fans at Memphis. He singled in his first at bat.

August 20, 1986, The Johnson City Cardinals, Appalachian League, lost after having won 23 straight games.

August 21, 1986, Willie Aikens completed his season with the Puebla Angeles with a .454 average, 46 home runs, and 154 RBIs. Three other Mexican League batters hit over .400. Many observers attributed the surge of offense in the league to its use of the Comando baseball, said to be much livelier.

September 1, 1986, Bo Jackson was promoted to Kansas City, after having hit .277 with seven homers for Memphis in the Southern League.

December 6, 1986, National Association President Johnny Johnson was re-elected, winning an election over Tidewater, International League, General Manager Dave Rosenfield.

1987

American League
President: Dr. Robert W. Brown

East Standings	W	L	Pct.	GB	Attend.	Manager
Detroit Tigers....................	98	64	.605	—	2,061,830	Sparky Anderson
Toronto Blue Jays..............	96	66	.593	2	2,778,429	Jimy Williams
Milwaukee Brewers...........	91	71	.562	7	1,909,244	Tom Trebelhorn
New York Yankees............	89	73	.549	9	2,427,672	Lou Piniella
Boston Red Sox	78	84	.481	20	2,231,551	John McNamara
Baltimore Orioles	67	95	.414	31	1,835,692	Cal Ripken, Sr.
Cleveland Indians	61	101	.377	37	1,077,898	Pat Corrales/Doc Edwards

West Standings	W	L	Pct.	GB	Attend.	Manager
Minnesota Twins	85	77	.525	—	2,081,976	Tom Kelly
Kansas City Royals............	83	79	.512	2	2,392,471	Billy Gardner/John Wathan
Oakland Athletics	81	81	.500	4	1,678,921	Tony LaRussa
Seattle Mariners	78	84	.481	7	1,134,255	Dick Williams
Chicago White Sox	77	85	.475	8	1,208,060	Jim Fregosi
California Angels...............	75	87	.463	10	2,696,299	Gene Mauch
Texas Rangers....................	75	87	.463	10	1,763,053	Bobby Valentine

Playoff: Minnesota 4 games, Detroit 1.

BA: Wade Boggs, Boston, .363
Runs: Paul Molitor, Milwaukee, 114
Hits: Kirby Puckett, Minnesota, 207
　　　　Kevin Seitzer, Kansas City, 207
RBIs: George Bell, Toronto, 134
HRs: Mark McGwire, Oakland, 49

Wins: Roger Clemens, Boston, 20
　　　　Dave Stewart, Oakland, 20
SOs: Mark Langston, Seattle, 262
ERA: Jimmy Key, Toronto, 2.76
Pct: Roger Clemens, Boston, .690, 20-9
Saves: Tom Henke, Toronto, 34

National League
President: A. Bartlett Giamatti

East Standings	W	L	Pct.	GB	Attend.	Manager
St. Louis Cardinals	95	67	.586	—	3,072,122	Whitey Herzog
New York Mets	92	70	.568	3	3,034,129	Davey Johnson
Montreal Expos	91	71	.562	4	1,850,324	Buck Rodgers
Philadelphia Phillies	80	82	.494	15	2,100,110	John Felske
Pittsburgh Pirates	80	82	.494	15	1,161,193	Jim Leyland
Chicago Cubs	76	85	.472	18½	2,035,130	Gene Michael/Frank Lucchesi

West Standings	W	L	Pct.	GB	Attend.	Manager
San Francisco Giants	90	72	.556	—	1,917,168	Roger Craig
Cincinnati Reds.................	84	78	.519	6	2,185,205	Pete Rose
Houston Astros	76	86	.469	14	1,909,902	Hal Lanier
Los Angeles Dodgers	73	89	.451	17	2,797,409	Tom Lasorda
Atlanta Braves	69	92	.429	20½	1,217,402	Chuck Tanner
San Diego Padres...............	65	97	.401	25	1,454,061	Larry Bowa

Playoff: St. Louis 4 games, San Francisco 3.

BA: Tony Gwynn, San Diego, .370
Runs: Tim Raines, Montreal, 123
Hits: Tony Gwynn, San Diego, 218
RBIs: Andre Dawson, Chicago, 137
HRs: Andre Dawson, Chicago, 49

Wins: Rick Sutcliffe, Chicago, 18
SOs: Nolan Ryan, Houston, 270
ERA: Nolan Ryan, Houston, 2.76
Pct: Dwight Gooden, New York, .682, 15-7
Saves: Steve Bedrosian, Philadelphia, 40

AAA American Association
President: Joe Ryan

Standings	W	L	Pct.	GB	Attend.	Manager
Denver Zephyrs (8)...........	79	61	.564	—	314,549	Terry Bevington
Louisville Redbirds (24).....	78	62	.557	1	516,329	Mike Jorgensen
Indianapolis Indians (20)....	74	64	.536	4	250,250	Joe Sparks
Oklahoma City 89ers (13) ..	69	71	.493	10	277,722	Toby Harrah
Buffalo Bisons (5)	66	74	.471	13	495,760	Orlando Gomez/ Steve Swisher
Iowa Cubs (16)	64	74	.464	14	257,857	Larry Cox
Omaha Royals (7)...............	64	76	.457	15	251,995	John Wathan/Frank Funk
Nashville Sounds (17)	64	76	.457	15	378,715	Jack Lind

Playoffs: Denver 3 games, Oklahoma City 2; Indianapolis 3 games, Louisville 2.
Finals: Indianapolis 4 games, Denver 1.

All-Star Team: 1B-Jack Daugherty, Indianapolis; **2B**-Bill Bates, Denver; **SS**-Luis Rivera, Indianapolis; **3B**-Steve Kiefer, Denver; **OF**-Dave Clark, Buffalo; Dallas Williams, Indianapolis; Lance Johnson, Louisville; **C**-Tom Pagnozzi, Louisville; Damon Berryhill, Iowa; **DH**-Joey Meyer, Denver; **P**-Pascual Perez, Indianapolis; Paul Cherry, Louisville; **MVP**-Lance Johnson, Louisville; **Manager**-Joe Sparks, Indianapolis.

BA: Dallas Williams, Indianapolis, .357
Runs: Bill Bates, Denver, 117
Hits: Steve Stanicek, Denver, 167
RBIs: Wade Rowdon, Iowa, 113
HRs: Brad Komminsk, Denver, 32
Wins: Bill Taylor, Oklahoma City, 12
SOs: Sergio Valdez, Indianapolis, 128
ERA: Pascual Perez, Indianapolis, 3.79

AAA International League
President: Harold Cooper

Standings	W	L	Pct.	GB	Attend.	Manager
Tidewater Tides (21)	81	59	.579	—	175,104	Mike Cubbage
Columbus Clippers (10)......	77	63	.550	4	570,599	Bucky Dent
Rochester Red Wings (1)....	74	65	.532	6½	315,807	John Hart
Pawtucket Red Sox (2).......	73	67	.521	8	220,838	Ed Nottle
Toledo Mud Hens (6)	70	70	.500	11	194,001	Leon Roberts
Syracuse Chiefs (14)...........	68	72	.486	13	211,315	Doug Ault
Maine Guides (22).............	60	80	.429	21	104,219	Bill Dancy
Richmond Braves (15)........	56	83	.403	24½	332,440	Roy Majtyka

Playoffs: Columbus 3 games, Rochester 0; Tidewater 3 games, Pawtucket 1.
Finals: Columbus 3 games, Tidewater 0.

All-Star Team: 1B-Randy Milligan, Tidewater; **2B**-Nelson Liriano, Syracuse; **SS**-Kevin Elster, Tidewater; **3B**-Jeff Moronko, Columbus; **OF**-Jay Buhner, Columbus; Mark Carreon, Tidewater; Roberto Kelly, Columbus; **DH**-Sam Horn, Pawtucket; **C**-Rey Palacios, Toledo; **P**-Brad Arnsberg, Columbus; Don Gordon, Syracuse; **MVP**-Randy Milligan, Tidewater; **Manager**-Ed Nottle, Pawtucket.

BA: Randy Milligan, Tidewater, .326
Runs: Randy Milligan, Tidewater, 99
Hits: Kevin Elster, Tidewater, 170
RBIs: Randy Milligan, Tidewater, 103
HRs: Jay Buhner, Columbus, 31
Wins: Paul Gibson, Toledo, 14
SOs: Odell Jones, Syracuse, 147
ERA: DeWayne Vaughn, Tidewater, 2.66

AAA Mexican League
President: Pedro Treto Cisneros

North Standings	W	L	Pct.	GB	Attend.	Manager
Monterrey Sultanes.............	67	58	.536	—	201,603	Manuel Magallon/ Roberto Castellon
Aguascalientes Rieleros......	65	60	.520	2	158,020	Sergio Robles
Dos Laredos Tecolotes	61	59	.508	3½	195,713	Jose Guerrero/Marcelo Juarez
Monclova Acereros............	63	61	.508	3½	205,312	Alfredo Rios/Carlos Paz
San Luis Potosi Tuneros......	60	67	.472	8	215,247	Gregorio Luque
Union Laguna Algodoneros	58	69	.457	10	188,507	Ramon Montoya
Saltillo Saraperos...............	41	81	.336	24½	155,726	Victor Favela/Felipe Leal

South Standings	W	L	Pct.	GB	Attend.	Manager
Mexico City Diablos Rojos	75	49	.605	—	170,522	Ben Reyes
Puebla Angeles	71	52	.577	3½	125,213	Rodolfo Sandoval/ Roberto Mendez
Mexico City Tigres	68	58	.540	8	165,215	Roberto Mendez/ Alfredo Ortiz
Leon Bravos......................	65	56	.537	8½	137,512	Obed Plascencia
Campeche Piratas	58	57	.504	12½	130,000	Francisco Estrada
Tabasco Ganaderos............	60	62	.492	14	160,415	Miguel Sotelo/Arturo Rubio
Yucatan Leones	51	74	.408	24½	250,513	Carlos Paz/Francisco Chavez/ Leonel Aldama

Playoffs: Monclova 4 games, Monterrey 1; Dos Laredos 4 games, Aguascalientes 1; MC Diablos Rojos 4 games, Leon 0; MC Tigres 4 games, Puebla 2. Dos Laredos 4 games, Monclova 1; MC Diablos Rojos 4 games, MC Tigres 3.
Finals: MC Diablos Rojos 4 games, Dos Laredos 1.

BA: Orlando Sanchez, Puebla, .415
Runs: Enrique Aguilar, Aguascalientes, 108
Hits: Orlando Sanchez, Puebla, 182
RBIs: Nelson Barrera, MC Diablos Rojos, 134
HRs: Nelson Barrera, MC Diablos Rojos, 42
Wins: Jesus Rios, MC Tigres, 16
　　　　Hilario Renteria, Union Laguna, 16
　　　　Luis Fernando Mendez, MC Diablos Rojos, 16
SOs: Jesus Rios, MC Tigres, 200
ERA: Robin Fernandez Fuson, Dos Laredos, 2.67

AAA Pacific Coast League
President: Bill Cutler

North Standings	W	L	Pct.	GB	Attend.	Manager
Calgary Cannons**(12)......	84	57	.596	—	304,897	Bill Plummer
Tacoma Tigers**(11)	78	65	.545	7	293,366	Keith Lieppman
Vancouver Canadians (23) .	72	72	.500	13½	338,614	Rocky Bridges
Edmonton Trappers (3).......	69	74	.483	16	229,381	Tom Kotchman
Portland Beavers (9)	45	96	.319	39	154,989	Charlie Manuel

South Standings	W	L	Pct.	GB	Attend.	Manager
Albuquerque Dukes*(19) ...	77	65	.542	—	300,035	Terry Collins
Phoenix Firebirds (26).......	77	67	.535	1	183,798	Wendell Kim
Tucson Toros (18)	75	67	.528	2	157,744	Bob Didier
Las Vegas Stars**(25)........	69	73	.486	8	299,198	Jack Krol
Hawaii Islanders (4)...........	65	75	.464	11	116,107	Bob Bailey

Playoffs: Albuquerque 3 games, Las Vegas 0; Calgary 3 games, Tacoma 2.
Finals: Albuquerque 3 games, Calgary 1.

All-Star Team: 1B-Jim Eppard, Edmonton; **2B**-Jose Lind, Vancouver; **SS**-Brad Wellman,

*Won first-half　　**Won second-half　　***Won both halves
Numbers after nicknames indicate farm system.
Affiliation listed at end of year.

584

Albuquerque; **3B**-Edgar Martinez, Calgary; **OF**-Jim Weaver, Calgary; Gerald Young, Tucson; David Hengel, Calgary; **C**-Mackey Sasser, Phoenix/Vancouver; **DH**-Francisco Melendez, Phoenix; **P**-Mike Campbell, Calgary; Ray Hayward, Las Vegas; Todd Simmons, Las Vegas; **MVP**-Mike Campbell, Calgary; **Manager**-Keith Lieppman, Tacoma.

BA: Jim Eppard, Edmonton, .341
Runs: Gary Jones, Tacoma, 102
Hits: Francisco Melendez, Phoenix, 168
RBIs: David Hengel, Calgary, 103

HRs: David Hengel, Calgary, 23
Wins: Mike Campbell, Calgary, 15
SOs: Vicente Palacios, Vancouver, 148
ERA: Vicente Palacios, Vancouver, 2.58

AA Eastern League
President: Charles E. Eshbach

Standings	W	L	Pct.	GB	Attend.	Manager
Pittsfield Cubs (16)	87	51	.630	—	51,551	Jim Essian
Harrisburg Senators (23)	77	63	.550	11	212,141	Dave Trembley
Reading Phillies (22)	76	63	.547	11½	100,895	George Culver
Vermont Reds (17)	73	67	.521	15	85,621	Tom Runnells
Albany-Colonie Yankees (10)	64	75	.460	23½	285,016	Tommy Jones
New Britain Red Sox (2)	61	79	.436	27	83,338	Dave Holt
Williamsport Bills (5)	60	79	.432	27½	77,140	Steve Swisher/Orlando Gomez
Glens Falls Tigers (6)	58	79	.423	28½	79,303	Tom Burgess/Tom Gamboa/Paul Felix

Playoffs: Harrisburg 3 games, Reading 2; Vermont 3 games, Pittsfield 1.
Finals: Harrisburg 3 games, Vermont 1.

All-Star Team: 1B-Mark Grace, Pittsfield; **2B**-Tommy Barrett, Reading; **SS**-Ken Jackson, Reading; **3B**-Doug Strange, Glens Falls; **OF**-Tommy Gregg, Harrisburg; Darren Reed, Albany-Colonie; Dwight Smith, Pittsfield; **DH**-Mark Higgins, Williamsport; **C**-Tom Prince, Harrisburg; **P**-Rob Lopez, Vermont; Rich Sauveur, Harrisburg; Todd Frohwirth, Reading; **MVP**-Mark Grace, Pittsfield; **Pitcher of the Year**-Rob Lopez, Vermont; **Manager**-Dave Trembley, Harrisburg.

BA: Tommy Gregg, Harrisburg, .371
Runs: Dwight Smith, Pittsfield, 111
Hits: Hal Morris, Albany-Colonie, 173
RBIs: Mark Grace, Pittsfield, 101

HRs: Bernardo Brito, Williamsport, 24
Wins: Bob Scanlan, Reading, 15
SOs: Rich Sauveur, Harrisburg, 160
ERA: Rob Lopez, Vermont, 2.40

AA Southern League
President: Jimmy Bragan

East Standings	W	L	Pct.	GB	Attend.	Manager
Jacksonville Expos**(20)	85	59	.590	—	190,456	Tommy Thompson
Charlotte O's*(1)	85	60	.586	½	129,246	Greg Biagini
Greenville Braves (15)	70	74	.486	15	206,468	Jim Beauchamp
Columbus Astros (18)	67	76	.469	17½	128,845	Tom Wiedenbauer
Orlando Twins (9)	61	82	.427	23½	69,656	George Mitterwald

West Standings	W	L	Pct.	GB	Attend.	Manager
Huntsville Stars**(11)	74	70	.514	—	256,090	Brad Fischer
Memphis Chicks (7)	72	71	.503	1½	215,749	Bob Schaefer
Chattanooga Lookouts (12)	68	75	.476	5½	110,893	Sal Rende
Birmingham Barons*(4)	68	75	.476	5½	147,279	Rico Petrocelli
Knoxville Blue Jays (14)	68	76	.472	6	124,231	Glenn Ezell

Playoffs: Birmingham 3 games, Huntsville 0; Charlotte 3 games, Jacksonville 2.
Finals: Birmingham 3 games, Charlotte 1.

All-Star Team: 1B-Dave Falcon, Charlotte; **2B**-Ron Gant, Greenville; **SS**-Walt Weiss, Huntsville; **3B**-Ken Caminiti, Columbus; **OF**-Geronimo Berroa, Knoxville; Larry Walker, Jacksonville; Rondal Rollin, Birmingham; Matt Winters, Memphis; Mike Berger, Jacksonville; **C**-Nelson Santovenia, Jacksonville; **DH**-Tom Dodd, Charlotte; **P**-Brian Holman, Jacksonville; Rob Mallicoat, Columbus; Kevin Price, Jacksonville; **MVP**-Tom Dodd, Charlotte; **Manager**-Tommy Thompson, Jacksonville.

BA: Dave Myers, Chattanooga, .328
Runs: Bernardo Tatis, Knoxville, 101
Hits: Dave Myers, Chattanooga, 160
RBIs: Tom Dodd, Charlotte, 127

HRs: Rondal Rollin, Birmingham, 39
Wins: John Trautwein, Knoxville, 15
SOs: Randy Johnson, Jacksonville, 163
ERA: Brian Holman, Jacksonville, 2.50

AA Texas League
President: Carl Sawatski

East Standings	W	L	Pct.	GB	Attend.	Manager
Shreveport Captains*(26)	78	57	.578	—	233,524	Jack Mull
Arkansas Travelers (24)	72	63	.533	6	256,365	Jim Riggleman
Jackson Mets**(21)	70	66	.515	8½	131,248	Tucker Ashford
Tulsa Drillers (13)	52	84	.382	26½	170,932	Bill Stearns

West Standings	W	L	Pct.	GB	Attend.	Manager
El Paso Diablos**(8)	75	59	.560	—	180,633	Duffy Dyer
Midland Angels (3)	75	61	.551	1	137,910	Max Oliveras
Wichita Pilots*(25)	69	65	.515	6	150,952	Steve Smith
San Antonio Dodgers (19)	50	86	.368	26	122,277	Gary LaRocque

Playoffs: Jackson 2 games, Shreveport 1; Wichita 2 games, El Paso 1.
Finals: Wichita 4 games, Jackson 2.

All-Star Team: 1B-Brad Pounders, Wichita; **2B**-Luis Alicea, Arkansas; **SS**-Gregg Jefferies, Jackson; **3B**-Joe Redfield, Midland; **OF**-Joaquin Contreras, Jackson; Lavell Freeman, El Paso; Mike Devereaux, San Antonio; **C**-Sandy Alomar, Jr., Wichita; Joe Szekely, San Antonio; **DH**-Doug Jennings, Midland; **P**-John Burkett, Shreveport; Dennis Cook, Shreveport; David West, Jackson; Steve Peters, Arkansas; Charles McGrath,

Arkansas; **MVP**-Doug Jennings, Midland; **Pitcher of the Year**-Dennis Cook, Shreveport; **Manager**-Duffy Dyer, El Paso.

BA: Lavell Freeman, El Paso, .395
Runs: Lavell Freeman, El Paso, 117
Hits: Lavell Freeman, El Paso, 208
RBIs: Mike Fitzgerald, Arkansas, 108
Joe Redfield, Midland, 108

HRs: Stan Holmes, Midland, 30
Doug Jennings, Midland, 30
Joe Redfield, Midland, 30
Wins: John Burkett, Shreveport, 14
Martin Reed, Midland, 14
SOs: David West, Jackson, 186
ERA: Charles McGrath, Arkansas, 2.85

A California League
President: Joe Gagliardi

North Standings	W	L	Pct.	GB	Attend.	Manager
Stockton Ports*(8)	94	48	.662	—	61,794	Dave Machemer
Modesto A's (11)	79	63	.556	15	78,357	Tommie Reynolds
Reno Padres**(25)	76	66	.535	18	109,002	Pat Kelly
Salinas Spurs (12)	64	78	.451	30	42,552	Greg Mahlberg
San Jose Bees	33	109	.232	61	69,120	Mike Verdi

South Standings	W	L	Pct.	GB	Attend.	Manager
Fresno Giants***(26)	80	63	.559	—	107,908	R.J. Harrison
Bakersfield Dodgers (19)	78	65	.545	2	109,120	Kevin Kennedy
San Bernardino Spirit	70	72	.493	9½	158,896	Rich Dauer
Palm Springs Angels (3)	69	73	.486	10½	52,313	Bill Lachemann
Visalia Oaks (9)	68	74	.479	11½	60,818	Dan Schmitz

Playoff: Reno 2 games, Stockton 0.
Finals: Fresno 4 games, Reno 3.

All-Star Team: 1B-Lee Stevens, Palm Springs; **2B**-Kenny Grant, Palm Springs; **SS**-Gary Sheffield, Stockton; **3B**-Tony Pellegrino, Reno; **OF**-Darryl Hamilton, Stockton; Jerome Nelson, Modesto; Daniel Grunhard, Palm Springs; **DH**-Chris Calvert, Visalia; **C**-Luis Lopez, Bakersfield; **P**-Taketo Kamei, San Jose; Mike Pitz, Bakersfield; Tim Burcham, Palm Springs; Mike Mills, Reno; **MVP**-Luis Lopez, Bakersfield; **Pitcher of the Year**-Taketo Kamei, San Jose; **Manager**-Dave Machemer, Stockton.

BA: Jim Lester, Reno, .331
Runs: Jeff Carter, Fresno, 109
Hits: Luis Lopez, Bakersfield, 181
RBIs: Gary Sheffield, Stockton, 103

HRs: Bill Stevenson, Reno, 21
Wins: Tim Burcham, Palm Springs, 17
SOs: Park Pittman, Visalia, 198
ERA: David Snell, Salinas, 1.96

A Carolina League
President: John Hopkins

North Standings	W	L	Pct.	GB	Attend.	Manager
Salem Buccaneers**(23)	80	59	.576	—	111,661	Steve Demeter
Hagerstown Suns*(1)	72	68	.514	8½	135,059	Glenn Gulliver
Prince William Yankees (10)	66	74	.471	14½	105,749	Wally Moon
Lynchburg Mets (21)	63	76	.453	17	88,370	John Tamargo

South Standings	W	L	Pct.	GB	Attend.	Manager
Kinston Indians**(5)	75	65	.536	—	68,199	Mike Hargrove
Winston-Salem Spirits*(16)	72	68	.514	3	133,263	Jay Loviglio
Peninsula White Sox (4)	66	74	.471	9	88,620	Marv Foley
Durham Bulls (15)	65	75	.464	10	217,012	Brian Snitker

Playoffs: Kinston 2 games, Winston-Salem 0; Salem 2 games, Hagerstown 0.
Finals: Salem 3 games, Kinston 1.

All-Star Team: 1B-Rob Sepanek, Prince William; **2B**-Mark Lemke, Durham; **SS**-Jim Bullinger, Winston-Salem; **3B**-Leo Gomez, Hagerstown; **OF**-Tony Chance, Salem; Alex Smith, Durham; Mark Davis, Peninsula; **DH**-Casey Webster, Kinston; **C**-Joe Girardi, Winston-Salem; **P**-Blaine Beatty, Hagerstown; David Miller, Durham; **MVP**-Casey Webster, Kinston; **Pitcher of the Year**-Blaine Beatty, Hagerstown; **Manager**-Mike Hargrove, Kinston.

BA: Leo Gomez, Hagerstown, .326
Runs: Milt Harper, Kinston, 100
Hits: Tony Chance, Salem, 167
RBIs: Casey Webster, Kinston, 111

HRs: Hensley Meulens, Prince William, 28
Wins: David Miller, Durham, 15
SOs: David Miller, Durham, 155
ERA: Charles Scott, Kinston, 2.69

A Florida State League
President: George MacDonald, Jr.

North Standings	W	L	Pct.	GB	Attend.	Manager
St. Petersburg Cardinals (24)	85	57	.599	—	121,732	Dave Bialas
Dunedin Blue Jays (14)	76	64	.543	8	29,905	Bob Bailor
Clearwater Phillies (22)	66	70	.485	16	55,370	Rollie DeArmas
Charlotte Rangers (13)	69	74	.483	16½	100,238	Jim Skaalen
Tampa Tarpons (17)	64	76	.457	20	62,394	Marc Bombard
Ft. Myers Royals (7)	54	87	.383	30½	27,369	Jerry Terrell

South Standings	W	L	Pct.	GB	Attend.	Manager
Ft. Lauderdale Yankees (10)	85	53	.616	—	50,074	Buck Showalter
West Palm Beach Expos (20)	75	63	.543	10	110,633	Felipe Alou
Vero Beach Dodgers (19)	62	76	.449	23	82,676	John Shoemaker
Miami Marlins	44	89	.331	38½	35,934	Dan Norman

Central Standings	W	L	Pct.	GB	Attend.	Manager
Osceola Astros (18)	80	59	.576	—	38,068	Ken Bolek
Lakeland Tigers (6)	74	61	.548	4	61,255	John Wockenfuss
Daytona Beach Admirals (4)	69	70	.496	11	54,132	Marc Hill
Winter Haven Red Sox (2)	67	71	.486	12½	30,711	Doug Camilli

Playoffs: Ft. Lauderdale 2 games, Lakeland 0; Osceola 2 games, St. Petersburg 0.
Finals: Ft. Lauderdale 3 games, Osceola 1.

All-Star Team: 1B-Terry Jones, Ft. Myers; **2B**-Andy Stankiewicz, Ft. Lauderdale; **SS**-Jerry Bertolani, Daytona Beach; **3B**-John Toale, Winter Haven; **OF**-Bernie Anderson, Lakeland; Mauricio Nunez, St. Petersburg; Jeff Baldwin, Osceola; **C**-Jim Leyritz, Ft. Lauderdale; Mike Fox, St. Petersburg; **DH**-Kevin Maas, Ft. Lauderdale; **P**-Jose Cano, Osceola; Ramon Martinez, Vero Beach; Rob Livechak, Osceola; Wayne Edwards, Daytona Beach; Brian Meyer, Osceola; Dana Ridenour, Ft. Lauderdale; **MVP**-Jose Cano, Osceola; **Manager**-Dave Bialas, St. Petersburg.

BA: Charles Culberson, Ft. Myers, .320
Runs: Pat Austin, Lakeland, 92
Hits: Jesus Mendez, St. Petersburg, 159
RBIs: Pat Sipe, West Palm Beach, 84
HRs: Pat Sipe, West Palm Beach, 17
Wins: Steve Cummings, Dunedin, 18
SOs: Dan Gabriele, Winter Haven, 150
ERA: Jose Cano, Osceola, 1.94

A Midwest League
President: George Spelius

North Standings	W	L	Pct.	GB	Attend.	Manager
Kenosha Twins (9)	82	58	.586	—	58,197	Don Leppert
Appleton Foxes (7)	71	69	.507	11	81,208	Ken Berry
Madison Muskies (11)	63	77	.450	19	84,381	Jim Nettles
Wausau Timbers (12)	57	83	.407	25	61,342	Bobby Cuellar

Central Standings	W	L	Pct.	GB	Attend.	Manager
Beloit Brewers (8)	76	64	.543	—	87,419	Gomer Hodge
Clinton Giants (26)	72	67	.518	3½	112,826	Bill Evers
Waterloo Indians (5)	72	68	.514	4	68,081	Glenn Adams
Cedar Rapids Reds (17)	70	70	.500	6	144,279	Paul Kirsch

South Standings	W	L	Pct.	GB	Attend.	Manager
Springfield Cardinals (24)	94	46	.671	—	154,148	Gaylen Pitts
Peoria Chiefs (16)	71	69	.507	23	195,832	Jim Tracy
Burlington Expos (20)	62	75	.453	30½	71,098	J.R. Miner
Quad City Angels (3)	47	91	.341	46	60,999	Eddie Rodriguez

Playoffs: Kenosha 2 games, Beloit 1; Springfield 2 games, Clinton 1.
Finals: Kenosha 3 games, Springfield 1.

All-Star Team: 1B-Mark Leonard, Clinton; **2B**-Francisco Laureano, Appleton; **SS**-Bienvenido Figueroa, Springfield; **3B**-Keith Lockhart, Cedar Rapids; **OF**-Greg Vaughn, Beloit; Gregg Ritchie, Clinton; Jerome Walton, Peoria; **C**-Todd Zeile, Springfield; **DH**-Victor Garcia, Peoria; **P**-Trevor Wilson, Clinton; Bob Faron, Springfield; Robert Glisson, Springfield; Mike Perez, Springfield; **MVP**-Greg Vaughn, Beloit; Todd Zeile, Springfield; **Manager**-Don Leppert, Kenosha.

BA: Chip Hale, Kenosha, .345
Runs: Greg Vaughn, Beloit, 120
Hits: Michael Randle, Kenosha, 166
RBIs: Todd Zeile, Springfield, 106
HRs: Greg Vaughn, Beloit, 33
Wins: Bob Faron, Springfield, 19
SOs: Paul McClellan, Clinton, 209
ERA: Keith Brown, Cedar Rapids, 1.59

A New York-Pennsylvania League
President: Leo A. Pinckney

East Standings	W	L	Pct.	GB	Attend.	Manager
Watertown Pirates (23)	44	32	.579	—	33,004	Jeff Cox
Oneonta Yankees (10)	41	34	.547	2½	48,903	Gary Allenson
Auburn Astros (18)	39	36	.520	4½	29,740	Gary Tuck
Little Falls Mets (21)	38	36	.514	5	32,536	Rich Miller
Utica Blue Sox (22)	31	43	.419	12	51,435	Tony Taylor
Elmira Pioneers (2)	26	50	.342	18	49,848	Bill Limoncelli

West Standings	W	L	Pct.	GB	Attend.	Manager
Geneva Cubs (16)	48	28	.632	—	19,918	Tom Spencer
Jamestown Expos (20)	44	33	.571	4½	46,324	Gene Glynn
Newark Orioles (1)	42	32	.568	5	21,489	Mike Hart
St. Catharines Blue Jays (14)	41	36	.532	7½	48,015	Joe Lonnett
Erie Cardinals (24)	36	39	.480	11½	59,698	Joe Rigoli
Batavia Trojans	23	54	.299	25½	25,339	Art Mazmanian

Playoff: Geneva 2 games, Watertown 0.

All-Star Team: 1B-Jaime Barragan, Utica; Ernie Young, Newark; **2B**-William Suero, St. Catharines; **SS**-Marty Rivero, Geneva; **3B**-Jack Voigt, Newark; **OF**-Dan Nyssen, Auburn; Steve Finley, Newark; Steve Kirkpatrick, Utica; Jeff Ahr, Newark; **C**-Rick Wilkins, Geneva; **DH**-Luc Berube, Oneonta; **P**-Doug Royalty, Auburn; Alex Sanchez, St. Catharines; Chris Pollack, Jamestown; Jerry Daniels, Erie; **Manager**-Tom Spencer, Geneva.

BA: Jack Voigt, Newark, .320
Runs: Don Buford, Jr., Newark, 68
Hits: Dan Nyssen, Auburn, 96
RBIs: Boi Rodriguez, Jamestown, 65
HRs: Craig Faulkner, Batavia, 16
Wins: Doug Royalty, Auburn, 10
SOs: Alex Sanchez, St. Catharines, 116
ERA: Bob Wishnevski, St. Catharines, 1.53

A Northwest League
President: Jack Cain

North Standings	W	L	Pct.	GB	Attend.	Manager
Spokane Indians (25)	54	22	.711	—	113,865	Rob Picciolo
Bend Bucks (x)	33	42	.440	20½	36,131	Mel Roberts
Medford A's (11)	31	45	.408	23	72,729	Dave Hudgens
Boise Hawks	26	50	.342	28	71,344	Derrel Thomas/Mal Fichman

South Standings	W	L	Pct.	GB	Attend.	Manager
Everett Giants (26)	49	26	.653	—	58,823	Joe Strain
Eugene Emeralds (7)	45	30	.600	4	132,819	Rich Mathews
Salem Angels (3)	34	41	.453	15	34,181	Chris Smith
Bellingham Mariners (12)	30	46	.395	19½	22,183	Rick Sweet

Playoff: Spokane 2 games, Everett 1.

All-Star Team: 1B-Steve Hendricks, Spokane; **2B**-Paul Faries, Spokane; **SS**-Jose Valentin, Spokane; **3B**-Mark Owens, Eugene; **OF**-Ken Griffey, Jr., Bellingham; Jeff Mace, Boise; **DH**-Jorge Pedre, Eugene; **C**-Andy Skeels, Spokane; **P**-Mike Erb, Salem; Jim Campbell, Eugene; **MVP**-Steve Hendricks, Spokane; **Manager**-Rob Picciolo, Spokane.

BA: Bob Moore, Eugene, .374
Runs: Paul Faries, Spokane, 67
Hits: Steve Hendricks, Spokane, 108
RBIs: Steve Hendricks, Spokane, 75
HRs: Mark Owens, Everett, 16
Wins: Tom Gordon, Eugene, 9
Tom Hostetler, Everett, 9
SOs: Eric Gunderson, Everett, 99
ERA: Jim Campbell, Eugene, 0.73
Pct: Tom Gordon, Eugene, 1.000, 9-0

A South Atlantic League
President: John H. Moss

North Standings	W	L	Pct.	GB	Attend.	Manager
Asheville Tourists***(18)	91	48	.655	—	104,060	Keith Bodie
Charleston (WV) Wheelers (x)	66	73	.475	25	97,563	Hal Dyer
Spartanburg Phillies (22)	66	74	.471	25½	36,286	Ramon Aviles
Fayetteville Generals (6)	65	74	.468	26	95,008	John Lipon
Gastonia Rangers (13)	58	82	.414	33½	71,110	Chino Cadahia
Greensboro Hornets (2)	55	85	.393	36½	166,208	Dick Berardino

South Standings	W	L	Pct.	GB	Attend.	Manager
Myrtle Beach Blue Jays***(14)	83	56	.597	—	74,179	Barry Foote
Sumter Braves (15)	75	62	.547	7	26,081	Buddy Bailey
Macon Pirates (23)	73	64	.533	9	41,728	Dennis Rogers
Savannah Cardinals (24)	69	69	.500	13½	33,363	Mark DeJohn
Charleston (SC) Rainbows (25)	68	71	.489	15	87,185	Tony Torchia
Columbia Mets (21)	64	75	.460	19	92,855	Butch Hobson

Playoff: Myrtle Beach 3 games, Asheville 2.

All-Star Team: 1B-Mike Simms, Asheville; **2B**-Carlos Baerga, Charleston (SC); Geronimo Pena, Savannah; **SS**-Lou Frazier, Asheville; **3B**-Ed Whited, Asheville; **OF**-Junior Felix, Myrtle Beach; Mark Whiten, Myrtle Beach; Vince Holyfield, Spartanburg; **C**-Phil Clark, Fayetteville; **DH**-John Love, Macon; **P**-Doug Linton, Myrtle Beach; Chuck McElroy, Spartanburg; **MVP**-Ed Whited, Asheville; **Manager**-Keith Bodie, Asheville.

BA: Ed Whited, Asheville, .323
Runs: Bert Hunter, Asheville, 105
Hits: John Love, Macon, 161
RBIs: Ed Whited, Asheville, 126
HRs: Mike Simms, Asheville, 39
Wins: Michael York, Macon, 17
SOs: Curt Schilling, Greensboro, 189
ERA: Doug Linton, Myrtle Beach, 1.55

R Appalachian League
President: Bill Halstead

North Standings	W	L	Pct.	GB	Attend.	Manager
Burlington Indians (5)	51	19	.729	—	76,653	Tom Chandler
Pulaski Braves (15)	39	31	.557	12	14,468	Grady Little
Bluefield Orioles (1)	37	32	.536	13½	35,867	Jim Pamlayne
Wytheville Cubs (16)	32	38	.457	19	18,122	Brad Mills

South Standings	W	L	Pct.	GB	Attend.	Manager
Johnson City Cardinals (24)	42	27	.609	—	22,271	Dan Radison
Elizabethton Twins (9)	29	40	.420	13	13,101	Ray Smith
Kingsport Mets (21)	28	42	.400	14½	28,453	Bobby Floyd
Bristol Tigers (6)	20	49	.290	22	15,337	Rick Magnante

Playoff: Burlington 2 games, Johnson City 0.

All-Star Team: 1B-Troy Neel, Burlington; **2B**-Rich Casarotti, Pulaski; **SS**-Bill Narleski, Burlington; **3B**-Brian Champion, Pulaski; **OF**-Beau Allred, Burlington; Tracy Pancoski, Bluefield; Ray Lankford, Johnson City; **C**-Dan Simon, Bluefield; **DH**-Terry Brown, Bluefield; **P**-Frank Castillo, Wytheville; Rocky Elli, Kingsport; **Player of the Year**-Frank Castillo, Wytheville; **Manager**-Tom Chandler, Burlington.

BA: Beau Allred, Burlington, .341
Runs: Bill Narleski, Burlington, 55
Hits: Jossy Rosario, Wytheville, 84
RBIs: Charles Fulton, Johnson City, 59
Troy Neel, Burlington, 59
HRs: Terry Brown, Bluefield, 14
Wins: Frank Castillo, Wytheville, 10
SOs: Pat Tilmon, Pulaski, 101
ERA: Pat Tilmon, Pulaski, 1.56

R Gulf Coast League
President: Thomas J. Saffell

North Standings	W	L	Pct.	GB	Manager
Dodgers (19)	43	20	.683	—	Jose Alvarez
Pirates (23)	33	30	.516	10	Woody Huyke
Yankees (10)	31	32	.492	12	Fred Ferreira
Expos (20)	21	42	.333	22	Jethro McIntyre
Braves (15)	20	43	.317	23	Pedro Gonzalez

South Standings	W	L	Pct.	GB	Manager
Royals (7)	40	23	.635	—	Luis Silverio
White Sox (4)	39	24	.619	1	Steve Dillard
Astros (18)	32	30	.516	7½	Julio Linares
Reds (17)	32	31	.508	8	Sam Mejias
Rangers (13)	23	39	.371	16½	Stan Hough

Games played at Sarasota and Bradenton, Florida.

Playoff: Dodgers 1 game, Royals 0.

All-Star Team: 1B-Ben Shelton, Pirates; **2B**-Jose Munoz, Dodgers; **SS**-Jose Vizcaino, Dodgers; **3B**-Bob Knecht, Royals; **OF**-Eric Anthony, Astros; Mark Merchant, Pirates; Lynn Robinson, Braves; **C**-Ruben Pujols, Royals; **P**-Danny Newman, Astros; Scott Jeffery, Reds; **Manager**-Luis Silverio, Royals.

BA: Henry Rodriguez, Dodgers, .331
Runs: Bob Knecht, Royals, 55
Hits: Luke Sable, Rangers, 69
RBIs: Eric Anthony, Astros, 46
HRs: Eric Anthony, Astros, 10

Wins: Bruce Colsom, Reds, 7
Greg Karklins, Royals, 7
Danny Newman, Astros, 7
Carl Nordstrom, Reds, 7
SOs: Chris Cerny, Dodgers, 72
ERA: Chris Lee, Astros, 1.15

R Pioneer League
President: Ralph C. Nelles

North Standings	W	L	Pct.	GB	Attend.	Manager
Helena Brewers (8)	46	24	.657	—	27,020	Dave Huppert
Billings Mustangs (17)	44	25	.638	1½	104,732	Dave Keller

	W	L	Pct.	GB	Attend.	Manager
Great Falls Dodgers (19)	35	34	.507	10½	64,226	Tim Johnson
Medicine Hat Blue Jays (14)...	26	43	.377	19½	25,948	Eddie Dennis

South Standings	W	L	Pct.	GB	Attend.	Manager
Salt Lake City Trappers	49	21	.700	—	170,134	Jim Gilligan
Idaho Falls Braves (15).......	36	34	.514	13	52,164	Rod Gilbreath
Pocatello Giants (26)	23	47	.329	26	18,790	Rafael Landestoy
Butte Copper Kings (x).......	19	50	.275	29½	19,669	Ernest Rodriguez

Playoff: Salt Lake City 3 games, Helena 1.

All-Star Team: 1B-Greg Vella, Medicine Hat; **2B**-Bryan Foster, Helena; **SS**-Andres Santana, Pocatello; **3B**-Alan Lewis, Great Falls; **OF**-Bernie Walker, Billings; Michael Malinak, Salt Lake City; John Mitchell, Idaho Falls; **C**-Frank Colston, Salt Lake City; **DH**-Matt Huff, Salt Lake City; **P**-Sherman Collins, Great Falls; Tim Peters, Salt Lake City; Jaime Navarro, Helena; **Manager**-Tim Johnson, Great Falls.

BA: Matt Huff, Salt Lake City, .417
Runs: Tony Blackmon, Salt Lake City, 61
Hits: John Mitchell, Idaho Falls, 92
RBIs: Bill Carlson, Pocatello, 67

HRs: Michael Malinak, Salt Lake City, 12
Wins: Steve Monson, Helena, 10
SOs: A.J. Waznik, Idaho Falls, 102
ERA: Samuel Chavez, Billings, 1.98

1987 Interleague Post Season Play

World Series
Minnesota (American) 4 games, St. Louis (National) 3

1987 Major League Farm Systems

American League

1. Baltimore (5): Rochester, Charlotte, Hagerstown, Newark, Bluefield.
2. Boston (5): Pawtucket, New Britain, Winter Haven, Greensboro, Elmira.
3. California (5): Edmonton, Midland, Palm Springs, Quad City, Salem (OR).
4. Chicago (5): Hawaii, Birmingham, Daytona Beach, Peninsula, Gulf Coast.
5. Cleveland (5): Buffalo, Williamsport, Kinston, Waterloo, Burlington (NC).
6. Detroit (5): Toledo, Glens Falls, Lakeland, Fayetteville, Bristol.
7. Kansas City (6): Omaha, Memphis, Ft. Myers, Appleton, Eugene, Gulf Coast.
8. Milwaukee (5): Denver, El Paso, Stockton, Beloit, Helena.
9. Minnesota (5): Portland, Orlando, Visalia, Kenosha, Elizabethton.
10. New York (6): Columbus (OH), Albany-Colonie, Prince William, Ft. Lauderdale, Oneonta, Gulf Coast.
11. Oakland (5): Tacoma, Huntsville, Modesto, Madison, Medford.
12. Seattle (5): Calgary, Chattanooga, Salinas, Wausau, Bellingham.
13. Texas (5): Oklahoma City, Tulsa, Port Charlotte, Gastonia, Gulf Coast.
14. Toronto (6): Syracuse, Knoxville, Dunedin, Myrtle Beach, St. Catharines, Medicine Hat.

National League

15. Atlanta (7): Richmond, Greenville, Durham, Sumter, Pulaski, Idaho Falls, Gulf Coast.
16. Chicago (6): Iowa, Pittsfield, Winston-Salem, Peoria, Geneva, Wytheville.
17. Cincinnati (6): Nashville, Vermont, Tampa, Cedar Rapids, Billings, Gulf Coast.
18. Houston (6): Tucson, Columbus (GA), Osceola, Asheville, Auburn, Gulf Coast.
19. Los Angeles (6): Albuquerque, San Antonio, Bakersfield, Vero Beach, Great Falls, Gulf Coast.
20. Montreal (6): Indianapolis, Jacksonville, West Palm Beach, Burlington (IA), Jamestown, Gulf Coast.
21. New York (6): Tidewater, Jackson, Lynchburg, Columbia, Little Falls, Kingsport.
22. Philadelphia (6): Maine, Reading, Clearwater, Spartanburg, Utica.
23. Pittsburgh (6): Vancouver, Harrisburg, Salem (VA), Macon, Watertown, Gulf Coast.
24. St. Louis (7): Louisville, Arkansas, St. Petersburg, Springfield, Savannah, Erie, Johnson City.
25. San Diego (5): Las Vegas, Wichita, Reno, Charleston (SC), Spokane.
26. San Francisco (6): Phoenix, Shreveport, Fresno, Clinton, Everett, Pocatello.

Co-op (x): Bend, Charleston (WV), Butte.
Independent: San Jose, San Bernardino, Miami, Batavia, Boise, Salt Lake City.

1987 No-Hitters

Date	Pitcher	Team	League	Opponent	Score
4-15	Juan Nieves	Milwaukee	American	Baltimore	7-0
5-17	Armando Pruneda	Monclova	Mexican	MC Tigres	1-0 (7)
5-24	Isaac Jimenez	Yucatan	Mexican	San Luis Potosi	6-0
5-28	Bob Milacki/				
	Rich Rice	Charlotte	Southern	Chattanooga	2-1 (11)
6-1	Park Pittman/				
	Tim O'Connor	Visalia	California	Palm Springs	1-0
6-3	Danny Weems	Charleston	South Atlantic	Greensboro	3-0 (7)
6-6	Matt Kinzer	Arkansas	Texas	Tulsa	10-0
7-6	Steve Curry	Pawtucket	International	Richmond	11-0
7-10	Jeff Schwarz	Peoria	Midwest	Kenosha	4-0
7-24	Dave Johnson	Vancouver	Pacific Coast	Portland	3-0
7-27	Paul Miller	Pirates	Gulf Coast	Reds	2-0
8-12	Sherm Collins/				
	Mike Munoz	Bakersfield	California	San Jose	4-0 (7)
8-12	Tim Fortugno	Salinas	California	Modesto	6-0 (7)
8-14	Bill Krueger	Albuquerque	Pacific Coast	Phoenix	2-0 (7)
8-14	Joseph Law	Modesto	California	Stockton	1-0
8-25	Greg W. Harris	Wichita	Texas	Midland	7-0

Number in parentheses indicates innings if other than nine.

THIS DATE IN MINOR LEAGUE HISTORY

April 8, 1987, Charleston, West Virginia, was scheduled to return to professional baseball in the South Atlantic League. Their home opener, however, was snowed out.

May 16, 1987, Dwight Gooden, on drug rehabilitation, returned to pitch for the Lynchburg Mets of the Carolina League, where he went 19-4 with 300 strikeouts in 1983. Gooden allowed two hits against Durham in four innings of work. A crowd of 5,342 was on hand.

June 9, 1987, Designated hitter Wade Rowdon tied an American Association record when he hit four home runs to spark the Iowa Cubs to an 18-12 victory over Louisville at Sec Taylor Stadium in Des Moines.

June 27, 1987, When Bend, managed by Mel Roberts, and Boise, managed by Derrel Thomas, met in a Northwest League game, it marked the first time in the history of Organized Ball in the United States that two black managers had faced each other.

July 22, 1987, Second baseman Jim Reboulet, Harrisburg, Eastern League, failed to connect after hitting safely in 32 straight games.

July 24, 1987, The Salt Lake City Trappers, Pioneer League, matched baseball's longest streak of 27 consecutive triumphs with a 7-2 win over Pocatello. The victory,

before 7,657 fans, matched the record set in 1902 by the Corsicana Oilers, Texas League, and the 1921 Baltimore Orioles, International League.

August 30, 1987, The final regular season game was played at historic Rickwood Field, home of the Birmingham Barons since 1910. The Barons would move into a new facility in suburban Hoover, Alabama, for the 1988 season.

August 30, 1987, The final game was played at "The Rockpile", Buffalo's War Memorial Stadium. War Memorial, primarily a football facility, replaced beloved Offerman Stadium in 1960, causing Buffalo's baseball fortunes to sag. New Pilot Field in downtown Buffalo would seat 19,500 fans.

August 31, 1987, Dave Bresnahan, reserve catcher for Williamsport of the Eastern League, substituted a peeled potato for a baseball and then hurled the potato into left field in an apparent pickoff attempt. The runner on third base raced home and was tagged out by Bresnahan with the real baseball. The umpire called the runner safe and ejected Bresnahan from the game. One day later, the Cleveland Indians gave Bresnahan his outright release.

September 28, 1987, The American Association and the International League announced the formation of the AAA Alliance and interleague play beginning in 1988.

1988

American League
President: Dr. Robert W. Brown

East Standings	W	L	Pct.	GB	Attend.	Manager
Boston Red Sox	89	73	.549	—	2,464,851	John McNamara/Joe Morgan
Detroit Tigers	88	74	.543	1	2,081,162	Sparky Anderson
Milwaukee Brewers	87	75	.537	2	1,923,238	Tom Trebelhorn
Toronto Blue Jays	87	75	.537	2	2,595,175	Jimy Williams
New York Yankees	85	76	.528	3½	2,633,701	Billy Martin/Lou Piniella
Cleveland Indians	78	84	.481	11	1,411,610	Doc Edwards
Baltimore Orioles	54	107	.335	34½	1,660,738	Cal Ripken, Sr./ Frank Robinson

West Standings	W	L	Pct.	GB	Attend.	Manager
Oakland Athletics	104	58	.642	—	2,287,335	Tony LaRussa
Minnesota Twins	91	71	.562	13	3,030,672	Tom Kelly
Kansas City Royals	84	77	.522	19½	2,350,181	John Wathan
California Angels	75	87	.463	29	2,340,925	Cookie Rojas/Moose Stubing
Chicago White Sox	71	90	.441	32½	1,115,749	Jim Fregosi
Texas Rangers	70	91	.435	33½	1,581,901	Bobby Valentine
Seattle Mariners	68	93	.422	35½	1,022,398	Dick Williams/Jimmy Snyder

Playoff: Oakland 4 games, Boston 0.

BA: Wade Boggs, Boston, .366
Runs: Wade Boggs, Boston, 128
Hits: Kirby Puckett, Minnesota, 234
RBIs: Jose Canseco, Oakland, 124
HRs: Jose Canseco, Oakland, 42

Wins: Frank Viola, Minnesota, 24
SOs: Roger Clemens, Boston, 291
ERA: Allan Anderson, Minnesota, 2.45
Pct: Frank Viola, Minnesota, .774, 24-7
Saves: Dennis Eckersley, Oakland, 45

National League
President: A. Bartlett Giamatti

East Standings	W	L	Pct.	GB	Attend.	Manager
New York Mets	100	60	.625	—	3,055,445	Davey Johnson
Pittsburgh Pirates	85	75	.531	15	1,866,713	Jim Leyland
Montreal Expos	81	81	.500	19	1,478,659	Buck Rodgers
Chicago Cubs	77	85	.475	23	2,089,034	Don Zimmer
St. Louis Cardinals	76	86	.469	24	2,892,799	Whitey Herzog
Philadelphia Phillies	65	96	.404	35½	1,990,041	Lee Elia/John Vukovich

West Standings	W	L	Pct.	GB	Attend.	Manager
Los Angeles Dodgers	94	67	.584	—	2,980,262	Tom Lasorda
Cincinnati Reds	87	74	.540	7	2,072,528	Pete Rose/Tommy Helms
San Diego Padres	83	78	.516	11	1,506,896	Larry Bowa/Jack McKeon
San Francisco Giants	83	79	.512	11½	1,785,297	Roger Craig
Houston Astros	82	80	.506	12½	1,933,505	Hal Lanier
Atlanta Braves	54	106	.338	39½	848,089	Chuck Tanner/Russ Nixon

Playoff: Los Angeles 4 games, New York 3.

BA: Tony Gwynn, San Diego, .313
Runs: Brett Butler, San Francisco, 109
Hits: Andres Galarraga, Montreal, 184
RBIs: Will Clark, San Francisco, 109
HRs: Darryl Strawberry, New York, 39

Wins: Danny Jackson, Cincinnati, 23
Orel Hershiser, Los Angeles, 23
SOs: Nolan Ryan, Houston, 228
ERA: Joe Magrane, St. Louis, 2.18
Pct: David Cone, New York, .870, 20-3
Saves: John Franco, Cincinnati, 39

AAA American Association
President: Ken Grandquist

East Standings	W	L	Pct.	GB	Attend.	Manager
Indianapolis Indians (20)	89	53	.627	—	293,721	Joe Sparks
Nashville Sounds (17)	73	69	.514	16	317,695	Jack Lind/Wayne Garland/ Jim Hoff/George Scherger/ Frank Lucchesi
Buffalo Bisons (23)	72	70	.507	17	1,147,651	Rocky Bridges
Louisville Redbirds (24)	63	79	.444	26	574,852	Mike Jorgensen

West Standings	W	L	Pct.	GB	Attend.	Manager
Omaha Royals (7)	81	61	.570	—	287,096	Glenn Ezell
Iowa Cubs (16)	78	64	.549	3	266,845	Pete Mackanin
Denver Zephyrs (8)	72	69	.511	8½	357,003	Duffy Dyer
Oklahoma City 89ers (13)	67	74	.475	13½	260,363	Toby Harrah

Played an interlocking schedule with the International League known as AAA Alliance.

Playoff: Indianapolis 3 games, Omaha 1.

All-Star Team: 1B-Luis de los Santos, Omaha; **2B**-Johnny Paredes, Indianapolis; **3B**-Tom O'Malley, Oklahoma City; **SS**-Felix Fermin, Buffalo; **OF**-Billy Moore, Indianapolis; Rolando Roomes, Iowa; Van Snider, Nashville; **C**-Bill Bathe, Iowa; **P**-Dorn Taylor, Buffalo; Norm Charlton, Nashville; **MVP**-Luis de los Santos, Omaha; **Pitcher of the Year**-Bob Sebra, Indianapolis; **Manager**-Joe Sparks, Indianapolis.

BA: Lavell Freeman, Denver, .318
Runs: Billy Moore, Indianapolis, 88
Hits: Luis de los Santos, Omaha, 164
RBIs: Luis de los Santos, Omaha, 87
German Rivera, Denver, 87

HRs: Van Snider, Nashville, 23
Wins: Dave Johnson, Buffalo, 15
SOs: Norm Charlton, Nashville, 161
ERA: Dorn Taylor, Buffalo, 2.14

AAA International League
President: Harold Cooper

East Standings	W	L	Pct.	GB	Attend.	Manager
Tidewater Tides (21)	77	64	.546	—	194,089	Mike Cubbage
Richmond Braves (15)	66	75	.468	11	355,704	Jim Beauchamp
Pawtucket Red Sox (2)	63	79	.444	14½	246,940	Ed Nottle
Maine Phillies (22)	62	80	.437	15½	80,071	George Culver

West Standings	W	L	Pct.	GB	Attend.	Manager
Rochester Red Wings (1)	77	64	.546	—	300,794	Johnny Oates
Syracuse Chiefs (14)	70	71	.496	7	184,910	Bob Bailor
Columbus Clippers (10)	65	77	.458	12½	536,171	Bucky Dent
Toledo Mud Hens (6)	58	84	.408	19½	193,097	Pat Corrales

Played an interlocking schedule with the American Association known as AAA Alliance.

Playoff: Rochester 3 games, Tidewater 1.

All-Star Team: 1B-Dave Griffin, Richmond; **2B**-Tommy Barrett, Maine; **3B**-Craig Worthington, Rochester; **SS**-Randy Velarde, Columbus; **OF**-Steve Finley, Rochester; Carlos Quintana, Pawtucket; Mark Carreon, Tidewater; **C**-Bob Geren, Columbus; **DH**-Lonnie Smith, Richmond; **P**-Steve Searcy, Toledo; Mark Huismann, Toledo; **MVP**-Craig Worthington, Rochester; **Pitcher of the Year**-Steve Searcy, Toledo; **Manager**-Johnny Oates, Rochester.

BA: Steve Finley, Rochester, .314
Runs: Tommy Barrett, Maine, 69
Jeff Wetherby, Richmond, 69
Eric Yelding, Syracuse, 69
Hits: Steve Finley, Rochester, 143
RBIs: Ron Jones, Maine, 75

HRs: Dave Griffin, Richmond, 21
Wins: Steve Searcy, Toledo, 13
Scott Nielsen, Columbus, 13
SOs: Steve Searcy, Toledo, 176
ERA: David West, Tidewater, 1.80

AAA Mexican League
President: Pedro Treto Cisneros

North Standings	W	L	Pct.	GB	Attend.	Manager
Dos Laredos Tecolotes	77	51	.602	—	160,253	Jose Guerrero
San Luis Potosi Tuneros	64	62	.508	12	220,853	Gregorio Luque
Monterrey Sultanes	62	69	.473	16½	141,258	Lee Sigman/Derek Bryant
Saltillo Saraperos	59	68	.465	17½	152,580	Victor Favela/Sergio Robles/ Jose Pena
Union Laguna Algodoneros	59	69	.461	18	178,831	Alfredo Rios/ Mark Weidemaier
Aguascalientes Rieleros	54	72	.461	22	120,000	Sergio Robles/Ramon Montoya
Monclova Aceleros	47	84	.359	31½	145,980	Miguel Sotelo/ Aurelio Monteagudo

South Standings	W	L	Pct.	GB	Attend.	Manager
Mexico City Diablos Rojos	82	45	.646	—	153,460	Ben Reyes
Jalisco Charros	75	55	.577	8½	270,500	Carlos Paz
Mexico City Tigres	72	56	.563	10½	155,580	Alfredo Ortiz
Yucatan Leones	70	56	.556	11½	285,569	Roberto Castellon
Leon Bravos	68	63	.519	16	151,635	Obed Plascencia/ Javier Espinoza/Agustin Enriquez/ Manuel Magallon
Campeche Piratas	62	65	.488	20	144,321	Francisco Estrada
Tabasco Ganaderos	46	82	.359	36½	115,148	Francisco Chavez/Arturo Rubio/ Miguel Gaspar/Javier Espinoza/ Miguel Solis

Playoffs: Monterrey 4 games, San Luis Potosi 1; Saltillo 4 games, Dos Laredos 2; MC Diablos Rojos 4 games, Yucatan 1; Jalisco 4 games, MC Tigres 2. Saltillo 4 games, Monterrey 1; MC Diablos Rojos 4 games, Jalisco 0.
Finals: MC Diablos Rojos 4 games, Saltillo 1.

BA: Nick Castaneda, Yucatan, .374
Runs: Dave Stockstill, Jalisco, 121
Hits: Harold Perkins, Leon, 184
RBIs: Nelson Barrera, MC Diablos Rojos, 124

HRs: Leo Hernandez, Union Laguna, 36
Wins: Jesus Rios, MC Tigres, 21
SOs: Jesus Rios, MC Tigres, 195
ERA: Dave Walsh, Dos Laredos, 1.73

AAA Pacific Coast League
President: Bill Cutler

North Standings	W	L	Pct.	GB	Attend.	Manager
Vancouver Canadians***(4)	85	57	.599	—	386,220	Terry Bevington
Portland Beavers (9)	76	66	.535	9	207,605	Jim Mahoney/Jim Shellenback
Calgary Cannons (12)	68	74	.479	17	332,590	Bill Plummer/Marty Martinez
Edmonton Trappers (3)	61	80	.433	23½	243,419	Tom Kotchman
Tacoma Tigers (11)	62	82	.431	24	280,168	Brad Fischer

*Won first-half **Won second-half ***Won both halves
Numbers after nicknames indicate farm system.
Affiliation listed at end of year.

588

South Standings	W	L	Pct.	GB	Attend.	Manager
Albuquerque Dukes**(19)	86	56	.606	—	314,186	Terry Collins
Las Vegas Stars*(25)	74	66	.526	11	305,622	Steve Smith
Tucson Toros (18)	68	75	.476	18½	173,889	Bob Didier
Phoenix Firebirds (26)	67	76	.469	19½	171,030	Wendell Kim
Colorado Springs Sky Sox (5)	62	77	.446	22½	168,248	Steve Swisher

Playoffs: Vancouver 3 games, Portland 0; Las Vegas 3 games, Albuquerque 0.
Finals: Las Vegas 3 games, Vancouver 1.

All-Star Team: 1B-Francisco Melendez, Phoenix; **2B-**Mike Woodard, Vancouver; **3B-**Edgar Martinez, Calgary; **SS-**Mike Brumley, Las Vegas; **OF-**Mike Devereaux, Albuquerque; Luis Medina, Colorado Springs; Cameron Drew, Tucson; **C-**Sandy Alomar, Jr., Las Vegas; **DH-**George Hinshaw, Albuquerque; Rod Allen, Colorado Springs; **P-**Bill Brennan, Albuquerque; Bill Krueger, Albuquerque; Karl Best, Portland/Phoenix; **MVP-**Sandy Alomar, Jr., Las Vegas; **Manager-**Terry Collins, Albuquerque.

BA: Edgar Martinez, Calgary, .363
Runs: Craig Smajstrla, Tucson, 89
Hits: Vic Rodriguez, Portland, 162
RBIs: Rod Allen, Colorado Springs, 100
HRs: Luis Medina, Colorado Springs, 28
Wins: Bill Krueger, Albuquerque, 15
SOs: Erik Hanson, Calgary, 154
ERA: Bill Krueger, Albuquerque, 3.01

AA Eastern League
President: Charles E. Eshbach

Standings	W	L	Pct.	GB	Attend.	Manager
Glens Falls Tigers (6)	80	57	.584	—	57,314	John Wockenfuss
Vermont Mariners (12)	79	60	.568	2	68,894	Rich Morales
Pittsfield Cubs (16)	75	63	.543	5½	53,121	Jim Essian
Albany-Colonie Yankees (10)	72	66	.522	8½	214,663	Tommy Jones/Stump Merrill
Reading Phillies (22)	67	69	.493	12½	144,107	Bill Dancy
Williamsport Bills (5)	66	73	.475	15	100,586	Mike Hargrove
Harrisburg Senators (23)	65	73	.471	15½	216,940	Dave Trembley
New Britain Red Sox (2)	47	90	.343	33	77,965	Dave Holt

Playoffs: Vermont 3 games, Pittsfield 1; Albany 3 games, Glens Falls 1.
Finals: Albany 3 games, Vermont 1.

All-Star Team: 1B-Kevin Maas, Albany-Colonie; **2B-**Andy Stankiewicz, Albany-Colonie; **3B-**Shane Turner, Reading; **SS-**Omar Vizquel, Vermont; **OF-**Rob Richie, Glens Falls; Jerome Walton, Pittsfield; Oscar Azocar, Albany-Colonie; **C-**Chris Hoiles, Glens Falls; **DH-**Jim Wilson, Vermont; **P-**Cesar Mejia, Glens Falls; Ken Williams, Glens Falls; Dean Wilkins, Pittsfield; **MVP-**Rob Richie, Glens Falls; **Pitcher of the Year-**Cesar Mejia, Glens Falls; **Manager-**Rich Morales, Vermont.

BA: Jerome Walton, Pittsfield, .331
Runs: Ced Landrum, Pittsfield, 82
Hits: Rob Richie, Glens Falls, 155
RBIs: Rob Richie, Glens Falls, 82
HRs: Chris Hoiles, Glens Falls, 17
Jim Wilson, Vermont, 17
Wins: Mike Walker, Williamsport, 15
SOs: Mike Walker, Williamsport, 144
ERA: Paul Wenson, Glens Falls, 2.04

AA Southern League
President: Jimmy Bragan

East Standings	W	L	Pct.	GB	Attend.	Manager
Greenville Braves***(15)	87	57	.604	—	209,791	Russ Nixon/Buddy Bailey
Jacksonville Expos (20)	69	73	.486	17	175,396	Tommy Thompson
Columbus Astros (18)	69	74	.483	17½	110,621	Tom Wiedenbauer
Charlotte Knights (1)	69	75	.479	18	102,467	Greg Biagini
Orlando Twins (9)	66	75	.468	19½	68,904	Duane Gustavson

West Standings	W	L	Pct.	GB	Attend.	Manager
Chattanooga Lookouts(17)	81	62	.566	—	136,921	Tom Runnells
Memphis Chicks**(7)	79	64	.552	2	205,568	Sal Rende
Knoxville Blue Jays (14)	75	69	.521	6½	87,434	Barry Foote
Birmingham Barons (4)	62	82	.431	19½	269,831	Rico Petrocelli
Huntsville Stars (11)	59	85	.410	22½	185,811	Tommie Reynolds

Playoffs: Chattanooga 3 games, Memphis 1; Greenville 3 games, Jacksonville 2.
Finals: Chattanooga 3 games, Greenville 0.

All-Star Team: 1B-Drew Denson, Greenville; **2B-**Mark Lemke, Greenville; **3B-**Carlo Colombino, Columbus; **SS-**Mike Bordick, Huntsville; **OF-**Rafael DeLima, Orlando; Barry Jones, Greenville; Bernardo Brito, Orlando; Butch Davis, Charlotte; **C-**Francisco Cabrera, Knoxville; **DH-**Matt Winters, Memphis; **P-**Chris Hammond, Chattanooga; Alex Sanchez, Knoxville; **MVP-**Matt Winters, Memphis; **Pitcher of the Year-**German Gonzalez, Orlando; **Manager-**Buddy Bailey, Greenville.

BA: Butch Davis, Charlotte, .301
Runs: Rafel Skeete, Charlotte, 89
Hits: Mark Lemke, Greenville, 153
RBIs: Matt Winters, Memphis, 91
HRs: Matt Winters, Memphis, 25
Wins: Chris Hammond, Chattanooga, 16
SOs: Alex Sanchez, Knoxville, 166
ERA: Chris Hammond, Chattanooga, 1.72

AA Texas League
President: Carl Sawatski

East Standings	W	L	Pct.	GB	Attend.	Manager
Shreveport Captains*(26)	74	62	.544	—	234,587	Jack Mull
Tulsa Drillers**(13)	71	65	.522	3	188,375	Jim Skaalen
Arkansas Travelers (24)	67	69	.493	7	251,892	Jim Riggleman/Darold Knowles/Gaylen Pitts
Jackson Mets (21)	61	75	.449	13	134,967	Tucker Ashford

West Standings	W	L	Pct.	GB	Attend.	Manager
El Paso Diablos**(8)	74	60	.552	—	207,236	Dave Machemer
San Antonio Missions*(19)	73	60	.549	½	130,899	Kevin Kennedy
Midland Angels (3)	61	74	.452	13½	133,105	Max Oliveras
Wichita Pilots (25)	60	76	.441	15	70,525	Pat Kelly

Playoffs: El Paso 2 games, San Antonio 0; Tulsa 2 games, Shreveport 0.
Finals: Tulsa 4 games, El Paso 2.

All-Star Team: 1B-Jim McCollom, Midland; **2B-**Frank Mattox, El Paso; **3B-**Jeff Manto, Midland; **SS-**Gary Sheffield, El Paso; **OF-**Greg Vaughn, El Paso; Mike Huff, San Antonio; Jeff Yurtin, Wichita; **C-**Todd Zeile, Arkansas; Chad Kreuter, Tulsa; **DH-**Mario Monico, El Paso; **Util-**Domingo Michel, San Antonio; **P-**Blaine Beatty, Jackson; Kevin Brown, Tulsa; Mike Munoz, San Antonio; Joe Olker, Shreveport; Steve Wilson, Tulsa; **MVP-**Jeff Manto, Midland; **Pitcher of the Year-**Blaine Beatty, Jackson; **Manager-**Jim Skaalen, Tulsa.

BA: Jim McCollom, Midland, .343
Runs: Greg Vaughn, El Paso, 104
Hits: Alan Hayden, Jackson, 156
RBIs: Greg Vaughn, El Paso, 105
HRs: Greg Vaughn, El Paso, 28
Wins: Blaine Beatty, Jackson, 16
SOs: Brian Givens, Jackson, 156
ERA: Mickey Weston, Jackson, 2.23

A California League
President: Joe Gagliardi

North Standings	W	L	Pct.	GB	Attend.	Manager
Stockton Ports*(8)	94	49	.657	—	58,586	Dave Huppert
San Jose Giants**(26)	91	52	.636	3	108,386	Duane Espy
Modesto A's (11)	54	88	.380	39½	71,500	Jeff Newman
Fresno Suns (x)	53	89	.373	40½	34,734	Dean Treanor
Reno Silver Sox (x)	39	103	.275	54½	85,624	Nate Oliver

South Standings	W	L	Pct.	GB	Attend.	Manager
Riverside Red Wave**(25)	85	57	.599	—	60,509	Tony Torchia
Visalia Oaks (9)	80	62	.563	5	47,593	Scott Ullger
San Bernardino Spirit (12)	74	68	.521	11	154,653	Ralph Dick
Bakersfield Dodgers (19)	71	71	.500	14	92,360	Gary LaRocque
Palm Springs Angels*(3)	70	72	.493	15	60,222	Bill Lachemann

Playoffs: Riverside 3 games, Palm Springs 2; Stockton 3 games, San Jose 2.
Finals: Riverside 3 games, Stockton 0.

All-Star Team: 1B-Rich Aldrete, San Jose; **2B-**Paul Faries, Riverside; **3B-**Dave Hollins, Riverside; **SS-**Tom LeVasseur, Riverside; **OF-**Mark Leonard, San Jose; Warren Newson, Riverside; Ken Griffey, Jr., San Bernardino; **C-**Tim McIntosh, Stockton; **DH-**Adam Brown, Bakersfield; **P-**Colin Charland, Palm Springs; Doug Robertson, San Jose; Eric Gunderson, San Jose; Steve Monson, Stockton; **MVP-**Paul Faries, Riverside; **Pitcher of the Year-**Colin Charland, Palm Springs; Doug Robertson, San Jose; **Manager-**Dave Huppert, Stockton.

BA: Adam Brown, Bakersfield, .352
Runs: Greg Ritchie, San Jose, 118
Hits: Marty Lanoux, Visalia, 185
RBIs: Mark Leonard, San Jose, 118
HRs: Warren Newson, Riverside, 22
Wins: Colin Charland, Palm Springs, 17
Tom Meagher, San Jose, 17
SOs: Paul Abbott, Visalia, 205
ERA: Richard Holsman, Riverside, 2.38

A Carolina League
President: John Hopkins

North Standings	W	L	Pct.	GB	Attend.	Manager
Hagerstown Suns (1)	79	61	.564	—	135,380	Mike Hart
Salem Buccaneers*(23)	73	66	.525	5½	119,966	Jay Ward
Lynchburg Red Sox**(2)	68	72	.486	11	81,197	Dick Berardino
Prince William Yankees (10)	55	84	.396	23½	114,403	Wally Moon/Gene Tenace

South Standings	W	L	Pct.	GB	Attend.	Manager
Kinston Indians***(5)	88	52	.629	—	80,623	Glenn Adams
Durham Bulls (15)	82	58	.586	6	271,650	Buddy Bailey/Grady Little
Winston-Salem Spirits (16)	73	67	.521	15	79,999	Jay Loviglio
Virginia Generals#(x)	41	99	.293	47	91,324	Joe Breeden

#represented Newport News-Hampton, Virginia.

Playoff: Lynchburg 2 games, Salem 1.
Finals: Kinston 3 games, Lynchburg 2.

All-Star Team: 1B-Jim Orsag, Lynchburg; **2B-**Greg Smith, Winston-Salem; **3B-**Scott Cooper, Lynchburg; **SS-**Ever Magallanes, Kinston; **OF-**Bernie Williams, Prince William; Mickey Pina, Lynchburg; Bob Zupcic, Lynchburg; **C-**Mike Eberle, Hagerstown; **DH-**Mitch Lyden, Prince William; **Util-**Mike Twardoski, Kinston; Derrick May, Winston-Salem; Mike Westbrook, Kinston; **P-**Bill Kazmierczak, Winston-Salem; Shawn Boskie, Winston-Salem; Kent Mercker, Durham; **MVP-**Mickey Pina, Lynchburg; **Pitcher of the Year-**Kent Mercker, Durham; Kevin Bearse, Kinston; **Manager-**Dick Berardino, Lynchburg.

BA: Bernie Williams, Prince William, .335
Runs: Don Buford, Jr., Hagerstown, 91
Jim Orsag, Lynchburg, 91
Mickey Pina, Lynchburg, 91
Hits: Scott Cooper, Lynchburg, 148
Derrick May, Winston-Salem, 148
RBIs: Mickey Pina, Lynchburg, 108
HRs: Mickey Pina, Lynchburg, 21
Wins: Brian Dubois, Virginia/Hagerstown, 14
Phil Harrison, Winston-Salem, 14
Michael Sander, Hagerstown, 14
SOs: Phil Harrison, Winston-Salem, 169
ERA: Kent Mercker, Durham, 2.75

A Florida State League

President: George MacDonald, Jr.

East Standings	W	L	Pct.	GB	Attend.	Manager
Vero Beach Dodgers*(19)..	75	62	.547	—	81,831	John Shoemaker
St. Lucie Mets**(21).........	74	65	.532	2	68,150	Clint Hurdle
West Palm Beach Expos (20)..	71	63	.530	2½	85,733	Felipe Alou
Ft. Lauderdale Yankees (10) ...	69	65	.519	4½	43,885	Buck Showalter
Miami Marlins..................	55	79	.410	18½	28,927	Jose Santiago
West Standings	**W**	**L**	**Pct.**	**GB**	**Attend.**	**Manager**
Tampa White Sox***(4)	71	59	.546	—	55,900	Marv Foley
Charlotte Rangers (13)........	72	65	.526	3½	117,275	Bobby Jones
St. Petersburg Cardinals (24)...	68	68	.500	6	170,534	Dave Bialas
Dunedin Blue Jays (14)	65	75	.464	11	33,540	Doug Ault
Clearwater Phillies (22)......	52	86	.377	23	50,456	Granny Hamner
Central Standings	**W**	**L**	**Pct.**	**GB**	**Attend.**	**Manager**
Osceola Astros*(18)	83	54	.606	—	44,023	Keith Bodie
Baseball City Royals#(7)....	79	60	.568	5	63,746	Luis Silverio
Lakeland Tigers**(6)	77	61	.558	6½	53,818	John Lipon
Winter Haven Red Sox (2) .	45	94	.324	39	27,746	Doug Camilli

#represented Davenport, Florida.

Playoffs: West Palm Beach 2 games, Vero Beach 0; St. Lucie 2 games, Lakeland 1. Osceola 2 games, West Palm Beach 0; St. Lucie 2 games, Tampa 0.
Finals: St. Lucie 2 games, Osceola 0.

All-Star Team: 1B-Mike Simms, Osceola; **2B-**Lou Frazier, Osceola; **3B-**Dave Hansen, Vero Beach; **SS-**Rey Sanchez, Charlotte; **OF-**Pedro Munoz, Dunedin; Milt Cuyler, Lakeland; Mike White, Vero Beach; **C-**Phil Clark, Lakeland; Carlos Escalera, Baseball City; **DH-**Brian Morrison, Miami; **P-**Jerry Kutzler, Tampa; Chris Nichting, Vero Beach; Darren Hursey, Lakeland; Masahiro Yamamoto, Vero Beach; Aguedo Vasquez, Baseball City; Greg Everson, Lakeland; **MVP-**Aguedo Vasquez, Baseball City; **Manager-**Marv Foley, Tampa.

BA: Mike White, Vero Beach, .340
Runs: Milt Cuyler, Lakeland, 100
Hits: Dave Hansen, Vero Beach, 149
RBIs: Dave Hansen, Vero Beach, 81
HRs: Brian Morrison, Miami, 17
Wins: Jerry Kutzler, Tampa, 16
SOs: Chris Nichting, Vero Beach, 151
ERA: Kevin Brown, St. Lucie, 1.81

A Midwest League

President: George Spelius

North Standings	W	L	Pct.	GB	Attend.	Manager
Rockford Expos**(20)	84	56	.600	—	158,674	Alan Bannister
Kenosha Twins*(9)............	81	59	.579	3	64,285	Ron Gardenhire
Beloit Brewers (8)	66	74	.471	18	96,616	Gomer Hodge
Madison Muskies (11)........	65	75	.464	19	88,343	Jim Nettles
South Bend White Sox (4)..	59	81	.421	25	171,444	Steve Dillard
Appleton Foxes (7)............	58	82	.414	26	85,310	Brian Poldberg
Wausau Timbers (12)	52	88	.371	32	55,255	Rick Sweet
South Standings	**W**	**L**	**Pct.**	**GB**	**Attend.**	**Manager**
Cedar Rapids Reds*(17).....	87	53	.321	—	166,121	Marc Bombard
Springfield Cardinals**(24) ..	81	58	.583	5½	155,416	Mark DeJohn
Clinton Giants (26)...........	78	62	.557	9	127,251	Bill Evers
Waterloo Indians (5)...........	78	62	.557	9	87,819	Ken Bolek
Peoria Chiefs (16)..............	70	70	.500	17	207,294	Jim Tracy
Quad City Angels (3)..........	60	79	.432	26½	115,459	Eddie Rodriguez
Burlington Braves (15).......	60	80	.429	27	78,308	Grady Little/Rick Albert

Playoffs: Kenosha 2 games, Rockford 0; Cedar Rapids 2 games, Springfield 0.
Finals: Cedar Rapids 3 games, Kenosha 1.

All-Star Team: 1B-Reggie Jefferson, Cedar Rapids; **2B-**Rich Casarotti, Burlington; **3B-**Bobby Rose, Quad City; **SS-**Shawn Gilbert, Kenosha; **OF-**Jarvis Brown, Kenosha; Jamie Cooper, Clinton; Jeff Forney, Cedar Rapids; **C-**Lenny Webster, Kenosha; **DH-**Bobby Knecht, Appleton; **P-**Butch Henry, Cedar Rapids; Tom Gordon, Appleton; Greg Becker, Springfield; Pete Delkus, Kenosha; **MVP-**Lenny Webster, Kenosha; **Manager-**Marc Bombard, Cedar Rapids.

BA: Ruben Gonzalez, Wausau, .314
Runs: Jarvis Brown, Kenosha, 108
Hits: Jarvis Brown, Kenosha, 156
RBIs: Reggie Jefferson, Cedar Rapids, 90
HRs: Brian Hunter, Burlington, 22
Steve Davis, Cedar Rapids, 22
Wins: Pat Bangston, Kenosha, 17
SOs: Tom Gordon, Appleton, 172
ERA: Mark Dewey, Clinton, 1.43

A New York-Pennsylvania League

President: Leo A. Pinckney

McNamara Standings	W	L	Pct.	GB	Attend.	Manager
Oneonta Yankees (10)	48	28	.632	—	53,187	Gary Allenson
Utica Blue Sox (4)	47	29	.618	1	65,384	Rick Patterson
Auburn Astros (18)............	42	33	.560	5½	37,973	Frank Cacciatore
Little Falls Mets (21).........	39	36	.520	8½	30,126	Bill Stein
Watertown Pirates (23)........	35	39	.473	12	19,649	Stan Cliburn
Elmira Pioneers (2)............	28	48	.368	20	48,978	Bill Limoncelli
Stedler Standings	**W**	**L**	**Pct.**	**GB**	**Attend.**	**Manager**
Jamestown Expos (20)........	47	29	.618	—	52,177	Roger LaFrancois
Erie Orioles (1)	46	31	.597	1½	47,589	Bobby Tolan
Hamilton Redbirds (24)......	36	39	.480	10½	60,380	Dan Radison
Batavia Clippers (22)..........	31	44	.413	15½	31,230	Don McCormick
St. Catharines Blue Jays (14)...	27	46	.370	18½	34,786	Eddie Dennis
Geneva Cubs (16)	27	51	.346	21	24,654	Bill Hayes

Playoff: Oneonta 2 games, Jamestown 0.

All-Star Team: 1B-Andy Mota, Auburn; **2B-**Pat Kelly, Oneonta; **3B-**Radhames Polanco, Little Falls; **SS-**Bob DeJardin, Oneonta; **OF-**Marquis Grissom, Jamestown; Derek Lee, Utica; Darwin Pennye, Watertown; Titi Roche, Little Falls; **C-**Luis Paulino, Erie; John Massarelli, Auburn; Todd Hundley, Little Falls; **DH-**John Furch, Utica; **P-**Dan Freed, Jamestown; Woody Williams, St. Catharines; Wally Trice, Auburn; Chris Hill, Little Falls; **Manager-**Roger LaFrancois, Jamestown.

BA: Andy Mota, Auburn, .351
Runs: Marquis Grissom, Jamestown, 69
Hits: Andy Mota, Auburn, 95
RBIs: Terry Brown, Erie, 49
HRs: Terry Brown, Erie, 13
Brian Cummings, Batavia, 13
Wins: Dan Freed, Jamestown, 13
SOs: Mike Sodders, Geneva, 119
ERA: Dan Freed, Jamestown, 0.67

A Northwest League

President: Jack Cain

North Standings	W	L	Pct.	GB	Attend.	Manager
Spokane Indians (25)..........	42	34	.553	—	113,143	Steve Lubratich
Everett Giants (26).............	42	34	.553	—	63,887	Joe Strain
Boise Hawks......................	30	46	.395	12	67,524	Mal Fichman
Bellingham Mariners (12) ..	25	51	.329	17	15,015	P.J. Carey
South Standings	**W**	**L**	**Pct.**	**GB**	**Attend.**	**Manager**
Southern Oregon A's#(11) .	46	30	.605	—	64,974	Lenn Sakata
Salem Dodgers (19)...........	43	33	.566	3	34,927	Tom Beyers
Bend Bucks (3)..................	38	38	.500	8	43,587	Don Long
Eugene Emeralds (7)	38	38	.500	8	137,372	Paul Kirsch

#represented Medford, Oregon.

Playoff: Spokane was declared division winner under league tie breaking rules.
Finals: Spokane 2 games, Southern Oregon 1.

All-Star Team: 1B-Bob Hamelin, Eugene; **2B-**Scott Bigham, Spokane; **3B-**Stan Royer, Southern Oregon; **SS-**Rafael Bournigal, Salem; **OF-**Shannon Coppell, Everett; Jeff Mace, Boise; Braulio Castillo, Salem; **C-**Eddie Tucker, Everett; **DH-**John Kuehl, Spokane; **P-**Tony Floyd, Southern Oregon; Kevin MacLeod, Southern Oregon; **MVP-**Stan Royer, Southern Oregon; **Manager-**Lenn Sakata, Southern Oregon.

BA: Scott Bigham, Spokane, .334
Runs: Mike Humphreys, Spokane, 67
Hits: Scott Bigham, Spokane, 105
RBIs: John Kuehl, Spokane, 65
HRs: Bob Hamelin, Eugene, 17
Wins: Doug Messer, Everett, 11
SOs: Tony Ariola, Southern Oregon, 107
ERA: Wes Bliven, Bend, 2.04

A South Atlantic League

President: John H. Moss

North Standings	W	L	Pct.	GB	Attend.	Manager
Greensboro Hornets**(17) .	79	60	.568	—	168,675	Dave Miley
Spartanburg Phillies*(22)...	69	69	.500	9½	61,108	Mel Roberts
Asheville Tourists (18).......	65	75	.464	14½	95,252	Gary Tuck/Jim Coveney
Fayetteville Generals (6)	62	73	.459	15	57,543	Leon Roberts
Charleston (WV) Wheelers (16).	51	86	.372	27	125,998	Brad Mills
Gastonia Rangers (13)	47	90	.343	31	50,212	Orlando Gomez
South Standings	**W**	**L**	**Pct.**	**GB**	**Attend.**	**Manager**
Charleston (SC) Rainbows**(25)	85	53	.616	—	55,909	Jack Krol
Myrtle Beach Blue Jays*(14)..	83	56	.597	2½	78,212	Richie Hebner
Augusta Pirates (23)	78	60	.565	7	123,626	Jeff Cox/Woody Huyke
Columbia Mets (21)............	74	63	.540	10½	114,172	Butch Hobson
Savannah Cardinals (24).....	68	67	.504	15½	58,311	Keith Champion
Sumter Braves (15)............	64	73	.467	20½	35,067	Ned Yost

Playoffs: Spartanburg 2 games, Greensboro 0; Charleston (SC) 2 games, Myrtle Beach 1.
Finals: Spartanburg 3 games, Charleston (SC) 0.

All-Star Team: 1B-Guillermo Velazquez, Charleston (SC); **2B-**William Suero, Myrtle Beach; **3B-**Brian Lane, Greensboro; **SS-**Luis Sojo, Myrtle Beach; **OF-**Derek Bell, Myrtle Beach; Jim Vatcher, Spartanburg; Moises Alou, Augusta; **C-**Eddie Taubensee, Greensboro; **DH-**Brant Alyea, Gastonia; **P-**Jimmy Rogers, Myrtle Beach; Denis Boucher, Myrtle Beach; **MVP-**Brant Alyea, Gastonia; **Pitcher of the Year-**Jimmy Rogers, Myrtle Beach; **Manager-**Richie Hebner, Myrtle Beach.

BA: Derek Bell, Myrtle Beach, .344
Runs: Jim Vatcher, Spartanburg, 90
Hits: Luis Sojo, Myrtle Beach, 155
RBIs: Brant Alyea, Gastonia, 98
HRs: Eric Anthony, Asheville, 29
Wins: Jimmy Rogers, Myrtle Beach, 18
SOs: Jimmy Rogers, Myrtle Beach, 198
ERA: Joe Pacholec, Augusta, 2.06

R Appalachian League

President: Bill Halstead

North Standings	W	L	Pct.	GB	Attend.	Manager
Burlington Indians (5)	37	32	.536	—	71,466	Mike Bucci
Pulaski Braves (15)...........	35	35	.500	2½	15,209	Cloyd Boyer
Princeton Pirates (23)	33	37	.471	4½	31,275	Jim Thrift
Martinsville Phillies (22)....	29	41	.414	8½	48,980	Rollie DeArmas
Bluefield Orioles (1)..........	24	47	.338	14	25,683	Glenn Gulliver
South Standings	**W**	**L**	**Pct.**	**GB**	**Attend.**	**Manager**
Kingsport Mets (21)...........	47	26	.644	—	41,044	Bobby Floyd
Bristol Tigers (6)	46	27	.630	1	20,224	Rick Magnante
Johnson City Cardinals (24)....	41	31	.569	5½	21,549	Jorge Aranzamendi/Gaylen Pitts
Elizabethton Twins (9)	33	37	.471	12½	14,670	Ray Smith
Wytheville Cubs (16)..........	28	40	.412	16½	20,331	Steve Roadcap

Playoff: Kingsport defeated Bristol in a one game playoff for the South title.
Finals: Kingsport 2 games, Burlington 0.

All-Star Team: 1B-Vince Zawaski, Kingsport; **2B**-Rodolfo Hernandez, Kingsport; **3B**-Jim Morrisette, Kingsport; **SS**-Mark Lewis, Burlington; **OF**-Wayne Weinheimer, Wytheville; Glen Gardner, Pulaski; Curtis Pride, Kingsport; **C**-Jeff Champ, Bluefield; **DH**-Tom Aldrich, Bristol; **P**-Rusty Meacham, Bristol; Steve Avery, Pulaski; **MVP**-Vince Zawaski, Kingsport; **Manager**-Bobby Floyd, Kingsport.

BA: Wayne Weinheimer, Wytheville, .355
Runs: Curtis Pride, Kingsport, 59
Hits: Rodolfo Hernandez, Kingsport, 84
RBIs: Vince Zawaski, Kingsport, 67
HRs: Vince Zawaski, Kingsport, 16
Wins: Danny Furmanik, Kingsport, 9
Rusty Meacham, Bristol, 9
Andrew Reich, Kingsport, 9
SOs: Mike Jones, Bristol, 100
ERA: Rusty Meacham, Bristol, 1.43

R Arizona League
President: Bob Richmond

Standings	W	L	Pct.	GB	Manager
Brewers (8)	40	18	.690	—	Alex Taveras
Athletics (11)	34	24	.586	6	Dave Hudgens
Padres (25)	31	28	.525	9½	Jaime Moreno
Red Sox/Mariners (2, 12)	12	47	.203	28½	Mike Verdi & Myron Pines

Games played at Peoria and Scottsdale, Arizona.

Playoffs: None.

All-Star Team: 1B-Leon Glenn, Brewers; **2B**-Matt Witkowski, Padres; **3B**-Frank Bolick, Brewers; **SS**-Luis Mateo, Athletics; **OF**-Tim McWilliam, Padres; Ed Ricks, Athletics; Osvaldo Sanchez, Padres; **C**-Gerald Cifarelli, Padres; **DH**-Robert Muhammed, Brewers; **P**-Joe Murdock, Padres; Jeff Hart, Padres; Will Love, Athletics; Marty Willis, Brewers; **MVP**-Ed Ricks, Athletics; **Manager**-Alex Taveras, Brewers.

BA: Tim McWilliam, Padres, .451
Runs: Sylvester Love, Brewers, 72
Hits: Tim McWilliam, Padres, 82
RBIs: Leon Glenn, Brewers, 53
HRs: Leon Glenn, Brewers, 8
Ed Ricks, Athletics, 8
Wins: Bruce Wegman, Brewers, 9
SOs: Larry Carter, Brewers, 65
ERA: Jeff Hart, Padres, 2.07

R Gulf Coast League
President: Thomas J. Saffell

North Standings	W	L	Pct.	GB	Manager
Royals (7)	39	24	.619	—	Carlos Tosca
Indians (5)	38	25	.603	1	Billy Williams
Astros (18)	28	35	.444	11	Julio Linares
Reds (17)	21	42	.333	18	Sam Mejias

South Standings	W	L	Pct.	GB	Manager
Yankees (10)	45	18	.714	—	Brian Butterfield
Dodgers (19)	43	20	.683	2	Jose Alvarez
White Sox (4)	42	21	.667	3	Art Kusyner
Rangers (13)	35	28	.556	10	Chino Cadahia

Pirates (23)	26	37	.413	19	Julio Garcia
Expos (20)	24	39	.381	21	Dave Jauss
Mets (21)	21	42	.333	24	John Tamargo
Braves (15)	16	47	.254	29	Pedro Gonzalez

Games played at Bradenton, Sarasota, Baseball City and Kissimmee, Florida.

Playoff: Yankees 1 game, Royals 0.

All-Star Team: 1B-Marc Tepper, Indians; **2B**-Javier Murillo, Indians; **3B**-Dennis Walker, White Sox; **SS**-Dino Ebel, Dodgers; **OF**-Brian Davis, White Sox; Mike Rhodes, Yankees; Scott Tedder, White Sox; **C**-James Harris, Mets; **P**-Lenny Brutcher, White Sox; Brett Marshall, White Sox; **Manager**-Brian Butterfield, Yankees.

BA: Scott Tedder, White Sox, .341
Runs: Darrin Campbell, Indians, 45
Hits: Scott Tedder, White Sox, 73
RBIs: Marc Tepper, Indians, 45
HRs: Steve Lemuth, Expos, 8
Wins: Robin Nina, Dodgers, 10
SOs: Cullen Hartzog, Yankees, 82
ERA: Garland Kiser, Indians, 1.29

R Pioneer League
President: Ralph C. Nelles

North Standings	W	L	Pct.	GB	Attend.	Manager
Great Falls Dodgers (19)	52	17	.754	—	71,497	Tim Johnson
Helena Brewers (8)	41	29	.586	11½	26,892	Dusty Rhodes
Billings Mustangs (17)	35	34	.507	17	87,762	Dave Keller
Medicine Hat Blue Jays (14)	12	58	.171	40½	10,553	Ralph "Rocket" Wheeler

South Standings	W	L	Pct.	GB	Attend.	Manager
Butte Copper Kings (13)	44	26	.629	—	28,338	Bump Wills
Salt Lake City Trappers (13)	41	29	.586	3	176,217	Barry Moss
Idaho Falls Braves (15)	28	42	.400	16	64,672	Jim Procopio
Pocatello Giants (26)	26	44	.371	18	20,785	Jack Hiatt

Playoff: Great Falls 3 games, Butte 2.

All-Star Team: 1B-Rob Maurer, Butte; **2B**-Kelly Zane, Salt Lake City; **3B**-Michael Songini, Billings; **SS**-Jose Offerman, Great Falls; **OF**-Trey McCoy, Butte; Ben Colvard, Billings; Donovan Campbell, Idaho Falls; **C**-Bert Heffernan, Helena; **DH**-Mando Verdugo, Salt Lake City; **P**-Sean Snedeker, Great Falls; Richard Nowak, Medicine Hat; Steve Reed, Pocatello; **Manager**-Tim Johnson, Great Falls.

BA: Rob Maurer, Butte, .391
Runs: Rod Morris, Butte, 77
Hits: Jerry Brooks, Great Falls, 99
RBIs: Trey McCoy, Butte, 80
HRs: Mando Verdugo, Salt Lake City, 17
Wins: Willie Ambos, Salt Lake City, 9
SOs: Jeff Hartsock, Great Falls, 108
ERA: Sean Snedeker, Great Falls, 2.20

1988 Interleague Post Season Play

World Series
Los Angeles (National) 4 games, Oakland (American) 1

AAA Classic
Indianapolis (American Association) 4 games, Rochester (International) 2

1988 Major League Farm Systems

American League
1 Baltimore (5): Rochester, Charlotte, Hagerstown, Erie, Bluefield.
2 Boston (6): Pawtucket, New Britain, Lynchburg, Winter Haven, Elmira, Arizona.
3 California (5): Edmonton, Midland, Palm Springs, Quad City, Bend.
4 Chicago (6): Vancouver, Birmingham, Tampa, South Bend, Utica, Gulf Coast.
5 Cleveland (6): Colorado Springs, Williamsport, Kinston, Waterloo, Burlington (NC), Gulf Coast.
6 Detroit (5): Toledo, Glens Falls, Lakeland, Fayetteville, Bristol.
7 Kansas City (6): Omaha, Memphis, Baseball City, Appleton, Eugene, Gulf Coast.
8 Milwaukee (6): Denver, El Paso, Stockton, Beloit, Helena, Arizona.
9 Minnesota (6): Portland, Orlando, Visalia, Kenosha, Elizabethton.
10 New York (6): Columbus (OH), Albany-Colonie, Prince William, Ft. Lauderdale, Oneonta, Gulf Coast.
11 Oakland (6): Tacoma, Huntsville, Modesto, Madison, Southern Oregon, Arizona.
12 Seattle (6): Calgary, Vermont, San Bernardino, Wausau, Bellingham, Arizona.
13 Texas (6): Oklahoma City, Tulsa, Port Charlotte, Gastonia, Butte, Gulf Coast.
14 Toronto (6): Syracuse, Knoxville, Dunedin, Myrtle Beach, St. Catharines, Medicine Hat.

Co-op (x): Fresno, Reno, Virginia.
Independent: Miami, Boise, Salt Lake City.

National League
15 Atlanta (8): Richmond, Greenville, Durham, Burlington (IA), Sumter, Pulaski, Idaho Falls, Gulf Coast.
16 Chicago (7): Iowa, Pittsfield, Winston-Salem, Charleston (WV), Peoria, Geneva, Wytheville.
17 Cincinnati (6): Nashville, Chattanooga, Cedar Rapids, Greensboro, Billings, Gulf Coast.
18 Houston (6): Tucson, Columbus (GA), Osceola, Asheville, Auburn, Gulf Coast.
19 Los Angeles (7): Albuquerque, San Antonio, Vero Beach, Bakersfield, Salem (OR), Great Falls, Gulf Coast.
20 Montreal (6): Indianapolis, Jacksonville, West Palm Beach, Rockford, Jamestown, Gulf Coast.
21 New York (7): Tidewater, Jackson, St. Lucie, Columbia, Little Falls, Kingsport, Gulf Coast.
22 Philadelphia (6): Maine, Reading, Clearwater, Spartanburg, Batavia, Martinsville.
23 Pittsburgh (7): Buffalo, Harrisburg, Salem (VA), Augusta, Watertown, Princeton, Gulf Coast.
24 St. Louis (7): Louisville, Arkansas, St. Petersburg, Springfield, Savannah, Hamilton, Johnson City.
25 San Diego (6): Las Vegas, Wichita, Riverside, Charleston (SC), Spokane, Arizona.
26 San Francisco (6): Phoenix, Shreveport, San Jose, Clinton, Everett, Pocatello.

1988 No-Hitters

Date	Pitcher	Team	League	Opponent	Score
4-13	Bill Kazmierczak	Winston-Salem	Carolina	Salem	1-0 (8)
4-15	Robert Rowen/				
	Atsushi Tagi	Fresno	California	Stockton	3-1 (11)
4-17	Cesar Mejia	Glens Falls	Eastern	Albany-Colonie	3-0
5-1	Vince Horsman/				
	Robert Watts	Dunedin	Florida State	Miami	5-1
5-10	Pat Hentgen/Willie Blair/				
	Enrique Burgos	Dunedin	Florida State	Osceola	2-1
5-14	Darrin Reichle	Charleston (SC)	South Atlantic	Charleston (WV)	9-0
5-15	Isidro Morales	San Luis Potosi	Mexican	Tabasco	2-0 (7)
5-18	Bill Risley	Greensboro	South Atlantic	Columbia	4-0
5-20	Scott Scudder	Cedar Rapids	Midwest	Wausau	4-0
5-20	Bill Kazmierczak	Winston-Salem	Carolina	Virginia	11-0
5-30	Darrin Reichle	Charleston (SC)	South Atlantic	Fayetteville	1-0
6-8	Scott Nielsen	Columbus	International	Maine	3-0
6-20	Luis Aquino	Omaha	American Assoc.	Columbus	2-0
6-23	Mike Redding	Kenosha	Midwest	Quad City	3-0
6-26	Paul Abbott	Visalia	California	Palm Springs	3-0 (7)
6-27	John Mitchell	Tidewater	International	Indianapolis	4-0 (P, 7)
7-7	Terry Griffin	Little Falls	New York-Penn.	Utica	1-0
7-8	Marcos Betances	Bristol	Appalachian	Pulaski	2-0
7-8	Kris Roth	Pittsfield	Eastern	Harrisburg	3-0
7-13	Jose Ventura	White Sox	Gulf Coast	Pirates	5-0
7-18	Jeff Hart	Padres	Arizona	Brewers	3-0
7-28	Marvin Freeman	Maine	International	Richmond	6-0 (7)
7-31	Freddie Arroyo	MC Diablos Rojos	Mexican	Campeche	1-2 (8)
8-6	Randy Johnson/				
	Pat Pacillo	Indianapolis	American Assoc.	Nashville	0-1
8-7	Jack Armstrong	Nashville	American Assoc.	Indianapolis	4-0
8-9	Michael Aspray	Peoria	Midwest	Waterloo	5-0
8-10	Allen Collins	West Palm Beach	Florida State	Miami	3-0
8-12	Dean Hartgraves	Asheville	South Atlantic	Myrtle Beach	3-0
8-18	Andrew Carter	Spartanburg	South Atlantic	Augusta	4-0
8-21	Erik Hanson	Calgary	Pacific Coast	Las Vegas	5-0 (7)
8-22	Mike Girouard	South Bend	Midwest	Appleton	5-1
8-23	Kevin MacLeod/				
	Tony Floyd	Southern Oregon	Northwest	Everett	4-1
8-24	Marty Willis	Brewers	Arizona	Red Sox/Mariners	7-0 (7)
9-16	Tom Browning	Cincinnati	National	Los Angeles	1-0 (P)

Number in parentheses indicates innings if other than nine; "P" indicates perfect game.

THIS DATE IN MINOR LEAGUE HISTORY

January 12, 1988, Johnny Johnson, President of the National Association, died after a long battle with cancer. He was 66.

March 16, 1988, Arnold "Jigger" Statz, 90, an outfielder who played in 683 major league games, but spent the bulk of his career with the Los Angeles Angels, Pacific Coast League, died in Corona Del Mar, California. Statz played in 3,473 professional baseball games, batting 13,242 times in his professional career. The 5-foot-7, 145-pound contact hitter off the Holy Cross College campus compiled a composite average of .309 in the major and minor leagues. He played a record 18 years for one minor league club, the Los Angeles Angels. He had 3,356 minor league hits for a batting average of .315. Statz had ten 200-hit seasons.

April 14, 1988, Pilot Field, built at a cost of $43 million, opened in downtown Buffalo. A sellout crowd in excess of 19,000 was on hand.

April 26, 1988, Sal Artiaga was elected president of the National Association. Artiaga, 41, a former Reds farm administrator, had been administrator of the National Association for six years.

April 27, 1988, Alphonse "Tommy" Thomas, 88, a lefthanded pitcher who compiled a 117-128 record with five major league clubs in the 1920s and 1930s but enjoyed his greatest success as a pitcher, manager and general manager with the Baltimore clubs of the International League, died in York County, Pennsylvania. Thomas pitched for five of the seven successive pennant winners put together by manager Jack Dunn of the Orioles, winning 32 games in 1925.

May 20, 1988, Winston-Salem's Bill Kazmierczak became the first pitcher in the history of the Carolina League to throw two no-hitters in one season.

June 18, 1988, Colorado Springs of the Pacific Coast League played its first home game in Sky Sox Stadium after playing its first eight home games in Yuma, Arizona, and the next 22 at a high school park in Colorado Springs.

June 20, 1988, Ron Simms, an infielder for the Gulf Coast League Braves, was blinded in his left eye when he was hit by a pitch in his first professional game. The eye had to be removed.

June 20, 1988, The Arizona League, a complex league modeled after the Gulf Coast League, began play. Games were played in the morning at spring training complexes and no admission was charged.

June 24, 1988, Bluefield defeated Burlington 3-2, in a 27-inning Appalachian League contest. The game lasted eight hours and 15 minutes, ending at 3:27 AM.

June 25, 1988, The movie "Bull Durham" opened. Filmed primarily at Durham (NC) Athletic Park and using minor league baseball as its backdrop, the film would become one of 1988's major hits.

July 6, 1988, William "Bill" Sisler, 87, a player, coach and manager in the minor leagues from 1924 to 1950, died in St. Petersburg, Florida. Sisler was a pitcher-outfielder who played with more than 25 different minor league clubs and reportedly signed more than 50 minor league contracts. He later operated summer youth baseball schools in Canada, Delaware and Florida.

July 9, 1988, The Geneva Cubs snapped an 18-game New York-Pennsylvania League losing streak with a 5-2 victory over Watertown.

July 13, 1988, The first Triple-A All-Star Game, played between the stars of the National League AAA affiliates and those of the American League AAA affiliates, was held in Buffalo. Before a crowd of 19,500, the American League won 2-1.

August 16, 1988, Burlington forfeited the second game of a doubleheader to Wytheville when Manager Mike Bucci pulled his club off the field, although the Indians were leading 1-0. Several beanballs had been thrown and a Wytheville coach had threatened star shortstop Mark Lewis, the second pick in the 1988 draft, saying Lewis would not "walk off the field under his own power."

September 1, 1988, Buffalo ended its season with a new minor league single season attendance record. A total of 1,147,651 fans attended Bisons games, breaking the prior mark of 1,052,438 set by Louisville in 1983.

September 22, 1988, Barney Deary, adminstrator of baseball's Umpire Development Program since 1969, died of a heart attack at age 62.

1989

American League
President: Dr. Robert W. Brown

East Standings	W	L	Pct.	GB	Attend.	Manager
Toronto Blue Jays	89	73	.549	—	3,375,883	Jimy Williams/Cito Gaston
Baltimore Orioles	87	75	.537	2	2,535,208	Frank Robinson
Boston Red Sox	83	79	.512	6	2,510,012	Joe Morgan
Milwaukee Brewers	81	81	.500	8	1,970,735	Tom Trebelhorn
New York Yankees	74	87	.460	14½	2,170,485	Dallas Green/Bucky Dent
Cleveland Indians	73	89	.451	16	1,285,542	Doc Edwards/John Hart
Detroit Tigers	59	103	.364	30	1,543,656	Sparky Anderson

West Standings	W	L	Pct.	GB	Attend.	Manager
Oakland Athletics	99	63	.611	—	2,667,225	Tony LaRussa
Kansas City Royals	92	70	.568	7	2,477,700	John Wathan
California Angels	91	71	.562	8	2,647,291	Doug Rader
Texas Rangers	83	79	.512	16	2,043,993	Bobby Valentine
Minnesota Twins	80	82	.494	19	2,277,438	Tom Kelly
Seattle Mariners	73	89	.451	26	1,298,443	Jim Lefebvre
Chicago White Sox	69	92	.429	29½	1,045,651	Jeff Torborg

Playoff: Oakland 4 games, Toronto 1.

BA: Kirby Puckett, Minnesota, .339
Runs: Rickey Henderson, New York/Oakland, 113
Wade Boggs, Boston, 113
Hits: Kirby Puckett, Minnesota, 215
RBIs: Ruben Sierra, Texas, 119
HRs: Fred McGriff, Toronto, 36
Wins: Bret Saberhagen, Kansas City, 23
SOs: Nolan Ryan, Texas, 301
ERA: Bret Saberhagen, Kansas City, 2.16
Pct: Bret Saberhagen, Kansas City, .793, 23-6
Saves: Jeff Russell, Texas, 38

National League
President: William White

East Standings	W	L	Pct.	GB	Attend.	Manager
Chicago Cubs	93	69	.574	—	2,491,942	Don Zimmer
New York Mets	87	75	.537	6	2,918,710	Davey Johnson
St. Louis Cardinals	86	76	.531	7	3,080,980	Whitey Herzog
Montreal Expos	81	81	.500	12	1,783,533	Buck Rodgers
Pittsburgh Pirates	74	88	.457	19	1,374,141	Jim Leyland
Philadelphia Phillies	67	95	.414	26	1,861,985	Nick Leyva

West Standings	W	L	Pct.	GB	Attend.	Manager
San Francisco Giants	92	70	.568	—	2,059,701	Roger Craig
San Diego Padres	89	73	.549	3	2,009,031	Jack McKeon
Houston Astros	86	76	.531	6	1,834,908	Art Howe
Los Angeles Dodgers	77	83	.481	14	2,944,653	Tom Lasorda
Cincinnati Reds	75	87	.463	17	1,979,320	Pete Rose/Tommy Helms
Atlanta Braves	63	97	.394	28	984,930	Russ Nixon

Playoff: San Francisco 4 games, Chicago 1.

BA: Tony Gwynn, San Diego, .336
Runs: Howard Johnson, New York, 104
Ryne Sandberg, Chicago, 104
Will Clark, San Francisco, 104
Hits: Tony Gwynn, San Diego, 203
RBIs: Kevin Mitchell, San Francisco, 125
HRs: Kevin Mitchell, San Francisco, 47
Wins: Mike Scott, Houston, 20
SOs: Jose DeLeon, St. Louis, 201
ERA: Scott Garrelts, San Francisco, 2.28
Pct: Mike Bielecki, Chicago, .720, 18-7
Saves: Mark Davis, San Diego, 44

AAA American Association
President: Joe Ryan

East Standings	W	L	Pct.	GB	Attend.	Manager
Indianapolis Indians (20)	87	59	.596	—	287,595	Tom Runnells
Buffalo Bisons (23)	80	62	.563	5	1,116,441	Terry Collins
Nashville Sounds (17)	74	72	.507	13	441,500	Frank Lucchesi
Louisville Redbirds (24)	71	74	.490	15½	580,270	Mike Jorgensen

West Standings	W	L	Pct.	GB	Attend.	Manager
Omaha Royals (7)	74	72	.507	—	314,683	Sal Rende
Denver Zephyrs (8)	69	77	.473	5	335,082	Dave Machemer
Iowa Cubs (16)	62	82	.431	11	252,289	Pete Mackanin
Oklahoma City 89ers (13)	59	86	.407	14½	250,850	Jim Skaalen

Played an interlocking schedule with the International League known as AAA Alliance.

Playoff: Indianapolis 3 games, Omaha 2.

All-Star Team: 1B-Luis de los Santos, Omaha; 2B-Junior Noboa, Indianapolis; 3B-Scott Coolbaugh, Oklahoma City; SS-Jeff Huson, Indianapolis; OF-Skeeter Barnes, Nashville; Greg Vaughn, Denver; Larry Walker, Indianapolis; C-Todd Zeile, Louisville; DH-Steve Henderson, Buffalo; P-Mark Gardner, Indianapolis; Morris Madden, Buffalo; MVP-Greg Vaughn, Denver; Pitcher of the Year-Mark Gardner, Indianapolis; Manager -Tom Runnells, Indianapolis.

BA: Junior Noboa, Indianapolis, .340
Runs: Nick Capra, Omaha, 84
Hits: Junior Noboa, Indianapolis, 159
RBIs: Greg Vaughn, Denver, 92
HRs: Greg Vaughn, Denver, 26
Wins: Steve Fireovid, Omaha, 13
Jack Armstrong, Nashville, 13
Kevin Blankenship, Iowa, 13
Bob Tewksbury, Louisville, 13
SOs: Mark Gardner, Indianapolis, 175
ERA: Rich Thompson, Indianapolis, 2.06

AAA International League
President: Harold Cooper

East Standings	W	L	Pct.	GB	Attend.	Manager
Syracuse Chiefs (14)	83	62	.572	—	226,244	Bob Bailor
Rochester Red Wings (1)	72	73	.497	11	284,394	Greg Biagini
Scranton-Wilkes-Barre Red Barons (22)	64	79	.448	18	434,106	Bill Dancy
Pawtucket Red Sox (2)	62	84	.425	21½	271,025	Ed Nottle

West Standings	W	L	Pct.	GB	Attend.	Manager
Richmond Braves (15)	81	65	.555	—	424,265	Jim Beauchamp
Columbus Clippers (10)	77	69	.527	4	504,224	Bucky Dent/Rick Down
Tidewater Tides (21)	77	69	.527	4	210,258	Mike Cubbage
Toledo Mud Hens (6)	69	76	.476	11½	172,454	John Wockenfuss

Played an interlocking schedule with the American Association known as AAA Alliance.

Playoff: Richmond 3 games, Syracuse 1.

All-Star Team: 1B-Hal Morris, Columbus; 2B-Mark Lemke, Richmond; 3B-Tom O'Malley, Tidewater; SS-Randy Velarde, Columbus; OF-Butch Davis, Rochester; Glenallen Hill, Syracuse; Greg Tubbs, Richmond; C-Francisco Cabrera, Syracuse/Richmond; DH-Kevin Maas, Columbus; P-Alex Sanchez, Syracuse; Mark Eichhorn, Richmond; MVP-Tom O'Malley, Tidewater; Pitcher of the Year-Alex Sanchez, Syracuse; Manager-Bob Bailor, Syracuse.

BA: Hal Morris, Columbus, .326
Runs: Glenallen Hill, Syracuse, 86
Hits: Glenallen Hill, Syracuse, 155
RBIs: Tom O'Malley, Tidewater, 84
HRs: Glenallen Hill, Syracuse, 21
Wins: Gary Eave, Richmond, 13
Alex Sanchez, Syracuse, 13
Curt Schilling, Rochester, 13
SOs: Kent Mercker, Richmond, 144
ERA: Jose Nunez, Syracuse, 2.21

AAA Mexican League
President: Pedro Treto Cisneros

North Standings	W	L	Pct.	GB	Attend.	Manager
Dos Laredos Tecolotes	82	50	.621	—	164,525	Jose Guerrero
Union Laguna Algodoneros	73	59	.553	9	152,831	Marco Antonio Vazquez
Saltillo Saraperos	70	59	.543	10½	175,123	Marcelo Juarez/Jose Pena
Monterrey Sultanes	67	65	.508	15	131,213	Miguel Sotelo/Leobardo Figueroa
San Luis Potosi Tuneros	63	67	.485	18	195,230	Gregorio Luque
Monclova Acereros	58	73	.443	23½	120,515	Alfredo Rios
Monterrey Industriales	50	80	.385	31	110,213	Manuel Magallon/Miguel Solis/Carlos Paz/Juan Navarrete

South Standings	W	L	Pct.	GB	Attend.	Manager
Campeche Pirates	75	52	.591	—	196,515	Rodolfo Sandoval
Leon Bravos	73	57	.562	3½	135,318	Francisco Estrada
Yucatan Leones	69	59	.539	6½	310,715	Roberto Castellon/Roberto Mendez
Mexico City Diablos Rojos	68	63	.519	9	136,215	Ben Reyes
Mexico City Tigres	59	71	.454	17½	120,944	Alfredo Ortiz/Domingo Rivera/Javier Espinoza
Tabasco Ganaderos	57	71	.445	18½	131,513	Ramon Montoya
Aguascalientes Rieleros	46	84	.354	30½	91,530	Aurelio Monteagudo

Playoffs: Dos Laredos 4 games, Monterrey 3; Saltillo 4 games, Union Laguna 1; Campeche 4 games, MC Diablos Rojos 0; Yucatan 4 games, Leon 2. Dos Laredos 4 games, Saltillo 3; Yucatan 4 games, Campeche 2.
Finals: Dos Laredos 4 games, Yucatan 2.

BA: Willie Aikens, Leon, .395
Runs: Willie Aikens, Leon, 108
Mike Cole, Tabasco, 108
Hits: Donald Cosey, Monclova, 183
RBIs: Willie Aikens, Leon, 131
HRs: Leo Hernandez, Campeche, 39
Wins: Ildefonso Velazquez, Campeche, 20
SOs: Adolfo Navarro, Monterrey, 150
ERA: Mercedes Esquer, Yucatan, 1.98

AAA Pacific Coast League
President: Bill Cutler

North Standings	W	L	Pct.	GB	Attend.	Manager
Tacoma Tigers (11)	77	66	.538	—	313,007	Brad Fischer
Vancouver Canadians*(4)	73	69	.514	3½	281,812	Marv Foley
Portland Beavers (9)	72	72	.500	5½	188,459	Phil Roof
Calgary Cannons**(12)	70	72	.493	6½	316,616	Rich Morales
Edmonton Trappers (3)	65	76	.461	11	230,728	Tom Kotchman

*Won first-half   **Won second-half   ***Won both halves
Numbers after nicknames indicate farm system.
Affiliation listed at end of each year.

593

South Standings

	W	L	Pct.	GB	Attend.	Manager
Albuquerque Dukes**(19)	80	62	.563	—	318,896	Kevin Kennedy
Colorado Springs Sky Sox*(5)	78	64	.549	2	203,955	Mike Hargrove
Las Vegas Stars (25)	74	69	.517	6½	315,517	Steve Smith
Phoenix Firebirds (26)	67	76	.469	13½	199,157	Gordy MacKenzie
Tucson Toros (18)	56	86	.394	24	186,270	Bob Skinner

Playoffs: Albuquerque 3 games, Colorado Springs 2; Vancouver 3 games, Calgary 0.
Finals: Vancouver 3 games, Albuquerque 1.

All-Star Team: 1B-Kelvin Torve, Portland; **2B**-Joey Cora, Las Vegas; **3B**-Matt Williams, Phoenix; **SS**-Paul Zuvella, Colorado Springs; **OF**-Bruce Fields, Calgary; Jerald Clark, Las Vegas; Mike Huff, Albuquerque; **C**-Sandy Alomar, Jr., Las Vegas; **DH**-Jim Wilson, Calgary; **P**-Ramon Martinez, Albuquerque; Bryan Clark, Tacoma; Steve Olin, Colorado Springs; **MVP**-Sandy Alomar, Jr., Las Vegas; **Manager**-Mike Hargrove, Colorado Springs.

BA: Bruce Fields, Calgary, .351
Runs: Doug Jennings, Tacoma, 99
Hits: Jim Wilson, Calgary, 163
RBIs: Jim Wilson, Calgary, 133
HRs: Denny Gonzalez, Colorado Springs, 27
Wins: Bryan Clark, Tacoma, 15
SOs: Mike Fetters, Edmonton, 144
ERA: Jeff Bittiger, Vancouver, 2.12

AA Eastern League
President: Charles E. Eshbach

Standings	W	L	Pct.	GB	Attend.	Manager
Albany-Colonie Yankees (10)	92	48	.657	—	192,862	Buck Showalter
Harrisburg Senators (23)	71	65	.522	19	200,196	Dave Trembley
Canton-Akron Indians (5)	70	69	.504	21½	203,986	Bob Molinaro
Reading Phillies (22)	68	71	.489	23½	178,734	Mike Hart
Hagerstown Suns (1)	67	72	.482	24½	161,630	Jim Schaffer
London Tigers (6)	63	76	.453	28½	167,679	Chris Chambliss
Williamsport Bills (12)	63	77	.450	29	66,767	Jay Ward
New Britain Red Sox (2)	60	76	.441	30	100,943	Butch Hobson

Playoffs: Albany-Colonie 3 games, Reading 1; Harrisburg 3 games, Canton 2.
Finals: Albany-Colonie 3 games, Harrisburg 1.

All-Star Team: 1B-Rob Sepanek, Albany-Colonie; **2B**-Andy Stankiewicz, Albany-Colonie; **3B**-Leo Gomez, Hagerstown; **SS**-Travis Fryman, London; **OF**-Wes Chamberlain, Harrisburg; Beau Allred, Canton-Akron; Joey Belle, Canton-Akron; **C**-None; **DH**-Troy Neel, Canton-Akron; **P**-Rodney Imes, Albany-Colonie; Steve Adkins, Albany-Colonie; Daryl Irvine, New Britain; **MVP**-Wes Chamberlain, Harrisburg; **Pitcher of the Year**-Rodney Imes, Albany-Colonie; **Manager**-Buck Showalter, Albany-Colonie.

BA: Jim Leyritz, Albany-Colonie, .315
Runs: Andy Stankiewicz, Albany-Colonie, 74
Hits: Wes Chamberlain, Harrisburg, 144
RBIs: Wes Chamberlain, Harrisburg, 87
HRs: Rob Sepanek, Albany-Colonie, 22
Wins: Rodney Imes, Albany-Colonie, 177
SOs: Scott Kamieniecki, Albany-Colonie, 140
ERA: Steve Adkins, Albany-Colonie, 2.07

AA Southern League
President: Jimmy Bragan

East Standings	W	L	Pct.	GB	Attend.	Manager
Orlando Twins*(9)	79	65	.549	—	93,034	Ron Gardenhire
Greenville Braves**(15)	70	69	.504	6½	208,117	Buddy Bailey
Columbus Mudcats (18)	71	72	.497	7½	95,689	Tom Wiedenbauer
Charlotte Knights (16)	70	73	.490	8½	157,720	Jim Essian
Jacksonville Expos (20)	68	76	.472	11	220,803	Alan Bannister

West Standings	W	L	Pct.	GB	Attend.	Manager
Birmingham Barons*(4)	88	55	.615	—	270,793	Ken Berry
Huntsville Stars**(11)	82	61	.573	6	217,948	Jeff Newman
Knoxville Blue Jays (14)	67	76	.469	21	69,776	Barry Foote
Chattanooga Lookouts (17)	58	81	.417	28	156,677	Jim Tracy
Memphis Chicks (7)	59	84	.413	29	175,334	Jeff Cox

Playoffs: Birmingham 3 games, Huntsville 1; Greenville 3 games, Orlando 1.
Finals: Birmingham 3 games, Greenville 0.

All-Star Team: 1B-Paul Sorrento, Orlando; **2B**-Greg Smith, Charlotte; **3B**-Robin Ventura, Birmingham; **SS**-Scott Leius, Orlando; **OF**-Eric Anthony, Columbus; Harvey Pulliam, Memphis; Marquis Grissom, Jacksonville; Derrick May, Charlotte; Dann Howitt, Huntsville; **C**-Kelly Mann, Charlotte; Jimmy Kremers, Greenville; **DH**-Bob Hamelin, Memphis; **P**-Mark Guthrie, Orlando; Wayne Edwards, Birmingham; Darryl Kile, Columbus; Joe Klink, Huntsville; **MVP**-Eric Anthony, Columbus; **Pitcher of the Year**-Laddie Renfroe, Charlotte; **Manager**-Jeff Newman, Huntsville.

BA: Scott Leius, Orlando, .303
Runs: Richie Amaral, Birmingham, 90
Hits: Craig Grebeck, Birmingham, 153
RBIs: Paul Sorrento, Orlando, 112
HRs: Eric Anthony, Columbus, 28
Wins: Laddie Renfroe, Charlotte, 19
SOs: Shawn Boskie, Charlotte, 164
ERA: Pete Delkus, Orlando, 1.87

AA Texas League
President: Carl Sawatski

East Standings	W	L	Pct.	GB	Attend.	Manager
Arkansas Travelers*(24)	79	56	.585	—	296,428	Gaylen Pitts
Shreveport Captains*(26)	75	61	.551	4½	210,669	Bill Evers
Tulsa Drillers (13)	73	63	.537	6½	218,755	Tommy Thompson
Jackson Mets (21)	61	74	.452	18	87,153	Steve Swisher

West Standings	W	L	Pct.	GB	Attend.	Manager
Wichita Wranglers***(25)	73	63	.537	—	176,424	Pat Kelly
Midland Angels (3)	70	66	.515	3	135,518	Max Oliveras
El Paso Diablos (8)	63	73	.463	10	228,261	Marc Bombard
San Antonio Missions (19)	49	87	.360	24	158,402	John Shoemaker

Playoff: Arkansas 2 games, Shreveport 0.
Finals: Arkansas 4 games, Wichita 3.

All-Star Team: 1B-Chris Cron, Midland; **2B**-Geronimo Pena, Arkansas; **3B**-Dean Palmer, Tulsa; **SS**-Gary DiSarcina, Midland; **OF**-Ray Lankford, Arkansas; Juan Gonzalez, Tulsa; Warren Newson, Wichita; **C**-Tim McIntosh, El Paso; Carlos Hernandez, San Antonio; **DH**-Bobby Rose, Midland; **Util**-Craig Colbert, Shreveport; **P**-Andy Benes, Wichita; Omar Olivares, Arkansas; Mike Perez, Arkansas; Dave Osteen, Arkansas; Julio Valera, Jackson; **MVP**-Ray Lankford, Arkansas; **Pitcher of the Year**-Andy Benes, Wichita; **Manager**-Gaylen Pitts, Arkansas.

BA: Bobby Rose, Midland, .359
Runs: Bernard Gilkey, Arkansas, 104
Hits: Ray Lankford, Arkansas, 158
RBIs: Chris Cron, Midland, 103
HRs: Dean Palmer, Tulsa, 25
Wins: Dave Osteen, Arkansas, 15
SOs: Chris Nichting, San Antonio, 136
ERA: Julio Valera, Jackson, 2.49
Saves: Mike Perez, Arkansas, 33

A California League
President: Joe Gagliardi

North Standings	W	L	Pct.	GB	Attend.	Manager
Stockton Ports**(8)	89	53	.627	—	72,734	Dave Huppert
San Jose Giants*(26)	81	61	.570	8	108,458	Duane Espy
Reno Silver Sox	68	74	.479	21	75,842	Eli Grba
Modesto A's (11)	56	86	.394	33	87,256	Lenn Sakata/Ted Kubiak
Salinas Spurs (x)	51	91	.359	38	47,609	Tim Ireland

South Standings	W	L	Pct.	GB	Attend.	Manager
San Bernardino Spirit**(12)	83	59	.585	—	184,791	Ralph Dick
Bakersfield Dodgers*(19)	82	60	.577	1	123,572	Tim Johnson
Visalia Oaks (9)	76	66	.535	7	83,946	Scott Ullger
Riverside Red Wave (25)	64	78	.451	19	80,154	Steve Lubratich
Palm Springs Angels (3)	60	82	.423	23	69,129	Bill Lachemann

Playoffs: Bakersfield 3 games, San Bernardino 1; Stockton 3 games, San Jose 2.
Finals: Bakersfield 3 games, Stockton 0.

All-Star Team: 1B-John Jaha, Stockton; Eric Karros, Bakersfield; **2B**-Steve Hecht, San Jose; **3B**-Ernie Carr, Bakersfield; **SS**-Jose Offerman, Bakersfield; **OF**-Braulio Castillo, Bakersfield; Jerry Brooks, Bakersfield; Mike Humphreys, Riverside; **C**-Jim Campanis, San Bernardino; **DH**-Ruben Gonzalez, San Bernardino; **P**-Steve Lienhard, San Jose; Jim Blueberg, San Bernardino; Jim Wray, Bakersfield; Rafael Valdez, Riverside; **MVP**-John Jaha, Stockton; **Pitcher of the Year**-Steve Lienhard, San Jose; **Manager**-Duane Espy, San Jose.

BA: Ruben Gonzalez, San Bernardino, .308
Runs: Jarvis Brown, Visalia, 95
Hits: Eric Karros, Bakersfield, 165
RBIs: Ruben Gonzalez, San Bernardino, 101
HRs: Ruben Gonzalez, San Bernardino, 27
Wins: Steve Sparks, Stockton, 13
Joe Slusarski, Modesto, 13
Johnny Ard, Visalia, 13
SOs: Willie Banks, Visalia, 173
ERA: Steve Lienhard, San Jose, 1.79

A Carolina League
President: John Hopkins

North Standings	W	L	Pct.	GB	Attend.	Manager
Frederick Keys (1)	73	65	.529	—	165,930	Jerry Narron
Prince William Cannons**(10)	72	66	.522	1	175,077	Mark Weidemaier/Stump Merrill
Lynchburg Red Sox*(2)	70	66	.515	2	74,375	Gary Allenson
Salem Buccaneers (23)	63	75	.457	10	121,581	Rocky Bridges

South Standings	W	L	Pct.	GB	Attend.	Manager
Durham Bulls***(15)	84	54	.609	—	272,202	Grady Little
Kinston Indians (5)	76	60	.559	7	88,154	Ken Bolek
Winston-Salem Spirits (16)	64	71	.474	18½	89,360	Jay Loviglio
Peninsula Pilots	44	89	.331	37½	20,059	Jim Thrift

Playoff: Prince William 2 games, Lynchburg 1.
Finals: Prince William 3 games, Durham 1.

All-Star Team: 1B-David Segui, Frederick; **2B**-Luis Mercedes, Frederick; **3B**-John Wehner, Salem; **SS**-Mark Lewis, Kinston; **OF**-Phil Plantier, Lynchburg; Moises Alou, Salem; Andy Tomberlin, Durham; Al Martin, Durham; **C**-Brian Deak, Durham; **DH**-Don Sparks, Prince William; **P**-Mike Draper, Prince William; Pat Gomez, Winston-Salem; Randy Tomlin, Salem; **MVP**-Phil Plantier, Lynchburg; **Pitcher of the Year**-Charles Nagy, Kinston; **Manager**-Grady Little, Durham.

BA: Luis Mercedes, Frederick, .309
Runs: Al Martin, Durham, 84
Hits: John Wehner, Salem, 155
RBIs: Phil Plantier, Lynchburg, 105
HRs: Phil Plantier, Lynchburg, 27
Wins: Mike Draper, Prince William, 14
SOs: Derek Livernois, Lynchburg, 151
ERA: Ray Mullino, Winston-Salem, 2.32

A Florida State League
President: George MacDonald, Jr.

East Standings	W	L	Pct.	GB	Attend.	Manager
St. Lucie Mets***(21)	79	55	.589	—	66,041	Clint Hurdle
West Palm Beach Expos (20)	74	64	.536	7	84,316	Felipe Alou
Vero Beach Dodgers (19)	69	66	.511	10½	87,178	Joe Alvarez
Ft. Lauderdale Yankees (10)	61	77	.442	20	43,307	Clete Boyer
Miami Miracle	43	91	.321	36	14,972	Jim Gattis

West Standings	W	L	Pct.	GB	Attend.	Manager
Sarasota White Sox**(4)	79	57	.581	—	52,061	Tony Franklin
St. Petersburg Cardinals (24)	75	64	.540	5½	202,383	Dave Bialas
Charlotte Rangers*(13)	75	64	.540	5½	122,060	Bobby Jones

	W	L	Pct.	GB	Attend.	Manager
Dunedin Blue Jays (14)	69	71	.493	12	41,231	Doug Ault
Clearwater Phillies (22)	57	79	.419	22	68,591	Glenn Gulliver

Central Standings	W	L	Pct.	GB	Attend.	Manager
Lakeland Tigers**(6)	77	59	.566	—	54,409	John Lipon
Baseball City Royals*(7)	78	61	.561	½	39,220	Luis Silverio
Osceola Astros (18)	72	65	.526	5½	53,566	Rick Sweet
Winter Haven Red Sox (2)	52	87	.374	26½	28,009	Dave Holt

Playoffs: Charlotte 2 games, Sarasota 1; St. Petersburg 2 games, Baseball City 0. Charlotte 2 games, St. Lucie 1; St. Petersburg 2 games, Lakeland 1.
Finals: Charlotte 2 games, St. Petersburg 1.

All-Star Team: 1B-Henry Rodriguez, Vero Beach; **2B**-Paco Burgos, Charlotte; **3B**-Chris Donnels, St. Lucie; **SS**-Wil Cordero, West Palm Beach; **OF**-Rodney McCray, Sarasota; Jim Vatcher, Clearwater; Jaime Roseboro, St. Lucie; **C**-Jim Baxter, Lakeland; Ed Fulton, St. Petersburg; **DH**-Vincent Degifico, Winter Haven; **P**-Mike Miller, St. Lucie; Ron Stephens, Sarasota; Wally Trice, Osceola; Rheal Cormier, St. Petersburg; Mark Grater, St. Petersburg; Jim Poole, Vero Beach; **MVP**-Chris Donnels, St. Lucie; **Manager**-John Lipon, Lakeland.

BA: Andy Mota, Osceola, .319
Runs: Bobby Moore, Baseball City, 85
Hits: Andy Mota, Osceola, 161
RBIs: Chris Donnels, St. Lucie, 78
HRs: Julian Yan, Dunedin, 24
Wins: Wally Trice, Osceola, 16
SOs: Nate Cromwell, Dunedin, 161
ERA: Ron Stephens, Sarasota, 1.47

A Midwest League
President: George Spelius

North Standings	W	L	Pct.	GB	Attend.	Manager
South Bend White Sox*(4)	85	47	.644	—	203,197	Rick Patterson
Rockford Expos**(20)	74	59	.556	11½	139,338	Mike Quade
Appleton Foxes (7)	67	68	.496	19½	76,223	Brian Poldberg
Wausau Timbers (12)	66	68	.493	20	49,302	Tommy Jones
Kenosha Twins (9)	63	66	.488	20½	63,392	Steve Liddle
Beloit Brewers (8)	62	72	.463	24	93,166	Alex Taveras
Madison Muskies (11)	59	72	.450	25½	84,064	Jim Nettles

South Standings	W	L	Pct.	GB	Attend.	Manager
Cedar Rapids Reds*(17)	80	57	.584	—	181,189	Dave Miley
Peoria Chiefs (16)	80	59	.576	1	225,757	Brad Mills
Springfield Cardinals**(24)	73	62	.541	6	164,012	Dan Radison
Quad City Angels (3)	72	63	.533	7	191,825	Eddie Rodriguez
Burlington Braves (15)	60	77	.438	20	82,936	Jim Saul
Clinton Giants (26)	55	84	.396	26	68,487	Keith Bodie
Waterloo Diamonds (x)	47	89	.346	32½	93,555	Jaime Moreno

Playoffs: Springfield 2 games, Cedar Rapids 0; South Bend 2 games, Rockford 0.
Finals: South Bend 3 games, Springfield 0.

All-Star Team: 1B-Adam Casillas, Cedar Rapids; **2B**-Cesar Bernhardt, South Bend; **3B**-Tom Redington, Burlington; **SS**-Jeff Branson, Cedar Rapids; **OF**-Derek Lee, South Bend; Terrel Hansen, Rockford; J.T. Bruett, Kenosha; **C**-Bert Heffernan, Beloit; **DH**-Rob Lukachyk, South Bend; **P**-Sam Chavez, South Bend; Glenn Carter, Quad City; Scott Radinsky, South Bend; Dale Kisten, Springfield; **MVP**-Tom Redington, Burlington; **Manager**-Dave Miley, Cedar Rapids.

BA: Adam Casillas, Cedar Rapids, .321
Runs: Derek Lee, South Bend, 89
Hits: Cesar Bernhardt, South Bend, 148
RBIs: Terrel Hansen, Rockford, 81
Cesar Bernhardt, South Bend, 81
HRs: Tom Redington, Burlington, 17
Wins: Marcos Lopez, Peoria, 18
SOs: Glenn Carter, Quad City, 190
ERA: Jose Ventura, South Bend, 1.57

A New York-Pennsylvania League
President: Leo A. Pinckney

McNamara Standings	W	L	Pct.	GB	Attend.	Manager
Pittsfield Mets (21)	53	23	.697	—	96,931	Tim Blackwell
Oneonta Yankees (10)	48	27	.640	4½	52,955	Brian Butterfield
Watertown Indians (5)	47	30	.610	6½	63,928	Brian Graham
Utica Blue Sox (4)	39	39	.500	15	56,836	Ron Vaughn
Geneva Cubs (16)	36	39	.480	16½	32,252	Bill Hayes
Auburn Astros (18)	35	42	.455	18½	38,155	Reggie Waller
Elmira Pioneers (2)	30	46	.395	23	56,595	Mike Verdi

Stedler Standings	W	L	Pct.	GB	Attend.	Manager
Jamestown Expos (20)	44	32	.579	—	35,039	Don Werner
Niagara Falls Rapids (6)	43	33	.566	1	54,138	Rick Magnante
Batavia Clippers (22)	37	39	.487	7	38,704	Don McCormack
Welland Pirates (23)	32	44	.421	12	41,217	U.L. Washington
Hamilton Redbirds (24)	32	44	.421	12	60,192	Joe Pettini
St. Catharines Blue Jays (14)	31	45	.408	13	31,594	Bob Shirley
Erie Orioles (1)	25	49	.338	18	56,025	Bobby Tolan

Playoff: Jamestown 2 games, Pittsfield 1.

All-Star Team: 1B-Howard Prager, Auburn; **2B**-Eduardo Ortega, Batavia; Mica Lewis, Auburn; **3B**-Fabio Gomez, Watertown; **SS**-William White, Geneva; **OF**-Sherman Obando, Oneonta; Brian Cornelius, Niagara Falls; Angel Gonzalez, Niagara Falls; **C**-Carlos Mota, Watertown; Eric Albright, Niagara Falls; **DH**-Marc Tepper, Watertown; **P**-John Johnstone, Pittsfield; Shannon Jones, Geneva; Greg Langbehn, Pittsfield; Mike Gardella, Oneonta; **Manager**-Tim Blackwell, Pittsfield.

BA: Marc Tepper, Watertown, .347
Runs: Fabio Gomez, Watertown, 63
Hits: Fabio Gomez, Watertown, 98
RBIs: Howard Prager, Auburn, 58
HRs: Jeff Kent, St. Catharines, 13
Wins: John Johnstone, Pittsfield, 11
SOs: Shannon Jones, Geneva, 114
ERA: Art Canestro, Oneonta, 1.06

A Northwest League
President: Jack Cain

North Standings	W	L	Pct.	GB	Attend.	Manager
Spokane Indians (25)	41	34	.547	—	124,844	Bruce Bochy
Boise Hawks	35	40	.467	6	127,594	Mal Fichman
Bellingham Mariners (12)	32	43	.427	9	31,685	P.J. Carey
Everett Giants (26)	31	44	.413	10	70,714	Joe Strain

South Standings	W	L	Pct.	GB	Attend.	Manager
Southern Oregon A's (11)	45	30	.600	—	69,641	Grady Fuson
Eugene Emeralds (7)	43	33	.566	2½	141,314	Paul Kirsch
Salem Dodgers (19)	41	35	.539	4½	30,049	Tom Beyers
Bend Bucks (3)	33	42	.440	12	40,526	Don Long

Playoff: Spokane 2 games, Southern Oregon 1.

All-Star Team: 1B-Fred Cooley, Southern Oregon; **2B**-Kevin Higgins, Spokane; **3B**-Craig Paquette, Southern Oregon; **SS**-Tim Wallace, Boise; **OF**-Kevin Long, Eugene; Darrell Sherman, Spokane; Steve Hosey, Everett; **C**-Mike Piazza, Salem; **DH**-Dave Staton, Spokane; **P**-Rick Davis, Spokane; Kerry Knox, Spokane; **Manager**-Bruce Bochy, Spokane.

BA: Dave Staton, Spokane, .362
Runs: Darrell Sherman, Spokane, 70
Hits: Kevin Higgins, Spokane, 98
RBIs: Dave Staton, Spokane, 72
HRs: Dave Staton, Spokane, 17
Wins: Darin Kracl, Southern Oregon, 10
SOs: Rick Davis, Spokane, 106
ERA: Rick Davis, Spokane, 1.35

A South Atlantic League
President: John H. Moss

North Standings	W	L	Pct.	GB	Attend.	Manager
Gastonia Rangers***(13)	92	48	.657	—	51,290	Orlando Gomez
Greensboro Hornets (17)	78	60	.565	13	157,927	Gary Denbo
Fayetteville Generals (6)	70	69	.504	21½	65,931	Gene Roof
Asheville Tourists (18)	68	70	.493	23	96,178	Jim Coveney
Spartanburg Phillies (22)	62	79	.440	30½	94,120	Mel Roberts
Charleston (WV) Wheelers (16)	58	76	.433	31	130,293	Greg Mahlberg

South Standings	W	L	Pct.	GB	Attend.	Manager
Augusta Pirates*(23)	77	67	.535	—	119,153	Stan Cliburn
Columbia Mets (21)	73	67	.521	2	85,862	Bill Stein
Charleston (SC) Rainbows**(25)	72	68	.514	3	78,438	Jack Krol
Savannah Cardinals (24)	69	70	.496	5½	76,287	Keith Champion
Sumter Braves (15)	60	81	.426	15½	36,706	Ned Yost
Myrtle Beach Blue Jays (14)	59	83	.415	17	68,779	Mike Fischlin

Playoff: Augusta 2 games, Charleston (SC) 1.
Finals: Augusta 3 games, Gastonia 1.

All-Star Team: 1B-Mike Mulvaney, Greensboro; **2B**-Jeff Frye, Gastonia; **3B**-Keith Raisanen, Augusta; **SS**-Andujar Cedeno, Asheville; Reggie Sanders, Greensboro; **OF**-Willie Ansley, Asheville; Kevin Belcher, Gastonia; Mauricio Nunez, Savannah; **C**-Todd Hundley, Columbia; **DH**-Trey McCoy, Charleston (SC); **P**-John Ericks, Savannah; Pedro Martinez, Charleston (SC); **MVP**-Mike Mulvaney, Greensboro; **Pitcher of the Year**-Pedro Martinez, Charleston (SC); **Manager**-Orlando Gomez, Gastonia.

BA: Jeff Frye, Gastonia, .313
Runs: Mark Young, Myrtle Beach, 94
Hits: Andujar Cedeno, Asheville, 146
RBIs: Mike Mulvaney, Greensboro, 112
HRs: Doug Cronk, Gastonia, 22
Wins: Francisco Valdez, Gastonia, 14
SOs: John Ericks, Savannah, 211
ERA: Pedro Martinez, Charleston (SC), 1.97

R Appalachian League
President: Bill Halstead

North Standings	W	L	Pct.	GB	Attend.	Manager
Pulaski Braves (15)	42	26	.618	—	11,284	Fred Koenig
Princeton Pirates (23)	32	37	.464	10½	33,754	Julio Garcia
Burlington Indians (5)	31	37	.456	11	55,695	Jim Gabella
Martinsville Phillies (22)	29	38	.433	12½	58,189	Rollie DeArmas
Bluefield Orioles (1)	27	41	.397	15	25,548	Mike Young

South Standings	W	L	Pct.	GB	Attend.	Manager
Elizabethton Twins (9)	47	21	.691	—	17,952	Ray Smith
Johnson City Cardinals (24)	38	32	.543	10	33,450	Mark DeJohn
Wytheville Cubs (16)	34	35	.493	13½	16,839	Steve Roadcap
Kingsport Mets (21)	35	37	.486	14	38,791	Jim Eschen
Bristol Tigers (6)	28	39	.418	18½	20,008	Ruben Amaro

Playoff: Elizabethton 2 games, Pulaski 0.

All-Star Team: 1B-Tom Hardgrove, Martinsville; **2B**-Bruce Schreiber, Princeton; **3B**-T.R. Lewis, Bluefield; **SS**-Manny Alexander, Bluefield; **OF**-Rex Delanuez, Elizabethton; Mike House, Elizabethton; Melvin Nieves, Pulaski; **C**-Brook Fordyce, Kingsport; **DH**-James Harris, Kingsport; **P**-Mike Misuraca, Elizabethton; Roger Hailey, Pulaski; **MVP**-Mike House, Elizabethton; **Manager**-Ray Smith, Elizabethton.

BA: Mike House, Elizabethton, .376
Runs: Alberto Diaz, Kingsport, 55
    Pedro Castellano, Wytheville, 55
Hits: Manny Alexander, Bluefield, 85
RBIs: Mike House, Elizabethton, 68

HRs: Tom Hardgrove, Martinsville, 13
Wins: Phil Wiese, Elizabethton, 10
    Mike Misuraca, Elizabethton, 10
SOs: Jac Gelb, Wytheville, 110
ERA: Roger Hailey, Pulaski, 1.41

R Arizona League
President: Bob Richmond

Standings	W	L	Pct.	GB	Manager
Brewers (8)	40	15	.732	—	Jeff Nate
Athletics (11)	28	25	.518	11	Casey Parsons
Mariners (12)	26	26	.500	12½	Dave Myers
Padres (25)	23	29	.446	15½	Lonnie Keeter
Cardinals (24)	22	31	.436	17	Luis Melendez
Angels (3)	20	33	.364	19	Nate Oliver

Games played at Peoria, Scottsdale, Tempe, and Mesa, Arizona.

Playoffs: None.

All-Star Team: 1B-Leon Glenn, Brewers; **2B**-Henry Reynoso, Brewers; **3B**-Luis Lanfranco, Athletics; **SS**-Justin McCray, Brewers; **OF**-Sean Twitty, Mariners; Kelvin Thomas, Mariners; Brian Stephens, Mariners; Francisco Garcia, Cardinals; **C**-Troy Clemons, Cardinals; **DH**-Scott Henry, Athletics; **P**-Jeff Kinder, Brewers; Russell Garside, Padres; Rob Callistro, Mariners; Manuel Furcal, Mariners; Reggie Leslie, Brewers; **MVP**-Leon Glenn, Brewers; **Manager** -Casey Parsons, Athletics; Dave Myers, Mariners.

BA: Leon Glenn, Brewers, .379
Runs: Brent Hendley, Athletics, 54
Hits: Leon Glenn, Brewers, 79
RBIs: Leon Glenn, Brewers, 50

HRs: Leon Glenn, Brewers, 9
Wins: Luis Lluberes, Brewers, 8
SOs: Rob Callistro, Mariners, 78
ERA: Luis Lluberes, Brewers, 1.33

R Gulf Coast League
President: Thomas J. Saffell

North Standings	W	L	Pct.	GB	Manager
Dodgers (19)	40	23	.635	—	Jerry Royster
Reds (17)	37	26	.587	3	Sam Mejias
Royals (7)	35	28	.556	5	Carlos Tosca
Indians (5)	34	29	.540	6	Mike Bucci
Red Sox (2)	27	36	.429	13	Felix Maldonado
Astros (18)	16	47	.254	24	Julio Linares

South Standings	W	L	Pct.	GB	Manager
Yankees (10)	41	22	.651	—	Jack Gillis
White Sox (4)	40	23	.635	1½	Ed Pebley
Braves (15)	37	26	.587	4	Jim Procopio
Rangers (13)	33	30	.524	8	Chino Cadahia
Expos (20)	28	35	.444	13	Jerry Weinstein
Twins (9)	27	36	.429	14	Joel Lepel
Mets (21)	25	38	.397	16	John Tamargo
Pirates (23)	21	42	.333	20	Woody Huyke

Games played at Sarasota, Bradenton, Baseball City, Kissimmee, Plant City and Port Charlotte, Florida.

Playoff: Yankees 2 games, Dodgers 1.

All-Star Team: 1B-Harry Guanchez, Royals; **2B**-Ossie Apolinario, Braves; **3B**-Butch Huskey, Mets; **SS**-Andres Rodriguez, Yankees; **OF**-Kenneth Powell, Rangers; Greg Blosser, Red Sox; Ken Ramos, Indians; **C**-Pedro Matilla, Red Sox; **DH**-Fred Gonzalez, Dodgers; **P**-Pedro Astacio, Dodgers; Sterling Hitchcock, Yankees; Mike Soper, Indians; **Manager**-Jack Gillis, Yankees.

BA: Fred Gonzalez, Dodgers, .380
Runs: Ossie Apolinario, Braves, 54
Hits: Ossie Apolinario, Braves, 74
RBIs: Ramon Jimenez, Yankees, 46

HRs: Ramon Jimenez, Yankees, 7
Wins: Sterling Hitchcock, Yankees, 9
SOs: Sterling Hitchcock, Yankees, 98
ERA: Mike Shepherd, Braves, 1.43

R Pioneer League
President: Ralph C. Nelles

North Standings	W	L	Pct.	GB	Attend.	Manager
Great Falls Dodgers (19)	53	14	.791	—	69,637	Joe Vavra
Helena Brewers (8)	38	30	.559	15½	39,645	Dusty Rhodes
Billings Mustangs (17)	26	41	.388	27	77,405	Dave Keller
Medicine Hat Blue Jays (14)	23	46	.333	31	13,624	Ralph "Rocket" Wheeler

South Standings	W	L	Pct.	GB	Attend.	Manager
Butte Copper Kings (13)	41	25	.621	—	26,711	Bump Wills
Salt Lake City Trappers	33	36	.478	9½	173,256	Barry Moss
Pocatello Giants (26)	29	38	.433	12½	17,117	Deron McCue
Idaho Falls Braves (15)	27	40	.403	14½	65,773	Cloyd Boyer

Playoff: Great Falls 3 games, Butte 0.

All-Star Team: 1B-Bo Dodson, Helena; **2B**-Ramces Guerrero, Idaho Falls; **3B**-Mike Grace, Salt Lake City; **SS**-Tim Barker, Great Falls; **OF**-Scott Pose, Billings; Dan Peltier, Butte; Shawn Holtzclaw, Medicine Hat; **C**-Barry Winford, Butte; **DH**-Tom Goodwin, Great Falls; **P**-Kiki Jones, Great Falls; Jamie McAndrew, Great Falls; Tony Valle, Idaho Falls.

BA: Barry Winford, Butte, .359
Runs: Tom Goodwin, Great Falls, 55
Hits: Troy O'Leary, Helena, 89
RBIs: Troy O'Leary, Helena, 56

HRs: Ramces Guerrero, Idaho Falls, 13
Wins: Jamie McAndrew, Great Falls, 11
SOs: Jason Brosnan, Great Falls, 89
ERA: Rob Taylor, Pocatello, 1.25

1989 Interleague Post Season Play

World Series
Oakland (American) 4 games, San Francisco (National) 0

AAA Classic
Indianapolis (American Association) 4 games, Richmond (International) 0

1989 Major League Farm Systems

American League

1 Baltimore (5): Rochester, Hagerstown, Frederick, Erie, Bluefield.
2 Boston (6): Pawtucket, New Britain, Lynchburg, Winter Haven, Elmira, Gulf Coast.
3 California (6): Edmonton, Midland, Palm Springs, Quad City, Bend, Arizona.
4 Chicago (6): Vancouver, Birmingham, Sarasota, South Bend, Utica, Gulf Coast.
5 Cleveland (6): Colorado Springs, Canton-Akron, Kinston, Watertown, Burlington (NC), Gulf Coast.
6 Detroit (6): Toledo, London, Lakeland, Fayetteville, Niagara Falls, Bristol.
7 Kansas City (6): Omaha, Memphis, Baseball City, Appleton, Eugene, Gulf Coast.
8 Milwaukee (6): Denver, El Paso, Stockton, Beloit, Helena, Arizona.
9 Minnesota (6): Portland, Orlando, Visalia, Kenosha, Elizabethton, Gulf Coast.
10 New York (6): Columbus (OH), Albany-Colonie, Prince William, Ft. Lauderdale, Oneonta, Gulf Coast.
11 Oakland (6): Tacoma, Huntsville, Modesto, Madison, Southern Oregon, Arizona.
12 Seattle (6): Calgary, Williamsport, San Bernardino, Wausau, Bellingham, Arizona.
13 Texas (6): Oklahoma City, Tulsa, Port Charlotte, Gastonia, Butte, Gulf Coast.
14 Toronto (6): Syracuse, Knoxville, Dunedin, Myrtle Beach, St. Catharines, Medicine Hat.

Co-op (x): Salinas, Waterloo.
Independent: Reno, Peninsula, Miami, Boise, Salt Lake City.

National League

15 Atlanta (8): Richmond, Greenville, Durham, Burlington (IA), Sumter, Pulaski, Idaho Falls, Gulf Coast.
16 Chicago (7): Iowa, Charlotte, Winston-Salem, Charleston (WV), Peoria, Geneva, Wytheville.
17 Cincinnati (6): Nashville, Chattanooga, Cedar Rapids, Greensboro, Billings, Gulf Coast.
18 Houston (6): Tucson, Columbus (GA), Osceola, Asheville, Auburn, Gulf Coast.
19 Los Angeles (7): Albuquerque, San Antonio, Bakersfield, Vero Beach, Salem (OR), Great Falls, Gulf Coast.
20 Montreal (6): Indianapolis, Jacksonville, West Palm Beach, Rockford, Jamestown, Gulf Coast.
21 New York (7): Tidewater, Jackson, St. Lucie, Columbia, Pittsfield, Kingsport, Gulf Coast.
22 Philadelphia (6): Scranton-Wilkes-Barre, Reading, Clearwater, Spartanburg, Batavia, Martinsville.
23 Pittsburgh (7): Buffalo, Harrisburg, Salem (VA), Augusta, Welland, Princeton, Gulf Coast.
24 St. Louis (8): Louisville, Arkansas, St. Petersburg, Springfield, Savannah, Hamilton, Johnson City, Arizona.
25 San Diego (6): Las Vegas, Wichita, Riverside, Charleston (SC), Spokane, Arizona.
26 San Francisco (6): Phoenix, Shreveport, San Jose, Clinton, Everett, Pocatello.

1989 No-Hitters

Date	Pitcher	Team	League	Opponent	Score
4-9	Dennis Burlingame	Durham	Carolina	Frederick	4-0 (P)
4-14	Bob Haas	Lakeland	Florida State	Clearwater	5-0
4-21	Dan Gabriele	New Britain	Eastern	Williamsport	1-0
4-22	Darrin Reichle/				
	Bill Marx	Riverside	California	Modesto	5-0
5-1	Ramon Manon	Ft. Lauderdale	Florida State	Dunedin	3-0
5-3	Jason Grimsley	Reading	Eastern	Harrisburg	3-0
5-23	Tom Drees	Vancouver	Pacific Coast	Calgary	1-0
5-24	Willie Banks	Visalia	California	Palm Springs	1-0
5-26	Curt Krippner	Beloit	Midwest	Madison	1-0
5-28	Tom Drees	Vancouver	Pacific Coast	Edmonton	1-0 (C, 7)
5-28	Randy Tomlin	Salem	Carolina	Kinston	1-0
6-2	Meredith Sanford	Greensboro	South Atlantic	Myrtle Beach	7-0
6-12	Jeff Fassero	Arkansas	Texas	Jackson	5-0
6-13	Timothy Dell	Spartanburg	South Atlantic	Greensboro	2-0 (7)
7-2	Francisco Valdez	Gastonia	South Atlantic	Asheville	7-0
7-2	Wayne Helm	Bend	Northwest	Everett	10-0
7-12	Josias Manzanillo	New Britain	Eastern	Reading	3-0
7-20	Rafael Valdez	Riverside	California	Reno	2-0 (P)
7-20	Marcos Garcia	Mariners	Arizona	Padres	4-0
7-21	Maximo Aleys	Everett	Northwest	Bend	4-1
7-25	Daniel Kite	Winter Haven	Florida State	Dunedin	14-0
7-27	Mike Anderson	Greensboro	South Atlantic	Columbia	5-0 (6)
7-29	Jody Ryan	Wausau	Midwest	Clinton	2-0
8-3	Ramon Garcia	White Sox	Gulf Coast	Mets	2-0
8-16	Tom Drees	Vancouver	Pacific Coast	Las Vegas	5-0 (7)
8-20	Roger Mason	Tucson	Pacific Coast	Las Vegas	0-1 (11)
8-21	Dean Hartgraves	Osceola	Florida State	Winter Haven	3-0 (6)
8-22	Clyde Keller	Savannah	South Atlantic	Augusta	4-0
8-26	Doug Marcero	Niagara Falls	New York-Penn.	Elmira	5-0
8-28	Raymond Doss	Welland	New York-Penn.	Batavia	1-0
8-30	Tim Mauser	Reading	Eastern	New Britain	9-0

Number in parentheses indicates innings if other than nine; "P" indicates perfect game; "C" indicates no-hitters in consecutive starts.

THIS DATE IN MINOR LEAGUE HISTORY

April 4, 1989, Manuel Magallon, manager of the Monterrey Industriales of the Mexican League, died of a heart attack at age 63.

April 8, 1989, Three new cities began play in the Eastern League with Canton-Akron, Hagerstown, and London, Ontario replacing Burlington, Vt., Glens Falls, N.Y., and Pittsfield, Mass.

April 9, 1989, Durham's Dennis Burlingame pitched a perfect game in game one of the Carolina League club's opening day doubleheader, a 4-0 win over Frederick. In game two, Steve Avery pitched a two-hit, 1-0 shutout for Durham.

May 28, 1989, Vancouver's Tom Drees pitched his second consecutive no-hitter, beating Edmonton 1-0.

June 29, 1989, Mal Fichman, manager for Boise, Northwest League, was thrown out of a game after an argument with the umpires. He went to the clubhouse, where he dressed in the Hawks' mascot suit and then returned to the field. He led fans in cheers and continued to direct his team. League President Jack Cain fined Fichman and suspended him for one game.

July 6, 1989, Vancouver forteited a Pacific Coast League game at Albuquerque. The team refused to take the field when their paychecks, due July 1, did not arrive. The Vancouver front office flew the checks to Albuquerque the next day, and the Canadians took the field.

July 11, 1989, The equipment of the Quad City Angels of the Midwest League was seized by the sheriff after a game in South Bend. The seizure resulted from a dispute over a prior year's hotel bill. The equipment was bailed out by farm director Bill Bavasi of the parent California Angels.

August 16, 1989, Tom Drees of Vancouver threw his third no-hitter of the season, beating Las Vegas 5-0. He became the first pitcher to throw three no-hitters in a season since Bill Bell of Bristol, Appalachian League, in 1952. Walter Justus pitched four no-hitters in 1908 for Lancaster of the Ohio State League.

August 17, 1989, Waterloo defeated Clinton 4-3 in a 25-inning Midwest League game. The contest began on July 6 but was suspended after 20 innings. Waterloo batters struck out 31 times. The time of game was seven hours and 37 minutes.

August 30, 1989, Great Falls of the Pioneer League ended the season with a 53-14 record and a .791 winning percentage, the third highest percentage in the history of the minors.

September 1, 1989, Buffalo of the American Association drew over 1 million fans for the second consecutive season.

September 28, 1989, College Park, home of the Charleston (SC) Rainbows of the South Atlantic League, was heavily damaged by Hurricane Hugo. $600,000 in insurance money and federal disaster funds would repair the park in time for the 1990 season. The hurricane also damaged parks in Sumter, S.C., and Gastonia, N.C.

November 8, 1989, Umpire Pam Postema was released by the AAA Alliance after 13 years of umpiring in the minors. She would later file a gender discrimination suit against major league baseball.

1990

American League
President: Dr. Robert W. Brown

East Standings	W	L	Pct.	GB	Attend.	Manager
Boston Red Sox	88	74	.543	—	2,528,986	Joe Morgan
Toronto Blue Jays	86	76	.531	2	3,885,284	Cito Gaston
Detroit Tigers	79	83	.488	9	1,495,785	Sparky Anderson
Cleveland Indians	77	85	.475	11	1,225,240	John McNamara
Baltimore Orioles	76	85	.472	11½	2,415,189	Frank Robinson
Milwaukee Brewers	74	88	.457	14	1,752,900	Tom Trebelhorn
New York Yankees	67	95	.414	21	2,006,436	Bucky Dent/Stump Merrill

West Standings	W	L	Pct.	GB	Attend.	Manager
Oakland Athletics	103	59	.636	—	2,900,217	Tony LaRussa
Chicago White Sox	94	68	.580	9	2,002,357	Jeff Torborg
Texas Rangers	83	79	.512	20	2,057,911	Bobby Valentine
California Angels	80	82	.494	23	2,555,688	Doug Rader
Seattle Mariners	77	85	.475	26	1,509,727	Jim Lefebvre
Kansas City Royals	75	86	.466	27½	2,244,956	John Wathan
Minnesota Twins	74	88	.457	29	1,751,584	Tom Kelly

Playoff: Oakland 4 games, Boston 0.

BA: George Brett, Kansas City, .329
Runs: Rickey Henderson, Oakland, 119
Hits: Rafael Palmeiro, Texas, 191
RBIs: Cecil Fielder, Detroit, 132
HRs: Cecil Fielder, Detroit, 51

Wins: Bob Welch, Oakland, 27
SOs: Nolan Ryan, Texas, 232
ERA: Roger Clemens, Boston, 1.93
Pct: Bob Welch, Oakland, .818, 27-6
Saves: Bobby Thigpen, Chicago, 57

National League
President: William White

East Standings	W	L	Pct.	GB	Attend.	Manager
Pittsburgh Pirates	95	67	.586	—	2,049,908	Jim Leyland
New York Mets	91	71	.562	4	2,732,745	Davey Johnson/Bud Harrelson
Montreal Expos	85	77	.525	10	1,373,087	Buck Rodgers
Chicago Cubs	77	85	.475	18	2,243,791	Don Zimmer
Philadelphia Phillies	77	85	.475	18	1,992,484	Nick Leyva
St. Louis Cardinals	70	92	.432	25	2,573,225	Whitey Herzog/Red Schoendienst/Joe Torre

West Standings	W	L	Pct.	GB	Attend.	Manager
Cincinnati Reds	91	71	.562	—	2,400,892	Lou Piniella
Los Angeles Dodgers	86	76	.531	5	3,002,396	Tom Lasorda
San Francisco Giants	85	77	.525	6	1,975,528	Roger Craig
Houston Astros	75	87	.463	16	1,310,927	Art Howe
San Diego Padres	75	87	.463	16	1,856,396	Jack McKeon/Greg Riddoch
Atlanta Braves	65	97	.401	26	980,129	Russ Nixon/Bobby Cox

Playoff: Cincinnati 4 games, Pittsburgh 2.

BA: Willie McGee, St. Louis, .335
Runs: Ryne Sandberg, Chicago, 116
Hits: Brett Butler, San Francisco, 192
Lenny Dykstra, Philadelphia, 192
RBIs: Matt Williams, San Francisco, 122
HRs: Ryne Sandberg, Chicago, 40

Wins: Doug Drabek, Pittsburgh, 22
SOs: David Cone, New York, 233
ERA: Danny Darwin, Houston, 2.21
Pct: Doug Drabek, Pittsburgh, .786, 22-6
Saves: John Franco, New York, 33

AAA American Association
President: Randy Mobley

East Standings	W	L	Pct.	GB	Attend.	Manager
Nashville Sounds (17)	86	61	.585	—	556,250	Pete Mackanin
Buffalo Bisons (23)	85	62	.578	1	1,174,358	Terry Collins
Louisville Redbirds (24)	74	72	.507	11½	616,687	Gaylen Pitts
Indianapolis Indians (20)	61	85	.418	24½	314,264	Tim Johnson

West Standings	W	L	Pct.	GB	Attend.	Manager
Omaha Royals (7)	86	60	.589	—	341,129	Sal Rende
Iowa Cubs (16)	72	74	.493	14	270,215	Jim Essian
Denver Zephyrs (8)	68	78	.466	18	433,880	Dave Machemer
Oklahoma City 89ers (13)	58	87	.400	27½	282,773	Steve Smith

Played an interlocking schedule with the International League known as AAA Alliance.

Playoffs: Nashville defeated Buffalo in a one game playoff for the East title. Omaha 3 games, Nashville 2.

All-Star Team: 1B-Orlando Merced, Buffalo; **2B-**Jeff Small, Iowa; **3B-**Joe Redfield, Denver; **SS-**Paul Zuvella, Omaha; **OF-**Bernard Gilkey, Louisville; Juan Gonzalez, Oklahoma City; Ray Lankford, Louisville; **C-**Tim McIntosh, Denver; **DH-**Mark Ryal, Buffalo; **P-**Dorn Taylor, Buffalo; Chris Hammond, Nashville; **MVP-**Chris Hammond, Nashville; **Pitcher of the Year-**Chris Hammond, Nashville; **Manager-**Sal Rende, Omaha.

BA: Mark Ryal, Buffalo, .334
Runs: Joe Redfield, Denver, 87
Hits: Skeeter Barnes, Nashville, 156
RBIs: Juan Gonzalez, Oklahoma City, 101
HRs: Juan Gonzalez, Oklahoma City, 29

Wins: Chris Hammond, Nashville, 15
SOs: Chris Hammond, Nashville, 149
ERA: Chris Hammond, Nashville, 2.17
Pct: Chris Hammond, Nashville, .938, 15-1

AAA International League
President: Randy Mobley

East Standings	W	L	Pct.	GB	Attend.	Manager
Rochester Red Wings (1)	89	56	.614	—	331,927	Greg Biagini
Scranton-Wilkes-Barre Red Barons (22)	68	78	.466	21½	545,844	Bill Dancy
Syracuse Chiefs (14)	62	83	.428	27	245,045	Bob Bailor
Pawtucket Red Sox (2)	62	84	.425	27½	290,953	Ed Nottle/Johnny Pesky

West Standings	W	L	Pct.	GB	Attend.	Manager
Columbus Clippers (10)	87	59	.596	—	584,010	Stump Merrill/Rick Down
Tidewater Tides (21)	79	67	.541	8	193,055	Steve Swisher
Richmond Braves (15)	71	74	.490	15½	427,552	Jim Beauchamp
Toledo Mud Hens (6)	58	86	.403	28	159,009	John Wockenfuss/Tom Gamboa

Played an interlocking schedule with the American Association known as AAA Alliance.

Playoff: Rochester 3 games, Columbus 2.

All-Star Team: 1B-David Segui, Rochester; **2B-**Luis Sojo, Syracuse; **3B-**Leo Gomez, Rochester; **SS-**Tim Naehring, Pawtucket; **OF-**Hensley Meulens, Columbus; Phil Plantier, Pawtucket; Mark Whiten, Syracuse; **C-**Brian Dorsett, Columbus; **DH-**Chris Hoiles, Rochester; **P-**Dave Eiland, Columbus; Todd Frohwirth, Scranton-Wilkes-Barre; **MVP-**Hensley Meulens, Columbus; **Pitcher of the Year-**Dave Eiland, Columbus; **Manager-**Greg Biagini, Rochester.

BA: Jim Eppard, Syracuse, .310
Runs: Leo Gomez, Rochester, 97
Hits: Jim Eppard, Syracuse, 143
RBIs: Leo Gomez, Rochester, 97

HRs: Phil Plantier, Pawtucket, 33
Wins: Dave Eiland, Columbus, 16
SOs: Manny Hernandez, Tidewater, 157
ERA: Paul Marak, Richmond, 2.49

AAA Mexican League
President: Pedro Treto Cisneros

North Standings	W	L	Pct.	GB	Attend.	Manager
Dos Laredos Tecolotes	81	50	.618	—	183,500	Jose Guerrero
Union Laguna Algodoneros	71	54	.568	7	210,147	Marco Antonio Vazquez
Monterrey Sultanes	70	62	.560	11½	160,066	Leobardo Figueroa/Aurelio Rodriguez
Monclova Acereros	63	66	.488	17	230,554	Gregorio Luque
Saltillo Saraperos	64	68	.485	17½	197,528	Aurelio Monteagudo/Marcelo Juarez
Monterrey Industriales	49	82	.374	32	171,364	Hector Espino
San Luis Potosi Tuneros	42	87	.326	38	195,502	Rodolfo Sandoval

South Standings	W	L	Pct.	GB	Attend.	Manager
Mexico City Tigres	73	50	.593	—	181,758	Oswaldo Alvarez
Mexico City Diablos Rojos	72	54	.571	2½	190,753	Ben Reyes
Leon Bravos	74	57	.565	3	195,538	Francisco Estrada
Campeche Piratas	66	57	.537	7	198,885	Roberto Mendez/Sergio Robles
Yucatan Leones	65	64	.504	11	250,358	Roberto Castellon
Aguascalientes Rieleros	54	69	.439	19	182,750	Carlos Paz/Alfredo Ortiz
Tabasco Olmecas	52	76	.406	23½	194,972	Miguel Sotelo/Joel Serna

Playoffs: Union Laguna 4 games, Monterrey Sultanes 2; Dos Laredos 4 games, Monclova 3; Leon 4 games, MC Diablos Rojos 1; Campeche 4 games, MC Tigres 2. Union Laguna 4 games, Dos Laredos 2; Leon 4 games, Campeche 2.
Finals: Leon 4 games, Union Laguna 1.

BA: Nick Castaneda, Yucatan, .388
Runs: Danny Fernandez, MC Diablos Rojos, 113
Hits: Trench Davis, Saltillo, 189
RBIs: Dave Stockstill, Union Laguna, 109

HRs: Alejandro Sanchez, San Luis Potosi, 28
Wins: Armando Reynoso, Saltillo, 20
SOs: Armando Reynoso, Saltillo, 170
ERA: Guy Normand, Monclova, 2.08

AAA Pacific Coast League
President: Bill Cutler

North Standings	W	L	Pct.	GB	Attend.	Manager
Edmonton Trappers**(3)	78	63	.553	—	229,437	Max Oliveras
Tacoma Tigers*(11)	75	67	.528	3½	309,210	Brad Fischer
Vancouver Canadians (4)	74	67	.525	4	281,540	Marv Foley
Calgary Cannons (12)	66	77	.462	13	312,416	Tom Jones
Portland Beavers (9)	56	83	.403	21	150,054	Phil Roof

South Standings	W	L	Pct.	GB	Attend.	Manager
Albuquerque Dukes***(19)	91	51	.641	—	324,046	Kevin Kennedy
Colorado Springs Sky Sox (5)	76	67	.531	15½	201,642	Ed Molinaro/Charlie Manuel
Tucson Toros (18)	71	71	.500	20	238,629	Bob Skinner
Phoenix Firebirds (26)	63	76	.453	26½	248,660	Duane Espy
Las Vegas Stars (25)	58	86	.403	34	312,522	Pat Kelly

*Won first-half   **Won second-half   ***Won both halves
Numbers after nicknames indicate farm system.
Affiliation listed at end of each year.

598

Playoffs: Albuquerque 3 games, Colorado Springs 2; Edmonton 3 games, Tacoma 2.
Finals: Albuquerque 3 games, Edmonton 0.

All-Star Team: 1B-Tino Martinez, Calgary; **2B**-Todd Haney, Calgary; **3B**-Dave Hansen, Albuquerque; **SS**-Jose Offerman, Albuquerque; **OF**-Mark Leonard, Phoenix; Mike Huff, Albuquerque; Butch Davis, Albuquerque; **C**-Jerry Willard, Vancouver; **DH**-Tom Dodd, Calgary; **P**-Scott Chiamparino, Tacoma; Grady Hall, Vancouver; Joe Bitker, Tacoma; **MVP**-Jose Offerman, Albuquerque; **Manager**-Kevin Kennedy, Albuquerque.

BA: Luis Lopez, Albuquerque, .353
Runs: Paul Faries, Las Vegas, 109
Hits: Paul Faries, Las Vegas, 172
RBIs: Tom Dodd, Calgary, 114

HRs: Bernardo Brito, Portland, 25
Wins: Jeff Bittiger, Albuquerque, 15
SOs: Ray Young, Tacoma, 137
ERA: Mike Cook, Portland, 3.20

AA Eastern League
President: Charles E. Eshbach

Standings	W	L	Pct.	GB	Attend.	Manager
Albany-Colonie Yankees (10)	79	60	.568	—	203,423	Rick Down/Dan Radison
London Tigers (6)	76	63	.547	3	167,694	Chris Chambliss
Canton-Akron Indians (5)	76	64	.543	3½	204,193	Ken Bolek
New Britain Red Sox (2)	72	67	.518	7	123,017	Butch Hobson
Harrisburg Senators (23)	69	69	.500	9½	223,033	Marc Bombard
Hagerstown Suns (1)	67	71	.486	11½	167,725	Jerry Narron
Williamsport Bills (12)	61	79	.436	18½	76,779	Rich Morales
Reading Phillies (22)	55	82	.401	23	204,240	Don McCormack

Playoffs: New Britain 3 games, Albany-Colonie 2; London 3 games, Canton-Akron 2.
Finals: London 3 games, New Britain 0.

All-Star Team: 1B-Rico Brogna, London; **2B**-Pat Kelly, Albany-Colonie; **3B**-Jeff Bagwell, New Britain; **SS**-Mark Lewis, Canton-Akron; **OF**-Scott Meadows, Hagerstown; Luis Mercedes, Hagerstown; Bernie Williams, Albany-Colonie; **C**-Mitch Lyden, Albany-Colonie; **DH**-Jeff Grotewold, Reading; **P**-Mike Gardiner, Williamsport; Randy Tomlin, Harrisburg; Darrin Chapin, Albany-Colonie; **MVP**-Jeff Bagwell, New Britain; **Pitcher of the Year**-Mike Gardiner, Williamsport; **Manager**-Chris Chambliss, London.

BA: Luis Mercedes, Hagerstown, .334
Runs: Bernie Williams, Albany-Colonie, 91
Hits: Jeff Bagwell, New Britain, 160
RBIs: Rico Brogna, London, 77
Greg Sparks, Albany-Colonie, 77

HRs: Rico Brogna, London, 21
Wins: Rusty Meacham, London, 15
SOs: Mike Gardiner, Williamsport, 149
ERA: Mike Gardiner, Williamsport, 1.90

AA Southern League
President: Jimmy Bragan

East Standings	W	L	Pct.	GB	Attend.	Manager
Orlando SunRays*(9)	85	59	.590	—	147,070	Ron Gardenhire
Jacksonville Expos**(20)	84	60	.583	1	244,494	Jerry Manuel
Columbus Mudcats (18)	67	77	.465	18	94,265	Rick Sweet
Charlotte Knights (16)	65	79	.451	20	271,502	Tommy Helms/Jay Loviglio
Greenville Braves (15)	57	87	.396	28	204,929	Buddy Bailey

West Standings	W	L	Pct.	GB	Attend.	Manager
Huntsville Stars (11)	79	65	.549	—	228,821	Jeff Newman
Birmingham Barons**(4)	77	67	.535	2	256,227	Ken Berry
Memphis Chicks*(7)	73	71	.507	6	193,758	Jeff Cox
Knoxville Blue Jays (14)	67	77	.465	12	82,676	John Stearns
Chattanooga Lookouts (17)	66	78	.458	13	135,825	Jim Tracy

Playoffs: Memphis 3 games, Birmingham 1; Orlando 3 games, Jacksonville 1.
Finals: Memphis 3 games, Orlando 2.

All-Star Team: 1B-Jeff Conine, Memphis; **2B**-William Suero, Knoxville; **3B**-Sean Berry, Memphis; **SS**-Eddie Zosky, Knoxville; **OF**-Terrel Hansen, Jacksonville; Adam Casillas, Chattanooga; Bobby Moore, Memphis; **C**-Greg Colbrunn, Jacksonville; **DH**-Matt Stark, Birmingham; **P**-Scott Erickson, Orlando; Brian Barnes, Jacksonville; Steve Chitren, Huntsville; **MVP**-Jeff Conine, Memphis; **Pitcher of the Year**-Brian Barnes, Jacksonville; **Manager**-Ron Gardenhire, Orlando; Jerry Manuel, Jacksonville.

BA: Adam Casillas, Chattanooga, .336
Runs: Jarvis Brown, Orlando, 104
Hits: Scott Brosius, Huntsville, 162
RBIs: Matt Stark, Birmingham, 109

HRs: Luis Gonzalez, Columbus, 24
Terrel Hansen, Jacksonville, 24
Wins: Doug Simons, Orlando, 15
SOs: Brian Barnes, Jacksonville, 213
ERA: Jeff Carter, Jacksonville, 1.84

AA Texas League
President: Carl Sawatski

East Standings	W	L	Pct.	GB	Attend.	Manager
Jackson Mets**(21)	73	62	.541	—	124,142	Clint Hurdle
Tulsa Drillers (13)	68	68	.500	5½	226,461	Tommy Thompson
Shreveport Captains*(26)	65	68	.489	7	204,872	Bill Evers
Arkansas Travelers (24)	56	80	.412	17½	256,074	Dave Bialas

West Standings	W	L	Pct.	GB	Attend.	Manager
San Antonio Missions**(19)	78	56	.582	—	180,931	John Shoemaker
El Paso Diablos*(8)	77	58	.570	1½	201,068	Dave Huppert
Wichita Wranglers (25)	67	68	.496	11½	218,109	Steve Lubratich
Midland Angels (3)	56	80	.412	23	168,742	Eddie Rodriguez

Playoffs: San Antonio 2 games, El Paso 1; Shreveport 2 games, Jackson 0.
Finals: Shreveport 4 games, San Antonio 2.

All-Star Team: 1B-Eric Karros, San Antonio; **2B**-Dean Kelley, Wichita; **3B**-Steve Finken, San Antonio; **SS**-Charlie Montoyo, El Paso; **OF**-Henry Rodriguez, San Antonio; Tom Goodwin, San Antonio; Mike Humphreys, Wichita; **C**-Steve Decker, Shreveport; Bill Haselman, Tulsa; **DH**-Jesus Alfaro, El Paso; **Util**-Dave Patterson, Shreveport; **P**-Anthony Young, Jackson; Pete Schourek, Jackson; Terry Bross, Jackson; Mike James, San Antonio; Ricky Bones, Wichita; **MVP**-Henry Rodriguez, San Antonio; **Pitcher of the Year**-Anthony Young, Jackson; **Manager**-Clint Hurdle, Jackson.

BA: Eric Karros, San Antonio, .352
Runs: Mike Humphreys, Wichita, 92
Hits: Eric Karros, San Antonio, 179
RBIs: Henry Rodriguez, San Antonio, 109

HRs: Henry Rodriguez, San Antonio, 28
Wins: Anthony Young, Jackson, 15
SOs: Tom Hostetler, Shreveport, 112
ERA: Anthony Young, Jackson, 1.65

A California League
President: Joe Gagliardi

North Standings	W	L	Pct.	GB	Attend.	Manager
Stockton Ports*(8)	82	59	.582	—	85,436	Chris Bando
San Jose Giants**(26)	74	68	.521	8½	108,478	Tom Spencer
Reno Silver Sox	71	68	.511	10	87,048	Mike Brown
Modesto A's (11)	59	82	.418	23	62,089	Ted Kubiak
Salinas Spurs	47	93	.336	34½	33,465	Hide Koga

South Standings	W	L	Pct.	GB	Attend.	Manager
Visalia Oaks***(9)	90	51	.638	—	78,212	Scott Ullger
Bakersfield Dodgers (19)	80	62	.563	10½	142,281	Tom Beyers
San Bernardino Spirit (12)	77	65	.542	13½	190,890	Keith Bodie
Riverside Red Wave (25)	64	78	.451	26½	82,420	Bruce Bochy
Palm Springs Angels (3)	62	80	.437	28½	76,462	Nate Oliver

Playoffs: Stockton 3 games, San Jose 1; Bakersfield 3 games, Visalia 2.
Finals: Stockton 3 games, Bakersfield 2.

All-Star Team: 1B-Bo Dodson, Stockton; **2B**-John Patterson, San Jose; **3B**-Frank Bolick, Stockton/San Bernardino; **SS**-Royce Clayton, San Jose; **OF**-Darrell Sherman, Riverside; Tom Eiterman, Reno; J.T. Bruett, Visalia; **C**-Bryan Baar, Bakersfield; **DH**-Brett Magnusson, Bakersfield; **P**-Dan Rambo, San Jose; Rich Garces, Visalia; George Tsamis, Visalia; Jason Brosnan, Bakersfield; Jamie McAndrew, Bakersfield; Chris Johnson, Stockton; **MVP**-Frank Bolick, Stockton/San Bernardino, San Jose; **Pitcher of the Year**-Dan Rambo, San Jose; **Manager**-Scott Ullger, Visalia.

BA: Tom Eiterman, Reno, .331
Runs: Pat Listach, Stockton, 116
Hits: Joel Chimelis, Reno/Modesto, 161
RBIs: Frank Bolick, Stockton/San Bernardino, 102

HRs: Ken Whitfield, Reno, 24
Wins: George Tsamis, Visalia, 17
SOs: Kevin Rogers, San Jose, 186
ERA: Dan Rambo, San Jose, 2.19

A Carolina League
President: John Hopkins

North Standings	W	L	Pct.	GB	Attend.	Manager
Frederick Keys***(1)	74	62	.544	—	277,802	Wally Moon
Prince William Cannons (10)	64	75	.460	11½	210,262	Gary Denbo
Lynchburg Red Sox (2)	58	80	.420	17	92,607	Gary Allenson
Salem Buccaneers (23)	55	84	.396	20½	126,121	Stan Cliburn

South Standings	W	L	Pct.	GB	Attend.	Manager
Kinston Indians***(5)	88	47	.652	—	106,219	Brian Graham
Winston-Salem Spirits (16)	86	54	.614	4½	102,558	Brad Mills
Durham Bulls (15)	71	68	.511	19	300,499	Grady Little
Peninsula Pilots (12)	57	83	.407	33½	70,647	Jim Nettles

Playoff: Frederick 3 games, Kinston 2.

All-Star Team: 1B-J.T. Snow, Prince William; **2B**-Rouglas Odor, Kinston; **3B**-Gary Scott, Winston-Salem; **SS**-Ricky Gutierrez, Frederick; **OF**-Greg Blosser, Lynchburg; Keith Mitchell, Durham; Ken Ramos, Kinston; **C**-Armando Romero, Salem; **DH**-Doug Welch, Winston-Salem; **P**-Frank Seminara, Prince William; Mike Gardella, Prince William; **MVP**-Gary Scott, Winston-Salem; **Pitcher of the Year**-Frank Seminara, Prince William; **Manager**-Wally Moon, Frederick.

BA: Ken Ramos, Kinston, .345
Runs: Greg Sims, Salem, 91
Hits: Bruce Schreiber, Salem, 160
RBIs: Armando Romero, Salem, 90

HRs: Greg Blosser, Lynchburg, 18
Wins: Frank Seminara, Prince William, 16
SOs: Mike Oquist, Frederick, 170
ERA: Frank Seminara, Prince William, 1.90

A Florida State League
President: Chuck Murphy

East Standings	W	L	Pct.	GB	Attend.	Manager
West Palm Beach Expos***(20)	92	40	.697	—	83,673	Felipe Alou
Vero Beach Dodgers (19)	79	56	.585	14½	94,832	Joe Alvarez
St. Lucie Mets (21)	76	58	.567	17	65,597	Tim Blackwell
Ft. Lauderdale Yankees (10)	62	75	.453	32½	34,826	Mike Hart
Miami Miracle#	44	93	.321	50½	43,580	Mike Easler/Fredi Gonzalez

West Standings	W	L	Pct.	GB	Attend.	Manager
Dunedin Blue Jays*(14)	84	52	.618	—	65,348	Dennis Holmberg
Charlotte Rangers**(13)	85	53	.616	—	122,478	Bobby Jones
Sarasota White Sox (4)	63	75	.457	22	51,775	Tony Franklin
St. Petersburg Cardinals (24)	60	74	.448	23	190,146	Joe Pettini
Clearwater Phillies (22)	50	87	.365	37½	91,040	Lee Elia

Central Standings	W	L	Pct.	GB	Attend.	Manager
Lakeland Tigers***(6)	83	49	.629	—	57,967	John Lipon
Osceola Astros (18)	72	66	.522	14	46,421	Sal Butera
Baseball City Royals (7)	60	78	.435	26	18,884	Brian Poldberg
Winter Haven Red Sox (2)	40	94	.299	44	23,008	Dave Holt

#played home games in Pompano Beach, Florida.

Playoffs: Charlotte 2 games, Dunedin 0; Vero Beach 2 games, St. Lucie 1; West Palm Beach 2 games, Lakeland 1; Vero Beach 2 games, Charlotte 1.
Finals: Vero Beach 2 games, West Palm Beach 1.

All-Star Team: 1B-Nikco Riesgo, St. Lucie; **2B**-Jeff Kent, Dunedin; **3B**-Fred Samson, Charlotte; **SS**-Keith Kimberlin, Lakeland; **OF**-D.J. Dozier, St. Lucie; Kenny Lofton, Osceola; Jacob Brumfield, Baseball City; **C**-Ivan Rodriguez, Charlotte; Jason Townley, Dunedin; **DH**-Greg O'Halloran, Dunedin; **P**-John Johnstone, St. Lucie; Ramon Taveras, Vero Beach; Anthony Ward, Dunedin; Chris Pollack, West Palm Beach; Barry Manuel, Charlotte; Larry Stanford, Ft. Lauderdale; **MVP**-Nikco Riesgo, St. Lucie; **Manager**-Felipe Alou, West Palm Beach.

BA: Jacob Brumfield, Baseball City, .336
Runs: Eric Young, Vero Beach, 101
Hits: Kenny Lofton, Osceola, 159
RBIs: Nikco Riesgo, St. Lucie, 94
HRs: Ray Giannelli, Dunedin, 18

Wins: John Johnstone, St. Lucie, 15
SOs: Anthony Ward, Dunedin, 137
ERA: Rob Brown, Charlotte, 1.90
Saves: Barry Manuel, Charlotte, 36

A Midwest League
President: George Spelius

North Standings	W	L	Pct.	GB	Attend.	Manager
South Bend White Sox**(4)....	77	57	.575	—	212,485	Rick Patterson
Madison Muskies*(11).....	74	61	.548	3½	82,490	Casey Parsons
Beloit Brewers (8)	72	63	.533	5½	95,876	Bob Derksen
Appleton Foxes (7)............	62	71	.466	14½	84,396	Joe Breeden
Kenosha Twins (9).............	61	77	.442	18	53,373	Steve Liddle
Rockford Expos (20).........	56	80	.412	22	140,864	Mike Quade
Wausau Timbers (1)	49	87	.360	29	56,434	Mike Young
South Standings	**W**	**L**	**Pct.**	**GB**	**Attend.**	**Manager**
Cedar Rapids Reds*(17).....	88	46	.657	—	121,340	Dave Miley
Quad City Angels**(3).......	81	59	.579	10	204,889	Don Long
Burlington Braves (15)......	78	59	.569	11½	81,230	Jim Saul
Clinton Giants (26)...........	76	58	.567	12	75,325	Jack Mull
Springfield Cardinals (24) ..	63	76	.453	27½	161,271	Keith Champion
Waterloo Diamonds (25)	60	76	.441	29	82,451	Bryan Little
Peoria Chiefs (16)	55	82	.401	34½	195,671	Greg Mahlberg

Playoffs: Quad City 2 games, Cedar Rapids 0; South Bend 2 games, Madison 0.
Finals: Quad City 3 games, South Bend 1.

All-Star Team: 1B-Rich Tunison, Appleton; **2B**-Chad Curtis, Quad City; **3B**-John Byington, Beloit; **SS**-Damion Easley, Quad City; **OF**-Reggie Sanders, Cedar Rapids; Troy O'Leary, Beloit; Scott Bryant, Cedar Rapids; **C**-Eddie Taubensee, Cedar Rapids; **DH**-Fred Cooley, Madison; **P**-Alan Newman, Kenosha; Darin Kracl, Madison; Mike Hook, Quad City; Clyde Keller, Springfield; **MVP**-Reggie Sanders, Cedar Rapids; **Manager**-Don Long, Quad City.

BA: Scott Cepicky, South Bend, .312
Runs: Kerwin Moore, Appleton, 93
Hits: Chad Curtis, Quad City, 151
RBIs: John Byington, Beloit, 89

HRs: Fred Cooley, Madison, 22
Wins: Marcus Moore, Quad City, 16
SOs: Fili Martinez, Quad City, 195
ERA: Alan Newman, Kenosha, 1.64

A New York-Pennsylvania League
President: Leo A. Pinckney

McNamara East Standings	W	L	Pct.	GB	Attend.	Manager
Oneonta Yankees (10)	52	26	.667	—	58,742	Trey Hillman
Watertown Indians (5)........	43	34	.558	8½	51,992	Jim Gabella
Pittsfield Mets (21).............	43	34	.558	8½	101,110	Jim Eschen
Utica Blue Sox (4)	31	47	.397	21	52,074	Tommy Thompson
McNamara West Standings	**W**	**L**	**Pct.**	**GB**	**Attend.**	**Manager**
Geneva Cubs (16)	51	26	.662	—	35,032	Bill Hayes
Batavia Clippers (22).........	41	35	.539	9½	39,257	Dave Cash/Ramon Aviles
Elmira Pioneers (2)	32	45	.416	19	66,204	Mike Verdi
Auburn Astros (18).............	31	46	.403	20	45,475	Ricky Peters
Stedler Standings	**W**	**L**	**Pct.**	**GB**	**Attend.**	**Manager**
Erie Sailors	44	33	.571	—	61,606	Mal Fichman
Jamestown Expos (20).........	41	36	.532	3	35,364	Pat Daugherty
Welland Pirates (23)	36	42	.462	8½	37,331	Jim Mallon
Niagara Falls Rapids (6)	35	42	.455	9	56,157	Juan Lopez
Hamilton Redbirds (24)......	30	46	.395	13½	74,744	Luis Melendez
St. Catharines Blue Jays (14)	29	47	.382	14½	29,742	Doug Ault

Playoffs: Erie 2 games, Jamestown 0; Oneonta 2 games, Geneva 0.
Finals: Oneonta 2 games, Erie 1.

All-Star Team: 1B-Mike Brown, Welland; **2B**-Kevin Jordan, Oneonta; **3B**-Mike Songini, Erie; **SS**-Andy Postema, Erie; **OF**-Robbie Katzaroff, Jamestown; Jeff McNeely, Elmira; Jalal Leach, Oneonta; Scott Bullett, Welland; **C**-Carlos Delgado, St. Catharines; Rob Fitzpatrick, Jamestown; **DH**-Andy Hartung, Geneva; **P**-Jessie Hollins, Geneva; Sam Militello, Oneonta; Kirt Ojala, Oneonta; Alan Botkin, Hamilton; **Manager**-Trey Hillman, Oneonta.

BA: Robbie Katzaroff, Jamestown, .364
Runs: Mike Songini, Erie, 61
Hits: Robbie Katzaroff, Jamestown, 101
RBIs: Andy Hartung, Geneva, 70
HRs: Sean Ryan, Batavia, 16

Wins: Jessie Hollins, Geneva, 10
Edgardo Vazquez, Pittsfield, 10
Bill Wertz, Watertown, 10
SOs: Sam Militello, Oneonta, 119
ERA: Bobby Ryan, Watertown, 0.73

A Northwest League
President: Jack Cain

North Standings	W	L	Pct.	GB	Attend.	Manager
Spokane Indians (25).........	49	27	.645	—	129,999	Gene Glynn
Yakima Bears (19).............	36	40	.474	13	71,892	Jerry Royster
Everett Giants (26).............	35	41	.461	14	74,577	Deron McCue
Bellingham Mariners (12) ..	32	44	.421	17	52,461	P.J. Carey
South Standings	**W**	**L**	**Pct.**	**GB**	**Attend.**	**Manager**
Boise Hawks (3)	53	23	.697	—	124,270	Tom Kotchman
Southern Oregon A's (11) ..	40	36	.526	13	69,247	Grady Fuson
Eugene Emeralds (7)	30	46	.395	23	128,831	Paul Kirsch
Bend Bucks (x)	29	47	.382	24	40,849	Mike Bubalo

Playoff: Spokane 2 games, Boise 1.

All-Star Team: 1B-Jay Gainer, Spokane; **2B**-Giovanni Miranda, Eugene; **3B**-Mike Galle, Yakima; **SS**-Kevin Farlow, Spokane; **OF**-Matt Mieske, Spokane; Eric Booker, Southern Oregon; Mark Dalesandro, Boise; **C**-Eric Helfand, Southern Oregon; **DH**-Brian Stephens, Bellingham; **P**-Hilly Hathaway, Boise; Randy Powers, Boise; **MVP**-Matt Mieske, Spokane; **Manager**-Gene Glynn, Spokane.

BA: Jay Gainer, Spokane, .356
Runs: Matt Mieske, Spokane, 59
Hits: Jay Gainer, Spokane, 100
RBIs: Matt Mieske, Spokane, 63

HRs: Matt Mieske, Spokane, 12
Wins: Danny Henrikson, Bend/Everett, 10
SOs: Hilly Hathaway, Boise, 113
ERA: David Adam, Bellingham, 1.43

A South Atlantic League
President: John H. Moss

North Standings	W	L	Pct.	GB	Attend.	Manager
Gastonia Rangers (13)	82	61	.573	—	48,767	Orlando Gomez
Fayetteville Generals*(6) ...	82	61	.573	—	95,040	Gene Roof
Charleston (WV) Wheelers**(17)	77	66	.538	5	152,350	Jim Lett
Asheville Tourists (18).......	66	77	.462	16	101,193	Frank Cacciatore
Spartanburg Phillies (22)...	63	78	.447	18	45,104	Mel Roberts
Greensboro Hornets (10)	59	85	.410	23½	153,232	Brian Butterfield
South Standings	**W**	**L**	**Pct.**	**GB**	**Attend.**	**Manager**
Columbia Mets*(21)...........	83	60	.580	—	99,385	Bill Stein
Myrtle Beach Blue Jays (14)	77	63	.550	4½	71,598	Mike Fischlin
Savannah Cardinals**(24)..	73	68	.518	9	94,686	Rick Colbert
Sumter Braves (15)	73	69	.514	9½	37,412	Ned Yost
Augusta Pirates (23)	73	70	.510	10	125,105	Lee Driggers
Charleston (SC) Rainbows (25) .	46	96	.324	36½	76,133	Jack Krol

Playoffs: Charleston (WV) 2 games, Fayetteville 0; Savannah 2 games, Columbia 0.
Finals: Charleston (WV) 3 games, Savannah 0.

All-Star Team: 1B-Ryan Klesko, Sumter; **2B**-David Hajek, Asheville; **3B**-Tim Howard, Columbia; **SS**-Tito Navarro, Columbia; **OF**-Pat Howell, Columbia; Scott Pose, Charleston (WV); Tony Scruggs, Gastonia; **C**-Brook Fordyce, Columbia; **DH**-Mike Burton, Gastonia; **P**-Tim Pugh, Charleston (WV); Randy Marshall, Fayetteville; **MVP**-Tim Howard, Columbia; **Pitcher of the Year**-Randy Marshall, Fayetteville; **Manager**-Bill Stein, Columbia.

BA: Tim Howard, Columbia, .323
Runs: Scott Pose, Charleston (WV), 106
Hits: Tim Howard, Columbia, 163
RBIs: Tim Howard, Columbia, 89

HRs: Cliff Brannon, Savannah, 18
Wins: Tim Pugh, Charleston (WV), 15
SOs: Sterling Hitchcock, Greensboro, 171
ERA: Jeffery Hoffman, Greensboro, 1.47

R Appalachian League
President: Bill Halstead

Standings	W	L	Pct.	GB	Attend.	Manager
Elizabethton Twins (9)	51	16	.761	—	17,013	Ray Smith
Huntington Cubs (16)	40	29	.580	12	66,042	Steve Roadcap
Kingsport Mets (21)..........	41	31	.569	12½	37,363	Jim Thrift
Bluefield Orioles (1)..........	38	32	.543	14½	33,354	Gus Gil
Pulaski Braves (15)............	37	35	.514	16½	17,673	Randy Ingle
Burlington Indians (5)	35	37	.486	18½	66,330	Dave Keller
Princeton Patriots (x)	31	36	.463	20	26,620	Eli Grba
Johnson City Cardinals (24)...	28	42	.400	24½	24,163	Mark DeJohn
Martinsville Phillies (22)....	25	44	.362	27	69,182	Rollie DeArmas
Bristol Tigers (6)	22	46	.324	29½	26,026	Ken Cunningham

Playoffs: None.

All-Star Team: 1B-Pat Dando, Pulaski; **2B**-Jeff Borgese, Martinsville; **3B**-Jose Viera, Huntington; **SS**-Aaron Ledesma, Kingsport; **OF**-Tracy Sanders, Burlington; Brian Kowitz, Pulaski; Rich Becker, Elizabethton; **C**-Greg Zaun, Bluefield; **P**-Brad Hassinger, Princeton; Roger Dixon, Elizabethton; Tom Benson, Elizabethton; **MVP**-Paul Russo, Elizabethton; **Manager**-Ray Smith, Elizabethton.

BA: Pat Dando, Pulaski, .360
Runs: Paul Russo, Elizabethton, 58
Hits: Pat Dando, Pulaski, 91
RBIs: Paul Russo, Elizabethton, 67

HRs: Paul Russo, Elizabethton, 22
Wins: Tyson Godfrey, Huntington, 9
SOs: J.J. Munoz, Martinsville, 126
ERA: Rob Carpenter, Kingsport, 1.76

R Arizona League
President: Bob Richmond

Standings	W	L	Pct.	GB	Manager
Brewers (Peoria) (8)	36	17	.679	—	Alex Taveras
Mariners (Tempe) (12)	32	21	.604	4	Dave Myers

	W	L	Pct.	GB	
Cardinals (Peoria) (24)	28	24	.538	7½	Larry Milbourne
Athletics (Scottsdale) (11)..	26	27	.491	10	Gary Jones
Padres (Scottsdale) (25)......	19	35	.352	17½	Jaime Moreno
Angels (Mesa) (3)..............	19	36	.345	18	Bill Lachemann

Playoffs: None.

All-Star Team: 1B-Marc Newfield, Mariners; **2B**-Julian Salazar, Brewers; Carlos Polanco, Angels; **3B**-John Halland, Mariners; **SS**-Israel Seda, Mariners; **OF**-Orlando Barrios, Brewers; Jose Velez, Cardinals; Tony Pritchett, Athletics; **C**-Don Pryblinski, Cardinals; Jose Stella, Angels; **DH**-Paul Brannon, Mariners; **P**-Phil Angelos, Brewers; Derron Spiller, Cardinals; Bill Kostich, Mariners; Victor Rojas, Angels; **MVP**-Marc Newfield, Mariners; **Manager**-Jaime Moreno, Padres; Bill Lachemann, Angels.

BA: Tommy Boudreau, Mariners, .378
Runs: Jonas Hamlin, Cardinals, 45
Hits: Jonas Hamlin, Cardinals, 76
RBIs: Brian Spears, Brewers, 45
HRs: Jonas Hamlin, Cardinals, 9

Wins: Phil Angelos, Brewers, 7
    Mike Hampton, Mariners, 7
SOs: Mike Lynch, Brewers, 69
ERA: Bill Kostich, Mariners, 0.40

R Gulf Coast League
President: Thomas J. Saffell

North Standings	W	L	Pct.	GB	Manager
Dodgers (Kissimmee) (19) .	38	25	.603	—	Ivan DeJesus
Reds (Plant City) (17).........	36	27	.571	2	Sam Mejias
Red Sox (Winter Haven) (2)....	34	29	.540	4	Felix Maldonado
Astros (Kissimmee) (18)	33	30	.524	5	Julio Linares
Royals (Baseball City) (7)..	25	38	.397	13	Carlos Tosca
Indians (Winter Haven) (5).	23	40	.365	15	Dean Treanor

South Standings	W	L	Pct.	GB	Manager
Expos (Bradenton) (20)	40	23	.635	—	Lorenzo Bundy
Rangers (Port Charlotte) (13)..	36	27	.571	4	Chino Cadahia
Braves (Bradenton) (15)	33	29	.532	6½	Jim Procopio
Yankees (Sarasota) (10)......	32	30	.516	7½	Glenn Sherlock
Twins (Sarasota) (9)	32	30	.516	7½	Joel Lepel
Mets (Sarasota) (21)	29	30	.492	9	John Tamargo
Pirates (Bradenton) (23)	25	37	.403	14½	Julio Garcia
White Sox (Sarasota) (4)	21	42	.333	19	Mike Gellinger

Playoff: Dodgers 2 games, Expos 0.

All-Star Team: 1B-Peter Laake, Rangers; **2B**-Claudio Ozario, Expos; **3B**-David Lowery, Rangers; **SS**-Tom Nevers, Astros; **OF**-Rondell White, Expos; Raul Robinson, Braves; Domingo Mota, Dodgers; **C**-Jose Valdez, Dodgers; **P**-John Roper, Reds; Tony Bouton, Rangers; **Manager**-Sam Mejias, Reds.

BA: Tom Houk, Twins, .344
Runs: Domingo Mota, Dodgers, 46
    Amadoz Arias, Reds, 46
Hits: Domingo Mota, Dodgers, 73
RBIs: Jose Valdez, Dodgers, 43

HRs: James Dismuke, Reds, 7
Wins: Melvin Gonzales, Red Sox, 9
SOs: Jose Martinez, Mets, 90
ERA: Mariano Rivera, Yankees, 0.17

R Pioneer League
President: Ralph C. Nelles

North Standings	W	L	Pct.	GB	Attend.	Manager
Great Falls Dodgers (19)	48	20	.706	—	72,609	Joe Vavra
Helena Brewers (8).............	37	28	.569	9½	40,524	Gary Calhoun
Billings Mustangs (17)	32	34	.485	15	94,245	Gerry Groninger
Medicine Hat Blue Jays (14)..	20	46	.303	27	13,350	Garth Iorg

South Standings	W	L	Pct.	GB	Attend.	Manager
Salt Lake City Trappers......	42	26	.618	—	192,366	Nick Belmonte
Idaho Falls Braves (15).......	39	31	.557	4	77,942	Steve Curry
Butte Copper Kings (13).....	37	30	.552	4½	30,116	Bump Wills
Gate City Pioneers#(x)	15	55	.214	28	20,926	Ed Creech

#represented Pocatello, Idaho.

Playoff: Great Falls 3 games, Salt Lake City 0.

All-Star Team: 1B-Mike Busch, Great Falls; **2B**-Vince Castaldo, Helena; **3B**-Tom Duffin, Salt Lake City; **SS**-Chris Brittain, Idaho Falls; **OF**-David Hulse, Butte; K.C. Gillum, Billings; Raul Mondesi, Great Falls; **C**-Todd Guggiana, Butte; **DH**-Kevin McMullan, Salt Lake City; **P**-Pedro Martinez, Great Falls; Willie Ambos, Salt Lake City; Michael Ferry, Billings; **Manager**-Steve Curry, Idaho Falls.

BA: David Hulse, Butte, .358
Runs: Mike Moberg, Salt Lake City, 64
Hits: David Hulse, Butte, 92
RBIs: Tim Carter, Helena, 58**HRs:** Mike Busch, Great Falls, 13

Wins: Scott Ryder, Idaho Falls, 9
SOs: Mark Mimbs, Great Falls, 94
ERA: Willie Ambos, Salt Lake City, 2.57

1990 Interleague Post Season Play

World Series
Cincinnati (National) 4 games, Oakland (American) 0

AAA Classic
Omaha (American Association) 4 games, Rochester (International) 1

1990 Major League Farm Systems

American League

1. Baltimore (5): Rochester, Hagerstown, Frederick, Wausau, Bluefield.
2. Boston (6): Pawtucket, New Britain, Lynchburg, Winter Haven, Elmira, Gulf Coast.
3. California (6): Edmonton, Midland, Palm Springs, Quad City, Boise, Arizona.
4. Chicago (6): Vancouver, Birmingham, Sarasota, South Bend, Utica, Gulf Coast.
5. Cleveland (6): Colorado Springs, Canton-Akron, Kinston, Watertown, Burlington (NC), Gulf Coast.
6. Detroit (6): Toledo, London, Lakeland, Fayetteville, Niagara Falls, Bristol.
7. Kansas City (6): Omaha, Memphis, Baseball City, Appleton, Eugene, Gulf Coast.
8. Milwaukee (6): Denver, El Paso, Stockton, Beloit, Helena, Arizona.
9. Minnesota (6): Portland, Orlando, Visalia, Kenosha, Elizabethton, Gulf Coast.
10. New York (7): Columbus (OH), Albany-Colonie, Prince William, Ft. Lauderdale, Greensboro, Oneonta, Gulf Coast.
11. Oakland (6): Tacoma, Huntsville, Modesto, Madison, Southern Oregon, Arizona.
12. Seattle (6): Calgary, Williamsport, San Bernardino, Peninsula, Bellingham, Arizona.
13. Texas (6): Oklahoma City, Tulsa, Port Charlotte, Gastonia, Butte, Gulf Coast.
14. Toronto (6): Syracuse, Knoxville, Dunedin, Myrtle Beach, St. Catharines, Medicine Hat.

Co-op (x): Bend, Princeton, Gate City.
Independent: Reno, Salinas, Miami, Erie, Salt Lake City.

National League

15. Atlanta (8): Richmond, Greenville, Durham, Sumter, Burlington (IA), Pulaski, Idaho Falls, Gulf Coast.
16. Chicago (6): Iowa, Charlotte, Winston-Salem, Peoria, Geneva, Huntington.
17. Cincinnati (6): Nashville, Chattanooga, Charleston (WV), Cedar Rapids, Billings, Gulf Coast.
18. Houston (6): Tucson, Columbus (GA), Osceola, Asheville, Auburn, Gulf Coast.
19. Los Angeles (7): Albuquerque, San Antonio, Bakersfield, Vero Beach, Yakima, Great Falls, Gulf Coast.
20. Montreal (6): Indianapolis, Jacksonville, West Palm Beach, Rockford, Jamestown, Gulf Coast.
21. New York (7): Tidewater, Jackson, St. Lucie, Columbia, Pittsfield, Kingsport, Gulf Coast.
22. Philadelphia (6): Scranton-Wilkes-Barre, Reading, Clearwater, Spartanburg, Batavia, Martinsville.
23. Pittsburgh (6): Buffalo, Harrisburg, Salem, Augusta, Welland, Gulf Coast.
24. St. Louis (8): Louisville, Arkansas, St. Petersburg, Springfield, Savannah, Hamilton, Johnson City, Arizona.
25. San Diego (7): Las Vegas, Wichita, Riverside, Waterloo, Charleston (SC), Spokane, Arizona.
26. San Francisco (5): Phoenix, Shreveport, San Jose, Clinton, Everett.

1990 No-Hitters

Date	Pitcher	Team	League	Opponent	Score
4-11	Mark Langston/				
	Mike Witt	California	American	Seattle	1-0
4-15	Michael Ignasiak/				
	Doug Henry	Stockton	California	San Jose	6-3 (7)
5-6	Mike Dunne	Las Vegas	Pacific Coast	Portland	2-0
5-19	Carl Randle	Gastonia	South Atlantic	Greensboro	4-0
5-24	Chris Czarnik	Durham	Carolina	Winston-Salem	2-3 (14)
5-25	Wally Ritchie	Scranton-	International	Syracuse	1-0 (8)
		Wilkes-Barre			
6-2	Randy Johnson	Seattle	American	Detroit	2-0
6-4	Robert Wishnevski	Knoxville	Southern	Charlotte	3-0 (7)
6-5	Linty Ingram	Fayetteville	South Atlantic	Charleston (WV)	7-0 (7)
6-11	Nolan Ryan	Texas	American	Oakland	5-0
6-12	Clayton Daniel	Miami	Florida State	Ft. Lauderdale	7-0 (7)
6-16	Rick Balabon	Peninsula	Carolina	Frederick	4-0 (7)
6-17	Kent Bottenfield	Jacksonville	Southern	Orlando	1-0
6-29	Dave Stewart	Oakland	American	Toronto	5-0
6-29	Fernando Valenzuela	Los Angeles	National	St. Louis	6-0
7-1	Andy Hawkins	New York	American	Chicago	0-4 (8)
7-4	Israel Velazquez	Leon	Mexican	MC Tigres	5-0 (7)
7-6	Earl Jewett	Sumter	South Atlantic	Spartanburg	1-0
7-13	Frank Castillo	Charlotte	Southern	Huntsville	4-0 (7)
7-13	Gene Walter	Omaha	American Assoc.	Iowa	3-0 (7)
7-16	Sterling Hitchcock	Greensboro	South Atlantic	Sumter	1-0
7-20	Armando Reynoso	Saltillo	Mexican	Industriales	1-0 (7)
7-21	Michael Draper	Ft. Lauderdale	Florida State	St. Petersburg	6-0
7-23	Daniel Boone	Rochester	International	Syracuse	2-0 (7)
7-24	Ottis Smith	Mets	Gulf Coast	Twins	1-0
7-26	John Conner/				
	John Smith	Appleton	Midwest	Wausau	8-0
7-31	Tom Wegmann	Kingsport	Appalachian	Pulaski	7-0 (P, 7)
8-2	Lauro Cervantes	Union Laguna	Mexican	Industriales	4-0
8-5	Scott Ryder	Idaho Falls	Pioneer	Medicine Hat	2-1
8-9	Peter Blohm	Knoxville	Southern	Greenville	2-0 (6)
8-15	Terry Mulholland	Philadelphia	National	San Francisco	6-0
8-21	Timothy Nedin	Kenosha	Midwest	Burlington	1-0 (7)
8-25	Kevin Morton	New Britain	Eastern	Reading	1-0 (P, 7)
8-29	Shawn Turri/				
	Bob Undorf	Niagara Falls	New York-Penn.	Elmira	6-1 (7)
8-30	Johnny Ard	Orlando	Southern	Chattanooga	2-0 (7)
8-31	Mariano Rivera	Yankees	Gulf Coast	Pirates	3-0 (7)
9-2	Dave Stieb	Toronto	American	Detroit	3-0

Number in parentheses indicates innings if other than nine; "P" indicates perfect game.

THIS DATE IN MINOR LEAGUE HISTORY

January 18, 1990, Boardwalk and Baseball in Davenport, Florida, was shut down by its owners, Busch Entertainment. The unprofitable theme park's closing would not affect the Kansas City Royals' spring training complex or the Baseball City, Florida State League, franchise which operated at the site.

February 20, 1990, The Birmingham Barons of the Southern League were purchased by the Suntory Corporation, Japan's largest privately owned company. The club was sold for a reported $3.6 million. The old ownership group was headed by Art Clarkson, general manager and president of the club.

April 6, 1990, Five of the six home openers in the Midwest League were postponed due to cold weather.

May 1, 1990, An option was taken for the sale of the Durham Bulls of the Carolina League. The selling price was reported to be in excess of $3 million.

May 14, 1990, Ronaldo Romero of the South Atlantic League's Gastonia Rangers collapsed and died in the dugout during a game at Fayetteville. Romero had pitched the first two innings of the game when he complained to the Gastonia trainer about his rapid heartbeat. He then was stricken. An autopsy revealed an enlarged and weakened heart wall.

June 4, 1990, The major league free agent draft was held, and for the first time in many years, a minor league club participated extensively. The independent Miami Miracle of the Florida State League drafted 16 players. Major league officials were not pleased, and in December the new Professional Baseball Agreement prohibited minor league clubs from taking part in the draft.

June 10, 1990, Lakeland's John Lipon won his 2,000th game as a minor league manager. He was in his 27th season as a minor league skipper.

June 13, 1990, Cohen Stadium opened in El Paso, Texas. The $6.8 million facility, named for former players Syd and Andy Cohen, replaced ancient Dudley Field. The "Dudley Dome" had housed El Paso baseball for 66 years.

June 27, 1990, Longtime minor league manager Ed Nottle was fired by the Boston Red Sox from his post as manager of Pawtucket of the International League.

July 11, 1990, The National League beat the American League 8-5 in the third annual Triple-A All-Star Game. It was played in Las Vegas before a crowd of 10,323.

August 25, 1990, Charlie Rogers tied a Florida State League record by striking out 20 batters as he pitched Miami to a 10-1 victory over Baseball City. Miami, an independent club, drafted Rogers in the 18th round of the free agent draft the previous June.

August 30, 1990, Charlotte's Barry Manuel set a Florida State League record with 37 saves, breaking the previous mark of 33 set in 1988 by Baseball City's Aquedo Vasquez.

November 1, 1990, When major and minor league negotiators failed to reach accord on a new Professional Baseball Agreement (PBA), the major leagues announced they would not attend the annual winter meetings in Los Angeles. They would hold their own meetings in Chicago. It was the first time since 1966 that the two groups had not met jointly.

December 15, 1990, With the major leagues threatening to form their own new minor leagues, the leagues of the National Association barely ratified a new PBA that gave new wide ranging power to the major league commissioner in dealing with the minors.

American League
President: Dr. Robert W. Brown

East Standings

	W	L	Pct.	GB	Attend.	Manager
Toronto Blue Jays	91	71	.562	—	4,001,527	Cito Gaston
Boston Red Sox	84	78	.519	7	2,562,435	Joe Morgan
Detroit Tigers	84	78	.519	7	1,641,661	Sparky Anderson
Milwaukee Brewers	83	79	.512	8	1,478,729	Tom Trebelhorn
New York Yankees	71	91	.438	20	1,863,733	Stump Merrill
Baltimore Orioles	67	95	.414	24	2,552,753	Frank Robinson/Johnny Oates
Cleveland Indians	57	105	.352	34	1,051,863	John McNamara/Mike Hargrove

West Standings

	W	L	Pct.	GB	Attend.	Manager
Minnesota Twins	95	67	.586	—	2,293,842	Tom Kelly
Chicago White Sox	87	75	.537	8	2,934,154	Jeff Torborg
Texas Rangers	85	77	.525	10	2,297,720	Bobby Valentine
Oakland Athletics	84	78	.519	11	2,713,493	Tony LaRussa
Seattle Mariners	83	79	.512	12	2,147,905	Jim Lefebvre
Kansas City Royals	82	80	.506	13	2,161,537	John Wathan/Bob Schaefer/Hal McRae
California Angels	81	81	.500	14	2,416,236	Doug Rader/Buck Rodgers

Playoff: Minnesota 4 games, Toronto 1.

BA: Julio Franco, Texas, .341
Runs: Paul Molitor, Milwaukee, 133
Hits: Paul Molitor, Milwaukee, 216
RBIs: Cecil Fielder, Detroit, 133
HRs: Jose Canseco, Oakland, 44
Cecil Fielder, Detroit, 44

Wins: Scott Erickson, Minnesota, 20
Don Gullickson, Detroit, 20
SOs: Roger Clemens, Boston, 241
ERA: Roger Clemens, Boston, 2.62
Pct: Scott Erickson, Minnesota, .714, 20-8
Saves: Bryan Harvey, California, 46

National League
President: William White

East Standings

	W	L	Pct.	GB	Attend.	Manager
Pittsburgh Pirates	98	64	.605	—	2,065,302	Jim Leyland
St. Louis Cardinals	84	78	.519	14	2,448,699	Joe Torre
Philadelphia Phillies	78	84	.481	20	2,050,012	Nick Leyva/Jim Fregosi
Chicago Cubs	77	83	.481	20	2,314,250	Don Zimmer/Joe Altobelli/Jim Essian
New York Mets	77	84	.478	20½	2,284,484	Bud Harrelson/Mike Cubbage
Montreal Expos	71	90	.441	26½	934,742	Buck Rodgers/Tom Runnells

West Standings

	W	L	Pct.	GB	Attend.	Manager
Atlanta Braves	94	68	.580	—	2,140,217	Bobby Cox
Los Angeles Dodgers	93	69	.574	1	3,348,170	Tom Lasorda
San Diego Padres	84	78	.519	10	1,804,289	Greg Riddoch
San Francisco Giants	75	87	.463	19	1,737,478	Roger Craig
Cincinnati Reds	74	88	.457	20	2,372,377	Lou Piniella
Houston Astros	65	97	.401	29	1,196,152	Art Howe

Playoff: Atlanta 4 games, Pittsburgh 3.

BA: Terry Pendleton, Atlanta, .319
Runs: Brett Butler, Los Angeles, 112
Hits: Terry Pendleton, Atlanta, 187
RBIs: Howard Johnson, New York, 117
HRs: Howard Johnson, New York, 38

Wins: Tom Glavine, Atlanta, 20
John Smiley, Pittsburgh, 20
SOs: David Cone, New York, 241
ERA: Dennis Martinez, Montreal, 2.39
Pct: John Smiley, Pittsburgh, .714, 20-8
Jose Rijo, Cincinnati, .714, 15-6
Saves: Lee Smith, Chicago, 47

AAA American Association
President: Randy Mobley

East Standings

	W	L	Pct.	GB	Attend.	Manager
Buffalo Bisons (23)	81	62	.566	—	1,188,972	Terry Collins
Indianapolis Indians (20)	75	68	.524	6	348,089	Jerry Manuel/Pat Kelly
Nashville Sounds (17)	65	78	.455	16	454,575	Pete Mackanin
Louisville Redbirds (24)	51	92	.357	30	565,716	Mark DeJohn

West Standings

	W	L	Pct.	GB	Attend.	Manager
Denver Zephyrs (8)	79	65	.549	—	550,135	Tony Muser
Iowa Cubs (16)	78	66	.542	1	308,814	Jim Essian/Mick Kelleher
Omaha Royals (7)	73	71	.507	6	329,797	Sal Rende
Oklahoma City 89ers (13)	52	92	.361	27	347,427	Tommy Thompson

Played an interlocking schedule with the International League known as AAA Alliance.

Playoff: Denver 3 games, Buffalo 2.

All-Star Team: 1B-Rob Maurer, Oklahoma City; **2B-**Todd Haney, Indianapolis; **3B-**Dean Palmer, Oklahoma City; **SS-**Rey Sanchez, Iowa; **OF-**Mickey Brantley, Denver; Jim Olander, Denver; John VanderWal, Indianapolis; **C-**Tim Spehr, Omaha; **DH-**Terry Lee, Nashville; **P-**Rick Reed, Buffalo; Bob Buchanan, Omaha; **MVP-**Jim Olander, Denver; **Pitcher of the Year-**Rick Reed, Buffalo; **Manager-**Tony Muser, Denver.

BA: Jim Olander, Denver, .325
Runs: Jim Olander, Denver, 89
Hits: Jim Olander, Denver, 162
RBIs: Tim McIntosh, Denver, 91

HRs: Dean Palmer, Oklahoma City, 22
Wins: Rick Reed, Buffalo, 14
SOs: Cal Eldred, Denver, 168
ERA: Rick Reed, Buffalo, 2.15

AAA International League
President: Randy Mobley

East Standings

	W	L	Pct.	GB	Attend.	Manager
Pawtucket Red Sox (2)	79	64	.552	—	349,338	Butch Hobson
Rochester Red Wings (1)	76	68	.528	3½	345,167	Greg Biagini
Syracuse Chiefs (14)	73	71	.507	6½	307,993	Bob Bailor
Scranton-Wilkes-Barre Red Barons (22)	65	78	.455	14	535,725	Bill Dancy

West Standings

	W	L	Pct.	GB	Attend.	Manager
Columbus Clippers (10)	85	59	.590	—	570,605	Rick Down
Tidewater Tides (21)	77	65	.542	7	196,998	Steve Swisher
Toledo Mud Hens (6)	74	70	.514	11	217,662	Joe Sparks
Richmond Braves (15)	65	79	.451	20	434,994	Phil Niekro

Played an interlocking schedule with the American Association known as AAA Alliance.

Playoff: Columbus 3 games, Pawtucket 0.

All-Star Team: 1B-Domingo Martinez, Syracuse; **2B-**Jeff Gardner, Tidewater; **3B-**Scott Cooper, Pawtucket; **SS-**Eddie Zosky, Syracuse; **OF-**Derek Bell, Syracuse; Phil Plantier, Pawtucket; Luis Mercedes, Rochester; **C-**Todd Hundley, Tidewater; **DH-**Mitch Lyden, Toledo; **P-**Mike Mussina, Rochester; Daryl Irvine, Pawtucket; **MVP-**Derek Bell, Syracuse; **Pitcher of the Year-**Mike Mussina, Rochester; **Manager-**Butch Hobson, Pawtucket.

BA: Derek Bell, Syracuse, .346
Runs: Derek Bell, Syracuse, 89
Hits: Derek Bell, Syracuse, 158
RBIs: Derek Bell, Syracuse, 93
HRs: Rick Lancellotti, Pawtucket, 21

Wins: John Shea, Syracuse, 12
Mickey Weston, Syracuse, 12
Blaine Beatty, Tidewater, 12
Mark Dewey, Tidewater, 12
Anthony Telford, Rochester, 12
Yorkis Perez, Richmond, 12
SOs: Pat Hentgen, Syracuse, 155
ERA: Armando Reynoso, Richmond, 2.61

AAA Mexican League
President: Pedro Treto Cisneros

North Standings

	W	L	Pct.	GB	Attend.	Manager
Monterrey Sultanes	82	38	.683	—	138,218	Aurelio Rodriguez
Dos Laredos Tecolotes	67	54	.554	15½	163,111	Jose Guerrero
Monterrey Industriales	61	56	.521	19½	132,740	Hector Espino/Marcelo Juarez
Jalisco Charros	57	62	.479	24½	171,564	Roberto Castellon
Union Laguna Algodoneros	57	63	.475	25	175,471	Marco Antonio Vazquez
Saltillo Saraperos	55	68	.447	28½	118,853	Juan Navarrete
Monclova Acereros	49	71	.408	33	170,221	Gregorio Luque
San Luis Potosi Reales	47	74	.388	35½	137,170	Rodolfo Sandoval

South Standings

	W	L	Pct.	GB	Attend.	Manager
Mexico City Diablos Rojos	74	44	.627	—	149,524	Ben Reyes/Ramon Montoya
Leon Bravos	73	45	.619	1	134,815	Francisco Estrada
Campeche Piratas	70	50	.583	5	155,254	Sergio Robles/Jorge Tellaeche
Yucatan Leones	70	52	.574	6	215,693	Fernando Villaescusa
Mexico City Tigres	62	56	.525	12	156,330	Oswaldo Alvarez
Cordoba Cafeteros	48	68	.414	25	139,721	Bernardo Calvo
Tabasco Olmecas	46	72	.390	28	134,294	Joel Serna/Armando Barajas/Rusty Tillman
Aguascalientes Rieleros	36	81	.308	37½	126,588	Alfredo Ortiz/Alfredo Rios

Playoffs: Monterrey Sultanes 4 games, Jalisco 1; Monterrey Industriales 4 games, Dos Laredos 0; MC Diablos Rojos 4 games, Yucatan 0; Leon 4 games, Campeche 1. MC Diablos Rojos 4 games, Leon 3; Monterrey Sultanes 4 games, Monterrey Industriales 2. **Finals:** Monterrey Sultanes 4 games, MC Diablos Rojos 3.

BA: Rich Renteria, Jalisco, .442
Runs: James Steels, MC Diablos Rojos, 131
Hits: James Steels, MC Diablos Rojos, 175
RBIs: Larry See, MC Diablos Rojos, 129

HRs: Roy Johnson, Campeche, 37
Wins: Juan Palafox, Union Laguna, 17
SOs: Ben Morrow, Saltillo, 144
ERA: Odell Jones, Monterrey Industriales, 2.67

AAA Pacific Coast League
President: Bill Cutler

North Standings

	W	L	Pct.	GB	Attend.	Manager
Calgary Cannons**(12)	72	64	.529	—	325,965	Keith Bodie
Edmonton Trappers (3)	70	66	.515	2	252,813	Max Oliveras
Portland Beavers*(9)	70	68	.507	3	181,116	Russ Nixon
Tacoma Tigers (11)	63	73	.463	9	293,418	Jeff Newman
Vancouver Canadians (4)	49	86	.363	22½	288,978	Marv Foley/Rick Renick

*Won first-half **Won second-half ***Won both halves
Numbers after nicknames indicate farm system.
Affiliation listed at end of each year.

South Standings

South Standings	W	L	Pct.	GB	Attend.	Manager
Albuquerque Dukes (19)	80	58	.580	—	340,685	Kevin Kennedy
Tucson Toros*(18)	79	61	.564	2	317,347	Bob Skinner
Colorado Springs Sky Sox**(5).	72	67	.518	8½	174,731	Charlie Manuel
Phoenix Firebirds (26)........	68	70	.493	12	247,791	Duane Espy
Las Vegas Stars (25)...........	65	75	.464	16	330,699	Jim Riggleman

Playoffs: Calgary 3 games, Portland 0; Tucson 3 games, Colorado Springs 1.
Finals: Tucson 3 games, Calgary 2.

All-Star Team: 1B-Tino Martinez, Calgary; **2B**-Andres Santana, Phoenix; **3B**-Gary Cooper, Tucson; **SS**-Andujar Cedeno, Tucson; **OF**-Kenny Lofton, Tucson; Ruben Amaro, Edmonton; Geronimo Berroa, Colorado Springs; **C**-Carlos Hernandez, Albuquerque; **DH**-Luis Medina, Colorado Springs; **P**-Kyle Abbott, Edmonton; Tom Edens, Portland; Dean Wilkins, Tucson; **MVP**-Tino Martinez, Calgary; **Manager**-Bob Skinner, Tucson.

BA: Rich Amaral, Calgary, .346
Runs: Ruben Amaro, Edmonton, 95
Hits: Kenny Lofton, Tucson, 168
RBIs: Ted Wood, Phoenix, 109

HRs: Luis Medina, Colorado Springs, 27
Bernardo Brito, Portland, 27
Wins: Kyle Abbott, Edmonton, 14
Terry Clark, Tucson, 14
SOs: Jeff Hartsock, Albuquerque, 123
ERA: Gil Heredia, Phoenix, 2.82

AA Eastern League
President: Charles E. Eshbach

Standings	W	L	Pct.	GB	Attend.	Manager
Harrisburg Senators (20)	87	53	.621	—	233,423	Mike Quade
Hagerstown Suns (1)	81	59	.579	6	193,753	Jerry Narron
Albany-Colonie Yankees (10).	76	64	.543	11	171,146	Dan Radison
Canton-Akron Indians (5)...	75	65	.536	12	218,397	Ken Bolek
Reading Phillies (22)	72	68	.514	15	250,610	Don McCormack
London Tigers (6)..............	61	78	.439	25½	150,435	Gene Roof
Williamsport Bills (21).......	60	79	.432	26½	96,711	Clint Hurdle
New Britain Red Sox (2)	47	93	.336	40	146,632	Gary Allenson

Playoffs: Harrisburg 3 games, Canton 1; Albany-Colonie 3 games, Hagerstown 0.
Finals: Albany-Colonie 3 games, Harrisburg 0.

All-Star Team: 1B-J.T. Snow, Albany-Colonie; **2B**-Rodney Lofton, Hagerstown; **3B**-Jim Thome, Canton-Akron; **SS**-Dave Silvestri, Albany-Colonie; **OF**-Rob Katzaroff, Harrisburg; Bruce Dostal, Reading; Jeromy Burnitz, Williamsport; **C**-Bob Natal, Harrisburg; **DH**-Carlos Martinez, Canton-Akron; **Util**-Matt Stairs, Harrisburg; **P**-Ed Martel, Albany-Colonie; Arthur Rhodes, Hagerstown; Larry Stanford, Albany-Colonie; **MVP**-Matt Stairs, Harrisburg; **Pitcher of the Year**-Arthur Rhodes, Hagerstown; **Manager**-Mike Quade, Harrisburg.

BA: Matt Stairs, Harrisburg, .333
Runs: Dave Silvestri, Albany-Colonie, 97
Hits: Matt Stairs, Harrisburg, 168
RBIs: Vince Phillips, Albany-Colonie, 85
Jeromy Burnitz, Williamsport, 85

HRs: Jeromy Burnitz, Williamsport, 31
Wins: Ed Martel, Albany-Colonie, 13
Dave Telgheder, Williamsport, 13
SOs: Ed Martel, Albany-Colonie, 141
ERA: Jeff Mutis, Canton-Akron, 1.80

AA Southern League
President: Jimmy Bragan

East Standings	W	L	Pct.	GB	Attend.	Manager
Greenville Braves*(15).......	88	56	.611	—	222,038	Chris Chambliss
Orlando SunRays**(9)	77	67	.535	11	110,131	Scott Ullger
Jacksonville Suns (12)........	74	69	.517	13½	231,139	Jim Nettles
Charlotte Knights (16)........	74	70	.514	14	313,791	Jay Loviglio
Carolina Mudcats#(23).......	66	76	.465	21	218,054	Marc Bombard

West Standings	W	L	Pct.	GB	Attend.	Manager
Birmingham Barons*(4).....	77	66	.538	—	313,412	Tony Franklin
Chattanooga Lookouts (17)	72	72	.500	5½	186,285	Jim Tracy
Knoxville Blue Jays**(14).	67	77	.465	10½	123,361	John Stearns
Memphis Chicks (7)...........	61	83	.424	16½	185,409	Jeff Cox
Huntsville Stars (11)..........	61	83	.424	16½	224,208	Casey Parsons

#represented Zebulon, North Carolina.

Playoffs: Orlando 3 games, Greenville 0; Birmingham 3 games, Knoxville 1.
Finals: Orlando 3 games, Birmingham 1.

All-Star Team: 1B-Elvin Paulino, Charlotte; **2B**-Bret Boone, Jacksonville; **3B**-Cheo Garcia, Orlando; **SS**-Alex Arias, Charlotte; **OF**-Reggie Sanders, Chattanooga; Fernando Ramsey, Charlotte; Kevin Koslofski, Memphis; Keith Mitchell, Greenville; **C**-Jim Campanis, Jacksonville; **DH**-Troy Neel, Huntsville; **Util**-Vinny Castilla, Greenville; **P**-Pat Mahomes, Orlando; Wilson Alvarez, Birmingham; **MVP**-Ryan Klesko, Greenville; **Pitcher of the Year**-Mark Wohlers, Greenville; **Manager**-Chris Chambliss, Greenville.

BA: Jim Bowie, Jacksonville, .310
Runs: Ron Coomer, Birmingham, 81
Hits: Fernando Ramsey, Charlotte, 151
RBIs: Elvin Paulino, Charlotte, 81

HRs: Elvin Paulino, Charlotte, 24
Wins: Napoleon Robinson, Greenville, 16
SOs: Mike Trombley, Orlando, 175
ERA: Pat Mahomes, Orlando, 1.78

AA Texas League
President: Carl Sawatski

East Standings	W	L	Pct.	GB	Attend.	Manager
Shreveport Captains***(26) .	86	50	.632	—	206,540	Bill Evers
Jackson Generals (18)........	70	66	.515	16	114,660	Rick Sweet

	W	L	Pct.	GB	Attend.	Manager
Tulsa Drillers (13)	58	78	.426	28	260,864	Bobby Jones
Arkansas Travelers (24)......	49	87	.360	37	265,268	Joe Pettini

West Standings	W	L	Pct.	GB	Attend.	Manager
El Paso Diablos*(8)............	81	55	.596	—	273,438	Dave Huppert
Wichita Wranglers (25)	71	64	.526	9½	200,217	Steve Lubratich
Midland Angels**(3)..........	67	68	.496	13½	180,616	Don Long
San Antonio Missions (19).	61	75	.449	20	185,336	John Shoemaker

Playoff: El Paso 2 games, Midland 0.
Finals: Shreveport 4 games, El Paso 2.

All-Star Team: 1B-John Jaha, El Paso; **2B**-John Patterson, Shreveport; **3B**-Juan Guerrero, Shreveport; **SS**-Royce Clayton, Shreveport; **OF**-Shon Ashley, El Paso; Ruben Escalera, El Paso; Steve Hosey, Shreveport; **C**-Dave Nilsson, El Paso; Ivan Rodriguez, Tulsa; **DH**-Mark Howie, Midland; **Util**-Jim Tatum, El Paso; **P**-Frank Seminara, Wichita; Don Vidmar, Midland; Paul McClellan, Shreveport; Chris Gardner, Jackson; Larry Carter, Shreveport; **MVP**-John Jaha, El Paso; **Pitcher of the Year**-Paul McClellan, Shreveport; **Manager**-Don Long, Midland.

BA: Mark Howie, Midland, .364
Runs: John Jaha, El Paso, 121
Hits: Mark Howie, Midland, 188
RBIs: John Jaha, El Paso, 134

HRs: John Jaha, El Paso, 30
Wins: Frank Seminara, Wichita, 15
SOs: Dennis Springer, San Antonio, 138
ERA: Larry Carter, Shreveport, 2.95

A California League
President: Joe Gagliardi

North Standings	W	L	Pct.	GB	Attend.	Manager
San Jose Giants***(26)......	92	44	.676	—	123,905	Ron Wotus
Stockton Ports (8).............	71	65	.522	21	90,126	Chris Bando
Modesto A's (11)...............	68	68	.500	24	77,287	Ted Kubiak
Reno Silver Sox	59	77	.434	33	76,045	Mal Fichman
Salinas Spurs....................	55	81	.404	37	66,079	Hide Koga

South Standings	W	L	Pct.	GB	Attend.	Manager
Bakersfield Dodgers*(19)...	85	51	.625	—	147,655	Tom Beyers
High Desert Mavericks##**(25)	73	63	.537	12	204,438	Bruce Bochy
Palm Springs Angels (3).....	65	71	.478	20	64,871	Nate Oliver
Visalia Oaks (9)	58	78	.426	27	67,386	Steve Liddle
San Bernardino Spirit (12)..	54	82	.397	31	187,895	Tommy Jones

#represented Adelanto, California.

Playoffs: Stockton 3 games, San Jose 1; High Desert 3 games, Bakersfield 0.
Finals: High Desert 3 games, Stockton 2.

All-Star Team: 1B-Jay Gainer, High Desert; **2B**-Frank Carey, San Jose; **3B**-Jim Bishop, Salinas; **SS**-Ron Maurer, Bakersfield; **OF**-Matt Mieske, High Desert; Marc Newfield, San Bernardino; J.D. Noland, High Desert; **C**-Mike Piazza, Bakersfield; **DH**-Chris Delarwelle, Visalia; **P**-Rich Huisman, San Jose; Greg Hansell, Bakersfield; Gary Sharko, San Jose; Timber Mead, Reno; **MVP**-Matt Mieske, High Desert; **Pitcher of the Year**-Rich Huisman, San Jose; **Manager**-Ron Wotus, San Jose.

BA: Matt Mieske, High Desert, .341
Runs: J.D. Noland, High Desert, 114
Hits: Matt Mieske, High Desert, 168
RBIs: Jay Gainer, High Desert, 120

HRs: Jay Gainer, High Desert, 32
Wins: Rich Huisman, San Jose, 16
SOs: Rich Huisman, San Jose, 216
ERA: Rich Huisman, San Jose, 1.83

A Carolina League
President: John Hopkins

North Standings	W	L	Pct.	GB	Attend.	Manager
Prince William Cannons*(10).	71	68	.511	—	207,103	Mike Hart
Lynchburg Red Sox**(2) ...	67	72	.482	4	88,897	Buddy Bailey
Salem Buccaneers (23)	63	77	.450	8½	131,582	Stan Cliburn
Frederick Keys (1).............	58	82	.414	13½	318,354	Wally Moon

South Standings	W	L	Pct.	GB	Attend.	Manager
Kinston Indians***(5)........	89	49	.645	—	100,857	Brian Graham
Winston-Salem Spirits (16)	83	57	.593	7	111,333	Brad Mills
Durham Bulls (15)..............	79	58	.577	9½	301,240	Grady Little
Peninsula Pilots (12)..........	46	93	.331	43½	41,107	Steve Smith

Playoff: Lynchburg 2 games, Prince William 0.
Finals: Kinston 3 games, Lynchburg 0.

All-Star Team: 1B-Willie Tatum, Lynchburg; **2B**-Miguel Flores, Kinston; **3B**-Pete Castellano, Winston-Salem; **SS**-Manny Alexander, Frederick; **OF**-Brian Giles, Kinston; Jeff McNeely, Lynchburg; Tracy Sanders, Kinston; **C**-Javy Lopez, Durham; **DH**-Chris Ebright, Winston-Salem; **Util**-Ramon Caraballo, Durham; John Jensen, Winston-Salem; **P**-Sam Militello, Prince William; Mike Soper, Kinston; **MVP**-Pete Castellano, Winston-Salem; **Pitcher of the Year**-Sam Militello, Prince William; **Manager**-Brian Graham, Kinston.

BA: Jeff McNeely, Lynchburg, .322
Runs: Jerrone Williams, Winston-Salem, 81
Manny Alexander, Frederick, 81
Hits: Manny Alexander, Frederick, 143
RBIs: Pete Castellano, Winston-Salem, 88
HRs: Tracy Sanders, Kinston, 18

Wins: Ryan Hawblitzel, Winston-Salem, 15
Curt Leskanic, Kinston, 15
SOs: Curt Leskanic, Kinston, 163
ERA: Tim Smith, Lynchburg, 2.16
Saves: Mike Soper, Kinston, 41

A Florida State League
President: Chuck Murphy

East Standings	W	L	Pct.	GB	Attend.	Manager
Vero Beach Dodgers*(19)	79	52	.603	—	95,900	Jerry Royster
St. Lucie Mets**(21)	72	59	.550	7	79,961	John Tamargo
West Palm Beach Expos (20)	72	59	.550	7	105,787	Felipe Alou
Miami Miracle#(x)	63	67	.485	15½	56,557	Fredi Gonzalez
Ft. Lauderdale Yankees (10)	59	69	.461	18½	51,362	Glenn Sherlock

West Standings	W	L	Pct.	GB	Attend.	Manager
Clearwater Phillies***(22)	81	49	.623	—	82,631	Lee Elia
Sarasota White Sox (4)	75	56	.573	6½	84,951	Rick Patterson
Charlotte Rangers (13)	62	70	.470	20	97,399	Bobby Molinaro
Dunedin Blue Jays (14)	59	72	.450	22½	67,040	Dennis Holmberg
St. Petersburg Cardinals (24)	47	84	.359	34½	155,946	Dave Bialas

Central Standings	W	L	Pct.	GB	Attend.	Manager
Lakeland Tigers***(6)	72	56	.563	—	51,464	John Lipon
Osceola Astros (18)	64	63	.504	7½	48,341	Sal Butera
Baseball City Royals (7)	62	69	.473	11½	21,174	Carlos Tosca
Winter Haven Red Sox (2)	43	85	.336	29	20,323	Mike Verdi

#played home games in Pompano Beach, Florida.

Playoffs: West Palm Beach 2 games, Vero Beach 1; St. Lucie 2 games, Sarasota 1; West Palm Beach 2 games, Lakeland 0; Clearwater 2 games, St. Lucie 0.
Finals: West Palm Beach 2 games, Clearwater 0.

All-Star Team: 1B-Scott Cepicky, Sarasota; **2B**-Matt Howard, Vero Beach; **3B**-Rey Noriega, Ft. Lauderdale; **SS**-Troy Paulsen, Clearwater; **OF**-Robert Perez, Dunedin; Nigel Wilson, Dunedin; Rusty Greer, Charlotte; **C**-Brook Fordyce, St. Lucie; Miah Bradbury, Miami; **DH**-John Deutsch, Vero Beach; **Util**-Mike Lansing, Miami; John Thomas, St. Petersburg; **P**-Tom Michno, Miami; Elliott Gray, Clearwater; Todd Douma, St. Lucie; Michael Mimbs, Vero Beach; Richard Batcheler, Ft. Lauderdale; Julian Vasquez, St. Lucie; **MVP**-Scott Cepicky, Sarasota; **Manager**-Lee Elia, Clearwater.

BA: Robert Perez, Dunedin, .302
Runs: Kevin Castleberry, Miami/Sarasota, 82
Hits: Robert Perez, Dunedin, 145
RBIs: Scott Cepicky, Sarasota, 76

HRs: Jose Oliva, Charlotte, 14
Rey Noriega, Ft. Lauderdale, 14
Wins: Doug Bochtler, West Palm Beach, 12
Michael Mimbs, Vero Beach, 12
SOs: Tom Michno, Miami, 190
ERA: Bill Wengert, Vero Beach, 2.06

A Midwest League
President: George Spelius

North Standings	W	L	Pct.	GB	Attend.	Manager
Madison Muskies*(11)	77	61	.558	—	92,663	Gary Jones
Rockford Expos (20)	76	61	.555	½	66,524	Pat Kelly/Rob Leary
Beloit Brewers (8)	70	67	.511	6½	77,487	Rob Derksen
Kane County Cougars#**(1)	68	67	.504	7½	240,290	Bob Miscik
South Bend White Sox (4)	69	70	.496	8½	221,071	Tommy Thompson
Kenosha Twins (9)	63	74	.460	13½	59,331	Joel Lepel
Appleton Foxes (7)	58	81	.417	19½	72,601	Joe Breeden

South Standings	W	L	Pct.	GB	Attend.	Manager
Clinton Giants**(26)	81	58	.583	—	83,943	Jack Mull
Waterloo Diamonds (25)	75	63	.543	5½	58,859	Bryan Little
Quad City Angels (3)	74	63	.540	6	242,322	Mitch Seoane
Burlington Astros*(18)	67	70	.489	13	81,811	Tim Tolman
Cedar Rapids Reds (17)	66	74	.471	18	132,820	Frank Funk
Peoria Chiefs (16)	62	76	.449	18½	212,159	Bill Hayes
Springfield Cardinals (24)	58	79	.423	22	175,017	Mike Ramsey

#represented Geneva, Illinois.

Playoffs: Madison 2 games, Kane County 0; Clinton 2 games, Burlington 1.
Finals: Clinton 3 games, Madison 0.

All-Star Team: 1B-Roberto Arredondo, Waterloo; **2B**-Fletcher Thompson, Burlington; **3B**-Paul Russo, Kenosha; **SS**-Brandon Wilson, South Bend; **OF**-Darius Gash, Waterloo; Phil Dauphin, Peoria; Chris Hatcher, Burlington; **C**-Eric Christopherson, Clinton; **DH**-Jeff Kipila, Quad City; **P**-Lance Painter, Waterloo; Salomon Torres, Clinton; Wally Trice, Burlington; Rod Huffman, Clinton; **MVP**-Salomon Torres, Clinton; **Manager**-Gary Jones, Madison.

BA: Midre Cummings, Kenosha, .322
Runs: Lee Sammons, Madison, 104
Hits: Darius Gash, Waterloo, 154
RBIs: Paul Russo, Kenosha, 100
HRs: Paul Russo, Kenosha, 20

Wins: Salomon Torres, Clinton, 16
Dan Carlson, Clinton, 16
SOs: Salomon Torres, Clinton, 214
ERA: Salomon Torres, Clinton, 1.41

A New York-Pennsylvania League
President: Leo A. Pinckney

McNamara East Standings	W	L	Pct.	GB	Attend.	Manager
Pittsfield Mets (21)	51	26	.662	—	62,525	Jim Thrift
Oneonta Yankees (10)	42	35	.545	9	52,657	Jack Gillis
Utica Blue Sox (4)	39	37	.513	11½	70,150	Mike Gellinger
Watertown Indians (5)	27	50	.351	24	58,394	Gary Tuck

McNamara West Standings	W	L	Pct.	GB	Attend.	Manager
Elmira Pioneers (2)	47	30	.610	—	79,414	Dave Holt
Auburn Astros (18)	38	39	.494	9	58,233	Steve Dillard
Batavia Clippers (22)	38	40	.487	9½	43,247	Ramon Aviles
Geneva Cubs (16)	35	43	.449	12½	35,676	Greg Mahlberg

Stedler Standings	W	L	Pct.	GB	Attend.	Manager
Jamestown Expos (20)	51	27	.654	—	40,276	Ed Creech
Erie Sailors (x)	37	41	.474	14	70,546	Barry Moss
Niagara Falls Rapids (6)	36	42	.462	15	62,157	Gary Calhoun
St. Catharines Blue Jays (14)	35	42	.455	15½	35,562	Doug Ault
Hamilton Redbirds (24)	35	42	.455	15½	69,872	Rick Colbert
Welland Pirates (23)	30	47	.390	20½	37,476	Lee Driggers

Playoffs: Jamestown 1 game, Erie 0; Pittsfield 1 game, Elmira 0.
Finals: Jamestown 2 games, Pittsfield 0.

All-Star Team: 1B-Derrick White, Jamestown; **2B**-Rick Juday, Erie; **3B**-Rob Grable, Niagara Falls; **SS**-Frank Rodriguez, Elmira; **OF**-Robert Butler, St. Catharines; Lyle Mouton, Oneonta; Jim Austin, Jamestown; John Mabry, Hamilton; **C**-Mike Daniel, Jamestown; Jim Robinson, Geneva; **DH**-Eric Martinez, Auburn; **Util**-Tim Flannelly, Oneonta; **P**-Mark Loughlin, Auburn; Brian Looney, Jamestown; Chris Davis, Elmira; Heath Haynes, Jamestown; **MVP**-Robert Butler, St. Catharines; **Manager**-Ed Creech, Jamestown.

BA: Rick Juday, Erie, .338
Runs: Randy Curtis, Pittsfield, 72
Hits: Robert Butler, St. Catharines, 105
RBIs: Mike Daniel, Jamestown, 62

HRs: Ossie Timmons, Geneva, 12
Felix Colon, Elmira, 12
Wins: Heath Haynes, Jamestown, 10
Chris Shanahan, Pittsfield, 10
SOs: Mike Lynch, Erie, 102
ERA: Brian Looney, Jamestown, 1.16

A Northwest League
President: Bob Richmond

North Standings	W	L	Pct.	GB	Attend.	Manager
Yakima Bears (19)	44	32	.579	—	81,835	Joe Vavra
Everett Giants (26)	37	39	.487	7	89,906	Rob Ellis/Mike Bubalo
Bellingham Mariners (12)	37	39	.487	7	60,484	Dave Myers
Spokane Indians (25)	24	52	.316	20	130,111	Gene Glynn

South Standings	W	L	Pct.	GB	Attend.	Manager
Boise Hawks (3)	50	26	.658	—	132,611	Tom Kotchman
Eugene Emeralds (7)	42	34	.553	8	130,939	Tom Poquette
Southern Oregon A's (11)	40	36	.526	10	70,164	Grady Fuson
Bend Bucks (x)	30	46	.395	20	47,018	Bill Stein

Playoff: Boise 2 games, Yakima 0.

All-Star Team: 1B-Murph Proctor, Yakima; **2B**-Eddy Diaz, Bellingham; **3B**-Joe Randa, Eugene; **SS**-Brent Gates, Southern Oregon; **OF**-Mike Neill, Southern Oregon; Matt Brewer, Everett; Mark Johnson, Eugene; **C**-Frank Charles, Everett; **DH**-Leon Glenn, Bend; **P**-Mike Hampton, Bellingham; Julian Heredia, Boise; Ken Grundt, Everett; Troy Percival, Boise; **MVP**-Joe Randa, Eugene; **Manager**-Tom Poquette, Eugene.

BA: Mike Neill, Southern Oregon, .350
Runs: Vernon Spearman, Yakima, 63
Hits: Joe Randa, Eugene, 93
RBIs: Murph Proctor, Yakima, 61
HRs: Leon Glenn, Bend, 15

Wins: Julian Heredia, Boise, 8
Lenny Ayers, Everett, 8
Shawn Purdy, Boise, 8
Bill VanLandingham, Everett, 8
David Baumann, Yakima, 8
SOs: Julian Heredia, Boise, 99
ERA: Julian Heredia, Boise, 1.05

A South Atlantic League
President: John H. Moss

North Standings	W	L	Pct.	GB	Attend.	Manager
Charleston (WV) Wheelers***(17)	92	50	.648	—	185,310	P.J. Carey/Dave Miley
Greensboro Hornets (10)	73	68	.518	18½	191,048	Trey Hillman
Spartanburg Phillies (22)	70	70	.500	21	54,489	Mel Roberts
Gastonia Rangers (13)	69	73	.486	23	44,060	Bump Wills
Sumter Flyers (20)	64	75	.460	26½	45,639	Lorenzo Bundy
Fayetteville Generals (6)	58	79	.423	31½	88,380	Gerry Groninger
Asheville Tourists (18)	55	83	.399	35	117,625	Frank Cacciatore

South Standings	W	L	Pct.	GB	Attend.	Manager
Columbia Mets*(21)	86	54	.614	—	79,564	Tim Blackwell
Macon Braves**(15)	83	58	.589	3½	107,059	Roy Majtyka
Columbus Indians (5)	73	69	.514	14	96,736	Mike Brown
Charleston (SC) Rainbows (25)	69	72	.489	17½	119,080	Dave Trembley
Augusta Pirates (23)	68	74	.479	19	100,141	Don Werner
Savannah Cardinals (24)	61	77	.442	24	99,399	Larry Milbourne
Myrtle Beach Hurricanes (14)	60	79	.432	25½	62,885	Garth Iorg

Playoff: Columbia 2 games, Macon 0.
Finals: Columbia 3 games, Charleston (WV) 0.

All-Star Team: 1B-Tom Raffo, Charleston (WV); **2B**-Joe Sondrini, Augusta; **3B**-Butch Huskey, Columbia; **SS**-Chipper Jones, Macon; **OF**-Kyle Washington, Columbus; Steve Gibralter, Charleston (WV); Rondell White, Sumter; **C/DH**-Kiki Hernandez, Greensboro; **Util**-Howard Battle, Myrtle Beach; Jason Hardtke, Columbus; Troy Hughes, Macon; **P**-Jose Martinez, Columbia; Rafael Quirico, Greensboro; **MVP**-Kiki Hernandez, Greensboro; **Pitcher of the Year**-Jose Martinez, Columbia.

BA: Kyle Washington, Columbus, .343
Runs: Chipper Jones, Macon, 104
Jason Hardtke, Columbus, 104
Hits: Jason Hardtke, Columbus, 155
RBIs: Butch Huskey, Columbia, 99

HRs: Butch Huskey, Columbia, 26
Wins: Jose Martinez, Columbia, 20
SOs: John Roper, Charleston (WV), 189
ERA: Jose Martinez, Columbia, 1.49

R Appalachian League
President: Bill Halstead

North Standings	W	L	Pct.	GB	Attend.	Manager
Burlington Indians (5)	40	27	.597	—	57,613	Dave Keller
Bluefield Orioles (1)	36	31	.537	4	55,373	Gus Gil
Martinsville Phillies (22)	27	41	.397	13½	72,703	Rollie DeArmas
Princeton Reds (17)	24	40	.375	14½	25,203	Sam Mejias
Huntington Cubs (16)	25	42	.373	15	59,860	Steve Roadcap

South Standings	W	L	Pct.	GB	Attend.	Manager
Pulaski Braves (15)	45	23	.662	—	24,656	Randy Ingle
Johnson City Cardinals (24)	40	26	.606	4	31,442	Chris Maloney
Elizabethton Twins (9)	39	29	.574	6	18,115	Ray Smith
Kingsport Mets (21)	36	31	.537	8½	31,721	Andre David
Bristol Tigers (6)	22	44	.333	22	26,901	Juan Lopez

Playoff: Pulaski 2 games, Burlington 0.

All-Star Team: 1B-Lance Marks, Pulaski; **2B**-Quilvio Veras, Kingsport; **3B**-Andy Bruce, Johnson City; **SS**-Manny Jimenez, Pulaski; **OF**-Ricky Otero, Kingsport; Manny Ramirez, Burlington; Clayton Byrne, Bluefield; **C**-Pedro Grifol, Elizabethton; **DH**-Tom Mezzanotte, Bristol; **Util**-Ken Arnold, Huntington; Don Robinson, Pulaski; **P**-Kevin Lomon, Pulaski; David Sartain, Elizabethton; Chris Lemp, Bluefield; **MVP**-Manny Ramirez, Burlington; **Manager**-Ray Smith, Elizabethton.

BA: Ricky Otero, Kingsport, .345
Runs: Quilvio Veras, Kingsport, 54
Hits: Ricky Otero, Kingsport, 81
RBIs: Manny Ramirez, Burlington, 63
HRs: Manny Ramirez, Burlington, 19
Wins: David Sartain, Elizabethton, 9
SOs: Eddie Guardado, Elizabethton, 106
ERA: Steve Jones, Johnson City, 1.47

R Arizona League
President: Bob Richmond

Standings	W	L	Pct.	GB	Manager
Athletics (Scottsdale) (11)	39	21	.650	—	Dickie Scott
Brewers (Peoria) (8)	34	26	.567	5	Wayne Krenchicki
Mariners (Tempe) (12)	33	27	.550	6	Myron Pines
Padres (Scottsdale) (25)	31	29	.517	8	Ken Berry
Cardinals (Peoria) (24)	29	30	.492	9½	Keith Champion
Angels (Mesa) (3)	29	30	.492	9½	Bill Lachemann
Giants (Scottsdale) (26)	14	46	.233	25	Nelson Rood

Playoffs: None.

All-Star Team: 1B-David Mowry, Padres; **2B**-Lino Connell, Angels; **3B**-Jason Imperial, Brewers; **SS**-Manuel Cora, Padres; **OF**-Luinis Aracena, Athletics; Howard House, Brewers; Dennis McCaffery, Angels; **C**-James Bonnici, Mariners; **DH**-Steve Cerio, Cardinals; **P**-Mike Hancock, Brewers; George Glinatsis, Mariners; Charles O'Laughlin, Brewers; Troy Koneman, Cardinals; **MVP**-Howard House, Brewers; **Manager**-Dickie Scott, Athletics.

BA: Michael Stefanski, Brewers, .364
Runs: Luinis Aracena, Athletics, 58
Hits: Steve Cerio, Cardinals, 80
RBIs: Steve Cerio, Cardinals, 47
HRs: Steve Cerio, Cardinals, 9
Wins: George Glinatsis, Mariners, 10
SOs: George Glinatsis, Mariners, 80
ERA: George Glinatsis, Mariners, 2.19

R Gulf Coast League
President: Thomas J. Saffell

North Standings	W	L	Pct.	GB	Manager
Red Sox (Winter Haven) (2)	33	27	.550	—	Felix Maldonado
Royals (Baseball City) (7)	31	29	.517	2	Bob Herold
Dodgers (Kissimmee) (19)	29	31	.483	4	Ivan DeJesus
Astros (Kissimmee) (18)	27	33	.450	6	Julio Linares

Central Standings	W	L	Pct.	GB	Manager
Expos (Bradenton) (20)	32	28	.533	—	Keith Snider
White Sox (Sarasota) (4)	30	29	.508	1½	Jaime Garcia
Pirates (Bradenton) (23)	30	29	.508	1½	Woody Huyke
Braves (Bradenton) (15)	30	29	.508	1½	Jim Saul
Yankees (Tampa) (10)	27	32	.458	4½	Ken Dominguez

South Standings	W	L	Pct.	GB	Manager
Orioles (Sarasota) (1)	35	24	.593	—	Ed Napoleon
Blue Jays (Port Charlotte) (14)	31	28	.525	4	Omar Malave
Rangers (Port Charlotte) (13)	30	29	.508	5	Chino Cadahia
Twins (Ft. Myers) (9)	27	33	.450	8½	Dan Rohn
Mets (Sarasota) (21)	24	35	.407	11	Junior Roman

Playoff: Expos 1 game, Red Sox 0.
Finals: Expos 2 games, Orioles 1.

All-Star Team: 1B-Joe Calder, Pirates; **2B**-Ed Alfonzo, Mets; **3B**-Elston Hansen, Yankees; **SS**-Keith Legree, Twins; **OF**-Abdiel Cumberbatch, Yankees; Angel Dotel, Dodgers; Duane Thomas, Orioles; **C**-Yabanne DeLeon, Royals; **P**-Rick Forney, Orioles; Bob Adkins, Blue Jays; **Manager**-Ed Napoleon, Orioles.

BA: Angel Dotel, Dodgers, .400
Runs: Elston Hansen, Yankees, 45
Hits: Elston Hansen, Yankees, 68
RBIs: Joe Calder, Pirates, 45
HRs: Duane Thomas, Orioles, 10
Wins: Young Chul Sohn, Dodgers, 7
Rick Forney, Orioles, 7
Candy Berson, Royals, 7
SOs: Mike Bovee, Royals, 76
ERA: Ihosvany Marquez, Orioles, 1.12

R Pioneer League
President: Ralph C. Nelles

North Standings	W	L	Pct.	GB	Attend.	Manager
Great Falls Dodgers (19)	46	24	.657	—	79,176	Glenn Hoffman
Helena Brewers (8)	44	26	.629	2	31,187	Harry Dunlop
Billings Mustangs (17)	25	44	.362	20½	80,242	P.J. Carey
Medicine Hat Blue Jays (14)	24	45	.348	21½	14,722	J.J. Cannon

South Standings	W	L	Pct.	GB	Attend.	Manager
Salt Lake City Trappers	49	21	.700	—	200,599	Nick Belmonte
Idaho Falls Braves (15)	39	30	.565	9½	71,292	Steve Curry
Butte Copper Kings (13)	29	41	.414	20	29,684	Dick Egan
Pocatello Pioneers (x)	21	46	.313	26½	25,468	Rich Morales

Playoff: Salt Lake City 2 games, Great Falls 1.

All-Star Team: 1B-Andy Fairman, Helena; **2B**-Dario Paulino, Idaho Falls; **3B**-Jeff Cirillo, Helena; **SS**-Tony Graffagnino, Idaho Falls; **OF**-Rick Hirtensteiner, Salt Lake City; Kevin Grijak, Idaho Falls; Terrell Lowery, Butte; **C**-Ken Huckaby, Great Falls; **DH**-D.J. Boston, Medicine Hat; **P**-Jake Botts, Great Falls; Tyrone Hill, Helena; Brad Woodall, Idaho Falls; **Manager**-P.J. Carey, Billings.

BA: Andy Fairman, Helena, .373
Runs: Rick Hirtensteiner, Salt Lake City, 77
Hits: Rick Hirtensteiner, Salt Lake City, 105
RBIs: Rick Hirtensteiner, Salt Lake City, 71
HRs: Rick Hirtensteiner, Salt Lake City, 11
Wins: Brian Souza, Helena, 8
Ross Farnsworth, Great Falls, 8
David Marcon, Salt Lake City, 8
SOs: Mark Stephens, Salt Lake City, 89
ERA: John Gilligan, Salt Lake City, 1.71

1991 Interleague Post Season Play

World Series
Minnesota (American) 4 games, Atlanta (National) 3

AAA Classic
Denver (American Association) 4 games, Columbus (International) 1

1991 Major League Farm Systems

American League

1 Baltimore (6): Rochester, Hagerstown, Frederick, Kane County, Bluefield, Gulf Coast.
2 Boston (6): Pawtucket, New Britain, Lynchburg, Winter Haven, Elmira, Gulf Coast.
3 California (6): Edmonton, Midland, Palm Springs, Quad City, Boise, Arizona.
4 Chicago (6): Vancouver, Birmingham, Sarasota, South Bend, Utica, Gulf Coast.
5 Cleveland (6): Colorado Springs, Canton-Akron, Kinston, Columbus (GA), Watertown, Burlington (NC).
6 Detroit (6): Toledo, London, Lakeland, Fayetteville, Niagara Falls, Bristol.
7 Kansas City (6): Omaha, Memphis, Baseball City, Appleton, Eugene, Gulf Coast.
8 Milwaukee (6): Denver, El Paso, Stockton, Beloit, Helena, Arizona.
9 Minnesota (6): Portland, Orlando, Visalia, Kenosha, Elizabethton, Gulf Coast.
10 New York (7): Columbus (OH), Albany-Colonie, Prince William, Ft. Lauderdale, Greensboro, Oneonta, Gulf Coast.
11 Oakland (6): Tacoma, Huntsville, Modesto, Madison, Southern Oregon, Arizona.
12 Seattle (6): Calgary, Jacksonville, San Bernardino, Peninsula, Bellingham, Arizona.
13 Texas (6): Oklahoma City, Tulsa, Port Charlotte, Gastonia, Butte, Gulf Coast.
14 Toronto (7): Syracuse, Knoxville, Dunedin, Myrtle Beach, St. Catharines, Medicine Hat, Gulf Coast.

National League

15 Atlanta (7): Richmond, Greenville, Durham, Macon, Pulaski, Idaho Falls, Gulf Coast.
16 Chicago (6): Iowa, Charlotte, Winston-Salem, Peoria, Geneva, Huntington.
17 Cincinnati (6): Nashville, Chattanooga, Charleston (WV), Cedar Rapids, Billings, Princeton.
18 Houston (7): Tucson, Jackson, Osceola, Asheville, Burlington (IA), Auburn, Gulf Coast.
19 Los Angeles (7): Albuquerque, San Antonio, Bakersfield, Vero Beach, Yakima, Great Falls, Gulf Coast.
20 Montreal (7): Indianapolis, Harrisburg, West Palm Beach, Rockford, Sumter, Jamestown, Gulf Coast.
21 New York (7): Tidewater, Williamsport, St. Lucie, Columbia, Pittsfield, Kingsport, Gulf Coast.
22 Philadelphia (6): Scranton-Wilkes-Barre, Reading, Clearwater, Spartanburg, Batavia, Martinsville.
23 Pittsburgh (6): Buffalo, Carolina, Salem, Augusta, Welland, Gulf Coast.
24 St. Louis (8): Louisville, Arkansas, St. Petersburg, Springfield, Savannah, Hamilton, Johnson City, Arizona.
25 San Diego (7): Las Vegas, Wichita, High Desert, Waterloo, Charleston (SC), Spokane, Arizona.
26 San Francisco (6): Phoenix, Shreveport, San Jose, Clinton, Everett, Arizona.

Co-op (x): Miami, Erie, Bend, Pocatello.
Independent: Reno, Salinas, Salt Lake City.

1991 No-Hitters

Date	Pitcher	Team	League	Opponent	Score
4-17	Roger Pavlik/				
	Steve Peters	Oklahoma City	American Assoc.	Indianapolis	0-1
4-18	Jose Ventura/Chris Howard/				
	John Hudek	Birmingham	Southern	Charlotte	4-1
4-18	Cedric Shaw/Everett Cunningham/				
	Barry Manuel	Tulsa	Texas	Arkansas	2-0
4-21	Danny Cox/				
	Bob Gaddy	Clearwater	Florida State	Baseball City	4-0
4-22	Don Vidmar	Palm Springs	California	Bakersfield	2-0 (7)
5-1	Nolan Ryan	Texas	American	Toronto	3-0
5-23	Tommy Greene	Philadelphia	National	Montreal	2-0
5-25	Fili Martinez	Palm Springs	California	Bakersfield	4-0
5-31	Mike Hampton	San Bernardino	California	Visalia	6-0
5-17	Kerry Knox	Wichita	Texas	Tulsa	1-0 (7)
5-22	Brian Conroy	New Britain	Eastern	Reading	2-0
5-26	Oscar Munoz	Kinston	Carolina	Prince William	1-0
5-31	Troy Mooney	Augusta	South Atlantic	Savannah	1-0 (7)
6-5	Antonio Felix	MC Diablos Rojos	Mexican	Sultanes	7-0
6-10	Pat Wernig	Tacoma	Pacific Coast	Vancouver	1-0
6-14	Johnny Ruffin	Sarasota	Florida State	Charlotte	6-1 (7)
6-18	Marcos Vazquez	Macon	South Atlantic	Sumter	8-0 (7)
6-18	Geoff Kellogg	Beloit	Midwest	Appleton	6-0
7-3	Erik Schullstrom	Frederick	Carolina	Kinston	2-0
7-5	Kevin Mmahat	Columbus	International	Louisville	6-0
7-12	Steve Trachsel	Winston-Salem	Carolina	Peninsula	4-2 (7)
7-13	Bob Milacki/Mike Flanagan/Mark Williamson/				
	Gregg Olson	Baltimore	American	Oakland	2-0
7-13	Scott Francis	Pulaski	Appalachian	Huntington	9-0
7-17	Doug Johns	Madison	Midwest	Burlington	3-0
7-21	Rafael Quirico	Greensboro	South Atlantic	Charleston (SC)	2-0
7-26	Mark Gardner	Montreal	National	Los Angeles	0-1 (10)
7-28	Dennis Martinez	Montreal	National	Los Angeles	2-0 (P)
8-2	Paul Gibbs	Bristol	Appalachian	Bluefield	8-2
8-3	Fred Dabney	Sarasota	Florida State	Baseball City	6-0
8-6	Jim Neidlinger	Albuquerque	Pacific Coast	Las Vegas	3-0 (5)
8-8	Mike Trombley	Orlando	Southern	Knoxville	3-0 (7)
8-11	Wilson Alvarez	Chicago	American	Baltimore	7-0
8-23	Paul Byrd/Scott Morgan/				
	Mike Soper	Kinston	Carolina	Prince William	1-0
8-26	Bret Saberhagen	Kansas City	American	Chicago	7-0
8-26	Eddie Guardado	Elizabethton	Appalachian	Pulaski	5-0
8-26	Danny Matznick	Sarasota	Florida State	Charlotte	1-0
8-28	Sean Snedeker	Vero Beach	Florida State	St. Lucie	3-0 (P, 7)
8-29	Keith Millay/Charlie Morgan/				
	Tony Fults	Athletics	Arizona	Angels	9-0
9-11	Kent Mercker/Mark Wohlers/				
	Alejandro Pena	Atlanta	National	San Diego	1-0

Number in parentheses indicates innings if other than nine; "P" indicates perfect game.

THIS DATE IN MINOR LEAGUE HISTORY

January 27, 1991, Dale Long, National Association Field Representative, and a former major leaguer, died at age 64. In 1956 he set a major league record by hitting home runs in eight straight games.

March 15, 1991, Commissioner Fay Vincent banned the use of chewing tobacco and snuff in the Appalachian, Gulf Coast, New York-Pennsylvania, Northwest and Pioneer Leagues.

March 20, 1991, The Mexican League season opened with the Monterrey teams playing in a new 32,000-seat stadium.

April 3, 1991, Commissioner Fay Vincent blocked the attempt of Miami, Florida State League, to sign 68-year old Minnie Minoso. Club President Mike Veeck, son of former big league owner Bill Veeck, had hoped to have Minoso become the first player ever to play professionally in six decades.

May 30, 1991, Walter Dilbeck, former owner of the Louisville International League franchise, died. In 1970, Dilbeck tried to start a third major league, the Global Baseball League, with franchises in Venezuela, Mexico, Puerto Rico, Japan, and U.S. teams in Mobile and Jersey City. The league never played a game.

July 3, 1991, The Southern League's Carolina Mudcats finally moved into their new home in Zebulon, North Carolina. For the first three months of the season, the club's home games were played at Fleming Stadium in nearby Wilson.

July 9, 1991, Directors of the International League voted to end the AAA Alliance, ending four years of interleague play with the American Association, after the 1991 season. Association directors favored continuing the Alliance.

July 10, 1991, In the first ever Double-A All-Star Game, the stars of the American League affiliates defeated the National League stars 8-2 before 4,022 fans in Huntsville, Alabama.

July 25, 1991, National Association President Sal Artiaga announced that he would not seek re-election in December at the conclusion of his three year term. His decision was an outgrowth of the bitter fight with the major leagues over the Professional Baseball Agreement negotiations.

August 19, 1991, Ted Norbert, who hit 314 home runs in 19 minor league seasons, died in Puerto Rico at the age of 84. Most of his career was spent in the Pacific Coast League.

September 1, 1991, The Peninsula Pilots set a new Carolina League record by losing 22 consecutive games. The prior mark of 19 was set by Fayetteville in 1950.

September 2, 1991, Mike Soper of Kinston, Carolina League, tied the minor league record of 41 saves set in 1987 by Mike Perez of Springfield in the Midwest League.

September 28, 1991, Charlotte and Ottawa were awarded Class AAA expansion franchises at the AAA meetings in Palm Springs. The two teams were to begin play in 1993.

November 10, 1991, Branch Rickey III was named president of the American Association. The grandson of baseball pioneer Branch Rickey, he had previously been a farm director for Cincinnati and Pittsburgh.

November 24, 1991, Carl Sawatski, president of the Texas League and a former major leaguer, died of leukemia in Little Rock at age 64.

December 11, 1991, Mike Moore was elected president of the National Association. Moore, a longtime minor league general manager and assistant to former president Sal Artiaga, was elected unanimously on the third ballot after Eastern League President Charles Eshbach withdrew his candidacy in the name of unity.

THE BOOM 1992 - 1996

Coming into the 1992 season, minor league operators had reason to doubt economic prospects for the future. The minors had been in a decade-long growth curve, one of the longest periods of prosperity in what had been a very fickle business, However, the major leagues, rather than pleased by this prosperity, seemed to show only resentment and jealousy.

Coming out of the acrimonious Professional Baseball Agreement negotiations, the major league owners gave every indication that they wanted fewer minor league clubs with more control of the few that remained. The PBA that had sustained the minors for some 30 years was dramatically changed.

The minors viewed a 5 percent tax on ticket revenue, control of all logos by Major League Baseball Properties, and new stadium standards that seemed impossible to achieve, as the most burdensome sections of the new document. Doom-sayers were everywhere, and few saw any reason for optimism in what was viewed as an extremely harsh contract By the end of six years, it became clear that the 1991 PBA was perhaps the best thing that ever had happened to minor league baseball. Major league owners' motives may not have been altruistic, but minor league baseball was one of the few bright spots in a decade of major league baseball strife.

The taking of 5 percent of minor league ticket revenue forced the minor leagues into a standardized accounting and control system. Clubs had to keep detailed records and report them annually to the National Association. Suddenly minor league baseball was no longer a loosely aligned group of mom and pop stores but now a multi-million dollar enterprise that had financial statements to prove it. National advertising contracts started coming to minor league baseball through the National Association, opening new sources of revenue to minor league clubs.

The control of logos and the marketing of them by Major League Properties forced the minor leagues to look at their marks and control them. Trademarks were taken, and a national system of licensing and distribution was started for minor league properties. In five years national sales of minor league paraphernalia went from $3 million dollars to over $50 million.

The major leagues' new standards for minor league facilities dictated almost every aspect of a ballpark, a far cry from the earlier controls of lighting and playing conditions. The costs for upgrading stadiums ran into the millions of dollars, and minor league operators, unable to pay for these improvements themselves, went to local and state government for help. Shockingly, the almost universal response from the public sector was to find the funds for these upgrades. The stadium boom which had started in the late 1980's took off, and civic pride entered into the equation as funds for minor league stadiums reached unprecedented heights. $10 million to $20 million was not too much to expect for the new palaces being built, and the only difference in many of the new minor league parks from the Camden Yards and Jacobs Fields of the major leagues was seating capacity. All the other amenities such as luxury boxes, huge clubhouses, and stadium clubs were part of the new minor league look.

Attendance continued to grow in most minor league cities, and front-office staffs of 10 to 20 were the norm rather than the exception. The name of the game was now entertainment, and clubs began to send their people to professional seminars to learn the proper way to serve and entertain the public.There were purists who complained that the game was being lost in a surfeit of between-innings contests and high-tech music, but the economic strength of the minors had never been better.

Another outgrowth of the PBA negotiations was the revival of independent baseball. Several long-time minor league operators, worried and tired of major league control, became part of a revived Northern League. The Northern League had been the last of the old minor leagues to fail, disbanding after the 1971 season. Independent baseball had not been successful on a league-wide basis since the late 1940s, and most expected this latest attempt to fail. But it was a success in its first season, and within three years a dozen other independent leagues had started. Few enjoyed the total success of the Northern, but independent baseball proved that many cities had a hunger for professional baseball that the 150 major league working agreements could not satisfy.

As minor league baseball entered the 21st century, it was the strongest it had been in its 100-year history. The facilities, the attendance, and the value of franchises all pointed to a healthy future. Forces outside the control of the minors had always had a huge impact on the state of the game, and wars, depressions and major league health could all change the current pattern. Still the minors were confident as they moved toward a new century.

1992

American League
President: Dr. Robert Brown

East Standings	W	L	Pct.	GB	Attend.	Manager
Toronto Blue Jays	96	66	.593	—	4,028,318	Cito Gaston
Milwaukee Brewers	92	70	.568	4	1,857,351	Phil Garner
Baltimore Orioles	89	73	.549	7	3,567,819	Johnny Oates
Cleveland Indians	76	86	.469	20	1,224,094	Mike Hargrove
New York Yankees	76	86	.469	20	1,748,737	Buck Showalter
Detroit Tigers	75	87	.463	21	1,423,963	Sparky Anderson
Boston Red Sox	73	89	.451	23	2,468,574	Butch Hobson

West Standings	W	L	Pct.	GB	Attend.	Manager
Oakland Athletics	96	66	.593	—	2,494,160	Tony LaRussa
Minnesota Twins	90	72	.556	6	2,482,428	Tom Kelly
Chicago White Sox	86	76	.531	10	2,681,156	Gene Lamont
Texas Rangers	77	85	.475	19	2,198,231	Bobby Valentine/Toby Harrah
California Angels	72	90	.444	24	2,065,444	Buck Rodgers/John Wathan
Kansas City Royals	72	90	.444	24	1,867,689	Hal McRae
Seattle Mariners	64	98	.395	32	1,651,367	Bill Plummer

Playoff: Toronto 4 games, Oakland 2.

BA: Edgar Martinez, Seattle, .343
Runs: Tony Phillips, Detroit, 114
Hits: Kirby Puckett, Minnesota, 210
RBIs: Cecil Fielder, Detroit, 124
HRs: Juan Gonzalez, Texas, 43

Wins: Jack Morris, Toronto, 21
Kevin Brown, Texas, 21
SOs: Randy Johnson, Seattle, 241
ERA: Roger Clemens, Boston, 2.41
Pct: Mike Mussina, Baltimore, .783, 18-5
Saves: Dennis Eckersley, Oakland, 51

National League
President: William White

East Standings	W	L	Pct.	GB	Attend.	Manager
Pittsburgh Pirates	96	66	.593	—	1,829,395	Jim Leyland
Montreal Expos	87	76	.537	9	1,669,127	Tom Runnells/Felipe Alou
St. Louis Cardinals	83	79	.512	13	2,418,483	Joe Torre
Chicago Cubs	78	84	.481	18	2,126,720	Jim Lefebvre
New York Mets	72	90	.444	24	1,779,534	Jeff Torborg
Philadelphia Phillies	70	92	.432	26	1,927,448	Jim Fregosi

West Standings	W	L	Pct.	GB	Attend.	Manager
Atlanta Braves	98	64	.605	—	3,077,400	Bobby Cox
Cincinnati Reds	90	72	.556	8	2,315,946	Lou Piniella
San Diego Padres	82	80	.506	16	1,721,406	Greg Riddoch/Jim Riggleman
Houston Astros	81	81	.500	17	1,211,412	Art Howe
San Francisco Giants	72	90	.444	26	1,560,998	Roger Craig
Los Angeles Dodgers	63	99	.389	35	2,473,266	Tom Lasorda

Playoff: Atlanta 4 games, Pittsburgh 3.

BA: Gary Sheffield, San Diego, .330
Runs: Barry Bonds, Pittsburgh, 109
Hits: Terry Pendleton, Atlanta, 199
Andy Van Slyke, Pittsburgh, 199
RBIs: Darren Daulton, Philadelphia, 109
HRs: Fred McGriff, San Diego, 35

Wins: Tom Glavine, Atlanta, 20
Greg Maddux, Chicago, 20
SOs: John Smoltz, Atlanta, 215
ERA: Bill Swift, San Francisco, 2.08
Pct: Bob Tewksbury, St. Louis, .762, 16-5
Saves: Lee Smith, St. Louis, 43

AAA American Association
President: Branch B. Rickey

East Standings	W	L	Pct.	GB	Attend.	Manager
Buffalo Bisons (25)	87	57	.604	—	1,117,867	Marc Bombard
Indianapolis Indians (22)	83	61	.576	4	332,941	Pat Kelly
Louisville Redbirds (26)	73	70	.510	13½	646,951	Jack Krol
Nashville Sounds (17)	67	77	.465	20	489,962	Pete Mackanin/Dave Miley

West Standings	W	L	Pct.	GB	Attend.	Manager
Oklahoma City 89ers (13)	74	70	.514	—	362,394	Tommy Thompson
Denver Zephyrs (8)	73	71	.507	1	347,616	Tony Muser
Omaha Royals (7)	67	77	.465	7	407,249	Jeff Cox
Iowa Cubs (16)	51	92	.357	22½	453,386	Brad Mills

Playoff: Oklahoma City 4 games, Buffalo 0.

All-Star Team: 1B-Jeff Conine, Omaha; **2B**-Jeff Frye, Oklahoma City; **3B**-Jim Tatum, Denver; **SS**-Carlos Garcia, Buffalo; **OF**-Al Martin, Buffalo; Geronimo Berroa, Nashville; Chuck Carr, Louisville; **C**-Bob Natal, Indianapolis; **DH**-Steve Balboni, Oklahoma City; **P**-Rene Arocha, Louisville; Dennis Moeller, Omaha; David Wainhouse, Indianapolis; **MVP**-Jim Tatum, Denver; **Rookie of the Year**-Kevin Young, Buffalo; **Manager**-Marc Bombard, Buffalo.

BA: Jim Tatum, Denver, .329
Runs: Kevin Young, Buffalo, 91
Hits: Jim Tatum, Denver, 162
RBIs: Steve Balboni, Oklahoma City, 104
HRs: Steve Balboni, Oklahoma City, 30

Wins: Keith Brown, Nashville, 12
Rene Arocha, Louisville, 12
Jeff Ballard, Louisville, 12
Tim Pugh, Nashville, 12
Kent Bottenfield, Indianapolis, 12
SOs: Mark Kiefer, Denver, 145
ERA: Dennis Moeller, Omaha, 2.46

AAA International League
President: Randy Mobley

East Standings	W	L	Pct.	GB	Attend.	Manager
Scranton-Wilkes-Barre Red Barons (24)	84	58	.592	—	560,464	Lee Elia
Pawtucket Red Sox (2)	71	72	.497	13½	358,318	Rico Petrocelli
Rochester Red Wings (1)	70	74	.486	15	305,205	Jerry Narron
Syracuse Chiefs (14)	60	83	.420	24½	269,067	Nick Leyva

West Standings	W	L	Pct.	GB	Attend.	Manager
Columbus Clippers (10)	95	49	.660	—	583,918	Rick Down
Richmond Braves (15)	73	71	.507	22	453,915	Chris Chambliss
Toledo Mud Hens (6)	64	80	.444	31	242,692	Joe Sparks
Tidewater Tides (23)	56	86	.394	38	174,362	Clint Hurdle

Playoffs: Columbus 3 games, Richmond 0; Scranton-Wilkes-Barre 3, Pawtucket 1. **Finals:** Columbus 3 games, Scranton-Wilkes-Barre 2.

All-Star Team: 1B-J.T. Snow, Columbus; **2B**-Steve Scarsone, Scranton-Wilkes-Barre/Rochester; **3B**-Hensley Meulens, Columbus; **SS**-Dave Silvestri, Columbus; **OF**-Butch Davis, Syracuse; Bernie Williams, Columbus; Gerald Williams, Columbus; **C**-Rich Rowland, Toledo; **DH**-Torey Lovullo, Columbus; **P**-Sam Militello, Columbus; Mike Draper, Columbus; **MVP**-J.T. Snow, Columbus; **Pitcher of the Year**-Sam Militello, Columbus; **Manager**-Lee Elia, Scranton-Wilkes-Barre.

BA: J.T. Snow, Columbus, .313
Luis Mercedes, Rochester, .313
Runs: Hensley Meulens, Columbus, 96
Hits: Gerald Williams, Columbus, 156
RBIs: Hensley Meulens, Columbus, 100

HRs: Hensley Meulens, Columbus, 26
Wins: David Nied, Richmond, 14
SOs: David Nied, Richmond, 159
ERA: Sam Militello, Columbus, 2.29

AAA Mexican League
President: Pedro Treto Cisneros

North Standings	W	L	Pct.	GB	Attend.	Manager
Dos Laredos Tecolotes	71	61	.538	—	184,391	Jose Guerrero
Union Laguna Algodoneros	71	63	.530	1	166,832	Marco Antonio Vazquez/Dave Stockstill
Monterrey Industriales	69	63	.523	2	137,942	Marcelo Juarez/Jose Manuel Ortiz/Miguel Solis/Gregorio Luque
Saltillo Saraperos	69	64	.519	2½	154,149	Juan Navarrete/Alfredo Rios
Aguascalientes Rieleros	67	66	.504	4½	149,806	Gregorio Luque/Francisco Rodriguez
Monterrey Sultanes	65	68	.489	6½	136,820	Aurelio Rodriguez/Carlos Paz
Monclova Acereros	58	73	.443	12½	128,435	Jose Soto/Jaime Corella
Jalisco Charros	56	74	.431	14	161,800	Roberto Castellon/Roberto Mendez/Marcelo Juarez

South Standings	W	L	Pct.	GB	Attend.	Manager
Mexico City Tigres	76	52	.594	—	171,102	Gerardo Gutierrez
Mexico City Diablos Rojos	71	56	.559	4½	173,897	Ramon Montoya
Minatitlan Petroleros	72	58	.554	5	151,234	Francisco Estrada
Yucatan Leones	70	61	.534	7½	246,042	Fernando Villaescusa
Campeche Piratas	64	64	.500	12	181,632	Jorge Tellaeche/Herminio Dominguez
Veracruz Aguila	62	70	.470	16	163,627	Jack Pierce
Tabasco Olmecas	56	75	.427	21½	152,000	Rodolfo Sandoval/Juan Raul Castillo
Cordoba Cafeteros	50	79	.388	26½	139,997	Bernardo Calvo

Playoffs: Dos Laredos 4 games, Saltillo 2; Union Laguna 4 games, Monterrey Industriales 3; MC Tigres 4 games, Yucatan 0; Minatitlan 4 games, MC Diablos Rojos 3. Dos Laredos 4 games, Union Laguna 2; MC Tigres 4 games, Minatitlan 2. **Finals:** MC Tigres 4 games, Dos Laredos 2.

BA: Raul Perez Tovar, Monclova, .416
Runs: Ty Gainey, MC Diablos Rojos, 114
Hits: Raul Perez Tovar, Monclova, 201
RBIs: Ty Gainey, MC Diablos Rojos, 133

HRs: Ty Gainey, MC Diablos Rojos, 47
Wins: Julio Parata, Minatitlan, 20
SOs: Jesus Rios, MC Tigres, 186
ERA: Mercedes Esquer, Yucatan, 2.24

AAA Pacific Coast League
President: Bill Cutler

North Standings	W	L	Pct.	GB	Attend.	Manager
Portland Beavers**(9)	83	61	.576	—	184,097	Scott Ullger
Vancouver Canadians*(4)	81	61	.570	1	333,564	Rick Renick
Edmonton Trappers (3)	74	69	.517	8½	257,146	Max Oliveras

*Won first-half   **Won second-half   ***Won both halves
Numbers after nicknames indicate farm system.
Affiliation listed at end of each year.

610

	W	L	Pct.	GB	Attend.	Manager
Calgary Cannons (12)..........	60	78	.435	20	277,307	Keith Bodie
Tacoma Tigers (11)	56	87	.392	26½	329,000	Bob Boone

South Standings	W	L	Pct.	GB	Attend.	Manager
Colorado Springs Sky Sox**(5).	84	57	.596	—	187,645	Charlie Manuel
Las Vegas Stars*(27)	74	70	.514	11½	382,838	Jim Riggleman
Tucson Toros (20)	70	74	.486	15½	330,134	Bob Skinner
Phoenix Firebirds (28)........	66	78	.458	19½	278,798	Bill Evers
Albuquerque Dukes (21)	65	78	.455	20	362,283	Bill Russell

Playoffs: Colorado Springs 3 games, Las Vegas 2; Vancouver 3 games, Portland 2.
Finals: Colorado Springs 3 games, Vancouver 0.

All-Star Team: 1B-Guillermo Velasquez, Las Vegas; **2B**-Bret Boone, Calgary; **3B**-Mike Blowers, Calgary; **SS**-Alvaro Espinoza, Colorado Springs; **OF**-Tim Salmon, Edmonton; Wayne Kirby, Colorado Springs; Bernardo Brito, Portland; **C**-Mike Piazza, Albuquerque; **DH**-Troy Neel, Tacoma; **P**-Rod Bolton, Vancouver; Denis Boucher, Colorado Springs; Brian Drahman, Vancouver; **MVP**-Tim Salmon, Edmonton; **Manager**-Charlie Manuel, Colorado Springs.

BA: Troy Neel, Tacoma, .351
Runs: Tim Salmon, Edmonton, 101
    Wayne Kirby, Colorado Springs, 101
Hits: Wayne Kirby, Colorado Springs, 162
RBIs: Tim Salmon, Edmonton, 105

HRs: Tim Salmon, Edmonton, 29
Wins: Zak Shinall, Albuquerque, 13
    George Tsamis, Portland, 13
SOs: Mike Trombley, Portland, 138
ERA: Mike Dunne, Vancouver, 2.78

AA Eastern League
President: Charles E. Eshbach

Standings	W	L	Pct.	GB	Attend.	Manager
Canton-Akron Indians (5)..	80	58	.580	—	194,662	Brian Graham
Binghamton Mets (23)........	79	59	.572	1	259,284	Steve Swisher
Harrisburg Senators (22)	78	59	.569	1½	209,159	Mike Quade
Albany-Colonie Yankees (10).	71	68	.511	9½	145,930	Dan Radison
London Tigers (6)..............	67	70	.489	12½	113,735	Mark DeJohn
Reading Phillies (24)	61	77	.442	19	287,078	Don McCormack
Hagerstown Suns (1)	59	80	.424	21½	130,331	Don Buford
New Britain Red Sox (2)	58	82	.414	23	125,393	Jim Pankovits

Playoffs: Binghamton 3 games, Harrisburg 1; Canton-Akron 3 games, Albany-Colonie 0.
Finals: Binghamton 3 games, Canton-Akron 2.

All-Star Team: 1B-Ivan Cruz, London; **2B**-Hector Vargas, Albany-Colonie; **3B**-Russ Davis, Albany-Colonie; **SS**-Mike Lansing, Harrisburg; **OF**-Ken Ramos, Canton-Akron; Mark Smith, Hagerstown; Tracy Sanders, Canton-Akron; **C**-Mike Lieberthal, Reading; **DH**-Greg Sparks, London; **P**-Bobby Jones, Binghamton; Ed Riley, New Britain; Len Picota, Harrisburg; **MVP**-Russ Davis, Albany-Colonie; **Pitcher of the Year**-Bobby Jones, Binghamton; **Manager**-Steve Swisher, Binghamton.

BA: Ken Ramos, Canton-Akron, .339
Runs: Ken Ramos, Canton-Akron, 94
Hits: Don Sparks, Albany-Colonie, 157
RBIs: Ivan Cruz, London, 104

HRs: Greg Sparks, London, 25
Wins: Paul Byrd, Canton-Akron, 14
SOs: Sterling Hitchcock, Albany-Colonie, 156
ERA: Bobby Jones, Binghamton, 1.88

AA Southern League
President: Jimmy Bragan

East Standings	W	L	Pct.	GB	Attend.	Manager
Greenville Braves***(15).	100	43	.699	—	247,798	Grady Little
Charlotte Knights (16)........	70	73	.490	30	338,047	Marv Foley
Jacksonville Suns (12)........	68	75	.476	32	226,273	Bob Hartsfield
Orlando SunRays (9)	60	82	.423	39½	154,965	Phil Roof
Carolina Mudcats (25)........	52	92	.361	48½	263,141	Don Werner

West Standings	W	L	Pct.	GB	Attend.	Manager
Chattanooga Lookouts***(17)...	90	53	.629	—	269,688	Dave Miley/Ron Oester
Huntsville Stars (11)........	81	63	.563	9½	252,010	Casey Parsons
Memphis Chicks (7)	71	73	.493	19½	212,768	Brian Poldberg
Birmingham Barons (4)......	68	74	.479	21½	263,323	Tony Franklin
Knoxville Blue Jays (14)	56	88	.389	34½	90,387	Garth Iorg

Playoffs: Greenville 3 games, Charlotte 0; Chattanooga 3 games, Huntsville 1.
Finals: Greenville 3 games, Chattanooga 2.

All-Star Team: 1B-Marcos Armas, Huntsville; Tim Costo, Chattanooga; **2B**-Brian Turang, Jacksonville; **3B**-Phil Hiatt, Memphis; **SS**-Chipper Jones, Greenville; **OF**-Scott Pose, Chattanooga; Juan de la Rosa, Knoxville; Melvin Nieves, Greenville; Scott Lydy, Huntsville; **C**-Javy Lopez, Greenville; **DH**-Nigel Wilson, Knoxville; **P**-Nate Minchey, Greenville; Larry Thomas, Birmingham; **MVP**-Javy Lopez, Greenville; **Pitcher of the Year**-Jim Converse, Jacksonville; Jerry Spradlin, Chattanooga; **Manager**-Grady Little, Greenville.

BA: Scott Pose, Chattanooga, .342
Runs: Scott Pose, Chattanooga, 87
Hits: Scott Pose, Chattanooga, 180
RBIs: Scott Cepicky, Birmingham, 87
HRs: Tim Costo, Chattanooga, 28

Wins: Bronswell Patrick, Huntsville, 13
    Mike Anderson, Chattanooga, 13
    Steve Trachsel, Charlotte, 13
    Nate Minchey, Greenville, 13
SOs: Jim Converse, Jacksonville, 157
ERA: Larry Thomas, Birmingham, 1.94

AA Texas League
President: Tom Kayser

East Standings	W	L	Pct.	GB	Attend.	Manager
Tulsa Drillers**(13)	77	59	.566	—	290,393	Bobby Jones
Shreveport Captains*(28)	77	59	.566	—	207,925	Bill Robinson

	W	L	Pct.	GB	Attend.	Manager
Jackson Generals (20)........	61	74	.452	15½	140,040	Rick Sweet
Arkansas Travelers (26)......	59	73	.447	16	265,984	Joe Pettini

West Standings	W	L	Pct.	GB	Attend.	Manager
El Paso Diablos**(8)	73	63	.537	—	262,727	Chris Bando
Wichita Wranglers*(27)	70	66	.515	3	210,990	Bruce Bochy
Midland Angels (3)............	61	72	.459	10½	195,629	Don Long
San Antonio Missions (21).	62	74	.456	11	177,365	Jerry Royster

Playoffs: Wichita 2 games, El Paso 1; Shreveport 2 games, Tulsa 0.
Finals: Wichita 4 games, Shreveport 0.

All-Star Team: 1B-Jay Gainer, Wichita; **2B**-Jon Shave, Tulsa; **3B**-Adell Davenport, Shreveport; **SS**-Edgar Caceres, El Paso; **OF**-Troy O'Leary, El Paso; Billy Ashley, San Antonio; Jeff Kipila, Midland; **C**-Tony Eusebio, Jackson; **DH**-Jose Oliva, Tulsa; **P**-Dan Smith, Tulsa; Dan Carlson, Shreveport; Todd Jones, Jackson; Kevin Meier, Arkansas; Rick Huisman, Shreveport; Tim Worrell, Wichita; **MVP**-Troy O'Leary, El Paso; **Pitcher of the Year**-Dan Smith, Tulsa; **Manager**-Bobby Jones, Tulsa.

BA: Troy O'Leary, El Paso, .334
Runs: Troy O'Leary, El Paso, 92
Hits: Troy O'Leary, El Paso, 169
RBIs: Adell Davenport, Shreveport, 88

HRs: Billy Ashley, San Antonio, 24
Wins: Dan Carlson, Shreveport, 15
SOs: Dan Carlson, Shreveport, 157
ERA: Dan Smith, Tulsa, 2.52

A California League
President: Joe Gagliardi

North Standings	W	L	Pct.	GB	Attend.	Manager
Stockton Ports***(8) ..	83	53	.610	—	112,348	Tim Ireland
Modesto A's (11)................	79	57	.581	4	104,671	Ted Kubiak
San Jose Giants (28)	78	58	.574	5	135,891	Ron Wotus
Reno Silver Sox (11)	65	71	.478	18	105,346	Gary Jones
Salinas Spurs....................	36	99	.267	46½	54,256	Hide Koga

South Standings	W	L	Pct.	GB	Attend.	Manager
Visalia Oaks**(9)............	75	61	.551	—	86,209	Steve Liddle
Palm Springs Angels*(3)....	72	63	.533	2½	89,645	Mario Mendoza
High Desert Mavericks (27)....	71	65	.522	4	218,482	Bryan Little
Bakersfield Dodgers (21)...	68	68	.500	7	156,233	Tom Beyers
San Bernardino Spirit (12)..	52	84	.382	23	106,469	Ivan DeJesus

Playoffs: Stockton 3 games, Modesto 2; Visalia 3 games, Palm Springs 1.
Finals: Stockton 3 games, Visalia 1.

All-Star Team: 1B-Steve Dunn, Visalia; **2B**-Brent Gates, Modesto; **3B**-Fabio Gomez, Reno; **SS**-Denny Hocking, Visalia; **OF**-Rich Becker, Visalia; Marty Cordova, Visalia; Mike Neill, Reno; **C**-Mike Durant, Visalia; Eric Helfand, Modesto; **DH**-Billy Hall, High Desert; **P**-Rafael Chaves, High Desert; Mike Farrell, Stockton; Joe Rosselli, San Jose; Curtis Shaw, Modesto; Tim Smith, Reno; **MVP**-Marty Cordova, Visalia; **Pitcher of the Year**-Joe Rosselli, San Jose; **Manager**-Tim Ireland, Stockton.

BA: Billy Hall, High Desert, .356
Runs: Rich Becker, Visalia, 118
Hits: Denny Hocking, Visalia, 182
RBIs: Marty Cordova, Visalia, 131
HRs: Marty Cordova, Visalia, 28

Wins: Brian Hancock, Stockton, 14
SOs: Curtis Shaw, Modesto, 154
ERA: Joe Rosselli, San Jose, 2.41
Saves: Rafael Chaves, High Desert, 34

A Carolina League
President: John Hopkins

North Standings	W	L	Pct.	GB	Attend.	Manager
Lynchburg Red Sox***(2).	77	58	.570	—	92,720	Buddy Bailey
Frederick Keys (1)............	69	71	.493	10½	329,592	Bob Miscik
Prince William Cannons (10)..	69	71	.493	10½	208,416	Mike Hart
Salem Buccaneers (25)........	64	76	.457	15½	134,598	John Wockenfuss

South Standings	W	L	Pct.	GB	Attend.	Manager
Peninsula Pilots***(12)......	74	64	.536	—	59,093	Marc Hill
Durham Bulls (15)	70	70	.500	5	280,994	Leon Roberts
Kinston Indians (5)	65	71	.478	8	105,090	Dave Keller
Winston-Salem Spirits (16)	66	73	.475	8½	159,316	Bill Hayes

Playoff: Peninsula defeated Durham in a one game playoff for the first half title.
Finals: Peninsula 3 games, Lynchburg 2.

All-Star Team: 1B-Bubba Smith, Peninsula; **2B**-Kevin Jordan, Prince William; **3B**-Jose Viera, Winston-Salem; **SS**-Ramon Martinez, Salem; **OF**-Darren Bragg, Peninsula; Stanton Cameron, Frederick; Brian Kowitz, Durham; **C**-Miah Bradbury, Peninsula; **DH**-Andy Hartung, Winston-Salem; **P**-John Cummings, Peninsula; Joe Caruso, Lynchburg; **MVP**-Bubba Smith, Peninsula; **Manager**-Marc Hill, Peninsula.

BA: Corey Kapano, Winston-Salem, .318
Runs: Darren Bragg, Peninsula, 82
Hits: Ramon Martinez, Salem, 154
RBIs: Andy Hartung, Winston-Salem, 94

HRs: Bubba Smith, Peninsula, 32
Wins: John Cummings, Peninsula, 16
SOs: John Cummings, Peninsula, 144
ERA: Joe Caruso, Lynchburg, 1.98

A Florida State League
President: Chuck Murphy

East Standings	W	L	Pct.	GB	Attend.	Manager
West Palm Beach Expos*(22).	76	61	.555	—	121,574	Dave Jauss
St. Lucie Mets**(23)	74	62	.544	1½	66,899	John Tamargo
Ft. Lauderdale Yankees (10).	59	76	.437	16	111,907	Brian Butterfield
Vero Beach Dodgers (21)...	53	82	.393	22	79,447	Glenn Hoffman

Central Standings	W	L	Pct.	GB	Attend.	Manager
Baseball City Royals (7)....	71	60	.542	—	17,406	Ron Johnson
Osceola Astros*(20)	72	62	.537	½	49,870	Sal Butera

Lakeland Tigers**(6)	70	62	.530	1½	56,951	John Lipon
Winter Haven Red Sox (2)	51	86	.372	23	16,082	Felix Maldonado

West Standings	W	L	Pct.	GB	Attend.	Manager
Sarasota White Sox*(4)	85	48	.639	—	91,574	Rick Patterson
Dunedin Blue Jays**(14)	78	59	.569	9	74,983	Dennis Holmberg
Clearwater Phillies (24)	75	59	.560	10½	91,834	Bill Dancy
Charlotte Rangers (13)	73	62	.541	13	92,996	Bump Wills
St. Petersburg Cardinals (26)	57	76	.429	28	121,763	Dave Bialas
Ft. Myers Miracle (x)	46	85	.351	38	105,578	Dan Rohn

Playoffs: Baseball City 2 games, Sarasota 0; Osceola 2 games, St. Lucie 1; Clearwater 2 games, Dunedin 0; Lakeland 2 games, West Palm Beach 0. Lakeland 2 games, Clearwater 0; Baseball City 2 games, Osceola 1.
Finals: Lakeland 2 games, Baseball City 0.

All-Star Team: 1B-Roberto Petagine, Osceola; **2B**-Fernando Vina, St. Lucie; **3B**-Howard Battle, Dunedin; **SS**-Brandon Wilson, Sarasota; **OF**-Rondell White, West Palm Beach; Rob Butler, Dunedin; Anthony Lewis, St. Petersburg; **C**-Carlos Delgado, Dunedin; Lance Jennings, Baseball City; **DH**-Jay Kirkpatrick, Vero Beach; **P**-Tavo Alvarez, West Palm Beach; Steve Schrenk, Sarasota; Chris Hill, Osceola; Brien Taylor, Ft. Lauderdale; John Kelly, St. Petersburg; Jim Dougherty, Osceola; **MVP**-Carlos Delgado, Dunedin; **Manager**-Rick Patterson, Sarasota.

BA: Rob Butler, Dunedin, .358
Runs: James Mouton, Osceola, 110
Hits: Carlos Delgado, Dunedin, 157
RBIs: Carlos Delgado, Dunedin, 100
HRs: Carlos Delgado, Dunedin, 30
Wins: Chris Hill, Osceola, 16
SOs: Brien Taylor, Ft. Lauderdale, 187
ERA: Tavo Alvarez, West Palm Beach, 1.49

A Midwest League

President: George Spelius

North Standings	W	L	Pct.	GB	Attend.	Manager
Beloit Brewers**(8)	77	58	.570	—	60,999	Wayne Krenchicki
South Bend White Sox (4)	73	64	.533	5	213,951	Terry Francona
Appleton Foxes*(7)	70	62	.530	5½	46,576	Tom Poquette
Rockford Expos (22)	66	70	.485	11½	50,900	Rob Leary
Kenosha Twins (9)	63	70	.474	13	45,349	Jim Dwyer
Kane County Cougars (1)	61	76	.445	17	323,769	Joel Youngblood
Madison Muskies (11)	59	75	.440	17½	95,846	Dick Scott

South Standings	W	L	Pct.	GB	Attend.	Manager
Quad City River Bandits**(3)	91	46	.664	—	250,745	Mitch Seoane
Springfield Cardinals (26)	84	56	.600	8½	152,942	Rick Colbert
Cedar Rapids Reds*(17)	82	56	.594	9½	133,899	Mark Berry
Peoria Chiefs (16)	62	74	.456	28½	172,560	Steve Roadcap
Waterloo Diamonds (27)	59	78	.431	32	48,074	Keith Champion
Clinton Giants (28)	59	79	.428	32½	79,374	Bill Stein
Burlington Astros (20)	47	89	.346	43½	69,679	Steve Curry

Playoffs: Cedar Rapids 2 games, Quad City 0; Beloit 2 games, Appleton 1.
Finals: Cedar Rapids 3 games, Beloit 2.

All-Star Team: 1B-Chris Pritchett, Quad City; **2B**-Jason Hardtke, Waterloo; **3B**-Dmitri Young, Springfield; **SS**-Shane Halter, Appleton; **OF**-Steve Gibralter, Cedar Rapids; Orlando Palmeiro, Quad City; Alex Ochoa, Kane County; **C**-Damian Miller, Kenosha; **DH**-Andre Keene, Clinton; **P**-Tyrone Hill, Beloit; James Baldwin, South Bend; Ken Grundt, Clinton; Gerald Santos, Springfield; **MVP**-Steve Gibralter, Cedar Rapids; **Manager**-Tom Poquette, Appleton.

BA: Orlando Palmeiro, Quad City, .317
Runs: Steve Gibralter, Cedar Rapids, 92
Hits: Steve Gibralter, Cedar Rapids, 162
RBIs: Steve Gibralter, Cedar Rapids, 99
HRs: Steve Gibralter, Cedar Rapids, 19
Wins: John Fritz, Quad City, 20
SOs: Gabe White, Rockford, 176
ERA: Bobby Chouinard, Kane County, 2.08
Saves: Gerald Santos, Springfield, 35

A New York-Pennsylvania League

President: Robert Julian

McNamara Standings	W	L	Pct.	GB	Attend.	Manager
Utica Blue Sox (4)	42	32	.568	—	73,464	Fred Kendall
Pittsfield Mets (23)	37	37	.500	5	52,967	Jim Thrift
Oneonta Yankees (10)	37	38	.493	5½	50,534	Jack Gillis
Watertown Indians (5)	37	39	.487	6	42,762	Shawn Pender

Pinckney Standings	W	L	Pct.	GB	Attend.	Manager
Geneva Cubs (16)	41	34	.547	—	32,075	Greg Mahlberg
Batavia Clippers (24)	36	34	.514	2½	39,385	Ramon Aviles
Auburn Astros (20)	32	41	.438	8	21,193	Steve Dillard
Elmira Pioneers (2)	31	44	.413	10	63,473	Dave Holt

Stedler Standings	W	L	Pct.	GB	Attend.	Manager
Hamilton Redbirds (26)	56	20	.737	—	65,584	Chris Maloney
Erie Sailors (19)	40	37	.519	16½	79,245	Fredi Gonzalez
Niagara Falls Rapids (6)	39	39	.500	18	48,698	Larry Parrish
Jamestown Expos (22)	34	43	.442	22½	40,269	Q.V. Lowe
St. Catharines Blue Jays (14)	33	42	.440	22½	36,066	J.J. Cannon
Welland Pirates (25)	31	46	.403	25½	38,210	Trent Jewett

Playoffs: Geneva 1 game, Utica 0; Erie 1 game, Hamilton 0.
Finals: Geneva 2 games, Erie 0.

All-Star Team: 1B-Todd Pridy, Erie; **2B**-Chad Tredaway, Geneva; **3B**-Lou Lucca, Erie; **SS**-Edgar Alfonzo, Pittsfield; **OF**-Jose Malave, Elmira; Robin Jennings, Geneva; Scot McCloughan, St. Catharines; Byron Mathews, Utica; **C**-Donnie Leshnock, Oneonta; Jeff Murphy, Hamilton; **DH**-Dave Duplessis, Watertown; **P**-Tim Crabtree, St. Catharines; Jamie Cochran, Hamilton; Dave Oehrlein, Hamilton; Bill Pulsipher, Pittsfield; **Manager**-Chris Maloney, Hamilton.

BA: Edgar Alfonzo, Pittsfield, .356
Runs: Shawn Wills, Batavia, 53
Hits: Edgar Alfonzo, Pittsfield, 106
RBIs: Todd Pridy, Erie, 61
HRs: Todd Pridy, Erie, 14
Wins: T.J. Mathews, Hamilton, 10
Dave Oehrlein, Hamilton, 10
SOs: Dave Oehrlein, Hamilton, 99
ERA: Tim Crabtree, St. Catharines, 1.57
Pct: T.J. Mathews, Hamilton, .909, 10-1
Dave Oehrlein, Hamilton, .909, 10-1

A Northwest League

President: Bob Richmond

North Standings	W	L	Pct.	GB	Attend.	Manager
Bellingham Mariners (12)	43	33	.566	—	68,928	Dave Myers
Yakima Bears (21)	36	40	.474	7	65,684	Joe Vavra
Everett Giants (28)	35	41	.461	8	85,936	Norm Sherry
Spokane Indians (27)	32	44	.421	11	111,607	Ed Romero

South Standings	W	L	Pct.	GB	Attend.	Manager
Bend Rockies (18)	43	33	.566	—	58,777	Gene Glynn
Boise Hawks (3)	40	36	.526	3	145,138	Tom Kotchman
Southern Oregon A's (11)	39	37	.513	4	77,098	Grady Fuson
Eugene Emeralds (7)	36	40	.474	7	109,163	Bobby Meacham

Playoff: Bellingham 2 games, Bend 0.

All-Star Team: 1B-Larry Sutton, Eugene; **2B**-Steve Sisco, Eugene; **3B**-Mark Sobolewski, Southern Oregon; **SS**-Jason Bates, Bend; **OF**-Terance Frazier, Southern Oregon; Papo Ramos, Everett; Bill Robbs, Spokane; **C**-Chris Abbe, Yakima; **DH**-Fred McNair, Bellingham; **P**-Mike Butler, Boise; Mark Thompson, Bend; Chris Eddy, Eugene; John Pricher, Boise; **MVP**-Larry Sutton, Eugene; **Manager**-Tom Kotchman, Boise.

BA: Sandy Martinez, Yakima, .333
Runs: Jason Bates, Bend, 57
Hits: Steve Sisco, Eugene, 86
RBIs: Larry Sutton, Eugene, 58
HRs: Larry Sutton, Eugene, 15
Wins: Mike Butler, Boise, 9
SOs: Mark Thompson, Bend, 102
ERA: Mark Thompson, Bend, 1.95

A South Atlantic League

President: John H. Moss

North Standings	W	L	Pct.	GB	Attend.	Manager
Columbia Mets (23)	79	59	.572	—	124,508	Tim Blackwell
Charleston (WV) Wheelers*(17)	77	64	.546	3½	135,010	P.J. Carey
Asheville Tourists (20)	74	66	.529	6	119,115	Tim Tolman
Greensboro Hornets (10)	74	67	.525	6½	156,387	Trey Hillman
Fayetteville Generals (6)	74	67	.525	6½	100,226	Gerry Groninger
Spartanburg Phillies**(22)	70	68	.507	9	47,274	Roy Majtyka
Gastonia Rangers (13)	66	70	.485	12	32,931	Walt Williams

South Standings	W	L	Pct.	GB	Attend.	Manager
Columbus RedStixx*(5)	77	62	.554	—	118,243	Mike Brown
Myrtle Beach Hurricanes**(14)	71	65	.522	4½	61,120	Doug Ault
Albany Polecats (22)	72	70	.507	6½	97,810	Lorenzo Bundy
Augusta Pirates (25)	67	74	.475	11	83,247	Scott Little
Savannah Cardinals (26)	62	78	.443	15½	79,589	Mike Ramsey
Macon Braves (15)	58	81	.417	19	88,833	Brian Snitker
Charleston (SC) Rainbows (27)	55	85	.393	22½	103,824	Dave Trembley

Playoffs: Myrtle Beach 2 games, Columbus 0; Charleston (WV) 2 games, Spartanburg 0.
Finals: Myrtle Beach 3 games, Charleston (WV) 0.

All-Star Team: 1B-Jamie Dismuke, Charleston (WV); **2B**-Quilvio Veras, Columbia; **3B**-Shane Andrews, Albany; **SS**-Benji Gil, Gastonia; **OF**-Gary Mota, Asheville; Cliff Floyd, Albany; William Canate, Columbus; **C**-Tommy Eason, Spartanburg; **DH**-Antonio Mitchell, Augusta/Columbus; **P**-Ron Blazier, Spartanburg; Paul Spoljaric, Myrtle Beach; **MVP**-Gary Mota, Asheville; **Pitcher of the Year**-Paul Spoljaric, Myrtle Beach; **Manager**-Mike Brown, Columbus.

BA: Quilvio Veras, Columbia, .319
Runs: William Canate, Columbus, 111
Hits: William Canate, Columbus, 168
RBIs: Cliff Floyd, Albany, 97
HRs: Shane Andrews, Albany, 25
Wins: Ron Blazier, Spartanburg, 14
Keith Garagozzo, Greensboro, 14
SOs: Jason Hisey, Savannah, 182
ERA: Travis Baptist, Myrtle Beach, 1.44

R Appalachian League

President: Bill Halstead

North Standings	W	L	Pct.	GB	Attend.	Manager
Bluefield Orioles (1)	37	25	.597	—	39,339	Mike O'Berry
Burlington Indians (5)	35	31	.530	4	67,276	Minnie Mendoza
Princeton Reds (17)	34	31	.523	4½	18,642	Sam Mejias
Huntington Cubs (16)	28	34	.452	9	42,129	Phil Hannon
Martinsville Phillies (24)	22	43	.338	16½	66,695	Rollie DeArmas

South Standings	W	L	Pct.	GB	Attend.	Manager
Elizabethton Twins (9)	49	17	.742	—	15,451	Ray Smith
Johnson City Cardinals (26)	33	32	.508	15½	42,868	Steve Turco
Bristol Tigers (6)	33	35	.485	17	29,185	Mark Wagner
Kingsport Mets (23)	27	35	.435	20	23,786	Andre David
Pulaski Braves (15)	23	38	.377	23½	16,993	Randy Ingle

Playoff: Bluefield 2 games, Elizabethton 1.

All-Star Team: 1B-Ken Tirpack, Elizabethton; **2B**-Marlon Nava, Elizabethton; **3B**-Dan Frye, Princeton; **SS**-David Fisher, Martinsville; **OF**-Derek Hacopian, Burlington; Roy Hodge, Bluefield; Basil Shabazz, Johnson City; **C**-Marco Manrique, Bluefield; **DH**-Aldo Pecorilli, Johnson City; **P**-Mike D'Andrea, Pulaski; Mike Matthews, Burlington; Gus Gandarillas, Elizabethton; **MVP**-Dan Frye, Princeton; **Manager**-Ray Smith, Elizabethton.

BA: Tim Stutheit, Huntington, .338
Runs: Dan Frye, Princeton, 50
Hits: Dan Frye, Princeton, 79
RBIs: Dan Frye, Princeton, 59
HRs: Dan Frye, Princeton, 15

Wins: Jose Cabrera, Burlington, 8
Blas Cedeno, Bristol, 8
Scott Moten, Elizabethton, 8
Mike D'Andrea, Pulaski, 8
SOs: Amaury Telemaco, Huntington, 93
ERA: Mike Matthews, Burlington, 1.01
Pct: Mike Matthews, Burlington, 1.000, 7-0
Kevin Legault, Elizabethton, 1.000, 7-0

R Arizona League
President: Bob Richmond

Standings	W	L	Pct.	GB	Manager
Athletics (Scottsdale) (11)	34	22	.607	—	Bruce Hines
Mariners (Tempe) (12)	32	24	.571	2	Carlos Lezcano
Giants (Scottsdale) (28)	32	24	.571	2	Alan Bannister
Brewers (Chandler) (8)	31	25	.554	3	Tommy Jones
Angels (Mesa) (3)	29	27	.518	5	Bill Lachemann
Cardinals (Chandler) (26)	28	28	.500	6	Joe Cunningham
Padres (Scottsdale) (27)	20	36	.357	14	Ken Berry
Rockies-Cubs (Mesa) (16, 18)	18	38	.321	16	Paul Zuvella

Playoffs: None.

BA: Brian Rupp, Cardinals, .386
Runs: Joe McEwing, Cardinals, 55
Hits: Brian Rupp, Cardinals, 80
RBIs: Brian Rupp, Cardinals, 40

HRs: Mark Pooschke, Giants, 3
Hiram Ramirez, Giants, 3
Jason Imperial, Brewers, 3
Greg Boyd, Rockies, 3
Brian Guzik, Angels, 3
Wins: Jeff Martin, Giants, 7
William Urbina, Athletics, 7
SOs: Stacy Hollins, Athletics, 93
ERA: Frankie Rodriguez, Brewers, 1.10

R Gulf Coast League
President: Thomas J. Saffell

East Standings	W	L	Pct.	GB	Manager
Expos (West Palm Beach) (22)	35	24	.593	—	Nelson Norman
Dodgers (Port St. Lucie) (21)	32	27	.542	3	John Shoemaker
Mets (Port St. Lucie) (23)	29	30	.492	6	Junior Roman
Braves (West Palm Beach) (15)	22	37	.373	13	Jim Saul
Central Standings	W	L	Pct.	GB	Manager
Royals (Baseball City) (7)	41	18	.695	—	Mike Jirschele
Marlins (Kissimmee) (19)	33	27	.550	8½	Carlos Tosca
Astros (Kissimmee) (20)	27	33	.450	14½	Julio Linares
Pirates (Bradenton) (25)	23	37	.383	18½	Woody Huyke
Red Sox (Winter Haven) (2)	18	41	.305	23	Frank White
West Standings	W	L	Pct.	GB	Manager
Blue Jays (Dunedin) (14)	35	24	.593	—	Omar Malave

	W	L	Pct.	GB		Manager
Yankees (Tampa) (10)	31	28	.525	4		Gary Denbo
Twins (Lee County) (9)	30	28	.517	4½		Jim Lemon
White Sox (Sarasota) (4)	30	29	.508	5		Mike Rojas
Orioles (Sarasota) (1)	29	29	.500	5½		Phillip Wellman
Rangers (Port Charlotte) (13)	28	31	.475	7		Chino Cadahia

Playoff: Expos 1 game, Blue Jays 0.
Finals: Royals 2 games, Expos 1.

All-Star Team: 1B-Chris Burr, Rangers; **2B**-Jose Vidro, Expos; **3B**-Tilson Brito, Blue Jays; **SS**-Brandon Cromer, Blue Jays; **OF**-Danny Clyburn, Pirates; Johnny Damon, Royals; Edgar Herrera, Twins; **C**-Jaime Torres, Yankees; **P**-Fernando DaSilva, Expos; Bart Rich, Blue Jays; **Manager**-Mike Jirschele, Royals.

BA: Johnny Damon, Royals, .349
Runs: Johnny Damon, Royals, 58
Hits: Chris Burr, Rangers, 70
RBIs: Chris Burr, Rangers, 47
HRs: Chris Burr, Rangers, 6

Wins: Fernando DaSilva, Expos, 10
SOs: Fernando DaSilva, Expos, 86
ERA: Jeff Cindrich, Yankees, 0.80
Pct: Fernando DaSilva, Expos, .909, 10-1

R Pioneer League
President: Ralph C. Nelles

North Standings	W	L	Pct.	GB	Attend.	Manager
Billings Mustangs (17)	53	23	.697	—	100,788	Donnie Scott
Great Falls Dodgers (21)	38	35	.521	13½	70,413	Jon Debus
Lethbridge Mounties (x)	24	50	.324	28	21,669	Larry Milbourne
Medicine Hat Blue Jays (14)	23	52	.307	29½	16,897	Jim Nettles
South Standings	W	L	Pct.	GB	Attend.	Manager
Salt Lake City Trappers	53	23	.697	—	217,263	Nick Belmonte
Helena Brewers (8)	50	26	.658	3	49,654	Harry Dunlop
Butte Copper Kings (13)	33	43	.434	20	24,551	Victor Ramirez
Idaho Falls Braves (15)	27	49	.355	26	46,209	Dave Hilton

Playoff: Billings 2 games, Salt Lake City 0.

All-Star Team: 1B-Tim Belk, Billings; **2B**-Demetrish Jenkins, Billings; **3B**-Tim Unroe, Helena; **SS**-Wes Weger, Helena; **OF**-Roger Cedeno, Great Falls; Tim Clark, Salt Lake City; Miguel Correa, Idaho Falls; **C**-Brian Hostetler, Helena; **DH**-Micah Franklin, Billings; **P**-Jason Kummerfeldt, Billings; Scott Karl, Helena; Bo Loftin, Billings; **Manager**-Donnie Scott, Billings.

BA: Tim Clark, Salt Lake City, .357
Runs: Cecil Rodrigues, Helena, 63
Hits: Tim Clark, Salt Lake City, 97
RBIs: Mike Welch, Butte, 62
HRs: Tim Unroe, Helena, 16

Wins: George Kerfut, Salt Lake City, 10
SOs: Rich Longford, Billings, 95
ERA: Scott Karl, Helena, 1.46
Pct: Scott Karl, Helena, 1.000, 7-0

1992 Interleague Post Season Play

World Series
Toronto (American) 4 games, Atlanta (National) 2

1992 Major League Farm Systems

American League
1 Baltimore (6): Rochester, Hagerstown, Frederick, Kane County, Gulf Coast, Bluefield.
2 Boston (6): Pawtucket, New Britain, Lynchburg, Winter Haven, Elmira, Gulf Coast.
3 California (6): Edmonton, Midland, Palm Springs, Quad City, Boise, Arizona.
4 Chicago (6): Vancouver, Birmingham, Sarasota, South Bend, Utica, Arizona.
5 Cleveland (6): Colorado Springs, Canton-Akron, Kinston, Columbus (GA), Watertown, Burlington (NC).
6 Detroit (6): Toledo, London, Lakeland, Fayetteville, Niagara Falls, Bristol.
7 Kansas City (6): Omaha, Memphis, Baseball City, Appleton, Eugene, Gulf Coast.
8 Milwaukee (6): Denver, El Paso, Stockton, Beloit, Helena, Arizona.
9 Minnesota (6): Portland, Orlando, Visalia, Kenosha, Elizabethton, Gulf Coast.
10 New York (7): Columbus (OH), Albany-Colonie, Prince William, Ft. Lauderdale, Greensboro, Oneonta, Gulf Coast.
11 Oakland (7): Tacoma, Huntsville, Modesto, Reno, Madison, Southern Oregon, Arizona.
12 Seattle (6): Calgary, Jacksonville, San Bernardino, Peninsula, Bellingham, Arizona.
13 Texas (6): Oklahoma City, Tulsa, Port Charlotte, Gastonia, Butte, Gulf Coast.
14 Toronto (7): Syracuse, Knoxville, Dunedin, Myrtle Beach, St. Catharines, Medicine Hat, Gulf Coast.

Co-op (x): Ft. Myers, Lethbridge.
Independent: Salinas, Salt Lake City.

National League
15 Atlanta (7): Richmond, Greenville, Durham, Macon, Pulaski, Idaho Falls, Gulf Coast.
16 Chicago (7): Iowa, Charlotte, Winston-Salem, Peoria, Geneva, Huntington, Arizona.
17 Cincinnati (6): Nashville, Chattanooga, Charleston (WV), Cedar Rapids, Princeton, Billings.
18 Colorado (2): Bend, Arizona.
19 Florida (2): Erie, Gulf Coast.
20 Houston (7): Tucson, Jackson, Osceola, Asheville, Burlington (IA), Auburn, Gulf Coast.
21 Los Angeles (7): Albuquerque, San Antonio, Bakersfield, Vero Beach, Yakima, Great Falls, Gulf Coast.
22 Montreal (7): Indianapolis, Harrisburg, West Palm Beach, Rockford, Albany (GA), amestown, Gulf Coast.
23 New York (7): Tidewater, Binghamton, St. Lucie, Columbia, Pittsfield, Kingsport, Gulf Coast.
24 Philadelphia (6): Scranton-Wilkes-Barre, Reading, Clearwater, Spartanburg, Batavia, Martinsville.
25 Pittsburgh (6): Buffalo, Carolina, Salem, Augusta, Welland, Gulf Coast.
26 St. Louis (8): Louisville, Arkansas, St. Petersburg, Springfield, Savannah, Hamilton, Johnson City, Arizona.
27 San Diego (7): Las Vegas, Wichita, High Desert, Waterloo, Charleston (SC), Spokane, Arizona.
28 San Francisco (6): Phoenix, Shreveport, San Jose, Clinton, Everett, Arizona.

1992 No-Hitters

Date	Pitcher	Team	League	Opponent	Score
3-31	Ernesto Barraza	Nuevo Laredo	Mexican	Cordoba	5-0
4-9	Greg Bicknell/				
	Chuck Wiley	Peninsula	Carolina	Salem	1-0
4-12	Matt Young	Boston	American	Cleveland	1-2 (8)
4-13	Mike Hostetler/Barry Chiles/Mike Potts/				
	Dave Williams	Durham	Carolina	Peninsula	9-0
4-30	Francisco Rodriguez/				
	Joe Caruso	Lynchburg	Carolina	Winston-Salem	3-0
5-2	Pete Smith	Richmond	International	Rochester	1-0 (P, 7)
5-5	Tom Singer	Dunedin	Florida State	Ft. Myers	2-0
5-8	Mike Zimmerman/				
	Dennis Tafoya	Carolina	Southern	Chattanooga	1-0 (8)
5-14	Chuck Wanke	Clinton	Midwest	Peoria	5-3
5-15	Dave Telgheder	Tidewater	International	Pawtucket	1-0
6-1	Tim Vanegmond	Lynchburg	Carolina	Prince William	2-0
6-2	Don Heinkel	Campeche	Mexican	MC Diablos Rojos	7-0 (P)
6-4	Ben Blomdahl	Fayetteville	South Atlantic	Spartanburg	1-0 (7)
6-7	David West/Larry Casian/				
	Greg Johnson	Portland	Pacific Coast	Vancouver	5-0
6-16	Joey Eischen	West Palm Beach	Florida State	Vero Beach	5-0 (7)
7-17	Eric Weaver	Vero Beach	Florida State	Ft. Lauderdale	2-1
7-18	Andres Cruz	Yucatan	Mexican	Jalisco	8-0
7-24	Jim McCready/				
	Todd Fiegel	Columbia	South Atlantic	Fayetteville	6-0
7-25	Ben Rivera	Scranton-Wilkes-Barre	International	Pawtucket	2-0 (10)
8-3	Dana Allison/Roger Smithberg/				
	Todd Revenig	Huntsville	Southern	Birmingham	1-0 (10)
8-10	Dave Oehrlein	Hamilton	New York-Penn.	Auburn	7-0 (5)
8-10	Hut Smith	Orioles	Gulf Coast	Blue Jays	3-0 (7)
8-13	David Sartain	Kenosha	Midwest	Clinton	1-0 (7)
8-14	Fernando DaSilva	Expos	Gulf Coast	Braves	2-0
8-17	Kevin Gross	Los Angeles	National	San Francisco	2-0
8-23	Andrew Carter	Clearwater	Florida State	Winter Haven	1-0
8-23	Scott Bakkum	Winter Haven	Florida State	Clearwater	0-1
8-24	Jeff Cindrich	Yankees	Gulf Coast	Rangers	2-0 (7)
8-28	John Roper	Chattanooga	Southern	Birmingham	1-0 (7)
9-5	Tim Worrell	Las Vegas	Pacific Coast	Phoenix	2-0

Number in parentheses indicates innings if other than nine; "P" indicates perfect game.

THIS DATE IN MINOR LEAGUE HISTORY

April 1, 1992, The Jalisco Charros of the Mexican League signed former big league pitcher Fernando Valenzuela.

April 12, 1992, The Iowa Cubs, American Association, opened new Sec Taylor Stadium, which had undergone a $12 million renovation.

May 2, 1992, Pete Smith of Richmond, International League, pitched a seven-inning perfect game, beating Rochester 1-0.

July 14, 1992, Toronto East, a Blue Jays affiliate in the Dominican Summer League, won 37 straight games. The club had not lost a game. They finished the season 68-2, but lost in the first round of the playoffs.

August 4, 1992, A chemical spill at a DuPont plant behind the left field wall forced the postponement of the Tidewater at Rochester game in the International League.

August 6, 1992, An Arkansas Travelers front office intern shot a co-worker and then killed himself on the infield at Ray Winder Field in Little Rock. It was on off day for the team and no players were present.

August 20, 1992, Gerardo Sanchez of Nuevo Laredo, Mexican League, finished the 1992 season with a streak of 997 consecutive games played. The league record of 1,166 was set by Rolando Camarero from 1968 to 1976.

August 22, 1992, With Idaho Falls leading Butte 4-3 in the seventh inning at Butte, the game was suspended due to snow. Players complained that they couldn't see the ball through the large flakes. It was the first August snowout in Pioneer League history.

August 23, 1992, For the first time in the 73 year history of the Florida State League, both pitchers threw no-hitters in one game. Andy Carter of Clearwater beat Scott Bakkum of Winter Haven 1-0 as Clearwater scored on two walks and two sacrifice bunts.

August 24, 1992, Hurricane Andrew caused extensive damage to the stadium at Homestead, Florida, spring training home of the Cleveland Indians and their minor league affiliates.

September 2, 1992, John Lipon of Lakeland, Florida State League, retired after his 30th year of managing. He had won 2,176 games, fifth on the all-time minor league managerial win list.

September 5, 1992, The Greenville Braves ended the season with 100 wins, becoming the first minor league team to win 100 games in a season since Peninsula did it in the Carolina League in 1980. It was a new Southern League record for wins in a season.

September 7, 1992, Steve Reed set a new National Association record for saves in a season with 43. He had split the season between Shreveport, Texas League, and Phoenix, Pacific Coast League.

1993

American League
President: Dr. Robert Brown

East Standings	W	L	Pct.	GB	Attend.	Manager
Toronto Blue Jays	95	67	.586	—	4,057,947	Cito Gaston
New York Yankees	88	74	.543	7	2,416,942	Buck Showalter
Baltimore Orioles	85	77	.525	10	3,644,965	Johnny Oates
Detroit Tigers	85	77	.525	10	1,970,791	Sparky Anderson
Boston Red Sox	80	82	.494	15	2,422,021	Butch Hobson
Cleveland Indians	76	86	.469	19	2,177,908	Mike Hargrove
Milwaukee Brewers	69	93	.426	26	1,688,080	Phil Garner

West Standings	W	L	Pct.	GB	Attend.	Manager
Chicago White Sox	94	68	.580	—	2,581,091	Gene Lamont
Texas Rangers	86	76	.531	8	2,244,616	Kevin Kennedy
Kansas City Royals	84	78	.519	10	1,934,578	Hal McRae
Seattle Mariners	82	80	.506	12	2,052,638	Lou Piniella
California Angels	71	91	.438	23	2,057,460	Buck Rodgers
Minnesota Twins	71	91	.438	23	2,048,673	Tom Kelly
Oakland Athletics	68	94	.420	26	2,035,025	Tony LaRussa

Playoff: Toronto 4 games, Chicago 2.

BA: John Olerud, Toronto, .363
Runs: Rafael Palmeiro, Texas, 124
Hits: Paul Molitor, Toronto, 211
RBIs: Albert Belle, Cleveland, 129
HRs: Juan Gonzalez, Texas, 46
Wins: Jack McDowell, Chicago, 22

SOs: Randy Johnson, Seattle, 308
ERA: Kevin Appier, Kansas City, 2.56
Pct: Juan Guzman, Toronto, .824, 14-3
Saves: Duane Ward, Toronto, 45
Jeff Montgomery, Kansas City, 45

National League
President: William White

East Standings	W	L	Pct.	GB	Attend.	Manager
Philadelphia Phillies	97	65	.599	—	3,137,539	Jim Fregosi
Montreal Expos	94	68	.580	3	1,641,437	Felipe Alou
St. Louis Cardinals	87	75	.537	10	2,841,028	Joe Torre
Chicago Cubs	84	78	.519	13	2,653,763	Jim Lefebvre
Pittsburgh Pirates	75	87	.463	22	1,650,593	Jim Leyland
Florida Marlins	64	98	.395	33	3,064,847	Rene Lachemann
New York Mets	59	103	.364	38	1,873,183	Jeff Torborg/Dallas Green

West Standings	W	L	Pct.	GB	Attend.	Manager
Atlanta Braves	104	58	.642	—	3,884,720	Bobby Cox
San Francisco Giants	103	59	.636	1	2,606,354	Dusty Baker
Houston Astros	85	77	.525	19	2,084,528	Art Howe
Los Angeles Dodgers	81	81	.500	23	3,162,576	Tom Lasorda
Cincinnati Reds	73	89	.451	31	2,453,232	Tony Perez/Davey Johnson
Colorado Rockies	67	95	.414	37	4,483,270	Don Baylor
San Diego Padres	61	101	.377	43	1,375,432	Jim Riggleman

Playoff: Philadelphia 4 games, Atlanta 2.

BA: Andres Galarraga, Colorado, .370
Runs: Lenny Dykstra, Philadelphia, 143
Hits: Lenny Dykstra, Philadelphia, 194
RBIs: Barry Bonds, San Francisco, 123
HRs: Barry Bonds, San Francisco, 46

Wins: Tom Glavine, Atlanta, 22
John Burkett, San Francisco, 22
SOs: Jose Rijo, Cincinnati, 227
ERA: Greg Maddux, Atlanta, 2.36
Pct: Mark Portugal, Houston, .818, 18-4
Saves: Randy Myers, Chicago, 53

AAA American Association
President: Branch B. Rickey

East Standings	W	L	Pct.	GB	Attend.	Manager
Nashville Sounds (4)	81	62	.566	—	438,745	Rick Renick
Buffalo Bisons (25)	71	71	.493	10½	1,058,620	Doc Edwards
Louisville Redbirds (26)	68	76	.472	13½	643,833	Jack Krol
Indianapolis Indians (17)	66	77	.462	15	300,397	Marc Bombard

West Standings	W	L	Pct.	GB	Attend.	Manager
Iowa Cubs (16)	85	59	.590	—	446,860	Marv Foley
New Orleans Zephyrs (8)	80	64	.556	5	161,846	Chris Bando
Omaha Royals (7)	70	74	.486	15	384,972	Jeff Cox
Oklahoma City 89ers (13)	54	90	.375	31	364,673	Bobby Jones

Playoff: Iowa 4 games, Nashville 3.

All-Star Team: 1B-Bob Hamelin, Omaha; **2B**-Norberto Martin, Nashville; **3B**-Keith Lockhart, Louisville; **SS**-Esteban Beltre, Nashville; **OF**-Eddie Zambrano, Iowa; Karl Rhodes, Omaha/Iowa; Rob Ducey, Oklahoma City; **C**-Matt Walbeck, Iowa; **DH**-Steve Balboni, Oklahoma City; **P**-Roy Smith, Buffalo; Blaise Ilsley, Iowa; Tony Menendez, Buffalo; **MVP**-Eddie Zambrano, Iowa; **Manager**-Rick Renick, Nashville.

BA: Matt Merullo, Nashville, .332
Runs: Karl Rhodes, Iowa, 112
Hits: Norberto Martin, Nashville, 179
RBIs: Eddie Zambrano, Iowa, 115

HRs: Steve Balboni, Oklahoma City, 36
Wins: Bill Brennan, Iowa, 15
SOs: Bill Brennan, Iowa, 143
ERA: Rod Bolton, Nashville, 2.88

AAA International League
President: Randy Mobley

East Standings	W	L	Pct.	GB	Attend.	Manager
Rochester Red Wings (1)	74	67	.525	—	361,676	Bob Miscik
Ottawa Lynx (22)	73	69	.514	1½	663,926	Mike Quade
Scranton-Wilkes-Barre Red Barons (24)	62	82	.423	12½	531,620	George Culver
Pawtucket Red Sox (2)	60	82	.423	14½	466,428	Buddy Bailey
Syracuse Chiefs (14)	59	82	.418	15	262,760	Nick Leyva/Bob Didier

West Standings	W	L	Pct.	GB	Attend.	Manager
Charlotte Knights (5)	86	55	.610	—	403,029	Charlie Manuel
Richmond Braves (15)	80	62	.563	6½	533,076	Grady Little
Columbus Clippers (10)	78	62	.557	7½	580,570	Stump Merrill
Norfolk Tides (23)	70	71	.496	16	529,708	Clint Hurdle
Toledo Mud Hens (6)	65	77	.458	31½	274,047	Joe Sparks

Playoffs: Rochester 3 games, Ottawa 2; Charlotte 3 games, Richmond 1.
Finals: Charlotte 3 games, Rochester 2.

All-Star Team: 1B-Ryan Klesko, Richmond; **2B**-Tommy Hinzo, Rochester; **3B**-Jim Thome, Charlotte; **SS**-Chipper Jones, Richmond; **OF**-Tony Longmire, Scranton-Wilkes-Barre; Billy Masse, Columbus; Tony Tarasco, Richmond; **C**-Javy Lopez, Richmond; **DH**-Sam Horn, Charlotte; **P**-Aaron Sele, Pawtucket; Billy Taylor, Richmond; **MVP**-Jim Thome, Charlotte; **Pitcher of the Year**-Aaron Sele, Pawtucket; **Manager**-Mike Quade, Ottawa.

BA: Jim Thome, Charlotte, .332
Runs: Chipper Jones, Richmond, 97
Hits: Chipper Jones, Richmond, 174
RBIs: Jim Thome, Charlotte, 102
HRs: Sam Horn, Charlotte, 38

Wins: Chad Ogea, Charlotte, 13
Mike Birkbeck, Richmond, 13
SOs: Mike Birkbeck, Richmond, 136
John DeSilva, Toledo, 136
ERA: Kevin McGehee, Rochester, 2.96

AAA Mexican League
President: Pedro Treto Cisneros

North Standings	W	L	Pct.	GB	Attend.	Manager
Dos Laredos Tecolotes**	76	53	.589	—	181,392	Dan Firova
Monterrey Sultanes*	75	55	.577	1½	159,998	Jose Guerrero
Monclova Acereros	73	57	.562	3½	170,823	Joel Serna
Aguascalientes Rieleros	67	64	.511	10	160,389	Francisco Rodriguez/Francisco Garcia
Jalisco Charros	61	65	.484	13½	173,526	Marcelo Juarez
Monterrey Industriales	61	67	.477	14½	150,943	Domingo Carrasquel/Miguel Solis
Union Laguna Algodoneros	61	70	.466	16	169,715	Dave Stockstill
Saltillo Saraperos	51	80	.389	26	164,413	Aurelio Rodriguez/Alfredo Rios

South Standings	W	L	Pct.	GB	Attend.	Manager
Mexico City Diablos Rojos***	81	47	.633	—	183,798	Marco Antonio Vazquez
Mexico City Tigres	74	54	.578	7	180,120	Gerardo Gutierrez
Tabasco Olmecas	66	59	.528	13½	187,876	Juan Navarrete
Veracruz Aguila	65	66	.496	17½	170,213	Jack Pierce/Jorge Tellaeche
Minatitlan Petroleros	60	66	.476	20	165,672	Francisco Estrada
Yucatan Leones	51	72	.415	27½	199,589	Fernando Villaescusa
Puebla Pericos	52	74	.413	28	152,905	Bernardo Calvo/Miguel Gaspar/Gregorio Luque
Campeche Piratas	49	74	.398	29½	167,937	Alfredo Ortiz/Javier Martinez

Playoffs: Monterrey Sultanes 4 games, Monclova 1; Dos Laredos 4 games, Aguascalientes 1; MC Diablos Rojos 4 games, Veracruz 0; Tabasco 4 games, MC Tigres 3. Dos Laredos 4 games, Monterrey Sultanes 1; Tabasco 4 games, MC Diablos Rojos 1.
Finals: Tabasco 4 games, Dos Laredos 1.

BA: Nelson Simmons, Jalisco, .382
Runs: Matias Carrillo, MC Tigres, 113
Hits: Ruben Avila, Union Laguna, 169
RBIs: Matias Carrillo, MC Tigres, 125
HRs: Matias Carrillo, MC Tigres, 38

Wins: Urbano Lugo, Jalisco, 17
Jesus Moreno, Saltillo, 17
SOs: Urbano Lugo, Jalisco, 164
ERA: Manuel Hernandez, Aguila, 2.20

AAA Pacific Coast League
President: Bill Cutler

North Standings	W	L	Pct.	GB	Attend.	Manager
Portland Beavers***(9)	87	56	.608	—	186,010	Scott Ullger
Vancouver Canadians (3)	72	68	.514	13½	349,726	Max Olivares
Edmonton Trappers (19)	72	69	.511	14	261,361	Sal Rende
Calgary Cannons (12)	68	72	.486	17½	278,140	Keith Bodie
Tacoma Tigers (11)	69	74	.483	18	316,475	Bob Boone

South Standings	W	L	Pct.	GB	Attend.	Manager
Tucson Toros***(20)	83	60	.580	—	307,791	Rick Sweet
Albuquerque Dukes (21)	71	72	.497	12	390,652	Bill Russell
Colorado Springs Sky Sox (18)	66	75	.468	16	189,293	Brad Mills
Phoenix Firebirds (28)	64	79	.448	19	246,414	Carlos Alfonso
Las Vegas Stars (27)	58	85	.406	25	386,310	Russ Nixon

Playoff: Tucson 4 games, Portland 2.

*Won first-half   **Won second-half   ***Won both halves
Numbers after nicknames indicate farm system.
Affiliation listed at end of year.

All-Star Team: 1B-J.R. Phillips, Phoenix; **2B**-James Mouton, Tucson; **3B**-Eddie Perez, Vancouver; **SS**-Kurt Abbott, Tacoma; **OF**-Billy Ashley, Albuquerque; Rikkert Faneyte, Phoenix; Nigel Wilson, Edmonton; **C**-Brian Johnson, Las Vegas; **DH**-Bernardo Brito, Portland; **P**-Dave Weathers, Edmonton; Carlos Pulido, Portland; Todd Williams, Albuquerque; **MVP**-James Mouton, Tacoma; **Manager**-Scott Ullger, Portland.

BA: Jim Lindeman, Tucson, .362
Runs: James Mouton, Tucson, 126
Hits: James Mouton, Tucson, 172
RBIs: Billy Ashley, Albuquerque, 100
HRs: J.R. Phillips, Phoenix, 27
Wins: Tom Drees, Portland, 15
SOs: Scott Sanders, Las Vegas, 161
ERA: Pat Mahomes, Portland, 3.03

AA Eastern League
President: John Levenda

Standings	W	L	Pct.	GB	Attend.	Manager
Harrisburg Senators (22)	94	44	.681	—	250,476	Jim Tracy
Canton-Akron Indians (5)...	75	63	.543	19	237,639	Brian Graham
Bowie Baysox (1)	72	68	.514	23	254,861	Don Buford
Albany-Colonie Yankees (10).	70	68	.507	24	137,541	Mike Hart/Bill Evers
Binghamton Mets (23)........	68	72	.486	27	225,467	Steve Swisher
London Tigers (6).............	63	75	.457	31	103,840	Tom Runnells
Reading Phillies (24).........	62	78	.443	33	313,083	Don McCormack
New Britain Red Sox (2)	52	88	.371	43	140,915	Jim Pankovits

Playoffs: Harrisburg 3 games, Albany-Colonie 1; Canton-Akron 3 games, Bowie 2. **Finals:** Harrisburg 3 games, Canton-Akron 2.

All-Star Team: 1B-Cliff Floyd, Harrisburg; **2B**-Quilvio Veras, Binghamton; **3B**-Butch Huskey, Harrisburg; **SS**-Robert Eenhoorn, Albany-Colonie; **OF**-Manny Ramirez, Canton-Akron; Omar Ramirez, Canton-Akron; Rondell White, Harrisburg; **C**-Greg Zaun, Bowie; **DH**-T.R. Lewis, Bowie; Alan Zinter, Binghamton; **P**-Albie Lopez, Canton-Akron; Felipe Lira, London; Gabe White, Harrisburg; **MVP**-Cliff Floyd, Harrisburg; **Pitcher of the Year**-Joey Eischen, Harrisburg; **Manager**-Jim Tracy, Harrisburg.

BA: Manny Ramirez, Canton-Akron, .340
Runs: Omar Ramirez, Canton-Akron, 116
Hits: Omar Ramirez, Canton-Akron, 162
RBIs: Cliff Floyd, Harrisburg, 101
HRs: Cliff Floyd, Harrisburg, 26
Glenn Murray, Harrisburg, 26
Wins: Joey Eischen, Harrisburg, 14
SOs: Tim Vanegmond, New Britain, 163
ERA: Denny Harriger, Binghamton, 2.95

AA Southern League
President: Jimmy Bragan

East Standings	W	L	Pct.	GB	Attend.	Manager
Greenville Braves*(15).......	75	67	.528	—	232,369	Bruce Kimm
Carolina Mudcats (25).......	74	67	.525	½	328,207	Spin Williams/John Wockenfuss
Orlando Cubs (16)	71	70	.504	3½	217,716	Tommy Jones
Knoxville Smokies**(14)...	71	71	.500	4	140,868	Garth Iorg
Jacksonville Suns (12)........	59	81	.421	15	250,002	Marc Hill

West Standings	W	L	Pct.	GB	Attend.	Manager
Birmingham Barons**(4)....	78	64	.549	—	277,096	Terry Francona
Chattanooga Lookouts (17)..	72	69	.511	5½	270,671	Pat Kelly
Nashville Xpress*(9).........	72	70	.507	6	178,737	Phil Roof
Huntsville Stars (11)..........	71	70	.504	6½	282,731	Casey Parsons
Memphis Chicks (7)	63	77	.450	14	230,181	Tom Poquette

Playoffs: Birmingham 3 games, Nashville 1; Knoxville 3 games, Greenville 2. **Finals:** Birmingham 3 games, Nashville 1.

All-Star Team: 1B-Jim Bowie, Huntsville; **2B**-Ruben Santana, Jacksonville; **3B**-Joe Randa, Memphis; **SS**-Alex Gonzalez, Knoxville; **OF**-Jerry Wolak, Birmingham; Les Norman, Memphis; Rich Becker, Nashville; Marc Newfield, Jacksonville; **C**-Carlos Delgado, Knoxville; George Williams, Huntsville; **DH**-Jamie Dismuke, Chattanooga; **P**-Scott Ruffcorn, Birmingham; Huck Flener, Knoxville; Chris Bushing, Chattanooga; **MVP**-Carlos Delgado, Knoxville; **Pitcher of the Year**-Oscar Munoz, Nashville; **Manager**-Terry Francona, Birmingham.

BA: Jim Bowie, Huntsville, .333
Runs: Rich Becker, Nashville, 93
Alex Gonzalez, Knoxville, 93
Hits: Jim Bowie, Huntsville, 167
RBIs: Carlos Delgado, Knoxville, 102
HRs: Carlos Delgado, Knoxville, 25
Wins: Mike Ferry, Chattanooga, 13
Huck Flener, Knoxville, 13
SOs: Scott Ruffcorn, Birmingham, 141
ERA: James Baldwin, Birmingham, 2.25

AA Texas League
President: Tom Kayser

East Standings	W	L	Pct.	GB	Attend.	Manager
Jackson Generals*(20)...	73	62	.541	—	148,230	Sal Butera
Arkansas Travelers (26)...	67	69	.493	6½	285,757	Joe Pettini
Tulsa Drillers (13)	66	69	.489	7	325,135	Stan Cliburn
Shreveport Captains**(28).	66	70	.485	7½	203,479	Ron Wotus

West Standings	W	L	Pct.	GB	Attend.	Manager
El Paso Diablos***(8).......	76	59	.563	—	306,948	Tim Ireland
Wichita Wranglers (27)...	68	68	.500	8½	236,378	Dave Trembley
Midland Angels (3)...........	67	68	.496	9	196,464	Don Long
San Antonio Missions (21).	58	76	.433	17½	189,251	Glenn Hoffman

Playoffs: El Paso 3 games, Wichita 1; Jackson 3 games, Shreveport 1. **Finals:** Jackson 3 games, El Paso 1.

All-Star Team: 1B-Roberto Petagine, Jackson; **2B**-P.J. Forbes, Midland; **3B**-Cris Colon, Tulsa; **SS**-Wes Weger, El Paso; **OF**-Brian Hunter, Jackson; Dwayne Hosey, Wichita; John Mabry, Arkansas; **C**-Jorge Fabregas, Midland; **DH**-Trey McCoy, Tulsa; **Util**-Frank Kellner, Jackson; **P**-Ben VanRyn, San Antonio; Jim Dougherty, Jackson; Rick Helling, Tulsa; Scott Karl, El Paso; Rick Gorecki, San Antonio; Bryce Florie, Wichita; **MVP**-

Roberto Petagine, Jackson; **Pitcher of the Year**-Ben VanRyn, San Antonio; **Manager**-Sal Butera, Jackson.

BA: Roberto Petagine, Jackson, .334
Runs: P.J. Forbes, Midland, 90
Hits: Orlando Palmeiro, Midland, 163
RBIs: Trey McCoy, Tulsa, 95
HRs: Trey McCoy, Tulsa, 29
Wins: Ben VanRyn, San Antonio, 14
SOs: Rick Helling, Tulsa, 188
ERA: Ben VanRyn, San Antonio, 2.21

A California League
President: Joe Gagliardi

North Standings	W	L	Pct.	GB	Attend.	Manager
Stockton Ports**(8)	79	57	.581	—	108,629	Lamar Johnson
San Jose Giants (28).........	79	57	.581	—	133,138	Dick Dietz
Modesto A's*(11).............	72	64	.529	7	100,016	Ted Kubiak
Central Valley Rockies#(18).	61	75	.449	18	77,547	Paul Zuvella
Bakersfield Dodgers (21)....	42	94	.309	37	149,095	Rick Dempsey

South Standings	W	L	Pct.	GB	Attend.	Manager
High Desert Mavericks***(19)	85	52	.620	—	191,697	Fredi Gonzalez
Riverside Pilots (12).........	76	61	.555	9	68,821	Dave Myers
Rancho Cucamonga Quakes (27)	64	72	.471	20½	331,005	Keith Champion
San Bernardino Spirit (x)....	62	74	.456	22½	88,468	Greg Mahlberg
Palm Springs Angels (3).....	61	75	.449	23½	105,039	Mario Mendoza

#represented Visalia, California.

Playoffs: High Desert defeated Riverside in a one game playoff for the second half championship. Modesto 3 games, Stockton 1; High Desert 3 games, Riverside 1. **Finals:** High Desert 3 games, Modesto 2.

All-Star Team: 1B-John Toale, High Desert; **2B**-Arquimedez Pozo, Riverside; **3B**-Bryn Kosco, High Desert; **SS**-Kurt Ehmann, San Jose; **OF**-Tim Clark, High Desert; Ira Smith, Rancho Cucamonga; Ernie Young, Modesto; **C**-Izzy Molina, Modesto; **DH**-Kevin Riggs, Stockton; **P**-Sid Roberson, Stockton; John Pricher, Palm Springs; Russ Brock, Modesto; John Burke, Central Valley; **MVP**-Tim Clark, High Desert; **Pitcher of the Year**-Sid Roberson, Stockton; **Manager**-Fredi Gonzalez, High Desert.

BA: Tim Clark, High Desert, .363
Runs: Kerwin Moore, High Desert, 120
Hits: Tim Clark, High Desert, 185
RBIs: Tim Clark, High Desert, 126
HRs: John Toale, High Desert, 28
Wins: Keith Morrison, Palm Springs, 14
Bill VanLandingham, San Jose, 14
SOs: Bill VanLandingham, San Jose, 171
ERA: Sid Roberson, Stockton, 2.60

A Carolina League
President: John Hopkins

North Standings	W	L	Pct.	GB	Attend.	Manager
Frederick Keys**(1)	78	62	.557	—	351,146	Pete Mackanin
Wilmington Blue Rocks*(7)....	74	65	.532	3½	332,132	Ron Johnson
Prince William Cannons (10)..	67	73	.479	11	209,273	Trey Hillman
Lynchburg Red Sox (2)	65	74	.468	12½	100,113	Mark Meleski

South Standings	W	L	Pct.	GB	Attend.	Manager
Kinston Indians*(5)	71	67	.514	—	134,506	Dave Keller
Winston-Salem Spirits**(17)..	72	68	.514	—	164,509	Mark Berry
Durham Bulls (15)...........	69	69	.500	2	305,692	Leon Roberts
Salem Buccaneers (25).......	61	79	.436	11	145,657	Scott Little

Playoffs: Wilmington 2 games, Frederick 0; Winston-Salem 2 games, Kinston 1. **Finals:** Winston-Salem 3 games, Wilmington 1.

All-Star Team: 1B-Tate Seefried, Prince William; **2B**-Tony Graffanino, Durham; **3B**-Scott McClain, Frederick; **SS**-Eric Owens, Winston-Salem; **OF**-Curtis Goodwin, Frederick; Chad Mottola, Winston-Salem; Alex Ochoa, Frederick; **C**-Jorge Posada, Prince William; **DH**-Bubba Smith, Winston-Salem; **P**-Julian Tavarez, Kinston; Ian Doyle, Kinston; **MVP**-Bubba Smith, Winston-Salem; **Manager**-Dave Keller, Kinston; Pete Mackanin, Frederick.

BA: Felix Colon, Lynchburg, .320
Runs: Curtis Goodwin, Frederick, 98
Hits: Tim Belk, Winston-Salem, 156
Curtis Goodwin, Frederick, 156
RBIs: Chad Mottola, Winston-Salem, 91
HRs: Bubba Smith, Winston-Salem, 27
Wins: Rick Forney, Frederick, 14
SOs: Joel Bennett, Lynchburg, 221
ERA: Jason Fronio, Kinston, 2.41

A Florida State League
President: Chuck Murphy

East Standings	W	L	Pct.	GB	Attend.	Manager
St. Lucie Mets**(23)	78	52	.600	—	69,078	John Tamargo
Lakeland Tigers*(6)	65	63	.508	12	25,248	Gerry Groninger
West Palm Beach Expos (22)..	69	67	.507	12	69,289	Rob Leary
Osceola Astros (20)	56	74	.431	22	51,527	Tim Tolman
Daytona Cubs (16)...........	57	76	.429	22½	95,089	Bill Hayes
Vero Beach Dodgers (21)..	56	77	.421	23½	72,861	Joe Vavra
Ft. Lauderdale Red Sox (2).	46	85	.351	32½	28,240	DeMarlo Hale

West Standings	W	L	Pct.	GB	Attend.	Manager
Charlotte Rangers (13).......	84	49	.632	—	90,792	Tommy Thompson
Sarasota White Sox*(4)......	77	57	.575	7½	91,883	Dave Huppert
Clearwater Phillies (24)......	75	60	.556	10	86,508	Bill Dancy
St. Petersburg Cardinals (26)..	75	58	.564	9	123,275	Terry Kennedy
Dunedin Blue Jays**(14)....	68	64	.515	15½	77,382	Dennis Holmberg
Ft. Myers Miracle (9).........	55	79	.410	29½	95,054	Steve Liddle

Playoffs: Clearwater 2 games, Charlotte 1; St. Lucie 2 games, Lakeland 1. **Finals:** Clearwater 3 games, St. Lucie 1.

All-Star Team: 1B-Chris Weinke, Dunedin; **2B**-Chris Demetral, Vero Beach; **3B**-Eduardo Lantigua, Vero Beach; **SS**-Edgardo Alfonzo, St. Lucie; **OF**-Rich Butler, Dunedin; Randy Curtis, St. Lucie; Rick Holifield, Dunedin; **C**-Jason Moler, Clearwater; Ken Huckaby, Vero Beach; **DH**-Doug Radziewicz, St. Petersburg; **P**-Rodney Henderson, West Palm Beach; John Dettmer, Charlotte; Chris Roberts, St. Lucie; B.J. Wallace, West Palm Beach; Clint Davis, St. Petersburg; Jim McCready, St. Lucie; **MVP**-Randy Curtis, St. Lucie; **Manager**-John Tamargo, St. Lucie.

BA: Doug Radziewicz, St. Petersburg, .342
Runs: Randy Curtis, St. Lucie, 91
Hits: Omar Garcia, St. Lucie, 156
    Desi Wilson, Charlotte, 156
RBIs: Chris Weinke, Dunedin, 98

HRs: Rick Holifield, Dunedin, 20
Wins: John Dettmer, Charlotte, 16
SOs: Alan Levine, Sarasota, 129
ERA: Rich Linares, Vero Beach, 1.81

A Midwest League
President: George Spelius

North Standings	W	L	Pct.	GB	Attend.	Manager
Rockford Royals*(7)	78	54	.597	—	68,206	Mike Jirschele
Madison Muskies (11)	77	58	.574	2½	101,219	Gary Jones
South Bend White Sox**(4)	77	59	.566	3	229,883	Tony Franklin
Kane County Cougars (19)	75	62	.547	5½	354,327	Carlos Tosca
Fort Wayne Wizards (9)	68	67	.504	11½	318,506	Jim Dwyer
Appleton Foxes (12)	62	73	.459	17½	56,036	Carlos Lezcano
Beloit Brewers (8)	60	74	.448	19	65,728	Wayne Krenchicki

South Standings	W	L	Pct.	GB	Attend.	Manager
Clinton Giants**(28)	80	54	.597	—	62,872	Jack Mull
Springfield Cardinals*(26)	78	58	.574	3	110,189	Mike Ramsey
Burlington Bees (22)	64	71	.474	16½	77,492	Lorenzo Bundy
Quad City River Bandits (20)	56	74	.431	22	103,797	Steve Dillard
Peoria Chiefs (16)	59	79	.428	23	100,811	Steve Roadcap
Waterloo Diamonds (27)	54	79	.406	25½	51,329	Ed Romero
Cedar Rapids Kernels (3)	54	80	.403	26	114,105	Mitch Seoane

Playoffs: South Bend 2 games, Rockford 0; Clinton 2 games, Springfield 0.
Finals: South Bend 3 games, Clinton 1.

All-Star Team: 1B-Ken Tirpack, Fort Wayne; **2B**-Joe Biasucci, Springfield; **3B**-Mike Gulan, Springfield; **SS**-Chad Fonville, Clinton; **OF**-Anthony Byrd, Fort Wayne; Johnny Damon, Rockford; Carmine Cappuccio, South Bend; **C**-Charles Johnson, Kane County; **DH**-Scott Talanoa, Beloit; **P**-Ugueth Urbina, Burlington; Tim Davis, Appleton; Vic Darensbourg, Kane County; Kirk Bullinger, Springfield; **MVP**-Joe Biasucci, Springfield; **Manager**-Jack Mull, Clinton.

BA: Homer Bush, Waterloo, .322
Runs: Essex Burton, South Bend, 91
Hits: Homer Bush, Waterloo, 152
RBIs: Charles Johnson, Kane County, 94
HRs: Joe Biasucci, Springfield, 26

Wins: LaTroy Hawkins, Fort Wayne, 15
    Mike Call, South Bend, 15
SOs: LaTroy Hawkins, Fort Wayne, 179
ERA: LaTroy Hawkins, Fort Wayne, 2.06

A New York-Pennsylvania League
President: Robert Julian

McNamara Standings	W	L	Pct.	GB	Attend.	Manager
Pittsfield Mets (23)	40	35	.533	—	46,682	Howard Freiling
Utica Blue Sox (2)	38	38	.500	2½	77,645	Dave Holt
Glens Falls Redbirds (26)	37	40	.481	4	78,725	Steve Turco
Oneonta Yankees (10)	36	40	.474	4½	55,144	Mark Newman

Pinckney Standings	W	L	Pct.	GB	Attend.	Manager
Watertown Indians (5)	46	32	.590	—	40,082	Mike Young
Geneva Cubs (16)	43	34	.558	2½	34,634	Jerry Weinstein
Elmira Pioneers (19)	31	44	.413	13½	65,106	Lynn Jones
Auburn Astros (20)	30	46	.395	15	30,325	Manny Acta

Stedler Standings	W	L	Pct.	GB	Attend.	Manager
St. Catharines Blue Jays (14)	49	29	.628	—	46,535	J.J. Cannon
Niagara Falls Rapids (6)	47	31	.603	2	50,190	Larry Parrish
Batavia Clippers (24)	38	39	.494	10½	41,539	Al LeBoeuf
Erie Sailors (13)	36	41	.468	12½	65,316	Doug Sisson
Welland Pirates (25)	35	42	.455	13½	35,664	Larry Smith
Jamestown Expos (22)	31	46	.403	17½	40,588	Tim Torricelli

Playoffs: Niagara Falls 1 game, St. Catharines 0; Pittsfield 1 game, Watertown 0.
Finals: Niagara Falls 2 games, Pittsfield 0.

All-Star Team: 1B-Greg Thomas, Watertown; **2B**-T.J. O'Donnell, Utica; **3B**-Adam Melhuse, St. Catharines; **SS**-Mike Neal, Watertown; **OF**-Ruben Rivera, Oneonta; Noel Rodriguez, Auburn; Jermaine Allensworth, Welland; Ron Brown, Elmira; **C**-Wes Shook, Erie; Ramsey Koeyers, Jamestown; **DH**-Wes Shook, Erie; **P**-Joshua Neese, Niagara Falls; Adam Meinershagen, St. Catharines; Casey Whitten, Watertown; Silvio Censale, Batavia; **MVP**-Ruben Rivera, Oneonta; **Manager**-J.J. Cannon, St. Catharines.

BA: Eric Danapilis, Niagara Falls, .341
Runs: Richard Prieto, Watertown, 53
    Shannon Stewart, St. Catharines, 53
Hits: Mike Wiseley, Niagara Falls, 92
RBIs: Greg Thomas, Watertown, 63

HRs: Wes Shook, Erie, 17
Wins: Joshua Neese, Niagara Falls, 12
SOs: Jason Isringhausen, Pittsfield, 104
ERA: Adam Meinershagen, St. Catharines, 1.88

A Northwest League
President: Bob Richmond

North Standings	W	L	Pct.	GB	Attend.	Manager
Bellingham Mariners (12)	44	32	.579	—	74,900	Mike Goff
Everett Giants (28)	42	34	.553	2	87,874	Norm Sherry
Spokane Indians (27)	35	41	.461	9	126,028	Tim Flannery
Yakima Bears (21)	30	46	.395	14	86,822	John Shoemaker

South Standings	W	L	Pct.	GB	Attend.	Manager
Boise Hawks (3)	41	35	.539	—	151,080	Tom Kotchman
Eugene Emeralds (7)	40	36	.526	1	121,283	John Mizerock
Southern Oregon A's (11)	37	39	.487	4	78,202	Dick Scott
Bend Rockies (18)	35	41	.461	6	60,612	Howie Bedell

Playoff: Boise 2 games, Bellingham 0.

All-Star Team: 1B-Jason Thompson, Spokane; **2B**-Mark Simmons, Boise; **3B**-Doug Newstrom, Yakima; **SS**-Brett King, Everett; **OF**-Todd Greene, Boise; Aaron Iatarola, Boise; Keith Williams, Everett; **C**-Mike Sweeney, Eugene; **DH**-Sal Fasano, Eugene; **P**-Bob Wolcott, Bellingham; Glenn Dishman, Spokane; Matt Mantei, Bellingham; Steve Day, Everett; **MVP**-Todd Greene, Boise; **Manager**-Dick Scott, Southern Oregon.

BA: Mark Simmons, Boise, .304
Runs: Chris Prieto, Spokane, 64
Hits: Keith Williams, Everett, 87
RBIs: Todd Greene, Boise, 71

HRs: Todd Greene, Boise, 15
Wins: Steve Day, Everett, 9
SOs: Bryan Harris, Boise, 96
ERA: Kris Franko, Everett, 1.47

A South Atlantic League
President: John H. Moss

North Standings	W	L	Pct.	GB	Attend.	Manager
Greensboro Hornets*(10)	85	56	.603	—	201,222	Bill Evers/Gary Denbo
Charleston (WV) Wheelers (17)	76	64	.543	8½	110,118	Tom Nieto
Fayetteville Generals**(6)	75	66	.532	10	100,321	Mark Wagner
Hagerstown Suns (14)	74	68	.521	11½	95,702	Jim Nettles
Spartanburg Phillies (24)	62	80	.437	23½	53,975	Roy Majtyka
Hickory Crawdads (4)	52	88	.371	32½	283,727	Fred Kendall
Asheville Tourists (20)	51	88	.367	33	121,573	Bobby Ramos

South Standings	W	L	Pct.	GB	Attend.	Manager
Savannah Cardinals***(26)	94	48	.662	—	106,287	Chris Maloney
Columbus RedStixx (5)	86	56	.606	8	122,137	Mike Brown
Macon Braves (15)	74	67	.525	19½	96,450	Randy Ingle
Albany Polecats (1)	71	71	.500	23	140,140	Mike O'Berry
Charleston (SC) Rainbows (13)	65	77	.458	29	98,670	Walt Williams
Capital City Bombers#(23)	64	77	.454	29½	144,054	Ron Washington
Augusta Pirates (25)	59	82	.418	34½	115,051	Trent Jewett

#represented Columbia, South Carolina.

Playoff: Greensboro 2 games, Fayetteville 1.
Finals: Savannah 3 games, Greensboro 2.

All-Star Team: 1B-D.J. Boston, Hagerstown; **2B**-Donovan Mitchell, Asheville; **3B**-Eric Chavez, Albany; **SS**-Derek Jeter, Greensboro; **OF**-Jose Herrera, Hagerstown; Matt Luke, Greensboro; Derek Hacopian, Columbus; **C**-Jason Kendall, Augusta; **DH**-Nick Delvecchio, Greensboro; **P**-J.J. Thobe, Columbus; Ryan Karp, Greensboro; **MVP**-D.J. Boston, Savannah; **Manager**-Chris Maloney, Savannah.

BA: Brian Rupp, Savannah, .320
Runs: Joe McEwing, Savannah, 94
Hits: Matt Luke, Greensboro, 157
    Aldo Pecorilli, Savannah, 157
RBIs: Alan Burke, Spartanburg, 96

HRs: Derek Hacopian, Columbus, 24
Wins: John Carter, Columbus, 17
SOs: Chuck York, Columbus, 182
ERA: J.J. Thobe, Columbus, 1.91
Saves: Jamie Cochran, Savannah, 46

R Appalachian League
President: Bill Halstead

North Standings	W	L	Pct.	GB	Attend.	Manager
Burlington Indians (5)	44	24	.647	—	61,088	Jim Gabella
Bluefield Orioles (1)	44	24	.647	—	47,281	Andy Etchebarren
Danville Braves (15)	38	30	.559	6	80,539	Bruce Benedict
Princeton Reds (17)	26	42	.382	18	32,606	Tommy Dunbar
Martinsville Phillies (24)	22	46	.324	22	58,368	Ramon Henderson

South Standings	W	L	Pct.	GB	Attend.	Manager
Elizabethton Twins (9)	37	30	.552	—	18,422	Ray Smith
Johnson City Cardinals (26)	37	31	.544	½	37,751	Joe Cunningham
Huntington Cubs (16)	33	35	.485	4½	51,365	Steve Kolinsky
Kingsport Mets (23)	30	38	.441	7½	25,467	Ron Gideon
Bristol Tigers (6)	28	39	.418	9	29,868	Ruben Amaro

Playoff: Burlington 2 games, Elizabethton 0.

All-Star Team: 1B-Bryan Link, Bluefield; **2B**-Jesus Azuaje, Burlington; **3B**-Myles Barnden, Bluefield; **SS**-Enrique Wilson, Elizabethton; **OF**-Andre King, Danville; Randy Warner, Kingsport; Damon Hollins, Danville; **C**-Cesar Diaz, Kingsport; **DH**-Sean Wooten, Bristol; **P**-Calvin Maduro, Bluefield; Javier DeJesus, Elizabethton; Cesar Ramos, Burlington; **MVP**-Bryan Link, Bluefield; **Manager**-Joe Cunningham, Johnson City.

BA: Sean Wooten, Bristol, .350
Runs: Bryan Link, Bluefield, 64
Hits: Bryan Link, Bluefield, 90
RBIs: Bryan Link, Bluefield, 60
HRs: Preston Wilson, Kingsport, 16

Wins: Javier DeJesus, Elizabethton, 9
    Calvin Maduro, Bluefield, 9
SOs: Calvin Maduro, Bluefield, 83
ERA: Roger Etheridge, Princeton, 1.49
Pct: Javier DeJesus, Elizabethton, 1.000, 9-0

R Arizona League
President: Bob Richmond

Standings	W	L	Pct.	GB	Manager
Athletics (Scottsdale) (11)	35	20	.636	—	Bruce Hines
Cardinals (Chandler) (26)	31	22	.585	3	Roy Silver
Giants (Scottsdale) (28)	31	24	.564	4	Alan Bannister
Angels (Mesa) (3)	29	26	.527	6	Bill Lachemann

Brewers (Chandler) (8)....... 29 27 .518   6½   Ralph Dickenson
Padres (Peoria) (27)........... 24 31 .436   11   Ken Berry
Rockies (Mesa) (18) .... 21 32 .396   13   P.J. Carey
Mariners (Peoria) (12) .... 18 36 .333   16½ Marty Martinez

Playoffs: None.

All-Star Team: 1B-Harold Herdocia, Angels; **2B**-Franklin Garcia, Brewers; **3B**-Dave Madsen, Cardinals; **SS**-Juan Henderson, Angels; **OF**-Tony Dermendziev, Rockies; Jason Herrick, Angels; Alex Rivera, Padres; **C**-Joel Galarza, Giants; **DH**-John Jones, Athletics; **P**-Jason Myers, Giants; Gustavo Gil, Athletics; Bret Morfin, Giants; Jose Carrasco, Angels; **MVP**-Jason Myers, Giants; **Manager**-Roy Silver, Cardinals.

BA: John Jones, Athletics, .341
Runs: Julio Vargas, Athletics, 46
Hits: Franklin Garcia, Brewers, 74
RBIs: Jay Canizaro, Giants, 41

HRs: Leon Hamburg, Athletics, 5
John Jones, Athletics, 5
Fred Soriano, Athletics, 5
Wins: Jason Myers, Giants, 8
SOs: Jason Myers, Giants, 105
ERA: Jason Myers, Giants, 1.69

R Gulf Coast League
President: Thomas J. Saffell

East Standings	W	L	Pct.	GB	Manager
Mets (Port St. Lucie) (23)	39	20	.661	—	Junior Roman
Braves (West Palm Beach) (15)	32	26	.552	6½	Jim Saul
Expos (West Palm Beach) (22)	27	31	.466	11½	Nelson Norman
Cubs (Port St. Lucie) (16)	19	40	.322	20	Butch Hughes

North Standings	W	L	Pct.	GB	Manager
Astros (Kissimmee) (20)	35	24	.593	—	Julio Linares
Marlins (Kissimmee) (19)	32	28	.533	3½	Jim Hendry
Yankees (Tampa) (10)	30	29	.508	5	Glenn Sherlock
Blue Jays (Dunedin) (14)	22	38	.367	13½	Hector Torres

West Standings	W	L	Pct.	GB	Manager
Rangers (Port Charlotte) (13)	40	20	.667	—	Chino Cadahia
White Sox (Sarasota) (4)	32	27	.542	7½	Mike Rojas
Red Sox (Ft. Myers) (2)	32	28	.533	8	Felix Maldonado
Orioles (Sarasota) (1)	30	28	.517	9	Oneri Fleita
Royals (Lee County) (7)	29	30	.492	10½	Bob Herold
Twins (Lee County) (9)	23	36	.390	16½	Jose Marzan
Pirates (Bradenton) (25)	21	38	.356	18½	Woody Huyke

Playoff: Astros 1 game, Mets 0.
Finals: Rangers 2 games, Astros 0.

All-Star Team: 1B-David Catlett, Braves; **2B**-Carlos Cabrera, Blue Jays; **3B**-Mike Bell, Rangers; **SS**-Gavin Jackson, Red Sox; **OF**-Charles Peterson, Pirates; Juan Ramirez, Mets; Romulo Vizcaino, Twins; **C**-Larry Ephan, Rangers; **P**-John Lombardi, Orioles; Julio Santana, Rangers; **Manager**-Chino Cadahia, Rangers.

BA: Larry Ephan, Rangers, .350
Runs: Tomas Arvelo, Mets, 50
Hits: Mike Bell, Rangers, 73
RBIs: Larry Ephan, Rangers, 38
HRs: Marc Niethammer, Expos, 6

Wins: John Lombardi, Orioles, 7
Joe Atwater, Mets, 7
Kevin Hodges, Royals, 7
Ryan Creek, Astros, 7
SOs: Jason Tatar, Twins, 73
ERA: John Lombardi, Orioles, 0.92

R Pioneer League
President: Ralph C. Nelles

North Standings	W	L	Pct.	GB	Attend.	Manager
Billings Mustangs (17)	49	26	.653	—	101,490	Donnie Scott
Medicine Hat Blue Jays (14)	39	34	.534	9	25,102	Omar Malave
Great Falls Dodgers (21)	37	35	.514	10½	59,924	Jon Debus
Lethbridge Mounties (x)	29	44	.397	19	28,053	Phillip Wellman

South Standings	W	L	Pct.	GB	Attend.	Manager
Helena Brewers (8)	43	30	.589	—	39,211	Mike Epstein/Harry Dunlop
Pocatello Posse	37	38	.493	7	45,638	Ernest Rodriguez/John Stein
Idaho Falls Braves (15)	36	40	.474	8½	37,385	Paul Runge
Butte Copper Kings (x)	26	49	.347	18	19,750	John Shelby

Playoff: Billings 2 games, Helena 1.

All-Star Team: 1B-Will Fitzpatrick, Pocatello; **2B**-Mike Eaglin, Idaho Falls; **3B**-Adam Burton, Idaho Falls; **SS**-Jeff Patzke, Medicine Hat; **OF**-Willie Brown, Lethbridge; Derek Vaughn, Pocatello; Marty Watson, Butte; **C**-Paul Bako, Billings; **DH**-Todd Takayoshi, Pocatello; **P**-Daniel Camacho, Great Falls; Todd Etler, Billings; Fabian Salmon, Helena; **Manager**-Harry Dunlop, Helena.

BA: Todd Takayoshi, Pocatello, .358
Runs: Chris Sexton, Billings, 63
Hits: Derek Vaughn, Pocatello, 93
RBIs: Will Fitzpatrick, Pocatello, 58
HRs: Willie Brown, Lethbridge, 16

Wins: Todd Etler, Billings, 8
Cory Lidle, Pocatello, 8
Fabian Salmon, Helena, 8
SOs: Gene Caruso, Pocatello, 163
ERA: Daniel Camacho, Great Falls, 1.38

Ind Frontier League
President: Bud Bickel

East Standings	W	L	Pct.	GB	Attend.	Manager
Ohio Valley Redcoats#**	29	22	.569	—	16,535	Lee Mrowicki
Kentucky Rifles@*	27	23	.540	1½	6,105	Roy Cutwright
Portsmouth Explorers	20	31	.392	9	11,539	Keith Throckmorton
West Virginia Coal Sox+	3	7	.300	NA		Don Croche

West Standings	W	L	Pct.	GB	Attend.	Manager
Zanesville Greys***	35	17	.673	—	21,547	Tom Venditelli
Chillicothe Paints	25	27	.481	10	20,453	Mark Jones
Lancaster Scouts	22	33	.400	14½	6,436	Scott Simms
Tri-State Tomahawks$	5	6	.455	NA		Jody Hamilton

#represented Parkersburg, West Virginia.
@represented Paintsville and Pikeville, Kentucky.
+represented Wayne, West Virginia; franchise disbanded July 12.
$represented Ashland, Kentucky; franchise disbanded July 12.

Playoff: Ohio Valley defeated Kentucky for East championship.
Finals: Zanesville 2 games, Ohio Valley 0.

BA: Kyle Shade, Zanesville, .378
Runs: Kyle Shade, Zanesville, 42
Hits: Kyle Shade, Zanesville, 73
RBIs: Kyle Shade, Zanesville, 42
Tim Kerns, Ohio Valley, 42

HRs: James Wambach, Zanesville, 10
Wins: Upi Puente, Zanesville, 8
SOs: Tom Crowley, Zanesville, 78
ERA: Tom Crowley, Zanesville, 2.05

Ind Northern League
President: Miles Wolff

Standings	W	L	Pct.	GB	Attend.	Manager
St. Paul Saints**	42	29	.592	—	167,956	Tim Blackwell
Rochester Aces*	38	34	.528	4½	50,803	Doug Simunic
Thunder Bay Whiskey Jacks	36	35	.507	6	127,581	Dan Shwam
Sioux Falls Canaries	34	38	.472	8½	86,187	Frank Verdi
Sioux City Explorers	34	38	.472	8½	112,971	Ed Nottle
Duluth-Superior Dukes	31	41	.431	11½	105,954	Mal Fichman

Playoff: St. Paul 3 games, Rochester 1.

All-Star Team: 1B-Warren Sawkiw, Rochester; **2B**-J.D. Ramirez, Sioux City; **3B**-Santy Gallone, Sioux Falls; **SS**-Kevin Farlow, Sioux City; **OF**-Kash Beauchamp, Rochester; Scott Meadows, St. Paul; Theron Todd, Sioux Falls; **C**-Gary Resetar, Duluth-Superior; **DH**-Leon Durham, St. Paul; **P**-Tim Cain, Rochester; Mike Garcia, Rochester; Joe Kraemer, Sioux City; Michael Mimbs, St. Paul; Pat Tilmon, Thunder Bay; **Manager**-Ed Nottle, Sioux City; Tim Blackwell, St. Paul; Doug Simunic, Rochester.

BA: Kash Beauchamp, Rochester, .367
Runs: Rick Hirtensteiner, St. Paul, 52
Hits: Theron Todd, Sioux Falls, 97
RBIs: Leon Durham, St. Paul, 59

HRs: Leon Durham, St. Paul, 11
Ty Griffin, Thunder Bay, 11
Wins: Joe Kraemer, Sioux City, 10
SOs: Mike Garcia, Rochester, 100
ERA: Jim Manfred, St. Paul, 2.06

1993 Interleague Post Season Play

World Series
Toronto (American) 4 games, Philadelphia (National) 2

1993 Major League Farm Systems

American League

1 Baltimore (6): Rochester, Bowie, Frederick, Albany (GA), Bluefield, Gulf Coast.
2 Boston (6): Pawtucket, New Britain, Lynchburg, Ft. Lauderdale, Utica, Gulf Coast.
3 California (6): Vancouver, Midland, Palm Springs, Cedar Rapids, Boise, Arizona.
4 Chicago (6): Nashville, Birmingham, Sarasota, Hickory, South Bend, Gulf Coast.
5 Cleveland (6): Charlotte, Canton-Akron, Kinston, Columbus (GA), Watertown, Burlington (NC).
6 Detroit (6): Toledo, London, Lakeland, Fayetteville, Niagara Falls, Bristol.
7 Kansas City (6): Omaha, Memphis, Wilmington, Rockford, Eugene, Gulf Coast.
8 Milwaukee (6): New Orleans, El Paso, Stockton, Beloit, Helena, Arizona.
9 Minnesota (6): Portland, Nashville, Ft. Myers, Fort Wayne, Elizabethton, Gulf Coast.
10 New York (6): Columbus (OH), Albany-Colonie, Prince William, Greensboro, Oneonta, Gulf Coast.
11 Oakland (6): Tacoma, Huntsville, Modesto, Madison, Southern Oregon, Arizona.
12 Seattle (6): Calgary, Jacksonville, Riverside, Appleton, Bellingham, Arizona.
13 Texas (6): Oklahoma City, Tulsa, Port Charlotte, Charleston (SC), Erie, Gulf Coast.
14 Toronto (7): Syracuse, Knoxville, Dunedin, Hagerstown, St. Catharines, Medicine Hat, Gulf Coast.

Co-op (x): San Bernardino, Lethbridge, Butte.
Independent: Pocatello.

National League

15 Atlanta (7): Richmond, Greenville, Durham, Macon, Danville, Idaho Falls, Gulf Coast.
16 Chicago (7): Iowa, Orlando, Daytona, Peoria, Geneva, Huntington, Gulf Coast.
17 Cincinnati (6): Indianapolis, Chattanooga, Winston-Salem, Charleston (WV), Billings, Princeton.
18 Colorado (4): Colorado Springs, Central Valley, Bend, Arizona.
19 Florida (5): Edmonton, High Desert, Kane County, Elmira, Gulf Coast.
20 Houston (7): Tucson, Jackson, Osceola, Quad City, Asheville, Auburn, Gulf Coast.
21 Los Angeles (6): Albuquerque, San Antonio, Bakersfield, Vero Beach, Yakima, Great Falls.
22 Montreal (6): Ottawa, Harrisburg, West Palm Beach, Burlington (IA), Jamestown, Gulf Coast.
23 New York (7): Norfolk, Binghamton, St. Lucie, Capital City, Pittsfield, Kingsport, Gulf Coast.
24 Philadelphia (6): Scranton-Wilkes-Barre, Reading, Clearwater, Spartanburg, Batavia, Martinsville.
25 Pittsburgh (6): Buffalo, Carolina, Salem, Augusta, Welland, Gulf Coast.
26 St. Louis (8): Louisville, Arkansas, St. Petersburg, Springfield, Savannah, Glens Falls, Johnson City, Arizona.
27 San Diego (6): Las Vegas, Wichita, Rancho Cucamonga, Waterloo, Spokane, Arizona.
28 San Francisco (6): Phoenix, Shreveport, San Jose, Clinton, Everett, Arizona.

1993 No-Hitters

Date	Pitcher	Team	League	Opponent	Score
3-21	Arturo Olmos	Saltillo	Mexican	Aguascalientes	2-0
4-22	Chris Bosio	Seattle	American	Boston	7-0
4-28	Scott Gardner/ Tony Lee	Peoria	Midwest	Springfield	2-1
5-15	Wayne Lindemann	Hickory	South Atlantic	Albany	1-0
5-24	Chris Nabholz/ Bruce Walton	Ottawa	International	Richmond	4-0
6-1	Tim Brown	Syracuse	International	Toledo	2-0 (P, 7)
6-9	Garrett Stephenson	Albany	South Atlantic	Macon	1-0
6-13	Leobardo Meza	Veracruz	Mexican	Nuevo Laredo	3-0
6-13	Tanyon Sturtze	Huntsville	Southern	Chattanooga	5-0
6-19	Israel Velazquez	Minatitlan	Mexican	Campeche	2-0
6-23	Matt Apana/Greg Theron/ Matt Mantei	Bellingham	Northwest	Spokane	4-0
6-30	Greg Twiggs	Geneva	New York-Penn.	Auburn	5-0 (7)
7-4	Tyler Green	Scranton-Wilkes-Barre	International	Ottawa	3-1 (7)
7-7	Stacy Hollins	Madison	Midwest	Springfield	3-0
7-11	Craig Costello/ Dan Camacho	Great Falls	Pioneer	Lethbridge	8-0
7-16	Ramiro Martinez	Charleston (SC)	South Atlantic	Macon	1-0 (5)
7-17	Glenn Dishman	Spokane	Northwest	Yakima	1-0
7-21	Carey Paige/Will Havens/ Matt Byrd	Danville	Appalachian	Bristol	4-0
7-25	Andy Larkin	Elmira	New York-Penn.	Welland	6-0
8-3	Clint Sodowsky/Blas Cedeno/Rich Navarro/ Sam Arguto	Fayetteville	South Atlantic	Greensboro	8-0
8-4	Jason Green/Bill Falle/ Charlie Gann	Braves	Gulf Coast	Expos	3-0
8-8	Rodney Myers	Memphis	Southern	Knoxville	3-0 (7)
8-13	David Sartain	Kenosha	Midwest	Clinton	1-0 (7)
8-13	T.J. Mathews	Springfield	Midwest	Burlington	4-0
8-28	Felix Rodriguez	Vero Beach	Florida State	Sarasota	11-0
9-1	Pete Agostinelli	Batavia	New York-Penn.	Welland	4-0 (7)
9-4	Jim Abbott	New York	American	Cleveland	4-0
9-4	Mike Romano/Scott Kennedy/ Jeff Leystra	Medicine Hat	Pioneer	Lethbridge	4-1
9-4	Craig Holman/Greg Brown/Toby Borland/ Ricky Bottalico	Reading	Eastern	New Britain	2-0 (7)
9-8	Darryl Kile	Houston	National	New York	7-1

Number in parentheses indicates innings if other than nine; "P" indicates perfect game.

THIS DATE IN MINOR LEAGUE HISTORY

February 26, 1993, The Baseball City franchise in the Florida State League was sold to Jordan Kobritz, who moved the team to Daytona and had just 44 days to be ready for the season opener. An invitation to first daughter Chelsea Clinton to throw out the first pitch at the home opener was declined. Kobritz and President Bill Clinton had been classmates at Georgetown.

March 15, 1993, 500 fans camped out to by tickets for the home opener of the Rancho Cucamonga Quakes, a new California League club. The game would sell out in three hours, and the club would go on to set a new league record for total season attendance.

April 8, 1993, The Southern League opened with the former Charlotte franchise settled in Nashville. The Xpress shared Herschel Greer Stadium with the American Association's Nashville Sounds. The wayward franchise, forced from Charlotte when that city was granted a Triple-A expansion team, could not find another suitable home. It marked the first time a city hosted two minor league clubs since 1972, when Charlotte, ironically, hosted two Minnesota Twins affiliates.

April 8, 1993, At opening night in Louisville, a fan won $50,000 in a promotion when Redbirds Ozzie Canseco and Van Snider hit back-to-back home runs in the first inning.

April 11, 1993, In an Easter Sunday promotion, a Las Vegas radio station sponsored an Easter egg hunt before the Stars' Pacific Coast League game against Edmonton. 2,000 pounds of chocolate eggs on the field melted in the 80-degree sun, leaving a brown stain in left field.

April 16, 1993, The Bowie Baysox of the Eastern League opened their inaugural season playing at Baltimore's Memorial Stadium, formerly the home of the Baltimore Orioles and the NFL Colts, as their new park in Bowie was not completed. The club would also open the 1994 season at temporary sites before being able to move into the new park.

April 17, 1993, San Antonio hosted Wichita at 9 a.m. in a Texas League game. The game time was moved due to the annual St. Mary's University Oyster Bake, which drew 65,000 people that day. Over 2,000 fans attended the game, and the first 1,000 received a commemorative cereal bowl, a box of cereal and a carton of milk.

April 19, 1993, In a Pacific Coast League game at Colorado Springs, the Sky Sox hosted Las Vegas in a steady snow. At game's end, the windchill factor was measured at -7.

April 29, 1993, Birmingham pitchers Scott Ruffcorn (15) and Jeff Pierce (5) combined to strike out 20 Chattanooga hitters, setting a new Southern League record. The Barons also had no assists, tying a mark last achieved in 1987.

May 2, 1993, The Buffalo at Iowa game in the American Association was postponed due to a toxic cloud emitting from a fire in an abandoned warehouse four blocks from Sec Taylor Stadium. The south side of downtown Des Moines was evacuated.

May 20, 1993, Savannah batboy Tommy McCoy, 14, was fired due to federal child labor laws. A newspaper story had brought his work schedule to the attention of the local labor department. A week later, McCoy returned after the national flap moved U.S. Labor Secretary Robert Reich to exempt batboys and batgirls from the laws.

May 28, 1993, Fort Wayne's Rene Lopez went 6-for-6 to set a new Midwest League record for consecutive hits with 10. The next day, he would walk in his first trip to reach base in his 11th straight at bat, also a new league mark.

June 15, 1993, The reborn Northern League began its first season as an independent circuit. The league's success would spawn the formation of numerous other independent leagues in subsequent seasons, with varying degrees of success.

June 15, 1993, A ban on the use of all tobacco products in all National Association leagues, mandated by Major League Baseball, took effect. Violators and their managers would be subject to ejections and fines.

August 28, 1993, Pocatello General Manager John Stein took over as manager of the Posse, as Ernest Rodriguez had to depart to return to his job as a teacher in Los Angeles. The club went 3-4 under Stein.

September 4, 1993, Ottawa completed its first season in the International League with total attendance of 663,926, a new IL record. The previous mark of 620,726 was set by Baltimore in 1946. Ottawa had been without pro baseball since 1954.

September 6, 1993, The minor league regular season concluded with total attendance of over 30 million fans, the first time that mark had been reached since 1950. Average per game attendance of 3,316 set an all-time record for the minors. Eight leagues set new records for total attendance.

1994

American League
Presidents: Dr. Bobby Brown/Gene Budig

East Standings	W	L	Pct.	GB	Attend.	Manager
New York Yankees............	70	43	.619	—	1,675,557	Buck Showalter
Baltimore Orioles	63	49	.563	6½	2,535,359	Johnny Oates
Toronto Blue Jays..............	55	60	.478	16	2,907,933	Cito Gaston
Boston Red Sox	54	61	.470	17	1,775,826	Butch Hobson
Detroit Tigers.....................	53	62	.461	18	1,184,763	Sparky Anderson

Central Standings	W	L	Pct.	GB	Attend.	Manager
Chicago White Sox	67	46	.593	—	1,697,398	Gene Lamont
Cleveland Indians	66	47	.584	1	1,995,174	Mike Hargrove
Kansas City Royals	64	51	.557	4	1,400,494	Hal McRae
Minnesota Twins	53	60	.469	14	1,398,565	Tom Kelly
Milwaukee Brewers	53	62	.461	15	1,268,397	Phil Garner

West Standings	W	L	Pct.	GB	Attend.	Manager
Texas Rangers....................	52	62	.456	—	2,502,538	Kevin Kennedy
Oakland Athletics	51	63	.447	1	1,242,692	Tony LaRussa
Seattle Mariners.................	49	63	.438	2	1,103,798	Lou Piniella
California Angels...............	47	68	.409	5½	1,512,622	Buck Rodgers/ Marcel Lachemann

Playoffs: None due to player strike August 12.

BA: Paul O'Neill, New York, .359
Runs: Frank Thomas, Chicago, 106
Hits: Kenny Lofton, Cleveland, 160
RBIs: Kirby Puckett, Minnesota, 112
HRs: Ken Griffey, Seattle, 40
Wins: Jimmy Key, New York, 17
SOs: Randy Johnson, Seattle, 204
ERA: Steve Ontiveros, Oakland, 2.65
Pct: Jason Bere, Chicago, .857, 12-2
Saves: Lee Smith, Baltimore, 33

National League
President: Leonard Coleman

East Standings	W	L	Pct.	GB	Attend.	Manager
Montreal Expos	74	40	.649	—	1,276,250	Felipe Alou
Atlanta Braves	68	46	.596	6	2,539,240	Bobby Cox
New York Mets	55	58	.487	18½	1,151,471	Dallas Green
Philadelphia Phillies	54	61	.470	20½	2,290,971	Jim Fregosi
Florida Marlins	51	64	.443	23½	1,937,467	Rene Lachemann

Central Standings	W	L	Pct.	GB	Attend.	Manager
Cincinnati Reds..................	66	48	.579	—	1,897,681	Davey Johnson
Houston Astros	66	49	.574	½	1,561,136	Terry Collins
Pittsburgh Pirates	53	61	.465	13	1,222,517	Jim Leyland
St. Louis Cardinals	53	61	.465	13	1,866,544	Joe Torre
Chicago Cubs	49	64	.434	16½	1,845,208	Tom Trebelhorn

West Standings	W	L	Pct.	GB	Attend.	Manager
Los Angeles Dodgers..........	58	56	.509	—	2,279,421	Tom Lasorda
San Francisco Giants	55	60	.478	3½	1,704,614	Dusty Baker
Colorado Rockies	53	64	.453	6½	3,281,511	Don Baylor
San Diego Padres	47	70	.402	12½	953,857	Jim Riggleman

Playoff: None due to player strike August 12.

BA: Tony Gwynn, San Diego, .394
Runs: Jeff Bagwell, Houston, 104
Hits: Tony Gwynn, San Diego, 165
RBIs: Jeff Bagwell, Houston, 116
HRs: Matt Williams, San Francisco, 43
Wins: Ken Hill, Montreal, 16 / Greg Maddux, Atlanta, 16
SOs: Andy Benes, San Diego, 189
ERA: Greg Maddux, Atlanta, 1.56
Pct: Marvin Freeman, Colorado, .833, 10-2
Saves: John Franco, New York, 30

AAA American Association
President: Branch B. Rickey

Standings	W	L	Pct.	GB	Attend.	Manager
Indianapolis Indians (17)....	86	57	.601	—	339,208	Marc Bombard
Nashville Sounds (4)	83	61	.576	3½	300,827	Rick Renick
New Orleans Zephyrs (8) ...	78	66	.542	8½	186,806	Chris Bando
Louisville Redbirds (26).....	74	68	.521	11½	573,174	Joe Pettini
Iowa Cubs (16)	69	74	.483	17	485,734	Rick Patterson
Omaha Royals (7)...............	68	76	.472	18½	439,277	Jeff Cox
Oklahoma City 89ers (13) ..	61	83	.424	25½	327,044	Bobby Jones
Buffalo Bisons (25)	55	89	.382	31½	982,493	Doc Edwards

Playoffs: Indianapolis 3 games, Louisville 0; Nashville 3 games, New Orleans 0.
Finals: Indianapolis 3 games, Nashville 1.

All-Star Team: 1B-Joe Vitiello, Omaha; 2B-Ray Durham, Nashville; 3B-Willie Greene, Indianapolis; SS-Tripp Cromer, Louisville; OF-Allen Battle, Louisville; Dwayne Hosey, Omaha; Doug Jennings, Indianapolis; C-Barry Lyons, Nashville; DH-Drew Denson, Nashville; P-Scott Ruffcorn, Nashville; Dennis Rasmussen, Omaha; Willie Smith, Louisville; MVP-Dwayne Hosey, Omaha; Manager-Marc Bombard, Indianapolis.

BA: Joe Vitiello, Omaha, .344
Runs: Allen Battle, Louisville, 104
Hits: Scott Bullett, Iowa, 163 / Allen Battle, Louisville, 163
RBIs: Drew Denson, Nashville, 103
HRs: Drew Denson, Nashville, 30
Wins: Scott Ruffcorn, Nashville, 15
SOs: James Baldwin, Nashville, 156
ERA: Matt Grott, Indianapolis, 2.55

AAA International League
President: Randy Mobley

East Standings	W	L	Pct.	GB	Attend.	Manager
Pawtucket Red Sox (2)	78	64	.549	—	469,029	Buddy Bailey
Syracuse Chiefs (14)..........	71	71	.500	7	329,594	Bob Didier
Ottawa Lynx (22)...............	70	72	.493	8	596,858	Jim Tracy
Rochester Red Wings (1)....	67	74	.475	10½	364,188	Bob Miscik
Scranton-Wilkes-Barre Red Barons (24)...............	62	80	.437	16	476,053	Mike Quade

West Standings	W	L	Pct.	GB	Attend.	Manager
Richmond Braves (15)........	80	61	.567	—	507,322	Grady Little
Charlotte Knights (5)..........	77	65	.542	3½	391,730	Brian Graham
Columbus Clippers (10)......	74	68	.521	6½	535,145	Stump Merrill
Norfolk Tides (23).............	67	75	.472	13½	546,826	Bobby Valentine
Toledo Mud Hens (6)	63	79	.444	17½	293,124	Joe Sparks/Larry Parrish

Playoffs: Syracuse 3 games, Pawtucket 1; Richmond 3 games, Charlotte 1.
Finals: Richmond 3 games, Syracuse 0.

All-Star Team: 1B-Herbert Perry, Charlotte; 2B-Shannon Penn, Toledo; 3B-Jeff Manto, Norfolk/Rochester; SS-Alex Gonzalez, Syracuse; OF-Brian Giles, Charlotte; Shawn Green, Syracuse; Sherman Obando, Rochester; C-Tim Laker, Ottawa; DH-Luis Lopez, Richmond; P-Brad Woodall, Richmond; Randy St. Claire, Syracuse; MVP-Jeff Manto, Norfolk/Rochester; Pitcher of the Year-Brad Woodall, Richmond; Manager-Grady Little, Richmond.

BA: Shawn Green, Syracuse, .344
Runs: Damon Buford, Rochester, 89
Hits: Luis Lopez, Richmond, 159
RBIs: Jeff Manto, Norfolk/Rochester, 100
HRs: Jeff Manto, Norfolk/Rochester, 31
Wins: Brad Woodall, Richmond, 15 / Julian Tavarez, Charlotte, 15
SOs: Frank Rodriguez, Pawtucket, 160
ERA: Brad Woodall, Richmond, 2.42

AAA Mexican League
President: Pedro Treto Cisneros

North Standings	W	L	Pct.	GB	Attend.	Manager
Monterrey Sultanes............	79	51	.608	—	191,118	Jose Guerrero/Alex Trevino
Saltillo Saraperos*	76	53	.589	2½	179,759	Roberto Castellon
Monterrey Industriales**....	74	54	.578	4	189,163	Aurelio Rodriguez
Union Laguna Algodoneros	72	57	.558	6½	184,975	Gregorio Luque
Monclova Acereros............	69	62	.527	10½	171,028	Joel Serna
Dos Laredos Tecolotes	64	67	.489	15½	179,086	Dan Firova
Jalisco Charros..................	51	77	.398	27	187,064	Ramon Montoya/Urbano Lugo/ Roberto Mendez
Aguascalientes Rieleros......	48	82	.369	31	179,009	Francisco Garcia/Angel Ruiz/ Marcelo Juarez

South Standings	W	L	Pct.	GB	Attend.	Manager
Mexico City Diablos Rojos***	82	45	.646	—	202,903	Marco Antonio Vazquez
Veracruz Aguila	64	56	.533	14½	184,123	Jorge Tellaeche/Ramon Arano
Yucatan Leones	66	58	.532	14½	310,941	Wilfredo Calvino
Campeche Piratas	64	57	.529	15	186,352	Javier Martinez
Mexico City Tigres.............	61	66	.480	21	186,386	Gerardo Gutierrez/ Ossie Alvarez/Porfirio Mendoza
Tabasco Olmecas	59	67	.468	22½	179,728	Juan Navarrete
Minatitlan Petroleros	57	71	.445	25½	180,089	Francisco Estrada
Puebla Pericos...................	33	96	.256	50	153,270	Bernardo Calvo/Moises Camacho

Playoffs: Monterrey Sultanes 4, Union Laguna 0; Saltillo 4 games, Monterrey Industriales 1; MC Diablos Rojos 4 games, Yucatan 1; Veracruz 4 games, Campeche 3. Monterrey Sultanes 4 games, Saltillo 1; MC Diablos Rojos 4 games, Veracruz 0.
Finals: MC Diablos Rojos 4 games, Monterrey Sultanes 3.

BA: Adam Casillas, Monterrey Industriales, .367
Runs: Todd Trafton, Union Laguna, 93
Hits: Adam Casillas, Monterrey Industriales, 165
RBIs: Hector Villanueva, Puebla/MC Tigres, 108
HRs: Hector Villanueva, Puebla/MC Tigres, 30 / Marco Romero, Dos Laredos, 30
Wins: Francisco Montano, Monclova, 19
SOs: Raul Rodriguez, Saltillo, 136
ERA: Leobardo Meza, Aguascalientes, 1.67

AAA Pacific Coast League
President: Bill Cutler

North Standings	W	L	Pct.	GB	Attend.	Manager
Vancouver Canadians***(3) ...	77	65	.542	—	320,863	Don Long
Salt Lake Buzz (9)	74	70	.514	4	713,224	Scott Ullger
Calgary Cannons (12).........	71	72	.497	6½	297,981	Steve Smith

*Won first-half   **Won second-half   ***Won both halves
Numbers after nicknames indicate farm system.
Affiliation listed at end of each year.

620

	W	L	Pct.	GB	Attend.	Manager
Edmonton Trappers (19).....	67	75	.472	10	272,631	Sal Rende
Tacoma Tigers (11)	61	81	.430	16	347,719	Casey Parsons

South Standings	W	L	Pct.	GB	Attend.	Manager
Albuquerque Dukes**(21) .	83	56	.597	—	376,272	Rick Dempsey
Tucson Toros (20)	81	63	.563	4½	309,623	Rick Sweet
Colorado Springs Sky Sox*(18).	70	69	.504	13	211,671	Brad Mills
Phoenix Firebirds (28)........	70	72	.493	14½	315,859	Carlos Alfonso
Las Vegas Stars (27)...........	56	87	.392	29	338,834	Russ Nixon

Playoffs: Albuquerque 3 games, Colorado Springs 1; Vancouver 3 games, Salt Lake 2.
Finals: Albuquerque 3 games, Vancouver 2.

All-Star Team: 1B-J.R. Phillips, Phoenix; **2B**-Dave Hajek, Tucson; **3B**-Ron Coomer, Albuquerque; **SS**-Jason Bates, Colorado Springs; **OF**-Billy Ashley, Albuquerque; Brian L. Hunter, Tucson; Marc Newfield, Calgary; **C**-Tim McIntosh, Salt Lake; **DH**-Bernardo Brito, Salt Lake; **P**-Craig McMurtry, Tucson; Andrew Lorraine, Vancouver; Jim Dougherty, Tucson; **MVP**-Billy Ashley, Albuquerque; **Manager**-Rick Sweet, Tucson.

BA: Brian L. Hunter, Tucson, .372
Runs: Brian L. Hunter, Tucson, 113
Hits: Brian L. Hunter, Tucson, 191
RBIs: Ron Coomer, Albuquerque, 123
HRs: Billy Ashley, Albuquerque, 37
Wins: Dan Carlson, Phoenix, 13
SOs: Kerry Taylor, Las Vegas, 142
ERA: Doug Johns, Tacoma, 2.89

AA Eastern League
President: John Levenda

North Standings	W	L	Pct.	GB	Attend.	Manager
Binghamton Mets (23)........	82	59	.582	—	217,600	John Tamargo
New Haven Ravens (18).....	77	63	.550	4½	276,316	Paul Zuvella
Albany-Colonie Yankees (10).	71	70	.504	11	115,819	Bill Evers
Portland Sea Dogs (19)......	60	81	.426	22	375,197	Carlos Tosca
New Britain Red Sox (2) ...	59	81	.421	22½	129,696	Jim Pankovits

South Standings	W	L	Pct.	GB	Attend.	Manager
Harrisburg Senators (22) ...	88	51	.633	—	234,774	Dave Jauss
Bowie Baysox (1)	84	58	.592	5½	293,665	Pete Mackanin
Canton-Akron Indians (5)...	69	73	.486	20½	255,002	Ted Kubiak
Reading Phillies (24)	58	82	.414	30½	338,249	Bill Dancy
Trenton Thunder (6)	55	85	.393	33½	318,252	Tom Runnells

Playoffs: Binghamton 3 games, New Haven 0; Harrisburg 3 games, Bowie 2.
Finals: Binghamton 3 games, Harrisburg 1.

All-Star Team: 1B-Tate Seefried, Albany-Colonie; **2B**-Hector Vargas, Bowie; **3B**-Bryn Kosco, New Haven; **SS**-Mark Grudzielanek, Harrisburg; **OF**-Curtis Goodwin, Bowie; Jesse Malave, New Britain; Kevin Northrup, Harrisburg; **C**-Charles Johnson, Portland; **DH**-Tony Clark, Trenton; **P**-Jimmy Haynes, Bowie; Rod Pedraza, New Haven; Bill Pulsipher, Binghamton; Alberto Reyes, Harrisburg; **MVP**-Mark Grudzielanek, Harrisburg; **Pitcher of the Year**-Juan Acevedo, New Haven; **Manager**-Dave Jauss, Harrisburg.

BA: Kevin Northrup, Harrisburg, .331
Runs: Curtis Goodwin, Bowie, 105
Hits: Curtis Goodwin, Bowie, 171
RBIs: Jose Malave, New Britain, 92
HRs: Charles Johnson, Portland, 28
Wins: Juan Acevedo, New Haven, 17
SOs: Jimmy Haynes, Bowie, 177
ERA: Juan Acevedo, New Haven, 2.37

AA Southern League
President: Jimmy Bragan

East Standings	W	L	Pct.	GB	Attend.	Manager
Greenville Braves**(15).....	73	63	.537	—	244,171	Bruce Benedict
Carolina Mudcats*(25).......	74	66	.529	1	319,279	Bobby Meacham
Knoxville Smokies (14)......	64	76	.457	11	145,092	Garth Iorg
Jacksonville Suns (12)	60	77	.438	13½	240,580	Marc Hill
Orlando Cubs (16)	59	78	.431	14½	195,270	Dave Trembley

West Standings	W	L	Pct.	GB	Attend.	Manager
Huntsville Stars*(11)..........	81	57	.587	—	297,801	Gary Jones
Memphis Chicks (7)	75	62	.547	5½	258,311	Ron Johnson
Nashville Xpress (9)...........	74	66	.529	8	135,048	Phil Roof
Chattanooga Lookouts**(17)..	67	73	.479	15	292,920	Pat Kelly
Birmingham Barons (4)......	65	74	.468	16½	467,867	Terry Francona

Playoffs: Huntsville 3 games, Chattanooga 0; Carolina 3 games, Greenville 2.
Finals: Huntsville 3 games, Carolina 1.

All-Star Team: 1B-Tim Belk, Chattanooga; **2B**-Chris Stynes, Knoxville; **3B**-Chris Snopek, Birmingham; **SS**-Pokey Reese, Chattanooga; **OF**-Tony Barron, Carolina; Trey Beamon, Carolina; Terrel Hansen, Jacksonville; Phil Hiatt, Memphis; Ernie Young, Huntsville; **C**-Chris Widger, Jacksonville; **DH**-Mark Johnson, Carolina; **Util**-Jason Wood, Huntsville; **P**-Blaine Beatty, Chattanooga; Brad Radke, Nashville; Gary Wilson, Carolina; **MVP**-Mark Johnson, Carolina; **Pitcher of the Year**-Brad Clontz, Greenville; **Manager**-Gary Jones, Huntsville.

BA: Trey Beamon, Carolina, .323
Runs: Kerwin Moore, Huntsville, 97
Hits: Chris Stynes, Knoxville, 173
RBIs: Chris Weinke, Knoxville, 87
HRs: Mark Johnson, Carolina, 23
Wins: Blaine Beatty, Chattanooga, 14
SOs: Blaine Beatty, Chattanooga, 162
ERA: Blaine Beatty, Chattanooga, 2.38

AA Texas League
President: Tom Kayser

East Standings	W	L	Pct.	GB	Attend.	Manager
Jackson Generals**(20)..	74	61	.548	—	148,647	Sal Butera
Shreveport Captains*(28)...	73	63	.537	1½	199,465	Ron Wotus
Arkansas Travelers (26)....	68	67	.504	6	275,524	Chris Maloney
Tulsa Drillers (13)	63	73	.463	11½	344,764	Stan Cliburn

West Standings	W	L	Pct.	GB	Attend.	Manager
El Paso Diablos***(8)........	88	48	.647	—	327,542	Tim Ireland
San Antonio Missions (21).	62	74	.456	26	411,959	Tom Beyers
Midland Angels (3)............	61	75	.449	27	190,022	Mario Mendoza
Wichita Wranglers (27)	54	82	.397	34	210,482	Keith Champion

Playoff: Jackson 3 games, Shreveport 2.
Finals: El Paso 4 games, Jackson 0.

All-Star Team: 1B-Chris Pritchett, Midland; **2B**-Rodney Lofton, El Paso; **3B**-Tim Unroe, El Paso; **SS**-Juan Castro, San Antonio; **OF**-Terry Bradshaw, Arkansas; Danny Perez, El Paso; Ira Smith, Wichita; **C**-Mike Stefanski, El Paso; **DH**-Glenn Dishman, Wichita; Rich Huisman, Jackson; Doug Mlicki, Jackson; Sid Roberson, El Paso; Scott Simmons, Arkansas; **MVP**-Tim Unroe, El Paso; **Pitcher of the Year**-Sid Roberson, El Paso; **Manager**-Tim Ireland, El Paso.

BA: Rodney Lofton, El Paso, .331
Runs: Tim Unroe, El Paso, 97
Hits: Tim Unroe, El Paso, 147
RBIs: Tim Unroe, El Paso, 103
HRs: Scott Talanoa, El Paso, 28
Wins: Sid Roberson, El Paso, 15
SOs: Glenn Dishman, Wichita, 165
ERA: Scott Simmons, Arkansas, 2.72

A California League
President: Joe Gagliardi

North Standings	W	L	Pct.	GB	Attend.	Manager
Modesto A's***(11)...........	96	40	.706	—	109,314	Dick Scott
San Jose Giants (28)	74	62	.544	22	131,091	Dick Dietz
Bakersfield Dodgers (21)....	69	67	.507	27	141,505	John Shelby
Central Valley Rockies (18)..	65	71	.478	31	92,756	Bill Hayes
Stockton Ports (8)	54	82	.397	42	114,013	Lamar Johnson

South Standings	W	L	Pct.	GB	Attend.	Manager
Riverside Pilots***(12)......	87	49	.640	—	85,358	Dave Myers
Rancho Cucamonga Quakes (27)	77	59	.566	10	386,633	Tim Flannery
Lake Elsinore Storm (3)	65	71	.478	22	357,123	Mitch Seoane
San Bernardino Spirit (x)....	48	88	.353	39	101,710	Greg Mahlberg
High Desert Mavericks (x)...	45	91	.331	42	171,783	Phil Hannon

Playoffs: Modesto 3 games, San Jose 0; Rancho Cucamonga 3 games, Riverside 1.
Finals: Rancho Cucamonga 3 games, Modesto 1.

All-Star Team: 1B-Jason Thompson, Rancho Cucamonga; **2B**-Mike Smith, High Desert; **3B**-George Arias, Lake Elsinore; **SS**-Desi Relaford, Riverside; **OF**-Charles Gipson, Riverside; Lee Heath, High Desert; Terry Jones, Central Valley; **C**-Raul Casanova, Rancho Cucamonga; **P**-Matt Apana, Riverside; Steve Lemke, Modesto; Greg Keagle, Rancho Cucamonga; Todd Schmitt, Rancho Cucamonga; **MVP**-Todd Greene, Lake Elsinore; **Manager**-Dick Scott, Modesto.

BA: Raul Casanova, Rancho Cucamonga, .340
Runs: Charles Gipson, Riverside, 102
Hits: Raul Casanova, Rancho Cucamonga, 160
RBIs: Todd Greene, Lake Elsinore, 124
HRs: Todd Greene, Lake Elsinore, 35
Wins: Jose Prado, Bakersfield, 15
SOs: Shigeki Noguchi, Central Valley, 161
ERA: Steve Lemke, Modesto, 2.32

A Carolina League
President: John Hopkins

North Standings	W	L	Pct.	GB	Attend.	Manager
Wilmington Blue Rocks***(7)	94	44	.681	—	335,024	Mike Jirschele
Frederick Keys (1)	76	61	.555	17½	344,563	Mike O'Berry
Prince William Cannons (4)...	71	65	.522	22	210,401	Dave Huppert
Lynchburg Red Sox (2)	52	87	.374	42½	100,724	Mark Meleski

South Standings	W	L	Pct.	GB	Attend.	Manager
Winston-Salem Spirits*(17)..	67	70	.489	—	160,994	Mark Berry
Durham Bulls**(15)...........	66	70	.485	½	259,758	Matt West
Salem Buccaneers (25)	64	75	.460	4	153,575	Trent Jewett
Kinston Indians (5)	60	78	.435	7½	122,557	Dave Keller

Playoff: Winston-Salem 2 games, Durham 0.
Finals: Wilmington 3 games, Winston-Salem 0.

All-Star Team: 1B-Larry Sutton, Wilmington; **2B**-Essex Burton, Prince William; **3B**-Bill Selby, Lynchburg; **SS**-Craig Wilson, Prince William; **OF**-Pat Watkins, Winston-Salem; Johnny Damon, Wilmington; Jimmy Hurst, Prince William; **C**-B.J. Waszgis, Frederick; **DH**-Andy Stewart, Wilmington; **Util**-Chance Sanford, Salem; Kimera Bartee, Frederick; **P**-Bart Evans, Wilmington; Chris Lemp, Frederick; **MVP**-Larry Sutton, Wilmington; **Manager**-Mike Jirschele, Wilmington.

BA: Harry Berrios, Frederick, .348
Runs: Pat Watkins, Winston-Salem, 107
Hits: Pat Watkins, Winston-Salem, 152
RBIs: B.J. Waszgis, Frederick, 100
HRs: Toby Rumfield, Winston-Salem, 29
Wins: Sean Johnston, Prince William, 15
SOs: Jim Pittsley, Wilmington, 171
ERA: Mike Bovee, Wilmington, 2.65

A Florida State League
President: Chuck Murphy

East Standings	W	L	Pct.	GB	Attend.	Manager
Brevard County Manatees#*(19)	78	61	.561	—	144,688	Fredi Gonzalez
West Palm Beach Expos**(22)	71	60	.542	3	72,097	Rob Leary
St. Lucie Mets (23)	71	65	.522	5½	67,999	Rafael Landestoy
Daytona Cubs (16).............	61	73	.455	14½	96,756	Ken Bolek
Vero Beach Dodgers (21)...	60	75	.444	16	68,903	Jon Debus
Osceola Astros (20)	46	89	.341	30	38,496	Tim Tolman

West Standings	W	L	Pct.	GB	Attend.	Manager
Tampa Yankees*(10)..........	80	52	.606	—	60,855	Jake Gibbs
Clearwater Phillies (24)	72	62	.537	9	82,494	Don McCormack

St. Petersburg Cardinals (26) 74 65 .532 9½ 108,283 Mike Ramsey
Ft. Myers Miracle (9).......... 71 63 .530 10 95,688 Steve Liddle
Sarasota Red Sox**(2) .... 69 64 .519 11½ 68,781 DeMarlo Hale
Dunedin Blue Jays (14) ...... 65 68 .489 15½ 80,126 Jim Nettles
Lakeland Tigers (6) .... 63 68 .481 16½ 21,996 Gerry Groninger/Mark Wagner
Charlotte Rangers (13)........ 60 76 .441 22 77,821 Tommy Thompson

#represented Melbourne, Florida.

Playoffs: Tampa 2 games, Sarasota 1; Brevard County 2 games, West Palm Beach 0.
Finals: Tampa 3 games, Brevard County 1.

All-Star Team: 1B-Andrew Kontorinis, Ft. Myers; **2B-**David Doster, Clearwater; **3B-**Lou Lucca, Brevard County; **SS-**Derek Jeter, Tampa; **OF-**Don White, St. Lucie; Matt Lawton, Ft. Myers; Karim Garcia, Vero Beach; **C-**Angel Martinez, Dunedin; Mike Figga, Tampa; **DH-**Jason Friedman, Sarasota; **Util-**Rey Ordonez, St. Lucie; Steve Solomon, Clearwater; **P-**Keith Heberling, Tampa; Aaron Jersild, Dunedin; David Hutcheson, Daytona Beach; Jason Isringhausen, St. Lucie; Gus Gandarillas, Ft. Myers; Eric Miller, St. Petersburg; **MVP-**Derek Jeter, Tampa; **Manager-**Fredi Gonzalez, Brevard County.

BA: Jason Friedman, Sarasota, .328
Runs: Aaron Fuller, Sarasota, 89
Hits: Jason Friedman, Sarasota, 154
RBIs: Todd Pridy, Brevard County, 89
HRs: Karim Garcia, Vero Beach, 21

Wins: David Hutcheson, Daytona, 13
Jerry Martin, Charlotte, 13
Jeff Suppan, Sarasota, 13
Ron Blazier, Clearwater, 13
SOs: Jeff Suppan, Sarasota, 173
ERA: Jerry Martin, Charlotte, 2.08

A Midwest League
President: George Spelius

North Standings	W	L	Pct.	GB	Attend.	Manager
Rockford Royals***(7)	89	50	.640	—	70,527	John Mizerock
Beloit Brewers (8)	76	64	.543	13½	60,650	Wayne Krenchicki
Appleton Foxes (12)	75	64	.540	14	76,281	Carlos Lezcano
West Michigan Whitecaps#(11).	74	65	.532	15	475,212	Jim Colborn
South Bend Silver Hawks (4) ..	72	67	.518	17	258,424	Mike Gellinger
Kane County Cougars (19) ..	71	68	.511	18	417,744	Lynn Jones
Fort Wayne Wizards (9)	66	73	.475	23	266,670	Jim Dwyer

South Standings	W	L	Pct.	GB	Attend.	Manager
Cedar Rapids Kernels**(3) ..	77	62	.554	—	137,795	Tom Lawless
Springfield Sultans*(27).....	69	71	.493	8½	54,214	Ed Romero
Peoria Chiefs (16).............	68	70	.493	8½	176,703	Steve Roadcap
Madison Hatters (26)	66	73	.475	11	69,060	Joe Cunningham
Quad City River Bandits (20)..	57	81	.413	19½	260,471	Steve Dillard
Clinton Lumber Kings (28) ..	57	82	.410	20	62,317	Jack Mull
Burlington Bees (22)	55	82	.401	21	83,927	Lorenzo Bundy

#represented Grand Rapids, Michigan.

Playoffs: Rockford 2 games, West Michigan 0; Cedar Rapids 2 games, Springfield 0.
Finals: Cedar Rapids 3 games, Rockford 1.

All-Star Team: 1B-Kevin Millar, Kane County; **2B-**Bob Morris, Peoria; **3B-**Lino Diaz, Rockford; **SS-**Alex Rodriguez, Appleton; **OF-**Richard Hidalgo, Quad City; Joe McEwing, Madison; Billy McMillon, Kane County; **C-**Sal Fasano, Rockford; **DH-**Alex Cabrera, Peoria; **P-**Mike Sirotka, South Bend; Jay Witasick, Madison; Hank Tagle, South Bend; Matt Mantei, Appleton; **MVP-**Sal Fasano, Rockford; **Manager-**John Mizerock, Rockford.

BA: Carlos Mendez, Rockford, .355
Runs: Ralph Milliard, Kane County, 97
Hits: Mike Barger, Appleton, 160
RBIs: Billy McMillon, Kane County, 101

HRs: Matt Raleigh, Burlington, 34
Wins: Jim Cole, Beloit, 18
SOs: Billy Wagner, Quad City, 204
ERA: Will Cunnane, Kane County, 1.43

A New York-Pennsylvania League
President: Robert Julian

McNamara Standings	W	L	Pct.	GB	Attend.	Manager
New Jersey Cardinals#(26).	43	32	.573	—	156,477	Roy Silver
Vermont Expos@(22).........	42	33	.560	1	114,179	Terry Kennedy
Hudson Valley Renegades+(13).	37	37	.500	5½	138,116	Doug Sisson
Pittsfield Mets (23)	37	38	.493	6	59,122	Howie Freiling

Pinckney Standings	W	L	Pct.	GB	Attend.	Manager
Watertown Indians (5)........	48	26	.649	—	57,089	Jeff Datz
Auburn Astros (20)............	45	31	.592	4	31,544	Manny Acta
Utica Blue Sox (2)	35	37	.486	12	72,006	Dave Holt
Elmira Pioneers (19)	30	43	.411	17½	60,464	Jim Hendry
Oneonta Yankees (10)	30	45	.400	18½	48,712	Ken Dominguez
Williamsport Cubs (16)	26	49	.347	22½	57,624	Jerry Weinstein

Stedler Standings	W	L	Pct.	GB	Attend.	Manager
Jamestown Jammers (6)......	42	32	.568	—	49,706	Dave Anderson
Batavia Clippers (24)..........	40	34	.541	2	41,502	Al LeBoeuf
St. Catharines Blue Jays (14)...	35	39	.473	7	31,539	J.J. Cannon
Welland Pirates (25)	30	44	.405	12	34,668	Jeff Banister

#represented Augusta, New Jersey.
@represented Burlington, Vermont.
+represented Fishkill, New York.

Playoffs: Auburn 2 games, Watertown 0; New Jersey 2 games, Jamestown 1.
Finals: New Jersey 2 games, Auburn 0.

All-Star Team: 1B-Mike Taylor, New Jersey; **2B-**Trace Coquillette, Vermont; **3B-**Chris

Truby, Auburn; **SS-**Geoff Blum, Vermont; **OF-**Jim Betzsold, Watertown; Marty Gazarek, Williamsport; Jay Payton, Pittsfield; Wes Pratt, Auburn; **C-**Jeff Ladd, St. Catharines; Brian Silvia, New Jersey; **DH-**Todd Betts, Watertown; **Util-**Todd Whitehurst, Pittsfield; **P-**Igor Oropeza, Watertown; Julien Tucker, Auburn; Steve Arffa, Pittsfield; Greg Whiteman, Jamestown; **MVP-**Chris Truby, Auburn; **Manager-**Dave Anderson, Jamestown.

BA: Jay Payton, Pittsfield, .365
Runs: Chris Truby, Auburn, 56
Hits: Chris Truby, Auburn, 91
RBIs: Chris Truby, Auburn, 61
HRs: Freddy Garcia, St. Catharines, 13

Wins: Jason Durocher, Vermont, 9
Scott Cunningham, New Jersey, 9
SOs: Brian Grant, St. Catharines, 90
ERA: Matt Drews, Oneonta, 2.10

A Northwest League
President: Bob Richmond

North Standings	W	L	Pct.	GB	Attend.	Manager
Yakima Bears (21).............	49	27	.645	—	85,483	Joe Vavra
Bellingham Mariners (12) ..	42	34	.553	7	71,256	Mike Goff
Everett Giants (28)............	37	39	.487	12	94,421	Mike Hart
Spokane Indians (27).........	30	46	.395	19	156,092	Tye Waller

South Standings	W	L	Pct.	GB	Attend.	Manager
Boise Hawks (3)	44	32	.579	—	156,950	Tom Kotchman
Southern Oregon A's (11) ..	38	38	.500	6	88,363	Tom Dunton
Eugene Emeralds (7)	35	41	.461	9	133,860	Brian Poldberg
Bend Rockies (18).............	29	47	.382	15	69,225	Rudy Jaramillo

Playoff: Boise 2 games, Yakima 1.

All-Star Team: 1B-John Donati, Boise; **2B-**Chris Dean, Bellingham; **3B-**Greg Morris, Boise; **SS-**Eric Martins, Southern Oregon; **OF-**Ben Grieve, Southern Oregon; Chris Latham, Yakima; Dante Powell, Everett; **C-**Bret Hemphill, Boise; **DH-**Pookie Jones, Bend; **P-**John Vanhof, Bellingham; Marino Santana, Bellingham; Bubba Dixon, Spokane; Tim Grieve, Eugene; **MVP-**John Donati, Boise; **Manager-**Joe Vavra, Yakima.

BA: Chris Latham, Yakima, .340
Runs: Chris Latham, Yakima, 70
Hits: Chris Latham, Yakima, 98
RBIs: Paul Konerko, Yakima, 58

HRs: Derrick Gibson, Bend, 12
Don Denbow, Everett, 12
Wins: Craig Scheffler, Yakima, 8
SOs: John Vanhof, Bellingham, 97
ERA: DeVohn Duncan, Spokane, 1.48

A South Atlantic League
President: John H. Moss

North Standings	W	L	Pct.	GB	Attend.	Manager
Hickory Crawdads**(4)	86	54	.614	—	270,880	Fred Kendall
Hagerstown Suns*(14)	80	56	.588	4	111,660	Omar Malave
Greensboro Bats (10)..........	71	69	.507	15	218,410	Trey Hillman
Spartanburg Phillies**(24)...	67	72	.482	18½	58,138	Roy Majtyka
Charleston (WV) Wheelers*(17)	65	75	.464	21	103,985	Tom Nieto
Fayetteville Generals (6)	62	75	.453	22½	104,379	Dwight Lowry
Asheville Tourists (18)	60	73	.451	22½	118,146	Tony Torchia

South Standings	W	L	Pct.	GB	Attend.	Manager
Columbus RedStixx**(5) ...	87	51	.630	—	133,351	Mike Young
Savannah Cardinals*(26).....	82	55	.599	4½	111,143	Luis Melendez
Macon Braves (15)	73	64	.533	13½	83,597	Leon Roberts
Albany Polecats (1)	63	74	.460	23½	124,520	Butch Wynegar
Capital City Bombers (23)...	59	76	.437	26½	146,676	Ron Washington
Charleston (SC) RiverDogs (13)	56	81	.409	30½	105,791	Walt Williams
Augusta GreenJackets (25).	50	86	.368	36	115,909	Scott Little

Playoffs: Hagerstown 2 games, Hickory 0; Savannah 2 games, Columbus 0.
Finals: Savannah 3 games, Hagerstown 0.

All-Star Team: 1B-Harold Williams, Hickory; **2B-**Frank Catalanotto, Fayetteville; **3B-**Scott Rolen, Spartanburg; **SS-**Enrique Wilson, Columbus; **OF-**Jermaine Dye, Macon; Jeremy Kendall, Spartanburg; Ruben Rivera, Greensboro; **C-**Einar Diaz, Columbus; **DH-**Joe Durso, Hagerstown; **Util-**Jeff Berblinger, Savannah; **P-**Chris Cumberland, Greensboro; Matt Arrandale, Savannah; **MVP-**Ruben Rivera, Greensboro; **Pitcher of the Year-**Matt Arrandale, Savannah; **Manager-**Fred Kendall, Hickory.

BA: Ben Boulware, Hickory, .332
Runs: Harold Williams, Hickory, 99
Hits: Harold Williams, Hickory, 162
RBIs: Harold Williams, Hickory, 104

HRs: Ruben Rivera, Greensboro, 28
Nate Holdren, Asheville, 28
Wins: Steve Kline, Columbus, 18
SOs: Steve Kline, Columbus, 174
ERA: Matt Arrandale, Savannah, 1.76

R Appalachian League
President: Bill Halstead

North Standings	W	L	Pct.	GB	Attend.	Manager
Princeton Reds (17)	41	25	.621	—	39,426	John Stearns
Bluefield Orioles (1)...........	39	29	.574	3	39,169	Andy Etchebarren
Martinsville Phillies (24)....	32	36	.471	10	56,595	Ramon Henderson
Danville Braves (15)..........	28	39	.418	13½	70,862	Paul Runge
Burlington Indians (5)	23	42	.354	17½	48,329	Jim Gabella

South Standings	W	L	Pct.	GB	Attend.	Manager
Johnson City Cardinals (26)	42	26	.618	—	48,038	Steve Turco
Elizabethton Twins (9)	36	30	.545	5	20,009	Ray Smith
Kingsport Mets (23)...........	36	30	.545	5	34,124	Ron Gideon
Bristol Tigers (6)	27	36	.429	12½	23,929	Kevin Bradshaw
Huntington Cubs (16)	28	39	.418	13½	57,589	Steve Kolinsky

Playoff: Princeton 2 games, Johnson City 1.

All-Star Team: 1B-Jacob Patterson, Elizabethton; **2B**-Johnny Carvajal, Princeton; **3B**-Rick Short, Bluefield; **SS**-Luis Ordaz, Princeton; **OF**-Decomba Conner, Princeton; Adrian Gordon, Elizabethton; Shane Pullen, Martinsville; **C**-Troy Fortin, Elizabethton; **DH**-Chan Perry, Burlington; **P**-Trevor Cobb, Elizabethton; Damon Callahan, Princeton; Darren Fidge, Elizabethton; **MVP**-Decomba Conner, Princeton; **Manager**-John Stearns, Princeton.

BA: Shane Pullen, Martinsville, .339
Runs: Romulo Vizcaino, Elizabethton, 51
Hits: Shane Pullen, Martinsville, 75
RBIs: Jacob Patterson, Elizabethton, 53
HRs: Jacob Patterson, Elizabethton, 18
Wins: Trevor Cobb, Elizabethton, 9
SOs: Carlos Chavez, Bluefield, 92
ERA: Cedric Allen, Princeton, 1.36

R Arizona League
President: Bob Richmond

Standings	W	L	Pct.	GB	Manager
Cardinals (Chandler) (26)...	34	22	.607	—	Scott Melvin
Athletics (Scottsdale) (11)..	32	24	.571	2	Tony DeFrancesco
Brewers (Chandler) (8).......	32	24	.571	2	Ralph Dickenson
Giants (Scottsdale) (28)......	29	26	.527	4½	Alan Bannister
Padres (Peoria) (27)...........	28	27	.509	5½	Barry Moss
Angels (Mesa) (3)...............	23	32	.418	10½	Bill Lachemann
Rockies (Chandler) (18)......	23	32	.418	10½	P.J. Carey
Mariners (Peoria) (12)	21	35	.375	13	Marty Martinez

Playoffs: None.

All-Star Team: 1B-Jon Valenti, Athletics; **2B**-Scott Swift, Giants; **3B**-Carlos Villalobos, Mariners; **SS**-Juan Melo, Padres; **OF**-Mike Burrows, Mariners; Jose Lugo, Cardinals; Anton French, Cardinals; **C**-Alex Rondon, Athletics; **DH**-Nate Dishington, Cardinals; **P**-Arthur Davis, Angels; Domingo Guzman, Padres; Jhonny Gonzalez, Rockies; Frank Garcia, Cardinals; **MVP**-Juan Melo, Padres; Alfonso Mota, Angels; **Manager**-Scott Melvin, Cardinals.

BA: Wilson Delgado, Mariners, .376
Runs: Alfonso Mota, Angels, 37
    Wilson Soto, Brewers, 37
    Anthony Iapoce, Brewers, 37
Hits: Jose Lugo, Cardinals, 70
RBIs: Nate Dishington, Cardinals, 36
HRs: Darren Tawwater, Cardinals, 5
Wins: Steve Woodard, Brewers, 8
    Domingo Guzman, Padres, 8
    Matt Clement, Padres, 8
SOs: Luis Silva, Athletics, 88
ERA: Derek Bieniasz, Mariners, 1.39

R Gulf Coast League
President: Thomas J. Saffell

East Standings	W	L	Pct.	GB	Manager
Marlins (Melbourne) (19)...	38	21	.644	—	Juan Bustabad
Expos (West Palm Beach) (22)..	35	24	.593	3	Nelson Norman
Mets (Port St. Lucie) (23)..	32	27	.542	6	Junior Roman
Braves (West Palm Beach) (15).	13	46	.220	25	Jim Saul
North Standings	**W**	**L**	**Pct.**	**GB**	**Manager**
Astros (Kissimmee) (20) ..	41	18	.695	—	Bobby Ramos
Yankees (Tampa) (10)........	26	32	.448	14½	Hector Lopez
Blue Jays (Dunedin) (14)....	26	34	.433	15½	Doug Ault
Cubs (Kissimmee) (16).......	25	34	.424	16	Phil Bradley
West Standings	**W**	**L**	**Pct.**	**GB**	**Manager**
Royals (Lee County) (7)......	47	12	.797	—	Bob Herold
Red Sox (Ft. Myers) (2)......	40	20	.667	7½	Felix Maldonado
Rangers (Port Charlotte) (13)..	32	28	.533	15½	Chino Cadahia
Pirates (Bradenton) (25)	25	35	.417	22½	Woody Huyke
Orioles (Sarasota) (1)..........	23	36	.390	24	Oneri Fleita
Twins (Lee County) (9)	22	38	.367	25½	Jose Marzan
White Sox (Sarasota) (4)	20	40	.333	27½	Mike Rojas

Playoff: Astros 1 game, Marlins 0.
Finals: Astros 2 games, Royals 1.

All-Star Team: 1B-Andy Rice, Pirates; **2B**-Sergio Nunez, Royals; **3B**-Fernando Tatis, Rangers; **SS**-Mendy Lopez, Royals; **OF**-Junior Braddy, Red Sox; Rodney Mangham, Astros; Rodolfo Mendez, Royals; **C**-Wikelman Gonzalez, Pirates; **P**-Rodney Nelson, Royals; Welnis Bonilla, Red Sox; **Manager**-Bobby Ramos, Astros.

BA: Sergio Nunez, Royals, .397
Runs: Sergio Nunez, Royals, 64
Hits: Sergio Nunez, Royals, 92
RBIs: Mendy Lopez, Royals, 50
HRs: Daniel Vasquez, Rangers, 9
Wins: Rodney Nelson, Royals, 9
SOs: Tony Mounce, Astros, 72
ERA: Jose Rosado, Royals, 1.25

R Pioneer League
President: Jim McCurdy

North Standings	W	L	Pct.	GB	Attend.	Manager
Billings Mustangs (17)	50	22	.694	—	100,556	Donnie Scott
Medicine Hat Blue Jays (14)...	36	36	.500	14	30,028	Darren Balsley
Great Falls Dodgers (21)...	34	38	.472	16	62,564	Ron Roenicke
Lethbridge Mounties (x).....	29	43	.403	21	42,967	Phillip Wellman
South Standings	**W**	**L**	**Pct.**	**GB**	**Attend.**	**Manager**
Helena Brewers (8).............	44	28	.611	—	45,424	Dub Kilgo
Ogden Raptors	41	31	.569	3	57,707	Willie Ambos
Idaho Falls Braves (15).......	30	42	.417	14	53,180	Max Venable
Butte Copper Kings (x).......	24	48	.333	20	22,592	Bruce Crabbe

Playoff: Billings 3 games, Helena 2.

All-Star Team: 1B-Jeremy Winget, Ogden; **2B**-James Lofton, Billings; **3B**-Aaron Boone,

---

Billings; **SS**-Mark Duncan, Lethbridge; **OF**-Alex Ascencio, Great Falls; Scott Krause, Helena; Chris Priest, Lethbridge; **C**-Julio Mosquera, Billings; **DH**-Nate Olmstead, Butte; **P**-Eddie Priest, Billings; Jason Robbins, Billings; Mike Toney, Medicine Hat; **MVP**-Ray Brown, Billings; **Manager**-Willie Ambos, Ogden.

BA: Jeremy Winget, Ogden, .372
Runs: Tim Gavello, Ogden, 68
Hits: Jeremy Winget, Ogden, 103
RBIs: Jeremy Winget, Ogden, 74
HRs: Nick Morrow, Billings, 14
    Chris Priest, Lethbridge, 14
Wins: Jason Robbins, Billings, 11
SOs: Brian Reed, Butte, 108
ERA: Jeff Kramer, Helena, 2.05

Ind Frontier League
President: Steve Sturgill

North Standings	W	L	Pct.	GB	Attend.	Manager
Ohio Valley Redcoats*** ...	50	17	.735	—	24,402	Greg LeMaster
Erie Sailors	42	25	.627	8	64,355	Mal Fichman
Zanesville Greys	35	28	.556	13	19,178	Tom Vendetelli
Newark Buffalos................	26	37	.413	22	44,910	Mike Hannah
South Standings	**W**	**L**	**Pct.**	**GB**	**Attend.**	**Manager**
Chillicothe Paints***	33	34	.493	—	32,808	Roger Hanners
Lancaster Scouts	25	39	.391	6½	7,055	George Spencer
Portsmouth Explorers	24	38	.387	6½	10,717	Ralph Cole
Kentucky Rifles#	24	41	.369	8	12,803	Wayne Albury

#represented Pikeville, Kentucky.

Playoffs: Erie 2 games, Ohio Valley 0; Lancaster 2 games, Chillicothe 1.
Finals: Erie 2 games, Lancaster 0.

All-Star Team: 1B-Darrell Fatzinger, Portsmouth; **2B**-Dan Bartolomeo, Portsmouth; **3B**-Steve Ruckman, Newark; **SS**-Andy Sreboski, Ohio Valley; **OF**-Joe Miller, Portsmouth; Corey Morris, Ohio Valley; Scott Pagano, Ohio Valley; **C**-Jason Moore, Chillicothe; **DH**-Robbie Robertson, Erie; **P**-Joe Fushey, Newark; Jim Knight, Erie; Brad Keely, Ohio Valley; **MVP**-Corey Morris, Ohio Valley; **Pitcher of the Year**-Jim Knight, Erie; **Manager**-Greg LeMaster, Ohio Valley.

BA: Joe Miller, Portsmouth, .402
Runs: Corey Morris, Ohio Valley, 67
Hits: Corey Morris, Ohio Valley, 91
RBIs: Corey Morris, Ohio Valley, 63
HRs: Corey Morris, Ohio Valley, 19
Wins: Jim Knight, Erie, 9
SOs: Jeff Markosky, Lancaster, 70
ERA: Matt Seymour, Zanesville, 1.81

Ind Great Central League
President: Dick Jacobson

Standings	W	L	Pct.	GB	Attend.	Manager
Lafayette Leopards	44	24	.647	—	11,682	Jim Gonzales
Champaign-Urbana Bandits	31	26	.559	7½		Brett Robinson
Minneapolis Millers...........	30	33	.476	11½	3,000	George Scott
Mason City Bats	19	41	.317	21		Tom Waelchi

Ind North Central League
President: George Vedder

East Standings	W	L	Pct.	GB	Attend.	Manager
Brainerd Bears	40	32	.556	—	35,150	Mitch Zwolensky
Minneapolis Loons	39	33	.542	1	24,601	Greg Olson
Marshall Mallards	26	44	.371	13	6,483	Mike Taylor
West Standings	**W**	**L**	**Pct.**	**GB**	**Attend.**	**Manager**
Regina Cyclones	44	25	.638	—	48,892	Jason Felice
Saskatoon Riot	32	38	.457	12½	47,544	Ron Malcolm
Huron Heaters...................	30	39	.435	14	13,648	Glenn Gulliver

Playoff: Brainerd 3 games, Regina 2.

BA: Jason Felice, Regina, .343
Runs: Dennis Hood, Regina, 69
    Tommy Griffith, Regina, 69
Hits: Dennis Hood, Regina, 93
RBIs: Jason Felice, Regina, 73
HRs: Jason Felice, Regina, 17
Wins: Russ Fandell, Minneapolis, 11
SOs: Jim Campbell, Saskatoon, 102
ERA: Linc Mikkelsen, Brainerd, 1.22
Saves: Juan Berenguer, Minneapolis, 21

Ind Northern League
President: Miles Wolff

Standings	W	L	Pct.	GB	Attend.	Manager
Sioux City Explorers*	52	28	.650	—	140,224	Ed Nottle
Sioux Falls Canaries	47	33	.586	5	99,752	Frank Verdi/Harry Stavrenos
St. Paul Saints	43	36	.544	8½	241,069	Tim Blackwell
Winnipeg Goldeyes**	43	37	.538	9	212,571	Doug Simunic
Thunder Bay Whiskey Jacks.	35	45	.438	17	133,081	Dan Shwam
Duluth-Superior Dukes.......	19	60	.241	32½	84,234	Howie Bedell

Playoff: Winnipeg 3 games, Sioux City 1.

All-Star Team: 1B-Rob Leary, Sioux City; **2B**-Lance Robbins, Sioux City; **3B**-Vince Castaldo, St. Paul; **SS**-Mike Hankins, Winnipeg; **OF**-Ben Castillo, St. Paul; Steve Dailey, Duluth-Superior/Winnipeg; Chris Powell, Sioux Falls; **C**-Carl Nichols, Sioux Falls; **DH**-Pedro Guerrero, Sioux Falls; **P**-Mike Lewis, St. Paul; Rod Steph, Thunder Bay; Rob Andrakin, Sioux Falls; **MVP**-Vince Castaldo, St. Paul; **Manager**-Ed Nottle, Sioux City.

BA: Chris Powell, Sioux Falls, .357
Runs: Lance Robbins, Sioux City, 61
Hits: Lance Robbins, Sioux City, 112
RBIs: Carl Nichols, Sioux Falls, 70
HRs: Pete Kuld, Thunder Bay, 27
Wins: Jamie Ybarra, Sioux Falls, 11
SOs: Jamie Ybarra, Sioux Falls, 109
ERA: Rob Andrakin, Sioux Falls, 1.12

Ind Texas-Louisiana League
President: Byron Pierce

East Standings	W	L	Pct.	GB	Attend.	Manager
Alexandria Aces***	53	35	.602	—	71,744	Pete Falcone
Tyler Wildcatters	42	46	.477	11	55,914	Bill Stein
Beaumont Bullfrogs	40	48	.455	13	31,997	Charley Kerfeld
Mobile Baysharks	34	54	.386	19	125,856	Ed Jurak

West Standings	W	L	Pct.	GB	Attend.	Manager
Corpus Christi Barracudas***	58	30	.659	—	92,068	Mark Wasinger
Amarillo Dillas	48	40	.545	10	134,539	Ross Grimsley
Rio Grande Valley WhiteWings#	40	48	.455	18	65,832	Alan Ashby
San Antonio Tejanos	37	51	.420	21	25,204	Jose Cruz

#represented Harlingen, Texas.

Playoff: Corpus Christi 4 games, Alexandria 1.

All-Star Team: 1B-John O'Brien, Rio Grande Valley; 2B-Marvin Cole, Alexandria; 3B-Mike Fernandez, Amarillo; SS-Gary Hagy, Corpus Christi; OF-Jay Andrews, Alexandria; Clay Gould, Tyler; Ron Reams, Corpus Christi; C-Paul Williams, Alexandria; DH-Steve DeAngelis, Corpus Christi; P-Alan Newman, Alexandria; Jason Pfaff, San Antonio; Ruben Felix, Corpus Christi.

BA: Mike Fernandez, Amarillo, .362
Runs: Vince Harris, Beaumont, 81
Hits: Kyle Shade, Alexandria, 119
RBIs: Ron Reams, Corpus Christi, 82
HRs: Steve DeAngelis, Corpus Christi, 23

Wins: Tony Mack, Corpus Christi, 14
SOs: Carlos Castillo, Alexandria, 140
ERA: Jason Pfaff, San Antonio, 2.69
Pct: Tony Mack, Corpus Christi, .824, 14-3
Saves: Ruben Felix, Corpus Christi, 14

1994 Major League Farm Systems

American League

1 Baltimore (6): Rochester, Bowie, Frederick, Albany (GA), Bluefield, Gulf Coast.
2 Boston (6): Pawtucket, New Britain, Lynchburg, Sarasota, Utica, Gulf Coast.
3 California (6): Vancouver, Midland, Lake Elsinore, Cedar Rapids, Boise, Arizona.
4 Chicago (6): Nashville, Birmingham, Prince William, South Bend, Hickory, Gulf Coast.
5 Cleveland (6): Charlotte, Canton-Akron, Kinston, Columbus (GA), Watertown, Burlington (NC).
6 Detroit (6): Toledo, Trenton, Lakeland, Fayetteville, Jamestown, Bristol.
7 Kansas City (6): Omaha, Memphis, Wilmington, Rockford, Eugene, Gulf Coast.
8 Milwaukee (6): New Orleans, El Paso, Stockton, Beloit, Helena, Arizona.
9 Minnesota (6): Salt Lake City, Nashville, Ft. Myers, Fort Wayne, Elizabethton, Gulf Coast.
10 New York (6): Columbus (OH), Albany-Colonie, Tampa, Greensboro, Oneonta, Gulf Coast.
11 Oakland (6): Tacoma, Huntsville, Modesto, West Michigan, Southern Oregon, Arizona.
12 Seattle (6): Calgary, Jacksonville, Riverside, Appleton, Bellingham, Arizona.
13 Texas (6): Oklahoma City, Tulsa, Port Charlotte, Charleston (SC), Hudson Valley, Gulf Coast.
14 Toronto (7): Syracuse, Knoxville, Dunedin, Hagerstown, St. Catharines, Medicine Hat, Gulf Coast.

National League

15 Atlanta (7): Richmond, Greenville, Durham, Macon, Danville, Idaho Falls, Gulf Coast.
16 Chicago (7): Iowa, Orlando, Daytona, Peoria, Williamsport, Huntington, Gulf Coast.
17 Cincinnati (6): Indianapolis, Chattanooga, Winston-Salem, Charleston (WV), Princeton, Billings.
18 Colorado (6): Colorado Springs, New Haven, Central Valley, Asheville, Bend, Arizona.
19 Florida (6): Edmonton, Portland, Brevard County, Kane County, Elmira, Gulf Coast.
20 Houston (6): Tucson, Jackson, Osceola, Quad City, Auburn, Gulf Coast.
21 Los Angeles (6): Albuquerque, San Antonio, Bakersfield, Vero Beach, Yakima, Great Falls.
22 Montreal (6): Ottawa, Harrisburg, West Palm Beach, Burlington (IA), Vermont, Gulf Coast.
23 New York (7): Norfolk, Binghamton, St. Lucie, Capital City, Pittsfield, Kingsport, Gulf Coast.
24 Philadelphia (6): Scranton-Wilkes-Barre, Reading, Clearwater, Spartanburg, Batavia, Martinsville.
25 Pittsburgh (6): Buffalo, Carolina, Salem, Augusta, Welland, Gulf Coast.
26 St. Louis (8): Louisville, Arkansas, St. Petersburg, Madison, Savannah, New Jersey, Johnson City, Arizona.
27 San Diego (6): Las Vegas, Wichita, Rancho Cucamonga, Springfield, Spokane, Arizona.
28 San Francisco (6): Phoenix, Shreveport, San Jose, Clinton, Everett, Arizona.

Co-op (x): San Bernardino, High Desert, Butte, Lethbridge.
Independent: Ogden.

1994 No-Hitters

Date	Pitcher	Team	League	Opponent	Score
4-8	Kent Mercker	Atlanta	National	Los Angeles	6-0
4-10	Rigo Beltran	Arkansas	Texas	Shreveport	2-0
4-10	Kevin Gallaher/ Jimmy Daspit	Jackson	Texas	Tulsa	3-0 (7)
4-14	Kris Hanson/ Cesar Ramos	Columbus	South Atlantic	Macon	6-1
4-27	Scott Erickson	Minnesota	American	Milwaukee	6-0
5-4	Felipe Lira	Toledo	International	Columbus	4-0 (7)
5-16	Mark Petkovsek	Tucson	Pacific Coast	Colorado Springs	5-0
5-17	Inigo Montano	Monclova	Mexican	Industriales	3-0
5-28	Shad Williams	Midland	Texas	Arkansas	7-0 (7)
6-22	Mercedes Esquer	Yucatan	Mexican	Saltillo	3-1
6-26	Damian Moss	Danville	Appalachian	Bluefield	6-0
6-28	Brett Hinchliffe	Appleton	Midwest	Cedar Rapids	13-0
7-4	Kym Ashworth	Bakersfield	California	San Jose	6-0
7-16	Oscar Rojo/Juan Tejeda/Mike Browning/ Herminio Dominguez	Campeche	Mexican	Yucatan	3-2
7-28	Kenny Rogers	Texas	American	California	4-0 (P)
7-30	Rick Forney	Bowie	Eastern	Trenton	8-0 (7)
8-1	Jason Robbins	Billings	Pioneer	Medicine Hat	5-0 (P)
8-1	Jerry Martin/ Luis Garcia	Charlotte	Florida State	Clearwater	4-0
8-3	James Brower	Charleston (SC)	South Atlantic	Columbus	3-0
8-4	Dave Hutcheson	Daytona Beach	Florida State	St. Petersburg	8-0
8-5	Mark Sievert	St. Catharines	New York-Penn.	Utica	2-0 (7)
8-7	Glendon Rusch	Rockford	Midwest	Kane County	9-0
8-12	Scott Taylor	New Orleans	American Assoc.	Buffalo	6-0
8-12	Derrin Ebert	Braves	Gulf Coast	Marlins	6-0 (7)
8-17	Jose Lima	Toledo	International	Pawtucket	3-0
8-19	Carlos Chavez	Bluefield	Appalachian	Bristol	6-0
8-19	Niuman Loiz	Astros	Gulf Coast	Cubs	2-0 (7)
9-13	Bill Pulsipher	Binghamton	Eastern	Harrisburg	2-0 (PO)

Number in parentheses indicates innings if other than nine; "P" indicates perfect game; "PO" indicates playoff game.

THIS DATE IN MINOR LEAGUE HISTORY

February 12, 1994, Hall of Famer Ray Dandridge died at age 79. A veteran of the minor leagues, Negro Leagues, and Latin American leagues, he was widely regarded as the best third baseman never to play in the majors.

April 7, 1994, The Southern League's Birmingham Barons opened their season with basketball star-turned-outfielder Michael Jordan on their roster. Jordan, who had not played since high school, would hit .202 on the season, after which he returned to basketball. Predictably, the league was swamped by fan and media interest throughout the season.

April 8, 1994, Springfield began its Midwest League season just two weeks after relocating from Waterloo. The Iowa city, which had hosted pro ball for 90 seasons, had to move when it could not secure a stadium lease. Springfield wore San Diego Padres uniforms on the road until they opened at home on April 19.

April 23, 1994, The Colorado Silver Bullets women's professional team played its first game against a National Association team, a 2-0, three inning loss at Memphis.

April 26, 1994, New Orleans righthander Mike Ignasiak's scoreless innings streak was snapped at 53-2/3 frames. He had last allowed a run on May 8, 1993.

June 12-13, 1994, The Texas League and Mexican League renewed their all-star series for the first time since 1961. In Monterrey, The Mexican Leaguers won the first game 4-3. The next night, in San Antonio, the Texas League stars won 5-1.

July 18, 1994, Rockford of the Midwest League began a 15-game winning streak, the longest in pro ball in 1994.

September 4, 1994, Lakeland ended its Florida State League season with 17 of 70 scheduled home dates lost to rainouts.

September 5, 1994, The Salt Lake Buzz completed its first season in the Pacific Coast League with attendance of 713,224, a new league record. The prior mark of 670,563 was set by the San Francisco Seals in 1946.

1995

American League
President: Gene Budig

East Standings	W	L	Pct.	GB	Attend.	Manager
Boston Red Sox	86	58	.597	—	2,164,378	Kevin Kennedy
New York Yankees#	79	65	.549	7	1,705,257	Buck Showalter
Baltimore Orioles	71	73	.493	15	3,098,475	Phil Regan
Detroit Tigers	60	84	.417	26	1,180,979	Sparky Anderson
Toronto Blue Jays	56	88	.389	30	2,826,483	Cito Gaston

Central Standings	W	L	Pct.	GB	Attend.	Manager
Cleveland Indians	100	44	.694	—	2,842,725	Mike Hargrove
Kansas City Royals	70	74	.486	30	1,232,969	Bob Boone
Chicago White Sox	68	76	.472	32	1,609,773	Gene Lamont/Terry Bevington
Milwaukee Brewers	65	79	.451	35	1,087,560	Phil Garner
Minnesota Twins	56	88	.389	44	1,057,667	Tom Kelly

West Standings	W	L	Pct.	GB	Attend.	Manager
Seattle Mariners	79	66	.545	—	1,640,992	Lou Piniella
California Angels	78	67	.538	1	1,748,680	Marcel Lachemann
Texas Rangers	74	70	.514	5½	1,985,910	Johnny Oates
Oakland Athletics	67	77	.465	11½	1,174,310	Tony LaRussa

#wild card representative.

Playoffs: Seattle defeated California in a one game playoff for the West Division title. Seattle 3 games, New York 2; Cleveland 3 games, Boston 0.
Finals: Cleveland 4 games, Seattle 2.

BA: Edgar Martinez, Seattle, .356
Runs: Edgar Martinez, Seattle, 121
Albert Belle, Cleveland, 121
Hits: Lance Johnson, Chicago, 186
RBIs: Albert Belle, Cleveland, 126
Mo Vaughn, Boston, 126

HRs: Albert Belle, Cleveland, 50
Wins: Mike Mussina, Baltimore, 19
SOs: Randy Johnson, Seattle, 294
ERA: Randy Johnson, Seattle, 2.48
Pct: Randy Johnson, Seattle, .900, 18-2
Saves: Jose Mesa, Cleveland, 46

National League
President: Leonard Coleman

East Standings	W	L	Pct.	GB	Attend.	Manager
Atlanta Braves	90	54	.625	—	2,561,831	Bobby Cox
New York Mets	69	75	.479	21	1,254,307	Dallas Green
Philadelphia Phillies	69	75	.479	21	2,043,588	Jim Fregosi
Florida Marlins	67	76	.468	22½	1,670,255	Rene Lachemann
Montreal Expos	66	78	.458	24	1,292,764	Felipe Alou

Central Standings	W	L	Pct.	GB	Attend.	Manager
Cincinnati Reds	85	59	.590	—	1,843,649	Davey Johnson
Houston Astros	76	68	.527	9	1,363,801	Terry Collins
Chicago Cubs	73	71	.507	12	1,893,925	Jim Riggleman
St. Louis Cardinals	62	81	.434	22½	1,727,536	Joe Torre/Mike Jorgensen
Pittsburgh Pirates	58	86	.403	27	905,517	Jim Leyland

West Standings	W	L	Pct.	GB	Attend.	Manager
Los Angeles Dodgers	78	66	.542	—	2,766,251	Tom Lasorda
Colorado Rockies#	77	67	.535	1	3,341,998	Don Baylor
San Diego Padres	70	74	.486	8	1,019,728	Bruce Bochy
San Francisco Giants	67	77	.465	11	1,241,497	Dusty Baker

#wild card representative.

Playoffs: Atlanta 3 games, Colorado 1; Cincinnati 3 games, Los Angeles 0.
Finals: Atlanta 4 games, Cincinnati 0.

BA: Tony Gwynn, San Diego, .368
Runs: Craig Biggio, Houston, 123
Hits: Tony Gwynn, San Diego, 197
Dante Bichette, Colorado, 197
RBIs: Dante Bichette, Colorado, 128
HRs: Dante Bichette, Colorado, 40

Wins: Greg Maddux, Atlanta, 19
SOs: Hideo Nomo, Los Angeles, 236
ERA: Greg Maddux, Atlanta, 1.63
Pct: Greg Maddux, Atlanta, .905, 19-2
Saves: Randy Myers, Chicago, 36
Tom Henke, St. Louis, 36

AAA American Association
President: Branch B. Rickey

Standings	W	L	Pct.	GB	Attend.	Manager
Indianapolis Indians (17)	88	56	.611	—	366,254	Marc Bombard
Buffalo Bisons (5)	82	62	.569	6	900,782	Brian Graham
Omaha Royals (7)	76	68	.528	12	404,156	Mike Jirschele
Louisville Redbirds (26)	74	70	.514	14	556,211	Joe Pettini
Iowa Cubs (16)	69	74	.483	18½	466,320	Ron Clark
Nashville Sounds (4)	68	76	.472	20	355,133	Rick Renick
New Orleans Zephyrs (8)	63	79	.444	24	143,728	Chris Bando
Oklahoma City 89ers (13)	54	89	.378	33½	259,518	Greg Biagini

Playoffs: Louisville 3 games, Indianapolis 0; Buffalo 3 games, Omaha 1.
Finals: Louisville 3 games, Buffalo 2.

All-Star Team: 1B-Jeff Grotewold, Omaha; 2B-Eric Owens, Indianapolis; 3B-Tracy Woodson, Louisville; SS-Mark Loretta, New Orleans; OF-Steve Gibralter, Indianapolis; Brian Giles, Buffalo; Brooks Kieschnick, Iowa; C-John Marzano, Oklahoma City; DH-Drew Denson, Indianapolis; P-Joe Roa, Buffalo; Eric Bell, Buffalo; Cory Bailey, Louisville; MVP-Eric Owens, Indianapolis; Manager-Marc Bombard, Indianapolis.

BA: Michael Carter, Iowa, .325
Runs: Eric Owens, Indianapolis, 86
Hits: Brooks Kieschnick, Iowa, 149
RBIs: Jeromy Burnitz, Buffalo, 85

HRs: Brooks Kieschnick, Iowa, 23
Wins: Joe Roa, Buffalo, 17
SOs: Paul Abbott, Iowa, 127
ERA: Rod Bolton, Nashville, 2.88

AAA International League
President: Randy Mobley

East Standings	W	L	Pct.	GB	Attend.	Manager
Rochester Red Wings (1)	73	69	.514	—	394,035	Marv Foley
Ottawa Lynx (22)	72	70	.507	1	482,144	Pete Mackanin
Pawtucket Red Sox (2)	70	71	.496	2½	479,126	Buddy Bailey
Scranton-Wilkes-Barre Red Barons (24)	70	72	.493	3	479,030	Mike Quade
Syracuse Chiefs (14)	59	82	.418	13½	303,208	Bob Didier/Richie Hebner

West Standings	W	L	Pct.	GB	Attend.	Manager
Norfolk Tides (23)	86	56	.606	—	560,211	Toby Harrah
Richmond Braves (15)	75	66	.532	10½	510,118	Grady Little
Columbus Clippers (10)	71	68	.511	13½	541,451	Bill Evers
Toledo Mud Hens (6)	71	71	.500	15	297,672	Tom Runnells
Charlotte Knights (19)	59	81	.421	26	330,496	Sal Rende

Playoffs: Norfolk 3 games, Richmond 2; Ottawa 3 games, Rochester 2.
Finals: Ottawa 3 games, Norfolk 1.

All-Star Team: 1B-Don Sparks, Columbus; 2B-Kevin Jordan, Scranton-Wilkes-Barre; 3B-Butch Huskey, Norfolk; SS-Derek Jeter, Columbus; OF-Robert Perez, Syracuse; Alex Ochoa, Rochester/Norfolk; Mark Smith, Rochester; C-Jorge Posada, Columbus; DH-Carlos Delgado, Syracuse; P-Jason Isringhausen, Norfolk; Rod Nichols, Richmond; MVP-Butch Huskey, Norfolk; Pitcher of the Year-Jason Isringhausen, Norfolk; Manager-Toby Harrah, Norfolk.

BA: Robert Perez, Syracuse, .343
Runs: Derek Jeter, Columbus, 96
Hits: Robert Perez, Syracuse, 172
RBIs: Don Sparks, Columbus, 90
HRs: Butch Huskey, Norfolk, 28

Wins: Jimmy Haynes, Rochester, 12
Jimmy Williams, Norfolk/Rochester, 12
SOs: Jimmy Haynes, Rochester, 140
ERA: Jason Schmidt, Richmond, 2.25

AAA Mexican League
President: Pedro Treto Cisneros

North Standings	W	L	Pct.	GB	Attend.	Manager
Reynosa Broncos***	73	40	.646	—	190,022	Aurelio Rodriguez
Monterrey Sultanes	65	49	.570	8½	156,145	Joel Serna/Derek Bryant
Saltillo Saraperos	63	53	.543	11½	127,933	Roberto Castellon
Nuevo Laredo Tecolotes	62	54	.534	12½	135,330	Andres Mora
Aguascalientes Rieleros	57	55	.509	15½	137,124	Jose Guerrero
Union Laguna Algodoneros	56	57	.496	17	110,568	Francisco Galindo/Herminio Saiz
Monclova Acereros	46	69	.400	28	164,962	Gerardo Gutierrez/Ramon Montoya
Jalisco Charros	30	82	.268	42½	109,455	Fernando Villaescusa/Francisco Garcia/Domingo Rivera

South Standings	W	L	Pct.	GB	Attend.	Manager
Mexico City Diablos Rojos***	80	33	.708	—	223,387	Marco Antonio Vazquez
Tabasco Olmecas	61	50	.550	18	152,567	Bernardo Calvo/Alexis Infante
Mexico City Tigres	62	54	.534	19½	229,732	Dan Firova/Jorge Calvo
Campeche Piratas	60	54	.526	20½	110,951	Javier Martinez/Leonel Carreon
Yucatan Leones	59	55	.518	21½	261,179	Carlos Paz/Roberto Perez
Puebla Pericos	52	63	.452	29	104,572	Francisco Estrada
Veracruz Aguila	45	71	.388	36½	100,287	Raul Cano
Minatitlan Petroleros	41	73	.360	39½	102,982	Ruben Amaro/Francisco Chavez

Playoffs: Reynosa 4 games, Nuevo Laredo 3; Monterrey 4 games, Saltillo 1; MC Diablos Rojos 4 games, Campeche 2; MC Tigres 4 games, Tabasco 1. Monterrey 4 games, Reynosa 2; MC Diablos Rojos 4 games, MC Tigres 2.
Finals: Monterrey 4 games, MC Diablos Rojos 0.

BA: Ty Gainey, MC Diablos Rojos, .411
Runs: Javier Robles, MC Tigres, 93
Hits: Alonso Tellez, Reynosa, 144
RBIs: Ty Gainey, MC Diablos Rojos, 115

HRs: Ty Gainey, MC Diablos Rojos, 27
Wins: Angel Moreno, Nuevo Laredo, 16
SOs: Angel Moreno, Nuevo Laredo, 108
ERA: Cecilio Ruiz, Tabasco, 1.71

*Won first-half   **Won second-half   ***Won both halves
Numbers after nicknames indicate farm system.
Affiliation listed at end of each year.

AAA Pacific Coast League
President: Bill Cutler

North Standings	W	L	Pct.	GB	Attend.	Manager
Vancouver Canadians*(3)	81	60	.574	—	305,739	Don Long
Salt Lake Buzz**(9)	79	65	.549	3½	637,332	Phil Roof
Edmonton Trappers (11)	68	76	.472	14½	426,012	Gary Jones
Tacoma Rainiers (12)	68	76	.472	14½	316,103	Steve Smith
Calgary Cannons (25)	58	83	.411	23	279,054	Bobby Meacham

South Standings	W	L	Pct.	GB	Attend.	Manager
Tucson Toros**(20)	87	56	.608	—	301,963	Rick Sweet
Colorado Springs Sky Sox*(18)	77	66	.538	10	195,375	Brad Mills
Albuquerque Dukes (21)	75	69	.521	12½	340,050	Rick Dempsey
Phoenix Firebirds (28)	62	82	.431	25½	282,370	Keith Bodie/Jim Davenport
Las Vegas Stars (27)	61	83	.424	26½	330,869	Tim Flannery

Playoffs: Salt Lake 3 games, Vancouver 1; Colorado Springs 3 games, Tucson 1.
Finals: Colorado Springs 3 games, Salt Lake 2.

All-Star Team: 1B-Mike Busch, Albuquerque; **2B**-Dave Hajek, Tucson; **3B**-Ron Coomer, Albuquerque; **SS**-Fausto Cruz, Edmonton; **OF**-Karim Garcia, Albuquerque; Trinidad Hubbard, Colorado Springs; Riccardo Ingram, Salt Lake; **C**-George Williams, Edmonton; **DH**-Harvey Pulliam, Colorado Springs; **P**-Donne Wall, Tucson; Glenn Dishman, Las Vegas; Scott Watkins, Salt Lake; **MVP**-Donne Wall, Tucson; **Manager**-Don Long, Vancouver.

BA: Riccardo Ingram, Salt Lake, .348
Runs: Trenidad Hubbard, Colorado Springs, 102
Hits: Riccardo Ingram, Salt Lake, 166
RBIs: Harvey Pulliam, Colorado Springs, 91

HRs: Harvey Pulliam, Colorado Springs, 25
Wins: Donne Wall, Tucson, 17
SOs: Donne Wall, Tucson, 119
ERA: Donne Wall, Tucson, 3.30

AA Eastern League
President: John Levenda

North Standings	W	L	Pct.	GB	Attend.	Manager
Portland Sea Dogs (19)	86	56	.606	—	429,763	Carlos Tosca
New Haven Ravens (18)	79	63	.556	7	283,766	Paul Zuvella
Norwich Navigators (10)	70	71	.496	15½	281,473	Jimmy Johnson
Binghamton Mets (23)	67	75	.472	19	200,077	John Tamargo
Hardware City Rock Cats#(9)	65	77	.458	21	124,560	Sal Butera

South Standings	W	L	Pct.	GB	Attend.	Manager
Reading Phillies (24)	73	69	.514	—	383,984	Bill Dancy
Trenton Thunder (2)	73	69	.514	—	453,915	Ken Macha
Bowie Baysox (1)	68	74	.479	5	463,976	Bob Miscik
Canton-Akron Indians (5)	67	75	.472	6	195,049	Ted Kubiak
Harrisburg Senators (22)	61	80	.433	11½	240,488	Pat Kelly

#represented New Britain, Connecticut.

Playoffs: New Haven 3 games, Portland 1; Reading 3 games, Trenton 0.
Finals: Reading 3 games, New Haven 2.

All-Star Team: 1B-David Kennedy, New Haven; **2B**-Todd Walker, Hardware City; **3B**-Rob Grable, Reading; **SS**-Nomar Garciaparra, Trenton; **OF**-Angel Echevarria, New Haven; Billy McMillon, Portland; Jay Payton, Binghamton; **C**-Mike Figga, Norwich; **DH**-Clyde "Pork Chop" Pough, Trenton; **P**-Eric Ludwick, Binghamton; Jay Powell, Portland; Dan Serafini, Hardware City; Paul Wilson, Binghamton; **MVP**-Jay Payton, Binghamton; **Pitcher of the Year**-Paul Wilson, Binghamton; **Manager**-Bill Dancy, Reading.

BA: Jay Payton, Binghamton, .345
Runs: Ralph Milliard, Portland, 104
Hits: Billy McMillon, Portland, 162
RBIs: Angel Echevarria, New Haven, 100

HRs: Fred McNair, Reading, 23
Wins: Joel Moore, New Haven, 14
SOs: Rafael Orellano, Trenton, 160
ERA: Paul Wilson, Binghamton, 2.17

AA Southern League
President: Arnold Fielkow

East Standings	W	L	Pct.	GB	Attend.	Manager
Carolina Mudcats***(25)	89	55	.618	—	317,802	Trent Jewett
Orlando Suns (16)	76	67	.531	12½	191,080	Bruce Kimm
Jacksonville Suns (6)	75	69	.521	14	237,433	Bill Plummer
Port City Roosters#(12)	62	80	.437	26	110,233	Dave Myers
Greenville Braves (15)	59	83	.415	29	223,225	Bruce Benedict

West Standings	W	L	Pct.	GB	Attend.	Manager
Chattanooga Lookouts**(17)	83	60	.580	—	290,002	Dave Miley
Birmingham Barons (4)	80	64	.556	3½	303,066	Terry Francona
Huntsville Stars (11)	70	74	.486	13½	243,179	Dick Scott
Memphis Chicks*(27)	68	74	.479	14½	221,302	Jerry Royster
Knoxville Smokies (14)	54	90	.375	29½	123,428	Garth Iorg

#represented Wilmington, North Carolina.

Playoffs: Carolina 3 games, Orlando 2; Chattanooga 3 games, Memphis 2.
Finals: Carolina 3 games, Chattanooga 2.

All-Star Team: 1B-James Bonnici, Port City; **2B**-Brian Koelling, Chattanooga; **3B**-Scott Spiezio, Huntsville; **SS**-Desi Relaford, Port City; **OF**-Jermaine Dye, Greenville; Robin Jennings, Orlando; Charles Poe, Birmingham; Pedro Valdes, Orlando; **C**-Jason Kendall, Carolina; **DH**-Ivan Cruz, Jacksonville; **P**-Luis Andujar, Birmingham; Elmer Dessens, Carolina; Matt Ruebel, Carolina; **MVP**-Jason Kendall, Carolina; **Manager**-Bruce Kimm, Orlando.

BA: Kevin Coughlin, Birmingham, .385
Runs: Essex Burton, Birmingham, 95
Hits: Ruben Santana, Chattanooga, 163
RBIs: George Canale, Carolina, 102

HRs: Ivan Cruz, Jacksonville, 31
Wins: Elmer Dessens, Carolina, 15
SOs: Osvaldo Fernandez, Port City, 160
ERA: Elmer Dessens, Carolina, 2.49

AA Texas League
President: Tom Kayser

East Standings	W	L	Pct.	GB	Attend.	Manager
Shreveport Captains***(28)	88	47	.652	—	173,996	Ron Wotus
Arkansas Travelers (26)	70	65	.519	18	248,340	Mike Ramsey
Jackson Generals (20)	62	73	.459	26	171,508	Tim Tolman
Tulsa Drillers (13)	52	83	.385	36	321,662	Bobby Jones

West Standings	W	L	Pct.	GB	Attend.	Manager
Wichita Wranglers**(7)	72	64	.603	—	203,134	Ron Johnson
El Paso Diablos (8)	68	68	.500	4	329,233	Tim Ireland
Midland Angels*(3)	66	70	.485	6	202,830	Mario Mendoza
San Antonio Missions (21)	64	72	.471	8	387,090	John Shelby

Playoff: Midland 3 games, Wichita 2.
Finals: Shreveport 4 games, Midland 1.

All-Star Team: 1B-Todd Landry, El Paso; **2B**-Jeff Berblinger, Arkansas; **3B**-George Arias, Midland; **SS**-Wilton Guerrero, San Antonio; **OF**-Brian Banks, El Paso; Jacob Cruz, Shreveport; Johnny Damon, Wichita; **C**-Todd Greene, Midland; **DH**-Oreste Marrero, San Antonio; **P**-Steve Bourgeois, Shreveport; Edwin Corps, Shreveport; Steve Montgomery, Arkansas; David Pyc, San Antonio; Gary Rath, San Antonio; Billy Wagner, Jackson; **MVP**-Johnny Damon, Wichita; **Pitcher of the Year**-Steve Bourgeois, Shreveport; **Manager**-Ron Johnson, Wichita.

BA: Wilton Guerrero, San Antonio, .348
Runs: George Arias, Midland, 91
Hits: Rod Myers, Wichita, 153
RBIs: George Arias, Midland, 104
HRs: George Arias, Midland, 30

Wins: Gary Rath, San Antonio, 13
Edwin Corps, Shreveport, 13
SOs: Frankie Rodriguez, El Paso, 129
ERA: Gary Rath, San Antonio, 2.77

A California League
President: Joe Gagliardi

North Standings	W	L	Pct.	GB	Attend.	Manager
Modesto A's*(11)	78	62	.557	—	100,108	Glenn Ezell
San Jose Giants**(28)	77	63	.550	1	140,976	Carlos Lezcano
Stockton Ports (8)	74	65	.532	3½	107,140	Bob Mariano
Bakersfield Dodgers (x)	58	82	.414	20	105,890	Greg Mahlberg
Visalia Oaks (x)	58	82	.414	20	71,513	Lyle Yates

South Standings	W	L	Pct.	GB	Attend.	Manager
San Bernardino Spirit*(21)	84	54	.609	—	119,463	Ron Roenicke
Lake Elsinore Storm**(3)	81	57	.587	3	383,297	Mitch Seoane
Riverside Pilots (12)	72	67	.518	12½	56,601	Dave Brundage
Rancho Cucamonga Quakes (27)	68	70	.493	16	446,146	Marty Barrett
High Desert Mavericks (1)	46	94	.329	39	146,355	Tim Blackwell

Playoffs: San Jose 2 games, Stockton 0; Lake Elsinore 2 games, Riverside 1; San Jose 3 games, Modesto 0; San Bernardino 3 games, Lake Elsinore 0.
Finals: San Bernardino 3 games, San Jose 0.

All-Star Team: 1B-Steve Cox, Modesto; **2B**-Adam Riggs, San Bernardino; **3B**-Rick Ladjevich, Riverside; **SS**-Greg LaRocca, Rancho Cucamonga; **OF**-Alex Ramirez, Bakersfield; Armando Rios, San Jose; Greg Shockey, Lake Elsinore; **C**-Raul Ibanez, Riverside; **DH**-Rod McCall, Bakersfield; **P**-Matt Beaumont, Lake Elsinore; Carlos Castillo, Lake Elsinore; Keith Foulke, San Jose; Doug Webb, Stockton; **MVP**-Adam Riggs, San Bernardino; **Manager**-Ron Roenicke, San Bernardino.

BA: Adam Riggs, San Bernardino, .362
Runs: Adam Riggs, San Bernardino, 111
Hits: Adam Riggs, San Bernardino, 196
RBIs: Steve Cox, Modesto, 110

HRs: Steve Cox, Modesto, 30
Wins: Matt Beaumont, Lake Elsinore, 16
SOs: Masataka Endo, Visalia, 178
ERA: Tom Price, San Bernardino, 2.20

A Carolina League
President: John Hopkins

North Standings	W	L	Pct.	GB	Attend.	Manager
Wilmington Blue Rocks**(7)	83	55	.601	—	358,766	John Mizerock
Lynchburg Hillcats (25)	67	71	.486	16	111,654	Marc Hill
Prince William Cannons*(4)	64	76	.457	20	215,250	Dave Huppert
Frederick Keys (1)	58	79	.449	24½	300,968	Mike O'Berry

South Standings	W	L	Pct.	GB	Attend.	Manager
Kinston Indians***(5)	81	56	.591	—	140,116	Gordy MacKenzie
Winston-Salem Warthogs (17)	69	68	.504	12	158,842	Mark Berry
Salem Avalanche (18)	68	72	.486	14½	140,111	Bill Hayes
Durham Bulls (15)	63	76	.453	19	390,486	Matt West

Playoff: Wilmington 2 games, Prince William 0.
Finals: Kinston 3 games, Wilmington 0.

All-Star Team: 1B-Richie Sexson, Kinston; **2B**-Ricky Gutierrez, Kinston; **3B**-Aaron Boone, Winston-Salem; **SS**-Enrique Wilson, Kinston; **OF**-Jim Betzsold, Kinston; Charles Peterson, Lynchburg; Edgard Velasquez, Salem; **C**-Mike Sweeney, Wilmington; **DH**-Reed Secrist, Lynchburg; **Util**-Anthony Medrano, Wilmington; **P**-Bartolo Colon, Kinston; Danny Graves, Kinston; **MVP**-Richie Sexson, Kinston; **Pitcher of the Year**-Bartolo Colon, Kinston; **Manager**-John Mizerock, Wilmington.

BA: Mike Sweeney, Wilmington, .310
Runs: Chris Sexton, Winston-Salem/Salem, 84
Hits: Richie Sexson, Kinston, 151
RBIs: Richie Sexson, Kinston, 85

HRs: Juan Thomas, Prince William, 26
Wins: Glendon Rusch, Wilmington, 14
SOs: Bartolo Colon, Kinston, 152
ERA: Glendon Rusch, Wilmington, 1.74

A Florida State League
President: Chuck Murphy

East Standings	W	L	Pct.	GB	Attend.	Manager
Daytona Cubs***(16)	87	48	.644	—	90,071	Dave Trembley
Vero Beach Dodgers (21)	74	59	.556	12	42,702	Jon Debus
St. Lucie Mets (23)	61	73	.455	25½	80,734	Rafael Landestoy
Brevard County Manatees (19)	61	74	.452	26	140,109	Fredi Gonzalez
Kissimmee Cobras (20)	55	81	.404	32½	41,091	Dave Engle
West Palm Beach Expos (22)	54	81	.400	33	71,446	Gomer Hodge/Rick Sofield

West Standings	W	L	Pct.	GB	Attend.	Manager
Ft. Myers Miracle**(9)	75	55	.577	—	78,431	Al Newman
Clearwater Phillies (24)	79	59	.572	—	71,761	Don McCormack
Tampa Yankees*(10)	72	64	.529	6	48,958	Jake Gibbs
Charlotte Rangers (13)	65	67	.492	11	60,000	Butch Wynegar
Sarasota Red Sox (2)	65	68	.489	11½	65,223	Tommy Barrett
St. Petersburg Cardinals (26)	64	67	.489	11½	100,035	Chris Maloney
Lakeland Tigers (6)	64	69	.481	12½	21,633	Dave Anderson
Dunedin Blue Jays (14)	63	74	.460	15½	65,764	Jim Nettles

Playoff: Ft. Myers 2 games, Tampa 1.
Finals: Daytona 3 games, Ft. Myers 2.

All-Star Team: 1B-Dan Held, Clearwater; **2B**-Bobby Morris, Daytona; **3B**-Gary Caraballo, Ft. Myers; **SS**-Jason Maxwell, Daytona; **OF**-Shane Spencer, Tampa; Wendell Magee, Clearwater; Scott Samuels, Daytona; **C**-Robert Estalella, Clearwater; **DH**-Bubba Trammell, Lakeland; **P**-Troy Carrasco, Ft. Myers; Benj Sampson, Ft. Myers; Shane Bowers, Ft. Myers; Matt Drews, Tampa; **MVP**-Shane Spencer, Tampa; **Manager**-Dave Trembley, Daytona.

BA: Wendell Magee, Clearwater, .353
Runs: Scott Samuels, Daytona, 92
Hits: Shane Spencer, Tampa, 150
RBIs: Shane Spencer, Tampa, 88

HRs: Dan Held, Clearwater, 21
Wins: Matt Drews, Tampa, 15
SOs: Kris Detmers, St. Petersburg, 150
ERA: Kevin Pincavitch, Vero Beach, 1.66

A Midwest League
President: George Spelius

East Standings	W	L	Pct.	GB	Attend.	Manager
Michigan Battle Cats#*(2)	75	62	.547	—	171,794	DeMarlo Hale
Fort Wayne Wizards**(9)	75	65	.536	1½	253,568	Dan Rohn
West Michigan Whitecaps (11)	67	69	.493	7½	507,989	Jim Colborn
South Bend Silver Hawks (4)	66	69	.489	8	225,999	Fred Kendall

Central Standings	W	L	Pct.	GB	Attend.	Manager
Beloit Snappers***(8)	88	51	.633	—	60,816	Dub Kilgo
Rockford Cubbies (16)	75	65	.536	13½	110,025	Steve Roadcap
Kane County Cougars (1)	69	69	.500	18½	477,550	Lynn Jones
Wisconsin Timber Rattlers@(12)	63	75	.457	24½	209,159	Mike Goff

West Standings	W	L	Pct.	GB	Attend.	Manager
Quad City River Bandits*(20)	76	61	.555	—	257,501	Jim Pankovits
Cedar Rapids Kernels**(3)	76	62	.551	½	135,840	Tom Lawless
Springfield Sultans (7)	65	74	.468	12	39,467	Brian Poldberg
Peoria Chiefs (26)	62	72	.463	12½	195,056	Roy Silver
Burlington Bees (28)	54	81	.400	21	69,412	Mike Hart
Clinton Lumber Kings (27)	51	86	.372	25	50,126	Ed Romero

#represented Battle Creek, Michigan.
@represented Appleton, Wisconsin.

Playoffs: Beloit 2 games, Rockford 0; Quad City 2 games, Cedar Rapids 1; Michigan 2 games, Fort Wayne 0; West Michigan 2 games, Kane County 1. Beloit 2 games, Quad City 1; Michigan 2 games, West Michigan 1.
Finals: Beloit 3 games, Michigan 0.

All-Star Team: 1B-Jesse Ibarra, Burlington; **2B**-Luis Castillo, Kane County; **3B**-Sean McNally, Springfield; **SS**-Donnie Sadler, Michigan; **OF**-Todd Dunwoody, Kane County; Ryan Jackson, Kane County; Demond Smith, Cedar Rapids/West Michigan; **C**-Jose Valentin, Fort Wayne; **DH**-Derek Hacopian, Beloit; **P**-Tony Mounce, Quad City; Jeff D'Amico, Beloit; Jeff Keith, Burlington; Travis Welch, Peoria; **MVP**-Jesse Ibarra, Burlington; **Manager**-DeMarlo Hale, Michigan.

BA: Demond Smith, Cedar Rapids/West Michigan, .338
Runs: Donnie Sadler, Michigan, 103
Hits: Nilson Robledo, South Bend, 153
RBIs: Nilson Robledo, South Bend, 108

HRs: Jesse Ibarra, Burlington, 34
Wins: Tony Mounce, Quad City, 16
SOs: Charles Smith, South Bend, 145
ERA: Cory Corrigan, Peoria, 2.32

A New York-Pennsylvania League
President: Robert Julian

McNamara Standings	W	L	Pct.	GB	Attend.	Manager
Vermont Expos (22)	49	27	.645	—	120,917	Jim Gabella
Hudson Valley Renegades (13)	47	27	.635	1	161,673	Bump Wills
New Jersey Cardinals (26)	35	41	.461	14	176,788	Luis Melendez
Pittsfield Mets (23)	34	42	.447	15	73,273	Ron Gideon

Pinckney Standings	W	L	Pct.	GB	Attend.	Manager
Watertown Indians (5)	46	27	.630	—	45,202	Joel Skinner
Auburn Astros (20)	40	34	.541	6½	58,972	Manny Acta

	W	L	Pct.	GB	Attend.	Manager
Williamsport Cubs (16)	37	39	.487	10½	63,192	Oneri Fleita
Oneonta Yankees (10)	34	41	.453	13	53,990	Rob Thomson
Utica Blue Sox (2)	33	40	.452	13	64,487	Bob Geren
Elmira Pioneers (19)	25	51	.329	22½	43,759	Paul Kirsch

Stedler Standings	W	L	Pct.	GB	Attend.	Manager
Batavia Clippers (24)	41	34	.547	—	38,313	Al LeBoeuf
St. Catharines Stompers (14)	38	37	.507	3	50,528	J.J. Cannon
Erie SeaWolves (25)	34	41	.453	7	181,815	Scott Little
Jamestown Jammers (6)	32	44	.421	9½	48,938	Bruce Fields

Playoffs: Watertown 2 games, Batavia 1; Vermont 2 games, Hudson Valley 0.
Finals: Watertown 2 games, Vermont 1.

All-Star Team: 1B-Steve Carver, Batavia; **2B**-Marlon Anderson, Batavia; **3B**-Cliff Brumbaugh, Hudson Valley; **SS**-Tim Giles, Auburn; **OF**-Ed Bady, Vermont; Fletcher Bates, Pittsfield; Jose Guillen, Erie; Luke Wilcox, Oneonta; **C**-Ramon Castro, Auburn; Scott Vieira, Williamsport; **DH**-Virgil Chevalier, Utica; **P**-Scott Mudd, Hudson Valley; Chris Weidert, Vermont; Bryan Link, Hudson Valley; Michael Venafro, Hudson Valley; **MVP**-Cliff Brumbaugh, Hudson Valley; **Manager**-Joel Skinner, Watertown.

BA: Cliff Brumbaugh, Hudson Valley, .358
Runs: Omar Sanchez, St. Catharines, 62
Hits: Cliff Brumbaugh, Hudson Valley, 101
RBIs: Rob Daly, Pittsfield, 60

HRs: Jose Guillen, Erie, 12
Wins: Chris Weidert, Vermont, 11
SOs: Bob St. Pierre, Oneonta, 91
ERA: Chris Weidert, Vermont, 1.79

A Northwest League
President: Bob Richmond

North Standings	W	L	Pct.	GB	Attend.	Manager
Bellingham Giants (28)	43	33	.566	—	54,104	Glenn Tufts
Everett AquaSox (12)	37	39	.487	6	89,950	Orlando Gomez
Spokane Indians (7)	36	39	.480	6½	162,344	Al Pedrique
Yakima Bears (21)	27	48	.360	15½	81,570	Joe Vavra

South Standings	W	L	Pct.	GB	Attend.	Manager
Boise Hawks (3)	48	27	.640	—	165,255	Tom Kotchman
Portland Rockies (18)	41	34	.547	7	249,696	P.J. Carey
Eugene Emeralds (15)	37	39	.487	11½	134,878	Paul Runge
Southern Oregon A's (11)	33	43	.434	15½	84,682	Tony DeFrancesco

Playoff: Boise 2 games, Bellingham 1.

All-Star Team: 1B-Danny Buxbaum, Boise; **2B**-Jon Watson, Bellingham; **3B**-Ryan Kane, Boise; **SS**-Miguel Tejada, Southern Oregon; **OF**-Kevin Gibbs, Yakima; Kevin Ham, Boise; Joe Trippy, Eugene; **C**-Patrick Hallmark, Spokane; **DH**-James Vida, Spokane; **P**-Marc D'Alessandro, Portland; Travis Thurmond, Boise; Adam Butler, Eugene; Grant Vermillion, Boise; **MVP**-Danny Buxbaum, Boise; **Manager**-Glenn Tufts, Bellingham.

BA: Danny Buxbaum, Boise, .329
Runs: Tony Miranda, Spokane, 53
Hits: James Vida, Spokane, 94
RBIs: Ryan Kane, Boise, 59

HRs: Ryan Kane, Boise, 14
Wins: Grant Vermillion, Boise, 12
SOs: Travis Thurmond, Boise, 93
ERA: Scott Randall, Portland, 1.99

A South Atlantic League
President: John H. Moss

North Standings	W	L	Pct.	GB	Attend.	Manager
Fayetteville Generals (6)	86	55	.610	—	121,051	Dwight Lowry
Piedmont Phillies#(24)	82	58	.586	3½	115,649	Roy Majtyka
Asheville Tourists**(18)	76	63	.547	9	138,148	Bill McGuire
Charleston (WV) Alley Cats (17)	77	65	.542	9½	106,530	Razor Shines
Hagerstown Suns (14)	73	68	.518	13	113,438	Omar Malave
Greensboro Bats (10)	70	70	.500	15½	170,444	Trey Hillman
Hickory Crawdads (4)	49	89	.355	35½	265,017	Mike Rojas

South Standings	W	L	Pct.	GB	Attend.	Manager
Columbus RedStixx**(5)	80	62	.563	—	128,816	Jeff Datz
Augusta GreenJackets*(25)	76	62	.551	2	171,166	Jeff Banister
Capital City Bombers (23)	72	68	.514	7	152,207	Howie Freiling
Macon Braves (15)	71	70	.504	8½	113,825	Nelson Norman
Albany Polecats (22)	62	78	.443	17	91,289	Doug Sisson
Savannah Cardinals (26)	56	83	.403	22½	113,849	Scott Melvin
Charleston (SC) RiverDogs (13)	50	89	.360	28½	101,280	Mike Berger

#represented Kannapolis, North Carolina.

Playoffs: Piedmont 2 games, Asheville 1; Augusta 2 games, Columbus 0.
Finals: Augusta 3 games, Piedmont 0.

All-Star Team: 1B-Daryle Ward, Fayetteville; **2B**-Julio Zorrilla, Columbia; **3B**-Wes Helms, Macon; **SS**-Hiram Bocachica, Albany; **OF**-Derrick Gibson, Asheville; Vladimir Guerrero, Albany; Andruw Jones, Macon; **C**-Julio Mosquera, Hagerstown; **DH**-Jeff Ladd, Hagerstown; **P**-Brent Crowther, Asheville; Larry Wimberly, Piedmont; **MVP**-Andruw Jones, Macon; **Pitcher of the Year**-Larry Wimberly, Piedmont; **Manager**-Roy Majtyka, Piedmont.

BA: Vladimir Guerrero, Albany, .333
Runs: Andruw Jones, Macon, 104
Hits: Brad Fullmer, Albany, 151; Fernando Tatis, Charleston (SC), 151
RBIs: Derrick Gibson, Asheville, 115

HRs: Derrick Gibson, Asheville, 32; Ron Wright, Macon, 32
Wins: Derrin Ebert, Macon, 14
SOs: Jesus Sanchez, Columbia, 177; Damian Moss, Macon, 177
ERA: Mike Kusiewicz, Asheville, 2.06

R Appalachian League
President: Bill Halstead

North Standings	W	L	Pct.	GB	Attend.	Manager
Bluefield Orioles (1)	49	16	.754	—	45,127	Andy Etchebarren
Princeton Reds (17)	31	32	.492	17	29,021	Brad Kelley
Martinsville Phillies (24)	30	37	.448	20	46,155	Ramon Henderson
Burlington Indians (5)	26	38	.406	22½	32,648	Harry Spilman
Danville Braves (15)	27	40	.403	23	63,905	Max Venable

South Standings	W	L	Pct.	GB	Attend.	Manager
Kingsport Mets (23)	48	18	.727	—	35,891	John Gibbons
Elizabethton Twins (9)	33	31	.516	14	18,982	John Russell
Johnson City Cardinals (26)	35	33	.515	14	41,449	Steve Turco
Bristol White Sox (4)	28	39	.418	20½	29,691	Chris Cron
River City Rumblers#(x)	22	45	.328	26½	20,631	Phillip Wellman

#represented Huntington, West Virginia.

Playoff: Kingsport 2 games, Bluefield 1.

All-Star Team: 1B-Jarrod Patterson, Kingsport; **2B**-Kevin Hooker, Martinsville; **3B**-Carlos Lee, Bristol; **SS**-Eddy Martinez, Bluefield; **OF**-Darron Ingram, Princeton; Johnny Isom, Bluefield; Jeramie Simpson, Kingsport; **C**-A.J. Pierzynski, Elizabethton; **DH**-Tony Boyette, Princeton; **P**-Chris Fussell, Bluefield; Chris Murphy, Princeton; Manuel Mendez, Johnson City; **MVP**-Jarrod Patterson, Kingsport; **Manager**-John Gibbons, Kingsport.

BA: Juan Munoz, Johnson City, .347	**HRs:** Darron Ingram, Princeton, 14
Runs: Carlos Mendoza, Kingsport, 56	**Wins:** Chris Fussell, Bluefield, 9
Hits: Carlos Lee, Bristol, 93	**SOs:** Chris Fussell, Bluefield, 98
RBIs: Jarrod Patterson, Kingsport, 57	**ERA:** Chris Murphy, Princeton, 1.55

R Arizona League
President: Bob Richmond

Standings	W	L	Pct.	GB	Manager
Athletics (Scottsdale) (11)	37	19	.661	—	Juan Navarrete
Angels (Mesa) (3)	35	21	.625	2	Bruce Hines
Brewers (Chandler) (8)	34	22	.607	3	Ralph Dickenson
Padres (Peoria) (27)	24	31	.436	12½	Dan Norman
Mariners (Peoria) (12)	24	32	.429	13	Tom LeVasseur
Rockies (Chandler) (18)	13	42	.236	23½	Jack Maloof

Playoffs: None.

All-Star Team: 1B-David Arias, Mariners; **2B**-Dionys Cesar, Athletics; **3B**-Juan Polanco, Athletics; **SS**-Edward Lara, Athletics; **OF**-Salvador Duverge, Rockies; Juan Rodriguez, Angels; Rich Stuart, Angels; **C**-Ramon Hernandez, Athletics; **DH**-Daryl Rutherford, Padres; **P**-Keith Volkman, Angels; Jose Paulino, Athletics; Bob Kazmirski, Athletics; **MVP**-Ramon Hernandez, Athletics; **Manager**-Ralph Dickenson, Brewers; Juan Navarrete, Athletics.

BA: Ramon Hernandez, Athletics, .364	**HRs:** Daryl Rutherford, Padres, 5
Runs: Larry Barnes, Angels, 42	Pete Paciorek, Padres, 5
Rich Stuart, Angels, 42	**Wins:** Jose Paulino, Athletics, 9
Hits: Juan Rodriguez, Angels, 64	Gabe Ishee, Brewers, 9
RBIs: Ramon Hernandez, Athletics, 37	**SOs:** Josh Bishop, Brewers, 134
David Arias, Mariners, 37	**ERA:** Tommy Darrell, Angels, 1.71
Larry Barnes, Angels, 37	

R Gulf Coast League
President: Thomas J. Saffell

East Standings	W	L	Pct.	GB	Manager
Marlins (Melbourne) (19)	40	16	.714	—	Juan Bustabad
Mets (Port St. Lucie) (23)	38	19	.667	2½	John Stephenson
Expos (West Palm Beach) (22)	21	35	.375	19	Luis Dorante
Braves (West Palm Beach) (15)	14	43	.246	26½	Jim Saul

North Standings	W	L	Pct.	GB	Manager
Tigers (Lakeland) (6)	33	24	.579	—	Kevin Bradshaw
Yankees (Tampa) (10)	32	26	.552	1½	Hector Lopez
Astros (Kissimmee) (20)	32	26	.552	1½	Bobby Ramos
Blue Jays (Dunedin) (14)	19	40	.322	15	Ralph "Rocket" Wheeler

Northwest Standings	W	L	Pct.	GB	Manager
White Sox (Sarasota) (4)	36	22	.621	—	Mike Gellinger
Orioles (Sarasota) (1)	34	25	.576	2½	Julio Garcia
Rangers (Port Charlotte) (13)	24	34	.414	12	Chino Cadahia
Pirates (Bradenton) (25)	23	36	.390	13½	Woody Huyke

Southwest Standings	W	L	Pct.	GB	Manager
Royals (Lee County) (7)	37	20	.649	—	Bob Herold
Cubs (Ft. Myers) (16)	35	22	.614	2	Sandy Alomar Sr.
Red Sox (Ft. Myers) (2)	21	36	.368	16	Felix Maldonado
Twins (Lee County) (9)	20	35	.364	16	Mike Boulanger

Playoffs: Tigers 1 game, Marlins 0; Royals 1 game, White Sox 0.
Finals: Royals 2 games, Tigers 0.

All-Star Team: 1B-Gary Coffee, Royals; **2B**-Elinton Jasco, Cubs; **3B**-Jose Cepeda, Royals; **SS**-Alex Gonzalez, Marlins; **OF**-Jose Camilo, Marlins; Carlos de la Cruz, Tigers; Thomas Peck, Blue Jays; **C**-Brian Downs, White Sox; **P**-Octavio Dotel, Mets; Brent Stentz, Tigers.

BA: Jose Cepeda, Royals, .348	**Wins:** Octavio Dotel, Mets, 7
Runs: Thomas Peck, Blue Jays, 42	James Nichols, White Sox, 7
Hits: Shawn Gallagher, Rangers, 71	**SOs:** Octavio Dotel, Mets, 86
RBIs: Gary Coffee, Royals, 45	**ERA:** Jeffrey Martin, Royals, 1.47
HRs: Gary Coffee, Royals, 11	

R Pioneer League
President: Jim McCurdy

North Standings	W	L	Pct.	GB	Attend.	Manager
Billings Mustangs***(17)	49	20	.710	—	103,758	Donnie Scott
Medicine Hat Blue Jays (14)	35	37	.486	15½	19,603	Darren Balsley
Great Falls Dodgers (21)	31	38	.449	18	62,312	John Shoemaker
Lethbridge Mounties (x)	25	47	.347	25½	47,607	Dan Simonds

South Standings	W	L	Pct.	GB	Attend.	Manager
Helena Brewers**(8)	49	22	.690	—	36,224	Alex Morales
Idaho Falls Braves*(27)	42	29	.592	7	57,620	Mike Basso
Ogden Raptors	32	38	.457	16½	56,630	Willie Ambos
Butte Copper Kings (x)	19	51	.271	29½	19,658	Billy Gardner, Jr.

Playoffs: Helena 2 games, Idaho Falls 1; Medicine Hat 2 games, Billings 1.
Finals: Helena 2 games, Medicine Hat 0.

All-Star Team: 1B-Sean Watkins, Idaho Falls; **2B**-Rick Gama, Idaho Falls; **3B**-Mike Kinkade, Helena; **SS**-Mickey Lopez, Helena; **OF**-Manuel Gonzalez, Great Falls; Jamie Lopiccolo, Ogden; Christian Rojas, Billings; **C**-Ben Davis, Idaho Falls; **DH**-Shane Jones, Ogden; Gerald Parent, Helena; **P**-Damon Callahan, Billings; Justin Atchley, Billings; John Mitchell, Medicine Hat; **MVP**-Jamie Lopiccolo, Ogden; **Manager**-Mike Basso, Idaho Falls.

BA: Jamie Lopiccolo, Ogden, .388	**HRs:** Sean Watkins, Idaho Falls, 13
Runs: Mike Kinkade, Helena, 76	**Wins:** Justin Atchley, Billings, 10
Hits: Jamie Lopiccolo, Ogden, 101	**SOs:** Casey Kirkman, Lethbridge, 91
RBIs: Shane Jones, Ogden, 69	**ERA:** Jay Veniard, Medicine Hat, 2.71

Ind Atlantic Coast League
President: Patrick Gaffney

Standings	W	L	Pct.	GB	Attend.	Manager
Gaston King Cougars#	12	3	.800	—	3,644	Jamie Nelson
Spartanburg Alley Cats	7	8	.467	5	1,793	Buzz Capra
Florence Flame	7	10	.412	6	6,282	Mark McKnight
Greenwood Grizzlies	6	11	.353	7	2,643	Mark Johnston

#represented Gastonia, North Carolina.

The league disbanded June 30.

BA: Eric Burroughs, Spartanburg, .345	**HRs:** Roberto Singer, Gaston, 8
Runs: Roberto Singer, Gaston, 18	Edwin Salceda, Gaston, 8
Hits: Tippy Passaeu, Florence, 22	**Wins:** Ruben Niebla, Gaston, 3
Ryan Ferby, Florence, 22	**SOs:** Adam Butler, Florence, 24
RBIs: Roberto Singer, Gaston, 17	**ERA:** Jeff Thomas, Gaston, 0.00

Ind Frontier League
President: Bill Lee

North Standings	W	L	Pct.	GB	Attend.	Manager
Johnstown Steal	46	23	.667	—	67,167	Mal Fichman
Newark Bison	39	29	.574	6½	21,309	John Pacella
Zanesville Greys	37	31	.544	8½	25,515	Eric Welch
Richmond Roosters	38	32	.543	8½	47,714	Larry Nolen
Ohio Valley Redcoats	36	34	.514	10½	21,093	Greg Tagert
Evansville Otters	31	38	.449	15	90,943	Boots Day
Portsmouth Explorers	28	41	.406	18	11,931	Wayne Albury/Dale Hagy
Chillicothe Paints	21	48	.304	25	31,128	Roger Hanners

Playoffs: Johnstown 2 games, Richmond 0; Zanesville 2 games, Newark 0.
Finals: Johnstown 2 games, Zanesville 0.

All-Star Team: 1B-Morgan Burkhardt, Richmond; **2B**-Mark Johnson, Newark; **3B**-Steve Ruckman, Richmond; **SS**-Robert Camarillo, Portsmouth; **OF**-Thurston Rockmore, Johnstown; Jeff Snyder, Portsmouth; Mark Soto, Johnstown; **C**-Stoney Burke, Richmond; **DH**-Johnny Booker, Richmond; **P**-Sean Hogan, Johnstown; Don Wolfe, Zanesville; **MVP**-Mark Soto, Johnstown; **Pitcher of the Year**-Don Wolfe, Zanesville; **Manager**-John Pacella, Newark.

BA: Jeff Snyder, Portsmouth, .398	**HRs:** Mark Soto, Johnstown, 12
Runs: Mark Soto, Johnstown, 62	**Wins:** Billy Williams, Johnstown, 9
Hits: Morgan Burkhardt, Richmond, 93	**SOs:** Fernando Mercado, Ohio Valley, 91
RBIs: Morgan Burkhardt, Richmond, 70	**ERA:** Ralph Bonelli, Newark, 2.45

Ind Golden State League
President: Bob Weinstein

Standings	W	L	Pct.	GB	Attend.	Manager
Imperial Valley Brahmas#	8	1	.889	—	1,803	Marty Berson
Yuma Desert Dawgs	7	3	.700	1½	7,766	Selwyn Young
Southern Nomadic Miners@	4	7	.364	5	2,337	Mark Webb
Antelope Valley Ravens+	1	9	.100	7½	1,516	Ellis Valentine/Tate Young

#represented Rosamond, California.
@represented Brawley, California.

#the Miners played most home games in Yuma, Arizona.
The league disbanded July 4.

BA: Malcolm Cepeda, Yuma, .476
Runs: Felix Pagan, Imperial Valley, 11
Hits: Anthony Banks, Yuma, 13
    Jermaine Swinton, Yuma, 13
HRs: Damon Auchard, Imperial Valley, 4
    Gilberto Bermudez, Imperial Valley, 4

Wins: Carlos Carrasco, Yuma, 3
    Brian Schmidt, Imperial Valley, 3
SOs: Carlos Carrasco, Yuma, 26
ERA: Carlos Carrasco, Yuma, 0.72

Ind Mid-America League
President: Jim Gonzales

Standings	W	L	Pct.	GB	Attend.	Manager
Lafayette Leopards	33	24	.579	—	7,624	Jim Gonzales
Anderson Lawmen	33	26	.559	1	12,579	Jay Welker
Merrillville Muddogs	27	31	.466	6½	18,351	Ron Kittle
East Chicago Conquistadors	23	35	.397	10½	5,444	Ron D'Auteuil

Playoffs: None.

MVP-Brian Heigle, Anderson; **Pitcher of the Year**-Javier Gomez, Merrillville; **Manager**-Jay Welker, Anderson.

BA: Brandon Allen, Lafayette, .391
Runs: Derek Alferman, Anderson, 48
Hits: Kadir Villalona, Lafayette, 86
RBIs: Brian Heigle, Anderson, 51

HRs: Brian Heigle, Anderson, 6
Wins: Dustin Riggs, Anderson, 8
SOs: Dustin Riggs, Anderson, 83
ERA: Javier Gomez, Merrillville, 2.43

Ind North Atlantic League
President: Edward Broidy

Standings	W	L	Pct.	GB	Attend.	Manager
Newark Barge Bandits	37	21	.638	—	15,005	Dave Keylin
Welland Aquaducks	32	27	.542	5½	2,653	Ellis Williams
Nashua Hawks	28	31	.475	9½	14,339	Allan Cupper
Niagara Falls Mallards	20	38	.345	17	17,398	Ken Barna

Playoffs: None.

All-Star Team: 1B-Doug Spofford, Nashua; **2B**-Erick Eckstein, Newark; **3B**-Rob Aziz, Nashua; **SS**-William Bellanger, Welland; **OF**-Keith Qualter, Nashua; Doug Shumway, Welland; Chris Neill, Welland; **C**-Rob Zachmann, Newark; **P**-Jon Hinkle, Niagara Falls; Jerry Hunter, Newark; Tim McKenna, Newark; **Manager** -Ellis Williams, Welland.

BA: Keith Qualter, Nashua, .354
Runs: Keith Qualter, Nashua, 37
    John Telford, Niagara Falls, 37
Hits: William Bellanger, Welland, 66
RBIs: Keith Qualter, Nashua, 37

HRs: Rob Zachmann, Newark, 5
Wins: Germaine Hunter, Newark, 8
    Jon Hinkle, Niagara Falls, 8
SOs: Germaine Hunter, Newark, 117
ERA: Germaine Hunter, Newark, 1.08

Ind North Central League
President: George Vedder

Standings	W	L	Pct.	GB	Attend.	Manager
Chaska Valley Buccaneers	8	6	.571	—		Glenn Gulliver
Brainerd Bears	12	10	.545	—	4,860	Bryan Clutterbuck
Minnesota Skeeters#	9	11	.450	2	6,634	Casey Waller
Will County Claws@	8	10	.444	2	2,181	Mike Taylor

#represented Hibbing, Minnesota.
@represented Romeoville, Illinois.

The league disbanded in mid-July.

BA: Ernesto Castro, Chaska Valley, .444
Runs: Casey Waller, Minnesota, 23
Hits: Menno Wickey, Brainerd, 30
RBIs: Ernesto Castro, Chaska Valley, 20
HRs: Bo Durkac, Will County, 6

Wins: Doug Martin, Chaska Valley, 3
    Ryan Frace, Brainerd, 3
    Jim Brantley, Will County, 3
    Mark Stephens, Brainerd, 3
SOs: Jim Brantley, Will County, 24
    Mark Stephens, Brainerd, 24
ERA: Doug Martin, Chaska Valley, 0.75

Ind Northeast League
President: Denise Byrd

Standings	W	L	Pct.	GB	Attend.	Manager
Albany Diamond Dogs	52	18	.743	—	60,084	Doc Edwards
Mohawk Valley Landsharks#	47	23	.671	5	12,507	Dan Shwam
Adirondack Lumberjacks@	42	27	.609	9½	51,543	Dave LaPoint
Newburgh Nighthawks	28	41	.406	23½	21,978	Ron LeFlore
Sullivan Mountain Lions+	23	43	.348	27	34,143	Ken Oberkfell
Yonkers Hoot Owls	12	52	.188	37	5,216	Paul Blair

#represented Little Falls, New York.
@represented Glens Falls, New York.
+represented Mountaindale, New York.

Playoff: Adirondack 2 games, Albany 1.

MVP-Hugh Walker, Mohawk Valley; **Pitcher of the Year**-Jeff Letourneau, Albany; **Manager**-Doc Edwards, Albany.

BA: Chris Kokinda, Sullivan, .370
Runs: Hugh Walker, Mohawk Valley, 55
    Jeff Cooke, Adirondack, 55
    Sean Gilliam, Albany, 55
Hits: Sean Gilliam, Albany, 93
RBIs: Sean Gilliam, Albany, 64

HRs: Sean Gilliam, Albany, 13
    Hugh Walker, Mohawk Valley, 13
Wins: Kenyatta Fleet, Albany, 11
SOs: Alan Sontag, Albany, 102
ERA: Jeff Letourneau, Albany, 1.50

Ind Northern League
President: Miles Wolff

Standings	W	L	Pct.	GB	Attend.	Manager
St. Paul Saints***	53	31	.631	—	258,297	Marty Scott
Winnipeg Goldeyes	47	38	.553	6½	196,460	Doug Simunic
Sioux City Explorers	46	39	.541	7½	149,770	Ed Nottle
Thunder Bay Whiskey Jacks	38	46	.452	15	100,211	Doug Ault
Sioux Falls Canaries	38	46	.452	15	102,328	Frank Verdi/Dick Dietz
Duluth-Superior Dukes	31	53	.369	22	81,514	Tommy Thompson

Playoff: St. Paul 3 games, Winnipeg 1.

All-Star Team: 1B-Dan Peltier, St. Paul; **2B**-Tommy Houk, Duluth-Superior; **3B**-Frank Valdez, Sioux Falls; **SS**-Greg D'Alexander, St. Paul; **OF**-Kevin Dattola, Winnipeg; Darryl Motley, St. Paul; Doug O'Neill, St. Paul; **C**-Hank Manning, Winnipeg; **DH**-Kevin Garner, Sioux Falls; **P**-Jeff Alkire, St. Paul; David Harris, Sioux City; Bruce Walton, St. Paul; **MVP**-Terry Lee, Winnipeg; **Rookie of the Year**-Bobby Post, Sioux Falls; **Manager**-Ed Nottle, Sioux City.

BA: Terry Lee, Winnipeg, .373
Runs: Doug O'Neill, St. Paul, 75
Hits: Dan Peltier, St. Paul, 119
RBIs: Terry Lee, Winnipeg, 73

HRs: Pete Kuld, Thunder Bay/
    Duluth-Superior, 24
Wins: David Harris, Sioux City, 11
SOs: Jeff Bittiger, Winnipeg, 106
ERA: David Harris, Sioux City, 3.01

Ind Prairie League
President: David Ferguson

American Standings	W	L	Pct.	GB	Attend.	Manager
Aberdeen Pheasants	56	13	.812	—	40,036	Bob Flori
Minneapolis Loons	43	26	.623	13	32,351	Greg Olson
Dakota Rattlers#	30	42	.417	27½	28,042	John King
Minot Mallards	24	47	.338	33	31,666	Mark Hebbeler

Canadian Standings	W	L	Pct.	GB	Attend.	Manager
Moose Jaw Diamond Dogs	44	28	.611	—	75,345	Mike Brocki
Regina Cyclones	40	30	.571	3	49,223	Jason Felice
Saskatoon Riot	26	45	.366	17½	38,711	George Scott
Brandon Grey Owls	19	51	.271	24	24,757	Greg McVey/Bryan Clutterbuck

#represented Bismarck, North Dakota.

Playoffs: Regina 2 games, Moose Jaw 1; Aberdeen 2 games, Minneapolis 0.
Finals: Regina 3 games, Aberdeen 1.

All-Star Team: 1B-Ken Tirpack, Aberdeen; **2B**-Enrique Duncan, Aberdeen; **3B**-Shawn Wooten, Aberdeen; **SS**-Bobby Holley, Aberdeen; **OF**-Brian Cornelius, Moose Jaw; Jason Felice, Regina; Ed Gerald, Aberdeen; **C**-Brad Gay, Aberdeen; **DH**-Boo Moore, Dakota; **P**-Chris Schmitt, Aberdeen; Darrin Reichle, Aberdeen; Juan Berenguer, Minneapolis; **MVP**-Ken Tirpack, Aberdeen; **Pitcher of the Year**-Darrin Reichle, Aberdeen; **Manager**-Bob Flori, Aberdeen.

BA: Brian Cornelius, Moose Jaw, .403
Runs: Brian Cornelius, Moose Jaw, 82
Hits: Brian Cornelius, Moose Jaw, 124
RBIs: Boo Moore, Dakota, 82

HRs: Butch Smith, Minot, 25
Wins: Darrin Reichle, Aberdeen, 14
SOs: Kerry Ligtenberg, Minneapolis, 100
ERA: Gary Painter, Aberdeen, 2.23

Ind Texas-Louisiana League
President: Doug Theodore

North Standings	W	L	Pct.	GB	Attend.	Manager
Amarillo Dillas**	64	36	.640	—	156,926	Ross Grimsley
Lubbock Crickets*	53	47	.530	11	94,367	Greg Minton
Tyler Wildcatters	48	52	.480	16	55,251	Wayne Krenchicki
Abilene Prairie Dogs	40	60	.400	24	73,954	Charley Kerfeld
Pueblo Bighorns#	21	29	.420	NA	11,474	Jim Essian

South Standings	W	L	Pct.	GB	Attend.	Manager
Alexandria Aces***	57	43	.570	—	57,791	Stan Cliburn
Corpus Christi Barracudas	55	44	.556	1½	61,793	Mark Wasinger
Rio Grande Valley WhiteWings	53	46	.535	3½	71,818	Alan Ashby
Mobile Baysharks	40	59	.404	16½	81,378	Butch Hobson
Laredo Apaches#	17	32	.347	NA	15,973	Jose Cruz

#Pueblo and Laredo disbanded July 17.

Playoff: Lubbock 2 games, Amarillo 1.
Finals: Lubbock 3 games, Alexandria 2.

All-Star Team: 1B-Mike Cantu, Corpus Christi; **2B**-Jorge Alvarez, Laredo/Amarillo; **3B**-Fletcher Thompson, Alexandria; **SS**-Rouglas Odor, Laredo/Lubbock; **OF**-Dennis Hood, Amarillo; Lonnie Maclin, Amarillo; Kyle Shade, Alexandria; **C**-Kevin Tahan, Amarillo; **DH**-Joe Ronca, Alexandria; **Util**-Lino Connell, Corpus Christi; **P**-Daren Brown, Amarillo; Gary Eave, Corpus Christi; Kevin Henthorne, Corpus Christi; Jerry Santos, Corpus Christi; **MVP**-Dennis Hood, Amarillo; **Pitcher of the Year**-Daren Brown, Amarillo; **Manager**-Ross Grimsley, Amarillo.

BA: Dennis Hood, Amarillo, .372
Runs: Fletcher Thompson, Alexandria, 106
Hits: Dennis Hood, Amarillo, 140
RBIs: Kevin Tahan, Amarillo, 95

HRs: Mike Cantu, Corpus Christi, 24
  Chris Cassels, Rio Grande Valley, 24
Wins: Daren Brown, Amarillo, 15
SOs: Alan Newman, Alexandria, 129
ERA: Dan Rambo, Tyler, 1.90

#represented Pasco-Kennewick-Richland, Washington.
@represented Aberdeen-Hoquiam, Washington.
+represented Rohnert Park, California.

Playoffs: Long Beach 2 games, Salinas 0; Tri-City 2 games, Surrey 0.
Finals: Long Beach 3 games, Tri-City 1.

MVP-Kyle Washington, Sonoma County; **Pitcher of the Year**-John Weglarz, Tri-City; **Manager**-Dave Holt, Salinas.

Ind Western League
President: Bruce Engel

North Standings	W	L	Pct.	GB	Attend.	Manager
Bend Bandits....................	48	43	.527	—	53,465	Al Gallagher
Tri-City Posse#**	45	46	.495	3	98,246	Tom Trebelhorn
Surrey Glaciers*	38	52	.422	9½	53,769	Dick Phillips
Grays Harbor Gulls@	31	59	.344	16½	82,450	Nate Colbert

South Standings	W	L	Pct.	GB	Attend.	Manager
Salinas Peppers***	60	30	.667	—	56,579	Dave Holt
Long Beach Barracuda/Riptide	52	38	.578	8	61,120	Jeff Burroughs
Sonoma County Crushers+.	44	46	.489	16	84,173	Paul Deese
Palm Springs Suns..............	43	47	.478	17	61,595	Bill Sudakis

BA: Kyle Washington, Sonoma County, .370
Runs: Scott Tedder, Bend, 68
  Jim Koehler, Bend, 68
  Don Robinson, Long Beach, 68
Hits: Scott Tedder, Bend, 119

RBIs: Paul Williams, Gray Harbor, 79
HRs: Paul Williams, Gray Harbor, 22
Wins: Kevin Reardon, Salinas, 14
SOs: John Weglarz, Tri-City, 162
ERA: John Weglarz, Tri-City, 1.87

1995 Interleague Post Season Play

World Series
Atlanta (National) 4 games, Cleveland (American) 2

1995 Major League Farm Systems

American League

1 Baltimore (6): Rochester, Bowie, Frederick, High Desert, Bluefield, Gulf Coast.
2 Boston (6): Pawtucket, Trenton, Sarasota, Michigan, Utica, Gulf Coast.
3 California (6): Vancouver, Midland, Lake Elsinore, Cedar Rapids, Boise, Arizona.
4 Chicago (7): Nashville, Birmingham, Prince William, South Bend, Hickory, Bristol, Gulf Coast.
5 Cleveland (6): Buffalo, Canton-Akron, Kinston, Columbus (GA), Watertown, Burlington (NC).
6 Detroit (6): Toledo, Jacksonville, Lakeland, Fayetteville, Jamestown, Gulf Coast.
7 Kansas City (6): Omaha, Wichita, Wilmington, Springfield, Spokane, Gulf Coast.
8 Milwaukee (6): New Orleans, El Paso, Stockton, Beloit, Helena, Arizona.
9 Minnesota (6): Salt Lake City, Hardware City, Ft. Myers, Fort Wayne, Elizabethton, Gulf Coast.
10 New York (6): Columbus (OH), Norwich, Tampa, Greensboro, Oneonta, Gulf Coast.
11 Oakland (6): Edmonton, Huntsville, Modesto, West Michigan, Southern Oregon, Arizona.
12 Seattle (6): Tacoma, Port City, Riverside, Wisconsin, Everett, Arizona.
13 Texas (6): Oklahoma City, Tulsa, Port Charlotte, Charleston (SC), Hudson Valley, Gulf Coast.
14 Toronto (7): Syracuse, Knoxville, Dunedin, Hagerstown, St. Catharines, Medicine Hat, Gulf Coast.

Co-op (x): Bakersfield, Visalia, River City, Lethbridge, Butte.
Independent: Ogden.

National League

15 Atlanta (7): Richmond, Greenville, Durham, Macon, Eugene, Danville, Gulf Coast.
16 Chicago (6): Iowa, Orlando, Daytona, Rockford, Williamsport, Gulf Coast.
17 Cincinnati (6): Indianapolis, Chattanooga, Winston-Salem, Charleston (WV), Billings, Princeton.
18 Colorado (6): Colorado Springs, New Haven, Salem, Asheville, Portland (OR), Arizona.
19 Florida (6): Charlotte, Portland (ME), Brevard County, Kane County, Elmira, Gulf Coast.
20 Houston (6): Tucson, Jackson, Kissimmee, Quad City, Auburn, Gulf Coast.
21 Los Angeles (6): Albuquerque, San Antonio, Vero Beach, San Bernardino, Yakima, Great Falls.
22 Montreal (6): Ottawa, Harrisburg, West Palm Beach, Albany (GA), Vermont, Gulf Coast.
23 New York (7): Norfolk, Binghamton, St. Lucie, Capital City, Pittsfield, Kingsport, Gulf Coast.
24 Philadelphia (6): Scranton-Wilkes-Barre, Reading, Clearwater, Piedmont, Batavia, Martinsville.
25 Pittsburgh (6): Calgary, Carolina, Lynchburg, Augusta, Erie, Gulf Coast.
26 St. Louis (7): Louisville, Arkansas, St. Petersburg, Peoria, Savannah, New Jersey, Johnson City.
27 San Diego (6): Las Vegas, Memphis, Rancho Cucamonga, Clinton, Idaho Falls, Arizona.
28 San Francisco (5): Phoenix, Shreveport, San Jose, Burlington (IA), Bellingham.

1995 No-Hitters

Date	Pitcher	Team	League	Opponent	Score
4-8	Brian Woods/				
	Archie Vazquez	Prince William	Carolina	Salem	8-0
4-15	Jose Rosado/				
	Pat Flury	Wilmington	Carolina	Winston-Salem	3-0
4-20	Eric Moody	Charlotte	Florida State	Sarasota	11-0
4-30	Tommy Harrison/				
	Earl Nelson	Durham	Carolina	Prince William	4-0
5-2	Jaret Wright/Wilmer Montoya/Noe Najera/				
	Scot Donovan	Columbus	South Atlantic	Fayetteville	4-1
5-19	Rich Pratt	Prince William	Carolina	Frederick	3-0 (7)
5-28	Clemente Nunez	Brevard County	Florida State	West Palm Beach	2-0
6-6	Roberto Ramirez	MC Diablos Rojos	Mexican	Tabasco	2-0
6-13	Mike Milchin	Albuquerque	Pacific Coast	Vancouver	2-0 (7)
6-20	Julio Hernandez	Veracruz	Mexican	MC Diablos Rojos	1-0 (7)
6-22	Cedric Allen/Pete Magre/				
	Emilio Giron	Charleston (WV)	South Atlantic	Hagerstown	4-0
6-23	Jake Bremington	Idaho Falls	Pioneer	Helena	6-0 (7)
6-25	Rob Ricketts/Kyle Farnsworth/				
	Barret Markey	Cubs	Gulf Coast	Royals	8-0
6-26	Mariano Rivera	Columbus	International	Rochester	3-0 (5)
6-28	Rafael Roque	St. Lucie	Florida State	Dunedin	6-1
6-28	Roberto Duran/Ronald Hillis/				
	Joe Jacobsen	Vero Beach	Florida State	West Palm Beach	3-0
7-1	Jon Henry	Puebla	Mexican	Veracruz	3-0 (7)
7-2	Winston Abreu	Danville	Appalachian	Burlington	7-1 (7)
7-2	Bernardo Cuervo	Campeche	Mexican	Minatitlan	4-0 (7)
7-11	Jason Stockstill	Angels	Arizona	Brewers	3-0
7-14	Ramon Martinez	Los Angeles	National	Florida	7-0
7-20	Kelvim Escobar	Medicine Hat	Pioneer	Ogden	2-0 (7)
7-26	John Dillinger/				
	Jason Pfaff	Lynchburg	Carolina	Kinston	4-0
8-3	Ty Young	River City	Appalachian	Elizabethton	4-0 (7)
8-8	Luis Andujar	Birmingham	Southern	Memphis	1-0
8-18	Brian Powell/Jeff Siler/Adam Housley/				
	Brandon Reed	Fayetteville	South Atlantic	Capital City	4-1
8-24	Elvin Hernandez	Erie	New York-Penn.	Oneonta	7-0
9-2	Robbie Beckett	Memphis	Southern	Chattanooga	0-1 (7)

Number in parentheses indicates innings if other than nine; "P" indicates perfect game.

THIS DATE IN MINOR LEAGUE HISTORY

April 6, 1995, The Durham Bulls played their first home game at new Durham Bulls Athletic Park, in front of 10,886 fans. The park was slated to open in 1994, but construction delays forced the club to play another season at historic Durham Athletic Park.

April 12, 1995, Reading pitcher Wayne Gomes balked six times in 4-2/3 innings pitched in an Eastern League game against Norwich. It was the first six-balk game in the minors since 1951.

April 15, 1995, Third baseman Rick Ladjevich, Riverside, California League, ripped a homer, two doubles and three singles to go 6-for-6 in a 16-1 win over High Desert.

May 6, 1995, Mark Mimbs of Albuquerque, Pacific Coast League, shut out Phoenix on one hit in six innings pitched. On the same day, his twin brother Mike compiled the same pitching line for the Philadelphia Phillies against Atlanta.

June 26, 1995, High winds during a thunderstorm split a light pole at Holman Stadium, home of the Florida State League's Vero Beach Dodgers, 40 minutes before the gates were scheduled to open. The pole ended up in the third base stands. No one was injured, and the game was postponed.

August 7, 1995, Scott Gardner of Fayetteville, South Atlantic League, struck out five Savannah batters in one inning, two of them reaching base on third-strike wild pitches. Gardner tied the professional record achieved three times previously.

August 29, 1995, The independent Northern League's Winnipeg Goldeyes drew 20,749 fans for their final regular season home game, a new short-season minor league record. Portland of the Northwest League had drawn a crowd of 20,600 earlier in the season.

September 1, 1995, Two California Leaguers hit for the cycle on the same day. Modesto's Gary Hust performed the feat, as did Stockton's Brad Seitzer.

1996

American League
President: Gene Budig

East Standings	W	L	Pct.	GB	Attend.	Manager
New York Yankees	92	70	.568	—	2,250,124	Joe Torre
Baltimore Orioles#	88	74	.543	4	3,646,950	Davey Johnson
Boston Red Sox	85	77	.525	7	2,315,233	Kevin Kennedy
Toronto Blue Jays	74	88	.457	18	2,559,563	Cito Gaston
Detroit Tigers	53	109	.327	39	1,168,610	Buddy Bell

Central Standings	W	L	Pct.	GB	Attend.	Manager
Cleveland Indians	99	62	.615	—	3,318,174	Mike Hargrove
Chicago White Sox	85	77	.525	14½	1,676,416	Terry Bevington
Milwaukee Brewers	80	82	.494	19½	1,327,155	Phil Garner
Minnesota Twins	78	84	.481	21½	1,437,352	Tom Kelly
Kansas City Royals	75	86	.466	24	1,436,007	Bob Boone

West Standings	W	L	Pct.	GB	Attend.	Manager
Texas Rangers	90	72	.556	—	2,888,920	Johnny Oates
Seattle Mariners	85	76	.528	4½	2,722,054	Lou Piniella
Oakland Athletics	78	84	.481	12	1,148,382	Art Howe
California Angels	70	91	.435	19½	1,820,532	Marcel Lachemann/ John McNamara

#wild card representative.

Playoffs: New York 3 games, Texas 1; Baltimore 3 games, Cleveland 1.
Finals: New York 4 games, Baltimore 1.

BA: Alex Rodriguez, Seattle, .358
Runs: Alex Rodriguez, Seattle, 141
Hits: Paul Molitor, Minnesota, 225
RBIs: Albert Belle, Cleveland, 148
HRs: Mark McGwire, Oakland, 52

Wins: Andy Pettitte, New York, 21
SOs: Roger Clemens, Boston, 257
ERA: Juan Guzman, Toronto, 2.93
Saves: John Wetteland, New York, 43

National League
President: Leonard Coleman

East Standings	W	L	Pct.	GB	Attend.	Manager
Atlanta Braves	96	66	.593	—	2,901,242	Bobby Cox
Montreal Expos	88	74	.543	8	1,618,573	Felipe Alou
Florida Marlins	80	82	.494	16	1,746,757	Rene Lachemann/John Boles
New York Mets	71	91	.438	25	1,588,323	Dallas Green/Bobby Valentine
Philadelphia Phillies	67	95	.414	29	1,801,677	Jim Fregosi

Central Standings	W	L	Pct.	GB	Attend.	Manager
St. Louis Cardinals	88	74	.543	—	2,659,251	Tony LaRussa
Houston Astros	82	80	.506	6	1,975,888	Terry Collins
Cincinnati Reds	81	81	.500	7	1,861,428	Ray Knight
Chicago Cubs	76	86	.469	12	2,219,110	Jim Riggleman
Pittsburgh Pirates	73	89	.451	15	1,332,150	Jim Leyland

West Standings	W	L	Pct.	GB	Attend.	Manager
San Diego Padres	91	71	.562	—	2,187,884	Bruce Bochy
Los Angeles Dodgers#	90	72	.556	1	3,188,454	Tom Lasorda/Bill Russell
Colorado Rockies	83	79	.512	8	3,891,014	Don Baylor
San Francisco Giants	68	94	.420	23	1,413,687	Dusty Baker

#wild card representative.

Playoffs: St. Louis 3 games, San Diego 0; Atlanta 3 games, Los Angeles 0.
Finals: Atlanta 4 games, St. Louis 3.

BA: Tony Gwynn, San Diego, .353
Runs: Ellis Burks, Colorado, 142
Hits: Lance Johnson, New York, 227
RBIs: Andres Galarraga, Colorado, 150
HRs: Andres Galarraga, Colorado, 47

Wins: John Smoltz, Atlanta, 24
SOs: John Smoltz, Atlanta, 276
ERA: Kevin Brown, Florida, 1.89
Saves: Jeff Brantley, Cincinnati, 44
Todd Worrell, Los Angeles, 44

AAA American Association
President: Branch B. Rickey

East Standings	W	L	Pct.	GB	Attend.	Manager
Buffalo Bisons (5)	84	60	.583	—	825,530	Brian Graham
Indianapolis Indians (17)	78	66	.542	6	544,592	Dave Miley
Nashville Sounds (4)	77	67	.535	7	303,407	Rick Renick
Louisville Redbirds (26)	60	84	.417	24	494,929	Joe Pettini

West Standings	W	L	Pct.	GB	Attend.	Manager
Omaha Royals (7)	79	65	.549	—	422,481	Mike Jirschele
Oklahoma City 89ers (13)	74	70	.514	5	267,724	Greg Biagini
Iowa Cubs (16)	64	78	.451	14	453,630	Ron Clark
New Orleans Zephyrs (8)	58	84	.408	20	180,520	Tim Ireland

Playoffs: Indianapolis 3 games, Buffalo 1; Oklahoma City 3 games, Omaha 1.
Finals: Oklahoma City 3 games, Indianapolis 1.

All-Star Team: 1B-Dmitri Young, Louisville; **2B**-Casey Candaele, Buffalo; **3B**-Eduardo

Perez, Indianapolis; **SS**-Damian Jackson, Buffalo; **OF**-Jeff Abbott, Nashville; Brian Giles, Buffalo; Nigel Wilson, Buffalo; **C**-Kelly Stinnett, New Orleans; **DH**-Lee Stevens, Oklahoma City; **P**-Brian Anderson, Buffalo; Rick Helling, Oklahoma City; Jaime Bluma, Omaha; **MVP**-Lee Stevens, Oklahoma City; **Rookie of the Year**-Jeff Abbott, Nashville; **Manager**-Rick Renick, Nashville.

BA: Dmitri Young, Louisville, .333
Runs: Dmitri Young, Louisville, 90
Hits: Luis Ortiz, Oklahoma City, 159
RBIs: Nigel Wilson, Buffalo, 95

HRs: Lee Stevens, Oklahoma City, 32
Wins: Scott Ruffcorn, Nashville, 13
SOs: Rick Helling, Oklahoma City, 157
ERA: Rick Helling, Oklahoma City, 2.96

AAA International League
President: Randy Mobley

East Standings	W	L	Pct.	GB	Attend.	Manager
Pawtucket Red Sox (2)	78	64	.549	—	360,005	Buddy Bailey
Rochester Red Wings (1)	72	69	.511	5½	366,479	Marv Foley
Scranton-Wilkes-Barre Red Barons (24)	70	72	.493	8	458,033	Butch Hobson/Ramon Aviles
Syracuse Chiefs (14)	67	75	.472	11	300,320	Richie Hebner
Ottawa Lynx (22)	60	82	.423	18	333,401	Pete Mackanin

West Standings	W	L	Pct.	GB	Attend.	Manager
Columbus Clippers (10)	85	57	.599	—	520,099	Stump Merrill
Norfolk Tides (23)	82	59	.582	2½	500,038	Bobby Valentine/Bruce Benedict
Toledo Mud Hens (6)	70	72	.493	15	306,847	Tom Runnells
Richmond Braves (15)	62	79	.440	22½	476,046	Bill Dancy
Charlotte Knights (19)	62	79	.440	22½	319,854	Sal Rende

Playoffs: Rochester 3 games, Pawtucket 1; Columbus 3 games, Norfolk 0.
Finals: Columbus 3 games, Rochester 0.

All-Star Team: 1B-Ivan Cruz, Columbus; **2B**-Jason Hardtke, Norfolk; **3B**-Phil Hiatt, Toledo; **SS**-Clay Bellinger, Rochester; **OF**-Phil Clark, Pawtucket; Billy McMillon, Charlotte; Rudy Pemberton, Pawtucket; **C**-Jorge Posada, Columbus; **DH**-Jerry Brooks, Charlotte; **P**-Mike Fyhrie, Norfolk; Derek Wallace, Norfolk; **MVP**-Phil Hiatt, Toledo; **Pitcher of the Year**-Mike Fyhrie, Norfolk; **Rookie of the Year**-Billy McMillon, Charlotte; **Manager**-Buddy Bailey, Pawtucket.

BA: Billy McMillon, Charlotte, .352
Runs: Phil Hiatt, Toledo, 99
Hits: Matt Franco, Norfolk, 164
RBIs: Phil Hiatt, Toledo, 119

HRs: Phil Hiatt, Toledo, 42
Wins: Mike Fyhrie, Norfolk, 15
SOs: Jeff Suppan, Pawtucket, 142
ERA: Mike Fyhrie, Norfolk, 3.04

AAA Mexican League
President: Pedro Treto Cisneros

North Standings	W	L	Pct.	GB	Attend.	Manager
Monterrey Sultanes***	82	33	.713	—	211,333	Derek Bryant
Monclova Acereros	58	56	.509	23½	290,994	Ramon Montoya/Marcelo Juarez
Reynosa Broncos	56	56	.500	24½	125,371	Aurelio Rodriguez/ Leo Clayton & Raul Montoya & Antonio Pollorena
Union Laguna Algodoneros	50	62	.446	30½	83,594	Herminio Saiz/Jose Guerrero
Nuevo Laredo Tecolotes	48	65	.425	33	80,522	Andres Mora
Saltillo Saraperos	41	70	.369	39	100,736	Roberto Castellon/Miguel Solis

Central Standings	W	L	Pct.	GB	Attend.	Manager
Mexico City Diablos Rojos**	70	43	.619	—	144,618	Marco Antonio Vazquez
Mexico City Tigres*	68	45	.602	2	154,764	Jorge Calvo
Poza Rica Petroleros	63	50	.558	7	200,226	Raul Cano/Bernardo Calvo/ Jesus Sommers
Aguascalientes Rieleros	58	57	.504	13	125,371	Jose Guerrero/Enrique Aguilar
Oaxaca Guerreros	46	64	.418	22½	201,719	Alfredo Ortiz

South Standings	W	L	Pct.	GB	Attend.	Manager
Yucatan Leones**	58	56	.509	—	199,433	Javier Martinez Marquez
Quintana Roo Langosteros#	55	55	.500	1	139,736	Francisco Estrada
Campeche Piratas*	53	59	.473	4	113,785	Fernando Villaescusa/ Leonel Carreon
Tabasco Olmecas	48	63	.432	8½	149,328	Alexis Infante/ Gerardo Gutierrez
Minatitlan Potros	45	65	.409	11	64,673	Carlos Paz/Eddy Castro

#represented Cancun, Mexico.

Playoffs: MC Diablos Rojos 4 games, Aguascalientes 3; MC Tigres 4 games, Poza Rica 1; Monterrey 4 games, Monclova 2; Yucatan 4 games, Campeche 1. MC Diablos Rojos 4 games, MC Tigres 2; Monterrey 4 games, Yucatan 1.
Finals: Monterrey 4 games, MC Diablos Rojos 1.

BA: Matias Carrillo, MC Tigres, .368
Runs: Cornelio Garcia, Monterrey, 87
Hits: Tony Chance, Monclova, 147
RBIs: Guillermo Velasquez, Monterrey, 112
HRs: Sam Horn, Union Laguna, 30

Wins: Emigdio Lopez, Tabasco, 15
Fernando Figueroa, Union Laguna, 15
SOs: Will Flynt, Oaxaca, 137
ERA: Sixto Baez, Poza Rica, 1.54

*Won first-half **Won second-half ***Won both halves
Numbers after nicknames indicate farm system.
Affiliation listed at end of each year.

AAA Pacific Coast League
President: Bill Cutler

North Standings	W	L	Pct.	GB	Attend.	Manager
Edmonton Trappers***(11)..	84	58	.592	—	463,684	Gary Jones
Salt Lake Buzz (9)	78	66	.542	7	621,027	Phil Roof
Calgary Cannons (25).........	74	68	.521	10	273,545	Trent Jewett
Vancouver Canadians (3)....	68	70	.493	14	334,800	Don Long
Tacoma Rainiers (12)	69	73	.486	15	338,500	Dave Myers

South Standings	W	L	Pct.	GB	Attend.	Manager
Las Vegas Stars**(27).......	73	67	.521	—	313,212	Jerry Royster
Tucson Toros (20)	70	74	.486	5	307,082	Tim Tolman
Phoenix Firebirds*(28).......	69	75	.479	6	267,649	Ron Wotus
Albuquerque Dukes (21)	67	76	.469	7½	307,445	Phil Regan
Colorado Springs Sky Sox (18)..	58	83	.411	15½	237,826	Brad Mills

Playoffs: Edmonton 3 games, Salt Lake 1; Phoenix 3 games, Las Vegas 0.
Finals: Edmonton 3 games, Phoenix 1.

All-Star Team: 1B-Jason Thompson, Las Vegas; **2B**-Brian Raabe, Salt Lake; **3B**-Todd Walker, Salt Lake; **SS**-Neifi Perez, Colorado Springs; **OF**-Jermaine Allensworth, Calgary; Brent Brede, Salt Lake; Ray Montgomery, Tucson; **C**-Angelo Encarnacion, Calgary; **DH**-James Bonnici, Tacoma; **P**-Shawn Estes, Phoenix; Bob Milacki, Tacoma; Steve Mintz, Phoenix; **MVP**-Steve Mintz, Phoenix; **Manager**-Gary Jones, Edmonton.

BA: Brian Raabe, Salt Lake, .351
Runs: Brian Raabe, Salt Lake, 103
Hits: Todd Walker, Salt Lake, 187
RBIs: Todd Walker, Salt Lake, 111
HRs: Todd Walker, Salt Lake, 28

Wins: Dan Carlson, Phoenix, 13
Bob Milacki, Tacoma, 13
SOs: Travis Miller, Salt Lake, 143
ERA: Bob Milacki, Tacoma, 2.74

AA Eastern League
President: John Levenda

North Standings	W	L	Pct.	GB	Attend.	Manager
Portland Sea Dogs (19).......	83	58	.589	—	408,497	Carlos Tosca
Binghamton Mets (23)........	76	66	.535	7½	202,461	John Tamargo
Norwich Navigators (10)....	71	70	.504	12	269,029	Jim Essian
New Haven Ravens (18).....	66	75	.468	17	254,074	Bill Hayes
Hardware City Rock Cats (9) ..	61	81	.430	22½	160,765	Al Newman

South Standings	W	L	Pct.	GB	Attend.	Manager
Trenton Thunder (2)	86	56	.606	—	437,446	Ken Macha
Harrisburg Senators (22)	74	68	.521	12	230,744	Pat Kelly
Canton-Akron Indians (5)...	71	71	.500	15	213,278	Jeff Datz
Reading Phillies (24).........	66	75	.468	19½	375,326	Bill Robinson
Bowie Baysox (1)	54	88	.380	32	396,086	Bob Miscik/Tim Blackwell

Playoffs: Portland 3 games, Binghamton 2; Harrisburg 3 games, Trenton 1.
Finals: Harrisburg 3 games, Portland 1.

All-Star Team: 1B-Todd Helton, New Haven; **2B**-Luis Castillo, Portland; **3B**-Scott Rolen, Reading; **SS**-Enrique Wilson, Canton-Akron; **OF**-Todd Dunwoody, Portland; Vladimir Guerrero, Harrisburg; Adam Hyzdu, Trenton; **C**-Walt McKeel, Trenton; **DH**-Rod McCall, Canton-Akron; **P**-Matt Beech, Reading; Carl Pavano, Trenton; Tony Saunders, Portland; Mike Welch, Binghamton; **MVP**-Vladimir Guerrero, Harrisburg; **Pitcher of the Year**-Carl Pavano, Trenton; **Rookie of the Year**-Vladimir Guerrero, Harrisburg; **Manager**-Carlos Tosca, Portland.

BA: Vladimir Guerrero, Harrisburg, .360
Runs: Jon Saffer, Harrisburg, 96
Hits: Alex Ramirez, Canton-Akron, 169
RBIs: Chris Saunders, Binghamton, 105

HRs: Shane Spencer, Norwich, 29
Wins: Carl Pavano, Trenton, 16
SOs: Tony Saunders, Portland, 156
ERA: Carl Pavano, Trenton, 2.63

AA Southern League
President: Arnold Fielkow

East Standings	W	L	Pct.	GB	Attend.	Manager
Jacksonville Suns***(6)......	75	63	.543	—	218,000	Bill Plummer/Larry Parrish
Carolina Mudcats (25)........	70	69	.504	5½	278,361	Marc Hill
Orlando Cubs (16)	60	78	.439	15	175,399	Bruce Kimm
Greenville Braves (15).......	58	82	.414	18	230,124	Jeff Cox
Port City Roosters (12)	56	84	.400	20	68,463	Orlando Gomez

West Standings	W	L	Pct.	GB	Attend.	Manager
Memphis Chicks*(27)	81	58	.583	—	197,084	Ed Romero
Chattanooga Lookouts**(17)..	81	59	.579	½	227,885	Mark Berry
Knoxville Smokies (14)......	75	65	.536	6½	142,537	Omar Malave
Birmingham Barons (4)	74	65	.532	7	296,131	Mike Heath
Huntsville Stars (11)..........	66	74	.471	15½	260,313	Dick Scott

Playoffs: Jacksonville 3 games, Carolina 2; Chattanooga 3 games, Memphis 1.
Finals: Jacksonville 3 games, Chattanooga 1.

All-Star Team: 1B-Derrek Lee, Memphis; **2B**-Frank Catalanotto, Jacksonville; **3B**-Aaron Boone, Chattanooga; **SS**-Lou Collier, Carolina; **OF**-Mike Cameron, Birmingham; T.J. Staton, Carolina; Bubba Trammell, Jacksonville; **C**-Willie Morales, Huntsville; **DH**-Dan Rohrmeier, Memphis; **Util**-Tony Beasley, Carolina; **P**-Heath Murray, Memphis; Curt Lyons, Chattanooga; **MVP**-Derrek Lee, Memphis; **Pitcher of the Year**-Curt Lyons, Chattanooga; **Manager**-Mark Berry, Chattanooga.

BA: Dan Rohrmeier, Memphis, .344
Runs: Mike Cameron, Birmingham, 120
Hits: Dan Rohrmeier, Memphis, 162
RBIs: Derrek Lee, Memphis, 104

HRs: Derrek Lee, Memphis, 34
Wins: Brian Moehler, Jacksonville, 15
SOs: Curt Lyons, Chattanooga, 176
ERA: Shane Dennis, Memphis, 2.27

AA Texas League
President: Tom Kayser

East Standings	W	L	Pct.	GB	Attend.	Manager
Tulsa Drillers**(13)	75	64	.540	—	343,196	Bobby Jones
Shreveport Captains (28)....	73	66	.525	2	179,584	Frank Cacciatore
Jackson Generals*(20).......	70	70	.500	5½	179,423	Dave Engle
Arkansas Travelers (26)......	67	73	.479	8½	209,535	Rick Mahler

West Standings	W	L	Pct.	GB	Attend.	Manager
El Paso Diablos**(8)	76	63	.547	—	292,074	Dave Machemer
Wichita Wranglers*(7)	70	70	.500	6½	186,084	Ron Johnson
San Antonio Missions (21).	69	70	.496	7	381,001	John Shelby
Midland Angels (3).............	58	82	.414	18½	203,011	Mario Mendoza

Playoffs: Jackson 3 games, Tulsa 1; Wichita 3 games, El Paso 1.
Finals: Jackson 4 games, Wichita 0.

All-Star Team: 1B-Paul Konerko, San Antonio; **2B**-Ronnie Belliard, El Paso; **3B**-Brad Seitzer, El Paso; **SS**-Russ Johnson, Jackson; **OF**-Todd Dunn, El Paso; Richard Hidalgo, Jackson; Bo Ortiz, Midland; **C**-Eli Marrero, Arkansas; **DH**-Bubba Smith, Tulsa; **Util**-Jeff Berblinger, Arkansas; Jonas Hamlin, El Paso; **P**-Kris Detmers, Arkansas; Keith Foulke, Shreveport; Jonathan Johnson, Tulsa; Sean Maloney, El Paso; Matt Morris, Arkansas; Brady Raggio, Arkansas; Eric Weaver, San Antonio; **Player of the Year**-Bubba Smith, Tulsa; **Pitcher of the Year**-Keith Foulke, Shreveport; **Manager**-Dave Machemer, El Paso.

BA: Todd Dunn, El Paso, .340
Runs: Dante Powell, Shreveport, 92
Hits: Russ Johnson, Jackson, 154
RBIs: Bubba Smith, Tulsa, 94
Jonas Hamlin, El Paso, 94

HRs: Bubba Smith, Tulsa, 32
Wins: Jonathan Johnson, Tulsa, 13
SOs: Matt Beaumont, Midland, 132
ERA: Keith Foulke, Shreveport, 2.76

A California League
President: Joe Gagliardi

North Standings	W	L	Pct.	GB	Attend.	Manager
San Jose Giants***(28)	89	51	.636	—	144,782	Carlos Lezcano
Modesto A's (11)................	82	58	.586	7	98,757	Jim Colborn
Stockton Ports (8)	79	61	.584	10	101,568	Greg Mahlberg
Visalia Oaks (6, 29)...........	50	90	.357	39	67,798	Tim Torricelli
Bakersfield Blaze (x).........	39	101	.279	50	83,307	Graig Nettles

South Standings	W	L	Pct.	GB	Attend.	Manager
High Desert Mavericks**(1)...	76	64	.543	—	143,882	Joe Ferguson
Lake Elsinore Storm (3)	75	65	.536	1	360,393	Mitch Seoane
Lancaster JetHawks (12)	71	69	.507	5	316,611	Dave Brundage
San Bernardino Stampede (21)................	70	70	.500	6	148,363	Del Crandall
Rancho Cucamonga Quakes*(27)...................	69	71	.493	7	410,214	Mike Basso

Playoffs: Stockton 2 games, Modesto 0; Lake Elsinore 2 games, Rancho Cucamonga 1. San Jose 3 games, Stockton 1; Lake Elsinore 3 games, High Desert 0.
Finals: Lake Elsinore 3 games, San Jose 2.

All-Star Team: 1B-Chris Kirgan, High Desert; **2B**-Jason Cook, Lancaster; **3B**-Mike Berry, High Desert; **SS**-Miguel Tejada, Modesto; **OF**-Ben Grieve, Modesto; Mike Neill, Modesto; Mike Rennhack, Stockton; **C**-Craig Mayes, San Jose; **DH**-D.T. Cromer, Modesto; **P**-Darin Blood, San Jose; Ken Cloude, Lancaster; Bill King, Modesto; Rich Linares, San Bernardino; **MVP**-D.T. Cromer, Modesto; **Pitcher of the Year**-Darin Blood, San Jose; **Rookie of the Year**-Darin Blood, San Jose; **Manager**-Carlos Lezcano, San Jose.

BA: Mike Berry, High Desert, .361
Runs: David Roberts, Visalia, 112
Hits: Tim Garland, San Jose, 171
RBIs: Chris Kirgan, High Desert, 131

HRs: Chris Kirgan, High Desert, 35
Wins: Darin Blood, San Jose, 17
SOs: Darin Blood, San Jose, 193
ERA: Darin Blood, San Jose, 2.65

A Carolina League
President: John Hopkins

North Standings	W	L	Pct.	GB	Attend.	Manager
Wilmington Blue Rocks***(7)	80	60	.571	—	331,562	John Mizerock
Frederick Keys (1).............	67	72	.482	12½	258,427	Tim Blackwell/Julio Garcia
Lynchburg Hillcats (5).......	65	74	.468	14½	100,016	Jeff Banister
Prince William Cannons (4).	58	80	.420	21	190,055	Dave Huppert

South Standings	W	L	Pct.	GB	Attend.	Manager
Kinston Indians (5)	76	62	.551	—	145,493	Jack Mull
Winston-Salem Warthogs (17)	74	65	.532	2½	154,132	Phillip Wellman
Durham Bulls (15).............	73	66	.525	3½	365,445	Randy Ingle
Salem Avalanche (18)	62	76	.449	14	173,703	Bill McGuire

Playoff: Kinston 2 games, Durham 1.
Finals: Wilmington 3 games, Kinston 1.

All-Star Team: 1B-Sean Casey, Kinston; **2B**-Sergio Nunez, Wilmington; **3B**-Freddy Garcia, Lynchburg; **SS**-Alejandro Prieto, Wilmington; **OF**-Decomba Conner, Winston-Salem; Jose Guillen, Lynchburg; Johnny Isom, Frederick; **C**-Blake Barthol, Salem; **DH**-Juan Thomas, Prince William; **Util IF**-Rick Short, Frederick; **Util OF**-Mike Asche, Lynchburg; **P**-Noe Najera, Kinston; Steve Prihoda, Wilmington; **MVP**-Jose Guillen, Lynchburg; **Pitcher of the Year**-Noe Najera, Kinston; **Manager**-Jack Mull, Kinston.

BA: Sean Casey, Kinston, .331
Runs: Juan Thomas, Prince William, 88
Hits: Jose Guillen, Lynchburg, 170
RBIs: Johnny Isom, Frederick, 104

HRs: Freddy Garcia, Lynchburg, 21
Jose Guillen, Lynchburg, 21
Wins: David Caldwell, Kinston, 13
SOs: Russ Herbert, Prince William, 148
ERA: Noe Najera, Kinston, 2.70

A Florida State League
President: Chuck Murphy

East Standings	W	L	Pct.	GB	Attend.	Manager
St. Lucie Mets**(23)	71	62	.534	—	74,728	John Gibbons
Daytona Cubs (16)	71	66	.518	2	97,098	Dave Trembley
West Palm Beach Expos (22)	68	67	.504	4	70,579	Rick Sofield
Vero Beach Dodgers*(21)	65	66	.496	5	75,753	Jon Debus
Kissimmee Cobras (20)	60	75	.444	12	29,533	Alan Ashby
Brevard County Manatees (19)	47	92	.338	27	140,724	Fredi Gonzalez

West Standings	W	L	Pct.	GB	Attend.	Manager
Tampa Yankees**(10)	84	50	.627	—	115,532	Trey Hillman
Ft. Myers Miracle (9)	79	58	.577	6½	77,181	John Russell
Clearwater Phillies*(24)	75	62	.547	10½	75,118	Al LeBoeuf
St. Petersburg Cardinals (26)	75	63	.543	11	124,174	Chris Maloney
Sarasota Red Sox (2)	67	69	.493	18	69,414	DeMarlo Hale
Dunedin Blue Jays (14)	67	70	.489	18½	66,567	Dennis Holmberg
Charlotte Rangers (13)	63	76	.453	23½	70,289	Butch Wynegar
Lakeland Tigers (6)	61	77	.442	25	35,256	Dave Anderson

Playoffs: St. Lucie 2 games, Vero Beach 0; Clearwater 2 games, Tampa 0.
Finals: St. Lucie 3 games, Clearwater 1.

All-Star Team: 1B-Chris Richard, St. Petersburg; **2B**-Richard Almanzar, Lakeland; **3B**-Jose Lopez, St. Lucie; **SS**-Mike Coolbaugh, Charlotte; **OF**-Aaron Fuller, Sarasota; Mike Murphy, Charlotte; Anthony Sanders, Dunedin; **C**-Pat Cline, Daytona; Paul LoDuca, Vero Beach; **DH**-Daryle Ward, Lakeland; **Util IF**-Placido Polanco, St. Petersburg; **Util OF**-Kurt Bierek, Tampa; **P**-Tony Mounce, Kissimmee; Tommy Phelps, West Palm Beach; Roy Halladay, Dunedin; Blake Stein, St. Petersburg; Curtis King, St. Petersburg; Jay Tessmer, Tampa; **MVP**-Jay Tessmer, Tampa; **Manager**-Trey Hillman, Tampa.

BA: Mike Murphy, Charlotte, .332
Runs: Richard Almanzar, Lakeland, 81
Hits: Placido Polanco, St. Petersburg, 157
RBIs: Kevin Ellis, Daytona, 89
HRs: John Curl, Dunedin, 18

Wins: Blake Stein, St. Petersburg, 16
Billy Neal, Vero Beach, 16
SOs: Blake Stein, St. Petersburg, 159
ERA: Blake Stein, St. Petersburg, 2.15

A Midwest League
President: George Spelius

East Standings	W	L	Pct.	GB	Attend.	Manager
West Michigan Whitecaps***(11)	77	61	.558	—	547,401	Mike Quade
Fort Wayne Wizards (9)	69	67	.507	7	224,131	Dan Rohn
Lansing Lugnuts**(7)	68	71	.489	9½	538,326	Brian Poldberg
Michigan Battle Cats (2)	60	78	.435	17	162,029	Tommy Barrett
South Bend Silver Hawks (4)	54	82	.397	22	214,721	Dave Keller

Central Standings	W	L	Pct.	GB	Attend.	Manager
Peoria Chiefs**(26)	79	57	.581	—	187,283	Roy Silver
Wisconsin Timber Rattlers*(12)	77	58	.570	1½	233,797	Mike Goff
Rockford Cubbies (16)	70	65	.519	8½	102,479	Steve Roadcap
Beloit Snappers (8)	69	67	.507	10	73,633	Luis Salazar
Kane County Cougars (19)	65	68	.489	12½	436,076	Lynn Jones

West Standings	W	L	Pct.	GB	Attend.	Manager
Quad City River Bandits***(20)	70	61	.534	—	209,513	Jim Pankovits
Clinton Lumber Kings (27)	64	70	.478	7½	56,493	Mike Ramsey
Burlington Bees (28)	65	73	.471	8½	52,726	Glenn Tufts
Cedar Rapids Kernels (3)	63	72	.467	9	127,369	Tom Lawless

Playoffs: West Michigan 2 games, Lansing 1; Wisconsin 2 games, Peoria 1; Quad City 2 games, Cedar Rapids 1; Rockford 2 games, Beloit 1. West Michigan 2 games, Rockford 0; Wisconsin 2 games, Quad City 1.
Finals: West Michigan 3 games, Wisconsin 1.

All-Star Team: 1B-Larry Barnes, Cedar Rapids; **2B**-Andy Hall, Peoria; **3B**-Mike Kinkade, Beloit; **SS**-Deivi Cruz, Burlington; **OF**-Don Denbow, Burlington; Kerry Robinson, Peoria; Brian Simmons, South Bend; **C**-Ramon Hernandez, West Michigan; **DH**-Jeff Liefer, South Bend; **P**-Valerio de los Santos, Beloit; Britt Reames, Peoria; Armando Almanza, Peoria; Santos Hernandez, Burlington; **MVP**-Larry Barnes, Cedar Rapids; **Manager**-Roy Silver, Peoria.

BA: Kerry Robinson, Peoria, .359
Runs: Mike Kinkade, Beloit, 105
Hits: Jose Cepeda, Lansing, 161
RBIs: Larry Barnes, Cedar Rapids, 112

HRs: Larry Barnes, Cedar Rapids, 27
Wins: Brandon Kolb, Clinton, 16
SOs: Britt Reames, Peoria, 167
ERA: Britt Reames, Peoria, 1.90

A New York-Pennsylvania League
President: Bob Julian

McNamara Standings	W	L	Pct.	GB	Attend.	Manager
Vermont Expos (22)	48	26	.649	—	124,496	Kevin Higgins
Pittsfield Mets (23)	46	29	.613	2½	63,534	Doug Davis
Lowell Spinners (2)	33	41	.446	15	98,039	Billy Gardner, Jr.
Hudson Valley Renegades (13, 30)	32	44	.421	17	152,626	Bump Wills
New Jersey Cardinals (26)	28	47	.373	20½	172,304	Scott Melvin

Pinckney Standings	W	L	Pct.	GB	Attend.	Manager
Watertown Indians (5)	45	30	.600	—	40,711	Ted Kubiak
Williamsport (16)	43	32	.573	2	65,089	Ruben Amaro, Sr.
Auburn Astros (20)	37	39	.487	8½	44,813	Manny Acta
Oneonta Yankees (10)	31	45	.408	14½	49,689	Gary Tuck
Utica Blue Marlins (19)	29	47	.382	16½	51,432	Steve McFarland

Stedler Standings	W	L	Pct.	GB	Attend.	Manager
St. Catharines Stompers (14)	44	32	.579	—	56,546	Ralph "Rocket" Wheeler
Batavia Clippers (24)	42	33	.560	1½	39,037	Floyd Rayford
Jamestown Jammers (6)	39	36	.520	4½	58,630	Bruce Fields
Erie SeaWolves (25)	30	46	.395	14	187,794	Jeff Richardson

Playoffs: Vermont 2 games, Pittsfield 0; St. Catharines 2 games, Watertown 0.
Finals: Vermont 2 games, St. Catharines 1.

All-Star Team: 1B-Kevin Burns, Auburn; **2B**-Will Skett, St. Catharines; **3B**-Aramis Ramirez, Erie; **SS**-Abraham Nunez, St. Catharines; **OF**-Donzell McDonald, Oneonta; Danny Ramirez, Pittsfield; Chris Stowers, Vermont; Chris Wakeland, Jamestown; **C**-Wilson Antigua, Erie; Mike Rose, Auburn; **DH**-Joe Pomierski, Hudson Valley; **Util IF**-Simon Pond, Vermont; **P**-Jared Camp, Watertown; Courtney Duncan, Williamsport; Derek Dace, Auburn; Tim Young, Vermont; **MVP**-Chris Stowers, Vermont; **Manager**-Ralph "Rocket" Wheeler, St. Catharines.

BA: Joe Freitas, New Jersey, .344
Runs: Chris Stowers, Vermont, 58
Hits: Chris Stowers, Vermont, 90
RBIs: Kevin Burns, Auburn, 55

HRs: Will Skett, St. Catharines, 15
Wins: Courtney Duncan, Williamsport, 11
SOs: Bobby Rodgers, Lowell, 108
ERA: Ken Raines, Hudson Valley, 1.07

A Northwest League
President: Bob Richmond

North Standings	W	L	Pct.	GB	Attend.	Manager
Yakima Bears (21)	40	36	.526	—	82,313	Joe Vavra
Bellingham Giants (28)	39	36	.520	½	48,417	Ozzie Virgil, Sr./Shane Turner
Spokane Indians (7)	37	39	.487	3	180,903	Bob Herold
Everett AquaSox (12)	33	42	.440	6½	87,846	Roger Hansen

South Standings	W	L	Pct.	GB	Attend.	Manager
Eugene Emeralds (15)	49	27	.645	—	148,282	Jim Saul
Boise Hawks (3)	43	33	.566	6	164,243	Tom Kotchman
Portland Rockies (18)	33	43	.434	16	249,995	Ron Gideon
Southern Oregon Timberjacks (11)	29	47	.382	20	77,437	Tony DeFrancesco

Playoff: Yakima 2 games, Eugene 0.

All-Star Team: 1B-Rob Zachmann, Everett; **2B**-Doug Livingston, Portland; Tony Zuniga, Bellingham; **3B**-Brian Rust, Eugene; **SS**-Mike Caruso, Bellingham; **OF**-Justin Bowles, Southern Oregon; Adam Johnson, Eugene; Nate Murphy, Boise; **C**-Matt Curtis, Boise; Dax Norris, Eugene; **DH**-Steve Hacker, Eugene; **P**-Ken Vining, Bellingham; Brandon Leese, Bellingham; Jeff Kubenka, Yakima; Mick Pageler, Bellingham; **MVP**-Rob Zachmann, Everett; **Manager**-Joe Vavra, Yakima.

BA: Adam Johnson, Eugene, .314
Runs: Nate Murphy, Boise, 58
Adam Johnson, Eugene, 58
Jeremy Giambi, Spokane, 58
Hits: Adam Johnson, Eugene, 100

RBIs: Kit Pellow, Spokane, 66
HRs: Steve Hacker, Eugene, 21
Wins: Tommy Darrell, Boise, 8
SOs: Brandon Leese, Bellingham, 90
ERA: Blake Mayo, Yakima, 1.20

A South Atlantic League
President: John Moss

North Standings	W	L	Pct.	GB	Attend.	Manager
Delmarva Shorebirds#*(22)	83	59	.585	—	314,963	Doug Sisson
Fayetteville Generals**(6)	76	63	.547	5½	73,340	Dwight Lowry
Hagerstown Suns (14)	70	71	.496	12½	102,765	J.J. Cannon
Charleston (WV) Alley Cats (17)	58	84	.408	25	87,179	Tommy Thompson/Donnie Scott

Central Standings	W	L	Pct.	GB	Attend.	Manager
Asheville Tourists*(18)	84	52	.618	—	145,798	P.J. Carey
Capital City Bombers**(23)	82	57	.590	3½	156,921	Howie Freiling
Piedmont Boll Weevils (24)	72	66	.522	13	102,983	Roy Majtyka
Charleston (SC) RiverDogs (13)	63	78	.447	23½	100,428	Gary Allenson
Greensboro Bats (10)	56	86	.394	31	167,281	Rick Patterson/Jimmy Johnson
Hickory Crawdads (4)	55	85	.393	31	207,069	Chris Cron

South Standings	W	L	Pct.	GB	Attend.	Manager
Columbus RedStixx**(5)	79	63	.556	—	45,010	Joel Skinner
Savannah Sand Gnats (21)	72	69	.511	6½	122,448	John Shoemaker
Augusta GreenJackets*(25)	71	70	.504	7½	157,487	Jay Loviglio
Macon Braves (15)	61	79	.436	17	117,042	Paul Runge

#represented Salisbury, Maryland.

Playoffs: Delmarva 2 games, Fayetteville 0; Asheville 2 games, Capital City 0; Columbus 2 games, Augusta 1; Savannah 2 games, Piedmont 0. Savannah 2 games, Columbus 0; Delmarva 2 games, Asheville 1.
Finals: Savannah 3 games, Delmarva 1.

All-Star Team: 1B-Darren Stumberger, Columbus; **2B**-Orlando Cabrera, Delmarva; **3B**-Russell Branyan, Columbus; **SS**-Chad Hermansen, Augusta; **OF**-David Feuerstein, Asheville; Gabe Kapler, Fayetteville; Scott Morgan, Columbus; **C**-Ben Petrick, Asheville; **DH**-Mike Whitlock, Hagerstown; **Util IF**-Carlos Lee, Hickory; **Util OF**-Eric Stuckenschneider, Savannah; **P**-Ethan McEntire, Capital City; Nelson Figueroa, Capital City; **MVP**-Russell Branyan, Columbus; **Pitcher of the Year**-Nelson Figueroa, Capital City; **Manager**-P.J. Carey, Asheville.

BA: Carlos Mendoza, Capital City, .336
Runs: Eric Stuckenschneider, Savannah, 111
Hits: Gabe Kapler, Fayetteville, 157
RBIs: Russell Branyan, Columbus, 106

HRs: Russell Branyan, Columbus, 40
Wins: Elvin Hernandez, Augusta, 17
SOs: Nelson Figueroa, Capital City, 200
ERA: Nelson Figueroa, Capital City, 2.04

R Appalachian League
President: Lee Landers

East Standings	W	L	Pct.	GB	Attend.	Manager
Bluefield Orioles (1)	42	26	.618	—	37,758	Bobby Dickerson
Danville Braves (15)	37	29	.561	4	66,825	Brian Snitker
Burlington Indians (5)	29	38	.433	12½	43,596	Harry Spilman
Princeton Reds (17)	28	40	.412	14	26,162	Mark Wagner
Martinsville Phillies (24)	20	47	.299	21½	42,153	Ramon Henderson

West Standings	W	L	Pct.	GB	Attend.	Manager
Kingsport Mets (23)	48	19	.716	—	33,188	John Stephenson
Johnson City Cardinals (26)	42	26	.618	6½	37,475	Steve Turco
Elizabethton Twins (9)	40	27	.597	8	16,711	Jose Marzan
Bristol White Sox (4)	17	51	.250	31½	25,262	Nick Capra

Playoff: Bluefield 2 games, Kingsport 1.

All-Star Team: 1B-Calvin Pickering, Bluefield; **2B**-Carlos Casimiro, Bluefield; **3B**-Matt Buczkowski, Martinsville; **SS**-Brent Butler, Johnson City; **OF**-Todd Hogan, Johnson City; Brandon O'Hearn, Princeton; Tyrone Pendergrass, Danville; **C**-Pee Wee Lopez, Kingsport; **DH**-Freddy Reyes, Elizabethton; **Util IF**-Cleatus Davidson, Elizabethton; **Util OF**-Tim Bishop, Kingsport; **P**-Mike Bacsik, Burlington; Brett Herbison, Kingsport; Jose DeLeon, Johnson City; **MVP**-Brent Butler, Johnson City; **Pitcher of the Year**-Andy Zwirchitz, Kingsport; **Manager**-Steve Turco, Johnson City.

BA: Rodger Harris, Johnson City, .369
Runs: Cleatus Davidson, Elizabethton, 53
   Pee Wee Lopez, Kingsport, 53
Hits: Brent Butler, Johnson City, 85
RBIs: Calvin Pickering, Bluefield, 66

HRs: Calvin Pickering, Bluefield, 18
Wins: Grant Roberts, Kingsport, 9
SOs: Grant Roberts, Kingsport, 92
ERA: Kevin McGlinchy, Danville, 1.13

R Arizona League
President: Bob Richmond

Standings	W	L	Pct.	GB	Manager
Padres (Peoria)	36	20	.643	—	Larry See
Athletics (Phoenix)	33	23	.589	3	Juan Navarrete
Mariners (Peoria)	29	27	.518	7	Tom LeVasseur
Rockies (Chandler)	26	30	.464	10	Jim Eppard
Angels (Mesa)	24	32	.429	12	Bruce Hines
Diamondbacks (Phoenix)	20	36	.357	16	Dwayne Murphy

Playoffs: None.

All-Star Team: 1B-Mike Petersen, Rockies; **2B**-Brian Smith, Mariners; **3B**-Monte Davis, Athletics; **SS**-Jose Ortiz, Athletics; **OF**-Gary Gordon, Rockies; Marcus Knight, Angels; Hipolito Martinez, Athletics; Jacob Ruotsinoja, Padres; Jhensy Sandoval, Diamondbacks; **C**-Danny Serrano, Angels; **DH**-Shane Cronin, Padres; **P**-Nick Bierbrodt, Diamondbacks; Steve Hoff, Padres; John Nicholson, Rockies; Ramon Ortiz, Angels; Greg Winkleman, Athletics; Jeromy Palki, Mariners; **MVP**-Shane Cronin, Padres; **Manager**-Tom LeVasseur, Mariners; Juan Navarrete, Athletics.

BA: Brad Schwartzbauer, Rockies, .344
Runs: Jose Ortiz, Athletics, 43
Hits: Shane Cronin, Padres, 68
RBIs: Shane Cronin, Padres, 54
HRs: Shane Cronin, Padres, 9

Wins: Steve Hoff, Padres, 8
   Josef Thompson, Padres, 8
SOs: Steve Hoff, Padres, 104
ERA: Shawn Chacon, Rockies, 1.60

R Gulf Coast League
President: Thomas J. Saffell

East Standings	W	L	Pct.	GB	Manager
Expos (22) (West Palm Beach)	41	18	.695	—	Jim Gabella
Marlins (19) (Melbourne)	34	25	.576	7	Juan Bustabad
Mets (23) (Port St. Lucie)	29	30	.492	12	Mickey Brantley
Braves (15) (W. Palm Beach)	14	45	.237	27	Robert Lucas/Chino Cadahia

North Standings	W	L	Pct.	GB	Manager
Yankees (10) (Tampa)	37	21	.638	—	Ken Dominguez
Astros (20) (Kissimmee)	31	28	.525	6½	Bobby Ramos
Tigers (6) (Lakeland)	26	34	.433	12	Kevin Bradshaw
Devil Rays (30)(St. Pete)	24	35	.407	13½	Bill Evers

Northwest Standings	W	L	Pct.	GB	Manager
Rangers (13) (Port Charlotte)	37	23	.617	—	James Byrd
Orioles (1) (Sarasota)	36	24	.600	1	Tommy Shields
Pirates (25) (Bradenton)	28	31	.475	8½	Woody Huyke
White Sox (4) (Sarasota)	20	40	.333	17	Hector Rincones

Southwest Standings	W	L	Pct.	GB	Manager
Cubs (16) (Ft. Myers)	34	26	.567	—	Sandy Alomar, Sr.
Royals (7) (Ft. Myers)	30	29	.508	3½	Al Pedrique
Twins (9) (Ft. Myers)	30	30	.500	4	Mike Boulanger
Red Sox (2) (Ft. Myers)	24	36	.400	10	Bob Geren

Playoffs: Yankees 1 game, Expos 0; Rangers 1 game, Cubs 0.
Finals: Yankees 2 games, Rangers 0.

All-Star Team: 1B-Franky Figueroa, Orioles; **2B**-Dean Robertson, Orioles; **3B**-Derrick

Bly, Cubs; **SS**-Franklin Font, Cubs; **OF**-Fernando Nova, White Sox; Alex Sanchez, Devil Rays; Alexis Zapata, Tigers; **C**-Donny Leon, Yankees; **P**-Peter Fortune, Expos; Bobby Styles, Rangers; **Manager**-Ken Dominguez, Yankees.

BA: Donny Leon, Yankees, .361
Runs: Aaron Miles, Astros, 48
Hits: Franklin Font, Cubs, 72
RBIs: Donny Leon, Yankees, 46

HRs: Derrick Bly, Cubs, 13
Wins: Jonathan Widerski, Marlins, 8
SOs: Jeriome Robertson, Astros, 98
ERA: Antonio Gholar, Twins, 1.72

R Pioneer League
President: Jim McCurdy

North Standings	W	L	Pct.	GB	Attend.	Manager
Lethbridge						
Black Diamonds**(29)	50	22	.694	—	49,093	Chris Speier
Helena Brewers*(8)	43	29	.597	7	44,886	Alex Morales
Great Falls Dodgers (21)	33	39	.458	17	68,532	Mickey Hatcher
Medicine Hat Blue Jays (14)	22	50	.306	28	41,942	Marty Pevey

South Standings	W	L	Pct.	GB	Attend.	Manager
Ogden Raptors*(8)	42	30	.583	—	62,120	Bernie Moncallo
Idaho Falls Braves (27)	38	34	.528	4	53,755	Don Werner
Butte Copper Kings**(30)	37	35	.514	5	37,317	Tom Foley
Billings Mustangs (17)	23	49	.319	19	83,588	Matt Martin

Playoffs: Helena 2 games, Lethbridge 1; Ogden 2 games, Butte 1.
Finals: Helena 2 games, Ogden 0.

All-Star Team: 1B-Jonathan Tucker, Great Falls; **2B**-Wylie Campbell, Billings; **3B**-Steven Chavez, Idaho Falls; **SS**-Ben Reynoso, Idaho Falls; **OF**-Marcus McCain, Butte; Kevin Sweeney, Lethbridge; Jason Weekley, Great Falls; **C**-Matt Quatraro, Butte; **DH**-Miguel Rodriguez, Ogden; **P**-Brian Passini, Helena; Vladimir Nunez, Lethbridge; David Bleazard, Medicine Hat; **MVP**-Kevin Sweeney, Lethbridge; **Manager**-Tom Foley, Butte.

BA: Kevin Sweeney, Lethbridge, .424
Runs: Kevin Sweeney, Lethbridge, 72
Hits: Brian McClure, Idaho Falls, 99
RBIs: Kevin Sweeney, Lethbridge, 72
   Ronald Hartman, Lethbridge, 72

HRs: David Hayman, Lethbridge, 17
   Darron Ingram, Billings, 17
   Miguel Rodriguez, Ogden, 17
Wins: Vladimir Nunez, Lethbridge, 10
SOs: Vladimir Nunez, Lethbridge, 93
ERA: Vladimir Nunez, Lethbridge, 2.22

Ind Big South League
President: Dick King

Standings	W	L	Pct.	GB	Attend.	Manager
Pine Bluff Locomotives	42	30	.583	—	35,693	Bob Lacey/Bobby Clark
Columbia Mules	40	31	.563	1½	39,229	Barry Lyons
Tennessee Tomahawks#	40	31	.563	1½	57,086	Mike O'Berry
Greenville Bluesmen	35	36	.493	6½	36,532	Lyle Yates
Clarksville Coyotes	31	41	.431	11	31,287	Nate Colbert
Meridian Brakemen	26	45	.366	15½	37,339	Jose Santiago

#represented Winchester, Tennessee.

Playoffs: Greenville 2 games, Pine Bluff 1; Columbia 2 games, Tennessee 1.
Finals: Greenville 3 games, Columbia 0.

All-Star Team: 1B-Andre Keene, Meridian/Greenville; **2B**-Jose Serra, Greenville; **3B**-Tony Gonzalez, Clarksville; **SS**-Jeff Michael, Tennessee; **OF**-Tony Bellinato, Meridian; Stanton Cameron, Meridian/Columbia; John Graham, Greenville; Tom McKinnon, Pine Bluff; **C**-Tim Graham, Greenville; Jason Townley, Pine Bluff; **P**-John Dopson, Tennessee; Les Lancaster, Pine Bluff; Shane Majors, Tennessee; John Mitchell, Columbia; Charlie Mitchell, Columbia; **MVP**-Les Lancaster, Pine Bluff; **Pitcher of the Year**-Les Lancaster, Pine Bluff; **Rookie of the Year**-Tony Bellinato, Meridian; **Manager**-Barry Lyons, Columbia.

BA: Jason Townley, Pine Bluff, .362
Runs: Erick Corps, Greenville, 64
   Tom McKinnon, Pine Bluff, 64
Hits: Tom McKinnon, Pine Bluff, 99
RBIs: Stanton Cameron, Meridian/Columbia, 78

HRs: Stanton Cameron, Meridian/Columbia, 21
Wins: Les Lancaster, Pine Bluff, 12
SOs: John Dopson, Tennessee, 99
ERA: John Dopson, Tennessee, 2.95

Ind Frontier League
President: Bill Lee

East Standings	W	L	Pct.	GB	Attend.	Manager
Chillicothe Paints***	48	26	.647	—	51,419	Roger Hanners
Johnstown Steal	41	33	.554	7	61,575	Jim Coffman
Zanesville Greys	41	33	.554	7	24,190	Eric Welch
Ohio Valley Redcoats	30	44	.405	18	30,248	Jim Procopio

West Standings	W	L	Pct.	GB	Attend.	Manager
Richmond Roosters**	39	35	.527	—	55,510	John Cate
Springfield Capitals*	39	35	.527	—	47,854	Mal Fichman
Evansville Otters	34	40	.459	5	84,492	Doc Edwards
Kalamazoo Kodiaks	24	50	.324	15	62,331	Glenn Gulliver

Playoffs: Springfield 2 games, Richmond 1; Chillicothe 2, Johnstown 1.
Finals: Springfield 2 games, Chillicothe 0.

All-Star Team: 1B-Morgan Burkhardt, Richmond; **2B**-Joe Pass, Richmond; **3B**-Mitch House, Chillicothe; **SS**-Matt Riemer, Chillicothe; **OF**-Gerald Bolden, Johnstown; Jackie Jempson, Chillicothe; Marty Watson, Evansville; **C**-Jorge Melendez, Springfield; **DH**-Scott

Pinoni, Chillicothe; **P**-Matt Baxter, Zanesville; Terry Pearson, Zanesville; **MVP**-Morgan Burkhardt, Richmond; **Most Valuable Pitcher**-Matt Baxter, Zanesville; **Manager**-Roger Hanners, Chillicothe.

BA: Scott Pinoni, Chillicothe, .384
Runs: Marty Watson, Evansville, 66
Hits: Scott Pinoni, Chillicothe, 108
RBIs: Scott Pinoni, Chillicothe, 65
HRs: Mitch House, Chillicothe, 18

Wins: Reenn Edmondson, Chillicothe, 9
Matt Baxter, Zanesville, 9
SOs: Jeff Leystra, Evansville, 109
ERA: Matt Baxter, Zanesville, 2.47

Ind Heartland League
President: S. Allen Wolf

Standings	W	L	Pct.	GB	Attend.	Manager
Lafayette Leopards	32	27	.542	—	12,193	Paul Hoines
Anderson Lawmen	32	28	.533	½	9,611	Jay Walker
Will County Cheetahs	28	31	.475	4	6,378	Gregg Slutsky
Dubois County Dragons#	27	33	.450	5½	33,203	R.C. Lichtenstein

#represented Huntingburg, Indiana.

Playoffs: Anderson 2 games, Will County 1; Lafayette 2 games, Dubois County 1.
Finals: Lafayette 3 games, Anderson 2.

BA: Mike Stevenson, Will County, .361
Runs: Toby Ricard, Anderson, 59
Hits: Toby Ricard, Anderson, 83
RBIs: Gary Kamphouse, Lafayette, 52

HRs: Juan Price, Dubois County, 13
Wins: Johnny Oestreich, Dubois County, 8
SOs: Johnny Oestreich, Dubois County, 96
ERA: Mark Olson, Will County, 1.11

Ind North Atlantic League
President: Ed Broidy

Standings	W	L	Pct.	GB	Attend.	Manager
Massachusetts Mad Dogs#	56	21	.727	—	52,384	George Scott
Catskill Cougars@	43	35	.551	13½	27,917	Al Lopez
Newark Barge Bandits	41	37	.526	15½	12,676	Kenneth Gardner
Altoona Rail Kings	36	42	.462	20½	33,019	Virgil Christof
Welland Aquaducks	33	44	.429	23	6,877	Ellis Williams
Nashua Hawks	23	53	.303	32½	13,556	Harry Ayotte

#represented Lynn, Massachusetts.
@represented Moutaindale, New York.

Playoff: Catskill 2 games, Massachusetts 0.

All-Star Team: 1B-Doug Spofford, Massachusetts; **2B**-Billy Reed, Altoona; **3B**-Felix Colon, Massachusetts; **SS**-Karun Jackson, Altoona; **OF**-Jose DeLeon, Nashua; Dan Dillingham, Welland; Roy Marsh, Massachusetts; **C**-Chris Hasty, Welland; **P**-Germaine Hunter, Newark; Jay Murphy, Massachusetts; Ray Schmittle, Altoona; Tom Singer, Catskill; Joe Nestor, Catskill; **MVP**-Roy Marsh, Massachusetts; **Manager**-George Scott, Massachusetts.

BA: Doug Spofford, Massachusetts, .380
Runs: Roy Marsh, Massachusetts, 87
Hits: Roy Marsh, Massachusetts, 107
RBIs: Felix Colon, Massachusetts, 64
HRs: Manny Garcia, Catskill, 8

Wins: Jay Murphy, Massachusetts, 12
Germaine Hunter, Newark, 12
SOs: Germaine Hunter, Newark, 116
ERA: Jay Murphy, Massachusetts, 1.11

Ind Northeast League
President: Jeffrey Kunion

Standings	W	L	Pct.	GB	Attend.	Manager
Albany Diamond Dogs*	55	25	.688	—	57,171	John Wockenfuss
Newburgh Night Hawks**	55	25	.688	—	41,161	Dan Shwam
Bangor Blue Ox	46	33	.582	8½	35,652	Dick Phillips
Elmira Pioneers	34	45	.430	20½	41,501	Ken Oberkfell
Adirondack Lumberjacks	30	50	.375	25	56,341	Dave LaPoint
Rhode Island Tigersharks#	19	61	.238	36	8,290	Michael Palermo

#represented West Warwick, Rhode Island.

Playoff: Albany 3 games, Newburgh 1.

All-Star Team: 1B-Ron Lockett, Albany; **2B**-Lonnie Goldberg, Bangor; **3B**-Mike Miller, Newburgh; **SS**-Felix DeLeon, Albany; **OF**-Angelo Cox, Bangor; Rich Lemons, Newburgh; Timmie Morrow, Bangor; Jerome Tolliver, Albany; **DH**-John Mueller, Adirondack; **P**-Joel Bennett, Newburgh; Oil Can Boyd, Bangor; Gene Caruso, Newburgh; **MVP**-Paul Reinisch, Albany; **Pitcher of the Year**-Ed Riley, Albany; **Manager**-Dan Shwam, Newburgh.

BA: Paul Reinisch, Albany, .360
Runs: Mike Miller, Newburgh, 62
Hits: Paul Reinisch, Albany, 108
RBIs: Paul Reinisch, Albany, 61
Rich Lemons, Newburgh, 61

HRs: John Mueller, Adirondack, 18
Wins: Ed Riley, Albany, 11
SOs: Gene Caruso, Newburgh, 121
ERA: Jerry Hasler, Albany, 1.72
Pct: Oil Can Boyd, Bangor, 1.000, 10-0

Ind Northern League
President: Miles Wolff

East Standings	W	L	Pct.	GB	Attend.	Manager
St. Paul Saints***	45	40	.529	—	267,009	Marty Scott
Madison Black Wolf	44	41	.518	1	83,573	Wayne Krenchicki
Duluth-Superior Dukes	42	42	.500	2½	77,294	George Mitterwald
Thunder Bay Whiskey Jacks	33	51	.393	11½	50,429	Jason Felice/Jay Ward

---

West Standings	W	L	Pct.	GB	Attend.	Manager
Fargo-Moorhead						
RedHawks***	53	31	.631	—	155,052	Doug Simunic
Winnipeg Goldeyes	50	34	.595	3	171,351	Hal Lanier
Sioux Falls Canaries	44	40	.524	9	100,958	John Zizzo
Sioux City Explorers	26	58	.310	27	147,062	Ed Nottle

Playoffs: St. Paul defeated Madison 7-6 in a one game playoff for the first half title. St. Paul 2 games, Madison 0; Fargo-Moorhead 2 games, Winnipeg 1.
Finals: St. Paul 3 games, Fargo-Moorhead 0.

All-Star Team: 1B-Terry Lee, Winnipeg; **2B**-Casey Waller, Thunder Bay; **3B**-Jose Peguero, Sioux City; **SS**-Matt Davis, Sioux Falls; **OF**-Sean Hearn, Thunder Bay; Anthony Johnson, Duluth-Superior; Darryl Motley, Fargo-Moorhead; **C**-Mitch Lyden, Madison; **DH**-Kevin Garner, St. Paul/Sioux City; **P**-Jamie Ybarra, Sioux Falls/Winnipeg; Matt Jarvis, Winnipeg; Paul Romanoli, St. Paul; **Player of the Year**-Terry Lee, Winnipeg; **Rookie of the Year**-Chris Kokinda, Winnipeg; **Manager**-Doug Simunic, Fargo-Moorhead.

BA: Jose Peguero, Sioux City, .366
Runs: Chad Akers, Fargo-Moorhead, 84
Hits: Jose Peguero, Sioux City, 122
RBIs: Darryl Motley, Fargo-Moorhead, 103
HRs: Mitch Lyden, Madison, 29

Wins: Jeremy McGarity, Duluth-Superior, 12
Jim Manfred, St. Paul, 12
SOs: Jamie Ybarra, Sioux Falls/Winnipeg, 119
ERA: Jack Morris, St. Paul, 2.61

Ind Prairie League
President: Chris Ferguson, Sr.

North Standings	W	L	Pct.	GB	Attend.	Manager
Moose Jaw						
Diamond Dogs***	50	29	.633	—	76,696	Darryl Robinson/Scott Douglas
Grand Forks Varmints	45	34	.570	5	35,619	Mark Schlemmer/Mike Verdi
Regina Cyclones	37	41	.474	12½	33,370	George Zabala/Daryl Boston
Saskatoon Smokin' Guns	30	47	.390	19	22,991	Andre Johnson
Brandon Grey Owls	26	53	.329	24	10,967	Mike Sodders

South Standings	W	L	Pct.	GB	Attend.	Manager
Aberdeen Pheasants**	54	24	.692	—	29,552	Bob Flori
Minot Mallards*	54	26	.675	1	28,361	Mitch Zwolensky
Southern Minny Stars#	34	45	.430	20½	31,548	Greg Olson
Dakota Rattlers	33	44	.429	20½	25,702	Bill Sharp
Green Bay Sultans	28	46	.378	24	16,038	Dennis Ruh
Brainerd Bobcats@	7	9	.438	NA	2,646	Greg Tagert

#represented Austin, Minnesota.
@Brainerd disbanded June 19.

Playoffs: Minot 2 games, Aberdeen 0; Grand Forks 2 games, Moose Jaw 1.
Finals: Minot 3 games, Grand Forks 1.

All-Star Team: 1B-Ken Tirpack, Aberdeen; **2B**-Gordon Powell, Grand Forks; **3B**-Randy Kapano, Moose Jaw; **SS**-Sean McKamie, Southern Minny; **OF**-Gary Collum, Minot; Brian Cornelius, Moose Jaw; Ty Griffin, Grand Forks; **C**-Kevin Schula, Moose Jaw; **DH**-Lou List, Minot; **P**-Linc Mikkelsen, Minot; Leonel Vasquez, Aberdeen; Mike Toney, Moose Jaw; **MVP**-Brian Cornelius, Moose Jaw; **Rookie of the Year**-Leonel Vasquez, Aberdeen; **Manager**-Mike Verdi, Grand Forks; Mitch Zwolensky, Minot.

BA: Ken Tirpack, Aberdeen, .404
Runs: Ed Gerald, Aberdeen, 86
Hits: Ken Tirpack, Aberdeen, 120
RBIs: Ken Tirpack, Aberdeen, 84

HRs: Brad Strauss, Minot, 27
Wins: Collin Kerley, Minot, 14
SOs: Linc Mikkelsen, Minot, 118
ERA: Linc Mikkelsen, Minot, 1.26

Ind Texas-Louisiana League
President: Byron Pierce

Standings	W	L	Pct.	GB	Attend.	Manager
Abilene Prairie Dogs***	67	31	.683	—	68,297	Phil Stephenson
Lubbock Crickets	59	40	.596	8½	81,257	Greg Minton
Rio Grande Valley						
WhiteWings	50	48	.510	17	81,884	John Pacella
Amarillo Dillas	43	57	.430	25	135,881	Jim Nettles
Alexandria Aces	42	58	.420	26	76,414	Stan Cliburn
Tyler Wildcatters	36	63	.364	31½	58,572	Dave Hilton

Playoffs: Abilene 2 games, Amarillo 0; Lubbock 2 games, Rio Grande Valley 0.
Finals: Abilene 3 games, Lubbock 0.

All-Star Team: 1B-John O'Brien, Rio Grande Valley; **2B**-Jorge Alvarez, Amarillo; **3B**-Manny Gagliano, Abilene; **SS**-Lipso Nava, Rio Grande Valley; **OF**-Rod Brewer, Abilene; Sean Collins, Tyler; Malvin Matos, Alexandria; **C**-Jack Johnson, Abilene; **DH**-Joe Ronca, Alexandria; **Util**-Mike Hardge, Lubbock; **P**-David Haas, Abilene; Kerry Knox, Abilene; Daren Brown, Amarillo; Steve Duda, Lubbock; Ron Gerstein, Lubbock; Ken Winkle, Abilene; **MVP**-Rod Brewer, Abilene; **Most Valuable Pitcher**-David Haas, Abilene.

BA: Jorge Alvarez, Amarillo, .357
Runs: Mike Hardge, Lubbock, 77
Hits: Jorge Alvarez, Amarillo, 133
RBIs: Rod Brewer, Abilene, 87

HRs: John O'Brien, Rio Grande Valley, 25
Wins: Ron Gerstein, Lubbock, 14
SOs: Daren Brown, Amarillo, 143
ERA: David Haas, Abilene, 2.43

Ind Western League
President: Bruce Engel

North Standings	W	L	Pct.	GB	Attend.	Manager
Reno Chukars*	48	42	.533	—	52,113	Butch Hughes
Tri-City Posse**	44	45	.494	3½	96,061	Bobo Brayton

Grays Harbor Gulls	40	50	.444	8	37,045	Charley Kerfeld
Bend Bandits	39	50	.433	8½	52,946	Al Gallagher

South Standings	W	L	Pct.	GB	Attend.	Manager
Long Beach Riptide**	54	36	.600	—	74,440	Jeff Burroughs
Salinas Peppers*	54	36	.600	—	47,363	Dave Holt
Palm Springs Suns	46	44	.511	8	31,241	Jamie Nelson
Sonoma County Crushers	34	56	.378	20	92,020	Dick Dietz

Playoffs: Long Beach 2 games, Salinas 1; Tri-City 2 games, Reno 0.
Finals: Long Beach 3 games, Tri-City 1.

All-Star Team: 1B-Todd Pridy, Salinas; **2B**-Chris Grubb, Grays Harbor; **3B**-Frank Valdez, Palm Springs; **SS**-Ryan Rutz, Tri-City; **OF**-Ray Harvey, Grays Harbor; Shawn Scott, Tri-City; Sam Taylor, Salinas; **C**-Carl Nichols, Reno; **DH**-David Mowry, Sonoma County; **Util**-Rick Prieto, Salinas; **P**-Paul Anderson, Long Beach; Tim Gower, Salinas; Jose

Salcedo, Tri-City; Mark Tranberg, Long Beach; Ben Weber, Salinas; **Player of the Year**-Rick Prieto, Salinas; **Pitcher of the Year**-Paul Anderson, Long Beach; **Manager**-Butch Hughes, Reno.

BA: Chris Grubb, Grays Harbor, .365
Runs: Rick Prieto, Salinas, 83
Hits: Rick Prieto, Salinas, 123
RBIs: Carl Nichols, Reno, 89
HRs: Todd Pridy, Salinas, 21

Wins: Paul Anderson, Long Beach, 12
Ben Weber, Salinas, 12
SOs: Chris Sheehan, Tri-City, 135
ERA: Jose Salcedo, Tri-City, 2.11

1996 Interleague Post Season Play

World Series
New York (American) 4 games, Atlanta (National) 2

1996 Major League Farm Systems

American League

1 Baltimore (6): Rochester, Bowie, Frederick, High Desert, Bluefield, Gulf Coast.
2 Boston (6): Pawtucket, Trenton, Sarasota, Michigan, Lowell, Gulf Coast.
3 California (6): Vancouver, Midland, Lake Elsinore, Cedar Rapids, Boise, Arizona.
4 Chicago (7): Nashville, Birmingham, Prince William, South Bend, Hickory, Bristol, Gulf Coast.
5 Cleveland (6): Buffalo, Canton-Akron, Kinston, Columbus (GA), Watertown, Burlington (NC).
6 Detroit (7): Toledo, Jacksonville, Lakeland, Visalia, Fayetteville, Jamestown, Gulf Coast.
7 Kansas City (6): Omaha, Wichita, Wilmington, Lansing, Spokane, Gulf Coast.
8 Milwaukee (6): New Orleans, El Paso, Stockton, Beloit, Helena, Ogden.
9 Minnesota (6): Salt Lake, Hardware City, Ft. Myers, Fort Wayne, Elizabethton, Gulf Coast.
10 New York (6): Columbus (OH), Norwich, Tampa, Greensboro, Oneonta, Gulf Coast.
11 Oakland (6): Edmonton, Huntsville, Modesto, West Michigan, Southern Oregon, Arizona.
12 Seattle (6): Tacoma, Port City, Lancaster, Wisconsin, Everett, Arizona.
13 Texas (6): Oklahoma City, Tulsa, Port Charlotte, Charleston (SC), Hudson Valley, Gulf Coast.
14 Toronto (6): Syracuse, Knoxville, Dunedin, Hagerstown, St. Catharines, Medicine Hat.

National League

15 Atlanta (7): Richmond, Greenville, Durham, Macon, Eugene, Danville, Gulf Coast.
16 Chicago (6): Iowa, Orlando, Daytona, Rockford, Williamsport, Gulf Coast.
17 Cincinnati (6): Indianapolis, Chattanooga, Winston-Salem, Charleston (WV), Billings, Princeton.
18 Colorado (6): Colorado Springs, New Haven, Salem, Asheville, Portland (OR), Arizona.
19 Florida (6): Charlotte, Portland (ME), Brevard County, Kane County, Utica, Gulf Coast.
20 Houston (6): Tucson, Jackson, Kissimmee, Quad City, Auburn, Gulf Coast.
21 Los Angeles (7): Albuquerque, San Antonio, Vero Beach, San Bernardino, Savannah, Yakima, Great Falls.
22 Montreal (6): Ottawa, Harrisburg, West Palm Beach, Delmarva, Vermont, Gulf Coast.
23 New York (7): Norfolk, Binghamton, St. Lucie, Capital City, Pittsfield, Kingsport, Gulf Coast.
24 Philadelphia (6): Scranton-Wilkes-Barre, Reading, Clearwater, Piedmont, Batavia, Martinsville.
25 Pittsburgh (6): Calgary, Carolina, Lynchburg, Augusta, Erie, Gulf Coast.
26 St. Louis (6): Louisville, Arkansas, St. Petersburg, Peoria, New Jersey, Johnson City.
27 San Diego (6): Las Vegas, Memphis, Rancho Cucamonga, Clinton, Idaho Falls, Arizona.
28 San Francisco (5): Phoenix, Shreveport, San Jose, Burlington (IA), Bellingham.

Expansion Teams

29 Arizona (3): Visalia, Lethbridge, Arizona.
30 Tampa Bay (3): Hudson Valley, Butte, Gulf Coast.

Co-op(x): Bakersfield.

1996 No-Hitters

Date	Pitcher	Team	League	Opponent	Score
4-30	Rob Burger	Piedmont	South Atlantic	Augusta	1-0
5-5	Joe Crawford	Binghamton	Eastern	Trenton	1-0 (7)
5-11	Al Leiter	Florida	National	Colorado	11-0
5-14	Dwight Gooden	New York	American	Seattle	2-0
5-28	Calvin Maduro	Bowie	Eastern	Portland	5-0 (7)
6-1	Travis Buckley	Chattanooga	Southern	Huntsville	6-0
6-9	John Rocker	Macon	South Atlantic	Charleston (SC)	2-0 (7)
6-10	Joe Atwater	St. Lucie	Florida State	Daytona	1-0 (7)
6-11	Sean Leslie	Delmarva	South Atlantic	Greensboro	9-0 (7)
6-12	Dan Kolb	Charleston (SC)	South Atlantic	Columbus	3-0 (6)
6-25	Aaron Lane	Bowie	Eastern	Norwich	2-0 (7)
7-17	Scott Randall	Asheville	South Atlantic	Fayetteville	4-0
7-17	Americo Peguero/Scott Eibey/Gabe Molina	Bluefield	Appalachian	Elizabethton	3-0
7-26	Jason Dawsey	Beloit	Midwest	Burlington	5-0
7-28	Kerry Wood/Jairo Diaz/ Darold Brown	Daytona	Florida State	Tampa	5-1
7-28	Luis de los Santos	Oneonta	New York-Penn.	Batavia	4-0
8-4	Luther Hackman	Salem	Carolina	Kinston	4-1
8-4	Jim Sak/Todd Bussa	Clinton	Midwest	Burlington	3-0
8-5	Jason Grote	Burlington	Midwest	Clinton	8-0 (8)
8-6	Edgar Ramos	Jackson	Texas	Shreveport	3-0
8-8	Aaron Small	Edmonton	Pacific Coast	Vancouver	6-0
8-13	Rick Helling	Oklahoma City	American Assoc.	Nashville	4-0 (P)
8-14	Scott Randall	Asheville	South Atlantic	Augusta	2-1 (11)
8-15	Domingo Guzman	Idaho Falls	Pioneer	Butte	6-0
8-21	Chris Corn/Jay Tessmer	Tampa	Florida State	Clearwater	2-1
8-24	Kerry Wood/Darold Brown/ Brandon Hammack	Daytona	Florida State	Vero Beach	3-0
9-3	Dennis Martinez, Jr./Sean DePaula/Matt Minter/Ken Wagner	Watertown	New York-Penn.	Utica	3-0
9-17	Hideo Nomo	Los Angeles	National	Colorado	9-0
	Roberto Ramirez	MC Diablos Rojos	Mexican	Tabasco	2-0

Number in parentheses indicates innings pitched if other than nine; "P" indicates perfect game.

THIS DATE IN MINOR LEAGUE HISTORY

April 15, 1996, Macon reliever Adam Butler began a streak of 36 consecutive scoreless innings pitched. Butler would move up to Durham and then to Greenville before the streak ended in July.

May 24, 1996, Jason Cook of Lancaster, California League, completed a run of 16 consecutive times reaching base over four days. He had five hits, five walks, three fielder's choices, and was hit by a pitch three times.

June 28, 1996, Huntsville's Demond Smith hit two grand slams against Orlando in Southern League action.

July 3, 1996, Lowell's Bobby Rodgers struck out 16 Utica batters in 7-2/3 innings pitched in a New York-Pennsylvania League game.

July 4, 1996, El Paso's Sean Maloney began a string of 14 consecutive appearances in which he would earn a save.

July 24, 1996, Steve Prihoda of Wilmington, Carolina League, struck out eight Lynchburg batters in succession.

August 6, 1996, Kevin Manley of the Gulf Coast League Mets threw six wild pitches in one inning in a game with the GCL Braves.

August 14, 1996, Asheville defeated Augusta 2-1 in a 19-inning South Atlantic League contest. Asheville starter Scott Randall held Augusta hitless for 11 innings before being relieved.

August 25, 1996, Colorado Springs' Neifi Perez collected seven hits in a 13-inning Pacific Coast League game against Salt Lake.

September 1, 1996, The Bakersfield Blaze of the California League ended the season with its 22nd consecutive loss. The club also had a 12-game losing skein earlier in the season.

IV
ACHIEVEMENTS

ACTIVE LEAGUE RECORDS

INACTIVE LEAGUE RECORDS

ALL TIME LEADERS

AWARDS

ACTIVE LEAGUE RECORDS

AMERICAN ASSOCIATION
Class A 1903-1911; Class AA 1912-1945;
Class AAA 1946-1962, 1969-

Batting
Games: 171, Maurice Shannon, Louisville, 1923
171, Charles Pechous, Toledo, 1923
171, Fred Maguire, Toledo, 1927
171, Leo Durocher, St. Paul, 1927
BA: .405, George Stone, Milwaukee, 1904
At Bats: 730, Jay Kirke, Sr., Louisville, 1921
Runs: 175, Joe Mowry, Minneapolis, 1932
Hits: 282, Jay Kirke, Sr., Louisville, 1921
RBIs: 191, Bunny Brief, Kansas City, 1921
2Bs: 69, Bill Knickerbocker, Toledo, 1932
3Bs: 28, Bert Daniels, Louisville, 1915
28, Lance Richbourg, Milwaukee, 1926
HRs: 69, Joe Hauser, Minneapolis, 1933
EBHs: 108, Joe Hauser, Minneapolis, 1933
TBs: 439, Joe Hauser, Minneapolis, 1933
Streak: 43, Eddie Marshall, Milwaukee, 1935
43, Howie Bedell, Louisville, 1961
SBs: 101, Vince Coleman, Louisville, 1984
Sac: 61, David Altizer, Minneapolis, 1910
BBs: 147, Nick Polly, Louisville, 1944
SOs: 174, Jim McDaniel, Denver, 1961

Pitching
Games: 85, George Spencer, Charleston, 1959
CGs: 35, Dave Danforth, Columbus, 1921
Wins: 31, Thomas Hughes, Minneapolis, 1910
31, Tom Sheehan, St. Paul, 1923
Losses: 26, Jim Durham, Kansas City, 1904
Pct: 1.000, 9-0, Ben Tincup, Louisville, 1921
.933, 14-1, Roy Parmelee, Columbus, 1932
ERA: 1.50, George Merritt, St. Paul, 1918
1.50, Gene Dale, Indianapolis, 1918
IP: 446, Stony McGlynn, Milwaukee, 1909
Win Streak: 16, Charley Hall, St. Paul, 1915
ShOs: 14, Stony McGlynn, Milwaukee, 1909
ShO Streak: 42, Mike Jackson, Omaha, 1972
SOs: 330, Herb Score, Indianapolis, 1954
Saves: 34, Jay Baller, Indianapolis, 1990
BBs: 173, Harry Weaver, Indianapolis, 1922

APPALACHIAN LEAGUE
(SHORT SEASON)
Class D 1957-1962, Rookie 1963-
(see also Appalachian League (long season) under Inactive Leagues)

Batting
Games: 73, Martin Boer, Covington, 1968
73, Larry Mansfield, Covington, 1968
73, Glenn Braggs, Paintsville, 1983
73, Jim Walewander, Bristol, 1983
BA: .410, Tony Oliva, Wytheville, 1961
At Bats: 296, David Heintz, Salem, 1964
Runs: 72, Ross Moschitto, Johnson City, 1964
Hits: 114, Mark Corey, Bluefield, 1976
RBIs: 84, James Walrath, Johnson City, 1964
2Bs: 23, Hosken Powell, Elizabethton, 1975
23, Mike Williams, Bristol, 1981
23, Darrell Deak, Johnson City, 1991
3Bs: 11, Jerry Pritchard, Wytheville, 1962
HRs: 22, Paul Russo, Elizabethton, 1990
EBHs: 38, Gary Fancher, Bluefield, 1964
TBs: 191, Mark Corey, Bluefield, 1976
SBs: 53, Steve Blomberg, Kingsport, 1973
BBs: 76, Jose Alvarez, Johnson City, 1974
SOs: 122, Mark Thomas, Princeton, 1988

Pitching
Games: 43, Dennis McMillian, Bluefield, 1974
CGs: 10, held by many
Wins: 13, Arthur Thompson, Morristown, 1959
Losses: 10, held by many
Pct: 1.000, 11-0, Bob Sykes, Bristol, 1974
ERA: 1.07, Bob Sykes, Bristol, 1974
IP: 124, Arthur Thompson, Morristown, 1959
Win Streak: 11, Bob Sykes, Bristol, 1974
ShOs: 6, Bob Sykes, Bristol, 1974
SOs: 180, Arne Thorsland, Bluefield, 1959
Saves: 17, Manuel Mendez, Johnson City 1995
WP: 25, Steve Dalkowski, Kingsport, 1957
BBs: 129, Steve Dalkowski, Kingsport, 1957

ARIZONA LEAGUE
Rookie 1988-

Batting
Games: 59, Rob Leary, Athletics, 1991
59, Mark Simmons, Angels, 1991
BA: .451, Timothy McWilliam, Padres, 1988
At Bats: 236, Franklin Garcia, Brewers, 1993
Runs: 72, Sylvester Love, Brewers, 1988
Hits: 82, Timothy McWilliam, Padres, 1988
RBIs: 54, Shane Cronin, Padres, 1996
2Bs: 20 Brian Rupp, Caridnals, 1992
3Bs: 10 Leon Glenn, Brewers, 1988
10, Lino Connell, Angels, 1991
HRs: 9, Leon Glenn, Brewers, 1989
9, Jonas Hamlin, Cardinals, 1990
9, Steve Cerio, Cardinals, 1991
9, Shane Cronin, Padres, 1996
EBHs: 31, Leon Glenn, Brewers, 1988
TBs: 129, Leon Glenn, Brewers, 1988
Sac: 7, Ruben Cephas, Brewers, 1993
SBs: 36, Franklin Garcia, Brewers, 1993
BBs: 56, Brett Hendley, Athletics, 1989
HBP: 15, Derrick Cantrell, Brewers, 1993
SOs: 66, Chad Bieri, Brewers, 1993

Pitching
Games: 29, Mark Tolbert, Cardinals, 1989
29, Matthew Tomso, Cardinals, 1990
CGs: 5, Jose Aguirre, Angels, 1993
Wins: 10, George Glinatsis, Mariners, 1991
Losses: 10, Richard Delgado, Co-op, 1988
Pct: .889, 8-1, Jason Myers, Giants, 1993
ERA: 0.40, William Kostich, Mariners, 1990
IP: 96.1, Bronswell Patrick, Athletics, 1988
Win Streak: 8, Luis Luebbers, Brewers, 1989
ShOs: 4, Ray Davis, Cardinals, 1992
SOs: 134, Josh Bishop, Rockies, 1995
Saves: 18, Frank Garcia, Cardinals, 1994

CALIFORNIA LEAGUE
Class C 1941-1942, 1946-1962; Class A 1963-

Batting
Games: 147, held by many
BA: .436, Francis Boniar, Reno, 1957
At Bats: 625, Melvin Nelson, Fresno, 1955
Runs: 167, Jess Pike, Bakersfield, 1949
Hits: 209, Benjamin Valenzuela, Fresno, 1955
209, Vada Pinson, Visalia, 1957
RBIs: 172, Harry Heslet, Visalia, 1956
2Bs: 55, Richard Wilson, Modesto, 1951
3Bs: 22, Bobby Smith, Fresno, 1954
HRs: 51, Harry Heslet, Visalia, 1956
EBHs: 97, Richard Wilson, Modesto, 1951
TBs: 384, Richard Wilson, Modesto, 1951
Streak: 35, Brent Gates, Modesto, 1992
SBs: 144, Donnell Nixon, Bakersfield, 1983
BBs: 194, Jess Pike, Bakersfield, 1949
SOs: 220, Wesley Kent, San Jose, 1984
HBP: 27, Chris Cron, Palm Springs, 1988

Pitching
Games: 69, Robert Arrighi, Reno, 1960
69, Tracy Harris, San Jose/Santa Clara, 1979
CGs: 32, Robert Thorpe, Stockton, 1954
Wins: 28, Earl Escalante, Baskerfield, 1949
28, Larry Jackson, Fresno, 1952
28, Robert Thorpe, Stockton, 1954
Losses: 22, Tom King, Visalia, 1954
Pct: 1.000, 16-0, Charles Beamon, Stockton, 1955
ERA: 1.30, Bill Wegman, Stockton, 1983
IP: 300⅓, Robert Thorpe, Stockton, 1954
Win Streak: 16, Charles Beamon, Stockton, 1955
16, Alvin Spearman, Stockton, 1956
ShOs: 8, Mark Ferguson, Modesto, 1982
ShO Streak: 40, William Dial, San Jose, 1957
40, Gary DeBenedetti, San Jose, 1970
SOs: 351, Larry Jackson, Fresno, 1952
Saves: 32, Carlos Castillo, Lake Elsinore, 1995
BBs: 262, Steve Dalkowski, Stockton, 1960
HB: 32, Robert Dunn, Visalia, 1957
WP: 33, Raymond Gault, Bakersfield, 1978

CAROLINA LEAGUE
Class C 1945-1948; Class B 1949-1962; Class A 1963-

Batting
Games: 154, Andy Pieski, Reidsville, 1950
154, Curt Flood, High Point-Thomasville, 1956
154, Karl Kuehl, High Point-Thomasville, 1956
154, Doug Hubacek, Greensboro, 1956
BA: .391, Harry Sullivan, Raleigh, 1947
At Bats: 624, Mike Hafenecker, Burlington, 1950
Runs: 161, Woody Fair, Durham, 1946
Hits: 208, Oswaldo Olivares, Salem, 1977
RBIs: 166, Leon Wagner, Danville, 1956
2Bs: 51, Woody Fair, Durham, 1946
3Bs: 17, David Arrington, Salem, 1968
HRs: 55, Leo "Muscle" Shoals, Reidsville, 1949
Grand Slams: 7, Chuck Weatherspoon, Wilson, 1961
EBHs: 82, Woody Fair, Durham, 1946
TBs: 365, Leo "Muscle" Shoals, Reidsville, 1949
Streak: 31, Orge "Pat" Cooper, Martinsville, 1948
SBs: 105, Lenny Dykstra, Lynchburg, 1983
BBs: 161, Gerald Davis, Salem, 1981
SOs: 211, Glenallen Hill, Kinston, 1985
HBP: 24, Rusty Crockett, Winston-Salem, 1989

Pitching
Games: 78, Mike Brown, Rocky Mount, 1980
CGs: 31, Frank Paulin, Leaksville-Spray-Draper, 1946
Wins: 25, Lewis Hester, Reidsville, 1948
25, Eddie Neville, Durham, 1949
Losses: 21, Charles Miller, Raleigh, 1950
Pct: .921, 13-1, Jim Wright, Peninsula, 1980
ERA: 1.16, Peter Manos, Peninsula, 1976
IP: 303, Frank Paulin, Leaksville-Spray-Draper, 1946
Win Streak: 16, Lamar Inman Chambers, Burlington, 1947
16, James Minshall, Salem 1972
ShOs: 9, Leonard Matarazzo, Fayetteville, 1952
ShO Streak: 42, Mike Brown, Winston-Salem, 1981
SOs: 300, Dwight Gooden, Lynchburg, 1983
BBs: 170, Andrew Rubilotta, Portsmouth, 1964
Saves: 41, Mike Soper, Kinston, 1991
HB: 30, Bill MacLeod, Winston-Salem, 1961
WP: 32, Wally Wolf, Peninsula, 1965

EASTERN LEAGUE
Class A 1923-1962; Class AA 1963-
(New York-Pennsylvania League 1923-1937)

Batting
Games: 149, Bob Bowman, Schenectady, 1953
149, Dan Schell, Schenectady, 1953
BA: .400, Joe Munson (Carlson), Harrisburg, 1925
At Bats: 609, Granny Hamner, Utica, 1947
Runs: 134, Larry Fischer, Harrisburg, 1934
Hits: 214, Don Brown, York, 1930
RBIs: 138, Ken Harrelson, Binghamton, 1962
2Bs: 54, Dewey Steffens, York, 1924
3Bs: 28, Al Gionfriddo, Albany, 1944
HRs: 41, Ken Strong, Hazleton, 1930
41, Rick Lancellotti, Buffalo, 1979
TBs: 355, Joe Munson (Carlson), Harrisburg, 1925
Streak: 38, Hubert Mason, Binghamton, 1925
SBs: 96, Larry Lintz, Quebec City, 1972
BBs: 151, Pinky May, Albany, 1947
151, Herschel Held, Albany, 1949
SOs: 165, Ezell King, Allentown, 1959
HBP: 23, Nick Delvecchio, Norwich, 1995

Pitching
Games: 67, Carlos Medrano, York, 1964
67, Wayne Gomes, Reading, 1996
CGs: 31, Hugh Mulcahy, Hazleton, 1936
Wins: 27, Thomas "Lefty" George, York, 1925
Losses: 24, Ernest Walters, Elmira, 1923
Pct: 1.000, 18-0, Bill MacLeod, Pittsfield, 1965
ERA: 1.30, Mel Parnell, Scranton, 1946
IP: 325, Hugh Mulcahy, Hazleton, 1936
Win Streak: 18, Bill MacLeod, Pittsfield, 1965
ShOs: 11, Allie Reynolds, Wilkes-Barre, 1942
SOs: 258, Fred Norman, Binghamton, 1963
Saves: 34, Alberto Reyes, Harrisburg, 1994
BBs: 180, Richard Rozak, Wilkes-Barre, 1948
HB: 21, Dudley Foulk, Williamsport, 1928
21, Ted Pritchard, Elmira, 1928

ACTIVE LEAGUE RECORDS

FLORIDA STATE LEAGUE
Class D 1936-1941, 1946-1962; Class A 1963-

Batting

Games: 146, Luis Gonzalez, St. Petersburg, 1973
BA: .400, Dan Keith, Sanford/Daytona Beach, 1955
At Bats: 606, Bob Truss, Daytona Beach, 1951
Runs: 150, Jesse Cade, DeLand, 1952
Hits: 217, Bruce Barnes, Orlando, 1950
RBIs: 140, Bernard Lake, Sanford, 1946
2Bs: 48, Curtis Burke, Daytona, 1983
3Bs: 30, Pete Rose, Tampa, 1961
HRs: 33, Ed Levy, Sanford, 1950
　　　　33, Jim Fuller, Miami, 1971
EBHs: 73, Robert Truss, Daytona Beach, 1951
TBs: 332, Robert Truss, Daytona Beach, 1951
Streak: 36, Joe Altobelli, Daytona Beach, 1951
SBs: 116, Allan Lewis, Leesburg, 1966
BBs: 153, Lyle Judy, St. Augustine, 1950
SOs: 200, Gerald Lyscio, Cocoa, 1965
HBP: 20, John Paszek, Leesburg, 1948

Pitching

Games: 68, Bill Boyette, West Palm Beach, 1955
　　　　68, Jay Tessmer, Tampa, 1996
CGs: 32, Wally Gaddis, Daytona Beach, 1948
Wins: 29, Stan Karpinski, St. Augustine, 1949
Losses: 23, Ballard Branham, Leesburg, 1948
Pct: .938, 15-1, David Morgan, St. Petersburg, 1964
ERA: 0.90, Earl Willoughby, Ft. Lauderdale, 1965
IP: 340, Jake Bunch, Leesburg, 1938
Win Streak: 17, James Dean, Sanford, 1939
ShOs: 9, Stan Karpinski, St. Augustine, 1949
　　　　9, Paul Gilliford, Miami, 1966
ShO Streak: 48 1/3, Paul Gilliford, Miami, 1966
SOs: 302, John Ivory Smith, Daytona Beach, 1955
Saves: 38, Barry Manuel, Charlotte, 1990
　　　　38, John Kelly, St. Petersburg, 1992
BBs: 205, Ernest Crammer, Daytona Beach, 1953

GULF COAST LEAGUE
Rookie 1964-
(Sarasota Rookie League 1964, Florida Rookie League 1965)

Batting

Games: 65, Reggie West, Royals Gold, 1981
BA: .400, Angel Dotel, Dodgers, 1991
At Bats: 266, Ronald Johnson, Royals Blue, 1980
Runs: 64, Sergio Nunez, Royals, 1994
Hits: 92, Sergio Nunez, Royals, 1994
RBIs: 53, Jeff Newman, Indians, 1970
2Bs: 20, Drew Denson, Braves, 1984
3Bs: 11, Irvin Abad, Blue Jays, 1994
HRs: 13, Derrick Bly, Cubs, 1996
TBs: 133, Drew Denson, Braves, 1984
Sac: 11, Gary D'Onofrio, Astros Blue, 1980
SBs: 50, Alexis Marte, Blue Jays, 1981
BBs: 58, Gary Gloede, Indians, 1970
　　　　58, Kevin Schoendienst, Cubs, 1980
SOs: 83, Tim McMillan, Pirates, 1984

Pitching

Games: 33, Ysidro Giron, Yankees, 1986
CGs: 9, Alexander Bonci, Braves, 1964
Wins: 10, held by many
Losses: 9, held by many
Pct: 1.000, held by many
ERA: 0.17, Mariano Rivera, Yankees, 1990
IP: 105, Fernando Santana, Blue Jays, 1984
ShOs: 4, Tom Hall, Twins, 1966
　　　　4, Fernando DaSilva, Expos, 1992
SOs: 108, Harold McClain, White Sox, 1970
BBs: 67, Kelly Phipps, Reds, 1972

INTERNATIONAL LEAGUE
Class A 1902-1911; Class AA 1912-1945; Class AAA 1946-
(Eastern League 1902-1911)

Batting

Games: 170, Al Moore, Buffalo, 1928
BA: .412, Jack Bentley, Baltimore, 1920
At Bats: 685, Joe Rabbit, Toronto, 1929

Runs: 173, Joe Hauser, Baltimore, 1930
Hits: 246, Jack Bentley, Baltimore, 1921
RBIs: 180, James "Rip" Collins, Rochester, 1930
2Bs: 57, Jim Holt, Jersey City, 1924
3Bs: 29, Guy Tutweiler, Providence, 1914
HRs: 63, Joe Hauser, Baltimore, 1930
EBHs: 113, Joe Hauser, Baltimore, 1930
TBs: 443, Joe Hauser, Baltimore, 1930
Streak: 36, Bill Sweeney, Baltimore, 1935
SBs: 94, Otis Nixon, Columbus, 1983
Sac: 64, Clifford Brady, Rochester, 1923
BBs: 167, Blas Monaco, Baltimore, 1944
SOs: 199, Dave Nicholson, Richmond, 1968

Pitching

CGs: 33, John Ogden, Baltimore, 1921
　　　　33, John Wisner, Rochester, 1923
Wins: 33, Rube Parnham, Baltimore, 1923
Losses: 29, Frank Leary, Rochester, 1903
　　　　29, Charles Swaney, Reading, 1926
Pct: .929, 13-1, Tony Jacobs, Rochester, 1954
ERA: 1.31, Urban Shocker, Toronto, 1916
IP: 422, Joe McGinnity, Newark, 1909
Win Streak: 20, Jim Parnham, Baltimore, 1923
ShOs: 11, Joe McGinnity, Newark, 1909
ShO Streak: 54, Urban Shocker, Toronto, 1916
SOs: 330, Lefty Grove, Baltimore, 1923
BBs: 186, Lefty Grove, Baltimore, 1923
Saves: 37, Mike Draper, Columbus, 1992

MEXICAN LEAGUE
Independent 1937-1954; Class AA 1955-1966; Class AAA 1967-

Batting

Games: 161, Rolando Camerero, Veracruz, 1969
BA: .454, Willie Aikens, Puebla, 1986
At Bats: 649, Pedro Cardenal, Laredo, 1959
Runs: 141, Nick Castaneda, San Luis Potosi, 1986
Hits: 227, Miguel Suarez Lopez, MC Diablos Rojos, 1977
RBIs: 154, Willie Aikens, Puebla, 1986
2Bs: 49, Vinicio Garcia, Monterrey, 1961
　　　　49, Roberto Vizcarro, Leon, 1991
3Bs: 19, Albino Diaz, Poza Rica, 1975
　　　　19, Leonardo Valenzuela, Monterrey, 1979
HRs: 54, Jack Pierce, Leon, 1986
Grand Slams: 6, Balthazar Valdez, Monclova, 1986
EBHs: 89, Nick Castaneda, San Luis Potosi, 1986
TBs: 384, Willie Aikens, Puebla, 1986
Streak: 44, Ruben Saldana, Monterrey, 1975
SBs: 100, Mike Cole, Tabasco, 1989
CS: 33, Mike Cole, Tabasco, 1989
Sac: 27, George Hausmann, Monterrey, 1947
SacF: 17, Antonio Martinez, MC Tigres/Veracruz, 1972
BBs: 152, Altar Greene, Monclova, 1986
IBBs: 53, Hector Espino, Monterrey, 1969
SOs: 131, Bill Parlier, Jalisco, 1970
HBP: 24, Wilfredo Arano, MC Diablos Rojos, 1967

Pitching

Games: 73, Aurelio Lopez, MC Diablos Rojos, 1977
Starts: 39, Bill Jefferson, Monterrey, 1960
　　　　39, Salvador Sanchez, Reynosa, 1970
CGs: 30, Jim Horsford, Monterrey, 1969
Wins: 30, Ramon Bragana, Veracruz, 1944
Losses: 21, Roman Ramos, Veracruz, 1957
Pct: .917, 22-2, Silvano Quezada, Tampico, 1973
　　　　1.000, 12-0, Aurelio Monteagudo, Puebla, 1974
ERA: 0.71, Henry Miller, Torreon, 1950
IP: 325, Ramon Bragana, Veracruz, 1944
Win Streak: 16, Silvano Quezada, Tampico, 1973
ShOs: 10, Gary Ryersen, Tampico, 1976
　　　　10, Luis Mere, MC Diablos Rojos, 1977
　　　　10, Vincente Romo, Coatzacoalcos, 1979
ShO Streak: 51, Jim Horsford, Reynosa, 1968
SOs: 309, Jose Ramon Lopez, Monterrey, 1966
Saves: 34, Mike Browning, Campeche, 1991
BBs: 176, Booker McDaniels, San Luis Potosi, 1946
WP: 30, Rafael Garcia, Aguascalientes, 1988
HBP: 31, Anibal Diaz, Coatzacoalcos, 1982

MIDWEST LEAGUE
Class D 1947-1962; Class A 1963-
(Illinois State League 1947-1948, Mississippi-Ohio Valley League 1949-1955)

Batting

Games: 140, James Christensen, Wisconsin Rapids, 1980
　　　　140, Keith Lockhart, Cedar Rapids, 1987
BA: .409, Grover "Deacon" Jones, Dubuque, 1956
At Bats: 567, James Christensen, Wisconsin Rapids, 1980
Runs: 133, James Belz, West Frankfort, 1950
Hits: 203, Eddie Logan, Mattoon, 1956
RBIs: 136, James Zaap, Paris, 1952
2Bs: 47, Richard Hidalgo, Quad City, 1994
3Bs: 19, John Wyre, Clinton, 1954
HRs: 42, Jeff Jones, Cedar Rapids, 1982
Grand Slams: 4, Pete Koegel, Burlington, 1966
EBHs: 70, Clinton McCord, Paris, 1952
　　　　70, Jeff Jones, Cedar Rapids, 1982
　　　　70, Greg Vaughn, Beloit, 1987
TBs: 313, Eddie Logan, Mattoon, 1956
Streak: 33, Frank Toups, Waterloo, 1977
SBs: 98, Ramon Sambo, Cedar Rapids, 1988
SOs: 195, Josh Booty, Kane County, 1996
BB: 150, Vanity Rushing, Waterloo, 1902
HBP: 27, Charles Gipson, Appleton, 1993

Pitching

Games: 65, Frank Cimorelli, Springfield, 1992
CGs: 26, Joel McDaniel, Decatur, 1959
Wins: 22, Eugene Pisarski, Centralia, 1950
　　　　22, Kenneth Gohn, Danville, 1962
　　　　22, John Baumgarner, Decatur, 1954
　　　　22, Arturo Miro, Clinton, 1956
　　　　22, Joel McDaniel, Decatur, 1959
Losses: 17, Steven Duckhorn, Cedar Rapids, 1979
　　　　17, Scott Kannenberg, Quad Cities, 1987
Pct: 1.000, 11-0, Bryan Hickerson, Clinton, 1987
ERA: 1.13, Vern Geishert, Quad City, 1966
IP: 249 2/3, Ronald Hagler, Hannibal, 1955
Win Streak: 19, Arturo Miro, Clinton, 1956
　　　　19, Robert Freels, Bellville, 1947
ShOs: 9, Joel McDaniel, Decatur, 1959
　　　　9, Robert DeLong, Decatur, 1967
ShO Streak: 42, Mark Grant, Clinton, 1982
SOs: 274, Danny Morris, Wisconsin Rapids, 1965
BBs: 176, James Michalec, West Frankfort, 1949
Saves: 41, Mike Perez, Springfield, 1989

NEW YORK-PENN. LEAGUE
(SHORT SEASON)
Class A 1967-
(see also New York-Pennsylvania League (long season) under Inactive Leagues)

Batting

Games: 78, Jim Bullinger, Geneva, 1986
BA: .402, Jack Maloof, Auburn, 1971
At Bats: 320, Santiago Escobar, St. Catharines, 1986
Runs: 83, Mark Gilbert, Geneva, 1978
Hits: 107, Rob Katzaroff, Jamestown, 1991
RBIs: 77, Gary Holle, Newark, 1977
　　　　77, Dennis Carter, Erie, 1985
2Bs: 26, Demetrius Dowler, Geneva, 1993
3Bs: 11, Darrell Jones, Oneonta, 1972
　　　　11, Terry Whitfield, Oneonta, 1972
　　　　11, Matt Winters, Oneonta, 1978
HRs: 23, John Hennell, Utica, 1982
Grand Slams: 3, held by many
EBHs: 41, John Hennell, Utica, 1982
TBs: 185, Don Jacoby, Utica, 1983
SBs: 66, Geoff Dogget, Geneva, 1982
BBs: 76, John Buszka, Batavia, 1976
SOs: 117, Dave Cochrane, Little Falls, 1982
HBP: 17, Charlie Foster, Auburn, 1968

Pitching

Games: 42, Roy Moretti, Utica, 1982
CGs: 14, Robert Jajczan, Oneonta, 1973
　　　　14, Mark Wiley, Auburn, 1970
Wins: 13, Robert Parker, Geneva, 1978

13, Daniel Freed, Jamestown, 1988
Losses: 11, Kyle Channing, Watertown, 1985
Pct: 1.000, 11-0, Neal Mersch, Oneonta, 1973
ERA: 0.67, Daniel Freed, Jamestown, 1988
IP: 132, Jervis Bell, Newark, 1969
Win Streak: 11, Neal Mersch, Oneonta, 1973
ShOs: 5, Mark Wiley, Auburn, 1970
SOs: 144, Mark Wiley, Auburn, 1970
Saves: 22, Mark Davis, Little Falls, 1982

NORTHERN LEAGUE
(SHORT SEASON)
Class A 1965-1971; Independent 1993-
(see also Northern League (long season) under Inactive Leagues)

Batting
Games: 85, held by many
BA: .373, Terry Lee, Winnipeg, 1995
At Bats: 356, Doug O'Neill, St. Paul, 1995
Runs: 84, Chad Akers, Fargo-Moorhead, 1996
Hits: 122, Jose Peguero, Sioux City, 1996
RBIs: 103, Darryl Motley, Fargo-Moorhead, 1996
2Bs: 34, Tony Marabella, Madison, 1996
29, Benny Castillo, Sioux Falls, 1995
3Bs: 10, Jose Peguero, Sioux City, 1996
HRs: 29, Mitch Lyden, Madison, 1996
TBs: 215, Darryl Motley, Fargo-Moorhead, 1996
Streak: 22, Matt Stark, St. Paul, 1994
Sac: 12, Greg D'Alexander, St. Paul, 1994
SBs: 46, Chris Powell, Sioux Falls/Fargo-Moorhead, 1996
BBs: 87, Frank Cappiello, St. Cloud, 1971
87, Larry Lintz, Watertown, 1971
SOs: 97, Jim Cartlidge, Sioux Falls, 1966
HBP: 13, Alan Barsoom, Duluth-Superior, 1995

Pitching
Games: 46, Aaron Quinn, Thunder Bay, 1996
CGs: 12, David Langrock, Duluth, 1965
Wins: 12, Steve Christopher, St. Cloud, 1967
12, Jeremy McGarity, Duluth-Superior, 1996
12, Jim Manfred, St. Paul, 1996
Losses: 11, Scott Freeman, Duluth/Winnipeg, 1994
11, Steve Lyons, Duluth, 1995
11, Chris Gogolewski, Sioux City, 1996
11, Reese Murdaugh, Sioux City, 1996
Pct: .909, 10-1, Michael Colin, St. Cloud, 1966
ERA: 1.12, Rob Andrakin, Sioux Falls, 1994
IP: 134⅓, Dan Rambo, Madison, 1996
ShOs: 5, Steve Spanich, Duluth-Superior, 1969
SOs: 174, Bob Castiglione, St. Cloud, 1966
Saves: 28, Bruce Walton, St. Paul, 1995
BBs: 90, Bob Galasso, Aberdeen, 1971

NORTHWEST LEAGUE
(SHORT SEASON)
Class A 1966-
(see also Northwest League (long season) under Inactive Leagues)

Batting
Games: 86, Nick Van Lue, Eugene, 1967
BA: .403, Ron McNelly, Boise, 1976
At Bats: 322, Robert Leatherwood, Eugene, 1967
Runs: 81, Bob Beall, Walla Walla, 1970
Hits: 113, Jim Buckner, Lewiston, 1972
RBIs: 83, Robert Davis, Tri-City, 1971
2Bs: 27, Donald Hyman, Victoria, 1980
3Bs: 13, Jim Buckner, Lewiston, 1972
HRs: 25, Willie Darkis, Central Oregon, 1980
EBHs: 48, Jim Buckner, Lewiston, 1972
TBs: 208, Jim Buckner, Lewiston, 1972
Streak: 26, Tony Laurenzi, Medford, 1982
SBs: 72, Reggie Thomas, Portland, 1974
BBs: 95, Bob Beall, Walla Walla, 1970
SOs: 106, Lee Tinsley, Southern Oregon, 1988
HBP: 22, Rick Ladjevich, Bellingham, 1994

Pitching
Games: 41, Chris Limbach, Bend, 1987
CGs: 16, Francis Hrischy, Grays Harbor, 1978
Wins: 13, Robert Wolf, Coos Bay-North Bend, 1971
13, David Jannusch, Grays Harbor, 1978
Losses: 12, Steven Jentsch, Tri-Cities, 1974
Pct: 1.000, 13-0, Robert Wolf, Coos Bay-North Bend, 1971
ERA: 0.73, James Campbell, Eugene, 1987

IP: 149, Francis Hirschy, Grays Harbor, 1978
Win Streak: 13, Robert Wolf, Coos Bay-North Bend, 1971
ShOs: 4, held by many
ShO Streak: 32, Joe Carboni, Eugene, 1966
SOs: 150, David Paynter, Walla Walla, 1972
Saves: 23, John Pricher, Boise, 1992

PACIFIC COAST LEAGUE
Class A 1903-1911; Class AA 1912-1945; Class AAA
1946-1951, 1958-; Open Classification 1952-1957

Batting
Games: 227, Bill Dunleavy, Oakland, 1905
BA: .414, Oscar "Ox" Eckhardt, Mission, 1933
At Bats: 941, George Van Haltren, Seattle, 1904
Runs: 202, Tony Lazzeri, Salt Lake City, 1925
Hits: 325, Paul Strand, Salt Lake City, 1923
RBIs: 222, Tony Lazzeri, Salt Lake City, 1925
2Bs: 75, Paul Waner, San Francisco, 1925
3Bs: 26, Willie Davis, Spokane, 1960
HRs: 60, Tony Lazzeri, Salt Lake City, 1925
Grand Slams: 4, Eric Soderholm, Portland, 1971
TBs: 553, Ike Boone, Mission, 1929
Streak: 61, Joe DiMaggio, San Francisco, 1933
SBs: 124, James Johnston, San Francisco, 1913
Sac: 74, Clyde "Buzzy" Wares, Oakland, 1903
BBs: 201, Max West, San Diego, 1949
SOs: 175, Gorman Thomas, Sacramento, 1974
175, Rob Deer, Phoenix, 1984
HBP: 23, Charles Irwin, San Francisco, 1903
23, George Wheeler, Los Angeles, 1903

Pitching
Games: 88, Kenneth Rowe, Spokane, 1964
CGs: 48, Cack Henley, San Francisco, 1910
Wins: 39, Doc Newton, Los Angeles, 1904
39, Harry "Rube" Vickers, Seattle, 1906
Losses: 31, Isaac Butler, Portland, 1903
31, Isaac Butler, Portland, 1904
Pct: 1.000, 11-0, Walter Nagle, Los Angeles, 1905
.938, 15-1, Luis Tiant, Portland, 1964
ERA: 1.57, Larry Jansen, San Francisco, 1946
IP: 526, Rube Vickers, Seattle, 1906
Win Streak: 16, Frank Browning, San Francisco, 1909
ShOs: 14, Vean Gregg, Portland, 1910
ShO Streak: 47, James Whalen, San Francisco, 1904-05
SOs: 408, Harry "Rube" Vickers, Seattle, 1906
BBs: 234, Oscar Graham, Oakland, 1903
Saves: 27, Steve Mintz, Phoenix, 1996

PIONEER LEAGUE
(SHORT SEASON)
Rookie 1964-
(see also Pioneer League (long season) under Inactive Leagues)

Batting
Games: 74, John Mahalik, Butte, 1993
BA: .462, Gary Redus, Billings, 1978
At Bats: 308, Brian McClure, Idaho Falls, 1996
Runs: 100, Gary Redus, Billings, 1978
Hits: 117, Gary Redus, Billings, 1978
RBIs: 83, Willie Darkis, Helena, 1979
2Bs: 28, Cecil Fielder, Butte, 1982
3Bs: 11, Charles Heist, Idaho Falls/Salt Lake City, 1985
HRs: 21, Mike Zouras, Lethbridge, 1977
EBHs: 48, Cecil Fielder, Butte, 1982
TBs: 199, Gary Redus, Billings, 1978
Streak: 27, K.C. Gillum, Billings, 1990
SBs: 60, Tom Goodwin, Great Falls, 1989
BBs: 86, Steve Staggs, Billings, 1971
SOs: 109, Willie Darkis, Helena, 1979
HBP: 17, Mark Duncan, Lethbridge, 1994

Pitching
Games: 38, Tim Peters, Salt Lake City, 1987
CGs: 13, Richard Zinniger, Salt Lake City, 1969
Wins: 14, Gene Vance, Ogden, 1968
14, Mark Dempsey, Great Falls, 1980
Losses: 10, held by many
Pct: 1.000, 13-0, Richard Lange, Idaho Falls, 1970
ERA: 1.115, Richard Rodas, Lethbridge, 1979
1.118, Todd Fischer, Idaho Falls, 1982
IP: 124, Paul O'Hearn, Ogden, 1994
Win Streak: 13, Richard Lange, Idaho Falls, 1970

ShOs: 4, held by many
ShO Streak: 38 2/3, Ray Brown, Billings, 1971
SOs: 186, Robert O'Brien, Odgen, 1969
Saves: 18, Mike Toney, Medicine Hat, 1994

SOUTH ATLANTIC LEAGUE
Class D 1960-1963; Class A 1964-
(Western Carolinas League 1960-1979)

Batting
Games: 143, Tim Thiessen, Gastonia, 1983
143, Ramon Jiminez, Greensboro, 1990
BA: .402, Aaron Pointer, Salisbury, 1961
At Bats: 575, Candido Ventura, Charleston, 1977
Runs: 128, Jose Leiva, Spartanburg, 1983
Hits: 194, Pat Putnam, Asheville, 1976
RBIs: 142, Pat Putnam, Asheville, 1976
2Bs: 45, Gabe Kapler, Fayetteville, 1996
3Bs: 16, Cliff Floyd, Albany, 1992
HRs: 40, Russell Branyan, Columbus, 1996
Grand Slams: 4, Earl Williams, Greenwood, 1969
4, Ed Whited, Asheville, 1987
TBs: 305, Pat Putnam, Asheville, 1976
Streak: 29, Charles Truesdale, Statesville, 1962
SBs: 145, Vince Coleman, Macon, 1983
BBs: 142, Jeff Gardner, Columbia, 1985
SOs: 208, Darryl Landrum, Florence, 1985
208, Al Shirley, Columbia, 1994
HBP: 30, Jim Ferguson, Savannah, 1989

Pitching
Games: 73, Roy Bailey, Savannah, 1991
CGs: 24, Danny Hayling, Hickory, 1960
Wins: 22, Danny Hayling, Hickory, 1960
Losses: 17, Charlie Thompson, Charleston, 1990
Pct: 1.000 (13-0), Randy Marshall, Fayetteville, 1990
ERA: 1.35, Bill Bethea, Lexington, 1960
IP: 246, Roy Searcy, Rutherford County, 1960
Win Streak: 14, Gary Putnam, Greenville, 1966
14, Matt Arrandale, Savannah, 1994
SO Streak: 39 2/3, Henry Carson, Savannah, 1984
ShOs: 6, John Penn, Spartanburg, 1966
SOs: 313, Mike Szemplenski, Statesville, 1963
Saves: 46, Jamie Cochran, Savannah, 1993

SOUTHERN LEAGUE
Class AA 1964-

Batting
Games: 146, Doug Baker, Birmingham, 1983
146, Jesus Alfaro, Charlotte, 1984
BA: .385, Kevin Coughlin, Birmingham, 1995
At Bats: 588, Stan Younger, Birmingham, 1981
Runs: 123, Mike Reinbach, Asheville, 1972
Hits: 187, Kevin Rhomberg, Chattanooga, 1981
RBIs: 132, Terry Steinbach, Huntsville, 1986
2Bs: 44, Aaron Boone, Chattanooga, 1996
3Bs: 19, Alan Trammell, Montgomery, 1977
HRs: 42, Tim Laudner, Orlando, 1981
EBHs: 72, Geronimo Berroa, Knoxville, 1987
TBs: 301, Mike Reinbach, Asheville, 1972
Streak: 33, Greg Tubbs, Greenville, 1987
SBs: 102, Donnell Nixon, Chattanooga, 1984
BBs: 129, Gary Jones, Huntsville, 1986
SOs: 218, Rondal Rollin, Birmingham, 1987
HBP: 32, Rusty Crockett, Charlotte, 1990

Pitching
Games: 78, Laddie Renfroe, Charlotte, 1989
CGs: 20, Ken Dixon, Charlotte, 1984
Wins: 20, Manly Johnson, Lynchburg, 1964
Losses: 17, Kent Bottenfield, Jacksonville, 1989
Pct: .917, 11-1, Mike Skinner, Charlotte, 1985
ERA: 1.57, Dave Rozema, Montgomery, 1976
IP: 240, Ken Dixon, Charlotte, 1984
Win Streak: 12, Bill Edgerton, Mobile, 1966
12, Bill Zepp, Charlotte, 1969
12, Andy McGaffigan, Nashville, 1980
ShOs: 6, Chuck Swanson, Montgomery, 1973
6, George Cappuzzello, Montgomery, 1980
ShO Streak: 40 1/3, Curt Wardle, Orlando, 1984
SOs: 225, Chris Floethe, Birmingham, 1971
BBs: 146, Scott Elam, Knoxville, 1982
Saves: 34, Jerry Spradlin, Chattanooga, 1992

ACTIVE LEAGUE RECORDS

TEXAS LEAGUE

1888-1890; Class D 1902-1903, 1906; Class C 1904-1905, 1907-1910; Class B 1911-1920; Class A 1921-1935; Class A1 1936-1942; Class AA 1946-
(South Texas League, 1903-1906)

Batting
Games: 168, Randolph Moore, Dallas, 1929
168, Irvin Jeffries, Dallas, 1929
BA: .444, Al McBride, Austin, 1896
.402, Ike Boone, San Antonio, 1923
At Bats: 686, Ed Hock, Houston, 1929
686, Tony Governor, Galveston, 1935
Runs: 171, Jimmy Slagle, Houston, 1896
150, Clarence "Big Boy" Kraft, Ft. Worth, 1924
Hits: 245, Randolph Moore, Dallas, 1929
RBIs: 196, Clarence "Big Boy" Kraft, Ft. Worth, 1924

2Bs: 70, Rhino Williams, Dallas, 1929
3Bs: 30, Eddie Moore, Ft. Worth, 1929
HRs: 62, Ken Guettler, Shreveport, 1956
Grand Slams: 6, Roy Ostergaard, Galveston, 1923
EBHs: 96, Clarence "Big Boy" Kraft, Ft. Worth, 1924
TBs: 414, Clarence "Big Boy" Kraft, Ft. Worth, 1924
Streak: 37, Ike Boone, San Antonio, 1923
37, Bobby Trevino, El Paso, 1969
SBs: 103, Will Blakey, Galveston, 1895
90, Tony Thebo, Shreveport, 1908
BBs: 153, Ed Lake, Houston, 1939
SOs: 186, Willie Crawford, Albuquerque, 1966
HBP: 27, Eddie Miller, Galveston, 1916

Pitching
Games: 77, Chief Waters, Ft. Worth, 1955
CGs: 34, Bob Couchman, Galveston, 1920
Wins: 34, Al McFarland, Ft. Worth, 1895
31, Ash Hillin, Oklahoma City, 1937
Losses: 28, Bill Doyle, Temple, 1907
Pct: 1.000, 12-0, Ted Thiem, Tulsa, 1960
ERA: 1.06, Hickory Dickson, Houston, 1916
IP: 382, Emmett Munsell, San Antonio, 1915
Win Streak: 19, Snipe Conley, Dallas, 1917
ShOs: 11, Dizzy Dean, Houston, 1931
SOs: 325, Harry Ables, San Antonio, 1910
BBs: 185, Bill Bailey, Beaumont, 1919
Saves: 38, Sean Maloney, El Paso, 1996
HB: 32, George Crabble, Galveston, 1909
WP: 21, Ovid Mullins, Dallas, 1914

INACTIVE LEAGUE RECORDS

ALABAMA-FLORIDA LEAGUE
Class D 1936-1941, 1946-1962
(Alabama State League 1940-1941, 1946-1950)

Batting
Games: 138, held by many, 1947
BA: .432, Neal Cobb, Crestview, 1954
At Bats: 586, Perry Roberts, Greenville, 1947
Runs: 149, Frank Tepedino, Andalusia, 1954
Hits: 228, Perry Roberts, Greenville, 1947
RBIs: 152, Perry Roberts, Greenville, 1947
2Bs: 49, Oscar Martin, Tallahassee, 1940
49, Perry Roberts, Greenville, 1947
3Bs: 25, Steve Summerhill, Union, 1937
HRs: 37, Charles Grant, Donalsonville, 1955
EBHs: 75, John Ostrowski, Troy, 1940
TBs: 334, Perry Roberts, Greenville, 1947
SBs: 76, Joe Harper, Headland, 1950
BBs: 140, Nesbit Wilson, Crestview, 1955
HBP: 21, Manuel Russo, Geneva, 1947
SOs: 168, James Murrya, Troy, 1946

Pitching
Games: 54, Charles Hertzberger, Dothan, 1963
CGs: 29, Max Peterson, Greenville, 1947
Wins: 27, Max Peterson, Greenville, 1947
27, Russell Harris, Ozark, 1952
Losses: 21, Bruno Shedis, Evergreen, 1937
Pct: .909, 10-1, John Koneff, Andalusia, 1939
.900, 27-3, Russell Harris, Ozark, 1952
ERA: 1.21, Spencer Davis, Dothan, 1953
IP: 299, Max Peterson, Greenville, 1947
SOs: 418, Virgil Trucks, Andalusia, 1938
BBs: 194, Harry Clifton, Headland, 1951

APPALACHIAN LEAGUE
(LONG SEASON)
Class D 1911-1914, 1921-1925, 1937-1955
(see also Appalachian League (short season) under Active Leagues)

Batting
Games: 131, Dominick Commisso, Bristol, 1951
BA: .418, Lew Flick, Elizabethton, 1941
At Bats: 531, Dominick Commisso, Bristol, 1951
Runs: 169, Ray Rudisill, Pulaski, 1946
Hits: 210, Lew Flick, Elizabethton, 1941
RBIs: 139, Ralph Davis, New River, 1947
2Bs: 51, Russell "Red" Mincy, Pulaski/Kingsport, 1946
3Bs: 23, Lew Flick, Elizabethton, 1941
HRs: 32, Leo "Muscle" Shoals, Kingsport, 1947
EBHs: 73, Russell "Red" Mincy, Pulaski/Kingsport, 1946
TBs: 333, Leo "Muscle" Shoals, Johnson City, 1939
Sac: 59, E.A. Sherrill, Morristown, 1911
SBs: 68, Herbert Mancini, Pulaski, 1950
BBs: 130, Ray Rudisill, Pulaski, 1947
SOs: 129, Harold Martin, Greenville, 1941

Pitching
Games: 58, Dempsey Cheatwood, Bluefield, 1953
CGs: 26, Melvin Nee, Kingsport, 1951
Wins: 27, Doug Clark, Elizabethton, 1950
Losses: 19, Richard Maher, New River, 1947
Pct: .947, 18-1, Jim Akard, Kingsport, 1945
ERA: 1.41, Paul Minner, Elizabethton, 1942
IP: 269, Doug Clark, Elizabethton, 1950
Win Streak: 19, Shannon Hardwick, New River, 1946
SOs: 249, Howie Nunn, Johnson City, 1955
BBs: 188, Bill Arrildt, Pulaski, 1947

ARIZONA-TEXAS LEAGUE
Class D 1928-1932, 1937-1939, Class C 1940-1941, 1947-1950, 1952-1958
(Arizona State League 1928-1930, Arizona-Mexico League 1955-1958)

Batting
Games: 150, held by many
BA: .430, Tony Antista, Bisbee, 1930
.430, Len Rodriguez, Cananea, 1954
At Bats: 661, Donald Mason, El Paso, 1950
Runs: 193, Ken Toothman, Phoenix, 1954
Hits: 259, Len Rodriguez, Cananea, 1954
RBIs: 195, Earl Smith, Phoenix, 1954
2Bs: 62, Len Rodriguez, Cananea, 1954
3Bs: 29, Burl Horton, El Paso, 1941

HRs: 47, Claudio Solano, Cananea, 1954
EBHs: 97, Claudio Solano, Cananea, 1954
TBs: 394, Claudio Solano, Cananea, 1954
Streak: 34, Jim Bynon, Bisbee, 1947
Sac: 26, Willie Reyes, Albuquerque, 1939
SBs: 71, Ramon Mendoza, Juarez/El Paso, 1949
BBs: 207, Pete Hughes, Phoenix, 1948
SOs: 170, Douglas Smith, Tucson, 1941

Pitching
Games: 55, Whitey Wietelmann, Yuma, 1955
CGs: 34, Ron Smith, Bisbee-Douglas, 1953
Wins: 29, LeRoy Reddell, Tucson, 1953
Losses: 22, Ron Smith, Bisbee-Douglas, 1953
Pct: .857, 14-2, Al McNeeley, Bisbee, 1930
ERA: 2.37, Jesse Flores, Bisbee, 1938
IP: 330, Ron Smith, Bisbee-Douglas, 1953
SOs: 322, James Peete, Tucson, 1955
BBs: 211, Tom Entwisle, El Paso, 1948

ARKANSAS-MISSOURI LEAGUE
Class D 1934-1940
(Arkansas State League 1934-1935)

Batting
Games: 127, Gerald Priddy, Rogers, 1937
BA: .392, Cyril Moran, Rogers, 1938
At Bats: 501, Joe Szuch, Fayetteville, 1939
Runs: 130, Kermit Lewis, Siloam Springs, 1936
Hits: 183, Paul Fugit, Fayetteville, 1937
RBIs: 132, Adolph Arlitt, Carthage, 1938
2Bs: 43, Cyril Moran, Rogers, 1938
3Bs: 16, Hans Krueger, Fayetteville, 1938
HRs: 28, Kermit Lewis, Siloam Springs, 1936
EBHs: 77, Cyril Moran, Rogers, 1938
TBs: 293, Kermit Lewis, Siloam Springs, 1936
Sac: 38, Clois Watson, Cassville/Bentonville, 1935
SBs: 76, Steve Luby, Neosho, 1938
BB: 100, Cliff Van Sickel, Monett, 1938
HBP: 19, Roy Fowler, Monett, 1938
SOs: 121, Joe Skeber, Neosho, 1938

Pitching
Games: 40, Erwin Gansauer, Cassville, 1935
CGs: 24, George Bender, Fayetteville, 1939
Wins: 23, Clint Raper, Siloam Springs, 1936
Losses: 18, Russ Wieneke, Monett, 1939
Pct: .870, 20-3, Bill Gill, Neosho, 1938
ERA: 1.35, John Murray, Siloam Springs, 1936
IP: 249, Harrel Toenes, Rogers, 1938
ShOs: 4, Bill Gill, Neosho, 1938
SOs: 266, Bill Gill, Neosho, 1938
BBs: 170, C.J. Ordneal, Siloam Springs, 1937

BI-STATE LEAGUE (NC-VA)
Class D 1934-1942

Batting
Games: 125, Nick Witek, Bassett, 1936
125, Cecil Payne, Leaksville-Draper-Spray, 1942
BA: .403, Eugene Handley, Mt. Airy, 1936
At Bats: 529, George Biershenk, Rocky Mount, 1942
Runs: 145, Jim Gruzdis, Leaksville-Spray-Draper, 1939
Hits: 199, Sam Gentile, Danville, 1939
RBIs: 147, Ray Scantling, Reidsville, 1938
2Bs: 54, Sam Gentile, Danville, 1939
3Bs: 17, Herb Freeman, Danville-Schoolfield, 1940
HRs: 34, Woodrow Traylor, Danville, 1936
EBHs: 82, Ken Keltner, Fieldale, 1936
TBs: 335, Ken Keltner, Fieldale, 1936
Sac: 26, Walter Novalk, Bassett, 1938
SBs: 46, James Gruzdis, Leaksville-Spray-Draper, 1939
BBs: 106, Harry Pletersek, Martinsville, 1939
HBP: 16, H. Briggs, Danville/Reidsville, 1935
16, Jim Gruzdis, Leaksville-Spray-Draper, 1939

Pitching
Games: 46, Murray Wade, South Boston, 1938
CGs: 27, Paige Dennis, Reidsville/Mt. Airy, 1940
27, Charlie Cuellar, Leaksville-Spray-Draper, 1942
Wins: 25, Fred Pipgras, Danville, 1935
25, Ernie Jenkins, Bassett, 1936
Losses: 18, Murray Wade, South Boston, 1938
Pct: .833, 25-5, Ernie Jenkins, Bassett, 1936
ERA: 1.67, Charlie Cuellar, Leaksville-Draper-Spray, 1942

IP: 280, Paige Dennis, Reidsville/Mt. Airy, 1940
SOs: 222, Jeff Jeffcoat, Leaksville-Spray-Draper, 1935
BBs: 160, Ramon Voight, Reidsville, 1938

BIG STATE LEAGUE
Class B 1947-1957

Batting
Games: 156, Buck Frierson, Sherman-Denison, 1947
156, Lloyd Rigby, Paris, 1947
BA: .446, Francis Saucier, Wichita Falls, 1949
At Bats: 667, Lloyd Rigby, Paris, 1947
Runs: 188, Buck Frierson, Sherman-Denison, 1947
Hits: 248, Buck Frierson, Sherman-Denison, 1947
RBIs: 197, Buck Frierson, Sherman-Denison, 1947
2Bs: 58, Leslie "Lon" Goldstein, Gainesville, 1948
3Bs: 23, Nelson Daehn, Temple, 1954
HRs: 58, Buck Frierson, Sherman-Denison, 1947
EBHs: 100, Buck Frierson, Sherman-Denison, 1947
TBs: 470, Buck Frierson, Sherman-Denison, 1947
SBs: 62, Edwin Palmer, Greenville, 1947
BBs: 135, Lou Fitzgerald, Texarkana, 1950
SOs: 152, Eugene Hurych, Wichita Falls, 1956

Pitching
Games: 61, John Bumgarner, Texarkana, 1953
CGs: 29, John Andre, Austin, 1952
Wins: 28, Rene Vega, Corpus Christi, 1955
Losses: 23, Marvin Hatcher, Temple, 1954
Pct: .909, 10-1, Bob Heinz, Sherman-Denison, 1948
ERA: 1.95, Dave Wickersham, Beaumont, 1957
IP: 301, Dean Franks, Austin, 1953
ShOs: 7, James Vitter, Wichita Falls, 1953
SOs: 275, Bill Pierro, Waco, 1949
BBs: 162, Orel Dryden, Longview, 1952

BLUE GRASS LEAGUE
Class D 1908-1912, 1922-1924

Batting
Games: 132, Kunkle, Maysville/Mt. Sterling, 1912
BA: .401, Danning Harrell, Paris, 1912
At Bats: 506, Ovid Nicholson, Frankfort, 1912
Runs: 128, Ovid Nicholson, Frankfort, 1912
Hits: 188, Norman Munn, Richmond, 1912
2Bs: 36, J.F. Whitaker, Richmond, 1911
3Bs: 17, Edward Coleman, Winchester, 1911
HRs: 22, Norman Munn, Richmond, 1912
EBHs: 65, Norman Munn, Richmond, 1912
TBs: 304, Norman Munn, Richmond, 1912
Sac: 51, George Kircher, Maysville/Winchester, 1910
SBs: 111, Ovid Nicholson, Frankfort, 1912
BBs: 70, Ollie Gfroerer, Frankfort, 1912
SOs: 99, Elmer Locke, Paris, 1912

Pitching
Games: 44, Howie Camnitz, Lexington, 1912
Wins: 25, Curtis Burden, Winchester, 1909
Losses: 21, Buckholtz, Mansfield, 1907
Pct: .850, 17-3, Milton McCormick, Paris, 1910
IP: 290, James Hauser, Paris, 1912
Win Streak: 12, John Scheneberg, Paris, 1911
SOs: 253, Frank Romine, Maysville, 1911
HB: 28, Claude Monhollen, Lexington/Cynthiana, 1922
BBs: 97, Lester Cornell, Frankfort, 1910

BLUE RIDGE LEAGUE
Class D 1915-1918, 1920-1930

Batting
Games: 118, Raymond Zorman, Hanover, 1929
118, Dan Tapson, Hanover, 1929
BA: .406, Roger "Doc" Cramer, Martinsburg, 1929
At Bats: 466, Babe Phelps, Hagerstown, 1930
Runs: 104, George Rawlings, Martinsburg, 1923
Hits: 175, Babe Phelps, Hagerstown, 1930
2Bs: 41, Holmes Diehl, Hagerstown, 1925
3Bs: 24, Joe Vosmik, Frederick, 1929
HRs: 30, Hack Wilson, Martinsburg, 1922
EBHs: 62, Babe Phelps, Hagerstown, 1930
62, Joe Vosmik, Frederick 1929
TBs: 296, Babe Phelps, Hagerstown, 1930
Sac: 39, John Boyle, Hagerstown, 1925
SBs: 47, Walter Kimmick, Waynesboro, 1921

BBs: 100, George Scheminant, Hagerstown, 1925
SOs: 89, Herbert Young, Frederick, 1928

Pitching
Games: 39, Halley, Frederick, 1929
CGs: 22, Frank Ulrich, Waynesboro, 1923
Wins: 25, Earl Howard, Hagerstown, 1917
    25, Alan Clarke, Waynesboro, 1921
Losses: 17, Stephen Woodgie, Chambersburg, 1922
Pct: .889, 16-2, Lester Shatzer, Chambersburg, 1927
IP: 274, Alan Clarke, Waynesboro, 1921
Win Streak: 8, Abe Weicher, Hagerstown, 1915
SOs: 258, Alan Clarke, Waynesboro, 1921
HB: 29, Alan Clarke, Waynesboro, 1921
BBs: 163, Joe Zubris, Hagerstown, 1925

BLUE RIDGE LEAGUE
Class D 1946-1950

Batting
Games: 124, Doug Shores, North Wilkesboro, 1948
BA: .403, Edward Wayne, Lenoir, 1946
At Bats: 524, Clifton Haywood, Radford, 1948
Runs: 127, Richard Kalal, Lenoir, 1946
Hits: 175, Clifton Haywood, Radford, 1948
RBIs: 127, Edwin Morgan, Mt. Airy-Galax, 1946
2Bs: 42, Edwin Morgan, Mt. Airy-Galax, 1947
3Bs: 16, Donald Levigne, Wytheville, 1949
HRs: 16, Edwin Morgan, Mt. Airy-Galax, 1946
EBHs: 62, Vern Shetler, New Bern, 1946
TBs: 259, Vern Shetler, New Bern, 1946
Sac: 16, Steve Sloboda, Radford, 1950
SBs: 59, Kenneth Howard, North Wilkesboro, 1948
BBs: 100, Edwin Morgan, Mt. Airy-Galax, 1947
SOs: 125, Tom Campbell, Galax, 1947

Pitching
Games: 40, Sid Weinbach, Galax, 1947
CGs: 27, Eurice "Pete" Treece, Mt. Airy, 1947
Wins: 21, Cecil Warren, Galax, 1948
    21, Eurice "Pete" Treece, Mt. Airy, 1949
Losses: 14, Peter Bakaitis, Radford, 1949
    14, Worth Cuthbertson, North Wilkesboro/
    Wytheville, 1949
Pct: .842, 16-3, David Powers, Elkin, 1950
ERA: 1.56, George Greene, Abingdon, 1948
IP: 269, Eurice "Pete" Treece, Mt. Airy, 1947
SOs: 234, Eurice "Pete" Treece, Mt. Airy, 1947

BORDER LEAGUE
Class C 1946-1951

Batting
Games: 130, held by many, 1949
BA: .397, Bob Dill, Ogdensburg/Auburn, 1946
At Bats: 542, Irvin Schupp, Ogdensburg, 1950
Runs: 122, Tony Gudaitis, Ogdensburg, 1947
Hits: 177, Bill Scally, Ogdensburg, 1948
RBIs: 125, Peter Kousagan, Geneva, 1950
2Bs: 40, Jim Heximer, Kinston, 1946
3Bs: 23, Fred Gerken, Watertown, 1947
HRs: 31, Peter Kousagan, Geneva, 1950
TBs: 290, Fred Gerken, Watertown, 1947
Sac: 23, George Pelati, Ogdensburg, 1948
SBs: 65, Jim Massar, Geneva, 1948
BBs: 135, Morris Tortoriello, Ogdensburg, 1948
SOs: 111, Peter Kousagan, Geneva, 1950

Pitching
Games: 43, Leon St. Dennis, Ottawa/Geneva 1947
CGs: 28, Arthur Cook, Kingston, 1948
Wins: 21, Larry Seamon, Ottawa, 1948
    21, Arnold Jarrell, Kingston, 1946
    21, Arthur Cook, Kinston, 1948
Losses: 17, Bill Gates, Watertown, 1948
Pct: .842, 16-3, Frank Fanovich, Watertown, 1947
ERA: 1.96, Edward Flanagan, Ottawa, 1950
IP: 176, Arthur Cook, Kingston, 1948
ShOs: 6, Larry Seamon, Ottawa, 1948
SOs: 232, Bill Gates, Watertown, 1948
BBs: 185, Bill Gates, Watertown, 1948
WP: 20, Bill Gates, Watertown, 1948

CANADIAN LEAGUE
Class D 1905, 1911; Class C 1912-1913;
Class B 1914-1915

Batting
Games: 125, Frank Dolan, Ottawa, 1914
BA: .398, Jack Shaffer, Guelph, 1913
At Bats: 446, Frank Shaughnessy, Ottawa, 1914
Runs: 104, Merlin Kopp, St. Thomas, 1913
Hits: 152, Bill Wright, Guelph, 1913
2Bs: 28, Hackenbush, Hamilton, 1911
3Bs: 16, E.T. Rogers, Ottawa, 1913
HRs: 10, Bill Wright, Guelph, 1913
EBHs: 44, Bill Wright, Guelph, 1913
TBs: 231, Bill Wright, Guelph, 1913
Sac: 36, Matty Matteson, London, 1913
    36, A.E. Schwind, Ottawa, 1912
SBs: 63, Merlin Kopp, St. Thomas, 1913
BBs: 83, Merlin Kopp, St. Thomas, 1913
SOs: 71, George Deneau, London, 1913

Pitching
Games: 36, Urban Shocker, Ottawa, 1914
CGs: 26, Ernest Chase, Brantford, 1914
Wins: 25, Ray Keating, Hamilton, 1913
Losses: 20, Howick, St. Thomas, 1915
Pct: .800, 24-6, Bob Heck, London, 1913
IP: 303, Urban Shocker, Ottawa, 1915
Win Streak: 14, Joe McManus, Ottawa, 1912
SOs: 186, Urban Shocker, Ottawa, 1915
BBs: 140, Joe Lill, Ottawa/Brantford, 1913

CANADIAN-AMERICAN LEAGUE
Class C 1936-1942, 1946-1951

Batting
Games: 142, David Jaska, Rome, 1947
BA: .406, August Knickerbocker, Oneonta, 1941
At Bats: 565, George Clark, Jr., Trois Rivieres, 1949
Runs: 145, Frank "Chick" Genovese, Oneonta, 1941
Hits: 202, August Knickerbocker, Oneonta, 1941
RBIs: 150, Maurice Van Robays, Ogdensburg, 1937
2Bs: 53, Eddie Sawyer, Amsterdam, 1939
3Bs: 26, Frank Malzone, Oneonta, 1949
HRs: 43, Maurice Van Robays, Ogdensburg, 1937
EBHs: 80, Maurice Van Robays, Ogdensburg, 1937
TBs: 334, Maurice Van Robays, Ogdensburg, 1937
Streak: 28, Dale Long, Oneonta, 1947
Sac: 29, Oscar Fleischman, Oswego, 1939
SBs: 64, Jim Whaley, Ottawa, 1939
BBs: 168, Garland Lawing, Quebec, 1950
SOs: 135, Arnold Spence, Gloversville-Johnstown, 1949

Pitching
Games: 56, Loren Stewart, Gloversville-Johnstown, 1950
CGs: 27, Frank Rochevot, Ottawa/Cornwall, 1937
    27 John Dickenson, Cornwall, 1938
    27, Hary Kuntashian, Oswego, 1940
Wins: 24, George McPhail, Oneonta, 1951
Losses: 20, William Hutchinson, Gloversville, 1939:
Pct: .909, 10-1, Roy Partlow, Three Rivers, 1946
ERA: 1.56, Xavier Rescigno, Smiths Falls, 1937
IP: 278⅔, Frank Rochevot, Ottawa/Cornwall, 1938
Win Streak: 13, Albert "Duke" Farrington, Amsterdam, 1938
ShOs: 7, John Masuga, Pittsfield, 1949
SOs: 280, Harry Markell, Schenectady, 1948
BBs: Frank Rochevot, Ottawa/Cornwall, 1938
HB: 25, Edward Carr, Ottawa, 1937
WP: 37, Mike Naymick, Oswego, 1938

CAPE BRETON COLLIERY LEAGUE
Class D 1937-1938; Class C 1939

Batting
Games: 57, held by many, 1939
BA: .394, Guido Panciera, Sydney, 1937
At Bats: 233, Gerard Kiley, New Waterford, 1938
    233, Raymond Ross, Glace Bay, 1939
Runs: 44, Raymond Ross, Glace Bay, 1937
Hits: 80, Guido Panciera, Sydney, 1937
RBIs: 48, Guido Panciera, Sydney, 1937
2Bs: 17, Guido Panciera, Sydney, 1937
3Bs: 11, Rex Wright, Sydney, 1937
HRs: 9, Lester Crabb, Glace Bay, 1939

EBHs: 23, Guido Panciera, Sydney, 1937
TBs: 111, Guido Panciera, Sydney, 1937
Sac: 13, Albert Mandeville, Glace Bay, 1937
    13, Mike DeAngelus, Sydney, 1939
SBs: 17, Raymond Ross, Glace Bay, 1939
    17, Mike DeAngelus, Sydney, 1939
BBs: 41, Ulric Millette, New Waterford, 1938
SOs: 45, John Sheehan, Glace Bay, 1937
    45, Stanley Pisiak, Dominion, 1937

Pitching
Games: 22, Tom Musil, Newe Waterford, 1938
    22, Roy Maxwell, Dominion, 1937
CGs: 16, Bernard Pearlman, Sydney, 1939
Wins: 14, Roy Moore, Glace Bay, 1937
Losses: 13, Herbert Hammerstrom, Sydney Mines/
    Glace Bay, 1939
Pct: .824, 14-3, Roy Moore, Glace Bay, 1937
ERA: 1.33, Roy Moore, Glace Bay, 1937
IP: 153, Bill Jarvis, Sydney, 1938
SOs: 114, Bill Jarvis, Sydney, 1937
BBs: 96, Tom Musil, New Waterford, 1938

CENTRAL LEAGUE
Class B 1903-1917, 1920-1922, 1926, 1928-1930, 1932, 1934, Class A 1948-1951

Batting
Games: 159, Tom Smith, Grand Rapids, 1906
BA: .419, Albert "Ab" Wright, Fort Wayne, 1930
At Bats: 619, John Reider, Fort Wayne, 1930
Runs: 162, Leroy "Cowboy" Jones, Fort Wayne, 1930
Hits: 228, Albert "Ab" Wright, Fort Wayne, 1930
RBIs: 169, Albert "Ab" Wright, Fort Wayne, 1930
2Bs: 52, John Reider, Fort Wayne, 1930
3Bs: 22, Curtis Elston, Fort Wayne, 1908
HRs: 52, Albert "Ab" Wright, Fort Wayne, 1930
EBHs: 94, John Reider, Fort Wayne, 1930
TBs: 425, Albert, "Ab" Wright, Fort Wayne, 1930
Sac: 66, Frank Matthews, Evansville, 1914
SBs: 87, Midge Craven, South Bend, 1909
BBs: 118, Louis Urcho, Muskegan, 1950
HBP: 15, Frank Kelleher, Muskegon, 1920
SOs: 128, Charles Bell, Muskegon, 1951

Pitching
Games: 48, Paul Watchel, Dayton/Muskegon, 1916
    48, Beeler, Richmond, 1930
CGs: 38, Dave Martin, Terre Haute, 1906
Wins: 28, Buck Sterzer, Evansville, 1910
Losses: 27, Dave Martin, Terre Haute, 1906
Pct: .857, 12-2, Roy Hale, Dayton, 1906
    .852, 23-4, Marvin Duke, Erie, 1932
ERA: 1.38, Art Nehf, Terre Haute, 1915
IP: 427, Ralph Willis, Canton, 1906
ShOs: 11, Ralph Willis, Canton, 1906
SOs: 249, Paul Fittery, Evansville, 1914
BBs: 220, Robert L. Harrison, Dayton/Flint, 1951

CENTRAL ASSOCIATION
Class D 1904-1917 (Iowa State League 1904-1907)

Batting
Games: 143, John Corriden, Keokuk, 1909
    143, Ed Reichle, Keokuk, 1909
BA: .375, George Manush, Ottumwa, 1912
At Bats: 567, Hartman, Quincy, 1910
Runs: 108, George Watson, Burlington, 1911
Hits: 178, Herbert Ellison, Muscatine, 1916
2Bs: 46, Herbert Ellison, Muscatine, 1916
3Bs: 17, C.B. Lewis, Kewanee, 1909
HRs: 21, John Sullivan, Ottumwa, 1912
EBHs: 76, Herbert Ellison, Muscatine, 1916
TBs: 268, Herbert Ellison, Muscatine, 1916
Sac: 56, Jim McAuley, Waterloo, 1916
SBs: 79, A. J. Ahring, Muscatine, 1911
BBs: 87, Joseph Wilkes, Clinton, 1916
SOs: 90, Ernie Menne, Clinton, 1915

Pitching
Games: 51, Charles Fanning, Galesburg, 1910
CGs: 43, C.R. Garrett, Mason City, 1915
Wins: 32, Harry Gaspar, Waterloo, 1908
Losses: 25, R.E. McCullough, Keokuk, 1914

Pct: .889, 32-4, Harry Gaspar, Waterloo, 1908
ERA: 1.25, Frank Ulch, La Crosse/Cedar Rapids, 1917
IP: 387, Charles Fanning, Galesburg, 1910
SOs: 320, Charles Fanning, Galesburg, 1910
BBs: 155, Adams, Galesburg/Muscatine, 1912
HB: 36, Phil Slattery, Marshalltown, 1916
WP: 15, Guy Beard, Marshalltown, 1915

CENTRAL ASSOCIATION
Class C 1947-1949

Batting
Games: 130, held by many, 1948
BA: .387, Ed Wiltsee, Clinton, 1947
At Bats: 544, George Sopko, Keokuk, 1949
Runs: 121, Roy Sievers, Hannibal, 1947
Hits: 167, Billy Klaus, Clinton, 1948
RBIs: 147, Roy Sievers, Hannibal, 1947
2Bs: 35, Billy Klaus, Clinton, 1948
3Bs: 20, David "Gus" Bell, Keokuk, 1948
HRs: 37, Jack Tanner, Cedar Rapids, 1949
EBHs: 61, Frank Pawlik, Rockford, 1947
TBs: 293, Roy Sievers, Hannibal, 1947
SBs: 41, Bruno Poveromo, Clinton, 1949
BBs: 180, Jim King, Keokuk, 1949
SOs: 106, John Addison, Kewanee, 1949

Pitching
Games: 38, Deryle Harris, Rockford, 1947
    38, Bob Howe, Rockford, 1947
CGs: 25, Deryle Harris, Rockford, 1948
Wins: 19, Charles Funk, Hannibal, 1947
Losses: 15, held by many
Pct: .818, 18-4, Calvin Howe, Clinton, 1948
ERA: 1.32, Harry Pritts, Keokuk, 1949
IP: 230, Deryle Harris, Rockford, 1948
ShOs: 5, Ron McLeland, Hannibal, 1948
    5, Calvin Howe, Clinton, 1948
SOs: 164, John Graney, Clinton, 1949
BBs: 150, Charles Funk, Hannibal, 1947

CENTRAL KANSAS LEAGUE
Class D 1908-1914
(Kansas State League 1913-1914)

Batting
Games: 90, held by many, 1912
BA: .403, A.B. Conley, Abilene, 1910
At Bats: 397, John Singleton, Clay Center, 1913
Runs: 88, Burnham Smith, Manhattan, 1912
Hits: 133, John Singleton, Clay Center, 1913
Sac: 34, John Misse, Salina, 1910
SBs: 57, Lee Gramley, Clay Center, 1910

Pitching
Wins: 21, G.H. Jepson, Junction City, 1911
Losses: 17, Seth Fowler, Salina, 1912
    17, T.E. Cox, Concordia, 1910
Pct: .826, 19-4, Ora Williams, Abilene, 1909
Win Streak: 9, C.H. Riley, Great Bend, 1913
ShOs: 7, Paul Stokesberry, Clay Center, 1909
    7, E. Gober, Minneapolis, 1910
SOs: 178, Ora Williams, Abilene, 1909
BBs: 71, Claude Hendrix, Salina, 1909

COASTAL PLAIN LEAGUE
Class D 1937-1941, 1946-1952

Batting
Games: 140, held by many
BA: .383, Valentine Gonzalez, Roanoke Rapids, 1948
At Bats: 579, Irv Dickens, Wilson, 1948
    579, Leo Katkaveck, Roanoke Rapids, 1950
Runs: 138, Grover Fowler, Rocky Mount, 1948
Hits: 207, Quentin Martin, Rocky Mount, 1948
RBIs: 148, Warriner Bass, Roanoke Rapids, 1948
2Bs: 42, Clyde Whlitener, Goldsboro, 1949
3Bs: 18, Lister Rock, Williamston, 1940
HRs: 35, John Hanley, Rocky Mount, 1948
TBs: 328, Fred "Pop" Williams, Kinston/Rocky Mount, 1948
SBs: 92, William Bevill, New Bern, 1949

BBs: 159, Kenneth Andrews, Tarboro, 1948
SOs: 117, Cornelius Hartbarger, Tarboro, 1949

Pitching
Games: 49, Tony Napoles, Tarboro, 1948
CGs: 32, Horace "Red" Benton, Rocky Mount, 1948
Wins: 28, Bill Kennedy, Rocky Mount, 1946
    28, Edward Neville, Tarboro, 1947
    28, Horace "Red" Benton, Rocky Mount, 1948
    28, Alton Brown, Roanoke Rapids, 1950
Losses: 21, Joe Alamo, Greenville, 1947
Pct: .903, 28-3, Bill Kennedy, Rocky Mount, 1946
ERA: 1.03, Bill Kennedy, Rocky Mount, 1946
IP: 339, Horace "Red" Benton, Rocky Mount, 1948
SOs: 456, Bill Kennedy, Rocky Mount, 1946
BBs: 196, Harry Helmer, Rocky Mount, 1948

COLONIAL LEAGUE
Class B 1947-1950

Batting
Games: 134, held by many, 1948
BA: .393, Connie Creedon, Port Chester, 1947
At Bats: 535, John Stefanik, Waterbury, 1948
Runs: 136, Carlos Bernier, Bristol, 1949
Hits: 183, George Handy, Bridgeport, 1949
RBIs: 123, Frank Lamanna, Waterbury, 1947
2Bs: 32, Joe Biros, Bridgeport, 1947
3Bs: 13, Dan Pavone, Stamford, 1949
HRs: 26, Leo Eastham, Waterbury, 1949
EBHs: 56, Frank Lamanna, Waterbury, 1947
TBs: 283, George Handy, Bridgeport, 1949
Sac: 16, Gary Rutkay, Port Chester, 1948
SBs: 89, Carlos Bernier, Bristol, 1949
BBs: 116, Leo Eastham, Waterbury, 1948
HBP: 14, Zaven Arakelian, Bridgeport, 1948
SOs: 92, Bob Nagle, Bridgeport, 1949

Pitching
Games: 43, Richard Blow, Stamford, 1948
CGs: 23, Mike Kash (Kaiserski), Waterbury, 1947
Wins: 20, Mike Kash (Kaiserski), Waterbury, 1947
Losses: 16, Edwin Moran, Poughkeepsie, 1949
Pct: .870, 20-3, Mike Kash (Kaiserski), Waterbury, 1947
ERA: 2.01, Emil Moscowitz, Stamford, 1949
IP: 234, Ernest Sawyer, Waterbury, 1949
ShOs: 4, Joe Murray, Port Chester/Bridgeport, 1947
    4, Walter Graham, Kingston/Bridgeport, 1949
SOs: 234, Edward Hrabscak, Stamford, 1949
BBs: 162, Bill Sahlin, Port Chester, 1947

CONNECTICUT STATE LEAGUE
Class D 1902-1904; Class B 1905-1914
(Eastern Association 1913-1914)

Batting
Games: 138, Tom Stankard, Meriden/Springfield, 1913
BA: .385, Claude Rossman, Holyoke, 1903
At Bats: 531, Swander, Springfield, 1913
Runs: 110, George Turner, Norwich, 1902
Hits: 176, Jim McCabe, New Britain, 1909
    176, Benny Kauff, Hartford, 1913
2Bs: 41, Elmer Smith, Waterbury, 1914
3Bs: 20, Ben Hilt, Bridgeport, 1909
HRs: 23, Cy Perkins, Hartford, 1909
EBHs: 58, Elmer Smith, Waterbury, 1914
TBs: 250, Jim McCabe, New Britain, 1909
SBs: 75, Tom Bannon, New London, 1902

Pitching
Games: 49, Fred Gibbs, Bridgeport, 1909
CGs: 42, Frank Green, Holyoke, 1912
Wins: 31, W. Booth Hopper, New Haven, 1913
    31, Otto Hess, Springfield, 1906
Losses: 25, Fred Gibbs, Bridgeport, 1909
Pct: .846, 22-4, M.J. Parker, Springfield, 1908
ERA: 1.81, M.J. Parker, New Britain, 1910
ShOs: 9, Otto Hess, Springfield, 1906
SOs: 264, Bucky O'Brien, Hartford, 1910
BBs: 146, Files, Holyoke, 1909

COTTON STATES LEAGUE
Class D 1902-1908, 1910-1913, 1921-1932;
Class C 1933-1941, 1947-1955
(Mississippi State League 1921, Dixie League 1933, East Dixie League 1934-1935)

Batting
Games: 142, Buford Rhea, Helena, 1936
    142, Ham Schulte, Greenville, 1936
BA: .401, Carlos Smith, Hattiesburg, 1911
At Bats: 599, John Ferretti, Marshall/El Dorado, 1941
Runs: 155, James Powell, Tyler, 1933
Hits: 223, Herbert Adams, Hot Springs, 1948
RBIs: 157, Ed Zydowski, Hot Springs, 1940
2Bs: 58, Jack Grantham, Clarksdale, 1940
3Bs: 23, Edwin Amelung, Greenwood, 1939
HRs: 41, Harold Martin, Hot Springs, 1953
EBHs: 86, Harold Martin, Hot Springs, 1953
TBs: 350, Harold Martin, Hot Springs, 1953
Sac: 60, Bob Murch, Gulfport, 1908
SBs: 79, Buford Rhea, Helena, 1938
BBs: 155, John Gabos, Hot Springs, 1951
SOs: 130, Paul Dobkowski, El Dorado, 1950

Pitching
Games: 58, Eddie Albrecht, Pine Bluff, 1949
CGs: 30, Eddie Albrecht, Pine Bluff, 1949
Wins: 29, Eddie Albrecht, Pine Bluff, 1949
Losses: 28, Jackson Ryan, Gulfport, 1907
Pct: 1.000, 12-0, Walter Hirsch, Meridian, 1912
    .895, 17-2, Tom Perry, Monroe, 1938
ERA: 1.34, Labe Dean, Greenwood, 1948
IP: 332, Eddie Albrecht, Pine Bluff, 1949
Win Streak: 12, Walter Hirsch, Meridian, 1912
SOs: 389, Eddie Albrecht, Pine Bluff, 1949
BBs: 178, Earl Harrist, El Dorado, 1939

DAKOTA LEAGUE
Class D 1920-1923
(South Dakota League 1920, 1923)

Batting
Games: 101, Edward Aaron, Fargo, 1922
    101, Wick, Jamestown, 1922
BA: .402, Harry Wingfield, Jamestown, 1923
At Bats: 425, Earl Chesbro, Aberdeen, 1922
Runs: 121, Albert Nolt, Mitchell, 1921
Hits: 154, Albert Nolt, Mitchell, 1921
2Bs: 32, Oscar "Bud" Stanage, Wahpeton-Breckenridge, 1922
3Bs: 18, Arthur Jahn, Sioux Falls, 1922
    18, Albert Nolt, Mitchell, 1921
    18, Gordon McGuire, Sioux Falls, 1921
HRs: 17, Lyman Nason, Wahpeton-Breckenridge, 1922
EBHs: 56, Lyman Nason, Wahpeton-Breckenridge, 1922
TBs: 235, Lyman Nason, Wahpeton-Breckenridge, 1922
Sac: 37, L.M. Hollecker, Mitchell, 1921
SBs: 38, Gordon McGuire, Sioux Falls, 1921
BBs: 84, Albert Nolt, Mitchell, 1921

Pitching
Games: 39, George Stueland, Sioux Falls, 1921
Wins: 22, George Stueland, Sioux Falls, 1920
    22, George Stueland, Sioux Falls, 1921
Losses: 16, Enger, Valley City, 1922
Pct: .909, 20-2, Earl Keiser, Mitchell, 1921
IP: 291, George Stueland, Sioux Falls, 1921
SOs: 212, George Stueland, Sioux Falls, 1920
BBs: 162, Fred Hagar, Redfield, 1921
HB: 16, Earl Keiser, Mitchell, 1921
WP: 11, George Stueland, Sioux Falls, 1921

EAST TEXAS LEAGUE
Class D 1916, 1923-1929, 1931;
Class C 1934-1940, 1946-1950
(Lone Star League 1927-1929, 1947-1948, West Dixie League 1934-1935)

Batting
Games: 142, Ruether Jones, Tyler, 1947
BA: .433, Joe Kracher, Kilgore, 1948

INACTIVE LEAGUE RECORDS

At Bats: 598, Bob Marquis, Lufkin, 1947
Runs: 145, Bob Marquis, Lufkin, 1947
Hits: 224, John Stone, Henderson, 1947
RBIs: 185, John Stone, Henderson, 1947
2Bs: 61, Emil DeJonghe, Henderson, 1937
3Bs: 22, David Short, Longview, 1939
HRs: 62, John "Moose" Clabaugh, Tyler, 1926
EBHs: 90, John Stone, Henderson, 1947
TBs: 390, John Stone, Henderson, 1947
Sac: 48, Joe Longnecker, Tyler, 1924
SBs: 60, Tom Tatum, Henderson, 1939
BBs: 143, Floyd Brooks, Lufkin, 1947
SOs: 146, Bob Neighbors, 1938

Pitching
Games: 51, Japhet "Red" Lynn, Jacksonville, 1937
CGs: 31, Elton Davis, Henderson, 1946
31, George Yanen, Paris, 1949
Wins: 31, Japhet "Red" Lynn, Jacksonville, 1937
Losses: 20, Paul Cook, Bryan, 1947
Pct: .885, 23-3, Ralph Pate, Longview, 1948
ERA: 1.80, Hugo Klaerner, Longview, 1935
IP: 312, Japhet "Red" Lynn, Jacksonville, 1937
SOs: 269, Walt Schafer, Henderson, 1937
BBs: 183, Andrew Davis, Jacksonville, 1938
ShOs: 6, held by many

EASTERN LEAGUE
Class B 1916-1918, Class A 1919-1932

Batting
Games: 175, Harry Hesse, Allentown, 1930
175, William Jarrett, Allentown, 1930
BA: .382, Jim Blakesley, New Haven, 1928
At Bats: 665, Gerald Fitzgerald, Albany, 1930
Runs: 150, Edward Gill, Albany, 1929
Hits: 232, Edward Gill, Albany, 1929
RBIs: 170, Harold Yordy, Albany, 1929
2Bs: 63, Edward Gill, Albany, 1929
3Bs: 24, Adolph Schinkle, Bridgeport, 1929
HRs: 44, Walter Simpson, Springfield, 1923
TBs: 386, Bruce Caldwell, New Haven, 1929
Sac: 64, Bill Yale, Northampton, 1916
SBs: 61, Ollie Sax, Scranton, 1927
BBs: 120, Bill Dresen, Springfield, 1930
SOs: 96, Henry Bosse, Springfield, 1927

Pitching
Games: 50, Gerald Kahn, Waterbury, 1926
CGs: 30, Charles "Chief" Bender, New Haven, 1920
Wins: 26, Steve Stryker, Worcester, 1923
Losses: 24, Axel Lindstrom, Fitchburg/Worcester, 1922
Pct: .895, 17-2, L. Earl Mattingly, Hartford, 1931
ERA: 1.25, Harry Weaver, New Haven, 1917
IP: 350, Earl Johnson, Hartford, 1925
SOs: 252, Charles "Chief" Bender, New Haven, 1920
BBs: 152, Dominick Mulrennan, New Haven/Worcester, 1922
ShOs: 8, John Krider, Hartford, 1931

EASTERN CAROLINA LEAGUE
Class D 1908-1910, 1928-1929

Batting
Games: 121, Tom Young, Fayetteville, 1929
BA: .387, Frank Roscoe, Wilmington, 1928
At Bats: 480, Orvin, Kinston, 1928
Runs: 101, Charles Hamel, Goldsboro, 1928
Hits: 154, Roland Robins, Wilmington, 1929
154, Frank Roscoe, Wilmington, 1928
RBIs: 101, Frank Roscoe, Wilmington, 1928
2Bs: 43, Roland Robins, Wilmington, 1929
3Bs: 15, Vance, Rocky Mount, 1929
HRs: 36, Frank Roscoe, Wilmington, 1928
EBHs: 61, Roland Robins, Wilmington, 1929
TBs: 286, Frank Roscoe, Wilmington, 1928
Sac: 34, Jimmy Teague, Goldsboro, 1928
SBs: 46, Sam Fayonsky, Rocky Mount, 1929
BBs: 100, Sam Fayonsky, Rocky Mount, 1929
SOs: 84, B. Baker, Wilmington, 1928

Pitching
Games: 42, J.T. "Deacon" Jolliff, Greenville, 1928
Wins: 19, Harry "Cannonball" Otis, Goldsboro, 1909
Losses: 15, R.L. Howard, Wilmington, 1909
Pct: .944, 17-1, Ralph Carver, Goldsboro, 1928

ERA: 2.37, Edward Heller, Goldsboro, 1929
IP: 299, J.T. "Deacon" Jolliff, Greenville, 1928
SOs: 135, Henry Thormahlen, Wilmington, 1929

EASTERN SHORE LEAGUE
Class D 1922-1928, 1937-1941, 1946-1949

Batting
Games: 127, Harold Contini, Salisbury, 1946
BA: .388, Harvey McDonald, Dover, 1923
.388, Tony Rensa, Crisfield, 1926
At Bats: 518, Charles Wilhelm, Federalsburg, 1947
Runs: 132, Jimmy Stevens, Centreville, 1946
Hits: 172, Ray Jablonski, Milford, 1948
RBIs: 138, Norm Zauchin, Milford, 1948
2Bs: 44, Norm Zauchin, Milford, 1948
3Bs: 15, Tom Clancy, Dover, 1925
HRs: 33, Norm Zauchin, Milford, 1948
EBHs: 82, Norm Zauchin, Milford, 1948
TBs: 323, Norm Zauchin, Milford, 1948
Sac: 22, Whitey Koppenhaver, Salisbury, 1948
SBs: 82, Don Nicholas, Cambridge, 1948
BBs: 133, Bobby Tripp, Dover, 1947
HBP: 37, William McKnight, Pocomoke City, 1922
SOs: 137, Hal Harrigan, Milford, 1939

Pitching
Games: 41, Leonard Baker, Federalsburg, 1949
CGs: 29, John Andre, Seaford, 1948
29, Les Hinckle, Federalsburg, 1939
Wins: 27, Les Hinckle, Federalsburg, 1939
Losses: 17, Newell Valentine, Pocomoke City, 1939
17, Howard Smith, Cambridge, 1940
Pct: .986, 25-1, Joe Kohlman, Salisbury, 1937
ERA: 1.56, John Thompson, Centreville, 1940
IP: 298, Ken Raffensberger, Cambridge, 1937
Win Streak: 20, George Corneilius, Salisbury, 1937
ShOs: 9, Chris Van Cuyk, Cambridge, 1947
SOs: 309, Les Hinckle, Federalsburg, 1939
BBs: 165, Andrew Schultz, Salisbury, 1949
HB: 20, Steve Colosky, Cambridge, 1940
WP: 21, Bill Fogg, Dover, 1947

EVANGELINE LEAGUE
Class D 1934-1942, 1946-1948; Class C 1949-1957

Batting
Games: 141, held by many, 1954
BA: .410, Bill Dossey, Thibodaux
At Bats: 601, John Millard, New Iberia, 1950
Runs: 169, Kenneth Huff, Alexandria, 1936
Hits: 221, Harry Elliott, Alexandria, 1951
RBIs: 185, Cecil "Dynamite" Dunn, Alexandria, 1936
2Bs: 55, Jerry Witte, Lafayette, 1939
3Bs: 22, Ike Livingston, Opelousas, 1935
22, Melvin Clark, Baton Rouge, 1948
HRs: 47, Cecil "Dynamite" Dunn, Alexandria, 1936
EBHs: 105, Cecil "Dynamite" Dunn, Alexandria, 1936
TBs: 431, Cecil "Dynamite" Dunn, Alexandria, 1936
Streak: 31, Roy Sanner, Houma, 1948
Sac: 34, Bill Ebranyi, Lafayette, 1939
SBs: 84, Charles Brewster, Abbeville, 1937
BBs: 158, Bob Akenhead, Thibodaux, 1949
SOs: 135, Victor Oehler, Lafayette, 1937

Pitching
Games: 59, James Stuart, New Iberia, 1954
CGs: 33, Bill Thomas, Houma, 1946
Wins: 35, Bill Thomas, Houma, 1946
Losses: 20, Joe Allen, Natchez/Rayne, 1940
Pct: 1.000, 20-0, Bob Riesener, Alexandria, 1957
ERA: 1.04, Tom Spears, Lafayette, 1949
IP: 353, Bill Thomas, Houma, 1946
Win Streak: 20, Bob Riesener, Alexandria, 1957
ShOs: 7, Fred Baczewski, Alexandria, 1947
SOs: 344, Roy Price, Houma, 1951
BBs: 200, Marshall O'Coine, Thibodaux, 1950

FAR WEST LEAGUE
Class D 1948-1951

Batting
Games: 140, Charles Terrazus, Eugene, 1950
BA: .411, Ray Perry, Redding, 1948

At Bats: 549, Donald Williams, Medford, 1950
Runs: 162, Ray Perry, Redding, 1950
Hits: 188, Ted "Pinky" Hesse, Klamath Falls, 1949
RBIs: 170, Ray Perry, Redding, 1950
2Bs: 39, Miguel Rivera, Willows, 1949
3Bs: 21, Stan Roseboro, Klamath Falls, 1951
HRs: 45, Ray Perry, Redding, 1949
EBHs: 78, Ray Perry, Redding, 1950
TBs: 339, Ray Perry, Redding, 1950
Sac: 21, William Murphy, Redding, 1951
SBs: 44, Jim Hudgens, 1948
BBs: 180, Ray Perry, Redding, 1951
SOs: 129, Charles Terrazas, Eugene, 1950

Pitching
Games: 51, William Seward, Reno, 1950
CGs: 23, Elwood Clear, Willows, 1948
Wins: 22, Larry Shepard, Medford, 1948
22, Andy Sierra, Klamath Falls, 1950
Losses: 18, Lavere Hermann, Medford, 1950
Pct: .882, 15-2, Blair Simpson, Pittsburg, 1949
ERA: 2.53, Ronald Lee, Medford, 1948
IP: 241, Lavere Hermann, Medford, 1950
ShOs: 4, William LaThorpe, Santa Rosa, 1948
4, Henry Pippen, Reno, 1951
SOs: 258, Andy Sierra, Klamath Falls, 1950
BBs: 181, Garrett "Ben" Scott, Redding, 1950

FLORIDA INTERNATIONAL LEAGUE
Class D 1940-1942, Class C 1946-1948; Class B 1949-1954
(Florida East Coast League 1940-1942)

Batting
Games: 155, held by many
BA: .385, John Douglas, Miami, 1941
At Bats: 643, Byron Bridges, Miami, 1948
Runs: 124, E.M. "Bitsy" Mott, Tampa, 1947
Hits: 210, Buster Kinard, Ft. Lauderdale, 1941
RBIs: 136, John Davis, Ft. Lauderdale, 1953
2Bs: 44, Gilberto Torrres, Havana, 1948
3Bs: 21, Carlos Bernier, Tampa, 1951
HRs: 35, John Davis, Ft. Lauderdale, 1953
TBs: 324, Buster Kinard, Ft. Lauderdale, 1941
Streak: 26, Peter Kantor, Lakeland, 1948
Sac: 27, George Spears, Tampa, 1949
SBs: 58, Carlos DeSouze, Tampa, 1949
BBs: 143, Gene Hassell, St. Petersburg, 1953
SOs: 120, Willard Davis, Miami, 1953

Pitching
Games: 57, Antonio Garcia, Lakeland, 1947
CGs: 30, Albert Reitz, West Palm Beach, 1941
Wins: 28, Chet Covington, Tampa, 1946
Losses: 23, Charles Miller, Ft. Lauderdale, 1948
Pct: .938, 15-1, Charles Morant, Miami Beach, 1952
ERA: 0.83, William Harris, Miami, 1952
0.86, Gilberto Torres, Miami, 1952
IP: 339, William Stanton, Miami, 1948
Win Streak: 17, Vicente Lopez, Miami, 1950
ShOs: 12, William Harris, Miami, 1952
12, Gilberto Torres, Miami, 1952
SOs: 275, Antonio Lorenzo, Havana, 1948
BBs: 178, Leonard Goicoechea, St. Petersburg, 1948

GEORGIA STATE LEAGUE
Class D 1948-1956

Batting
Games: 147, Mike Milosevich, Tifton, 1949
BA: .400, Jim Stoyle, Sparta, 1949
.400, Edgar Hartness, Eastman, 1950
At Bats: 627, Jack Collins, Sparta, 1949
Runs: 150, Sam Buell, Dublin, 1954
Hits: 207, Alvin Jenkins, Jesup, 1951
RBIs: 159, Van Davis, Douglas, 1953
2Bs: 48, Edgar Hartness, Eastman, 1950
3Bs: 24, Ted Paterson, Sparta, 1949
HRs: 45, Van Davis, Douglas, 1953
TBs: 331, Edgar Hartness, Eastman, 1950
Sac: 23, Jerome Silverman, Vidalia-Lyons, 1949
SBs: 80, Charles Ridgeway, Fitzgerald, 1948
BBs: 165, Robert Reid, Eastman, 1953
SOs: 152, Sam Buell, Dublin, 1954

INACTIVE LEAGUE RECORDS

Pitching
Games: 75, Cecil Hutson, Jesup, 1953
CGs: 32, Mike Rossi, Vidalia-Lyons, 1949
Wins: 28, Don Rudolph, Jesup, 1951
Losses: 20, Raul Villamea, Dublin, 1952
Pct: .929, 13-1, Jim Harden, Eastman, 1948
ERA: 1.36, Jim Harden, Eastman, 1948
IP: 325, Mike Rossi, Vidalia, 1949
ShOs: 9, Paul Brock, Sparta, 1949
SOs: 270, Paul Brock, Sparta, 1949
BBs: 187, Ralph Hisey, Dublin/Eastman, 1949

GEORGIA-ALABAMA LEAGUE
Class D 1913-1917, 1928-1930, 1946-1951

Batting
Games: 129, Jake Daniel, Valley/La Grange, 1946
129, John Allen, La Grange, 1946
BA: .422, Bernard Lewis, Lindale, 1930
At Bats: 526, McDonald Turner, Newnan, 1948
Runs: 149, Fred DeSouza, Carrollton, 1950
Hits: 184, Malvern Morgan, Lanett, 1947
RBIs: 151, Eugene Solt, Carrollton, 1950
2Bs: 39, John Stowe, Rome, 1951
3Bs: 17, Earl Persons, Gadsden, 1929
HRs: 38, Eugene Solt, Carrollton, 1950
EBHs: 69, Bernard Lewis, Lindale, 1930
TBs: 311, Eugene Solt, Carrollton, 1950
Sac: 21, Jack Shipley, Cedartown, 1929
SBs: 85, John Heusman, Alexander City, 1949
BBs: 165, Fred DeSouza, Carrollton, 1950
SOs: 118, Ted Przeworski, La Grange/Carrollton, 1948

Pitching
Games: 51, Marvin Chappell, Alexander City, 1949
CGs: 28, Paul Brock, Newnan, 1947
Wins: 23, Bill Kallaher, Opelika, 1948
23, Paul Brock, Newnan, 1948
23, Gene Doerflinger, Carrollton, 1948
Losses: 17, Claude Jackson, Opelika, 1949
Pct: .933, 12-1, John Nabors, Talladega/Newnan, 1915
.913, 21-2, Paul Fittery, Carrollton, 1928
ERA: 1.60, Paul Fittery, Carrollton, 1928
IP: 313, Paul Brock, Newnan, 1947
ShOs: 6, Marvin Chappell, Alexander City, 1949
SOs: 233, Gene Doerflinger, Carrollton, 1948
BBs: 149, Mickey Mihalik, Newnan, 1948

GEORGIA-FLORIDA LEAGUE
Class D 1935-1942, 1946-1958, 1962; Class A 1963

Batting
Games: 142, Ralph Lageman, Albany, 1950
BA: .388, Dale Alexander, Thomasville, 1940
At Bats: 615, Paul Smith, Tallahassee, 1950
Runs: 147, David Williams, Waycross, 1950
Hits: 221, Edward Kazak, Albany, 1941
RBIs: 142, Chase Riddle, Albany, 1956
2Bs: 47, Marvin Leib(ovitz), Valdosta, 1948
3Bs: 23, David Pluss, Valdosta, 1942
HRs: 32, Bob Boyer, Albany, 1958
TBs: 296, Bob Wellman, Moultrie, 1956
Sac: 42, John Kelly, Waycross, 1942
SBs: 69, Edward Trojanowski, Americus, 1949
BBs: 150, Edward Trojanowski, Americus, 1949
150, Bob Bird, Dublin, 1958
SOs: 190, Arthur DeVany, Brunswick, 1956

Pitching
Games: 58, Siebert Scott, Thomasville, 1957
CGs: 31, Harry Raulerson, Waycross, 1951
Wins: 26, Ellwood Lawson, Waycross, 1940
26, Ace Adams, Cordele, 1937
Losses: 22, John Lindstrom, Moultrie, 1940
Pct: .882, 15-2, Robert Koczwara, Thomasville, 1953
ERA: 1.26, Tony Sarmiento, Tifton, 1952
IP: 339, Ace Adams, Cordele, 1937
ShOs: 8, Tony Sarmiento, Tifton, 1952
SOs: 294, Art Ceccarelli, Valdosta, 1949
BBs: 190, Fred Green, Brunswick, 1952

GULF COAST LEAGUE
Class C 1950; Class B 1951-1953

Batting
Games: 154, Herb Nauert, Harlingen, 1951
BA: .389, Bill Radulovich, Port Arthur, 1952
At Bats: 651, John Faucett, Galveston, 1952
Runs: 148, Bill Radulovich, Brownsville, 1952
Hits: 212, Arthur Edinger, Jacksonville, 1950
212, Bill Radulovich, Port Arthur, 1952
RBIs: 179, Walt Sessi, Brownsville, 1952
2Bs: 54, Bill Radulovich, Port Arthur, 1952
3Bs: 19, Warren Schroeder, Port Arthur, 1953
HRs: 45, Walt Sessi, Brownsville, 1952
TBs: 380, Walt Sessi, Brownsville, 1952
Sac: 18, Jack Terrill, Lufkin/Leesville, 1950
SBs: 50, Eugene Depperschmidt, Port Arthur, 1953
BBs: 128, Walt Sessi, Brownsville, 1952
SOs: 119, Claudio Barcello, Port Arthur, 1952

Pitching
Games: 54, Leslie Kash, Port Arthur, 1953
CGs: 31, Vallie Eaves, Lufkin/Leesville, 1950
Wins: 30, G.T. Walters, Crowley, 1950
Losses: 19, Dempsey Sterling, Port Arthur, 1950
Pct: .857, 24-4, James Price, Harlingen, 1953
ERA: 1.93, James Price, Harlingen, 1953
IP: 326, Bob Upton, Jacksonville, 1950
ShOs: 6, James Hagan, Jacksonville, 1950
6, James Price, Harlingen, 1953
SOs: 346, Bob Upton, Jacksonville, 1950
BBs: 183, G.T. Walters, Crowley, 1950

ILLINOIS-MISSOURI LEAGUE
Class D 1908-1914

Batting
Games: 130, Joe Anderson, Canton, 1909
BA: .405, A.J. Holzhouser, Kankakee, 1913
At Bats: 530, Will Johnston, Monmouth, 1909
Runs: 94, Will Lindberg, Clinton, 1911
Hits: 164, Roy Wolfe, Lincoln, 1912
2Bs: 33, Frank "Cy" Forsythe, Pekin, 1909
3Bs: 14, Andy Lotshaw, Beardstown, 1909
14, Gus Williams, Monmouth, 1909
14, Andy Lotshaw, Champaign, 1914
HRs: 29, Andy Lotshaw, Canton, 1911
EBHs: 68, Andy Lotshaw, Beardstown, 1911
TBs: 297, Andy Lotshaw, Beardstown, 1911
Sac: 46, H.J. Fleming, Champaign-Urbana, 1911
46, Joe Anderson, Pekin, 1911
SBs: 72, Roy Wolfe, Lincoln, 1912
SOs: 119, Fred Perry, Lincoln/LaSalle, 1914

Pitching
Games: 46, Joab McManus, Canton, 1911
46, Clarence Vaught, Lincoln, 1911
CGs: 32, Earl Hill, Macomb/Canton, 1908
Wins: 32, Joab McManus, Canton, 1911
Losses: 19, Fred Witte, Champaign, 1912
Pct: .938, 15-1, Grover Baichley, Champaign, 1914
IP: 381, Omar Hargrove, Monmouth, 1909
ShOs: 9, Henry Rossbach, Galesburg, 1908
SOs: 249, Charles Fanning, Canton, 1909
BBs: 120, Charles Delair, Monmouth, 1909
WP: 18, Charles Delair, Monmouth, 1909
HB: 23, William Jacobs, Kankakee, 1912

INTERSTATE LEAGUE
Class C 1939; Class B 1940-1952

Batting
Games: 142, Steve Filipowicz, Sunbury, 1947
BA: .404, David Kelly, Sunbury, 1939
At Bats: 593, Robert Mays, Hagerstown, 1943
Runs: 128, Nellie Fox, Lancaster, 1945
128, Richard Burgett, Allentown, 1946
Hits: 220, George Kell, Lancaster, 1943
RBIs: 144, Edward Sanicki, Wilmington, 1946
2Bs: 52, Bob Maier, Hagerstown, 1943

3Bs: 24, Harold Bamberger, Trenton, 1947
24, Charley Neal, Lancaster, 1951
HRs: 37, Ed Sanicki, Wilmington, 1947
EBHs: 73, John Capra, Allentown, 1944
TBs: 320, Del Ennis, Trenton, 1943
Streak: 22, Harold Nerino, Sunbury, 1940
22, Bill Cox, Harrisburg, 1941
22, Edward Nowak, Hagerstown, 1945
Sac: 24, Harvey Johnson, Harrisburg, 1941
SBs: 47, Joseph Scheldt, Wilmington, 1946
BBs: 130, Guy Glaser, Wilmington, 1945
HBP: 23, Nellie Fox, Lancaster, 1945
SOs: 123, Peyton Rambin, Trenton, 1949

Pitching
Games: 49, George Eyrick, Wilmington, 1948
CGs: 29, Charles Bowles, Lancaster, 1943
29, Norman Shope, York, 1944
Wins: 22, George Estock, Wilmington, 1945
22, Anderson Bush, Hagerstown, 1951
Losses: 21, William Emmerick, Allentown, 1943
Pct: .880, 22-3, Anderson Bush, Hagerstown, 1951
ERA: 1.44, Royce Lint, Harrisburg, 1942
IP: 260, Charles Miller, Hagerstown, 1943
Win Streak: 13, Woody Wheaton, Lancaster, 1943
ShOs: 7, John Burrows, Wilmington, 1942
SOs: 278, Andy Tomasic, Trenton, 1947
BBs: 165, Dick Libby, Sunbury, 1948
WP: 19, Joseph Slotter, Hagerstown, 1944

KANSAS STATE LEAGUE
Class D 1905-1911
(Oklahoma-Arkansas-Kansas League 1907,
Oklahoma-Kansas League 1908)

Batting
Games: 123, Dave White, Bartlesville, 1907
123, F.W. Hutchinson, Bartlesville, 1907
BA: .362, Joe Riggert, Lyons, 1910
At Bats: 492, Dave White, Bartlesville, 1907
Runs: 132, Charles Weisner, Lyons, 1910
Hits: 141, Bill Zink, Hutchinson, 1910
2Bs: 24, Charles Weisner, Lyons, 1909
3Bs: 19, Harriott, Larned, 1910
HRs: 13, Joe Riggert, Lyons, 1910
TBs: 228, Joe Riggert, Lyons, 1910
Sac: 36, W.J. Roth, Bartlesville, 1907
SBs: 57, F.W. Hutchinson, Bartlesville, 1907

Pitching
Games: 37, Bob Hassler, Lyons, 1909
Wins: 25, Bob Hassler, Lyons, 1909
Losses: 20, Henry Grohs, Great Bend/Wellington, 1910
Pct: 1.000, 10-0, Harry Womack, Coffeyville, 1906
.793, 23-6, P. Stanley, Hutchinson, 1909
Win Streak: 10, Harry Womack, Coffeyville, 1906
SOs: 205, Rolla Maple, Great Bend, 1910
BBs: 117, Henry Grohs, Great Bend/Wellington, 1910

KANSAS-OKLAHOMA-MISSOURI LEAGUE
(KOM LEAGUE)

Class D 1946-1952

Batting
Games: 127, Paul Weeks, Iola, 1952
127, Leroy Coulter, Iola, 1952
BA: .365, Jack Denison, Ponca City, 1951
At Bats: 530, Al Solenberger, Bartlesville, 1947
Runs: 133, Jack Denison, Ponca City, 1951
Hits: 185, Loren Packard, Miami, 1947
RBIs: 124, Loren Packard, Miami, 1947
2Bs: 44, Adolph Arlitt, Carthage, 1946
3Bs: 16, Jim Pisoni, Pittsburg, 1950
HRs: 24, Don Ervin, Miami, 1952
TBs: 259, R.T. Upright, Bartlesville, 1948
SBs: 103, Paul Weeks, Iola, 1952
BBs: 133, William Schreier, Iola, 1952
SOs: 169, Willard Davis, Ponca City, 1950

INACTIVE LEAGUE RECORDS

Pitching

Games: 48, Joe Vilk, Iola, 1952
CGs: 25, John Waltman, Pittsburg, 1949
Wins: 26, Joe Vilk, Iola, 1952
Losses: 20, Lawrence Jaros, Chanute/Iola, 1950
Pct: .900, 18-2, Joe Tufteland, Ponca City, 1948
ERA: 1.69, Conrad Swensson, Ponca City, 1949
IP: 287, Joe Vilk, Iola, 1952
ShOs: 6, Bill Pierro, Bartlesville, 1948
SOs: 300, Bill Pierro, Bartlesville, 1948
     300, James Owens, Miami, 1952
BBs: 212, Bob Wiesler, Independence, 1949

KENTUCKY-ILLINOIS-TENNESSEE LEAGUE
(KITTY LEAGUE)

Class D 1903-1906, 1910-1914, 1916, 1922-1924, 1935-1942, 1946-1955

Batting

Games: 130, held by many, 1938
BA: .429, Earle Browne, Owenboro, 1946
At Bats: 566, Carol Peterson, Fulton, 1941
Runs: 141, Vincent Mullen, Fulton, 1940
Hits: 208, Frank McElyea, Owensboro, 1940
RBIs: 159, Ned Waldrop, Fulton, 1954
2Bs: 60, Ellis "Mike" Powers, Bowling Green, 1940
3Bs: 24, Andy Lotshaw, Jacksonville, 1906
HRs: 34, Edward Urban, Owensboro, 1940
TBs: 323, Vern Stephens, Mayfield, 1939
Sac: 51, Bill Roland, Cairo, 1906
SBs: 84, Don Hazelton, Owensboro, 1949
BBs: 154, Wayne Blackburn, Owensboro, 1951
SOs: 147, Francis Babrys, Madisonville, 1949

Pitching

Games: 56, Elmer Weening, Fulton, 1937
CGs: 29, Ellis Kinder, Jackson, 1940
Wins: 26, Carl Gaiser, Jackson, 1941
Losses: 19, Paul Gehringer, Fulton, 1949
Pct: .905, 19-2, Carl Dunagan, Dyersburg, 1924
ERA: 1.29, Bill Howard, Paducah, 1951
IP: 294, Cecil Hutson, Lexington, 1938
ShOs: 6, Alvin Brown, Fulton, 1952
SOs: 361, Bob Schultz, Fulton, 1946
BBs: 224, Mike Conovan, Jackson, 1952

LONGHORN LEAGUE

Class D 1947-1950; Class C 1951-1955; Class B 1956-1957
(Southwestern League 1956-1957)

Batting

Games: 153, William Peeler, Vernon, 1950
BA: .429, Jim Prince, Midland, 1947
At Bats: 642, Felix Gomez, Big Spring, 1950
Runs: 188, Joe Bauman, Roswell, 1954
Hits: 231, Roberto Fernandez, Roswell, 1956
RBIs: 224, Joe Bauman, Roswell, 1954
2Bs: 69, Tom Jordan, Artesia, 1955
3Bs: 24, Roman Loyko, Odessa, 1952
HRs: 72, Joe Bauman, Roswell, 1954
EBHs: 110, Joe Bauman, Roswell, 1954
TBs: 456, Joe Bauman, Roswell, 1954
Streak: 43, Orlando Moreno, Big Spring, 1947
Sac: 22, Tony Guerrero, Odessa/San Angelo, 1950
SBs: 53, Duane White, Roswell, 1955
BBs: 170, Leo Eastham, Odessa, 1950
SOs: 142, Joe Calderon, Artesia, 1953

Pitching

Games: 60, George Payte, Carlsbad/Roswell, 1956
CGs: 30, Dean Franks, Roswell, 1951
     30, Jodie Phipps, San Angelo, 1956
Wins: 30, Dean Franks, Roswell, 1951
Losses: 22, Lloyd Wallis, Vernon, 1952
Pct: .917, 11-1, Roy Sims, Odessa, 1951
     .846, 22-4, Julio Ramos, Big Spring, 1949
Lowest Pct: .048, 1-20, Charles Rogers, Ballinger, 1950
ERA: 1.77, Humberto Garcia, Big Spring, 1949
IP: 338, Eddie Jacome, Midland, 1951
ShOs: 7, Billy Russell, Vernon, 1950

SOs: 262, Julio Ramos, Big Spring, 1949
BBs: 192, Lee Zamora, Sweetwater, 1950

MEXICAN CENTER LEAGUE

Class D 1956-1957, 1960; Class C 1961-1962; Class A 1963-1978
(Centre Mexican League 1956-1957)

Batting

Games: 143, Roberto Mendez, Fresnillo, 1965
BA: .445, Heriberto Vargas, Guanajuato, 1966
At Bats: 568, Javier Hernandez de la F., Guanajuato, 1965
Runs: 168, Heriberto Vargas, Guanajuato, 1966
Hits: 224, Alfonso Preciado, Guanajuato, 1965
RBIs: 174, Heriberto Vargas, Guanajuato, 1966
2Bs: 48, Alfonso Preciado, Guanajuato, 1965
3Bs: 20, Wilfredo Arano, Fresnillo, 1962
HRs: 59, Ramon Caballero, Guanajuato, 1962
TBs: 417, Pedro Hernandez, Guanajuato, 1966
SBs: 90, Guillermo Murello, Torreon, 1969
BBs: 126, Ramiro Caballero, Leon, 1965
SOs: 125, Rogelio Montoya, Fresnillo, 1966

Pitching

Games: 52, Crispin Salcedo, Ciudad Madero, 1970
CGs: 20, Alfredo Ortiz, Fresnillo, 1962
     20, Gustavo Guerrero, Aguascalientes, 1966
Wins: 21, Cesar Guiterrez, Aguascalientes, 1961
Losses: 17, held by many
Pct: .867, 13-2, Ricardo Vasquez, Leon, 1962
ERA: 1.65, Saul Montoya, Tampico, 1969
     0.58, Regio Moroyoqui, Ciudad Valles, 1974 (short season)
IP: 243, Antonio Dicocheu, Chihuahua, 1957
ShOs: 7, Luis Mere, Ciudad Madero, 1969
SOs: 234, Raul Gomez, San Luis Potosi, 1965
BBs: 171, Francisco Moreno, Zacatecas, 1965

MEXICAN SOUTHEAST LEAGUE

Class A 1964-1970

Batting

Games: 120, Lucas Buye, Campeche, 1969
     120, Angel Scull, Campeche, 1969
BA: .448, Celerino Sanchez, Campeche, 1966
At Bats: 471, Hilario Pena, Campeche, 1969
Runs: 75, Maximo Garcia, Campeche, 1966
Hits: 165, Arturo Bernal, Carmen, 1969
RBIs: 106, Francisco "Pancho" Herrera, Carmen, 1969
2Bs: 61, Hilario Pena, Campeche, 1967
3Bs: 21, Celerino Sanchez, Campeche, 1966
HRs: 39, Francisco "Pancho" Herrera, Carmen, 1969
TBs: 273, Celerino Sanchez, Campeche, 1966
SBs: 56, Victor Orozco, Campeche, 1967
BBs: 106, Francisco "Pancho" Herrera, Carmen, 1969
SOs: 87, Carlos Vigen, Puerto Mexico, 1968

Pitching

Games: 51, Domingo Hernandez, Campeche, 1966
CGs: 20, Julio Imbert, Yucatan, 1969
Wins: 22, Julio Imbert, Yucatan, 1969
Losses: 14, Rosario Reyes, Yucatan, 1969
Pct: .867, 13-2, Eusebio Elizalde, Campeche, 1966
ERA: 1.08, Eusebio Elizalde, Campeche, 1966
IP: 230, Julio Imbert, Yucatan, 1969
ShOs: 6, Ruben Soqui, Tabasco, 1966
     6, Pablo Montes de Oca, Campeche, 1968
SOs: 170, Julio Imbert, Yucatan, 1969
BBs: 105, Alejo Ahumuda, Carmen, 1967

MICHIGAN STATE LEAGUE
Class D 1902, 1910-1914
(West Michigan League 1910)

Batting

Games: 124, Zick Taillon, Manistee, 1913
     124, Ray Anderson, Manistee, 1913
     124, Adams, Ludington/Cadillac, 1913
BA: .367, Alfred Platte, Cadillac, 1911
At Bats: 482, Bunny Brief, Traverse City, 1912
Runs: 120, Otto Pfeifer, Traverse City, 1911
Hits: 169, Bunny Brief, Traverse City, 1911

2Bs: 37, Zick Taillon, Manistee, 1913
3Bs: 15, Jay Sharrock, Cadillac, 1914
HRs: 14, Grover Prough, Manistee, 1913
EBHs: 55, Bunny Brief, Traverse City, 1911
TBs: 244, Bunny Brief, Traverse City, 1912
Sac: 50, Henry Collett, Traverse City, 1911
SBs: 85, Otto Pfeifer, Traverse City, 1911
BBs: 79, Bill Varley, Boyne City, 1913
SOs: 79, Tom Stevenson, Muskegon, 1913

Pitching

Games: 46, Ross Mooney, Cadillac, 1912
CGs: 31, L. Walker, Ludington, 1914
Wins: 25, Ray Williams, Manistee, 1911
Losses: 20, Ross Mooney, Cadillac, 1912
Pct: .857, 18-3, LaRue Kirby, Traverse City, 1912
IP: 299, Abe Bowman, Muskegon, 1912
SOs: 235, John Walter Radloff, Manistee, 1913
BBs: 111, Roy Road, Ludington, 1914

MICHIGAN-ONTARIO LEAGUE
Class B 1919-1926

Batting

Games: 143, William "Dutch" Ussat, Saginaw, 1925
BA: .410, Jack Shaefer, London, 1922
At Bats: 564, Art Tefry, Flint, 1925
Runs: 111, Frank McGee, Hamilton, 1924
Hits: 178, Jack Cross, London, 1925
RBIs: 112, Guy Froman, Hamilton, 1925
2Bs: 46, Ernest "Tex" Jeanes, Saginaw, 1923
3Bs: 32, Jack Cross, London, 1925
HRs: 28, Ernest Calbert, Hamilton, 1922
TBs: 308, Ernest Calbert, Hamilton, 1922
Sac: 53, Andrew Getsie, London, 1923
SBs: 76, Clifford Hegedern, Bay City, 1923
BBs: 111, Albert Bashang, Saginaw, 192
SOs: 98, Frank "Dutch" Wright, Flint, 1920

Pitching

Games: 42, Hughes, Kalamazoo, 1924
CGs: 26, Will Coogin, London, 1925
Wins: 26, George Carmen, London, 1920
Losses: 20, Horan, Grand Rapids, 1923
     20, Feigert, Flint, 1922
Pct: .929, 26-2, George Carmen, London, 1920
ERA: 1.33, Charles "Pete" Behan, Hamilton, 1921
IP: 302, John Saladna, Brantford, 1922
SOs: 213, John Glasier, Hamilton, 1919
BBs: 151, Oscar Nossett, Kitchener, 1925

MIDDLE ATLANTIC LEAGUE
Class C 1925-1942, 1946-1951

Batting

Games: 140, Joe Beran, Johnstown, 1949
BA: .419, Joe Medwick, Scottdale, 1930
At Bats: 581, Charles Segale, Butler, 1949
Runs: 150, Oscar Grimes, Zanesville, 1936
Hits: 209, Whitey Kurowski, Portsmouth, 1938
RBIs: 187, Jeff Heath, Zanesville, 1936
2Bs: 54, James Wasdell, Zanesville, 1935
3Bs: 24, James Ripple, Jeannette, 1929
HRs: 38, Frank Welch, Beckley, 1931
TBs: 367, Jeff Heath, Zanesville, 1936
Sac: 36, Anthony Cyran, Fairmont, 1930
SBs: 72, Eugene Bilo, New Castle, 1950
BBs: 152, Bill Palumbo, Johnstown, 1949
SOs: 153, Joe Beran, Johnstown, 1949

Pitching

Games: 55, Howard Kiser, Niagara Falls, 1946
CGs: 25, John Kucab, Youngstown, 1949
Wins: 24, Richard Proctor, Clarksburg, 1930
Losses: 22, Charles Trader, Beaver Falls, 1931
Pct: .923, 12-1, John Kucab, Youngstown, 1941
     .909, 10-1, Paul Secrist, Cumberland, 1925
ERA: 1.33, Charles "Chief" Bender, Johnstown, 1928
IP: 307, Jope Drugmond, Charleroi, 1928
SOs: 299, Mike Martynik, Huntington, 1935
BBs: 195, Clarence "Hooks" Iott, Youngstown, 1940
HB: 21, Melvin Miller, Charleston, 1931
WP: 23, Ralph Waite, Canton, 1939

INACTIVE LEAGUE RECORDS

MINK LEAGUE
(MISSOURI-IOWA-NEBRASKA-KANSAS)
Class D 1910-1913

Batting
Games: 99, Harry Ries, Clarinda, 1911
BA: .349, Joe Stricker, Clarinda, 1912
At Bats: 408, Harry Mayfield, Nebraska City, 1910
Runs: 78, Leslie Mann, Nebraska City, 1911
Hits: 128, Joe Stricker, Clarinda, 1912
2Bs: 25, Ledger Free, Auburn, 1912
3Bs: 12, Sporer, Nebraska City, 1912
   12, Ledger Free, Auburn, 1912
HRs: 7, Howard Marshall, Nebraska City, 1912
Sac: 25, E.A. Rygert, Auburn, 1912
   25, Howard Marshall, Nebraska City, 1912
SBs: 56, Steve Brewer, Auburn, 1912
BBs: 56, Dallas Bradshaw, Nebraska City, 1912

Pitching
Games: 44, Vern Hirsch, Auburn, 1910
CGs: 25, Vern Hirsch, Auburn, 1910
Wins: 25, Vern Hirsch, Auburn, 1910
Losses: 19, Vern Hirsch, Auburn, 1910
Pct: .750, 12-4, Lawrence Casey, Clarinda, 1910
SOs: 175, George Zonderman, Auburn, 1912
BBs: 68, Herman Walters, Falls City, 1912

MISSISSIPPI VALLEY LEAGUE
Class D 1922-1932; Class B 1933

Batting
Games: 134, E. J. Hyde, Dubuque, 1923
BA: .407, Como Cotelle, Davenport, 1933
At Bats: 547, Jack Frost, Waterloo, 1929
Runs: 130, George Meyer, Davenport, 1933
Hits: 185, Bob Worthington, Waterloo, 1926
RBIs: 151, Ed Hall, Davenport, 1933
2Bs: 52, Ed Farber, Rock Island, 1925
3Bs: 25, Fred Schulte, Waterloo, 1924
HRs: 28, Ed Hall, Davenport, 1933
EBHs: 67, Ken Storme, Davenport, 1931
   67, Ed Hall, Davenport, 1933
TBs: 290, Len Koenecke, Moline, 1928
Sac: 36, Conrad, Marshalltown, 1926
SBs: 84, John Kerr, Cedar Rapids, 1930
BBs: 113, Cletus Dixon, Davenport, 1933
HBP: 22, Manchester, Dubuque/Rock Island, 1930
SOs: 96, Newton, Burlington, 1926

Pitching
Games: 44, Holmes, Moline, 1930
   44, Keil, Ottumwa, 1923
Wins: 26, George Valentine, Cedar Rapids, 1925
Losses: 23, Hamilton, Marshalltown, 1923
Pct: .862, 25-4, Allan Bauer, Ottumwa, 1926
ERA: 2.21, Guilford Paulsen, Burlington, 1931
IP: 317, J. Johnson, Cedar Rapids, 1923
SOs: 228, Edward Linke, Davenport, 1932
BBs: 170, Clarence "Steamer" Struss, Rock Island, 1932
HB: 35, Irvin, Marshalltown/Rock Island, 1923

MOUNTAIN STATE LEAGUE
Class D 1937-1942

Batting
Games: 130, John Sweetko, Logan, 1939
BA: .439, Murray Franklin, Beckley, 1938
At Bats: 540, John Sweetko, Logan, 1939
Runs: 136, Don Manno, Welch, 1942
Hits: 185, John Streza, Williamson, 1939
RBIs: 147, Harrison Wickel, Williamson, 1941
2Bs: 53, Harrison Wickel, Williamson, 1941
3Bs: 21, Bill Shewey, Williamson, 1940
HRs: 34, Don Manno, Welch, 1942
TBs: 336, Don Manno, Welch, 1942
Sac: 26, Andrew Ograin, Welch, 1937
SBs: 85, Edison Guinther, Ashland, 1941
BBs: 113, Edison Guinther, Logan, 1939
SOs: 97, Tony Kvedar, Logan, 1939

Pitching
Games: 40, Steve Milnarsik, Logan, 1939
   40, Ernest Clark, Huntington, 1941
CGs: 25, Frank Mahon, Huntington, 1938
Wins: 21, Joe Pennington, Logan, 1941
Losses: 19, Ralph Holland, 1939
Pct: .900, 18-2, Earl Brinegar, Welch, 1938
ERA: 2.24, Vernon Koehler, Logan, 1938
IP: 254, Steve Milnarsik, Logan, 1939
SOs: 297, Russell Meers, Huntington, 1939
BBs: 191, Russell Meers, Huntington, 1939

MOUNTAIN STATES LEAGUE
Class D 1948-1953; Class C 1954

Batting
Games: 126, George Kennis, Morristown, 1950
   126, Clifton Patrick, Harlan, 1953
BA: .427, Leo "Muscle" Shoals, Kingsport, 1953
At Bats: 526, Lew Flick, Big Stone Gap, 1951
Runs: 165, Hugh Hamil, Maryville-Alcoa, 1953
Hits: 216, Leonard Feriancek, Pennington Gap, 1951
RBIs: 164, Willie Kirkland, Maryville, 1953
2Bs: 54, Max Macon, Hazard, 1951
3Bs: 24, Willie Kirkland, Maryville, 1953
HRs: 40, Len Cross, Big Stone Gap, 1952
EBHs: 79, Walt Dixon, Norton, 1953
   79, Willie Kirkland, Maryville, 1953
TBs: 357, Walt Dixon, Norton, 1953
Streak: 22, Earl Motsinger, Big Stone Gap, 1951
Sac: 23, Ceferino Sanabria, Newport, 1950
SBs: 76, Carl Lucas, Kingsport, 1953
BBs: 197, Ken Johnson, Hazard, 1952
SOs: 145, Armenio Badea, Kingsport, 1953

Pitching
Games: 47, James Mays, Jenkins, 1949
CGs: 35, James Tugerson, Knoxville, 1953
Wins: 29, James Tugerson, Knoxville, 1953
Losses: 21, John Perechinsky, Jenkins, 1951
Pct: .905, 19-2, Mike Hudak, Big Stone Gap, 1950
ERA: 1.67, Johnny Podres, Hazard, 1951
IP: 330, James Tugerson, Knoxville, 1953
Win Streak: 19, Dan Hayling, Hazard, 1951
ShOs: 5, Michael Del Piano, Harlan, 1952
   5, James Tugerson, Knoxville, 1953
SOs: 286, James Tugerson, Knoxville, 1953
BBs: 178, Eric Doughtie, Norton, 1953

NEBRASKA STATE LEAGUE
Class D 1910-1915, 1922-1924, 1928-1941
(Tri-State League 1924,
Western League 1939-1941)

Batting
Games: 138, L. Metz, Grand Island, 1923
BA: .410, John Stoneham, McCook, 1923
At Bats: 530, Dick Cleveland, Lincoln, 1923
Runs: 139, Bob Dillinger, Lincoln, 1939
Hits: 194, Herbert Pember, McCook, 1929
RBIs: 140, Harold Schmiel, Sioux Falls, 1937
2Bs: 49, T.W. Rouse, Norfolk, 1922
3Bs: 25, Ted Kakaloris, Lincoln, 1939
HRs: 29, William James, Norfolk, 1936
TBs: 298, Bert Haas, Beatrice, 1936
Sac: 46, Paul Garzee, Hastings, 1910
SBs: 91, Charlie Block, Fremont, 1912
BBs: 118, Lee Riley, Beatrice, 1937
SOs: 138, Harold Freeman, Beatrice, 1937

Pitching
Games: 45, Cliff Homstad, Norfolk, 1936
Wins: 26, Joe Lotz, Kearney, 1912
Losses: 23, Foulk, Grand Island, 1922
Pct: .905, 19-2, Jim Cameron, McCook, 1930
ERA: 1.71, Nelson Potter, Lincoln, 1934
IP: 297, A.M. Stokes, Lincoln, 1923
SOs: 323, Winifred Noyes, Kearney, 1910
BBs: 176, Cliff Homstad, Norfolk, 1936

NEBRASKA STATE LEAGUE
(SHORT SEASON)

Class D 1956-1959

Batting
Games: 64, held by many
BA: .393, Ronald Debus, Grand Island, 1958
At Bats: 258, Keith Williams, North Platte, 1958
Runs: 70, Deron Johnson, Kearney, 1956
Hits: 87, Jimmie Hall, Superior, 1956
RBIs: 78, Deron Johnson, Kearney, 1956
2Bs: 18, William Palka, North Platte, 1956
3Bs: 12, Donald Dantoni, Superior, 1956
   12, Arthur Cole, Hastings, 1959
HRs: 24, Deron Johnson, Kearney, 1956
TBs: 167, Deron Johnson, Kearney, 1956
Sac: 9, Thomas Mieczkowski, Superior, 1956
SBs: 32, Fred Knapp, Grand Island, 1957
BBs: 70, Thomas Jaskowski, Grand Island, 1956
SOs: 79, William Rozich, Holdrege, 1956

Pitching
Games: 44, Raymond Searcy, Paris, 1957
CGs: 12, James Perry, North Platte, 1956
Wins: 11, held by many
Losses: 10, Robert Botto, North Platte, 1957
Pct: .917, 11-1, Theodore Ellis, Lexington, 1956
ERA: 1.68, Leonardo Ferguson, Kearney, 1957
IP: 128, Gary Peters, Holdrege, 1956
ShOs: 3, Leonardo Ferguson, Kearney, 1957
   3, Raymond Brunton, Grand Island, 1958
SOs: 149, Leonardo Ferguson, Kearney, 1957
BBs: 81, Benedict Birsa, Holdrege, 1956

NEW ENGLAND LEAGUE
Class B 1902-1915, 1919, 1926-1930,
1933-1934, 1946-1949
(Northeastern League 1934)

Batting
Games: 132, Elbert Slayback, Manchester, 1929
BA: .423, Bob Montag, Pawtucket, 1949
At Bats: 536, Joe Dwyer, Lynn, 1929
Runs: 139, Bob Montag, Pawtucket, 1949
Hits: 192, Joe Dwyer, Lynn, 1929
   192, Bob Montag, Pawtucket, 1949
RBIs: 145, Russ Saunders, Portland, 1929
2Bs: 42, Ted Bartz (Barczuk), Nashua, 1948
3Bs: 19, Sol Mishkin, Manchester, 1929
   19, Albert Touchette, Worcester, 1933
HRs: 30, Jim Pokel, Portland, 1948
EBHs: 75, Bob Montag, Pawtucket, 1949
TBs: 327, Bob Montag, Pawtucket, 1949
Sac: 57, Ed McLane, Brockton, 1909
SBs: 76, John Flynn, Lawrence, 1908
BBs: 116, Bob Montag, Pawtucket, 1949
HBP: 20, Paddy Driscoll, New Bedford, 1929
SOs: 121, Bill Reardon, Pawtucket, 1947

Pitching
Games: 45, A.G. Abbott, Lowell, 1906
CGs: 28, John Pomorski, Attleboro, 1928
Wins: 31, Marty O'Toole, Brockton, 1908
Losses: 24, A.E. Sweeney, Brockton, 1910
Pct: .875, 14-2, Joe Finneran, Lowell, 1913
ERA: 1.19, Bill Diehl, Lewiston, 1928
IP: 375, Fred Klobedanz, New Bedford, 1904
Win Streak: 10, George Martin, Portland, 1915
ShOs: 6, John Miller, Manchester, 1928
SOs: 243, Dan Bankhead, Nashua, 1948
BBs: 158, John Prudhomme, Lawrence, 1926

NEW YORK STATE LEAGUE
Class B 1902-1917

Batting
Games: 146, George Hunter, Wilkes-Barre, 1911
   146, Cranston, Wilkes-Barre, 1911
BA: .378, Bill Kay, Binghamton, 1915
At Bats: 576, John Duffy, Troy, 1911
Runs: 107, George Anderson, Wilkes-Barre, 1912

Hits: 185, Bill Kay, Albany, 1909
185, Del Drake, Wilkes-Barre, 1909
2Bs: 34, Bill Kay, Albany, 1909
3Bs: 25, Bill Kay, Binghamton, 1915
HRs: 13, Otis Johnson, Elmira, 1914
EBHs: 54, Bill Kay, Binghamton, 1915
TBs: 262, Bill Kay, Binghamton, 1915
Sac: 55, Bill Lauterborn, Syracuse, 1904
SBs: 105, Bill Zimmerman, Utica, 1910
BBs: 89, George Hunter, Elmira, 1914
SOs: 98, Richard Kaufman, Elmira, 1913

Pitching

Games: 43, Grover Alexander, Syracuse, 1910
43, Fred Walker, Utica/Reading, 1916
43, Jimmy Ring, Utica, 1916
Wins: 31, Howard Ehmke, Syracuse, 1916
Losses: 26, Jesse Buckles, Scranton, 1917
Pct: .816, 31-7, Howard Ehmke, Syracuse, 1916
IP: 311, Grover Alexander, Syracuse, 1910
ShOs: 12, Grover Alexander, Syracuse, 1910
SOs: 238, George Pearce, Scranton, 1912
BBs: 121, Marty Beretski, Wilkes-Barre, 1916
HB: 25, Harvey Teal, Syracuse, 1912
WP: 15, W.R. Hall, Scranton, 1914

NEW YORK-PENNSYLVANIA LEAGUE
(LONG SEASON)
Class D 1939-1962; Class A 1963-66
(PONY League 1939-1956)
(see also New York-Pennsylvania League (short season)
under Active Leagues)

Batting

Games: 130, held by many
BA: .435, Fran Bonair, Hornell, 1955
At Bats: 551, Chuck Harmon, Olean, 1950
Runs: 146, Don Zimmer, Hornell, 1950
Hits: 206, Chuck Harmon, Olean, 1950
RBIs: 144, Ted Sepkowski, Wellsville, 1954
2Bs: 49, George Scherger, Olean, 1948
3Bs: 23, Don Hasenmayer, Bradford, 1944
HRs: 45, Ted Sepkowski, Wellsville, 1954
TBs: 339, Chuck Harmon, Olean, 1950
Streak: 38, Paul Owens, Olean, 1951
Sac: 23, Joey Lawrence, Hornell, 1956
SBs: 88, Cesar Tovar, Geneva, 1961
BBs: 167, Bill Dowling, Olean, 1950
SOs: 196, Dick Snider, Geneva, 1958

Pitching

Games: 61, Gene Baker, Geneva, 1966
CGs: 27, Ralph Butler, Hornell, 1950
Wins: 25, Bob Christophel, Lockport, 1948
Losses: 17, John Smith, Lockport, 1942
17, Carroll Berger, Corning, 1951
Pct: .929, 13-1, Tom Keating, Hamilton, 1950
ERA: 1.40, Louis Palmisiano, Batavia, 1945
IP: 280, Phil Poole, Lockport, 1944
Win Streak: 15, Hayden Shupe, Olean, 1939
15, George Patte, Batavia, 1945
ShOs: 8, Gary Geiger, Hamilton, 1955
SOs: 258, John "Bubber" Moore, Wellsville, 1942
258, Jerry Kleinsmith, Jamestown, 1948
BBs: 169, Don Woerner, Olean, 1954

NORTH ATLANTIC LEAGUE
Class D 1946-1950

Batting

Games: 140, Barney Lutz, Carbondale, 1949
BA: .406, Walter Forwood, Carbondale, 1946
At Bats: 563, J.C. Dunn, Lebanon, 1949
Runs: 141, J.C. Dunn, Lebanon, 1949
Hits: 216, J.C. Dunn, Lebanon, 1949
RBIs: 163, Clarence "Buck" Etchison, Mahanoy City, 1947
2Bs: 43, Walter Forwood, Carbondale, 1946
43, George Rhoads, Carbondale, 1950
3Bs: 24, Walter Kowalski, Kingston, 1949
HRs: 34, Carl Sawatski, Bloomingdale, 1947
TBs: 334, J.C. Dunn, Lebanon, 1949

SBs: 46, Tom Ambrose, Mahanoy City, 1949
BBs: 121, Wayne Kreidler, Carbondale, 1947
SOs: 118, Chester Krajeski, Stroudsburg, 1950

Pitching

Games: 44, Al Gardella, Peekskill, 1949
44, Roland Burt, Mahanoy City/Stroudsburg, 1950
CGs: 28, Frank Radler, Stroudsburg, 1948
28, Clarence Heffelfinger, Bangor, 1949
Wins: 22, Tony Napoles, Peekskill, 1946
Losses: 16, George Keister, Mahoney City, 1950
Pct: 1.000, 22-0, Tony Napoles, Peekskill, 1946
ERA: 1.59, Frank Radler, Stroudsburg, 1949
IP: 263, Clarence Heffelfinger, Bangor, 1949
Win Streak: 22, Tony Napoles, Peekskill, 1946
ShOs: 7, Dale Melms, Stroudsburg, 1949
SOs: 237, Joe Seber, Stroudsburg, 1947
BBs: 151, Mike McCarron, Peekskill, 1949

NORTH CAROLINA STATE LEAGUE
Class D 1937-1942, 1945-1954
(Tar Heel League 1953-1954)

Batting

Games: 127, David Pierce, Statesville, 1951
127, Richard Hidalgo, Hi-Toms, 1951
BA: .425, D.C. "Pud" Miller, Hickory, 1951
At Bats: 567, Hillard Nance, Hi-Toms, 1951
Runs: 140, John Allen, Hickory, 1945
Hits: 189, John Lybrand, Thomasville, 1951
RBIs: 152, Norman Small, Mooresville, 1949
2Bs: 52, Darr Shealy, Thomasville, 1938
3Bs: 19, Bob Barker, Marion, 1953
HRs: 41, Norman Small, Mooresville, 1949
EBHs: 78, Norman Small, Hickory, 1951
TBs: 335, D.C. "Pud" Miller, Hickory, 1951
Sac: 26, Jim Layton, Newton-Conover, 1937
SBs: 80, George Silvey, Gastonia, 1938
BBs: 105, Charles Knight, Mooresville, 1949
SOs: 162, Doug Marvel, Salisbury, 1951

Pitching

Games: 52, Kelly Jack Swift, Marion, 1953
CGs: 28, Paige Dennis, Thomasville, 1938
Wins: 30, Kelly Jack Swift, Marion, 1953
Losses: 21, Hal Griggs, Hickory, 1950
Pct: .955, 21-1, Lynn Southworth, Thomasville, 1949
.933, 28-2, Paige Dennis, Thomasville, 1938
ERA: 1.05, Bob Ennis, Concord, 1946
IP: 287, Kelly Jack Swift, Marion, 1953
ShOs: 8, Bob Ennis, Concord, 1946
SOs: 321, Kelly Jack Swift, Marion, 1953
BBs: 170, John Hargrove, Lexington, 1948

NORTHEAST ARKANSAS LEAGUE
Class D 1909-1911, 1936-1941

Batting

Games: 122, Chandler Duncan, Newport, 1940
122, Clarence Harris, Newport, 1939
BA: .390, Charles Valci, Newport, 1936
At Bats: 497, Joe Marco, Paragould, 1940
Runs: 125, George "Whitey" Kurowski, Caruthersville, 1937
Hits: 166, Joe Marco, Paragould, 1940
RBIs: 124, Harrison Wickel, Caruthersville, 1937
2Bs: 37, Allen "Zeke" Zarilla, Batesville, 1938
37, Louis Leiter, Jonesboro, 1939
3Bs: 16, James Walker, Paragould, 1938
HRs: 23, Joe Rayne, Paragould, 1939
TBs: 251, D.C. O'Neill, Jonesboro, 1940
Sac: 17, Andrew Pasierb, Jonesboro, 1936
SBs: 62, Tom Woodruff, Paragould, 1939
BBs: 103, Hans Duda, Batesville, 1941
SOs: 116, George Ogorek, Jonesboro, 1941

Pitching

Games: 51, Russell May, Newport, 1938
CGs: 27, Edward Hughes, Newport, 1939
27, Johnny Sain, Newport, 1939
Wins: 23, Ernest Bingham, Osceola, 1936
Losses: 15, held by many

Pct: .929, 13-1, Harry Feldman, Blytheville, 1938
ERA: 1.73, Bob Eisiminger, Batesville, 1941
IP: 282, Russell May, Newport, 1938
SOs: 267, Joe Coveleskie, Paragould, 1941
BBs: 142, Tom Graham, Caruthersville/Newport, 1937

NORTHERN LEAGUE
(LONG SEASON)
Class D 1903-1905, 1917, 1933-1940; Class C 1913-1916, 1941-1942, 1946-1962; Class A 1963-1964
(see also Northern League (short season) under Active Leagues)

Batting

Games: 142, Steve Jankowski, Fargo-Moorhead, 1954
BA: .441, Robert Schmidt, Duluth, 1939
At Bats: 545, Bill Bruton, Eau Claire, 1950
545, Mitchell June, Fargo-Moorhead, 1954
Runs: 154, Cal Lahman, Jamestown, 1936
Hits: 194, Robert Schmidt, Duluth, 1939
RBIs: 174, Frank Gravino, Fargo-Moorhead, 1953
2Bs: 43, Morris Arnovich, Superior, 1934
3Bs: 20, Bob Latshaw, Crookston, 1936
20, Bill Polubiatka, Sioux Falls, 1947
HRs: 56, Frank Gravino, Fargo-Moorhead, 1954
TBs: 374, Cal Lahman, Jamestown, 1936
Streak: 32, Robert Schmidt, Duluth, 1939
Sac: 32, John Schenck, Fargo-Moorhead, 1946
SBs: 66, Bill Bruton, Eau Claire, 1950
BBs: 137, Vince LaSala, St. Cloud, 1951
SOs: 153, Gil Carter, St. Cloud, 1960

Pitching

Games: 58, William Harvey, St. Cloud, 1963
CGs: 26, Joe Hatten, Crookston, 1939
Wins: 25, Milton Goemer, Grand Forks, 1948
Losses: 20, Glenn Brickey, Superior, 1953
Pct: .933, 14-1, Eddie Watt, Aberdeen, 1964
ERA: 1.29, Danny Horton, Grand Forks, 1940
IP: 292, Otto Davis, Brandon, 1933
Win Streak: 15, Lloyd Sterling, Winnipeg, 1935
ShOs: 5, held by many
SOs: 304, Hugh Orphan, Wausau, 1940
BBs: 175, Chester Dickey, Grand Forks, 1954

NORTHWEST LEAGUE
(LONG SEASON)
Class B 1937-1942, 1946-1951, 1955-1962; Class A 1952-1954, 1963-1965
(Western International League 1937-1942, 1946-1954)

(see also Northwest League (short season) under Active Leagues)

Batting

Games: 166, Gene Petralli, Spokane, 1948
BA: .391, Hillis Layne, Lewiston, 1955
At Bats: 703, Edo Vanni, Spokane, 1948
Runs: 152, Jim Warner, Wenatchee, 1949
Hits: 244, Archie Wilson, Victoria, 1948
RBIs: 181, Smead Jolley, Spokane, 1940
2Bs: 56, Smead Jolley, Spokane, 1940
3Bs: 26, Archie Wilson, Victoria, 1948
HRs: 43, Jim Warner, Wenatchee, 1949
TBs: 408, Archie Wilson, Victoria, 1948
Streak: 36, Harold Rhyne, Wenatchee, 1949
SBs: 90, Ed Murphy, Spokane, 1951
BBs: 160, Cecil Garriott, Victoria, 1952
SOs: 167, Vic Pagel, Salem, 1962

Pitching

Games: 62, David Morgan, Salem, 1965
CGs: 32, Thornton Kipper, Lewiston, 1958
Wins: 27, Robert Snyder, Vancouver, 1951
Losses: 25, Frank Dasso, Wenatchee, 1952
Pct: .875, 14-2, Dewey Soriano, Yakima, 1949
ERA: 1.63, Don Osborn, Vancouver, 1942
IP: 303, Robert Snyder, Vancouver, 1951
Win Streak: 12, Frank Nelson, Spokane, 1948
12, Bob Kerrigan, Tacoma, 1950
12, Edward Robertson, Vancouver, 1950
ShOs: 9, Bobby Bolin, Eugene, 1959

INACTIVE LEAGUE RECORDS

SO Streak: 32, Larry Loughlin, Eugene, 1965
SOs: 296, Robert Jensen, Victoria, 1946
BBs: 209, Don Ferrarese, Wenatchee, 1950

OHIO STATE LEAGUE
Class D 1936-1941, 1944-1951
(Ohio-Indiana League 1948-1951)

Batting
Games: 141, Bill Henry, Springfield, 1946
141, Joe Pattison, Springfield, 1946
BA: .419, John Zipay, Fostoria, 1936
At Bats: 585, Andrew Rellick, Springfield, 1950
Runs: 158, Marvin Stender, Marion, 1951
Hits: 209, Henry Edwards, Mansfield, 1939
RBIs: 150, John Cindric, Lima, 1940
2Bs: 62, Jim Engleman, Newark, 1950
3Bs: 20, Charles Frey, Marion, 1946
20, Keith Jones, Richmond, 1950
HRs: 39, John Cindric, Lima, 1940
TBs: 350, Jim Engleman, Newark, 1950
SBs: 110, Maynard DeWitt, Zanesville, 1946
BBs: 142, Wayne Yoder, Springfield, 1949
SOs: 136, Charles Hopkins, Newark, 1947

Pitching
Games: 55, Richard McEvoy, Newark, 1948
CGs: 31, Joe Bielemeier, Zanesville, 1945
Wins: 25, Ray Janikowski, Middleton, 1945
Losses: 19, Bob Jenkins, Newark, 1944
19, Bob McCormick, Zanesville, 1945
Pct: 1.000, 15-0, Merle Settlemire, Lima, 1940
ERA: 1.21, Ned Garver, Newark, 1944
IP: 307, Merlin Williams, Lima, 1946
Win Streak: 15, Merle Settlemire, Lima, 1940
ShOs: 7, Joe Bielemeier, Zanesville, 1945
SOs: 275, Merlin Williams, Lima, 1946
BBs: 182, Bob Purcell, Springfield, 1950

OHIO-PENNSYLVANIA LEAGUE
Class C 1905-1911; Class D 1912

Batting
Games: 139, Kerr, Sharon, 1906
139, Del Drake, Marion, 1907
139, Bert Biery, Mansfield, 1907
BA: .370, Wilbur Good, Akron, 1908
At Bats: 545, Fred Abbott, Lancaster, 1906
545, Del Drake, Marion, 1907
Runs: 96, Ezra Midkiff, Akron, 1911
Hits: 164, Del Drake, Mansfield, 1907
2Bs: 47, Roy Miller, Akron, 1911
3Bs: 15, Fred Corbin, Akron, 1911
HRs: 23, Hugh Tate, Youngstown, 1911
TBs: 260, Del Drake, Mansfield, 1907
Sac: 63, F.E. Heller, Lancaster, 1906
SBs: 75, Charles Starr, Youngstown, 1907

Pitching
Games: 43, Fred Ehman, Akron, 1907
CGs: 40, Fred Ehman, Akron, 1907
Wins: 29, Fred Ehman, Akron, 1907
Losses: 25, Bud Scanlon, Mansfield, 1906
Pct: .818, William Phillips, East Liverpool, 1908
SOs: 284, Fred Wilhelm, Canton, 1910
BBs: 112, Fred Wilhelm, Canton, 1910

PENNSYLVANIA STATE ASSOCIATION
Class D 1934-1942

Batting
Games: 115, Harold Reitz, Jeanette, 1936
BA: .393, John Russian, Butler, 1937
At Bats: 484, M.A. Sambolich, Oil City, 1941
Runs: 129, Howard Murdeski, Johnstown, 1941
Hits: 166, Floyd Peters, Oil City, 1941
166, Ray Scott, Warren, 1941
RBIs: 139, Howard Murdeski, Johnstown, 1941
2Bs: 34, John Jerina, Butler, 1942
3Bs: 18, Carl Huffman, Monessen, 1934
HRs: 38, Howard Murdeski, Johnstown, 1941
TBs: 281, Howard Murdeski, Johnstown, 1941

SBs: 64, Arnold Evans, Butler, 1939
BBs: 86, Howard Murdeski, Johnstown, 1941
SOs: 118, Alfred Vaverka, Warren, 1940

Pitching
Games: 43, Mike Yurocko, Monessen, 1937
Wins: 20, Ken Heintzelman, Jeanette, 1936
20, Bill Sample, Johnstown, 1940
20, Joe Smolko, Johnstown, 1941
Losses: 19, Stanley Ferens, Greensburg, 1939
Pct: .938, 15-1, Joe Murray, Butler, 1942
ERA: 2.01, Ralph Ifft, Beaver Falls, 1940
IP: 260, Stanley Ferens, Greensburg, 1939
ShOs: 5, Bill Sample, Johnstown, 1940
SOs: 229, Ken Heintzelman, Jeanette, 1936
BBs: 143, Earl Jones, Beaver Falls, 1939

PIEDMONT LEAGUE
Class D 1920; Class C 1921-1931; Class B 1932-1955

Batting
Games: 149, Jack Mallonee, Durham, 1926
BA: .419, Danny Boone, High Point, 1928
At Bats: 596, Jimmy Brown, Greensboro, 1933
Runs: 149, Jack Lindley, Durham, 1930
Hits: 214, Danny Boone, High Point, 1926
RBIs: 154, Tom Wolfe, Durham, 1930
2Bs: 52, Bobby Goff, Henderson, 1930
3Bs: 25, Carr Smith, Raleigh, 1923
HRs: 46, Danny Boone, High Point, 1929
EBHs: 96, Fred Tauby, Durham, 1930
96, Jack Lindley, Durham, 1930
TBs: 379, Jack Lindley, Durham, 1930
Sac: 50, Sam Crane, Greensboro, 1914
SBs: 88, Dave Mann, York, 1954
BBs: 163, Nick Purchia, Richmond, 1951
SOs: 127, Edward Jabb, Portsmouth, 1936

Pitching
Games: 62, Vernon Gray, Lynchburg, 1955
CGs: 32, William Harris, Winston-Salem, 1922
32, Raymond Phelps, High Point, 1926
Wins: 26, Rube Eldridge, High Point, 1922
Losses: 24, Gene Rumple, Winston-Salem, 1933
Pct: .947, 18-1, Bill Yocke, Norfolk, 1921
ERA: 0.74, Garland Braxton, Norfolk, 1943
IP: 308, Henry Gornicki, Asheville, 1938
ShOs: 7, Jake Levy, Portsmouth, 1943
SOs: 301, Stan Williams, Newport News, 1955
BBs: 264, Edward Frenick, High Point, 1923

PIONEER LEAGUE
(LONG SEASON)
Class C 1939-1942, 1946-1962, Class A 1963
(see also Pioneer League (short season) under Active Leagues)

Batting
Games: 140, Olney Patterson, Idaho Falls, 1951
BA: .416, Oscar Sardinas, Great Falls, 1953
At Bats: 589, Earl Silverthorn, Idaho Falls, 1947
Runs: 168, Tony Robello, Pocatello, 1939
Hits: 205, Tony Robello, Pocatello, 1939
RBIs: 179, Tony Robello, Pocatello, 1939
2Bs: 46, Jay Kirke, Jr., Pocatello, 1939
3Bs: 25, Gordon Duff, Ogden, 1940
25, Earl Silverthorn, Great Falls, 1952
HRs: 58, Tony Robello, Pocatello, 1939
EBHs: 98, Tony Robello, Pocatello, 1939
TBs: 426, Tony Robello, Pocatello, 1939
Streak: 32, Herbert Harlow, Ogden, 1950
SBs: 60, Earl Silverthorn, Idaho Falls, 1947
BBs: 203, Leonard Schuermann, Great Falls, 1954
SOs: 216, James Lankford, Ogden, 1954

Pitching
Games: 63, Clifford Politte, Billings, 1963
CGs: 31, Ken Kimball, Idaho Falls, 1952
Wins: 26, Larry Manier, Great Falls, 1951
26, Ken Kimball, Idaho Falls, 1952
Losses: 19, Edward Schaack, Magic Valley, 1953
Pct: .875, 21-3, Les Bass, Boise, 1959
Lowest Pct: .000, 0-15, Granville Stone, Pocatello, 1947
ERA: 1.52, Bob Chesnes, Salt Lake City, 1946
IP: 291, Ken Kimball, Idaho Falls, 1952

Win Streak: 15, Bob Drilling, Salt Lake City, 1947
ShOs: 6, Harry Perkowski, Ogden, 1946
6, James Arnold, Twin Falls, 1946
SOs: 296, James Russell, Twin Falls, 1951
BBs: 213, John Hahn, Great Falls, 1951

PROVINCIAL LEAGUE
Class B 1922-23, 1940; Class D 1924; Class C 1950-1955
(Eastern Canada League 1922-23, Quebec-Ontario-Vermont League 1924, Quebec Provincial League 1940)

Batting
Games: 130, held by many
BA: .417, Ralph "Buck" Fraser, Rutland/Quebec, 1924
At Bats: 531, Alphonso Brathwaite, St. Hyacinthe, 1952
Runs: 115, Hector Lopez, St. Hyacinthe, 1953
Hits: 182, John Waters, Sherbrooke, 1953
RBIs: 123, Frank Gravino, St. Jean, 1951
2Bs: 43, Robert Stephens, Sherbrooke, 1954
3Bs: 16, Frank LaFontaine, Trois Rivieres, 1922
HRs: 42, Frank Gravino, St. Jean, 1951
TBs: 305, Al Pinkston, St. Hyacinthe, 1952
Sac: 32, George "Andy" Anderson, Ottawa, 1922
SBs: 60, Leonard Pecou, St. Hyacinthe, 1950
BBs: 134, Dominic Bertocci, Trois Rivieres, 1953
SOs: 133, David Mann, Thetford Mines, 1953
133, Francis Glamp, St. Jean, 1955

Pitching
Games: 56, William Anderson, Drummondville, 1953
CGs: 26, Connie Johnson, St. Hyacinthe, 1951
Wins: 20, held by many
Losses: 17, George Crowe, Ottawa, 1924
Pct: .867, 13-2, Walter Keay, Quebec, 1924
.867, 13-2, John H. Williams, Quebec, 1924
ERA: 1.67, Lou Lepine, Quebec, 1940
IP: 267, Mike Munsinger, St. Hyacinthe, 1953
ShOs: 5, Ruben Gomez, St. Jean, 1950
SOs: 220, Matt Peoples, Quebec, 1954
BBs: 164, Robert Long, St. Jean, 1952

RIO GRANDE VALLEY LEAGUE
Class D 1910-1911, 1927-1928, 1931, 1938, 1949; Class C 1950
(Texas Valley League 1927-1928, 1938, Southwest Texas League 1910-1911)

Batting
Games: 147, Jess "Jake" McClain, Harlingen, 1950
147, Ted Squillante, Harlingen, 1950
BA: .383, Lloyd Pearson, Corpus Christi, 1950
At Bats: 617, Manuel Cavazos, Robstown/McAllen, 1950
617, Bernard Pardue, Corpus Christi, 1949
Runs: 181, Joe Koppe, Corpus Christi, 1950
Hits: 207, Steve Carter, Harlingen, 1938
207, Lloyd Pearson, Corpus Christi, 1950
207, Jess "Jake" McClain, Harlingen, 1950
RBIs: 173, Jess "Jake" McClain, Harlingen, 1950
2Bs: 54, Herbert Fash, Taft, 1938
3Bs: 21, John Scolinas, Corpus Christi, 1938
HRs: 53, Jess "Jake" McLain, Harlingen, 1950
TBs: 410, Jess "Jake" McLain, Harlingen, 1950
Sac: 22, Leo Najo, McAllen, 1938
SBs: 94, J. P. Sheffield, Victoria, 1910
BBs: 161, Walter Graham, Laredo, 1950
SOs: 132, Lewis Hull, McAllen, 1949

Pitching
Games: 52, Simon Luna, McAllen/Laredo, 1950
CGs: 31, Eugene Hinrichs, Harlingen, 1938
Wins: 27, Eugene Hinrichs, Harlingen, 1938
Losses: 17, Edwardo Beltran, Robstown, 1949
17, Miguel Martin, Brownsville/Robstown, 1949
Pct: .850, 17-3, Roy Morton, Brownsville, 1910
ERA: 2.75, Tom Finger, Corpus Christi, 1938
IP: 310, Eugene Hinrichs, Harlingen, 1938
SOs: 223, Eugene Hinrichs, Harlingen, 1938
BBs: 228, Charles Kelsey, Harlingen/McAllen, 1950

INACTIVE LEAGUE RECORDS

SOONER STATE LEAGUE
Class D 1947-1957

Batting
Games: 143, Don Leppert, McAlester, 1949
BA: .432, Russ Snyder, McAlester, 1953
At Bats: 612, Jim England, Ada, 1952
Runs: 179, Joe Nodar, Ardmore, 1951
Hits: 240, Russ Snyder, McAlester, 1953
RBIs: 162, Stephen Molinari, Ada, 1950
2Bs: 58, Glen Snyder, Ardmore, 1951
3Bs: 25, Charles Buck, McAlester, 1948
HRs: 39, Stephen Molinari, Ada, 1950
    39, Gene Oliver, Ardmore, 1956
TBs: 356, Al Viotta, Ardmore, 1953
Grand Slams: 4, William Krueger, Ada, 1950
Streak: 33, Rod Kanehl, McAlester, 1954
Sac: 33, Marty Dooley, Pauls Valley, 1951
SBs: 86, A.B. Everett, McAlester, 1947
BBs: 183, Bunny Mick, McAlester, 1954
HBP: 32, Joe Dembrosky, Lawton, 1953
SOs: 173, Doug Davidson, Lawton, 1953

Pitching
Games: 59, Vic Stryska, Chickasha, 1948
CGs: 31, Andy Pane, Pauls Valley, 1951
Wins: 27, Dee Sanders, McAlester, 1951
    27, Kenny Hemphill, Pauls Valley, 1951
Losses: 19, Bill Winters, Pauls Valley, 1954
Pct: .944, 17-1, Buddy Yount, McAlester, 1948
ERA: 1.67, Dee Sanders, McAlester, 1951
IP: 302, Andy Pane, Pauls Valley, 1951
Win Streak: 17, Buddy Yount, McAlester, 1948
ShOs: 6, Charles Seymour, McAlester, 1952
ShO Streak: 26 2/3, Dee Sanders, McAlester, 1951
SOs: 341, Armin Somonte, Ardmore, 1951
BBs: 235, Andy Pane, Pauls Valley, 1950
HBP: 21, Dodson Stokes, Duncan, 1946
    21, Jim Farmer, Ardmore, 1953
WP: 25, Gene Fedak, Lawton, 1953
Balks: 15, John Francis, Seminole, 1950

SOPHOMORE LEAGUE
Class D 1958-1961

Batting
Games: 130, Damaso Blanco, El Paso, 1961
    130, Jose Calero, El Paso, 1961
BA: .387, Tommie Martz, Hobbs, 1961
At Bats: 534, Jesus Alou, Artesia, 1960
Runs: 159, Jose Cardenal, El Paso, 1961
Hits: 188, Jesus Alou, Artesia, 1960
RBIs: 119, Bob Carruthers, Plainview, 1959
2Bs: 39, Jose Cardenal, El Paso, 1961
3Bs: 19, Dick McLaughlin, Odessa, 1960
HRs: 35, Jose Cardenal, El Paso, 1961
TBs: 336, Jose Cardenal, El Paso, 1961
SBs: 64, Jose Cardenal, El Paso, 1961
BBs: 159, Dick Dietz, El Paso, 1961
SOs: 147, Gil Carter, Carlsbad, 1959

Pitching
Games: 54, Jack Warner, Carlsbad, 1959
CGs: 29, Don Schwall, Alpine, 1959
    29, Lynn Rube, Hobbs, 1959
Wins: 23, Don Schwall, Alpine, 1959
Losses: 16, James Doyle, Plainview, 1959
Pct: .889, 16-2, Les Bass, Midland, 1958
ERA: 2.41, Jack Warner, Carlsbad, 1959
IP: 241, Gary Modrell, Alpine, 1959
ShOs: 4, Dennis O'Melia, Plainview, 1959
    4, John Hanes, Albuquerque, 1960
SOs: 217, Jose Santiago, Albuquerque, 1960
BBs: 156, James Acton, Artesia, 1961

SOUTH ATLANTIC LEAGUE
(SALLY LEAGUE)
Class C 1904-1917, 1919-1920; Class B 1921-1930, 1936-1942; Class A 1946-1962; Class AA 1963

Batting
Games: 157, Don LeJohn, Macon, 1957
BA: .404, George Rhinehardt, Greenville, 1924
At Bats: 645, Russell Scarritt, Greenville, 1926

Runs: 150, Russell Scarritt, Greenville, 1926
Hits: 243, Russell Scarritt, Greenville, 1926
RBIs: 152, Ray Sanders, Columbus, 1940
2Bs: 58, Bob Winters, Columbia, 1939
3Bs: 30, Dusty Cooke, Asheville, 1928
HRs: 39, Bob Barrett, Knoxville, 1927
    39, Jim Hudgens, Greenville, 1930
TBs: 375, Russell Scarritt, Greenville, 1926
Streak: 36, Al Pinkston, Savannah, 1954
SBs: 80, Tom Raftery, Charleston, 1907
BBs: 148, Banks McDowell, Montgomery, 1951
SOs: 166, Roger Repoz, Augusta, 1963
HBP: 36, Ernest Vache, Charleston, 1922

Pitching
Games: 70, Willie Powell, Knoxville, 1958
CGs: 29, Irvin Stein, Charleston, 1941
Wins: 35, Bugs Raymond, Charleston, 1907
Losses: 26, Dick Robertson, Savannah, 1911
Pct: .950, 19-1, Frank Marino, Macon, 1941
ERA: 1.51, John Tsitouris, Augusta, 1956
IP: 376, Reid Zellars, Macon, 1916
Win Streak: 17, Wilcy Moore, Greenville, 1926
ShOs: 9, Harry Kane, Savannah, 1906
SOs: 335, Bugs Raymond, Charleston, 1907
BBs: 203, George Burpo, Columbia, 1947

SOUTHEASTERN LEAGUE
Class B 1926-1930, 1932, 1937-1942, 1946-1950

Batting
Games: 156, Mel Simons, Montgomery, 1927
BA: .404, Jack Kloza, Albany, 1927
At Bats: 614, Tom McBride, Jackson, 1940
Runs: 139, Jim Rivera, Pensacola, 1950
    139, Frank DiPrima, Montgomery, 1950
Hits: 210, Grover Bowers, Gadsden, 1947
RBIs: 163, Nesbit Wilson, Pensacola, 1950
2Bs: 65, George Jansco, Jackson, 1939
3Bs: 28, George Biggerstaff, Montgomery, 1930
HRs: 39, Henry "Prince" Oana, Jackson, 1939
EBHs: 80, George Jansco, Jackson, 1939
TBs: 339, Roy Pinkston, Gadsden, 1946
Streak: 42, Herbert Chapman, Gadsden, 1950
Sac: 51, Harry Collenberger, Selma, 1929
    51, Dan Seremba, Jacksonville, 1930
SBs: 78, Bill Martin, Montgomery, 1947
BBs: 141, Banks McDowell, Jackson, 1950
SOs: 138, Bill Serena, Montgomery, 1946

Pitching
Games: 61, Sid Nethery, Meridan, 1938
CGs: 30, Ambrose Palica, Meridian, 1949
Wins: 26, Floyd Van Pelt, Montgomery, 1928
    26, Roy Appleton, Pensacola, 1928
Losses: 24, Sharp, Pensacola, 1930
Pct: .889, 16-2, Joe Demoran, Montgomery, 1948
ERA: 1.62, Joe Ed Kirkland, Pensacola, 1949
IP: 350, Stewart, Pensacola, 1928
ShOs: 8, George Dockins, Mobile, 1941
SOs: 220, Ray Scarborough, Selma, 1941
BBs: 195, Norcum Rauch, Savannah, 1927

SOUTHERN ASSOCIATION
Class A 1901-1935; Class A1 1936-1945; Class AA 1946-1961
(Southern League prior to 1920)

Batting
Games: 161, Roy Ellam, Birmingham, 1915
BA: .416, Hugh Hill, Nashville, 1902
    .414, Les Fleming, Nashville, 1941
At Bats: 685, Gene Paulette, Nashville, 1915
Runs: 178, Charles Gilbert, Nashville, 1948
Hits: 236, Wilbur Good, Atlanta, 1925
RBIs: 182, Charles Workman, Nashville, 1948
2Bs: 65, Joe Dwyer, Nashville, 1936
3Bs: 28, Gil Coan, Chattanooga, 1945
HRs: 64, Bob Lennon, Nashville, 1954
EBHs: 103, Bob Lennon, Nashville, 1954
TBs: 447, Bob Lennon, Nashville, 1954
Streak: 49, Harry Chozen, Mobile, 1945
Sac: 63, James Fox, Atlanta, 1907
SBs: 84, Don Nicholas, Memphis, 1952

BBs: 155, Charles Gilbert, Nashville, 1948
SOs: 149, Dave Nicholson, Little Rock, 1961

Pitching
Games: 74, Jerry Lock, Memphis, 1960
CGs: 45, Glenn Liebhardt, Memphis, 1906
Wins: 35, Glenn Liebhardt, Memphis, 1906
Losses: 27, Ray Roberts, Mobile, 1921
Pct: 1.000, 12-0, Roman "Pete" Brunswick, Memphis, 1948
    .938, 15-1, Larry Brunke, Chattanooga, 1945
ERA: 1.56, Hub Perdue, New Orleans, 1919
IP: 375, Tom Sheehan, Atlanta, 1920
Win Streak: 17, Al Milnar, New Orleans, 1935
ShOs: 11, Irving Wilhelm, Birmingham, 1907
SOs: 251, Pete Richert, Atlanta, 1960
BBs: 173, Dick Weik, Chattanooga, 1948
HB: 24, Earle Flaherity, Nashville, 1913
WP: 18, Phil Morrison, Birmingham, 1921

SOUTHERN MICHIGAN LEAGUE
Class D 1906-1910, 1912-1913; Class C 1911, 1914-1915
(Southern Michigan Association 1910-1915)

Batting
Games: 148, Roy Richards, Battle Creek, 1914
BA: .386, Joe "Moon" Harris, Bay City, 1914
At Bats: 581, Joe Campbell, Saginaw, 1911
Runs: 140, Dan Jenkins, Bay City, 1914
Hits: 197, Joe "Moon" Harris, Bay City, 1914
2Bs: 55, John "Buck" Connors, Jackson, 1911
    55, J.J. Kutina, Saginaw, 1911
3Bs: 25, John "Bash" Compton, Battle Creek, 1911
HRs: 25, Al "Bull" Durham, Bay City/Lansing, 1912
TBs: 310, Joe "Moon" Harris, Bay City, 1914
Sac: 59, Carl Vandagrift, Adrian, 1910
SBs: 76, Dan Jenkins, Adrian, 1911
BBs: 89, A.V. Thebo, Flint, 1914
SOs: 116, Edward Hoffman, Flint, 1914

Pitching
Games: 50, John Loomis, Battle Creek, 1914
CGs: 37, Robert Troy, Adrian, 1912
Wins: 26, A.L. Jacobson, Kalamazoo, 1911
    26, Homer Warner, Lansing, 1911
    26, Walter Scott, Saginaw, 1914
Losses: 22, Turner, Toledo, 1914
Pct: .852, 23-3, J.W. Jenkins, Bay City, 1914
IP: 386, John Loomis, Battle Creek, 1914
ShOs: 9, B.L. Method, Kalamazoo, 1908
SOs: 338, Russell Robbins, Saginaw, 1914
BBs: 176, Frank Gordon, Flint, 1911

SOUTHWESTERN LEAGUE
Class D 1921, 1924-1926; Class C 1922-1923

Batting
Games: 141, Bill Bagwell, Salina/Independence, 1922
BA: .444, Bill Diester, Salina, 1926
At Bats: 580, Joe Rabbitt, Muskogee, 1922
Runs: 143, Morris "Moe" Solomon, Hutchinson, 1923
Hits: 222, Morris "Moe" Solomon, Hutchinson, 1923
2Bs: 43, John Paul Jones, Hutchinson, 1922
3Bs: 27, Bill Bagwell, Pittsburg, 1921
HRs: 49, Morris "Moe" Solomon, Hutchinson, 1923
EBHs: 104, Morris "Moe" Solomon, Hutchinson, 1923
TBs: 439, Morris "Moe" Solomon, Hutchinson, 1923
SBs: 98, Bill "Red" Lowrence, Independence, 1921
Sac: 37, Edward Stewart, Independence, 1921
    37, Louis Bachantz, Coffeyville, 1923
BBs: 98, L.T. Willis, Sapulpa, 1922
SOs: 98, Rowe, Coffeyville, 1923

Pitching
Games: 59, Joe Kling, Newton, 1924
Wins: 28, Happy Campbell, Independence, 1921
Losses: 21, Charles Humphrey, Bartlesville, 1921
    21, Delmar Lundgren, Salina, 1922
Pct: .833, 10-2, Bill Doak, Independence, 1924
ERA: 1.88, Andy Rush, Muskogee, 1922
IP: 353, Joe Kling, Newton, 1924
SOs: 263, Jake Beedle, Pittsburg, 1921
BBs: 163, D. Walker, Salina, 1923

INACTIVE LEAGUE RECORDS

SUNSET LEAGUE
Class C 1947-1952
(Southwest International League 1951-1952)

Batting

Games: 146, Earl Hochstatter, Porterville, 1950
146, Chris Remo, Porterville, 1950
BA: .411, Frosty Kennedy, Riverside, 1949
At Bats: 618, Eduardo Cruz, Juarez, 1951
Runs: 173, Calvin Felix, Las Vegas, 1947
Hits: 236, Calvin Felix, Las Vegas, 1947
RBIs: 188, Richard Wilson, Mexicali, 1948
2Bs: 57, Dick Steinhauer, Phoenix, 1951
3Bs: 23, Martin Krug, Jr., Las Vegas, 1948
HRs: 52, Calvin Felix, Las Vegas, 1947
TBs: 443, Calvin Felix, Las Vegas, 1947
Sac: 28, Ray Alderete, Ontario, 1947
SBs: 67, Don Jameson, Riverside, 1948
BBs: 210, Pete Hughes, Las Vegas, 1949
SOs: 149, Bob Bockman, Riverside, 1948

Pitching

Games: 61, William Stites, El Paso, 1951
CGs: 38, Tony Ponce, Phoenix, 1951
Wins: 32, Wenceslao Gonzalez, Juarez, 1951
Losses: 18, Wilbert Pender, Bisbee-Douglas, 1951
Pct: .875, 21-3, Forrest Orrill, Tijuana, 1952
ERA: 2.01, Forrest Orrill, Tijuana, 1952
IP: 352, Tony Ponce, Phoenix, 1951
ShOs: 6, Tony Ponce, Phoenix, 1951
SOs: 333, Manuel Echeverria, Mexicali, 1950
BBs: 237, Bob Schulte, Riverside, 1948

THREE-I LEAGUE
(ILLINOIS-IOWA-INDIANA)
Class B 1902-1917, 1919-1932, 1935, 1937-1942, 1946-1961

Batting

Games: 144, Otto Vogel, Rock Island, 1910
144, Harry Kelly, Rock Island, 1910
BA: .397, Joe Vosmik, Terre Haute, 1930
At Bats: 591, Sam Goody, Peoria, 1954
Runs: 136, Hubert Walker, Evansville, 1930
Hits: 198, Guy Dunning, Terre Haute, 1923
RBIs: 154, John "Moose" Clabaugh, Quincy, 1930
2Bs: 45, Frank Howard, Cedar Rapids, 1938
3Bs: 26, Ray Fritz, Evansville, 1930
HRs: 38, John Romano, Waterloo, 1955
TBs: 325, William Mizeur, Peoria, 1927
Streak: 50, Otto Pahlman, Danville, 1922
Sac: 75, Pete Hughes, Evansville, 1922
SBs: 79, Russell Fountain, Peoria, 1914
BBs: 137, Richard Beall, Topeka, 1959
SOs: 148, Olney Patterson, Quincy, 1948
148, Robert Seltzer, Springfield, 1949
148, Richard Smith, Green Bay, 1960

Pitching

Games: 68, George Bielik, Cedar Rapids, 1957
CGs: 32, Cicero Littrell, Rockford, 1921
Wins: 28, Roy Beecher, Springfield, 1907
Losses: 26, Bert Grimm, Terre Haute, 1919
Pct: .889, 16-2, Warren Gill, Cedar Rapids, 1903
ERA: 1.13, Frank Romine, Peoria, 1915
IP: 367, John Middleton, Davenport, 1913
Win Streak: 20, Charles Bomar, Decatur, 1907
ShOs: 7, Warren Spahn, Evansville, 1941
SOs: 297, Claude Elliott, Rockford, 1901
288, Paul Stuffel, Terre Haute, 1949
BBs: 210, Frank Oberlin, Springfield, 1905
210, Andrew Varga, Decatur, 1950
HB: 32, Ben Dyer, Decatur, 1913
BBs: 210, Andy Varga, Decatur, 1950

TOBACCO STATE LEAGUE
Class D 1946-1950

Batting

Games: 141, Orville Nesselrode, Sanford, 1948
BA: .408, Joe Roseberry, Fayetteville, 1949
At Bats: 605, James Wilson, Sanford, 1948
Runs: 146, Pierre Ethier, Lumberton, 1950
Hits: 212, James Wilson, Sanford, 1948
RBIs: 166, Orville Nesselrode, Sanford, 1947

2Bs: 46, Orville Nesselrode, Sanford, 1948
3Bs: 24, Joe Mangini, Red Springs, 1948
HRs: 32, Orville Nesselrode, Sanford, 1947
EBHs: 77, Orville Nesselrode, Sanford, 1948
TBs: 334, Orville Nesselrode, Sanford, 1948
Sac: 21, John Piccone, Clinton, 1948
SBs: 66, James Wilson, Sanford, 1947
BBs: 180, Bill Kay, Clinton, 1950
SOs: 117, Tom McGhee, Warsaw, 1947

Pitching

Games: 41, Aaron Osofsky, Smithfield-Selma, 1948
CGs: 28, Howard Auman, Sanford, 1946
Wins: 24, Aaron Osofsky, Smithfield-Selma, 1948
24, Hoyt Clegg, Sanford, 1950
Losses: 17, Hampton Conn, Warsaw, 1947
17, Wallace Ammons, Red Springs, 1948
Pct: .875, 21-3, John Logan, Lumberton, 1950
ERA: 2.19, Leslie Price, Clinton, 1949
IP: 271, Aaron Osofsky, Smithfield-Selma, 1948
SOs: 264, Clarence Condit, Dunn-Erwin, 1949
BBs: 176, Hugh Holder, Red Springs, 1950

TRI-STATE LEAGUE (NC)
Class B 1946-1955

Batting

Games: 150, Joe Fuller, Spartanburg, 1953
150, James Finn, Spartanburg, 1953
BA: .406, Bob Cheverill, Knoxville, 1948
At Bats: 666, Joe Fuller, Spartanburg, 1953
Runs: 145, Norman Koney, Asheville, 1948
Hits: 230, Bob Churchill, Knoxville, 1948
RBIs: 154, Albert Neil, Spartanburg, 1951
2Bs: 48, Fred Leonard, Gastonia, 1953
3Bs: 28, Bob Churchill, Knoxville, 1948
HRs: 44, Albert Neil, Spartanburg, 1951
EBHs: 86, Albert Neil, Spartanburg, 1951
TBs: 345, Albert Neil, Spartanburg, 1951
Streak: 29, Ralph Ellis, Greenwood, 1951
Sac: 23, Harold Kollar, Knoxville, 1946
SBs: 62, Ziggy Jasinski, Knoxville, 1949
BBs: 162, Pete Meachini, Charlotte, 1952
HBP: 14, Woody Quintano, Anderson, 1953
SOs: 140, Jack Maupin, Knoxville, 1949

Pitching

Games: 55, Melvin Fisher, Florence, 1949
CGs: 29, Melvin Fisher, Florence, 1950
29, Eurice "Pete" Treece, Rock Hill, 1954
Wins: 27, Melvin Fisher, Florence, 1949
Losses: 20, Melvin Fisher, Florence, 1950
Pct: .818, 18-4, Bob Spicer, Fayetteville, 1948
ERA: 1.41, Alex Zukowski, Charlotte, 1946
IP: 351, Melvin Fisher, Florence, 1949
Win Streak: 16, Al Aber, Spartanburg, 1949
ShOs: 8, Eugene Law, Spartanburg, 1953
SOs: 239, Murphy Murszewski, Spartanburg, 1952
BBs: 212, William Miller, Knoxville, 1949

UNION ASSOCIATION
Class D 1911-1914

Batting

Games: 143, Bill Orr, Salt Lake City, 1911
BA: .423, James Lacke, Salt Lake City, 1913
At Bats: 616, Howard Murphy, Great Falls, 1912
Runs: 46, Howard Murphy, Great Falls, 1912
Hits: 240, Howard Murphy, Great Falls, 1912
RBIs: 126, Frank Huelsman, Salt Lake City, 1913
2Bs: 52, Bill Orr, Salt Lake City, 1911
3Bs: 25, Mike Killilay, Helena, 1912
HRs: 23, Frank Huelsman, Salt Lake City, 1914
TBs: 342, Frank Huelsman, Salt Lake City, 1913
Sac: 58, John Misse, Great Falls, 1912
SBs: 61, A.E. Spencer, Salt Lake City, 1913

Pitching

Games: 58, Carl Zamloch, Missoula, 1912
Wins: 30, Roswell Hildebrand, Great Falls, 1911
Losses: 24, James Jachs, Salt Lake City/Missoula, 1911
Pct: .813, 13-3, Leo Dressen, Salt Lake City, 1911
IP: 357, Roswell Hildebrand, Great Falls, 1911
SOs: 267, Amos Morgan, Salt Lake City, 1911
BBs: 205, Pat Bohan, Missoula, 1913

WP: 39, Pat Bohan, Missoula, 1913
HB: 29, A. Kelley, Butte, 1913

UTAH-IDAHO LEAGUE
Class C 1926-1928

Batting

Games: 124, Dan Crowley, Salt Lake City, 1926
BA: .402, Charles King, Logan, 1926
At Bats: 491, Ray Molle, Salt Lake City, 1926
491, Harry Benjamin, Pocatello, 1926
Runs: 133, Roy Johnson, Idaho Falls, 1926
Hits: 177, Eddie Rose, Idaho Falls, 1926
2Bs: 41, Dan Jessee, Salt Lake City, 1927
3Bs: 20, Eddie Rose, Idaho Falls, 1926
HRs: 26, Ed Coleman, Boise/Twin Falls, 1928
EBHs: 69, Roy Johnson, Idaho Falls, 1926
TBs: 297, Ed Coleman, Boise/Twin Falls, 1928
Sac: 34, Don McShane, Ogden, 1928
SBs: 51, Phil Apperson, Twin Falls, 1926
BBs: 81, Dolph Camilli, Salt Lake City, 1928
HBP: 19, Mal Stevens, Ogden, 1928
SOs: 99, Arthur Parker, Pocatello, 1928

Pitching

Games: 35, Bruce Cunningham, Pocatello, 1926
35, Ed Auercamp, Ogden, 1926
CGs: 24, Daglia, Twin Falls, 1926
Wins: 20, Larman Cox, Ogden, 1926
Losses: 14, Orville McMurty, Salt Lake City, 1926
14, Dave Salazar, Pocatello, 1927
14, Lefty Gomez, Salt Lake City, 1928
Pct: .833, 15-3, John Walters, Salt Lake City/Twin Falls, 1928
ERA: 2.83, John Morrison, Idaho Falls, 1926
IP: 250 2/3, Bruce Cunningham, Pocatello, 1926
SOs: 172, Lefty Gomez, Salt Lake City, 1928
BBs: 126, James Walp, Salt Lake City, 1926

VIRGINIA LEAGUE
Class C 1906-1919; Class B 1920-1928

Batting

Games: 156, Eddie Mooers, Richmond, 1926
156, Ben Mallonee, Richmond, 1926
BA: .422, Rasty Walters, Wilson, 1922
At Bats: 638, Eddie Mooers, Richmond, 1926
Runs: 154, Dick Attreau, Norfolk, 1926
Hits: 225, Dick Attreau, Norfolk, 1926
RBIs: 127, Davis Robertson, Norfolk, 1926
2Bs: 50, Ben Spencer, Rocky Mount, 1921
3Bs: 18, Angel Aragon, Richmond, 1921
HRs: 44, Stanley "Pete" Stack, Richmond, 1926
TBs: 369, Stanley "Pete" Stack, Richmond, 1926
Sac: 54, R.W. Reeve, Richmond, 1907
SBs: 74, George Kircher, Norfolk, 1913
BBs: 93, Harry Snyder, Rocky Mount, 1924
SOs: 102, Fred Henry, Suffolk, 1915

Pitching

Games: 59, Jimmy Lavender, Danville, 1907
CGs: 32, Clifford Markle, Norfolk, 1914
32, Frank Dodson, Richmond, 1924
Wins: 31, Clifford Markle, Norfolk, 1914
Losses: 23, R.W. McCleary, Portsmouth, 1914
Pct: 1.000, 14-0, John Picus Quinn, Richmond, 1908
1.000, 11-0, J.G. Vance, Petersburg, 1911
1.000, 11-0, Alex Peterson, Norfolk, 1925
.935, 29-2, Charles "Chief" Bender, Richmond, 1919
ERA: 1.01, Rion Mitchell, Norfolk, 1919
IP: 380, Walter Doane, Roanoke, 1909
380, J.J. Efird, Roanoke, 1913
Win Streak: 14, John Picus Quinn, Richmond, 1908
SOs: 390, Yancey Ayers, Richmond, 1913
BBs: 144, Claral Gillenwater, Petersburg, 1924

VIRGINIA LEAGUE
Class D 1939-1940; 1948-1951; Class C 1941-1942

Batting

Games: 142, Arthur Jacobs, Emporia, 1948
BA: .394, Morris "Smut" Aderholt, Emporia, 1948
At Bats: 547, Gordon Bragg, Blackstone, 1948
Runs: 147, Arthur Jacobs, Emporia, 1948
Hits: 185, Morris "Smut" Aderholt, Emporia, 1948

RBIs: 150, Vernon "Moose" Shetler, Franklin, 1948
2Bs: 46, Paul "Buck" Varner, Petersburg, 1948
3Bs: 18, Gordon Bragg, Blackstone, 1948
HRs: 34, Kenneth Hatcher, Petersburg, 1951
EBHs: 80, Morris "Smut" Aderholt, Emporia, 1948
TBs: 334, Morris "Smut" Aderholt, Emporia, 1948
Sac: 22, Bill Sheridan, Staunton, 1939
SBs: 70, Morris "Smut" Aderholt, Emporia, 1948
BBs: 127, John Zontini, Franklin, 1948
HBP: 14, William Burgos, Newport News, 1942
SOs: 110, Bruno Cassanova, Lawrenceville, 1948

Pitching
Games: 70, Cecil Hutson, Suffolk, 1948
CGs: 29, John Brockwell, Petersburg, 1951
Wins: 25, John Brockwell, Petersburg, 1951
Losses: 23, George Sumey, Staunton, 1942
Pct: .952, 21-1, Al Tefft, Blackstone, 1948
ERA: 1.57, Al Tefft, Blackstone, 1948
IP: 296, Joe Kania, Newport News, 1942
Win Streak: 20, Al Tefft, Blackstone, 1948
ShOs: 6, Al Tefft, Blackstone, 1948
SOs: 212, George Blair, Petersburg, 1948
BBs: 198, Dick Brockwell, Petersburg, 1948

WASHINGTON STATE LEAGUE
Class D 1903-1912
(Southwest Washington League
1903-1906, 1912)

Batting
Games: 58, Miller, Chehalis-Centralia, 1911
BA: .358, Fielder Jones, Chehalis, 1910
At Bats: 228, Miller, Chehalis-Centralia, 1911
228, Tate Berry, Chehalis, 1911
Runs: 48, White McBride, Chehalis, 1910
Hits: 72, H. Guynn, Centralia, 1911
2Bs: 36, H. Guynn, Centralia, 1911
3Bs: 8, Murray, Chehalis, 1911
HRs: 8, C.D. Wineholt, Raymond/Chehalis, 1911
EBHs: 43, C.D. Wineholt, Raymond/Chehalis, 1911
43, Miller, Chehalis-Centralia, 1911
TBs: 127, C.D. Wineholt, Raymond/Chehalis, 1911
Sac: 21, Fitzgerald, Raymond, 1910
SBs: 37, Ira Harmon, Raymond, 1910

Pitching
Games: 26, James Jachs, Raymond, 1910
Wins: 15, James Jachs, Raymond, 1910
Losses: 9, Ray Baker, Raymond, 1911
Pct: .909, 10-1, Walt Frink, Chehalis, 1911
SOs: 164, James Jachs, Raymond, 1910
BBs: 72, Fitchner, Chehalis, 1911

WEST TEXAS LEAGUE
Class D 1920-1923, 1928-1929
(Panhandle-Pecos Valley League 1923)

Batting
BA: .433, Edward Kallina, Midland, 1929
Runs: 136, Julian Flowers, Midland, 1929
Hits: 181, Alfred Anderson, Abilene, 1929
2Bs: 43, John King, Midland, 1929
3Bs: 19, Cameron Best, Coleman, 1929
HRs: 44, Edward Kallina, Midland, 1929
EBHs: 79, Edward Kallina, Midland, 1929
TBs: 333, Edward Kallina, Midland, 1929
Sac: 33, Grady White, Abilene, 1920
SBs: 63, Dan Lynch, Ballinger, 1929
BBs: 73, John Norek, Abilene, 1929
SOs: 103, Grover Seitz, Big Spring, 1929

Pitching
Games: 39, Gene Moore, Midland, 1929
CGs: 23, Steve Myers, Coleman, 1929
Wins: 23, Steve Myers, Coleman, 1929
Losses: 14, held by many
Pct: .867, 13-2, Tom Blake, Midland, 1929
ERA: 3.30, Jim Parker, Ballinger, 1929
IP: 270, Kolzelnik, Cisco, 1920

SOs: 186, Alvin Betts, San Angelo, 1929
BBs: 116, Joe Blackwell, San Angelo, 1929

WEST TEXAS-NEW MEXICO LEAGUE
Class D 1937-1942; Class C 1946-1954; Class B 1955

Batting
Games: 146, Art Cuitti, Albuquerque, 1950
BA: .426, Don Stokes, Plainview, 1953
At Bats: 635, Redic Otey, Pampa, 1948
Runs: 185, Bob Crues, Amarillo, 1948
Hits: 242, Don Stokes, Plainview, 1953
RBIs: 254, Bob Crues, Amarillo, 1948
2Bs: 66, Douglas Lewis, Pampa, 1953
3Bs: 22, Len Attyd, Albuquerque, 1948
HRs: 69, Bob Crues, Amarillo, 1948
EBHs: 110, Bob Crues, Amarillo, 1948
TBs: 479, Bob Crues, Amarillo, 1948
Streak: 40, Frosty Kennedy, Plainview, 1953
Sac: 38, Curdele Lloyd, Big Spring, 1939
SBs: 67, Bob Decker, Big Spring, 1954
BBs: 183, Verdun Gilchrist, Borger, 1947
HBP: 27, Delmont Balinger, Midland, 1938
SOs: 176, Robert Bailey, Wink, 1937

Pitching
Games: 58, Andres Alonso, Abilene, 1954
CGs: 33, Willard Ramsdell, Big Spring/Odessa, 1940
Wins: 28, Carroll Dial, Clovis, 1953
28, Carroll Dial, Clovis, 1954
Losses: 23, Mike Gazella, Abilene, 1953
Pct: 1.000, 17-0, Kenneth Wyatt, Clovis, 1942
1.000, 14-0, George Sucha, Albuquerque, 1953
ERA: 1.81, John Isenhart, Lubbock, 1954
IP: 351, Willard Ramsdell, Big Spring/Odessa, 1940
Win Streak: 17, Kenneth Wyatt, Clovis, 1942
17, Jess Priest, Albuquerque, 1951
ShOs: 6, Leonard Ruyle, Amarillo, 1954
SOs: 297, William Evans, Amarillo, 1946
BBs: 205, John Kelly, Abilene, 1948

WESTERN ASSOCIATION
Class C 1902-1911, 1922-1932, 1934-1942, 1946-1954; Class D 1914-1917, 1920-1921
(Missouri Valley League 1902-1904)

Batting
Games: 163, Everett Booe, Ft. Smith, 1926
BA: .410, David Minor, Okmulgee, 1927
At Bats: 676, Cecil "Stormy" Davis, Okmulgee, 1924
Runs: 195, Leo Najo, Okmulgee, 1925
Hits: 260, Wilbur Davis, Okmulgee, 1924
RBIs: 190, Wilbur Davis, Okmulgee, 1924
2Bs: 63, Jim Hudgens, Ft. Smith, 1925
3Bs: 29, Jo Jo White, Ft. Smith, 1928
HRs: 51, Wilbur Davis, Okmulgee, 1924
51, Cecil "Stormy" Davis, Okmulgee, 1924
EBHs: 112, Wilbur Davis, Okmulgee, 1924
TBs: 487, Wilbur Davis, Okmulgee, 1924
Sac: 53, Joe Humphreys, McAlester, 1916
SBs: 107, Lyle Judy, Springfield, 1935
BBs: 149, Butch Nieman, Topeka, 1950
SOs: 164, Joe Beran, Hutchinson, 1953

Pitching
Games: 56, Winlow Johnson, Topeka, 1948
CGs: 41, Robert Groom, Springfield, 1905
41, Blaine Durbin, Joplin, 1906
Wins: 32, Amos Morgan, Iola, 1904
32, Henry Gehring, Wichita, 1905
32, Blaine Durbin, Joplin, 1906
Losses: 24, Andrew Jelsma, Drumwright/Henryetta, 1921
Pct: 1.000, 13-0, Ray Fagan, Oklahoma City, 1915
.944, 17-1, Lloyd Brown, Ardmore, 1925
ERA: 1.15, Ray Fagan, Oklahoma City, 1915
1.60, A. G. McGuire, Enid, 1920
IP: 393, Robert Groom, Springfield, 1905
Win Streak: 13, Ray Fagan, Oklahoma City, 1915
ShOs: 10, Henry Gehring, Wichita, 1905
9, Roger Sawyer, Hutchinson, 1953
ShO Streak: 53, Henry Gehring, Wichita, 1905

SOs: 304, Blix Donnelley, Springfield, 1941
BBs: 225, Gene Snyder, Salina, 1951

WESTERN LEAGUE
Class A 1902-1937, 1947-1958

Batting
Games: 171, held by many
BA: .422, Joe Wilhoit, Wichita, 1919
At Bats: 723, Ed Hemingway, Sioux City, 1922
Runs: 184, Royce "Mule" Washburn, Tulsa, 1924
Hits: 274, Jack Lelivelt, Omaha, 1921
RBIs: 160, Stanley Keyes, Des Moines, 1931
2Bs: 100, Lyman Lamb, Tulsa, 1924
3Bs: 30, Walter Shaner, Lincoln, 1925
HRs: 66, Dick Stuart, Lincoln, 1956
EBHs: 123, Lyman Lamb, Tulsa, 1924
TBs: 458, Royce "Mule" Washburn, Tulsa, 1924
Streak: 69, Joe Wilhoit, Wichita, 1919
Sac: 75, Bill Davidson, Sioux City, 1914
SBs: 88, Bill Fischer, Omaha, 1909
BBs: 137, Dallas "Moose" Womack, Lincoln, 1953
SOs: 171, Dick Stuart, Lincoln, 1956

Pitching
Games: 73, Frank Tubbs, Oklahoma City, 1928
CGs: 28, Harold Turpin, Des Moines, 1936
28, John Kucab, Lincoln, 1950
Wins: 38, George Boehler, Tulsa, 1922
Losses: 30, Pat Paige, Denver, 1906
Pct: .938, 15-1, Lou Ciola, Omaha, 1952
ERA: 1.75, Paul Musser, Des Moines, 1917
IP: 441, George Boehler, Tulsa, 1922
Win Streak: 17, Frank Lamanski, Davenport, 1934
ShOs: 9, Jack Pfeister, Omaha, 1905
SOs: 337, Paul Musser, Des Moines, 1917
BBs: 237, Oscar Roettger, Sioux City, 1922

WESTERN CANADA LEAGUE
Class D 1907-1914; Class C 1919; Class B 1920-1921

Batting
Games: 131, Les Wilson, Saskatoon, 1914
131, Tom Herriott, Regina, 1914
BA: .377, Jack Fournier, Moose Jaw, 1911
At Bats: 503, Jack Smith, Regina, 1914
Runs: 111, Phil Apperson, Edmonton, 1921
Hits: 161, Nelson Hawks, Calgary, 1920
RBIs: 80, Ernest Vache, Regina, 1920
2Bs: 30, Floyd "Babe" Herman, Edmonton, 1921
3Bs: 19, Jack Smith, Regina, 1914
19, Jack Fournier, Moose Jaw, 1911
HRs: 13, Bradley Hollis, Calgary, 1913
EBHs: 52, Jack Fournier, Moose Jaw, 1911
TBs: 230, Jack Fournier, Moose Jaw, 1911
Sac: 42, Henry, Regina, 1914
SBs: 72, Hap Morse, Edmonton, 1910

Pitching
Games: 44, Jesse Buckles, Medicine Hat, 1914
Wins: 26, Del Manning, Calgary, 1910
26, Ralph Works, Medicine Hat, 1907
Losses: 19, Sheridan, Saskatoon, 1911
Pct: .824, 14-3, Albert Zweifel, Regina, 1920
ERA: 1.55, Albert Zweifel, Regina, 1920
IP: 334, Jesse Buckles, Medicine Hat, 1914
SOs: 217, Ralph Works, Medicine Hat, 1907
BBs: 129, Ralph Works, Medicine Hat, 1907

WESTERN CAROLINA LEAGUE
Class D 1948-1952

Batting
Games: 113, Robert Peters, Lincolnton, 1951
BA: .425, Wes Ferrell, Marion, 1948
At Bats: 490, Lester Bangs, Hendersonville, 1948
Runs: 139, Edwin Yount, Newton-Conover, 1948
Hits: 179, Henry Miller, Shelby, 1951
RBIs: 157, Edward Bass, Shelby, 1951
2Bs: 47, Charles Ballard, Shelby, 1951

INACTIVE LEAGUE RECORDS

3Bs: 20, Junior Dogin, Lincolnton, 1950
HRs: 43, Edwin Yount, Newton-Conover, 1948
TBs: 342, Edwin Yount, Newton-Conover, 1948
SBs: 48, James Sharpe, Newton-Conover, 1949
BBs: 122, Tom Marino, Lenoir, 1950
SOs: 100, Bill McKenney, Rutherford County, 1950
100, Manuel Rojas, Shelby, 1952

Pitching

Games: 46, Eurice "Pete" Treece, Morganton, 1951
CGs: 27, Eurice "Pete" Treece, Morganton, 1951
Wins: 25, Eurice "Pete" Treece, Morganton, 1951
Losses: 16, Efrid Gwaltney, Hickory, 1952
16, Wade Brown, Shelby/Gastonia/Lincolnton, 1950
Pct: .867, 13-2, George Long, Rutherford County, 1951
ERA: 2.12, George Long, Rutherford County, 1951
IP: 292, Eurice "Pete" Treece, Morganton, 1951
ShOs: 7, Joe Sheppard, Shelby, 1952
SOs: 264, Eurice "Pete" Treece, Morganton, 1951
BBs: 158, Maurice Gross, Morganton, 1950

WESTERN TRI-STATE LEAGUE
Class D 1902, 1908, 1912-1914
(Inland Empire League 1902, 1908)

Batting

Games: 119, Earl Sheeley, Walla Walla, 1913
BA: .349, George Pembroke, Pendleton, 1914
At Bats: 477, M.E. Reams, Boise, 1913
Runs: 93, Henry Martini, Walla Walla, 1913
Hits: 136, M.E. Reams, Boise, 1913
2Bs: 35, Henry Martini, Walla Walla, 1913
3Bs: 16, Bob Davis, Walla Walla, 1913
HRs: 16, Henry Martini, Walla Walla, 1913
TBs: 220, Bob Davis, Walla Walla, 1913
Sac: 33, Wallace Childer, Walla Walla, 1913
SBs: 54, Nick Fuller, North Yakima, 1913

Pitching

Games: 40, Carl Mays, Boise, 1912
CGs: 29, Al Bonner, Boise, 1913

29, Berger, Pendleton, 1913
Wins: 22, Carl Mays, Boise, 1912
Losses: 16, Berger, Pendleton, 1913
Pct: .792, 19-5, E.E. "Tiny" Leonard, Walla Walla, 1913
SOs: 206, Clyde Schroedre, Pendleton, 1914
ShOs: 5, E.E. "Tiny" Leonard, Walla Walla, 1913
BBs: 101, Fred Kile, North Yakima, 1913

WISCONSIN STATE LEAGUE
Class D 1940-1942, 1946-1953

Batting

Games: 126, held by many
BA: .396, Bill Deininger, Sheboygan, 1942
At Bats: 506, Joe Barracato, Sheboygan, 1950
Runs: 138, Walt Moryn, Sheboygan, 1948
Hits: 170, Joe Tuminelli, Fond du Lac, 1953
RBIs: 148, Joe Tuminelli, Fond du Lac, 1953
2Bs: 40, Bob Pascal, Oshkosh, 1950
3Bs: 18, Edward Waytula, Appleton, 1947
HRs: 32, Fred Collins, Fond du Lac, 1948
TBs: 300, Ray Shearer, Sheboygan, 1950
Streak: 29, Bill Deininger, Sheboygan, 1942
SBs: 64, Harold Gordon, Fond du Lac, 1953
BBs: 164, Tom Bartos, Sheboygan, 1947
SOs: 138, Allen Mugford, Sheboygan, 1953

Pitching

Games: 56, Robert Zimmerman, Appleton, 1949
CGs: 27, Eugene Josalene, Janesville, 1941
Wins: 24, Connie Grob, Sheboygan, 1952
Losses: 17, James Warmouth, Appleton, 1953
Pct: .944, 17-1, Bill "Red" Rose, Fond du Lac, 1946
ERA: 1.81, Mervin Hensley, La Crosse, 1940
IP: 251, Connie Grob, Sheboygan, 1952
Win Streak: 16, Bill "Red" Rose, Fond du Lac, 1946
ShOs: 5, Dick Grabowski, Sheybogen, 1952
5, Wilber Striker, Green Bay, 1952
SOs: 292, Dick Grabowski, Appleton, 1952
BBs: 177, Lowell Grosskopf, Sheboygan, 1949

WISCONSIN-ILLINOIS LEAGUE
Class D 1905-1909; Class C 1910-1915
(Wisconsin State League/Wisconsin Association
1905-1907)

Batting

Games: 127, Fred Thomas, Green Bay, 1913
127, H.P. Hadley, Madison, 1913
BA: .383, Ward Miller, Wausau, 1908
At Bats: 506, T. Chouinard, Green Bay, 1909
Runs: 104, George Brautigan, Appleton, 1912
Hits: 177, Harry Sylvester, Appleton, 1912
2Bs: 34, Rube Vinson, Madison, 1914
3Bs: 13, Fred Thomas, Green Bay, 1913
HRs: 26, Al "Bull" Durham, Oshkosh, 1913
TBs: 225, Al "Bull" Durham, Oshkosh, 1913
Sac: 54, G.H. Ives, Freeport, 1906
SBs: 81, Harold Irelan, Freeport, 1907
BBs: 79, Al "Bull" Durham, Oshkosh, 1914
SOs: 106, E. Morrison, Appleton, 1914

Pitching

Games: 40, James Jachs, Fond du Lac, 1913
40, Cy Boothby, Rockford, 1913
40, Frank Baille, Wausau, 1913
40, Joe Lotz, Oshkosh, 1914
CGs: 35, James Jachs, Fond du Lac, 1913
35, Bruce Noel, Fond du Lac, 1913
Wins: 32, Mike Murphy, Appleton, 1910
Losses: 22, George Palmer, Madison, 1910
22, Frank Carroll, Wausau, 1913
Pct: .842, 32-6, Mike Murphy, Appleton, 1910
IP: 325, Jack Warhop, Freeport, 1907
ShOs: 13, Jack Warhop, Freeport, 1907
SOs: 339, Jack Warhop, Freeport, 1907
BBs: 116, Joe Lotz, Oshkosh, 1914

ALL-TIME LEADERS, INDIVIDUAL, SINGLE SEASON

Batting Average (200 at bats)

Player	Avg	Team	League	Year
Gary Redus	.462	Billings	Pioneer	1978
Bill Krieg	.452	Rockford	Western Association	1896
Ike Boone	.448	Mission	Pacific Coast	1930
Frank Saucier	.446	Wichita Falls	Big State	1949
Willie Aikens	.443	Puebla/Tidewater	Mexican/International	1986
Angel Aragon	.443	Newark/Long Branch	Atlantic	1914
Billy O'Connell	.442	Richmond	Blue Grass	1912
Robert Schmidt	.441	Duluth	Northern	1939
Murray Franklin	.439	Beckley	Mountain State	1938
Hediberto Vargas	.438	Veracruz/Guanajuato	Mexican/Mexican Center	1966
Jimmie Collins	.438	Chihuahua	Mexican	1979
Francis Boniar	.436	Reno	California	1957
Francis Boniar	.435	Hornell	PONY	1956
Bill Diester	.434	Salina/Tulsa	Southwestern/Western	1926
Ollie Tucker	.434	Cedartown	Georgia State	1921
Carl East	.433	Anniston	Georgia-Alabama	1926
T.P. Osborne	.432	Mt. Pleasant	East Texas	1924
Russ Snyder	.432	McAlester	Sooner State	1953
Neal Cobb	.432	Crestview	Alabama-Florida	1954
Kelly	.431	Poughkeepsie	Atlantic	1914
Tony Antista	.430	Bisbee	Arizona State	1930
Len Rodriguez	.430	Cananea	Arizona-Texas	1954

Runs

Player	Runs	Team	League	Year
Tony Lazzeri	202	Salt Lake City	Pacific Coast	1925
Gus Suhr	196	San Francisco	Pacific Coast	1929
Leo Najo	195	Okmulgee	Western Association	1925
Ike Boone	195	Mission	Pacific Coast	1929
Ken Toothman	193	Phoenix	Arizona-Texas	1954
Frank Demaree	190	Los Angeles	Pacific Coast	1934
Buck Frierson	188	Sherman-Denison	Big State	1947
Joe Bauman	188	Roswell	Longhorn	1954
Stormy Davis	187	Okmulgee	Western Association	1924
Orlando Moreno	186	Big Spring	Longhorn	1947
Bob Crues	185	Amarillo	West Texas-New Mexico	1947

Hits

Player	Hits	Team	League	Year
Paul Strand	325	Salt Lake City	Pacific Coast	1923
Ike Boone	323	Mission	Pacific Coast	1929
Oscar "Ox" Eckhardt	315	Mission	Pacific Coast	1933
Smead Jolley	314	San Francisco	Pacific Coast	1929
Jay Kirke, Sr.	282	Louisville	American Association	1921

Doubles

Player	2Bs	Team	League	Year
Lyman Lamb	100	Tulsa	Western	1924
Paul Waner	75	San Francisco	Pacific Coast	1925
Roy Leslie	73	Salt Lake City	Pacific Coast	1924
Leslie Sheehan	72	Salt Lake City	Pacific Coast	1923
Robert Holland	72	Seattle	Pacific Coast	1930
Ervin Beck	71	Toledo	Interstate	1900
Lyman Lamb	71	Tulsa	Western	1923
Roy Eldred	71	Seattle	Pacific Coast	1923
Roy Eldred	71	Seattle	Pacific Coast	1924
Jack Lelivelt	70	Omaha	Western	1921
Rhino Williams	70	Dallas	Texas	1925
Buzz Arlett	70	Oakland	Pacific Coast	1929

Triples

Player	3Bs	Team	League	Year
Jack Cross	32	London	Michigan-Ontario	1925
Walter Shaner	30	Lincoln	Western	1925
Dusty Cooke	30	Asheville	South Atlantic	1928
Eddie Moore	30	Ft. Worth	Texas	1929
Pete Rose	30	Tampa	Florida State	1961
Guy Tutweiler	29	Providence	International	1914
Jo Jo White	29	Ft. Smith	Western Assoc.	1929
Burl Horton	29	El Paso	Arizona-Texas	1941

Home Runs

Player	HRs	Team	League	Year
Joe Bauman	72	Roswell	Longhorn	1954
Joe Hauser	69	Minneapolis	American Association	1933
Bob Crues	69	Amarillo	West Texas-New Mexico	1948
Dick Stuart	66	Lincoln	Western	1956
Bob Lennon	64	Nashville	Southern Association	1954
Joe Hauser	63	Baltimore	International	1930
Moose Clabaugh	62	Tyler	East Texas	1926
Ken Guettler	62	Shreveport	Texas	1956
Tony Lazzeri	60	Salt Lake City	Pacific Coast	1925
Forrest "Frosty" Kennedy	60	Plainview	Southwestern	1956

Runs Batted In

Player	RBIs	Team	League	Year
Bob Crues	254	Amarillo	West Texas-New Mexico	1948
Joe Bauman	224	Roswell	Longhorn	1954
Tony Lazzeri	222	Salt Lake City	Pacific Coast	1925
Ike Boone	218	Mission	Pacific Coast	1929
Buck Frierson	197	Sherman-Denison	Big State	1947
Glenn Burns	197	Lamesa	West Texas-New Mexico	1951
Clarence Kraft	196	Ft. Worth	Texas	1924
D.C. "Pud" Miller	196	Wichita Falls	Big State	1947
Virg Richardson	196	Lubbock	West Texas-New Mexico	1948
Earl Smith	195	Phoenix	Arizona-Texas	1954

Stolen Bases

Player	SBs	Team	League	Year
Vince Coleman	145	Macon	South Atlantic	1983
Donell Nixon	144	Bakersfield	California	1983
James Johnston	124	San Francisco	Pacific Coast	1913
Jeff Stone	123	Spartanburg	South Atlantic	1981
Alan Wiggins	120	Lodi	California	1980
Allan Lewis	116	Leesburg	Florida State	1966
Ovid Nicholson	111	Frankfort	Blue Grass	1912
Maynard DeWitt	110	Zanesville	Ohio State	1946
Otis Nixon	108	Columbus (49)	American Association	1982
		Nashville (59)	Southern Association	
Lyle Judy	107	Springfield	Western Association	1935

Strikeouts

Player	SOs	Team	League	Year
Grover Lowdermilk	465	Decatur	Three I	1907
		Mattoon	Eastern Illinois	
Bill Kennedy	456	Rocky Mount	Coastal Plain	1946
Virgil Trucks	418	Andalusia	Alabama-Florida	1938
Harry Vickers	409	Seattle	Pacific Coast	1906
Yancey Ayers	390	Richmond	Virginia	1913
Eddie Albrecht	389	Pine Bluff	Cotton States	1949
Vean Gregg	376	Portland	Pacific Coast	1910
Bob Schultz	361	Fulton	Kitty	1946
Larry Jackson	351	Fresno	California	1952
Bob Upton	346	Jacksonville	Gulf Coast	1950
Mike Conovan	345	Jackson	Kitty	1952

Wins (since 1902)

Player	Wins	Team	League	Year
Doc Newton	39	Los Angeles	Pacific Coast	1904
Harry Vickers	39	Seattle	Pacific Coast	1906
George Boehler	38	Tulsa	Western	1922
Oscar Jones	37	Los Angeles	California	1902
Glenn Liebhardt	35	Memphis	Southern Association	1906
Bugs Raymond	35	Charleston	South Atlantic	1907
Jackie May	35	Vernon	Pacific Coast	1922
Bill Thomas	35	Houma	Evangeline	1946

ALL-TIME LEADERS, INDIVIDUAL CAREER

BATTING

Batting Average

Player	
Ike Boone	.370
Oscar "Ox" Eckhardt	.367
Smead Jolley	.366
Don Stokes	.365
Carl East	.364
Bill Bagwell	.360
Claudio Solano	.360
Bill George	.358
Dan Boone	.356
Jack Bentley	.354
Al Pinkston	.352
Tom Pyle	.354
Dean Stafford	.351
Bill Wright	.351
Pete Hughes	.350

Runs

Player	
Spencer Harris	2287
George Hogriever	2046
Eddie Hock	2007
Arnold "Jigger" Statz	1996
George Whiteman	1885
Ernest "Kid" Mohler	1812
Bernard "Frenchy" Uhalt	1786
Bunny Brief	1776
Ray French	1769
Charles "Buster" Chatham	1739

Hits

Player	
Spencer Harris	3617
Harry Strohm	3486
Eddie Hock	3474
George Whiteman	3388
Fred "Snake" Henry	3384
Arnold "Jigger" Statz	3356
Ray French	3254
Jesus Sommers	3247
Chet Chadbourne	3216
Hugh Luby	3169
Ray O'Brien	3152
Jay Kirke, Sr.	3165
Jim Poole	3150
John Gill	3141
Bernard "Frenchy" Uhalt	3120
Vinicio Garcia	3116
Charles "Buster" Chatham	3067

Larry Barton	3045
Smead Jolley	3037
Mel Simons	3031

Doubles

Player	
Spencer Harris	743
Fred "Snake" Henry	675
George Whiteman	673
Johnny Gill	667
Jim Poole	662
Harry Strohm	658
Ray O'Brien	642
Larry Barton	634
Smead Jolley	612
Lyman Lamb	608

Triples

Player	
Joe Riggert	228
Fred "Snake" Henry	200
George Whiteman	196
Fred Nicholson	195
Leon Riley	195
Jim Murray	191
Ray O'Brien	186
Stanley Keyes	185
Ray Powell	183
Charles "Buster" Chatham	182

Home Runs

Player	
Hector Espino	484
Andres Mora	444
Buzz Arlett	432
Nick Cullop	420
Merv Connors	400
Joe Hauser	399
Bobby Prescott	398
Jack Pierce	395
Jack Graham	384
Ted Gullic	370
Gordon Nell	365
Leo "Muscle" Shoals	362

Runs Batted In

Player	
Nick Cullop	1857
Buzz Arlett	1786
Jim Poole	1785

Spencer Harris	1769
Larry Barton	1751
Johnny Gill	1743
George Ferrell	1716
Hector Espino	1678
Jesus Sommers	1662
Smead Jolley	1631
Merv Connors	1629

Stolen Bases

Player	
George Hogriever	948
Ernest "Kid" Mohler	776
Michael Cole	702
Charles "Count" Campau	682
Alex Reilley	676
Bill Lane	670
John Duffy	626
Merlin Kopp	604
Dave Mann	601
Carlos Bernier	594
Tony Thebo	593

Batting Titles

Player	
Smead Jolley	6
Ike Boone	5
Moose Clabaugh	5
Oscar "Ox" Eckhardt	5
Frank Huelsman	5
Sheldon Lejeune	5
Hector Espino	5
Al Pinkston	5

200-Hit Seasons

Player	
Arnold "Jigger" Statz	11
Buzz Arlett	7
Bunny Brief	7
Chet Chadbourne	7
Smead Jolley	7
Don Stokes	7
Edward Mulligan	6

100-RBI Seasons

Player	
Buzz Arlett	12
Merv Connors	11
Smead Jolley	9
Pete Hughes	9

Dean Stafford	9
Bunny Brief	8
Gordon Nell	8
Ray Perry	8
Ollie Tucker	8
Ab Wright	8
Isaac Palmer	8

Home Run Titles

Player	
Ken Guettler	8
Bunny Brief	7
Ray Perry	7
Leo "Muscle" Shoals	7
Norman Small	7
Merv Connors	6
Ted Norbert	6

20-Home Run Seasons

Player	
Merv Connors	12
Nick Cullop	12
Hector Espino	12
Jack Graham	12
Buzz Arlett	11
Joe Hauser	10

30-Home Run Seasons

Player	
Buzz Arlett	8
Joe Bauman	6
Jack Graham	6
Joe Hauser	6
Gordon Nell	6
Norman Small	6

40-Home Run Seasons

Player	
Joe Bauman	5
Gordon Nell	5

50-Home Run Seasons

Player	
Joe Bauman	3
Joe Hauser	2
Bob Crues	2
D.C. "Pud" Miller	2
Frank Gravino	2
Steve Bilko	2

PITCHING

Games

Player	
Bill Thomas	1015
Jack Brillheart	956
George Payne	900
Ken Penner	869
Alex McColl	865
Earl Caldwell	859
Walter Tauscher	856
Bobby Tiefenauer	849
Joe Martina	833
Ramon Arano	817
Karl Black	814

Wins

Player	Won-Lost
Bill Thomas	383-346
Joe Martina	349-277
George Payne	348-262
Tony Freitas	342-238
Ramon Arano	335-266
Alex McColl	332-263
Ken Penner	330-284
Lefty George	327-285
Dick "Kewpie" Barrett	325-257
Spider Baum	325-280
Earl Caldwell	321-277
Willard Mains	318-179
Paul Wachtel	317-221

Frank Shellenback	315-192
Clyde Barfoot	314-243
Jack Brillheart	309-266
Sam Gibson	307-200
Bill Hughes	302-248
Harry Smythe	301-221
Harry Krause	300-249

Strikeouts

Player	
George Brunet	3175
Joe Martina	2770
Jackie Reid	2694
Clarence "Hooks" Iott	2561
Dick "Kewpie" Barrett	2512
Jodie Phipps	2447
Woody Rich	2405
Ramon Arano	2380
Bill Bailey	2375
Aurelio Monteagudo	2361
Paul Fittery	2359

20-Win Seasons

Player	
Spider Baum	9
Tony Freitas	9
Dick "Kewpie" Barrett	8
Joe Pate	7
Joe Martina	7
Charles "Sea Lion" Hall	7

George Boehler	7
Herschel Prough	7
Willard Mains	7
Doc Crandall	6

Sam Gibson	6
John Ogden	6
Paul Wachtel	6
James Middleton	6

LIFETIME PITCHING PERCENTAGE LEADERS

Pitcher	Dates	Won Lost	Pct.
John Ogden	1918-1934	213-103	.674
Joe Pate	1911-1932	257-134	.657
Willard Mains	1887-1906	318-179	.640
Chet Covington	1939-1953	220-126	.636
Bobby Tiefenauer	1948-1969	162-96	.628
Stony McGlynn	1902-1915	182-109	.625
Frank Shellenback	1917-1938	315-192	.621
Rube Parnham	1914-1927	167-102	.621
Rube Vickers	1902-1914	217-134	.618
Jodie Phipps	1939-1957	275-172	.615
Jimmy Walkup	1915-1934	259-164	.612
Tom Sheehan	1913-1934	260-166	.610
Sam Gibson	1923-1949	307-200	.606
Doc Crandall	1906-1929	249-163	.604
Jimmy Zinn	1915-1939	295-198	.598
Cliff Markle	1913-1928	211-144	.594

AWARDS

THE SPORTING NEWS AWARD WINNERS

MINOR LEAGUE PLAYER OF THE YEAR

1936	John Vander Meer, Durham, Piedmont League
1937	Charlie Keller, Newark, International League
1938	Fred Hutchinson, Seattle, Pacific Coast League
1939	Lou Novikoff, Tulsa, Pacific Coast League
1940	Phil Rizzuto, Kansas City, American Association
1941	John Lindell, Newark, International League
1942	Dick Barrett, Seattle, Pacific Coast League
1943	Chet Covington, Scranton, Eastern League
1944	Rip Collins, Albany, Eastern League
1945	Gil Coan, Chattanooga, Southern Association
1946	Sibby Sisti, Indianapolis, American Association
1947	Hank Sauer, Syracuse, International League
1948	Gene Woodling, San Francisco, Pacific Coast League
1949	Orie Arntzen, Albany, Eastern League
1950	Frank Saucier, San Antonio, Texas League
1951	Gene Conley, Hartford, Eastern League
1952	Bill Skowron, Kansas City, American Association
1953	Gene Conley, Toledo, American Association
1954	Herb Score, Indianapolis, American Association
1955	John Murff, Dallas, Texas League
1956	Steve Bilko, Los Angeles, Pacific Coast League
1957	Norm Siebern, Denver, American Association
1958	Jim O'Toole, Nashville, Southern Association
1959	Frank Howard, Victoria/Spokane, Pacific Coast League
1960	Willie Davis, Spokane, Pacific Coast League
1961	Howie Koplitz, Birmingham, Southern Association
1962	Bob Bailey, Columbus, International League
1963	Don Buford, Indianapolis, International League
1964	Mel Stottlemyre, Richmond, International League
1965	Joe Foy, Toronto, International League
1966	Mike Epstein, Rochester, International League
1967	Johnny Bench, Buffalo, International League
1968	Merv Rettenmund, Rochester, International League
1969	Danny Walton, Oklahoma City, American Association
1970	Don Baylor, Rochester, International League
1971	Bobby Grich, Rochester, International League
1972	Tom Paciorek, Albuquerque, Pacific Coast League
1973	Steve Ontiveros, Phoenix, Pacific Coast League
1974	Jim Rice, Pawtucket, International League
1975	Hector Cruz, Tulsa, American Association
1976	Pat Putnam, Asheville, West Carolinas League
1977	Ken Landreaux, Salt Lake City, Pacific Coast League/El Paso, Texas League
1978	Champ Summers, Indianapolis, American Association
1979	Mark Bomback, Vancouver, Pacific Coast League
1980	Tim Raines, Denver, American Association
1981	Mike Marshall, Albuquerque, Pacific Coast League
1982	Ron Kittle, Edmonton, Pacific Coast League
1983	Kevin McReynolds, Las Vegas, Pacific Coast League
1984	Alan Knicely, Wichita, American Association
1985	Jose Canseco, Huntington, Southern League/Tacoma, Pacific Coast League
1986	Tim Pyznarski, Las Vegas, Pacific Coast League
1987	Randy Milligan, Tidewater, International League
1988	Sandy Alomar, Jr., Las Vegas, Pacific Coast League
	Gary Sheffield, Denver, American Association
1989	Sandy Alomar, Jr., Las Vegas, Pacific Coast League
1990	Jose Offerman, Albuquerque, Pacific Coast League
1991	Pedro Martinez, Albuquerque, Pacific Coast League
1992	Tim Salmon, Edmonton, Pacific Coast League
1993	Cliff Floyd, Harrisburg, Eastern League
1994	Derek Jeter, Columbus, International League
1995	Karim Garcia, Albany, Pacific Coast League
1996	Vladimir Guerrero, Harrisburg, Eastern League

MINOR LEAGUE MANAGER OF THE YEAR

1936	Al Sothoron, Milwaukee, American Association
1937	Jake Flowers, Salisbury, Eastern Shore League
1938	Paul Richards, Atlanta, Southern Association
1939	Bill Meyer, Kansas City, American Association
1940	Larry Gilbert, Nashville, Southern Association
1941	Burt Shotton, Columbus, American Association
1942	Eddie Dyer, Columbus, American Association
1943	Nick Cullop, Columbus, American Association
1944	Al Thomas, Baltimore, International League
1945	Lefty O'Doul, San Francisco, Pacific Coast League
1946	Clay Hoper, Montreal, International League
1947	Nick Cullop, Milwaukee, American Association
1948	Casey Stengel, Oakland, Pacific Coast League
1949	Fred Haney, Hollywood, Pacific Coast League
1950	Rollie Hemsley, Columbus, American Association
1951	Charlie Grimm, Milwaukee, American Association
1952	Luke Appling, Memphis, Southern Association
1953	Bobby Bragan, Hollywood, Pacific Coast League
1954	Kerby Farrell, Indianapolis, American Association
1955	Bill Rigney, Minneapolis, American Association
1956	Kerby Farrell, Indianapolis, American Association
1957	Ben Geraghty, Wichita, American Association
1958	Cal Ermer, Birmingham, Southern Association
1959	Pete Reiser, Victoria, Texas League
1960	Mel McGaha, Toronto, International League
1961	Kerby Farrell, Buffalo, International League
1962	Ben Geraghty, Jacksonville, International League
1963	Rollie Hemsley, Indianapolis, International League
1964	Harry Walker, Jacksonville, International League
1965	Grady Hatton, Oklahoma City, Pacific Coast League
1966	Bob Lemon, Seattle, Pacific Coast League
1967	Bob Skinner, San Diego, Pacific Coast League
1968	Jack Tighe, Toledo, International League
1969	Clyde McCullough, Tidewater, International League
1970	Tom Lasorda, Spokane, Pacific Coast League
1971	Del Rice, Salt Lake City, Pacific Coast League
1972	Hank Bauer, Tidewater, International League
1973	Joe Morgan, Charleston, International League
1974	Joe Altobelli, Rochester, International League
1975	Joe Frazier, Tidewater, International League
1976	Vern Rapp, Denver, American Association
1977	Tommy Thompson, Arkansas, Texas League
1978	Les Moss, Evansville, American Association
1979	Vern Benson, syracuse, International League
1980	Hal Lanier, Springfield, American Association
1981	Del Crandall, Albuquerque, Pacific Coast League
1982	George Scherger, Indianapolis, American Association
1983	Bill Dancy, Reading, Eastern League
1984	Bob Rodgers, Indianapolis, American Association
1985	Jim Fregosi, Louisville, American Association
1986	Joe Sparks, Indianapolis, American Association
1987	Terry Collins, Albuquerque, Pacific Coast League
1988	Joe Sparks, Indianapolis, American Association
1989	Bob Bailor, Syracuse, International League
1990	Sal Rende, Omaha, American Association
1991	Chris Chambliss, Greenville, Southern League
1992	Grady Little, Greenville, Southern League
1993	Jim Tracy, Harrisburg, Eastern League
1994	Mike Jirschele, Wilmington, Carolinas League
1995	Pete Mackanin, Ottawa, International League
1996	John Mizerock, Wilmington, Carolina League

AWARDS

THE SPORTING NEWS AWARD WINNERS

MINOR LEAGUE EXECUTIVE OF THE YEAR
(Restricted to Class AAA 1963-1990)

1936 Earl Mann, Atlanta, Southern League
1937 Robert LaMotte, Savannah, South Atlantic League
1938 Louis McKenna, St. Paul, American Association
1939 Bruce Dudley, Louisville, American Association
1940 Roy Hamey, Kansas City, American Association
1941 Emil Sick, Seattle, Pacific Coast League
1942 Bill Veeck, Milwaukee, American Association
1943 Clarence Rowland, Los Angeles, Pacific Coast League
1944 William Mulligan, Seattle, Pacific Coast League
1945 Bruce Dudley, Louisville, American Association
1946 Earl Mann, Atlanta, Southern League
1947 William Purnhage, Waterloo, Three-I League
1948 Edward Glennon, Birmingham, Southern League
1949 Ted Sullivan, Indianapolis, American Association
1950 Clarence "Brick" Laws, Oakland, Pacific Coast League
1951 Robert Howsam, Denver, Western League
1952 Jack Cooke, Toronto, International League
1953 Richard Burnett, Dallas, Texas League
1954 Edward Stumpf, Indianapolis, American Association
1955 Dewey Soriano, Seattle, Pacific Coast League
1956 Robert Howsam, Denver, American Association
1957 John Stiglmeier, Buffalo, International League
1958 Edward Glennon, Birmingham, Southern League
1959 Edward Leishman, Salt Lake City, Pacific Coast League
1960 Ray Winder, Little Rock, Southern League
1961 Elten Schiller, Omaha, American Association
1962 George Sisler Jr., Rochester, International League
1963 Lewis Matlin, Hawaii, Pacific Coast League
1964 Edward Leishman, San Diego, Pacific Coast League
1965 Harold Cooper, Columbus, International League
1966 John Quinn Jr., Hawaii, Pacific Coast League
1967 Hillman Lyons, Richmond, International League
1968 Gabe Paul Jr., Tulsa, Pacific Coast League
1969 Bill Gardner, Louisville, International League
1970 Dick King, Wichita, American Association
1971 Carl Steinfeldt Jr., Rochester, International League
1972 Don Labbruzzo, Evansville, American Association
1973 Merle Miller, Tucson, Pacific Coast League
1974 John Carbray, Sacramento, Pacific Coast League
1975 Stan Naccarato, Tacoma, Pacific Coast League
1976 Art Teece, Salt Lake City, Pacific Coast League
1977 George Sisler Jr., Columbus, International League
1978 Willie Sanchez, Albuquerque, Pacific Coast League
1979 George Sisler Jr., Columbus, International League
1980 Jim Burris, Denver, American Association
1981 Pat McKernan, Albuquerque, Pacific Coast League
1982 A. Ray Smith, Louisville, American Association
1983 A. Ray Smith, Louisville, American Association
1984 Mike Tamburro, Pawtucket, International League
1985 Patty Cox Hampton, Oklahoma City, American Association
1986 Bob Goughan, Rochester, International League
1987 Stu Kehoe, Vancouver, Pacific Coast League
1988 Bob Rich, Buffalo, American Association
1989 Larry Schmittou, Nashville, American Association
1990 Greg Corns, Phoenix, Pacific Coast League
1991 Tom Maloney, Denver, American Association
1992 Lou Schwechheimer, Pawtucket, International League
1993 Todd Vander Woude, Harrisburg, Eastern League
1994 Scott Lane, West Michigan, Midwest League
1995 Jack and Mary Cain, Portland, Northwest League
1996 Wayne Hodes, Trenton, Eastern League

MINOR LEAGUE EXECUTIVE OF THE YEAR
(Lower Classifications)

1950 H. Cooper, Hutchinson, Western Association
1951 O. W. "Bill" Hayes, Temple, Big State League
1952 Hillman Lyons, Danville, Mississippi-Ohio Valley League
1953 Carl Roth, Peoria, Three-I League
1954 James Meagham, Cedar Rapids, Three-I League
1955 John Petrakis, Dubuque, Mississippi-Ohio Valley League
1956 Marvin Milkes, Fresno, California League

1957 Richard Wagner, Lincoln, Western League
1958 Gerald Waring, Macon, South Atlantic League
1959 Clay Dennis, Des Moines, Three-I League
1960 Hub Kittle, Yakima, Northwest League
1961 David Steele, Fresno, California League
1962 John Quinn Jr., San Jose, California League

MINOR LEAGUE EXECUTIVE OF THE YEAR
(Class AA)

1963 Hugh Finnerty, Tulsa, Texas League
1964 Glynn West, Birmingham, Southern League
1965 Dick Butler, Dallas-Ft. Worth, Texas League
1966 Tom Fleming, Evansville, Southern League
1967 Robert Quinn, Reading, Eastern League
1968 Phil Howser, Charlotte, Southern League
1969 Charlie Blaney, Albuquerque, Texas League
1970 Carl Sawatski, Arkansas, Texas League
1971 Miles Wolff, Savannah, Dixie Association
1972 John Begzos, San Antonio, Texas League
1973 Dick Kravitz, Jacksonville, Southern League
1974 Jim Paul, El Paso, Texas League
1975 Jim Paul, El Paso, Texas League
1976 Woodrow Reid, Chattanooga, Southern League
1977 Jim Paul, El Paso, Texas League
1978 Larry Schmittou, Nashville, Southern League
1979 Bill Rigney Jr., Midland, Texas League
1980 Frances Crockett, Charlotte, Southern League
1981 Allie Prescott, Memphis, Southern League
1982 Art Clarkson, Birmingham, Southern League
1983 Edward Kenney, New Britain, Eastern League
1984 Bruce Baldwin, Greenville, Southern League
1985 Ben Bernard, Albany-Colonie, Eastern League
1986 Bill Davidson, Midland, Texas League
1987 Joe Preseren, Tulsa, Texas League
1988 Bill Valentine, Arkansas, Texas League
1989 Chuck Domino, Reading, Eastern League
1990 Joe Preseren, Tulsa, Texas League

MINOR LEAGUE EXECUTIVE OF THE YEAR
(Class A)

1963 Ben Jewell, Magic Valley, Pioneer League
1964 James Bayens, Rock Hill, Western Carolinas League
1965 Ken Blackman, Quad Cities, Midwest League
1966 Cappy Harada, Lodi, California League
1967 Pat Williams, Spartanburg, Western Carolinas League
1968 Merle Miller, Burlington, Midwest League
1969 Bill Gorman, Visalia, California League
1970 Bob Williams, Bakersfield, California League
1971 Ed Holtz, Appleton, Midwest League
1972 Bob Piccinini, Modesto, California League
1973 Fritz Colschen, Clinton, Midwest League
1974 Bing Russell, Portland, Northwest League
1975 Cordy Jensen, Eugene, Northwest League
1976 Don Buchheister, Cedar Rapids, Midwest League
1977 Harry Pells, Quad City, Midwest League
1978 Dave Hersh, Appleton, Midwest League
1979 Tom Romenesko, Greensboro, Western Carolinas League
1980 Tom Romenesko, Greensboro, South Atlantic League
1981 Dan Overstreet, Hagerstown, Carolina League
1982 Bob Carruesco, Stockton, California League
1983 Terry Reynolds, Vero Beach, Florida State League
1984 Dave Tarrolly, Beloit, Midwest League
1985 Pete Vonachen, Peoria, Midwest League
1986 Rob Dlugozima, Durham, Carolina League
1987 Skip Weisman, Greensboro, South Atlantic League
1988 Dennis Bastien, Charleston (WV), South Atlantic League
1989 John Baxter, South Bend, Midwest League
1990 Dan Chapman, Stockton, California League

MINOR LEAGUE EXECUTIVE OF THE YEAR
(Class A Short Season)

1988 Bob Beban, Eugene, Northwest League
1989 Bill Pereira, Boise, Northwest League
1990 Dave Baggott, Salt Lake City, Pioneer League

AWARDS

NATIONAL ASSOCIATION AWARD WINNERS

RAWLINGS AWARD
(Outstanding Female Executive)

1976 Alice Neighbors, Tulsa (A.A.)
1977 Mary Anne Whitacre, Hawaii (PCL)
1978 Patty Cox, Oklahoma City (A.A.)
1979 Doris Krucker, (MWL)
1980 Frances Crockett, Charlotte (SOU)
1982 Linda Pereira, San Jose (CAL)
1983 Karen Paul, El Paso (TEX)
1984 Mildred Boyenga, Waterloo (MID)
1985 Frances Crockett, Charlotte (SOU)
1987 Leslie Leary, Auburn (NYP)
1988 Mindy Rich, Buffalo (A.A.)
1989 Pat Hamilton, Toledo (INT)
1990 Leanne Pagliai, High Desert (CAL)
1991 Marta Hiczewski, Buffalo (A.A.)
1992 Tammy Felker-White, Portland (PCL)
1993 Shereen Samonds, Orlando (SOU)
1994 Naomi Silver, Rochester (INT)
1995 Mary Cain, Portland (NWL)
1996 Audrey Zielinski, Detroit (AL)

WARREN GILES AWARD
(Outstanding League President)

1984 Charles Eshbach, Eastern League
1985 Bill Walters, Midwest League
1986 Joe Ryan, American Association
1987 Carl Sawatski, Texas League
1988 Harold Cooper, International League
1989 Jimmy Bragan, Southern League
1990 Joe Gagliardi, California League
1991 Chuck Murphy, Florida State League
1992 Bill Cutler, Pacific Coast League
1993 John Moss, South Atlantic League
1994 Randy Mobley, International League
1995 John Hopkins, Carolina League
1996 Freddy Jana, Dominican Summer League

JOHN H. JOHNSON PRESIDENT'S TROPHY
(Outstanding Club Operations)

1974 Edward Barnowski, Rochester
1975 Stan Naccarato, Tacoma
1976 Angel Vasquez, Mexico City
1977 Soup Carothers, Fresno
1978 Ray Johnston, Iowa
1979 Jim Burris, Denver
1980 Roger Crow, Quad-City
1981 Logan Hurlbert, Great Falls
1982 Stan Naccarato, Tacoma
1983 A. Ray Smith, Louisville
1984 Pat McKernan Albuquerque
1985 Larry Koentopp, Las Vegas
1986 Jim Paul, El Paso
1987 Tex Simone, Syracuse
1988 Max Schumacher, Indianapolis
1989 Miles Wolff, Durham
1990 Ben Mondor, Pawtucket
1991 Pat McKernan Albuquerque
1992 Mike Billoni, Buffalo
1993 Dave Rosenfield, Norfolk
1994 Bob Wilson, Billings
1995 Ken Schnacke, Columbus
1996 Joe Buzas, Salt Lake City

LARRY MacPHAIL TROPHY
(Outstanding Club Promotion)

1966 Spartanburg, Western Carolinas
1967 Rochester, International
1968 Cocoa, Florida State
1969 Hawaii, Pacific Coast
1970 Wichita, American Association/Hawaii, Pacific Coast (Tie)
1971 Oklahoma City, American Association
1972 San Antonio, Texas
1973 Tucson, Pacific Coast
1974 West Palm Beach, Florida State

1975 Tacoma, Pacific Coast
1976 El Paso, Texas/Cedar Rapids, Midwest (Tie)
1977 Columbus, OH, International
1978 Nashville, Southern
1979 Columbus, OH, International
1980 Nashville, Southern
1981 Nashville, Southern
1982 El Paso, Texas
1983 Arkansas, Texas
1984 Columbus, OH, International/Billings, Pioneer (Tie)
1985 Richmond, International
1986 Iowa, American Association
1987 Albuquerque, Pacific Coast
1988 Birmingham, Southern
1989 Buffalo, American Association
1990 Richmond, International
1991 Salt Lake City, Pioneer
1992 Ft Meyers, Florida State
1993 El Paso, Texas
1994 Reading, Eastern
1995 Kane County, Midwest
1996 Wilmington, Carolina

THE "KING OF BASEBALL" AWARD
(Presented at Winter Meetings site listed after name)

1951 Clarence "Pants" Rowland, Columbus, OH
1952 J. Alvin Gardner, Phoenix, AZ
1953 Frank Shaughnessy, Atlanta, GA
1954 Shelby Pease, Houston, TX
1955 Herman White, Columbus, OH
1956 Tommy Richardson, Jacksonville, FL
1957 Charles Hurth, Colorado Springs, CO
1958 (not awarded), Washington, D.C.
1959 Bonneau Peters, St. Petersburg, FL
1960 Joe Engel, Louisville, KY
1961 Rosy Ryan, Tampa, FL
1962 Phil Howser, Rochester, NY
1963 Donnie Bush, San Diego, CA
1964 Eddie Mulligan, Houston, TX
1965 Ray Winder, Ft. Lauderdale, FL
1966 Eddie Leishmann, Columbus, OH
1967 Alejo Peralta, Mexico City, MEX
1968 Dewey Soriano, San Francisco, CA
1969 Chauncy DeVault, Ft. Lauderdale, FL
1970 George MacDonald, Sr., Los Angeles, CA
1971 Phil Piton, Phoenix, AZ
1972 Vince McNamara, Honolulu, HI
1973 Ray Johnston, Houston, TX
1974 Fred Haney, New Orleans, LA
1975 Joe Buzas, Hollywood, FL
1976 Don Avery, Los Angeles, CA
1977 Bill Weiss, Honolulu, HI
1978 Zinn Beck, Orlando, FL
1979 Harry Simmons, Toronto, CAN
1980 Billy Hitchcock, Dallas, TX
1981 Jack Schwarz, Hollywood, FL
1982 Sy Berger, Honolulu, HI
1983 Oscar Roettger, Nashville, TN
1984 Donald Davidson, Houston, TX
1985 Stan Wasiak, San Diego, CA
1986 Leftey Gomez, Hollywood, FL
1987 Bill Schweppe, Dallas, TX
1988 Max Patkin, Atlanta, GA
1989 George Sisler, Jr., Nashville, TN
1990 John Moss, Los Angeles, CA
1991 George Pfister, Miami Beach, FL
1992 John Lipon, Louisville, KY
1993 George Kissell, Atlanta, GA
1994 Jimmy Bragan, Dallas, TX
1995 Gene DaCosse, Los Angeles, CA
1996 Sheldon "Chief" Bender, Boston, MA

AWARDS

BASEBALL AMERICA AWARD WINNERS

MINOR LEAGUE PLAYER OF THE YEAR

1981	Mike Marshall, Albuquerque
1982	Ron Kittle, Edmonton
1983	Dwight Gooden, Lynchburg
1984	Mike Bielecki, Hawaii
1985	Jose Canseco, Huntsville/Tacoma
1986	Gregg Jefferies, Columbia/Lynchburg
1987	Gregg Jefferies, Jackson/Tidewater
1988	Tom Gordon, Appleton/Memphis/Omaha
1989	Sandy Alomar, Jr., Las Vegas
1990	Frank Thomas, Birmingham
1991	Derek Bell, Syracuse
1992	Tim Salmon, Edmonton
1993	Manny Ramirez, Canton, Charlotte
1994	Derek Jeter, Tampa, Albany, Columbus
1995	Andruw Jones, Macon
1996	Andruw Jones, Durham, Greenville, Richmond

MINOR LEAGUE MANAGER OF THE YEAR

1981	Ed Nottle, Tacoma
1982	Eddie Haas, Richmond
1983	Bill Dancy, Reading
1984	Sam Perlozzo, Jackson
1985	Jim Lefebvre, Phoenix
1986	Brad Fischer, Huntsville
1987	Dave Trembley, Harrisburg
1988	Joe Sparks, Indianapolis
1989	Buck Showalter, Albany
1990	Kevin Kennedy, Albuquerque
1991	Butch Hobson, Pawtucket
1992	Grady Little, Greenville
1993	Terry Francona, Birmingham
1994	Tim Ireland, El Paso
1995	Marc Bombard, Indianapolis
1996	Carlos Tosca, Portland

ORGANIZATION OF THE YEAR

1982	Oakland A's
1983	New York Mets
1984	New York Mets
1985	Milwaukee Brewers
1986	Milwaukee Brewers
1987	Milwaukee Brewers
1988	Montreal Expos
1989	Texas Rangers
1990	Montreal Expos
1991	Atlanta Braves
1992	Cleveland Indians
1993	Toronto Blue Jays
1994	Kansas City Royals
1995	New York Mets
1996	Atlanta Braves

BOB FREITAS AWARD
(Outstanding Minor League Organization)

Triple A

1989	Columbus, International League
1990	Pawtucket, International League
1991	Buffalo, American Association
1992	Iowa, American Association
1993	Richmond, International League
1994	Norfolk, International League
1995	Albuquerque, Pacific Coast League
1996	Indianapolis, American Association

Double A

1989	El Paso, Texas League
1990	Arkansas, Texas League
1991	Reading, Eastern League
1992	Tulsa, Texas League
1993	Harrisburg, Eastern League
1994	San Antonio, Texas League
1995	Midland, Texas League
1996	Carolina, Southern League

Class A

1989	Durham, Carolina League
1990	San Jose, California League
1991	Asheville, South Atlantic League
1992	Springfield, Midwest League
1993	South Bend, Midwest League
1994	Kinston, Carolina League
1995	Kane County, Midwest League
1996	Wisconsin, Midwest League

Short Season A

1989	Eugene, Northwest League
1990	Salt Lake City, Pioneer League
1991	Spokane, Northwest League
1992	Boise, Northwest League
1993	Billings, Pioneer League
1994	Everett, Northwest League
1995	Great Falls, Pioneer League
1996	Bluefield, Appalachian League

V
BIBLIOGRAPHY

BIBLIOGRAPHY
Selected Minor League Baseball Bibliography

═══ Books ═══

Anderson, Will. Was Baseball Really Invented In Maine. Will Anderson Publishing, 1992.

Benson, Michael. Ballparks of North America. Jefferson, North Carolina: McFarland & Company, 1989

Beverage, Richard E. The Angels. Los Angeles in the Pacific Coast League, 1919-1957. Placentia, California: Deacon Press, 1981.

Beverage, Richard E. The Hollywood Stars. Placentia, California: Deacon Press, 1984.

Blatnick, Judith; and Schulz, Phillip S. Mud Hens and Mavericks. Viking Penguin, 1995.

Brooks, Ken. The Last Rebel Yell. Lynn Haven, Florida: Seneca Press, 1986.

Bryson, Bill and Leighton Housh. Through the years with the Western League, since 1885. Washington: Western League, 1951.

Cauz, Louis. Baseball's Back In Town. Toronto, Canada: Controlled Media Corporation, 1977.

Chrisman, David. The History of the International League. David Chrisman, 1983

Chrisman, David. The History of the Piedmont League. David Chrisman, 1986

Chrisman, David. The History of the Virginia League. David Chrisman, 1988.

Clifton, Merritt. Disorganized Baseball, vol. 1: The Quebec Provincial League. Richford, Vermont: Samisdat, 1983.

Clifton, Merritt. Disorganized Baseball, vol. 2: Baseball in Vermont, 1887-1935. Richford, Vermont: Samisdat, 1983.

Clifton, Merritt. Disorganized Baseball, vol. 3: Baseball in Vermont, 1935-1988 & Player Records. Richford, Vermont: Samisdat, 1983.

Davids, L. Robert, ed. Minor League Stars: vol. III. Cleveland: Society for American Baseball Research, 1992.

Davids, L. Robert, ed. Minor League Stars: vol. II. Cooperstown: Society for American Baseball Research, 1985.

Davids, L. Robert, ed. Minor League Stars. Cooperstown: Society for American Baseball Research, 1978, rev. ed. 1984.

Dews, Robert P. Southeastern Organized Baseball (SOB). Edison, Georgia: Rebel Books, 1987

Dews, Robert P. The Georgia-Florida League 1935-1958. Edison, Georgia: Rebel Books, 1985

Dolson, Frank. Beating the Bushes: Life in the Minor Leagues. South Bend, Indiana: Icarus Press, 1983.

Dowling, John R. The III League, 1901-1961. Watseka, Illinois: John Dowling, 1992.

Fatsis. Stefan. Wild and Outside. New York: Walker and Co., 1995.

Filichia, Peter. Professional Baseball Franchises: From the Abbeville Athletics to the Zanesville Indians. New York: Facts on Files, 1993.

Finch, Robert L.; L. H. Addington; and Ben M. Morgan, The Story of Minor League Baseball: A History of the Game of Professional Baseball in the United States with Particular Reference to Its Growth and Development in the Smaller Cities and Towns of the Nation. The Record of Championship Performances from 1901 to 1952. Columbus, Ohio: National Association of Professional Leagues, 1952.

French, Robert A. Fifty Golden Years in the American Association of Professional Baseball Clubs: 1902-1951. Minneapolis: American Association, 1951.

Friend, J. P. Cotton State League Golden Anniversary, 1902-1951. Blytheville, Arkansas: Cotton States League, 1951.

Gammon, Wirt. Your Chattanooga Lookouts Since 1885. Chattanooga: Chattanooga Publishing Co., 1953.

Gaunt, Robert H. We Could Have Played Forever: The Story of the Coastal Plains Baseball League. 1996.

Hockenbury, Russell. A Sketch History of the Middle Atlantic League, 1925-1947. Scottdale, Pennsylvania: Middle Atlantic League, 1947.

Hoie, Robert. "The Minor Leagues." Total Baseball. New York: Warner Books, 1989.

Hoie, Robert. "The Farm System." Total Baseball. New York: Warner Books, 1991.

Humber, William. Cheering for the Home Team: The Story of Baseball in Canada. Erin, Ontario: Boston Mills Press, 1983.

Hurth, Charles A. Baseball Records, The Southern Association, 1901-1947. New Orleans: The Southern Association, 1947.

Jimenez, Jr., Jose Jesus. Archivo de Baseball. Santiago, Dominican Republic, 1985.

Johnson, Arthur. Minor League Baseball and Local Economic Development. Champaign, Illinois: University of Illinois Press, 1993.

Johnson, W. Lloyd. Minor League Register. Durham, N.C.: Baseball America, 1994.

Kahn, Roger. Good Enough to Dream, Garden City, New York: Doubleday and Company, 1985

Keetz, Frank M. Class "C" Baseball: A Case Study of the Schenectady Blue Jays in the Canadian-American League 1946-1950. Schenectady, New York: Frank Keetz, 1988.

Kirkland, Bill. Eddie Neville of the Durham Bulls. Jefferson, N.C.: McFarland and Co., Inc., 1993.

Lamb, David. Stolen Season. New York: Random House, 1991.

Lange, Fred W. History of Baseball in California and Pacific Coast Leagues, 1847-1938. Oakland: privately published, 1938.

Lin Weber, Ralph. The Toledo Baseball Guide of the Mud Hens: 1883-1943. Toledo: Toledo Mud Hens Baseball Co., 1944.

Lindthurst, Randy. The 1938 Newark Bears. Trenton, New Jersey: Randy Lindthurst, 1984.

Lundquist, Carl, ed. 70 Nights in a Ball Park: An all new promotion Guide for Baseball Executives. Columbus, Ohio: National Association of Professional Baseball Leagues. 1958.

Lyttle, Richard. A Year in the Minors: Baseball's Untold Story. Garden City, New York: Doubleday, 1975.

Mackey, R. Scott. Barbary Baseball: The Pacific Coast League of the 1920's. Jefferson, N.C.: McFarland and Co., 1995.

Mayer, Ronald A. Mayer, The 1937 Newark Bears: A Baseball Legend. East Hanover, New Jersey: Vintage Press, 1985

Maywar, James P. The 1926 Port Huron Saints. Port Huron, Michigan: James Maywar, 1984.

McCombs, Wayne. Let's Gooooooooo Tulsa: The History and Record Book of Professional Baseball in Tulsa, Oklahoma, 1905-1989.

Mandelaro, Jim; and Pitaniak, Scott. Silver Seasons: The Story of the Rochester Red Wings. Syracuse, N.Y.: Syracuse University Press, 1996.

Moss, Earle W. The Leagues and League Cities of Professional Baseball, 1910-1941. Fort Wayne: Heilbroner Baseball Bureau, 1941.

Mowbray, William W. The Eastern Shore Baseball League. Centreville, Maryland: Tidewater Publishers, 1989.

O'Neal, Bill. The Texas League: A Century of Baseball, 1888-1987. Austin, Texas: Eakin Press, 1987.

O'Neal, Bill. The Pacific Coast League: 1903-1988. Austin, Texas: Eakin Press, 1990.

O'Neal, Bill. The International League: A Baseball History, 1884-1992. Austin, Texas: Eakin Press, 1992.

O'Neal, Bill. The American Association: A Baseball History, 1902-1991. Austin, Texas: Eakin Press, 1991.

O'Neal, Bill. The Southern League: Baseball in Dixie, 1885-1994. Austin: Eakin Press, 1994.

Obojski, Robert. Bush League, A Colorful, Factual Account of Minor League Baseball from 1877 to the Present. New York: Macmillan, 1975.

Overfield, Joseph M. The 100 Seasons of Buffalo Baseball. Kenmore, New York: Partner's Press, 1985

Paradis, Jean-Marc. 100 Ans de Baseball a Trois-Rivieres. Quebec: Trois-Rivieres, 1989.

Perlstein, Steve. Rebel Baseball. Minneapolis: Onion Press, 1994.

Pietrusza, David. Baseball's Canadian-American League: A History of Its Inception, Franchises, Participants, Locales, Statistics, Demise and Legacy, 1936-1951. Jefferson, North Carolina: McFarland & Company, 1990.

Puff, Richard A. Albany Senators: 1986 Old Timer's Day, July 12, 1986. Albany, New York: Old Timer's Day Committee, 1986.

Reddick, David B. and Ken M. Rogers. The Magic of Indians Baseball. Indianapolis: Indianapolis Indians, Inc.

Reidenbaugh, Lowell. Take Me Out to the Ball Park. The Sporting News, 1983.

Remington, John. The Red Wings - A Love Story: A Pictorial History of

BIBLIOGRAPHY

Professional Baseball in Rochester, New York. Rochester: Christopher Press, 1969.

Ruggles, William B. The History of the Texas League of Professional Baseball Clubs, 1888-1951. Dallas, The Texas League, 1951.

Ryan, Robert. Wait Till I Make the Show: Baseball in the Minor Leagues. Boston: Little, Brown and Company, 1972.

Schott, Arthur. 70 Years with the Pelicans. New Orleans: Arthur Schott, 1957.

Seymour, Harold. Baseball: The People's Game. New York: Oxford University Press, 1990.

Seymour, Harold. Baseball: The Early Years. New York: Oxford University Press, 1960.

Seymour, Harold. Baseball: The Golden Age. New York: Oxford University Press, 1971.

Snelling, Dennis. The Pacific Coast League: A Statistical History 1903-1957. McFarland and Co., 1995.

Stadler, Ken. The Pacific Coast League: One's Man's Memories, 1938-1957. Los Angeles: Marbek Publishers, 1984.

Sullivan Neil. The Minors. New York: St. Martins Press, 1990.

Summer, Jim. Separating the Men from the Boys; the First Half-Century of the Carolina League. Winston-Salem, N.C.: John Blair, 1994.

Sumner, Jim. "The North Carolina State Professional Baseball League of 1902." The North Carolina Historical Review, vol. 64, no. 3, July, 1987.

Sumner, Jim and Dave Kemp, ed. Minor League History Journal, vol.1. Cleveland: Society for American Baseball Research, 1991.

Temperly, Kevin. 1991 Midwest League Yearbook: First Collector's Edition. Clinton, Iowa: Midwest Baseball League, 1991.

Thornley, Stew. On to Nicollet: The Glory and Fame of the Minneapolis Millers. Minneapolis: Nodin Press, 1988.

Violanti, Anthony. Buffalo: How The Dream of Baseball Revived a City. New York: St, Martin's Press, 1991.

Waddingham, Gary. The Seattle Rainiers, 1938-1942. Seattle: Gary Waddingham, 1987.

Guides, Serials, Encyclopedias and Official Publications

American Association Record Book. Published by the league.

Baseball Blue Book, 1909-1996. Lexington, Kentucky: Sportsource, Inc.

Baseball Research Journal, 1972-1996. Cleveland: Society for American Baseball Research.

Baseball America Statistics Report, 1983-1987, Durham: Baseball America, Inc.

Baseball America Directory, 1983-1996, Durham: Baseball America, Inc.

Baseball America Almanac, 1988-1997, Durham: Baseball America, Inc.

Carolina League Record Book, 1948-1996, Durham, N.C.

Darby, Cecil, ed. South Atlantic League Dope Book - 1948, 1951.

Eastern League Pilot: Media Guide and Record Book. Published by the league.

Enciclopedia del Beisbol Mexicano, 1996. Monterrey, Mexico: Revista Deportivas, S.A. de C.V. (REDSA).

Florida State League Media Guide and Record Book. Published by the league.

Howe News Bureau. Western Carolinas League Record Book.

Howe Sportsdata International. South Atlantic League Record Book.

Howe Sportsdata International. Midwest League Record Book. Boston: Midwest Baseball League.

Howe Sportsdata International. Florida State League Media Guide and Record Book. Daytona Beach: Florida State League.

Journal of Sport History, 1974-1992. University Park, Pennsylvania: North American Society for Sport History.

Keys, Tom. 1986 International League of Professional Baseball Clubs Record Book. Grove City, Ohio: International Baseball League, 1986.

Keyser, Tim, ed. Texas League Media Guide and Record Book. 1996.

King, Dick. Baseball '76: Official Bi-Centennial Edition (NAPBBL). St. Petersburg: National Association of Professional Baseball Leagues, 1976.

Kramer, Charles F. The Middle Atlantic League, 25th Anniversary, 1925-1949, Souvenir Book. Johnstown, Pennsylvania: Middle Atlantic League, 1949.

Minor League Digest, 1941-1951. Fort Wayne, Indiana:Heilbroner Baseball Bureau.

Minor League Digest, 1952-1996. Fort Wayne and St. Petersburg: Baseball Blue Book, Inc.

Murnane, Timothy. National Association Baseball Guide, 1903-1910. Auburn, New York: National Association of Professional Baseball Clubs.

New York-Pennsylvania Record Book. Published by the league.

Official Baseball Guide, 1940-1997. St. Louis: The Sporting News.

Official American League Baseball Guide, 1883-1939. Philadelphia: Alfred J. Reach Company.

Official Guide of the National Association of Professional Baseball Leagues, 1902-1919. New York: American Sports Publishing Company.

Official Baseball Guide, 1877-1939. New York: American Sports Publishing Company.

Reichler, Joseph L., ed. The Baseball Encyclopedia, 1969-1988. New York: Macmillan Publishing Co.

Southern League Record Book. Published by the league,

Spalding's Minor League Guide, 1889-1910. New York: American Sports Publishing Company.

Sparks, Robert, ed. National Association Orange Book: Official Publication of the National Association of Professional Baseball Leagues. St. Petersburg: National Association of Professional Baseball Leagues.

The National Pastime, 1984-1996 Cleveland: Society for American Baseball Research.

Thorn, John and Pete Palmer, ed. Total Baseball, 1989-1993. New York: Warner Books.

Weiss, William J. ed. California League Record Book.

Weiss, William J. ed. Northwest League Record Book: Northwest Baseball League.

Weiss, William J. ed. Pacific Coast League Record Book: Pacific Coast Baseball League..

Weiss, William J. ed. Pioneer League Record Book: Pioneer Baseball League.

Wolff, Rick, ed. The Baseball Encyclopedia. New York: MacMillan Publishing Co.

Collections and Manuscripts

Arnold Springer Minor League manuscript

Bob McConnell Minor League Baseball Collection

John Pardon Minor League Baseball Collection

Player contract cards at the National Baseball Library

Player contract cards at The Sporting News

Ray Nemec Baseball Collection

Robert Hoie Pacific Coast Baseball Collection